***Bill James* presents . . .**

# STATS™ 1991 Major League Handbook

## STATS, Inc. • Bill James

Published by Sports Team Analysis & Tracking Systems, Inc.
Dr. Richard Cramer, Chairman • John Dewan, President

Cover by Brian Dempsey



First Edition: November, 1990

Printed in the United States of America

ISBN 0-9625581-1-7

**This book is dedicated to the memory of Comiskey Park,
Home of the Chicago White Sox, 1910 - 1990.**

**A "Field of Dreams" for the young and old . . .**

**Thanks for the memories.**

# Acknowledgments

We at the STATS' office like to think of this book as a pioneering effort in the world of baseball statistics, making this season's information available as quickly as possible. It's the only book of its kind to come out while fans are still trying to locate their cars in the parking lot after the last World Series game. How do we get this all done? It takes a lot of extra effort on the part of many people, namely . . .

Dr. Richard Cramer, the founder and Chairman of STATS, designed and continually improves upon our innovative System that seems to do everything except swing the bat. A look at the Player Profile section in this book will give you just a glimpse of the extent of information this System tracks on a daily basis.

John Dewan, President and CEO, has been directing STATS to make this baseball information available to teams, media and fans in new and creative ways. It is primarily through his organization and vision that STATS is able to get this information from the System and into the tangible book you hold while the last sip of champagne is taken in celebration of the World Series.

Arthur Ashley, Assistant Vice-President, adds a new section to the book this year, fielding. Among his many other jobs, Art also had the complex job of making sure that every game was covered, from not one but two angles. It takes a lot of coordination and perseverance to get the best possible coverage, but it brings to you the best and most accurate statistics.

Bob Mecca, Senior Statistician, developed the categories for the Leaders Boards and used his extensive baseball and system expertise to produce the Player Profiles. He has a special knack for looking at the numbers and separating the interesting from the obscure. You can also find his creative handiwork in many of the periodicals that STATS supports.

The core staff of the office, Matt Greenberger, Dave Klotz, Marge Morra and Ross Schaufelberger kept the daily operations going, along with turning new projects into reality. Not only does it take hard work, but creativity, ingenuity and a sense of humor. David Pinto helped bring STATS information into your living rooms nightly with his creative and detailed support for ESPN broadcasts. Don Zminda also added his baseball expertise to the Sunday night broadcasts along with directing the publication of ***The Scouting Report: 1991*** and ***The STATS Baseball Scoreboard: 1991***. Craig Wright once again used his talents to oversee our Major League operations.

The STATS Reporters throughout the country have proven their baseball skills by providing exceptional play-by-play coverage of every game. Their accurate scoring this year has helped to make our jobs in the office easier. Thanks.

Minor league information is provided by the folks at *Howe Sportsdata International*. Nice work, guys.

Thanks to Cleo for waiting patiently those long nights while we worked on the book.

Special thanks to Rob Neyer who worked on the Minor League Equivalencies used in the 1991 Projections.

And once again, thanks to Bill James for his consultation and support. This book certainly wouldn't be here without him.

— Sue Dewan
Vice President

# Table of Contents

# Introduction

Welcome to the *1991 Handbook!* This is now the second year of the most timely baseball book there is. We've done a lot of new things this year.

We've expanded the career section to include minor league statistics courtesy of *Howe Sportsdata International.* We've added more biographical info on each player. And we've even improved on what was already near-flawless data accuracy. The first printing of last year's book had some birth date errors that were corrected in the second printing. This year we've checked, doubled-checked and triple-checked all the data printed in the career section. We compared our biographical info against Howe's and against biographical data from SABR. We've researched all differences against individual team media guides and called major league teams for additional clarification. It is safe to say that the career data printed here, except for the unoffical nature of the 1990 stats, are more accurate than any other publication you could find including *The Baseball Encyclopedia* or *Total Baseball.*

We've added sections for team statistics and fielding statistics. We had a lot of people tell us they loved last year's book but would like to see these two sections added. So we did.

We've modified and improved our projection system. Be sure to read Bill James' write-up on the projections in the last section of this book. He discusses how accurate we were last year and how we've modified the system for this year.

We've expanded the Leader Boards. Last year we had 72 tables. We've more than tripled that this year.

We've developed Player Profiles like you've never seen before. Bob Mecca had our computer standing on it's head spitting out numbers until we told him to stop. Ignoring that, he had the computer dancing around the office doing cartwheels after everyone left the office at night. As Ed McMahon might say, "Everything you could possibly want to know about Doug Drabek, Dennis Eckersley, Carlton Fisk or Ryne Sandberg is in this book, right Johnny?" Well, probably not. But it's not for lack of trying.

As I mentioned last year, I call this book a "No-nonsense" baseball stat book because it's baseball statistics, pure and simple. Every statistic is not for everyone, but we hope that the stuff **YOU** want to see is here.

And don't forget, the 1992 edition will be ready in November 1991!

## What's Official and What's Not

The stats in this book are technically unofficial. The Official Major League Baseball Averages are not released until December. But we couldn't wait that long. However, if you take the effort to compare these stats with those that come out in December, you'll find no major differences. The only possible changes between now and December would involve official scoring changes made to the stats in that time period. I would be shocked to find even one batting average different from the official numbers when they come out.

This year we want to point out a couple of differences between our stats and those printed by the MLB-IBM system and the USA Today in early October. We have an extra game played at second base by David Rohde and one less for Karl Rhodes, both of Houston. This was clearly a case of mistaken spelling on the last day of the season by the MLB-IBM scorer. Both of our reporters reported Rohde as a defensive replacement at second. If Rhodes had actually played second, it would have been his only game of the season at second with Rohde, a true second basemen, on the bench during the game!

Other differences to point out (hopefully the official averages will contain these corrections): Cal Ripken was intentionally walked by Charles Nagy in the 3rd inning of the second game on September 30 according to our records; this was not reported in the October MLB-IBM stats. Also, Billy Spiers of Milwaukee was inadvertantly credited with an extra strikeout by the MLB-IBM system on the last day of the season; this strikeout should go to George Canale.

As mentioned in its section, our fielding stats are "more" unofficial than our batting and pitching stats. No one keeps fielding stats as meticulously as batting and pitching, with good reason. They're just not as important. You will find some differences between ours and the official statistics when they're published in December. But unless you can actually count toothpicks as well as Dustin Hoffman in *Rainman*, these minor differences are insignificant.

## Player Ages

When we give a **player's age** in this book, it's what we call his seasonal age. This is the age that a player would tell you if you asked him on July 1, 1991. By choosing this particular date, almost exactly mid-season, you get the age at which the player will have played the most during the 1991 season.

— John Dewan

# Career Stats

The biggest addition we've made to the career stats this year is minor league data. We now show minor league career info back to 1984 for any player who made his major league debut within the last two years (1989 or 1990). We've also added position (Pos) played. The most common position is listed first. Any other postion where a player played in at least 10 games is also shown. One caveat though—the player must also have appeared offensively in those 10 games. Height and weight appear for the first time this year too. Finally, one subtle change from last year is if a player played for more than one team in a season, we now list the teams in the order he played for them.

Some notes:

- **Age** is seasonal age based on July 1, 1991.
- **Hm** and **Rd** in the batters' tables stand for home runs hit at home and home runs hit on the road, respectively.
- **TBB** and **IBB** are Total Bases and Intentional Bases on Balls.
- **SB%** is Stolen Base Percentage (stolen bases divided by attempts). **OBP** and **SLG** are On-Base Percentage and Slugging Percentage.
- **BFP**, **Bk** and **ShO** are Batters Faced Pitcher, Balks and Shut-outs.
- For pitchers, thirds of an inning were not officially kept prior to 1982. Therefore, you'll see no thirds of an inning for 1981 and prior for older pitchers.
- For a player who played for more than one major league team in a season, his stats for each team are shown just above the bottom line career totals.

## Don Aase

**Pitches:** Right **Bats:** Right **Pos:** RP **Ht:** 6' 3" **Wt:** 222 **Born:** 09/08/54 **Age:** 36

| | | HOW MUCH HE PITCHED | | | | | | WHAT HE GAVE UP | | | | | | | | | | | | THE RESULTS | | | | | |
|---|---|---|---|---|---|---|---|---|---|---|---|---|---|---|---|---|---|---|---|---|---|---|---|---|---|
| Year Team | Lg | G | GS | CG | GF | IP | BFP | H | R | ER | HR | SH | SF | HB | TBB | IBB | SO | WP | Bk | W | L | Pct. | ShO | Sv | ERA |
| 1977 Boston | AL | 13 | 13 | 4 | 0 | 92 | 373 | 85 | 36 | 32 | 6 | 2 | 3 | 1 | 19 | 1 | 49 | 0 | 0 | 6 | 2 | .750 | 2 | 0 | 3.13 |
| 1978 California | AL | 29 | 29 | 6 | 0 | 179 | 773 | 185 | 88 | 80 | 14 | 5 | 1 | 2 | 80 | 4 | 93 | 3 | 0 | 11 | 8 | .579 | 1 | 0 | 4.02 |
| 1979 California | AL | 37 | 28 | 7 | 4 | 185 | 817 | 200 | 104 | 99 | 19 | 8 | 8 | 1 | 77 | 7 | 96 | 5 | 0 | 9 | 10 | .474 | 1 | 2 | 4.82 |
| 1980 California | AL | 40 | 21 | 5 | 6 | 175 | 761 | 193 | 83 | 79 | 13 | 12 | 9 | 1 | 66 | 3 | 74 | 2 | 1 | 8 | 13 | .381 | 1 | 2 | 4.06 |
| 1981 California | AL | 39 | 0 | 0 | 31 | 65 | 265 | 56 | 17 | 17 | 4 | 1 | 1 | 0 | 24 | 2 | 38 | 1 | 0 | 4 | 4 | .500 | 0 | 11 | 2.35 |
| 1982 California | AL | 24 | 0 | 0 | 18 | 52 | 212 | 45 | 20 | 20 | 5 | 4 | 0 | 0 | 23 | 2 | 40 | 2 | 0 | 3 | 3 | .500 | 0 | 4 | 3.46 |
| 1984 California | AL | 23 | 0 | 0 | 17 | 39 | 160 | 30 | 7 | 7 | 1 | 3 | 2 | 0 | 19 | 5 | 28 | 0 | 0 | 4 | 1 | .800 | 0 | 8 | 1.62 |
| 1985 Baltimore | AL | 54 | 0 | 0 | 43 | 88 | 366 | 83 | 44 | 37 | 6 | 5 | 3 | 1 | 35 | 7 | 67 | 0 | 1 | 10 | 6 | .625 | 0 | 14 | 3.78 |
| 1986 Baltimore | AL | 66 | 0 | 0 | 58 | 81.2 | 337 | 71 | 29 | 27 | 6 | 3 | 2 | 0 | 28 | 2 | 67 | 4 | 0 | 6 | 7 | .462 | 0 | 34 | 2.98 |
| 1987 Baltimore | AL | 7 | 0 | 0 | 6 | 8 | 33 | 8 | 2 | 2 | 1 | 0 | 0 | 0 | 4 | 0 | 3 | 0 | 0 | 1 | 0 | 1.000 | 0 | 2 | 2.25 |
| 1988 Baltimore | AL | 35 | 0 | 0 | 16 | 46.2 | 209 | 40 | 22 | 21 | 4 | 3 | 2 | 0 | 37 | 5 | 28 | 1 | 0 | 0 | 0 | .000 | 0 | 0 | 4.05 |
| 1989 New York | NL | 49 | 0 | 0 | 22 | 59.1 | 261 | 56 | 27 | 26 | 5 | 2 | 3 | 1 | 26 | 3 | 34 | 0 | 1 | 1 | 5 | .167 | 0 | 2 | 3.94 |
| 1990 Los Angeles | NL | 32 | 0 | 0 | 13 | 38 | 163 | 33 | 24 | 21 | 5 | 2 | 0 | 0 | 19 | 4 | 24 | 3 | 0 | 3 | 1 | .750 | 0 | 3 | 4.97 |
| 13 ML YEARS | | 448 | 91 | 22 | 234 | 1108.2 | 4730 | 1085 | 503 | 468 | 89 | 50 | 34 | 7 | 457 | 45 | 641 | 21 | 3 | 66 | 60 | .524 | 5 | 82 | 3.80 |

## Jim Abbott

**Pitches:** Left **Bats:** Left **Pos:** SP **Ht:** 6' 3" **Wt:** 200 **Born:** 09/19/67 **Age:** 23

| | | HOW MUCH HE PITCHED | | | | | | WHAT HE GAVE UP | | | | | | | | | | | | THE RESULTS | | | | | |
|---|---|---|---|---|---|---|---|---|---|---|---|---|---|---|---|---|---|---|---|---|---|---|---|---|---|
| Year Team | Lg | G | GS | CG | GF | IP | BFP | H | R | ER | HR | SH | SF | HB | TBB | IBB | SO | WP | Bk | W | L | Pct. | ShO | Sv | ERA |
| 1989 California | AL | 29 | 29 | 4 | 0 | 181.1 | 788 | 190 | 95 | 79 | 13 | 11 | 5 | 4 | 74 | 3 | 115 | 8 | 2 | 12 | 12 | .500 | 2 | 0 | 3.92 |
| 1990 California | AL | 33 | 33 | 4 | 0 | 211.2 | 925 | 246 | 116 | 106 | 16 | 9 | 6 | 5 | 72 | 6 | 105 | 4 | 3 | 10 | 14 | .417 | 1 | 0 | 4.51 |
| 2 ML YEARS | | 62 | 62 | 8 | 0 | 393 | 1713 | 436 | 211 | 185 | 29 | 20 | 11 | 9 | 146 | 9 | 220 | 12 | 5 | 22 | 26 | .458 | 3 | 0 | 4.24 |

## Paul Abbott

**Pitches:** Right **Bats:** Right **Pos:** SP **Ht:** 6' 3" **Wt:** 185 **Born:** 09/15/67 **Age:** 23

| | | HOW MUCH HE PITCHED | | | | | | WHAT HE GAVE UP | | | | | | | | | | | | THE RESULTS | | | | | |
|---|---|---|---|---|---|---|---|---|---|---|---|---|---|---|---|---|---|---|---|---|---|---|---|---|---|
| Year Team | Lg | G | GS | CG | GF | IP | BFP | H | R | ER | HR | SH | SF | HB | TBB | IBB | SO | WP | Bk | W | L | Pct. | ShO | Sv | ERA |
| 1985 Elizabethtn | R | 10 | 10 | 1 | 0 | 35 | 172 | 33 | 32 | 27 | 3 | 1 | 0 | 0 | 32 | 0 | 34 | 7 | 1 | 1 | 5 | .167 | 0 | 0 | 6.94 |
| 1986 Kenosha | A | 25 | 15 | 1 | 7 | 98 | 462 | 102 | 62 | 49 | 13 | 3 | 2 | 2 | 73 | 3 | 73 | 7 | 0 | 6 | 10 | .375 | 0 | 0 | 4.50 |
| 1987 Kenosha | A | 26 | 25 | 1 | 0 | 145.1 | 620 | 102 | 76 | 59 | 11 | 5 | 6 | 3 | 103 | 0 | 138 | 11 | 2 | 13 | 6 | .684 | 0 | 0 | 3.65 |
| 1988 Visalia | A | 28 | 28 | 4 | 0 | 172.1 | 799 | 141 | 95 | 80 | 9 | 8 | 6 | 4 | 143 | 5 | 205 | 12 | 9 | 11 | 9 | .550 | 2 | 0 | 4.18 |
| 1989 Orlando | AA | 17 | 17 | 1 | 0 | 90.2 | 389 | 71 | 48 | 44 | 6 | 2 | 1 | 0 | 48 | 0 | 102 | 7 | 7 | 9 | 3 | .750 | 0 | 0 | 4.37 |
| 1990 Portland | AAA | 23 | 23 | 4 | 0 | 128.1 | 568 | 110 | 75 | 65 | 9 | 3 | 3 | 1 | 82 | 0 | 129 | 8 | 5 | 5 | 14 | .263 | 1 | 0 | 4.56 |
| 1990 Minnesota | AL | 7 | 7 | 0 | 0 | 34.2 | 162 | 37 | 24 | 23 | 0 | 1 | 1 | 1 | 28 | 0 | 25 | 1 | 0 | 0 | 5 | .000 | 0 | 0 | 5.97 |

## Shawn Abner

**Bats:** Right **Throws:** Right **Pos:** CF/LF **Ht:** 6' 1" **Wt:** 190 **Born:** 06/17/66 **Age:** 25

| | | BATTING | | | | | | | | | | | | | | | | | BASERUNNING | | | | PERCENTAGES | | |
|---|---|---|---|---|---|---|---|---|---|---|---|---|---|---|---|---|---|---|---|---|---|---|---|---|---|
| Year Team | Lg | G | AB | H | 2B | 3B | HR | (Hm | Rd) | TB | R | RBI | TBB | IBB | SO | HBP | SH | SF | SB | CS | SB% | GDP | Avg | OBP | SLG |
| 1987 San Diego | NL | 16 | 47 | 13 | 3 | 1 | 2 | (1 | 1) | 24 | 5 | 7 | 2 | 0 | 8 | 0 | 0 | 0 | 1 | 0 | 1.00 | 0 | .277 | .306 | .511 |
| 1988 San Diego | NL | 37 | 83 | 15 | 3 | 0 | 2 | (2 | 0) | 24 | 6 | 5 | 4 | 1 | 19 | 1 | 0 | 1 | 0 | 1 | .00 | 1 | .181 | .225 | .289 |
| 1989 San Diego | NL | 57 | 102 | 18 | 4 | 0 | 2 | (1 | 1) | 28 | 13 | 14 | 5 | 2 | 20 | 0 | 0 | 1 | 1 | 0 | 1.00 | 1 | .176 | .213 | .275 |
| 1990 San Diego | NL | 91 | 184 | 45 | 9 | 0 | 1 | (1 | 0) | 57 | 17 | 15 | 9 | 1 | 28 | 2 | 2 | 1 | 2 | 3 | .40 | 3 | .245 | .286 | .310 |
| 4 ML YEARS | | 201 | 416 | 91 | 19 | 1 | 7 | (5 | 2) | 133 | 41 | 41 | 20 | 4 | 75 | 3 | 2 | 3 | 4 | 4 | .50 | 5 | .219 | .258 | .320 |

## Jim Acker

**Pitches:** Right **Bats:** Right **Pos:** RP **Ht:** 6' 2" **Wt:** 212 **Born:** 09/24/58 **Age:** 32

| | | HOW MUCH HE PITCHED | | | | | | WHAT HE GAVE UP | | | | | | | | | | | | THE RESULTS | | | | | |
|---|---|---|---|---|---|---|---|---|---|---|---|---|---|---|---|---|---|---|---|---|---|---|---|---|---|
| Year Team | Lg | G | GS | CG | GF | IP | BFP | H | R | ER | HR | SH | SF | HB | TBB | IBB | SO | WP | Bk | W | L | Pct. | ShO | Sv | ERA |
| 1983 Toronto | AL | 38 | 5 | 0 | 8 | 97.2 | 426 | 103 | 52 | 47 | 7 | 1 | 2 | 8 | 38 | 1 | 44 | 1 | 0 | 5 | 1 | .833 | 0 | 1 | 4.33 |
| 1984 Toronto | AL | 32 | 3 | 0 | 9 | 72 | 312 | 79 | 39 | 35 | 3 | 4 | 1 | 6 | 25 | 3 | 33 | 5 | 0 | 3 | 5 | .375 | 0 | 1 | 4.38 |
| 1985 Toronto | AL | 61 | 0 | 0 | 26 | 86.1 | 370 | 86 | 35 | 31 | 7 | 1 | 2 | 3 | 43 | 1 | 42 | 2 | 0 | 7 | 2 | .778 | 0 | 10 | 3.23 |
| 1986 2 ML Teams | | 44 | 19 | 0 | 9 | 155 | 661 | 163 | 81 | 69 | 13 | 12 | 9 | 3 | 48 | 6 | 69 | 5 | 1 | 5 | 12 | .294 | 0 | 0 | 4.01 |
| 1987 Atlanta | NL | 68 | 0 | 0 | 41 | 114.2 | 491 | 109 | 57 | 53 | 11 | 3 | 3 | 4 | 51 | 4 | 68 | 1 | 0 | 4 | 9 | .308 | 0 | 14 | 4.16 |
| 1988 Atlanta | NL | 21 | 1 | 0 | 7 | 42 | 184 | 45 | 26 | 22 | 6 | 5 | 3 | 1 | 14 | 3 | 25 | 2 | 0 | 0 | 4 | .000 | 0 | 0 | 4.71 |
| 1989 2 ML Teams | | 73 | 0 | 0 | 26 | 126 | 499 | 108 | 36 | 34 | 6 | 6 | 3 | 2 | 32 | 11 | 92 | 3 | 0 | 2 | 7 | .222 | 0 | 2 | 2.43 |
| 1990 Toronto | AL | 59 | 0 | 0 | 19 | 91.2 | 403 | 103 | 49 | 39 | 9 | 3 | 1 | 3 | 30 | 5 | 54 | 4 | 1 | 4 | 4 | .500 | 0 | 1 | 3.83 |
| 1986 Toronto | AL | 23 | 5 | 0 | 6 | 60 | 259 | 63 | 34 | 29 | 6 | 6 | 5 | 2 | 22 | 3 | 32 | 3 | 1 | 2 | 4 | .333 | 0 | 0 | 4.35 |
| Atlanta | NL | 21 | 14 | 0 | 3 | 95 | 402 | 100 | 47 | 40 | 7 | 6 | 4 | 1 | 26 | 3 | 37 | 2 | 0 | 3 | 8 | .273 | 0 | 0 | 3.79 |
| 1989 Atlanta | NL | 59 | 0 | 0 | 23 | 97.2 | 383 | 84 | 29 | 29 | 5 | 5 | 3 | 1 | 20 | 8 | 68 | 2 | 0 | 0 | 6 | .000 | 0 | 2 | 2.67 |
| Toronto | AL | 14 | 0 | 0 | 3 | 28.1 | 116 | 24 | 7 | 5 | 1 | 1 | 0 | 1 | 12 | 3 | 24 | 1 | 0 | 2 | 1 | .667 | 0 | 0 | 1.59 |
| 8 ML YEARS | | 396 | 28 | 0 | 145 | 785.1 | 3346 | 796 | 375 | 330 | 62 | 35 | 24 | 30 | 281 | 34 | 427 | 23 | 2 | 30 | 44 | .405 | 0 | 29 | 3.78 |

## Steve Adkins

**Pitches:** Left **Bats:** Right **Pos:** SP **Ht:** 6' 6" **Wt:** 200 **Born:** 10/26/64 **Age:** 26

| | | HOW MUCH HE PITCHED | | | | | | WHAT HE GAVE UP | | | | | | | | | | | | THE RESULTS | | | | | |
|---|---|---|---|---|---|---|---|---|---|---|---|---|---|---|---|---|---|---|---|---|---|---|---|---|---|
| Year Team | Lg | G | GS | CG | GF | IP | BFP | H | R | ER | HR | SH | SF | HB | TBB | IBB | SO | WP | Bk | W | L | Pct. | ShO | Sv | ERA |
| 1986 Oneonta | A | 14 | 12 | 2 | 1 | 80.1 | 325 | 59 | 23 | 15 | 1 | 6 | 0 | 0 | 36 | 2 | 74 | 8 | 0 | 8 | 2 | .800 | 1 | 1 | 1.68 |
| 1987 Ft.Laudrdle | A | 5 | 3 | 0 | 1 | 21.1 | 91 | 26 | 11 | 11 | 2 | 1 | 1 | 0 | 8 | 0 | 7 | 3 | 1 | 1 | 1 | .500 | 0 | 0 | 4.64 |
| Pr William | A | 21 | 20 | 0 | 0 | 115.2 | 527 | 120 | 72 | 62 | 11 | 3 | 3 | 3 | 70 | 1 | 84 | 12 | 1 | 9 | 8 | .529 | 0 | 0 | 4.82 |
| 1988 Pr William | A | 31 | 6 | 2 | 13 | 94.1 | 404 | 88 | 44 | 35 | 6 | 6 | 3 | 3 | 40 | 4 | 92 | 5 | 4 | 6 | 4 | .600 | 1 | 0 | 3.34 |
| 1989 Ft.Laudrdle | A | 11 | 4 | 0 | 4 | 45.2 | 185 | 40 | 15 | 12 | 2 | 1 | 2 | 1 | 14 | 0 | 48 | 2 | 1 | 3 | 3 | .500 | 0 | 3 | 2.36 |
| Albany | AA | 16 | 16 | 7 | 0 | 117.2 | 467 | 67 | 31 | 27 | 5 | 3 | 0 | 1 | 58 | 1 | 132 | 2 | 0 | 12 | 1 | .923 | 5 | 0 | 2.07 |
| 1990 Columbus | AAA | 27 | 27 | 6 | 0 | 177 | 764 | 153 | 72 | 57 | 9 | 4 | 6 | 5 | 98 | 0 | 138 | 4 | 1 | 15 | 7 | .682 | 2 | 0 | 2.90 |
| 1990 New York | AL | 5 | 5 | 0 | 0 | 24 | 115 | 19 | 18 | 17 | 4 | 1 | 1 | 0 | 29 | 0 | 14 | 2 | 0 | 1 | 2 | .333 | 0 | 0 | 6.38 |

## Troy Afenir

**Bats:** Right **Throws:** Right **Pos:** C **Ht:** 6' 4" **Wt:** 200 **Born:** 09/21/63 **Age:** 27

| | | BATTING | | | | | | | | | | | | | | | | | BASERUNNING | | | | PERCENTAGES | | |
|---|---|---|---|---|---|---|---|---|---|---|---|---|---|---|---|---|---|---|---|---|---|---|---|---|---|
| Year Team | Lg | G | AB | H | 2B | 3B | HR | (Hm | Rd) | TB | R | RBI | TBB | IBB | SO | HBP | SH | SF | SB | CS | SB% | GDP | Avg | OBP | SLG |
| 1987 Houston | NL | 10 | 20 | 6 | 1 | 0 | 0 | (0 | 0) | 7 | 1 | 1 | 0 | 0 | 12 | 0 | 0 | 0 | 0 | 0 | .00 | 0 | .300 | .300 | .350 |
| 1990 Oakland | AL | 14 | 14 | 2 | 0 | 0 | 0 | (0 | 0) | 2 | 0 | 2 | 0 | 0 | 6 | 0 | 0 | 1 | 0 | 0 | .00 | 0 | .143 | .133 | .143 |
| 2 ML YEARS | | 24 | 34 | 8 | 1 | 0 | 0 | (0 | 0) | 9 | 1 | 3 | 0 | 0 | 18 | 0 | 0 | 1 | 0 | 0 | .00 | 0 | .235 | .229 | .265 |

## Juan Agosto

**Pitches:** Left **Bats:** Left **Pos:** RP **Ht:** 6' 2" **Wt:** 190 **Born:** 02/23/58 **Age:** 33

| | | HOW MUCH HE PITCHED | | | | | | WHAT HE GAVE UP | | | | | | | | | | | | THE RESULTS | | | | | |
|---|---|---|---|---|---|---|---|---|---|---|---|---|---|---|---|---|---|---|---|---|---|---|---|---|---|
| Year Team | Lg | G | GS | CG | GF | IP | BFP | H | R | ER | HR | SH | SF | HB | TBB | IBB | SO | WP | Bk | W | L | Pct. | ShO | Sv | ERA |
| 1981 Chicago | AL | 2 | 0 | 0 | 1 | 6 | 22 | 5 | 3 | 3 | 1 | 0 | 0 | 1 | 0 | 0 | 3 | 0 | 0 | 0 | 0 | .000 | 0 | 0 | 4.50 |
| 1982 Chicago | AL | 1 | 0 | 0 | 1 | 2 | 13 | 7 | 4 | 4 | 0 | 0 | 0 | 0 | 0 | 0 | 1 | 0 | 0 | 0 | 0 | .000 | 0 | 0 | 18.00 |
| 1983 Chicago | AL | 39 | 0 | 0 | 13 | 41.2 | 166 | 41 | 20 | 19 | 2 | 5 | 4 | 1 | 11 | 1 | 29 | 2 | 0 | 2 | 2 | .500 | 0 | 7 | 4.10 |
| 1984 Chicago | AL | 49 | 0 | 0 | 18 | 55.1 | 243 | 54 | 20 | 19 | 2 | 5 | 1 | 3 | 34 | 7 | 26 | 1 | 0 | 2 | 1 | .667 | 0 | 7 | 3.09 |
| 1985 Chicago | AL | 54 | 0 | 0 | 21 | 60.1 | 246 | 45 | 27 | 24 | 3 | 3 | 3 | 3 | 23 | 1 | 39 | 0 | 0 | 4 | 3 | .571 | 0 | 1 | 3.58 |
| 1986 2 ML Teams | | 26 | 1 | 0 | 4 | 25 | 139 | 49 | 30 | 24 | 1 | 2 | 0 | 2 | 18 | 0 | 12 | 1 | 0 | 1 | 4 | .200 | 0 | 1 | 8.64 |
| 1987 Houston | NL | 27 | 0 | 0 | 13 | 27.1 | 118 | 26 | 12 | 8 | 1 | 3 | 0 | 0 | 10 | 1 | 6 | 1 | 0 | 1 | 1 | .500 | 0 | 2 | 2.63 |
| 1988 Houston | NL | 75 | 0 | 0 | 33 | 91.2 | 371 | 74 | 27 | 23 | 6 | 9 | 5 | 0 | 30 | 13 | 33 | 3 | 5 | 10 | 2 | .833 | 0 | 4 | 2.26 |
| 1989 Houston | NL | 71 | 0 | 0 | 28 | 83 | 361 | 81 | 32 | 27 | 3 | 5 | 6 | 2 | 32 | 10 | 46 | 4 | 1 | 4 | 5 | .444 | 0 | 1 | 2.93 |
| 1990 Houston | NL | 82 | 0 | 0 | 29 | 92.1 | 404 | 91 | 46 | 44 | 4 | 7 | 2 | 7 | 39 | 8 | 50 | 1 | 0 | 9 | 8 | .529 | 0 | 4 | 4.29 |
| 1986 Chicago | AL | 9 | 0 | 0 | 1 | 4.2 | 24 | 6 | 5 | 4 | 0 | 0 | 0 | 0 | 4 | 0 | 3 | 0 | 0 | 0 | 2 | .000 | 0 | 0 | 7.71 |
| Minnesota | AL | 17 | 1 | 0 | 3 | 20.1 | 115 | 43 | 25 | 20 | 1 | 2 | 0 | 2 | 14 | 0 | 9 | 1 | 0 | 1 | 2 | .333 | 0 | 1 | 8.85 |
| 10 ML YEARS | | 426 | 1 | 0 | 161 | 484.2 | 2083 | 473 | 221 | 195 | 23 | 39 | 21 | 19 | 197 | 41 | 245 | 13 | 6 | 33 | 26 | .559 | 0 | 27 | 3.62 |

## Rick Aguilera

**Pitches:** Right **Bats:** Right **Pos:** RP **Ht:** 6' 5" **Wt:** 200 **Born:** 12/31/61 **Age:** 29

| | | HOW MUCH HE PITCHED | | | | | | WHAT HE GAVE UP | | | | | | | | | | | | THE RESULTS | | | | | |
|---|---|---|---|---|---|---|---|---|---|---|---|---|---|---|---|---|---|---|---|---|---|---|---|---|---|
| Year Team | Lg | G | GS | CG | GF | IP | BFP | H | R | ER | HR | SH | SF | HB | TBB | IBB | SO | WP | Bk | W | L | Pct. | ShO | Sv | ERA |
| 1985 New York | NL | 21 | 19 | 2 | 1 | 122.1 | 507 | 118 | 49 | 44 | 8 | 7 | 4 | 2 | 37 | 2 | 74 | 5 | 2 | 10 | 7 | .588 | 0 | 0 | 3.24 |
| 1986 New York | NL | 28 | 20 | 2 | 2 | 141.2 | 605 | 145 | 70 | 61 | 15 | 6 | 5 | 7 | 36 | 1 | 104 | 5 | 3 | 10 | 7 | .588 | 0 | 0 | 3.88 |
| 1987 New York | NL | 18 | 17 | 1 | 0 | 115 | 494 | 124 | 53 | 46 | 12 | 7 | 2 | 3 | 33 | 2 | 77 | 9 | 0 | 11 | 3 | .786 | 0 | 0 | 3.60 |
| 1988 New York | NL | 11 | 3 | 0 | 2 | 24.2 | 111 | 29 | 20 | 19 | 2 | 2 | 0 | 1 | 10 | 2 | 16 | 1 | 1 | 0 | 4 | .000 | 0 | 0 | 6.93 |
| 1989 2 ML Teams | | 47 | 11 | 3 | 19 | 145 | 594 | 130 | 51 | 45 | 8 | 7 | 1 | 3 | 38 | 4 | 137 | 4 | 3 | 9 | 11 | .450 | 0 | 7 | 2.79 |
| 1990 Minnesota | AL | 56 | 0 | 0 | 54 | 65.1 | 268 | 55 | 27 | 20 | 5 | 0 | 0 | 4 | 19 | 6 | 61 | 3 | 0 | 5 | 3 | .625 | 0 | 32 | 2.76 |
| 1989 New York | NL | 36 | 0 | 0 | 19 | 69.1 | 284 | 59 | 19 | 18 | 3 | 5 | 1 | 2 | 21 | 3 | 80 | 3 | 3 | 6 | 6 | .500 | 0 | 7 | 2.34 |
| Minnesota | AL | 11 | 11 | 3 | 0 | 75.2 | 310 | 71 | 32 | 27 | 5 | 2 | 0 | 1 | 17 | 1 | 57 | 1 | 0 | 3 | 5 | .375 | 0 | 0 | 3.21 |
| 6 ML YEARS | | 181 | 70 | 8 | 78 | 614 | 2579 | 601 | 270 | 235 | 50 | 29 | 12 | 20 | 173 | 17 | 469 | 27 | 9 | 45 | 35 | .563 | 0 | 39 | 3.44 |

## Darrel Akerfelds

**Pitches:** Right **Bats:** Right **Pos:** RP **Ht:** 6' 2" **Wt:** 210 **Born:** 06/12/62 **Age:** 29

| | | HOW MUCH HE PITCHED | | | | | | WHAT HE GAVE UP | | | | | | | | | | | | THE RESULTS | | | | | |
|---|---|---|---|---|---|---|---|---|---|---|---|---|---|---|---|---|---|---|---|---|---|---|---|---|---|
| Year Team | Lg | G | GS | CG | GF | IP | BFP | H | R | ER | HR | SH | SF | HB | TBB | IBB | SO | WP | Bk | W | L | Pct. | ShO | Sv | ERA |
| 1986 Oakland | AL | 2 | 0 | 0 | 2 | 5.1 | 26 | 7 | 5 | 4 | 2 | 0 | 0 | 0 | 3 | 1 | 5 | 2 | 0 | 0 | 0 | .000 | 0 | 0 | 6.75 |
| 1987 Cleveland | AL | 16 | 13 | 1 | 0 | 74.2 | 347 | 84 | 60 | 56 | 18 | 2 | 4 | 7 | 38 | 1 | 42 | 7 | 0 | 2 | 6 | .250 | 0 | 0 | 6.75 |
| 1989 Texas | AL | 6 | 0 | 0 | 2 | 11 | 50 | 11 | 6 | 4 | 1 | 0 | 1 | 0 | 5 | 2 | 9 | 1 | 0 | 0 | 1 | .000 | 0 | 0 | 3.27 |
| 1990 Philadelphia | NL | 71 | 0 | 0 | 18 | 93 | 395 | 65 | 45 | 39 | 10 | 9 | 5 | 3 | 54 | 8 | 42 | 7 | 1 | 5 | 2 | .714 | 0 | 3 | 3.77 |
| 4 ML YEARS | | 95 | 13 | 1 | 22 | 184 | 818 | 167 | 116 | 103 | 31 | 11 | 10 | 10 | 100 | 12 | 98 | 17 | 1 | 7 | 9 | .438 | 0 | 3 | 5.04 |

## Scott Aldred

**Pitches:** Left **Bats:** Left **Pos:** SP **Ht:** 6' 4" **Wt:** 195 **Born:** 06/12/68 **Age:** 23

| | | HOW MUCH HE PITCHED | | | | | | WHAT HE GAVE UP | | | | | | | | | | | | THE RESULTS | | | | | |
|---|---|---|---|---|---|---|---|---|---|---|---|---|---|---|---|---|---|---|---|---|---|---|---|---|---|
| Year Team | Lg | G | GS | CG | GF | IP | BFP | H | R | ER | HR | SH | SF | HB | TBB | IBB | SO | WP | Bk | W | L | Pct. | ShO | Sv | ERA |
| 1987 Fayettevlle | A | 21 | 20 | 0 | 0 | 111 | 485 | 101 | 56 | 44 | 5 | 2 | 7 | 3 | 69 | 0 | 91 | 8 | 1 | 4 | 9 | .308 | 0 | 0 | 3.57 |
| 1988 Lakeland | A | 25 | 25 | 1 | 0 | 131.1 | 583 | 122 | 61 | 52 | 6 | 3 | 3 | 8 | 72 | 1 | 102 | 5 | 4 | 8 | 7 | .533 | 1 | 0 | 3.56 |
| 1989 London | AA | 20 | 20 | 3 | 0 | 122 | 513 | 98 | 55 | 52 | 11 | 3 | 3 | 5 | 59 | 0 | 97 | 9 | 2 | 10 | 6 | .625 | 1 | 0 | 3.84 |
| 1990 Toledo | AAA | 29 | 29 | 2 | 0 | 158 | 687 | 145 | 93 | 86 | 16 | 2 | 10 | 4 | 81 | 1 | 133 | 9 | 4 | 6 | 15 | .286 | 0 | 0 | 4.90 |
| 1990 Detroit | AL | 4 | 3 | 0 | 0 | 14.1 | 63 | 13 | 6 | 6 | 0 | 2 | 1 | 1 | 10 | 1 | 7 | 0 | 0 | 1 | 2 | .333 | 0 | 0 | 3.77 |

## Mike Aldrete

**Bats:** Left **Throws:** Left **Pos:** LF/1B **Ht:** 5'11" **Wt:** 185 **Born:** 01/29/61 **Age:** 30

| | | BATTING | | | | | | | | | | | | | | | | | BASERUNNING | | | | PERCENTAGES | | |
|---|---|---|---|---|---|---|---|---|---|---|---|---|---|---|---|---|---|---|---|---|---|---|---|---|---|
| Year Team | Lg | G | AB | H | 2B | 3B | HR | (Hm | Rd) | TB | R | RBI | TBB | IBB | SO | HBP | SH | SF | SB | CS | SB% | GDP | Avg | OBP | SLG |
| 1986 San Francisco | NL | 84 | 216 | 54 | 18 | 3 | 2 | (1 | 1) | 84 | 27 | 25 | 33 | 4 | 34 | 2 | 4 | 1 | 1 | 3 | .25 | 3 | .250 | .353 | .389 |
| 1987 San Francisco | NL | 126 | 357 | 116 | 18 | 2 | 9 | (7 | 2) | 165 | 50 | 51 | 43 | 5 | 50 | 0 | 4 | 2 | 6 | 0 | 1.00 | 6 | .325 | .396 | .462 |
| 1988 San Francisco | NL | 139 | 389 | 104 | 15 | 0 | 3 | (3 | 0) | 128 | 44 | 50 | 56 | 13 | 65 | 0 | 1 | 3 | 6 | 5 | .55 | 10 | .267 | .357 | .329 |
| 1989 Montreal | NL | 76 | 136 | 30 | 8 | 1 | 1 | (0 | 1) | 43 | 12 | 12 | 19 | 0 | 30 | 1 | 1 | 2 | 1 | 3 | .25 | 4 | .221 | .316 | .316 |
| 1990 Montreal | NL | 96 | 161 | 39 | 7 | 1 | 1 | (0 | 1) | 51 | 22 | 18 | 37 | 2 | 31 | 1 | 0 | 1 | 1 | 2 | .33 | 2 | .242 | .385 | .317 |
| 5 ML YEARS | | 521 | 1259 | 343 | 66 | 7 | 16 | (11 | 5) | 471 | 155 | 156 | 188 | 24 | 210 | 4 | 10 | 9 | 15 | 13 | .54 | 25 | .272 | .366 | .374 |

## Jay Aldrich

**Pitches:** Right **Bats:** Right **Pos:** RP **Ht:** 6' 3" **Wt:** 210 **Born:** 04/14/61 **Age:** 30

| | | HOW MUCH HE PITCHED | | | | | | WHAT HE GAVE UP | | | | | | | | | | | | THE RESULTS | | | | | |
|---|---|---|---|---|---|---|---|---|---|---|---|---|---|---|---|---|---|---|---|---|---|---|---|---|---|
| Year Team | Lg | G | GS | CG | GF | IP | BFP | H | R | ER | HR | SH | SF | HB | TBB | IBB | SO | WP | Bk | W | L | Pct. | ShO | Sv | ERA |
| 1987 Milwaukee | AL | 31 | 0 | 0 | 9 | 58.1 | 253 | 71 | 33 | 32 | 8 | 3 | 3 | 2 | 13 | 3 | 22 | 1 | 1 | 3 | 1 | .750 | 0 | 0 | 4.94 |
| 1989 2 ML Teams | | 24 | 0 | 0 | 10 | 38.1 | 160 | 31 | 16 | 14 | 3 | 2 | 1 | 1 | 19 | 3 | 19 | 2 | 0 | 2 | 2 | .500 | 0 | 1 | 3.29 |
| 1990 Baltimore | AL | 7 | 0 | 0 | 2 | 12 | 61 | 17 | 13 | 11 | 1 | 2 | 0 | 0 | 7 | 3 | 5 | 0 | 1 | 1 | 2 | .333 | 0 | 1 | 8.25 |
| 1989 Milwaukee | AL | 16 | 0 | 0 | 8 | 26 | 110 | 24 | 11 | 11 | 3 | 1 | 0 | 1 | 13 | 2 | 12 | 2 | 0 | 1 | 0 | 1.000 | 0 | 1 | 3.81 |
| Atlanta | NL | 8 | 0 | 0 | 2 | 12.1 | 50 | 7 | 5 | 3 | 0 | 1 | 1 | 0 | 6 | 1 | 7 | 0 | 0 | 1 | 2 | .333 | 0 | 0 | 2.19 |
| 3 ML YEARS | | 62 | 0 | 0 | 21 | 108.2 | 474 | 119 | 62 | 57 | 12 | 7 | 4 | 3 | 39 | 9 | 46 | 3 | 2 | 6 | 5 | .545 | 0 | 2 | 4.72 |

## Gerald Alexander

**Pitches:** Right **Bats:** Right **Pos:** SP **Ht:** 5'11" **Wt:** 190 **Born:** 03/26/68 **Age:** 23

| | | HOW MUCH HE PITCHED | | | | | | WHAT HE GAVE UP | | | | | | | | | | | | THE RESULTS | | | | | |
|---|---|---|---|---|---|---|---|---|---|---|---|---|---|---|---|---|---|---|---|---|---|---|---|---|---|
| Year Team | Lg | G | GS | CG | GF | IP | BFP | H | R | ER | HR | SH | SF | HB | TBB | IBB | SO | WP | Bk | W | L | Pct. | ShO | Sv | ERA |
| 1989 Rangers | R | 6 | 0 | 0 | 5 | 6.1 | 19 | 3 | 0 | 0 | 0 | 0 | 0 | 0 | 0 | 0 | 9 | 0 | 0 | 0 | 0 | .000 | 0 | 4 | 0.00 |
| Charlotte | A | 14 | 6 | 0 | 5 | 53 | 215 | 36 | 12 | 10 | 1 | 2 | 1 | 2 | 16 | 0 | 41 | 5 | 0 | 2 | 3 | .400 | 0 | 2 | 1.70 |
| 1990 Charlotte | A | 7 | 7 | 0 | 0 | 42.2 | 163 | 24 | 7 | 3 | 0 | 0 | 0 | 1 | 14 | 0 | 39 | 2 | 0 | 6 | 1 | .857 | 0 | 0 | 0.63 |
| Okla City | AAA | 20 | 20 | 2 | 0 | 118.2 | 510 | 126 | 58 | 54 | 6 | 2 | 4 | 3 | 45 | 0 | 94 | 6 | 1 | 13 | 2 | .867 | 1 | 0 | 4.10 |
| 1990 Texas | AL | 3 | 2 | 0 | 1 | 7 | 39 | 14 | 6 | 6 | 0 | 0 | 1 | 1 | 5 | 0 | 8 | 0 | 0 | 0 | 0 | .000 | 0 | 0 | 7.71 |

## Beau Allred

**Bats:** Left **Throws:** Left **Pos:** CF **Ht:** 6' 0" **Wt:** 193 **Born:** 06/04/65 **Age:** 26

| | | BATTING | | | | | | | | | | | | | | | | | BASERUNNING | | | | PERCENTAGES | | |
|---|---|---|---|---|---|---|---|---|---|---|---|---|---|---|---|---|---|---|---|---|---|---|---|---|---|
| Year Team | Lg | G | AB | H | 2B | 3B | HR | (Hm | Rd) | TB | R | RBI | TBB | IBB | SO | HBP | SH | SF | SB | CS | SB% | GDP | Avg | OBP | SLG |
| 1987 Burlington | R | 54 | 167 | 57 | 14 | 1 | 10 | -- | -- | 103 | 39 | 38 | 35 | 3 | 33 | 1 | 2 | 4 | 4 | 0 | 1.00 | 1 | .341 | .449 | .617 |
| 1988 Kinston | A | 126 | 397 | 100 | 23 | 3 | 15 | -- | -- | 174 | 66 | 74 | 59 | 4 | 112 | 5 | 0 | 8 | 6 | 0 | 1.00 | 5 | .252 | .350 | .438 |
| 1989 Canton-Akrn | AA | 118 | 412 | 125 | 23 | 5 | 14 | -- | -- | 200 | 67 | 75 | 56 | 2 | 88 | 2 | 2 | 8 | 16 | 5 | .76 | 8 | .303 | .383 | .485 |
| Colo Sprngs | AAA | 11 | 47 | 13 | 3 | 0 | 1 | -- | -- | 19 | 8 | 4 | 2 | 1 | 10 | 0 | 0 | 0 | 0 | 3 | .00 | 2 | .277 | .306 | .404 |
| 1990 Colo Sprngs | AAA | 115 | 378 | 105 | 23 | 6 | 13 | -- | -- | 179 | 79 | 74 | 60 | 1 | 54 | 4 | 2 | 7 | 6 | 3 | .67 | 5 | .278 | .376 | .474 |
| 1989 Cleveland | AL | 13 | 24 | 6 | 3 | 0 | 0 | (0 | 0) | 9 | 0 | 1 | 2 | 0 | 10 | 0 | 0 | 0 | 0 | 0 | .00 | 0 | .250 | .308 | .375 |
| 1990 Cleveland | AL | 4 | 16 | 3 | 1 | 0 | 1 | (0 | 1) | 7 | 2 | 2 | 2 | 0 | 3 | 0 | 0 | 0 | 0 | 0 | .00 | 0 | .188 | .278 | .438 |
| 2 ML YEARS | | 17 | 40 | 9 | 4 | 0 | 1 | (0 | 1) | 16 | 2 | 3 | 4 | 0 | 13 | 0 | 0 | 0 | 0 | 0 | .00 | 0 | .225 | .295 | .400 |

## Roberto Alomar

**Bats:** Both **Throws:** Right **Pos:** 2B **Ht:** 6' 0" **Wt:** 175 **Born:** 02/05/68 **Age:** 23

| | | BATTING | | | | | | | | | | | | | | | | | BASERUNNING | | | | PERCENTAGES | | |
|---|---|---|---|---|---|---|---|---|---|---|---|---|---|---|---|---|---|---|---|---|---|---|---|---|---|
| Year Team | Lg | G | AB | H | 2B | 3B | HR | (Hm | Rd) | TB | R | RBI | TBB | IBB | SO | HBP | SH | SF | SB | CS | SB% | GDP | Avg | OBP | SLG |
| 1988 San Diego | NL | 143 | 545 | 145 | 24 | 6 | 9 | (5 | 4) | 208 | 84 | 41 | 47 | 5 | 83 | 3 | 16 | 0 | 24 | 6 | .80 | 15 | .266 | .328 | .382 |
| 1989 San Diego | NL | 158 | 623 | 184 | 27 | 1 | 7 | (3 | 4) | 234 | 82 | 56 | 53 | 4 | 76 | 1 | 17 | 8 | 42 | 17 | .71 | 10 | .295 | .347 | .376 |
| 1990 San Diego | NL | 147 | 586 | 168 | 27 | 5 | 6 | (4 | 2) | 223 | 80 | 60 | 48 | 1 | 72 | 2 | 5 | 5 | 24 | 7 | .77 | 16 | .287 | .340 | .381 |
| 3 ML YEARS | | 448 | 1754 | 497 | 78 | 12 | 22 | (12 | 10) | 665 | 246 | 157 | 148 | 10 | 231 | 6 | 38 | 13 | 90 | 30 | .75 | 41 | .283 | .339 | .379 |

## Sandy Alomar Jr

**Bats:** Right **Throws:** Right **Pos:** C **Ht:** 6' 5" **Wt:** 200 **Born:** 06/18/66 **Age:** 25

| BATTING | | | | | | | | | | | | | | | | | | | BASERUNNING | | | | PERCENTAGES | | |
|---|---|---|---|---|---|---|---|---|---|---|---|---|---|---|---|---|---|---|---|---|---|---|---|---|---|
| Year Team | Lg | G | AB | H | 2B | 3B | HR | (Hm | Rd) | TB | R | RBI | TBB | IBB | SO | HBP | SH | SF | SB | CS | SB% | GDP | Avg | OBP | SLG |
| 1988 San Diego | NL | 1 | 1 | 0 | 0 | 0 | 0 | (0 | 0) | 0 | 0 | 0 | 0 | 0 | 1 | 0 | 0 | 0 | 0 | 0 | .00 | 0 | .000 | .000 | .000 |
| 1989 San Diego | NL | 7 | 19 | 4 | 1 | 0 | 1 | (1 | 0) | 8 | 1 | 6 | 3 | 1 | 3 | 0 | 0 | 0 | 0 | 0 | .00 | 1 | .211 | .318 | .421 |
| 1990 Cleveland | AL | 132 | 445 | 129 | 26 | 2 | 9 | (5 | 4) | 186 | 60 | 66 | 25 | 2 | 46 | 2 | 5 | 6 | 4 | 1 | .80 | 10 | .290 | .326 | .418 |
| 3 ML YEARS | | 140 | 465 | 133 | 27 | 2 | 10 | (6 | 4) | 194 | 61 | 72 | 28 | 3 | 50 | 2 | 5 | 6 | 4 | 1 | .80 | 11 | .286 | .325 | .417 |

## Moises Alou

**Bats:** Right **Throws:** Right **Pos:** LF **Ht:** 6' 3" **Wt:** 175 **Born:** 07/03/66 **Age:** 24

| BATTING | | | | | | | | | | | | | | | | | | | BASERUNNING | | | | PERCENTAGES | | |
|---|---|---|---|---|---|---|---|---|---|---|---|---|---|---|---|---|---|---|---|---|---|---|---|---|---|
| Year Team | Lg | G | AB | H | 2B | 3B | HR | (Hm | Rd) | TB | R | RBI | TBB | IBB | SO | HBP | SH | SF | SB | CS | SB% | GDP | Avg | OBP | SLG |
| 1986 Watertown | A | 69 | 254 | 60 | 9 | 8 | 6 | -- | -- | 103 | 30 | 35 | 22 | 1 | 72 | 1 | 0 | 0 | 14 | 8 | .64 | 5 | .236 | .300 | .406 |
| 1987 Macon | A | 4 | 8 | 1 | 0 | 0 | 0 | -- | -- | 1 | 1 | 0 | 2 | 0 | 4 | 0 | 0 | 0 | 0 | 0 | .00 | 0 | .125 | .300 | .125 |
| Watertown | A | 39 | 117 | 25 | 6 | 2 | 4 | -- | -- | 47 | 20 | 18 | 16 | 0 | 36 | 4 | 0 | 2 | 6 | 3 | .67 | 0 | .214 | .324 | .402 |
| 1988 Augusta | A | 105 | 358 | 112 | 23 | 5 | 7 | -- | -- | 166 | 58 | 62 | 51 | 4 | 84 | 5 | 0 | 7 | 24 | 12 | .67 | 5 | .313 | .399 | .464 |
| 1989 Salem | A | 86 | 321 | 97 | 29 | 2 | 14 | -- | -- | 172 | 50 | 53 | 35 | 2 | 69 | 3 | 0 | 2 | 12 | 5 | .71 | 6 | .302 | .374 | .536 |
| Harrisburg | AA | 54 | 205 | 60 | 5 | 2 | 3 | -- | -- | 78 | 36 | 19 | 17 | 1 | 38 | 0 | 0 | 2 | 8 | 4 | .67 | 1 | .293 | .344 | .380 |
| 1990 Harrisburg | AA | 36 | 132 | 39 | 12 | 2 | 3 | -- | -- | 64 | 19 | 22 | 16 | 3 | 21 | 1 | 0 | 1 | 7 | 4 | .64 | 5 | .295 | .373 | .485 |
| Buffalo | AAA | 75 | 271 | 74 | 4 | 6 | 5 | -- | -- | 105 | 38 | 31 | 30 | 0 | 43 | 2 | 2 | 4 | 9 | 4 | .69 | 8 | .273 | .345 | .387 |
| Indianapolis | AAA | 15 | 55 | 12 | 1 | 0 | 0 | -- | -- | 13 | 6 | 6 | 3 | 0 | 7 | 0 | 0 | 1 | 4 | 3 | .57 | 0 | .218 | .254 | .236 |
| 1990 2 ML Teams | | 16 | 20 | 4 | 0 | 1 | 0 | (0 | 0) | 6 | 4 | 0 | 0 | 0 | 3 | 0 | 1 | 0 | 0 | 0 | .00 | 1 | .200 | .200 | .300 |
| 1990 Pittsburgh | NL | 2 | 5 | 1 | 0 | 0 | 0 | (0 | 0) | 1 | 0 | 0 | 0 | 0 | 0 | 0 | 0 | 0 | 0 | 0 | .00 | 1 | .200 | .200 | .200 |
| Montreal | NL | 14 | 15 | 3 | 0 | 1 | 0 | (0 | 0) | 5 | 4 | 0 | 0 | 0 | 3 | 0 | 1 | 0 | 0 | 0 | .00 | 0 | .200 | .200 | .333 |

## Larry Andersen

**Pitches:** Right **Bats:** Right **Pos:** RP **Ht:** 6' 3" **Wt:** 205 **Born:** 05/06/53 **Age:** 38

| HOW MUCH HE PITCHED | | | | | | | | WHAT HE GAVE UP | | | | | | | | | | | | THE RESULTS | | | | | |
|---|---|---|---|---|---|---|---|---|---|---|---|---|---|---|---|---|---|---|---|---|---|---|---|---|---|
| Year Team | Lg | G | GS | CG | GF | IP | BFP | H | R | ER | HR | SH | SF | HB | TBB | IBB | SO | WP | Bk | W | L | Pct. | ShO | Sv | ERA |
| 1975 Cleveland | AL | 3 | 0 | 0 | 1 | 6 | 23 | 4 | 3 | 3 | 0 | 0 | 1 | 0 | 2 | 0 | 4 | 2 | 0 | 0 | 0 | .000 | 0 | 0 | 4.50 |
| 1977 Cleveland | AL | 11 | 0 | 0 | 7 | 14 | 62 | 10 | 7 | 5 | 1 | 3 | 0 | 0 | 9 | 3 | 8 | 1 | 0 | 0 | 1 | .000 | 0 | 0 | 3.21 |
| 1979 Cleveland | AL | 8 | 0 | 0 | 4 | 17 | 77 | 25 | 14 | 14 | 3 | 1 | 2 | 0 | 4 | 0 | 7 | 0 | 0 | 0 | 0 | .000 | 0 | 0 | 7.41 |
| 1981 Seattle | AL | 41 | 0 | 0 | 23 | 68 | 273 | 57 | 27 | 20 | 4 | 0 | 3 | 2 | 18 | 2 | 40 | 0 | 0 | 3 | 3 | .500 | 0 | 5 | 2.65 |
| 1982 Seattle | AL | 40 | 1 | 0 | 14 | 79.2 | 354 | 100 | 56 | 53 | 16 | 2 | 3 | 4 | 23 | 1 | 32 | 2 | 0 | 0 | 0 | .000 | 0 | 1 | 5.99 |
| 1983 Philadelphia | NL | 17 | 0 | 0 | 4 | 26.1 | 106 | 19 | 7 | 7 | 0 | 1 | 1 | 0 | 9 | 1 | 14 | 1 | 1 | 1 | 0 | 1.000 | 0 | 0 | 2.39 |
| 1984 Philadelphia | NL | 64 | 0 | 0 | 25 | 90.2 | 376 | 85 | 32 | 24 | 5 | 4 | 4 | 0 | 25 | 6 | 54 | 2 | 1 | 3 | 7 | .300 | 0 | 4 | 2.38 |
| 1985 Philadelphia | NL | 57 | 0 | 0 | 19 | 73 | 318 | 78 | 41 | 35 | 5 | 3 | 1 | 3 | 26 | 4 | 50 | 1 | 1 | 3 | 3 | .500 | 0 | 3 | 4.32 |
| 1986 2 ML Teams | | 48 | 0 | 0 | 8 | 77.1 | 323 | 83 | 30 | 26 | 2 | 10 | 5 | 1 | 26 | 10 | 42 | 1 | 0 | 2 | 1 | .667 | 0 | 1 | 3.03 |
| 1987 Houston | NL | 67 | 0 | 0 | 31 | 101.2 | 440 | 95 | 46 | 39 | 7 | 7 | 4 | 2 | 41 | 10 | 94 | 1 | 0 | 9 | 5 | .643 | 0 | 5 | 3.45 |
| 1988 Houston | NL | 53 | 0 | 0 | 25 | 82.2 | 350 | 82 | 29 | 27 | 3 | 3 | 3 | 1 | 20 | 8 | 66 | 1 | 2 | 2 | 4 | .333 | 0 | 5 | 2.94 |
| 1989 Houston | NL | 60 | 0 | 0 | 21 | 87.2 | 351 | 63 | 19 | 15 | 2 | 4 | 5 | 0 | 24 | 4 | 85 | 2 | 1 | 4 | 4 | .500 | 0 | 3 | 1.54 |
| 1990 2 ML Teams | | 65 | 0 | 0 | 24 | 95.2 | 387 | 79 | 22 | 19 | 2 | 5 | 5 | 2 | 27 | 5 | 93 | 4 | 0 | 5 | 2 | .714 | 0 | 7 | 1.79 |
| 1986 Philadelphia | NL | 10 | 0 | 0 | 1 | 12.2 | 55 | 19 | 8 | 6 | 0 | 2 | 1 | 0 | 3 | 0 | 9 | 0 | 0 | 0 | 0 | .000 | 0 | 0 | 4.26 |
| Houston | NL | 38 | 0 | 0 | 7 | 64.2 | 268 | 64 | 22 | 20 | 2 | 8 | 4 | 1 | 23 | 10 | 33 | 1 | 0 | 2 | 1 | .667 | 0 | 1 | 2.78 |
| 1990 Houston | NL | 50 | 0 | 0 | 20 | 73.2 | 301 | 61 | 19 | 16 | 2 | 5 | 5 | 1 | 24 | 5 | 68 | 2 | 0 | 5 | 2 | .714 | 0 | 6 | 1.95 |
| Boston | AL | 15 | 0 | 0 | 4 | 22 | 86 | 18 | 3 | 3 | 0 | 0 | 0 | 1 | 3 | 0 | 25 | 2 | 0 | 0 | 0 | .000 | 0 | 1 | 1.23 |
| 13 ML YEARS | | 534 | 1 | 0 | 206 | 819.2 | 3440 | 780 | 333 | 287 | 50 | 43 | 37 | 15 | 254 | 54 | 589 | 18 | 6 | 32 | 30 | .516 | 0 | 34 | 3.15 |

## Allan Anderson

**Pitches:** Left **Bats:** Left **Pos:** SP **Ht:** 6' 0" **Wt:** 194 **Born:** 01/07/64 **Age:** 27

| HOW MUCH HE PITCHED | | | | | | | | WHAT HE GAVE UP | | | | | | | | | | | | THE RESULTS | | | | | |
|---|---|---|---|---|---|---|---|---|---|---|---|---|---|---|---|---|---|---|---|---|---|---|---|---|---|
| Year Team | Lg | G | GS | CG | GF | IP | BFP | H | R | ER | HR | SH | SF | HB | TBB | IBB | SO | WP | Bk | W | L | Pct. | ShO | Sv | ERA |
| 1986 Minnesota | AL | 21 | 10 | 1 | 3 | 84.1 | 371 | 106 | 54 | 52 | 11 | 2 | 3 | 1 | 30 | 3 | 51 | 2 | 2 | 3 | 6 | .333 | 0 | 0 | 5.55 |
| 1987 Minnesota | AL | 4 | 2 | 0 | 0 | 12.1 | 61 | 20 | 15 | 15 | 3 | 0 | 0 | 0 | 10 | 2 | 3 | 0 | 0 | 1 | 0 | 1.000 | 0 | 0 | 10.95 |
| 1988 Minnesota | AL | 30 | 30 | 3 | 0 | 202.1 | 815 | 199 | 70 | 55 | 14 | 3 | 5 | 7 | 37 | 1 | 83 | 1 | 4 | 16 | 9 | .640 | 1 | 0 | 2.45 |
| 1989 Minnesota | AL | 33 | 33 | 4 | 0 | 196.2 | 846 | 214 | 97 | 83 | 15 | 4 | 5 | 7 | 53 | 1 | 69 | 5 | 0 | 17 | 10 | .630 | 1 | 0 | 3.80 |
| 1990 Minnesota | AL | 31 | 31 | 5 | 0 | 188.2 | 797 | 214 | 106 | 95 | 20 | 4 | 8 | 5 | 39 | 1 | 82 | 4 | 3 | 7 | 18 | .280 | 1 | 0 | 4.53 |
| 5 ML YEARS | | 119 | 106 | 13 | 3 | 684.1 | 2890 | 753 | 342 | 300 | 63 | 13 | 21 | 20 | 169 | 8 | 288 | 12 | 9 | 44 | 43 | .506 | 3 | 0 | 3.95 |

## Brady Anderson

**Bats:** Left **Throws:** Left **Pos:** LF/CF **Ht:** 6' 1" **Wt:** 186 **Born:** 01/18/64 **Age:** 27

| BATTING | | | | | | | | | | | | | | | | | | | BASERUNNING | | | | PERCENTAGES | | |
|---|---|---|---|---|---|---|---|---|---|---|---|---|---|---|---|---|---|---|---|---|---|---|---|---|---|
| Year Team | Lg | G | AB | H | 2B | 3B | HR | (Hm | Rd) | TB | R | RBI | TBB | IBB | SO | HBP | SH | SF | SB | CS | SB% | GDP | Avg | OBP | SLG |
| 1988 2 ML Teams | | 94 | 325 | 69 | 13 | 4 | 1 | (1 | 0) | 93 | 31 | 21 | 23 | 0 | 75 | 4 | 11 | 1 | 10 | 6 | .63 | 3 | .212 | .272 | .286 |
| 1989 Baltimore | AL | 94 | 266 | 55 | 12 | 2 | 4 | (2 | 2) | 83 | 44 | 16 | 43 | 6 | 45 | 3 | 5 | 0 | 16 | 4 | .80 | 4 | .207 | .324 | .312 |

| Year Team | Lg | G | AB | H | 2B | 3B | HR | (Hm | Rd) | TB | R | RBI | TBB | IBB | SO | HBP | SH | SF | SB | CS | SB% | GDP | Avg | OBP | SLG |
|---|---|---|---|---|---|---|---|---|---|---|---|---|---|---|---|---|---|---|---|---|---|---|---|---|---|
| 1990 Baltimore | AL | 89 | 234 | 54 | 5 | 2 | 3 | (1 | 2) | 72 | 24 | 24 | 31 | 2 | 46 | 5 | 4 | 5 | 15 | 2 | .88 | 5 | .231 | .327 | .308 |
| 1988 Boston | AL | 41 | 148 | 34 | 5 | 3 | 0 | (0 | 0) | 45 | 14 | 12 | 15 | 0 | 35 | 4 | 4 | 1 | 4 | 2 | .67 | 2 | .230 | .315 | .304 |
| Baltimore | AL | 53 | 177 | 35 | 8 | 1 | 1 | (1 | 0) | 48 | 17 | 9 | 8 | 0 | 40 | 0 | 7 | 0 | 6 | 4 | .60 | 1 | .198 | .232 | .271 |
| 3 ML YEARS | | 277 | 825 | 178 | 30 | 8 | 8 | (4 | 4) | 248 | 99 | 61 | 97 | 8 | 166 | 12 | 20 | 6 | 41 | 12 | .77 | 12 | .216 | .305 | .301 |

## Dave Anderson

**Bats:** Right **Throws:** Right **Pos:** SS/2B **Ht:** 6' 2" **Wt:** 191 **Born:** 08/01/60 **Age:** 30

| | | | | | BATTING | | | | | | | | | | | | | | BASERUNNING | | | | PERCENTAGES | | |
|---|---|---|---|---|---|---|---|---|---|---|---|---|---|---|---|---|---|---|---|---|---|---|---|---|---|
| Year Team | Lg | G | AB | H | 2B | 3B | HR | (Hm | Rd) | TB | R | RBI | TBB | IBB | SO | HBP | SH | SF | SB | CS | SB% | GDP | Avg | OBP | SLG |
| 1983 Los Angeles | NL | 61 | 115 | 19 | 4 | 2 | 1 | (1 | 0) | 30 | 12 | 2 | 12 | 1 | 15 | 0 | 4 | 0 | 6 | 3 | .67 | 1 | .165 | .244 | .261 |
| 1984 Los Angeles | NL | 121 | 374 | 94 | 16 | 2 | 3 | (2 | 1) | 123 | 51 | 34 | 45 | 4 | 55 | 2 | 7 | 5 | 15 | 5 | .75 | 8 | .251 | .331 | .329 |
| 1985 Los Angeles | NL | 77 | 221 | 44 | 6 | 0 | 4 | (1 | 3) | 62 | 24 | 18 | 35 | 3 | 42 | 1 | 4 | 1 | 5 | 4 | .56 | 4 | .199 | .310 | .281 |
| 1986 Los Angeles | NL | 92 | 216 | 53 | 9 | 0 | 1 | (0 | 1) | 65 | 31 | 15 | 22 | 1 | 39 | 0 | 2 | 1 | 5 | 1 | .83 | 11 | .245 | .314 | .301 |
| 1987 Los Angeles | NL | 108 | 265 | 62 | 12 | 3 | 1 | (0 | 1) | 83 | 32 | 13 | 24 | 1 | 43 | 1 | 6 | 1 | 9 | 5 | .64 | 2 | .234 | .299 | .313 |
| 1988 Los Angeles | NL | 116 | 285 | 71 | 10 | 2 | 2 | (1 | 1) | 91 | 31 | 20 | 32 | 4 | 45 | 1 | 5 | 2 | 4 | 2 | .67 | 9 | .249 | .325 | .319 |
| 1989 Los Angeles | NL | 87 | 140 | 32 | 2 | 0 | 1 | (1 | 0) | 37 | 15 | 14 | 17 | 1 | 26 | 0 | 5 | 1 | 2 | 0 | 1.00 | 1 | .229 | .310 | .264 |
| 1990 San Francisco | NL | 60 | 100 | 35 | 5 | 1 | 1 | (1 | 0) | 45 | 14 | 6 | 3 | 0 | 20 | 0 | 1 | 0 | 1 | 2 | .33 | 2 | .350 | .369 | .450 |
| 8 ML YEARS | | 722 | 1716 | 410 | 64 | 10 | 14 | (7 | 7) | 536 | 210 | 122 | 190 | 15 | 285 | 5 | 34 | 11 | 47 | 22 | .68 | 38 | .239 | .315 | .312 |

## Kent Anderson

**Bats:** Right **Throws:** Right **Pos:** SS/3B **Ht:** 6' 1" **Wt:** 180 **Born:** 08/12/63 **Age:** 27

| | | | | | BATTING | | | | | | | | | | | | | | BASERUNNING | | | | PERCENTAGES | | |
|---|---|---|---|---|---|---|---|---|---|---|---|---|---|---|---|---|---|---|---|---|---|---|---|---|---|
| Year Team | Lg | G | AB | H | 2B | 3B | HR | (Hm | Rd) | TB | R | RBI | TBB | IBB | SO | HBP | SH | SF | SB | CS | SB% | GDP | Avg | OBP | SLG |
| 1984 Peoria | A | 67 | 223 | 50 | 9 | 1 | 1 | -- | -- | 64 | 24 | 16 | 23 | 1 | 34 | 1 | 2 | 0 | 6 | 3 | .67 | 3 | .224 | .300 | .287 |
| 1985 Redwood | A | 117 | 420 | 105 | 17 | 1 | 1 | -- | -- | 127 | 53 | 47 | 40 | 1 | 66 | 2 | 10 | 2 | 4 | 7 | .36 | 8 | .250 | .317 | .302 |
| 1986 Palm Sprngs | A | 69 | 240 | 67 | 14 | 0 | 2 | -- | -- | 87 | 37 | 35 | 14 | 0 | 28 | 3 | 2 | 3 | 4 | 3 | .57 | 3 | .279 | .323 | .363 |
| 1987 Edmonton | AAA | 57 | 181 | 42 | 4 | 5 | 3 | -- | -- | 65 | 27 | 20 | 19 | 0 | 26 | 3 | 5 | 1 | 2 | 1 | .67 | 2 | .232 | .314 | .359 |
| 1988 Edmonton | AAA | 113 | 374 | 94 | 22 | 3 | 2 | -- | -- | 128 | 50 | 39 | 26 | 0 | 67 | 3 | 4 | 6 | 10 | 3 | .77 | 12 | .251 | .301 | .342 |
| 1989 Edmonton | AAA | 4 | 12 | 4 | 0 | 0 | 0 | -- | -- | 4 | 3 | 1 | 4 | 0 | 1 | 0 | 1 | 0 | 1 | 0 | 1.00 | 1 | .333 | .500 | .333 |
| 1990 Edmonton | AAA | 18 | 59 | 16 | 6 | 1 | 0 | -- | -- | 24 | 10 | 7 | 8 | 0 | 8 | 2 | 2 | 0 | 1 | 1 | .50 | 2 | .271 | .377 | .407 |
| 1989 California | AL | 86 | 223 | 51 | 6 | 1 | 0 | (0 | 0) | 59 | 27 | 17 | 17 | 0 | 42 | 1 | 6 | 1 | 1 | 2 | .33 | 4 | .229 | .285 | .265 |
| 1990 California | AL | 49 | 143 | 44 | 6 | 1 | 1 | (1 | 0) | 55 | 16 | 5 | 13 | 1 | 19 | 1 | 4 | 0 | 0 | 2 | .00 | 4 | .308 | .369 | .385 |
| 2 ML YEARS | | 135 | 366 | 95 | 12 | 2 | 1 | (1 | 0) | 114 | 43 | 22 | 30 | 1 | 61 | 2 | 10 | 1 | 1 | 4 | .20 | 8 | .260 | .318 | .311 |

## Scott Anderson

**Pitches:** Right **Bats:** Right **Pos:** SP **Ht:** 6' 6" **Wt:** 190 **Born:** 05/01/62 **Age:** 29

| | | HOW MUCH HE PITCHED | | | | | | WHAT HE GAVE UP | | | | | | | | | | | THE RESULTS | | | | | |
|---|---|---|---|---|---|---|---|---|---|---|---|---|---|---|---|---|---|---|---|---|---|---|---|---|
| Year Team | Lg | G | GS | CG | GF | IP | BFP | H | R | ER | HR | SH | SF | HB | TBB | IBB | SO | WP | Bk | W | L | Pct. | ShO | Sv | ERA |
| 1987 Texas | AL | 8 | 0 | 0 | 2 | 11.1 | 59 | 17 | 12 | 12 | 0 | 1 | 0 | 1 | 8 | 2 | 6 | 2 | 0 | 0 | 1 | .000 | 0 | 0 | 9.53 |
| 1990 Montreal | NL | 4 | 3 | 0 | 1 | 18 | 71 | 12 | 6 | 6 | 1 | 1 | 1 | 0 | 5 | 0 | 16 | 0 | 0 | 0 | 1 | .000 | 0 | 0 | 3.00 |
| 2 ML YEARS | | 12 | 3 | 0 | 3 | 29.1 | 130 | 29 | 18 | 18 | 1 | 2 | 1 | 1 | 13 | 2 | 22 | 2 | 0 | 0 | 2 | .000 | 0 | 0 | 5.52 |

## Eric Anthony

**Bats:** Left **Throws:** Left **Pos:** RF/LF **Ht:** 6' 2" **Wt:** 195 **Born:** 11/08/67 **Age:** 23

| | | | | | BATTING | | | | | | | | | | | | | | BASERUNNING | | | | PERCENTAGES | | |
|---|---|---|---|---|---|---|---|---|---|---|---|---|---|---|---|---|---|---|---|---|---|---|---|---|---|
| Year Team | Lg | G | AB | H | 2B | 3B | HR | (Hm | Rd) | TB | R | RBI | TBB | IBB | SO | HBP | SH | SF | SB | CS | SB% | GDP | Avg | OBP | SLG |
| 1986 Astros | R | 13 | 12 | 3 | 0 | 0 | 0 | -- | -- | 3 | 2 | 0 | 5 | 0 | 5 | 1 | 0 | 0 | 1 | 0 | 1.00 | 1 | .250 | .500 | .250 |
| 1987 Astros | R | 60 | 216 | 57 | 11 | 6 | 10 | -- | -- | 110 | 38 | 46 | 26 | 3 | 58 | 2 | 0 | 1 | 2 | 2 | .50 | 4 | .264 | .347 | .509 |
| 1988 Asheville | A | 115 | 439 | 120 | 36 | 1 | 29 | -- | -- | 245 | 73 | 89 | 40 | 5 | 101 | 3 | 0 | 3 | 10 | 4 | .71 | 10 | .273 | .336 | .558 |
| 1989 Columbus | AA | 107 | 403 | 121 | 16 | 2 | 28 | -- | -- | 225 | 67 | 79 | 35 | 5 | 127 | 3 | 0 | 3 | 14 | 9 | .61 | 3 | .300 | .358 | .558 |
| Tucson | AAA | 12 | 46 | 10 | 3 | 0 | 3 | -- | -- | 22 | 10 | 11 | 6 | 0 | 11 | 0 | 0 | 0 | 0 | 0 | .00 | 2 | .217 | .308 | .478 |
| 1990 Columbus | AA | 4 | 12 | 2 | 0 | 0 | 1 | -- | -- | 5 | 2 | 3 | 3 | 0 | 4 | 0 | 0 | 0 | 0 | 0 | .00 | 0 | .167 | .333 | .417 |
| Tucson | AAA | 40 | 161 | 46 | 10 | 2 | 6 | -- | -- | 78 | 28 | 26 | 17 | 0 | 41 | 1 | 0 | 3 | 8 | 3 | .73 | 4 | .286 | .352 | .484 |
| 1989 Houston | NL | 25 | 61 | 11 | 2 | 0 | 4 | (2 | 2) | 25 | 7 | 7 | 9 | 2 | 16 | 0 | 0 | 0 | 0 | 0 | .00 | 1 | .180 | .286 | .410 |
| 1990 Houston | NL | 84 | 239 | 46 | 8 | 0 | 10 | (5 | 5) | 84 | 26 | 29 | 29 | 3 | 78 | 2 | 1 | 6 | 5 | 0 | 1.00 | 4 | .192 | .279 | .351 |
| 2 ML YEARS | | 109 | 300 | 57 | 10 | 0 | 14 | (7 | 7) | 109 | 33 | 36 | 38 | 5 | 94 | 2 | 1 | 6 | 5 | 0 | 1.00 | 5 | .190 | .280 | .363 |

## Kevin Appier

**Pitches:** Right **Bats:** Right **Pos:** SP/RP **Ht:** 6' 2" **Wt:** 180 **Born:** 12/06/67 **Age:** 23

| | | HOW MUCH HE PITCHED | | | | | | WHAT HE GAVE UP | | | | | | | | | | | THE RESULTS | | | | | |
|---|---|---|---|---|---|---|---|---|---|---|---|---|---|---|---|---|---|---|---|---|---|---|---|---|
| Year Team | Lg | G | GS | CG | GF | IP | BFP | H | R | ER | HR | SH | SF | HB | TBB | IBB | SO | WP | Bk | W | L | Pct. | ShO | Sv | ERA |
| 1987 Eugene | A | 15 | 15 | 0 | 0 | 77 | 340 | 81 | 43 | 26 | 2 | 0 | 1 | 2 | 29 | 0 | 72 | 7 | 1 | 5 | 2 | .714 | 0 | 0 | 3.04 |
| 1988 Baseball Cy | A | 24 | 24 | 1 | 0 | 147.1 | 601 | 134 | 58 | 45 | 1 | 4 | 6 | 2 | 39 | 5 | 112 | 7 | 4 | 10 | 9 | .526 | 0 | 0 | 2.75 |
| Memphis | AA | 3 | 3 | 0 | 0 | 19.2 | 75 | 11 | 5 | 4 | 0 | 0 | 1 | 0 | 7 | 0 | 18 | 1 | 0 | 2 | 0 | 1.000 | 0 | 0 | 1.83 |
| 1989 Omaha | AAA | 22 | 22 | 3 | 0 | 139 | 594 | 141 | 70 | 61 | 6 | 2 | 4 | 2 | 42 | 1 | 109 | 5 | 1 | 8 | 8 | .500 | 2 | 0 | 3.95 |
| 1990 Omaha | AAA | 3 | 3 | 0 | 0 | 18 | 69 | 15 | 3 | 3 | 0 | 0 | 0 | 1 | 3 | 0 | 17 | 0 | 0 | 2 | 0 | 1.000 | 0 | 0 | 1.50 |
| 1989 Kansas City | AL | 6 | 5 | 0 | 0 | 21.2 | 106 | 34 | 22 | 22 | 3 | 0 | 3 | 0 | 12 | 1 | 10 | 0 | 0 | 1 | 4 | .200 | 0 | 0 | 9.14 |

| Year Team | Lg | G | GS | CG | GF | IP | BFP | H | R | ER | HR | SH | SF | HB | TBB | IBB | SO | WP | Bk | W | L | Pct. | ShO | Sv | ERA |
|---|---|---|---|---|---|---|---|---|---|---|---|---|---|---|---|---|---|---|---|---|---|---|---|---|---|
| 1990 Kansas City | AL | 32 | 24 | 3 | 1 | 185.2 | 784 | 179 | 67 | 57 | 13 | 5 | 9 | 6 | 54 | 2 | 127 | 6 | 1 | 12 | 8 | .600 | 3 | 0 | 2.76 |
| 2 ML YEARS | | 38 | 29 | 3 | 1 | 207.1 | 890 | 213 | 89 | 79 | 16 | 5 | 12 | 6 | 66 | 3 | 137 | 6 | 1 | 13 | 12 | .520 | 3 | 0 | 3.43 |

## Luis Aquino

**Pitches:** Right **Bats:** Right **Pos:** RP/SP **Ht:** 6' 1" **Wt:** 175 **Born:** 05/19/65 **Age:** 26

| HOW MUCH HE PITCHED | | | | | | | | WHAT HE GAVE UP | | | | | | | | | | | | THE RESULTS | | | | | |
|---|---|---|---|---|---|---|---|---|---|---|---|---|---|---|---|---|---|---|---|---|---|---|---|---|---|
| Year Team | Lg | G | GS | CG | GF | IP | BFP | H | R | ER | HR | SH | SF | HB | TBB | IBB | SO | WP | Bk | W | L | Pct. | ShO | Sv | ERA |
| 1986 Toronto | AL | 7 | 0 | 0 | 3 | 11.1 | 50 | 14 | 8 | 8 | 2 | 0 | 1 | 0 | 3 | 1 | 5 | 1 | 0 | 1 | 1 | .500 | 0 | 0 | 6.35 |
| 1988 Kansas City | AL | 7 | 5 | 1 | 0 | 29 | 136 | 33 | 15 | 9 | 1 | 0 | 1 | 1 | 17 | 0 | 11 | 1 | 1 | 1 | 0 | 1.000 | 1 | 0 | 2.79 |
| 1989 Kansas City | AL | 34 | 16 | 2 | 7 | 141.1 | 591 | 148 | 62 | 55 | 6 | 2 | 4 | 4 | 35 | 4 | 68 | 4 | 0 | 6 | 8 | .429 | 1 | 0 | 3.50 |
| 1990 Kansas City | AL | 20 | 3 | 1 | 3 | 68.1 | 287 | 59 | 25 | 24 | 6 | 5 | 2 | 4 | 27 | 6 | 28 | 3 | 1 | 4 | 1 | .800 | 0 | 0 | 3.16 |
| 4 ML YEARS | | 68 | 24 | 4 | 13 | 250 | 1064 | 254 | 110 | 96 | 15 | 7 | 8 | 9 | 82 | 11 | 112 | 9 | 2 | 12 | 10 | .545 | 2 | 0 | 3.46 |

## Jack Armstrong

**Pitches:** Right **Bats:** Right **Pos:** SP **Ht:** 6' 5" **Wt:** 220 **Born:** 03/07/65 **Age:** 26

| HOW MUCH HE PITCHED | | | | | | | | WHAT HE GAVE UP | | | | | | | | | | | | THE RESULTS | | | | | |
|---|---|---|---|---|---|---|---|---|---|---|---|---|---|---|---|---|---|---|---|---|---|---|---|---|---|
| Year Team | Lg | G | GS | CG | GF | IP | BFP | H | R | ER | HR | SH | SF | HB | TBB | IBB | SO | WP | Bk | W | L | Pct. | ShO | Sv | ERA |
| 1988 Cincinnati | NL | 14 | 13 | 0 | 0 | 65.1 | 293 | 63 | 44 | 42 | 8 | 4 | 5 | 0 | 38 | 2 | 45 | 3 | 2 | 4 | 7 | .364 | 0 | 0 | 5.79 |
| 1989 Cincinnati | NL | 9 | 8 | 0 | 1 | 42.2 | 187 | 40 | 24 | 22 | 5 | 2 | 1 | 0 | 21 | 4 | 23 | 0 | 0 | 2 | 3 | .400 | 0 | 0 | 4.64 |
| 1990 Cincinnati | NL | 29 | 27 | 2 | 1 | 166 | 704 | 151 | 72 | 63 | 9 | 8 | 5 | 6 | 59 | 7 | 110 | 7 | 5 | 12 | 9 | .571 | 1 | 0 | 3.42 |
| 3 ML YEARS | | 52 | 48 | 2 | 2 | 274 | 1184 | 254 | 140 | 127 | 22 | 14 | 11 | 6 | 118 | 13 | 178 | 10 | 7 | 18 | 19 | .486 | 1 | 0 | 4.17 |

## Brad Arnsberg

**Pitches:** Right **Bats:** Right **Pos:** RP **Ht:** 6' 4" **Wt:** 215 **Born:** 08/20/63 **Age:** 27

| HOW MUCH HE PITCHED | | | | | | | | WHAT HE GAVE UP | | | | | | | | | | | | THE RESULTS | | | | | |
|---|---|---|---|---|---|---|---|---|---|---|---|---|---|---|---|---|---|---|---|---|---|---|---|---|---|
| Year Team | Lg | G | GS | CG | GF | IP | BFP | H | R | ER | HR | SH | SF | HB | TBB | IBB | SO | WP | Bk | W | L | Pct. | ShO | Sv | ERA |
| 1986 New York | AL | 2 | 1 | 0 | 1 | 8 | 39 | 13 | 3 | 3 | 1 | 0 | 0 | 0 | 1 | 0 | 3 | 0 | 0 | 0 | 0 | .000 | 0 | 0 | 3.38 |
| 1987 New York | AL | 6 | 2 | 0 | 2 | 19.1 | 91 | 22 | 12 | 12 | 5 | 0 | 2 | 0 | 13 | 3 | 14 | 1 | 0 | 1 | 3 | .250 | 0 | 0 | 5.59 |
| 1989 Texas | AL | 16 | 1 | 0 | 3 | 48 | 209 | 45 | 27 | 22 | 6 | 1 | 1 | 3 | 22 | 0 | 26 | 6 | 2 | 2 | 1 | .667 | 0 | 1 | 4.13 |
| 1990 Texas | AL | 53 | 0 | 0 | 20 | 62.2 | 277 | 56 | 20 | 15 | 4 | 2 | 2 | 2 | 33 | 1 | 44 | 8 | 0 | 6 | 1 | .857 | 0 | 5 | 2.15 |
| 4 ML YEARS | | 77 | 4 | 0 | 26 | 138 | 616 | 136 | 62 | 52 | 16 | 3 | 5 | 5 | 69 | 4 | 87 | 15 | 2 | 9 | 5 | .643 | 0 | 6 | 3.39 |

## Paul Assenmacher

**Pitches:** Left **Bats:** Left **Pos:** RP **Ht:** 6' 3" **Wt:** 200 **Born:** 12/10/60 **Age:** 30

| HOW MUCH HE PITCHED | | | | | | | | WHAT HE GAVE UP | | | | | | | | | | | | THE RESULTS | | | | | |
|---|---|---|---|---|---|---|---|---|---|---|---|---|---|---|---|---|---|---|---|---|---|---|---|---|---|
| Year Team | Lg | G | GS | CG | GF | IP | BFP | H | R | ER | HR | SH | SF | HB | TBB | IBB | SO | WP | Bk | W | L | Pct. | ShO | Sv | ERA |
| 1986 Atlanta | NL | 61 | 0 | 0 | 27 | 68.1 | 287 | 61 | 23 | 19 | 5 | 7 | 1 | 0 | 26 | 4 | 56 | 2 | 3 | 7 | 3 | .700 | 0 | 7 | 2.50 |
| 1987 Atlanta | NL | 52 | 0 | 0 | 10 | 54.2 | 251 | 58 | 41 | 31 | 8 | 2 | 1 | 1 | 24 | 4 | 39 | 0 | 0 | 1 | 1 | .500 | 0 | 2 | 5.10 |
| 1988 Atlanta | NL | 64 | 0 | 0 | 32 | 79.1 | 329 | 72 | 28 | 27 | 4 | 8 | 1 | 1 | 32 | 11 | 71 | 7 | 0 | 8 | 7 | .533 | 0 | 5 | 3.06 |
| 1989 2 ML Teams | | 63 | 0 | 0 | 17 | 76.2 | 331 | 74 | 37 | 34 | 3 | 9 | 3 | 1 | 28 | 8 | 79 | 3 | 1 | 3 | 4 | .429 | 0 | 0 | 3.99 |
| 1990 Chicago | NL | 74 | 1 | 0 | 21 | 103 | 426 | 90 | 33 | 32 | 10 | 10 | 3 | 1 | 36 | 8 | 95 | 2 | 0 | 7 | 2 | .778 | 0 | 10 | 2.80 |
| 1989 Atlanta | NL | 49 | 0 | 0 | 14 | 57.2 | 247 | 55 | 26 | 23 | 2 | 7 | 2 | 1 | 16 | 7 | 64 | 3 | 1 | 1 | 3 | .250 | 0 | 0 | 3.59 |
| Chicago | NL | 14 | 0 | 0 | 3 | 19 | 84 | 19 | 11 | 11 | 1 | 2 | 1 | 0 | 12 | 1 | 15 | 0 | 0 | 2 | 1 | .667 | 0 | 0 | 5.21 |
| 5 ML YEARS | | 314 | 1 | 0 | 107 | 382 | 1624 | 355 | 162 | 143 | 30 | 36 | 9 | 4 | 146 | 35 | 340 | 14 | 4 | 26 | 17 | .605 | 0 | 24 | 3.37 |

## Don August

**Pitches:** Right **Bats:** Right **Pos:** RP **Ht:** 6' 3" **Wt:** 190 **Born:** 07/03/63 **Age:** 27

| HOW MUCH HE PITCHED | | | | | | | | WHAT HE GAVE UP | | | | | | | | | | | | THE RESULTS | | | | | |
|---|---|---|---|---|---|---|---|---|---|---|---|---|---|---|---|---|---|---|---|---|---|---|---|---|---|
| Year Team | Lg | G | GS | CG | GF | IP | BFP | H | R | ER | HR | SH | SF | HB | TBB | IBB | SO | WP | Bk | W | L | Pct. | ShO | Sv | ERA |
| 1988 Milwaukee | AL | 24 | 22 | 6 | 0 | 148.1 | 614 | 137 | 55 | 51 | 12 | 4 | 3 | 0 | 48 | 6 | 66 | 5 | 0 | 13 | 7 | .650 | 1 | 0 | 3.09 |
| 1989 Milwaukee | AL | 31 | 25 | 2 | 2 | 142.1 | 648 | 175 | 93 | 84 | 17 | 2 | 7 | 2 | 58 | 2 | 51 | 3 | 1 | 12 | 12 | .500 | 1 | 0 | 5.31 |
| 1990 Milwaukee | AL | 5 | 0 | 0 | 1 | 11 | 51 | 13 | 10 | 8 | 0 | 2 | 0 | 0 | 5 | 0 | 2 | 2 | 0 | 0 | 3 | .000 | 0 | 0 | 6.55 |
| 3 ML YEARS | | 60 | 47 | 8 | 3 | 301.2 | 1313 | 325 | 158 | 143 | 29 | 8 | 10 | 2 | 111 | 8 | 119 | 10 | 1 | 25 | 22 | .532 | 2 | 0 | 4.27 |

## Steve Avery

**Pitches:** Left **Bats:** Left **Pos:** SP **Ht:** 6' 4" **Wt:** 180 **Born:** 04/14/70 **Age:** 21

| HOW MUCH HE PITCHED | | | | | | | | WHAT HE GAVE UP | | | | | | | | | | | | THE RESULTS | | | | | |
|---|---|---|---|---|---|---|---|---|---|---|---|---|---|---|---|---|---|---|---|---|---|---|---|---|---|
| Year Team | Lg | G | GS | CG | GF | IP | BFP | H | R | ER | HR | SH | SF | HB | TBB | IBB | SO | WP | Bk | W | L | Pct. | ShO | Sv | ERA |
| 1988 Pulaski | R | 10 | 10 | 3 | 0 | 66 | 249 | 38 | 16 | 11 | 2 | 1 | 1 | 1 | 19 | 0 | 80 | 5 | 1 | 7 | 1 | .875 | 2 | 0 | 1.50 |
| 1989 Durham | A | 13 | 13 | 3 | 0 | 86.2 | 337 | 59 | 22 | 14 | 5 | 5 | 0 | 1 | 20 | 1 | 90 | 4 | 1 | 6 | 4 | .600 | 1 | 0 | 1.45 |
| Greenville | AA | 13 | 13 | 1 | 0 | 84.1 | 341 | 68 | 32 | 26 | 3 | 4 | 1 | 1 | 34 | 0 | 75 | 4 | 0 | 6 | 3 | .667 | 0 | 0 | 2.77 |
| 1990 Richmond | AAA | 13 | 13 | 3 | 0 | 82.1 | 343 | 85 | 35 | 32 | 7 | 6 | 2 | 2 | 21 | 0 | 69 | 5 | 0 | 5 | 5 | .500 | 0 | 0 | 3.50 |
| 1990 Atlanta | NL | 21 | 20 | 1 | 1 | 99 | 466 | 121 | 79 | 62 | 7 | 14 | 4 | 2 | 45 | 2 | 75 | 5 | 1 | 3 | 11 | .214 | 1 | 0 | 5.64 |

## Oscar Azocar

**Bats:** Left **Throws:** Left **Pos:** LF/RF **Ht:** 6' 1" **Wt:** 170 **Born:** 02/21/65 **Age:** 26

| BATTING | | | | | | | | | | | | | | | | | | | BASERUNNING | | | | PERCENTAGES | | |
|---|---|---|---|---|---|---|---|---|---|---|---|---|---|---|---|---|---|---|---|---|---|---|---|---|---|
| Year Team | Lg | G | AB | H | 2B | 3B | HR | (Hm | Rd) | TB | R | RBI | TBB | IBB | SO | HBP | SH | SF | SB | CS | SB% | GDP | Avg | OBP | SLG |
| 1987 Ft.Laudrdle | A | 53 | 192 | 69 | 11 | 3 | 6 | -- | -- | 104 | 25 | 39 | 3 | 0 | 18 | 0 | 0 | 0 | 5 | 5 | .50 | 6 | .359 | .369 | .542 |
| 1988 Albany | AA | 138 | 543 | 148 | 22 | 9 | 6 | -- | -- | 206 | 60 | 66 | 12 | 6 | 48 | 2 | 4 | 4 | 21 | 6 | .78 | 15 | .273 | .289 | .379 |
| 1989 Albany | AA | 92 | 362 | 101 | 15 | 2 | 4 | -- | -- | 132 | 50 | 47 | 10 | 4 | 31 | 0 | 8 | 4 | 11 | 6 | .65 | 6 | .279 | .295 | .365 |
| Columbus | AAA | 37 | 130 | 38 | 9 | 3 | 1 | -- | -- | 56 | 14 | 12 | 7 | 0 | 10 | 1 | 1 | 0 | 3 | 1 | .75 | 1 | .292 | .333 | .431 |
| 1990 Columbus | AAA | 94 | 374 | 109 | 20 | 5 | 5 | -- | -- | 154 | 49 | 52 | 9 | 2 | 26 | 2 | 4 | 7 | 8 | 8 | .50 | 15 | .291 | .306 | .412 |
| 1990 New York | AL | 65 | 214 | 53 | 8 | 0 | 5 | (3 | 2) | 76 | 18 | 19 | 2 | 0 | 15 | 1 | 0 | 1 | 7 | 0 | 1.00 | 1 | .248 | .257 | .355 |

## Wally Backman

**Bats:** Both **Throws:** Right **Pos:** 3B/2B **Ht:** 5' 9" **Wt:** 168 **Born:** 09/22/59 **Age:** 31

| BATTING | | | | | | | | | | | | | | | | | | | BASERUNNING | | | | PERCENTAGES | | |
|---|---|---|---|---|---|---|---|---|---|---|---|---|---|---|---|---|---|---|---|---|---|---|---|---|---|
| Year Team | Lg | G | AB | H | 2B | 3B | HR | (Hm | Rd) | TB | R | RBI | TBB | IBB | SO | HBP | SH | SF | SB | CS | SB% | GDP | Avg | OBP | SLG |
| 1980 New York | NL | 27 | 93 | 30 | 1 | 1 | 0 | (0 | 0) | 33 | 12 | 9 | 11 | 1 | 14 | 1 | 4 | 1 | 2 | 3 | .40 | 3 | .323 | .396 | .355 |
| 1981 New York | NL | 26 | 36 | 10 | 2 | 0 | 0 | (0 | 0) | 12 | 5 | 0 | 4 | 0 | 7 | 0 | 2 | 0 | 1 | 0 | 1.00 | 0 | .278 | .350 | .333 |
| 1982 New York | NL | 96 | 261 | 71 | 13 | 2 | 3 | (1 | 2) | 97 | 37 | 22 | 49 | 1 | 47 | 0 | 2 | 0 | 8 | 7 | .53 | 6 | .272 | .387 | .372 |
| 1983 New York | NL | 26 | 42 | 7 | 0 | 1 | 0 | (0 | 0) | 9 | 6 | 3 | 2 | 0 | 8 | 0 | 1 | 0 | 0 | 0 | .00 | 2 | .167 | .205 | .214 |
| 1984 New York | NL | 128 | 436 | 122 | 19 | 2 | 1 | (0 | 1) | 148 | 68 | 26 | 56 | 2 | 63 | 0 | 5 | 2 | 32 | 9 | .78 | 13 | .280 | .360 | .339 |
| 1985 New York | NL | 145 | 520 | 142 | 24 | 5 | 1 | (0 | 1) | 179 | 77 | 38 | 36 | 1 | 72 | 1 | 14 | 3 | 30 | 12 | .71 | 3 | .273 | .320 | .344 |
| 1986 New York | NL | 124 | 387 | 124 | 18 | 2 | 1 | (1 | 0) | 149 | 67 | 27 | 36 | 1 | 32 | 0 | 14 | 3 | 13 | 7 | .65 | 3 | .320 | .376 | .385 |
| 1987 New York | NL | 94 | 300 | 75 | 6 | 1 | 1 | (0 | 1) | 86 | 43 | 23 | 25 | 0 | 43 | 0 | 9 | 1 | 11 | 3 | .79 | 5 | .250 | .307 | .287 |
| 1988 New York | NL | 99 | 294 | 89 | 12 | 0 | 0 | (0 | 0) | 101 | 44 | 17 | 41 | 1 | 49 | 1 | 9 | 2 | 9 | 5 | .64 | 6 | .303 | .388 | .344 |
| 1989 Minnesota | AL | 87 | 299 | 69 | 9 | 2 | 1 | (0 | 1) | 85 | 33 | 26 | 32 | 0 | 45 | 1 | 4 | 1 | 1 | 1 | .50 | 4 | .231 | .306 | .284 |
| 1990 Pittsburgh | NL | 104 | 315 | 92 | 21 | 3 | 2 | (0 | 2) | 125 | 62 | 28 | 42 | 1 | 53 | 1 | 0 | 3 | 6 | 3 | .67 | 5 | .292 | .374 | .397 |
| 11 ML YEARS | | 956 | 2983 | 831 | 125 | 19 | 10 | (2 | 8) | 1024 | 454 | 219 | 334 | 8 | 433 | 5 | 64 | 16 | 113 | 50 | .69 | 50 | .279 | .351 | .343 |

## Carlos Baerga

**Bats:** Both **Throws:** Right **Pos:** 3B/SS **Ht:** 5'11" **Wt:** 165 **Born:** 11/04/68 **Age:** 22

| BATTING | | | | | | | | | | | | | | | | | | | BASERUNNING | | | | PERCENTAGES | | |
|---|---|---|---|---|---|---|---|---|---|---|---|---|---|---|---|---|---|---|---|---|---|---|---|---|---|
| Year Team | Lg | G | AB | H | 2B | 3B | HR | (Hm | Rd) | TB | R | RBI | TBB | IBB | SO | HBP | SH | SF | SB | CS | SB% | GDP | Avg | OBP | SLG |
| 1986 Charleston | A | 111 | 378 | 102 | 14 | 4 | 7 | -- | -- | 145 | 57 | 41 | 26 | 1 | 60 | 5 | 2 | 5 | 6 | 1 | .86 | 4 | .270 | .321 | .384 |
| 1987 Chston-Sc | A | 134 | 515 | 157 | 23 | 9 | 7 | -- | -- | 219 | 83 | 50 | 38 | 7 | 107 | 12 | 6 | 2 | 26 | 21 | .55 | 10 | .305 | .365 | .425 |
| 1988 Wichita | AA | 122 | 444 | 121 | 28 | 1 | 12 | -- | -- | 187 | 67 | 65 | 31 | 2 | 83 | 9 | 0 | 3 | 4 | 4 | .50 | 8 | .273 | .331 | .421 |
| 1989 Las Vegas | AAA | 132 | 520 | 143 | 28 | 2 | 10 | -- | -- | 205 | 63 | 74 | 30 | 5 | 98 | 6 | 0 | 6 | 6 | 6 | .50 | 10 | .275 | .319 | .394 |
| 1990 Colo Sprngs | AAA | 12 | 50 | 19 | 2 | 1 | 1 | -- | -- | 26 | 11 | 11 | 5 | 2 | 4 | 0 | 0 | 0 | 1 | 0 | 1.00 | 4 | .380 | .436 | .520 |
| 1990 Cleveland | AL | 108 | 312 | 81 | 17 | 2 | 7 | (3 | 4) | 123 | 46 | 47 | 16 | 2 | 57 | 4 | 1 | 5 | 0 | 2 | .00 | 4 | .260 | .300 | .394 |

## Kevin Baez

**Bats:** Right **Throws:** Right **Pos:** SS **Ht:** 6' 0" **Wt:** 160 **Born:** 01/10/67 **Age:** 24

| BATTING | | | | | | | | | | | | | | | | | | | BASERUNNING | | | | PERCENTAGES | | |
|---|---|---|---|---|---|---|---|---|---|---|---|---|---|---|---|---|---|---|---|---|---|---|---|---|---|
| Year Team | Lg | G | AB | H | 2B | 3B | HR | (Hm | Rd) | TB | R | RBI | TBB | IBB | SO | HBP | SH | SF | SB | CS | SB% | GDP | Avg | OBP | SLG |
| 1988 Little Fls | A | 70 | 218 | 58 | 7 | 1 | 1 | -- | -- | 70 | 23 | 19 | 32 | 1 | 30 | 2 | 2 | 3 | 7 | 3 | .70 | 3 | .266 | .361 | .321 |
| 1989 Columbia | A | 123 | 426 | 108 | 25 | 1 | 5 | -- | -- | 150 | 59 | 44 | 58 | 3 | 53 | 6 | 9 | 3 | 11 | 9 | .55 | 5 | .254 | .349 | .352 |
| 1990 Jackson | AA | 106 | 327 | 76 | 11 | 0 | 2 | -- | -- | 93 | 29 | 29 | 37 | 4 | 44 | 2 | 11 | 2 | 3 | 4 | .43 | 7 | .232 | .313 | .284 |
| 1990 New York | NL | 5 | 12 | 2 | 1 | 0 | 0 | (0 | 0) | 3 | 0 | 0 | 0 | 0 | 0 | 0 | 0 | 0 | 0 | 0 | .00 | 2 | .167 | .167 | .250 |

## Scott Bailes

**Pitches:** Left **Bats:** Left **Pos:** RP **Ht:** 6' 2" **Wt:** 184 **Born:** 12/18/62 **Age:** 28

| HOW MUCH HE PITCHED | | | | | | | | WHAT HE GAVE UP | | | | | | | | | | | | THE RESULTS | | | | | |
|---|---|---|---|---|---|---|---|---|---|---|---|---|---|---|---|---|---|---|---|---|---|---|---|---|---|
| Year Team | Lg | G | GS | CG | GF | IP | BFP | H | R | ER | HR | SH | SF | HB | TBB | IBB | SO | WP | Bk | W | L | Pct. | ShO | Sv | ERA |
| 1986 Cleveland | AL | 62 | 10 | 0 | 22 | 112.2 | 500 | 123 | 70 | 62 | 12 | 7 | 4 | 1 | 43 | 5 | 60 | 4 | 2 | 10 | 10 | .500 | 0 | 7 | 4.95 |
| 1987 Cleveland | AL | 39 | 17 | 0 | 15 | 120.1 | 551 | 145 | 75 | 62 | 21 | 4 | 6 | 4 | 47 | 1 | 65 | 3 | 0 | 7 | 8 | .467 | 0 | 6 | 4.64 |
| 1988 Cleveland | AL | 37 | 21 | 5 | 7 | 145 | 617 | 149 | 89 | 79 | 22 | 5 | 4 | 2 | 46 | 0 | 53 | 2 | 3 | 9 | 14 | .391 | 2 | 0 | 4.90 |
| 1989 Cleveland | AL | 34 | 11 | 0 | 9 | 113.2 | 473 | 116 | 57 | 54 | 7 | 5 | 5 | 3 | 29 | 4 | 47 | 3 | 0 | 5 | 9 | .357 | 0 | 0 | 4.28 |
| 1990 California | AL | 27 | 0 | 0 | 6 | 35.1 | 173 | 46 | 30 | 25 | 8 | 1 | 5 | 1 | 20 | 0 | 16 | 0 | 0 | 2 | 0 | 1.000 | 0 | 0 | 6.37 |
| 5 ML YEARS | | 199 | 59 | 5 | 59 | 527 | 2314 | 579 | 321 | 282 | 70 | 22 | 24 | 11 | 185 | 10 | 241 | 12 | 5 | 33 | 41 | .446 | 2 | 13 | 4.82 |

## Mark Bailey

**Bats:** Both **Throws:** Right **Pos:** C **Ht:** 6' 3" **Wt:** 200 **Born:** 11/04/61 **Age:** 29

| BATTING | | | | | | | | | | | | | | | | | | | BASERUNNING | | | | PERCENTAGES | | |
|---|---|---|---|---|---|---|---|---|---|---|---|---|---|---|---|---|---|---|---|---|---|---|---|---|---|
| Year Team | Lg | G | AB | H | 2B | 3B | HR | (Hm | Rd) | TB | R | RBI | TBB | IBB | SO | HBP | SH | SF | SB | CS | SB% | GDP | Avg | OBP | SLG |
| 1984 Houston | NL | 108 | 344 | 73 | 16 | 1 | 9 | (7 | 2) | 118 | 38 | 34 | 53 | 4 | 71 | 2 | 1 | 3 | 0 | 1 | .00 | 7 | .212 | .318 | .343 |

| Year Team | Lg | G | AB | H | 2B | 3B | HR | (Hm | Rd) | TB | R | RBI | TBB | IBB | SO | HBP | SH | SF | SB | CS | SB% | GDP | Avg | OBP | SLG |
|---|---|---|---|---|---|---|---|---|---|---|---|---|---|---|---|---|---|---|---|---|---|---|---|---|---|
| 1985 Houston | NL | 114 | 332 | 88 | 14 | 0 | 10 | (4 | 6) | 132 | 47 | 45 | 67 | 13 | 70 | 1 | 1 | 1 | 0 | 2 | .00 | 16 | .265 | .389 | .398 |
| 1986 Houston | NL | 57 | 153 | 27 | 5 | 0 | 4 | (1 | 3) | 44 | 9 | 15 | 28 | 6 | 45 | 0 | 0 | 1 | 1 | 1 | .50 | 7 | .176 | .302 | .288 |
| 1987 Houston | NL | 35 | 64 | 13 | 1 | 0 | 0 | (0 | 0) | 14 | 5 | 3 | 10 | 0 | 21 | 0 | 1 | 0 | 1 | 0 | 1.00 | 3 | .203 | .311 | .219 |
| 1988 Houston | NL | 8 | 23 | 3 | 0 | 0 | 0 | (0 | 0) | 3 | 1 | 0 | 5 | 0 | 6 | 0 | 0 | 0 | 0 | 1 | .00 | 1 | .130 | .286 | .130 |
| 1990 San Francisco | NL | 5 | 7 | 1 | 0 | 0 | 1 | (0 | 1) | 4 | 1 | 3 | 0 | 0 | 2 | 0 | 0 | 0 | 0 | 0 | .00 | 0 | .143 | .143 | .571 |
| 6 ML YEARS | | 327 | 923 | 205 | 36 | 1 | 24 | (12 | 12) | 315 | 101 | 100 | 163 | 23 | 215 | 3 | 3 | 5 | 2 | 5 | .29 | 34 | .222 | .339 | .341 |

## Harold Baines

**Bats:** Left **Throws:** Left **Pos:** DH **Ht:** 6' 2" **Wt:** 195 **Born:** 03/15/59 **Age:** 32

| | | BATTING | | | | | | | | | | | | | | | | | BASERUNNING | | | | PERCENTAGES | | |
|---|---|---|---|---|---|---|---|---|---|---|---|---|---|---|---|---|---|---|---|---|---|---|---|---|---|
| Year Team | Lg | G | AB | H | 2B | 3B | HR | (Hm | Rd) | TB | R | RBI | TBB | IBB | SO | HBP | SH | SF | SB | CS | SB% | GDP | Avg | OBP | SLG |
| 1980 Chicago | AL | 141 | 491 | 125 | 23 | 6 | 13 | (3 | 10) | 199 | 55 | 49 | 19 | 7 | 65 | 1 | 2 | 5 | 2 | 4 | .33 | 15 | .255 | .281 | .405 |
| 1981 Chicago | AL | 82 | 280 | 80 | 11 | 7 | 10 | (3 | 7) | 135 | 42 | 41 | 12 | 4 | 41 | 2 | 0 | 2 | 6 | 2 | .75 | 6 | .286 | .318 | .482 |
| 1982 Chicago | AL | 161 | 608 | 165 | 29 | 8 | 25 | (11 | 14) | 285 | 89 | 105 | 49 | 10 | 95 | 0 | 2 | 9 | 10 | 3 | .77 | 12 | .271 | .321 | .469 |
| 1983 Chicago | AL | 156 | 596 | 167 | 33 | 2 | 20 | (12 | 8) | 264 | 76 | 99 | 49 | 13 | 85 | 1 | 3 | 6 | 7 | 5 | .58 | 15 | .280 | .333 | .443 |
| 1984 Chicago | AL | 147 | 569 | 173 | 28 | 10 | 29 | (16 | 13) | 308 | 72 | 94 | 54 | 9 | 75 | 0 | 1 | 5 | 1 | 2 | .33 | 12 | .304 | .361 | .541 |
| 1985 Chicago | AL | 160 | 640 | 198 | 29 | 3 | 22 | (13 | 9) | 299 | 86 | 113 | 42 | 8 | 89 | 1 | 0 | 10 | 1 | 1 | .50 | 23 | .309 | .348 | .467 |
| 1986 Chicago | AL | 145 | 570 | 169 | 29 | 2 | 21 | (8 | 13) | 265 | 72 | 88 | 38 | 9 | 89 | 2 | 0 | 8 | 2 | 1 | .67 | 14 | .296 | .338 | .465 |
| 1987 Chicago | AL | 132 | 505 | 148 | 26 | 4 | 20 | (12 | 8) | 242 | 59 | 93 | 46 | 2 | 82 | 1 | 0 | 2 | 0 | 0 | .00 | 12 | .293 | .352 | .479 |
| 1988 Chicago | AL | 158 | 599 | 166 | 39 | 1 | 13 | (5 | 8) | 246 | 55 | 81 | 67 | 14 | 109 | 1 | 0 | 7 | 0 | 0 | .00 | 21 | .277 | .347 | .411 |
| 1989 2 ML Teams | | 146 | 505 | 156 | 29 | 1 | 16 | (5 | 11) | 235 | 73 | 72 | 73 | 13 | 79 | 1 | 0 | 4 | 0 | 3 | .00 | 15 | .309 | .395 | .465 |
| 1990 2 ML Teams | | 135 | 415 | 118 | 15 | 1 | 16 | (9 | 7) | 183 | 52 | 65 | 67 | 10 | 80 | 0 | 0 | 7 | 0 | 3 | .00 | 17 | .284 | .378 | .441 |
| 1989 Chicago | AL | 96 | 333 | 107 | 20 | 1 | 13 | (4 | 9) | 168 | 55 | 56 | 60 | 13 | 52 | 1 | 0 | 3 | 0 | 1 | .00 | 11 | .321 | .423 | .505 |
| Texas | AL | 50 | 172 | 49 | 9 | 0 | 3 | (1 | 2) | 67 | 18 | 16 | 13 | 0 | 27 | 0 | 0 | 1 | 0 | 2 | .00 | 4 | .285 | .333 | .390 |
| 1990 Texas | AL | 103 | 321 | 93 | 10 | 1 | 13 | (6 | 7) | 144 | 41 | 44 | 47 | 9 | 63 | 0 | 0 | 3 | 0 | 1 | .00 | 13 | .290 | .377 | .449 |
| Oakland | AL | 32 | 94 | 25 | 5 | 0 | 3 | (3 | 0) | 39 | 11 | 21 | 20 | 1 | 17 | 0 | 0 | 4 | 0 | 2 | .00 | 4 | .266 | .381 | .415 |
| 11 ML YEARS | | 1563 | 5778 | 1665 | 291 | 45 | 205 | (97 | 108) | 2661 | 731 | 900 | 516 | 99 | 889 | 10 | 8 | 65 | 29 | 24 | .55 | 162 | .288 | .344 | .461 |

## Doug Bair

**Pitches:** Right **Bats:** Right **Pos:** RP **Ht:** 6' 0" **Wt:** 180 **Born:** 08/22/49 **Age:** 41

| | | HOW MUCH HE PITCHED | | | | | | WHAT HE GAVE UP | | | | | | | | | | | | THE RESULTS | | | | | |
|---|---|---|---|---|---|---|---|---|---|---|---|---|---|---|---|---|---|---|---|---|---|---|---|---|---|
| Year Team | Lg | G | GS | CG | GF | IP | BFP | H | R | ER | HR | SH | SF | HB | TBB | IBB | SO | WP | Bk | W | L | Pct. | ShO | Sv | ERA |
| 1976 Pittsburgh | NL | 4 | 0 | 0 | 1 | 6 | 28 | 4 | 4 | 4 | 0 | 0 | 0 | 0 | 5 | 1 | 4 | 0 | 0 | 0 | 0 | .000 | 0 | 0 | 6.00 |
| 1977 Oakland | AL | 45 | 0 | 0 | 28 | 83 | 377 | 78 | 39 | 32 | 11 | 6 | 6 | 0 | 57 | 9 | 68 | 6 | 0 | 4 | 6 | .400 | 0 | 8 | 3.47 |
| 1978 Cincinnati | NL | 70 | 0 | 0 | 56 | 100 | 416 | 87 | 23 | 22 | 6 | 6 | 3 | 0 | 38 | 3 | 91 | 1 | 0 | 7 | 6 | .538 | 0 | 28 | 1.98 |
| 1979 Cincinnati | NL | 65 | 0 | 0 | 42 | 94 | 430 | 93 | 47 | 45 | 7 | 10 | 3 | 3 | 51 | 12 | 86 | 3 | 0 | 11 | 7 | .611 | 0 | 16 | 4.31 |
| 1980 Cincinnati | NL | 61 | 0 | 0 | 38 | 85 | 377 | 91 | 42 | 40 | 7 | 4 | 4 | 1 | 39 | 10 | 62 | 5 | 0 | 3 | 6 | .333 | 0 | 6 | 4.24 |
| 1981 2 ML Teams | | 35 | 0 | 0 | 20 | 54.2 | 234 | 55 | 34 | 31 | 5 | 2 | 0 | 0 | 19 | 4 | 30 | 3 | 0 | 4 | 2 | .667 | 0 | 1 | 5.10 |
| 1982 St. Louis | NL | 63 | 0 | 0 | 33 | 91.2 | 372 | 69 | 27 | 26 | 7 | 4 | 4 | 1 | 36 | 13 | 68 | 2 | 0 | 5 | 3 | .625 | 0 | 8 | 2.55 |
| 1983 2 ML Teams | | 53 | 1 | 0 | 19 | 85.1 | 355 | 75 | 38 | 34 | 12 | 3 | 1 | 1 | 32 | 7 | 60 | 1 | 0 | 8 | 4 | .667 | 0 | 5 | 3.59 |
| 1984 Detroit | AL | 47 | 1 | 0 | 12 | 93.2 | 387 | 82 | 42 | 39 | 10 | 3 | 4 | 0 | 36 | 2 | 57 | 3 | 0 | 5 | 3 | .625 | 0 | 4 | 3.75 |
| 1985 2 ML Teams | | 23 | 3 | 0 | 5 | 51 | 232 | 55 | 38 | 34 | 3 | 2 | 4 | 1 | 27 | 5 | 30 | 6 | 1 | 2 | 0 | 1.000 | 0 | 0 | 6.00 |
| 1986 Oakland | AL | 31 | 0 | 0 | 17 | 45 | 189 | 37 | 15 | 15 | 5 | 3 | 3 | 0 | 18 | 0 | 40 | 2 | 0 | 2 | 3 | .400 | 0 | 4 | 3.00 |
| 1987 Philadelphia | NL | 11 | 0 | 0 | 2 | 13.2 | 61 | 17 | 9 | 9 | 4 | 0 | 1 | 0 | 5 | 0 | 10 | 0 | 0 | 2 | 0 | 1.000 | 0 | 0 | 5.93 |
| 1988 Toronto | AL | 10 | 0 | 0 | 4 | 13.1 | 55 | 14 | 6 | 6 | 2 | 2 | 0 | 0 | 3 | 0 | 8 | 1 | 0 | 0 | 0 | .000 | 0 | 0 | 4.05 |
| 1989 Pittsburgh | NL | 44 | 0 | 0 | 17 | 67.1 | 276 | 52 | 19 | 17 | 4 | 1 | 1 | 0 | 28 | 10 | 56 | 7 | 0 | 2 | 3 | .400 | 0 | 1 | 2.27 |
| 1990 Pittsburgh | NL | 22 | 0 | 0 | 5 | 24.1 | 112 | 30 | 15 | 13 | 3 | 3 | 0 | 0 | 11 | 1 | 19 | 3 | 1 | 0 | 0 | .000 | 0 | 0 | 4.81 |
| 1981 Cincinnati | NL | 24 | 0 | 0 | 12 | 39 | 174 | 42 | 28 | 25 | 5 | 2 | 0 | 0 | 17 | 4 | 16 | 3 | 0 | 2 | 2 | .500 | 0 | 0 | 5.77 |
| St. Louis | NL | 11 | 0 | 0 | 8 | 15.2 | 60 | 13 | 6 | 6 | 0 | 0 | 0 | 0 | 2 | 0 | 14 | 0 | 0 | 2 | 0 | 1.000 | 0 | 1 | 3.45 |
| 1983 St. Louis | NL | 26 | 0 | 0 | 9 | 29.2 | 122 | 24 | 11 | 10 | 4 | 1 | 1 | 0 | 13 | 3 | 21 | 1 | 0 | 1 | 1 | .500 | 0 | 1 | 3.03 |
| Detroit | AL | 27 | 1 | 0 | 10 | 55.2 | 233 | 51 | 27 | 24 | 8 | 2 | 0 | 1 | 19 | 4 | 39 | 0 | 0 | 7 | 3 | .700 | 0 | 4 | 3.88 |
| 1985 Detroit | AL | 21 | 3 | 0 | 4 | 49 | 224 | 54 | 38 | 34 | 3 | 2 | 4 | 1 | 25 | 5 | 30 | 6 | 1 | 2 | 0 | 1.000 | 0 | 0 | 6.24 |
| St. Louis | NL | 2 | 0 | 0 | 1 | 2 | 8 | 1 | 0 | 0 | 0 | 0 | 0 | 0 | 2 | 0 | 0 | 0 | 0 | 0 | 0 | .000 | 0 | 0 | 0.00 |
| 15 ML YEARS | | 584 | 5 | 0 | 299 | 908 | 3901 | 839 | 398 | 367 | 86 | 49 | 34 | 7 | 405 | 77 | 689 | 43 | 2 | 55 | 43 | .561 | 0 | 81 | 3.64 |

## Doug Baker

**Bats:** Both **Throws:** Right **Pos:** 2B **Ht:** 5' 9" **Wt:** 165 **Born:** 04/03/61 **Age:** 30

| | | BATTING | | | | | | | | | | | | | | | | | BASERUNNING | | | | PERCENTAGES | | |
|---|---|---|---|---|---|---|---|---|---|---|---|---|---|---|---|---|---|---|---|---|---|---|---|---|---|
| Year Team | Lg | G | AB | H | 2B | 3B | HR | (Hm | Rd) | TB | R | RBI | TBB | IBB | SO | HBP | SH | SF | SB | CS | SB% | GDP | Avg | OBP | SLG |
| 1984 Detroit | AL | 43 | 108 | 20 | 4 | 1 | 0 | (0 | 0) | 26 | 15 | 12 | 7 | 0 | 22 | 1 | 2 | 0 | 3 | 0 | 1.00 | 1 | .185 | .241 | .241 |
| 1985 Detroit | AL | 15 | 27 | 5 | 1 | 0 | 0 | (0 | 0) | 6 | 4 | 1 | 0 | 0 | 9 | 0 | 0 | 0 | 0 | 0 | .00 | 0 | .185 | .185 | .222 |
| 1986 Detroit | AL | 13 | 24 | 3 | 1 | 0 | 0 | (0 | 0) | 4 | 1 | 0 | 2 | 0 | 7 | 0 | 4 | 0 | 0 | 0 | .00 | 0 | .125 | .192 | .167 |
| 1987 Detroit | AL | 8 | 1 | 0 | 0 | 0 | 0 | (0 | 0) | 0 | 0 | 0 | 0 | 0 | 1 | 0 | 0 | 0 | 0 | 0 | .00 | 0 | .000 | .000 | .000 |
| 1988 Minnesota | AL | 11 | 7 | 0 | 0 | 0 | 0 | (0 | 0) | 0 | 1 | 0 | 0 | 0 | 5 | 0 | 0 | 0 | 0 | 0 | .00 | 0 | .000 | .000 | .000 |
| 1989 Minnesota | AL | 43 | 78 | 23 | 5 | 1 | 0 | (0 | 0) | 30 | 17 | 9 | 9 | 0 | 18 | 2 | 2 | 1 | 0 | 0 | .00 | 0 | .295 | .378 | .385 |
| 1990 Minnesota | AL | 3 | 1 | 0 | 0 | 0 | 0 | (0 | 0) | 0 | 0 | 0 | 0 | 0 | 0 | 0 | 0 | 0 | 0 | 0 | .00 | 0 | .000 | .000 | .000 |
| 7 ML YEARS | | 136 | 246 | 51 | 11 | 2 | 0 | (0 | 0) | 66 | 38 | 22 | 18 | 0 | 62 | 3 | 8 | 1 | 3 | 0 | 1.00 | 1 | .207 | .269 | .268 |

## Steve Balboni

**Bats:** Right **Throws:** Right **Pos:** DH/1B **Ht:** 6' 3" **Wt:** 225 **Born:** 01/16/57 **Age:** 34

| BATTING | | | | | | | | | | | | | | | | | | | | BASERUNNING | | | | PERCENTAGES | | |
|---|---|---|---|---|---|---|---|---|---|---|---|---|---|---|---|---|---|---|---|---|---|---|---|---|---|---|
| Year Team | Lg | G | AB | H | 2B | 3B | HR | (Hm | Rd) | TB | R | RBI | TBB | IBB | SO | HBP | SH | SF | SB | CS | SB% | GDP | Avg | OBP | SLG |
| 1981 New York | AL | 4 | 7 | 2 | 1 | 1 | 0 | (0 | 0) | 5 | 2 | 2 | 1 | 0 | 4 | 0 | 0 | 0 | 0 | 0 | .00 | 0 | .286 | .375 | .714 |
| 1982 New York | AL | 33 | 107 | 20 | 2 | 1 | 2 | (0 | 2) | 30 | 8 | 4 | 6 | 0 | 34 | 0 | 0 | 1 | 0 | 0 | .00 | 1 | .187 | .228 | .280 |
| 1983 New York | AL | 32 | 86 | 20 | 2 | 0 | 5 | (0 | 5) | 37 | 8 | 17 | 8 | 0 | 23 | 0 | 0 | 1 | 0 | 0 | .00 | 2 | .233 | .295 | .430 |
| 1984 Kansas City | AL | 126 | 438 | 107 | 23 | 2 | 28 | (10 | 18) | 218 | 58 | 77 | 45 | 5 | 139 | 4 | 0 | 1 | 0 | 0 | .00 | 9 | .244 | .320 | .498 |
| 1985 Kansas City | AL | 160 | 600 | 146 | 28 | 2 | 36 | (17 | 19) | 286 | 74 | 88 | 52 | 4 | 166 | 5 | 0 | 5 | 1 | 1 | .50 | 14 | .243 | .307 | .477 |
| 1986 Kansas City | AL | 138 | 512 | 117 | 25 | 1 | 29 | (10 | 19) | 231 | 54 | 88 | 43 | 2 | 146 | 1 | 0 | 6 | 0 | 0 | .00 | 8 | .229 | .286 | .451 |
| 1987 Kansas City | AL | 121 | 386 | 80 | 11 | 1 | 24 | (8 | 16) | 165 | 44 | 60 | 34 | 1 | 97 | 2 | 0 | 3 | 0 | 0 | .00 | 11 | .207 | .273 | .427 |
| 1988 2 ML Teams | | 118 | 413 | 97 | 17 | 1 | 23 | (15 | 8) | 185 | 46 | 66 | 24 | 2 | 87 | 1 | 0 | 2 | 0 | 1 | .00 | 8 | .235 | .277 | .448 |
| 1989 New York | AL | 110 | 300 | 71 | 12 | 2 | 17 | (7 | 10) | 138 | 33 | 59 | 25 | 5 | 67 | 3 | 0 | 6 | 0 | 0 | .00 | 10 | .237 | .296 | .460 |
| 1990 New York | AL | 116 | 266 | 51 | 6 | 0 | 17 | (8 | 9) | 108 | 24 | 34 | 35 | 2 | 91 | 3 | 1 | 2 | 0 | 0 | .00 | 4 | .192 | .291 | .406 |
| 1988 Kansas City | AL | 21 | 63 | 9 | 2 | 0 | 2 | (1 | 1) | 17 | 2 | 5 | 1 | 0 | 20 | 0 | 0 | 0 | 0 | 0 | .00 | 0 | .143 | .156 | .270 |
| Seattle | AL | 97 | 350 | 88 | 15 | 1 | 21 | (14 | 7) | 168 | 44 | 61 | 23 | 2 | 67 | 1 | 0 | 2 | 0 | 1 | .00 | 8 | .251 | .298 | .480 |
| 10 ML YEARS | | 958 | 3115 | 711 | 127 | 11 | 181 | (75 | 106) | 1403 | 351 | 495 | 273 | 21 | 854 | 19 | 1 | 27 | 1 | 2 | .33 | 67 | .228 | .292 | .450 |

## Jeff Baldwin

**Bats:** Left **Throws:** Left **Pos:** LF **Ht:** 6' 1" **Wt:** 180 **Born:** 09/05/65 **Age:** 25

| BATTING | | | | | | | | | | | | | | | | | | | | BASERUNNING | | | | PERCENTAGES | | |
|---|---|---|---|---|---|---|---|---|---|---|---|---|---|---|---|---|---|---|---|---|---|---|---|---|---|---|
| Year Team | Lg | G | AB | H | 2B | 3B | HR | (Hm | Rd) | TB | R | RBI | TBB | IBB | SO | HBP | SH | SF | SB | CS | SB% | GDP | Avg | OBP | SLG |
| 1985 Astros | R | 47 | 138 | 36 | 2 | 2 | 0 | -- | -- | 42 | 17 | 12 | 23 | 0 | 22 | 2 | 1 | 2 | 5 | 3 | .63 | 1 | .261 | .370 | .304 |
| 1986 Asheville | A | 118 | 346 | 94 | 14 | 3 | 13 | -- | -- | 153 | 66 | 69 | 69 | 0 | 64 | 5 | 1 | 5 | 5 | 6 | .45 | 5 | .272 | .395 | .442 |
| 1987 Osceola | A | 127 | 437 | 133 | 20 | 5 | 1 | -- | -- | 166 | 70 | 56 | 83 | 9 | 49 | 1 | 3 | 8 | 5 | 7 | .42 | 12 | .304 | .410 | .380 |
| 1988 Columbus | AA | 39 | 91 | 20 | 1 | 0 | 0 | -- | -- | 21 | 7 | 6 | 12 | 2 | 19 | 1 | 0 | 0 | 2 | 1 | .67 | 1 | .220 | .317 | .231 |
| Osceola | A | 55 | 168 | 45 | 8 | 1 | 1 | -- | -- | 58 | 23 | 25 | 22 | 1 | 23 | 2 | 0 | 2 | 2 | 3 | .40 | 1 | .268 | .356 | .345 |
| 1989 Columbus | AA | 96 | 256 | 70 | 13 | 0 | 1 | -- | -- | 86 | 31 | 23 | 39 | 3 | 54 | 2 | 0 | 1 | 3 | 6 | .33 | 9 | .273 | .372 | .336 |
| 1990 Tucson | AAA | 19 | 37 | 5 | 1 | 0 | 0 | -- | -- | 6 | 4 | 5 | 7 | 2 | 11 | 0 | 0 | 0 | 0 | 0 | .00 | 1 | .135 | .273 | .162 |
| Columbus | AA | 77 | 250 | 79 | 11 | 1 | 7 | -- | -- | 113 | 43 | 37 | 33 | 4 | 34 | 3 | 0 | 4 | 0 | 1 | .00 | 8 | .316 | .397 | .452 |
| 1990 Houston | NL | 7 | 8 | 0 | 0 | 0 | 0 | (0 | 0) | 0 | 1 | 0 | 1 | 0 | 2 | 0 | 0 | 0 | 0 | 0 | .00 | 0 | .000 | .111 | .000 |

## Jeff Ballard

**Pitches:** Left **Bats:** Left **Pos:** RP/SP **Ht:** 6' 2" **Wt:** 198 **Born:** 08/13/63 **Age:** 27

| HOW MUCH HE PITCHED | | | | | | | | WHAT HE GAVE UP | | | | | | | | | | | | THE RESULTS | | | | | |
|---|---|---|---|---|---|---|---|---|---|---|---|---|---|---|---|---|---|---|---|---|---|---|---|---|---|
| Year Team | Lg | G | GS | CG | GF | IP | BFP | H | R | ER | HR | SH | SF | HB | TBB | IBB | SO | WP | Bk | W | L | Pct. | ShO | Sv | ERA |
| 1987 Baltimore | AL | 14 | 14 | 0 | 0 | 69.2 | 327 | 100 | 60 | 51 | 15 | 0 | 1 | 0 | 35 | 1 | 27 | 0 | 1 | 2 | 8 | .200 | 0 | 0 | 6.59 |
| 1988 Baltimore | AL | 25 | 25 | 6 | 0 | 153.1 | 654 | 167 | 83 | 75 | 15 | 3 | 3 | 6 | 42 | 2 | 41 | 2 | 2 | 8 | 12 | .400 | 1 | 0 | 4.40 |
| 1989 Baltimore | AL | 35 | 35 | 4 | 0 | 215.1 | 912 | 240 | 95 | 82 | 16 | 10 | 5 | 4 | 57 | 5 | 62 | 3 | 0 | 18 | 8 | .692 | 1 | 0 | 3.43 |
| 1990 Baltimore | AL | 44 | 17 | 0 | 6 | 133.1 | 578 | 152 | 79 | 73 | 22 | 5 | 2 | 3 | 42 | 6 | 50 | 2 | 1 | 2 | 11 | .154 | 0 | 0 | 4.93 |
| 4 ML YEARS | | 118 | 91 | 10 | 6 | 571.2 | 2471 | 659 | 317 | 281 | 68 | 18 | 11 | 13 | 176 | 14 | 180 | 7 | 4 | 30 | 39 | .435 | 2 | 0 | 4.42 |

## Jay Baller

**Pitches:** Right **Bats:** Right **Pos:** RP **Ht:** 6' 7" **Wt:** 225 **Born:** 10/06/60 **Age:** 30

| HOW MUCH HE PITCHED | | | | | | | | WHAT HE GAVE UP | | | | | | | | | | | | THE RESULTS | | | | | |
|---|---|---|---|---|---|---|---|---|---|---|---|---|---|---|---|---|---|---|---|---|---|---|---|---|---|
| Year Team | Lg | G | GS | CG | GF | IP | BFP | H | R | ER | HR | SH | SF | HB | TBB | IBB | SO | WP | Bk | W | L | Pct. | ShO | Sv | ERA |
| 1982 Philadelphia | NL | 4 | 1 | 0 | 1 | 8 | 35 | 7 | 4 | 3 | 1 | 1 | 0 | 1 | 2 | 0 | 7 | 0 | 1 | 0 | 0 | .000 | 0 | 0 | 3.38 |
| 1985 Chicago | NL | 20 | 4 | 0 | 4 | 52 | 223 | 52 | 21 | 20 | 8 | 4 | 1 | 1 | 17 | 7 | 31 | 2 | 0 | 2 | 3 | .400 | 0 | 1 | 3.46 |
| 1986 Chicago | NL | 36 | 0 | 0 | 16 | 53.2 | 248 | 58 | 37 | 32 | 7 | 4 | 3 | 2 | 28 | 4 | 42 | 2 | 4 | 2 | 4 | .333 | 0 | 5 | 5.37 |
| 1987 Chicago | NL | 23 | 0 | 0 | 9 | 29.1 | 139 | 38 | 22 | 22 | 4 | 2 | 0 | 0 | 20 | 2 | 27 | 5 | 2 | 0 | 1 | .000 | 0 | 0 | 6.75 |
| 1990 Kansas City | AL | 3 | 0 | 0 | 2 | 2.1 | 14 | 4 | 4 | 4 | 1 | 0 | 0 | 1 | 2 | 1 | 1 | 1 | 0 | 0 | 1 | .000 | 0 | 0 | 15.43 |
| 5 ML YEARS | | 86 | 5 | 0 | 32 | 145.1 | 659 | 159 | 88 | 81 | 21 | 11 | 4 | 5 | 69 | 14 | 108 | 10 | 7 | 4 | 9 | .308 | 0 | 6 | 5.02 |

## Scott Bankhead

**Pitches:** Right **Bats:** Right **Pos:** SP **Ht:** 5'10" **Wt:** 185 **Born:** 07/31/63 **Age:** 27

| HOW MUCH HE PITCHED | | | | | | | | WHAT HE GAVE UP | | | | | | | | | | | | THE RESULTS | | | | | |
|---|---|---|---|---|---|---|---|---|---|---|---|---|---|---|---|---|---|---|---|---|---|---|---|---|---|
| Year Team | Lg | G | GS | CG | GF | IP | BFP | H | R | ER | HR | SH | SF | HB | TBB | IBB | SO | WP | Bk | W | L | Pct. | ShO | Sv | ERA |
| 1986 Kansas City | AL | 24 | 17 | 0 | 2 | 121 | 517 | 121 | 66 | 62 | 14 | 5 | 5 | 3 | 37 | 7 | 94 | 1 | 0 | 8 | 9 | .471 | 0 | 0 | 4.61 |
| 1987 Seattle | AL | 27 | 25 | 2 | 1 | 149.1 | 642 | 168 | 96 | 90 | 35 | 3 | 6 | 3 | 37 | 0 | 95 | 2 | 2 | 9 | 8 | .529 | 0 | 0 | 5.42 |
| 1988 Seattle | AL | 21 | 21 | 2 | 0 | 135 | 557 | 115 | 53 | 46 | 8 | 3 | 1 | 1 | 38 | 5 | 102 | 3 | 1 | 7 | 9 | .438 | 1 | 0 | 3.07 |
| 1989 Seattle | AL | 33 | 33 | 3 | 0 | 210.1 | 862 | 187 | 84 | 78 | 19 | 4 | 8 | 3 | 63 | 1 | 140 | 2 | 0 | 14 | 6 | .700 | 2 | 0 | 3.34 |
| 1990 Seattle | AL | 4 | 4 | 0 | 0 | 13 | 63 | 18 | 16 | 16 | 2 | 0 | 2 | 0 | 7 | 0 | 10 | 1 | 0 | 0 | 2 | .000 | 0 | 0 | 11.08 |
| 5 ML YEARS | | 109 | 100 | 7 | 3 | 628.2 | 2641 | 609 | 315 | 292 | 78 | 15 | 22 | 10 | 182 | 13 | 441 | 9 | 3 | 38 | 34 | .528 | 3 | 0 | 4.18 |

## Jesse Barfield

**Bats:** Right **Throws:** Right **Pos:** RF **Ht:** 6' 1" **Wt:** 200 **Born:** 10/29/59 **Age:** 31

| | | BATTING | | | | | | | | | | | | | | | | | BASERUNNING | | | | PERCENTAGES | | |
|---|---|---|---|---|---|---|---|---|---|---|---|---|---|---|---|---|---|---|---|---|---|---|---|---|---|
| Year Team | Lg | G | AB | H | 2B | 3B | HR | (Hm | Rd) | TB | R | RBI | TBB | IBB | SO | HBP | SH | SF | SB | CS | SB% | GDP | Avg | OBP | SLG |
| 1981 Toronto | AL | 25 | 95 | 22 | 3 | 2 | 2 | (1 | 1) | 35 | 7 | 9 | 4 | 0 | 19 | 1 | 0 | 0 | 4 | 3 | .57 | 4 | .232 | .270 | .368 |
| 1982 Toronto | AL | 139 | 394 | 97 | 13 | 2 | 18 | (11 | 7) | 168 | 54 | 58 | 42 | 3 | 79 | 3 | 6 | 1 | 1 | 4 | .20 | 7 | .246 | .323 | .426 |
| 1983 Toronto | AL | 128 | 388 | 98 | 13 | 3 | 27 | (22 | 5) | 198 | 58 | 68 | 22 | 0 | 110 | 4 | 1 | 5 | 2 | 5 | .29 | 8 | .253 | .296 | .510 |
| 1984 Toronto | AL | 110 | 320 | 91 | 14 | 1 | 14 | (10 | 4) | 149 | 51 | 49 | 35 | 5 | 81 | 2 | 1 | 2 | 8 | 2 | .80 | 5 | .284 | .357 | .466 |
| 1985 Toronto | AL | 155 | 539 | 156 | 34 | 9 | 27 | (15 | 12) | 289 | 94 | 84 | 66 | 5 | 143 | 4 | 0 | 3 | 22 | 8 | .73 | 14 | .289 | .369 | .536 |
| 1986 Toronto | AL | 158 | 589 | 170 | 35 | 2 | 40 | (16 | 24) | 329 | 107 | 108 | 69 | 5 | 146 | 8 | 0 | 5 | 8 | 8 | .50 | 9 | .289 | .368 | .559 |
| 1987 Toronto | AL | 159 | 590 | 155 | 25 | 3 | 28 | (11 | 17) | 270 | 89 | 84 | 58 | 7 | 141 | 3 | 1 | 2 | 3 | 5 | .38 | 13 | .263 | .331 | .458 |
| 1988 Toronto | AL | 137 | 468 | 114 | 21 | 5 | 18 | (12 | 6) | 199 | 62 | 56 | 41 | 6 | 108 | 1 | 4 | 6 | 7 | 3 | .70 | 10 | .244 | .302 | .425 |
| 1989 2 ML Teams | | 150 | 521 | 122 | 23 | 1 | 23 | (7 | 16) | 216 | 79 | 67 | 87 | 6 | 150 | 3 | 1 | 3 | 5 | 5 | .50 | 8 | .234 | .345 | .415 |
| 1990 New York | AL | 153 | 476 | 117 | 21 | 2 | 25 | (12 | 13) | 217 | 69 | 78 | 82 | 4 | 150 | 5 | 2 | 5 | 4 | 3 | .57 | 6 | .246 | .359 | .456 |
| 1989 Toronto | AL | 21 | 80 | 16 | 4 | 0 | 5 | (1 | 4) | 35 | 8 | 11 | 5 | 0 | 28 | 1 | 0 | 0 | 0 | 2 | .00 | 0 | .200 | .256 | .438 |
| New York | AL | 129 | 441 | 106 | 19 | 1 | 18 | (6 | 12) | 181 | 71 | 56 | 82 | 6 | 122 | 2 | 1 | 3 | 5 | 3 | .63 | 8 | .240 | .360 | .410 |
| 10 ML YEARS | | 1314 | 4380 | 1142 | 202 | 30 | 222 | (117 | 105) | 2070 | 670 | 661 | 506 | 41 | 1127 | 34 | 16 | 32 | 64 | 46 | .58 | 84 | .261 | .340 | .473 |

## John Barfield

**Pitches:** Left **Bats:** Left **Pos:** RP **Ht:** 6' 1" **Wt:** 185 **Born:** 10/15/64 **Age:** 26

| | | HOW MUCH HE PITCHED | | | | | | WHAT HE GAVE UP | | | | | | | | | | | | THE RESULTS | | | | | |
|---|---|---|---|---|---|---|---|---|---|---|---|---|---|---|---|---|---|---|---|---|---|---|---|---|---|
| Year Team | Lg | G | GS | CG | GF | IP | BFP | H | R | ER | HR | SH | SF | HB | TBB | IBB | SO | WP | Bk | W | L | Pct. | ShO | Sv | ERA |
| 1986 Daytona Bch | A | 3 | 3 | 0 | 0 | 17.1 | 69 | 14 | 9 | 8 | 0 | 0 | 0 | 1 | 1 | 0 | 13 | 0 | 0 | 1 | 1 | .500 | 0 | 0 | 4.15 |
| Salem | A | 13 | 11 | 0 | 0 | 56 | 250 | 71 | 43 | 31 | 7 | 2 | 0 | 1 | 22 | 0 | 39 | 3 | 1 | 2 | 5 | .286 | 0 | 0 | 4.98 |
| 1987 Charlotte | A | 25 | 25 | 3 | 0 | 153.2 | 654 | 145 | 75 | 63 | 3 | 1 | 8 | 3 | 55 | 0 | 79 | 6 | 3 | 10 | 7 | .588 | 2 | 0 | 3.69 |
| 1988 Tulsa | AA | 24 | 24 | 5 | 0 | 169 | 702 | 159 | 69 | 54 | 8 | 6 | 2 | 3 | 66 | 2 | 125 | 13 | 2 | 9 | 9 | .500 | 0 | 0 | 2.88 |
| 1989 Okla City | AAA | 28 | 28 | 7 | 0 | 175.1 | 739 | 178 | 93 | 79 | 14 | 6 | 6 | 2 | 68 | 2 | 58 | 11 | 1 | 10 | 8 | .556 | 3 | 0 | 4.06 |
| 1990 Okla City | AAA | 19 | 3 | 0 | 2 | 43.1 | 182 | 44 | 21 | 17 | 3 | 6 | 0 | 1 | 21 | 3 | 25 | 0 | 2 | 1 | 6 | .143 | 0 | 1 | 3.53 |
| 1989 Texas | AL | 4 | 2 | 0 | 1 | 11.2 | 52 | 15 | 10 | 8 | 0 | 1 | 0 | 0 | 4 | 0 | 9 | 1 | 0 | 0 | 1 | .000 | 0 | 0 | 6.17 |
| 1990 Texas | AL | 33 | 0 | 0 | 10 | 44.1 | 178 | 42 | 25 | 23 | 2 | 3 | 4 | 1 | 13 | 3 | 17 | 1 | 1 | 4 | 3 | .571 | 0 | 1 | 4.67 |
| 2 ML YEARS | | 37 | 2 | 0 | 11 | 56 | 230 | 57 | 35 | 31 | 2 | 4 | 4 | 1 | 17 | 3 | 26 | 2 | 1 | 4 | 4 | .500 | 0 | 1 | 4.98 |

## Brian Barnes

**Pitches:** Left **Bats:** Left **Pos:** SP **Ht:** 5' 9" **Wt:** 170 **Born:** 03/25/67 **Age:** 24

| | | HOW MUCH HE PITCHED | | | | | | WHAT HE GAVE UP | | | | | | | | | | | | THE RESULTS | | | | | |
|---|---|---|---|---|---|---|---|---|---|---|---|---|---|---|---|---|---|---|---|---|---|---|---|---|---|
| Year Team | Lg | G | GS | CG | GF | IP | BFP | H | R | ER | HR | SH | SF | HB | TBB | IBB | SO | WP | Bk | W | L | Pct. | ShO | Sv | ERA |
| 1989 Jamestown | A | 2 | 2 | 0 | 0 | 9 | 33 | 4 | 1 | 1 | 0 | 0 | 0 | 0 | 3 | 0 | 15 | 1 | 1 | 1 | 0 | 1.000 | 0 | 0 | 1.00 |
| Wst Plm Bch | A | 7 | 7 | 4 | 0 | 50 | 187 | 25 | 9 | 4 | 0 | 3 | 1 | 0 | 16 | 0 | 67 | 4 | 0 | 4 | 3 | .571 | 3 | 0 | 0.72 |
| Indianapols | AAA | 1 | 1 | 0 | 0 | 6 | 24 | 5 | 1 | 1 | 0 | 0 | 0 | 0 | 2 | 0 | 5 | 0 | 0 | 1 | 0 | 1.000 | 0 | 0 | 1.50 |
| 1990 Jacksnville | AA | 29 | 28 | 3 | 0 | 201.1 | 828 | 144 | 78 | 62 | 12 | 7 | 5 | 9 | 87 | 2 | 213 | 8 | 1 | 13 | 7 | .650 | 1 | 0 | 2.77 |
| 1990 Montreal | NL | 4 | 4 | 1 | 0 | 28 | 115 | 25 | 10 | 9 | 2 | 2 | 0 | 0 | 7 | 0 | 23 | 2 | 0 | 1 | 1 | .500 | 0 | 0 | 2.89 |

## Marty Barrett

**Bats:** Right **Throws:** Right **Pos:** 2B **Ht:** 5'10" **Wt:** 175 **Born:** 06/23/58 **Age:** 33

| | | BATTING | | | | | | | | | | | | | | | | | BASERUNNING | | | | PERCENTAGES | | |
|---|---|---|---|---|---|---|---|---|---|---|---|---|---|---|---|---|---|---|---|---|---|---|---|---|---|
| Year Team | Lg | G | AB | H | 2B | 3B | HR | (Hm | Rd) | TB | R | RBI | TBB | IBB | SO | HBP | SH | SF | SB | CS | SB% | GDP | Avg | OBP | SLG |
| 1982 Boston | AL | 8 | 18 | 1 | 0 | 0 | 0 | (0 | 0) | 1 | 0 | 0 | 0 | 0 | 1 | 0 | 0 | 0 | 0 | 0 | .00 | 1 | .056 | .056 | .056 |
| 1983 Boston | AL | 33 | 44 | 10 | 1 | 1 | 0 | (0 | 0) | 13 | 7 | 2 | 3 | 0 | 1 | 0 | 0 | 1 | 0 | 0 | .00 | 1 | .227 | .271 | .295 |
| 1984 Boston | AL | 139 | 475 | 144 | 23 | 3 | 3 | (1 | 2) | 182 | 56 | 45 | 42 | 2 | 25 | 1 | 4 | 4 | 5 | 3 | .63 | 9 | .303 | .358 | .383 |
| 1985 Boston | AL | 156 | 534 | 142 | 26 | 0 | 5 | (3 | 2) | 183 | 59 | 56 | 56 | 3 | 50 | 2 | 12 | 4 | 7 | 5 | .58 | 14 | .266 | .336 | .343 |
| 1986 Boston | AL | 158 | 625 | 179 | 39 | 4 | 4 | (4 | 0) | 238 | 94 | 60 | 65 | 0 | 31 | 1 | 18 | 4 | 15 | 7 | .68 | 13 | .286 | .353 | .381 |
| 1987 Boston | AL | 137 | 559 | 164 | 23 | 0 | 3 | (2 | 1) | 196 | 72 | 43 | 51 | 0 | 38 | 1 | 22 | 5 | 15 | 2 | .88 | 11 | .293 | .351 | .351 |
| 1988 Boston | AL | 150 | 612 | 173 | 28 | 1 | 1 | (1 | 0) | 206 | 83 | 65 | 40 | 1 | 35 | 7 | 20 | 8 | 7 | 3 | .70 | 16 | .283 | .330 | .337 |
| 1989 Boston | AL | 86 | 336 | 86 | 18 | 0 | 1 | (0 | 1) | 107 | 31 | 27 | 32 | 0 | 12 | 2 | 15 | 5 | 4 | 1 | .80 | 12 | .256 | .320 | .318 |
| 1990 Boston | AL | 62 | 159 | 36 | 4 | 0 | 0 | (0 | 0) | 40 | 15 | 13 | 15 | 1 | 13 | 1 | 11 | 2 | 4 | 0 | 1.00 | 4 | .226 | .294 | .252 |
| 9 ML YEARS | | 929 | 3362 | 935 | 162 | 9 | 17 | (11 | 6) | 1166 | 417 | 311 | 304 | 7 | 206 | 15 | 102 | 33 | 57 | 21 | .73 | 81 | .278 | .338 | .347 |

## Kevin Bass

**Bats:** Both **Throws:** Right **Pos:** RF **Ht:** 6' 0" **Wt:** 180 **Born:** 05/12/59 **Age:** 32

| | | BATTING | | | | | | | | | | | | | | | | | BASERUNNING | | | | PERCENTAGES | | |
|---|---|---|---|---|---|---|---|---|---|---|---|---|---|---|---|---|---|---|---|---|---|---|---|---|---|
| Year Team | Lg | G | AB | H | 2B | 3B | HR | (Hm | Rd) | TB | R | RBI | TBB | IBB | SO | HBP | SH | SF | SB | CS | SB% | GDP | Avg | OBP | SLG |
| 1982 2 ML Teams | | 30 | 33 | 1 | 0 | 0 | 0 | (0 | 0) | 1 | 6 | 1 | 1 | 0 | 9 | 0 | 1 | 0 | 0 | 0 | .00 | 1 | .030 | .059 | .030 |
| 1983 Houston | NL | 88 | 195 | 46 | 7 | 3 | 2 | (2 | 0) | 65 | 25 | 18 | 6 | 1 | 27 | 0 | 4 | 1 | 2 | 2 | .50 | 2 | .236 | .257 | .333 |
| 1984 Houston | NL | 121 | 331 | 86 | 17 | 5 | 2 | (1 | 1) | 119 | 33 | 29 | 6 | 1 | 57 | 3 | 2 | 0 | 5 | 5 | .50 | 2 | .260 | .279 | .360 |
| 1985 Houston | NL | 150 | 539 | 145 | 27 | 5 | 16 | (9 | 7) | 230 | 72 | 68 | 31 | 1 | 63 | 6 | 4 | 2 | 19 | 8 | .70 | 10 | .269 | .315 | .427 |
| 1986 Houston | NL | 157 | 591 | 184 | 33 | 5 | 20 | (5 | 15) | 287 | 83 | 79 | 38 | 11 | 72 | 6 | 1 | 4 | 22 | 13 | .63 | 15 | .311 | .357 | .486 |

| | | | | | | | | | | | | | | | | | | | | | | | | | |
|---|---|---|---|---|---|---|---|---|---|---|---|---|---|---|---|---|---|---|---|---|---|---|---|---|---|
| 1987 Houston | NL | 157 | 592 | 168 | 31 | 5 | 19 | (10 | 9) | 266 | 83 | 85 | 53 | 13 | 77 | 4 | 0 | 5 | 21 | 8 | .72 | 15 | .284 | .344 | .449 |
| 1988 Houston | NL | 157 | 541 | 138 | 27 | 2 | 14 | (5 | 9) | 211 | 57 | 72 | 42 | 10 | 65 | 6 | 3 | 3 | 31 | 6 | .84 | 16 | .255 | .314 | .390 |
| 1989 Houston | NL | 87 | 313 | 94 | 19 | 4 | 5 | (2 | 3) | 136 | 42 | 44 | 29 | 3 | 44 | 1 | 1 | 4 | 11 | 4 | .73 | 2 | .300 | .357 | .435 |
| 1990 San Francisco | NL | 61 | 214 | 54 | 9 | 1 | 7 | (3 | 4) | 86 | 25 | 32 | 14 | 3 | 26 | 2 | 2 | 1 | 2 | 2 | .50 | 5 | .252 | .303 | .402 |
| 1982 Milwaukee | AL | 18 | 9 | 0 | 0 | 0 | 0 | (0 | 0) | 0 | 4 | 0 | 1 | 0 | 1 | 0 | 1 | 0 | 0 | 0 | .00 | 0 | .000 | .100 | .000 |
| Houston | NL | 12 | 24 | 1 | 0 | 0 | 0 | (0 | 0) | 1 | 2 | 1 | 0 | 0 | 8 | 0 | 0 | 0 | 0 | 0 | .00 | 1 | .042 | .042 | .042 |
| 9 ML YEARS | | 1008 | 3349 | 916 | 170 | 30 | 85 | (37 | 48) | 1401 | 426 | 428 | 220 | 43 | 440 | 28 | 18 | 20 | 113 | 48 | .70 | 68 | .274 | .322 | .418 |

## Billy Bates

**Bats:** Left **Throws:** Right **Pos:** 2B **Ht:** 5' 7" **Wt:** 165 **Born:** 12/07/63 **Age:** 27

| BATTING | | | | | | | | | | | | | | | | | | | BASERUNNING | | | | PERCENTAGES | | |
|---|---|---|---|---|---|---|---|---|---|---|---|---|---|---|---|---|---|---|---|---|---|---|---|---|---|
| Year Team | Lg | G | AB | H | 2B | 3B | HR | (Hm | Rd) | TB | R | RBI | TBB | IBB | SO | HBP | SH | SF | SB | CS | SB% | GDP | Avg | OBP | SLG |
| 1985 Stockton | A | 59 | 218 | 65 | 8 | 1 | 3 | -- | -- | 84 | 36 | 31 | 35 | 0 | 27 | 1 | 2 | 1 | 18 | 5 | .78 | 7 | .298 | .396 | .385 |
| 1986 El Paso | AA | 122 | 511 | 151 | 26 | 4 | 8 | -- | -- | 209 | 104 | 75 | 72 | 0 | 64 | 2 | 3 | 0 | 23 | 10 | .70 | 9 | .295 | .385 | .409 |
| 1987 Denver | AAA | 130 | 506 | 160 | 25 | 5 | 3 | -- | -- | 204 | 117 | 62 | 73 | 1 | 52 | 0 | 4 | 8 | 51 | 13 | .80 | 9 | .316 | .397 | .403 |
| 1988 Denver | AAA | 119 | 472 | 122 | 16 | 12 | 2 | -- | -- | 168 | 74 | 44 | 51 | 2 | 49 | 2 | 4 | 3 | 29 | 8 | .78 | 15 | .258 | .331 | .356 |
| 1989 Denver | AAA | 95 | 363 | 99 | 11 | 2 | 1 | -- | -- | 117 | 50 | 38 | 36 | 1 | 26 | 2 | 5 | 2 | 13 | 5 | .72 | 12 | .273 | .340 | .322 |
| 1990 Denver | AAA | 25 | 101 | 33 | 2 | 1 | 0 | -- | -- | 37 | 18 | 14 | 8 | 0 | 7 | 0 | 2 | 2 | 3 | 2 | .60 | 2 | .327 | .369 | .366 |
| Nashville | AAA | 73 | 261 | 73 | 13 | 2 | 0 | -- | -- | 90 | 33 | 20 | 21 | 2 | 21 | 0 | 3 | 1 | 12 | 6 | .67 | 2 | .280 | .332 | .345 |
| 1989 Milwaukee | AL | 7 | 14 | 3 | 0 | 0 | 0 | (0 | 0) | 3 | 3 | 0 | 0 | 0 | 1 | 0 | 0 | 0 | 2 | 0 | 1.00 | 2 | .214 | .214 | .214 |
| 1990 2 ML Teams | | 22 | 34 | 3 | 1 | 0 | 0 | (0 | 0) | 4 | 8 | 2 | 4 | 0 | 9 | 0 | 1 | 1 | 6 | 1 | .86 | 0 | .088 | .179 | .118 |
| 1990 Milwaukee | AL | 14 | 29 | 3 | 1 | 0 | 0 | (0 | 0) | 4 | 6 | 2 | 4 | 0 | 7 | 0 | 1 | 1 | 4 | 0 | 1.00 | 0 | .103 | .206 | .138 |
| Cincinnati | NL | 8 | 5 | 0 | 0 | 0 | 0 | (0 | 0) | 0 | 2 | 0 | 0 | 0 | 2 | 0 | 0 | 0 | 2 | 1 | .67 | 0 | .000 | .000 | .000 |
| 2 ML YEARS | | 29 | 48 | 6 | 1 | 0 | 0 | (0 | 0) | 7 | 11 | 2 | 4 | 0 | 10 | 0 | 1 | 1 | 8 | 1 | .89 | 2 | .125 | .189 | .146 |

## Bill Bathe

**Bats:** Right **Throws:** Right **Pos:** C **Ht:** 6' 2" **Wt:** 200 **Born:** 10/14/60 **Age:** 30

| BATTING | | | | | | | | | | | | | | | | | | | BASERUNNING | | | | PERCENTAGES | | |
|---|---|---|---|---|---|---|---|---|---|---|---|---|---|---|---|---|---|---|---|---|---|---|---|---|---|
| Year Team | Lg | G | AB | H | 2B | 3B | HR | (Hm | Rd) | TB | R | RBI | TBB | IBB | SO | HBP | SH | SF | SB | CS | SB% | GDP | Avg | OBP | SLG |
| 1986 Oakland | AL | 39 | 103 | 19 | 3 | 0 | 5 | (4 | 1) | 37 | 9 | 11 | 2 | 0 | 20 | 1 | 6 | 0 | 0 | 0 | .00 | 2 | .184 | .208 | .359 |
| 1989 San Francisco | NL | 30 | 32 | 9 | 1 | 0 | 0 | (0 | 0) | 10 | 3 | 6 | 0 | 0 | 7 | 0 | 0 | 1 | 0 | 0 | .00 | 0 | .281 | .273 | .313 |
| 1990 San Francisco | NL | 52 | 48 | 11 | 0 | 1 | 3 | (1 | 2) | 22 | 3 | 12 | 7 | 2 | 12 | 0 | 0 | 1 | 0 | 0 | .00 | 2 | .229 | .321 | .458 |
| 3 ML YEARS | | 121 | 183 | 39 | 4 | 1 | 8 | (5 | 3) | 69 | 15 | 29 | 9 | 2 | 39 | 1 | 6 | 2 | 0 | 0 | .00 | 4 | .213 | .251 | .377 |

## Jose Bautista

**Pitches:** Right **Bats:** Right **Pos:** RP **Ht:** 6' 2" **Wt:** 210 **Born:** 07/25/64 **Age:** 26

| HOW MUCH HE PITCHED | | | | | | | | WHAT HE GAVE UP | | | | | | | | | | | | THE RESULTS | | | | | |
|---|---|---|---|---|---|---|---|---|---|---|---|---|---|---|---|---|---|---|---|---|---|---|---|---|---|
| Year Team | Lg | G | GS | CG | GF | IP | BFP | H | R | ER | HR | SH | SF | HB | TBB | IBB | SO | WP | Bk | W | L | Pct. | ShO | Sv | ERA |
| 1988 Baltimore | AL | 33 | 25 | 3 | 5 | 171.2 | 721 | 171 | 86 | 82 | 21 | 2 | 3 | 7 | 45 | 3 | 76 | 4 | 5 | 6 | 15 | .286 | 0 | 0 | 4.30 |
| 1989 Baltimore | AL | 15 | 10 | 0 | 4 | 78 | 325 | 84 | 46 | 46 | 17 | 1 | 1 | 1 | 15 | 0 | 30 | 0 | 0 | 3 | 4 | .429 | 0 | 0 | 5.31 |
| 1990 Baltimore | AL | 22 | 0 | 0 | 9 | 26.2 | 112 | 28 | 15 | 12 | 4 | 1 | 1 | 0 | 7 | 3 | 15 | 2 | 0 | 1 | 0 | 1.000 | 0 | 0 | 4.05 |
| 3 ML YEARS | | 70 | 35 | 3 | 18 | 276.1 | 1158 | 283 | 147 | 140 | 42 | 4 | 5 | 8 | 67 | 6 | 121 | 6 | 5 | 10 | 19 | .345 | 0 | 0 | 4.56 |

## Kevin Bearse

**Pitches:** Left **Bats:** Left **Pos:** SP **Ht:** 6' 2" **Wt:** 195 **Born:** 11/07/65 **Age:** 25

| HOW MUCH HE PITCHED | | | | | | | | WHAT HE GAVE UP | | | | | | | | | | | | THE RESULTS | | | | | |
|---|---|---|---|---|---|---|---|---|---|---|---|---|---|---|---|---|---|---|---|---|---|---|---|---|---|
| Year Team | Lg | G | GS | CG | GF | IP | BFP | H | R | ER | HR | SH | SF | HB | TBB | IBB | SO | WP | Bk | W | L | Pct. | ShO | Sv | ERA |
| 1987 Burlington | R | 22 | 3 | 0 | 18 | 63 | 249 | 45 | 13 | 12 | 1 | 0 | 0 | 1 | 15 | 1 | 81 | 2 | 0 | 7 | 1 | .875 | 0 | 8 | 1.71 |
| 1988 Kinston | A | 62 | 0 | 0 | 56 | 103 | 405 | 76 | 19 | 15 | 1 | 8 | 3 | 2 | 28 | 4 | 127 | 3 | 1 | 10 | 8 | .556 | 0 | 22 | 1.31 |
| 1989 Canton-Akrn | AA | 14 | 14 | 6 | 0 | 101 | 400 | 90 | 29 | 23 | 2 | 2 | 0 | 1 | 16 | 1 | 67 | 2 | 1 | 9 | 3 | .750 | 2 | 0 | 2.05 |
| Colo Sprngs | AAA | 13 | 13 | 2 | 0 | 89 | 376 | 87 | 44 | 39 | 9 | 3 | 1 | 2 | 32 | 0 | 51 | 1 | 1 | 5 | 2 | .714 | 2 | 0 | 3.94 |
| 1990 Colo Sprngs | AAA | 25 | 24 | 6 | 0 | 145.2 | 648 | 170 | 92 | 81 | 17 | 4 | 7 | 8 | 49 | 1 | 79 | 12 | 1 | 11 | 9 | .550 | 2 | 0 | 5.00 |
| 1990 Cleveland | AL | 3 | 3 | 0 | 0 | 7.2 | 45 | 16 | 11 | 11 | 2 | 0 | 0 | 2 | 5 | 0 | 2 | 0 | 0 | 0 | 2 | .000 | 0 | 0 | 12.91 |

## Steve Bedrosian

**Pitches:** Right **Bats:** Right **Pos:** RP **Ht:** 6' 3" **Wt:** 205 **Born:** 12/06/57 **Age:** 33

| HOW MUCH HE PITCHED | | | | | | | | WHAT HE GAVE UP | | | | | | | | | | | | THE RESULTS | | | | | |
|---|---|---|---|---|---|---|---|---|---|---|---|---|---|---|---|---|---|---|---|---|---|---|---|---|---|
| Year Team | Lg | G | GS | CG | GF | IP | BFP | H | R | ER | HR | SH | SF | HB | TBB | IBB | SO | WP | Bk | W | L | Pct. | ShO | Sv | ERA |
| 1981 Atlanta | NL | 15 | 1 | 0 | 5 | 24 | 106 | 15 | 14 | 12 | 2 | 0 | 1 | 1 | 15 | 2 | 9 | 0 | 0 | 1 | 2 | .333 | 0 | 0 | 4.50 |
| 1982 Atlanta | NL | 64 | 3 | 0 | 30 | 137.2 | 567 | 102 | 39 | 37 | 7 | 9 | 2 | 4 | 57 | 5 | 123 | 0 | 0 | 8 | 6 | .571 | 0 | 11 | 2.42 |
| 1983 Atlanta | NL | 70 | 1 | 0 | 52 | 120 | 504 | 100 | 50 | 48 | 11 | 8 | 4 | 4 | 51 | 8 | 114 | 2 | 0 | 9 | 10 | .474 | 0 | 19 | 3.60 |
| 1984 Atlanta | NL | 40 | 4 | 0 | 28 | 83.2 | 345 | 65 | 23 | 22 | 5 | 1 | 1 | 1 | 33 | 5 | 81 | 4 | 0 | 9 | 6 | .600 | 0 | 11 | 2.37 |
| 1985 Atlanta | NL | 37 | 37 | 0 | 0 | 206.2 | 907 | 198 | 101 | 88 | 17 | 6 | 7 | 5 | 111 | 6 | 134 | 6 | 0 | 7 | 15 | .318 | 0 | 0 | 3.83 |
| 1986 Philadelphia | NL | 68 | 0 | 0 | 56 | 90.1 | 381 | 79 | 39 | 34 | 12 | 3 | 3 | 0 | 34 | 10 | 82 | 5 | 2 | 8 | 6 | .571 | 0 | 29 | 3.39 |
| 1987 Philadelphia | NL | 65 | 0 | 0 | 56 | 89 | 366 | 79 | 31 | 28 | 11 | 2 | 1 | 1 | 28 | 5 | 74 | 3 | 1 | 5 | 3 | .625 | 0 | 40 | 2.83 |
| 1988 Philadelphia | NL | 57 | 0 | 0 | 49 | 74.1 | 322 | 75 | 34 | 31 | 6 | 0 | 3 | 0 | 27 | 5 | 61 | 0 | 0 | 6 | 6 | .500 | 0 | 28 | 3.75 |
| 1989 2 ML Teams | | 68 | 0 | 0 | 60 | 84.2 | 342 | 56 | 31 | 27 | 12 | 1 | 4 | 1 | 39 | 5 | 58 | 2 | 0 | 3 | 7 | .300 | 0 | 23 | 2.87 |

| Year | Team | Lg | G | GS | CG | GF | IP | BFP | H | R | ER | HR | SH | SF | HB | TBB | IBB | SO | WP | Bk | W | L | Pct. | ShO | Sv | ERA |
|---|---|---|---|---|---|---|---|---|---|---|---|---|---|---|---|---|---|---|---|---|---|---|---|---|---|---|
| 1990 | San Francisco | NL | 68 | 0 | 0 | 53 | 79.1 | 349 | 72 | 40 | 37 | 6 | 3 | 1 | 2 | 44 | 9 | 43 | 3 | 0 | 9 | 9 | .500 | 0 | 17 | 4.20 |
| 1989 | Philadelphia | NL | 28 | 0 | 0 | 27 | 33.2 | 135 | 21 | 13 | 12 | 7 | 0 | 2 | 1 | 17 | 1 | 24 | 0 | 0 | 2 | 3 | .400 | 0 | 6 | 3.21 |
| | San Francisco | NL | 40 | 0 | 0 | 33 | 51 | 207 | 35 | 18 | 15 | 5 | 1 | 2 | 0 | 22 | 4 | 34 | 2 | 0 | 1 | 4 | .200 | 0 | 17 | 2.65 |
| 10 ML YEARS | | | 552 | 46 | 0 | 389 | 989.2 | 4189 | 841 | 402 | 364 | 89 | 33 | 27 | 19 | 439 | 60 | 779 | 25 | 3 | 65 | 70 | .481 | 0 | 178 | 3.31 |

## Kevin Belcher

**Bats:** Right **Throws:** Right **Pos:** CF **Ht:** 6' 0" **Wt:** 170 **Born:** 08/08/67 **Age:** 23

| BATTING | | | | | | | | | | | | | | | | | | | | BASERUNNING | | | | PERCENTAGES | | |
|---|---|---|---|---|---|---|---|---|---|---|---|---|---|---|---|---|---|---|---|---|---|---|---|---|---|---|
| Year | Team | Lg | G | AB | H | 2B | 3B | HR | (Hm | Rd) | TB | R | RBI | TBB | IBB | SO | HBP | SH | SF | SB | CS | SB% | GDP | Avg | OBP | SLG |
| 1987 | Rangers | R | 58 | 215 | 45 | 8 | 2 | 2 | -- | -- | 63 | 32 | 10 | 32 | 0 | 38 | 2 | 0 | 0 | 10 | 7 | .59 | 5 | .209 | .317 | .293 |
| 1988 | Gastonia | A | 105 | 392 | 96 | 13 | 1 | 8 | -- | -- | 135 | 56 | 44 | 40 | 1 | 81 | 4 | 4 | 3 | 22 | 11 | .67 | 4 | .245 | .319 | .344 |
| 1989 | Gastonia | A | 93 | 338 | 100 | 21 | 1 | 14 | -- | -- | 165 | 61 | 59 | 31 | 0 | 62 | 5 | 4 | 7 | 13 | 11 | .54 | 6 | .296 | .357 | .488 |
| 1990 | Tulsa | AA | 110 | 423 | 124 | 17 | 7 | 11 | -- | -- | 188 | 66 | 43 | 55 | 3 | 88 | 5 | 0 | 1 | 29 | 14 | .67 | 11 | .293 | .380 | .444 |
| 1990 | Texas | AL | 16 | 15 | 2 | 1 | 0 | 0 | (0 | 0) | 3 | 4 | 0 | 2 | 0 | 6 | 0 | 0 | 0 | 0 | 0 | .00 | 0 | .133 | .235 | .200 |

## Tim Belcher

**Pitches:** Right **Bats:** Right **Pos:** SP **Ht:** 6' 3" **Wt:** 210 **Born:** 10/19/61 **Age:** 29

| HOW MUCH HE PITCHED | | | | | | | | | WHAT HE GAVE UP | | | | | | | | | | | | THE RESULTS | | | | | |
|---|---|---|---|---|---|---|---|---|---|---|---|---|---|---|---|---|---|---|---|---|---|---|---|---|---|---|
| Year | Team | Lg | G | GS | CG | GF | IP | BFP | H | R | ER | HR | SH | SF | HB | TBB | IBB | SO | WP | Bk | W | L | Pct. | ShO | Sv | ERA |
| 1987 | Los Angeles | NL | 6 | 5 | 0 | 1 | 34 | 135 | 30 | 11 | 9 | 2 | 2 | 1 | 0 | 7 | 0 | 23 | 0 | 1 | 4 | 2 | .667 | 0 | 0 | 2.38 |
| 1988 | Los Angeles | NL | 36 | 27 | 4 | 5 | 179.2 | 719 | 143 | 65 | 58 | 8 | 6 | 1 | 2 | 51 | 7 | 152 | 4 | 0 | 12 | 6 | .667 | 1 | 4 | 2.91 |
| 1989 | Los Angeles | NL | 39 | 30 | 10 | 6 | 230 | 937 | 182 | 81 | 72 | 20 | 6 | 6 | 7 | 80 | 5 | 200 | 7 | 2 | 15 | 12 | .556 | 8 | 1 | 2.82 |
| 1990 | Los Angeles | NL | 24 | 24 | 5 | 0 | 153 | 627 | 136 | 76 | 68 | 17 | 5 | 6 | 2 | 48 | 0 | 102 | 6 | 1 | 9 | 9 | .500 | 2 | 0 | 4.00 |
| 4 ML YEARS | | | 105 | 86 | 19 | 12 | 596.2 | 2418 | 491 | 233 | 207 | 47 | 19 | 14 | 11 | 186 | 12 | 477 | 17 | 4 | 40 | 29 | .580 | 11 | 5 | 3.12 |

## Stan Belinda

**Pitches:** Right **Bats:** Right **Pos:** RP **Ht:** 6' 3" **Wt:** 185 **Born:** 08/06/66 **Age:** 24

| HOW MUCH HE PITCHED | | | | | | | | | WHAT HE GAVE UP | | | | | | | | | | | | THE RESULTS | | | | | |
|---|---|---|---|---|---|---|---|---|---|---|---|---|---|---|---|---|---|---|---|---|---|---|---|---|---|---|
| Year | Team | Lg | G | GS | CG | GF | IP | BFP | H | R | ER | HR | SH | SF | HB | TBB | IBB | SO | WP | Bk | W | L | Pct. | ShO | Sv | ERA |
| 1986 | Pirates | R | 17 | 0 | 0 | 15 | 20.1 | 84 | 23 | 12 | 6 | 1 | 1 | 2 | 1 | 2 | 0 | 17 | 0 | 0 | 3 | 2 | .600 | 0 | 7 | 2.66 |
| | Watertown | A | 5 | 0 | 0 | 5 | 8 | 29 | 5 | 3 | 3 | 1 | 0 | 0 | 0 | 2 | 0 | 5 | 0 | 0 | 0 | 0 | .000 | 0 | 2 | 3.38 |
| 1987 | Macon | A | 50 | 0 | 0 | 45 | 82 | 329 | 59 | 26 | 19 | 4 | 3 | 5 | 4 | 27 | 1 | 75 | 4 | 0 | 6 | 4 | .600 | 0 | 16 | 2.09 |
| 1988 | Salem | A | 53 | 0 | 0 | 42 | 71.2 | 308 | 54 | 33 | 22 | 9 | 8 | 3 | 2 | 32 | 4 | 63 | 4 | 0 | 6 | 4 | .600 | 0 | 14 | 2.76 |
| 1989 | Harrisburg | AA | 32 | 0 | 0 | 28 | 38.2 | 171 | 32 | 13 | 10 | 1 | 3 | 1 | 1 | 25 | 3 | 33 | 4 | 2 | 1 | 4 | .200 | 0 | 13 | 2.33 |
| | Buffalo | AAA | 19 | 0 | 0 | 15 | 28.1 | 114 | 13 | 5 | 3 | 1 | 3 | 1 | 2 | 13 | 3 | 28 | 1 | 1 | 2 | 2 | .500 | 0 | 9 | 0.95 |
| 1990 | Buffalo | AAA | 15 | 0 | 0 | 10 | 23.2 | 96 | 20 | 8 | 5 | 1 | 2 | 1 | 1 | 8 | 1 | 25 | 0 | 1 | 3 | 1 | .750 | 0 | 5 | 1.90 |
| 1989 | Pittsburgh | NL | 8 | 0 | 0 | 2 | 10.1 | 46 | 13 | 8 | 7 | 0 | 0 | 0 | 0 | 2 | 0 | 10 | 1 | 0 | 0 | 1 | .000 | 0 | 0 | 6.10 |
| 1990 | Pittsburgh | NL | 55 | 0 | 0 | 17 | 58.1 | 245 | 48 | 23 | 23 | 4 | 2 | 2 | 1 | 29 | 3 | 55 | 1 | 0 | 3 | 4 | .429 | 0 | 8 | 3.55 |
| 2 ML YEARS | | | 63 | 0 | 0 | 19 | 68.2 | 291 | 61 | 31 | 30 | 4 | 2 | 2 | 1 | 31 | 3 | 65 | 2 | 0 | 3 | 5 | .375 | 0 | 8 | 3.93 |

## George Bell

**Bats:** Right **Throws:** Right **Pos:** LF/DH **Ht:** 6' 1" **Wt:** 202 **Born:** 10/21/59 **Age:** 31

| BATTING | | | | | | | | | | | | | | | | | | | | BASERUNNING | | | | PERCENTAGES | | |
|---|---|---|---|---|---|---|---|---|---|---|---|---|---|---|---|---|---|---|---|---|---|---|---|---|---|---|
| Year | Team | Lg | G | AB | H | 2B | 3B | HR | (Hm | Rd) | TB | R | RBI | TBB | IBB | SO | HBP | SH | SF | SB | CS | SB% | GDP | Avg | OBP | SLG |
| 1981 | Toronto | AL | 60 | 163 | 38 | 2 | 1 | 5 | (3 | 2) | 57 | 19 | 12 | 5 | 1 | 27 | 0 | 0 | 0 | 3 | 2 | .60 | 1 | .233 | .256 | .350 |
| 1983 | Toronto | AL | 39 | 112 | 30 | 5 | 4 | 2 | (1 | 1) | 49 | 5 | 17 | 4 | 1 | 17 | 2 | 0 | 0 | 1 | 1 | .50 | 4 | .268 | .305 | .438 |
| 1984 | Toronto | AL | 159 | 606 | 177 | 39 | 4 | 26 | (12 | 14) | 302 | 85 | 87 | 24 | 2 | 86 | 8 | 0 | 3 | 11 | 2 | .85 | 14 | .292 | .326 | .498 |
| 1985 | Toronto | AL | 157 | 607 | 167 | 28 | 6 | 28 | (10 | 18) | 291 | 87 | 95 | 43 | 6 | 90 | 8 | 0 | 8 | 21 | 6 | .78 | 8 | .275 | .327 | .479 |
| 1986 | Toronto | AL | 159 | 641 | 198 | 38 | 6 | 31 | (15 | 16) | 341 | 101 | 108 | 41 | 3 | 62 | 2 | 0 | 6 | 7 | 8 | .47 | 15 | .309 | .349 | .532 |
| 1987 | Toronto | AL | 156 | 610 | 188 | 32 | 4 | 47 | (19 | 28) | 369 | 111 | 134 | 39 | 9 | 75 | 7 | 0 | 9 | 5 | 1 | .83 | 17 | .308 | .352 | .605 |
| 1988 | Toronto | AL | 156 | 614 | 165 | 27 | 5 | 24 | (9 | 15) | 274 | 78 | 97 | 34 | 5 | 66 | 1 | 0 | 8 | 4 | 2 | .67 | 21 | .269 | .304 | .446 |
| 1989 | Toronto | AL | 153 | 613 | 182 | 41 | 2 | 18 | (8 | 10) | 281 | 88 | 104 | 33 | 3 | 60 | 4 | 0 | 14 | 4 | 3 | .57 | 18 | .297 | .330 | .458 |
| 1990 | Toronto | AL | 142 | 562 | 149 | 25 | 0 | 21 | (11 | 10) | 237 | 67 | 86 | 32 | 7 | 80 | 3 | 0 | 11 | 3 | 2 | .60 | 14 | .265 | .303 | .422 |
| 9 ML YEARS | | | 1181 | 4528 | 1294 | 237 | 32 | 202 | (88 | 114) | 2201 | 641 | 740 | 255 | 37 | 563 | 35 | 0 | 59 | 59 | 27 | .69 | 112 | .286 | .325 | .486 |

## Jay Bell

**Bats:** Right **Throws:** Right **Pos:** SS **Ht:** 6' 1" **Wt:** 180 **Born:** 12/11/65 **Age:** 25

| BATTING | | | | | | | | | | | | | | | | | | | | BASERUNNING | | | | PERCENTAGES | | |
|---|---|---|---|---|---|---|---|---|---|---|---|---|---|---|---|---|---|---|---|---|---|---|---|---|---|---|
| Year | Team | Lg | G | AB | H | 2B | 3B | HR | (Hm | Rd) | TB | R | RBI | TBB | IBB | SO | HBP | SH | SF | SB | CS | SB% | GDP | Avg | OBP | SLG |
| 1986 | Cleveland | AL | 5 | 14 | 5 | 2 | 0 | 1 | (0 | 1) | 10 | 3 | 4 | 2 | 0 | 3 | 0 | 0 | 0 | 0 | 0 | .00 | 0 | .357 | .438 | .714 |
| 1987 | Cleveland | AL | 38 | 125 | 27 | 9 | 1 | 2 | (1 | 1) | 44 | 14 | 13 | 8 | 0 | 31 | 1 | 3 | 0 | 2 | 0 | 1.00 | 0 | .216 | .269 | .352 |
| 1988 | Cleveland | AL | 73 | 211 | 46 | 5 | 1 | 2 | (2 | 0) | 59 | 23 | 21 | 21 | 0 | 53 | 1 | 1 | 2 | 4 | 2 | .67 | 3 | .218 | .289 | .280 |
| 1989 | Pittsburgh | NL | 78 | 271 | 70 | 13 | 3 | 2 | (1 | 1) | 95 | 33 | 27 | 19 | 0 | 47 | 1 | 10 | 2 | 5 | 3 | .63 | 9 | .258 | .307 | .351 |
| 1990 | Pittsburgh | NL | 159 | 583 | 148 | 28 | 7 | 7 | (1 | 6) | 211 | 93 | 52 | 65 | 0 | 109 | 3 | 39 | 6 | 10 | 6 | .63 | 14 | .254 | .329 | .362 |
| 5 ML YEARS | | | 353 | 1204 | 296 | 57 | 12 | 14 | (5 | 9) | 419 | 166 | 117 | 115 | 0 | 243 | 6 | 53 | 10 | 21 | 11 | .66 | 26 | .246 | .312 | .348 |

## Juan Bell

**Bats:** Both **Throws:** Right **Pos:** SS **Ht:** 5'11" **Wt:** 172 **Born:** 03/29/68 **Age:** 23

| BATTING | | | | | | | | | | | | | | | | | | | | BASERUNNING | | | | PERCENTAGES | | |
|---|---|---|---|---|---|---|---|---|---|---|---|---|---|---|---|---|---|---|---|---|---|---|---|---|---|---|
| Year | Team | Lg | G | AB | H | 2B | 3B | HR | (Hm | Rd) | TB | R | RBI | TBB | IBB | SO | HBP | SH | SF | SB | CS | SB% | GDP | Avg | OBP | SLG |
| 1989 | Baltimore | AL | 8 | 4 | 0 | 0 | 0 | 0 | (0 | 0) | 0 | 2 | 0 | 0 | 0 | 1 | 0 | 0 | 0 | 1 | 0 | 1.00 | 0 | .000 | .000 | .000 |
| 1990 | Baltimore | AL | 5 | 2 | 0 | 0 | 0 | 0 | (0 | 0) | 0 | 1 | 0 | 0 | 0 | 1 | 0 | 0 | 0 | 0 | 0 | .00 | 0 | .000 | .000 | .000 |
| | 2 ML YEARS | | 13 | 6 | 0 | 0 | 0 | 0 | (0 | 0) | 0 | 3 | 0 | 0 | 0 | 2 | 0 | 0 | 0 | 1 | 0 | 1.00 | 0 | .000 | .000 | .000 |

## Mike Bell

**Bats:** Left **Throws:** Left **Pos:** 1B **Ht:** 6' 1" **Wt:** 175 **Born:** 04/22/68 **Age:** 23

| BATTING | | | | | | | | | | | | | | | | | | | | BASERUNNING | | | | PERCENTAGES | | |
|---|---|---|---|---|---|---|---|---|---|---|---|---|---|---|---|---|---|---|---|---|---|---|---|---|---|---|
| Year | Team | Lg | G | AB | H | 2B | 3B | HR | (Hm | Rd) | TB | R | RBI | TBB | IBB | SO | HBP | SH | SF | SB | CS | SB% | GDP | Avg | OBP | SLG |
| 1987 | Sumter | A | 133 | 443 | 108 | 17 | 3 | 5 | -- | -- | 146 | 54 | 51 | 54 | 3 | 95 | 3 | 0 | 1 | 11 | 9 | .55 | 10 | .244 | .329 | .330 |
| 1988 | Durham | A | 126 | 440 | 113 | 18 | 3 | 17 | -- | -- | 188 | 72 | 84 | 58 | 3 | 91 | 6 | 2 | 6 | 11 | 3 | .79 | 5 | .257 | .347 | .427 |
| | Greenville | AA | 4 | 12 | 3 | 1 | 0 | 0 | -- | -- | 4 | 1 | 4 | 1 | 0 | 1 | 0 | 0 | 0 | 0 | 0 | .00 | 0 | .250 | .308 | .333 |
| 1989 | Greenville | AA | 132 | 472 | 115 | 26 | 3 | 6 | -- | -- | 165 | 63 | 57 | 62 | 6 | 91 | 2 | 1 | 1 | 10 | 5 | .67 | 8 | .244 | .333 | .350 |
| 1990 | Greenville | AA | 106 | 405 | 118 | 24 | 2 | 6 | -- | -- | 164 | 50 | 42 | 41 | 6 | 63 | 5 | 4 | 2 | 10 | 4 | .71 | 3 | .291 | .362 | .405 |
| 1990 | Atlanta | NL | 36 | 45 | 11 | 5 | 1 | 1 | (0 | 1) | 21 | 8 | 5 | 2 | 0 | 9 | 1 | 0 | 0 | 0 | 1 | .00 | 4 | .244 | .292 | .467 |

## Joey Belle

**Bats:** Right **Throws:** Right **Pos:** DH **Ht:** 6' 2" **Wt:** 200 **Born:** 08/25/66 **Age:** 24

| BATTING | | | | | | | | | | | | | | | | | | | | BASERUNNING | | | | PERCENTAGES | | |
|---|---|---|---|---|---|---|---|---|---|---|---|---|---|---|---|---|---|---|---|---|---|---|---|---|---|---|
| Year | Team | Lg | G | AB | H | 2B | 3B | HR | (Hm | Rd) | TB | R | RBI | TBB | IBB | SO | HBP | SH | SF | SB | CS | SB% | GDP | Avg | OBP | SLG |
| 1987 | Kinston | A | 10 | 37 | 12 | 2 | 0 | 3 | -- | -- | 23 | 5 | 9 | 8 | 0 | 16 | 0 | 0 | 0 | 0 | 1 | .00 | 1 | .324 | .444 | .622 |
| 1988 | Kinston | A | 41 | 153 | 46 | 16 | 0 | 8 | -- | -- | 86 | 21 | 39 | 18 | 1 | 45 | 0 | 0 | 0 | 2 | 0 | 1.00 | 4 | .301 | .374 | .562 |
| | Waterloo | A | 9 | 28 | 7 | 1 | 0 | 1 | -- | -- | 11 | 2 | 2 | 1 | 0 | 9 | 0 | 0 | 0 | 0 | 0 | .00 | 1 | .250 | .276 | .393 |
| 1989 | Canton-Akrn | AA | 89 | 312 | 88 | 20 | 0 | 20 | -- | -- | 168 | 48 | 69 | 32 | 5 | 82 | 4 | 0 | 2 | 8 | 4 | .67 | 6 | .282 | .354 | .538 |
| 1990 | Colo Sprngs | AAA | 24 | 96 | 33 | 3 | 1 | 5 | -- | -- | 53 | 16 | 19 | 5 | 0 | 16 | 0 | 0 | 0 | 4 | 3 | .57 | 4 | .344 | .376 | .552 |
| | Canton-Akrn | AA | 9 | 32 | 8 | 1 | 0 | 0 | -- | -- | 9 | 4 | 3 | 3 | 1 | 7 | 0 | 0 | 0 | 0 | 0 | .00 | 2 | .250 | .314 | .281 |
| 1989 | Cleveland | AL | 62 | 218 | 49 | 8 | 4 | 7 | (3 | 4) | 86 | 22 | 37 | 12 | 0 | 55 | 2 | 0 | 2 | 2 | 2 | .50 | 4 | .225 | .269 | .394 |
| 1990 | Cleveland | AL | 9 | 23 | 4 | 0 | 0 | 1 | (1 | 0) | 7 | 1 | 3 | 1 | 0 | 6 | 0 | 1 | 0 | 0 | 0 | .00 | 1 | .174 | .208 | .304 |
| | 2 ML YEARS | | 71 | 241 | 53 | 8 | 4 | 8 | (4 | 4) | 93 | 23 | 40 | 13 | 0 | 61 | 2 | 1 | 2 | 2 | 2 | .50 | 5 | .220 | .264 | .386 |

## Rafael Belliard

**Bats:** Right **Throws:** Right **Pos:** 2B **Ht:** 5' 6" **Wt:** 160 **Born:** 10/24/61 **Age:** 29

| BATTING | | | | | | | | | | | | | | | | | | | | BASERUNNING | | | | PERCENTAGES | | |
|---|---|---|---|---|---|---|---|---|---|---|---|---|---|---|---|---|---|---|---|---|---|---|---|---|---|---|
| Year | Team | Lg | G | AB | H | 2B | 3B | HR | (Hm | Rd) | TB | R | RBI | TBB | IBB | SO | HBP | SH | SF | SB | CS | SB% | GDP | Avg | OBP | SLG |
| 1982 | Pittsburgh | NL | 9 | 2 | 1 | 0 | 0 | 0 | (0 | 0) | 1 | 3 | 0 | 0 | 0 | 0 | 0 | 0 | 0 | 1 | 0 | 1.00 | 0 | .500 | .500 | .500 |
| 1983 | Pittsburgh | NL | 4 | 1 | 0 | 0 | 0 | 0 | (0 | 0) | 0 | 1 | 0 | 0 | 0 | 1 | 0 | 0 | 0 | 0 | 0 | .00 | 0 | .000 | .000 | .000 |
| 1984 | Pittsburgh | NL | 20 | 22 | 5 | 0 | 0 | 0 | (0 | 0) | 5 | 3 | 0 | 0 | 0 | 1 | 0 | 0 | 0 | 4 | 1 | .80 | 0 | .227 | .227 | .227 |
| 1985 | Pittsburgh | NL | 17 | 20 | 4 | 0 | 0 | 0 | (0 | 0) | 4 | 1 | 1 | 0 | 0 | 5 | 0 | 0 | 0 | 0 | 0 | .00 | 0 | .200 | .200 | .200 |
| 1986 | Pittsburgh | NL | 117 | 309 | 72 | 5 | 2 | 0 | (0 | 0) | 81 | 33 | 31 | 26 | 6 | 54 | 3 | 11 | 1 | 12 | 2 | .86 | 8 | .233 | .298 | .262 |
| 1987 | Pittsburgh | NL | 81 | 203 | 42 | 4 | 3 | 1 | (0 | 1) | 55 | 26 | 15 | 20 | 6 | 25 | 3 | 2 | 1 | 5 | 1 | .83 | 4 | .207 | .286 | .271 |
| 1988 | Pittsburgh | NL | 122 | 286 | 61 | 0 | 4 | 0 | (0 | 0) | 69 | 28 | 11 | 26 | 3 | 47 | 4 | 5 | 0 | 7 | 1 | .88 | 10 | .213 | .288 | .241 |
| 1989 | Pittsburgh | NL | 67 | 154 | 33 | 4 | 0 | 0 | (0 | 0) | 37 | 10 | 8 | 8 | 2 | 22 | 0 | 3 | 0 | 5 | 2 | .71 | 1 | .214 | .253 | .240 |
| 1990 | Pittsburgh | NL | 47 | 54 | 11 | 3 | 0 | 0 | (0 | 0) | 14 | 10 | 6 | 5 | 0 | 13 | 1 | 1 | 0 | 1 | 2 | .33 | 2 | .204 | .283 | .259 |
| | 9 ML YEARS | | 484 | 1051 | 229 | 16 | 9 | 1 | (0 | 1) | 266 | 115 | 72 | 85 | 17 | 168 | 11 | 22 | 2 | 35 | 9 | .80 | 25 | .218 | .283 | .253 |

## Andy Benes

**Pitches:** Right **Bats:** Right **Pos:** SP **Ht:** 6' 6" **Wt:** 235 **Born:** 08/20/67 **Age:** 23

| HOW MUCH HE PITCHED | | | | | | | | | WHAT HE GAVE UP | | | | | | | | | | | | THE RESULTS | | | | | |
|---|---|---|---|---|---|---|---|---|---|---|---|---|---|---|---|---|---|---|---|---|---|---|---|---|---|---|
| Year | Team | Lg | G | GS | CG | GF | IP | BFP | H | R | ER | HR | SH | SF | HB | TBB | IBB | SO | WP | Bk | W | L | Pct. | ShO | Sv | ERA |
| 1989 | Wichita | AA | 16 | 16 | 5 | 0 | 108.1 | 437 | 79 | 32 | 26 | 6 | 5 | 2 | 2 | 39 | 1 | 115 | 1 | 2 | 8 | 4 | .667 | 3 | 0 | 2.16 |
| | Las Vegas | AAA | 5 | 5 | 0 | 0 | 26.2 | 133 | 41 | 29 | 24 | 8 | 2 | 0 | 0 | 12 | 0 | 29 | 2 | 2 | 2 | 1 | .667 | 0 | 0 | 8.10 |
| 1989 | San Diego | NL | 10 | 10 | 0 | 0 | 66.2 | 280 | 51 | 28 | 26 | 7 | 6 | 2 | 1 | 31 | 0 | 66 | 0 | 3 | 6 | 3 | .667 | 0 | 0 | 3.51 |
| 1990 | San Diego | NL | 32 | 31 | 2 | 1 | 192.1 | 811 | 177 | 87 | 77 | 18 | 5 | 6 | 1 | 69 | 5 | 140 | 2 | 5 | 10 | 11 | .476 | 0 | 0 | 3.60 |
| | 2 ML YEARS | | 42 | 41 | 2 | 1 | 259 | 1091 | 228 | 115 | 103 | 25 | 11 | 8 | 2 | 100 | 5 | 206 | 2 | 8 | 16 | 14 | .533 | 0 | 0 | 3.58 |

## Mike Benjamin

**Bats:** Right **Throws:** Right **Pos:** SS **Ht:** 6' 3" **Wt:** 195 **Born:** 11/22/65 **Age:** 25

| BATTING | | | | | | | | | | | | | | | | | | | | BASERUNNING | | | | PERCENTAGES | | |
|---|---|---|---|---|---|---|---|---|---|---|---|---|---|---|---|---|---|---|---|---|---|---|---|---|---|---|
| Year | Team | Lg | G | AB | H | 2B | 3B | HR | (Hm | Rd) | TB | R | RBI | TBB | IBB | SO | HBP | SH | SF | SB | CS | SB% | GDP | Avg | OBP | SLG |
| 1987 | Fresno | A | 64 | 212 | 51 | 6 | 4 | 6 | -- | -- | 83 | 25 | 24 | 24 | 1 | 71 | 2 | 2 | 0 | 6 | 2 | .75 | 1 | .241 | .324 | .392 |
| 1988 | Shreveport | AA | 89 | 309 | 73 | 19 | 5 | 6 | -- | -- | 120 | 48 | 37 | 22 | 1 | 63 | 0 | 5 | 2 | 14 | 6 | .70 | 5 | .236 | .285 | .388 |
| | Phoenix | AAA | 37 | 106 | 18 | 4 | 1 | 0 | -- | -- | 24 | 13 | 6 | 13 | 0 | 32 | 2 | 2 | 1 | 2 | 1 | .67 | 3 | .170 | .270 | .226 |

| Year | Team | Lg | G | AB | H | 2B | 3B | HR | (Hm | Rd) | TB | R | RBI | TBB | IBB | SO | HBP | SH | SF | SB | CS | SB% | GDP | Avg | OBP | SLG |
|---|---|---|---|---|---|---|---|---|---|---|---|---|---|---|---|---|---|---|---|---|---|---|---|---|---|---|
| 1989 | Phoenix | AAA | 113 | 363 | 94 | 17 | 6 | 3 | -- | -- | 132 | 44 | 36 | 18 | 1 | 82 | 6 | 12 | 2 | 10 | 4 | .71 | 6 | .259 | .303 | .364 |
| 1990 | Phoenix | AAA | 118 | 419 | 105 | 21 | 7 | 5 | -- | -- | 155 | 61 | 39 | 25 | 3 | 89 | 5 | 2 | 5 | 13 | 7 | .65 | 6 | .251 | .297 | .370 |
| 1989 | San Francisco | NL | 14 | 6 | 1 | 0 | 0 | 0 | (0 | 0) | 1 | 6 | 0 | 0 | 0 | 1 | 0 | 0 | 0 | 0 | 0 | .00 | 0 | .167 | .167 | .167 |
| 1990 | San Francisco | NL | 22 | 56 | 12 | 3 | 1 | 2 | (2 | 0) | 23 | 7 | 3 | 3 | 1 | 10 | 0 | 0 | 0 | 1 | 0 | 1.00 | 2 | .214 | .254 | .411 |
| | 2 ML YEARS | | 36 | 62 | 13 | 3 | 1 | 2 | (2 | 0) | 24 | 13 | 3 | 3 | 1 | 11 | 0 | 0 | 0 | 1 | 0 | 1.00 | 2 | .210 | .246 | .387 |

## Todd Benzinger

**Bats:** Both **Throws:** Right **Pos:** 1B **Ht:** 6' 1" **Wt:** 190 **Born:** 02/11/63 **Age:** 28

| | | | BATTING | | | | | | | | | | | | | | | | | BASERUNNING | | | | PERCENTAGES | | |
|---|---|---|---|---|---|---|---|---|---|---|---|---|---|---|---|---|---|---|---|---|---|---|---|---|---|---|
| Year | Team | Lg | G | AB | H | 2B | 3B | HR | (Hm | Rd) | TB | R | RBI | TBB | IBB | SO | HBP | SH | SF | SB | CS | SB% | GDP | Avg | OBP | SLG |
| 1987 | Boston | AL | 73 | 223 | 62 | 11 | 1 | 8 | (5 | 3) | 99 | 36 | 43 | 22 | 3 | 41 | 2 | 3 | 3 | 5 | 4 | .56 | 5 | .278 | .344 | .444 |
| 1988 | Boston | AL | 120 | 405 | 103 | 28 | 1 | 13 | (6 | 7) | 172 | 47 | 70 | 22 | 4 | 80 | 1 | 6 | 2 | 2 | 3 | .40 | 8 | .254 | .293 | .425 |
| 1989 | Cincinnati | NL | 161 | 628 | 154 | 28 | 3 | 17 | (6 | 11) | 239 | 79 | 76 | 44 | 13 | 120 | 2 | 4 | 8 | 3 | 7 | .30 | 5 | .245 | .293 | .381 |
| 1990 | Cincinnati | NL | 118 | 376 | 95 | 14 | 2 | 5 | (4 | 1) | 128 | 35 | 46 | 19 | 4 | 69 | 4 | 2 | 7 | 3 | 4 | .43 | 3 | .253 | .291 | .340 |
| | 4 ML YEARS | | 472 | 1632 | 414 | 81 | 7 | 43 | (21 | 22) | 638 | 197 | 235 | 107 | 24 | 310 | 9 | 15 | 20 | 13 | 18 | .42 | 21 | .254 | .300 | .391 |

## Juan Berenguer

**Pitches:** Right **Bats:** Right **Pos:** RP **Ht:** 5'11" **Wt:** 223 **Born:** 11/30/54 **Age:** 36

| | | | HOW MUCH HE PITCHED | | | | | | WHAT HE GAVE UP | | | | | | | | | | | | THE RESULTS | | | | | |
|---|---|---|---|---|---|---|---|---|---|---|---|---|---|---|---|---|---|---|---|---|---|---|---|---|---|---|
| Year | Team | Lg | G | GS | CG | GF | IP | BFP | H | R | ER | HR | SH | SF | HB | TBB | IBB | SO | WP | Bk | W | L | Pct. | ShO | Sv | ERA |
| 1978 | New York | NL | 5 | 3 | 0 | 1 | 13 | 65 | 17 | 12 | 12 | 1 | 0 | 1 | 1 | 11 | 0 | 8 | 0 | 0 | 0 | 2 | .000 | 0 | 0 | 8.31 |
| 1979 | New York | NL | 5 | 5 | 0 | 0 | 31 | 126 | 28 | 13 | 10 | 2 | 1 | 1 | 1 | 12 | 0 | 25 | 0 | 2 | 1 | 1 | .500 | 0 | 0 | 2.90 |
| 1980 | New York | NL | 6 | 0 | 0 | 4 | 9 | 46 | 9 | 9 | 6 | 1 | 0 | 0 | 0 | 10 | 2 | 7 | 0 | 0 | 0 | 1 | .000 | 0 | 0 | 6.00 |
| 1981 | 2 ML Teams | | 20 | 14 | 1 | 4 | 91 | 405 | 84 | 62 | 53 | 11 | 2 | 7 | 5 | 51 | 1 | 49 | 2 | 0 | 2 | 13 | .133 | 0 | 0 | 5.24 |
| 1982 | Detroit | AL | 2 | 1 | 0 | 0 | 6.2 | 34 | 5 | 5 | 5 | 0 | 0 | 0 | 0 | 9 | 1 | 8 | 0 | 0 | 0 | 0 | .000 | 0 | 0 | 6.75 |
| 1983 | Detroit | AL | 37 | 19 | 2 | 7 | 157.2 | 650 | 110 | 58 | 55 | 19 | 1 | 2 | 6 | 71 | 3 | 129 | 3 | 1 | 9 | 5 | .643 | 1 | 1 | 3.14 |
| 1984 | Detroit | AL | 31 | 27 | 2 | 0 | 168.1 | 720 | 146 | 75 | 65 | 14 | 2 | 6 | 5 | 79 | 2 | 118 | 7 | 2 | 11 | 10 | .524 | 1 | 0 | 3.48 |
| 1985 | Detroit | AL | 31 | 13 | 0 | 9 | 95 | 424 | 96 | 67 | 59 | 12 | 1 | 4 | 1 | 48 | 3 | 82 | 4 | 1 | 5 | 6 | .455 | 0 | 0 | 5.59 |
| 1986 | San Francisco | NL | 46 | 4 | 0 | 17 | 73.1 | 314 | 64 | 23 | 22 | 4 | 2 | 1 | 2 | 44 | 3 | 72 | 4 | 2 | 2 | 3 | .400 | 0 | 4 | 2.70 |
| 1987 | Minnesota | AL | 47 | 6 | 0 | 13 | 112 | 473 | 100 | 51 | 49 | 10 | 2 | 4 | 0 | 47 | 7 | 110 | 6 | 0 | 8 | 1 | .889 | 0 | 4 | 3.94 |
| 1988 | Minnesota | AL | 57 | 1 | 0 | 27 | 100 | 428 | 74 | 44 | 44 | 7 | 5 | 4 | 1 | 61 | 7 | 99 | 3 | 5 | 8 | 4 | .667 | 0 | 2 | 3.96 |
| 1989 | Minnesota | AL | 56 | 0 | 0 | 17 | 106 | 452 | 96 | 44 | 41 | 11 | 7 | 5 | 2 | 47 | 0 | 93 | 5 | 3 | 9 | 3 | .750 | 0 | 3 | 3.48 |
| 1990 | Minnesota | AL | 51 | 0 | 0 | 13 | 100.1 | 434 | 85 | 43 | 38 | 9 | 5 | 2 | 2 | 58 | 4 | 77 | 5 | 0 | 8 | 5 | .615 | 0 | 0 | 3.41 |
| 1981 | Kansas City | AL | 8 | 3 | 0 | 4 | 20 | 97 | 22 | 21 | 19 | 4 | 0 | 3 | 2 | 16 | 0 | 20 | 1 | 0 | 0 | 4 | .000 | 0 | 0 | 8.55 |
| | Toronto | AL | 12 | 11 | 1 | 0 | 71 | 308 | 62 | 41 | 34 | 7 | 2 | 4 | 3 | 35 | 1 | 29 | 1 | 0 | 2 | 9 | .182 | 0 | 0 | 4.31 |
| | 13 ML YEARS | | 394 | 93 | 5 | 112 | 1063.1 | 4571 | 914 | 506 | 459 | 101 | 28 | 37 | 26 | 548 | 33 | 877 | 39 | 16 | 63 | 54 | .538 | 2 | 14 | 3.88 |

## Dave Bergman

**Bats:** Left **Throws:** Left **Pos:** DH/1B **Ht:** 6' 2" **Wt:** 190 **Born:** 06/06/53 **Age:** 38

| | | | BATTING | | | | | | | | | | | | | | | | | BASERUNNING | | | | PERCENTAGES | | |
|---|---|---|---|---|---|---|---|---|---|---|---|---|---|---|---|---|---|---|---|---|---|---|---|---|---|---|
| Year | Team | Lg | G | AB | H | 2B | 3B | HR | (Hm | Rd) | TB | R | RBI | TBB | IBB | SO | HBP | SH | SF | SB | CS | SB% | GDP | Avg | OBP | SLG |
| 1975 | New York | AL | 7 | 17 | 0 | 0 | 0 | 0 | (0 | 0) | 0 | 0 | 0 | 2 | 0 | 4 | 0 | 0 | 0 | 0 | 0 | .00 | 0 | .000 | .105 | .000 |
| 1977 | New York | NL | 5 | 4 | 1 | 0 | 0 | 0 | (0 | 0) | 1 | 1 | 1 | 0 | 0 | 0 | 0 | 0 | 1 | 0 | 0 | .00 | 0 | .250 | .200 | .250 |
| 1978 | Houston | NL | 104 | 186 | 43 | 5 | 1 | 0 | (0 | 0) | 50 | 15 | 12 | 39 | 9 | 32 | 0 | 1 | 2 | 2 | 0 | 1.00 | 5 | .231 | .361 | .269 |
| 1979 | Houston | NL | 13 | 15 | 6 | 0 | 0 | 1 | (0 | 1) | 9 | 4 | 2 | 0 | 0 | 3 | 0 | 0 | 0 | 0 | 0 | .00 | 0 | .400 | .400 | .600 |
| 1980 | Houston | NL | 90 | 78 | 20 | 6 | 1 | 0 | (0 | 0) | 28 | 12 | 3 | 10 | 2 | 10 | 0 | 3 | 0 | 1 | 0 | 1.00 | 1 | .256 | .341 | .359 |
| 1981 | 2 ML Teams | | 69 | 151 | 38 | 9 | 0 | 4 | (1 | 3) | 59 | 17 | 14 | 19 | 3 | 18 | 0 | 2 | 1 | 2 | 0 | 1.00 | 4 | .252 | .333 | .391 |
| 1982 | San Francisco | NL | 100 | 121 | 33 | 3 | 1 | 4 | (2 | 2) | 50 | 22 | 14 | 18 | 3 | 11 | 0 | 0 | 1 | 3 | 0 | 1.00 | 1 | .273 | .364 | .413 |
| 1983 | San Francisco | NL | 90 | 140 | 40 | 4 | 1 | 6 | (3 | 3) | 64 | 16 | 24 | 24 | 2 | 21 | 1 | 2 | 0 | 2 | 1 | .67 | 5 | .286 | .394 | .457 |
| 1984 | Detroit | AL | 120 | 271 | 74 | 8 | 5 | 7 | (4 | 3) | 113 | 42 | 44 | 33 | 2 | 40 | 3 | 3 | 6 | 3 | 4 | .43 | 4 | .273 | .351 | .417 |
| 1985 | Detroit | AL | 69 | 140 | 25 | 2 | 0 | 3 | (2 | 1) | 36 | 8 | 7 | 14 | 0 | 15 | 0 | 1 | 2 | 0 | 0 | .00 | 6 | .179 | .250 | .257 |
| 1986 | Detroit | AL | 65 | 130 | 30 | 6 | 1 | 1 | (0 | 1) | 41 | 14 | 9 | 21 | 0 | 16 | 0 | 0 | 0 | 0 | 0 | .00 | 3 | .231 | .338 | .315 |
| 1987 | Detroit | AL | 91 | 172 | 47 | 7 | 3 | 6 | (4 | 2) | 78 | 25 | 22 | 30 | 4 | 23 | 1 | 1 | 3 | 0 | 1 | .00 | 1 | .273 | .379 | .453 |
| 1988 | Detroit | AL | 116 | 289 | 85 | 14 | 0 | 5 | (4 | 1) | 114 | 37 | 35 | 38 | 2 | 34 | 0 | 2 | 4 | 0 | 2 | .00 | 7 | .294 | .372 | .394 |
| 1989 | Detroit | AL | 137 | 385 | 103 | 13 | 1 | 7 | (6 | 1) | 139 | 38 | 37 | 44 | 3 | 44 | 2 | 4 | 1 | 1 | 3 | .25 | 5 | .268 | .345 | .361 |
| 1990 | Detroit | AL | 100 | 205 | 57 | 10 | 1 | 2 | (1 | 1) | 75 | 21 | 26 | 33 | 3 | 17 | 0 | 1 | 2 | 3 | 2 | .60 | 7 | .278 | .375 | .366 |
| 1981 | Houston | NL | 6 | 6 | 1 | 0 | 0 | 1 | (0 | 1) | 4 | 1 | 1 | 0 | 0 | 0 | 0 | 0 | 0 | 0 | 0 | .00 | 0 | .167 | .167 | .667 |
| | San Francisco | NL | 63 | 145 | 37 | 9 | 0 | 3 | (1 | 2) | 55 | 16 | 13 | 19 | 3 | 18 | 0 | 2 | 1 | 2 | 0 | 1.00 | 4 | .255 | .339 | .379 |
| | 15 ML YEARS | | 1176 | 2304 | 602 | 87 | 15 | 46 | (27 | 19) | 857 | 272 | 250 | 325 | 33 | 288 | 7 | 20 | 23 | 17 | 13 | .57 | 49 | .261 | .351 | .372 |

## Geronimo Berroa

**Bats:** Right **Throws:** Right **Pos:** LF **Ht:** 6' 0" **Wt:** 165 **Born:** 03/18/65 **Age:** 26

| | | | BATTING | | | | | | | | | | | | | | | | | BASERUNNING | | | | PERCENTAGES | | |
|---|---|---|---|---|---|---|---|---|---|---|---|---|---|---|---|---|---|---|---|---|---|---|---|---|---|---|
| Year | Team | Lg | G | AB | H | 2B | 3B | HR | (Hm | Rd) | TB | R | RBI | TBB | IBB | SO | HBP | SH | SF | SB | CS | SB% | GDP | Avg | OBP | SLG |
| 1989 | Atlanta | NL | 81 | 136 | 36 | 4 | 0 | 2 | (1 | 1) | 46 | 7 | 9 | 7 | 1 | 32 | 0 | 0 | 0 | 0 | 1 | .00 | 2 | .265 | .301 | .338 |
| 1990 | Atlanta | NL | 7 | 4 | 0 | 0 | 0 | 0 | (0 | 0) | 0 | 0 | 0 | 1 | 1 | 1 | 0 | 0 | 0 | 0 | 0 | .00 | 0 | .000 | .200 | .000 |
| | 2 ML YEARS | | 88 | 140 | 36 | 4 | 0 | 2 | (1 | 1) | 46 | 7 | 9 | 8 | 2 | 33 | 0 | 0 | 0 | 0 | 1 | .00 | 2 | .257 | .297 | .329 |

## Sean Berry

**Bats:** Right **Throws:** Right **Pos:** 3B **Ht:** 5'11" **Wt:** 200 **Born:** 03/22/66 **Age:** 25

| BATTING | | | | | | | | | | | | | | | | | | | BASERUNNING | | | | PERCENTAGES | | |
|---|---|---|---|---|---|---|---|---|---|---|---|---|---|---|---|---|---|---|---|---|---|---|---|---|---|
| Year Team | Lg | G | AB | H | 2B | 3B | HR | (Hm | Rd) | TB | R | RBI | TBB | IBB | SO | HBP | SH | SF | SB | CS | SB% | GDP | Avg | OBP | SLG |
| 1986 Eugene | A | 65 | 238 | 76 | 20 | 2 | 5 | -- | -- | 115 | 53 | 44 | 44 | 0 | 73 | 5 | 1 | 2 | 10 | 1 | .91 | 2 | .319 | .433 | .483 |
| 1987 Ft. Myers | A | 66 | 205 | 52 | 7 | 2 | 2 | -- | -- | 69 | 26 | 30 | 43 | 2 | 65 | 3 | 1 | 1 | 4 | 4 | .50 | 1 | .254 | .389 | .337 |
| 1988 Baseball Cy | A | 94 | 304 | 71 | 6 | 4 | 4 | -- | -- | 97 | 34 | 30 | 31 | 1 | 62 | 2 | 3 | 3 | 24 | 11 | .69 | 3 | .234 | .306 | .319 |
| 1989 Baseball Cy | A | 116 | 399 | 106 | 19 | 7 | 4 | -- | -- | 151 | 67 | 44 | 44 | 1 | 68 | 6 | 5 | 5 | 37 | 11 | .77 | 6 | .266 | .344 | .378 |
| 1990 Memphis | AA | 135 | 487 | 142 | 25 | 4 | 14 | -- | -- | 217 | 73 | 77 | 44 | 1 | 89 | 5 | 7 | 5 | 18 | 9 | .67 | 10 | .292 | .353 | .446 |
| 1990 Kansas City | AL | 8 | 23 | 5 | 1 | 1 | 0 | (0 | 0) | 8 | 2 | 4 | 2 | 0 | 5 | 0 | 0 | 0 | 0 | 0 | .00 | 0 | .217 | .280 | .348 |

## Damon Berryhill

**Bats:** Both **Throws:** Right **Pos:** C **Ht:** 6' 0" **Wt:** 205 **Born:** 12/03/63 **Age:** 27

| BATTING | | | | | | | | | | | | | | | | | | | BASERUNNING | | | | PERCENTAGES | | |
|---|---|---|---|---|---|---|---|---|---|---|---|---|---|---|---|---|---|---|---|---|---|---|---|---|---|
| Year Team | Lg | G | AB | H | 2B | 3B | HR | (Hm | Rd) | TB | R | RBI | TBB | IBB | SO | HBP | SH | SF | SB | CS | SB% | GDP | Avg | OBP | SLG |
| 1987 Chicago | NL | 12 | 28 | 5 | 1 | 0 | 0 | (0 | 0) | 6 | 2 | 1 | 3 | 0 | 5 | 0 | 0 | 0 | 0 | 1 | .00 | 1 | .179 | .258 | .214 |
| 1988 Chicago | NL | 95 | 309 | 80 | 19 | 1 | 7 | (5 | 2) | 122 | 19 | 38 | 17 | 5 | 56 | 0 | 3 | 3 | 1 | 0 | 1.00 | 11 | .259 | .295 | .395 |
| 1989 Chicago | NL | 91 | 334 | 86 | 13 | 0 | 5 | (2 | 3) | 114 | 37 | 41 | 16 | 4 | 54 | 2 | 4 | 5 | 1 | 0 | 1.00 | 13 | .257 | .291 | .341 |
| 1990 Chicago | NL | 17 | 53 | 10 | 4 | 0 | 1 | (1 | 0) | 17 | 6 | 9 | 5 | 1 | 14 | 0 | 0 | 1 | 0 | 0 | .00 | 3 | .189 | .254 | .321 |
| 4 ML YEARS | | 215 | 724 | 181 | 37 | 1 | 13 | (8 | 5) | 259 | 64 | 89 | 41 | 10 | 129 | 2 | 7 | 9 | 2 | 1 | .67 | 28 | .250 | .289 | .358 |

## Dante Bichette

**Bats:** Right **Throws:** Right **Pos:** RF/LF/CF **Ht:** 6' 3" **Wt:** 215 **Born:** 11/18/63 **Age:** 27

| BATTING | | | | | | | | | | | | | | | | | | | BASERUNNING | | | | PERCENTAGES | | |
|---|---|---|---|---|---|---|---|---|---|---|---|---|---|---|---|---|---|---|---|---|---|---|---|---|---|
| Year Team | Lg | G | AB | H | 2B | 3B | HR | (Hm | Rd) | TB | R | RBI | TBB | IBB | SO | HBP | SH | SF | SB | CS | SB% | GDP | Avg | OBP | SLG |
| 1988 California | AL | 21 | 46 | 12 | 2 | 0 | 0 | (0 | 0) | 14 | 1 | 8 | 0 | 0 | 7 | 0 | 0 | 4 | 0 | 0 | .00 | 0 | .261 | .240 | .304 |
| 1989 California | AL | 48 | 138 | 29 | 7 | 0 | 3 | (2 | 1) | 45 | 13 | 15 | 6 | 0 | 24 | 0 | 0 | 2 | 3 | 0 | 1.00 | 3 | .210 | .240 | .326 |
| 1990 California | AL | 109 | 349 | 89 | 15 | 1 | 15 | (8 | 7) | 151 | 40 | 53 | 16 | 1 | 79 | 3 | 1 | 2 | 5 | 2 | .71 | 9 | .255 | .292 | .433 |
| 3 ML YEARS | | 178 | 533 | 130 | 24 | 1 | 18 | (10 | 8) | 210 | 54 | 76 | 22 | 1 | 110 | 3 | 1 | 8 | 8 | 2 | .80 | 12 | .244 | .274 | .394 |

## Mike Bielecki

**Pitches:** Right **Bats:** Right **Pos:** SP/RP **Ht:** 6' 3" **Wt:** 195 **Born:** 07/31/59 **Age:** 31

| HOW MUCH HE PITCHED | | | | | | | | WHAT HE GAVE UP | | | | | | | | | | | | THE RESULTS | | | | | |
|---|---|---|---|---|---|---|---|---|---|---|---|---|---|---|---|---|---|---|---|---|---|---|---|---|---|
| Year Team | Lg | G | GS | CG | GF | IP | BFP | H | R | ER | HR | SH | SF | HB | TBB | IBB | SO | WP | Bk | W | L | Pct. | ShO | Sv | ERA |
| 1984 Pittsburgh | NL | 4 | 0 | 0 | 1 | 4.1 | 17 | 4 | 0 | 0 | 0 | 1 | 0 | 0 | 0 | 0 | 1 | 0 | 1 | 0 | 0 | .000 | 0 | 0 | 0.00 |
| 1985 Pittsburgh | NL | 12 | 7 | 0 | 1 | 45.2 | 211 | 45 | 26 | 23 | 5 | 4 | 0 | 1 | 31 | 1 | 22 | 1 | 1 | 2 | 3 | .400 | 0 | 0 | 4.53 |
| 1986 Pittsburgh | NL | 31 | 27 | 0 | 0 | 148.2 | 667 | 149 | 87 | 77 | 10 | 7 | 6 | 2 | 83 | 3 | 83 | 7 | 5 | 6 | 11 | .353 | 0 | 0 | 4.66 |
| 1987 Pittsburgh | NL | 8 | 8 | 2 | 0 | 45.2 | 192 | 43 | 25 | 24 | 6 | 5 | 2 | 1 | 12 | 0 | 25 | 3 | 0 | 2 | 3 | .400 | 0 | 0 | 4.73 |
| 1988 Chicago | NL | 19 | 5 | 0 | 7 | 48.1 | 215 | 55 | 22 | 18 | 4 | 1 | 4 | 0 | 16 | 1 | 33 | 3 | 3 | 2 | 2 | .500 | 0 | 0 | 3.35 |
| 1989 Chicago | NL | 33 | 33 | 4 | 0 | 212.1 | 882 | 187 | 82 | 74 | 16 | 9 | 3 | 0 | 81 | 8 | 147 | 9 | 4 | 18 | 7 | .720 | 3 | 0 | 3.14 |
| 1990 Chicago | NL | 36 | 29 | 0 | 6 | 168 | 749 | 188 | 101 | 92 | 13 | 16 | 4 | 5 | 70 | 11 | 103 | 11 | 0 | 8 | 11 | .421 | 0 | 1 | 4.93 |
| 7 ML YEARS | | 143 | 109 | 6 | 15 | 673 | 2933 | 671 | 343 | 308 | 54 | 43 | 19 | 9 | 293 | 24 | 414 | 34 | 14 | 38 | 37 | .507 | 3 | 1 | 4.12 |

## Craig Biggio

**Bats:** Right **Throws:** Right **Pos:** C/LF/CF **Ht:** 5'11" **Wt:** 180 **Born:** 12/14/65 **Age:** 25

| BATTING | | | | | | | | | | | | | | | | | | | BASERUNNING | | | | PERCENTAGES | | |
|---|---|---|---|---|---|---|---|---|---|---|---|---|---|---|---|---|---|---|---|---|---|---|---|---|---|
| Year Team | Lg | G | AB | H | 2B | 3B | HR | (Hm | Rd) | TB | R | RBI | TBB | IBB | SO | HBP | SH | SF | SB | CS | SB% | GDP | Avg | OBP | SLG |
| 1988 Houston | NL | 50 | 123 | 26 | 6 | 1 | 3 | (1 | 2) | 43 | 14 | 5 | 7 | 2 | 29 | 0 | 1 | 0 | 6 | 1 | .86 | 1 | .211 | .254 | .350 |
| 1989 Houston | NL | 134 | 443 | 114 | 21 | 2 | 13 | (6 | 7) | 178 | 64 | 60 | 49 | 8 | 64 | 6 | 6 | 5 | 21 | 3 | .88 | 7 | .257 | .336 | .402 |
| 1990 Houston | NL | 150 | 555 | 153 | 24 | 2 | 4 | (2 | 2) | 193 | 53 | 42 | 53 | 1 | 79 | 3 | 9 | 1 | 25 | 11 | .69 | 11 | .276 | .342 | .348 |
| 3 ML YEARS | | 334 | 1121 | 293 | 51 | 5 | 20 | (9 | 11) | 414 | 131 | 107 | 109 | 11 | 172 | 9 | 16 | 6 | 52 | 15 | .78 | 19 | .261 | .330 | .369 |

## Dann Bilardello

**Bats:** Right **Throws:** Right **Pos:** C **Ht:** 6' 0" **Wt:** 190 **Born:** 05/26/59 **Age:** 32

| BATTING | | | | | | | | | | | | | | | | | | | BASERUNNING | | | | PERCENTAGES | | |
|---|---|---|---|---|---|---|---|---|---|---|---|---|---|---|---|---|---|---|---|---|---|---|---|---|---|
| Year Team | Lg | G | AB | H | 2B | 3B | HR | (Hm | Rd) | TB | R | RBI | TBB | IBB | SO | HBP | SH | SF | SB | CS | SB% | GDP | Avg | OBP | SLG |
| 1983 Cincinnati | NL | 109 | 298 | 71 | 18 | 0 | 9 | (7 | 2) | 116 | 27 | 38 | 15 | 3 | 49 | 1 | 2 | 4 | 2 | 1 | .67 | 9 | .238 | .274 | .389 |
| 1984 Cincinnati | NL | 68 | 182 | 38 | 7 | 0 | 2 | (2 | 0) | 51 | 16 | 10 | 19 | 3 | 34 | 1 | 4 | 0 | 0 | 1 | .00 | 6 | .209 | .287 | .280 |
| 1985 Cincinnati | NL | 42 | 102 | 17 | 0 | 0 | 1 | (1 | 0) | 20 | 6 | 9 | 4 | 1 | 15 | 1 | 1 | 0 | 0 | 0 | .00 | 5 | .167 | .206 | .196 |
| 1986 Montreal | NL | 79 | 191 | 37 | 5 | 0 | 4 | (1 | 3) | 54 | 12 | 17 | 14 | 3 | 32 | 0 | 7 | 0 | 1 | 0 | 1.00 | 5 | .194 | .249 | .283 |
| 1989 Pittsburgh | NL | 33 | 80 | 18 | 6 | 0 | 2 | (1 | 1) | 30 | 11 | 8 | 2 | 0 | 18 | 0 | 1 | 0 | 1 | 2 | .33 | 1 | .225 | .244 | .375 |
| 1990 Pittsburgh | NL | 19 | 37 | 2 | 0 | 0 | 0 | (0 | 0) | 2 | 1 | 3 | 4 | 1 | 10 | 0 | 2 | 0 | 0 | 0 | .00 | 0 | .054 | .146 | .054 |
| 6 ML YEARS | | 350 | 890 | 183 | 36 | 0 | 18 | (12 | 6) | 273 | 73 | 85 | 58 | 11 | 158 | 3 | 17 | 4 | 4 | 4 | .50 | 26 | .206 | .255 | .307 |

## Tim Birtsas

**Pitches:** Left **Bats:** Left **Pos:** RP **Ht:** 6' 7" **Wt:** 240 **Born:** 09/05/60 **Age:** 30

| | | HOW MUCH HE PITCHED | | | | | | WHAT HE GAVE UP | | | | | | | | | | | | THE RESULTS | | | | | |
|---|---|---|---|---|---|---|---|---|---|---|---|---|---|---|---|---|---|---|---|---|---|---|---|---|---|
| Year Team | Lg | G | GS | CG | GF | IP | BFP | H | R | ER | HR | SH | SF | HB | TBB | IBB | SO | WP | Bk | W | L | Pct. | ShO | Sv | ERA |
| 1985 Oakland | AL | 29 | 25 | 2 | 4 | 141.1 | 624 | 124 | 72 | 63 | 18 | 4 | 5 | 3 | 91 | 0 | 94 | 6 | 0 | 10 | 6 | .625 | 0 | 0 | 4.01 |
| 1986 Oakland | AL | 2 | 0 | 0 | 2 | 2 | 12 | 2 | 5 | 5 | 1 | 1 | 0 | 0 | 4 | 1 | 1 | 0 | 0 | 0 | 0 | .000 | 0 | 0 | 22.50 |
| 1988 Cincinnati | NL | 36 | 4 | 0 | 8 | 64.1 | 277 | 61 | 34 | 30 | 6 | 3 | 3 | 3 | 24 | 5 | 38 | 0 | 3 | 1 | 3 | .250 | 0 | 0 | 4.20 |
| 1989 Cincinnati | NL | 42 | 1 | 0 | 12 | 69.2 | 300 | 68 | 33 | 29 | 5 | 3 | 6 | 3 | 27 | 8 | 57 | 3 | 3 | 2 | 2 | .500 | 0 | 1 | 3.75 |
| 1990 Cincinnati | NL | 29 | 0 | 0 | 8 | 51.1 | 239 | 69 | 24 | 22 | 7 | 1 | 1 | 1 | 24 | 6 | 41 | 4 | 0 | 1 | 3 | .250 | 0 | 0 | 3.86 |
| 5 ML YEARS | | 138 | 30 | 2 | 34 | 328.2 | 1452 | 324 | 168 | 149 | 37 | 12 | 15 | 10 | 170 | 20 | 231 | 13 | 6 | 14 | 14 | .500 | 0 | 1 | 4.08 |

## Joe Bitker

**Pitches:** Right **Bats:** Right **Pos:** RP **Ht:** 6' 1" **Wt:** 175 **Born:** 02/12/64 **Age:** 27

| | | HOW MUCH HE PITCHED | | | | | | WHAT HE GAVE UP | | | | | | | | | | | | THE RESULTS | | | | | |
|---|---|---|---|---|---|---|---|---|---|---|---|---|---|---|---|---|---|---|---|---|---|---|---|---|---|
| Year Team | Lg | G | GS | CG | GF | IP | BFP | H | R | ER | HR | SH | SF | HB | TBB | IBB | SO | WP | Bk | W | L | Pct. | ShO | Sv | ERA |
| 1984 Spokane | A | 14 | 14 | 2 | 0 | 87 | 0 | 85 | 48 | 33 | 2 | 0 | 0 | 2 | 33 | 0 | 60 | 8 | 0 | 4 | 4 | .500 | 0 | 0 | 3.41 |
| 1985 Charleston | A | 13 | 13 | 6 | 0 | 90.1 | 380 | 74 | 35 | 26 | 3 | 4 | 3 | 2 | 31 | 0 | 85 | 3 | 3 | 9 | 3 | .750 | 4 | 0 | 2.59 |
| Beaumont | AA | 15 | 14 | 4 | 0 | 98 | 422 | 91 | 43 | 34 | 3 | 3 | 4 | 2 | 41 | 2 | 64 | 3 | 1 | 8 | 1 | .889 | 1 | 0 | 3.12 |
| 1986 Beaumont | AA | 18 | 17 | 2 | 1 | 114.2 | 497 | 114 | 55 | 45 | 2 | 5 | 4 | 6 | 52 | 4 | 91 | 4 | 1 | 7 | 7 | .500 | 2 | 0 | 3.53 |
| Las Vegas | AAA | 5 | 4 | 0 | 0 | 27.1 | 112 | 24 | 10 | 10 | 3 | 2 | 0 | 2 | 9 | 0 | 19 | 4 | 0 | 2 | 0 | 1.000 | 0 | 0 | 3.29 |
| 1987 Las Vegas | AAA | 36 | 27 | 3 | 2 | 160.1 | 736 | 184 | 97 | 86 | 14 | 9 | 3 | 7 | 79 | 1 | 80 | 9 | 1 | 11 | 9 | .550 | 0 | 1 | 4.83 |
| 1988 Las Vegas | AAA | 28 | 27 | 3 | 0 | 178.1 | 769 | 195 | 98 | 71 | 11 | 7 | 10 | 4 | 41 | 3 | 106 | 4 | 4 | 8 | 10 | .444 | 1 | 0 | 3.58 |
| 1989 Las Vegas | AAA | 18 | 0 | 0 | 10 | 22.2 | 104 | 29 | 12 | 10 | 1 | 2 | 1 | 0 | 8 | 1 | 11 | 1 | 1 | 0 | 1 | .000 | 0 | 2 | 3.97 |
| Tacoma | AAA | 24 | 2 | 0 | 6 | 51 | 207 | 38 | 26 | 20 | 3 | 3 | 0 | 3 | 12 | 1 | 37 | 3 | 0 | 3 | 3 | .500 | 0 | 1 | 3.53 |
| 1990 Tacoma | AAA | 48 | 0 | 0 | 43 | 56.1 | 235 | 51 | 22 | 20 | 6 | 3 | 1 | 0 | 20 | 0 | 52 | 2 | 0 | 2 | 3 | .400 | 0 | 26 | 3.20 |
| 1990 2 ML Teams | | 6 | 0 | 0 | 5 | 12 | 48 | 8 | 3 | 3 | 0 | 0 | 1 | 1 | 4 | 0 | 8 | 0 | 0 | 0 | 0 | .000 | 0 | 0 | 2.25 |
| 1990 Oakland | AL | 1 | 0 | 0 | 1 | 3 | 10 | 1 | 0 | 0 | 0 | 0 | 0 | 0 | 1 | 0 | 2 | 0 | 0 | 0 | 0 | .000 | 0 | 0 | 0.00 |
| Texas | AL | 5 | 0 | 0 | 4 | 9 | 38 | 7 | 3 | 3 | 0 | 0 | 1 | 1 | 3 | 0 | 6 | 0 | 0 | 0 | 0 | .000 | 0 | 0 | 3.00 |

## Bud Black

**Pitches:** Left **Bats:** Left **Pos:** SP **Ht:** 6' 2" **Wt:** 185 **Born:** 06/30/57 **Age:** 34

| | | HOW MUCH HE PITCHED | | | | | | WHAT HE GAVE UP | | | | | | | | | | | | THE RESULTS | | | | | |
|---|---|---|---|---|---|---|---|---|---|---|---|---|---|---|---|---|---|---|---|---|---|---|---|---|---|
| Year Team | Lg | G | GS | CG | GF | IP | BFP | H | R | ER | HR | SH | SF | HB | TBB | IBB | SO | WP | Bk | W | L | Pct. | ShO | Sv | ERA |
| 1981 Seattle | AL | 2 | 0 | 0 | 0 | 1 | 7 | 2 | 0 | 0 | 0 | 0 | 0 | 0 | 3 | 1 | 0 | 1 | 0 | 0 | 0 | .000 | 0 | 0 | 0.00 |
| 1982 Kansas City | AL | 22 | 14 | 0 | 2 | 88.1 | 386 | 92 | 48 | 45 | 10 | 4 | 3 | 3 | 34 | 6 | 40 | 4 | 7 | 4 | 6 | .400 | 0 | 0 | 4.58 |
| 1983 Kansas City | AL | 24 | 24 | 3 | 0 | 161.1 | 672 | 159 | 75 | 68 | 19 | 4 | 5 | 2 | 43 | 1 | 58 | 4 | 0 | 10 | 7 | .588 | 0 | 0 | 3.79 |
| 1984 Kansas City | AL | 35 | 35 | 8 | 0 | 257 | 1045 | 226 | 99 | 89 | 22 | 6 | 1 | 4 | 64 | 2 | 140 | 2 | 2 | 17 | 12 | .586 | 1 | 0 | 3.12 |
| 1985 Kansas City | AL | 33 | 33 | 5 | 0 | 205.2 | 885 | 216 | 111 | 99 | 17 | 8 | 4 | 8 | 59 | 4 | 122 | 9 | 1 | 10 | 15 | .400 | 2 | 0 | 4.33 |
| 1986 Kansas City | AL | 56 | 4 | 0 | 26 | 121 | 503 | 100 | 49 | 43 | 14 | 4 | 4 | 7 | 43 | 5 | 68 | 2 | 2 | 5 | 10 | .333 | 0 | 9 | 3.20 |
| 1987 Kansas City | AL | 29 | 18 | 0 | 4 | 122.1 | 520 | 126 | 63 | 49 | 16 | 1 | 3 | 5 | 35 | 2 | 61 | 6 | 0 | 8 | 6 | .571 | 0 | 1 | 3.60 |
| 1988 2 ML Teams | | 33 | 7 | 0 | 9 | 81 | 358 | 82 | 47 | 45 | 8 | 6 | 3 | 4 | 34 | 3 | 63 | 5 | 6 | 4 | 4 | .500 | 0 | 1 | 5.00 |
| 1989 Cleveland | AL | 33 | 32 | 6 | 0 | 222.1 | 912 | 213 | 95 | 83 | 14 | 9 | 5 | 1 | 52 | 0 | 88 | 13 | 5 | 12 | 11 | .522 | 3 | 0 | 3.36 |
| 1990 2 ML Teams | | 32 | 31 | 5 | 1 | 206.2 | 857 | 181 | 86 | 82 | 19 | 6 | 7 | 5 | 61 | 1 | 106 | 6 | 1 | 13 | 11 | .542 | 2 | 0 | 3.57 |
| 1988 Kansas City | AL | 17 | 0 | 0 | 5 | 22 | 98 | 23 | 12 | 12 | 2 | 1 | 0 | 0 | 11 | 2 | 19 | 0 | 2 | 2 | 1 | .667 | 0 | 0 | 4.91 |
| Cleveland | AL | 16 | 7 | 0 | 4 | 59 | 260 | 59 | 35 | 33 | 6 | 5 | 3 | 4 | 23 | 1 | 44 | 5 | 4 | 2 | 3 | .400 | 0 | 1 | 5.03 |
| 1990 Cleveland | AL | 29 | 29 | 5 | 0 | 191 | 796 | 171 | 79 | 75 | 17 | 4 | 5 | 4 | 58 | 1 | 103 | 6 | 1 | 11 | 10 | .524 | 2 | 0 | 3.53 |
| Toronto | AL | 3 | 2 | 0 | 1 | 15.2 | 61 | 10 | 7 | 7 | 2 | 2 | 2 | 1 | 3 | 0 | 3 | 0 | 0 | 2 | 1 | .667 | 0 | 0 | 4.02 |
| 10 ML YEARS | | 299 | 198 | 27 | 42 | 1466.2 | 6145 | 1397 | 673 | 603 | 139 | 48 | 35 | 39 | 428 | 25 | 746 | 52 | 24 | 83 | 82 | .503 | 8 | 11 | 3.70 |

## Willie Blair

**Pitches:** Right **Bats:** Right **Pos:** RP/SP **Ht:** 6' 1" **Wt:** 185 **Born:** 12/18/65 **Age:** 25

| | | HOW MUCH HE PITCHED | | | | | | WHAT HE GAVE UP | | | | | | | | | | | | THE RESULTS | | | | | |
|---|---|---|---|---|---|---|---|---|---|---|---|---|---|---|---|---|---|---|---|---|---|---|---|---|---|
| Year Team | Lg | G | GS | CG | GF | IP | BFP | H | R | ER | HR | SH | SF | HB | TBB | IBB | SO | WP | Bk | W | L | Pct. | ShO | Sv | ERA |
| 1986 St.Cathrnes | A | 21 | 0 | 0 | 18 | 53.2 | 204 | 32 | 10 | 10 | 1 | 1 | 0 | 0 | 20 | 1 | 55 | 3 | 0 | 5 | 0 | 1.000 | 0 | 12 | 1.68 |
| 1987 Dunedin | A | 50 | 0 | 0 | 45 | 85.1 | 375 | 99 | 51 | 42 | 5 | 5 | 6 | 1 | 29 | 0 | 72 | 9 | 0 | 2 | 9 | .182 | 0 | 13 | 4.43 |
| 1988 Dunedin | A | 4 | 0 | 0 | 1 | 6.2 | 26 | 5 | 2 | 2 | 0 | 1 | 0 | 0 | 4 | 1 | 5 | 2 | 0 | 2 | 0 | 1.000 | 0 | 0 | 2.70 |
| Knoxville | AA | 34 | 9 | 0 | 14 | 102 | 429 | 94 | 49 | 41 | 7 | 1 | 5 | 4 | 35 | 2 | 76 | 4 | 2 | 5 | 5 | .500 | 0 | 3 | 3.62 |
| 1989 Syracuse | AAA | 19 | 17 | 3 | 2 | 106.2 | 451 | 94 | 55 | 47 | 10 | 2 | 2 | 2 | 38 | 1 | 76 | 1 | 2 | 5 | 6 | .455 | 1 | 0 | 3.97 |
| 1990 Syracuse | AAA | 3 | 3 | 1 | 0 | 19 | 83 | 20 | 13 | 10 | 1 | 1 | 1 | 0 | 8 | 1 | 6 | 0 | 0 | 0 | 2 | .000 | 0 | 0 | 4.74 |
| 1990 Toronto | AL | 27 | 6 | 0 | 8 | 68.2 | 297 | 66 | 33 | 31 | 4 | 0 | 4 | 1 | 28 | 4 | 43 | 3 | 0 | 3 | 5 | .375 | 0 | 0 | 4.06 |

## Kevin Blankenship

**Pitches:** Right **Bats:** Right **Pos:** SP **Ht:** 6' 0" **Wt:** 185 **Born:** 01/26/63 **Age:** 28

| | | HOW MUCH HE PITCHED | | | | | | WHAT HE GAVE UP | | | | | | | | | | | | THE RESULTS | | | | | |
|---|---|---|---|---|---|---|---|---|---|---|---|---|---|---|---|---|---|---|---|---|---|---|---|---|---|
| Year Team | Lg | G | GS | CG | GF | IP | BFP | H | R | ER | HR | SH | SF | HB | TBB | IBB | SO | WP | Bk | W | L | Pct. | ShO | Sv | ERA |
| 1988 2 ML Teams | | 3 | 3 | 0 | 0 | 15.2 | 67 | 14 | 8 | 8 | 2 | 0 | 0 | 1 | 8 | 0 | 9 | 0 | 0 | 1 | 1 | .500 | 0 | 0 | 4.60 |

| | | | | | | | | | | | | | | | | | | | | | | | | |
|---|---|---|---|---|---|---|---|---|---|---|---|---|---|---|---|---|---|---|---|---|---|---|---|---|
| 1989 Chicago | NL | 2 | 0 | 0 | 1 | 5.1 | 22 | 4 | 1 | 1 | 0 | 0 | 0 | 0 | 2 | 0 | 2 | 0 | 0 | 0 | 0 | .000 | 0 | 0 | 1.69 |
| 1990 Chicago | NL | 3 | 2 | 0 | 0 | 12.1 | 57 | 13 | 10 | 8 | 1 | 0 | 2 | 0 | 6 | 0 | 5 | 1 | 0 | 0 | 2 | .000 | 0 | 0 | 5.84 |
| 1988 Atlanta | NL | 2 | 2 | 0 | 0 | 10.2 | 44 | 7 | 4 | 4 | 0 | 0 | 0 | 1 | 7 | 0 | 5 | 0 | 0 | 0 | 1 | .000 | 0 | 0 | 3.38 |
| Chicago | NL | 1 | 1 | 0 | 0 | 5 | 23 | 7 | 4 | 4 | 2 | 0 | 0 | 0 | 1 | 0 | 4 | 0 | 0 | 1 | 0 | 1.000 | 0 | 0 | 7.20 |
| 3 ML YEARS | | 8 | 5 | 0 | 1 | 33.1 | 146 | 31 | 19 | 17 | 3 | 0 | 2 | 1 | 16 | 0 | 16 | 1 | 0 | 1 | 3 | .250 | 0 | 0 | 4.59 |

## Lance Blankenship

**Bats:** Right **Throws:** Right **Pos:** 3B/2B/RF **Ht:** 6' 0" **Wt:** 185 **Born:** 12/06/63 **Age:** 27

| | | BATTING | | | | | | | | | | | | | | | | | BASERUNNING | | | | PERCENTAGES | | |
|---|---|---|---|---|---|---|---|---|---|---|---|---|---|---|---|---|---|---|---|---|---|---|---|---|---|
| Year Team | Lg | G | AB | H | 2B | 3B | HR | (Hm | Rd) | TB | R | RBI | TBB | IBB | SO | HBP | SH | SF | SB | CS | SB% | GDP | Avg | OBP | SLG |
| 1988 Oakland | AL | 10 | 3 | 0 | 0 | 0 | 0 | (0 | 0) | 0 | 1 | 0 | 0 | 0 | 1 | 0 | 0 | 0 | 0 | 1 | .00 | 0 | .000 | .000 | .000 |
| 1989 Oakland | AL | 58 | 125 | 29 | 5 | 1 | 1 | (1 | 0) | 39 | 22 | 4 | 8 | 0 | 31 | 0 | 3 | 1 | 5 | 1 | .83 | 0 | .232 | .276 | .312 |
| 1990 Oakland | AL | 86 | 136 | 26 | 3 | 0 | 0 | (0 | 0) | 29 | 18 | 10 | 20 | 0 | 23 | 0 | 6 | 0 | 3 | 1 | .75 | 6 | .191 | .295 | .213 |
| 3 ML YEARS | | 154 | 264 | 55 | 8 | 1 | 1 | (1 | 0) | 68 | 41 | 14 | 28 | 0 | 55 | 0 | 9 | 1 | 8 | 3 | .73 | 6 | .208 | .283 | .258 |

## Jeff Blauser

**Bats:** Right **Throws:** Right **Pos:** SS/2B **Ht:** 6' 0" **Wt:** 170 **Born:** 11/08/65 **Age:** 25

| | | BATTING | | | | | | | | | | | | | | | | | BASERUNNING | | | | PERCENTAGES | | |
|---|---|---|---|---|---|---|---|---|---|---|---|---|---|---|---|---|---|---|---|---|---|---|---|---|---|
| Year Team | Lg | G | AB | H | 2B | 3B | HR | (Hm | Rd) | TB | R | RBI | TBB | IBB | SO | HBP | SH | SF | SB | CS | SB% | GDP | Avg | OBP | SLG |
| 1987 Atlanta | NL | 51 | 165 | 40 | 6 | 3 | 2 | (1 | 1) | 58 | 11 | 15 | 18 | 1 | 34 | 3 | 1 | 0 | 7 | 3 | .70 | 4 | .242 | .328 | .352 |
| 1988 Atlanta | NL | 18 | 67 | 16 | 3 | 1 | 2 | (2 | 0) | 27 | 7 | 7 | 2 | 0 | 11 | 1 | 3 | 1 | 0 | 1 | .00 | 1 | .239 | .268 | .403 |
| 1989 Atlanta | NL | 142 | 456 | 123 | 24 | 2 | 12 | (5 | 7) | 187 | 63 | 46 | 38 | 2 | 101 | 1 | 8 | 4 | 5 | 2 | .71 | 7 | .270 | .325 | .410 |
| 1990 Atlanta | NL | 115 | 386 | 104 | 24 | 3 | 8 | (3 | 5) | 158 | 46 | 39 | 35 | 1 | 70 | 5 | 3 | 0 | 3 | 5 | .38 | 4 | .269 | .338 | .409 |
| 4 ML YEARS | | 326 | 1074 | 283 | 57 | 9 | 24 | (11 | 13) | 430 | 127 | 107 | 93 | 4 | 216 | 10 | 15 | 5 | 15 | 11 | .58 | 16 | .264 | .327 | .400 |

## Mike Blowers

**Bats:** Right **Throws:** Right **Pos:** 3B **Ht:** 6' 2" **Wt:** 190 **Born:** 04/24/65 **Age:** 26

| | | BATTING | | | | | | | | | | | | | | | | | BASERUNNING | | | | PERCENTAGES | | |
|---|---|---|---|---|---|---|---|---|---|---|---|---|---|---|---|---|---|---|---|---|---|---|---|---|---|
| Year Team | Lg | G | AB | H | 2B | 3B | HR | (Hm | Rd) | TB | R | RBI | TBB | IBB | SO | HBP | SH | SF | SB | CS | SB% | GDP | Avg | OBP | SLG |
| 1986 Jamestown | A | 32 | 95 | 24 | 9 | 2 | 1 | -- | -- | 40 | 13 | 6 | 17 | 2 | 18 | 3 | 2 | 0 | 3 | 2 | .60 | 4 | .253 | .383 | .421 |
| Expos | R | 31 | 115 | 25 | 3 | 1 | 2 | -- | -- | 36 | 14 | 17 | 15 | 0 | 25 | 0 | 2 | 0 | 2 | 0 | 1.00 | 4 | .217 | .308 | .313 |
| 1987 Wst Plm Bch | A | 136 | 491 | 124 | 30 | 3 | 16 | -- | -- | 208 | 68 | 71 | 48 | 0 | 118 | 0 | 0 | 3 | 4 | 4 | .50 | 11 | .253 | .317 | .424 |
| 1988 Jacksnville | AA | 137 | 460 | 115 | 20 | 6 | 15 | -- | -- | 192 | 58 | 60 | 68 | 3 | 114 | 2 | 1 | 0 | 6 | 4 | .60 | 11 | .250 | .349 | .417 |
| 1989 Indianapols | AAA | 131 | 461 | 123 | 29 | 6 | 14 | -- | -- | 206 | 49 | 56 | 41 | 4 | 109 | 2 | 1 | 3 | 3 | 2 | .60 | 10 | .267 | .327 | .447 |
| 1990 Columbus | AAA | 62 | 230 | 78 | 20 | 6 | 6 | -- | -- | 128 | 30 | 50 | 29 | 1 | 40 | 1 | 0 | 4 | 3 | 0 | 1.00 | 8 | .339 | .409 | .557 |
| 1989 New York | AL | 13 | 38 | 10 | 0 | 0 | 0 | (0 | 0) | 10 | 2 | 3 | 3 | 0 | 13 | 0 | 0 | 0 | 0 | 0 | .00 | 1 | .263 | .317 | .263 |
| 1990 New York | AL | 48 | 144 | 27 | 4 | 0 | 5 | (1 | 4) | 46 | 16 | 21 | 12 | 1 | 50 | 1 | 0 | 0 | 1 | 0 | 1.00 | 3 | .188 | .255 | .319 |
| 2 ML YEARS | | 61 | 182 | 37 | 4 | 0 | 5 | (1 | 4) | 56 | 18 | 24 | 15 | 1 | 63 | 1 | 0 | 0 | 1 | 0 | 1.00 | 4 | .203 | .268 | .308 |

## Bert Blyleven

**Pitches:** Right **Bats:** Right **Pos:** SP **Ht:** 6' 3" **Wt:** 205 **Born:** 04/06/51 **Age:** 40

| | | HOW MUCH HE PITCHED | | | | | | WHAT HE GAVE UP | | | | | | | | | | | | THE RESULTS | | | | | |
|---|---|---|---|---|---|---|---|---|---|---|---|---|---|---|---|---|---|---|---|---|---|---|---|---|---|
| Year Team | Lg | G | GS | CG | GF | IP | BFP | H | R | ER | HR | SH | SF | HB | TBB | IBB | SO | WP | Bk | W | L | Pct. | ShO | Sv | ERA |
| 1970 Minnesota | AL | 27 | 25 | 5 | 1 | 164 | 675 | 143 | 66 | 58 | 17 | 8 | 2 | 2 | 47 | 6 | 135 | 2 | 3 | 10 | 9 | .526 | 1 | 0 | 3.18 |
| 1971 Minnesota | AL | 38 | 38 | 17 | 0 | 278 | 1126 | 267 | 95 | 87 | 21 | 12 | 3 | 5 | 59 | 1 | 224 | 5 | 1 | 16 | 15 | .516 | 5 | 0 | 2.82 |
| 1972 Minnesota | AL | 39 | 38 | 11 | 1 | 287 | 1158 | 247 | 93 | 87 | 22 | 14 | 6 | 10 | 69 | 7 | 228 | 7 | 1 | 17 | 17 | .500 | 3 | 0 | 2.73 |
| 1973 Minnesota | AL | 40 | 40 | 25 | 0 | 325 | 1321 | 296 | 109 | 91 | 16 | 11 | 13 | 9 | 67 | 4 | 258 | 7 | 2 | 20 | 17 | .541 | 9 | 0 | 2.52 |
| 1974 Minnesota | AL | 37 | 37 | 19 | 0 | 281 | 1149 | 244 | 99 | 83 | 14 | 13 | 5 | 9 | 77 | 3 | 249 | 3 | 0 | 17 | 17 | .500 | 3 | 0 | 2.66 |
| 1975 Minnesota | AL | 35 | 35 | 20 | 0 | 276 | 1104 | 219 | 104 | 92 | 24 | 10 | 8 | 4 | 84 | 2 | 233 | 7 | 0 | 15 | 10 | .600 | 3 | 0 | 3.00 |
| 1976 2 ML Teams | | 36 | 36 | 18 | 0 | 297 | 1225 | 283 | 106 | 95 | 14 | 18 | 6 | 12 | 81 | 6 | 219 | 7 | 2 | 13 | 16 | .448 | 6 | 0 | 2.88 |
| 1977 Texas | AL | 30 | 30 | 15 | 0 | 235 | 935 | 181 | 81 | 71 | 20 | 10 | 5 | 7 | 69 | 1 | 182 | 8 | 0 | 14 | 12 | .538 | 5 | 0 | 2.72 |
| 1978 Pittsburgh | NL | 34 | 34 | 11 | 0 | 244 | 1011 | 217 | 94 | 82 | 17 | 13 | 2 | 6 | 66 | 5 | 182 | 6 | 2 | 14 | 10 | .583 | 4 | 0 | 3.02 |
| 1979 Pittsburgh | NL | 37 | 37 | 4 | 0 | 237 | 1018 | 238 | 102 | 95 | 21 | 14 | 9 | 6 | 92 | 8 | 172 | 9 | 0 | 12 | 5 | .706 | 0 | 0 | 3.61 |
| 1980 Pittsburgh | NL | 34 | 32 | 5 | 1 | 217 | 907 | 219 | 102 | 92 | 20 | 10 | 2 | 0 | 59 | 5 | 168 | 2 | 1 | 8 | 13 | .381 | 2 | 0 | 3.82 |
| 1981 Cleveland | AL | 20 | 20 | 9 | 0 | 159 | 644 | 145 | 52 | 51 | 9 | 3 | 3 | 5 | 40 | 1 | 107 | 3 | 1 | 11 | 7 | .611 | 1 | 0 | 2.89 |
| 1982 Cleveland | AL | 4 | 4 | 0 | 0 | 20.1 | 89 | 16 | 14 | 11 | 2 | 0 | 2 | 0 | 11 | 0 | 19 | 0 | 0 | 2 | 2 | .500 | 0 | 0 | 4.87 |
| 1983 Cleveland | AL | 24 | 24 | 5 | 0 | 156.1 | 660 | 160 | 74 | 68 | 8 | 2 | 5 | 10 | 44 | 4 | 123 | 5 | 1 | 7 | 10 | .412 | 0 | 0 | 3.91 |
| 1984 Cleveland | AL | 33 | 32 | 12 | 0 | 245 | 1004 | 204 | 86 | 78 | 19 | 6 | 8 | 6 | 74 | 4 | 170 | 6 | 0 | 19 | 7 | .731 | 4 | 0 | 2.87 |
| 1985 2 ML Teams | | 37 | 37 | 24 | 0 | 293.2 | 1203 | 264 | 121 | 103 | 23 | 5 | 8 | 9 | 75 | 1 | 206 | 4 | 1 | 17 | 16 | .515 | 5 | 0 | 3.16 |
| 1986 Minnesota | AL | 36 | 36 | 16 | 0 | 271.2 | 1126 | 262 | 134 | 121 | 50 | 5 | 4 | 10 | 58 | 4 | 215 | 4 | 0 | 17 | 14 | .548 | 3 | 0 | 4.01 |
| 1987 Minnesota | AL | 37 | 37 | 8 | 0 | 267 | 1122 | 249 | 132 | 119 | 46 | 4 | 6 | 9 | 101 | 4 | 196 | 13 | 0 | 15 | 12 | .556 | 1 | 0 | 4.01 |
| 1988 Minnesota | AL | 33 | 33 | 7 | 0 | 207.1 | 895 | 240 | 128 | 125 | 21 | 6 | 6 | 16 | 51 | 1 | 145 | 5 | 3 | 10 | 17 | .370 | 0 | 0 | 5.43 |
| 1989 California | AL | 33 | 33 | 8 | 0 | 241 | 973 | 225 | 76 | 73 | 14 | 7 | 7 | 8 | 44 | 2 | 131 | 2 | 0 | 17 | 5 | .773 | 5 | 0 | 2.73 |
| 1990 California | AL | 23 | 23 | 2 | 0 | 134 | 578 | 163 | 85 | 78 | 15 | 2 | 6 | 7 | 25 | 0 | 69 | 6 | 0 | 8 | 7 | .533 | 0 | 0 | 5.24 |
| 1976 Minnesota | AL | 12 | 12 | 4 | 0 | 95 | 406 | 101 | 39 | 33 | 3 | 7 | 3 | 4 | 35 | 5 | 75 | 0 | 2 | 4 | 5 | .444 | 0 | 0 | 3.13 |
| Texas | AL | 24 | 24 | 14 | 0 | 202 | 819 | 182 | 67 | 62 | 11 | 11 | 3 | 8 | 46 | 1 | 144 | 7 | 0 | 9 | 11 | .450 | 6 | 0 | 2.76 |
| 1985 Cleveland | AL | 23 | 23 | 15 | 0 | 179.2 | 743 | 163 | 76 | 65 | 14 | 4 | 4 | 7 | 49 | 1 | 129 | 1 | 1 | 9 | 11 | .450 | 4 | 0 | 3.26 |

| Year Team | Lg | G | GS | CG | GF | IP | BFP | H | R | ER | HR | SH | SF | HB | TBB | IBB | SO | WP | Bk | W | L | Pct. | ShO | Sv | ERA |
|---|---|---|---|---|---|---|---|---|---|---|---|---|---|---|---|---|---|---|---|---|---|---|---|---|---|
| Minnesota | AL | 14 | 14 | 9 | 0 | 114 | 460 | 101 | 45 | 38 | 9 | 1 | 4 | 2 | 26 | 0 | 77 | 3 | 0 | 8 | 5 | .615 | 1 | 0 | 3.00 |
| 21 ML YEARS | | 667 | 661 | 241 | 3 | 4836.1 | 19923 | 4482 | 1953 | 1760 | 413 | 173 | 116 | 150 | 1293 | 69 | 3631 | 111 | 18 | 279 | 238 | .540 | 60 | 0 | 3.28 |

## Mike Boddicker

**Pitches:** Right **Bats:** Right **Pos:** SP **Ht:** 5'11" **Wt:** 186 **Born:** 08/23/57 **Age:** 33

| | | HOW MUCH HE PITCHED | | | | | | WHAT HE GAVE UP | | | | | | | | | | | | THE RESULTS | | | | | |
|---|---|---|---|---|---|---|---|---|---|---|---|---|---|---|---|---|---|---|---|---|---|---|---|---|---|
| Year Team | Lg | G | GS | CG | GF | IP | BFP | H | R | ER | HR | SH | SF | HB | TBB | IBB | SO | WP | Bk | W | L | Pct. | ShO | Sv | ERA |
| 1980 Baltimore | AL | 1 | 1 | 0 | 0 | 7 | 34 | 6 | 6 | 5 | 1 | 0 | 0 | 0 | 5 | 0 | 4 | 0 | 0 | 0 | 1 | .000 | 0 | 0 | 6.43 |
| 1981 Baltimore | AL | 2 | 0 | 0 | 1 | 6 | 25 | 6 | 4 | 3 | 1 | 0 | 0 | 0 | 2 | 0 | 2 | 2 | 0 | 0 | 0 | .000 | 0 | 0 | 4.50 |
| 1982 Baltimore | AL | 7 | 0 | 0 | 4 | 25.2 | 110 | 25 | 10 | 10 | 2 | 1 | 0 | 0 | 12 | 2 | 20 | 0 | 0 | 1 | 0 | 1.000 | 0 | 0 | 3.51 |
| 1983 Baltimore | AL | 27 | 26 | 10 | 1 | 179 | 711 | 141 | 65 | 55 | 13 | 4 | 3 | 0 | 52 | 1 | 120 | 5 | 0 | 16 | 8 | .667 | 5 | 0 | 2.77 |
| 1984 Baltimore | AL | 34 | 34 | 16 | 0 | 261.1 | 1051 | 218 | 95 | 81 | 23 | 2 | 7 | 5 | 81 | 1 | 128 | 6 | 1 | 20 | 11 | .645 | 4 | 0 | 2.79 |
| 1985 Baltimore | AL | 32 | 32 | 9 | 0 | 203.1 | 899 | 227 | 104 | 92 | 13 | 9 | 2 | 5 | 89 | 7 | 135 | 5 | 0 | 12 | 17 | .414 | 2 | 0 | 4.07 |
| 1986 Baltimore | AL | 33 | 33 | 7 | 0 | 218.1 | 934 | 214 | 125 | 114 | 30 | 3 | 6 | 11 | 74 | 4 | 175 | 7 | 0 | 14 | 12 | .538 | 0 | 0 | 4.70 |
| 1987 Baltimore | AL | 33 | 33 | 7 | 0 | 226 | 950 | 212 | 114 | 105 | 29 | 7 | 4 | 7 | 78 | 4 | 152 | 10 | 0 | 10 | 12 | .455 | 2 | 0 | 4.18 |
| 1988 2 ML Teams | | 36 | 35 | 5 | 0 | 236 | 1001 | 234 | 102 | 89 | 17 | 4 | 12 | 14 | 77 | 6 | 156 | 6 | 4 | 13 | 15 | .464 | 1 | 0 | 3.39 |
| 1989 Boston | AL | 34 | 34 | 3 | 0 | 211.2 | 912 | 217 | 101 | 94 | 19 | 8 | 10 | 10 | 71 | 4 | 145 | 4 | 1 | 15 | 11 | .577 | 2 | 0 | 4.00 |
| 1990 Boston | AL | 34 | 34 | 4 | 0 | 228 | 956 | 225 | 92 | 85 | 16 | 3 | 1 | 10 | 69 | 6 | 143 | 10 | 0 | 17 | 8 | .680 | 0 | 0 | 3.36 |
| 1988 Baltimore | AL | 21 | 21 | 4 | 0 | 147 | 636 | 149 | 72 | 63 | 14 | 3 | 8 | 11 | 51 | 5 | 100 | 3 | 4 | 6 | 12 | .333 | 0 | 0 | 3.86 |
| Boston | AL | 15 | 14 | 1 | 0 | 89 | 365 | 85 | 30 | 26 | 3 | 1 | 4 | 3 | 26 | 1 | 56 | 3 | 0 | 7 | 3 | .700 | 1 | 0 | 2.63 |
| 11 ML YEARS | | 273 | 262 | 61 | 6 | 1802.1 | 7583 | 1725 | 818 | 733 | 164 | 41 | 45 | 62 | 610 | 35 | 1180 | 55 | 6 | 118 | 95 | .554 | 16 | 0 | 3.66 |

## Joe Boever

**Pitches:** Right **Bats:** Right **Pos:** RP **Ht:** 6' 1" **Wt:** 200 **Born:** 10/04/60 **Age:** 30

| | | HOW MUCH HE PITCHED | | | | | | WHAT HE GAVE UP | | | | | | | | | | | | THE RESULTS | | | | | |
|---|---|---|---|---|---|---|---|---|---|---|---|---|---|---|---|---|---|---|---|---|---|---|---|---|---|
| Year Team | Lg | G | GS | CG | GF | IP | BFP | H | R | ER | HR | SH | SF | HB | TBB | IBB | SO | WP | Bk | W | L | Pct. | ShO | Sv | ERA |
| 1985 St. Louis | NL | 13 | 0 | 0 | 5 | 16.1 | 69 | 17 | 8 | 8 | 3 | 1 | 1 | 0 | 4 | 1 | 20 | 1 | 0 | 0 | 0 | .000 | 0 | 0 | 4.41 |
| 1986 St. Louis | NL | 11 | 0 | 0 | 4 | 21.2 | 93 | 19 | 5 | 4 | 2 | 0 | 0 | 0 | 11 | 0 | 8 | 1 | 0 | 0 | 1 | .000 | 0 | 0 | 1.66 |
| 1987 Atlanta | NL | 14 | 0 | 0 | 10 | 18.1 | 93 | 29 | 15 | 15 | 4 | 1 | 1 | 0 | 12 | 1 | 18 | 1 | 0 | 1 | 0 | 1.000 | 0 | 0 | 7.36 |
| 1988 Atlanta | NL | 16 | 0 | 0 | 13 | 20.1 | 70 | 12 | 4 | 4 | 1 | 2 | 0 | 1 | 1 | 0 | 7 | 0 | 0 | 0 | 2 | .000 | 0 | 1 | 1.77 |
| 1989 Atlanta | NL | 66 | 0 | 0 | 53 | 82.1 | 349 | 78 | 37 | 36 | 6 | 5 | 0 | 1 | 34 | 5 | 68 | 5 | 0 | 4 | 11 | .267 | 0 | 21 | 3.94 |
| 1990 2 ML Teams | | 67 | 0 | 0 | 34 | 88.1 | 388 | 77 | 35 | 33 | 6 | 4 | 2 | 0 | 51 | 12 | 75 | 3 | 2 | 3 | 6 | .333 | 0 | 14 | 3.36 |
| 1990 Atlanta | NL | 33 | 0 | 0 | 21 | 42.1 | 198 | 40 | 23 | 22 | 6 | 2 | 2 | 0 | 35 | 10 | 35 | 2 | 0 | 1 | 3 | .250 | 0 | 8 | 4.68 |
| Philadelphia | NL | 34 | 0 | 0 | 13 | 46 | 190 | 37 | 12 | 11 | 0 | 2 | 0 | 0 | 16 | 2 | 40 | 1 | 2 | 2 | 3 | .400 | 0 | 6 | 2.15 |
| 6 ML YEARS | | 187 | 0 | 0 | 119 | 247.1 | 1062 | 232 | 104 | 100 | 22 | 13 | 4 | 2 | 113 | 19 | 196 | 11 | 2 | 8 | 20 | .286 | 0 | 36 | 3.64 |

## Wade Boggs

**Bats:** Left **Throws:** Right **Pos:** 3B **Ht:** 6' 2" **Wt:** 197 **Born:** 06/15/58 **Age:** 33

| | | BATTING | | | | | | | | | | | | | | | | | BASERUNNING | | | | PERCENTAGES | | |
|---|---|---|---|---|---|---|---|---|---|---|---|---|---|---|---|---|---|---|---|---|---|---|---|---|---|
| Year Team | Lg | G | AB | H | 2B | 3B | HR | (Hm Rd) | TB | R | RBI | TBB | IBB | SO | HBP | SH | SF | SB | CS | SB% | GDP | Avg | OBP | SLG |
| 1982 Boston | AL | 104 | 338 | 118 | 14 | 1 | 5 | (4 1) | 149 | 51 | 44 | 35 | 4 | 21 | 0 | 4 | 4 | 1 | 0 | 1.00 | 9 | .349 | .406 | .441 |
| 1983 Boston | AL | 153 | 582 | 210 | 44 | 7 | 5 | (2 3) | 283 | 100 | 74 | 92 | 2 | 36 | 1 | 3 | 7 | 3 | 3 | .50 | 15 | .361 | .444 | .486 |
| 1984 Boston | AL | 158 | 625 | 203 | 31 | 4 | 6 | (5 1) | 260 | 109 | 55 | 89 | 6 | 44 | 0 | 8 | 4 | 3 | 2 | .60 | 13 | .325 | .407 | .416 |
| 1985 Boston | AL | 161 | 653 | 240 | 42 | 3 | 8 | (6 2) | 312 | 107 | 78 | 96 | 5 | 61 | 4 | 3 | 2 | 2 | 1 | .67 | 20 | .368 | .450 | .478 |
| 1986 Boston | AL | 149 | 580 | 207 | 47 | 2 | 8 | (3 5) | 282 | 107 | 71 | 105 | 14 | 44 | 0 | 4 | 4 | 0 | 4 | .00 | 11 | .357 | .453 | .486 |
| 1987 Boston | AL | 147 | 551 | 200 | 40 | 6 | 24 | (10 14) | 324 | 108 | 89 | 105 | 19 | 48 | 2 | 1 | 8 | 1 | 3 | .25 | 13 | .363 | .461 | .588 |
| 1988 Boston | AL | 155 | 584 | 214 | 45 | 6 | 5 | (4 1) | 286 | 128 | 58 | 125 | 18 | 34 | 3 | 0 | 7 | 2 | 3 | .40 | 23 | .366 | .476 | .490 |
| 1989 Boston | AL | 156 | 621 | 205 | 51 | 7 | 3 | (2 1) | 279 | 113 | 54 | 107 | 19 | 51 | 7 | 0 | 7 | 2 | 6 | .25 | 19 | .330 | .430 | .449 |
| 1990 Boston | AL | 155 | 619 | 187 | 44 | 5 | 6 | (3 3) | 259 | 89 | 63 | 87 | 19 | 68 | 1 | 0 | 6 | 0 | 0 | .00 | 14 | .302 | .386 | .418 |
| 9 ML YEARS | | 1338 | 5153 | 1784 | 358 | 41 | 70 | (39 31) | 2434 | 912 | 586 | 841 | 106 | 407 | 18 | 23 | 49 | 14 | 22 | .39 | 137 | .346 | .436 | .472 |

## Brian Bohanon

**Pitches:** Left **Bats:** Left **Pos:** SP/RP **Ht:** 6' 2" **Wt:** 205 **Born:** 08/01/68 **Age:** 22

| | | HOW MUCH HE PITCHED | | | | | | WHAT HE GAVE UP | | | | | | | | | | | | THE RESULTS | | | | | |
|---|---|---|---|---|---|---|---|---|---|---|---|---|---|---|---|---|---|---|---|---|---|---|---|---|---|
| Year Team | Lg | G | GS | CG | GF | IP | BFP | H | R | ER | HR | SH | SF | HB | TBB | IBB | SO | WP | Bk | W | L | Pct. | ShO | Sv | ERA |
| 1987 Rangers | R | 5 | 4 | 0 | 0 | 21 | 84 | 15 | 13 | 11 | 1 | 0 | 0 | 0 | 5 | 0 | 21 | 2 | 0 | 0 | 2 | .000 | 0 | 0 | 4.71 |
| 1988 Charlotte | A | 2 | 2 | 0 | 0 | 6.2 | 31 | 6 | 4 | 4 | 0 | 0 | 0 | 0 | 5 | 0 | 9 | 0 | 1 | 0 | 1 | .000 | 0 | 0 | 5.40 |
| 1989 Charlotte | A | 11 | 7 | 0 | 3 | 54.2 | 213 | 40 | 16 | 11 | 1 | 1 | 1 | 2 | 20 | 0 | 33 | 1 | 1 | 0 | 3 | .000 | 0 | 1 | 1.81 |
| Tulsa | AA | 11 | 11 | 1 | 0 | 73.2 | 297 | 59 | 20 | 18 | 3 | 3 | 2 | 3 | 27 | 0 | 44 | 2 | 1 | 5 | 0 | 1.000 | 1 | 0 | 2.20 |
| 1990 Okla City | AAA | 14 | 4 | 0 | 4 | 32 | 135 | 35 | 16 | 13 | 0 | 2 | 1 | 0 | 8 | 0 | 22 | 2 | 1 | 1 | 2 | .333 | 0 | 1 | 3.66 |
| 1990 Texas | AL | 11 | 6 | 0 | 1 | 34 | 158 | 40 | 30 | 25 | 6 | 0 | 3 | 2 | 18 | 0 | 15 | 1 | 0 | 0 | 3 | .000 | 0 | 0 | 6.62 |

## Tom Bolton

**Pitches:** Left **Bats:** Left **Pos:** SP/RP **Ht:** 6' 3" **Wt:** 175 **Born:** 05/06/62 **Age:** 29

| HOW MUCH HE PITCHED | | | | | | | | | WHAT HE GAVE UP | | | | | | | | | | | | THE RESULTS | | | | | |
|---|---|---|---|---|---|---|---|---|---|---|---|---|---|---|---|---|---|---|---|---|---|---|---|---|---|---|
| Year | Team | Lg | G | GS | CG | GF | IP | BFP | H | R | ER | HR | SH | SF | HB | TBB | IBB | SO | WP | Bk | W | L | Pct. | ShO | Sv | ERA |
| 1987 | Boston | AL | 29 | 0 | 0 | 5 | 61.2 | 287 | 83 | 33 | 30 | 5 | 3 | 3 | 2 | 27 | 2 | 49 | 3 | 0 | 1 | 0 | 1.000 | 0 | 0 | 4.38 |
| 1988 | Boston | AL | 28 | 0 | 0 | 8 | 30.1 | 140 | 35 | 17 | 16 | 1 | 2 | 1 | 0 | 14 | 1 | 21 | 2 | 1 | 1 | 3 | .250 | 0 | 1 | 4.75 |
| 1989 | Boston | AL | 4 | 4 | 0 | 0 | 17.1 | 83 | 21 | 18 | 16 | 1 | 0 | 1 | 0 | 10 | 1 | 9 | 1 | 0 | 0 | 4 | .000 | 0 | 0 | 8.31 |
| 1990 | Boston | AL | 21 | 16 | 3 | 2 | 119.2 | 501 | 111 | 46 | 45 | 6 | 3 | 5 | 3 | 47 | 3 | 65 | 1 | 1 | 10 | 5 | .667 | 0 | 0 | 3.38 |
| | 4 ML YEARS | | 82 | 20 | 3 | 15 | 229 | 1011 | 250 | 114 | 107 | 13 | 8 | 10 | 5 | 98 | 7 | 144 | 7 | 2 | 12 | 12 | .500 | 0 | 1 | 4.21 |

## Barry Bonds

**Bats:** Left **Throws:** Left **Pos:** LF **Ht:** 6' 1" **Wt:** 185 **Born:** 07/24/64 **Age:** 26

| BATTING | | | | | | | | | | | | | | | | | | | | BASERUNNING | | | | PERCENTAGES | | |
|---|---|---|---|---|---|---|---|---|---|---|---|---|---|---|---|---|---|---|---|---|---|---|---|---|---|---|
| Year | Team | Lg | G | AB | H | 2B | 3B | HR | (Hm | Rd) | TB | R | RBI | TBB | IBB | SO | HBP | SH | SF | SB | CS | SB% | GDP | Avg | OBP | SLG |
| 1986 | Pittsburgh | NL | 113 | 413 | 92 | 26 | 3 | 16 | (9 | 7) | 172 | 72 | 48 | 65 | 2 | 102 | 2 | 2 | 2 | 36 | 7 | .84 | 4 | .223 | .330 | .416 |
| 1987 | Pittsburgh | NL | 150 | 551 | 144 | 34 | 9 | 25 | (12 | 13) | 271 | 99 | 59 | 54 | 3 | 88 | 3 | 0 | 3 | 32 | 10 | .76 | 4 | .261 | .329 | .492 |
| 1988 | Pittsburgh | NL | 144 | 538 | 152 | 30 | 5 | 24 | (14 | 10) | 264 | 97 | 58 | 72 | 14 | 82 | 2 | 0 | 2 | 17 | 11 | .61 | 3 | .283 | .368 | .491 |
| 1989 | Pittsburgh | NL | 159 | 580 | 144 | 34 | 6 | 19 | (7 | 12) | 247 | 96 | 58 | 93 | 22 | 93 | 1 | 1 | 4 | 32 | 10 | .76 | 9 | .248 | .351 | .426 |
| 1990 | Pittsburgh | NL | 151 | 519 | 156 | 32 | 3 | 33 | (14 | 19) | 293 | 104 | 114 | 93 | 15 | 83 | 3 | 0 | 6 | 52 | 13 | .80 | 8 | .301 | .406 | .565 |
| | 5 ML YEARS | | 717 | 2601 | 688 | 156 | 26 | 117 | (56 | 61) | 1247 | 468 | 337 | 377 | 56 | 448 | 11 | 3 | 17 | 169 | 51 | .77 | 28 | .265 | .358 | .479 |

## Bobby Bonilla

**Bats:** Both **Throws:** Right **Pos:** RF/3B **Ht:** 6' 3" **Wt:** 230 **Born:** 02/23/63 **Age:** 28

| BATTING | | | | | | | | | | | | | | | | | | | | BASERUNNING | | | | PERCENTAGES | | |
|---|---|---|---|---|---|---|---|---|---|---|---|---|---|---|---|---|---|---|---|---|---|---|---|---|---|---|
| Year | Team | Lg | G | AB | H | 2B | 3B | HR | (Hm | Rd) | TB | R | RBI | TBB | IBB | SO | HBP | SH | SF | SB | CS | SB% | GDP | Avg | OBP | SLG |
| 1986 | 2 ML Teams | | 138 | 426 | 109 | 16 | 4 | 3 | (2 | 1) | 142 | 55 | 43 | 62 | 3 | 88 | 2 | 5 | 1 | 8 | 5 | .62 | 9 | .256 | .352 | .333 |
| 1987 | Pittsburgh | NL | 141 | 466 | 140 | 33 | 3 | 15 | (7 | 8) | 224 | 58 | 77 | 39 | 4 | 64 | 2 | 0 | 8 | 3 | 5 | .38 | 8 | .300 | .351 | .481 |
| 1988 | Pittsburgh | NL | 159 | 584 | 160 | 32 | 7 | 24 | (9 | 15) | 278 | 87 | 100 | 85 | 19 | 82 | 4 | 0 | 8 | 3 | 5 | .38 | 4 | .274 | .366 | .476 |
| 1989 | Pittsburgh | NL | 163 | 616 | 173 | 37 | 10 | 24 | (13 | 11) | 302 | 96 | 86 | 76 | 20 | 93 | 1 | 0 | 5 | 8 | 8 | .50 | 10 | .281 | .358 | .490 |
| 1990 | Pittsburgh | NL | 160 | 625 | 175 | 39 | 7 | 32 | (13 | 19) | 324 | 112 | 120 | 45 | 9 | 103 | 1 | 0 | 15 | 4 | 3 | .57 | 10 | .280 | .322 | .518 |
| 1986 | Chicago | AL | 75 | 234 | 63 | 10 | 2 | 2 | (2 | 0) | 83 | 27 | 26 | 33 | 2 | 49 | 1 | 2 | 1 | 4 | 1 | .80 | 4 | .269 | .361 | .355 |
| | Pittsburgh | NL | 63 | 192 | 46 | 6 | 2 | 1 | (0 | 1) | 59 | 28 | 17 | 29 | 1 | 39 | 1 | 3 | 0 | 4 | 4 | .50 | 5 | .240 | .342 | .307 |
| | 5 ML YEARS | | 761 | 2717 | 757 | 157 | 31 | 98 | (44 | 54) | 1270 | 408 | 426 | 307 | 55 | 430 | 10 | 5 | 37 | 26 | 26 | .50 | 41 | .279 | .350 | .467 |

## Greg Booker

**Pitches:** Right **Bats:** Right **Pos:** RP **Ht:** 6' 6" **Wt:** 245 **Born:** 06/22/60 **Age:** 31

| HOW MUCH HE PITCHED | | | | | | | | | WHAT HE GAVE UP | | | | | | | | | | | | THE RESULTS | | | | | |
|---|---|---|---|---|---|---|---|---|---|---|---|---|---|---|---|---|---|---|---|---|---|---|---|---|---|---|
| Year | Team | Lg | G | GS | CG | GF | IP | BFP | H | R | ER | HR | SH | SF | HB | TBB | IBB | SO | WP | Bk | W | L | Pct. | ShO | Sv | ERA |
| 1983 | San Diego | NL | 6 | 1 | 0 | 1 | 11.2 | 58 | 18 | 10 | 10 | 2 | 1 | 0 | 0 | 9 | 0 | 5 | 0 | 0 | 0 | 1 | .000 | 0 | 0 | 7.71 |
| 1984 | San Diego | NL | 32 | 1 | 0 | 12 | 57.1 | 262 | 67 | 27 | 21 | 4 | 6 | 2 | 0 | 27 | 4 | 28 | 6 | 0 | 1 | 1 | .500 | 0 | 0 | 3.30 |
| 1985 | San Diego | NL | 17 | 0 | 0 | 9 | 22.1 | 102 | 20 | 17 | 17 | 3 | 1 | 2 | 1 | 17 | 2 | 7 | 5 | 0 | 0 | 1 | .000 | 0 | 0 | 6.85 |
| 1986 | San Diego | NL | 9 | 0 | 0 | 4 | 11 | 47 | 10 | 5 | 2 | 0 | 0 | 0 | 0 | 4 | 2 | 7 | 0 | 0 | 1 | 0 | 1.000 | 0 | 0 | 1.64 |
| 1987 | San Diego | NL | 44 | 0 | 0 | 16 | 68.1 | 288 | 62 | 29 | 24 | 5 | 2 | 1 | 3 | 30 | 1 | 17 | 1 | 1 | 1 | 1 | .500 | 0 | 1 | 3.16 |
| 1988 | San Diego | NL | 34 | 2 | 0 | 11 | 63.2 | 272 | 68 | 31 | 24 | 5 | 3 | 4 | 1 | 19 | 2 | 43 | 2 | 0 | 2 | 2 | .500 | 0 | 0 | 3.39 |
| 1989 | 2 ML Teams | | 17 | 0 | 0 | 6 | 27.2 | 117 | 26 | 14 | 13 | 3 | 2 | 0 | 0 | 12 | 1 | 11 | 3 | 0 | 0 | 1 | .000 | 0 | 0 | 4.23 |
| 1990 | San Francisco | NL | 2 | 0 | 0 | 1 | 2 | 13 | 7 | 3 | 3 | 0 | 0 | 0 | 0 | 0 | 0 | 1 | 0 | 1 | 0 | 0 | .000 | 0 | 0 | 13.50 |
| 1989 | San Diego | NL | 11 | 0 | 0 | 4 | 19 | 79 | 15 | 10 | 9 | 2 | 2 | 0 | 0 | 10 | 1 | 8 | 1 | 0 | 0 | 1 | .000 | 0 | 0 | 4.26 |
| | Minnesota | AL | 6 | 0 | 0 | 2 | 8.2 | 38 | 11 | 4 | 4 | 1 | 0 | 0 | 0 | 2 | 0 | 3 | 2 | 0 | 0 | 0 | .000 | 0 | 0 | 4.15 |
| | 8 ML YEARS | | 161 | 4 | 0 | 60 | 264 | 1159 | 278 | 136 | 114 | 22 | 15 | 9 | 5 | 118 | 12 | 119 | 17 | 2 | 5 | 7 | .417 | 0 | 1 | 3.89 |

## Rod Booker

**Bats:** Left **Throws:** Right **Pos:** SS/2B **Ht:** 6' 0" **Wt:** 175 **Born:** 09/04/58 **Age:** 32

| BATTING | | | | | | | | | | | | | | | | | | | | BASERUNNING | | | | PERCENTAGES | | |
|---|---|---|---|---|---|---|---|---|---|---|---|---|---|---|---|---|---|---|---|---|---|---|---|---|---|---|
| Year | Team | Lg | G | AB | H | 2B | 3B | HR | (Hm | Rd) | TB | R | RBI | TBB | IBB | SO | HBP | SH | SF | SB | CS | SB% | GDP | Avg | OBP | SLG |
| 1987 | St. Louis | NL | 44 | 47 | 13 | 1 | 1 | 0 | (0 | 0) | 16 | 9 | 8 | 7 | 1 | 7 | 0 | 2 | 0 | 2 | 0 | 1.00 | 0 | .277 | .370 | .340 |
| 1988 | St. Louis | NL | 18 | 35 | 12 | 3 | 0 | 0 | (0 | 0) | 15 | 6 | 3 | 4 | 0 | 3 | 0 | 0 | 0 | 2 | 2 | .50 | 0 | .343 | .410 | .429 |
| 1989 | St. Louis | NL | 10 | 8 | 2 | 0 | 0 | 0 | (0 | 0) | 2 | 1 | 0 | 0 | 0 | 1 | 0 | 0 | 0 | 0 | 0 | .00 | 0 | .250 | .250 | .250 |
| 1990 | Philadelphia | NL | 73 | 131 | 29 | 5 | 2 | 0 | (0 | 0) | 38 | 19 | 10 | 15 | 7 | 26 | 0 | 2 | 0 | 3 | 1 | .75 | 7 | .221 | .301 | .290 |
| | 4 ML YEARS | | 145 | 221 | 56 | 9 | 3 | 0 | (0 | 0) | 71 | 35 | 21 | 26 | 8 | 37 | 0 | 4 | 0 | 7 | 3 | .70 | 7 | .253 | .332 | .321 |

## Bob Boone

**Bats:** Right **Throws:** Right **Pos:** C **Ht:** 6' 2" **Wt:** 207 **Born:** 11/19/47 **Age:** 43

| BATTING | | | | | | | | | | | | | | | | | | | | BASERUNNING | | | | PERCENTAGES | | |
|---|---|---|---|---|---|---|---|---|---|---|---|---|---|---|---|---|---|---|---|---|---|---|---|---|---|---|
| Year | Team | Lg | G | AB | H | 2B | 3B | HR | (Hm | Rd) | TB | R | RBI | TBB | IBB | SO | HBP | SH | SF | SB | CS | SB% | GDP | Avg | OBP | SLG |
| 1972 | Philadelphia | NL | 16 | 51 | 14 | 1 | 0 | 1 | (0 | 1) | 18 | 4 | 4 | 5 | 2 | 7 | 0 | 0 | 1 | 1 | 0 | 1.00 | 2 | .275 | .333 | .353 |
| 1973 | Philadelphia | NL | 145 | 521 | 136 | 20 | 2 | 10 | (4 | 6) | 190 | 42 | 61 | 41 | 8 | 36 | 0 | 5 | 8 | 3 | 4 | .43 | 7 | .261 | .311 | .365 |

| | | | | | | | | | | | | | | | | | | | | | | | | | |
|---|---|---|---|---|---|---|---|---|---|---|---|---|---|---|---|---|---|---|---|---|---|---|---|---|---|
| 1974 Philadelphia | NL | 146 | 488 | 118 | 24 | 3 | 3 | (3 | 0) | 157 | 41 | 52 | 35 | 9 | 29 | 4 | 9 | 5 | 3 | 1 | .75 | 16 | .242 | .295 | .322 |
| 1975 Philadelphia | NL | 97 | 289 | 71 | 14 | 2 | 2 | (0 | 2) | 95 | 28 | 20 | 32 | 6 | 14 | 1 | 6 | 1 | 1 | 3 | .25 | 8 | .246 | .322 | .329 |
| 1976 Philadelphia | NL | 121 | 361 | 98 | 18 | 2 | 4 | (3 | 1) | 132 | 40 | 54 | 45 | 14 | 44 | 1 | 4 | 7 | 2 | 5 | .29 | 10 | .271 | .348 | .366 |
| 1977 Philadelphia | NL | 132 | 440 | 125 | 26 | 4 | 11 | (7 | 4) | 192 | 55 | 66 | 42 | 5 | 54 | 2 | 3 | 8 | 5 | 5 | .50 | 8 | .284 | .343 | .436 |
| 1978 Philadelphia | NL | 132 | 435 | 123 | 18 | 4 | 12 | (8 | 4) | 185 | 48 | 62 | 46 | 10 | 37 | 1 | 5 | 8 | 2 | 5 | .29 | 13 | .283 | .347 | .425 |
| 1979 Philadelphia | NL | 119 | 398 | 114 | 21 | 3 | 9 | (4 | 5) | 168 | 38 | 58 | 49 | 9 | 33 | 2 | 4 | 1 | 1 | 4 | .20 | 9 | .286 | .367 | .422 |
| 1980 Philadelphia | NL | 141 | 480 | 110 | 23 | 1 | 9 | (5 | 4) | 162 | 34 | 55 | 48 | 12 | 41 | 1 | 4 | 2 | 3 | 4 | .43 | 9 | .229 | .299 | .338 |
| 1981 Philadelphia | NL | 76 | 227 | 48 | 7 | 0 | 4 | (2 | 2) | 67 | 19 | 24 | 22 | 2 | 16 | 0 | 2 | 2 | 2 | 2 | .50 | 6 | .211 | .279 | .295 |
| 1982 California | AL | 143 | 472 | 121 | 17 | 0 | 7 | (5 | 2) | 159 | 42 | 58 | 39 | 2 | 34 | 0 | 23 | 5 | 0 | 2 | .00 | 9 | .256 | .310 | .337 |
| 1983 California | AL | 142 | 468 | 120 | 18 | 0 | 9 | (6 | 3) | 165 | 46 | 52 | 24 | 1 | 42 | 0 | 10 | 7 | 4 | 3 | .57 | 19 | .256 | .289 | .353 |
| 1984 California | AL | 139 | 450 | 91 | 16 | 1 | 3 | (1 | 2) | 118 | 33 | 32 | 25 | 1 | 45 | 0 | 6 | 5 | 3 | 3 | .50 | 11 | .202 | .242 | .262 |
| 1985 California | AL | 150 | 460 | 114 | 17 | 0 | 5 | (0 | 5) | 146 | 37 | 55 | 37 | 2 | 35 | 3 | 16 | 4 | 1 | 2 | .33 | 12 | .248 | .306 | .317 |
| 1986 California | AL | 144 | 442 | 98 | 12 | 2 | 7 | (1 | 6) | 135 | 48 | 49 | 43 | 1 | 30 | 0 | 12 | 6 | 1 | 0 | 1.00 | 15 | .222 | .287 | .305 |
| 1987 California | AL | 128 | 389 | 94 | 18 | 0 | 3 | (1 | 2) | 121 | 42 | 33 | 35 | 0 | 36 | 1 | 14 | 3 | 0 | 2 | .00 | 10 | .242 | .304 | .311 |
| 1988 California | AL | 122 | 352 | 104 | 17 | 0 | 5 | (3 | 2) | 136 | 38 | 39 | 29 | 2 | 26 | 2 | 9 | 0 | 2 | 2 | .50 | 9 | .295 | .352 | .386 |
| 1989 Kansas City | AL | 131 | 405 | 111 | 13 | 2 | 1 | (1 | 0) | 131 | 33 | 43 | 49 | 4 | 37 | 2 | 8 | 5 | 3 | 2 | .60 | 16 | .274 | .351 | .323 |
| 1990 Kansas City | AL | 40 | 117 | 28 | 3 | 0 | 0 | (0 | 0) | 31 | 11 | 9 | 17 | 0 | 12 | 0 | 2 | 0 | 1 | 1 | .50 | 2 | .239 | .336 | .265 |
| 19 ML YEARS | | 2264 | 7245 | 1838 | 303 | 26 | 105 | (54 | 51) | 2508 | 679 | 826 | 663 | 90 | 608 | 20 | 142 | 78 | 38 | 50 | .43 | 191 | .254 | .315 | .346 |

## Dan Boone

**Pitches:** Left **Bats:** Left **Pos:** RP **Ht:** 5' 8" **Wt:** 140 **Born:** 01/14/54 **Age:** 37

| HOW MUCH HE PITCHED | | | | | | | | WHAT HE GAVE UP | | | | | | | | | | | | THE RESULTS | | | | | |
|---|---|---|---|---|---|---|---|---|---|---|---|---|---|---|---|---|---|---|---|---|---|---|---|---|---|
| Year Team | Lg | G | GS | CG | GF | IP | BFP | H | R | ER | HR | SH | SF | HB | TBB | IBB | SO | WP | Bk | W | L | Pct. | ShO | Sv | ERA |
| 1981 San Diego | NL | 37 | 0 | 0 | 8 | 63 | 262 | 63 | 23 | 20 | 2 | 2 | 2 | 1 | 21 | 7 | 43 | 1 | 5 | 1 | 0 | 1.000 | 0 | 2 | 2.86 |
| 1982 2 ML Teams | | 20 | 0 | 0 | 8 | 28.2 | 116 | 28 | 16 | 15 | 3 | 2 | 1 | 0 | 7 | 1 | 12 | 1 | 0 | 1 | 1 | .500 | 0 | 2 | 4.71 |
| 1990 Baltimore | AL | 4 | 1 | 0 | 0 | 9.2 | 43 | 12 | 3 | 3 | 1 | 0 | 0 | 1 | 3 | 0 | 2 | 1 | 0 | 0 | 0 | .000 | 0 | 0 | 2.79 |
| 1982 San Diego | NL | 10 | 0 | 0 | 4 | 16 | 69 | 21 | 10 | 10 | 2 | 1 | 0 | 0 | 3 | 0 | 8 | 0 | 0 | 1 | 0 | 1.000 | 0 | 1 | 5.63 |
| Houston | NL | 10 | 0 | 0 | 4 | 12.2 | 47 | 7 | 6 | 5 | 1 | 1 | 1 | 0 | 4 | 1 | 4 | 1 | 0 | 0 | 1 | .000 | 0 | 1 | 3.55 |
| 3 ML YEARS | | 61 | 1 | 0 | 16 | 101.1 | 421 | 103 | 42 | 38 | 6 | 4 | 3 | 2 | 31 | 8 | 57 | 3 | 5 | 2 | 1 | .667 | 0 | 4 | 3.38 |

## Pat Borders

**Bats:** Right **Throws:** Right **Pos:** C **Ht:** 6' 2" **Wt:** 205 **Born:** 05/14/63 **Age:** 28

| BATTING | | | | | | | | | | | | | | | | | | | BASERUNNING | | | | PERCENTAGES | | |
|---|---|---|---|---|---|---|---|---|---|---|---|---|---|---|---|---|---|---|---|---|---|---|---|---|---|
| Year Team | Lg | G | AB | H | 2B | 3B | HR | (Hm | Rd) | TB | R | RBI | TBB | IBB | SO | HBP | SH | SF | SB | CS | SB% | GDP | Avg | OBP | SLG |
| 1988 Toronto | AL | 56 | 154 | 42 | 6 | 3 | 5 | (2 | 3) | 69 | 15 | 21 | 3 | 0 | 24 | 0 | 2 | 1 | 0 | 0 | .00 | 5 | .273 | .285 | .448 |
| 1989 Toronto | AL | 94 | 241 | 62 | 11 | 1 | 3 | (1 | 2) | 84 | 22 | 29 | 11 | 2 | 45 | 1 | 1 | 2 | 2 | 1 | .67 | 7 | .257 | .290 | .349 |
| 1990 Toronto | AL | 125 | 346 | 99 | 24 | 2 | 15 | (10 | 5) | 172 | 36 | 49 | 18 | 2 | 57 | 0 | 1 | 3 | 0 | 1 | .00 | 17 | .286 | .319 | .497 |
| 3 ML YEARS | | 275 | 741 | 203 | 41 | 6 | 23 | (13 | 10) | 325 | 73 | 99 | 32 | 4 | 126 | 1 | 4 | 6 | 2 | 2 | .50 | 29 | .274 | .303 | .439 |

## Mike Bordick

**Bats:** Right **Throws:** Right **Pos:** 3B **Ht:** 5'11" **Wt:** 170 **Born:** 07/21/65 **Age:** 25

| BATTING | | | | | | | | | | | | | | | | | | | BASERUNNING | | | | PERCENTAGES | | |
|---|---|---|---|---|---|---|---|---|---|---|---|---|---|---|---|---|---|---|---|---|---|---|---|---|---|
| Year Team | Lg | G | AB | H | 2B | 3B | HR | (Hm | Rd) | TB | R | RBI | TBB | IBB | SO | HBP | SH | SF | SB | CS | SB% | GDP | Avg | OBP | SLG |
| 1986 Medford | A | 46 | 187 | 48 | 3 | 1 | 0 | -- | -- | 53 | 30 | 19 | 40 | 0 | 21 | 1 | 1 | 1 | 6 | 0 | 1.00 | 5 | .257 | .389 | .283 |
| 1987 Modesto | A | 133 | 497 | 133 | 17 | 0 | 3 | -- | -- | 159 | 73 | 75 | 87 | 3 | 92 | 5 | 4 | 8 | 8 | 8 | .50 | 13 | .268 | .377 | .320 |
| 1988 Huntsville | AA | 132 | 481 | 130 | 13 | 2 | 0 | -- | -- | 147 | 48 | 38 | 87 | 0 | 50 | 4 | 9 | 3 | 7 | 9 | .44 | 11 | .270 | .384 | .306 |
| 1989 Tacoma | AAA | 136 | 487 | 117 | 17 | 1 | 1 | -- | -- | 139 | 55 | 43 | 58 | 0 | 51 | 7 | 15 | 2 | 4 | 9 | .31 | 14 | .240 | .329 | .285 |
| 1990 Tacoma | AAA | 111 | 348 | 79 | 16 | 1 | 2 | -- | -- | 103 | 49 | 30 | 46 | 0 | 40 | 3 | 7 | 2 | 3 | 0 | 1.00 | 6 | .227 | .321 | .296 |
| 1990 Oakland | AL | 25 | 14 | 1 | 0 | 0 | 0 | (0 | 0) | 1 | 0 | 0 | 1 | 0 | 4 | 0 | 0 | 0 | 0 | 0 | .00 | 0 | .071 | .133 | .071 |

## Chris Bosio

**Pitches:** Right **Bats:** Right **Pos:** SP **Ht:** 6' 3" **Wt:** 225 **Born:** 04/03/63 **Age:** 28

| HOW MUCH HE PITCHED | | | | | | | | WHAT HE GAVE UP | | | | | | | | | | | | THE RESULTS | | | | | |
|---|---|---|---|---|---|---|---|---|---|---|---|---|---|---|---|---|---|---|---|---|---|---|---|---|---|
| Year Team | Lg | G | GS | CG | GF | IP | BFP | H | R | ER | HR | SH | SF | HB | TBB | IBB | SO | WP | Bk | W | L | Pct. | ShO | Sv | ERA |
| 1986 Milwaukee | AL | 10 | 4 | 0 | 3 | 34.2 | 154 | 41 | 27 | 27 | 9 | 1 | 0 | 0 | 13 | 0 | 29 | 2 | 1 | 0 | 4 | .000 | 0 | 0 | 7.01 |
| 1987 Milwaukee | AL | 46 | 19 | 2 | 8 | 170 | 734 | 187 | 102 | 99 | 18 | 3 | 3 | 1 | 50 | 3 | 150 | 14 | 2 | 11 | 8 | .579 | 1 | 2 | 5.24 |
| 1988 Milwaukee | AL | 38 | 22 | 9 | 15 | 182 | 766 | 190 | 80 | 68 | 13 | 7 | 9 | 2 | 38 | 6 | 84 | 1 | 2 | 7 | 15 | .318 | 1 | 6 | 3.36 |
| 1989 Milwaukee | AL | 33 | 33 | 8 | 0 | 234.2 | 969 | 225 | 90 | 77 | 16 | 5 | 5 | 6 | 48 | 1 | 173 | 4 | 2 | 15 | 10 | .600 | 2 | 0 | 2.95 |
| 1990 Milwaukee | AL | 20 | 20 | 4 | 0 | 132.2 | 557 | 131 | 67 | 59 | 15 | 4 | 4 | 3 | 38 | 1 | 76 | 7 | 0 | 4 | 9 | .308 | 1 | 0 | 4.00 |
| 5 ML YEARS | | 147 | 98 | 23 | 26 | 754 | 3180 | 774 | 366 | 330 | 71 | 20 | 21 | 12 | 187 | 11 | 512 | 28 | 7 | 37 | 46 | .446 | 5 | 8 | 3.94 |

## Shawn Boskie

**Pitches:** Right **Bats:** Right **Pos:** SP **Ht:** 6' 3" **Wt:** 205 **Born:** 03/28/67 **Age:** 24

| HOW MUCH HE PITCHED | | | | | | | | WHAT HE GAVE UP | | | | | | | | | | | | THE RESULTS | | | | | |
|---|---|---|---|---|---|---|---|---|---|---|---|---|---|---|---|---|---|---|---|---|---|---|---|---|---|
| Year Team | Lg | G | GS | CG | GF | IP | BFP | H | R | ER | HR | SH | SF | HB | TBB | IBB | SO | WP | Bk | W | L | Pct. | ShO | Sv | ERA |
| 1986 Wytheville | R | 14 | 12 | 1 | 0 | 54 | 268 | 42 | 41 | 32 | 4 | 0 | 1 | 7 | 57 | 1 | 40 | 15 | 0 | 4 | 4 | .500 | 0 | 0 | 5.33 |
| 1987 Peoria | A | 26 | 25 | 1 | 0 | 149 | 657 | 149 | 91 | 72 | 12 | 4 | 5 | 17 | 56 | 2 | 100 | 7 | 5 | 9 | 11 | .450 | 0 | 0 | 4.35 |

| Year Team | Lg | G | GS | CG | GF | IP | BFP | H | R | ER | HR | SH | SF | HB | TBB | IBB | SO | WP | Bk | W | L | Pct. | ShO | Sv | ERA |
|---|---|---|---|---|---|---|---|---|---|---|---|---|---|---|---|---|---|---|---|---|---|---|---|---|---|
| 1988 Winston-Sal | A | 27 | 27 | 4 | 0 | 186 | 825 | 176 | 83 | 70 | 9 | 4 | 7 | 17 | 89 | 1 | 164 | 14 | 4 | 12 | 7 | .632 | 2 | 0 | 3.39 |
| 1989 Charlotte | AA | 28 | 28 | 5 | 0 | 181 | 813 | 196 | 105 | 88 | 10 | 3 | 8 | 19 | 84 | 3 | 164 | 11 | 1 | 11 | 8 | .579 | 0 | 0 | 4.38 |
| 1990 Iowa | AAA | 8 | 8 | 1 | 0 | 51 | 217 | 46 | 22 | 18 | 1 | 2 | 1 | 2 | 21 | 1 | 51 | 1 | 0 | 4 | 2 | .667 | 0 | 0 | 3.18 |
| 1990 Chicago | NL | 15 | 15 | 1 | 0 | 97.2 | 415 | 99 | 42 | 40 | 8 | 8 | 2 | 1 | 31 | 3 | 49 | 3 | 2 | 5 | 6 | .455 | 0 | 0 | 3.69 |

## Thad Bosley

**Bats:** Left **Throws:** Left **Pos:** LF **Ht:** 6' 3" **Wt:** 175 **Born:** 09/17/56 **Age:** 34

| BATTING | | | | | | | | | | | | | | | | | | | BASERUNNING | | | | PERCENTAGES | | |
|---|---|---|---|---|---|---|---|---|---|---|---|---|---|---|---|---|---|---|---|---|---|---|---|---|---|
| Year Team | Lg | G | AB | H | 2B | 3B | HR | (Hm | Rd) | TB | R | RBI | TBB | IBB | SO | HBP | SH | SF | SB | CS | SB% | GDP | Avg | OBP | SLG |
| 1977 California | AL | 58 | 212 | 63 | 10 | 2 | 0 | (0 | 0) | 77 | 19 | 19 | 16 | 0 | 32 | 1 | 4 | 2 | 5 | 4 | .56 | 4 | .297 | .346 | .363 |
| 1978 Chicago | AL | 66 | 219 | 59 | 5 | 1 | 2 | (1 | 1) | 72 | 25 | 13 | 13 | 1 | 32 | 0 | 2 | 2 | 12 | 11 | .52 | 4 | .269 | .308 | .329 |
| 1979 Chicago | AL | 36 | 77 | 24 | 1 | 1 | 1 | (1 | 0) | 30 | 13 | 8 | 9 | 0 | 14 | 0 | 0 | 0 | 4 | 1 | .80 | 1 | .312 | .384 | .390 |
| 1980 Chicago | AL | 70 | 147 | 33 | 2 | 0 | 2 | (2 | 0) | 41 | 12 | 14 | 10 | 3 | 27 | 0 | 4 | 1 | 3 | 2 | .60 | 5 | .224 | .272 | .279 |
| 1981 Milwaukee | AL | 42 | 105 | 24 | 2 | 0 | 0 | (0 | 0) | 26 | 11 | 3 | 6 | 0 | 13 | 0 | 1 | 0 | 2 | 1 | .67 | 4 | .229 | .270 | .248 |
| 1982 Seattle | AL | 22 | 46 | 8 | 1 | 0 | 0 | (0 | 0) | 9 | 3 | 2 | 4 | 0 | 8 | 0 | 0 | 0 | 3 | 1 | .75 | 1 | .174 | .240 | .196 |
| 1983 Chicago | NL | 43 | 72 | 21 | 4 | 1 | 2 | (1 | 1) | 33 | 12 | 12 | 10 | 1 | 12 | 0 | 0 | 1 | 1 | 1 | .50 | 0 | .292 | .373 | .458 |
| 1984 Chicago | NL | 55 | 98 | 29 | 2 | 2 | 2 | (0 | 2) | 41 | 17 | 14 | 13 | 2 | 22 | 0 | 0 | 1 | 5 | 1 | .83 | 1 | .296 | .375 | .418 |
| 1985 Chicago | NL | 108 | 180 | 59 | 6 | 3 | 7 | (4 | 3) | 92 | 25 | 27 | 20 | 1 | 29 | 0 | 0 | 2 | 5 | 1 | .83 | 3 | .328 | .391 | .511 |
| 1986 Chicago | NL | 87 | 120 | 33 | 4 | 1 | 1 | (0 | 1) | 42 | 15 | 9 | 18 | 3 | 24 | 0 | 1 | 0 | 3 | 0 | 1.00 | 3 | .275 | .370 | .350 |
| 1987 Kansas City | AL | 80 | 140 | 39 | 6 | 1 | 1 | (0 | 1) | 50 | 13 | 16 | 9 | 2 | 26 | 0 | 1 | 2 | 0 | 0 | .00 | 2 | .279 | .318 | .357 |
| 1988 2 ML Teams | | 50 | 96 | 25 | 5 | 0 | 0 | (0 | 0) | 30 | 10 | 9 | 8 | 1 | 18 | 0 | 1 | 4 | 1 | 1 | .50 | 2 | .260 | .306 | .313 |
| 1989 Texas | AL | 37 | 40 | 9 | 2 | 0 | 1 | (1 | 0) | 14 | 5 | 9 | 3 | 0 | 11 | 0 | 0 | 1 | 2 | 0 | 1.00 | 2 | .225 | .273 | .350 |
| 1990 Texas | AL | 30 | 29 | 4 | 0 | 0 | 1 | (1 | 0) | 7 | 3 | 3 | 4 | 1 | 7 | 0 | 0 | 0 | 1 | 0 | 1.00 | 1 | .138 | .242 | .241 |
| 1988 Kansas City | AL | 15 | 21 | 4 | 0 | 0 | 0 | (0 | 0) | 4 | 1 | 2 | 2 | 1 | 6 | 0 | 0 | 1 | 0 | 0 | .00 | 0 | .190 | .250 | .190 |
| California | AL | 35 | 75 | 21 | 5 | 0 | 0 | (0 | 0) | 26 | 9 | 7 | 6 | 0 | 12 | 0 | 1 | 3 | 1 | 1 | .50 | 2 | .280 | .321 | .347 |
| 14 ML YEARS | | 784 | 1581 | 430 | 50 | 12 | 20 | (11 | 9) | 564 | 183 | 158 | 143 | 15 | 275 | 1 | 14 | 16 | 47 | 24 | .66 | 33 | .272 | .330 | .357 |

## Daryl Boston

**Bats:** Left **Throws:** Left **Pos:** CF **Ht:** 6' 3" **Wt:** 203 **Born:** 01/04/63 **Age:** 28

| BATTING | | | | | | | | | | | | | | | | | | | BASERUNNING | | | | PERCENTAGES | | |
|---|---|---|---|---|---|---|---|---|---|---|---|---|---|---|---|---|---|---|---|---|---|---|---|---|---|
| Year Team | Lg | G | AB | H | 2B | 3B | HR | (Hm | Rd) | TB | R | RBI | TBB | IBB | SO | HBP | SH | SF | SB | CS | SB% | GDP | Avg | OBP | SLG |
| 1984 Chicago | AL | 35 | 83 | 14 | 3 | 1 | 0 | (0 | 0) | 19 | 8 | 3 | 4 | 0 | 20 | 0 | 0 | 0 | 6 | 0 | 1.00 | 0 | .169 | .207 | .229 |
| 1985 Chicago | AL | 95 | 232 | 53 | 13 | 1 | 3 | (1 | 2) | 77 | 20 | 15 | 14 | 1 | 44 | 0 | 1 | 1 | 8 | 6 | .57 | 3 | .228 | .271 | .332 |
| 1986 Chicago | AL | 56 | 199 | 53 | 11 | 3 | 5 | (1 | 4) | 85 | 29 | 22 | 21 | 3 | 33 | 0 | 3 | 1 | 9 | 5 | .64 | 4 | .266 | .335 | .427 |
| 1987 Chicago | AL | 103 | 337 | 87 | 21 | 2 | 10 | (5 | 5) | 142 | 51 | 29 | 25 | 2 | 68 | 0 | 4 | 3 | 12 | 6 | .67 | 5 | .258 | .307 | .421 |
| 1988 Chicago | AL | 105 | 281 | 61 | 12 | 2 | 15 | (6 | 9) | 122 | 37 | 31 | 21 | 5 | 44 | 0 | 2 | 1 | 9 | 3 | .75 | 5 | .217 | .271 | .434 |
| 1989 Chicago | AL | 101 | 218 | 55 | 3 | 4 | 5 | (3 | 2) | 81 | 34 | 23 | 24 | 3 | 31 | 0 | 4 | 1 | 7 | 2 | .78 | 1 | .252 | .325 | .372 |
| 1990 2 ML Teams | | 120 | 367 | 100 | 21 | 2 | 12 | (4 | 8) | 161 | 65 | 45 | 28 | 2 | 50 | 2 | 0 | 0 | 19 | 7 | .73 | 7 | .272 | .327 | .439 |
| 1990 Chicago | AL | 5 | 1 | 0 | 0 | 0 | 0 | (0 | 0) | 0 | 0 | 0 | 0 | 0 | 0 | 0 | 0 | 0 | 1 | 0 | 1.00 | 0 | .000 | .000 | .000 |
| New York | NL | 115 | 366 | 100 | 21 | 2 | 12 | (4 | 8) | 161 | 65 | 45 | 28 | 2 | 50 | 2 | 0 | 0 | 18 | 7 | .72 | 7 | .273 | .328 | .440 |
| 7 ML YEARS | | 615 | 1717 | 423 | 84 | 15 | 50 | (20 | 30) | 687 | 244 | 168 | 137 | 16 | 290 | 2 | 14 | 7 | 70 | 29 | .71 | 25 | .246 | .302 | .400 |

## Oil Can Boyd

**Pitches:** Right **Bats:** Right **Pos:** SP **Ht:** 6' 1" **Wt:** 160 **Born:** 10/06/59 **Age:** 31

| HOW MUCH HE PITCHED | | | | | | | | WHAT HE GAVE UP | | | | | | | | | | | | THE RESULTS | | | | | |
|---|---|---|---|---|---|---|---|---|---|---|---|---|---|---|---|---|---|---|---|---|---|---|---|---|---|
| Year Team | Lg | G | GS | CG | GF | IP | BFP | H | R | ER | HR | SH | SF | HB | TBB | IBB | SO | WP | Bk | W | L | Pct. | ShO | Sv | ERA |
| 1982 Boston | AL | 3 | 1 | 0 | 0 | 8.1 | 37 | 11 | 5 | 5 | 2 | 0 | 0 | 0 | 2 | 0 | 2 | 1 | 0 | 0 | 1 | .000 | 0 | 0 | 5.40 |
| 1983 Boston | AL | 15 | 13 | 5 | 2 | 98.2 | 413 | 103 | 46 | 36 | 9 | 1 | 5 | 1 | 23 | 0 | 43 | 3 | 1 | 4 | 8 | .333 | 0 | 0 | 3.28 |
| 1984 Boston | AL | 29 | 26 | 10 | 2 | 197.2 | 835 | 207 | 109 | 96 | 18 | 4 | 8 | 1 | 53 | 5 | 134 | 5 | 1 | 12 | 12 | .500 | 3 | 0 | 4.37 |
| 1985 Boston | AL | 35 | 35 | 13 | 0 | 272.1 | 1132 | 273 | 117 | 112 | 26 | 9 | 7 | 4 | 67 | 3 | 154 | 1 | 1 | 15 | 13 | .536 | 3 | 0 | 3.70 |
| 1986 Boston | AL | 30 | 30 | 10 | 0 | 214.1 | 893 | 222 | 99 | 90 | 32 | 3 | 6 | 2 | 45 | 1 | 129 | 3 | 0 | 16 | 10 | .615 | 0 | 0 | 3.78 |
| 1987 Boston | AL | 7 | 7 | 0 | 0 | 36.2 | 167 | 47 | 31 | 24 | 6 | 4 | 3 | 2 | 9 | 1 | 12 | 0 | 2 | 1 | 3 | .250 | 0 | 0 | 5.89 |
| 1988 Boston | AL | 23 | 23 | 1 | 0 | 129.2 | 561 | 147 | 82 | 77 | 25 | 3 | 6 | 2 | 41 | 2 | 71 | 0 | 5 | 9 | 7 | .563 | 0 | 0 | 5.34 |
| 1989 Boston | AL | 10 | 10 | 0 | 0 | 59 | 246 | 57 | 31 | 29 | 8 | 0 | 2 | 0 | 19 | 0 | 26 | 2 | 0 | 3 | 2 | .600 | 0 | 0 | 4.42 |
| 1990 Montreal | NL | 31 | 31 | 3 | 0 | 190.2 | 774 | 164 | 64 | 62 | 19 | 12 | 4 | 3 | 52 | 10 | 113 | 3 | 3 | 10 | 6 | .625 | 3 | 0 | 2.93 |
| 9 ML YEARS | | 183 | 176 | 42 | 4 | 1207.1 | 5058 | 1231 | 584 | 531 | 145 | 36 | 41 | 15 | 311 | 22 | 684 | 18 | 13 | 70 | 62 | .530 | 9 | 0 | 3.96 |

## Phil Bradley

**Bats:** Right **Throws:** Right **Pos:** LF/CF **Ht:** 6' 0" **Wt:** 185 **Born:** 03/11/59 **Age:** 32

| BATTING | | | | | | | | | | | | | | | | | | | BASERUNNING | | | | PERCENTAGES | | |
|---|---|---|---|---|---|---|---|---|---|---|---|---|---|---|---|---|---|---|---|---|---|---|---|---|---|
| Year Team | Lg | G | AB | H | 2B | 3B | HR | (Hm | Rd) | TB | R | RBI | TBB | IBB | SO | HBP | SH | SF | SB | CS | SB% | GDP | Avg | OBP | SLG |
| 1983 Seattle | AL | 23 | 67 | 18 | 2 | 0 | 0 | (0 | 0) | 20 | 8 | 5 | 8 | 0 | 5 | 0 | 1 | 1 | 3 | 1 | .75 | 0 | .269 | .342 | .299 |
| 1984 Seattle | AL | 124 | 322 | 97 | 12 | 4 | 0 | (0 | 0) | 117 | 49 | 24 | 34 | 2 | 61 | 3 | 11 | 0 | 21 | 8 | .72 | 6 | .301 | .373 | .363 |
| 1985 Seattle | AL | 159 | 641 | 192 | 33 | 8 | 26 | (15 | 11) | 319 | 100 | 88 | 55 | 4 | 129 | 12 | 4 | 2 | 22 | 9 | .71 | 14 | .300 | .365 | .498 |
| 1986 Seattle | AL | 143 | 526 | 163 | 27 | 4 | 12 | (5 | 7) | 234 | 88 | 50 | 77 | 1 | 134 | 8 | 1 | 2 | 21 | 12 | .64 | 9 | .310 | .405 | .445 |
| 1987 Seattle | AL | 158 | 603 | 179 | 38 | 10 | 14 | (12 | 2) | 279 | 101 | 67 | 84 | 2 | 119 | 8 | 1 | 5 | 40 | 10 | .80 | 18 | .297 | .387 | .463 |
| 1988 Philadelphia | NL | 154 | 569 | 150 | 30 | 5 | 11 | (8 | 3) | 223 | 77 | 56 | 54 | 0 | 106 | 16 | 3 | 6 | 11 | 9 | .55 | 11 | .264 | .341 | .392 |

| Year Team | Lg | G | AB | H | 2B | 3B | HR | (Hm | Rd) | TB | R | RBI | TBB | IBB | SO | HBP | SH | SF | SB | CS | SB% | GDP | Avg | OBP | SLG |
|---|---|---|---|---|---|---|---|---|---|---|---|---|---|---|---|---|---|---|---|---|---|---|---|---|---|
| 1989 Baltimore | AL | 144 | 545 | 151 | 23 | 10 | 11 | (3 | 8) | 227 | 83 | 55 | 70 | 4 | 103 | 7 | 4 | 4 | 20 | 6 | .77 | 12 | .277 | .364 | .417 |
| 1990 2 ML Teams | | 117 | 422 | 108 | 14 | 2 | 4 | (4 | 0) | 138 | 59 | 31 | 50 | 5 | 61 | 11 | 11 | 1 | 17 | 7 | .71 | 11 | .256 | .349 | .327 |
| 1990 Baltimore | AL | 72 | 289 | 78 | 9 | 1 | 4 | (4 | 0) | 101 | 39 | 26 | 30 | 2 | 35 | 7 | 6 | 1 | 10 | 4 | .71 | 9 | .270 | .352 | .349 |
| Chicago | AL | 45 | 133 | 30 | 5 | 1 | 0 | (0 | 0) | 37 | 20 | 5 | 20 | 3 | 26 | 4 | 5 | 0 | 7 | 3 | .70 | 2 | .226 | .344 | .278 |
| 8 ML YEARS | | 1022 | 3695 | 1058 | 179 | 43 | 78 | (47 | 31) | 1557 | 565 | 376 | 432 | 18 | 718 | 65 | 36 | 21 | 155 | 62 | .71 | 81 | .286 | .369 | .421 |

## Scott Bradley

**Bats:** Left **Throws:** Right **Pos:** C **Ht:** 5'11" **Wt:** 185 **Born:** 03/22/60 **Age:** 31

| BATTING | | | | | | | | | | | | | | | | | | | BASERUNNING | | | | PERCENTAGES | | |
|---|---|---|---|---|---|---|---|---|---|---|---|---|---|---|---|---|---|---|---|---|---|---|---|---|---|
| Year Team | Lg | G | AB | H | 2B | 3B | HR | (Hm | Rd) | TB | R | RBI | TBB | IBB | SO | HBP | SH | SF | SB | CS | SB% | GDP | Avg | OBP | SLG |
| 1984 New York | AL | 9 | 21 | 6 | 1 | 0 | 0 | (0 | 0) | 7 | 3 | 2 | 1 | 0 | 1 | 0 | 0 | 0 | 0 | 0 | .00 | 0 | .286 | .318 | .333 |
| 1985 New York | AL | 19 | 49 | 8 | 2 | 1 | 0 | (0 | 0) | 12 | 4 | 1 | 1 | 0 | 5 | 1 | 0 | 0 | 0 | 0 | .00 | 2 | .163 | .196 | .245 |
| 1986 2 ML Teams | | 77 | 220 | 66 | 8 | 3 | 5 | (4 | 1) | 95 | 20 | 28 | 13 | 4 | 7 | 4 | 2 | 2 | 1 | 2 | .33 | 13 | .300 | .347 | .432 |
| 1987 Seattle | AL | 102 | 342 | 95 | 15 | 1 | 5 | (5 | 0) | 127 | 34 | 43 | 15 | 1 | 18 | 3 | 2 | 4 | 0 | 1 | .00 | 13 | .278 | .310 | .371 |
| 1988 Seattle | AL | 103 | 335 | 86 | 17 | 1 | 4 | (3 | 1) | 117 | 45 | 33 | 17 | 1 | 16 | 2 | 3 | 2 | 1 | 1 | .50 | 11 | .257 | .295 | .349 |
| 1989 Seattle | AL | 103 | 270 | 74 | 16 | 0 | 3 | (1 | 2) | 99 | 21 | 37 | 21 | 4 | 23 | 1 | 1 | 6 | 1 | 1 | .50 | 5 | .274 | .322 | .367 |
| 1990 Seattle | AL | 101 | 233 | 52 | 9 | 0 | 1 | (1 | 0) | 64 | 11 | 28 | 15 | 2 | 20 | 0 | 3 | 6 | 0 | 1 | .00 | 6 | .223 | .264 | .275 |
| 1986 Chicago | AL | 9 | 21 | 6 | 0 | 0 | 0 | (0 | 0) | 6 | 3 | 0 | 1 | 0 | 0 | 2 | 0 | 0 | 0 | 2 | .00 | 1 | .286 | .375 | .286 |
| Seattle | AL | 68 | 199 | 60 | 8 | 3 | 5 | (4 | 1) | 89 | 17 | 28 | 12 | 4 | 7 | 2 | 2 | 2 | 1 | 0 | 1.00 | 12 | .302 | .344 | .447 |
| 7 ML YEARS | | 514 | 1470 | 387 | 68 | 6 | 18 | (14 | 4) | 521 | 138 | 172 | 83 | 12 | 90 | 11 | 11 | 20 | 3 | 6 | .33 | 50 | .263 | .304 | .354 |

## Glenn Braggs

**Bats:** Right **Throws:** Right **Pos:** RF/LF **Ht:** 6' 3" **Wt:** 210 **Born:** 10/17/62 **Age:** 28

| BATTING | | | | | | | | | | | | | | | | | | | BASERUNNING | | | | PERCENTAGES | | |
|---|---|---|---|---|---|---|---|---|---|---|---|---|---|---|---|---|---|---|---|---|---|---|---|---|---|
| Year Team | Lg | G | AB | H | 2B | 3B | HR | (Hm | Rd) | TB | R | RBI | TBB | IBB | SO | HBP | SH | SF | SB | CS | SB% | GDP | Avg | OBP | SLG |
| 1986 Milwaukee | AL | 58 | 215 | 51 | 8 | 2 | 4 | (2 | 2) | 75 | 19 | 18 | 11 | 0 | 47 | 1 | 2 | 3 | 1 | 1 | .50 | 6 | .237 | .274 | .349 |
| 1987 Milwaukee | AL | 132 | 505 | 136 | 28 | 7 | 13 | (4 | 9) | 217 | 67 | 77 | 47 | 7 | 96 | 4 | 2 | 7 | 12 | 5 | .71 | 20 | .269 | .332 | .430 |
| 1988 Milwaukee | AL | 72 | 272 | 71 | 14 | 0 | 10 | (6 | 4) | 115 | 30 | 42 | 14 | 0 | 60 | 5 | 1 | 2 | 6 | 4 | .60 | 6 | .261 | .307 | .423 |
| 1989 Milwaukee | AL | 144 | 514 | 127 | 12 | 3 | 15 | (8 | 7) | 190 | 77 | 66 | 42 | 4 | 111 | 4 | 3 | 7 | 17 | 5 | .77 | 13 | .247 | .305 | .370 |
| 1990 2 ML Teams | | 109 | 314 | 88 | 14 | 1 | 9 | (5 | 4) | 131 | 39 | 41 | 38 | 3 | 64 | 6 | 0 | 4 | 8 | 7 | .53 | 4 | .280 | .365 | .417 |
| 1990 Milwaukee | AL | 37 | 113 | 28 | 5 | 0 | 3 | (1 | 2) | 42 | 17 | 13 | 12 | 2 | 21 | 3 | 0 | 3 | 5 | 3 | .63 | 1 | .248 | .328 | .372 |
| Cincinnati | NL | 72 | 201 | 60 | 9 | 1 | 6 | (4 | 2) | 89 | 22 | 28 | 26 | 1 | 43 | 3 | 0 | 1 | 3 | 4 | .43 | 3 | .299 | .385 | .443 |
| 5 ML YEARS | | 515 | 1820 | 473 | 76 | 13 | 51 | (25 | 26) | 728 | 232 | 244 | 152 | 14 | 378 | 20 | 8 | 23 | 44 | 22 | .67 | 49 | .260 | .320 | .400 |

## Jeff Brantley

**Pitches:** Right **Bats:** Right **Pos:** RP **Ht:** 5'11" **Wt:** 180 **Born:** 09/05/63 **Age:** 27

| HOW MUCH HE PITCHED | | | | | | | | WHAT HE GAVE UP | | | | | | | | | | | | THE RESULTS | | | | | |
|---|---|---|---|---|---|---|---|---|---|---|---|---|---|---|---|---|---|---|---|---|---|---|---|---|---|
| Year Team | Lg | G | GS | CG | GF | IP | BFP | H | R | ER | HR | SH | SF | HB | TBB | IBB | SO | WP | Bk | W | L | Pct. | ShO | Sv | ERA |
| 1988 San Francisco | NL | 9 | 1 | 0 | 2 | 20.2 | 88 | 22 | 13 | 13 | 2 | 1 | 0 | 1 | 6 | 1 | 11 | 0 | 1 | 0 | 1 | .000 | 0 | 1 | 5.66 |
| 1989 San Francisco | NL | 59 | 1 | 0 | 15 | 97.1 | 422 | 101 | 50 | 44 | 10 | 7 | 3 | 2 | 37 | 8 | 69 | 3 | 2 | 7 | 1 | .875 | 0 | 0 | 4.07 |
| 1990 San Francisco | NL | 55 | 0 | 0 | 32 | 86.2 | 361 | 77 | 18 | 15 | 3 | 2 | 2 | 3 | 33 | 6 | 61 | 0 | 3 | 5 | 3 | .625 | 0 | 19 | 1.56 |
| 3 ML YEARS | | 123 | 2 | 0 | 49 | 204.2 | 871 | 200 | 81 | 72 | 15 | 10 | 5 | 6 | 76 | 15 | 141 | 3 | 6 | 12 | 5 | .706 | 0 | 20 | 3.17 |

## Sid Bream

**Bats:** Left **Throws:** Left **Pos:** 1B **Ht:** 6' 4" **Wt:** 220 **Born:** 08/03/60 **Age:** 30

| BATTING | | | | | | | | | | | | | | | | | | | BASERUNNING | | | | PERCENTAGES | | |
|---|---|---|---|---|---|---|---|---|---|---|---|---|---|---|---|---|---|---|---|---|---|---|---|---|---|
| Year Team | Lg | G | AB | H | 2B | 3B | HR | (Hm | Rd) | TB | R | RBI | TBB | IBB | SO | HBP | SH | SF | SB | CS | SB% | GDP | Avg | OBP | SLG |
| 1983 Los Angeles | NL | 15 | 11 | 2 | 0 | 0 | 0 | (0 | 0) | 2 | 0 | 2 | 2 | 0 | 2 | 0 | 0 | 0 | 0 | 0 | .00 | 1 | .182 | .308 | .182 |
| 1984 Los Angeles | NL | 27 | 49 | 9 | 3 | 0 | 0 | (0 | 0) | 12 | 2 | 6 | 6 | 2 | 9 | 0 | 1 | 2 | 1 | 0 | 1.00 | 1 | .184 | .263 | .245 |
| 1985 2 ML Teams | | 50 | 148 | 34 | 7 | 0 | 6 | (2 | 4) | 59 | 18 | 21 | 18 | 5 | 24 | 0 | 3 | 2 | 0 | 2 | .00 | 4 | .230 | .310 | .399 |
| 1986 Pittsburgh | NL | 154 | 522 | 140 | 37 | 5 | 16 | (5 | 11) | 235 | 73 | 77 | 60 | 5 | 73 | 1 | 1 | 7 | 13 | 7 | .65 | 14 | .268 | .341 | .450 |
| 1987 Pittsburgh | NL | 149 | 516 | 142 | 25 | 3 | 13 | (10 | 3) | 212 | 64 | 65 | 49 | 11 | 69 | 0 | 3 | 4 | 9 | 8 | .53 | 19 | .275 | .336 | .411 |
| 1988 Pittsburgh | NL | 148 | 462 | 122 | 37 | 0 | 10 | (6 | 4) | 189 | 50 | 65 | 47 | 6 | 64 | 1 | 4 | 8 | 9 | 9 | .50 | 11 | .264 | .328 | .409 |
| 1989 Pittsburgh | NL | 19 | 36 | 8 | 3 | 0 | 0 | (0 | 0) | 11 | 3 | 4 | 12 | 0 | 10 | 0 | 2 | 0 | 0 | 4 | .00 | 0 | .222 | .417 | .306 |
| 1990 Pittsburgh | NL | 147 | 389 | 105 | 23 | 2 | 15 | (8 | 7) | 177 | 39 | 67 | 48 | 5 | 65 | 2 | 4 | 5 | 8 | 4 | .67 | 6 | .270 | .349 | .455 |
| 1985 Los Angeles | NL | 24 | 53 | 7 | 0 | 0 | 3 | (2 | 1) | 16 | 4 | 6 | 7 | 3 | 10 | 0 | 2 | 1 | 0 | 0 | .00 | 0 | .132 | .230 | .302 |
| Pittsburgh | NL | 26 | 95 | 27 | 7 | 0 | 3 | (0 | 3) | 43 | 14 | 15 | 11 | 2 | 14 | 0 | 1 | 1 | 0 | 2 | .00 | 4 | .284 | .355 | .453 |
| 8 ML YEARS | | 709 | 2133 | 562 | 135 | 10 | 60 | (31 | 29) | 897 | 249 | 307 | 242 | 34 | 316 | 4 | 18 | 28 | 40 | 34 | .54 | 56 | .263 | .336 | .421 |

## George Brett

**Bats:** Left **Throws:** Right **Pos:** 1B/DH **Ht:** 6' 0" **Wt:** 200 **Born:** 05/15/53 **Age:** 38

| BATTING | | | | | | | | | | | | | | | | | | | BASERUNNING | | | | PERCENTAGES | | |
|---|---|---|---|---|---|---|---|---|---|---|---|---|---|---|---|---|---|---|---|---|---|---|---|---|---|
| Year Team | Lg | G | AB | H | 2B | 3B | HR | (Hm | Rd) | TB | R | RBI | TBB | IBB | SO | HBP | SH | SF | SB | CS | SB% | GDP | Avg | OBP | SLG |
| 1973 Kansas City | AL | 13 | 40 | 5 | 2 | 0 | 0 | (0 | 0) | 7 | 2 | 0 | 0 | 0 | 5 | 0 | 1 | 0 | 0 | 0 | .00 | 0 | .125 | .125 | .175 |
| 1974 Kansas City | AL | 133 | 457 | 129 | 21 | 5 | 2 | (0 | 2) | 166 | 49 | 47 | 21 | 3 | 38 | 0 | 6 | 2 | 8 | 5 | .62 | 9 | .282 | .313 | .363 |
| 1975 Kansas City | AL | 159 | 634 | 195 | 35 | 13 | 11 | (2 | 9) | 289 | 84 | 89 | 46 | 6 | 49 | 2 | 9 | 6 | 13 | 10 | .57 | 8 | .308 | .353 | .456 |
| 1976 Kansas City | AL | 159 | 645 | 215 | 34 | 14 | 7 | (6 | 1) | 298 | 94 | 67 | 49 | 4 | 36 | 1 | 2 | 8 | 21 | 11 | .66 | 8 | .333 | .377 | .462 |
| 1977 Kansas City | AL | 139 | 564 | 176 | 32 | 13 | 22 | (9 | 13) | 300 | 105 | 88 | 55 | 9 | 24 | 2 | 3 | 3 | 14 | 12 | .54 | 12 | .312 | .373 | .532 |

| Year | Team | Lg | G | AB | H | 2B | 3B | HR | (Hm | Rd) | TB | R | RBI | TBB | IBB | SO | HBP | SH | SF | SB | CS | SB% | GDP | Avg | OBP | SLG |
|---|---|---|---|---|---|---|---|---|---|---|---|---|---|---|---|---|---|---|---|---|---|---|---|---|---|---|
| 1978 | Kansas City | AL | 128 | 510 | 150 | 45 | 8 | 9 | (4 | 5) | 238 | 79 | 62 | 39 | 6 | 35 | 1 | 3 | 5 | 23 | 7 | .77 | 6 | .294 | .342 | .467 |
| 1979 | Kansas City | AL | 154 | 645 | 212 | 42 | 20 | 23 | (11 | 12) | 363 | 119 | 107 | 51 | 14 | 36 | 0 | 1 | 4 | 17 | 10 | .63 | 8 | .329 | .376 | .563 |
| 1980 | Kansas City | AL | 117 | 449 | 175 | 33 | 9 | 24 | (13 | 11) | 298 | 87 | 118 | 58 | 16 | 22 | 1 | 0 | 7 | 15 | 6 | .71 | 11 | .390 | .454 | .664 |
| 1981 | Kansas City | AL | 89 | 347 | 109 | 27 | 7 | 6 | (2 | 4) | 168 | 42 | 43 | 27 | 7 | 23 | 1 | 0 | 4 | 14 | 6 | .70 | 7 | .314 | .361 | .484 |
| 1982 | Kansas City | AL | 144 | 552 | 166 | 32 | 9 | 21 | (9 | 12) | 279 | 101 | 82 | 71 | 14 | 51 | 1 | 0 | 5 | 6 | 1 | .86 | 12 | .301 | .378 | .505 |
| 1983 | Kansas City | AL | 123 | 464 | 144 | 38 | 2 | 25 | (7 | 18) | 261 | 90 | 93 | 57 | 13 | 39 | 1 | 0 | 3 | 0 | 1 | .00 | 9 | .310 | .385 | .563 |
| 1984 | Kansas City | AL | 104 | 377 | 107 | 21 | 3 | 13 | (6 | 7) | 173 | 42 | 69 | 38 | 6 | 37 | 0 | 0 | 7 | 0 | 2 | .00 | 11 | .284 | .344 | .459 |
| 1985 | Kansas City | AL | 155 | 550 | 184 | 38 | 5 | 30 | (15 | 15) | 322 | 108 | 112 | 103 | 31 | 49 | 3 | 0 | 9 | 9 | 1 | .90 | 12 | .335 | .436 | .585 |
| 1986 | Kansas City | AL | 124 | 441 | 128 | 28 | 4 | 16 | (8 | 8) | 212 | 70 | 73 | 80 | 18 | 45 | 4 | 0 | 4 | 1 | 2 | .33 | 6 | .290 | .401 | .481 |
| 1987 | Kansas City | AL | 115 | 427 | 124 | 18 | 2 | 22 | (14 | 8) | 212 | 71 | 78 | 72 | 14 | 47 | 1 | 0 | 8 | 6 | 3 | .67 | 10 | .290 | .388 | .496 |
| 1988 | Kansas City | AL | 157 | 589 | 180 | 42 | 3 | 24 | (13 | 11) | 300 | 90 | 103 | 82 | 15 | 51 | 3 | 0 | 7 | 14 | 3 | .82 | 15 | .306 | .389 | .509 |
| 1989 | Kansas City | AL | 124 | 457 | 129 | 26 | 3 | 12 | (3 | 9) | 197 | 67 | 80 | 59 | 14 | 47 | 3 | 0 | 9 | 14 | 4 | .78 | 18 | .282 | .362 | .431 |
| 1990 | Kansas City | AL | 142 | 544 | 179 | 45 | 7 | 14 | (3 | 11) | 280 | 82 | 87 | 56 | 14 | 63 | 0 | 0 | 7 | 9 | 2 | .82 | 17 | .329 | .387 | .515 |
| 18 ML YEARS | | | 2279 | 8692 | 2707 | 559 | 127 | 281 | (125 | 156) | 4363 | 1382 | 1398 | 964 | 204 | 697 | 24 | 25 | 98 | 184 | 86 | .68 | 179 | .311 | .378 | .502 |

## Rod Brewer

**Bats:** Left **Throws:** Left **Pos:** 1B **Ht:** 6' 3" **Wt:** 210 **Born:** 02/24/66 **Age:** 25

| BATTING | | | | | | | | | | | | | | | | | | | | BASERUNNING | | | | PERCENTAGES | | |
|---|---|---|---|---|---|---|---|---|---|---|---|---|---|---|---|---|---|---|---|---|---|---|---|---|---|---|
| Year | Team | Lg | G | AB | H | 2B | 3B | HR | (Hm | Rd) | TB | R | RBI | TBB | IBB | SO | HBP | SH | SF | SB | CS | SB% | GDP | Avg | OBP | SLG |
| 1987 | Johnson Cty | R | 67 | 238 | 60 | 11 | 2 | 10 | -- | -- | 105 | 33 | 42 | 36 | 5 | 40 | 3 | 0 | 2 | 2 | 2 | .50 | 4 | .252 | .355 | .441 |
| 1988 | Springfield | A | 133 | 457 | 136 | 25 | 2 | 8 | -- | -- | 189 | 57 | 64 | 63 | 7 | 52 | 5 | 1 | 4 | 6 | 4 | .60 | 22 | .298 | .386 | .414 |
| 1989 | Arkansas | AA | 128 | 470 | 130 | 25 | 2 | 10 | -- | -- | 189 | 71 | 93 | 46 | 3 | 46 | 7 | 0 | 3 | 2 | 3 | .40 | 8 | .277 | .348 | .402 |
| 1990 | Louisville | AAA | 144 | 514 | 129 | 15 | 5 | 12 | -- | -- | 190 | 60 | 83 | 54 | 7 | 62 | 9 | 0 | 6 | 0 | 2 | .00 | 9 | .251 | .329 | .370 |
| 1990 | St. Louis | NL | 14 | 25 | 6 | 1 | 0 | 0 | (0 | 0) | 7 | 4 | 2 | 0 | 0 | 4 | 0 | 0 | 0 | 0 | 0 | .00 | 1 | .240 | .240 | .280 |

## Greg Briley

**Bats:** Left **Throws:** Right **Pos:** RF/LF **Ht:** 5' 8" **Wt:** 165 **Born:** 05/24/65 **Age:** 26

| BATTING | | | | | | | | | | | | | | | | | | | | BASERUNNING | | | | PERCENTAGES | | |
|---|---|---|---|---|---|---|---|---|---|---|---|---|---|---|---|---|---|---|---|---|---|---|---|---|---|---|
| Year | Team | Lg | G | AB | H | 2B | 3B | HR | (Hm | Rd) | TB | R | RBI | TBB | IBB | SO | HBP | SH | SF | SB | CS | SB% | GDP | Avg | OBP | SLG |
| 1988 | Seattle | AL | 13 | 36 | 9 | 2 | 0 | 1 | (0 | 1) | 14 | 6 | 4 | 5 | 1 | 6 | 0 | 0 | 1 | 0 | 1 | .00 | 0 | .250 | .333 | .389 |
| 1989 | Seattle | AL | 115 | 394 | 105 | 22 | 4 | 13 | (5 | 8) | 174 | 52 | 52 | 39 | 1 | 82 | 5 | 1 | 5 | 11 | 5 | .69 | 9 | .266 | .336 | .442 |
| 1990 | Seattle | AL | 126 | 337 | 83 | 18 | 2 | 5 | (4 | 1) | 120 | 40 | 29 | 37 | 0 | 48 | 1 | 1 | 4 | 16 | 4 | .80 | 6 | .246 | .319 | .356 |
| 3 ML YEARS | | | 254 | 767 | 197 | 42 | 6 | 19 | (9 | 10) | 308 | 98 | 85 | 81 | 2 | 136 | 6 | 2 | 10 | 27 | 10 | .73 | 15 | .257 | .329 | .402 |

## Greg Brock

**Bats:** Left **Throws:** Right **Pos:** 1B **Ht:** 6' 3" **Wt:** 205 **Born:** 06/14/57 **Age:** 34

| BATTING | | | | | | | | | | | | | | | | | | | | BASERUNNING | | | | PERCENTAGES | | |
|---|---|---|---|---|---|---|---|---|---|---|---|---|---|---|---|---|---|---|---|---|---|---|---|---|---|---|
| Year | Team | Lg | G | AB | H | 2B | 3B | HR | (Hm | Rd) | TB | R | RBI | TBB | IBB | SO | HBP | SH | SF | SB | CS | SB% | GDP | Avg | OBP | SLG |
| 1982 | Los Angeles | NL | 18 | 17 | 2 | 1 | 0 | 0 | (0 | 0) | 3 | 1 | 1 | 1 | 1 | 5 | 0 | 0 | 0 | 0 | 0 | .00 | 0 | .118 | .167 | .176 |
| 1983 | Los Angeles | NL | 146 | 455 | 102 | 14 | 2 | 20 | (14 | 6) | 180 | 64 | 66 | 83 | 12 | 81 | 1 | 0 | 4 | 5 | 1 | .83 | 13 | .224 | .343 | .396 |
| 1984 | Los Angeles | NL | 88 | 271 | 61 | 6 | 0 | 14 | (8 | 6) | 109 | 33 | 34 | 39 | 3 | 37 | 0 | 0 | 3 | 8 | 0 | 1.00 | 6 | .225 | .319 | .402 |
| 1985 | Los Angeles | NL | 129 | 438 | 110 | 19 | 0 | 21 | (7 | 14) | 192 | 64 | 66 | 54 | 4 | 72 | 0 | 2 | 2 | 4 | 2 | .67 | 9 | .251 | .332 | .438 |
| 1986 | Los Angeles | NL | 115 | 325 | 76 | 13 | 0 | 16 | (5 | 11) | 137 | 33 | 52 | 37 | 5 | 60 | 0 | 1 | 4 | 2 | 5 | .29 | 5 | .234 | .309 | .422 |
| 1987 | Milwaukee | AL | 141 | 532 | 159 | 29 | 3 | 13 | (5 | 8) | 233 | 81 | 85 | 57 | 4 | 63 | 6 | 4 | 3 | 5 | 4 | .56 | 9 | .299 | .371 | .438 |
| 1988 | Milwaukee | AL | 115 | 364 | 77 | 16 | 1 | 6 | (4 | 2) | 113 | 53 | 50 | 63 | 16 | 48 | 3 | 3 | 4 | 6 | 2 | .75 | 11 | .212 | .329 | .310 |
| 1989 | Milwaukee | AL | 107 | 373 | 99 | 16 | 0 | 12 | (7 | 5) | 151 | 40 | 52 | 43 | 8 | 49 | 3 | 2 | 1 | 6 | 1 | .86 | 10 | .265 | .345 | .405 |
| 1990 | Milwaukee | AL | 123 | 367 | 91 | 23 | 0 | 7 | (3 | 4) | 135 | 42 | 50 | 43 | 9 | 45 | 2 | 2 | 8 | 4 | 2 | .67 | 6 | .248 | .324 | .368 |
| 9 ML YEARS | | | 982 | 3142 | 777 | 137 | 6 | 109 | (53 | 56) | 1253 | 411 | 456 | 420 | 62 | 460 | 15 | 14 | 29 | 40 | 17 | .70 | 69 | .247 | .336 | .399 |

## Tom Brookens

**Bats:** Right **Throws:** Right **Pos:** 3B/2B **Ht:** 5'10" **Wt:** 170 **Born:** 08/10/53 **Age:** 37

| BATTING | | | | | | | | | | | | | | | | | | | | BASERUNNING | | | | PERCENTAGES | | |
|---|---|---|---|---|---|---|---|---|---|---|---|---|---|---|---|---|---|---|---|---|---|---|---|---|---|---|
| Year | Team | Lg | G | AB | H | 2B | 3B | HR | (Hm | Rd) | TB | R | RBI | TBB | IBB | SO | HBP | SH | SF | SB | CS | SB% | GDP | Avg | OBP | SLG |
| 1979 | Detroit | AL | 60 | 190 | 50 | 5 | 2 | 4 | (3 | 1) | 71 | 23 | 21 | 11 | 0 | 40 | 2 | 4 | 1 | 10 | 3 | .77 | 3 | .263 | .309 | .374 |
| 1980 | Detroit | AL | 151 | 509 | 140 | 25 | 9 | 10 | (7 | 3) | 213 | 64 | 66 | 32 | 3 | 71 | 1 | 2 | 7 | 13 | 11 | .54 | 10 | .275 | .315 | .418 |
| 1981 | Detroit | AL | 71 | 239 | 58 | 10 | 1 | 4 | (3 | 1) | 82 | 19 | 25 | 14 | 0 | 43 | 2 | 4 | 6 | 5 | 3 | .63 | 5 | .243 | .284 | .343 |
| 1982 | Detroit | AL | 140 | 398 | 92 | 15 | 3 | 9 | (4 | 5) | 140 | 40 | 58 | 27 | 0 | 63 | 0 | 2 | 5 | 5 | 9 | .36 | 9 | .231 | .277 | .352 |
| 1983 | Detroit | AL | 138 | 332 | 71 | 13 | 3 | 6 | (5 | 1) | 108 | 50 | 32 | 29 | 2 | 46 | 2 | 5 | 6 | 10 | 4 | .71 | 3 | .214 | .276 | .325 |
| 1984 | Detroit | AL | 113 | 224 | 55 | 11 | 4 | 5 | (4 | 1) | 89 | 32 | 26 | 19 | 0 | 33 | 1 | 8 | 1 | 6 | 6 | .50 | 2 | .246 | .306 | .397 |
| 1985 | Detroit | AL | 156 | 485 | 115 | 34 | 6 | 7 | (3 | 4) | 182 | 54 | 47 | 27 | 0 | 78 | 0 | 9 | 1 | 14 | 5 | .74 | 8 | .237 | .277 | .375 |
| 1986 | Detroit | AL | 98 | 281 | 76 | 11 | 2 | 3 | (2 | 1) | 100 | 42 | 25 | 20 | 0 | 42 | 1 | 6 | 2 | 11 | 8 | .58 | 4 | .270 | .319 | .356 |
| 1987 | Detroit | AL | 143 | 444 | 107 | 15 | 3 | 13 | (6 | 7) | 167 | 59 | 59 | 33 | 3 | 63 | 2 | 9 | 2 | 7 | 4 | .64 | 8 | .241 | .295 | .376 |
| 1988 | Detroit | AL | 136 | 441 | 107 | 23 | 5 | 5 | (4 | 1) | 155 | 62 | 38 | 44 | 2 | 74 | 3 | 6 | 4 | 4 | 4 | .50 | 9 | .243 | .313 | .351 |
| 1989 | New York | AL | 66 | 168 | 38 | 6 | 0 | 4 | (0 | 4) | 56 | 14 | 14 | 11 | 1 | 27 | 0 | 3 | 1 | 1 | 3 | .25 | 3 | .226 | .272 | .333 |
| 1990 | Cleveland | AL | 64 | 154 | 41 | 7 | 2 | 1 | (0 | 1) | 55 | 18 | 20 | 14 | 1 | 25 | 0 | 1 | 3 | 0 | 0 | .00 | 3 | .266 | .322 | .357 |
| 12 ML YEARS | | | 1336 | 3865 | 950 | 175 | 40 | 71 | (41 | 30) | 1418 | 477 | 431 | 281 | 12 | 605 | 14 | 59 | 39 | 86 | 60 | .59 | 67 | .246 | .296 | .367 |

## Hubie Brooks

**Bats:** Right **Throws:** Right **Pos:** RF **Ht:** 6' 0" **Wt:** 205 **Born:** 09/24/56 **Age:** 34

| BATTING | | | | | | | | | | | | | | | | | | | | BASERUNNING | | | | PERCENTAGES | | |
|---|---|---|---|---|---|---|---|---|---|---|---|---|---|---|---|---|---|---|---|---|---|---|---|---|---|---|
| Year Team | Lg | G | AB | H | 2B | 3B | HR | (Hm | Rd) | TB | R | RBI | TBB | IBB | SO | HBP | SH | SF | | SB | CS | SB% | GDP | Avg | OBP | SLG |
| 1980 New York | NL | 24 | 81 | 25 | 2 | 1 | 1 | (0 | 1) | 32 | 8 | 10 | 5 | 0 | 9 | 2 | 1 | 0 | | 1 | 1 | .50 | 1 | .309 | .364 | .395 |
| 1981 New York | NL | 98 | 358 | 110 | 21 | 2 | 4 | (2 | 2) | 147 | 34 | 38 | 23 | 2 | 65 | 1 | 1 | 6 | | 9 | 5 | .64 | 9 | .307 | .345 | .411 |
| 1982 New York | NL | 126 | 457 | 114 | 21 | 2 | 2 | (1 | 1) | 145 | 40 | 40 | 28 | 5 | 76 | 5 | 3 | 5 | | 6 | 3 | .67 | 11 | .249 | .297 | .317 |
| 1983 New York | NL | 150 | 586 | 147 | 18 | 4 | 5 | (4 | 1) | 188 | 53 | 58 | 24 | 2 | 96 | 4 | 7 | 3 | | 6 | 4 | .60 | 14 | .251 | .284 | .321 |
| 1984 New York | NL | 153 | 561 | 159 | 23 | 2 | 16 | (12 | 4) | 234 | 61 | 73 | 48 | 15 | 79 | 2 | 0 | 2 | | 6 | 5 | .55 | 17 | .283 | .341 | .417 |
| 1985 Montreal | NL | 156 | 605 | 163 | 34 | 7 | 13 | (4 | 9) | 250 | 67 | 100 | 34 | 6 | 79 | 5 | 0 | 8 | | 6 | 9 | .40 | 20 | .269 | .310 | .413 |
| 1986 Montreal | NL | 80 | 306 | 104 | 18 | 5 | 14 | (3 | 11) | 174 | 50 | 58 | 25 | 3 | 60 | 2 | 0 | 5 | | 4 | 2 | .67 | 11 | .340 | .388 | .569 |
| 1987 Montreal | NL | 112 | 430 | 113 | 22 | 3 | 14 | (9 | 5) | 183 | 57 | 72 | 24 | 2 | 72 | 1 | 0 | 4 | | 4 | 3 | .57 | 7 | .263 | .301 | .426 |
| 1988 Montreal | NL | 151 | 588 | 164 | 35 | 2 | 20 | (9 | 11) | 263 | 61 | 90 | 35 | 3 | 108 | 1 | 0 | 4 | | 7 | 3 | .70 | 21 | .279 | .318 | .447 |
| 1989 Montreal | NL | 148 | 542 | 145 | 30 | 1 | 14 | (7 | 7) | 219 | 56 | 70 | 39 | 2 | 108 | 4 | 0 | 8 | | 6 | 11 | .35 | 15 | .268 | .317 | .404 |
| 1990 Los Angeles | NL | 153 | 568 | 151 | 28 | 1 | 20 | (9 | 11) | 241 | 74 | 91 | 33 | 10 | 108 | 6 | 0 | 11 | | 2 | 5 | .29 | 13 | .266 | .307 | .424 |
| 11 ML YEARS | | 1351 | 5082 | 1395 | 252 | 30 | 123 | (60 | 63) | 2076 | 561 | 700 | 318 | 50 | 860 | 33 | 12 | 56 | | 57 | 51 | .53 | 139 | .274 | .318 | .409 |

## Keith Brown

**Pitches:** Right **Bats:** Right **Pos:** RP **Ht:** 6' 4" **Wt:** 205 **Born:** 02/14/64 **Age:** 27

| HOW MUCH HE PITCHED | | | | | | | | WHAT HE GAVE UP | | | | | | | | | | | | THE RESULTS | | | | | |
|---|---|---|---|---|---|---|---|---|---|---|---|---|---|---|---|---|---|---|---|---|---|---|---|---|---|
| Year Team | Lg | G | GS | CG | GF | IP | BFP | H | R | ER | HR | SH | SF | HB | TBB | IBB | SO | WP | Bk | W | L | Pct. | ShO | Sv | ERA |
| 1988 Cincinnati | NL | 4 | 3 | 0 | 1 | 16.1 | 63 | 14 | 5 | 5 | 1 | 0 | 0 | 0 | 4 | 0 | 6 | 1 | 0 | 2 | 1 | .667 | 0 | 0 | 2.76 |
| 1990 Cincinnati | NL | 8 | 0 | 0 | 2 | 11.1 | 46 | 12 | 6 | 6 | 2 | 1 | 0 | 0 | 3 | 0 | 8 | 0 | 0 | 0 | 0 | .000 | 0 | 0 | 4.76 |
| 2 ML YEARS | | 12 | 3 | 0 | 3 | 27.2 | 109 | 26 | 11 | 11 | 3 | 1 | 0 | 0 | 7 | 0 | 14 | 1 | 0 | 2 | 1 | .667 | 0 | 0 | 3.58 |

## Kevin Brown

**Pitches:** Right **Bats:** Right **Pos:** SP **Ht:** 6' 4" **Wt:** 198 **Born:** 03/14/65 **Age:** 26

| HOW MUCH HE PITCHED | | | | | | | | WHAT HE GAVE UP | | | | | | | | | | | | THE RESULTS | | | | | |
|---|---|---|---|---|---|---|---|---|---|---|---|---|---|---|---|---|---|---|---|---|---|---|---|---|---|
| Year Team | Lg | G | GS | CG | GF | IP | BFP | H | R | ER | HR | SH | SF | HB | TBB | IBB | SO | WP | Bk | W | L | Pct. | ShO | Sv | ERA |
| 1986 Texas | AL | 1 | 1 | 0 | 0 | 5 | 19 | 6 | 2 | 2 | 0 | 0 | 0 | 0 | 0 | 0 | 4 | 0 | 0 | 1 | 0 | 1.000 | 0 | 0 | 3.60 |
| 1988 Texas | AL | 4 | 4 | 1 | 0 | 23.1 | 110 | 33 | 15 | 11 | 2 | 1 | 0 | 1 | 8 | 0 | 12 | 1 | 0 | 1 | 1 | .500 | 0 | 0 | 4.24 |
| 1989 Texas | AL | 28 | 28 | 7 | 0 | 191 | 798 | 167 | 81 | 71 | 10 | 3 | 6 | 4 | 70 | 2 | 104 | 7 | 2 | 12 | 9 | .571 | 0 | 0 | 3.35 |
| 1990 Texas | AL | 26 | 26 | 6 | 0 | 180 | 757 | 175 | 84 | 72 | 13 | 2 | 7 | 3 | 60 | 3 | 88 | 9 | 2 | 12 | 10 | .545 | 2 | 0 | 3.60 |
| 4 ML YEARS | | 59 | 59 | 14 | 0 | 399.1 | 1684 | 381 | 182 | 156 | 25 | 6 | 13 | 8 | 138 | 5 | 208 | 17 | 4 | 26 | 20 | .565 | 2 | 0 | 3.52 |

## Kevin D. Brown

**Pitches:** Left **Bats:** Left **Pos:** RP/SP **Ht:** 6' 1" **Wt:** 185 **Born:** 03/05/66 **Age:** 25

| HOW MUCH HE PITCHED | | | | | | | | WHAT HE GAVE UP | | | | | | | | | | | | THE RESULTS | | | | | |
|---|---|---|---|---|---|---|---|---|---|---|---|---|---|---|---|---|---|---|---|---|---|---|---|---|---|
| Year Team | Lg | G | GS | CG | GF | IP | BFP | H | R | ER | HR | SH | SF | HB | TBB | IBB | SO | WP | Bk | W | L | Pct. | ShO | Sv | ERA |
| 1986 Idaho Falls | R | 12 | 12 | 1 | 0 | 68 | 0 | 65 | 48 | 38 | 5 | 0 | 0 | 0 | 41 | 0 | 44 | 2 | 0 | 3 | 6 | .333 | 0 | 0 | 5.03 |
| 1987 Sumter | A | 9 | 9 | 0 | 0 | 56 | 232 | 53 | 14 | 12 | 2 | 2 | 1 | 1 | 19 | 0 | 45 | 5 | 0 | 7 | 1 | .875 | 0 | 0 | 1.93 |
| Durham | A | 13 | 12 | 1 | 1 | 72.2 | 330 | 78 | 46 | 42 | 6 | 0 | 1 | 0 | 42 | 0 | 48 | 5 | 2 | 4 | 4 | .500 | 0 | 0 | 5.20 |
| 1988 Jackson | AA | 5 | 5 | 1 | 0 | 32.2 | 129 | 24 | 9 | 8 | 1 | 1 | 2 | 0 | 11 | 0 | 24 | 2 | 0 | 1 | 2 | .333 | 1 | 0 | 2.20 |
| St. Lucie | A | 20 | 20 | 5 | 0 | 134 | 533 | 96 | 42 | 27 | 4 | 3 | 2 | 6 | 37 | 1 | 113 | 10 | 2 | 5 | 7 | .417 | 1 | 0 | 1.81 |
| 1989 Jackson | AA | 8 | 8 | 2 | 0 | 51.2 | 216 | 51 | 15 | 13 | 0 | 1 | 1 | 4 | 11 | 0 | 40 | 4 | 4 | 5 | 2 | .714 | 2 | 0 | 2.26 |
| Tidewater | AAA | 13 | 13 | 4 | 0 | 75 | 326 | 81 | 41 | 37 | 2 | 3 | 1 | 0 | 31 | 0 | 46 | 2 | 0 | 6 | 6 | .500 | 0 | 0 | 4.44 |
| 1990 Tidewater | AAA | 26 | 24 | 3 | 0 | 134.1 | 592 | 138 | 71 | 53 | 4 | 7 | 0 | 2 | 60 | 0 | 109 | 3 | 2 | 10 | 6 | .625 | 0 | 0 | 3.55 |
| 1990 2 ML Teams | | 7 | 3 | 0 | 2 | 23 | 96 | 16 | 7 | 6 | 1 | 1 | 1 | 1 | 8 | 1 | 12 | 2 | 0 | 1 | 1 | .500 | 0 | 0 | 2.35 |
| 1990 New York | NL | 2 | 0 | 0 | 1 | 2 | 9 | 2 | 0 | 0 | 0 | 0 | 0 | 0 | 1 | 0 | 0 | 0 | 0 | 0 | 0 | .000 | 0 | 0 | 0.00 |
| Milwaukee | AL | 5 | 3 | 0 | 1 | 21 | 87 | 14 | 7 | 6 | 1 | 1 | 1 | 1 | 7 | 1 | 12 | 2 | 0 | 1 | 1 | .500 | 0 | 0 | 2.57 |

## Marty Brown

**Bats:** Right **Throws:** Right **Pos:** 2B **Ht:** 6' 1" **Wt:** 195 **Born:** 01/23/63 **Age:** 28

| BATTING | | | | | | | | | | | | | | | | | | | BASERUNNING | | | | PERCENTAGES | | |
|---|---|---|---|---|---|---|---|---|---|---|---|---|---|---|---|---|---|---|---|---|---|---|---|---|---|
| Year Team | Lg | G | AB | H | 2B | 3B | HR | (Hm | Rd) | TB | R | RBI | TBB | IBB | SO | HBP | SH | SF | SB | CS | SB% | GDP | Avg | OBP | SLG |
| 1988 Cincinnati | NL | 10 | 16 | 3 | 1 | 0 | 0 | (0 | 0) | 4 | 0 | 2 | 1 | 0 | 2 | 0 | 0 | 0 | 0 | 1 | .00 | 0 | .188 | .235 | .250 |
| 1989 Cincinnati | NL | 16 | 30 | 5 | 1 | 0 | 0 | (0 | 0) | 6 | 2 | 4 | 4 | 0 | 9 | 0 | 0 | 1 | 0 | 0 | .00 | 0 | .167 | .257 | .200 |
| 1990 Baltimore | AL | 9 | 15 | 3 | 0 | 0 | 0 | (0 | 0) | 3 | 1 | 0 | 1 | 0 | 7 | 0 | 0 | 0 | 0 | 0 | .00 | 1 | .200 | .250 | .200 |
| 3 ML YEARS | | 35 | 61 | 11 | 2 | 0 | 0 | (0 | 0) | 13 | 3 | 6 | 6 | 0 | 18 | 0 | 0 | 1 | 0 | 1 | .00 | 1 | .180 | .250 | .213 |

## Jerry Browne

**Bats:** Both **Throws:** Right **Pos:** 2B **Ht:** 5'10" **Wt:** 170 **Born:** 02/13/66 **Age:** 25

| BATTING | | | | | | | | | | | | | | | | | | | BASERUNNING | | | | PERCENTAGES | | |
|---|---|---|---|---|---|---|---|---|---|---|---|---|---|---|---|---|---|---|---|---|---|---|---|---|---|
| Year Team | Lg | G | AB | H | 2B | 3B | HR | (Hm | Rd) | TB | R | RBI | TBB | IBB | SO | HBP | SH | SF | SB | CS | SB% | GDP | Avg | OBP | SLG |
| 1986 Texas | AL | 12 | 24 | 10 | 2 | 0 | 0 | (0 | 0) | 12 | 6 | 3 | 1 | 0 | 4 | 0 | 0 | 0 | 0 | 2 | .00 | 0 | .417 | .440 | .500 |

| | | | | | | | | | | | | | | | | | | | | | | | | | |
|---|---|---|---|---|---|---|---|---|---|---|---|---|---|---|---|---|---|---|---|---|---|---|---|---|---|
| 1987 Texas | AL | 132 | 454 | 123 | 16 | 6 | 1 | (1 | 0) | 154 | 63 | 38 | 61 | 0 | 50 | 2 | 7 | 2 | 27 | 17 | .61 | 6 | .271 | .358 | .339 |
| 1988 Texas | AL | 73 | 214 | 49 | 9 | 2 | 1 | (1 | 0) | 65 | 26 | 17 | 25 | 0 | 32 | 0 | 3 | 1 | 7 | 5 | .58 | 5 | .229 | .308 | .304 |
| 1989 Cleveland | AL | 153 | 598 | 179 | 31 | 4 | 5 | (1 | 4) | 233 | 83 | 45 | 68 | 10 | 64 | 1 | 14 | 4 | 14 | 6 | .70 | 9 | .299 | .370 | .390 |
| 1990 Cleveland | AL | 140 | 513 | 137 | 26 | 5 | 6 | (2 | 4) | 191 | 92 | 50 | 72 | 1 | 46 | 2 | 12 | 11 | 12 | 7 | .63 | 12 | .267 | .353 | .372 |
| 5 ML YEARS | | 510 | 1803 | 498 | 84 | 17 | 13 | (5 | 8) | 655 | 270 | 153 | 227 | 11 | 196 | 5 | 36 | 18 | 60 | 37 | .62 | 32 | .276 | .356 | .363 |

## Tom Browning

**Pitches:** Left **Bats:** Left **Pos:** SP **Ht:** 6' 1" **Wt:** 190 **Born:** 04/28/60 **Age:** 31

| | | HOW MUCH HE PITCHED | | | | | | WHAT HE GAVE UP | | | | | | | | | | | | THE RESULTS | | | | | |
|---|---|---|---|---|---|---|---|---|---|---|---|---|---|---|---|---|---|---|---|---|---|---|---|---|---|
| Year Team | Lg | G | GS | CG | GF | IP | BFP | H | R | ER | HR | SH | SF | HB | TBB | IBB | SO | WP | Bk | W | L | Pct. | ShO | Sv | ERA |
| 1984 Cincinnati | NL | 3 | 3 | 0 | 0 | 23.1 | 95 | 27 | 4 | 4 | 0 | 1 | 0 | 0 | 5 | 0 | 14 | 1 | 0 | 1 | 0 | 1.000 | 0 | 0 | 1.54 |
| 1985 Cincinnati | NL | 38 | 38 | 6 | 0 | 261.1 | 1083 | 242 | 111 | 103 | 29 | 13 | 7 | 3 | 73 | 8 | 155 | 2 | 0 | 20 | 9 | .690 | 4 | 0 | 3.55 |
| 1986 Cincinnati | NL | 39 | 39 | 4 | 0 | 243.1 | 1016 | 225 | 123 | 103 | 26 | 14 | 12 | 1 | 70 | 6 | 147 | 3 | 0 | 14 | 13 | .519 | 2 | 0 | 3.81 |
| 1987 Cincinnati | NL | 32 | 31 | 2 | 1 | 183 | 791 | 201 | 107 | 102 | 27 | 10 | 7 | 5 | 61 | 7 | 117 | 2 | 4 | 10 | 13 | .435 | 0 | 0 | 5.02 |
| 1988 Cincinnati | NL | 36 | 36 | 5 | 0 | 250.2 | 1001 | 205 | 98 | 95 | 36 | 6 | 8 | 7 | 64 | 3 | 124 | 2 | 4 | 18 | 5 | .783 | 2 | 0 | 3.41 |
| 1989 Cincinnati | NL | 37 | 37 | 9 | 0 | 249.2 | 1031 | 241 | 109 | 94 | 31 | 12 | 6 | 3 | 64 | 10 | 118 | 2 | 1 | 15 | 12 | .556 | 2 | 0 | 3.39 |
| 1990 Cincinnati | NL | 35 | 35 | 2 | 0 | 227.2 | 957 | 235 | 98 | 96 | 24 | 13 | 5 | 5 | 52 | 13 | 99 | 5 | 1 | 15 | 9 | .625 | 1 | 0 | 3.80 |
| 7 ML YEARS | | 220 | 219 | 28 | 1 | 1439 | 5974 | 1376 | 650 | 597 | 173 | 69 | 45 | 24 | 389 | 47 | 774 | 17 | 10 | 93 | 61 | .604 | 11 | 0 | 3.73 |

## Mike Brumley

**Bats:** Both **Throws:** Right **Pos:** SS **Ht:** 5'10" **Wt:** 165 **Born:** 04/09/63 **Age:** 28

| | | BATTING | | | | | | | | | | | | | | | | | BASERUNNING | | | | PERCENTAGES | | |
|---|---|---|---|---|---|---|---|---|---|---|---|---|---|---|---|---|---|---|---|---|---|---|---|---|---|
| Year Team | Lg | G | AB | H | 2B | 3B | HR | (Hm | Rd) | TB | R | RBI | TBB | IBB | SO | HBP | SH | SF | SB | CS | SB% | GDP | Avg | OBP | SLG |
| 1987 Chicago | NL | 39 | 104 | 21 | 2 | 2 | 1 | (0 | 1) | 30 | 8 | 9 | 10 | 1 | 30 | 1 | 1 | 1 | 7 | 1 | .88 | 2 | .202 | .276 | .288 |
| 1989 Detroit | AL | 92 | 212 | 42 | 5 | 2 | 1 | (1 | 0) | 54 | 33 | 11 | 14 | 0 | 45 | 1 | 3 | 0 | 8 | 4 | .67 | 4 | .198 | .251 | .255 |
| 1990 Seattle | AL | 62 | 147 | 33 | 5 | 4 | 0 | (0 | 0) | 46 | 19 | 7 | 10 | 0 | 22 | 0 | 4 | 1 | 2 | 0 | 1.00 | 5 | .224 | .272 | .313 |
| 3 ML YEARS | | 193 | 463 | 96 | 12 | 8 | 2 | (1 | 1) | 130 | 60 | 27 | 34 | 1 | 97 | 2 | 8 | 2 | 17 | 5 | .77 | 11 | .207 | .263 | .281 |

## Tom Brunansky

**Bats:** Right **Throws:** Right **Pos:** RF **Ht:** 6' 4" **Wt:** 216 **Born:** 08/20/60 **Age:** 30

| | | BATTING | | | | | | | | | | | | | | | | | BASERUNNING | | | | PERCENTAGES | | |
|---|---|---|---|---|---|---|---|---|---|---|---|---|---|---|---|---|---|---|---|---|---|---|---|---|---|
| Year Team | Lg | G | AB | H | 2B | 3B | HR | (Hm | Rd) | TB | R | RBI | TBB | IBB | SO | HBP | SH | SF | SB | CS | SB% | GDP | Avg | OBP | SLG |
| 1981 California | AL | 11 | 33 | 5 | 0 | 0 | 3 | (1 | 2) | 14 | 7 | 6 | 8 | 0 | 10 | 0 | 0 | 0 | 1 | 0 | 1.00 | 0 | .152 | .317 | .424 |
| 1982 Minnesota | AL | 127 | 463 | 126 | 30 | 1 | 20 | (10 | 10) | 218 | 77 | 46 | 71 | 0 | 101 | 8 | 1 | 2 | 1 | 2 | .33 | 12 | .272 | .377 | .471 |
| 1983 Minnesota | AL | 151 | 542 | 123 | 24 | 5 | 28 | (8 | 20) | 241 | 70 | 82 | 61 | 4 | 95 | 4 | 1 | 3 | 2 | 5 | .29 | 13 | .227 | .308 | .445 |
| 1984 Minnesota | AL | 155 | 567 | 144 | 21 | 0 | 32 | (14 | 18) | 261 | 75 | 85 | 57 | 2 | 94 | 0 | 0 | 4 | 4 | 5 | .44 | 15 | .254 | .320 | .460 |
| 1985 Minnesota | AL | 157 | 567 | 137 | 28 | 4 | 27 | (12 | 15) | 254 | 71 | 90 | 71 | 7 | 86 | 0 | 0 | 13 | 5 | 3 | .63 | 12 | .242 | .320 | .448 |
| 1986 Minnesota | AL | 157 | 593 | 152 | 28 | 1 | 23 | (15 | 8) | 251 | 69 | 75 | 53 | 4 | 98 | 1 | 1 | 7 | 12 | 4 | .75 | 15 | .256 | .315 | .423 |
| 1987 Minnesota | AL | 155 | 532 | 138 | 22 | 2 | 32 | (19 | 13) | 260 | 83 | 85 | 74 | 5 | 104 | 4 | 0 | 4 | 11 | 11 | .50 | 12 | .259 | .352 | .489 |
| 1988 2 ML Teams | | 157 | 572 | 137 | 23 | 4 | 23 | (7 | 16) | 237 | 74 | 85 | 86 | 6 | 93 | 4 | 1 | 6 | 17 | 8 | .68 | 17 | .240 | .340 | .414 |
| 1989 St. Louis | NL | 158 | 556 | 133 | 29 | 3 | 20 | (4 | 16) | 228 | 67 | 85 | 59 | 3 | 107 | 2 | 0 | 5 | 5 | 9 | .36 | 10 | .239 | .312 | .410 |
| 1990 2 ML Teams | | 148 | 518 | 132 | 27 | 5 | 16 | (13 | 3) | 217 | 66 | 73 | 66 | 7 | 115 | 4 | 0 | 9 | 5 | 10 | .33 | 13 | .255 | .338 | .419 |
| 1988 Minnesota | AL | 14 | 49 | 9 | 1 | 0 | 1 | (0 | 1) | 13 | 5 | 6 | 7 | 0 | 11 | 0 | 0 | 0 | 1 | 2 | .33 | 0 | .184 | .286 | .265 |
| St. Louis | NL | 143 | 523 | 128 | 22 | 4 | 22 | (7 | 15) | 224 | 69 | 79 | 79 | 6 | 82 | 4 | 1 | 6 | 16 | 6 | .73 | 17 | .245 | .345 | .428 |
| 1990 St. Louis | NL | 19 | 57 | 9 | 3 | 0 | 1 | (0 | 1) | 15 | 5 | 2 | 12 | 0 | 10 | 1 | 0 | 1 | 0 | 0 | .00 | 1 | .158 | .310 | .263 |
| Boston | AL | 129 | 461 | 123 | 24 | 5 | 15 | (13 | 2) | 202 | 61 | 71 | 54 | 7 | 105 | 3 | 0 | 8 | 5 | 10 | .33 | 12 | .267 | .342 | .438 |
| 10 ML YEARS | | 1376 | 4943 | 1227 | 232 | 25 | 224 | (103 | 121) | 2181 | 659 | 712 | 606 | 38 | 903 | 27 | 4 | 53 | 63 | 57 | .53 | 119 | .248 | .330 | .441 |

## Bill Buckner

**Bats:** Left **Throws:** Left **Pos:** 1B **Ht:** 6' 1" **Wt:** 195 **Born:** 12/14/49 **Age:** 41

| | | BATTING | | | | | | | | | | | | | | | | | BASERUNNING | | | | PERCENTAGES | | |
|---|---|---|---|---|---|---|---|---|---|---|---|---|---|---|---|---|---|---|---|---|---|---|---|---|---|
| Year Team | Lg | G | AB | H | 2B | 3B | HR | (Hm | Rd) | TB | R | RBI | TBB | IBB | SO | HBP | SH | SF | SB | CS | SB% | GDP | Avg | OBP | SLG |
| 1969 Los Angeles | NL | 1 | 1 | 0 | 0 | 0 | 0 | (0 | 0) | 0 | 0 | 0 | 0 | 0 | 0 | 0 | 0 | 0 | 0 | 0 | .00 | 0 | .000 | .000 | .000 |
| 1970 Los Angeles | NL | 28 | 68 | 13 | 3 | 1 | 0 | (0 | 0) | 18 | 6 | 4 | 3 | 1 | 7 | 0 | 0 | 0 | 0 | 1 | .00 | 0 | .191 | .225 | .265 |
| 1971 Los Angeles | NL | 108 | 358 | 99 | 15 | 1 | 5 | (2 | 3) | 131 | 37 | 41 | 11 | 4 | 18 | 5 | 7 | 2 | 4 | 1 | .80 | 6 | .277 | .306 | .366 |
| 1972 Los Angeles | NL | 105 | 383 | 122 | 14 | 3 | 5 | (1 | 4) | 157 | 47 | 37 | 17 | 2 | 13 | 1 | 3 | 1 | 10 | 3 | .77 | 13 | .319 | .348 | .410 |
| 1973 Los Angeles | NL | 140 | 575 | 158 | 20 | 0 | 8 | (4 | 4) | 202 | 68 | 46 | 17 | 5 | 34 | 3 | 6 | 5 | 12 | 2 | .86 | 15 | .275 | .297 | .351 |
| 1974 Los Angeles | NL | 145 | 580 | 182 | 30 | 3 | 7 | (3 | 4) | 239 | 83 | 58 | 30 | 10 | 24 | 4 | 4 | 2 | 31 | 13 | .70 | 13 | .314 | .351 | .412 |
| 1975 Los Angeles | NL | 92 | 288 | 70 | 11 | 2 | 6 | (3 | 3) | 103 | 30 | 31 | 17 | 7 | 15 | 2 | 4 | 4 | 8 | 3 | .73 | 11 | .243 | .286 | .358 |
| 1976 Los Angeles | NL | 154 | 642 | 193 | 28 | 4 | 7 | (4 | 3) | 250 | 76 | 60 | 26 | 6 | 26 | 1 | 6 | 5 | 28 | 9 | .76 | 8 | .301 | .326 | .389 |
| 1977 Chicago | NL | 122 | 426 | 121 | 27 | 0 | 11 | (7 | 4) | 181 | 40 | 60 | 21 | 2 | 23 | 1 | 2 | 7 | 7 | 5 | .58 | 16 | .284 | .314 | .425 |
| 1978 Chicago | NL | 117 | 446 | 144 | 26 | 1 | 5 | (3 | 2) | 187 | 47 | 74 | 18 | 5 | 17 | 0 | 1 | 5 | 7 | 5 | .58 | 16 | .323 | .345 | .419 |
| 1979 Chicago | NL | 149 | 591 | 168 | 34 | 7 | 14 | (8 | 6) | 258 | 72 | 66 | 30 | 6 | 28 | 2 | 1 | 4 | 9 | 4 | .69 | 16 | .284 | .319 | .437 |
| 1980 Chicago | NL | 145 | 578 | 187 | 41 | 3 | 10 | (3 | 7) | 264 | 69 | 68 | 30 | 11 | 18 | 0 | 0 | 6 | 1 | 2 | .33 | 13 | .324 | .353 | .457 |
| 1981 Chicago | NL | 106 | 421 | 131 | 35 | 3 | 10 | (7 | 3) | 202 | 45 | 75 | 26 | 9 | 16 | 1 | 0 | 5 | 5 | 2 | .71 | 17 | .311 | .349 | .480 |
| 1982 Chicago | NL | 161 | 657 | 201 | 34 | 5 | 15 | (9 | 6) | 290 | 93 | 105 | 36 | 7 | 26 | 5 | 1 | 10 | 15 | 5 | .75 | 14 | .306 | .342 | .441 |
| 1983 Chicago | NL | 153 | 626 | 175 | 38 | 6 | 16 | (6 | 10) | 273 | 79 | 66 | 25 | 5 | 30 | 5 | 4 | 5 | 12 | 4 | .75 | 10 | .280 | .310 | .436 |

| Year Team | Lg | G | AB | H | 2B | 3B | HR | (Hm | Rd) | TB | R | RBI | TBB | IBB | SO | HBP | SH | SF | SB | CS | SB% | GDP | Avg | OBP | SLG |
|---|---|---|---|---|---|---|---|---|---|---|---|---|---|---|---|---|---|---|---|---|---|---|---|---|---|
| 1984 2 ML Teams | | 135 | 482 | 131 | 21 | 2 | 11 | (6 | 5) | 189 | 54 | 69 | 25 | 6 | 39 | 6 | 0 | 4 | 2 | 2 | .50 | 12 | .272 | .313 | .392 |
| 1985 Boston | AL | 162 | 673 | 201 | 46 | 3 | 16 | (6 | 10) | 301 | 89 | 110 | 30 | 5 | 36 | 2 | 2 | 11 | 18 | 4 | .82 | 16 | .299 | .325 | .447 |
| 1986 Boston | AL | 153 | 629 | 168 | 39 | 2 | 18 | (8 | 10) | 265 | 73 | 102 | 40 | 9 | 25 | 4 | 0 | 8 | 6 | 4 | .60 | 25 | .267 | .311 | .421 |
| 1987 2 ML Teams | | 132 | 469 | 134 | 18 | 2 | 5 | (2 | 3) | 171 | 39 | 74 | 22 | 2 | 26 | 0 | 1 | 6 | 2 | 3 | .40 | 13 | .286 | .314 | .365 |
| 1988 2 ML Teams | | 108 | 285 | 71 | 14 | 0 | 3 | (0 | 3) | 94 | 19 | 43 | 17 | 5 | 19 | 0 | 4 | 5 | 5 | 1 | .83 | 8 | .249 | .287 | .330 |
| 1989 Kansas City | AL | 79 | 176 | 38 | 4 | 1 | 1 | (0 | 1) | 47 | 7 | 16 | 6 | 2 | 11 | 0 | 0 | 1 | 1 | 0 | 1.00 | 4 | .216 | .240 | .267 |
| 1990 Boston | AL | 22 | 43 | 8 | 0 | 0 | 1 | (1 | 0) | 11 | 4 | 3 | 3 | 2 | 2 | 0 | 1 | 1 | 0 | 0 | .00 | 1 | .186 | .234 | .256 |
| 1984 Chicago | NL | 21 | 43 | 9 | 0 | 0 | 0 | (0 | 0) | 9 | 3 | 2 | 1 | 1 | 1 | 1 | 0 | 1 | 0 | 0 | .00 | 1 | .209 | .239 | .209 |
| Boston | AL | 114 | 439 | 122 | 21 | 2 | 11 | (6 | 5) | 180 | 51 | 67 | 24 | 5 | 38 | 5 | 0 | 3 | 2 | 2 | .50 | 11 | .278 | .321 | .410 |
| 1987 Boston | AL | 75 | 286 | 78 | 6 | 1 | 2 | (0 | 2) | 92 | 23 | 42 | 13 | 1 | 19 | 0 | 0 | 5 | 1 | 3 | .25 | 10 | .273 | .299 | .322 |
| California | AL | 57 | 183 | 56 | 12 | 1 | 3 | (2 | 1) | 79 | 16 | 32 | 9 | 1 | 7 | 0 | 1 | 1 | 1 | 0 | 1.00 | 3 | .306 | .337 | .432 |
| 1988 California | AL | 19 | 43 | 9 | 0 | 0 | 0 | (0 | 0) | 9 | 1 | 9 | 4 | 0 | 0 | 0 | 0 | 1 | 2 | 0 | 1.00 | 2 | .209 | .271 | .209 |
| Kansas City | AL | 89 | 242 | 62 | 14 | 0 | 3 | (0 | 3) | 85 | 18 | 34 | 13 | 5 | 19 | 0 | 4 | 4 | 3 | 1 | .75 | 6 | .256 | .290 | .351 |
| 22 ML YEARS | | 2517 | 9397 | 2715 | 498 | 49 | 174 | (83 | 91) | 3833 | 1077 | 1208 | 450 | 111 | 453 | 42 | 47 | 97 | 183 | 73 | .71 | 247 | .289 | .321 | .408 |

## Steve Buechele

**Bats:** Right **Throws:** Right **Pos:** 3B **Ht:** 6' 2" **Wt:** 190 **Born:** 09/26/61 **Age:** 29

| BATTING | | | | | | | | | | | | | | | | | | | BASERUNNING | | | | PERCENTAGES | | |
|---|---|---|---|---|---|---|---|---|---|---|---|---|---|---|---|---|---|---|---|---|---|---|---|---|---|
| Year Team | Lg | G | AB | H | 2B | 3B | HR | (Hm | Rd) | TB | R | RBI | TBB | IBB | SO | HBP | SH | SF | SB | CS | SB% | GDP | Avg | OBP | SLG |
| 1985 Texas | AL | 69 | 219 | 48 | 6 | 3 | 6 | (5 | 1) | 78 | 22 | 21 | 14 | 2 | 38 | 2 | 0 | 1 | 3 | 2 | .60 | 11 | .219 | .271 | .356 |
| 1986 Texas | AL | 153 | 461 | 112 | 19 | 2 | 18 | (6 | 12) | 189 | 54 | 54 | 35 | 1 | 98 | 5 | 9 | 3 | 5 | 8 | .38 | 10 | .243 | .302 | .410 |
| 1987 Texas | AL | 136 | 363 | 86 | 20 | 0 | 13 | (6 | 7) | 145 | 45 | 50 | 28 | 3 | 66 | 1 | 4 | 4 | 2 | 2 | .50 | 7 | .237 | .290 | .399 |
| 1988 Texas | AL | 155 | 503 | 126 | 21 | 4 | 16 | (8 | 8) | 203 | 68 | 58 | 65 | 6 | 79 | 5 | 6 | 0 | 2 | 4 | .33 | 8 | .250 | .342 | .404 |
| 1989 Texas | AL | 155 | 486 | 114 | 22 | 2 | 16 | (7 | 9) | 188 | 60 | 59 | 36 | 0 | 107 | 5 | 2 | 1 | 1 | 3 | .25 | 21 | .235 | .294 | .387 |
| 1990 Texas | AL | 91 | 251 | 54 | 10 | 0 | 7 | (5 | 2) | 85 | 30 | 30 | 27 | 1 | 63 | 2 | 7 | 2 | 1 | 0 | 1.00 | 5 | .215 | .294 | .339 |
| 6 ML YEARS | | 759 | 2283 | 540 | 98 | 11 | 76 | (37 | 39) | 888 | 279 | 272 | 205 | 13 | 451 | 20 | 28 | 11 | 14 | 19 | .42 | 62 | .237 | .304 | .389 |

## Jay Buhner

**Bats:** Right **Throws:** Right **Pos:** RF **Ht:** 6' 3" **Wt:** 205 **Born:** 08/13/64 **Age:** 26

| BATTING | | | | | | | | | | | | | | | | | | | BASERUNNING | | | | PERCENTAGES | | |
|---|---|---|---|---|---|---|---|---|---|---|---|---|---|---|---|---|---|---|---|---|---|---|---|---|---|
| Year Team | Lg | G | AB | H | 2B | 3B | HR | (Hm | Rd) | TB | R | RBI | TBB | IBB | SO | HBP | SH | SF | SB | CS | SB% | GDP | Avg | OBP | SLG |
| 1987 New York | AL | 7 | 22 | 5 | 2 | 0 | 0 | (0 | 0) | 7 | 0 | 1 | 1 | 0 | 6 | 0 | 0 | 0 | 0 | 0 | .00 | 1 | .227 | .261 | .318 |
| 1988 2 ML Teams | | 85 | 261 | 56 | 13 | 1 | 13 | (8 | 5) | 110 | 36 | 38 | 28 | 1 | 93 | 6 | 1 | 3 | 1 | 1 | .50 | 5 | .215 | .302 | .421 |
| 1989 Seattle | AL | 58 | 204 | 56 | 15 | 1 | 9 | (7 | 2) | 100 | 27 | 33 | 19 | 0 | 55 | 2 | 0 | 1 | 1 | 4 | .20 | 0 | .275 | .341 | .490 |
| 1990 Seattle | AL | 51 | 163 | 45 | 12 | 0 | 7 | (2 | 5) | 78 | 16 | 33 | 17 | 1 | 50 | 4 | 0 | 1 | 2 | 2 | .50 | 6 | .276 | .357 | .479 |
| 1988 New York | AL | 25 | 69 | 13 | 0 | 0 | 3 | (1 | 2) | 22 | 8 | 13 | 3 | 0 | 25 | 3 | 0 | 1 | 0 | 0 | .00 | 1 | .188 | .250 | .319 |
| Seattle | AL | 60 | 192 | 43 | 13 | 1 | 10 | (7 | 3) | 88 | 28 | 25 | 25 | 1 | 68 | 3 | 1 | 2 | 1 | 1 | .50 | 4 | .224 | .320 | .458 |
| 4 ML YEARS | | 201 | 650 | 162 | 42 | 2 | 29 | (17 | 12) | 295 | 79 | 105 | 65 | 2 | 204 | 12 | 1 | 5 | 4 | 7 | .36 | 12 | .249 | .327 | .454 |

## Eric Bullock

**Bats:** Left **Throws:** Left **Pos:** PH **Ht:** 5'11" **Wt:** 185 **Born:** 02/16/60 **Age:** 31

| BATTING | | | | | | | | | | | | | | | | | | | BASERUNNING | | | | PERCENTAGES | | |
|---|---|---|---|---|---|---|---|---|---|---|---|---|---|---|---|---|---|---|---|---|---|---|---|---|---|
| Year Team | Lg | G | AB | H | 2B | 3B | HR | (Hm | Rd) | TB | R | RBI | TBB | IBB | SO | HBP | SH | SF | SB | CS | SB% | GDP | Avg | OBP | SLG |
| 1985 Houston | NL | 18 | 25 | 7 | 2 | 0 | 0 | (0 | 0) | 9 | 3 | 2 | 1 | 0 | 3 | 0 | 0 | 0 | 0 | 1 | .00 | 0 | .280 | .308 | .360 |
| 1986 Houston | NL | 6 | 21 | 1 | 0 | 0 | 0 | (0 | 0) | 1 | 0 | 1 | 0 | 0 | 3 | 0 | 0 | 0 | 2 | 0 | 1.00 | 0 | .048 | .048 | .048 |
| 1988 Minnesota | AL | 16 | 17 | 5 | 0 | 0 | 0 | (0 | 0) | 5 | 3 | 3 | 3 | 0 | 1 | 0 | 0 | 0 | 1 | 0 | 1.00 | 0 | .294 | .400 | .294 |
| 1989 Philadelphia | NL | 6 | 4 | 0 | 0 | 0 | 0 | (0 | 0) | 0 | 1 | 0 | 0 | 0 | 2 | 0 | 0 | 0 | 0 | 0 | .00 | 0 | .000 | .000 | .000 |
| 1990 Montreal | NL | 4 | 2 | 1 | 0 | 0 | 0 | (0 | 0) | 1 | 0 | 0 | 0 | 0 | 0 | 0 | 0 | 0 | 0 | 0 | .00 | 0 | .500 | .500 | .500 |
| 5 ML YEARS | | 50 | 69 | 14 | 2 | 0 | 0 | (0 | 0) | 16 | 7 | 6 | 4 | 0 | 9 | 0 | 0 | 0 | 3 | 1 | .75 | 0 | .203 | .247 | .232 |

## Dave Burba

**Pitches:** Right **Bats:** Right **Pos:** RP **Ht:** 6' 4" **Wt:** 220 **Born:** 07/07/66 **Age:** 24

| HOW MUCH HE PITCHED | | | | | | | | WHAT HE GAVE UP | | | | | | | | | | | | THE RESULTS | | | | | |
|---|---|---|---|---|---|---|---|---|---|---|---|---|---|---|---|---|---|---|---|---|---|---|---|---|---|
| Year Team | Lg | G | GS | CG | GF | IP | BFP | H | R | ER | HR | SH | SF | HB | TBB | IBB | SO | WP | Bk | W | L | Pct. | ShO | Sv | ERA |
| 1987 Bellingham | A | 5 | 5 | 0 | 0 | 23.1 | 97 | 20 | 10 | 5 | 0 | 0 | 0 | 0 | 3 | 0 | 24 | 4 | 0 | 3 | 1 | .750 | 0 | 0 | 1.93 |
| Salinas | A | 9 | 9 | 0 | 0 | 54.2 | 246 | 53 | 31 | 28 | 3 | 3 | 2 | 2 | 29 | 0 | 46 | 3 | 0 | 1 | 6 | .143 | 0 | 0 | 4.61 |
| 1988 San Berndno | A | 20 | 20 | 1 | 0 | 114 | 485 | 106 | 41 | 34 | 4 | 4 | 2 | 4 | 54 | 1 | 102 | 5 | 2 | 5 | 7 | .417 | 0 | 0 | 2.68 |
| 1989 Williamsprt | AA | 25 | 25 | 5 | 0 | 156.2 | 651 | 138 | 69 | 55 | 7 | 5 | 3 | 3 | 55 | 0 | 89 | 4 | 5 | 11 | 7 | .611 | 1 | 0 | 3.16 |
| 1990 Calgary | AAA | 31 | 18 | 1 | 8 | 113.2 | 493 | 124 | 64 | 59 | 11 | 4 | 3 | 2 | 45 | 0 | 47 | 5 | 3 | 10 | 6 | .625 | 0 | 2 | 4.67 |
| 1990 Seattle | AL | 6 | 0 | 0 | 2 | 8 | 35 | 8 | 6 | 4 | 0 | 2 | 0 | 1 | 2 | 0 | 4 | 0 | 0 | 0 | 0 | .000 | 0 | 0 | 4.50 |

## Tim Burke

**Pitches:** Right **Bats:** Right **Pos:** RP **Ht:** 6' 3" **Wt:** 200 **Born:** 02/19/59 **Age:** 32

| HOW MUCH HE PITCHED | | | | | | | | WHAT HE GAVE UP | | | | | | | | | | | | THE RESULTS | | | | | |
|---|---|---|---|---|---|---|---|---|---|---|---|---|---|---|---|---|---|---|---|---|---|---|---|---|---|
| Year Team | Lg | G | GS | CG | GF | IP | BFP | H | R | ER | HR | SH | SF | HB | TBB | IBB | SO | WP | Bk | W | L | Pct. | ShO | Sv | ERA |
| 1985 Montreal | NL | 78 | 0 | 0 | 31 | 120.1 | 483 | 86 | 32 | 32 | 9 | 8 | 3 | 7 | 44 | 14 | 87 | 7 | 0 | 9 | 4 | .692 | 0 | 8 | 2.39 |
| 1986 Montreal | NL | 68 | 2 | 0 | 25 | 101.1 | 451 | 103 | 37 | 33 | 7 | 6 | 2 | 4 | 46 | 13 | 82 | 4 | 0 | 9 | 7 | .563 | 0 | 4 | 2.93 |
| 1987 Montreal | NL | 55 | 0 | 0 | 30 | 91 | 354 | 64 | 18 | 12 | 3 | 8 | 2 | 0 | 17 | 6 | 58 | 2 | 0 | 7 | 0 | 1.000 | 0 | 18 | 1.19 |

| Year Team | Lg | G | GS | CG | GF | IP | BFP | H | R | ER | HR | SH | SF | HB | TBB | IBB | SO | WP | Bk | W | L | Pct. | ShO | Sv | ERA |
|---|---|---|---|---|---|---|---|---|---|---|---|---|---|---|---|---|---|---|---|---|---|---|---|---|---|
| 1988 Montreal | NL | 61 | 0 | 0 | 39 | 82 | 350 | 84 | 36 | 31 | 7 | 8 | 5 | 3 | 25 | 13 | 42 | 3 | 1 | 3 | 5 | .375 | 0 | 18 | 3.40 |
| 1989 Montreal | NL | 68 | 0 | 0 | 52 | 84.2 | 333 | 68 | 24 | 24 | 6 | 4 | 5 | 0 | 22 | 7 | 54 | 1 | 0 | 9 | 3 | .750 | 0 | 28 | 2.55 |
| 1990 Montreal | NL | 58 | 0 | 0 | 35 | 75 | 316 | 71 | 29 | 21 | 6 | 3 | 3 | 2 | 21 | 6 | 47 | 1 | 1 | 3 | 3 | .500 | 0 | 20 | 2.52 |
| 6 ML YEARS | | 388 | 2 | 0 | 212 | 554.1 | 2287 | 476 | 176 | 153 | 38 | 37 | 20 | 16 | 175 | 59 | 370 | 18 | 2 | 40 | 22 | .645 | 0 | 96 | 2.48 |

## John Burkett

**Pitches:** Right **Bats:** Right **Pos:** SP **Ht:** 6' 2" **Wt:** 180 **Born:** 11/28/64 **Age:** 26

| | | HOW MUCH HE PITCHED | | | | | | WHAT HE GAVE UP | | | | | | | | | | | | THE RESULTS | | | | | |
|---|---|---|---|---|---|---|---|---|---|---|---|---|---|---|---|---|---|---|---|---|---|---|---|---|---|
| Year Team | Lg | G | GS | CG | GF | IP | BFP | H | R | ER | HR | SH | SF | HB | TBB | IBB | SO | WP | Bk | W | L | Pct. | ShO | Sv | ERA |
| 1987 San Francisco | NL | 3 | 0 | 0 | 1 | 6 | 28 | 7 | 4 | 3 | 2 | 1 | 0 | 1 | 3 | 0 | 5 | 0 | 0 | 0 | 0 | .000 | 0 | 0 | 4.50 |
| 1990 San Francisco | NL | 33 | 32 | 2 | 1 | 204 | 857 | 201 | 92 | 86 | 18 | 6 | 5 | 4 | 61 | 7 | 118 | 3 | 3 | 14 | 7 | .667 | 0 | 1 | 3.79 |
| 2 ML YEARS | | 36 | 32 | 2 | 2 | 210 | 885 | 208 | 96 | 89 | 20 | 7 | 5 | 5 | 64 | 7 | 123 | 3 | 3 | 14 | 7 | .667 | 0 | 1 | 3.81 |

## Ellis Burks

**Bats:** Right **Throws:** Right **Pos:** CF **Ht:** 6' 2" **Wt:** 188 **Born:** 09/11/64 **Age:** 26

| | | BATTING | | | | | | | | | | | | | | | | | BASERUNNING | | | | PERCENTAGES | | |
|---|---|---|---|---|---|---|---|---|---|---|---|---|---|---|---|---|---|---|---|---|---|---|---|---|---|
| Year Team | Lg | G | AB | H | 2B | 3B | HR | (Hm | Rd) | TB | R | RBI | TBB | IBB | SO | HBP | SH | SF | SB | CS | SB% | GDP | Avg | OBP | SLG |
| 1987 Boston | AL | 133 | 558 | 152 | 30 | 2 | 20 | (11 | 9) | 246 | 94 | 59 | 41 | 0 | 98 | 2 | 4 | 1 | 27 | 6 | .82 | 1 | .272 | .324 | .441 |
| 1988 Boston | AL | 144 | 540 | 159 | 37 | 5 | 18 | (8 | 10) | 260 | 93 | 92 | 62 | 1 | 89 | 3 | 4 | 6 | 25 | 9 | .74 | 8 | .294 | .367 | .481 |
| 1989 Boston | AL | 97 | 399 | 121 | 19 | 6 | 12 | (6 | 6) | 188 | 73 | 61 | 36 | 2 | 52 | 5 | 2 | 4 | 21 | 5 | .81 | 8 | .303 | .365 | .471 |
| 1990 Boston | AL | 152 | 588 | 174 | 33 | 8 | 21 | (10 | 11) | 286 | 89 | 89 | 48 | 4 | 82 | 1 | 2 | 2 | 9 | 11 | .45 | 18 | .296 | .349 | .486 |
| 4 ML YEARS | | 526 | 2085 | 606 | 119 | 21 | 71 | (35 | 36) | 980 | 349 | 301 | 187 | 7 | 321 | 11 | 12 | 13 | 82 | 31 | .73 | 35 | .291 | .350 | .470 |

## Todd Burns

**Pitches:** Right **Bats:** Right **Pos:** RP **Ht:** 6' 2" **Wt:** 186 **Born:** 07/06/63 **Age:** 27

| | | HOW MUCH HE PITCHED | | | | | | WHAT HE GAVE UP | | | | | | | | | | | | THE RESULTS | | | | | |
|---|---|---|---|---|---|---|---|---|---|---|---|---|---|---|---|---|---|---|---|---|---|---|---|---|---|
| Year Team | Lg | G | GS | CG | GF | IP | BFP | H | R | ER | HR | SH | SF | HB | TBB | IBB | SO | WP | Bk | W | L | Pct. | ShO | Sv | ERA |
| 1988 Oakland | AL | 17 | 14 | 2 | 3 | 102.2 | 425 | 93 | 38 | 36 | 8 | 2 | 2 | 1 | 34 | 1 | 57 | 3 | 6 | 8 | 2 | .800 | 0 | 1 | 3.16 |
| 1989 Oakland | AL | 50 | 2 | 0 | 22 | 96.1 | 374 | 66 | 27 | 24 | 3 | 7 | 1 | 1 | 28 | 5 | 49 | 4 | 0 | 6 | 5 | .545 | 0 | 8 | 2.24 |
| 1990 Oakland | AL | 43 | 2 | 0 | 9 | 78.2 | 337 | 78 | 28 | 26 | 8 | 5 | 3 | 0 | 32 | 4 | 43 | 5 | 0 | 3 | 3 | .500 | 0 | 3 | 2.97 |
| 3 ML YEARS | | 110 | 18 | 2 | 34 | 277.2 | 1136 | 237 | 93 | 86 | 19 | 14 | 6 | 2 | 94 | 10 | 149 | 12 | 6 | 17 | 10 | .630 | 0 | 12 | 2.79 |

## Randy Bush

**Bats:** Left **Throws:** Left **Pos:** RF/DH **Ht:** 6' 1" **Wt:** 184 **Born:** 10/05/58 **Age:** 32

| | | BATTING | | | | | | | | | | | | | | | | | BASERUNNING | | | | PERCENTAGES | | |
|---|---|---|---|---|---|---|---|---|---|---|---|---|---|---|---|---|---|---|---|---|---|---|---|---|---|
| Year Team | Lg | G | AB | H | 2B | 3B | HR | (Hm | Rd) | TB | R | RBI | TBB | IBB | SO | HBP | SH | SF | SB | CS | SB% | GDP | Avg | OBP | SLG |
| 1982 Minnesota | AL | 55 | 119 | 29 | 6 | 1 | 4 | (2 | 2) | 49 | 13 | 13 | 8 | 0 | 28 | 3 | 0 | 1 | 0 | 0 | .00 | 1 | .244 | .305 | .412 |
| 1983 Minnesota | AL | 124 | 373 | 93 | 24 | 3 | 11 | (4 | 7) | 156 | 43 | 56 | 34 | 8 | 51 | 7 | 0 | 1 | 0 | 1 | .00 | 7 | .249 | .323 | .418 |
| 1984 Minnesota | AL | 113 | 311 | 69 | 17 | 1 | 11 | (8 | 3) | 121 | 46 | 43 | 31 | 6 | 60 | 4 | 0 | 10 | 1 | 2 | .33 | 1 | .222 | .292 | .389 |
| 1985 Minnesota | AL | 97 | 234 | 56 | 13 | 3 | 10 | (5 | 5) | 105 | 26 | 35 | 24 | 1 | 30 | 5 | 0 | 2 | 3 | 0 | 1.00 | 3 | .239 | .321 | .449 |
| 1986 Minnesota | AL | 130 | 357 | 96 | 19 | 7 | 7 | (6 | 1) | 150 | 50 | 45 | 39 | 2 | 63 | 4 | 1 | 1 | 5 | 3 | .63 | 7 | .269 | .347 | .420 |
| 1987 Minnesota | AL | 122 | 293 | 74 | 10 | 2 | 11 | (3 | 8) | 121 | 46 | 46 | 43 | 5 | 49 | 3 | 5 | 5 | 10 | 3 | .77 | 6 | .253 | .349 | .413 |
| 1988 Minnesota | AL | 136 | 394 | 103 | 20 | 3 | 14 | (10 | 4) | 171 | 51 | 51 | 58 | 14 | 49 | 9 | 0 | 5 | 8 | 6 | .57 | 8 | .261 | .365 | .434 |
| 1989 Minnesota | AL | 141 | 391 | 103 | 17 | 4 | 14 | (6 | 8) | 170 | 60 | 54 | 48 | 6 | 73 | 3 | 0 | 2 | 5 | 8 | .38 | 16 | .263 | .347 | .435 |
| 1990 Minnesota | AL | 73 | 181 | 44 | 8 | 0 | 6 | (4 | 2) | 70 | 17 | 18 | 21 | 2 | 27 | 6 | 0 | 2 | 0 | 3 | .00 | 2 | .243 | .338 | .387 |
| 9 ML YEARS | | 991 | 2653 | 667 | 134 | 24 | 88 | (48 | 40) | 1113 | 352 | 361 | 306 | 44 | 430 | 44 | 6 | 29 | 32 | 26 | .55 | 51 | .251 | .335 | .420 |

## Brett Butler

**Bats:** Left **Throws:** Left **Pos:** CF **Ht:** 5'10" **Wt:** 170 **Born:** 06/15/57 **Age:** 34

| | | BATTING | | | | | | | | | | | | | | | | | BASERUNNING | | | | PERCENTAGES | | |
|---|---|---|---|---|---|---|---|---|---|---|---|---|---|---|---|---|---|---|---|---|---|---|---|---|---|
| Year Team | Lg | G | AB | H | 2B | 3B | HR | (Hm | Rd) | TB | R | RBI | TBB | IBB | SO | HBP | SH | SF | SB | CS | SB% | GDP | Avg | OBP | SLG |
| 1981 Atlanta | NL | 40 | 126 | 32 | 2 | 3 | 0 | (0 | 0) | 40 | 17 | 4 | 19 | 0 | 17 | 0 | 0 | 0 | 9 | 1 | .90 | 0 | .254 | .352 | .317 |
| 1982 Atlanta | NL | 89 | 240 | 52 | 2 | 0 | 0 | (0 | 0) | 54 | 35 | 7 | 25 | 0 | 35 | 0 | 3 | 0 | 21 | 8 | .72 | 1 | .217 | .291 | .225 |
| 1983 Atlanta | NL | 151 | 549 | 154 | 21 | 13 | 5 | (4 | 1) | 216 | 84 | 37 | 54 | 3 | 56 | 2 | 3 | 5 | 39 | 23 | .63 | 5 | .281 | .344 | .393 |
| 1984 Cleveland | AL | 159 | 602 | 162 | 25 | 9 | 3 | (1 | 2) | 214 | 108 | 49 | 86 | 1 | 62 | 4 | 11 | 6 | 52 | 22 | .70 | 6 | .269 | .361 | .355 |
| 1985 Cleveland | AL | 152 | 591 | 184 | 28 | 14 | 5 | (1 | 4) | 255 | 106 | 50 | 63 | 2 | 42 | 1 | 8 | 3 | 47 | 20 | .70 | 8 | .311 | .377 | .431 |
| 1986 Cleveland | AL | 161 | 587 | 163 | 17 | 14 | 4 | (0 | 4) | 220 | 92 | 51 | 70 | 1 | 65 | 4 | 17 | 5 | 32 | 15 | .68 | 8 | .278 | .356 | .375 |
| 1987 Cleveland | AL | 137 | 522 | 154 | 25 | 8 | 9 | (4 | 5) | 222 | 91 | 41 | 91 | 0 | 55 | 1 | 2 | 2 | 33 | 16 | .67 | 3 | .295 | .399 | .425 |
| 1988 San Francisco | NL | 157 | 568 | 163 | 27 | 9 | 6 | (1 | 5) | 226 | 109 | 43 | 97 | 4 | 64 | 4 | 8 | 2 | 43 | 20 | .68 | 2 | .287 | .393 | .398 |
| 1989 San Francisco | NL | 154 | 594 | 168 | 22 | 4 | 4 | (2 | 2) | 210 | 100 | 36 | 59 | 2 | 69 | 3 | 13 | 3 | 31 | 16 | .66 | 4 | .283 | .349 | .354 |
| 1990 San Francisco | NL | 160 | 622 | 192 | 20 | 9 | 3 | (3 | 0) | 239 | 108 | 44 | 90 | 1 | 62 | 6 | 7 | 7 | 51 | 19 | .73 | 3 | .309 | .397 | .384 |
| 10 ML YEARS | | 1360 | 5001 | 1424 | 189 | 83 | 39 | (16 | 23) | 1896 | 850 | 362 | 654 | 14 | 527 | 25 | 72 | 33 | 358 | 160 | .69 | 40 | .285 | .368 | .379 |

## Francisco Cabrera

**Bats:** Right **Throws:** Right **Pos:** 1B **Ht:** 6' 4" **Wt:** 195 **Born:** 10/10/66 **Age:** 24

| BATTING | | | | | | | | | | | | | | | | | | | | | BASERUNNING | | | | PERCENTAGES | | |
|---|---|---|---|---|---|---|---|---|---|---|---|---|---|---|---|---|---|---|---|---|---|---|---|---|---|---|---|
| Year | Team | Lg | G | AB | H | 2B | 3B | HR | (Hm | Rd) | TB | R | RBI | TBB | IBB | SO | HBP | SH | SF | SB | CS | SB% | GDP | Avg | OBP | SLG |
| 1986 | Ventura | A | 6 | 12 | 2 | 1 | 0 | 0 | -- | -- | 3 | 2 | 3 | 0 | 0 | 4 | 0 | 0 | 0 | 1 | 0 | 1.00 | 0 | .167 | .167 | .250 |
| | St.Cathrnes | A | 68 | 246 | 73 | 13 | 2 | 6 | -- | -- | 108 | 31 | 35 | 16 | 1 | 48 | 4 | 1 | 1 | 7 | 4 | .64 | 6 | .297 | .348 | .439 |
| 1987 | Myrtle Bch | A | 129 | 449 | 124 | 27 | 1 | 14 | -- | -- | 195 | 61 | 72 | 40 | 6 | 82 | 3 | 0 | 6 | 4 | 2 | .67 | 12 | .276 | .335 | .434 |
| 1988 | Dunedin | A | 9 | 35 | 14 | 4 | 0 | 1 | -- | -- | 21 | 2 | 9 | 1 | 0 | 2 | 0 | 0 | 0 | 0 | 0 | .00 | 0 | .400 | .417 | .600 |
| | Knoxville | AA | 119 | 429 | 122 | 19 | 1 | 20 | -- | -- | 203 | 59 | 54 | 26 | 2 | 75 | 2 | 2 | 5 | 4 | 3 | .57 | 13 | .284 | .325 | .473 |
| 1989 | Syracuse | AAA | 113 | 428 | 128 | 30 | 5 | 9 | -- | -- | 195 | 59 | 71 | 20 | 2 | 72 | 3 | 1 | 7 | 4 | 4 | .50 | 11 | .299 | .330 | .456 |
| | Richmond | AAA | 3 | 6 | 2 | 1 | 0 | 0 | -- | -- | 3 | 0 | 1 | 0 | 0 | 0 | 0 | 0 | 1 | 0 | 0 | .00 | 0 | .333 | .286 | .500 |
| 1990 | Richmond | AAA | 35 | 132 | 30 | 3 | 1 | 7 | -- | -- | 56 | 12 | 20 | 7 | 0 | 23 | 1 | 0 | 2 | 2 | 0 | 1.00 | 3 | .227 | .268 | .424 |
| 1989 | 2 ML Teams | | 7 | 26 | 5 | 3 | 0 | 0 | (0 | 0) | 8 | 1 | 0 | 1 | 0 | 6 | 0 | 0 | 0 | 0 | 0 | .00 | 0 | .192 | .222 | .308 |
| 1990 | Atlanta | NL | 63 | 137 | 38 | 5 | 1 | 7 | (4 | 3) | 66 | 14 | 25 | 5 | 0 | 21 | 0 | 0 | 1 | 1 | 0 | 1.00 | 4 | .277 | .301 | .482 |
| 1989 | Toronto | AL | 3 | 12 | 2 | 1 | 0 | 0 | (0 | 0) | 3 | 1 | 0 | 1 | 0 | 3 | 0 | 0 | 0 | 0 | 0 | .00 | 0 | .167 | .231 | .250 |
| | Atlanta | NL | 4 | 14 | 3 | 2 | 0 | 0 | (0 | 0) | 5 | 0 | 0 | 0 | 0 | 3 | 0 | 0 | 0 | 0 | 0 | .00 | 0 | .214 | .214 | .357 |
| | 2 ML YEARS | | 70 | 163 | 43 | 8 | 1 | 7 | (4 | 3) | 74 | 15 | 25 | 6 | 0 | 27 | 0 | 0 | 1 | 1 | 0 | 1.00 | 4 | .264 | .288 | .454 |

## Greg Cadaret

**Pitches:** Left **Bats:** Left **Pos:** RP/SP **Ht:** 6' 3" **Wt:** 205 **Born:** 02/27/62 **Age:** 29

| HOW MUCH HE PITCHED | | | | | | | | | WHAT HE GAVE UP | | | | | | | | | | | | THE RESULTS | | | | | |
|---|---|---|---|---|---|---|---|---|---|---|---|---|---|---|---|---|---|---|---|---|---|---|---|---|---|---|
| Year | Team | Lg | G | GS | CG | GF | IP | BFP | H | R | ER | HR | SH | SF | HB | TBB | IBB | SO | WP | Bk | W | L | Pct. | ShO | Sv | ERA |
| 1987 | Oakland | AL | 29 | 0 | 0 | 7 | 39.2 | 176 | 37 | 22 | 20 | 6 | 2 | 2 | 1 | 24 | 1 | 30 | 1 | 0 | 6 | 2 | .750 | 0 | 0 | 4.54 |
| 1988 | Oakland | AL | 58 | 0 | 0 | 16 | 71.2 | 311 | 60 | 26 | 23 | 2 | 5 | 3 | 1 | 36 | 1 | 64 | 5 | 3 | 5 | 2 | .714 | 0 | 3 | 2.89 |
| 1989 | 2 ML Teams | | 46 | 13 | 3 | 7 | 120 | 531 | 130 | 62 | 54 | 7 | 3 | 5 | 2 | 57 | 4 | 80 | 6 | 2 | 5 | 5 | .500 | 1 | 0 | 4.05 |
| 1990 | New York | AL | 54 | 6 | 0 | 9 | 121.1 | 525 | 120 | 62 | 56 | 8 | 9 | 4 | 1 | 64 | 5 | 80 | 14 | 0 | 5 | 4 | .556 | 0 | 3 | 4.15 |
| 1989 | Oakland | AL | 26 | 0 | 0 | 6 | 27.2 | 119 | 21 | 9 | 7 | 0 | 0 | 2 | 0 | 19 | 3 | 14 | 0 | 0 | 0 | 0 | .000 | 0 | 0 | 2.28 |
| | New York | AL | 20 | 13 | 3 | 1 | 92.1 | 412 | 109 | 53 | 47 | 7 | 3 | 3 | 2 | 38 | 1 | 66 | 6 | 2 | 5 | 5 | .500 | 1 | 0 | 4.58 |
| | 4 ML YEARS | | 187 | 19 | 3 | 39 | 352.2 | 1543 | 347 | 172 | 153 | 23 | 19 | 14 | 5 | 181 | 11 | 254 | 26 | 5 | 21 | 13 | .618 | 1 | 6 | 3.90 |

## Ivan Calderon

**Bats:** Right **Throws:** Right **Pos:** LF/DH **Ht:** 6' 1" **Wt:** 221 **Born:** 03/19/62 **Age:** 29

| BATTING | | | | | | | | | | | | | | | | | | | | | BASERUNNING | | | | PERCENTAGES | | |
|---|---|---|---|---|---|---|---|---|---|---|---|---|---|---|---|---|---|---|---|---|---|---|---|---|---|---|---|
| Year | Team | Lg | G | AB | H | 2B | 3B | HR | (Hm | Rd) | TB | R | RBI | TBB | IBB | SO | HBP | SH | SF | SB | CS | SB% | GDP | Avg | OBP | SLG |
| 1984 | Seattle | AL | 11 | 24 | 5 | 1 | 0 | 1 | (0 | 1) | 9 | 2 | 1 | 2 | 0 | 5 | 0 | 0 | 0 | 1 | 0 | 1.00 | 3 | .208 | .269 | .375 |
| 1985 | Seattle | AL | 67 | 210 | 60 | 16 | 4 | 8 | (6 | 2) | 108 | 37 | 28 | 19 | 1 | 45 | 2 | 1 | 1 | 4 | 2 | .67 | 10 | .286 | .349 | .514 |
| 1986 | 2 ML Teams | | 50 | 164 | 41 | 7 | 1 | 2 | (1 | 1) | 56 | 16 | 15 | 9 | 1 | 39 | 1 | 0 | 0 | 3 | 1 | .75 | 1 | .250 | .293 | .341 |
| 1987 | Chicago | AL | 144 | 542 | 159 | 38 | 2 | 28 | (15 | 13) | 285 | 93 | 83 | 60 | 6 | 109 | 1 | 0 | 4 | 10 | 5 | .67 | 13 | .293 | .362 | .526 |
| 1988 | Chicago | AL | 73 | 264 | 56 | 14 | 0 | 14 | (6 | 8) | 112 | 40 | 35 | 34 | 2 | 66 | 0 | 0 | 3 | 4 | 4 | .50 | 6 | .212 | .299 | .424 |
| 1989 | Chicago | AL | 157 | 622 | 178 | 34 | 9 | 14 | (2 | 12) | 272 | 83 | 87 | 43 | 7 | 94 | 3 | 2 | 6 | 7 | 1 | .88 | 20 | .286 | .332 | .437 |
| 1990 | Chicago | AL | 158 | 607 | 166 | 44 | 2 | 14 | (6 | 8) | 256 | 85 | 74 | 51 | 7 | 79 | 1 | 0 | 8 | 32 | 16 | .67 | 26 | .273 | .327 | .422 |
| 1986 | Seattle | AL | 37 | 131 | 31 | 5 | 0 | 2 | (1 | 1) | 42 | 13 | 13 | 6 | 0 | 33 | 1 | 0 | 0 | 3 | 1 | .75 | 1 | .237 | .275 | .321 |
| | Chicago | AL | 13 | 33 | 10 | 2 | 1 | 0 | (0 | 0) | 14 | 3 | 2 | 3 | 1 | 6 | 0 | 0 | 0 | 0 | 0 | .00 | 0 | .303 | .361 | .424 |
| | 7 ML YEARS | | 660 | 2433 | 665 | 154 | 18 | 81 | (36 | 45) | 1098 | 356 | 323 | 218 | 24 | 437 | 8 | 3 | 22 | 61 | 29 | .68 | 79 | .273 | .332 | .451 |

## Ernie Camacho

**Pitches:** Right **Bats:** Right **Pos:** RP **Ht:** 6' 1" **Wt:** 180 **Born:** 02/01/56 **Age:** 35

| HOW MUCH HE PITCHED | | | | | | | | | WHAT HE GAVE UP | | | | | | | | | | | | THE RESULTS | | | | | |
|---|---|---|---|---|---|---|---|---|---|---|---|---|---|---|---|---|---|---|---|---|---|---|---|---|---|---|
| Year | Team | Lg | G | GS | CG | GF | IP | BFP | H | R | ER | HR | SH | SF | HB | TBB | IBB | SO | WP | Bk | W | L | Pct. | ShO | Sv | ERA |
| 1980 | Oakland | AL | 5 | 0 | 0 | 2 | 12 | 61 | 20 | 9 | 9 | 2 | 0 | 0 | 1 | 5 | 0 | 9 | 2 | 0 | 0 | 0 | .000 | 0 | 0 | 6.75 |
| 1981 | Pittsburgh | NL | 7 | 3 | 0 | 2 | 22 | 96 | 23 | 13 | 12 | 0 | 1 | 2 | 0 | 15 | 1 | 11 | 2 | 3 | 0 | 1 | .000 | 0 | 0 | 4.91 |
| 1983 | Cleveland | AL | 4 | 0 | 0 | 1 | 5.1 | 23 | 5 | 3 | 3 | 1 | 0 | 0 | 1 | 2 | 0 | 2 | 0 | 0 | 0 | 1 | .000 | 0 | 0 | 5.06 |
| 1984 | Cleveland | AL | 69 | 0 | 0 | 49 | 100 | 411 | 83 | 31 | 27 | 6 | 7 | 4 | 1 | 37 | 5 | 48 | 3 | 1 | 5 | 9 | .357 | 0 | 23 | 2.43 |
| 1985 | Cleveland | AL | 2 | 0 | 0 | 1 | 3.1 | 15 | 4 | 3 | 3 | 0 | 0 | 2 | 0 | 1 | 0 | 2 | 1 | 0 | 0 | 1 | .000 | 0 | 0 | 8.10 |
| 1986 | Cleveland | AL | 51 | 0 | 0 | 37 | 57.1 | 267 | 60 | 26 | 26 | 1 | 5 | 6 | 2 | 31 | 6 | 36 | 3 | 1 | 2 | 4 | .333 | 0 | 20 | 4.08 |
| 1987 | Cleveland | AL | 15 | 0 | 0 | 10 | 13.2 | 69 | 21 | 14 | 14 | 1 | 1 | 0 | 3 | 5 | 1 | 9 | 4 | 0 | 0 | 1 | .000 | 0 | 1 | 9.22 |
| 1988 | Houston | NL | 13 | 0 | 0 | 6 | 17.2 | 85 | 25 | 15 | 15 | 1 | 2 | 0 | 0 | 12 | 2 | 13 | 4 | 3 | 0 | 3 | .000 | 0 | 1 | 7.64 |
| 1989 | San Francisco | NL | 13 | 0 | 0 | 5 | 16.1 | 70 | 10 | 5 | 5 | 1 | 2 | 0 | 0 | 11 | 2 | 14 | 3 | 1 | 3 | 0 | 1.000 | 0 | 0 | 2.76 |
| 1990 | 2 ML Teams | | 14 | 0 | 0 | 6 | 15.2 | 72 | 17 | 10 | 9 | 3 | 0 | 2 | 0 | 9 | 1 | 15 | 2 | 0 | 0 | 0 | .000 | 0 | 0 | 5.17 |
| 1990 | San Francisco | NL | 8 | 0 | 0 | 3 | 10 | 42 | 10 | 4 | 4 | 1 | 0 | 0 | 0 | 3 | 0 | 8 | 1 | 0 | 0 | 0 | .000 | 0 | 0 | 3.60 |
| | St. Louis | NL | 6 | 0 | 0 | 3 | 5.2 | 30 | 7 | 6 | 5 | 2 | 0 | 2 | 0 | 6 | 1 | 7 | 1 | 0 | 0 | 0 | .000 | 0 | 0 | 7.94 |
| | 10 ML YEARS | | 193 | 3 | 0 | 119 | 263.1 | 1169 | 268 | 129 | 123 | 16 | 18 | 16 | 8 | 128 | 18 | 159 | 24 | 9 | 10 | 20 | .333 | 0 | 45 | 4.20 |

## Ken Caminiti

**Bats:** Both **Throws:** Right **Pos:** 3B **Ht:** 6' 0" **Wt:** 200 **Born:** 04/21/63 **Age:** 28

| BATTING | | | | | | | | | | | | | | | | | | | BASERUNNING | | | | PERCENTAGES | | |
|---|---|---|---|---|---|---|---|---|---|---|---|---|---|---|---|---|---|---|---|---|---|---|---|---|---|
| Year Team | Lg | G | AB | H | 2B | 3B | HR | (Hm | Rd) | TB | R | RBI | TBB | IBB | SO | HBP | SH | SF | SB | CS | SB% | GDP | Avg | OBP | SLG |
| 1987 Houston | NL | 63 | 203 | 50 | 7 | 1 | 3 | (2 | 1) | 68 | 10 | 23 | 12 | 1 | 44 | 0 | 2 | 1 | 0 | 0 | .00 | 6 | .246 | .287 | .335 |
| 1988 Houston | NL | 30 | 83 | 15 | 2 | 0 | 1 | (0 | 1) | 20 | 5 | 7 | 5 | 0 | 18 | 0 | 0 | 1 | 0 | 0 | .00 | 3 | .181 | .225 | .241 |
| 1989 Houston | NL | 161 | 585 | 149 | 31 | 3 | 10 | (3 | 7) | 216 | 71 | 72 | 51 | 9 | 93 | 3 | 3 | 4 | 4 | 1 | .80 | 8 | .255 | .316 | .369 |
| 1990 Houston | NL | 153 | 541 | 131 | 20 | 2 | 4 | (2 | 2) | 167 | 52 | 51 | 48 | 7 | 97 | 0 | 3 | 4 | 9 | 4 | .69 | 14 | .242 | .302 | .309 |
| 4 ML YEARS | | 407 | 1412 | 345 | 60 | 6 | 18 | (7 | 11) | 471 | 138 | 153 | 116 | 17 | 252 | 3 | 8 | 10 | 13 | 5 | .72 | 31 | .244 | .301 | .334 |

## Jim Campbell

**Pitches:** Left **Bats:** Left **Pos:** SP **Ht:** 5'11" **Wt:** 175 **Born:** 05/19/66 **Age:** 25

| HOW MUCH HE PITCHED | | | | | | | | WHAT HE GAVE UP | | | | | | | | | | | | THE RESULTS | | | | | |
|---|---|---|---|---|---|---|---|---|---|---|---|---|---|---|---|---|---|---|---|---|---|---|---|---|---|
| Year Team | Lg | G | GS | CG | GF | IP | BFP | H | R | ER | HR | SH | SF | HB | TBB | IBB | SO | WP | Bk | W | L | Pct. | ShO | Sv | ERA |
| 1987 Eugene | A | 32 | 0 | 0 | 21 | 62 | 229 | 32 | 5 | 5 | 1 | 5 | 1 | 1 | 12 | 3 | 75 | 3 | 0 | 6 | 0 | 1.000 | 0 | 10 | 0.73 |
| 1988 Memphis | AA | 53 | 0 | 0 | 27 | 85 | 356 | 80 | 39 | 34 | 6 | 3 | 4 | 2 | 25 | 1 | 81 | 2 | 1 | 4 | 3 | .571 | 0 | 8 | 3.60 |
| 1989 Memphis | AA | 49 | 9 | 0 | 25 | 104 | 444 | 96 | 58 | 52 | 5 | 1 | 4 | 6 | 38 | 1 | 78 | 1 | 2 | 7 | 10 | .412 | 0 | 2 | 4.50 |
| 1990 Memphis | AA | 40 | 12 | 0 | 8 | 99.2 | 405 | 78 | 38 | 27 | 7 | 5 | 1 | 4 | 32 | 0 | 79 | 1 | 2 | 5 | 5 | .500 | 0 | 0 | 2.44 |
| Omaha | AAA | 4 | 4 | 1 | 0 | 27.1 | 111 | 25 | 4 | 4 | 0 | 1 | 0 | 1 | 10 | 0 | 19 | 0 | 1 | 2 | 2 | .500 | 1 | 0 | 1.32 |
| 1990 Kansas City | AL | 2 | 2 | 0 | 0 | 9.2 | 44 | 15 | 9 | 9 | 1 | 0 | 0 | 0 | 1 | 0 | 2 | 0 | 0 | 1 | 0 | 1.000 | 0 | 0 | 8.38 |

## Sil Campusano

**Bats:** Right **Throws:** Right **Pos:** CF **Ht:** 6' 0" **Wt:** 175 **Born:** 12/31/66 **Age:** 24

| BATTING | | | | | | | | | | | | | | | | | | | BASERUNNING | | | | PERCENTAGES | | |
|---|---|---|---|---|---|---|---|---|---|---|---|---|---|---|---|---|---|---|---|---|---|---|---|---|---|
| Year Team | Lg | G | AB | H | 2B | 3B | HR | (Hm | Rd) | TB | R | RBI | TBB | IBB | SO | HBP | SH | SF | SB | CS | SB% | GDP | Avg | OBP | SLG |
| 1988 Toronto | AL | 73 | 142 | 31 | 10 | 2 | 2 | (1 | 1) | 51 | 14 | 12 | 9 | 0 | 33 | 4 | 2 | 1 | 0 | 0 | .00 | 0 | .218 | .282 | .359 |
| 1990 Philadelphia | NL | 66 | 85 | 18 | 1 | 1 | 2 | (2 | 0) | 27 | 10 | 9 | 6 | 0 | 16 | 1 | 0 | 1 | 1 | 0 | 1.00 | 1 | .212 | .269 | .318 |
| 2 ML YEARS | | 139 | 227 | 49 | 11 | 3 | 4 | (3 | 1) | 78 | 24 | 21 | 15 | 0 | 49 | 5 | 2 | 2 | 1 | 0 | 1.00 | 1 | .216 | .277 | .344 |

## George Canale

**Bats:** Left **Throws:** Right **Pos:** 1B **Ht:** 6' 1" **Wt:** 190 **Born:** 08/11/65 **Age:** 25

| BATTING | | | | | | | | | | | | | | | | | | | BASERUNNING | | | | PERCENTAGES | | |
|---|---|---|---|---|---|---|---|---|---|---|---|---|---|---|---|---|---|---|---|---|---|---|---|---|---|
| Year Team | Lg | G | AB | H | 2B | 3B | HR | (Hm | Rd) | TB | R | RBI | TBB | IBB | SO | HBP | SH | SF | SB | CS | SB% | GDP | Avg | OBP | SLG |
| 1986 Helena | R | 65 | 221 | 72 | 19 | 0 | 9 | -- | -- | 118 | 48 | 49 | 54 | 0 | 65 | 0 | 2 | 5 | 6 | 4 | .60 | 2 | .326 | .450 | .534 |
| 1987 Stockton | A | 66 | 246 | 69 | 18 | 1 | 7 | -- | -- | 110 | 42 | 48 | 38 | 3 | 59 | 1 | 2 | 2 | 5 | 4 | .56 | 8 | .280 | .376 | .447 |
| El Paso | AA | 65 | 253 | 65 | 10 | 2 | 7 | -- | -- | 100 | 38 | 36 | 20 | 1 | 69 | 2 | 0 | 0 | 3 | 2 | .60 | 4 | .257 | .316 | .395 |
| 1988 El Paso | AA | 132 | 496 | 120 | 23 | 2 | 23 | -- | -- | 216 | 77 | 93 | 59 | 5 | 152 | 2 | 0 | 2 | 9 | 3 | .75 | 12 | .242 | .324 | .435 |
| 1989 Denver | AAA | 144 | 503 | 140 | 33 | 9 | 18 | -- | -- | 245 | 80 | 71 | 71 | 1 | 134 | 2 | 2 | 6 | 5 | 8 | .38 | 3 | .278 | .366 | .487 |
| 1990 Denver | AAA | 134 | 468 | 119 | 18 | 6 | 12 | -- | -- | 185 | 76 | 60 | 69 | 4 | 103 | 1 | 3 | 3 | 12 | 5 | .71 | 10 | .254 | .349 | .395 |
| 1989 Milwaukee | AL | 13 | 26 | 5 | 1 | 0 | 1 | (0 | 1) | 9 | 5 | 3 | 2 | 0 | 3 | 0 | 1 | 0 | 0 | 1 | .00 | 0 | .192 | .250 | .346 |
| 1990 Milwaukee | AL | 10 | 13 | 1 | 1 | 0 | 0 | (0 | 0) | 2 | 4 | 0 | 2 | 0 | 6 | 0 | 0 | 0 | 0 | 1 | .00 | 0 | .077 | .200 | .154 |
| 2 ML YEARS | | 23 | 39 | 6 | 2 | 0 | 1 | (0 | 1) | 11 | 9 | 3 | 4 | 0 | 9 | 0 | 1 | 0 | 0 | 2 | .00 | 0 | .154 | .233 | .282 |

## Casey Candaele

**Bats:** Both **Throws:** Right **Pos:** 2B/LF **Ht:** 5' 7" **Wt:** 165 **Born:** 01/12/61 **Age:** 30

| BATTING | | | | | | | | | | | | | | | | | | | BASERUNNING | | | | PERCENTAGES | | |
|---|---|---|---|---|---|---|---|---|---|---|---|---|---|---|---|---|---|---|---|---|---|---|---|---|---|
| Year Team | Lg | G | AB | H | 2B | 3B | HR | (Hm | Rd) | TB | R | RBI | TBB | IBB | SO | HBP | SH | SF | SB | CS | SB% | GDP | Avg | OBP | SLG |
| 1986 Montreal | NL | 30 | 104 | 24 | 4 | 1 | 0 | (0 | 0) | 30 | 9 | 6 | 5 | 0 | 15 | 0 | 0 | 1 | 3 | 5 | .38 | 3 | .231 | .264 | .288 |
| 1987 Montreal | NL | 138 | 449 | 122 | 23 | 4 | 1 | (1 | 0) | 156 | 62 | 23 | 38 | 3 | 28 | 2 | 4 | 2 | 7 | 10 | .41 | 5 | .272 | .330 | .347 |
| 1988 2 ML Teams | | 57 | 147 | 25 | 8 | 1 | 0 | (0 | 0) | 35 | 11 | 5 | 11 | 1 | 17 | 0 | 3 | 0 | 1 | 1 | .50 | 7 | .170 | .228 | .238 |
| 1990 Houston | NL | 130 | 262 | 75 | 8 | 6 | 3 | (1 | 2) | 104 | 30 | 22 | 31 | 5 | 42 | 1 | 4 | 0 | 7 | 5 | .58 | 4 | .286 | .364 | .397 |
| 1988 Montreal | NL | 36 | 116 | 20 | 5 | 1 | 0 | (0 | 0) | 27 | 9 | 4 | 10 | 1 | 11 | 0 | 2 | 0 | 1 | 0 | 1.00 | 7 | .172 | .238 | .233 |
| Houston | NL | 21 | 31 | 5 | 3 | 0 | 0 | (0 | 0) | 8 | 2 | 1 | 1 | 0 | 6 | 0 | 1 | 0 | 0 | 1 | .00 | 0 | .161 | .188 | .258 |
| 4 ML YEARS | | 355 | 962 | 246 | 43 | 12 | 4 | (2 | 2) | 325 | 112 | 56 | 85 | 9 | 102 | 3 | 11 | 3 | 18 | 21 | .46 | 19 | .256 | .317 | .338 |

## John Candelaria

**Pitches:** Left **Bats:** Right **Pos:** RP/SP **Ht:** 6' 6" **Wt:** 225 **Born:** 11/06/53 **Age:** 37

| HOW MUCH HE PITCHED | | | | | | | | WHAT HE GAVE UP | | | | | | | | | | | | THE RESULTS | | | | | |
|---|---|---|---|---|---|---|---|---|---|---|---|---|---|---|---|---|---|---|---|---|---|---|---|---|---|
| Year Team | Lg | G | GS | CG | GF | IP | BFP | H | R | ER | HR | SH | SF | HB | TBB | IBB | SO | WP | Bk | W | L | Pct. | ShO | Sv | ERA |
| 1975 Pittsburgh | NL | 18 | 18 | 4 | 0 | 121 | 497 | 95 | 47 | 37 | 8 | 6 | 4 | 2 | 36 | 9 | 95 | 1 | 0 | 8 | 6 | .571 | 1 | 0 | 2.75 |
| 1976 Pittsburgh | NL | 32 | 31 | 11 | 1 | 220 | 881 | 173 | 87 | 77 | 22 | 13 | 6 | 2 | 60 | 5 | 138 | 0 | 0 | 16 | 7 | .696 | 4 | 1 | 3.15 |
| 1977 Pittsburgh | NL | 33 | 33 | 6 | 0 | 231 | 917 | 197 | 64 | 60 | 29 | 9 | 6 | 2 | 50 | 2 | 133 | 1 | 2 | 20 | 5 | .800 | 1 | 0 | 2.34 |
| 1978 Pittsburgh | NL | 30 | 29 | 3 | 1 | 189 | 796 | 191 | 73 | 68 | 15 | 8 | 2 | 5 | 49 | 6 | 94 | 3 | 3 | 12 | 11 | .522 | 1 | 1 | 3.24 |
| 1979 Pittsburgh | NL | 33 | 30 | 8 | 2 | 207 | 850 | 201 | 83 | 74 | 25 | 4 | 7 | 3 | 41 | 6 | 101 | 2 | 0 | 14 | 9 | .609 | 0 | 0 | 3.22 |
| 1980 Pittsburgh | NL | 35 | 34 | 7 | 1 | 233 | 969 | 246 | 114 | 104 | 14 | 14 | 12 | 3 | 50 | 4 | 97 | 0 | 2 | 11 | 14 | .440 | 0 | 1 | 4.02 |

| Year Team | Lg | G | GS | CG | GF | IP | BFP | H | R | ER | HR | SH | SF | HB | TBB | IBB | SO | WP | Bk | W | L | Pct. | ShO | Sv | ERA |
|---|---|---|---|---|---|---|---|---|---|---|---|---|---|---|---|---|---|---|---|---|---|---|---|---|---|
| 1981 Pittsburgh | NL | 6 | 6 | 0 | 0 | 41 | 168 | 42 | 17 | 16 | 3 | 1 | 1 | 0 | 11 | 1 | 14 | 0 | 0 | 2 | 2 | .500 | 0 | 0 | 3.51 |
| 1982 Pittsburgh | NL | 31 | 30 | 1 | 1 | 174.2 | 704 | 166 | 62 | 57 | 13 | 5 | 6 | 4 | 37 | 3 | 133 | 1 | 0 | 12 | 7 | .632 | 1 | 1 | 2.94 |
| 1983 Pittsburgh | NL | 33 | 32 | 2 | 0 | 197.2 | 797 | 191 | 73 | 71 | 15 | 4 | 4 | 2 | 45 | 3 | 157 | 3 | 2 | 15 | 8 | .652 | 0 | 0 | 3.23 |
| 1984 Pittsburgh | NL | 33 | 28 | 3 | 4 | 185.1 | 751 | 179 | 69 | 56 | 19 | 10 | 6 | 1 | 34 | 3 | 133 | 1 | 1 | 12 | 11 | .522 | 1 | 2 | 2.72 |
| 1985 2 ML Teams | | 50 | 13 | 1 | 26 | 125.1 | 530 | 127 | 56 | 52 | 14 | 7 | 7 | 4 | 38 | 3 | 100 | 2 | 0 | 9 | 7 | .563 | 1 | 9 | 3.73 |
| 1986 California | AL | 16 | 16 | 1 | 0 | 91.2 | 365 | 68 | 30 | 26 | 4 | 3 | 3 | 3 | 26 | 2 | 81 | 2 | 1 | 10 | 2 | .833 | 1 | 0 | 2.55 |
| 1987 2 ML Teams | | 23 | 23 | 0 | 0 | 129 | 544 | 144 | 78 | 69 | 18 | 8 | 6 | 1 | 23 | 0 | 84 | 0 | 1 | 10 | 6 | .625 | 0 | 0 | 4.81 |
| 1988 New York | AL | 25 | 24 | 6 | 1 | 157 | 640 | 150 | 69 | 59 | 18 | 4 | 6 | 2 | 23 | 2 | 121 | 2 | 12 | 13 | 7 | .650 | 2 | 1 | 3.38 |
| 1989 2 ML Teams | | 22 | 6 | 1 | 3 | 65.1 | 274 | 66 | 36 | 34 | 11 | 3 | 5 | 0 | 16 | 3 | 51 | 2 | 1 | 3 | 5 | .375 | 0 | 0 | 4.68 |
| 1990 2 ML Teams | | 47 | 3 | 0 | 15 | 79.2 | 345 | 87 | 36 | 35 | 11 | 2 | 6 | 2 | 20 | 5 | 63 | 5 | 0 | 7 | 6 | .538 | 0 | 5 | 3.95 |
| 1985 Pittsburgh | NL | 37 | 0 | 0 | 26 | 54.1 | 229 | 57 | 23 | 22 | 7 | 3 | 4 | 1 | 14 | 2 | 47 | 0 | 0 | 2 | 4 | .333 | 0 | 9 | 3.64 |
| California | AL | 13 | 13 | 1 | 0 | 71 | 301 | 70 | 33 | 30 | 7 | 4 | 3 | 3 | 24 | 1 | 53 | 2 | 0 | 7 | 3 | .700 | 1 | 0 | 3.80 |
| 1987 California | AL | 20 | 20 | 0 | 0 | 116.2 | 487 | 127 | 70 | 61 | 17 | 6 | 5 | 1 | 20 | 0 | 74 | 0 | 0 | 8 | 6 | .571 | 0 | 0 | 4.71 |
| New York | NL | 3 | 3 | 0 | 0 | 12.1 | 57 | 17 | 8 | 8 | 1 | 2 | 1 | 0 | 3 | 0 | 10 | 0 | 1 | 2 | 0 | 1.000 | 0 | 0 | 5.84 |
| 1989 New York | AL | 10 | 6 | 1 | 1 | 49 | 206 | 49 | 28 | 28 | 8 | 2 | 2 | 0 | 12 | 1 | 37 | 2 | 1 | 3 | 3 | .500 | 0 | 0 | 5.14 |
| Montreal | NL | 12 | 0 | 0 | 2 | 16.1 | 68 | 17 | 8 | 6 | 3 | 1 | 3 | 0 | 4 | 2 | 14 | 0 | 0 | 0 | 2 | .000 | 0 | 0 | 3.31 |
| 1990 Minnesota | AL | 34 | 1 | 0 | 10 | 58.1 | 239 | 55 | 23 | 22 | 9 | 2 | 3 | 0 | 9 | 2 | 44 | 3 | 0 | 7 | 3 | .700 | 0 | 4 | 3.39 |
| Toronto | AL | 13 | 2 | 0 | 5 | 21.1 | 106 | 32 | 13 | 13 | 2 | 0 | 3 | 2 | 11 | 3 | 19 | 2 | 0 | 0 | 3 | .000 | 0 | 1 | 5.48 |
| 16 ML YEARS | | 467 | 356 | 54 | 55 | 2447.2 | 10028 | 2323 | 994 | 895 | 239 | 101 | 87 | 36 | 559 | 57 | 1595 | 25 | 25 | 174 | 113 | .606 | 13 | 21 | 3.29 |

## Tom Candiotti

**Pitches:** Right **Bats:** Right **Pos:** SP **Ht:** 6' 2" **Wt:** 200 **Born:** 08/31/57 **Age:** 33

| | | HOW MUCH HE PITCHED | | | | | | WHAT HE GAVE UP | | | | | | | | | | | | THE RESULTS | | | | | |
|---|---|---|---|---|---|---|---|---|---|---|---|---|---|---|---|---|---|---|---|---|---|---|---|---|---|
| Year Team | Lg | G | GS | CG | GF | IP | BFP | H | R | ER | HR | SH | SF | HB | TBB | IBB | SO | WP | Bk | W | L | Pct. | ShO | Sv | ERA |
| 1983 Milwaukee | AL | 10 | 8 | 2 | 1 | 55.2 | 233 | 62 | 21 | 20 | 4 | 0 | 2 | 2 | 16 | 0 | 21 | 0 | 0 | 4 | 4 | .500 | 1 | 0 | 3.23 |
| 1984 Milwaukee | AL | 8 | 6 | 0 | 0 | 32.1 | 147 | 38 | 21 | 19 | 5 | 0 | 0 | 0 | 10 | 0 | 23 | 1 | 0 | 2 | 2 | .500 | 0 | 0 | 5.29 |
| 1986 Cleveland | AL | 36 | 34 | 17 | 1 | 252.1 | 1078 | 234 | 112 | 100 | 18 | 3 | 9 | 8 | 106 | 0 | 167 | 12 | 4 | 16 | 12 | .571 | 3 | 0 | 3.57 |
| 1987 Cleveland | AL | 32 | 32 | 7 | 0 | 201.2 | 888 | 193 | 132 | 107 | 28 | 8 | 10 | 4 | 93 | 2 | 111 | 13 | 2 | 7 | 18 | .280 | 2 | 0 | 4.78 |
| 1988 Cleveland | AL | 31 | 31 | 11 | 0 | 216.2 | 903 | 225 | 86 | 79 | 15 | 12 | 5 | 6 | 53 | 3 | 137 | 5 | 7 | 14 | 8 | .636 | 1 | 0 | 3.28 |
| 1989 Cleveland | AL | 31 | 31 | 4 | 0 | 206 | 847 | 188 | 80 | 71 | 10 | 6 | 4 | 4 | 55 | 5 | 124 | 4 | 8 | 13 | 10 | .565 | 0 | 0 | 3.10 |
| 1990 Cleveland | AL | 31 | 29 | 3 | 1 | 202 | 856 | 207 | 92 | 82 | 23 | 4 | 3 | 6 | 55 | 1 | 128 | 9 | 3 | 15 | 11 | .577 | 1 | 0 | 3.65 |
| 7 ML YEARS | | 179 | 171 | 44 | 3 | 1166.2 | 4952 | 1147 | 544 | 478 | 103 | 33 | 33 | 30 | 388 | 11 | 711 | 44 | 24 | 71 | 65 | .522 | 8 | 0 | 3.69 |

## John Cangelosi

**Bats:** Both **Throws:** Left **Pos:** CF **Ht:** 5' 8" **Wt:** 150 **Born:** 03/10/63 **Age:** 28

| | | BATTING | | | | | | | | | | | | | | | | | BASERUNNING | | | | PERCENTAGES | | |
|---|---|---|---|---|---|---|---|---|---|---|---|---|---|---|---|---|---|---|---|---|---|---|---|---|---|
| Year Team | Lg | G | AB | H | 2B | 3B | HR | (Hm | Rd) | TB | R | RBI | TBB | IBB | SO | HBP | SH | SF | SB | CS | SB% | GDP | Avg | OBP | SLG |
| 1985 Chicago | AL | 5 | 2 | 0 | 0 | 0 | 0 | (0 | 0) | 0 | 2 | 0 | 0 | 0 | 1 | 1 | 1 | 0 | 0 | 0 | .00 | 0 | .000 | .333 | .000 |
| 1986 Chicago | AL | 137 | 438 | 103 | 16 | 3 | 2 | (1 | 1) | 131 | 65 | 32 | 71 | 0 | 61 | 7 | 6 | 3 | 50 | 17 | .75 | 5 | .235 | .349 | .299 |
| 1987 Pittsburgh | NL | 104 | 182 | 50 | 8 | 3 | 4 | (2 | 2) | 76 | 44 | 18 | 46 | 1 | 33 | 3 | 1 | 1 | 21 | 6 | .78 | 3 | .275 | .427 | .418 |
| 1988 Pittsburgh | NL | 75 | 118 | 30 | 4 | 1 | 0 | (0 | 0) | 36 | 18 | 8 | 17 | 0 | 16 | 1 | 3 | 0 | 9 | 4 | .69 | 0 | .254 | .353 | .305 |
| 1989 Pittsburgh | NL | 112 | 160 | 35 | 4 | 2 | 0 | (0 | 0) | 43 | 18 | 9 | 35 | 2 | 20 | 3 | 1 | 2 | 11 | 8 | .58 | 1 | .219 | .365 | .269 |
| 1990 Pittsburgh | NL | 58 | 76 | 15 | 2 | 0 | 0 | (0 | 0) | 17 | 13 | 1 | 11 | 0 | 12 | 1 | 2 | 0 | 7 | 2 | .78 | 2 | .197 | .307 | .224 |
| 6 ML YEARS | | 491 | 976 | 233 | 34 | 9 | 6 | (3 | 3) | 303 | 160 | 68 | 180 | 3 | 143 | 16 | 14 | 6 | 98 | 37 | .73 | 11 | .239 | .364 | .310 |

## Jose Canseco

**Bats:** Right **Throws:** Right **Pos:** RF/DH **Ht:** 6' 3" **Wt:** 240 **Born:** 07/02/64 **Age:** 26

| | | BATTING | | | | | | | | | | | | | | | | | BASERUNNING | | | | PERCENTAGES | | |
|---|---|---|---|---|---|---|---|---|---|---|---|---|---|---|---|---|---|---|---|---|---|---|---|---|---|
| Year Team | Lg | G | AB | H | 2B | 3B | HR | (Hm | Rd) | TB | R | RBI | TBB | IBB | SO | HBP | SH | SF | SB | CS | SB% | GDP | Avg | OBP | SLG |
| 1985 Oakland | AL | 29 | 96 | 29 | 3 | 0 | 5 | (4 | 1) | 47 | 16 | 13 | 4 | 0 | 31 | 0 | 0 | 0 | 1 | 1 | .50 | 1 | .302 | .330 | .490 |
| 1986 Oakland | AL | 157 | 600 | 144 | 29 | 1 | 33 | (14 | 19) | 274 | 85 | 117 | 65 | 1 | 175 | 8 | 0 | 9 | 15 | 7 | .68 | 12 | .240 | .318 | .457 |
| 1987 Oakland | AL | 159 | 630 | 162 | 35 | 3 | 31 | (16 | 15) | 296 | 81 | 113 | 50 | 2 | 157 | 2 | 0 | 9 | 15 | 3 | .83 | 16 | .257 | .310 | .470 |
| 1988 Oakland | AL | 158 | 610 | 187 | 34 | 0 | 42 | (16 | 26) | 347 | 120 | 124 | 78 | 10 | 128 | 10 | 1 | 6 | 40 | 16 | .71 | 15 | .307 | .391 | .569 |
| 1989 Oakland | AL | 65 | 227 | 61 | 9 | 1 | 17 | (8 | 9) | 123 | 40 | 57 | 23 | 4 | 69 | 2 | 0 | 6 | 6 | 3 | .67 | 4 | .269 | .333 | .542 |
| 1990 Oakland | AL | 131 | 481 | 132 | 14 | 2 | 37 | (18 | 19) | 261 | 83 | 101 | 72 | 8 | 158 | 5 | 0 | 5 | 19 | 10 | .66 | 9 | .274 | .371 | .543 |
| 6 ML YEARS | | 699 | 2644 | 715 | 124 | 7 | 165 | (76 | 89) | 1348 | 425 | 525 | 292 | 25 | 718 | 27 | 1 | 35 | 96 | 40 | .71 | 57 | .270 | .345 | .510 |

## Ozzie Canseco

**Bats:** Right **Throws:** Right **Pos:** DH **Ht:** 6' 3" **Wt:** 220 **Born:** 07/02/64 **Age:** 26

| | | BATTING | | | | | | | | | | | | | | | | | BASERUNNING | | | | PERCENTAGES | | |
|---|---|---|---|---|---|---|---|---|---|---|---|---|---|---|---|---|---|---|---|---|---|---|---|---|---|
| Year Team | Lg | G | AB | H | 2B | 3B | HR | (Hm | Rd) | TB | R | RBI | TBB | IBB | SO | HBP | SH | SF | SB | CS | SB% | GDP | Avg | OBP | SLG |
| 1984 Greensboro | A | 8 | 1 | 0 | 0 | 0 | 0 | -- | -- | 0 | 1 | 0 | 0 | 0 | 0 | 0 | 0 | 0 | 0 | 0 | .00 | 0 | .000 | .000 | .000 |
| 1985 Yankees | R | 20 | 39 | 7 | 0 | 1 | 1 | -- | -- | 12 | 2 | 5 | 2 | 0 | 18 | 0 | 0 | 0 | 0 | 0 | .00 | 0 | .179 | .220 | .308 |
| 1986 Yankees | R | 7 | 15 | 2 | 1 | 0 | 1 | -- | -- | 6 | 3 | 3 | 5 | 0 | 9 | 0 | 0 | 0 | 0 | 0 | .00 | 0 | .133 | .350 | .400 |
| Madison | A | 42 | 128 | 20 | 1 | 1 | 3 | -- | -- | 32 | 17 | 17 | 22 | 0 | 47 | 0 | 0 | 3 | 1 | 1 | .50 | 2 | .156 | .275 | .250 |
| 1987 Madison | A | 92 | 309 | 82 | 12 | 4 | 11 | -- | -- | 135 | 64 | 54 | 67 | 3 | 104 | 1 | 0 | 1 | 6 | 7 | .46 | 6 | .265 | .397 | .437 |

| Year Team | Lg | G | AB | H | 2B | 3B | HR | (Hm | Rd) | TB | R | RBI | TBB | IBB | SO | HBP | SH | SF | SB | CS | SB% | GDP | Avg | OBP | SLG |
|---|---|---|---|---|---|---|---|---|---|---|---|---|---|---|---|---|---|---|---|---|---|---|---|---|---|
| 1988 Madison | A | 99 | 359 | 98 | 17 | 7 | 12 | -- | -- | 165 | 63 | 68 | 49 | 3 | 84 | 3 | 1 | 7 | 15 | 8 | .65 | 8 | .273 | .359 | .460 |
| Huntsville | AA | 27 | 99 | 22 | 7 | 0 | 3 | -- | -- | 38 | 6 | 12 | 6 | 1 | 31 | 0 | 0 | 0 | 3 | 0 | 1.00 | 1 | .222 | .267 | .384 |
| 1989 Huntsville | AA | 91 | 317 | 74 | 17 | 2 | 12 | -- | -- | 131 | 52 | 52 | 51 | 0 | 88 | 5 | 2 | 4 | 1 | 2 | .33 | 4 | .233 | .345 | .413 |
| 1990 Huntsville | AA | 97 | 325 | 73 | 21 | 0 | 20 | -- | -- | 154 | 50 | 67 | 47 | 2 | 103 | 7 | 2 | 2 | 2 | 2 | .50 | 5 | .225 | .333 | .474 |
| 1990 Oakland | AL | 9 | 19 | 2 | 1 | 0 | 0 | (0 | 0) | 3 | 1 | 1 | 1 | 0 | 10 | 0 | 0 | 0 | 0 | 0 | .00 | 0 | .105 | .150 | .158 |

## Mike Capel

**Pitches:** Right **Bats:** Right **Pos:** RP **Ht:** 6' 2" **Wt:** 175 **Born:** 10/13/61 **Age:** 29

| HOW MUCH HE PITCHED | | | | | | | | WHAT HE GAVE UP | | | | | | | | | | | | THE RESULTS | | | | | |
|---|---|---|---|---|---|---|---|---|---|---|---|---|---|---|---|---|---|---|---|---|---|---|---|---|---|
| Year Team | Lg | G | GS | CG | GF | IP | BFP | H | R | ER | HR | SH | SF | HB | TBB | IBB | SO | WP | Bk | W | L | Pct. | ShO | Sv | ERA |
| 1988 Chicago | NL | 22 | 0 | 0 | 11 | 29.1 | 134 | 34 | 19 | 16 | 5 | 2 | 0 | 3 | 13 | 2 | 19 | 5 | 0 | 2 | 1 | .667 | 0 | 0 | 4.91 |
| 1990 Milwaukee | AL | 2 | 0 | 0 | 0 | 0.1 | 9 | 6 | 6 | 5 | 0 | 0 | 0 | 1 | 1 | 0 | 1 | 0 | 0 | 0 | 0 | .000 | 0 | 0 | 99.99 |
| 2 ML YEARS | | 24 | 0 | 0 | 11 | 29.2 | 143 | 40 | 25 | 21 | 5 | 2 | 0 | 4 | 14 | 2 | 20 | 5 | 0 | 2 | 1 | .667 | 0 | 0 | 6.37 |

## Don Carman

**Pitches:** Left **Bats:** Left **Pos:** RP **Ht:** 6' 3" **Wt:** 195 **Born:** 08/14/59 **Age:** 31

| HOW MUCH HE PITCHED | | | | | | | | WHAT HE GAVE UP | | | | | | | | | | | | THE RESULTS | | | | | |
|---|---|---|---|---|---|---|---|---|---|---|---|---|---|---|---|---|---|---|---|---|---|---|---|---|---|
| Year Team | Lg | G | GS | CG | GF | IP | BFP | H | R | ER | HR | SH | SF | HB | TBB | IBB | SO | WP | Bk | W | L | Pct. | ShO | Sv | ERA |
| 1983 Philadelphia | NL | 1 | 0 | 0 | 1 | 1 | 3 | 0 | 0 | 0 | 0 | 0 | 0 | 0 | 0 | 0 | 0 | 0 | 0 | 0 | 0 | .000 | 0 | 1 | 0.00 |
| 1984 Philadelphia | NL | 11 | 0 | 0 | 9 | 13.1 | 61 | 14 | 9 | 8 | 2 | 0 | 0 | 0 | 6 | 4 | 16 | 3 | 0 | 0 | 1 | .000 | 0 | 0 | 5.40 |
| 1985 Philadelphia | NL | 71 | 0 | 0 | 33 | 86.1 | 342 | 52 | 25 | 20 | 6 | 5 | 5 | 2 | 38 | 3 | 87 | 1 | 0 | 9 | 4 | .692 | 0 | 7 | 2.08 |
| 1986 Philadelphia | NL | 50 | 14 | 2 | 13 | 134.1 | 545 | 113 | 50 | 48 | 11 | 5 | 3 | 3 | 52 | 11 | 98 | 6 | 2 | 10 | 5 | .667 | 1 | 1 | 3.22 |
| 1987 Philadelphia | NL | 35 | 35 | 3 | 0 | 211 | 886 | 194 | 110 | 99 | 34 | 11 | 5 | 5 | 69 | 7 | 125 | 3 | 1 | 13 | 11 | .542 | 2 | 0 | 4.22 |
| 1988 Philadelphia | NL | 36 | 32 | 2 | 0 | 201.1 | 873 | 211 | 101 | 96 | 20 | 9 | 8 | 4 | 70 | 6 | 116 | 8 | 3 | 10 | 14 | .417 | 0 | 0 | 4.29 |
| 1989 Philadelphia | NL | 49 | 20 | 0 | 5 | 149.1 | 683 | 152 | 98 | 87 | 21 | 5 | 5 | 3 | 86 | 6 | 81 | 7 | 3 | 5 | 15 | .250 | 0 | 0 | 5.24 |
| 1990 Philadelphia | NL | 59 | 1 | 0 | 11 | 86.2 | 368 | 69 | 43 | 40 | 13 | 6 | 4 | 4 | 38 | 7 | 58 | 6 | 1 | 6 | 2 | .750 | 0 | 1 | 4.15 |
| 8 ML YEARS | | 312 | 102 | 7 | 72 | 883.1 | 3761 | 805 | 436 | 398 | 107 | 41 | 30 | 21 | 359 | 44 | 581 | 34 | 10 | 53 | 52 | .505 | 3 | 10 | 4.06 |

## Cris Carpenter

**Pitches:** Right **Bats:** Right **Pos:** RP **Ht:** 6' 1" **Wt:** 185 **Born:** 04/05/65 **Age:** 26

| HOW MUCH HE PITCHED | | | | | | | | WHAT HE GAVE UP | | | | | | | | | | | | THE RESULTS | | | | | |
|---|---|---|---|---|---|---|---|---|---|---|---|---|---|---|---|---|---|---|---|---|---|---|---|---|---|
| Year Team | Lg | G | GS | CG | GF | IP | BFP | H | R | ER | HR | SH | SF | HB | TBB | IBB | SO | WP | Bk | W | L | Pct. | ShO | Sv | ERA |
| 1988 St. Louis | NL | 8 | 8 | 1 | 0 | 47.2 | 203 | 56 | 27 | 25 | 3 | 1 | 4 | 1 | 9 | 2 | 24 | 1 | 0 | 2 | 3 | .400 | 0 | 0 | 4.72 |
| 1989 St. Louis | NL | 36 | 5 | 0 | 10 | 68 | 303 | 70 | 30 | 24 | 4 | 4 | 4 | 2 | 26 | 9 | 35 | 1 | 0 | 4 | 4 | .500 | 0 | 0 | 3.18 |
| 1990 St. Louis | NL | 4 | 0 | 0 | 1 | 8 | 32 | 5 | 4 | 4 | 2 | 0 | 0 | 0 | 2 | 1 | 6 | 0 | 0 | 0 | 0 | .000 | 0 | 0 | 4.50 |
| 3 ML YEARS | | 48 | 13 | 1 | 11 | 123.2 | 538 | 131 | 61 | 53 | 9 | 5 | 8 | 3 | 37 | 12 | 65 | 2 | 0 | 6 | 7 | .462 | 0 | 0 | 3.86 |

## Chuck Carr

**Bats:** Both **Throws:** Right **Pos:** PH **Ht:** 5'10" **Wt:** 160 **Born:** 08/10/68 **Age:** 22

| BATTING | | | | | | | | | | | | | | | | | | | BASERUNNING | | | | PERCENTAGES | | |
|---|---|---|---|---|---|---|---|---|---|---|---|---|---|---|---|---|---|---|---|---|---|---|---|---|---|
| Year Team | Lg | G | AB | H | 2B | 3B | HR | (Hm | Rd) | TB | R | RBI | TBB | IBB | SO | HBP | SH | SF | SB | CS | SB% | GDP | Avg | OBP | SLG |
| 1986 Reds | R | 44 | 123 | 21 | 5 | 0 | 0 | -- | -- | 26 | 13 | 10 | 10 | 0 | 27 | 0 | 5 | 2 | 9 | 1 | .90 | 2 | .171 | .230 | .211 |
| 1987 Bellingham | A | 44 | 165 | 40 | 1 | 1 | 1 | -- | -- | 46 | 31 | 11 | 12 | 0 | 38 | 1 | 3 | 0 | 20 | 1 | .95 | 2 | .242 | .298 | .279 |
| 1988 Wausau | A | 82 | 304 | 91 | 14 | 2 | 6 | -- | -- | 127 | 58 | 30 | 14 | 0 | 49 | 1 | 3 | 5 | 41 | 11 | .79 | 3 | .299 | .327 | .418 |
| Vermont | AA | 41 | 159 | 39 | 4 | 2 | 1 | -- | -- | 50 | 26 | 13 | 8 | 0 | 33 | 0 | 3 | 1 | 21 | 9 | .70 | 0 | .245 | .280 | .314 |
| 1989 Jackson | AA | 116 | 444 | 107 | 13 | 1 | 0 | -- | -- | 122 | 45 | 22 | 27 | 2 | 66 | 1 | 7 | 2 | 47 | 20 | .70 | 3 | .241 | .285 | .275 |
| 1990 Tidewater | AAA | 20 | 81 | 21 | 5 | 1 | 0 | -- | -- | 28 | 13 | 8 | 4 | 0 | 12 | 0 | 0 | 2 | 6 | 4 | .60 | 0 | .259 | .287 | .346 |
| Jackson | AA | 93 | 360 | 93 | 20 | 9 | 3 | -- | -- | 140 | 60 | 24 | 44 | 2 | 77 | 2 | 3 | 2 | 47 | 15 | .76 | 2 | .258 | .341 | .389 |
| 1990 New York | NL | 4 | 2 | 0 | 0 | 0 | 0 | (0 | 0) | 0 | 0 | 0 | 0 | 0 | 2 | 0 | 0 | 0 | 1 | 0 | 1.00 | 0 | .000 | .000 | .000 |

## Mark Carreon

**Bats:** Right **Throws:** Left **Pos:** CF/LF/RF **Ht:** 6' 0" **Wt:** 194 **Born:** 07/19/63 **Age:** 27

| BATTING | | | | | | | | | | | | | | | | | | | BASERUNNING | | | | PERCENTAGES | | |
|---|---|---|---|---|---|---|---|---|---|---|---|---|---|---|---|---|---|---|---|---|---|---|---|---|---|
| Year Team | Lg | G | AB | H | 2B | 3B | HR | (Hm | Rd) | TB | R | RBI | TBB | IBB | SO | HBP | SH | SF | SB | CS | SB% | GDP | Avg | OBP | SLG |
| 1987 New York | NL | 9 | 12 | 3 | 0 | 0 | 0 | (0 | 0) | 3 | 0 | 1 | 1 | 0 | 1 | 0 | 0 | 0 | 0 | 1 | .00 | 0 | .250 | .308 | .250 |
| 1988 New York | NL | 7 | 9 | 5 | 2 | 0 | 1 | (0 | 1) | 10 | 5 | 1 | 2 | 0 | 1 | 0 | 0 | 0 | 0 | 0 | .00 | 0 | .556 | .636 | 1.111 |
| 1989 New York | NL | 68 | 133 | 41 | 6 | 0 | 6 | (4 | 2) | 65 | 20 | 16 | 12 | 0 | 17 | 1 | 0 | 0 | 2 | 3 | .40 | 1 | .308 | .370 | .489 |
| 1990 New York | NL | 82 | 188 | 47 | 12 | 0 | 10 | (1 | 9) | 89 | 30 | 26 | 15 | 0 | 29 | 2 | 0 | 0 | 1 | 0 | 1.00 | 1 | .250 | .312 | .473 |
| 4 ML YEARS | | 166 | 342 | 96 | 20 | 0 | 17 | (5 | 12) | 167 | 55 | 44 | 30 | 0 | 48 | 3 | 0 | 0 | 3 | 4 | .43 | 2 | .281 | .344 | .488 |

## Gary Carter

**Bats:** Right **Throws:** Right **Pos:** C **Ht:** 6' 2" **Wt:** 210 **Born:** 04/08/54 **Age:** 37

| BATTING | | | | | | | | | | | | | | | | | | | BASERUNNING | | | | PERCENTAGES | | |
|---|---|---|---|---|---|---|---|---|---|---|---|---|---|---|---|---|---|---|---|---|---|---|---|---|---|
| Year Team | Lg | G | AB | H | 2B | 3B | HR | (Hm | Rd) | TB | R | RBI | TBB | IBB | SO | HBP | SH | SF | SB | CS | SB% | GDP | Avg | OBP | SLG |
| 1974 Montreal | NL | 9 | 27 | 11 | 0 | 1 | 1 | (1 | 0) | 16 | 5 | 6 | 1 | 0 | 2 | 0 | 0 | 1 | 2 | 0 | 1.00 | 0 | .407 | .414 | .593 |
| 1975 Montreal | NL | 144 | 503 | 136 | 20 | 1 | 17 | (9 | 8) | 209 | 58 | 68 | 72 | 8 | 83 | 1 | 10 | 4 | 5 | 2 | .71 | 7 | .270 | .360 | .416 |

| Year Team | Lg | G | AB | H | 2B | 3B | HR | (Hm | Rd) | TB | R | RBI | TBB | IBB | SO | HBP | SH | SF | SB | CS | SB% | GDP | Avg | OBP | SLG |
|---|---|---|---|---|---|---|---|---|---|---|---|---|---|---|---|---|---|---|---|---|---|---|---|---|---|
| 1976 Montreal | NL | 91 | 311 | 68 | 8 | 1 | 6 | (5 | 1) | 96 | 31 | 38 | 30 | 2 | 43 | 1 | 2 | 3 | 0 | 2 | .00 | 7 | .219 | .287 | .309 |
| 1977 Montreal | NL | 154 | 522 | 148 | 29 | 2 | 31 | (22 | 9) | 274 | 86 | 84 | 58 | 5 | 103 | 5 | 3 | 7 | 5 | 5 | .50 | 9 | .284 | .356 | .525 |
| 1978 Montreal | NL | 157 | 533 | 136 | 27 | 1 | 20 | (7 | 13) | 225 | 76 | 72 | 62 | 11 | 70 | 5 | 2 | 5 | 10 | 6 | .63 | 10 | .255 | .336 | .422 |
| 1979 Montreal | NL | 141 | 505 | 143 | 26 | 5 | 22 | (12 | 10) | 245 | 74 | 75 | 40 | 3 | 62 | 5 | 2 | 7 | 3 | 2 | .60 | 11 | .283 | .338 | .485 |
| 1980 Montreal | NL | 154 | 549 | 145 | 25 | 5 | 29 | (12 | 17) | 267 | 76 | 101 | 58 | 11 | 78 | 1 | 1 | 8 | 3 | 2 | .60 | 9 | .264 | .331 | .486 |
| 1981 Montreal | NL | 100 | 374 | 94 | 20 | 2 | 16 | (7 | 9) | 166 | 48 | 68 | 35 | 4 | 35 | 1 | 3 | 6 | 1 | 5 | .17 | 6 | .251 | .313 | .444 |
| 1982 Montreal | NL | 154 | 557 | 163 | 32 | 1 | 29 | (16 | 13) | 284 | 91 | 97 | 78 | 11 | 64 | 6 | 4 | 8 | 2 | 5 | .29 | 16 | .293 | .381 | .510 |
| 1983 Montreal | NL | 145 | 541 | 146 | 37 | 3 | 17 | (6 | 11) | 240 | 63 | 79 | 51 | 7 | 57 | 7 | 2 | 8 | 1 | 1 | .50 | 14 | .270 | .336 | .444 |
| 1984 Montreal | NL | 159 | 596 | 175 | 32 | 1 | 27 | (14 | 13) | 290 | 75 | 106 | 64 | 9 | 57 | 6 | 0 | 3 | 2 | 2 | .50 | 8 | .294 | .366 | .487 |
| 1985 New York | NL | 149 | 555 | 156 | 17 | 1 | 32 | (12 | 20) | 271 | 83 | 100 | 69 | 16 | 46 | 6 | 0 | 3 | 1 | 1 | .50 | 18 | .281 | .365 | .488 |
| 1986 New York | NL | 132 | 490 | 125 | 14 | 2 | 24 | (13 | 11) | 215 | 81 | 105 | 62 | 9 | 63 | 6 | 0 | 15 | 1 | 0 | 1.00 | 21 | .255 | .337 | .439 |
| 1987 New York | NL | 139 | 523 | 123 | 18 | 2 | 20 | (9 | 11) | 205 | 55 | 83 | 42 | 1 | 73 | 1 | 1 | 6 | 0 | 0 | .00 | 14 | .235 | .290 | .392 |
| 1988 New York | NL | 130 | 455 | 110 | 16 | 2 | 11 | (5 | 6) | 163 | 39 | 46 | 34 | 1 | 52 | 7 | 1 | 6 | 0 | 2 | .00 | 8 | .242 | .301 | .358 |
| 1989 New York | NL | 50 | 153 | 28 | 8 | 0 | 2 | (1 | 1) | 42 | 14 | 15 | 12 | 0 | 15 | 0 | 0 | 1 | 0 | 0 | .00 | 5 | .183 | .241 | .275 |
| 1990 San Francisco | NL | 92 | 244 | 62 | 10 | 0 | 9 | (6 | 3) | 99 | 24 | 27 | 25 | 3 | 31 | 1 | 0 | 2 | 1 | 1 | .50 | 2 | .254 | .324 | .406 |
| 17 ML YEARS | | 2100 | 7438 | 1969 | 339 | 30 | 313 | (157 | 156) | 3307 | 979 | 1170 | 793 | 101 | 934 | 59 | 31 | 93 | 37 | 36 | .51 | 165 | .265 | .337 | .445 |

## Joe Carter

**Bats:** Right **Throws:** Right **Pos:** CF/1B/LF **Ht:** 6' 3" **Wt:** 215 **Born:** 03/07/60 **Age:** 31

| | | BATTING | | | | | | | | | | | | | | | | | BASERUNNING | | | | PERCENTAGES | | |
|---|---|---|---|---|---|---|---|---|---|---|---|---|---|---|---|---|---|---|---|---|---|---|---|---|---|
| Year Team | Lg | G | AB | H | 2B | 3B | HR | (Hm | Rd) | TB | R | RBI | TBB | IBB | SO | HBP | SH | SF | SB | CS | SB% | GDP | Avg | OBP | SLG |
| 1983 Chicago | NL | 23 | 51 | 9 | 1 | 1 | 0 | (0 | 0) | 12 | 6 | 1 | 0 | 0 | 21 | 0 | 1 | 0 | 1 | 0 | 1.00 | 1 | .176 | .176 | .235 |
| 1984 Cleveland | AL | 66 | 244 | 67 | 6 | 1 | 13 | (9 | 4) | 114 | 32 | 41 | 11 | 0 | 48 | 1 | 0 | 1 | 2 | 4 | .33 | 2 | .275 | .307 | .467 |
| 1985 Cleveland | AL | 143 | 489 | 128 | 27 | 0 | 15 | (5 | 10) | 200 | 64 | 59 | 25 | 2 | 74 | 2 | 3 | 4 | 24 | 6 | .80 | 9 | .262 | .298 | .409 |
| 1986 Cleveland | AL | 162 | 663 | 200 | 36 | 9 | 29 | (14 | 15) | 341 | 108 | 121 | 32 | 3 | 95 | 5 | 1 | 8 | 29 | 7 | .81 | 8 | .302 | .335 | .514 |
| 1987 Cleveland | AL | 149 | 588 | 155 | 27 | 2 | 32 | (9 | 23) | 282 | 83 | 106 | 27 | 6 | 105 | 9 | 1 | 4 | 31 | 6 | .84 | 8 | .264 | .304 | .480 |
| 1988 Cleveland | AL | 157 | 621 | 168 | 36 | 6 | 27 | (16 | 11) | 297 | 85 | 98 | 35 | 6 | 82 | 7 | 1 | 6 | 27 | 5 | .84 | 6 | .271 | .314 | .478 |
| 1989 Cleveland | AL | 162 | 651 | 158 | 32 | 4 | 35 | (16 | 19) | 303 | 84 | 105 | 39 | 8 | 112 | 8 | 2 | 5 | 13 | 5 | .72 | 6 | .243 | .292 | .465 |
| 1990 San Diego | NL | 162 | 634 | 147 | 27 | 1 | 24 | (12 | 12) | 248 | 79 | 115 | 48 | 18 | 93 | 7 | 0 | 8 | 22 | 6 | .79 | 12 | .232 | .290 | .391 |
| 8 ML YEARS | | 1024 | 3941 | 1032 | 192 | 24 | 175 | (81 | 94) | 1797 | 541 | 646 | 217 | 43 | 630 | 39 | 9 | 36 | 149 | 39 | .79 | 52 | .262 | .304 | .456 |

## Steve Carter

**Bats:** Left **Throws:** Right **Pos:** CF **Ht:** 6' 4" **Wt:** 200 **Born:** 12/03/64 **Age:** 26

| | | BATTING | | | | | | | | | | | | | | | | | BASERUNNING | | | | PERCENTAGES | | |
|---|---|---|---|---|---|---|---|---|---|---|---|---|---|---|---|---|---|---|---|---|---|---|---|---|---|
| Year Team | Lg | G | AB | H | 2B | 3B | HR | (Hm | Rd) | TB | R | RBI | TBB | IBB | SO | HBP | SH | SF | SB | CS | SB% | GDP | Avg | OBP | SLG |
| 1987 Watertown | A | 66 | 242 | 75 | 18 | 1 | 0 | -- | -- | 95 | 50 | 30 | 33 | 2 | 37 | 4 | 0 | 3 | 24 | 8 | .75 | 1 | .310 | .397 | .393 |
| 1988 Harrisburg | AA | 9 | 35 | 10 | 2 | 0 | 0 | -- | -- | 12 | 7 | 2 | 1 | 0 | 6 | 0 | 0 | 0 | 3 | 0 | 1.00 | 0 | .286 | .306 | .343 |
| Augusta | A | 74 | 278 | 83 | 18 | 6 | 3 | -- | -- | 122 | 47 | 43 | 31 | 5 | 59 | 2 | 1 | 4 | 22 | 8 | .73 | 5 | .299 | .368 | .439 |
| Salem | A | 6 | 21 | 6 | 0 | 0 | 0 | -- | -- | 6 | 4 | 1 | 0 | 0 | 1 | 0 | 0 | 0 | 2 | 0 | 1.00 | 0 | .286 | .286 | .286 |
| 1989 Buffalo | AAA | 100 | 356 | 105 | 24 | 6 | 1 | -- | -- | 144 | 53 | 43 | 27 | 5 | 62 | 2 | 1 | 3 | 17 | 9 | .65 | 4 | .295 | .345 | .404 |
| 1990 Buffalo | AAA | 120 | 426 | 129 | 19 | 12 | 8 | -- | -- | 196 | 62 | 45 | 25 | 3 | 61 | 9 | 2 | 0 | 10 | 10 | .50 | 11 | .303 | .354 | .460 |
| 1989 Pittsburgh | NL | 9 | 16 | 2 | 1 | 0 | 1 | (1 | 0) | 6 | 2 | 3 | 2 | 1 | 5 | 0 | 0 | 0 | 0 | 0 | .00 | 0 | .125 | .222 | .375 |
| 1990 Pittsburgh | NL | 5 | 5 | 1 | 0 | 0 | 0 | (0 | 0) | 1 | 0 | 0 | 0 | 0 | 1 | 0 | 0 | 0 | 0 | 0 | .00 | 0 | .200 | .200 | .200 |
| 2 ML YEARS | | 14 | 21 | 3 | 1 | 0 | 1 | (1 | 0) | 7 | 2 | 3 | 2 | 1 | 6 | 0 | 0 | 0 | 0 | 0 | .00 | 0 | .143 | .217 | .333 |

## Chuck Cary

**Pitches:** Left **Bats:** Left **Pos:** SP **Ht:** 6' 4" **Wt:** 210 **Born:** 03/03/60 **Age:** 31

| | | HOW MUCH HE PITCHED | | | | | | WHAT HE GAVE UP | | | | | | | | | | | | THE RESULTS | | | | | |
|---|---|---|---|---|---|---|---|---|---|---|---|---|---|---|---|---|---|---|---|---|---|---|---|---|---|
| Year Team | Lg | G | GS | CG | GF | IP | BFP | H | R | ER | HR | SH | SF | HB | TBB | IBB | SO | WP | Bk | W | L | Pct. | ShO | Sv | ERA |
| 1985 Detroit | AL | 16 | 0 | 0 | 6 | 23.2 | 95 | 16 | 9 | 9 | 2 | 0 | 1 | 2 | 8 | 1 | 22 | 0 | 0 | 0 | 1 | .000 | 0 | 2 | 3.42 |
| 1986 Detroit | AL | 22 | 0 | 0 | 6 | 31.2 | 140 | 33 | 18 | 12 | 3 | 2 | 2 | 0 | 15 | 4 | 21 | 1 | 1 | 1 | 2 | .333 | 0 | 0 | 3.41 |
| 1987 Atlanta | NL | 13 | 0 | 0 | 6 | 16.2 | 70 | 17 | 7 | 7 | 3 | 1 | 0 | 1 | 4 | 3 | 15 | 1 | 0 | 1 | 1 | .500 | 0 | 1 | 3.78 |
| 1988 Atlanta | NL | 7 | 0 | 0 | 1 | 8.1 | 39 | 8 | 6 | 6 | 1 | 2 | 0 | 1 | 4 | 0 | 7 | 1 | 0 | 0 | 0 | .000 | 0 | 0 | 6.48 |
| 1989 New York | AL | 22 | 11 | 2 | 4 | 99.1 | 404 | 78 | 42 | 36 | 13 | 1 | 1 | 0 | 29 | 6 | 79 | 6 | 1 | 4 | 4 | .500 | 0 | 0 | 3.26 |
| 1990 New York | AL | 28 | 27 | 2 | 1 | 156.2 | 661 | 155 | 77 | 73 | 21 | 3 | 5 | 1 | 55 | 1 | 134 | 11 | 2 | 6 | 12 | .333 | 0 | 0 | 4.19 |
| 6 ML YEARS | | 108 | 38 | 4 | 24 | 336.1 | 1409 | 307 | 159 | 143 | 43 | 9 | 9 | 5 | 115 | 15 | 278 | 20 | 4 | 12 | 20 | .375 | 0 | 3 | 3.83 |

## Larry Casian

**Pitches:** Left **Bats:** Right **Pos:** SP **Ht:** 6' 0" **Wt:** 170 **Born:** 10/28/65 **Age:** 25

| | | HOW MUCH HE PITCHED | | | | | | WHAT HE GAVE UP | | | | | | | | | | | | THE RESULTS | | | | | |
|---|---|---|---|---|---|---|---|---|---|---|---|---|---|---|---|---|---|---|---|---|---|---|---|---|---|
| Year Team | Lg | G | GS | CG | GF | IP | BFP | H | R | ER | HR | SH | SF | HB | TBB | IBB | SO | WP | Bk | W | L | Pct. | ShO | Sv | ERA |
| 1987 Visalia | A | 18 | 15 | 2 | 3 | 97 | 400 | 89 | 35 | 27 | 3 | 1 | 2 | 7 | 49 | 0 | 96 | 7 | 0 | 10 | 3 | .769 | 1 | 2 | 2.51 |
| 1988 Orlando | AA | 27 | 26 | 4 | 0 | 174 | 723 | 165 | 72 | 57 | 14 | 6 | 4 | 7 | 62 | 1 | 104 | 12 | 8 | 9 | 9 | .500 | 1 | 0 | 2.95 |
| Portland | AAA | 1 | 0 | 0 | 1 | 2.2 | 14 | 5 | 3 | 0 | 1 | 1 | 0 | 0 | 0 | 0 | 2 | 0 | 0 | 0 | 1 | .000 | 0 | 0 | 0.00 |

| Year Team | Lg | G | GS | CG | GF | IP | BFP | H | R | ER | HR | SH | SF | HB | TBB | IBB | SO | WP | Bk | W | L | Pct. | ShO | Sv | ERA |
|---|---|---|---|---|---|---|---|---|---|---|---|---|---|---|---|---|---|---|---|---|---|---|---|---|---|
| 1989 Portland | AAA | 28 | 27 | 0 | 0 | 169.1 | 738 | 201 | 97 | 85 | 13 | 5 | 6 | 6 | 63 | 0 | 65 | 5 | 2 | 7 | 12 | .368 | 0 | 0 | 4.52 |
| 1990 Portland | AAA | 37 | 23 | 1 | 4 | 156.2 | 682 | 171 | 90 | 78 | 14 | 8 | 4 | 3 | 59 | 5 | 89 | 2 | 2 | 9 | 9 | .500 | 0 | 0 | 4.48 |
| 1990 Minnesota | AL | 5 | 3 | 0 | 1 | 22.1 | 90 | 26 | 9 | 8 | 2 | 0 | 1 | 0 | 4 | 0 | 11 | 0 | 0 | 2 | 1 | .667 | 0 | 0 | 3.22 |

## Carmen Castillo

**Bats:** Right **Throws:** Right **Pos:** DH/RF **Ht:** 6' 1" **Wt:** 190 **Born:** 06/08/58 **Age:** 33

| BATTING | | | | | | | | | | | | | | | | | | | BASERUNNING | | | | PERCENTAGES | | |
|---|---|---|---|---|---|---|---|---|---|---|---|---|---|---|---|---|---|---|---|---|---|---|---|---|---|
| Year Team | Lg | G | AB | H | 2B | 3B | HR | (Hm | Rd) | TB | R | RBI | TBB | IBB | SO | HBP | SH | SF | SB | CS | SB% | GDP | Avg | OBP | SLG |
| 1982 Cleveland | AL | 47 | 120 | 25 | 4 | 0 | 2 | (2 | 0) | 35 | 11 | 11 | 6 | 2 | 17 | 2 | 1 | 0 | 0 | 0 | .00 | 2 | .208 | .258 | .292 |
| 1983 Cleveland | AL | 23 | 36 | 10 | 2 | 1 | 1 | (1 | 0) | 17 | 9 | 3 | 4 | 0 | 6 | 1 | 0 | 0 | 1 | 1 | .50 | 0 | .278 | .366 | .472 |
| 1984 Cleveland | AL | 87 | 211 | 55 | 9 | 2 | 10 | (7 | 3) | 98 | 36 | 36 | 21 | 0 | 32 | 2 | 0 | 3 | 1 | 3 | .25 | 7 | .261 | .329 | .464 |
| 1985 Cleveland | AL | 67 | 184 | 45 | 5 | 1 | 11 | (4 | 7) | 85 | 27 | 25 | 11 | 0 | 40 | 3 | 0 | 0 | 3 | 0 | 1.00 | 6 | .245 | .298 | .462 |
| 1986 Cleveland | AL | 85 | 205 | 57 | 9 | 0 | 8 | (4 | 4) | 90 | 34 | 32 | 9 | 0 | 48 | 1 | 1 | 1 | 2 | 1 | .67 | 9 | .278 | .310 | .439 |
| 1987 Cleveland | AL | 89 | 220 | 55 | 17 | 0 | 11 | (8 | 3) | 105 | 27 | 31 | 16 | 0 | 52 | 0 | 1 | 4 | 1 | 1 | .50 | 0 | .250 | .296 | .477 |
| 1988 Cleveland | AL | 66 | 176 | 48 | 8 | 0 | 4 | (2 | 2) | 68 | 12 | 14 | 5 | 1 | 31 | 1 | 0 | 0 | 6 | 2 | .75 | 4 | .273 | .297 | .386 |
| 1989 Minnesota | AL | 94 | 218 | 56 | 13 | 3 | 8 | (2 | 6) | 99 | 23 | 33 | 15 | 1 | 40 | 1 | 4 | 2 | 1 | 2 | .33 | 5 | .257 | .305 | .454 |
| 1990 Minnesota | AL | 64 | 137 | 30 | 4 | 0 | 0 | (0 | 0) | 34 | 11 | 12 | 3 | 1 | 23 | 1 | 0 | 1 | 0 | 1 | .00 | 1 | .219 | .239 | .248 |
| 9 ML YEARS | | 622 | 1507 | 381 | 71 | 7 | 55 | (30 | 25) | 631 | 190 | 197 | 90 | 5 | 289 | 12 | 7 | 11 | 15 | 11 | .58 | 34 | .253 | .298 | .419 |

## Tony Castillo

**Pitches:** Left **Bats:** Left **Pos:** RP/SP **Ht:** 5'10" **Wt:** 177 **Born:** 03/01/63 **Age:** 28

| HOW MUCH HE PITCHED | | | | | | | | WHAT HE GAVE UP | | | | | | | | | | | | THE RESULTS | | | | | |
|---|---|---|---|---|---|---|---|---|---|---|---|---|---|---|---|---|---|---|---|---|---|---|---|---|---|
| Year Team | Lg | G | GS | CG | GF | IP | BFP | H | R | ER | HR | SH | SF | HB | TBB | IBB | SO | WP | Bk | W | L | Pct. | ShO | Sv | ERA |
| 1988 Toronto | AL | 14 | 0 | 0 | 6 | 15 | 54 | 10 | 5 | 5 | 2 | 0 | 2 | 0 | 2 | 0 | 14 | 0 | 0 | 1 | 0 | 1.000 | 0 | 0 | 3.00 |
| 1989 2 ML Teams | | 29 | 0 | 0 | 9 | 27 | 127 | 31 | 19 | 17 | 0 | 3 | 4 | 1 | 14 | 6 | 15 | 3 | 0 | 1 | 2 | .333 | 0 | 1 | 5.67 |
| 1990 Atlanta | NL | 52 | 3 | 0 | 7 | 76.2 | 337 | 93 | 41 | 36 | 5 | 4 | 4 | 1 | 20 | 3 | 64 | 2 | 2 | 5 | 1 | .833 | 0 | 1 | 4.23 |
| 1989 Toronto | AL | 17 | 0 | 0 | 8 | 17.2 | 86 | 23 | 14 | 12 | 0 | 2 | 4 | 1 | 10 | 5 | 10 | 3 | 0 | 1 | 1 | .500 | 0 | 1 | 6.11 |
| Atlanta | NL | 12 | 0 | 0 | 1 | 9.1 | 41 | 8 | 5 | 5 | 0 | 1 | 0 | 0 | 4 | 1 | 5 | 0 | 0 | 0 | 1 | .000 | 0 | 0 | 4.82 |
| 3 ML YEARS | | 95 | 3 | 0 | 22 | 118.2 | 518 | 134 | 65 | 58 | 7 | 7 | 10 | 2 | 36 | 9 | 93 | 5 | 2 | 7 | 3 | .700 | 0 | 2 | 4.40 |

## Andujar Cedeno

**Bats:** Right **Throws:** Right **Pos:** SS **Ht:** 6' 1" **Wt:** 170 **Born:** 08/21/69 **Age:** 21

| BATTING | | | | | | | | | | | | | | | | | | | BASERUNNING | | | | PERCENTAGES | | |
|---|---|---|---|---|---|---|---|---|---|---|---|---|---|---|---|---|---|---|---|---|---|---|---|---|---|
| Year Team | Lg | G | AB | H | 2B | 3B | HR | (Hm | Rd) | TB | R | RBI | TBB | IBB | SO | HBP | SH | SF | SB | CS | SB% | GDP | Avg | OBP | SLG |
| 1988 Astros | R | 46 | 165 | 47 | 5 | 2 | 1 | -- | -- | 59 | 25 | 20 | 11 | 0 | 34 | 1 | 0 | 4 | 10 | 4 | .71 | 1 | .285 | .326 | .358 |
| 1989 Asheville | A | 126 | 487 | 146 | 23 | 6 | 14 | -- | -- | 223 | 76 | 93 | 29 | 0 | 124 | 1 | 2 | 5 | 23 | 10 | .70 | 10 | .300 | .337 | .458 |
| 1990 Columbus | AA | 132 | 495 | 119 | 21 | 11 | 19 | -- | -- | 219 | 57 | 64 | 33 | 1 | 135 | 6 | 7 | 5 | 6 | 10 | .38 | 11 | .240 | .293 | .442 |
| 1990 Houston | NL | 7 | 8 | 0 | 0 | 0 | 0 | (0 | 0) | 0 | 0 | 0 | 0 | 0 | 5 | 0 | 0 | 0 | 0 | 0 | .00 | 0 | .000 | .000 | .000 |

## Rick Cerone

**Bats:** Right **Throws:** Right **Pos:** C **Ht:** 5'11" **Wt:** 195 **Born:** 05/19/54 **Age:** 37

| BATTING | | | | | | | | | | | | | | | | | | | BASERUNNING | | | | PERCENTAGES | | |
|---|---|---|---|---|---|---|---|---|---|---|---|---|---|---|---|---|---|---|---|---|---|---|---|---|---|
| Year Team | Lg | G | AB | H | 2B | 3B | HR | (Hm | Rd) | TB | R | RBI | TBB | IBB | SO | HBP | SH | SF | SB | CS | SB% | GDP | Avg | OBP | SLG |
| 1975 Cleveland | AL | 7 | 12 | 3 | 1 | 0 | 0 | (0 | 0) | 4 | 1 | 0 | 1 | 0 | 0 | 0 | 1 | 0 | 0 | 0 | .00 | 0 | .250 | .308 | .333 |
| 1976 Cleveland | AL | 7 | 16 | 2 | 0 | 0 | 0 | (0 | 0) | 2 | 1 | 1 | 0 | 0 | 2 | 0 | 0 | 0 | 0 | 0 | .00 | 0 | .125 | .125 | .125 |
| 1977 Toronto | AL | 31 | 100 | 20 | 4 | 0 | 1 | (0 | 1) | 27 | 7 | 10 | 6 | 0 | 12 | 0 | 1 | 0 | 0 | 0 | .00 | 3 | .200 | .245 | .270 |
| 1978 Toronto | AL | 88 | 282 | 63 | 8 | 2 | 3 | (2 | 1) | 84 | 25 | 20 | 23 | 0 | 32 | 1 | 4 | 0 | 0 | 3 | .00 | 7 | .223 | .284 | .298 |
| 1979 Toronto | AL | 136 | 469 | 112 | 27 | 4 | 7 | (3 | 4) | 168 | 47 | 61 | 37 | 1 | 40 | 1 | 3 | 4 | 1 | 4 | .20 | 5 | .239 | .294 | .358 |
| 1980 New York | AL | 147 | 519 | 144 | 30 | 4 | 14 | (7 | 7) | 224 | 70 | 85 | 32 | 2 | 56 | 6 | 8 | 10 | 1 | 3 | .25 | 14 | .277 | .321 | .432 |
| 1981 New York | AL | 71 | 234 | 57 | 13 | 2 | 2 | (2 | 0) | 80 | 23 | 21 | 12 | 0 | 24 | 0 | 4 | 4 | 0 | 2 | .00 | 10 | .244 | .276 | .342 |
| 1982 New York | AL | 89 | 300 | 68 | 10 | 0 | 5 | (1 | 4) | 93 | 29 | 28 | 19 | 1 | 27 | 1 | 4 | 5 | 0 | 2 | .00 | 12 | .227 | .271 | .310 |
| 1983 New York | AL | 80 | 246 | 54 | 7 | 0 | 2 | (0 | 2) | 67 | 18 | 22 | 15 | 1 | 29 | 1 | 4 | 0 | 0 | 0 | .00 | 5 | .220 | .267 | .272 |
| 1984 New York | AL | 38 | 120 | 25 | 3 | 0 | 2 | (0 | 2) | 34 | 8 | 13 | 9 | 0 | 15 | 1 | 2 | 0 | 1 | 0 | 1.00 | 5 | .208 | .269 | .283 |
| 1985 Atlanta | NL | 96 | 282 | 61 | 9 | 0 | 3 | (3 | 0) | 79 | 15 | 25 | 29 | 1 | 25 | 1 | 0 | 4 | 0 | 3 | .00 | 15 | .216 | .288 | .280 |
| 1986 Milwaukee | AL | 68 | 216 | 56 | 14 | 0 | 4 | (3 | 1) | 82 | 22 | 18 | 15 | 0 | 28 | 1 | 5 | 5 | 1 | 1 | .50 | 5 | .259 | .304 | .380 |
| 1987 New York | AL | 113 | 284 | 69 | 12 | 1 | 4 | (1 | 3) | 95 | 28 | 23 | 30 | 0 | 46 | 4 | 5 | 4 | 0 | 1 | .00 | 8 | .243 | .320 | .335 |
| 1988 Boston | AL | 84 | 264 | 71 | 13 | 1 | 3 | (3 | 0) | 95 | 31 | 27 | 20 | 0 | 32 | 3 | 1 | 1 | 0 | 0 | .00 | 6 | .269 | .326 | .360 |
| 1989 Boston | AL | 102 | 296 | 72 | 16 | 1 | 4 | (2 | 2) | 102 | 28 | 48 | 34 | 1 | 40 | 2 | 4 | 5 | 0 | 0 | .00 | 10 | .243 | .320 | .345 |
| 1990 New York | AL | 49 | 139 | 42 | 6 | 0 | 2 | (1 | 1) | 54 | 12 | 11 | 5 | 0 | 13 | 0 | 1 | 1 | 0 | 0 | .00 | 4 | .302 | .324 | .388 |
| 16 ML YEARS | | 1206 | 3779 | 919 | 173 | 15 | 56 | (28 | 28) | 1290 | 365 | 413 | 287 | 7 | 421 | 22 | 47 | 43 | 4 | 19 | .17 | 109 | .243 | .297 | .341 |

## John Cerutti

**Pitches:** Left **Bats:** Left **Pos:** SP/RP **Ht:** 6' 2" **Wt:** 200 **Born:** 04/28/60 **Age:** 31

| HOW MUCH HE PITCHED | | | | | | | | WHAT HE GAVE UP | | | | | | | | | | | | THE RESULTS | | | | | |
|---|---|---|---|---|---|---|---|---|---|---|---|---|---|---|---|---|---|---|---|---|---|---|---|---|---|
| Year Team | Lg | G | GS | CG | GF | IP | BFP | H | R | ER | HR | SH | SF | HB | TBB | IBB | SO | WP | Bk | W | L | Pct. | ShO | Sv | ERA |
| 1985 Toronto | AL | 4 | 1 | 0 | 1 | 6.2 | 36 | 10 | 7 | 4 | 1 | 0 | 0 | 1 | 4 | 0 | 5 | 2 | 0 | 0 | 2 | .000 | 0 | 0 | 5.40 |

| | | | | | | | | | | | | | | | | | | | | | | | | | |
|---|---|---|---|---|---|---|---|---|---|---|---|---|---|---|---|---|---|---|---|---|---|---|---|---|---|
| 1986 Toronto | AL | 34 | 20 | 2 | 3 | 145.1 | 616 | 150 | 73 | 67 | 25 | 4 | 5 | 1 | 47 | 2 | 89 | 8 | 0 | 9 | 4 | .692 | 1 | 1 | 4.15 |
| 1987 Toronto | AL | 44 | 21 | 2 | 6 | 151.1 | 638 | 144 | 75 | 74 | 30 | 3 | 2 | 1 | 59 | 5 | 92 | 5 | 1 | 11 | 4 | .733 | 0 | 0 | 4.40 |
| 1988 Toronto | AL | 46 | 12 | 0 | 11 | 123.2 | 524 | 120 | 56 | 43 | 12 | 8 | 3 | 3 | 42 | 6 | 65 | 7 | 3 | 6 | 7 | .462 | 0 | 1 | 3.13 |
| 1989 Toronto | AL | 33 | 31 | 3 | 1 | 205.1 | 856 | 214 | 90 | 70 | 19 | 7 | 5 | 6 | 53 | 2 | 69 | 4 | 2 | 11 | 11 | .500 | 1 | 0 | 3.07 |
| 1990 Toronto | AL | 30 | 23 | 0 | 1 | 140 | 609 | 162 | 77 | 74 | 23 | 5 | 5 | 4 | 49 | 3 | 49 | 4 | 1 | 9 | 9 | .500 | 0 | 0 | 4.76 |
| 6 ML YEARS | | 191 | 108 | 7 | 23 | 772.1 | 3279 | 800 | 378 | 332 | 110 | 27 | 20 | 16 | 254 | 18 | 369 | 30 | 7 | 46 | 37 | .554 | 2 | 2 | 3.87 |

## Wes Chamberlain

**Bats:** Right **Throws:** Right **Pos:** LF **Ht:** 6' 2" **Wt:** 210 **Born:** 04/13/66 **Age:** 25

| BATTING | | | | | | | | | | | | | | | | | | | BASERUNNING | | | | PERCENTAGES | | |
|---|---|---|---|---|---|---|---|---|---|---|---|---|---|---|---|---|---|---|---|---|---|---|---|---|---|
| Year Team | Lg | G | AB | H | 2B | 3B | HR | (Hm | Rd) | TB | R | RBI | TBB | IBB | SO | HBP | SH | SF | SB | CS | SB% | GDP | Avg | OBP | SLG |
| 1987 Watertown | A | 66 | 258 | 67 | 13 | 4 | 5 | -- | -- | 103 | 50 | 35 | 25 | 2 | 48 | 1 | 0 | 3 | 22 | 7 | .76 | 6 | .260 | .324 | .399 |
| 1988 Augusta | A | 27 | 107 | 36 | 7 | 2 | 1 | -- | -- | 50 | 22 | 17 | 11 | 0 | 11 | 1 | 2 | 0 | 1 | 3 | .25 | 4 | .336 | .403 | .467 |
| Salem | A | 92 | 365 | 100 | 15 | 1 | 11 | -- | -- | 150 | 66 | 50 | 38 | 2 | 59 | 0 | 0 | 2 | 14 | 4 | .78 | 7 | .274 | .341 | .411 |
| 1989 Harrisburg | AA | 129 | 471 | 144 | 26 | 3 | 21 | -- | -- | 239 | 65 | 87 | 32 | 4 | 82 | 2 | 0 | 7 | 11 | 10 | .52 | 14 | .306 | .348 | .507 |
| 1990 Buffalo | AAA | 123 | 416 | 104 | 24 | 2 | 6 | -- | -- | 150 | 43 | 52 | 34 | 0 | 58 | 8 | 2 | 5 | 14 | 19 | .42 | 19 | .250 | .315 | .361 |
| 1990 Philadelphia | NL | 18 | 46 | 13 | 3 | 0 | 2 | (0 | 2) | 22 | 9 | 4 | 1 | 0 | 9 | 0 | 0 | 0 | 4 | 0 | 1.00 | 0 | .283 | .298 | .478 |

## Norm Charlton

**Pitches:** Left **Bats:** Both **Pos:** RP/SP **Ht:** 6' 3" **Wt:** 195 **Born:** 01/06/63 **Age:** 28

| HOW MUCH HE PITCHED | | | | | | | | WHAT HE GAVE UP | | | | | | | | | | | | THE RESULTS | | | | | |
|---|---|---|---|---|---|---|---|---|---|---|---|---|---|---|---|---|---|---|---|---|---|---|---|---|---|
| Year Team | Lg | G | GS | CG | GF | IP | BFP | H | R | ER | HR | SH | SF | HB | TBB | IBB | SO | WP | Bk | W | L | Pct. | ShO | Sv | ERA |
| 1988 Cincinnati | NL | 10 | 10 | 0 | 0 | 61.1 | 259 | 60 | 27 | 27 | 6 | 1 | 2 | 2 | 20 | 2 | 39 | 3 | 2 | 4 | 5 | .444 | 0 | 0 | 3.96 |
| 1989 Cincinnati | NL | 69 | 0 | 0 | 27 | 95.1 | 393 | 67 | 38 | 31 | 5 | 9 | 2 | 2 | 40 | 7 | 98 | 2 | 4 | 8 | 3 | .727 | 0 | 0 | 2.93 |
| 1990 Cincinnati | NL | 56 | 16 | 1 | 13 | 154.1 | 650 | 131 | 53 | 47 | 10 | 7 | 2 | 4 | 70 | 4 | 117 | 9 | 1 | 12 | 9 | .571 | 1 | 2 | 2.74 |
| 3 ML YEARS | | 135 | 26 | 1 | 40 | 311 | 1302 | 258 | 118 | 105 | 21 | 17 | 6 | 8 | 130 | 13 | 254 | 14 | 7 | 24 | 17 | .585 | 1 | 2 | 3.04 |

## Scott Chiamparino

**Pitches:** Right **Bats:** Left **Pos:** SP **Ht:** 6' 2" **Wt:** 195 **Born:** 08/22/66 **Age:** 24

| HOW MUCH HE PITCHED | | | | | | | | WHAT HE GAVE UP | | | | | | | | | | | | THE RESULTS | | | | | |
|---|---|---|---|---|---|---|---|---|---|---|---|---|---|---|---|---|---|---|---|---|---|---|---|---|---|
| Year Team | Lg | G | GS | CG | GF | IP | BFP | H | R | ER | HR | SH | SF | HB | TBB | IBB | SO | WP | Bk | W | L | Pct. | ShO | Sv | ERA |
| 1987 Medford | A | 13 | 11 | 3 | 1 | 67.2 | 288 | 64 | 29 | 19 | 2 | 1 | 3 | 3 | 20 | 0 | 65 | 6 | 0 | 5 | 4 | .556 | 1 | 0 | 2.53 |
| 1988 Modesto | A | 16 | 16 | 5 | 0 | 106.2 | 456 | 89 | 40 | 32 | 1 | 2 | 2 | 0 | 56 | 0 | 117 | 17 | 4 | 5 | 7 | .417 | 3 | 0 | 2.70 |
| Huntsville | AA | 13 | 13 | 4 | 0 | 84 | 365 | 88 | 36 | 30 | 3 | 1 | 7 | 1 | 26 | 2 | 49 | 5 | 1 | 4 | 5 | .444 | 0 | 0 | 3.21 |
| 1989 Huntsville | AA | 17 | 17 | 2 | 0 | 101.2 | 440 | 109 | 60 | 52 | 8 | 4 | 3 | 4 | 29 | 0 | 87 | 8 | 0 | 8 | 6 | .571 | 1 | 0 | 4.60 |
| 1990 Tacoma | AAA | 26 | 26 | 4 | 0 | 173 | 744 | 174 | 79 | 63 | 10 | 5 | 4 | 5 | 72 | 1 | 110 | 9 | 1 | 13 | 9 | .591 | 2 | 0 | 3.28 |
| 1990 Texas | AL | 6 | 6 | 0 | 0 | 37.2 | 160 | 36 | 14 | 11 | 1 | 1 | 1 | 2 | 12 | 0 | 19 | 5 | 0 | 1 | 2 | .333 | 0 | 0 | 2.63 |

## Steve Chitren

**Pitches:** Right **Bats:** Right **Pos:** RP **Ht:** 6' 0" **Wt:** 180 **Born:** 06/08/67 **Age:** 24

| HOW MUCH HE PITCHED | | | | | | | | WHAT HE GAVE UP | | | | | | | | | | | | THE RESULTS | | | | | |
|---|---|---|---|---|---|---|---|---|---|---|---|---|---|---|---|---|---|---|---|---|---|---|---|---|---|
| Year Team | Lg | G | GS | CG | GF | IP | BFP | H | R | ER | HR | SH | SF | HB | TBB | IBB | SO | WP | Bk | W | L | Pct. | ShO | Sv | ERA |
| 1989 Sou Oregon | A | 2 | 0 | 0 | 1 | 5 | 20 | 3 | 2 | 1 | 0 | 0 | 1 | 0 | 2 | 0 | 3 | 0 | 0 | 0 | 0 | .000 | 0 | 0 | 1.80 |
| Madison | A | 20 | 0 | 0 | 18 | 22.2 | 85 | 13 | 3 | 3 | 1 | 0 | 2 | 2 | 4 | 0 | 17 | 0 | 0 | 2 | 1 | .667 | 0 | 7 | 1.19 |
| 1990 Huntsville | AA | 48 | 0 | 0 | 39 | 53.2 | 218 | 32 | 18 | 10 | 4 | 0 | 0 | 3 | 22 | 1 | 61 | 2 | 0 | 2 | 4 | .333 | 0 | 27 | 1.68 |
| Tacoma | AAA | 1 | 0 | 0 | 1 | 0.2 | 3 | 1 | 0 | 0 | 0 | 0 | 0 | 0 | 0 | 0 | 2 | 0 | 0 | 0 | 0 | .000 | 0 | 0 | 0.00 |
| 1990 Oakland | AL | 8 | 0 | 0 | 4 | 17.2 | 64 | 7 | 2 | 2 | 0 | 0 | 0 | 0 | 4 | 0 | 19 | 2 | 0 | 1 | 0 | 1.000 | 0 | 0 | 1.02 |

## Jim Clancy

**Pitches:** Right **Bats:** Right **Pos:** RP/SP **Ht:** 6' 4" **Wt:** 220 **Born:** 12/18/55 **Age:** 35

| HOW MUCH HE PITCHED | | | | | | | | WHAT HE GAVE UP | | | | | | | | | | | | THE RESULTS | | | | | |
|---|---|---|---|---|---|---|---|---|---|---|---|---|---|---|---|---|---|---|---|---|---|---|---|---|---|
| Year Team | Lg | G | GS | CG | GF | IP | BFP | H | R | ER | HR | SH | SF | HB | TBB | IBB | SO | WP | Bk | W | L | Pct. | ShO | Sv | ERA |
| 1977 Toronto | AL | 13 | 13 | 4 | 0 | 77 | 346 | 80 | 47 | 43 | 7 | 6 | 7 | 0 | 47 | 1 | 44 | 4 | 0 | 4 | 9 | .308 | 1 | 0 | 5.03 |
| 1978 Toronto | AL | 31 | 30 | 7 | 0 | 194 | 846 | 199 | 96 | 88 | 10 | 8 | 10 | 1 | 91 | 1 | 106 | 10 | 0 | 10 | 12 | .455 | 0 | 0 | 4.08 |
| 1979 Toronto | AL | 12 | 11 | 2 | 0 | 64 | 278 | 65 | 44 | 39 | 8 | 3 | 5 | 0 | 31 | 0 | 33 | 2 | 0 | 2 | 7 | .222 | 0 | 0 | 5.48 |
| 1980 Toronto | AL | 34 | 34 | 15 | 0 | 251 | 1075 | 217 | 108 | 92 | 19 | 9 | 4 | 2 | 128 | 4 | 152 | 10 | 0 | 13 | 16 | .448 | 2 | 0 | 3.30 |
| 1981 Toronto | AL | 22 | 22 | 2 | 0 | 125 | 556 | 126 | 77 | 68 | 12 | 2 | 4 | 5 | 64 | 0 | 56 | 12 | 0 | 6 | 12 | .333 | 0 | 0 | 4.90 |
| 1982 Toronto | AL | 40 | 40 | 11 | 0 | 266.2 | 1100 | 251 | 122 | 110 | 26 | 5 | 4 | 2 | 77 | 1 | 139 | 6 | 0 | 16 | 14 | .533 | 3 | 0 | 3.71 |
| 1983 Toronto | AL | 34 | 34 | 11 | 0 | 223 | 955 | 238 | 115 | 97 | 23 | 4 | 12 | 1 | 61 | 0 | 99 | 3 | 0 | 15 | 11 | .577 | 1 | 0 | 3.91 |
| 1984 Toronto | AL | 36 | 36 | 5 | 0 | 219.2 | 966 | 249 | 132 | 125 | 25 | 4 | 4 | 3 | 88 | 2 | 118 | 10 | 0 | 13 | 15 | .464 | 0 | 0 | 5.12 |
| 1985 Toronto | AL | 23 | 23 | 1 | 0 | 128.2 | 527 | 117 | 54 | 54 | 15 | 0 | 5 | 0 | 37 | 0 | 66 | 2 | 0 | 9 | 6 | .600 | 0 | 0 | 3.78 |
| 1986 Toronto | AL | 34 | 34 | 6 | 0 | 219.1 | 913 | 202 | 100 | 96 | 24 | 5 | 9 | 4 | 63 | 0 | 126 | 4 | 0 | 14 | 14 | .500 | 3 | 0 | 3.94 |
| 1987 Toronto | AL | 37 | 37 | 5 | 0 | 241.1 | 1008 | 234 | 103 | 95 | 24 | 5 | 4 | 1 | 80 | 5 | 180 | 12 | 1 | 15 | 11 | .577 | 1 | 0 | 3.54 |
| 1988 Toronto | AL | 36 | 31 | 4 | 5 | 196.1 | 827 | 207 | 106 | 98 | 26 | 7 | 4 | 9 | 47 | 3 | 118 | 7 | 0 | 11 | 13 | .458 | 0 | 1 | 4.49 |
| 1989 Houston | NL | 33 | 26 | 1 | 3 | 147 | 655 | 155 | 100 | 83 | 13 | 9 | 4 | 0 | 66 | 15 | 91 | 6 | 3 | 7 | 14 | .333 | 0 | 0 | 5.08 |
| 1990 Houston | NL | 33 | 10 | 0 | 8 | 76 | 352 | 100 | 58 | 55 | 4 | 1 | 4 | 3 | 33 | 9 | 44 | 3 | 0 | 2 | 8 | .200 | 0 | 1 | 6.51 |
| 14 ML YEARS | | 418 | 381 | 74 | 16 | 2429 | 10404 | 2440 | 1262 | 1143 | 236 | 68 | 80 | 31 | 913 | 41 | 1372 | 91 | 4 | 137 | 162 | .458 | 11 | 2 | 4.24 |

## Bryan Clark

**Pitches:** Left **Bats:** Left **Pos:** RP **Ht:** 6' 2" **Wt:** 200 **Born:** 07/12/56 **Age:** 34

| | | HOW MUCH HE PITCHED | | | | | | WHAT HE GAVE UP | | | | | | | | | | | | THE RESULTS | | | | | |
|---|---|---|---|---|---|---|---|---|---|---|---|---|---|---|---|---|---|---|---|---|---|---|---|---|---|
| Year Team | Lg | G | GS | CG | GF | IP | BFP | H | R | ER | HR | SH | SF | HB | TBB | IBB | SO | WP | Bk | W | L | Pct. | ShO | Sv | ERA |
| 1981 Seattle | AL | 29 | 9 | 1 | 5 | 93 | 421 | 92 | 54 | 45 | 3 | 9 | 4 | 1 | 55 | 4 | 52 | 7 | 3 | 2 | 5 | .286 | 0 | 2 | 4.35 |
| 1982 Seattle | AL | 37 | 5 | 1 | 2 | 114.2 | 491 | 104 | 44 | 35 | 6 | 0 | 2 | 0 | 58 | 2 | 70 | 4 | 0 | 5 | 2 | .714 | 1 | 0 | 2.75 |
| 1983 Seattle | AL | 41 | 17 | 2 | 7 | 162.1 | 697 | 160 | 82 | 71 | 14 | 6 | 3 | 3 | 72 | 6 | 76 | 10 | 0 | 7 | 10 | .412 | 0 | 0 | 3.94 |
| 1984 Toronto | AL | 20 | 3 | 0 | 8 | 45.2 | 221 | 66 | 33 | 30 | 6 | 4 | 1 | 1 | 22 | 2 | 21 | 7 | 0 | 1 | 2 | .333 | 0 | 0 | 5.91 |
| 1985 Cleveland | AL | 31 | 3 | 0 | 10 | 62.2 | 290 | 78 | 47 | 44 | 8 | 3 | 2 | 0 | 34 | 2 | 24 | 5 | 0 | 3 | 4 | .429 | 0 | 2 | 6.32 |
| 1986 Chicago | AL | 5 | 0 | 0 | 2 | 8 | 31 | 8 | 4 | 4 | 0 | 0 | 0 | 0 | 2 | 0 | 5 | 0 | 0 | 0 | 0 | .000 | 0 | 0 | 4.50 |
| 1987 Chicago | AL | 11 | 0 | 0 | 5 | 18.2 | 77 | 19 | 5 | 5 | 1 | 3 | 2 | 0 | 8 | 0 | 8 | 2 | 0 | 0 | 0 | .000 | 0 | 0 | 2.41 |
| 1990 Seattle | AL | 12 | 0 | 0 | 2 | 11 | 48 | 9 | 4 | 4 | 0 | 0 | 0 | 0 | 10 | 0 | 3 | 1 | 0 | 2 | 0 | 1.000 | 0 | 0 | 3.27 |
| 8 ML YEARS | | 186 | 37 | 4 | 41 | 516 | 2276 | 536 | 273 | 238 | 38 | 25 | 14 | 5 | 261 | 16 | 259 | 36 | 3 | 20 | 23 | .465 | 1 | 4 | 4.15 |

## Dave Clark

**Bats:** Left **Throws:** Right **Pos:** LF **Ht:** 6' 2" **Wt:** 200 **Born:** 09/03/62 **Age:** 28

| | | BATTING | | | | | | | | | | | | | | | | | BASERUNNING | | | | PERCENTAGES | | |
|---|---|---|---|---|---|---|---|---|---|---|---|---|---|---|---|---|---|---|---|---|---|---|---|---|---|
| Year Team | Lg | G | AB | H | 2B | 3B | HR | (Hm | Rd) | TB | R | RBI | TBB | IBB | SO | HBP | SH | SF | SB | CS | SB% | GDP | Avg | OBP | SLG |
| 1986 Cleveland | AL | 18 | 58 | 16 | 1 | 0 | 3 | (1 | 2) | 26 | 10 | 9 | 7 | 0 | 11 | 0 | 2 | 1 | 1 | 0 | 1.00 | 1 | .276 | .348 | .448 |
| 1987 Cleveland | AL | 29 | 87 | 18 | 5 | 0 | 3 | (1 | 2) | 32 | 11 | 12 | 2 | 0 | 24 | 0 | 0 | 0 | 1 | 0 | 1.00 | 4 | .207 | .225 | .368 |
| 1988 Cleveland | AL | 63 | 156 | 41 | 4 | 1 | 3 | (2 | 1) | 56 | 11 | 18 | 17 | 2 | 28 | 0 | 0 | 1 | 0 | 2 | .00 | 8 | .263 | .333 | .359 |
| 1989 Cleveland | AL | 102 | 253 | 60 | 12 | 0 | 8 | (4 | 4) | 96 | 21 | 29 | 30 | 5 | 63 | 0 | 1 | 1 | 0 | 2 | .00 | 7 | .237 | .317 | .379 |
| 1990 Chicago | NL | 84 | 171 | 47 | 4 | 2 | 5 | (3 | 2) | 70 | 22 | 20 | 8 | 1 | 40 | 0 | 0 | 2 | 7 | 1 | .88 | 4 | .275 | .304 | .409 |
| 5 ML YEARS | | 296 | 725 | 182 | 26 | 3 | 22 | (11 | 11) | 280 | 75 | 88 | 64 | 8 | 166 | 0 | 3 | 5 | 9 | 5 | .64 | 24 | .251 | .310 | .386 |

## Jack Clark

**Bats:** Right **Throws:** Right **Pos:** 1B **Ht:** 6' 3" **Wt:** 205 **Born:** 11/10/55 **Age:** 35

| | | BATTING | | | | | | | | | | | | | | | | | BASERUNNING | | | | PERCENTAGES | | |
|---|---|---|---|---|---|---|---|---|---|---|---|---|---|---|---|---|---|---|---|---|---|---|---|---|---|
| Year Team | Lg | G | AB | H | 2B | 3B | HR | (Hm | Rd) | TB | R | RBI | TBB | IBB | SO | HBP | SH | SF | SB | CS | SB% | GDP | Avg | OBP | SLG |
| 1975 San Francisco | NL | 8 | 17 | 4 | 0 | 0 | 0 | (0 | 0) | 4 | 3 | 2 | 1 | 0 | 2 | 0 | 0 | 1 | 1 | 0 | 1.00 | 0 | .235 | .263 | .235 |
| 1976 San Francisco | NL | 26 | 102 | 23 | 6 | 2 | 2 | (2 | 0) | 39 | 14 | 10 | 8 | 0 | 18 | 0 | 3 | 2 | 6 | 2 | .75 | 0 | .225 | .277 | .382 |
| 1977 San Francisco | NL | 136 | 413 | 104 | 17 | 4 | 13 | (7 | 6) | 168 | 64 | 51 | 49 | 2 | 73 | 2 | 1 | 3 | 12 | 4 | .75 | 7 | .252 | .332 | .407 |
| 1978 San Francisco | NL | 156 | 592 | 181 | 46 | 8 | 25 | (10 | 15) | 318 | 90 | 98 | 50 | 8 | 72 | 3 | 3 | 9 | 15 | 11 | .58 | 15 | .306 | .358 | .537 |
| 1979 San Francisco | NL | 143 | 527 | 144 | 25 | 2 | 26 | (10 | 16) | 251 | 84 | 86 | 63 | 6 | 95 | 1 | 1 | 6 | 11 | 8 | .58 | 9 | .273 | .348 | .476 |
| 1980 San Francisco | NL | 127 | 437 | 124 | 20 | 8 | 22 | (8 | 14) | 226 | 77 | 82 | 74 | 13 | 52 | 2 | 1 | 10 | 2 | 5 | .29 | 12 | .284 | .382 | .517 |
| 1981 San Francisco | NL | 99 | 385 | 103 | 19 | 2 | 17 | (7 | 10) | 177 | 60 | 53 | 45 | 6 | 45 | 1 | 0 | 6 | 1 | 1 | .50 | 12 | .268 | .341 | .460 |
| 1982 San Francisco | NL | 157 | 563 | 154 | 30 | 3 | 27 | (9 | 18) | 271 | 90 | 103 | 90 | 7 | 91 | 1 | 0 | 5 | 6 | 9 | .40 | 20 | .274 | .372 | .481 |
| 1983 San Francisco | NL | 135 | 492 | 132 | 25 | 0 | 20 | (11 | 9) | 217 | 82 | 66 | 74 | 6 | 79 | 1 | 0 | 7 | 5 | 3 | .63 | 14 | .268 | .361 | .441 |
| 1984 San Francisco | NL | 57 | 203 | 65 | 9 | 1 | 11 | (4 | 7) | 109 | 33 | 44 | 43 | 7 | 29 | 0 | 0 | 3 | 1 | 1 | .50 | 9 | .320 | .434 | .537 |
| 1985 St. Louis | NL | 126 | 442 | 124 | 26 | 3 | 22 | (8 | 14) | 222 | 71 | 87 | 83 | 14 | 88 | 2 | 0 | 5 | 1 | 4 | .20 | 10 | .281 | .393 | .502 |
| 1986 St. Louis | NL | 65 | 232 | 55 | 12 | 2 | 9 | (4 | 5) | 98 | 34 | 23 | 45 | 4 | 61 | 1 | 0 | 1 | 1 | 1 | .50 | 4 | .237 | .362 | .422 |
| 1987 St. Louis | NL | 131 | 419 | 120 | 23 | 1 | 35 | (17 | 18) | 250 | 93 | 106 | 136 | 13 | 139 | 0 | 0 | 3 | 1 | 2 | .33 | 5 | .286 | .459 | .597 |
| 1988 New York | AL | 150 | 496 | 120 | 14 | 0 | 27 | (13 | 14) | 215 | 81 | 93 | 113 | 6 | 141 | 2 | 0 | 5 | 3 | 2 | .60 | 14 | .242 | .381 | .433 |
| 1989 San Diego | NL | 142 | 455 | 110 | 19 | 1 | 26 | (11 | 15) | 209 | 76 | 94 | 132 | 18 | 145 | 1 | 0 | 5 | 6 | 2 | .75 | 10 | .242 | .410 | .459 |
| 1990 San Diego | NL | 115 | 334 | 89 | 12 | 1 | 25 | (16 | 9) | 178 | 59 | 62 | 104 | 11 | 91 | 2 | 0 | 2 | 4 | 3 | .57 | 13 | .266 | .441 | .533 |
| 16 ML YEARS | | 1773 | 6109 | 1652 | 303 | 38 | 307 | (137 | 170) | 2952 | 1011 | 1060 | 1110 | 121 | 1221 | 19 | 9 | 73 | 76 | 58 | .57 | 154 | .270 | .380 | .483 |

## Jerald Clark

**Bats:** Right **Throws:** Right **Pos:** 1B **Ht:** 6' 4" **Wt:** 189 **Born:** 08/10/63 **Age:** 27

| | | BATTING | | | | | | | | | | | | | | | | | BASERUNNING | | | | PERCENTAGES | | |
|---|---|---|---|---|---|---|---|---|---|---|---|---|---|---|---|---|---|---|---|---|---|---|---|---|---|
| Year Team | Lg | G | AB | H | 2B | 3B | HR | (Hm | Rd) | TB | R | RBI | TBB | IBB | SO | HBP | SH | SF | SB | CS | SB% | GDP | Avg | OBP | SLG |
| 1988 San Diego | NL | 6 | 15 | 3 | 1 | 0 | 0 | (0 | 0) | 4 | 0 | 3 | 0 | 0 | 4 | 0 | 0 | 0 | 0 | 0 | .00 | 0 | .200 | .200 | .267 |
| 1989 San Diego | NL | 17 | 41 | 8 | 2 | 0 | 1 | (1 | 0) | 13 | 5 | 7 | 3 | 0 | 9 | 0 | 0 | 0 | 0 | 1 | .00 | 0 | .195 | .250 | .317 |
| 1990 San Diego | NL | 52 | 101 | 27 | 4 | 1 | 5 | (2 | 3) | 48 | 12 | 11 | 5 | 0 | 24 | 0 | 0 | 1 | 0 | 0 | .00 | 3 | .267 | .299 | .475 |
| 3 ML YEARS | | 75 | 157 | 38 | 7 | 1 | 6 | (3 | 3) | 65 | 17 | 21 | 8 | 0 | 37 | 0 | 0 | 1 | 0 | 1 | .00 | 3 | .242 | .277 | .414 |

## Terry Clark

**Pitches:** Right **Bats:** Right **Pos:** SP **Ht:** 6' 2" **Wt:** 196 **Born:** 10/10/60 **Age:** 30

| | | HOW MUCH HE PITCHED | | | | | | WHAT HE GAVE UP | | | | | | | | | | | | THE RESULTS | | | | | |
|---|---|---|---|---|---|---|---|---|---|---|---|---|---|---|---|---|---|---|---|---|---|---|---|---|---|
| Year Team | Lg | G | GS | CG | GF | IP | BFP | H | R | ER | HR | SH | SF | HB | TBB | IBB | SO | WP | Bk | W | L | Pct. | ShO | Sv | ERA |
| 1988 California | AL | 15 | 15 | 2 | 0 | 94 | 410 | 120 | 54 | 53 | 8 | 2 | 5 | 0 | 31 | 6 | 39 | 5 | 2 | 6 | 6 | .500 | 1 | 0 | 5.07 |
| 1989 California | AL | 4 | 2 | 0 | 2 | 11 | 48 | 13 | 8 | 6 | 0 | 2 | 1 | 0 | 3 | 0 | 7 | 2 | 1 | 0 | 2 | .000 | 0 | 0 | 4.91 |
| 1990 Houston | NL | 1 | 1 | 0 | 0 | 4 | 25 | 9 | 7 | 6 | 0 | 1 | 0 | 0 | 3 | 0 | 2 | 0 | 0 | 0 | 0 | .000 | 0 | 0 | 13.50 |
| 3 ML YEARS | | 20 | 18 | 2 | 2 | 109 | 483 | 142 | 69 | 65 | 8 | 5 | 6 | 0 | 37 | 6 | 48 | 7 | 3 | 6 | 8 | .429 | 1 | 0 | 5.37 |

## Will Clark

**Bats:** Left **Throws:** Left **Pos:** 1B **Ht:** 6' 1" **Wt:** 190 **Born:** 03/13/64 **Age:** 27

| BATTING | | | | | | | | | | | | | | | | | | | | BASERUNNING | | | | PERCENTAGES | | |
|---|---|---|---|---|---|---|---|---|---|---|---|---|---|---|---|---|---|---|---|---|---|---|---|---|---|---|
| Year | Team | Lg | G | AB | H | 2B | 3B | HR | (Hm | Rd) | TB | R | RBI | TBB | IBB | SO | HBP | SH | SF | SB | CS | SB% | GDP | Avg | OBP | SLG |
| 1986 | San Francisco | NL | 111 | 408 | 117 | 27 | 2 | 11 | (7 | 4) | 181 | 66 | 41 | 34 | 10 | 76 | 3 | 9 | 4 | 4 | 7 | .36 | 3 | .287 | .343 | .444 |
| 1987 | San Francisco | NL | 150 | 529 | 163 | 29 | 5 | 35 | (22 | 13) | 307 | 89 | 91 | 49 | 11 | 98 | 5 | 3 | 2 | 5 | 17 | .23 | 2 | .308 | .371 | .580 |
| 1988 | San Francisco | NL | 162 | 575 | 162 | 31 | 6 | 29 | (14 | 15) | 292 | 102 | 109 | 100 | 27 | 129 | 4 | 0 | 10 | 9 | 1 | .90 | 9 | .282 | .386 | .508 |
| 1989 | San Francisco | NL | 159 | 588 | 196 | 38 | 9 | 23 | (9 | 14) | 321 | 104 | 111 | 74 | 14 | 103 | 5 | 0 | 8 | 8 | 3 | .73 | 6 | .333 | .407 | .546 |
| 1990 | San Francisco | NL | 154 | 600 | 177 | 25 | 5 | 19 | (8 | 11) | 269 | 91 | 95 | 62 | 9 | 97 | 3 | 0 | 13 | 8 | 2 | .80 | 7 | .295 | .357 | .448 |
| 5 ML YEARS | | | 736 | 2700 | 815 | 150 | 27 | 117 | (60 | 57) | 1370 | 452 | 447 | 319 | 71 | 503 | 20 | 12 | 37 | 34 | 30 | .53 | 27 | .302 | .375 | .507 |

## Stan Clarke

**Pitches:** Left **Bats:** Left **Pos:** RP **Ht:** 6' 1" **Wt:** 180 **Born:** 08/09/60 **Age:** 30

| HOW MUCH HE PITCHED | | | | | | | | | WHAT HE GAVE UP | | | | | | | | | | | | THE RESULTS | | | | | |
|---|---|---|---|---|---|---|---|---|---|---|---|---|---|---|---|---|---|---|---|---|---|---|---|---|---|---|
| Year | Team | Lg | G | GS | CG | GF | IP | BFP | H | R | ER | HR | SH | SF | HB | TBB | IBB | SO | WP | Bk | W | L | Pct. | ShO | Sv | ERA |
| 1983 | Toronto | AL | 10 | 0 | 0 | 5 | 11 | 46 | 10 | 4 | 4 | 2 | 1 | 1 | 0 | 5 | 0 | 7 | 0 | 1 | 1 | 1 | .500 | 0 | 0 | 3.27 |
| 1985 | Toronto | AL | 4 | 0 | 0 | 2 | 4 | 16 | 3 | 2 | 2 | 1 | 0 | 0 | 0 | 2 | 0 | 2 | 0 | 0 | 0 | 0 | .000 | 0 | 0 | 4.50 |
| 1986 | Toronto | AL | 10 | 0 | 0 | 6 | 12.2 | 62 | 18 | 13 | 13 | 4 | 3 | 1 | 0 | 10 | 1 | 9 | 0 | 2 | 0 | 1 | .000 | 0 | 0 | 9.24 |
| 1987 | Seattle | AL | 22 | 0 | 0 | 9 | 23 | 107 | 31 | 14 | 14 | 7 | 1 | 3 | 0 | 10 | 1 | 13 | 3 | 0 | 2 | 2 | .500 | 0 | 0 | 5.48 |
| 1989 | Kansas City | AL | 2 | 2 | 0 | 0 | 7 | 36 | 14 | 12 | 12 | 2 | 0 | 0 | 0 | 4 | 0 | 2 | 1 | 0 | 0 | 2 | .000 | 0 | 0 | 15.43 |
| 1990 | St. Louis | NL | 2 | 0 | 0 | 2 | 3.1 | 12 | 2 | 1 | 1 | 0 | 0 | 0 | 0 | 0 | 0 | 3 | 0 | 0 | 0 | 0 | .000 | 0 | 0 | 2.70 |
| 6 ML YEARS | | | 50 | 2 | 0 | 24 | 61 | 279 | 78 | 46 | 46 | 16 | 5 | 5 | 0 | 31 | 2 | 36 | 4 | 3 | 3 | 6 | .333 | 0 | 0 | 6.79 |

## Martin Clary

**Pitches:** Right **Bats:** Right **Pos:** RP/SP **Ht:** 6' 4" **Wt:** 190 **Born:** 04/03/62 **Age:** 29

| HOW MUCH HE PITCHED | | | | | | | | | WHAT HE GAVE UP | | | | | | | | | | | | THE RESULTS | | | | | |
|---|---|---|---|---|---|---|---|---|---|---|---|---|---|---|---|---|---|---|---|---|---|---|---|---|---|---|
| Year | Team | Lg | G | GS | CG | GF | IP | BFP | H | R | ER | HR | SH | SF | HB | TBB | IBB | SO | WP | Bk | W | L | Pct. | ShO | Sv | ERA |
| 1987 | Atlanta | NL | 7 | 1 | 0 | 2 | 14.2 | 68 | 20 | 13 | 10 | 2 | 1 | 1 | 1 | 4 | 0 | 7 | 0 | 0 | 0 | 1 | .000 | 0 | 0 | 6.14 |
| 1989 | Atlanta | NL | 18 | 17 | 2 | 0 | 108.2 | 452 | 103 | 47 | 38 | 6 | 4 | 3 | 1 | 31 | 3 | 30 | 5 | 0 | 4 | 3 | .571 | 1 | 0 | 3.15 |
| 1990 | Atlanta | NL | 33 | 14 | 0 | 5 | 101.2 | 466 | 128 | 72 | 64 | 9 | 5 | 5 | 1 | 39 | 4 | 44 | 5 | 1 | 1 | 10 | .091 | 0 | 0 | 5.67 |
| 3 ML YEARS | | | 58 | 32 | 2 | 7 | 225 | 986 | 251 | 132 | 112 | 17 | 10 | 9 | 3 | 74 | 7 | 81 | 10 | 1 | 5 | 14 | .263 | 1 | 0 | 4.48 |

## Mark Clear

**Pitches:** Right **Bats:** Right **Pos:** RP **Ht:** 6' 4" **Wt:** 215 **Born:** 05/27/56 **Age:** 35

| HOW MUCH HE PITCHED | | | | | | | | | WHAT HE GAVE UP | | | | | | | | | | | | THE RESULTS | | | | | |
|---|---|---|---|---|---|---|---|---|---|---|---|---|---|---|---|---|---|---|---|---|---|---|---|---|---|---|
| Year | Team | Lg | G | GS | CG | GF | IP | BFP | H | R | ER | HR | SH | SF | HB | TBB | IBB | SO | WP | Bk | W | L | Pct. | ShO | Sv | ERA |
| 1979 | California | AL | 52 | 0 | 0 | 37 | 109 | 481 | 87 | 48 | 44 | 6 | 7 | 5 | 3 | 68 | 5 | 98 | 9 | 1 | 11 | 5 | .688 | 0 | 14 | 3.63 |
| 1980 | California | AL | 58 | 0 | 0 | 41 | 106 | 461 | 82 | 51 | 39 | 2 | 8 | 3 | 5 | 65 | 9 | 105 | 4 | 0 | 11 | 11 | .500 | 0 | 9 | 3.31 |
| 1981 | Boston | AL | 34 | 0 | 0 | 20 | 77 | 346 | 69 | 36 | 35 | 11 | 4 | 0 | 2 | 51 | 2 | 82 | 6 | 0 | 8 | 3 | .727 | 0 | 9 | 4.09 |
| 1982 | Boston | AL | 55 | 0 | 0 | 44 | 105 | 467 | 92 | 39 | 35 | 11 | 7 | 5 | 7 | 61 | 6 | 109 | 1 | 1 | 14 | 9 | .609 | 0 | 14 | 3.00 |
| 1983 | Boston | AL | 48 | 0 | 0 | 33 | 96 | 448 | 101 | 71 | 67 | 10 | 1 | 6 | 3 | 68 | 5 | 81 | 2 | 0 | 4 | 5 | .444 | 0 | 4 | 6.28 |
| 1984 | Boston | AL | 47 | 0 | 0 | 27 | 67 | 318 | 47 | 38 | 30 | 2 | 3 | 6 | 2 | 70 | 3 | 76 | 6 | 0 | 8 | 3 | .727 | 0 | 8 | 4.03 |
| 1985 | Boston | AL | 41 | 0 | 0 | 30 | 55.2 | 259 | 45 | 26 | 23 | 1 | 2 | 2 | 5 | 50 | 10 | 55 | 8 | 0 | 1 | 3 | .250 | 0 | 3 | 3.72 |
| 1986 | Milwaukee | AL | 59 | 0 | 0 | 52 | 73.2 | 306 | 53 | 23 | 18 | 4 | 1 | 4 | 1 | 36 | 2 | 85 | 8 | 2 | 5 | 5 | .500 | 0 | 16 | 2.20 |
| 1987 | Milwaukee | AL | 58 | 1 | 0 | 37 | 78.1 | 360 | 70 | 46 | 39 | 9 | 2 | 5 | 5 | 55 | 3 | 81 | 3 | 0 | 8 | 5 | .615 | 0 | 6 | 4.48 |
| 1988 | Milwaukee | AL | 25 | 0 | 0 | 16 | 29 | 130 | 23 | 12 | 9 | 4 | 0 | 2 | 0 | 21 | 0 | 26 | 1 | 4 | 1 | 0 | 1.000 | 0 | 0 | 2.79 |
| 1990 | California | AL | 4 | 0 | 0 | 1 | 7.2 | 38 | 5 | 7 | 5 | 0 | 0 | 2 | 2 | 9 | 0 | 6 | 1 | 0 | 0 | 0 | .000 | 0 | 0 | 5.87 |
| 11 ML YEARS | | | 481 | 1 | 0 | 338 | 804.1 | 3614 | 674 | 397 | 344 | 60 | 35 | 40 | 35 | 554 | 45 | 804 | 49 | 8 | 71 | 49 | .592 | 0 | 83 | 3.85 |

## Roger Clemens

**Pitches:** Right **Bats:** Right **Pos:** SP **Ht:** 6' 4" **Wt:** 220 **Born:** 08/04/62 **Age:** 28

| HOW MUCH HE PITCHED | | | | | | | | | WHAT HE GAVE UP | | | | | | | | | | | | THE RESULTS | | | | | |
|---|---|---|---|---|---|---|---|---|---|---|---|---|---|---|---|---|---|---|---|---|---|---|---|---|---|---|
| Year | Team | Lg | G | GS | CG | GF | IP | BFP | H | R | ER | HR | SH | SF | HB | TBB | IBB | SO | WP | Bk | W | L | Pct. | ShO | Sv | ERA |
| 1984 | Boston | AL | 21 | 20 | 5 | 0 | 133.1 | 575 | 146 | 67 | 64 | 13 | 2 | 3 | 2 | 29 | 3 | 126 | 4 | 0 | 9 | 4 | .692 | 1 | 0 | 4.32 |
| 1985 | Boston | AL | 15 | 15 | 3 | 0 | 98.1 | 407 | 83 | 38 | 36 | 5 | 1 | 2 | 3 | 37 | 0 | 74 | 1 | 3 | 7 | 5 | .583 | 1 | 0 | 3.29 |
| 1986 | Boston | AL | 33 | 33 | 10 | 0 | 254 | 997 | 179 | 77 | 70 | 21 | 4 | 6 | 4 | 67 | 0 | 238 | 11 | 3 | 24 | 4 | .857 | 1 | 0 | 2.48 |
| 1987 | Boston | AL | 36 | 36 | 18 | 0 | 281.2 | 1157 | 248 | 100 | 93 | 19 | 6 | 4 | 9 | 83 | 4 | 256 | 4 | 3 | 20 | 9 | .690 | 7 | 0 | 2.97 |
| 1988 | Boston | AL | 35 | 35 | 14 | 0 | 264 | 1063 | 217 | 93 | 86 | 17 | 6 | 3 | 6 | 62 | 4 | 291 | 4 | 7 | 18 | 12 | .600 | 8 | 0 | 2.93 |
| 1989 | Boston | AL | 35 | 35 | 8 | 0 | 253.1 | 1044 | 215 | 101 | 88 | 20 | 9 | 5 | 8 | 93 | 5 | 230 | 7 | 0 | 17 | 11 | .607 | 3 | 0 | 3.13 |
| 1990 | Boston | AL | 31 | 31 | 7 | 0 | 228.1 | 920 | 193 | 59 | 49 | 7 | 7 | 5 | 7 | 54 | 3 | 209 | 8 | 0 | 21 | 6 | .778 | 4 | 0 | 1.93 |
| 7 ML YEARS | | | 206 | 205 | 65 | 0 | 1513 | 6163 | 1281 | 535 | 486 | 102 | 35 | 28 | 39 | 425 | 19 | 1424 | 39 | 16 | 116 | 51 | .695 | 25 | 0 | 2.89 |

## Pat Clements

**Pitches:** Left **Bats:** Right **Pos:** RP **Ht:** 6' 0" **Wt:** 180 **Born:** 02/02/62 **Age:** 29

| | | | HOW MUCH HE PITCHED | | | | | | WHAT HE GAVE UP | | | | | | | | | | | | THE RESULTS | | | | | |
|---|---|---|---|---|---|---|---|---|---|---|---|---|---|---|---|---|---|---|---|---|---|---|---|---|---|---|
| Year | Team | Lg | G | GS | CG | GF | IP | BFP | H | R | ER | HR | SH | SF | HB | TBB | IBB | SO | WP | Bk | W | L | Pct. | ShO | Sv | ERA |
| 1985 | 2 ML Teams | | 68 | 0 | 0 | 19 | 96.1 | 400 | 86 | 37 | 37 | 6 | 6 | 1 | 2 | 40 | 5 | 36 | 3 | 0 | 5 | 2 | .714 | 0 | 3 | 3.46 |
| 1986 | Pittsburgh | NL | 65 | 0 | 0 | 19 | 61 | 256 | 53 | 20 | 19 | 1 | 7 | 4 | 2 | 32 | 6 | 31 | 2 | 0 | 0 | 4 | .000 | 0 | 2 | 2.80 |
| 1987 | New York | AL | 55 | 0 | 0 | 20 | 80 | 347 | 91 | 45 | 44 | 4 | 6 | 4 | 3 | 30 | 2 | 36 | 8 | 2 | 3 | 3 | .500 | 0 | 7 | 4.95 |
| 1988 | New York | AL | 6 | 1 | 0 | 1 | 8.1 | 41 | 12 | 8 | 6 | 1 | 0 | 2 | 0 | 4 | 0 | 3 | 1 | 0 | 0 | 0 | .000 | 0 | 0 | 6.48 |
| 1989 | San Diego | NL | 23 | 1 | 0 | 8 | 39 | 167 | 39 | 17 | 17 | 4 | 5 | 1 | 0 | 15 | 5 | 18 | 1 | 0 | 4 | 1 | .800 | 0 | 0 | 3.92 |
| 1990 | San Diego | NL | 9 | 0 | 0 | 3 | 13 | 63 | 20 | 9 | 6 | 1 | 0 | 0 | 0 | 7 | 1 | 6 | 1 | 0 | 0 | 0 | .000 | 0 | 0 | 4.15 |
| 1985 | California | AL | 41 | 0 | 0 | 12 | 62 | 247 | 47 | 23 | 23 | 4 | 4 | 0 | 2 | 25 | 2 | 19 | 1 | 0 | 5 | 0 | 1.000 | 0 | 1 | 3.34 |
| | Pittsburgh | NL | 27 | 0 | 0 | 7 | 34.1 | 153 | 39 | 14 | 14 | 2 | 2 | 1 | 0 | 15 | 3 | 17 | 2 | 0 | 0 | 2 | .000 | 0 | 2 | 3.67 |
| | 6 ML YEARS | | 226 | 2 | 0 | 70 | 297.2 | 1274 | 301 | 136 | 129 | 17 | 24 | 12 | 7 | 128 | 19 | 130 | 16 | 2 | 12 | 10 | .545 | 0 | 12 | 3.90 |

## Pete Coachman

**Bats:** Right **Throws:** Right **Pos:** 3B **Ht:** 5' 9" **Wt:** 175 **Born:** 11/11/61 **Age:** 29

| | | | BATTING | | | | | | | | | | | | | | | | BASERUNNING | | | | PERCENTAGES | | |
|---|---|---|---|---|---|---|---|---|---|---|---|---|---|---|---|---|---|---|---|---|---|---|---|---|---|
| Year | Team | Lg | G | AB | H | 2B | 3B | HR | (Hm | Rd) | TB | R | RBI | TBB | IBB | SO | HBP | SH | SF | SB | CS | SB% | GDP | Avg | OBP | SLG |
| 1984 | Salem | A | 65 | 231 | 60 | 10 | 2 | 0 | -- | -- | 74 | 44 | 21 | 44 | 3 | 28 | 1 | 2 | 3 | 22 | 8 | .73 | 3 | .260 | .376 | .320 |
| 1985 | Quad City | A | 135 | 530 | 140 | 21 | 4 | 1 | -- | -- | 172 | 93 | 38 | 74 | 1 | 77 | 12 | 4 | 2 | 69 | 16 | .81 | 9 | .264 | .366 | .325 |
| 1986 | Palm Sprngs | A | 68 | 274 | 85 | 12 | 4 | 3 | -- | -- | 114 | 74 | 41 | 51 | 0 | 35 | 2 | 2 | 4 | 29 | 7 | .81 | 3 | .310 | .417 | .416 |
| | Midland | AA | 61 | 249 | 87 | 17 | 3 | 5 | -- | -- | 125 | 53 | 35 | 21 | 0 | 34 | 6 | 3 | 1 | 10 | 6 | .63 | 7 | .349 | .412 | .502 |
| 1987 | Edmonton | AAA | 115 | 440 | 136 | 26 | 3 | 4 | -- | -- | 180 | 82 | 43 | 44 | 0 | 33 | 5 | 2 | 2 | 9 | 5 | .64 | 8 | .309 | .377 | .409 |
| 1988 | Edmonton | AAA | 129 | 486 | 128 | 21 | 2 | 6 | -- | -- | 171 | 80 | 61 | 53 | 2 | 63 | 6 | 0 | 4 | 17 | 7 | .71 | 6 | .263 | .341 | .352 |
| 1989 | Edmonton | AAA | 127 | 477 | 136 | 17 | 10 | 2 | -- | -- | 179 | 69 | 43 | 51 | 1 | 62 | 1 | 0 | 5 | 14 | 4 | .78 | 7 | .285 | .352 | .375 |
| 1990 | Edmonton | AAA | 111 | 419 | 122 | 15 | 2 | 5 | -- | -- | 156 | 78 | 51 | 74 | 1 | 49 | 6 | 2 | 5 | 27 | 4 | .87 | 10 | .291 | .401 | .372 |
| 1990 | California | AL | 16 | 45 | 14 | 3 | 0 | 0 | (0 | 0) | 17 | 3 | 5 | 1 | 0 | 7 | 2 | 1 | 0 | 0 | 1 | .00 | 1 | .311 | .354 | .378 |

## Dave Cochrane

**Bats:** Both **Throws:** Right **Pos:** 3B **Ht:** 6' 2" **Wt:** 180 **Born:** 01/31/63 **Age:** 28

| | | | BATTING | | | | | | | | | | | | | | | | BASERUNNING | | | | PERCENTAGES | | |
|---|---|---|---|---|---|---|---|---|---|---|---|---|---|---|---|---|---|---|---|---|---|---|---|---|---|
| Year | Team | Lg | G | AB | H | 2B | 3B | HR | (Hm | Rd) | TB | R | RBI | TBB | IBB | SO | HBP | SH | SF | SB | CS | SB% | GDP | Avg | OBP | SLG |
| 1986 | Chicago | AL | 19 | 62 | 12 | 2 | 0 | 1 | (1 | 0) | 17 | 4 | 2 | 5 | 1 | 22 | 0 | 1 | 0 | 0 | 0 | .00 | 2 | .194 | .254 | .274 |
| 1989 | Seattle | AL | 54 | 102 | 24 | 4 | 1 | 3 | (3 | 0) | 39 | 13 | 7 | 14 | 0 | 27 | 1 | 0 | 0 | 0 | 2 | .00 | 2 | .235 | .333 | .382 |
| 1990 | Seattle | AL | 15 | 20 | 3 | 0 | 0 | 0 | (0 | 0) | 3 | 0 | 0 | 0 | 0 | 8 | 0 | 0 | 0 | 0 | 0 | .00 | 0 | .150 | .150 | .150 |
| | 3 ML YEARS | | 88 | 184 | 39 | 6 | 1 | 4 | (4 | 0) | 59 | 17 | 9 | 19 | 1 | 57 | 1 | 1 | 0 | 0 | 2 | .00 | 4 | .212 | .289 | .321 |

## Chris Codiroli

**Pitches:** Right **Bats:** Right **Pos:** RP **Ht:** 6' 1" **Wt:** 160 **Born:** 03/26/58 **Age:** 33

| | | | HOW MUCH HE PITCHED | | | | | | WHAT HE GAVE UP | | | | | | | | | | | | THE RESULTS | | | | | |
|---|---|---|---|---|---|---|---|---|---|---|---|---|---|---|---|---|---|---|---|---|---|---|---|---|---|---|
| Year | Team | Lg | G | GS | CG | GF | IP | BFP | H | R | ER | HR | SH | SF | HB | TBB | IBB | SO | WP | Bk | W | L | Pct. | ShO | Sv | ERA |
| 1982 | Oakland | AL | 3 | 3 | 0 | 0 | 16.2 | 70 | 16 | 8 | 8 | 1 | 1 | 0 | 0 | 4 | 0 | 5 | 0 | 0 | 1 | 2 | .333 | 0 | 0 | 4.32 |
| 1983 | Oakland | AL | 37 | 31 | 7 | 3 | 205.2 | 884 | 208 | 115 | 102 | 17 | 10 | 6 | 7 | 72 | 4 | 85 | 2 | 2 | 12 | 12 | .500 | 2 | 1 | 4.46 |
| 1984 | Oakland | AL | 28 | 14 | 1 | 5 | 89.1 | 406 | 111 | 67 | 58 | 16 | 2 | 2 | 3 | 34 | 4 | 44 | 2 | 0 | 6 | 4 | .600 | 0 | 1 | 5.84 |
| 1985 | Oakland | AL | 37 | 37 | 4 | 0 | 226 | 975 | 228 | 125 | 112 | 23 | 4 | 8 | 3 | 78 | 2 | 111 | 8 | 1 | 14 | 14 | .500 | 0 | 0 | 4.46 |
| 1986 | Oakland | AL | 16 | 16 | 1 | 0 | 91.2 | 406 | 91 | 54 | 41 | 15 | 1 | 1 | 2 | 38 | 2 | 43 | 4 | 0 | 5 | 8 | .385 | 0 | 0 | 4.03 |
| 1987 | Oakland | AL | 3 | 3 | 0 | 0 | 11.1 | 54 | 12 | 11 | 11 | 1 | 1 | 0 | 1 | 8 | 0 | 4 | 2 | 0 | 0 | 2 | .000 | 0 | 0 | 8.74 |
| 1988 | Cleveland | AL | 14 | 2 | 0 | 4 | 19.1 | 101 | 32 | 22 | 20 | 2 | 2 | 0 | 3 | 10 | 2 | 12 | 2 | 0 | 0 | 4 | .000 | 0 | 1 | 9.31 |
| 1990 | Kansas City | AL | 6 | 2 | 0 | 1 | 10.1 | 61 | 13 | 11 | 11 | 1 | 0 | 0 | 4 | 17 | 1 | 8 | 2 | 0 | 0 | 1 | .000 | 0 | 0 | 9.58 |
| | 8 ML YEARS | | 144 | 108 | 13 | 13 | 670.1 | 2957 | 711 | 413 | 363 | 76 | 21 | 17 | 23 | 261 | 15 | 312 | 22 | 3 | 38 | 47 | .447 | 2 | 3 | 4.87 |

## Kevin Coffman

**Pitches:** Right **Bats:** Right **Pos:** RP **Ht:** 6' 3" **Wt:** 206 **Born:** 01/19/65 **Age:** 26

| | | | HOW MUCH HE PITCHED | | | | | | WHAT HE GAVE UP | | | | | | | | | | | | THE RESULTS | | | | | |
|---|---|---|---|---|---|---|---|---|---|---|---|---|---|---|---|---|---|---|---|---|---|---|---|---|---|---|
| Year | Team | Lg | G | GS | CG | GF | IP | BFP | H | R | ER | HR | SH | SF | HB | TBB | IBB | SO | WP | Bk | W | L | Pct. | ShO | Sv | ERA |
| 1987 | Atlanta | NL | 5 | 5 | 0 | 0 | 25.1 | 126 | 31 | 14 | 13 | 2 | 1 | 1 | 3 | 22 | 0 | 14 | 1 | 1 | 2 | 3 | .400 | 0 | 0 | 4.62 |
| 1988 | Atlanta | NL | 18 | 11 | 0 | 2 | 67 | 311 | 62 | 52 | 43 | 3 | 3 | 3 | 4 | 54 | 2 | 24 | 11 | 1 | 2 | 6 | .250 | 0 | 0 | 5.78 |
| 1990 | Chicago | NL | 8 | 2 | 0 | 0 | 18.1 | 100 | 26 | 24 | 23 | 0 | 2 | 1 | 0 | 19 | 0 | 9 | 4 | 0 | 0 | 2 | .000 | 0 | 0 | 11.29 |
| | 3 ML YEARS | | 31 | 18 | 0 | 2 | 110.2 | 537 | 119 | 90 | 79 | 5 | 6 | 5 | 7 | 95 | 2 | 47 | 16 | 2 | 4 | 11 | .267 | 0 | 0 | 6.42 |

## Alex Cole

**Bats:** Left **Throws:** Left **Pos:** CF **Ht:** 6' 2" **Wt:** 183 **Born:** 08/17/65 **Age:** 25

| Year Team | Lg | G | AB | H | 2B | 3B | HR | (Hm | Rd) | TB | R | RBI | TBB | IBB | SO | HBP | SH | SF | SB | CS | SB% | GDP | Avg | OBP | SLG |
|---|---|---|---|---|---|---|---|---|---|---|---|---|---|---|---|---|---|---|---|---|---|---|---|---|---|
| | BATTING | | | | | | | | | | | | | | | | | | BASERUNNING | | | | PERCENTAGES | | |
| 1985 Johnson Cty | R | 66 | 232 | 61 | 5 | 1 | 1 | -- | -- | 71 | 60 | 13 | 30 | 0 | 27 | 1 | 0 | 1 | 46 | 8 | .85 | 4 | .263 | .348 | .306 |
| 1986 St. Pete | A | 74 | 286 | 98 | 9 | 1 | 0 | -- | -- | 109 | 76 | 26 | 54 | 1 | 37 | 2 | 2 | 1 | 56 | 22 | .72 | 2 | .343 | .449 | .381 |
| Louisville | AAA | 63 | 200 | 50 | 2 | 4 | 1 | -- | -- | 63 | 25 | 16 | 17 | 0 | 30 | 1 | 0 | 1 | 24 | 13 | .65 | 3 | .250 | .311 | .315 |
| 1987 Arkansas | AA | 125 | 477 | 122 | 12 | 4 | 2 | -- | -- | 148 | 68 | 27 | 44 | 5 | 55 | 0 | 5 | 1 | 68 | 29 | .70 | 3 | .256 | .318 | .310 |
| 1988 Louisville | AAA | 120 | 392 | 91 | 7 | 8 | 0 | -- | -- | 114 | 44 | 24 | 42 | 1 | 59 | 1 | 6 | 1 | 40 | 15 | .73 | 2 | .232 | .307 | .291 |
| 1989 St.Pete | A | 8 | 32 | 6 | 0 | 0 | 0 | -- | -- | 6 | 2 | 1 | 3 | 0 | 7 | 0 | 0 | 0 | 4 | 1 | .80 | 1 | .188 | .257 | .188 |
| Louisville | AAA | 127 | 455 | 128 | 5 | 5 | 2 | -- | -- | 149 | 75 | 29 | 71 | 1 | 76 | 1 | 4 | 1 | 47 | 19 | .71 | 3 | .281 | .379 | .327 |
| 1990 Las Vegas | AAA | 90 | 341 | 99 | 7 | 4 | 0 | -- | -- | 114 | 58 | 28 | 47 | 1 | 62 | 1 | 8 | 2 | 32 | 15 | .68 | 4 | .290 | .376 | .334 |
| Colo Sprngs | AAA | 14 | 49 | 21 | 2 | 0 | 0 | -- | -- | 23 | 13 | 3 | 8 | 0 | 7 | 0 | 0 | 0 | 6 | 4 | .60 | 1 | .429 | .509 | .469 |
| 1990 Cleveland | AL | 63 | 227 | 68 | 5 | 4 | 0 | (0 | 0) | 81 | 43 | 13 | 28 | 0 | 38 | 1 | 0 | 0 | 40 | 9 | .82 | 2 | .300 | .379 | .357 |

## Vince Coleman

**Bats:** Both **Throws:** Right **Pos:** LF **Ht:** 6' 0" **Wt:** 170 **Born:** 09/22/61 **Age:** 29

| Year Team | Lg | G | AB | H | 2B | 3B | HR | (Hm | Rd) | TB | R | RBI | TBB | IBB | SO | HBP | SH | SF | SB | CS | SB% | GDP | Avg | OBP | SLG |
|---|---|---|---|---|---|---|---|---|---|---|---|---|---|---|---|---|---|---|---|---|---|---|---|---|---|
| | BATTING | | | | | | | | | | | | | | | | | | BASERUNNING | | | | PERCENTAGES | | |
| 1985 St. Louis | NL | 151 | 636 | 170 | 20 | 10 | 1 | (1 | 0) | 213 | 107 | 40 | 50 | 1 | 115 | 0 | 5 | 1 | 110 | 25 | .81 | 3 | .267 | .320 | .335 |
| 1986 St. Louis | NL | 154 | 600 | 139 | 13 | 8 | 0 | (0 | 0) | 168 | 94 | 29 | 60 | 0 | 98 | 2 | 3 | 5 | 107 | 14 | .88 | 4 | .232 | .301 | .280 |
| 1987 St. Louis | NL | 151 | 623 | 180 | 14 | 10 | 3 | (3 | 0) | 223 | 121 | 43 | 70 | 0 | 126 | 3 | 5 | 1 | 109 | 22 | .83 | 7 | .289 | .363 | .358 |
| 1988 St. Louis | NL | 153 | 616 | 160 | 20 | 10 | 3 | (2 | 1) | 209 | 77 | 38 | 49 | 4 | 111 | 1 | 8 | 5 | 81 | 27 | .75 | 4 | .260 | .313 | .339 |
| 1989 St. Louis | NL | 145 | 563 | 143 | 21 | 9 | 2 | (1 | 1) | 188 | 94 | 28 | 50 | 0 | 90 | 2 | 7 | 2 | 65 | 10 | .87 | 4 | .254 | .316 | .334 |
| 1990 St. Louis | NL | 124 | 497 | 145 | 18 | 9 | 6 | (5 | 1) | 199 | 73 | 39 | 35 | 1 | 88 | 2 | 4 | 1 | 77 | 17 | .82 | 6 | .292 | .340 | .400 |
| 6 ML YEARS | | 878 | 3535 | 937 | 106 | 56 | 15 | (12 | 3) | 1200 | 566 | 217 | 314 | 6 | 628 | 10 | 32 | 15 | 549 | 115 | .83 | 28 | .265 | .326 | .339 |

## Darnell Coles

**Bats:** Right **Throws:** Right **Pos:** RF/3B/DH **Ht:** 6' 1" **Wt:** 185 **Born:** 06/02/62 **Age:** 29

| Year Team | Lg | G | AB | H | 2B | 3B | HR | (Hm | Rd) | TB | R | RBI | TBB | IBB | SO | HBP | SH | SF | SB | CS | SB% | GDP | Avg | OBP | SLG |
|---|---|---|---|---|---|---|---|---|---|---|---|---|---|---|---|---|---|---|---|---|---|---|---|---|---|
| | BATTING | | | | | | | | | | | | | | | | | | BASERUNNING | | | | PERCENTAGES | | |
| 1983 Seattle | AL | 27 | 92 | 26 | 7 | 0 | 1 | (0 | 1) | 36 | 9 | 6 | 7 | 0 | 12 | 0 | 1 | 0 | 0 | 3 | .00 | 8 | .283 | .333 | .391 |
| 1984 Seattle | AL | 48 | 143 | 23 | 3 | 1 | 0 | (0 | 0) | 28 | 15 | 6 | 17 | 0 | 26 | 2 | 3 | 0 | 2 | 1 | .67 | 5 | .161 | .259 | .196 |
| 1985 Seattle | AL | 27 | 59 | 14 | 4 | 0 | 1 | (0 | 1) | 21 | 8 | 5 | 9 | 0 | 17 | 1 | 0 | 2 | 0 | 1 | .00 | 0 | .237 | .338 | .356 |
| 1986 Detroit | AL | 142 | 521 | 142 | 30 | 2 | 20 | (12 | 8) | 236 | 67 | 86 | 45 | 3 | 84 | 6 | 7 | 8 | 6 | 2 | .75 | 8 | .273 | .333 | .453 |
| 1987 2 ML Teams | | 93 | 268 | 54 | 13 | 1 | 10 | (8 | 2) | 99 | 34 | 39 | 34 | 3 | 43 | 3 | 5 | 3 | 1 | 4 | .20 | 4 | .201 | .295 | .369 |
| 1988 2 ML Teams | | 123 | 406 | 106 | 23 | 2 | 15 | (10 | 5) | 178 | 52 | 70 | 37 | 1 | 67 | 7 | 2 | 10 | 4 | 3 | .57 | 8 | .261 | .326 | .438 |
| 1989 Seattle | AL | 146 | 535 | 135 | 21 | 3 | 10 | (4 | 6) | 192 | 54 | 59 | 27 | 1 | 61 | 6 | 2 | 3 | 5 | 4 | .56 | 13 | .252 | .294 | .359 |
| 1990 2 ML Teams | | 89 | 215 | 45 | 7 | 1 | 3 | (3 | 0) | 63 | 22 | 20 | 16 | 2 | 38 | 1 | 1 | 2 | 0 | 4 | .00 | 4 | .209 | .265 | .293 |
| 1987 Detroit | AL | 53 | 149 | 27 | 5 | 1 | 4 | (3 | 1) | 46 | 14 | 15 | 15 | 1 | 23 | 2 | 2 | 1 | 0 | 1 | .00 | 1 | .181 | .263 | .309 |
| Pittsburgh | NL | 40 | 119 | 27 | 8 | 0 | 6 | (5 | 1) | 53 | 20 | 24 | 19 | 2 | 20 | 1 | 3 | 2 | 1 | 3 | .25 | 3 | .227 | .333 | .445 |
| 1988 Pittsburgh | NL | 68 | 211 | 49 | 13 | 1 | 5 | (1 | 4) | 79 | 20 | 36 | 20 | 1 | 41 | 3 | 0 | 7 | 1 | 1 | .50 | 3 | .232 | .299 | .374 |
| Seattle | AL | 55 | 195 | 57 | 10 | 1 | 10 | (9 | 1) | 99 | 32 | 34 | 17 | 0 | 26 | 4 | 2 | 3 | 3 | 2 | .60 | 5 | .292 | .356 | .508 |
| 1990 Seattle | AL | 37 | 107 | 23 | 5 | 1 | 2 | (2 | 0) | 36 | 9 | 16 | 4 | 1 | 17 | 1 | 0 | 1 | 0 | 0 | .00 | 1 | .215 | .248 | .336 |
| Detroit | AL | 52 | 108 | 22 | 2 | 0 | 1 | (1 | 0) | 27 | 13 | 4 | 12 | 1 | 21 | 0 | 1 | 1 | 0 | 4 | .00 | 3 | .204 | .281 | .250 |
| 8 ML YEARS | | 695 | 2239 | 545 | 108 | 10 | 60 | (37 | 23) | 853 | 261 | 291 | 192 | 10 | 348 | 26 | 21 | 28 | 18 | 22 | .45 | 50 | .243 | .307 | .381 |

## Dave Collins

**Bats:** Both **Throws:** Left **Pos:** 1B **Ht:** 5'10" **Wt:** 175 **Born:** 10/20/52 **Age:** 38

| Year Team | Lg | G | AB | H | 2B | 3B | HR | (Hm | Rd) | TB | R | RBI | TBB | IBB | SO | HBP | SH | SF | SB | CS | SB% | GDP | Avg | OBP | SLG |
|---|---|---|---|---|---|---|---|---|---|---|---|---|---|---|---|---|---|---|---|---|---|---|---|---|---|
| | BATTING | | | | | | | | | | | | | | | | | | BASERUNNING | | | | PERCENTAGES | | |
| 1975 California | AL | 93 | 319 | 85 | 13 | 4 | 3 | (1 | 2) | 115 | 41 | 29 | 36 | 1 | 55 | 1 | 3 | 3 | 24 | 10 | .71 | 4 | .266 | .340 | .361 |
| 1976 California | AL | 99 | 365 | 96 | 12 | 1 | 4 | (1 | 3) | 122 | 45 | 28 | 40 | 2 | 55 | 0 | 7 | 1 | 32 | 19 | .63 | 2 | .263 | .335 | .334 |
| 1977 Seattle | AL | 120 | 402 | 96 | 9 | 3 | 5 | (2 | 3) | 126 | 46 | 28 | 33 | 0 | 66 | 3 | 6 | 3 | 25 | 10 | .71 | 2 | .239 | .299 | .313 |
| 1978 Cincinnati | NL | 102 | 102 | 22 | 1 | 0 | 0 | (0 | 0) | 23 | 13 | 7 | 15 | 0 | 18 | 0 | 1 | 2 | 7 | 7 | .50 | 2 | .216 | .311 | .225 |
| 1979 Cincinnati | NL | 122 | 396 | 126 | 16 | 4 | 3 | (0 | 3) | 159 | 59 | 35 | 27 | 2 | 48 | 2 | 3 | 1 | 16 | 9 | .64 | 6 | .318 | .364 | .402 |
| 1980 Cincinnati | NL | 144 | 551 | 167 | 20 | 4 | 3 | (3 | 0) | 204 | 94 | 35 | 53 | 2 | 68 | 3 | 3 | 3 | 79 | 21 | .79 | 5 | .303 | .366 | .370 |
| 1981 Cincinnati | NL | 95 | 360 | 98 | 18 | 6 | 3 | (1 | 2) | 137 | 63 | 23 | 41 | 1 | 41 | 6 | 3 | 2 | 26 | 10 | .72 | 6 | .272 | .355 | .381 |
| 1982 New York | AL | 111 | 348 | 88 | 12 | 3 | 3 | (2 | 1) | 115 | 41 | 25 | 28 | 3 | 49 | 5 | 9 | 3 | 13 | 8 | .62 | 6 | .253 | .315 | .330 |
| 1983 Toronto | AL | 118 | 402 | 109 | 12 | 4 | 1 | (0 | 1) | 132 | 55 | 34 | 43 | 1 | 67 | 2 | 2 | 2 | 31 | 7 | .82 | 7 | .271 | .343 | .328 |
| 1984 Toronto | AL | 128 | 441 | 136 | 24 | 15 | 2 | (2 | 0) | 196 | 59 | 44 | 33 | 0 | 41 | 9 | 6 | 3 | 60 | 14 | .81 | 0 | .308 | .366 | .444 |
| 1985 Oakland | AL | 112 | 379 | 95 | 16 | 4 | 4 | (1 | 3) | 131 | 52 | 29 | 29 | 2 | 37 | 1 | 5 | 4 | 29 | 8 | .78 | 6 | .251 | .303 | .346 |
| 1986 Detroit | AL | 124 | 419 | 113 | 18 | 2 | 1 | (0 | 1) | 138 | 44 | 27 | 44 | 0 | 49 | 2 | 9 | 2 | 27 | 12 | .69 | 9 | .270 | .340 | .329 |
| 1987 Cincinnati | NL | 57 | 85 | 25 | 5 | 0 | 0 | (0 | 0) | 30 | 19 | 5 | 11 | 0 | 12 | 2 | 2 | 0 | 9 | 0 | 1.00 | 1 | .294 | .388 | .353 |

| | | | | | | | | | | | | | | | | | | | | | | | | | | |
|---|---|---|---|---|---|---|---|---|---|---|---|---|---|---|---|---|---|---|---|---|---|---|---|---|---|---|
| 1988 Cincinnati | NL | 99 | 174 | 41 | 6 | 2 | 0 | (0 | 0) | 51 | 12 | 14 | 11 | 0 | 27 | 2 | 0 | 2 | 7 | 2 | .78 | 0 | .236 | .286 | .293 |
| 1989 Cincinnati | NL | 78 | 106 | 25 | 4 | 0 | 0 | (0 | 0) | 29 | 12 | 7 | 10 | 0 | 17 | 0 | 2 | 0 | 3 | 1 | .75 | 2 | .236 | .302 | .274 |
| 1990 St. Louis | NL | 99 | 58 | 13 | 1 | 0 | 0 | (0 | 0) | 14 | 12 | 3 | 13 | 2 | 10 | 0 | 3 | 0 | 7 | 1 | .88 | 1 | .224 | .366 | .241 |
| 16 ML YEARS | | 1701 | 4907 | 1335 | 187 | 52 | 32 | (13 | 19) | 1722 | 667 | 373 | 467 | 16 | 660 | 38 | 64 | 31 | 395 | 139 | .74 | 59 | .272 | .338 | .351 |

## Pat Combs

**Pitches:** Left **Bats:** Left **Pos:** SP **Ht:** 6' 4" **Wt:** 205 **Born:** 10/29/66 **Age:** 24

| | | HOW MUCH HE PITCHED | | | | | | WHAT HE GAVE UP | | | | | | | | | | | | THE RESULTS | | | | | |
|---|---|---|---|---|---|---|---|---|---|---|---|---|---|---|---|---|---|---|---|---|---|---|---|---|---|
| Year Team | Lg | G | GS | CG | GF | IP | BFP | H | R | ER | HR | SH | SF | HB | TBB | IBB | SO | WP | Bk | W | L | Pct. | ShO | Sv | ERA |
| 1989 Clearwater | A | 6 | 6 | 0 | 0 | 41.2 | 165 | 35 | 8 | 6 | 0 | 3 | 0 | 1 | 11 | 0 | 24 | 0 | 1 | 2 | 1 | .667 | 0 | 0 | 1.30 |
| Reading | AA | 19 | 19 | 4 | 0 | 125 | 512 | 104 | 57 | 47 | 16 | 6 | 2 | 4 | 40 | 2 | 77 | 5 | 2 | 8 | 7 | .533 | 0 | 0 | 3.38 |
| Scr Wil-Bar | AAA | 3 | 3 | 2 | 0 | 24.1 | 94 | 15 | 4 | 1 | 0 | 0 | 1 | 0 | 7 | 0 | 20 | 1 | 0 | 3 | 0 | 1.000 | 1 | 0 | 0.37 |
| 1989 Philadelphia | NL | 6 | 6 | 1 | 0 | 38.2 | 153 | 36 | 10 | 9 | 2 | 2 | 0 | 0 | 6 | 1 | 30 | 5 | 0 | 4 | 0 | 1.000 | 1 | 0 | 2.09 |
| 1990 Philadelphia | NL | 32 | 31 | 3 | 0 | 183.1 | 800 | 179 | 90 | 83 | 12 | 7 | 7 | 4 | 86 | 7 | 108 | 9 | 1 | 10 | 10 | .500 | 2 | 0 | 4.07 |
| 2 ML YEARS | | 38 | 37 | 4 | 0 | 222 | 953 | 215 | 100 | 92 | 14 | 9 | 7 | 4 | 92 | 8 | 138 | 14 | 1 | 14 | 10 | .583 | 3 | 0 | 3.73 |

## Keith Comstock

**Pitches:** Left **Bats:** Left **Pos:** RP **Ht:** 6' 0" **Wt:** 174 **Born:** 12/23/55 **Age:** 35

| | | HOW MUCH HE PITCHED | | | | | | WHAT HE GAVE UP | | | | | | | | | | | | THE RESULTS | | | | | |
|---|---|---|---|---|---|---|---|---|---|---|---|---|---|---|---|---|---|---|---|---|---|---|---|---|---|
| Year Team | Lg | G | GS | CG | GF | IP | BFP | H | R | ER | HR | SH | SF | HB | TBB | IBB | SO | WP | Bk | W | L | Pct. | ShO | Sv | ERA |
| 1984 Minnesota | AL | 4 | 0 | 0 | 2 | 6.1 | 28 | 6 | 6 | 6 | 2 | 1 | 0 | 0 | 4 | 0 | 2 | 0 | 0 | 0 | 0 | .000 | 0 | 0 | 8.53 |
| 1987 2 ML Teams | | 41 | 0 | 0 | 15 | 56.2 | 244 | 52 | 30 | 29 | 5 | 3 | 4 | 0 | 31 | 5 | 59 | 6 | 1 | 2 | 1 | .667 | 0 | 1 | 4.61 |
| 1988 San Diego | NL | 7 | 0 | 0 | 3 | 8 | 35 | 8 | 6 | 6 | 1 | 0 | 0 | 0 | 3 | 1 | 9 | 2 | 1 | 0 | 0 | .000 | 0 | 0 | 6.75 |
| 1989 Seattle | AL | 31 | 0 | 0 | 7 | 25.2 | 111 | 26 | 8 | 8 | 2 | 2 | 2 | 0 | 10 | 2 | 22 | 2 | 0 | 1 | 2 | .333 | 0 | 0 | 2.81 |
| 1990 Seattle | AL | 60 | 0 | 0 | 19 | 56 | 228 | 40 | 22 | 18 | 4 | 5 | 3 | 0 | 26 | 5 | 50 | 2 | 1 | 7 | 4 | .636 | 0 | 2 | 2.89 |
| 1987 San Francisco | NL | 15 | 0 | 0 | 3 | 20.2 | 87 | 19 | 8 | 7 | 1 | 1 | 1 | 0 | 10 | 2 | 21 | 3 | 1 | 2 | 0 | 1.000 | 0 | 1 | 3.05 |
| San Diego | NL | 26 | 0 | 0 | 12 | 36 | 157 | 33 | 22 | 22 | 4 | 2 | 3 | 0 | 21 | 3 | 38 | 3 | 0 | 0 | 1 | .000 | 0 | 0 | 5.50 |
| 5 ML YEARS | | 143 | 0 | 0 | 46 | 152.2 | 646 | 132 | 72 | 67 | 14 | 11 | 9 | 0 | 74 | 13 | 142 | 12 | 3 | 10 | 7 | .588 | 0 | 3 | 3.95 |

## David Cone

**Pitches:** Right **Bats:** Left **Pos:** SP **Ht:** 6' 1" **Wt:** 185 **Born:** 01/02/63 **Age:** 28

| | | HOW MUCH HE PITCHED | | | | | | WHAT HE GAVE UP | | | | | | | | | | | | THE RESULTS | | | | | |
|---|---|---|---|---|---|---|---|---|---|---|---|---|---|---|---|---|---|---|---|---|---|---|---|---|---|
| Year Team | Lg | G | GS | CG | GF | IP | BFP | H | R | ER | HR | SH | SF | HB | TBB | IBB | SO | WP | Bk | W | L | Pct. | ShO | Sv | ERA |
| 1986 Kansas City | AL | 11 | 0 | 0 | 5 | 22.2 | 108 | 29 | 14 | 14 | 2 | 0 | 0 | 1 | 13 | 1 | 21 | 3 | 0 | 0 | 0 | .000 | 0 | 0 | 5.56 |
| 1987 New York | NL | 21 | 13 | 1 | 3 | 99.1 | 420 | 87 | 46 | 41 | 11 | 4 | 3 | 5 | 44 | 1 | 68 | 2 | 4 | 5 | 6 | .455 | 0 | 1 | 3.71 |
| 1988 New York | NL | 35 | 28 | 8 | 0 | 231.1 | 936 | 178 | 67 | 57 | 10 | 11 | 5 | 4 | 80 | 7 | 213 | 10 | 10 | 20 | 3 | .870 | 4 | 0 | 2.22 |
| 1989 New York | NL | 34 | 33 | 7 | 0 | 219.2 | 910 | 183 | 92 | 86 | 20 | 6 | 4 | 4 | 74 | 6 | 190 | 14 | 4 | 14 | 8 | .636 | 2 | 0 | 3.52 |
| 1990 New York | NL | 31 | 30 | 6 | 1 | 211.2 | 860 | 177 | 84 | 76 | 21 | 4 | 6 | 1 | 65 | 1 | 233 | 10 | 4 | 14 | 10 | .583 | 2 | 0 | 3.23 |
| 5 ML YEARS | | 132 | 104 | 22 | 9 | 784.2 | 3234 | 654 | 303 | 274 | 64 | 25 | 18 | 15 | 276 | 16 | 725 | 39 | 22 | 53 | 27 | .663 | 8 | 1 | 3.14 |

## Jeff Conine

**Bats:** Right **Throws:** Right **Pos:** 1B **Ht:** 6' 1" **Wt:** 205 **Born:** 06/27/66 **Age:** 25

| | | BATTING | | | | | | | | | | | | | | | | | BASERUNNING | | | | PERCENTAGES | | |
|---|---|---|---|---|---|---|---|---|---|---|---|---|---|---|---|---|---|---|---|---|---|---|---|---|---|
| Year Team | Lg | G | AB | H | 2B | 3B | HR | (Hm | Rd) | TB | R | RBI | TBB | IBB | SO | HBP | SH | SF | SB | CS | SB% | GDP | Avg | OBP | SLG |
| 1988 Baseball Cy | A | 118 | 415 | 113 | 23 | 9 | 10 | -- | -- | 184 | 63 | 59 | 46 | 1 | 77 | 0 | 5 | 4 | 26 | 12 | .68 | 6 | .272 | .342 | .443 |
| 1989 Baseball Cy | A | 113 | 425 | 116 | 12 | 7 | 14 | -- | -- | 184 | 68 | 60 | 40 | 2 | 91 | 3 | 0 | 3 | 32 | 13 | .71 | 14 | .273 | .338 | .433 |
| 1990 Memphis | AA | 137 | 487 | 156 | 37 | 8 | 15 | -- | -- | 254 | 89 | 95 | 94 | 6 | 88 | 1 | 0 | 8 | 21 | 6 | .78 | 10 | .320 | .425 | .522 |
| 1990 Kansas City | AL | 9 | 20 | 5 | 2 | 0 | 0 | (0 | 0) | 7 | 3 | 2 | 2 | 0 | 5 | 0 | 0 | 0 | 0 | 0 | .00 | 1 | .250 | .318 | .350 |

## Dennis Cook

**Pitches:** Left **Bats:** Left **Pos:** RP/SP **Ht:** 6' 3" **Wt:** 185 **Born:** 10/04/62 **Age:** 28

| | | HOW MUCH HE PITCHED | | | | | | WHAT HE GAVE UP | | | | | | | | | | | | THE RESULTS | | | | | |
|---|---|---|---|---|---|---|---|---|---|---|---|---|---|---|---|---|---|---|---|---|---|---|---|---|---|
| Year Team | Lg | G | GS | CG | GF | IP | BFP | H | R | ER | HR | SH | SF | HB | TBB | IBB | SO | WP | Bk | W | L | Pct. | ShO | Sv | ERA |
| 1988 San Francisco | NL | 4 | 4 | 1 | 0 | 22 | 86 | 9 | 8 | 7 | 1 | 0 | 3 | 0 | 11 | 1 | 13 | 1 | 0 | 2 | 1 | .667 | 1 | 0 | 2.86 |
| 1989 2 ML Teams | | 23 | 18 | 2 | 1 | 121 | 499 | 110 | 59 | 50 | 18 | 5 | 2 | 2 | 38 | 6 | 67 | 4 | 2 | 7 | 8 | .467 | 1 | 0 | 3.72 |
| 1990 2 ML Teams | | 47 | 16 | 2 | 4 | 156 | 663 | 155 | 74 | 68 | 20 | 7 | 7 | 2 | 56 | 9 | 64 | 6 | 3 | 9 | 4 | .692 | 1 | 1 | 3.92 |
| 1989 San Francisco | NL | 2 | 2 | 1 | 0 | 15 | 58 | 13 | 3 | 3 | 1 | 0 | 0 | 0 | 5 | 0 | 9 | 1 | 0 | 1 | 0 | 1.000 | 0 | 0 | 1.80 |
| Philadelphia | NL | 21 | 16 | 1 | 1 | 106 | 441 | 97 | 56 | 47 | 17 | 5 | 2 | 2 | 33 | 6 | 58 | 3 | 2 | 6 | 8 | .429 | 1 | 0 | 3.99 |
| 1990 Philadelphia | NL | 42 | 13 | 2 | 4 | 141.2 | 594 | 132 | 61 | 56 | 13 | 5 | 5 | 2 | 54 | 9 | 58 | 6 | 3 | 8 | 3 | .727 | 1 | 1 | 3.56 |
| Los Angeles | NL | 5 | 3 | 0 | 0 | 14.1 | 69 | 23 | 13 | 12 | 7 | 2 | 2 | 0 | 2 | 0 | 6 | 0 | 0 | 1 | 1 | .500 | 0 | 0 | 7.53 |
| 3 ML YEARS | | 74 | 38 | 5 | 5 | 299 | 1248 | 274 | 141 | 125 | 39 | 12 | 12 | 4 | 105 | 16 | 144 | 11 | 5 | 18 | 13 | .581 | 3 | 1 | 3.76 |

## Scott Coolbaugh

**Bats:** Right **Throws:** Right **Pos:** 3B **Ht:** 5'11" **Wt:** 185 **Born:** 06/13/66 **Age:** 25

| | | BATTING | | | | | | | | | | | | | | | | | BASERUNNING | | | | PERCENTAGES | | |
|---|---|---|---|---|---|---|---|---|---|---|---|---|---|---|---|---|---|---|---|---|---|---|---|---|---|
| Year Team | Lg | G | AB | H | 2B | 3B | HR | (Hm | Rd) | TB | R | RBI | TBB | IBB | SO | HBP | SH | SF | SB | CS | SB% | GDP | Avg | OBP | SLG |
| 1987 Charlotte | A | 66 | 233 | 64 | 21 | 0 | 2 | -- | -- | 91 | 27 | 20 | 24 | 1 | 56 | 0 | 1 | 2 | 0 | 1 | .00 | 5 | .275 | .340 | .391 |

| | | | | | | | | | | | | | | | | | | | | | | | | | |
|---|---|---|---|---|---|---|---|---|---|---|---|---|---|---|---|---|---|---|---|---|---|---|---|---|---|
| 1988 Tulsa | AA | 136 | 470 | 127 | 15 | 4 | 13 | -- | -- | 189 | 52 | 75 | 76 | 4 | 79 | 1 | 2 | 8 | 2 | 4 | .33 | 14 | .270 | .368 | .402 |
| 1989 Okla City | AAA | 144 | 527 | 137 | 28 | 0 | 18 | -- | -- | 219 | 66 | 74 | 57 | 5 | 93 | 2 | 2 | 3 | 1 | 2 | .33 | 13 | .260 | .333 | .416 |
| 1990 Okla City | AAA | 76 | 293 | 66 | 17 | 2 | 6 | -- | -- | 105 | 39 | 30 | 27 | 2 | 62 | 1 | 0 | 3 | 0 | 1 | .00 | 6 | .225 | .290 | .358 |
| 1989 Texas | AL | 25 | 51 | 14 | 1 | 0 | 2 | (1 | 1) | 21 | 7 | 7 | 4 | 0 | 12 | 0 | 1 | 1 | 0 | 0 | .00 | 2 | .275 | .321 | .412 |
| 1990 Texas | AL | 67 | 180 | 36 | 6 | 0 | 2 | (1 | 1) | 48 | 21 | 13 | 15 | 0 | 47 | 1 | 4 | 1 | 1 | 0 | 1.00 | 2 | .200 | .264 | .267 |
| 2 ML YEARS | | 92 | 231 | 50 | 7 | 0 | 4 | (2 | 2) | 69 | 28 | 20 | 19 | 0 | 59 | 1 | 5 | 2 | 1 | 0 | 1.00 | 4 | .216 | .277 | .299 |

## Scott Cooper

**Bats:** Left **Throws:** Right **Pos:** PH **Ht:** 6' 3" **Wt:** 200 **Born:** 10/13/67 **Age:** 23

| BATTING | | | | | | | | | | | | | | | | | | | BASERUNNING | | | | PERCENTAGES | | |
|---|---|---|---|---|---|---|---|---|---|---|---|---|---|---|---|---|---|---|---|---|---|---|---|---|---|
| Year Team | Lg | G | AB | H | 2B | 3B | HR | (Hm | Rd) | TB | R | RBI | TBB | IBB | SO | HBP | SH | SF | SB | CS | SB% | GDP | Avg | OBP | SLG |
| 1986 Elmira | A | 51 | 191 | 55 | 9 | 0 | 9 | -- | -- | 91 | 23 | 43 | 19 | 2 | 32 | 0 | 1 | 4 | 1 | 4 | .20 | 6 | .288 | .346 | .476 |
| 1987 Greensboro | A | 119 | 370 | 93 | 21 | 2 | 15 | -- | -- | 163 | 52 | 63 | 58 | 7 | 69 | 2 | 0 | 6 | 1 | 0 | 1.00 | 5 | .251 | .351 | .441 |
| 1988 Lynchburg | A | 130 | 497 | 148 | 45 | 7 | 9 | -- | -- | 234 | 90 | 73 | 58 | 0 | 74 | 2 | 2 | 4 | 0 | 0 | .00 | 11 | .298 | .371 | .471 |
| 1989 New Britain | AA | 124 | 421 | 104 | 24 | 2 | 7 | -- | -- | 153 | 50 | 39 | 55 | 2 | 84 | 6 | 5 | 5 | 1 | 1 | .50 | 5 | .247 | .339 | .363 |
| 1990 Pawtucket | AAA | 124 | 433 | 115 | 17 | 1 | 12 | -- | -- | 170 | 56 | 44 | 39 | 3 | 75 | 7 | 4 | 3 | 2 | 0 | 1.00 | 9 | .266 | .334 | .393 |
| 1990 Boston | AL | 2 | 1 | 0 | 0 | 0 | 0 | (0 | 0) | 0 | 0 | 0 | 0 | 0 | 1 | 0 | 0 | 0 | 0 | 0 | .00 | 0 | .000 | .000 | .000 |

## Joey Cora

**Bats:** Both **Throws:** Right **Pos:** SS/2B **Ht:** 5' 8" **Wt:** 150 **Born:** 05/14/65 **Age:** 26

| BATTING | | | | | | | | | | | | | | | | | | | BASERUNNING | | | | PERCENTAGES | | |
|---|---|---|---|---|---|---|---|---|---|---|---|---|---|---|---|---|---|---|---|---|---|---|---|---|---|
| Year Team | Lg | G | AB | H | 2B | 3B | HR | (Hm | Rd) | TB | R | RBI | TBB | IBB | SO | HBP | SH | SF | SB | CS | SB% | GDP | Avg | OBP | SLG |
| 1987 San Diego | NL | 77 | 241 | 57 | 7 | 2 | 0 | (0 | 0) | 68 | 23 | 13 | 28 | 1 | 26 | 1 | 5 | 1 | 15 | 11 | .58 | 4 | .237 | .317 | .282 |
| 1989 San Diego | NL | 12 | 19 | 6 | 1 | 0 | 0 | (0 | 0) | 7 | 5 | 1 | 1 | 0 | 0 | 0 | 0 | 0 | 1 | 0 | 1.00 | 0 | .316 | .350 | .368 |
| 1990 San Diego | NL | 51 | 100 | 27 | 3 | 0 | 0 | (0 | 0) | 30 | 12 | 2 | 6 | 1 | 9 | 0 | 0 | 0 | 8 | 3 | .73 | 1 | .270 | .311 | .300 |
| 3 ML YEARS | | 140 | 360 | 90 | 11 | 2 | 0 | (0 | 0) | 105 | 40 | 16 | 35 | 2 | 35 | 1 | 5 | 1 | 24 | 14 | .63 | 5 | .250 | .317 | .292 |

## Sherman Corbett

**Pitches:** Left **Bats:** Left **Pos:** RP **Ht:** 6' 4" **Wt:** 203 **Born:** 11/03/62 **Age:** 28

| HOW MUCH HE PITCHED | | | | | | | | WHAT HE GAVE UP | | | | | | | | | | | | THE RESULTS | | | | | |
|---|---|---|---|---|---|---|---|---|---|---|---|---|---|---|---|---|---|---|---|---|---|---|---|---|---|
| Year Team | Lg | G | GS | CG | GF | IP | BFP | H | R | ER | HR | SH | SF | HB | TBB | IBB | SO | WP | Bk | W | L | Pct. | ShO | Sv | ERA |
| 1988 California | AL | 34 | 0 | 0 | 7 | 45.2 | 204 | 47 | 23 | 21 | 2 | 4 | 5 | 0 | 23 | 3 | 28 | 2 | 0 | 2 | 1 | .667 | 0 | 1 | 4.14 |
| 1989 California | AL | 4 | 0 | 0 | 2 | 5.1 | 20 | 3 | 2 | 2 | 1 | 0 | 0 | 0 | 1 | 0 | 3 | 0 | 0 | 0 | 0 | .000 | 0 | 0 | 3.38 |
| 1990 California | AL | 4 | 0 | 0 | 2 | 5 | 26 | 8 | 5 | 5 | 0 | 0 | 1 | 0 | 3 | 0 | 2 | 0 | 0 | 0 | 0 | .000 | 0 | 0 | 9.00 |
| 3 ML YEARS | | 42 | 0 | 0 | 11 | 56 | 250 | 58 | 30 | 28 | 3 | 4 | 6 | 0 | 27 | 3 | 33 | 2 | 0 | 2 | 1 | .667 | 0 | 1 | 4.50 |

## John Costello

**Pitches:** Right **Bats:** Right **Pos:** RP **Ht:** 6' 1" **Wt:** 180 **Born:** 12/24/60 **Age:** 30

| HOW MUCH HE PITCHED | | | | | | | | WHAT HE GAVE UP | | | | | | | | | | | | THE RESULTS | | | | | |
|---|---|---|---|---|---|---|---|---|---|---|---|---|---|---|---|---|---|---|---|---|---|---|---|---|---|
| Year Team | Lg | G | GS | CG | GF | IP | BFP | H | R | ER | HR | SH | SF | HB | TBB | IBB | SO | WP | Bk | W | L | Pct. | ShO | Sv | ERA |
| 1988 St. Louis | NL | 36 | 0 | 0 | 15 | 49.2 | 214 | 44 | 15 | 10 | 3 | 1 | 1 | 0 | 25 | 4 | 38 | 0 | 1 | 5 | 2 | .714 | 0 | 1 | 1.81 |
| 1989 St. Louis | NL | 48 | 0 | 0 | 11 | 62.1 | 252 | 48 | 24 | 23 | 5 | 0 | 5 | 2 | 20 | 7 | 40 | 0 | 0 | 5 | 4 | .556 | 0 | 3 | 3.32 |
| 1990 2 ML Teams | | 8 | 0 | 0 | 4 | 10.2 | 47 | 12 | 8 | 7 | 3 | 0 | 1 | 1 | 2 | 1 | 2 | 0 | 1 | 0 | 0 | .000 | 0 | 0 | 5.91 |
| 1990 St. Louis | NL | 4 | 0 | 0 | 3 | 4.1 | 21 | 7 | 3 | 3 | 1 | 0 | 0 | 1 | 1 | 1 | 1 | 0 | 0 | 0 | 0 | .000 | 0 | 0 | 6.23 |
| Montreal | NL | 4 | 0 | 0 | 1 | 6.1 | 26 | 5 | 5 | 4 | 2 | 0 | 1 | 0 | 1 | 0 | 1 | 0 | 1 | 0 | 0 | .000 | 0 | 0 | 5.68 |
| 3 ML YEARS | | 92 | 0 | 0 | 30 | 122.2 | 513 | 104 | 47 | 40 | 11 | 1 | 7 | 3 | 47 | 12 | 80 | 0 | 2 | 10 | 6 | .625 | 0 | 4 | 2.93 |

## Henry Cotto

**Bats:** Right **Throws:** Right **Pos:** RF/LF/CF **Ht:** 6' 2" **Wt:** 180 **Born:** 01/05/61 **Age:** 30

| BATTING | | | | | | | | | | | | | | | | | | | BASERUNNING | | | | PERCENTAGES | | |
|---|---|---|---|---|---|---|---|---|---|---|---|---|---|---|---|---|---|---|---|---|---|---|---|---|---|
| Year Team | Lg | G | AB | H | 2B | 3B | HR | (Hm | Rd) | TB | R | RBI | TBB | IBB | SO | HBP | SH | SF | SB | CS | SB% | GDP | Avg | OBP | SLG |
| 1984 Chicago | NL | 105 | 146 | 40 | 5 | 0 | 0 | (0 | 0) | 45 | 24 | 8 | 10 | 2 | 23 | 1 | 3 | 0 | 9 | 3 | .75 | 1 | .274 | .325 | .308 |
| 1985 New York | AL | 34 | 56 | 17 | 1 | 0 | 1 | (0 | 1) | 21 | 4 | 6 | 3 | 0 | 12 | 0 | 1 | 0 | 1 | 1 | .50 | 1 | .304 | .339 | .375 |
| 1986 New York | AL | 35 | 80 | 17 | 3 | 0 | 1 | (0 | 1) | 23 | 11 | 6 | 2 | 0 | 17 | 0 | 0 | 1 | 3 | 0 | 1.00 | 3 | .213 | .229 | .288 |
| 1987 New York | AL | 68 | 149 | 35 | 10 | 0 | 5 | (5 | 0) | 60 | 21 | 20 | 6 | 0 | 35 | 1 | 0 | 0 | 4 | 2 | .67 | 7 | .235 | .269 | .403 |
| 1988 Seattle | AL | 133 | 386 | 100 | 18 | 1 | 8 | (5 | 3) | 144 | 50 | 33 | 23 | 0 | 53 | 2 | 4 | 3 | 27 | 3 | .90 | 8 | .259 | .302 | .373 |
| 1989 Seattle | AL | 100 | 295 | 78 | 11 | 2 | 9 | (5 | 4) | 120 | 44 | 33 | 12 | 3 | 44 | 3 | 0 | 0 | 10 | 4 | .71 | 4 | .264 | .300 | .407 |
| 1990 Seattle | AL | 127 | 355 | 92 | 14 | 3 | 4 | (2 | 2) | 124 | 40 | 33 | 22 | 2 | 52 | 4 | 6 | 3 | 21 | 3 | .88 | 13 | .259 | .307 | .349 |
| 7 ML YEARS | | 602 | 1467 | 379 | 62 | 6 | 28 | (17 | 11) | 537 | 194 | 139 | 78 | 7 | 236 | 11 | 14 | 7 | 75 | 16 | .82 | 37 | .258 | .299 | .366 |

## Steve Crawford

**Pitches:** Right **Bats:** Right **Pos:** RP **Ht:** 6' 5" **Wt:** 225 **Born:** 04/29/58 **Age:** 33

| HOW MUCH HE PITCHED | | | | | | | | WHAT HE GAVE UP | | | | | | | | | | | | THE RESULTS | | | | | |
|---|---|---|---|---|---|---|---|---|---|---|---|---|---|---|---|---|---|---|---|---|---|---|---|---|---|
| Year Team | Lg | G | GS | CG | GF | IP | BFP | H | R | ER | HR | SH | SF | HB | TBB | IBB | SO | WP | Bk | W | L | Pct. | ShO | Sv | ERA |
| 1980 Boston | AL | 6 | 4 | 2 | 1 | 32 | 142 | 41 | 14 | 13 | 3 | 0 | 0 | 0 | 8 | 2 | 10 | 0 | 0 | 2 | 0 | 1.000 | 0 | 0 | 3.66 |
| 1981 Boston | AL | 14 | 11 | 0 | 2 | 58 | 257 | 69 | 38 | 32 | 10 | 3 | 4 | 3 | 18 | 0 | 29 | 2 | 0 | 0 | 5 | .000 | 0 | 0 | 4.97 |
| 1982 Boston | AL | 5 | 0 | 0 | 4 | 9 | 41 | 14 | 3 | 2 | 0 | 0 | 0 | 0 | 0 | 0 | 2 | 0 | 0 | 1 | 0 | 1.000 | 0 | 0 | 2.00 |

| Year Team | Lg | G | GS | CG | GF | IP | BFP | H | R | ER | HR | SH | SF | HB | TBB | IBB | SO | WP | Bk | W | L | Pct. | ShO | Sv | ERA |
|---|---|---|---|---|---|---|---|---|---|---|---|---|---|---|---|---|---|---|---|---|---|---|---|---|---|
| 1984 Boston | AL | 35 | 0 | 0 | 19 | 62 | 268 | 69 | 31 | 23 | 6 | 1 | 4 | 1 | 21 | 5 | 21 | 2 | 0 | 5 | 0 | 1.000 | 0 | 1 | 3.34 |
| 1985 Boston | AL | 44 | 1 | 0 | 26 | 91 | 394 | 103 | 47 | 38 | 5 | 6 | 3 | 0 | 28 | 8 | 58 | 5 | 0 | 6 | 5 | .545 | 0 | 12 | 3.76 |
| 1986 Boston | AL | 40 | 0 | 0 | 15 | 57.1 | 248 | 69 | 29 | 25 | 5 | 3 | 2 | 0 | 19 | 7 | 32 | 2 | 0 | 0 | 2 | .000 | 0 | 4 | 3.92 |
| 1987 Boston | AL | 29 | 0 | 0 | 7 | 72.2 | 324 | 91 | 48 | 43 | 13 | 0 | 0 | 2 | 32 | 2 | 43 | 2 | 0 | 5 | 4 | .556 | 0 | 0 | 5.33 |
| 1989 Kansas City | AL | 25 | 0 | 0 | 5 | 54 | 224 | 48 | 19 | 17 | 2 | 3 | 1 | 3 | 19 | 3 | 33 | 0 | 0 | 3 | 1 | .750 | 0 | 0 | 2.83 |
| 1990 Kansas City | AL | 46 | 0 | 0 | 14 | 80 | 341 | 79 | 38 | 37 | 7 | 2 | 2 | 3 | 23 | 3 | 54 | 1 | 0 | 5 | 4 | .556 | 0 | 1 | 4.16 |
| 9 ML YEARS | | 244 | 16 | 2 | 93 | 516 | 2239 | 583 | 267 | 230 | 51 | 18 | 16 | 12 | 168 | 30 | 282 | 14 | 0 | 27 | 21 | .563 | 0 | 18 | 4.01 |

## Tim Crews

**Pitches:** Right **Bats:** Right **Pos:** RP **Ht:** 6' 0" **Wt:** 190 **Born:** 04/03/61 **Age:** 30

| | | HOW MUCH HE PITCHED | | | | | | WHAT HE GAVE UP | | | | | | | | | | | | THE RESULTS | | | | | |
|---|---|---|---|---|---|---|---|---|---|---|---|---|---|---|---|---|---|---|---|---|---|---|---|---|---|
| Year Team | Lg | G | GS | CG | GF | IP | BFP | H | R | ER | HR | SH | SF | HB | TBB | IBB | SO | WP | Bk | W | L | Pct. | ShO | Sv | ERA |
| 1987 Los Angeles | NL | 20 | 0 | 0 | 7 | 29 | 124 | 30 | 9 | 8 | 2 | 1 | 1 | 2 | 8 | 1 | 20 | 0 | 0 | 1 | 1 | .500 | 0 | 3 | 2.48 |
| 1988 Los Angeles | NL | 42 | 0 | 0 | 12 | 71.2 | 301 | 77 | 29 | 25 | 3 | 3 | 5 | 0 | 16 | 7 | 45 | 1 | 0 | 4 | 0 | 1.000 | 0 | 0 | 3.14 |
| 1989 Los Angeles | NL | 44 | 0 | 0 | 16 | 61.2 | 275 | 69 | 27 | 22 | 7 | 7 | 0 | 2 | 23 | 9 | 56 | 1 | 0 | 0 | 1 | .000 | 0 | 1 | 3.21 |
| 1990 Los Angeles | NL | 66 | 2 | 0 | 18 | 107.1 | 440 | 98 | 40 | 33 | 9 | 1 | 3 | 1 | 24 | 6 | 76 | 2 | 0 | 4 | 5 | .444 | 0 | 5 | 2.77 |
| 4 ML YEARS | | 172 | 2 | 0 | 53 | 269.2 | 1140 | 274 | 105 | 88 | 21 | 12 | 9 | 5 | 71 | 23 | 197 | 4 | 0 | 9 | 7 | .563 | 0 | 9 | 2.94 |

## Chuck Crim

**Pitches:** Right **Bats:** Right **Pos:** RP **Ht:** 6' 0" **Wt:** 185 **Born:** 07/23/61 **Age:** 29

| | | HOW MUCH HE PITCHED | | | | | | WHAT HE GAVE UP | | | | | | | | | | | | THE RESULTS | | | | | |
|---|---|---|---|---|---|---|---|---|---|---|---|---|---|---|---|---|---|---|---|---|---|---|---|---|---|
| Year Team | Lg | G | GS | CG | GF | IP | BFP | H | R | ER | HR | SH | SF | HB | TBB | IBB | SO | WP | Bk | W | L | Pct. | ShO | Sv | ERA |
| 1987 Milwaukee | AL | 53 | 5 | 0 | 18 | 130 | 549 | 133 | 60 | 53 | 15 | 6 | 1 | 3 | 39 | 5 | 56 | 2 | 1 | 6 | 8 | .429 | 0 | 12 | 3.67 |
| 1988 Milwaukee | AL | 70 | 0 | 0 | 25 | 105 | 425 | 95 | 38 | 34 | 11 | 5 | 6 | 2 | 28 | 3 | 58 | 9 | 2 | 7 | 6 | .538 | 0 | 9 | 2.91 |
| 1989 Milwaukee | AL | 76 | 0 | 0 | 31 | 117.2 | 487 | 114 | 42 | 37 | 7 | 3 | 6 | 2 | 36 | 9 | 59 | 5 | 0 | 9 | 7 | .563 | 0 | 7 | 2.83 |
| 1990 Milwaukee | AL | 67 | 0 | 0 | 25 | 85.2 | 367 | 88 | 39 | 33 | 7 | 1 | 4 | 2 | 23 | 4 | 39 | 0 | 1 | 3 | 5 | .375 | 0 | 11 | 3.47 |
| 4 ML YEARS | | 266 | 5 | 0 | 99 | 438.1 | 1828 | 430 | 179 | 157 | 40 | 15 | 17 | 9 | 126 | 21 | 212 | 16 | 4 | 25 | 26 | .490 | 0 | 39 | 3.22 |

## Steve Cummings

**Pitches:** Right **Bats:** Both **Pos:** RP **Ht:** 6' 2" **Wt:** 200 **Born:** 07/15/64 **Age:** 26

| | | HOW MUCH HE PITCHED | | | | | | WHAT HE GAVE UP | | | | | | | | | | | | THE RESULTS | | | | | |
|---|---|---|---|---|---|---|---|---|---|---|---|---|---|---|---|---|---|---|---|---|---|---|---|---|---|
| Year Team | Lg | G | GS | CG | GF | IP | BFP | H | R | ER | HR | SH | SF | HB | TBB | IBB | SO | WP | Bk | W | L | Pct. | ShO | Sv | ERA |
| 1986 St.Cathrnes | A | 18 | 18 | 2 | 0 | 110.1 | 444 | 80 | 36 | 25 | 2 | 1 | 0 | 6 | 34 | 0 | 86 | 0 | 1 | 9 | 5 | .643 | 0 | 0 | 2.04 |
| 1987 Dunedin | A | 32 | 29 | 2 | 1 | 186.2 | 797 | 189 | 80 | 61 | 8 | 1 | 5 | 2 | 60 | 0 | 111 | 12 | 1 | 18 | 8 | .692 | 2 | 0 | 2.94 |
| 1988 Knoxville | AA | 35 | 33 | 3 | 0 | 212.2 | 894 | 206 | 88 | 65 | 5 | 7 | 5 | 5 | 64 | 3 | 131 | 10 | 6 | 14 | 11 | .560 | 1 | 0 | 2.75 |
| 1989 Syracuse | AAA | 19 | 17 | 3 | 1 | 106 | 437 | 97 | 46 | 37 | 7 | 3 | 4 | 1 | 41 | 2 | 60 | 6 | 3 | 7 | 5 | .583 | 1 | 0 | 3.14 |
| 1990 Syracuse | AAA | 16 | 13 | 4 | 0 | 81 | 342 | 76 | 31 | 28 | 3 | 1 | 2 | 1 | 37 | 0 | 34 | 1 | 0 | 5 | 3 | .625 | 0 | 0 | 3.11 |
| 1989 Toronto | AL | 5 | 2 | 0 | 2 | 21 | 90 | 18 | 9 | 7 | 1 | 0 | 0 | 1 | 11 | 0 | 8 | 1 | 0 | 2 | 0 | 1.000 | 0 | 0 | 3.00 |
| 1990 Toronto | AL | 6 | 2 | 0 | 2 | 12.1 | 58 | 22 | 7 | 7 | 4 | 1 | 0 | 1 | 5 | 0 | 4 | 0 | 0 | 0 | 0 | .000 | 0 | 0 | 5.11 |
| 2 ML YEARS | | 11 | 4 | 0 | 4 | 33.1 | 148 | 40 | 16 | 14 | 5 | 1 | 0 | 2 | 16 | 0 | 12 | 1 | 0 | 2 | 0 | 1.000 | 0 | 0 | 3.78 |

## Milt Cuyler

**Bats:** Both **Throws:** Right **Pos:** CF **Ht:** 5'10" **Wt:** 175 **Born:** 10/07/68 **Age:** 22

| | | BATTING | | | | | | | | | | | | | | | | | BASERUNNING | | | | PERCENTAGES | | |
|---|---|---|---|---|---|---|---|---|---|---|---|---|---|---|---|---|---|---|---|---|---|---|---|---|---|
| Year Team | Lg | G | AB | H | 2B | 3B | HR | (Hm | Rd) | TB | R | RBI | TBB | IBB | SO | HBP | SH | SF | SB | CS | SB% | GDP | Avg | OBP | SLG |
| 1986 Bristol | R | 45 | 174 | 40 | 3 | 5 | 1 | -- | -- | 56 | 24 | 11 | 15 | 0 | 35 | 5 | 2 | 0 | 12 | 4 | .75 | 1 | .230 | .309 | .322 |
| 1987 Fayettevlle | A | 94 | 366 | 107 | 8 | 4 | 2 | -- | -- | 129 | 65 | 34 | 34 | 4 | 78 | 7 | 17 | 2 | 27 | 13 | .68 | 3 | .292 | .362 | .352 |
| 1988 Lakeland | A | 132 | 483 | 143 | 11 | 3 | 2 | -- | -- | 166 | 100 | 32 | 71 | 2 | 83 | 4 | 14 | 1 | 50 | 25 | .67 | 3 | .296 | .390 | .344 |
| 1989 Toledo | AAA | 24 | 83 | 14 | 3 | 2 | 0 | -- | -- | 21 | 4 | 6 | 8 | 0 | 27 | 0 | 3 | 1 | 4 | 1 | .80 | 1 | .169 | .239 | .253 |
| London | AA | 98 | 366 | 96 | 8 | 7 | 7 | -- | -- | 139 | 69 | 34 | 47 | 2 | 74 | 4 | 4 | 0 | 32 | 5 | .86 | 2 | .262 | .353 | .380 |
| 1990 Toledo | AAA | 124 | 461 | 119 | 11 | 8 | 2 | -- | -- | 152 | 77 | 42 | 60 | 1 | 77 | 5 | 7 | 2 | 52 | 14 | .79 | 6 | .258 | .348 | .330 |
| 1990 Detroit | AL | 19 | 51 | 13 | 3 | 1 | 0 | (0 | 0) | 18 | 8 | 8 | 5 | 0 | 10 | 0 | 2 | 1 | 1 | 2 | .33 | 1 | .255 | .316 | .353 |

## Kal Daniels

**Bats:** Left **Throws:** Right **Pos:** LF **Ht:** 5'11" **Wt:** 195 **Born:** 08/20/63 **Age:** 27

| | | BATTING | | | | | | | | | | | | | | | | | BASERUNNING | | | | PERCENTAGES | | |
|---|---|---|---|---|---|---|---|---|---|---|---|---|---|---|---|---|---|---|---|---|---|---|---|---|---|
| Year Team | Lg | G | AB | H | 2B | 3B | HR | (Hm | Rd) | TB | R | RBI | TBB | IBB | SO | HBP | SH | SF | SB | CS | SB% | GDP | Avg | OBP | SLG |
| 1986 Cincinnati | NL | 74 | 181 | 58 | 10 | 4 | 6 | (3 | 3) | 94 | 34 | 23 | 22 | 1 | 30 | 2 | 1 | 1 | 15 | 2 | .88 | 4 | .320 | .398 | .519 |
| 1987 Cincinnati | NL | 108 | 368 | 123 | 24 | 1 | 26 | (13 | 13) | 227 | 73 | 64 | 60 | 11 | 62 | 1 | 1 | 0 | 26 | 8 | .76 | 6 | .334 | .429 | .617 |
| 1988 Cincinnati | NL | 140 | 495 | 144 | 29 | 1 | 18 | (12 | 6) | 229 | 95 | 64 | 87 | 10 | 94 | 3 | 0 | 4 | 27 | 6 | .82 | 11 | .291 | .397 | .463 |
| 1989 2 ML Teams | | 55 | 171 | 42 | 13 | 0 | 4 | (2 | 2) | 67 | 33 | 17 | 43 | 1 | 33 | 2 | 0 | 2 | 9 | 4 | .69 | 2 | .246 | .399 | .392 |
| 1990 Los Angeles | NL | 130 | 450 | 133 | 23 | 1 | 27 | (12 | 15) | 239 | 81 | 94 | 68 | 1 | 104 | 3 | 2 | 3 | 4 | 3 | .57 | 10 | .296 | .389 | .531 |
| 1989 Cincinnati | NL | 44 | 133 | 29 | 11 | 0 | 2 | (1 | 1) | 46 | 26 | 9 | 36 | 1 | 28 | 2 | 0 | 1 | 6 | 4 | .60 | 1 | .218 | .390 | .346 |
| Los Angeles | NL | 11 | 38 | 13 | 2 | 0 | 2 | (1 | 1) | 21 | 7 | 8 | 7 | 0 | 5 | 0 | 0 | 1 | 3 | 0 | 1.00 | 1 | .342 | .435 | .553 |
| 5 ML YEARS | | 507 | 1665 | 500 | 99 | 7 | 81 | (42 | 39) | 856 | 316 | 262 | 280 | 24 | 323 | 11 | 4 | 10 | 81 | 23 | .78 | 33 | .300 | .402 | .514 |

## Ron Darling

**Pitches:** Right **Bats:** Right **Pos:** SP/RP **Ht:** 6' 3" **Wt:** 195 **Born:** 08/19/60 **Age:** 30

| | | | HOW MUCH HE PITCHED | | | | | | WHAT HE GAVE UP | | | | | | | | | | | | THE RESULTS | | | | | |
|---|---|---|---|---|---|---|---|---|---|---|---|---|---|---|---|---|---|---|---|---|---|---|---|---|---|---|
| Year | Team | Lg | G | GS | CG | GF | IP | BFP | H | R | ER | HR | SH | SF | HB | TBB | IBB | SO | WP | Bk | W | L | Pct. | ShO | Sv | ERA |
| 1983 | New York | NL | 5 | 5 | 1 | 0 | 35.1 | 148 | 31 | 11 | 11 | 0 | 3 | 0 | 3 | 17 | 1 | 23 | 3 | 2 | 1 | 3 | .250 | 0 | 0 | 2.80 |
| 1984 | New York | NL | 33 | 33 | 2 | 0 | 205.2 | 884 | 179 | 97 | 87 | 17 | 7 | 6 | 5 | 104 | 2 | 136 | 7 | 1 | 12 | 9 | .571 | 2 | 0 | 3.81 |
| 1985 | New York | NL | 36 | 35 | 4 | 1 | 248 | 1043 | 214 | 93 | 80 | 21 | 13 | 4 | 3 | 114 | 1 | 167 | 7 | 1 | 16 | 6 | .727 | 2 | 0 | 2.90 |
| 1986 | New York | NL | 34 | 34 | 4 | 0 | 237 | 967 | 203 | 84 | 74 | 21 | 10 | 6 | 3 | 81 | 2 | 184 | 7 | 3 | 15 | 6 | .714 | 2 | 0 | 2.81 |
| 1987 | New York | NL | 32 | 32 | 2 | 0 | 207.2 | 891 | 183 | 111 | 99 | 24 | 5 | 3 | 3 | 96 | 3 | 167 | 6 | 3 | 12 | 8 | .600 | 0 | 0 | 4.29 |
| 1988 | New York | NL | 34 | 34 | 7 | 0 | 240.2 | 971 | 218 | 97 | 87 | 24 | 10 | 8 | 5 | 60 | 2 | 161 | 7 | 2 | 17 | 9 | .654 | 4 | 0 | 3.25 |
| 1989 | New York | NL | 33 | 33 | 4 | 0 | 217.1 | 922 | 214 | 100 | 85 | 19 | 7 | 13 | 3 | 70 | 7 | 153 | 12 | 4 | 14 | 14 | .500 | 0 | 0 | 3.52 |
| 1990 | New York | NL | 33 | 18 | 1 | 3 | 126 | 554 | 135 | 73 | 63 | 20 | 7 | 3 | 5 | 44 | 4 | 99 | 5 | 1 | 7 | 9 | .438 | 0 | 0 | 4.50 |
| 8 ML YEARS | | | 240 | 224 | 25 | 4 | 1517.2 | 6380 | 1377 | 666 | 586 | 146 | 62 | 43 | 30 | 586 | 22 | 1090 | 54 | 17 | 94 | 64 | .595 | 10 | 0 | 3.48 |

## Danny Darwin

**Pitches:** Right **Bats:** Right **Pos:** RP/SP **Ht:** 6' 3" **Wt:** 190 **Born:** 10/25/55 **Age:** 35

| | | | HOW MUCH HE PITCHED | | | | | | WHAT HE GAVE UP | | | | | | | | | | | | THE RESULTS | | | | | |
|---|---|---|---|---|---|---|---|---|---|---|---|---|---|---|---|---|---|---|---|---|---|---|---|---|---|---|
| Year | Team | Lg | G | GS | CG | GF | IP | BFP | H | R | ER | HR | SH | SF | HB | TBB | IBB | SO | WP | Bk | W | L | Pct. | ShO | Sv | ERA |
| 1978 | Texas | AL | 3 | 1 | 0 | 2 | 9 | 36 | 11 | 4 | 4 | 0 | 0 | 1 | 0 | 1 | 0 | 8 | 0 | 0 | 1 | 0 | 1.000 | 0 | 0 | 4.00 |
| 1979 | Texas | AL | 20 | 6 | 1 | 4 | 78 | 313 | 50 | 36 | 35 | 5 | 3 | 6 | 5 | 30 | 2 | 58 | 0 | 1 | 4 | 4 | .500 | 0 | 0 | 4.04 |
| 1980 | Texas | AL | 53 | 2 | 0 | 35 | 110 | 468 | 98 | 37 | 32 | 4 | 5 | 7 | 2 | 50 | 7 | 104 | 3 | 0 | 13 | 4 | .765 | 0 | 8 | 2.62 |
| 1981 | Texas | AL | 22 | 22 | 6 | 0 | 146 | 601 | 115 | 67 | 59 | 12 | 8 | 3 | 6 | 57 | 5 | 98 | 1 | 0 | 9 | 9 | .500 | 2 | 0 | 3.64 |
| 1982 | Texas | AL | 56 | 1 | 0 | 41 | 89 | 394 | 95 | 38 | 34 | 6 | 10 | 5 | 2 | 37 | 8 | 61 | 2 | 1 | 10 | 8 | .556 | 0 | 7 | 3.44 |
| 1983 | Texas | AL | 28 | 26 | 9 | 0 | 183 | 780 | 175 | 86 | 71 | 9 | 7 | 7 | 3 | 62 | 3 | 92 | 2 | 0 | 8 | 13 | .381 | 2 | 0 | 3.49 |
| 1984 | Texas | AL | 35 | 32 | 5 | 2 | 223.2 | 955 | 249 | 110 | 98 | 19 | 3 | 3 | 4 | 54 | 2 | 123 | 3 | 0 | 8 | 12 | .400 | 1 | 0 | 3.94 |
| 1985 | Milwaukee | AL | 39 | 29 | 11 | 8 | 217.2 | 919 | 212 | 112 | 92 | 34 | 7 | 9 | 4 | 65 | 4 | 125 | 6 | 0 | 8 | 18 | .308 | 1 | 2 | 3.80 |
| 1986 | 2 ML Teams | | 39 | 22 | 6 | 6 | 184.2 | 759 | 170 | 81 | 65 | 16 | 6 | 9 | 3 | 44 | 1 | 120 | 7 | 1 | 11 | 10 | .524 | 1 | 0 | 3.17 |
| 1987 | Houston | NL | 33 | 30 | 3 | 0 | 195.2 | 833 | 184 | 87 | 78 | 17 | 8 | 3 | 5 | 69 | 12 | 134 | 3 | 1 | 9 | 10 | .474 | 1 | 0 | 3.59 |
| 1988 | Houston | NL | 44 | 20 | 3 | 9 | 192 | 804 | 189 | 86 | 82 | 20 | 10 | 9 | 7 | 48 | 9 | 129 | 1 | 2 | 8 | 13 | .381 | 0 | 3 | 3.84 |
| 1989 | Houston | NL | 68 | 0 | 0 | 26 | 122 | 482 | 92 | 34 | 32 | 8 | 8 | 5 | 2 | 33 | 9 | 104 | 2 | 3 | 11 | 4 | .733 | 0 | 7 | 2.36 |
| 1990 | Houston | NL | 48 | 17 | 3 | 14 | 162.2 | 646 | 136 | 42 | 40 | 11 | 4 | 2 | 4 | 31 | 4 | 109 | 0 | 2 | 11 | 4 | .733 | 0 | 2 | 2.21 |
| 1986 | Milwaukee | AL | 27 | 14 | 5 | 4 | 130.1 | 537 | 120 | 62 | 51 | 13 | 5 | 6 | 3 | 35 | 1 | 80 | 5 | 0 | 6 | 8 | .429 | 1 | 0 | 3.52 |
| | Houston | NL | 12 | 8 | 1 | 2 | 54.1 | 222 | 50 | 19 | 14 | 3 | 1 | 3 | 0 | 9 | 0 | 40 | 2 | 1 | 5 | 2 | .714 | 0 | 0 | 2.32 |
| 13 ML YEARS | | | 488 | 208 | 47 | 147 | 1913.1 | 7990 | 1776 | 820 | 722 | 161 | 79 | 69 | 47 | 581 | 66 | 1265 | 30 | 11 | 111 | 109 | .505 | 8 | 29 | 3.40 |

## Doug Dascenzo

**Bats:** Both **Throws:** Left **Pos:** CF/LF/RF **Ht:** 5' 8" **Wt:** 160 **Born:** 06/30/64 **Age:** 27

| | | | BATTING | | | | | | | | | | | | | | | | | BASERUNNING | | | | PERCENTAGES | | |
|---|---|---|---|---|---|---|---|---|---|---|---|---|---|---|---|---|---|---|---|---|---|---|---|---|---|---|
| Year | Team | Lg | G | AB | H | 2B | 3B | HR | (Hm | Rd) | TB | R | RBI | TBB | IBB | SO | HBP | SH | SF | SB | CS | SB% | GDP | Avg | OBP | SLG |
| 1988 | Chicago | NL | 26 | 75 | 16 | 3 | 0 | 0 | (0 | 0) | 19 | 9 | 4 | 9 | 1 | 4 | 0 | 1 | 0 | 6 | 1 | .86 | 2 | .213 | .298 | .253 |
| 1989 | Chicago | NL | 47 | 139 | 23 | 1 | 0 | 1 | (0 | 1) | 27 | 20 | 12 | 13 | 0 | 13 | 0 | 3 | 2 | 6 | 3 | .67 | 2 | .165 | .234 | .194 |
| 1990 | Chicago | NL | 113 | 241 | 61 | 9 | 5 | 1 | (1 | 0) | 83 | 27 | 26 | 21 | 2 | 18 | 1 | 5 | 3 | 15 | 6 | .71 | 3 | .253 | .312 | .344 |
| 3 ML YEARS | | | 186 | 455 | 100 | 13 | 5 | 2 | (1 | 1) | 129 | 56 | 42 | 43 | 3 | 35 | 1 | 9 | 5 | 27 | 10 | .73 | 7 | .220 | .286 | .284 |

## Jack Daugherty

**Bats:** Both **Throws:** Left **Pos:** LF/1B/DH **Ht:** 6' 0" **Wt:** 185 **Born:** 06/03/60 **Age:** 31

| | | | BATTING | | | | | | | | | | | | | | | | | BASERUNNING | | | | PERCENTAGES | | |
|---|---|---|---|---|---|---|---|---|---|---|---|---|---|---|---|---|---|---|---|---|---|---|---|---|---|---|
| Year | Team | Lg | G | AB | H | 2B | 3B | HR | (Hm | Rd) | TB | R | RBI | TBB | IBB | SO | HBP | SH | SF | SB | CS | SB% | GDP | Avg | OBP | SLG |
| 1987 | Montreal | NL | 11 | 10 | 1 | 1 | 0 | 0 | (0 | 0) | 2 | 1 | 1 | 0 | 0 | 3 | 0 | 2 | 0 | 0 | 0 | .00 | 0 | .100 | .100 | .200 |
| 1989 | Texas | AL | 52 | 106 | 32 | 4 | 2 | 1 | (1 | 0) | 43 | 15 | 10 | 11 | 0 | 21 | 1 | 0 | 3 | 2 | 1 | .67 | 1 | .302 | .364 | .406 |
| 1990 | Texas | AL | 125 | 310 | 93 | 20 | 2 | 6 | (5 | 1) | 135 | 36 | 47 | 22 | 0 | 49 | 2 | 2 | 3 | 0 | 0 | .00 | 4 | .300 | .347 | .435 |
| 3 ML YEARS | | | 188 | 426 | 126 | 25 | 4 | 7 | (6 | 1) | 180 | 52 | 58 | 33 | 0 | 73 | 3 | 4 | 6 | 2 | 1 | .67 | 5 | .296 | .346 | .423 |

## Darren Daulton

**Bats:** Left **Throws:** Right **Pos:** C **Ht:** 6' 2" **Wt:** 190 **Born:** 01/03/62 **Age:** 29

| | | | BATTING | | | | | | | | | | | | | | | | | BASERUNNING | | | | PERCENTAGES | | |
|---|---|---|---|---|---|---|---|---|---|---|---|---|---|---|---|---|---|---|---|---|---|---|---|---|---|---|
| Year | Team | Lg | G | AB | H | 2B | 3B | HR | (Hm | Rd) | TB | R | RBI | TBB | IBB | SO | HBP | SH | SF | SB | CS | SB% | GDP | Avg | OBP | SLG |
| 1983 | Philadelphia | NL | 2 | 3 | 1 | 0 | 0 | 0 | (0 | 0) | 1 | 1 | 0 | 1 | 0 | 1 | 0 | 0 | 0 | 0 | 0 | .00 | 0 | .333 | .500 | .333 |
| 1985 | Philadelphia | NL | 36 | 103 | 21 | 3 | 1 | 4 | (0 | 4) | 38 | 14 | 11 | 16 | 0 | 37 | 0 | 0 | 0 | 3 | 0 | 1.00 | 1 | .204 | .311 | .369 |
| 1986 | Philadelphia | NL | 49 | 138 | 31 | 4 | 0 | 8 | (4 | 4) | 59 | 18 | 21 | 38 | 3 | 41 | 1 | 2 | 2 | 2 | 3 | .40 | 1 | .225 | .391 | .428 |
| 1987 | Philadelphia | NL | 53 | 129 | 25 | 6 | 0 | 3 | (1 | 2) | 40 | 10 | 13 | 16 | 1 | 37 | 0 | 4 | 1 | 0 | 0 | .00 | 0 | .194 | .281 | .310 |
| 1988 | Philadelphia | NL | 58 | 144 | 30 | 6 | 0 | 1 | (0 | 1) | 39 | 13 | 12 | 17 | 1 | 26 | 0 | 0 | 2 | 2 | 1 | .67 | 2 | .208 | .288 | .271 |
| 1989 | Philadelphia | NL | 131 | 368 | 74 | 12 | 2 | 8 | (2 | 6) | 114 | 29 | 44 | 52 | 8 | 58 | 2 | 1 | 1 | 2 | 1 | .67 | 4 | .201 | .303 | .310 |
| 1990 | Philadelphia | NL | 143 | 459 | 123 | 30 | 1 | 12 | (5 | 7) | 191 | 62 | 57 | 72 | 9 | 72 | 2 | 3 | 4 | 7 | 1 | .88 | 6 | .268 | .367 | .416 |
| 7 ML YEARS | | | 472 | 1344 | 305 | 61 | 4 | 36 | (12 | 24) | 482 | 147 | 158 | 212 | 22 | 272 | 5 | 10 | 10 | 16 | 6 | .73 | 14 | .227 | .332 | .359 |

## Mark Davidson

**Bats:** Right **Throws:** Right **Pos:** RF/LF **Ht:** 6' 2" **Wt:** 190 **Born:** 02/15/61 **Age:** 30

| | | BATTING | | | | | | | | | | | | | | | | | BASERUNNING | | | | PERCENTAGES | | |
|---|---|---|---|---|---|---|---|---|---|---|---|---|---|---|---|---|---|---|---|---|---|---|---|---|---|
| Year Team | Lg | G | AB | H | 2B | 3B | HR | (Hm | Rd) | TB | R | RBI | TBB | IBB | SO | HBP | SH | SF | SB | CS | SB% | GDP | Avg | OBP | SLG |
| 1986 Minnesota | AL | 36 | 68 | 8 | 3 | 0 | 0 | (0 | 0) | 11 | 5 | 2 | 6 | 0 | 22 | 0 | 3 | 0 | 2 | 3 | .40 | 1 | .118 | .189 | .162 |
| 1987 Minnesota | AL | 102 | 150 | 40 | 4 | 1 | 1 | (0 | 1) | 49 | 32 | 14 | 13 | 1 | 26 | 0 | 4 | 2 | 9 | 2 | .82 | 4 | .267 | .321 | .327 |
| 1988 Minnesota | AL | 100 | 106 | 23 | 7 | 0 | 1 | (0 | 1) | 33 | 22 | 10 | 10 | 0 | 20 | 1 | 1 | 1 | 3 | 3 | .50 | 3 | .217 | .288 | .311 |
| 1989 Houston | NL | 33 | 65 | 13 | 2 | 1 | 1 | (0 | 1) | 20 | 7 | 5 | 7 | 0 | 14 | 0 | 1 | 0 | 1 | 0 | 1.00 | 1 | .200 | .278 | .308 |
| 1990 Houston | NL | 57 | 130 | 38 | 5 | 1 | 1 | (0 | 1) | 48 | 12 | 11 | 10 | 1 | 18 | 0 | 1 | 1 | 0 | 3 | .00 | 1 | .292 | .340 | .369 |
| 5 ML YEARS | | 328 | 519 | 122 | 21 | 3 | 4 | (0 | 4) | 161 | 78 | 42 | 46 | 2 | 100 | 1 | 10 | 4 | 15 | 11 | .58 | 10 | .235 | .296 | .310 |

## Alvin Davis

**Bats:** Left **Throws:** Right **Pos:** DH/1B **Ht:** 6' 1" **Wt:** 190 **Born:** 09/09/60 **Age:** 30

| | | BATTING | | | | | | | | | | | | | | | | | BASERUNNING | | | | PERCENTAGES | | |
|---|---|---|---|---|---|---|---|---|---|---|---|---|---|---|---|---|---|---|---|---|---|---|---|---|---|
| Year Team | Lg | G | AB | H | 2B | 3B | HR | (Hm | Rd) | TB | R | RBI | TBB | IBB | SO | HBP | SH | SF | SB | CS | SB% | GDP | Avg | OBP | SLG |
| 1984 Seattle | AL | 152 | 567 | 161 | 34 | 3 | 27 | (15 | 12) | 282 | 80 | 116 | 97 | 16 | 78 | 7 | 0 | 7 | 5 | 4 | .56 | 7 | .284 | .391 | .497 |
| 1985 Seattle | AL | 155 | 578 | 166 | 33 | 1 | 18 | (11 | 7) | 255 | 78 | 78 | 90 | 7 | 71 | 2 | 0 | 7 | 1 | 2 | .33 | 14 | .287 | .381 | .441 |
| 1986 Seattle | AL | 135 | 479 | 130 | 18 | 1 | 18 | (14 | 4) | 204 | 66 | 72 | 76 | 10 | 68 | 3 | 2 | 2 | 0 | 3 | .00 | 11 | .271 | .373 | .426 |
| 1987 Seattle | AL | 157 | 580 | 171 | 37 | 2 | 29 | (18 | 11) | 299 | 86 | 100 | 72 | 6 | 84 | 2 | 0 | 8 | 0 | 0 | .00 | 17 | .295 | .370 | .516 |
| 1988 Seattle | AL | 140 | 478 | 141 | 24 | 1 | 18 | (12 | 6) | 221 | 67 | 69 | 95 | 13 | 53 | 4 | 0 | 5 | 1 | 1 | .50 | 14 | .295 | .412 | .462 |
| 1989 Seattle | AL | 142 | 498 | 152 | 30 | 1 | 21 | (13 | 8) | 247 | 84 | 95 | 101 | 15 | 49 | 6 | 0 | 6 | 0 | 1 | .00 | 15 | .305 | .424 | .496 |
| 1990 Seattle | AL | 140 | 494 | 140 | 21 | 0 | 17 | (12 | 5) | 212 | 63 | 68 | 85 | 10 | 68 | 4 | 0 | 9 | 0 | 2 | .00 | 9 | .283 | .387 | .429 |
| 7 ML YEARS | | 1021 | 3674 | 1061 | 197 | 9 | 148 | (95 | 53) | 1720 | 524 | 598 | 616 | 77 | 471 | 28 | 2 | 44 | 7 | 13 | .35 | 87 | .289 | .391 | .468 |

## Chili Davis

**Bats:** Both **Throws:** Right **Pos:** DH/LF **Ht:** 6' 3" **Wt:** 210 **Born:** 01/17/60 **Age:** 31

| | | BATTING | | | | | | | | | | | | | | | | | BASERUNNING | | | | PERCENTAGES | | |
|---|---|---|---|---|---|---|---|---|---|---|---|---|---|---|---|---|---|---|---|---|---|---|---|---|---|
| Year Team | Lg | G | AB | H | 2B | 3B | HR | (Hm | Rd) | TB | R | RBI | TBB | IBB | SO | HBP | SH | SF | SB | CS | SB% | GDP | Avg | OBP | SLG |
| 1981 San Francisco | NL | 8 | 15 | 2 | 0 | 0 | 0 | (0 | 0) | 2 | 1 | 0 | 1 | 0 | 2 | 0 | 0 | 0 | 2 | 0 | 1.00 | 1 | .133 | .188 | .133 |
| 1982 San Francisco | NL | 154 | 641 | 167 | 27 | 6 | 19 | (6 | 13) | 263 | 86 | 76 | 45 | 2 | 115 | 2 | 7 | 6 | 24 | 13 | .65 | 13 | .261 | .308 | .410 |
| 1983 San Francisco | NL | 137 | 486 | 113 | 21 | 2 | 11 | (7 | 4) | 171 | 54 | 59 | 55 | 6 | 108 | 0 | 3 | 9 | 10 | 12 | .45 | 9 | .233 | .305 | .352 |
| 1984 San Francisco | NL | 137 | 499 | 157 | 21 | 6 | 21 | (7 | 14) | 253 | 87 | 81 | 42 | 6 | 74 | 1 | 2 | 2 | 12 | 8 | .60 | 13 | .315 | .368 | .507 |
| 1985 San Francisco | NL | 136 | 481 | 130 | 25 | 2 | 13 | (7 | 6) | 198 | 53 | 56 | 62 | 12 | 74 | 0 | 1 | 7 | 15 | 7 | .68 | 16 | .270 | .349 | .412 |
| 1986 San Francisco | NL | 153 | 526 | 146 | 28 | 3 | 13 | (7 | 6) | 219 | 71 | 70 | 84 | 23 | 96 | 1 | 2 | 5 | 16 | 13 | .55 | 11 | .278 | .375 | .416 |
| 1987 San Francisco | NL | 149 | 500 | 125 | 22 | 1 | 24 | (9 | 15) | 221 | 80 | 76 | 72 | 15 | 109 | 2 | 0 | 4 | 16 | 9 | .64 | 8 | .250 | .344 | .442 |
| 1988 California | AL | 158 | 600 | 161 | 29 | 3 | 21 | (11 | 10) | 259 | 81 | 93 | 56 | 14 | 118 | 0 | 1 | 10 | 9 | 10 | .47 | 13 | .268 | .326 | .432 |
| 1989 California | AL | 154 | 560 | 152 | 24 | 1 | 22 | (6 | 16) | 244 | 81 | 90 | 61 | 12 | 109 | 0 | 3 | 6 | 3 | 0 | 1.00 | 21 | .271 | .340 | .436 |
| 1990 California | AL | 113 | 412 | 109 | 17 | 1 | 12 | (10 | 2) | 164 | 58 | 58 | 61 | 4 | 89 | 0 | 0 | 3 | 1 | 2 | .33 | 14 | .265 | .357 | .398 |
| 10 ML YEARS | | 1299 | 4720 | 1262 | 214 | 25 | 156 | (70 | 86) | 1994 | 652 | 659 | 539 | 94 | 894 | 6 | 19 | 52 | 108 | 74 | .59 | 119 | .267 | .340 | .422 |

## Eric Davis

**Bats:** Right **Throws:** Right **Pos:** CF/LF **Ht:** 6' 3" **Wt:** 185 **Born:** 05/29/62 **Age:** 29

| | | BATTING | | | | | | | | | | | | | | | | | BASERUNNING | | | | PERCENTAGES | | |
|---|---|---|---|---|---|---|---|---|---|---|---|---|---|---|---|---|---|---|---|---|---|---|---|---|---|
| Year Team | Lg | G | AB | H | 2B | 3B | HR | (Hm | Rd) | TB | R | RBI | TBB | IBB | SO | HBP | SH | SF | SB | CS | SB% | GDP | Avg | OBP | SLG |
| 1984 Cincinnati | NL | 57 | 174 | 39 | 10 | 1 | 10 | (3 | 7) | 81 | 33 | 30 | 24 | 0 | 48 | 1 | 0 | 1 | 10 | 2 | .83 | 1 | .224 | .320 | .466 |
| 1985 Cincinnati | NL | 56 | 122 | 30 | 3 | 3 | 8 | (1 | 7) | 63 | 26 | 18 | 7 | 0 | 39 | 0 | 2 | 0 | 16 | 3 | .84 | 1 | .246 | .287 | .516 |
| 1986 Cincinnati | NL | 132 | 415 | 115 | 15 | 3 | 27 | (12 | 15) | 217 | 97 | 71 | 68 | 5 | 100 | 1 | 0 | 3 | 80 | 11 | .88 | 6 | .277 | .378 | .523 |
| 1987 Cincinnati | NL | 129 | 474 | 139 | 23 | 4 | 37 | (17 | 20) | 281 | 120 | 100 | 84 | 8 | 134 | 1 | 0 | 3 | 50 | 6 | .89 | 6 | .293 | .399 | .593 |
| 1988 Cincinnati | NL | 135 | 472 | 129 | 18 | 3 | 26 | (14 | 12) | 231 | 81 | 93 | 65 | 10 | 124 | 3 | 0 | 3 | 35 | 3 | .92 | 11 | .273 | .363 | .489 |
| 1989 Cincinnati | NL | 131 | 462 | 130 | 14 | 2 | 34 | (15 | 19) | 250 | 74 | 101 | 68 | 12 | 116 | 1 | 0 | 11 | 21 | 7 | .75 | 16 | .281 | .367 | .541 |
| 1990 Cincinnati | NL | 127 | 453 | 118 | 26 | 2 | 24 | (13 | 11) | 220 | 84 | 86 | 60 | 6 | 100 | 2 | 0 | 3 | 21 | 3 | .88 | 7 | .260 | .347 | .486 |
| 7 ML YEARS | | 767 | 2572 | 700 | 109 | 18 | 166 | (75 | 91) | 1343 | 515 | 499 | 376 | 41 | 661 | 9 | 2 | 24 | 233 | 35 | .87 | 48 | .272 | .364 | .522 |

## Glenn Davis

**Bats:** Right **Throws:** Right **Pos:** 1B **Ht:** 6' 3" **Wt:** 210 **Born:** 03/28/61 **Age:** 30

| | | BATTING | | | | | | | | | | | | | | | | | BASERUNNING | | | | PERCENTAGES | | |
|---|---|---|---|---|---|---|---|---|---|---|---|---|---|---|---|---|---|---|---|---|---|---|---|---|---|
| Year Team | Lg | G | AB | H | 2B | 3B | HR | (Hm | Rd) | TB | R | RBI | TBB | IBB | SO | HBP | SH | SF | SB | CS | SB% | GDP | Avg | OBP | SLG |
| 1984 Houston | NL | 18 | 61 | 13 | 5 | 0 | 2 | (1 | 1) | 24 | 6 | 8 | 4 | 0 | 12 | 0 | 2 | 1 | 0 | 0 | .00 | 0 | .213 | .258 | .393 |
| 1985 Houston | NL | 100 | 350 | 95 | 11 | 0 | 20 | (8 | 12) | 166 | 51 | 64 | 27 | 6 | 68 | 7 | 2 | 4 | 0 | 0 | .00 | 12 | .271 | .332 | .474 |
| 1986 Houston | NL | 158 | 574 | 152 | 32 | 3 | 31 | (17 | 14) | 283 | 91 | 101 | 64 | 6 | 72 | 9 | 0 | 7 | 3 | 1 | .75 | 11 | .265 | .344 | .493 |
| 1987 Houston | NL | 151 | 578 | 145 | 35 | 2 | 27 | (12 | 15) | 265 | 70 | 93 | 47 | 10 | 84 | 5 | 0 | 5 | 4 | 1 | .80 | 16 | .251 | .310 | .458 |
| 1988 Houston | NL | 152 | 561 | 152 | 26 | 0 | 30 | (15 | 15) | 268 | 78 | 99 | 53 | 20 | 77 | 11 | 0 | 9 | 4 | 3 | .57 | 11 | .271 | .341 | .478 |
| 1989 Houston | NL | 158 | 581 | 156 | 26 | 1 | 34 | (15 | 19) | 286 | 87 | 89 | 69 | 17 | 123 | 7 | 0 | 6 | 4 | 2 | .67 | 9 | .269 | .350 | .492 |
| 1990 Houston | NL | 93 | 327 | 82 | 15 | 4 | 22 | (4 | 18) | 171 | 44 | 64 | 46 | 17 | 54 | 8 | 0 | 0 | 8 | 3 | .73 | 5 | .251 | .357 | .523 |
| 7 ML YEARS | | 830 | 3032 | 795 | 150 | 10 | 166 | (72 | 94) | 1463 | 427 | 518 | 310 | 76 | 490 | 47 | 4 | 32 | 23 | 10 | .70 | 64 | .262 | .337 | .483 |

## Jody Davis

**Bats:** Right **Throws:** Right **Pos:** 1B **Ht:** 6' 3" **Wt:** 210 **Born:** 11/12/56 **Age:** 34

| | | BATTING | | | | | | | | | | | | | | | | | BASERUNNING | | | | PERCENTAGES | | |
|---|---|---|---|---|---|---|---|---|---|---|---|---|---|---|---|---|---|---|---|---|---|---|---|---|---|
| Year Team | Lg | G | AB | H | 2B | 3B | HR | (Hm | Rd) | TB | R | RBI | TBB | IBB | SO | HBP | SH | SF | SB | CS | SB% | GDP | Avg | OBP | SLG |
| 1981 Chicago | NL | 56 | 180 | 46 | 5 | 1 | 4 | (4 | 0) | 65 | 14 | 21 | 21 | 3 | 28 | 1 | 3 | 2 | 0 | 1 | .00 | 6 | .256 | .333 | .361 |
| 1982 Chicago | NL | 130 | 418 | 109 | 20 | 2 | 12 | (6 | 6) | 169 | 41 | 52 | 36 | 4 | 92 | 1 | 4 | 7 | 0 | 1 | .00 | 6 | .261 | .316 | .404 |
| 1983 Chicago | NL | 151 | 510 | 138 | 31 | 2 | 24 | (15 | 9) | 245 | 56 | 84 | 33 | 5 | 93 | 2 | 0 | 5 | 0 | 2 | .00 | 16 | .271 | .315 | .480 |
| 1984 Chicago | NL | 150 | 523 | 134 | 25 | 2 | 19 | (13 | 6) | 220 | 55 | 94 | 47 | 15 | 99 | 1 | 1 | 7 | 5 | 6 | .45 | 20 | .256 | .315 | .421 |
| 1985 Chicago | NL | 142 | 482 | 112 | 30 | 0 | 17 | (10 | 7) | 193 | 47 | 58 | 48 | 5 | 83 | 0 | 2 | 4 | 1 | 0 | 1.00 | 14 | .232 | .300 | .400 |
| 1986 Chicago | NL | 148 | 528 | 132 | 27 | 2 | 21 | (14 | 7) | 226 | 61 | 74 | 41 | 4 | 110 | 0 | 4 | 8 | 0 | 1 | .00 | 14 | .250 | .300 | .428 |
| 1987 Chicago | NL | 125 | 428 | 106 | 12 | 2 | 19 | (7 | 12) | 179 | 57 | 51 | 52 | 2 | 91 | 2 | 1 | 2 | 1 | 2 | .33 | 14 | .248 | .331 | .418 |
| 1988 2 ML Teams | | 90 | 257 | 59 | 9 | 0 | 7 | (3 | 4) | 89 | 21 | 36 | 29 | 3 | 52 | 1 | 2 | 3 | 0 | 3 | .00 | 7 | .230 | .307 | .346 |
| 1989 Atlanta | NL | 78 | 231 | 39 | 5 | 0 | 4 | (1 | 3) | 56 | 12 | 19 | 23 | 3 | 61 | 1 | 1 | 1 | 0 | 0 | .00 | 8 | .169 | .246 | .242 |
| 1990 Atlanta | NL | 12 | 28 | 2 | 0 | 0 | 0 | (0 | 0) | 2 | 0 | 1 | 3 | 0 | 3 | 0 | 0 | 0 | 0 | 0 | .00 | 1 | .071 | .161 | .071 |
| 1988 Chicago | NL | 88 | 249 | 57 | 9 | 0 | 6 | (3 | 3) | 84 | 19 | 33 | 29 | 3 | 51 | 1 | 2 | 3 | 0 | 3 | .00 | 7 | .229 | .309 | .337 |
| Atlanta | NL | 2 | 8 | 2 | 0 | 0 | 1 | (0 | 1) | 5 | 2 | 3 | 0 | 0 | 1 | 0 | 0 | 0 | 0 | 0 | .00 | 0 | .250 | .250 | .625 |
| 10 ML YEARS | | 1082 | 3585 | 877 | 164 | 11 | 127 | (73 | 54) | 1444 | 364 | 490 | 333 | 44 | 712 | 9 | 18 | 39 | 7 | 16 | .30 | 106 | .245 | .307 | .403 |

## John Davis

**Pitches:** Right **Bats:** Right **Pos:** RP **Ht:** 6' 7" **Wt:** 215 **Born:** 01/05/63 **Age:** 28

| | | HOW MUCH HE PITCHED | | | | | | WHAT HE GAVE UP | | | | | | | | | | | THE RESULTS | | | | | |
|---|---|---|---|---|---|---|---|---|---|---|---|---|---|---|---|---|---|---|---|---|---|---|---|---|
| Year Team | Lg | G | GS | CG | GF | IP | BFP | H | R | ER | HR | SH | SF | HB | TBB | IBB | SO | WP | Bk | W | L | Pct. | ShO | Sv | ERA |
| 1987 Kansas City | AL | 27 | 0 | 0 | 12 | 43.2 | 181 | 29 | 13 | 11 | 0 | 0 | 4 | 2 | 26 | 4 | 24 | 2 | 0 | 5 | 2 | .714 | 0 | 2 | 2.27 |
| 1988 Chicago | AL | 34 | 1 | 0 | 10 | 63.2 | 319 | 77 | 58 | 47 | 5 | 2 | 4 | 4 | 50 | 10 | 37 | 6 | 3 | 2 | 5 | .286 | 0 | 1 | 6.64 |
| 1989 Chicago | AL | 4 | 0 | 0 | 3 | 6 | 25 | 5 | 4 | 3 | 2 | 0 | 0 | 0 | 2 | 0 | 5 | 0 | 0 | 0 | 1 | .000 | 0 | 1 | 4.50 |
| 1990 San Diego | NL | 6 | 0 | 0 | 5 | 9.1 | 39 | 9 | 7 | 6 | 1 | 0 | 0 | 0 | 4 | 0 | 7 | 0 | 0 | 0 | 1 | .000 | 0 | 0 | 5.79 |
| 4 ML YEARS | | 71 | 1 | 0 | 30 | 122.2 | 564 | 120 | 82 | 67 | 8 | 2 | 8 | 6 | 82 | 14 | 73 | 8 | 3 | 7 | 9 | .438 | 0 | 4 | 4.92 |

## Mark Davis

**Pitches:** Left **Bats:** Left **Pos:** RP/SP **Ht:** 6' 4" **Wt:** 200 **Born:** 10/19/60 **Age:** 30

| | | HOW MUCH HE PITCHED | | | | | | WHAT HE GAVE UP | | | | | | | | | | | THE RESULTS | | | | | |
|---|---|---|---|---|---|---|---|---|---|---|---|---|---|---|---|---|---|---|---|---|---|---|---|---|
| Year Team | Lg | G | GS | CG | GF | IP | BFP | H | R | ER | HR | SH | SF | HB | TBB | IBB | SO | WP | Bk | W | L | Pct. | ShO | Sv | ERA |
| 1980 Philadelphia | NL | 2 | 1 | 0 | 0 | 7 | 30 | 4 | 2 | 2 | 0 | 0 | 0 | 0 | 5 | 0 | 5 | 0 | 0 | 0 | 0 | .000 | 0 | 0 | 2.57 |
| 1981 Philadelphia | NL | 9 | 9 | 0 | 0 | 43 | 194 | 49 | 37 | 37 | 7 | 2 | 4 | 0 | 24 | 0 | 29 | 1 | 1 | 1 | 4 | .200 | 0 | 0 | 7.74 |
| 1983 San Francisco | NL | 20 | 20 | 2 | 0 | 111 | 469 | 93 | 51 | 43 | 14 | 2 | 4 | 3 | 50 | 4 | 83 | 8 | 1 | 6 | 4 | .600 | 2 | 0 | 3.49 |
| 1984 San Francisco | NL | 46 | 27 | 1 | 6 | 174.2 | 766 | 201 | 113 | 104 | 25 | 10 | 10 | 5 | 54 | 12 | 124 | 8 | 4 | 5 | 17 | .227 | 0 | 0 | 5.36 |
| 1985 San Francisco | NL | 77 | 1 | 0 | 38 | 114.1 | 465 | 89 | 49 | 45 | 13 | 13 | 1 | 3 | 41 | 7 | 131 | 6 | 1 | 5 | 12 | .294 | 0 | 7 | 3.54 |
| 1986 San Francisco | NL | 67 | 2 | 0 | 20 | 84.1 | 342 | 63 | 33 | 28 | 6 | 5 | 5 | 1 | 34 | 7 | 90 | 3 | 0 | 5 | 7 | .417 | 0 | 4 | 2.99 |
| 1987 2 ML Teams | | 63 | 11 | 1 | 18 | 133 | 566 | 123 | 64 | 59 | 14 | 7 | 2 | 6 | 59 | 8 | 98 | 6 | 2 | 9 | 8 | .529 | 0 | 2 | 3.99 |
| 1988 San Diego | NL | 62 | 0 | 0 | 52 | 98.1 | 402 | 70 | 24 | 22 | 2 | 7 | 1 | 0 | 42 | 11 | 102 | 9 | 1 | 5 | 10 | .333 | 0 | 28 | 2.01 |
| 1989 San Diego | NL | 70 | 0 | 0 | 65 | 92.2 | 370 | 66 | 21 | 19 | 6 | 3 | 4 | 2 | 31 | 1 | 92 | 8 | 0 | 4 | 3 | .571 | 0 | 44 | 1.85 |
| 1990 Kansas City | AL | 53 | 3 | 0 | 28 | 68.2 | 334 | 71 | 43 | 39 | 9 | 2 | 2 | 4 | 52 | 3 | 73 | 6 | 0 | 2 | 7 | .222 | 0 | 6 | 5.11 |
| 1987 San Francisco | NL | 20 | 11 | 1 | 1 | 70.2 | 301 | 72 | 38 | 37 | 9 | 3 | 2 | 4 | 28 | 1 | 51 | 4 | 2 | 4 | 5 | .444 | 0 | 0 | 4.71 |
| San Diego | NL | 43 | 0 | 0 | 17 | 62.1 | 265 | 51 | 26 | 22 | 5 | 4 | 0 | 2 | 31 | 7 | 47 | 2 | 0 | 5 | 3 | .625 | 0 | 2 | 3.18 |
| 10 ML YEARS | | 469 | 74 | 4 | 227 | 927 | 3938 | 829 | 437 | 398 | 96 | 51 | 33 | 24 | 392 | 53 | 827 | 55 | 10 | 42 | 72 | .368 | 2 | 91 | 3.86 |

## Storm Davis

**Pitches:** Right **Bats:** Right **Pos:** SP **Ht:** 6' 4" **Wt:** 200 **Born:** 12/26/61 **Age:** 29

| | | HOW MUCH HE PITCHED | | | | | | WHAT HE GAVE UP | | | | | | | | | | | THE RESULTS | | | | | |
|---|---|---|---|---|---|---|---|---|---|---|---|---|---|---|---|---|---|---|---|---|---|---|---|---|
| Year Team | Lg | G | GS | CG | GF | IP | BFP | H | R | ER | HR | SH | SF | HB | TBB | IBB | SO | WP | Bk | W | L | Pct. | ShO | Sv | ERA |
| 1982 Baltimore | AL | 29 | 8 | 1 | 9 | 100.2 | 412 | 96 | 40 | 39 | 8 | 4 | 6 | 0 | 28 | 4 | 67 | 2 | 1 | 8 | 4 | .667 | 0 | 0 | 3.49 |
| 1983 Baltimore | AL | 34 | 29 | 6 | 0 | 200.1 | 831 | 180 | 90 | 80 | 14 | 5 | 4 | 2 | 64 | 4 | 125 | 7 | 2 | 13 | 7 | .650 | 1 | 0 | 3.59 |
| 1984 Baltimore | AL | 35 | 31 | 10 | 3 | 225 | 923 | 205 | 86 | 78 | 7 | 7 | 9 | 5 | 71 | 6 | 105 | 6 | 1 | 14 | 9 | .609 | 2 | 1 | 3.12 |
| 1985 Baltimore | AL | 31 | 28 | 8 | 0 | 175 | 750 | 172 | 92 | 88 | 11 | 3 | 3 | 1 | 70 | 5 | 93 | 2 | 1 | 10 | 8 | .556 | 1 | 0 | 4.53 |
| 1986 Baltimore | AL | 25 | 25 | 2 | 0 | 154 | 657 | 166 | 70 | 62 | 16 | 3 | 2 | 0 | 49 | 2 | 96 | 5 | 0 | 9 | 12 | .429 | 0 | 0 | 3.62 |
| 1987 2 ML Teams | | 26 | 15 | 0 | 5 | 93 | 420 | 98 | 61 | 54 | 8 | 2 | 3 | 2 | 47 | 6 | 65 | 9 | 1 | 3 | 8 | .273 | 0 | 0 | 5.23 |
| 1988 Oakland | AL | 33 | 33 | 1 | 0 | 201.2 | 872 | 211 | 86 | 83 | 16 | 3 | 8 | 1 | 91 | 2 | 127 | 16 | 2 | 16 | 7 | .696 | 0 | 0 | 3.70 |
| 1989 Oakland | AL | 31 | 31 | 1 | 0 | 169.1 | 733 | 187 | 91 | 82 | 19 | 5 | 7 | 3 | 68 | 1 | 91 | 8 | 1 | 19 | 7 | .731 | 0 | 0 | 4.36 |
| 1990 Kansas City | AL | 21 | 20 | 0 | 0 | 112 | 498 | 129 | 66 | 59 | 9 | 1 | 3 | 0 | 35 | 1 | 62 | 8 | 1 | 7 | 10 | .412 | 0 | 0 | 4.74 |
| 1987 San Diego | NL | 21 | 10 | 0 | 5 | 62.2 | 292 | 70 | 48 | 43 | 5 | 2 | 2 | 2 | 36 | 6 | 37 | 7 | 1 | 2 | 7 | .222 | 0 | 0 | 6.18 |
| Oakland | AL | 5 | 5 | 0 | 0 | 30.1 | 128 | 28 | 13 | 11 | 3 | 0 | 1 | 0 | 11 | 0 | 28 | 2 | 0 | 1 | 1 | .500 | 0 | 0 | 3.26 |
| 9 ML YEARS | | 265 | 220 | 29 | 17 | 1431 | 6096 | 1444 | 682 | 625 | 108 | 33 | 45 | 14 | 523 | 31 | 831 | 63 | 10 | 99 | 72 | .579 | 4 | 1 | 3.93 |

## Andre Dawson

**Bats:** Right **Throws:** Right **Pos:** RF **Ht:** 6' 3" **Wt:** 195 **Born:** 07/10/54 **Age:** 36

| | | BATTING | | | | | | | | | | | | | | | | | BASERUNNING | | | | PERCENTAGES | | |
|---|---|---|---|---|---|---|---|---|---|---|---|---|---|---|---|---|---|---|---|---|---|---|---|---|---|
| Year Team | Lg | G | AB | H | 2B | 3B | HR | (Hm | Rd) | TB | R | RBI | TBB | IBB | SO | HBP | SH | SF | SB | CS | SB% | GDP | Avg | OBP | SLG |
| 1976 Montreal | NL | 24 | 85 | 20 | 4 | 1 | 0 | (0 | 0) | 26 | 9 | 7 | 5 | 1 | 13 | 0 | 2 | 0 | 1 | 2 | .33 | 0 | .235 | .278 | .306 |

| | | | | | | | | | | | | | | | | | | | | | | | | |
|---|---|---|---|---|---|---|---|---|---|---|---|---|---|---|---|---|---|---|---|---|---|---|---|---|
| 1977 Montreal | NL | 139 | 525 | 148 | 26 | 9 | 19 | (7 | 12) | 249 | 64 | 65 | 34 | 4 | 93 | 2 | 1 | 4 | 21 | 7 | .75 | 6 | .282 | .326 | .474 |
| 1978 Montreal | NL | 157 | 609 | 154 | 24 | 8 | 25 | (12 | 13) | 269 | 84 | 72 | 30 | 3 | 128 | 12 | 4 | 5 | 28 | 11 | .72 | 7 | .253 | .299 | .442 |
| 1979 Montreal | NL | 155 | 639 | 176 | 24 | 12 | 25 | (13 | 12) | 299 | 90 | 92 | 27 | 5 | 115 | 6 | 8 | 4 | 35 | 10 | .78 | 10 | .275 | .309 | .468 |
| 1980 Montreal | NL | 151 | 577 | 178 | 41 | 7 | 17 | (7 | 10) | 284 | 96 | 87 | 44 | 7 | 69 | 6 | 1 | 10 | 34 | 9 | .79 | 9 | .308 | .358 | .492 |
| 1981 Montreal | NL | 103 | 394 | 119 | 21 | 3 | 24 | (9 | 15) | 218 | 71 | 64 | 35 | 14 | 50 | 7 | 0 | 5 | 26 | 4 | .87 | 6 | .302 | .365 | .553 |
| 1982 Montreal | NL | 148 | 608 | 183 | 37 | 7 | 23 | (9 | 14) | 303 | 107 | 83 | 34 | 4 | 96 | 8 | 4 | 6 | 39 | 10 | .80 | 8 | .301 | .343 | .498 |
| 1983 Montreal | NL | 159 | 633 | 189 | 36 | 10 | 32 | (10 | 22) | 341 | 104 | 113 | 38 | 12 | 81 | 9 | 0 | 18 | 25 | 11 | .69 | 14 | .299 | .338 | .539 |
| 1984 Montreal | NL | 138 | 533 | 132 | 23 | 6 | 17 | (6 | 11) | 218 | 73 | 86 | 41 | 2 | 80 | 2 | 1 | 6 | 13 | 5 | .72 | 12 | .248 | .301 | .409 |
| 1985 Montreal | NL | 139 | 529 | 135 | 27 | 2 | 23 | (11 | 12) | 235 | 65 | 91 | 29 | 8 | 92 | 4 | 1 | 7 | 13 | 4 | .76 | 12 | .255 | .295 | .444 |
| 1986 Montreal | NL | 130 | 496 | 141 | 32 | 2 | 20 | (11 | 9) | 237 | 65 | 78 | 37 | 11 | 79 | 6 | 1 | 6 | 18 | 12 | .60 | 13 | .284 | .338 | .478 |
| 1987 Chicago | NL | 153 | 621 | 178 | 24 | 2 | 49 | (27 | 22) | 353 | 90 | 137 | 32 | 7 | 103 | 7 | 0 | 2 | 11 | 3 | .79 | 15 | .287 | .328 | .568 |
| 1988 Chicago | NL | 157 | 591 | 179 | 31 | 8 | 24 | (12 | 12) | 298 | 78 | 79 | 37 | 12 | 73 | 4 | 1 | 7 | 12 | 4 | .75 | 13 | .303 | .344 | .504 |
| 1989 Chicago | NL | 118 | 416 | 105 | 18 | 6 | 21 | (6 | 15) | 198 | 62 | 77 | 35 | 13 | 62 | 1 | 0 | 7 | 8 | 5 | .62 | 16 | .252 | .307 | .476 |
| 1990 Chicago | NL | 147 | 529 | 164 | 28 | 5 | 27 | (14 | 13) | 283 | 72 | 100 | 42 | 21 | 65 | 2 | 0 | 8 | 16 | 2 | .89 | 12 | .310 | .358 | .535 |
| 15 ML YEARS | | 2018 | 7785 | 2201 | 396 | 88 | 346 | (154 | 192) | 3811 | 1130 | 1231 | 500 | 124 | 1199 | 76 | 24 | 95 | 300 | 99 | .75 | 153 | .283 | .328 | .490 |

## Ken Dayley

**Pitches:** Left **Bats:** Left **Pos:** RP **Ht:** 6' 0" **Wt:** 180 **Born:** 02/25/59 **Age:** 32

| | | HOW MUCH HE PITCHED | | | | | | WHAT HE GAVE UP | | | | | | | | | | | | THE RESULTS | | | | | |
|---|---|---|---|---|---|---|---|---|---|---|---|---|---|---|---|---|---|---|---|---|---|---|---|---|---|
| Year Team | Lg | G | GS | CG | GF | IP | BFP | H | R | ER | HR | SH | SF | HB | TBB | IBB | SO | WP | Bk | W | L | Pct. | ShO | Sv | ERA |
| 1982 Atlanta | NL | 20 | 11 | 0 | 3 | 71.1 | 313 | 79 | 39 | 36 | 9 | 7 | 5 | 0 | 25 | 2 | 34 | 2 | 0 | 5 | 6 | .455 | 0 | 0 | 4.54 |
| 1983 Atlanta | NL | 24 | 16 | 0 | 3 | 104.2 | 436 | 100 | 59 | 50 | 12 | 3 | 3 | 2 | 39 | 2 | 70 | 3 | 0 | 5 | 8 | .385 | 0 | 0 | 4.30 |
| 1984 2 ML Teams | | 7 | 6 | 0 | 1 | 23.2 | 124 | 44 | 28 | 21 | 6 | 4 | 0 | 1 | 11 | 1 | 10 | 0 | 0 | 0 | 5 | .000 | 0 | 0 | 7.99 |
| 1985 St. Louis | NL | 57 | 0 | 0 | 27 | 65.1 | 271 | 65 | 24 | 20 | 2 | 4 | 2 | 0 | 18 | 9 | 62 | 4 | 0 | 4 | 4 | .500 | 0 | 11 | 2.76 |
| 1986 St. Louis | NL | 31 | 0 | 0 | 13 | 38.2 | 170 | 42 | 19 | 14 | 1 | 4 | 1 | 1 | 11 | 3 | 33 | 0 | 0 | 0 | 3 | .000 | 0 | 5 | 3.26 |
| 1987 St. Louis | NL | 53 | 0 | 0 | 29 | 61 | 260 | 52 | 21 | 18 | 2 | 2 | 1 | 2 | 33 | 8 | 63 | 5 | 0 | 9 | 5 | .643 | 0 | 4 | 2.66 |
| 1988 St. Louis | NL | 54 | 0 | 0 | 21 | 55.1 | 226 | 48 | 20 | 17 | 2 | 4 | 1 | 1 | 19 | 7 | 38 | 2 | 0 | 2 | 7 | .222 | 0 | 5 | 2.77 |
| 1989 St. Louis | NL | 71 | 0 | 0 | 28 | 75.1 | 310 | 63 | 26 | 24 | 3 | 3 | 1 | 0 | 30 | 10 | 40 | 2 | 1 | 4 | 3 | .571 | 0 | 12 | 2.87 |
| 1990 St. Louis | NL | 58 | 0 | 0 | 17 | 73.1 | 307 | 63 | 32 | 29 | 5 | 2 | 5 | 0 | 30 | 7 | 51 | 6 | 0 | 4 | 4 | .500 | 0 | 2 | 3.56 |
| 1984 Atlanta | NL | 4 | 4 | 0 | 0 | 18.2 | 92 | 28 | 18 | 11 | 5 | 3 | 0 | 1 | 6 | 1 | 10 | 0 | 0 | 0 | 3 | .000 | 0 | 0 | 5.30 |
| St. Louis | NL | 3 | 2 | 0 | 1 | 5 | 32 | 16 | 10 | 10 | 1 | 1 | 0 | 0 | 5 | 0 | 0 | 0 | 0 | 0 | 2 | .000 | 0 | 0 | 18.00 |
| 9 ML YEARS | | 375 | 33 | 0 | 142 | 568.2 | 2417 | 556 | 268 | 229 | 42 | 33 | 19 | 7 | 216 | 49 | 401 | 24 | 1 | 33 | 45 | .423 | 0 | 39 | 3.62 |

## Steve Decker

**Bats:** Right **Throws:** Right **Pos:** C **Ht:** 6' 3" **Wt:** 205 **Born:** 10/25/65 **Age:** 25

| | | BATTING | | | | | | | | | | | | | | | | | BASERUNNING | | | | PERCENTAGES | | |
|---|---|---|---|---|---|---|---|---|---|---|---|---|---|---|---|---|---|---|---|---|---|---|---|---|---|
| Year Team | Lg | G | AB | H | 2B | 3B | HR | (Hm | Rd) | TB | R | RBI | TBB | IBB | SO | HBP | SH | SF | SB | CS | SB% | GDP | Avg | OBP | SLG |
| 1988 Everett | A | 13 | 42 | 22 | 2 | 0 | 2 | -- | -- | 30 | 11 | 13 | 7 | 0 | 5 | 1 | 0 | 3 | 0 | 0 | .00 | 1 | .524 | .566 | .714 |
| San Jose | A | 47 | 175 | 56 | 9 | 0 | 4 | -- | -- | 77 | 31 | 34 | 21 | 1 | 21 | 1 | 1 | 0 | 0 | 2 | .00 | 4 | .320 | .396 | .440 |
| 1989 San Jose | A | 64 | 225 | 65 | 12 | 0 | 3 | -- | -- | 86 | 27 | 46 | 44 | 3 | 36 | 0 | 0 | 5 | 8 | 5 | .62 | 9 | .289 | .398 | .382 |
| Shreveport | AA | 44 | 142 | 46 | 8 | 0 | 1 | -- | -- | 57 | 19 | 18 | 11 | 0 | 24 | 0 | 1 | 1 | 0 | 3 | .00 | 5 | .324 | .370 | .401 |
| 1990 Shreveport | AA | 116 | 403 | 118 | 22 | 1 | 15 | -- | -- | 187 | 52 | 80 | 40 | 2 | 64 | 2 | 0 | 7 | 3 | 7 | .30 | 11 | .293 | .354 | .464 |
| 1990 San Francisco | NL | 15 | 54 | 16 | 2 | 0 | 3 | (1 | 2) | 27 | 5 | 8 | 1 | 0 | 10 | 0 | 1 | 0 | 0 | 0 | .00 | 1 | .296 | .309 | .500 |

## Rob Deer

**Bats:** Right **Throws:** Right **Pos:** RF/1B **Ht:** 6' 3" **Wt:** 210 **Born:** 09/29/60 **Age:** 30

| | | BATTING | | | | | | | | | | | | | | | | | BASERUNNING | | | | PERCENTAGES | | |
|---|---|---|---|---|---|---|---|---|---|---|---|---|---|---|---|---|---|---|---|---|---|---|---|---|---|
| Year Team | Lg | G | AB | H | 2B | 3B | HR | (Hm | Rd) | TB | R | RBI | TBB | IBB | SO | HBP | SH | SF | SB | CS | SB% | GDP | Avg | OBP | SLG |
| 1984 San Francisco | NL | 13 | 24 | 4 | 0 | 0 | 3 | (2 | 1) | 13 | 5 | 3 | 7 | 0 | 10 | 1 | 0 | 0 | 1 | 1 | .50 | 0 | .167 | .375 | .542 |
| 1985 San Francisco | NL | 78 | 162 | 30 | 5 | 1 | 8 | (5 | 3) | 61 | 22 | 20 | 23 | 0 | 71 | 0 | 0 | 2 | 0 | 1 | .00 | 0 | .185 | .283 | .377 |
| 1986 Milwaukee | AL | 134 | 466 | 108 | 17 | 3 | 33 | (19 | 14) | 230 | 75 | 86 | 72 | 3 | 179 | 3 | 2 | 3 | 5 | 2 | .71 | 4 | .232 | .336 | .494 |
| 1987 Milwaukee | AL | 134 | 474 | 113 | 15 | 2 | 28 | (11 | 17) | 216 | 71 | 80 | 86 | 6 | 186 | 5 | 0 | 1 | 12 | 4 | .75 | 4 | .238 | .360 | .456 |
| 1988 Milwaukee | AL | 135 | 492 | 124 | 24 | 0 | 23 | (12 | 11) | 217 | 71 | 85 | 51 | 4 | 153 | 7 | 0 | 5 | 9 | 5 | .64 | 4 | .252 | .328 | .441 |
| 1989 Milwaukee | AL | 130 | 466 | 98 | 18 | 2 | 26 | (15 | 11) | 198 | 72 | 65 | 60 | 5 | 158 | 4 | 0 | 2 | 4 | 8 | .33 | 8 | .210 | .305 | .425 |
| 1990 Milwaukee | AL | 134 | 440 | 92 | 15 | 1 | 27 | (11 | 16) | 190 | 57 | 69 | 64 | 6 | 147 | 4 | 0 | 3 | 2 | 3 | .40 | 0 | .209 | .313 | .432 |
| 7 ML YEARS | | 758 | 2524 | 569 | 94 | 9 | 148 | (75 | 73) | 1125 | 373 | 408 | 363 | 24 | 904 | 24 | 2 | 16 | 33 | 24 | .58 | 20 | .225 | .327 | .446 |

## Jose DeJesus

**Pitches:** Right **Bats:** Right **Pos:** SP **Ht:** 6' 5" **Wt:** 175 **Born:** 01/06/65 **Age:** 26

| | | HOW MUCH HE PITCHED | | | | | | WHAT HE GAVE UP | | | | | | | | | | | | THE RESULTS | | | | | |
|---|---|---|---|---|---|---|---|---|---|---|---|---|---|---|---|---|---|---|---|---|---|---|---|---|---|
| Year Team | Lg | G | GS | CG | GF | IP | BFP | H | R | ER | HR | SH | SF | HB | TBB | IBB | SO | WP | Bk | W | L | Pct. | ShO | Sv | ERA |
| 1988 Kansas City | AL | 2 | 1 | 0 | 0 | 2.2 | 19 | 6 | 10 | 8 | 0 | 0 | 0 | 0 | 5 | 1 | 2 | 0 | 0 | 0 | 1 | .000 | 0 | 0 | 27.00 |
| 1989 Kansas City | AL | 3 | 1 | 0 | 1 | 8 | 37 | 7 | 4 | 4 | 1 | 0 | 0 | 0 | 8 | 0 | 2 | 0 | 0 | 0 | 0 | .000 | 0 | 0 | 4.50 |
| 1990 Philadelphia | NL | 22 | 22 | 3 | 0 | 130 | 544 | 97 | 63 | 54 | 10 | 8 | 0 | 2 | 73 | 3 | 87 | 4 | 0 | 7 | 8 | .467 | 1 | 0 | 3.74 |
| 3 ML YEARS | | 27 | 24 | 3 | 1 | 140.2 | 600 | 110 | 77 | 66 | 11 | 8 | 0 | 2 | 86 | 4 | 91 | 4 | 0 | 7 | 9 | .438 | 1 | 0 | 4.22 |

## Jose DeLeon

**Pitches:** Right **Bats:** Right **Pos:** SP **Ht:** 6' 3" **Wt:** 211 **Born:** 12/20/60 **Age:** 30

| | | | HOW MUCH HE PITCHED | | | | | | WHAT HE GAVE UP | | | | | | | | | | | | THE RESULTS | | | | | |
|---|---|---|---|---|---|---|---|---|---|---|---|---|---|---|---|---|---|---|---|---|---|---|---|---|---|---|
| Year | Team | Lg | G | GS | CG | GF | IP | BFP | H | R | ER | HR | SH | SF | HB | TBB | IBB | SO | WP | Bk | W | L | Pct. | ShO | Sv | ERA |
| 1983 | Pittsburgh | NL | 15 | 15 | 3 | 0 | 108 | 438 | 75 | 36 | 34 | 5 | 4 | 3 | 1 | 47 | 2 | 118 | 5 | 2 | 7 | 3 | .700 | 2 | 0 | 2.83 |
| 1984 | Pittsburgh | NL | 30 | 28 | 5 | 0 | 192.1 | 795 | 147 | 86 | 80 | 10 | 7 | 7 | 3 | 92 | 5 | 153 | 6 | 2 | 7 | 13 | .350 | 1 | 0 | 3.74 |
| 1985 | Pittsburgh | NL | 31 | 25 | 1 | 5 | 162.2 | 700 | 138 | 93 | 85 | 15 | 7 | 4 | 3 | 89 | 3 | 149 | 7 | 1 | 2 | 19 | .095 | 0 | 3 | 4.70 |
| 1986 | 2 ML Teams | | 22 | 14 | 1 | 5 | 95.1 | 408 | 66 | 46 | 41 | 9 | 5 | 1 | 5 | 59 | 3 | 79 | 7 | 0 | 5 | 8 | .385 | 0 | 1 | 3.87 |
| 1987 | Chicago | AL | 33 | 31 | 2 | 0 | 206 | 889 | 177 | 106 | 92 | 24 | 6 | 6 | 10 | 97 | 4 | 153 | 6 | 1 | 11 | 12 | .478 | 0 | 0 | 4.02 |
| 1988 | St. Louis | NL | 34 | 34 | 3 | 0 | 225.1 | 940 | 198 | 95 | 92 | 13 | 10 | 7 | 2 | 86 | 7 | 208 | 10 | 0 | 13 | 10 | .565 | 1 | 0 | 3.67 |
| 1989 | St. Louis | NL | 36 | 36 | 5 | 0 | 244.2 | 972 | 173 | 96 | 83 | 16 | 5 | 3 | 6 | 80 | 5 | 201 | 2 | 0 | 16 | 12 | .571 | 3 | 0 | 3.05 |
| 1990 | St. Louis | NL | 32 | 32 | 0 | 0 | 182.2 | 793 | 168 | 96 | 90 | 15 | 11 | 8 | 5 | 86 | 9 | 164 | 5 | 0 | 7 | 19 | .269 | 0 | 0 | 4.43 |
| 1986 | Pittsburgh | NL | 9 | 1 | 0 | 5 | 16.1 | 83 | 17 | 16 | 15 | 2 | 1 | 0 | 1 | 17 | 3 | 11 | 1 | 0 | 1 | 3 | .250 | 0 | 1 | 8.27 |
| | Chicago | AL | 13 | 13 | 1 | 0 | 79 | 325 | 49 | 30 | 26 | 7 | 4 | 1 | 4 | 42 | 0 | 68 | 6 | 0 | 4 | 5 | .444 | 0 | 0 | 2.96 |
| | 8 ML YEARS | | 233 | 215 | 20 | 10 | 1417 | 5935 | 1142 | 654 | 597 | 107 | 55 | 39 | 35 | 636 | 38 | 1225 | 48 | 6 | 68 | 96 | .415 | 7 | 4 | 3.79 |

## Rich Delucia

**Pitches:** Right **Bats:** Right **Pos:** SP **Ht:** 6' 0" **Wt:** 180 **Born:** 10/07/64 **Age:** 26

| | | | HOW MUCH HE PITCHED | | | | | | WHAT HE GAVE UP | | | | | | | | | | | | THE RESULTS | | | | | |
|---|---|---|---|---|---|---|---|---|---|---|---|---|---|---|---|---|---|---|---|---|---|---|---|---|---|---|
| Year | Team | Lg | G | GS | CG | GF | IP | BFP | H | R | ER | HR | SH | SF | HB | TBB | IBB | SO | WP | Bk | W | L | Pct. | ShO | Sv | ERA |
| 1986 | Bellingham | A | 13 | 11 | 1 | 1 | 74 | 0 | 44 | 20 | 14 | 4 | 0 | 0 | 1 | 24 | 0 | 69 | 3 | 0 | 8 | 2 | .800 | 1 | 0 | 1.70 |
| 1988 | San Berndno | A | 22 | 22 | 0 | 0 | 127.2 | 541 | 110 | 57 | 44 | 4 | 2 | 6 | 7 | 59 | 3 | 118 | 6 | 2 | 7 | 8 | .467 | 0 | 0 | 3.10 |
| 1989 | Williamsprt | AA | 10 | 10 | 0 | 0 | 54.2 | 234 | 59 | 28 | 23 | 5 | 3 | 2 | 1 | 13 | 0 | 41 | 5 | 0 | 3 | 4 | .429 | 0 | 0 | 3.79 |
| 1990 | San Berndno | A | 5 | 5 | 1 | 0 | 30.2 | 116 | 19 | 9 | 7 | 4 | 1 | 0 | 4 | 3 | 0 | 35 | 1 | 0 | 4 | 1 | .800 | 0 | 0 | 2.05 |
| | Williamsprt | AA | 18 | 18 | 2 | 0 | 115 | 447 | 92 | 30 | 27 | 7 | 3 | 3 | 2 | 30 | 2 | 76 | 1 | 0 | 6 | 6 | .500 | 1 | 0 | 2.11 |
| | Calgary | AAA | 5 | 5 | 1 | 0 | 32.1 | 139 | 30 | 17 | 13 | 2 | 0 | 3 | 2 | 12 | 0 | 23 | 3 | 0 | 2 | 2 | .500 | 0 | 0 | 3.62 |
| 1990 | Seattle | AL | 5 | 5 | 1 | 0 | 36 | 144 | 30 | 9 | 8 | 2 | 2 | 0 | 0 | 9 | 0 | 20 | 0 | 0 | 1 | 2 | .333 | 0 | 0 | 2.00 |

## Rick Dempsey

**Bats:** Right **Throws:** Right **Pos:** C **Ht:** 6' 0" **Wt:** 184 **Born:** 09/13/49 **Age:** 41

| | | | BATTING | | | | | | | | | | | | | | | | | BASERUNNING | | | | PERCENTAGES | | |
|---|---|---|---|---|---|---|---|---|---|---|---|---|---|---|---|---|---|---|---|---|---|---|---|---|---|---|
| Year | Team | Lg | G | AB | H | 2B | 3B | HR | (Hm | Rd) | TB | R | RBI | TBB | IBB | SO | HBP | SH | SF | SB | CS | SB% | GDP | Avg | OBP | SLG |
| 1969 | Minnesota | AL | 5 | 6 | 3 | 1 | 0 | 0 | (0 | 0) | 4 | 1 | 0 | 1 | 0 | 0 | 0 | 0 | 0 | 0 | 0 | .00 | 0 | .500 | .571 | .667 |
| 1970 | Minnesota | AL | 5 | 7 | 0 | 0 | 0 | 0 | (0 | 0) | 0 | 1 | 0 | 1 | 0 | 1 | 0 | 0 | 0 | 0 | 0 | .00 | 1 | .000 | .125 | .000 |
| 1971 | Minnesota | AL | 6 | 13 | 4 | 1 | 0 | 0 | (0 | 0) | 5 | 2 | 0 | 1 | 0 | 1 | 0 | 0 | 0 | 0 | 0 | .00 | 1 | .308 | .357 | .385 |
| 1972 | Minnesota | AL | 25 | 40 | 8 | 1 | 0 | 0 | (0 | 0) | 9 | 0 | 0 | 6 | 0 | 8 | 0 | 1 | 0 | 0 | 0 | .00 | 2 | .200 | .304 | .225 |
| 1973 | New York | AL | 6 | 11 | 2 | 0 | 0 | 0 | (0 | 0) | 2 | 0 | 0 | 1 | 0 | 3 | 0 | 1 | 0 | 0 | 0 | .00 | 1 | .182 | .250 | .182 |
| 1974 | New York | AL | 43 | 109 | 26 | 3 | 0 | 2 | (1 | 1) | 35 | 12 | 12 | 8 | 0 | 7 | 0 | 1 | 1 | 1 | 0 | 1.00 | 5 | .239 | .288 | .321 |
| 1975 | New York | AL | 71 | 145 | 38 | 8 | 0 | 1 | (0 | 1) | 49 | 18 | 11 | 21 | 1 | 15 | 0 | 3 | 1 | 0 | 0 | .00 | 5 | .262 | .353 | .338 |
| 1976 | 2 ML Teams | | 80 | 216 | 42 | 2 | 0 | 0 | (0 | 0) | 44 | 12 | 12 | 18 | 0 | 21 | 2 | 4 | 0 | 1 | 1 | .50 | 2 | .194 | .263 | .204 |
| 1977 | Baltimore | AL | 91 | 270 | 61 | 7 | 4 | 3 | (1 | 2) | 85 | 27 | 34 | 34 | 1 | 34 | 2 | 5 | 3 | 2 | 3 | .40 | 9 | .226 | .314 | .315 |
| 1978 | Baltimore | AL | 136 | 441 | 114 | 25 | 0 | 6 | (4 | 2) | 157 | 41 | 32 | 48 | 2 | 54 | 0 | 3 | 6 | 7 | 3 | .70 | 11 | .259 | .327 | .356 |
| 1979 | Baltimore | AL | 124 | 368 | 88 | 23 | 0 | 6 | (1 | 5) | 129 | 48 | 41 | 38 | 1 | 37 | 0 | 3 | 4 | 0 | 1 | .00 | 12 | .239 | .307 | .351 |
| 1980 | Baltimore | AL | 119 | 362 | 95 | 26 | 3 | 9 | (5 | 4) | 154 | 51 | 40 | 36 | 1 | 45 | 3 | 4 | 1 | 3 | 1 | .75 | 11 | .262 | .333 | .425 |
| 1981 | Baltimore | AL | 92 | 251 | 54 | 10 | 1 | 6 | (4 | 2) | 84 | 24 | 15 | 32 | 1 | 36 | 1 | 3 | 0 | 0 | 1 | .00 | 5 | .215 | .306 | .335 |
| 1982 | Baltimore | AL | 125 | 344 | 88 | 15 | 1 | 5 | (2 | 3) | 120 | 35 | 36 | 46 | 1 | 37 | 0 | 7 | 5 | 0 | 3 | .00 | 10 | .256 | .339 | .349 |
| 1983 | Baltimore | AL | 128 | 347 | 80 | 16 | 2 | 4 | (3 | 1) | 112 | 33 | 32 | 40 | 1 | 54 | 3 | 5 | 5 | 1 | 1 | .50 | 9 | .231 | .311 | .323 |
| 1984 | Baltimore | AL | 109 | 330 | 76 | 11 | 0 | 11 | (6 | 5) | 120 | 37 | 34 | 40 | 0 | 58 | 1 | 5 | 4 | 1 | 2 | .33 | 11 | .230 | .312 | .364 |
| 1985 | Baltimore | AL | 132 | 362 | 92 | 19 | 0 | 12 | (4 | 8) | 147 | 54 | 52 | 50 | 0 | 87 | 1 | 5 | 2 | 0 | 1 | .00 | 2 | .254 | .345 | .406 |
| 1986 | Baltimore | AL | 122 | 327 | 68 | 15 | 1 | 13 | (7 | 6) | 124 | 42 | 29 | 45 | 0 | 78 | 3 | 7 | 0 | 1 | 0 | 1.00 | 5 | .208 | .309 | .379 |
| 1987 | Cleveland | AL | 60 | 141 | 25 | 10 | 0 | 1 | (1 | 0) | 38 | 16 | 9 | 23 | 0 | 29 | 1 | 4 | 1 | 0 | 0 | .00 | 4 | .177 | .295 | .270 |
| 1988 | Los Angeles | NL | 77 | 167 | 42 | 13 | 0 | 7 | (3 | 4) | 76 | 25 | 30 | 25 | 0 | 44 | 0 | 0 | 6 | 1 | 0 | 1.00 | 4 | .251 | .338 | .455 |
| 1989 | Los Angeles | NL | 79 | 151 | 27 | 7 | 0 | 4 | (2 | 2) | 46 | 16 | 16 | 30 | 3 | 37 | 1 | 1 | 0 | 1 | 0 | 1.00 | 5 | .179 | .319 | .305 |
| 1990 | Los Angeles | NL | 62 | 128 | 25 | 5 | 0 | 2 | (2 | 0) | 36 | 13 | 15 | 23 | 0 | 29 | 0 | 0 | 0 | 1 | 0 | 1.00 | 8 | .195 | .318 | .281 |
| 1976 | New York | AL | 21 | 42 | 5 | 0 | 0 | 0 | (0 | 0) | 5 | 1 | 2 | 5 | 0 | 4 | 0 | 1 | 0 | 0 | 0 | .00 | 0 | .119 | .213 | .119 |
| | Baltimore | AL | 59 | 174 | 37 | 2 | 0 | 0 | (0 | 0) | 39 | 11 | 10 | 13 | 0 | 17 | 2 | 3 | 0 | 1 | 1 | .50 | 2 | .213 | .275 | .224 |
| | 22 ML YEARS | | 1697 | 4536 | 1058 | 218 | 12 | 92 | (46 | 46) | 1576 | 508 | 450 | 567 | 12 | 715 | 18 | 62 | 39 | 20 | 17 | .54 | 123 | .233 | .318 | .347 |

## Jim Deshaies

**Pitches:** Left **Bats:** Left **Pos:** SP **Ht:** 6' 4" **Wt:** 222 **Born:** 06/23/60 **Age:** 31

| | | | HOW MUCH HE PITCHED | | | | | | WHAT HE GAVE UP | | | | | | | | | | | | THE RESULTS | | | | | |
|---|---|---|---|---|---|---|---|---|---|---|---|---|---|---|---|---|---|---|---|---|---|---|---|---|---|---|
| Year | Team | Lg | G | GS | CG | GF | IP | BFP | H | R | ER | HR | SH | SF | HB | TBB | IBB | SO | WP | Bk | W | L | Pct. | ShO | Sv | ERA |
| 1984 | New York | AL | 2 | 2 | 0 | 0 | 7 | 40 | 14 | 9 | 9 | 1 | 0 | 1 | 0 | 7 | 0 | 5 | 0 | 0 | 0 | 1 | .000 | 0 | 0 | 11.57 |
| 1985 | Houston | NL | 2 | 0 | 0 | 0 | 3 | 10 | 1 | 0 | 0 | 0 | 0 | 0 | 0 | 0 | 0 | 2 | 0 | 0 | 0 | 0 | .000 | 0 | 0 | 0.00 |
| 1986 | Houston | NL | 26 | 26 | 1 | 0 | 144 | 599 | 124 | 58 | 52 | 16 | 4 | 3 | 2 | 59 | 2 | 128 | 0 | 7 | 12 | 5 | .706 | 1 | 0 | 3.25 |
| 1987 | Houston | NL | 26 | 25 | 1 | 0 | 152 | 648 | 149 | 81 | 78 | 22 | 9 | 3 | 0 | 57 | 7 | 104 | 4 | 5 | 11 | 6 | .647 | 0 | 0 | 4.62 |

| Year | Team | Lg | G | GS | CG | GF | IP | BFP | H | R | ER | HR | SH | SF | HB | TBB | IBB | SO | WP | Bk | W | L | Pct. | ShO | Sv | ERA |
|---|---|---|---|---|---|---|---|---|---|---|---|---|---|---|---|---|---|---|---|---|---|---|---|---|---|---|
| 1988 | Houston | NL | 31 | 31 | 3 | 0 | 207 | 847 | 164 | 77 | 69 | 20 | 8 | 13 | 2 | 72 | 5 | 127 | 1 | 6 | 11 | 14 | .440 | 2 | 0 | 3.00 |
| 1989 | Houston | NL | 34 | 34 | 6 | 0 | 225.2 | 928 | 180 | 80 | 73 | 15 | 11 | 5 | 4 | 79 | 8 | 153 | 8 | 1 | 15 | 10 | .600 | 3 | 0 | 2.91 |
| 1990 | Houston | NL | 34 | 34 | 2 | 0 | 209.1 | 881 | 186 | 93 | 88 | 21 | 17 | 12 | 8 | 84 | 9 | 119 | 3 | 3 | 7 | 12 | .368 | 0 | 0 | 3.78 |
| | 7 ML YEARS | | 155 | 152 | 13 | 0 | 948 | 3953 | 818 | 398 | 369 | 95 | 49 | 37 | 16 | 358 | 31 | 638 | 16 | 22 | 56 | 48 | .538 | 6 | 0 | 3.50 |

## Delino DeShields

**Bats:** Left **Throws:** Right **Pos:** 2B **Ht:** 6' 1" **Wt:** 170 **Born:** 01/15/69 **Age:** 22

| BATTING | | | | | | | | | | | | | | | | | | | BASERUNNING | | | | PERCENTAGES | | |
|---|---|---|---|---|---|---|---|---|---|---|---|---|---|---|---|---|---|---|---|---|---|---|---|---|---|
| Year Team | Lg | G | AB | H | 2B | 3B | HR | (Hm | Rd) | TB | R | RBI | TBB | IBB | SO | HBP | SH | SF | SB | CS | SB% | GDP | Avg | OBP | SLG |
| 1987 Expos | R | 31 | 111 | 24 | 5 | 2 | 1 | -- | -- | 36 | 17 | 4 | 21 | 0 | 30 | 2 | 0 | 0 | 16 | 5 | .76 | 0 | .216 | .351 | .324 |
| Jamestown | A | 34 | 96 | 21 | 1 | 2 | 1 | -- | -- | 29 | 16 | 5 | 24 | 1 | 28 | 1 | 2 | 1 | 14 | 4 | .78 | 0 | .219 | .377 | .302 |
| 1988 Rockford | A | 129 | 460 | 116 | 26 | 6 | 12 | -- | -- | 190 | 97 | 46 | 95 | 3 | 110 | 2 | 2 | 3 | 59 | 18 | .77 | 4 | .252 | .380 | .413 |
| 1989 Jacksnville | AA | 93 | 307 | 83 | 10 | 6 | 3 | -- | -- | 114 | 55 | 35 | 76 | 0 | 80 | 1 | 4 | 3 | 37 | 12 | .76 | 3 | .270 | .413 | .371 |
| Indianapols | AAA | 47 | 181 | 47 | 8 | 4 | 2 | -- | -- | 69 | 29 | 14 | 16 | 0 | 53 | 0 | 1 | 0 | 16 | 7 | .70 | 0 | .260 | .320 | .381 |
| 1990 Montreal | NL | 129 | 499 | 144 | 28 | 6 | 4 | (3 | 1) | 196 | 69 | 45 | 66 | 3 | 96 | 4 | 1 | 2 | 42 | 22 | .66 | 10 | .289 | .375 | .393 |

## Mike Devereaux

**Bats:** Right **Throws:** Right **Pos:** CF **Ht:** 6' 0" **Wt:** 195 **Born:** 04/10/63 **Age:** 28

| BATTING | | | | | | | | | | | | | | | | | | | BASERUNNING | | | | PERCENTAGES | | |
|---|---|---|---|---|---|---|---|---|---|---|---|---|---|---|---|---|---|---|---|---|---|---|---|---|---|
| Year Team | Lg | G | AB | H | 2B | 3B | HR | (Hm | Rd) | TB | R | RBI | TBB | IBB | SO | HBP | SH | SF | SB | CS | SB% | GDP | Avg | OBP | SLG |
| 1987 Los Angeles | NL | 19 | 54 | 12 | 3 | 0 | 0 | (0 | 0) | 15 | 7 | 4 | 3 | 0 | 10 | 0 | 1 | 0 | 3 | 1 | .75 | 0 | .222 | .263 | .278 |
| 1988 Los Angeles | NL | 30 | 43 | 5 | 1 | 0 | 0 | (0 | 0) | 6 | 4 | 2 | 2 | 0 | 10 | 0 | 0 | 0 | 0 | 1 | .00 | 0 | .116 | .156 | .140 |
| 1989 Baltimore | AL | 122 | 391 | 104 | 14 | 3 | 8 | (4 | 4) | 148 | 55 | 46 | 36 | 0 | 60 | 2 | 2 | 3 | 22 | 11 | .67 | 7 | .266 | .329 | .379 |
| 1990 Baltimore | AL | 108 | 367 | 88 | 18 | 1 | 12 | (6 | 6) | 144 | 48 | 49 | 28 | 0 | 48 | 0 | 4 | 4 | 13 | 12 | .52 | 10 | .240 | .291 | .392 |
| 4 ML YEARS | | 279 | 855 | 209 | 36 | 4 | 20 | (10 | 10) | 313 | 114 | 101 | 69 | 0 | 128 | 2 | 7 | 7 | 38 | 25 | .60 | 17 | .244 | .300 | .366 |

## Mark Dewey

**Pitches:** Right **Bats:** Right **Pos:** RP **Ht:** 6' 0" **Wt:** 185 **Born:** 01/03/65 **Age:** 26

| HOW MUCH HE PITCHED | | | | | | | WHAT HE GAVE UP | | | | | | | | | | | | THE RESULTS | | | | | |
|---|---|---|---|---|---|---|---|---|---|---|---|---|---|---|---|---|---|---|---|---|---|---|---|---|
| Year Team | Lg | G | GS | CG | GF | IP | BFP | H | R | ER | HR | SH | SF | HB | TBB | IBB | SO | WP | Bk | W | L | Pct. | ShO | Sv | ERA |
| 1987 Everett | A | 19 | 10 | 1 | 5 | 84.2 | 365 | 88 | 39 | 31 | 2 | 2 | 6 | 2 | 26 | 1 | 67 | 1 | 2 | 7 | 3 | .700 | 0 | 1 | 3.30 |
| 1988 Clinton | A | 37 | 7 | 1 | 11 | 119.1 | 474 | 95 | 36 | 19 | 5 | 2 | 1 | 8 | 14 | 0 | 76 | 1 | 5 | 10 | 4 | .714 | 0 | 7 | 1.43 |
| 1989 San Jose | A | 59 | 0 | 0 | 57 | 68.2 | 301 | 62 | 35 | 24 | 2 | 5 | 1 | 7 | 23 | 5 | 60 | 3 | 0 | 1 | 6 | .143 | 0 | 30 | 3.15 |
| 1990 Shreveport | AA | 33 | 0 | 0 | 32 | 38.1 | 157 | 37 | 11 | 8 | 1 | 3 | 0 | 1 | 10 | 2 | 23 | 1 | 0 | 1 | 5 | .167 | 0 | 13 | 1.88 |
| Phoenix | AAA | 19 | 0 | 0 | 17 | 30.1 | 130 | 26 | 14 | 9 | 2 | 2 | 1 | 2 | 10 | 2 | 27 | 1 | 0 | 2 | 3 | .400 | 0 | 8 | 2.67 |
| 1990 San Francisco | NL | 14 | 0 | 0 | 5 | 22.2 | 92 | 22 | 7 | 7 | 1 | 2 | 0 | 0 | 5 | 1 | 11 | 0 | 1 | 1 | 1 | .500 | 0 | 0 | 2.78 |

## Carlos Diaz

**Bats:** Right **Throws:** Right **Pos:** C **Ht:** 6' 3" **Wt:** 195 **Born:** 12/24/64 **Age:** 26

| BATTING | | | | | | | | | | | | | | | | | | | BASERUNNING | | | | PERCENTAGES | | |
|---|---|---|---|---|---|---|---|---|---|---|---|---|---|---|---|---|---|---|---|---|---|---|---|---|---|
| Year Team | Lg | G | AB | H | 2B | 3B | HR | (Hm | Rd) | TB | R | RBI | TBB | IBB | SO | HBP | SH | SF | SB | CS | SB% | GDP | Avg | OBP | SLG |
| 1986 Ventura | A | 2 | 5 | 2 | 1 | 0 | 0 | -- | -- | 3 | 1 | 0 | 1 | 0 | 2 | 0 | 0 | 0 | 0 | 0 | .00 | 0 | .400 | .500 | .600 |
| Medicne Hat | R | 20 | 83 | 26 | 5 | 2 | 0 | -- | -- | 35 | 11 | 16 | 6 | 0 | 17 | 0 | 0 | 1 | 1 | 0 | 1.00 | 1 | .313 | .356 | .422 |
| St.Cathrnes | A | 24 | 74 | 13 | 3 | 1 | 1 | -- | -- | 21 | 9 | 5 | 7 | 2 | 18 | 2 | 0 | 1 | 1 | 0 | 1.00 | 1 | .176 | .262 | .284 |
| 1987 Dunedin | A | 73 | 230 | 53 | 6 | 0 | 0 | -- | -- | 59 | 24 | 27 | 22 | 0 | 41 | 1 | 1 | 1 | 3 | 2 | .60 | 3 | .230 | .299 | .257 |
| 1988 Knoxville | AA | 7 | 23 | 5 | 1 | 0 | 0 | -- | -- | 6 | 2 | 0 | 2 | 0 | 4 | 0 | 0 | 0 | 0 | 1 | .00 | 1 | .217 | .280 | .261 |
| Dunedin | A | 68 | 235 | 46 | 11 | 0 | 6 | -- | -- | 75 | 20 | 23 | 20 | 0 | 56 | 2 | 2 | 1 | 2 | 2 | .50 | 8 | .196 | .264 | .319 |
| Syracuse | AAA | 27 | 83 | 14 | 5 | 0 | 1 | -- | -- | 22 | 4 | 8 | 1 | 0 | 23 | 0 | 2 | 1 | 0 | 0 | .00 | 0 | .169 | .176 | .265 |
| 1989 Knoxville | AA | 100 | 320 | 80 | 12 | 1 | 6 | -- | -- | 112 | 28 | 36 | 17 | 0 | 55 | 3 | 4 | 3 | 3 | 1 | .75 | 6 | .250 | .292 | .350 |
| 1990 Syracuse | AAA | 77 | 251 | 51 | 10 | 0 | 1 | -- | -- | 64 | 18 | 19 | 17 | 1 | 51 | 0 | 5 | 2 | 2 | 2 | .50 | 9 | .203 | .252 | .255 |
| 1990 Toronto | AL | 9 | 3 | 1 | 0 | 0 | 0 | (0 | 0) | 1 | 1 | 0 | 0 | 0 | 2 | 0 | 1 | 0 | 0 | 0 | .00 | 0 | .333 | .333 | .333 |

## Edgar Diaz

**Bats:** Right **Throws:** Right **Pos:** SS **Ht:** 6' 0" **Wt:** 160 **Born:** 02/08/64 **Age:** 27

| BATTING | | | | | | | | | | | | | | | | | | | BASERUNNING | | | | PERCENTAGES | | |
|---|---|---|---|---|---|---|---|---|---|---|---|---|---|---|---|---|---|---|---|---|---|---|---|---|---|
| Year Team | Lg | G | AB | H | 2B | 3B | HR | (Hm | Rd) | TB | R | RBI | TBB | IBB | SO | HBP | SH | SF | SB | CS | SB% | GDP | Avg | OBP | SLG |
| 1986 Milwaukee | AL | 5 | 13 | 3 | 0 | 0 | 0 | (0 | 0) | 3 | 0 | 0 | 1 | 0 | 3 | 0 | 0 | 0 | 0 | 0 | .00 | 0 | .231 | .286 | .231 |
| 1990 Milwaukee | AL | 86 | 218 | 59 | 2 | 2 | 0 | (0 | 0) | 65 | 27 | 14 | 21 | 0 | 32 | 1 | 5 | 0 | 3 | 2 | .60 | 3 | .271 | .338 | .298 |
| 2 ML YEARS | | 91 | 231 | 62 | 2 | 2 | 0 | (0 | 0) | 68 | 27 | 14 | 22 | 0 | 35 | 1 | 5 | 0 | 3 | 2 | .60 | 3 | .268 | .335 | .294 |

## Mario Diaz

**Bats:** Right **Throws:** Right **Pos:** SS **Ht:** 5'10" **Wt:** 160 **Born:** 01/10/62 **Age:** 29

| BATTING | | | | | | | | | | | | | | | | | | | BASERUNNING | | | | PERCENTAGES | | |
|---|---|---|---|---|---|---|---|---|---|---|---|---|---|---|---|---|---|---|---|---|---|---|---|---|---|
| Year Team | Lg | G | AB | H | 2B | 3B | HR | (Hm | Rd) | TB | R | RBI | TBB | IBB | SO | HBP | SH | SF | SB | CS | SB% | GDP | Avg | OBP | SLG |
| 1987 Seattle | AL | 11 | 23 | 7 | 0 | 1 | 0 | (0 | 0) | 9 | 4 | 3 | 0 | 0 | 4 | 0 | 0 | 0 | 0 | 0 | .00 | 0 | .304 | .304 | .391 |
| 1988 Seattle | AL | 28 | 72 | 22 | 5 | 0 | 0 | (0 | 0) | 27 | 6 | 9 | 3 | 0 | 5 | 0 | 0 | 1 | 0 | 0 | .00 | 3 | .306 | .329 | .375 |

| Year Team | Lg | G | AB | H | 2B | 3B | HR | (Hm | Rd) | TB | R | RBI | TBB | IBB | SO | HBP | SH | SF | SB | CS | SB% | GDP | Avg | OBP | SLG |
|---|---|---|---|---|---|---|---|---|---|---|---|---|---|---|---|---|---|---|---|---|---|---|---|---|---|
| 1989 Seattle | AL | 52 | 74 | 10 | 0 | 0 | 1 | (0 | 1) | 13 | 9 | 7 | 7 | 0 | 7 | 0 | 5 | 0 | 0 | 0 | .00 | 2 | .135 | .210 | .176 |
| 1990 New York | NL | 16 | 22 | 3 | 1 | 0 | 0 | (0 | 0) | 4 | 0 | 1 | 0 | 0 | 3 | 0 | 0 | 1 | 0 | 0 | .00 | 0 | .136 | .130 | .182 |
| 4 ML YEARS | | 107 | 191 | 42 | 6 | 1 | 1 | (0 | 1) | 53 | 19 | 20 | 10 | 0 | 19 | 0 | 5 | 2 | 0 | 0 | .00 | 5 | .220 | .256 | .277 |

## Rob Dibble

**Pitches:** Right **Bats:** Left **Pos:** RP **Ht:** 6' 4" **Wt:** 235 **Born:** 01/24/64 **Age:** 27

| | | HOW MUCH HE PITCHED | | | | | | WHAT HE GAVE UP | | | | | | | | | | | | THE RESULTS | | | | | |
|---|---|---|---|---|---|---|---|---|---|---|---|---|---|---|---|---|---|---|---|---|---|---|---|---|---|
| Year Team | Lg | G | GS | CG | GF | IP | BFP | H | R | ER | HR | SH | SF | HB | TBB | IBB | SO | WP | Bk | W | L | Pct. | ShO | Sv | ERA |
| 1988 Cincinnati | NL | 37 | 0 | 0 | 6 | 59.1 | 235 | 43 | 12 | 12 | 2 | 2 | 3 | 1 | 21 | 5 | 59 | 3 | 2 | 1 | 1 | .500 | 0 | 0 | 1.82 |
| 1989 Cincinnati | NL | 74 | 0 | 0 | 18 | 99 | 401 | 62 | 23 | 23 | 4 | 3 | 4 | 3 | 39 | 11 | 141 | 7 | 0 | 10 | 5 | .667 | 0 | 2 | 2.09 |
| 1990 Cincinnati | NL | 68 | 0 | 0 | 29 | 98 | 384 | 62 | 22 | 19 | 3 | 4 | 6 | 1 | 34 | 3 | 136 | 3 | 1 | 8 | 3 | .727 | 0 | 11 | 1.74 |
| 3 ML YEARS | | 179 | 0 | 0 | 53 | 256.1 | 1020 | 167 | 57 | 54 | 9 | 9 | 13 | 5 | 94 | 19 | 336 | 13 | 3 | 19 | 9 | .679 | 0 | 13 | 1.90 |

## Lance Dickson

**Pitches:** Left **Bats:** Right **Pos:** SP **Ht:** 6' 0" **Wt:** 180 **Born:** 01/01/70 **Age:** 21

| | | HOW MUCH HE PITCHED | | | | | | WHAT HE GAVE UP | | | | | | | | | | | | THE RESULTS | | | | | |
|---|---|---|---|---|---|---|---|---|---|---|---|---|---|---|---|---|---|---|---|---|---|---|---|---|---|
| Year Team | Lg | G | GS | CG | GF | IP | BFP | H | R | ER | HR | SH | SF | HB | TBB | IBB | SO | WP | Bk | W | L | Pct. | ShO | Sv | ERA |
| 1990 Geneva | A | 3 | 3 | 0 | 0 | 17 | 56 | 5 | 1 | 1 | 1 | 0 | 0 | 0 | 4 | 0 | 29 | 0 | 0 | 2 | 1 | .667 | 0 | 0 | 0.53 |
| Peoria | A | 5 | 5 | 1 | 0 | 35.2 | 138 | 22 | 9 | 6 | 1 | 1 | 0 | 0 | 11 | 0 | 54 | 2 | 4 | 3 | 1 | .750 | 0 | 0 | 1.51 |
| Charlotte | AA | 3 | 3 | 1 | 0 | 23.2 | 87 | 13 | 1 | 1 | 0 | 1 | 0 | 0 | 3 | 0 | 28 | 2 | 0 | 2 | 1 | .667 | 1 | 0 | 0.38 |
| 1990 Chicago | NL | 3 | 3 | 0 | 0 | 13.2 | 61 | 20 | 12 | 11 | 2 | 2 | 1 | 0 | 4 | 1 | 4 | 0 | 1 | 0 | 3 | .000 | 0 | 0 | 7.24 |

## Frank DePino

**Pitches:** Left **Bats:** Left **Pos:** RP **Ht:** 6' 0" **Wt:** 180 **Born:** 10/22/56 **Age:** 34

| | | HOW MUCH HE PITCHED | | | | | | WHAT HE GAVE UP | | | | | | | | | | | | THE RESULTS | | | | | |
|---|---|---|---|---|---|---|---|---|---|---|---|---|---|---|---|---|---|---|---|---|---|---|---|---|---|
| Year Team | Lg | G | GS | CG | GF | IP | BFP | H | R | ER | HR | SH | SF | HB | TBB | IBB | SO | WP | Bk | W | L | Pct. | ShO | Sv | ERA |
| 1981 Milwaukee | AL | 2 | 0 | 0 | 2 | 2 | 10 | 0 | 0 | 0 | 0 | 0 | 0 | 0 | 3 | 0 | 3 | 0 | 0 | 0 | 0 | .000 | 0 | 0 | 0.00 |
| 1982 Houston | NL | 6 | 6 | 0 | 0 | 28.1 | 122 | 32 | 20 | 19 | 1 | 3 | 2 | 0 | 11 | 1 | 25 | 0 | 0 | 2 | 2 | .500 | 0 | 0 | 6.04 |
| 1983 Houston | NL | 53 | 0 | 0 | 32 | 71.1 | 279 | 52 | 21 | 21 | 2 | 1 | 3 | 1 | 20 | 5 | 67 | 3 | 0 | 3 | 4 | .429 | 0 | 20 | 2.65 |
| 1984 Houston | NL | 57 | 0 | 0 | 44 | 75.1 | 329 | 74 | 32 | 28 | 3 | 5 | 2 | 1 | 36 | 11 | 65 | 3 | 1 | 4 | 9 | .308 | 0 | 14 | 3.35 |
| 1985 Houston | NL | 54 | 0 | 0 | 29 | 76 | 329 | 69 | 44 | 34 | 7 | 3 | 3 | 2 | 43 | 6 | 49 | 4 | 1 | 3 | 7 | .300 | 0 | 6 | 4.03 |
| 1986 2 ML Teams | | 61 | 0 | 0 | 26 | 80.1 | 345 | 74 | 45 | 39 | 11 | 9 | 3 | 2 | 30 | 6 | 70 | 3 | 0 | 3 | 7 | .300 | 0 | 3 | 4.37 |
| 1987 Chicago | NL | 69 | 0 | 0 | 20 | 80 | 343 | 75 | 31 | 28 | 7 | 6 | 4 | 1 | 34 | 2 | 61 | 5 | 0 | 3 | 3 | .500 | 0 | 4 | 3.15 |
| 1988 Chicago | NL | 63 | 0 | 0 | 23 | 90.1 | 398 | 102 | 54 | 50 | 6 | 2 | 6 | 0 | 32 | 7 | 69 | 6 | 1 | 2 | 3 | .400 | 0 | 6 | 4.98 |
| 1989 St. Louis | NL | 67 | 0 | 0 | 8 | 88.1 | 347 | 73 | 26 | 24 | 6 | 1 | 5 | 0 | 20 | 7 | 44 | 2 | 0 | 9 | 0 | 1.000 | 0 | 0 | 2.45 |
| 1990 St. Louis | NL | 62 | 0 | 0 | 24 | 81 | 360 | 92 | 45 | 41 | 8 | 8 | 7 | 1 | 31 | 12 | 49 | 2 | 1 | 5 | 2 | .714 | 0 | 3 | 4.56 |
| 1986 Houston | NL | 31 | 0 | 0 | 14 | 40.1 | 167 | 27 | 18 | 16 | 5 | 5 | 1 | 2 | 16 | 1 | 27 | 0 | 0 | 1 | 3 | .250 | 0 | 3 | 3.57 |
| Chicago | NL | 30 | 0 | 0 | 12 | 40 | 178 | 47 | 27 | 23 | 6 | 4 | 2 | 0 | 14 | 5 | 43 | 3 | 0 | 2 | 4 | .333 | 0 | 0 | 5.18 |
| 10 ML YEARS | | 494 | 6 | 0 | 208 | 673 | 2862 | 643 | 318 | 284 | 51 | 38 | 35 | 8 | 260 | 57 | 502 | 28 | 4 | 34 | 37 | .479 | 0 | 56 | 3.80 |

## Gary Disarcina

**Bats:** Right **Throws:** Right **Pos:** SS **Ht:** 6' 1" **Wt:** 170 **Born:** 11/19/67 **Age:** 23

| | | BATTING | | | | | | | | | | | | | | | | | BASERUNNING | | | | PERCENTAGES | | |
|---|---|---|---|---|---|---|---|---|---|---|---|---|---|---|---|---|---|---|---|---|---|---|---|---|---|
| Year Team | Lg | G | AB | H | 2B | 3B | HR | (Hm | Rd) | TB | R | RBI | TBB | IBB | SO | HBP | SH | SF | SB | CS | SB% | GDP | Avg | OBP | SLG |
| 1988 Bend | A | 71 | 295 | 90 | 11 | 5 | 2 | -- | -- | 117 | 40 | 39 | 27 | 1 | 34 | 2 | 4 | 4 | 7 | 4 | .64 | 6 | .305 | .363 | .397 |
| 1989 Midland | AA | 126 | 441 | 126 | 18 | 7 | 4 | -- | -- | 170 | 65 | 54 | 24 | 3 | 54 | 4 | 7 | 5 | 11 | 6 | .65 | 17 | .286 | .325 | .385 |
| 1990 Edmonton | AAA | 97 | 330 | 70 | 12 | 2 | 4 | -- | -- | 98 | 46 | 37 | 25 | 0 | 46 | 4 | 5 | 2 | 5 | 3 | .63 | 6 | .212 | .274 | .297 |
| 1989 California | AL | 2 | 0 | 0 | 0 | 0 | 0 | (0 | 0) | 0 | 0 | 0 | 0 | 0 | 0 | 0 | 0 | 0 | 0 | 0 | .00 | 0 | .000 | .000 | .000 |
| 1990 California | AL | 18 | 57 | 8 | 1 | 1 | 0 | (0 | 0) | 11 | 8 | 0 | 3 | 0 | 10 | 0 | 1 | 0 | 1 | 0 | 1.00 | 3 | .140 | .183 | .193 |
| 2 ML YEARS | | 20 | 57 | 8 | 1 | 1 | 0 | (0 | 0) | 11 | 8 | 0 | 3 | 0 | 10 | 0 | 1 | 0 | 1 | 0 | 1.00 | 3 | .140 | .183 | .193 |

## John Dopson

**Pitches:** Right **Bats:** Left **Pos:** SP **Ht:** 6' 4" **Wt:** 225 **Born:** 07/14/63 **Age:** 27

| | | HOW MUCH HE PITCHED | | | | | | WHAT HE GAVE UP | | | | | | | | | | | | THE RESULTS | | | | | |
|---|---|---|---|---|---|---|---|---|---|---|---|---|---|---|---|---|---|---|---|---|---|---|---|---|---|
| Year Team | Lg | G | GS | CG | GF | IP | BFP | H | R | ER | HR | SH | SF | HB | TBB | IBB | SO | WP | Bk | W | L | Pct. | ShO | Sv | ERA |
| 1985 Montreal | NL | 4 | 3 | 0 | 0 | 13 | 70 | 25 | 17 | 16 | 4 | 0 | 0 | 0 | 4 | 0 | 4 | 2 | 0 | 0 | 2 | .000 | 0 | 0 | 11.08 |
| 1988 Montreal | NL | 26 | 26 | 1 | 0 | 168.2 | 704 | 150 | 69 | 57 | 15 | 5 | 2 | 1 | 58 | 3 | 101 | 3 | 1 | 3 | 11 | .214 | 0 | 0 | 3.04 |
| 1989 Boston | AL | 29 | 28 | 2 | 0 | 169.1 | 727 | 166 | 84 | 75 | 14 | 5 | 4 | 2 | 69 | 0 | 95 | 7 | 15 | 12 | 8 | .600 | 0 | 0 | 3.99 |
| 1990 Boston | AL | 4 | 4 | 0 | 0 | 17.2 | 75 | 13 | 7 | 4 | 2 | 0 | 1 | 0 | 9 | 0 | 9 | 0 | 0 | 0 | 0 | .000 | 0 | 0 | 2.04 |
| 4 ML YEARS | | 63 | 61 | 3 | 0 | 368.2 | 1576 | 354 | 177 | 152 | 35 | 10 | 7 | 3 | 140 | 3 | 209 | 12 | 16 | 15 | 21 | .417 | 0 | 0 | 3.71 |

## Billy Doran

**Bats:** Both **Throws:** Right **Pos:** 2B **Ht:** 6' 0" **Wt:** 175 **Born:** 05/28/58 **Age:** 33

| | | BATTING | | | | | | | | | | | | | | | | | BASERUNNING | | | | PERCENTAGES | | |
|---|---|---|---|---|---|---|---|---|---|---|---|---|---|---|---|---|---|---|---|---|---|---|---|---|---|
| Year Team | Lg | G | AB | H | 2B | 3B | HR | (Hm | Rd) | TB | R | RBI | TBB | IBB | SO | HBP | SH | SF | SB | CS | SB% | GDP | Avg | OBP | SLG |
| 1982 Houston | NL | 26 | 97 | 27 | 3 | 0 | 0 | (0 | 0) | 30 | 11 | 6 | 4 | 0 | 11 | 0 | 0 | 1 | 5 | 0 | 1.00 | 0 | .278 | .304 | .309 |
| 1983 Houston | NL | 154 | 535 | 145 | 12 | 7 | 8 | (1 | 7) | 195 | 70 | 39 | 86 | 11 | 67 | 0 | 7 | 1 | 12 | 12 | .50 | 6 | .271 | .371 | .364 |

| | | | | | | | | | | | | | | | | | | | | | | | | | |
|---|---|---|---|---|---|---|---|---|---|---|---|---|---|---|---|---|---|---|---|---|---|---|---|---|---|
| 1984 Houston | NL | 147 | 548 | 143 | 18 | 11 | 4 | (2 | 2) | 195 | 92 | 41 | 66 | 7 | 69 | 2 | 7 | 3 | 21 | 12 | .64 | 6 | .261 | .341 | .356 |
| 1985 Houston | NL | 148 | 578 | 166 | 31 | 6 | 14 | (5 | 9) | 251 | 84 | 59 | 71 | 6 | 69 | 0 | 3 | 5 | 23 | 15 | .61 | 10 | .287 | .362 | .434 |
| 1986 Houston | NL | 145 | 550 | 152 | 29 | 3 | 6 | (3 | 3) | 205 | 92 | 37 | 81 | 7 | 57 | 2 | 4 | 5 | 42 | 19 | .69 | 10 | .276 | .368 | .373 |
| 1987 Houston | NL | 162 | 625 | 177 | 23 | 3 | 16 | (7 | 9) | 254 | 82 | 79 | 82 | 3 | 64 | 3 | 2 | 7 | 31 | 11 | .74 | 11 | .283 | .365 | .406 |
| 1988 Houston | NL | 132 | 480 | 119 | 18 | 1 | 7 | (2 | 5) | 160 | 66 | 53 | 65 | 3 | 60 | 1 | 4 | 2 | 17 | 4 | .81 | 7 | .248 | .338 | .333 |
| 1989 Houston | NL | 142 | 507 | 111 | 25 | 2 | 8 | (3 | 5) | 164 | 65 | 58 | 59 | 2 | 63 | 2 | 3 | 3 | 22 | 3 | .88 | 8 | .219 | .301 | .323 |
| 1990 2 ML Teams | | 126 | 403 | 121 | 29 | 2 | 7 | (4 | 3) | 175 | 59 | 37 | 79 | 2 | 58 | 0 | 1 | 5 | 23 | 9 | .72 | 3 | .300 | .411 | .434 |
| 1990 Houston | NL | 109 | 344 | 99 | 21 | 2 | 6 | (3 | 3) | 142 | 49 | 32 | 71 | 1 | 53 | 0 | 1 | 5 | 18 | 9 | .67 | 2 | .288 | .405 | .413 |
| Cincinnati | NL | 17 | 59 | 22 | 8 | 0 | 1 | (1 | 0) | 33 | 10 | 5 | 8 | 1 | 5 | 0 | 0 | 0 | 5 | 0 | 1.00 | 1 | .373 | .448 | .559 |
| 9 ML YEARS | | 1182 | 4323 | 1161 | 188 | 35 | 70 | (27 | 43) | 1629 | 621 | 409 | 593 | 41 | 518 | 10 | 31 | 32 | 196 | 85 | .70 | 61 | .269 | .356 | .377 |

## Brian Dorsett

**Bats:** Right **Throws:** Right **Pos:** C **Ht:** 6' 3" **Wt:** 215 **Born:** 04/09/61 **Age:** 30

| BATTING | | | | | | | | | | | | | | | | | | | BASERUNNING | | | | PERCENTAGES | | |
|---|---|---|---|---|---|---|---|---|---|---|---|---|---|---|---|---|---|---|---|---|---|---|---|---|---|
| Year Team | Lg | G | AB | H | 2B | 3B | HR | (Hm | Rd) | TB | R | RBI | TBB | IBB | SO | HBP | SH | SF | SB | CS | SB% | GDP | Avg | OBP | SLG |
| 1987 Cleveland | AL | 5 | 11 | 3 | 0 | 0 | 1 | (1 | 0) | 6 | 2 | 3 | 0 | 0 | 3 | 1 | 0 | 0 | 0 | 0 | .00 | 0 | .273 | .333 | .545 |
| 1988 California | AL | 7 | 11 | 1 | 0 | 0 | 0 | (0 | 0) | 1 | 0 | 2 | 1 | 0 | 5 | 0 | 0 | 0 | 0 | 0 | .00 | 0 | .091 | .167 | .091 |
| 1989 New York | AL | 8 | 22 | 8 | 1 | 0 | 0 | (0 | 0) | 9 | 3 | 4 | 1 | 0 | 3 | 0 | 0 | 0 | 0 | 0 | .00 | 0 | .364 | .391 | .409 |
| 1990 New York | AL | 14 | 35 | 5 | 2 | 0 | 0 | (0 | 0) | 7 | 2 | 0 | 2 | 0 | 4 | 0 | 0 | 0 | 0 | 0 | .00 | 2 | .143 | .189 | .200 |
| 4 ML YEARS | | 34 | 79 | 17 | 3 | 0 | 1 | (1 | 0) | 23 | 7 | 9 | 4 | 0 | 15 | 1 | 0 | 0 | 0 | 0 | .00 | 2 | .215 | .262 | .291 |

## Rich Dotson

**Pitches:** Right **Bats:** Right **Pos:** SP **Ht:** 6' 0" **Wt:** 203 **Born:** 01/10/59 **Age:** 32

| HOW MUCH HE PITCHED | | | | | | | WHAT HE GAVE UP | | | | | | | | | | | | THE RESULTS | | | | | |
|---|---|---|---|---|---|---|---|---|---|---|---|---|---|---|---|---|---|---|---|---|---|---|---|---|
| Year Team | Lg | G | GS | CG | GF | IP | BFP | H | R | ER | HR | SH | SF | HB | TBB | IBB | SO | WP | Bk | W | L | Pct. | ShO | Sv | ERA |
| 1979 Chicago | AL | 5 | 5 | 1 | 0 | 24 | 107 | 28 | 13 | 10 | 0 | 1 | 2 | 0 | 6 | 0 | 13 | 0 | 0 | 2 | 0 | 1.000 | 1 | 0 | 3.75 |
| 1980 Chicago | AL | 33 | 32 | 8 | 1 | 198 | 863 | 185 | 105 | 94 | 20 | 15 | 7 | 6 | 87 | 2 | 109 | 6 | 2 | 12 | 10 | .545 | 0 | 0 | 4.27 |
| 1981 Chicago | AL | 24 | 24 | 5 | 0 | 141 | 599 | 145 | 67 | 59 | 13 | 4 | 5 | 4 | 49 | 0 | 73 | 3 | 2 | 9 | 8 | .529 | 4 | 0 | 3.77 |
| 1982 Chicago | AL | 34 | 31 | 3 | 3 | 196.2 | 867 | 219 | 97 | 84 | 19 | 7 | 6 | 5 | 73 | 4 | 109 | 2 | 1 | 11 | 15 | .423 | 1 | 0 | 3.84 |
| 1983 Chicago | AL | 35 | 35 | 8 | 0 | 240 | 997 | 209 | 92 | 86 | 19 | 4 | 7 | 8 | 106 | 1 | 137 | 7 | 0 | 22 | 7 | .759 | 1 | 0 | 3.22 |
| 1984 Chicago | AL | 32 | 32 | 14 | 0 | 245.2 | 1035 | 216 | 110 | 98 | 24 | 8 | 10 | 7 | 103 | 5 | 120 | 4 | 1 | 14 | 15 | .483 | 1 | 0 | 3.59 |
| 1985 Chicago | AL | 9 | 9 | 0 | 0 | 52.1 | 226 | 53 | 30 | 26 | 5 | 1 | 2 | 3 | 17 | 1 | 33 | 0 | 0 | 3 | 4 | .429 | 0 | 0 | 4.47 |
| 1986 Chicago | AL | 34 | 34 | 3 | 0 | 197 | 861 | 226 | 125 | 120 | 24 | 4 | 4 | 2 | 69 | 2 | 110 | 10 | 0 | 10 | 17 | .370 | 1 | 0 | 5.48 |
| 1987 Chicago | AL | 31 | 31 | 7 | 0 | 211.1 | 900 | 201 | 109 | 98 | 24 | 4 | 3 | 0 | 86 | 2 | 114 | 5 | 0 | 11 | 12 | .478 | 2 | 0 | 4.17 |
| 1988 New York | AL | 32 | 29 | 4 | 0 | 171 | 755 | 178 | 103 | 95 | 27 | 3 | 7 | 4 | 72 | 3 | 77 | 3 | 3 | 12 | 9 | .571 | 0 | 0 | 5.00 |
| 1989 2 ML Teams | | 28 | 26 | 2 | 2 | 151.1 | 685 | 181 | 84 | 75 | 16 | 7 | 4 | 1 | 58 | 3 | 69 | 2 | 3 | 5 | 12 | .294 | 0 | 0 | 4.46 |
| 1990 Kansas City | AL | 8 | 7 | 0 | 1 | 28.2 | 139 | 43 | 29 | 27 | 3 | 0 | 4 | 0 | 14 | 1 | 9 | 4 | 0 | 0 | 4 | .000 | 0 | 0 | 8.48 |
| 1989 New York | AL | 11 | 9 | 1 | 2 | 51.2 | 239 | 69 | 33 | 32 | 8 | 1 | 2 | 1 | 17 | 0 | 14 | 0 | 3 | 2 | 5 | .286 | 0 | 0 | 5.57 |
| Chicago | AL | 17 | 17 | 1 | 0 | 99.2 | 446 | 112 | 51 | 43 | 8 | 6 | 2 | 0 | 41 | 3 | 55 | 2 | 0 | 3 | 7 | .300 | 0 | 0 | 3.88 |
| 12 ML YEARS | | 305 | 295 | 55 | 7 | 1857 | 8034 | 1884 | 964 | 872 | 194 | 58 | 61 | 40 | 740 | 24 | 973 | 46 | 12 | 111 | 113 | .496 | 11 | 0 | 4.23 |

## Brian Downing

**Bats:** Right **Throws:** Right **Pos:** DH **Ht:** 5'10" **Wt:** 194 **Born:** 10/09/50 **Age:** 40

| BATTING | | | | | | | | | | | | | | | | | | | BASERUNNING | | | | PERCENTAGES | | |
|---|---|---|---|---|---|---|---|---|---|---|---|---|---|---|---|---|---|---|---|---|---|---|---|---|---|
| Year Team | Lg | G | AB | H | 2B | 3B | HR | (Hm | Rd) | TB | R | RBI | TBB | IBB | SO | HBP | SH | SF | SB | CS | SB% | GDP | Avg | OBP | SLG |
| 1973 Chicago | AL | 34 | 73 | 13 | 1 | 0 | 2 | (1 | 1) | 20 | 5 | 4 | 10 | 1 | 17 | 0 | 2 | 0 | 0 | 0 | .00 | 3 | .178 | .277 | .274 |
| 1974 Chicago | AL | 108 | 293 | 66 | 12 | 1 | 10 | (6 | 4) | 110 | 41 | 39 | 51 | 3 | 72 | 2 | 4 | 0 | 0 | 1 | .00 | 11 | .225 | .344 | .375 |
| 1975 Chicago | AL | 138 | 420 | 101 | 12 | 1 | 7 | (5 | 2) | 136 | 58 | 41 | 76 | 5 | 75 | 3 | 11 | 6 | 13 | 4 | .76 | 12 | .240 | .356 | .324 |
| 1976 Chicago | AL | 104 | 317 | 81 | 14 | 0 | 3 | (0 | 3) | 104 | 38 | 30 | 40 | 0 | 55 | 1 | 4 | 3 | 7 | 3 | .70 | 2 | .256 | .338 | .328 |
| 1977 Chicago | AL | 69 | 169 | 48 | 4 | 2 | 4 | (1 | 3) | 68 | 28 | 25 | 34 | 0 | 21 | 2 | 5 | 4 | 1 | 2 | .33 | 3 | .284 | .402 | .402 |
| 1978 California | AL | 133 | 412 | 105 | 15 | 0 | 7 | (2 | 5) | 141 | 42 | 46 | 52 | 2 | 47 | 6 | 4 | 2 | 3 | 2 | .60 | 14 | .255 | .345 | .342 |
| 1979 California | AL | 148 | 509 | 166 | 27 | 3 | 12 | (3 | 9) | 235 | 87 | 75 | 77 | 4 | 57 | 5 | 3 | 2 | 3 | 3 | .50 | 17 | .326 | .418 | .462 |
| 1980 California | AL | 30 | 93 | 27 | 6 | 0 | 2 | (2 | 0) | 39 | 5 | 25 | 12 | 1 | 12 | 0 | 1 | 2 | 0 | 2 | .00 | 5 | .290 | .364 | .419 |
| 1981 California | AL | 93 | 317 | 79 | 14 | 0 | 9 | (6 | 3) | 120 | 47 | 41 | 46 | 1 | 35 | 4 | 3 | 0 | 1 | 1 | .50 | 11 | .249 | .351 | .379 |
| 1982 California | AL | 158 | 623 | 175 | 37 | 2 | 28 | (15 | 13) | 300 | 109 | 84 | 86 | 1 | 58 | 5 | 3 | 8 | 2 | 1 | .67 | 14 | .281 | .368 | .482 |
| 1983 California | AL | 113 | 403 | 99 | 15 | 1 | 19 | (10 | 9) | 173 | 68 | 53 | 62 | 4 | 59 | 5 | 1 | 2 | 1 | 2 | .33 | 8 | .246 | .352 | .429 |
| 1984 California | AL | 156 | 539 | 148 | 28 | 2 | 23 | (9 | 14) | 249 | 65 | 91 | 70 | 3 | 66 | 7 | 3 | 9 | 0 | 4 | .00 | 18 | .275 | .360 | .462 |
| 1985 California | AL | 150 | 520 | 137 | 23 | 1 | 20 | (10 | 10) | 222 | 80 | 85 | 78 | 3 | 61 | 13 | 5 | 4 | 5 | 3 | .63 | 12 | .263 | .371 | .427 |
| 1986 California | AL | 152 | 513 | 137 | 27 | 4 | 20 | (13 | 7) | 232 | 90 | 95 | 90 | 2 | 84 | 17 | 3 | 8 | 4 | 4 | .50 | 14 | .267 | .389 | .452 |
| 1987 California | AL | 155 | 567 | 154 | 29 | 3 | 29 | (11 | 18) | 276 | 110 | 77 | 106 | 6 | 85 | 17 | 2 | 3 | 5 | 5 | .50 | 10 | .272 | .400 | .487 |
| 1988 California | AL | 135 | 484 | 117 | 18 | 2 | 25 | (11 | 14) | 214 | 80 | 64 | 81 | 5 | 63 | 14 | 5 | 6 | 3 | 4 | .43 | 12 | .242 | .362 | .442 |
| 1989 California | AL | 142 | 544 | 154 | 25 | 2 | 14 | (10 | 4) | 225 | 59 | 59 | 56 | 3 | 87 | 6 | 0 | 4 | 0 | 2 | .00 | 6 | .283 | .354 | .414 |
| 1990 California | AL | 96 | 330 | 90 | 18 | 2 | 14 | (11 | 3) | 154 | 47 | 51 | 50 | 2 | 45 | 6 | 0 | 4 | 0 | 0 | .00 | 11 | .273 | .374 | .467 |
| 18 ML YEARS | | 2114 | 7126 | 1897 | 325 | 26 | 248 | (126 | 122) | 3018 | 1059 | 985 | 1077 | 46 | 999 | 113 | 59 | 67 | 48 | 43 | .53 | 183 | .266 | .368 | .424 |

## Kelly Downs

**Pitches:** Right **Bats:** Right **Pos:** SP **Ht:** 6' 4" **Wt:** 200 **Born:** 10/25/60 **Age:** 30

| HOW MUCH HE PITCHED | | | | | | | | WHAT HE GAVE UP | | | | | | | | | | | | THE RESULTS | | | | | |
|---|---|---|---|---|---|---|---|---|---|---|---|---|---|---|---|---|---|---|---|---|---|---|---|---|---|
| Year Team | Lg | G | GS | CG | GF | IP | BFP | H | R | ER | HR | SH | SF | HB | TBB | IBB | SO | WP | Bk | W | L | Pct. | ShO | Sv | ERA |
| 1986 San Francisco | NL | 14 | 14 | 1 | 0 | 88.1 | 372 | 78 | 29 | 27 | 5 | 4 | 4 | 3 | 30 | 7 | 64 | 3 | 2 | 4 | 4 | .500 | 0 | 0 | 2.75 |
| 1987 San Francisco | NL | 41 | 28 | 4 | 4 | 186 | 797 | 185 | 83 | 75 | 14 | 7 | 1 | 4 | 67 | 11 | 137 | 12 | 4 | 12 | 9 | .571 | 3 | 1 | 3.63 |
| 1988 San Francisco | NL | 27 | 26 | 6 | 0 | 168 | 685 | 140 | 67 | 62 | 11 | 4 | 9 | 3 | 47 | 8 | 118 | 7 | 4 | 13 | 9 | .591 | 3 | 0 | 3.32 |
| 1989 San Francisco | NL | 18 | 15 | 0 | 1 | 82.2 | 349 | 82 | 47 | 44 | 7 | 4 | 4 | 1 | 26 | 4 | 49 | 3 | 3 | 4 | 8 | .333 | 0 | 0 | 4.79 |
| 1990 San Francisco | NL | 13 | 9 | 0 | 1 | 63 | 265 | 56 | 26 | 24 | 2 | 2 | 1 | 2 | 20 | 4 | 31 | 2 | 1 | 3 | 2 | .600 | 0 | 0 | 3.43 |
| 5 ML YEARS | | 113 | 92 | 11 | 6 | 588 | 2468 | 541 | 252 | 232 | 39 | 21 | 19 | 13 | 190 | 34 | 399 | 27 | 14 | 36 | 32 | .529 | 6 | 1 | 3.55 |

## Doug Drabek

**Pitches:** Right **Bats:** Right **Pos:** SP **Ht:** 6' 1" **Wt:** 185 **Born:** 07/25/62 **Age:** 28

| HOW MUCH HE PITCHED | | | | | | | | WHAT HE GAVE UP | | | | | | | | | | | | THE RESULTS | | | | | |
|---|---|---|---|---|---|---|---|---|---|---|---|---|---|---|---|---|---|---|---|---|---|---|---|---|---|
| Year Team | Lg | G | GS | CG | GF | IP | BFP | H | R | ER | HR | SH | SF | HB | TBB | IBB | SO | WP | Bk | W | L | Pct. | ShO | Sv | ERA |
| 1986 New York | AL | 27 | 21 | 0 | 2 | 131.2 | 561 | 126 | 64 | 60 | 13 | 5 | 2 | 3 | 50 | 1 | 76 | 2 | 0 | 7 | 8 | .467 | 0 | 0 | 4.10 |
| 1987 Pittsburgh | NL | 29 | 28 | 1 | 0 | 176.1 | 721 | 165 | 86 | 76 | 22 | 3 | 4 | 0 | 46 | 2 | 120 | 5 | 1 | 11 | 12 | .478 | 1 | 0 | 3.88 |
| 1988 Pittsburgh | NL | 33 | 32 | 3 | 0 | 219.1 | 880 | 194 | 83 | 75 | 21 | 7 | 5 | 6 | 50 | 4 | 127 | 4 | 1 | 15 | 7 | .682 | 1 | 0 | 3.08 |
| 1989 Pittsburgh | NL | 35 | 34 | 8 | 1 | 244.1 | 994 | 215 | 83 | 76 | 21 | 13 | 7 | 3 | 69 | 3 | 123 | 3 | 0 | 14 | 12 | .538 | 5 | 0 | 2.80 |
| 1990 Pittsburgh | NL | 33 | 33 | 9 | 0 | 231.1 | 918 | 190 | 78 | 71 | 15 | 10 | 3 | 3 | 56 | 2 | 131 | 6 | 0 | 22 | 6 | .786 | 3 | 0 | 2.76 |
| 5 ML YEARS | | 157 | 148 | 21 | 3 | 1003 | 4074 | 890 | 394 | 358 | 92 | 38 | 21 | 15 | 271 | 12 | 577 | 20 | 2 | 69 | 45 | .605 | 10 | 0 | 3.21 |

## Tim Drummond

**Pitches:** Right **Bats:** Right **Pos:** RP/SP **Ht:** 6' 3" **Wt:** 170 **Born:** 12/24/64 **Age:** 26

| HOW MUCH HE PITCHED | | | | | | | | WHAT HE GAVE UP | | | | | | | | | | | | THE RESULTS | | | | | |
|---|---|---|---|---|---|---|---|---|---|---|---|---|---|---|---|---|---|---|---|---|---|---|---|---|---|
| Year Team | Lg | G | GS | CG | GF | IP | BFP | H | R | ER | HR | SH | SF | HB | TBB | IBB | SO | WP | Bk | W | L | Pct. | ShO | Sv | ERA |
| 1987 Pittsburgh | NL | 6 | 0 | 0 | 2 | 6 | 26 | 5 | 3 | 3 | 0 | 1 | 0 | 0 | 3 | 0 | 5 | 1 | 0 | 0 | 0 | .000 | 0 | 0 | 4.50 |
| 1989 Minnesota | AL | 8 | 0 | 0 | 2 | 16.1 | 75 | 16 | 7 | 7 | 0 | 0 | 0 | 2 | 8 | 1 | 9 | 0 | 1 | 0 | 0 | .000 | 0 | 1 | 3.86 |
| 1990 Minnesota | AL | 35 | 4 | 0 | 14 | 91 | 399 | 104 | 46 | 44 | 8 | 4 | 5 | 1 | 36 | 1 | 49 | 2 | 0 | 3 | 5 | .375 | 0 | 1 | 4.35 |
| 3 ML YEARS | | 49 | 4 | 0 | 18 | 113.1 | 500 | 125 | 56 | 54 | 8 | 5 | 5 | 3 | 47 | 2 | 63 | 3 | 1 | 3 | 5 | .375 | 0 | 2 | 4.29 |

## Brian DuBois

**Pitches:** Left **Bats:** Left **Pos:** SP **Ht:** 5'10" **Wt:** 170 **Born:** 04/18/67 **Age:** 24

| HOW MUCH HE PITCHED | | | | | | | | WHAT HE GAVE UP | | | | | | | | | | | | THE RESULTS | | | | | |
|---|---|---|---|---|---|---|---|---|---|---|---|---|---|---|---|---|---|---|---|---|---|---|---|---|---|
| Year Team | Lg | G | GS | CG | GF | IP | BFP | H | R | ER | HR | SH | SF | HB | TBB | IBB | SO | WP | Bk | W | L | Pct. | ShO | Sv | ERA |
| 1985 Bluefield | R | 10 | 9 | 2 | 1 | 57.2 | 231 | 42 | 23 | 16 | 1 | 3 | 1 | 2 | 20 | 0 | 67 | 5 | 0 | 5 | 4 | .556 | 1 | 0 | 2.50 |
| 1986 Hagerstown | A | 5 | 5 | 0 | 0 | 20.1 | 95 | 29 | 19 | 16 | 1 | 1 | 1 | 1 | 11 | 0 | 17 | 2 | 1 | 1 | 2 | .333 | 0 | 0 | 7.08 |
| Bluefield | R | 3 | 1 | 0 | 0 | 9.1 | 37 | 8 | 2 | 1 | 0 | 0 | 0 | 0 | 2 | 0 | 8 | 1 | 1 | 1 | 1 | .500 | 0 | 0 | 0.96 |
| 1987 Hagerstown | A | 27 | 25 | 3 | 0 | 155 | 662 | 162 | 81 | 67 | 13 | 7 | 5 | 5 | 73 | 2 | 96 | 5 | 0 | 8 | 9 | .471 | 0 | 0 | 3.89 |
| 1988 Virginia | A | 9 | 9 | 0 | 0 | 48.2 | 228 | 66 | 42 | 30 | 2 | 1 | 1 | 0 | 20 | 0 | 35 | 2 | 1 | 2 | 5 | .286 | 0 | 0 | 5.55 |
| Hagerstown | A | 19 | 19 | 7 | 0 | 135 | 556 | 129 | 71 | 55 | 5 | 4 | 2 | 0 | 30 | 0 | 112 | 6 | 3 | 12 | 4 | .750 | 1 | 0 | 3.67 |
| 1989 Hagerstown | AA | 15 | 15 | 6 | 0 | 112 | 440 | 93 | 36 | 31 | 5 | 6 | 1 | 1 | 18 | 0 | 82 | 4 | 0 | 6 | 4 | .600 | 2 | 0 | 2.49 |
| Rochester | AAA | 4 | 4 | 0 | 0 | 30 | 121 | 24 | 8 | 6 | 3 | 0 | 0 | 0 | 12 | 0 | 16 | 2 | 0 | 3 | 1 | .750 | 0 | 0 | 1.80 |
| Toledo | AAA | 3 | 3 | 0 | 0 | 24 | 93 | 17 | 6 | 6 | 3 | 0 | 1 | 0 | 6 | 0 | 13 | 0 | 0 | 1 | 1 | .500 | 0 | 0 | 2.25 |
| 1990 Toledo | AAA | 13 | 10 | 2 | 2 | 69.2 | 297 | 67 | 27 | 21 | 6 | 2 | 2 | 2 | 26 | 1 | 47 | 2 | 0 | 5 | 4 | .556 | 1 | 0 | 2.71 |
| 1989 Detroit | AL | 6 | 5 | 0 | 1 | 36 | 153 | 29 | 14 | 7 | 2 | 0 | 1 | 2 | 17 | 3 | 13 | 0 | 1 | 0 | 4 | .000 | 0 | 1 | 1.75 |
| 1990 Detroit | AL | 12 | 11 | 0 | 0 | 58.1 | 255 | 70 | 37 | 33 | 9 | 2 | 4 | 1 | 22 | 1 | 34 | 5 | 1 | 3 | 5 | .375 | 0 | 0 | 5.09 |
| 2 ML YEARS | | 18 | 16 | 0 | 1 | 94.1 | 408 | 99 | 51 | 40 | 11 | 2 | 5 | 3 | 39 | 4 | 47 | 5 | 2 | 3 | 9 | .250 | 0 | 1 | 3.82 |

## Rob Ducey

**Bats:** Left **Throws:** Right **Pos:** LF **Ht:** 6' 2" **Wt:** 175 **Born:** 05/24/65 **Age:** 26

| BATTING | | | | | | | | | | | | | | | | | | | BASERUNNING | | | | PERCENTAGES | | |
|---|---|---|---|---|---|---|---|---|---|---|---|---|---|---|---|---|---|---|---|---|---|---|---|---|---|
| Year Team | Lg | G | AB | H | 2B | 3B | HR | (Hm | Rd) | TB | R | RBI | TBB | IBB | SO | HBP | SH | SF | SB | CS | SB% | GDP | Avg | OBP | SLG |
| 1987 Toronto | AL | 34 | 48 | 9 | 1 | 0 | 1 | (1 | 0) | 13 | 12 | 6 | 8 | 0 | 10 | 0 | 0 | 1 | 2 | 0 | 1.00 | 0 | .188 | .298 | .271 |
| 1988 Toronto | AL | 27 | 54 | 17 | 4 | 1 | 0 | (0 | 0) | 23 | 15 | 6 | 5 | 0 | 7 | 0 | 2 | 2 | 1 | 0 | 1.00 | 1 | .315 | .361 | .426 |
| 1989 Toronto | AL | 41 | 76 | 16 | 4 | 0 | 0 | (0 | 0) | 20 | 5 | 7 | 9 | 1 | 25 | 0 | 1 | 0 | 2 | 1 | .67 | 2 | .211 | .294 | .263 |
| 1990 Toronto | AL | 19 | 53 | 16 | 5 | 0 | 0 | (0 | 0) | 21 | 7 | 7 | 7 | 0 | 15 | 1 | 0 | 1 | 1 | 1 | .50 | 0 | .302 | .387 | .396 |
| 4 ML YEARS | | 121 | 231 | 58 | 14 | 1 | 1 | (1 | 0) | 77 | 39 | 26 | 29 | 1 | 57 | 1 | 3 | 4 | 6 | 2 | .75 | 3 | .251 | .332 | .333 |

## Mariano Duncan

**Bats:** Both **Throws:** Right **Pos:** 2B/SS **Ht:** 6' 0" **Wt:** 185 **Born:** 03/13/63 **Age:** 28

| BATTING | | | | | | | | | | | | | | | | | | | BASERUNNING | | | | PERCENTAGES | | |
|---|---|---|---|---|---|---|---|---|---|---|---|---|---|---|---|---|---|---|---|---|---|---|---|---|---|
| Year Team | Lg | G | AB | H | 2B | 3B | HR | (Hm | Rd) | TB | R | RBI | TBB | IBB | SO | HBP | SH | SF | SB | CS | SB% | GDP | Avg | OBP | SLG |
| 1985 Los Angeles | NL | 142 | 562 | 137 | 24 | 6 | 6 | (1 | 5) | 191 | 74 | 39 | 38 | 4 | 113 | 3 | 13 | 4 | 38 | 8 | .83 | 9 | .244 | .293 | .340 |
| 1986 Los Angeles | NL | 109 | 407 | 93 | 7 | 0 | 8 | (2 | 6) | 124 | 47 | 30 | 30 | 1 | 78 | 2 | 5 | 1 | 48 | 13 | .79 | 6 | .229 | .284 | .305 |
| 1987 Los Angeles | NL | 76 | 261 | 56 | 8 | 1 | 6 | (3 | 3) | 84 | 31 | 18 | 17 | 1 | 62 | 2 | 6 | 1 | 11 | 1 | .92 | 4 | .215 | .267 | .322 |
| 1989 2 ML Teams | | 94 | 258 | 64 | 15 | 2 | 3 | (2 | 1) | 92 | 32 | 21 | 8 | 0 | 51 | 5 | 2 | 0 | 9 | 5 | .64 | 3 | .248 | .284 | .357 |
| 1990 Cincinnati | NL | 125 | 435 | 133 | 22 | 11 | 10 | (5 | 5) | 207 | 67 | 55 | 24 | 4 | 67 | 4 | 4 | 4 | 13 | 7 | .65 | 10 | .306 | .345 | .476 |

| 1989 Los Angeles | NL | 49 | 84 | 21 | 5 | 1 | 0 | (0 | 0) | 28 | 9 | 8 | 0 | 0 | 15 | 2 | 1 | 0 | 3 | 3 | .50 | 1 | .250 | .267 | .333 |
|---|---|---|---|---|---|---|---|---|---|---|---|---|---|---|---|---|---|---|---|---|---|---|---|---|---|
| Cincinnati | NL | 45 | 174 | 43 | 10 | 1 | 3 | (2 | 1) | 64 | 23 | 13 | 8 | 0 | 36 | 3 | 1 | 0 | 6 | 2 | .75 | 2 | .247 | .292 | .368 |
| 5 ML YEARS | | 546 | 1923 | 483 | 76 | 20 | 33 | (13 | 20) | 698 | 251 | 163 | 117 | 10 | 371 | 16 | 30 | 10 | 119 | 34 | .78 | 32 | .251 | .298 | .363 |

## Mike Dunne

**Pitches:** Right **Bats:** Right **Pos:** SP **Ht:** 6' 4" **Wt:** 200 **Born:** 10/27/62 **Age:** 28

| HOW MUCH HE PITCHED | | | | | | | | WHAT HE GAVE UP | | | | | | | | | | | | THE RESULTS | | | | | |
|---|---|---|---|---|---|---|---|---|---|---|---|---|---|---|---|---|---|---|---|---|---|---|---|---|---|
| Year Team | Lg | G | GS | CG | GF | IP | BFP | H | R | ER | HR | SH | SF | HB | TBB | IBB | SO | WP | Bk | W | L | Pct. | ShO | Sv | ERA |
| 1987 Pittsburgh | NL | 23 | 23 | 5 | 0 | 163.1 | 680 | 143 | 66 | 55 | 10 | 11 | 4 | 1 | 68 | 8 | 72 | 6 | 4 | 13 | 6 | .684 | 1 | 0 | 3.03 |
| 1988 Pittsburgh | NL | 30 | 28 | 1 | 1 | 170 | 752 | 163 | 88 | 74 | 15 | 11 | 8 | 5 | 88 | 3 | 70 | 12 | 7 | 7 | 11 | .389 | 0 | 0 | 3.92 |
| 1989 2 ML Teams | | 18 | 18 | 1 | 0 | 99.2 | 461 | 125 | 73 | 62 | 8 | 4 | 5 | 3 | 46 | 2 | 42 | 8 | 1 | 3 | 10 | .231 | 0 | 0 | 5.60 |
| 1990 San Diego | NL | 10 | 6 | 0 | 0 | 28.2 | 134 | 28 | 21 | 18 | 4 | 1 | 0 | 0 | 17 | 0 | 15 | 4 | 1 | 0 | 3 | .000 | 0 | 0 | 5.65 |
| 1989 Pittsburgh | NL | 3 | 3 | 0 | 0 | 14.1 | 75 | 21 | 12 | 12 | 1 | 1 | 0 | 1 | 9 | 1 | 4 | 1 | 0 | 1 | 1 | .500 | 0 | 0 | 7.53 |
| Seattle | AL | 15 | 15 | 1 | 0 | 85.1 | 386 | 104 | 61 | 50 | 7 | 3 | 5 | 2 | 37 | 1 | 38 | 7 | 1 | 2 | 9 | .182 | 0 | 0 | 5.27 |
| 4 ML YEARS | | 81 | 75 | 7 | 1 | 461.2 | 2027 | 459 | 248 | 209 | 37 | 27 | 17 | 9 | 219 | 13 | 199 | 30 | 13 | 23 | 30 | .434 | 1 | 0 | 4.07 |

## Shawon Dunston

**Bats:** Right **Throws:** Right **Pos:** SS **Ht:** 6' 1" **Wt:** 175 **Born:** 03/21/63 **Age:** 28

| BATTING | | | | | | | | | | | | | | | | | | | BASERUNNING | | | | PERCENTAGES | | |
|---|---|---|---|---|---|---|---|---|---|---|---|---|---|---|---|---|---|---|---|---|---|---|---|---|---|
| Year Team | Lg | G | AB | H | 2B | 3B | HR | (Hm | Rd) | TB | R | RBI | TBB | IBB | SO | HBP | SH | SF | SB | CS | SB% | GDP | Avg | OBP | SLG |
| 1985 Chicago | NL | 74 | 250 | 65 | 12 | 4 | 4 | (3 | 1) | 97 | 40 | 18 | 19 | 3 | 42 | 0 | 1 | 2 | 11 | 3 | .79 | 3 | .260 | .310 | .388 |
| 1986 Chicago | NL | 150 | 581 | 145 | 37 | 3 | 17 | (10 | 7) | 239 | 66 | 68 | 21 | 5 | 114 | 3 | 4 | 2 | 13 | 11 | .54 | 5 | .250 | .278 | .411 |
| 1987 Chicago | NL | 95 | 346 | 85 | 18 | 3 | 5 | (3 | 2) | 124 | 40 | 22 | 10 | 1 | 68 | 1 | 0 | 2 | 12 | 3 | .80 | 6 | .246 | .267 | .358 |
| 1988 Chicago | NL | 155 | 575 | 143 | 23 | 6 | 9 | (5 | 4) | 205 | 69 | 56 | 16 | 8 | 108 | 2 | 4 | 2 | 30 | 9 | .77 | 6 | .249 | .271 | .357 |
| 1989 Chicago | NL | 138 | 471 | 131 | 20 | 6 | 9 | (3 | 6) | 190 | 52 | 60 | 30 | 15 | 86 | 1 | 6 | 4 | 19 | 11 | .63 | 7 | .278 | .320 | .403 |
| 1990 Chicago | NL | 146 | 545 | 143 | 22 | 8 | 17 | (7 | 10) | 232 | 73 | 66 | 15 | 1 | 87 | 3 | 4 | 6 | 25 | 5 | .83 | 9 | .262 | .283 | .426 |
| 6 ML YEARS | | 758 | 2768 | 712 | 132 | 30 | 61 | (31 | 30) | 1087 | 340 | 290 | 111 | 33 | 505 | 10 | 19 | 18 | 110 | 42 | .72 | 36 | .257 | .287 | .393 |

## Jim Dwyer

**Bats:** Left **Throws:** Left **Pos:** DH **Ht:** 5'10" **Wt:** 186 **Born:** 01/03/50 **Age:** 41

| BATTING | | | | | | | | | | | | | | | | | | | BASERUNNING | | | | PERCENTAGES | | |
|---|---|---|---|---|---|---|---|---|---|---|---|---|---|---|---|---|---|---|---|---|---|---|---|---|---|
| Year Team | Lg | G | AB | H | 2B | 3B | HR | (Hm | Rd) | TB | R | RBI | TBB | IBB | SO | HBP | SH | SF | SB | CS | SB% | GDP | Avg | OBP | SLG |
| 1973 St. Louis | NL | 28 | 57 | 11 | 1 | 1 | 0 | (0 | 0) | 14 | 7 | 0 | 1 | 0 | 5 | 0 | 0 | 0 | 0 | 0 | .00 | 4 | .193 | .207 | .246 |
| 1974 St. Louis | NL | 74 | 86 | 24 | 1 | 0 | 2 | (1 | 1) | 31 | 13 | 11 | 11 | 2 | 16 | 1 | 0 | 2 | 0 | 0 | .00 | 1 | .279 | .360 | .360 |
| 1975 2 ML Teams | | 81 | 206 | 56 | 8 | 1 | 3 | (3 | 0) | 75 | 26 | 21 | 27 | 0 | 36 | 0 | 12 | 2 | 4 | 1 | .80 | 1 | .272 | .353 | .364 |
| 1976 2 ML Teams | | 61 | 105 | 19 | 3 | 1 | 0 | (0 | 0) | 24 | 9 | 5 | 13 | 2 | 11 | 0 | 0 | 1 | 0 | 0 | .00 | 3 | .181 | .269 | .229 |
| 1977 St. Louis | NL | 13 | 31 | 7 | 1 | 0 | 0 | (0 | 0) | 8 | 3 | 2 | 4 | 0 | 5 | 2 | 0 | 0 | 0 | 0 | .00 | 0 | .226 | .351 | .258 |
| 1978 2 ML Teams | | 107 | 238 | 53 | 12 | 2 | 6 | (3 | 3) | 87 | 30 | 26 | 37 | 4 | 32 | 1 | 3 | 4 | 7 | 0 | 1.00 | 2 | .223 | .325 | .366 |
| 1979 Boston | AL | 76 | 113 | 30 | 7 | 0 | 2 | (2 | 0) | 43 | 19 | 14 | 17 | 1 | 9 | 1 | 0 | 2 | 3 | 1 | .75 | 7 | .265 | .361 | .381 |
| 1980 Boston | AL | 93 | 260 | 74 | 11 | 1 | 9 | (1 | 8) | 114 | 41 | 38 | 28 | 5 | 23 | 2 | 1 | 1 | 3 | 2 | .60 | 4 | .285 | .357 | .438 |
| 1981 Baltimore | AL | 68 | 134 | 30 | 0 | 1 | 3 | (3 | 0) | 41 | 16 | 10 | 20 | 0 | 19 | 0 | 0 | 3 | 0 | 2 | .00 | 2 | .224 | .318 | .306 |
| 1982 Baltimore | AL | 71 | 148 | 45 | 4 | 3 | 6 | (4 | 2) | 73 | 28 | 15 | 27 | 4 | 24 | 0 | 1 | 2 | 2 | 0 | 1.00 | 0 | .304 | .407 | .493 |
| 1983 Baltimore | AL | 100 | 196 | 56 | 17 | 1 | 8 | (3 | 5) | 99 | 37 | 38 | 31 | 3 | 29 | 0 | 1 | 1 | 1 | 1 | .50 | 3 | .286 | .382 | .505 |
| 1984 Baltimore | AL | 76 | 161 | 41 | 9 | 1 | 2 | (1 | 1) | 58 | 22 | 21 | 23 | 0 | 24 | 0 | 5 | 6 | 0 | 2 | .00 | 2 | .255 | .337 | .360 |
| 1985 Baltimore | AL | 101 | 233 | 58 | 8 | 3 | 7 | (1 | 6) | 93 | 35 | 36 | 37 | 2 | 31 | 1 | 2 | 1 | 0 | 3 | .00 | 5 | .249 | .353 | .399 |
| 1986 Baltimore | AL | 94 | 160 | 39 | 13 | 1 | 8 | (5 | 3) | 78 | 18 | 31 | 23 | 1 | 31 | 2 | 0 | 4 | 0 | 2 | .00 | 2 | .244 | .339 | .488 |
| 1987 Baltimore | AL | 92 | 241 | 66 | 7 | 1 | 15 | (3 | 12) | 120 | 54 | 33 | 37 | 4 | 57 | 1 | 1 | 1 | 4 | 1 | .80 | 4 | .274 | .371 | .498 |
| 1988 2 ML Teams | | 55 | 94 | 24 | 1 | 0 | 2 | (2 | 0) | 31 | 9 | 18 | 25 | 4 | 19 | 1 | 0 | 2 | 0 | 0 | .00 | 1 | .255 | .410 | .330 |
| 1989 2 ML Teams | | 101 | 235 | 74 | 12 | 0 | 3 | (2 | 1) | 95 | 35 | 25 | 29 | 1 | 24 | 0 | 0 | 1 | 2 | 0 | 1.00 | 6 | .315 | .389 | .404 |
| 1990 Minnesota | AL | 37 | 63 | 12 | 0 | 0 | 1 | (0 | 1) | 15 | 7 | 5 | 12 | 1 | 7 | 0 | 0 | 0 | 0 | 0 | .00 | 2 | .190 | .320 | .238 |
| 1975 St. Louis | NL | 21 | 31 | 6 | 1 | 0 | 0 | (0 | 0) | 7 | 4 | 1 | 4 | 0 | 6 | 0 | 1 | 0 | 0 | 0 | .00 | 1 | .194 | .286 | .226 |
| Montreal | NL | 60 | 175 | 50 | 7 | 1 | 3 | (3 | 0) | 68 | 22 | 20 | 23 | 0 | 30 | 0 | 11 | 2 | 4 | 1 | .80 | 0 | .286 | .365 | .389 |
| 1976 Montreal | NL | 50 | 92 | 17 | 3 | 1 | 0 | (0 | 0) | 22 | 7 | 5 | 11 | 1 | 10 | 0 | 0 | 1 | 0 | 0 | .00 | 3 | .185 | .269 | .239 |
| New York | NL | 11 | 13 | 2 | 0 | 0 | 0 | (0 | 0) | 2 | 2 | 0 | 2 | 1 | 1 | 0 | 0 | 0 | 0 | 0 | .00 | 0 | .154 | .267 | .154 |
| 1978 St. Louis | NL | 34 | 65 | 14 | 3 | 0 | 1 | (0 | 1) | 20 | 8 | 4 | 9 | 1 | 3 | 1 | 0 | 0 | 1 | 0 | 1.00 | 1 | .215 | .320 | .308 |
| San Francisco | NL | 73 | 173 | 39 | 9 | 2 | 5 | (3 | 2) | 67 | 22 | 22 | 28 | 3 | 29 | 0 | 3 | 4 | 6 | 0 | 1.00 | 1 | .225 | .327 | .387 |
| 1988 Baltimore | AL | 35 | 53 | 12 | 0 | 0 | 0 | (0 | 0) | 12 | 3 | 3 | 12 | 3 | 11 | 0 | 0 | 1 | 0 | 0 | .00 | 0 | .226 | .364 | .226 |
| Minnesota | AL | 20 | 41 | 12 | 1 | 0 | 2 | (2 | 0) | 19 | 6 | 15 | 13 | 1 | 8 | 1 | 0 | 1 | 0 | 0 | .00 | 1 | .293 | .464 | .463 |
| 1989 Minnesota | AL | 88 | 225 | 71 | 11 | 0 | 3 | (2 | 1) | 91 | 34 | 23 | 28 | 1 | 23 | 0 | 0 | 1 | 2 | 0 | 1.00 | 6 | .316 | .390 | .404 |
| Montreal | NL | 13 | 10 | 3 | 1 | 0 | 0 | (0 | 0) | 4 | 1 | 2 | 1 | 0 | 1 | 0 | 0 | 0 | 0 | 0 | .00 | 0 | .300 | .364 | .400 |
| 18 ML YEARS | | 1328 | 2761 | 719 | 115 | 17 | 77 | (34 | 43) | 1099 | 409 | 349 | 402 | 34 | 402 | 12 | 26 | 33 | 26 | 15 | .63 | 49 | .260 | .353 | .398 |

## Lenny Dykstra

**Bats:** Left **Throws:** Left **Pos:** CF **Ht:** 5'10" **Wt:** 170 **Born:** 02/10/63 **Age:** 28

| BATTING | | | | | | | | | | | | | | | | | | | BASERUNNING | | | | PERCENTAGES | | |
|---|---|---|---|---|---|---|---|---|---|---|---|---|---|---|---|---|---|---|---|---|---|---|---|---|---|
| Year Team | Lg | G | AB | H | 2B | 3B | HR | (Hm | Rd) | TB | R | RBI | TBB | IBB | SO | HBP | SH | SF | SB | CS | SB% | GDP | Avg | OBP | SLG |
| 1985 New York | NL | 83 | 236 | 60 | 9 | 3 | 1 | (0 | 1) | 78 | 40 | 19 | 30 | 0 | 24 | 1 | 4 | 2 | 15 | 2 | .88 | 4 | .254 | .338 | .331 |
| 1986 New York | NL | 147 | 431 | 127 | 27 | 7 | 8 | (4 | 4) | 192 | 77 | 45 | 58 | 1 | 55 | 0 | 7 | 2 | 31 | 7 | .82 | 4 | .295 | .377 | .445 |

| | | | | | | | | | | | | | | | | | | | | | | | | |
|---|---|---|---|---|---|---|---|---|---|---|---|---|---|---|---|---|---|---|---|---|---|---|---|---|
| 1987 New York | NL | 132 | 431 | 123 | 37 | 3 | 10 | (7 | 3) | 196 | 86 | 43 | 40 | 3 | 67 | 4 | 4 | 0 | 27 | 7 | .79 | 1 | .285 | .352 | .455 |
| 1988 New York | NL | 126 | 429 | 116 | 19 | 3 | 8 | (3 | 5) | 165 | 57 | 33 | 30 | 2 | 43 | 3 | 2 | 2 | 30 | 8 | .79 | 3 | .270 | .321 | .385 |
| 1989 2 ML Teams | | 146 | 511 | 121 | 32 | 4 | 7 | (5 | 2) | 182 | 66 | 32 | 60 | 1 | 53 | 3 | 5 | 5 | 30 | 12 | .71 | 7 | .237 | .318 | .356 |
| 1990 Philadelphia | NL | 149 | 590 | 192 | 35 | 3 | 9 | (6 | 3) | 260 | 106 | 60 | 89 | 14 | 48 | 7 | 2 | 3 | 33 | 5 | .87 | 5 | .325 | .418 | .441 |
| 1989 New York | NL | 56 | 159 | 43 | 12 | 1 | 3 | (2 | 1) | 66 | 27 | 13 | 23 | 0 | 15 | 2 | 4 | 4 | 13 | 1 | .93 | 2 | .270 | .362 | .415 |
| Philadelphia | NL | 90 | 352 | 78 | 20 | 3 | 4 | (3 | 1) | 116 | 39 | 19 | 37 | 1 | 38 | 1 | 1 | 1 | 17 | 11 | .61 | 5 | .222 | .297 | .330 |
| 6 ML YEARS | | 783 | 2628 | 739 | 159 | 23 | 43 | (25 | 18) | 1073 | 432 | 232 | 307 | 21 | 290 | 18 | 24 | 14 | 166 | 41 | .80 | 24 | .281 | .359 | .408 |

## Gary Eave

**Pitches:** Right **Bats:** Right **Pos:** SP **Ht:** 6' 4" **Wt:** 190 **Born:** 07/22/63 **Age:** 27

| | | HOW MUCH HE PITCHED | | | | | | WHAT HE GAVE UP | | | | | | | | | | | | THE RESULTS | | | | | |
|---|---|---|---|---|---|---|---|---|---|---|---|---|---|---|---|---|---|---|---|---|---|---|---|---|---|
| Year Team | Lg | G | GS | CG | GF | IP | BFP | H | R | ER | HR | SH | SF | HB | TBB | IBB | SO | WP | Bk | W | L | Pct. | ShO | Sv | ERA |
| 1988 Atlanta | NL | 5 | 0 | 0 | 4 | 5 | 24 | 7 | 5 | 5 | 0 | 0 | 0 | 0 | 3 | 0 | 0 | 0 | 0 | 0 | 0 | .000 | 0 | 0 | 9.00 |
| 1989 Atlanta | NL | 3 | 3 | 0 | 0 | 20.2 | 88 | 15 | 3 | 3 | 0 | 0 | 0 | 1 | 12 | 0 | 9 | 1 | 1 | 2 | 0 | 1.000 | 0 | 0 | 1.31 |
| 1990 Seattle | AL | 8 | 5 | 0 | 1 | 30 | 134 | 27 | 16 | 14 | 5 | 0 | 0 | 2 | 20 | 1 | 16 | 0 | 0 | 0 | 3 | .000 | 0 | 0 | 4.20 |
| 3 ML YEARS | | 16 | 8 | 0 | 5 | 55.2 | 246 | 49 | 24 | 22 | 5 | 0 | 0 | 3 | 35 | 1 | 25 | 1 | 1 | 2 | 3 | .400 | 0 | 0 | 3.56 |

## Dennis Eckersley

**Pitches:** Right **Bats:** Right **Pos:** RP **Ht:** 6' 2" **Wt:** 195 **Born:** 10/03/54 **Age:** 36

| | | HOW MUCH HE PITCHED | | | | | | WHAT HE GAVE UP | | | | | | | | | | | | THE RESULTS | | | | | |
|---|---|---|---|---|---|---|---|---|---|---|---|---|---|---|---|---|---|---|---|---|---|---|---|---|---|
| Year Team | Lg | G | GS | CG | GF | IP | BFP | H | R | ER | HR | SH | SF | HB | TBB | IBB | SO | WP | Bk | W | L | Pct. | ShO | Sv | ERA |
| 1975 Cleveland | AL | 34 | 24 | 6 | 5 | 187 | 794 | 147 | 61 | 54 | 16 | 6 | 7 | 7 | 90 | 8 | 152 | 4 | 2 | 13 | 7 | .650 | 2 | 2 | 2.60 |
| 1976 Cleveland | AL | 36 | 30 | 9 | 3 | 199 | 821 | 155 | 82 | 76 | 13 | 10 | 4 | 5 | 78 | 2 | 200 | 6 | 1 | 13 | 12 | .520 | 3 | 1 | 3.44 |
| 1977 Cleveland | AL | 33 | 33 | 12 | 0 | 247 | 1006 | 214 | 100 | 97 | 31 | 11 | 6 | 7 | 54 | 11 | 191 | 3 | 0 | 14 | 13 | .519 | 3 | 0 | 3.53 |
| 1978 Boston | AL | 35 | 35 | 16 | 0 | 268 | 1121 | 258 | 99 | 89 | 30 | 7 | 8 | 7 | 71 | 8 | 162 | 3 | 0 | 20 | 8 | .714 | 3 | 0 | 2.99 |
| 1979 Boston | AL | 33 | 33 | 17 | 0 | 247 | 1018 | 234 | 89 | 82 | 29 | 10 | 6 | 6 | 59 | 4 | 150 | 1 | 1 | 17 | 10 | .630 | 2 | 0 | 2.99 |
| 1980 Boston | AL | 30 | 30 | 8 | 0 | 198 | 818 | 188 | 101 | 94 | 25 | 7 | 8 | 2 | 44 | 7 | 121 | 0 | 0 | 12 | 14 | .462 | 0 | 0 | 4.27 |
| 1981 Boston | AL | 23 | 23 | 8 | 0 | 154 | 649 | 160 | 82 | 73 | 9 | 6 | 5 | 3 | 35 | 2 | 79 | 0 | 0 | 9 | 8 | .529 | 2 | 0 | 4.27 |
| 1982 Boston | AL | 33 | 33 | 11 | 0 | 224.1 | 926 | 228 | 101 | 93 | 31 | 4 | 4 | 2 | 43 | 3 | 127 | 1 | 0 | 13 | 13 | .500 | 3 | 0 | 3.73 |
| 1983 Boston | AL | 28 | 28 | 2 | 0 | 176.1 | 787 | 223 | 119 | 110 | 27 | 1 | 5 | 6 | 39 | 4 | 77 | 1 | 0 | 9 | 13 | .409 | 0 | 0 | 5.61 |
| 1984 2 ML Teams | | 33 | 33 | 4 | 0 | 225 | 932 | 223 | 97 | 90 | 21 | 11 | 9 | 5 | 49 | 9 | 114 | 3 | 2 | 14 | 12 | .538 | 0 | 0 | 3.60 |
| 1985 Chicago | NL | 25 | 25 | 6 | 0 | 169.1 | 664 | 145 | 61 | 58 | 15 | 6 | 2 | 3 | 19 | 4 | 117 | 0 | 3 | 11 | 7 | .611 | 2 | 0 | 3.08 |
| 1986 Chicago | NL | 33 | 32 | 1 | 0 | 201 | 862 | 226 | 109 | 102 | 21 | 13 | 10 | 3 | 43 | 3 | 137 | 2 | 5 | 6 | 11 | .353 | 0 | 0 | 4.57 |
| 1987 Oakland | AL | 54 | 2 | 0 | 33 | 115.2 | 460 | 99 | 41 | 39 | 11 | 3 | 3 | 3 | 17 | 3 | 113 | 1 | 0 | 6 | 8 | .429 | 0 | 16 | 3.03 |
| 1988 Oakland | AL | 60 | 0 | 0 | 53 | 72.2 | 279 | 52 | 20 | 19 | 5 | 1 | 3 | 1 | 11 | 2 | 70 | 0 | 2 | 4 | 2 | .667 | 0 | 45 | 2.35 |
| 1989 Oakland | AL | 51 | 0 | 0 | 46 | 57.2 | 206 | 32 | 10 | 10 | 5 | 0 | 4 | 1 | 3 | 0 | 55 | 0 | 0 | 4 | 0 | 1.000 | 0 | 33 | 1.56 |
| 1990 Oakland | AL | 63 | 0 | 0 | 61 | 73.1 | 262 | 41 | 9 | 5 | 2 | 0 | 1 | 0 | 4 | 1 | 73 | 0 | 0 | 4 | 2 | .667 | 0 | 48 | 0.61 |
| 1984 Boston | AL | 9 | 9 | 2 | 0 | 64.2 | 270 | 71 | 38 | 36 | 10 | 3 | 3 | 1 | 13 | 2 | 33 | 2 | 0 | 4 | 4 | .500 | 0 | 0 | 5.01 |
| Chicago | NL | 24 | 24 | 2 | 0 | 160.1 | 662 | 152 | 59 | 54 | 11 | 8 | 6 | 4 | 36 | 7 | 81 | 1 | 2 | 10 | 8 | .556 | 0 | 0 | 3.03 |
| 16 ML YEARS | | 604 | 361 | 100 | 201 | 2815.1 | 11605 | 2625 | 1181 | 1091 | 291 | 96 | 85 | 61 | 659 | 71 | 1938 | 25 | 16 | 169 | 140 | .547 | 20 | 145 | 3.49 |

## Tom Edens

**Pitches:** Right **Bats:** Right **Pos:** RP/SP **Ht:** 6' 3" **Wt:** 185 **Born:** 06/09/61 **Age:** 30

| | | HOW MUCH HE PITCHED | | | | | | WHAT HE GAVE UP | | | | | | | | | | | | THE RESULTS | | | | | |
|---|---|---|---|---|---|---|---|---|---|---|---|---|---|---|---|---|---|---|---|---|---|---|---|---|---|
| Year Team | Lg | G | GS | CG | GF | IP | BFP | H | R | ER | HR | SH | SF | HB | TBB | IBB | SO | WP | Bk | W | L | Pct. | ShO | Sv | ERA |
| 1987 New York | NL | 2 | 2 | 0 | 0 | 8 | 42 | 15 | 6 | 6 | 2 | 2 | 0 | 0 | 4 | 0 | 4 | 2 | 0 | 0 | 0 | .000 | 0 | 0 | 6.75 |
| 1990 Milwaukee | AL | 35 | 6 | 0 | 9 | 89 | 387 | 89 | 52 | 44 | 8 | 6 | 4 | 4 | 33 | 3 | 40 | 1 | 0 | 4 | 5 | .444 | 0 | 2 | 4.45 |
| 2 ML YEARS | | 37 | 8 | 0 | 9 | 97 | 429 | 104 | 58 | 50 | 10 | 8 | 4 | 4 | 37 | 3 | 44 | 3 | 0 | 4 | 5 | .444 | 0 | 2 | 4.64 |

## Wayne Edwards

**Pitches:** Left **Bats:** Left **Pos:** RP/SP **Ht:** 6' 5" **Wt:** 185 **Born:** 03/07/64 **Age:** 27

| | | HOW MUCH HE PITCHED | | | | | | WHAT HE GAVE UP | | | | | | | | | | | | THE RESULTS | | | | | |
|---|---|---|---|---|---|---|---|---|---|---|---|---|---|---|---|---|---|---|---|---|---|---|---|---|---|
| Year Team | Lg | G | GS | CG | GF | IP | BFP | H | R | ER | HR | SH | SF | HB | TBB | IBB | SO | WP | Bk | W | L | Pct. | ShO | Sv | ERA |
| 1985 White Sox | R | 11 | 11 | 3 | 0 | 68.2 | 274 | 52 | 26 | 19 | 0 | 1 | 1 | 3 | 18 | 0 | 61 | 2 | 0 | 7 | 3 | .700 | 0 | 0 | 2.49 |
| 1986 Peninsula | A | 24 | 21 | 0 | 2 | 128.1 | 574 | 149 | 80 | 60 | 10 | 6 | 2 | 2 | 68 | 1 | 86 | 8 | 2 | 8 | 8 | .500 | 0 | 0 | 4.21 |
| 1987 Daytona Bch | A | 29 | 28 | 15 | 0 | 199.2 | 862 | 211 | 91 | 80 | 4 | 5 | 6 | 9 | 68 | 3 | 121 | 17 | 0 | 16 | 8 | .667 | 2 | 0 | 3.61 |
| 1988 Birmingham | AA | 27 | 27 | 6 | 0 | 167 | 762 | 176 | 108 | 91 | 9 | 5 | 10 | 5 | 92 | 3 | 136 | 16 | 7 | 9 | 12 | .429 | 1 | 0 | 4.90 |
| Vancouver | AAA | 2 | 0 | 0 | 1 | 3 | 9 | 0 | 0 | 0 | 0 | 0 | 0 | 0 | 0 | 0 | 2 | 0 | 0 | 0 | 0 | .000 | 0 | 0 | 0.00 |
| 1989 Birmingham | AA | 24 | 19 | 5 | 1 | 158 | 660 | 131 | 69 | 56 | 6 | 4 | 1 | 5 | 65 | 1 | 122 | 6 | 4 | 10 | 4 | .714 | 0 | 1 | 3.19 |
| 1989 Chicago | AL | 7 | 0 | 0 | 2 | 7.1 | 30 | 7 | 3 | 3 | 1 | 0 | 1 | 0 | 3 | 0 | 9 | 0 | 0 | 0 | 0 | .000 | 0 | 0 | 3.68 |
| 1990 Chicago | AL | 42 | 5 | 0 | 8 | 95 | 396 | 81 | 39 | 34 | 6 | 4 | 2 | 3 | 41 | 2 | 63 | 1 | 0 | 5 | 3 | .625 | 0 | 2 | 3.22 |
| 2 ML YEARS | | 49 | 5 | 0 | 10 | 102.1 | 426 | 88 | 42 | 37 | 7 | 4 | 3 | 3 | 44 | 2 | 72 | 1 | 0 | 5 | 3 | .625 | 0 | 2 | 3.25 |

## Mark Eichhorn

**Pitches:** Right **Bats:** Right **Pos:** RP **Ht:** 6' 3" **Wt:** 200 **Born:** 11/21/60 **Age:** 30

| | | | HOW MUCH HE PITCHED | | | | | | WHAT HE GAVE UP | | | | | | | | | | | | THE RESULTS | | | | | |
|---|---|---|---|---|---|---|---|---|---|---|---|---|---|---|---|---|---|---|---|---|---|---|---|---|---|---|
| Year | Team | Lg | G | GS | CG | GF | IP | BFP | H | R | ER | HR | SH | SF | HB | TBB | IBB | SO | WP | Bk | W | L | Pct. | ShO | Sv | ERA |
| 1982 | Toronto | AL | 7 | 7 | 0 | 0 | 38 | 171 | 40 | 28 | 23 | 4 | 1 | 2 | 0 | 14 | 1 | 16 | 3 | 0 | 0 | 3 | .000 | 0 | 0 | 5.45 |
| 1986 | Toronto | AL | 69 | 0 | 0 | 38 | 157 | 612 | 105 | 32 | 30 | 8 | 9 | 2 | 7 | 45 | 14 | 166 | 2 | 1 | 14 | 6 | .700 | 0 | 10 | 1.72 |
| 1987 | Toronto | AL | 89 | 0 | 0 | 27 | 127.2 | 540 | 110 | 47 | 45 | 14 | 7 | 4 | 6 | 52 | 13 | 96 | 3 | 1 | 10 | 6 | .625 | 0 | 4 | 3.17 |
| 1988 | Toronto | AL | 37 | 0 | 0 | 17 | 66.2 | 302 | 79 | 32 | 31 | 3 | 8 | 1 | 6 | 27 | 4 | 28 | 3 | 6 | 0 | 3 | .000 | 0 | 1 | 4.18 |
| 1989 | Atlanta | NL | 45 | 0 | 0 | 13 | 68.1 | 286 | 70 | 36 | 33 | 6 | 7 | 4 | 1 | 19 | 8 | 49 | 0 | 1 | 5 | 5 | .500 | 0 | 0 | 4.35 |
| 1990 | California | AL | 60 | 0 | 0 | 40 | 84.2 | 374 | 98 | 36 | 29 | 2 | 2 | 4 | 6 | 23 | 0 | 69 | 2 | 0 | 2 | 5 | .286 | 0 | 13 | 3.08 |
| | 6 ML YEARS | | 307 | 7 | 0 | 135 | 542.1 | 2285 | 502 | 211 | 191 | 37 | 34 | 17 | 26 | 180 | 40 | 424 | 13 | 9 | 31 | 28 | .525 | 0 | 28 | 3.17 |

## Dave Eiland

**Pitches:** Right **Bats:** Right **Pos:** SP **Ht:** 6' 3" **Wt:** 210 **Born:** 07/05/66 **Age:** 24

| | | | HOW MUCH HE PITCHED | | | | | | WHAT HE GAVE UP | | | | | | | | | | | | THE RESULTS | | | | | |
|---|---|---|---|---|---|---|---|---|---|---|---|---|---|---|---|---|---|---|---|---|---|---|---|---|---|---|
| Year | Team | Lg | G | GS | CG | GF | IP | BFP | H | R | ER | HR | SH | SF | HB | TBB | IBB | SO | WP | Bk | W | L | Pct. | ShO | Sv | ERA |
| 1988 | New York | AL | 3 | 3 | 0 | 0 | 12.2 | 57 | 15 | 9 | 9 | 6 | 0 | 0 | 2 | 4 | 0 | 7 | 0 | 0 | 0 | 0 | .000 | 0 | 0 | 6.39 |
| 1989 | New York | AL | 6 | 6 | 0 | 0 | 34.1 | 152 | 44 | 25 | 22 | 5 | 1 | 2 | 2 | 13 | 3 | 11 | 0 | 0 | 1 | 3 | .250 | 0 | 0 | 5.77 |
| 1990 | New York | AL | 5 | 5 | 0 | 0 | 30.1 | 127 | 31 | 14 | 12 | 2 | 0 | 0 | 0 | 5 | 0 | 16 | 0 | 0 | 2 | 1 | .667 | 0 | 0 | 3.56 |
| | 3 ML YEARS | | 14 | 14 | 0 | 0 | 77.1 | 336 | 90 | 48 | 43 | 13 | 1 | 2 | 4 | 22 | 3 | 34 | 0 | 0 | 3 | 4 | .429 | 0 | 0 | 5.00 |

## Jim Eisenreich

**Bats:** Left **Throws:** Left **Pos:** LF/CF/RF **Ht:** 5'11" **Wt:** 195 **Born:** 04/18/59 **Age:** 32

| | | | BATTING | | | | | | | | | | | | | | | | | BASERUNNING | | | | PERCENTAGES | | |
|---|---|---|---|---|---|---|---|---|---|---|---|---|---|---|---|---|---|---|---|---|---|---|---|---|---|---|
| Year | Team | Lg | G | AB | H | 2B | 3B | HR | (Hm | Rd) | TB | R | RBI | TBB | IBB | SO | HBP | SH | SF | SB | CS | SB% | GDP | Avg | OBP | SLG |
| 1982 | Minnesota | AL | 34 | 99 | 30 | 6 | 0 | 2 | (1 | 1) | 42 | 10 | 9 | 11 | 0 | 13 | 1 | 0 | 0 | 0 | 0 | .00 | 1 | .303 | .378 | .424 |
| 1983 | Minnesota | AL | 2 | 7 | 2 | 1 | 0 | 0 | (0 | 0) | 3 | 1 | 0 | 1 | 0 | 1 | 0 | 0 | 0 | 0 | 0 | .00 | 0 | .286 | .375 | .429 |
| 1984 | Minnesota | AL | 12 | 32 | 7 | 1 | 0 | 0 | (0 | 0) | 8 | 1 | 3 | 2 | 1 | 4 | 0 | 0 | 2 | 2 | 0 | 1.00 | 1 | .219 | .250 | .250 |
| 1987 | Kansas City | AL | 44 | 105 | 25 | 8 | 2 | 4 | (3 | 1) | 49 | 10 | 21 | 7 | 2 | 13 | 0 | 0 | 3 | 1 | 1 | .50 | 2 | .238 | .278 | .467 |
| 1988 | Kansas City | AL | 82 | 202 | 44 | 8 | 1 | 1 | (0 | 1) | 57 | 26 | 19 | 6 | 1 | 31 | 0 | 2 | 4 | 9 | 3 | .75 | 2 | .218 | .236 | .282 |
| 1989 | Kansas City | AL | 134 | 475 | 139 | 33 | 7 | 9 | (4 | 5) | 213 | 64 | 59 | 37 | 9 | 44 | 0 | 3 | 4 | 27 | 8 | .77 | 8 | .293 | .341 | .448 |
| 1990 | Kansas City | AL | 142 | 496 | 139 | 29 | 7 | 5 | (2 | 3) | 197 | 61 | 51 | 42 | 2 | 51 | 1 | 2 | 4 | 12 | 14 | .46 | 7 | .280 | .335 | .397 |
| | 7 ML YEARS | | 450 | 1416 | 386 | 86 | 17 | 21 | (10 | 11) | 569 | 173 | 162 | 106 | 15 | 157 | 2 | 7 | 17 | 51 | 26 | .66 | 21 | .273 | .321 | .402 |

## Kevin Elster

**Bats:** Right **Throws:** Right **Pos:** SS **Ht:** 6' 2" **Wt:** 195 **Born:** 08/03/64 **Age:** 26

| | | | BATTING | | | | | | | | | | | | | | | | | BASERUNNING | | | | PERCENTAGES | | |
|---|---|---|---|---|---|---|---|---|---|---|---|---|---|---|---|---|---|---|---|---|---|---|---|---|---|---|
| Year | Team | Lg | G | AB | H | 2B | 3B | HR | (Hm | Rd) | TB | R | RBI | TBB | IBB | SO | HBP | SH | SF | SB | CS | SB% | GDP | Avg | OBP | SLG |
| 1986 | New York | NL | 19 | 30 | 5 | 1 | 0 | 0 | (0 | 0) | 6 | 3 | 0 | 3 | 1 | 8 | 0 | 0 | 0 | 0 | 0 | .00 | 0 | .167 | .242 | .200 |
| 1987 | New York | NL | 5 | 10 | 4 | 2 | 0 | 0 | (0 | 0) | 6 | 1 | 1 | 0 | 0 | 1 | 0 | 0 | 0 | 0 | 0 | .00 | 1 | .400 | .400 | .600 |
| 1988 | New York | NL | 149 | 406 | 87 | 11 | 1 | 9 | (6 | 3) | 127 | 41 | 37 | 35 | 12 | 47 | 3 | 6 | 0 | 2 | 0 | 1.00 | 5 | .214 | .282 | .313 |
| 1989 | New York | NL | 151 | 458 | 106 | 25 | 2 | 10 | (5 | 5) | 165 | 52 | 55 | 34 | 11 | 77 | 2 | 6 | 8 | 4 | 3 | .57 | 13 | .231 | .283 | .360 |
| 1990 | New York | NL | 92 | 314 | 65 | 20 | 1 | 9 | (2 | 7) | 114 | 36 | 45 | 30 | 2 | 54 | 1 | 1 | 6 | 2 | 0 | 1.00 | 4 | .207 | .274 | .363 |
| | 5 ML YEARS | | 416 | 1218 | 267 | 59 | 4 | 28 | (13 | 15) | 418 | 133 | 138 | 102 | 26 | 187 | 6 | 13 | 14 | 8 | 3 | .73 | 23 | .219 | .280 | .343 |

## Narciso Elvira

**Pitches:** Left **Bats:** Left **Pos:** RP **Ht:** 5'10" **Wt:** 160 **Born:** 10/29/67 **Age:** 23

| | | | HOW MUCH HE PITCHED | | | | | | WHAT HE GAVE UP | | | | | | | | | | | | THE RESULTS | | | | | |
|---|---|---|---|---|---|---|---|---|---|---|---|---|---|---|---|---|---|---|---|---|---|---|---|---|---|---|
| Year | Team | Lg | G | GS | CG | GF | IP | BFP | H | R | ER | HR | SH | SF | HB | TBB | IBB | SO | WP | Bk | W | L | Pct. | ShO | Sv | ERA |
| 1987 | Beloit | A | 4 | 4 | 1 | 0 | 27 | 102 | 15 | 5 | 4 | 1 | 1 | 0 | 0 | 12 | 0 | 29 | 3 | 0 | 3 | 0 | 1.000 | 1 | 0 | 1.33 |
| 1988 | Stockton | A | 25 | 23 | 0 | 1 | 135.1 | 563 | 87 | 49 | 44 | 6 | 6 | 7 | 7 | 79 | 1 | 161 | 10 | 4 | 7 | 6 | .538 | 0 | 0 | 2.93 |
| 1989 | El Paso | AA | 7 | 7 | 0 | 0 | 33 | 157 | 48 | 34 | 28 | 4 | 0 | 1 | 1 | 23 | 0 | 18 | 4 | 3 | 2 | 2 | .500 | 0 | 0 | 7.64 |
| | Stockton | A | 17 | 17 | 6 | 0 | 115.1 | 470 | 92 | 45 | 39 | 5 | 3 | 1 | 5 | 43 | 0 | 135 | 11 | 1 | 8 | 5 | .615 | 2 | 0 | 3.04 |
| 1990 | Beloit | A | 8 | 7 | 0 | 1 | 38.1 | 160 | 37 | 16 | 10 | 1 | 1 | 2 | 0 | 9 | 0 | 45 | 2 | 0 | 3 | 2 | .600 | 0 | 1 | 2.35 |
| | El Paso | AA | 4 | 4 | 0 | 0 | 18 | 77 | 17 | 11 | 9 | 4 | 0 | 0 | 0 | 6 | 0 | 12 | 0 | 0 | 0 | 2 | .000 | 0 | 0 | 4.50 |
| 1990 | Milwaukee | AL | 4 | 0 | 0 | 2 | 5 | 25 | 6 | 3 | 3 | 0 | 0 | 0 | 0 | 5 | 0 | 6 | 0 | 0 | 0 | 0 | .000 | 0 | 0 | 5.40 |

## Luis Encarnacion

**Pitches:** Right **Bats:** Right **Pos:** RP **Ht:** 5'10" **Wt:** 180 **Born:** 10/20/63 **Age:** 27

| | | | HOW MUCH HE PITCHED | | | | | | WHAT HE GAVE UP | | | | | | | | | | | | THE RESULTS | | | | | |
|---|---|---|---|---|---|---|---|---|---|---|---|---|---|---|---|---|---|---|---|---|---|---|---|---|---|---|
| Year | Team | Lg | G | GS | CG | GF | IP | BFP | H | R | ER | HR | SH | SF | HB | TBB | IBB | SO | WP | Bk | W | L | Pct. | ShO | Sv | ERA |
| 1984 | Batavia | A | 21 | 1 | 0 | 17 | 60.2 | 266 | 48 | 25 | 21 | 7 | 3 | 1 | 3 | 33 | 2 | 65 | 1 | 0 | 5 | 2 | .714 | 0 | 6 | 3.12 |
| 1985 | Waterloo | A | 53 | 0 | 0 | 49 | 92 | 373 | 63 | 31 | 27 | 8 | 3 | 2 | 3 | 36 | 3 | 108 | 3 | 0 | 8 | 5 | .615 | 0 | 24 | 2.64 |
| 1986 | Waterbury | AA | 46 | 0 | 0 | 39 | 67.2 | 307 | 58 | 38 | 30 | 6 | 8 | 3 | 2 | 42 | 5 | 75 | 5 | 0 | 8 | 9 | .471 | 0 | 10 | 3.99 |

| | | | | | | | | | | | | | | | | | | | | | | | | | |
|---|---|---|---|---|---|---|---|---|---|---|---|---|---|---|---|---|---|---|---|---|---|---|---|---|---|
| 1987 Williamsprt | AA | 43 | 1 | 0 | 35 | 55.1 | 247 | 61 | 24 | 24 | 5 | 3 | 3 | 6 | 22 | 5 | 34 | 1 | 2 | 4 | 5 | .444 | 0 | 12 | 3.90 |
| 1988 Memphis | AA | 49 | 0 | 0 | 36 | 78 | 316 | 60 | 27 | 24 | 7 | 1 | 3 | 2 | 28 | 1 | 64 | 4 | 0 | 4 | 3 | .571 | 0 | 22 | 2.77 |
| 1989 Memphis | AA | 20 | 0 | 0 | 9 | 47.1 | 198 | 32 | 21 | 11 | 4 | 5 | 1 | 1 | 20 | 1 | 44 | 3 | 0 | 4 | 4 | .500 | 0 | 2 | 2.09 |
| Omaha | AAA | 31 | 0 | 0 | 25 | 50.2 | 207 | 39 | 10 | 10 | 2 | 3 | 1 | 0 | 18 | 6 | 41 | 1 | 0 | 3 | 5 | .375 | 0 | 5 | 1.78 |
| 1990 Omaha | AAA | 44 | 0 | 0 | 21 | 76 | 323 | 70 | 30 | 25 | 9 | 4 | 2 | 0 | 30 | 5 | 62 | 0 | 1 | 6 | 5 | .545 | 0 | 7 | 2.96 |
| 1990 Kansas City | AL | 4 | 0 | 0 | 2 | 10.1 | 49 | 14 | 10 | 9 | 1 | 0 | 0 | 0 | 4 | 0 | 8 | 1 | 0 | 0 | 0 | .000 | 0 | 0 | 7.84 |

## Jim Eppard

**Bats:** Left **Throws:** Left **Pos:** PH **Ht:** 6' 2" **Wt:** 180 **Born:** 04/27/60 **Age:** 31

| BATTING | | | | | | | | | | | | | | | | | | | BASERUNNING | | | | PERCENTAGES | | |
|---|---|---|---|---|---|---|---|---|---|---|---|---|---|---|---|---|---|---|---|---|---|---|---|---|---|
| Year Team | Lg | G | AB | H | 2B | 3B | HR | (Hm | Rd) | TB | R | RBI | TBB | IBB | SO | HBP | SH | SF | SB | CS | SB% | GDP | Avg | OBP | SLG |
| 1987 California | AL | 8 | 9 | 3 | 0 | 0 | 0 | (0 | 0) | 3 | 2 | 0 | 2 | 0 | 0 | 0 | 0 | 0 | 0 | 0 | .00 | 1 | .333 | .455 | .333 |
| 1988 California | AL | 56 | 113 | 32 | 3 | 1 | 0 | (0 | 0) | 37 | 7 | 14 | 11 | 0 | 15 | 0 | 2 | 0 | 0 | 0 | .00 | 4 | .283 | .347 | .327 |
| 1989 California | AL | 12 | 12 | 3 | 0 | 0 | 0 | (0 | 0) | 3 | 0 | 2 | 1 | 0 | 4 | 0 | 0 | 0 | 0 | 0 | .00 | 0 | .250 | .308 | .250 |
| 1990 Toronto | AL | 6 | 5 | 1 | 0 | 0 | 0 | (0 | 0) | 1 | 0 | 0 | 0 | 0 | 2 | 1 | 0 | 0 | 0 | 0 | .00 | 0 | .200 | .333 | .200 |
| 4 ML YEARS | | 82 | 139 | 39 | 3 | 1 | 0 | (0 | 0) | 44 | 9 | 16 | 14 | 0 | 21 | 1 | 2 | 0 | 0 | 0 | .00 | 5 | .281 | .351 | .317 |

## Scott Erickson

**Pitches:** Right **Bats:** Right **Pos:** SP **Ht:** 6' 0" **Wt:** 190 **Born:** 02/02/68 **Age:** 23

| HOW MUCH HE PITCHED | | | | | | | | WHAT HE GAVE UP | | | | | | | | | | | | THE RESULTS | | | | | |
|---|---|---|---|---|---|---|---|---|---|---|---|---|---|---|---|---|---|---|---|---|---|---|---|---|---|
| Year Team | Lg | G | GS | CG | GF | IP | BFP | H | R | ER | HR | SH | SF | HB | TBB | IBB | SO | WP | Bk | W | L | Pct. | ShO | Sv | ERA |
| 1989 Visalia | A | 12 | 12 | 2 | 0 | 78.2 | 320 | 79 | 29 | 26 | 3 | 0 | 0 | 0 | 22 | 0 | 59 | 3 | 4 | 3 | 4 | .429 | 0 | 0 | 2.97 |
| 1990 Orlando | AA | 15 | 15 | 3 | 0 | 101 | 397 | 75 | 38 | 34 | 3 | 1 | 2 | 5 | 24 | 0 | 69 | 4 | 1 | 8 | 3 | .727 | 1 | 0 | 3.03 |
| 1990 Minnesota | AL | 19 | 17 | 1 | 1 | 113 | 485 | 108 | 49 | 36 | 9 | 5 | 2 | 5 | 51 | 4 | 53 | 3 | 0 | 8 | 4 | .667 | 0 | 0 | 2.87 |

## Nick Esasky

**Bats:** Right **Throws:** Right **Pos:** 1B **Ht:** 6' 3" **Wt:** 215 **Born:** 02/24/60 **Age:** 31

| BATTING | | | | | | | | | | | | | | | | | | | BASERUNNING | | | | PERCENTAGES | | |
|---|---|---|---|---|---|---|---|---|---|---|---|---|---|---|---|---|---|---|---|---|---|---|---|---|---|
| Year Team | Lg | G | AB | H | 2B | 3B | HR | (Hm | Rd) | TB | R | RBI | TBB | IBB | SO | HBP | SH | SF | SB | CS | SB% | GDP | Avg | OBP | SLG |
| 1983 Cincinnati | NL | 85 | 302 | 80 | 10 | 5 | 12 | (5 | 7) | 136 | 41 | 46 | 27 | 1 | 99 | 3 | 0 | 3 | 6 | 2 | .75 | 5 | .265 | .328 | .450 |
| 1984 Cincinnati | NL | 113 | 322 | 62 | 10 | 5 | 10 | (5 | 5) | 112 | 30 | 45 | 52 | 3 | 103 | 0 | 3 | 5 | 1 | 2 | .33 | 6 | .193 | .301 | .348 |
| 1985 Cincinnati | NL | 125 | 413 | 108 | 21 | 0 | 21 | (7 | 14) | 192 | 61 | 66 | 41 | 3 | 102 | 4 | 3 | 3 | 3 | 4 | .43 | 9 | .262 | .332 | .465 |
| 1986 Cincinnati | NL | 102 | 330 | 76 | 17 | 2 | 12 | (9 | 3) | 133 | 35 | 41 | 47 | 0 | 97 | 1 | 1 | 4 | 0 | 2 | .00 | 8 | .230 | .325 | .403 |
| 1987 Cincinnati | NL | 100 | 346 | 94 | 19 | 2 | 22 | (10 | 12) | 183 | 48 | 59 | 29 | 3 | 76 | 0 | 2 | 1 | 0 | 0 | .00 | 10 | .272 | .327 | .529 |
| 1988 Cincinnati | NL | 122 | 391 | 95 | 17 | 2 | 15 | (7 | 8) | 161 | 40 | 62 | 48 | 4 | 104 | 4 | 0 | 7 | 7 | 2 | .78 | 6 | .243 | .327 | .412 |
| 1989 Boston | AL | 154 | 564 | 156 | 26 | 5 | 30 | (15 | 15) | 282 | 79 | 108 | 66 | 9 | 117 | 3 | 0 | 0 | 1 | 2 | .33 | 11 | .277 | .355 | .500 |
| 1990 Atlanta | NL | 9 | 35 | 6 | 0 | 0 | 0 | (0 | 0) | 6 | 2 | 0 | 4 | 0 | 14 | 0 | 0 | 0 | 0 | 0 | .00 | 0 | .171 | .256 | .171 |
| 8 ML YEARS | | 810 | 2703 | 677 | 120 | 21 | 122 | (58 | 64) | 1205 | 336 | 427 | 314 | 23 | 712 | 15 | 9 | 23 | 18 | 14 | .56 | 55 | .250 | .329 | .446 |

## Alvaro Espinoza

**Bats:** Right **Throws:** Right **Pos:** SS **Ht:** 6' 0" **Wt:** 170 **Born:** 02/19/62 **Age:** 29

| BATTING | | | | | | | | | | | | | | | | | | | BASERUNNING | | | | PERCENTAGES | | |
|---|---|---|---|---|---|---|---|---|---|---|---|---|---|---|---|---|---|---|---|---|---|---|---|---|---|
| Year Team | Lg | G | AB | H | 2B | 3B | HR | (Hm | Rd) | TB | R | RBI | TBB | IBB | SO | HBP | SH | SF | SB | CS | SB% | GDP | Avg | OBP | SLG |
| 1985 Minnesota | AL | 32 | 57 | 15 | 2 | 0 | 0 | (0 | 0) | 17 | 5 | 9 | 1 | 0 | 9 | 1 | 3 | 0 | 0 | 1 | .00 | 2 | .263 | .288 | .298 |
| 1986 Minnesota | AL | 37 | 42 | 9 | 1 | 0 | 0 | (0 | 0) | 10 | 4 | 1 | 1 | 0 | 10 | 0 | 2 | 0 | 0 | 1 | .00 | 0 | .214 | .233 | .238 |
| 1988 New York | AL | 3 | 3 | 0 | 0 | 0 | 0 | (0 | 0) | 0 | 0 | 0 | 0 | 0 | 0 | 0 | 0 | 0 | 0 | 0 | .00 | 0 | .000 | .000 | .000 |
| 1989 New York | AL | 146 | 503 | 142 | 23 | 1 | 0 | (0 | 0) | 167 | 51 | 41 | 14 | 1 | 60 | 1 | 23 | 3 | 3 | 3 | .50 | 14 | .282 | .301 | .332 |
| 1990 New York | AL | 150 | 438 | 98 | 12 | 2 | 2 | (0 | 2) | 120 | 31 | 20 | 16 | 0 | 54 | 5 | 11 | 2 | 1 | 2 | .33 | 13 | .224 | .258 | .274 |
| 5 ML YEARS | | 368 | 1043 | 264 | 38 | 3 | 2 | (0 | 2) | 314 | 91 | 71 | 32 | 1 | 133 | 7 | 39 | 5 | 4 | 7 | .36 | 29 | .253 | .279 | .301 |

## Cecil Espy

**Bats:** Both **Throws:** Right **Pos:** CF **Ht:** 6' 3" **Wt:** 195 **Born:** 01/20/63 **Age:** 28

| BATTING | | | | | | | | | | | | | | | | | | | BASERUNNING | | | | PERCENTAGES | | |
|---|---|---|---|---|---|---|---|---|---|---|---|---|---|---|---|---|---|---|---|---|---|---|---|---|---|
| Year Team | Lg | G | AB | H | 2B | 3B | HR | (Hm | Rd) | TB | R | RBI | TBB | IBB | SO | HBP | SH | SF | SB | CS | SB% | GDP | Avg | OBP | SLG |
| 1983 Los Angeles | NL | 20 | 11 | 3 | 1 | 0 | 0 | (0 | 0) | 4 | 4 | 1 | 1 | 0 | 2 | 0 | 0 | 0 | 0 | 0 | .00 | 0 | .273 | .333 | .364 |
| 1987 Texas | AL | 14 | 8 | 0 | 0 | 0 | 0 | (0 | 0) | 0 | 1 | 0 | 1 | 0 | 3 | 0 | 0 | 0 | 2 | 0 | 1.00 | 1 | .000 | .111 | .000 |
| 1988 Texas | AL | 123 | 347 | 86 | 17 | 6 | 2 | (2 | 0) | 121 | 46 | 39 | 20 | 1 | 83 | 1 | 5 | 3 | 33 | 10 | .77 | 2 | .248 | .288 | .349 |
| 1989 Texas | AL | 142 | 475 | 122 | 12 | 7 | 3 | (2 | 1) | 157 | 65 | 31 | 38 | 2 | 99 | 2 | 10 | 2 | 45 | 20 | .69 | 2 | .257 | .313 | .331 |
| 1990 Texas | AL | 52 | 71 | 9 | 0 | 0 | 0 | (0 | 0) | 9 | 10 | 1 | 10 | 0 | 20 | 0 | 1 | 0 | 11 | 5 | .69 | 1 | .127 | .235 | .127 |
| 5 ML YEARS | | 351 | 912 | 220 | 30 | 13 | 5 | (4 | 1) | 291 | 126 | 72 | 70 | 3 | 207 | 3 | 16 | 5 | 91 | 35 | .72 | 6 | .241 | .296 | .319 |

## Dwight Evans

**Bats:** Right **Throws:** Right **Pos:** DH **Ht:** 6' 3" **Wt:** 208 **Born:** 11/03/51 **Age:** 39

| BATTING | | | | | | | | | | | | | | | | | | | BASERUNNING | | | | PERCENTAGES | | |
|---|---|---|---|---|---|---|---|---|---|---|---|---|---|---|---|---|---|---|---|---|---|---|---|---|---|
| Year Team | Lg | G | AB | H | 2B | 3B | HR | (Hm | Rd) | TB | R | RBI | TBB | IBB | SO | HBP | SH | SF | SB | CS | SB% | GDP | Avg | OBP | SLG |
| 1972 Boston | AL | 18 | 57 | 15 | 3 | 1 | 1 | (1 | 0) | 23 | 2 | 6 | 7 | 0 | 13 | 0 | 0 | 0 | 0 | 0 | .00 | 2 | .263 | .344 | .404 |

| | | | | | | | | | | | | | | | | | | | | | | | | | |
|---|---|---|---|---|---|---|---|---|---|---|---|---|---|---|---|---|---|---|---|---|---|---|---|---|---|
| 1973 Boston | AL | 119 | 282 | 63 | 13 | 1 | 10 | (6 | 4) | 108 | 46 | 32 | 40 | 2 | 52 | 1 | 3 | 2 | 5 | 0 | 1.00 | 8 | .223 | .320 | .383 |
| 1974 Boston | AL | 133 | 463 | 130 | 19 | 8 | 10 | (7 | 3) | 195 | 60 | 70 | 38 | 2 | 77 | 2 | 6 | 5 | 4 | 4 | .50 | 9 | .281 | .335 | .421 |
| 1975 Boston | AL | 128 | 412 | 113 | 24 | 6 | 13 | (8 | 5) | 188 | 61 | 56 | 47 | 3 | 60 | 4 | 5 | 2 | 3 | 4 | .43 | 10 | .274 | .353 | .456 |
| 1976 Boston | AL | 146 | 501 | 121 | 34 | 5 | 17 | (9 | 8) | 216 | 61 | 62 | 57 | 4 | 92 | 6 | 3 | 4 | 6 | 7 | .46 | 11 | .242 | .324 | .431 |
| 1977 Boston | AL | 73 | 230 | 66 | 9 | 2 | 14 | (9 | 5) | 121 | 39 | 36 | 28 | 0 | 58 | 0 | 6 | 1 | 4 | 2 | .67 | 3 | .287 | .363 | .526 |
| 1978 Boston | AL | 147 | 497 | 123 | 24 | 2 | 24 | (13 | 11) | 223 | 75 | 63 | 65 | 2 | 119 | 2 | 6 | 2 | 8 | 5 | .62 | 15 | .247 | .336 | .449 |
| 1979 Boston | AL | 152 | 489 | 134 | 24 | 1 | 21 | (12 | 9) | 223 | 69 | 58 | 69 | 7 | 76 | 1 | 3 | 1 | 6 | 9 | .40 | 14 | .274 | .364 | .456 |
| 1980 Boston | AL | 148 | 463 | 123 | 37 | 5 | 18 | (11 | 7) | 224 | 72 | 60 | 64 | 6 | 98 | 5 | 6 | 4 | 3 | 1 | .75 | 5 | .266 | .358 | .484 |
| 1981 Boston | AL | 108 | 412 | 122 | 19 | 4 | 22 | (15 | 7) | 215 | 84 | 71 | 85 | 1 | 85 | 1 | 3 | 3 | 3 | 2 | .60 | 8 | .296 | .415 | .522 |
| 1982 Boston | AL | 162 | 609 | 178 | 37 | 7 | 32 | (19 | 13) | 325 | 122 | 98 | 112 | 1 | 125 | 1 | 3 | 2 | 3 | 2 | .60 | 17 | .292 | .402 | .534 |
| 1983 Boston | AL | 126 | 470 | 112 | 19 | 4 | 22 | (12 | 10) | 205 | 74 | 58 | 70 | 5 | 97 | 2 | 0 | 2 | 3 | 0 | 1.00 | 12 | .238 | .338 | .436 |
| 1984 Boston | AL | 162 | 630 | 186 | 37 | 8 | 32 | (15 | 17) | 335 | 121 | 104 | 96 | 2 | 115 | 4 | 1 | 7 | 3 | 1 | .75 | 19 | .295 | .388 | .532 |
| 1985 Boston | AL | 159 | 617 | 162 | 29 | 1 | 29 | (14 | 15) | 280 | 110 | 78 | 114 | 4 | 105 | 5 | 1 | 7 | 7 | 2 | .78 | 16 | .263 | .378 | .454 |
| 1986 Boston | AL | 152 | 529 | 137 | 33 | 2 | 26 | (8 | 18) | 252 | 86 | 97 | 97 | 4 | 117 | 6 | 2 | 6 | 3 | 3 | .50 | 11 | .259 | .376 | .476 |
| 1987 Boston | AL | 154 | 541 | 165 | 37 | 2 | 34 | (14 | 20) | 308 | 109 | 123 | 106 | 6 | 98 | 3 | 0 | 7 | 4 | 6 | .40 | 10 | .305 | .417 | .569 |
| 1988 Boston | AL | 149 | 559 | 164 | 31 | 7 | 21 | (11 | 10) | 272 | 96 | 111 | 76 | 3 | 99 | 1 | 2 | 7 | 5 | 1 | .83 | 16 | .293 | .375 | .487 |
| 1989 Boston | AL | 146 | 520 | 148 | 27 | 3 | 20 | (8 | 12) | 241 | 82 | 100 | 99 | 1 | 84 | 3 | 1 | 7 | 3 | 3 | .50 | 16 | .285 | .397 | .463 |
| 1990 Boston | AL | 123 | 445 | 111 | 18 | 3 | 13 | (7 | 6) | 174 | 66 | 63 | 67 | 5 | 73 | 4 | 0 | 6 | 3 | 4 | .43 | 18 | .249 | .349 | .391 |
| 19 ML YEARS | | 2505 | 8726 | 2373 | 474 | 72 | 379 | (199 | 180) | 4128 | 1435 | 1346 | 1337 | 58 | 1643 | 51 | 51 | 75 | 76 | 56 | .58 | 220 | .272 | .369 | .473 |

## Paul Faries

**Bats:** Right **Throws:** Right **Pos:** 2B **Ht:** 5'10" **Wt:** 165 **Born:** 02/20/65 **Age:** 26

| BATTING | | | | | | | | | | | | | | | | | | | BASERUNNING | | | | PERCENTAGES | | |
|---|---|---|---|---|---|---|---|---|---|---|---|---|---|---|---|---|---|---|---|---|---|---|---|---|---|
| Year Team | Lg | G | AB | H | 2B | 3B | HR | (Hm | Rd) | TB | R | RBI | TBB | IBB | SO | HBP | SH | SF | SB | CS | SB% | GDP | Avg | OBP | SLG |
| 1987 Spokane | A | 74 | 280 | 86 | 9 | 3 | 0 | -- | -- | 101 | 67 | 27 | 36 | 0 | 25 | 5 | 4 | 5 | 30 | 9 | .77 | 7 | .307 | .390 | .361 |
| 1988 Riverside | A | 141 | 579 | 183 | 39 | 4 | 2 | -- | -- | 236 | 108 | 77 | 72 | 1 | 79 | 8 | 7 | 7 | 65 | 30 | .68 | 14 | .316 | .395 | .408 |
| 1989 Wichita | AA | 130 | 513 | 136 | 25 | 8 | 6 | -- | -- | 195 | 79 | 52 | 47 | 0 | 52 | 2 | 2 | 1 | 41 | 13 | .76 | 13 | .265 | .329 | .380 |
| 1990 Las Vegas | AAA | 137 | 552 | 172 | 29 | 3 | 5 | -- | -- | 222 | 109 | 64 | 75 | 1 | 60 | 6 | 7 | 1 | 48 | 15 | .76 | 16 | .312 | .399 | .402 |
| 1990 San Diego | NL | 14 | 37 | 7 | 1 | 0 | 0 | (0 | 0) | 8 | 4 | 2 | 4 | 0 | 7 | 1 | 2 | 1 | 0 | 1 | .00 | 0 | .189 | .279 | .216 |

## Howard Farmer

**Pitches:** Right **Bats:** Right **Pos:** SP **Ht:** 6' 3" **Wt:** 190 **Born:** 01/18/66 **Age:** 25

| HOW MUCH HE PITCHED | | | | | | | | WHAT HE GAVE UP | | | | | | | | | | | | THE RESULTS | | | | | |
|---|---|---|---|---|---|---|---|---|---|---|---|---|---|---|---|---|---|---|---|---|---|---|---|---|---|
| Year Team | Lg | G | GS | CG | GF | IP | BFP | H | R | ER | HR | SH | SF | HB | TBB | IBB | SO | WP | Bk | W | L | Pct. | ShO | Sv | ERA |
| 1987 Jamestown | A | 15 | 15 | 3 | 0 | 96.1 | 404 | 93 | 42 | 35 | 4 | 1 | 2 | 3 | 30 | 0 | 63 | 4 | 2 | 9 | 6 | .600 | 1 | 0 | 3.27 |
| 1988 Rockford | A | 27 | 25 | 8 | 0 | 193.2 | 774 | 153 | 70 | 54 | 10 | 3 | 5 | 8 | 58 | 2 | 145 | 10 | 9 | 15 | 7 | .682 | 2 | 0 | 2.51 |
| 1989 Jacksnville | AA | 26 | 26 | 5 | 0 | 184 | 724 | 122 | 59 | 45 | 5 | 7 | 4 | 4 | 50 | 0 | 151 | 6 | 10 | 12 | 9 | .571 | 2 | 0 | 2.20 |
| Indianapols | AAA | 1 | 1 | 0 | 0 | 7 | 28 | 3 | 1 | 0 | 0 | 0 | 0 | 0 | 3 | 0 | 3 | 0 | 0 | 1 | 0 | 1.000 | 0 | 0 | 0.00 |
| 1990 Indianapols | AAA | 26 | 26 | 4 | 0 | 148 | 640 | 150 | 84 | 64 | 12 | 4 | 4 | 6 | 48 | 2 | 99 | 5 | 2 | 7 | 9 | .438 | 2 | 0 | 3.89 |
| 1990 Montreal | NL | 6 | 4 | 0 | 0 | 23 | 99 | 26 | 18 | 18 | 9 | 2 | 1 | 0 | 10 | 1 | 14 | 1 | 0 | 0 | 3 | .000 | 0 | 0 | 7.04 |

## Steve Farr

**Pitches:** Right **Bats:** Right **Pos:** RP/SP **Ht:** 5'11" **Wt:** 200 **Born:** 12/12/56 **Age:** 34

| HOW MUCH HE PITCHED | | | | | | | | WHAT HE GAVE UP | | | | | | | | | | | | THE RESULTS | | | | | |
|---|---|---|---|---|---|---|---|---|---|---|---|---|---|---|---|---|---|---|---|---|---|---|---|---|---|
| Year Team | Lg | G | GS | CG | GF | IP | BFP | H | R | ER | HR | SH | SF | HB | TBB | IBB | SO | WP | Bk | W | L | Pct. | ShO | Sv | ERA |
| 1984 Cleveland | AL | 31 | 16 | 0 | 4 | 116 | 488 | 106 | 61 | 59 | 14 | 2 | 3 | 5 | 46 | 3 | 83 | 2 | 2 | 3 | 11 | .214 | 0 | 1 | 4.58 |
| 1985 Kansas City | AL | 16 | 3 | 0 | 5 | 37.2 | 164 | 34 | 15 | 13 | 2 | 1 | 2 | 2 | 20 | 4 | 36 | 3 | 0 | 2 | 1 | .667 | 0 | 1 | 3.11 |
| 1986 Kansas City | AL | 56 | 0 | 0 | 33 | 109.1 | 443 | 90 | 39 | 38 | 10 | 3 | 2 | 4 | 39 | 8 | 83 | 4 | 1 | 8 | 4 | .667 | 0 | 8 | 3.13 |
| 1987 Kansas City | AL | 47 | 0 | 0 | 19 | 91 | 408 | 97 | 47 | 42 | 9 | 0 | 3 | 2 | 44 | 4 | 88 | 2 | 0 | 4 | 3 | .571 | 0 | 1 | 4.15 |
| 1988 Kansas City | AL | 62 | 1 | 0 | 49 | 82.2 | 344 | 74 | 25 | 23 | 5 | 1 | 3 | 2 | 30 | 6 | 72 | 4 | 2 | 5 | 4 | .556 | 0 | 20 | 2.50 |
| 1989 Kansas City | AL | 51 | 2 | 0 | 40 | 63.1 | 279 | 75 | 35 | 29 | 5 | 0 | 3 | 1 | 22 | 5 | 56 | 2 | 0 | 2 | 5 | .286 | 0 | 18 | 4.12 |
| 1990 Kansas City | AL | 57 | 6 | 1 | 20 | 127 | 515 | 99 | 32 | 28 | 6 | 10 | 1 | 5 | 48 | 9 | 94 | 2 | 0 | 13 | 7 | .650 | 1 | 1 | 1.98 |
| 7 ML YEARS | | 320 | 28 | 1 | 170 | 627 | 2641 | 575 | 254 | 232 | 51 | 17 | 17 | 21 | 249 | 39 | 512 | 19 | 5 | 37 | 35 | .514 | 1 | 50 | 3.33 |

## John Farrell

**Pitches:** Right **Bats:** Right **Pos:** SP **Ht:** 6' 4" **Wt:** 210 **Born:** 08/04/62 **Age:** 28

| HOW MUCH HE PITCHED | | | | | | | | WHAT HE GAVE UP | | | | | | | | | | | | THE RESULTS | | | | | |
|---|---|---|---|---|---|---|---|---|---|---|---|---|---|---|---|---|---|---|---|---|---|---|---|---|---|
| Year Team | Lg | G | GS | CG | GF | IP | BFP | H | R | ER | HR | SH | SF | HB | TBB | IBB | SO | WP | Bk | W | L | Pct. | ShO | Sv | ERA |
| 1987 Cleveland | AL | 10 | 9 | 1 | 1 | 69 | 297 | 68 | 29 | 26 | 7 | 3 | 1 | 5 | 22 | 1 | 28 | 1 | 1 | 5 | 1 | .833 | 0 | 0 | 3.39 |
| 1988 Cleveland | AL | 31 | 30 | 4 | 0 | 210.1 | 895 | 216 | 106 | 99 | 15 | 9 | 6 | 9 | 67 | 3 | 92 | 2 | 3 | 14 | 10 | .583 | 0 | 0 | 4.24 |
| 1989 Cleveland | AL | 31 | 31 | 7 | 0 | 208 | 895 | 196 | 97 | 84 | 14 | 8 | 6 | 7 | 71 | 4 | 132 | 4 | 0 | 9 | 14 | .391 | 2 | 0 | 3.63 |
| 1990 Cleveland | AL | 17 | 17 | 1 | 0 | 96.2 | 418 | 108 | 49 | 46 | 10 | 5 | 2 | 1 | 33 | 1 | 44 | 1 | 0 | 4 | 5 | .444 | 0 | 0 | 4.28 |
| 4 ML YEARS | | 89 | 87 | 13 | 1 | 584 | 2505 | 588 | 281 | 255 | 46 | 25 | 15 | 22 | 193 | 9 | 296 | 8 | 4 | 32 | 30 | .516 | 2 | 0 | 3.93 |

## Mike Felder

**Bats:** Both **Throws:** Right **Pos:** LF/CF/RF **Ht:** 5' 8" **Wt:** 160 **Born:** 11/18/62 **Age:** 28

| BATTING | | | | | | | | | | | | | | | | | | | | BASERUNNING | | | | PERCENTAGES | | |
|---|---|---|---|---|---|---|---|---|---|---|---|---|---|---|---|---|---|---|---|---|---|---|---|---|---|---|
| Year Team | Lg | G | AB | H | 2B | 3B | HR | (Hm | Rd) | TB | R | RBI | TBB | IBB | SO | HBP | SH | SF | | SB | CS | SB% | GDP | Avg | OBP | SLG |
| 1985 Milwaukee | AL | 15 | 56 | 11 | 1 | 0 | 0 | (0 | 0) | 12 | 8 | 0 | 5 | 0 | 6 | 0 | 1 | 0 | | 4 | 1 | .80 | 2 | .196 | .262 | .214 |
| 1986 Milwaukee | AL | 44 | 155 | 37 | 2 | 4 | 1 | (1 | 0) | 50 | 24 | 13 | 13 | 1 | 16 | 0 | 1 | 5 | | 16 | 2 | .89 | 2 | .239 | .289 | .323 |
| 1987 Milwaukee | AL | 108 | 289 | 77 | 5 | 7 | 2 | (1 | 1) | 102 | 48 | 31 | 28 | 0 | 23 | 0 | 9 | 2 | | 34 | 8 | .81 | 3 | .266 | .329 | .353 |
| 1988 Milwaukee | AL | 50 | 81 | 14 | 1 | 0 | 0 | (0 | 0) | 15 | 14 | 5 | 0 | 0 | 11 | 1 | 3 | 0 | | 8 | 2 | .80 | 1 | .173 | .183 | .185 |
| 1989 Milwaukee | AL | 117 | 315 | 76 | 11 | 3 | 3 | (1 | 2) | 102 | 50 | 23 | 23 | 2 | 38 | 0 | 7 | 0 | | 26 | 5 | .84 | 4 | .241 | .293 | .324 |
| 1990 Milwaukee | AL | 121 | 237 | 65 | 7 | 2 | 3 | (1 | 2) | 85 | 38 | 27 | 22 | 0 | 17 | 0 | 8 | 5 | | 20 | 9 | .69 | 0 | .274 | .330 | .359 |
| 6 ML YEARS | | 455 | 1133 | 280 | 27 | 16 | 9 | (4 | 5) | 366 | 182 | 99 | 91 | 3 | 111 | 1 | 29 | 12 | | 108 | 27 | .80 | 12 | .247 | .301 | .323 |

## Junior Felix

**Bats:** Both **Throws:** Right **Pos:** RF/CF **Ht:** 5'11" **Wt:** 165 **Born:** 10/03/67 **Age:** 23

| BATTING | | | | | | | | | | | | | | | | | | | | BASERUNNING | | | | PERCENTAGES | | |
|---|---|---|---|---|---|---|---|---|---|---|---|---|---|---|---|---|---|---|---|---|---|---|---|---|---|---|
| Year Team | Lg | G | AB | H | 2B | 3B | HR | (Hm | Rd) | TB | R | RBI | TBB | IBB | SO | HBP | SH | SF | | SB | CS | SB% | GDP | Avg | OBP | SLG |
| 1986 Medicne Hat | R | 67 | 263 | 75 | 9 | 3 | 4 | -- | -- | 102 | 57 | 28 | 35 | 1 | 84 | 6 | 0 | 0 | | 37 | 9 | .80 | 4 | .285 | .382 | .388 |
| 1987 Myrtle Bch | A | 124 | 466 | 135 | 15 | 9 | 12 | -- | -- | 204 | 70 | 51 | 43 | 8 | 124 | 10 | 2 | 2 | | 64 | 28 | .70 | 2 | .290 | .361 | .438 |
| 1988 Knoxville | AA | 93 | 360 | 91 | 16 | 5 | 3 | -- | -- | 126 | 52 | 25 | 20 | 2 | 82 | 3 | 2 | 1 | | 40 | 16 | .71 | 4 | .253 | .297 | .350 |
| 1989 Syracuse | AAA | 21 | 87 | 24 | 4 | 2 | 1 | -- | -- | 35 | 17 | 10 | 9 | 0 | 18 | 0 | 1 | 1 | | 13 | 3 | .81 | 2 | .276 | .340 | .402 |
| 1989 Toronto | AL | 110 | 415 | 107 | 14 | 8 | 9 | (4 | 5) | 164 | 62 | 46 | 33 | 2 | 101 | 3 | 0 | 3 | | 18 | 12 | .60 | 5 | .258 | .315 | .395 |
| 1990 Toronto | AL | 127 | 463 | 122 | 23 | 7 | 15 | (7 | 8) | 204 | 73 | 65 | 45 | 0 | 99 | 2 | 2 | 5 | | 13 | 8 | .62 | 4 | .263 | .328 | .441 |
| 2 ML YEARS | | 237 | 878 | 229 | 37 | 15 | 24 | (11 | 13) | 368 | 135 | 111 | 78 | 2 | 200 | 5 | 2 | 8 | | 31 | 20 | .61 | 9 | .261 | .322 | .419 |

## Felix Fermin

**Bats:** Right **Throws:** Right **Pos:** SS **Ht:** 5'11" **Wt:** 170 **Born:** 10/09/63 **Age:** 27

| BATTING | | | | | | | | | | | | | | | | | | | | BASERUNNING | | | | PERCENTAGES | | |
|---|---|---|---|---|---|---|---|---|---|---|---|---|---|---|---|---|---|---|---|---|---|---|---|---|---|---|
| Year Team | Lg | G | AB | H | 2B | 3B | HR | (Hm | Rd) | TB | R | RBI | TBB | IBB | SO | HBP | SH | SF | | SB | CS | SB% | GDP | Avg | OBP | SLG |
| 1987 Pittsburgh | NL | 23 | 68 | 17 | 0 | 0 | 0 | (0 | 0) | 17 | 6 | 4 | 4 | 1 | 9 | 1 | 2 | 0 | | 0 | 0 | .00 | 3 | .250 | .301 | .250 |
| 1988 Pittsburgh | NL | 43 | 87 | 24 | 0 | 2 | 0 | (0 | 0) | 28 | 9 | 2 | 8 | 1 | 10 | 3 | 1 | 1 | | 3 | 1 | .75 | 3 | .276 | .354 | .322 |
| 1989 Cleveland | AL | 156 | 484 | 115 | 9 | 1 | 0 | (0 | 0) | 126 | 50 | 21 | 41 | 0 | 27 | 4 | 32 | 1 | | 6 | 4 | .60 | 15 | .238 | .302 | .260 |
| 1990 Cleveland | AL | 148 | 414 | 106 | 13 | 2 | 1 | (1 | 0) | 126 | 47 | 40 | 26 | 0 | 22 | 0 | 13 | 5 | | 3 | 3 | .50 | 13 | .256 | .297 | .304 |
| 4 ML YEARS | | 370 | 1053 | 262 | 22 | 5 | 1 | (1 | 0) | 297 | 112 | 67 | 79 | 2 | 68 | 8 | 48 | 7 | | 12 | 8 | .60 | 34 | .249 | .304 | .282 |

## Alex Fernandez

**Pitches:** Right **Bats:** Right **Pos:** SP **Ht:** 6' 0" **Wt:** 190 **Born:** 01/01/70 **Age:** 21

| HOW MUCH HE PITCHED | | | | | | | | WHAT HE GAVE UP | | | | | | | | | | | | THE RESULTS | | | | | |
|---|---|---|---|---|---|---|---|---|---|---|---|---|---|---|---|---|---|---|---|---|---|---|---|---|---|
| Year Team | Lg | G | GS | CG | GF | IP | BFP | H | R | ER | HR | SH | SF | HB | TBB | IBB | SO | WP | Bk | W | L | Pct. | ShO | Sv | ERA |
| 1990 White Sox | R | 2 | 2 | 0 | 0 | 10 | 43 | 11 | 4 | 4 | 0 | 0 | 1 | 2 | 1 | 0 | 16 | 1 | 2 | 1 | 0 | 1.000 | 0 | 0 | 3.60 |
| Sarasota | A | 2 | 2 | 0 | 0 | 14.2 | 59 | 8 | 4 | 3 | 0 | 0 | 1 | 0 | 3 | 0 | 23 | 0 | 1 | 1 | 1 | .500 | 0 | 0 | 1.84 |
| Birmingham | AA | 4 | 4 | 0 | 0 | 25 | 99 | 20 | 7 | 3 | 0 | 0 | 0 | 0 | 6 | 0 | 27 | 0 | 0 | 3 | 0 | 1.000 | 0 | 0 | 1.08 |
| 1990 Chicago | AL | 13 | 13 | 3 | 0 | 87.2 | 378 | 89 | 40 | 37 | 6 | 5 | 0 | 3 | 34 | 0 | 61 | 1 | 0 | 5 | 5 | .500 | 0 | 0 | 3.80 |

## Sid Fernandez

**Pitches:** Left **Bats:** Left **Pos:** SP **Ht:** 6' 1" **Wt:** 230 **Born:** 10/12/62 **Age:** 28

| HOW MUCH HE PITCHED | | | | | | | | WHAT HE GAVE UP | | | | | | | | | | | | THE RESULTS | | | | | |
|---|---|---|---|---|---|---|---|---|---|---|---|---|---|---|---|---|---|---|---|---|---|---|---|---|---|
| Year Team | Lg | G | GS | CG | GF | IP | BFP | H | R | ER | HR | SH | SF | HB | TBB | IBB | SO | WP | Bk | W | L | Pct. | ShO | Sv | ERA |
| 1983 Los Angeles | NL | 2 | 1 | 0 | 0 | 6 | 33 | 7 | 4 | 4 | 0 | 0 | 0 | 1 | 7 | 0 | 9 | 0 | 0 | 0 | 1 | .000 | 0 | 0 | 6.00 |
| 1984 New York | NL | 15 | 15 | 0 | 0 | 90 | 371 | 74 | 40 | 35 | 8 | 5 | 5 | 0 | 34 | 3 | 62 | 1 | 4 | 6 | 6 | .500 | 0 | 0 | 3.50 |
| 1985 New York | NL | 26 | 26 | 3 | 0 | 170.1 | 685 | 108 | 56 | 53 | 14 | 4 | 3 | 2 | 80 | 3 | 180 | 3 | 2 | 9 | 9 | .500 | 0 | 0 | 2.80 |
| 1986 New York | NL | 32 | 31 | 2 | 1 | 204.1 | 855 | 161 | 82 | 80 | 13 | 9 | 7 | 2 | 91 | 1 | 200 | 6 | 0 | 16 | 6 | .727 | 1 | 1 | 3.52 |
| 1987 New York | NL | 28 | 27 | 3 | 0 | 156 | 665 | 130 | 75 | 66 | 16 | 3 | 6 | 8 | 67 | 8 | 134 | 2 | 0 | 12 | 8 | .600 | 1 | 0 | 3.81 |
| 1988 New York | NL | 31 | 31 | 1 | 0 | 187 | 751 | 127 | 69 | 63 | 15 | 2 | 7 | 6 | 70 | 1 | 189 | 4 | 9 | 12 | 10 | .545 | 1 | 0 | 3.03 |
| 1989 New York | NL | 35 | 32 | 6 | 0 | 219.1 | 883 | 157 | 73 | 69 | 21 | 4 | 4 | 6 | 75 | 3 | 198 | 1 | 3 | 14 | 5 | .737 | 2 | 0 | 2.83 |
| 1990 New York | NL | 30 | 30 | 2 | 0 | 179.1 | 735 | 130 | 79 | 69 | 18 | 7 | 6 | 5 | 67 | 4 | 181 | 1 | 0 | 9 | 14 | .391 | 1 | 0 | 3.46 |
| 8 ML YEARS | | 199 | 193 | 17 | 1 | 1212.1 | 4978 | 894 | 478 | 439 | 105 | 34 | 38 | 30 | 491 | 23 | 1153 | 18 | 18 | 78 | 59 | .569 | 6 | 1 | 3.26 |

## Tony Fernandez

**Bats:** Both **Throws:** Right **Pos:** SS **Ht:** 6' 2" **Wt:** 170 **Born:** 06/30/62 **Age:** 29

| BATTING | | | | | | | | | | | | | | | | | | | | BASERUNNING | | | | PERCENTAGES | | |
|---|---|---|---|---|---|---|---|---|---|---|---|---|---|---|---|---|---|---|---|---|---|---|---|---|---|---|
| Year Team | Lg | G | AB | H | 2B | 3B | HR | (Hm | Rd) | TB | R | RBI | TBB | IBB | SO | HBP | SH | SF | | SB | CS | SB% | GDP | Avg | OBP | SLG |
| 1983 Toronto | AL | 15 | 34 | 9 | 1 | 1 | 0 | (0 | 0) | 12 | 5 | 2 | 2 | 0 | 2 | 1 | 1 | 0 | | 0 | 1 | .00 | 1 | .265 | .324 | .353 |
| 1984 Toronto | AL | 88 | 233 | 63 | 5 | 3 | 3 | (1 | 2) | 83 | 29 | 19 | 17 | 0 | 15 | 0 | 2 | 2 | | 5 | 7 | .42 | 3 | .270 | .317 | .356 |
| 1985 Toronto | AL | 161 | 564 | 163 | 31 | 10 | 2 | (1 | 1) | 220 | 71 | 51 | 43 | 2 | 41 | 2 | 7 | 2 | | 13 | 6 | .68 | 12 | .289 | .340 | .390 |
| 1986 Toronto | AL | 163 | 687 | 213 | 33 | 9 | 10 | (4 | 6) | 294 | 91 | 65 | 27 | 0 | 52 | 4 | 5 | 4 | | 25 | 12 | .68 | 8 | .310 | .338 | .428 |

| | | | | | | | | | | | | | | | | | | | | | | | | | |
|---|---|---|---|---|---|---|---|---|---|---|---|---|---|---|---|---|---|---|---|---|---|---|---|---|---|
| 1987 Toronto | AL | 146 | 578 | 186 | 29 | 8 | 5 | (1 | 4) | 246 | 90 | 67 | 51 | 3 | 48 | 5 | 4 | 4 | 32 | 12 | .73 | 14 | .322 | .379 | .426 |
| 1988 Toronto | AL | 154 | 648 | 186 | 41 | 4 | 5 | (3 | 2) | 250 | 76 | 70 | 45 | 3 | 65 | 4 | 3 | 4 | 15 | 5 | .75 | 9 | .287 | .335 | .386 |
| 1989 Toronto | AL | 140 | 573 | 147 | 25 | 9 | 11 | (2 | 9) | 223 | 64 | 64 | 29 | 1 | 51 | 3 | 2 | 10 | 22 | 6 | .79 | 9 | .257 | .291 | .389 |
| 1990 Toronto | AL | 161 | 635 | 175 | 27 | 17 | 4 | (2 | 2) | 248 | 84 | 66 | 71 | 4 | 70 | 7 | 2 | 6 | 26 | 13 | .67 | 17 | .276 | .352 | .391 |
| 8 ML YEARS | | 1028 | 3952 | 1142 | 192 | 61 | 40 | (14 | 26) | 1576 | 510 | 404 | 285 | 13 | 344 | 26 | 26 | 32 | 138 | 62 | .69 | 73 | .289 | .338 | .399 |

## Mike Fetters

**Pitches:** Right **Bats:** Right **Pos:** RP **Ht:** 6' 4" **Wt:** 200 **Born:** 12/19/64 **Age:** 26

| HOW MUCH HE PITCHED | | | | | | | | WHAT HE GAVE UP | | | | | | | | | | | THE RESULTS | | | | | |
|---|---|---|---|---|---|---|---|---|---|---|---|---|---|---|---|---|---|---|---|---|---|---|---|---|
| Year Team | Lg | G | GS | CG | GF | IP | BFP | H | R | ER | HR | SH | SF | HB | TBB | IBB | SO | WP | Bk | W | L | Pct. | ShO | Sv | ERA |
| 1986 Salem | A | 12 | 12 | 1 | 0 | 72 | 0 | 60 | 39 | 27 | 4 | 0 | 0 | 3 | 51 | 0 | 72 | 4 | 1 | 4 | 2 | .667 | 0 | 0 | 3.38 |
| 1987 Palm Sprngs | A | 19 | 19 | 2 | 1 | 116 | 518 | 106 | 62 | 46 | 2 | 4 | 5 | 6 | 73 | 0 | 105 | 22 | 1 | 9 | 7 | .563 | 0 | 0 | 3.57 |
| 1988 Midland | AA | 20 | 20 | 2 | 0 | 114 | 522 | 116 | 78 | 75 | 10 | 2 | 4 | 7 | 67 | 3 | 101 | 18 | 14 | 8 | 8 | .500 | 0 | 0 | 5.92 |
| Edmonton | AAA | 2 | 2 | 1 | 0 | 14 | 57 | 8 | 3 | 3 | 0 | 0 | 0 | 0 | 10 | 0 | 11 | 2 | 0 | 2 | 0 | 1.000 | 0 | 0 | 1.93 |
| 1989 Edmonton | AAA | 26 | 26 | 6 | 0 | 168 | 704 | 160 | 80 | 71 | 11 | 1 | 1 | 7 | 72 | 2 | 144 | 16 | 2 | 12 | 8 | .600 | 2 | 0 | 3.80 |
| 1990 Edmonton | AAA | 5 | 5 | 1 | 0 | 27.1 | 116 | 22 | 9 | 3 | 0 | 1 | 0 | 1 | 13 | 0 | 26 | 2 | 1 | 1 | 1 | .500 | 1 | 0 | 0.99 |
| 1989 California | AL | 1 | 0 | 0 | 0 | 3.1 | 16 | 5 | 4 | 3 | 1 | 0 | 0 | 0 | 1 | 0 | 4 | 2 | 0 | 0 | 0 | .000 | 0 | 0 | 8.10 |
| 1990 California | AL | 26 | 2 | 0 | 10 | 67.2 | 291 | 77 | 33 | 31 | 9 | 1 | 0 | 2 | 20 | 0 | 35 | 3 | 0 | 1 | 1 | .500 | 0 | 1 | 4.12 |
| 2 ML YEARS | | 27 | 2 | 0 | 10 | 71 | 307 | 82 | 37 | 34 | 10 | 1 | 0 | 2 | 21 | 0 | 39 | 5 | 0 | 1 | 1 | .500 | 0 | 1 | 4.31 |

## Cecil Fielder

**Bats:** Right **Throws:** Right **Pos:** 1B/DH **Ht:** 6' 3" **Wt:** 230 **Born:** 09/21/63 **Age:** 27

| BATTING | | | | | | | | | | | | | | | | | | | BASERUNNING | | | | PERCENTAGES | | |
|---|---|---|---|---|---|---|---|---|---|---|---|---|---|---|---|---|---|---|---|---|---|---|---|---|---|
| Year Team | Lg | G | AB | H | 2B | 3B | HR | (Hm | Rd) | TB | R | RBI | TBB | IBB | SO | HBP | SH | SF | SB | CS | SB% | GDP | Avg | OBP | SLG |
| 1985 Toronto | AL | 30 | 74 | 23 | 4 | 0 | 4 | (2 | 2) | 39 | 6 | 16 | 6 | 0 | 16 | 0 | 0 | 1 | 0 | 0 | .00 | 2 | .311 | .358 | .527 |
| 1986 Toronto | AL | 34 | 83 | 13 | 2 | 0 | 4 | (0 | 4) | 27 | 7 | 13 | 6 | 0 | 27 | 1 | 0 | 0 | 0 | 0 | .00 | 3 | .157 | .222 | .325 |
| 1987 Toronto | AL | 82 | 175 | 47 | 7 | 1 | 14 | (10 | 4) | 98 | 30 | 32 | 20 | 2 | 48 | 1 | 0 | 1 | 0 | 1 | .00 | 6 | .269 | .345 | .560 |
| 1988 Toronto | AL | 74 | 174 | 40 | 6 | 1 | 9 | (6 | 3) | 75 | 24 | 23 | 14 | 0 | 53 | 1 | 0 | 1 | 0 | 1 | .00 | 6 | .230 | .289 | .431 |
| 1990 Detroit | AL | 159 | 573 | 159 | 25 | 1 | 51 | (25 | 26) | 339 | 104 | 132 | 90 | 11 | 182 | 5 | 0 | 5 | 0 | 1 | .00 | 15 | .277 | .377 | .592 |
| 5 ML YEARS | | 379 | 1079 | 282 | 44 | 3 | 82 | (43 | 39) | 578 | 171 | 216 | 136 | 13 | 326 | 8 | 0 | 8 | 0 | 3 | .00 | 32 | .261 | .346 | .536 |

## Tom Filer

**Pitches:** Right **Bats:** Right **Pos:** SP **Ht:** 6' 1" **Wt:** 198 **Born:** 12/01/56 **Age:** 34

| HOW MUCH HE PITCHED | | | | | | | | WHAT HE GAVE UP | | | | | | | | | | | THE RESULTS | | | | | |
|---|---|---|---|---|---|---|---|---|---|---|---|---|---|---|---|---|---|---|---|---|---|---|---|---|
| Year Team | Lg | G | GS | CG | GF | IP | BFP | H | R | ER | HR | SH | SF | HB | TBB | IBB | SO | WP | Bk | W | L | Pct. | ShO | Sv | ERA |
| 1982 Chicago | NL | 8 | 8 | 0 | 0 | 40.2 | 187 | 50 | 25 | 25 | 5 | 3 | 0 | 0 | 18 | 2 | 15 | 2 | 0 | 1 | 2 | .333 | 0 | 0 | 5.53 |
| 1985 Toronto | AL | 11 | 9 | 0 | 0 | 48.2 | 192 | 38 | 21 | 21 | 6 | 2 | 1 | 0 | 18 | 0 | 24 | 0 | 1 | 7 | 0 | 1.000 | 0 | 0 | 3.88 |
| 1988 Milwaukee | AL | 19 | 16 | 2 | 0 | 101.2 | 431 | 108 | 54 | 50 | 8 | 5 | 7 | 1 | 33 | 4 | 39 | 5 | 0 | 5 | 8 | .385 | 1 | 0 | 4.43 |
| 1989 Milwaukee | AL | 13 | 13 | 0 | 0 | 72.1 | 302 | 74 | 30 | 29 | 6 | 2 | 0 | 4 | 23 | 1 | 20 | 1 | 0 | 7 | 3 | .700 | 0 | 0 | 3.61 |
| 1990 Milwaukee | AL | 7 | 4 | 0 | 1 | 22 | 99 | 26 | 17 | 15 | 2 | 0 | 0 | 0 | 9 | 0 | 8 | 2 | 0 | 2 | 3 | .400 | 0 | 0 | 6.14 |
| 5 ML YEARS | | 58 | 50 | 2 | 1 | 285.1 | 1211 | 296 | 147 | 140 | 27 | 12 | 8 | 5 | 101 | 7 | 106 | 10 | 1 | 22 | 16 | .579 | 1 | 0 | 4.42 |

## Pete Filson

**Pitches:** Left **Bats:** Both **Pos:** SP **Ht:** 6' 2" **Wt:** 185 **Born:** 09/28/58 **Age:** 32

| HOW MUCH HE PITCHED | | | | | | | | WHAT HE GAVE UP | | | | | | | | | | | THE RESULTS | | | | | |
|---|---|---|---|---|---|---|---|---|---|---|---|---|---|---|---|---|---|---|---|---|---|---|---|---|
| Year Team | Lg | G | GS | CG | GF | IP | BFP | H | R | ER | HR | SH | SF | HB | TBB | IBB | SO | WP | Bk | W | L | Pct. | ShO | Sv | ERA |
| 1982 Minnesota | AL | 5 | 3 | 0 | 1 | 12.1 | 63 | 17 | 12 | 12 | 2 | 0 | 2 | 0 | 8 | 1 | 10 | 0 | 2 | 0 | 2 | .000 | 0 | 0 | 8.76 |
| 1983 Minnesota | AL | 26 | 8 | 0 | 10 | 90 | 378 | 87 | 34 | 34 | 9 | 1 | 2 | 1 | 29 | 0 | 49 | 1 | 2 | 4 | 1 | .800 | 0 | 1 | 3.40 |
| 1984 Minnesota | AL | 55 | 7 | 0 | 13 | 118.2 | 514 | 106 | 56 | 54 | 14 | 9 | 3 | 3 | 54 | 7 | 59 | 2 | 1 | 6 | 5 | .545 | 0 | 1 | 4.10 |
| 1985 Minnesota | AL | 40 | 6 | 1 | 12 | 95.2 | 406 | 93 | 42 | 39 | 13 | 3 | 2 | 0 | 30 | 4 | 42 | 1 | 1 | 4 | 5 | .444 | 0 | 2 | 3.67 |
| 1986 2 ML Teams | | 7 | 1 | 0 | 4 | 18 | 89 | 27 | 13 | 12 | 5 | 0 | 0 | 1 | 7 | 0 | 8 | 1 | 0 | 0 | 1 | .000 | 0 | 0 | 6.00 |
| 1987 New York | AL | 7 | 2 | 0 | 3 | 22 | 99 | 26 | 10 | 8 | 2 | 2 | 0 | 1 | 9 | 1 | 10 | 0 | 0 | 1 | 0 | 1.000 | 0 | 0 | 3.27 |
| 1990 Kansas City | AL | 8 | 7 | 0 | 0 | 35 | 165 | 42 | 31 | 23 | 6 | 0 | 1 | 2 | 13 | 0 | 9 | 0 | 1 | 0 | 4 | .000 | 0 | 0 | 5.91 |
| 1986 Minnesota | AL | 4 | 0 | 0 | 2 | 6.1 | 35 | 13 | 4 | 4 | 1 | 0 | 0 | 1 | 2 | 0 | 4 | 0 | 0 | 0 | 0 | .000 | 0 | 0 | 5.68 |
| Chicago | AL | 3 | 1 | 0 | 2 | 11.2 | 54 | 14 | 9 | 8 | 4 | 0 | 0 | 0 | 5 | 0 | 4 | 1 | 0 | 0 | 1 | .000 | 0 | 0 | 6.17 |
| 7 ML YEARS | | 148 | 34 | 1 | 43 | 391.2 | 1714 | 398 | 198 | 182 | 51 | 15 | 10 | 8 | 150 | 13 | 187 | 5 | 7 | 15 | 18 | .455 | 0 | 4 | 4.18 |

## Chuck Finley

**Pitches:** Left **Bats:** Left **Pos:** SP **Ht:** 6' 6" **Wt:** 215 **Born:** 11/26/62 **Age:** 28

| HOW MUCH HE PITCHED | | | | | | | | WHAT HE GAVE UP | | | | | | | | | | | THE RESULTS | | | | | |
|---|---|---|---|---|---|---|---|---|---|---|---|---|---|---|---|---|---|---|---|---|---|---|---|---|
| Year Team | Lg | G | GS | CG | GF | IP | BFP | H | R | ER | HR | SH | SF | HB | TBB | IBB | SO | WP | Bk | W | L | Pct. | ShO | Sv | ERA |
| 1986 California | AL | 25 | 0 | 0 | 7 | 46.1 | 198 | 40 | 17 | 17 | 2 | 4 | 0 | 1 | 23 | 1 | 37 | 2 | 0 | 3 | 1 | .750 | 0 | 0 | 3.30 |
| 1987 California | AL | 35 | 3 | 0 | 17 | 90.2 | 405 | 102 | 54 | 47 | 7 | 2 | 2 | 3 | 43 | 3 | 63 | 4 | 3 | 2 | 7 | .222 | 0 | 0 | 4.67 |
| 1988 California | AL | 31 | 31 | 2 | 0 | 194.1 | 831 | 191 | 95 | 90 | 15 | 7 | 10 | 6 | 82 | 7 | 111 | 5 | 8 | 9 | 15 | .375 | 0 | 0 | 4.17 |
| 1989 California | AL | 29 | 29 | 9 | 0 | 199.2 | 827 | 171 | 64 | 57 | 13 | 7 | 3 | 2 | 82 | 0 | 156 | 4 | 2 | 16 | 9 | .640 | 1 | 0 | 2.57 |
| 1990 California | AL | 32 | 32 | 7 | 0 | 236 | 962 | 210 | 77 | 63 | 17 | 12 | 3 | 2 | 81 | 3 | 177 | 9 | 0 | 18 | 9 | .667 | 2 | 0 | 2.40 |
| 5 ML YEARS | | 152 | 95 | 18 | 24 | 767 | 3223 | 714 | 307 | 274 | 54 | 32 | 18 | 14 | 311 | 14 | 544 | 24 | 13 | 48 | 41 | .539 | 3 | 0 | 3.22 |

## Steve Finley

**Bats:** Left **Throws:** Left **Pos:** RF/LF/CF **Ht:** 6' 2" **Wt:** 175 **Born:** 05/12/65 **Age:** 26

| BATTING | | | | | | | | | | | | | | | | | | | | BASERUNNING | | | | PERCENTAGES | | |
|---|---|---|---|---|---|---|---|---|---|---|---|---|---|---|---|---|---|---|---|---|---|---|---|---|---|---|
| Year Team | Lg | G | AB | H | 2B | 3B | HR | (Hm | Rd) | TB | R | RBI | TBB | IBB | SO | HBP | SH | SF | SB | CS | SB% | GDP | Avg | OBP | SLG |
| 1987 Newark | A | 54 | 222 | 65 | 13 | 2 | 3 | -- | -- | 91 | 40 | 33 | 22 | 0 | 24 | 2 | 1 | 2 | 26 | 5 | .84 | 4 | .293 | .359 | .410 |
| Hagerstown | A | 15 | 65 | 22 | 3 | 2 | 1 | -- | -- | 32 | 9 | 5 | 1 | 0 | 6 | 0 | 0 | 0 | 7 | 2 | .78 | 2 | .338 | .348 | .492 |
| 1988 Hagerstown | A | 8 | 28 | 6 | 2 | 0 | 0 | -- | -- | 8 | 2 | 3 | 4 | 0 | 3 | 0 | 0 | 0 | 4 | 0 | 1.00 | 2 | .214 | .313 | .286 |
| Charlotte | AA | 10 | 40 | 12 | 4 | 2 | 1 | -- | -- | 23 | 7 | 6 | 4 | 0 | 3 | 1 | 0 | 0 | 2 | 0 | 1.00 | 1 | .300 | .378 | .575 |
| Rochester | AAA | 120 | 456 | 143 | 19 | 7 | 5 | -- | -- | 191 | 61 | 54 | 28 | 5 | 55 | 0 | 8 | 2 | 20 | 11 | .65 | 4 | .314 | .352 | .419 |
| 1989 Rochester | AAA | 7 | 25 | 4 | 0 | 0 | 0 | -- | -- | 4 | 2 | 2 | 1 | 0 | 5 | 0 | 0 | 0 | 3 | 0 | 1.00 | 0 | .160 | .192 | .160 |
| Hagerstown | AA | 11 | 48 | 20 | 3 | 1 | 0 | -- | -- | 25 | 11 | 7 | 4 | 0 | 3 | 0 | 0 | 1 | 4 | 0 | 1.00 | 0 | .417 | .453 | .521 |
| 1989 Baltimore | AL | 81 | 217 | 54 | 5 | 2 | 2 | (0 | 2) | 69 | 35 | 25 | 15 | 1 | 30 | 1 | 6 | 2 | 17 | 3 | .85 | 3 | .249 | .298 | .318 |
| 1990 Baltimore | AL | 142 | 464 | 119 | 16 | 4 | 3 | (1 | 2) | 152 | 46 | 37 | 32 | 3 | 53 | 2 | 10 | 5 | 22 | 9 | .71 | 8 | .256 | .304 | .328 |
| 2 ML YEARS | | 223 | 681 | 173 | 21 | 6 | 5 | (1 | 4) | 221 | 81 | 62 | 47 | 4 | 83 | 3 | 16 | 7 | 39 | 12 | .76 | 11 | .254 | .302 | .325 |

## Brian Fisher

**Pitches:** Right **Bats:** Right **Pos:** RP **Ht:** 6' 4" **Wt:** 210 **Born:** 03/18/62 **Age:** 29

| HOW MUCH HE PITCHED | | | | | | | | WHAT HE GAVE UP | | | | | | | | | | | | THE RESULTS | | | | | |
|---|---|---|---|---|---|---|---|---|---|---|---|---|---|---|---|---|---|---|---|---|---|---|---|---|---|
| Year Team | Lg | G | GS | CG | GF | IP | BFP | H | R | ER | HR | SH | SF | HB | TBB | IBB | SO | WP | Bk | W | L | Pct. | ShO | Sv | ERA |
| 1985 New York | AL | 55 | 0 | 0 | 23 | 98.1 | 391 | 77 | 32 | 26 | 4 | 3 | 2 | 0 | 29 | 3 | 85 | 3 | 0 | 4 | 4 | .500 | 0 | 14 | 2.38 |
| 1986 New York | AL | 62 | 0 | 0 | 26 | 96.2 | 424 | 105 | 61 | 53 | 14 | 5 | 2 | 1 | 37 | 2 | 67 | 2 | 0 | 9 | 5 | .643 | 0 | 6 | 4.93 |
| 1987 Pittsburgh | NL | 37 | 26 | 6 | 1 | 185.1 | 792 | 185 | 99 | 93 | 27 | 6 | 5 | 4 | 72 | 7 | 117 | 3 | 3 | 11 | 9 | .550 | 3 | 0 | 4.52 |
| 1988 Pittsburgh | NL | 33 | 22 | 1 | 3 | 146.1 | 645 | 157 | 78 | 75 | 13 | 10 | 6 | 5 | 57 | 4 | 66 | 0 | 4 | 8 | 10 | .444 | 1 | 1 | 4.61 |
| 1989 Pittsburgh | NL | 9 | 3 | 0 | 3 | 17 | 88 | 25 | 17 | 15 | 2 | 1 | 1 | 0 | 10 | 3 | 8 | 1 | 0 | 0 | 3 | .000 | 0 | 1 | 7.94 |
| 1990 Houston | NL | 4 | 0 | 0 | 3 | 5 | 24 | 9 | 5 | 4 | 1 | 0 | 2 | 0 | 0 | 0 | 1 | 0 | 0 | 0 | 0 | .000 | 0 | 0 | 7.20 |
| 6 ML YEARS | | 200 | 51 | 7 | 59 | 548.2 | 2364 | 558 | 292 | 266 | 61 | 25 | 18 | 10 | 205 | 19 | 344 | 9 | 7 | 32 | 31 | .508 | 4 | 22 | 4.36 |

## Carlton Fisk

**Bats:** Right **Throws:** Right **Pos:** C/DH **Ht:** 6' 2" **Wt:** 225 **Born:** 12/26/47 **Age:** 43

| BATTING | | | | | | | | | | | | | | | | | | | | BASERUNNING | | | | PERCENTAGES | | |
|---|---|---|---|---|---|---|---|---|---|---|---|---|---|---|---|---|---|---|---|---|---|---|---|---|---|---|
| Year Team | Lg | G | AB | H | 2B | 3B | HR | (Hm | Rd) | TB | R | RBI | TBB | IBB | SO | HBP | SH | SF | SB | CS | SB% | GDP | Avg | OBP | SLG |
| 1969 Boston | AL | 2 | 5 | 0 | 0 | 0 | 0 | (0 | 0) | 0 | 0 | 0 | 0 | 0 | 2 | 0 | 0 | 0 | 0 | 0 | .00 | 0 | .000 | .000 | .000 |
| 1971 Boston | AL | 14 | 48 | 15 | 2 | 1 | 2 | (0 | 2) | 25 | 7 | 6 | 1 | 0 | 10 | 0 | 0 | 0 | 0 | 0 | .00 | 1 | .313 | .327 | .521 |
| 1972 Boston | AL | 131 | 457 | 134 | 28 | 9 | 22 | (13 | 9) | 246 | 74 | 61 | 52 | 6 | 83 | 4 | 1 | 0 | 5 | 2 | .71 | 11 | .293 | .370 | .538 |
| 1973 Boston | AL | 135 | 508 | 125 | 21 | 0 | 26 | (16 | 10) | 224 | 65 | 71 | 37 | 2 | 99 | 10 | 1 | 2 | 7 | 2 | .78 | 11 | .246 | .309 | .441 |
| 1974 Boston | AL | 52 | 187 | 56 | 12 | 1 | 11 | (5 | 6) | 103 | 36 | 26 | 24 | 2 | 23 | 2 | 2 | 1 | 5 | 1 | .83 | 5 | .299 | .383 | .551 |
| 1975 Boston | AL | 79 | 263 | 87 | 14 | 4 | 10 | (6 | 4) | 139 | 47 | 52 | 27 | 4 | 32 | 2 | 0 | 2 | 4 | 3 | .57 | 7 | .331 | .395 | .529 |
| 1976 Boston | AL | 134 | 487 | 124 | 17 | 5 | 17 | (10 | 7) | 202 | 76 | 58 | 56 | 3 | 71 | 6 | 3 | 5 | 12 | 5 | .71 | 11 | .255 | .336 | .415 |
| 1977 Boston | AL | 152 | 536 | 169 | 26 | 3 | 26 | (15 | 11) | 279 | 106 | 102 | 75 | 3 | 85 | 9 | 2 | 10 | 7 | 6 | .54 | 9 | .315 | .402 | .521 |
| 1978 Boston | AL | 157 | 571 | 162 | 39 | 5 | 20 | (8 | 12) | 271 | 94 | 88 | 71 | 6 | 83 | 7 | 3 | 6 | 7 | 2 | .78 | 10 | .284 | .366 | .475 |
| 1979 Boston | AL | 91 | 320 | 87 | 23 | 2 | 10 | (5 | 5) | 144 | 49 | 42 | 10 | 0 | 38 | 6 | 1 | 3 | 3 | 0 | 1.00 | 9 | .272 | .304 | .450 |
| 1980 Boston | AL | 131 | 478 | 138 | 25 | 3 | 18 | (12 | 6) | 223 | 73 | 62 | 36 | 6 | 62 | 13 | 0 | 3 | 11 | 5 | .69 | 12 | .289 | .353 | .467 |
| 1981 Chicago | AL | 96 | 338 | 89 | 12 | 0 | 7 | (4 | 3) | 122 | 44 | 45 | 38 | 3 | 37 | 12 | 1 | 5 | 3 | 2 | .60 | 9 | .263 | .354 | .361 |
| 1982 Chicago | AL | 135 | 476 | 127 | 17 | 3 | 14 | (7 | 7) | 192 | 66 | 65 | 46 | 7 | 60 | 6 | 4 | 4 | 17 | 2 | .89 | 12 | .267 | .336 | .403 |
| 1983 Chicago | AL | 138 | 488 | 141 | 26 | 4 | 26 | (17 | 9) | 253 | 85 | 86 | 46 | 3 | 88 | 6 | 2 | 3 | 9 | 6 | .60 | 8 | .289 | .355 | .518 |
| 1984 Chicago | AL | 102 | 359 | 83 | 20 | 1 | 21 | (11 | 10) | 168 | 54 | 43 | 26 | 4 | 60 | 5 | 1 | 4 | 6 | 0 | 1.00 | 7 | .231 | .289 | .468 |
| 1985 Chicago | AL | 153 | 543 | 129 | 23 | 1 | 37 | (20 | 17) | 265 | 85 | 107 | 52 | 12 | 81 | 17 | 2 | 6 | 17 | 9 | .65 | 9 | .238 | .320 | .488 |
| 1986 Chicago | AL | 125 | 457 | 101 | 11 | 0 | 14 | (5 | 9) | 154 | 42 | 63 | 22 | 2 | 92 | 6 | 0 | 6 | 2 | 4 | .33 | 10 | .221 | .263 | .337 |
| 1987 Chicago | AL | 135 | 454 | 116 | 22 | 1 | 23 | (5 | 18) | 209 | 68 | 71 | 39 | 8 | 72 | 8 | 1 | 6 | 1 | 4 | .20 | 9 | .256 | .321 | .460 |
| 1988 Chicago | AL | 76 | 253 | 70 | 8 | 1 | 19 | (9 | 10) | 137 | 37 | 50 | 37 | 9 | 40 | 5 | 1 | 2 | 0 | 0 | .00 | 6 | .277 | .377 | .542 |
| 1989 Chicago | AL | 103 | 375 | 110 | 25 | 2 | 13 | (4 | 9) | 178 | 47 | 68 | 36 | 8 | 60 | 3 | 0 | 5 | 1 | 0 | 1.00 | 15 | .293 | .356 | .475 |
| 1990 Chicago | AL | 137 | 452 | 129 | 21 | 0 | 18 | (5 | 13) | 204 | 65 | 65 | 61 | 8 | 73 | 7 | 0 | 1 | 7 | 2 | .78 | 12 | .285 | .378 | .451 |
| 21 ML YEARS | | 2278 | 8055 | 2192 | 392 | 46 | 354 | (177 | 177) | 3738 | 1220 | 1231 | 792 | 96 | 1251 | 134 | 25 | 74 | 124 | 55 | .69 | 183 | .272 | .344 | .464 |

## Mike Fitzgerald

**Bats:** Right **Throws:** Right **Pos:** C **Ht:** 5'11" **Wt:** 190 **Born:** 07/13/60 **Age:** 30

| BATTING | | | | | | | | | | | | | | | | | | | | BASERUNNING | | | | PERCENTAGES | | |
|---|---|---|---|---|---|---|---|---|---|---|---|---|---|---|---|---|---|---|---|---|---|---|---|---|---|---|
| Year Team | Lg | G | AB | H | 2B | 3B | HR | (Hm | Rd) | TB | R | RBI | TBB | IBB | SO | HBP | SH | SF | SB | CS | SB% | GDP | Avg | OBP | SLG |
| 1983 New York | NL | 8 | 20 | 2 | 0 | 0 | 1 | (0 | 1) | 5 | 1 | 2 | 3 | 1 | 6 | 0 | 0 | 0 | 0 | 0 | .00 | 0 | .100 | .217 | .250 |
| 1984 New York | NL | 112 | 360 | 87 | 15 | 1 | 2 | (2 | 0) | 110 | 20 | 33 | 24 | 7 | 71 | 1 | 5 | 4 | 1 | 0 | 1.00 | 17 | .242 | .288 | .306 |
| 1985 Montreal | NL | 108 | 295 | 61 | 7 | 1 | 5 | (3 | 2) | 85 | 25 | 34 | 38 | 12 | 55 | 2 | 1 | 5 | 5 | 3 | .63 | 8 | .207 | .297 | .288 |
| 1986 Montreal | NL | 73 | 209 | 59 | 13 | 1 | 6 | (1 | 5) | 92 | 20 | 37 | 27 | 6 | 34 | 1 | 4 | 2 | 3 | 2 | .60 | 4 | .282 | .364 | .440 |
| 1987 Montreal | NL | 107 | 287 | 69 | 11 | 0 | 3 | (1 | 2) | 89 | 32 | 36 | 42 | 7 | 54 | 1 | 3 | 1 | 3 | 4 | .43 | 10 | .240 | .338 | .310 |
| 1988 Montreal | NL | 63 | 155 | 42 | 6 | 1 | 5 | (3 | 2) | 65 | 17 | 23 | 19 | 0 | 22 | 0 | 4 | 2 | 2 | 2 | .50 | 4 | .271 | .347 | .419 |

| Year Team | Lg | G | AB | H | 2B | 3B | HR | (Hm | Rd) | TB | R | RBI | TBB | IBB | SO | HBP | SH | SF | SB | CS | SB% | GDP | Avg | OBP | SLG |
|---|---|---|---|---|---|---|---|---|---|---|---|---|---|---|---|---|---|---|---|---|---|---|---|---|---|
| 1989 Montreal | NL | 100 | 290 | 69 | 18 | 2 | 7 | (3 | 4) | 112 | 33 | 42 | 35 | 3 | 61 | 2 | 2 | 2 | 3 | 4 | .43 | 8 | .238 | .322 | .386 |
| 1990 Montreal | NL | 111 | 313 | 76 | 18 | 1 | 9 | (2 | 7) | 123 | 36 | 41 | 60 | 2 | 60 | 2 | 5 | 3 | 8 | 1 | .89 | 5 | .243 | .365 | .393 |
| 8 ML YEARS | | 682 | 1929 | 465 | 88 | 7 | 38 | (15 | 23) | 681 | 184 | 248 | 248 | 38 | 363 | 9 | 24 | 19 | 25 | 16 | .61 | 56 | .241 | .327 | .353 |

## Mike Flanagan

**Pitches:** Left **Bats:** Left **Pos:** SP **Ht:** 6' 0" **Wt:** 195 **Born:** 12/16/51 **Age:** 39

| | | HOW MUCH HE PITCHED | | | | | | WHAT HE GAVE UP | | | | | | | | | | | | THE RESULTS | | | | | |
|---|---|---|---|---|---|---|---|---|---|---|---|---|---|---|---|---|---|---|---|---|---|---|---|---|---|
| Year Team | Lg | G | GS | CG | GF | IP | BFP | H | R | ER | HR | SH | SF | HB | TBB | IBB | SO | WP | Bk | W | L | Pct. | ShO | Sv | ERA |
| 1975 Baltimore | AL | 2 | 1 | 0 | 0 | 10 | 42 | 9 | 4 | 3 | 0 | 0 | 0 | 0 | 6 | 1 | 7 | 0 | 0 | 0 | 1 | .000 | 0 | 0 | 2.70 |
| 1976 Baltimore | AL | 20 | 10 | 4 | 7 | 85 | 358 | 83 | 41 | 39 | 7 | 2 | 4 | 0 | 33 | 0 | 56 | 2 | 1 | 3 | 5 | .375 | 0 | 0 | 4.13 |
| 1977 Baltimore | AL | 36 | 33 | 15 | 2 | 235 | 974 | 235 | 100 | 95 | 17 | 10 | 7 | 2 | 70 | 5 | 149 | 5 | 0 | 15 | 10 | .600 | 2 | 1 | 3.64 |
| 1978 Baltimore | AL | 40 | 40 | 17 | 0 | 281 | 1160 | 271 | 128 | 126 | 22 | 10 | 5 | 3 | 87 | 2 | 167 | 8 | 1 | 19 | 15 | .559 | 2 | 0 | 4.04 |
| 1979 Baltimore | AL | 39 | 38 | 16 | 0 | 266 | 1085 | 245 | 107 | 91 | 23 | 9 | 4 | 3 | 70 | 1 | 190 | 6 | 0 | 23 | 9 | .719 | 5 | 0 | 3.08 |
| 1980 Baltimore | AL | 37 | 37 | 12 | 0 | 251 | 1065 | 278 | 121 | 115 | 27 | 10 | 12 | 2 | 71 | 3 | 128 | 12 | 1 | 16 | 13 | .552 | 2 | 0 | 4.12 |
| 1981 Baltimore | AL | 20 | 20 | 3 | 0 | 116 | 482 | 108 | 55 | 54 | 11 | 0 | 0 | 2 | 37 | 1 | 72 | 6 | 0 | 9 | 6 | .600 | 2 | 0 | 4.19 |
| 1982 Baltimore | AL | 36 | 35 | 11 | 1 | 236 | 991 | 233 | 110 | 104 | 24 | 5 | 6 | 4 | 76 | 5 | 103 | 9 | 2 | 15 | 11 | .577 | 1 | 0 | 3.97 |
| 1983 Baltimore | AL | 20 | 20 | 3 | 0 | 125.1 | 528 | 135 | 53 | 46 | 10 | 4 | 6 | 2 | 31 | 2 | 50 | 1 | 0 | 12 | 4 | .750 | 1 | 0 | 3.30 |
| 1984 Baltimore | AL | 34 | 34 | 10 | 0 | 226.2 | 947 | 213 | 103 | 89 | 24 | 8 | 6 | 1 | 81 | 5 | 115 | 8 | 0 | 13 | 13 | .500 | 2 | 0 | 3.53 |
| 1985 Baltimore | AL | 15 | 15 | 1 | 0 | 86 | 379 | 101 | 49 | 49 | 14 | 7 | 2 | 2 | 28 | 0 | 42 | 3 | 0 | 4 | 5 | .444 | 0 | 0 | 5.13 |
| 1986 Baltimore | AL | 29 | 28 | 2 | 0 | 172 | 747 | 179 | 95 | 81 | 15 | 10 | 6 | 1 | 66 | 4 | 96 | 8 | 1 | 7 | 11 | .389 | 0 | 0 | 4.24 |
| 1987 2 ML Teams | | 23 | 23 | 4 | 0 | 144 | 619 | 148 | 72 | 65 | 12 | 6 | 1 | 0 | 51 | 4 | 93 | 3 | 0 | 6 | 8 | .429 | 0 | 0 | 4.06 |
| 1988 Toronto | AL | 34 | 34 | 2 | 0 | 211 | 916 | 220 | 106 | 98 | 23 | 14 | 4 | 6 | 80 | 1 | 99 | 3 | 4 | 13 | 13 | .500 | 1 | 0 | 4.18 |
| 1989 Toronto | AL | 30 | 30 | 1 | 0 | 171.2 | 726 | 186 | 82 | 75 | 10 | 8 | 8 | 5 | 47 | 0 | 47 | 4 | 0 | 8 | 10 | .444 | 1 | 0 | 3.93 |
| 1990 Toronto | AL | 5 | 5 | 0 | 0 | 20.1 | 94 | 28 | 14 | 12 | 3 | 1 | 0 | 0 | 8 | 0 | 5 | 0 | 0 | 2 | 2 | .500 | 0 | 0 | 5.31 |
| 1987 Baltimore | AL | 16 | 16 | 4 | 0 | 94.2 | 410 | 102 | 57 | 52 | 9 | 6 | 1 | 0 | 36 | 1 | 50 | 1 | 0 | 3 | 6 | .333 | 0 | 0 | 4.94 |
| Toronto | AL | 7 | 7 | 0 | 0 | 49.1 | 209 | 46 | 15 | 13 | 3 | 0 | 0 | 0 | 15 | 3 | 43 | 2 | 0 | 3 | 2 | .600 | 0 | 0 | 2.37 |
| 16 ML YEARS | | 420 | 403 | 101 | 10 | 2637 | 11113 | 2672 | 1240 | 1142 | 242 | 104 | 71 | 33 | 842 | 34 | 1419 | 78 | 10 | 165 | 136 | .548 | 19 | 1 | 3.90 |

## Darrin Fletcher

**Bats:** Left **Throws:** Right **Pos:** C **Ht:** 6' 2" **Wt:** 195 **Born:** 10/03/66 **Age:** 24

| | | BATTING | | | | | | | | | | | | | | | | | BASERUNNING | | | | PERCENTAGES | | |
|---|---|---|---|---|---|---|---|---|---|---|---|---|---|---|---|---|---|---|---|---|---|---|---|---|---|
| Year Team | Lg | G | AB | H | 2B | 3B | HR | (Hm | Rd) | TB | R | RBI | TBB | IBB | SO | HBP | SH | SF | SB | CS | SB% | GDP | Avg | OBP | SLG |
| 1987 Vero Beach | A | 43 | 124 | 33 | 7 | 0 | 0 | -- | -- | 40 | 13 | 15 | 22 | 3 | 12 | 1 | 0 | 4 | 0 | 2 | .00 | 6 | .266 | .371 | .323 |
| 1988 San Antonio | AA | 89 | 279 | 58 | 8 | 0 | 1 | -- | -- | 69 | 19 | 20 | 17 | 5 | 42 | 3 | 6 | 2 | 2 | 6 | .25 | 6 | .208 | .259 | .247 |
| 1989 Albuquerque | AAA | 100 | 315 | 86 | 16 | 1 | 5 | -- | -- | 119 | 34 | 44 | 30 | 0 | 38 | 2 | 2 | 6 | 1 | 5 | .17 | 12 | .273 | .334 | .378 |
| 1990 Albuquerque | AAA | 105 | 350 | 102 | 23 | 1 | 13 | -- | -- | 166 | 58 | 65 | 40 | 6 | 37 | 5 | 3 | 6 | 1 | 1 | .50 | 11 | .291 | .367 | .474 |
| 1989 Los Angeles | NL | 5 | 8 | 4 | 0 | 0 | 1 | (1 | 0) | 7 | 1 | 2 | 1 | 0 | 0 | 0 | 0 | 0 | 0 | 0 | .00 | 0 | .500 | .556 | .875 |
| 1990 2 ML Teams | | 11 | 23 | 3 | 1 | 0 | 0 | (0 | 0) | 4 | 3 | 1 | 1 | 0 | 6 | 0 | 0 | 0 | 0 | 0 | .00 | 0 | .130 | .167 | .174 |
| 1990 Los Angeles | NL | 2 | 1 | 0 | 0 | 0 | 0 | (0 | 0) | 0 | 0 | 0 | 0 | 0 | 1 | 0 | 0 | 0 | 0 | 0 | .00 | 0 | .000 | .000 | .000 |
| Philadelphia | NL | 9 | 22 | 3 | 1 | 0 | 0 | (0 | 0) | 4 | 3 | 1 | 1 | 0 | 5 | 0 | 0 | 0 | 0 | 0 | .00 | 0 | .136 | .174 | .182 |
| 2 ML YEARS | | 16 | 31 | 7 | 1 | 0 | 1 | (1 | 0) | 11 | 4 | 3 | 2 | 0 | 6 | 0 | 0 | 0 | 0 | 0 | .00 | 0 | .226 | .273 | .355 |

## Scott Fletcher

**Bats:** Right **Throws:** Right **Pos:** 2B **Ht:** 5'11" **Wt:** 173 **Born:** 07/30/58 **Age:** 32

| | | BATTING | | | | | | | | | | | | | | | | | BASERUNNING | | | | PERCENTAGES | | |
|---|---|---|---|---|---|---|---|---|---|---|---|---|---|---|---|---|---|---|---|---|---|---|---|---|---|
| Year Team | Lg | G | AB | H | 2B | 3B | HR | (Hm | Rd) | TB | R | RBI | TBB | IBB | SO | HBP | SH | SF | SB | CS | SB% | GDP | Avg | OBP | SLG |
| 1981 Chicago | NL | 19 | 46 | 10 | 4 | 0 | 0 | (0 | 0) | 14 | 6 | 1 | 2 | 0 | 4 | 0 | 0 | 0 | 0 | 0 | .00 | 0 | .217 | .250 | .304 |
| 1982 Chicago | NL | 11 | 24 | 4 | 0 | 0 | 0 | (0 | 0) | 4 | 4 | 1 | 4 | 0 | 5 | 0 | 0 | 0 | 1 | 0 | 1.00 | 0 | .167 | .286 | .167 |
| 1983 Chicago | AL | 114 | 262 | 62 | 16 | 5 | 3 | (1 | 2) | 97 | 42 | 31 | 29 | 0 | 22 | 2 | 7 | 2 | 5 | 1 | .83 | 8 | .237 | .315 | .370 |
| 1984 Chicago | AL | 149 | 456 | 114 | 13 | 3 | 3 | (2 | 1) | 142 | 46 | 35 | 46 | 2 | 46 | 8 | 9 | 2 | 10 | 4 | .71 | 5 | .250 | .328 | .311 |
| 1985 Chicago | AL | 119 | 301 | 77 | 8 | 1 | 2 | (0 | 2) | 93 | 38 | 31 | 35 | 0 | 47 | 0 | 11 | 1 | 5 | 5 | .50 | 9 | .256 | .332 | .309 |
| 1986 Texas | AL | 147 | 530 | 159 | 34 | 5 | 3 | (2 | 1) | 212 | 82 | 50 | 47 | 0 | 59 | 4 | 10 | 3 | 12 | 11 | .52 | 10 | .300 | .360 | .400 |
| 1987 Texas | AL | 156 | 588 | 169 | 28 | 4 | 5 | (4 | 1) | 220 | 82 | 63 | 61 | 3 | 66 | 5 | 12 | 2 | 13 | 12 | .52 | 14 | .287 | .358 | .374 |
| 1988 Texas | AL | 140 | 515 | 142 | 19 | 4 | 0 | (0 | 0) | 169 | 59 | 47 | 62 | 1 | 34 | 12 | 15 | 5 | 8 | 5 | .62 | 13 | .276 | .364 | .328 |
| 1989 2 ML Teams | | 142 | 546 | 138 | 25 | 2 | 1 | (0 | 1) | 170 | 77 | 43 | 64 | 1 | 60 | 3 | 11 | 5 | 2 | 1 | .67 | 12 | .253 | .332 | .311 |
| 1990 Chicago | AL | 151 | 509 | 123 | 18 | 3 | 4 | (1 | 3) | 159 | 54 | 56 | 45 | 3 | 63 | 3 | 11 | 5 | 1 | 3 | .25 | 10 | .242 | .304 | .312 |
| 1989 Texas | AL | 83 | 314 | 75 | 14 | 1 | 0 | (0 | 0) | 91 | 47 | 22 | 38 | 1 | 41 | 2 | 2 | 2 | 1 | 0 | 1.00 | 8 | .239 | .323 | .290 |
| Chicago | AL | 59 | 232 | 63 | 11 | 1 | 1 | (0 | 1) | 79 | 30 | 21 | 26 | 0 | 19 | 1 | 9 | 3 | 1 | 1 | .50 | 4 | .272 | .344 | .341 |
| 10 ML YEARS | | 1148 | 3777 | 998 | 165 | 27 | 21 | (10 | 11) | 1280 | 490 | 358 | 395 | 10 | 406 | 37 | 86 | 25 | 57 | 42 | .58 | 81 | .264 | .338 | .339 |

## Tom Foley

**Bats:** Left **Throws:** Right **Pos:** SS/2B **Ht:** 6' 1" **Wt:** 180 **Born:** 09/09/59 **Age:** 31

| | | BATTING | | | | | | | | | | | | | | | | | BASERUNNING | | | | PERCENTAGES | | |
|---|---|---|---|---|---|---|---|---|---|---|---|---|---|---|---|---|---|---|---|---|---|---|---|---|---|
| Year Team | Lg | G | AB | H | 2B | 3B | HR | (Hm | Rd) | TB | R | RBI | TBB | IBB | SO | HBP | SH | SF | SB | CS | SB% | GDP | Avg | OBP | SLG |
| 1983 Cincinnati | NL | 68 | 98 | 20 | 4 | 1 | 0 | (0 | 0) | 26 | 7 | 9 | 13 | 2 | 17 | 0 | 2 | 0 | 1 | 0 | 1.00 | 1 | .204 | .297 | .265 |
| 1984 Cincinnati | NL | 106 | 277 | 70 | 8 | 3 | 5 | (2 | 3) | 99 | 26 | 27 | 24 | 7 | 36 | 0 | 1 | 2 | 3 | 2 | .60 | 2 | .253 | .310 | .357 |
| 1985 2 ML Teams | | 89 | 250 | 60 | 13 | 1 | 3 | (2 | 1) | 84 | 24 | 23 | 19 | 8 | 34 | 0 | 0 | 0 | 2 | 3 | .40 | 2 | .240 | .294 | .336 |
| 1986 2 ML Teams | | 103 | 263 | 70 | 15 | 3 | 1 | (1 | 0) | 94 | 26 | 23 | 30 | 6 | 37 | 0 | 2 | 4 | 10 | 3 | .77 | 4 | .266 | .337 | .357 |

| Year | Team | Lg | G | AB | H | 2B | 3B | HR | (Hm | Rd) | TB | R | RBI | TBB | IBB | SO | HBP | SH | SF | SB | CS | SB% | GDP | Avg | OBP | SLG |
|---|---|---|---|---|---|---|---|---|---|---|---|---|---|---|---|---|---|---|---|---|---|---|---|---|---|---|
| 1987 | Montreal | NL | 106 | 280 | 82 | 18 | 3 | 5 | (3 | 2) | 121 | 35 | 28 | 11 | 0 | 40 | 1 | 1 | 0 | 6 | 10 | .38 | 6 | .293 | .322 | .432 |
| 1988 | Montreal | NL | 127 | 377 | 100 | 21 | 3 | 5 | (3 | 2) | 142 | 33 | 43 | 30 | 10 | 49 | 1 | 0 | 3 | 2 | 7 | .22 | 11 | .265 | .319 | .377 |
| 1989 | Montreal | NL | 122 | 375 | 86 | 19 | 2 | 7 | (4 | 3) | 130 | 34 | 39 | 45 | 4 | 53 | 3 | 4 | 4 | 2 | 3 | .40 | 2 | .229 | .314 | .347 |
| 1990 | Montreal | NL | 73 | 164 | 35 | 2 | 1 | 0 | (0 | 0) | 39 | 11 | 12 | 12 | 2 | 22 | 0 | 1 | 1 | 0 | 1 | .00 | 4 | .213 | .266 | .238 |
| 1985 | Cincinnati | NL | 43 | 92 | 18 | 5 | 1 | 0 | (0 | 0) | 25 | 7 | 6 | 6 | 1 | 16 | 0 | 0 | 0 | 1 | 0 | 1.00 | 0 | .196 | .245 | .272 |
| | Philadelphia | NL | 46 | 158 | 42 | 8 | 0 | 3 | (2 | 1) | 59 | 17 | 17 | 13 | 7 | 18 | 0 | 0 | 0 | 1 | 3 | .25 | 2 | .266 | .322 | .373 |
| 1986 | Philadelphia | NL | 39 | 61 | 18 | 2 | 1 | 0 | (0 | 0) | 22 | 8 | 5 | 10 | 1 | 11 | 0 | 0 | 1 | 2 | 0 | 1.00 | 1 | .295 | .389 | .361 |
| | Montreal | NL | 64 | 202 | 52 | 13 | 2 | 1 | (1 | 0) | 72 | 18 | 18 | 20 | 5 | 26 | 0 | 2 | 3 | 8 | 3 | .73 | 3 | .257 | .320 | .356 |
| 8 | ML YEARS | | 794 | 2084 | 523 | 100 | 17 | 26 | (15 | 11) | 735 | 196 | 204 | 184 | 39 | 288 | 5 | 11 | 14 | 26 | 29 | .47 | 32 | .251 | .311 | .353 |

## Curt Ford

**Bats:** Left **Throws:** Right **Pos:** RF **Ht:** 5'10" **Wt:** 150 **Born:** 10/11/60 **Age:** 30

| | | | BATTING | | | | | | | | | | | | | | | | | BASERUNNING | | | | PERCENTAGES | | |
|---|---|---|---|---|---|---|---|---|---|---|---|---|---|---|---|---|---|---|---|---|---|---|---|---|---|---|
| Year | Team | Lg | G | AB | H | 2B | 3B | HR | (Hm | Rd) | TB | R | RBI | TBB | IBB | SO | HBP | SH | SF | SB | CS | SB% | GDP | Avg | OBP | SLG |
| 1985 | St. Louis | NL | 11 | 12 | 6 | 2 | 0 | 0 | (0 | 0) | 8 | 2 | 3 | 4 | 0 | 1 | 0 | 0 | 0 | 1 | 0 | 1.00 | 0 | .500 | .625 | .667 |
| 1986 | St. Louis | NL | 85 | 214 | 53 | 15 | 2 | 2 | (0 | 2) | 78 | 30 | 29 | 23 | 2 | 29 | 0 | 1 | 2 | 13 | 5 | .72 | 1 | .248 | .318 | .364 |
| 1987 | St. Louis | NL | 89 | 228 | 65 | 9 | 5 | 3 | (1 | 2) | 93 | 32 | 26 | 14 | 0 | 32 | 1 | 1 | 3 | 11 | 8 | .58 | 5 | .285 | .325 | .408 |
| 1988 | St. Louis | NL | 91 | 128 | 25 | 6 | 0 | 1 | (0 | 1) | 34 | 11 | 18 | 8 | 1 | 26 | 0 | 1 | 2 | 6 | 1 | .86 | 4 | .195 | .239 | .266 |
| 1989 | Philadelphia | NL | 108 | 142 | 31 | 5 | 1 | 1 | (0 | 1) | 41 | 13 | 13 | 16 | 0 | 33 | 1 | 0 | 2 | 5 | 3 | .63 | 4 | .218 | .298 | .289 |
| 1990 | Philadelphia | NL | 22 | 18 | 2 | 0 | 0 | 0 | (0 | 0) | 2 | 0 | 0 | 1 | 0 | 5 | 0 | 0 | 0 | 0 | 0 | .00 | 1 | .111 | .158 | .111 |
| 6 | ML YEARS | | 406 | 742 | 182 | 37 | 8 | 7 | (1 | 6) | 256 | 88 | 89 | 66 | 3 | 126 | 2 | 3 | 9 | 36 | 17 | .68 | 15 | .245 | .305 | .345 |

## Tony Fossas

**Pitches:** Left **Bats:** Left **Pos:** RP **Ht:** 6' 0" **Wt:** 180 **Born:** 09/23/57 **Age:** 33

| | | | HOW MUCH HE PITCHED | | | | | | WHAT HE GAVE UP | | | | | | | | | | | | THE RESULTS | | | | | |
|---|---|---|---|---|---|---|---|---|---|---|---|---|---|---|---|---|---|---|---|---|---|---|---|---|---|---|
| Year | Team | Lg | G | GS | CG | GF | IP | BFP | H | R | ER | HR | SH | SF | HB | TBB | IBB | SO | WP | Bk | W | L | Pct. | ShO | Sv | ERA |
| 1988 | Texas | AL | 5 | 0 | 0 | 1 | 5.2 | 28 | 11 | 3 | 3 | 0 | 0 | 0 | 0 | 2 | 0 | 0 | 1 | 0 | 0 | 0 | .000 | 0 | 0 | 4.76 |
| 1989 | Milwaukee | AL | 51 | 0 | 0 | 16 | 61 | 256 | 57 | 27 | 24 | 3 | 7 | 3 | 1 | 22 | 7 | 42 | 1 | 3 | 2 | 2 | .500 | 0 | 1 | 3.54 |
| 1990 | Milwaukee | AL | 32 | 0 | 0 | 9 | 29.1 | 146 | 44 | 23 | 21 | 5 | 2 | 1 | 0 | 10 | 2 | 24 | 0 | 0 | 2 | 3 | .400 | 0 | 0 | 6.44 |
| 3 | ML YEARS | | 88 | 0 | 0 | 26 | 96 | 430 | 112 | 53 | 48 | 8 | 9 | 4 | 1 | 34 | 9 | 66 | 2 | 3 | 4 | 5 | .444 | 0 | 1 | 4.50 |

## John Franco

**Pitches:** Left **Bats:** Left **Pos:** RP **Ht:** 5'10" **Wt:** 185 **Born:** 09/17/60 **Age:** 30

| | | | HOW MUCH HE PITCHED | | | | | | WHAT HE GAVE UP | | | | | | | | | | | | THE RESULTS | | | | | |
|---|---|---|---|---|---|---|---|---|---|---|---|---|---|---|---|---|---|---|---|---|---|---|---|---|---|---|
| Year | Team | Lg | G | GS | CG | GF | IP | BFP | H | R | ER | HR | SH | SF | HB | TBB | IBB | SO | WP | Bk | W | L | Pct. | ShO | Sv | ERA |
| 1984 | Cincinnati | NL | 54 | 0 | 0 | 30 | 79.1 | 335 | 74 | 28 | 23 | 3 | 4 | 4 | 2 | 36 | 4 | 55 | 2 | 0 | 6 | 2 | .750 | 0 | 4 | 2.61 |
| 1985 | Cincinnati | NL | 67 | 0 | 0 | 33 | 99 | 407 | 83 | 27 | 24 | 5 | 11 | 1 | 1 | 40 | 8 | 61 | 4 | 0 | 12 | 3 | .800 | 0 | 12 | 2.18 |
| 1986 | Cincinnati | NL | 74 | 0 | 0 | 52 | 101 | 429 | 90 | 40 | 33 | 7 | 8 | 3 | 2 | 44 | 12 | 84 | 4 | 2 | 6 | 6 | .500 | 0 | 29 | 2.94 |
| 1987 | Cincinnati | NL | 68 | 0 | 0 | 60 | 82 | 344 | 76 | 26 | 23 | 6 | 5 | 2 | 0 | 27 | 6 | 61 | 1 | 0 | 8 | 5 | .615 | 0 | 32 | 2.52 |
| 1988 | Cincinnati | NL | 70 | 0 | 0 | 61 | 86 | 336 | 60 | 18 | 15 | 3 | 5 | 1 | 0 | 27 | 3 | 46 | 1 | 2 | 6 | 6 | .500 | 0 | 39 | 1.57 |
| 1989 | Cincinnati | NL | 60 | 0 | 0 | 50 | 80.2 | 345 | 77 | 35 | 28 | 3 | 7 | 3 | 0 | 36 | 8 | 60 | 3 | 2 | 4 | 8 | .333 | 0 | 32 | 3.12 |
| 1990 | New York | NL | 55 | 0 | 0 | 48 | 67.2 | 287 | 66 | 22 | 19 | 4 | 3 | 1 | 0 | 21 | 2 | 56 | 7 | 2 | 5 | 3 | .625 | 0 | 33 | 2.53 |
| 7 | ML YEARS | | 448 | 0 | 0 | 334 | 595.2 | 2483 | 526 | 196 | 165 | 31 | 43 | 15 | 5 | 231 | 43 | 423 | 22 | 8 | 47 | 33 | .588 | 0 | 181 | 2.49 |

## Julio Franco

**Bats:** Right **Throws:** Right **Pos:** 2B **Ht:** 6' 0" **Wt:** 165 **Born:** 08/23/61 **Age:** 29

| | | | BATTING | | | | | | | | | | | | | | | | | BASERUNNING | | | | PERCENTAGES | | |
|---|---|---|---|---|---|---|---|---|---|---|---|---|---|---|---|---|---|---|---|---|---|---|---|---|---|---|
| Year | Team | Lg | G | AB | H | 2B | 3B | HR | (Hm | Rd) | TB | R | RBI | TBB | IBB | SO | HBP | SH | SF | SB | CS | SB% | GDP | Avg | OBP | SLG |
| 1982 | Philadelphia | NL | 16 | 29 | 8 | 1 | 0 | 0 | (0 | 0) | 9 | 3 | 3 | 2 | 1 | 4 | 0 | 1 | 0 | 0 | 2 | .00 | 1 | .276 | .323 | .310 |
| 1983 | Cleveland | AL | 149 | 560 | 153 | 24 | 8 | 8 | (6 | 2) | 217 | 68 | 80 | 27 | 1 | 50 | 2 | 3 | 6 | 32 | 12 | .73 | 21 | .273 | .306 | .388 |
| 1984 | Cleveland | AL | 160 | 658 | 188 | 22 | 5 | 3 | (1 | 2) | 229 | 82 | 79 | 43 | 1 | 68 | 6 | 1 | 10 | 19 | 10 | .66 | 23 | .286 | .331 | .348 |
| 1985 | Cleveland | AL | 160 | 636 | 183 | 33 | 4 | 6 | (3 | 3) | 242 | 97 | 90 | 54 | 2 | 74 | 4 | 0 | 9 | 13 | 9 | .59 | 26 | .288 | .343 | .381 |
| 1986 | Cleveland | AL | 149 | 599 | 183 | 30 | 5 | 10 | (4 | 6) | 253 | 80 | 74 | 32 | 1 | 66 | 0 | 0 | 5 | 10 | 7 | .59 | 28 | .306 | .338 | .422 |
| 1987 | Cleveland | AL | 128 | 495 | 158 | 24 | 3 | 8 | (5 | 3) | 212 | 86 | 52 | 57 | 2 | 56 | 3 | 0 | 5 | 32 | 9 | .78 | 23 | .319 | .389 | .428 |
| 1988 | Cleveland | AL | 152 | 613 | 186 | 23 | 6 | 10 | (3 | 7) | 251 | 88 | 54 | 56 | 4 | 72 | 2 | 1 | 4 | 25 | 11 | .69 | 17 | .303 | .361 | .409 |
| 1989 | Texas | AL | 150 | 548 | 173 | 31 | 5 | 13 | (9 | 4) | 253 | 80 | 92 | 66 | 11 | 69 | 1 | 0 | 6 | 21 | 3 | .88 | 27 | .316 | .386 | .462 |
| 1990 | Texas | AL | 157 | 582 | 172 | 27 | 1 | 11 | (4 | 7) | 234 | 96 | 69 | 82 | 3 | 83 | 2 | 2 | 2 | 31 | 10 | .76 | 12 | .296 | .383 | .402 |
| 9 | ML YEARS | | 1221 | 4720 | 1404 | 215 | 37 | 69 | (35 | 34) | 1900 | 680 | 593 | 419 | 26 | 542 | 20 | 8 | 47 | 183 | 73 | .71 | 178 | .297 | .354 | .403 |

## Terry Francona

**Bats:** Left **Throws:** Left **Pos:** 1B **Ht:** 6' 1" **Wt:** 175 **Born:** 04/22/59 **Age:** 32

| | | | BATTING | | | | | | | | | | | | | | | | | BASERUNNING | | | | PERCENTAGES | | |
|---|---|---|---|---|---|---|---|---|---|---|---|---|---|---|---|---|---|---|---|---|---|---|---|---|---|---|
| Year | Team | Lg | G | AB | H | 2B | 3B | HR | (Hm | Rd) | TB | R | RBI | TBB | IBB | SO | HBP | SH | SF | SB | CS | SB% | GDP | Avg | OBP | SLG |
| 1981 | Montreal | NL | 34 | 95 | 26 | 0 | 1 | 1 | (1 | 0) | 31 | 11 | 8 | 5 | 1 | 6 | 1 | 3 | 0 | 1 | 0 | 1.00 | 0 | .274 | .317 | .326 |
| 1982 | Montreal | NL | 46 | 131 | 42 | 3 | 0 | 0 | (0 | 0) | 45 | 14 | 9 | 8 | 0 | 11 | 0 | 5 | 0 | 2 | 3 | .40 | 2 | .321 | .360 | .344 |
| 1983 | Montreal | NL | 120 | 230 | 59 | 11 | 1 | 3 | (1 | 2) | 81 | 21 | 22 | 6 | 2 | 20 | 0 | 0 | 2 | 0 | 2 | .00 | 7 | .257 | .273 | .352 |

| | | | | | | | | | | | | | | | | | | | | | | | | | | |
|---|---|---|---|---|---|---|---|---|---|---|---|---|---|---|---|---|---|---|---|---|---|---|---|---|---|---|
| 1984 Montreal | NL | 58 | 214 | 74 | 19 | 2 | 1 | (1 | 0) | 100 | 18 | 18 | 5 | 3 | 12 | 1 | 1 | 2 | 0 | 0 | .00 | 4 | .346 | .360 | .467 |
| 1985 Montreal | NL | 107 | 281 | 75 | 15 | 1 | 2 | (0 | 2) | 98 | 19 | 31 | 12 | 4 | 12 | 1 | 2 | 0 | 5 | 5 | .50 | 1 | .267 | .299 | .349 |
| 1986 Chicago | NL | 86 | 124 | 31 | 3 | 0 | 2 | (0 | 2) | 40 | 13 | 8 | 6 | 0 | 8 | 1 | 0 | 2 | 0 | 1 | .00 | 3 | .250 | .286 | .323 |
| 1987 Cincinnati | NL | 102 | 207 | 47 | 5 | 0 | 3 | (2 | 1) | 61 | 16 | 12 | 10 | 1 | 12 | 1 | 1 | 0 | 2 | 0 | 1.00 | 5 | .227 | .266 | .295 |
| 1988 Cleveland | AL | 62 | 212 | 66 | 8 | 0 | 1 | (1 | 0) | 77 | 24 | 12 | 5 | 1 | 18 | 0 | 2 | 2 | 0 | 0 | .00 | 4 | .311 | .324 | .363 |
| 1989 Milwaukee | AL | 90 | 233 | 54 | 10 | 1 | 3 | (1 | 2) | 75 | 26 | 23 | 8 | 3 | 20 | 0 | 1 | 2 | 2 | 1 | .67 | 4 | .232 | .255 | .322 |
| 1990 Milwaukee | AL | 3 | 4 | 0 | 0 | 0 | 0 | (0 | 0) | 0 | 1 | 0 | 0 | 0 | 0 | 0 | 0 | 0 | 0 | 0 | .00 | 0 | .000 | .000 | .000 |
| 10 ML YEARS | | 708 | 1731 | 474 | 74 | 6 | 16 | (7 | 9) | 608 | 163 | 143 | 65 | 15 | 119 | 5 | 15 | 10 | 12 | 12 | .50 | 30 | .274 | .300 | .351 |

## Willie Fraser

**Pitches:** Right **Bats:** Right **Pos:** RP **Ht:** 6' 1" **Wt:** 208 **Born:** 05/26/64 **Age:** 27

| | | HOW MUCH HE PITCHED | | | | | | WHAT HE GAVE UP | | | | | | | | | | | | THE RESULTS | | | | | |
|---|---|---|---|---|---|---|---|---|---|---|---|---|---|---|---|---|---|---|---|---|---|---|---|---|---|
| Year Team | Lg | G | GS | CG | GF | IP | BFP | H | R | ER | HR | SH | SF | HB | TBB | IBB | SO | WP | Bk | W | L | Pct. | ShO | Sv | ERA |
| 1986 California | AL | 1 | 1 | 0 | 0 | 4.1 | 20 | 6 | 4 | 4 | 0 | 1 | 1 | 0 | 1 | 0 | 2 | 0 | 0 | 0 | 0 | .000 | 0 | 0 | 8.31 |
| 1987 California | AL | 36 | 23 | 5 | 6 | 176.2 | 744 | 160 | 85 | 77 | 26 | 5 | 4 | 6 | 63 | 3 | 106 | 12 | 1 | 10 | 10 | .500 | 1 | 1 | 3.92 |
| 1988 California | AL | 34 | 32 | 2 | 0 | 194.2 | 861 | 203 | 129 | 117 | 33 | 2 | 9 | 9 | 80 | 7 | 86 | 12 | 6 | 12 | 13 | .480 | 0 | 0 | 5.41 |
| 1989 California | AL | 44 | 0 | 0 | 21 | 91.2 | 375 | 80 | 33 | 33 | 6 | 4 | 3 | 5 | 23 | 4 | 46 | 5 | 0 | 4 | 7 | .364 | 0 | 2 | 3.24 |
| 1990 California | AL | 45 | 0 | 0 | 20 | 76 | 315 | 69 | 29 | 26 | 4 | 2 | 3 | 0 | 24 | 3 | 32 | 1 | 0 | 5 | 4 | .556 | 0 | 2 | 3.08 |
| 5 ML YEARS | | 160 | 56 | 7 | 47 | 543.1 | 2315 | 518 | 280 | 257 | 69 | 14 | 20 | 20 | 191 | 17 | 272 | 30 | 7 | 31 | 34 | .477 | 1 | 5 | 4.26 |

## Marvin Freeman

**Pitches:** Right **Bats:** Right **Pos:** RP/SP **Ht:** 6' 7" **Wt:** 200 **Born:** 04/10/63 **Age:** 28

| | | HOW MUCH HE PITCHED | | | | | | WHAT HE GAVE UP | | | | | | | | | | | | THE RESULTS | | | | | |
|---|---|---|---|---|---|---|---|---|---|---|---|---|---|---|---|---|---|---|---|---|---|---|---|---|---|
| Year Team | Lg | G | GS | CG | GF | IP | BFP | H | R | ER | HR | SH | SF | HB | TBB | IBB | SO | WP | Bk | W | L | Pct. | ShO | Sv | ERA |
| 1986 Philadelphia | NL | 3 | 3 | 0 | 0 | 16 | 61 | 6 | 4 | 4 | 0 | 0 | 1 | 0 | 10 | 0 | 8 | 1 | 0 | 2 | 0 | 1.000 | 0 | 0 | 2.25 |
| 1988 Philadelphia | NL | 11 | 11 | 0 | 0 | 51.2 | 249 | 55 | 36 | 35 | 2 | 5 | 1 | 1 | 43 | 2 | 37 | 3 | 1 | 2 | 3 | .400 | 0 | 0 | 6.10 |
| 1989 Philadelphia | NL | 1 | 1 | 0 | 0 | 3 | 16 | 2 | 2 | 2 | 0 | 0 | 0 | 0 | 5 | 0 | 0 | 0 | 1 | 0 | 0 | .000 | 0 | 0 | 6.00 |
| 1990 2 ML Teams | | 25 | 3 | 0 | 5 | 48 | 207 | 41 | 24 | 23 | 5 | 2 | 0 | 5 | 17 | 2 | 38 | 4 | 0 | 1 | 2 | .333 | 0 | 1 | 4.31 |
| 1990 Philadelphia | NL | 16 | 3 | 0 | 4 | 32.1 | 147 | 34 | 21 | 20 | 5 | 1 | 0 | 3 | 14 | 2 | 26 | 4 | 0 | 0 | 2 | .000 | 0 | 1 | 5.57 |
| Atlanta | NL | 9 | 0 | 0 | 1 | 15.2 | 60 | 7 | 3 | 3 | 0 | 1 | 0 | 2 | 3 | 0 | 12 | 0 | 0 | 1 | 0 | 1.000 | 0 | 0 | 1.72 |
| 4 ML YEARS | | 40 | 18 | 0 | 5 | 118.2 | 533 | 104 | 66 | 64 | 7 | 7 | 2 | 6 | 75 | 4 | 83 | 8 | 2 | 5 | 5 | .500 | 0 | 1 | 4.85 |

## Steve Frey

**Pitches:** Left **Bats:** Left **Pos:** RP **Ht:** 5' 9" **Wt:** 170 **Born:** 07/29/63 **Age:** 27

| | | HOW MUCH HE PITCHED | | | | | | WHAT HE GAVE UP | | | | | | | | | | | | THE RESULTS | | | | | |
|---|---|---|---|---|---|---|---|---|---|---|---|---|---|---|---|---|---|---|---|---|---|---|---|---|---|
| Year Team | Lg | G | GS | CG | GF | IP | BFP | H | R | ER | HR | SH | SF | HB | TBB | IBB | SO | WP | Bk | W | L | Pct. | ShO | Sv | ERA |
| 1984 Ft.Laudrdle | A | 47 | 0 | 0 | 25 | 64.2 | 281 | 46 | 26 | 15 | 2 | 1 | 3 | 0 | 34 | 2 | 66 | 4 | 0 | 4 | 2 | .667 | 0 | 4 | 2.09 |
| 1985 Ft.Laudrdle | A | 19 | 0 | 0 | 13 | 22.1 | 89 | 11 | 4 | 3 | 0 | 1 | 0 | 1 | 12 | 0 | 15 | 0 | 0 | 1 | 1 | .500 | 0 | 7 | 1.21 |
| Albany | AA | 40 | 0 | 0 | 14 | 61.1 | 261 | 53 | 30 | 26 | 4 | 2 | 0 | 3 | 25 | 5 | 54 | 0 | 0 | 4 | 7 | .364 | 0 | 3 | 3.82 |
| 1986 Columbus | AAA | 11 | 0 | 0 | 2 | 19 | 93 | 29 | 17 | 17 | 3 | 0 | 2 | 0 | 10 | 1 | 11 | 0 | 0 | 0 | 2 | .000 | 0 | 0 | 8.05 |
| Albany | AA | 40 | 0 | 0 | 26 | 73 | 287 | 50 | 25 | 17 | 5 | 2 | 4 | 2 | 18 | 1 | 62 | 2 | 0 | 3 | 4 | .429 | 0 | 4 | 2.10 |
| 1987 Albany | AA | 14 | 0 | 0 | 10 | 28 | 111 | 20 | 6 | 6 | 0 | 1 | 0 | 0 | 7 | 1 | 19 | 1 | 0 | 0 | 2 | .000 | 0 | 1 | 1.93 |
| Columbus | AAA | 23 | 0 | 0 | 11 | 47.1 | 196 | 45 | 19 | 16 | 2 | 1 | 3 | 0 | 10 | 0 | 35 | 4 | 0 | 2 | 1 | .667 | 0 | 6 | 3.04 |
| 1988 Tidewater | AAA | 58 | 1 | 0 | 22 | 54.2 | 230 | 38 | 23 | 19 | 3 | 4 | 2 | 3 | 25 | 6 | 58 | 1 | 3 | 6 | 3 | .667 | 0 | 6 | 3.13 |
| 1989 Indianapols | AAA | 21 | 0 | 0 | 8 | 25.1 | 97 | 18 | 7 | 5 | 1 | 2 | 0 | 0 | 6 | 1 | 23 | 0 | 0 | 2 | 1 | .667 | 0 | 3 | 1.78 |
| 1990 Indianapols | AAA | 2 | 0 | 0 | 1 | 3 | 10 | 0 | 0 | 0 | 0 | 0 | 0 | 0 | 1 | 0 | 3 | 0 | 0 | 0 | 0 | .000 | 0 | 1 | 0.00 |
| 1989 Montreal | NL | 20 | 0 | 0 | 11 | 21.1 | 103 | 29 | 15 | 13 | 4 | 0 | 2 | 1 | 11 | 1 | 15 | 1 | 1 | 3 | 2 | .600 | 0 | 0 | 5.48 |
| 1990 Montreal | NL | 51 | 0 | 0 | 21 | 55.2 | 236 | 44 | 15 | 13 | 4 | 3 | 2 | 1 | 29 | 6 | 29 | 0 | 0 | 8 | 2 | .800 | 0 | 9 | 2.10 |
| 2 ML YEARS | | 71 | 0 | 0 | 32 | 77 | 339 | 73 | 30 | 26 | 8 | 3 | 4 | 2 | 40 | 7 | 44 | 1 | 1 | 11 | 4 | .733 | 0 | 9 | 3.04 |

## Todd Frohwirth

**Pitches:** Right **Bats:** Right **Pos:** RP **Ht:** 6' 4" **Wt:** 195 **Born:** 09/28/62 **Age:** 28

| | | HOW MUCH HE PITCHED | | | | | | WHAT HE GAVE UP | | | | | | | | | | | | THE RESULTS | | | | | |
|---|---|---|---|---|---|---|---|---|---|---|---|---|---|---|---|---|---|---|---|---|---|---|---|---|---|
| Year Team | Lg | G | GS | CG | GF | IP | BFP | H | R | ER | HR | SH | SF | HB | TBB | IBB | SO | WP | Bk | W | L | Pct. | ShO | Sv | ERA |
| 1987 Philadelphia | NL | 10 | 0 | 0 | 2 | 11 | 43 | 12 | 0 | 0 | 0 | 0 | 0 | 0 | 2 | 0 | 9 | 0 | 0 | 1 | 0 | 1.000 | 0 | 0 | 0.00 |
| 1988 Philadelphia | NL | 12 | 0 | 0 | 6 | 12 | 62 | 16 | 11 | 11 | 2 | 1 | 1 | 0 | 11 | 6 | 11 | 1 | 0 | 1 | 2 | .333 | 0 | 0 | 8.25 |
| 1989 Philadelphia | NL | 45 | 0 | 0 | 11 | 62.2 | 258 | 56 | 26 | 25 | 4 | 3 | 1 | 3 | 18 | 0 | 39 | 1 | 1 | 1 | 0 | 1.000 | 0 | 0 | 3.59 |
| 1990 Philadelphia | NL | 5 | 0 | 0 | 0 | 1 | 12 | 3 | 2 | 2 | 0 | 0 | 0 | 0 | 6 | 2 | 1 | 1 | 0 | 0 | 1 | .000 | 0 | 0 | 18.00 |
| 4 ML YEARS | | 72 | 0 | 0 | 19 | 86.2 | 375 | 87 | 39 | 38 | 6 | 4 | 2 | 3 | 37 | 8 | 60 | 3 | 1 | 3 | 3 | .500 | 0 | 0 | 3.95 |

## Travis Fryman

**Bats:** Right **Throws:** Right **Pos:** 3B/SS **Ht:** 6' 2" **Wt:** 190 **Born:** 03/25/69 **Age:** 22

| | | BATTING | | | | | | | | | | | | | | | | | BASERUNNING | | | | PERCENTAGES | | |
|---|---|---|---|---|---|---|---|---|---|---|---|---|---|---|---|---|---|---|---|---|---|---|---|---|---|
| Year Team | Lg | G | AB | H | 2B | 3B | HR | (Hm | Rd) | TB | R | RBI | TBB | IBB | SO | HBP | SH | SF | SB | CS | SB% | GDP | Avg | OBP | SLG |
| 1987 Bristol | R | 67 | 248 | 58 | 9 | 0 | 2 | -- | -- | 73 | 25 | 20 | 22 | 0 | 40 | 1 | 0 | 2 | 5 | 2 | .71 | 12 | .234 | .297 | .294 |
| 1988 Fayetteville | A | 123 | 411 | 96 | 17 | 4 | 0 | -- | -- | 121 | 44 | 47 | 24 | 0 | 83 | 10 | 8 | 5 | 18 | 5 | .78 | 6 | .234 | .289 | .294 |

| Year Team | Lg | G | AB | H | 2B | 3B | HR | (Hm | Rd) | TB | R | RBI | TBB | IBB | SO | HBP | SH | SF | SB | CS | SB% | GDP | Avg | OBP | SLG |
|---|---|---|---|---|---|---|---|---|---|---|---|---|---|---|---|---|---|---|---|---|---|---|---|---|---|
| 1989 London | AA | 118 | 426 | 113 | 30 | 1 | 9 | -- | -- | 172 | 52 | 56 | 19 | 0 | 78 | 8 | 2 | 4 | 5 | 3 | .63 | 5 | .265 | .306 | .404 |
| 1990 Toledo | AAA | 87 | 327 | 84 | 22 | 2 | 10 | -- | -- | 140 | 38 | 53 | 17 | 0 | 59 | 2 | 2 | 3 | 4 | 7 | .36 | 7 | .257 | .295 | .428 |
| 1990 Detroit | AL | 66 | 232 | 69 | 11 | 1 | 9 | (5 | 4) | 109 | 32 | 27 | 17 | 0 | 51 | 1 | 1 | 0 | 3 | 3 | .50 | 3 | .297 | .348 | .470 |

## Gary Gaetti

**Bats:** Right **Throws:** Right **Pos:** 3B **Ht:** 6' 0" **Wt:** 200 **Born:** 08/19/58 **Age:** 32

| BATTING | | | | | | | | | | | | | | | | | | | BASERUNNING | | | | PERCENTAGES | | |
|---|---|---|---|---|---|---|---|---|---|---|---|---|---|---|---|---|---|---|---|---|---|---|---|---|---|
| Year Team | Lg | G | AB | H | 2B | 3B | HR | (Hm | Rd) | TB | R | RBI | TBB | IBB | SO | HBP | SH | SF | SB | CS | SB% | GDP | Avg | OBP | SLG |
| 1981 Minnesota | AL | 9 | 26 | 5 | 0 | 0 | 2 | (1 | 1) | 11 | 4 | 3 | 0 | 0 | 6 | 0 | 0 | 0 | 0 | 0 | .00 | 1 | .192 | .192 | .423 |
| 1982 Minnesota | AL | 145 | 508 | 117 | 25 | 4 | 25 | (15 | 10) | 225 | 59 | 84 | 37 | 2 | 107 | 3 | 4 | 13 | 0 | 4 | .00 | 16 | .230 | .280 | .443 |
| 1983 Minnesota | AL | 157 | 584 | 143 | 30 | 3 | 21 | (7 | 14) | 242 | 81 | 78 | 54 | 2 | 121 | 4 | 0 | 8 | 7 | 1 | .88 | 18 | .245 | .309 | .414 |
| 1984 Minnesota | AL | 162 | 588 | 154 | 29 | 4 | 5 | (2 | 3) | 206 | 55 | 65 | 44 | 1 | 81 | 4 | 3 | 5 | 11 | 5 | .69 | 9 | .262 | .315 | .350 |
| 1985 Minnesota | AL | 160 | 560 | 138 | 31 | 0 | 20 | (10 | 10) | 229 | 71 | 63 | 37 | 3 | 89 | 7 | 3 | 1 | 13 | 5 | .72 | 15 | .246 | .301 | .409 |
| 1986 Minnesota | AL | 157 | 596 | 171 | 34 | 1 | 34 | (16 | 18) | 309 | 91 | 108 | 52 | 4 | 108 | 6 | 1 | 6 | 14 | 15 | .48 | 18 | .287 | .347 | .518 |
| 1987 Minnesota | AL | 154 | 584 | 150 | 36 | 2 | 31 | (18 | 13) | 283 | 95 | 109 | 37 | 7 | 92 | 3 | 1 | 3 | 10 | 7 | .59 | 25 | .257 | .303 | .485 |
| 1988 Minnesota | AL | 133 | 468 | 141 | 29 | 2 | 28 | (9 | 19) | 258 | 66 | 88 | 36 | 5 | 85 | 5 | 1 | 6 | 7 | 4 | .64 | 10 | .301 | .353 | .551 |
| 1989 Minnesota | AL | 130 | 498 | 125 | 11 | 4 | 19 | (10 | 9) | 201 | 63 | 75 | 25 | 5 | 87 | 3 | 1 | 9 | 6 | 2 | .75 | 12 | .251 | .286 | .404 |
| 1990 Minnesota | AL | 154 | 577 | 132 | 27 | 5 | 16 | (7 | 9) | 217 | 61 | 85 | 36 | 1 | 101 | 3 | 1 | 8 | 6 | 1 | .86 | 22 | .229 | .274 | .376 |
| 10 ML YEARS | | 1361 | 4989 | 1276 | 252 | 25 | 201 | (95 | 106) | 2181 | 646 | 758 | 358 | 30 | 877 | 38 | 15 | 59 | 74 | 44 | .63 | 146 | .256 | .307 | .437 |

## Greg Gagne

**Bats:** Right **Throws:** Right **Pos:** SS **Ht:** 5'11" **Wt:** 177 **Born:** 11/12/61 **Age:** 29

| BATTING | | | | | | | | | | | | | | | | | | | BASERUNNING | | | | PERCENTAGES | | |
|---|---|---|---|---|---|---|---|---|---|---|---|---|---|---|---|---|---|---|---|---|---|---|---|---|---|
| Year Team | Lg | G | AB | H | 2B | 3B | HR | (Hm | Rd) | TB | R | RBI | TBB | IBB | SO | HBP | SH | SF | SB | CS | SB% | GDP | Avg | OBP | SLG |
| 1983 Minnesota | AL | 10 | 27 | 3 | 1 | 0 | 0 | (0 | 0) | 4 | 2 | 3 | 0 | 0 | 6 | 0 | 0 | 2 | 0 | 0 | .00 | 0 | .111 | .103 | .148 |
| 1984 Minnesota | AL | 2 | 1 | 0 | 0 | 0 | 0 | (0 | 0) | 0 | 0 | 0 | 0 | 0 | 0 | 0 | 0 | 0 | 0 | 0 | .00 | 0 | .000 | .000 | .000 |
| 1985 Minnesota | AL | 114 | 293 | 66 | 15 | 3 | 2 | (0 | 2) | 93 | 37 | 23 | 20 | 0 | 57 | 3 | 3 | 3 | 10 | 4 | .71 | 5 | .225 | .279 | .317 |
| 1986 Minnesota | AL | 156 | 472 | 118 | 22 | 6 | 12 | (10 | 2) | 188 | 63 | 54 | 30 | 0 | 108 | 6 | 13 | 3 | 12 | 10 | .55 | 4 | .250 | .301 | .398 |
| 1987 Minnesota | AL | 137 | 437 | 116 | 28 | 7 | 10 | (7 | 3) | 188 | 68 | 40 | 25 | 0 | 84 | 4 | 10 | 2 | 6 | 6 | .50 | 3 | .265 | .310 | .430 |
| 1988 Minnesota | AL | 149 | 461 | 109 | 20 | 6 | 14 | (5 | 9) | 183 | 70 | 48 | 27 | 2 | 110 | 7 | 11 | 1 | 15 | 7 | .68 | 13 | .236 | .288 | .397 |
| 1989 Minnesota | AL | 149 | 460 | 125 | 29 | 7 | 9 | (5 | 4) | 195 | 69 | 48 | 17 | 0 | 80 | 2 | 7 | 5 | 11 | 4 | .73 | 10 | .272 | .298 | .424 |
| 1990 Minnesota | AL | 138 | 388 | 91 | 22 | 3 | 7 | (3 | 4) | 140 | 38 | 38 | 24 | 0 | 76 | 1 | 8 | 2 | 8 | 8 | .50 | 5 | .235 | .280 | .361 |
| 8 ML YEARS | | 855 | 2539 | 628 | 137 | 32 | 54 | (30 | 24) | 991 | 347 | 254 | 143 | 2 | 521 | 23 | 52 | 18 | 62 | 39 | .61 | 40 | .247 | .292 | .390 |

## Andres Galarraga

**Bats:** Right **Throws:** Right **Pos:** 1B **Ht:** 6' 3" **Wt:** 235 **Born:** 06/18/61 **Age:** 30

| BATTING | | | | | | | | | | | | | | | | | | | BASERUNNING | | | | PERCENTAGES | | |
|---|---|---|---|---|---|---|---|---|---|---|---|---|---|---|---|---|---|---|---|---|---|---|---|---|---|
| Year Team | Lg | G | AB | H | 2B | 3B | HR | (Hm | Rd) | TB | R | RBI | TBB | IBB | SO | HBP | SH | SF | SB | CS | SB% | GDP | Avg | OBP | SLG |
| 1985 Montreal | NL | 24 | 75 | 14 | 1 | 0 | 2 | (0 | 2) | 21 | 9 | 4 | 3 | 0 | 18 | 1 | 0 | 0 | 1 | 2 | .33 | 0 | .187 | .228 | .280 |
| 1986 Montreal | NL | 105 | 321 | 87 | 13 | 0 | 10 | (4 | 6) | 130 | 39 | 42 | 30 | 5 | 79 | 3 | 1 | 1 | 6 | 5 | .55 | 8 | .271 | .338 | .405 |
| 1987 Montreal | NL | 147 | 551 | 168 | 40 | 3 | 13 | (7 | 6) | 253 | 72 | 90 | 41 | 13 | 127 | 10 | 0 | 4 | 7 | 10 | .41 | 11 | .305 | .361 | .459 |
| 1988 Montreal | NL | 157 | 609 | 184 | 42 | 8 | 29 | (14 | 15) | 329 | 99 | 92 | 39 | 9 | 153 | 10 | 0 | 3 | 13 | 4 | .76 | 12 | .302 | .352 | .540 |
| 1989 Montreal | NL | 152 | 572 | 147 | 30 | 1 | 23 | (13 | 10) | 248 | 76 | 85 | 48 | 10 | 158 | 13 | 0 | 3 | 12 | 5 | .71 | 12 | .257 | .327 | .434 |
| 1990 Montreal | NL | 155 | 579 | 148 | 29 | 0 | 20 | (6 | 14) | 237 | 65 | 87 | 40 | 8 | 169 | 4 | 0 | 5 | 10 | 1 | .91 | 14 | .256 | .306 | .409 |
| 6 ML YEARS | | 740 | 2707 | 748 | 155 | 12 | 97 | (44 | 53) | 1218 | 360 | 400 | 201 | 45 | 704 | 41 | 1 | 16 | 49 | 27 | .64 | 57 | .276 | .334 | .450 |

## Dave Gallagher

**Bats:** Right **Throws:** Right **Pos:** CF/LF **Ht:** 6' 0" **Wt:** 180 **Born:** 09/20/60 **Age:** 30

| BATTING | | | | | | | | | | | | | | | | | | | BASERUNNING | | | | PERCENTAGES | | |
|---|---|---|---|---|---|---|---|---|---|---|---|---|---|---|---|---|---|---|---|---|---|---|---|---|---|
| Year Team | Lg | G | AB | H | 2B | 3B | HR | (Hm | Rd) | TB | R | RBI | TBB | IBB | SO | HBP | SH | SF | SB | CS | SB% | GDP | Avg | OBP | SLG |
| 1987 Cleveland | AL | 15 | 36 | 4 | 1 | 1 | 0 | (0 | 0) | 7 | 2 | 1 | 2 | 0 | 5 | 0 | 1 | 0 | 2 | 0 | 1.00 | 1 | .111 | .158 | .194 |
| 1988 Chicago | AL | 101 | 347 | 105 | 15 | 3 | 5 | (1 | 4) | 141 | 59 | 31 | 29 | 3 | 40 | 0 | 6 | 2 | 5 | 4 | .56 | 8 | .303 | .354 | .406 |
| 1989 Chicago | AL | 161 | 601 | 160 | 22 | 2 | 1 | (1 | 0) | 189 | 74 | 46 | 46 | 1 | 79 | 2 | 16 | 2 | 5 | 6 | .45 | 9 | .266 | .320 | .314 |
| 1990 2 ML Teams | | 67 | 126 | 32 | 4 | 1 | 0 | (0 | 0) | 38 | 12 | 7 | 7 | 0 | 12 | 1 | 7 | 1 | 1 | 2 | .33 | 3 | .254 | .296 | .302 |
| 1990 Chicago | AL | 44 | 75 | 21 | 3 | 1 | 0 | (0 | 0) | 26 | 5 | 5 | 3 | 0 | 9 | 1 | 5 | 0 | 0 | 1 | .00 | 3 | .280 | .316 | .347 |
| Baltimore | AL | 23 | 51 | 11 | 1 | 0 | 0 | (0 | 0) | 12 | 7 | 2 | 4 | 0 | 3 | 0 | 2 | 1 | 1 | 1 | .50 | 0 | .216 | .268 | .235 |
| 4 ML YEARS | | 344 | 1110 | 301 | 42 | 7 | 6 | (2 | 4) | 375 | 147 | 85 | 84 | 4 | 136 | 3 | 30 | 5 | 13 | 12 | .52 | 21 | .271 | .323 | .338 |

## Mike Gallego

**Bats:** Right **Throws:** Right **Pos:** 2B/3B/SS **Ht:** 5' 8" **Wt:** 160 **Born:** 10/31/60 **Age:** 30

| BATTING | | | | | | | | | | | | | | | | | | | BASERUNNING | | | | PERCENTAGES | | |
|---|---|---|---|---|---|---|---|---|---|---|---|---|---|---|---|---|---|---|---|---|---|---|---|---|---|
| Year Team | Lg | G | AB | H | 2B | 3B | HR | (Hm | Rd) | TB | R | RBI | TBB | IBB | SO | HBP | SH | SF | SB | CS | SB% | GDP | Avg | OBP | SLG |
| 1985 Oakland | AL | 76 | 77 | 16 | 5 | 1 | 1 | (0 | 1) | 26 | 13 | 9 | 12 | 0 | 14 | 1 | 2 | 1 | 1 | 1 | .50 | 2 | .208 | .319 | .338 |
| 1986 Oakland | AL | 20 | 37 | 10 | 2 | 0 | 0 | (0 | 0) | 12 | 2 | 4 | 1 | 0 | 6 | 0 | 2 | 0 | 0 | 2 | .00 | 0 | .270 | .289 | .324 |
| 1987 Oakland | AL | 72 | 124 | 31 | 6 | 0 | 2 | (0 | 2) | 43 | 18 | 14 | 12 | 0 | 21 | 1 | 5 | 1 | 0 | 1 | .00 | 5 | .250 | .319 | .347 |
| 1988 Oakland | AL | 129 | 277 | 58 | 8 | 0 | 2 | (2 | 0) | 72 | 38 | 20 | 34 | 0 | 53 | 1 | 8 | 0 | 2 | 3 | .40 | 6 | .209 | .298 | .260 |
| 1989 Oakland | AL | 133 | 357 | 90 | 14 | 2 | 3 | (2 | 1) | 117 | 45 | 30 | 35 | 0 | 43 | 6 | 8 | 3 | 7 | 5 | .58 | 10 | .252 | .327 | .328 |

| 1990 Oakland | AL | 140 | 389 | 80 | 13 | 2 | 3 | (1 | 2) | 106 | 36 | 34 | 35 | 0 | 50 | 4 | 17 | 2 | 5 | 5 | .50 | 13 | .206 | .277 | .272 |
|---|---|---|---|---|---|---|---|---|---|---|---|---|---|---|---|---|---|---|---|---|---|---|---|---|---|
| 6 ML YEARS | | 570 | 1261 | 285 | 48 | 5 | 11 | (5 | 6) | 376 | 152 | 111 | 129 | 0 | 187 | 13 | 42 | 7 | 15 | 17 | .47 | 36 | .226 | .303 | .298 |

## Ron Gant

**Bats:** Right **Throws:** Right **Pos:** CF/LF **Ht:** 6' 0" **Wt:** 172 **Born:** 03/02/65 **Age:** 26

| BATTING | | | | | | | | | | | | | | | | | | | BASERUNNING | | | | PERCENTAGES | | |
|---|---|---|---|---|---|---|---|---|---|---|---|---|---|---|---|---|---|---|---|---|---|---|---|---|---|
| Year Team | Lg | G | AB | H | 2B | 3B | HR | (Hm | Rd) | TB | R | RBI | TBB | IBB | SO | HBP | SH | SF | SB | CS | SB% | GDP | Avg | OBP | SLG |
| 1987 Atlanta | NL | 21 | 83 | 22 | 4 | 0 | 2 | (1 | 1) | 32 | 9 | 9 | 1 | 0 | 11 | 0 | 1 | 1 | 4 | 2 | .67 | 3 | .265 | .271 | .386 |
| 1988 Atlanta | NL | 146 | 563 | 146 | 28 | 8 | 19 | (7 | 12) | 247 | 85 | 60 | 46 | 4 | 118 | 3 | 2 | 4 | 19 | 10 | .66 | 7 | .259 | .317 | .439 |
| 1989 Atlanta | NL | 75 | 260 | 46 | 8 | 3 | 9 | (5 | 4) | 87 | 26 | 25 | 20 | 0 | 63 | 1 | 2 | 2 | 9 | 6 | .60 | 0 | .177 | .237 | .335 |
| 1990 Atlanta | NL | 152 | 575 | 174 | 34 | 3 | 32 | (18 | 14) | 310 | 107 | 84 | 50 | 0 | 86 | 1 | 1 | 4 | 33 | 16 | .67 | 8 | .303 | .357 | .539 |
| 4 ML YEARS | | 394 | 1481 | 388 | 74 | 14 | 62 | (31 | 31) | 676 | 227 | 178 | 117 | 4 | 278 | 5 | 6 | 11 | 65 | 34 | .66 | 18 | .262 | .316 | .456 |

## Jim Gantner

**Bats:** Left **Throws:** Right **Pos:** 2B **Ht:** 5'11" **Wt:** 175 **Born:** 01/05/54 **Age:** 37

| BATTING | | | | | | | | | | | | | | | | | | | BASERUNNING | | | | PERCENTAGES | | |
|---|---|---|---|---|---|---|---|---|---|---|---|---|---|---|---|---|---|---|---|---|---|---|---|---|---|
| Year Team | Lg | G | AB | H | 2B | 3B | HR | (Hm | Rd) | TB | R | RBI | TBB | IBB | SO | HBP | SH | SF | SB | CS | SB% | GDP | Avg | OBP | SLG |
| 1976 Milwaukee | AL | 26 | 69 | 17 | 1 | 0 | 0 | (0 | 0) | 18 | 6 | 7 | 6 | 0 | 11 | 1 | 3 | 0 | 1 | 0 | 1.00 | 1 | .246 | .316 | .261 |
| 1977 Milwaukee | AL | 14 | 47 | 14 | 1 | 0 | 1 | (0 | 1) | 18 | 4 | 2 | 2 | 0 | 5 | 0 | 0 | 0 | 2 | 1 | .67 | 1 | .298 | .327 | .383 |
| 1978 Milwaukee | AL | 43 | 97 | 21 | 1 | 0 | 1 | (0 | 1) | 25 | 14 | 8 | 5 | 0 | 10 | 2 | 1 | 0 | 2 | 0 | 1.00 | 0 | .216 | .269 | .258 |
| 1979 Milwaukee | AL | 70 | 208 | 59 | 10 | 3 | 2 | (0 | 2) | 81 | 29 | 22 | 16 | 1 | 17 | 2 | 5 | 3 | 3 | 5 | .38 | 3 | .284 | .336 | .389 |
| 1980 Milwaukee | AL | 132 | 415 | 117 | 21 | 3 | 4 | (1 | 3) | 156 | 47 | 40 | 30 | 5 | 29 | 1 | 8 | 3 | 11 | 10 | .52 | 8 | .282 | .330 | .376 |
| 1981 Milwaukee | AL | 107 | 352 | 94 | 14 | 1 | 2 | (0 | 2) | 116 | 35 | 33 | 29 | 5 | 29 | 3 | 9 | 4 | 3 | 6 | .33 | 6 | .267 | .325 | .330 |
| 1982 Milwaukee | AL | 132 | 447 | 132 | 17 | 2 | 4 | (2 | 2) | 165 | 48 | 43 | 26 | 3 | 36 | 2 | 7 | 3 | 6 | 3 | .67 | 6 | .295 | .335 | .369 |
| 1983 Milwaukee | AL | 161 | 603 | 170 | 23 | 8 | 11 | (5 | 6) | 242 | 85 | 74 | 38 | 5 | 46 | 6 | 11 | 4 | 5 | 6 | .45 | 10 | .282 | .329 | .401 |
| 1984 Milwaukee | AL | 153 | 613 | 173 | 27 | 1 | 3 | (0 | 3) | 211 | 61 | 56 | 30 | 0 | 51 | 3 | 2 | 10 | 6 | 5 | .55 | 16 | .282 | .314 | .344 |
| 1985 Milwaukee | AL | 143 | 523 | 133 | 15 | 4 | 5 | (4 | 1) | 171 | 63 | 44 | 33 | 7 | 42 | 3 | 10 | 4 | 11 | 8 | .58 | 13 | .254 | .300 | .327 |
| 1986 Milwaukee | AL | 139 | 497 | 136 | 25 | 1 | 7 | (4 | 3) | 184 | 58 | 38 | 26 | 2 | 50 | 6 | 6 | 7 | 13 | 7 | .65 | 13 | .274 | .313 | .370 |
| 1987 Milwaukee | AL | 81 | 265 | 72 | 14 | 0 | 4 | (0 | 4) | 98 | 37 | 30 | 19 | 2 | 22 | 5 | 4 | 1 | 6 | 2 | .75 | 7 | .272 | .331 | .370 |
| 1988 Milwaukee | AL | 155 | 539 | 149 | 28 | 2 | 0 | (0 | 0) | 181 | 67 | 47 | 34 | 1 | 50 | 3 | 18 | 2 | 20 | 8 | .71 | 9 | .276 | .322 | .336 |
| 1989 Milwaukee | AL | 116 | 409 | 112 | 18 | 3 | 0 | (0 | 0) | 136 | 51 | 34 | 21 | 2 | 33 | 10 | 8 | 5 | 20 | 6 | .77 | 10 | .274 | .321 | .333 |
| 1990 Milwaukee | AL | 88 | 323 | 85 | 8 | 5 | 0 | (0 | 0) | 103 | 36 | 25 | 29 | 0 | 19 | 2 | 4 | 0 | 18 | 3 | .86 | 10 | .263 | .328 | .319 |
| 15 ML YEARS | | 1560 | 5407 | 1484 | 223 | 33 | 44 | (16 | 28) | 1905 | 641 | 503 | 344 | 33 | 450 | 49 | 96 | 46 | 127 | 70 | .64 | 113 | .274 | .321 | .352 |

## Rich Garces

**Pitches:** Right **Bats:** Right **Pos:** RP **Ht:** 6' 1" **Wt:** 187 **Born:** 05/18/71 **Age:** 20

| HOW MUCH HE PITCHED | | | | | | | | WHAT HE GAVE UP | | | | | | | | | | | | THE RESULTS | | | | | |
|---|---|---|---|---|---|---|---|---|---|---|---|---|---|---|---|---|---|---|---|---|---|---|---|---|---|
| Year Team | Lg | G | GS | CG | GF | IP | BFP | H | R | ER | HR | SH | SF | HB | TBB | IBB | SO | WP | Bk | W | L | Pct. | ShO | Sv | ERA |
| 1988 Elizabethtn | R | 17 | 3 | 1 | 10 | 59 | 254 | 51 | 22 | 15 | 1 | 2 | 1 | 1 | 27 | 2 | 69 | 7 | 0 | 5 | 4 | .556 | 0 | 5 | 2.29 |
| 1989 Kenosha | A | 24 | 24 | 4 | 0 | 142.2 | 596 | 117 | 70 | 54 | 5 | 5 | 5 | 5 | 62 | 1 | 84 | 5 | 6 | 9 | 10 | .474 | 1 | 0 | 3.41 |
| 1990 Visalia | A | 47 | 0 | 0 | 42 | 54.2 | 212 | 33 | 14 | 11 | 2 | 1 | 1 | 1 | 16 | 0 | 75 | 6 | 0 | 2 | 2 | .500 | 0 | 28 | 1.81 |
| Orlando | AA | 15 | 0 | 0 | 14 | 17.1 | 81 | 17 | 4 | 4 | 0 | 1 | 0 | 0 | 14 | 2 | 22 | 2 | 0 | 2 | 1 | .667 | 0 | 8 | 2.08 |
| 1990 Minnesota | AL | 5 | 0 | 0 | 3 | 5.2 | 24 | 4 | 2 | 1 | 0 | 0 | 0 | 0 | 4 | 0 | 1 | 0 | 0 | 0 | 0 | .000 | 0 | 2 | 1.59 |

## Carlos Garcia

**Bats:** Right **Throws:** Right **Pos:** SS **Ht:** 6' 1" **Wt:** 185 **Born:** 10/15/67 **Age:** 23

| BATTING | | | | | | | | | | | | | | | | | | | BASERUNNING | | | | PERCENTAGES | | |
|---|---|---|---|---|---|---|---|---|---|---|---|---|---|---|---|---|---|---|---|---|---|---|---|---|---|
| Year Team | Lg | G | AB | H | 2B | 3B | HR | (Hm | Rd) | TB | R | RBI | TBB | IBB | SO | HBP | SH | SF | SB | CS | SB% | GDP | Avg | OBP | SLG |
| 1987 Macon | A | 110 | 373 | 95 | 14 | 3 | 3 | -- | -- | 124 | 44 | 38 | 23 | 2 | 80 | 6 | 2 | 2 | 20 | 10 | .67 | 6 | .255 | .307 | .332 |
| 1988 Augusta | A | 73 | 269 | 78 | 13 | 2 | 1 | -- | -- | 98 | 32 | 45 | 22 | 0 | 46 | 1 | 2 | 1 | 11 | 6 | .65 | 5 | .290 | .345 | .364 |
| Salem | A | 62 | 236 | 65 | 9 | 3 | 1 | -- | -- | 83 | 21 | 28 | 10 | 0 | 32 | 1 | 0 | 3 | 8 | 2 | .80 | 9 | .275 | .304 | .352 |
| 1989 Salem | A | 81 | 304 | 86 | 12 | 4 | 7 | -- | -- | 127 | 45 | 49 | 18 | 0 | 51 | 4 | 1 | 5 | 19 | 6 | .76 | 3 | .283 | .326 | .418 |
| Harrisburg | AA | 54 | 188 | 53 | 5 | 5 | 3 | -- | -- | 77 | 28 | 25 | 8 | 0 | 36 | 0 | 0 | 1 | 6 | 4 | .60 | 4 | .282 | .310 | .410 |
| 1990 Harrisburg | AA | 65 | 242 | 67 | 11 | 2 | 5 | -- | -- | 97 | 36 | 25 | 16 | 0 | 36 | 3 | 1 | 1 | 12 | 1 | .92 | 6 | .277 | .328 | .401 |
| Buffalo | AAA | 63 | 197 | 52 | 10 | 0 | 5 | -- | -- | 77 | 23 | 18 | 16 | 2 | 40 | 2 | 1 | 2 | 7 | 4 | .64 | 5 | .264 | .323 | .391 |
| 1990 Pittsburgh | NL | 4 | 4 | 2 | 0 | 0 | 0 | (0 | 0) | 2 | 1 | 0 | 0 | 0 | 2 | 0 | 0 | 0 | 0 | 0 | .00 | 0 | .500 | .500 | .500 |

## Mike Gardiner

**Pitches:** Right **Bats:** Both **Pos:** SP **Ht:** 6' 0" **Wt:** 185 **Born:** 10/19/65 **Age:** 25

| HOW MUCH HE PITCHED | | | | | | | | WHAT HE GAVE UP | | | | | | | | | | | | THE RESULTS | | | | | |
|---|---|---|---|---|---|---|---|---|---|---|---|---|---|---|---|---|---|---|---|---|---|---|---|---|---|
| Year Team | Lg | G | GS | CG | GF | IP | BFP | H | R | ER | HR | SH | SF | HB | TBB | IBB | SO | WP | Bk | W | L | Pct. | ShO | Sv | ERA |
| 1987 Bellingham | A | 2 | 1 | 0 | 0 | 10 | 35 | 6 | 0 | 0 | 0 | 0 | 0 | 0 | 1 | 0 | 11 | 0 | 0 | 2 | 0 | 1.000 | 0 | 0 | 0.00 |
| Wausau | A | 13 | 13 | 2 | 0 | 81 | 368 | 91 | 54 | 47 | 9 | 2 | 5 | 3 | 33 | 2 | 80 | 3 | 1 | 3 | 5 | .375 | 1 | 0 | 5.22 |
| 1988 Wausau | A | 11 | 6 | 0 | 4 | 31.1 | 132 | 31 | 16 | 11 | 1 | 0 | 0 | 1 | 13 | 0 | 24 | 1 | 1 | 2 | 1 | .667 | 0 | 1 | 3.16 |
| 1989 Wausau | A | 15 | 1 | 0 | 11 | 30.1 | 120 | 21 | 5 | 2 | 0 | 2 | 0 | 1 | 11 | 0 | 48 | 0 | 0 | 4 | 0 | 1.000 | 0 | 7 | 0.59 |
| Williamsprt | AA | 30 | 3 | 1 | 14 | 63.1 | 274 | 54 | 25 | 20 | 6 | 1 | 3 | 1 | 32 | 6 | 60 | 4 | 1 | 4 | 6 | .400 | 0 | 2 | 2.84 |

| Year Team | Lg | G | GS | CG | GF | IP | BFP | H | R | ER | HR | SH | SF | HB | TBB | IBB | SO | WP | Bk | W | L | Pct. | ShO | Sv | ERA |
|---|---|---|---|---|---|---|---|---|---|---|---|---|---|---|---|---|---|---|---|---|---|---|---|---|---|
| 1990 Williamsprt | AA | 26 | 26 | 5 | 0 | 179.2 | 697 | 136 | 47 | 38 | 8 | 4 | 3 | 1 | 29 | 1 | 149 | 4 | 1 | 12 | 8 | .600 | 1 | 0 | 1.90 |
| 1990 Seattle | AL | 5 | 3 | 0 | 1 | 12.2 | 66 | 22 | 17 | 15 | 1 | 0 | 1 | 2 | 5 | 0 | 6 | 0 | 0 | 0 | 2 | .000 | 0 | 0 | 10.66 |

## Mark Gardner

**Pitches:** Right **Bats:** Right **Pos:** SP **Ht:** 6' 1" **Wt:** 190 **Born:** 03/01/62 **Age:** 29

| | | HOW MUCH HE PITCHED | | | | | | WHAT HE GAVE UP | | | | | | | | | | | | THE RESULTS | | | | | |
|---|---|---|---|---|---|---|---|---|---|---|---|---|---|---|---|---|---|---|---|---|---|---|---|---|---|
| Year Team | Lg | G | GS | CG | GF | IP | BFP | H | R | ER | HR | SH | SF | HB | TBB | IBB | SO | WP | Bk | W | L | Pct. | ShO | Sv | ERA |
| 1985 Jamestown | A | 3 | 3 | 0 | 0 | 13 | 54 | 9 | 4 | 4 | 0 | 1 | 0 | 1 | 4 | 0 | 16 | 0 | 1 | 0 | 0 | .000 | 0 | 0 | 2.77 |
| Wst Plm Bch | A | 10 | 9 | 4 | 1 | 60.2 | 257 | 54 | 24 | 16 | 4 | 3 | 2 | 2 | 18 | 1 | 44 | 6 | 1 | 5 | 4 | .556 | 0 | 0 | 2.37 |
| 1986 Jacksnville | AA | 29 | 28 | 3 | 1 | 168.2 | 726 | 144 | 88 | 72 | 8 | 5 | 5 | 8 | 90 | 1 | 140 | 15 | 1 | 10 | 11 | .476 | 1 | 0 | 3.84 |
| 1987 Indianapols | AAA | 9 | 9 | 0 | 0 | 46 | 207 | 48 | 32 | 29 | 8 | 0 | 1 | 1 | 28 | 1 | 41 | 2 | 1 | 3 | 3 | .500 | 0 | 0 | 5.67 |
| Jacksnville | AA | 17 | 17 | 1 | 0 | 101 | 434 | 101 | 50 | 47 | 13 | 5 | 3 | 0 | 42 | 0 | 78 | 4 | 0 | 4 | 6 | .400 | 0 | 0 | 4.19 |
| 1988 Jacksnville | AA | 15 | 15 | 4 | 0 | 112.1 | 443 | 72 | 24 | 20 | 4 | 3 | 1 | 5 | 36 | 0 | 130 | 2 | 0 | 6 | 3 | .667 | 2 | 0 | 1.60 |
| Indianapols | AAA | 13 | 13 | 3 | 0 | 84.1 | 351 | 65 | 30 | 26 | 5 | 6 | 1 | 5 | 32 | 0 | 71 | 3 | 1 | 4 | 2 | .667 | 1 | 0 | 2.77 |
| 1989 Indianapols | AAA | 24 | 23 | 4 | 1 | 163.1 | 660 | 122 | 51 | 43 | 3 | 9 | 6 | 5 | 59 | 1 | 175 | 7 | 1 | 12 | 4 | .750 | 2 | 0 | 2.37 |
| 1989 Montreal | NL | 7 | 4 | 0 | 1 | 26.1 | 117 | 26 | 16 | 15 | 2 | 0 | 0 | 2 | 11 | 1 | 21 | 0 | 0 | 0 | 3 | .000 | 0 | 0 | 5.13 |
| 1990 Montreal | NL | 27 | 26 | 3 | 1 | 152.2 | 642 | 129 | 62 | 58 | 13 | 4 | 7 | 9 | 61 | 5 | 135 | 2 | 4 | 7 | 9 | .438 | 3 | 0 | 3.42 |
| 2 ML YEARS | | 34 | 30 | 3 | 2 | 179 | 759 | 155 | 78 | 73 | 15 | 4 | 7 | 11 | 72 | 6 | 156 | 2 | 4 | 7 | 12 | .368 | 3 | 0 | 3.67 |

## Wes Gardner

**Pitches:** Right **Bats:** Right **Pos:** RP/SP **Ht:** 6' 4" **Wt:** 203 **Born:** 04/29/61 **Age:** 30

| | | HOW MUCH HE PITCHED | | | | | | WHAT HE GAVE UP | | | | | | | | | | | | THE RESULTS | | | | | |
|---|---|---|---|---|---|---|---|---|---|---|---|---|---|---|---|---|---|---|---|---|---|---|---|---|---|
| Year Team | Lg | G | GS | CG | GF | IP | BFP | H | R | ER | HR | SH | SF | HB | TBB | IBB | SO | WP | Bk | W | L | Pct. | ShO | Sv | ERA |
| 1984 New York | NL | 21 | 0 | 0 | 12 | 25.1 | 116 | 34 | 19 | 18 | 0 | 1 | 1 | 0 | 8 | 2 | 19 | 1 | 0 | 1 | 1 | .500 | 0 | 1 | 6.39 |
| 1985 New York | NL | 9 | 0 | 0 | 8 | 12 | 61 | 18 | 14 | 7 | 1 | 4 | 1 | 0 | 8 | 2 | 11 | 1 | 0 | 0 | 2 | .000 | 0 | 0 | 5.25 |
| 1986 Boston | AL | 1 | 0 | 0 | 0 | 1 | 4 | 1 | 1 | 1 | 0 | 0 | 1 | 0 | 0 | 0 | 1 | 0 | 0 | 0 | 0 | .000 | 0 | 0 | 9.00 |
| 1987 Boston | AL | 49 | 1 | 0 | 29 | 89.2 | 401 | 98 | 55 | 54 | 17 | 4 | 2 | 2 | 42 | 7 | 70 | 4 | 0 | 3 | 6 | .333 | 0 | 10 | 5.42 |
| 1988 Boston | AL | 36 | 18 | 1 | 12 | 149 | 620 | 119 | 61 | 58 | 17 | 5 | 6 | 3 | 64 | 2 | 106 | 5 | 0 | 8 | 6 | .571 | 0 | 2 | 3.50 |
| 1989 Boston | AL | 22 | 16 | 0 | 2 | 86 | 393 | 97 | 64 | 57 | 10 | 3 | 4 | 1 | 47 | 7 | 81 | 3 | 0 | 3 | 7 | .300 | 0 | 0 | 5.97 |
| 1990 Boston | AL | 34 | 9 | 0 | 9 | 77.1 | 340 | 77 | 43 | 42 | 6 | 4 | 2 | 2 | 35 | 0 | 58 | 2 | 1 | 3 | 7 | .300 | 0 | 0 | 4.89 |
| 7 ML YEARS | | 172 | 44 | 1 | 72 | 440.1 | 1935 | 444 | 257 | 237 | 51 | 21 | 17 | 8 | 204 | 20 | 346 | 16 | 1 | 18 | 29 | .383 | 0 | 13 | 4.84 |

## Scott Garrelts

**Pitches:** Right **Bats:** Right **Pos:** SP **Ht:** 6' 4" **Wt:** 205 **Born:** 10/30/61 **Age:** 29

| | | HOW MUCH HE PITCHED | | | | | | WHAT HE GAVE UP | | | | | | | | | | | | THE RESULTS | | | | | |
|---|---|---|---|---|---|---|---|---|---|---|---|---|---|---|---|---|---|---|---|---|---|---|---|---|---|
| Year Team | Lg | G | GS | CG | GF | IP | BFP | H | R | ER | HR | SH | SF | HB | TBB | IBB | SO | WP | Bk | W | L | Pct. | ShO | Sv | ERA |
| 1982 San Francisco | NL | 1 | 0 | 0 | 1 | 2 | 11 | 3 | 3 | 3 | 0 | 0 | 0 | 0 | 2 | 0 | 4 | 0 | 0 | 0 | 0 | .000 | 0 | 0 | 13.50 |
| 1983 San Francisco | NL | 5 | 5 | 1 | 0 | 35.2 | 154 | 33 | 11 | 10 | 4 | 3 | 0 | 2 | 19 | 4 | 16 | 4 | 1 | 2 | 2 | .500 | 1 | 0 | 2.52 |
| 1984 San Francisco | NL | 21 | 3 | 0 | 5 | 43 | 206 | 45 | 33 | 27 | 6 | 5 | 2 | 1 | 34 | 1 | 32 | 3 | 0 | 2 | 3 | .400 | 0 | 0 | 5.65 |
| 1985 San Francisco | NL | 74 | 0 | 0 | 44 | 105.2 | 454 | 76 | 37 | 27 | 2 | 6 | 3 | 3 | 58 | 12 | 106 | 7 | 1 | 9 | 6 | .600 | 0 | 13 | 2.30 |
| 1986 San Francisco | NL | 53 | 18 | 2 | 27 | 173.2 | 717 | 144 | 65 | 60 | 17 | 10 | 7 | 2 | 74 | 11 | 125 | 9 | 1 | 13 | 9 | .591 | 0 | 10 | 3.11 |
| 1987 San Francisco | NL | 64 | 0 | 0 | 43 | 106.1 | 428 | 70 | 41 | 38 | 10 | 7 | 2 | 0 | 55 | 4 | 127 | 5 | 1 | 11 | 7 | .611 | 0 | 12 | 3.22 |
| 1988 San Francisco | NL | 65 | 0 | 0 | 40 | 98 | 413 | 80 | 42 | 39 | 3 | 9 | 2 | 2 | 46 | 10 | 86 | 6 | 4 | 5 | 9 | .357 | 0 | 13 | 3.58 |
| 1989 San Francisco | NL | 30 | 29 | 2 | 0 | 193.1 | 766 | 149 | 58 | 49 | 11 | 9 | 7 | 0 | 46 | 3 | 119 | 7 | 2 | 14 | 5 | .737 | 1 | 0 | 2.28 |
| 1990 San Francisco | NL | 31 | 31 | 4 | 0 | 182 | 786 | 190 | 91 | 84 | 16 | 10 | 5 | 3 | 70 | 8 | 80 | 7 | 0 | 12 | 11 | .522 | 2 | 0 | 4.15 |
| 9 ML YEARS | | 344 | 86 | 9 | 160 | 939.2 | 3935 | 790 | 381 | 337 | 69 | 59 | 28 | 13 | 404 | 53 | 695 | 48 | 10 | 68 | 52 | .567 | 4 | 48 | 3.23 |

## Rich Gedman

**Bats:** Left **Throws:** Right **Pos:** C **Ht:** 6' 0" **Wt:** 215 **Born:** 09/26/59 **Age:** 31

| | | BATTING | | | | | | | | | | | | | | | | | BASERUNNING | | | | PERCENTAGES | | |
|---|---|---|---|---|---|---|---|---|---|---|---|---|---|---|---|---|---|---|---|---|---|---|---|---|---|
| Year Team | Lg | G | AB | H | 2B | 3B | HR | (Hm | Rd) | TB | R | RBI | TBB | IBB | SO | HBP | SH | SF | SB | CS | SB% | GDP | Avg | OBP | SLG |
| 1980 Boston | AL | 9 | 24 | 5 | 0 | 0 | 0 | (0 | 0) | 5 | 2 | 1 | 0 | 0 | 5 | 0 | 0 | 0 | 0 | 0 | .00 | 1 | .208 | .208 | .208 |
| 1981 Boston | AL | 62 | 205 | 59 | 15 | 0 | 5 | (3 | 2) | 89 | 22 | 26 | 9 | 1 | 31 | 1 | 1 | 3 | 0 | 0 | .00 | 9 | .288 | .317 | .434 |
| 1982 Boston | AL | 92 | 289 | 72 | 17 | 2 | 4 | (1 | 3) | 105 | 30 | 26 | 10 | 2 | 37 | 2 | 4 | 0 | 0 | 1 | .00 | 13 | .249 | .279 | .363 |
| 1983 Boston | AL | 81 | 204 | 60 | 16 | 1 | 2 | (0 | 2) | 84 | 21 | 18 | 15 | 6 | 37 | 1 | 3 | 0 | 0 | 1 | .00 | 4 | .294 | .345 | .412 |
| 1984 Boston | AL | 133 | 449 | 121 | 26 | 4 | 24 | (16 | 8) | 227 | 54 | 72 | 29 | 8 | 72 | 1 | 2 | 5 | 0 | 0 | .00 | 5 | .269 | .312 | .506 |
| 1985 Boston | AL | 144 | 498 | 147 | 30 | 5 | 18 | (9 | 9) | 241 | 66 | 80 | 50 | 11 | 79 | 3 | 3 | 2 | 2 | 0 | 1.00 | 12 | .295 | .362 | .484 |
| 1986 Boston | AL | 135 | 462 | 119 | 29 | 0 | 16 | (2 | 14) | 196 | 49 | 65 | 37 | 13 | 61 | 4 | 1 | 5 | 1 | 0 | 1.00 | 15 | .258 | .315 | .424 |
| 1987 Boston | AL | 52 | 151 | 31 | 8 | 0 | 1 | (1 | 0) | 42 | 11 | 13 | 10 | 2 | 24 | 0 | 1 | 3 | 0 | 0 | .00 | 2 | .205 | .250 | .278 |
| 1988 Boston | AL | 95 | 299 | 69 | 14 | 0 | 9 | (5 | 4) | 110 | 33 | 39 | 18 | 2 | 49 | 3 | 9 | 3 | 0 | 0 | .00 | 6 | .231 | .279 | .368 |
| 1989 Boston | AL | 93 | 260 | 55 | 9 | 0 | 4 | (2 | 2) | 76 | 24 | 16 | 23 | 1 | 47 | 0 | 3 | 3 | 0 | 1 | .00 | 8 | .212 | .273 | .292 |
| 1990 2 ML Teams | | 50 | 119 | 24 | 7 | 0 | 1 | (0 | 1) | 34 | 7 | 10 | 20 | 6 | 30 | 1 | 2 | 1 | 0 | 0 | .00 | 3 | .202 | .319 | .286 |
| 1990 Boston | AL | 10 | 15 | 3 | 0 | 0 | 0 | (0 | 0) | 3 | 3 | 0 | 5 | 0 | 6 | 1 | 0 | 0 | 0 | 0 | .00 | 1 | .200 | .429 | .200 |
| Houston | NL | 40 | 104 | 21 | 7 | 0 | 1 | (0 | 1) | 31 | 4 | 10 | 15 | 6 | 24 | 0 | 2 | 1 | 0 | 0 | .00 | 2 | .202 | .300 | .298 |
| 11 ML YEARS | | 946 | 2960 | 762 | 171 | 12 | 84 | (39 | 45) | 1209 | 319 | 366 | 221 | 52 | 472 | 16 | 29 | 25 | 3 | 3 | .50 | 78 | .257 | .310 | .408 |

## Bob Geren

**Bats:** Right **Throws:** Right **Pos:** C **Ht:** 6' 3" **Wt:** 205 **Born:** 09/22/61 **Age:** 29

| | | BATTING | | | | | | | | | | | | | | | | | BASERUNNING | | | | PERCENTAGES | | |
|---|---|---|---|---|---|---|---|---|---|---|---|---|---|---|---|---|---|---|---|---|---|---|---|---|---|
| Year Team | Lg | G | AB | H | 2B | 3B | HR | (Hm | Rd) | TB | R | RBI | TBB | IBB | SO | HBP | SH | SF | SB | CS | SB% | GDP | Avg | OBP | SLG |
| 1988 New York | AL | 10 | 10 | 1 | 0 | 0 | 0 | (0 | 0) | 1 | 0 | 0 | 2 | 0 | 3 | 0 | 0 | 0 | 0 | 0 | .00 | 0 | .100 | .250 | .100 |
| 1989 New York | AL | 65 | 205 | 59 | 5 | 1 | 9 | (4 | 5) | 93 | 26 | 27 | 12 | 0 | 44 | 1 | 6 | 1 | 0 | 0 | .00 | 10 | .288 | .329 | .454 |
| 1990 New York | AL | 110 | 277 | 59 | 7 | 0 | 8 | (4 | 4) | 90 | 21 | 31 | 13 | 1 | 73 | 5 | 6 | 2 | 0 | 0 | .00 | 7 | .213 | .259 | .325 |
| 3 ML YEARS | | 185 | 492 | 119 | 12 | 1 | 17 | (8 | 9) | 184 | 47 | 58 | 27 | 1 | 120 | 6 | 12 | 3 | 0 | 0 | .00 | 17 | .242 | .288 | .374 |

## Kirk Gibson

**Bats:** Left **Throws:** Left **Pos:** CF/LF **Ht:** 6' 3" **Wt:** 215 **Born:** 05/28/57 **Age:** 34

| | | BATTING | | | | | | | | | | | | | | | | | BASERUNNING | | | | PERCENTAGES | | |
|---|---|---|---|---|---|---|---|---|---|---|---|---|---|---|---|---|---|---|---|---|---|---|---|---|---|
| Year Team | Lg | G | AB | H | 2B | 3B | HR | (Hm | Rd) | TB | R | RBI | TBB | IBB | SO | HBP | SH | SF | SB | CS | SB% | GDP | Avg | OBP | SLG |
| 1979 Detroit | AL | 12 | 38 | 9 | 3 | 0 | 1 | (0 | 1) | 15 | 3 | 4 | 1 | 0 | 3 | 0 | 0 | 0 | 3 | 3 | .50 | 0 | .237 | .256 | .395 |
| 1980 Detroit | AL | 51 | 175 | 46 | 2 | 1 | 9 | (3 | 6) | 77 | 23 | 16 | 10 | 0 | 45 | 1 | 1 | 2 | 4 | 7 | .36 | 0 | .263 | .303 | .440 |
| 1981 Detroit | AL | 83 | 290 | 95 | 11 | 3 | 9 | (4 | 5) | 139 | 41 | 40 | 18 | 1 | 64 | 2 | 1 | 2 | 17 | 5 | .77 | 9 | .328 | .369 | .479 |
| 1982 Detroit | AL | 69 | 266 | 74 | 16 | 2 | 8 | (4 | 4) | 118 | 34 | 35 | 25 | 2 | 41 | 1 | 1 | 1 | 9 | 7 | .56 | 2 | .278 | .341 | .444 |
| 1983 Detroit | AL | 128 | 401 | 91 | 12 | 9 | 15 | (5 | 10) | 166 | 60 | 51 | 53 | 3 | 96 | 4 | 5 | 4 | 14 | 3 | .82 | 2 | .227 | .320 | .414 |
| 1984 Detroit | AL | 149 | 531 | 150 | 23 | 10 | 27 | (11 | 16) | 274 | 92 | 91 | 63 | 6 | 103 | 8 | 3 | 6 | 29 | 9 | .76 | 4 | .282 | .363 | .516 |
| 1985 Detroit | AL | 154 | 581 | 167 | 37 | 5 | 29 | (18 | 11) | 301 | 96 | 97 | 71 | 16 | 137 | 5 | 3 | 10 | 30 | 4 | .88 | 5 | .287 | .364 | .518 |
| 1986 Detroit | AL | 119 | 441 | 118 | 11 | 2 | 28 | (15 | 13) | 217 | 84 | 86 | 68 | 4 | 107 | 7 | 1 | 4 | 34 | 6 | .85 | 8 | .268 | .371 | .492 |
| 1987 Detroit | AL | 128 | 487 | 135 | 25 | 3 | 24 | (14 | 10) | 238 | 95 | 79 | 71 | 8 | 117 | 5 | 1 | 4 | 26 | 7 | .79 | 5 | .277 | .372 | .489 |
| 1988 Los Angeles | NL | 150 | 542 | 157 | 28 | 1 | 25 | (14 | 11) | 262 | 106 | 76 | 73 | 14 | 120 | 7 | 3 | 7 | 31 | 4 | .89 | 8 | .290 | .377 | .483 |
| 1989 Los Angeles | NL | 71 | 253 | 54 | 8 | 2 | 9 | (4 | 5) | 93 | 35 | 28 | 35 | 5 | 55 | 2 | 0 | 2 | 12 | 3 | .80 | 5 | .213 | .312 | .368 |
| 1990 Los Angeles | NL | 89 | 315 | 82 | 20 | 0 | 8 | (2 | 6) | 126 | 59 | 38 | 39 | 0 | 65 | 3 | 0 | 2 | 26 | 2 | .93 | 4 | .260 | .345 | .400 |
| 12 ML YEARS | | 1203 | 4320 | 1178 | 196 | 38 | 192 | (94 | 98) | 2026 | 728 | 641 | 527 | 59 | 953 | 45 | 19 | 44 | 235 | 60 | .80 | 52 | .273 | .355 | .469 |

## Paul Gibson

**Pitches:** Left **Bats:** Right **Pos:** RP **Ht:** 6' 0" **Wt:** 165 **Born:** 01/04/60 **Age:** 31

| | | HOW MUCH HE PITCHED | | | | | | WHAT HE GAVE UP | | | | | | | | | | | | THE RESULTS | | | | | |
|---|---|---|---|---|---|---|---|---|---|---|---|---|---|---|---|---|---|---|---|---|---|---|---|---|---|
| Year Team | Lg | G | GS | CG | GF | IP | BFP | H | R | ER | HR | SH | SF | HB | TBB | IBB | SO | WP | Bk | W | L | Pct. | ShO | Sv | ERA |
| 1988 Detroit | AL | 40 | 1 | 0 | 18 | 92 | 390 | 83 | 33 | 30 | 6 | 3 | 5 | 2 | 34 | 8 | 50 | 3 | 1 | 4 | 2 | .667 | 0 | 0 | 2.93 |
| 1989 Detroit | AL | 45 | 13 | 0 | 16 | 132 | 573 | 129 | 71 | 68 | 11 | 7 | 5 | 6 | 57 | 12 | 77 | 4 | 1 | 4 | 8 | .333 | 0 | 0 | 4.64 |
| 1990 Detroit | AL | 61 | 0 | 0 | 17 | 97.1 | 422 | 99 | 36 | 33 | 10 | 4 | 5 | 1 | 44 | 12 | 56 | 1 | 1 | 5 | 4 | .556 | 0 | 3 | 3.05 |
| 3 ML YEARS | | 146 | 14 | 0 | 51 | 321.1 | 1385 | 311 | 140 | 131 | 27 | 14 | 15 | 9 | 135 | 32 | 183 | 8 | 3 | 13 | 14 | .481 | 0 | 3 | 3.67 |

## Brett Gideon

**Pitches:** Right **Bats:** Right **Pos:** RP **Ht:** 6' 2" **Wt:** 195 **Born:** 08/08/63 **Age:** 27

| | | HOW MUCH HE PITCHED | | | | | | WHAT HE GAVE UP | | | | | | | | | | | | THE RESULTS | | | | | |
|---|---|---|---|---|---|---|---|---|---|---|---|---|---|---|---|---|---|---|---|---|---|---|---|---|---|
| Year Team | Lg | G | GS | CG | GF | IP | BFP | H | R | ER | HR | SH | SF | HB | TBB | IBB | SO | WP | Bk | W | L | Pct. | ShO | Sv | ERA |
| 1987 Pittsburgh | NL | 29 | 0 | 0 | 17 | 36.2 | 153 | 34 | 22 | 19 | 6 | 2 | 0 | 1 | 10 | 3 | 31 | 2 | 0 | 1 | 5 | .167 | 0 | 3 | 4.66 |
| 1989 Montreal | NL | 4 | 0 | 0 | 1 | 4.2 | 22 | 5 | 1 | 1 | 1 | 0 | 0 | 0 | 5 | 1 | 2 | 0 | 0 | 0 | 0 | .000 | 0 | 0 | 1.93 |
| 1990 Montreal | NL | 1 | 0 | 0 | 0 | 1 | 8 | 2 | 1 | 1 | 0 | 0 | 0 | 0 | 4 | 1 | 0 | 0 | 0 | 0 | 0 | .000 | 0 | 0 | 9.00 |
| 3 ML YEARS | | 34 | 0 | 0 | 18 | 42.1 | 183 | 41 | 24 | 21 | 7 | 2 | 0 | 1 | 19 | 5 | 33 | 2 | 0 | 1 | 5 | .167 | 0 | 3 | 4.46 |

## Brian Giles

**Bats:** Right **Throws:** Right **Pos:** SS **Ht:** 6' 0" **Wt:** 160 **Born:** 04/27/60 **Age:** 31

| | | BATTING | | | | | | | | | | | | | | | | | BASERUNNING | | | | PERCENTAGES | | |
|---|---|---|---|---|---|---|---|---|---|---|---|---|---|---|---|---|---|---|---|---|---|---|---|---|---|
| Year Team | Lg | G | AB | H | 2B | 3B | HR | (Hm | Rd) | TB | R | RBI | TBB | IBB | SO | HBP | SH | SF | SB | CS | SB% | GDP | Avg | OBP | SLG |
| 1981 New York | NL | 9 | 7 | 0 | 0 | 0 | 0 | (0 | 0) | 0 | 0 | 0 | 0 | 0 | 3 | 0 | 1 | 0 | 0 | 0 | .00 | 0 | .000 | .000 | .000 |
| 1982 New York | NL | 45 | 138 | 29 | 5 | 0 | 3 | (0 | 3) | 43 | 14 | 10 | 12 | 1 | 29 | 0 | 0 | 2 | 6 | 1 | .86 | 0 | .210 | .270 | .312 |
| 1983 New York | NL | 145 | 400 | 98 | 15 | 0 | 2 | (1 | 1) | 119 | 39 | 27 | 36 | 1 | 77 | 2 | 4 | 3 | 17 | 10 | .63 | 8 | .245 | .308 | .298 |
| 1985 Milwaukee | AL | 34 | 58 | 10 | 1 | 0 | 1 | (1 | 0) | 14 | 6 | 1 | 7 | 0 | 16 | 0 | 0 | 0 | 2 | 1 | .67 | 1 | .172 | .262 | .241 |
| 1986 Chicago | AL | 9 | 11 | 3 | 0 | 0 | 0 | (0 | 0) | 3 | 0 | 1 | 0 | 0 | 2 | 0 | 0 | 0 | 0 | 0 | .00 | 1 | .273 | .273 | .273 |
| 1990 Seattle | AL | 45 | 95 | 22 | 6 | 0 | 4 | (2 | 2) | 40 | 15 | 11 | 15 | 0 | 24 | 0 | 0 | 0 | 2 | 1 | .67 | 1 | .232 | .336 | .421 |
| 6 ML YEARS | | 287 | 709 | 162 | 27 | 0 | 10 | (4 | 6) | 219 | 74 | 50 | 70 | 2 | 151 | 2 | 5 | 5 | 27 | 13 | .68 | 11 | .228 | .298 | .309 |

## Bernard Gilkey

**Bats:** Right **Throws:** Right **Pos:** LF **Ht:** 6' 0" **Wt:** 170 **Born:** 09/24/66 **Age:** 24

| | | BATTING | | | | | | | | | | | | | | | | | BASERUNNING | | | | PERCENTAGES | | |
|---|---|---|---|---|---|---|---|---|---|---|---|---|---|---|---|---|---|---|---|---|---|---|---|---|---|
| Year Team | Lg | G | AB | H | 2B | 3B | HR | (Hm | Rd) | TB | R | RBI | TBB | IBB | SO | HBP | SH | SF | SB | CS | SB% | GDP | Avg | OBP | SLG |
| 1985 Erie | A | 77 | 294 | 60 | 9 | 1 | 7 | -- | -- | 92 | 57 | 27 | 55 | 1 | 57 | 3 | 4 | 2 | 34 | 10 | .77 | 4 | .204 | .333 | .313 |
| 1986 Savannah | A | 105 | 374 | 88 | 15 | 4 | 6 | -- | -- | 129 | 64 | 36 | 84 | 1 | 57 | 2 | 3 | 3 | 32 | 15 | .68 | 6 | .235 | .376 | .345 |
| 1987 Springfield | A | 46 | 162 | 37 | 5 | 0 | 0 | -- | -- | 42 | 30 | 9 | 39 | 1 | 28 | 2 | 2 | 2 | 18 | 5 | .78 | 3 | .228 | .380 | .259 |
| 1988 Springfield | A | 125 | 491 | 120 | 18 | 7 | 6 | -- | -- | 170 | 84 | 36 | 65 | 1 | 53 | 4 | 2 | 2 | 56 | 18 | .76 | 10 | .244 | .336 | .346 |
| 1989 Arkansas | AA | 131 | 500 | 139 | 25 | 3 | 6 | -- | -- | 188 | 104 | 57 | 70 | 2 | 54 | 2 | 8 | 5 | 53 | 22 | .71 | 9 | .278 | .366 | .376 |

| Year Team | Lg | G | AB | H | 2B | 3B | HR | (Hm | Rd) | TB | R | RBI | TBB | IBB | SO | HBP | SH | SF | SB | CS | SB% | GDP | Avg | OBP | SLG |
|---|---|---|---|---|---|---|---|---|---|---|---|---|---|---|---|---|---|---|---|---|---|---|---|---|---|
| 1990 Louisville | AAA | 132 | 499 | 147 | 26 | 8 | 3 | -- | -- | 198 | 83 | 46 | 75 | 3 | 49 | 2 | 1 | 1 | 45 | 32 | .58 | 11 | .295 | .388 | .397 |
| 1990 St. Louis | NL | 18 | 64 | 19 | 5 | 2 | 1 | (0 | 1) | 31 | 11 | 3 | 8 | 0 | 5 | 0 | 0 | 0 | 6 | 1 | .86 | 1 | .297 | .375 | .484 |

## Tom Gilles

**Pitches:** Right **Bats:** Right **Pos:** RP **Ht:** 6' 1" **Wt:** 187 **Born:** 07/02/62 **Age:** 28

| | | HOW MUCH HE PITCHED | | | | | | WHAT HE GAVE UP | | | | | | | | | | | | THE RESULTS | | | | | |
|---|---|---|---|---|---|---|---|---|---|---|---|---|---|---|---|---|---|---|---|---|---|---|---|---|---|
| Year Team | Lg | G | GS | CG | GF | IP | BFP | H | R | ER | HR | SH | SF | HB | TBB | IBB | SO | WP | Bk | W | L | Pct. | ShO | Sv | ERA |
| 1987 Appleton | A | 1 | 1 | 0 | 0 | 3 | 12 | 2 | 0 | 0 | 0 | 0 | 0 | 0 | 2 | 0 | 1 | 0 | 0 | 0 | 0 | .000 | 0 | 0 | 0.00 |
| 1988 Kenosha | A | 21 | 11 | 1 | 3 | 89.2 | 359 | 77 | 40 | 33 | 4 | 3 | 6 | 2 | 15 | 0 | 41 | 0 | 3 | 6 | 3 | .667 | 0 | 1 | 3.31 |
| Orlando | AA | 7 | 3 | 1 | 2 | 25.2 | 107 | 27 | 13 | 11 | 3 | 0 | 1 | 1 | 5 | 0 | 7 | 2 | 1 | 3 | 0 | 1.000 | 0 | 0 | 3.86 |
| 1989 Knoxville | AA | 12 | 4 | 0 | 4 | 52 | 209 | 42 | 21 | 17 | 1 | 2 | 0 | 3 | 14 | 1 | 27 | 2 | 1 | 5 | 1 | .833 | 0 | 0 | 2.94 |
| Syracuse | AAA | 29 | 8 | 2 | 12 | 83.2 | 356 | 85 | 38 | 33 | 5 | 2 | 2 | 2 | 28 | 2 | 41 | 6 | 0 | 4 | 4 | .500 | 1 | 1 | 3.55 |
| 1990 Syracuse | AAA | 43 | 0 | 0 | 25 | 71.1 | 285 | 58 | 22 | 17 | 6 | 3 | 3 | 2 | 20 | 2 | 44 | 4 | 0 | 3 | 3 | .500 | 0 | 5 | 2.14 |
| 1990 Toronto | AL | 2 | 0 | 0 | 1 | 1.1 | 6 | 2 | 1 | 1 | 0 | 0 | 0 | 0 | 0 | 0 | 1 | 0 | 0 | 1 | 0 | 1.000 | 0 | 0 | 6.75 |

## Joe Girardi

**Bats:** Right **Throws:** Right **Pos:** C **Ht:** 5'11" **Wt:** 195 **Born:** 10/14/64 **Age:** 26

| | | BATTING | | | | | | | | | | | | | | | | | BASERUNNING | | | | PERCENTAGES | | |
|---|---|---|---|---|---|---|---|---|---|---|---|---|---|---|---|---|---|---|---|---|---|---|---|---|---|
| Year Team | Lg | G | AB | H | 2B | 3B | HR | (Hm | Rd) | TB | R | RBI | TBB | IBB | SO | HBP | SH | SF | SB | CS | SB% | GDP | Avg | OBP | SLG |
| 1986 Peoria | A | 68 | 230 | 71 | 13 | 1 | 3 | -- | -- | 95 | 36 | 28 | 17 | 1 | 36 | 3 | 2 | 3 | 6 | 3 | .67 | 8 | .309 | .360 | .413 |
| 1987 Winston-Sal | A | 99 | 364 | 102 | 9 | 8 | 8 | -- | -- | 151 | 51 | 46 | 33 | 2 | 64 | 2 | 2 | 1 | 9 | 2 | .82 | 11 | .280 | .343 | .415 |
| 1988 Pittsfield | AA | 104 | 357 | 97 | 14 | 1 | 7 | -- | -- | 134 | 44 | 41 | 29 | 2 | 51 | 3 | 2 | 2 | 7 | 4 | .64 | 10 | .272 | .330 | .375 |
| 1989 Iowa | AAA | 32 | 110 | 27 | 4 | 2 | 2 | -- | -- | 41 | 12 | 11 | 5 | 1 | 19 | 0 | 0 | 0 | 3 | 1 | .75 | 0 | .245 | .278 | .373 |
| 1989 Chicago | NL | 59 | 157 | 39 | 10 | 0 | 1 | (0 | 1) | 52 | 15 | 14 | 11 | 5 | 26 | 2 | 1 | 1 | 2 | 1 | .67 | 4 | .248 | .304 | .331 |
| 1990 Chicago | NL | 133 | 419 | 113 | 24 | 2 | 1 | (1 | 0) | 144 | 36 | 38 | 17 | 11 | 50 | 3 | 4 | 4 | 8 | 3 | .73 | 13 | .270 | .300 | .344 |
| 2 ML YEARS | | 192 | 576 | 152 | 34 | 2 | 2 | (1 | 1) | 196 | 51 | 52 | 28 | 16 | 76 | 5 | 5 | 5 | 10 | 4 | .71 | 17 | .264 | .301 | .340 |

## Dan Gladden

**Bats:** Right **Throws:** Right **Pos:** LF **Ht:** 5'11" **Wt:** 181 **Born:** 07/07/57 **Age:** 33

| | | BATTING | | | | | | | | | | | | | | | | | BASERUNNING | | | | PERCENTAGES | | |
|---|---|---|---|---|---|---|---|---|---|---|---|---|---|---|---|---|---|---|---|---|---|---|---|---|---|
| Year Team | Lg | G | AB | H | 2B | 3B | HR | (Hm | Rd) | TB | R | RBI | TBB | IBB | SO | HBP | SH | SF | SB | CS | SB% | GDP | Avg | OBP | SLG |
| 1983 San Francisco | NL | 18 | 63 | 14 | 2 | 0 | 1 | (1 | 0) | 19 | 6 | 9 | 5 | 0 | 11 | 0 | 3 | 1 | 4 | 3 | .57 | 3 | .222 | .275 | .302 |
| 1984 San Francisco | NL | 86 | 342 | 120 | 17 | 2 | 4 | (4 | 0) | 153 | 71 | 31 | 33 | 2 | 37 | 2 | 6 | 1 | 31 | 16 | .66 | 3 | .351 | .410 | .447 |
| 1985 San Francisco | NL | 142 | 502 | 122 | 15 | 8 | 7 | (6 | 1) | 174 | 64 | 41 | 40 | 1 | 78 | 7 | 10 | 2 | 32 | 15 | .68 | 10 | .243 | .307 | .347 |
| 1986 San Francisco | NL | 102 | 351 | 97 | 16 | 1 | 4 | (1 | 3) | 127 | 55 | 29 | 39 | 3 | 59 | 5 | 7 | 0 | 27 | 10 | .73 | 5 | .276 | .357 | .362 |
| 1987 Minnesota | AL | 121 | 438 | 109 | 21 | 2 | 8 | (4 | 4) | 158 | 69 | 38 | 38 | 2 | 72 | 3 | 1 | 2 | 25 | 9 | .74 | 8 | .249 | .312 | .361 |
| 1988 Minnesota | AL | 141 | 576 | 155 | 32 | 6 | 11 | (8 | 3) | 232 | 91 | 62 | 46 | 4 | 74 | 4 | 2 | 5 | 28 | 8 | .78 | 9 | .269 | .325 | .403 |
| 1989 Minnesota | AL | 121 | 461 | 136 | 23 | 3 | 8 | (1 | 7) | 189 | 69 | 46 | 23 | 3 | 53 | 5 | 5 | 7 | 23 | 7 | .77 | 6 | .295 | .331 | .410 |
| 1990 Minnesota | AL | 136 | 534 | 147 | 27 | 6 | 5 | (2 | 3) | 201 | 64 | 40 | 26 | 2 | 67 | 6 | 1 | 4 | 25 | 9 | .74 | 17 | .275 | .314 | .376 |
| 8 ML YEARS | | 867 | 3267 | 900 | 153 | 28 | 48 | (27 | 21) | 1253 | 489 | 296 | 250 | 17 | 451 | 32 | 35 | 22 | 195 | 77 | .72 | 61 | .275 | .331 | .384 |

## Tom Glavine

**Pitches:** Left **Bats:** Left **Pos:** SP **Ht:** 6' 0" **Wt:** 175 **Born:** 03/25/66 **Age:** 25

| | | HOW MUCH HE PITCHED | | | | | | WHAT HE GAVE UP | | | | | | | | | | | | THE RESULTS | | | | | |
|---|---|---|---|---|---|---|---|---|---|---|---|---|---|---|---|---|---|---|---|---|---|---|---|---|---|
| Year Team | Lg | G | GS | CG | GF | IP | BFP | H | R | ER | HR | SH | SF | HB | TBB | IBB | SO | WP | Bk | W | L | Pct. | ShO | Sv | ERA |
| 1987 Atlanta | NL | 9 | 9 | 0 | 0 | 50.1 | 238 | 55 | 34 | 31 | 5 | 2 | 3 | 3 | 33 | 4 | 20 | 1 | 1 | 2 | 4 | .333 | 0 | 0 | 5.54 |
| 1988 Atlanta | NL | 34 | 34 | 1 | 0 | 195.1 | 844 | 201 | 111 | 99 | 12 | 17 | 11 | 8 | 63 | 7 | 84 | 2 | 2 | 7 | 17 | .292 | 0 | 0 | 4.56 |
| 1989 Atlanta | NL | 29 | 29 | 6 | 0 | 186 | 766 | 172 | 88 | 76 | 20 | 11 | 4 | 2 | 40 | 3 | 90 | 2 | 0 | 14 | 8 | .636 | 4 | 0 | 3.68 |
| 1990 Atlanta | NL | 33 | 33 | 1 | 0 | 214.1 | 929 | 232 | 111 | 102 | 18 | 21 | 2 | 1 | 78 | 10 | 129 | 8 | 1 | 10 | 12 | .455 | 0 | 0 | 4.28 |
| 4 ML YEARS | | 105 | 105 | 8 | 0 | 646 | 2777 | 660 | 344 | 308 | 55 | 51 | 20 | 14 | 214 | 24 | 323 | 13 | 4 | 33 | 41 | .446 | 4 | 0 | 4.29 |

## Jerry Don Gleaton

**Pitches:** Left **Bats:** Left **Pos:** RP **Ht:** 6' 3" **Wt:** 210 **Born:** 09/14/57 **Age:** 33

| | | HOW MUCH HE PITCHED | | | | | | WHAT HE GAVE UP | | | | | | | | | | | | THE RESULTS | | | | | |
|---|---|---|---|---|---|---|---|---|---|---|---|---|---|---|---|---|---|---|---|---|---|---|---|---|---|
| Year Team | Lg | G | GS | CG | GF | IP | BFP | H | R | ER | HR | SH | SF | HB | TBB | IBB | SO | WP | Bk | W | L | Pct. | ShO | Sv | ERA |
| 1979 Texas | AL | 5 | 2 | 0 | 1 | 10 | 45 | 15 | 7 | 7 | 0 | 1 | 1 | 1 | 2 | 0 | 2 | 1 | 0 | 0 | 1 | .000 | 0 | 0 | 6.30 |
| 1980 Texas | AL | 5 | 0 | 0 | 2 | 7 | 30 | 5 | 2 | 2 | 0 | 0 | 2 | 0 | 4 | 0 | 2 | 0 | 0 | 0 | 0 | .000 | 0 | 0 | 2.57 |
| 1981 Seattle | AL | 20 | 13 | 1 | 3 | 85 | 369 | 88 | 50 | 45 | 10 | 3 | 4 | 2 | 38 | 2 | 31 | 3 | 0 | 4 | 7 | .364 | 0 | 0 | 4.76 |
| 1982 Seattle | AL | 3 | 0 | 0 | 1 | 4.2 | 24 | 7 | 7 | 7 | 3 | 0 | 0 | 1 | 2 | 0 | 1 | 0 | 0 | 0 | 0 | .000 | 0 | 0 | 13.50 |
| 1984 Chicago | AL | 11 | 1 | 0 | 4 | 18.1 | 81 | 20 | 12 | 7 | 2 | 0 | 4 | 1 | 6 | 0 | 4 | 4 | 0 | 1 | 2 | .333 | 0 | 2 | 3.44 |
| 1985 Chicago | AL | 31 | 0 | 0 | 9 | 29.2 | 135 | 37 | 19 | 19 | 3 | 4 | 1 | 0 | 13 | 3 | 22 | 3 | 0 | 1 | 0 | 1.000 | 0 | 1 | 5.76 |
| 1987 Kansas City | AL | 48 | 0 | 0 | 22 | 50.2 | 210 | 38 | 28 | 24 | 4 | 3 | 3 | 0 | 28 | 3 | 44 | 4 | 1 | 4 | 4 | .500 | 0 | 5 | 4.26 |
| 1988 Kansas City | AL | 42 | 0 | 0 | 20 | 38 | 164 | 33 | 17 | 15 | 2 | 2 | 0 | 3 | 17 | 1 | 29 | 2 | 0 | 0 | 4 | .000 | 0 | 3 | 3.55 |
| 1989 Kansas City | AL | 15 | 0 | 0 | 5 | 14.1 | 66 | 20 | 10 | 9 | 0 | 0 | 2 | 0 | 6 | 0 | 9 | 0 | 1 | 0 | 0 | .000 | 0 | 0 | 5.65 |
| 1990 Detroit | AL | 57 | 0 | 0 | 34 | 82.2 | 325 | 62 | 27 | 27 | 5 | 2 | 4 | 3 | 25 | 2 | 56 | 2 | 1 | 1 | 3 | .250 | 0 | 13 | 2.94 |
| 10 ML YEARS | | 237 | 16 | 1 | 101 | 340.1 | 1449 | 325 | 179 | 162 | 29 | 15 | 21 | 11 | 141 | 11 | 200 | 19 | 3 | 11 | 21 | .344 | 0 | 24 | 4.28 |

## Jerry Goff

**Bats:** Left **Throws:** Right **Pos:** C **Ht:** 6' 3" **Wt:** 205 **Born:** 04/12/64 **Age:** 27

| | | BATTING | | | | | | | | | | | | | | | | | BASERUNNING | | | | PERCENTAGES | | |
|---|---|---|---|---|---|---|---|---|---|---|---|---|---|---|---|---|---|---|---|---|---|---|---|---|---|
| Year Team | Lg | G | AB | H | 2B | 3B | HR | (Hm | Rd) | TB | R | RBI | TBB | IBB | SO | HBP | SH | SF | SB | CS | SB% | GDP | Avg | OBP | SLG |
| 1986 Bellingham | A | 54 | 168 | 32 | 7 | 2 | 7 | -- | -- | 64 | 26 | 25 | 42 | 1 | 55 | 4 | 1 | 3 | 4 | 3 | .57 | 4 | .190 | .359 | .381 |
| 1987 Wausau | A | 109 | 336 | 78 | 17 | 2 | 13 | -- | -- | 138 | 51 | 47 | 65 | 3 | 87 | 8 | 1 | 2 | 4 | 7 | .36 | 4 | .232 | .367 | .411 |
| 1988 San Berndno | A | 65 | 215 | 62 | 11 | 0 | 13 | -- | -- | 112 | 38 | 43 | 53 | 6 | 59 | 3 | 0 | 2 | 2 | 3 | .40 | 0 | .288 | .432 | .521 |
| Vermont | AA | 63 | 195 | 41 | 7 | 1 | 7 | -- | -- | 71 | 27 | 23 | 23 | 1 | 58 | 4 | 0 | 0 | 2 | 3 | .40 | 1 | .210 | .306 | .364 |
| 1989 Williamsprt | AA | 33 | 119 | 22 | 5 | 0 | 3 | -- | -- | 36 | 9 | 8 | 14 | 2 | 42 | 1 | 0 | 0 | 1 | 1 | .50 | 3 | .185 | .276 | .303 |
| Calgary | AAA | 76 | 253 | 59 | 16 | 0 | 11 | -- | -- | 108 | 40 | 50 | 23 | 1 | 62 | 3 | 1 | 2 | 1 | 0 | 1.00 | 4 | .233 | .302 | .427 |
| 1990 Indianapols | AAA | 39 | 143 | 41 | 10 | 2 | 5 | -- | -- | 70 | 23 | 26 | 24 | 3 | 33 | 0 | 0 | 0 | 3 | 1 | .75 | 1 | .287 | .389 | .490 |
| 1990 Montreal | NL | 52 | 119 | 27 | 1 | 0 | 3 | (0 | 3) | 37 | 14 | 7 | 21 | 4 | 36 | 0 | 1 | 0 | 0 | 2 | .00 | 0 | .227 | .343 | .311 |

## Leo Gomez

**Bats:** Right **Throws:** Right **Pos:** 3B **Ht:** 6' 0" **Wt:** 180 **Born:** 03/02/67 **Age:** 24

| | | BATTING | | | | | | | | | | | | | | | | | BASERUNNING | | | | PERCENTAGES | | |
|---|---|---|---|---|---|---|---|---|---|---|---|---|---|---|---|---|---|---|---|---|---|---|---|---|---|
| Year Team | Lg | G | AB | H | 2B | 3B | HR | (Hm | Rd) | TB | R | RBI | TBB | IBB | SO | HBP | SH | SF | SB | CS | SB% | GDP | Avg | OBP | SLG |
| 1986 Bluefield | R | 27 | 88 | 31 | 7 | 1 | 7 | -- | -- | 61 | 23 | 28 | 25 | 0 | 27 | 1 | 0 | 3 | 1 | 0 | 1.00 | 1 | .352 | .487 | .693 |
| 1987 Hagerstown | A | 131 | 466 | 152 | 38 | 2 | 19 | -- | -- | 251 | 94 | 110 | 95 | 3 | 85 | 2 | 1 | 10 | 6 | 2 | .75 | 8 | .326 | .435 | .539 |
| 1988 Charlotte | AA | 24 | 89 | 26 | 5 | 0 | 1 | -- | -- | 34 | 6 | 10 | 10 | 0 | 17 | 0 | 0 | 0 | 1 | 2 | .33 | 2 | .292 | .364 | .382 |
| 1989 Hagerstown | AA | 134 | 448 | 126 | 23 | 3 | 18 | -- | -- | 209 | 71 | 78 | 89 | 6 | 102 | 5 | 0 | 5 | 2 | 2 | .50 | 8 | .281 | .402 | .467 |
| 1990 Rochester | AAA | 131 | 430 | 119 | 26 | 4 | 26 | -- | -- | 231 | 97 | 97 | 89 | 4 | 89 | 6 | 0 | 7 | 2 | 2 | .50 | 11 | .277 | .402 | .537 |
| 1990 Baltimore | AL | 12 | 39 | 9 | 0 | 0 | 0 | (0 | 0) | 9 | 3 | 1 | 8 | 0 | 7 | 0 | 1 | 0 | 0 | 0 | .00 | 2 | .231 | .362 | .231 |

## Rene Gonzales

**Bats:** Right **Throws:** Right **Pos:** 2B **Ht:** 6' 2" **Wt:** 191 **Born:** 09/03/61 **Age:** 29

| | | BATTING | | | | | | | | | | | | | | | | | BASERUNNING | | | | PERCENTAGES | | |
|---|---|---|---|---|---|---|---|---|---|---|---|---|---|---|---|---|---|---|---|---|---|---|---|---|---|
| Year Team | Lg | G | AB | H | 2B | 3B | HR | (Hm | Rd) | TB | R | RBI | TBB | IBB | SO | HBP | SH | SF | SB | CS | SB% | GDP | Avg | OBP | SLG |
| 1984 Montreal | NL | 29 | 30 | 7 | 1 | 0 | 0 | (0 | 0) | 8 | 5 | 2 | 2 | 0 | 5 | 1 | 0 | 0 | 0 | 0 | .00 | 0 | .233 | .303 | .267 |
| 1986 Montreal | NL | 11 | 26 | 3 | 0 | 0 | 0 | (0 | 0) | 3 | 1 | 0 | 2 | 0 | 7 | 0 | 0 | 0 | 0 | 2 | .00 | 0 | .115 | .179 | .115 |
| 1987 Baltimore | AL | 37 | 60 | 16 | 2 | 1 | 1 | (1 | 0) | 23 | 14 | 7 | 3 | 0 | 11 | 0 | 2 | 0 | 1 | 0 | 1.00 | 2 | .267 | .302 | .383 |
| 1988 Baltimore | AL | 92 | 237 | 51 | 6 | 0 | 2 | (1 | 1) | 63 | 13 | 15 | 13 | 0 | 32 | 3 | 5 | 2 | 2 | 0 | 1.00 | 5 | .215 | .263 | .266 |
| 1989 Baltimore | AL | 71 | 166 | 36 | 4 | 0 | 1 | (0 | 1) | 43 | 16 | 11 | 12 | 0 | 30 | 0 | 6 | 1 | 5 | 3 | .63 | 6 | .217 | .268 | .259 |
| 1990 Baltimore | AL | 67 | 103 | 22 | 3 | 1 | 1 | (1 | 0) | 30 | 13 | 12 | 12 | 0 | 14 | 0 | 6 | 0 | 1 | 2 | .33 | 3 | .214 | .296 | .291 |
| 6 ML YEARS | | 307 | 622 | 135 | 16 | 2 | 5 | (3 | 2) | 170 | 62 | 47 | 44 | 0 | 99 | 4 | 19 | 3 | 9 | 7 | .56 | 16 | .217 | .272 | .273 |

## Jose Gonzalez

**Bats:** Right **Throws:** Right **Pos:** LF/CF/RF **Ht:** 6' 2" **Wt:** 196 **Born:** 11/23/64 **Age:** 26

| | | BATTING | | | | | | | | | | | | | | | | | BASERUNNING | | | | PERCENTAGES | | |
|---|---|---|---|---|---|---|---|---|---|---|---|---|---|---|---|---|---|---|---|---|---|---|---|---|---|
| Year Team | Lg | G | AB | H | 2B | 3B | HR | (Hm | Rd) | TB | R | RBI | TBB | IBB | SO | HBP | SH | SF | SB | CS | SB% | GDP | Avg | OBP | SLG |
| 1985 Los Angeles | NL | 23 | 11 | 3 | 2 | 0 | 0 | (0 | 0) | 5 | 6 | 0 | 1 | 0 | 3 | 0 | 0 | 0 | 1 | 1 | .50 | 1 | .273 | .333 | .455 |
| 1986 Los Angeles | NL | 57 | 93 | 20 | 5 | 1 | 2 | (1 | 1) | 33 | 15 | 6 | 7 | 0 | 29 | 0 | 2 | 0 | 4 | 3 | .57 | 0 | .215 | .270 | .355 |
| 1987 Los Angeles | NL | 19 | 16 | 3 | 2 | 0 | 0 | (0 | 0) | 5 | 2 | 1 | 1 | 0 | 2 | 0 | 0 | 1 | 5 | 0 | 1.00 | 0 | .188 | .222 | .313 |
| 1988 Los Angeles | NL | 37 | 24 | 2 | 1 | 0 | 0 | (0 | 0) | 3 | 7 | 0 | 2 | 0 | 10 | 0 | 0 | 0 | 3 | 0 | 1.00 | 0 | .083 | .154 | .125 |
| 1989 Los Angeles | NL | 95 | 261 | 70 | 11 | 2 | 3 | (2 | 1) | 94 | 31 | 18 | 23 | 5 | 53 | 0 | 1 | 1 | 9 | 3 | .75 | 2 | .268 | .326 | .360 |
| 1990 Los Angeles | NL | 106 | 99 | 23 | 5 | 3 | 2 | (2 | 0) | 40 | 15 | 8 | 6 | 1 | 27 | 1 | 1 | 1 | 3 | 1 | .75 | 1 | .232 | .280 | .404 |
| 6 ML YEARS | | 337 | 504 | 121 | 26 | 6 | 7 | (5 | 2) | 180 | 76 | 33 | 40 | 6 | 124 | 1 | 4 | 3 | 25 | 8 | .76 | 4 | .240 | .296 | .357 |

## Juan Gonzalez

**Bats:** Right **Throws:** Right **Pos:** CF **Ht:** 6' 3" **Wt:** 175 **Born:** 10/16/69 **Age:** 21

| | | BATTING | | | | | | | | | | | | | | | | | BASERUNNING | | | | PERCENTAGES | | |
|---|---|---|---|---|---|---|---|---|---|---|---|---|---|---|---|---|---|---|---|---|---|---|---|---|---|
| Year Team | Lg | G | AB | H | 2B | 3B | HR | (Hm | Rd) | TB | R | RBI | TBB | IBB | SO | HBP | SH | SF | SB | CS | SB% | GDP | Avg | OBP | SLG |
| 1986 Rangers | R | 60 | 233 | 56 | 4 | 1 | 0 | -- | -- | 62 | 24 | 36 | 21 | 0 | 57 | 1 | 1 | 3 | 7 | 5 | .58 | 9 | .240 | .302 | .266 |
| 1987 Gastonia | A | 127 | 509 | 135 | 21 | 2 | 14 | -- | -- | 202 | 69 | 74 | 30 | 2 | 92 | 5 | 1 | 4 | 9 | 4 | .69 | 14 | .265 | .310 | .397 |
| 1988 Charlotte | A | 77 | 277 | 71 | 14 | 3 | 8 | -- | -- | 115 | 25 | 43 | 25 | 3 | 64 | 4 | 0 | 2 | 5 | 2 | .71 | 7 | .256 | .325 | .415 |
| 1989 Tulsa | AA | 133 | 502 | 147 | 30 | 7 | 21 | -- | -- | 254 | 73 | 85 | 31 | 3 | 98 | 9 | 1 | 4 | 1 | 8 | .11 | 8 | .293 | .342 | .506 |
| 1990 Okla City | AAA | 128 | 496 | 128 | 29 | 4 | 29 | -- | -- | 252 | 78 | 101 | 32 | 2 | 109 | 1 | 0 | 8 | 2 | 2 | .50 | 11 | .258 | .300 | .508 |
| 1989 Texas | AL | 24 | 60 | 9 | 3 | 0 | 1 | (1 | 0) | 15 | 6 | 7 | 6 | 0 | 17 | 0 | 2 | 0 | 0 | 0 | .00 | 4 | .150 | .227 | .250 |
| 1990 Texas | AL | 25 | 90 | 26 | 7 | 1 | 4 | (3 | 1) | 47 | 11 | 12 | 2 | 0 | 18 | 2 | 0 | 1 | 0 | 1 | .00 | 2 | .289 | .316 | .522 |
| 2 ML YEARS | | 49 | 150 | 35 | 10 | 1 | 5 | (4 | 1) | 62 | 17 | 19 | 8 | 0 | 35 | 2 | 2 | 1 | 0 | 1 | .00 | 6 | .233 | .280 | .413 |

## Luis Gonzalez

**Bats:** Left **Throws:** Right **Pos:** 3B **Ht:** 6' 2" **Wt:** 180 **Born:** 09/03/67 **Age:** 23

| | | | BATTING | | | | | | | | | | | | | | | | | BASERUNNING | | | | PERCENTAGES | | |
|---|---|---|---|---|---|---|---|---|---|---|---|---|---|---|---|---|---|---|---|---|---|---|---|---|---|---|
| Year | Team | Lg | G | AB | H | 2B | 3B | HR | (Hm | Rd) | TB | R | RBI | TBB | IBB | SO | HBP | SH | SF | SB | CS | SB% | GDP | Avg | OBP | SLG |
| 1988 | Auburn | A | 39 | 157 | 49 | 10 | 3 | 5 | -- | -- | 80 | 32 | 27 | 12 | 1 | 19 | 1 | 1 | 5 | 2 | 0 | 1.00 | 1 | .312 | .354 | .510 |
| | Asheville | A | 31 | 115 | 29 | 7 | 1 | 2 | -- | -- | 44 | 13 | 14 | 12 | 0 | 17 | 2 | 0 | 0 | 2 | 2 | .50 | 4 | .252 | .333 | .383 |
| 1989 | Osceola | A | 86 | 287 | 82 | 16 | 7 | 6 | -- | -- | 130 | 46 | 38 | 37 | 5 | 49 | 4 | 1 | 4 | 2 | 1 | .67 | 3 | .286 | .370 | .453 |
| 1990 | Columbus | AA | 138 | 495 | 131 | 30 | 6 | 24 | -- | -- | 245 | 86 | 89 | 54 | 9 | 100 | 6 | 1 | 12 | 27 | 9 | .75 | 6 | .265 | .337 | .495 |
| 1990 | Houston | NL | 12 | 21 | 4 | 2 | 0 | 0 | (0 | 0) | 6 | 1 | 0 | 2 | 1 | 5 | 0 | 0 | 0 | 0 | 0 | .00 | 0 | .190 | .261 | .286 |

## Dwight Gooden

**Pitches:** Right **Bats:** Right **Pos:** SP **Ht:** 6' 3" **Wt:** 210 **Born:** 11/16/64 **Age:** 26

| | | | HOW MUCH HE PITCHED | | | | | | WHAT HE GAVE UP | | | | | | | | | | | | THE RESULTS | | | | | |
|---|---|---|---|---|---|---|---|---|---|---|---|---|---|---|---|---|---|---|---|---|---|---|---|---|---|---|
| Year | Team | Lg | G | GS | CG | GF | IP | BFP | H | R | ER | HR | SH | SF | HB | TBB | IBB | SO | WP | Bk | W | L | Pct. | ShO | Sv | ERA |
| 1984 | New York | NL | 31 | 31 | 7 | 0 | 218 | 879 | 161 | 72 | 63 | 7 | 3 | 2 | 2 | 73 | 2 | 276 | 3 | 7 | 17 | 9 | .654 | 3 | 0 | 2.60 |
| 1985 | New York | NL | 35 | 35 | 16 | 0 | 276.2 | 1065 | 198 | 51 | 47 | 13 | 6 | 2 | 2 | 69 | 4 | 268 | 6 | 2 | 24 | 4 | .857 | 8 | 0 | 1.53 |
| 1986 | New York | NL | 33 | 33 | 12 | 0 | 250 | 1020 | 197 | 92 | 79 | 17 | 10 | 8 | 4 | 80 | 3 | 200 | 4 | 4 | 17 | 6 | .739 | 2 | 0 | 2.84 |
| 1987 | New York | NL | 25 | 25 | 7 | 0 | 179.2 | 730 | 162 | 68 | 64 | 11 | 5 | 5 | 2 | 53 | 2 | 148 | 1 | 1 | 15 | 7 | .682 | 3 | 0 | 3.21 |
| 1988 | New York | NL | 34 | 34 | 10 | 0 | 248.1 | 1024 | 242 | 98 | 88 | 8 | 10 | 6 | 6 | 57 | 4 | 175 | 5 | 5 | 18 | 9 | .667 | 3 | 0 | 3.19 |
| 1989 | New York | NL | 19 | 17 | 0 | 1 | 118.1 | 497 | 93 | 42 | 38 | 9 | 4 | 3 | 2 | 47 | 2 | 101 | 7 | 5 | 9 | 4 | .692 | 0 | 1 | 2.89 |
| 1990 | New York | NL | 34 | 34 | 2 | 0 | 232.2 | 983 | 229 | 106 | 99 | 10 | 10 | 7 | 7 | 70 | 3 | 223 | 6 | 3 | 19 | 7 | .731 | 1 | 0 | 3.83 |
| | 7 ML YEARS | | 211 | 209 | 54 | 1 | 1523.2 | 6198 | 1282 | 529 | 478 | 75 | 48 | 33 | 25 | 449 | 20 | 1391 | 32 | 27 | 119 | 46 | .721 | 20 | 1 | 2.82 |

## Tom Gordon

**Pitches:** Right **Bats:** Right **Pos:** SP **Ht:** 5' 9" **Wt:** 160 **Born:** 11/18/67 **Age:** 23

| | | | HOW MUCH HE PITCHED | | | | | | WHAT HE GAVE UP | | | | | | | | | | | | THE RESULTS | | | | | |
|---|---|---|---|---|---|---|---|---|---|---|---|---|---|---|---|---|---|---|---|---|---|---|---|---|---|---|
| Year | Team | Lg | G | GS | CG | GF | IP | BFP | H | R | ER | HR | SH | SF | HB | TBB | IBB | SO | WP | Bk | W | L | Pct. | ShO | Sv | ERA |
| 1988 | Kansas City | AL | 5 | 2 | 0 | 0 | 15.2 | 67 | 16 | 9 | 9 | 1 | 0 | 0 | 0 | 7 | 0 | 18 | 0 | 0 | 0 | 2 | .000 | 0 | 0 | 5.17 |
| 1989 | Kansas City | AL | 49 | 16 | 1 | 16 | 163 | 677 | 122 | 67 | 66 | 10 | 4 | 4 | 1 | 86 | 4 | 153 | 12 | 0 | 17 | 9 | .654 | 1 | 1 | 3.64 |
| 1990 | Kansas City | AL | 32 | 32 | 6 | 0 | 195.1 | 858 | 192 | 99 | 81 | 17 | 8 | 2 | 3 | 99 | 1 | 175 | 11 | 0 | 12 | 11 | .522 | 1 | 0 | 3.73 |
| | 3 ML YEARS | | 86 | 50 | 7 | 16 | 374 | 1602 | 330 | 175 | 156 | 28 | 12 | 6 | 4 | 192 | 5 | 346 | 23 | 0 | 29 | 22 | .569 | 2 | 1 | 3.75 |

## Jim Gott

**Pitches:** Right **Bats:** Right **Pos:** RP **Ht:** 6' 4" **Wt:** 220 **Born:** 08/03/59 **Age:** 31

| | | | HOW MUCH HE PITCHED | | | | | | WHAT HE GAVE UP | | | | | | | | | | | | THE RESULTS | | | | | |
|---|---|---|---|---|---|---|---|---|---|---|---|---|---|---|---|---|---|---|---|---|---|---|---|---|---|---|
| Year | Team | Lg | G | GS | CG | GF | IP | BFP | H | R | ER | HR | SH | SF | HB | TBB | IBB | SO | WP | Bk | W | L | Pct. | ShO | Sv | ERA |
| 1982 | Toronto | AL | 30 | 23 | 1 | 4 | 136 | 600 | 134 | 76 | 67 | 15 | 3 | 2 | 3 | 66 | 0 | 82 | 8 | 0 | 5 | 10 | .333 | 1 | 0 | 4.43 |
| 1983 | Toronto | AL | 34 | 30 | 6 | 2 | 176.2 | 776 | 195 | 103 | 93 | 15 | 4 | 3 | 5 | 68 | 5 | 121 | 2 | 0 | 9 | 14 | .391 | 1 | 0 | 4.74 |
| 1984 | Toronto | AL | 35 | 12 | 1 | 11 | 109.2 | 464 | 93 | 54 | 49 | 7 | 7 | 6 | 3 | 49 | 3 | 73 | 1 | 0 | 7 | 6 | .538 | 1 | 2 | 4.02 |
| 1985 | San Francisco | NL | 26 | 26 | 2 | 0 | 148.1 | 629 | 144 | 73 | 64 | 10 | 6 | 4 | 1 | 51 | 3 | 78 | 3 | 2 | 7 | 10 | .412 | 0 | 0 | 3.88 |
| 1986 | San Francisco | NL | 9 | 2 | 0 | 3 | 13 | 66 | 16 | 12 | 11 | 0 | 1 | 1 | 0 | 13 | 2 | 9 | 1 | 1 | 0 | 0 | .000 | 0 | 1 | 7.62 |
| 1987 | 2 ML Teams | | 55 | 3 | 0 | 30 | 87 | 382 | 81 | 43 | 33 | 4 | 2 | 1 | 2 | 40 | 7 | 90 | 5 | 0 | 1 | 2 | .333 | 0 | 13 | 3.41 |
| 1988 | Pittsburgh | NL | 67 | 0 | 0 | 59 | 77.1 | 314 | 68 | 30 | 30 | 9 | 7 | 3 | 2 | 22 | 5 | 76 | 1 | 6 | 6 | 6 | .500 | 0 | 34 | 3.49 |
| 1989 | Pittsburgh | NL | 1 | 0 | 0 | 0 | 0.2 | 4 | 1 | 0 | 0 | 0 | 0 | 0 | 0 | 1 | 0 | 1 | 0 | 0 | 0 | 0 | .000 | 0 | 0 | 0.00 |
| 1990 | Los Angeles | NL | 50 | 0 | 0 | 24 | 62 | 270 | 59 | 27 | 20 | 5 | 2 | 4 | 0 | 34 | 7 | 44 | 4 | 0 | 3 | 5 | .375 | 0 | 3 | 2.90 |
| 1987 | San Francisco | NL | 30 | 3 | 0 | 8 | 56 | 253 | 53 | 32 | 28 | 4 | 1 | 1 | 2 | 32 | 5 | 63 | 3 | 0 | 1 | 0 | 1.000 | 0 | 0 | 4.50 |
| | Pittsburgh | NL | 25 | 0 | 0 | 22 | 31 | 129 | 28 | 11 | 5 | 0 | 1 | 0 | 0 | 8 | 2 | 27 | 2 | 0 | 0 | 2 | .000 | 0 | 13 | 1.45 |
| | 9 ML YEARS | | 307 | 96 | 10 | 133 | 810.2 | 3505 | 791 | 418 | 367 | 65 | 32 | 24 | 16 | 344 | 32 | 574 | 25 | 9 | 38 | 53 | .418 | 3 | 53 | 4.07 |

## Mauro Gozzo

**Pitches:** Right **Bats:** Right **Pos:** RP **Ht:** 6' 3" **Wt:** 212 **Born:** 03/07/66 **Age:** 25

| | | | HOW MUCH HE PITCHED | | | | | | WHAT HE GAVE UP | | | | | | | | | | | | THE RESULTS | | | | | |
|---|---|---|---|---|---|---|---|---|---|---|---|---|---|---|---|---|---|---|---|---|---|---|---|---|---|---|
| Year | Team | Lg | G | GS | CG | GF | IP | BFP | H | R | ER | HR | SH | SF | HB | TBB | IBB | SO | WP | Bk | W | L | Pct. | ShO | Sv | ERA |
| 1984 | Little Fls | A | 24 | 0 | 0 | 8 | 38.1 | 176 | 40 | 27 | 24 | 3 | 0 | 2 | 0 | 28 | 4 | 30 | 7 | 1 | 4 | 3 | .571 | 0 | 2 | 5.63 |
| 1985 | Columbia | A | 49 | 0 | 0 | 42 | 78 | 330 | 62 | 22 | 22 | 2 | 3 | 5 | 2 | 39 | 7 | 66 | 4 | 1 | 11 | 4 | .733 | 0 | 14 | 2.54 |
| 1986 | Lynchburg | A | 60 | 0 | 0 | 46 | 78.1 | 341 | 80 | 30 | 27 | 3 | 5 | 2 | 2 | 35 | 3 | 50 | 4 | 1 | 9 | 4 | .692 | 0 | 9 | 3.10 |
| 1987 | Memphis | AA | 19 | 14 | 1 | 2 | 91.1 | 400 | 95 | 58 | 46 | 13 | 1 | 2 | 4 | 36 | 2 | 56 | 3 | 3 | 6 | 5 | .545 | 0 | 0 | 4.53 |
| 1988 | Memphis | AA | 33 | 12 | 0 | 9 | 92.2 | 430 | 127 | 64 | 59 | 9 | 2 | 7 | 1 | 36 | 1 | 48 | 14 | 3 | 4 | 9 | .308 | 0 | 3 | 5.73 |
| 1989 | Knoxville | AA | 18 | 6 | 2 | 6 | 60.1 | 245 | 59 | 27 | 20 | 1 | 0 | 5 | 1 | 12 | 1 | 37 | 2 | 1 | 7 | 0 | 1.000 | 1 | 0 | 2.98 |
| | Syracuse | AAA | 12 | 7 | 2 | 2 | 62 | 251 | 56 | 22 | 19 | 3 | 1 | 1 | 0 | 19 | 0 | 34 | 2 | 0 | 5 | 1 | .833 | 1 | 2 | 2.76 |
| 1990 | Syracuse | AAA | 34 | 10 | 0 | 19 | 98 | 409 | 87 | 46 | 39 | 5 | 3 | 1 | 3 | 44 | 3 | 62 | 2 | 1 | 3 | 8 | .273 | 0 | 7 | 3.58 |
| 1989 | Toronto | AL | 9 | 3 | 0 | 2 | 31.2 | 133 | 35 | 19 | 17 | 1 | 0 | 2 | 1 | 9 | 1 | 10 | 0 | 0 | 4 | 1 | .800 | 0 | 0 | 4.83 |
| 1990 | Cleveland | AL | 2 | 0 | 0 | 1 | 3 | 13 | 2 | 0 | 0 | 0 | 0 | 0 | 0 | 2 | 0 | 2 | 0 | 0 | 0 | 0 | .000 | 0 | 0 | 0.00 |
| | 2 ML YEARS | | 11 | 3 | 0 | 3 | 34.2 | 146 | 37 | 19 | 17 | 1 | 0 | 2 | 1 | 11 | 1 | 12 | 0 | 0 | 4 | 1 | .800 | 0 | 0 | 4.41 |

## Mark Grace

**Bats:** Left **Throws:** Left **Pos:** 1B **Ht:** 6' 2" **Wt:** 190 **Born:** 06/28/64 **Age:** 27

| | | BATTING | | | | | | | | | | | | | | | | | BASERUNNING | | | | PERCENTAGES | | |
|---|---|---|---|---|---|---|---|---|---|---|---|---|---|---|---|---|---|---|---|---|---|---|---|---|---|
| Year Team | Lg | G | AB | H | 2B | 3B | HR | (Hm | Rd) | TB | R | RBI | TBB | IBB | SO | HBP | SH | SF | SB | CS | SB% | GDP | Avg | OBP | SLG |
| 1988 Chicago | NL | 134 | 486 | 144 | 23 | 4 | 7 | (0 | 7) | 196 | 65 | 57 | 60 | 5 | 43 | 0 | 0 | 4 | 3 | 3 | .50 | 12 | .296 | .371 | .403 |
| 1989 Chicago | NL | 142 | 510 | 160 | 28 | 3 | 13 | (8 | 5) | 233 | 74 | 79 | 80 | 13 | 42 | 0 | 3 | 3 | 14 | 7 | .67 | 13 | .314 | .405 | .457 |
| 1990 Chicago | NL | 157 | 589 | 182 | 32 | 1 | 9 | (4 | 5) | 243 | 72 | 82 | 59 | 5 | 54 | 5 | 1 | 8 | 15 | 6 | .71 | 10 | .309 | .372 | .413 |
| 3 ML YEARS | | 433 | 1585 | 486 | 83 | 8 | 29 | (12 | 17) | 672 | 211 | 218 | 199 | 23 | 139 | 5 | 4 | 15 | 32 | 16 | .67 | 35 | .307 | .382 | .424 |

## Joe Grahe

**Pitches:** Right **Bats:** Right **Pos:** SP **Ht:** 6' 0" **Wt:** 195 **Born:** 08/14/67 **Age:** 23

| | | HOW MUCH HE PITCHED | | | | | | WHAT HE GAVE UP | | | | | | | | | | | | THE RESULTS | | | | | |
|---|---|---|---|---|---|---|---|---|---|---|---|---|---|---|---|---|---|---|---|---|---|---|---|---|---|
| Year Team | Lg | G | GS | CG | GF | IP | BFP | H | R | ER | HR | SH | SF | HB | TBB | IBB | SO | WP | Bk | W | L | Pct. | ShO | Sv | ERA |
| 1990 Midland | AA | 18 | 18 | 1 | 0 | 119 | 519 | 145 | 75 | 68 | 10 | 2 | 2 | 4 | 34 | 1 | 58 | 10 | 1 | 7 | 5 | .583 | 0 | 0 | 5.14 |
| Edmonton | AAA | 5 | 5 | 2 | 0 | 40 | 159 | 35 | 10 | 6 | 4 | 0 | 0 | 0 | 11 | 0 | 21 | 0 | 0 | 3 | 0 | 1.000 | 0 | 0 | 1.35 |
| 1990 California | AL | 8 | 8 | 0 | 0 | 43.1 | 200 | 51 | 30 | 24 | 3 | 0 | 0 | 3 | 23 | 1 | 25 | 1 | 0 | 3 | 4 | .429 | 0 | 0 | 4.98 |

## Mark Grant

**Pitches:** Right **Bats:** Right **Pos:** RP **Ht:** 6' 2" **Wt:** 205 **Born:** 10/24/63 **Age:** 27

| | | HOW MUCH HE PITCHED | | | | | | WHAT HE GAVE UP | | | | | | | | | | | | THE RESULTS | | | | | |
|---|---|---|---|---|---|---|---|---|---|---|---|---|---|---|---|---|---|---|---|---|---|---|---|---|---|
| Year Team | Lg | G | GS | CG | GF | IP | BFP | H | R | ER | HR | SH | SF | HB | TBB | IBB | SO | WP | Bk | W | L | Pct. | ShO | Sv | ERA |
| 1984 San Francisco | NL | 11 | 10 | 0 | 1 | 53.2 | 231 | 56 | 40 | 38 | 6 | 2 | 3 | 1 | 19 | 0 | 32 | 3 | 0 | 1 | 4 | .200 | 0 | 1 | 6.37 |
| 1986 San Francisco | NL | 4 | 1 | 0 | 3 | 10 | 39 | 6 | 4 | 4 | 0 | 0 | 0 | 0 | 5 | 0 | 5 | 0 | 1 | 0 | 1 | .000 | 0 | 0 | 3.60 |
| 1987 2 ML Teams | | 33 | 25 | 2 | 2 | 163.1 | 720 | 170 | 88 | 77 | 22 | 15 | 1 | 1 | 73 | 8 | 90 | 8 | 3 | 7 | 9 | .438 | 1 | 1 | 4.24 |
| 1988 San Diego | NL | 33 | 11 | 0 | 9 | 97.2 | 410 | 97 | 41 | 40 | 14 | 6 | 4 | 2 | 36 | 6 | 61 | 5 | 0 | 2 | 8 | .200 | 0 | 0 | 3.69 |
| 1989 San Diego | NL | 50 | 0 | 0 | 19 | 116.1 | 466 | 105 | 45 | 43 | 11 | 5 | 2 | 3 | 32 | 6 | 69 | 2 | 0 | 8 | 2 | .800 | 0 | 2 | 3.33 |
| 1990 2 ML Teams | | 59 | 1 | 0 | 21 | 91.1 | 411 | 108 | 53 | 48 | 9 | 6 | 5 | 1 | 37 | 11 | 69 | 2 | 1 | 2 | 3 | .400 | 0 | 3 | 4.73 |
| 1987 San Francisco | NL | 16 | 8 | 0 | 2 | 61 | 264 | 66 | 29 | 24 | 6 | 7 | 1 | 1 | 21 | 5 | 32 | 2 | 2 | 1 | 2 | .333 | 0 | 1 | 3.54 |
| San Diego | NL | 17 | 17 | 2 | 0 | 102.1 | 456 | 104 | 59 | 53 | 16 | 8 | 0 | 0 | 52 | 3 | 58 | 6 | 1 | 6 | 7 | .462 | 1 | 0 | 4.66 |
| 1990 San Diego | NL | 26 | 0 | 0 | 5 | 39 | 180 | 47 | 23 | 21 | 5 | 4 | 3 | 0 | 19 | 8 | 29 | 1 | 1 | 1 | 1 | .500 | 0 | 0 | 4.85 |
| Atlanta | NL | 33 | 1 | 0 | 16 | 52.1 | 231 | 61 | 30 | 27 | 4 | 2 | 2 | 1 | 18 | 3 | 40 | 1 | 0 | 1 | 2 | .333 | 0 | 3 | 4.64 |
| 6 ML YEARS | | 190 | 48 | 2 | 55 | 532.1 | 2277 | 542 | 271 | 250 | 62 | 34 | 15 | 8 | 202 | 31 | 326 | 20 | 5 | 20 | 27 | .426 | 1 | 7 | 4.23 |

## Jeff Gray

**Pitches:** Right **Bats:** Right **Pos:** RP **Ht:** 6' 1" **Wt:** 175 **Born:** 04/10/63 **Age:** 28

| | | HOW MUCH HE PITCHED | | | | | | WHAT HE GAVE UP | | | | | | | | | | | | THE RESULTS | | | | | |
|---|---|---|---|---|---|---|---|---|---|---|---|---|---|---|---|---|---|---|---|---|---|---|---|---|---|
| Year Team | Lg | G | GS | CG | GF | IP | BFP | H | R | ER | HR | SH | SF | HB | TBB | IBB | SO | WP | Bk | W | L | Pct. | ShO | Sv | ERA |
| 1988 Cincinnati | NL | 5 | 0 | 0 | 1 | 9.1 | 45 | 12 | 4 | 4 | 0 | 3 | 2 | 0 | 4 | 2 | 5 | 0 | 0 | 0 | 0 | .000 | 0 | 0 | 3.86 |
| 1990 Boston | AL | 41 | 0 | 0 | 28 | 50.2 | 217 | 53 | 27 | 25 | 3 | 2 | 1 | 1 | 15 | 3 | 50 | 2 | 0 | 2 | 4 | .333 | 0 | 9 | 4.44 |
| 2 ML YEARS | | 46 | 0 | 0 | 29 | 60 | 262 | 65 | 31 | 29 | 3 | 5 | 3 | 1 | 19 | 5 | 55 | 2 | 0 | 2 | 4 | .333 | 0 | 9 | 4.35 |

## Craig Grebeck

**Bats:** Right **Throws:** Right **Pos:** 3B/SS **Ht:** 5' 8" **Wt:** 160 **Born:** 12/29/64 **Age:** 26

| | | BATTING | | | | | | | | | | | | | | | | | BASERUNNING | | | | PERCENTAGES | | |
|---|---|---|---|---|---|---|---|---|---|---|---|---|---|---|---|---|---|---|---|---|---|---|---|---|---|
| Year Team | Lg | G | AB | H | 2B | 3B | HR | (Hm | Rd) | TB | R | RBI | TBB | IBB | SO | HBP | SH | SF | SB | CS | SB% | GDP | Avg | OBP | SLG |
| 1987 Peninsula | A | 104 | 378 | 106 | 22 | 3 | 15 | -- | -- | 179 | 63 | 67 | 37 | 0 | 62 | 1 | 2 | 4 | 3 | 6 | .33 | 8 | .280 | .343 | .474 |
| 1988 Birmingham | AA | 133 | 450 | 126 | 21 | 1 | 9 | -- | -- | 176 | 57 | 53 | 65 | 3 | 72 | 2 | 7 | 3 | 5 | 7 | .42 | 10 | .280 | .371 | .391 |
| 1989 Birmingham | AA | 143 | 533 | 153 | 25 | 4 | 5 | -- | -- | 201 | 85 | 80 | 63 | 4 | 77 | 4 | 11 | 7 | 14 | 15 | .48 | 15 | .287 | .362 | .377 |
| 1990 Vancouver | AAA | 12 | 41 | 8 | 0 | 0 | 1 | -- | -- | 11 | 8 | 3 | 6 | 0 | 7 | 0 | 0 | 0 | 1 | 0 | 1.00 | 2 | .195 | .298 | .268 |
| 1990 Chicago | AL | 59 | 119 | 20 | 3 | 1 | 1 | (1 | 0) | 28 | 7 | 9 | 8 | 0 | 24 | 2 | 3 | 3 | 0 | 0 | .00 | 2 | .168 | .227 | .235 |

## Gary Green

**Bats:** Right **Throws:** Right **Pos:** SS **Ht:** 6' 3" **Wt:** 170 **Born:** 01/14/62 **Age:** 29

| | | BATTING | | | | | | | | | | | | | | | | | BASERUNNING | | | | PERCENTAGES | | |
|---|---|---|---|---|---|---|---|---|---|---|---|---|---|---|---|---|---|---|---|---|---|---|---|---|---|
| Year Team | Lg | G | AB | H | 2B | 3B | HR | (Hm | Rd) | TB | R | RBI | TBB | IBB | SO | HBP | SH | SF | SB | CS | SB% | GDP | Avg | OBP | SLG |
| 1986 San Diego | NL | 13 | 33 | 7 | 1 | 0 | 0 | (0 | 0) | 8 | 2 | 2 | 1 | 0 | 11 | 0 | 1 | 0 | 0 | 0 | .00 | 0 | .212 | .235 | .242 |
| 1989 San Diego | NL | 15 | 27 | 7 | 3 | 0 | 0 | (0 | 0) | 10 | 4 | 0 | 1 | 0 | 1 | 0 | 0 | 0 | 0 | 1 | .00 | 0 | .259 | .286 | .370 |
| 1990 Texas | AL | 62 | 88 | 19 | 3 | 0 | 0 | (0 | 0) | 22 | 10 | 8 | 6 | 0 | 18 | 0 | 4 | 1 | 1 | 1 | .50 | 2 | .216 | .263 | .250 |
| 3 ML YEARS | | 90 | 148 | 33 | 7 | 0 | 0 | (0 | 0) | 40 | 16 | 10 | 8 | 0 | 30 | 0 | 5 | 1 | 1 | 2 | .33 | 2 | .223 | .261 | .270 |

## Tommy Greene

**Pitches:** Right **Bats:** Right **Pos:** SP/RP **Ht:** 6' 5" **Wt:** 225 **Born:** 04/06/67 **Age:** 24

| | | HOW MUCH HE PITCHED | | | | | | WHAT HE GAVE UP | | | | | | | | | | | | THE RESULTS | | | | | |
|---|---|---|---|---|---|---|---|---|---|---|---|---|---|---|---|---|---|---|---|---|---|---|---|---|---|
| Year Team | Lg | G | GS | CG | GF | IP | BFP | H | R | ER | HR | SH | SF | HB | TBB | IBB | SO | WP | Bk | W | L | Pct. | ShO | Sv | ERA |
| 1985 Pulaski | R | 12 | 12 | 1 | 0 | 50.2 | 226 | 49 | 45 | 43 | 7 | 1 | 1 | 2 | 27 | 0 | 32 | 4 | 0 | 2 | 5 | .286 | 1 | 0 | 7.64 |
| 1986 Sumter | A | 28 | 28 | 5 | 0 | 174.2 | 758 | 162 | 95 | 91 | 17 | 4 | 3 | 8 | 82 | 3 | 169 | 15 | 7 | 11 | 7 | .611 | 3 | 0 | 4.69 |

| Year Team | Lg | | | | | | | | | | | | | | | | | | | | | | | | |
|---|---|---|---|---|---|---|---|---|---|---|---|---|---|---|---|---|---|---|---|---|---|---|---|---|---|
| 1987 Greenville | AA | 23 | 23 | 4 | 0 | 142.1 | 590 | 103 | 60 | 52 | 13 | 4 | 2 | 4 | 66 | 1 | 101 | 7 | 2 | 11 | 8 | .579 | 2 | 0 | 3.29 |
| 1988 Richmond | AAA | 29 | 29 | 4 | 0 | 177.1 | 765 | 169 | 98 | 94 | 10 | 7 | 8 | 3 | 70 | 1 | 130 | 5 | 8 | 7 | 17 | .292 | 3 | 0 | 4.77 |
| 1989 Richmond | AAA | 26 | 26 | 2 | 0 | 152 | 638 | 136 | 74 | 61 | 9 | 9 | 5 | 2 | 50 | 0 | 125 | 10 | 0 | 9 | 12 | .429 | 1 | 0 | 3.61 |
| 1990 Richmond | AAA | 19 | 18 | 2 | 0 | 109 | 459 | 88 | 49 | 45 | 5 | 5 | 3 | 0 | 65 | 3 | 65 | 8 | 3 | 5 | 8 | .385 | 0 | 0 | 3.72 |
| Scr Wil-Bar | AAA | 1 | 1 | 0 | 0 | 7 | 27 | 5 | 0 | 0 | 0 | 0 | 0 | 0 | 2 | 0 | 4 | 0 | 0 | 0 | 0 | .000 | 0 | 0 | 0.00 |
| 1989 Atlanta | NL | 4 | 4 | 1 | 0 | 26.1 | 103 | 22 | 12 | 12 | 5 | 1 | 2 | 0 | 6 | 1 | 17 | 1 | 0 | 1 | 2 | .333 | 1 | 0 | 4.10 |
| 1990 2 ML Teams | | 15 | 9 | 0 | 1 | 51.1 | 227 | 50 | 31 | 29 | 8 | 5 | 0 | 1 | 26 | 1 | 21 | 1 | 0 | 3 | 3 | .500 | 0 | 0 | 5.08 |
| 1990 Atlanta | NL | 5 | 2 | 0 | 0 | 12.1 | 61 | 14 | 11 | 11 | 3 | 2 | 0 | 1 | 9 | 0 | 4 | 0 | 0 | 1 | 0 | 1.000 | 0 | 0 | 8.03 |
| Philadelphia | NL | 10 | 7 | 0 | 1 | 39 | 166 | 36 | 20 | 18 | 5 | 3 | 0 | 0 | 17 | 1 | 17 | 1 | 0 | 2 | 3 | .400 | 0 | 0 | 4.15 |
| 2 ML YEARS | | 19 | 13 | 1 | 1 | 77.2 | 330 | 72 | 43 | 41 | 13 | 6 | 2 | 1 | 32 | 2 | 38 | 2 | 0 | 4 | 5 | .444 | 1 | 0 | 4.75 |

## Mike Greenwell

**Bats:** Left **Throws:** Right **Pos:** LF **Ht:** 6' 0" **Wt:** 195 **Born:** 07/18/63 **Age:** 27

| BATTING | | | | | | | | | | | | | | | | | | | BASERUNNING | | | | PERCENTAGES | | |
|---|---|---|---|---|---|---|---|---|---|---|---|---|---|---|---|---|---|---|---|---|---|---|---|---|---|
| Year Team | Lg | G | AB | H | 2B | 3B | HR | (Hm | Rd) | TB | R | RBI | TBB | IBB | SO | HBP | SH | SF | SB | CS | SB% | GDP | Avg | OBP | SLG |
| 1985 Boston | AL | 17 | 31 | 10 | 1 | 0 | 4 | (1 | 3) | 23 | 7 | 8 | 3 | 1 | 4 | 0 | 0 | 0 | 1 | 0 | 1.00 | 0 | .323 | .382 | .742 |
| 1986 Boston | AL | 31 | 35 | 11 | 2 | 0 | 0 | (0 | 0) | 13 | 4 | 4 | 5 | 0 | 7 | 0 | 0 | 0 | 0 | 0 | .00 | 1 | .314 | .400 | .371 |
| 1987 Boston | AL | 125 | 412 | 135 | 31 | 6 | 19 | (8 | 11) | 235 | 71 | 89 | 35 | 1 | 40 | 6 | 0 | 3 | 5 | 4 | .56 | 7 | .328 | .386 | .570 |
| 1988 Boston | AL | 158 | 590 | 192 | 39 | 8 | 22 | (12 | 10) | 313 | 86 | 119 | 87 | 18 | 38 | 9 | 0 | 7 | 16 | 8 | .67 | 11 | .325 | .416 | .531 |
| 1989 Boston | AL | 145 | 578 | 178 | 36 | 0 | 14 | (6 | 8) | 256 | 87 | 95 | 56 | 15 | 44 | 3 | 0 | 4 | 13 | 5 | .72 | 21 | .308 | .370 | .443 |
| 1990 Boston | AL | 159 | 610 | 181 | 30 | 6 | 14 | (6 | 8) | 265 | 71 | 73 | 65 | 12 | 43 | 4 | 0 | 3 | 8 | 7 | .53 | 19 | .297 | .367 | .434 |
| 6 ML YEARS | | 635 | 2256 | 707 | 139 | 20 | 73 | (33 | 40) | 1105 | 326 | 388 | 251 | 47 | 176 | 22 | 0 | 17 | 43 | 24 | .64 | 59 | .313 | .385 | .490 |

## Tommy Gregg

**Bats:** Left **Throws:** Left **Pos:** 1B/RF **Ht:** 6' 1" **Wt:** 190 **Born:** 07/29/63 **Age:** 27

| BATTING | | | | | | | | | | | | | | | | | | | BASERUNNING | | | | PERCENTAGES | | |
|---|---|---|---|---|---|---|---|---|---|---|---|---|---|---|---|---|---|---|---|---|---|---|---|---|---|
| Year Team | Lg | G | AB | H | 2B | 3B | HR | (Hm | Rd) | TB | R | RBI | TBB | IBB | SO | HBP | SH | SF | SB | CS | SB% | GDP | Avg | OBP | SLG |
| 1987 Pittsburgh | NL | 10 | 8 | 2 | 1 | 0 | 0 | (0 | 0) | 3 | 3 | 0 | 0 | 0 | 2 | 0 | 0 | 0 | 0 | 0 | .00 | 2 | .250 | .250 | .375 |
| 1988 2 ML Teams | | 25 | 44 | 13 | 4 | 0 | 1 | (0 | 1) | 20 | 5 | 7 | 3 | 1 | 6 | 0 | 0 | 1 | 0 | 1 | .00 | 1 | .295 | .333 | .455 |
| 1989 Atlanta | NL | 102 | 276 | 67 | 8 | 0 | 6 | (2 | 4) | 93 | 24 | 23 | 18 | 2 | 45 | 0 | 3 | 1 | 3 | 4 | .43 | 4 | .243 | .288 | .337 |
| 1990 Atlanta | NL | 124 | 239 | 63 | 13 | 1 | 5 | (2 | 3) | 93 | 18 | 32 | 20 | 4 | 39 | 1 | 0 | 1 | 4 | 3 | .57 | 2 | .264 | .322 | .389 |
| 1988 Pittsburgh | NL | 14 | 15 | 3 | 1 | 0 | 1 | (0 | 1) | 7 | 4 | 3 | 1 | 0 | 4 | 0 | 0 | 1 | 0 | 1 | .00 | 0 | .200 | .235 | .467 |
| Atlanta | NL | 11 | 29 | 10 | 3 | 0 | 0 | (0 | 0) | 13 | 1 | 4 | 2 | 1 | 2 | 0 | 0 | 0 | 0 | 0 | .00 | 1 | .345 | .387 | .448 |
| 4 ML YEARS | | 261 | 567 | 145 | 26 | 1 | 12 | (4 | 8) | 209 | 50 | 62 | 41 | 7 | 92 | 1 | 3 | 3 | 7 | 8 | .47 | 9 | .256 | .306 | .369 |

## Ken Griffey Jr

**Bats:** Left **Throws:** Left **Pos:** CF **Ht:** 6' 3" **Wt:** 195 **Born:** 11/21/69 **Age:** 21

| BATTING | | | | | | | | | | | | | | | | | | | BASERUNNING | | | | PERCENTAGES | | |
|---|---|---|---|---|---|---|---|---|---|---|---|---|---|---|---|---|---|---|---|---|---|---|---|---|---|
| Year Team | Lg | G | AB | H | 2B | 3B | HR | (Hm | Rd) | TB | R | RBI | TBB | IBB | SO | HBP | SH | SF | SB | CS | SB% | GDP | Avg | OBP | SLG |
| 1987 Bellingham | A | 54 | 182 | 57 | 9 | 1 | 14 | -- | -- | 110 | 43 | 40 | 44 | 3 | 42 | 0 | 1 | 1 | 13 | 6 | .68 | 2 | .313 | .445 | .604 |
| 1988 San Berndno | A | 58 | 219 | 74 | 13 | 3 | 11 | -- | -- | 126 | 50 | 42 | 34 | 5 | 39 | 2 | 1 | 0 | 32 | 9 | .78 | 3 | .338 | .431 | .575 |
| Vermont | AA | 17 | 61 | 17 | 5 | 1 | 2 | -- | -- | 30 | 10 | 10 | 5 | 0 | 12 | 2 | 0 | 0 | 4 | 2 | .67 | 3 | .279 | .353 | .492 |
| 1989 Seattle | AL | 127 | 455 | 120 | 23 | 0 | 16 | (10 | 6) | 191 | 61 | 61 | 44 | 8 | 83 | 2 | 1 | 4 | 16 | 7 | .70 | 4 | .264 | .329 | .420 |
| 1990 Seattle | AL | 155 | 597 | 179 | 28 | 7 | 22 | (8 | 14) | 287 | 91 | 80 | 63 | 12 | 81 | 2 | 0 | 4 | 16 | 11 | .59 | 12 | .300 | .366 | .481 |
| 2 ML YEARS | | 282 | 1052 | 299 | 51 | 7 | 38 | (18 | 20) | 478 | 152 | 141 | 107 | 20 | 164 | 4 | 1 | 8 | 32 | 18 | .64 | 16 | .284 | .350 | .454 |

## Ken Griffey Sr

**Bats:** Left **Throws:** Left **Pos:** LF **Ht:** 6' 0" **Wt:** 210 **Born:** 04/10/50 **Age:** 41

| BATTING | | | | | | | | | | | | | | | | | | | BASERUNNING | | | | PERCENTAGES | | |
|---|---|---|---|---|---|---|---|---|---|---|---|---|---|---|---|---|---|---|---|---|---|---|---|---|---|
| Year Team | Lg | G | AB | H | 2B | 3B | HR | (Hm | Rd) | TB | R | RBI | TBB | IBB | SO | HBP | SH | SF | SB | CS | SB% | GDP | Avg | OBP | SLG |
| 1973 Cincinnati | NL | 25 | 86 | 33 | 5 | 1 | 3 | (2 | 1) | 49 | 19 | 14 | 6 | 0 | 10 | 0 | 0 | 0 | 4 | 2 | .67 | 0 | .384 | .424 | .570 |
| 1974 Cincinnati | NL | 88 | 227 | 57 | 9 | 5 | 2 | (2 | 0) | 82 | 24 | 19 | 27 | 2 | 43 | 1 | 1 | 0 | 9 | 4 | .69 | 2 | .251 | .333 | .361 |
| 1975 Cincinnati | NL | 132 | 463 | 141 | 15 | 9 | 4 | (1 | 3) | 186 | 95 | 46 | 67 | 2 | 67 | 1 | 6 | 3 | 16 | 7 | .70 | 10 | .305 | .391 | .402 |
| 1976 Cincinnati | NL | 148 | 562 | 189 | 28 | 9 | 6 | (2 | 4) | 253 | 111 | 74 | 62 | 0 | 65 | 1 | 0 | 3 | 34 | 11 | .76 | 3 | .336 | .401 | .450 |
| 1977 Cincinnati | NL | 154 | 585 | 186 | 35 | 8 | 12 | (4 | 8) | 273 | 117 | 57 | 69 | 2 | 84 | 0 | 1 | 2 | 17 | 8 | .68 | 12 | .318 | .389 | .467 |
| 1978 Cincinnati | NL | 158 | 614 | 177 | 33 | 8 | 10 | (7 | 3) | 256 | 90 | 63 | 54 | 1 | 70 | 0 | 9 | 3 | 23 | 5 | .82 | 6 | .288 | .344 | .417 |
| 1979 Cincinnati | NL | 95 | 380 | 120 | 27 | 4 | 8 | (3 | 5) | 179 | 62 | 32 | 36 | 3 | 39 | 1 | 0 | 3 | 12 | 5 | .71 | 7 | .316 | .374 | .471 |
| 1980 Cincinnati | NL | 146 | 544 | 160 | 28 | 10 | 13 | (9 | 4) | 247 | 89 | 85 | 62 | 4 | 77 | 1 | 3 | 5 | 23 | 1 | .96 | 4 | .294 | .364 | .454 |
| 1981 Cincinnati | NL | 101 | 396 | 123 | 21 | 6 | 2 | (0 | 2) | 162 | 65 | 34 | 39 | 6 | 42 | 1 | 2 | 4 | 12 | 4 | .75 | 9 | .311 | .370 | .409 |
| 1982 New York | AL | 127 | 484 | 134 | 23 | 2 | 12 | (8 | 4) | 197 | 70 | 54 | 39 | 1 | 58 | 0 | 1 | 3 | 10 | 4 | .71 | 10 | .277 | .329 | .407 |
| 1983 New York | AL | 118 | 458 | 140 | 21 | 3 | 11 | (8 | 3) | 200 | 60 | 46 | 34 | 3 | 45 | 2 | 3 | 2 | 6 | 1 | .86 | 3 | .306 | .355 | .437 |
| 1984 New York | AL | 120 | 399 | 109 | 20 | 1 | 7 | (5 | 2) | 152 | 44 | 56 | 29 | 2 | 32 | 1 | 3 | 4 | 2 | 2 | .50 | 7 | .273 | .321 | .381 |
| 1985 New York | AL | 127 | 438 | 120 | 28 | 4 | 10 | (6 | 4) | 186 | 68 | 69 | 41 | 4 | 51 | 0 | 0 | 8 | 7 | 7 | .50 | 2 | .274 | .331 | .425 |
| 1986 2 ML Teams | | 139 | 490 | 150 | 22 | 3 | 21 | (14 | 7) | 241 | 69 | 58 | 35 | 4 | 67 | 1 | 1 | 5 | 14 | 9 | .61 | 9 | .306 | .350 | .492 |
| 1987 Atlanta | NL | 122 | 399 | 114 | 24 | 1 | 14 | (8 | 6) | 182 | 65 | 64 | 46 | 11 | 54 | 1 | 1 | 4 | 4 | 7 | .36 | 12 | .286 | .358 | .456 |
| 1988 2 ML Teams | | 94 | 243 | 62 | 6 | 0 | 4 | (3 | 1) | 80 | 26 | 23 | 19 | 3 | 31 | 0 | 0 | 2 | 1 | 3 | .25 | 5 | .255 | .307 | .329 |
| 1989 Cincinnati | NL | 106 | 236 | 62 | 8 | 3 | 8 | (2 | 6) | 100 | 26 | 30 | 29 | 3 | 42 | 1 | 0 | 0 | 4 | 2 | .67 | 2 | .263 | .346 | .424 |

| Year | Team | Lg | G | AB | H | 2B | 3B | HR | (Hm | Rd) | TB | R | RBI | TBB | IBB | SO | HBP | SH | SF | SB | CS | SB% | GDP | Avg | OBP | SLG |
|---|---|---|---|---|---|---|---|---|---|---|---|---|---|---|---|---|---|---|---|---|---|---|---|---|---|---|
| 1990 | 2 ML Teams | | 67 | 140 | 42 | 4 | 0 | 4 | (2 | 2) | 58 | 19 | 26 | 12 | 0 | 8 | 1 | 0 | 3 | 2 | 1 | .67 | 1 | .300 | .353 | .414 |
| 1986 | New York | AL | 59 | 198 | 60 | 7 | 0 | 9 | (5 | 4) | 94 | 33 | 26 | 15 | 0 | 24 | 1 | 1 | 4 | 2 | 2 | .50 | 7 | .303 | .349 | .475 |
| | Atlanta | NL | 80 | 292 | 90 | 15 | 3 | 12 | (9 | 3) | 147 | 36 | 32 | 20 | 4 | 43 | 0 | 0 | 1 | 12 | 7 | .63 | 2 | .308 | .351 | .503 |
| 1988 | Atlanta | NL | 69 | 193 | 48 | 5 | 0 | 2 | (2 | 0) | 59 | 21 | 19 | 17 | 2 | 26 | 0 | 0 | 2 | 1 | 3 | .25 | 5 | .249 | .307 | .306 |
| | Cincinnati | NL | 25 | 50 | 14 | 1 | 0 | 2 | (1 | 1) | 21 | 5 | 4 | 2 | 1 | 5 | 0 | 0 | 0 | 0 | 0 | .00 | 0 | .280 | .308 | .420 |
| 1990 | Cincinnati | NL | 46 | 63 | 13 | 2 | 0 | 1 | (1 | 0) | 18 | 6 | 8 | 2 | 0 | 5 | 1 | 0 | 2 | 2 | 1 | .67 | 0 | .206 | .235 | .286 |
| | Seattle | AL | 21 | 77 | 29 | 2 | 0 | 3 | (1 | 2) | 40 | 13 | 18 | 10 | 0 | 3 | 0 | 0 | 1 | 0 | 0 | .00 | 1 | .377 | .443 | .519 |
| | 18 ML YEARS | | 2067 | 7144 | 2119 | 357 | 77 | 151 | (86 | 65) | 3083 | 1119 | 850 | 706 | 51 | 885 | 13 | 31 | 54 | 200 | 83 | .71 | 104 | .297 | .358 | .432 |

## Alfredo Griffin

**Bats:** Both **Throws:** Right **Pos:** SS **Ht:** 5'11" **Wt:** 165 **Born:** 03/06/57 **Age:** 34

| | | | BATTING | | | | | | | | | | | | | | | | | BASERUNNING | | | | PERCENTAGES | | |
|---|---|---|---|---|---|---|---|---|---|---|---|---|---|---|---|---|---|---|---|---|---|---|---|---|---|---|
| Year | Team | Lg | G | AB | H | 2B | 3B | HR | (Hm | Rd) | TB | R | RBI | TBB | IBB | SO | HBP | SH | SF | SB | CS | SB% | GDP | Avg | OBP | SLG |
| 1976 | Cleveland | AL | 12 | 4 | 1 | 0 | 0 | 0 | (0 | 0) | 1 | 0 | 0 | 0 | 0 | 2 | 0 | 0 | 0 | 0 | 1 | .00 | 0 | .250 | .250 | .250 |
| 1977 | Cleveland | AL | 14 | 41 | 6 | 1 | 0 | 0 | (0 | 0) | 7 | 5 | 3 | 3 | 0 | 5 | 0 | 0 | 0 | 2 | 2 | .50 | 1 | .146 | .205 | .171 |
| 1978 | Cleveland | AL | 5 | 4 | 2 | 1 | 0 | 0 | (0 | 0) | 3 | 1 | 0 | 2 | 0 | 1 | 0 | 0 | 0 | 0 | 0 | .00 | 0 | .500 | .667 | .750 |
| 1979 | Toronto | AL | 153 | 624 | 179 | 22 | 10 | 2 | (2 | 0) | 227 | 81 | 31 | 40 | 0 | 59 | 5 | 16 | 4 | 21 | 16 | .57 | 10 | .287 | .333 | .364 |
| 1980 | Toronto | AL | 155 | 653 | 166 | 26 | 15 | 2 | (1 | 1) | 228 | 63 | 41 | 24 | 2 | 58 | 4 | 10 | 5 | 18 | 23 | .44 | 8 | .254 | .283 | .349 |
| 1981 | Toronto | AL | 101 | 388 | 81 | 19 | 6 | 0 | (0 | 0) | 112 | 30 | 21 | 17 | 1 | 38 | 1 | 6 | 2 | 8 | 12 | .40 | 6 | .209 | .243 | .289 |
| 1982 | Toronto | AL | 162 | 539 | 130 | 20 | 8 | 1 | (0 | 1) | 169 | 57 | 48 | 22 | 0 | 48 | 0 | 11 | 4 | 10 | 8 | .56 | 7 | .241 | .269 | .314 |
| 1983 | Toronto | AL | 162 | 528 | 132 | 22 | 9 | 4 | (2 | 2) | 184 | 62 | 47 | 27 | 0 | 44 | 3 | 11 | 3 | 8 | 11 | .42 | 5 | .250 | .289 | .348 |
| 1984 | Toronto | AL | 140 | 419 | 101 | 8 | 2 | 4 | (1 | 3) | 125 | 53 | 30 | 4 | 0 | 33 | 1 | 13 | 4 | 11 | 3 | .79 | 5 | .241 | .248 | .298 |
| 1985 | Oakland | AL | 162 | 614 | 166 | 18 | 7 | 2 | (0 | 2) | 204 | 75 | 64 | 20 | 1 | 50 | 0 | 5 | 7 | 24 | 9 | .73 | 6 | .270 | .290 | .332 |
| 1986 | Oakland | AL | 162 | 594 | 169 | 23 | 6 | 4 | (1 | 3) | 216 | 74 | 51 | 35 | 6 | 52 | 2 | 12 | 6 | 33 | 16 | .67 | 5 | .285 | .323 | .364 |
| 1987 | Oakland | AL | 144 | 494 | 130 | 23 | 5 | 3 | (2 | 1) | 172 | 69 | 60 | 28 | 2 | 41 | 4 | 10 | 3 | 26 | 13 | .67 | 9 | .263 | .306 | .348 |
| 1988 | Los Angeles | NL | 95 | 316 | 63 | 8 | 3 | 1 | (0 | 1) | 80 | 39 | 27 | 24 | 7 | 30 | 2 | 11 | 1 | 7 | 5 | .58 | 3 | .199 | .259 | .253 |
| 1989 | Los Angeles | NL | 136 | 506 | 125 | 27 | 2 | 0 | (0 | 0) | 156 | 49 | 29 | 29 | 2 | 57 | 0 | 11 | 1 | 10 | 7 | .59 | 5 | .247 | .287 | .308 |
| 1990 | Los Angeles | NL | 141 | 461 | 97 | 11 | 3 | 1 | (0 | 1) | 117 | 38 | 35 | 29 | 11 | 65 | 2 | 6 | 4 | 6 | 3 | .67 | 5 | .210 | .258 | .254 |
| | 15 ML YEARS | | 1744 | 6185 | 1548 | 229 | 76 | 24 | (9 | 15) | 2001 | 696 | 487 | 304 | 32 | 583 | 24 | 122 | 44 | 184 | 129 | .59 | 75 | .250 | .286 | .324 |

## Jason Grimsley

**Pitches:** Right **Bats:** Right **Pos:** SP **Ht:** 6' 3" **Wt:** 180 **Born:** 08/07/67 **Age:** 23

| | | | HOW MUCH HE PITCHED | | | | | | WHAT HE GAVE UP | | | | | | | | | | | | THE RESULTS | | | | | |
|---|---|---|---|---|---|---|---|---|---|---|---|---|---|---|---|---|---|---|---|---|---|---|---|---|---|---|
| Year | Team | Lg | G | GS | CG | GF | IP | BFP | H | R | ER | HR | SH | SF | HB | TBB | IBB | SO | WP | Bk | W | L | Pct. | ShO | Sv | ERA |
| 1985 | Bend | A | 6 | 1 | 0 | 2 | 11.1 | 0 | 12 | 21 | 17 | 0 | 0 | 0 | 1 | 25 | 0 | 10 | 3 | 0 | 0 | 1 | .000 | 0 | 0 | 13.50 |
| 1986 | Utica | A | 14 | 14 | 3 | 0 | 64.2 | 342 | 63 | 61 | 46 | 3 | 1 | 2 | 11 | 77 | 0 | 46 | 18 | 0 | 1 | 10 | .091 | 0 | 0 | 6.40 |
| 1987 | Spartanburg | A | 23 | 9 | 3 | 7 | 88.1 | 380 | 59 | 48 | 31 | 4 | 2 | 5 | 6 | 54 | 2 | 98 | 12 | 0 | 7 | 4 | .636 | 0 | 0 | 3.16 |
| 1988 | Clearwater | A | 16 | 15 | 2 | 1 | 101.1 | 422 | 80 | 48 | 42 | 2 | 4 | 4 | 9 | 37 | 1 | 90 | 12 | 2 | 4 | 7 | .364 | 0 | 0 | 3.73 |
| | Reading | AA | 5 | 4 | 0 | 1 | 21.1 | 98 | 20 | 19 | 17 | 1 | 1 | 1 | 1 | 13 | 1 | 14 | 1 | 0 | 1 | 3 | .250 | 0 | 0 | 7.17 |
| 1989 | Reading | AA | 26 | 26 | 8 | 0 | 172 | 727 | 121 | 65 | 57 | 13 | 6 | 3 | 10 | 109 | 4 | 134 | 12 | 0 | 11 | 8 | .579 | 2 | 0 | 2.98 |
| 1990 | Scr Wil-Bar | AAA | 22 | 22 | 0 | 0 | 128.1 | 563 | 111 | 68 | 56 | 7 | 4 | 6 | 4 | 78 | 1 | 99 | 18 | 3 | 8 | 5 | .615 | 0 | 0 | 3.93 |
| 1989 | Philadelphia | NL | 4 | 4 | 0 | 0 | 18.1 | 91 | 19 | 13 | 12 | 2 | 1 | 0 | 0 | 19 | 1 | 7 | 2 | 0 | 1 | 3 | .250 | 0 | 0 | 5.89 |
| 1990 | Philadelphia | NL | 11 | 11 | 0 | 0 | 57.1 | 255 | 47 | 21 | 21 | 1 | 2 | 1 | 2 | 43 | 0 | 41 | 6 | 1 | 3 | 2 | .600 | 0 | 0 | 3.30 |
| | 2 ML YEARS | | 15 | 15 | 0 | 0 | 75.2 | 346 | 66 | 34 | 33 | 3 | 3 | 1 | 2 | 62 | 1 | 48 | 8 | 1 | 4 | 5 | .444 | 0 | 0 | 3.93 |

## Marquis Grissom

**Bats:** Right **Throws:** Right **Pos:** RF/LF/CF **Ht:** 5'11" **Wt:** 190 **Born:** 04/17/67 **Age:** 24

| | | | BATTING | | | | | | | | | | | | | | | | | BASERUNNING | | | | PERCENTAGES | | |
|---|---|---|---|---|---|---|---|---|---|---|---|---|---|---|---|---|---|---|---|---|---|---|---|---|---|---|
| Year | Team | Lg | G | AB | H | 2B | 3B | HR | (Hm | Rd) | TB | R | RBI | TBB | IBB | SO | HBP | SH | SF | SB | CS | SB% | GDP | Avg | OBP | SLG |
| 1988 | Jamestown | A | 74 | 291 | 94 | 14 | 7 | 8 | -- | -- | 146 | 69 | 39 | 35 | 2 | 39 | 2 | 2 | 5 | 23 | 7 | .77 | 2 | .323 | .393 | .502 |
| 1989 | Jacksonville | AA | 78 | 278 | 83 | 15 | 4 | 3 | -- | -- | 115 | 43 | 31 | 24 | 1 | 31 | 7 | 1 | 3 | 24 | 6 | .80 | 1 | .299 | .365 | .414 |
| | Indianapols | AAA | 49 | 187 | 52 | 10 | 4 | 2 | -- | -- | 76 | 28 | 21 | 14 | 0 | 23 | 0 | 0 | 1 | 16 | 4 | .80 | 2 | .278 | .327 | .406 |
| 1990 | Indianapols | AAA | 5 | 22 | 4 | 0 | 0 | 2 | -- | -- | 10 | 3 | 3 | 0 | 0 | 5 | 0 | 0 | 0 | 1 | 0 | 1.00 | 0 | .182 | .182 | .455 |
| 1989 | Montreal | NL | 26 | 74 | 19 | 2 | 0 | 1 | (0 | 1) | 24 | 16 | 2 | 12 | 0 | 21 | 0 | 1 | 0 | 1 | 0 | 1.00 | 1 | .257 | .360 | .324 |
| 1990 | Montreal | NL | 98 | 288 | 74 | 14 | 2 | 3 | (2 | 1) | 101 | 42 | 29 | 27 | 2 | 40 | 0 | 4 | 1 | 22 | 2 | .92 | 3 | .257 | .320 | .351 |
| | 2 ML YEARS | | 124 | 362 | 93 | 16 | 2 | 4 | (2 | 2) | 125 | 58 | 31 | 39 | 2 | 61 | 0 | 5 | 1 | 23 | 2 | .92 | 4 | .257 | .328 | .345 |

## Kevin Gross

**Pitches:** Right **Bats:** Right **Pos:** SP/RP **Ht:** 6' 5" **Wt:** 215 **Born:** 06/08/61 **Age:** 30

| | | | HOW MUCH HE PITCHED | | | | | | WHAT HE GAVE UP | | | | | | | | | | | | THE RESULTS | | | | | |
|---|---|---|---|---|---|---|---|---|---|---|---|---|---|---|---|---|---|---|---|---|---|---|---|---|---|---|
| Year | Team | Lg | G | GS | CG | GF | IP | BFP | H | R | ER | HR | SH | SF | HB | TBB | IBB | SO | WP | Bk | W | L | Pct. | ShO | Sv | ERA |
| 1983 | Philadelphia | NL | 17 | 17 | 1 | 0 | 96 | 418 | 100 | 46 | 38 | 13 | 2 | 1 | 3 | 35 | 3 | 66 | 4 | 1 | 4 | 6 | .400 | 1 | 0 | 3.56 |
| 1984 | Philadelphia | NL | 44 | 14 | 1 | 9 | 129 | 566 | 140 | 66 | 59 | 8 | 9 | 3 | 5 | 44 | 4 | 84 | 4 | 4 | 8 | 5 | .615 | 0 | 1 | 4.12 |
| 1985 | Philadelphia | NL | 38 | 31 | 6 | 0 | 205.2 | 873 | 194 | 86 | 78 | 11 | 7 | 5 | 7 | 81 | 6 | 151 | 2 | 0 | 15 | 13 | .536 | 2 | 0 | 3.41 |
| 1986 | Philadelphia | NL | 37 | 36 | 7 | 0 | 241.2 | 1040 | 240 | 115 | 108 | 28 | 8 | 5 | 8 | 94 | 2 | 154 | 2 | 1 | 12 | 12 | .500 | 2 | 0 | 4.02 |
| 1987 | Philadelphia | NL | 34 | 33 | 3 | 1 | 200.2 | 878 | 205 | 107 | 97 | 26 | 8 | 6 | 10 | 87 | 7 | 110 | 3 | 7 | 9 | 16 | .360 | 1 | 0 | 4.35 |
| 1988 | Philadelphia | NL | 33 | 33 | 5 | 0 | 231.2 | 989 | 209 | 101 | 95 | 18 | 9 | 4 | 11 | 89 | 5 | 162 | 5 | 7 | 12 | 14 | .462 | 1 | 0 | 3.69 |
| 1989 | Montreal | NL | 31 | 31 | 4 | 0 | 201.1 | 867 | 188 | 105 | 98 | 20 | 10 | 3 | 6 | 88 | 6 | 158 | 5 | 5 | 11 | 12 | .478 | 3 | 0 | 4.38 |

| Year Team | Lg | G | GS | CG | GF | IP | BFP | H | R | ER | HR | SH | SF | HB | TBB | IBB | SO | WP | Bk | W | L | Pct. | ShO | Sv | ERA |
|---|---|---|---|---|---|---|---|---|---|---|---|---|---|---|---|---|---|---|---|---|---|---|---|---|---|
| 1990 Montreal | NL | 31 | 26 | 2 | 3 | 163.1 | 712 | 171 | 86 | 83 | 9 | 6 | 9 | 4 | 65 | 7 | 111 | 4 | 1 | 9 | 12 | .429 | 1 | 0 | 4.57 |
| 8 ML YEARS | | 265 | 221 | 29 | 13 | 1469.1 | 6343 | 1447 | 712 | 656 | 133 | 59 | 36 | 54 | 583 | 40 | 996 | 29 | 26 | 80 | 90 | .471 | 11 | 1 | 4.02 |

## Kip Gross

**Pitches:** Right **Bats:** Right **Pos:** RP **Ht:** 6' 2" **Wt:** 195 **Born:** 08/24/64 **Age:** 26

| | | HOW MUCH HE PITCHED | | | | | | WHAT HE GAVE UP | | | | | | | | | | | | THE RESULTS | | | | | |
|---|---|---|---|---|---|---|---|---|---|---|---|---|---|---|---|---|---|---|---|---|---|---|---|---|---|
| Year Team | Lg | G | GS | CG | GF | IP | BFP | H | R | ER | HR | SH | SF | HB | TBB | IBB | SO | WP | Bk | W | L | Pct. | ShO | Sv | ERA |
| 1987 Lynchburg | A | 16 | 15 | 2 | 0 | 89.1 | 379 | 92 | 37 | 27 | 1 | 2 | 3 | 6 | 22 | 1 | 39 | 1 | 1 | 7 | 4 | .636 | 0 | 0 | 2.72 |
| 1988 St. Lucie | A | 28 | 27 | 7 | 1 | 178.1 | 736 | 153 | 72 | 52 | 1 | 1 | 3 | 7 | 53 | 6 | 124 | 10 | 11 | 13 | 9 | .591 | 3 | 0 | 2.62 |
| 1989 Jackson | AA | 16 | 16 | 4 | 0 | 112 | 444 | 96 | 47 | 31 | 9 | 4 | 2 | 2 | 13 | 0 | 60 | 4 | 4 | 6 | 5 | .545 | 0 | 0 | 2.49 |
| Tidewater | AAA | 12 | 12 | 0 | 0 | 70.1 | 289 | 72 | 33 | 31 | 3 | 5 | 2 | 1 | 17 | 0 | 39 | 1 | 1 | 4 | 4 | .500 | 0 | 0 | 3.97 |
| 1990 Nashville | AAA | 40 | 11 | 2 | 11 | 127 | 521 | 113 | 54 | 47 | 6 | 6 | 2 | 7 | 47 | 3 | 62 | 6 | 3 | 12 | 7 | .632 | 1 | 3 | 3.33 |
| 1990 Cincinnati | NL | 5 | 0 | 0 | 2 | 6.1 | 25 | 6 | 3 | 3 | 0 | 0 | 1 | 0 | 2 | 0 | 3 | 0 | 0 | 0 | 0 | .000 | 0 | 0 | 4.26 |

## Kelly Gruber

**Bats:** Right **Throws:** Right **Pos:** 3B **Ht:** 6' 0" **Wt:** 185 **Born:** 02/26/62 **Age:** 29

| | | BATTING | | | | | | | | | | | | | | | | BASERUNNING | | | | PERCENTAGES | | |
|---|---|---|---|---|---|---|---|---|---|---|---|---|---|---|---|---|---|---|---|---|---|---|---|---|
| Year Team | Lg | G | AB | H | 2B | 3B | HR | (Hm | Rd) | TB | R | RBI | TBB | IBB | SO | HBP | SH | SF | SB | CS | SB% | GDP | Avg | OBP | SLG |
| 1984 Toronto | AL | 15 | 16 | 1 | 0 | 0 | 1 | (0 | 1) | 4 | 1 | 2 | 0 | 0 | 5 | 0 | 0 | 0 | 0 | 0 | .00 | 1 | .063 | .063 | .250 |
| 1985 Toronto | AL | 5 | 13 | 3 | 0 | 0 | 0 | (0 | 0) | 3 | 0 | 1 | 0 | 0 | 3 | 0 | 0 | 0 | 0 | 0 | .00 | 0 | .231 | .231 | .231 |
| 1986 Toronto | AL | 87 | 143 | 28 | 4 | 1 | 5 | (4 | 1) | 49 | 20 | 15 | 5 | 0 | 27 | 0 | 2 | 2 | 2 | 5 | .29 | 4 | .196 | .220 | .343 |
| 1987 Toronto | AL | 138 | 341 | 80 | 14 | 3 | 12 | (5 | 7) | 136 | 50 | 36 | 17 | 2 | 70 | 7 | 1 | 2 | 12 | 2 | .86 | 11 | .235 | .283 | .399 |
| 1988 Toronto | AL | 158 | 569 | 158 | 33 | 5 | 16 | (5 | 11) | 249 | 75 | 81 | 38 | 1 | 92 | 7 | 5 | 4 | 23 | 5 | .82 | 20 | .278 | .328 | .438 |
| 1989 Toronto | AL | 135 | 545 | 158 | 24 | 4 | 18 | (8 | 10) | 244 | 83 | 73 | 30 | 0 | 60 | 3 | 0 | 5 | 10 | 5 | .67 | 13 | .290 | .328 | .448 |
| 1990 Toronto | AL | 150 | 592 | 162 | 36 | 6 | 31 | (23 | 8) | 303 | 92 | 118 | 48 | 2 | 94 | 8 | 1 | 13 | 14 | 2 | .88 | 14 | .274 | .330 | .512 |
| 7 ML YEARS | | 688 | 2219 | 590 | 111 | 19 | 83 | (45 | 38) | 988 | 321 | 326 | 138 | 5 | 351 | 25 | 9 | 26 | 61 | 19 | .76 | 63 | .266 | .313 | .445 |

## Cecilio Guante

**Pitches:** Right **Bats:** Right **Pos:** RP **Ht:** 6' 3" **Wt:** 205 **Born:** 02/02/60 **Age:** 31

| | | HOW MUCH HE PITCHED | | | | | | WHAT HE GAVE UP | | | | | | | | | | | | THE RESULTS | | | | | |
|---|---|---|---|---|---|---|---|---|---|---|---|---|---|---|---|---|---|---|---|---|---|---|---|---|---|
| Year Team | Lg | G | GS | CG | GF | IP | BFP | H | R | ER | HR | SH | SF | HB | TBB | IBB | SO | WP | Bk | W | L | Pct. | ShO | Sv | ERA |
| 1982 Pittsburgh | NL | 10 | 0 | 0 | 1 | 27 | 117 | 28 | 16 | 10 | 1 | 0 | 4 | 2 | 5 | 0 | 26 | 0 | 0 | 0 | 0 | .000 | 0 | 0 | 3.33 |
| 1983 Pittsburgh | NL | 49 | 0 | 0 | 19 | 100.1 | 431 | 90 | 45 | 37 | 5 | 7 | 2 | 2 | 46 | 6 | 82 | 3 | 0 | 2 | 6 | .250 | 0 | 9 | 3.32 |
| 1984 Pittsburgh | NL | 27 | 0 | 0 | 15 | 41.1 | 166 | 32 | 12 | 12 | 3 | 2 | 3 | 2 | 16 | 2 | 30 | 0 | 1 | 2 | 3 | .400 | 0 | 2 | 2.61 |
| 1985 Pittsburgh | NL | 63 | 0 | 0 | 31 | 109 | 445 | 84 | 34 | 33 | 5 | 4 | 3 | 5 | 40 | 9 | 92 | 5 | 0 | 4 | 6 | .400 | 0 | 5 | 2.72 |
| 1986 Pittsburgh | NL | 52 | 0 | 0 | 24 | 78 | 326 | 65 | 32 | 29 | 11 | 3 | 2 | 3 | 29 | 3 | 63 | 2 | 1 | 5 | 2 | .714 | 0 | 4 | 3.35 |
| 1987 New York | AL | 23 | 0 | 0 | 9 | 44 | 195 | 42 | 30 | 28 | 8 | 0 | 4 | 1 | 20 | 0 | 46 | 3 | 0 | 3 | 2 | .600 | 0 | 1 | 5.73 |
| 1988 2 ML Teams | | 63 | 0 | 0 | 40 | 79.2 | 331 | 67 | 26 | 25 | 11 | 2 | 1 | 5 | 26 | 4 | 65 | 0 | 3 | 5 | 6 | .455 | 0 | 12 | 2.82 |
| 1989 Texas | AL | 50 | 0 | 0 | 19 | 69 | 311 | 66 | 35 | 30 | 7 | 2 | 4 | 4 | 36 | 10 | 69 | 1 | 0 | 6 | 6 | .500 | 0 | 2 | 3.91 |
| 1990 Cleveland | AL | 26 | 1 | 0 | 6 | 46.2 | 197 | 38 | 26 | 26 | 10 | 1 | 2 | 3 | 18 | 4 | 30 | 0 | 0 | 2 | 3 | .400 | 0 | 0 | 5.01 |
| 1988 New York | AL | 56 | 0 | 0 | 37 | 75 | 307 | 59 | 25 | 24 | 10 | 2 | 1 | 5 | 22 | 3 | 61 | 0 | 3 | 5 | 6 | .455 | 0 | 11 | 2.88 |
| Texas | AL | 7 | 0 | 0 | 3 | 4.2 | 24 | 8 | 1 | 1 | 1 | 0 | 0 | 0 | 4 | 1 | 4 | 0 | 0 | 0 | 0 | .000 | 0 | 1 | 1.93 |
| 9 ML YEARS | | 363 | 1 | 0 | 164 | 595 | 2519 | 512 | 256 | 230 | 61 | 21 | 25 | 27 | 236 | 38 | 503 | 14 | 5 | 29 | 34 | .460 | 0 | 35 | 3.48 |

## Mark Gubicza

**Pitches:** Right **Bats:** Right **Pos:** SP **Ht:** 6' 5" **Wt:** 220 **Born:** 08/14/62 **Age:** 28

| | | HOW MUCH HE PITCHED | | | | | | WHAT HE GAVE UP | | | | | | | | | | | | THE RESULTS | | | | | |
|---|---|---|---|---|---|---|---|---|---|---|---|---|---|---|---|---|---|---|---|---|---|---|---|---|---|
| Year Team | Lg | G | GS | CG | GF | IP | BFP | H | R | ER | HR | SH | SF | HB | TBB | IBB | SO | WP | Bk | W | L | Pct. | ShO | Sv | ERA |
| 1984 Kansas City | AL | 29 | 29 | 4 | 0 | 189 | 800 | 172 | 90 | 85 | 13 | 4 | 9 | 5 | 75 | 0 | 111 | 3 | 1 | 10 | 14 | .417 | 2 | 0 | 4.05 |
| 1985 Kansas City | AL | 29 | 28 | 0 | 0 | 177.1 | 760 | 160 | 88 | 80 | 14 | 1 | 6 | 5 | 77 | 0 | 99 | 12 | 0 | 14 | 10 | .583 | 0 | 0 | 4.06 |
| 1986 Kansas City | AL | 35 | 24 | 3 | 2 | 180.2 | 765 | 155 | 77 | 73 | 8 | 4 | 8 | 5 | 84 | 2 | 118 | 15 | 0 | 12 | 6 | .667 | 2 | 0 | 3.64 |
| 1987 Kansas City | AL | 35 | 35 | 10 | 0 | 241.2 | 1036 | 231 | 114 | 107 | 18 | 6 | 11 | 6 | 120 | 3 | 166 | 14 | 1 | 13 | 18 | .419 | 2 | 0 | 3.98 |
| 1988 Kansas City | AL | 35 | 35 | 8 | 0 | 269.2 | 1111 | 237 | 94 | 81 | 11 | 3 | 6 | 6 | 83 | 3 | 183 | 12 | 4 | 20 | 8 | .714 | 4 | 0 | 2.70 |
| 1989 Kansas City | AL | 36 | 36 | 8 | 0 | 255 | 1060 | 252 | 100 | 86 | 10 | 11 | 8 | 5 | 63 | 8 | 173 | 9 | 0 | 15 | 11 | .577 | 2 | 0 | 3.04 |
| 1990 Kansas City | AL | 16 | 16 | 2 | 0 | 94 | 409 | 101 | 48 | 47 | 5 | 6 | 4 | 4 | 38 | 4 | 71 | 2 | 1 | 4 | 7 | .364 | 0 | 0 | 4.50 |
| 7 ML YEARS | | 215 | 203 | 35 | 2 | 1407.1 | 5941 | 1308 | 611 | 559 | 79 | 35 | 52 | 36 | 540 | 20 | 921 | 67 | 7 | 88 | 74 | .543 | 12 | 0 | 3.57 |

## Pedro Guerrero

**Bats:** Right **Throws:** Right **Pos:** 1B **Ht:** 6' 0" **Wt:** 195 **Born:** 06/29/56 **Age:** 35

| | | BATTING | | | | | | | | | | | | | | | | BASERUNNING | | | | PERCENTAGES | | |
|---|---|---|---|---|---|---|---|---|---|---|---|---|---|---|---|---|---|---|---|---|---|---|---|---|
| Year Team | Lg | G | AB | H | 2B | 3B | HR | (Hm | Rd) | TB | R | RBI | TBB | IBB | SO | HBP | SH | SF | SB | CS | SB% | GDP | Avg | OBP | SLG |
| 1978 Los Angeles | NL | 5 | 8 | 5 | 0 | 1 | 0 | (0 | 0) | 7 | 3 | 1 | 0 | 0 | 0 | 0 | 0 | 0 | 0 | 0 | .00 | 0 | .625 | .625 | .875 |
| 1979 Los Angeles | NL | 25 | 62 | 15 | 2 | 0 | 2 | (0 | 2) | 23 | 7 | 9 | 1 | 1 | 14 | 0 | 0 | 1 | 2 | 0 | 1.00 | 1 | .242 | .250 | .371 |
| 1980 Los Angeles | NL | 75 | 183 | 59 | 9 | 1 | 7 | (3 | 4) | 91 | 27 | 31 | 12 | 3 | 31 | 0 | 1 | 3 | 2 | 1 | .67 | 2 | .322 | .359 | .497 |
| 1981 Los Angeles | NL | 98 | 347 | 104 | 17 | 2 | 12 | (5 | 7) | 161 | 46 | 48 | 34 | 3 | 57 | 2 | 3 | 1 | 5 | 9 | .36 | 12 | .300 | .365 | .464 |
| 1982 Los Angeles | NL | 150 | 575 | 175 | 27 | 5 | 32 | (15 | 17) | 308 | 87 | 100 | 65 | 16 | 89 | 5 | 4 | 3 | 22 | 5 | .81 | 7 | .304 | .378 | .536 |

| Year | Team | Lg | G | AB | H | 2B | 3B | HR | (Hm | Rd) | TB | R | RBI | TBB | IBB | SO | HBP | SH | SF | SB | CS | SB% | GDP | Avg | OBP | SLG |
|---|---|---|---|---|---|---|---|---|---|---|---|---|---|---|---|---|---|---|---|---|---|---|---|---|---|---|
| 1983 | Los Angeles | NL | 160 | 584 | 174 | 28 | 6 | 32 | (13 | 19) | 310 | 87 | 103 | 72 | 12 | 110 | 2 | 0 | 6 | 23 | 7 | .77 | 11 | .298 | .373 | .531 |
| 1984 | Los Angeles | NL | 144 | 535 | 162 | 29 | 4 | 16 | (7 | 9) | 247 | 85 | 72 | 49 | 7 | 105 | 1 | 1 | 8 | 9 | 8 | .53 | 7 | .303 | .358 | .462 |
| 1985 | Los Angeles | NL | 137 | 487 | 156 | 22 | 2 | 33 | (13 | 20) | 281 | 99 | 87 | 83 | 14 | 68 | 6 | 0 | 5 | 12 | 4 | .75 | 13 | .320 | .422 | .577 |
| 1986 | Los Angeles | NL | 31 | 61 | 15 | 3 | 0 | 5 | (1 | 4) | 33 | 7 | 10 | 2 | 0 | 19 | 1 | 0 | 0 | 0 | 0 | .00 | 1 | .246 | .281 | .541 |
| 1987 | Los Angeles | NL | 152 | 545 | 184 | 25 | 2 | 27 | (12 | 15) | 294 | 89 | 89 | 74 | 18 | 85 | 4 | 0 | 7 | 9 | 7 | .56 | 16 | .338 | .416 | .539 |
| 1988 | 2 ML Teams | | 103 | 364 | 104 | 14 | 2 | 10 | (5 | 5) | 152 | 40 | 65 | 46 | 9 | 59 | 5 | 0 | 7 | 4 | 1 | .80 | 5 | .286 | .367 | .418 |
| 1989 | St. Louis | NL | 162 | 570 | 177 | 42 | 1 | 17 | (3 | 14) | 272 | 60 | 117 | 79 | 13 | 84 | 4 | 0 | 12 | 2 | 0 | 1.00 | 17 | .311 | .391 | .477 |
| 1990 | St. Louis | NL | 136 | 498 | 140 | 31 | 1 | 13 | (8 | 5) | 212 | 42 | 80 | 44 | 14 | 70 | 1 | 0 | 11 | 1 | 1 | .50 | 14 | .281 | .334 | .426 |
| 1988 | Los Angeles | NL | 59 | 215 | 64 | 7 | 1 | 5 | (3 | 2) | 88 | 24 | 35 | 25 | 2 | 33 | 3 | 0 | 3 | 2 | 1 | .67 | 2 | .298 | .374 | .409 |
| | St. Louis | NL | 44 | 149 | 40 | 7 | 1 | 5 | (2 | 3) | 64 | 16 | 30 | 21 | 7 | 26 | 2 | 0 | 4 | 2 | 0 | 1.00 | 3 | .268 | .358 | .430 |
| | 13 ML YEARS | | 1378 | 4819 | 1470 | 249 | 27 | 206 | (85 | 121) | 2391 | 679 | 812 | 561 | 110 | 791 | 31 | 9 | 64 | 91 | 43 | .68 | 106 | .305 | .377 | .496 |

## Lee Guetterman

**Pitches:** Left **Bats:** Left **Pos:** RP **Ht:** 6' 8" **Wt:** 225 **Born:** 11/22/58 **Age:** 32

| | | | HOW MUCH HE PITCHED | | | | | | WHAT HE GAVE UP | | | | | | | | | | | | THE RESULTS | | | | | |
|---|---|---|---|---|---|---|---|---|---|---|---|---|---|---|---|---|---|---|---|---|---|---|---|---|---|---|
| Year | Team | Lg | G | GS | CG | GF | IP | BFP | H | R | ER | HR | SH | SF | HB | TBB | IBB | SO | WP | Bk | W | L | Pct. | ShO | Sv | ERA |
| 1984 | Seattle | AL | 3 | 0 | 0 | 1 | 4.1 | 22 | 9 | 2 | 2 | 0 | 0 | 0 | 0 | 2 | 0 | 2 | 1 | 0 | 0 | 0 | .000 | 0 | 0 | 4.15 |
| 1986 | Seattle | AL | 41 | 4 | 1 | 8 | 76 | 353 | 108 | 67 | 62 | 7 | 3 | 5 | 4 | 30 | 3 | 38 | 2 | 0 | 0 | 4 | .000 | 0 | 0 | 7.34 |
| 1987 | Seattle | AL | 25 | 17 | 2 | 3 | 113.1 | 483 | 117 | 60 | 48 | 13 | 2 | 5 | 2 | 35 | 2 | 42 | 3 | 0 | 11 | 4 | .733 | 1 | 0 | 3.81 |
| 1988 | New York | AL | 20 | 2 | 0 | 7 | 40.2 | 177 | 49 | 21 | 21 | 2 | 1 | 1 | 1 | 14 | 0 | 15 | 2 | 0 | 1 | 2 | .333 | 0 | 0 | 4.65 |
| 1989 | New York | AL | 70 | 0 | 0 | 38 | 103 | 412 | 98 | 31 | 28 | 6 | 4 | 2 | 0 | 26 | 9 | 51 | 4 | 0 | 5 | 5 | .500 | 0 | 13 | 2.45 |
| 1990 | New York | AL | 64 | 0 | 0 | 21 | 93 | 376 | 80 | 37 | 35 | 6 | 8 | 3 | 0 | 26 | 7 | 48 | 1 | 1 | 11 | 7 | .611 | 0 | 2 | 3.39 |
| | 6 ML YEARS | | 223 | 23 | 3 | 78 | 430.1 | 1823 | 461 | 218 | 196 | 34 | 18 | 16 | 7 | 133 | 21 | 196 | 13 | 1 | 28 | 22 | .560 | 1 | 15 | 4.10 |

## Ozzie Guillen

**Bats:** Left **Throws:** Right **Pos:** SS **Ht:** 5'11" **Wt:** 153 **Born:** 01/20/64 **Age:** 27

| | | | BATTING | | | | | | | | | | | | | | | | | BASERUNNING | | | | PERCENTAGES | | |
|---|---|---|---|---|---|---|---|---|---|---|---|---|---|---|---|---|---|---|---|---|---|---|---|---|---|---|
| Year | Team | Lg | G | AB | H | 2B | 3B | HR | (Hm | Rd) | TB | R | RBI | TBB | IBB | SO | HBP | SH | SF | SB | CS | SB% | GDP | Avg | OBP | SLG |
| 1985 | Chicago | AL | 150 | 491 | 134 | 21 | 9 | 1 | (1 | 0) | 176 | 71 | 33 | 12 | 1 | 36 | 1 | 8 | 1 | 7 | 4 | .64 | 5 | .273 | .291 | .358 |
| 1986 | Chicago | AL | 159 | 547 | 137 | 19 | 4 | 2 | (1 | 1) | 170 | 58 | 47 | 12 | 1 | 52 | 1 | 12 | 5 | 8 | 4 | .67 | 14 | .250 | .265 | .311 |
| 1987 | Chicago | AL | 149 | 560 | 156 | 22 | 7 | 2 | (2 | 0) | 198 | 64 | 51 | 22 | 2 | 52 | 1 | 13 | 8 | 25 | 8 | .76 | 10 | .279 | .303 | .354 |
| 1988 | Chicago | AL | 156 | 566 | 148 | 16 | 7 | 0 | (0 | 0) | 178 | 58 | 39 | 25 | 3 | 40 | 2 | 10 | 3 | 25 | 13 | .66 | 14 | .261 | .294 | .314 |
| 1989 | Chicago | AL | 155 | 597 | 151 | 20 | 8 | 1 | (0 | 1) | 190 | 63 | 54 | 15 | 3 | 48 | 0 | 11 | 3 | 36 | 17 | .68 | 8 | .253 | .270 | .318 |
| 1990 | Chicago | AL | 160 | 516 | 144 | 21 | 4 | 1 | (1 | 0) | 176 | 61 | 58 | 26 | 8 | 37 | 1 | 15 | 5 | 13 | 17 | .43 | 6 | .279 | .312 | .341 |
| | 6 ML YEARS | | 929 | 3277 | 870 | 119 | 39 | 7 | (5 | 2) | 1088 | 375 | 282 | 112 | 18 | 265 | 6 | 69 | 25 | 114 | 63 | .64 | 57 | .265 | .289 | .332 |

## Bill Gullickson

**Pitches:** Right **Bats:** Right **Pos:** SP **Ht:** 6' 3" **Wt:** 220 **Born:** 02/20/59 **Age:** 32

| | | | HOW MUCH HE PITCHED | | | | | | WHAT HE GAVE UP | | | | | | | | | | | | THE RESULTS | | | | | |
|---|---|---|---|---|---|---|---|---|---|---|---|---|---|---|---|---|---|---|---|---|---|---|---|---|---|---|
| Year | Team | Lg | G | GS | CG | GF | IP | BFP | H | R | ER | HR | SH | SF | HB | TBB | IBB | SO | WP | Bk | W | L | Pct. | ShO | Sv | ERA |
| 1979 | Montreal | NL | 1 | 0 | 0 | 1 | 1 | 4 | 2 | 0 | 0 | 0 | 0 | 0 | 0 | 0 | 0 | 0 | 0 | 0 | 0 | 0 | .000 | 0 | 0 | 0.00 |
| 1980 | Montreal | NL | 24 | 19 | 5 | 1 | 141 | 593 | 127 | 53 | 47 | 6 | 3 | 4 | 2 | 50 | 2 | 120 | 5 | 0 | 10 | 5 | .667 | 2 | 0 | 3.00 |
| 1981 | Montreal | NL | 22 | 22 | 3 | 0 | 157 | 640 | 142 | 54 | 49 | 3 | 5 | 2 | 4 | 34 | 4 | 115 | 4 | 0 | 7 | 9 | .438 | 2 | 0 | 2.81 |
| 1982 | Montreal | NL | 34 | 34 | 6 | 0 | 236.2 | 990 | 231 | 101 | 94 | 25 | 9 | 6 | 4 | 61 | 2 | 155 | 11 | 3 | 12 | 14 | .462 | 0 | 0 | 3.57 |
| 1983 | Montreal | NL | 34 | 34 | 10 | 0 | 242.1 | 990 | 230 | 108 | 101 | 19 | 4 | 7 | 4 | 59 | 4 | 120 | 4 | 1 | 17 | 12 | .586 | 1 | 0 | 3.75 |
| 1984 | Montreal | NL | 32 | 32 | 3 | 0 | 226.2 | 919 | 230 | 100 | 91 | 27 | 8 | 4 | 1 | 37 | 7 | 100 | 5 | 0 | 12 | 9 | .571 | 0 | 0 | 3.61 |
| 1985 | Montreal | NL | 29 | 29 | 4 | 0 | 181.1 | 759 | 187 | 78 | 71 | 8 | 12 | 8 | 1 | 47 | 9 | 68 | 1 | 1 | 14 | 12 | .538 | 1 | 0 | 3.52 |
| 1986 | Cincinnati | NL | 37 | 37 | 6 | 0 | 244.2 | 1014 | 245 | 103 | 92 | 24 | 12 | 13 | 2 | 60 | 10 | 121 | 3 | 0 | 15 | 12 | .556 | 2 | 0 | 3.38 |
| 1987 | 2 ML Teams | | 35 | 35 | 4 | 0 | 213 | 896 | 218 | 128 | 115 | 40 | 8 | 8 | 3 | 50 | 7 | 117 | 4 | 1 | 14 | 13 | .519 | 1 | 0 | 4.86 |
| 1990 | Houston | NL | 32 | 32 | 2 | 0 | 193.1 | 846 | 221 | 100 | 82 | 21 | 6 | 8 | 2 | 61 | 14 | 73 | 3 | 2 | 10 | 14 | .417 | 1 | 0 | 3.82 |
| 1987 | Cincinnati | NL | 27 | 27 | 3 | 0 | 165 | 698 | 172 | 99 | 89 | 33 | 6 | 6 | 2 | 39 | 6 | 89 | 4 | 1 | 10 | 11 | .476 | 1 | 0 | 4.85 |
| | New York | AL | 8 | 8 | 1 | 0 | 48 | 198 | 46 | 29 | 26 | 7 | 2 | 2 | 1 | 11 | 1 | 28 | 0 | 0 | 4 | 2 | .667 | 0 | 0 | 4.88 |
| | 10 ML YEARS | | 280 | 274 | 43 | 2 | 1837 | 7651 | 1833 | 825 | 742 | 173 | 67 | 60 | 23 | 459 | 59 | 989 | 40 | 8 | 111 | 100 | .526 | 10 | 0 | 3.64 |

## Eric Gunderson

**Pitches:** Left **Bats:** Right **Pos:** SP **Ht:** 6' 0" **Wt:** 175 **Born:** 03/29/66 **Age:** 25

| | | | HOW MUCH HE PITCHED | | | | | | WHAT HE GAVE UP | | | | | | | | | | | | THE RESULTS | | | | | |
|---|---|---|---|---|---|---|---|---|---|---|---|---|---|---|---|---|---|---|---|---|---|---|---|---|---|---|
| Year | Team | Lg | G | GS | CG | GF | IP | BFP | H | R | ER | HR | SH | SF | HB | TBB | IBB | SO | WP | Bk | W | L | Pct. | ShO | Sv | ERA |
| 1987 | Everett | A | 15 | 15 | 5 | 0 | 98.2 | 406 | 80 | 34 | 27 | 4 | 2 | 2 | 3 | 34 | 1 | 99 | 4 | 3 | 8 | 4 | .667 | 3 | 0 | 2.46 |
| 1988 | San Jose | A | 20 | 20 | 5 | 0 | 149.1 | 640 | 131 | 56 | 44 | 2 | 7 | 3 | 17 | 52 | 0 | 151 | 14 | 6 | 12 | 5 | .706 | 4 | 0 | 2.65 |
| | Shreveport | AA | 7 | 6 | 0 | 1 | 36.2 | 166 | 45 | 25 | 21 | 1 | 1 | 1 | 1 | 13 | 0 | 28 | 0 | 1 | 1 | 2 | .333 | 0 | 0 | 5.15 |
| 1989 | Shreveport | AA | 11 | 11 | 2 | 0 | 72.2 | 298 | 68 | 24 | 22 | 1 | 1 | 3 | 1 | 23 | 0 | 61 | 1 | 1 | 8 | 2 | .800 | 1 | 0 | 2.72 |
| | Phoenix | AAA | 14 | 14 | 2 | 0 | 85.2 | 375 | 93 | 51 | 48 | 7 | 5 | 6 | 2 | 36 | 2 | 56 | 7 | 1 | 2 | 4 | .333 | 1 | 0 | 5.04 |
| 1990 | Phoenix | AAA | 16 | 16 | 0 | 0 | 82 | 418 | 137 | 87 | 75 | 11 | 5 | 3 | 3 | 46 | 1 | 41 | 4 | 2 | 5 | 7 | .417 | 0 | 0 | 8.23 |
| | Shreveport | AA | 8 | 8 | 1 | 0 | 52.2 | 225 | 51 | 24 | 19 | 7 | 1 | 3 | 2 | 17 | 1 | 44 | 1 | 0 | 2 | 2 | .500 | 1 | 0 | 3.25 |
| 1990 | San Francisco | NL | 7 | 4 | 0 | 1 | 19.2 | 94 | 24 | 14 | 12 | 2 | 1 | 0 | 0 | 11 | 1 | 14 | 0 | 0 | 1 | 2 | .333 | 0 | 0 | 5.49 |

## Mark Guthrie

**Pitches:** Left **Bats:** Both **Pos:** SP **Ht:** 6' 4" **Wt:** 202 **Born:** 09/22/65 **Age:** 25

| | | HOW MUCH HE PITCHED | | | | | | WHAT HE GAVE UP | | | | | | | | | | | | THE RESULTS | | | | | |
|---|---|---|---|---|---|---|---|---|---|---|---|---|---|---|---|---|---|---|---|---|---|---|---|---|---|
| Year Team | Lg | G | GS | CG | GF | IP | BFP | H | R | ER | HR | SH | SF | HB | TBB | IBB | SO | WP | Bk | W | L | Pct. | ShO | Sv | ERA |
| 1987 Visalia | A | 4 | 1 | 0 | 1 | 12 | 48 | 10 | 7 | 6 | 0 | 2 | 0 | 0 | 5 | 1 | 9 | 2 | 0 | 2 | 1 | .667 | 0 | 0 | 4.50 |
| 1988 Visalia | A | 25 | 25 | 4 | 0 | 171.1 | 742 | 169 | 81 | 63 | 6 | 5 | 3 | 3 | 86 | 1 | 182 | 14 | 7 | 12 | 9 | .571 | 1 | 0 | 3.31 |
| 1989 Orlando | AA | 14 | 14 | 0 | 0 | 96 | 382 | 75 | 32 | 21 | 4 | 4 | 0 | 2 | 38 | 0 | 103 | 3 | 6 | 8 | 3 | .727 | 0 | 0 | 1.97 |
| Portland | AAA | 7 | 7 | 1 | 0 | 44.1 | 189 | 45 | 21 | 18 | 4 | 1 | 3 | 0 | 16 | 0 | 35 | 2 | 0 | 3 | 4 | .429 | 0 | 0 | 3.65 |
| 1990 Portland | AAA | 9 | 8 | 1 | 1 | 42.1 | 178 | 47 | 19 | 14 | 1 | 1 | 1 | 2 | 12 | 0 | 39 | 0 | 1 | 1 | 3 | .250 | 0 | 0 | 2.98 |
| 1989 Minnesota | AL | 13 | 8 | 0 | 2 | 57.1 | 254 | 66 | 32 | 29 | 7 | 1 | 5 | 1 | 21 | 1 | 38 | 1 | 0 | 2 | 4 | .333 | 0 | 0 | 4.55 |
| 1990 Minnesota | AL | 24 | 21 | 3 | 0 | 144.2 | 603 | 154 | 65 | 61 | 8 | 6 | 0 | 1 | 39 | 3 | 101 | 9 | 0 | 7 | 9 | .438 | 1 | 0 | 3.79 |
| 2 ML YEARS | | 37 | 29 | 3 | 2 | 202 | 857 | 220 | 97 | 90 | 15 | 7 | 5 | 2 | 60 | 4 | 139 | 10 | 0 | 9 | 13 | .409 | 1 | 0 | 4.01 |

## Chris Gwynn

**Bats:** Left **Throws:** Left **Pos:** LF **Ht:** 6' 0" **Wt:** 200 **Born:** 10/13/64 **Age:** 26

| | | BATTING | | | | | | | | | | | | | | | | | BASERUNNING | | | | PERCENTAGES | | |
|---|---|---|---|---|---|---|---|---|---|---|---|---|---|---|---|---|---|---|---|---|---|---|---|---|---|
| Year Team | Lg | G | AB | H | 2B | 3B | HR | (Hm | Rd) | TB | R | RBI | TBB | IBB | SO | HBP | SH | SF | SB | CS | SB% | GDP | Avg | OBP | SLG |
| 1987 Los Angeles | NL | 17 | 32 | 7 | 1 | 0 | 0 | (0 | 0) | 8 | 2 | 2 | 1 | 0 | 7 | 0 | 1 | 0 | 0 | 0 | .00 | 0 | .219 | .242 | .250 |
| 1988 Los Angeles | NL | 12 | 11 | 2 | 0 | 0 | 0 | (0 | 0) | 2 | 1 | 0 | 1 | 0 | 2 | 0 | 0 | 0 | 0 | 0 | .00 | 0 | .182 | .250 | .182 |
| 1989 Los Angeles | NL | 32 | 68 | 16 | 4 | 1 | 0 | (0 | 0) | 22 | 8 | 7 | 2 | 0 | 9 | 0 | 2 | 1 | 1 | 0 | 1.00 | 1 | .235 | .254 | .324 |
| 1990 Los Angeles | NL | 101 | 141 | 40 | 2 | 1 | 5 | (0 | 5) | 59 | 19 | 22 | 7 | 2 | 28 | 0 | 0 | 3 | 0 | 1 | .00 | 2 | .284 | .311 | .418 |
| 4 ML YEARS | | 162 | 252 | 65 | 7 | 2 | 5 | (0 | 5) | 91 | 30 | 31 | 11 | 2 | 46 | 0 | 3 | 4 | 1 | 1 | .50 | 3 | .258 | .285 | .361 |

## Tony Gwynn

**Bats:** Left **Throws:** Left **Pos:** RF **Ht:** 5'11" **Wt:** 199 **Born:** 05/09/60 **Age:** 31

| | | BATTING | | | | | | | | | | | | | | | | | BASERUNNING | | | | PERCENTAGES | | |
|---|---|---|---|---|---|---|---|---|---|---|---|---|---|---|---|---|---|---|---|---|---|---|---|---|---|
| Year Team | Lg | G | AB | H | 2B | 3B | HR | (Hm | Rd) | TB | R | RBI | TBB | IBB | SO | HBP | SH | SF | SB | CS | SB% | GDP | Avg | OBP | SLG |
| 1982 San Diego | NL | 54 | 190 | 55 | 12 | 2 | 1 | (0 | 1) | 74 | 33 | 17 | 14 | 0 | 16 | 0 | 4 | 1 | 8 | 3 | .73 | 5 | .289 | .337 | .389 |
| 1983 San Diego | NL | 86 | 304 | 94 | 12 | 2 | 1 | (0 | 1) | 113 | 34 | 37 | 23 | 5 | 21 | 0 | 4 | 3 | 7 | 4 | .64 | 9 | .309 | .355 | .372 |
| 1984 San Diego | NL | 158 | 606 | 213 | 21 | 10 | 5 | (3 | 2) | 269 | 88 | 71 | 59 | 13 | 23 | 2 | 6 | 2 | 33 | 18 | .65 | 15 | .351 | .410 | .444 |
| 1985 San Diego | NL | 154 | 622 | 197 | 29 | 5 | 6 | (3 | 3) | 254 | 90 | 46 | 45 | 4 | 33 | 2 | 1 | 1 | 14 | 11 | .56 | 17 | .317 | .364 | .408 |
| 1986 San Diego | NL | 160 | 642 | 211 | 33 | 7 | 14 | (8 | 6) | 300 | 107 | 59 | 52 | 11 | 35 | 3 | 2 | 2 | 37 | 9 | .80 | 20 | .329 | .381 | .467 |
| 1987 San Diego | NL | 157 | 589 | 218 | 36 | 13 | 7 | (5 | 2) | 301 | 119 | 54 | 82 | 26 | 35 | 3 | 2 | 4 | 56 | 12 | .82 | 13 | .370 | .447 | .511 |
| 1988 San Diego | NL | 133 | 521 | 163 | 22 | 5 | 7 | (3 | 4) | 216 | 64 | 70 | 51 | 13 | 40 | 0 | 4 | 2 | 26 | 11 | .70 | 11 | .313 | .373 | .415 |
| 1989 San Diego | NL | 158 | 604 | 203 | 27 | 7 | 4 | (3 | 1) | 256 | 82 | 62 | 56 | 16 | 30 | 1 | 11 | 7 | 40 | 16 | .71 | 12 | .336 | .389 | .424 |
| 1990 San Diego | NL | 141 | 573 | 177 | 29 | 10 | 4 | (2 | 2) | 238 | 79 | 72 | 44 | 20 | 23 | 1 | 7 | 4 | 17 | 8 | .68 | 13 | .309 | .357 | .415 |
| 9 ML YEARS | | 1201 | 4651 | 1531 | 221 | 61 | 49 | (27 | 22) | 2021 | 696 | 488 | 426 | 108 | 256 | 12 | 41 | 26 | 238 | 92 | .72 | 115 | .329 | .385 | .435 |

## John Habyan

**Pitches:** Right **Bats:** Right **Pos:** RP **Ht:** 6' 2" **Wt:** 198 **Born:** 01/29/64 **Age:** 27

| | | HOW MUCH HE PITCHED | | | | | | WHAT HE GAVE UP | | | | | | | | | | | | THE RESULTS | | | | | |
|---|---|---|---|---|---|---|---|---|---|---|---|---|---|---|---|---|---|---|---|---|---|---|---|---|---|
| Year Team | Lg | G | GS | CG | GF | IP | BFP | H | R | ER | HR | SH | SF | HB | TBB | IBB | SO | WP | Bk | W | L | Pct. | ShO | Sv | ERA |
| 1985 Baltimore | AL | 2 | 0 | 0 | 1 | 2.2 | 12 | 3 | 1 | 0 | 0 | 0 | 0 | 0 | 0 | 0 | 2 | 0 | 0 | 1 | 0 | 1.000 | 0 | 0 | 0.00 |
| 1986 Baltimore | AL | 6 | 5 | 0 | 1 | 26.1 | 117 | 24 | 17 | 13 | 3 | 2 | 1 | 0 | 18 | 2 | 14 | 1 | 0 | 1 | 3 | .250 | 0 | 0 | 4.44 |
| 1987 Baltimore | AL | 27 | 13 | 0 | 4 | 116.1 | 493 | 110 | 67 | 62 | 20 | 4 | 4 | 2 | 40 | 1 | 64 | 3 | 0 | 6 | 7 | .462 | 0 | 1 | 4.80 |
| 1988 Baltimore | AL | 7 | 0 | 0 | 1 | 14.2 | 68 | 22 | 10 | 7 | 2 | 0 | 2 | 0 | 4 | 0 | 4 | 1 | 1 | 1 | 0 | 1.000 | 0 | 0 | 4.30 |
| 1990 New York | AL | 6 | 0 | 0 | 1 | 8.2 | 37 | 10 | 2 | 2 | 0 | 0 | 0 | 1 | 2 | 0 | 4 | 1 | 0 | 0 | 0 | .000 | 0 | 0 | 2.08 |
| 5 ML YEARS | | 48 | 18 | 0 | 8 | 168.2 | 727 | 169 | 97 | 84 | 25 | 6 | 7 | 3 | 64 | 3 | 88 | 6 | 1 | 9 | 10 | .474 | 0 | 1 | 4.48 |

## Chip Hale

**Bats:** Left **Throws:** Right **Pos:** 2B **Ht:** 5'11" **Wt:** 180 **Born:** 12/02/64 **Age:** 26

| | | BATTING | | | | | | | | | | | | | | | | | BASERUNNING | | | | PERCENTAGES | | |
|---|---|---|---|---|---|---|---|---|---|---|---|---|---|---|---|---|---|---|---|---|---|---|---|---|---|
| Year Team | Lg | G | AB | H | 2B | 3B | HR | (Hm | Rd) | TB | R | RBI | TBB | IBB | SO | HBP | SH | SF | SB | CS | SB% | GDP | Avg | OBP | SLG |
| 1987 Kenosha | A | 87 | 339 | 117 | 12 | 7 | 7 | -- | -- | 164 | 65 | 65 | 33 | 4 | 26 | 4 | 0 | 7 | 3 | 3 | .50 | 4 | .345 | .402 | .484 |
| 1988 Orlando | AA | 133 | 482 | 126 | 20 | 1 | 11 | -- | -- | 181 | 62 | 65 | 64 | 3 | 31 | 3 | 5 | 3 | 8 | 3 | .73 | 12 | .261 | .350 | .376 |
| 1989 Portland | AAA | 108 | 411 | 112 | 16 | 9 | 2 | -- | -- | 152 | 49 | 34 | 35 | 2 | 55 | 1 | 5 | 2 | 3 | 2 | .60 | 11 | .273 | .330 | .370 |
| 1990 Portland | AAA | 130 | 479 | 134 | 24 | 2 | 3 | -- | -- | 171 | 71 | 40 | 68 | 3 | 57 | 1 | 7 | 7 | 6 | 6 | .50 | 16 | .280 | .366 | .357 |
| 1989 Minnesota | AL | 28 | 67 | 14 | 3 | 0 | 0 | (0 | 0) | 17 | 6 | 4 | 1 | 0 | 6 | 0 | 1 | 2 | 0 | 0 | .00 | 0 | .209 | .214 | .254 |
| 1990 Minnesota | AL | 1 | 2 | 0 | 0 | 0 | 0 | (0 | 0) | 0 | 0 | 2 | 0 | 0 | 1 | 0 | 0 | 2 | 0 | 0 | .00 | 0 | .000 | .000 | .000 |
| 2 ML YEARS | | 29 | 69 | 14 | 3 | 0 | 0 | (0 | 0) | 17 | 6 | 6 | 1 | 0 | 7 | 0 | 1 | 4 | 0 | 0 | .00 | 0 | .203 | .203 | .246 |

## Drew Hall

**Pitches:** Left **Bats:** Left **Pos:** RP **Ht:** 6' 4" **Wt:** 220 **Born:** 03/27/63 **Age:** 28

| | | HOW MUCH HE PITCHED | | | | | | WHAT HE GAVE UP | | | | | | | | | | | | THE RESULTS | | | | | |
|---|---|---|---|---|---|---|---|---|---|---|---|---|---|---|---|---|---|---|---|---|---|---|---|---|---|
| Year Team | Lg | G | GS | CG | GF | IP | BFP | H | R | ER | HR | SH | SF | HB | TBB | IBB | SO | WP | Bk | W | L | Pct. | ShO | Sv | ERA |
| 1986 Chicago | NL | 5 | 4 | 1 | 1 | 23.2 | 101 | 24 | 12 | 12 | 3 | 1 | 0 | 0 | 10 | 0 | 21 | 0 | 0 | 1 | 2 | .333 | 0 | 1 | 4.56 |
| 1987 Chicago | NL | 21 | 0 | 0 | 7 | 32.2 | 147 | 40 | 31 | 25 | 4 | 1 | 2 | 0 | 14 | 0 | 20 | 1 | 0 | 1 | 1 | .500 | 0 | 0 | 6.89 |
| 1988 Chicago | NL | 19 | 0 | 0 | 8 | 22.1 | 103 | 26 | 20 | 19 | 4 | 3 | 2 | 1 | 9 | 2 | 22 | 0 | 0 | 1 | 1 | .500 | 0 | 1 | 7.66 |

| Year | Team | Lg | G | GS | CG | GF | IP | BFP | H | R | ER | HR | SH | SF | HB | TBB | IBB | SO | WP | Bk | W | L | Pct. | ShO | Sv | ERA |
|---|---|---|---|---|---|---|---|---|---|---|---|---|---|---|---|---|---|---|---|---|---|---|---|---|---|---|
| 1989 | Texas | AL | 38 | 0 | 0 | 6 | 58.1 | 242 | 42 | 24 | 24 | 3 | 2 | 1 | 3 | 33 | 1 | 45 | 1 | 0 | 2 | 1 | .667 | 0 | 0 | 3.70 |
| 1990 | Montreal | NL | 42 | 0 | 0 | 13 | 58.1 | 254 | 52 | 35 | 33 | 6 | 6 | 4 | 0 | 29 | 5 | 40 | 3 | 0 | 4 | 7 | .364 | 0 | 3 | 5.09 |
| | 5 ML YEARS | | 125 | 4 | 1 | 35 | 195.1 | 847 | 184 | 122 | 113 | 20 | 13 | 9 | 4 | 95 | 8 | 148 | 5 | 0 | 9 | 12 | .429 | 0 | 5 | 5.21 |

## Mel Hall

**Bats:** Left **Throws:** Left **Pos:** DH/LF/RF **Ht:** 6' 1" **Wt:** 205 **Born:** 09/16/60 **Age:** 30

| | | | BATTING | | | | | | | | | | | | | | | | | BASERUNNING | | | | PERCENTAGES | | |
|---|---|---|---|---|---|---|---|---|---|---|---|---|---|---|---|---|---|---|---|---|---|---|---|---|---|---|
| Year | Team | Lg | G | AB | H | 2B | 3B | HR | (Hm | Rd) | TB | R | RBI | TBB | IBB | SO | HBP | SH | SF | SB | CS | SB% | GDP | Avg | OBP | SLG |
| 1981 | Chicago | NL | 10 | 11 | 1 | 0 | 0 | 1 | (1 | 0) | 4 | 1 | 2 | 1 | 0 | 4 | 0 | 0 | 0 | 0 | 0 | .00 | 0 | .091 | .167 | .364 |
| 1982 | Chicago | NL | 24 | 80 | 21 | 3 | 2 | 0 | (0 | 0) | 28 | 6 | 4 | 5 | 1 | 17 | 2 | 0 | 1 | 0 | 1 | .00 | 0 | .263 | .318 | .350 |
| 1983 | Chicago | NL | 112 | 410 | 116 | 23 | 5 | 17 | (6 | 11) | 200 | 60 | 56 | 42 | 6 | 101 | 3 | 1 | 2 | 6 | 6 | .50 | 4 | .283 | .352 | .488 |
| 1984 | 2 ML Teams | | 131 | 407 | 108 | 24 | 4 | 11 | (7 | 4) | 173 | 68 | 52 | 47 | 8 | 78 | 2 | 0 | 7 | 3 | 2 | .60 | 5 | .265 | .339 | .425 |
| 1985 | Cleveland | AL | 23 | 66 | 21 | 6 | 0 | 0 | (0 | 0) | 27 | 7 | 12 | 8 | 0 | 12 | 0 | 0 | 1 | 0 | 1 | .00 | 2 | .318 | .387 | .409 |
| 1986 | Cleveland | AL | 140 | 442 | 131 | 29 | 2 | 18 | (8 | 10) | 218 | 68 | 77 | 33 | 8 | 65 | 2 | 0 | 3 | 6 | 2 | .75 | 8 | .296 | .346 | .493 |
| 1987 | Cleveland | AL | 142 | 485 | 136 | 21 | 1 | 18 | (8 | 10) | 213 | 57 | 76 | 20 | 6 | 68 | 1 | 0 | 2 | 5 | 4 | .56 | 7 | .280 | .309 | .439 |
| 1988 | Cleveland | AL | 150 | 515 | 144 | 32 | 4 | 6 | (3 | 3) | 202 | 69 | 71 | 28 | 12 | 50 | 0 | 2 | 8 | 7 | 3 | .70 | 8 | .280 | .312 | .392 |
| 1989 | New York | AL | 113 | 361 | 94 | 9 | 0 | 17 | (11 | 6) | 154 | 54 | 58 | 21 | 4 | 37 | 0 | 1 | 8 | 0 | 0 | .00 | 9 | .260 | .295 | .427 |
| 1990 | New York | AL | 113 | 360 | 93 | 23 | 2 | 12 | (3 | 9) | 156 | 41 | 46 | 6 | 2 | 46 | 2 | 0 | 3 | 0 | 0 | .00 | 7 | .258 | .272 | .433 |
| 1984 | Chicago | NL | 48 | 150 | 42 | 11 | 3 | 4 | (3 | 1) | 71 | 25 | 22 | 12 | 3 | 23 | 0 | 0 | 2 | 2 | 1 | .67 | 2 | .280 | .329 | .473 |
| | Cleveland | AL | 83 | 257 | 66 | 13 | 1 | 7 | (4 | 3) | 102 | 43 | 30 | 35 | 5 | 55 | 2 | 0 | 5 | 1 | 1 | .50 | 3 | .257 | .344 | .397 |
| | 10 ML YEARS | | 958 | 3137 | 865 | 170 | 20 | 100 | (47 | 53) | 1375 | 431 | 454 | 211 | 47 | 478 | 12 | 4 | 35 | 27 | 19 | .59 | 50 | .276 | .320 | .438 |

## Daryl Hamilton

**Bats:** Left **Throws:** Right **Pos:** LF/RF **Ht:** 6' 1" **Wt:** 180 **Born:** 12/03/64 **Age:** 26

| | | | BATTING | | | | | | | | | | | | | | | | | BASERUNNING | | | | PERCENTAGES | | |
|---|---|---|---|---|---|---|---|---|---|---|---|---|---|---|---|---|---|---|---|---|---|---|---|---|---|---|
| Year | Team | Lg | G | AB | H | 2B | 3B | HR | (Hm | Rd) | TB | R | RBI | TBB | IBB | SO | HBP | SH | SF | SB | CS | SB% | GDP | Avg | OBP | SLG |
| 1988 | Milwaukee | AL | 44 | 103 | 19 | 4 | 0 | 1 | (1 | 0) | 26 | 14 | 11 | 12 | 0 | 9 | 1 | 0 | 1 | 7 | 3 | .70 | 2 | .184 | .274 | .252 |
| 1990 | Milwaukee | AL | 89 | 156 | 46 | 5 | 0 | 1 | (1 | 0) | 54 | 27 | 18 | 9 | 0 | 12 | 0 | 3 | 0 | 10 | 3 | .77 | 2 | .295 | .333 | .346 |
| | 2 ML YEARS | | 133 | 259 | 65 | 9 | 0 | 2 | (2 | 0) | 80 | 41 | 29 | 21 | 0 | 21 | 1 | 3 | 1 | 17 | 6 | .74 | 4 | .251 | .309 | .309 |

## Jeff Hamilton

**Bats:** Right **Throws:** Right **Pos:** 3B **Ht:** 6' 3" **Wt:** 214 **Born:** 03/19/64 **Age:** 27

| | | | BATTING | | | | | | | | | | | | | | | | | BASERUNNING | | | | PERCENTAGES | | |
|---|---|---|---|---|---|---|---|---|---|---|---|---|---|---|---|---|---|---|---|---|---|---|---|---|---|---|
| Year | Team | Lg | G | AB | H | 2B | 3B | HR | (Hm | Rd) | TB | R | RBI | TBB | IBB | SO | HBP | SH | SF | SB | CS | SB% | GDP | Avg | OBP | SLG |
| 1986 | Los Angeles | NL | 71 | 147 | 33 | 5 | 0 | 5 | (2 | 3) | 53 | 22 | 19 | 2 | 1 | 43 | 0 | 0 | 2 | 0 | 0 | .00 | 3 | .224 | .232 | .361 |
| 1987 | Los Angeles | NL | 35 | 83 | 18 | 3 | 0 | 0 | (0 | 0) | 21 | 5 | 1 | 7 | 2 | 22 | 1 | 0 | 0 | 0 | 1 | .00 | 0 | .217 | .286 | .253 |
| 1988 | Los Angeles | NL | 111 | 309 | 73 | 14 | 2 | 6 | (4 | 2) | 109 | 34 | 33 | 10 | 1 | 51 | 4 | 2 | 2 | 0 | 2 | .00 | 8 | .236 | .268 | .353 |
| 1989 | Los Angeles | NL | 151 | 548 | 134 | 35 | 1 | 12 | (8 | 4) | 207 | 45 | 56 | 20 | 5 | 71 | 3 | 4 | 6 | 0 | 0 | .00 | 10 | .245 | .272 | .378 |
| 1990 | Los Angeles | NL | 7 | 24 | 3 | 0 | 0 | 0 | (0 | 0) | 3 | 1 | 1 | 0 | 0 | 3 | 0 | 0 | 0 | 0 | 0 | .00 | 1 | .125 | .125 | .125 |
| | 5 ML YEARS | | 375 | 1111 | 261 | 57 | 3 | 23 | (14 | 9) | 393 | 107 | 110 | 39 | 9 | 190 | 8 | 6 | 10 | 0 | 3 | .00 | 22 | .235 | .264 | .354 |

## Atlee Hammaker

**Pitches:** Left **Bats:** Both **Pos:** RP/SP **Ht:** 6' 2" **Wt:** 200 **Born:** 01/24/58 **Age:** 33

| | | | HOW MUCH HE PITCHED | | | | | | WHAT HE GAVE UP | | | | | | | | | | | | THE RESULTS | | | | | |
|---|---|---|---|---|---|---|---|---|---|---|---|---|---|---|---|---|---|---|---|---|---|---|---|---|---|---|
| Year | Team | Lg | G | GS | CG | GF | IP | BFP | H | R | ER | HR | SH | SF | HB | TBB | IBB | SO | WP | Bk | W | L | Pct. | ShO | Sv | ERA |
| 1981 | Kansas City | AL | 10 | 6 | 0 | 2 | 39 | 169 | 44 | 24 | 24 | 2 | 2 | 1 | 0 | 12 | 1 | 11 | 0 | 1 | 1 | 3 | .250 | 0 | 0 | 5.54 |
| 1982 | San Francisco | NL | 29 | 27 | 4 | 0 | 175 | 725 | 189 | 86 | 80 | 16 | 12 | 4 | 2 | 28 | 8 | 102 | 2 | 4 | 12 | 8 | .600 | 1 | 0 | 4.11 |
| 1983 | San Francisco | NL | 23 | 23 | 8 | 0 | 172.1 | 695 | 147 | 57 | 43 | 9 | 10 | 4 | 3 | 32 | 12 | 127 | 6 | 2 | 10 | 9 | .526 | 3 | 0 | 2.25 |
| 1984 | San Francisco | NL | 6 | 6 | 0 | 0 | 33 | 139 | 32 | 10 | 8 | 2 | 3 | 2 | 0 | 9 | 1 | 24 | 0 | 2 | 2 | 0 | 1.000 | 0 | 0 | 2.18 |
| 1985 | San Francisco | NL | 29 | 29 | 1 | 0 | 170.2 | 713 | 161 | 81 | 71 | 17 | 8 | 6 | 0 | 47 | 5 | 100 | 4 | 4 | 5 | 12 | .294 | 1 | 0 | 3.74 |
| 1987 | San Francisco | NL | 31 | 27 | 2 | 1 | 168.1 | 706 | 159 | 73 | 67 | 22 | 3 | 3 | 3 | 57 | 10 | 107 | 8 | 7 | 10 | 10 | .500 | 0 | 0 | 3.58 |
| 1988 | San Francisco | NL | 43 | 17 | 3 | 11 | 144.2 | 607 | 136 | 68 | 60 | 11 | 10 | 4 | 3 | 41 | 9 | 65 | 1 | 2 | 9 | 9 | .500 | 1 | 5 | 3.73 |
| 1989 | San Francisco | NL | 28 | 9 | 0 | 5 | 76.2 | 322 | 78 | 34 | 32 | 5 | 6 | 4 | 1 | 23 | 2 | 30 | 1 | 2 | 6 | 6 | .500 | 0 | 0 | 3.76 |
| 1990 | 2 ML Teams | | 34 | 7 | 0 | 8 | 86.2 | 363 | 85 | 44 | 42 | 8 | 4 | 4 | 0 | 27 | 5 | 44 | 4 | 2 | 4 | 9 | .308 | 0 | 0 | 4.36 |
| 1990 | San Francisco | NL | 25 | 6 | 0 | 5 | 67.1 | 282 | 69 | 33 | 32 | 7 | 4 | 4 | 0 | 21 | 4 | 28 | 3 | 1 | 4 | 5 | .444 | 0 | 0 | 4.28 |
| | San Diego | NL | 9 | 1 | 0 | 3 | 19.1 | 81 | 16 | 11 | 10 | 1 | 0 | 0 | 0 | 6 | 1 | 16 | 1 | 1 | 0 | 4 | .000 | 0 | 0 | 4.66 |
| | 9 ML YEARS | | 233 | 151 | 18 | 27 | 1066.1 | 4439 | 1031 | 477 | 427 | 92 | 58 | 32 | 12 | 276 | 53 | 610 | 26 | 26 | 59 | 66 | .472 | 6 | 5 | 3.60 |

## Chris Hammond

**Pitches:** Left **Bats:** Left **Pos:** SP **Ht:** 6' 1" **Wt:** 190 **Born:** 01/21/66 **Age:** 25

| | | | HOW MUCH HE PITCHED | | | | | | WHAT HE GAVE UP | | | | | | | | | | | | THE RESULTS | | | | | |
|---|---|---|---|---|---|---|---|---|---|---|---|---|---|---|---|---|---|---|---|---|---|---|---|---|---|---|
| Year | Team | Lg | G | GS | CG | GF | IP | BFP | H | R | ER | HR | SH | SF | HB | TBB | IBB | SO | WP | Bk | W | L | Pct. | ShO | Sv | ERA |
| 1986 | Reds | R | 7 | 7 | 1 | 0 | 41.2 | 176 | 27 | 21 | 13 | 0 | 1 | 0 | 0 | 17 | 1 | 53 | 5 | 0 | 3 | 2 | .600 | 0 | 0 | 2.81 |
| | Tampa | A | 5 | 5 | 0 | 0 | 21.2 | 100 | 25 | 8 | 8 | 0 | 0 | 0 | 1 | 13 | 1 | 5 | 1 | 0 | 0 | 2 | .000 | 0 | 0 | 3.32 |
| 1987 | Tampa | A | 25 | 24 | 6 | 1 | 170 | 745 | 174 | 81 | 67 | 10 | 4 | 4 | 3 | 60 | 1 | 126 | 6 | 3 | 11 | 11 | .500 | 0 | 0 | 3.55 |
| 1988 | Chattanooga | AA | 26 | 26 | 4 | 0 | 182.2 | 743 | 127 | 48 | 35 | 2 | 1 | 3 | 3 | 77 | 3 | 127 | 5 | 4 | 16 | 5 | .762 | 2 | 0 | 1.72 |
| 1989 | Nashville | AAA | 24 | 24 | 3 | 0 | 157.1 | 697 | 144 | 69 | 59 | 7 | 6 | 4 | 3 | 96 | 1 | 142 | 9 | 2 | 11 | 7 | .611 | 1 | 0 | 3.38 |

| Year Team | Lg | G | GS | CG | GF | IP | BFP | H | R | ER | HR | SH | SF | HB | TBB | IBB | SO | WP | Bk | W | L | Pct. | ShO | Sv | ERA |
|---|---|---|---|---|---|---|---|---|---|---|---|---|---|---|---|---|---|---|---|---|---|---|---|---|---|
| 1990 Nashville | AAA | 24 | 24 | 5 | 0 | 149 | 611 | 118 | 43 | 36 | 7 | 1 | 3 | 5 | 63 | 1 | 149 | 8 | 7 | 15 | 1 | .938 | 3 | 0 | 2.17 |
| 1990 Cincinnati | NL | 3 | 3 | 0 | 0 | 11.1 | 56 | 13 | 9 | 8 | 2 | 1 | 0 | 0 | 12 | 1 | 4 | 1 | 3 | 0 | 2 | .000 | 0 | 0 | 6.35 |

## Dave Hansen

**Bats:** Left **Throws:** Right **Pos:** 3B **Ht:** 6' 0" **Wt:** 180 **Born:** 11/24/68 **Age:** 22

| | | BATTING | | | | | | | | | | | | | | | | | BASERUNNING | | | | PERCENTAGES | | |
|---|---|---|---|---|---|---|---|---|---|---|---|---|---|---|---|---|---|---|---|---|---|---|---|---|---|
| Year Team | Lg | G | AB | H | 2B | 3B | HR | (Hm | Rd) | TB | R | RBI | TBB | IBB | SO | HBP | SH | SF | SB | CS | SB% | GDP | Avg | OBP | SLG |
| 1986 Great Falls | R | 61 | 204 | 61 | 7 | 3 | 1 | -- | -- | 77 | 39 | 36 | 27 | 0 | 28 | 0 | 1 | 0 | 9 | 3 | .75 | 6 | .299 | .381 | .377 |
| 1987 Bakersfield | A | 132 | 432 | 113 | 22 | 1 | 3 | -- | -- | 146 | 68 | 38 | 65 | 1 | 61 | 4 | 6 | 1 | 4 | 2 | .67 | 11 | .262 | .363 | .338 |
| 1988 Vero Beach | A | 135 | 512 | 149 | 28 | 6 | 7 | -- | -- | 210 | 68 | 81 | 56 | 6 | 46 | 4 | 1 | 9 | 2 | 2 | .50 | 9 | .291 | .360 | .410 |
| 1989 San Antonio | AA | 121 | 464 | 138 | 21 | 4 | 6 | -- | -- | 185 | 72 | 52 | 50 | 5 | 44 | 2 | 0 | 5 | 3 | 2 | .60 | 18 | .297 | .365 | .399 |
| Albuquerque | AAA | 6 | 30 | 8 | 1 | 0 | 2 | -- | -- | 15 | 6 | 10 | 2 | 0 | 3 | 0 | 0 | 0 | 0 | 0 | .00 | 1 | .267 | .313 | .500 |
| 1990 Albuquerque | AAA | 135 | 487 | 154 | 20 | 3 | 11 | -- | -- | 213 | 90 | 92 | 90 | 4 | 54 | 3 | 0 | 9 | 9 | 4 | .69 | 12 | .316 | .419 | .437 |
| 1990 Los Angeles | NL | 5 | 7 | 1 | 0 | 0 | 0 | (0 | 0) | 1 | 0 | 1 | 0 | 0 | 3 | 0 | 0 | 0 | 0 | 0 | .00 | 0 | .143 | .143 | .143 |

## Erik Hanson

**Pitches:** Right **Bats:** Right **Pos:** SP **Ht:** 6' 6" **Wt:** 205 **Born:** 05/18/65 **Age:** 26

| | | HOW MUCH HE PITCHED | | | | | | WHAT HE GAVE UP | | | | | | | | | | | | THE RESULTS | | | | | |
|---|---|---|---|---|---|---|---|---|---|---|---|---|---|---|---|---|---|---|---|---|---|---|---|---|---|
| Year Team | Lg | G | GS | CG | GF | IP | BFP | H | R | ER | HR | SH | SF | HB | TBB | IBB | SO | WP | Bk | W | L | Pct. | ShO | Sv | ERA |
| 1988 Seattle | AL | 6 | 6 | 0 | 0 | 41.2 | 168 | 35 | 17 | 15 | 4 | 3 | 0 | 1 | 12 | 1 | 36 | 2 | 2 | 2 | 3 | .400 | 0 | 0 | 3.24 |
| 1989 Seattle | AL | 17 | 17 | 1 | 0 | 113.1 | 465 | 103 | 44 | 40 | 7 | 4 | 1 | 5 | 32 | 1 | 75 | 3 | 0 | 9 | 5 | .643 | 0 | 0 | 3.18 |
| 1990 Seattle | AL | 33 | 33 | 5 | 0 | 236 | 964 | 205 | 88 | 85 | 15 | 5 | 6 | 2 | 68 | 6 | 211 | 10 | 1 | 18 | 9 | .667 | 1 | 0 | 3.24 |
| 3 ML YEARS | | 56 | 56 | 6 | 0 | 391 | 1597 | 343 | 149 | 140 | 26 | 12 | 7 | 8 | 112 | 8 | 322 | 15 | 3 | 29 | 17 | .630 | 1 | 0 | 3.22 |

## Mike Harkey

**Pitches:** Right **Bats:** Right **Pos:** SP **Ht:** 6' 5" **Wt:** 220 **Born:** 10/25/66 **Age:** 24

| | | HOW MUCH HE PITCHED | | | | | | WHAT HE GAVE UP | | | | | | | | | | | | THE RESULTS | | | | | |
|---|---|---|---|---|---|---|---|---|---|---|---|---|---|---|---|---|---|---|---|---|---|---|---|---|---|
| Year Team | Lg | G | GS | CG | GF | IP | BFP | H | R | ER | HR | SH | SF | HB | TBB | IBB | SO | WP | Bk | W | L | Pct. | ShO | Sv | ERA |
| 1988 Chicago | NL | 5 | 5 | 0 | 0 | 34.2 | 155 | 33 | 14 | 10 | 0 | 5 | 0 | 2 | 15 | 3 | 18 | 2 | 1 | 0 | 3 | .000 | 0 | 0 | 2.60 |
| 1990 Chicago | NL | 27 | 27 | 2 | 0 | 173.2 | 728 | 153 | 71 | 63 | 14 | 5 | 4 | 7 | 59 | 8 | 94 | 8 | 1 | 12 | 6 | .667 | 1 | 0 | 3.26 |
| 2 ML YEARS | | 32 | 32 | 2 | 0 | 208.1 | 883 | 186 | 85 | 73 | 14 | 10 | 4 | 9 | 74 | 11 | 112 | 10 | 2 | 12 | 9 | .571 | 1 | 0 | 3.15 |

## Pete Harnisch

**Pitches:** Right **Bats:** Right **Pos:** SP **Ht:** 6' 0" **Wt:** 195 **Born:** 09/23/66 **Age:** 24

| | | HOW MUCH HE PITCHED | | | | | | WHAT HE GAVE UP | | | | | | | | | | | | THE RESULTS | | | | | |
|---|---|---|---|---|---|---|---|---|---|---|---|---|---|---|---|---|---|---|---|---|---|---|---|---|---|
| Year Team | Lg | G | GS | CG | GF | IP | BFP | H | R | ER | HR | SH | SF | HB | TBB | IBB | SO | WP | Bk | W | L | Pct. | ShO | Sv | ERA |
| 1988 Baltimore | AL | 2 | 2 | 0 | 0 | 13 | 61 | 13 | 8 | 8 | 1 | 2 | 0 | 0 | 9 | 1 | 10 | 1 | 0 | 0 | 2 | .000 | 0 | 0 | 5.54 |
| 1989 Baltimore | AL | 18 | 17 | 2 | 1 | 103.1 | 468 | 97 | 55 | 53 | 10 | 4 | 5 | 5 | 64 | 3 | 70 | 5 | 1 | 5 | 9 | .357 | 0 | 0 | 4.62 |
| 1990 Baltimore | AL | 31 | 31 | 3 | 0 | 188.2 | 821 | 189 | 96 | 91 | 17 | 6 | 5 | 1 | 86 | 5 | 122 | 2 | 2 | 11 | 11 | .500 | 0 | 0 | 4.34 |
| 3 ML YEARS | | 51 | 50 | 5 | 1 | 305 | 1350 | 299 | 159 | 152 | 28 | 12 | 10 | 6 | 159 | 9 | 202 | 8 | 3 | 16 | 22 | .421 | 0 | 0 | 4.49 |

## Brian Harper

**Bats:** Right **Throws:** Right **Pos:** C **Ht:** 6' 2" **Wt:** 195 **Born:** 10/16/59 **Age:** 31

| | | BATTING | | | | | | | | | | | | | | | | | BASERUNNING | | | | PERCENTAGES | | |
|---|---|---|---|---|---|---|---|---|---|---|---|---|---|---|---|---|---|---|---|---|---|---|---|---|---|
| Year Team | Lg | G | AB | H | 2B | 3B | HR | (Hm | Rd) | TB | R | RBI | TBB | IBB | SO | HBP | SH | SF | SB | CS | SB% | GDP | Avg | OBP | SLG |
| 1979 California | AL | 1 | 2 | 0 | 0 | 0 | 0 | (0 | 0) | 0 | 0 | 0 | 0 | 0 | 1 | 0 | 0 | 0 | 0 | 0 | .00 | 0 | .000 | .000 | .000 |
| 1981 California | AL | 4 | 11 | 3 | 0 | 0 | 0 | (0 | 0) | 3 | 1 | 1 | 0 | 0 | 0 | 0 | 0 | 1 | 1 | 0 | 1.00 | 0 | .273 | .250 | .273 |
| 1982 Pittsburgh | NL | 20 | 29 | 8 | 1 | 0 | 2 | (0 | 2) | 15 | 4 | 4 | 1 | 1 | 4 | 0 | 1 | 0 | 0 | 0 | .00 | 1 | .276 | .300 | .517 |
| 1983 Pittsburgh | NL | 61 | 131 | 29 | 4 | 1 | 7 | (5 | 2) | 56 | 16 | 20 | 2 | 0 | 15 | 1 | 2 | 4 | 0 | 0 | .00 | 3 | .221 | .232 | .427 |
| 1984 Pittsburgh | NL | 46 | 112 | 29 | 4 | 0 | 2 | (1 | 1) | 39 | 4 | 11 | 5 | 0 | 11 | 2 | 1 | 1 | 0 | 0 | .00 | 4 | .259 | .300 | .348 |
| 1985 St. Louis | NL | 43 | 52 | 13 | 4 | 0 | 0 | (0 | 0) | 17 | 5 | 8 | 2 | 0 | 3 | 0 | 0 | 1 | 0 | 0 | .00 | 2 | .250 | .273 | .327 |
| 1986 Detroit | AL | 19 | 36 | 5 | 1 | 0 | 0 | (0 | 0) | 6 | 2 | 3 | 3 | 0 | 3 | 0 | 1 | 1 | 0 | 0 | .00 | 1 | .139 | .200 | .167 |
| 1987 Oakland | AL | 11 | 17 | 4 | 1 | 0 | 0 | (0 | 0) | 5 | 1 | 3 | 0 | 0 | 4 | 0 | 1 | 1 | 0 | 0 | .00 | 1 | .235 | .222 | .294 |
| 1988 Minnesota | AL | 60 | 166 | 49 | 11 | 1 | 3 | (0 | 3) | 71 | 15 | 20 | 10 | 1 | 12 | 3 | 2 | 1 | 0 | 3 | .00 | 12 | .295 | .344 | .428 |
| 1989 Minnesota | AL | 126 | 385 | 125 | 24 | 0 | 8 | (4 | 4) | 173 | 43 | 57 | 13 | 3 | 16 | 6 | 4 | 4 | 2 | 4 | .33 | 11 | .325 | .353 | .449 |
| 1990 Minnesota | AL | 134 | 479 | 141 | 42 | 3 | 6 | (1 | 5) | 207 | 61 | 54 | 19 | 2 | 27 | 7 | 0 | 4 | 3 | 2 | .60 | 20 | .294 | .328 | .432 |
| 11 ML YEARS | | 525 | 1420 | 406 | 92 | 5 | 28 | (11 | 17) | 592 | 152 | 181 | 55 | 7 | 96 | 19 | 12 | 18 | 6 | 9 | .40 | 55 | .286 | .317 | .417 |

## Gene Harris

**Pitches:** Right **Bats:** Right **Pos:** RP **Ht:** 5'11" **Wt:** 190 **Born:** 12/05/64 **Age:** 26

| | | HOW MUCH HE PITCHED | | | | | | WHAT HE GAVE UP | | | | | | | | | | | | THE RESULTS | | | | | |
|---|---|---|---|---|---|---|---|---|---|---|---|---|---|---|---|---|---|---|---|---|---|---|---|---|---|
| Year Team | Lg | G | GS | CG | GF | IP | BFP | H | R | ER | HR | SH | SF | HB | TBB | IBB | SO | WP | Bk | W | L | Pct. | ShO | Sv | ERA |
| 1986 Jamestown | A | 4 | 4 | 0 | 0 | 20.1 | 86 | 15 | 8 | 5 | 0 | 0 | 2 | 0 | 11 | 0 | 16 | 0 | 1 | 0 | 2 | .000 | 0 | 0 | 2.21 |
| Burlington | A | 7 | 6 | 4 | 0 | 53.1 | 210 | 37 | 12 | 8 | 1 | 0 | 3 | 1 | 15 | 0 | 32 | 2 | 2 | 4 | 2 | .667 | 3 | 0 | 1.35 |
| Wst Plm Bch | A | 2 | 2 | 0 | 0 | 11 | 52 | 14 | 7 | 5 | 0 | 2 | 1 | 0 | 7 | 0 | 5 | 0 | 0 | 0 | 0 | .000 | 0 | 0 | 4.09 |

| Year Team | Lg | G | GS | CG | GF | IP | BFP | H | R | ER | HR | SH | SF | HB | TBB | IBB | SO | WP | Bk | W | L | Pct. | ShO | Sv | ERA |
|---|---|---|---|---|---|---|---|---|---|---|---|---|---|---|---|---|---|---|---|---|---|---|---|---|---|
| 1987 Wst Plm Bch | A | 26 | 26 | 7 | 0 | 179 | 773 | 178 | 101 | 87 | 7 | 5 | 4 | 2 | 77 | 1 | 121 | 11 | 3 | 9 | 7 | .563 | 1 | 0 | 4.37 |
| 1988 Jacksnville | AA | 18 | 18 | 7 | 0 | 126.2 | 500 | 95 | 43 | 37 | 4 | 2 | 2 | 2 | 45 | 0 | 103 | 7 | 4 | 9 | 5 | .643 | 0 | 0 | 2.63 |
| 1989 Indianapols | AAA | 6 | 0 | 0 | 4 | 11 | 46 | 4 | 0 | 0 | 0 | 4 | 0 | 0 | 10 | 1 | 9 | 0 | 0 | 2 | 0 | 1.000 | 0 | 2 | 0.00 |
| Calgary | AAA | 5 | 0 | 0 | 4 | 6 | 20 | 4 | 0 | 0 | 0 | 0 | 0 | 0 | 1 | 0 | 4 | 0 | 0 | 0 | 0 | .000 | 0 | 2 | 0.00 |
| 1990 Calgary | AAA | 6 | 0 | 0 | 6 | 7.2 | 30 | 7 | 2 | 2 | 0 | 0 | 0 | 0 | 4 | 0 | 9 | 2 | 0 | 3 | 0 | 1.000 | 0 | 2 | 2.35 |
| 1989 2 ML Teams | | 21 | 6 | 0 | 9 | 53.1 | 236 | 63 | 38 | 35 | 4 | 7 | 4 | 1 | 25 | 1 | 25 | 3 | 0 | 2 | 5 | .286 | 0 | 1 | 5.91 |
| 1990 Seattle | AL | 25 | 0 | 0 | 12 | 38 | 176 | 31 | 25 | 20 | 5 | 0 | 2 | 1 | 30 | 5 | 43 | 2 | 0 | 1 | 2 | .333 | 0 | 0 | 4.74 |
| 1989 Montreal | NL | 11 | 0 | 0 | 7 | 20 | 84 | 16 | 11 | 11 | 1 | 7 | 1 | 0 | 10 | 0 | 11 | 3 | 0 | 1 | 1 | .500 | 0 | 0 | 4.95 |
| Seattle | AL | 10 | 6 | 0 | 2 | 33.1 | 152 | 47 | 27 | 24 | 3 | 0 | 3 | 1 | 15 | 1 | 14 | 0 | 0 | 1 | 4 | .200 | 0 | 1 | 6.48 |
| 2 ML YEARS | | 46 | 6 | 0 | 21 | 91.1 | 412 | 94 | 63 | 55 | 9 | 7 | 6 | 2 | 55 | 6 | 68 | 5 | 0 | 3 | 7 | .300 | 0 | 1 | 5.42 |

## Greg Harris

**Pitches:** Right **Bats:** Both **Pos:** SP **Ht:** 5'11" **Wt:** 165 **Born:** 11/02/55 **Age:** 35

| | | HOW MUCH HE PITCHED | | | | | | WHAT HE GAVE UP | | | | | | | | | | | | THE RESULTS | | | | | |
|---|---|---|---|---|---|---|---|---|---|---|---|---|---|---|---|---|---|---|---|---|---|---|---|---|---|
| Year Team | Lg | G | GS | CG | GF | IP | BFP | H | R | ER | HR | SH | SF | HB | TBB | IBB | SO | WP | Bk | W | L | Pct. | ShO | Sv | ERA |
| 1981 New York | NL | 16 | 14 | 0 | 2 | 69 | 300 | 65 | 36 | 34 | 8 | 4 | 1 | 2 | 28 | 2 | 54 | 3 | 2 | 3 | 5 | .375 | 0 | 1 | 4.43 |
| 1982 Cincinnati | NL | 34 | 10 | 1 | 9 | 91.1 | 398 | 96 | 56 | 49 | 12 | 5 | 3 | 2 | 37 | 1 | 67 | 2 | 2 | 2 | 6 | .250 | 0 | 1 | 4.83 |
| 1983 San Diego | NL | 1 | 0 | 0 | 0 | 1 | 9 | 2 | 3 | 3 | 0 | 1 | 0 | 1 | 3 | 2 | 1 | 0 | 0 | 0 | 0 | .000 | 0 | 0 | 27.00 |
| 1984 2 ML Teams | | 34 | 1 | 0 | 14 | 54.1 | 226 | 38 | 18 | 15 | 3 | 2 | 3 | 4 | 25 | 1 | 45 | 3 | 0 | 2 | 2 | .500 | 0 | 3 | 2.48 |
| 1985 Texas | AL | 58 | 0 | 0 | 35 | 113 | 450 | 74 | 35 | 31 | 7 | 3 | 2 | 5 | 43 | 3 | 111 | 2 | 1 | 5 | 4 | .556 | 0 | 11 | 2.47 |
| 1986 Texas | AL | 73 | 0 | 0 | 63 | 111.1 | 462 | 103 | 40 | 35 | 12 | 3 | 6 | 1 | 42 | 6 | 95 | 2 | 1 | 10 | 8 | .556 | 0 | 20 | 2.83 |
| 1987 Texas | AL | 42 | 19 | 0 | 14 | 140.2 | 629 | 157 | 92 | 76 | 18 | 7 | 3 | 4 | 56 | 3 | 106 | 4 | 2 | 5 | 10 | .333 | 0 | 0 | 4.86 |
| 1988 Philadelphia | NL | 66 | 1 | 0 | 19 | 107 | 446 | 80 | 34 | 28 | 7 | 6 | 2 | 4 | 52 | 14 | 71 | 8 | 2 | 4 | 6 | .400 | 0 | 1 | 2.36 |
| 1989 2 ML Teams | | 59 | 0 | 0 | 24 | 103.1 | 442 | 85 | 46 | 38 | 8 | 4 | 3 | 2 | 58 | 9 | 76 | 12 | 0 | 4 | 4 | .500 | 0 | 1 | 3.31 |
| 1990 Boston | AL | 34 | 30 | 1 | 3 | 184.1 | 803 | 186 | 90 | 82 | 13 | 8 | 9 | 6 | 77 | 7 | 117 | 7 | 1 | 13 | 9 | .591 | 0 | 0 | 4.00 |
| 1984 Montreal | NL | 15 | 0 | 0 | 4 | 17.2 | 68 | 10 | 4 | 4 | 0 | 1 | 0 | 2 | 7 | 1 | 15 | 0 | 0 | 0 | 1 | .000 | 0 | 2 | 2.04 |
| San Diego | NL | 19 | 1 | 0 | 10 | 36.2 | 158 | 28 | 14 | 11 | 3 | 1 | 3 | 2 | 18 | 0 | 30 | 3 | 0 | 2 | 1 | .667 | 0 | 1 | 2.70 |
| 1989 Philadelphia | NL | 44 | 0 | 0 | 17 | 75.1 | 324 | 64 | 34 | 30 | 7 | 3 | 2 | 2 | 43 | 7 | 51 | 10 | 0 | 2 | 2 | .500 | 0 | 1 | 3.58 |
| Boston | AL | 15 | 0 | 0 | 7 | 28 | 118 | 21 | 12 | 8 | 1 | 1 | 1 | 0 | 15 | 2 | 25 | 2 | 0 | 2 | 2 | .500 | 0 | 0 | 2.57 |
| 10 ML YEARS | | 417 | 75 | 2 | 183 | 975.1 | 4165 | 886 | 450 | 391 | 88 | 43 | 32 | 31 | 421 | 48 | 743 | 43 | 11 | 48 | 54 | .471 | 0 | 38 | 3.61 |

## Greg W. Harris

**Pitches:** Right **Bats:** Right **Pos:** RP **Ht:** 6' 2" **Wt:** 190 **Born:** 12/01/63 **Age:** 27

| | | HOW MUCH HE PITCHED | | | | | | WHAT HE GAVE UP | | | | | | | | | | | | THE RESULTS | | | | | |
|---|---|---|---|---|---|---|---|---|---|---|---|---|---|---|---|---|---|---|---|---|---|---|---|---|---|
| Year Team | Lg | G | GS | CG | GF | IP | BFP | H | R | ER | HR | SH | SF | HB | TBB | IBB | SO | WP | Bk | W | L | Pct. | ShO | Sv | ERA |
| 1988 San Diego | NL | 3 | 1 | 1 | 2 | 18 | 68 | 13 | 3 | 3 | 0 | 0 | 0 | 0 | 3 | 0 | 15 | 0 | 0 | 2 | 0 | 1.000 | 0 | 0 | 1.50 |
| 1989 San Diego | NL | 56 | 8 | 0 | 25 | 135 | 554 | 106 | 43 | 39 | 8 | 5 | 2 | 2 | 52 | 9 | 106 | 3 | 3 | 8 | 9 | .471 | 0 | 6 | 2.60 |
| 1990 San Diego | NL | 73 | 0 | 0 | 33 | 117.1 | 488 | 92 | 35 | 30 | 6 | 9 | 7 | 4 | 49 | 13 | 97 | 2 | 3 | 8 | 8 | .500 | 0 | 9 | 2.30 |
| 3 ML YEARS | | 132 | 9 | 1 | 60 | 270.1 | 1110 | 211 | 81 | 72 | 14 | 14 | 9 | 6 | 104 | 22 | 218 | 5 | 6 | 18 | 17 | .514 | 0 | 15 | 2.40 |

## Lenny Harris

**Bats:** Left **Throws:** Right **Pos:** 3B/2B **Ht:** 5'10" **Wt:** 195 **Born:** 10/28/64 **Age:** 26

| | | BATTING | | | | | | | | | | | | | | | | | BASERUNNING | | | | PERCENTAGES | | |
|---|---|---|---|---|---|---|---|---|---|---|---|---|---|---|---|---|---|---|---|---|---|---|---|---|---|
| Year Team | Lg | G | AB | H | 2B | 3B | HR | (Hm | Rd) | TB | R | RBI | TBB | IBB | SO | HBP | SH | SF | SB | CS | SB% | GDP | Avg | OBP | SLG |
| 1988 Cincinnati | NL | 16 | 43 | 16 | 1 | 0 | 0 | (0 | 0) | 17 | 7 | 8 | 5 | 0 | 4 | 0 | 1 | 2 | 4 | 1 | .80 | 0 | .372 | .420 | .395 |
| 1989 2 ML Teams | | 115 | 335 | 79 | 10 | 1 | 3 | (1 | 2) | 100 | 36 | 26 | 20 | 0 | 33 | 2 | 1 | 0 | 14 | 9 | .61 | 14 | .236 | .283 | .299 |
| 1990 Los Angeles | NL | 137 | 431 | 131 | 16 | 4 | 2 | (0 | 2) | 161 | 61 | 29 | 29 | 2 | 31 | 1 | 3 | 1 | 15 | 10 | .60 | 8 | .304 | .348 | .374 |
| 1989 Cincinnati | NL | 61 | 188 | 42 | 4 | 0 | 2 | (0 | 2) | 52 | 17 | 11 | 9 | 0 | 20 | 1 | 1 | 0 | 10 | 6 | .63 | 5 | .223 | .263 | .277 |
| Los Angeles | NL | 54 | 147 | 37 | 6 | 1 | 1 | (1 | 0) | 48 | 19 | 15 | 11 | 0 | 13 | 1 | 0 | 0 | 4 | 3 | .57 | 9 | .252 | .308 | .327 |
| 3 ML YEARS | | 268 | 809 | 226 | 27 | 5 | 5 | (1 | 4) | 278 | 104 | 63 | 54 | 2 | 68 | 3 | 5 | 3 | 33 | 20 | .62 | 22 | .279 | .326 | .344 |

## Reggie Harris

**Pitches:** Right **Bats:** Right **Pos:** RP **Ht:** 6' 1" **Wt:** 180 **Born:** 08/12/68 **Age:** 22

| | | HOW MUCH HE PITCHED | | | | | | WHAT HE GAVE UP | | | | | | | | | | | | THE RESULTS | | | | | |
|---|---|---|---|---|---|---|---|---|---|---|---|---|---|---|---|---|---|---|---|---|---|---|---|---|---|
| Year Team | Lg | G | GS | CG | GF | IP | BFP | H | R | ER | HR | SH | SF | HB | TBB | IBB | SO | WP | Bk | W | L | Pct. | ShO | Sv | ERA |
| 1987 Elmira | A | 9 | 8 | 1 | 0 | 46.2 | 212 | 50 | 29 | 26 | 3 | 1 | 1 | 6 | 22 | 0 | 25 | 3 | 0 | 2 | 3 | .400 | 1 | 0 | 5.01 |
| 1988 Lynchburg | A | 17 | 11 | 0 | 2 | 64 | 310 | 86 | 60 | 53 | 8 | 0 | 3 | 4 | 34 | 5 | 48 | 5 | 7 | 1 | 8 | .111 | 0 | 0 | 7.45 |
| Elmira | A | 10 | 10 | 0 | 0 | 54.1 | 237 | 56 | 37 | 32 | 5 | 1 | 3 | 2 | 28 | 0 | 46 | 1 | 2 | 3 | 6 | .333 | 0 | 0 | 5.30 |
| 1989 Winter Havn | A | 29 | 26 | 1 | 2 | 153.1 | 670 | 144 | 81 | 68 | 6 | 5 | 11 | 7 | 77 | 2 | 85 | 7 | 4 | 10 | 13 | .435 | 0 | 0 | 3.99 |
| 1990 Huntsville | AA | 5 | 5 | 0 | 0 | 29.2 | 131 | 26 | 12 | 10 | 3 | 1 | 1 | 4 | 16 | 0 | 34 | 4 | 0 | 0 | 2 | .000 | 0 | 0 | 3.03 |
| 1990 Oakland | AL | 16 | 1 | 0 | 9 | 41.1 | 168 | 25 | 16 | 16 | 5 | 1 | 2 | 2 | 21 | 1 | 31 | 2 | 0 | 1 | 0 | 1.000 | 0 | 0 | 3.48 |

## Mike Hartley

**Pitches:** Right **Bats:** Right **Pos:** RP/SP **Ht:** 6' 1" **Wt:** 192 **Born:** 08/31/61 **Age:** 29

| | | HOW MUCH HE PITCHED | | | | | | WHAT HE GAVE UP | | | | | | | | | | | | THE RESULTS | | | | | |
|---|---|---|---|---|---|---|---|---|---|---|---|---|---|---|---|---|---|---|---|---|---|---|---|---|---|
| Year Team | Lg | G | GS | CG | GF | IP | BFP | H | R | ER | HR | SH | SF | HB | TBB | IBB | SO | WP | Bk | W | L | Pct. | ShO | Sv | ERA |
| 1984 St. Pete | A | 31 | 23 | 4 | 1 | 139.1 | 622 | 142 | 81 | 65 | 3 | 7 | 2 | 4 | 84 | 10 | 88 | 16 | 2 | 8 | 14 | .364 | 1 | 0 | 4.20 |
| 1985 Springfield | A | 33 | 12 | 0 | 10 | 114.1 | 516 | 119 | 77 | 65 | 9 | 7 | 6 | 8 | 62 | 2 | 100 | 9 | 0 | 2 | 7 | .222 | 0 | 0 | 5.12 |

| | | | | | | | | | | | | | | | | | | | | | | | | |
|---|---|---|---|---|---|---|---|---|---|---|---|---|---|---|---|---|---|---|---|---|---|---|---|---|
| 1986 Springfield | A | 8 | 0 | 0 | 5 | 15 | 82 | 22 | 17 | 16 | 4 | 0 | 1 | 1 | 14 | 1 | 10 | 2 | 0 | 0 | 0 | .000 | 0 | 1 | 9.60 |
| Savannah | A | 39 | 0 | 0 | 25 | 56 | 248 | 38 | 31 | 18 | 0 | 0 | 1 | 7 | 37 | 1 | 55 | 9 | 0 | 5 | 7 | .417 | 0 | 8 | 2.89 |
| 1987 Bakersfield | A | 33 | 0 | 0 | 27 | 56 | 236 | 44 | 19 | 16 | 3 | 4 | 2 | 4 | 24 | 5 | 72 | 7 | 0 | 5 | 4 | .556 | 0 | 14 | 2.57 |
| San Antonio | AA | 25 | 0 | 0 | 19 | 41 | 161 | 21 | 8 | 6 | 2 | 4 | 1 | 2 | 18 | 5 | 37 | 6 | 0 | 3 | 4 | .429 | 0 | 3 | 1.32 |
| Albuquerque | AAA | 2 | 0 | 0 | 0 | 2.2 | 14 | 5 | 3 | 2 | 0 | 0 | 0 | 0 | 3 | 1 | 3 | 0 | 0 | 0 | 1 | .000 | 0 | 0 | 6.75 |
| 1988 San Antonio | AA | 30 | 0 | 0 | 25 | 45 | 177 | 25 | 5 | 4 | 2 | 1 | 1 | 2 | 18 | 3 | 57 | 1 | 1 | 5 | 1 | .833 | 0 | 9 | 0.80 |
| Albuquerque | AAA | 18 | 0 | 0 | 11 | 20.2 | 99 | 22 | 11 | 10 | 1 | 4 | 0 | 2 | 12 | 1 | 16 | 0 | 1 | 2 | 2 | .500 | 0 | 3 | 4.35 |
| 1989 Albuquerque | AAA | 58 | 0 | 0 | 50 | 77.1 | 315 | 53 | 31 | 24 | 4 | 3 | 3 | 2 | 34 | 2 | 76 | 4 | 1 | 7 | 4 | .636 | 0 | 18 | 2.79 |
| 1990 Albuquerque | AAA | 3 | 0 | 0 | 2 | 3 | 14 | 3 | 0 | 0 | 0 | 0 | 0 | 0 | 2 | 0 | 3 | 0 | 0 | 0 | 0 | .000 | 0 | 2 | 0.00 |
| 1989 Los Angeles | NL | 5 | 0 | 0 | 3 | 6 | 20 | 2 | 1 | 1 | 0 | 0 | 0 | 0 | 0 | 0 | 4 | 0 | 0 | 0 | 1 | .000 | 0 | 0 | 1.50 |
| 1990 Los Angeles | NL | 32 | 6 | 1 | 8 | 79.1 | 325 | 58 | 32 | 26 | 7 | 2 | 1 | 2 | 30 | 2 | 76 | 3 | 0 | 6 | 3 | .667 | 1 | 1 | 2.95 |
| 2 ML YEARS | | 37 | 6 | 1 | 11 | 85.1 | 345 | 60 | 33 | 27 | 7 | 2 | 1 | 2 | 30 | 2 | 80 | 3 | 0 | 6 | 4 | .600 | 1 | 1 | 2.85 |

## Bryan Harvey

**Pitches:** Right **Bats:** Right **Pos:** RP **Ht:** 6' 2" **Wt:** 212 **Born:** 06/02/63 **Age:** 28

| | | HOW MUCH HE PITCHED | | | | | | WHAT HE GAVE UP | | | | | | | | | | | | THE RESULTS | | | | | |
|---|---|---|---|---|---|---|---|---|---|---|---|---|---|---|---|---|---|---|---|---|---|---|---|---|---|
| Year Team | Lg | G | GS | CG | GF | IP | BFP | H | R | ER | HR | SH | SF | HB | TBB | IBB | SO | WP | Bk | W | L | Pct. | ShO | Sv | ERA |
| 1987 California | AL | 3 | 0 | 0 | 2 | 5 | 22 | 6 | 0 | 0 | 0 | 0 | 0 | 0 | 2 | 0 | 3 | 3 | 0 | 0 | 0 | .000 | 0 | 0 | 0.00 |
| 1988 California | AL | 50 | 0 | 0 | 38 | 76 | 303 | 59 | 22 | 18 | 4 | 3 | 3 | 1 | 20 | 6 | 67 | 4 | 1 | 7 | 5 | .583 | 0 | 17 | 2.13 |
| 1989 California | AL | 51 | 0 | 0 | 42 | 55 | 245 | 36 | 21 | 21 | 6 | 5 | 2 | 0 | 41 | 1 | 78 | 5 | 0 | 3 | 3 | .500 | 0 | 25 | 3.44 |
| 1990 California | AL | 54 | 0 | 0 | 47 | 64.1 | 267 | 45 | 24 | 23 | 4 | 4 | 4 | 0 | 35 | 6 | 82 | 7 | 1 | 4 | 4 | .500 | 0 | 25 | 3.22 |
| 4 ML YEARS | | 158 | 0 | 0 | 129 | 200.1 | 837 | 146 | 67 | 62 | 14 | 12 | 9 | 1 | 98 | 13 | 230 | 19 | 2 | 14 | 12 | .538 | 0 | 67 | 2.79 |

## Bill Haselman

**Bats:** Right **Throws:** Right **Pos:** DH **Ht:** 6' 3" **Wt:** 200 **Born:** 05/25/66 **Age:** 25

| | | BATTING | | | | | | | | | | | | | | | | | BASERUNNING | | | | PERCENTAGES | | |
|---|---|---|---|---|---|---|---|---|---|---|---|---|---|---|---|---|---|---|---|---|---|---|---|---|---|
| Year Team | Lg | G | AB | H | 2B | 3B | HR | (Hm | Rd) | TB | R | RBI | TBB | IBB | SO | HBP | SH | SF | SB | CS | SB% | GDP | Avg | OBP | SLG |
| 1987 Gastonia | A | 61 | 235 | 72 | 13 | 1 | 8 | -- | -- | 111 | 35 | 33 | 19 | 0 | 46 | 1 | 0 | 1 | 1 | 2 | .33 | 3 | .306 | .359 | .472 |
| 1988 Charlotte | A | 122 | 453 | 111 | 17 | 2 | 10 | -- | -- | 162 | 56 | 54 | 45 | 3 | 99 | 3 | 1 | 2 | 8 | 5 | .62 | 10 | .245 | .316 | .358 |
| 1989 Tulsa | AA | 107 | 352 | 95 | 17 | 2 | 7 | -- | -- | 137 | 38 | 36 | 40 | 0 | 88 | 3 | 1 | 2 | 5 | 10 | .33 | 7 | .270 | .348 | .389 |
| 1990 Tulsa | AA | 120 | 430 | 137 | 38 | 2 | 18 | -- | -- | 233 | 68 | 80 | 43 | 1 | 96 | 6 | 3 | 3 | 3 | 7 | .30 | 11 | .319 | .386 | .542 |
| 1990 Texas | AL | 7 | 13 | 2 | 0 | 0 | 0 | (0 | 0) | 2 | 0 | 3 | 1 | 0 | 5 | 0 | 0 | 0 | 0 | 0 | .00 | 0 | .154 | .214 | .154 |

## Ron Hassey

**Bats:** Left **Throws:** Right **Pos:** C/DH **Ht:** 6' 2" **Wt:** 195 **Born:** 02/27/53 **Age:** 38

| | | BATTING | | | | | | | | | | | | | | | | | BASERUNNING | | | | PERCENTAGES | | |
|---|---|---|---|---|---|---|---|---|---|---|---|---|---|---|---|---|---|---|---|---|---|---|---|---|---|
| Year Team | Lg | G | AB | H | 2B | 3B | HR | (Hm | Rd) | TB | R | RBI | TBB | IBB | SO | HBP | SH | SF | SB | CS | SB% | GDP | Avg | OBP | SLG |
| 1978 Cleveland | AL | 25 | 74 | 15 | 0 | 0 | 2 | (1 | 1) | 21 | 5 | 9 | 5 | 0 | 7 | 1 | 1 | 2 | 2 | 0 | 1.00 | 1 | .203 | .256 | .284 |
| 1979 Cleveland | AL | 75 | 223 | 64 | 14 | 0 | 4 | (2 | 2) | 90 | 20 | 32 | 19 | 2 | 19 | 0 | 4 | 3 | 1 | 0 | 1.00 | 8 | .287 | .339 | .404 |
| 1980 Cleveland | AL | 130 | 390 | 124 | 18 | 4 | 8 | (5 | 3) | 174 | 43 | 65 | 49 | 3 | 51 | 1 | 1 | 6 | 0 | 2 | .00 | 13 | .318 | .390 | .446 |
| 1981 Cleveland | AL | 61 | 190 | 44 | 4 | 0 | 1 | (0 | 1) | 51 | 8 | 25 | 17 | 0 | 11 | 2 | 3 | 3 | 0 | 1 | .00 | 5 | .232 | .297 | .268 |
| 1982 Cleveland | AL | 113 | 323 | 81 | 18 | 0 | 5 | (2 | 3) | 114 | 33 | 34 | 53 | 5 | 32 | 1 | 3 | 2 | 3 | 2 | .60 | 10 | .251 | .356 | .353 |
| 1983 Cleveland | AL | 117 | 341 | 92 | 21 | 0 | 6 | (4 | 2) | 131 | 48 | 42 | 38 | 2 | 35 | 2 | 2 | 5 | 2 | 2 | .50 | 11 | .270 | .342 | .384 |
| 1984 2 ML Teams | | 67 | 182 | 49 | 5 | 1 | 2 | (1 | 1) | 62 | 16 | 24 | 19 | 3 | 32 | 0 | 0 | 1 | 1 | 1 | .50 | 5 | .269 | .337 | .341 |
| 1985 New York | AL | 92 | 267 | 79 | 16 | 1 | 13 | (3 | 10) | 136 | 31 | 42 | 28 | 4 | 21 | 3 | 0 | 0 | 0 | 0 | .00 | 7 | .296 | .369 | .509 |
| 1986 2 ML Teams | | 113 | 341 | 110 | 25 | 1 | 9 | (5 | 4) | 164 | 45 | 49 | 46 | 3 | 27 | 3 | 1 | 2 | 1 | 1 | .50 | 15 | .323 | .406 | .481 |
| 1987 Chicago | AL | 49 | 145 | 31 | 9 | 0 | 3 | (1 | 2) | 49 | 15 | 12 | 17 | 2 | 11 | 2 | 0 | 1 | 0 | 0 | .00 | 9 | .214 | .303 | .338 |
| 1988 Oakland | AL | 107 | 323 | 83 | 15 | 0 | 7 | (3 | 4) | 119 | 32 | 45 | 30 | 1 | 42 | 4 | 3 | 5 | 2 | 0 | 1.00 | 9 | .257 | .323 | .368 |
| 1989 Oakland | AL | 97 | 268 | 61 | 12 | 0 | 5 | (3 | 2) | 88 | 29 | 23 | 24 | 2 | 45 | 1 | 1 | 4 | 1 | 0 | 1.00 | 9 | .228 | .290 | .328 |
| 1990 Oakland | AL | 94 | 254 | 54 | 7 | 0 | 5 | (2 | 3) | 76 | 18 | 22 | 27 | 3 | 29 | 1 | 1 | 3 | 0 | 0 | .00 | 3 | .213 | .288 | .299 |
| 1984 Cleveland | AL | 48 | 149 | 38 | 5 | 1 | 0 | (0 | 0) | 45 | 11 | 19 | 15 | 2 | 26 | 0 | 0 | 1 | 1 | 0 | 1.00 | 4 | .255 | .321 | .302 |
| Chicago | NL | 19 | 33 | 11 | 0 | 0 | 2 | (1 | 1) | 17 | 5 | 5 | 4 | 1 | 6 | 0 | 0 | 0 | 0 | 1 | .00 | 1 | .333 | .405 | .515 |
| 1986 New York | AL | 64 | 191 | 57 | 14 | 0 | 6 | (2 | 4) | 89 | 23 | 29 | 24 | 1 | 16 | 2 | 1 | 1 | 1 | 1 | .50 | 8 | .298 | .381 | .466 |
| Chicago | AL | 49 | 150 | 53 | 11 | 1 | 3 | (3 | 0) | 75 | 22 | 20 | 22 | 2 | 11 | 1 | 0 | 1 | 0 | 0 | .00 | 7 | .353 | .437 | .500 |
| 13 ML YEARS | | 1140 | 3321 | 887 | 164 | 7 | 70 | (32 | 38) | 1275 | 343 | 424 | 372 | 30 | 362 | 21 | 20 | 37 | 13 | 9 | .59 | 105 | .267 | .341 | .384 |

## Billy Hatcher

**Bats:** Right **Throws:** Right **Pos:** LF/CF **Ht:** 5' 9" **Wt:** 175 **Born:** 10/04/60 **Age:** 30

| | | BATTING | | | | | | | | | | | | | | | | | BASERUNNING | | | | PERCENTAGES | | |
|---|---|---|---|---|---|---|---|---|---|---|---|---|---|---|---|---|---|---|---|---|---|---|---|---|---|
| Year Team | Lg | G | AB | H | 2B | 3B | HR | (Hm | Rd) | TB | R | RBI | TBB | IBB | SO | HBP | SH | SF | SB | CS | SB% | GDP | Avg | OBP | SLG |
| 1984 Chicago | NL | 8 | 9 | 1 | 0 | 0 | 0 | (0 | 0) | 1 | 1 | 0 | 1 | 1 | 0 | 0 | 0 | 0 | 2 | 0 | 1.00 | 0 | .111 | .200 | .111 |
| 1985 Chicago | NL | 53 | 163 | 40 | 12 | 1 | 2 | (2 | 0) | 60 | 24 | 10 | 8 | 0 | 12 | 3 | 2 | 2 | 2 | 4 | .33 | 9 | .245 | .290 | .368 |
| 1986 Houston | NL | 127 | 419 | 108 | 15 | 4 | 6 | (2 | 4) | 149 | 55 | 36 | 22 | 1 | 52 | 5 | 6 | 1 | 38 | 14 | .73 | 3 | .258 | .302 | .356 |
| 1987 Houston | NL | 141 | 564 | 167 | 28 | 3 | 11 | (3 | 8) | 234 | 96 | 63 | 42 | 1 | 70 | 9 | 7 | 5 | 53 | 9 | .85 | 11 | .296 | .352 | .415 |
| 1988 Houston | NL | 145 | 530 | 142 | 25 | 4 | 7 | (3 | 4) | 196 | 79 | 52 | 37 | 4 | 56 | 8 | 8 | 8 | 32 | 13 | .71 | 6 | .268 | .321 | .370 |
| 1989 2 ML Teams | | 135 | 481 | 111 | 19 | 3 | 4 | (0 | 4) | 148 | 59 | 51 | 30 | 2 | 62 | 2 | 3 | 4 | 24 | 7 | .77 | 4 | .231 | .277 | .308 |
| 1990 Cincinnati | NL | 139 | 504 | 139 | 28 | 5 | 5 | (2 | 3) | 192 | 68 | 25 | 33 | 5 | 42 | 6 | 1 | 1 | 30 | 10 | .75 | 4 | .276 | .327 | .381 |

| Year Team | Lg | G | AB | H | 2B | 3B | HR | (Hm | Rd) | TB | R | RBI | TBB | IBB | SO | HBP | SH | SF | SB | CS | SB% | GDP | Avg | OBP | SLG |
|---|---|---|---|---|---|---|---|---|---|---|---|---|---|---|---|---|---|---|---|---|---|---|---|---|---|
| 1989 Houston | NL | 108 | 395 | 90 | 15 | 3 | 3 | (0 | 3) | 120 | 49 | 44 | 30 | 2 | 53 | 1 | 3 | 4 | 22 | 6 | .79 | 3 | .228 | .281 | .304 |
| Pittsburgh | NL | 27 | 86 | 21 | 4 | 0 | 1 | (0 | 1) | 28 | 10 | 7 | 0 | 0 | 9 | 1 | 0 | 0 | 2 | 1 | .67 | 1 | .244 | .253 | .326 |
| 7 ML YEARS | | 748 | 2670 | 708 | 127 | 20 | 35 | (12 | 23) | 980 | 382 | 237 | 173 | 14 | 294 | 33 | 27 | 21 | 181 | 57 | .76 | 37 | .265 | .315 | .367 |

## Mickey Hatcher

**Bats:** Right **Throws:** Right **Pos:** 1B **Ht:** 6' 2" **Wt:** 202 **Born:** 03/15/55 **Age:** 36

| | | BATTING | | | | | | | | | | | | | | | | | BASERUNNING | | | | PERCENTAGES | | |
|---|---|---|---|---|---|---|---|---|---|---|---|---|---|---|---|---|---|---|---|---|---|---|---|---|---|
| Year Team | Lg | G | AB | H | 2B | 3B | HR | (Hm | Rd) | TB | R | RBI | TBB | IBB | SO | HBP | SH | SF | SB | CS | SB% | GDP | Avg | OBP | SLG |
| 1979 Los Angeles | NL | 33 | 93 | 25 | 4 | 1 | 1 | (0 | 1) | 34 | 9 | 5 | 7 | 0 | 12 | 1 | 1 | 0 | 1 | 3 | .25 | 5 | .269 | .327 | .366 |
| 1980 Los Angeles | NL | 57 | 84 | 19 | 2 | 0 | 1 | (1 | 0) | 24 | 4 | 5 | 2 | 1 | 12 | 0 | 4 | 0 | 0 | 2 | .00 | 6 | .226 | .244 | .286 |
| 1981 Minnesota | AL | 99 | 377 | 96 | 23 | 2 | 3 | (3 | 0) | 132 | 36 | 37 | 15 | 2 | 29 | 2 | 5 | 3 | 3 | 1 | .75 | 10 | .255 | .285 | .350 |
| 1982 Minnesota | AL | 84 | 277 | 69 | 13 | 2 | 3 | (2 | 1) | 95 | 23 | 26 | 8 | 1 | 27 | 0 | 0 | 1 | 0 | 2 | .00 | 12 | .249 | .269 | .343 |
| 1983 Minnesota | AL | 106 | 375 | 119 | 15 | 3 | 9 | (6 | 3) | 167 | 50 | 47 | 14 | 0 | 19 | 1 | 3 | 2 | 2 | 0 | 1.00 | 12 | .317 | .342 | .445 |
| 1984 Minnesota | AL | 152 | 576 | 174 | 35 | 5 | 5 | (4 | 1) | 234 | 61 | 69 | 37 | 3 | 34 | 2 | 1 | 8 | 0 | 1 | .00 | 17 | .302 | .342 | .406 |
| 1985 Minnesota | AL | 116 | 444 | 125 | 28 | 0 | 3 | (1 | 2) | 162 | 46 | 49 | 16 | 1 | 23 | 2 | 3 | 2 | 0 | 0 | .00 | 15 | .282 | .308 | .365 |
| 1986 Minnesota | AL | 115 | 317 | 88 | 13 | 3 | 3 | (1 | 2) | 116 | 40 | 32 | 19 | 2 | 26 | 0 | 0 | 4 | 2 | 1 | .67 | 8 | .278 | .315 | .366 |
| 1987 Los Angeles | NL | 101 | 287 | 81 | 19 | 1 | 7 | (4 | 3) | 123 | 27 | 42 | 20 | 4 | 19 | 1 | 3 | 3 | 2 | 3 | .40 | 6 | .282 | .328 | .429 |
| 1988 Los Angeles | NL | 88 | 191 | 56 | 8 | 0 | 1 | (0 | 1) | 67 | 22 | 25 | 7 | 3 | 7 | 2 | 0 | 2 | 0 | 0 | .00 | 7 | .293 | .322 | .351 |
| 1989 Los Angeles | NL | 94 | 224 | 66 | 9 | 2 | 2 | (0 | 2) | 85 | 18 | 25 | 13 | 3 | 16 | 1 | 0 | 6 | 1 | 2 | .33 | 7 | .295 | .328 | .379 |
| 1990 Los Angeles | NL | 85 | 132 | 28 | 3 | 1 | 0 | (0 | 0) | 33 | 12 | 13 | 6 | 1 | 22 | 1 | 0 | 2 | 0 | 0 | .00 | 1 | .212 | .248 | .250 |
| 12 ML YEARS | | 1130 | 3377 | 946 | 172 | 20 | 38 | (22 | 16) | 1272 | 348 | 375 | 164 | 21 | 246 | 13 | 20 | 33 | 11 | 15 | .42 | 106 | .280 | .313 | .377 |

## Andy Hawkins

**Pitches:** Right **Bats:** Right **Pos:** SP **Ht:** 6' 3" **Wt:** 217 **Born:** 01/21/60 **Age:** 31

| | | HOW MUCH HE PITCHED | | | | | | WHAT HE GAVE UP | | | | | | | | | | | | THE RESULTS | | | | | |
|---|---|---|---|---|---|---|---|---|---|---|---|---|---|---|---|---|---|---|---|---|---|---|---|---|---|
| Year Team | Lg | G | GS | CG | GF | IP | BFP | H | R | ER | HR | SH | SF | HB | TBB | IBB | SO | WP | Bk | W | L | Pct. | ShO | Sv | ERA |
| 1982 San Diego | NL | 15 | 10 | 1 | 2 | 63.2 | 281 | 66 | 33 | 29 | 4 | 6 | 5 | 2 | 27 | 3 | 25 | 2 | 3 | 2 | 5 | .286 | 0 | 0 | 4.10 |
| 1983 San Diego | NL | 21 | 19 | 4 | 1 | 119.2 | 501 | 106 | 50 | 39 | 8 | 10 | 4 | 5 | 48 | 4 | 59 | 4 | 1 | 5 | 7 | .417 | 1 | 0 | 2.93 |
| 1984 San Diego | NL | 36 | 22 | 2 | 9 | 146 | 650 | 143 | 90 | 76 | 13 | 10 | 4 | 2 | 72 | 2 | 77 | 1 | 2 | 8 | 9 | .471 | 1 | 0 | 4.68 |
| 1985 San Diego | NL | 33 | 33 | 5 | 0 | 228.2 | 953 | 229 | 88 | 80 | 18 | 13 | 12 | 4 | 65 | 8 | 69 | 3 | 3 | 18 | 8 | .692 | 2 | 0 | 3.15 |
| 1986 San Diego | NL | 37 | 35 | 3 | 0 | 209.1 | 905 | 218 | 111 | 100 | 24 | 7 | 6 | 5 | 75 | 7 | 117 | 6 | 2 | 10 | 8 | .556 | 1 | 0 | 4.30 |
| 1987 San Diego | NL | 24 | 20 | 0 | 2 | 117.2 | 516 | 131 | 71 | 66 | 16 | 5 | 3 | 2 | 49 | 2 | 51 | 2 | 3 | 3 | 10 | .231 | 0 | 0 | 5.05 |
| 1988 San Diego | NL | 33 | 33 | 4 | 0 | 217.2 | 906 | 196 | 88 | 81 | 16 | 14 | 6 | 6 | 76 | 4 | 91 | 1 | 3 | 14 | 11 | .560 | 2 | 0 | 3.35 |
| 1989 New York | AL | 34 | 34 | 5 | 0 | 208.1 | 908 | 238 | 127 | 111 | 23 | 3 | 3 | 6 | 76 | 6 | 98 | 1 | 2 | 15 | 15 | .500 | 2 | 0 | 4.80 |
| 1990 New York | AL | 28 | 26 | 2 | 1 | 157.2 | 692 | 156 | 101 | 94 | 20 | 4 | 5 | 2 | 82 | 3 | 74 | 2 | 1 | 5 | 12 | .294 | 1 | 0 | 5.37 |
| 9 ML YEARS | | 261 | 232 | 26 | 15 | 1468.2 | 6312 | 1483 | 759 | 676 | 142 | 72 | 48 | 34 | 570 | 39 | 661 | 22 | 20 | 80 | 85 | .485 | 10 | 0 | 4.14 |

## Charlie Hayes

**Bats:** Right **Throws:** Right **Pos:** 3B **Ht:** 6' 0" **Wt:** 190 **Born:** 05/29/65 **Age:** 26

| | | BATTING | | | | | | | | | | | | | | | | | BASERUNNING | | | | PERCENTAGES | | |
|---|---|---|---|---|---|---|---|---|---|---|---|---|---|---|---|---|---|---|---|---|---|---|---|---|---|
| Year Team | Lg | G | AB | H | 2B | 3B | HR | (Hm | Rd) | TB | R | RBI | TBB | IBB | SO | HBP | SH | SF | SB | CS | SB% | GDP | Avg | OBP | SLG |
| 1988 San Francisco | NL | 7 | 11 | 1 | 0 | 0 | 0 | (0 | 0) | 1 | 0 | 0 | 0 | 0 | 3 | 0 | 0 | 0 | 0 | 0 | .00 | 0 | .091 | .091 | .091 |
| 1989 2 ML Teams | | 87 | 304 | 78 | 15 | 1 | 8 | (3 | 5) | 119 | 26 | 43 | 11 | 1 | 50 | 0 | 2 | 3 | 3 | 1 | .75 | 6 | .257 | .280 | .391 |
| 1990 Philadelphia | NL | 152 | 561 | 145 | 20 | 0 | 10 | (3 | 7) | 195 | 56 | 57 | 28 | 3 | 91 | 2 | 0 | 6 | 4 | 4 | .50 | 12 | .258 | .293 | .348 |
| 1989 San Francisco | NL | 3 | 5 | 1 | 0 | 0 | 0 | (0 | 0) | 1 | 0 | 0 | 0 | 0 | 1 | 0 | 0 | 0 | 0 | 0 | .00 | 0 | .200 | .200 | .200 |
| Philadelphia | NL | 84 | 299 | 77 | 15 | 1 | 8 | (3 | 5) | 118 | 26 | 43 | 11 | 1 | 49 | 0 | 2 | 3 | 3 | 1 | .75 | 6 | .258 | .281 | .395 |
| 3 ML YEARS | | 246 | 876 | 224 | 35 | 1 | 18 | (6 | 12) | 315 | 82 | 100 | 39 | 4 | 144 | 2 | 2 | 9 | 7 | 5 | .58 | 18 | .256 | .286 | .360 |

## Von Hayes

**Bats:** Left **Throws:** Right **Pos:** RF/LF **Ht:** 6' 5" **Wt:** 180 **Born:** 08/31/58 **Age:** 32

| | | BATTING | | | | | | | | | | | | | | | | | BASERUNNING | | | | PERCENTAGES | | |
|---|---|---|---|---|---|---|---|---|---|---|---|---|---|---|---|---|---|---|---|---|---|---|---|---|---|
| Year Team | Lg | G | AB | H | 2B | 3B | HR | (Hm | Rd) | TB | R | RBI | TBB | IBB | SO | HBP | SH | SF | SB | CS | SB% | GDP | Avg | OBP | SLG |
| 1981 Cleveland | AL | 43 | 109 | 28 | 8 | 2 | 1 | (0 | 1) | 43 | 21 | 17 | 14 | 1 | 10 | 2 | 4 | 2 | 8 | 1 | .89 | 2 | .257 | .346 | .394 |
| 1982 Cleveland | AL | 150 | 527 | 132 | 25 | 3 | 14 | (3 | 11) | 205 | 65 | 82 | 42 | 3 | 63 | 4 | 8 | 2 | 32 | 13 | .71 | 10 | .250 | .310 | .389 |
| 1983 Philadelphia | NL | 124 | 351 | 93 | 9 | 5 | 6 | (3 | 3) | 130 | 45 | 32 | 36 | 7 | 55 | 3 | 0 | 2 | 20 | 12 | .63 | 11 | .265 | .337 | .370 |
| 1984 Philadelphia | NL | 152 | 561 | 164 | 27 | 6 | 16 | (10 | 6) | 251 | 85 | 67 | 59 | 4 | 84 | 0 | 0 | 2 | 48 | 13 | .79 | 10 | .292 | .359 | .447 |
| 1985 Philadelphia | NL | 152 | 570 | 150 | 30 | 4 | 13 | (12 | 1) | 227 | 76 | 70 | 61 | 6 | 99 | 0 | 2 | 4 | 21 | 8 | .72 | 6 | .263 | .332 | .398 |
| 1986 Philadelphia | NL | 158 | 610 | 186 | 46 | 2 | 19 | (11 | 8) | 293 | 107 | 98 | 74 | 9 | 77 | 1 | 1 | 4 | 24 | 12 | .67 | 14 | .305 | .379 | .480 |
| 1987 Philadelphia | NL | 158 | 556 | 154 | 36 | 5 | 21 | (14 | 7) | 263 | 84 | 84 | 121 | 12 | 77 | 0 | 0 | 4 | 16 | 7 | .70 | 12 | .277 | .404 | .473 |
| 1988 Philadelphia | NL | 104 | 367 | 100 | 28 | 2 | 6 | (2 | 4) | 150 | 43 | 45 | 49 | 5 | 59 | 1 | 1 | 5 | 20 | 9 | .69 | 3 | .272 | .355 | .409 |
| 1989 Philadelphia | NL | 154 | 540 | 140 | 27 | 2 | 26 | (15 | 11) | 249 | 93 | 78 | 101 | 14 | 103 | 4 | 0 | 7 | 28 | 7 | .80 | 7 | .259 | .376 | .461 |
| 1990 Philadelphia | NL | 129 | 467 | 122 | 14 | 3 | 17 | (10 | 7) | 193 | 70 | 73 | 87 | 16 | 81 | 4 | 0 | 10 | 16 | 7 | .70 | 10 | .261 | .375 | .413 |
| 10 ML YEARS | | 1324 | 4658 | 1269 | 250 | 34 | 139 | (80 | 59) | 2004 | 689 | 646 | 644 | 77 | 708 | 19 | 16 | 42 | 233 | 89 | .72 | 85 | .272 | .360 | .430 |

## Mike Heath

**Bats:** Right **Throws:** Right **Pos:** C **Ht:** 5'11" **Wt:** 180 **Born:** 02/05/55 **Age:** 36

| | | BATTING | | | | | | | | | | | | | | | | | BASERUNNING | | | | PERCENTAGES | | |
|---|---|---|---|---|---|---|---|---|---|---|---|---|---|---|---|---|---|---|---|---|---|---|---|---|---|
| Year Team | Lg | G | AB | H | 2B | 3B | HR | (Hm | Rd) | TB | R | RBI | TBB | IBB | SO | HBP | SH | SF | SB | CS | SB% | GDP | Avg | OBP | SLG |
| 1978 New York | AL | 33 | 92 | 21 | 3 | 1 | 0 | (0 | 0) | 26 | 6 | 8 | 4 | 0 | 9 | 1 | 1 | 1 | 0 | 0 | .00 | 1 | .228 | .265 | .283 |
| 1979 Oakland | AL | 74 | 258 | 66 | 8 | 0 | 3 | (2 | 1) | 83 | 19 | 27 | 17 | 1 | 18 | 3 | 3 | 5 | 1 | 0 | 1.00 | 14 | .256 | .304 | .322 |
| 1980 Oakland | AL | 92 | 305 | 74 | 10 | 2 | 1 | (1 | 0) | 91 | 27 | 33 | 16 | 2 | 28 | 0 | 7 | 1 | 3 | 3 | .50 | 7 | .243 | .280 | .298 |
| 1981 Oakland | AL | 84 | 301 | 71 | 7 | 1 | 8 | (4 | 4) | 104 | 26 | 30 | 13 | 1 | 36 | 1 | 5 | 1 | 3 | 3 | .50 | 9 | .236 | .269 | .346 |
| 1982 Oakland | AL | 101 | 318 | 77 | 18 | 4 | 3 | (3 | 0) | 112 | 43 | 39 | 27 | 3 | 36 | 0 | 2 | 4 | 8 | 3 | .73 | 3 | .242 | .298 | .352 |
| 1983 Oakland | AL | 96 | 345 | 97 | 17 | 0 | 6 | (5 | 1) | 132 | 45 | 33 | 18 | 4 | 59 | 1 | 1 | 1 | 3 | 4 | .43 | 9 | .281 | .318 | .383 |
| 1984 Oakland | AL | 140 | 475 | 118 | 21 | 5 | 13 | (8 | 5) | 188 | 49 | 64 | 26 | 2 | 72 | 1 | 2 | 4 | 7 | 4 | .64 | 14 | .248 | .287 | .396 |
| 1985 Oakland | AL | 138 | 436 | 109 | 18 | 6 | 13 | (8 | 5) | 178 | 71 | 55 | 41 | 0 | 63 | 1 | 10 | 4 | 7 | 7 | .50 | 13 | .250 | .313 | .408 |
| 1986 2 ML Teams | | 95 | 288 | 65 | 11 | 1 | 8 | (4 | 4) | 102 | 30 | 36 | 27 | 4 | 53 | 1 | 1 | 2 | 6 | 4 | .60 | 6 | .226 | .292 | .354 |
| 1987 Detroit | AL | 93 | 270 | 76 | 16 | 0 | 8 | (8 | 0) | 116 | 34 | 33 | 21 | 0 | 42 | 3 | 1 | 1 | 1 | 5 | .17 | 5 | .281 | .339 | .430 |
| 1988 Detroit | AL | 86 | 219 | 54 | 7 | 2 | 5 | (4 | 1) | 80 | 24 | 18 | 18 | 0 | 32 | 1 | 3 | 0 | 1 | 0 | 1.00 | 6 | .247 | .307 | .365 |
| 1989 Detroit | AL | 122 | 396 | 104 | 16 | 2 | 10 | (5 | 5) | 154 | 38 | 43 | 24 | 2 | 71 | 4 | 1 | 4 | 7 | 1 | .88 | 18 | .263 | .308 | .389 |
| 1990 Detroit | AL | 122 | 370 | 100 | 18 | 2 | 7 | (3 | 4) | 143 | 46 | 38 | 19 | 0 | 71 | 4 | 2 | 3 | 7 | 6 | .54 | 12 | .270 | .311 | .386 |
| 1986 St. Louis | NL | 65 | 190 | 39 | 8 | 1 | 4 | (1 | 3) | 61 | 19 | 25 | 23 | 4 | 36 | 1 | 1 | 1 | 2 | 3 | .40 | 5 | .205 | .293 | .321 |
| Detroit | AL | 30 | 98 | 26 | 3 | 0 | 4 | (3 | 1) | 41 | 11 | 11 | 4 | 0 | 17 | 0 | 0 | 1 | 4 | 1 | .80 | 1 | .265 | .291 | .418 |
| 13 ML YEARS | | 1276 | 4073 | 1032 | 170 | 26 | 85 | (55 | 30) | 1509 | 458 | 457 | 271 | 19 | 590 | 21 | 39 | 31 | 54 | 40 | .57 | 117 | .253 | .301 | .370 |

## Neal Heaton

**Pitches:** Left **Bats:** Left **Pos:** SP/RP **Ht:** 6' 1" **Wt:** 195 **Born:** 03/03/60 **Age:** 31

| | | HOW MUCH HE PITCHED | | | | | | WHAT HE GAVE UP | | | | | | | | | | | | THE RESULTS | | | | | |
|---|---|---|---|---|---|---|---|---|---|---|---|---|---|---|---|---|---|---|---|---|---|---|---|---|---|
| Year Team | Lg | G | GS | CG | GF | IP | BFP | H | R | ER | HR | SH | SF | HB | TBB | IBB | SO | WP | Bk | W | L | Pct. | ShO | Sv | ERA |
| 1982 Cleveland | AL | 8 | 4 | 0 | 0 | 31 | 142 | 32 | 21 | 18 | 1 | 1 | 2 | 0 | 16 | 0 | 14 | 4 | 0 | 0 | 2 | .000 | 0 | 0 | 5.23 |
| 1983 Cleveland | AL | 39 | 16 | 4 | 19 | 149.1 | 637 | 157 | 79 | 69 | 11 | 3 | 5 | 1 | 44 | 10 | 75 | 1 | 0 | 11 | 7 | .611 | 3 | 7 | 4.16 |
| 1984 Cleveland | AL | 38 | 34 | 4 | 2 | 198.2 | 880 | 231 | 128 | 115 | 21 | 6 | 10 | 0 | 75 | 5 | 75 | 3 | 1 | 12 | 15 | .444 | 1 | 0 | 5.21 |
| 1985 Cleveland | AL | 36 | 33 | 5 | 2 | 207.2 | 921 | 244 | 119 | 113 | 19 | 7 | 8 | 7 | 80 | 2 | 82 | 2 | 2 | 9 | 17 | .346 | 1 | 0 | 4.90 |
| 1986 2 ML Teams | | 33 | 29 | 5 | 2 | 198.2 | 850 | 201 | 102 | 90 | 26 | 6 | 5 | 2 | 81 | 8 | 90 | 4 | 0 | 7 | 15 | .318 | 0 | 1 | 4.08 |
| 1987 Montreal | NL | 32 | 32 | 3 | 0 | 193.1 | 807 | 207 | 103 | 97 | 25 | 5 | 5 | 3 | 37 | 3 | 105 | 2 | 5 | 13 | 10 | .565 | 1 | 0 | 4.52 |
| 1988 Montreal | NL | 32 | 11 | 0 | 7 | 97.1 | 415 | 98 | 54 | 54 | 14 | 5 | 3 | 3 | 43 | 5 | 43 | 1 | 5 | 3 | 10 | .231 | 0 | 2 | 4.99 |
| 1989 Pittsburgh | NL | 42 | 18 | 1 | 5 | 147.1 | 620 | 127 | 55 | 50 | 12 | 12 | 3 | 6 | 55 | 12 | 67 | 4 | 5 | 6 | 7 | .462 | 0 | 0 | 3.05 |
| 1990 Pittsburgh | NL | 30 | 24 | 0 | 2 | 146 | 599 | 143 | 66 | 56 | 17 | 10 | 6 | 2 | 38 | 1 | 68 | 4 | 1 | 12 | 9 | .571 | 0 | 0 | 3.45 |
| 1986 Cleveland | AL | 12 | 12 | 2 | 0 | 74.1 | 324 | 73 | 42 | 35 | 8 | 2 | 0 | 1 | 34 | 4 | 24 | 2 | 0 | 3 | 6 | .333 | 0 | 0 | 4.24 |
| Minnesota | AL | 21 | 17 | 3 | 2 | 124.1 | 526 | 128 | 60 | 55 | 18 | 4 | 5 | 1 | 47 | 4 | 66 | 2 | 0 | 4 | 9 | .308 | 0 | 1 | 3.98 |
| 9 ML YEARS | | 290 | 201 | 22 | 39 | 1369.1 | 5871 | 1440 | 727 | 662 | 146 | 55 | 47 | 24 | 469 | 46 | 619 | 25 | 19 | 73 | 92 | .442 | 6 | 10 | 4.35 |

## Danny Heep

**Bats:** Left **Throws:** Left **Pos:** RF **Ht:** 5'11" **Wt:** 177 **Born:** 07/03/57 **Age:** 33

| | | BATTING | | | | | | | | | | | | | | | | | BASERUNNING | | | | PERCENTAGES | | |
|---|---|---|---|---|---|---|---|---|---|---|---|---|---|---|---|---|---|---|---|---|---|---|---|---|---|
| Year Team | Lg | G | AB | H | 2B | 3B | HR | (Hm | Rd) | TB | R | RBI | TBB | IBB | SO | HBP | SH | SF | SB | CS | SB% | GDP | Avg | OBP | SLG |
| 1979 Houston | NL | 14 | 14 | 2 | 0 | 0 | 0 | (0 | 0) | 2 | 0 | 2 | 1 | 1 | 4 | 0 | 0 | 2 | 0 | 0 | .00 | 0 | .143 | .176 | .143 |
| 1980 Houston | NL | 33 | 87 | 24 | 8 | 0 | 0 | (0 | 0) | 32 | 6 | 6 | 8 | 0 | 9 | 1 | 0 | 1 | 0 | 0 | .00 | 0 | .276 | .340 | .368 |
| 1981 Houston | NL | 33 | 96 | 24 | 3 | 0 | 0 | (0 | 0) | 27 | 6 | 11 | 10 | 2 | 11 | 0 | 0 | 0 | 0 | 0 | .00 | 3 | .250 | .321 | .281 |
| 1982 Houston | NL | 85 | 198 | 47 | 14 | 1 | 4 | (1 | 3) | 75 | 16 | 22 | 21 | 3 | 31 | 1 | 0 | 2 | 0 | 2 | .00 | 5 | .237 | .311 | .379 |
| 1983 New York | NL | 115 | 253 | 64 | 12 | 0 | 8 | (6 | 2) | 100 | 30 | 21 | 29 | 6 | 40 | 1 | 1 | 5 | 3 | 3 | .50 | 5 | .253 | .326 | .395 |
| 1984 New York | NL | 99 | 199 | 46 | 9 | 2 | 1 | (1 | 0) | 62 | 36 | 12 | 27 | 3 | 22 | 1 | 1 | 5 | 3 | 1 | .75 | 9 | .231 | .319 | .312 |
| 1985 New York | NL | 95 | 271 | 76 | 17 | 0 | 7 | (2 | 5) | 114 | 26 | 42 | 27 | 1 | 27 | 1 | 0 | 6 | 2 | 2 | .50 | 12 | .280 | .341 | .421 |
| 1986 New York | NL | 86 | 195 | 55 | 8 | 2 | 5 | (3 | 2) | 82 | 24 | 33 | 30 | 5 | 31 | 1 | 0 | 1 | 1 | 4 | .20 | 3 | .282 | .379 | .421 |
| 1987 Los Angeles | NL | 60 | 98 | 16 | 4 | 0 | 0 | (0 | 0) | 20 | 7 | 9 | 8 | 0 | 10 | 0 | 1 | 0 | 1 | 0 | 1.00 | 6 | .163 | .226 | .204 |
| 1988 Los Angeles | NL | 95 | 149 | 36 | 2 | 0 | 0 | (0 | 0) | 38 | 14 | 11 | 22 | 0 | 13 | 1 | 0 | 1 | 2 | 0 | 1.00 | 4 | .242 | .341 | .255 |
| 1989 Boston | AL | 113 | 320 | 96 | 17 | 0 | 5 | (1 | 4) | 128 | 36 | 49 | 29 | 4 | 26 | 1 | 1 | 4 | 0 | 1 | .00 | 13 | .300 | .356 | .400 |
| 1990 Boston | AL | 41 | 69 | 12 | 1 | 1 | 0 | (0 | 0) | 15 | 3 | 8 | 7 | 0 | 14 | 1 | 0 | 1 | 0 | 0 | .00 | 0 | .174 | .256 | .217 |
| 12 ML YEARS | | 869 | 1949 | 498 | 95 | 6 | 30 | (14 | 16) | 695 | 204 | 226 | 219 | 25 | 238 | 9 | 4 | 28 | 12 | 13 | .48 | 60 | .256 | .329 | .357 |

## Scott Hemond

**Bats:** Right **Throws:** Right **Pos:** 3B **Ht:** 6' 0" **Wt:** 205 **Born:** 11/18/65 **Age:** 25

| | | BATTING | | | | | | | | | | | | | | | | | BASERUNNING | | | | PERCENTAGES | | |
|---|---|---|---|---|---|---|---|---|---|---|---|---|---|---|---|---|---|---|---|---|---|---|---|---|---|
| Year Team | Lg | G | AB | H | 2B | 3B | HR | (Hm | Rd) | TB | R | RBI | TBB | IBB | SO | HBP | SH | SF | SB | CS | SB% | GDP | Avg | OBP | SLG |
| 1986 Madison | A | 22 | 85 | 26 | 2 | 0 | 2 | -- | -- | 34 | 9 | 13 | 5 | 0 | 19 | 0 | 0 | 1 | 2 | 1 | .67 | 0 | .306 | .341 | .400 |
| 1987 Madison | A | 90 | 343 | 99 | 21 | 4 | 8 | -- | -- | 152 | 60 | 52 | 40 | 1 | 79 | 1 | 0 | 2 | 27 | 12 | .69 | 10 | .289 | .363 | .443 |
| Huntsville | AA | 33 | 110 | 20 | 3 | 1 | 1 | -- | -- | 28 | 10 | 8 | 4 | 0 | 30 | 0 | 1 | 0 | 5 | 1 | .83 | 3 | .182 | .211 | .255 |
| 1988 Huntsville | AA | 133 | 482 | 106 | 22 | 4 | 9 | -- | -- | 163 | 51 | 53 | 48 | 1 | 114 | 3 | 1 | 7 | 29 | 8 | .78 | 7 | .220 | .291 | .338 |
| 1989 Huntsville | AA | 132 | 490 | 130 | 26 | 6 | 5 | -- | -- | 183 | 89 | 62 | 62 | 0 | 77 | 7 | 13 | 6 | 45 | 17 | .73 | 11 | .265 | .352 | .373 |

| Year Team | Lg | G | AB | H | 2B | 3B | HR | (Hm | Rd) | TB | R | RBI | TBB | IBB | SO | HBP | SH | SF | SB | CS | SB% | GDP | Avg | OBP | SLG |
|---|---|---|---|---|---|---|---|---|---|---|---|---|---|---|---|---|---|---|---|---|---|---|---|---|---|
| 1990 Tacoma | AAA | 72 | 218 | 53 | 11 | 0 | 8 | -- | -- | 88 | 32 | 35 | 24 | 3 | 52 | 1 | 3 | 3 | 10 | 5 | .67 | 7 | .243 | .317 | .404 |
| 1989 Oakland | AL | 4 | 0 | 0 | 0 | 0 | 0 | (0 | 0) | 0 | 2 | 0 | 0 | 0 | 0 | 0 | 0 | 0 | 0 | 0 | .00 | 0 | .000 | .000 | .000 |
| 1990 Oakland | AL | 7 | 13 | 2 | 0 | 0 | 0 | (0 | 0) | 2 | 0 | 1 | 0 | 0 | 5 | 0 | 0 | 0 | 0 | 0 | .00 | 0 | .154 | .154 | .154 |
| 2 ML YEARS | | 11 | 13 | 2 | 0 | 0 | 0 | (0 | 0) | 2 | 2 | 1 | 0 | 0 | 5 | 0 | 0 | 0 | 0 | 0 | .00 | 0 | .154 | .154 | .154 |

## Dave Henderson

**Bats:** Right **Throws:** Right **Pos:** CF **Ht:** 6' 2" **Wt:** 210 **Born:** 07/21/58 **Age:** 32

| BATTING | | | | | | | | | | | | | | | | | | | BASERUNNING | | | | PERCENTAGES | | |
|---|---|---|---|---|---|---|---|---|---|---|---|---|---|---|---|---|---|---|---|---|---|---|---|---|---|
| Year Team | Lg | G | AB | H | 2B | 3B | HR | (Hm | Rd) | TB | R | RBI | TBB | IBB | SO | HBP | SH | SF | SB | CS | SB% | GDP | Avg | OBP | SLG |
| 1981 Seattle | AL | 59 | 126 | 21 | 3 | 0 | 6 | (5 | 1) | 42 | 17 | 13 | 16 | 1 | 24 | 1 | 1 | 1 | 2 | 1 | .67 | 4 | .167 | .264 | .333 |
| 1982 Seattle | AL | 104 | 324 | 82 | 17 | 1 | 14 | (8 | 6) | 143 | 47 | 48 | 36 | 2 | 67 | 0 | 1 | 1 | 2 | 5 | .29 | 5 | .253 | .327 | .441 |
| 1983 Seattle | AL | 137 | 484 | 130 | 24 | 5 | 17 | (9 | 8) | 215 | 50 | 55 | 28 | 3 | 93 | 1 | 2 | 6 | 9 | 3 | .75 | 5 | .269 | .306 | .444 |
| 1984 Seattle | AL | 112 | 350 | 98 | 23 | 0 | 14 | (8 | 6) | 163 | 42 | 43 | 19 | 0 | 56 | 2 | 2 | 1 | 5 | 5 | .50 | 4 | .280 | .320 | .466 |
| 1985 Seattle | AL | 139 | 502 | 121 | 28 | 2 | 14 | (8 | 6) | 195 | 70 | 68 | 48 | 2 | 104 | 3 | 1 | 2 | 6 | 1 | .86 | 11 | .241 | .310 | .388 |
| 1986 2 ML Teams | | 139 | 388 | 103 | 22 | 4 | 15 | (10 | 5) | 178 | 59 | 47 | 39 | 4 | 110 | 2 | 2 | 1 | 2 | 3 | .40 | 6 | .265 | .335 | .459 |
| 1987 2 ML Teams | | 90 | 205 | 48 | 12 | 0 | 8 | (4 | 4) | 84 | 32 | 26 | 30 | 0 | 53 | 0 | 1 | 2 | 3 | 1 | .75 | 3 | .234 | .329 | .410 |
| 1988 Oakland | AL | 146 | 507 | 154 | 38 | 1 | 24 | (12 | 12) | 266 | 100 | 94 | 47 | 1 | 92 | 4 | 5 | 7 | 2 | 4 | .33 | 14 | .304 | .363 | .525 |
| 1989 Oakland | AL | 152 | 579 | 145 | 24 | 3 | 15 | (10 | 5) | 220 | 77 | 80 | 54 | 1 | 131 | 3 | 1 | 6 | 8 | 5 | .62 | 13 | .250 | .315 | .380 |
| 1990 Oakland | AL | 127 | 450 | 122 | 28 | 0 | 20 | (11 | 9) | 210 | 65 | 63 | 40 | 1 | 105 | 1 | 1 | 2 | 3 | 1 | .75 | 5 | .271 | .331 | .467 |
| 1986 Seattle | AL | 103 | 337 | 93 | 19 | 4 | 14 | (10 | 4) | 162 | 51 | 44 | 37 | 4 | 95 | 2 | 1 | 1 | 1 | 3 | .25 | 5 | .276 | .350 | .481 |
| Boston | AL | 36 | 51 | 10 | 3 | 0 | 1 | (0 | 1) | 16 | 8 | 3 | 2 | 0 | 15 | 0 | 1 | 0 | 1 | 0 | 1.00 | 1 | .196 | .226 | .314 |
| 1987 Boston | AL | 75 | 184 | 43 | 10 | 0 | 8 | (4 | 4) | 77 | 30 | 25 | 22 | 0 | 48 | 0 | 1 | 2 | 1 | 1 | .50 | 3 | .234 | .313 | .418 |
| San Francisco | NL | 15 | 21 | 5 | 2 | 0 | 0 | (0 | 0) | 7 | 2 | 1 | 8 | 0 | 5 | 0 | 0 | 0 | 2 | 0 | 1.00 | 0 | .238 | .448 | .333 |
| 10 ML YEARS | | 1205 | 3915 | 1024 | 219 | 16 | 147 | (85 | 62) | 1716 | 559 | 537 | 357 | 15 | 835 | 17 | 17 | 29 | 42 | 29 | .59 | 70 | .262 | .324 | .438 |

## Rickey Henderson

**Bats:** Right **Throws:** Left **Pos:** LF/DH **Ht:** 5'10" **Wt:** 195 **Born:** 12/25/58 **Age:** 32

| BATTING | | | | | | | | | | | | | | | | | | | BASERUNNING | | | | PERCENTAGES | | |
|---|---|---|---|---|---|---|---|---|---|---|---|---|---|---|---|---|---|---|---|---|---|---|---|---|---|
| Year Team | Lg | G | AB | H | 2B | 3B | HR | (Hm | Rd) | TB | R | RBI | TBB | IBB | SO | HBP | SH | SF | SB | CS | SB% | GDP | Avg | OBP | SLG |
| 1979 Oakland | AL | 89 | 351 | 96 | 13 | 3 | 1 | (1 | 0) | 118 | 49 | 26 | 34 | 0 | 39 | 2 | 8 | 3 | 33 | 11 | .75 | 4 | .274 | .338 | .336 |
| 1980 Oakland | AL | 158 | 591 | 179 | 22 | 4 | 9 | (3 | 6) | 236 | 111 | 53 | 117 | 7 | 54 | 5 | 6 | 3 | 100 | 26 | .79 | 6 | .303 | .420 | .399 |
| 1981 Oakland | AL | 108 | 423 | 135 | 18 | 7 | 6 | (5 | 1) | 185 | 89 | 35 | 64 | 4 | 68 | 2 | 0 | 4 | 56 | 22 | .72 | 7 | .319 | .408 | .437 |
| 1982 Oakland | AL | 149 | 536 | 143 | 24 | 4 | 10 | (5 | 5) | 205 | 119 | 51 | 116 | 1 | 94 | 2 | 0 | 2 | 130 | 42 | .76 | 5 | .267 | .398 | .382 |
| 1983 Oakland | AL | 145 | 513 | 150 | 25 | 7 | 9 | (5 | 4) | 216 | 105 | 48 | 103 | 8 | 80 | 4 | 1 | 1 | 108 | 19 | .85 | 11 | .292 | .414 | .421 |
| 1984 Oakland | AL | 142 | 502 | 147 | 27 | 4 | 16 | (7 | 9) | 230 | 113 | 58 | 86 | 1 | 81 | 5 | 1 | 3 | 66 | 18 | .79 | 7 | .293 | .399 | .458 |
| 1985 New York | AL | 143 | 547 | 172 | 28 | 5 | 24 | (8 | 16) | 282 | 146 | 72 | 99 | 1 | 65 | 3 | 0 | 5 | 80 | 10 | .89 | 8 | .314 | .419 | .516 |
| 1986 New York | AL | 153 | 608 | 160 | 31 | 5 | 28 | (13 | 15) | 285 | 130 | 74 | 89 | 2 | 81 | 2 | 0 | 2 | 87 | 18 | .83 | 12 | .263 | .358 | .469 |
| 1987 New York | AL | 95 | 358 | 104 | 17 | 3 | 17 | (10 | 7) | 178 | 78 | 37 | 80 | 1 | 52 | 2 | 0 | 0 | 41 | 8 | .84 | 10 | .291 | .423 | .497 |
| 1988 New York | AL | 140 | 554 | 169 | 30 | 2 | 6 | (2 | 4) | 221 | 118 | 50 | 82 | 1 | 54 | 3 | 2 | 6 | 93 | 13 | .88 | 6 | .305 | .394 | .399 |
| 1989 2 ML Teams | | 150 | 541 | 148 | 26 | 3 | 12 | (7 | 5) | 216 | 113 | 57 | 126 | 5 | 68 | 3 | 0 | 4 | 77 | 14 | .85 | 8 | .274 | .411 | .399 |
| 1990 Oakland | AL | 136 | 489 | 159 | 33 | 3 | 28 | (8 | 20) | 282 | 119 | 61 | 97 | 2 | 60 | 4 | 2 | 2 | 65 | 10 | .87 | 13 | .325 | .439 | .577 |
| 1989 New York | AL | 65 | 235 | 58 | 13 | 1 | 3 | (1 | 2) | 82 | 41 | 22 | 56 | 0 | 29 | 1 | 0 | 1 | 25 | 8 | .76 | 0 | .247 | .392 | .349 |
| Oakland | AL | 85 | 306 | 90 | 13 | 2 | 9 | (6 | 3) | 134 | 72 | 35 | 70 | 5 | 39 | 2 | 0 | 3 | 52 | 6 | .90 | 8 | .294 | .425 | .438 |
| 12 ML YEARS | | 1608 | 6013 | 1762 | 294 | 50 | 166 | (74 | 92) | 2654 | 1290 | 622 | 1093 | 33 | 796 | 37 | 20 | 35 | 936 | 211 | .82 | 97 | .293 | .403 | .441 |

## Tom Henke

**Pitches:** Right **Bats:** Right **Pos:** RP **Ht:** 6' 5" **Wt:** 225 **Born:** 12/21/57 **Age:** 33

| HOW MUCH HE PITCHED | | | | | | | | WHAT HE GAVE UP | | | | | | | | | | | | THE RESULTS | | | | | |
|---|---|---|---|---|---|---|---|---|---|---|---|---|---|---|---|---|---|---|---|---|---|---|---|---|---|
| Year Team | Lg | G | GS | CG | GF | IP | BFP | H | R | ER | HR | SH | SF | HB | TBB | IBB | SO | WP | Bk | W | L | Pct. | ShO | Sv | ERA |
| 1982 Texas | AL | 8 | 0 | 0 | 6 | 15.2 | 67 | 14 | 2 | 2 | 0 | 1 | 0 | 1 | 8 | 2 | 9 | 0 | 0 | 1 | 0 | 1.000 | 0 | 0 | 1.15 |
| 1983 Texas | AL | 8 | 0 | 0 | 5 | 16 | 65 | 16 | 6 | 6 | 1 | 0 | 0 | 0 | 4 | 0 | 17 | 0 | 0 | 1 | 0 | 1.000 | 0 | 1 | 3.38 |
| 1984 Texas | AL | 25 | 0 | 0 | 13 | 28.1 | 141 | 36 | 21 | 20 | 0 | 1 | 4 | 1 | 20 | 2 | 25 | 2 | 2 | 1 | 1 | .500 | 0 | 2 | 6.35 |
| 1985 Toronto | AL | 28 | 0 | 0 | 22 | 40 | 153 | 29 | 12 | 9 | 4 | 2 | 2 | 0 | 8 | 2 | 42 | 0 | 0 | 3 | 3 | .500 | 0 | 13 | 2.03 |
| 1986 Toronto | AL | 63 | 0 | 0 | 51 | 91.1 | 370 | 63 | 39 | 34 | 6 | 2 | 6 | 1 | 32 | 4 | 118 | 3 | 1 | 9 | 5 | .643 | 0 | 27 | 3.35 |
| 1987 Toronto | AL | 72 | 0 | 0 | 62 | 94 | 363 | 62 | 27 | 26 | 10 | 3 | 5 | 0 | 25 | 3 | 128 | 5 | 0 | 0 | 6 | .000 | 0 | 34 | 2.49 |
| 1988 Toronto | AL | 52 | 0 | 0 | 44 | 68 | 285 | 60 | 23 | 22 | 6 | 4 | 2 | 2 | 24 | 3 | 66 | 0 | 0 | 4 | 4 | .500 | 0 | 25 | 2.91 |
| 1989 Toronto | AL | 64 | 0 | 0 | 56 | 89 | 356 | 66 | 20 | 19 | 5 | 4 | 3 | 2 | 25 | 4 | 116 | 2 | 0 | 8 | 3 | .727 | 0 | 20 | 1.92 |
| 1990 Toronto | AL | 61 | 0 | 0 | 58 | 74.2 | 297 | 58 | 18 | 18 | 8 | 4 | 1 | 1 | 19 | 2 | 75 | 6 | 0 | 2 | 4 | .333 | 0 | 32 | 2.17 |
| 9 ML YEARS | | 381 | 0 | 0 | 317 | 517 | 2097 | 404 | 168 | 156 | 40 | 21 | 23 | 8 | 165 | 22 | 596 | 18 | 3 | 29 | 26 | .527 | 0 | 154 | 2.72 |

## Mike Henneman

**Pitches:** Right **Bats:** Right **Pos:** RP **Ht:** 6' 4" **Wt:** 195 **Born:** 12/11/61 **Age:** 29

| HOW MUCH HE PITCHED | | | | | | | | WHAT HE GAVE UP | | | | | | | | | | | | THE RESULTS | | | | | |
|---|---|---|---|---|---|---|---|---|---|---|---|---|---|---|---|---|---|---|---|---|---|---|---|---|---|
| Year Team | Lg | G | GS | CG | GF | IP | BFP | H | R | ER | HR | SH | SF | HB | TBB | IBB | SO | WP | Bk | W | L | Pct. | ShO | Sv | ERA |
| 1987 Detroit | AL | 55 | 0 | 0 | 28 | 96.2 | 399 | 86 | 36 | 32 | 8 | 2 | 2 | 3 | 30 | 5 | 75 | 7 | 0 | 11 | 3 | .786 | 0 | 7 | 2.98 |
| 1988 Detroit | AL | 65 | 0 | 0 | 51 | 91.1 | 364 | 72 | 23 | 19 | 7 | 5 | 2 | 2 | 24 | 10 | 58 | 8 | 1 | 9 | 6 | .600 | 0 | 22 | 1.87 |

| Year Team | Lg | G | GS | CG | GF | IP | BFP | H | R | ER | HR | SH | SF | HB | TBB | IBB | SO | WP | Bk | W | L | Pct. | ShO | Sv | ERA |
|---|---|---|---|---|---|---|---|---|---|---|---|---|---|---|---|---|---|---|---|---|---|---|---|---|---|
| 1989 Detroit | AL | 60 | 0 | 0 | 35 | 90 | 401 | 84 | 46 | 37 | 4 | 7 | 3 | 5 | 51 | 15 | 69 | 0 | 1 | 11 | 4 | .733 | 0 | 8 | 3.70 |
| 1990 Detroit | AL | 69 | 0 | 0 | 53 | 94.1 | 399 | 90 | 36 | 32 | 4 | 5 | 2 | 3 | 33 | 12 | 50 | 3 | 0 | 8 | 6 | .571 | 0 | 22 | 3.05 |
| 4 ML YEARS | | 249 | 0 | 0 | 167 | 372.1 | 1563 | 332 | 141 | 120 | 23 | 19 | 9 | 13 | 138 | 42 | 252 | 18 | 2 | 39 | 19 | .672 | 0 | 59 | 2.90 |

## Randy Hennis

**Pitches:** Right **Bats:** Right **Pos:** RP **Ht:** 6' 4" **Wt:** 220 **Born:** 12/16/65 **Age:** 25

| | | HOW MUCH HE PITCHED | | | | | | WHAT HE GAVE UP | | | | | | | | | | | | THE RESULTS | | | | | |
|---|---|---|---|---|---|---|---|---|---|---|---|---|---|---|---|---|---|---|---|---|---|---|---|---|---|
| Year Team | Lg | G | GS | CG | GF | IP | BFP | H | R | ER | HR | SH | SF | HB | TBB | IBB | SO | WP | Bk | W | L | Pct. | ShO | Sv | ERA |
| 1987 Auburn | A | 13 | 12 | 3 | 0 | 72.2 | 320 | 67 | 41 | 37 | 2 | 6 | 1 | 2 | 33 | 3 | 40 | 6 | 1 | 3 | 9 | .250 | 0 | 0 | 4.58 |
| 1988 Osceola | A | 14 | 14 | 2 | 0 | 82.2 | 341 | 64 | 34 | 22 | 2 | 0 | 1 | 3 | 28 | 2 | 48 | 7 | 5 | 7 | 3 | .700 | 1 | 0 | 2.40 |
| 1989 Columbus | AA | 28 | 28 | 2 | 0 | 171 | 723 | 151 | 75 | 68 | 6 | 8 | 7 | 6 | 78 | 1 | 101 | 11 | 1 | 9 | 9 | .500 | 0 | 0 | 3.58 |
| 1990 Tucson | AAA | 28 | 28 | 3 | 0 | 159.1 | 695 | 153 | 87 | 78 | 6 | 2 | 8 | 3 | 92 | 3 | 101 | 10 | 2 | 10 | 8 | .556 | 1 | 0 | 4.41 |
| 1990 Houston | NL | 3 | 1 | 0 | 1 | 9.2 | 34 | 1 | 0 | 0 | 0 | 0 | 0 | 1 | 3 | 0 | 4 | 0 | 0 | 0 | 0 | .000 | 0 | 0 | 0.00 |

## Dwayne Henry

**Pitches:** Right **Bats:** Right **Pos:** RP **Ht:** 6' 3" **Wt:** 205 **Born:** 02/16/62 **Age:** 29

| | | HOW MUCH HE PITCHED | | | | | | WHAT HE GAVE UP | | | | | | | | | | | | THE RESULTS | | | | | |
|---|---|---|---|---|---|---|---|---|---|---|---|---|---|---|---|---|---|---|---|---|---|---|---|---|---|
| Year Team | Lg | G | GS | CG | GF | IP | BFP | H | R | ER | HR | SH | SF | HB | TBB | IBB | SO | WP | Bk | W | L | Pct. | ShO | Sv | ERA |
| 1984 Texas | AL | 3 | 0 | 0 | 1 | 4.1 | 25 | 5 | 4 | 4 | 0 | 1 | 0 | 0 | 7 | 0 | 2 | 0 | 0 | 0 | 1 | .000 | 0 | 0 | 8.31 |
| 1985 Texas | AL | 16 | 0 | 0 | 10 | 21 | 86 | 16 | 7 | 6 | 0 | 2 | 1 | 0 | 7 | 0 | 20 | 1 | 0 | 2 | 2 | .500 | 0 | 3 | 2.57 |
| 1986 Texas | AL | 19 | 0 | 0 | 4 | 19.1 | 93 | 14 | 11 | 10 | 1 | 1 | 2 | 1 | 22 | 0 | 17 | 7 | 1 | 1 | 0 | 1.000 | 0 | 0 | 4.66 |
| 1987 Texas | AL | 5 | 0 | 0 | 1 | 10 | 50 | 12 | 10 | 10 | 2 | 0 | 0 | 0 | 9 | 0 | 7 | 1 | 0 | 0 | 0 | .000 | 0 | 0 | 9.00 |
| 1988 Texas | AL | 11 | 0 | 0 | 5 | 10.1 | 59 | 15 | 10 | 10 | 1 | 0 | 1 | 3 | 9 | 1 | 10 | 3 | 1 | 0 | 1 | .000 | 0 | 1 | 8.71 |
| 1989 Atlanta | NL | 12 | 0 | 0 | 6 | 12.2 | 55 | 12 | 6 | 6 | 2 | 2 | 0 | 0 | 5 | 1 | 16 | 1 | 0 | 0 | 2 | .000 | 0 | 1 | 4.26 |
| 1990 Atlanta | NL | 34 | 0 | 0 | 14 | 38.1 | 176 | 41 | 26 | 24 | 3 | 0 | 1 | 0 | 25 | 0 | 34 | 2 | 1 | 2 | 2 | .500 | 0 | 0 | 5.63 |
| 7 ML YEARS | | 100 | 0 | 0 | 41 | 116 | 544 | 115 | 74 | 70 | 9 | 6 | 5 | 4 | 84 | 2 | 106 | 15 | 3 | 5 | 8 | .385 | 0 | 5 | 5.43 |

## Carlos Hernandez

**Bats:** Right **Throws:** Right **Pos:** C **Ht:** 5'11" **Wt:** 185 **Born:** 05/24/67 **Age:** 24

| | | BATTING | | | | | | | | | | | | | | | | | BASERUNNING | | | | PERCENTAGES | | |
|---|---|---|---|---|---|---|---|---|---|---|---|---|---|---|---|---|---|---|---|---|---|---|---|---|---|
| Year Team | Lg | G | AB | H | 2B | 3B | HR | (Hm | Rd) | TB | R | RBI | TBB | IBB | SO | HBP | SH | SF | SB | CS | SB% | GDP | Avg | OBP | SLG |
| 1985 Dodgers | R | 22 | 49 | 12 | 1 | 0 | 0 | -- | -- | 13 | 3 | 6 | 3 | 0 | 8 | 0 | 0 | 0 | 0 | 0 | .00 | 4 | .245 | .288 | .265 |
| 1986 Dodgers | R | 57 | 205 | 64 | 7 | 0 | 1 | -- | -- | 74 | 19 | 31 | 5 | 2 | 18 | 2 | 1 | 1 | 1 | 2 | .33 | 7 | .312 | .333 | .361 |
| 1987 Bakersfield | A | 48 | 162 | 37 | 6 | 1 | 3 | -- | -- | 54 | 22 | 22 | 14 | 0 | 23 | 3 | 1 | 2 | 8 | 4 | .67 | 6 | .228 | .298 | .333 |
| 1988 Bakersfield | A | 92 | 333 | 103 | 15 | 2 | 5 | -- | -- | 137 | 37 | 52 | 16 | 2 | 39 | 1 | 3 | 4 | 3 | 2 | .60 | 18 | .309 | .339 | .411 |
| Albuquerque | AAA | 3 | 8 | 1 | 0 | 0 | 0 | -- | -- | 1 | 0 | 1 | 0 | 0 | 0 | 0 | 0 | 0 | 0 | 0 | .00 | 1 | .125 | .125 | .125 |
| 1989 San Antonio | AA | 99 | 370 | 111 | 16 | 3 | 8 | -- | -- | 157 | 37 | 41 | 12 | 0 | 46 | 7 | 1 | 3 | 2 | 3 | .40 | 12 | .300 | .332 | .424 |
| Albuquerque | AAA | 4 | 14 | 3 | 0 | 0 | 0 | -- | -- | 3 | 1 | 1 | 2 | 1 | 1 | 0 | 0 | 0 | 0 | 0 | .00 | 1 | .214 | .313 | .214 |
| 1990 Albuquerque | AAA | 52 | 143 | 45 | 8 | 1 | 0 | -- | -- | 55 | 11 | 16 | 8 | 1 | 25 | 1 | 0 | 3 | 2 | 2 | .50 | 5 | .315 | .348 | .385 |
| 1990 Los Angeles | NL | 10 | 20 | 4 | 1 | 0 | 0 | (0 | 0) | 5 | 2 | 1 | 0 | 0 | 2 | 0 | 0 | 0 | 0 | 0 | .00 | 0 | .200 | .200 | .250 |

## Keith Hernandez

**Bats:** Left **Throws:** Left **Pos:** 1B **Ht:** 6' 0" **Wt:** 205 **Born:** 10/20/53 **Age:** 37

| | | BATTING | | | | | | | | | | | | | | | | | BASERUNNING | | | | PERCENTAGES | | |
|---|---|---|---|---|---|---|---|---|---|---|---|---|---|---|---|---|---|---|---|---|---|---|---|---|---|
| Year Team | Lg | G | AB | H | 2B | 3B | HR | (Hm | Rd) | TB | R | RBI | TBB | IBB | SO | HBP | SH | SF | SB | CS | SB% | GDP | Avg | OBP | SLG |
| 1974 St. Louis | NL | 14 | 34 | 10 | 1 | 2 | 0 | (0 | 0) | 15 | 3 | 2 | 7 | 0 | 8 | 0 | 0 | 0 | 0 | 0 | .00 | 1 | .294 | .415 | .441 |
| 1975 St. Louis | NL | 64 | 188 | 47 | 8 | 2 | 3 | (0 | 3) | 68 | 20 | 20 | 17 | 2 | 26 | 0 | 0 | 2 | 0 | 1 | .00 | 5 | .250 | .309 | .362 |
| 1976 St. Louis | NL | 129 | 374 | 108 | 21 | 5 | 7 | (4 | 3) | 160 | 54 | 46 | 49 | 5 | 53 | 3 | 2 | 0 | 4 | 2 | .67 | 8 | .289 | .376 | .428 |
| 1977 St. Louis | NL | 161 | 560 | 163 | 41 | 4 | 15 | (5 | 10) | 257 | 90 | 91 | 79 | 11 | 88 | 1 | 3 | 2 | 7 | 7 | .50 | 17 | .291 | .379 | .459 |
| 1978 St. Louis | NL | 159 | 542 | 138 | 32 | 4 | 11 | (4 | 7) | 211 | 90 | 64 | 82 | 11 | 68 | 2 | 1 | 6 | 13 | 5 | .72 | 12 | .255 | .351 | .389 |
| 1979 St. Louis | NL | 161 | 610 | 210 | 48 | 11 | 11 | (5 | 6) | 313 | 116 | 105 | 80 | 5 | 78 | 1 | 0 | 7 | 11 | 6 | .65 | 9 | .344 | .417 | .513 |
| 1980 St. Louis | NL | 159 | 595 | 191 | 39 | 8 | 16 | (8 | 8) | 294 | 111 | 99 | 86 | 4 | 73 | 4 | 1 | 4 | 14 | 8 | .64 | 14 | .321 | .408 | .494 |
| 1981 St. Louis | NL | 103 | 376 | 115 | 27 | 4 | 8 | (4 | 4) | 174 | 65 | 48 | 61 | 6 | 45 | 2 | 0 | 5 | 12 | 5 | .71 | 9 | .306 | .401 | .463 |
| 1982 St. Louis | NL | 160 | 579 | 173 | 33 | 6 | 7 | (4 | 3) | 239 | 79 | 94 | 100 | 19 | 67 | 2 | 1 | 12 | 19 | 11 | .63 | 10 | .299 | .397 | .413 |
| 1983 2 ML Teams | | 150 | 538 | 160 | 23 | 7 | 12 | (10 | 2) | 233 | 77 | 63 | 88 | 14 | 72 | 2 | 2 | 3 | 9 | 5 | .64 | 7 | .297 | .396 | .433 |
| 1984 New York | NL | 154 | 550 | 171 | 31 | 0 | 15 | (10 | 5) | 247 | 83 | 94 | 97 | 12 | 89 | 1 | 0 | 9 | 2 | 3 | .40 | 9 | .311 | .409 | .449 |
| 1985 New York | NL | 158 | 593 | 183 | 34 | 4 | 10 | (4 | 6) | 255 | 87 | 91 | 77 | 15 | 59 | 2 | 0 | 10 | 3 | 3 | .50 | 14 | .309 | .384 | .430 |
| 1986 New York | NL | 149 | 551 | 171 | 34 | 1 | 13 | (6 | 7) | 246 | 94 | 83 | 94 | 9 | 69 | 4 | 0 | 3 | 2 | 1 | .67 | 14 | .310 | .413 | .446 |
| 1987 New York | NL | 154 | 587 | 170 | 28 | 2 | 18 | (6 | 12) | 256 | 87 | 89 | 81 | 8 | 104 | 4 | 0 | 4 | 0 | 2 | .00 | 15 | .290 | .377 | .436 |
| 1988 New York | NL | 95 | 348 | 96 | 16 | 0 | 11 | (2 | 9) | 145 | 43 | 55 | 31 | 3 | 57 | 1 | 0 | 4 | 2 | 1 | .67 | 11 | .276 | .333 | .417 |
| 1989 New York | NL | 75 | 215 | 50 | 8 | 0 | 4 | (2 | 2) | 70 | 18 | 19 | 27 | 3 | 39 | 2 | 0 | 0 | 0 | 3 | .00 | 4 | .233 | .324 | .326 |
| 1990 Cleveland | AL | 43 | 130 | 26 | 2 | 0 | 1 | (0 | 1) | 31 | 7 | 8 | 14 | 3 | 17 | 1 | 0 | 0 | 0 | 0 | .00 | 2 | .200 | .283 | .238 |
| 1983 St. Louis | NL | 55 | 218 | 62 | 15 | 4 | 3 | (2 | 1) | 94 | 34 | 26 | 24 | 5 | 30 | 0 | 0 | 2 | 1 | 1 | .50 | 2 | .284 | .352 | .431 |
| New York | NL | 95 | 320 | 98 | 8 | 3 | 9 | (8 | 1) | 139 | 43 | 37 | 64 | 9 | 42 | 2 | 2 | 1 | 8 | 4 | .67 | 5 | .306 | .424 | .434 |
| 17 ML YEARS | | 2088 | 7370 | 2182 | 426 | 60 | 162 | (74 | 88) | 3214 | 1124 | 1071 | 1070 | 130 | 1012 | 32 | 10 | 71 | 98 | 63 | .61 | 161 | .296 | .384 | .436 |

## Xavier Hernandez

**Pitches:** Right **Bats:** Left **Pos:** RP **Ht:** 6' 2" **Wt:** 185 **Born:** 08/16/65 **Age:** 25

| | | | HOW MUCH HE PITCHED | | | | | | WHAT HE GAVE UP | | | | | | | | | | | | THE RESULTS | | | | | |
|---|---|---|---|---|---|---|---|---|---|---|---|---|---|---|---|---|---|---|---|---|---|---|---|---|---|---|
| Year | Team | Lg | G | GS | CG | GF | IP | BFP | H | R | ER | HR | SH | SF | HB | TBB | IBB | SO | WP | Bk | W | L | Pct. | ShO | Sv | ERA |
| 1986 | St.Cathrnes | A | 13 | 10 | 1 | 3 | 70.2 | 284 | 55 | 27 | 21 | 6 | 1 | 0 | 6 | 16 | 0 | 69 | 5 | 2 | 5 | 5 | .500 | 1 | 0 | 2.67 |
| 1987 | St.Cathrnes | A | 13 | 11 | 0 | 0 | 55 | 242 | 57 | 39 | 31 | 4 | 1 | 1 | 4 | 16 | 0 | 49 | 2 | 0 | 3 | 3 | .500 | 0 | 0 | 5.07 |
| 1988 | Myrtle Bch | A | 23 | 22 | 2 | 1 | 148 | 585 | 116 | 52 | 42 | 5 | 1 | 3 | 7 | 28 | 1 | 111 | 10 | 4 | 13 | 6 | .684 | 2 | 0 | 2.55 |
| | Knoxville | AA | 11 | 11 | 2 | 0 | 68.1 | 290 | 73 | 32 | 22 | 3 | 2 | 1 | 3 | 15 | 0 | 33 | 2 | 1 | 2 | 4 | .333 | 0 | 0 | 2.90 |
| 1989 | Knoxville | AA | 4 | 4 | 1 | 0 | 24 | 112 | 25 | 11 | 11 | 0 | 0 | 1 | 1 | 11 | 0 | 17 | 1 | 0 | 1 | 1 | .500 | 1 | 0 | 4.13 |
| | Syracuse | AAA | 15 | 15 | 2 | 0 | 99.1 | 411 | 95 | 42 | 39 | 7 | 4 | 4 | 2 | 22 | 0 | 47 | 4 | 2 | 5 | 6 | .455 | 1 | 0 | 3.53 |
| 1989 | Toronto | AL | 7 | 0 | 0 | 2 | 22.2 | 101 | 25 | 15 | 12 | 2 | 0 | 2 | 1 | 8 | 0 | 7 | 1 | 0 | 1 | 0 | 1.000 | 0 | 0 | 4.76 |
| 1990 | Houston | NL | 34 | 1 | 0 | 10 | 62.1 | 268 | 60 | 34 | 32 | 8 | 2 | 4 | 4 | 24 | 5 | 24 | 6 | 0 | 2 | 1 | .667 | 0 | 0 | 4.62 |
| | 2 ML YEARS | | 41 | 1 | 0 | 12 | 85 | 369 | 85 | 49 | 44 | 10 | 2 | 6 | 5 | 32 | 5 | 31 | 7 | 0 | 3 | 1 | .750 | 0 | 0 | 4.66 |

## Tommy Herr

**Bats:** Both **Throws:** Right **Pos:** 2B **Ht:** 6' 0" **Wt:** 185 **Born:** 04/04/56 **Age:** 35

| | | | BATTING | | | | | | | | | | | | | | | | | BASERUNNING | | | | PERCENTAGES | | |
|---|---|---|---|---|---|---|---|---|---|---|---|---|---|---|---|---|---|---|---|---|---|---|---|---|---|---|
| Year | Team | Lg | G | AB | H | 2B | 3B | HR | (Hm | Rd) | TB | R | RBI | TBB | IBB | SO | HBP | SH | SF | SB | CS | SB% | GDP | Avg | OBP | SLG |
| 1979 | St. Louis | NL | 14 | 10 | 2 | 0 | 0 | 0 | (0 | 0) | 2 | 4 | 1 | 2 | 0 | 2 | 0 | 0 | 0 | 1 | 0 | 1.00 | 0 | .200 | .333 | .200 |
| 1980 | St. Louis | NL | 76 | 222 | 55 | 12 | 5 | 0 | (0 | 0) | 77 | 29 | 15 | 16 | 5 | 21 | 1 | 1 | 2 | 9 | 2 | .82 | 8 | .248 | .299 | .347 |
| 1981 | St. Louis | NL | 103 | 411 | 110 | 14 | 9 | 0 | (0 | 0) | 142 | 50 | 46 | 39 | 3 | 30 | 1 | 6 | 5 | 23 | 7 | .77 | 9 | .268 | .329 | .345 |
| 1982 | St. Louis | NL | 135 | 493 | 131 | 19 | 4 | 0 | (0 | 0) | 158 | 83 | 36 | 57 | 2 | 56 | 2 | 3 | 5 | 25 | 12 | .68 | 5 | .266 | .341 | .320 |
| 1983 | St. Louis | NL | 89 | 313 | 101 | 14 | 4 | 2 | (1 | 1) | 129 | 43 | 31 | 43 | 2 | 27 | 1 | 8 | 3 | 6 | 8 | .43 | 7 | .323 | .403 | .412 |
| 1984 | St. Louis | NL | 145 | 558 | 154 | 23 | 2 | 4 | (1 | 3) | 193 | 67 | 49 | 49 | 2 | 56 | 2 | 10 | 3 | 13 | 7 | .65 | 11 | .276 | .335 | .346 |
| 1985 | St. Louis | NL | 159 | 596 | 180 | 38 | 3 | 8 | (4 | 4) | 248 | 97 | 110 | 80 | 5 | 55 | 2 | 5 | 13 | 31 | 3 | .91 | 6 | .302 | .379 | .416 |
| 1986 | St. Louis | NL | 152 | 559 | 141 | 30 | 4 | 2 | (1 | 1) | 185 | 48 | 61 | 73 | 10 | 75 | 5 | 6 | 4 | 22 | 8 | .73 | 8 | .252 | .342 | .331 |
| 1987 | St. Louis | NL | 141 | 510 | 134 | 29 | 0 | 2 | (1 | 1) | 169 | 73 | 83 | 68 | 3 | 62 | 3 | 4 | 12 | 19 | 4 | .83 | 12 | .263 | .346 | .331 |
| 1988 | 2 ML Teams | | 101 | 354 | 93 | 16 | 0 | 2 | (1 | 1) | 115 | 46 | 24 | 51 | 4 | 51 | 0 | 3 | 0 | 13 | 3 | .81 | 10 | .263 | .356 | .325 |
| 1989 | Philadelphia | NL | 151 | 561 | 161 | 25 | 6 | 2 | (0 | 2) | 204 | 65 | 37 | 54 | 2 | 63 | 3 | 6 | 2 | 10 | 7 | .59 | 9 | .287 | .352 | .364 |
| 1990 | 2 ML Teams | | 146 | 547 | 143 | 26 | 3 | 5 | (4 | 1) | 190 | 48 | 60 | 50 | 4 | 58 | 2 | 6 | 2 | 7 | 1 | .88 | 11 | .261 | .324 | .347 |
| 1988 | St. Louis | NL | 15 | 50 | 13 | 0 | 0 | 1 | (1 | 0) | 16 | 4 | 3 | 11 | 3 | 4 | 0 | 2 | 0 | 3 | 0 | 1.00 | 1 | .260 | .393 | .320 |
| | Minnesota | AL | 86 | 304 | 80 | 16 | 0 | 1 | (0 | 1) | 99 | 42 | 21 | 40 | 1 | 47 | 0 | 1 | 0 | 10 | 3 | .77 | 9 | .263 | .349 | .326 |
| 1990 | Philadelphia | NL | 119 | 447 | 118 | 21 | 3 | 4 | (3 | 1) | 157 | 39 | 50 | 36 | 4 | 47 | 2 | 6 | 2 | 7 | 1 | .88 | 10 | .264 | .320 | .351 |
| | New York | NL | 27 | 100 | 25 | 5 | 0 | 1 | (1 | 0) | 33 | 9 | 10 | 14 | 0 | 11 | 0 | 0 | 0 | 0 | 0 | .00 | 1 | .250 | .342 | .330 |
| | 12 ML YEARS | | 1412 | 5134 | 1405 | 246 | 40 | 27 | (13 | 14) | 1812 | 653 | 553 | 582 | 42 | 556 | 22 | 58 | 51 | 179 | 62 | .74 | 96 | .274 | .347 | .353 |

## Orel Hershiser

**Pitches:** Right **Bats:** Right **Pos:** SP **Ht:** 6' 3" **Wt:** 190 **Born:** 09/16/58 **Age:** 32

| | | | HOW MUCH HE PITCHED | | | | | | WHAT HE GAVE UP | | | | | | | | | | | | THE RESULTS | | | | | |
|---|---|---|---|---|---|---|---|---|---|---|---|---|---|---|---|---|---|---|---|---|---|---|---|---|---|---|
| Year | Team | Lg | G | GS | CG | GF | IP | BFP | H | R | ER | HR | SH | SF | HB | TBB | IBB | SO | WP | Bk | W | L | Pct. | ShO | Sv | ERA |
| 1983 | Los Angeles | NL | 8 | 0 | 0 | 4 | 8 | 37 | 7 | 6 | 3 | 1 | 1 | 0 | 0 | 6 | 0 | 5 | 1 | 0 | 0 | 0 | .000 | 0 | 1 | 3.38 |
| 1984 | Los Angeles | NL | 45 | 20 | 8 | 10 | 189.2 | 771 | 160 | 65 | 56 | 9 | 2 | 3 | 4 | 50 | 8 | 150 | 8 | 1 | 11 | 8 | .579 | 4 | 2 | 2.66 |
| 1985 | Los Angeles | NL | 36 | 34 | 9 | 1 | 239.2 | 953 | 179 | 72 | 54 | 8 | 5 | 4 | 6 | 68 | 5 | 157 | 5 | 0 | 19 | 3 | .864 | 5 | 0 | 2.03 |
| 1986 | Los Angeles | NL | 35 | 35 | 8 | 0 | 231.1 | 988 | 213 | 112 | 99 | 13 | 14 | 6 | 5 | 86 | 11 | 153 | 12 | 3 | 14 | 14 | .500 | 1 | 0 | 3.85 |
| 1987 | Los Angeles | NL | 37 | 35 | 10 | 2 | 264.2 | 1093 | 247 | 105 | 90 | 17 | 8 | 2 | 9 | 74 | 5 | 190 | 11 | 2 | 16 | 16 | .500 | 1 | 1 | 3.06 |
| 1988 | Los Angeles | NL | 35 | 34 | 15 | 1 | 267 | 1068 | 208 | 73 | 67 | 18 | 9 | 6 | 4 | 73 | 10 | 178 | 6 | 5 | 23 | 8 | .742 | 8 | 1 | 2.26 |
| 1989 | Los Angeles | NL | 35 | 33 | 8 | 0 | 256.2 | 1047 | 226 | 75 | 66 | 9 | 19 | 6 | 3 | 77 | 14 | 178 | 8 | 4 | 15 | 15 | .500 | 4 | 0 | 2.31 |
| 1990 | Los Angeles | NL | 4 | 4 | 0 | 0 | 25.1 | 106 | 26 | 12 | 12 | 1 | 1 | 0 | 1 | 4 | 0 | 16 | 0 | 1 | 1 | 1 | .500 | 0 | 0 | 4.26 |
| | 8 ML YEARS | | 235 | 195 | 58 | 18 | 1482.1 | 6063 | 1266 | 520 | 447 | 76 | 59 | 27 | 32 | 438 | 53 | 1027 | 51 | 16 | 99 | 65 | .604 | 23 | 5 | 2.71 |

## Joe Hesketh

**Pitches:** Left **Bats:** Left **Pos:** RP **Ht:** 6' 2" **Wt:** 170 **Born:** 02/15/59 **Age:** 32

| | | | HOW MUCH HE PITCHED | | | | | | WHAT HE GAVE UP | | | | | | | | | | | | THE RESULTS | | | | | |
|---|---|---|---|---|---|---|---|---|---|---|---|---|---|---|---|---|---|---|---|---|---|---|---|---|---|---|
| Year | Team | Lg | G | GS | CG | GF | IP | BFP | H | R | ER | HR | SH | SF | HB | TBB | IBB | SO | WP | Bk | W | L | Pct. | ShO | Sv | ERA |
| 1984 | Montreal | NL | 11 | 5 | 1 | 2 | 45 | 182 | 38 | 12 | 9 | 2 | 2 | 2 | 0 | 15 | 3 | 32 | 1 | 3 | 2 | 2 | .500 | 1 | 1 | 1.80 |
| 1985 | Montreal | NL | 25 | 25 | 2 | 0 | 155.1 | 618 | 125 | 52 | 43 | 10 | 8 | 2 | 0 | 45 | 2 | 113 | 3 | 3 | 10 | 5 | .667 | 1 | 0 | 2.49 |
| 1986 | Montreal | NL | 15 | 15 | 0 | 0 | 82.2 | 362 | 92 | 46 | 46 | 11 | 2 | 2 | 2 | 31 | 4 | 67 | 4 | 3 | 6 | 5 | .545 | 0 | 0 | 5.01 |
| 1987 | Montreal | NL | 18 | 0 | 0 | 3 | 28.2 | 128 | 23 | 12 | 10 | 2 | 2 | 0 | 2 | 15 | 3 | 31 | 1 | 0 | 0 | 0 | .000 | 0 | 1 | 3.14 |
| 1988 | Montreal | NL | 60 | 0 | 0 | 23 | 72.2 | 304 | 63 | 30 | 23 | 1 | 5 | 4 | 0 | 35 | 9 | 64 | 5 | 1 | 4 | 3 | .571 | 0 | 9 | 2.85 |
| 1989 | Montreal | NL | 43 | 0 | 0 | 17 | 48.1 | 219 | 54 | 34 | 31 | 5 | 6 | 2 | 0 | 26 | 6 | 44 | 1 | 3 | 6 | 4 | .600 | 0 | 3 | 5.77 |
| 1990 | 3 ML Teams | | 45 | 2 | 0 | 19 | 59.2 | 269 | 69 | 35 | 30 | 7 | 0 | 1 | 1 | 25 | 2 | 50 | 8 | 0 | 1 | 6 | .143 | 0 | 5 | 4.53 |
| 1990 | Montreal | NL | 2 | 0 | 0 | 0 | 3 | 12 | 2 | 0 | 0 | 0 | 0 | 0 | 0 | 2 | 1 | 3 | 0 | 0 | 1 | 0 | 1.000 | 0 | 0 | 0.00 |
| | Atlanta | NL | 31 | 0 | 0 | 15 | 31 | 135 | 30 | 23 | 20 | 5 | 0 | 1 | 1 | 12 | 0 | 21 | 5 | 0 | 0 | 2 | .000 | 0 | 5 | 5.81 |
| | Boston | AL | 12 | 2 | 0 | 4 | 25.2 | 122 | 37 | 12 | 10 | 2 | 0 | 0 | 0 | 11 | 1 | 26 | 3 | 0 | 0 | 4 | .000 | 0 | 0 | 3.51 |
| | 7 ML YEARS | | 217 | 47 | 3 | 64 | 492.1 | 2082 | 464 | 221 | 192 | 38 | 25 | 13 | 5 | 192 | 29 | 401 | 23 | 13 | 29 | 25 | .537 | 2 | 19 | 3.51 |

## Eric Hetzel

**Pitches:** Right **Bats:** Right **Pos:** SP **Ht:** 6' 3" **Wt:** 175 **Born:** 09/25/63 **Age:** 27

| HOW MUCH HE PITCHED | | | | | | | | WHAT HE GAVE UP | | | | | | | | | | | | THE RESULTS | | | | | |
|---|---|---|---|---|---|---|---|---|---|---|---|---|---|---|---|---|---|---|---|---|---|---|---|---|---|
| Year Team | Lg | G | GS | CG | GF | IP | BFP | H | R | ER | HR | SH | SF | HB | TBB | IBB | SO | WP | Bk | W | L | Pct. | ShO | Sv | ERA |
| 1985 Greensboro | A | 15 | 15 | 1 | 0 | 76 | 361 | 87 | 54 | 47 | 9 | 3 | 2 | 0 | 48 | 0 | 82 | 8 | 1 | 7 | 5 | .583 | 0 | 0 | 5.57 |
| 1987 Winter Havn | A | 26 | 26 | 11 | 0 | 192.2 | 834 | 186 | 94 | 76 | 6 | 10 | 7 | 1 | 87 | 1 | 136 | 12 | 3 | 10 | 12 | .455 | 0 | 0 | 3.55 |
| 1988 Pawtucket | AAA | 22 | 22 | 2 | 0 | 127.1 | 550 | 129 | 67 | 56 | 14 | 4 | 6 | 2 | 51 | 1 | 122 | 2 | 3 | 6 | 10 | .375 | 1 | 0 | 3.96 |
| 1989 Pawtucket | AAA | 12 | 12 | 4 | 0 | 80 | 326 | 65 | 27 | 22 | 5 | 1 | 4 | 1 | 32 | 2 | 79 | 4 | 0 | 4 | 4 | .500 | 1 | 0 | 2.47 |
| 1990 Pawtucket | AAA | 19 | 18 | 3 | 0 | 108.2 | 489 | 85 | 51 | 44 | 7 | 4 | 7 | 4 | 74 | 1 | 90 | 10 | 2 | 6 | 5 | .545 | 0 | 0 | 3.64 |
| 1989 Boston | AL | 12 | 11 | 0 | 0 | 50.1 | 239 | 61 | 39 | 35 | 7 | 1 | 2 | 2 | 28 | 1 | 33 | 2 | 1 | 2 | 3 | .400 | 0 | 0 | 6.26 |
| 1990 Boston | AL | 9 | 8 | 0 | 1 | 35 | 163 | 39 | 28 | 23 | 3 | 1 | 1 | 1 | 21 | 0 | 20 | 2 | 0 | 1 | 4 | .200 | 0 | 0 | 5.91 |
| 2 ML YEARS | | 21 | 19 | 0 | 1 | 85.1 | 402 | 100 | 67 | 58 | 10 | 2 | 3 | 3 | 49 | 1 | 53 | 4 | 1 | 3 | 7 | .300 | 0 | 0 | 6.12 |

## Greg Hibbard

**Pitches:** Left **Bats:** Left **Pos:** SP **Ht:** 6' 0" **Wt:** 180 **Born:** 09/13/64 **Age:** 26

| HOW MUCH HE PITCHED | | | | | | | | WHAT HE GAVE UP | | | | | | | | | | | | THE RESULTS | | | | | |
|---|---|---|---|---|---|---|---|---|---|---|---|---|---|---|---|---|---|---|---|---|---|---|---|---|---|
| Year Team | Lg | G | GS | CG | GF | IP | BFP | H | R | ER | HR | SH | SF | HB | TBB | IBB | SO | WP | Bk | W | L | Pct. | ShO | Sv | ERA |
| 1986 Eugene | A | 26 | 1 | 0 | 15 | 39 | 0 | 30 | 23 | 15 | 2 | 0 | 0 | 2 | 19 | 0 | 44 | 0 | 0 | 5 | 2 | .714 | 0 | 5 | 3.46 |
| 1987 Appleton | A | 9 | 9 | 2 | 0 | 64.2 | 265 | 53 | 17 | 8 | 3 | 1 | 0 | 2 | 18 | 3 | 61 | 2 | 0 | 7 | 2 | .778 | 1 | 0 | 1.11 |
| Ft. Myers | A | 3 | 3 | 3 | 0 | 24 | 92 | 20 | 5 | 5 | 0 | 2 | 0 | 1 | 3 | 0 | 20 | 0 | 0 | 2 | 1 | .667 | 1 | 0 | 1.88 |
| Memphis | AA | 16 | 16 | 3 | 0 | 106 | 431 | 102 | 48 | 38 | 7 | 3 | 3 | 2 | 21 | 1 | 56 | 1 | 0 | 7 | 6 | .538 | 1 | 0 | 3.23 |
| 1988 Vancouver | AAA | 25 | 24 | 4 | 0 | 144.1 | 617 | 155 | 74 | 66 | 7 | 7 | 5 | 4 | 44 | 4 | 65 | 6 | 2 | 11 | 11 | .500 | 1 | 0 | 4.12 |
| 1989 Vancouver | AAA | 9 | 9 | 2 | 0 | 58 | 231 | 47 | 24 | 17 | 3 | 1 | 3 | 1 | 11 | 0 | 45 | 5 | 0 | 2 | 3 | .400 | 1 | 0 | 2.64 |
| 1989 Chicago | AL | 23 | 23 | 2 | 0 | 137.1 | 581 | 142 | 58 | 49 | 5 | 5 | 4 | 2 | 41 | 0 | 55 | 4 | 0 | 6 | 7 | .462 | 0 | 0 | 3.21 |
| 1990 Chicago | AL | 33 | 33 | 3 | 0 | 211 | 871 | 202 | 80 | 74 | 11 | 8 | 10 | 6 | 55 | 2 | 92 | 2 | 1 | 14 | 9 | .609 | 1 | 0 | 3.16 |
| 2 ML YEARS | | 56 | 56 | 5 | 0 | 348.1 | 1452 | 344 | 138 | 123 | 16 | 13 | 14 | 8 | 96 | 2 | 147 | 6 | 1 | 20 | 16 | .556 | 1 | 0 | 3.18 |

## Kevin Hickey

**Pitches:** Left **Bats:** Left **Pos:** RP **Ht:** 6' 1" **Wt:** 195 **Born:** 02/25/56 **Age:** 35

| HOW MUCH HE PITCHED | | | | | | | | WHAT HE GAVE UP | | | | | | | | | | | | THE RESULTS | | | | | |
|---|---|---|---|---|---|---|---|---|---|---|---|---|---|---|---|---|---|---|---|---|---|---|---|---|---|
| Year Team | Lg | G | GS | CG | GF | IP | BFP | H | R | ER | HR | SH | SF | HB | TBB | IBB | SO | WP | Bk | W | L | Pct. | ShO | Sv | ERA |
| 1981 Chicago | AL | 41 | 0 | 0 | 14 | 44 | 188 | 38 | 22 | 18 | 3 | 3 | 2 | 1 | 18 | 5 | 17 | 1 | 0 | 0 | 2 | .000 | 0 | 3 | 3.68 |
| 1982 Chicago | AL | 60 | 0 | 0 | 20 | 78 | 327 | 73 | 32 | 26 | 4 | 6 | 4 | 2 | 30 | 6 | 38 | 0 | 0 | 4 | 4 | .500 | 0 | 6 | 3.00 |
| 1983 Chicago | AL | 23 | 0 | 0 | 13 | 20.2 | 98 | 23 | 14 | 12 | 5 | 0 | 0 | 0 | 11 | 2 | 8 | 1 | 0 | 1 | 2 | .333 | 0 | 5 | 5.23 |
| 1989 Baltimore | AL | 51 | 0 | 0 | 17 | 49.1 | 199 | 38 | 16 | 16 | 3 | 2 | 0 | 1 | 23 | 4 | 28 | 3 | 2 | 2 | 3 | .400 | 0 | 2 | 2.92 |
| 1990 Baltimore | AL | 37 | 0 | 0 | 9 | 26.1 | 113 | 26 | 16 | 15 | 3 | 1 | 1 | 0 | 13 | 2 | 17 | 1 | 0 | 1 | 3 | .250 | 0 | 1 | 5.13 |
| 5 ML YEARS | | 212 | 0 | 0 | 73 | 218.1 | 925 | 198 | 100 | 87 | 18 | 12 | 7 | 4 | 95 | 19 | 108 | 6 | 2 | 8 | 14 | .364 | 0 | 17 | 3.59 |

## Ted Higuera

**Pitches:** Left **Bats:** Both **Pos:** SP **Ht:** 5'10" **Wt:** 180 **Born:** 11/09/58 **Age:** 32

| HOW MUCH HE PITCHED | | | | | | | | WHAT HE GAVE UP | | | | | | | | | | | | THE RESULTS | | | | | |
|---|---|---|---|---|---|---|---|---|---|---|---|---|---|---|---|---|---|---|---|---|---|---|---|---|---|
| Year Team | Lg | G | GS | CG | GF | IP | BFP | H | R | ER | HR | SH | SF | HB | TBB | IBB | SO | WP | Bk | W | L | Pct. | ShO | Sv | ERA |
| 1985 Milwaukee | AL | 32 | 30 | 7 | 2 | 212.1 | 874 | 186 | 105 | 92 | 22 | 5 | 10 | 3 | 63 | 0 | 127 | 4 | 3 | 15 | 8 | .652 | 2 | 0 | 3.90 |
| 1986 Milwaukee | AL | 34 | 34 | 15 | 0 | 248.1 | 1031 | 226 | 84 | 77 | 26 | 7 | 11 | 3 | 74 | 5 | 207 | 3 | 0 | 20 | 11 | .645 | 4 | 0 | 2.79 |
| 1987 Milwaukee | AL | 35 | 35 | 14 | 0 | 261.2 | 1084 | 236 | 120 | 112 | 24 | 6 | 9 | 2 | 87 | 2 | 240 | 4 | 2 | 18 | 10 | .643 | 3 | 0 | 3.85 |
| 1988 Milwaukee | AL | 31 | 31 | 8 | 0 | 227.1 | 895 | 168 | 66 | 62 | 15 | 10 | 7 | 6 | 59 | 4 | 192 | 0 | 6 | 16 | 9 | .640 | 1 | 0 | 2.45 |
| 1989 Milwaukee | AL | 22 | 22 | 2 | 0 | 135.1 | 567 | 125 | 56 | 52 | 9 | 6 | 5 | 4 | 48 | 2 | 91 | 0 | 1 | 9 | 6 | .600 | 1 | 0 | 3.46 |
| 1990 Milwaukee | AL | 27 | 27 | 4 | 0 | 170 | 720 | 167 | 80 | 71 | 16 | 10 | 4 | 3 | 50 | 2 | 129 | 2 | 1 | 11 | 10 | .524 | 1 | 0 | 3.76 |
| 6 ML YEARS | | 181 | 179 | 50 | 2 | 1255 | 5171 | 1108 | 511 | 466 | 112 | 44 | 46 | 21 | 381 | 15 | 986 | 13 | 13 | 89 | 54 | .622 | 12 | 0 | 3.34 |

## Donnie Hill

**Bats:** Both **Throws:** Right **Pos:** 2B/3B/SS **Ht:** 5'10" **Wt:** 160 **Born:** 11/12/60 **Age:** 30

| BATTING | | | | | | | | | | | | | | | | | | | BASERUNNING | | | | PERCENTAGES | | |
|---|---|---|---|---|---|---|---|---|---|---|---|---|---|---|---|---|---|---|---|---|---|---|---|---|---|
| Year Team | Lg | G | AB | H | 2B | 3B | HR | (Hm | Rd) | TB | R | RBI | TBB | IBB | SO | HBP | SH | SF | SB | CS | SB% | GDP | Avg | OBP | SLG |
| 1983 Oakland | AL | 53 | 158 | 42 | 7 | 0 | 2 | (1 | 1) | 55 | 20 | 15 | 4 | 0 | 21 | 0 | 5 | 2 | 1 | 1 | .50 | 3 | .266 | .280 | .348 |
| 1984 Oakland | AL | 73 | 174 | 40 | 6 | 0 | 2 | (0 | 2) | 52 | 21 | 16 | 5 | 0 | 12 | 0 | 4 | 2 | 1 | 1 | .50 | 3 | .230 | .249 | .299 |
| 1985 Oakland | AL | 123 | 393 | 112 | 13 | 2 | 3 | (0 | 3) | 138 | 45 | 48 | 23 | 2 | 33 | 0 | 16 | 4 | 9 | 4 | .69 | 7 | .285 | .321 | .351 |
| 1986 Oakland | AL | 108 | 339 | 96 | 16 | 2 | 4 | (0 | 4) | 128 | 37 | 29 | 23 | 1 | 38 | 0 | 4 | 0 | 5 | 2 | .71 | 9 | .283 | .329 | .378 |
| 1987 Chicago | AL | 111 | 410 | 98 | 14 | 6 | 9 | (1 | 8) | 151 | 57 | 46 | 30 | 1 | 35 | 1 | 4 | 4 | 1 | 0 | 1.00 | 11 | .239 | .290 | .368 |
| 1988 Chicago | AL | 83 | 221 | 48 | 6 | 1 | 2 | (1 | 1) | 62 | 17 | 20 | 26 | 1 | 32 | 0 | 3 | 3 | 3 | 1 | .75 | 3 | .217 | .296 | .281 |
| 1990 California | AL | 102 | 352 | 93 | 18 | 2 | 3 | (0 | 3) | 124 | 36 | 32 | 29 | 1 | 27 | 1 | 6 | 4 | 1 | 2 | .33 | 10 | .264 | .319 | .352 |
| 7 ML YEARS | | 653 | 2047 | 529 | 80 | 13 | 25 | (3 | 22) | 710 | 233 | 206 | 140 | 6 | 198 | 2 | 42 | 19 | 21 | 11 | .66 | 46 | .258 | .304 | .347 |

## Glenallen Hill

**Bats:** Right **Throws:** Right **Pos:** RF/LF/DH **Ht:** 6' 2" **Wt:** 210 **Born:** 03/22/65 **Age:** 26

| | | | BATTING | | | | | | | | | | | | | | | | | | BASERUNNING | | | | PERCENTAGES | | |
|---|---|---|---|---|---|---|---|---|---|---|---|---|---|---|---|---|---|---|---|---|---|---|---|---|---|---|---|
| Year | Team | Lg | G | AB | H | 2B | 3B | HR | (Hm | Rd) | TB | R | RBI | TBB | IBB | SO | HBP | SH | SF | SB | CS | SB% | GDP | Avg | OBP | SLG |
| 1983 | Medcine Hat | R | 46 | 133 | 34 | 3 | 4 | 6 | -- | -- | 63 | 26 | 27 | 17 | 0 | 49 | 1 | 2 | 0 | 4 | 4 | .50 | 3 | .256 | .344 | .474 |
| 1984 | Florence | A | 129 | 440 | 105 | 19 | 5 | 16 | -- | -- | 182 | 75 | 64 | 63 | 3 | 150 | 3 | 0 | 6 | 30 | 15 | .67 | 6 | .239 | .334 | .414 |
| 1985 | Kinston | A | 131 | 466 | 98 | 13 | 0 | 20 | -- | -- | 171 | 57 | 56 | 57 | 0 | 211 | 1 | 2 | 4 | 42 | 15 | .74 | 7 | .210 | .295 | .367 |
| 1986 | Knoxville | AA | 141 | 570 | 159 | 23 | 6 | 31 | -- | -- | 287 | 87 | 96 | 39 | 3 | 153 | 1 | 0 | 13 | 18 | 18 | .50 | 10 | .279 | .319 | .504 |
| 1987 | Syracuse | AAA | 137 | 536 | 126 | 25 | 6 | 16 | -- | -- | 211 | 65 | 77 | 25 | 1 | 152 | 1 | 1 | 5 | 22 | 9 | .71 | 10 | .235 | .268 | .394 |
| 1988 | Syracuse | AAA | 51 | 172 | 40 | 7 | 0 | 4 | -- | -- | 59 | 21 | 19 | 15 | 3 | 59 | 2 | 0 | 3 | 7 | 2 | .78 | 2 | .233 | .297 | .343 |
| | Knoxville | AA | 79 | 269 | 71 | 13 | 2 | 12 | -- | -- | 124 | 37 | 38 | 28 | 1 | 75 | 2 | 0 | 3 | 10 | 4 | .71 | 4 | .264 | .334 | .461 |
| 1989 | Syracuse | AAA | 125 | 483 | 155 | 31 | 15 | 21 | -- | -- | 279 | 86 | 72 | 34 | 0 | 107 | 5 | 3 | 4 | 21 | 7 | .75 | 4 | .321 | .369 | .578 |
| 1989 | Toronto | AL | 19 | 52 | 15 | 0 | 0 | 1 | (1 | 0) | 18 | 4 | 7 | 3 | 0 | 12 | 0 | 0 | 0 | 2 | 1 | .67 | 0 | .288 | .327 | .346 |
| 1990 | Toronto | AL | 84 | 260 | 60 | 11 | 3 | 12 | (7 | 5) | 113 | 47 | 32 | 18 | 0 | 62 | 0 | 0 | 0 | 8 | 3 | .73 | 5 | .231 | .281 | .435 |
| | 2 ML YEARS | | 103 | 312 | 75 | 11 | 3 | 13 | (8 | 5) | 131 | 51 | 39 | 21 | 0 | 74 | 0 | 0 | 0 | 10 | 4 | .71 | 5 | .240 | .288 | .420 |

## Ken Hill

**Pitches:** Right **Bats:** Right **Pos:** SP **Ht:** 6' 2" **Wt:** 175 **Born:** 12/14/65 **Age:** 25

| | | | HOW MUCH HE PITCHED | | | | | | WHAT HE GAVE UP | | | | | | | | | | | | THE RESULTS | | | | | |
|---|---|---|---|---|---|---|---|---|---|---|---|---|---|---|---|---|---|---|---|---|---|---|---|---|---|---|
| Year | Team | Lg | G | GS | CG | GF | IP | BFP | H | R | ER | HR | SH | SF | HB | TBB | IBB | SO | WP | Bk | W | L | Pct. | ShO | Sv | ERA |
| 1988 | St. Louis | NL | 4 | 1 | 0 | 0 | 14 | 62 | 16 | 9 | 8 | 0 | 0 | 0 | 0 | 6 | 0 | 6 | 1 | 0 | 0 | 1 | .000 | 0 | 0 | 5.14 |
| 1989 | St. Louis | NL | 33 | 33 | 2 | 0 | 196.2 | 862 | 186 | 92 | 83 | 9 | 14 | 5 | 5 | 99 | 6 | 112 | 11 | 2 | 7 | 15 | .318 | 1 | 0 | 3.80 |
| 1990 | St. Louis | NL | 17 | 14 | 1 | 1 | 78.2 | 343 | 79 | 49 | 48 | 7 | 5 | 5 | 1 | 33 | 1 | 58 | 5 | 0 | 5 | 6 | .455 | 0 | 0 | 5.49 |
| | 3 ML YEARS | | 54 | 48 | 3 | 1 | 289.1 | 1267 | 281 | 150 | 139 | 16 | 19 | 10 | 6 | 138 | 7 | 176 | 17 | 2 | 12 | 22 | .353 | 1 | 0 | 4.32 |

## Shawn Hillegas

**Pitches:** Right **Bats:** Right **Pos:** RP **Ht:** 6' 2" **Wt:** 223 **Born:** 08/21/64 **Age:** 26

| | | | HOW MUCH HE PITCHED | | | | | | WHAT HE GAVE UP | | | | | | | | | | | | THE RESULTS | | | | | |
|---|---|---|---|---|---|---|---|---|---|---|---|---|---|---|---|---|---|---|---|---|---|---|---|---|---|---|
| Year | Team | Lg | G | GS | CG | GF | IP | BFP | H | R | ER | HR | SH | SF | HB | TBB | IBB | SO | WP | Bk | W | L | Pct. | ShO | Sv | ERA |
| 1987 | Los Angeles | NL | 12 | 10 | 0 | 1 | 58 | 252 | 52 | 27 | 23 | 5 | 4 | 1 | 0 | 31 | 0 | 51 | 4 | 0 | 4 | 3 | .571 | 0 | 0 | 3.57 |
| 1988 | 2 ML Teams | | 17 | 16 | 0 | 0 | 96.2 | 405 | 84 | 42 | 40 | 9 | 1 | 4 | 4 | 35 | 1 | 56 | 3 | 0 | 6 | 6 | .500 | 0 | 0 | 3.72 |
| 1989 | Chicago | AL | 50 | 13 | 0 | 12 | 119.2 | 533 | 132 | 67 | 63 | 12 | 4 | 2 | 3 | 51 | 4 | 76 | 4 | 1 | 7 | 11 | .389 | 0 | 3 | 4.74 |
| 1990 | Chicago | AL | 7 | 0 | 0 | 3 | 11.1 | 43 | 4 | 1 | 1 | 0 | 1 | 1 | 0 | 5 | 1 | 5 | 2 | 0 | 0 | 0 | .000 | 0 | 0 | 0.79 |
| 1988 | Los Angeles | NL | 11 | 10 | 0 | 0 | 56.2 | 239 | 54 | 26 | 26 | 5 | 1 | 2 | 3 | 17 | 1 | 30 | 3 | 0 | 3 | 4 | .429 | 0 | 0 | 4.13 |
| | Chicago | AL | 6 | 6 | 0 | 0 | 40 | 166 | 30 | 16 | 14 | 4 | 0 | 2 | 1 | 18 | 0 | 26 | 0 | 0 | 3 | 2 | .600 | 0 | 0 | 3.15 |
| | 4 ML YEARS | | 86 | 39 | 0 | 16 | 285.2 | 1233 | 272 | 137 | 127 | 26 | 10 | 8 | 7 | 122 | 6 | 188 | 13 | 1 | 17 | 20 | .459 | 0 | 3 | 4.00 |

## Howard Hilton

**Pitches:** Right **Bats:** Right **Pos:** RP **Ht:** 6' 3" **Wt:** 230 **Born:** 01/03/64 **Age:** 27

| | | | HOW MUCH HE PITCHED | | | | | | WHAT HE GAVE UP | | | | | | | | | | | | THE RESULTS | | | | | |
|---|---|---|---|---|---|---|---|---|---|---|---|---|---|---|---|---|---|---|---|---|---|---|---|---|---|---|
| Year | Team | Lg | G | GS | CG | GF | IP | BFP | H | R | ER | HR | SH | SF | HB | TBB | IBB | SO | WP | Bk | W | L | Pct. | ShO | Sv | ERA |
| 1985 | Erie | A | 24 | 5 | 0 | 13 | 65.1 | 301 | 73 | 46 | 31 | 6 | 4 | 2 | 2 | 26 | 8 | 66 | 5 | 1 | 3 | 7 | .300 | 0 | 7 | 4.27 |
| 1986 | St. Pete | A | 36 | 1 | 0 | 19 | 62.2 | 267 | 53 | 21 | 17 | 1 | 3 | 3 | 1 | 28 | 5 | 49 | 0 | 0 | 4 | 5 | .444 | 0 | 3 | 2.44 |
| 1987 | Springfield | A | 62 | 0 | 0 | 26 | 107.1 | 418 | 77 | 33 | 25 | 11 | 6 | 3 | 2 | 17 | 5 | 107 | 4 | 1 | 8 | 6 | .571 | 0 | 7 | 2.10 |
| 1988 | Arkansas | AA | 66 | 0 | 0 | 34 | 102 | 439 | 90 | 39 | 30 | 6 | 5 | 2 | 4 | 46 | 11 | 90 | 5 | 10 | 8 | 7 | .533 | 0 | 7 | 2.65 |
| 1989 | Louisville | AAA | 70 | 0 | 0 | 22 | 96.1 | 405 | 86 | 44 | 40 | 7 | 5 | 2 | 1 | 42 | 7 | 77 | 2 | 1 | 12 | 5 | .706 | 0 | 1 | 3.74 |
| 1990 | Louisville | AAA | 56 | 1 | 0 | 20 | 80 | 343 | 73 | 40 | 32 | 8 | 5 | 2 | 1 | 34 | 1 | 55 | 4 | 2 | 4 | 3 | .571 | 0 | 0 | 3.60 |
| 1990 | St. Louis | NL | 2 | 0 | 0 | 1 | 3 | 14 | 2 | 0 | 0 | 0 | 0 | 0 | 0 | 3 | 0 | 2 | 0 | 0 | 0 | 0 | .000 | 0 | 0 | 0.00 |

## Chris Hoiles

**Bats:** Right **Throws:** Right **Pos:** 1B **Ht:** 6' 0" **Wt:** 195 **Born:** 03/20/65 **Age:** 26

| | | | BATTING | | | | | | | | | | | | | | | | | | BASERUNNING | | | | PERCENTAGES | | |
|---|---|---|---|---|---|---|---|---|---|---|---|---|---|---|---|---|---|---|---|---|---|---|---|---|---|---|---|
| Year | Team | Lg | G | AB | H | 2B | 3B | HR | (Hm | Rd) | TB | R | RBI | TBB | IBB | SO | HBP | SH | SF | SB | CS | SB% | GDP | Avg | OBP | SLG |
| 1986 | Bristol | R | 68 | 253 | 81 | 19 | 2 | 13 | -- | -- | 143 | 42 | 57 | 30 | 3 | 20 | 1 | 0 | 2 | 10 | 1 | .91 | 9 | .320 | .392 | .565 |
| 1987 | Glens Falls | AA | 108 | 380 | 105 | 12 | 0 | 13 | -- | -- | 156 | 47 | 53 | 35 | 4 | 37 | 3 | 4 | 3 | 1 | 5 | .17 | 10 | .276 | .340 | .411 |
| 1988 | Toledo | AAA | 22 | 69 | 11 | 1 | 0 | 2 | -- | -- | 18 | 4 | 6 | 2 | 0 | 12 | 2 | 0 | 0 | 1 | 0 | 1.00 | 4 | .159 | .205 | .261 |
| | Glens Falls | AA | 103 | 360 | 102 | 21 | 3 | 17 | -- | -- | 180 | 67 | 73 | 50 | 4 | 57 | 7 | 3 | 3 | 4 | 3 | .57 | 5 | .283 | .379 | .500 |
| 1989 | Rochester | AAA | 96 | 322 | 79 | 19 | 1 | 10 | -- | -- | 130 | 41 | 51 | 31 | 1 | 58 | 4 | 2 | 4 | 1 | 2 | .33 | 10 | .245 | .316 | .404 |
| 1990 | Rochester | AAA | 74 | 247 | 86 | 20 | 1 | 18 | -- | -- | 162 | 52 | 56 | 44 | 4 | 48 | 1 | 1 | 1 | 4 | 2 | .67 | 7 | .348 | .447 | .656 |
| 1989 | Baltimore | AL | 6 | 9 | 1 | 1 | 0 | 0 | (0 | 0) | 2 | 0 | 1 | 1 | 0 | 3 | 0 | 0 | 0 | 0 | 0 | .00 | 0 | .111 | .200 | .222 |
| 1990 | Baltimore | AL | 23 | 63 | 12 | 3 | 0 | 1 | (1 | 0) | 18 | 7 | 6 | 5 | 1 | 12 | 0 | 0 | 0 | 0 | 0 | .00 | 0 | .190 | .250 | .286 |
| | 2 ML YEARS | | 29 | 72 | 13 | 4 | 0 | 1 | (1 | 0) | 20 | 7 | 7 | 6 | 1 | 15 | 0 | 0 | 0 | 0 | 0 | .00 | 0 | .181 | .244 | .278 |

## Dave Hollins

**Bats:** Both **Throws:** Right **Pos:** 3B **Ht:** 6' 1" **Wt:** 195 **Born:** 05/25/66 **Age:** 25

| | | BATTING | | | | | | | | | | | | | | | | | BASERUNNING | | | | PERCENTAGES | | |
|---|---|---|---|---|---|---|---|---|---|---|---|---|---|---|---|---|---|---|---|---|---|---|---|---|---|
| Year Team | Lg | G | AB | H | 2B | 3B | HR | (Hm | Rd) | TB | R | RBI | TBB | IBB | SO | HBP | SH | SF | SB | CS | SB% | GDP | Avg | OBP | SLG |
| 1987 Spokane | A | 75 | 278 | 86 | 14 | 4 | 2 | -- | -- | 114 | 52 | 44 | 53 | 7 | 36 | 2 | 3 | 4 | 20 | 5 | .80 | 3 | .309 | .418 | .410 |
| 1988 Riverside | A | 139 | 516 | 157 | 32 | 1 | 9 | -- | -- | 218 | 90 | 92 | 82 | 2 | 67 | 1 | 0 | 9 | 13 | 11 | .54 | 15 | .304 | .395 | .422 |
| 1989 Wichita | AA | 131 | 459 | 126 | 29 | 4 | 9 | -- | -- | 190 | 69 | 79 | 63 | 4 | 88 | 5 | 1 | 10 | 8 | 3 | .73 | 4 | .275 | .361 | .414 |
| 1990 Philadelphia | NL | 72 | 114 | 21 | 0 | 0 | 5 | (2 | 3) | 36 | 14 | 15 | 10 | 3 | 28 | 1 | 0 | 2 | 0 | 0 | .00 | 1 | .184 | .252 | .316 |

## Brian Holman

**Pitches:** Right **Bats:** Right **Pos:** SP **Ht:** 6' 4" **Wt:** 185 **Born:** 01/25/65 **Age:** 26

| | | HOW MUCH HE PITCHED | | | | | | WHAT HE GAVE UP | | | | | | | | | | | | THE RESULTS | | | | | |
|---|---|---|---|---|---|---|---|---|---|---|---|---|---|---|---|---|---|---|---|---|---|---|---|---|---|
| Year Team | Lg | G | GS | CG | GF | IP | BFP | H | R | ER | HR | SH | SF | HB | TBB | IBB | SO | WP | Bk | W | L | Pct. | ShO | Sv | ERA |
| 1988 Montreal | NL | 18 | 16 | 1 | 1 | 100.1 | 422 | 101 | 39 | 36 | 3 | 4 | 1 | 0 | 34 | 2 | 58 | 2 | 0 | 4 | 8 | .333 | 1 | 0 | 3.23 |
| 1989 2 ML Teams | | 33 | 25 | 6 | 1 | 191.1 | 833 | 194 | 86 | 78 | 11 | 6 | 4 | 7 | 77 | 6 | 105 | 8 | 1 | 9 | 12 | .429 | 2 | 0 | 3.67 |
| 1990 Seattle | AL | 28 | 28 | 3 | 0 | 189.2 | 804 | 188 | 92 | 85 | 17 | 1 | 7 | 6 | 66 | 2 | 121 | 8 | 2 | 11 | 11 | .500 | 0 | 0 | 4.03 |
| 1989 Montreal | NL | 10 | 3 | 0 | 0 | 31.2 | 145 | 34 | 18 | 17 | 2 | 2 | 1 | 1 | 15 | 0 | 23 | 3 | 1 | 1 | 2 | .333 | 0 | 0 | 4.83 |
| Seattle | AL | 23 | 22 | 6 | 1 | 159.2 | 688 | 160 | 68 | 61 | 9 | 4 | 3 | 6 | 62 | 6 | 82 | 5 | 0 | 8 | 10 | .444 | 2 | 0 | 3.44 |
| 3 ML YEARS | | 79 | 69 | 10 | 2 | 481.1 | 2059 | 483 | 217 | 199 | 31 | 11 | 12 | 13 | 177 | 10 | 284 | 18 | 3 | 24 | 31 | .436 | 3 | 0 | 3.72 |

## Darren Holmes

**Pitches:** Right **Bats:** Right **Pos:** RP **Ht:** 6' 0" **Wt:** 199 **Born:** 04/25/66 **Age:** 25

| | | HOW MUCH HE PITCHED | | | | | | WHAT HE GAVE UP | | | | | | | | | | | | THE RESULTS | | | | | |
|---|---|---|---|---|---|---|---|---|---|---|---|---|---|---|---|---|---|---|---|---|---|---|---|---|---|
| Year Team | Lg | G | GS | CG | GF | IP | BFP | H | R | ER | HR | SH | SF | HB | TBB | IBB | SO | WP | Bk | W | L | Pct. | ShO | Sv | ERA |
| 1984 Great Falls | R | 18 | 6 | 1 | 4 | 44.2 | 0 | 53 | 41 | 33 | 5 | 0 | 0 | 2 | 30 | 1 | 29 | 3 | 3 | 2 | 5 | .286 | 0 | 0 | 6.65 |
| 1985 Vero Beach | A | 33 | 0 | 0 | 20 | 63.2 | 277 | 57 | 31 | 22 | 0 | 4 | 5 | 0 | 35 | 2 | 46 | 6 | 1 | 4 | 3 | .571 | 0 | 2 | 3.11 |
| 1986 Vero Beach | A | 11 | 10 | 0 | 1 | 64.2 | 288 | 55 | 30 | 21 | 0 | 3 | 0 | 3 | 39 | 2 | 59 | 5 | 0 | 3 | 6 | .333 | 0 | 0 | 2.92 |
| 1987 Vero Beach | A | 19 | 19 | 1 | 0 | 99.2 | 455 | 111 | 60 | 50 | 4 | 4 | 6 | 1 | 53 | 0 | 46 | 5 | 1 | 6 | 4 | .600 | 1 | 0 | 4.52 |
| 1988 Albuquerque | AAA | 2 | 1 | 0 | 0 | 5.1 | 22 | 6 | 3 | 3 | 0 | 0 | 0 | 0 | 1 | 0 | 1 | 0 | 0 | 0 | 1 | .000 | 0 | 0 | 5.06 |
| 1989 San Antonio | AA | 17 | 16 | 3 | 1 | 110.1 | 471 | 102 | 59 | 47 | 5 | 2 | 4 | 3 | 44 | 2 | 81 | 8 | 6 | 5 | 8 | .385 | 2 | 1 | 3.83 |
| Albuquerque | AAA | 9 | 8 | 0 | 1 | 38.2 | 177 | 50 | 32 | 32 | 8 | 0 | 2 | 0 | 18 | 1 | 31 | 2 | 0 | 1 | 4 | .200 | 0 | 0 | 7.45 |
| 1990 Albuquerque | AAA | 56 | 0 | 0 | 30 | 92.2 | 389 | 78 | 34 | 32 | 3 | 0 | 4 | 4 | 39 | 2 | 99 | 5 | 2 | 12 | 2 | .857 | 0 | 13 | 3.11 |
| 1990 Los Angeles | NL | 14 | 0 | 0 | 1 | 17.1 | 77 | 15 | 10 | 10 | 1 | 1 | 2 | 0 | 11 | 3 | 19 | 1 | 0 | 0 | 1 | .000 | 0 | 0 | 5.19 |

## Brian Holton

**Pitches:** Right **Bats:** Right **Pos:** RP **Ht:** 6' 0" **Wt:** 195 **Born:** 11/29/59 **Age:** 31

| | | HOW MUCH HE PITCHED | | | | | | WHAT HE GAVE UP | | | | | | | | | | | | THE RESULTS | | | | | |
|---|---|---|---|---|---|---|---|---|---|---|---|---|---|---|---|---|---|---|---|---|---|---|---|---|---|
| Year Team | Lg | G | GS | CG | GF | IP | BFP | H | R | ER | HR | SH | SF | HB | TBB | IBB | SO | WP | Bk | W | L | Pct. | ShO | Sv | ERA |
| 1985 Los Angeles | NL | 3 | 0 | 0 | 0 | 4 | 21 | 9 | 7 | 4 | 0 | 0 | 0 | 0 | 1 | 0 | 1 | 1 | 0 | 1 | 1 | .500 | 0 | 0 | 9.00 |
| 1986 Los Angeles | NL | 12 | 3 | 0 | 4 | 24.1 | 106 | 28 | 13 | 12 | 1 | 2 | 1 | 1 | 6 | 2 | 24 | 1 | 0 | 2 | 3 | .400 | 0 | 0 | 4.44 |
| 1987 Los Angeles | NL | 53 | 1 | 0 | 26 | 83.1 | 360 | 87 | 39 | 36 | 11 | 2 | 3 | 0 | 32 | 11 | 58 | 0 | 4 | 3 | 2 | .600 | 0 | 2 | 3.89 |
| 1988 Los Angeles | NL | 45 | 0 | 0 | 11 | 84.2 | 339 | 69 | 19 | 16 | 1 | 7 | 3 | 1 | 26 | 7 | 49 | 1 | 6 | 7 | 3 | .700 | 0 | 1 | 1.70 |
| 1989 Baltimore | AL | 39 | 12 | 0 | 8 | 116.1 | 514 | 140 | 63 | 52 | 11 | 2 | 5 | 1 | 39 | 1 | 51 | 5 | 1 | 5 | 7 | .417 | 0 | 0 | 4.02 |
| 1990 Baltimore | AL | 33 | 0 | 0 | 13 | 58 | 257 | 68 | 31 | 29 | 7 | 1 | 2 | 0 | 21 | 6 | 27 | 2 | 2 | 2 | 3 | .400 | 0 | 0 | 4.50 |
| 6 ML YEARS | | 185 | 16 | 0 | 62 | 370.2 | 1597 | 401 | 172 | 149 | 31 | 14 | 14 | 3 | 125 | 27 | 210 | 10 | 13 | 20 | 19 | .513 | 0 | 3 | 3.62 |

## Rick Honeycutt

**Pitches:** Left **Bats:** Left **Pos:** RP **Ht:** 6' 1" **Wt:** 190 **Born:** 06/29/54 **Age:** 37

| | | HOW MUCH HE PITCHED | | | | | | WHAT HE GAVE UP | | | | | | | | | | | | THE RESULTS | | | | | |
|---|---|---|---|---|---|---|---|---|---|---|---|---|---|---|---|---|---|---|---|---|---|---|---|---|---|
| Year Team | Lg | G | GS | CG | GF | IP | BFP | H | R | ER | HR | SH | SF | HB | TBB | IBB | SO | WP | Bk | W | L | Pct. | ShO | Sv | ERA |
| 1977 Seattle | AL | 10 | 3 | 0 | 3 | 29 | 125 | 26 | 16 | 14 | 7 | 0 | 2 | 3 | 11 | 2 | 17 | 2 | 1 | 0 | 1 | .000 | 0 | 0 | 4.34 |
| 1978 Seattle | AL | 26 | 24 | 4 | 0 | 134 | 594 | 150 | 81 | 73 | 12 | 9 | 7 | 3 | 49 | 5 | 50 | 3 | 0 | 5 | 11 | .313 | 1 | 0 | 4.90 |
| 1979 Seattle | AL | 33 | 28 | 8 | 2 | 194 | 839 | 201 | 103 | 87 | 22 | 11 | 6 | 6 | 67 | 7 | 83 | 5 | 1 | 11 | 12 | .478 | 1 | 0 | 4.04 |
| 1980 Seattle | AL | 30 | 30 | 9 | 0 | 203 | 871 | 221 | 99 | 89 | 22 | 11 | 7 | 3 | 60 | 7 | 79 | 4 | 0 | 10 | 17 | .370 | 1 | 0 | 3.95 |
| 1981 Texas | AL | 20 | 20 | 8 | 0 | 128 | 509 | 120 | 49 | 47 | 12 | 5 | 0 | 0 | 17 | 1 | 40 | 1 | 0 | 11 | 6 | .647 | 2 | 0 | 3.30 |
| 1982 Texas | AL | 30 | 26 | 4 | 3 | 164 | 728 | 201 | 103 | 96 | 20 | 4 | 8 | 3 | 54 | 4 | 64 | 3 | 1 | 5 | 17 | .227 | 1 | 0 | 5.27 |
| 1983 2 ML Teams | | 34 | 32 | 6 | 0 | 213.2 | 865 | 214 | 85 | 72 | 15 | 5 | 6 | 8 | 50 | 6 | 74 | 1 | 3 | 16 | 11 | .593 | 2 | 0 | 3.03 |
| 1984 Los Angeles | NL | 29 | 28 | 6 | 0 | 183.2 | 762 | 180 | 72 | 58 | 11 | 6 | 5 | 2 | 51 | 11 | 75 | 1 | 2 | 10 | 9 | .526 | 2 | 0 | 2.84 |
| 1985 Los Angeles | NL | 31 | 25 | 1 | 2 | 142 | 600 | 141 | 71 | 54 | 9 | 5 | 4 | 1 | 49 | 7 | 67 | 2 | 0 | 8 | 12 | .400 | 0 | 1 | 3.42 |
| 1986 Los Angeles | NL | 32 | 28 | 0 | 2 | 171 | 713 | 164 | 71 | 63 | 9 | 6 | 1 | 3 | 45 | 4 | 100 | 4 | 1 | 11 | 9 | .550 | 0 | 0 | 3.32 |
| 1987 2 ML Teams | | 34 | 24 | 1 | 1 | 139.1 | 631 | 158 | 91 | 73 | 13 | 1 | 3 | 4 | 54 | 4 | 102 | 5 | 1 | 3 | 16 | .158 | 1 | 0 | 4.72 |
| 1988 Oakland | AL | 55 | 0 | 0 | 17 | 79.2 | 330 | 74 | 36 | 31 | 6 | 3 | 6 | 3 | 25 | 2 | 47 | 3 | 8 | 3 | 2 | .600 | 0 | 7 | 3.50 |
| 1989 Oakland | AL | 64 | 0 | 0 | 24 | 76.2 | 305 | 56 | 26 | 20 | 5 | 5 | 2 | 1 | 26 | 3 | 52 | 6 | 1 | 2 | 2 | .500 | 0 | 12 | 2.35 |
| 1990 Oakland | AL | 63 | 0 | 0 | 13 | 63.1 | 256 | 46 | 23 | 19 | 2 | 2 | 6 | 1 | 22 | 2 | 38 | 1 | 1 | 2 | 2 | .500 | 0 | 7 | 2.70 |
| 1983 Texas | AL | 25 | 25 | 5 | 0 | 174.2 | 693 | 168 | 59 | 47 | 9 | 3 | 6 | 6 | 37 | 2 | 56 | 1 | 2 | 14 | 8 | .636 | 2 | 0 | 2.42 |

| Year | Team | Lg | G | GS | CG | GF | IP | BFP | H | R | ER | HR | SH | SF | HB | TBB | IBB | SO | WP | Bk | W | L | Pct. | ShO | Sv | ERA |
|---|---|---|---|---|---|---|---|---|---|---|---|---|---|---|---|---|---|---|---|---|---|---|---|---|---|---|
| | Los Angeles | NL | 9 | 7 | 1 | 0 | 39 | 172 | 46 | 26 | 25 | 6 | 2 | 0 | 2 | 13 | 4 | 18 | 0 | 1 | 2 | 3 | .400 | 0 | 0 | 5.77 |
| 1987 | Los Angeles | NL | 27 | 20 | 1 | 0 | 115.2 | 525 | 133 | 74 | 59 | 10 | 0 | 0 | 2 | 45 | 4 | 92 | 4 | 0 | 2 | 12 | .143 | 1 | 0 | 4.59 |
| | Oakland | AL | 7 | 4 | 0 | 1 | 23.2 | 106 | 25 | 17 | 14 | 3 | 1 | 3 | 2 | 9 | 0 | 10 | 1 | 1 | 1 | 4 | .200 | 0 | 0 | 5.32 |
| 14 ML YEARS | | | 491 | 268 | 47 | 67 | 1921.1 | 8128 | 1952 | 926 | 796 | 165 | 73 | 63 | 41 | 580 | 65 | 888 | 41 | 20 | 97 | 127 | .433 | 11 | 27 | 3.73 |

## John Hoover

**Pitches:** Right **Bats:** Right **Pos:** RP **Ht:** 6' 2" **Wt:** 195 **Born:** 11/22/62 **Age:** 28

| | | | HOW MUCH HE PITCHED | | | | | | WHAT HE GAVE UP | | | | | | | | | | | | THE RESULTS | | | | | |
|---|---|---|---|---|---|---|---|---|---|---|---|---|---|---|---|---|---|---|---|---|---|---|---|---|---|---|
| Year | Team | Lg | G | GS | CG | GF | IP | BFP | H | R | ER | HR | SH | SF | HB | TBB | IBB | SO | WP | Bk | W | L | Pct. | ShO | Sv | ERA |
| 1990 | Texas | AL | 2 | 0 | 0 | 1 | 4.2 | 26 | 8 | 6 | 6 | 0 | 1 | 0 | 0 | 3 | 0 | 0 | 0 | 0 | 0 | 0 | .000 | 0 | 0 | 11.57 |

## Sam Horn

**Bats:** Left **Throws:** Left **Pos:** DH **Ht:** 6' 5" **Wt:** 240 **Born:** 11/02/63 **Age:** 27

| | | | BATTING | | | | | | | | | | | | | | | | | BASERUNNING | | | | PERCENTAGES | | |
|---|---|---|---|---|---|---|---|---|---|---|---|---|---|---|---|---|---|---|---|---|---|---|---|---|---|---|
| Year | Team | Lg | G | AB | H | 2B | 3B | HR | (Hm | Rd) | TB | R | RBI | TBB | IBB | SO | HBP | SH | SF | SB | CS | SB% | GDP | Avg | OBP | SLG |
| 1987 | Boston | AL | 46 | 158 | 44 | 7 | 0 | 14 | (6 | 8) | 93 | 31 | 34 | 17 | 0 | 55 | 2 | 0 | 0 | 0 | 1 | .00 | 5 | .278 | .356 | .589 |
| 1988 | Boston | AL | 24 | 61 | 9 | 0 | 0 | 2 | (2 | 0) | 15 | 4 | 8 | 11 | 3 | 20 | 0 | 0 | 1 | 0 | 0 | .00 | 1 | .148 | .274 | .246 |
| 1989 | Boston | AL | 33 | 54 | 8 | 2 | 0 | 0 | (0 | 0) | 10 | 1 | 4 | 8 | 1 | 16 | 0 | 0 | 0 | 0 | 0 | .00 | 4 | .148 | .258 | .185 |
| 1990 | Baltimore | AL | 79 | 246 | 61 | 13 | 0 | 14 | (8 | 6) | 116 | 30 | 45 | 32 | 1 | 62 | 0 | 0 | 2 | 0 | 0 | .00 | 8 | .248 | .332 | .472 |
| 4 ML YEARS | | | 182 | 519 | 122 | 22 | 0 | 30 | (16 | 14) | 234 | 66 | 91 | 68 | 5 | 153 | 2 | 0 | 3 | 0 | 1 | .00 | 18 | .235 | .324 | .451 |

## Ricky Horton

**Pitches:** Left **Bats:** Left **Pos:** RP **Ht:** 6' 2" **Wt:** 197 **Born:** 07/30/59 **Age:** 31

| | | | HOW MUCH HE PITCHED | | | | | | WHAT HE GAVE UP | | | | | | | | | | | | THE RESULTS | | | | | |
|---|---|---|---|---|---|---|---|---|---|---|---|---|---|---|---|---|---|---|---|---|---|---|---|---|---|---|
| Year | Team | Lg | G | GS | CG | GF | IP | BFP | H | R | ER | HR | SH | SF | HB | TBB | IBB | SO | WP | Bk | W | L | Pct. | ShO | Sv | ERA |
| 1984 | St. Louis | NL | 37 | 18 | 1 | 7 | 125.2 | 537 | 140 | 53 | 48 | 14 | 3 | 3 | 1 | 39 | 2 | 76 | 5 | 6 | 9 | 4 | .692 | 1 | 1 | 3.44 |
| 1985 | St. Louis | NL | 49 | 3 | 0 | 10 | 89.2 | 382 | 84 | 30 | 29 | 5 | 8 | 3 | 3 | 34 | 13 | 59 | 3 | 2 | 3 | 2 | .600 | 0 | 1 | 2.91 |
| 1986 | St. Louis | NL | 42 | 9 | 1 | 12 | 100.1 | 387 | 77 | 25 | 25 | 7 | 3 | 3 | 1 | 26 | 7 | 49 | 1 | 0 | 4 | 3 | .571 | 0 | 3 | 2.24 |
| 1987 | St. Louis | NL | 67 | 6 | 0 | 24 | 125 | 533 | 127 | 58 | 53 | 15 | 6 | 3 | 0 | 42 | 10 | 55 | 3 | 4 | 8 | 3 | .727 | 0 | 7 | 3.82 |
| 1988 | 2 ML Teams | | 64 | 9 | 1 | 13 | 118.1 | 512 | 131 | 71 | 64 | 8 | 12 | 9 | 5 | 38 | 4 | 36 | 0 | 3 | 7 | 11 | .389 | 0 | 2 | 4.87 |
| 1989 | 2 ML Teams | | 34 | 8 | 0 | 7 | 72.1 | 314 | 85 | 39 | 39 | 3 | 6 | 4 | 4 | 21 | 4 | 26 | 0 | 0 | 0 | 3 | .000 | 0 | 0 | 4.85 |
| 1990 | St. Louis | NL | 32 | 0 | 0 | 8 | 42 | 193 | 52 | 25 | 23 | 3 | 4 | 1 | 1 | 22 | 7 | 18 | 1 | 1 | 1 | 1 | .500 | 0 | 1 | 4.93 |
| 1988 | Chicago | AL | 52 | 9 | 1 | 12 | 109.1 | 471 | 120 | 64 | 59 | 6 | 10 | 8 | 5 | 36 | 4 | 28 | 0 | 3 | 6 | 10 | .375 | 0 | 2 | 4.86 |
| | Los Angeles | NL | 12 | 0 | 0 | 1 | 9 | 41 | 11 | 7 | 5 | 2 | 2 | 1 | 0 | 2 | 0 | 8 | 0 | 0 | 1 | 1 | .500 | 0 | 0 | 5.00 |
| 1989 | Los Angeles | NL | 23 | 0 | 0 | 6 | 26.2 | 120 | 35 | 15 | 15 | 1 | 4 | 2 | 1 | 11 | 2 | 12 | 0 | 0 | 0 | 0 | .000 | 0 | 0 | 5.06 |
| | St. Louis | NL | 11 | 8 | 0 | 1 | 45.2 | 194 | 50 | 24 | 24 | 2 | 2 | 2 | 3 | 10 | 2 | 14 | 0 | 0 | 0 | 3 | .000 | 0 | 0 | 4.73 |
| 7 ML YEARS | | | 325 | 53 | 3 | 81 | 673.1 | 2858 | 696 | 301 | 281 | 55 | 42 | 26 | 15 | 222 | 47 | 319 | 13 | 16 | 32 | 27 | .542 | 1 | 15 | 3.76 |

## Charlie Hough

**Pitches:** Right **Bats:** Right **Pos:** SP **Ht:** 6' 2" **Wt:** 190 **Born:** 01/05/48 **Age:** 43

| | | | HOW MUCH HE PITCHED | | | | | | WHAT HE GAVE UP | | | | | | | | | | | | THE RESULTS | | | | | |
|---|---|---|---|---|---|---|---|---|---|---|---|---|---|---|---|---|---|---|---|---|---|---|---|---|---|---|
| Year | Team | Lg | G | GS | CG | GF | IP | BFP | H | R | ER | HR | SH | SF | HB | TBB | IBB | SO | WP | Bk | W | L | Pct. | ShO | Sv | ERA |
| 1970 | Los Angeles | NL | 8 | 0 | 0 | 5 | 17 | 79 | 18 | 11 | 10 | 7 | 0 | 0 | 0 | 11 | 0 | 8 | 0 | 0 | 0 | 0 | .000 | 0 | 2 | 5.29 |
| 1971 | Los Angeles | NL | 4 | 0 | 0 | 3 | 4 | 19 | 3 | 3 | 2 | 1 | 1 | 0 | 0 | 3 | 0 | 4 | 0 | 0 | 0 | 0 | .000 | 0 | 0 | 4.50 |
| 1972 | Los Angeles | NL | 2 | 0 | 0 | 2 | 3 | 13 | 2 | 1 | 1 | 0 | 0 | 0 | 1 | 2 | 0 | 4 | 0 | 0 | 0 | 0 | .000 | 0 | 0 | 3.00 |
| 1973 | Los Angeles | NL | 37 | 0 | 0 | 18 | 72 | 309 | 52 | 24 | 22 | 3 | 4 | 3 | 6 | 45 | 2 | 70 | 2 | 0 | 4 | 2 | .667 | 0 | 5 | 2.75 |
| 1974 | Los Angeles | NL | 49 | 0 | 0 | 16 | 96 | 389 | 65 | 45 | 40 | 12 | 6 | 8 | 4 | 40 | 2 | 63 | 4 | 0 | 9 | 4 | .692 | 0 | 1 | 3.75 |
| 1975 | Los Angeles | NL | 38 | 0 | 0 | 24 | 61 | 266 | 43 | 25 | 20 | 3 | 3 | 0 | 8 | 34 | 0 | 34 | 4 | 1 | 3 | 7 | .300 | 0 | 4 | 2.95 |
| 1976 | Los Angeles | NL | 77 | 0 | 0 | 55 | 143 | 600 | 102 | 43 | 35 | 6 | 4 | 1 | 8 | 77 | 3 | 81 | 9 | 0 | 12 | 8 | .600 | 0 | 18 | 2.20 |
| 1977 | Los Angeles | NL | 70 | 1 | 0 | 53 | 127 | 551 | 98 | 53 | 47 | 10 | 10 | 4 | 7 | 70 | 6 | 105 | 8 | 0 | 6 | 12 | .333 | 0 | 22 | 3.33 |
| 1978 | Los Angeles | NL | 55 | 0 | 0 | 31 | 93 | 390 | 69 | 38 | 34 | 6 | 0 | 0 | 5 | 48 | 4 | 66 | 6 | 0 | 5 | 5 | .500 | 0 | 7 | 3.29 |
| 1979 | Los Angeles | NL | 42 | 14 | 0 | 10 | 151 | 662 | 152 | 88 | 80 | 16 | 9 | 4 | 8 | 66 | 2 | 76 | 9 | 1 | 7 | 5 | .583 | 0 | 0 | 4.77 |
| 1980 | 2 ML Teams | | 35 | 3 | 2 | 12 | 93 | 426 | 91 | 51 | 47 | 6 | 7 | 4 | 5 | 58 | 2 | 72 | 11 | 0 | 3 | 5 | .375 | 1 | 1 | 4.55 |
| 1981 | Texas | AL | 21 | 5 | 2 | 9 | 82 | 330 | 61 | 30 | 27 | 4 | 1 | 1 | 3 | 31 | 1 | 69 | 4 | 0 | 4 | 1 | .800 | 0 | 1 | 2.96 |
| 1982 | Texas | AL | 34 | 34 | 12 | 0 | 228 | 954 | 217 | 111 | 100 | 21 | 7 | 4 | 7 | 72 | 5 | 128 | 9 | 0 | 16 | 13 | .552 | 2 | 0 | 3.95 |
| 1983 | Texas | AL | 34 | 33 | 11 | 1 | 252 | 1030 | 219 | 96 | 89 | 22 | 5 | 5 | 3 | 95 | 0 | 152 | 6 | 1 | 15 | 13 | .536 | 3 | 0 | 3.18 |
| 1984 | Texas | AL | 36 | 36 | 17 | 0 | 266 | 1133 | 260 | 127 | 111 | 26 | 5 | 7 | 9 | 94 | 3 | 164 | 12 | 2 | 16 | 14 | .533 | 1 | 0 | 3.76 |
| 1985 | Texas | AL | 34 | 34 | 14 | 0 | 250.1 | 1018 | 198 | 102 | 92 | 23 | 1 | 7 | 7 | 83 | 1 | 141 | 11 | 3 | 14 | 16 | .467 | 1 | 0 | 3.31 |
| 1986 | Texas | AL | 33 | 33 | 7 | 0 | 230.1 | 958 | 188 | 115 | 97 | 32 | 9 | 1 | 9 | 89 | 2 | 146 | 16 | 0 | 17 | 10 | .630 | 2 | 0 | 3.79 |
| 1987 | Texas | AL | 40 | 40 | 13 | 0 | 285.1 | 1231 | 238 | 159 | 120 | 36 | 5 | 14 | 19 | 124 | 1 | 223 | 12 | 9 | 18 | 13 | .581 | 0 | 0 | 3.79 |
| 1988 | Texas | AL | 34 | 34 | 10 | 0 | 252 | 1067 | 202 | 111 | 93 | 20 | 8 | 8 | 12 | 126 | 1 | 174 | 10 | 10 | 15 | 16 | .484 | 0 | 0 | 3.32 |
| 1989 | Texas | AL | 30 | 30 | 5 | 0 | 182 | 795 | 168 | 97 | 88 | 28 | 3 | 6 | 6 | 95 | 2 | 94 | 7 | 5 | 10 | 13 | .435 | 1 | 0 | 4.35 |
| 1990 | Texas | AL | 32 | 32 | 5 | 0 | 218.2 | 950 | 190 | 108 | 99 | 24 | 2 | 11 | 11 | 119 | 2 | 114 | 4 | 0 | 12 | 12 | .500 | 0 | 0 | 4.07 |
| 1980 | Los Angeles | NL | 19 | 1 | 0 | 5 | 32 | 156 | 37 | 21 | 20 | 4 | 3 | 3 | 2 | 21 | 0 | 25 | 3 | 0 | 1 | 3 | .250 | 0 | 1 | 5.63 |
| | Texas | AL | 16 | 2 | 2 | 7 | 61 | 270 | 54 | 30 | 27 | 2 | 4 | 1 | 3 | 37 | 2 | 47 | 8 | 0 | 2 | 2 | .500 | 1 | 0 | 3.98 |
| 21 ML YEARS | | | 745 | 329 | 98 | 239 | 3106.2 | 13170 | 2636 | 1438 | 1254 | 306 | 90 | 88 | 138 | 1382 | 39 | 1988 | 144 | 32 | 186 | 169 | .524 | 11 | 61 | 3.63 |

## Steve Howard

**Bats:** Right **Throws:** Right **Pos:** RF **Ht:** 6' 2" **Wt:** 205 **Born:** 12/07/63 **Age:** 27

| BATTING | | | | | | | | | | | | | | | | | | | BASERUNNING | | | | PERCENTAGES | | |
|---|---|---|---|---|---|---|---|---|---|---|---|---|---|---|---|---|---|---|---|---|---|---|---|---|---|
| Year Team | Lg | G | AB | H | 2B | 3B | HR | (Hm | Rd) | TB | R | RBI | TBB | IBB | SO | HBP | SH | SF | SB | CS | SB% | GDP | Avg | OBP | SLG |
| 1984 Madison | A | 44 | 123 | 21 | 4 | 0 | 2 | -- | -- | 31 | 13 | 14 | 21 | 0 | 56 | 7 | 1 | 1 | 4 | 4 | .50 | 2 | .171 | .322 | .252 |
| Medford | A | 53 | 185 | 39 | 4 | 1 | 4 | -- | -- | 57 | 26 | 24 | 43 | 1 | 89 | 4 | 0 | 1 | 15 | 6 | .71 | 0 | .211 | .369 | .308 |
| 1985 Modesto | A | 110 | 349 | 77 | 15 | 3 | 14 | -- | -- | 140 | 59 | 64 | 67 | 0 | 138 | 8 | 1 | 2 | 10 | 9 | .53 | 9 | .221 | .357 | .401 |
| 1986 Modesto | A | 98 | 302 | 70 | 11 | 4 | 9 | -- | -- | 116 | 64 | 53 | 100 | 0 | 128 | 5 | 0 | 4 | 13 | 7 | .65 | 8 | .232 | .426 | .384 |
| 1987 Huntsville | AA | 133 | 439 | 112 | 17 | 4 | 13 | -- | -- | 176 | 79 | 66 | 76 | 2 | 142 | 12 | 5 | 6 | 9 | 8 | .53 | 11 | .255 | .375 | .401 |
| 1988 Huntsville | AA | 128 | 461 | 114 | 19 | 6 | 17 | -- | -- | 196 | 70 | 78 | 64 | 3 | 134 | 2 | 0 | 8 | 29 | 7 | .81 | 18 | .247 | .336 | .425 |
| 1989 Tacoma | AAA | 107 | 341 | 83 | 10 | 2 | 13 | -- | -- | 136 | 51 | 60 | 64 | 1 | 135 | 11 | 1 | 7 | 15 | 4 | .79 | 6 | .243 | .374 | .399 |
| 1990 Tacoma | AAA | 97 | 330 | 89 | 18 | 4 | 10 | -- | -- | 145 | 55 | 45 | 42 | 1 | 100 | 8 | 1 | 3 | 17 | 5 | .77 | 6 | .270 | .363 | .439 |
| 1990 Oakland | AL | 21 | 52 | 12 | 4 | 0 | 0 | (0 | 0) | 16 | 5 | 1 | 4 | 1 | 17 | 0 | 0 | 0 | 0 | 0 | .00 | 0 | .231 | .286 | .308 |

## Thomas Howard

**Bats:** Both **Throws:** Right **Pos:** LF **Ht:** 6' 0" **Wt:** 198 **Born:** 12/11/64 **Age:** 26

| BATTING | | | | | | | | | | | | | | | | | | | BASERUNNING | | | | PERCENTAGES | | |
|---|---|---|---|---|---|---|---|---|---|---|---|---|---|---|---|---|---|---|---|---|---|---|---|---|---|
| Year Team | Lg | G | AB | H | 2B | 3B | HR | (Hm | Rd) | TB | R | RBI | TBB | IBB | SO | HBP | SH | SF | SB | CS | SB% | GDP | Avg | OBP | SLG |
| 1986 Spokane | A | 13 | 55 | 23 | 3 | 3 | 2 | -- | -- | 38 | 16 | 17 | 3 | 0 | 9 | 1 | 0 | 0 | 2 | 1 | .67 | 0 | .418 | .458 | .691 |
| Reno | A | 61 | 223 | 57 | 7 | 3 | 10 | -- | -- | 100 | 35 | 39 | 34 | 1 | 49 | 0 | 1 | 3 | 10 | 2 | .83 | 3 | .256 | .350 | .448 |
| 1987 Wichita | AA | 113 | 401 | 133 | 27 | 4 | 14 | -- | -- | 210 | 72 | 60 | 36 | 9 | 72 | 1 | 8 | 1 | 26 | 8 | .76 | 8 | .332 | .387 | .524 |
| 1988 Las Vegas | AAA | 44 | 167 | 42 | 9 | 1 | 0 | -- | -- | 53 | 29 | 15 | 12 | 2 | 31 | 1 | 1 | 0 | 3 | 4 | .43 | 5 | .251 | .306 | .317 |
| Wichita | AA | 29 | 103 | 31 | 9 | 2 | 0 | -- | -- | 44 | 15 | 16 | 13 | 0 | 14 | 0 | 0 | 0 | 6 | 3 | .67 | 3 | .301 | .379 | .427 |
| 1989 Las Vegas | AAA | 80 | 303 | 91 | 18 | 3 | 3 | -- | -- | 124 | 45 | 31 | 30 | 1 | 56 | 0 | 3 | 1 | 22 | 11 | .67 | 6 | .300 | .362 | .409 |
| 1990 Las Vegas | AAA | 89 | 341 | 112 | 26 | 8 | 5 | -- | -- | 169 | 58 | 51 | 44 | 5 | 63 | 0 | 4 | 4 | 27 | 5 | .84 | 5 | .328 | .401 | .496 |
| 1990 San Diego | NL | 20 | 44 | 12 | 2 | 0 | 0 | (0 | 0) | 14 | 4 | 0 | 0 | 0 | 11 | 0 | 1 | 0 | 0 | 1 | .00 | 1 | .273 | .273 | .318 |

## Jack Howell

**Bats:** Left **Throws:** Right **Pos:** 3B **Ht:** 6' 0" **Wt:** 201 **Born:** 08/18/61 **Age:** 29

| BATTING | | | | | | | | | | | | | | | | | | | BASERUNNING | | | | PERCENTAGES | | |
|---|---|---|---|---|---|---|---|---|---|---|---|---|---|---|---|---|---|---|---|---|---|---|---|---|---|
| Year Team | Lg | G | AB | H | 2B | 3B | HR | (Hm | Rd) | TB | R | RBI | TBB | IBB | SO | HBP | SH | SF | SB | CS | SB% | GDP | Avg | OBP | SLG |
| 1985 California | AL | 43 | 137 | 27 | 4 | 0 | 5 | (2 | 3) | 46 | 19 | 18 | 16 | 2 | 33 | 0 | 4 | 1 | 1 | 1 | .50 | 1 | .197 | .279 | .336 |
| 1986 California | AL | 63 | 151 | 41 | 14 | 2 | 4 | (1 | 3) | 71 | 26 | 21 | 19 | 0 | 28 | 0 | 3 | 2 | 2 | 0 | 1.00 | 1 | .272 | .349 | .470 |
| 1987 California | AL | 138 | 449 | 110 | 18 | 5 | 23 | (15 | 8) | 207 | 64 | 64 | 57 | 4 | 118 | 2 | 1 | 2 | 4 | 3 | .57 | 7 | .245 | .331 | .461 |
| 1988 California | AL | 154 | 500 | 127 | 32 | 2 | 16 | (9 | 7) | 211 | 59 | 63 | 46 | 8 | 130 | 6 | 4 | 2 | 2 | 6 | .25 | 8 | .254 | .323 | .422 |
| 1989 California | AL | 144 | 474 | 108 | 19 | 4 | 20 | (9 | 11) | 195 | 56 | 52 | 52 | 9 | 125 | 3 | 3 | 1 | 0 | 3 | .00 | 8 | .228 | .308 | .411 |
| 1990 California | AL | 105 | 316 | 72 | 19 | 1 | 8 | (3 | 5) | 117 | 35 | 33 | 46 | 5 | 61 | 1 | 1 | 2 | 3 | 0 | 1.00 | 3 | .228 | .326 | .370 |
| 6 ML YEARS | | 647 | 2027 | 485 | 106 | 14 | 76 | (39 | 37) | 847 | 259 | 251 | 236 | 28 | 495 | 12 | 16 | 10 | 12 | 13 | .48 | 28 | .239 | .321 | .418 |

## Jay Howell

**Pitches:** Right **Bats:** Right **Pos:** RP **Ht:** 6' 3" **Wt:** 205 **Born:** 11/26/55 **Age:** 35

| HOW MUCH HE PITCHED | | | | | | | | WHAT HE GAVE UP | | | | | | | | | | | | THE RESULTS | | | | | |
|---|---|---|---|---|---|---|---|---|---|---|---|---|---|---|---|---|---|---|---|---|---|---|---|---|---|
| Year Team | Lg | G | GS | CG | GF | IP | BFP | H | R | ER | HR | SH | SF | HB | TBB | IBB | SO | WP | Bk | W | L | Pct. | ShO | Sv | ERA |
| 1980 Cincinnati | NL | 5 | 0 | 0 | 1 | 3 | 19 | 8 | 5 | 5 | 0 | 0 | 1 | 1 | 0 | 0 | 1 | 0 | 0 | 0 | 0 | .000 | 0 | 0 | 15.00 |
| 1981 Chicago | NL | 10 | 2 | 0 | 1 | 22 | 97 | 23 | 13 | 12 | 3 | 1 | 1 | 2 | 10 | 2 | 10 | 0 | 0 | 2 | 0 | 1.000 | 0 | 0 | 4.91 |
| 1982 New York | AL | 6 | 6 | 0 | 0 | 28 | 138 | 42 | 25 | 24 | 1 | 0 | 2 | 0 | 13 | 0 | 21 | 1 | 0 | 2 | 3 | .400 | 0 | 0 | 7.71 |
| 1983 New York | AL | 19 | 12 | 2 | 3 | 82 | 368 | 89 | 53 | 49 | 7 | 1 | 5 | 3 | 35 | 0 | 61 | 2 | 1 | 1 | 5 | .167 | 0 | 0 | 5.38 |
| 1984 New York | AL | 61 | 1 | 0 | 23 | 103.2 | 426 | 86 | 33 | 31 | 5 | 3 | 3 | 0 | 34 | 3 | 109 | 4 | 0 | 9 | 4 | .692 | 0 | 7 | 2.69 |
| 1985 Oakland | AL | 63 | 0 | 0 | 58 | 98 | 414 | 98 | 32 | 31 | 5 | 3 | 4 | 1 | 31 | 3 | 68 | 4 | 1 | 9 | 8 | .529 | 0 | 29 | 2.85 |
| 1986 Oakland | AL | 38 | 0 | 0 | 33 | 53.1 | 230 | 53 | 23 | 20 | 3 | 3 | 1 | 1 | 23 | 4 | 42 | 4 | 0 | 3 | 6 | .333 | 0 | 16 | 3.38 |
| 1987 Oakland | AL | 36 | 0 | 0 | 27 | 44.1 | 200 | 48 | 30 | 29 | 6 | 3 | 2 | 1 | 21 | 1 | 35 | 4 | 0 | 3 | 4 | .429 | 0 | 16 | 5.89 |
| 1988 Los Angeles | NL | 50 | 0 | 0 | 38 | 65 | 262 | 44 | 16 | 15 | 1 | 3 | 3 | 1 | 21 | 2 | 70 | 2 | 2 | 5 | 3 | .625 | 0 | 21 | 2.08 |
| 1989 Los Angeles | NL | 56 | 0 | 0 | 41 | 79.2 | 312 | 60 | 15 | 14 | 3 | 4 | 2 | 0 | 22 | 6 | 55 | 1 | 0 | 5 | 3 | .625 | 0 | 28 | 1.58 |
| 1990 Los Angeles | NL | 45 | 0 | 0 | 35 | 66 | 271 | 59 | 17 | 16 | 5 | 1 | 0 | 6 | 20 | 3 | 59 | 4 | 1 | 5 | 5 | .500 | 0 | 16 | 2.18 |
| 11 ML YEARS | | 389 | 21 | 2 | 260 | 645 | 2737 | 610 | 262 | 246 | 39 | 22 | 24 | 16 | 230 | 24 | 531 | 26 | 5 | 44 | 41 | .518 | 0 | 133 | 3.43 |

## Ken Howell

**Pitches:** Right **Bats:** Right **Pos:** SP **Ht:** 6' 3" **Wt:** 228 **Born:** 11/28/60 **Age:** 30

| HOW MUCH HE PITCHED | | | | | | | | WHAT HE GAVE UP | | | | | | | | | | | | THE RESULTS | | | | | |
|---|---|---|---|---|---|---|---|---|---|---|---|---|---|---|---|---|---|---|---|---|---|---|---|---|---|
| Year Team | Lg | G | GS | CG | GF | IP | BFP | H | R | ER | HR | SH | SF | HB | TBB | IBB | SO | WP | Bk | W | L | Pct. | ShO | Sv | ERA |
| 1984 Los Angeles | NL | 32 | 1 | 0 | 19 | 51.1 | 207 | 51 | 21 | 19 | 1 | 2 | 4 | 1 | 9 | 4 | 54 | 0 | 0 | 5 | 5 | .500 | 0 | 6 | 3.33 |
| 1985 Los Angeles | NL | 56 | 0 | 0 | 31 | 86 | 356 | 66 | 41 | 36 | 8 | 4 | 0 | 0 | 35 | 3 | 85 | 4 | 2 | 4 | 7 | .364 | 0 | 12 | 3.77 |
| 1986 Los Angeles | NL | 62 | 0 | 0 | 36 | 97.2 | 437 | 86 | 48 | 42 | 7 | 8 | 3 | 3 | 63 | 9 | 104 | 4 | 0 | 6 | 12 | .333 | 0 | 12 | 3.87 |
| 1987 Los Angeles | NL | 40 | 2 | 0 | 17 | 55 | 239 | 54 | 32 | 30 | 7 | 6 | 0 | 0 | 29 | 2 | 60 | 5 | 1 | 3 | 4 | .429 | 0 | 1 | 4.91 |
| 1988 Los Angeles | NL | 4 | 1 | 0 | 2 | 12.2 | 55 | 16 | 10 | 9 | 0 | 1 | 0 | 0 | 4 | 1 | 12 | 0 | 0 | 0 | 1 | .000 | 0 | 0 | 6.39 |

| Year Team | Lg | G | GS | CG | GF | IP | BFP | H | R | ER | HR | SH | SF | HB | TBB | IBB | SO | WP | Bk | W | L | Pct. | ShO | Sv | ERA |
|---|---|---|---|---|---|---|---|---|---|---|---|---|---|---|---|---|---|---|---|---|---|---|---|---|---|
| 1989 Philadelphia | NL | 33 | 32 | 1 | 0 | 204 | 827 | 155 | 84 | 78 | 11 | 8 | 9 | 2 | 86 | 6 | 164 | 21 | 1 | 12 | 12 | .500 | 1 | 0 | 3.44 |
| 1990 Philadelphia | NL | 18 | 18 | 2 | 0 | 106.2 | 467 | 106 | 60 | 55 | 12 | 7 | 1 | 3 | 49 | 6 | 70 | 8 | 0 | 8 | 7 | .533 | 0 | 0 | 4.64 |
| 7 ML YEARS | | 245 | 54 | 3 | 105 | 613.1 | 2588 | 534 | 296 | 269 | 46 | 36 | 17 | 9 | 275 | 31 | 549 | 42 | 4 | 38 | 48 | .442 | 1 | 31 | 3.95 |

## Dann Howitt

**Bats:** Left **Throws:** Right **Pos:** RF **Ht:** 6' 5" **Wt:** 205 **Born:** 02/13/64 **Age:** 27

| BATTING | | | | | | | | | | | | | | | | | | | BASERUNNING | | | | PERCENTAGES | | |
|---|---|---|---|---|---|---|---|---|---|---|---|---|---|---|---|---|---|---|---|---|---|---|---|---|---|
| Year Team | Lg | G | AB | H | 2B | 3B | HR | (Hm | Rd) | TB | R | RBI | TBB | IBB | SO | HBP | SH | SF | SB | CS | SB% | GDP | Avg | OBP | SLG |
| 1986 Medford | A | 66 | 208 | 66 | 9 | 2 | 6 | -- | -- | 97 | 36 | 37 | 49 | 3 | 37 | 1 | 1 | 1 | 5 | 1 | .83 | 7 | .317 | .448 | .466 |
| 1987 Modesto | A | 109 | 336 | 70 | 11 | 2 | 8 | -- | -- | 109 | 44 | 42 | 59 | 1 | 110 | 4 | 3 | 3 | 7 | 9 | .44 | 8 | .208 | .331 | .324 |
| 1988 Modesto | A | 132 | 480 | 121 | 20 | 2 | 18 | -- | -- | 199 | 75 | 86 | 81 | 3 | 106 | 2 | 0 | 2 | 11 | 5 | .69 | 9 | .252 | .361 | .415 |
| Tacoma | AAA | 4 | 15 | 2 | 1 | 0 | 0 | -- | -- | 3 | 1 | 0 | 0 | 0 | 4 | 0 | 0 | 0 | 0 | 0 | .00 | 0 | .133 | .133 | .200 |
| 1989 Huntsville | AA | 138 | 509 | 143 | 28 | 2 | 26 | -- | -- | 253 | 78 | 111 | 68 | 7 | 107 | 3 | 2 | 6 | 2 | 1 | .67 | 6 | .281 | .365 | .497 |
| 1990 Tacoma | AAA | 118 | 437 | 116 | 30 | 1 | 11 | -- | -- | 181 | 58 | 69 | 38 | 3 | 95 | 2 | 0 | 4 | 4 | 4 | .50 | 16 | .265 | .324 | .414 |
| 1989 Oakland | AL | 3 | 3 | 0 | 0 | 0 | 0 | (0 | 0) | 0 | 0 | 0 | 0 | 0 | 2 | 0 | 0 | 0 | 0 | 0 | .00 | 0 | .000 | .000 | .000 |
| 1990 Oakland | AL | 14 | 22 | 3 | 0 | 1 | 0 | (0 | 0) | 5 | 3 | 1 | 3 | 0 | 12 | 0 | 0 | 0 | 0 | 0 | .00 | 0 | .136 | .240 | .227 |
| 2 ML YEARS | | 17 | 25 | 3 | 0 | 1 | 0 | (0 | 0) | 5 | 3 | 1 | 3 | 0 | 14 | 0 | 0 | 0 | 0 | 0 | .00 | 0 | .120 | .214 | .200 |

## Kent Hrbek

**Bats:** Left **Throws:** Right **Pos:** 1B/DH **Ht:** 6' 4" **Wt:** 250 **Born:** 05/21/60 **Age:** 31

| BATTING | | | | | | | | | | | | | | | | | | | BASERUNNING | | | | PERCENTAGES | | |
|---|---|---|---|---|---|---|---|---|---|---|---|---|---|---|---|---|---|---|---|---|---|---|---|---|---|
| Year Team | Lg | G | AB | H | 2B | 3B | HR | (Hm | Rd) | TB | R | RBI | TBB | IBB | SO | HBP | SH | SF | SB | CS | SB% | GDP | Avg | OBP | SLG |
| 1981 Minnesota | AL | 24 | 67 | 16 | 5 | 0 | 1 | (0 | 1) | 24 | 5 | 7 | 5 | 1 | 9 | 1 | 0 | 0 | 0 | 0 | .00 | 0 | .239 | .301 | .358 |
| 1982 Minnesota | AL | 140 | 532 | 160 | 21 | 4 | 23 | (11 | 12) | 258 | 82 | 92 | 54 | 12 | 80 | 0 | 1 | 4 | 3 | 1 | .75 | 17 | .301 | .363 | .485 |
| 1983 Minnesota | AL | 141 | 515 | 153 | 41 | 5 | 16 | (7 | 9) | 252 | 75 | 84 | 57 | 5 | 71 | 3 | 0 | 7 | 4 | 6 | .40 | 12 | .297 | .366 | .489 |
| 1984 Minnesota | AL | 149 | 559 | 174 | 31 | 3 | 27 | (15 | 12) | 292 | 80 | 107 | 65 | 15 | 87 | 4 | 1 | 6 | 1 | 1 | .50 | 17 | .311 | .383 | .522 |
| 1985 Minnesota | AL | 158 | 593 | 165 | 31 | 2 | 21 | (10 | 11) | 263 | 78 | 93 | 67 | 12 | 87 | 2 | 0 | 4 | 1 | 1 | .50 | 12 | .278 | .351 | .444 |
| 1986 Minnesota | AL | 149 | 550 | 147 | 27 | 1 | 29 | (18 | 11) | 263 | 85 | 91 | 71 | 9 | 81 | 6 | 0 | 7 | 2 | 2 | .50 | 15 | .267 | .353 | .478 |
| 1987 Minnesota | AL | 143 | 477 | 136 | 20 | 1 | 34 | (20 | 14) | 260 | 85 | 90 | 84 | 12 | 60 | 0 | 0 | 5 | 5 | 2 | .71 | 13 | .285 | .389 | .545 |
| 1988 Minnesota | AL | 143 | 510 | 159 | 31 | 0 | 25 | (13 | 12) | 265 | 75 | 76 | 67 | 7 | 54 | 0 | 2 | 7 | 0 | 3 | .00 | 9 | .312 | .387 | .520 |
| 1989 Minnesota | AL | 109 | 375 | 102 | 17 | 0 | 25 | (17 | 8) | 194 | 59 | 84 | 53 | 4 | 35 | 1 | 1 | 4 | 3 | 0 | 1.00 | 6 | .272 | .360 | .517 |
| 1990 Minnesota | AL | 143 | 492 | 141 | 26 | 0 | 22 | (8 | 14) | 233 | 61 | 79 | 69 | 8 | 45 | 7 | 2 | 8 | 5 | 2 | .71 | 17 | .287 | .377 | .474 |
| 10 ML YEARS | | 1299 | 4670 | 1353 | 250 | 16 | 223 | (119 | 104) | 2304 | 685 | 803 | 592 | 85 | 609 | 24 | 7 | 52 | 24 | 18 | .57 | 118 | .290 | .369 | .493 |

## Rex Hudler

**Bats:** Right **Throws:** Right **Pos:** RF/LF **Ht:** 6' 2" **Wt:** 180 **Born:** 09/02/60 **Age:** 30

| BATTING | | | | | | | | | | | | | | | | | | | BASERUNNING | | | | PERCENTAGES | | |
|---|---|---|---|---|---|---|---|---|---|---|---|---|---|---|---|---|---|---|---|---|---|---|---|---|---|
| Year Team | Lg | G | AB | H | 2B | 3B | HR | (Hm | Rd) | TB | R | RBI | TBB | IBB | SO | HBP | SH | SF | SB | CS | SB% | GDP | Avg | OBP | SLG |
| 1984 New York | AL | 9 | 7 | 1 | 1 | 0 | 0 | (0 | 0) | 2 | 2 | 0 | 1 | 0 | 5 | 1 | 0 | 0 | 0 | 0 | .00 | 0 | .143 | .333 | .286 |
| 1985 New York | AL | 20 | 51 | 8 | 0 | 1 | 0 | (0 | 0) | 10 | 4 | 1 | 1 | 0 | 9 | 0 | 5 | 0 | 0 | 1 | .00 | 0 | .157 | .173 | .196 |
| 1986 Baltimore | AL | 14 | 1 | 0 | 0 | 0 | 0 | (0 | 0) | 0 | 1 | 0 | 0 | 0 | 0 | 0 | 0 | 0 | 1 | 0 | 1.00 | 0 | .000 | .000 | .000 |
| 1988 Montreal | NL | 77 | 216 | 59 | 14 | 2 | 4 | (1 | 3) | 89 | 38 | 14 | 10 | 6 | 34 | 0 | 1 | 2 | 29 | 7 | .81 | 2 | .273 | .303 | .412 |
| 1989 Montreal | NL | 92 | 155 | 38 | 7 | 0 | 6 | (3 | 3) | 63 | 21 | 13 | 6 | 2 | 23 | 1 | 0 | 0 | 15 | 4 | .79 | 2 | .245 | .278 | .406 |
| 1990 2 ML Teams | | 93 | 220 | 62 | 11 | 2 | 7 | (2 | 5) | 98 | 31 | 22 | 12 | 1 | 32 | 2 | 2 | 1 | 18 | 10 | .64 | 3 | .282 | .323 | .445 |
| 1990 Montreal | NL | 4 | 3 | 1 | 0 | 0 | 0 | (0 | 0) | 1 | 1 | 0 | 0 | 0 | 1 | 0 | 0 | 0 | 0 | 0 | .00 | 0 | .333 | .333 | .333 |
| St. Louis | NL | 89 | 217 | 61 | 11 | 2 | 7 | (2 | 5) | 97 | 30 | 22 | 12 | 1 | 31 | 2 | 2 | 1 | 18 | 10 | .64 | 3 | .281 | .323 | .447 |
| 6 ML YEARS | | 305 | 650 | 168 | 33 | 5 | 17 | (6 | 11) | 262 | 97 | 50 | 30 | 9 | 103 | 4 | 8 | 3 | 63 | 22 | .74 | 7 | .258 | .294 | .403 |

## Keith Hughes

**Bats:** Left **Throws:** Left **Pos:** LF **Ht:** 6' 3" **Wt:** 210 **Born:** 09/12/63 **Age:** 27

| BATTING | | | | | | | | | | | | | | | | | | | BASERUNNING | | | | PERCENTAGES | | |
|---|---|---|---|---|---|---|---|---|---|---|---|---|---|---|---|---|---|---|---|---|---|---|---|---|---|
| Year Team | Lg | G | AB | H | 2B | 3B | HR | (Hm | Rd) | TB | R | RBI | TBB | IBB | SO | HBP | SH | SF | SB | CS | SB% | GDP | Avg | OBP | SLG |
| 1987 2 ML Teams | | 41 | 80 | 20 | 2 | 0 | 0 | (0 | 0) | 22 | 8 | 10 | 7 | 0 | 13 | 1 | 0 | 0 | 0 | 0 | .00 | 1 | .250 | .318 | .275 |
| 1988 Baltimore | AL | 41 | 108 | 21 | 4 | 2 | 2 | (1 | 1) | 35 | 10 | 14 | 16 | 1 | 27 | 0 | 0 | 2 | 1 | 0 | 1.00 | 3 | .194 | .294 | .324 |
| 1990 New York | NL | 8 | 9 | 0 | 0 | 0 | 0 | (0 | 0) | 0 | 0 | 0 | 0 | 0 | 4 | 0 | 0 | 0 | 0 | 0 | .00 | 0 | .000 | .000 | .000 |
| 1987 New York | AL | 4 | 4 | 0 | 0 | 0 | 0 | (0 | 0) | 0 | 0 | 0 | 0 | 0 | 2 | 0 | 0 | 0 | 0 | 0 | .00 | 0 | .000 | .000 | .000 |
| Philadelphia | NL | 37 | 76 | 20 | 2 | 0 | 0 | (0 | 0) | 22 | 8 | 10 | 7 | 0 | 11 | 1 | 0 | 0 | 0 | 0 | .00 | 1 | .263 | .333 | .289 |
| 3 ML YEARS | | 90 | 197 | 41 | 6 | 2 | 2 | (1 | 1) | 57 | 18 | 24 | 23 | 1 | 44 | 1 | 0 | 2 | 1 | 0 | 1.00 | 4 | .208 | .291 | .289 |

## Mark Huismann

**Pitches:** Right **Bats:** Right **Pos:** RP **Ht:** 6' 3" **Wt:** 195 **Born:** 05/11/58 **Age:** 33

| HOW MUCH HE PITCHED | | | | | | | | WHAT HE GAVE UP | | | | | | | | | | | | THE RESULTS | | | | | |
|---|---|---|---|---|---|---|---|---|---|---|---|---|---|---|---|---|---|---|---|---|---|---|---|---|---|
| Year Team | Lg | G | GS | CG | GF | IP | BFP | H | R | ER | HR | SH | SF | HB | TBB | IBB | SO | WP | Bk | W | L | Pct. | ShO | Sv | ERA |
| 1983 Kansas City | AL | 13 | 0 | 0 | 5 | 30.2 | 135 | 29 | 20 | 19 | 1 | 1 | 1 | 0 | 17 | 3 | 20 | 4 | 1 | 2 | 1 | .667 | 0 | 0 | 5.58 |
| 1984 Kansas City | AL | 38 | 0 | 0 | 23 | 75 | 324 | 84 | 38 | 35 | 7 | 3 | 5 | 1 | 21 | 3 | 54 | 3 | 0 | 3 | 3 | .500 | 0 | 3 | 4.20 |
| 1985 Kansas City | AL | 9 | 0 | 0 | 6 | 18.2 | 70 | 14 | 4 | 4 | 1 | 1 | 2 | 0 | 3 | 0 | 9 | 0 | 0 | 1 | 0 | 1.000 | 0 | 0 | 1.93 |
| 1986 2 ML Teams | | 46 | 1 | 0 | 19 | 97.1 | 408 | 98 | 47 | 41 | 19 | 0 | 3 | 1 | 25 | 0 | 72 | 5 | 0 | 3 | 4 | .429 | 0 | 5 | 3.79 |

| | | | | | | | | | | | | | | | | | | | | | | | | | |
|---|---|---|---|---|---|---|---|---|---|---|---|---|---|---|---|---|---|---|---|---|---|---|---|---|---|
| 1987 2 ML Teams | | 26 | 0 | 0 | 11 | 50 | 212 | 48 | 32 | 28 | 7 | 4 | 3 | 2 | 12 | 0 | 38 | 3 | 0 | 2 | 3 | .400 | 0 | 2 | 5.04 |
| 1988 Detroit | AL | 5 | 0 | 0 | 2 | 5.1 | 23 | 6 | 3 | 3 | 0 | 0 | 0 | 0 | 2 | 1 | 6 | 0 | 0 | 1 | 0 | 1.000 | 0 | 0 | 5.06 |
| 1989 Baltimore | AL | 8 | 0 | 0 | 1 | 11.1 | 48 | 13 | 8 | 8 | 0 | 0 | 1 | 0 | 0 | 0 | 13 | 1 | 0 | 0 | 0 | .000 | 0 | 1 | 6.35 |
| 1990 Pittsburgh | NL | 2 | 0 | 0 | 0 | 3 | 15 | 6 | 5 | 3 | 2 | 0 | 0 | 1 | 1 | 0 | 2 | 1 | 0 | 1 | 0 | 1.000 | 0 | 0 | 9.00 |
| 1986 Kansas City | AL | 10 | 0 | 0 | 5 | 17.1 | 74 | 18 | 8 | 8 | 1 | 0 | 1 | 0 | 6 | 0 | 13 | 1 | 0 | 0 | 1 | .000 | 0 | 1 | 4.15 |
| Seattle | AL | 36 | 1 | 0 | 14 | 80 | 334 | 80 | 39 | 33 | 18 | 0 | 2 | 1 | 19 | 0 | 59 | 4 | 0 | 3 | 3 | .500 | 0 | 4 | 3.71 |
| 1987 Seattle | AL | 6 | 0 | 0 | 1 | 14.2 | 61 | 10 | 10 | 8 | 1 | 3 | 1 | 2 | 4 | 0 | 15 | 0 | 0 | 0 | 0 | .000 | 0 | 0 | 4.91 |
| Cleveland | AL | 20 | 0 | 0 | 10 | 35.1 | 151 | 38 | 22 | 20 | 6 | 1 | 2 | 0 | 8 | 0 | 23 | 3 | 0 | 2 | 3 | .400 | 0 | 2 | 5.09 |
| 8 ML YEARS | | 147 | 1 | 0 | 67 | 291.1 | 1235 | 298 | 157 | 141 | 37 | 9 | 15 | 5 | 81 | 7 | 214 | 17 | 1 | 13 | 11 | .542 | 0 | 11 | 4.36 |

## Tim Hulett

**Bats:** Right **Throws:** Right **Pos:** 3B/2B **Ht:** 6' 0" **Wt:** 185 **Born:** 01/12/60 **Age:** 31

| BATTING | | | | | | | | | | | | | | | | | | | BASERUNNING | | | | PERCENTAGES | | |
|---|---|---|---|---|---|---|---|---|---|---|---|---|---|---|---|---|---|---|---|---|---|---|---|---|---|
| Year Team | Lg | G | AB | H | 2B | 3B | HR | (Hm | Rd) | TB | R | RBI | TBB | IBB | SO | HBP | SH | SF | SB | CS | SB% | GDP | Avg | OBP | SLG |
| 1983 Chicago | AL | 6 | 5 | 1 | 0 | 0 | 0 | (0 | 0) | 1 | 0 | 0 | 0 | 0 | 0 | 0 | 0 | 0 | 1 | 0 | 1.00 | 0 | .200 | .200 | .200 |
| 1984 Chicago | AL | 8 | 7 | 0 | 0 | 0 | 0 | (0 | 0) | 0 | 1 | 0 | 1 | 0 | 4 | 0 | 0 | 0 | 1 | 0 | 1.00 | 0 | .000 | .125 | .000 |
| 1985 Chicago | AL | 141 | 395 | 106 | 19 | 4 | 5 | (2 | 3) | 148 | 52 | 37 | 30 | 1 | 81 | 4 | 4 | 3 | 6 | 4 | .60 | 8 | .268 | .324 | .375 |
| 1986 Chicago | AL | 150 | 520 | 120 | 16 | 5 | 17 | (7 | 10) | 197 | 53 | 44 | 21 | 0 | 91 | 1 | 6 | 4 | 4 | 1 | .80 | 11 | .231 | .260 | .379 |
| 1987 Chicago | AL | 68 | 240 | 52 | 10 | 0 | 7 | (3 | 4) | 83 | 20 | 28 | 10 | 1 | 41 | 0 | 5 | 2 | 0 | 2 | .00 | 6 | .217 | .246 | .346 |
| 1989 Baltimore | AL | 33 | 97 | 27 | 5 | 0 | 3 | (2 | 1) | 41 | 12 | 18 | 10 | 0 | 17 | 0 | 1 | 1 | 0 | 0 | .00 | 3 | .278 | .343 | .423 |
| 1990 Baltimore | AL | 53 | 153 | 39 | 7 | 1 | 3 | (2 | 1) | 57 | 16 | 16 | 15 | 0 | 41 | 0 | 1 | 0 | 1 | 0 | 1.00 | 2 | .255 | .321 | .373 |
| 7 ML YEARS | | 459 | 1417 | 345 | 57 | 10 | 35 | (16 | 19) | 527 | 154 | 143 | 87 | 2 | 275 | 5 | 17 | 10 | 13 | 7 | .65 | 30 | .243 | .288 | .372 |

## Todd Hundley

**Bats:** Both **Throws:** Right **Pos:** C **Ht:** 5'11" **Wt:** 170 **Born:** 05/27/69 **Age:** 22

| BATTING | | | | | | | | | | | | | | | | | | | BASERUNNING | | | | PERCENTAGES | | |
|---|---|---|---|---|---|---|---|---|---|---|---|---|---|---|---|---|---|---|---|---|---|---|---|---|---|
| Year Team | Lg | G | AB | H | 2B | 3B | HR | (Hm | Rd) | TB | R | RBI | TBB | IBB | SO | HBP | SH | SF | SB | CS | SB% | GDP | Avg | OBP | SLG |
| 1987 Little Fls | A | 34 | 103 | 15 | 4 | 0 | 1 | -- | -- | 22 | 12 | 10 | 12 | 2 | 27 | 3 | 0 | 0 | 0 | 0 | .00 | 2 | .146 | .254 | .214 |
| 1988 Little Fls | A | 52 | 176 | 33 | 8 | 0 | 2 | -- | -- | 47 | 23 | 18 | 16 | 1 | 31 | 4 | 2 | 1 | 1 | 1 | .50 | 2 | .188 | .269 | .267 |
| St. Lucie | A | 1 | 1 | 0 | 0 | 0 | 0 | -- | -- | 0 | 0 | 0 | 2 | 0 | 1 | 0 | 0 | 0 | 0 | 0 | .00 | 0 | .000 | .667 | .000 |
| 1989 Columbia | A | 125 | 439 | 118 | 23 | 4 | 11 | -- | -- | 182 | 67 | 66 | 54 | 10 | 67 | 8 | 1 | 5 | 6 | 3 | .67 | 20 | .269 | .356 | .415 |
| 1990 Jackson | AA | 81 | 279 | 74 | 12 | 2 | 1 | -- | -- | 93 | 27 | 35 | 34 | 3 | 44 | 1 | 0 | 3 | 5 | 3 | .63 | 5 | .265 | .344 | .333 |
| 1990 New York | NL | 36 | 67 | 14 | 6 | 0 | 0 | (0 | 0) | 20 | 8 | 2 | 6 | 0 | 18 | 0 | 1 | 0 | 0 | 0 | .00 | 1 | .209 | .274 | .299 |

## Bruce Hurst

**Pitches:** Left **Bats:** Left **Pos:** SP **Ht:** 6' 3" **Wt:** 215 **Born:** 03/24/58 **Age:** 33

| HOW MUCH HE PITCHED | | | | | | | | WHAT HE GAVE UP | | | | | | | | | | | | THE RESULTS | | | | | |
|---|---|---|---|---|---|---|---|---|---|---|---|---|---|---|---|---|---|---|---|---|---|---|---|---|---|
| Year Team | Lg | G | GS | CG | GF | IP | BFP | H | R | ER | HR | SH | SF | HB | TBB | IBB | SO | WP | Bk | W | L | Pct. | ShO | Sv | ERA |
| 1980 Boston | AL | 12 | 7 | 0 | 2 | 31 | 147 | 39 | 33 | 31 | 4 | 0 | 2 | 2 | 16 | 0 | 16 | 4 | 2 | 2 | 2 | .500 | 0 | 0 | 9.00 |
| 1981 Boston | AL | 5 | 5 | 0 | 0 | 23 | 104 | 23 | 11 | 11 | 1 | 0 | 2 | 1 | 12 | 2 | 11 | 2 | 0 | 2 | 0 | 1.000 | 0 | 0 | 4.30 |
| 1982 Boston | AL | 28 | 19 | 0 | 3 | 117 | 535 | 161 | 87 | 75 | 16 | 2 | 7 | 3 | 40 | 2 | 53 | 5 | 0 | 3 | 7 | .300 | 0 | 0 | 5.77 |
| 1983 Boston | AL | 33 | 32 | 6 | 0 | 211.1 | 903 | 241 | 102 | 96 | 22 | 3 | 4 | 3 | 62 | 5 | 115 | 1 | 2 | 12 | 12 | .500 | 2 | 0 | 4.09 |
| 1984 Boston | AL | 33 | 33 | 9 | 0 | 218 | 958 | 232 | 106 | 95 | 25 | 3 | 4 | 6 | 88 | 3 | 136 | 1 | 1 | 12 | 12 | .500 | 2 | 0 | 3.92 |
| 1985 Boston | AL | 35 | 31 | 6 | 0 | 229.1 | 973 | 243 | 123 | 115 | 31 | 6 | 4 | 3 | 70 | 4 | 189 | 3 | 4 | 11 | 13 | .458 | 1 | 0 | 4.51 |
| 1986 Boston | AL | 25 | 25 | 11 | 0 | 174.1 | 721 | 169 | 63 | 58 | 18 | 5 | 3 | 3 | 50 | 2 | 167 | 6 | 0 | 13 | 8 | .619 | 4 | 0 | 2.99 |
| 1987 Boston | AL | 33 | 33 | 15 | 0 | 238.2 | 1001 | 239 | 124 | 117 | 35 | 5 | 8 | 1 | 76 | 5 | 190 | 3 | 1 | 15 | 13 | .536 | 3 | 0 | 4.41 |
| 1988 Boston | AL | 33 | 32 | 7 | 0 | 216.2 | 922 | 222 | 98 | 88 | 21 | 8 | 5 | 2 | 65 | 1 | 166 | 5 | 3 | 18 | 6 | .750 | 1 | 0 | 3.66 |
| 1989 San Diego | NL | 33 | 33 | 10 | 0 | 244.2 | 990 | 214 | 84 | 73 | 16 | 18 | 3 | 0 | 66 | 7 | 179 | 8 | 0 | 15 | 11 | .577 | 2 | 0 | 2.69 |
| 1990 San Diego | NL | 33 | 33 | 9 | 0 | 223.2 | 903 | 188 | 85 | 78 | 21 | 15 | 1 | 1 | 63 | 5 | 162 | 7 | 1 | 11 | 9 | .550 | 4 | 0 | 3.14 |
| 11 ML YEARS | | 303 | 283 | 73 | 5 | 1927.2 | 8157 | 1971 | 916 | 837 | 210 | 65 | 43 | 25 | 608 | 36 | 1384 | 45 | 14 | 114 | 93 | .551 | 19 | 0 | 3.91 |

## Jeff Huson

**Bats:** Left **Throws:** Right **Pos:** SS/3B **Ht:** 6' 3" **Wt:** 170 **Born:** 08/15/64 **Age:** 26

| BATTING | | | | | | | | | | | | | | | | | | | BASERUNNING | | | | PERCENTAGES | | |
|---|---|---|---|---|---|---|---|---|---|---|---|---|---|---|---|---|---|---|---|---|---|---|---|---|---|
| Year Team | Lg | G | AB | H | 2B | 3B | HR | (Hm | Rd) | TB | R | RBI | TBB | IBB | SO | HBP | SH | SF | SB | CS | SB% | GDP | Avg | OBP | SLG |
| 1988 Montreal | NL | 20 | 42 | 13 | 2 | 0 | 0 | (0 | 0) | 15 | 7 | 3 | 4 | 2 | 3 | 0 | 0 | 0 | 2 | 1 | .67 | 2 | .310 | .370 | .357 |
| 1989 Montreal | NL | 32 | 74 | 12 | 5 | 0 | 0 | (0 | 0) | 17 | 1 | 2 | 6 | 3 | 6 | 0 | 3 | 0 | 3 | 0 | 1.00 | 6 | .162 | .225 | .230 |
| 1990 Texas | AL | 145 | 396 | 95 | 12 | 2 | 0 | (0 | 0) | 111 | 57 | 28 | 46 | 0 | 54 | 2 | 7 | 3 | 12 | 4 | .75 | 8 | .240 | .320 | .280 |
| 3 ML YEARS | | 197 | 512 | 120 | 19 | 2 | 0 | (0 | 0) | 143 | 65 | 33 | 56 | 5 | 63 | 2 | 10 | 3 | 17 | 5 | .77 | 16 | .234 | .311 | .279 |

## Pete Incaviglia

**Bats:** Right **Throws:** Right **Pos:** LF/CF **Ht:** 6' 1" **Wt:** 220 **Born:** 04/02/64 **Age:** 27

| BATTING | | | | | | | | | | | | | | | | | | | BASERUNNING | | | | PERCENTAGES | | |
|---|---|---|---|---|---|---|---|---|---|---|---|---|---|---|---|---|---|---|---|---|---|---|---|---|---|
| Year Team | Lg | G | AB | H | 2B | 3B | HR | (Hm | Rd) | TB | R | RBI | TBB | IBB | SO | HBP | SH | SF | SB | CS | SB% | GDP | Avg | OBP | SLG |
| 1986 Texas | AL | 153 | 540 | 135 | 21 | 2 | 30 | (17 | 13) | 250 | 82 | 88 | 55 | 2 | 185 | 4 | 0 | 7 | 3 | 2 | .60 | 9 | .250 | .320 | .463 |
| 1987 Texas | AL | 139 | 509 | 138 | 26 | 4 | 27 | (11 | 16) | 253 | 85 | 80 | 48 | 1 | 168 | 1 | 0 | 5 | 9 | 3 | .75 | 8 | .271 | .332 | .497 |

| Year Team | Lg | G | AB | H | 2B | 3B | HR | (Hm | Rd) | TB | R | RBI | TBB | IBB | SO | HBP | SH | SF | SB | CS | SB% | GDP | Avg | OBP | SLG |
|---|---|---|---|---|---|---|---|---|---|---|---|---|---|---|---|---|---|---|---|---|---|---|---|---|---|
| 1988 Texas | AL | 116 | 418 | 104 | 19 | 3 | 22 | (12 | 10) | 195 | 59 | 54 | 39 | 3 | 153 | 7 | 0 | 3 | 6 | 4 | .60 | 6 | .249 | .321 | .467 |
| 1989 Texas | AL | 133 | 453 | 107 | 27 | 4 | 21 | (13 | 8) | 205 | 48 | 81 | 32 | 0 | 136 | 6 | 0 | 4 | 5 | 7 | .42 | 12 | .236 | .293 | .453 |
| 1990 Texas | AL | 153 | 529 | 123 | 27 | 0 | 24 | (15 | 9) | 222 | 59 | 85 | 45 | 5 | 146 | 9 | 0 | 4 | 3 | 4 | .43 | 18 | .233 | .302 | .420 |
| 5 ML YEARS | | 694 | 2449 | 607 | 120 | 13 | 124 | (68 | 56) | 1125 | 333 | 388 | 219 | 11 | 788 | 27 | 0 | 23 | 26 | 20 | .57 | 53 | .248 | .314 | .459 |

## Alex Infante

**Bats:** Right **Throws:** Right **Pos:** 2B **Ht:** 5'11" **Wt:** 182 **Born:** 12/04/61 **Age:** 29

| | | BATTING | | | | | | | | | | | | | | | | | BASERUNNING | | | | PERCENTAGES | | |
|---|---|---|---|---|---|---|---|---|---|---|---|---|---|---|---|---|---|---|---|---|---|---|---|---|---|
| Year Team | Lg | G | AB | H | 2B | 3B | HR | (Hm | Rd) | TB | R | RBI | TBB | IBB | SO | HBP | SH | SF | SB | CS | SB% | GDP | Avg | OBP | SLG |
| 1987 Toronto | AL | 1 | 0 | 0 | 0 | 0 | 0 | (0 | 0) | 0 | 0 | 0 | 0 | 0 | 0 | 0 | 0 | 0 | 0 | 0 | .00 | 0 | .000 | .000 | .000 |
| 1988 Toronto | AL | 19 | 15 | 3 | 0 | 0 | 0 | (0 | 0) | 3 | 7 | 0 | 2 | 0 | 4 | 0 | 0 | 0 | 0 | 0 | .00 | 1 | .200 | .294 | .200 |
| 1989 Toronto | AL | 20 | 12 | 2 | 0 | 0 | 0 | (0 | 0) | 2 | 1 | 0 | 0 | 0 | 1 | 0 | 1 | 0 | 1 | 0 | 1.00 | 0 | .167 | .167 | .167 |
| 1990 Atlanta | NL | 20 | 28 | 1 | 1 | 0 | 0 | (0 | 0) | 2 | 3 | 0 | 0 | 0 | 7 | 1 | 3 | 0 | 0 | 0 | .00 | 2 | .036 | .069 | .071 |
| 4 ML YEARS | | 60 | 55 | 6 | 1 | 0 | 0 | (0 | 0) | 7 | 11 | 0 | 2 | 0 | 12 | 1 | 4 | 0 | 1 | 0 | 1.00 | 3 | .109 | .155 | .127 |

## Jeff Innis

**Pitches:** Right **Bats:** Right **Pos:** RP **Ht:** 6' 0" **Wt:** 170 **Born:** 07/05/62 **Age:** 28

| | | HOW MUCH HE PITCHED | | | | | | WHAT HE GAVE UP | | | | | | | | | | | | THE RESULTS | | | | | |
|---|---|---|---|---|---|---|---|---|---|---|---|---|---|---|---|---|---|---|---|---|---|---|---|---|---|
| Year Team | Lg | G | GS | CG | GF | IP | BFP | H | R | ER | HR | SH | SF | HB | TBB | IBB | SO | WP | Bk | W | L | Pct. | ShO | Sv | ERA |
| 1987 New York | NL | 17 | 1 | 0 | 8 | 25.2 | 109 | 29 | 9 | 9 | 5 | 0 | 0 | 1 | 4 | 1 | 28 | 1 | 1 | 0 | 1 | .000 | 0 | 0 | 3.16 |
| 1988 New York | NL | 12 | 0 | 0 | 7 | 19 | 80 | 19 | 6 | 4 | 0 | 1 | 1 | 0 | 2 | 1 | 14 | 0 | 0 | 1 | 1 | .500 | 0 | 0 | 1.89 |
| 1989 New York | NL | 29 | 0 | 0 | 12 | 39.2 | 160 | 38 | 16 | 14 | 2 | 1 | 1 | 1 | 8 | 0 | 16 | 0 | 0 | 0 | 1 | .000 | 0 | 0 | 3.18 |
| 1990 New York | NL | 18 | 0 | 0 | 12 | 26.1 | 104 | 19 | 9 | 7 | 4 | 0 | 2 | 1 | 10 | 3 | 12 | 1 | 1 | 1 | 3 | .250 | 0 | 1 | 2.39 |
| 4 ML YEARS | | 76 | 1 | 0 | 39 | 110.2 | 453 | 105 | 40 | 34 | 11 | 2 | 4 | 3 | 24 | 5 | 70 | 2 | 2 | 2 | 6 | .250 | 0 | 1 | 2.77 |

## Daryl Irvine

**Pitches:** Right **Bats:** Right **Pos:** RP **Ht:** 6' 3" **Wt:** 195 **Born:** 11/15/64 **Age:** 26

| | | HOW MUCH HE PITCHED | | | | | | WHAT HE GAVE UP | | | | | | | | | | | | THE RESULTS | | | | | |
|---|---|---|---|---|---|---|---|---|---|---|---|---|---|---|---|---|---|---|---|---|---|---|---|---|---|
| Year Team | Lg | G | GS | CG | GF | IP | BFP | H | R | ER | HR | SH | SF | HB | TBB | IBB | SO | WP | Bk | W | L | Pct. | ShO | Sv | ERA |
| 1985 Greensboro | A | 8 | 7 | 0 | 0 | 37 | 173 | 46 | 26 | 18 | 3 | 1 | 0 | 1 | 17 | 0 | 19 | 3 | 1 | 4 | 2 | .667 | 0 | 0 | 4.38 |
| 1986 Winter Havn | A | 26 | 24 | 3 | 0 | 161 | 702 | 162 | 73 | 57 | 2 | 9 | 3 | 7 | 67 | 3 | 73 | 13 | 1 | 9 | 8 | .529 | 0 | 0 | 3.19 |
| 1987 New Britain | AA | 37 | 16 | 3 | 8 | 127 | 588 | 156 | 101 | 75 | 7 | 9 | 6 | 2 | 59 | 4 | 70 | 16 | 9 | 4 | 13 | .235 | 0 | 0 | 5.31 |
| 1988 New Britain | AA | 39 | 14 | 4 | 13 | 125.1 | 536 | 113 | 62 | 43 | 4 | 5 | 2 | 5 | 57 | 4 | 82 | 8 | 7 | 5 | 11 | .313 | 1 | 0 | 3.09 |
| 1989 New Britain | AA | 54 | 1 | 0 | 45 | 91.1 | 366 | 74 | 24 | 13 | 0 | 5 | 0 | 3 | 23 | 2 | 50 | 9 | 0 | 4 | 6 | .400 | 0 | 16 | 1.28 |
| 1990 Pawtucket | AAA | 42 | 0 | 0 | 30 | 50 | 216 | 47 | 24 | 18 | 1 | 6 | 1 | 3 | 19 | 5 | 35 | 1 | 1 | 2 | 5 | .286 | 0 | 12 | 3.24 |
| 1990 Boston | AL | 11 | 0 | 0 | 6 | 17.1 | 75 | 15 | 10 | 9 | 0 | 1 | 3 | 0 | 10 | 3 | 9 | 1 | 1 | 1 | 1 | .500 | 0 | 0 | 4.67 |

## Bo Jackson

**Bats:** Right **Throws:** Right **Pos:** CF/LF **Ht:** 6' 1" **Wt:** 222 **Born:** 11/30/62 **Age:** 28

| | | BATTING | | | | | | | | | | | | | | | | | BASERUNNING | | | | PERCENTAGES | | |
|---|---|---|---|---|---|---|---|---|---|---|---|---|---|---|---|---|---|---|---|---|---|---|---|---|---|
| Year Team | Lg | G | AB | H | 2B | 3B | HR | (Hm | Rd) | TB | R | RBI | TBB | IBB | SO | HBP | SH | SF | SB | CS | SB% | GDP | Avg | OBP | SLG |
| 1986 Kansas City | AL | 25 | 82 | 17 | 2 | 1 | 2 | (1 | 1) | 27 | 9 | 9 | 7 | 0 | 34 | 2 | 0 | 0 | 3 | 1 | .75 | 1 | .207 | .286 | .329 |
| 1987 Kansas City | AL | 116 | 396 | 93 | 17 | 2 | 22 | (14 | 8) | 180 | 46 | 53 | 30 | 0 | 158 | 5 | 1 | 2 | 10 | 4 | .71 | 3 | .235 | .296 | .455 |
| 1988 Kansas City | AL | 124 | 439 | 108 | 16 | 4 | 25 | (10 | 15) | 207 | 63 | 68 | 25 | 6 | 146 | 1 | 1 | 2 | 27 | 6 | .82 | 6 | .246 | .287 | .472 |
| 1989 Kansas City | AL | 135 | 515 | 132 | 15 | 6 | 32 | (11 | 21) | 255 | 86 | 105 | 39 | 8 | 172 | 3 | 0 | 4 | 26 | 9 | .74 | 10 | .256 | .310 | .495 |
| 1990 Kansas City | AL | 111 | 405 | 110 | 16 | 1 | 28 | (12 | 16) | 212 | 74 | 78 | 44 | 2 | 128 | 2 | 0 | 5 | 15 | 9 | .63 | 10 | .272 | .342 | .523 |
| 5 ML YEARS | | 511 | 1837 | 460 | 66 | 14 | 109 | (48 | 61) | 881 | 278 | 313 | 145 | 16 | 638 | 13 | 2 | 13 | 81 | 29 | .74 | 30 | .250 | .308 | .480 |

## Danny Jackson

**Pitches:** Left **Bats:** Right **Pos:** SP **Ht:** 6' 0" **Wt:** 205 **Born:** 01/05/62 **Age:** 29

| | | HOW MUCH HE PITCHED | | | | | | WHAT HE GAVE UP | | | | | | | | | | | | THE RESULTS | | | | | |
|---|---|---|---|---|---|---|---|---|---|---|---|---|---|---|---|---|---|---|---|---|---|---|---|---|---|
| Year Team | Lg | G | GS | CG | GF | IP | BFP | H | R | ER | HR | SH | SF | HB | TBB | IBB | SO | WP | Bk | W | L | Pct. | ShO | Sv | ERA |
| 1983 Kansas City | AL | 4 | 3 | 0 | 0 | 19 | 87 | 26 | 12 | 11 | 1 | 1 | 0 | 0 | 6 | 0 | 9 | 0 | 0 | 1 | 1 | .500 | 0 | 0 | 5.21 |
| 1984 Kansas City | AL | 15 | 11 | 1 | 3 | 76 | 338 | 84 | 41 | 36 | 4 | 3 | 0 | 5 | 35 | 0 | 40 | 3 | 2 | 2 | 6 | .250 | 0 | 0 | 4.26 |
| 1985 Kansas City | AL | 32 | 32 | 4 | 0 | 208 | 893 | 209 | 94 | 79 | 7 | 5 | 4 | 6 | 76 | 2 | 114 | 4 | 2 | 14 | 12 | .538 | 3 | 0 | 3.42 |
| 1986 Kansas City | AL | 32 | 27 | 4 | 3 | 185.2 | 789 | 177 | 83 | 66 | 13 | 10 | 4 | 4 | 79 | 1 | 115 | 7 | 0 | 11 | 12 | .478 | 1 | 1 | 3.20 |
| 1987 Kansas City | AL | 36 | 34 | 11 | 1 | 224 | 981 | 219 | 115 | 100 | 11 | 8 | 7 | 7 | 109 | 1 | 152 | 5 | 0 | 9 | 18 | .333 | 2 | 0 | 4.02 |
| 1988 Cincinnati | NL | 35 | 35 | 15 | 0 | 260.2 | 1034 | 206 | 86 | 79 | 13 | 13 | 5 | 2 | 71 | 6 | 161 | 5 | 2 | 23 | 8 | .742 | 6 | 0 | 2.73 |
| 1989 Cincinnati | NL | 20 | 20 | 1 | 0 | 115.2 | 519 | 122 | 78 | 72 | 10 | 6 | 4 | 1 | 57 | 7 | 70 | 3 | 2 | 6 | 11 | .353 | 0 | 0 | 5.60 |
| 1990 Cincinnati | NL | 22 | 21 | 0 | 1 | 117.1 | 499 | 119 | 54 | 47 | 11 | 4 | 5 | 2 | 40 | 4 | 76 | 3 | 1 | 6 | 6 | .500 | 0 | 0 | 3.61 |
| 8 ML YEARS | | 196 | 183 | 36 | 8 | 1206.1 | 5140 | 1162 | 563 | 490 | 70 | 50 | 29 | 27 | 473 | 21 | 737 | 30 | 9 | 72 | 74 | .493 | 12 | 1 | 3.66 |

## Darrin Jackson

**Bats:** Right **Throws:** Right **Pos:** CF **Ht:** 6' 0" **Wt:** 185 **Born:** 08/22/63 **Age:** 27

| BATTING | | | | | | | | | | | | | | | | | | | BASERUNNING | | | | PERCENTAGES | | |
|---|---|---|---|---|---|---|---|---|---|---|---|---|---|---|---|---|---|---|---|---|---|---|---|---|---|
| Year Team | Lg | G | AB | H | 2B | 3B | HR | (Hm | Rd) | TB | R | RBI | TBB | IBB | SO | HBP | SH | SF | SB | CS | SB% | GDP | Avg | OBP | SLG |
| 1985 Chicago | NL | 5 | 11 | 1 | 0 | 0 | 0 | (0 | 0) | 1 | 0 | 0 | 0 | 0 | 3 | 0 | 0 | 0 | 0 | 0 | .00 | 0 | .091 | .091 | .091 |
| 1987 Chicago | NL | 7 | 5 | 4 | 1 | 0 | 0 | (0 | 0) | 5 | 2 | 0 | 0 | 0 | 0 | 0 | 0 | 0 | 0 | 0 | .00 | 0 | .800 | .800 | 1.000 |
| 1988 Chicago | NL | 100 | 188 | 50 | 11 | 3 | 6 | (3 | 3) | 85 | 29 | 20 | 5 | 1 | 28 | 1 | 2 | 1 | 4 | 1 | .80 | 3 | .266 | .287 | .452 |
| 1989 2 ML Teams | | 70 | 170 | 37 | 7 | 0 | 4 | (1 | 3) | 56 | 17 | 20 | 13 | 5 | 34 | 0 | 0 | 2 | 1 | 4 | .20 | 2 | .218 | .270 | .329 |
| 1990 San Diego | NL | 58 | 113 | 29 | 3 | 0 | 3 | (1 | 2) | 41 | 10 | 9 | 5 | 1 | 24 | 0 | 1 | 1 | 3 | 0 | 1.00 | 1 | .257 | .286 | .363 |
| 1989 Chicago | NL | 45 | 83 | 19 | 4 | 0 | 1 | (0 | 1) | 26 | 7 | 8 | 6 | 1 | 17 | 0 | 0 | 0 | 1 | 2 | .33 | 1 | .229 | .281 | .313 |
| San Diego | NL | 25 | 87 | 18 | 3 | 0 | 3 | (1 | 2) | 30 | 10 | 12 | 7 | 4 | 17 | 0 | 0 | 2 | 0 | 2 | .00 | 1 | .207 | .260 | .345 |
| 5 ML YEARS | | 240 | 487 | 121 | 22 | 3 | 13 | (5 | 8) | 188 | 58 | 49 | 23 | 7 | 89 | 1 | 3 | 4 | 8 | 5 | .62 | 6 | .248 | .282 | .386 |

## Mike Jackson

**Pitches:** Right **Bats:** Right **Pos:** RP **Ht:** 6' 0" **Wt:** 185 **Born:** 12/22/64 **Age:** 26

| HOW MUCH HE PITCHED | | | | | | | | WHAT HE GAVE UP | | | | | | | | | | | | THE RESULTS | | | | | |
|---|---|---|---|---|---|---|---|---|---|---|---|---|---|---|---|---|---|---|---|---|---|---|---|---|---|
| Year Team | Lg | G | GS | CG | GF | IP | BFP | H | R | ER | HR | SH | SF | HB | TBB | IBB | SO | WP | Bk | W | L | Pct. | ShO | Sv | ERA |
| 1986 Philadelphia | NL | 9 | 0 | 0 | 4 | 13.1 | 54 | 12 | 5 | 5 | 2 | 0 | 0 | 2 | 4 | 1 | 3 | 0 | 0 | 0 | 0 | .000 | 0 | 0 | 3.38 |
| 1987 Philadelphia | NL | 55 | 7 | 0 | 8 | 109.1 | 468 | 88 | 55 | 51 | 16 | 3 | 4 | 3 | 56 | 6 | 93 | 6 | 8 | 3 | 10 | .231 | 0 | 1 | 4.20 |
| 1988 Seattle | AL | 62 | 0 | 0 | 29 | 99.1 | 412 | 74 | 37 | 29 | 10 | 3 | 10 | 2 | 43 | 10 | 76 | 6 | 6 | 6 | 5 | .545 | 0 | 4 | 2.63 |
| 1989 Seattle | AL | 65 | 0 | 0 | 27 | 99.1 | 431 | 81 | 43 | 35 | 8 | 6 | 2 | 6 | 54 | 6 | 94 | 1 | 2 | 4 | 6 | .400 | 0 | 7 | 3.17 |
| 1990 Seattle | AL | 63 | 0 | 0 | 28 | 77.1 | 338 | 64 | 42 | 39 | 8 | 8 | 5 | 2 | 44 | 12 | 69 | 9 | 2 | 5 | 7 | .417 | 0 | 3 | 4.54 |
| 5 ML YEARS | | 254 | 7 | 0 | 96 | 398.2 | 1703 | 319 | 182 | 159 | 44 | 20 | 21 | 15 | 201 | 35 | 335 | 22 | 18 | 18 | 28 | .391 | 0 | 15 | 3.59 |

## Brook Jacoby

**Bats:** Right **Throws:** Right **Pos:** 3B/1B **Ht:** 5'11" **Wt:** 195 **Born:** 11/23/59 **Age:** 31

| BATTING | | | | | | | | | | | | | | | | | | | BASERUNNING | | | | PERCENTAGES | | |
|---|---|---|---|---|---|---|---|---|---|---|---|---|---|---|---|---|---|---|---|---|---|---|---|---|---|
| Year Team | Lg | G | AB | H | 2B | 3B | HR | (Hm | Rd) | TB | R | RBI | TBB | IBB | SO | HBP | SH | SF | SB | CS | SB% | GDP | Avg | OBP | SLG |
| 1981 Atlanta | NL | 11 | 10 | 2 | 0 | 0 | 0 | (0 | 0) | 2 | 0 | 1 | 0 | 0 | 3 | 0 | 0 | 0 | 0 | 0 | .00 | 1 | .200 | .200 | .200 |
| 1983 Atlanta | NL | 4 | 8 | 0 | 0 | 0 | 0 | (0 | 0) | 0 | 0 | 0 | 0 | 0 | 1 | 0 | 1 | 0 | 0 | 0 | .00 | 0 | .000 | .000 | .000 |
| 1984 Cleveland | AL | 126 | 439 | 116 | 19 | 3 | 7 | (2 | 5) | 162 | 64 | 40 | 32 | 0 | 73 | 3 | 2 | 7 | 3 | 2 | .60 | 13 | .264 | .314 | .369 |
| 1985 Cleveland | AL | 161 | 606 | 166 | 26 | 3 | 20 | (9 | 11) | 258 | 72 | 87 | 48 | 3 | 120 | 0 | 1 | 7 | 2 | 3 | .40 | 17 | .274 | .324 | .426 |
| 1986 Cleveland | AL | 158 | 583 | 168 | 30 | 4 | 17 | (10 | 7) | 257 | 83 | 80 | 56 | 5 | 137 | 0 | 1 | 1 | 2 | 1 | .67 | 15 | .288 | .350 | .441 |
| 1987 Cleveland | AL | 155 | 540 | 162 | 26 | 4 | 32 | (21 | 11) | 292 | 73 | 69 | 75 | 2 | 73 | 3 | 0 | 2 | 2 | 3 | .40 | 19 | .300 | .387 | .541 |
| 1988 Cleveland | AL | 152 | 552 | 133 | 25 | 0 | 9 | (3 | 6) | 185 | 59 | 49 | 48 | 2 | 101 | 1 | 0 | 5 | 2 | 3 | .40 | 12 | .241 | .300 | .335 |
| 1989 Cleveland | AL | 147 | 519 | 141 | 26 | 5 | 13 | (7 | 6) | 216 | 49 | 64 | 62 | 3 | 90 | 3 | 0 | 8 | 2 | 5 | .29 | 15 | .272 | .348 | .416 |
| 1990 Cleveland | AL | 155 | 553 | 162 | 24 | 4 | 14 | (10 | 4) | 236 | 77 | 75 | 63 | 6 | 58 | 2 | 2 | 4 | 1 | 4 | .20 | 20 | .293 | .365 | .427 |
| 9 ML YEARS | | 1069 | 3810 | 1050 | 176 | 23 | 112 | (62 | 50) | 1608 | 477 | 465 | 384 | 21 | 656 | 12 | 7 | 34 | 14 | 21 | .40 | 112 | .276 | .341 | .422 |

## Chris James

**Bats:** Right **Throws:** Right **Pos:** DH/LF **Ht:** 6' 1" **Wt:** 190 **Born:** 10/04/62 **Age:** 28

| BATTING | | | | | | | | | | | | | | | | | | | BASERUNNING | | | | PERCENTAGES | | |
|---|---|---|---|---|---|---|---|---|---|---|---|---|---|---|---|---|---|---|---|---|---|---|---|---|---|
| Year Team | Lg | G | AB | H | 2B | 3B | HR | (Hm | Rd) | TB | R | RBI | TBB | IBB | SO | HBP | SH | SF | SB | CS | SB% | GDP | Avg | OBP | SLG |
| 1986 Philadelphia | NL | 16 | 46 | 13 | 3 | 0 | 1 | (0 | 1) | 19 | 5 | 5 | 1 | 0 | 13 | 0 | 1 | 0 | 0 | 0 | .00 | 1 | .283 | .298 | .413 |
| 1987 Philadelphia | NL | 115 | 358 | 105 | 20 | 6 | 17 | (9 | 8) | 188 | 48 | 54 | 27 | 0 | 67 | 2 | 1 | 3 | 3 | 1 | .75 | 4 | .293 | .344 | .525 |
| 1988 Philadelphia | NL | 150 | 566 | 137 | 24 | 1 | 19 | (10 | 9) | 220 | 57 | 66 | 31 | 2 | 73 | 3 | 0 | 5 | 7 | 4 | .64 | 15 | .242 | .283 | .389 |
| 1989 2 ML Teams | | 132 | 482 | 117 | 17 | 2 | 13 | (7 | 6) | 177 | 55 | 65 | 26 | 2 | 68 | 1 | 4 | 3 | 5 | 2 | .71 | 20 | .243 | .281 | .367 |
| 1990 Cleveland | AL | 140 | 528 | 158 | 32 | 4 | 12 | (6 | 6) | 234 | 62 | 70 | 31 | 4 | 71 | 4 | 3 | 3 | 4 | 3 | .57 | 11 | .299 | .341 | .443 |
| 1989 Philadelphia | NL | 45 | 179 | 37 | 4 | 0 | 2 | (1 | 1) | 47 | 14 | 19 | 4 | 0 | 23 | 0 | 1 | 1 | 3 | 1 | .75 | 9 | .207 | .223 | .263 |
| San Diego | NL | 87 | 303 | 80 | 13 | 2 | 11 | (6 | 5) | 130 | 41 | 46 | 22 | 2 | 45 | 1 | 3 | 2 | 2 | 1 | .67 | 11 | .264 | .314 | .429 |
| 5 ML YEARS | | 553 | 1980 | 530 | 96 | 13 | 62 | (32 | 30) | 838 | 227 | 260 | 116 | 8 | 292 | 10 | 9 | 14 | 19 | 10 | .66 | 51 | .268 | .309 | .423 |

## Dion James

**Bats:** Left **Throws:** Left **Pos:** 1B/LF **Ht:** 6' 1" **Wt:** 170 **Born:** 11/09/62 **Age:** 28

| BATTING | | | | | | | | | | | | | | | | | | | BASERUNNING | | | | PERCENTAGES | | |
|---|---|---|---|---|---|---|---|---|---|---|---|---|---|---|---|---|---|---|---|---|---|---|---|---|---|
| Year Team | Lg | G | AB | H | 2B | 3B | HR | (Hm | Rd) | TB | R | RBI | TBB | IBB | SO | HBP | SH | SF | SB | CS | SB% | GDP | Avg | OBP | SLG |
| 1983 Milwaukee | AL | 11 | 20 | 2 | 0 | 0 | 0 | (0 | 0) | 2 | 1 | 1 | 2 | 0 | 2 | 0 | 0 | 0 | 1 | 0 | 1.00 | 0 | .100 | .182 | .100 |
| 1984 Milwaukee | AL | 128 | 387 | 114 | 19 | 5 | 1 | (1 | 0) | 146 | 52 | 30 | 32 | 1 | 41 | 3 | 6 | 3 | 10 | 10 | .50 | 7 | .295 | .351 | .377 |
| 1985 Milwaukee | AL | 18 | 49 | 11 | 1 | 0 | 0 | (0 | 0) | 12 | 5 | 3 | 6 | 0 | 6 | 0 | 0 | 0 | 0 | 0 | .00 | 0 | .224 | .309 | .245 |
| 1987 Atlanta | NL | 134 | 494 | 154 | 37 | 6 | 10 | (5 | 5) | 233 | 80 | 61 | 70 | 2 | 63 | 2 | 5 | 3 | 10 | 8 | .56 | 8 | .312 | .397 | .472 |
| 1988 Atlanta | NL | 132 | 386 | 99 | 17 | 5 | 3 | (1 | 2) | 135 | 46 | 30 | 58 | 5 | 59 | 1 | 2 | 2 | 9 | 9 | .50 | 12 | .256 | .353 | .350 |
| 1989 2 ML Teams | | 134 | 415 | 119 | 18 | 0 | 5 | (1 | 4) | 152 | 41 | 40 | 49 | 6 | 49 | 1 | 5 | 1 | 2 | 7 | .22 | 9 | .287 | .363 | .366 |
| 1990 Cleveland | AL | 87 | 248 | 68 | 15 | 2 | 1 | (0 | 1) | 90 | 28 | 22 | 27 | 3 | 23 | 1 | 3 | 1 | 5 | 3 | .63 | 6 | .274 | .347 | .363 |
| 1989 Atlanta | NL | 63 | 170 | 44 | 7 | 0 | 1 | (0 | 1) | 54 | 15 | 11 | 25 | 2 | 23 | 1 | 3 | 1 | 1 | 3 | .25 | 4 | .259 | .355 | .318 |

| Year Team | Lg | G | AB | H | 2B | 3B | HR | (Hm | Rd) | TB | R | RBI | TBB | IBB | SO | HBP | SH | SF | SB | CS | SB% | GDP | Avg | OBP | SLG |
|---|---|---|---|---|---|---|---|---|---|---|---|---|---|---|---|---|---|---|---|---|---|---|---|---|---|
| Cleveland | AL | 71 | 245 | 75 | 11 | 0 | 4 | (1 | 3) | 98 | 26 | 29 | 24 | 4 | 26 | 0 | 2 | 0 | 1 | 4 | .20 | 5 | .306 | .368 | .400 |
| 7 ML YEARS | | 644 | 1999 | 567 | 107 | 18 | 20 | (8 | 12) | 770 | 253 | 187 | 244 | 17 | 243 | 8 | 21 | 10 | 37 | 37 | .50 | 42 | .284 | .362 | .385 |

## Stan Javier

**Bats:** Both **Throws:** Right **Pos:** CF/RF **Ht:** 6' 0" **Wt:** 185 **Born:** 09/01/65 **Age:** 25

| BATTING | | | | | | | | | | | | | | | | | | | BASERUNNING | | | | PERCENTAGES | | |
|---|---|---|---|---|---|---|---|---|---|---|---|---|---|---|---|---|---|---|---|---|---|---|---|---|---|
| Year Team | Lg | G | AB | H | 2B | 3B | HR | (Hm | Rd) | TB | R | RBI | TBB | IBB | SO | HBP | SH | SF | SB | CS | SB% | GDP | Avg | OBP | SLG |
| 1984 New York | AL | 7 | 7 | 1 | 0 | 0 | 0 | (0 | 0) | 1 | 1 | 0 | 0 | 0 | 1 | 0 | 0 | 0 | 0 | 0 | .00 | 0 | .143 | .143 | .143 |
| 1986 Oakland | AL | 59 | 114 | 23 | 8 | 0 | 0 | (0 | 0) | 31 | 13 | 8 | 16 | 0 | 27 | 1 | 0 | 0 | 8 | 0 | 1.00 | 2 | .202 | .305 | .272 |
| 1987 Oakland | AL | 81 | 151 | 28 | 3 | 1 | 2 | (1 | 1) | 39 | 22 | 9 | 19 | 3 | 33 | 0 | 6 | 0 | 3 | 2 | .60 | 2 | .185 | .276 | .258 |
| 1988 Oakland | AL | 125 | 397 | 102 | 13 | 3 | 2 | (0 | 2) | 127 | 49 | 35 | 32 | 1 | 63 | 2 | 6 | 3 | 20 | 1 | .95 | 13 | .257 | .313 | .320 |
| 1989 Oakland | AL | 112 | 310 | 77 | 12 | 3 | 1 | (1 | 0) | 98 | 42 | 28 | 31 | 1 | 45 | 1 | 4 | 2 | 12 | 2 | .86 | 6 | .248 | .317 | .316 |
| 1990 2 ML Teams | | 123 | 309 | 92 | 9 | 6 | 3 | (1 | 2) | 122 | 60 | 27 | 40 | 2 | 50 | 0 | 6 | 2 | 15 | 7 | .68 | 6 | .298 | .376 | .395 |
| 1990 Oakland | AL | 19 | 33 | 8 | 0 | 2 | 0 | (0 | 0) | 12 | 4 | 3 | 3 | 0 | 6 | 0 | 0 | 0 | 0 | 0 | .00 | 0 | .242 | .306 | .364 |
| Los Angeles | NL | 104 | 276 | 84 | 9 | 4 | 3 | (1 | 2) | 110 | 56 | 24 | 37 | 2 | 44 | 0 | 6 | 2 | 15 | 7 | .68 | 6 | .304 | .384 | .399 |
| 6 ML YEARS | | 507 | 1288 | 323 | 45 | 13 | 8 | (3 | 5) | 418 | 187 | 107 | 138 | 7 | 219 | 4 | 22 | 7 | 58 | 12 | .83 | 29 | .251 | .324 | .325 |

## Mike Jeffcoat

**Pitches:** Left **Bats:** Left **Pos:** RP/SP **Ht:** 6' 2" **Wt:** 189 **Born:** 08/03/59 **Age:** 31

| HOW MUCH HE PITCHED | | | | | | | | WHAT HE GAVE UP | | | | | | | | | | | | THE RESULTS | | | | | |
|---|---|---|---|---|---|---|---|---|---|---|---|---|---|---|---|---|---|---|---|---|---|---|---|---|---|
| Year Team | Lg | G | GS | CG | GF | IP | BFP | H | R | ER | HR | SH | SF | HB | TBB | IBB | SO | WP | Bk | W | L | Pct. | ShO | Sv | ERA |
| 1983 Cleveland | AL | 11 | 2 | 0 | 1 | 32.2 | 140 | 32 | 13 | 12 | 1 | 1 | 0 | 1 | 13 | 1 | 9 | 1 | 1 | 1 | 3 | .250 | 0 | 0 | 3.31 |
| 1984 Cleveland | AL | 63 | 1 | 0 | 12 | 75.1 | 327 | 82 | 28 | 25 | 7 | 3 | 7 | 1 | 24 | 7 | 41 | 8 | 1 | 5 | 2 | .714 | 0 | 1 | 2.99 |
| 1985 2 ML Teams | | 28 | 1 | 0 | 10 | 31.2 | 143 | 35 | 18 | 16 | 5 | 4 | 3 | 2 | 12 | 4 | 14 | 1 | 0 | 0 | 2 | .000 | 0 | 0 | 4.55 |
| 1987 Texas | AL | 2 | 2 | 0 | 0 | 7 | 35 | 11 | 10 | 10 | 4 | 0 | 0 | 0 | 4 | 0 | 1 | 0 | 0 | 0 | 1 | .000 | 0 | 0 | 12.86 |
| 1988 Texas | AL | 5 | 2 | 0 | 2 | 10 | 52 | 19 | 13 | 13 | 1 | 1 | 0 | 2 | 5 | 1 | 5 | 0 | 0 | 0 | 2 | .000 | 0 | 0 | 11.70 |
| 1989 Texas | AL | 22 | 22 | 2 | 0 | 130.2 | 559 | 139 | 65 | 52 | 7 | 3 | 5 | 4 | 33 | 0 | 64 | 0 | 1 | 9 | 6 | .600 | 2 | 0 | 3.58 |
| 1990 Texas | AL | 44 | 12 | 1 | 11 | 110.2 | 466 | 122 | 57 | 55 | 12 | 3 | 2 | 2 | 28 | 5 | 58 | 1 | 0 | 5 | 6 | .455 | 0 | 5 | 4.47 |
| 1985 Cleveland | AL | 9 | 0 | 0 | 3 | 9.2 | 44 | 8 | 5 | 3 | 1 | 2 | 2 | 0 | 6 | 1 | 4 | 0 | 0 | 0 | 0 | .000 | 0 | 0 | 2.79 |
| San Francisco | NL | 19 | 1 | 0 | 7 | 22 | 99 | 27 | 13 | 13 | 4 | 2 | 1 | 2 | 6 | 3 | 10 | 1 | 0 | 0 | 2 | .000 | 0 | 0 | 5.32 |
| 7 ML YEARS | | 175 | 42 | 3 | 36 | 398 | 1722 | 440 | 204 | 183 | 37 | 15 | 17 | 12 | 119 | 18 | 192 | 11 | 3 | 20 | 22 | .476 | 2 | 6 | 4.14 |

## Gregg Jefferies

**Bats:** Both **Throws:** Right **Pos:** 2B/3B **Ht:** 5'10" **Wt:** 175 **Born:** 08/01/67 **Age:** 23

| BATTING | | | | | | | | | | | | | | | | | | | BASERUNNING | | | | PERCENTAGES | | |
|---|---|---|---|---|---|---|---|---|---|---|---|---|---|---|---|---|---|---|---|---|---|---|---|---|---|
| Year Team | Lg | G | AB | H | 2B | 3B | HR | (Hm | Rd) | TB | R | RBI | TBB | IBB | SO | HBP | SH | SF | SB | CS | SB% | GDP | Avg | OBP | SLG |
| 1987 New York | NL | 6 | 6 | 3 | 1 | 0 | 0 | (0 | 0) | 4 | 0 | 2 | 0 | 0 | 0 | 0 | 0 | 0 | 0 | 0 | .00 | 0 | .500 | .500 | .667 |
| 1988 New York | NL | 29 | 109 | 35 | 8 | 2 | 6 | (3 | 3) | 65 | 19 | 17 | 8 | 0 | 10 | 0 | 0 | 1 | 5 | 1 | .83 | 1 | .321 | .364 | .596 |
| 1989 New York | NL | 141 | 508 | 131 | 28 | 2 | 12 | (7 | 5) | 199 | 72 | 56 | 39 | 8 | 46 | 5 | 2 | 5 | 21 | 6 | .78 | 16 | .258 | .314 | .392 |
| 1990 New York | NL | 153 | 604 | 171 | 40 | 3 | 15 | (9 | 6) | 262 | 96 | 68 | 46 | 2 | 40 | 5 | 0 | 4 | 11 | 2 | .85 | 13 | .283 | .337 | .434 |
| 4 ML YEARS | | 329 | 1227 | 340 | 77 | 7 | 33 | (19 | 14) | 530 | 187 | 143 | 93 | 10 | 96 | 10 | 2 | 10 | 37 | 9 | .80 | 30 | .277 | .331 | .432 |

## Stan Jefferson

**Bats:** Both **Throws:** Right **Pos:** LF/CF **Ht:** 5'11" **Wt:** 175 **Born:** 12/04/62 **Age:** 28

| BATTING | | | | | | | | | | | | | | | | | | | BASERUNNING | | | | PERCENTAGES | | |
|---|---|---|---|---|---|---|---|---|---|---|---|---|---|---|---|---|---|---|---|---|---|---|---|---|---|
| Year Team | Lg | G | AB | H | 2B | 3B | HR | (Hm | Rd) | TB | R | RBI | TBB | IBB | SO | HBP | SH | SF | SB | CS | SB% | GDP | Avg | OBP | SLG |
| 1986 New York | NL | 14 | 24 | 5 | 1 | 0 | 1 | (1 | 0) | 9 | 6 | 3 | 2 | 0 | 8 | 1 | 0 | 0 | 0 | 0 | .00 | 1 | .208 | .296 | .375 |
| 1987 San Diego | NL | 116 | 422 | 97 | 8 | 7 | 8 | (5 | 3) | 143 | 59 | 29 | 39 | 2 | 92 | 2 | 3 | 3 | 34 | 11 | .76 | 6 | .230 | .296 | .339 |
| 1988 San Diego | NL | 49 | 111 | 16 | 1 | 2 | 1 | (1 | 0) | 24 | 16 | 4 | 9 | 0 | 22 | 1 | 2 | 2 | 5 | 1 | .83 | 3 | .144 | .211 | .216 |
| 1989 2 ML Teams | | 45 | 139 | 34 | 7 | 0 | 4 | (3 | 1) | 53 | 20 | 21 | 4 | 0 | 26 | 1 | 0 | 2 | 10 | 4 | .71 | 1 | .245 | .267 | .381 |
| 1990 2 ML Teams | | 59 | 117 | 27 | 8 | 0 | 2 | (1 | 1) | 41 | 22 | 10 | 10 | 0 | 26 | 2 | 1 | 3 | 9 | 4 | .69 | 2 | .231 | .295 | .350 |
| 1989 New York | AL | 10 | 12 | 1 | 0 | 0 | 0 | (0 | 0) | 1 | 1 | 1 | 0 | 0 | 4 | 0 | 0 | 0 | 1 | 1 | .50 | 0 | .083 | .083 | .083 |
| Baltimore | AL | 35 | 127 | 33 | 7 | 0 | 4 | (3 | 1) | 52 | 19 | 20 | 4 | 0 | 22 | 1 | 0 | 2 | 9 | 3 | .75 | 1 | .260 | .284 | .409 |
| 1990 Baltimore | AL | 10 | 19 | 0 | 0 | 0 | 0 | (0 | 0) | 0 | 1 | 0 | 2 | 0 | 8 | 0 | 0 | 0 | 1 | 0 | 1.00 | 0 | .000 | .095 | .000 |
| Cleveland | AL | 49 | 98 | 27 | 8 | 0 | 2 | (1 | 1) | 41 | 21 | 10 | 8 | 0 | 18 | 2 | 1 | 3 | 8 | 4 | .67 | 2 | .276 | .333 | .418 |
| 5 ML YEARS | | 283 | 813 | 179 | 25 | 9 | 16 | (11 | 5) | 270 | 123 | 67 | 64 | 2 | 174 | 7 | 6 | 10 | 58 | 20 | .74 | 13 | .220 | .280 | .332 |

## Chris Jelic

**Bats:** Right **Throws:** Right **Pos:** LF **Ht:** 5'11" **Wt:** 180 **Born:** 12/16/63 **Age:** 27

| BATTING | | | | | | | | | | | | | | | | | | | BASERUNNING | | | | PERCENTAGES | | |
|---|---|---|---|---|---|---|---|---|---|---|---|---|---|---|---|---|---|---|---|---|---|---|---|---|---|
| Year Team | Lg | G | AB | H | 2B | 3B | HR | (Hm | Rd) | TB | R | RBI | TBB | IBB | SO | HBP | SH | SF | SB | CS | SB% | GDP | Avg | OBP | SLG |
| 1985 Eugene | A | 42 | 144 | 45 | 7 | 3 | 2 | -- | -- | 64 | 24 | 22 | 37 | 0 | 24 | 0 | 0 | 1 | 7 | 3 | .70 | 1 | .313 | .451 | .444 |
| 1986 Ft. Myers | A | 108 | 348 | 89 | 11 | 5 | 5 | -- | -- | 125 | 50 | 50 | 83 | 5 | 52 | 4 | 4 | 2 | 13 | 6 | .68 | 9 | .256 | .403 | .359 |
| 1987 Lynchburg | A | 71 | 224 | 74 | 8 | 5 | 8 | -- | -- | 116 | 47 | 48 | 49 | 1 | 30 | 0 | 0 | 3 | 4 | 4 | .50 | 6 | .330 | .446 | .518 |
| Jackson | AA | 50 | 183 | 45 | 10 | 2 | 5 | -- | -- | 74 | 22 | 24 | 27 | 1 | 40 | 3 | 1 | 3 | 1 | 3 | .25 | 1 | .246 | .347 | .404 |
| 1988 Jackson | AA | 88 | 273 | 57 | 13 | 1 | 4 | -- | -- | 84 | 29 | 25 | 43 | 2 | 57 | 7 | 1 | 1 | 3 | 4 | .43 | 8 | .209 | .330 | .308 |
| 1989 Jackson | AA | 86 | 249 | 64 | 11 | 1 | 7 | -- | -- | 98 | 32 | 37 | 43 | 3 | 37 | 1 | 1 | 3 | 0 | 1 | .00 | 7 | .257 | .365 | .394 |

| Year Team | Lg | G | AB | H | 2B | 3B | HR | (Hm | Rd) | TB | R | RBI | TBB | IBB | SO | HBP | SH | SF | SB | CS | SB% | GDP | Avg | OBP | SLG |
|---|---|---|---|---|---|---|---|---|---|---|---|---|---|---|---|---|---|---|---|---|---|---|---|---|---|
| 1990 Tidewater | AAA | 92 | 265 | 81 | 21 | 1 | 4 | -- | -- | 116 | 39 | 49 | 48 | 1 | 52 | 2 | 3 | 8 | 2 | 1 | .67 | 9 | .306 | .406 | .438 |
| 1990 New York | NL | 4 | 11 | 1 | 0 | 0 | 1 | (0 | 1) | 4 | 2 | 1 | 0 | 0 | 3 | 0 | 0 | 0 | 0 | 0 | .00 | 0 | .091 | .091 | .364 |

## Steve Jeltz

**Bats:** Both **Throws:** Right **Pos:** 2B/SS **Ht:** 5'11" **Wt:** 180 **Born:** 05/28/59 **Age:** 32

| | | BATTING | | | | | | | | | | | | | | | | | BASERUNNING | | | | PERCENTAGES | | |
|---|---|---|---|---|---|---|---|---|---|---|---|---|---|---|---|---|---|---|---|---|---|---|---|---|---|
| Year Team | Lg | G | AB | H | 2B | 3B | HR | (Hm | Rd) | TB | R | RBI | TBB | IBB | SO | HBP | SH | SF | SB | CS | SB% | GDP | Avg | OBP | SLG |
| 1983 Philadelphia | NL | 13 | 8 | 1 | 0 | 1 | 0 | (0 | 0) | 3 | 0 | 1 | 1 | 0 | 2 | 0 | 1 | 0 | 0 | 0 | .00 | 2 | .125 | .222 | .375 |
| 1984 Philadelphia | NL | 28 | 68 | 14 | 0 | 1 | 1 | (0 | 1) | 19 | 7 | 7 | 7 | 1 | 11 | 0 | 1 | 1 | 2 | 1 | .67 | 3 | .206 | .276 | .279 |
| 1985 Philadelphia | NL | 89 | 196 | 37 | 4 | 1 | 0 | (0 | 0) | 43 | 17 | 12 | 26 | 4 | 55 | 0 | 5 | 1 | 1 | 1 | .50 | 6 | .189 | .283 | .219 |
| 1986 Philadelphia | NL | 145 | 439 | 96 | 11 | 4 | 0 | (0 | 0) | 115 | 44 | 36 | 65 | 9 | 97 | 1 | 3 | 2 | 6 | 3 | .67 | 9 | .219 | .320 | .262 |
| 1987 Philadelphia | NL | 114 | 293 | 68 | 9 | 6 | 0 | (0 | 0) | 89 | 37 | 12 | 39 | 4 | 54 | 1 | 4 | 0 | 1 | 2 | .33 | 13 | .232 | .324 | .304 |
| 1988 Philadelphia | NL | 148 | 379 | 71 | 11 | 4 | 0 | (0 | 0) | 90 | 39 | 27 | 59 | 8 | 58 | 0 | 10 | 2 | 3 | 0 | 1.00 | 11 | .187 | .295 | .237 |
| 1989 Philadelphia | NL | 116 | 263 | 64 | 7 | 3 | 4 | (3 | 1) | 89 | 28 | 25 | 45 | 6 | 44 | 1 | 6 | 0 | 4 | 2 | .67 | 6 | .243 | .356 | .338 |
| 1990 Kansas City | AL | 74 | 103 | 16 | 4 | 0 | 0 | (0 | 0) | 20 | 11 | 10 | 6 | 0 | 21 | 0 | 4 | 1 | 1 | 1 | .50 | 3 | .155 | .200 | .194 |
| 8 ML YEARS | | 727 | 1749 | 367 | 46 | 20 | 5 | (3 | 2) | 468 | 183 | 130 | 248 | 32 | 342 | 3 | 34 | 7 | 18 | 10 | .64 | 53 | .210 | .308 | .268 |

## Doug Jennings

**Bats:** Left **Throws:** Left **Pos:** LF/RF **Ht:** 5'10" **Wt:** 165 **Born:** 09/30/64 **Age:** 26

| | | BATTING | | | | | | | | | | | | | | | | | BASERUNNING | | | | PERCENTAGES | | |
|---|---|---|---|---|---|---|---|---|---|---|---|---|---|---|---|---|---|---|---|---|---|---|---|---|---|
| Year Team | Lg | G | AB | H | 2B | 3B | HR | (Hm | Rd) | TB | R | RBI | TBB | IBB | SO | HBP | SH | SF | SB | CS | SB% | GDP | Avg | OBP | SLG |
| 1988 Oakland | AL | 71 | 101 | 21 | 6 | 0 | 1 | (0 | 1) | 30 | 9 | 15 | 21 | 1 | 28 | 2 | 1 | 3 | 0 | 1 | .00 | 1 | .208 | .346 | .297 |
| 1989 Oakland | AL | 4 | 4 | 0 | 0 | 0 | 0 | (0 | 0) | 0 | 0 | 0 | 0 | 0 | 2 | 0 | 0 | 0 | 0 | 0 | .00 | 0 | .000 | .000 | .000 |
| 1990 Oakland | AL | 64 | 156 | 30 | 7 | 2 | 2 | (1 | 1) | 47 | 19 | 14 | 17 | 0 | 48 | 2 | 2 | 3 | 0 | 3 | .00 | 1 | .192 | .275 | .301 |
| 3 ML YEARS | | 139 | 261 | 51 | 13 | 2 | 3 | (1 | 2) | 77 | 28 | 29 | 38 | 1 | 78 | 4 | 3 | 6 | 0 | 4 | .00 | 2 | .195 | .301 | .295 |

## Dave Johnson

**Pitches:** Right **Bats:** Right **Pos:** SP **Ht:** 5'11" **Wt:** 180 **Born:** 10/24/59 **Age:** 31

| | | HOW MUCH HE PITCHED | | | | | | WHAT HE GAVE UP | | | | | | | | | | | | THE RESULTS | | | | | |
|---|---|---|---|---|---|---|---|---|---|---|---|---|---|---|---|---|---|---|---|---|---|---|---|---|---|
| Year Team | Lg | G | GS | CG | GF | IP | BFP | H | R | ER | HR | SH | SF | HB | TBB | IBB | SO | WP | Bk | W | L | Pct. | ShO | Sv | ERA |
| 1987 Pittsburgh | NL | 5 | 0 | 0 | 3 | 6.1 | 31 | 13 | 7 | 7 | 1 | 0 | 0 | 0 | 2 | 0 | 4 | 0 | 0 | 0 | 0 | .000 | 0 | 0 | 9.95 |
| 1989 Baltimore | AL | 14 | 14 | 4 | 0 | 89.1 | 378 | 90 | 44 | 42 | 11 | 3 | 3 | 4 | 28 | 1 | 26 | 0 | 2 | 4 | 7 | .364 | 0 | 0 | 4.23 |
| 1990 Baltimore | AL | 30 | 29 | 3 | 0 | 180 | 758 | 196 | 83 | 82 | 30 | 5 | 7 | 3 | 43 | 2 | 68 | 1 | 2 | 13 | 9 | .591 | 0 | 0 | 4.10 |
| 3 ML YEARS | | 49 | 43 | 7 | 3 | 275.2 | 1167 | 299 | 134 | 131 | 42 | 8 | 10 | 7 | 73 | 3 | 98 | 1 | 4 | 17 | 16 | .515 | 0 | 0 | 4.28 |

## Howard Johnson

**Bats:** Both **Throws:** Right **Pos:** 3B/SS **Ht:** 5'10" **Wt:** 195 **Born:** 11/29/60 **Age:** 30

| | | BATTING | | | | | | | | | | | | | | | | | BASERUNNING | | | | PERCENTAGES | | |
|---|---|---|---|---|---|---|---|---|---|---|---|---|---|---|---|---|---|---|---|---|---|---|---|---|---|
| Year Team | Lg | G | AB | H | 2B | 3B | HR | (Hm | Rd) | TB | R | RBI | TBB | IBB | SO | HBP | SH | SF | SB | CS | SB% | GDP | Avg | OBP | SLG |
| 1982 Detroit | AL | 54 | 155 | 49 | 5 | 0 | 4 | (1 | 3) | 66 | 23 | 14 | 16 | 1 | 30 | 1 | 1 | 0 | 7 | 4 | .64 | 3 | .316 | .384 | .426 |
| 1983 Detroit | AL | 27 | 66 | 14 | 0 | 0 | 3 | (2 | 1) | 23 | 11 | 5 | 7 | 0 | 10 | 1 | 0 | 0 | 0 | 0 | .00 | 1 | .212 | .297 | .348 |
| 1984 Detroit | AL | 116 | 355 | 88 | 14 | 1 | 12 | (4 | 8) | 140 | 43 | 50 | 40 | 1 | 67 | 1 | 4 | 2 | 10 | 6 | .63 | 6 | .248 | .324 | .394 |
| 1985 New York | NL | 126 | 389 | 94 | 18 | 4 | 11 | (5 | 6) | 153 | 38 | 46 | 34 | 10 | 78 | 0 | 1 | 4 | 6 | 4 | .60 | 6 | .242 | .300 | .393 |
| 1986 New York | NL | 88 | 220 | 54 | 14 | 0 | 10 | (5 | 5) | 98 | 30 | 39 | 31 | 8 | 64 | 1 | 1 | 0 | 8 | 1 | .89 | 2 | .245 | .341 | .445 |
| 1987 New York | NL | 157 | 554 | 147 | 22 | 1 | 36 | (13 | 23) | 279 | 93 | 99 | 83 | 18 | 113 | 5 | 0 | 3 | 32 | 10 | .76 | 8 | .265 | .364 | .504 |
| 1988 New York | NL | 148 | 495 | 114 | 21 | 1 | 24 | (9 | 15) | 209 | 85 | 68 | 86 | 25 | 104 | 3 | 2 | 8 | 23 | 7 | .77 | 6 | .230 | .343 | .422 |
| 1989 New York | NL | 153 | 571 | 164 | 41 | 3 | 36 | (19 | 17) | 319 | 104 | 101 | 77 | 8 | 126 | 1 | 0 | 6 | 41 | 8 | .84 | 4 | .287 | .369 | .559 |
| 1990 New York | NL | 154 | 590 | 144 | 37 | 3 | 23 | (13 | 10) | 256 | 89 | 90 | 69 | 12 | 100 | 0 | 0 | 9 | 34 | 8 | .81 | 7 | .244 | .319 | .434 |
| 9 ML YEARS | | 1023 | 3395 | 868 | 172 | 13 | 159 | (71 | 88) | 1543 | 516 | 512 | 443 | 83 | 692 | 13 | 9 | 32 | 161 | 48 | .77 | 43 | .256 | .341 | .454 |

## Lance Johnson

**Bats:** Left **Throws:** Left **Pos:** CF **Ht:** 5'11" **Wt:** 155 **Born:** 07/07/63 **Age:** 27

| | | BATTING | | | | | | | | | | | | | | | | | BASERUNNING | | | | PERCENTAGES | | |
|---|---|---|---|---|---|---|---|---|---|---|---|---|---|---|---|---|---|---|---|---|---|---|---|---|---|
| Year Team | Lg | G | AB | H | 2B | 3B | HR | (Hm | Rd) | TB | R | RBI | TBB | IBB | SO | HBP | SH | SF | SB | CS | SB% | GDP | Avg | OBP | SLG |
| 1987 St. Louis | NL | 33 | 59 | 13 | 2 | 1 | 0 | (0 | 0) | 17 | 4 | 7 | 4 | 1 | 6 | 0 | 0 | 0 | 6 | 1 | .86 | 2 | .220 | .270 | .288 |
| 1988 Chicago | AL | 33 | 124 | 23 | 4 | 1 | 0 | (0 | 0) | 29 | 11 | 6 | 6 | 0 | 11 | 0 | 2 | 0 | 6 | 2 | .75 | 1 | .185 | .223 | .234 |
| 1989 Chicago | AL | 50 | 180 | 54 | 8 | 2 | 0 | (0 | 0) | 66 | 28 | 16 | 17 | 0 | 24 | 0 | 2 | 0 | 16 | 3 | .84 | 1 | .300 | .360 | .367 |
| 1990 Chicago | AL | 151 | 541 | 154 | 18 | 9 | 1 | (0 | 1) | 193 | 76 | 51 | 33 | 2 | 45 | 1 | 8 | 4 | 36 | 22 | .62 | 12 | .285 | .325 | .357 |
| 4 ML YEARS | | 267 | 904 | 244 | 32 | 13 | 1 | (0 | 1) | 305 | 119 | 80 | 60 | 3 | 86 | 1 | 12 | 4 | 64 | 28 | .70 | 16 | .270 | .315 | .337 |

## Randy Johnson

**Pitches:** Left **Bats:** Right **Pos:** SP **Ht:** 6'10" **Wt:** 225 **Born:** 09/10/63 **Age:** 27

| | | HOW MUCH HE PITCHED | | | | | | WHAT HE GAVE UP | | | | | | | | | | | | THE RESULTS | | | | | |
|---|---|---|---|---|---|---|---|---|---|---|---|---|---|---|---|---|---|---|---|---|---|---|---|---|---|
| Year Team | Lg | G | GS | CG | GF | IP | BFP | H | R | ER | HR | SH | SF | HB | TBB | IBB | SO | WP | Bk | W | L | Pct. | ShO | Sv | ERA |
| 1988 Montreal | NL | 4 | 4 | 1 | 0 | 26 | 109 | 23 | 8 | 7 | 3 | 0 | 0 | 0 | 7 | 0 | 25 | 3 | 0 | 3 | 0 | 1.000 | 0 | 0 | 2.42 |
| 1989 2 ML Teams | | 29 | 28 | 2 | 1 | 160.2 | 715 | 147 | 100 | 86 | 13 | 10 | 13 | 3 | 96 | 2 | 130 | 7 | 7 | 7 | 13 | .350 | 0 | 0 | 4.82 |

| | | | | | | | | | | | | | | | | | | | | | | | | | |
|---|---|---|---|---|---|---|---|---|---|---|---|---|---|---|---|---|---|---|---|---|---|---|---|---|---|
| 1990 Seattle | AL | 33 | 33 | 5 | 0 | 219.2 | 944 | 174 | 103 | 89 | 26 | 7 | 6 | 5 | 120 | 2 | 194 | 4 | 2 | 14 | 11 | .560 | 2 | 0 | 3.65 |
| 1989 Montreal | NL | 7 | 6 | 0 | 1 | 29.2 | 143 | 29 | 25 | 22 | 2 | 3 | 4 | 0 | 26 | 1 | 26 | 2 | 2 | 0 | 4 | .000 | 0 | 0 | 6.67 |
| Seattle | AL | 22 | 22 | 2 | 0 | 131 | 572 | 118 | 75 | 64 | 11 | 7 | 9 | 3 | 70 | 1 | 104 | 5 | 5 | 7 | 9 | .438 | 0 | 0 | 4.40 |
| 3 ML YEARS | | 66 | 65 | 8 | 1 | 406.1 | 1768 | 344 | 211 | 182 | 42 | 17 | 19 | 8 | 223 | 4 | 349 | 14 | 9 | 24 | 24 | .500 | 2 | 0 | 4.03 |

## Wallace Johnson

**Bats:** Both **Throws:** Right **Pos:** 1B **Ht:** 5'11" **Wt:** 185 **Born:** 12/25/56 **Age:** 34

| BATTING | | | | | | | | | | | | | | | | | | | BASERUNNING | | | | PERCENTAGES | | |
|---|---|---|---|---|---|---|---|---|---|---|---|---|---|---|---|---|---|---|---|---|---|---|---|---|---|
| Year Team | Lg | G | AB | H | 2B | 3B | HR | (Hm | Rd) | TB | R | RBI | TBB | IBB | SO | HBP | SH | SF | SB | CS | SB% | GDP | Avg | OBP | SLG |
| 1981 Montreal | NL | 11 | 9 | 2 | 0 | 1 | 0 | (0 | 0) | 4 | 1 | 3 | 1 | 1 | 1 | 0 | 0 | 0 | 1 | 1 | .50 | 1 | .222 | .300 | .444 |
| 1982 Montreal | NL | 36 | 57 | 11 | 0 | 2 | 0 | (0 | 0) | 15 | 5 | 2 | 5 | 0 | 5 | 0 | 0 | 0 | 4 | 1 | .80 | 0 | .193 | .258 | .263 |
| 1983 2 ML Teams | | 10 | 10 | 2 | 0 | 0 | 0 | (0 | 0) | 2 | 1 | 1 | 1 | 0 | 0 | 0 | 0 | 0 | 1 | 0 | 1.00 | 0 | .200 | .273 | .200 |
| 1984 Montreal | NL | 17 | 24 | 5 | 0 | 0 | 0 | (0 | 0) | 5 | 3 | 4 | 5 | 0 | 4 | 0 | 0 | 0 | 0 | 0 | .00 | 0 | .208 | .345 | .208 |
| 1986 Montreal | NL | 61 | 127 | 36 | 3 | 1 | 1 | (1 | 0) | 44 | 13 | 10 | 7 | 0 | 9 | 0 | 0 | 0 | 6 | 3 | .67 | 2 | .283 | .321 | .346 |
| 1987 Montreal | NL | 75 | 85 | 21 | 5 | 0 | 1 | (0 | 1) | 29 | 7 | 14 | 7 | 0 | 6 | 0 | 0 | 2 | 5 | 0 | 1.00 | 0 | .247 | .298 | .341 |
| 1988 Montreal | NL | 86 | 94 | 29 | 5 | 1 | 0 | (0 | 0) | 36 | 7 | 3 | 12 | 1 | 15 | 0 | 1 | 0 | 0 | 2 | .00 | 2 | .309 | .387 | .383 |
| 1989 Montreal | NL | 85 | 114 | 31 | 3 | 1 | 2 | (0 | 2) | 42 | 9 | 17 | 7 | 0 | 12 | 0 | 2 | 2 | 1 | 0 | 1.00 | 2 | .272 | .309 | .368 |
| 1990 Montreal | NL | 47 | 49 | 8 | 1 | 0 | 1 | (0 | 1) | 12 | 6 | 5 | 7 | 2 | 6 | 1 | 0 | 0 | 1 | 0 | 1.00 | 1 | .163 | .281 | .245 |
| 1983 Montreal | NL | 3 | 2 | 1 | 0 | 0 | 0 | (0 | 0) | 1 | 1 | 0 | 1 | 0 | 0 | 0 | 0 | 0 | 1 | 0 | 1.00 | 0 | .500 | .667 | .500 |
| San Francisco | NL | 7 | 8 | 1 | 0 | 0 | 0 | (0 | 0) | 1 | 0 | 1 | 0 | 0 | 0 | 0 | 0 | 0 | 0 | 0 | .00 | 0 | .125 | .125 | .125 |
| 9 ML YEARS | | 428 | 569 | 145 | 17 | 6 | 5 | (1 | 4) | 189 | 52 | 59 | 52 | 4 | 58 | 1 | 3 | 4 | 19 | 7 | .73 | 8 | .255 | .316 | .332 |

## Barry Jones

**Pitches:** Right **Bats:** Right **Pos:** RP **Ht:** 6' 4" **Wt:** 225 **Born:** 02/15/63 **Age:** 28

| HOW MUCH HE PITCHED | | | | | | | | WHAT HE GAVE UP | | | | | | | | | | | | THE RESULTS | | | | | |
|---|---|---|---|---|---|---|---|---|---|---|---|---|---|---|---|---|---|---|---|---|---|---|---|---|---|
| Year Team | Lg | G | GS | CG | GF | IP | BFP | H | R | ER | HR | SH | SF | HB | TBB | IBB | SO | WP | Bk | W | L | Pct. | ShO | Sv | ERA |
| 1986 Pittsburgh | NL | 26 | 0 | 0 | 10 | 37.1 | 159 | 29 | 16 | 12 | 3 | 2 | 1 | 0 | 21 | 2 | 29 | 2 | 0 | 3 | 4 | .429 | 0 | 3 | 2.89 |
| 1987 Pittsburgh | NL | 32 | 0 | 0 | 10 | 43.1 | 203 | 55 | 34 | 27 | 6 | 3 | 2 | 0 | 23 | 6 | 28 | 3 | 0 | 2 | 4 | .333 | 0 | 1 | 5.61 |
| 1988 2 ML Teams | | 59 | 0 | 0 | 25 | 82.1 | 347 | 72 | 28 | 26 | 6 | 5 | 5 | 1 | 38 | 7 | 48 | 13 | 2 | 3 | 3 | .500 | 0 | 3 | 2.84 |
| 1989 Chicago | AL | 22 | 0 | 0 | 8 | 30.1 | 121 | 22 | 12 | 8 | 2 | 4 | 2 | 1 | 8 | 0 | 17 | 1 | 0 | 3 | 2 | .600 | 0 | 1 | 2.37 |
| 1990 Chicago | AL | 65 | 0 | 0 | 9 | 74 | 310 | 62 | 20 | 19 | 2 | 7 | 5 | 1 | 33 | 7 | 45 | 0 | 1 | 11 | 4 | .733 | 0 | 1 | 2.31 |
| 1988 Pittsburgh | NL | 42 | 0 | 0 | 15 | 56.1 | 241 | 57 | 21 | 19 | 3 | 5 | 4 | 1 | 21 | 6 | 31 | 7 | 1 | 1 | 1 | .500 | 0 | 2 | 3.04 |
| Chicago | AL | 17 | 0 | 0 | 10 | 26 | 106 | 15 | 7 | 7 | 3 | 0 | 1 | 0 | 17 | 1 | 17 | 6 | 1 | 2 | 2 | .500 | 0 | 1 | 2.42 |
| 5 ML YEARS | | 204 | 0 | 0 | 62 | 267.1 | 1140 | 240 | 110 | 92 | 19 | 21 | 15 | 3 | 123 | 22 | 167 | 19 | 3 | 22 | 17 | .564 | 0 | 9 | 3.10 |

## Doug Jones

**Pitches:** Right **Bats:** Right **Pos:** RP **Ht:** 6' 2" **Wt:** 195 **Born:** 06/24/57 **Age:** 34

| HOW MUCH HE PITCHED | | | | | | | | WHAT HE GAVE UP | | | | | | | | | | | | THE RESULTS | | | | | |
|---|---|---|---|---|---|---|---|---|---|---|---|---|---|---|---|---|---|---|---|---|---|---|---|---|---|
| Year Team | Lg | G | GS | CG | GF | IP | BFP | H | R | ER | HR | SH | SF | HB | TBB | IBB | SO | WP | Bk | W | L | Pct. | ShO | Sv | ERA |
| 1982 Milwaukee | AL | 4 | 0 | 0 | 2 | 2.2 | 14 | 5 | 3 | 3 | 1 | 0 | 0 | 0 | 1 | 0 | 1 | 0 | 0 | 0 | 0 | .000 | 0 | 0 | 10.13 |
| 1986 Cleveland | AL | 11 | 0 | 0 | 5 | 18 | 79 | 18 | 5 | 5 | 0 | 1 | 1 | 1 | 6 | 1 | 12 | 0 | 0 | 1 | 0 | 1.000 | 0 | 1 | 2.50 |
| 1987 Cleveland | AL | 49 | 0 | 0 | 29 | 91.1 | 400 | 101 | 45 | 32 | 4 | 5 | 5 | 6 | 24 | 5 | 87 | 0 | 0 | 6 | 5 | .545 | 0 | 8 | 3.15 |
| 1988 Cleveland | AL | 51 | 0 | 0 | 46 | 83.1 | 338 | 69 | 26 | 21 | 1 | 3 | 0 | 2 | 16 | 3 | 72 | 2 | 3 | 3 | 4 | .429 | 0 | 37 | 2.27 |
| 1989 Cleveland | AL | 59 | 0 | 0 | 53 | 80.2 | 331 | 76 | 25 | 21 | 4 | 8 | 6 | 1 | 13 | 4 | 65 | 1 | 1 | 7 | 10 | .412 | 0 | 32 | 2.34 |
| 1990 Cleveland | AL | 66 | 0 | 0 | 64 | 84.1 | 331 | 66 | 26 | 24 | 5 | 2 | 2 | 2 | 22 | 4 | 55 | 2 | 0 | 5 | 5 | .500 | 0 | 43 | 2.56 |
| 6 ML YEARS | | 240 | 0 | 0 | 199 | 360.1 | 1493 | 335 | 130 | 106 | 15 | 19 | 14 | 12 | 82 | 17 | 292 | 5 | 4 | 22 | 24 | .478 | 0 | 121 | 2.65 |

## Jimmy Jones

**Pitches:** Right **Bats:** Right **Pos:** RP/SP **Ht:** 6' 2" **Wt:** 190 **Born:** 04/20/64 **Age:** 27

| HOW MUCH HE PITCHED | | | | | | | | WHAT HE GAVE UP | | | | | | | | | | | | THE RESULTS | | | | | |
|---|---|---|---|---|---|---|---|---|---|---|---|---|---|---|---|---|---|---|---|---|---|---|---|---|---|
| Year Team | Lg | G | GS | CG | GF | IP | BFP | H | R | ER | HR | SH | SF | HB | TBB | IBB | SO | WP | Bk | W | L | Pct. | ShO | Sv | ERA |
| 1986 San Diego | NL | 3 | 3 | 1 | 0 | 18 | 65 | 10 | 6 | 5 | 1 | 1 | 0 | 0 | 3 | 0 | 15 | 0 | 0 | 2 | 0 | 1.000 | 1 | 0 | 2.50 |
| 1987 San Diego | NL | 30 | 22 | 2 | 4 | 145.2 | 639 | 154 | 85 | 67 | 14 | 5 | 5 | 5 | 54 | 2 | 51 | 3 | 2 | 9 | 7 | .563 | 1 | 0 | 4.14 |
| 1988 San Diego | NL | 29 | 29 | 3 | 0 | 179 | 760 | 192 | 98 | 82 | 14 | 11 | 9 | 3 | 44 | 3 | 82 | 4 | 1 | 9 | 14 | .391 | 0 | 0 | 4.12 |
| 1989 New York | AL | 11 | 6 | 0 | 3 | 48 | 211 | 56 | 29 | 28 | 7 | 1 | 1 | 2 | 16 | 1 | 25 | 1 | 0 | 2 | 1 | .667 | 0 | 0 | 5.25 |
| 1990 New York | AL | 17 | 7 | 0 | 9 | 50 | 238 | 72 | 42 | 35 | 8 | 1 | 4 | 1 | 23 | 0 | 25 | 3 | 0 | 1 | 2 | .333 | 0 | 0 | 6.30 |
| 5 ML YEARS | | 90 | 67 | 6 | 16 | 440.2 | 1913 | 484 | 260 | 217 | 44 | 19 | 19 | 11 | 140 | 6 | 198 | 11 | 3 | 23 | 24 | .489 | 2 | 0 | 4.43 |

## Ron Jones

**Bats:** Left **Throws:** Right **Pos:** LF **Ht:** 5'10" **Wt:** 200 **Born:** 06/11/64 **Age:** 27

| BATTING | | | | | | | | | | | | | | | | | | | BASERUNNING | | | | PERCENTAGES | | |
|---|---|---|---|---|---|---|---|---|---|---|---|---|---|---|---|---|---|---|---|---|---|---|---|---|---|
| Year Team | Lg | G | AB | H | 2B | 3B | HR | (Hm | Rd) | TB | R | RBI | TBB | IBB | SO | HBP | SH | SF | SB | CS | SB% | GDP | Avg | OBP | SLG |
| 1988 Philadelphia | NL | 33 | 124 | 36 | 6 | 1 | 8 | (5 | 3) | 68 | 15 | 26 | 2 | 0 | 14 | 0 | 0 | 3 | 0 | 0 | .00 | 2 | .290 | .295 | .548 |
| 1989 Philadelphia | NL | 12 | 31 | 9 | 0 | 0 | 2 | (1 | 1) | 15 | 7 | 4 | 9 | 1 | 1 | 0 | 0 | 0 | 1 | 0 | 1.00 | 2 | .290 | .450 | .484 |
| 1990 Philadelphia | NL | 24 | 58 | 16 | 2 | 0 | 3 | (2 | 1) | 27 | 5 | 7 | 9 | 0 | 9 | 0 | 0 | 0 | 0 | 1 | .00 | 1 | .276 | .373 | .466 |
| 3 ML YEARS | | 69 | 213 | 61 | 8 | 1 | 13 | (8 | 5) | 110 | 27 | 37 | 20 | 1 | 24 | 0 | 0 | 3 | 1 | 1 | .50 | 5 | .286 | .343 | .516 |

## Tim Jones

**Bats:** Left **Throws:** Right **Pos:** SS/2B **Ht:** 5'10" **Wt:** 172 **Born:** 12/01/62 **Age:** 28

| BATTING | | | | | | | | | | | | | | | | | | | BASERUNNING | | | | PERCENTAGES | | |
|---|---|---|---|---|---|---|---|---|---|---|---|---|---|---|---|---|---|---|---|---|---|---|---|---|---|
| Year Team | Lg | G | AB | H | 2B | 3B | HR | (Hm | Rd) | TB | R | RBI | TBB | IBB | SO | HBP | SH | SF | SB | CS | SB% | GDP | Avg | OBP | SLG |
| 1988 St. Louis | NL | 31 | 52 | 14 | 0 | 0 | 0 | (0 | 0) | 14 | 2 | 3 | 4 | 0 | 10 | 0 | 0 | 0 | 4 | 1 | .80 | 1 | .269 | .321 | .269 |
| 1989 St. Louis | NL | 42 | 75 | 22 | 6 | 0 | 0 | (0 | 0) | 28 | 11 | 7 | 7 | 1 | 8 | 1 | 1 | 2 | 1 | 0 | 1.00 | 2 | .293 | .353 | .373 |
| 1990 St. Louis | NL | 67 | 128 | 28 | 7 | 1 | 1 | (1 | 0) | 40 | 9 | 12 | 12 | 1 | 20 | 1 | 4 | 0 | 3 | 4 | .43 | 1 | .219 | .291 | .313 |
| 3 ML YEARS | | 140 | 255 | 64 | 13 | 1 | 1 | (1 | 0) | 82 | 22 | 22 | 23 | 2 | 38 | 2 | 5 | 2 | 8 | 5 | .62 | 4 | .251 | .316 | .322 |

## Tracy Jones

**Bats:** Right **Throws:** Right **Pos:** LF/DH **Ht:** 6' 3" **Wt:** 220 **Born:** 03/31/61 **Age:** 30

| BATTING | | | | | | | | | | | | | | | | | | | BASERUNNING | | | | PERCENTAGES | | |
|---|---|---|---|---|---|---|---|---|---|---|---|---|---|---|---|---|---|---|---|---|---|---|---|---|---|
| Year Team | Lg | G | AB | H | 2B | 3B | HR | (Hm | Rd) | TB | R | RBI | TBB | IBB | SO | HBP | SH | SF | SB | CS | SB% | GDP | Avg | OBP | SLG |
| 1986 Cincinnati | NL | 46 | 86 | 30 | 3 | 0 | 2 | (1 | 1) | 39 | 16 | 10 | 9 | 1 | 5 | 0 | 0 | 1 | 7 | 1 | .88 | 2 | .349 | .406 | .453 |
| 1987 Cincinnati | NL | 117 | 359 | 104 | 17 | 3 | 10 | (4 | 6) | 157 | 53 | 44 | 23 | 0 | 40 | 3 | 0 | 5 | 31 | 8 | .79 | 10 | .290 | .333 | .437 |
| 1988 2 ML Teams | | 90 | 224 | 66 | 6 | 1 | 3 | (0 | 3) | 83 | 29 | 24 | 20 | 3 | 18 | 2 | 3 | 0 | 18 | 6 | .75 | 5 | .295 | .358 | .371 |
| 1989 2 ML Teams | | 86 | 255 | 59 | 14 | 0 | 3 | (3 | 0) | 82 | 22 | 38 | 21 | 4 | 30 | 2 | 1 | 3 | 3 | 2 | .60 | 5 | .231 | .292 | .322 |
| 1990 2 ML Teams | | 75 | 204 | 53 | 8 | 1 | 6 | (3 | 3) | 81 | 23 | 24 | 9 | 0 | 25 | 5 | 2 | 0 | 1 | 2 | .33 | 7 | .260 | .307 | .397 |
| 1988 Cincinnati | NL | 37 | 83 | 19 | 1 | 0 | 1 | (0 | 1) | 23 | 9 | 9 | 8 | 2 | 6 | 1 | 0 | 0 | 9 | 0 | 1.00 | 4 | .229 | .304 | .277 |
| Montreal | NL | 53 | 141 | 47 | 5 | 1 | 2 | (0 | 2) | 60 | 20 | 15 | 12 | 1 | 12 | 1 | 3 | 0 | 9 | 6 | .60 | 1 | .333 | .390 | .426 |
| 1989 San Francisco | NL | 40 | 97 | 18 | 4 | 0 | 0 | (0 | 0) | 22 | 5 | 12 | 5 | 3 | 14 | 1 | 0 | 0 | 2 | 1 | .67 | 4 | .186 | .233 | .227 |
| Detroit | AL | 46 | 158 | 41 | 10 | 0 | 3 | (3 | 0) | 60 | 17 | 26 | 16 | 1 | 16 | 1 | 1 | 3 | 1 | 1 | .50 | 1 | .259 | .326 | .380 |
| 1990 Detroit | AL | 50 | 118 | 27 | 4 | 1 | 4 | (2 | 2) | 45 | 15 | 9 | 6 | 0 | 13 | 3 | 1 | 0 | 1 | 1 | .50 | 3 | .229 | .283 | .381 |
| Seattle | AL | 25 | 86 | 26 | 4 | 0 | 2 | (1 | 1) | 36 | 8 | 15 | 3 | 0 | 12 | 2 | 1 | 0 | 0 | 1 | .00 | 4 | .302 | .341 | .419 |
| 5 ML YEARS | | 414 | 1128 | 312 | 48 | 5 | 24 | (11 | 13) | 442 | 143 | 140 | 82 | 8 | 118 | 12 | 6 | 9 | 60 | 19 | .76 | 29 | .277 | .330 | .392 |

## Ricky Jordan

**Bats:** Right **Throws:** Right **Pos:** 1B **Ht:** 6' 3" **Wt:** 210 **Born:** 05/26/65 **Age:** 26

| BATTING | | | | | | | | | | | | | | | | | | | BASERUNNING | | | | PERCENTAGES | | |
|---|---|---|---|---|---|---|---|---|---|---|---|---|---|---|---|---|---|---|---|---|---|---|---|---|---|
| Year Team | Lg | G | AB | H | 2B | 3B | HR | (Hm | Rd) | TB | R | RBI | TBB | IBB | SO | HBP | SH | SF | SB | CS | SB% | GDP | Avg | OBP | SLG |
| 1988 Philadelphia | NL | 69 | 273 | 84 | 15 | 1 | 11 | (6 | 5) | 134 | 41 | 43 | 7 | 2 | 39 | 0 | 0 | 1 | 1 | 1 | .50 | 5 | .308 | .324 | .491 |
| 1989 Philadelphia | NL | 144 | 523 | 149 | 22 | 3 | 12 | (7 | 5) | 213 | 63 | 75 | 23 | 5 | 62 | 5 | 0 | 8 | 4 | 3 | .57 | 19 | .285 | .317 | .407 |
| 1990 Philadelphia | NL | 92 | 324 | 78 | 21 | 0 | 5 | (2 | 3) | 114 | 32 | 44 | 13 | 6 | 39 | 5 | 0 | 4 | 2 | 0 | 1.00 | 9 | .241 | .277 | .352 |
| 3 ML YEARS | | 305 | 1120 | 311 | 58 | 4 | 28 | (15 | 13) | 461 | 136 | 162 | 43 | 13 | 140 | 10 | 0 | 13 | 7 | 4 | .64 | 33 | .278 | .307 | .412 |

## Felix Jose

**Bats:** Both **Throws:** Right **Pos:** RF/LF/CF **Ht:** 6' 1" **Wt:** 190 **Born:** 05/08/65 **Age:** 26

| BATTING | | | | | | | | | | | | | | | | | | | BASERUNNING | | | | PERCENTAGES | | |
|---|---|---|---|---|---|---|---|---|---|---|---|---|---|---|---|---|---|---|---|---|---|---|---|---|---|
| Year Team | Lg | G | AB | H | 2B | 3B | HR | (Hm | Rd) | TB | R | RBI | TBB | IBB | SO | HBP | SH | SF | SB | CS | SB% | GDP | Avg | OBP | SLG |
| 1988 Oakland | AL | 8 | 6 | 2 | 1 | 0 | 0 | (0 | 0) | 3 | 2 | 1 | 0 | 0 | 1 | 0 | 0 | 0 | 1 | 0 | 1.00 | 0 | .333 | .333 | .500 |
| 1989 Oakland | AL | 20 | 57 | 11 | 2 | 0 | 0 | (0 | 0) | 13 | 3 | 5 | 4 | 0 | 13 | 0 | 0 | 0 | 0 | 1 | .00 | 2 | .193 | .246 | .228 |
| 1990 2 ML Teams | | 126 | 426 | 113 | 16 | 1 | 11 | (5 | 6) | 164 | 54 | 52 | 24 | 0 | 81 | 5 | 2 | 1 | 12 | 6 | .67 | 9 | .265 | .311 | .385 |
| 1990 Oakland | AL | 101 | 341 | 90 | 12 | 0 | 8 | (3 | 5) | 126 | 42 | 39 | 16 | 0 | 65 | 5 | 2 | 1 | 8 | 2 | .80 | 8 | .264 | .306 | .370 |
| St. Louis | NL | 25 | 85 | 23 | 4 | 1 | 3 | (2 | 1) | 38 | 12 | 13 | 8 | 0 | 16 | 0 | 0 | 0 | 4 | 4 | .50 | 1 | .271 | .333 | .447 |
| 3 ML YEARS | | 154 | 489 | 126 | 19 | 1 | 11 | (5 | 6) | 180 | 59 | 58 | 28 | 0 | 95 | 5 | 2 | 1 | 13 | 7 | .65 | 11 | .258 | .304 | .368 |

## Wally Joyner

**Bats:** Left **Throws:** Left **Pos:** 1B **Ht:** 6' 2" **Wt:** 198 **Born:** 06/16/62 **Age:** 29

| BATTING | | | | | | | | | | | | | | | | | | | BASERUNNING | | | | PERCENTAGES | | |
|---|---|---|---|---|---|---|---|---|---|---|---|---|---|---|---|---|---|---|---|---|---|---|---|---|---|
| Year Team | Lg | G | AB | H | 2B | 3B | HR | (Hm | Rd) | TB | R | RBI | TBB | IBB | SO | HBP | SH | SF | SB | CS | SB% | GDP | Avg | OBP | SLG |
| 1986 California | AL | 154 | 593 | 172 | 27 | 3 | 22 | (11 | 11) | 271 | 82 | 100 | 57 | 8 | 58 | 2 | 10 | 12 | 5 | 2 | .71 | 11 | .290 | .348 | .457 |
| 1987 California | AL | 149 | 564 | 161 | 33 | 1 | 34 | (19 | 15) | 298 | 100 | 117 | 72 | 12 | 64 | 5 | 2 | 10 | 8 | 2 | .80 | 14 | .285 | .366 | .528 |
| 1988 California | AL | 158 | 597 | 176 | 31 | 2 | 13 | (6 | 7) | 250 | 81 | 85 | 55 | 14 | 51 | 5 | 0 | 6 | 8 | 2 | .80 | 16 | .295 | .356 | .419 |
| 1989 California | AL | 159 | 593 | 167 | 30 | 2 | 16 | (8 | 8) | 249 | 78 | 79 | 46 | 7 | 58 | 6 | 1 | 8 | 3 | 2 | .60 | 15 | .282 | .335 | .420 |
| 1990 California | AL | 83 | 310 | 83 | 15 | 0 | 8 | (5 | 3) | 122 | 35 | 41 | 41 | 4 | 34 | 1 | 1 | 5 | 2 | 1 | .67 | 10 | .268 | .350 | .394 |
| 5 ML YEARS | | 703 | 2657 | 759 | 136 | 8 | 93 | (49 | 44) | 1190 | 376 | 422 | 271 | 45 | 265 | 19 | 14 | 41 | 26 | 9 | .74 | 66 | .286 | .351 | .448 |

## Dave Justice

**Bats:** Left **Throws:** Left **Pos:** 1B/RF **Ht:** 6' 3" **Wt:** 195 **Born:** 04/14/66 **Age:** 25

| BATTING | | | | | | | | | | | | | | | | | | | BASERUNNING | | | | PERCENTAGES | | |
|---|---|---|---|---|---|---|---|---|---|---|---|---|---|---|---|---|---|---|---|---|---|---|---|---|---|
| Year Team | Lg | G | AB | H | 2B | 3B | HR | (Hm | Rd) | TB | R | RBI | TBB | IBB | SO | HBP | SH | SF | SB | CS | SB% | GDP | Avg | OBP | SLG |
| 1985 Pulaski | R | 66 | 204 | 50 | 8 | 0 | 10 | -- | -- | 88 | 39 | 46 | 40 | 0 | 30 | 0 | 0 | 5 | 0 | 1 | .00 | 5 | .245 | .361 | .431 |
| 1986 Sumter | A | 61 | 220 | 66 | 16 | 0 | 10 | -- | -- | 112 | 48 | 61 | 48 | 2 | 28 | 5 | 0 | 7 | 10 | 2 | .83 | 7 | .300 | .425 | .509 |
| Durham | A | 67 | 229 | 64 | 9 | 1 | 12 | -- | -- | 111 | 47 | 44 | 46 | 5 | 24 | 7 | 1 | 1 | 2 | 4 | .33 | 4 | .279 | .413 | .485 |
| 1987 Greenville | AA | 93 | 348 | 79 | 12 | 4 | 6 | -- | -- | 117 | 38 | 40 | 53 | 6 | 48 | 0 | 1 | 3 | 3 | 2 | .60 | 9 | .227 | .327 | .336 |
| 1988 Richmond | AAA | 70 | 227 | 46 | 9 | 1 | 8 | -- | -- | 81 | 27 | 28 | 39 | 9 | 55 | 0 | 2 | 7 | 4 | 3 | .57 | 3 | .203 | .311 | .357 |
| Greenville | AA | 58 | 198 | 55 | 13 | 1 | 9 | -- | -- | 97 | 34 | 37 | 36 | 4 | 43 | 2 | 0 | 1 | 6 | 2 | .75 | 6 | .278 | .392 | .490 |
| 1989 Richmond | AAA | 115 | 391 | 102 | 24 | 3 | 12 | -- | -- | 168 | 47 | 58 | 59 | 4 | 66 | 3 | 1 | 3 | 12 | 8 | .60 | 4 | .261 | .360 | .430 |

| | | | | | | | | | | | | | | | | | | | | | | | | | | |
|---|---|---|---|---|---|---|---|---|---|---|---|---|---|---|---|---|---|---|---|---|---|---|---|---|---|---|
| 1990 Richmond | AAA | 12 | 45 | 16 | 5 | 1 | 2 | -- | -- | 29 | 7 | 7 | 7 | 2 | 6 | 0 | 0 | 0 | 0 | 0 | .00 | 2 | .356 | .442 | .644 |
| 1989 Atlanta | NL | 16 | 51 | 12 | 3 | 0 | 1 | (1 | 0) | 18 | 7 | 3 | 3 | 1 | 9 | 1 | 1 | 0 | 2 | 1 | .67 | 1 | .235 | .291 | .353 |
| 1990 Atlanta | NL | 127 | 439 | 124 | 23 | 2 | 28 | (19 | 9) | 235 | 76 | 78 | 64 | 4 | 92 | 0 | 0 | 1 | 11 | 6 | .65 | 2 | .282 | .373 | .535 |
| 2 ML YEARS | | 143 | 490 | 136 | 26 | 2 | 29 | (20 | 9) | 253 | 83 | 81 | 67 | 5 | 101 | 1 | 1 | 1 | 13 | 7 | .65 | 3 | .278 | .365 | .516 |

## Jeff Kaiser

**Pitches:** Left **Bats:** Right **Pos:** RP **Ht:** 6' 3" **Wt:** 195 **Born:** 07/24/60 **Age:** 30

| | | HOW MUCH HE PITCHED | | | | | | WHAT HE GAVE UP | | | | | | | | | | | | THE RESULTS | | | | | |
|---|---|---|---|---|---|---|---|---|---|---|---|---|---|---|---|---|---|---|---|---|---|---|---|---|---|
| Year Team | Lg | G | GS | CG | GF | IP | BFP | H | R | ER | HR | SH | SF | HB | TBB | IBB | SO | WP | Bk | W | L | Pct. | ShO | Sv | ERA |
| 1985 Oakland | AL | 15 | 0 | 0 | 4 | 16.2 | 97 | 25 | 32 | 27 | 6 | 1 | 2 | 1 | 20 | 2 | 10 | 2 | 0 | 0 | 0 | .000 | 0 | 0 | 14.58 |
| 1987 Cleveland | AL | 2 | 0 | 0 | 0 | 3.1 | 18 | 4 | 6 | 6 | 1 | 0 | 0 | 1 | 3 | 0 | 2 | 0 | 0 | 0 | 0 | .000 | 0 | 0 | 16.20 |
| 1988 Cleveland | AL | 3 | 0 | 0 | 1 | 2.2 | 11 | 2 | 0 | 0 | 0 | 2 | 1 | 0 | 1 | 0 | 0 | 0 | 0 | 0 | 0 | .000 | 0 | 0 | 0.00 |
| 1989 Cleveland | AL | 6 | 0 | 0 | 1 | 3.2 | 22 | 5 | 5 | 3 | 1 | 0 | 1 | 0 | 5 | 0 | 4 | 1 | 0 | 0 | 1 | .000 | 0 | 0 | 7.36 |
| 1990 Cleveland | AL | 5 | 0 | 0 | 0 | 12.2 | 60 | 16 | 5 | 5 | 2 | 0 | 1 | 0 | 7 | 1 | 9 | 0 | 0 | 0 | 0 | .000 | 0 | 0 | 3.55 |
| 5 ML YEARS | | 31 | 0 | 0 | 6 | 39 | 208 | 52 | 48 | 41 | 10 | 3 | 5 | 2 | 36 | 3 | 25 | 3 | 0 | 0 | 1 | .000 | 0 | 0 | 9.46 |

## Ron Karkovice

**Bats:** Right **Throws:** Right **Pos:** C **Ht:** 6' 1" **Wt:** 215 **Born:** 08/08/63 **Age:** 27

| | | BATTING | | | | | | | | | | | | | | | | | BASERUNNING | | | | PERCENTAGES | | |
|---|---|---|---|---|---|---|---|---|---|---|---|---|---|---|---|---|---|---|---|---|---|---|---|---|---|
| Year Team | Lg | G | AB | H | 2B | 3B | HR | (Hm | Rd) | TB | R | RBI | TBB | IBB | SO | HBP | SH | SF | SB | CS | SB% | GDP | Avg | OBP | SLG |
| 1986 Chicago | AL | 37 | 97 | 24 | 7 | 0 | 4 | (1 | 3) | 43 | 13 | 13 | 9 | 0 | 37 | 1 | 1 | 1 | 1 | 0 | 1.00 | 3 | .247 | .315 | .443 |
| 1987 Chicago | AL | 39 | 85 | 6 | 0 | 0 | 2 | (1 | 1) | 12 | 7 | 7 | 7 | 0 | 40 | 2 | 1 | 0 | 3 | 0 | 1.00 | 2 | .071 | .160 | .141 |
| 1988 Chicago | AL | 46 | 115 | 20 | 4 | 0 | 3 | (1 | 2) | 33 | 10 | 9 | 7 | 0 | 30 | 1 | 3 | 0 | 4 | 2 | .67 | 1 | .174 | .228 | .287 |
| 1989 Chicago | AL | 71 | 182 | 48 | 9 | 2 | 3 | (0 | 3) | 70 | 21 | 24 | 10 | 0 | 56 | 2 | 7 | 2 | 0 | 0 | .00 | 0 | .264 | .306 | .385 |
| 1990 Chicago | AL | 68 | 183 | 45 | 10 | 0 | 6 | (0 | 6) | 73 | 30 | 20 | 16 | 1 | 52 | 1 | 7 | 1 | 2 | 0 | 1.00 | 1 | .246 | .308 | .399 |
| 5 ML YEARS | | 261 | 662 | 143 | 30 | 2 | 18 | (3 | 15) | 231 | 81 | 73 | 49 | 1 | 215 | 7 | 19 | 4 | 10 | 2 | .83 | 7 | .216 | .276 | .349 |

## Roberto Kelly

**Bats:** Right **Throws:** Right **Pos:** CF/LF **Ht:** 6' 4" **Wt:** 185 **Born:** 10/01/64 **Age:** 26

| | | BATTING | | | | | | | | | | | | | | | | | BASERUNNING | | | | PERCENTAGES | | |
|---|---|---|---|---|---|---|---|---|---|---|---|---|---|---|---|---|---|---|---|---|---|---|---|---|---|
| Year Team | Lg | G | AB | H | 2B | 3B | HR | (Hm | Rd) | TB | R | RBI | TBB | IBB | SO | HBP | SH | SF | SB | CS | SB% | GDP | Avg | OBP | SLG |
| 1987 New York | AL | 23 | 52 | 14 | 3 | 0 | 1 | (0 | 1) | 20 | 12 | 7 | 5 | 0 | 15 | 0 | 1 | 1 | 9 | 3 | .75 | 0 | .269 | .328 | .385 |
| 1988 New York | AL | 38 | 77 | 19 | 4 | 1 | 1 | (1 | 0) | 28 | 9 | 7 | 3 | 0 | 15 | 0 | 3 | 1 | 5 | 2 | .71 | 0 | .247 | .272 | .364 |
| 1989 New York | AL | 137 | 441 | 133 | 18 | 3 | 9 | (2 | 7) | 184 | 65 | 48 | 41 | 3 | 89 | 6 | 8 | 0 | 35 | 12 | .74 | 9 | .302 | .369 | .417 |
| 1990 New York | AL | 162 | 641 | 183 | 32 | 4 | 15 | (5 | 10) | 268 | 85 | 61 | 33 | 0 | 148 | 4 | 4 | 4 | 42 | 17 | .71 | 7 | .285 | .323 | .418 |
| 4 ML YEARS | | 360 | 1211 | 349 | 57 | 8 | 26 | (8 | 18) | 500 | 171 | 123 | 82 | 3 | 267 | 10 | 16 | 6 | 91 | 34 | .73 | 16 | .288 | .337 | .413 |

## Terry Kennedy

**Bats:** Left **Throws:** Right **Pos:** C **Ht:** 6' 4" **Wt:** 224 **Born:** 06/04/56 **Age:** 35

| | | BATTING | | | | | | | | | | | | | | | | | BASERUNNING | | | | PERCENTAGES | | |
|---|---|---|---|---|---|---|---|---|---|---|---|---|---|---|---|---|---|---|---|---|---|---|---|---|---|
| Year Team | Lg | G | AB | H | 2B | 3B | HR | (Hm | Rd) | TB | R | RBI | TBB | IBB | SO | HBP | SH | SF | SB | CS | SB% | GDP | Avg | OBP | SLG |
| 1978 St. Louis | NL | 10 | 29 | 5 | 0 | 0 | 0 | (0 | 0) | 5 | 0 | 2 | 4 | 2 | 3 | 0 | 0 | 0 | 0 | 0 | .00 | 2 | .172 | .273 | .172 |
| 1979 St. Louis | NL | 33 | 109 | 31 | 7 | 0 | 2 | (2 | 0) | 44 | 11 | 17 | 6 | 2 | 20 | 0 | 0 | 1 | 0 | 0 | .00 | 2 | .284 | .319 | .404 |
| 1980 St. Louis | NL | 84 | 248 | 63 | 12 | 3 | 4 | (1 | 3) | 93 | 28 | 34 | 28 | 3 | 34 | 0 | 1 | 4 | 0 | 0 | .00 | 9 | .254 | .325 | .375 |
| 1981 San Diego | NL | 101 | 382 | 115 | 24 | 1 | 2 | (1 | 1) | 147 | 32 | 41 | 22 | 6 | 53 | 2 | 4 | 2 | 0 | 2 | .00 | 7 | .301 | .341 | .385 |
| 1982 San Diego | NL | 153 | 562 | 166 | 42 | 1 | 21 | (10 | 11) | 273 | 75 | 97 | 26 | 9 | 91 | 5 | 3 | 8 | 1 | 0 | 1.00 | 7 | .295 | .328 | .486 |
| 1983 San Diego | NL | 149 | 549 | 156 | 27 | 2 | 17 | (7 | 10) | 238 | 47 | 98 | 51 | 15 | 89 | 2 | 1 | 9 | 1 | 3 | .25 | 10 | .284 | .342 | .434 |
| 1984 San Diego | NL | 148 | 530 | 127 | 16 | 1 | 14 | (8 | 6) | 187 | 54 | 57 | 33 | 8 | 99 | 2 | 0 | 5 | 1 | 2 | .33 | 16 | .240 | .284 | .353 |
| 1985 San Diego | NL | 143 | 532 | 139 | 27 | 1 | 10 | (7 | 3) | 198 | 54 | 74 | 31 | 10 | 102 | 0 | 0 | 2 | 0 | 0 | .00 | 19 | .261 | .301 | .372 |
| 1986 San Diego | NL | 141 | 432 | 114 | 22 | 1 | 12 | (7 | 5) | 174 | 46 | 57 | 37 | 7 | 74 | 2 | 4 | 1 | 0 | 3 | .00 | 10 | .264 | .324 | .403 |
| 1987 Baltimore | AL | 143 | 512 | 128 | 13 | 1 | 18 | (11 | 7) | 197 | 51 | 62 | 35 | 6 | 112 | 1 | 1 | 0 | 1 | 0 | 1.00 | 13 | .250 | .299 | .385 |
| 1988 Baltimore | AL | 85 | 265 | 60 | 10 | 0 | 3 | (2 | 1) | 79 | 20 | 16 | 15 | 0 | 53 | 1 | 2 | 2 | 0 | 0 | .00 | 13 | .226 | .269 | .298 |
| 1989 San Francisco | NL | 125 | 355 | 85 | 15 | 0 | 5 | (1 | 4) | 115 | 19 | 34 | 35 | 7 | 56 | 0 | 3 | 2 | 1 | 3 | .25 | 6 | .239 | .306 | .324 |
| 1990 San Francisco | NL | 107 | 303 | 84 | 22 | 0 | 2 | (2 | 0) | 112 | 25 | 26 | 31 | 7 | 38 | 0 | 3 | 2 | 1 | 2 | .33 | 7 | .277 | .342 | .370 |
| 13 ML YEARS | | 1422 | 4808 | 1273 | 237 | 11 | 110 | (59 | 51) | 1862 | 462 | 615 | 354 | 82 | 824 | 15 | 22 | 38 | 6 | 15 | .29 | 121 | .265 | .315 | .387 |

## Charlie Kerfeld

**Pitches:** Right **Bats:** Right **Pos:** RP **Ht:** 6' 7" **Wt:** 250 **Born:** 09/28/63 **Age:** 27

| | | HOW MUCH HE PITCHED | | | | | | WHAT HE GAVE UP | | | | | | | | | | | | THE RESULTS | | | | | |
|---|---|---|---|---|---|---|---|---|---|---|---|---|---|---|---|---|---|---|---|---|---|---|---|---|---|
| Year Team | Lg | G | GS | CG | GF | IP | BFP | H | R | ER | HR | SH | SF | HB | TBB | IBB | SO | WP | Bk | W | L | Pct. | ShO | Sv | ERA |
| 1985 Houston | NL | 11 | 6 | 0 | 2 | 44.1 | 193 | 44 | 22 | 20 | 2 | 1 | 3 | 0 | 25 | 2 | 30 | 1 | 0 | 4 | 2 | .667 | 0 | 0 | 4.06 |
| 1986 Houston | NL | 61 | 0 | 0 | 29 | 93.2 | 390 | 71 | 32 | 27 | 5 | 6 | 7 | 2 | 42 | 3 | 77 | 7 | 2 | 11 | 2 | .846 | 0 | 7 | 2.59 |
| 1987 Houston | NL | 21 | 0 | 0 | 11 | 29.2 | 137 | 34 | 22 | 22 | 3 | 4 | 1 | 1 | 21 | 2 | 17 | 0 | 0 | 0 | 2 | .000 | 0 | 0 | 6.67 |
| 1990 2 ML Teams | | 30 | 0 | 0 | 11 | 34 | 168 | 40 | 28 | 25 | 2 | 5 | 2 | 0 | 29 | 4 | 31 | 1 | 0 | 3 | 3 | .500 | 0 | 2 | 6.62 |
| 1990 Houston | NL | 5 | 0 | 0 | 1 | 3.1 | 25 | 9 | 6 | 6 | 0 | 2 | 0 | 0 | 6 | 1 | 4 | 1 | 0 | 0 | 2 | .000 | 0 | 0 | 16.20 |
| Atlanta | NL | 25 | 0 | 0 | 10 | 30.2 | 143 | 31 | 22 | 19 | 2 | 3 | 2 | 0 | 23 | 3 | 27 | 0 | 0 | 3 | 1 | .750 | 0 | 2 | 5.58 |
| 4 ML YEARS | | 123 | 6 | 0 | 53 | 201.2 | 888 | 189 | 104 | 94 | 12 | 16 | 13 | 3 | 117 | 11 | 155 | 9 | 2 | 18 | 9 | .667 | 0 | 9 | 4.20 |

## Jimmy Key

**Pitches:** Left **Bats:** Right **Pos:** SP **Ht:** 6' 1" **Wt:** 190 **Born:** 04/22/61 **Age:** 30

| | | HOW MUCH HE PITCHED | | | | | | WHAT HE GAVE UP | | | | | | | | | | | | THE RESULTS | | | | | |
|---|---|---|---|---|---|---|---|---|---|---|---|---|---|---|---|---|---|---|---|---|---|---|---|---|---|
| Year Team | Lg | G | GS | CG | GF | IP | BFP | H | R | ER | HR | SH | SF | HB | TBB | IBB | SO | WP | Bk | W | L | Pct. | ShO | Sv | ERA |
| 1984 Toronto | AL | 63 | 0 | 0 | 24 | 62 | 285 | 70 | 37 | 32 | 8 | 6 | 1 | 1 | 32 | 8 | 44 | 3 | 1 | 4 | 5 | .444 | 0 | 10 | 4.65 |
| 1985 Toronto | AL | 35 | 32 | 3 | 0 | 212.2 | 856 | 188 | 77 | 71 | 22 | 5 | 5 | 2 | 50 | 1 | 85 | 6 | 1 | 14 | 6 | .700 | 0 | 0 | 3.00 |
| 1986 Toronto | AL | 36 | 35 | 4 | 0 | 232 | 959 | 222 | 98 | 92 | 24 | 10 | 6 | 3 | 74 | 1 | 141 | 3 | 0 | 14 | 11 | .560 | 2 | 0 | 3.57 |
| 1987 Toronto | AL | 36 | 36 | 8 | 0 | 261 | 1033 | 210 | 93 | 80 | 24 | 11 | 3 | 2 | 66 | 6 | 161 | 8 | 5 | 17 | 8 | .680 | 1 | 0 | 2.76 |
| 1988 Toronto | AL | 21 | 21 | 2 | 0 | 131.1 | 551 | 127 | 55 | 48 | 13 | 4 | 3 | 5 | 30 | 2 | 65 | 1 | 0 | 12 | 5 | .706 | 2 | 0 | 3.29 |
| 1989 Toronto | AL | 33 | 33 | 5 | 0 | 216 | 886 | 226 | 99 | 93 | 18 | 9 | 9 | 3 | 27 | 2 | 118 | 4 | 1 | 13 | 14 | .481 | 1 | 0 | 3.88 |
| 1990 Toronto | AL | 27 | 27 | 0 | 0 | 154.2 | 636 | 169 | 79 | 73 | 20 | 5 | 6 | 1 | 22 | 2 | 88 | 0 | 1 | 13 | 7 | .650 | 0 | 0 | 4.25 |
| 7 ML YEARS | | 251 | 184 | 22 | 24 | 1269.2 | 5206 | 1212 | 538 | 489 | 129 | 50 | 33 | 17 | 301 | 22 | 702 | 25 | 9 | 87 | 56 | .608 | 6 | 10 | 3.47 |

## Dana Kiecker

**Pitches:** Right **Bats:** Right **Pos:** SP/RP **Ht:** 6' 3" **Wt:** 180 **Born:** 02/25/61 **Age:** 30

| | | HOW MUCH HE PITCHED | | | | | | WHAT HE GAVE UP | | | | | | | | | | | | THE RESULTS | | | | | |
|---|---|---|---|---|---|---|---|---|---|---|---|---|---|---|---|---|---|---|---|---|---|---|---|---|---|
| Year Team | Lg | G | GS | CG | GF | IP | BFP | H | R | ER | HR | SH | SF | HB | TBB | IBB | SO | WP | Bk | W | L | Pct. | ShO | Sv | ERA |
| 1984 Winston-Sal | A | 29 | 19 | 5 | 8 | 137.2 | 615 | 142 | 86 | 67 | 12 | 2 | 3 | 1 | 55 | 2 | 82 | 12 | 2 | 6 | 11 | .353 | 1 | 1 | 4.38 |
| 1985 Winter Havn | A | 29 | 29 | 9 | 0 | 193.2 | 789 | 176 | 72 | 56 | 4 | 7 | 10 | 2 | 59 | 2 | 60 | 7 | 0 | 12 | 12 | .500 | 2 | 0 | 2.60 |
| 1986 New Britain | AA | 24 | 24 | 7 | 0 | 156.1 | 675 | 171 | 88 | 72 | 8 | 5 | 8 | 4 | 48 | 3 | 71 | 10 | 5 | 7 | 12 | .368 | 0 | 0 | 4.14 |
| 1987 New Britain | AA | 39 | 17 | 2 | 18 | 153 | 691 | 164 | 76 | 65 | 6 | 5 | 6 | 10 | 66 | 5 | 66 | 9 | 1 | 7 | 10 | .412 | 0 | 6 | 3.82 |
| 1988 New Britain | AA | 1 | 1 | 0 | 0 | 6 | 22 | 3 | 0 | 0 | 0 | 0 | 0 | 1 | 0 | 0 | 1 | 0 | 0 | 1 | 0 | 1.000 | 0 | 0 | 0.00 |
| Pawtucket | AAA | 23 | 22 | 4 | 1 | 132.1 | 556 | 120 | 65 | 54 | 7 | 2 | 2 | 6 | 46 | 2 | 74 | 5 | 7 | 7 | 7 | .500 | 1 | 0 | 3.67 |
| 1989 Pawtucket | AAA | 28 | 19 | 3 | 3 | 147.1 | 644 | 163 | 83 | 60 | 12 | 0 | 6 | 4 | 36 | 2 | 87 | 6 | 2 | 8 | 9 | .471 | 0 | 0 | 3.67 |
| 1990 Boston | AL | 32 | 25 | 0 | 3 | 152 | 641 | 145 | 74 | 67 | 7 | 1 | 5 | 9 | 54 | 2 | 93 | 9 | 1 | 8 | 9 | .471 | 0 | 0 | 3.97 |

## Paul Kilgus

**Pitches:** Left **Bats:** Left **Pos:** RP **Ht:** 6' 1" **Wt:** 175 **Born:** 02/02/62 **Age:** 29

| | | HOW MUCH HE PITCHED | | | | | | WHAT HE GAVE UP | | | | | | | | | | | | THE RESULTS | | | | | |
|---|---|---|---|---|---|---|---|---|---|---|---|---|---|---|---|---|---|---|---|---|---|---|---|---|---|
| Year Team | Lg | G | GS | CG | GF | IP | BFP | H | R | ER | HR | SH | SF | HB | TBB | IBB | SO | WP | Bk | W | L | Pct. | ShO | Sv | ERA |
| 1987 Texas | AL | 25 | 12 | 0 | 2 | 89.1 | 385 | 95 | 45 | 41 | 14 | 2 | 0 | 2 | 31 | 2 | 42 | 0 | 0 | 2 | 7 | .222 | 0 | 0 | 4.13 |
| 1988 Texas | AL | 32 | 32 | 5 | 0 | 203.1 | 871 | 190 | 105 | 94 | 18 | 4 | 4 | 10 | 71 | 2 | 88 | 6 | 4 | 12 | 15 | .444 | 3 | 0 | 4.16 |
| 1989 Chicago | NL | 35 | 23 | 0 | 5 | 145.2 | 642 | 164 | 90 | 71 | 9 | 5 | 4 | 5 | 49 | 6 | 61 | 3 | 2 | 6 | 10 | .375 | 0 | 2 | 4.39 |
| 1990 Toronto | AL | 11 | 0 | 0 | 4 | 16.1 | 74 | 19 | 11 | 11 | 2 | 1 | 3 | 1 | 7 | 1 | 7 | 0 | 0 | 0 | 0 | .000 | 0 | 0 | 6.06 |
| 4 ML YEARS | | 103 | 67 | 5 | 11 | 454.2 | 1972 | 468 | 251 | 217 | 43 | 12 | 11 | 18 | 158 | 11 | 198 | 9 | 6 | 20 | 32 | .385 | 3 | 2 | 4.30 |

## Eric King

**Pitches:** Right **Bats:** Right **Pos:** SP **Ht:** 6' 2" **Wt:** 180 **Born:** 04/10/64 **Age:** 27

| | | HOW MUCH HE PITCHED | | | | | | WHAT HE GAVE UP | | | | | | | | | | | | THE RESULTS | | | | | |
|---|---|---|---|---|---|---|---|---|---|---|---|---|---|---|---|---|---|---|---|---|---|---|---|---|---|
| Year Team | Lg | G | GS | CG | GF | IP | BFP | H | R | ER | HR | SH | SF | HB | TBB | IBB | SO | WP | Bk | W | L | Pct. | ShO | Sv | ERA |
| 1986 Detroit | AL | 33 | 16 | 3 | 9 | 138.1 | 579 | 108 | 54 | 54 | 11 | 6 | 1 | 8 | 63 | 3 | 79 | 4 | 3 | 11 | 4 | .733 | 1 | 3 | 3.51 |
| 1987 Detroit | AL | 55 | 4 | 0 | 26 | 116 | 513 | 111 | 67 | 63 | 15 | 3 | 3 | 4 | 60 | 10 | 89 | 5 | 1 | 6 | 9 | .400 | 0 | 9 | 4.89 |
| 1988 Detroit | AL | 23 | 5 | 0 | 8 | 68.2 | 303 | 60 | 28 | 26 | 5 | 5 | 2 | 5 | 34 | 2 | 45 | 4 | 2 | 4 | 1 | .800 | 0 | 3 | 3.41 |
| 1989 Chicago | AL | 25 | 25 | 1 | 0 | 159.1 | 666 | 144 | 69 | 60 | 13 | 3 | 4 | 4 | 64 | 1 | 72 | 5 | 4 | 9 | 10 | .474 | 1 | 0 | 3.39 |
| 1990 Chicago | AL | 25 | 25 | 2 | 0 | 151 | 623 | 135 | 59 | 55 | 10 | 6 | 1 | 6 | 40 | 0 | 70 | 2 | 3 | 12 | 4 | .750 | 2 | 0 | 3.28 |
| 5 ML YEARS | | 161 | 75 | 6 | 43 | 633.1 | 2684 | 558 | 277 | 258 | 54 | 23 | 11 | 27 | 261 | 16 | 355 | 20 | 13 | 42 | 28 | .600 | 4 | 15 | 3.67 |

## Jeff King

**Bats:** Right **Throws:** Right **Pos:** 3B **Ht:** 6' 1" **Wt:** 175 **Born:** 12/26/64 **Age:** 26

| | | BATTING | | | | | | | | | | | | | | | | | BASERUNNING | | | | PERCENTAGES | | |
|---|---|---|---|---|---|---|---|---|---|---|---|---|---|---|---|---|---|---|---|---|---|---|---|---|---|
| Year Team | Lg | G | AB | H | 2B | 3B | HR | (Hm | Rd) | TB | R | RBI | TBB | IBB | SO | HBP | SH | SF | SB | CS | SB% | GDP | Avg | OBP | SLG |
| 1986 Pr William | A | 37 | 132 | 31 | 4 | 1 | 6 | -- | -- | 55 | 18 | 20 | 19 | 2 | 34 | 1 | 0 | 0 | 1 | 1 | .50 | 4 | .235 | .336 | .417 |
| 1987 Salem | A | 90 | 310 | 86 | 9 | 1 | 26 | -- | -- | 175 | 68 | 71 | 61 | 2 | 88 | 1 | 0 | 2 | 6 | 2 | .75 | 7 | .277 | .396 | .565 |
| Harrisburg | AA | 26 | 100 | 24 | 7 | 0 | 2 | -- | -- | 37 | 12 | 25 | 4 | 0 | 27 | 0 | 0 | 4 | 0 | 1 | .00 | 2 | .240 | .259 | .370 |
| 1988 Harrisburg | AA | 117 | 411 | 105 | 21 | 1 | 14 | -- | -- | 170 | 49 | 66 | 46 | 3 | 87 | 0 | 2 | 8 | 5 | 4 | .56 | 5 | .255 | .325 | .414 |
| 1989 Buffalo | AAA | 51 | 169 | 43 | 5 | 2 | 6 | -- | -- | 70 | 26 | 29 | 13 | 0 | 22 | 0 | 2 | 5 | 7 | 1 | .88 | 5 | .254 | .299 | .414 |
| 1989 Pittsburgh | NL | 75 | 215 | 42 | 13 | 3 | 5 | (3 | 2) | 76 | 31 | 19 | 20 | 1 | 34 | 2 | 2 | 4 | 4 | 2 | .67 | 3 | .195 | .266 | .353 |
| 1990 Pittsburgh | NL | 127 | 371 | 91 | 17 | 1 | 14 | (9 | 5) | 152 | 46 | 53 | 21 | 1 | 50 | 1 | 2 | 7 | 3 | 3 | .50 | 12 | .245 | .283 | .410 |
| 2 ML YEARS | | 202 | 586 | 133 | 30 | 4 | 19 | (12 | 7) | 228 | 77 | 72 | 41 | 2 | 84 | 3 | 4 | 11 | 7 | 5 | .58 | 15 | .227 | .276 | .389 |

## Mike Kingery

**Bats:** Left **Throws:** Left **Pos:** RF/LF **Ht:** 6' 0" **Wt:** 180 **Born:** 03/29/61 **Age:** 30

| | | BATTING | | | | | | | | | | | | | | | | | BASERUNNING | | | | PERCENTAGES | | |
|---|---|---|---|---|---|---|---|---|---|---|---|---|---|---|---|---|---|---|---|---|---|---|---|---|---|
| Year Team | Lg | G | AB | H | 2B | 3B | HR | (Hm | Rd) | TB | R | RBI | TBB | IBB | SO | HBP | SH | SF | SB | CS | SB% | GDP | Avg | OBP | SLG |
| 1986 Kansas City | AL | 62 | 209 | 54 | 8 | 5 | 3 | (1 | 2) | 81 | 25 | 14 | 12 | 2 | 30 | 0 | 0 | 2 | 7 | 3 | .70 | 4 | .258 | .296 | .388 |
| 1987 Seattle | AL | 120 | 354 | 99 | 25 | 4 | 9 | (5 | 4) | 159 | 38 | 52 | 27 | 0 | 43 | 2 | 1 | 6 | 7 | 9 | .44 | 4 | .280 | .329 | .449 |
| 1988 Seattle | AL | 57 | 123 | 25 | 6 | 0 | 1 | (1 | 0) | 34 | 21 | 9 | 19 | 1 | 23 | 1 | 1 | 1 | 3 | 1 | .75 | 1 | .203 | .313 | .276 |

| | | | | | | | | | | | | | | | | | | | | | | | | | | |
|---|---|---|---|---|---|---|---|---|---|---|---|---|---|---|---|---|---|---|---|---|---|---|---|---|---|---|
| 1989 Seattle | AL | 31 | 76 | 17 | 3 | 0 | 2 | (2 | 0) | 26 | 14 | 6 | 7 | 0 | 14 | 0 | 0 | 1 | 1 | 1 | .50 | 2 | .224 | .286 | .342 |
| 1990 San Francisco | NL | 105 | 207 | 61 | 7 | 1 | 0 | (0 | 0) | 70 | 24 | 24 | 12 | 0 | 19 | 1 | 5 | 1 | 6 | 1 | .86 | 1 | .295 | .335 | .338 |
| 5 ML YEARS | | 375 | 969 | 256 | 49 | 10 | 15 | (9 | 6) | 370 | 122 | 105 | 77 | 3 | 129 | 4 | 7 | 11 | 24 | 15 | .62 | 12 | .264 | .318 | .382 |

## Matt Kinzer

**Pitches:** Right **Bats:** Right **Pos:** RP **Ht:** 6' 2" **Wt:** 210 **Born:** 06/17/63 **Age:** 28

| | | HOW MUCH HE PITCHED | | | | | | WHAT HE GAVE UP | | | | | | | | | | | | THE RESULTS | | | | | |
|---|---|---|---|---|---|---|---|---|---|---|---|---|---|---|---|---|---|---|---|---|---|---|---|---|---|
| Year Team | Lg | G | GS | CG | GF | IP | BFP | H | R | ER | HR | SH | SF | HB | TBB | IBB | SO | WP | Bk | W | L | Pct. | ShO | Sv | ERA |
| 1989 St. Louis | NL | 8 | 1 | 0 | 3 | 13.1 | 67 | 25 | 20 | 19 | 3 | 0 | 1 | 0 | 4 | 2 | 8 | 1 | 0 | 0 | 2 | .000 | 0 | 0 | 12.83 |
| 1990 Detroit | AL | 1 | 0 | 0 | 1 | 1.2 | 11 | 3 | 3 | 3 | 0 | 0 | 0 | 0 | 3 | 0 | 1 | 0 | 0 | 0 | 0 | .000 | 0 | 0 | 16.20 |
| 2 ML YEARS | | 9 | 1 | 0 | 4 | 15 | 78 | 28 | 23 | 22 | 3 | 0 | 1 | 0 | 7 | 2 | 9 | 1 | 0 | 0 | 2 | .000 | 0 | 0 | 13.20 |

## Bob Kipper

**Pitches:** Left **Bats:** Right **Pos:** RP **Ht:** 6' 2" **Wt:** 175 **Born:** 07/08/64 **Age:** 26

| | | HOW MUCH HE PITCHED | | | | | | WHAT HE GAVE UP | | | | | | | | | | | | THE RESULTS | | | | | |
|---|---|---|---|---|---|---|---|---|---|---|---|---|---|---|---|---|---|---|---|---|---|---|---|---|---|
| Year Team | Lg | G | GS | CG | GF | IP | BFP | H | R | ER | HR | SH | SF | HB | TBB | IBB | SO | WP | Bk | W | L | Pct. | ShO | Sv | ERA |
| 1985 2 ML Teams | | 7 | 5 | 0 | 1 | 28 | 124 | 28 | 24 | 22 | 5 | 1 | 3 | 0 | 10 | 0 | 13 | 0 | 0 | 1 | 3 | .250 | 0 | 0 | 7.07 |
| 1986 Pittsburgh | NL | 20 | 19 | 0 | 1 | 114 | 496 | 123 | 60 | 51 | 17 | 3 | 3 | 2 | 34 | 3 | 81 | 3 | 3 | 6 | 8 | .429 | 0 | 0 | 4.03 |
| 1987 Pittsburgh | NL | 24 | 20 | 1 | 0 | 110.2 | 493 | 117 | 74 | 73 | 25 | 4 | 3 | 2 | 52 | 4 | 83 | 5 | 0 | 5 | 9 | .357 | 1 | 0 | 5.94 |
| 1988 Pittsburgh | NL | 50 | 0 | 0 | 15 | 65 | 267 | 54 | 33 | 27 | 7 | 5 | 3 | 2 | 26 | 4 | 39 | 1 | 1 | 2 | 6 | .250 | 0 | 0 | 3.74 |
| 1989 Pittsburgh | NL | 52 | 0 | 0 | 15 | 83 | 334 | 55 | 29 | 27 | 5 | 5 | 3 | 0 | 33 | 6 | 58 | 5 | 2 | 3 | 4 | .429 | 0 | 4 | 2.93 |
| 1990 Pittsburgh | NL | 41 | 1 | 0 | 7 | 62.2 | 260 | 44 | 24 | 21 | 7 | 2 | 3 | 3 | 26 | 1 | 35 | 1 | 5 | 5 | 2 | .714 | 0 | 3 | 3.02 |
| 1985 California | AL | 2 | 1 | 0 | 0 | 3.1 | 20 | 7 | 8 | 8 | 1 | 0 | 2 | 0 | 3 | 0 | 0 | 0 | 0 | 0 | 1 | .000 | 0 | 0 | 21.60 |
| Pittsburgh | NL | 5 | 4 | 0 | 1 | 24.2 | 104 | 21 | 16 | 14 | 4 | 1 | 1 | 0 | 7 | 0 | 13 | 0 | 0 | 1 | 2 | .333 | 0 | 0 | 5.11 |
| 6 ML YEARS | | 194 | 45 | 1 | 39 | 463.1 | 1974 | 421 | 244 | 221 | 66 | 20 | 18 | 9 | 181 | 18 | 309 | 15 | 11 | 22 | 32 | .407 | 1 | 7 | 4.29 |

## Ron Kittle

**Bats:** Right **Throws:** Right **Pos:** DH/1B **Ht:** 6' 4" **Wt:** 220 **Born:** 01/05/58 **Age:** 33

| | | BATTING | | | | | | | | | | | | | | | | | BASERUNNING | | | | PERCENTAGES | | |
|---|---|---|---|---|---|---|---|---|---|---|---|---|---|---|---|---|---|---|---|---|---|---|---|---|---|
| Year Team | Lg | G | AB | H | 2B | 3B | HR | (Hm | Rd) | TB | R | RBI | TBB | IBB | SO | HBP | SH | SF | SB | CS | SB% | GDP | Avg | OBP | SLG |
| 1982 Chicago | AL | 20 | 29 | 7 | 2 | 0 | 1 | (0 | 1) | 12 | 3 | 7 | 3 | 0 | 12 | 0 | 0 | 0 | 0 | 0 | .00 | 0 | .241 | .313 | .414 |
| 1983 Chicago | AL | 145 | 520 | 132 | 19 | 3 | 35 | (18 | 17) | 262 | 75 | 100 | 39 | 8 | 150 | 8 | 0 | 3 | 8 | 3 | .73 | 10 | .254 | .314 | .504 |
| 1984 Chicago | AL | 139 | 466 | 100 | 15 | 0 | 32 | (17 | 15) | 211 | 67 | 74 | 49 | 5 | 137 | 6 | 0 | 4 | 3 | 6 | .33 | 7 | .215 | .295 | .453 |
| 1985 Chicago | AL | 116 | 379 | 87 | 12 | 0 | 26 | (12 | 14) | 177 | 51 | 58 | 31 | 1 | 92 | 5 | 0 | 2 | 1 | 4 | .20 | 12 | .230 | .295 | .467 |
| 1986 2 ML Teams | | 116 | 376 | 82 | 13 | 0 | 21 | (6 | 15) | 158 | 42 | 60 | 35 | 1 | 110 | 3 | 0 | 8 | 4 | 1 | .80 | 10 | .218 | .284 | .420 |
| 1987 New York | AL | 59 | 159 | 44 | 5 | 0 | 12 | (7 | 5) | 85 | 21 | 28 | 10 | 1 | 36 | 1 | 0 | 3 | 0 | 1 | .00 | 4 | .277 | .318 | .535 |
| 1988 Cleveland | AL | 75 | 225 | 58 | 8 | 0 | 18 | (7 | 11) | 120 | 31 | 43 | 16 | 1 | 65 | 8 | 0 | 5 | 0 | 0 | .00 | 0 | .258 | .323 | .533 |
| 1989 Chicago | AL | 51 | 169 | 51 | 10 | 0 | 11 | (6 | 5) | 94 | 26 | 37 | 22 | 1 | 42 | 1 | 0 | 4 | 0 | 1 | .00 | 2 | .302 | .378 | .556 |
| 1990 2 ML Teams | | 105 | 338 | 78 | 16 | 0 | 18 | (8 | 10) | 148 | 33 | 46 | 26 | 2 | 91 | 4 | 0 | 1 | 0 | 0 | .00 | 6 | .231 | .293 | .438 |
| 1986 Chicago | AL | 86 | 296 | 63 | 11 | 0 | 17 | (5 | 12) | 125 | 34 | 48 | 28 | 0 | 87 | 3 | 0 | 6 | 2 | 1 | .67 | 10 | .213 | .282 | .422 |
| New York | AL | 30 | 80 | 19 | 2 | 0 | 4 | (1 | 3) | 33 | 8 | 12 | 7 | 1 | 23 | 0 | 0 | 2 | 2 | 0 | 1.00 | 0 | .238 | .292 | .413 |
| 1990 Chicago | AL | 83 | 277 | 68 | 14 | 0 | 16 | (7 | 9) | 130 | 29 | 43 | 24 | 2 | 77 | 3 | 0 | 1 | 0 | 0 | .00 | 3 | .245 | .311 | .469 |
| Baltimore | AL | 22 | 61 | 10 | 2 | 0 | 2 | (1 | 1) | 18 | 4 | 3 | 2 | 0 | 14 | 1 | 0 | 0 | 0 | 0 | .00 | 3 | .164 | .203 | .295 |
| 9 ML YEARS | | 826 | 2661 | 639 | 100 | 3 | 174 | (81 | 93) | 1267 | 349 | 453 | 231 | 20 | 735 | 36 | 0 | 30 | 16 | 16 | .50 | 51 | .240 | .306 | .476 |

## Joe Klink

**Pitches:** Left **Bats:** Left **Pos:** RP **Ht:** 5'11" **Wt:** 175 **Born:** 02/03/62 **Age:** 29

| | | HOW MUCH HE PITCHED | | | | | | WHAT HE GAVE UP | | | | | | | | | | | | THE RESULTS | | | | | |
|---|---|---|---|---|---|---|---|---|---|---|---|---|---|---|---|---|---|---|---|---|---|---|---|---|---|
| Year Team | Lg | G | GS | CG | GF | IP | BFP | H | R | ER | HR | SH | SF | HB | TBB | IBB | SO | WP | Bk | W | L | Pct. | ShO | Sv | ERA |
| 1987 Minnesota | AL | 12 | 0 | 0 | 5 | 23 | 116 | 37 | 18 | 17 | 4 | 1 | 1 | 0 | 11 | 0 | 17 | 1 | 0 | 0 | 1 | .000 | 0 | 0 | 6.65 |
| 1990 Oakland | AL | 40 | 0 | 0 | 19 | 39.2 | 165 | 34 | 9 | 9 | 1 | 1 | 0 | 0 | 18 | 0 | 19 | 3 | 1 | 0 | 0 | .000 | 0 | 1 | 2.04 |
| 2 ML YEARS | | 52 | 0 | 0 | 24 | 62.2 | 281 | 71 | 27 | 26 | 5 | 2 | 1 | 0 | 29 | 0 | 36 | 4 | 1 | 0 | 1 | .000 | 0 | 1 | 3.73 |

## Brent Knackert

**Pitches:** Right **Bats:** Right **Pos:** RP **Ht:** 6' 4" **Wt:** 185 **Born:** 08/01/69 **Age:** 21

| | | HOW MUCH HE PITCHED | | | | | | WHAT HE GAVE UP | | | | | | | | | | | | THE RESULTS | | | | | |
|---|---|---|---|---|---|---|---|---|---|---|---|---|---|---|---|---|---|---|---|---|---|---|---|---|---|
| Year Team | Lg | G | GS | CG | GF | IP | BFP | H | R | ER | HR | SH | SF | HB | TBB | IBB | SO | WP | Bk | W | L | Pct. | ShO | Sv | ERA |
| 1987 White Sox | R | 12 | 11 | 1 | 0 | 72.2 | 288 | 55 | 28 | 23 | 2 | 0 | 5 | 4 | 15 | 0 | 60 | 4 | 2 | 6 | 2 | .750 | 1 | 0 | 2.85 |
| 1988 Tampa | A | 23 | 23 | 4 | 0 | 142 | 591 | 132 | 58 | 50 | 4 | 2 | 5 | 4 | 46 | 3 | 78 | 11 | 5 | 10 | 8 | .556 | 0 | 0 | 3.17 |
| 1989 Sarasota | A | 35 | 12 | 2 | 22 | 98 | 407 | 85 | 41 | 32 | 3 | 0 | 2 | 4 | 35 | 0 | 80 | 4 | 2 | 8 | 5 | .615 | 0 | 12 | 2.94 |
| 1990 Seattle | AL | 24 | 2 | 0 | 6 | 37.1 | 186 | 50 | 28 | 27 | 5 | 1 | 2 | 2 | 21 | 2 | 28 | 3 | 0 | 1 | 1 | .500 | 0 | 0 | 6.51 |

## Bob Knepper

**Pitches:** Left **Bats:** Left **Pos:** SP/RP **Ht:** 6' 2" **Wt:** 210 **Born:** 05/25/54 **Age:** 37

| | | | HOW MUCH HE PITCHED | | | | | | WHAT HE GAVE UP | | | | | | | | | | | | THE RESULTS | | | | | |
|---|---|---|---|---|---|---|---|---|---|---|---|---|---|---|---|---|---|---|---|---|---|---|---|---|---|---|
| Year | Team | Lg | G | GS | CG | GF | IP | BFP | H | R | ER | HR | SH | SF | HB | TBB | IBB | SO | WP | Bk | W | L | Pct. | ShO | Sv | ERA |
| 1976 | San Francisco | NL | 4 | 4 | 0 | 0 | 25 | 104 | 26 | 9 | 9 | 0 | 3 | 0 | 0 | 7 | 1 | 11 | 2 | 0 | 1 | 2 | .333 | 0 | 0 | 3.24 |
| 1977 | San Francisco | NL | 27 | 27 | 6 | 0 | 166 | 710 | 151 | 73 | 62 | 14 | 7 | 4 | 3 | 72 | 2 | 100 | 6 | 0 | 11 | 9 | .550 | 2 | 0 | 3.36 |
| 1978 | San Francisco | NL | 36 | 35 | 16 | 1 | 260 | 1062 | 218 | 85 | 76 | 10 | 11 | 9 | 4 | 85 | 11 | 147 | 6 | 0 | 17 | 11 | .607 | 6 | 0 | 2.63 |
| 1979 | San Francisco | NL | 34 | 34 | 6 | 0 | 207 | 926 | 241 | 117 | 107 | 30 | 10 | 3 | 3 | 77 | 8 | 123 | 6 | 1 | 9 | 12 | .429 | 2 | 0 | 4.65 |
| 1980 | San Francisco | NL | 35 | 33 | 8 | 1 | 215 | 943 | 242 | 114 | 98 | 15 | 9 | 5 | 8 | 61 | 10 | 103 | 2 | 1 | 9 | 16 | .360 | 1 | 0 | 4.10 |
| 1981 | Houston | NL | 22 | 22 | 6 | 0 | 157 | 617 | 128 | 41 | 38 | 5 | 6 | 3 | 4 | 38 | 1 | 75 | 0 | 0 | 9 | 5 | .643 | 5 | 0 | 2.18 |
| 1982 | Houston | NL | 33 | 29 | 4 | 1 | 180 | 770 | 193 | 100 | 89 | 14 | 6 | 6 | 3 | 60 | 4 | 108 | 8 | 0 | 5 | 15 | .250 | 0 | 1 | 4.45 |
| 1983 | Houston | NL | 35 | 29 | 4 | 2 | 203 | 867 | 202 | 93 | 72 | 12 | 9 | 8 | 4 | 71 | 3 | 125 | 3 | 2 | 6 | 13 | .316 | 3 | 0 | 3.19 |
| 1984 | Houston | NL | 35 | 34 | 11 | 0 | 233.2 | 954 | 223 | 93 | 83 | 26 | 7 | 4 | 1 | 55 | 5 | 140 | 2 | 0 | 15 | 10 | .600 | 3 | 0 | 3.20 |
| 1985 | Houston | NL | 37 | 37 | 4 | 0 | 241 | 1016 | 253 | 119 | 95 | 21 | 15 | 9 | 3 | 54 | 5 | 131 | 4 | 0 | 15 | 13 | .536 | 0 | 0 | 3.55 |
| 1986 | Houston | NL | 40 | 38 | 8 | 1 | 258 | 1053 | 232 | 100 | 90 | 19 | 22 | 5 | 4 | 62 | 13 | 143 | 5 | 0 | 17 | 12 | .586 | 5 | 0 | 3.14 |
| 1987 | Houston | NL | 33 | 31 | 1 | 1 | 177.2 | 792 | 226 | 118 | 104 | 26 | 7 | 4 | 4 | 54 | 3 | 76 | 4 | 0 | 8 | 17 | .320 | 0 | 0 | 5.27 |
| 1988 | Houston | NL | 27 | 27 | 3 | 0 | 175 | 726 | 156 | 70 | 61 | 13 | 10 | 5 | 2 | 67 | 2 | 103 | 6 | 2 | 14 | 5 | .737 | 2 | 0 | 3.14 |
| 1989 | 2 ML Teams | | 35 | 26 | 1 | 2 | 165 | 746 | 190 | 98 | 94 | 16 | 12 | 6 | 3 | 75 | 6 | 64 | 5 | 4 | 7 | 12 | .368 | 1 | 0 | 5.13 |
| 1990 | San Francisco | NL | 12 | 7 | 0 | 1 | 44.1 | 202 | 56 | 28 | 28 | 7 | 0 | 2 | 1 | 19 | 4 | 24 | 1 | 3 | 3 | 3 | .500 | 0 | 0 | 5.68 |
| 1989 | Houston | NL | 22 | 20 | 0 | 0 | 113 | 520 | 135 | 78 | 74 | 12 | 9 | 3 | 2 | 60 | 4 | 45 | 4 | 3 | 4 | 10 | .286 | 0 | 0 | 5.89 |
| | San Francisco | NL | 13 | 6 | 1 | 2 | 52 | 226 | 55 | 20 | 20 | 4 | 3 | 3 | 1 | 15 | 2 | 19 | 1 | 1 | 3 | 2 | .600 | 1 | 0 | 3.46 |
| | 15 ML YEARS | | 445 | 413 | 78 | 10 | 2707.2 | 11488 | 2737 | 1258 | 1106 | 228 | 134 | 73 | 47 | 857 | 78 | 1473 | 60 | 13 | 146 | 155 | .485 | 30 | 1 | 3.68 |

## Mark Knudson

**Pitches:** Right **Bats:** Right **Pos:** SP **Ht:** 6' 5" **Wt:** 215 **Born:** 10/28/60 **Age:** 30

| | | | HOW MUCH HE PITCHED | | | | | | WHAT HE GAVE UP | | | | | | | | | | | | THE RESULTS | | | | | |
|---|---|---|---|---|---|---|---|---|---|---|---|---|---|---|---|---|---|---|---|---|---|---|---|---|---|---|
| Year | Team | Lg | G | GS | CG | GF | IP | BFP | H | R | ER | HR | SH | SF | HB | TBB | IBB | SO | WP | Bk | W | L | Pct. | ShO | Sv | ERA |
| 1985 | Houston | NL | 2 | 2 | 0 | 0 | 11 | 53 | 21 | 11 | 11 | 0 | 1 | 0 | 0 | 3 | 0 | 4 | 0 | 0 | 0 | 2 | .000 | 0 | 0 | 9.00 |
| 1986 | 2 ML Teams | | 13 | 8 | 0 | 2 | 60.1 | 273 | 70 | 38 | 35 | 12 | 3 | 0 | 1 | 20 | 6 | 29 | 2 | 0 | 1 | 6 | .143 | 0 | 0 | 5.22 |
| 1987 | Milwaukee | AL | 15 | 8 | 1 | 3 | 62 | 288 | 88 | 46 | 37 | 7 | 3 | 5 | 0 | 14 | 1 | 26 | 1 | 0 | 4 | 4 | .500 | 0 | 0 | 5.37 |
| 1988 | Milwaukee | AL | 5 | 0 | 0 | 3 | 16 | 63 | 17 | 3 | 2 | 1 | 0 | 0 | 0 | 2 | 0 | 7 | 1 | 0 | 0 | 0 | .000 | 0 | 0 | 1.13 |
| 1989 | Milwaukee | AL | 40 | 7 | 1 | 16 | 123.2 | 499 | 110 | 50 | 46 | 15 | 2 | 1 | 3 | 29 | 2 | 47 | 2 | 0 | 8 | 5 | .615 | 0 | 0 | 3.35 |
| 1990 | Milwaukee | AL | 30 | 27 | 4 | 0 | 168.1 | 719 | 187 | 84 | 77 | 14 | 3 | 9 | 3 | 40 | 1 | 56 | 6 | 0 | 10 | 9 | .526 | 2 | 0 | 4.12 |
| 1986 | Houston | NL | 9 | 7 | 0 | 1 | 42.2 | 191 | 48 | 23 | 20 | 5 | 3 | 0 | 1 | 15 | 5 | 20 | 1 | 0 | 1 | 5 | .167 | 0 | 0 | 4.22 |
| | Milwaukee | AL | 4 | 1 | 0 | 1 | 17.2 | 82 | 22 | 15 | 15 | 7 | 0 | 0 | 0 | 5 | 1 | 9 | 1 | 0 | 0 | 1 | .000 | 0 | 0 | 7.64 |
| | 6 ML YEARS | | 105 | 52 | 6 | 24 | 441.1 | 1895 | 493 | 232 | 208 | 49 | 12 | 15 | 7 | 108 | 10 | 169 | 12 | 0 | 23 | 26 | .469 | 2 | 0 | 4.24 |

## Brad Komminsk

**Bats:** Right **Throws:** Right **Pos:** RF/CF **Ht:** 6' 2" **Wt:** 205 **Born:** 04/04/61 **Age:** 30

| | | | BATTING | | | | | | | | | | | | | | | | | BASERUNNING | | | | PERCENTAGES | | |
|---|---|---|---|---|---|---|---|---|---|---|---|---|---|---|---|---|---|---|---|---|---|---|---|---|---|---|
| Year | Team | Lg | G | AB | H | 2B | 3B | HR | (Hm | Rd) | TB | R | RBI | TBB | IBB | SO | HBP | SH | SF | SB | CS | SB% | GDP | Avg | OBP | SLG |
| 1983 | Atlanta | NL | 19 | 36 | 8 | 2 | 0 | 0 | (0 | 0) | 10 | 2 | 4 | 5 | 0 | 7 | 0 | 0 | 0 | 0 | 0 | .00 | 1 | .222 | .317 | .278 |
| 1984 | Atlanta | NL | 90 | 301 | 61 | 10 | 0 | 8 | (3 | 5) | 95 | 37 | 36 | 29 | 0 | 77 | 2 | 1 | 1 | 18 | 8 | .69 | 5 | .203 | .276 | .316 |
| 1985 | Atlanta | NL | 106 | 300 | 68 | 12 | 3 | 4 | (1 | 3) | 98 | 52 | 21 | 38 | 1 | 71 | 1 | 2 | 2 | 10 | 8 | .56 | 4 | .227 | .314 | .327 |
| 1986 | Atlanta | NL | 5 | 5 | 2 | 0 | 0 | 0 | (0 | 0) | 2 | 1 | 1 | 0 | 0 | 1 | 0 | 0 | 0 | 0 | 1 | .00 | 0 | .400 | .400 | .400 |
| 1987 | Milwaukee | AL | 7 | 15 | 1 | 0 | 0 | 0 | (0 | 0) | 1 | 0 | 0 | 1 | 0 | 7 | 0 | 1 | 0 | 1 | 0 | 1.00 | 0 | .067 | .125 | .067 |
| 1989 | Cleveland | AL | 71 | 198 | 47 | 8 | 2 | 8 | (6 | 2) | 83 | 27 | 33 | 24 | 0 | 55 | 1 | 1 | 3 | 8 | 2 | .80 | 4 | .237 | .319 | .419 |
| 1990 | 2 ML Teams | | 54 | 106 | 25 | 4 | 0 | 3 | (3 | 0) | 38 | 20 | 8 | 15 | 1 | 31 | 2 | 2 | 0 | 1 | 1 | .50 | 2 | .236 | .341 | .358 |
| 1990 | San Francisco | NL | 8 | 5 | 1 | 0 | 0 | 0 | (0 | 0) | 1 | 2 | 0 | 1 | 0 | 2 | 0 | 0 | 0 | 0 | 0 | .00 | 0 | .200 | .333 | .200 |
| | Baltimore | AL | 46 | 101 | 24 | 4 | 0 | 3 | (3 | 0) | 37 | 18 | 8 | 14 | 1 | 29 | 2 | 2 | 0 | 1 | 1 | .50 | 2 | .238 | .342 | .366 |
| | 7 ML YEARS | | 352 | 961 | 212 | 36 | 5 | 23 | (13 | 10) | 327 | 139 | 103 | 112 | 2 | 249 | 6 | 7 | 6 | 38 | 20 | .66 | 16 | .221 | .304 | .340 |

## Joe Kraemer

**Pitches:** Left **Bats:** Left **Pos:** RP **Ht:** 6' 2" **Wt:** 185 **Born:** 09/10/64 **Age:** 26

| | | | HOW MUCH HE PITCHED | | | | | | WHAT HE GAVE UP | | | | | | | | | | | | THE RESULTS | | | | | |
|---|---|---|---|---|---|---|---|---|---|---|---|---|---|---|---|---|---|---|---|---|---|---|---|---|---|---|
| Year | Team | Lg | G | GS | CG | GF | IP | BFP | H | R | ER | HR | SH | SF | HB | TBB | IBB | SO | WP | Bk | W | L | Pct. | ShO | Sv | ERA |
| 1985 | Wytheville | R | 22 | 3 | 1 | 12 | 45.2 | 207 | 33 | 21 | 17 | 3 | 0 | 1 | 1 | 36 | 4 | 52 | 5 | 2 | 4 | 2 | .667 | 0 | 4 | 3.35 |
| 1986 | Peoria | A | 45 | 0 | 0 | 34 | 66.1 | 268 | 50 | 17 | 8 | 1 | 2 | 1 | 2 | 19 | 2 | 78 | 6 | 0 | 6 | 3 | .667 | 0 | 14 | 1.09 |
| 1987 | Iowa | AAA | 5 | 0 | 0 | 1 | 2.2 | 21 | 8 | 8 | 8 | 4 | 0 | 0 | 0 | 5 | 1 | 2 | 0 | 0 | 1 | 0 | 1.000 | 0 | 0 | 27.00 |
| | Winston-Sal | A | 41 | 0 | 0 | 27 | 52.2 | 242 | 49 | 20 | 16 | 4 | 0 | 3 | 2 | 41 | 2 | 43 | 3 | 1 | 3 | 2 | .600 | 0 | 13 | 2.73 |
| 1988 | Iowa | AAA | 20 | 1 | 0 | 5 | 26 | 113 | 19 | 14 | 13 | 2 | 1 | 1 | 1 | 17 | 3 | 26 | 1 | 2 | 3 | 3 | .500 | 0 | 1 | 4.50 |
| | Pittsfield | AA | 15 | 15 | 2 | 0 | 95 | 406 | 84 | 37 | 29 | 3 | 8 | 6 | 3 | 43 | 0 | 47 | 8 | 1 | 5 | 5 | .500 | 1 | 0 | 2.75 |
| 1989 | Iowa | AAA | 27 | 27 | 7 | 0 | 181.2 | 756 | 180 | 81 | 70 | 7 | 6 | 5 | 4 | 50 | 0 | 113 | 5 | 4 | 8 | 10 | .444 | 3 | 0 | 3.47 |
| 1990 | Iowa | AAA | 20 | 20 | 3 | 0 | 122 | 506 | 113 | 56 | 51 | 11 | 8 | 1 | 3 | 40 | 4 | 84 | 4 | 1 | 7 | 6 | .538 | 0 | 0 | 3.76 |

| 1989 Chicago | NL | 1 | 1 | 0 | 0 | 3.2 | 21 | 7 | 6 | 2 | 0 | 0 | 0 | 0 | 2 | 1 | 5 | 0 | 0 | 0 | 1 | .000 | 0 | 0 | 4.91 |
|---|---|---|---|---|---|---|---|---|---|---|---|---|---|---|---|---|---|---|---|---|---|---|---|---|---|
| 1990 Chicago | NL | 18 | 0 | 0 | 8 | 25 | 119 | 31 | 25 | 20 | 2 | 1 | 2 | 2 | 14 | 2 | 16 | 2 | 1 | 0 | 0 | .000 | 0 | 0 | 7.20 |
| 2 ML YEARS | | 19 | 1 | 0 | 8 | 28.2 | 140 | 38 | 31 | 22 | 2 | 1 | 2 | 2 | 16 | 3 | 21 | 2 | 1 | 0 | 1 | .000 | 0 | 0 | 6.91 |

## Randy Kramer

**Pitches:** Right **Bats:** Right **Pos:** RP/SP **Ht:** 6' 2" **Wt:** 180 **Born:** 09/20/60 **Age:** 30

| | | HOW MUCH HE PITCHED | | | | | | WHAT HE GAVE UP | | | | | | | | | | | | THE RESULTS | | | | | |
|---|---|---|---|---|---|---|---|---|---|---|---|---|---|---|---|---|---|---|---|---|---|---|---|---|---|
| Year Team | Lg | G | GS | CG | GF | IP | BFP | H | R | ER | HR | SH | SF | HB | TBB | IBB | SO | WP | Bk | W | L | Pct. | ShO | Sv | ERA |
| 1988 Pittsburgh | NL | 5 | 1 | 0 | 1 | 10 | 42 | 12 | 6 | 6 | 1 | 1 | 1 | 1 | 1 | 0 | 7 | 1 | 0 | 1 | 2 | .333 | 0 | 0 | 5.40 |
| 1989 Pittsburgh | NL | 35 | 15 | 1 | 7 | 111.1 | 482 | 90 | 53 | 49 | 10 | 9 | 4 | 7 | 61 | 4 | 52 | 1 | 0 | 5 | 9 | .357 | 1 | 2 | 3.96 |
| 1990 2 ML Teams | | 22 | 4 | 0 | 6 | 46 | 207 | 47 | 25 | 23 | 6 | 5 | 0 | 3 | 21 | 6 | 27 | 0 | 0 | 0 | 3 | .000 | 0 | 0 | 4.50 |
| 1990 Pittsburgh | NL | 12 | 2 | 0 | 2 | 25.2 | 112 | 27 | 15 | 14 | 3 | 2 | 0 | 2 | 9 | 4 | 15 | 0 | 0 | 0 | 1 | .000 | 0 | 0 | 4.91 |
| Chicago | NL | 10 | 2 | 0 | 4 | 20.1 | 95 | 20 | 10 | 9 | 3 | 3 | 0 | 1 | 12 | 2 | 12 | 0 | 0 | 0 | 2 | .000 | 0 | 0 | 3.98 |
| 3 ML YEARS | | 62 | 20 | 1 | 14 | 167.1 | 731 | 149 | 84 | 78 | 17 | 15 | 5 | 11 | 83 | 10 | 86 | 2 | 0 | 6 | 14 | .300 | 1 | 2 | 4.20 |

## Jimmy Kremers

**Bats:** Left **Throws:** Right **Pos:** C **Ht:** 6' 3" **Wt:** 205 **Born:** 10/08/65 **Age:** 25

| | | BATTING | | | | | | | | | | | | | | | | | | BASERUNNING | | | | PERCENTAGES | | |
|---|---|---|---|---|---|---|---|---|---|---|---|---|---|---|---|---|---|---|---|---|---|---|---|---|---|---|
| Year Team | Lg | G | AB | H | 2B | 3B | HR | (Hm | Rd) | TB | R | RBI | TBB | IBB | SO | HBP | SH | SF | SB | CS | SB% | GDP | Avg | OBP | SLG |
| 1988 Sumter | A | 72 | 256 | 68 | 12 | 3 | 5 | -- | -- | 101 | 30 | 42 | 39 | 0 | 53 | 2 | 0 | 4 | 1 | 1 | .50 | 3 | .266 | .362 | .395 |
| 1989 Greenville | AA | 121 | 388 | 91 | 19 | 1 | 16 | -- | -- | 160 | 41 | 58 | 34 | 5 | 95 | 0 | 2 | 2 | 5 | 5 | .50 | 3 | .235 | .295 | .412 |
| 1990 Richmond | AAA | 63 | 190 | 44 | 8 | 0 | 6 | -- | -- | 70 | 25 | 24 | 35 | 1 | 47 | 1 | 0 | 1 | 1 | 0 | 1.00 | 4 | .232 | .352 | .368 |
| 1990 Atlanta | NL | 29 | 73 | 8 | 1 | 1 | 1 | (1 | 0) | 14 | 7 | 2 | 6 | 1 | 27 | 0 | 0 | 0 | 0 | 0 | .00 | 0 | .110 | .177 | .192 |

## Chad Kreuter

**Bats:** Right **Throws:** Right **Pos:** C **Ht:** 6' 2" **Wt:** 190 **Born:** 08/26/64 **Age:** 26

| | | BATTING | | | | | | | | | | | | | | | | | | BASERUNNING | | | | PERCENTAGES | | |
|---|---|---|---|---|---|---|---|---|---|---|---|---|---|---|---|---|---|---|---|---|---|---|---|---|---|---|
| Year Team | Lg | G | AB | H | 2B | 3B | HR | (Hm | Rd) | TB | R | RBI | TBB | IBB | SO | HBP | SH | SF | SB | CS | SB% | GDP | Avg | OBP | SLG |
| 1988 Texas | AL | 16 | 51 | 14 | 2 | 1 | 1 | (0 | 1) | 21 | 3 | 5 | 7 | 0 | 13 | 0 | 0 | 0 | 0 | 0 | .00 | 1 | .275 | .362 | .412 |
| 1989 Texas | AL | 87 | 158 | 24 | 3 | 0 | 5 | (2 | 3) | 42 | 16 | 9 | 27 | 0 | 40 | 0 | 6 | 1 | 0 | 1 | .00 | 4 | .152 | .274 | .266 |
| 1990 Texas | AL | 22 | 22 | 1 | 1 | 0 | 0 | (0 | 0) | 2 | 2 | 2 | 8 | 0 | 9 | 0 | 1 | 1 | 0 | 0 | .00 | 0 | .045 | .290 | .091 |
| 3 ML YEARS | | 125 | 231 | 39 | 6 | 1 | 6 | (2 | 4) | 65 | 21 | 16 | 42 | 0 | 62 | 0 | 7 | 2 | 0 | 1 | .00 | 5 | .169 | .295 | .281 |

## Bill Krueger

**Pitches:** Left **Bats:** Left **Pos:** SP/RP **Ht:** 6' 5" **Wt:** 210 **Born:** 04/24/58 **Age:** 33

| | | HOW MUCH HE PITCHED | | | | | | WHAT HE GAVE UP | | | | | | | | | | | | THE RESULTS | | | | | |
|---|---|---|---|---|---|---|---|---|---|---|---|---|---|---|---|---|---|---|---|---|---|---|---|---|---|
| Year Team | Lg | G | GS | CG | GF | IP | BFP | H | R | ER | HR | SH | SF | HB | TBB | IBB | SO | WP | Bk | W | L | Pct. | ShO | Sv | ERA |
| 1983 Oakland | AL | 17 | 16 | 2 | 0 | 109.2 | 473 | 104 | 54 | 44 | 7 | 0 | 5 | 2 | 53 | 1 | 58 | 1 | 1 | 7 | 6 | .538 | 0 | 0 | 3.61 |
| 1984 Oakland | AL | 26 | 24 | 1 | 0 | 142 | 647 | 156 | 95 | 75 | 9 | 4 | 8 | 2 | 85 | 2 | 61 | 5 | 1 | 10 | 10 | .500 | 0 | 0 | 4.75 |
| 1985 Oakland | AL | 32 | 23 | 2 | 4 | 151.1 | 674 | 165 | 95 | 76 | 13 | 1 | 5 | 2 | 69 | 1 | 56 | 6 | 3 | 9 | 10 | .474 | 0 | 0 | 4.52 |
| 1986 Oakland | AL | 11 | 3 | 0 | 4 | 34.1 | 149 | 40 | 25 | 23 | 4 | 1 | 2 | 0 | 13 | 0 | 10 | 3 | 1 | 1 | 2 | .333 | 0 | 1 | 6.03 |
| 1987 2 ML Teams | | 11 | 0 | 0 | 1 | 8 | 46 | 12 | 9 | 6 | 0 | 0 | 0 | 0 | 9 | 3 | 4 | 0 | 1 | 0 | 3 | .000 | 0 | 0 | 6.75 |
| 1988 Los Angeles | NL | 1 | 1 | 0 | 0 | 2.1 | 14 | 4 | 3 | 3 | 0 | 0 | 0 | 1 | 2 | 1 | 1 | 0 | 0 | 0 | 0 | .000 | 0 | 0 | 11.57 |
| 1989 Milwaukee | AL | 34 | 5 | 0 | 8 | 93.2 | 403 | 96 | 43 | 40 | 9 | 5 | 1 | 0 | 33 | 3 | 72 | 10 | 1 | 3 | 2 | .600 | 0 | 3 | 3.84 |
| 1990 Milwaukee | AL | 30 | 17 | 0 | 4 | 129 | 566 | 137 | 70 | 57 | 10 | 3 | 10 | 3 | 54 | 6 | 64 | 8 | 0 | 6 | 8 | .429 | 0 | 0 | 3.98 |
| 1987 Oakland | AL | 9 | 0 | 0 | 1 | 5.2 | 33 | 9 | 7 | 6 | 0 | 0 | 0 | 0 | 8 | 3 | 2 | 0 | 1 | 0 | 3 | .000 | 0 | 0 | 9.53 |
| Los Angeles | NL | 2 | 0 | 0 | 0 | 2.1 | 13 | 3 | 2 | 0 | 0 | 0 | 0 | 0 | 1 | 0 | 2 | 0 | 0 | 0 | 0 | .000 | 0 | 0 | 0.00 |
| 8 ML YEARS | | 162 | 89 | 5 | 21 | 670.1 | 2972 | 714 | 394 | 324 | 52 | 14 | 31 | 10 | 318 | 17 | 326 | 33 | 8 | 36 | 41 | .468 | 0 | 4 | 4.35 |

## John Kruk

**Bats:** Left **Throws:** Left **Pos:** LF/1B/RF **Ht:** 5'10" **Wt:** 195 **Born:** 02/09/61 **Age:** 30

| | | BATTING | | | | | | | | | | | | | | | | | | BASERUNNING | | | | PERCENTAGES | | |
|---|---|---|---|---|---|---|---|---|---|---|---|---|---|---|---|---|---|---|---|---|---|---|---|---|---|---|
| Year Team | Lg | G | AB | H | 2B | 3B | HR | (Hm | Rd) | TB | R | RBI | TBB | IBB | SO | HBP | SH | SF | SB | CS | SB% | GDP | Avg | OBP | SLG |
| 1986 San Diego | NL | 122 | 278 | 86 | 16 | 2 | 4 | (1 | 3) | 118 | 33 | 38 | 45 | 0 | 58 | 0 | 2 | 2 | 2 | 4 | .33 | 11 | .309 | .403 | .424 |
| 1987 San Diego | NL | 138 | 447 | 140 | 14 | 2 | 20 | (8 | 12) | 218 | 72 | 91 | 73 | 15 | 93 | 0 | 3 | 4 | 18 | 10 | .64 | 6 | .313 | .406 | .488 |
| 1988 San Diego | NL | 120 | 378 | 91 | 17 | 1 | 9 | (8 | 1) | 137 | 54 | 44 | 80 | 12 | 68 | 0 | 3 | 5 | 5 | 3 | .63 | 7 | .241 | .369 | .362 |
| 1989 2 ML Teams | | 112 | 357 | 107 | 13 | 6 | 8 | (6 | 2) | 156 | 53 | 44 | 44 | 2 | 53 | 0 | 2 | 3 | 3 | 0 | 1.00 | 10 | .300 | .374 | .437 |
| 1990 Philadelphia | NL | 142 | 443 | 129 | 25 | 8 | 7 | (2 | 5) | 191 | 52 | 67 | 69 | 16 | 70 | 0 | 2 | 1 | 10 | 5 | .67 | 11 | .291 | .386 | .431 |
| 1989 San Diego | NL | 31 | 76 | 14 | 0 | 0 | 3 | (2 | 1) | 23 | 7 | 6 | 17 | 0 | 14 | 0 | 1 | 0 | 0 | 0 | .00 | 5 | .184 | .333 | .303 |
| Philadelphia | NL | 81 | 281 | 93 | 13 | 6 | 5 | (4 | 1) | 133 | 46 | 38 | 27 | 2 | 39 | 0 | 1 | 3 | 3 | 0 | 1.00 | 5 | .331 | .386 | .473 |
| 5 ML YEARS | | 634 | 1903 | 553 | 85 | 19 | 48 | (25 | 23) | 820 | 264 | 284 | 311 | 45 | 342 | 0 | 12 | 15 | 38 | 22 | .63 | 45 | .291 | .388 | .431 |

## Jeff Kunkel

**Bats:** Right **Throws:** Right **Pos:** SS/3B **Ht:** 6' 2" **Wt:** 190 **Born:** 03/25/62 **Age:** 29

| | | BATTING | | | | | | | | | | | | | | | | | | BASERUNNING | | | | PERCENTAGES | | |
|---|---|---|---|---|---|---|---|---|---|---|---|---|---|---|---|---|---|---|---|---|---|---|---|---|---|---|
| Year Team | Lg | G | AB | H | 2B | 3B | HR | (Hm | Rd) | TB | R | RBI | TBB | IBB | SO | HBP | SH | SF | SB | CS | SB% | GDP | Avg | OBP | SLG |
| 1984 Texas | AL | 50 | 142 | 29 | 2 | 3 | 3 | (1 | 2) | 46 | 13 | 7 | 2 | 0 | 35 | 1 | 3 | 2 | 4 | 3 | .57 | 2 | .204 | .218 | .324 |

| | | | | | | | | | | | | | | | | | | | | | | | | | | |
|---|---|---|---|---|---|---|---|---|---|---|---|---|---|---|---|---|---|---|---|---|---|---|---|---|---|---|
| 1985 Texas | AL | 2 | 4 | 1 | 0 | 0 | 0 | (0 | 0) | 1 | 1 | 0 | 0 | 0 | 3 | 0 | 0 | 0 | 0 | 0 | .00 | 0 | .250 | .250 | .250 |
| 1986 Texas | AL | 8 | 13 | 3 | 0 | 0 | 1 | (1 | 0) | 6 | 3 | 2 | 0 | 0 | 2 | 0 | 0 | 0 | 0 | 0 | .00 | 0 | .231 | .231 | .462 |
| 1987 Texas | AL | 15 | 32 | 7 | 0 | 0 | 1 | (0 | 1) | 10 | 1 | 2 | 0 | 0 | 10 | 1 | 1 | 0 | 0 | 1 | .00 | 0 | .219 | .242 | .313 |
| 1988 Texas | AL | 55 | 154 | 35 | 8 | 3 | 2 | (2 | 0) | 55 | 14 | 15 | 4 | 1 | 35 | 1 | 1 | 1 | 0 | 1 | .00 | 5 | .227 | .250 | .357 |
| 1989 Texas | AL | 108 | 293 | 79 | 21 | 2 | 8 | (8 | 0) | 128 | 39 | 29 | 20 | 0 | 75 | 3 | 10 | 0 | 3 | 2 | .60 | 6 | .270 | .323 | .437 |
| 1990 Texas | AL | 99 | 200 | 34 | 11 | 1 | 3 | (1 | 2) | 56 | 17 | 17 | 11 | 0 | 66 | 2 | 5 | 0 | 2 | 1 | .67 | 7 | .170 | .221 | .280 |
| 7 ML YEARS | | 337 | 838 | 188 | 42 | 9 | 18 | (13 | 5) | 302 | 88 | 72 | 37 | 1 | 226 | 8 | 20 | 3 | 9 | 8 | .53 | 20 | .224 | .263 | .360 |

## Randy Kutcher

**Bats:** Right **Throws:** Right **Pos:** RF **Ht:** 5'11" **Wt:** 175 **Born:** 04/20/60 **Age:** 31

| BATTING | | | | | | | | | | | | | | | | | | | BASERUNNING | | | | PERCENTAGES | | |
|---|---|---|---|---|---|---|---|---|---|---|---|---|---|---|---|---|---|---|---|---|---|---|---|---|---|
| Year Team | Lg | G | AB | H | 2B | 3B | HR | (Hm | Rd) | TB | R | RBI | TBB | IBB | SO | HBP | SH | SF | SB | CS | SB% | GDP | Avg | OBP | SLG |
| 1986 San Francisco | NL | 71 | 186 | 44 | 9 | 1 | 7 | (5 | 2) | 76 | 28 | 16 | 11 | 0 | 41 | 0 | 6 | 0 | 6 | 5 | .55 | 3 | .237 | .279 | .409 |
| 1987 San Francisco | NL | 14 | 16 | 3 | 1 | 1 | 0 | (0 | 0) | 6 | 7 | 1 | 1 | 0 | 5 | 0 | 0 | 0 | 1 | 0 | 1.00 | 0 | .188 | .235 | .375 |
| 1988 Boston | AL | 19 | 12 | 2 | 1 | 0 | 0 | (0 | 0) | 3 | 2 | 0 | 0 | 0 | 2 | 0 | 0 | 0 | 0 | 1 | .00 | 0 | .167 | .167 | .250 |
| 1989 Boston | AL | 77 | 160 | 36 | 10 | 3 | 2 | (1 | 1) | 58 | 28 | 18 | 11 | 0 | 46 | 0 | 3 | 1 | 3 | 0 | 1.00 | 5 | .225 | .273 | .363 |
| 1990 Boston | AL | 63 | 74 | 17 | 4 | 1 | 1 | (0 | 1) | 26 | 18 | 5 | 13 | 0 | 18 | 0 | 3 | 0 | 3 | 3 | .50 | 2 | .230 | .345 | .351 |
| 5 ML YEARS | | 244 | 448 | 102 | 25 | 6 | 10 | (6 | 4) | 169 | 83 | 40 | 36 | 0 | 112 | 0 | 12 | 1 | 13 | 9 | .59 | 10 | .228 | .285 | .377 |

## Jerry Kutzler

**Pitches:** Right **Bats:** Left **Pos:** SP **Ht:** 6' 1" **Wt:** 175 **Born:** 03/25/65 **Age:** 26

| HOW MUCH HE PITCHED | | | | | | | | WHAT HE GAVE UP | | | | | | | | | | | | THE RESULTS | | | | | |
|---|---|---|---|---|---|---|---|---|---|---|---|---|---|---|---|---|---|---|---|---|---|---|---|---|---|
| Year Team | Lg | G | GS | CG | GF | IP | BFP | H | R | ER | HR | SH | SF | HB | TBB | IBB | SO | WP | Bk | W | L | Pct. | ShO | Sv | ERA |
| 1987 White Sox | R | 4 | 3 | 0 | 0 | 20 | 83 | 14 | 13 | 11 | 1 | 1 | 1 | 2 | 7 | 0 | 16 | 1 | 0 | 1 | 1 | .500 | 0 | 0 | 4.95 |
| Peninsula | A | 10 | 9 | 2 | 1 | 63.2 | 268 | 53 | 34 | 29 | 1 | 2 | 4 | 3 | 24 | 1 | 30 | 2 | 0 | 5 | 2 | .714 | 1 | 0 | 4.10 |
| 1988 Tampa | A | 26 | 26 | 12 | 0 | 184 | 733 | 154 | 73 | 57 | 10 | 3 | 2 | 6 | 39 | 1 | 100 | 9 | 2 | 16 | 7 | .696 | 4 | 0 | 2.79 |
| 1989 Birmingham | AA | 14 | 14 | 4 | 0 | 99.1 | 423 | 95 | 50 | 40 | 5 | 6 | 2 | 4 | 27 | 0 | 85 | 2 | 1 | 9 | 4 | .692 | 0 | 0 | 3.62 |
| Vancouver | AAA | 12 | 12 | 2 | 0 | 80 | 333 | 76 | 37 | 34 | 6 | 6 | 2 | 7 | 20 | 1 | 36 | 0 | 0 | 5 | 5 | .500 | 0 | 0 | 3.83 |
| 1990 Vancouver | AAA | 19 | 19 | 2 | 0 | 113.2 | 491 | 124 | 64 | 53 | 8 | 4 | 6 | 6 | 34 | 0 | 73 | 2 | 1 | 5 | 7 | .417 | 0 | 0 | 4.20 |
| 1990 Chicago | AL | 7 | 7 | 0 | 0 | 31.1 | 141 | 38 | 23 | 21 | 2 | 1 | 1 | 0 | 14 | 1 | 21 | 1 | 0 | 2 | 1 | .667 | 0 | 0 | 6.03 |

## Mike LaCoss

**Pitches:** Right **Bats:** Right **Pos:** SP **Ht:** 6' 4" **Wt:** 200 **Born:** 05/30/56 **Age:** 35

| HOW MUCH HE PITCHED | | | | | | | | WHAT HE GAVE UP | | | | | | | | | | | | THE RESULTS | | | | | |
|---|---|---|---|---|---|---|---|---|---|---|---|---|---|---|---|---|---|---|---|---|---|---|---|---|---|
| Year Team | Lg | G | GS | CG | GF | IP | BFP | H | R | ER | HR | SH | SF | HB | TBB | IBB | SO | WP | Bk | W | L | Pct. | ShO | Sv | ERA |
| 1978 Cincinnati | NL | 16 | 15 | 2 | 0 | 96 | 420 | 104 | 56 | 48 | 5 | 6 | 6 | 1 | 46 | 9 | 31 | 2 | 1 | 4 | 8 | .333 | 1 | 0 | 4.50 |
| 1979 Cincinnati | NL | 35 | 32 | 6 | 0 | 206 | 868 | 202 | 92 | 80 | 13 | 12 | 6 | 2 | 79 | 8 | 73 | 3 | 3 | 14 | 8 | .636 | 1 | 0 | 3.50 |
| 1980 Cincinnati | NL | 34 | 29 | 4 | 1 | 169 | 762 | 207 | 101 | 87 | 9 | 7 | 3 | 1 | 68 | 8 | 59 | 3 | 2 | 10 | 12 | .455 | 2 | 0 | 4.63 |
| 1981 Cincinnati | NL | 20 | 13 | 1 | 3 | 78 | 354 | 102 | 55 | 53 | 7 | 4 | 5 | 1 | 30 | 4 | 22 | 1 | 0 | 4 | 7 | .364 | 1 | 1 | 6.12 |
| 1982 Houston | NL | 41 | 8 | 0 | 11 | 115 | 488 | 107 | 41 | 37 | 3 | 5 | 0 | 4 | 54 | 6 | 51 | 5 | 1 | 6 | 6 | .500 | 0 | 0 | 2.90 |
| 1983 Houston | NL | 38 | 17 | 2 | 6 | 138 | 590 | 142 | 81 | 68 | 10 | 6 | 6 | 2 | 56 | 11 | 53 | 9 | 1 | 5 | 7 | .417 | 0 | 1 | 4.43 |
| 1984 Houston | NL | 39 | 18 | 2 | 6 | 132 | 565 | 132 | 64 | 59 | 3 | 3 | 2 | 0 | 55 | 5 | 86 | 9 | 1 | 7 | 5 | .583 | 1 | 3 | 4.02 |
| 1985 Kansas City | AL | 21 | 0 | 0 | 7 | 40.2 | 193 | 49 | 25 | 23 | 2 | 3 | 0 | 0 | 29 | 6 | 26 | 2 | 0 | 1 | 1 | .500 | 0 | 1 | 5.09 |
| 1986 San Francisco | NL | 37 | 31 | 4 | 1 | 204.1 | 842 | 179 | 99 | 81 | 14 | 16 | 3 | 6 | 70 | 8 | 86 | 5 | 5 | 10 | 13 | .435 | 1 | 0 | 3.57 |
| 1987 San Francisco | NL | 39 | 26 | 2 | 4 | 171 | 728 | 184 | 78 | 70 | 16 | 9 | 3 | 2 | 63 | 12 | 79 | 6 | 1 | 13 | 10 | .565 | 1 | 0 | 3.68 |
| 1988 San Francisco | NL | 19 | 19 | 1 | 0 | 114.1 | 477 | 99 | 55 | 46 | 5 | 5 | 1 | 1 | 47 | 3 | 70 | 6 | 2 | 7 | 7 | .500 | 1 | 0 | 3.62 |
| 1989 San Francisco | NL | 45 | 18 | 1 | 16 | 150.1 | 647 | 143 | 62 | 53 | 3 | 8 | 7 | 7 | 65 | 4 | 78 | 1 | 5 | 10 | 10 | .500 | 0 | 6 | 3.17 |
| 1990 San Francisco | NL | 13 | 12 | 1 | 0 | 77.2 | 337 | 75 | 37 | 34 | 5 | 4 | 4 | 0 | 39 | 2 | 39 | 1 | 1 | 6 | 4 | .600 | 0 | 0 | 3.94 |
| 13 ML YEARS | | 397 | 238 | 26 | 55 | 1692.1 | 7271 | 1725 | 846 | 739 | 95 | 88 | 46 | 27 | 701 | 86 | 753 | 53 | 23 | 97 | 98 | .497 | 9 | 12 | 3.93 |

## Mike Laga

**Bats:** Left **Throws:** Left **Pos:** 1B **Ht:** 6' 2" **Wt:** 210 **Born:** 06/14/60 **Age:** 31

| BATTING | | | | | | | | | | | | | | | | | | | BASERUNNING | | | | PERCENTAGES | | |
|---|---|---|---|---|---|---|---|---|---|---|---|---|---|---|---|---|---|---|---|---|---|---|---|---|---|
| Year Team | Lg | G | AB | H | 2B | 3B | HR | (Hm | Rd) | TB | R | RBI | TBB | IBB | SO | HBP | SH | SF | SB | CS | SB% | GDP | Avg | OBP | SLG |
| 1982 Detroit | AL | 27 | 88 | 23 | 9 | 0 | 3 | (3 | 0) | 41 | 6 | 11 | 4 | 0 | 23 | 0 | 0 | 0 | 1 | 0 | 1.00 | 1 | .261 | .293 | .466 |
| 1983 Detroit | AL | 12 | 21 | 4 | 0 | 0 | 0 | (0 | 0) | 4 | 2 | 2 | 1 | 0 | 9 | 0 | 0 | 0 | 0 | 0 | .00 | 1 | .190 | .227 | .190 |
| 1984 Detroit | AL | 9 | 11 | 6 | 0 | 0 | 0 | (0 | 0) | 6 | 1 | 1 | 1 | 0 | 2 | 0 | 0 | 0 | 0 | 0 | .00 | 0 | .545 | .583 | .545 |
| 1985 Detroit | AL | 9 | 36 | 6 | 1 | 0 | 2 | (0 | 2) | 13 | 3 | 6 | 0 | 0 | 9 | 0 | 0 | 0 | 0 | 0 | .00 | 1 | .167 | .167 | .361 |
| 1986 2 ML Teams | | 33 | 91 | 19 | 5 | 0 | 6 | (3 | 3) | 42 | 13 | 16 | 10 | 2 | 31 | 1 | 0 | 0 | 0 | 0 | .00 | 1 | .209 | .294 | .462 |
| 1987 St. Louis | NL | 17 | 29 | 4 | 1 | 0 | 1 | (0 | 1) | 8 | 4 | 4 | 2 | 1 | 7 | 0 | 0 | 2 | 0 | 0 | .00 | 1 | .138 | .182 | .276 |
| 1988 St. Louis | NL | 41 | 100 | 13 | 0 | 0 | 1 | (1 | 0) | 16 | 5 | 4 | 2 | 0 | 21 | 0 | 0 | 0 | 0 | 0 | .00 | 0 | .130 | .147 | .160 |
| 1989 San Francisco | NL | 17 | 20 | 4 | 1 | 0 | 1 | (0 | 1) | 8 | 1 | 7 | 1 | 0 | 6 | 0 | 0 | 0 | 0 | 0 | .00 | 0 | .200 | .238 | .400 |
| 1990 San Francisco | NL | 23 | 27 | 5 | 1 | 0 | 2 | (1 | 1) | 12 | 4 | 4 | 1 | 0 | 7 | 1 | 0 | 0 | 0 | 0 | .00 | 1 | .185 | .241 | .444 |
| 1986 Detroit | AL | 15 | 45 | 9 | 1 | 0 | 3 | (2 | 1) | 19 | 6 | 8 | 5 | 1 | 13 | 0 | 0 | 0 | 0 | 0 | .00 | 0 | .200 | .280 | .422 |
| St. Louis | NL | 18 | 46 | 10 | 4 | 0 | 3 | (1 | 2) | 23 | 7 | 8 | 5 | 1 | 18 | 1 | 0 | 0 | 0 | 0 | .00 | 1 | .217 | .308 | .500 |
| 9 ML YEARS | | 188 | 423 | 84 | 18 | 0 | 16 | (8 | 8) | 150 | 39 | 55 | 22 | 3 | 115 | 2 | 0 | 2 | 1 | 0 | 1.00 | 6 | .199 | .241 | .355 |

## Steve Lake

**Bats:** Right **Throws:** Right **Pos:** C **Ht:** 6' 1" **Wt:** 190 **Born:** 03/14/57 **Age:** 34

| | | BATTING | | | | | | | | | | | | | | | | | BASERUNNING | | | | PERCENTAGES | | |
|---|---|---|---|---|---|---|---|---|---|---|---|---|---|---|---|---|---|---|---|---|---|---|---|---|---|
| Year Team | Lg | G | AB | H | 2B | 3B | HR | (Hm | Rd) | TB | R | RBI | TBB | IBB | SO | HBP | SH | SF | SB | CS | SB% | GDP | Avg | OBP | SLG |
| 1983 Chicago | NL | 38 | 85 | 22 | 4 | 1 | 1 | (1 | 0) | 31 | 9 | 7 | 2 | 2 | 6 | 1 | 0 | 0 | 0 | 0 | .00 | 4 | .259 | .284 | .365 |
| 1984 Chicago | NL | 25 | 54 | 12 | 4 | 0 | 2 | (1 | 1) | 22 | 4 | 7 | 0 | 0 | 7 | 1 | 1 | 1 | 0 | 0 | .00 | 0 | .222 | .232 | .407 |
| 1985 Chicago | NL | 58 | 119 | 18 | 2 | 0 | 1 | (1 | 0) | 23 | 5 | 11 | 3 | 1 | 21 | 1 | 4 | 1 | 1 | 0 | 1.00 | 3 | .151 | .177 | .193 |
| 1986 2 ML Teams | | 36 | 68 | 20 | 2 | 0 | 2 | (0 | 2) | 28 | 8 | 14 | 3 | 1 | 7 | 0 | 1 | 0 | 0 | 0 | .00 | 3 | .294 | .324 | .412 |
| 1987 St. Louis | NL | 74 | 179 | 45 | 7 | 2 | 2 | (1 | 1) | 62 | 19 | 19 | 10 | 4 | 18 | 0 | 5 | 1 | 0 | 0 | .00 | 2 | .251 | .289 | .346 |
| 1988 St. Louis | NL | 36 | 54 | 15 | 3 | 0 | 1 | (1 | 0) | 21 | 5 | 4 | 3 | 0 | 15 | 2 | 0 | 0 | 0 | 0 | .00 | 0 | .278 | .339 | .389 |
| 1989 Philadelphia | NL | 58 | 155 | 39 | 5 | 1 | 2 | (1 | 1) | 52 | 9 | 14 | 12 | 4 | 20 | 0 | 1 | 1 | 0 | 0 | .00 | 6 | .252 | .304 | .335 |
| 1990 Philadelphia | NL | 29 | 80 | 20 | 2 | 0 | 0 | (0 | 0) | 22 | 4 | 6 | 3 | 1 | 12 | 1 | 0 | 0 | 0 | 0 | .00 | 1 | .250 | .286 | .275 |
| 1986 Chicago | NL | 10 | 19 | 8 | 1 | 0 | 0 | (0 | 0) | 9 | 4 | 4 | 1 | 1 | 2 | 0 | 1 | 0 | 0 | 0 | .00 | 1 | .421 | .450 | .474 |
| St. Louis | NL | 26 | 49 | 12 | 1 | 0 | 2 | (0 | 2) | 19 | 4 | 10 | 2 | 0 | 5 | 0 | 0 | 0 | 0 | 0 | .00 | 2 | .245 | .275 | .388 |
| 8 ML YEARS | | 354 | 794 | 191 | 29 | 4 | 11 | (6 | 5) | 261 | 63 | 82 | 36 | 13 | 106 | 6 | 12 | 4 | 1 | 0 | 1.00 | 19 | .241 | .277 | .329 |

## Dennis Lamp

**Pitches:** Right **Bats:** Right **Pos:** RP **Ht:** 6' 3" **Wt:** 215 **Born:** 09/23/52 **Age:** 38

| | | HOW MUCH HE PITCHED | | | | | | WHAT HE GAVE UP | | | | | | | | | | | | THE RESULTS | | | | | |
|---|---|---|---|---|---|---|---|---|---|---|---|---|---|---|---|---|---|---|---|---|---|---|---|---|---|
| Year Team | Lg | G | GS | CG | GF | IP | BFP | H | R | ER | HR | SH | SF | HB | TBB | IBB | SO | WP | Bk | W | L | Pct. | ShO | Sv | ERA |
| 1977 Chicago | NL | 11 | 3 | 0 | 4 | 30 | 137 | 43 | 21 | 21 | 3 | 1 | 1 | 2 | 8 | 4 | 12 | 0 | 1 | 0 | 2 | .000 | 0 | 0 | 6.30 |
| 1978 Chicago | NL | 37 | 36 | 6 | 0 | 224 | 928 | 221 | 96 | 82 | 16 | 10 | 3 | 4 | 56 | 8 | 73 | 2 | 2 | 7 | 15 | .318 | 3 | 0 | 3.29 |
| 1979 Chicago | NL | 38 | 32 | 6 | 3 | 200 | 843 | 223 | 96 | 78 | 14 | 9 | 5 | 5 | 46 | 9 | 86 | 1 | 0 | 11 | 10 | .524 | 1 | 0 | 3.51 |
| 1980 Chicago | NL | 41 | 37 | 2 | 3 | 203 | 921 | 259 | 123 | 117 | 16 | 17 | 4 | 1 | 82 | 7 | 83 | 10 | 0 | 10 | 14 | .417 | 1 | 0 | 5.19 |
| 1981 Chicago | AL | 27 | 10 | 3 | 5 | 127 | 514 | 103 | 41 | 34 | 4 | 5 | 0 | 1 | 43 | 1 | 71 | 4 | 1 | 7 | 6 | .538 | 0 | 0 | 2.41 |
| 1982 Chicago | AL | 44 | 27 | 3 | 11 | 189.2 | 817 | 206 | 96 | 84 | 9 | 12 | 2 | 6 | 59 | 3 | 78 | 5 | 0 | 11 | 8 | .579 | 2 | 5 | 3.99 |
| 1983 Chicago | AL | 49 | 5 | 1 | 31 | 116.1 | 483 | 123 | 52 | 48 | 6 | 2 | 1 | 4 | 29 | 7 | 44 | 0 | 0 | 7 | 7 | .500 | 0 | 15 | 3.71 |
| 1984 Toronto | AL | 56 | 4 | 0 | 37 | 85 | 387 | 97 | 53 | 43 | 9 | 7 | 1 | 1 | 38 | 7 | 45 | 2 | 0 | 8 | 8 | .500 | 0 | 9 | 4.55 |
| 1985 Toronto | AL | 53 | 1 | 0 | 11 | 105.2 | 426 | 96 | 42 | 39 | 7 | 5 | 6 | 0 | 27 | 3 | 68 | 5 | 0 | 11 | 0 | 1.000 | 0 | 2 | 3.32 |
| 1986 Toronto | AL | 40 | 2 | 0 | 11 | 73 | 329 | 93 | 50 | 41 | 5 | 4 | 1 | 0 | 23 | 6 | 30 | 2 | 0 | 2 | 6 | .250 | 0 | 2 | 5.05 |
| 1987 Oakland | AL | 36 | 5 | 0 | 10 | 56.2 | 262 | 76 | 38 | 32 | 5 | 3 | 3 | 1 | 22 | 3 | 36 | 4 | 0 | 1 | 3 | .250 | 0 | 0 | 5.08 |
| 1988 Boston | AL | 46 | 0 | 0 | 14 | 82.2 | 350 | 92 | 39 | 32 | 3 | 3 | 2 | 2 | 19 | 3 | 49 | 5 | 8 | 7 | 6 | .538 | 0 | 0 | 3.48 |
| 1989 Boston | AL | 42 | 0 | 0 | 14 | 112.1 | 445 | 96 | 37 | 29 | 4 | 5 | 5 | 0 | 27 | 6 | 61 | 1 | 1 | 4 | 2 | .667 | 0 | 2 | 2.32 |
| 1990 Boston | AL | 47 | 1 | 0 | 5 | 105.2 | 453 | 114 | 61 | 55 | 10 | 8 | 4 | 3 | 30 | 8 | 49 | 2 | 0 | 3 | 5 | .375 | 0 | 0 | 4.68 |
| 14 ML YEARS | | 567 | 163 | 21 | 159 | 1711 | 7295 | 1842 | 845 | 735 | 111 | 91 | 38 | 30 | 509 | 75 | 785 | 43 | 13 | 89 | 92 | .492 | 7 | 35 | 3.87 |

## Tom Lampkin

**Bats:** Left **Throws:** Right **Pos:** C **Ht:** 5'11" **Wt:** 185 **Born:** 03/04/64 **Age:** 27

| | | BATTING | | | | | | | | | | | | | | | | | BASERUNNING | | | | PERCENTAGES | | |
|---|---|---|---|---|---|---|---|---|---|---|---|---|---|---|---|---|---|---|---|---|---|---|---|---|---|
| Year Team | Lg | G | AB | H | 2B | 3B | HR | (Hm | Rd) | TB | R | RBI | TBB | IBB | SO | HBP | SH | SF | SB | CS | SB% | GDP | Avg | OBP | SLG |
| 1988 Cleveland | AL | 4 | 4 | 0 | 0 | 0 | 0 | (0 | 0) | 0 | 0 | 0 | 1 | 0 | 0 | 0 | 0 | 0 | 0 | 0 | .00 | 1 | .000 | .200 | .000 |
| 1990 San Diego | NL | 26 | 63 | 14 | 0 | 1 | 1 | (1 | 0) | 19 | 4 | 4 | 4 | 1 | 9 | 0 | 0 | 0 | 0 | 1 | .00 | 2 | .222 | .269 | .302 |
| 2 ML YEARS | | 30 | 67 | 14 | 0 | 1 | 1 | (1 | 0) | 19 | 4 | 4 | 5 | 1 | 9 | 0 | 0 | 0 | 0 | 1 | .00 | 3 | .209 | .264 | .284 |

## Les Lancaster

**Pitches:** Right **Bats:** Right **Pos:** RP/SP **Ht:** 6' 2" **Wt:** 200 **Born:** 04/21/62 **Age:** 29

| | | HOW MUCH HE PITCHED | | | | | | WHAT HE GAVE UP | | | | | | | | | | | | THE RESULTS | | | | | |
|---|---|---|---|---|---|---|---|---|---|---|---|---|---|---|---|---|---|---|---|---|---|---|---|---|---|
| Year Team | Lg | G | GS | CG | GF | IP | BFP | H | R | ER | HR | SH | SF | HB | TBB | IBB | SO | WP | Bk | W | L | Pct. | ShO | Sv | ERA |
| 1987 Chicago | NL | 27 | 18 | 0 | 4 | 132.1 | 578 | 138 | 76 | 72 | 14 | 5 | 6 | 1 | 51 | 5 | 78 | 7 | 8 | 8 | 3 | .727 | 0 | 0 | 4.90 |
| 1988 Chicago | NL | 44 | 3 | 1 | 15 | 85.2 | 371 | 89 | 42 | 36 | 4 | 3 | 7 | 1 | 34 | 7 | 36 | 3 | 3 | 4 | 6 | .400 | 0 | 5 | 3.78 |
| 1989 Chicago | NL | 42 | 0 | 0 | 15 | 72.2 | 288 | 60 | 12 | 11 | 2 | 3 | 4 | 0 | 15 | 1 | 56 | 2 | 1 | 4 | 2 | .667 | 0 | 8 | 1.36 |
| 1990 Chicago | NL | 55 | 6 | 1 | 26 | 109 | 479 | 121 | 57 | 56 | 11 | 6 | 5 | 1 | 40 | 8 | 65 | 7 | 0 | 9 | 5 | .643 | 1 | 6 | 4.62 |
| 4 ML YEARS | | 168 | 27 | 2 | 60 | 399.2 | 1716 | 408 | 187 | 175 | 31 | 17 | 22 | 3 | 140 | 21 | 235 | 19 | 12 | 25 | 16 | .610 | 1 | 19 | 3.94 |

## Rick Lancellotti

**Bats:** Left **Throws:** Left **Pos:** 1B **Ht:** 6' 3" **Wt:** 195 **Born:** 07/05/57 **Age:** 33

| | | BATTING | | | | | | | | | | | | | | | | | BASERUNNING | | | | PERCENTAGES | | |
|---|---|---|---|---|---|---|---|---|---|---|---|---|---|---|---|---|---|---|---|---|---|---|---|---|---|
| Year Team | Lg | G | AB | H | 2B | 3B | HR | (Hm | Rd) | TB | R | RBI | TBB | IBB | SO | HBP | SH | SF | SB | CS | SB% | GDP | Avg | OBP | SLG |
| 1982 San Diego | NL | 17 | 39 | 7 | 2 | 0 | 0 | (0 | 0) | 9 | 2 | 4 | 2 | 0 | 8 | 0 | 0 | 0 | 0 | 0 | .00 | 0 | .179 | .220 | .231 |
| 1986 San Francisco | NL | 15 | 18 | 4 | 0 | 0 | 2 | (0 | 2) | 10 | 2 | 6 | 0 | 0 | 7 | 0 | 0 | 0 | 0 | 0 | .00 | 0 | .222 | .222 | .556 |
| 1990 Boston | AL | 4 | 8 | 0 | 0 | 0 | 0 | (0 | 0) | 0 | 0 | 1 | 0 | 0 | 3 | 0 | 0 | 1 | 0 | 0 | .00 | 0 | .000 | .000 | .000 |
| 3 ML YEARS | | 36 | 65 | 11 | 2 | 0 | 2 | (0 | 2) | 19 | 4 | 11 | 2 | 0 | 18 | 0 | 0 | 1 | 0 | 0 | .00 | 0 | .169 | .191 | .292 |

## Bill Landrum

**Pitches:** Right **Bats:** Right **Pos:** RP **Ht:** 6' 2" **Wt:** 185 **Born:** 08/17/57 **Age:** 33

| | | HOW MUCH HE PITCHED | | | | | | WHAT HE GAVE UP | | | | | | | | | | | | THE RESULTS | | | | | |
|---|---|---|---|---|---|---|---|---|---|---|---|---|---|---|---|---|---|---|---|---|---|---|---|---|---|
| Year Team | Lg | G | GS | CG | GF | IP | BFP | H | R | ER | HR | SH | SF | HB | TBB | IBB | SO | WP | Bk | W | L | Pct. | ShO | Sv | ERA |
| 1986 Cincinnati | NL | 10 | 0 | 0 | 4 | 13.1 | 65 | 23 | 11 | 10 | 0 | 1 | 1 | 0 | 4 | 0 | 14 | 0 | 0 | 0 | 0 | .000 | 0 | 0 | 6.75 |
| 1987 Cincinnati | NL | 44 | 2 | 0 | 14 | 65 | 276 | 68 | 35 | 34 | 3 | 7 | 2 | 0 | 34 | 6 | 42 | 4 | 1 | 3 | 2 | .600 | 0 | 2 | 4.71 |
| 1988 Chicago | NL | 7 | 0 | 0 | 5 | 12.1 | 55 | 19 | 8 | 8 | 1 | 0 | 0 | 0 | 3 | 0 | 6 | 1 | 1 | 1 | 0 | 1.000 | 0 | 0 | 5.84 |
| 1989 Pittsburgh | NL | 56 | 0 | 0 | 40 | 81 | 325 | 60 | 18 | 15 | 2 | 3 | 2 | 0 | 28 | 8 | 51 | 2 | 0 | 2 | 3 | .400 | 0 | 26 | 1.67 |
| 1990 Pittsburgh | NL | 54 | 0 | 0 | 41 | 71.2 | 292 | 69 | 22 | 17 | 4 | 5 | 3 | 0 | 21 | 5 | 39 | 1 | 1 | 7 | 3 | .700 | 0 | 13 | 2.13 |
| 5 ML YEARS | | 171 | 2 | 0 | 104 | 243.1 | 1013 | 239 | 94 | 84 | 10 | 16 | 8 | 0 | 90 | 19 | 152 | 8 | 3 | 13 | 8 | .619 | 0 | 41 | 3.11 |

## Mark Langston

**Pitches:** Left **Bats:** Right **Pos:** SP **Ht:** 6' 2" **Wt:** 183 **Born:** 08/20/60 **Age:** 30

| | | HOW MUCH HE PITCHED | | | | | | WHAT HE GAVE UP | | | | | | | | | | | | THE RESULTS | | | | | |
|---|---|---|---|---|---|---|---|---|---|---|---|---|---|---|---|---|---|---|---|---|---|---|---|---|---|
| Year Team | Lg | G | GS | CG | GF | IP | BFP | H | R | ER | HR | SH | SF | HB | TBB | IBB | SO | WP | Bk | W | L | Pct. | ShO | Sv | ERA |
| 1984 Seattle | AL | 35 | 33 | 5 | 0 | 225 | 965 | 188 | 99 | 85 | 16 | 13 | 7 | 8 | 118 | 5 | 204 | 4 | 2 | 17 | 10 | .630 | 2 | 0 | 3.40 |
| 1985 Seattle | AL | 24 | 24 | 2 | 0 | 126.2 | 577 | 122 | 85 | 77 | 22 | 3 | 2 | 2 | 91 | 2 | 72 | 3 | 3 | 7 | 14 | .333 | 0 | 0 | 5.47 |
| 1986 Seattle | AL | 37 | 36 | 9 | 1 | 239.1 | 1057 | 234 | 142 | 129 | 30 | 5 | 8 | 4 | 123 | 1 | 245 | 10 | 3 | 12 | 14 | .462 | 0 | 0 | 4.85 |
| 1987 Seattle | AL | 35 | 35 | 14 | 0 | 272 | 1152 | 242 | 132 | 116 | 30 | 12 | 6 | 5 | 114 | 0 | 262 | 9 | 2 | 19 | 13 | .594 | 3 | 0 | 3.84 |
| 1988 Seattle | AL | 35 | 35 | 9 | 0 | 261.1 | 1078 | 222 | 108 | 97 | 32 | 6 | 5 | 3 | 110 | 2 | 235 | 7 | 4 | 15 | 11 | .577 | 3 | 0 | 3.34 |
| 1989 2 ML Teams | | 34 | 34 | 8 | 0 | 250 | 1037 | 198 | 87 | 76 | 16 | 9 | 7 | 4 | 112 | 6 | 235 | 6 | 4 | 16 | 14 | .533 | 5 | 0 | 2.74 |
| 1990 California | AL | 33 | 33 | 5 | 0 | 223 | 950 | 215 | 120 | 109 | 13 | 6 | 6 | 5 | 104 | 1 | 195 | 8 | 0 | 10 | 17 | .370 | 1 | 0 | 4.40 |
| 1989 Seattle | AL | 10 | 10 | 2 | 0 | 73.1 | 297 | 60 | 30 | 29 | 3 | 0 | 3 | 4 | 19 | 0 | 60 | 1 | 2 | 4 | 5 | .444 | 1 | 0 | 3.56 |
| Montreal | NL | 24 | 24 | 6 | 0 | 176.2 | 740 | 138 | 57 | 47 | 13 | 9 | 4 | 0 | 93 | 6 | 175 | 5 | 2 | 12 | 9 | .571 | 4 | 0 | 2.39 |
| 7 ML YEARS | | 233 | 230 | 52 | 1 | 1597.1 | 6816 | 1421 | 773 | 689 | 159 | 54 | 41 | 31 | 772 | 17 | 1448 | 47 | 18 | 96 | 93 | .508 | 14 | 0 | 3.88 |

## Ray Lankford

**Bats:** Left **Throws:** Left **Pos:** CF **Ht:** 5'11" **Wt:** 180 **Born:** 06/05/67 **Age:** 24

| | | BATTING | | | | | | | | | | | | | | | | | BASERUNNING | | | | PERCENTAGES | | |
|---|---|---|---|---|---|---|---|---|---|---|---|---|---|---|---|---|---|---|---|---|---|---|---|---|---|
| Year Team | Lg | G | AB | H | 2B | 3B | HR | (Hm | Rd) | TB | R | RBI | TBB | IBB | SO | HBP | SH | SF | SB | CS | SB% | GDP | Avg | OBP | SLG |
| 1987 Johnson Cty | R | 66 | 253 | 78 | 17 | 4 | 3 | -- | -- | 112 | 45 | 32 | 19 | 0 | 43 | 5 | 0 | 1 | 14 | 11 | .56 | 5 | .308 | .367 | .443 |
| 1988 Springfield | A | 135 | 532 | 151 | 26 | 16 | 11 | -- | -- | 242 | 90 | 66 | 60 | 2 | 92 | 10 | 1 | 2 | 33 | 17 | .66 | 4 | .284 | .366 | .455 |
| 1989 Arkansas | AA | 134 | 498 | 158 | 28 | 12 | 11 | -- | -- | 243 | 98 | 98 | 65 | 6 | 57 | 4 | 0 | 7 | 38 | 10 | .79 | 7 | .317 | .395 | .488 |
| 1990 Louisville | AAA | 132 | 473 | 123 | 25 | 8 | 10 | -- | -- | 194 | 61 | 72 | 72 | 9 | 81 | 5 | 0 | 2 | 29 | 7 | .81 | 8 | .260 | .362 | .410 |
| 1990 St. Louis | NL | 39 | 126 | 36 | 10 | 1 | 3 | (2 | 1) | 57 | 12 | 12 | 13 | 0 | 27 | 0 | 0 | 0 | 8 | 2 | .80 | 1 | .286 | .353 | .452 |

## Carney Lansford

**Bats:** Right **Throws:** Right **Pos:** 3B **Ht:** 6' 2" **Wt:** 195 **Born:** 02/07/57 **Age:** 34

| | | BATTING | | | | | | | | | | | | | | | | | BASERUNNING | | | | PERCENTAGES | | |
|---|---|---|---|---|---|---|---|---|---|---|---|---|---|---|---|---|---|---|---|---|---|---|---|---|---|
| Year Team | Lg | G | AB | H | 2B | 3B | HR | (Hm | Rd) | TB | R | RBI | TBB | IBB | SO | HBP | SH | SF | SB | CS | SB% | GDP | Avg | OBP | SLG |
| 1978 California | AL | 121 | 453 | 133 | 23 | 2 | 8 | (4 | 4) | 184 | 63 | 52 | 31 | 2 | 67 | 4 | 5 | 7 | 20 | 9 | .69 | 4 | .294 | .339 | .406 |
| 1979 California | AL | 157 | 654 | 188 | 30 | 5 | 19 | (5 | 14) | 285 | 114 | 79 | 39 | 2 | 115 | 3 | 12 | 4 | 20 | 8 | .71 | 16 | .287 | .329 | .436 |
| 1980 California | AL | 151 | 602 | 157 | 27 | 3 | 15 | (8 | 7) | 235 | 87 | 80 | 50 | 2 | 93 | 0 | 7 | 11 | 14 | 5 | .74 | 12 | .261 | .312 | .390 |
| 1981 Boston | AL | 102 | 399 | 134 | 23 | 3 | 4 | (1 | 3) | 175 | 61 | 52 | 34 | 3 | 28 | 2 | 1 | 2 | 15 | 10 | .60 | 6 | .336 | .389 | .439 |
| 1982 Boston | AL | 128 | 482 | 145 | 28 | 4 | 11 | (4 | 7) | 214 | 65 | 63 | 46 | 2 | 48 | 2 | 1 | 8 | 9 | 4 | .69 | 15 | .301 | .359 | .444 |
| 1983 Oakland | AL | 80 | 299 | 92 | 16 | 2 | 10 | (4 | 6) | 142 | 43 | 45 | 22 | 4 | 33 | 3 | 0 | 4 | 3 | 8 | .27 | 8 | .308 | .357 | .475 |
| 1984 Oakland | AL | 151 | 597 | 179 | 31 | 5 | 14 | (7 | 7) | 262 | 70 | 74 | 40 | 6 | 62 | 3 | 2 | 9 | 9 | 3 | .75 | 12 | .300 | .342 | .439 |
| 1985 Oakland | AL | 98 | 401 | 111 | 18 | 2 | 13 | (7 | 6) | 172 | 51 | 46 | 18 | 1 | 27 | 4 | 4 | 5 | 2 | 3 | .40 | 6 | .277 | .311 | .429 |
| 1986 Oakland | AL | 151 | 591 | 168 | 16 | 4 | 19 | (10 | 9) | 249 | 80 | 72 | 39 | 2 | 51 | 5 | 1 | 4 | 16 | 7 | .70 | 16 | .284 | .332 | .421 |
| 1987 Oakland | AL | 151 | 554 | 160 | 27 | 4 | 19 | (9 | 10) | 252 | 89 | 76 | 60 | 11 | 44 | 9 | 5 | 3 | 27 | 8 | .77 | 9 | .289 | .366 | .455 |
| 1988 Oakland | AL | 150 | 556 | 155 | 20 | 2 | 7 | (1 | 6) | 200 | 80 | 57 | 35 | 4 | 35 | 7 | 5 | 4 | 29 | 8 | .78 | 17 | .279 | .327 | .360 |
| 1989 Oakland | AL | 148 | 551 | 185 | 28 | 2 | 2 | (1 | 1) | 223 | 81 | 52 | 51 | 2 | 25 | 9 | 1 | 4 | 37 | 15 | .71 | 21 | .336 | .398 | .405 |
| 1990 Oakland | AL | 134 | 507 | 136 | 15 | 1 | 3 | (1 | 2) | 162 | 58 | 50 | 45 | 4 | 50 | 6 | 2 | 4 | 16 | 14 | .53 | 10 | .268 | .333 | .320 |
| 13 ML YEARS | | 1722 | 6646 | 1943 | 302 | 39 | 144 | (62 | 82) | 2755 | 942 | 798 | 510 | 45 | 678 | 57 | 46 | 69 | 217 | 102 | .68 | 152 | .292 | .345 | .415 |

## Dave LaPoint

**Pitches:** Left **Bats:** Left **Pos:** SP **Ht:** 6' 3" **Wt:** 215 **Born:** 07/29/59 **Age:** 31

| | | HOW MUCH HE PITCHED | | | | | | WHAT HE GAVE UP | | | | | | | | | | | | THE RESULTS | | | | | |
|---|---|---|---|---|---|---|---|---|---|---|---|---|---|---|---|---|---|---|---|---|---|---|---|---|---|
| Year Team | Lg | G | GS | CG | GF | IP | BFP | H | R | ER | HR | SH | SF | HB | TBB | IBB | SO | WP | Bk | W | L | Pct. | ShO | Sv | ERA |
| 1980 Milwaukee | AL | 5 | 3 | 0 | 1 | 15 | 75 | 17 | 14 | 10 | 2 | 2 | 2 | 0 | 13 | 1 | 5 | 0 | 1 | 1 | 0 | 1.000 | 0 | 1 | 6.00 |
| 1981 St. Louis | NL | 3 | 2 | 0 | 0 | 11 | 45 | 12 | 5 | 5 | 1 | 1 | 0 | 1 | 2 | 0 | 4 | 0 | 0 | 1 | 0 | 1.000 | 0 | 0 | 4.09 |
| 1982 St. Louis | NL | 42 | 21 | 0 | 6 | 152.2 | 656 | 170 | 63 | 58 | 8 | 9 | 5 | 3 | 52 | 8 | 81 | 4 | 2 | 9 | 3 | .750 | 0 | 0 | 3.42 |
| 1983 St. Louis | NL | 37 | 29 | 1 | 1 | 191.1 | 832 | 191 | 92 | 84 | 12 | 17 | 11 | 4 | 84 | 7 | 113 | 11 | 4 | 12 | 9 | .571 | 0 | 0 | 3.95 |
| 1984 St. Louis | NL | 33 | 33 | 2 | 0 | 193 | 827 | 205 | 94 | 85 | 9 | 8 | 3 | 1 | 77 | 8 | 130 | 15 | 3 | 12 | 10 | .545 | 1 | 0 | 3.96 |
| 1985 San Francisco | NL | 31 | 31 | 2 | 0 | 206.2 | 886 | 215 | 99 | 82 | 18 | 7 | 5 | 0 | 74 | 6 | 122 | 10 | 0 | 7 | 17 | .292 | 1 | 0 | 3.57 |

| Year | Team | Lg | | | | | | | | | | | | | | | | | | | | | | | | |
|---|---|---|---|---|---|---|---|---|---|---|---|---|---|---|---|---|---|---|---|---|---|---|---|---|---|---|
| 1986 | 2 ML Teams | | 40 | 12 | 0 | 6 | 129 | 588 | 152 | 86 | 72 | 19 | 9 | 2 | 1 | 56 | 7 | 77 | 3 | 5 | 4 | 10 | .286 | 0 | 0 | 5.02 |
| 1987 | 2 ML Teams | | 20 | 14 | 2 | 3 | 98.2 | 420 | 95 | 41 | 39 | 11 | 1 | 0 | 1 | 36 | 0 | 51 | 4 | 1 | 7 | 4 | .636 | 1 | 0 | 3.56 |
| 1988 | 2 ML Teams | | 33 | 33 | 2 | 0 | 213.1 | 892 | 205 | 87 | 77 | 14 | 13 | 4 | 2 | 57 | 3 | 98 | 1 | 7 | 14 | 13 | .519 | 1 | 0 | 3.25 |
| 1989 | New York | AL | 20 | 20 | 0 | 0 | 113.2 | 524 | 146 | 73 | 71 | 12 | 2 | 4 | 2 | 45 | 4 | 51 | 1 | 2 | 6 | 9 | .400 | 0 | 0 | 5.62 |
| 1990 | New York | AL | 28 | 27 | 2 | 0 | 157.2 | 694 | 180 | 84 | 72 | 11 | 8 | 11 | 1 | 57 | 3 | 67 | 4 | 0 | 7 | 10 | .412 | 0 | 0 | 4.11 |
| 1986 | Detroit | AL | 16 | 8 | 0 | 2 | 67.2 | 314 | 85 | 49 | 43 | 11 | 4 | 1 | 0 | 32 | 3 | 36 | 2 | 1 | 3 | 6 | .333 | 0 | 0 | 5.72 |
| | San Diego | NL | 24 | 4 | 0 | 4 | 61.1 | 274 | 67 | 37 | 29 | 8 | 5 | 1 | 1 | 24 | 4 | 41 | 1 | 4 | 1 | 4 | .200 | 0 | 0 | 4.26 |
| 1987 | St. Louis | NL | 6 | 2 | 0 | 3 | 16 | 79 | 26 | 12 | 12 | 4 | 0 | 0 | 0 | 5 | 0 | 8 | 1 | 1 | 1 | 1 | .500 | 0 | 0 | 6.75 |
| | Chicago | AL | 14 | 12 | 2 | 0 | 82.2 | 341 | 69 | 29 | 27 | 7 | 1 | 0 | 1 | 31 | 0 | 43 | 3 | 0 | 6 | 3 | .667 | 1 | 0 | 2.94 |
| 1988 | Chicago | AL | 25 | 25 | 1 | 0 | 161.1 | 677 | 151 | 69 | 61 | 10 | 8 | 3 | 2 | 47 | 1 | 79 | 1 | 5 | 10 | 11 | .476 | 1 | 0 | 3.40 |
| | Pittsburgh | NL | 8 | 8 | 1 | 0 | 52 | 215 | 54 | 18 | 16 | 4 | 5 | 1 | 0 | 10 | 2 | 19 | 0 | 2 | 4 | 2 | .667 | 0 | 0 | 2.77 |
| | 11 ML YEARS | | 292 | 225 | 11 | 17 | 1482 | 6439 | 1588 | 738 | 655 | 117 | 77 | 47 | 16 | 553 | 47 | 799 | 53 | 25 | 80 | 85 | .485 | 4 | 1 | 3.98 |

## Barry Larkin

**Bats:** Right **Throws:** Right **Pos:** SS **Ht:** 6' 0" **Wt:** 185 **Born:** 04/28/64 **Age:** 27

| | | | BATTING | | | | | | | | | | | | | | | | | BASERUNNING | | | | PERCENTAGES | | |
|---|---|---|---|---|---|---|---|---|---|---|---|---|---|---|---|---|---|---|---|---|---|---|---|---|---|---|
| Year | Team | Lg | G | AB | H | 2B | 3B | HR | (Hm | Rd) | TB | R | RBI | TBB | IBB | SO | HBP | SH | SF | SB | CS | SB% | GDP | Avg | OBP | SLG |
| 1986 | Cincinnati | NL | 41 | 159 | 45 | 4 | 3 | 3 | (3 | 0) | 64 | 27 | 19 | 9 | 1 | 21 | 0 | 0 | 1 | 8 | 0 | 1.00 | 2 | .283 | .320 | .403 |
| 1987 | Cincinnati | NL | 125 | 439 | 107 | 16 | 2 | 12 | (6 | 6) | 163 | 64 | 43 | 36 | 3 | 52 | 5 | 5 | 3 | 21 | 6 | .78 | 8 | .244 | .306 | .371 |
| 1988 | Cincinnati | NL | 151 | 588 | 174 | 32 | 5 | 12 | (9 | 3) | 252 | 91 | 56 | 41 | 3 | 24 | 8 | 10 | 5 | 40 | 7 | .85 | 7 | .296 | .347 | .429 |
| 1989 | Cincinnati | NL | 97 | 325 | 111 | 14 | 4 | 4 | (1 | 3) | 145 | 47 | 36 | 20 | 5 | 23 | 2 | 2 | 8 | 10 | 5 | .67 | 7 | .342 | .375 | .446 |
| 1990 | Cincinnati | NL | 158 | 614 | 185 | 25 | 6 | 7 | (4 | 3) | 243 | 85 | 67 | 49 | 3 | 49 | 7 | 7 | 4 | 30 | 5 | .86 | 14 | .301 | .358 | .396 |
| | 5 ML YEARS | | 572 | 2125 | 622 | 91 | 20 | 38 | (23 | 15) | 867 | 314 | 221 | 155 | 15 | 169 | 22 | 24 | 21 | 109 | 23 | .83 | 38 | .293 | .344 | .408 |

## Gene Larkin

**Bats:** Both **Throws:** Right **Pos:** RF/1B/DH **Ht:** 6' 3" **Wt:** 205 **Born:** 10/24/62 **Age:** 28

| | | | BATTING | | | | | | | | | | | | | | | | | BASERUNNING | | | | PERCENTAGES | | |
|---|---|---|---|---|---|---|---|---|---|---|---|---|---|---|---|---|---|---|---|---|---|---|---|---|---|---|
| Year | Team | Lg | G | AB | H | 2B | 3B | HR | (Hm | Rd) | TB | R | RBI | TBB | IBB | SO | HBP | SH | SF | SB | CS | SB% | GDP | Avg | OBP | SLG |
| 1987 | Minnesota | AL | 85 | 233 | 62 | 11 | 2 | 4 | (0 | 4) | 89 | 23 | 28 | 25 | 3 | 31 | 2 | 0 | 2 | 1 | 4 | .20 | 4 | .266 | .340 | .382 |
| 1988 | Minnesota | AL | 149 | 505 | 135 | 30 | 2 | 8 | (5 | 3) | 193 | 56 | 70 | 68 | 8 | 55 | 15 | 1 | 5 | 3 | 2 | .60 | 12 | .267 | .368 | .382 |
| 1989 | Minnesota | AL | 136 | 446 | 119 | 25 | 1 | 6 | (3 | 3) | 164 | 61 | 46 | 54 | 6 | 57 | 9 | 5 | 6 | 5 | 2 | .71 | 13 | .267 | .353 | .368 |
| 1990 | Minnesota | AL | 119 | 401 | 108 | 26 | 4 | 5 | (5 | 0) | 157 | 46 | 42 | 42 | 2 | 55 | 5 | 5 | 4 | 5 | 3 | .63 | 7 | .269 | .343 | .392 |
| | 4 ML YEARS | | 489 | 1585 | 424 | 92 | 9 | 23 | (13 | 10) | 603 | 186 | 186 | 189 | 19 | 198 | 31 | 11 | 17 | 14 | 11 | .56 | 36 | .268 | .353 | .380 |

## Mike LaValliere

**Bats:** Left **Throws:** Right **Pos:** C **Ht:** 5' 9" **Wt:** 190 **Born:** 08/18/60 **Age:** 30

| | | | BATTING | | | | | | | | | | | | | | | | | BASERUNNING | | | | PERCENTAGES | | |
|---|---|---|---|---|---|---|---|---|---|---|---|---|---|---|---|---|---|---|---|---|---|---|---|---|---|---|
| Year | Team | Lg | G | AB | H | 2B | 3B | HR | (Hm | Rd) | TB | R | RBI | TBB | IBB | SO | HBP | SH | SF | SB | CS | SB% | GDP | Avg | OBP | SLG |
| 1984 | Philadelphia | NL | 6 | 7 | 0 | 0 | 0 | 0 | (0 | 0) | 0 | 0 | 0 | 2 | 0 | 2 | 0 | 0 | 0 | 0 | 0 | .00 | 0 | .000 | .222 | .000 |
| 1985 | St. Louis | NL | 12 | 34 | 5 | 1 | 0 | 0 | (0 | 0) | 6 | 2 | 6 | 7 | 0 | 3 | 0 | 0 | 3 | 0 | 0 | .00 | 2 | .147 | .273 | .176 |
| 1986 | St. Louis | NL | 110 | 303 | 71 | 10 | 2 | 3 | (1 | 2) | 94 | 18 | 30 | 36 | 5 | 37 | 1 | 10 | 0 | 0 | 1 | .00 | 7 | .234 | .318 | .310 |
| 1987 | Pittsburgh | NL | 121 | 340 | 102 | 19 | 0 | 1 | (1 | 0) | 124 | 33 | 36 | 43 | 9 | 32 | 1 | 3 | 3 | 0 | 0 | .00 | 4 | .300 | .377 | .365 |
| 1988 | Pittsburgh | NL | 120 | 352 | 92 | 18 | 0 | 2 | (0 | 2) | 116 | 24 | 47 | 50 | 10 | 34 | 2 | 1 | 4 | 3 | 2 | .60 | 8 | .261 | .353 | .330 |
| 1989 | Pittsburgh | NL | 68 | 190 | 60 | 10 | 0 | 2 | (2 | 0) | 76 | 15 | 23 | 29 | 7 | 24 | 0 | 4 | 0 | 0 | 2 | .00 | 4 | .316 | .406 | .400 |
| 1990 | Pittsburgh | NL | 96 | 279 | 72 | 15 | 0 | 3 | (2 | 1) | 96 | 27 | 31 | 44 | 8 | 20 | 2 | 4 | 1 | 0 | 3 | .00 | 6 | .258 | .362 | .344 |
| | 7 ML YEARS | | 533 | 1505 | 402 | 73 | 2 | 11 | (6 | 5) | 512 | 119 | 173 | 211 | 39 | 152 | 6 | 22 | 11 | 3 | 8 | .27 | 31 | .267 | .357 | .340 |

## Tom Lawless

**Bats:** Right **Throws:** Right **Pos:** 3B **Ht:** 5'11" **Wt:** 165 **Born:** 12/19/56 **Age:** 34

| | | | BATTING | | | | | | | | | | | | | | | | | BASERUNNING | | | | PERCENTAGES | | |
|---|---|---|---|---|---|---|---|---|---|---|---|---|---|---|---|---|---|---|---|---|---|---|---|---|---|---|
| Year | Team | Lg | G | AB | H | 2B | 3B | HR | (Hm | Rd) | TB | R | RBI | TBB | IBB | SO | HBP | SH | SF | SB | CS | SB% | GDP | Avg | OBP | SLG |
| 1982 | Cincinnati | NL | 49 | 165 | 35 | 6 | 0 | 0 | (0 | 0) | 41 | 19 | 4 | 9 | 0 | 30 | 0 | 2 | 0 | 16 | 5 | .76 | 5 | .212 | .253 | .248 |
| 1984 | 2 ML Teams | | 54 | 97 | 23 | 3 | 0 | 1 | (0 | 1) | 29 | 11 | 2 | 8 | 1 | 16 | 0 | 1 | 0 | 7 | 3 | .70 | 4 | .237 | .295 | .299 |
| 1985 | St. Louis | NL | 47 | 58 | 12 | 3 | 1 | 0 | (0 | 0) | 17 | 8 | 8 | 5 | 0 | 4 | 0 | 1 | 0 | 2 | 1 | .67 | 0 | .207 | .270 | .293 |
| 1986 | St. Louis | NL | 46 | 39 | 11 | 1 | 0 | 0 | (0 | 0) | 12 | 5 | 3 | 2 | 0 | 8 | 0 | 2 | 1 | 8 | 1 | .89 | 0 | .282 | .310 | .308 |
| 1987 | St. Louis | NL | 19 | 25 | 2 | 1 | 0 | 0 | (0 | 0) | 3 | 5 | 0 | 3 | 0 | 5 | 0 | 1 | 0 | 2 | 0 | 1.00 | 1 | .080 | .179 | .120 |
| 1988 | St. Louis | NL | 54 | 65 | 10 | 2 | 1 | 1 | (0 | 1) | 17 | 9 | 3 | 7 | 0 | 9 | 0 | 7 | 0 | 6 | 0 | 1.00 | 1 | .154 | .236 | .262 |
| 1989 | Toronto | AL | 59 | 70 | 16 | 1 | 0 | 0 | (0 | 0) | 17 | 20 | 3 | 7 | 0 | 12 | 0 | 1 | 1 | 12 | 1 | .92 | 0 | .229 | .295 | .243 |
| 1990 | Toronto | AL | 15 | 12 | 1 | 0 | 0 | 0 | (0 | 0) | 1 | 1 | 1 | 0 | 0 | 1 | 0 | 0 | 0 | 0 | 2 | .00 | 0 | .083 | .083 | .083 |
| 1984 | Cincinnati | NL | 43 | 80 | 20 | 2 | 0 | 1 | (0 | 1) | 25 | 10 | 2 | 8 | 1 | 12 | 0 | 1 | 0 | 6 | 3 | .67 | 1 | .250 | .318 | .313 |
| | Montreal | NL | 11 | 17 | 3 | 1 | 0 | 0 | (0 | 0) | 4 | 1 | 0 | 0 | 0 | 4 | 0 | 0 | 0 | 1 | 0 | 1.00 | 3 | .176 | .176 | .235 |
| | 8 ML YEARS | | 343 | 531 | 110 | 17 | 2 | 2 | (0 | 2) | 137 | 78 | 24 | 41 | 1 | 85 | 0 | 15 | 2 | 53 | 13 | .80 | 11 | .207 | .263 | .258 |

## Tim Layana

**Pitches:** Right **Bats:** Right **Pos:** RP **Ht:** 6' 2" **Wt:** 195 **Born:** 03/02/64 **Age:** 27

| | | | HOW MUCH HE PITCHED | | | | | | WHAT HE GAVE UP | | | | | | | | | | | | THE RESULTS | | | | | |
|---|---|---|---|---|---|---|---|---|---|---|---|---|---|---|---|---|---|---|---|---|---|---|---|---|---|---|
| Year | Team | Lg | G | GS | CG | GF | IP | BFP | H | R | ER | HR | SH | SF | HB | TBB | IBB | SO | WP | Bk | W | L | Pct. | ShO | Sv | ERA |
| 1986 | Oneonta | A | 3 | 3 | 0 | 0 | 19 | 71 | 10 | 5 | 5 | 1 | 1 | 0 | 1 | 5 | 0 | 24 | 1 | 0 | 2 | 0 | 1.000 | 0 | 0 | 2.37 |
| | Ft.Laudrdle | A | 11 | 10 | 3 | 1 | 68.1 | 276 | 59 | 19 | 17 | 1 | 2 | 0 | 4 | 19 | 1 | 52 | 5 | 1 | 5 | 4 | .556 | 1 | 1 | 2.24 |
| 1987 | Albany | AA | 8 | 7 | 1 | 1 | 46.1 | 195 | 51 | 28 | 26 | 4 | 2 | 1 | 2 | 18 | 0 | 19 | 1 | 1 | 2 | 4 | .333 | 0 | 0 | 5.05 |
| | Pr William | A | 7 | 3 | 0 | 2 | 22.2 | 111 | 29 | 22 | 16 | 3 | 1 | 2 | 1 | 11 | 0 | 17 | 5 | 2 | 2 | 1 | .667 | 0 | 0 | 6.35 |
| | Columbus | AAA | 13 | 13 | 0 | 0 | 70 | 310 | 77 | 37 | 37 | 6 | 3 | 1 | 1 | 37 | 2 | 36 | 3 | 0 | 4 | 5 | .444 | 0 | 0 | 4.76 |
| 1988 | Albany | AA | 14 | 14 | 1 | 0 | 87 | 378 | 90 | 52 | 42 | 3 | 3 | 3 | 6 | 30 | 2 | 42 | 2 | 8 | 5 | 7 | .417 | 0 | 0 | 4.34 |
| | Columbus | AAA | 11 | 9 | 0 | 0 | 47.2 | 216 | 54 | 34 | 32 | 2 | 0 | 1 | 6 | 25 | 0 | 25 | 2 | 4 | 1 | 7 | .125 | 0 | 0 | 6.04 |
| 1989 | Albany | AA | 40 | 1 | 0 | 37 | 67.2 | 261 | 53 | 17 | 13 | 2 | 5 | 1 | 3 | 15 | 3 | 48 | 2 | 4 | 7 | 4 | .636 | 0 | 17 | 1.73 |
| 1990 | Cincinnati | NL | 55 | 0 | 0 | 17 | 80 | 344 | 71 | 33 | 31 | 7 | 4 | 3 | 2 | 44 | 6 | 53 | 5 | 4 | 5 | 3 | .625 | 0 | 2 | 3.49 |

## Rick Leach

**Bats:** Left **Throws:** Left **Pos:** RF **Ht:** 6' 0" **Wt:** 195 **Born:** 05/04/57 **Age:** 34

| | | | BATTING | | | | | | | | | | | | | | | | | BASERUNNING | | | | PERCENTAGES | | |
|---|---|---|---|---|---|---|---|---|---|---|---|---|---|---|---|---|---|---|---|---|---|---|---|---|---|---|
| Year | Team | Lg | G | AB | H | 2B | 3B | HR | (Hm | Rd) | TB | R | RBI | TBB | IBB | SO | HBP | SH | SF | SB | CS | SB% | GDP | Avg | OBP | SLG |
| 1981 | Detroit | AL | 54 | 83 | 16 | 3 | 1 | 1 | (1 | 0) | 24 | 9 | 11 | 16 | 1 | 15 | 0 | 1 | 1 | 0 | 1 | .00 | 5 | .193 | .320 | .289 |
| 1982 | Detroit | AL | 82 | 218 | 52 | 7 | 2 | 3 | (2 | 1) | 72 | 23 | 12 | 21 | 2 | 29 | 0 | 4 | 2 | 4 | 0 | 1.00 | 2 | .239 | .303 | .330 |
| 1983 | Detroit | AL | 99 | 242 | 60 | 17 | 0 | 3 | (1 | 2) | 86 | 22 | 26 | 19 | 1 | 21 | 1 | 0 | 0 | 2 | 2 | .50 | 6 | .248 | .305 | .355 |
| 1984 | Toronto | AL | 65 | 88 | 23 | 6 | 2 | 0 | (0 | 0) | 33 | 11 | 7 | 8 | 0 | 14 | 0 | 0 | 1 | 0 | 0 | .00 | 3 | .261 | .320 | .375 |
| 1985 | Toronto | AL | 16 | 35 | 7 | 0 | 1 | 0 | (0 | 0) | 9 | 2 | 1 | 3 | 1 | 9 | 0 | 0 | 0 | 0 | 0 | .00 | 0 | .200 | .263 | .257 |
| 1986 | Toronto | AL | 110 | 246 | 76 | 14 | 1 | 5 | (4 | 1) | 107 | 35 | 39 | 13 | 3 | 24 | 0 | 0 | 7 | 0 | 0 | .00 | 6 | .309 | .335 | .435 |
| 1987 | Toronto | AL | 98 | 195 | 55 | 13 | 1 | 3 | (3 | 0) | 79 | 26 | 25 | 25 | 2 | 25 | 3 | 0 | 1 | 0 | 1 | .00 | 3 | .282 | .371 | .405 |
| 1988 | Toronto | AL | 87 | 199 | 55 | 13 | 1 | 0 | (0 | 0) | 70 | 21 | 23 | 18 | 3 | 27 | 0 | 0 | 0 | 0 | 1 | .00 | 8 | .276 | .336 | .352 |
| 1989 | Texas | AL | 110 | 239 | 65 | 14 | 1 | 1 | (0 | 1) | 84 | 32 | 23 | 32 | 7 | 33 | 1 | 4 | 2 | 2 | 1 | .67 | 7 | .272 | .358 | .351 |
| 1990 | San Francisco | NL | 78 | 174 | 51 | 13 | 0 | 2 | (2 | 0) | 70 | 24 | 16 | 21 | 0 | 20 | 1 | 0 | 0 | 0 | 2 | .00 | 2 | .293 | .372 | .402 |
| | 10 ML YEARS | | 799 | 1719 | 460 | 100 | 10 | 18 | (13 | 5) | 634 | 205 | 183 | 176 | 20 | 217 | 6 | 9 | 14 | 8 | 8 | .50 | 42 | .268 | .335 | .369 |

## Terry Leach

**Pitches:** Right **Bats:** Right **Pos:** RP **Ht:** 6' 0" **Wt:** 191 **Born:** 03/13/54 **Age:** 37

| | | | HOW MUCH HE PITCHED | | | | | | WHAT HE GAVE UP | | | | | | | | | | | | THE RESULTS | | | | | |
|---|---|---|---|---|---|---|---|---|---|---|---|---|---|---|---|---|---|---|---|---|---|---|---|---|---|---|
| Year | Team | Lg | G | GS | CG | GF | IP | BFP | H | R | ER | HR | SH | SF | HB | TBB | IBB | SO | WP | Bk | W | L | Pct. | ShO | Sv | ERA |
| 1981 | New York | NL | 21 | 1 | 0 | 3 | 35 | 139 | 26 | 11 | 10 | 2 | 0 | 0 | 0 | 12 | 1 | 16 | 0 | 0 | 1 | 1 | .500 | 0 | 0 | 2.57 |
| 1982 | New York | NL | 21 | 1 | 1 | 12 | 45.1 | 194 | 46 | 22 | 21 | 2 | 5 | 1 | 0 | 18 | 5 | 30 | 0 | 0 | 2 | 1 | .667 | 1 | 3 | 4.17 |
| 1985 | New York | NL | 22 | 4 | 1 | 4 | 55.2 | 226 | 48 | 19 | 18 | 3 | 5 | 2 | 1 | 14 | 3 | 30 | 0 | 0 | 3 | 4 | .429 | 1 | 1 | 2.91 |
| 1986 | New York | NL | 6 | 0 | 0 | 1 | 6.2 | 30 | 6 | 3 | 2 | 0 | 0 | 0 | 0 | 3 | 0 | 4 | 0 | 0 | 0 | 0 | .000 | 0 | 0 | 2.70 |
| 1987 | New York | NL | 44 | 12 | 1 | 7 | 131.1 | 542 | 132 | 54 | 47 | 14 | 8 | 1 | 1 | 29 | 5 | 61 | 0 | 1 | 11 | 1 | .917 | 1 | 0 | 3.22 |
| 1988 | New York | NL | 52 | 0 | 0 | 21 | 92 | 392 | 95 | 32 | 26 | 5 | 8 | 3 | 3 | 24 | 4 | 51 | 0 | 0 | 7 | 2 | .778 | 0 | 3 | 2.54 |
| 1989 | 2 ML Teams | | 40 | 3 | 0 | 10 | 95 | 413 | 97 | 57 | 44 | 5 | 6 | 6 | 2 | 40 | 9 | 36 | 1 | 1 | 5 | 6 | .455 | 0 | 0 | 4.17 |
| 1990 | Minnesota | AL | 55 | 0 | 0 | 29 | 81.2 | 344 | 84 | 31 | 29 | 2 | 7 | 2 | 1 | 21 | 10 | 46 | 1 | 1 | 2 | 5 | .286 | 0 | 2 | 3.20 |
| 1989 | New York | NL | 10 | 0 | 0 | 4 | 21.1 | 85 | 19 | 11 | 10 | 1 | 0 | 2 | 1 | 4 | 0 | 2 | 0 | 0 | 0 | 0 | .000 | 0 | 0 | 4.22 |
| | Kansas City | AL | 30 | 3 | 0 | 6 | 73.2 | 328 | 78 | 46 | 34 | 4 | 6 | 4 | 1 | 36 | 9 | 34 | 1 | 1 | 5 | 6 | .455 | 0 | 0 | 4.15 |
| | 8 ML YEARS | | 261 | 21 | 3 | 87 | 542.2 | 2280 | 534 | 229 | 197 | 33 | 39 | 15 | 8 | 161 | 37 | 274 | 2 | 3 | 31 | 20 | .608 | 3 | 9 | 3.27 |

## Tim Leary

**Pitches:** Right **Bats:** Right **Pos:** SP **Ht:** 6' 3" **Wt:** 208 **Born:** 12/23/58 **Age:** 32

| | | | HOW MUCH HE PITCHED | | | | | | WHAT HE GAVE UP | | | | | | | | | | | | THE RESULTS | | | | | |
|---|---|---|---|---|---|---|---|---|---|---|---|---|---|---|---|---|---|---|---|---|---|---|---|---|---|---|
| Year | Team | Lg | G | GS | CG | GF | IP | BFP | H | R | ER | HR | SH | SF | HB | TBB | IBB | SO | WP | Bk | W | L | Pct. | ShO | Sv | ERA |
| 1981 | New York | NL | 1 | 1 | 0 | 0 | 2 | 7 | 0 | 0 | 0 | 0 | 0 | 0 | 0 | 1 | 0 | 3 | 1 | 0 | 0 | 0 | .000 | 0 | 0 | 0.00 |
| 1983 | New York | NL | 2 | 2 | 1 | 0 | 10.2 | 53 | 15 | 10 | 4 | 0 | 1 | 1 | 0 | 4 | 0 | 9 | 0 | 1 | 1 | 1 | .500 | 0 | 0 | 3.38 |
| 1984 | New York | NL | 20 | 7 | 0 | 3 | 53.2 | 237 | 61 | 28 | 24 | 2 | 1 | 2 | 2 | 18 | 3 | 29 | 2 | 3 | 3 | 3 | .500 | 0 | 0 | 4.02 |
| 1985 | Milwaukee | AL | 5 | 5 | 0 | 0 | 33.1 | 146 | 40 | 18 | 15 | 5 | 2 | 0 | 1 | 8 | 0 | 29 | 1 | 0 | 1 | 4 | .200 | 0 | 0 | 4.05 |
| 1986 | Milwaukee | AL | 33 | 30 | 3 | 2 | 188.1 | 817 | 216 | 97 | 88 | 20 | 4 | 6 | 7 | 53 | 4 | 110 | 7 | 0 | 12 | 12 | .500 | 2 | 0 | 4.21 |
| 1987 | Los Angeles | NL | 39 | 12 | 0 | 11 | 107.2 | 469 | 121 | 62 | 57 | 15 | 6 | 1 | 2 | 36 | 5 | 61 | 3 | 1 | 3 | 11 | .214 | 0 | 1 | 4.76 |
| 1988 | Los Angeles | NL | 35 | 34 | 9 | 0 | 228.2 | 932 | 201 | 87 | 74 | 13 | 7 | 3 | 6 | 56 | 4 | 180 | 9 | 6 | 17 | 11 | .607 | 6 | 0 | 2.91 |
| 1989 | 2 ML Teams | | 33 | 31 | 2 | 0 | 207 | 874 | 205 | 84 | 81 | 17 | 7 | 8 | 5 | 68 | 15 | 123 | 10 | 0 | 8 | 14 | .364 | 0 | 0 | 3.52 |
| 1990 | New York | AL | 31 | 31 | 6 | 0 | 208 | 881 | 202 | 105 | 95 | 18 | 7 | 4 | 7 | 78 | 1 | 138 | 23 | 0 | 9 | 19 | .321 | 1 | 0 | 4.11 |
| 1989 | Los Angeles | NL | 19 | 17 | 2 | 0 | 117.1 | 481 | 107 | 45 | 44 | 9 | 4 | 4 | 2 | 37 | 7 | 59 | 4 | 0 | 6 | 7 | .462 | 0 | 0 | 3.38 |
| | Cincinnati | NL | 14 | 14 | 0 | 0 | 89.2 | 393 | 98 | 39 | 37 | 8 | 3 | 4 | 3 | 31 | 8 | 64 | 6 | 0 | 2 | 7 | .222 | 0 | 0 | 3.71 |
| | 9 ML YEARS | | 199 | 153 | 21 | 16 | 1039.1 | 4416 | 1061 | 491 | 438 | 90 | 35 | 25 | 30 | 322 | 32 | 682 | 56 | 11 | 54 | 75 | .419 | 9 | 1 | 3.79 |

## Manny Lee

**Bats:** Both **Throws:** Right **Pos:** 2B **Ht:** 5' 9" **Wt:** 161 **Born:** 06/17/65 **Age:** 26

| | | BATTING | | | | | | | | | | | | | | | | | BASERUNNING | | | | PERCENTAGES | | |
|---|---|---|---|---|---|---|---|---|---|---|---|---|---|---|---|---|---|---|---|---|---|---|---|---|---|
| Year Team | Lg | G | AB | H | 2B | 3B | HR | (Hm | Rd) | TB | R | RBI | TBB | IBB | SO | HBP | SH | SF | SB | CS | SB% | GDP | Avg | OBP | SLG |
| 1985 Toronto | AL | 64 | 40 | 8 | 0 | 0 | 0 | (0 | 0) | 8 | 9 | 0 | 2 | 0 | 9 | 0 | 1 | 0 | 1 | 4 | .20 | 2 | .200 | .238 | .200 |
| 1986 Toronto | AL | 35 | 78 | 16 | 0 | 1 | 1 | (1 | 0) | 21 | 8 | 7 | 4 | 0 | 10 | 0 | 2 | 1 | 0 | 1 | .00 | 5 | .205 | .241 | .269 |
| 1987 Toronto | AL | 56 | 121 | 31 | 2 | 3 | 1 | (0 | 1) | 42 | 14 | 11 | 6 | 0 | 13 | 0 | 1 | 1 | 2 | 0 | 1.00 | 1 | .256 | .289 | .347 |
| 1988 Toronto | AL | 116 | 381 | 111 | 16 | 3 | 2 | (2 | 0) | 139 | 38 | 38 | 26 | 1 | 64 | 0 | 4 | 4 | 3 | 3 | .50 | 13 | .291 | .333 | .365 |
| 1989 Toronto | AL | 99 | 300 | 78 | 9 | 2 | 3 | (1 | 2) | 100 | 27 | 34 | 20 | 1 | 60 | 0 | 1 | 1 | 4 | 2 | .67 | 8 | .260 | .305 | .333 |
| 1990 Toronto | AL | 117 | 391 | 95 | 12 | 4 | 6 | (2 | 4) | 133 | 45 | 41 | 26 | 0 | 90 | 0 | 1 | 3 | 3 | 1 | .75 | 9 | .243 | .288 | .340 |
| 6 ML YEARS | | 487 | 1311 | 339 | 39 | 13 | 13 | (6 | 7) | 443 | 141 | 131 | 84 | 2 | 246 | 0 | 10 | 10 | 13 | 11 | .54 | 38 | .259 | .301 | .338 |

## Mark Lee

**Pitches:** Left **Bats:** Left **Pos:** RP **Ht:** 6' 3" **Wt:** 198 **Born:** 07/20/64 **Age:** 26

| | | HOW MUCH HE PITCHED | | | | | | WHAT HE GAVE UP | | | | | | | | | | | | THE RESULTS | | | | | |
|---|---|---|---|---|---|---|---|---|---|---|---|---|---|---|---|---|---|---|---|---|---|---|---|---|---|
| Year Team | Lg | G | GS | CG | GF | IP | BFP | H | R | ER | HR | SH | SF | HB | TBB | IBB | SO | WP | Bk | W | L | Pct. | ShO | Sv | ERA |
| 1988 Kansas City | AL | 4 | 0 | 0 | 4 | 5 | 21 | 6 | 2 | 2 | 0 | 0 | 0 | 0 | 1 | 0 | 0 | 0 | 0 | 0 | 0 | .000 | 0 | 0 | 3.60 |
| 1990 Milwaukee | AL | 11 | 0 | 0 | 1 | 21.1 | 85 | 20 | 5 | 5 | 1 | 1 | 2 | 0 | 4 | 0 | 14 | 0 | 0 | 1 | 0 | 1.000 | 0 | 0 | 2.11 |
| 2 ML YEARS | | 15 | 0 | 0 | 5 | 26.1 | 106 | 26 | 7 | 7 | 1 | 1 | 2 | 0 | 5 | 0 | 14 | 0 | 0 | 1 | 0 | 1.000 | 0 | 0 | 2.39 |

## Terry Lee

**Bats:** Right **Throws:** Right **Pos:** 1B **Ht:** 6' 5" **Wt:** 215 **Born:** 03/13/62 **Age:** 29

| | | BATTING | | | | | | | | | | | | | | | | | BASERUNNING | | | | PERCENTAGES | | |
|---|---|---|---|---|---|---|---|---|---|---|---|---|---|---|---|---|---|---|---|---|---|---|---|---|---|
| Year Team | Lg | G | AB | H | 2B | 3B | HR | (Hm | Rd) | TB | R | RBI | TBB | IBB | SO | HBP | SH | SF | SB | CS | SB% | GDP | Avg | OBP | SLG |
| 1984 Vermont | AA | 134 | 422 | 102 | 10 | 2 | 11 | -- | -- | 149 | 56 | 47 | 44 | 1 | 94 | 3 | 2 | 4 | 2 | 4 | .33 | 13 | .242 | .315 | .353 |
| 1985 Vermont | AA | 121 | 409 | 118 | 20 | 2 | 12 | -- | -- | 178 | 56 | 62 | 48 | 2 | 51 | 3 | 0 | 4 | 4 | 0 | 1.00 | 9 | .289 | .364 | .435 |
| 1986 Denver | AAA | 34 | 104 | 25 | 2 | 1 | 2 | -- | -- | 35 | 10 | 10 | 4 | 0 | 24 | 0 | 0 | 2 | 0 | 1 | .00 | 3 | .240 | .264 | .337 |
| 1988 Greensboro | A | 25 | 56 | 18 | 5 | 0 | 2 | -- | -- | 29 | 8 | 9 | 11 | 2 | 11 | 0 | 0 | 0 | 0 | 0 | .00 | 2 | .321 | .433 | .518 |
| 1989 Chattanooga | AA | 51 | 177 | 46 | 13 | 0 | 5 | -- | -- | 74 | 23 | 27 | 13 | 0 | 32 | 1 | 1 | 4 | 0 | 0 | .00 | 10 | .260 | .308 | .418 |
| Nashville | AAA | 13 | 47 | 11 | 4 | 0 | 0 | -- | -- | 15 | 5 | 3 | 3 | 0 | 8 | 1 | 1 | 0 | 0 | 0 | .00 | 2 | .234 | .294 | .319 |
| 1990 Chattanooga | AA | 43 | 156 | 51 | 8 | 1 | 8 | -- | -- | 85 | 25 | 20 | 20 | 1 | 27 | 2 | 1 | 2 | 4 | 1 | .80 | 5 | .327 | .406 | .545 |
| Nashville | AAA | 72 | 260 | 79 | 18 | 1 | 15 | -- | -- | 144 | 38 | 67 | 31 | 1 | 47 | 4 | 1 | 7 | 3 | 1 | .75 | 10 | .304 | .377 | .554 |
| 1990 Cincinnati | NL | 12 | 19 | 4 | 1 | 0 | 0 | (0 | 0) | 5 | 1 | 3 | 2 | 0 | 2 | 0 | 0 | 1 | 0 | 0 | .00 | 1 | .211 | .273 | .263 |

## Craig Lefferts

**Pitches:** Left **Bats:** Left **Pos:** RP **Ht:** 6' 1" **Wt:** 210 **Born:** 09/29/57 **Age:** 33

| | | HOW MUCH HE PITCHED | | | | | | WHAT HE GAVE UP | | | | | | | | | | | | THE RESULTS | | | | | |
|---|---|---|---|---|---|---|---|---|---|---|---|---|---|---|---|---|---|---|---|---|---|---|---|---|---|
| Year Team | Lg | G | GS | CG | GF | IP | BFP | H | R | ER | HR | SH | SF | HB | TBB | IBB | SO | WP | Bk | W | L | Pct. | ShO | Sv | ERA |
| 1983 Chicago | NL | 56 | 5 | 0 | 10 | 89 | 367 | 80 | 35 | 31 | 13 | 7 | 0 | 2 | 29 | 3 | 60 | 2 | 0 | 3 | 4 | .429 | 0 | 1 | 3.13 |
| 1984 San Diego | NL | 62 | 0 | 0 | 29 | 105.2 | 420 | 88 | 29 | 25 | 4 | 4 | 6 | 1 | 24 | 1 | 56 | 2 | 2 | 3 | 4 | .429 | 0 | 10 | 2.13 |
| 1985 San Diego | NL | 60 | 0 | 0 | 24 | 83.1 | 345 | 75 | 34 | 31 | 7 | 7 | 1 | 0 | 30 | 4 | 48 | 2 | 0 | 7 | 6 | .538 | 0 | 2 | 3.35 |
| 1986 San Diego | NL | 83 | 0 | 0 | 36 | 107.2 | 446 | 98 | 41 | 37 | 7 | 9 | 5 | 1 | 44 | 11 | 72 | 1 | 1 | 9 | 8 | .529 | 0 | 4 | 3.09 |
| 1987 2 ML Teams | | 77 | 0 | 0 | 22 | 98.2 | 416 | 92 | 47 | 42 | 13 | 6 | 2 | 2 | 33 | 11 | 57 | 6 | 3 | 5 | 5 | .500 | 0 | 6 | 3.83 |
| 1988 San Francisco | NL | 64 | 0 | 0 | 30 | 92.1 | 362 | 74 | 33 | 30 | 7 | 6 | 3 | 1 | 23 | 5 | 58 | 4 | 0 | 3 | 8 | .273 | 0 | 11 | 2.92 |
| 1989 San Francisco | NL | 70 | 0 | 0 | 32 | 107 | 430 | 93 | 38 | 32 | 11 | 4 | 4 | 1 | 22 | 5 | 71 | 4 | 1 | 2 | 4 | .333 | 0 | 20 | 2.69 |
| 1990 San Diego | NL | 56 | 0 | 0 | 44 | 78.2 | 327 | 68 | 26 | 22 | 10 | 5 | 1 | 1 | 22 | 4 | 60 | 1 | 0 | 7 | 5 | .583 | 0 | 23 | 2.52 |
| 1987 San Diego | NL | 33 | 0 | 0 | 8 | 51.1 | 225 | 56 | 29 | 25 | 9 | 2 | 0 | 2 | 15 | 5 | 39 | 5 | 2 | 2 | 2 | .500 | 0 | 2 | 4.38 |
| San Francisco | NL | 44 | 0 | 0 | 14 | 47.1 | 191 | 36 | 18 | 17 | 4 | 4 | 2 | 0 | 18 | 6 | 18 | 1 | 1 | 3 | 3 | .500 | 0 | 4 | 3.23 |
| 8 ML YEARS | | 528 | 5 | 0 | 227 | 762.1 | 3113 | 668 | 283 | 250 | 72 | 48 | 22 | 9 | 227 | 44 | 482 | 22 | 7 | 39 | 44 | .470 | 0 | 77 | 2.95 |

## Charlie Leibrandt

**Pitches:** Left **Bats:** Right **Pos:** SP **Ht:** 6' 3" **Wt:** 200 **Born:** 10/04/56 **Age:** 34

| | | HOW MUCH HE PITCHED | | | | | | WHAT HE GAVE UP | | | | | | | | | | | | THE RESULTS | | | | | |
|---|---|---|---|---|---|---|---|---|---|---|---|---|---|---|---|---|---|---|---|---|---|---|---|---|---|
| Year Team | Lg | G | GS | CG | GF | IP | BFP | H | R | ER | HR | SH | SF | HB | TBB | IBB | SO | WP | Bk | W | L | Pct. | ShO | Sv | ERA |
| 1979 Cincinnati | NL | 3 | 0 | 0 | 1 | 4 | 16 | 2 | 2 | 0 | 0 | 0 | 1 | 0 | 2 | 0 | 1 | 0 | 0 | 0 | 0 | .000 | 0 | 0 | 0.00 |
| 1980 Cincinnati | NL | 36 | 27 | 5 | 3 | 174 | 754 | 200 | 84 | 82 | 15 | 12 | 2 | 2 | 54 | 4 | 62 | 1 | 6 | 10 | 9 | .526 | 2 | 0 | 4.24 |
| 1981 Cincinnati | NL | 7 | 4 | 1 | 0 | 30 | 128 | 28 | 12 | 12 | 0 | 4 | 2 | 0 | 15 | 2 | 9 | 0 | 0 | 1 | 1 | .500 | 1 | 0 | 3.60 |
| 1982 Cincinnati | NL | 36 | 11 | 0 | 10 | 107.2 | 484 | 130 | 68 | 61 | 4 | 10 | 2 | 2 | 48 | 9 | 34 | 6 | 1 | 5 | 7 | .417 | 0 | 2 | 5.10 |
| 1984 Kansas City | AL | 23 | 23 | 0 | 0 | 143.2 | 621 | 158 | 65 | 58 | 11 | 3 | 7 | 3 | 38 | 2 | 53 | 5 | 1 | 11 | 7 | .611 | 0 | 0 | 3.63 |
| 1985 Kansas City | AL | 33 | 33 | 8 | 0 | 237.2 | 983 | 223 | 86 | 71 | 17 | 8 | 5 | 2 | 68 | 3 | 108 | 4 | 3 | 17 | 9 | .654 | 3 | 0 | 2.69 |
| 1986 Kansas City | AL | 35 | 34 | 8 | 0 | 231.1 | 975 | 238 | 112 | 105 | 18 | 14 | 5 | 4 | 63 | 0 | 108 | 2 | 1 | 14 | 11 | .560 | 1 | 0 | 4.09 |
| 1987 Kansas City | AL | 35 | 35 | 8 | 0 | 240.1 | 1015 | 235 | 104 | 91 | 23 | 5 | 5 | 1 | 74 | 2 | 151 | 9 | 3 | 16 | 11 | .593 | 3 | 0 | 3.41 |
| 1988 Kansas City | AL | 35 | 35 | 7 | 0 | 243 | 1002 | 244 | 98 | 86 | 20 | 5 | 7 | 4 | 62 | 3 | 125 | 10 | 4 | 13 | 12 | .520 | 2 | 0 | 3.19 |
| 1989 Kansas City | AL | 33 | 27 | 3 | 3 | 161 | 712 | 196 | 98 | 92 | 13 | 8 | 4 | 2 | 54 | 4 | 73 | 9 | 2 | 5 | 11 | .313 | 1 | 0 | 5.14 |

| Year Team | Lg | G | GS | CG | GF | IP | BFP | H | R | ER | HR | SH | SF | HB | TBB | IBB | SO | WP | Bk | W | L | Pct. | ShO | Sv | ERA |
|---|---|---|---|---|---|---|---|---|---|---|---|---|---|---|---|---|---|---|---|---|---|---|---|---|---|
| 1990 Atlanta | NL | 24 | 24 | 5 | 0 | 162.1 | 680 | 164 | 72 | 57 | 9 | 7 | 6 | 4 | 35 | 3 | 76 | 4 | 3 | 9 | 11 | .450 | 2 | 0 | 3.16 |
| 11 ML YEARS | | 300 | 253 | 45 | 17 | 1735 | 7370 | 1818 | 801 | 715 | 130 | 76 | 46 | 24 | 513 | 32 | 800 | 50 | 24 | 101 | 89 | .532 | 15 | 2 | 3.71 |

## John Leister

**Pitches:** Right **Bats:** Right **Pos:** SP **Ht:** 6' 2" **Wt:** 215 **Born:** 01/03/61 **Age:** 30

| | | HOW MUCH HE PITCHED | | | | | | WHAT HE GAVE UP | | | | | | | | | | | | THE RESULTS | | | | | |
|---|---|---|---|---|---|---|---|---|---|---|---|---|---|---|---|---|---|---|---|---|---|---|---|---|---|
| Year Team | Lg | G | GS | CG | GF | IP | BFP | H | R | ER | HR | SH | SF | HB | TBB | IBB | SO | WP | Bk | W | L | Pct. | ShO | Sv | ERA |
| 1987 Boston | AL | 8 | 6 | 0 | 0 | 30.1 | 146 | 49 | 31 | 31 | 9 | 0 | 1 | 0 | 12 | 1 | 16 | 1 | 0 | 0 | 2 | .000 | 0 | 0 | 9.20 |
| 1990 Boston | AL | 2 | 1 | 0 | 1 | 5.2 | 29 | 7 | 5 | 3 | 0 | 1 | 1 | 0 | 4 | 0 | 3 | 0 | 0 | 0 | 0 | .000 | 0 | 0 | 4.76 |
| 2 ML YEARS | | 10 | 7 | 0 | 1 | 36 | 175 | 56 | 36 | 34 | 9 | 1 | 2 | 0 | 16 | 1 | 19 | 1 | 0 | 0 | 2 | .000 | 0 | 0 | 8.50 |

## Al Leiter

**Pitches:** Left **Bats:** Left **Pos:** RP **Ht:** 6' 3" **Wt:** 210 **Born:** 10/23/65 **Age:** 25

| | | HOW MUCH HE PITCHED | | | | | | WHAT HE GAVE UP | | | | | | | | | | | | THE RESULTS | | | | | |
|---|---|---|---|---|---|---|---|---|---|---|---|---|---|---|---|---|---|---|---|---|---|---|---|---|---|
| Year Team | Lg | G | GS | CG | GF | IP | BFP | H | R | ER | HR | SH | SF | HB | TBB | IBB | SO | WP | Bk | W | L | Pct. | ShO | Sv | ERA |
| 1987 New York | AL | 4 | 4 | 0 | 0 | 22.2 | 104 | 24 | 16 | 16 | 2 | 1 | 0 | 0 | 15 | 0 | 28 | 4 | 0 | 2 | 2 | .500 | 0 | 0 | 6.35 |
| 1988 New York | AL | 14 | 14 | 0 | 0 | 57.1 | 251 | 49 | 27 | 25 | 7 | 1 | 0 | 5 | 33 | 0 | 60 | 1 | 4 | 4 | 4 | .500 | 0 | 0 | 3.92 |
| 1989 2 ML Teams | | 5 | 5 | 0 | 0 | 33.1 | 154 | 32 | 23 | 21 | 2 | 1 | 1 | 2 | 23 | 0 | 26 | 2 | 1 | 1 | 2 | .333 | 0 | 0 | 5.67 |
| 1990 Toronto | AL | 4 | 0 | 0 | 2 | 6.1 | 22 | 1 | 0 | 0 | 0 | 0 | 0 | 0 | 2 | 0 | 5 | 0 | 0 | 0 | 0 | .000 | 0 | 0 | 0.00 |
| 1989 New York | AL | 4 | 4 | 0 | 0 | 26.2 | 123 | 23 | 20 | 18 | 1 | 1 | 1 | 2 | 21 | 0 | 22 | 1 | 1 | 1 | 2 | .333 | 0 | 0 | 6.08 |
| Toronto | AL | 1 | 1 | 0 | 0 | 6.2 | 31 | 9 | 3 | 3 | 1 | 0 | 0 | 0 | 2 | 0 | 4 | 1 | 0 | 0 | 0 | .000 | 0 | 0 | 4.05 |
| 4 ML YEARS | | 27 | 23 | 0 | 2 | 119.2 | 531 | 106 | 66 | 62 | 11 | 3 | 1 | 7 | 73 | 0 | 119 | 7 | 5 | 7 | 8 | .467 | 0 | 0 | 4.66 |

## Mark Leiter

**Pitches:** Right **Bats:** Right **Pos:** RP/SP **Ht:** 6' 3" **Wt:** 210 **Born:** 04/13/63 **Age:** 28

| | | HOW MUCH HE PITCHED | | | | | | WHAT HE GAVE UP | | | | | | | | | | | | THE RESULTS | | | | | |
|---|---|---|---|---|---|---|---|---|---|---|---|---|---|---|---|---|---|---|---|---|---|---|---|---|---|
| Year Team | Lg | G | GS | CG | GF | IP | BFP | H | R | ER | HR | SH | SF | HB | TBB | IBB | SO | WP | Bk | W | L | Pct. | ShO | Sv | ERA |
| 1984 Hagerstown | A | 27 | 24 | 5 | 2 | 139.1 | 643 | 132 | 96 | 87 | 13 | 6 | 4 | 8 | 108 | 2 | 105 | 13 | 1 | 8 | 13 | .381 | 1 | 0 | 5.62 |
| 1985 Hagerstown | A | 34 | 6 | 1 | 22 | 83.1 | 351 | 77 | 44 | 32 | 2 | 4 | 4 | 7 | 29 | 3 | 82 | 3 | 0 | 2 | 8 | .200 | 0 | 8 | 3.46 |
| Charlotte | AA | 5 | 0 | 0 | 2 | 6.1 | 23 | 3 | 1 | 1 | 1 | 0 | 0 | 0 | 2 | 0 | 8 | 0 | 0 | 0 | 1 | .000 | 0 | 1 | 1.42 |
| 1989 Ft.Laudrdle | A | 6 | 4 | 1 | 1 | 35.1 | 143 | 27 | 9 | 6 | 1 | 0 | 1 | 2 | 5 | 0 | 22 | 0 | 1 | 2 | 2 | .500 | 0 | 1 | 1.53 |
| Columbus | AAA | 22 | 12 | 0 | 2 | 90 | 404 | 102 | 50 | 50 | 5 | 2 | 3 | 5 | 34 | 2 | 70 | 3 | 5 | 9 | 6 | .600 | 0 | 0 | 5.00 |
| 1990 Columbus | AAA | 30 | 14 | 2 | 6 | 122.2 | 508 | 114 | 56 | 49 | 5 | 2 | 3 | 1 | 27 | 0 | 115 | 7 | 0 | 9 | 4 | .692 | 1 | 1 | 3.60 |
| 1990 New York | AL | 8 | 3 | 0 | 2 | 26.1 | 119 | 33 | 20 | 20 | 5 | 2 | 1 | 2 | 9 | 0 | 21 | 0 | 0 | 1 | 1 | .500 | 0 | 0 | 6.84 |

## Scott Leius

**Bats:** Right **Throws:** Right **Pos:** SS **Ht:** 6' 3" **Wt:** 180 **Born:** 09/24/65 **Age:** 25

| | | BATTING | | | | | | | | | | | | | | | | | BASERUNNING | | | | PERCENTAGES | | |
|---|---|---|---|---|---|---|---|---|---|---|---|---|---|---|---|---|---|---|---|---|---|---|---|---|---|
| Year Team | Lg | G | AB | H | 2B | 3B | HR | (Hm | Rd) | TB | R | RBI | TBB | IBB | SO | HBP | SH | SF | SB | CS | SB% | GDP | Avg | OBP | SLG |
| 1986 Elizabethtn | R | 61 | 237 | 66 | 14 | 1 | 4 | -- | -- | 94 | 37 | 23 | 26 | 0 | 45 | 3 | 2 | 1 | 5 | 0 | 1.00 | 6 | .278 | .356 | .397 |
| 1987 Kenosha | A | 126 | 414 | 99 | 16 | 4 | 8 | -- | -- | 147 | 65 | 51 | 50 | 0 | 88 | 3 | 5 | 4 | 6 | 4 | .60 | 2 | .239 | .323 | .355 |
| 1988 Visalia | A | 93 | 308 | 73 | 14 | 4 | 3 | -- | -- | 104 | 44 | 46 | 42 | 0 | 50 | 3 | 8 | 1 | 3 | 1 | .75 | 11 | .237 | .333 | .338 |
| 1989 Orlando | AA | 99 | 346 | 105 | 22 | 2 | 4 | -- | -- | 143 | 49 | 45 | 38 | 0 | 74 | 0 | 3 | 2 | 3 | 2 | .60 | 4 | .303 | .370 | .413 |
| 1990 Portland | AAA | 103 | 353 | 81 | 13 | 5 | 2 | -- | -- | 110 | 34 | 23 | 35 | 0 | 66 | 0 | 4 | 0 | 5 | 3 | .63 | 8 | .229 | .299 | .312 |
| 1990 Minnesota | AL | 14 | 25 | 6 | 1 | 0 | 1 | (0 | 1) | 10 | 4 | 4 | 2 | 0 | 2 | 0 | 1 | 0 | 0 | 0 | .00 | 2 | .240 | .296 | .400 |

## Mark Lemke

**Bats:** Both **Throws:** Right **Pos:** 2B/3B **Ht:** 5' 9" **Wt:** 165 **Born:** 08/13/65 **Age:** 25

| | | BATTING | | | | | | | | | | | | | | | | | BASERUNNING | | | | PERCENTAGES | | |
|---|---|---|---|---|---|---|---|---|---|---|---|---|---|---|---|---|---|---|---|---|---|---|---|---|---|
| Year Team | Lg | G | AB | H | 2B | 3B | HR | (Hm | Rd) | TB | R | RBI | TBB | IBB | SO | HBP | SH | SF | SB | CS | SB% | GDP | Avg | OBP | SLG |
| 1988 Atlanta | NL | 16 | 58 | 13 | 4 | 0 | 0 | (0 | 0) | 17 | 8 | 2 | 4 | 0 | 5 | 0 | 2 | 0 | 0 | 2 | .00 | 1 | .224 | .274 | .293 |
| 1989 Atlanta | NL | 14 | 55 | 10 | 2 | 1 | 2 | (1 | 1) | 20 | 4 | 10 | 5 | 0 | 7 | 0 | 0 | 0 | 0 | 1 | .00 | 1 | .182 | .250 | .364 |
| 1990 Atlanta | NL | 102 | 239 | 54 | 13 | 0 | 0 | (0 | 0) | 67 | 22 | 21 | 21 | 3 | 22 | 0 | 4 | 2 | 0 | 1 | .00 | 6 | .226 | .286 | .280 |
| 3 ML YEARS | | 132 | 352 | 77 | 19 | 1 | 2 | (1 | 1) | 104 | 34 | 33 | 30 | 3 | 34 | 0 | 6 | 2 | 0 | 4 | .00 | 8 | .219 | .279 | .295 |

## Chet Lemon

**Bats:** Right **Throws:** Right **Pos:** RF **Ht:** 6' 0" **Wt:** 190 **Born:** 02/12/55 **Age:** 36

| | | BATTING | | | | | | | | | | | | | | | | | BASERUNNING | | | | PERCENTAGES | | |
|---|---|---|---|---|---|---|---|---|---|---|---|---|---|---|---|---|---|---|---|---|---|---|---|---|---|
| Year Team | Lg | G | AB | H | 2B | 3B | HR | (Hm | Rd) | TB | R | RBI | TBB | IBB | SO | HBP | SH | SF | SB | CS | SB% | GDP | Avg | OBP | SLG |
| 1975 Chicago | AL | 9 | 35 | 9 | 2 | 0 | 0 | (0 | 0) | 11 | 2 | 1 | 2 | 0 | 6 | 0 | 1 | 0 | 1 | 0 | 1.00 | 0 | .257 | .297 | .314 |
| 1976 Chicago | AL | 132 | 451 | 111 | 15 | 5 | 4 | (2 | 2) | 148 | 46 | 38 | 28 | 0 | 65 | 7 | 7 | 4 | 13 | 7 | .65 | 9 | .246 | .298 | .328 |
| 1977 Chicago | AL | 150 | 553 | 151 | 38 | 4 | 19 | (11 | 8) | 254 | 99 | 67 | 52 | 1 | 88 | 11 | 4 | 7 | 8 | 7 | .53 | 7 | .273 | .343 | .459 |
| 1978 Chicago | AL | 105 | 357 | 107 | 24 | 6 | 13 | (8 | 5) | 182 | 51 | 55 | 39 | 2 | 46 | 8 | 8 | 4 | 5 | 9 | .36 | 11 | .300 | .377 | .510 |
| 1979 Chicago | AL | 148 | 556 | 177 | 44 | 2 | 17 | (7 | 10) | 276 | 79 | 86 | 56 | 6 | 68 | 13 | 3 | 4 | 7 | 11 | .39 | 15 | .318 | .391 | .496 |
| 1980 Chicago | AL | 147 | 514 | 150 | 32 | 6 | 11 | (5 | 6) | 227 | 76 | 51 | 71 | 6 | 56 | 12 | 4 | 3 | 6 | 6 | .50 | 12 | .292 | .388 | .442 |
| 1981 Chicago | AL | 94 | 328 | 99 | 23 | 6 | 9 | (4 | 5) | 161 | 50 | 50 | 33 | 0 | 48 | 13 | 5 | 4 | 5 | 8 | .38 | 10 | .302 | .384 | .491 |

| 1982 | Detroit | AL | 125 | 436 | 116 | 20 | 1 | 19 | (12 | 7) | 195 | 75 | 52 | 56 | 2 | 69 | 15 | 4 | 1 | 1 | 4 | .20 | 13 | .266 | .368 | .447 |
|---|---|---|---|---|---|---|---|---|---|---|---|---|---|---|---|---|---|---|---|---|---|---|---|---|---|---|
| 1983 | Detroit | AL | 145 | 491 | 125 | 21 | 5 | 24 | (14 | 10) | 228 | 78 | 69 | 54 | 1 | 70 | 20 | 4 | 4 | 0 | 7 | .00 | 11 | .255 | .350 | .464 |
| 1984 | Detroit | AL | 141 | 509 | 146 | 34 | 6 | 20 | (12 | 8) | 252 | 77 | 76 | 51 | 9 | 83 | 7 | 2 | 4 | 5 | 5 | .50 | 16 | .287 | .357 | .495 |
| 1985 | Detroit | AL | 145 | 517 | 137 | 28 | 4 | 18 | (9 | 9) | 227 | 69 | 68 | 45 | 3 | 93 | 10 | 0 | 3 | 0 | 2 | .00 | 5 | .265 | .334 | .439 |
| 1986 | Detroit | AL | 126 | 403 | 101 | 21 | 3 | 12 | (7 | 5) | 164 | 45 | 53 | 39 | 3 | 53 | 8 | 3 | 4 | 2 | 1 | .67 | 15 | .251 | .326 | .407 |
| 1987 | Detroit | AL | 146 | 470 | 130 | 30 | 3 | 20 | (10 | 10) | 226 | 75 | 75 | 70 | 1 | 82 | 8 | 0 | 5 | 0 | 0 | .00 | 17 | .277 | .376 | .481 |
| 1988 | Detroit | AL | 144 | 512 | 135 | 29 | 4 | 17 | (12 | 5) | 223 | 67 | 64 | 59 | 6 | 65 | 7 | 1 | 3 | 1 | 2 | .33 | 18 | .264 | .346 | .436 |
| 1989 | Detroit | AL | 127 | 414 | 98 | 19 | 2 | 7 | (4 | 3) | 142 | 45 | 47 | 46 | 3 | 71 | 8 | 2 | 2 | 1 | 5 | .17 | 7 | .237 | .323 | .343 |
| 1990 | Detroit | AL | 104 | 322 | 83 | 16 | 4 | 5 | (2 | 3) | 122 | 39 | 32 | 48 | 3 | 61 | 4 | 2 | 2 | 3 | 2 | .60 | 8 | .258 | .359 | .379 |
| | 16 ML YEARS | | 1988 | 6868 | 1875 | 396 | 61 | 215 | (119 | 96) | 3038 | 973 | 884 | 749 | 46 | 1024 | 151 | 50 | 54 | 58 | 76 | .43 | 174 | .273 | .355 | .442 |

## Jeff Leonard

**Bats:** Right **Throws:** Right **Pos:** LF/DH **Ht:** 6' 4" **Wt:** 200 **Born:** 09/22/55 **Age:** 35

| BATTING | | | | | | | | | | | | | | | | | | | | BASERUNNING | | | | PERCENTAGES | | |
|---|---|---|---|---|---|---|---|---|---|---|---|---|---|---|---|---|---|---|---|---|---|---|---|---|---|---|
| Year | Team | Lg | G | AB | H | 2B | 3B | HR | (Hm | Rd) | TB | R | RBI | TBB | IBB | SO | HBP | SH | SF | SB | CS | SB% | GDP | Avg | OBP | SLG |
| 1977 | Los Angeles | NL | 11 | 10 | 3 | 0 | 1 | 0 | (0 | 0) | 5 | 1 | 2 | 1 | 0 | 4 | 0 | 0 | 0 | 0 | 0 | .00 | 1 | .300 | .364 | .500 |
| 1978 | Houston | NL | 8 | 26 | 10 | 2 | 0 | 0 | (0 | 0) | 12 | 2 | 4 | 1 | 0 | 2 | 0 | 0 | 0 | 0 | 1 | .00 | 0 | .385 | .407 | .462 |
| 1979 | Houston | NL | 134 | 411 | 119 | 15 | 5 | 0 | (0 | 0) | 144 | 47 | 47 | 46 | 7 | 68 | 2 | 3 | 5 | 23 | 10 | .70 | 11 | .290 | .360 | .350 |
| 1980 | Houston | NL | 88 | 216 | 46 | 7 | 5 | 3 | (3 | 0) | 72 | 29 | 20 | 19 | 2 | 46 | 0 | 1 | 2 | 4 | 1 | .80 | 8 | .213 | .274 | .333 |
| 1981 | 2 ML Teams | | 44 | 145 | 42 | 12 | 4 | 4 | (0 | 4) | 74 | 21 | 29 | 12 | 3 | 25 | 1 | 1 | 1 | 5 | 2 | .71 | 5 | .290 | .346 | .510 |
| 1982 | San Francisco | NL | 80 | 278 | 72 | 16 | 1 | 9 | (4 | 5) | 117 | 32 | 49 | 19 | 2 | 65 | 2 | 0 | 5 | 18 | 5 | .78 | 11 | .259 | .306 | .421 |
| 1983 | San Francisco | NL | 139 | 516 | 144 | 17 | 7 | 21 | (9 | 12) | 238 | 74 | 87 | 35 | 2 | 116 | 1 | 0 | 6 | 26 | 7 | .79 | 10 | .279 | .323 | .461 |
| 1984 | San Francisco | NL | 136 | 514 | 155 | 27 | 2 | 21 | (13 | 8) | 249 | 76 | 86 | 47 | 3 | 123 | 0 | 0 | 5 | 17 | 7 | .71 | 13 | .302 | .357 | .484 |
| 1985 | San Francisco | NL | 133 | 507 | 122 | 20 | 3 | 17 | (8 | 9) | 199 | 49 | 62 | 21 | 5 | 107 | 1 | 1 | 1 | 11 | 6 | .65 | 19 | .241 | .272 | .393 |
| 1986 | San Francisco | NL | 89 | 341 | 95 | 11 | 3 | 6 | (2 | 4) | 130 | 48 | 42 | 20 | 1 | 62 | 3 | 1 | 3 | 16 | 3 | .84 | 4 | .279 | .322 | .381 |
| 1987 | San Francisco | NL | 131 | 503 | 141 | 29 | 4 | 19 | (9 | 10) | 235 | 70 | 63 | 21 | 6 | 68 | 2 | 0 | 5 | 16 | 7 | .70 | 17 | .280 | .309 | .467 |
| 1988 | 2 ML Teams | | 138 | 534 | 129 | 27 | 1 | 10 | (5 | 5) | 188 | 57 | 64 | 25 | 2 | 92 | 3 | 1 | 6 | 17 | 9 | .65 | 15 | .242 | .276 | .352 |
| 1989 | Seattle | AL | 150 | 566 | 144 | 20 | 1 | 24 | (9 | 15) | 238 | 69 | 93 | 38 | 2 | 125 | 5 | 0 | 12 | 6 | 1 | .86 | 12 | .254 | .301 | .420 |
| 1990 | Seattle | AL | 134 | 478 | 120 | 20 | 0 | 10 | (7 | 3) | 170 | 39 | 75 | 37 | 6 | 97 | 3 | 0 | 7 | 4 | 2 | .67 | 20 | .251 | .305 | .356 |
| 1981 | Houston | NL | 7 | 18 | 3 | 1 | 1 | 0 | (0 | 0) | 6 | 1 | 3 | 0 | 0 | 4 | 0 | 0 | 1 | 1 | 0 | 1.00 | 0 | .167 | .158 | .333 |
| | San Francisco | NL | 37 | 127 | 39 | 11 | 3 | 4 | (0 | 4) | 68 | 20 | 26 | 12 | 3 | 21 | 1 | 1 | 0 | 4 | 2 | .67 | 5 | .307 | .371 | .535 |
| 1988 | San Francisco | NL | 44 | 160 | 41 | 8 | 1 | 2 | (0 | 2) | 57 | 12 | 20 | 9 | 1 | 24 | 0 | 0 | 2 | 7 | 5 | .58 | 5 | .256 | .292 | .356 |
| | Milwaukee | AL | 94 | 374 | 88 | 19 | 0 | 8 | (5 | 3) | 131 | 45 | 44 | 16 | 1 | 68 | 3 | 1 | 4 | 10 | 4 | .71 | 10 | .235 | .270 | .350 |
| | 14 ML YEARS | | 1415 | 5045 | 1342 | 223 | 37 | 144 | (69 | 75) | 2071 | 614 | 723 | 342 | 41 | 1000 | 23 | 8 | 58 | 163 | 61 | .73 | 146 | .266 | .312 | .411 |

## Mark Leonard

**Bats:** Left **Throws:** Right **Pos:** RF **Ht:** 6' 1" **Wt:** 195 **Born:** 08/14/64 **Age:** 26

| BATTING | | | | | | | | | | | | | | | | | | | | BASERUNNING | | | | PERCENTAGES | | |
|---|---|---|---|---|---|---|---|---|---|---|---|---|---|---|---|---|---|---|---|---|---|---|---|---|---|---|
| Year | Team | Lg | G | AB | H | 2B | 3B | HR | (Hm | Rd) | TB | R | RBI | TBB | IBB | SO | HBP | SH | SF | SB | CS | SB% | GDP | Avg | OBP | SLG |
| 1986 | Everett | A | 2 | 8 | 1 | 0 | 0 | 0 | -- | -- | 1 | 0 | 2 | 2 | 0 | 2 | 0 | 0 | 1 | 0 | 0 | .00 | 0 | .125 | .273 | .125 |
| | Tri-Cities | A | 36 | 120 | 32 | 6 | 0 | 4 | -- | -- | 50 | 21 | 15 | 25 | 0 | 19 | 1 | 0 | 0 | 4 | 2 | .67 | 7 | .267 | .397 | .417 |
| 1987 | Clinton | A | 128 | 413 | 132 | 31 | 2 | 15 | -- | -- | 212 | 57 | 80 | 71 | 3 | 61 | 5 | 0 | 3 | 5 | 8 | .38 | 7 | .320 | .423 | .513 |
| 1988 | San Jose | A | 142 | 510 | 176 | 50 | 6 | 15 | -- | -- | 283 | 102 | 118 | 118 | 13 | 82 | 5 | 0 | 11 | 11 | 6 | .65 | 10 | .345 | .464 | .555 |
| 1989 | Shreveport | AA | 63 | 219 | 68 | 15 | 3 | 10 | -- | -- | 119 | 29 | 52 | 33 | 8 | 40 | 3 | 0 | 3 | 1 | 5 | .17 | 7 | .311 | .403 | .543 |
| | Phoenix | AAA | 27 | 78 | 21 | 4 | 0 | 0 | -- | -- | 25 | 7 | 6 | 9 | 1 | 15 | 0 | 0 | 1 | 1 | 1 | .50 | 3 | .269 | .341 | .321 |
| 1990 | Phoenix | AAA | 109 | 390 | 130 | 22 | 2 | 19 | -- | -- | 213 | 76 | 82 | 76 | 1 | 81 | 4 | 0 | 4 | 6 | 3 | .67 | 7 | .333 | .443 | .546 |
| 1990 | San Francisco | NL | 11 | 17 | 3 | 1 | 0 | 1 | (0 | 1) | 7 | 3 | 2 | 3 | 0 | 8 | 0 | 0 | 0 | 0 | 0 | .00 | 0 | .176 | .300 | .412 |

## Darren Lewis

**Bats:** Right **Throws:** Right **Pos:** CF **Ht:** 6' 0" **Wt:** 175 **Born:** 08/28/67 **Age:** 23

| BATTING | | | | | | | | | | | | | | | | | | | | BASERUNNING | | | | PERCENTAGES | | |
|---|---|---|---|---|---|---|---|---|---|---|---|---|---|---|---|---|---|---|---|---|---|---|---|---|---|---|
| Year | Team | Lg | G | AB | H | 2B | 3B | HR | (Hm | Rd) | TB | R | RBI | TBB | IBB | SO | HBP | SH | SF | SB | CS | SB% | GDP | Avg | OBP | SLG |
| 1988 | Athletics | R | 5 | 15 | 5 | 3 | 0 | 0 | -- | -- | 8 | 8 | 4 | 6 | 0 | 5 | 1 | 1 | 1 | 4 | 0 | 1.00 | 1 | .333 | .522 | .533 |
| | Madison | A | 60 | 199 | 49 | 4 | 1 | 0 | -- | -- | 55 | 38 | 11 | 46 | 0 | 37 | 4 | 4 | 3 | 21 | 10 | .68 | 3 | .246 | .393 | .276 |
| 1989 | Modesto | A | 129 | 503 | 150 | 23 | 5 | 4 | -- | -- | 195 | 74 | 39 | 59 | 0 | 84 | 11 | 2 | 4 | 27 | 22 | .55 | 4 | .298 | .381 | .388 |
| | Huntsville | AA | 9 | 31 | 10 | 1 | 1 | 1 | -- | -- | 16 | 7 | 7 | 2 | 0 | 6 | 1 | 2 | 0 | 0 | 1 | .00 | 1 | .323 | .382 | .516 |
| 1990 | Huntsville | AA | 71 | 284 | 84 | 11 | 3 | 3 | -- | -- | 110 | 52 | 23 | 36 | 3 | 28 | 7 | 0 | 3 | 21 | 7 | .75 | 8 | .296 | .385 | .387 |
| | Tacoma | AAA | 60 | 247 | 72 | 5 | 2 | 2 | -- | -- | 87 | 32 | 26 | 16 | 0 | 35 | 1 | 4 | 2 | 16 | 6 | .73 | 2 | .291 | .335 | .352 |
| 1990 | Oakland | AL | 25 | 35 | 8 | 0 | 0 | 0 | (0 | 0) | 8 | 4 | 1 | 7 | 0 | 4 | 1 | 3 | 0 | 2 | 0 | 1.00 | 2 | .229 | .372 | .229 |

## Scott Lewis

**Pitches:** Right **Bats:** Right **Pos:** SP **Ht:** 6' 3" **Wt:** 190 **Born:** 12/05/65 **Age:** 25

| | | HOW MUCH HE PITCHED | | | | | | WHAT HE GAVE UP | | | | | | | | | | | | THE RESULTS | | | | | |
|---|---|---|---|---|---|---|---|---|---|---|---|---|---|---|---|---|---|---|---|---|---|---|---|---|---|
| Year Team | Lg | G | GS | CG | GF | IP | BFP | H | R | ER | HR | SH | SF | HB | TBB | IBB | SO | WP | Bk | W | L | Pct. | ShO | Sv | ERA |
| 1988 Bend | A | 9 | 9 | 2 | 0 | 61.2 | 262 | 63 | 33 | 24 | 3 | 1 | 3 | 5 | 12 | 0 | 53 | 3 | 2 | 5 | 3 | .625 | 0 | 0 | 3.50 |
| Quad City | A | 3 | 3 | 1 | 0 | 21.1 | 85 | 19 | 12 | 11 | 0 | 1 | 0 | 0 | 5 | 0 | 20 | 1 | 2 | 1 | 2 | .333 | 0 | 0 | 4.64 |
| Palm Sprngs | A | 2 | 1 | 0 | 0 | 8 | 37 | 12 | 5 | 5 | 3 | 0 | 0 | 0 | 2 | 0 | 7 | 0 | 0 | 0 | 1 | .000 | 0 | 0 | 5.63 |
| 1989 Midland | AA | 25 | 25 | 4 | 0 | 162.1 | 729 | 195 | 121 | 89 | 15 | 2 | 3 | 8 | 55 | 9 | 104 | 12 | 9 | 11 | 12 | .478 | 1 | 0 | 4.93 |
| 1990 Edmonton | AAA | 27 | 27 | 6 | 0 | 177.2 | 749 | 198 | 90 | 77 | 16 | 4 | 3 | 7 | 35 | 1 | 124 | 2 | 0 | 13 | 11 | .542 | 0 | 0 | 3.90 |
| 1990 California | AL | 2 | 2 | 1 | 0 | 16.1 | 60 | 10 | 4 | 4 | 2 | 0 | 0 | 0 | 2 | 0 | 9 | 0 | 0 | 1 | 1 | .500 | 0 | 0 | 2.20 |

## Jim Leyritz

**Bats:** Right **Throws:** Right **Pos:** 3B **Ht:** 6' 0" **Wt:** 195 **Born:** 12/27/63 **Age:** 27

| | | BATTING | | | | | | | | | | | | | | | | | BASERUNNING | | | | PERCENTAGES | | |
|---|---|---|---|---|---|---|---|---|---|---|---|---|---|---|---|---|---|---|---|---|---|---|---|---|---|
| Year Team | Lg | G | AB | H | 2B | 3B | HR | (Hm | Rd) | TB | R | RBI | TBB | IBB | SO | HBP | SH | SF | SB | CS | SB% | GDP | Avg | OBP | SLG |
| 1986 Ft.Laudrdle | A | 12 | 34 | 10 | 1 | 1 | 0 | -- | -- | 13 | 3 | 1 | 4 | 1 | 5 | 1 | 0 | 0 | 0 | 0 | .00 | 1 | .294 | .385 | .382 |
| Oneonta | A | 23 | 91 | 33 | 3 | 1 | 4 | -- | -- | 50 | 12 | 15 | 5 | 1 | 10 | 0 | 2 | 3 | 1 | 0 | 1.00 | 0 | .363 | .384 | .549 |
| 1987 Ft.Laudrdle | A | 102 | 374 | 115 | 22 | 0 | 6 | -- | -- | 155 | 48 | 51 | 38 | 1 | 54 | 6 | 7 | 4 | 2 | 1 | .67 | 8 | .307 | .377 | .414 |
| 1988 Albany | AA | 112 | 382 | 92 | 18 | 3 | 5 | -- | -- | 131 | 40 | 50 | 43 | 5 | 60 | 6 | 3 | 2 | 3 | 3 | .50 | 8 | .241 | .326 | .343 |
| 1989 Albany | AA | 114 | 375 | 118 | 18 | 2 | 10 | -- | -- | 170 | 53 | 66 | 65 | 5 | 51 | 9 | 2 | 5 | 2 | 1 | .67 | 8 | .315 | .423 | .453 |
| 1990 Columbus | AAA | 59 | 204 | 59 | 11 | 1 | 8 | -- | -- | 96 | 36 | 32 | 37 | 1 | 33 | 3 | 2 | 1 | 4 | 2 | .67 | 6 | .289 | .404 | .471 |
| 1990 New York | AL | 92 | 303 | 78 | 13 | 1 | 5 | (1 | 4) | 108 | 28 | 25 | 27 | 1 | 51 | 7 | 1 | 1 | 2 | 3 | .40 | 11 | .257 | .331 | .356 |

## Dave Liddell

**Bats:** Right **Throws:** Right **Pos:** PH **Ht:** 6' 2" **Wt:** 190 **Born:** 06/15/66 **Age:** 25

| | | BATTING | | | | | | | | | | | | | | | | | BASERUNNING | | | | PERCENTAGES | | |
|---|---|---|---|---|---|---|---|---|---|---|---|---|---|---|---|---|---|---|---|---|---|---|---|---|---|
| Year Team | Lg | G | AB | H | 2B | 3B | HR | (Hm | Rd) | TB | R | RBI | TBB | IBB | SO | HBP | SH | SF | SB | CS | SB% | GDP | Avg | OBP | SLG |
| 1984 Pikeville | R | 22 | 46 | 3 | 1 | 0 | 0 | -- | -- | 4 | 3 | 1 | 9 | 0 | 21 | 1 | 0 | 0 | 0 | 0 | .00 | 0 | .065 | .232 | .087 |
| 1985 Wytheville | R | 36 | 104 | 24 | 5 | 0 | 4 | -- | -- | 41 | 21 | 11 | 15 | 1 | 29 | 3 | 1 | 0 | 0 | 1 | .00 | 0 | .231 | .344 | .394 |
| 1986 Peoria | A | 37 | 125 | 33 | 4 | 1 | 3 | -- | -- | 48 | 12 | 15 | 15 | 2 | 42 | 4 | 1 | 0 | 0 | 1 | .00 | 2 | .264 | .361 | .384 |
| Columbia | A | 18 | 54 | 12 | 2 | 0 | 2 | -- | -- | 20 | 8 | 10 | 12 | 1 | 16 | 0 | 0 | 2 | 0 | 0 | .00 | 0 | .222 | .353 | .370 |
| Lynchburg | A | 9 | 29 | 3 | 0 | 0 | 1 | -- | -- | 6 | 5 | 3 | 3 | 0 | 8 | 1 | 0 | 0 | 0 | 0 | .00 | 1 | .103 | .212 | .207 |
| 1987 Columbia | A | 23 | 53 | 11 | 3 | 0 | 0 | -- | -- | 14 | 6 | 3 | 7 | 0 | 18 | 0 | 0 | 0 | 0 | 0 | .00 | 0 | .208 | .300 | .264 |
| Jackson | AA | 10 | 25 | 3 | 0 | 0 | 0 | -- | -- | 3 | 2 | 0 | 3 | 0 | 8 | 0 | 0 | 0 | 0 | 0 | .00 | 1 | .120 | .214 | .120 |
| Lynchburg | A | 31 | 102 | 26 | 6 | 0 | 4 | -- | -- | 44 | 18 | 17 | 7 | 1 | 30 | 4 | 1 | 1 | 1 | 1 | .50 | 1 | .255 | .325 | .431 |
| 1988 Reno | A | 26 | 70 | 23 | 8 | 0 | 0 | -- | -- | 31 | 11 | 12 | 21 | 0 | 13 | 0 | 1 | 1 | 1 | 3 | .25 | 1 | .329 | .478 | .443 |
| St. Lucie | A | 57 | 165 | 41 | 5 | 2 | 1 | -- | -- | 53 | 23 | 13 | 18 | 0 | 42 | 1 | 2 | 0 | 0 | 1 | .00 | 5 | .248 | .326 | .321 |
| 1989 Jackson | AA | 62 | 191 | 34 | 8 | 0 | 1 | -- | -- | 45 | 15 | 8 | 23 | 1 | 58 | 3 | 5 | 0 | 0 | 2 | .00 | 7 | .178 | .276 | .236 |
| Tidewater | AAA | 24 | 73 | 11 | 2 | 0 | 2 | -- | -- | 19 | 8 | 7 | 9 | 1 | 25 | 2 | 0 | 0 | 0 | 1 | .00 | 0 | .151 | .262 | .260 |
| 1990 Tidewater | AAA | 73 | 189 | 40 | 5 | 0 | 2 | -- | -- | 51 | 16 | 15 | 21 | 1 | 51 | 2 | 6 | 0 | 0 | 0 | .00 | 1 | .212 | .297 | .270 |
| 1990 New York | NL | 1 | 1 | 1 | 0 | 0 | 0 | (0 | 0) | 1 | 1 | 0 | 0 | 0 | 0 | 0 | 0 | 0 | 0 | 0 | .00 | 0 | 1.000 | 1.000 | 1.000 |

## Derek Lilliquist

**Pitches:** Left **Bats:** Left **Pos:** SP/RP **Ht:** 6' 0" **Wt:** 200 **Born:** 02/20/66 **Age:** 25

| | | HOW MUCH HE PITCHED | | | | | | WHAT HE GAVE UP | | | | | | | | | | | | THE RESULTS | | | | | |
|---|---|---|---|---|---|---|---|---|---|---|---|---|---|---|---|---|---|---|---|---|---|---|---|---|---|
| Year Team | Lg | G | GS | CG | GF | IP | BFP | H | R | ER | HR | SH | SF | HB | TBB | IBB | SO | WP | Bk | W | L | Pct. | ShO | Sv | ERA |
| 1987 Braves | R | 2 | 2 | 0 | 0 | 13 | 44 | 3 | 0 | 0 | 0 | 0 | 0 | 0 | 2 | 0 | 16 | 0 | 0 | 0 | 0 | .000 | 0 | 0 | 0.00 |
| Durham | A | 3 | 3 | 2 | 0 | 25 | 94 | 13 | 9 | 8 | 1 | 0 | 1 | 1 | 6 | 0 | 29 | 0 | 0 | 2 | 1 | .667 | 0 | 0 | 2.88 |
| 1988 Richmond | AAA | 28 | 28 | 2 | 0 | 170.2 | 716 | 179 | 70 | 64 | 11 | 6 | 7 | 1 | 36 | 1 | 80 | 5 | 6 | 10 | 12 | .455 | 0 | 0 | 3.38 |
| 1990 Richmond | AAA | 5 | 5 | 1 | 0 | 35 | 143 | 31 | 11 | 10 | 3 | 0 | 0 | 0 | 11 | 0 | 24 | 0 | 0 | 4 | 0 | 1.000 | 0 | 0 | 2.57 |
| 1989 Atlanta | NL | 32 | 30 | 0 | 0 | 165.2 | 718 | 202 | 87 | 73 | 16 | 8 | 3 | 2 | 34 | 5 | 79 | 4 | 3 | 8 | 10 | .444 | 0 | 0 | 3.97 |
| 1990 2 ML Teams | | 28 | 18 | 1 | 3 | 122 | 537 | 136 | 74 | 72 | 16 | 9 | 5 | 3 | 42 | 5 | 63 | 2 | 3 | 5 | 11 | .313 | 1 | 0 | 5.31 |
| 1990 Atlanta | NL | 12 | 11 | 0 | 1 | 61.2 | 279 | 75 | 45 | 43 | 10 | 6 | 4 | 1 | 19 | 4 | 34 | 0 | 2 | 2 | 8 | .200 | 0 | 0 | 6.28 |
| San Diego | NL | 16 | 7 | 1 | 2 | 60.1 | 258 | 61 | 29 | 29 | 6 | 3 | 1 | 2 | 23 | 1 | 29 | 2 | 1 | 3 | 3 | .500 | 1 | 0 | 4.33 |
| 2 ML YEARS | | 60 | 48 | 1 | 3 | 287.2 | 1255 | 338 | 161 | 145 | 32 | 17 | 8 | 5 | 76 | 10 | 142 | 6 | 6 | 13 | 21 | .382 | 1 | 0 | 4.54 |

## Jose Lind

**Bats:** Right **Throws:** Right **Pos:** 2B **Ht:** 5'11" **Wt:** 170 **Born:** 05/01/64 **Age:** 27

| | | BATTING | | | | | | | | | | | | | | | | | BASERUNNING | | | | PERCENTAGES | | |
|---|---|---|---|---|---|---|---|---|---|---|---|---|---|---|---|---|---|---|---|---|---|---|---|---|---|
| Year Team | Lg | G | AB | H | 2B | 3B | HR | (Hm | Rd) | TB | R | RBI | TBB | IBB | SO | HBP | SH | SF | SB | CS | SB% | GDP | Avg | OBP | SLG |
| 1987 Pittsburgh | NL | 35 | 143 | 46 | 8 | 4 | 0 | (0 | 0) | 62 | 21 | 11 | 8 | 1 | 12 | 0 | 6 | 0 | 2 | 1 | .67 | 5 | .322 | .358 | .434 |
| 1988 Pittsburgh | NL | 154 | 611 | 160 | 24 | 4 | 2 | (1 | 1) | 198 | 82 | 49 | 42 | 0 | 75 | 0 | 12 | 3 | 15 | 4 | .79 | 11 | .262 | .308 | .324 |
| 1989 Pittsburgh | NL | 153 | 578 | 134 | 21 | 3 | 2 | (2 | 0) | 167 | 52 | 48 | 39 | 7 | 64 | 2 | 13 | 5 | 15 | 1 | .94 | 13 | .232 | .280 | .289 |
| 1990 Pittsburgh | NL | 152 | 514 | 134 | 28 | 5 | 1 | (1 | 0) | 175 | 46 | 48 | 35 | 19 | 52 | 1 | 4 | 7 | 8 | 0 | 1.00 | 20 | .261 | .305 | .340 |
| 4 ML YEARS | | 494 | 1846 | 474 | 81 | 16 | 5 | (4 | 1) | 602 | 201 | 156 | 124 | 27 | 203 | 3 | 35 | 15 | 40 | 6 | .87 | 49 | .257 | .302 | .326 |

## Jim Lindeman

**Bats:** Right **Throws:** Right **Pos:** DH **Ht:** 6' 1" **Wt:** 200 **Born:** 01/10/62 **Age:** 29

| BATTING | | | | | | | | | | | | | | | | | | | BASERUNNING | | | | PERCENTAGES | | |
|---|---|---|---|---|---|---|---|---|---|---|---|---|---|---|---|---|---|---|---|---|---|---|---|---|---|
| Year Team | Lg | G | AB | H | 2B | 3B | HR | (Hm | Rd) | TB | R | RBI | TBB | IBB | SO | HBP | SH | SF | SB | CS | SB% | GDP | Avg | OBP | SLG |
| 1986 St. Louis | NL | 19 | 55 | 14 | 1 | 0 | 1 | (0 | 1) | 18 | 7 | 6 | 2 | 0 | 10 | 0 | 0 | 1 | 1 | 1 | .50 | 2 | .255 | .276 | .327 |
| 1987 St. Louis | NL | 75 | 207 | 43 | 13 | 0 | 8 | (2 | 6) | 80 | 20 | 28 | 11 | 0 | 56 | 3 | 2 | 4 | 3 | 1 | .75 | 4 | .208 | .253 | .386 |
| 1988 St. Louis | NL | 17 | 43 | 9 | 1 | 0 | 2 | (0 | 2) | 16 | 3 | 7 | 2 | 0 | 9 | 0 | 1 | 0 | 0 | 0 | .00 | 1 | .209 | .244 | .372 |
| 1989 St. Louis | NL | 73 | 45 | 5 | 1 | 0 | 0 | (0 | 0) | 6 | 8 | 2 | 3 | 0 | 18 | 0 | 1 | 1 | 0 | 0 | .00 | 2 | .111 | .163 | .133 |
| 1990 Detroit | AL | 12 | 32 | 7 | 1 | 0 | 2 | (2 | 0) | 14 | 5 | 8 | 2 | 0 | 13 | 0 | 0 | 0 | 0 | 0 | .00 | 0 | .219 | .265 | .438 |
| 5 ML YEARS | | 196 | 382 | 78 | 17 | 0 | 13 | (4 | 9) | 134 | 43 | 51 | 20 | 0 | 106 | 3 | 4 | 6 | 4 | 2 | .67 | 9 | .204 | .246 | .351 |

## Nelson Liriano

**Bats:** Both **Throws:** Right **Pos:** 2B **Ht:** 5'10" **Wt:** 165 **Born:** 06/03/64 **Age:** 27

| BATTING | | | | | | | | | | | | | | | | | | | BASERUNNING | | | | PERCENTAGES | | |
|---|---|---|---|---|---|---|---|---|---|---|---|---|---|---|---|---|---|---|---|---|---|---|---|---|---|
| Year Team | Lg | G | AB | H | 2B | 3B | HR | (Hm | Rd) | TB | R | RBI | TBB | IBB | SO | HBP | SH | SF | SB | CS | SB% | GDP | Avg | OBP | SLG |
| 1987 Toronto | AL | 37 | 158 | 38 | 6 | 2 | 2 | (1 | 1) | 54 | 29 | 10 | 16 | 2 | 22 | 0 | 2 | 0 | 13 | 2 | .87 | 3 | .241 | .310 | .342 |
| 1988 Toronto | AL | 99 | 276 | 73 | 6 | 2 | 3 | (0 | 3) | 92 | 36 | 23 | 11 | 0 | 40 | 2 | 5 | 1 | 12 | 5 | .71 | 4 | .264 | .297 | .333 |
| 1989 Toronto | AL | 132 | 418 | 110 | 26 | 3 | 5 | (3 | 2) | 157 | 51 | 53 | 43 | 0 | 51 | 2 | 10 | 5 | 16 | 7 | .70 | 10 | .263 | .331 | .376 |
| 1990 2 ML Teams | | 103 | 355 | 83 | 12 | 9 | 1 | (1 | 0) | 116 | 46 | 28 | 38 | 0 | 44 | 1 | 4 | 2 | 8 | 7 | .53 | 8 | .234 | .308 | .327 |
| 1990 Toronto | AL | 50 | 170 | 36 | 7 | 2 | 1 | (1 | 0) | 50 | 16 | 15 | 16 | 0 | 20 | 1 | 1 | 1 | 3 | 5 | .38 | 5 | .212 | .282 | .294 |
| Minnesota | AL | 53 | 185 | 47 | 5 | 7 | 0 | (0 | 0) | 66 | 30 | 13 | 22 | 0 | 24 | 0 | 3 | 1 | 5 | 2 | .71 | 3 | .254 | .332 | .357 |
| 4 ML YEARS | | 371 | 1207 | 304 | 50 | 16 | 11 | (5 | 6) | 419 | 162 | 114 | 108 | 2 | 157 | 5 | 21 | 8 | 49 | 21 | .70 | 25 | .252 | .314 | .347 |

## Greg Litton

**Bats:** Right **Throws:** Right **Pos:** RF/2B **Ht:** 6' 0" **Wt:** 175 **Born:** 07/13/64 **Age:** 26

| BATTING | | | | | | | | | | | | | | | | | | | BASERUNNING | | | | PERCENTAGES | | |
|---|---|---|---|---|---|---|---|---|---|---|---|---|---|---|---|---|---|---|---|---|---|---|---|---|---|
| Year Team | Lg | G | AB | H | 2B | 3B | HR | (Hm | Rd) | TB | R | RBI | TBB | IBB | SO | HBP | SH | SF | SB | CS | SB% | GDP | Avg | OBP | SLG |
| 1984 Everett | A | 62 | 243 | 57 | 12 | 2 | 4 | -- | -- | 85 | 29 | 26 | 27 | 0 | 47 | 1 | 0 | 0 | 2 | 1 | .67 | 4 | .235 | .314 | .350 |
| 1985 Fresno | A | 141 | 564 | 150 | 33 | 7 | 12 | -- | -- | 233 | 88 | 103 | 50 | 0 | 86 | 3 | 2 | 7 | 8 | 4 | .67 | 8 | .266 | .325 | .413 |
| 1986 Shreveport | AA | 131 | 455 | 112 | 30 | 3 | 10 | -- | -- | 178 | 46 | 55 | 52 | 4 | 77 | 4 | 5 | 2 | 1 | 2 | .33 | 13 | .246 | .327 | .391 |
| 1987 Shreveport | AA | 72 | 254 | 66 | 6 | 3 | 8 | -- | -- | 102 | 34 | 33 | 22 | 2 | 51 | 2 | 2 | 2 | 2 | 4 | .33 | 2 | .260 | .321 | .402 |
| Phoenix | AAA | 60 | 203 | 44 | 8 | 2 | 1 | -- | -- | 59 | 24 | 22 | 18 | 1 | 40 | 2 | 2 | 3 | 0 | 1 | .00 | 5 | .217 | .283 | .291 |
| 1988 Shreveport | AA | 116 | 432 | 120 | 35 | 5 | 11 | -- | -- | 198 | 58 | 64 | 37 | 2 | 84 | 5 | 1 | 7 | 2 | 2 | .50 | 8 | .278 | .337 | .458 |
| 1989 Phoenix | AAA | 30 | 89 | 16 | 4 | 2 | 2 | -- | -- | 30 | 6 | 6 | 8 | 0 | 24 | 0 | 0 | 2 | 1 | 3 | .25 | 3 | .180 | .242 | .337 |
| 1990 Phoenix | AAA | 6 | 22 | 6 | 1 | 0 | 0 | -- | -- | 7 | 3 | 4 | 2 | 0 | 7 | 0 | 0 | 1 | 0 | 0 | .00 | 0 | .273 | .320 | .318 |
| 1989 San Francisco | NL | 71 | 143 | 36 | 5 | 3 | 4 | (3 | 1) | 59 | 12 | 17 | 7 | 0 | 29 | 1 | 4 | 0 | 0 | 2 | .00 | 3 | .252 | .291 | .413 |
| 1990 San Francisco | NL | 93 | 204 | 50 | 9 | 1 | 1 | (0 | 1) | 64 | 17 | 24 | 11 | 0 | 45 | 1 | 2 | 2 | 1 | 0 | 1.00 | 5 | .245 | .284 | .314 |
| 2 ML YEARS | | 164 | 347 | 86 | 14 | 4 | 5 | (3 | 2) | 123 | 29 | 41 | 18 | 0 | 74 | 2 | 6 | 2 | 1 | 2 | .33 | 8 | .248 | .287 | .354 |

## Steve Lombardozzi

**Bats:** Right **Throws:** Right **Pos:** PH **Ht:** 6' 0" **Wt:** 183 **Born:** 04/26/60 **Age:** 31

| BATTING | | | | | | | | | | | | | | | | | | | BASERUNNING | | | | PERCENTAGES | | |
|---|---|---|---|---|---|---|---|---|---|---|---|---|---|---|---|---|---|---|---|---|---|---|---|---|---|
| Year Team | Lg | G | AB | H | 2B | 3B | HR | (Hm | Rd) | TB | R | RBI | TBB | IBB | SO | HBP | SH | SF | SB | CS | SB% | GDP | Avg | OBP | SLG |
| 1985 Minnesota | AL | 28 | 54 | 20 | 4 | 1 | 0 | (0 | 0) | 26 | 10 | 6 | 6 | 0 | 6 | 0 | 4 | 1 | 3 | 2 | .60 | 0 | .370 | .426 | .481 |
| 1986 Minnesota | AL | 156 | 453 | 103 | 20 | 5 | 8 | (6 | 2) | 157 | 53 | 33 | 52 | 2 | 76 | 1 | 9 | 0 | 3 | 1 | .75 | 8 | .227 | .308 | .347 |
| 1987 Minnesota | AL | 136 | 432 | 103 | 19 | 3 | 8 | (3 | 5) | 152 | 51 | 38 | 33 | 1 | 66 | 4 | 9 | 1 | 5 | 1 | .83 | 10 | .238 | .298 | .352 |
| 1988 Minnesota | AL | 103 | 287 | 60 | 15 | 2 | 3 | (3 | 0) | 88 | 34 | 27 | 35 | 2 | 48 | 2 | 6 | 5 | 2 | 5 | .29 | 2 | .209 | .295 | .307 |
| 1989 Houston | NL | 21 | 37 | 8 | 3 | 1 | 1 | (1 | 0) | 16 | 5 | 3 | 4 | 1 | 9 | 0 | 0 | 0 | 0 | 0 | .00 | 0 | .216 | .293 | .432 |
| 1990 Houston | NL | 2 | 1 | 0 | 0 | 0 | 0 | (0 | 0) | 0 | 0 | 0 | 1 | 0 | 1 | 0 | 0 | 0 | 0 | 0 | .00 | 0 | .000 | .500 | .000 |
| 6 ML YEARS | | 446 | 1264 | 294 | 61 | 12 | 20 | (13 | 7) | 439 | 153 | 107 | 131 | 6 | 206 | 7 | 28 | 7 | 13 | 9 | .59 | 20 | .233 | .307 | .347 |

## Bill Long

**Pitches:** Right **Bats:** Right **Pos:** RP **Ht:** 6' 0" **Wt:** 185 **Born:** 02/29/60 **Age:** 31

| HOW MUCH HE PITCHED | | | | | | | | WHAT HE GAVE UP | | | | | | | | | | | | THE RESULTS | | | | | |
|---|---|---|---|---|---|---|---|---|---|---|---|---|---|---|---|---|---|---|---|---|---|---|---|---|---|
| Year Team | Lg | G | GS | CG | GF | IP | BFP | H | R | ER | HR | SH | SF | HB | TBB | IBB | SO | WP | Bk | W | L | Pct. | ShO | Sv | ERA |
| 1985 Chicago | AL | 4 | 3 | 0 | 1 | 14 | 71 | 25 | 17 | 16 | 4 | 1 | 1 | 0 | 5 | 2 | 13 | 1 | 0 | 0 | 1 | .000 | 0 | 0 | 10.29 |
| 1987 Chicago | AL | 29 | 23 | 5 | 2 | 169 | 699 | 179 | 85 | 82 | 20 | 6 | 3 | 3 | 28 | 1 | 72 | 0 | 1 | 8 | 8 | .500 | 2 | 1 | 4.37 |
| 1988 Chicago | AL | 47 | 18 | 3 | 14 | 174 | 732 | 187 | 89 | 78 | 21 | 8 | 8 | 4 | 43 | 4 | 77 | 2 | 0 | 8 | 11 | .421 | 0 | 2 | 4.03 |
| 1989 Chicago | AL | 30 | 8 | 0 | 3 | 98.2 | 432 | 101 | 49 | 43 | 8 | 4 | 6 | 4 | 37 | 0 | 51 | 3 | 0 | 5 | 5 | .500 | 0 | 1 | 3.92 |
| 1990 2 ML Teams | | 46 | 0 | 0 | 21 | 61.1 | 270 | 72 | 34 | 31 | 10 | 4 | 0 | 1 | 23 | 4 | 34 | 1 | 0 | 6 | 2 | .750 | 0 | 5 | 4.55 |
| 1990 Chicago | AL | 4 | 0 | 0 | 0 | 5.2 | 26 | 6 | 5 | 4 | 2 | 1 | 0 | 0 | 2 | 0 | 2 | 0 | 0 | 0 | 1 | .000 | 0 | 0 | 6.35 |
| Chicago | NL | 42 | 0 | 0 | 21 | 55.2 | 244 | 66 | 29 | 27 | 8 | 3 | 0 | 1 | 21 | 4 | 32 | 1 | 0 | 6 | 1 | .857 | 0 | 5 | 4.37 |
| 5 ML YEARS | | 156 | 52 | 8 | 41 | 517 | 2204 | 564 | 274 | 250 | 63 | 23 | 18 | 12 | 136 | 11 | 247 | 7 | 1 | 27 | 27 | .500 | 2 | 9 | 4.35 |

## Luis Lopez

**Bats:** Right **Throws:** Right **Pos:** 1B **Ht:** 6' 1" **Wt:** 190 **Born:** 09/01/64 **Age:** 26

| | | | BATTING | | | | | | | | | | | | | | | | | BASERUNNING | | | | PERCENTAGES | | |
|---|---|---|---|---|---|---|---|---|---|---|---|---|---|---|---|---|---|---|---|---|---|---|---|---|---|---|
| Year | Team | Lg | G | AB | H | 2B | 3B | HR | (Hm | Rd) | TB | R | RBI | TBB | IBB | SO | HBP | SH | SF | SB | CS | SB% | GDP | Avg | OBP | SLG |
| 1984 | Great Falls | R | 68 | 275 | 90 | 15 | 5 | 6 | -- | -- | 133 | 60 | 61 | 27 | 1 | 15 | 5 | 1 | 2 | 4 | 4 | .50 | 10 | .327 | .395 | .484 |
| 1985 | Vero Beach | A | 120 | 382 | 106 | 18 | 2 | 1 | -- | -- | 131 | 47 | 43 | 25 | 3 | 41 | 6 | 3 | 3 | 2 | 2 | .50 | 19 | .277 | .329 | .343 |
| 1986 | Vero Beach | A | 122 | 434 | 124 | 21 | 3 | 1 | -- | -- | 154 | 52 | 60 | 33 | 3 | 25 | 2 | 2 | 4 | 5 | 7 | .42 | 21 | .286 | .336 | .355 |
| 1987 | Bakersfield | A | 142 | 550 | 181 | 43 | 2 | 16 | -- | -- | 276 | 89 | 96 | 38 | 3 | 49 | 9 | 5 | 6 | 6 | 6 | .50 | 9 | .329 | .378 | .502 |
| 1988 | San Antonio | AA | 124 | 470 | 116 | 16 | 3 | 7 | -- | -- | 159 | 56 | 65 | 32 | 5 | 33 | 13 | 5 | 7 | 3 | 4 | .43 | 12 | .247 | .308 | .338 |
| 1989 | San Antonio | AA | 99 | 327 | 87 | 17 | 0 | 10 | -- | -- | 134 | 46 | 51 | 38 | 4 | 39 | 5 | 0 | 2 | 1 | 0 | 1.00 | 14 | .266 | .349 | .410 |
| | Albuquerque | AAA | 19 | 75 | 37 | 7 | 0 | 2 | -- | -- | 50 | 17 | 16 | 6 | 0 | 7 | 1 | 0 | 2 | 1 | 0 | 1.00 | 1 | .493 | .524 | .667 |
| 1990 | Albuquerque | AAA | 128 | 448 | 158 | 23 | 2 | 11 | -- | -- | 218 | 65 | 81 | 47 | 4 | 49 | 4 | 0 | 2 | 3 | 3 | .50 | 12 | .353 | .417 | .487 |
| 1990 | Los Angeles | NL | 6 | 6 | 0 | 0 | 0 | 0 | (0 | 0) | 0 | 0 | 0 | 0 | 0 | 2 | 0 | 0 | 0 | 0 | 0 | .00 | 0 | .000 | .000 | .000 |

## Vance Lovelace

**Pitches:** Left **Bats:** Left **Pos:** RP **Ht:** 6' 5" **Wt:** 235 **Born:** 08/09/63 **Age:** 27

| | | | HOW MUCH HE PITCHED | | | | | WHAT HE GAVE UP | | | | | | | | | | | | THE RESULTS | | | | | |
|---|---|---|---|---|---|---|---|---|---|---|---|---|---|---|---|---|---|---|---|---|---|---|---|---|---|
| Year | Team | Lg | G | GS | CG | GF | IP | BFP | H | R | ER | HR | SH | SF | HB | TBB | IBB | SO | WP | Bk | W | L | Pct. | ShO | Sv | ERA |
| 1988 | California | AL | 3 | 0 | 0 | 2 | 1.1 | 8 | 2 | 2 | 2 | 1 | 0 | 0 | 0 | 3 | 0 | 0 | 0 | 0 | 0 | 0 | .000 | 0 | 0 | 13.50 |
| 1989 | California | AL | 1 | 0 | 0 | 1 | 1 | 4 | 0 | 0 | 0 | 0 | 0 | 0 | 0 | 1 | 1 | 1 | 0 | 0 | 0 | 0 | .000 | 0 | 0 | 0.00 |
| 1990 | Seattle | AL | 5 | 0 | 0 | 1 | 2.1 | 17 | 3 | 1 | 1 | 0 | 0 | 0 | 1 | 6 | 0 | 1 | 2 | 0 | 0 | 0 | .000 | 0 | 0 | 3.86 |
| | 3 ML YEARS | | 9 | 0 | 0 | 4 | 4.2 | 29 | 5 | 3 | 3 | 1 | 0 | 0 | 1 | 10 | 1 | 2 | 2 | 0 | 0 | 0 | .000 | 0 | 0 | 5.79 |

## Rick Luecken

**Pitches:** Right **Bats:** Right **Pos:** RP **Ht:** 6' 6" **Wt:** 210 **Born:** 11/15/60 **Age:** 30

| | | | HOW MUCH HE PITCHED | | | | | WHAT HE GAVE UP | | | | | | | | | | | | THE RESULTS | | | | | |
|---|---|---|---|---|---|---|---|---|---|---|---|---|---|---|---|---|---|---|---|---|---|---|---|---|---|
| Year | Team | Lg | G | GS | CG | GF | IP | BFP | H | R | ER | HR | SH | SF | HB | TBB | IBB | SO | WP | Bk | W | L | Pct. | ShO | Sv | ERA |
| 1983 | Bellingham | A | 14 | 12 | 2 | 1 | 78 | 0 | 70 | 39 | 31 | 4 | 0 | 0 | 0 | 37 | 0 | 83 | 5 | 0 | 5 | 4 | .556 | 0 | 0 | 3.58 |
| 1984 | Chattanooga | AA | 26 | 26 | 5 | 0 | 163.2 | 727 | 166 | 85 | 69 | 13 | 6 | 5 | 2 | 88 | 0 | 90 | 9 | 0 | 11 | 13 | .458 | 1 | 0 | 3.79 |
| 1985 | Calgary | AAA | 18 | 14 | 2 | 4 | 85.2 | 0 | 111 | 70 | 66 | 12 | 0 | 0 | 1 | 39 | 1 | 44 | 5 | 0 | 4 | 8 | .333 | 0 | 0 | 6.93 |
| 1986 | Chattanooga | AA | 17 | 14 | 4 | 0 | 88.2 | 401 | 106 | 57 | 52 | 10 | 3 | 3 | 2 | 42 | 3 | 55 | 2 | 0 | 6 | 7 | .462 | 2 | 0 | 5.28 |
| 1987 | Memphis | AA | 28 | 24 | 2 | 0 | 146 | 645 | 163 | 86 | 77 | 12 | 4 | 7 | 3 | 53 | 3 | 88 | 5 | 0 | 9 | 9 | .500 | 0 | 0 | 4.75 |
| 1988 | Memphis | AA | 21 | 0 | 0 | 19 | 24.2 | 99 | 17 | 8 | 6 | 0 | 1 | 1 | 1 | 7 | 2 | 30 | 1 | 1 | 4 | 1 | .800 | 0 | 5 | 2.19 |
| | Omaha | AAA | 26 | 0 | 0 | 22 | 40 | 175 | 45 | 10 | 9 | 1 | 1 | 1 | 1 | 15 | 3 | 27 | 2 | 0 | 5 | 0 | 1.000 | 0 | 9 | 2.03 |
| 1989 | Omaha | AAA | 36 | 0 | 0 | 29 | 46.2 | 193 | 33 | 14 | 12 | 0 | 2 | 3 | 1 | 22 | 0 | 39 | 6 | 0 | 4 | 1 | .800 | 0 | 16 | 2.31 |
| 1990 | Richmond | AAA | 8 | 0 | 0 | 6 | 13.1 | 61 | 11 | 3 | 2 | 0 | 0 | 1 | 0 | 8 | 4 | 15 | 0 | 0 | 1 | 1 | .500 | 0 | 4 | 1.35 |
| 1989 | Kansas City | AL | 19 | 0 | 0 | 12 | 23.2 | 104 | 23 | 9 | 9 | 3 | 2 | 0 | 0 | 13 | 4 | 16 | 0 | 1 | 2 | 1 | .667 | 0 | 1 | 3.42 |
| 1990 | 2 ML Teams | | 37 | 0 | 0 | 12 | 54 | 260 | 75 | 37 | 35 | 6 | 4 | 1 | 3 | 31 | 7 | 35 | 2 | 0 | 1 | 4 | .200 | 0 | 1 | 5.83 |
| 1990 | Atlanta | NL | 36 | 0 | 0 | 11 | 53 | 255 | 73 | 36 | 34 | 5 | 4 | 1 | 3 | 30 | 7 | 35 | 2 | 0 | 1 | 4 | .200 | 0 | 1 | 5.77 |
| | Toronto | AL | 1 | 0 | 0 | 1 | 1 | 5 | 2 | 1 | 1 | 1 | 0 | 0 | 0 | 1 | 0 | 0 | 0 | 0 | 0 | 0 | .000 | 0 | 0 | 9.00 |
| | 2 ML YEARS | | 56 | 0 | 0 | 24 | 77.2 | 364 | 98 | 46 | 44 | 9 | 6 | 1 | 3 | 44 | 11 | 51 | 2 | 1 | 3 | 5 | .375 | 0 | 2 | 5.10 |

## Urbano Lugo

**Pitches:** Right **Bats:** Right **Pos:** RP **Ht:** 5'11" **Wt:** 197 **Born:** 08/12/62 **Age:** 28

| | | | HOW MUCH HE PITCHED | | | | | WHAT HE GAVE UP | | | | | | | | | | | | THE RESULTS | | | | | |
|---|---|---|---|---|---|---|---|---|---|---|---|---|---|---|---|---|---|---|---|---|---|---|---|---|---|
| Year | Team | Lg | G | GS | CG | GF | IP | BFP | H | R | ER | HR | SH | SF | HB | TBB | IBB | SO | WP | Bk | W | L | Pct. | ShO | Sv | ERA |
| 1985 | California | AL | 20 | 10 | 1 | 5 | 83 | 351 | 86 | 36 | 34 | 10 | 2 | 2 | 4 | 29 | 1 | 42 | 2 | 0 | 3 | 4 | .429 | 0 | 0 | 3.69 |
| 1986 | California | AL | 6 | 3 | 0 | 0 | 21.1 | 86 | 21 | 9 | 9 | 4 | 1 | 0 | 0 | 6 | 0 | 9 | 0 | 0 | 1 | 1 | .500 | 0 | 0 | 3.80 |
| 1987 | California | AL | 7 | 5 | 0 | 0 | 28 | 143 | 42 | 34 | 29 | 8 | 0 | 1 | 0 | 18 | 0 | 24 | 3 | 0 | 0 | 2 | .000 | 0 | 0 | 9.32 |
| 1988 | California | AL | 1 | 0 | 0 | 0 | 2 | 9 | 2 | 2 | 2 | 1 | 0 | 0 | 0 | 1 | 0 | 1 | 0 | 0 | 0 | 0 | .000 | 0 | 0 | 9.00 |
| 1989 | Montreal | NL | 3 | 0 | 0 | 2 | 4 | 16 | 4 | 3 | 3 | 1 | 0 | 0 | 0 | 0 | 0 | 3 | 1 | 0 | 0 | 0 | .000 | 0 | 0 | 6.75 |
| 1990 | Detroit | AL | 13 | 1 | 0 | 4 | 24.1 | 116 | 30 | 19 | 19 | 9 | 4 | 0 | 3 | 13 | 1 | 12 | 2 | 0 | 2 | 0 | 1.000 | 0 | 0 | 7.03 |
| | 6 ML YEARS | | 50 | 19 | 1 | 11 | 162.2 | 721 | 185 | 103 | 96 | 33 | 7 | 3 | 7 | 67 | 2 | 91 | 8 | 0 | 6 | 7 | .462 | 0 | 0 | 5.31 |

## Scott Lusader

**Bats:** Left **Throws:** Left **Pos:** RF **Ht:** 5'10" **Wt:** 165 **Born:** 09/30/64 **Age:** 26

| | | | BATTING | | | | | | | | | | | | | | | | | BASERUNNING | | | | PERCENTAGES | | |
|---|---|---|---|---|---|---|---|---|---|---|---|---|---|---|---|---|---|---|---|---|---|---|---|---|---|---|
| Year | Team | Lg | G | AB | H | 2B | 3B | HR | (Hm | Rd) | TB | R | RBI | TBB | IBB | SO | HBP | SH | SF | SB | CS | SB% | GDP | Avg | OBP | SLG |
| 1987 | Detroit | AL | 23 | 47 | 15 | 3 | 1 | 1 | (1 | 0) | 23 | 8 | 8 | 5 | 1 | 7 | 0 | 1 | 1 | 1 | 0 | 1.00 | 0 | .319 | .377 | .489 |
| 1988 | Detroit | AL | 16 | 16 | 1 | 0 | 0 | 1 | (0 | 1) | 4 | 3 | 3 | 1 | 0 | 4 | 0 | 0 | 1 | 0 | 0 | .00 | 1 | .063 | .111 | .250 |
| 1989 | Detroit | AL | 40 | 103 | 26 | 4 | 0 | 1 | (1 | 0) | 33 | 15 | 8 | 9 | 0 | 21 | 0 | 0 | 1 | 3 | 0 | 1.00 | 2 | .252 | .310 | .320 |
| 1990 | Detroit | AL | 45 | 87 | 21 | 2 | 0 | 2 | (1 | 1) | 29 | 13 | 16 | 12 | 0 | 8 | 0 | 0 | 3 | 0 | 0 | .00 | 2 | .241 | .324 | .333 |
| | 4 ML YEARS | | 124 | 253 | 63 | 9 | 1 | 5 | (3 | 2) | 89 | 39 | 35 | 27 | 1 | 40 | 0 | 1 | 6 | 4 | 0 | 1.00 | 5 | .249 | .315 | .352 |

## Fred Lynn

**Bats:** Left **Throws:** Left **Pos:** LF **Ht:** 6' 1" **Wt:** 190 **Born:** 02/03/52 **Age:** 39

| BATTING | | | | | | | | | | | | | | | | | | | | | BASERUNNING | | | | PERCENTAGES | | |
|---|---|---|---|---|---|---|---|---|---|---|---|---|---|---|---|---|---|---|---|---|---|---|---|---|---|---|---|
| Year | Team | Lg | G | AB | H | 2B | 3B | HR | (Hm | Rd) | TB | R | RBI | TBB | IBB | SO | HBP | SH | SF | SB | CS | SB% | GDP | Avg | OBP | SLG |
| 1974 | Boston | AL | 15 | 43 | 18 | 2 | 2 | 2 | (1 | 1) | 30 | 5 | 10 | 6 | 2 | 6 | 1 | 0 | 1 | 0 | 0 | .00 | 0 | .419 | .490 | .698 |
| 1975 | Boston | AL | 145 | 528 | 175 | 47 | 7 | 21 | (9 | 12) | 299 | 103 | 105 | 62 | 10 | 90 | 3 | 6 | 6 | 10 | 5 | .67 | 11 | .331 | .401 | .566 |
| 1976 | Boston | AL | 132 | 507 | 159 | 32 | 8 | 10 | (4 | 6) | 237 | 76 | 65 | 48 | 2 | 67 | 1 | 0 | 10 | 14 | 9 | .61 | 9 | .314 | .367 | .467 |
| 1977 | Boston | AL | 129 | 497 | 129 | 29 | 5 | 18 | (10 | 8) | 222 | 81 | 76 | 51 | 2 | 63 | 3 | 5 | 8 | 2 | 3 | .40 | 14 | .260 | .327 | .447 |
| 1978 | Boston | AL | 150 | 541 | 161 | 33 | 3 | 22 | (11 | 11) | 266 | 75 | 82 | 75 | 11 | 50 | 1 | 4 | 6 | 3 | 6 | .33 | 9 | .298 | .380 | .492 |
| 1979 | Boston | AL | 147 | 531 | 177 | 42 | 1 | 39 | (28 | 11) | 338 | 116 | 122 | 82 | 4 | 79 | 4 | 0 | 5 | 2 | 2 | .50 | 9 | .333 | .423 | .637 |
| 1980 | Boston | AL | 110 | 415 | 125 | 32 | 3 | 12 | (6 | 6) | 199 | 67 | 61 | 58 | 3 | 39 | 0 | 0 | 5 | 12 | 0 | 1.00 | 10 | .301 | .383 | .480 |
| 1981 | California | AL | 76 | 256 | 56 | 8 | 1 | 5 | (3 | 2) | 81 | 28 | 31 | 38 | 4 | 42 | 3 | 1 | 4 | 1 | 2 | .33 | 7 | .219 | .322 | .316 |
| 1982 | California | AL | 138 | 472 | 141 | 38 | 1 | 21 | (13 | 8) | 244 | 89 | 86 | 58 | 4 | 72 | 3 | 5 | 7 | 7 | 8 | .47 | 9 | .299 | .374 | .517 |
| 1983 | California | AL | 117 | 437 | 119 | 20 | 3 | 22 | (14 | 8) | 211 | 56 | 74 | 55 | 10 | 83 | 2 | 0 | 6 | 2 | 2 | .50 | 7 | .272 | .352 | .483 |
| 1984 | California | AL | 142 | 517 | 140 | 28 | 4 | 23 | (16 | 7) | 245 | 84 | 79 | 77 | 8 | 97 | 2 | 2 | 2 | 2 | 2 | .50 | 14 | .271 | .366 | .474 |
| 1985 | Baltimore | AL | 124 | 448 | 118 | 12 | 1 | 23 | (14 | 9) | 201 | 59 | 68 | 53 | 6 | 100 | 1 | 0 | 6 | 7 | 3 | .70 | 7 | .263 | .339 | .449 |
| 1986 | Baltimore | AL | 112 | 397 | 114 | 13 | 1 | 23 | (13 | 10) | 198 | 67 | 67 | 53 | 1 | 59 | 2 | 0 | 4 | 2 | 2 | .50 | 20 | .287 | .371 | .499 |
| 1987 | Baltimore | AL | 111 | 396 | 100 | 24 | 0 | 23 | (11 | 12) | 193 | 49 | 60 | 39 | 6 | 72 | 1 | 0 | 2 | 3 | 7 | .30 | 8 | .253 | .320 | .487 |
| 1988 | 2 ML Teams | | 114 | 391 | 96 | 14 | 1 | 25 | (13 | 12) | 187 | 46 | 56 | 33 | 1 | 82 | 1 | 1 | 6 | 2 | 2 | .50 | 9 | .246 | .302 | .478 |
| 1989 | Detroit | AL | 117 | 353 | 85 | 11 | 1 | 11 | (9 | 2) | 131 | 44 | 46 | 47 | 1 | 71 | 1 | 0 | 5 | 1 | 1 | .50 | 5 | .241 | .328 | .371 |
| 1990 | San Diego | NL | 90 | 196 | 47 | 3 | 1 | 6 | (2 | 4) | 70 | 18 | 23 | 22 | 2 | 44 | 1 | 1 | 3 | 2 | 0 | 1.00 | 1 | .240 | .315 | .357 |
| 1988 | Baltimore | AL | 87 | 301 | 76 | 13 | 1 | 18 | (11 | 7) | 145 | 37 | 37 | 28 | 1 | 66 | 0 | 1 | 4 | 2 | 2 | .50 | 7 | .252 | .312 | .482 |
| | Detroit | AL | 27 | 90 | 20 | 1 | 0 | 7 | (2 | 5) | 42 | 9 | 19 | 5 | 0 | 16 | 1 | 0 | 2 | 0 | 0 | .00 | 2 | .222 | .265 | .467 |
| 17 ML YEARS | | | 1969 | 6925 | 1960 | 388 | 43 | 306 | (177 | 129) | 3352 | 1063 | 1111 | 857 | 77 | 1116 | 30 | 25 | 86 | 72 | 54 | .57 | 149 | .283 | .360 | .484 |

## Barry Lyons

**Bats:** Right **Throws:** Right **Pos:** C **Ht:** 6' 1" **Wt:** 205 **Born:** 06/03/60 **Age:** 31

| BATTING | | | | | | | | | | | | | | | | | | | | | BASERUNNING | | | | PERCENTAGES | | |
|---|---|---|---|---|---|---|---|---|---|---|---|---|---|---|---|---|---|---|---|---|---|---|---|---|---|---|---|
| Year | Team | Lg | G | AB | H | 2B | 3B | HR | (Hm | Rd) | TB | R | RBI | TBB | IBB | SO | HBP | SH | SF | SB | CS | SB% | GDP | Avg | OBP | SLG |
| 1986 | New York | NL | 6 | 9 | 0 | 0 | 0 | 0 | (0 | 0) | 0 | 1 | 2 | 1 | 1 | 2 | 0 | 0 | 0 | 0 | 0 | .00 | 0 | .000 | .100 | .000 |
| 1987 | New York | NL | 53 | 130 | 33 | 4 | 1 | 4 | (4 | 0) | 51 | 15 | 24 | 8 | 1 | 24 | 2 | 0 | 3 | 0 | 0 | .00 | 1 | .254 | .301 | .392 |
| 1988 | New York | NL | 50 | 91 | 21 | 7 | 1 | 0 | (0 | 0) | 30 | 5 | 11 | 3 | 0 | 12 | 0 | 3 | 1 | 0 | 0 | .00 | 3 | .231 | .253 | .330 |
| 1989 | New York | NL | 79 | 235 | 58 | 13 | 0 | 3 | (1 | 2) | 80 | 15 | 27 | 11 | 1 | 28 | 2 | 1 | 3 | 0 | 1 | .00 | 7 | .247 | .283 | .340 |
| 1990 | 2 ML Teams | | 27 | 85 | 20 | 0 | 0 | 3 | (1 | 2) | 29 | 9 | 9 | 2 | 0 | 10 | 1 | 0 | 0 | 0 | 0 | .00 | 2 | .235 | .261 | .341 |
| 1990 | New York | NL | 24 | 80 | 19 | 0 | 0 | 2 | (1 | 1) | 25 | 8 | 7 | 2 | 0 | 9 | 1 | 0 | 0 | 0 | 0 | .00 | 2 | .238 | .265 | .313 |
| | Los Angeles | NL | 3 | 5 | 1 | 0 | 0 | 1 | (0 | 1) | 4 | 1 | 2 | 0 | 0 | 1 | 0 | 0 | 0 | 0 | 0 | .00 | 0 | .200 | .200 | .800 |
| 5 ML YEARS | | | 215 | 550 | 132 | 24 | 2 | 10 | (6 | 4) | 190 | 45 | 73 | 25 | 3 | 76 | 5 | 4 | 7 | 0 | 1 | .00 | 13 | .240 | .276 | .345 |

## Steve Lyons

**Bats:** Left **Throws:** Right **Pos:** 1B/2B **Ht:** 6' 3" **Wt:** 195 **Born:** 06/03/60 **Age:** 31

| BATTING | | | | | | | | | | | | | | | | | | | | | BASERUNNING | | | | PERCENTAGES | | |
|---|---|---|---|---|---|---|---|---|---|---|---|---|---|---|---|---|---|---|---|---|---|---|---|---|---|---|---|
| Year | Team | Lg | G | AB | H | 2B | 3B | HR | (Hm | Rd) | TB | R | RBI | TBB | IBB | SO | HBP | SH | SF | SB | CS | SB% | GDP | Avg | OBP | SLG |
| 1985 | Boston | AL | 133 | 371 | 98 | 14 | 3 | 5 | (4 | 1) | 133 | 52 | 30 | 32 | 0 | 64 | 1 | 2 | 3 | 12 | 9 | .57 | 2 | .264 | .322 | .358 |
| 1986 | 2 ML Teams | | 101 | 247 | 56 | 9 | 3 | 1 | (1 | 0) | 74 | 30 | 20 | 19 | 2 | 47 | 1 | 4 | 4 | 4 | 6 | .40 | 4 | .227 | .280 | .300 |
| 1987 | Chicago | AL | 76 | 193 | 54 | 11 | 1 | 1 | (0 | 1) | 70 | 26 | 19 | 12 | 0 | 37 | 0 | 4 | 1 | 3 | 1 | .75 | 4 | .280 | .320 | .363 |
| 1988 | Chicago | AL | 146 | 472 | 127 | 28 | 3 | 5 | (1 | 4) | 176 | 59 | 45 | 32 | 1 | 59 | 1 | 15 | 6 | 1 | 2 | .33 | 6 | .269 | .313 | .373 |
| 1989 | Chicago | AL | 140 | 443 | 117 | 21 | 3 | 2 | (0 | 2) | 150 | 51 | 50 | 35 | 3 | 68 | 1 | 12 | 3 | 9 | 6 | .60 | 3 | .264 | .317 | .339 |
| 1990 | Chicago | AL | 93 | 146 | 28 | 6 | 1 | 1 | (0 | 1) | 39 | 22 | 11 | 10 | 1 | 41 | 1 | 4 | 2 | 1 | 0 | 1.00 | 1 | .192 | .245 | .267 |
| 1986 | Boston | AL | 59 | 124 | 31 | 7 | 2 | 1 | (1 | 0) | 45 | 20 | 14 | 12 | 2 | 23 | 0 | 1 | 2 | 2 | 3 | .40 | 3 | .250 | .312 | .363 |
| | Chicago | AL | 42 | 123 | 25 | 2 | 1 | 0 | (0 | 0) | 29 | 10 | 6 | 7 | 0 | 24 | 1 | 3 | 2 | 2 | 3 | .40 | 1 | .203 | .248 | .236 |
| 6 ML YEARS | | | 689 | 1872 | 480 | 89 | 14 | 15 | (6 | 9) | 642 | 240 | 175 | 140 | 7 | 316 | 5 | 41 | 19 | 30 | 24 | .56 | 20 | .256 | .307 | .343 |

## Kevin Maas

**Bats:** Left **Throws:** Left **Pos:** 1B/DH **Ht:** 6' 3" **Wt:** 205 **Born:** 01/20/65 **Age:** 26

| | | BATTING | | | | | | | | | | | | | | | | | BASERUNNING | | | | PERCENTAGES | | |
|---|---|---|---|---|---|---|---|---|---|---|---|---|---|---|---|---|---|---|---|---|---|---|---|---|---|
| Year Team | Lg | G | AB | H | 2B | 3B | HR | (Hm | Rd) | TB | R | RBI | TBB | IBB | SO | HBP | SH | SF | SB | CS | SB% | GDP | Avg | OBP | SLG |
| 1986 Oneonta | A | 28 | 101 | 36 | 10 | 0 | 0 | -- | -- | 46 | 14 | 18 | 7 | 1 | 9 | 0 | 0 | 1 | 5 | 1 | .83 | 1 | .356 | .394 | .455 |
| 1987 Ft.Laudrdle | A | 116 | 439 | 122 | 28 | 4 | 11 | -- | -- | 191 | 77 | 73 | 53 | 4 | 108 | 2 | 0 | 8 | 14 | 4 | .78 | 5 | .278 | .353 | .435 |
| 1988 Pr William | A | 29 | 108 | 32 | 7 | 0 | 12 | -- | -- | 75 | 24 | 35 | 17 | 1 | 28 | 4 | 0 | 4 | 3 | 1 | .75 | 0 | .296 | .398 | .694 |
| Albany | AA | 109 | 372 | 98 | 14 | 3 | 16 | -- | -- | 166 | 66 | 55 | 64 | 4 | 103 | 4 | 3 | 2 | 5 | 1 | .83 | 5 | .263 | .376 | .446 |
| 1989 Columbus | AAA | 83 | 291 | 93 | 23 | 2 | 6 | -- | -- | 138 | 42 | 45 | 40 | 0 | 73 | 1 | 0 | 4 | 2 | 3 | .40 | 3 | .320 | .399 | .474 |
| 1990 Columbus | AAA | 57 | 194 | 55 | 15 | 2 | 13 | -- | -- | 113 | 37 | 38 | 34 | 1 | 45 | 0 | 0 | 0 | 2 | 2 | .50 | 5 | .284 | .390 | .582 |
| 1990 New York | AL | 79 | 254 | 64 | 9 | 0 | 21 | (12 | 9) | 136 | 42 | 41 | 43 | 10 | 76 | 3 | 0 | 0 | 1 | 2 | .33 | 2 | .252 | .367 | .535 |

## Bob MacDonald

**Pitches:** Left **Bats:** Left **Pos:** RP **Ht:** 6' 2" **Wt:** 180 **Born:** 04/27/65 **Age:** 26

| | | HOW MUCH HE PITCHED | | | | | | WHAT HE GAVE UP | | | | | | | | | | | | THE RESULTS | | | | | |
|---|---|---|---|---|---|---|---|---|---|---|---|---|---|---|---|---|---|---|---|---|---|---|---|---|---|
| Year Team | Lg | G | GS | CG | GF | IP | BFP | H | R | ER | HR | SH | SF | HB | TBB | IBB | SO | WP | Bk | W | L | Pct. | ShO | Sv | ERA |
| 1987 St.Cathrnes | A | 1 | 1 | 0 | 0 | 4 | 20 | 8 | 4 | 2 | 0 | 0 | 0 | 0 | 0 | 0 | 4 | 0 | 0 | 0 | 0 | .000 | 0 | 0 | 4.50 |
| Medicne Hat | R | 13 | 0 | 0 | 9 | 24.2 | 109 | 22 | 13 | 8 | 0 | 1 | 0 | 1 | 12 | 1 | 26 | 5 | 0 | 3 | 1 | .750 | 0 | 2 | 2.92 |
| Myrtle Bch | A | 10 | 0 | 0 | 4 | 20.2 | 94 | 24 | 18 | 13 | 1 | 2 | 1 | 0 | 7 | 1 | 12 | 2 | 0 | 2 | 1 | .667 | 0 | 0 | 5.66 |
| 1988 Myrtle Bch | A | 52 | 0 | 0 | 48 | 53.1 | 222 | 42 | 13 | 10 | 2 | 3 | 1 | 0 | 18 | 3 | 43 | 2 | 0 | 3 | 4 | .429 | 0 | 15 | 1.69 |
| 1989 Knoxville | AA | 43 | 0 | 0 | 27 | 63 | 264 | 52 | 27 | 23 | 0 | 5 | 0 | 2 | 23 | 2 | 58 | 0 | 1 | 3 | 5 | .375 | 0 | 9 | 3.29 |
| Syracuse | AAA | 12 | 0 | 0 | 4 | 16 | 75 | 16 | 10 | 10 | 0 | 3 | 1 | 1 | 6 | 0 | 12 | 0 | 0 | 1 | 0 | 1.000 | 0 | 0 | 5.63 |
| 1990 Knoxville | AA | 36 | 0 | 0 | 29 | 57 | 237 | 37 | 17 | 12 | 2 | 9 | 1 | 0 | 29 | 4 | 54 | 3 | 0 | 1 | 2 | .333 | 0 | 15 | 1.89 |
| Syracuse | AAA | 9 | 0 | 0 | 5 | 8.1 | 35 | 4 | 5 | 5 | 1 | 0 | 0 | 0 | 9 | 0 | 6 | 0 | 0 | 0 | 2 | .000 | 0 | 2 | 5.40 |
| 1990 Toronto | AL | 4 | 0 | 0 | 1 | 2.1 | 8 | 0 | 0 | 0 | 0 | 0 | 0 | 0 | 2 | 0 | 0 | 0 | 0 | 0 | 0 | .000 | 0 | 0 | 0.00 |

## Mike Macfarlane

**Bats:** Right **Throws:** Right **Pos:** C **Ht:** 6' 1" **Wt:** 200 **Born:** 04/12/64 **Age:** 27

| | | BATTING | | | | | | | | | | | | | | | | | BASERUNNING | | | | PERCENTAGES | | |
|---|---|---|---|---|---|---|---|---|---|---|---|---|---|---|---|---|---|---|---|---|---|---|---|---|---|
| Year Team | Lg | G | AB | H | 2B | 3B | HR | (Hm | Rd) | TB | R | RBI | TBB | IBB | SO | HBP | SH | SF | SB | CS | SB% | GDP | Avg | OBP | SLG |
| 1987 Kansas City | AL | 8 | 19 | 4 | 1 | 0 | 0 | (0 | 0) | 5 | 0 | 3 | 2 | 0 | 2 | 0 | 0 | 0 | 0 | 0 | .00 | 1 | .211 | .286 | .263 |
| 1988 Kansas City | AL | 70 | 211 | 56 | 15 | 0 | 4 | (2 | 2) | 83 | 25 | 26 | 21 | 2 | 37 | 1 | 1 | 2 | 0 | 0 | .00 | 5 | .265 | .332 | .393 |
| 1989 Kansas City | AL | 69 | 157 | 35 | 6 | 0 | 2 | (0 | 2) | 47 | 13 | 19 | 7 | 0 | 27 | 2 | 0 | 1 | 0 | 0 | .00 | 8 | .223 | .263 | .299 |
| 1990 Kansas City | AL | 124 | 400 | 102 | 24 | 4 | 6 | (1 | 5) | 152 | 37 | 58 | 25 | 2 | 69 | 7 | 1 | 6 | 1 | 0 | 1.00 | 9 | .255 | .306 | .380 |
| 4 ML YEARS | | 271 | 787 | 197 | 46 | 4 | 12 | (3 | 9) | 287 | 75 | 106 | 55 | 4 | 135 | 10 | 2 | 9 | 1 | 0 | 1.00 | 23 | .250 | .304 | .365 |

## Julio Machado

**Pitches:** Right **Bats:** Right **Pos:** RP **Ht:** 5' 9" **Wt:** 160 **Born:** 12/01/65 **Age:** 25

| | | HOW MUCH HE PITCHED | | | | | | WHAT HE GAVE UP | | | | | | | | | | | | THE RESULTS | | | | | |
|---|---|---|---|---|---|---|---|---|---|---|---|---|---|---|---|---|---|---|---|---|---|---|---|---|---|
| Year Team | Lg | G | GS | CG | GF | IP | BFP | H | R | ER | HR | SH | SF | HB | TBB | IBB | SO | WP | Bk | W | L | Pct. | ShO | Sv | ERA |
| 1985 Spartanburg | A | 32 | 3 | 1 | 13 | 81.1 | 363 | 75 | 50 | 39 | 5 | 6 | 7 | 4 | 38 | 1 | 71 | 4 | 3 | 4 | 5 | .444 | 0 | 0 | 4.32 |
| 1986 Spartanburg | A | 43 | 5 | 2 | 28 | 79.2 | 366 | 68 | 39 | 33 | 1 | 5 | 6 | 8 | 52 | 3 | 81 | 5 | 1 | 2 | 5 | .286 | 1 | 7 | 3.73 |
| 1987 Clearwater | A | 7 | 5 | 0 | 1 | 34.2 | 153 | 31 | 11 | 10 | 2 | 1 | 2 | 2 | 19 | 2 | 32 | 0 | 2 | 2 | 0 | 1.000 | 0 | 0 | 2.60 |
| Reading | AA | 21 | 17 | 2 | 2 | 108.1 | 472 | 112 | 70 | 57 | 9 | 4 | 7 | 4 | 40 | 2 | 89 | 6 | 7 | 4 | 5 | .444 | 0 | 0 | 4.74 |
| 1988 Clearwater | A | 13 | 3 | 0 | 7 | 36.2 | 154 | 34 | 13 | 12 | 3 | 0 | 1 | 2 | 14 | 1 | 45 | 3 | 2 | 1 | 4 | .200 | 0 | 5 | 2.95 |
| Reading | AA | 26 | 5 | 0 | 9 | 63 | 291 | 69 | 41 | 38 | 1 | 6 | 6 | 5 | 34 | 3 | 52 | 3 | 2 | 6 | 1 | .857 | 0 | 3 | 5.43 |
| 1989 Peninsula | A | 4 | 0 | 0 | 3 | 3.2 | 17 | 2 | 0 | 0 | 0 | 1 | 0 | 1 | 2 | 0 | 1 | 0 | 0 | 1 | 0 | 1.000 | 0 | 2 | 0.00 |
| St.Lucie | A | 4 | 0 | 0 | 3 | 10.2 | 39 | 5 | 0 | 0 | 0 | 1 | 0 | 0 | 3 | 0 | 14 | 0 | 0 | 1 | 0 | 1.000 | 0 | 2 | 0.00 |
| Jackson | AA | 32 | 0 | 0 | 16 | 57 | 239 | 42 | 23 | 18 | 0 | 5 | 2 | 2 | 27 | 4 | 67 | 1 | 1 | 3 | 5 | .375 | 0 | 3 | 2.84 |
| Tidewater | AAA | 14 | 1 | 0 | 9 | 29 | 116 | 16 | 2 | 2 | 0 | 2 | 0 | 0 | 17 | 2 | 37 | 2 | 0 | 1 | 2 | .333 | 0 | 5 | 0.62 |
| 1990 Tidewater | AAA | 16 | 0 | 0 | 13 | 21.1 | 88 | 16 | 7 | 4 | 1 | 3 | 0 | 1 | 8 | 0 | 24 | 1 | 0 | 0 | 1 | .000 | 0 | 8 | 1.69 |
| 1989 New York | NL | 10 | 0 | 0 | 9 | 11 | 45 | 9 | 4 | 4 | 0 | 0 | 0 | 0 | 3 | 0 | 14 | 0 | 0 | 0 | 1 | .000 | 0 | 0 | 3.27 |
| 1990 2 ML Teams | | 37 | 0 | 0 | 21 | 47.1 | 207 | 41 | 14 | 13 | 4 | 1 | 3 | 2 | 25 | 6 | 39 | 3 | 0 | 4 | 1 | .800 | 0 | 3 | 2.47 |
| 1990 New York | NL | 27 | 0 | 0 | 14 | 34.1 | 151 | 32 | 13 | 12 | 4 | 1 | 2 | 2 | 17 | 4 | 27 | 3 | 0 | 4 | 1 | .800 | 0 | 0 | 3.15 |
| Milwaukee | AL | 10 | 0 | 0 | 7 | 13 | 56 | 9 | 1 | 1 | 0 | 0 | 1 | 0 | 8 | 2 | 12 | 0 | 0 | 0 | 0 | .000 | 0 | 3 | 0.69 |
| 2 ML YEARS | | 47 | 0 | 0 | 30 | 58.1 | 252 | 50 | 18 | 17 | 4 | 1 | 3 | 2 | 28 | 6 | 53 | 3 | 0 | 4 | 2 | .667 | 0 | 3 | 2.62 |

## Shane Mack

**Bats:** Right **Throws:** Right **Pos:** RF/LF/CF **Ht:** 6' 0" **Wt:** 185 **Born:** 12/07/63 **Age:** 27

| | | BATTING | | | | | | | | | | | | | | | | | BASERUNNING | | | | PERCENTAGES | | |
|---|---|---|---|---|---|---|---|---|---|---|---|---|---|---|---|---|---|---|---|---|---|---|---|---|---|
| Year Team | Lg | G | AB | H | 2B | 3B | HR | (Hm | Rd) | TB | R | RBI | TBB | IBB | SO | HBP | SH | SF | SB | CS | SB% | GDP | Avg | OBP | SLG |
| 1987 San Diego | NL | 105 | 238 | 57 | 11 | 3 | 4 | (2 | 2) | 86 | 28 | 25 | 18 | 0 | 47 | 3 | 6 | 2 | 4 | 6 | .40 | 11 | .239 | .299 | .361 |
| 1988 San Diego | NL | 56 | 119 | 29 | 3 | 0 | 0 | (0 | 0) | 32 | 13 | 12 | 14 | 0 | 21 | 3 | 3 | 1 | 5 | 1 | .83 | 2 | .244 | .336 | .269 |
| 1990 Minnesota | AL | 125 | 313 | 102 | 10 | 4 | 8 | (5 | 3) | 144 | 50 | 44 | 29 | 1 | 69 | 5 | 6 | 0 | 13 | 4 | .76 | 7 | .326 | .392 | .460 |
| 3 ML YEARS | | 286 | 670 | 188 | 24 | 7 | 12 | (7 | 5) | 262 | 91 | 81 | 61 | 1 | 137 | 11 | 15 | 3 | 22 | 11 | .67 | 20 | .281 | .349 | .391 |

## Greg Maddux

**Pitches:** Right **Bats:** Right **Pos:** SP **Ht:** 6' 0" **Wt:** 170 **Born:** 04/14/66 **Age:** 25

| | | HOW MUCH HE PITCHED | | | | | | WHAT HE GAVE UP | | | | | | | | | | | | THE RESULTS | | | | | |
|---|---|---|---|---|---|---|---|---|---|---|---|---|---|---|---|---|---|---|---|---|---|---|---|---|---|
| Year Team | Lg | G | GS | CG | GF | IP | BFP | H | R | ER | HR | SH | SF | HB | TBB | IBB | SO | WP | Bk | W | L | Pct. | ShO | Sv | ERA |
| 1986 Chicago | NL | 6 | 5 | 1 | 1 | 31 | 144 | 44 | 20 | 19 | 3 | 1 | 0 | 1 | 11 | 2 | 20 | 2 | 0 | 2 | 4 | .333 | 0 | 0 | 5.52 |
| 1987 Chicago | NL | 30 | 27 | 1 | 2 | 155.2 | 701 | 181 | 111 | 97 | 17 | 7 | 1 | 4 | 74 | 13 | 101 | 4 | 7 | 6 | 14 | .300 | 1 | 0 | 5.61 |
| 1988 Chicago | NL | 34 | 34 | 9 | 0 | 249 | 1047 | 230 | 97 | 88 | 13 | 11 | 2 | 9 | 81 | 16 | 140 | 3 | 6 | 18 | 8 | .692 | 3 | 0 | 3.18 |
| 1989 Chicago | NL | 35 | 35 | 7 | 0 | 238.1 | 1002 | 222 | 90 | 78 | 13 | 18 | 6 | 6 | 82 | 13 | 135 | 5 | 3 | 19 | 12 | .613 | 1 | 0 | 2.95 |
| 1990 Chicago | NL | 35 | 35 | 8 | 0 | 237 | 1011 | 242 | 116 | 91 | 11 | 18 | 5 | 4 | 71 | 10 | 144 | 3 | 3 | 15 | 15 | .500 | 2 | 0 | 3.46 |
| 5 ML YEARS | | 140 | 136 | 26 | 3 | 911 | 3905 | 919 | 434 | 373 | 57 | 55 | 14 | 24 | 319 | 54 | 540 | 17 | 19 | 60 | 53 | .531 | 7 | 0 | 3.68 |

## Mike Maddux

**Pitches:** Right **Bats:** Left **Pos:** RP **Ht:** 6' 2" **Wt:** 180 **Born:** 08/27/61 **Age:** 29

| | | HOW MUCH HE PITCHED | | | | | | WHAT HE GAVE UP | | | | | | | | | | | | THE RESULTS | | | | | |
|---|---|---|---|---|---|---|---|---|---|---|---|---|---|---|---|---|---|---|---|---|---|---|---|---|---|
| Year Team | Lg | G | GS | CG | GF | IP | BFP | H | R | ER | HR | SH | SF | HB | TBB | IBB | SO | WP | Bk | W | L | Pct. | ShO | Sv | ERA |
| 1986 Philadelphia | NL | 16 | 16 | 0 | 0 | 78 | 351 | 88 | 56 | 47 | 6 | 3 | 3 | 3 | 34 | 4 | 44 | 4 | 2 | 3 | 7 | .300 | 0 | 0 | 5.42 |
| 1987 Philadelphia | NL | 7 | 2 | 0 | 0 | 17 | 72 | 17 | 5 | 5 | 0 | 0 | 0 | 0 | 5 | 0 | 15 | 1 | 0 | 2 | 0 | 1.000 | 0 | 0 | 2.65 |
| 1988 Philadelphia | NL | 25 | 11 | 0 | 4 | 88.2 | 380 | 91 | 41 | 37 | 6 | 7 | 3 | 5 | 34 | 4 | 59 | 4 | 2 | 4 | 3 | .571 | 0 | 0 | 3.76 |
| 1989 Philadelphia | NL | 16 | 4 | 2 | 1 | 43.2 | 191 | 52 | 29 | 25 | 3 | 3 | 1 | 2 | 14 | 3 | 26 | 3 | 1 | 1 | 3 | .250 | 1 | 1 | 5.15 |
| 1990 Los Angeles | NL | 11 | 2 | 0 | 3 | 20.2 | 88 | 24 | 15 | 15 | 3 | 0 | 1 | 1 | 4 | 0 | 11 | 2 | 0 | 0 | 1 | .000 | 0 | 0 | 6.53 |
| 5 ML YEARS | | 75 | 35 | 2 | 8 | 248 | 1082 | 272 | 146 | 129 | 18 | 13 | 8 | 11 | 91 | 11 | 155 | 14 | 5 | 10 | 14 | .417 | 1 | 1 | 4.68 |

## Dave Magadan

**Bats:** Left **Throws:** Right **Pos:** 1B/3B **Ht:** 6' 3" **Wt:** 195 **Born:** 09/30/62 **Age:** 28

| | | BATTING | | | | | | | | | | | | | | | | | BASERUNNING | | | | PERCENTAGES | | |
|---|---|---|---|---|---|---|---|---|---|---|---|---|---|---|---|---|---|---|---|---|---|---|---|---|---|
| Year Team | Lg | G | AB | H | 2B | 3B | HR | (Hm | Rd) | TB | R | RBI | TBB | IBB | SO | HBP | SH | SF | SB | CS | SB% | GDP | Avg | OBP | SLG |
| 1986 New York | NL | 10 | 18 | 8 | 0 | 0 | 0 | (0 | 0) | 8 | 3 | 3 | 3 | 0 | 1 | 0 | 0 | 0 | 0 | 0 | .00 | 1 | .444 | .524 | .444 |
| 1987 New York | NL | 85 | 192 | 61 | 13 | 1 | 3 | (2 | 1) | 85 | 21 | 24 | 22 | 2 | 22 | 0 | 1 | 1 | 0 | 0 | .00 | 5 | .318 | .386 | .443 |
| 1988 New York | NL | 112 | 314 | 87 | 15 | 0 | 1 | (1 | 0) | 105 | 39 | 35 | 60 | 4 | 39 | 2 | 1 | 3 | 0 | 1 | .00 | 9 | .277 | .393 | .334 |
| 1989 New York | NL | 127 | 374 | 107 | 22 | 3 | 4 | (3 | 1) | 147 | 47 | 41 | 49 | 6 | 37 | 1 | 1 | 4 | 1 | 0 | 1.00 | 2 | .286 | .367 | .393 |
| 1990 New York | NL | 144 | 451 | 148 | 28 | 6 | 6 | (2 | 4) | 206 | 74 | 72 | 74 | 4 | 55 | 2 | 4 | 10 | 2 | 1 | .67 | 10 | .328 | .417 | .457 |
| 5 ML YEARS | | 478 | 1349 | 411 | 78 | 10 | 14 | (8 | 6) | 551 | 184 | 175 | 208 | 16 | 154 | 5 | 7 | 18 | 3 | 2 | .60 | 27 | .305 | .395 | .408 |

## Joe Magrane

**Pitches:** Left **Bats:** Right **Pos:** SP **Ht:** 6' 6" **Wt:** 230 **Born:** 07/02/64 **Age:** 26

| | | HOW MUCH HE PITCHED | | | | | | WHAT HE GAVE UP | | | | | | | | | | | | THE RESULTS | | | | | |
|---|---|---|---|---|---|---|---|---|---|---|---|---|---|---|---|---|---|---|---|---|---|---|---|---|---|
| Year Team | Lg | G | GS | CG | GF | IP | BFP | H | R | ER | HR | SH | SF | HB | TBB | IBB | SO | WP | Bk | W | L | Pct. | ShO | Sv | ERA |
| 1987 St. Louis | NL | 27 | 26 | 4 | 0 | 170.1 | 722 | 157 | 75 | 67 | 9 | 9 | 3 | 10 | 60 | 6 | 101 | 9 | 7 | 9 | 7 | .563 | 2 | 0 | 3.54 |
| 1988 St. Louis | NL | 24 | 24 | 4 | 0 | 165.1 | 677 | 133 | 57 | 40 | 6 | 8 | 4 | 2 | 51 | 4 | 100 | 8 | 8 | 5 | 9 | .357 | 3 | 0 | 2.18 |
| 1989 St. Louis | NL | 34 | 33 | 9 | 1 | 234.2 | 971 | 219 | 81 | 76 | 5 | 14 | 8 | 6 | 72 | 7 | 127 | 14 | 5 | 18 | 9 | .667 | 3 | 0 | 2.91 |
| 1990 St. Louis | NL | 31 | 31 | 3 | 0 | 203.1 | 855 | 204 | 86 | 81 | 10 | 8 | 6 | 8 | 59 | 7 | 100 | 11 | 1 | 10 | 17 | .370 | 2 | 0 | 3.59 |
| 4 ML YEARS | | 116 | 114 | 20 | 1 | 773.2 | 3225 | 713 | 299 | 264 | 30 | 39 | 21 | 26 | 242 | 24 | 428 | 42 | 21 | 42 | 42 | .500 | 10 | 0 | 3.07 |

## Rick Mahler

**Pitches:** Right **Bats:** Right **Pos:** RP/SP **Ht:** 6' 1" **Wt:** 202 **Born:** 08/05/53 **Age:** 37

| | | HOW MUCH HE PITCHED | | | | | | WHAT HE GAVE UP | | | | | | | | | | | | THE RESULTS | | | | | |
|---|---|---|---|---|---|---|---|---|---|---|---|---|---|---|---|---|---|---|---|---|---|---|---|---|---|
| Year Team | Lg | G | GS | CG | GF | IP | BFP | H | R | ER | HR | SH | SF | HB | TBB | IBB | SO | WP | Bk | W | L | Pct. | ShO | Sv | ERA |
| 1979 Atlanta | NL | 15 | 0 | 0 | 5 | 22 | 101 | 28 | 16 | 15 | 4 | 0 | 0 | 0 | 11 | 2 | 12 | 1 | 1 | 0 | 0 | .000 | 0 | 0 | 6.14 |
| 1980 Atlanta | NL | 2 | 0 | 0 | 0 | 4 | 13 | 2 | 1 | 1 | 0 | 0 | 0 | 0 | 0 | 0 | 1 | 0 | 0 | 0 | 0 | .000 | 0 | 0 | 2.25 |
| 1981 Atlanta | NL | 34 | 14 | 1 | 10 | 112 | 478 | 109 | 41 | 35 | 5 | 8 | 3 | 1 | 43 | 5 | 54 | 3 | 1 | 8 | 6 | .571 | 0 | 2 | 2.81 |
| 1982 Atlanta | NL | 39 | 33 | 5 | 0 | 205.1 | 857 | 213 | 105 | 96 | 18 | 6 | 6 | 1 | 62 | 5 | 105 | 8 | 2 | 9 | 10 | .474 | 2 | 0 | 4.21 |
| 1983 Atlanta | NL | 10 | 0 | 0 | 1 | 14.1 | 66 | 16 | 8 | 8 | 0 | 1 | 2 | 0 | 9 | 1 | 7 | 0 | 0 | 0 | 0 | .000 | 0 | 0 | 5.02 |
| 1984 Atlanta | NL | 38 | 29 | 9 | 1 | 222 | 918 | 209 | 86 | 77 | 13 | 13 | 8 | 3 | 62 | 7 | 106 | 3 | 1 | 13 | 10 | .565 | 1 | 0 | 3.12 |
| 1985 Atlanta | NL | 39 | 39 | 6 | 0 | 266.2 | 1110 | 272 | 116 | 103 | 24 | 10 | 5 | 2 | 79 | 8 | 107 | 3 | 1 | 17 | 15 | .531 | 1 | 0 | 3.48 |
| 1986 Atlanta | NL | 39 | 39 | 7 | 0 | 237.2 | 1056 | 283 | 139 | 129 | 25 | 10 | 8 | 3 | 95 | 10 | 137 | 5 | 1 | 14 | 18 | .438 | 1 | 0 | 4.88 |
| 1987 Atlanta | NL | 39 | 28 | 3 | 1 | 197 | 849 | 212 | 118 | 109 | 24 | 9 | 3 | 2 | 85 | 8 | 95 | 5 | 2 | 8 | 13 | .381 | 1 | 0 | 4.98 |
| 1988 Atlanta | NL | 39 | 34 | 5 | 2 | 249 | 1063 | 279 | 125 | 102 | 17 | 19 | 5 | 8 | 42 | 6 | 131 | 5 | 8 | 9 | 16 | .360 | 0 | 0 | 3.69 |
| 1989 Cincinnati | NL | 40 | 31 | 5 | 1 | 220.2 | 940 | 242 | 113 | 94 | 15 | 15 | 5 | 10 | 51 | 13 | 102 | 4 | 4 | 9 | 13 | .409 | 2 | 0 | 3.83 |
| 1990 Cincinnati | NL | 35 | 16 | 2 | 9 | 134.2 | 564 | 134 | 67 | 64 | 16 | 4 | 4 | 3 | 39 | 4 | 68 | 3 | 2 | 7 | 6 | .538 | 1 | 4 | 4.28 |
| 12 ML YEARS | | 369 | 263 | 43 | 30 | 1885.1 | 8015 | 1999 | 935 | 833 | 161 | 95 | 49 | 33 | 578 | 69 | 925 | 40 | 23 | 94 | 107 | .468 | 9 | 6 | 3.98 |

## Candy Maldonado

**Bats:** Right **Throws:** Right **Pos:** LF/RF/DH **Ht:** 6' 0" **Wt:** 195 **Born:** 09/05/60 **Age:** 30

| | | BATTING | | | | | | | | | | | | | | | | | BASERUNNING | | | | PERCENTAGES | | |
|---|---|---|---|---|---|---|---|---|---|---|---|---|---|---|---|---|---|---|---|---|---|---|---|---|---|
| Year Team | Lg | G | AB | H | 2B | 3B | HR | (Hm | Rd) | TB | R | RBI | TBB | IBB | SO | HBP | SH | SF | SB | CS | SB% | GDP | Avg | OBP | SLG |
| 1981 Los Angeles | NL | 11 | 12 | 1 | 0 | 0 | 0 | (0 | 0) | 1 | 0 | 0 | 0 | 0 | 5 | 0 | 0 | 0 | 0 | 0 | .00 | 0 | .083 | .083 | .083 |
| 1982 Los Angeles | NL | 6 | 4 | 0 | 0 | 0 | 0 | (0 | 0) | 0 | 0 | 0 | 1 | 1 | 2 | 0 | 0 | 0 | 0 | 0 | .00 | 0 | .000 | .200 | .000 |

| | | | | | | | | | | | | | | | | | | | | | | | | | | | |
|---|---|---|---|---|---|---|---|---|---|---|---|---|---|---|---|---|---|---|---|---|---|---|---|---|---|---|---|
| 1983 Los Angeles | NL | 42 | 62 | 12 | 1 | 1 | 1 | (1 | 0) | 18 | 5 | 6 | 5 | 0 | 14 | 0 | 1 | 0 | 0 | 0 | .00 | 1 | .194 | .254 | .290 |
| 1984 Los Angeles | NL | 116 | 254 | 68 | 14 | 0 | 5 | (1 | 4) | 97 | 25 | 28 | 19 | 0 | 29 | 1 | 1 | 3 | 0 | 3 | .00 | 6 | .268 | .318 | .382 |
| 1985 Los Angeles | NL | 121 | 213 | 48 | 7 | 1 | 5 | (2 | 3) | 72 | 20 | 19 | 19 | 4 | 40 | 0 | 2 | 1 | 1 | 1 | .50 | 3 | .225 | .288 | .338 |
| 1986 San Francisco | NL | 133 | 405 | 102 | 31 | 3 | 18 | (6 | 12) | 193 | 49 | 85 | 20 | 4 | 77 | 3 | 0 | 4 | 4 | 4 | .50 | 12 | .252 | .289 | .477 |
| 1987 San Francisco | NL | 118 | 442 | 129 | 28 | 4 | 20 | (14 | 6) | 225 | 69 | 85 | 34 | 4 | 78 | 6 | 0 | 7 | 8 | 8 | .50 | 9 | .292 | .346 | .509 |
| 1988 San Francisco | NL | 142 | 499 | 127 | 23 | 1 | 12 | (5 | 7) | 188 | 53 | 68 | 37 | 1 | 89 | 7 | 3 | 6 | 6 | 5 | .55 | 13 | .255 | .311 | .377 |
| 1989 San Francisco | NL | 129 | 345 | 75 | 23 | 0 | 9 | (1 | 8) | 125 | 39 | 41 | 37 | 4 | 69 | 3 | 1 | 3 | 4 | 1 | .80 | 8 | .217 | .296 | .362 |
| 1990 Cleveland | AL | 155 | 590 | 161 | 32 | 2 | 22 | (12 | 10) | 263 | 76 | 95 | 49 | 4 | 134 | 5 | 0 | 7 | 3 | 5 | .38 | 13 | .273 | .330 | .446 |
| 10 ML YEARS | | 973 | 2826 | 723 | 159 | 12 | 92 | (42 | 50) | 1182 | 336 | 427 | 221 | 22 | 537 | 25 | 8 | 31 | 26 | 27 | .49 | 65 | .256 | .312 | .418 |

## Carlos Maldonado

**Pitches:** Right **Bats:** Both **Pos:** RP **Ht:** 6' 2" **Wt:** 175 **Born:** 10/18/66 **Age:** 24

| HOW MUCH HE PITCHED | | | | | | | | WHAT HE GAVE UP | | | | | | | | | | | | THE RESULTS | | | | | |
|---|---|---|---|---|---|---|---|---|---|---|---|---|---|---|---|---|---|---|---|---|---|---|---|---|---|
| Year Team | Lg | G | GS | CG | GF | IP | BFP | H | R | ER | HR | SH | SF | HB | TBB | IBB | SO | WP | Bk | W | L | Pct. | ShO | Sv | ERA |
| 1986 Royals | R | 10 | 4 | 0 | 2 | 34.1 | 136 | 29 | 10 | 7 | 1 | 1 | 1 | 1 | 10 | 1 | 16 | 3 | 0 | 0 | 2 | .000 | 0 | 1 | 1.83 |
| 1987 Appleton | A | 2 | 0 | 0 | 1 | 2.1 | 13 | 4 | 3 | 3 | 0 | 0 | 1 | 0 | 3 | 0 | 4 | 1 | 0 | 0 | 0 | .000 | 0 | 0 | 11.57 |
| Royals | R | 20 | 0 | 0 | 8 | 58 | 223 | 32 | 18 | 16 | 2 | 2 | 0 | 2 | 19 | 2 | 56 | 2 | 1 | 5 | 1 | .833 | 0 | 4 | 2.48 |
| 1988 Baseball Cy | A | 16 | 7 | 0 | 2 | 52.2 | 242 | 46 | 35 | 31 | 5 | 2 | 1 | 7 | 39 | 0 | 44 | 3 | 0 | 1 | 5 | .167 | 0 | 0 | 5.30 |
| 1989 Baseball Cy | A | 28 | 0 | 0 | 19 | 76.2 | 300 | 47 | 14 | 10 | 3 | 3 | 1 | 1 | 24 | 4 | 66 | 2 | 0 | 11 | 3 | .786 | 0 | 9 | 1.17 |
| 1990 Memphis | AA | 55 | 0 | 0 | 48 | 77.1 | 325 | 61 | 29 | 25 | 5 | 3 | 4 | 1 | 39 | 0 | 77 | 5 | 0 | 4 | 5 | .444 | 0 | 20 | 2.91 |
| 1990 Kansas City | AL | 4 | 0 | 0 | 1 | 6 | 31 | 9 | 6 | 6 | 0 | 0 | 1 | 0 | 4 | 0 | 9 | 1 | 0 | 0 | 0 | .000 | 0 | 0 | 9.00 |

## Bob Malloy

**Pitches:** Right **Bats:** Right **Pos:** RP **Ht:** 6' 5" **Wt:** 200 **Born:** 11/24/64 **Age:** 26

| HOW MUCH HE PITCHED | | | | | | | | WHAT HE GAVE UP | | | | | | | | | | | | THE RESULTS | | | | | |
|---|---|---|---|---|---|---|---|---|---|---|---|---|---|---|---|---|---|---|---|---|---|---|---|---|---|
| Year Team | Lg | G | GS | CG | GF | IP | BFP | H | R | ER | HR | SH | SF | HB | TBB | IBB | SO | WP | Bk | W | L | Pct. | ShO | Sv | ERA |
| 1987 Texas | AL | 2 | 2 | 0 | 0 | 11 | 51 | 13 | 11 | 8 | 6 | 0 | 0 | 0 | 3 | 0 | 8 | 0 | 0 | 0 | 0 | .000 | 0 | 0 | 6.55 |
| 1990 Montreal | NL | 1 | 0 | 0 | 0 | 2 | 8 | 1 | 0 | 0 | 0 | 0 | 0 | 0 | 1 | 0 | 1 | 0 | 0 | 0 | 0 | .000 | 0 | 0 | 0.00 |
| 2 ML YEARS | | 3 | 2 | 0 | 0 | 13 | 59 | 14 | 11 | 8 | 6 | 0 | 0 | 0 | 4 | 0 | 9 | 0 | 0 | 0 | 0 | .000 | 0 | 0 | 5.54 |

## Chuck Malone

**Pitches:** Right **Bats:** Right **Pos:** RP **Ht:** 6' 7" **Wt:** 250 **Born:** 07/08/65 **Age:** 25

| HOW MUCH HE PITCHED | | | | | | | | WHAT HE GAVE UP | | | | | | | | | | | | THE RESULTS | | | | | |
|---|---|---|---|---|---|---|---|---|---|---|---|---|---|---|---|---|---|---|---|---|---|---|---|---|---|
| Year Team | Lg | G | GS | CG | GF | IP | BFP | H | R | ER | HR | SH | SF | HB | TBB | IBB | SO | WP | Bk | W | L | Pct. | ShO | Sv | ERA |
| 1986 Bend | A | 21 | 3 | 0 | 11 | 54.2 | 0 | 47 | 38 | 31 | 0 | 0 | 0 | 2 | 50 | 2 | 60 | 4 | 1 | 2 | 6 | .250 | 0 | 2 | 5.10 |
| 1987 Clearwater | A | 34 | 15 | 0 | 10 | 120 | 525 | 105 | 55 | 52 | 7 | 5 | 5 | 4 | 63 | 2 | 100 | 5 | 1 | 6 | 8 | .429 | 0 | 2 | 3.90 |
| 1988 Reading | AA | 22 | 21 | 2 | 0 | 126.2 | 559 | 107 | 63 | 53 | 7 | 3 | 3 | 4 | 88 | 0 | 117 | 7 | 3 | 12 | 7 | .632 | 0 | 0 | 3.77 |
| Maine | AAA | 6 | 6 | 1 | 0 | 27.2 | 135 | 28 | 27 | 21 | 2 | 1 | 1 | 1 | 24 | 2 | 38 | 4 | 0 | 1 | 4 | .200 | 0 | 0 | 6.83 |
| 1989 Reading | AA | 33 | 16 | 2 | 14 | 106 | 476 | 64 | 61 | 49 | 12 | 4 | 5 | 4 | 106 | 1 | 107 | 5 | 1 | 5 | 7 | .417 | 1 | 2 | 4.16 |
| 1990 Scr Wil-Bar | AAA | 26 | 11 | 0 | 3 | 76 | 355 | 47 | 57 | 54 | 9 | 0 | 7 | 7 | 78 | 0 | 79 | 7 | 2 | 4 | 3 | .571 | 0 | 0 | 6.39 |
| 1990 Philadelphia | NL | 7 | 0 | 0 | 3 | 7.1 | 34 | 3 | 4 | 3 | 1 | 0 | 0 | 0 | 11 | 0 | 7 | 1 | 0 | 1 | 0 | 1.000 | 0 | 0 | 3.68 |

## Kelly Mann

**Bats:** Right **Throws:** Right **Pos:** C **Ht:** 6' 3" **Wt:** 215 **Born:** 08/17/67 **Age:** 23

| BATTING | | | | | | | | | | | | | | | | | | | BASERUNNING | | | | PERCENTAGES | | |
|---|---|---|---|---|---|---|---|---|---|---|---|---|---|---|---|---|---|---|---|---|---|---|---|---|---|
| Year Team | Lg | G | AB | H | 2B | 3B | HR | (Hm | Rd) | TB | R | RBI | TBB | IBB | SO | HBP | SH | SF | SB | CS | SB% | GDP | Avg | OBP | SLG |
| 1985 Wytheville | R | 26 | 75 | 15 | 3 | 0 | 1 | -- | -- | 21 | 6 | 10 | 6 | 0 | 21 | 0 | 0 | 0 | 0 | 0 | .00 | 3 | .200 | .259 | .280 |
| 1986 Geneva | A | 60 | 191 | 37 | 1 | 0 | 2 | -- | -- | 44 | 17 | 15 | 18 | 0 | 38 | 5 | 0 | 1 | 3 | 2 | .60 | 4 | .194 | .279 | .230 |
| Peoria | A | 3 | 13 | 6 | 2 | 0 | 0 | -- | -- | 8 | 4 | 4 | 0 | 0 | 1 | 0 | 0 | 0 | 0 | 0 | .00 | 0 | .462 | .462 | .615 |
| 1987 Peoria | A | 95 | 287 | 73 | 16 | 1 | 4 | -- | -- | 103 | 24 | 45 | 23 | 0 | 66 | 4 | 3 | 4 | 1 | 1 | .50 | 9 | .254 | .314 | .359 |
| 1988 Winston-Sal | A | 94 | 307 | 84 | 11 | 0 | 8 | -- | -- | 119 | 32 | 40 | 24 | 3 | 46 | 8 | 4 | 4 | 5 | 1 | .83 | 10 | .274 | .338 | .388 |
| Pittsfield | AA | 22 | 51 | 10 | 3 | 0 | 0 | -- | -- | 13 | 7 | 3 | 3 | 1 | 14 | 1 | 4 | 1 | 0 | 0 | .00 | 0 | .196 | .250 | .255 |
| 1989 Charlotte | AA | 117 | 345 | 85 | 14 | 1 | 8 | -- | -- | 125 | 37 | 56 | 33 | 1 | 60 | 9 | 8 | 8 | 1 | 1 | .50 | 9 | .246 | .322 | .362 |
| 1990 Greenville | AA | 50 | 155 | 49 | 13 | 0 | 7 | -- | -- | 83 | 25 | 27 | 32 | 1 | 22 | 0 | 1 | 1 | 6 | 3 | .67 | 2 | .316 | .431 | .535 |
| Richmond | AAA | 63 | 203 | 41 | 13 | 0 | 3 | -- | -- | 63 | 18 | 20 | 16 | 1 | 36 | 4 | 3 | 1 | 1 | 0 | 1.00 | 6 | .202 | .272 | .310 |
| 1989 Atlanta | NL | 7 | 24 | 5 | 2 | 0 | 0 | (0 | 0) | 7 | 1 | 1 | 0 | 0 | 6 | 1 | 0 | 0 | 0 | 0 | .00 | 1 | .208 | .240 | .292 |
| 1990 Atlanta | NL | 11 | 28 | 4 | 1 | 0 | 1 | (0 | 1) | 8 | 2 | 2 | 0 | 0 | 6 | 0 | 0 | 0 | 0 | 0 | .00 | 2 | .143 | .143 | .286 |
| 2 ML YEARS | | 18 | 52 | 9 | 3 | 0 | 1 | (0 | 1) | 15 | 3 | 3 | 0 | 0 | 12 | 1 | 0 | 0 | 0 | 0 | .00 | 3 | .173 | .189 | .288 |

## Ramon Manon

**Pitches:** Right **Bats:** Right **Pos:** RP **Ht:** 6' 0" **Wt:** 170 **Born:** 01/20/68 **Age:** 23

| HOW MUCH HE PITCHED | | | | | | | | WHAT HE GAVE UP | | | | | | | | | | | | THE RESULTS | | | | | |
|---|---|---|---|---|---|---|---|---|---|---|---|---|---|---|---|---|---|---|---|---|---|---|---|---|---|
| Year Team | Lg | G | GS | CG | GF | IP | BFP | H | R | ER | HR | SH | SF | HB | TBB | IBB | SO | WP | Bk | W | L | Pct. | ShO | Sv | ERA |
| 1986 Yankees | R | 11 | 4 | 0 | 2 | 28 | 137 | 31 | 22 | 16 | 0 | 1 | 1 | 1 | 22 | 1 | 13 | 2 | 0 | 0 | 4 | .000 | 0 | 0 | 5.14 |
| 1987 Pr William | A | 23 | 3 | 0 | 4 | 39.1 | 198 | 45 | 36 | 32 | 1 | 1 | 2 | 0 | 41 | 0 | 28 | 7 | 2 | 2 | 3 | .400 | 0 | 1 | 7.32 |
| 1988 Ft.Laudrdle | A | 4 | 4 | 1 | 0 | 22.1 | 86 | 13 | 5 | 5 | 1 | 1 | 2 | 1 | 12 | 0 | 13 | 1 | 0 | 2 | 0 | 1.000 | 1 | 0 | 2.01 |

| Year | Team | Lg | G | GS | CG | GF | IP | BFP | H | R | ER | HR | SH | SF | HB | TBB | IBB | SO | WP | Bk | W | L | Pct. | ShO | Sv | ERA |
|---|---|---|---|---|---|---|---|---|---|---|---|---|---|---|---|---|---|---|---|---|---|---|---|---|---|---|
| 1989 | Ft.Laudrdle | A | 22 | 22 | 6 | 0 | 122.1 | 504 | 91 | 62 | 48 | 5 | 4 | 5 | 9 | 53 | 0 | 100 | 4 | 2 | 7 | 9 | .438 | 3 | 0 | 3.53 |
| 1990 | Albany | AA | 9 | 3 | 0 | 3 | 25.2 | 129 | 24 | 19 | 17 | 1 | 1 | 0 | 2 | 29 | 0 | 21 | 3 | 0 | 1 | 2 | .333 | 0 | 0 | 5.96 |
| | Ft.Laudrdle | A | 11 | 5 | 0 | 2 | 35.1 | 171 | 39 | 26 | 23 | 2 | 2 | 0 | 1 | 23 | 0 | 40 | 7 | 1 | 2 | 3 | .400 | 0 | 0 | 5.86 |
| 1990 | Texas | AL | 1 | 0 | 0 | 0 | 2 | 12 | 3 | 3 | 3 | 0 | 0 | 0 | 0 | 3 | 1 | 0 | 0 | 0 | 0 | 0 | .000 | 0 | 0 | 13.50 |

## Fred Manrique

**Bats:** Right **Throws:** Right **Pos:** 2B **Ht:** 6' 1" **Wt:** 175 **Born:** 11/05/61 **Age:** 29

| BATTING | | | | | | | | | | | | | | | | | | | | BASERUNNING | | | | PERCENTAGES | | |
|---|---|---|---|---|---|---|---|---|---|---|---|---|---|---|---|---|---|---|---|---|---|---|---|---|---|---|
| Year | Team | Lg | G | AB | H | 2B | 3B | HR | (Hm | Rd) | TB | R | RBI | TBB | IBB | SO | HBP | SH | SF | SB | CS | SB% | GDP | Avg | OBP | SLG |
| 1981 | Toronto | AL | 14 | 28 | 4 | 0 | 0 | 0 | (0 | 0) | 4 | 1 | 1 | 0 | 0 | 12 | 1 | 0 | 0 | 0 | 1 | .00 | 0 | .143 | .172 | .143 |
| 1984 | Toronto | AL | 10 | 9 | 3 | 0 | 0 | 0 | (0 | 0) | 3 | 0 | 1 | 0 | 0 | 1 | 0 | 0 | 0 | 0 | 0 | .00 | 1 | .333 | .333 | .333 |
| 1985 | Montreal | NL | 9 | 13 | 4 | 1 | 1 | 1 | (1 | 0) | 10 | 5 | 1 | 1 | 0 | 3 | 0 | 0 | 0 | 0 | 0 | .00 | 0 | .308 | .357 | .769 |
| 1986 | St. Louis | NL | 13 | 17 | 3 | 0 | 0 | 1 | (0 | 1) | 6 | 2 | 1 | 1 | 0 | 1 | 0 | 0 | 0 | 1 | 0 | 1.00 | 1 | .176 | .222 | .353 |
| 1987 | Chicago | AL | 115 | 298 | 77 | 13 | 3 | 4 | (2 | 2) | 108 | 30 | 29 | 19 | 1 | 69 | 1 | 9 | 3 | 5 | 3 | .63 | 4 | .258 | .302 | .362 |
| 1988 | Chicago | AL | 140 | 345 | 81 | 10 | 6 | 5 | (3 | 2) | 118 | 43 | 37 | 21 | 1 | 54 | 3 | 16 | 2 | 6 | 5 | .55 | 7 | .235 | .283 | .342 |
| 1989 | 2 ML Teams | | 119 | 378 | 111 | 25 | 1 | 4 | (1 | 3) | 150 | 46 | 52 | 17 | 1 | 63 | 2 | 13 | 2 | 4 | 5 | .44 | 9 | .294 | .326 | .397 |
| 1990 | Minnesota | AL | 69 | 228 | 54 | 10 | 0 | 5 | (3 | 2) | 79 | 22 | 29 | 4 | 0 | 35 | 2 | 1 | 2 | 2 | 0 | 1.00 | 8 | .237 | .254 | .346 |
| 1989 | Chicago | AL | 65 | 187 | 56 | 13 | 1 | 2 | (1 | 1) | 77 | 23 | 30 | 8 | 1 | 30 | 2 | 4 | 1 | 0 | 4 | .00 | 6 | .299 | .333 | .412 |
| | Texas | AL | 54 | 191 | 55 | 12 | 0 | 2 | (0 | 2) | 73 | 23 | 22 | 9 | 0 | 33 | 0 | 9 | 1 | 4 | 1 | .80 | 3 | .288 | .318 | .382 |
| | 8 ML YEARS | | 489 | 1316 | 337 | 59 | 11 | 20 | (10 | 10) | 478 | 149 | 151 | 63 | 3 | 238 | 9 | 39 | 9 | 18 | 14 | .56 | 30 | .256 | .293 | .363 |

## Jeff Manto

**Bats:** Right **Throws:** Right **Pos:** 1B **Ht:** 6' 3" **Wt:** 210 **Born:** 08/23/64 **Age:** 26

| BATTING | | | | | | | | | | | | | | | | | | | | BASERUNNING | | | | PERCENTAGES | | |
|---|---|---|---|---|---|---|---|---|---|---|---|---|---|---|---|---|---|---|---|---|---|---|---|---|---|---|
| Year | Team | Lg | G | AB | H | 2B | 3B | HR | (Hm | Rd) | TB | R | RBI | TBB | IBB | SO | HBP | SH | SF | SB | CS | SB% | GDP | Avg | OBP | SLG |
| 1985 | Quad City | A | 74 | 233 | 46 | 5 | 2 | 11 | -- | -- | 88 | 34 | 34 | 40 | 0 | 74 | 5 | 1 | 3 | 3 | 1 | .75 | 7 | .197 | .324 | .378 |
| 1986 | Quad City | A | 73 | 239 | 59 | 13 | 0 | 8 | -- | -- | 96 | 31 | 49 | 37 | 0 | 70 | 4 | 1 | 2 | 2 | 1 | .67 | 2 | .247 | .355 | .402 |
| 1987 | Palm Sprngs | A | 112 | 375 | 96 | 21 | 4 | 7 | -- | -- | 146 | 61 | 63 | 102 | 1 | 85 | 8 | 5 | 7 | 8 | 2 | .80 | 7 | .256 | .419 | .389 |
| 1988 | Midland | AA | 120 | 408 | 123 | 23 | 3 | 24 | -- | -- | 224 | 88 | 101 | 62 | 5 | 76 | 8 | 3 | 4 | 7 | 5 | .58 | 17 | .301 | .400 | .549 |
| 1989 | Edmonton | AAA | 127 | 408 | 113 | 25 | 3 | 23 | -- | -- | 213 | 89 | 67 | 91 | 5 | 81 | 9 | 3 | 4 | 4 | 4 | .50 | 12 | .277 | .416 | .522 |
| 1990 | Colo Sprngs | AAA | 96 | 316 | 94 | 27 | 1 | 18 | -- | -- | 177 | 73 | 82 | 78 | 2 | 65 | 9 | 1 | 3 | 10 | 3 | .77 | 9 | .297 | .446 | .560 |
| 1990 | Cleveland | AL | 30 | 76 | 17 | 5 | 1 | 2 | (1 | 1) | 30 | 12 | 14 | 21 | 1 | 18 | 0 | 0 | 0 | 0 | 1 | .00 | 0 | .224 | .392 | .395 |

## Kirt Manwaring

**Bats:** Right **Throws:** Right **Pos:** C **Ht:** 5'11" **Wt:** 185 **Born:** 07/15/65 **Age:** 25

| BATTING | | | | | | | | | | | | | | | | | | | | BASERUNNING | | | | PERCENTAGES | | |
|---|---|---|---|---|---|---|---|---|---|---|---|---|---|---|---|---|---|---|---|---|---|---|---|---|---|---|
| Year | Team | Lg | G | AB | H | 2B | 3B | HR | (Hm | Rd) | TB | R | RBI | TBB | IBB | SO | HBP | SH | SF | SB | CS | SB% | GDP | Avg | OBP | SLG |
| 1987 | San Francisco | NL | 6 | 7 | 1 | 0 | 0 | 0 | (0 | 0) | 1 | 0 | 0 | 0 | 0 | 1 | 1 | 0 | 0 | 0 | 0 | .00 | 1 | .143 | .250 | .143 |
| 1988 | San Francisco | NL | 40 | 116 | 29 | 7 | 0 | 1 | (0 | 1) | 39 | 12 | 15 | 2 | 0 | 21 | 3 | 1 | 1 | 0 | 1 | .00 | 1 | .250 | .279 | .336 |
| 1989 | San Francisco | NL | 85 | 200 | 42 | 4 | 2 | 0 | (0 | 0) | 50 | 14 | 18 | 11 | 1 | 28 | 4 | 7 | 1 | 2 | 1 | .67 | 5 | .210 | .264 | .250 |
| 1990 | San Francisco | NL | 8 | 13 | 2 | 0 | 1 | 0 | (0 | 0) | 4 | 0 | 1 | 0 | 0 | 3 | 0 | 0 | 0 | 0 | 0 | .00 | 0 | .154 | .154 | .308 |
| | 4 ML YEARS | | 139 | 336 | 74 | 11 | 3 | 1 | (0 | 1) | 94 | 26 | 34 | 13 | 1 | 53 | 8 | 8 | 2 | 2 | 2 | .50 | 7 | .220 | .265 | .280 |

## Paul Marak

**Pitches:** Right **Bats:** Right **Pos:** SP **Ht:** 6' 2" **Wt:** 180 **Born:** 08/02/65 **Age:** 25

| HOW MUCH HE PITCHED | | | | | | | | | WHAT HE GAVE UP | | | | | | | | | | | | THE RESULTS | | | | | |
|---|---|---|---|---|---|---|---|---|---|---|---|---|---|---|---|---|---|---|---|---|---|---|---|---|---|---|
| Year | Team | Lg | G | GS | CG | GF | IP | BFP | H | R | ER | HR | SH | SF | HB | TBB | IBB | SO | WP | Bk | W | L | Pct. | ShO | Sv | ERA |
| 1985 | Braves | R | 12 | 12 | 0 | 0 | 63 | 305 | 80 | 58 | 39 | 1 | 3 | 1 | 1 | 36 | 0 | 33 | 11 | 0 | 2 | 6 | .250 | 0 | 0 | 5.57 |
| 1986 | Idaho Falls | R | 12 | 12 | 1 | 0 | 61 | 0 | 82 | 57 | 34 | 6 | 0 | 0 | 4 | 25 | 1 | 52 | 12 | 1 | 2 | 5 | .286 | 0 | 0 | 5.02 |
| 1987 | Sumter | A | 50 | 6 | 0 | 14 | 118 | 495 | 101 | 50 | 41 | 6 | 5 | 3 | 6 | 44 | 1 | 98 | 9 | 0 | 12 | 5 | .706 | 0 | 2 | 3.13 |
| 1988 | Greenville | AA | 12 | 0 | 0 | 3 | 16.1 | 84 | 25 | 19 | 19 | 6 | 1 | 1 | 0 | 11 | 0 | 9 | 2 | 1 | 0 | 0 | .000 | 0 | 0 | 10.47 |
| | Durham | A | 32 | 7 | 3 | 7 | 100.2 | 419 | 90 | 40 | 30 | 5 | 4 | 5 | 0 | 33 | 3 | 84 | 6 | 3 | 7 | 4 | .636 | 1 | 0 | 2.68 |
| 1989 | Richmond | AAA | 2 | 1 | 0 | 0 | 4 | 23 | 8 | 4 | 4 | 1 | 0 | 0 | 0 | 4 | 1 | 2 | 1 | 0 | 0 | 1 | .000 | 0 | 0 | 9.00 |
| | Greenville | AA | 43 | 14 | 0 | 10 | 121.2 | 510 | 102 | 53 | 41 | 7 | 5 | 5 | 3 | 47 | 1 | 81 | 5 | 0 | 8 | 7 | .533 | 0 | 5 | 3.03 |
| 1990 | Richmond | AAA | 32 | 16 | 5 | 6 | 148 | 603 | 130 | 49 | 41 | 9 | 3 | 4 | 2 | 50 | 0 | 75 | 6 | 1 | 9 | 8 | .529 | 0 | 0 | 2.49 |
| 1990 | Atlanta | NL | 7 | 7 | 1 | 0 | 39 | 172 | 39 | 16 | 16 | 2 | 3 | 1 | 3 | 19 | 3 | 15 | 2 | 0 | 1 | 2 | .333 | 1 | 0 | 3.69 |

## Mike Marshall

**Bats:** Right **Throws:** Right **Pos:** 1B/DH **Ht:** 6' 5" **Wt:** 220 **Born:** 01/12/60 **Age:** 31

| BATTING | | | | | | | | | | | | | | | | | | | | BASERUNNING | | | | PERCENTAGES | | |
|---|---|---|---|---|---|---|---|---|---|---|---|---|---|---|---|---|---|---|---|---|---|---|---|---|---|---|
| Year | Team | Lg | G | AB | H | 2B | 3B | HR | (Hm | Rd) | TB | R | RBI | TBB | IBB | SO | HBP | SH | SF | SB | CS | SB% | GDP | Avg | OBP | SLG |
| 1981 | Los Angeles | NL | 14 | 25 | 5 | 3 | 0 | 0 | (0 | 0) | 8 | 2 | 1 | 1 | 0 | 4 | 1 | 0 | 0 | 0 | 0 | .00 | 1 | .200 | .259 | .320 |
| 1982 | Los Angeles | NL | 49 | 95 | 23 | 3 | 0 | 5 | (2 | 3) | 41 | 10 | 9 | 13 | 1 | 23 | 1 | 0 | 1 | 2 | 0 | 1.00 | 1 | .242 | .336 | .432 |
| 1983 | Los Angeles | NL | 140 | 465 | 132 | 17 | 1 | 17 | (9 | 8) | 202 | 47 | 65 | 43 | 4 | 127 | 5 | 0 | 5 | 7 | 3 | .70 | 8 | .284 | .347 | .434 |
| 1984 | Los Angeles | NL | 134 | 495 | 127 | 27 | 0 | 21 | (11 | 10) | 217 | 68 | 65 | 40 | 6 | 93 | 3 | 1 | 2 | 4 | 3 | .57 | 12 | .257 | .315 | .438 |
| 1985 | Los Angeles | NL | 135 | 518 | 152 | 27 | 2 | 28 | (15 | 13) | 267 | 72 | 95 | 37 | 6 | 137 | 3 | 2 | 4 | 3 | 10 | .23 | 8 | .293 | .342 | .515 |

| Year Team | Lg | G | AB | H | 2B | 3B | HR | (Hm | Rd) | TB | R | RBI | TBB | IBB | SO | HBP | SH | SF | SB | CS | SB% | GDP | Avg | OBP | SLG |
|---|---|---|---|---|---|---|---|---|---|---|---|---|---|---|---|---|---|---|---|---|---|---|---|---|---|
| 1986 Los Angeles | NL | 103 | 330 | 77 | 11 | 0 | 19 | (13 | 6) | 145 | 47 | 53 | 27 | 3 | 90 | 4 | 0 | 1 | 4 | 4 | .50 | 5 | .233 | .298 | .439 |
| 1987 Los Angeles | NL | 104 | 402 | 118 | 19 | 0 | 16 | (5 | 11) | 185 | 45 | 72 | 18 | 2 | 79 | 4 | 0 | 4 | 0 | 5 | .00 | 13 | .294 | .327 | .460 |
| 1988 Los Angeles | NL | 144 | 542 | 150 | 27 | 2 | 20 | (9 | 11) | 241 | 63 | 82 | 24 | 7 | 93 | 7 | 0 | 4 | 4 | 1 | .80 | 17 | .277 | .314 | .445 |
| 1989 Los Angeles | NL | 105 | 377 | 98 | 21 | 1 | 11 | (6 | 5) | 154 | 41 | 42 | 33 | 4 | 78 | 5 | 0 | 4 | 2 | 5 | .29 | 8 | .260 | .325 | .408 |
| 1990 2 ML Teams | | 83 | 275 | 71 | 14 | 2 | 10 | (7 | 3) | 119 | 34 | 39 | 11 | 0 | 66 | 4 | 0 | 3 | 0 | 2 | .00 | 4 | .258 | .294 | .433 |
| 1990 New York | NL | 53 | 163 | 39 | 8 | 1 | 6 | (4 | 2) | 67 | 24 | 27 | 7 | 0 | 40 | 3 | 0 | 3 | 0 | 2 | .00 | 2 | .239 | .278 | .411 |
| Boston | AL | 30 | 112 | 32 | 6 | 1 | 4 | (3 | 1) | 52 | 10 | 12 | 4 | 0 | 26 | 1 | 0 | 0 | 0 | 0 | .00 | 2 | .286 | .316 | .464 |
| 10 ML YEARS | | 1011 | 3524 | 953 | 169 | 8 | 147 | (77 | 70) | 1579 | 429 | 523 | 247 | 33 | 790 | 37 | 3 | 28 | 26 | 33 | .44 | 77 | .270 | .322 | .448 |

## Carlos Martinez

**Bats:** Right **Throws:** Right **Pos:** 1B **Ht:** 6' 5" **Wt:** 175 **Born:** 08/11/65 **Age:** 25

| | | BATTING | | | | | | | | | | | | | | | | | BASERUNNING | | | | PERCENTAGES | | |
|---|---|---|---|---|---|---|---|---|---|---|---|---|---|---|---|---|---|---|---|---|---|---|---|---|---|
| Year Team | Lg | G | AB | H | 2B | 3B | HR | (Hm | Rd) | TB | R | RBI | TBB | IBB | SO | HBP | SH | SF | SB | CS | SB% | GDP | Avg | OBP | SLG |
| 1988 Chicago | AL | 17 | 55 | 9 | 1 | 0 | 0 | (0 | 0) | 10 | 5 | 0 | 0 | 0 | 12 | 0 | 0 | 0 | 1 | 0 | 1.00 | 1 | .164 | .164 | .182 |
| 1989 Chicago | AL | 109 | 350 | 105 | 22 | 0 | 5 | (2 | 3) | 142 | 44 | 32 | 21 | 2 | 57 | 1 | 6 | 1 | 4 | 1 | .80 | 14 | .300 | .340 | .406 |
| 1990 Chicago | AL | 92 | 272 | 61 | 6 | 5 | 4 | (2 | 2) | 89 | 18 | 24 | 10 | 2 | 40 | 0 | 1 | 0 | 0 | 4 | .00 | 8 | .224 | .252 | .327 |
| 3 ML YEARS | | 218 | 677 | 175 | 29 | 5 | 9 | (4 | 5) | 241 | 67 | 56 | 31 | 4 | 109 | 1 | 7 | 1 | 5 | 5 | .50 | 23 | .258 | .292 | .356 |

## Carmelo Martinez

**Bats:** Right **Throws:** Right **Pos:** 1B/LF **Ht:** 6' 2" **Wt:** 220 **Born:** 07/28/60 **Age:** 30

| | | BATTING | | | | | | | | | | | | | | | | | BASERUNNING | | | | PERCENTAGES | | |
|---|---|---|---|---|---|---|---|---|---|---|---|---|---|---|---|---|---|---|---|---|---|---|---|---|---|
| Year Team | Lg | G | AB | H | 2B | 3B | HR | (Hm | Rd) | TB | R | RBI | TBB | IBB | SO | HBP | SH | SF | SB | CS | SB% | GDP | Avg | OBP | SLG |
| 1983 Chicago | NL | 29 | 89 | 23 | 3 | 0 | 6 | (2 | 4) | 44 | 8 | 16 | 4 | 0 | 19 | 0 | 0 | 1 | 0 | 0 | .00 | 3 | .258 | .287 | .494 |
| 1984 San Diego | NL | 149 | 488 | 122 | 28 | 2 | 13 | (6 | 7) | 193 | 64 | 66 | 68 | 4 | 82 | 4 | 0 | 10 | 1 | 3 | .25 | 7 | .250 | .340 | .395 |
| 1985 San Diego | NL | 150 | 514 | 130 | 28 | 1 | 21 | (15 | 6) | 223 | 64 | 72 | 87 | 4 | 82 | 3 | 2 | 4 | 0 | 4 | .00 | 10 | .253 | .362 | .434 |
| 1986 San Diego | NL | 113 | 244 | 58 | 10 | 0 | 9 | (6 | 3) | 95 | 28 | 25 | 35 | 2 | 46 | 1 | 1 | 2 | 1 | 1 | .50 | 9 | .238 | .333 | .389 |
| 1987 San Diego | NL | 139 | 447 | 122 | 21 | 2 | 15 | (10 | 5) | 192 | 59 | 70 | 70 | 5 | 82 | 3 | 1 | 4 | 5 | 5 | .50 | 11 | .273 | .372 | .430 |
| 1988 San Diego | NL | 121 | 365 | 86 | 12 | 0 | 18 | (11 | 7) | 152 | 48 | 65 | 35 | 3 | 57 | 0 | 3 | 2 | 1 | 1 | .50 | 10 | .236 | .301 | .416 |
| 1989 San Diego | NL | 111 | 267 | 59 | 12 | 2 | 6 | (2 | 4) | 93 | 23 | 39 | 32 | 3 | 54 | 0 | 0 | 2 | 0 | 0 | .00 | 12 | .221 | .302 | .348 |
| 1990 2 ML Teams | | 83 | 217 | 52 | 9 | 0 | 10 | (6 | 4) | 91 | 26 | 35 | 30 | 0 | 42 | 0 | 0 | 0 | 2 | 1 | .67 | 3 | .240 | .332 | .419 |
| 1990 Philadelphia | NL | 71 | 198 | 48 | 8 | 0 | 8 | (4 | 4) | 80 | 23 | 31 | 29 | 0 | 37 | 0 | 0 | 0 | 2 | 1 | .67 | 3 | .242 | .339 | .404 |
| Pittsburgh | NL | 12 | 19 | 4 | 1 | 0 | 2 | (2 | 0) | 11 | 3 | 4 | 1 | 0 | 5 | 0 | 0 | 0 | 0 | 0 | .00 | 0 | .211 | .250 | .579 |
| 8 ML YEARS | | 895 | 2631 | 652 | 123 | 7 | 98 | (58 | 40) | 1083 | 320 | 388 | 361 | 21 | 464 | 11 | 7 | 25 | 10 | 15 | .40 | 65 | .248 | .338 | .412 |

## Dave Martinez

**Bats:** Left **Throws:** Left **Pos:** CF/RF **Ht:** 5'10" **Wt:** 150 **Born:** 09/26/64 **Age:** 26

| | | BATTING | | | | | | | | | | | | | | | | | BASERUNNING | | | | PERCENTAGES | | |
|---|---|---|---|---|---|---|---|---|---|---|---|---|---|---|---|---|---|---|---|---|---|---|---|---|---|
| Year Team | Lg | G | AB | H | 2B | 3B | HR | (Hm | Rd) | TB | R | RBI | TBB | IBB | SO | HBP | SH | SF | SB | CS | SB% | GDP | Avg | OBP | SLG |
| 1986 Chicago | NL | 53 | 108 | 15 | 1 | 1 | 1 | (1 | 0) | 21 | 13 | 7 | 6 | 0 | 22 | 1 | 0 | 1 | 4 | 2 | .67 | 1 | .139 | .190 | .194 |
| 1987 Chicago | NL | 142 | 459 | 134 | 18 | 8 | 8 | (5 | 3) | 192 | 70 | 36 | 57 | 4 | 96 | 2 | 1 | 1 | 16 | 8 | .67 | 4 | .292 | .372 | .418 |
| 1988 2 ML Teams | | 138 | 447 | 114 | 13 | 6 | 6 | (2 | 4) | 157 | 51 | 46 | 38 | 8 | 94 | 2 | 2 | 5 | 23 | 9 | .72 | 3 | .255 | .313 | .351 |
| 1989 Montreal | NL | 126 | 361 | 99 | 16 | 7 | 3 | (1 | 2) | 138 | 41 | 27 | 27 | 2 | 57 | 0 | 7 | 1 | 23 | 4 | .85 | 1 | .274 | .324 | .382 |
| 1990 Montreal | NL | 118 | 391 | 109 | 13 | 5 | 11 | (5 | 6) | 165 | 60 | 39 | 24 | 2 | 48 | 1 | 3 | 2 | 13 | 11 | .54 | 8 | .279 | .321 | .422 |
| 1988 Chicago | NL | 75 | 256 | 65 | 10 | 1 | 4 | (2 | 2) | 89 | 27 | 34 | 21 | 5 | 46 | 2 | 0 | 4 | 7 | 3 | .70 | 2 | .254 | .311 | .348 |
| Montreal | NL | 63 | 191 | 49 | 3 | 5 | 2 | (0 | 2) | 68 | 24 | 12 | 17 | 3 | 48 | 0 | 2 | 1 | 16 | 6 | .73 | 1 | .257 | .316 | .356 |
| 5 ML YEARS | | 577 | 1766 | 471 | 61 | 27 | 29 | (14 | 15) | 673 | 235 | 155 | 152 | 16 | 317 | 6 | 13 | 10 | 79 | 34 | .70 | 17 | .267 | .325 | .381 |

## Dennis Martinez

**Pitches:** Right **Bats:** Right **Pos:** SP **Ht:** 6' 1" **Wt:** 183 **Born:** 05/14/55 **Age:** 36

| | | HOW MUCH HE PITCHED | | | | | | WHAT HE GAVE UP | | | | | | | | | | | | THE RESULTS | | | | | |
|---|---|---|---|---|---|---|---|---|---|---|---|---|---|---|---|---|---|---|---|---|---|---|---|---|---|
| Year Team | Lg | G | GS | CG | GF | IP | BFP | H | R | ER | HR | SH | SF | HB | TBB | IBB | SO | WP | Bk | W | L | Pct. | ShO | Sv | ERA |
| 1976 Baltimore | AL | 4 | 2 | 1 | 1 | 28 | 106 | 23 | 8 | 8 | 1 | 1 | 0 | 0 | 8 | 0 | 18 | 1 | 0 | 1 | 2 | .333 | 0 | 0 | 2.57 |
| 1977 Baltimore | AL | 42 | 13 | 5 | 19 | 167 | 709 | 157 | 86 | 76 | 10 | 8 | 8 | 8 | 64 | 5 | 107 | 5 | 0 | 14 | 7 | .667 | 0 | 4 | 4.10 |
| 1978 Baltimore | AL | 40 | 38 | 15 | 0 | 276 | 1140 | 257 | 121 | 108 | 20 | 8 | 7 | 3 | 93 | 4 | 142 | 8 | 0 | 16 | 11 | .593 | 2 | 0 | 3.52 |
| 1979 Baltimore | AL | 40 | 39 | 18 | 0 | 292 | 1206 | 279 | 129 | 119 | 28 | 12 | 12 | 1 | 78 | 1 | 132 | 9 | 2 | 15 | 16 | .484 | 3 | 0 | 3.67 |
| 1980 Baltimore | AL | 25 | 12 | 2 | 8 | 100 | 428 | 103 | 44 | 44 | 12 | 1 | 3 | 2 | 44 | 6 | 42 | 0 | 1 | 6 | 4 | .600 | 0 | 1 | 3.96 |
| 1981 Baltimore | AL | 25 | 24 | 9 | 0 | 179 | 753 | 173 | 84 | 66 | 10 | 2 | 5 | 2 | 62 | 1 | 88 | 6 | 1 | 14 | 5 | .737 | 2 | 0 | 3.32 |
| 1982 Baltimore | AL | 40 | 39 | 10 | 0 | 252 | 1093 | 262 | 123 | 118 | 30 | 11 | 7 | 7 | 87 | 2 | 111 | 7 | 1 | 16 | 12 | .571 | 2 | 0 | 4.21 |
| 1983 Baltimore | AL | 32 | 25 | 4 | 3 | 153 | 688 | 209 | 108 | 94 | 21 | 3 | 5 | 2 | 45 | 0 | 71 | 2 | 0 | 7 | 16 | .304 | 0 | 0 | 5.53 |
| 1984 Baltimore | AL | 34 | 20 | 2 | 4 | 141.2 | 599 | 145 | 81 | 79 | 26 | 0 | 5 | 5 | 37 | 2 | 77 | 13 | 0 | 6 | 9 | .400 | 0 | 0 | 5.02 |
| 1985 Baltimore | AL | 33 | 31 | 3 | 1 | 180 | 789 | 203 | 110 | 103 | 29 | 0 | 11 | 9 | 63 | 3 | 68 | 4 | 1 | 13 | 11 | .542 | 1 | 0 | 5.15 |
| 1986 2 ML Teams | | 23 | 15 | 1 | 2 | 104.2 | 449 | 114 | 57 | 55 | 11 | 8 | 2 | 3 | 30 | 4 | 65 | 3 | 2 | 3 | 6 | .333 | 1 | 0 | 4.73 |
| 1987 Montreal | NL | 22 | 22 | 2 | 0 | 144.2 | 599 | 133 | 59 | 53 | 9 | 4 | 3 | 6 | 40 | 2 | 84 | 4 | 2 | 11 | 4 | .733 | 1 | 0 | 3.30 |
| 1988 Montreal | NL | 34 | 34 | 9 | 0 | 235.1 | 968 | 215 | 94 | 71 | 21 | 2 | 6 | 6 | 55 | 3 | 120 | 5 | 10 | 15 | 13 | .536 | 2 | 0 | 2.72 |
| 1989 Montreal | NL | 34 | 33 | 5 | 1 | 232 | 950 | 227 | 88 | 82 | 21 | 8 | 2 | 7 | 49 | 4 | 142 | 5 | 2 | 16 | 7 | .696 | 2 | 0 | 3.18 |
| 1990 Montreal | NL | 32 | 32 | 7 | 0 | 226 | 908 | 191 | 80 | 74 | 16 | 11 | 3 | 6 | 49 | 9 | 156 | 1 | 1 | 10 | 11 | .476 | 2 | 0 | 2.95 |

| Year Team | Lg | G | GS | CG | GF | IP | BFP | H | R | ER | HR | SH | SF | HB | TBB | IBB | SO | WP | Bk | W | L | Pct. | ShO | Sv | ERA |
|---|---|---|---|---|---|---|---|---|---|---|---|---|---|---|---|---|---|---|---|---|---|---|---|---|---|
| 1986 Baltimore | AL | 4 | 0 | 0 | 1 | 6.2 | 33 | 11 | 5 | 5 | 0 | 0 | 1 | 0 | 2 | 0 | 2 | 1 | 0 | 0 | 0 | .000 | 0 | 0 | 6.75 |
| Montreal | NL | 19 | 15 | 1 | 1 | 98 | 416 | 103 | 52 | 50 | 11 | 8 | 1 | 3 | 28 | 4 | 63 | 2 | 2 | 3 | 6 | .333 | 1 | 0 | 4.59 |
| 15 ML YEARS | | 460 | 379 | 93 | 39 | 2711.1 | 11385 | 2691 | 1272 | 1150 | 265 | 79 | 79 | 67 | 804 | 46 | 1423 | 73 | 23 | 163 | 134 | .549 | 18 | 5 | 3.82 |

## Edgar Martinez

**Bats:** Right **Throws:** Right **Pos:** 3B **Ht:** 5'11" **Wt:** 175 **Born:** 01/02/63 **Age:** 28

| | | BATTING | | | | | | | | | | | | | | | | | BASERUNNING | | | | PERCENTAGES | | |
|---|---|---|---|---|---|---|---|---|---|---|---|---|---|---|---|---|---|---|---|---|---|---|---|---|---|
| Year Team | Lg | G | AB | H | 2B | 3B | HR | (Hm | Rd) | TB | R | RBI | TBB | IBB | SO | HBP | SH | SF | SB | CS | SB% | GDP | Avg | OBP | SLG |
| 1987 Seattle | AL | 13 | 43 | 16 | 5 | 2 | 0 | (0 | 0) | 25 | 6 | 5 | 2 | 0 | 5 | 1 | 0 | 0 | 0 | 0 | .00 | 0 | .372 | .413 | .581 |
| 1988 Seattle | AL | 14 | 32 | 9 | 4 | 0 | 0 | (0 | 0) | 13 | 0 | 5 | 4 | 0 | 7 | 0 | 1 | 1 | 0 | 0 | .00 | 0 | .281 | .351 | .406 |
| 1989 Seattle | AL | 65 | 171 | 41 | 5 | 0 | 2 | (0 | 2) | 52 | 20 | 20 | 17 | 1 | 26 | 3 | 2 | 3 | 2 | 1 | .67 | 3 | .240 | .314 | .304 |
| 1990 Seattle | AL | 144 | 487 | 147 | 27 | 2 | 11 | (3 | 8) | 211 | 71 | 49 | 74 | 3 | 62 | 5 | 1 | 3 | 1 | 4 | .20 | 13 | .302 | .397 | .433 |
| 4 ML YEARS | | 236 | 733 | 213 | 41 | 4 | 13 | (3 | 10) | 301 | 97 | 79 | 97 | 4 | 100 | 9 | 4 | 7 | 3 | 5 | .38 | 16 | .291 | .377 | .411 |

## Ramon Martinez

**Pitches:** Right **Bats:** Right **Pos:** SP **Ht:** 6' 4" **Wt:** 172 **Born:** 03/22/68 **Age:** 23

| | | HOW MUCH HE PITCHED | | | | | | WHAT HE GAVE UP | | | | | | | | | | | | THE RESULTS | | | | | |
|---|---|---|---|---|---|---|---|---|---|---|---|---|---|---|---|---|---|---|---|---|---|---|---|---|---|
| Year Team | Lg | G | GS | CG | GF | IP | BFP | H | R | ER | HR | SH | SF | HB | TBB | IBB | SO | WP | Bk | W | L | Pct. | ShO | Sv | ERA |
| 1988 Los Angeles | NL | 9 | 6 | 0 | 0 | 35.2 | 151 | 27 | 17 | 15 | 0 | 4 | 0 | 0 | 22 | 1 | 23 | 1 | 0 | 1 | 3 | .250 | 0 | 0 | 3.79 |
| 1989 Los Angeles | NL | 15 | 15 | 2 | 0 | 98.2 | 410 | 79 | 39 | 35 | 11 | 4 | 0 | 5 | 41 | 1 | 89 | 1 | 0 | 6 | 4 | .600 | 2 | 0 | 3.19 |
| 1990 Los Angeles | NL | 33 | 33 | 12 | 0 | 234.1 | 950 | 191 | 89 | 76 | 22 | 7 | 5 | 4 | 67 | 5 | 223 | 3 | 3 | 20 | 6 | .769 | 3 | 0 | 2.92 |
| 3 ML YEARS | | 57 | 54 | 14 | 0 | 368.2 | 1511 | 297 | 145 | 126 | 33 | 15 | 5 | 9 | 130 | 7 | 335 | 5 | 3 | 27 | 13 | .675 | 5 | 0 | 3.08 |

## Tino Martinez

**Bats:** Left **Throws:** Right **Pos:** 1B **Ht:** 6' 2" **Wt:** 205 **Born:** 12/07/67 **Age:** 23

| | | BATTING | | | | | | | | | | | | | | | | | BASERUNNING | | | | PERCENTAGES | | |
|---|---|---|---|---|---|---|---|---|---|---|---|---|---|---|---|---|---|---|---|---|---|---|---|---|---|
| Year Team | Lg | G | AB | H | 2B | 3B | HR | (Hm | Rd) | TB | R | RBI | TBB | IBB | SO | HBP | SH | SF | SB | CS | SB% | GDP | Avg | OBP | SLG |
| 1989 Williamsprt | AA | 137 | 509 | 131 | 29 | 2 | 13 | -- | -- | 203 | 51 | 64 | 59 | 13 | 54 | 0 | 1 | 8 | 7 | 1 | .88 | 11 | .257 | .330 | .399 |
| 1990 Calgary | AAA | 128 | 453 | 145 | 28 | 1 | 17 | -- | -- | 226 | 83 | 93 | 74 | 11 | 37 | 3 | 2 | 8 | 8 | 5 | .62 | 9 | .320 | .413 | .499 |
| 1990 Seattle | AL | 24 | 68 | 15 | 4 | 0 | 0 | (0 | 0) | 19 | 4 | 5 | 9 | 0 | 9 | 0 | 0 | 1 | 0 | 0 | .00 | 0 | .221 | .308 | .279 |

## John Marzano

**Bats:** Right **Throws:** Right **Pos:** C **Ht:** 5'11" **Wt:** 197 **Born:** 02/14/63 **Age:** 28

| | | BATTING | | | | | | | | | | | | | | | | | BASERUNNING | | | | PERCENTAGES | | |
|---|---|---|---|---|---|---|---|---|---|---|---|---|---|---|---|---|---|---|---|---|---|---|---|---|---|
| Year Team | Lg | G | AB | H | 2B | 3B | HR | (Hm | Rd) | TB | R | RBI | TBB | IBB | SO | HBP | SH | SF | SB | CS | SB% | GDP | Avg | OBP | SLG |
| 1987 Boston | AL | 52 | 168 | 41 | 11 | 0 | 5 | (4 | 1) | 67 | 20 | 24 | 7 | 0 | 41 | 3 | 2 | 2 | 0 | 1 | .00 | 3 | .244 | .283 | .399 |
| 1988 Boston | AL | 10 | 29 | 4 | 1 | 0 | 0 | (0 | 0) | 5 | 3 | 1 | 1 | 0 | 3 | 0 | 0 | 0 | 0 | 0 | .00 | 1 | .138 | .167 | .172 |
| 1989 Boston | AL | 7 | 18 | 8 | 3 | 0 | 1 | (1 | 0) | 14 | 5 | 3 | 0 | 0 | 2 | 0 | 1 | 1 | 0 | 0 | .00 | 1 | .444 | .421 | .778 |
| 1990 Boston | AL | 32 | 83 | 20 | 4 | 0 | 0 | (0 | 0) | 24 | 8 | 6 | 5 | 0 | 10 | 0 | 2 | 1 | 0 | 1 | .00 | 0 | .241 | .281 | .289 |
| 4 ML YEARS | | 101 | 298 | 73 | 19 | 0 | 6 | (5 | 1) | 110 | 36 | 34 | 13 | 0 | 56 | 3 | 5 | 4 | 0 | 2 | .00 | 5 | .245 | .280 | .369 |

## Greg Mathews

**Pitches:** Left **Bats:** Both **Pos:** SP **Ht:** 6' 2" **Wt:** 180 **Born:** 05/17/62 **Age:** 29

| | | HOW MUCH HE PITCHED | | | | | | WHAT HE GAVE UP | | | | | | | | | | | | THE RESULTS | | | | | |
|---|---|---|---|---|---|---|---|---|---|---|---|---|---|---|---|---|---|---|---|---|---|---|---|---|---|
| Year Team | Lg | G | GS | CG | GF | IP | BFP | H | R | ER | HR | SH | SF | HB | TBB | IBB | SO | WP | Bk | W | L | Pct. | ShO | Sv | ERA |
| 1986 St. Louis | NL | 23 | 22 | 1 | 1 | 145.1 | 591 | 139 | 61 | 59 | 15 | 7 | 1 | 2 | 44 | 3 | 67 | 5 | 6 | 11 | 8 | .579 | 0 | 0 | 3.65 |
| 1987 St. Louis | NL | 32 | 32 | 2 | 0 | 197.2 | 822 | 184 | 87 | 82 | 17 | 9 | 2 | 0 | 71 | 5 | 108 | 7 | 2 | 11 | 11 | .500 | 1 | 0 | 3.73 |
| 1988 St. Louis | NL | 13 | 13 | 1 | 0 | 68 | 286 | 61 | 34 | 32 | 4 | 1 | 3 | 2 | 33 | 5 | 31 | 4 | 4 | 4 | 6 | .400 | 0 | 0 | 4.24 |
| 1990 St. Louis | NL | 11 | 10 | 0 | 0 | 50.2 | 229 | 53 | 34 | 30 | 2 | 4 | 2 | 2 | 30 | 1 | 18 | 2 | 1 | 0 | 5 | .000 | 0 | 0 | 5.33 |
| 4 ML YEARS | | 79 | 77 | 4 | 1 | 461.2 | 1928 | 437 | 216 | 203 | 38 | 21 | 8 | 6 | 178 | 14 | 224 | 18 | 13 | 26 | 30 | .464 | 1 | 0 | 3.96 |

## Don Mattingly

**Bats:** Left **Throws:** Left **Pos:** 1B **Ht:** 6' 0" **Wt:** 175 **Born:** 04/20/61 **Age:** 30

| | | BATTING | | | | | | | | | | | | | | | | | BASERUNNING | | | | PERCENTAGES | | |
|---|---|---|---|---|---|---|---|---|---|---|---|---|---|---|---|---|---|---|---|---|---|---|---|---|---|
| Year Team | Lg | G | AB | H | 2B | 3B | HR | (Hm | Rd) | TB | R | RBI | TBB | IBB | SO | HBP | SH | SF | SB | CS | SB% | GDP | Avg | OBP | SLG |
| 1982 New York | AL | 7 | 12 | 2 | 0 | 0 | 0 | (0 | 0) | 2 | 0 | 1 | 0 | 0 | 1 | 0 | 0 | 1 | 0 | 0 | .00 | 2 | .167 | .154 | .167 |
| 1983 New York | AL | 91 | 279 | 79 | 15 | 4 | 4 | (0 | 4) | 114 | 34 | 32 | 21 | 5 | 31 | 1 | 2 | 2 | 0 | 0 | .00 | 8 | .283 | .333 | .409 |
| 1984 New York | AL | 153 | 603 | 207 | 44 | 2 | 23 | (12 | 11) | 324 | 91 | 110 | 41 | 8 | 33 | 1 | 8 | 9 | 1 | 1 | .50 | 15 | .343 | .381 | .537 |
| 1985 New York | AL | 159 | 652 | 211 | 48 | 3 | 35 | (22 | 13) | 370 | 107 | 145 | 56 | 13 | 41 | 2 | 2 | 15 | 2 | 2 | .50 | 15 | .324 | .371 | .567 |
| 1986 New York | AL | 162 | 677 | 238 | 53 | 2 | 31 | (17 | 14) | 388 | 117 | 113 | 53 | 11 | 35 | 1 | 1 | 10 | 0 | 0 | .00 | 17 | .352 | .394 | .573 |
| 1987 New York | AL | 141 | 569 | 186 | 38 | 2 | 30 | (17 | 13) | 318 | 93 | 115 | 51 | 13 | 38 | 1 | 0 | 8 | 1 | 4 | .20 | 16 | .327 | .378 | .559 |
| 1988 New York | AL | 144 | 599 | 186 | 37 | 0 | 18 | (11 | 7) | 277 | 94 | 88 | 41 | 14 | 29 | 3 | 0 | 8 | 1 | 0 | 1.00 | 13 | .311 | .353 | .462 |
| 1989 New York | AL | 158 | 631 | 191 | 37 | 2 | 23 | (19 | 4) | 301 | 79 | 113 | 51 | 18 | 30 | 1 | 0 | 10 | 3 | 0 | 1.00 | 15 | .303 | .351 | .477 |
| 1990 New York | AL | 102 | 394 | 101 | 16 | 0 | 5 | (4 | 1) | 132 | 40 | 42 | 28 | 13 | 20 | 3 | 0 | 3 | 1 | 0 | 1.00 | 13 | .256 | .308 | .335 |
| 9 ML YEARS | | 1117 | 4416 | 1401 | 288 | 15 | 169 | (102 | 67) | 2226 | 655 | 759 | 342 | 95 | 258 | 13 | 13 | 66 | 9 | 7 | .56 | 114 | .317 | .363 | .504 |

## Derrick May

**Bats:** Left **Throws:** Right **Pos:** LF **Ht:** 6' 4" **Wt:** 210 **Born:** 07/14/68 **Age:** 22

| BATTING | | | | | | | | | | | | | | | | | | | BASERUNNING | | | | PERCENTAGES | | |
|---|---|---|---|---|---|---|---|---|---|---|---|---|---|---|---|---|---|---|---|---|---|---|---|---|---|
| Year Team | Lg | G | AB | H | 2B | 3B | HR | (Hm | Rd) | TB | R | RBI | TBB | IBB | SO | HBP | SH | SF | SB | CS | SB% | GDP | Avg | OBP | SLG |
| 1986 Wytheville | R | 54 | 178 | 57 | 6 | 1 | 0 | -- | -- | 65 | 25 | 23 | 16 | 1 | 15 | 2 | 0 | 1 | 17 | 4 | .81 | 3 | .320 | .381 | .365 |
| 1987 Peoria | A | 128 | 439 | 131 | 19 | 8 | 9 | -- | -- | 193 | 60 | 52 | 42 | 4 | 106 | 1 | 0 | 5 | 5 | 7 | .42 | 5 | .298 | .357 | .440 |
| 1988 Winston-Sal | A | 130 | 485 | 148 | 29 | 9 | 8 | -- | -- | 219 | 76 | 65 | 37 | 4 | 82 | 5 | 0 | 5 | 13 | 8 | .62 | 3 | .305 | .357 | .452 |
| 1989 Charlotte | AA | 136 | 491 | 145 | 26 | 5 | 9 | -- | -- | 208 | 72 | 70 | 33 | 4 | 76 | 5 | 1 | 0 | 19 | 7 | .73 | 8 | .295 | .346 | .424 |
| 1990 Iowa | AAA | 119 | 459 | 136 | 27 | 1 | 8 | -- | -- | 189 | 55 | 69 | 23 | 4 | 50 | 0 | 1 | 6 | 5 | 6 | .45 | 11 | .296 | .326 | .412 |
| 1990 Chicago | NL | 17 | 61 | 15 | 3 | 0 | 1 | (1 | 0) | 21 | 8 | 11 | 2 | 0 | 7 | 0 | 0 | 0 | 1 | 0 | 1.00 | 1 | .246 | .270 | .344 |

## Brent Mayne

**Bats:** Left **Throws:** Right **Pos:** C **Ht:** 6' 1" **Wt:** 195 **Born:** 04/19/68 **Age:** 23

| BATTING | | | | | | | | | | | | | | | | | | | BASERUNNING | | | | PERCENTAGES | | |
|---|---|---|---|---|---|---|---|---|---|---|---|---|---|---|---|---|---|---|---|---|---|---|---|---|---|
| Year Team | Lg | G | AB | H | 2B | 3B | HR | (Hm | Rd) | TB | R | RBI | TBB | IBB | SO | HBP | SH | SF | SB | CS | SB% | GDP | Avg | OBP | SLG |
| 1989 Baseball Cy | A | 7 | 24 | 13 | 3 | 1 | 0 | -- | -- | 18 | 5 | 8 | 0 | 0 | 3 | 0 | 0 | 0 | 0 | 1 | .00 | 0 | .542 | .542 | .750 |
| 1990 Memphis | AA | 115 | 412 | 110 | 16 | 3 | 2 | -- | -- | 138 | 48 | 61 | 52 | 1 | 51 | 2 | 7 | 8 | 5 | 2 | .71 | 13 | .267 | .346 | .335 |
| 1990 Kansas City | AL | 5 | 13 | 3 | 0 | 0 | 0 | (0 | 0) | 3 | 2 | 1 | 3 | 0 | 3 | 0 | 0 | 0 | 0 | 1 | .00 | 0 | .231 | .375 | .231 |

## Randy McCament

**Pitches:** Right **Bats:** Right **Pos:** RP **Ht:** 6' 3" **Wt:** 180 **Born:** 07/29/62 **Age:** 28

| HOW MUCH HE PITCHED | | | | | | | | WHAT HE GAVE UP | | | | | | | | | | | | THE RESULTS | | | | | |
|---|---|---|---|---|---|---|---|---|---|---|---|---|---|---|---|---|---|---|---|---|---|---|---|---|---|
| Year Team | Lg | G | GS | CG | GF | IP | BFP | H | R | ER | HR | SH | SF | HB | TBB | IBB | SO | WP | Bk | W | L | Pct. | ShO | Sv | ERA |
| 1985 Everett | A | 14 | 14 | 5 | 0 | 105.2 | 0 | 98 | 46 | 34 | 6 | 0 | 0 | 5 | 20 | 0 | 66 | 5 | 0 | 7 | 3 | .700 | 2 | 0 | 2.90 |
| 1986 Fresno | A | 54 | 0 | 0 | 48 | 86.2 | 366 | 87 | 36 | 24 | 4 | 3 | 1 | 5 | 24 | 1 | 61 | 9 | 0 | 4 | 4 | .500 | 0 | 19 | 2.49 |
| Shreveport | AA | 8 | 0 | 0 | 6 | 19.1 | 74 | 16 | 7 | 6 | 1 | 0 | 0 | 0 | 4 | 2 | 16 | 1 | 0 | 2 | 1 | .667 | 0 | 2 | 2.79 |
| 1987 Shreveport | AA | 52 | 0 | 0 | 44 | 79.1 | 321 | 78 | 28 | 21 | 5 | 2 | 3 | 5 | 18 | 4 | 39 | 5 | 0 | 4 | 3 | .571 | 0 | 14 | 2.38 |
| 1988 Phoenix | AAA | 19 | 0 | 0 | 14 | 25 | 129 | 40 | 26 | 21 | 2 | 0 | 2 | 2 | 16 | 2 | 7 | 1 | 0 | 0 | 1 | .000 | 0 | 1 | 7.56 |
| Shreveport | AA | 24 | 0 | 0 | 10 | 42 | 194 | 56 | 29 | 25 | 6 | 2 | 2 | 1 | 14 | 2 | 15 | 4 | 0 | 3 | 4 | .429 | 0 | 2 | 5.36 |
| 1989 Shreveport | AA | 13 | 0 | 0 | 8 | 25.1 | 105 | 22 | 6 | 6 | 1 | 4 | 0 | 2 | 5 | 1 | 13 | 2 | 0 | 4 | 2 | .667 | 0 | 1 | 2.13 |
| Phoenix | AAA | 22 | 0 | 0 | 6 | 37.1 | 155 | 40 | 15 | 15 | 4 | 0 | 1 | 2 | 12 | 1 | 13 | 1 | 0 | 3 | 0 | 1.000 | 0 | 1 | 3.62 |
| 1990 Phoenix | AAA | 46 | 0 | 0 | 21 | 78.1 | 356 | 99 | 40 | 33 | 4 | 5 | 2 | 2 | 32 | 5 | 32 | 3 | 1 | 3 | 3 | .500 | 0 | 6 | 3.79 |
| 1989 San Francisco | NL | 25 | 0 | 0 | 10 | 36.2 | 159 | 32 | 22 | 16 | 4 | 1 | 1 | 1 | 23 | 2 | 12 | 1 | 1 | 1 | 1 | .500 | 0 | 0 | 3.93 |
| 1990 San Francisco | NL | 3 | 0 | 0 | 0 | 6 | 30 | 8 | 2 | 2 | 0 | 0 | 1 | 0 | 5 | 0 | 5 | 0 | 0 | 0 | 0 | .000 | 0 | 0 | 3.00 |
| 2 ML YEARS | | 28 | 0 | 0 | 10 | 42.2 | 189 | 40 | 24 | 18 | 4 | 1 | 2 | 1 | 28 | 2 | 17 | 1 | 1 | 1 | 1 | .500 | 0 | 0 | 3.80 |

## Kirk McCaskill

**Pitches:** Right **Bats:** Right **Pos:** SP **Ht:** 6' 1" **Wt:** 195 **Born:** 04/09/61 **Age:** 30

| HOW MUCH HE PITCHED | | | | | | | | WHAT HE GAVE UP | | | | | | | | | | | | THE RESULTS | | | | | |
|---|---|---|---|---|---|---|---|---|---|---|---|---|---|---|---|---|---|---|---|---|---|---|---|---|---|
| Year Team | Lg | G | GS | CG | GF | IP | BFP | H | R | ER | HR | SH | SF | HB | TBB | IBB | SO | WP | Bk | W | L | Pct. | ShO | Sv | ERA |
| 1985 California | AL | 30 | 29 | 6 | 0 | 189.2 | 807 | 189 | 105 | 99 | 23 | 2 | 5 | 4 | 64 | 1 | 102 | 5 | 0 | 12 | 12 | .500 | 1 | 0 | 4.70 |
| 1986 California | AL | 34 | 33 | 10 | 1 | 246.1 | 1013 | 207 | 98 | 92 | 19 | 6 | 5 | 5 | 92 | 1 | 202 | 10 | 2 | 17 | 10 | .630 | 2 | 0 | 3.36 |
| 1987 California | AL | 14 | 13 | 1 | 0 | 74.2 | 334 | 84 | 52 | 47 | 14 | 3 | 1 | 2 | 34 | 0 | 56 | 1 | 0 | 4 | 6 | .400 | 1 | 0 | 5.67 |
| 1988 California | AL | 23 | 23 | 4 | 0 | 146.1 | 635 | 155 | 78 | 70 | 9 | 1 | 6 | 1 | 61 | 3 | 98 | 13 | 2 | 8 | 6 | .571 | 2 | 0 | 4.31 |
| 1989 California | AL | 32 | 32 | 6 | 0 | 212 | 864 | 202 | 73 | 69 | 16 | 3 | 4 | 3 | 59 | 1 | 107 | 7 | 2 | 15 | 10 | .600 | 4 | 0 | 2.93 |
| 1990 California | AL | 29 | 29 | 2 | 0 | 174.1 | 738 | 161 | 77 | 63 | 9 | 3 | 1 | 2 | 72 | 1 | 78 | 6 | 1 | 12 | 11 | .522 | 1 | 0 | 3.25 |
| 6 ML YEARS | | 162 | 159 | 29 | 1 | 1043.1 | 4391 | 998 | 483 | 440 | 90 | 18 | 22 | 17 | 382 | 7 | 643 | 42 | 7 | 68 | 55 | .553 | 11 | 0 | 3.80 |

## Paul McClellan

**Pitches:** Right **Bats:** Right **Pos:** RP **Ht:** 6' 2" **Wt:** 180 **Born:** 02/08/66 **Age:** 25

| HOW MUCH HE PITCHED | | | | | | | | WHAT HE GAVE UP | | | | | | | | | | | | THE RESULTS | | | | | |
|---|---|---|---|---|---|---|---|---|---|---|---|---|---|---|---|---|---|---|---|---|---|---|---|---|---|
| Year Team | Lg | G | GS | CG | GF | IP | BFP | H | R | ER | HR | SH | SF | HB | TBB | IBB | SO | WP | Bk | W | L | Pct. | ShO | Sv | ERA |
| 1986 Everett | A | 13 | 13 | 2 | 0 | 86.1 | 0 | 71 | 39 | 32 | 2 | 0 | 0 | 0 | 46 | 0 | 74 | 8 | 0 | 5 | 4 | .556 | 0 | 0 | 3.34 |
| 1987 Clinton | A | 28 | 27 | 5 | 0 | 177.1 | 756 | 141 | 86 | 64 | 18 | 10 | 1 | 6 | 100 | 2 | 209 | 10 | 2 | 12 | 10 | .545 | 2 | 0 | 3.25 |
| 1988 Shreveport | AA | 27 | 27 | 4 | 0 | 167 | 701 | 146 | 89 | 75 | 11 | 7 | 5 | 4 | 62 | 4 | 128 | 3 | 22 | 10 | 12 | .455 | 1 | 0 | 4.04 |
| 1989 Shreveport | AA | 12 | 12 | 2 | 0 | 84.1 | 339 | 56 | 26 | 21 | 4 | 3 | 3 | 1 | 35 | 0 | 56 | 5 | 3 | 8 | 3 | .727 | 0 | 0 | 2.24 |
| Phoenix | AAA | 9 | 9 | 0 | 0 | 56.2 | 248 | 56 | 34 | 31 | 6 | 0 | 4 | 4 | 29 | 1 | 25 | 4 | 2 | 3 | 4 | .429 | 0 | 0 | 4.92 |
| 1990 Phoenix | AAA | 28 | 27 | 1 | 0 | 172.1 | 770 | 192 | 112 | 99 | 17 | 9 | 10 | 5 | 78 | 3 | 102 | 7 | 6 | 7 | 16 | .304 | 0 | 0 | 5.17 |
| 1990 San Francisco | NL | 4 | 1 | 0 | 2 | 7.2 | 44 | 14 | 10 | 10 | 3 | 1 | 0 | 1 | 6 | 0 | 2 | 0 | 0 | 0 | 1 | .000 | 0 | 0 | 11.74 |

## Lloyd McClendon

**Bats:** Right **Throws:** Right **Pos:** LF **Ht:** 5'11" **Wt:** 195 **Born:** 01/11/59 **Age:** 32

| BATTING | | | | | | | | | | | | | | | | | | | BASERUNNING | | | | PERCENTAGES | | |
|---|---|---|---|---|---|---|---|---|---|---|---|---|---|---|---|---|---|---|---|---|---|---|---|---|---|
| Year Team | Lg | G | AB | H | 2B | 3B | HR | (Hm | Rd) | TB | R | RBI | TBB | IBB | SO | HBP | SH | SF | SB | CS | SB% | GDP | Avg | OBP | SLG |
| 1987 Cincinnati | NL | 45 | 72 | 15 | 5 | 0 | 2 | (0 | 2) | 26 | 8 | 13 | 4 | 0 | 15 | 0 | 0 | 1 | 1 | 0 | 1.00 | 1 | .208 | .247 | .361 |
| 1988 Cincinnati | NL | 72 | 137 | 30 | 4 | 0 | 3 | (0 | 3) | 43 | 9 | 14 | 15 | 1 | 22 | 2 | 1 | 2 | 4 | 0 | 1.00 | 6 | .219 | .301 | .314 |

| | | | | | | | | | | | | | | | | | | | | | | | | | | | |
|---|---|---|---|---|---|---|---|---|---|---|---|---|---|---|---|---|---|---|---|---|---|---|---|---|---|---|---|
| 1989 | Chicago | NL | 92 | 259 | 74 | 12 | 1 | 12 | (9 | 3) | 124 | 47 | 40 | 37 | 3 | 31 | 1 | 1 | 7 | 6 | 4 | .60 | 3 | .286 | .368 | .479 |
| 1990 | 2 ML Teams | | 53 | 110 | 18 | 3 | 0 | 2 | (0 | 2) | 27 | 6 | 12 | 14 | 2 | 22 | 0 | 0 | 1 | 1 | 0 | 1.00 | 2 | .164 | .256 | .245 |
| 1990 | Chicago | NL | 49 | 107 | 17 | 3 | 0 | 1 | (0 | 1) | 23 | 5 | 10 | 14 | 2 | 21 | 0 | 0 | 1 | 1 | 0 | 1.00 | 2 | .159 | .254 | .215 |
| | Pittsburgh | NL | 4 | 3 | 1 | 0 | 0 | 1 | (0 | 1) | 4 | 1 | 2 | 0 | 0 | 1 | 0 | 0 | 0 | 0 | 0 | .00 | 0 | .333 | .333 | 1.333 |
| | 4 ML YEARS | | 262 | 578 | 137 | 24 | 1 | 19 | (9 | 10) | 220 | 70 | 79 | 70 | 6 | 90 | 3 | 2 | 11 | 12 | 4 | .75 | 12 | .237 | .317 | .381 |

## Bob McClure

**Pitches:** Left **Bats:** Right **Pos:** RP **Ht:** 5'11" **Wt:** 170 **Born:** 04/29/53 **Age:** 38

| | | | HOW MUCH HE PITCHED | | | | | | WHAT HE GAVE UP | | | | | | | | | | | | THE RESULTS | | | | | |
|---|---|---|---|---|---|---|---|---|---|---|---|---|---|---|---|---|---|---|---|---|---|---|---|---|---|---|
| Year | Team | Lg | G | GS | CG | GF | IP | BFP | H | R | ER | HR | SH | SF | HB | TBB | IBB | SO | WP | Bk | W | L | Pct. | ShO | Sv | ERA |
| 1975 | Kansas City | AL | 12 | 0 | 0 | 4 | 15 | 66 | 4 | 0 | 0 | 0 | 0 | 0 | 0 | 14 | 2 | 15 | 0 | 2 | 1 | 0 | 1.000 | 0 | 1 | 0.00 |
| 1976 | Kansas City | AL | 8 | 0 | 0 | 0 | 4 | 22 | 3 | 4 | 4 | 0 | 0 | 0 | 0 | 8 | 0 | 3 | 0 | 0 | 0 | 0 | .000 | 0 | 0 | 9.00 |
| 1977 | Milwaukee | AL | 68 | 0 | 0 | 31 | 71 | 302 | 64 | 25 | 20 | 2 | 5 | 5 | 1 | 34 | 5 | 57 | 1 | 2 | 2 | 1 | .667 | 0 | 6 | 2.54 |
| 1978 | Milwaukee | AL | 44 | 0 | 0 | 29 | 65 | 283 | 53 | 30 | 27 | 8 | 7 | 2 | 6 | 30 | 4 | 47 | 1 | 1 | 2 | 6 | .250 | 0 | 9 | 3.74 |
| 1979 | Milwaukee | AL | 36 | 0 | 0 | 16 | 51 | 229 | 53 | 29 | 22 | 6 | 2 | 3 | 3 | 24 | 0 | 37 | 5 | 0 | 5 | 2 | .714 | 0 | 5 | 3.88 |
| 1980 | Milwaukee | AL | 52 | 5 | 2 | 23 | 91 | 390 | 83 | 34 | 31 | 6 | 1 | 5 | 2 | 37 | 2 | 47 | 0 | 2 | 5 | 8 | .385 | 1 | 10 | 3.07 |
| 1981 | Milwaukee | AL | 4 | 0 | 0 | 1 | 8 | 34 | 7 | 3 | 3 | 1 | 0 | 0 | 0 | 4 | 1 | 6 | 0 | 0 | 0 | 0 | .000 | 0 | 0 | 3.38 |
| 1982 | Milwaukee | AL | 34 | 26 | 5 | 5 | 172.2 | 734 | 160 | 90 | 81 | 21 | 6 | 4 | 4 | 74 | 4 | 99 | 5 | 5 | 12 | 7 | .632 | 0 | 0 | 4.22 |
| 1983 | Milwaukee | AL | 24 | 23 | 4 | 0 | 142 | 625 | 152 | 75 | 71 | 11 | 0 | 4 | 5 | 68 | 1 | 68 | 4 | 6 | 9 | 9 | .500 | 0 | 0 | 4.50 |
| 1984 | Milwaukee | AL | 39 | 18 | 1 | 5 | 139.2 | 616 | 154 | 76 | 68 | 9 | 8 | 8 | 2 | 52 | 4 | 68 | 1 | 3 | 4 | 8 | .333 | 0 | 1 | 4.38 |
| 1985 | Milwaukee | AL | 38 | 1 | 0 | 12 | 85.2 | 370 | 91 | 43 | 41 | 10 | 3 | 2 | 3 | 30 | 2 | 57 | 5 | 0 | 4 | 1 | .800 | 0 | 3 | 4.31 |
| 1986 | 2 ML Teams | | 65 | 0 | 0 | 22 | 79 | 332 | 71 | 29 | 28 | 4 | 4 | 3 | 1 | 33 | 3 | 53 | 1 | 1 | 4 | 6 | .400 | 0 | 6 | 3.19 |
| 1987 | Montreal | NL | 52 | 0 | 0 | 16 | 52.1 | 222 | 47 | 30 | 20 | 8 | 5 | 2 | 0 | 20 | 3 | 33 | 0 | 1 | 6 | 1 | .857 | 0 | 5 | 3.44 |
| 1988 | 2 ML Teams | | 33 | 0 | 0 | 13 | 30 | 133 | 35 | 18 | 18 | 4 | 3 | 2 | 2 | 8 | 0 | 19 | 1 | 3 | 2 | 3 | .400 | 0 | 3 | 5.40 |
| 1989 | California | AL | 48 | 0 | 0 | 27 | 52.1 | 205 | 39 | 14 | 9 | 2 | 1 | 4 | 1 | 15 | 1 | 36 | 2 | 2 | 6 | 1 | .857 | 0 | 3 | 1.55 |
| 1990 | California | AL | 11 | 0 | 0 | 1 | 7 | 30 | 7 | 6 | 5 | 0 | 1 | 0 | 0 | 3 | 0 | 6 | 0 | 1 | 2 | 0 | 1.000 | 0 | 0 | 6.43 |
| 1986 | Milwaukee | AL | 13 | 0 | 0 | 7 | 16.1 | 75 | 18 | 7 | 7 | 2 | 1 | 1 | 0 | 10 | 1 | 11 | 0 | 0 | 2 | 1 | .667 | 0 | 0 | 3.86 |
| | Montreal | NL | 52 | 0 | 0 | 15 | 62.2 | 257 | 53 | 22 | 21 | 2 | 3 | 2 | 1 | 23 | 2 | 42 | 1 | 1 | 2 | 5 | .286 | 0 | 6 | 3.02 |
| 1988 | Montreal | NL | 19 | 0 | 0 | 8 | 19 | 87 | 23 | 13 | 13 | 3 | 3 | 2 | 1 | 6 | 0 | 12 | 0 | 3 | 1 | 3 | .250 | 0 | 2 | 6.16 |
| | New York | NL | 14 | 0 | 0 | 5 | 11 | 46 | 12 | 5 | 5 | 1 | 0 | 0 | 1 | 2 | 0 | 7 | 1 | 0 | 1 | 0 | 1.000 | 0 | 1 | 4.09 |
| | 16 ML YEARS | | 568 | 73 | 12 | 205 | 1065.2 | 4593 | 1023 | 506 | 448 | 92 | 46 | 44 | 30 | 454 | 32 | 651 | 26 | 29 | 64 | 53 | .547 | 1 | 52 | 3.78 |

## Rodney McCray

**Bats:** Right **Throws:** Right **Pos:** CF **Ht:** 5'10" **Wt:** 175 **Born:** 09/13/63 **Age:** 27

| | | | BATTING | | | | | | | | | | | | | | | | | BASERUNNING | | | | PERCENTAGES | | |
|---|---|---|---|---|---|---|---|---|---|---|---|---|---|---|---|---|---|---|---|---|---|---|---|---|---|---|
| Year | Team | Lg | G | AB | H | 2B | 3B | HR | (Hm | Rd) | TB | R | RBI | TBB | IBB | SO | HBP | SH | SF | SB | CS | SB% | GDP | Avg | OBP | SLG |
| 1984 | Spokane | A | 71 | 244 | 50 | 6 | 1 | 1 | -- | -- | 61 | 40 | 20 | 65 | 0 | 50 | 2 | 0 | 4 | 25 | 5 | .83 | 8 | .205 | .371 | .250 |
| 1985 | Charleston | A | 117 | 373 | 77 | 8 | 1 | 1 | -- | -- | 90 | 81 | 27 | 80 | 2 | 88 | 6 | 5 | 1 | 49 | 7 | .88 | 6 | .206 | .354 | .241 |
| 1986 | Charleston | A | 123 | 417 | 107 | 13 | 3 | 4 | -- | -- | 138 | 88 | 33 | 108 | 2 | 80 | 5 | 6 | 2 | 81 | 32 | .72 | 3 | .257 | .414 | .331 |
| 1987 | Reno | A | 117 | 413 | 87 | 11 | 5 | 0 | -- | -- | 108 | 69 | 26 | 69 | 3 | 96 | 10 | 9 | 3 | 65 | 16 | .80 | 4 | .211 | .335 | .262 |
| 1988 | South Bend | A | 107 | 306 | 65 | 10 | 2 | 1 | -- | -- | 82 | 48 | 24 | 56 | 0 | 72 | 10 | 7 | 2 | 55 | 12 | .82 | 5 | .212 | .350 | .268 |
| 1989 | Sarasota | A | 124 | 422 | 112 | 19 | 4 | 1 | -- | -- | 142 | 81 | 34 | 96 | 3 | 81 | 9 | 4 | 2 | 44 | 22 | .67 | 6 | .265 | .410 | .336 |
| 1990 | Birmingham | AA | 60 | 188 | 37 | 2 | 2 | 1 | -- | -- | 46 | 36 | 16 | 36 | 0 | 42 | 5 | 6 | 2 | 25 | 10 | .71 | 2 | .197 | .338 | .245 |
| | Vancouver | AAA | 19 | 53 | 12 | 4 | 2 | 0 | -- | -- | 20 | 7 | 6 | 10 | 0 | 20 | 2 | 1 | 0 | 4 | 3 | .57 | 0 | .226 | .369 | .377 |
| 1990 | Chicago | AL | 32 | 6 | 0 | 0 | 0 | 0 | (0 | 0) | 0 | 8 | 0 | 1 | 0 | 4 | 0 | 0 | 0 | 6 | 0 | 1.00 | 0 | .000 | .143 | .000 |

## Lance McCullers

**Pitches:** Right **Bats:** Both **Pos:** RP **Ht:** 6' 1" **Wt:** 218 **Born:** 03/08/64 **Age:** 27

| | | | HOW MUCH HE PITCHED | | | | | | WHAT HE GAVE UP | | | | | | | | | | | | THE RESULTS | | | | | |
|---|---|---|---|---|---|---|---|---|---|---|---|---|---|---|---|---|---|---|---|---|---|---|---|---|---|---|
| Year | Team | Lg | G | GS | CG | GF | IP | BFP | H | R | ER | HR | SH | SF | HB | TBB | IBB | SO | WP | Bk | W | L | Pct. | ShO | Sv | ERA |
| 1985 | San Diego | NL | 21 | 0 | 0 | 11 | 35 | 142 | 23 | 15 | 9 | 3 | 7 | 0 | 1 | 16 | 3 | 27 | 0 | 1 | 0 | 2 | .000 | 0 | 5 | 2.31 |
| 1986 | San Diego | NL | 70 | 7 | 0 | 29 | 136 | 550 | 103 | 46 | 42 | 12 | 8 | 3 | 4 | 58 | 9 | 92 | 5 | 3 | 10 | 10 | .500 | 0 | 5 | 2.78 |
| 1987 | San Diego | NL | 78 | 0 | 0 | 41 | 123.1 | 540 | 115 | 60 | 51 | 11 | 6 | 2 | 2 | 59 | 11 | 126 | 5 | 1 | 8 | 10 | .444 | 0 | 16 | 3.72 |
| 1988 | San Diego | NL | 60 | 0 | 0 | 39 | 97.2 | 407 | 70 | 29 | 27 | 8 | 7 | 3 | 0 | 55 | 12 | 81 | 4 | 2 | 3 | 6 | .333 | 0 | 10 | 2.49 |
| 1989 | New York | AL | 52 | 1 | 0 | 20 | 84.2 | 373 | 83 | 46 | 43 | 9 | 3 | 5 | 3 | 37 | 4 | 82 | 2 | 0 | 4 | 3 | .571 | 0 | 3 | 4.57 |
| 1990 | 2 ML Teams | | 20 | 1 | 0 | 14 | 44.2 | 186 | 32 | 19 | 15 | 4 | 0 | 3 | 0 | 19 | 3 | 31 | 5 | 0 | 2 | 0 | 1.000 | 0 | 0 | 3.02 |
| 1990 | New York | AL | 11 | 0 | 0 | 7 | 15 | 65 | 14 | 8 | 6 | 2 | 0 | 1 | 0 | 6 | 2 | 11 | 3 | 0 | 1 | 0 | 1.000 | 0 | 0 | 3.60 |
| | Detroit | AL | 9 | 1 | 0 | 7 | 29.2 | 121 | 18 | 11 | 9 | 2 | 0 | 2 | 0 | 13 | 1 | 20 | 2 | 0 | 1 | 0 | 1.000 | 0 | 0 | 2.73 |
| | 6 ML YEARS | | 301 | 9 | 0 | 154 | 521.1 | 2198 | 426 | 215 | 187 | 47 | 31 | 16 | 10 | 244 | 42 | 439 | 21 | 7 | 27 | 31 | .466 | 0 | 39 | 3.23 |

## Ben McDonald

**Pitches:** Right **Bats:** Right **Pos:** SP/RP **Ht:** 6' 7" **Wt:** 212 **Born:** 11/24/67 **Age:** 23

| | | | HOW MUCH HE PITCHED | | | | | | WHAT HE GAVE UP | | | | | | | | | | | | THE RESULTS | | | | | |
|---|---|---|---|---|---|---|---|---|---|---|---|---|---|---|---|---|---|---|---|---|---|---|---|---|---|---|
| Year | Team | Lg | G | GS | CG | GF | IP | BFP | H | R | ER | HR | SH | SF | HB | TBB | IBB | SO | WP | Bk | W | L | Pct. | ShO | Sv | ERA |
| 1989 | Frederick | A | 2 | 2 | 0 | 0 | 9 | 35 | 10 | 2 | 2 | 0 | 0 | 0 | 0 | 0 | 0 | 9 | 1 | 2 | 0 | 0 | .000 | 0 | 0 | 2.00 |
| 1990 | Hagerstown | AA | 3 | 3 | 0 | 0 | 11 | 48 | 11 | 8 | 8 | 1 | 0 | 0 | 1 | 3 | 0 | 15 | 0 | 1 | 0 | 1 | .000 | 0 | 0 | 6.55 |
| | Rochester | AAA | 7 | 7 | 0 | 0 | 44 | 183 | 33 | 18 | 14 | 4 | 2 | 0 | 2 | 21 | 1 | 37 | 4 | 0 | 3 | 3 | .500 | 0 | 0 | 2.86 |

| Year Team | Lg | G | GS | CG | GF | IP | BFP | H | R | ER | HR | SH | SF | HB | TBB | IBB | SO | WP | Bk | W | L | Pct. | ShO | Sv | ERA |
|---|---|---|---|---|---|---|---|---|---|---|---|---|---|---|---|---|---|---|---|---|---|---|---|---|---|
| 1989 Baltimore | AL | 6 | 0 | 0 | 2 | 7.1 | 33 | 8 | 7 | 7 | 2 | 0 | 1 | 0 | 4 | 0 | 3 | 1 | 1 | 1 | 0 | 1.000 | 0 | 0 | 8.59 |
| 1990 Baltimore | AL | 21 | 15 | 3 | 2 | 118.2 | 472 | 88 | 36 | 32 | 9 | 3 | 5 | 0 | 35 | 0 | 65 | 5 | 0 | 8 | 5 | .615 | 2 | 0 | 2.43 |
| 2 ML YEARS | | 27 | 15 | 3 | 4 | 126 | 505 | 96 | 43 | 39 | 11 | 3 | 6 | 0 | 39 | 0 | 68 | 6 | 1 | 9 | 5 | .643 | 2 | 0 | 2.79 |

## Jack McDowell

**Pitches:** Right **Bats:** Right **Pos:** SP **Ht:** 6' 5" **Wt:** 179 **Born:** 01/16/66 **Age:** 25

| | | HOW MUCH HE PITCHED | | | | | | WHAT HE GAVE UP | | | | | | | | | | | | THE RESULTS | | | | | |
|---|---|---|---|---|---|---|---|---|---|---|---|---|---|---|---|---|---|---|---|---|---|---|---|---|---|
| Year Team | Lg | G | GS | CG | GF | IP | BFP | H | R | ER | HR | SH | SF | HB | TBB | IBB | SO | WP | Bk | W | L | Pct. | ShO | Sv | ERA |
| 1987 Chicago | AL | 4 | 4 | 0 | 0 | 28 | 103 | 16 | 6 | 6 | 1 | 0 | 0 | 2 | 6 | 0 | 15 | 0 | 0 | 3 | 0 | 1.000 | 0 | 0 | 1.93 |
| 1988 Chicago | AL | 26 | 26 | 1 | 0 | 158.2 | 687 | 147 | 85 | 70 | 12 | 6 | 7 | 7 | 68 | 5 | 84 | 11 | 1 | 5 | 10 | .333 | 0 | 0 | 3.97 |
| 1990 Chicago | AL | 33 | 33 | 4 | 0 | 205 | 866 | 189 | 93 | 87 | 20 | 1 | 5 | 7 | 77 | 0 | 165 | 7 | 1 | 14 | 9 | .609 | 0 | 0 | 3.82 |
| 3 ML YEARS | | 63 | 63 | 5 | 0 | 391.2 | 1656 | 352 | 184 | 163 | 33 | 7 | 12 | 16 | 151 | 5 | 264 | 18 | 2 | 22 | 19 | .537 | 0 | 0 | 3.75 |

## Oddibe McDowell

**Bats:** Left **Throws:** Left **Pos:** CF/LF **Ht:** 5' 9" **Wt:** 160 **Born:** 08/25/62 **Age:** 28

| | | BATTING | | | | | | | | | | | | | | | | | | BASERUNNING | | | | PERCENTAGES | | |
|---|---|---|---|---|---|---|---|---|---|---|---|---|---|---|---|---|---|---|---|---|---|---|---|---|---|---|
| Year Team | Lg | G | AB | H | 2B | 3B | HR | (Hm | Rd) | TB | R | RBI | TBB | IBB | SO | HBP | SH | SF | SB | CS | SB% | GDP | Avg | OBP | SLG |
| 1985 Texas | AL | 111 | 406 | 97 | 14 | 5 | 18 | (10 | 8) | 175 | 63 | 42 | 36 | 2 | 85 | 3 | 5 | 2 | 25 | 7 | .78 | 6 | .239 | .304 | .431 |
| 1986 Texas | AL | 154 | 572 | 152 | 24 | 7 | 18 | (8 | 10) | 244 | 105 | 49 | 65 | 5 | 112 | 1 | 3 | 2 | 33 | 15 | .69 | 12 | .266 | .341 | .427 |
| 1987 Texas | AL | 128 | 407 | 98 | 26 | 4 | 14 | (5 | 9) | 174 | 65 | 52 | 51 | 0 | 99 | 0 | 3 | 2 | 24 | 2 | .92 | 8 | .241 | .324 | .428 |
| 1988 Texas | AL | 120 | 437 | 108 | 19 | 5 | 6 | (4 | 2) | 155 | 55 | 37 | 41 | 2 | 89 | 2 | 2 | 5 | 33 | 10 | .77 | 3 | .247 | .311 | .355 |
| 1989 2 ML Teams | | 145 | 519 | 138 | 23 | 6 | 10 | (3 | 7) | 203 | 89 | 46 | 52 | 3 | 73 | 1 | 4 | 2 | 27 | 15 | .64 | 3 | .266 | .333 | .391 |
| 1990 Atlanta | NL | 113 | 305 | 74 | 14 | 0 | 7 | (4 | 3) | 109 | 47 | 25 | 21 | 0 | 53 | 2 | 0 | 1 | 13 | 2 | .87 | 3 | .243 | .295 | .357 |
| 1989 Cleveland | AL | 69 | 239 | 53 | 5 | 2 | 3 | (1 | 2) | 71 | 33 | 22 | 25 | 0 | 36 | 1 | 3 | 2 | 12 | 5 | .71 | 3 | .222 | .296 | .297 |
| Atlanta | NL | 76 | 280 | 85 | 18 | 4 | 7 | (2 | 5) | 132 | 56 | 24 | 27 | 3 | 37 | 0 | 1 | 0 | 15 | 10 | .60 | 0 | .304 | .365 | .471 |
| 6 ML YEARS | | 771 | 2646 | 667 | 120 | 27 | 73 | (34 | 39) | 1060 | 424 | 251 | 266 | 12 | 511 | 9 | 17 | 14 | 155 | 51 | .75 | 35 | .252 | .321 | .401 |

## Roger McDowell

**Pitches:** Right **Bats:** Right **Pos:** RP **Ht:** 6' 1" **Wt:** 185 **Born:** 12/21/60 **Age:** 30

| | | HOW MUCH HE PITCHED | | | | | | WHAT HE GAVE UP | | | | | | | | | | | | THE RESULTS | | | | | |
|---|---|---|---|---|---|---|---|---|---|---|---|---|---|---|---|---|---|---|---|---|---|---|---|---|---|
| Year Team | Lg | G | GS | CG | GF | IP | BFP | H | R | ER | HR | SH | SF | HB | TBB | IBB | SO | WP | Bk | W | L | Pct. | ShO | Sv | ERA |
| 1985 New York | NL | 62 | 2 | 0 | 36 | 127.1 | 516 | 108 | 43 | 40 | 9 | 6 | 2 | 1 | 37 | 8 | 70 | 6 | 2 | 6 | 5 | .545 | 0 | 17 | 2.83 |
| 1986 New York | NL | 75 | 0 | 0 | 52 | 128 | 524 | 107 | 48 | 43 | 4 | 7 | 3 | 3 | 42 | 5 | 65 | 3 | 3 | 14 | 9 | .609 | 0 | 22 | 3.02 |
| 1987 New York | NL | 56 | 0 | 0 | 45 | 88.2 | 384 | 95 | 41 | 41 | 7 | 5 | 5 | 2 | 28 | 4 | 32 | 3 | 1 | 7 | 5 | .583 | 0 | 25 | 4.16 |
| 1988 New York | NL | 62 | 0 | 0 | 41 | 89 | 378 | 80 | 31 | 26 | 1 | 3 | 5 | 3 | 31 | 7 | 46 | 6 | 1 | 5 | 5 | .500 | 0 | 16 | 2.63 |
| 1989 2 ML Teams | | 69 | 0 | 0 | 56 | 92 | 387 | 79 | 36 | 20 | 3 | 6 | 1 | 3 | 38 | 8 | 47 | 3 | 1 | 4 | 8 | .333 | 0 | 23 | 1.96 |
| 1990 Philadelphia | NL | 72 | 0 | 0 | 60 | 86.1 | 373 | 92 | 41 | 37 | 2 | 10 | 4 | 2 | 35 | 9 | 39 | 1 | 1 | 6 | 8 | .429 | 0 | 22 | 3.86 |
| 1989 New York | NL | 25 | 0 | 0 | 15 | 35.1 | 156 | 34 | 21 | 13 | 1 | 3 | 1 | 2 | 16 | 3 | 15 | 3 | 1 | 1 | 5 | .167 | 0 | 4 | 3.31 |
| Philadelphia | NL | 44 | 0 | 0 | 41 | 56.2 | 231 | 45 | 15 | 7 | 2 | 3 | 0 | 1 | 22 | 5 | 32 | 0 | 0 | 3 | 3 | .500 | 0 | 19 | 1.11 |
| 6 ML YEARS | | 396 | 2 | 0 | 290 | 611.1 | 2562 | 561 | 240 | 207 | 26 | 37 | 20 | 14 | 211 | 41 | 299 | 22 | 9 | 42 | 40 | .512 | 0 | 125 | 3.05 |

## Charlie McElroy

**Pitches:** Left **Bats:** Left **Pos:** RP **Ht:** 6' 0" **Wt:** 160 **Born:** 10/01/67 **Age:** 23

| | | HOW MUCH HE PITCHED | | | | | | WHAT HE GAVE UP | | | | | | | | | | | | THE RESULTS | | | | | |
|---|---|---|---|---|---|---|---|---|---|---|---|---|---|---|---|---|---|---|---|---|---|---|---|---|---|
| Year Team | Lg | G | GS | CG | GF | IP | BFP | H | R | ER | HR | SH | SF | HB | TBB | IBB | SO | WP | Bk | W | L | Pct. | ShO | Sv | ERA |
| 1986 Utica | A | 14 | 14 | 5 | 0 | 94.2 | 386 | 85 | 40 | 31 | 4 | 8 | 2 | 2 | 28 | 0 | 91 | 2 | 0 | 4 | 6 | .400 | 1 | 0 | 2.95 |
| 1987 Spartanburg | A | 24 | 21 | 5 | 0 | 130.1 | 535 | 117 | 51 | 45 | 6 | 4 | 1 | 0 | 48 | 2 | 115 | 7 | 1 | 14 | 4 | .778 | 2 | 0 | 3.11 |
| Clearwater | A | 2 | 2 | 0 | 0 | 7.1 | 27 | 1 | 1 | 0 | 0 | 0 | 1 | 0 | 4 | 0 | 7 | 0 | 0 | 1 | 0 | 1.000 | 0 | 0 | 0.00 |
| 1988 Reading | AA | 28 | 26 | 4 | 0 | 160 | 698 | 173 | 89 | 80 | 9 | 2 | 6 | 2 | 70 | 2 | 92 | 4 | 1 | 9 | 12 | .429 | 2 | 0 | 4.50 |
| 1989 Reading | AA | 32 | 0 | 0 | 24 | 47 | 188 | 39 | 14 | 14 | 0 | 3 | 2 | 3 | 14 | 2 | 39 | 3 | 0 | 3 | 1 | .750 | 0 | 12 | 2.68 |
| Scr Wil-Bar | AAA | 14 | 0 | 0 | 9 | 15.1 | 68 | 13 | 6 | 5 | 1 | 1 | 1 | 1 | 11 | 1 | 12 | 0 | 0 | 1 | 2 | .333 | 0 | 3 | 2.93 |
| 1990 Scr Wil-Bar | AAA | 57 | 1 | 0 | 26 | 76 | 324 | 62 | 24 | 23 | 6 | 7 | 2 | 5 | 34 | 4 | 78 | 2 | 0 | 6 | 8 | .429 | 0 | 7 | 2.72 |
| 1989 Philadelphia | NL | 11 | 0 | 0 | 4 | 10.1 | 46 | 12 | 2 | 2 | 1 | 0 | 0 | 0 | 4 | 1 | 8 | 0 | 0 | 0 | 0 | .000 | 0 | 0 | 1.74 |
| 1990 Philadelphia | NL | 16 | 0 | 0 | 8 | 14 | 76 | 24 | 13 | 12 | 0 | 0 | 1 | 0 | 10 | 2 | 16 | 0 | 0 | 0 | 1 | .000 | 0 | 0 | 7.71 |
| 2 ML YEARS | | 27 | 0 | 0 | 12 | 24.1 | 122 | 36 | 15 | 14 | 1 | 0 | 1 | 0 | 14 | 3 | 24 | 0 | 0 | 0 | 1 | .000 | 0 | 0 | 5.18 |

## Andy McGaffigan

**Pitches:** Right **Bats:** Right **Pos:** RP/SP **Ht:** 6' 3" **Wt:** 190 **Born:** 10/25/56 **Age:** 34

| | | HOW MUCH HE PITCHED | | | | | | WHAT HE GAVE UP | | | | | | | | | | | | THE RESULTS | | | | | |
|---|---|---|---|---|---|---|---|---|---|---|---|---|---|---|---|---|---|---|---|---|---|---|---|---|---|
| Year Team | Lg | G | GS | CG | GF | IP | BFP | H | R | ER | HR | SH | SF | HB | TBB | IBB | SO | WP | Bk | W | L | Pct. | ShO | Sv | ERA |
| 1981 New York | AL | 2 | 0 | 0 | 0 | 7 | 31 | 5 | 3 | 2 | 1 | 1 | 2 | 0 | 3 | 0 | 2 | 0 | 1 | 0 | 0 | .000 | 0 | 0 | 2.57 |
| 1982 San Francisco | NL | 4 | 0 | 0 | 2 | 8 | 30 | 5 | 1 | 0 | 0 | 0 | 0 | 1 | 1 | 0 | 4 | 0 | 0 | 1 | 0 | 1.000 | 0 | 0 | 0.00 |
| 1983 San Francisco | NL | 43 | 16 | 0 | 11 | 134.1 | 560 | 131 | 67 | 64 | 17 | 5 | 2 | 1 | 39 | 5 | 93 | 8 | 7 | 3 | 9 | .250 | 0 | 2 | 4.29 |
| 1984 2 ML Teams | | 30 | 6 | 0 | 10 | 69 | 282 | 60 | 28 | 27 | 4 | 2 | 1 | 0 | 23 | 2 | 57 | 1 | 2 | 3 | 6 | .333 | 0 | 1 | 3.52 |
| 1985 Cincinnati | NL | 15 | 15 | 2 | 0 | 94.1 | 392 | 88 | 40 | 39 | 4 | 4 | 0 | 2 | 30 | 4 | 83 | 2 | 0 | 3 | 3 | .500 | 0 | 0 | 3.72 |
| 1986 Montreal | NL | 48 | 14 | 1 | 8 | 142.2 | 583 | 114 | 49 | 42 | 9 | 10 | 5 | 2 | 55 | 8 | 104 | 5 | 4 | 10 | 5 | .667 | 1 | 2 | 2.65 |

| | | | | | | | | | | | | | | | | | | | | | | | | | |
|---|---|---|---|---|---|---|---|---|---|---|---|---|---|---|---|---|---|---|---|---|---|---|---|---|---|
| 1987 Montreal | NL | 69 | 0 | 0 | 30 | 120.1 | 500 | 105 | 38 | 32 | 5 | 5 | 3 | 3 | 42 | 7 | 100 | 6 | 0 | 5 | 2 | .714 | 0 | 12 | 2.39 |
| 1988 Montreal | NL | 63 | 0 | 0 | 24 | 91.1 | 392 | 81 | 31 | 28 | 4 | 4 | 2 | 2 | 37 | 7 | 71 | 2 | 2 | 6 | 0 | 1.000 | 0 | 4 | 2.76 |
| 1989 Montreal | NL | 57 | 0 | 0 | 23 | 75 | 333 | 85 | 40 | 39 | 3 | 6 | 4 | 3 | 30 | 4 | 40 | 3 | 0 | 3 | 5 | .375 | 0 | 2 | 4.68 |
| 1990 2 ML Teams | | 28 | 11 | 0 | 3 | 83.1 | 363 | 85 | 49 | 36 | 8 | 2 | 2 | 2 | 32 | 1 | 53 | 3 | 0 | 4 | 3 | .571 | 0 | 1 | 3.89 |
| 1984 Montreal | NL | 21 | 3 | 0 | 8 | 46 | 184 | 37 | 14 | 13 | 2 | 0 | 1 | 0 | 15 | 2 | 39 | 1 | 2 | 3 | 4 | .429 | 0 | 1 | 2.54 |
| Cincinnati | NL | 9 | 3 | 0 | 2 | 23 | 98 | 23 | 14 | 14 | 2 | 2 | 0 | 0 | 8 | 0 | 18 | 0 | 0 | 0 | 2 | .000 | 0 | 0 | 5.48 |
| 1990 San Francisco | NL | 4 | 0 | 0 | 1 | 4.2 | 27 | 10 | 9 | 9 | 2 | 1 | 0 | 0 | 4 | 0 | 4 | 0 | 0 | 0 | 0 | .000 | 0 | 0 | 17.36 |
| Kansas City | AL | 24 | 11 | 0 | 2 | 78.2 | 336 | 75 | 40 | 27 | 6 | 1 | 2 | 2 | 28 | 1 | 49 | 3 | 0 | 4 | 3 | .571 | 0 | 1 | 3.09 |
| 10 ML YEARS | | 359 | 62 | 3 | 111 | 825.1 | 3466 | 759 | 346 | 309 | 55 | 39 | 21 | 16 | 292 | 38 | 607 | 30 | 16 | 38 | 33 | .535 | 1 | 24 | 3.37 |

## Willie McGee

**Bats:** Both **Throws:** Right **Pos:** CF **Ht:** 6' 1" **Wt:** 176 **Born:** 11/02/58 **Age:** 32

| BATTING | | | | | | | | | | | | | | | | | | | BASERUNNING | | | | PERCENTAGES | | |
|---|---|---|---|---|---|---|---|---|---|---|---|---|---|---|---|---|---|---|---|---|---|---|---|---|---|
| Year Team | Lg | G | AB | H | 2B | 3B | HR | (Hm | Rd) | TB | R | RBI | TBB | IBB | SO | HBP | SH | SF | SB | CS | SB% | GDP | Avg | OBP | SLG |
| 1982 St. Louis | NL | 123 | 422 | 125 | 12 | 8 | 4 | (2 | 2) | 165 | 43 | 56 | 12 | 2 | 58 | 2 | 2 | 1 | 24 | 12 | .67 | 9 | .296 | .318 | .391 |
| 1983 St. Louis | NL | 147 | 601 | 172 | 22 | 8 | 5 | (4 | 1) | 225 | 75 | 75 | 26 | 2 | 98 | 0 | 1 | 3 | 39 | 8 | .83 | 8 | .286 | .314 | .374 |
| 1984 St. Louis | NL | 145 | 571 | 166 | 19 | 11 | 6 | (2 | 4) | 225 | 82 | 50 | 29 | 2 | 80 | 1 | 0 | 3 | 43 | 10 | .81 | 12 | .291 | .325 | .394 |
| 1985 St. Louis | NL | 152 | 612 | 216 | 26 | 18 | 10 | (3 | 7) | 308 | 114 | 82 | 34 | 2 | 86 | 0 | 1 | 5 | 56 | 16 | .78 | 3 | .353 | .384 | .503 |
| 1986 St. Louis | NL | 124 | 497 | 127 | 22 | 7 | 7 | (7 | 0) | 184 | 65 | 48 | 37 | 7 | 82 | 1 | 0 | 4 | 19 | 16 | .54 | 8 | .256 | .306 | .370 |
| 1987 St. Louis | NL | 153 | 620 | 177 | 37 | 11 | 11 | (6 | 5) | 269 | 76 | 105 | 24 | 5 | 90 | 2 | 1 | 5 | 16 | 4 | .80 | 24 | .285 | .312 | .434 |
| 1988 St. Louis | NL | 137 | 562 | 164 | 24 | 6 | 3 | (1 | 2) | 209 | 73 | 50 | 32 | 5 | 84 | 1 | 2 | 3 | 41 | 6 | .87 | 10 | .292 | .329 | .372 |
| 1989 St. Louis | NL | 58 | 199 | 47 | 10 | 2 | 3 | (1 | 2) | 70 | 23 | 17 | 10 | 0 | 34 | 1 | 0 | 1 | 8 | 6 | .57 | 2 | .236 | .275 | .352 |
| 1990 2 ML Teams | | 154 | 614 | 199 | 35 | 7 | 3 | (1 | 2) | 257 | 99 | 77 | 48 | 6 | 104 | 1 | 0 | 2 | 31 | 9 | .78 | 13 | .324 | .373 | .419 |
| 1990 St. Louis | NL | 125 | 501 | 168 | 32 | 5 | 3 | (1 | 2) | 219 | 76 | 62 | 38 | 6 | 86 | 1 | 0 | 2 | 28 | 9 | .76 | 9 | .335 | .382 | .437 |
| Oakland | AL | 29 | 113 | 31 | 3 | 2 | 0 | (0 | 0) | 38 | 23 | 15 | 10 | 0 | 18 | 0 | 0 | 0 | 3 | 0 | 1.00 | 4 | .274 | .333 | .336 |
| 9 ML YEARS | | 1193 | 4698 | 1393 | 207 | 78 | 52 | (27 | 25) | 1912 | 650 | 560 | 252 | 31 | 716 | 9 | 7 | 27 | 277 | 87 | .76 | 89 | .297 | .332 | .407 |

## Fred McGriff

**Bats:** Left **Throws:** Left **Pos:** 1B **Ht:** 6' 3" **Wt:** 208 **Born:** 10/31/63 **Age:** 27

| BATTING | | | | | | | | | | | | | | | | | | | BASERUNNING | | | | PERCENTAGES | | |
|---|---|---|---|---|---|---|---|---|---|---|---|---|---|---|---|---|---|---|---|---|---|---|---|---|---|
| Year Team | Lg | G | AB | H | 2B | 3B | HR | (Hm | Rd) | TB | R | RBI | TBB | IBB | SO | HBP | SH | SF | SB | CS | SB% | GDP | Avg | OBP | SLG |
| 1986 Toronto | AL | 3 | 5 | 1 | 0 | 0 | 0 | (0 | 0) | 1 | 1 | 0 | 0 | 0 | 2 | 0 | 0 | 0 | 0 | 0 | .00 | 0 | .200 | .200 | .200 |
| 1987 Toronto | AL | 107 | 295 | 73 | 16 | 0 | 20 | (7 | 13) | 149 | 58 | 43 | 60 | 4 | 104 | 1 | 0 | 0 | 3 | 2 | .60 | 3 | .247 | .376 | .505 |
| 1988 Toronto | AL | 154 | 536 | 151 | 35 | 4 | 34 | (18 | 16) | 296 | 100 | 82 | 79 | 3 | 149 | 4 | 0 | 4 | 6 | 1 | .86 | 15 | .282 | .376 | .552 |
| 1989 Toronto | AL | 161 | 551 | 148 | 27 | 3 | 36 | (18 | 18) | 289 | 98 | 92 | 119 | 12 | 132 | 4 | 1 | 5 | 7 | 4 | .64 | 14 | .269 | .399 | .525 |
| 1990 Toronto | AL | 153 | 557 | 167 | 21 | 1 | 35 | (14 | 21) | 295 | 91 | 88 | 94 | 12 | 108 | 2 | 1 | 4 | 5 | 3 | .63 | 7 | .300 | .400 | .530 |
| 5 ML YEARS | | 578 | 1944 | 540 | 99 | 8 | 125 | (57 | 68) | 1030 | 348 | 305 | 352 | 31 | 495 | 11 | 2 | 13 | 21 | 10 | .68 | 39 | .278 | .389 | .530 |

## Terry McGriff

**Bats:** Right **Throws:** Right **Pos:** C **Ht:** 6' 2" **Wt:** 195 **Born:** 09/23/63 **Age:** 27

| BATTING | | | | | | | | | | | | | | | | | | | BASERUNNING | | | | PERCENTAGES | | |
|---|---|---|---|---|---|---|---|---|---|---|---|---|---|---|---|---|---|---|---|---|---|---|---|---|---|
| Year Team | Lg | G | AB | H | 2B | 3B | HR | (Hm | Rd) | TB | R | RBI | TBB | IBB | SO | HBP | SH | SF | SB | CS | SB% | GDP | Avg | OBP | SLG |
| 1987 Cincinnati | NL | 34 | 89 | 20 | 3 | 0 | 2 | (1 | 1) | 29 | 6 | 11 | 8 | 0 | 17 | 0 | 0 | 0 | 0 | 0 | .00 | 3 | .225 | .289 | .326 |
| 1988 Cincinnati | NL | 35 | 96 | 19 | 3 | 0 | 1 | (1 | 0) | 25 | 9 | 4 | 12 | 0 | 31 | 0 | 0 | 1 | 1 | 0 | 1.00 | 3 | .198 | .284 | .260 |
| 1989 Cincinnati | NL | 6 | 11 | 3 | 0 | 0 | 0 | (0 | 0) | 3 | 1 | 2 | 2 | 1 | 3 | 0 | 0 | 0 | 0 | 0 | .00 | 0 | .273 | .385 | .273 |
| 1990 2 ML Teams | | 6 | 9 | 0 | 0 | 0 | 0 | (0 | 0) | 0 | 0 | 0 | 0 | 0 | 1 | 0 | 0 | 0 | 0 | 0 | .00 | 0 | .000 | .000 | .000 |
| 1990 Cincinnati | NL | 2 | 4 | 0 | 0 | 0 | 0 | (0 | 0) | 0 | 0 | 0 | 0 | 0 | 1 | 0 | 0 | 0 | 0 | 0 | .00 | 0 | .000 | .000 | .000 |
| Houston | NL | 4 | 5 | 0 | 0 | 0 | 0 | (0 | 0) | 0 | 0 | 0 | 0 | 0 | 0 | 0 | 0 | 0 | 0 | 0 | .00 | 0 | .000 | .000 | .000 |
| 4 ML YEARS | | 81 | 205 | 42 | 6 | 0 | 3 | (2 | 1) | 57 | 16 | 17 | 22 | 1 | 52 | 0 | 0 | 1 | 1 | 0 | 1.00 | 6 | .205 | .281 | .278 |

## Mark McGwire

**Bats:** Right **Throws:** Right **Pos:** 1B **Ht:** 6' 5" **Wt:** 225 **Born:** 10/01/63 **Age:** 27

| BATTING | | | | | | | | | | | | | | | | | | | BASERUNNING | | | | PERCENTAGES | | |
|---|---|---|---|---|---|---|---|---|---|---|---|---|---|---|---|---|---|---|---|---|---|---|---|---|---|
| Year Team | Lg | G | AB | H | 2B | 3B | HR | (Hm | Rd) | TB | R | RBI | TBB | IBB | SO | HBP | SH | SF | SB | CS | SB% | GDP | Avg | OBP | SLG |
| 1986 Oakland | AL | 18 | 53 | 10 | 1 | 0 | 3 | (1 | 2) | 20 | 10 | 9 | 4 | 0 | 18 | 1 | 0 | 0 | 0 | 1 | .00 | 0 | .189 | .259 | .377 |
| 1987 Oakland | AL | 151 | 557 | 161 | 28 | 4 | 49 | (21 | 28) | 344 | 97 | 118 | 71 | 8 | 131 | 5 | 0 | 8 | 1 | 1 | .50 | 6 | .289 | .370 | .618 |
| 1988 Oakland | AL | 155 | 550 | 143 | 22 | 1 | 32 | (12 | 20) | 263 | 87 | 99 | 76 | 4 | 117 | 4 | 1 | 4 | 0 | 0 | .00 | 15 | .260 | .352 | .478 |
| 1989 Oakland | AL | 143 | 490 | 113 | 17 | 0 | 33 | (12 | 21) | 229 | 74 | 95 | 83 | 5 | 94 | 3 | 0 | 11 | 1 | 1 | .50 | 23 | .231 | .339 | .467 |
| 1990 Oakland | AL | 156 | 523 | 123 | 16 | 0 | 39 | (14 | 25) | 256 | 87 | 108 | 110 | 9 | 116 | 7 | 1 | 9 | 2 | 1 | .67 | 13 | .235 | .370 | .489 |
| 5 ML YEARS | | 623 | 2173 | 550 | 84 | 5 | 156 | (60 | 96) | 1112 | 355 | 429 | 344 | 26 | 476 | 20 | 2 | 32 | 4 | 4 | .50 | 57 | .253 | .356 | .512 |

## Tim McIntosh

**Bats:** Right **Throws:** Right **Pos:** C **Ht:** 5'11" **Wt:** 195 **Born:** 03/21/65 **Age:** 26

| BATTING | | | | | | | | | | | | | | | | | | | BASERUNNING | | | | PERCENTAGES | | |
|---|---|---|---|---|---|---|---|---|---|---|---|---|---|---|---|---|---|---|---|---|---|---|---|---|---|
| Year Team | Lg | G | AB | H | 2B | 3B | HR | (Hm | Rd) | TB | R | RBI | TBB | IBB | SO | HBP | SH | SF | SB | CS | SB% | GDP | Avg | OBP | SLG |
| 1986 Beloit | A | 49 | 173 | 45 | 3 | 2 | 4 | -- | -- | 64 | 26 | 21 | 18 | 0 | 33 | 2 | 0 | 3 | 0 | 0 | .00 | 3 | .260 | .332 | .370 |
| 1987 Beloit | A | 130 | 461 | 139 | 30 | 3 | 20 | -- | -- | 235 | 83 | 85 | 49 | 2 | 96 | 7 | 1 | 3 | 7 | 4 | .64 | 4 | .302 | .375 | .510 |
| 1988 Stockton | A | 138 | 519 | 147 | 32 | 6 | 15 | -- | -- | 236 | 81 | 92 | 57 | 1 | 96 | 11 | 6 | 5 | 10 | 5 | .67 | 6 | .283 | .363 | .455 |
| 1989 El Paso | AA | 120 | 463 | 139 | 30 | 3 | 17 | -- | -- | 226 | 72 | 93 | 29 | 3 | 72 | 8 | 2 | 9 | 5 | 4 | .56 | 8 | .300 | .346 | .488 |

| Year Team | Lg | G | AB | H | 2B | 3B | HR | (Hm | Rd) | TB | R | RBI | TBB | IBB | SO | HBP | SH | SF | SB | CS | SB% | GDP | Avg | OBP | SLG |
|---|---|---|---|---|---|---|---|---|---|---|---|---|---|---|---|---|---|---|---|---|---|---|---|---|---|
| 1990 Denver | AAA | 116 | 416 | 120 | 20 | 3 | 18 | -- | -- | 200 | 72 | 74 | 26 | 0 | 58 | 14 | 3 | 7 | 6 | 2 | .75 | 9 | .288 | .346 | .481 |
| 1990 Milwaukee | AL | 5 | 5 | 1 | 0 | 0 | 1 | (1 | 0) | 4 | 1 | 1 | 0 | 0 | 2 | 0 | 0 | 0 | 0 | 0 | .00 | 0 | .200 | .200 | .800 |

## Jeff McKnight

**Bats:** Both **Throws:** Right **Pos:** 1B **Ht:** 6' 0" **Wt:** 175 **Born:** 02/18/63 **Age:** 28

| | | BATTING | | | | | | | | | | | | | | | | | BASERUNNING | | | | PERCENTAGES | | |
|---|---|---|---|---|---|---|---|---|---|---|---|---|---|---|---|---|---|---|---|---|---|---|---|---|---|
| Year Team | Lg | G | AB | H | 2B | 3B | HR | (Hm | Rd) | TB | R | RBI | TBB | IBB | SO | HBP | SH | SF | SB | CS | SB% | GDP | Avg | OBP | SLG |
| 1984 Columbia | A | 95 | 251 | 64 | 10 | 1 | 1 | -- | -- | 79 | 31 | 27 | 26 | 2 | 17 | 1 | 1 | 1 | 9 | 1 | .90 | 5 | .255 | .326 | .315 |
| 1985 Columbia | A | 67 | 159 | 42 | 6 | 1 | 1 | -- | -- | 53 | 26 | 24 | 21 | 2 | 18 | 1 | 0 | 2 | 6 | 2 | .75 | 2 | .264 | .350 | .333 |
| Lynchburg | A | 49 | 150 | 33 | 6 | 1 | 0 | -- | -- | 41 | 19 | 21 | 29 | 0 | 19 | 0 | 4 | 3 | 0 | 0 | .00 | 1 | .220 | .341 | .273 |
| 1986 Jackson | AA | 132 | 469 | 118 | 24 | 3 | 4 | -- | -- | 160 | 71 | 55 | 76 | 3 | 58 | 3 | 5 | 9 | 5 | 2 | .71 | 10 | .252 | .354 | .341 |
| 1987 Jackson | AA | 16 | 59 | 12 | 3 | 0 | 2 | -- | -- | 21 | 5 | 8 | 4 | 0 | 12 | 1 | 0 | 0 | 1 | 1 | .50 | 3 | .203 | .266 | .356 |
| Tidewater | AAA | 87 | 184 | 47 | 7 | 3 | 2 | -- | -- | 66 | 21 | 25 | 24 | 1 | 22 | 1 | 1 | 4 | 0 | 1 | .00 | 6 | .255 | .338 | .359 |
| 1988 Tidewater | AAA | 113 | 345 | 88 | 14 | 0 | 2 | -- | -- | 108 | 36 | 25 | 36 | 5 | 32 | 0 | 1 | 3 | 0 | 4 | .00 | 3 | .255 | .323 | .313 |
| 1989 Tidewater | AAA | 116 | 425 | 106 | 19 | 2 | 9 | -- | -- | 156 | 84 | 48 | 79 | 1 | 56 | 1 | 3 | 1 | 3 | 0 | 1.00 | 13 | .249 | .368 | .367 |
| 1990 Rochester | AAA | 100 | 339 | 95 | 21 | 3 | 7 | -- | -- | 143 | 56 | 45 | 41 | 3 | 58 | 0 | 4 | 6 | 7 | 5 | .58 | 4 | .280 | .352 | .422 |
| 1989 New York | NL | 6 | 12 | 3 | 0 | 0 | 0 | (0 | 0) | 3 | 2 | 0 | 2 | 0 | 1 | 0 | 0 | 0 | 0 | 0 | .00 | 1 | .250 | .357 | .250 |
| 1990 Baltimore | AL | 29 | 75 | 15 | 2 | 0 | 1 | (1 | 0) | 20 | 11 | 4 | 5 | 0 | 17 | 1 | 3 | 0 | 0 | 0 | .00 | 0 | .200 | .259 | .267 |
| 2 ML YEARS | | 35 | 87 | 18 | 2 | 0 | 1 | (1 | 0) | 23 | 13 | 4 | 7 | 0 | 18 | 1 | 3 | 0 | 0 | 0 | .00 | 1 | .207 | .274 | .264 |

## Mark McLemore

**Bats:** Both **Throws:** Right **Pos:** 2B **Ht:** 5'11" **Wt:** 195 **Born:** 10/04/64 **Age:** 26

| | | BATTING | | | | | | | | | | | | | | | | | BASERUNNING | | | | PERCENTAGES | | |
|---|---|---|---|---|---|---|---|---|---|---|---|---|---|---|---|---|---|---|---|---|---|---|---|---|---|
| Year Team | Lg | G | AB | H | 2B | 3B | HR | (Hm | Rd) | TB | R | RBI | TBB | IBB | SO | HBP | SH | SF | SB | CS | SB% | GDP | Avg | OBP | SLG |
| 1986 California | AL | 5 | 4 | 0 | 0 | 0 | 0 | (0 | 0) | 0 | 0 | 0 | 1 | 0 | 2 | 0 | 1 | 0 | 0 | 1 | .00 | 0 | .000 | .200 | .000 |
| 1987 California | AL | 138 | 433 | 102 | 13 | 3 | 3 | (3 | 0) | 130 | 61 | 41 | 48 | 0 | 72 | 0 | 15 | 3 | 25 | 8 | .76 | 7 | .236 | .310 | .300 |
| 1988 California | AL | 77 | 233 | 56 | 11 | 2 | 2 | (1 | 1) | 77 | 38 | 16 | 25 | 0 | 28 | 0 | 5 | 2 | 13 | 7 | .65 | 6 | .240 | .312 | .330 |
| 1989 California | AL | 32 | 103 | 25 | 3 | 1 | 0 | (0 | 0) | 30 | 12 | 14 | 7 | 0 | 19 | 1 | 3 | 1 | 6 | 1 | .86 | 2 | .243 | .295 | .291 |
| 1990 2 ML Teams | | 28 | 60 | 9 | 2 | 0 | 0 | (0 | 0) | 11 | 6 | 2 | 4 | 0 | 15 | 0 | 1 | 0 | 1 | 0 | 1.00 | 1 | .150 | .203 | .183 |
| 1990 California | AL | 20 | 48 | 7 | 2 | 0 | 0 | (0 | 0) | 9 | 4 | 2 | 4 | 0 | 9 | 0 | 1 | 0 | 1 | 0 | 1.00 | 1 | .146 | .212 | .188 |
| Cleveland | AL | 8 | 12 | 2 | 0 | 0 | 0 | (0 | 0) | 2 | 2 | 0 | 0 | 0 | 6 | 0 | 0 | 0 | 0 | 0 | .00 | 0 | .167 | .167 | .167 |
| 5 ML YEARS | | 280 | 833 | 192 | 29 | 6 | 5 | (4 | 1) | 248 | 117 | 73 | 85 | 0 | 136 | 1 | 25 | 6 | 45 | 17 | .73 | 16 | .230 | .301 | .298 |

## Craig McMurtry

**Pitches:** Right **Bats:** Right **Pos:** RP/SP **Ht:** 6' 5" **Wt:** 195 **Born:** 11/05/59 **Age:** 31

| | | HOW MUCH HE PITCHED | | | | | | WHAT HE GAVE UP | | | | | | | | | | | | THE RESULTS | | | | | |
|---|---|---|---|---|---|---|---|---|---|---|---|---|---|---|---|---|---|---|---|---|---|---|---|---|---|
| Year Team | Lg | G | GS | CG | GF | IP | BFP | H | R | ER | HR | SH | SF | HB | TBB | IBB | SO | WP | Bk | W | L | Pct. | ShO | Sv | ERA |
| 1983 Atlanta | NL | 36 | 35 | 6 | 0 | 224.2 | 943 | 204 | 86 | 77 | 13 | 9 | 5 | 1 | 88 | 1 | 105 | 1 | 2 | 15 | 9 | .625 | 3 | 0 | 3.08 |
| 1984 Atlanta | NL | 37 | 30 | 0 | 1 | 183.1 | 811 | 184 | 100 | 88 | 16 | 12 | 9 | 1 | 102 | 4 | 99 | 4 | 3 | 9 | 17 | .346 | 0 | 0 | 4.32 |
| 1985 Atlanta | NL | 17 | 6 | 0 | 3 | 45 | 220 | 56 | 36 | 33 | 6 | 7 | 2 | 1 | 27 | 1 | 28 | 3 | 0 | 0 | 3 | .000 | 0 | 1 | 6.60 |
| 1986 Atlanta | NL | 37 | 5 | 0 | 5 | 79.2 | 356 | 82 | 46 | 42 | 7 | 0 | 2 | 2 | 43 | 5 | 50 | 2 | 0 | 1 | 6 | .143 | 0 | 0 | 4.74 |
| 1988 Texas | AL | 32 | 0 | 0 | 14 | 60 | 236 | 37 | 16 | 15 | 5 | 3 | 3 | 1 | 24 | 4 | 35 | 2 | 2 | 3 | 3 | .500 | 0 | 3 | 2.25 |
| 1989 Texas | AL | 19 | 0 | 0 | 4 | 23 | 111 | 29 | 21 | 19 | 3 | 1 | 2 | 2 | 13 | 1 | 14 | 1 | 1 | 0 | 0 | .000 | 0 | 0 | 7.43 |
| 1990 Texas | AL | 23 | 3 | 0 | 6 | 41.2 | 188 | 43 | 25 | 20 | 4 | 2 | 2 | 1 | 30 | 0 | 14 | 3 | 0 | 0 | 3 | .000 | 0 | 0 | 4.32 |
| 7 ML YEARS | | 201 | 79 | 6 | 33 | 657.1 | 2865 | 635 | 330 | 294 | 54 | 34 | 25 | 9 | 327 | 16 | 345 | 16 | 8 | 28 | 41 | .406 | 3 | 4 | 4.03 |

## Brian McRae

**Bats:** Both **Throws:** Right **Pos:** CF **Ht:** 6' 0" **Wt:** 180 **Born:** 08/27/67 **Age:** 23

| | | BATTING | | | | | | | | | | | | | | | | | BASERUNNING | | | | PERCENTAGES | | |
|---|---|---|---|---|---|---|---|---|---|---|---|---|---|---|---|---|---|---|---|---|---|---|---|---|---|
| Year Team | Lg | G | AB | H | 2B | 3B | HR | (Hm | Rd) | TB | R | RBI | TBB | IBB | SO | HBP | SH | SF | SB | CS | SB% | GDP | Avg | OBP | SLG |
| 1985 Royals | R | 60 | 217 | 58 | 6 | 5 | 0 | -- | -- | 74 | 40 | 23 | 28 | 0 | 34 | 2 | 4 | 2 | 27 | 12 | .69 | 7 | .267 | .353 | .341 |
| 1986 Eugene | A | 72 | 306 | 82 | 10 | 3 | 1 | -- | -- | 101 | 66 | 29 | 41 | 1 | 49 | 5 | 1 | 2 | 28 | 4 | .88 | 6 | .268 | .362 | .330 |
| 1987 Ft. Myers | A | 131 | 481 | 121 | 14 | 1 | 1 | -- | -- | 140 | 62 | 31 | 22 | 1 | 70 | 6 | 0 | 0 | 33 | 18 | .65 | 4 | .252 | .293 | .291 |
| 1988 Baseball Cy | A | 30 | 107 | 33 | 2 | 0 | 1 | -- | -- | 38 | 18 | 11 | 9 | 0 | 11 | 3 | 2 | 0 | 8 | 4 | .67 | 2 | .308 | .378 | .355 |
| Memphis | AA | 91 | 288 | 58 | 13 | 1 | 4 | -- | -- | 85 | 33 | 15 | 16 | 0 | 60 | 2 | 10 | 0 | 13 | 5 | .72 | 8 | .201 | .248 | .295 |
| 1989 Memphis | AA | 138 | 533 | 121 | 18 | 8 | 5 | -- | -- | 170 | 72 | 42 | 43 | 1 | 94 | 8 | 7 | 1 | 23 | 8 | .74 | 5 | .227 | .294 | .319 |
| 1990 Memphis | AA | 116 | 470 | 126 | 24 | 6 | 10 | -- | -- | 192 | 78 | 64 | 44 | 1 | 66 | 3 | 14 | 1 | 21 | 10 | .68 | 9 | .268 | .334 | .409 |
| 1990 Kansas City | AL | 46 | 168 | 48 | 8 | 3 | 2 | (1 | 1) | 68 | 21 | 23 | 9 | 0 | 29 | 0 | 3 | 2 | 4 | 3 | .57 | 5 | .286 | .318 | .405 |

## Kevin McReynolds

**Bats:** Right **Throws:** Right **Pos:** LF **Ht:** 6' 1" **Wt:** 215 **Born:** 10/16/59 **Age:** 31

| | | BATTING | | | | | | | | | | | | | | | | | BASERUNNING | | | | PERCENTAGES | | |
|---|---|---|---|---|---|---|---|---|---|---|---|---|---|---|---|---|---|---|---|---|---|---|---|---|---|
| Year Team | Lg | G | AB | H | 2B | 3B | HR | (Hm | Rd) | TB | R | RBI | TBB | IBB | SO | HBP | SH | SF | SB | CS | SB% | GDP | Avg | OBP | SLG |
| 1983 San Diego | NL | 39 | 140 | 31 | 3 | 1 | 4 | (3 | 1) | 48 | 15 | 14 | 12 | 1 | 29 | 0 | 0 | 3 | 2 | 1 | .67 | 1 | .221 | .277 | .343 |
| 1984 San Diego | NL | 147 | 525 | 146 | 26 | 6 | 20 | (10 | 10) | 244 | 68 | 75 | 34 | 8 | 69 | 0 | 3 | 9 | 3 | 6 | .33 | 14 | .278 | .317 | .465 |
| 1985 San Diego | NL | 152 | 564 | 132 | 24 | 4 | 15 | (6 | 9) | 209 | 61 | 75 | 43 | 6 | 81 | 3 | 2 | 4 | 4 | 0 | 1.00 | 17 | .234 | .290 | .371 |
| 1986 San Diego | NL | 158 | 560 | 161 | 31 | 6 | 26 | (14 | 12) | 282 | 89 | 96 | 66 | 6 | 83 | 1 | 5 | 9 | 8 | 6 | .57 | 9 | .288 | .358 | .504 |

| 1987 New York | NL | 151 | 590 | 163 | 32 | 5 | 29 | (18 | 11) | 292 | 86 | 95 | 39 | 5 | 70 | 1 | 1 | 8 | 14 | 1 | .93 | 13 | .276 | .318 | .495 |
|---|---|---|---|---|---|---|---|---|---|---|---|---|---|---|---|---|---|---|---|---|---|---|---|---|---|
| 1988 New York | NL | 147 | 552 | 159 | 30 | 2 | 27 | (13 | 14) | 274 | 82 | 99 | 38 | 3 | 56 | 4 | 1 | 5 | 21 | 0 | 1.00 | 6 | .288 | .336 | .496 |
| 1989 New York | NL | 148 | 545 | 148 | 25 | 3 | 22 | (12 | 10) | 245 | 74 | 85 | 46 | 10 | 74 | 1 | 0 | 7 | 15 | 7 | .68 | 8 | .272 | .326 | .450 |
| 1990 New York | NL | 147 | 521 | 140 | 23 | 1 | 24 | (11 | 13) | 237 | 75 | 82 | 71 | 11 | 61 | 1 | 0 | 8 | 9 | 2 | .82 | 8 | .269 | .353 | .455 |
| 8 ML YEARS | | 1089 | 3997 | 1080 | 194 | 28 | 167 | (87 | 80) | 1831 | 550 | 621 | 349 | 50 | 523 | 11 | 12 | 53 | 76 | 23 | .77 | 76 | .270 | .327 | .458 |

## Larry McWilliams

**Pitches:** Left **Bats:** Left **Pos:** RP **Ht:** 6' 5" **Wt:** 181 **Born:** 02/10/54 **Age:** 37

| | | HOW MUCH HE PITCHED | | | | | | WHAT HE GAVE UP | | | | | | | | | | | | THE RESULTS | | | | | |
|---|---|---|---|---|---|---|---|---|---|---|---|---|---|---|---|---|---|---|---|---|---|---|---|---|---|
| Year Team | Lg | G | GS | CG | GF | IP | BFP | H | R | ER | HR | SH | SF | HB | TBB | IBB | SO | WP | Bk | W | L | Pct. | ShO | Sv | ERA |
| 1978 Atlanta | NL | 15 | 15 | 3 | 0 | 99 | 417 | 84 | 38 | 31 | 11 | 5 | 0 | 2 | 35 | 4 | 42 | 2 | 0 | 9 | 3 | .750 | 1 | 0 | 2.82 |
| 1979 Atlanta | NL | 13 | 13 | 1 | 0 | 66 | 287 | 69 | 41 | 41 | 4 | 6 | 1 | 4 | 22 | 2 | 32 | 2 | 0 | 3 | 2 | .600 | 0 | 0 | 5.59 |
| 1980 Atlanta | NL | 30 | 30 | 4 | 0 | 164 | 715 | 188 | 97 | 90 | 27 | 8 | 2 | 7 | 39 | 2 | 77 | 5 | 1 | 9 | 14 | .391 | 1 | 0 | 4.94 |
| 1981 Atlanta | NL | 6 | 5 | 2 | 0 | 38 | 147 | 31 | 13 | 13 | 2 | 2 | 2 | 0 | 8 | 0 | 23 | 0 | 0 | 2 | 1 | .667 | 1 | 0 | 3.08 |
| 1982 2 ML Teams | | 46 | 20 | 2 | 6 | 159.1 | 678 | 158 | 79 | 68 | 12 | 9 | 3 | 6 | 44 | 6 | 118 | 3 | 1 | 8 | 8 | .500 | 2 | 1 | 3.84 |
| 1983 Pittsburgh | NL | 35 | 35 | 8 | 0 | 238 | 1002 | 205 | 99 | 86 | 19 | 13 | 6 | 3 | 87 | 7 | 199 | 9 | 4 | 15 | 8 | .652 | 4 | 0 | 3.25 |
| 1984 Pittsburgh | NL | 34 | 32 | 7 | 1 | 227.1 | 957 | 226 | 86 | 74 | 18 | 12 | 6 | 2 | 78 | 7 | 149 | 3 | 3 | 12 | 11 | .522 | 2 | 1 | 2.93 |
| 1985 Pittsburgh | NL | 30 | 19 | 2 | 2 | 126.1 | 568 | 139 | 70 | 66 | 9 | 4 | 3 | 7 | 62 | 11 | 52 | 4 | 0 | 7 | 9 | .438 | 0 | 0 | 4.70 |
| 1986 Pittsburgh | NL | 49 | 15 | 0 | 11 | 122.1 | 545 | 129 | 75 | 70 | 16 | 8 | 0 | 7 | 49 | 5 | 80 | 5 | 0 | 3 | 11 | .214 | 0 | 0 | 5.15 |
| 1987 Atlanta | NL | 9 | 2 | 0 | 4 | 20.1 | 95 | 25 | 15 | 13 | 2 | 2 | 1 | 2 | 7 | 1 | 13 | 1 | 0 | 0 | 1 | .000 | 0 | 0 | 5.75 |
| 1988 St. Louis | NL | 42 | 17 | 2 | 12 | 136 | 581 | 130 | 64 | 59 | 10 | 17 | 2 | 4 | 45 | 7 | 70 | 9 | 3 | 6 | 9 | .400 | 1 | 1 | 3.90 |
| 1989 2 ML Teams | | 48 | 21 | 3 | 6 | 153.1 | 667 | 154 | 82 | 70 | 5 | 11 | 5 | 7 | 57 | 5 | 78 | 8 | 3 | 4 | 13 | .235 | 1 | 0 | 4.11 |
| 1990 Kansas City | AL | 13 | 0 | 0 | 2 | 8.1 | 43 | 10 | 9 | 9 | 2 | 1 | 0 | 1 | 9 | 1 | 7 | 1 | 0 | 0 | 0 | .000 | 0 | 0 | 9.72 |
| 1982 Atlanta | NL | 27 | 2 | 0 | 5 | 37.2 | 185 | 52 | 30 | 26 | 3 | 3 | 1 | 2 | 20 | 5 | 24 | 1 | 1 | 2 | 3 | .400 | 0 | 0 | 6.21 |
| Pittsburgh | NL | 19 | 18 | 2 | 1 | 121.2 | 493 | 106 | 49 | 42 | 9 | 6 | 2 | 4 | 24 | 1 | 94 | 2 | 0 | 6 | 5 | .545 | 2 | 1 | 3.11 |
| 1989 Philadelphia | NL | 40 | 16 | 2 | 6 | 120.2 | 531 | 123 | 67 | 55 | 3 | 9 | 4 | 4 | 49 | 4 | 54 | 6 | 3 | 2 | 11 | .154 | 1 | 0 | 4.10 |
| Kansas City | AL | 8 | 5 | 1 | 0 | 32.2 | 136 | 31 | 15 | 15 | 2 | 2 | 1 | 3 | 8 | 1 | 24 | 2 | 0 | 2 | 2 | .500 | 0 | 0 | 4.13 |
| 13 ML YEARS | | 370 | 224 | 34 | 44 | 1558.1 | 6702 | 1548 | 768 | 690 | 137 | 98 | 31 | 52 | 542 | 58 | 940 | 52 | 15 | 78 | 90 | .464 | 13 | 3 | 3.99 |

## Louie Meadows

**Bats:** Left **Throws:** Left **Pos:** LF **Ht:** 5'11" **Wt:** 190 **Born:** 04/29/61 **Age:** 30

| | | BATTING | | | | | | | | | | | | | | | | | BASERUNNING | | | | PERCENTAGES | | |
|---|---|---|---|---|---|---|---|---|---|---|---|---|---|---|---|---|---|---|---|---|---|---|---|---|---|
| Year Team | Lg | G | AB | H | 2B | 3B | HR | (Hm | Rd) | TB | R | RBI | TBB | IBB | SO | HBP | SH | SF | SB | CS | SB% | GDP | Avg | OBP | SLG |
| 1986 Houston | NL | 6 | 6 | 2 | 0 | 0 | 0 | (0 | 0) | 2 | 1 | 0 | 0 | 0 | 0 | 0 | 0 | 0 | 1 | 0 | 1.00 | 0 | .333 | .333 | .333 |
| 1988 Houston | NL | 35 | 42 | 8 | 0 | 1 | 2 | (1 | 1) | 16 | 5 | 3 | 6 | 0 | 8 | 0 | 0 | 0 | 4 | 2 | .67 | 1 | .190 | .292 | .381 |
| 1989 Houston | NL | 31 | 51 | 9 | 0 | 0 | 3 | (3 | 0) | 18 | 5 | 10 | 1 | 0 | 14 | 0 | 0 | 1 | 1 | 2 | .33 | 0 | .176 | .189 | .353 |
| 1990 2 ML Teams | | 30 | 28 | 3 | 0 | 0 | 0 | (0 | 0) | 3 | 4 | 0 | 3 | 0 | 6 | 0 | 0 | 0 | 0 | 0 | .00 | 0 | .107 | .194 | .107 |
| 1990 Houston | NL | 15 | 14 | 2 | 0 | 0 | 0 | (0 | 0) | 2 | 3 | 0 | 2 | 0 | 4 | 0 | 0 | 0 | 0 | 0 | .00 | 0 | .143 | .250 | .143 |
| Philadelphia | NL | 15 | 14 | 1 | 0 | 0 | 0 | (0 | 0) | 1 | 1 | 0 | 1 | 0 | 2 | 0 | 0 | 0 | 0 | 0 | .00 | 0 | .071 | .133 | .071 |
| 4 ML YEARS | | 102 | 127 | 22 | 0 | 1 | 5 | (4 | 1) | 39 | 15 | 13 | 10 | 0 | 28 | 0 | 0 | 1 | 6 | 4 | .60 | 1 | .173 | .232 | .307 |

## Scott Medvin

**Pitches:** Right **Bats:** Right **Pos:** RP **Ht:** 6' 0" **Wt:** 190 **Born:** 09/16/61 **Age:** 29

| | | HOW MUCH HE PITCHED | | | | | | WHAT HE GAVE UP | | | | | | | | | | | | THE RESULTS | | | | | |
|---|---|---|---|---|---|---|---|---|---|---|---|---|---|---|---|---|---|---|---|---|---|---|---|---|---|
| Year Team | Lg | G | GS | CG | GF | IP | BFP | H | R | ER | HR | SH | SF | HB | TBB | IBB | SO | WP | Bk | W | L | Pct. | ShO | Sv | ERA |
| 1988 Pittsburgh | NL | 17 | 0 | 0 | 5 | 27.2 | 112 | 23 | 16 | 15 | 1 | 1 | 1 | 1 | 9 | 2 | 16 | 5 | 0 | 3 | 0 | 1.000 | 0 | 0 | 4.88 |
| 1989 Pittsburgh | NL | 6 | 0 | 0 | 2 | 6.1 | 30 | 6 | 5 | 4 | 0 | 0 | 0 | 0 | 5 | 2 | 4 | 1 | 1 | 0 | 1 | .000 | 0 | 0 | 5.68 |
| 1990 Seattle | AL | 5 | 0 | 0 | 3 | 4.1 | 22 | 7 | 4 | 3 | 0 | 0 | 0 | 1 | 2 | 0 | 1 | 1 | 0 | 0 | 1 | .000 | 0 | 0 | 6.23 |
| 3 ML YEARS | | 28 | 0 | 0 | 10 | 38.1 | 164 | 36 | 25 | 22 | 1 | 1 | 1 | 2 | 16 | 4 | 21 | 7 | 1 | 3 | 2 | .600 | 0 | 0 | 5.17 |

## Jose Melendez

**Pitches:** Right **Bats:** Right **Pos:** RP **Ht:** 6' 2" **Wt:** 175 **Born:** 09/02/65 **Age:** 25

| | | HOW MUCH HE PITCHED | | | | | | WHAT HE GAVE UP | | | | | | | | | | | | THE RESULTS | | | | | |
|---|---|---|---|---|---|---|---|---|---|---|---|---|---|---|---|---|---|---|---|---|---|---|---|---|---|
| Year Team | Lg | G | GS | CG | GF | IP | BFP | H | R | ER | HR | SH | SF | HB | TBB | IBB | SO | WP | Bk | W | L | Pct. | ShO | Sv | ERA |
| 1984 Watertown | A | 15 | 15 | 3 | 0 | 91 | 372 | 61 | 37 | 28 | 6 | 1 | 2 | 6 | 40 | 0 | 68 | 4 | 2 | 5 | 7 | .417 | 1 | 0 | 2.77 |
| 1985 Pr William | A | 9 | 8 | 1 | 1 | 44.1 | 180 | 25 | 17 | 12 | 2 | 0 | 3 | 0 | 26 | 0 | 41 | 2 | 0 | 3 | 2 | .600 | 0 | 1 | 2.44 |
| 1986 Pr William | A | 28 | 27 | 6 | 0 | 186.1 | 768 | 141 | 75 | 54 | 9 | 7 | 5 | 2 | 81 | 1 | 146 | 6 | 5 | 13 | 10 | .565 | 1 | 0 | 2.61 |
| 1987 Harrisburg | AA | 6 | 6 | 0 | 0 | 18.1 | 91 | 28 | 24 | 22 | 4 | 1 | 0 | 0 | 11 | 0 | 13 | 0 | 1 | 1 | 3 | .250 | 0 | 0 | 10.80 |
| Salem | A | 20 | 20 | 1 | 0 | 116.1 | 493 | 96 | 62 | 59 | 17 | 0 | 5 | 8 | 56 | 0 | 86 | 4 | 0 | 9 | 6 | .600 | 1 | 0 | 4.56 |
| 1988 Salem | A | 8 | 8 | 2 | 0 | 53.2 | 233 | 55 | 26 | 24 | 10 | 0 | 0 | 1 | 19 | 0 | 50 | 2 | 1 | 4 | 2 | .667 | 1 | 0 | 4.02 |
| Harrisburg | AA | 22 | 4 | 2 | 6 | 71.1 | 274 | 46 | 20 | 18 | 2 | 2 | 3 | 1 | 19 | 1 | 38 | 3 | 4 | 5 | 3 | .625 | 2 | 1 | 2.27 |
| 1989 Williamsprt | AA | 11 | 11 | 0 | 0 | 73.1 | 295 | 54 | 23 | 20 | 7 | 1 | 2 | 2 | 22 | 1 | 56 | 0 | 6 | 3 | 4 | .429 | 0 | 0 | 2.45 |
| Calgary | AAA | 17 | 2 | 0 | 4 | 40.2 | 184 | 42 | 27 | 26 | 6 | 2 | 3 | 3 | 19 | 2 | 24 | 1 | 0 | 1 | 2 | .333 | 0 | 0 | 5.75 |
| 1990 Calgary | AAA | 45 | 10 | 1 | 14 | 124.2 | 525 | 119 | 61 | 54 | 11 | 2 | 5 | 6 | 44 | 2 | 95 | 2 | 1 | 11 | 4 | .733 | 0 | 2 | 3.90 |
| 1990 Seattle | AL | 3 | 0 | 0 | 1 | 5.1 | 28 | 8 | 8 | 7 | 2 | 0 | 0 | 1 | 3 | 0 | 7 | 1 | 0 | 0 | 0 | .000 | 0 | 0 | 11.81 |

## Bob Melvin

**Bats:** Right **Throws:** Right **Pos:** C **Ht:** 6' 4" **Wt:** 205 **Born:** 10/28/61 **Age:** 29

| BATTING | | | | | | | | | | | | | | | | | | | BASERUNNING | | | | PERCENTAGES | | |
|---|---|---|---|---|---|---|---|---|---|---|---|---|---|---|---|---|---|---|---|---|---|---|---|---|---|
| Year Team | Lg | G | AB | H | 2B | 3B | HR | (Hm | Rd) | TB | R | RBI | TBB | IBB | SO | HBP | SH | SF | SB | CS | SB% | GDP | Avg | OBP | SLG |
| 1985 Detroit | AL | 41 | 82 | 18 | 4 | 1 | 0 | (0 | 0) | 24 | 10 | 4 | 3 | 0 | 21 | 0 | 2 | 0 | 0 | 0 | .00 | 1 | .220 | .247 | .293 |
| 1986 San Francisco | NL | 89 | 268 | 60 | 14 | 2 | 5 | (2 | 3) | 93 | 24 | 25 | 15 | 1 | 69 | 0 | 3 | 3 | 3 | 2 | .60 | 7 | .224 | .262 | .347 |
| 1987 San Francisco | NL | 84 | 246 | 49 | 8 | 0 | 11 | (6 | 5) | 90 | 31 | 31 | 17 | 3 | 44 | 0 | 0 | 2 | 0 | 4 | .00 | 7 | .199 | .249 | .366 |
| 1988 San Francisco | NL | 92 | 273 | 64 | 13 | 1 | 8 | (4 | 4) | 103 | 23 | 27 | 13 | 0 | 46 | 0 | 1 | 1 | 0 | 2 | .00 | 5 | .234 | .268 | .377 |
| 1989 Baltimore | AL | 85 | 278 | 67 | 10 | 1 | 1 | (0 | 1) | 82 | 22 | 32 | 15 | 3 | 53 | 0 | 7 | 1 | 1 | 4 | .20 | 10 | .241 | .279 | .295 |
| 1990 Baltimore | AL | 93 | 301 | 73 | 14 | 1 | 5 | (3 | 2) | 104 | 30 | 37 | 11 | 1 | 53 | 0 | 3 | 3 | 0 | 1 | .00 | 8 | .243 | .267 | .346 |
| 6 ML YEARS | | 484 | 1448 | 331 | 63 | 6 | 30 | (15 | 15) | 496 | 140 | 156 | 74 | 8 | 286 | 0 | 16 | 10 | 4 | 13 | .24 | 38 | .229 | .264 | .343 |

## Orlando Mercado

**Bats:** Right **Throws:** Right **Pos:** C **Ht:** 6' 0" **Wt:** 195 **Born:** 11/07/61 **Age:** 29

| BATTING | | | | | | | | | | | | | | | | | | | BASERUNNING | | | | PERCENTAGES | | |
|---|---|---|---|---|---|---|---|---|---|---|---|---|---|---|---|---|---|---|---|---|---|---|---|---|---|
| Year Team | Lg | G | AB | H | 2B | 3B | HR | (Hm | Rd) | TB | R | RBI | TBB | IBB | SO | HBP | SH | SF | SB | CS | SB% | GDP | Avg | OBP | SLG |
| 1982 Seattle | AL | 9 | 17 | 2 | 0 | 0 | 1 | (1 | 0) | 5 | 1 | 6 | 0 | 0 | 5 | 0 | 0 | 0 | 0 | 0 | .00 | 0 | .118 | .118 | .294 |
| 1983 Seattle | AL | 66 | 178 | 35 | 11 | 2 | 1 | (1 | 0) | 53 | 10 | 16 | 14 | 0 | 27 | 1 | 2 | 2 | 2 | 2 | .50 | 3 | .197 | .256 | .298 |
| 1984 Seattle | AL | 30 | 78 | 17 | 3 | 1 | 0 | (0 | 0) | 22 | 5 | 5 | 4 | 0 | 12 | 1 | 1 | 0 | 1 | 0 | 1.00 | 1 | .218 | .265 | .282 |
| 1986 Texas | AL | 46 | 102 | 24 | 1 | 1 | 1 | (1 | 0) | 30 | 7 | 7 | 6 | 0 | 13 | 1 | 1 | 2 | 0 | 1 | .00 | 5 | .235 | .279 | .294 |
| 1987 2 ML Teams | | 17 | 27 | 6 | 1 | 0 | 0 | (0 | 0) | 7 | 3 | 2 | 3 | 0 | 1 | 0 | 0 | 0 | 0 | 0 | .00 | 0 | .222 | .300 | .259 |
| 1988 Oakland | AL | 16 | 24 | 3 | 0 | 0 | 1 | (1 | 0) | 6 | 3 | 1 | 3 | 0 | 8 | 0 | 0 | 0 | 0 | 0 | .00 | 0 | .125 | .222 | .250 |
| 1989 Minnesota | AL | 19 | 38 | 4 | 0 | 0 | 0 | (0 | 0) | 4 | 1 | 1 | 4 | 0 | 4 | 0 | 0 | 0 | 1 | 0 | 1.00 | 0 | .105 | .190 | .105 |
| 1990 2 ML Teams | | 50 | 98 | 21 | 1 | 0 | 3 | (2 | 1) | 31 | 10 | 7 | 8 | 3 | 12 | 2 | 0 | 0 | 0 | 0 | .00 | 4 | .214 | .287 | .316 |
| 1987 Detroit | AL | 10 | 22 | 3 | 0 | 0 | 0 | (0 | 0) | 3 | 2 | 1 | 2 | 0 | 0 | 0 | 0 | 0 | 0 | 0 | .00 | 0 | .136 | .208 | .136 |
| Los Angeles | NL | 7 | 5 | 3 | 1 | 0 | 0 | (0 | 0) | 4 | 1 | 1 | 1 | 0 | 1 | 0 | 0 | 0 | 0 | 0 | .00 | 0 | .600 | .667 | .800 |
| 1990 New York | NL | 42 | 90 | 19 | 1 | 0 | 3 | (2 | 1) | 29 | 10 | 7 | 8 | 3 | 11 | 2 | 0 | 0 | 0 | 0 | .00 | 4 | .211 | .290 | .322 |
| Montreal | NL | 8 | 8 | 2 | 0 | 0 | 0 | (0 | 0) | 2 | 0 | 0 | 0 | 0 | 1 | 0 | 0 | 0 | 0 | 0 | .00 | 0 | .250 | .250 | .250 |
| 8 ML YEARS | | 253 | 562 | 112 | 17 | 4 | 7 | (6 | 1) | 158 | 40 | 45 | 42 | 3 | 82 | 5 | 4 | 4 | 4 | 3 | .57 | 13 | .199 | .259 | .281 |

## Orlando Merced

**Bats:** Both **Throws:** Right **Pos:** PH **Ht:** 6' 0" **Wt:** 190 **Born:** 11/02/66 **Age:** 24

| BATTING | | | | | | | | | | | | | | | | | | | BASERUNNING | | | | PERCENTAGES | | |
|---|---|---|---|---|---|---|---|---|---|---|---|---|---|---|---|---|---|---|---|---|---|---|---|---|---|
| Year Team | Lg | G | AB | H | 2B | 3B | HR | (Hm | Rd) | TB | R | RBI | TBB | IBB | SO | HBP | SH | SF | SB | CS | SB% | GDP | Avg | OBP | SLG |
| 1985 Pirates | R | 40 | 136 | 31 | 6 | 0 | 1 | -- | -- | 40 | 16 | 13 | 9 | 0 | 9 | 1 | 0 | 0 | 3 | 1 | .75 | 3 | .228 | .281 | .294 |
| 1986 Macon | A | 65 | 173 | 34 | 4 | 1 | 2 | -- | -- | 46 | 20 | 24 | 12 | 0 | 38 | 1 | 0 | 2 | 5 | 3 | .63 | 3 | .197 | .250 | .266 |
| Watertown | A | 27 | 89 | 16 | 0 | 1 | 3 | -- | -- | 27 | 12 | 9 | 14 | 2 | 21 | 2 | 0 | 1 | 6 | 2 | .75 | 2 | .180 | .302 | .303 |
| 1987 Macon | A | 4 | 4 | 0 | 0 | 0 | 0 | -- | -- | 0 | 1 | 0 | 1 | 0 | 3 | 0 | 0 | 0 | 0 | 0 | .00 | 0 | .000 | .200 | .000 |
| Watertown | A | 4 | 12 | 5 | 0 | 1 | 0 | -- | -- | 7 | 4 | 3 | 1 | 0 | 1 | 1 | 0 | 0 | 1 | 0 | 1.00 | 0 | .417 | .500 | .583 |
| 1988 Augusta | A | 37 | 136 | 36 | 6 | 3 | 1 | -- | -- | 51 | 19 | 17 | 7 | 1 | 20 | 2 | 0 | 1 | 2 | 0 | 1.00 | 2 | .265 | .308 | .375 |
| Salem | A | 80 | 298 | 87 | 12 | 7 | 7 | -- | -- | 134 | 47 | 42 | 27 | 1 | 64 | 1 | 1 | 5 | 13 | 3 | .81 | 7 | .292 | .347 | .450 |
| 1989 Harrisburg | AA | 95 | 341 | 82 | 16 | 4 | 6 | -- | -- | 124 | 43 | 48 | 32 | 6 | 65 | 2 | 1 | 4 | 13 | 3 | .81 | 6 | .240 | .306 | .364 |
| Buffalo | AAA | 35 | 129 | 44 | 5 | 3 | 1 | -- | -- | 58 | 18 | 16 | 7 | 1 | 26 | 0 | 2 | 1 | 0 | 1 | .00 | 2 | .341 | .372 | .450 |
| 1990 Buffalo | AAA | 101 | 378 | 99 | 12 | 6 | 9 | -- | -- | 150 | 52 | 55 | 46 | 3 | 63 | 0 | 1 | 1 | 14 | 5 | .74 | 8 | .262 | .341 | .397 |
| 1990 Pittsburgh | NL | 25 | 24 | 5 | 1 | 0 | 0 | (0 | 0) | 6 | 3 | 0 | 1 | 0 | 9 | 0 | 0 | 0 | 0 | 0 | .00 | 1 | .208 | .240 | .250 |

## Kent Mercker

**Pitches:** Left **Bats:** Left **Pos:** RP **Ht:** 6' 1" **Wt:** 175 **Born:** 02/01/68 **Age:** 23

| HOW MUCH HE PITCHED | | | | | | | WHAT HE GAVE UP | | | | | | | | | | | | THE RESULTS | | | | | | |
|---|---|---|---|---|---|---|---|---|---|---|---|---|---|---|---|---|---|---|---|---|---|---|---|---|---|
| Year Team | Lg | G | GS | CG | GF | IP | BFP | H | R | ER | HR | SH | SF | HB | TBB | IBB | SO | WP | Bk | W | L | Pct. | ShO | Sv | ERA |
| 1986 Braves | R | 9 | 8 | 0 | 1 | 47.1 | 203 | 37 | 21 | 13 | 1 | 2 | 0 | 0 | 16 | 1 | 42 | 0 | 1 | 4 | 3 | .571 | 0 | 0 | 2.47 |
| 1987 Durham | A | 3 | 3 | 0 | 0 | 11.2 | 49 | 11 | 8 | 7 | 1 | 0 | 0 | 0 | 6 | 0 | 14 | 1 | 0 | 0 | 1 | .000 | 0 | 0 | 5.40 |
| 1988 Durham | A | 19 | 19 | 5 | 0 | 127.2 | 527 | 102 | 44 | 39 | 5 | 0 | 1 | 2 | 47 | 0 | 159 | 7 | 1 | 11 | 4 | .733 | 0 | 0 | 2.75 |
| Greenville | AA | 9 | 9 | 0 | 0 | 48.1 | 207 | 36 | 20 | 18 | 2 | 1 | 0 | 1 | 26 | 1 | 60 | 2 | 2 | 3 | 1 | .750 | 0 | 0 | 3.35 |
| 1989 Richmond | AAA | 27 | 27 | 4 | 0 | 168.2 | 698 | 107 | 66 | 60 | 17 | 7 | 7 | 3 | 95 | 4 | 144 | 7 | 2 | 9 | 12 | .429 | 0 | 0 | 3.20 |
| 1990 Richmond | AAA | 12 | 10 | 0 | 1 | 58.1 | 260 | 60 | 30 | 23 | 1 | 0 | 1 | 1 | 27 | 1 | 69 | 5 | 1 | 5 | 4 | .556 | 0 | 1 | 3.55 |
| 1989 Atlanta | NL | 2 | 1 | 0 | 1 | 4.1 | 26 | 8 | 6 | 6 | 0 | 0 | 0 | 0 | 6 | 0 | 4 | 0 | 0 | 0 | 0 | .000 | 0 | 0 | 12.46 |
| 1990 Atlanta | NL | 36 | 0 | 0 | 28 | 48.1 | 211 | 43 | 22 | 17 | 6 | 1 | 2 | 2 | 24 | 3 | 39 | 2 | 0 | 4 | 7 | .364 | 0 | 7 | 3.17 |
| 2 ML YEARS | | 38 | 1 | 0 | 29 | 52.2 | 237 | 51 | 28 | 23 | 6 | 1 | 2 | 2 | 30 | 3 | 43 | 2 | 0 | 4 | 7 | .364 | 0 | 7 | 3.93 |

## Jose Mesa

**Pitches:** Right **Bats:** Right **Pos:** SP **Ht:** 6' 3" **Wt:** 210 **Born:** 05/22/66 **Age:** 25

| HOW MUCH HE PITCHED | | | | | | | WHAT HE GAVE UP | | | | | | | | | | | | THE RESULTS | | | | | | |
|---|---|---|---|---|---|---|---|---|---|---|---|---|---|---|---|---|---|---|---|---|---|---|---|---|---|
| Year Team | Lg | G | GS | CG | GF | IP | BFP | H | R | ER | HR | SH | SF | HB | TBB | IBB | SO | WP | Bk | W | L | Pct. | ShO | Sv | ERA |
| 1987 Baltimore | AL | 6 | 5 | 0 | 0 | 31.1 | 143 | 38 | 23 | 21 | 7 | 0 | 0 | 0 | 15 | 0 | 17 | 4 | 0 | 1 | 3 | .250 | 0 | 0 | 6.03 |
| 1990 Baltimore | AL | 7 | 7 | 0 | 0 | 46.2 | 202 | 37 | 20 | 20 | 2 | 2 | 2 | 1 | 27 | 2 | 24 | 1 | 1 | 3 | 2 | .600 | 0 | 0 | 3.86 |
| 2 ML YEARS | | 13 | 12 | 0 | 0 | 78 | 345 | 75 | 43 | 41 | 9 | 2 | 2 | 1 | 42 | 2 | 41 | 5 | 1 | 4 | 5 | .444 | 0 | 0 | 4.73 |

## Hensley Meulens

**Bats:** Right **Throws:** Right **Pos:** LF **Ht:** 6' 3" **Wt:** 190 **Born:** 06/23/67 **Age:** 24

| BATTING | | | | | | | | | | | | | | | | | | | BASERUNNING | | | | PERCENTAGES | | |
|---|---|---|---|---|---|---|---|---|---|---|---|---|---|---|---|---|---|---|---|---|---|---|---|---|---|
| Year Team | Lg | G | AB | H | 2B | 3B | HR | (Hm | Rd) | TB | R | RBI | TBB | IBB | SO | HBP | SH | SF | SB | CS | SB% | GDP | Avg | OBP | SLG |
| 1986 Yankees | R | 59 | 219 | 51 | 10 | 4 | 4 | -- | -- | 81 | 36 | 31 | 28 | 0 | 66 | 4 | 1 | 1 | 4 | 2 | .67 | 7 | .233 | .329 | .370 |
| 1987 Pr William | A | 116 | 430 | 129 | 23 | 2 | 28 | -- | -- | 240 | 76 | 103 | 53 | 3 | 124 | 9 | 0 | 6 | 14 | 3 | .82 | 7 | .300 | .384 | .558 |
| Ft.Laudrdle | A | 17 | 58 | 10 | 3 | 0 | 0 | -- | -- | 13 | 2 | 2 | 7 | 0 | 25 | 0 | 0 | 0 | 0 | 0 | .00 | 0 | .172 | .262 | .224 |
| 1988 Albany | AA | 79 | 278 | 68 | 9 | 1 | 13 | -- | -- | 118 | 50 | 40 | 37 | 2 | 97 | 1 | 0 | 0 | 3 | 3 | .50 | 7 | .245 | .335 | .424 |
| Columbus | AAA | 55 | 209 | 48 | 9 | 1 | 6 | -- | -- | 77 | 27 | 22 | 14 | 0 | 61 | 0 | 0 | 1 | 2 | 0 | 1.00 | 5 | .230 | .277 | .368 |
| 1989 Albany | AA | 104 | 335 | 86 | 8 | 2 | 11 | -- | -- | 131 | 55 | 45 | 61 | 0 | 108 | 9 | 0 | 1 | 3 | 2 | .60 | 6 | .257 | .384 | .391 |
| Columbus | AAA | 14 | 45 | 13 | 4 | 0 | 1 | -- | -- | 20 | 8 | 3 | 8 | 0 | 13 | 0 | 0 | 0 | 0 | 0 | .00 | 2 | .289 | .396 | .444 |
| 1990 Columbus | AAA | 136 | 480 | 137 | 20 | 5 | 26 | -- | -- | 245 | 81 | 96 | 66 | 4 | 132 | 7 | 1 | 5 | 6 | 4 | .60 | 12 | .285 | .376 | .510 |
| 1989 New York | AL | 8 | 28 | 5 | 0 | 0 | 0 | (0 | 0) | 5 | 2 | 1 | 2 | 0 | 8 | 0 | 0 | 0 | 0 | 1 | .00 | 2 | .179 | .233 | .179 |
| 1990 New York | AL | 23 | 83 | 20 | 7 | 0 | 3 | (2 | 1) | 36 | 12 | 10 | 9 | 0 | 25 | 3 | 0 | 0 | 1 | 0 | 1.00 | 3 | .241 | .337 | .434 |
| 2 ML YEARS | | 31 | 111 | 25 | 7 | 0 | 3 | (2 | 1) | 41 | 14 | 11 | 11 | 0 | 33 | 3 | 0 | 0 | 1 | 1 | .50 | 5 | .225 | .312 | .369 |

## Brian Meyer

**Pitches:** Right **Bats:** Right **Pos:** RP **Ht:** 6' 1" **Wt:** 190 **Born:** 01/29/63 **Age:** 28

| HOW MUCH HE PITCHED | | | | | | | | WHAT HE GAVE UP | | | | | | | | | | | | THE RESULTS | | | | | |
|---|---|---|---|---|---|---|---|---|---|---|---|---|---|---|---|---|---|---|---|---|---|---|---|---|---|
| Year Team | Lg | G | GS | CG | GF | IP | BFP | H | R | ER | HR | SH | SF | HB | TBB | IBB | SO | WP | Bk | W | L | Pct. | ShO | Sv | ERA |
| 1988 Houston | NL | 8 | 0 | 0 | 5 | 12.1 | 46 | 9 | 2 | 2 | 2 | 2 | 0 | 0 | 4 | 0 | 10 | 0 | 0 | 0 | 0 | .000 | 0 | 0 | 1.46 |
| 1989 Houston | NL | 12 | 0 | 0 | 2 | 18 | 82 | 16 | 13 | 9 | 0 | 0 | 1 | 1 | 13 | 3 | 13 | 0 | 1 | 0 | 1 | .000 | 0 | 1 | 4.50 |
| 1990 Houston | NL | 14 | 0 | 0 | 7 | 20.1 | 84 | 16 | 7 | 5 | 3 | 2 | 0 | 0 | 6 | 0 | 6 | 0 | 0 | 0 | 4 | .000 | 0 | 1 | 2.21 |
| 3 ML YEARS | | 34 | 0 | 0 | 14 | 50.2 | 212 | 41 | 22 | 16 | 5 | 4 | 1 | 1 | 23 | 3 | 29 | 0 | 1 | 0 | 5 | .000 | 0 | 2 | 2.84 |

## Gary Mielke

**Pitches:** Right **Bats:** Right **Pos:** RP **Ht:** 6' 3" **Wt:** 180 **Born:** 01/28/63 **Age:** 28

| HOW MUCH HE PITCHED | | | | | | | | WHAT HE GAVE UP | | | | | | | | | | | | THE RESULTS | | | | | |
|---|---|---|---|---|---|---|---|---|---|---|---|---|---|---|---|---|---|---|---|---|---|---|---|---|---|
| Year Team | Lg | G | GS | CG | GF | IP | BFP | H | R | ER | HR | SH | SF | HB | TBB | IBB | SO | WP | Bk | W | L | Pct. | ShO | Sv | ERA |
| 1987 Texas | AL | 3 | 0 | 0 | 1 | 3 | 14 | 3 | 2 | 2 | 2 | 1 | 0 | 0 | 1 | 0 | 3 | 0 | 0 | 0 | 0 | .000 | 0 | 0 | 6.00 |
| 1989 Texas | AL | 43 | 0 | 0 | 8 | 49.2 | 217 | 52 | 18 | 18 | 4 | 3 | 1 | 2 | 25 | 3 | 26 | 1 | 0 | 1 | 0 | 1.000 | 0 | 1 | 3.26 |
| 1990 Texas | AL | 33 | 0 | 0 | 8 | 41 | 174 | 42 | 17 | 17 | 4 | 2 | 0 | 2 | 15 | 5 | 13 | 1 | 0 | 0 | 3 | .000 | 0 | 0 | 3.73 |
| 3 ML YEARS | | 79 | 0 | 0 | 17 | 93.2 | 405 | 97 | 37 | 37 | 10 | 6 | 1 | 4 | 41 | 8 | 42 | 2 | 0 | 1 | 3 | .250 | 0 | 1 | 3.56 |

## Bob Milacki

**Pitches:** Right **Bats:** Right **Pos:** SP **Ht:** 6' 4" **Wt:** 220 **Born:** 07/28/64 **Age:** 26

| HOW MUCH HE PITCHED | | | | | | | | WHAT HE GAVE UP | | | | | | | | | | | | THE RESULTS | | | | | |
|---|---|---|---|---|---|---|---|---|---|---|---|---|---|---|---|---|---|---|---|---|---|---|---|---|---|
| Year Team | Lg | G | GS | CG | GF | IP | BFP | H | R | ER | HR | SH | SF | HB | TBB | IBB | SO | WP | Bk | W | L | Pct. | ShO | Sv | ERA |
| 1988 Baltimore | AL | 3 | 3 | 1 | 0 | 25 | 91 | 9 | 2 | 2 | 1 | 0 | 0 | 0 | 9 | 0 | 18 | 0 | 0 | 2 | 0 | 1.000 | 1 | 0 | 0.72 |
| 1989 Baltimore | AL | 37 | 36 | 3 | 1 | 243 | 1022 | 233 | 105 | 101 | 21 | 7 | 6 | 2 | 88 | 4 | 113 | 1 | 1 | 14 | 12 | .538 | 2 | 0 | 3.74 |
| 1990 Baltimore | AL | 27 | 24 | 1 | 0 | 135.1 | 594 | 143 | 73 | 67 | 18 | 5 | 5 | 0 | 61 | 2 | 60 | 2 | 1 | 5 | 8 | .385 | 1 | 0 | 4.46 |
| 3 ML YEARS | | 67 | 63 | 5 | 1 | 403.1 | 1707 | 385 | 180 | 170 | 40 | 12 | 11 | 2 | 158 | 6 | 191 | 3 | 2 | 21 | 20 | .512 | 4 | 0 | 3.79 |

## Keith Miller

**Bats:** Right **Throws:** Right **Pos:** CF **Ht:** 5'11" **Wt:** 180 **Born:** 06/12/63 **Age:** 28

| BATTING | | | | | | | | | | | | | | | | | | | BASERUNNING | | | | PERCENTAGES | | |
|---|---|---|---|---|---|---|---|---|---|---|---|---|---|---|---|---|---|---|---|---|---|---|---|---|---|
| Year Team | Lg | G | AB | H | 2B | 3B | HR | (Hm | Rd) | TB | R | RBI | TBB | IBB | SO | HBP | SH | SF | SB | CS | SB% | GDP | Avg | OBP | SLG |
| 1987 New York | NL | 25 | 51 | 19 | 2 | 2 | 0 | (0 | 0) | 25 | 14 | 1 | 2 | 0 | 6 | 1 | 3 | 0 | 8 | 1 | .89 | 1 | .373 | .407 | .490 |
| 1988 New York | NL | 40 | 70 | 15 | 1 | 1 | 1 | (1 | 0) | 21 | 9 | 5 | 6 | 0 | 10 | 0 | 3 | 0 | 0 | 5 | .00 | 1 | .214 | .276 | .300 |
| 1989 New York | NL | 57 | 143 | 33 | 7 | 0 | 1 | (0 | 1) | 43 | 15 | 7 | 5 | 0 | 27 | 1 | 3 | 0 | 6 | 0 | 1.00 | 3 | .231 | .262 | .301 |
| 1990 New York | NL | 88 | 233 | 60 | 8 | 0 | 1 | (1 | 0) | 71 | 42 | 12 | 23 | 1 | 46 | 2 | 2 | 2 | 16 | 3 | .84 | 2 | .258 | .327 | .305 |
| 4 ML YEARS | | 210 | 497 | 127 | 18 | 3 | 3 | (2 | 1) | 160 | 80 | 25 | 36 | 1 | 89 | 4 | 11 | 2 | 30 | 9 | .77 | 7 | .256 | .310 | .322 |

## Randy Milligan

**Bats:** Right **Throws:** Right **Pos:** 1B **Ht:** 6' 2" **Wt:** 225 **Born:** 11/27/61 **Age:** 29

| BATTING | | | | | | | | | | | | | | | | | | | BASERUNNING | | | | PERCENTAGES | | |
|---|---|---|---|---|---|---|---|---|---|---|---|---|---|---|---|---|---|---|---|---|---|---|---|---|---|
| Year Team | Lg | G | AB | H | 2B | 3B | HR | (Hm | Rd) | TB | R | RBI | TBB | IBB | SO | HBP | SH | SF | SB | CS | SB% | GDP | Avg | OBP | SLG |
| 1987 New York | NL | 3 | 1 | 0 | 0 | 0 | 0 | (0 | 0) | 0 | 0 | 0 | 1 | 0 | 1 | 0 | 0 | 0 | 0 | 0 | .00 | 0 | .000 | .500 | .000 |
| 1988 Pittsburgh | NL | 40 | 82 | 18 | 5 | 0 | 3 | (1 | 2) | 32 | 10 | 8 | 20 | 0 | 24 | 1 | 0 | 0 | 1 | 2 | .33 | 2 | .220 | .379 | .390 |
| 1989 Baltimore | AL | 124 | 365 | 98 | 23 | 5 | 12 | (6 | 6) | 167 | 56 | 45 | 74 | 2 | 75 | 3 | 0 | 2 | 9 | 5 | .64 | 12 | .268 | .394 | .458 |
| 1990 Baltimore | AL | 109 | 362 | 96 | 20 | 1 | 20 | (11 | 9) | 178 | 64 | 60 | 88 | 3 | 68 | 2 | 0 | 4 | 6 | 3 | .67 | 11 | .265 | .408 | .492 |
| 4 ML YEARS | | 276 | 810 | 212 | 48 | 6 | 35 | (18 | 17) | 377 | 130 | 113 | 183 | 5 | 168 | 6 | 0 | 6 | 16 | 10 | .62 | 25 | .262 | .399 | .465 |

## Alan Mills

**Pitches:** Right **Bats:** Both **Pos:** RP **Ht:** 6' 1" **Wt:** 190 **Born:** 10/18/66 **Age:** 24

| HOW MUCH HE PITCHED | | | | | | | | | WHAT HE GAVE UP | | | | | | | | | | | | THE RESULTS | | | | | |
|---|---|---|---|---|---|---|---|---|---|---|---|---|---|---|---|---|---|---|---|---|---|---|---|---|---|---|
| Year | Team | Lg | G | GS | CG | GF | IP | BFP | H | R | ER | HR | SH | SF | HB | TBB | IBB | SO | WP | Bk | W | L | Pct. | ShO | Sv | ERA |
| 1986 | Salem | A | 14 | 14 | 1 | 0 | 83.2 | 0 | 77 | 58 | 43 | 1 | 0 | 0 | 5 | 60 | 0 | 50 | 5 | 0 | 6 | 6 | .500 | 0 | 0 | 4.63 |
| 1987 | Pr William | A | 35 | 8 | 0 | 11 | 85.2 | 424 | 102 | 75 | 58 | 7 | 7 | 0 | 4 | 64 | 3 | 53 | 9 | 0 | 2 | 11 | .154 | 0 | 1 | 6.09 |
| 1988 | Pr William | A | 42 | 5 | 0 | 19 | 93.2 | 416 | 93 | 56 | 43 | 4 | 5 | 5 | 5 | 43 | 2 | 59 | 6 | 1 | 3 | 8 | .273 | 0 | 4 | 4.13 |
| 1989 | Ft.Laudrdle | A | 22 | 0 | 0 | 15 | 31 | 140 | 40 | 15 | 13 | 0 | 3 | 3 | 4 | 9 | 1 | 25 | 3 | 2 | 1 | 4 | .200 | 0 | 6 | 3.77 |
| | Pr William | A | 26 | 0 | 0 | 26 | 39.2 | 155 | 22 | 5 | 4 | 0 | 1 | 2 | 5 | 13 | 1 | 44 | 6 | 0 | 6 | 1 | .857 | 0 | 7 | 0.91 |
| 1990 | Columbus | AAA | 17 | 0 | 0 | 13 | 29.1 | 123 | 22 | 11 | 11 | 0 | 1 | 1 | 2 | 14 | 0 | 30 | 2 | 0 | 3 | 3 | .500 | 0 | 6 | 3.38 |
| 1990 | New York | AL | 36 | 0 | 0 | 18 | 41.2 | 200 | 48 | 21 | 19 | 4 | 4 | 1 | 1 | 33 | 6 | 24 | 3 | 0 | 1 | 5 | .167 | 0 | 0 | 4.10 |

## Greg Minton

**Pitches:** Right **Bats:** Both **Pos:** RP **Ht:** 6' 2" **Wt:** 207 **Born:** 07/29/51 **Age:** 39

| HOW MUCH HE PITCHED | | | | | | | | | WHAT HE GAVE UP | | | | | | | | | | | | THE RESULTS | | | | | |
|---|---|---|---|---|---|---|---|---|---|---|---|---|---|---|---|---|---|---|---|---|---|---|---|---|---|---|
| Year | Team | Lg | G | GS | CG | GF | IP | BFP | H | R | ER | HR | SH | SF | HB | TBB | IBB | SO | WP | Bk | W | L | Pct. | ShO | Sv | ERA |
| 1975 | San Francisco | NL | 4 | 2 | 0 | 0 | 17 | 79 | 19 | 14 | 13 | 1 | 1 | 0 | 1 | 11 | 3 | 6 | 2 | 1 | 1 | 1 | .500 | 0 | 0 | 6.88 |
| 1976 | San Francisco | NL | 10 | 2 | 0 | 5 | 26 | 117 | 32 | 18 | 14 | 0 | 1 | 2 | 1 | 12 | 1 | 7 | 3 | 1 | 0 | 3 | .000 | 0 | 0 | 4.85 |
| 1977 | San Francisco | NL | 2 | 2 | 0 | 0 | 14 | 57 | 14 | 8 | 7 | 0 | 0 | 0 | 0 | 4 | 0 | 5 | 2 | 1 | 1 | 1 | .500 | 0 | 0 | 4.50 |
| 1978 | San Francisco | NL | 11 | 0 | 0 | 3 | 16 | 76 | 22 | 14 | 14 | 3 | 1 | 1 | 1 | 8 | 1 | 6 | 0 | 0 | 0 | 1 | .000 | 0 | 0 | 7.88 |
| 1979 | San Francisco | NL | 46 | 0 | 0 | 18 | 80 | 314 | 59 | 25 | 16 | 0 | 9 | 1 | 2 | 27 | 7 | 33 | 8 | 2 | 4 | 3 | .571 | 0 | 4 | 1.80 |
| 1980 | San Francisco | NL | 68 | 0 | 0 | 38 | 91 | 377 | 81 | 28 | 25 | 0 | 8 | 1 | 0 | 34 | 6 | 42 | 7 | 1 | 4 | 6 | .400 | 0 | 19 | 2.47 |
| 1981 | San Francisco | NL | 55 | 0 | 0 | 44 | 84 | 359 | 84 | 28 | 27 | 0 | 6 | 2 | 0 | 36 | 8 | 29 | 2 | 2 | 4 | 5 | .444 | 0 | 21 | 2.89 |
| 1982 | San Francisco | NL | 78 | 0 | 0 | 66 | 123 | 496 | 108 | 29 | 25 | 5 | 6 | 4 | 2 | 42 | 17 | 58 | 7 | 0 | 10 | 4 | .714 | 0 | 30 | 1.83 |
| 1983 | San Francisco | NL | 73 | 0 | 0 | 52 | 106.2 | 476 | 117 | 51 | 42 | 6 | 10 | 5 | 0 | 47 | 13 | 38 | 5 | 0 | 7 | 11 | .389 | 0 | 22 | 3.54 |
| 1984 | San Francisco | NL | 74 | 1 | 0 | 43 | 124.1 | 556 | 130 | 60 | 52 | 6 | 7 | 6 | 0 | 57 | 20 | 48 | 5 | 0 | 4 | 9 | .308 | 0 | 19 | 3.76 |
| 1985 | San Francisco | NL | 68 | 0 | 0 | 36 | 96.2 | 424 | 98 | 42 | 38 | 6 | 6 | 4 | 0 | 54 | 18 | 37 | 2 | 0 | 5 | 4 | .556 | 0 | 4 | 3.54 |
| 1986 | San Francisco | NL | 48 | 0 | 0 | 28 | 68.2 | 296 | 63 | 35 | 30 | 4 | 7 | 3 | 1 | 34 | 15 | 34 | 3 | 0 | 4 | 4 | .500 | 0 | 5 | 3.93 |
| 1987 | 2 ML Teams | | 56 | 0 | 0 | 29 | 99.1 | 418 | 101 | 37 | 35 | 6 | 6 | 2 | 2 | 39 | 7 | 44 | 3 | 0 | 6 | 4 | .600 | 0 | 11 | 3.17 |
| 1988 | California | AL | 44 | 0 | 0 | 26 | 79 | 331 | 67 | 37 | 25 | 1 | 3 | 3 | 3 | 34 | 10 | 46 | 4 | 1 | 4 | 5 | .444 | 0 | 7 | 2.85 |
| 1989 | California | AL | 62 | 0 | 0 | 24 | 90 | 373 | 76 | 22 | 22 | 4 | 2 | 1 | 2 | 37 | 4 | 42 | 3 | 0 | 4 | 3 | .571 | 0 | 8 | 2.20 |
| 1990 | California | AL | 11 | 0 | 0 | 3 | 15.1 | 61 | 11 | 4 | 4 | 1 | 1 | 0 | 1 | 7 | 1 | 4 | 0 | 0 | 1 | 1 | .500 | 0 | 0 | 2.35 |
| 1987 | San Francisco | NL | 15 | 0 | 0 | 2 | 23.1 | 105 | 30 | 9 | 9 | 2 | 1 | 0 | 1 | 10 | 3 | 9 | 1 | 0 | 1 | 0 | 1.000 | 0 | 1 | 3.47 |
| | California | AL | 41 | 0 | 0 | 27 | 76 | 313 | 71 | 28 | 26 | 4 | 5 | 2 | 1 | 29 | 4 | 35 | 2 | 0 | 5 | 4 | .556 | 0 | 10 | 3.08 |
| | 16 ML YEARS | | 710 | 7 | 0 | 415 | 1131 | 4810 | 1082 | 452 | 389 | 43 | 74 | 35 | 16 | 483 | 131 | 479 | 56 | 9 | 59 | 65 | .476 | 0 | 150 | 3.10 |

## Gino Minutelli

**Pitches:** Left **Bats:** Left **Pos:** RP **Ht:** 6' 0" **Wt:** 180 **Born:** 05/23/64 **Age:** 27

| HOW MUCH HE PITCHED | | | | | | | | | WHAT HE GAVE UP | | | | | | | | | | | | THE RESULTS | | | | | |
|---|---|---|---|---|---|---|---|---|---|---|---|---|---|---|---|---|---|---|---|---|---|---|---|---|---|---|
| Year | Team | Lg | G | GS | CG | GF | IP | BFP | H | R | ER | HR | SH | SF | HB | TBB | IBB | SO | WP | Bk | W | L | Pct. | ShO | Sv | ERA |
| 1985 | Tri-Cities | A | 20 | 10 | 0 | 7 | 57 | 0 | 61 | 57 | 51 | 3 | 0 | 0 | 6 | 57 | 0 | 79 | 6 | 0 | 4 | 8 | .333 | 0 | 0 | 8.05 |
| 1986 | Cedar Rapds | A | 27 | 27 | 3 | 0 | 152.2 | 671 | 133 | 73 | 62 | 14 | 4 | 6 | 5 | 76 | 1 | 149 | 16 | 2 | 15 | 5 | .750 | 2 | 0 | 3.66 |
| 1987 | Tampa | A | 17 | 15 | 5 | 1 | 104.1 | 461 | 98 | 51 | 44 | 4 | 10 | 3 | 5 | 48 | 4 | 70 | 13 | 1 | 7 | 6 | .538 | 1 | 0 | 3.80 |
| | Vermont | AA | 6 | 6 | 0 | 0 | 39.2 | 168 | 34 | 15 | 14 | 3 | 0 | 0 | 2 | 16 | 0 | 39 | 2 | 1 | 4 | 1 | .800 | 0 | 0 | 3.18 |
| 1988 | Chattanooga | AA | 2 | 2 | 0 | 0 | 5.2 | 27 | 6 | 2 | 1 | 0 | 0 | 0 | 1 | 4 | 0 | 3 | 0 | 2 | 0 | 1 | .000 | 0 | 0 | 1.59 |
| 1989 | Reds | R | 1 | 1 | 0 | 0 | 1 | 4 | 0 | 0 | 0 | 0 | 0 | 0 | 0 | 1 | 0 | 0 | 0 | 1 | 0 | 0 | .000 | 0 | 0 | 0.00 |
| | Chattanooga | AA | 6 | 6 | 1 | 0 | 29 | 140 | 28 | 19 | 17 | 1 | 0 | 1 | 6 | 23 | 0 | 20 | 8 | 4 | 1 | 1 | .500 | 0 | 0 | 5.28 |
| 1990 | Chattanooga | AA | 17 | 17 | 5 | 0 | 108.1 | 467 | 106 | 52 | 48 | 9 | 5 | 2 | 2 | 46 | 1 | 75 | 5 | 13 | 9 | 5 | .643 | 0 | 0 | 3.99 |
| | Nashville | AAA | 11 | 11 | 3 | 0 | 78.1 | 315 | 65 | 34 | 28 | 5 | 1 | 1 | 1 | 31 | 0 | 61 | 1 | 0 | 5 | 2 | .714 | 0 | 0 | 3.22 |
| 1990 | Cincinnati | NL | 2 | 0 | 0 | 0 | 1 | 6 | 0 | 1 | 1 | 0 | 0 | 0 | 1 | 2 | 0 | 0 | 1 | 0 | 0 | 0 | .000 | 0 | 0 | 9.00 |

## Paul Mirabella

**Pitches:** Left **Bats:** Left **Pos:** RP **Ht:** 6' 2" **Wt:** 185 **Born:** 03/20/54 **Age:** 37

| HOW MUCH HE PITCHED | | | | | | | | | WHAT HE GAVE UP | | | | | | | | | | | | THE RESULTS | | | | | |
|---|---|---|---|---|---|---|---|---|---|---|---|---|---|---|---|---|---|---|---|---|---|---|---|---|---|---|
| Year | Team | Lg | G | GS | CG | GF | IP | BFP | H | R | ER | HR | SH | SF | HB | TBB | IBB | SO | WP | Bk | W | L | Pct. | ShO | Sv | ERA |
| 1978 | Texas | AL | 10 | 4 | 0 | 3 | 28 | 125 | 30 | 18 | 18 | 2 | 1 | 2 | 0 | 17 | 0 | 23 | 0 | 1 | 3 | 2 | .600 | 0 | 1 | 5.79 |
| 1979 | New York | AL | 10 | 1 | 0 | 0 | 14 | 71 | 16 | 15 | 14 | 3 | 2 | 0 | 1 | 10 | 1 | 4 | 3 | 0 | 0 | 4 | .000 | 0 | 0 | 9.00 |
| 1980 | Toronto | AL | 33 | 22 | 3 | 2 | 131 | 596 | 151 | 73 | 63 | 11 | 9 | 5 | 3 | 66 | 3 | 53 | 4 | 0 | 5 | 12 | .294 | 1 | 0 | 4.33 |
| 1981 | Toronto | AL | 8 | 1 | 0 | 2 | 15 | 73 | 20 | 16 | 12 | 2 | 0 | 1 | 1 | 7 | 0 | 9 | 0 | 0 | 0 | 0 | .000 | 0 | 0 | 7.20 |
| 1982 | Texas | AL | 40 | 0 | 0 | 19 | 50.2 | 217 | 46 | 28 | 27 | 4 | 1 | 1 | 2 | 22 | 5 | 29 | 2 | 0 | 1 | 1 | .500 | 0 | 3 | 4.80 |
| 1983 | Baltimore | AL | 3 | 2 | 0 | 1 | 9.2 | 45 | 9 | 6 | 6 | 1 | 1 | 0 | 0 | 7 | 0 | 4 | 0 | 0 | 0 | 0 | .000 | 0 | 0 | 5.59 |
| 1984 | Seattle | AL | 52 | 1 | 0 | 19 | 68 | 303 | 74 | 39 | 33 | 6 | 5 | 3 | 1 | 32 | 6 | 41 | 3 | 0 | 2 | 5 | .286 | 0 | 3 | 4.37 |
| 1985 | Seattle | AL | 10 | 0 | 0 | 1 | 13.2 | 57 | 9 | 4 | 2 | 0 | 1 | 2 | 2 | 4 | 1 | 8 | 0 | 0 | 0 | 0 | .000 | 0 | 0 | 1.32 |
| 1986 | Seattle | AL | 8 | 0 | 0 | 2 | 6.1 | 34 | 13 | 7 | 6 | 1 | 0 | 0 | 0 | 3 | 0 | 6 | 1 | 0 | 0 | 0 | .000 | 0 | 0 | 8.53 |
| 1987 | Milwaukee | AL | 29 | 0 | 0 | 9 | 29.1 | 133 | 30 | 20 | 16 | 0 | 2 | 3 | 0 | 16 | 3 | 14 | 2 | 0 | 2 | 1 | .667 | 0 | 2 | 4.91 |

| | | | | | | | | | | | | | | | | | | | | | | | | | |
|---|---|---|---|---|---|---|---|---|---|---|---|---|---|---|---|---|---|---|---|---|---|---|---|---|---|
| 1988 Milwaukee | AL | 38 | 0 | 0 | 13 | 60 | 241 | 44 | 12 | 11 | 3 | 2 | 2 | 0 | 21 | 5 | 33 | 1 | 0 | 2 | 2 | .500 | 0 | 4 | 1.65 |
| 1989 Milwaukee | AL | 13 | 0 | 0 | 7 | 15.1 | 74 | 18 | 14 | 13 | 1 | 1 | 3 | 1 | 7 | 3 | 6 | 0 | 0 | 0 | 0 | .000 | 0 | 0 | 7.63 |
| 1990 Milwaukee | AL | 44 | 2 | 0 | 10 | 59 | 267 | 66 | 32 | 26 | 9 | 1 | 2 | 2 | 27 | 2 | 28 | 1 | 0 | 4 | 2 | .667 | 0 | 0 | 3.97 |
| 13 ML YEARS | | 298 | 33 | 3 | 88 | 500 | 2236 | 526 | 284 | 247 | 43 | 26 | 24 | 13 | 239 | 29 | 258 | 17 | 1 | 19 | 29 | .396 | 1 | 13 | 4.45 |

## John Mitchell

**Pitches:** Right **Bats:** Right **Pos:** SP/RP **Ht:** 6' 2" **Wt:** 195 **Born:** 08/11/65 **Age:** 25

| | | HOW MUCH HE PITCHED | | | | | | WHAT HE GAVE UP | | | | | | | | | | | | THE RESULTS | | | | | |
|---|---|---|---|---|---|---|---|---|---|---|---|---|---|---|---|---|---|---|---|---|---|---|---|---|---|
| Year Team | Lg | G | GS | CG | GF | IP | BFP | H | R | ER | HR | SH | SF | HB | TBB | IBB | SO | WP | Bk | W | L | Pct. | ShO | Sv | ERA |
| 1986 New York | NL | 4 | 1 | 0 | 1 | 10 | 40 | 10 | 4 | 4 | 1 | 0 | 0 | 0 | 4 | 0 | 2 | 2 | 0 | 0 | 1 | .000 | 0 | 0 | 3.60 |
| 1987 New York | NL | 20 | 19 | 1 | 0 | 111.2 | 493 | 124 | 64 | 51 | 6 | 6 | 5 | 2 | 36 | 3 | 57 | 7 | 1 | 3 | 6 | .333 | 0 | 0 | 4.11 |
| 1988 New York | NL | 1 | 0 | 0 | 0 | 1 | 5 | 2 | 0 | 0 | 0 | 0 | 0 | 0 | 1 | 0 | 1 | 0 | 0 | 0 | 0 | .000 | 0 | 0 | 0.00 |
| 1989 New York | NL | 2 | 0 | 0 | 0 | 3 | 17 | 3 | 7 | 2 | 0 | 0 | 0 | 0 | 4 | 1 | 4 | 1 | 0 | 0 | 1 | .000 | 0 | 0 | 6.00 |
| 1990 Baltimore | AL | 24 | 17 | 0 | 2 | 114.1 | 509 | 133 | 63 | 59 | 7 | 6 | 8 | 3 | 48 | 3 | 43 | 3 | 0 | 6 | 6 | .500 | 0 | 0 | 4.64 |
| 5 ML YEARS | | 51 | 37 | 1 | 3 | 240 | 1064 | 272 | 138 | 116 | 14 | 12 | 13 | 5 | 93 | 7 | 107 | 13 | 1 | 9 | 14 | .391 | 0 | 0 | 4.35 |

## Kevin Mitchell

**Bats:** Right **Throws:** Right **Pos:** LF **Ht:** 5'11" **Wt:** 210 **Born:** 01/13/62 **Age:** 29

| | | BATTING | | | | | | | | | | | | | | | | | BASERUNNING | | | | PERCENTAGES | | |
|---|---|---|---|---|---|---|---|---|---|---|---|---|---|---|---|---|---|---|---|---|---|---|---|---|---|
| Year Team | Lg | G | AB | H | 2B | 3B | HR | (Hm | Rd) | TB | R | RBI | TBB | IBB | SO | HBP | SH | SF | SB | CS | SB% | GDP | Avg | OBP | SLG |
| 1984 New York | NL | 7 | 14 | 3 | 0 | 0 | 0 | (0 | 0) | 3 | 0 | 1 | 0 | 0 | 3 | 0 | 0 | 0 | 0 | 1 | .00 | 0 | .214 | .214 | .214 |
| 1986 New York | NL | 108 | 328 | 91 | 22 | 2 | 12 | (4 | 8) | 153 | 51 | 43 | 33 | 0 | 61 | 1 | 1 | 1 | 3 | 3 | .50 | 6 | .277 | .344 | .466 |
| 1987 2 ML Teams | | 131 | 464 | 130 | 20 | 2 | 22 | (9 | 13) | 220 | 68 | 70 | 48 | 4 | 88 | 2 | 0 | 1 | 9 | 6 | .60 | 10 | .280 | .350 | .474 |
| 1988 San Francisco | NL | 148 | 505 | 127 | 25 | 7 | 19 | (10 | 9) | 223 | 60 | 80 | 48 | 7 | 85 | 5 | 1 | 7 | 5 | 5 | .50 | 9 | .251 | .319 | .442 |
| 1989 San Francisco | NL | 154 | 543 | 158 | 34 | 6 | 47 | (22 | 25) | 345 | 100 | 125 | 87 | 32 | 115 | 3 | 0 | 7 | 3 | 4 | .43 | 6 | .291 | .388 | .635 |
| 1990 San Francisco | NL | 140 | 524 | 152 | 24 | 2 | 35 | (15 | 20) | 285 | 90 | 93 | 58 | 9 | 87 | 2 | 0 | 5 | 4 | 7 | .36 | 9 | .290 | .360 | .544 |
| 1987 San Diego | NL | 62 | 196 | 48 | 7 | 1 | 7 | (2 | 5) | 78 | 19 | 26 | 20 | 3 | 38 | 0 | 0 | 1 | 0 | 0 | .00 | 5 | .245 | .313 | .398 |
| San Francisco | NL | 69 | 268 | 82 | 13 | 1 | 15 | (7 | 8) | 142 | 49 | 44 | 28 | 1 | 50 | 2 | 0 | 0 | 9 | 6 | .60 | 5 | .306 | .376 | .530 |
| 6 ML YEARS | | 688 | 2378 | 661 | 125 | 19 | 135 | (60 | 75) | 1229 | 369 | 412 | 274 | 52 | 439 | 13 | 2 | 21 | 24 | 26 | .48 | 40 | .278 | .353 | .517 |

## Dale Mohorcic

**Pitches:** Right **Bats:** Right **Pos:** RP **Ht:** 6' 3" **Wt:** 220 **Born:** 01/25/56 **Age:** 35

| | | HOW MUCH HE PITCHED | | | | | | WHAT HE GAVE UP | | | | | | | | | | | | THE RESULTS | | | | | |
|---|---|---|---|---|---|---|---|---|---|---|---|---|---|---|---|---|---|---|---|---|---|---|---|---|---|
| Year Team | Lg | G | GS | CG | GF | IP | BFP | H | R | ER | HR | SH | SF | HB | TBB | IBB | SO | WP | Bk | W | L | Pct. | ShO | Sv | ERA |
| 1986 Texas | AL | 58 | 0 | 0 | 20 | 79 | 325 | 86 | 25 | 22 | 5 | 1 | 0 | 1 | 15 | 6 | 29 | 1 | 0 | 2 | 4 | .333 | 0 | 7 | 2.51 |
| 1987 Texas | AL | 74 | 0 | 0 | 54 | 99.1 | 390 | 88 | 34 | 33 | 11 | 7 | 2 | 2 | 19 | 6 | 48 | 3 | 4 | 7 | 6 | .538 | 0 | 16 | 2.99 |
| 1988 2 ML Teams | | 56 | 0 | 0 | 25 | 74.2 | 342 | 83 | 42 | 35 | 7 | 1 | 6 | 8 | 29 | 7 | 44 | 4 | 0 | 4 | 8 | .333 | 0 | 6 | 4.22 |
| 1989 New York | AL | 32 | 0 | 0 | 10 | 57.2 | 254 | 65 | 41 | 32 | 8 | 1 | 2 | 6 | 18 | 3 | 24 | 4 | 1 | 2 | 1 | .667 | 0 | 2 | 4.99 |
| 1990 Montreal | NL | 34 | 0 | 0 | 12 | 53 | 226 | 56 | 21 | 19 | 6 | 3 | 5 | 4 | 18 | 3 | 29 | 1 | 1 | 1 | 2 | .333 | 0 | 2 | 3.23 |
| 1988 Texas | AL | 43 | 0 | 0 | 21 | 52 | 240 | 62 | 35 | 28 | 6 | 0 | 5 | 5 | 20 | 5 | 25 | 2 | 0 | 2 | 6 | .250 | 0 | 5 | 4.85 |
| New York | AL | 13 | 0 | 0 | 4 | 22.2 | 102 | 21 | 7 | 7 | 1 | 1 | 1 | 3 | 9 | 2 | 19 | 2 | 0 | 2 | 2 | .500 | 0 | 1 | 2.78 |
| 5 ML YEARS | | 254 | 0 | 0 | 121 | 363.2 | 1537 | 378 | 163 | 141 | 37 | 13 | 15 | 21 | 99 | 25 | 174 | 13 | 6 | 16 | 21 | .432 | 0 | 33 | 3.49 |

## Paul Molitor

**Bats:** Right **Throws:** Right **Pos:** 2B/1B **Ht:** 6' 0" **Wt:** 185 **Born:** 08/22/56 **Age:** 34

| | | BATTING | | | | | | | | | | | | | | | | | BASERUNNING | | | | PERCENTAGES | | |
|---|---|---|---|---|---|---|---|---|---|---|---|---|---|---|---|---|---|---|---|---|---|---|---|---|---|
| Year Team | Lg | G | AB | H | 2B | 3B | HR | (Hm | Rd) | TB | R | RBI | TBB | IBB | SO | HBP | SH | SF | SB | CS | SB% | GDP | Avg | OBP | SLG |
| 1978 Milwaukee | AL | 125 | 521 | 142 | 26 | 4 | 6 | (4 | 2) | 194 | 73 | 45 | 19 | 2 | 54 | 4 | 7 | 5 | 30 | 12 | .71 | 6 | .273 | .301 | .372 |
| 1979 Milwaukee | AL | 140 | 584 | 188 | 27 | 16 | 9 | (3 | 6) | 274 | 88 | 62 | 48 | 5 | 48 | 2 | 6 | 5 | 33 | 13 | .72 | 9 | .322 | .372 | .469 |
| 1980 Milwaukee | AL | 111 | 450 | 137 | 29 | 2 | 9 | (2 | 7) | 197 | 81 | 37 | 48 | 4 | 48 | 3 | 6 | 5 | 34 | 7 | .83 | 9 | .304 | .372 | .438 |
| 1981 Milwaukee | AL | 64 | 251 | 67 | 11 | 0 | 2 | (1 | 1) | 84 | 45 | 19 | 25 | 1 | 29 | 3 | 5 | 0 | 10 | 6 | .63 | 3 | .267 | .341 | .335 |
| 1982 Milwaukee | AL | 160 | 666 | 201 | 26 | 8 | 19 | (9 | 10) | 300 | 136 | 71 | 69 | 1 | 93 | 1 | 10 | 5 | 41 | 9 | .82 | 9 | .302 | .366 | .450 |
| 1983 Milwaukee | AL | 152 | 608 | 164 | 28 | 6 | 15 | (9 | 6) | 249 | 95 | 47 | 59 | 4 | 74 | 2 | 7 | 6 | 41 | 8 | .84 | 12 | .270 | .333 | .410 |
| 1984 Milwaukee | AL | 13 | 46 | 10 | 1 | 0 | 0 | (0 | 0) | 11 | 3 | 6 | 2 | 0 | 8 | 0 | 0 | 1 | 1 | 0 | 1.00 | 0 | .217 | .245 | .239 |
| 1985 Milwaukee | AL | 140 | 576 | 171 | 28 | 3 | 10 | (6 | 4) | 235 | 93 | 48 | 54 | 6 | 80 | 1 | 7 | 4 | 21 | 7 | .75 | 12 | .297 | .356 | .408 |
| 1986 Milwaukee | AL | 105 | 437 | 123 | 24 | 6 | 9 | (5 | 4) | 186 | 62 | 55 | 40 | 0 | 81 | 0 | 2 | 3 | 20 | 5 | .80 | 9 | .281 | .340 | .426 |
| 1987 Milwaukee | AL | 118 | 465 | 164 | 41 | 5 | 16 | (7 | 9) | 263 | 114 | 75 | 69 | 2 | 67 | 2 | 5 | 1 | 45 | 10 | .82 | 4 | .353 | .438 | .566 |
| 1988 Milwaukee | AL | 154 | 609 | 190 | 34 | 6 | 13 | (9 | 4) | 275 | 115 | 60 | 71 | 8 | 54 | 2 | 5 | 3 | 41 | 10 | .80 | 10 | .312 | .384 | .452 |
| 1989 Milwaukee | AL | 155 | 615 | 194 | 35 | 4 | 11 | (6 | 5) | 270 | 84 | 56 | 64 | 4 | 67 | 4 | 4 | 9 | 27 | 11 | .71 | 11 | .315 | .379 | .439 |
| 1990 Milwaukee | AL | 103 | 418 | 119 | 27 | 6 | 12 | (6 | 6) | 194 | 64 | 45 | 37 | 4 | 51 | 1 | 0 | 2 | 18 | 3 | .86 | 7 | .285 | .343 | .464 |
| 13 ML YEARS | | 1540 | 6246 | 1870 | 337 | 66 | 131 | (67 | 64) | 2732 | 1053 | 626 | 605 | 41 | 754 | 25 | 64 | 49 | 362 | 101 | .78 | 101 | .299 | .361 | .437 |

## Rich Monteleone

**Pitches:** Right **Bats:** Right **Pos:** RP **Ht:** 6' 2" **Wt:** 217 **Born:** 03/22/63 **Age:** 28

| | | HOW MUCH HE PITCHED | | | | | | WHAT HE GAVE UP | | | | | | | | | | | | THE RESULTS | | | | | |
|---|---|---|---|---|---|---|---|---|---|---|---|---|---|---|---|---|---|---|---|---|---|---|---|---|---|
| Year Team | Lg | G | GS | CG | GF | IP | BFP | H | R | ER | HR | SH | SF | HB | TBB | IBB | SO | WP | Bk | W | L | Pct. | ShO | Sv | ERA |
| 1987 Seattle | AL | 3 | 0 | 0 | 1 | 7 | 34 | 10 | 5 | 5 | 2 | 0 | 0 | 1 | 4 | 0 | 2 | 0 | 0 | 0 | 0 | .000 | 0 | 0 | 6.43 |
| 1988 California | AL | 3 | 0 | 0 | 2 | 4.1 | 20 | 4 | 0 | 0 | 0 | 0 | 0 | 1 | 1 | 1 | 3 | 0 | 1 | 0 | 0 | .000 | 0 | 0 | 0.00 |
| 1989 California | AL | 24 | 0 | 0 | 8 | 39.2 | 170 | 39 | 15 | 14 | 3 | 1 | 2 | 1 | 13 | 1 | 27 | 2 | 0 | 2 | 2 | .500 | 0 | 0 | 3.18 |
| 1990 New York | AL | 5 | 0 | 0 | 2 | 7.1 | 31 | 8 | 5 | 5 | 0 | 0 | 0 | 0 | 2 | 0 | 8 | 0 | 0 | 0 | 1 | .000 | 0 | 0 | 6.14 |
| 4 ML YEARS | | 35 | 0 | 0 | 13 | 58.1 | 255 | 61 | 25 | 24 | 5 | 1 | 2 | 3 | 20 | 2 | 40 | 2 | 1 | 2 | 3 | .400 | 0 | 0 | 3.70 |

## Jeff Montgomery

**Pitches:** Right **Bats:** Right **Pos:** RP **Ht:** 5'11" **Wt:** 180 **Born:** 01/07/62 **Age:** 29

| | | HOW MUCH HE PITCHED | | | | | | WHAT HE GAVE UP | | | | | | | | | | | | THE RESULTS | | | | | |
|---|---|---|---|---|---|---|---|---|---|---|---|---|---|---|---|---|---|---|---|---|---|---|---|---|---|
| Year Team | Lg | G | GS | CG | GF | IP | BFP | H | R | ER | HR | SH | SF | HB | TBB | IBB | SO | WP | Bk | W | L | Pct. | ShO | Sv | ERA |
| 1987 Cincinnati | NL | 14 | 1 | 0 | 6 | 19.1 | 89 | 25 | 15 | 14 | 2 | 0 | 0 | 0 | 9 | 1 | 13 | 1 | 1 | 2 | 2 | .500 | 0 | 0 | 6.52 |
| 1988 Kansas City | AL | 45 | 0 | 0 | 13 | 62.2 | 271 | 54 | 25 | 24 | 6 | 3 | 2 | 2 | 30 | 1 | 47 | 3 | 6 | 7 | 2 | .778 | 0 | 1 | 3.45 |
| 1989 Kansas City | AL | 63 | 0 | 0 | 39 | 92 | 363 | 66 | 16 | 14 | 3 | 1 | 1 | 2 | 25 | 4 | 94 | 6 | 1 | 7 | 3 | .700 | 0 | 18 | 1.37 |
| 1990 Kansas City | AL | 73 | 0 | 0 | 59 | 94.1 | 400 | 81 | 36 | 25 | 6 | 2 | 2 | 5 | 34 | 8 | 94 | 3 | 0 | 6 | 5 | .545 | 0 | 24 | 2.39 |
| 4 ML YEARS | | 195 | 1 | 0 | 117 | 268.1 | 1123 | 226 | 92 | 77 | 17 | 6 | 5 | 9 | 98 | 14 | 248 | 13 | 8 | 22 | 12 | .647 | 0 | 43 | 2.58 |

## Brad Moore

**Pitches:** Right **Bats:** Right **Pos:** RP **Ht:** 6' 1" **Wt:** 185 **Born:** 06/21/64 **Age:** 27

| | | HOW MUCH HE PITCHED | | | | | | WHAT HE GAVE UP | | | | | | | | | | | | THE RESULTS | | | | | |
|---|---|---|---|---|---|---|---|---|---|---|---|---|---|---|---|---|---|---|---|---|---|---|---|---|---|
| Year Team | Lg | G | GS | CG | GF | IP | BFP | H | R | ER | HR | SH | SF | HB | TBB | IBB | SO | WP | Bk | W | L | Pct. | ShO | Sv | ERA |
| 1988 Philadelphia | NL | 5 | 0 | 0 | 2 | 5.2 | 21 | 4 | 0 | 0 | 0 | 2 | 0 | 0 | 4 | 1 | 2 | 0 | 0 | 0 | 0 | .000 | 0 | 0 | 0.00 |
| 1990 Philadelphia | NL | 3 | 0 | 0 | 3 | 2.2 | 13 | 4 | 1 | 1 | 0 | 0 | 1 | 0 | 2 | 1 | 1 | 1 | 0 | 0 | 0 | .000 | 0 | 0 | 3.38 |
| 2 ML YEARS | | 8 | 0 | 0 | 5 | 8.1 | 34 | 8 | 1 | 1 | 0 | 2 | 1 | 0 | 6 | 2 | 3 | 1 | 0 | 0 | 0 | .000 | 0 | 0 | 1.08 |

## Mike Moore

**Pitches:** Right **Bats:** Right **Pos:** SP **Ht:** 6' 4" **Wt:** 205 **Born:** 11/26/59 **Age:** 31

| | | HOW MUCH HE PITCHED | | | | | | WHAT HE GAVE UP | | | | | | | | | | | | THE RESULTS | | | | | |
|---|---|---|---|---|---|---|---|---|---|---|---|---|---|---|---|---|---|---|---|---|---|---|---|---|---|
| Year Team | Lg | G | GS | CG | GF | IP | BFP | H | R | ER | HR | SH | SF | HB | TBB | IBB | SO | WP | Bk | W | L | Pct. | ShO | Sv | ERA |
| 1982 Seattle | AL | 28 | 27 | 1 | 0 | 144.1 | 651 | 159 | 91 | 86 | 21 | 8 | 4 | 2 | 79 | 0 | 73 | 6 | 0 | 7 | 14 | .333 | 1 | 0 | 5.36 |
| 1983 Seattle | AL | 22 | 21 | 3 | 1 | 128 | 556 | 130 | 75 | 67 | 10 | 1 | 6 | 3 | 60 | 4 | 108 | 7 | 0 | 6 | 8 | .429 | 2 | 0 | 4.71 |
| 1984 Seattle | AL | 34 | 33 | 6 | 0 | 212 | 937 | 236 | 127 | 117 | 16 | 5 | 6 | 5 | 85 | 10 | 158 | 7 | 2 | 7 | 17 | .292 | 0 | 0 | 4.97 |
| 1985 Seattle | AL | 35 | 34 | 14 | 1 | 247 | 1016 | 230 | 100 | 95 | 18 | 2 | 7 | 4 | 70 | 2 | 155 | 10 | 3 | 17 | 10 | .630 | 2 | 0 | 3.46 |
| 1986 Seattle | AL | 38 | 37 | 11 | 1 | 266 | 1145 | 279 | 141 | 127 | 28 | 10 | 6 | 12 | 94 | 6 | 146 | 4 | 1 | 11 | 13 | .458 | 1 | 1 | 4.30 |
| 1987 Seattle | AL | 33 | 33 | 12 | 0 | 231 | 1020 | 268 | 145 | 121 | 29 | 9 | 8 | 0 | 84 | 3 | 115 | 4 | 2 | 9 | 19 | .321 | 0 | 0 | 4.71 |
| 1988 Seattle | AL | 37 | 32 | 9 | 3 | 228.2 | 918 | 196 | 104 | 96 | 24 | 3 | 3 | 3 | 63 | 6 | 182 | 4 | 3 | 9 | 15 | .375 | 3 | 1 | 3.78 |
| 1989 Oakland | AL | 35 | 35 | 6 | 0 | 241.2 | 976 | 193 | 82 | 70 | 14 | 5 | 6 | 2 | 83 | 1 | 172 | 17 | 0 | 19 | 11 | .633 | 3 | 0 | 2.61 |
| 1990 Oakland | AL | 33 | 33 | 3 | 0 | 199.1 | 862 | 204 | 113 | 103 | 14 | 4 | 7 | 3 | 84 | 2 | 73 | 13 | 0 | 13 | 15 | .464 | 0 | 0 | 4.65 |
| 9 ML YEARS | | 295 | 285 | 65 | 6 | 1898 | 8081 | 1895 | 978 | 882 | 174 | 47 | 53 | 34 | 702 | 34 | 1182 | 72 | 11 | 98 | 122 | .445 | 12 | 2 | 4.18 |

## Mickey Morandini

**Bats:** Left **Throws:** Right **Pos:** 2B **Ht:** 5'11" **Wt:** 170 **Born:** 04/22/66 **Age:** 25

| | | BATTING | | | | | | | | | | | | | | | | | BASERUNNING | | | | PERCENTAGES | | |
|---|---|---|---|---|---|---|---|---|---|---|---|---|---|---|---|---|---|---|---|---|---|---|---|---|---|
| Year Team | Lg | G | AB | H | 2B | 3B | HR | (Hm | Rd) | TB | R | RBI | TBB | IBB | SO | HBP | SH | SF | SB | CS | SB% | GDP | Avg | OBP | SLG |
| 1989 Spartanburg | A | 63 | 231 | 78 | 19 | 1 | 1 | -- | -- | 102 | 43 | 30 | 35 | 0 | 45 | 3 | 4 | 2 | 18 | 9 | .67 | 3 | .338 | .428 | .442 |
| Clearwater | A | 17 | 63 | 19 | 4 | 1 | 0 | -- | -- | 25 | 14 | 4 | 7 | 1 | 8 | 1 | 0 | 1 | 3 | 1 | .75 | 0 | .302 | .375 | .397 |
| Reading | AA | 48 | 188 | 66 | 12 | 1 | 5 | -- | -- | 95 | 39 | 29 | 23 | 4 | 32 | 1 | 1 | 0 | 5 | 5 | .50 | 2 | .351 | .425 | .505 |
| 1990 Scr Wil-Bar | AAA | 138 | 502 | 131 | 24 | 10 | 1 | -- | -- | 178 | 77 | 31 | 60 | 0 | 90 | 5 | 10 | 0 | 16 | 6 | .73 | 11 | .261 | .346 | .355 |
| 1990 Philadelphia | NL | 25 | 79 | 19 | 4 | 0 | 1 | (1 | 0) | 26 | 9 | 3 | 6 | 0 | 19 | 0 | 2 | 0 | 3 | 0 | 1.00 | 1 | .241 | .294 | .329 |

## Mike Morgan

**Pitches:** Right **Bats:** Right **Pos:** SP **Ht:** 6' 2" **Wt:** 215 **Born:** 10/08/59 **Age:** 31

| | | HOW MUCH HE PITCHED | | | | | | WHAT HE GAVE UP | | | | | | | | | | | | THE RESULTS | | | | | |
|---|---|---|---|---|---|---|---|---|---|---|---|---|---|---|---|---|---|---|---|---|---|---|---|---|---|
| Year Team | Lg | G | GS | CG | GF | IP | BFP | H | R | ER | HR | SH | SF | HB | TBB | IBB | SO | WP | Bk | W | L | Pct. | ShO | Sv | ERA |
| 1978 Oakland | AL | 3 | 3 | 1 | 0 | 12 | 60 | 19 | 12 | 10 | 1 | 1 | 0 | 0 | 8 | 0 | 0 | 0 | 0 | 0 | 3 | .000 | 0 | 0 | 7.50 |
| 1979 Oakland | AL | 13 | 13 | 2 | 0 | 77 | 368 | 102 | 57 | 51 | 7 | 4 | 4 | 3 | 50 | 0 | 17 | 7 | 0 | 2 | 10 | .167 | 0 | 0 | 5.96 |
| 1982 New York | AL | 30 | 23 | 2 | 2 | 150.1 | 661 | 167 | 77 | 73 | 15 | 2 | 4 | 2 | 67 | 5 | 71 | 6 | 0 | 7 | 11 | .389 | 0 | 0 | 4.37 |
| 1983 Toronto | AL | 16 | 4 | 0 | 2 | 45.1 | 198 | 48 | 26 | 26 | 6 | 0 | 1 | 0 | 21 | 0 | 22 | 3 | 0 | 0 | 3 | .000 | 0 | 0 | 5.16 |
| 1985 Seattle | AL | 2 | 2 | 0 | 0 | 6 | 33 | 11 | 8 | 8 | 2 | 0 | 0 | 0 | 5 | 0 | 2 | 1 | 0 | 1 | 1 | .500 | 0 | 0 | 12.00 |
| 1986 Seattle | AL | 37 | 33 | 9 | 2 | 216.1 | 951 | 243 | 122 | 109 | 24 | 7 | 3 | 4 | 86 | 3 | 116 | 8 | 1 | 11 | 17 | .393 | 1 | 1 | 4.53 |
| 1987 Seattle | AL | 34 | 31 | 8 | 2 | 207 | 898 | 245 | 117 | 107 | 25 | 8 | 5 | 5 | 53 | 3 | 85 | 11 | 0 | 12 | 17 | .414 | 2 | 0 | 4.65 |
| 1988 Baltimore | AL | 22 | 10 | 2 | 6 | 71.1 | 299 | 70 | 45 | 43 | 6 | 1 | 0 | 1 | 23 | 1 | 29 | 5 | 0 | 1 | 6 | .143 | 0 | 1 | 5.43 |

| Year Team | Lg | G | GS | CG | GF | IP | BFP | H | R | ER | HR | SH | SF | HB | TBB | IBB | SO | WP | Bk | W | L | Pct. | ShO | Sv | ERA |
|---|---|---|---|---|---|---|---|---|---|---|---|---|---|---|---|---|---|---|---|---|---|---|---|---|---|
| 1989 Los Angeles | NL | 40 | 19 | 0 | 7 | 152.2 | 604 | 130 | 51 | 43 | 6 | 8 | 6 | 2 | 33 | 8 | 72 | 6 | 0 | 8 | 11 | .421 | 0 | 0 | 2.53 |
| 1990 Los Angeles | NL | 33 | 33 | 6 | 0 | 211 | 891 | 216 | 100 | 88 | 19 | 11 | 4 | 5 | 60 | 5 | 106 | 4 | 1 | 11 | 15 | .423 | 4 | 0 | 3.75 |
| 10 ML YEARS | | 230 | 171 | 30 | 21 | 1149 | 4963 | 1251 | 615 | 558 | 111 | 42 | 27 | 22 | 406 | 25 | 520 | 51 | 2 | 53 | 94 | .361 | 7 | 2 | 4.37 |

## Russ Morman

**Bats:** Right **Throws:** Right **Pos:** LF **Ht:** 6' 4" **Wt:** 215 **Born:** 04/28/62 **Age:** 29

| | | BATTING | | | | | | | | | | | | | | | | BASERUNNING | | | | PERCENTAGES | | |
|---|---|---|---|---|---|---|---|---|---|---|---|---|---|---|---|---|---|---|---|---|---|---|---|---|
| Year Team | Lg | G | AB | H | 2B | 3B | HR | (Hm | Rd) | TB | R | RBI | TBB | IBB | SO | HBP | SH | SF | SB | CS | SB% | GDP | Avg | OBP | SLG |
| 1986 Chicago | AL | 49 | 159 | 40 | 5 | 0 | 4 | (1 | 3) | 57 | 18 | 17 | 16 | 0 | 36 | 2 | 1 | 2 | 1 | 0 | 1.00 | 5 | .252 | .324 | .358 |
| 1988 Chicago | AL | 40 | 75 | 18 | 2 | 0 | 0 | (0 | 0) | 20 | 8 | 3 | 3 | 0 | 17 | 0 | 2 | 0 | 0 | 0 | .00 | 5 | .240 | .269 | .267 |
| 1989 Chicago | AL | 37 | 58 | 13 | 2 | 0 | 0 | (0 | 0) | 15 | 5 | 8 | 6 | 1 | 16 | 0 | 2 | 1 | 1 | 0 | 1.00 | 1 | .224 | .292 | .259 |
| 1990 Kansas City | AL | 12 | 37 | 10 | 4 | 2 | 1 | (0 | 1) | 21 | 5 | 3 | 3 | 0 | 3 | 0 | 0 | 1 | 0 | 0 | .00 | 0 | .270 | .317 | .568 |
| 4 ML YEARS | | 138 | 329 | 81 | 13 | 2 | 5 | (1 | 4) | 113 | 36 | 31 | 28 | 1 | 72 | 2 | 5 | 4 | 2 | 0 | 1.00 | 11 | .246 | .306 | .343 |

## Hal Morris

**Bats:** Left **Throws:** Left **Pos:** 1B **Ht:** 6' 4" **Wt:** 200 **Born:** 04/09/65 **Age:** 26

| | | BATTING | | | | | | | | | | | | | | | | BASERUNNING | | | | PERCENTAGES | | |
|---|---|---|---|---|---|---|---|---|---|---|---|---|---|---|---|---|---|---|---|---|---|---|---|---|
| Year Team | Lg | G | AB | H | 2B | 3B | HR | (Hm | Rd) | TB | R | RBI | TBB | IBB | SO | HBP | SH | SF | SB | CS | SB% | GDP | Avg | OBP | SLG |
| 1988 New York | AL | 15 | 20 | 2 | 0 | 0 | 0 | (0 | 0) | 2 | 1 | 0 | 0 | 0 | 9 | 0 | 0 | 0 | 0 | 0 | .00 | 0 | .100 | .100 | .100 |
| 1989 New York | AL | 15 | 18 | 5 | 0 | 0 | 0 | (0 | 0) | 5 | 2 | 4 | 1 | 0 | 4 | 0 | 0 | 0 | 0 | 0 | .00 | 2 | .278 | .316 | .278 |
| 1990 Cincinnati | NL | 107 | 309 | 105 | 22 | 3 | 7 | (3 | 4) | 154 | 50 | 36 | 21 | 4 | 32 | 1 | 3 | 2 | 9 | 3 | .75 | 12 | .340 | .381 | .498 |
| 3 ML YEARS | | 137 | 347 | 112 | 22 | 3 | 7 | (3 | 4) | 161 | 53 | 40 | 22 | 4 | 45 | 1 | 3 | 2 | 9 | 3 | .75 | 14 | .323 | .363 | .464 |

## Jack Morris

**Pitches:** Right **Bats:** Right **Pos:** SP **Ht:** 6' 3" **Wt:** 200 **Born:** 05/16/55 **Age:** 36

| | | HOW MUCH HE PITCHED | | | | | | WHAT HE GAVE UP | | | | | | | | | | | | THE RESULTS | | | | | |
|---|---|---|---|---|---|---|---|---|---|---|---|---|---|---|---|---|---|---|---|---|---|---|---|---|---|
| Year Team | Lg | G | GS | CG | GF | IP | BFP | H | R | ER | HR | SH | SF | HB | TBB | IBB | SO | WP | Bk | W | L | Pct. | ShO | Sv | ERA |
| 1977 Detroit | AL | 7 | 6 | 1 | 0 | 46 | 189 | 38 | 20 | 19 | 4 | 3 | 1 | 0 | 23 | 0 | 28 | 2 | 0 | 1 | 1 | .500 | 0 | 0 | 3.72 |
| 1978 Detroit | AL | 28 | 7 | 0 | 10 | 106 | 469 | 107 | 57 | 51 | 8 | 8 | 9 | 3 | 49 | 5 | 48 | 4 | 0 | 3 | 5 | .375 | 0 | 0 | 4.33 |
| 1979 Detroit | AL | 27 | 27 | 9 | 0 | 198 | 806 | 179 | 76 | 72 | 19 | 3 | 6 | 4 | 59 | 4 | 113 | 9 | 1 | 17 | 7 | .708 | 1 | 0 | 3.27 |
| 1980 Detroit | AL | 36 | 36 | 11 | 0 | 250 | 1074 | 252 | 125 | 116 | 20 | 10 | 13 | 4 | 87 | 5 | 112 | 6 | 2 | 16 | 15 | .516 | 2 | 0 | 4.18 |
| 1981 Detroit | AL | 25 | 25 | 15 | 0 | 198 | 798 | 153 | 69 | 67 | 14 | 8 | 9 | 2 | 78 | 11 | 97 | 2 | 2 | 14 | 7 | .667 | 1 | 0 | 3.05 |
| 1982 Detroit | AL | 37 | 37 | 17 | 0 | 266.1 | 1107 | 247 | 131 | 120 | 37 | 4 | 5 | 0 | 96 | 7 | 135 | 10 | 0 | 17 | 16 | .515 | 3 | 0 | 4.06 |
| 1983 Detroit | AL | 37 | 37 | 20 | 0 | 293.2 | 1204 | 257 | 117 | 109 | 30 | 8 | 9 | 3 | 83 | 5 | 232 | 18 | 0 | 20 | 13 | .606 | 1 | 0 | 3.34 |
| 1984 Detroit | AL | 35 | 35 | 9 | 0 | 240.1 | 1015 | 221 | 108 | 96 | 20 | 5 | 3 | 2 | 87 | 7 | 148 | 14 | 0 | 19 | 11 | .633 | 1 | 0 | 3.60 |
| 1985 Detroit | AL | 35 | 35 | 13 | 0 | 257 | 1077 | 212 | 102 | 95 | 21 | 11 | 7 | 5 | 110 | 7 | 191 | 15 | 3 | 16 | 11 | .593 | 4 | 0 | 3.33 |
| 1986 Detroit | AL | 35 | 35 | 15 | 0 | 267 | 1092 | 229 | 105 | 97 | 40 | 7 | 3 | 0 | 82 | 7 | 223 | 12 | 0 | 21 | 8 | .724 | 6 | 0 | 3.27 |
| 1987 Detroit | AL | 34 | 34 | 13 | 0 | 266 | 1101 | 227 | 111 | 100 | 39 | 6 | 5 | 1 | 93 | 7 | 208 | 24 | 1 | 18 | 11 | .621 | 0 | 0 | 3.38 |
| 1988 Detroit | AL | 34 | 34 | 10 | 0 | 235 | 997 | 225 | 115 | 103 | 20 | 12 | 3 | 4 | 83 | 7 | 168 | 11 | 11 | 15 | 13 | .536 | 2 | 0 | 3.94 |
| 1989 Detroit | AL | 24 | 24 | 10 | 0 | 170.1 | 743 | 189 | 102 | 92 | 23 | 6 | 7 | 2 | 59 | 3 | 115 | 12 | 1 | 6 | 14 | .300 | 0 | 0 | 4.86 |
| 1990 Detroit | AL | 36 | 36 | 11 | 0 | 249.2 | 1073 | 231 | 144 | 125 | 26 | 7 | 10 | 6 | 97 | 13 | 162 | 16 | 2 | 15 | 18 | .455 | 3 | 0 | 4.51 |
| 14 ML YEARS | | 430 | 408 | 154 | 10 | 3043.1 | 12745 | 2767 | 1382 | 1262 | 321 | 98 | 90 | 36 | 1086 | 88 | 1980 | 155 | 23 | 198 | 150 | .569 | 24 | 0 | 3.73 |

## John Morris

**Bats:** Left **Throws:** Left **Pos:** RF **Ht:** 6' 1" **Wt:** 185 **Born:** 02/23/61 **Age:** 30

| | | BATTING | | | | | | | | | | | | | | | | BASERUNNING | | | | PERCENTAGES | | |
|---|---|---|---|---|---|---|---|---|---|---|---|---|---|---|---|---|---|---|---|---|---|---|---|---|
| Year Team | Lg | G | AB | H | 2B | 3B | HR | (Hm | Rd) | TB | R | RBI | TBB | IBB | SO | HBP | SH | SF | SB | CS | SB% | GDP | Avg | OBP | SLG |
| 1986 St. Louis | NL | 39 | 100 | 24 | 0 | 1 | 1 | (1 | 0) | 29 | 8 | 14 | 7 | 2 | 15 | 0 | 0 | 1 | 6 | 2 | .75 | 2 | .240 | .287 | .290 |
| 1987 St. Louis | NL | 101 | 157 | 41 | 6 | 4 | 3 | (1 | 2) | 64 | 22 | 23 | 11 | 4 | 22 | 1 | 1 | 0 | 5 | 2 | .71 | 2 | .261 | .314 | .408 |
| 1988 St. Louis | NL | 20 | 38 | 11 | 2 | 1 | 0 | (0 | 0) | 15 | 3 | 3 | 1 | 0 | 7 | 0 | 0 | 0 | 0 | 0 | .00 | 0 | .289 | .308 | .395 |
| 1989 St. Louis | NL | 96 | 117 | 28 | 4 | 1 | 2 | (2 | 0) | 40 | 8 | 14 | 4 | 0 | 22 | 0 | 3 | 0 | 1 | 0 | 1.00 | 4 | .239 | .264 | .342 |
| 1990 St. Louis | NL | 18 | 18 | 2 | 0 | 0 | 0 | (0 | 0) | 2 | 0 | 0 | 3 | 0 | 6 | 0 | 0 | 0 | 0 | 0 | .00 | 0 | .111 | .238 | .111 |
| 5 ML YEARS | | 274 | 430 | 106 | 12 | 7 | 6 | (4 | 2) | 150 | 41 | 54 | 26 | 6 | 72 | 1 | 4 | 1 | 12 | 4 | .75 | 8 | .247 | .290 | .349 |

## Lloyd Moseby

**Bats:** Left **Throws:** Right **Pos:** CF/LF **Ht:** 6' 3" **Wt:** 200 **Born:** 11/05/59 **Age:** 31

| | | BATTING | | | | | | | | | | | | | | | | BASERUNNING | | | | PERCENTAGES | | |
|---|---|---|---|---|---|---|---|---|---|---|---|---|---|---|---|---|---|---|---|---|---|---|---|---|
| Year Team | Lg | G | AB | H | 2B | 3B | HR | (Hm | Rd) | TB | R | RBI | TBB | IBB | SO | HBP | SH | SF | SB | CS | SB% | GDP | Avg | OBP | SLG |
| 1980 Toronto | AL | 114 | 389 | 89 | 24 | 1 | 9 | (4 | 5) | 142 | 44 | 46 | 25 | 4 | 85 | 4 | 10 | 2 | 4 | 6 | .40 | 11 | .229 | .281 | .365 |
| 1981 Toronto | AL | 100 | 378 | 88 | 16 | 2 | 9 | (3 | 6) | 135 | 36 | 43 | 24 | 3 | 86 | 1 | 5 | 4 | 11 | 8 | .58 | 4 | .233 | .278 | .357 |
| 1982 Toronto | AL | 147 | 487 | 115 | 20 | 9 | 9 | (4 | 5) | 180 | 51 | 52 | 33 | 3 | 106 | 8 | 3 | 2 | 11 | 7 | .61 | 10 | .236 | .294 | .370 |
| 1983 Toronto | AL | 151 | 539 | 170 | 31 | 7 | 18 | (13 | 5) | 269 | 104 | 81 | 51 | 4 | 85 | 5 | 3 | 6 | 27 | 8 | .77 | 10 | .315 | .376 | .499 |
| 1984 Toronto | AL | 158 | 592 | 166 | 28 | 15 | 18 | (10 | 8) | 278 | 97 | 92 | 78 | 9 | 122 | 8 | 3 | 7 | 39 | 9 | .81 | 8 | .280 | .368 | .470 |
| 1985 Toronto | AL | 152 | 584 | 151 | 30 | 7 | 18 | (11 | 7) | 249 | 92 | 70 | 76 | 4 | 91 | 4 | 1 | 5 | 37 | 15 | .71 | 12 | .259 | .345 | .426 |
| 1986 Toronto | AL | 152 | 589 | 149 | 24 | 5 | 21 | (11 | 10) | 246 | 89 | 86 | 64 | 3 | 122 | 6 | 2 | 7 | 32 | 11 | .74 | 7 | .253 | .329 | .418 |
| 1987 Toronto | AL | 155 | 592 | 167 | 27 | 4 | 26 | (15 | 11) | 280 | 106 | 96 | 70 | 4 | 124 | 2 | 3 | 3 | 39 | 7 | .85 | 11 | .282 | .358 | .473 |
| 1988 Toronto | AL | 128 | 472 | 113 | 17 | 7 | 10 | (2 | 8) | 174 | 77 | 42 | 70 | 6 | 93 | 6 | 1 | 3 | 31 | 8 | .79 | 8 | .239 | .343 | .369 |

| Year Team | Lg | G | AB | H | 2B | 3B | HR | (Hm | Rd) | TB | R | RBI | TBB | IBB | SO | HBP | SH | SF | SB | CS | SB% | GDP | Avg | OBP | SLG |
|---|---|---|---|---|---|---|---|---|---|---|---|---|---|---|---|---|---|---|---|---|---|---|---|---|---|
| 1989 Toronto | AL | 135 | 502 | 111 | 25 | 3 | 11 | (4 | 7) | 175 | 72 | 43 | 56 | 1 | 101 | 6 | 7 | 1 | 24 | 7 | .77 | 7 | .221 | .306 | .349 |
| 1990 Detroit | AL | 122 | 431 | 107 | 16 | 5 | 14 | (8 | 6) | 175 | 64 | 51 | 48 | 3 | 77 | 5 | 1 | 2 | 17 | 5 | .77 | 15 | .248 | .329 | .406 |
| 11 ML YEARS | | 1514 | 5555 | 1426 | 258 | 65 | 163 | (85 | 78) | 2303 | 832 | 702 | 595 | 44 | 1092 | 55 | 39 | 42 | 272 | 91 | .75 | 103 | .257 | .332 | .415 |

## John Moses

**Bats:** Both **Throws:** Left **Pos:** RF/LF/CF **Ht:** 5'10" **Wt:** 170 **Born:** 08/09/57 **Age:** 33

| BATTING | | | | | | | | | | | | | | | | | | | BASERUNNING | | | | PERCENTAGES | | |
|---|---|---|---|---|---|---|---|---|---|---|---|---|---|---|---|---|---|---|---|---|---|---|---|---|---|
| Year Team | Lg | G | AB | H | 2B | 3B | HR | (Hm | Rd) | TB | R | RBI | TBB | IBB | SO | HBP | SH | SF | SB | CS | SB% | GDP | Avg | OBP | SLG |
| 1982 Seattle | AL | 22 | 44 | 14 | 5 | 1 | 1 | (1 | 0) | 24 | 7 | 3 | 4 | 0 | 5 | 0 | 0 | 0 | 5 | 1 | .83 | 0 | .318 | .375 | .545 |
| 1983 Seattle | AL | 93 | 130 | 27 | 4 | 1 | 0 | (0 | 0) | 33 | 19 | 6 | 12 | 0 | 20 | 1 | 0 | 0 | 11 | 5 | .69 | 4 | .208 | .280 | .254 |
| 1984 Seattle | AL | 19 | 35 | 12 | 1 | 1 | 0 | (0 | 0) | 15 | 3 | 2 | 2 | 0 | 5 | 1 | 1 | 0 | 1 | 0 | 1.00 | 0 | .343 | .395 | .429 |
| 1985 Seattle | AL | 33 | 62 | 12 | 0 | 0 | 0 | (0 | 0) | 12 | 4 | 3 | 2 | 0 | 8 | 0 | 1 | 0 | 5 | 2 | .71 | 3 | .194 | .219 | .194 |
| 1986 Seattle | AL | 103 | 399 | 102 | 16 | 3 | 3 | (2 | 1) | 133 | 56 | 34 | 34 | 3 | 65 | 0 | 5 | 4 | 25 | 18 | .58 | 7 | .256 | .311 | .333 |
| 1987 Seattle | AL | 116 | 390 | 96 | 16 | 4 | 3 | (2 | 1) | 129 | 58 | 38 | 29 | 2 | 49 | 3 | 8 | 3 | 23 | 15 | .61 | 6 | .246 | .301 | .331 |
| 1988 Minnesota | AL | 105 | 206 | 65 | 10 | 3 | 2 | (0 | 2) | 87 | 33 | 12 | 15 | 2 | 21 | 2 | 1 | 1 | 11 | 6 | .65 | 4 | .316 | .366 | .422 |
| 1989 Minnesota | AL | 129 | 242 | 68 | 12 | 3 | 1 | (0 | 1) | 89 | 33 | 31 | 19 | 1 | 23 | 1 | 3 | 2 | 14 | 7 | .67 | 5 | .281 | .333 | .368 |
| 1990 Minnesota | AL | 115 | 172 | 38 | 3 | 1 | 1 | (0 | 1) | 46 | 26 | 14 | 19 | 1 | 19 | 2 | 0 | 2 | 2 | 3 | .40 | 4 | .221 | .303 | .267 |
| 9 ML YEARS | | 735 | 1680 | 434 | 67 | 17 | 11 | (5 | 6) | 568 | 239 | 143 | 136 | 9 | 215 | 10 | 19 | 12 | 97 | 57 | .63 | 33 | .258 | .316 | .338 |

## Jamie Moyer

**Pitches:** Left **Bats:** Left **Pos:** RP/SP **Ht:** 6' 0" **Wt:** 170 **Born:** 11/18/62 **Age:** 28

| HOW MUCH HE PITCHED | | | | | | | | WHAT HE GAVE UP | | | | | | | | | | | | THE RESULTS | | | | | |
|---|---|---|---|---|---|---|---|---|---|---|---|---|---|---|---|---|---|---|---|---|---|---|---|---|---|
| Year Team | Lg | G | GS | CG | GF | IP | BFP | H | R | ER | HR | SH | SF | HB | TBB | IBB | SO | WP | Bk | W | L | Pct. | ShO | Sv | ERA |
| 1986 Chicago | NL | 16 | 16 | 1 | 0 | 87.1 | 395 | 107 | 52 | 49 | 10 | 3 | 3 | 3 | 42 | 1 | 45 | 3 | 3 | 7 | 4 | .636 | 1 | 0 | 5.05 |
| 1987 Chicago | NL | 35 | 33 | 1 | 1 | 201 | 899 | 210 | 127 | 114 | 28 | 14 | 7 | 5 | 97 | 9 | 147 | 11 | 2 | 12 | 15 | .444 | 0 | 0 | 5.10 |
| 1988 Chicago | NL | 34 | 30 | 3 | 1 | 202 | 855 | 212 | 84 | 78 | 20 | 14 | 4 | 4 | 55 | 7 | 121 | 4 | 0 | 9 | 15 | .375 | 1 | 0 | 3.48 |
| 1989 Texas | AL | 15 | 15 | 1 | 0 | 76 | 337 | 84 | 51 | 41 | 10 | 1 | 4 | 2 | 33 | 0 | 44 | 1 | 0 | 4 | 9 | .308 | 0 | 0 | 4.86 |
| 1990 Texas | AL | 33 | 10 | 1 | 6 | 102.1 | 447 | 115 | 59 | 53 | 6 | 1 | 7 | 4 | 39 | 4 | 58 | 1 | 0 | 2 | 6 | .250 | 0 | 0 | 4.66 |
| 5 ML YEARS | | 133 | 104 | 7 | 8 | 668.2 | 2933 | 728 | 373 | 335 | 74 | 33 | 25 | 18 | 266 | 21 | 415 | 20 | 5 | 34 | 49 | .410 | 2 | 0 | 4.51 |

## Terry Mulholland

**Pitches:** Left **Bats:** Right **Pos:** SP/RP **Ht:** 6' 3" **Wt:** 200 **Born:** 03/09/63 **Age:** 28

| HOW MUCH HE PITCHED | | | | | | | | WHAT HE GAVE UP | | | | | | | | | | | | THE RESULTS | | | | | |
|---|---|---|---|---|---|---|---|---|---|---|---|---|---|---|---|---|---|---|---|---|---|---|---|---|---|
| Year Team | Lg | G | GS | CG | GF | IP | BFP | H | R | ER | HR | SH | SF | HB | TBB | IBB | SO | WP | Bk | W | L | Pct. | ShO | Sv | ERA |
| 1986 San Francisco | NL | 15 | 10 | 0 | 1 | 54.2 | 245 | 51 | 33 | 30 | 3 | 5 | 1 | 1 | 35 | 2 | 27 | 6 | 0 | 1 | 7 | .125 | 0 | 0 | 4.94 |
| 1988 San Francisco | NL | 9 | 6 | 2 | 1 | 46 | 191 | 50 | 20 | 19 | 3 | 5 | 0 | 1 | 7 | 0 | 18 | 1 | 0 | 2 | 1 | .667 | 1 | 0 | 3.72 |
| 1989 2 ML Teams | | 25 | 18 | 2 | 4 | 115.1 | 513 | 137 | 66 | 63 | 8 | 7 | 1 | 4 | 36 | 3 | 66 | 3 | 0 | 4 | 7 | .364 | 1 | 0 | 4.92 |
| 1990 Philadelphia | NL | 33 | 26 | 6 | 2 | 180.2 | 746 | 172 | 78 | 67 | 15 | 7 | 12 | 2 | 42 | 7 | 75 | 7 | 2 | 9 | 10 | .474 | 1 | 0 | 3.34 |
| 1989 San Francisco | NL | 5 | 1 | 0 | 2 | 11 | 51 | 15 | 5 | 5 | 0 | 0 | 0 | 0 | 4 | 0 | 6 | 0 | 0 | 0 | 0 | .000 | 0 | 0 | 4.09 |
| Philadelphia | NL | 20 | 17 | 2 | 2 | 104.1 | 462 | 122 | 61 | 58 | 8 | 7 | 1 | 4 | 32 | 3 | 60 | 3 | 0 | 4 | 7 | .364 | 1 | 0 | 5.00 |
| 4 ML YEARS | | 82 | 60 | 10 | 8 | 396.2 | 1695 | 410 | 197 | 179 | 29 | 24 | 14 | 8 | 120 | 12 | 186 | 17 | 2 | 16 | 25 | .390 | 3 | 0 | 4.06 |

## Rance Mulliniks

**Bats:** Left **Throws:** Right **Pos:** 3B **Ht:** 6' 0" **Wt:** 175 **Born:** 01/15/56 **Age:** 35

| BATTING | | | | | | | | | | | | | | | | | | | BASERUNNING | | | | PERCENTAGES | | |
|---|---|---|---|---|---|---|---|---|---|---|---|---|---|---|---|---|---|---|---|---|---|---|---|---|---|
| Year Team | Lg | G | AB | H | 2B | 3B | HR | (Hm | Rd) | TB | R | RBI | TBB | IBB | SO | HBP | SH | SF | SB | CS | SB% | GDP | Avg | OBP | SLG |
| 1977 California | AL | 78 | 271 | 73 | 13 | 2 | 3 | (2 | 1) | 99 | 36 | 21 | 23 | 2 | 36 | 1 | 8 | 0 | 1 | 1 | .50 | 2 | .269 | .329 | .365 |
| 1978 California | AL | 50 | 119 | 22 | 3 | 1 | 1 | (1 | 0) | 30 | 6 | 6 | 8 | 0 | 23 | 1 | 0 | 2 | 2 | 0 | 1.00 | 3 | .185 | .238 | .252 |
| 1979 California | AL | 22 | 68 | 10 | 0 | 0 | 1 | (0 | 1) | 13 | 7 | 8 | 4 | 0 | 14 | 1 | 0 | 5 | 0 | 0 | .00 | 2 | .147 | .192 | .191 |
| 1980 Kansas City | AL | 36 | 54 | 14 | 3 | 0 | 0 | (0 | 0) | 17 | 8 | 6 | 7 | 0 | 10 | 0 | 0 | 1 | 0 | 0 | .00 | 2 | .259 | .339 | .315 |
| 1981 Kansas City | AL | 24 | 44 | 10 | 3 | 0 | 0 | (0 | 0) | 13 | 6 | 5 | 2 | 0 | 7 | 0 | 0 | 0 | 0 | 1 | .00 | 2 | .227 | .261 | .295 |
| 1982 Toronto | AL | 112 | 311 | 76 | 25 | 0 | 4 | (2 | 2) | 113 | 32 | 35 | 37 | 1 | 49 | 1 | 3 | 1 | 3 | 2 | .60 | 10 | .244 | .326 | .363 |
| 1983 Toronto | AL | 129 | 364 | 100 | 34 | 3 | 10 | (4 | 6) | 170 | 54 | 49 | 57 | 5 | 43 | 1 | 3 | 2 | 0 | 2 | .00 | 14 | .275 | .373 | .467 |
| 1984 Toronto | AL | 125 | 343 | 111 | 21 | 5 | 3 | (1 | 2) | 151 | 41 | 42 | 33 | 3 | 44 | 1 | 0 | 2 | 2 | 3 | .40 | 5 | .324 | .383 | .440 |
| 1985 Toronto | AL | 129 | 366 | 108 | 26 | 1 | 10 | (4 | 6) | 166 | 55 | 57 | 55 | 2 | 54 | 0 | 1 | 5 | 2 | 0 | 1.00 | 10 | .295 | .383 | .454 |
| 1986 Toronto | AL | 117 | 348 | 90 | 22 | 0 | 11 | (5 | 6) | 145 | 50 | 45 | 43 | 1 | 60 | 1 | 1 | 2 | 1 | 1 | .50 | 12 | .259 | .340 | .417 |
| 1987 Toronto | AL | 124 | 332 | 103 | 28 | 1 | 11 | (6 | 5) | 166 | 37 | 44 | 34 | 1 | 55 | 0 | 3 | 3 | 1 | 1 | .50 | 10 | .310 | .371 | .500 |
| 1988 Toronto | AL | 119 | 337 | 101 | 21 | 1 | 12 | (7 | 5) | 160 | 49 | 48 | 56 | 3 | 57 | 0 | 2 | 4 | 1 | 0 | 1.00 | 10 | .300 | .395 | .475 |
| 1989 Toronto | AL | 103 | 273 | 65 | 11 | 2 | 3 | (1 | 2) | 89 | 25 | 29 | 34 | 6 | 40 | 0 | 0 | 2 | 0 | 0 | .00 | 12 | .238 | .320 | .326 |
| 1990 Toronto | AL | 57 | 97 | 28 | 4 | 0 | 2 | (1 | 1) | 38 | 11 | 16 | 22 | 2 | 19 | 0 | 0 | 1 | 2 | 1 | .67 | 2 | .289 | .417 | .392 |
| 14 ML YEARS | | 1225 | 3327 | 911 | 214 | 16 | 71 | (34 | 37) | 1370 | 417 | 411 | 415 | 26 | 511 | 7 | 21 | 30 | 15 | 12 | .56 | 96 | .274 | .353 | .412 |

## Mike Munoz

**Pitches:** Left **Bats:** Left **Pos:** RP **Ht:** 6' 2" **Wt:** 190 **Born:** 07/12/65 **Age:** 25

| HOW MUCH HE PITCHED | | | | | | | | WHAT HE GAVE UP | | | | | | | | | | | | THE RESULTS | | | | | |
|---|---|---|---|---|---|---|---|---|---|---|---|---|---|---|---|---|---|---|---|---|---|---|---|---|---|
| Year Team | Lg | G | GS | CG | GF | IP | BFP | H | R | ER | HR | SH | SF | HB | TBB | IBB | SO | WP | Bk | W | L | Pct. | ShO | Sv | ERA |
| 1986 Great Falls | R | 14 | 14 | 2 | 0 | 81.1 | 0 | 85 | 44 | 29 | 4 | 0 | 0 | 1 | 38 | 0 | 49 | 3 | 0 | 4 | 4 | .500 | 2 | 0 | 3.21 |
| 1987 Bakersfield | A | 52 | 12 | 2 | 23 | 118 | 524 | 125 | 68 | 49 | 5 | 11 | 2 | 0 | 43 | 3 | 80 | 6 | 1 | 8 | 7 | .533 | 0 | 8 | 3.74 |
| 1988 San Antonio | AA | 56 | 0 | 0 | 35 | 71.2 | 302 | 63 | 18 | 8 | 0 | 5 | 1 | 1 | 24 | 1 | 71 | 6 | 0 | 7 | 2 | .778 | 0 | 14 | 1.00 |
| 1989 Albuquerque | AAA | 60 | 0 | 0 | 27 | 79 | 345 | 72 | 32 | 27 | 2 | 6 | 3 | 0 | 40 | 8 | 81 | 6 | 0 | 6 | 4 | .600 | 0 | 6 | 3.08 |
| 1990 Albuquerque | AAA | 49 | 0 | 0 | 14 | 59.1 | 258 | 65 | 33 | 28 | 8 | 4 | 2 | 0 | 19 | 3 | 40 | 3 | 1 | 4 | 1 | .800 | 0 | 6 | 4.25 |
| 1989 Los Angeles | NL | 3 | 0 | 0 | 1 | 2.2 | 14 | 5 | 5 | 5 | 1 | 0 | 0 | 0 | 2 | 0 | 3 | 0 | 0 | 0 | 0 | .000 | 0 | 0 | 16.88 |
| 1990 Los Angeles | NL | 8 | 0 | 0 | 3 | 5.2 | 24 | 6 | 2 | 2 | 0 | 1 | 0 | 0 | 3 | 0 | 2 | 0 | 0 | 0 | 1 | .000 | 0 | 0 | 3.18 |
| 2 ML YEARS | | 11 | 0 | 0 | 4 | 8.1 | 38 | 11 | 7 | 7 | 1 | 1 | 0 | 0 | 5 | 0 | 5 | 0 | 0 | 0 | 1 | .000 | 0 | 0 | 7.56 |

## Pedro Munoz

**Bats:** Right **Throws:** Right **Pos:** RF **Ht:** 5'11" **Wt:** 170 **Born:** 09/19/68 **Age:** 22

| BATTING | | | | | | | | | | | | | | | | | | | BASERUNNING | | | | PERCENTAGES | | |
|---|---|---|---|---|---|---|---|---|---|---|---|---|---|---|---|---|---|---|---|---|---|---|---|---|---|
| Year Team | Lg | G | AB | H | 2B | 3B | HR | (Hm | Rd) | TB | R | RBI | TBB | IBB | SO | HBP | SH | SF | SB | CS | SB% | GDP | Avg | OBP | SLG |
| 1985 Blue Jays | R | 40 | 145 | 38 | 3 | 0 | 2 | -- | -- | 47 | 14 | 17 | 9 | 0 | 20 | 4 | 1 | 1 | 4 | 1 | .80 | 4 | .262 | .321 | .324 |
| 1986 Florence | A | 122 | 445 | 131 | 16 | 5 | 14 | -- | -- | 199 | 69 | 82 | 54 | 4 | 100 | 5 | 2 | 2 | 9 | 5 | .64 | 12 | .294 | .375 | .447 |
| 1987 Dunedin | A | 92 | 341 | 80 | 11 | 5 | 8 | -- | -- | 125 | 55 | 44 | 34 | 0 | 74 | 2 | 1 | 4 | 13 | 4 | .76 | 7 | .235 | .304 | .367 |
| 1988 Dunedin | A | 133 | 481 | 141 | 21 | 7 | 8 | -- | -- | 200 | 59 | 73 | 52 | 5 | 87 | 4 | 0 | 7 | 15 | 4 | .79 | 23 | .293 | .362 | .416 |
| 1989 Knoxville | AA | 122 | 442 | 118 | 15 | 4 | 19 | -- | -- | 198 | 54 | 65 | 20 | 2 | 85 | 2 | 0 | 4 | 10 | 4 | .71 | 11 | .267 | .299 | .448 |
| 1990 Syracuse | AAA | 86 | 317 | 101 | 22 | 3 | 7 | -- | -- | 150 | 41 | 56 | 24 | 3 | 64 | 1 | 1 | 3 | 16 | 7 | .70 | 12 | .319 | .365 | .473 |
| Portland | AAA | 30 | 110 | 35 | 4 | 0 | 5 | -- | -- | 54 | 19 | 21 | 15 | 1 | 18 | 4 | 0 | 0 | 8 | 4 | .67 | 1 | .318 | .419 | .491 |
| 1990 Minnesota | AL | 22 | 85 | 23 | 4 | 1 | 0 | (0 | 0) | 29 | 13 | 5 | 2 | 0 | 16 | 0 | 1 | 2 | 3 | 0 | 1.00 | 3 | .271 | .281 | .341 |

## Dale Murphy

**Bats:** Right **Throws:** Right **Pos:** RF **Ht:** 6' 4" **Wt:** 215 **Born:** 03/12/56 **Age:** 35

| BATTING | | | | | | | | | | | | | | | | | | | BASERUNNING | | | | PERCENTAGES | | |
|---|---|---|---|---|---|---|---|---|---|---|---|---|---|---|---|---|---|---|---|---|---|---|---|---|---|
| Year Team | Lg | G | AB | H | 2B | 3B | HR | (Hm | Rd) | TB | R | RBI | TBB | IBB | SO | HBP | SH | SF | SB | CS | SB% | GDP | Avg | OBP | SLG |
| 1976 Atlanta | NL | 19 | 65 | 17 | 6 | 0 | 0 | (0 | 0) | 23 | 3 | 9 | 7 | 0 | 9 | 0 | 0 | 0 | 0 | 0 | .00 | 0 | .262 | .333 | .354 |
| 1977 Atlanta | NL | 18 | 76 | 24 | 8 | 1 | 2 | (0 | 2) | 40 | 5 | 14 | 0 | 0 | 8 | 0 | 0 | 0 | 0 | 1 | .00 | 3 | .316 | .316 | .526 |
| 1978 Atlanta | NL | 151 | 530 | 120 | 14 | 3 | 23 | (17 | 6) | 209 | 66 | 79 | 42 | 3 | 145 | 3 | 3 | 5 | 11 | 7 | .61 | 15 | .226 | .284 | .394 |
| 1979 Atlanta | NL | 104 | 384 | 106 | 7 | 2 | 21 | (12 | 9) | 180 | 53 | 57 | 38 | 5 | 67 | 2 | 0 | 5 | 6 | 1 | .86 | 12 | .276 | .340 | .469 |
| 1980 Atlanta | NL | 156 | 569 | 160 | 27 | 2 | 33 | (17 | 16) | 290 | 98 | 89 | 59 | 9 | 133 | 1 | 2 | 2 | 9 | 6 | .60 | 8 | .281 | .349 | .510 |
| 1981 Atlanta | NL | 104 | 369 | 91 | 12 | 1 | 13 | (8 | 5) | 144 | 43 | 50 | 44 | 8 | 72 | 0 | 1 | 2 | 14 | 5 | .74 | 10 | .247 | .325 | .390 |
| 1982 Atlanta | NL | 162 | 598 | 168 | 23 | 2 | 36 | (24 | 12) | 303 | 113 | 109 | 93 | 9 | 134 | 3 | 0 | 4 | 23 | 11 | .68 | 10 | .281 | .378 | .507 |
| 1983 Atlanta | NL | 162 | 589 | 178 | 24 | 4 | 36 | (17 | 19) | 318 | 131 | 121 | 90 | 12 | 110 | 2 | 0 | 6 | 30 | 4 | .88 | 15 | .302 | .393 | .540 |
| 1984 Atlanta | NL | 162 | 607 | 176 | 32 | 8 | 36 | (18 | 18) | 332 | 94 | 100 | 79 | 20 | 134 | 2 | 0 | 3 | 19 | 7 | .73 | 13 | .290 | .372 | .547 |
| 1985 Atlanta | NL | 162 | 616 | 185 | 32 | 2 | 37 | (19 | 18) | 332 | 118 | 111 | 90 | 15 | 141 | 1 | 0 | 5 | 10 | 3 | .77 | 14 | .300 | .388 | .539 |
| 1986 Atlanta | NL | 160 | 614 | 163 | 29 | 7 | 29 | (17 | 12) | 293 | 89 | 83 | 75 | 5 | 141 | 2 | 0 | 1 | 7 | 7 | .50 | 10 | .265 | .347 | .477 |
| 1987 Atlanta | NL | 159 | 566 | 167 | 27 | 1 | 44 | (25 | 19) | 328 | 115 | 105 | 115 | 29 | 136 | 7 | 0 | 5 | 16 | 6 | .73 | 11 | .295 | .417 | .580 |
| 1988 Atlanta | NL | 156 | 592 | 134 | 35 | 4 | 24 | (14 | 10) | 249 | 77 | 77 | 74 | 16 | 125 | 2 | 0 | 3 | 3 | 5 | .38 | 24 | .226 | .313 | .421 |
| 1989 Atlanta | NL | 154 | 574 | 131 | 16 | 0 | 20 | (9 | 11) | 207 | 60 | 84 | 65 | 10 | 142 | 2 | 0 | 6 | 3 | 2 | .60 | 14 | .228 | .306 | .361 |
| 1990 2 ML Teams | | 154 | 563 | 138 | 23 | 1 | 24 | (9 | 15) | 235 | 60 | 83 | 61 | 14 | 130 | 1 | 0 | 4 | 9 | 3 | .75 | 22 | .245 | .318 | .417 |
| 1990 Atlanta | NL | 97 | 349 | 81 | 14 | 0 | 17 | (8 | 9) | 146 | 38 | 55 | 41 | 11 | 84 | 1 | 0 | 3 | 9 | 2 | .82 | 11 | .232 | .312 | .418 |
| Philadelphia | NL | 57 | 214 | 57 | 9 | 1 | 7 | (1 | 6) | 89 | 22 | 28 | 20 | 3 | 46 | 0 | 0 | 1 | 0 | 1 | .00 | 11 | .266 | .328 | .416 |
| 15 ML YEARS | | 1983 | 7312 | 1958 | 315 | 38 | 378 | (206 | 172) | 3483 | 1125 | 1171 | 932 | 155 | 1627 | 28 | 6 | 51 | 160 | 68 | .70 | 181 | .268 | .351 | .476 |

## Rob Murphy

**Pitches:** Left **Bats:** Left **Pos:** RP **Ht:** 6' 2" **Wt:** 205 **Born:** 05/26/60 **Age:** 31

| HOW MUCH HE PITCHED | | | | | | | | WHAT HE GAVE UP | | | | | | | | | | | | THE RESULTS | | | | | |
|---|---|---|---|---|---|---|---|---|---|---|---|---|---|---|---|---|---|---|---|---|---|---|---|---|---|
| Year Team | Lg | G | GS | CG | GF | IP | BFP | H | R | ER | HR | SH | SF | HB | TBB | IBB | SO | WP | Bk | W | L | Pct. | ShO | Sv | ERA |
| 1985 Cincinnati | NL | 2 | 0 | 0 | 2 | 3 | 12 | 2 | 2 | 2 | 1 | 0 | 0 | 0 | 2 | 0 | 1 | 0 | 0 | 0 | 0 | .000 | 0 | 0 | 6.00 |
| 1986 Cincinnati | NL | 34 | 0 | 0 | 12 | 50.1 | 195 | 26 | 4 | 4 | 0 | 3 | 3 | 0 | 21 | 2 | 36 | 5 | 0 | 6 | 0 | 1.000 | 0 | 1 | 0.72 |
| 1987 Cincinnati | NL | 87 | 0 | 0 | 21 | 100.2 | 415 | 91 | 37 | 34 | 7 | 1 | 2 | 0 | 32 | 5 | 99 | 1 | 0 | 8 | 5 | .615 | 0 | 3 | 3.04 |
| 1988 Cincinnati | NL | 76 | 0 | 0 | 28 | 84.2 | 350 | 69 | 31 | 29 | 3 | 9 | 1 | 1 | 38 | 6 | 74 | 5 | 1 | 0 | 6 | .000 | 0 | 3 | 3.08 |
| 1989 Boston | AL | 74 | 0 | 0 | 27 | 105 | 438 | 97 | 38 | 32 | 7 | 7 | 3 | 1 | 41 | 8 | 107 | 6 | 0 | 5 | 7 | .417 | 0 | 9 | 2.74 |
| 1990 Boston | AL | 68 | 0 | 0 | 20 | 57 | 285 | 85 | 46 | 40 | 10 | 4 | 4 | 1 | 32 | 3 | 54 | 4 | 0 | 0 | 6 | .000 | 0 | 7 | 6.32 |
| 6 ML YEARS | | 341 | 0 | 0 | 110 | 400.2 | 1695 | 370 | 158 | 141 | 28 | 24 | 13 | 3 | 166 | 24 | 371 | 21 | 1 | 19 | 24 | .442 | 0 | 23 | 3.17 |

## Eddie Murray

**Bats:** Both **Throws:** Right **Pos:** 1B **Ht:** 6' 2" **Wt:** 224 **Born:** 02/24/56 **Age:** 35

| | | BATTING | | | | | | | | | | | | | | | | | BASERUNNING | | | | PERCENTAGES | | |
|---|---|---|---|---|---|---|---|---|---|---|---|---|---|---|---|---|---|---|---|---|---|---|---|---|---|
| Year Team | Lg | G | AB | H | 2B | 3B | HR | (Hm | Rd) | TB | R | RBI | TBB | IBB | SO | HBP | SH | SF | SB | CS | SB% | GDP | Avg | OBP | SLG |
| 1977 Baltimore | AL | 160 | 611 | 173 | 29 | 2 | 27 | (14 | 13) | 287 | 81 | 88 | 48 | 6 | 104 | 1 | 0 | 6 | 0 | 1 | .00 | 22 | .283 | .333 | .470 |
| 1978 Baltimore | AL | 161 | 610 | 174 | 32 | 3 | 27 | (10 | 17) | 293 | 85 | 95 | 70 | 7 | 97 | 1 | 1 | 8 | 6 | 5 | .55 | 15 | .285 | .356 | .480 |
| 1979 Baltimore | AL | 159 | 606 | 179 | 30 | 2 | 25 | (10 | 15) | 288 | 90 | 99 | 72 | 9 | 78 | 2 | 1 | 6 | 10 | 2 | .83 | 16 | .295 | .369 | .475 |
| 1980 Baltimore | AL | 158 | 621 | 186 | 36 | 2 | 32 | (10 | 22) | 322 | 100 | 116 | 54 | 10 | 71 | 2 | 0 | 6 | 7 | 2 | .78 | 18 | .300 | .354 | .519 |
| 1981 Baltimore | AL | 99 | 378 | 111 | 21 | 2 | 22 | (12 | 10) | 202 | 57 | 78 | 40 | 10 | 43 | 1 | 0 | 3 | 2 | 3 | .40 | 10 | .294 | .360 | .534 |
| 1982 Baltimore | AL | 151 | 550 | 174 | 30 | 1 | 32 | (18 | 14) | 302 | 87 | 110 | 70 | 18 | 82 | 1 | 0 | 6 | 7 | 2 | .78 | 17 | .316 | .391 | .549 |
| 1983 Baltimore | AL | 156 | 582 | 178 | 30 | 3 | 33 | (16 | 17) | 313 | 115 | 111 | 86 | 13 | 90 | 3 | 0 | 9 | 5 | 1 | .83 | 13 | .306 | .393 | .538 |
| 1984 Baltimore | AL | 162 | 588 | 180 | 26 | 3 | 29 | (18 | 11) | 299 | 97 | 110 | 107 | 25 | 87 | 2 | 0 | 8 | 10 | 2 | .83 | 9 | .306 | .410 | .509 |
| 1985 Baltimore | AL | 156 | 583 | 173 | 37 | 1 | 31 | (15 | 16) | 305 | 111 | 124 | 84 | 12 | 68 | 2 | 0 | 8 | 5 | 2 | .71 | 8 | .297 | .383 | .523 |
| 1986 Baltimore | AL | 137 | 495 | 151 | 25 | 1 | 17 | (9 | 8) | 229 | 61 | 84 | 78 | 7 | 49 | 0 | 0 | 5 | 3 | 0 | 1.00 | 17 | .305 | .396 | .463 |
| 1987 Baltimore | AL | 160 | 618 | 171 | 28 | 3 | 30 | (14 | 16) | 295 | 89 | 91 | 73 | 6 | 80 | 0 | 0 | 3 | 1 | 2 | .33 | 15 | .277 | .352 | .477 |
| 1988 Baltimore | AL | 161 | 603 | 171 | 27 | 2 | 28 | (14 | 14) | 286 | 75 | 84 | 75 | 8 | 78 | 0 | 0 | 3 | 5 | 2 | .71 | 20 | .284 | .361 | .474 |
| 1989 Los Angeles | NL | 160 | 594 | 147 | 29 | 1 | 20 | (4 | 16) | 238 | 66 | 88 | 87 | 24 | 85 | 2 | 0 | 7 | 7 | 2 | .78 | 12 | .247 | .342 | .401 |
| 1990 Los Angeles | NL | 155 | 558 | 184 | 22 | 3 | 26 | (12 | 14) | 290 | 96 | 95 | 82 | 21 | 64 | 1 | 0 | 4 | 8 | 5 | .62 | 19 | .330 | .414 | .520 |
| 14 ML YEARS | | 2135 | 7997 | 2352 | 402 | 29 | 379 | (176 | 203) | 3949 | 1210 | 1373 | 1026 | 176 | 1076 | 18 | 2 | 82 | 76 | 31 | .71 | 211 | .294 | .372 | .494 |

## Jeff Musselman

**Pitches:** Left **Bats:** Left **Pos:** RP **Ht:** 6' 0" **Wt:** 185 **Born:** 06/21/63 **Age:** 28

| | | HOW MUCH HE PITCHED | | | | | | WHAT HE GAVE UP | | | | | | | | | | | | THE RESULTS | | | | | |
|---|---|---|---|---|---|---|---|---|---|---|---|---|---|---|---|---|---|---|---|---|---|---|---|---|---|
| Year Team | Lg | G | GS | CG | GF | IP | BFP | H | R | ER | HR | SH | SF | HB | TBB | IBB | SO | WP | Bk | W | L | Pct. | ShO | Sv | ERA |
| 1986 Toronto | AL | 6 | 0 | 0 | 0 | 5.1 | 29 | 8 | 7 | 6 | 1 | 0 | 0 | 0 | 5 | 1 | 4 | 0 | 0 | 0 | 0 | .000 | 0 | 0 | 10.13 |
| 1987 Toronto | AL | 68 | 1 | 0 | 14 | 89 | 381 | 75 | 43 | 41 | 7 | 7 | 1 | 3 | 54 | 12 | 54 | 5 | 3 | 12 | 5 | .706 | 0 | 3 | 4.15 |
| 1988 Toronto | AL | 15 | 15 | 0 | 0 | 85 | 354 | 80 | 34 | 30 | 4 | 1 | 2 | 3 | 30 | 2 | 39 | 1 | 2 | 8 | 5 | .615 | 0 | 0 | 3.18 |
| 1989 2 ML Teams | | 25 | 3 | 0 | 6 | 37.1 | 177 | 46 | 26 | 22 | 3 | 5 | 1 | 0 | 23 | 3 | 14 | 4 | 0 | 3 | 3 | .500 | 0 | 0 | 5.30 |
| 1990 New York | NL | 28 | 0 | 0 | 5 | 32 | 144 | 40 | 22 | 20 | 3 | 1 | 2 | 1 | 11 | 1 | 14 | 3 | 0 | 0 | 2 | .000 | 0 | 0 | 5.63 |
| 1989 Toronto | AL | 5 | 3 | 0 | 2 | 11 | 58 | 19 | 15 | 13 | 2 | 1 | 1 | 0 | 9 | 0 | 3 | 3 | 0 | 0 | 1 | .000 | 0 | 0 | 10.64 |
| New York | NL | 20 | 0 | 0 | 4 | 26.1 | 119 | 27 | 11 | 9 | 1 | 4 | 0 | 0 | 14 | 3 | 11 | 1 | 0 | 3 | 2 | .600 | 0 | 0 | 3.08 |
| 5 ML YEARS | | 142 | 19 | 0 | 25 | 248.2 | 1085 | 249 | 132 | 119 | 18 | 14 | 6 | 7 | 123 | 19 | 125 | 13 | 5 | 23 | 15 | .605 | 0 | 3 | 4.31 |

## Greg Myers

**Bats:** Left **Throws:** Right **Pos:** C **Ht:** 6' 2" **Wt:** 200 **Born:** 04/14/66 **Age:** 25

| | | BATTING | | | | | | | | | | | | | | | | | BASERUNNING | | | | PERCENTAGES | | |
|---|---|---|---|---|---|---|---|---|---|---|---|---|---|---|---|---|---|---|---|---|---|---|---|---|---|
| Year Team | Lg | G | AB | H | 2B | 3B | HR | (Hm | Rd) | TB | R | RBI | TBB | IBB | SO | HBP | SH | SF | SB | CS | SB% | GDP | Avg | OBP | SLG |
| 1987 Toronto | AL | 7 | 9 | 1 | 0 | 0 | 0 | (0 | 0) | 1 | 1 | 0 | 0 | 0 | 3 | 0 | 0 | 0 | 0 | 0 | .00 | 2 | .111 | .111 | .111 |
| 1989 Toronto | AL | 17 | 44 | 5 | 2 | 0 | 0 | (0 | 0) | 7 | 0 | 1 | 2 | 0 | 9 | 0 | 0 | 0 | 0 | 1 | .00 | 2 | .114 | .152 | .159 |
| 1990 Toronto | AL | 87 | 250 | 59 | 7 | 1 | 5 | (3 | 2) | 83 | 33 | 22 | 22 | 0 | 33 | 0 | 1 | 4 | 0 | 1 | .00 | 12 | .236 | .293 | .332 |
| 3 ML YEARS | | 111 | 303 | 65 | 9 | 1 | 5 | (3 | 2) | 91 | 34 | 23 | 24 | 0 | 45 | 0 | 1 | 4 | 0 | 2 | .00 | 16 | .215 | .269 | .300 |

## Randy Myers

**Pitches:** Left **Bats:** Left **Pos:** RP **Ht:** 6' 1" **Wt:** 208 **Born:** 09/19/62 **Age:** 28

| | | HOW MUCH HE PITCHED | | | | | | WHAT HE GAVE UP | | | | | | | | | | | | THE RESULTS | | | | | |
|---|---|---|---|---|---|---|---|---|---|---|---|---|---|---|---|---|---|---|---|---|---|---|---|---|---|
| Year Team | Lg | G | GS | CG | GF | IP | BFP | H | R | ER | HR | SH | SF | HB | TBB | IBB | SO | WP | Bk | W | L | Pct. | ShO | Sv | ERA |
| 1985 New York | NL | 1 | 0 | 0 | 1 | 2 | 7 | 0 | 0 | 0 | 0 | 0 | 0 | 0 | 1 | 0 | 2 | 0 | 0 | 0 | 0 | .000 | 0 | 0 | 0.00 |
| 1986 New York | NL | 10 | 0 | 0 | 5 | 10.2 | 53 | 11 | 5 | 5 | 1 | 0 | 0 | 1 | 9 | 1 | 13 | 0 | 0 | 0 | 0 | .000 | 0 | 0 | 4.22 |
| 1987 New York | NL | 54 | 0 | 0 | 18 | 75 | 314 | 61 | 36 | 33 | 6 | 7 | 6 | 0 | 30 | 5 | 92 | 3 | 0 | 3 | 6 | .333 | 0 | 6 | 3.96 |
| 1988 New York | NL | 55 | 0 | 0 | 44 | 68 | 261 | 45 | 15 | 13 | 5 | 3 | 2 | 2 | 17 | 2 | 69 | 2 | 0 | 7 | 3 | .700 | 0 | 26 | 1.72 |
| 1989 New York | NL | 65 | 0 | 0 | 47 | 84.1 | 349 | 62 | 23 | 22 | 4 | 6 | 2 | 0 | 40 | 4 | 88 | 3 | 0 | 7 | 4 | .636 | 0 | 24 | 2.35 |
| 1990 Cincinnati | NL | 66 | 0 | 0 | 59 | 86.2 | 353 | 59 | 24 | 20 | 6 | 4 | 2 | 3 | 38 | 8 | 98 | 2 | 1 | 4 | 6 | .400 | 0 | 31 | 2.08 |
| 6 ML YEARS | | 251 | 0 | 0 | 174 | 326.2 | 1337 | 238 | 103 | 93 | 22 | 20 | 12 | 6 | 135 | 20 | 362 | 10 | 1 | 21 | 19 | .525 | 0 | 87 | 2.56 |

## Chris Nabholz

**Pitches:** Left **Bats:** Left **Pos:** SP **Ht:** 6' 5" **Wt:** 210 **Born:** 01/05/67 **Age:** 24

| | | HOW MUCH HE PITCHED | | | | | | WHAT HE GAVE UP | | | | | | | | | | | | THE RESULTS | | | | | |
|---|---|---|---|---|---|---|---|---|---|---|---|---|---|---|---|---|---|---|---|---|---|---|---|---|---|
| Year Team | Lg | G | GS | CG | GF | IP | BFP | H | R | ER | HR | SH | SF | HB | TBB | IBB | SO | WP | Bk | W | L | Pct. | ShO | Sv | ERA |
| 1989 Rockford | A | 24 | 23 | 3 | 0 | 161.1 | 654 | 132 | 54 | 39 | 6 | 5 | 4 | 0 | 41 | 0 | 149 | 11 | 2 | 13 | 5 | .722 | 3 | 0 | 2.18 |
| 1990 Jacksonville | AA | 11 | 11 | 0 | 0 | 74.1 | 304 | 62 | 28 | 25 | 6 | 1 | 1 | 0 | 27 | 0 | 77 | 6 | 1 | 7 | 2 | .778 | 0 | 0 | 3.03 |
| Indianapols | AAA | 10 | 10 | 0 | 0 | 63.1 | 274 | 66 | 38 | 34 | 7 | 1 | 6 | 1 | 28 | 0 | 44 | 3 | 0 | 0 | 6 | .000 | 0 | 0 | 4.83 |
| 1990 Montreal | NL | 11 | 11 | 1 | 0 | 70 | 282 | 43 | 23 | 22 | 6 | 1 | 2 | 2 | 32 | 1 | 53 | 1 | 1 | 6 | 2 | .750 | 1 | 0 | 2.83 |

## Tim Naehring

**Bats:** Right **Throws:** Right **Pos:** SS **Ht:** 6' 2" **Wt:** 190 **Born:** 02/01/67 **Age:** 24

| BATTING | | | | | | | | | | | | | | | | | | | | BASERUNNING | | | | PERCENTAGES | | |
|---|---|---|---|---|---|---|---|---|---|---|---|---|---|---|---|---|---|---|---|---|---|---|---|---|---|---|
| Year Team | Lg | G | AB | H | 2B | 3B | HR | (Hm | Rd) | TB | R | RBI | TBB | IBB | SO | HBP | SH | SF | | SB | CS | SB% | GDP | Avg | OBP | SLG |
| 1988 Elmira | A | 19 | 59 | 18 | 3 | 0 | 1 | -- | -- | 24 | 6 | 13 | 8 | 0 | 11 | 1 | 1 | 4 | | 0 | 0 | .00 | 1 | .305 | .375 | .407 |
| Winter Havn | A | 42 | 141 | 32 | 7 | 0 | 0 | -- | -- | 39 | 17 | 10 | 19 | 1 | 24 | 3 | 0 | 1 | | 1 | 1 | .50 | 1 | .227 | .329 | .277 |
| 1989 Lynchburg | A | 56 | 209 | 63 | 7 | 1 | 4 | -- | -- | 84 | 24 | 37 | 23 | 0 | 30 | 0 | 1 | 3 | | 2 | 0 | 1.00 | 7 | .301 | .366 | .402 |
| Pawtucket | AAA | 79 | 273 | 75 | 16 | 1 | 3 | -- | -- | 102 | 32 | 31 | 27 | 1 | 41 | 3 | 2 | 7 | | 2 | 3 | .40 | 6 | .275 | .339 | .374 |
| 1990 Pawtucket | AAA | 82 | 290 | 78 | 16 | 1 | 15 | -- | -- | 141 | 45 | 47 | 37 | 2 | 56 | 3 | 2 | 3 | | 0 | 1 | .00 | 6 | .269 | .354 | .486 |
| 1990 Boston | AL | 24 | 85 | 23 | 6 | 0 | 2 | (2 | 0) | 35 | 10 | 12 | 8 | 1 | 15 | 0 | 0 | 0 | | 0 | 0 | .00 | 2 | .271 | .333 | .412 |

## Charles Nagy

**Pitches:** Right **Bats:** Left **Pos:** SP **Ht:** 6' 3" **Wt:** 200 **Born:** 05/05/67 **Age:** 24

| HOW MUCH HE PITCHED | | | | | | | | WHAT HE GAVE UP | | | | | | | | | | | THE RESULTS | | | | | |
|---|---|---|---|---|---|---|---|---|---|---|---|---|---|---|---|---|---|---|---|---|---|---|---|---|
| Year Team | Lg | G | GS | CG | GF | IP | BFP | H | R | ER | HR | SH | SF | HB | TBB | IBB | SO | WP | Bk | W | L | Pct. | ShO | Sv | ERA |
| 1989 Kinston | A | 13 | 13 | 6 | 0 | 95.1 | 373 | 69 | 22 | 16 | 0 | 1 | 3 | 4 | 24 | 0 | 99 | 3 | 0 | 8 | 4 | .667 | 4 | 0 | 1.51 |
| Canton-Akrn | AA | 15 | 14 | 2 | 0 | 94 | 400 | 102 | 44 | 35 | 4 | 3 | 2 | 2 | 32 | 0 | 65 | 7 | 0 | 4 | 5 | .444 | 0 | 0 | 3.35 |
| 1990 Canton-Akrn | AA | 23 | 23 | 9 | 0 | 175 | 694 | 132 | 62 | 49 | 9 | 4 | 4 | 6 | 39 | 0 | 99 | 3 | 3 | 13 | 8 | .619 | 0 | 0 | 2.52 |
| 1990 Cleveland | AL | 9 | 8 | 0 | 1 | 45.2 | 208 | 58 | 31 | 30 | 7 | 1 | 1 | 1 | 21 | 1 | 26 | 1 | 1 | 2 | 4 | .333 | 0 | 0 | 5.91 |

## Jaime Navarro

**Pitches:** Right **Bats:** Right **Pos:** SP/RP **Ht:** 6' 4" **Wt:** 210 **Born:** 03/27/67 **Age:** 24

| HOW MUCH HE PITCHED | | | | | | | | WHAT HE GAVE UP | | | | | | | | | | | THE RESULTS | | | | | |
|---|---|---|---|---|---|---|---|---|---|---|---|---|---|---|---|---|---|---|---|---|---|---|---|---|
| Year Team | Lg | G | GS | CG | GF | IP | BFP | H | R | ER | HR | SH | SF | HB | TBB | IBB | SO | WP | Bk | W | L | Pct. | ShO | Sv | ERA |
| 1987 Helena | R | 13 | 13 | 3 | 0 | 85.2 | 356 | 87 | 37 | 34 | 5 | 2 | 2 | 1 | 18 | 1 | 95 | 5 | 1 | 4 | 3 | .571 | 0 | 0 | 3.57 |
| 1988 Stockton | A | 26 | 26 | 4 | 0 | 174.2 | 727 | 148 | 70 | 60 | 6 | 4 | 1 | 6 | 74 | 1 | 151 | 22 | 2 | 15 | 5 | .750 | 1 | 0 | 3.09 |
| 1989 El Paso | AA | 11 | 11 | 1 | 0 | 76.2 | 316 | 61 | 29 | 21 | 3 | 1 | 0 | 1 | 35 | 1 | 78 | 5 | 1 | 5 | 2 | .714 | 0 | 0 | 2.47 |
| Denver | AAA | 3 | 3 | 1 | 1 | 20 | 87 | 24 | 8 | 8 | 0 | 1 | 1 | 0 | 7 | 2 | 17 | 0 | 0 | 1 | 1 | .500 | 0 | 0 | 3.60 |
| 1990 Denver | AAA | 6 | 6 | 1 | 0 | 40.2 | 176 | 41 | 27 | 19 | 1 | 1 | 0 | 0 | 14 | 0 | 28 | 2 | 1 | 2 | 3 | .400 | 0 | 0 | 4.20 |
| 1989 Milwaukee | AL | 19 | 17 | 1 | 1 | 109.2 | 470 | 119 | 47 | 38 | 6 | 5 | 2 | 1 | 32 | 3 | 56 | 3 | 0 | 7 | 8 | .467 | 0 | 0 | 3.12 |
| 1990 Milwaukee | AL | 32 | 22 | 3 | 2 | 149.1 | 654 | 176 | 83 | 74 | 11 | 4 | 5 | 4 | 41 | 3 | 75 | 6 | 5 | 8 | 7 | .533 | 0 | 1 | 4.46 |
| 2 ML YEARS | | 51 | 39 | 4 | 3 | 259 | 1124 | 295 | 130 | 112 | 17 | 9 | 7 | 5 | 73 | 6 | 131 | 9 | 5 | 15 | 15 | .500 | 0 | 1 | 3.89 |

## Jim Neidlinger

**Pitches:** Right **Bats:** Both **Pos:** SP **Ht:** 6' 4" **Wt:** 180 **Born:** 09/24/64 **Age:** 26

| HOW MUCH HE PITCHED | | | | | | | | WHAT HE GAVE UP | | | | | | | | | | | THE RESULTS | | | | | |
|---|---|---|---|---|---|---|---|---|---|---|---|---|---|---|---|---|---|---|---|---|---|---|---|---|
| Year Team | Lg | G | GS | CG | GF | IP | BFP | H | R | ER | HR | SH | SF | HB | TBB | IBB | SO | WP | Bk | W | L | Pct. | ShO | Sv | ERA |
| 1984 Macon | A | 25 | 25 | 2 | 0 | 166 | 707 | 138 | 65 | 51 | 6 | 4 | 5 | 0 | 85 | 2 | 113 | 4 | 1 | 9 | 8 | .529 | 0 | 0 | 2.77 |
| 1985 Pr William | A | 26 | 26 | 4 | 0 | 165.1 | 713 | 141 | 86 | 79 | 14 | 7 | 11 | 7 | 83 | 0 | 143 | 8 | 0 | 8 | 13 | .381 | 0 | 0 | 4.30 |
| 1986 Nashua | AA | 22 | 22 | 8 | 0 | 163.2 | 663 | 135 | 57 | 44 | 6 | 6 | 3 | 3 | 44 | 0 | 98 | 5 | 1 | 12 | 7 | .632 | 2 | 0 | 2.42 |
| Hawaii | AAA | 4 | 4 | 1 | 0 | 27.2 | 124 | 33 | 14 | 12 | 3 | 2 | 0 | 1 | 9 | 0 | 14 | 0 | 0 | 2 | 1 | .667 | 0 | 0 | 3.90 |
| 1987 Harrisburg | AA | 26 | 26 | 7 | 0 | 170.2 | 737 | 183 | 92 | 75 | 9 | 3 | 5 | 5 | 61 | 4 | 96 | 6 | 1 | 11 | 8 | .579 | 0 | 0 | 3.96 |
| 1988 Harrisburg | AA | 40 | 11 | 0 | 15 | 124.2 | 531 | 135 | 54 | 39 | 3 | 9 | 4 | 5 | 25 | 3 | 88 | 2 | 2 | 5 | 8 | .385 | 0 | 2 | 2.82 |
| Buffalo | AAA | 3 | 0 | 0 | 1 | 4.1 | 22 | 7 | 3 | 3 | 0 | 0 | 0 | 0 | 1 | 0 | 4 | 1 | 0 | 0 | 0 | .000 | 0 | 0 | 6.23 |
| 1989 Albuquerque | AAA | 34 | 18 | 1 | 5 | 139.2 | 604 | 164 | 77 | 63 | 8 | 5 | 3 | 1 | 37 | 1 | 97 | 2 | 1 | 8 | 6 | .571 | 0 | 1 | 4.06 |
| 1990 Albuquerque | AAA | 20 | 18 | 4 | 2 | 119.2 | 516 | 129 | 70 | 57 | 13 | 2 | 2 | 1 | 34 | 3 | 81 | 2 | 0 | 8 | 5 | .615 | 1 | 0 | 4.29 |
| 1990 Los Angeles | NL | 12 | 12 | 0 | 0 | 74 | 301 | 67 | 30 | 27 | 4 | 4 | 3 | 1 | 15 | 1 | 46 | 0 | 1 | 5 | 3 | .625 | 0 | 0 | 3.28 |

## Gene Nelson

**Pitches:** Right **Bats:** Right **Pos:** RP **Ht:** 6' 0" **Wt:** 172 **Born:** 12/03/60 **Age:** 30

| HOW MUCH HE PITCHED | | | | | | | | WHAT HE GAVE UP | | | | | | | | | | | THE RESULTS | | | | | |
|---|---|---|---|---|---|---|---|---|---|---|---|---|---|---|---|---|---|---|---|---|---|---|---|---|
| Year Team | Lg | G | GS | CG | GF | IP | BFP | H | R | ER | HR | SH | SF | HB | TBB | IBB | SO | WP | Bk | W | L | Pct. | ShO | Sv | ERA |
| 1981 New York | AL | 8 | 7 | 0 | 0 | 39 | 179 | 40 | 24 | 21 | 5 | 0 | 2 | 1 | 23 | 1 | 16 | 2 | 0 | 3 | 1 | .750 | 0 | 0 | 4.85 |
| 1982 Seattle | AL | 22 | 19 | 2 | 2 | 122.2 | 545 | 133 | 70 | 63 | 16 | 4 | 2 | 2 | 60 | 1 | 71 | 4 | 2 | 6 | 9 | .400 | 1 | 0 | 4.62 |
| 1983 Seattle | AL | 10 | 5 | 1 | 2 | 32 | 153 | 38 | 29 | 28 | 6 | 2 | 0 | 1 | 21 | 2 | 11 | 1 | 0 | 0 | 3 | .000 | 0 | 0 | 7.88 |
| 1984 Chicago | AL | 20 | 9 | 2 | 4 | 74.2 | 304 | 72 | 38 | 37 | 9 | 1 | 2 | 1 | 17 | 0 | 36 | 4 | 1 | 3 | 5 | .375 | 0 | 1 | 4.46 |
| 1985 Chicago | AL | 46 | 18 | 1 | 11 | 145.2 | 643 | 144 | 74 | 69 | 23 | 9 | 2 | 7 | 67 | 4 | 101 | 11 | 1 | 10 | 10 | .500 | 0 | 2 | 4.26 |
| 1986 Chicago | AL | 54 | 1 | 0 | 26 | 114.2 | 488 | 118 | 52 | 49 | 7 | 7 | 1 | 3 | 41 | 5 | 70 | 3 | 0 | 6 | 6 | .500 | 0 | 6 | 3.85 |
| 1987 Oakland | AL | 54 | 6 | 0 | 15 | 123.2 | 530 | 120 | 58 | 54 | 12 | 3 | 5 | 5 | 35 | 0 | 94 | 7 | 0 | 6 | 5 | .545 | 0 | 3 | 3.93 |
| 1988 Oakland | AL | 54 | 1 | 0 | 20 | 111.2 | 456 | 93 | 42 | 38 | 9 | 3 | 4 | 3 | 38 | 4 | 67 | 4 | 6 | 9 | 6 | .600 | 0 | 3 | 3.06 |
| 1989 Oakland | AL | 50 | 0 | 0 | 15 | 80 | 335 | 60 | 33 | 29 | 5 | 3 | 4 | 2 | 30 | 3 | 70 | 5 | 0 | 3 | 5 | .375 | 0 | 3 | 3.26 |
| 1990 Oakland | AL | 51 | 0 | 0 | 17 | 74.2 | 291 | 55 | 14 | 13 | 5 | 1 | 5 | 3 | 17 | 1 | 38 | 1 | 0 | 3 | 3 | .500 | 0 | 5 | 1.57 |
| 10 ML YEARS | | 369 | 66 | 6 | 112 | 918.2 | 3924 | 873 | 434 | 401 | 97 | 33 | 27 | 28 | 349 | 21 | 574 | 42 | 10 | 49 | 53 | .480 | 1 | 23 | 3.93 |

## Rob Nelson

**Bats:** Left **Throws:** Left **Pos:** PH **Ht:** 6' 4" **Wt:** 215 **Born:** 05/17/64 **Age:** 27

| | | BATTING | | | | | | | | | | | | | | | | | BASERUNNING | | | | PERCENTAGES | | |
|---|---|---|---|---|---|---|---|---|---|---|---|---|---|---|---|---|---|---|---|---|---|---|---|---|---|
| Year Team | Lg | G | AB | H | 2B | 3B | HR | (Hm | Rd) | TB | R | RBI | TBB | IBB | SO | HBP | SH | SF | SB | CS | SB% | GDP | Avg | OBP | SLG |
| 1986 Oakland | AL | 5 | 9 | 2 | 1 | 0 | 0 | (0 | 0) | 3 | 1 | 0 | 1 | 0 | 4 | 0 | 0 | 0 | 0 | 0 | .00 | 0 | .222 | .300 | .333 |
| 1987 2 ML Teams | | 17 | 35 | 5 | 1 | 0 | 0 | (0 | 0) | 6 | 1 | 1 | 1 | 0 | 20 | 0 | 1 | 0 | 0 | 0 | .00 | 0 | .143 | .167 | .171 |
| 1988 San Diego | NL | 7 | 21 | 4 | 0 | 0 | 1 | (1 | 0) | 7 | 4 | 3 | 2 | 0 | 9 | 0 | 0 | 0 | 0 | 0 | .00 | 0 | .190 | .261 | .333 |
| 1989 San Diego | NL | 42 | 82 | 16 | 0 | 1 | 3 | (1 | 2) | 27 | 6 | 7 | 20 | 1 | 29 | 0 | 0 | 0 | 1 | 3 | .25 | 2 | .195 | .353 | .329 |
| 1990 San Diego | NL | 5 | 5 | 0 | 0 | 0 | 0 | (0 | 0) | 0 | 0 | 0 | 0 | 0 | 4 | 0 | 0 | 0 | 0 | 0 | .00 | 0 | .000 | .000 | .000 |
| 1987 Oakland | AL | 7 | 24 | 4 | 1 | 0 | 0 | (0 | 0) | 5 | 1 | 0 | 0 | 0 | 12 | 0 | 1 | 0 | 0 | 0 | .00 | 0 | .167 | .167 | .208 |
| San Diego | NL | 10 | 11 | 1 | 0 | 0 | 0 | (0 | 0) | 1 | 0 | 1 | 1 | 0 | 8 | 0 | 0 | 0 | 0 | 0 | .00 | 0 | .091 | .167 | .091 |
| 5 ML YEARS | | 76 | 152 | 27 | 2 | 1 | 4 | (2 | 2) | 43 | 12 | 11 | 24 | 1 | 66 | 0 | 1 | 0 | 1 | 3 | .25 | 2 | .178 | .290 | .283 |

## Al Newman

**Bats:** Both **Throws:** Right **Pos:** 2B/3B/SS **Ht:** 5' 9" **Wt:** 183 **Born:** 06/30/60 **Age:** 31

| | | BATTING | | | | | | | | | | | | | | | | | BASERUNNING | | | | PERCENTAGES | | |
|---|---|---|---|---|---|---|---|---|---|---|---|---|---|---|---|---|---|---|---|---|---|---|---|---|---|
| Year Team | Lg | G | AB | H | 2B | 3B | HR | (Hm | Rd) | TB | R | RBI | TBB | IBB | SO | HBP | SH | SF | SB | CS | SB% | GDP | Avg | OBP | SLG |
| 1985 Montreal | NL | 25 | 29 | 5 | 1 | 0 | 0 | (0 | 0) | 6 | 7 | 1 | 3 | 0 | 4 | 0 | 0 | 0 | 2 | 1 | .67 | 0 | .172 | .250 | .207 |
| 1986 Montreal | NL | 95 | 185 | 37 | 3 | 0 | 1 | (0 | 1) | 43 | 23 | 8 | 21 | 2 | 20 | 0 | 4 | 2 | 11 | 11 | .50 | 4 | .200 | .279 | .232 |
| 1987 Minnesota | AL | 110 | 307 | 68 | 15 | 5 | 0 | (0 | 0) | 93 | 44 | 29 | 34 | 0 | 27 | 0 | 7 | 1 | 15 | 11 | .58 | 5 | .221 | .298 | .303 |
| 1988 Minnesota | AL | 105 | 260 | 58 | 7 | 0 | 0 | (0 | 0) | 65 | 35 | 19 | 29 | 0 | 34 | 0 | 6 | 0 | 12 | 3 | .80 | 4 | .223 | .301 | .250 |
| 1989 Minnesota | AL | 141 | 446 | 113 | 18 | 2 | 0 | (0 | 0) | 135 | 62 | 38 | 59 | 0 | 46 | 2 | 10 | 4 | 25 | 12 | .68 | 3 | .253 | .341 | .303 |
| 1990 Minnesota | AL | 144 | 388 | 94 | 14 | 0 | 0 | (0 | 0) | 108 | 43 | 30 | 33 | 0 | 34 | 2 | 8 | 2 | 13 | 6 | .68 | 7 | .242 | .304 | .278 |
| 6 ML YEARS | | 620 | 1615 | 375 | 58 | 7 | 1 | (0 | 1) | 450 | 214 | 125 | 179 | 2 | 165 | 4 | 35 | 9 | 78 | 44 | .64 | 23 | .232 | .309 | .279 |

## Carl Nichols

**Bats:** Right **Throws:** Right **Pos:** C **Ht:** 6' 0" **Wt:** 192 **Born:** 10/14/62 **Age:** 28

| | | BATTING | | | | | | | | | | | | | | | | | BASERUNNING | | | | PERCENTAGES | | |
|---|---|---|---|---|---|---|---|---|---|---|---|---|---|---|---|---|---|---|---|---|---|---|---|---|---|
| Year Team | Lg | G | AB | H | 2B | 3B | HR | (Hm | Rd) | TB | R | RBI | TBB | IBB | SO | HBP | SH | SF | SB | CS | SB% | GDP | Avg | OBP | SLG |
| 1986 Baltimore | AL | 5 | 5 | 0 | 0 | 0 | 0 | (0 | 0) | 0 | 0 | 0 | 1 | 1 | 4 | 0 | 0 | 0 | 0 | 0 | .00 | 0 | .000 | .167 | .000 |
| 1987 Baltimore | AL | 13 | 21 | 8 | 1 | 0 | 0 | (0 | 0) | 9 | 4 | 3 | 1 | 0 | 4 | 0 | 1 | 0 | 0 | 0 | .00 | 0 | .381 | .409 | .429 |
| 1988 Baltimore | AL | 18 | 47 | 9 | 1 | 0 | 0 | (0 | 0) | 10 | 2 | 1 | 3 | 0 | 10 | 0 | 1 | 1 | 0 | 0 | .00 | 3 | .191 | .235 | .213 |
| 1989 Houston | NL | 8 | 13 | 1 | 0 | 0 | 0 | (0 | 0) | 1 | 0 | 2 | 0 | 0 | 3 | 0 | 0 | 0 | 0 | 0 | .00 | 0 | .077 | .077 | .077 |
| 1990 Houston | NL | 32 | 49 | 10 | 3 | 0 | 0 | (0 | 0) | 13 | 7 | 11 | 8 | 1 | 11 | 1 | 1 | 2 | 0 | 0 | .00 | 1 | .204 | .317 | .265 |
| 5 ML YEARS | | 76 | 135 | 28 | 5 | 0 | 0 | (0 | 0) | 33 | 13 | 17 | 13 | 2 | 32 | 1 | 3 | 3 | 0 | 0 | .00 | 4 | .207 | .276 | .244 |

## Rod Nichols

**Pitches:** Right **Bats:** Right **Pos:** SP **Ht:** 6' 2" **Wt:** 190 **Born:** 12/29/64 **Age:** 26

| | | HOW MUCH HE PITCHED | | | | | | WHAT HE GAVE UP | | | | | | | | | | | | THE RESULTS | | | | | |
|---|---|---|---|---|---|---|---|---|---|---|---|---|---|---|---|---|---|---|---|---|---|---|---|---|---|
| Year Team | Lg | G | GS | CG | GF | IP | BFP | H | R | ER | HR | SH | SF | HB | TBB | IBB | SO | WP | Bk | W | L | Pct. | ShO | Sv | ERA |
| 1988 Cleveland | AL | 11 | 10 | 3 | 1 | 69.1 | 297 | 73 | 41 | 39 | 5 | 2 | 2 | 2 | 23 | 1 | 31 | 2 | 3 | 1 | 7 | .125 | 0 | 0 | 5.06 |
| 1989 Cleveland | AL | 15 | 11 | 0 | 2 | 71.2 | 315 | 81 | 42 | 35 | 9 | 3 | 2 | 2 | 24 | 0 | 42 | 0 | 0 | 4 | 6 | .400 | 0 | 0 | 4.40 |
| 1990 Cleveland | AL | 4 | 2 | 0 | 0 | 16 | 79 | 24 | 14 | 14 | 5 | 1 | 0 | 2 | 6 | 0 | 3 | 0 | 0 | 0 | 3 | .000 | 0 | 0 | 7.88 |
| 3 ML YEARS | | 30 | 23 | 3 | 3 | 157 | 691 | 178 | 97 | 88 | 19 | 6 | 4 | 6 | 53 | 1 | 76 | 2 | 3 | 5 | 16 | .238 | 0 | 0 | 5.04 |

## Tom Niedenfuer

**Pitches:** Right **Bats:** Right **Pos:** RP **Ht:** 6' 5" **Wt:** 224 **Born:** 08/13/59 **Age:** 31

| | | HOW MUCH HE PITCHED | | | | | | WHAT HE GAVE UP | | | | | | | | | | | | THE RESULTS | | | | | |
|---|---|---|---|---|---|---|---|---|---|---|---|---|---|---|---|---|---|---|---|---|---|---|---|---|---|
| Year Team | Lg | G | GS | CG | GF | IP | BFP | H | R | ER | HR | SH | SF | HB | TBB | IBB | SO | WP | Bk | W | L | Pct. | ShO | Sv | ERA |
| 1981 Los Angeles | NL | 17 | 0 | 0 | 8 | 26 | 107 | 25 | 11 | 11 | 1 | 2 | 1 | 1 | 6 | 2 | 12 | 0 | 0 | 3 | 1 | .750 | 0 | 2 | 3.81 |
| 1982 Los Angeles | NL | 55 | 0 | 0 | 24 | 69.2 | 299 | 71 | 22 | 21 | 3 | 5 | 3 | 2 | 25 | 8 | 60 | 1 | 0 | 3 | 4 | .429 | 0 | 9 | 2.71 |
| 1983 Los Angeles | NL | 66 | 0 | 0 | 38 | 94.2 | 366 | 55 | 22 | 20 | 6 | 7 | 5 | 1 | 29 | 11 | 66 | 1 | 0 | 8 | 3 | .727 | 0 | 11 | 1.90 |
| 1984 Los Angeles | NL | 33 | 0 | 0 | 21 | 47.1 | 203 | 39 | 14 | 13 | 3 | 6 | 0 | 2 | 23 | 7 | 45 | 1 | 1 | 2 | 5 | .286 | 0 | 11 | 2.47 |
| 1985 Los Angeles | NL | 64 | 0 | 0 | 43 | 106.1 | 415 | 86 | 32 | 32 | 6 | 1 | 3 | 1 | 24 | 5 | 102 | 0 | 0 | 7 | 9 | .438 | 0 | 19 | 2.71 |
| 1986 Los Angeles | NL | 60 | 0 | 0 | 27 | 80 | 345 | 86 | 35 | 33 | 11 | 5 | 3 | 1 | 29 | 15 | 55 | 2 | 0 | 6 | 6 | .500 | 0 | 11 | 3.71 |
| 1987 2 ML Teams | | 60 | 0 | 0 | 47 | 68.2 | 303 | 68 | 37 | 34 | 12 | 0 | 4 | 2 | 31 | 4 | 47 | 3 | 0 | 4 | 5 | .444 | 0 | 14 | 4.46 |
| 1988 Baltimore | AL | 52 | 0 | 0 | 42 | 59 | 252 | 59 | 23 | 23 | 8 | 2 | 1 | 2 | 19 | 3 | 40 | 0 | 0 | 3 | 4 | .429 | 0 | 18 | 3.51 |
| 1989 Seattle | AL | 25 | 0 | 0 | 14 | 36.1 | 171 | 46 | 29 | 27 | 7 | 4 | 2 | 1 | 15 | 5 | 15 | 3 | 0 | 0 | 3 | .000 | 0 | 0 | 6.69 |
| 1990 St. Louis | NL | 52 | 0 | 0 | 12 | 65 | 276 | 66 | 26 | 25 | 3 | 1 | 5 | 0 | 25 | 7 | 32 | 3 | 0 | 0 | 6 | .000 | 0 | 2 | 3.46 |
| 1987 Los Angeles | NL | 15 | 0 | 0 | 8 | 16.1 | 70 | 13 | 5 | 5 | 1 | 0 | 1 | 1 | 9 | 1 | 10 | 1 | 0 | 1 | 0 | 1.000 | 0 | 1 | 2.76 |
| Baltimore | AL | 45 | 0 | 0 | 39 | 52.1 | 233 | 55 | 32 | 29 | 11 | 0 | 3 | 1 | 22 | 3 | 37 | 2 | 0 | 3 | 5 | .375 | 0 | 13 | 4.99 |
| 10 ML YEARS | | 484 | 0 | 0 | 276 | 653 | 2737 | 601 | 251 | 239 | 60 | 33 | 27 | 13 | 226 | 67 | 474 | 14 | 1 | 36 | 46 | .439 | 0 | 97 | 3.29 |

## Tom Nieto

**Bats:** Right **Throws:** Right **Pos:** C **Ht:** 6' 1" **Wt:** 205 **Born:** 10/27/60 **Age:** 30

| | | BATTING | | | | | | | | | | | | | | | | | BASERUNNING | | | | PERCENTAGES | | |
|---|---|---|---|---|---|---|---|---|---|---|---|---|---|---|---|---|---|---|---|---|---|---|---|---|---|
| Year Team | Lg | G | AB | H | 2B | 3B | HR | (Hm | Rd) | TB | R | RBI | TBB | IBB | SO | HBP | SH | SF | SB | CS | SB% | GDP | Avg | OBP | SLG |
| 1984 St. Louis | NL | 33 | 86 | 24 | 4 | 0 | 3 | (2 | 1) | 37 | 7 | 12 | 5 | 2 | 18 | 0 | 0 | 2 | 0 | 0 | .00 | 3 | .279 | .312 | .430 |
| 1985 St. Louis | NL | 95 | 253 | 57 | 10 | 2 | 0 | (0 | 0) | 71 | 15 | 34 | 26 | 8 | 37 | 3 | 6 | 0 | 0 | 2 | .00 | 9 | .225 | .305 | .281 |
| 1986 Montreal | NL | 30 | 65 | 13 | 3 | 1 | 1 | (1 | 0) | 21 | 5 | 7 | 6 | 1 | 21 | 1 | 0 | 0 | 0 | 1 | .00 | 3 | .200 | .278 | .323 |
| 1987 Minnesota | AL | 41 | 105 | 21 | 7 | 1 | 1 | (0 | 1) | 33 | 7 | 12 | 8 | 0 | 24 | 3 | 5 | 0 | 0 | 0 | .00 | 1 | .200 | .276 | .314 |
| 1988 Minnesota | AL | 24 | 60 | 4 | 0 | 0 | 0 | (0 | 0) | 4 | 1 | 0 | 1 | 0 | 17 | 1 | 0 | 0 | 0 | 0 | .00 | 2 | .067 | .097 | .067 |
| 1989 Philadelphia | NL | 11 | 20 | 3 | 0 | 0 | 0 | (0 | 0) | 3 | 1 | 0 | 6 | 0 | 7 | 1 | 0 | 0 | 0 | 0 | .00 | 0 | .150 | .370 | .150 |
| 1990 Philadelphia | NL | 17 | 30 | 5 | 0 | 0 | 0 | (0 | 0) | 5 | 1 | 4 | 3 | 0 | 11 | 1 | 0 | 0 | 0 | 0 | .00 | 2 | .167 | .265 | .167 |
| 7 ML YEARS | | 251 | 619 | 127 | 24 | 4 | 5 | (3 | 2) | 174 | 37 | 69 | 55 | 11 | 135 | 10 | 11 | 2 | 0 | 3 | .00 | 20 | .205 | .280 | .281 |

## Al Nipper

**Pitches:** Right **Bats:** Right **Pos:** SP **Ht:** 6' 0" **Wt:** 194 **Born:** 04/02/59 **Age:** 32

| | | HOW MUCH HE PITCHED | | | | | | WHAT HE GAVE UP | | | | | | | | | | | | THE RESULTS | | | | | |
|---|---|---|---|---|---|---|---|---|---|---|---|---|---|---|---|---|---|---|---|---|---|---|---|---|---|
| Year Team | Lg | G | GS | CG | GF | IP | BFP | H | R | ER | HR | SH | SF | HB | TBB | IBB | SO | WP | Bk | W | L | Pct. | ShO | Sv | ERA |
| 1983 Boston | AL | 3 | 2 | 1 | 1 | 16 | 67 | 17 | 4 | 4 | 0 | 0 | 1 | 1 | 7 | 0 | 5 | 0 | 0 | 1 | 1 | .500 | 0 | 0 | 2.25 |
| 1984 Boston | AL | 29 | 24 | 6 | 3 | 182.2 | 777 | 183 | 86 | 79 | 18 | 3 | 2 | 7 | 52 | 1 | 84 | 7 | 1 | 11 | 6 | .647 | 0 | 0 | 3.89 |
| 1985 Boston | AL | 25 | 25 | 5 | 0 | 162 | 713 | 157 | 83 | 73 | 14 | 4 | 4 | 9 | 82 | 3 | 85 | 3 | 1 | 9 | 12 | .429 | 0 | 0 | 4.06 |
| 1986 Boston | AL | 26 | 26 | 3 | 0 | 159 | 702 | 186 | 108 | 95 | 24 | 4 | 5 | 4 | 47 | 2 | 79 | 1 | 1 | 10 | 12 | .455 | 0 | 0 | 5.38 |
| 1987 Boston | AL | 30 | 30 | 6 | 0 | 174 | 777 | 196 | 115 | 105 | 30 | 8 | 9 | 7 | 62 | 1 | 89 | 5 | 0 | 11 | 12 | .478 | 0 | 0 | 5.43 |
| 1988 Chicago | NL | 22 | 12 | 0 | 3 | 80 | 341 | 72 | 37 | 27 | 9 | 1 | 1 | 3 | 34 | 2 | 27 | 1 | 1 | 2 | 4 | .333 | 0 | 1 | 3.04 |
| 1990 Cleveland | AL | 9 | 5 | 0 | 1 | 24 | 125 | 35 | 19 | 18 | 2 | 0 | 5 | 2 | 19 | 0 | 12 | 6 | 0 | 2 | 3 | .400 | 0 | 0 | 6.75 |
| 7 ML YEARS | | 144 | 124 | 21 | 8 | 797.2 | 3502 | 846 | 452 | 401 | 97 | 20 | 27 | 33 | 303 | 9 | 381 | 23 | 4 | 46 | 50 | .479 | 0 | 1 | 4.52 |

## Donell Nixon

**Bats:** Right **Throws:** Right **Pos:** LF **Ht:** 6' 1" **Wt:** 185 **Born:** 12/31/61 **Age:** 29

| | | BATTING | | | | | | | | | | | | | | | | | BASERUNNING | | | | PERCENTAGES | | |
|---|---|---|---|---|---|---|---|---|---|---|---|---|---|---|---|---|---|---|---|---|---|---|---|---|---|
| Year Team | Lg | G | AB | H | 2B | 3B | HR | (Hm | Rd) | TB | R | RBI | TBB | IBB | SO | HBP | SH | SF | SB | CS | SB% | GDP | Avg | OBP | SLG |
| 1987 Seattle | AL | 46 | 132 | 33 | 4 | 0 | 3 | (2 | 1) | 46 | 17 | 12 | 13 | 0 | 28 | 2 | 4 | 0 | 21 | 7 | .75 | 3 | .250 | .327 | .348 |
| 1988 San Francisco | NL | 59 | 78 | 27 | 3 | 0 | 0 | (0 | 0) | 30 | 15 | 6 | 10 | 0 | 12 | 0 | 1 | 0 | 11 | 8 | .58 | 1 | .346 | .420 | .385 |
| 1989 San Francisco | NL | 95 | 166 | 44 | 2 | 0 | 1 | (0 | 1) | 49 | 23 | 15 | 11 | 1 | 30 | 0 | 0 | 0 | 10 | 3 | .77 | 4 | .265 | .311 | .295 |
| 1990 Baltimore | AL | 8 | 20 | 5 | 2 | 0 | 0 | (0 | 0) | 7 | 1 | 2 | 1 | 0 | 7 | 0 | 0 | 0 | 5 | 0 | 1.00 | 0 | .250 | .286 | .350 |
| 4 ML YEARS | | 208 | 396 | 109 | 11 | 0 | 4 | (2 | 2) | 132 | 56 | 35 | 35 | 1 | 77 | 2 | 5 | 0 | 47 | 18 | .72 | 8 | .275 | .337 | .333 |

## Otis Nixon

**Bats:** Both **Throws:** Right **Pos:** CF/LF **Ht:** 6' 2" **Wt:** 180 **Born:** 01/09/59 **Age:** 32

| | | BATTING | | | | | | | | | | | | | | | | | BASERUNNING | | | | PERCENTAGES | | |
|---|---|---|---|---|---|---|---|---|---|---|---|---|---|---|---|---|---|---|---|---|---|---|---|---|---|
| Year Team | Lg | G | AB | H | 2B | 3B | HR | (Hm | Rd) | TB | R | RBI | TBB | IBB | SO | HBP | SH | SF | SB | CS | SB% | GDP | Avg | OBP | SLG |
| 1983 New York | AL | 13 | 14 | 2 | 0 | 0 | 0 | (0 | 0) | 2 | 2 | 0 | 1 | 0 | 5 | 0 | 0 | 0 | 2 | 0 | 1.00 | 0 | .143 | .200 | .143 |
| 1984 Cleveland | AL | 49 | 91 | 14 | 0 | 0 | 0 | (0 | 0) | 14 | 16 | 1 | 8 | 0 | 11 | 0 | 3 | 1 | 12 | 6 | .67 | 2 | .154 | .220 | .154 |
| 1985 Cleveland | AL | 104 | 162 | 38 | 4 | 0 | 3 | (1 | 2) | 51 | 34 | 9 | 8 | 0 | 27 | 0 | 4 | 0 | 20 | 11 | .65 | 2 | .235 | .271 | .315 |
| 1986 Cleveland | AL | 105 | 95 | 25 | 4 | 1 | 0 | (0 | 0) | 31 | 33 | 8 | 13 | 0 | 12 | 0 | 2 | 0 | 23 | 6 | .79 | 1 | .263 | .352 | .326 |
| 1987 Cleveland | AL | 19 | 17 | 1 | 0 | 0 | 0 | (0 | 0) | 1 | 2 | 1 | 3 | 0 | 4 | 0 | 0 | 0 | 2 | 3 | .40 | 0 | .059 | .200 | .059 |
| 1988 Montreal | NL | 90 | 271 | 66 | 8 | 2 | 0 | (0 | 0) | 78 | 47 | 15 | 28 | 0 | 42 | 0 | 4 | 2 | 46 | 13 | .78 | 0 | .244 | .312 | .288 |
| 1989 Montreal | NL | 126 | 258 | 56 | 7 | 2 | 0 | (0 | 0) | 67 | 41 | 21 | 33 | 1 | 36 | 0 | 2 | 0 | 37 | 12 | .76 | 4 | .217 | .306 | .260 |
| 1990 Montreal | NL | 119 | 231 | 58 | 6 | 2 | 1 | (0 | 1) | 71 | 46 | 20 | 28 | 0 | 33 | 0 | 3 | 1 | 50 | 13 | .79 | 2 | .251 | .331 | .307 |
| 8 ML YEARS | | 625 | 1139 | 260 | 29 | 7 | 4 | (1 | 3) | 315 | 221 | 75 | 122 | 1 | 170 | 0 | 18 | 4 | 192 | 64 | .75 | 11 | .228 | .302 | .277 |

## Junior Noboa

**Bats:** Right **Throws:** Right **Pos:** 2B **Ht:** 5' 9" **Wt:** 160 **Born:** 11/10/64 **Age:** 26

| | | BATTING | | | | | | | | | | | | | | | | | BASERUNNING | | | | PERCENTAGES | | |
|---|---|---|---|---|---|---|---|---|---|---|---|---|---|---|---|---|---|---|---|---|---|---|---|---|---|
| Year Team | Lg | G | AB | H | 2B | 3B | HR | (Hm | Rd) | TB | R | RBI | TBB | IBB | SO | HBP | SH | SF | SB | CS | SB% | GDP | Avg | OBP | SLG |
| 1984 Cleveland | AL | 23 | 11 | 4 | 0 | 0 | 0 | (0 | 0) | 4 | 3 | 0 | 0 | 0 | 2 | 0 | 1 | 0 | 1 | 0 | 1.00 | 1 | .364 | .364 | .364 |
| 1987 Cleveland | AL | 39 | 80 | 18 | 2 | 1 | 0 | (0 | 0) | 22 | 7 | 7 | 3 | 1 | 6 | 0 | 5 | 0 | 1 | 0 | 1.00 | 1 | .225 | .253 | .275 |
| 1988 California | AL | 21 | 16 | 1 | 0 | 0 | 0 | (0 | 0) | 1 | 4 | 0 | 0 | 0 | 1 | 0 | 0 | 0 | 0 | 0 | .00 | 2 | .063 | .063 | .063 |
| 1989 Montreal | NL | 21 | 44 | 10 | 0 | 0 | 0 | (0 | 0) | 10 | 3 | 1 | 1 | 0 | 3 | 0 | 0 | 0 | 0 | 0 | .00 | 0 | .227 | .244 | .227 |
| 1990 Montreal | NL | 81 | 158 | 42 | 7 | 2 | 0 | (0 | 0) | 53 | 15 | 14 | 7 | 2 | 14 | 1 | 3 | 4 | 4 | 1 | .80 | 2 | .266 | .294 | .335 |
| 5 ML YEARS | | 185 | 309 | 75 | 9 | 3 | 0 | (0 | 0) | 90 | 32 | 22 | 11 | 3 | 26 | 1 | 9 | 4 | 6 | 1 | .86 | 6 | .243 | .268 | .291 |

# Paul Noce

**Bats:** Right **Throws:** Right **Pos:** PH **Ht:** 5'11" **Wt:** 170 **Born:** 12/16/59 **Age:** 31

| BATTING | | | | | | | | | | | | | | | | | | | | BASERUNNING | | | | PERCENTAGES | | |
|---|---|---|---|---|---|---|---|---|---|---|---|---|---|---|---|---|---|---|---|---|---|---|---|---|---|---|
| Year | Team | Lg | G | AB | H | 2B | 3B | HR | (Hm | Rd) | TB | R | RBI | TBB | IBB | SO | HBP | SH | SF | SB | CS | SB% | GDP | Avg | OBP | SLG |
| 1987 | Chicago | NL | 70 | 180 | 41 | 9 | 2 | 3 | (3 | 0) | 63 | 17 | 14 | 6 | 1 | 49 | 2 | 4 | 0 | 5 | 3 | .63 | 2 | .228 | .261 | .350 |
| 1990 | Cincinnati | NL | 1 | 1 | 1 | 0 | 0 | 0 | (0 | 0) | 1 | 0 | 0 | 0 | 0 | 0 | 0 | 0 | 0 | 0 | 0 | .00 | 0 | 1.000 | 1.000 | 1.000 |
| | 2 ML YEARS | | 71 | 181 | 42 | 9 | 2 | 3 | (3 | 0) | 64 | 17 | 14 | 6 | 1 | 49 | 2 | 4 | 0 | 5 | 3 | .63 | 2 | .232 | .265 | .354 |

# Matt Nokes

**Bats:** Left **Throws:** Right **Pos:** C/DH **Ht:** 6' 1" **Wt:** 185 **Born:** 10/31/63 **Age:** 27

| BATTING | | | | | | | | | | | | | | | | | | | | BASERUNNING | | | | PERCENTAGES | | |
|---|---|---|---|---|---|---|---|---|---|---|---|---|---|---|---|---|---|---|---|---|---|---|---|---|---|---|
| Year | Team | Lg | G | AB | H | 2B | 3B | HR | (Hm | Rd) | TB | R | RBI | TBB | IBB | SO | HBP | SH | SF | SB | CS | SB% | GDP | Avg | OBP | SLG |
| 1985 | San Francisco | NL | 19 | 53 | 11 | 2 | 0 | 2 | (1 | 1) | 19 | 3 | 5 | 1 | 0 | 9 | 1 | 0 | 0 | 0 | 0 | .00 | 2 | .208 | .236 | .358 |
| 1986 | Detroit | AL | 7 | 24 | 8 | 1 | 0 | 1 | (0 | 1) | 12 | 2 | 2 | 1 | 1 | 1 | 0 | 0 | 0 | 0 | 0 | .00 | 1 | .333 | .360 | .500 |
| 1987 | Detroit | AL | 135 | 461 | 133 | 14 | 2 | 32 | (14 | 18) | 247 | 69 | 87 | 35 | 2 | 70 | 6 | 3 | 3 | 2 | 1 | .67 | 13 | .289 | .345 | .536 |
| 1988 | Detroit | AL | 122 | 382 | 96 | 18 | 0 | 16 | (9 | 7) | 162 | 53 | 53 | 34 | 3 | 58 | 1 | 6 | 2 | 0 | 1 | .00 | 11 | .251 | .313 | .424 |
| 1989 | Detroit | AL | 87 | 268 | 67 | 10 | 0 | 9 | (7 | 2) | 104 | 15 | 39 | 17 | 1 | 37 | 2 | 1 | 2 | 1 | 0 | 1.00 | 7 | .250 | .298 | .388 |
| 1990 | 2 ML Teams | | 136 | 351 | 87 | 9 | 1 | 11 | (4 | 7) | 131 | 33 | 40 | 24 | 6 | 47 | 6 | 0 | 1 | 2 | 2 | .50 | 11 | .248 | .306 | .373 |
| 1990 | Detroit | AL | 44 | 111 | 30 | 5 | 1 | 3 | (1 | 2) | 46 | 12 | 8 | 4 | 3 | 14 | 2 | 0 | 1 | 0 | 0 | .00 | 5 | .270 | .305 | .414 |
| | New York | AL | 92 | 240 | 57 | 4 | 0 | 8 | (3 | 5) | 85 | 21 | 32 | 20 | 3 | 33 | 4 | 0 | 0 | 2 | 2 | .50 | 6 | .238 | .307 | .354 |
| | 6 ML YEARS | | 506 | 1539 | 402 | 54 | 3 | 71 | (35 | 36) | 675 | 175 | 226 | 112 | 13 | 222 | 16 | 10 | 8 | 5 | 4 | .56 | 45 | .261 | .316 | .439 |

# Dickie Noles

**Pitches:** Right **Bats:** Right **Pos:** RP **Ht:** 6' 2" **Wt:** 190 **Born:** 11/19/56 **Age:** 34

| HOW MUCH HE PITCHED | | | | | | | | | WHAT HE GAVE UP | | | | | | | | | | | | THE RESULTS | | | | | |
|---|---|---|---|---|---|---|---|---|---|---|---|---|---|---|---|---|---|---|---|---|---|---|---|---|---|---|
| Year | Team | Lg | G | GS | CG | GF | IP | BFP | H | R | ER | HR | SH | SF | HB | TBB | IBB | SO | WP | Bk | W | L | Pct. | ShO | Sv | ERA |
| 1979 | Philadelphia | NL | 14 | 14 | 0 | 0 | 90 | 377 | 80 | 40 | 38 | 6 | 8 | 4 | 2 | 38 | 2 | 42 | 1 | 2 | 3 | 4 | .429 | 0 | 0 | 3.80 |
| 1980 | Philadelphia | NL | 48 | 3 | 0 | 20 | 81 | 367 | 80 | 42 | 35 | 5 | 7 | 2 | 1 | 42 | 11 | 57 | 2 | 0 | 1 | 4 | .200 | 0 | 6 | 3.89 |
| 1981 | Philadelphia | NL | 13 | 8 | 0 | 1 | 58 | 249 | 57 | 30 | 27 | 2 | 2 | 2 | 3 | 23 | 2 | 34 | 3 | 3 | 2 | 2 | .500 | 0 | 0 | 4.19 |
| 1982 | Chicago | NL | 31 | 30 | 2 | 1 | 171 | 744 | 180 | 99 | 84 | 11 | 11 | 10 | 5 | 61 | 2 | 85 | 4 | 6 | 10 | 13 | .435 | 2 | 0 | 4.42 |
| 1983 | Chicago | NL | 24 | 18 | 1 | 2 | 116.1 | 506 | 133 | 69 | 61 | 9 | 2 | 2 | 1 | 37 | 3 | 59 | 3 | 1 | 5 | 10 | .333 | 1 | 0 | 4.72 |
| 1984 | 2 ML Teams | | 39 | 7 | 0 | 12 | 108.1 | 480 | 120 | 67 | 62 | 10 | 0 | 2 | 6 | 46 | 1 | 53 | 4 | 1 | 4 | 5 | .444 | 0 | 0 | 5.15 |
| 1985 | Texas | AL | 28 | 13 | 0 | 3 | 110.1 | 488 | 129 | 67 | 62 | 11 | 2 | 0 | 6 | 33 | 1 | 59 | 1 | 0 | 4 | 8 | .333 | 0 | 1 | 5.06 |
| 1986 | Cleveland | AL | 32 | 0 | 0 | 9 | 54.2 | 251 | 56 | 33 | 31 | 9 | 3 | 5 | 5 | 30 | 4 | 32 | 1 | 1 | 3 | 2 | .600 | 0 | 0 | 5.10 |
| 1987 | 2 ML Teams | | 45 | 1 | 0 | 19 | 66.1 | 294 | 61 | 32 | 26 | 1 | 5 | 1 | 5 | 28 | 1 | 33 | 4 | 2 | 4 | 2 | .667 | 0 | 4 | 3.53 |
| 1988 | Baltimore | AL | 2 | 2 | 0 | 0 | 3.1 | 23 | 11 | 10 | 9 | 2 | 0 | 0 | 1 | 0 | 0 | 1 | 0 | 0 | 0 | 2 | .000 | 0 | 0 | 24.30 |
| 1990 | Philadelphia | NL | 1 | 0 | 0 | 1 | 0.1 | 3 | 2 | 1 | 1 | 0 | 0 | 0 | 0 | 0 | 0 | 0 | 0 | 0 | 0 | 1 | .000 | 0 | 0 | 27.00 |
| 1984 | Chicago | NL | 21 | 1 | 0 | 6 | 50.2 | 216 | 60 | 29 | 29 | 4 | 0 | 2 | 1 | 16 | 1 | 14 | 1 | 0 | 2 | 2 | .500 | 0 | 0 | 5.15 |
| | Texas | AL | 18 | 6 | 0 | 6 | 57.2 | 264 | 60 | 38 | 33 | 6 | 0 | 0 | 5 | 30 | 0 | 39 | 3 | 1 | 2 | 3 | .400 | 0 | 0 | 5.15 |
| 1987 | Chicago | NL | 41 | 1 | 0 | 16 | 64.1 | 285 | 59 | 31 | 25 | 1 | 5 | 1 | 5 | 27 | 1 | 33 | 4 | 2 | 4 | 2 | .667 | 0 | 2 | 3.50 |
| | Detroit | AL | 4 | 0 | 0 | 3 | 2 | 9 | 2 | 1 | 1 | 0 | 0 | 0 | 0 | 1 | 0 | 0 | 0 | 0 | 0 | 0 | .000 | 0 | 2 | 4.50 |
| | 11 ML YEARS | | 277 | 96 | 3 | 68 | 859.2 | 3782 | 909 | 490 | 436 | 66 | 40 | 28 | 35 | 338 | 27 | 455 | 23 | 16 | 36 | 53 | .404 | 3 | 11 | 4.56 |

# Mike Norris

**Pitches:** Right **Bats:** Right **Pos:** RP **Ht:** 6' 2" **Wt:** 190 **Born:** 03/19/55 **Age:** 36

| HOW MUCH HE PITCHED | | | | | | | | | WHAT HE GAVE UP | | | | | | | | | | | | THE RESULTS | | | | | |
|---|---|---|---|---|---|---|---|---|---|---|---|---|---|---|---|---|---|---|---|---|---|---|---|---|---|---|
| Year | Team | Lg | G | GS | CG | GF | IP | BFP | H | R | ER | HR | SH | SF | HB | TBB | IBB | SO | WP | Bk | W | L | Pct. | ShO | Sv | ERA |
| 1975 | Oakland | AL | 4 | 3 | 1 | 0 | 17 | 65 | 6 | 2 | 0 | 0 | 0 | 1 | 0 | 8 | 0 | 5 | 0 | 0 | 1 | 0 | 1.000 | 1 | 0 | 0.00 |
| 1976 | Oakland | AL | 24 | 19 | 1 | 1 | 96 | 430 | 91 | 53 | 51 | 10 | 4 | 4 | 2 | 56 | 2 | 44 | 4 | 0 | 4 | 5 | .444 | 1 | 0 | 4.78 |
| 1977 | Oakland | AL | 16 | 12 | 1 | 2 | 77 | 335 | 77 | 45 | 41 | 14 | 2 | 2 | 4 | 31 | 1 | 35 | 4 | 0 | 2 | 7 | .222 | 1 | 0 | 4.79 |
| 1978 | Oakland | AL | 14 | 5 | 1 | 1 | 49 | 230 | 46 | 35 | 30 | 2 | 4 | 2 | 3 | 35 | 1 | 36 | 1 | 0 | 0 | 5 | .000 | 0 | 0 | 5.51 |
| 1979 | Oakland | AL | 29 | 18 | 3 | 3 | 146 | 669 | 146 | 87 | 78 | 11 | 6 | 9 | 9 | 94 | 9 | 96 | 10 | 1 | 5 | 8 | .385 | 0 | 0 | 4.81 |
| 1980 | Oakland | AL | 33 | 33 | 24 | 0 | 284 | 1135 | 215 | 88 | 80 | 18 | 9 | 7 | 6 | 83 | 2 | 180 | 9 | 4 | 22 | 9 | .710 | 1 | 0 | 2.54 |
| 1981 | Oakland | AL | 23 | 23 | 12 | 0 | 173 | 721 | 145 | 77 | 72 | 17 | 6 | 7 | 10 | 63 | 0 | 78 | 14 | 5 | 12 | 9 | .571 | 2 | 0 | 3.75 |
| 1982 | Oakland | AL | 28 | 28 | 7 | 0 | 166.1 | 735 | 154 | 103 | 88 | 25 | 6 | 3 | 6 | 84 | 1 | 83 | 7 | 4 | 7 | 11 | .389 | 1 | 0 | 4.76 |
| 1983 | Oakland | AL | 16 | 16 | 2 | 0 | 88.2 | 365 | 68 | 42 | 37 | 11 | 5 | 2 | 3 | 36 | 0 | 63 | 1 | 1 | 4 | 5 | .444 | 0 | 0 | 3.76 |
| 1990 | Oakland | AL | 14 | 0 | 0 | 9 | 27 | 113 | 24 | 10 | 9 | 0 | 2 | 1 | 2 | 9 | 0 | 16 | 3 | 2 | 1 | 0 | 1.000 | 0 | 0 | 3.00 |
| | 10 ML YEARS | | 201 | 157 | 52 | 16 | 1124 | 4798 | 972 | 542 | 486 | 108 | 44 | 38 | 45 | 499 | 16 | 636 | 53 | 17 | 58 | 59 | .496 | 7 | 0 | 3.89 |

# Randy Nosek

**Pitches:** Right **Bats:** Right **Pos:** SP **Ht:** 6' 4" **Wt:** 215 **Born:** 01/08/67 **Age:** 24

| HOW MUCH HE PITCHED | | | | | | | | | WHAT HE GAVE UP | | | | | | | | | | | | THE RESULTS | | | | | |
|---|---|---|---|---|---|---|---|---|---|---|---|---|---|---|---|---|---|---|---|---|---|---|---|---|---|---|
| Year | Team | Lg | G | GS | CG | GF | IP | BFP | H | R | ER | HR | SH | SF | HB | TBB | IBB | SO | WP | Bk | W | L | Pct. | ShO | Sv | ERA |
| 1986 | Gastonia | A | 12 | 10 | 0 | 1 | 52.1 | 256 | 56 | 41 | 35 | 4 | 1 | 2 | 2 | 49 | 0 | 37 | 11 | 1 | 4 | 5 | .444 | 0 | 0 | 6.02 |
| | Bristol | R | 11 | 11 | 2 | 0 | 63.1 | 289 | 58 | 38 | 32 | 1 | 3 | 1 | 4 | 45 | 0 | 48 | 12 | 0 | 6 | 4 | .600 | 0 | 0 | 4.55 |

| Year Team | Lg | G | GS | CG | GF | IP | BFP | H | R | ER | HR | SH | SF | HB | TBB | IBB | SO | WP | Bk | W | L | Pct. | ShO | Sv | ERA |
|---|---|---|---|---|---|---|---|---|---|---|---|---|---|---|---|---|---|---|---|---|---|---|---|---|---|
| 1987 Lakeland | A | 10 | 10 | 0 | 0 | 39 | 204 | 63 | 40 | 32 | 4 | 0 | 3 | 1 | 30 | 0 | 16 | 6 | 1 | 2 | 4 | .333 | 0 | 0 | 7.38 |
| Fayettevlle | A | 16 | 16 | 0 | 0 | 77.2 | 375 | 69 | 63 | 40 | 1 | 1 | 4 | 7 | 63 | 0 | 57 | 12 | 2 | 4 | 11 | .267 | 0 | 0 | 4.64 |
| 1988 Lakeland | A | 8 | 8 | 0 | 0 | 30.2 | 137 | 29 | 17 | 13 | 0 | 1 | 0 | 0 | 16 | 0 | 11 | 4 | 3 | 0 | 4 | .000 | 0 | 0 | 3.82 |
| 1989 Toledo | AAA | 1 | 1 | 0 | 0 | 1 | 9 | 2 | 4 | 4 | 0 | 0 | 0 | 0 | 4 | 0 | 0 | 0 | 0 | 0 | 0 | .000 | 0 | 0 | 36.00 |
| London | AA | 22 | 22 | 3 | 0 | 123.2 | 569 | 113 | 75 | 68 | 5 | 4 | 6 | 3 | 100 | 1 | 62 | 14 | 1 | 8 | 10 | .444 | 1 | 0 | 4.95 |
| 1990 Toledo | AAA | 22 | 19 | 0 | 1 | 109.1 | 499 | 112 | 70 | 63 | 4 | 3 | 0 | 4 | 66 | 0 | 55 | 10 | 2 | 5 | 8 | .385 | 0 | 0 | 5.19 |
| 1989 Detroit | AL | 2 | 2 | 0 | 0 | 5.1 | 31 | 7 | 8 | 8 | 2 | 0 | 0 | 0 | 10 | 0 | 4 | 0 | 0 | 0 | 2 | .000 | 0 | 0 | 13.50 |
| 1990 Detroit | AL | 3 | 2 | 0 | 0 | 7 | 35 | 7 | 7 | 6 | 1 | 0 | 1 | 0 | 9 | 1 | 3 | 1 | 0 | 1 | 1 | .500 | 0 | 0 | 7.71 |
| 2 ML YEARS | | 5 | 4 | 0 | 0 | 12.1 | 66 | 14 | 15 | 14 | 3 | 0 | 1 | 0 | 19 | 1 | 7 | 1 | 0 | 1 | 3 | .250 | 0 | 0 | 10.22 |

## Rafael Novoa

**Pitches:** Left **Bats:** Left **Pos:** RP **Ht:** 6' 0" **Wt:** 180 **Born:** 10/26/67 **Age:** 23

| | | HOW MUCH HE PITCHED | | | | | | WHAT HE GAVE UP | | | | | | | | | | | | THE RESULTS | | | | | |
|---|---|---|---|---|---|---|---|---|---|---|---|---|---|---|---|---|---|---|---|---|---|---|---|---|---|
| Year Team | Lg | G | GS | CG | GF | IP | BFP | H | R | ER | HR | SH | SF | HB | TBB | IBB | SO | WP | Bk | W | L | Pct. | ShO | Sv | ERA |
| 1989 Everett | A | 3 | 3 | 0 | 0 | 15 | 73 | 20 | 11 | 8 | 2 | 0 | 0 | 1 | 8 | 0 | 20 | 3 | 1 | 0 | 1 | .000 | 0 | 0 | 4.80 |
| Clinton | A | 13 | 10 | 0 | 0 | 63.2 | 267 | 58 | 20 | 18 | 1 | 9 | 1 | 4 | 18 | 1 | 61 | 1 | 6 | 5 | 4 | .556 | 0 | 0 | 2.54 |
| 1990 Clinton | A | 15 | 14 | 3 | 0 | 97.2 | 397 | 73 | 32 | 26 | 6 | 2 | 3 | 4 | 30 | 0 | 113 | 2 | 2 | 9 | 2 | .818 | 1 | 0 | 2.40 |
| Shreveport | AA | 11 | 10 | 2 | 1 | 71.2 | 297 | 60 | 21 | 21 | 3 | 1 | 2 | 3 | 25 | 0 | 66 | 1 | 0 | 5 | 4 | .556 | 1 | 0 | 2.64 |
| 1990 San Francisco | NL | 7 | 2 | 0 | 2 | 18.2 | 88 | 21 | 14 | 14 | 3 | 0 | 1 | 0 | 13 | 1 | 14 | 0 | 0 | 0 | 1 | .000 | 0 | 1 | 6.75 |

## Edwin Nunez

**Pitches:** Right **Bats:** Right **Pos:** RP **Ht:** 6' 5" **Wt:** 240 **Born:** 05/27/63 **Age:** 28

| | | HOW MUCH HE PITCHED | | | | | | WHAT HE GAVE UP | | | | | | | | | | | | THE RESULTS | | | | | |
|---|---|---|---|---|---|---|---|---|---|---|---|---|---|---|---|---|---|---|---|---|---|---|---|---|---|
| Year Team | Lg | G | GS | CG | GF | IP | BFP | H | R | ER | HR | SH | SF | HB | TBB | IBB | SO | WP | Bk | W | L | Pct. | ShO | Sv | ERA |
| 1982 Seattle | AL | 8 | 5 | 0 | 0 | 35.1 | 153 | 36 | 18 | 18 | 7 | 3 | 0 | 0 | 16 | 0 | 27 | 0 | 2 | 1 | 2 | .333 | 0 | 0 | 4.58 |
| 1983 Seattle | AL | 14 | 5 | 0 | 4 | 37 | 170 | 40 | 21 | 18 | 3 | 1 | 0 | 3 | 22 | 1 | 35 | 0 | 2 | 0 | 4 | .000 | 0 | 0 | 4.38 |
| 1984 Seattle | AL | 37 | 0 | 0 | 23 | 67.2 | 280 | 55 | 26 | 24 | 8 | 1 | 3 | 3 | 21 | 2 | 57 | 1 | 0 | 2 | 2 | .500 | 0 | 7 | 3.19 |
| 1985 Seattle | AL | 70 | 0 | 0 | 53 | 90.1 | 378 | 79 | 36 | 31 | 13 | 4 | 3 | 0 | 34 | 5 | 58 | 2 | 1 | 7 | 3 | .700 | 0 | 16 | 3.09 |
| 1986 Seattle | AL | 14 | 1 | 0 | 6 | 21.2 | 93 | 25 | 15 | 14 | 5 | 0 | 0 | 0 | 5 | 1 | 17 | 0 | 0 | 1 | 2 | .333 | 0 | 0 | 5.82 |
| 1987 Seattle | AL | 48 | 0 | 0 | 40 | 47.1 | 198 | 45 | 20 | 20 | 7 | 3 | 4 | 1 | 18 | 3 | 34 | 2 | 0 | 3 | 4 | .429 | 0 | 12 | 3.80 |
| 1988 2 ML Teams | | 24 | 3 | 0 | 6 | 43.1 | 210 | 66 | 40 | 33 | 5 | 2 | 4 | 2 | 17 | 3 | 27 | 1 | 1 | 2 | 4 | .333 | 0 | 0 | 6.85 |
| 1989 Detroit | AL | 27 | 0 | 0 | 12 | 54 | 238 | 49 | 33 | 25 | 6 | 6 | 3 | 0 | 36 | 13 | 41 | 2 | 1 | 3 | 4 | .429 | 0 | 1 | 4.17 |
| 1990 Detroit | AL | 42 | 0 | 0 | 15 | 80.1 | 343 | 65 | 26 | 20 | 4 | 5 | 1 | 2 | 37 | 6 | 66 | 4 | 0 | 3 | 1 | .750 | 0 | 6 | 2.24 |
| 1988 Seattle | AL | 14 | 3 | 0 | 2 | 29.1 | 145 | 45 | 33 | 26 | 4 | 2 | 4 | 2 | 14 | 3 | 19 | 0 | 1 | 1 | 4 | .200 | 0 | 0 | 7.98 |
| New York | NL | 10 | 0 | 0 | 4 | 14 | 65 | 21 | 7 | 7 | 1 | 0 | 0 | 0 | 3 | 0 | 8 | 1 | 0 | 1 | 0 | 1.000 | 0 | 0 | 4.50 |
| 9 ML YEARS | | 284 | 14 | 0 | 159 | 477 | 2063 | 460 | 235 | 203 | 58 | 25 | 18 | 11 | 206 | 34 | 362 | 12 | 7 | 22 | 26 | .458 | 0 | 42 | 3.83 |

## Jose Nunez

**Pitches:** Right **Bats:** Right **Pos:** RP/SP **Ht:** 6' 3" **Wt:** 185 **Born:** 01/13/64 **Age:** 27

| | | HOW MUCH HE PITCHED | | | | | | WHAT HE GAVE UP | | | | | | | | | | | | THE RESULTS | | | | | |
|---|---|---|---|---|---|---|---|---|---|---|---|---|---|---|---|---|---|---|---|---|---|---|---|---|---|
| Year Team | Lg | G | GS | CG | GF | IP | BFP | H | R | ER | HR | SH | SF | HB | TBB | IBB | SO | WP | Bk | W | L | Pct. | ShO | Sv | ERA |
| 1987 Toronto | AL | 37 | 9 | 0 | 13 | 97 | 427 | 91 | 57 | 54 | 12 | 8 | 5 | 0 | 58 | 8 | 99 | 3 | 1 | 5 | 2 | .714 | 0 | 0 | 5.01 |
| 1988 Toronto | AL | 13 | 2 | 0 | 3 | 29.1 | 127 | 28 | 11 | 10 | 3 | 1 | 0 | 1 | 17 | 3 | 18 | 2 | 1 | 0 | 1 | .000 | 0 | 0 | 3.07 |
| 1989 Toronto | AL | 6 | 1 | 0 | 3 | 10.2 | 42 | 8 | 3 | 3 | 0 | 0 | 0 | 0 | 2 | 0 | 14 | 2 | 0 | 0 | 0 | .000 | 0 | 0 | 2.53 |
| 1990 Chicago | NL | 21 | 10 | 0 | 4 | 60.2 | 274 | 61 | 47 | 44 | 5 | 11 | 3 | 0 | 34 | 4 | 40 | 2 | 2 | 4 | 7 | .364 | 0 | 0 | 6.53 |
| 4 ML YEARS | | 77 | 22 | 0 | 23 | 197.2 | 870 | 188 | 118 | 111 | 20 | 20 | 8 | 1 | 111 | 15 | 171 | 9 | 4 | 9 | 10 | .474 | 0 | 0 | 5.05 |

## Charlie O'Brien

**Bats:** Right **Throws:** Right **Pos:** C **Ht:** 6' 2" **Wt:** 190 **Born:** 05/01/61 **Age:** 30

| | | BATTING | | | | | | | | | | | | | | | | | BASERUNNING | | | | PERCENTAGES | | |
|---|---|---|---|---|---|---|---|---|---|---|---|---|---|---|---|---|---|---|---|---|---|---|---|---|---|
| Year Team | Lg | G | AB | H | 2B | 3B | HR | (Hm | Rd) | TB | R | RBI | TBB | IBB | SO | HBP | SH | SF | SB | CS | SB% | GDP | Avg | OBP | SLG |
| 1985 Oakland | AL | 16 | 11 | 3 | 1 | 0 | 0 | (0 | 0) | 4 | 3 | 1 | 3 | 0 | 3 | 0 | 0 | 0 | 0 | 0 | .00 | 0 | .273 | .429 | .364 |
| 1987 Milwaukee | AL | 10 | 35 | 7 | 3 | 1 | 0 | (0 | 0) | 12 | 2 | 0 | 4 | 0 | 4 | 0 | 1 | 0 | 0 | 1 | .00 | 0 | .200 | .282 | .343 |
| 1988 Milwaukee | AL | 40 | 118 | 26 | 6 | 0 | 2 | (2 | 0) | 38 | 12 | 9 | 5 | 0 | 16 | 0 | 4 | 0 | 0 | 1 | .00 | 3 | .220 | .252 | .322 |
| 1989 Milwaukee | AL | 62 | 188 | 44 | 10 | 0 | 6 | (4 | 2) | 72 | 22 | 35 | 21 | 1 | 11 | 9 | 8 | 0 | 0 | 0 | .00 | 11 | .234 | .339 | .383 |
| 1990 2 ML Teams | | 74 | 213 | 38 | 10 | 2 | 0 | (0 | 0) | 52 | 17 | 20 | 21 | 3 | 34 | 3 | 10 | 2 | 0 | 0 | .00 | 4 | .178 | .259 | .244 |
| 1990 Milwaukee | AL | 46 | 145 | 27 | 7 | 2 | 0 | (0 | 0) | 38 | 11 | 11 | 11 | 1 | 26 | 2 | 8 | 0 | 0 | 0 | .00 | 3 | .186 | .253 | .262 |
| New York | NL | 28 | 68 | 11 | 3 | 0 | 0 | (0 | 0) | 14 | 6 | 9 | 10 | 2 | 8 | 1 | 2 | 2 | 0 | 0 | .00 | 1 | .162 | .272 | .206 |
| 5 ML YEARS | | 202 | 565 | 118 | 30 | 3 | 8 | (6 | 2) | 178 | 56 | 65 | 54 | 4 | 68 | 12 | 23 | 2 | 0 | 2 | .00 | 18 | .209 | .291 | .315 |

## Pete O'Brien

**Bats:** Left **Throws:** Left **Pos:** 1B **Ht:** 6' 2" **Wt:** 205 **Born:** 02/09/58 **Age:** 33

| | | BATTING | | | | | | | | | | | | | | | | | BASERUNNING | | | | PERCENTAGES | | |
|---|---|---|---|---|---|---|---|---|---|---|---|---|---|---|---|---|---|---|---|---|---|---|---|---|---|
| Year Team | Lg | G | AB | H | 2B | 3B | HR | (Hm | Rd) | TB | R | RBI | TBB | IBB | SO | HBP | SH | SF | SB | CS | SB% | GDP | Avg | OBP | SLG |
| 1982 Texas | AL | 20 | 67 | 16 | 4 | 1 | 4 | (2 | 2) | 34 | 13 | 13 | 6 | 0 | 8 | 0 | 0 | 1 | 1 | 0 | 1.00 | 0 | .239 | .297 | .507 |
| 1983 Texas | AL | 154 | 524 | 124 | 24 | 5 | 8 | (4 | 4) | 182 | 53 | 53 | 58 | 2 | 62 | 1 | 3 | 2 | 5 | 4 | .56 | 12 | .237 | .313 | .347 |
| 1984 Texas | AL | 142 | 520 | 149 | 26 | 2 | 18 | (7 | 11) | 233 | 57 | 80 | 53 | 8 | 50 | 0 | 1 | 7 | 3 | 5 | .38 | 11 | .287 | .348 | .448 |
| 1985 Texas | AL | 159 | 573 | 153 | 34 | 3 | 22 | (12 | 10) | 259 | 69 | 92 | 69 | 4 | 53 | 1 | 3 | 9 | 5 | 10 | .33 | 18 | .267 | .342 | .452 |

| Year Team | Lg | G | AB | H | 2B | 3B | HR | (Hm | Rd) | TB | R | RBI | TBB | IBB | SO | HBP | SH | SF | SB | CS | SB% | GDP | Avg | OBP | SLG |
|---|---|---|---|---|---|---|---|---|---|---|---|---|---|---|---|---|---|---|---|---|---|---|---|---|---|
| 1986 Texas | AL | 156 | 551 | 160 | 23 | 3 | 23 | (11 | 12) | 258 | 86 | 90 | 87 | 11 | 66 | 0 | 0 | 3 | 4 | 4 | .50 | 19 | .290 | .385 | .468 |
| 1987 Texas | AL | 159 | 569 | 163 | 26 | 1 | 23 | (9 | 14) | 260 | 84 | 88 | 59 | 6 | 61 | 0 | 0 | 10 | 0 | 4 | .00 | 9 | .286 | .348 | .457 |
| 1988 Texas | AL | 156 | 547 | 149 | 24 | 1 | 16 | (6 | 10) | 223 | 57 | 71 | 72 | 9 | 73 | 0 | 1 | 8 | 1 | 4 | .20 | 12 | .272 | .352 | .408 |
| 1989 Cleveland | AL | 155 | 554 | 144 | 24 | 1 | 12 | (5 | 7) | 206 | 75 | 55 | 83 | 17 | 48 | 2 | 2 | 5 | 3 | 1 | .75 | 10 | .260 | .356 | .372 |
| 1990 Seattle | AL | 108 | 366 | 82 | 18 | 0 | 5 | (3 | 2) | 115 | 32 | 27 | 44 | 1 | 33 | 2 | 1 | 4 | 0 | 0 | .00 | 12 | .224 | .308 | .314 |
| 9 ML YEARS | | 1209 | 4271 | 1140 | 203 | 17 | 131 | (59 | 72) | 1770 | 526 | 569 | 531 | 58 | 454 | 6 | 11 | 49 | 22 | 32 | .41 | 103 | .267 | .345 | .414 |

## Tom O'Malley

**Bats:** Left **Throws:** Right **Pos:** 3B **Ht:** 6' 0" **Wt:** 190 **Born:** 12/25/60 **Age:** 30

| | | BATTING | | | | | | | | | | | | | | | | | BASERUNNING | | | | PERCENTAGES | | |
|---|---|---|---|---|---|---|---|---|---|---|---|---|---|---|---|---|---|---|---|---|---|---|---|---|---|
| Year Team | Lg | G | AB | H | 2B | 3B | HR | (Hm | Rd) | TB | R | RBI | TBB | IBB | SO | HBP | SH | SF | SB | CS | SB% | GDP | Avg | OBP | SLG |
| 1982 San Francisco | NL | 92 | 291 | 80 | 12 | 4 | 2 | (0 | 2) | 106 | 26 | 27 | 33 | 9 | 39 | 1 | 1 | 1 | 0 | 3 | .00 | 11 | .275 | .350 | .364 |
| 1983 San Francisco | NL | 135 | 410 | 106 | 16 | 1 | 5 | (3 | 2) | 139 | 40 | 45 | 52 | 4 | 47 | 4 | 4 | 3 | 2 | 4 | .33 | 12 | .259 | .345 | .339 |
| 1984 2 ML Teams | | 25 | 41 | 5 | 0 | 0 | 0 | (0 | 0) | 5 | 2 | 3 | 2 | 0 | 7 | 0 | 0 | 0 | 0 | 0 | .00 | 1 | .122 | .163 | .122 |
| 1985 Baltimore | AL | 8 | 14 | 1 | 0 | 0 | 1 | (0 | 1) | 4 | 1 | 2 | 0 | 0 | 2 | 0 | 0 | 0 | 0 | 0 | .00 | 1 | .071 | .071 | .286 |
| 1986 Baltimore | AL | 56 | 181 | 46 | 9 | 0 | 1 | (1 | 0) | 58 | 19 | 18 | 17 | 1 | 21 | 0 | 1 | 1 | 0 | 1 | .00 | 4 | .254 | .317 | .320 |
| 1987 Texas | AL | 45 | 117 | 32 | 8 | 0 | 1 | (0 | 1) | 43 | 10 | 12 | 15 | 1 | 9 | 0 | 0 | 2 | 0 | 0 | .00 | 7 | .274 | .351 | .368 |
| 1988 Montreal | NL | 14 | 27 | 7 | 0 | 0 | 0 | (0 | 0) | 7 | 3 | 2 | 3 | 1 | 4 | 0 | 0 | 1 | 0 | 0 | .00 | 0 | .259 | .323 | .259 |
| 1989 New York | NL | 9 | 11 | 6 | 2 | 0 | 0 | (0 | 0) | 8 | 2 | 8 | 0 | 0 | 2 | 0 | 0 | 0 | 0 | 0 | .00 | 0 | .545 | .545 | .727 |
| 1990 New York | NL | 82 | 121 | 27 | 7 | 0 | 3 | (1 | 2) | 43 | 14 | 14 | 11 | 1 | 20 | 0 | 0 | 1 | 0 | 0 | .00 | 1 | .223 | .286 | .355 |
| 1984 San Francisco | NL | 13 | 25 | 3 | 0 | 0 | 0 | (0 | 0) | 3 | 2 | 0 | 2 | 0 | 2 | 0 | 0 | 0 | 0 | 0 | .00 | 0 | .120 | .185 | .120 |
| Chicago | AL | 12 | 16 | 2 | 0 | 0 | 0 | (0 | 0) | 2 | 0 | 3 | 0 | 0 | 5 | 0 | 0 | 0 | 0 | 0 | .00 | 1 | .125 | .125 | .125 |
| 9 ML YEARS | | 466 | 1213 | 310 | 54 | 5 | 13 | (5 | 8) | 413 | 117 | 131 | 133 | 17 | 151 | 5 | 6 | 9 | 2 | 8 | .20 | 37 | .256 | .329 | .340 |

## Randy O'Neal

**Pitches:** Right **Bats:** Right **Pos:** RP **Ht:** 6' 2" **Wt:** 195 **Born:** 08/30/60 **Age:** 30

| | | HOW MUCH HE PITCHED | | | | | | WHAT HE GAVE UP | | | | | | | | | | | | THE RESULTS | | | | | |
|---|---|---|---|---|---|---|---|---|---|---|---|---|---|---|---|---|---|---|---|---|---|---|---|---|---|
| Year Team | Lg | G | GS | CG | GF | IP | BFP | H | R | ER | HR | SH | SF | HB | TBB | IBB | SO | WP | Bk | W | L | Pct. | ShO | Sv | ERA |
| 1984 Detroit | AL | 4 | 3 | 0 | 0 | 18.2 | 78 | 16 | 7 | 7 | 0 | 0 | 0 | 0 | 6 | 0 | 12 | 1 | 0 | 2 | 1 | .667 | 0 | 0 | 3.38 |
| 1985 Detroit | AL | 28 | 12 | 1 | 8 | 94.1 | 388 | 82 | 42 | 34 | 8 | 1 | 7 | 2 | 36 | 3 | 52 | 5 | 0 | 5 | 5 | .500 | 0 | 1 | 3.24 |
| 1986 Detroit | AL | 37 | 11 | 1 | 9 | 122.2 | 522 | 121 | 69 | 59 | 13 | 3 | 6 | 3 | 44 | 9 | 68 | 8 | 0 | 3 | 7 | .300 | 0 | 2 | 4.33 |
| 1987 2 ML Teams | | 17 | 11 | 0 | 2 | 66 | 300 | 81 | 42 | 39 | 12 | 2 | 2 | 2 | 26 | 3 | 37 | 10 | 0 | 4 | 2 | .667 | 0 | 0 | 5.32 |
| 1988 St. Louis | NL | 10 | 8 | 0 | 0 | 53 | 222 | 57 | 29 | 27 | 7 | 2 | 0 | 2 | 10 | 1 | 20 | 4 | 0 | 2 | 3 | .400 | 0 | 0 | 4.58 |
| 1989 Philadelphia | NL | 20 | 1 | 0 | 1 | 39 | 167 | 46 | 28 | 27 | 5 | 2 | 3 | 0 | 9 | 2 | 29 | 5 | 1 | 0 | 1 | .000 | 0 | 0 | 6.23 |
| 1990 San Francisco | NL | 26 | 0 | 0 | 4 | 47 | 208 | 58 | 23 | 20 | 3 | 3 | 2 | 0 | 18 | 4 | 30 | 4 | 1 | 1 | 0 | 1.000 | 0 | 0 | 3.83 |
| 1987 Atlanta | NL | 16 | 10 | 0 | 2 | 61 | 279 | 79 | 41 | 38 | 12 | 1 | 2 | 2 | 24 | 3 | 33 | 9 | 0 | 4 | 2 | .667 | 0 | 0 | 5.61 |
| St. Louis | NL | 1 | 1 | 0 | 0 | 5 | 21 | 2 | 1 | 1 | 0 | 1 | 0 | 0 | 2 | 0 | 4 | 1 | 0 | 0 | 0 | .000 | 0 | 0 | 1.80 |
| 7 ML YEARS | | 142 | 46 | 2 | 24 | 440.2 | 1885 | 461 | 240 | 213 | 48 | 13 | 20 | 9 | 149 | 22 | 248 | 37 | 2 | 17 | 19 | .472 | 0 | 3 | 4.35 |

## Paul O'Neill

**Bats:** Left **Throws:** Left **Pos:** RF **Ht:** 6' 4" **Wt:** 210 **Born:** 02/25/63 **Age:** 28

| | | BATTING | | | | | | | | | | | | | | | | | BASERUNNING | | | | PERCENTAGES | | |
|---|---|---|---|---|---|---|---|---|---|---|---|---|---|---|---|---|---|---|---|---|---|---|---|---|---|
| Year Team | Lg | G | AB | H | 2B | 3B | HR | (Hm | Rd) | TB | R | RBI | TBB | IBB | SO | HBP | SH | SF | SB | CS | SB% | GDP | Avg | OBP | SLG |
| 1985 Cincinnati | NL | 5 | 12 | 4 | 1 | 0 | 0 | (0 | 0) | 5 | 1 | 1 | 0 | 0 | 2 | 0 | 0 | 0 | 0 | 0 | .00 | 0 | .333 | .333 | .417 |
| 1986 Cincinnati | NL | 3 | 2 | 0 | 0 | 0 | 0 | (0 | 0) | 0 | 0 | 0 | 1 | 0 | 1 | 0 | 0 | 0 | 0 | 0 | .00 | 0 | .000 | .333 | .000 |
| 1987 Cincinnati | NL | 84 | 160 | 41 | 14 | 1 | 7 | (4 | 3) | 78 | 24 | 28 | 18 | 1 | 29 | 0 | 0 | 0 | 2 | 1 | .67 | 3 | .256 | .331 | .488 |
| 1988 Cincinnati | NL | 145 | 485 | 122 | 25 | 3 | 16 | (12 | 4) | 201 | 58 | 73 | 38 | 5 | 65 | 2 | 3 | 5 | 8 | 6 | .57 | 7 | .252 | .306 | .414 |
| 1989 Cincinnati | NL | 117 | 428 | 118 | 24 | 2 | 15 | (11 | 4) | 191 | 49 | 74 | 46 | 8 | 64 | 2 | 0 | 4 | 20 | 5 | .80 | 7 | .276 | .346 | .446 |
| 1990 Cincinnati | NL | 145 | 503 | 136 | 28 | 0 | 16 | (10 | 6) | 212 | 59 | 78 | 53 | 13 | 103 | 2 | 1 | 5 | 13 | 11 | .54 | 12 | .270 | .339 | .421 |
| 6 ML YEARS | | 499 | 1590 | 421 | 92 | 6 | 54 | (37 | 17) | 687 | 191 | 254 | 156 | 27 | 264 | 6 | 4 | 14 | 43 | 23 | .65 | 29 | .265 | .330 | .432 |

## Ken Oberkfell

**Bats:** Left **Throws:** Right **Pos:** 3B/2B **Ht:** 6' 1" **Wt:** 210 **Born:** 05/04/56 **Age:** 35

| | | BATTING | | | | | | | | | | | | | | | | | BASERUNNING | | | | PERCENTAGES | | |
|---|---|---|---|---|---|---|---|---|---|---|---|---|---|---|---|---|---|---|---|---|---|---|---|---|---|
| Year Team | Lg | G | AB | H | 2B | 3B | HR | (Hm | Rd) | TB | R | RBI | TBB | IBB | SO | HBP | SH | SF | SB | CS | SB% | GDP | Avg | OBP | SLG |
| 1977 St. Louis | NL | 9 | 9 | 1 | 0 | 0 | 0 | (0 | 0) | 1 | 0 | 1 | 0 | 0 | 3 | 0 | 0 | 0 | 0 | 0 | .00 | 0 | .111 | .111 | .111 |
| 1978 St. Louis | NL | 24 | 50 | 6 | 1 | 0 | 0 | (0 | 0) | 7 | 7 | 0 | 3 | 0 | 1 | 0 | 1 | 0 | 0 | 0 | .00 | 1 | .120 | .170 | .140 |
| 1979 St. Louis | NL | 135 | 369 | 111 | 19 | 5 | 1 | (1 | 0) | 143 | 53 | 35 | 57 | 9 | 35 | 4 | 1 | 4 | 4 | 1 | .80 | 9 | .301 | .396 | .388 |
| 1980 St. Louis | NL | 116 | 422 | 128 | 27 | 6 | 3 | (0 | 3) | 176 | 58 | 46 | 51 | 8 | 23 | 1 | 9 | 3 | 4 | 4 | .50 | 11 | .303 | .377 | .417 |
| 1981 St. Louis | NL | 102 | 376 | 110 | 12 | 6 | 2 | (0 | 2) | 140 | 43 | 45 | 37 | 6 | 28 | 0 | 3 | 4 | 13 | 5 | .72 | 11 | .293 | .353 | .372 |
| 1982 St. Louis | NL | 137 | 470 | 136 | 22 | 5 | 2 | (1 | 1) | 174 | 55 | 34 | 40 | 6 | 31 | 1 | 3 | 2 | 11 | 9 | .55 | 11 | .289 | .345 | .370 |
| 1983 St. Louis | NL | 151 | 488 | 143 | 26 | 5 | 3 | (0 | 3) | 188 | 62 | 38 | 61 | 5 | 27 | 1 | 4 | 3 | 12 | 6 | .67 | 12 | .293 | .371 | .385 |
| 1984 2 ML Teams | | 100 | 324 | 87 | 19 | 2 | 1 | (1 | 0) | 113 | 38 | 21 | 31 | 3 | 27 | 1 | 3 | 3 | 2 | 5 | .29 | 7 | .269 | .331 | .349 |
| 1985 Atlanta | NL | 134 | 412 | 112 | 19 | 4 | 3 | (2 | 1) | 148 | 30 | 35 | 51 | 6 | 38 | 6 | 1 | 2 | 1 | 2 | .33 | 10 | .272 | .359 | .359 |
| 1986 Atlanta | NL | 151 | 503 | 136 | 24 | 3 | 5 | (2 | 3) | 181 | 62 | 48 | 83 | 6 | 40 | 2 | 4 | 4 | 7 | 4 | .64 | 11 | .270 | .373 | .360 |
| 1987 Atlanta | NL | 135 | 508 | 142 | 29 | 2 | 3 | (2 | 1) | 184 | 59 | 48 | 48 | 5 | 29 | 2 | 5 | 3 | 3 | 3 | .50 | 13 | .280 | .342 | .362 |

| Year Team | Lg | G | AB | H | 2B | 3B | HR | (Hm | Rd) | TB | R | RBI | TBB | IBB | SO | HBP | SH | SF | SB | CS | SB% | GDP | Avg | OBP | SLG |
|---|---|---|---|---|---|---|---|---|---|---|---|---|---|---|---|---|---|---|---|---|---|---|---|---|---|
| 1988 2 ML Teams | | 140 | 476 | 129 | 22 | 4 | 3 | (1 | 2) | 168 | 49 | 42 | 37 | 7 | 34 | 2 | 6 | 8 | 4 | 5 | .44 | 8 | .271 | .321 | .353 |
| 1989 2 ML Teams | | 97 | 156 | 42 | 6 | 1 | 2 | (1 | 1) | 56 | 19 | 17 | 10 | 0 | 10 | 2 | 2 | 3 | 0 | 1 | .00 | 4 | .269 | .316 | .359 |
| 1990 Houston | NL | 77 | 150 | 31 | 6 | 1 | 1 | (0 | 1) | 42 | 10 | 12 | 15 | 1 | 17 | 1 | 1 | 1 | 1 | 1 | .50 | 3 | .207 | .281 | .280 |
| 1984 St. Louis | NL | 50 | 152 | 47 | 11 | 1 | 0 | (0 | 0) | 60 | 17 | 11 | 16 | 2 | 10 | 1 | 0 | 0 | 1 | 2 | .33 | 3 | .309 | .379 | .395 |
| Atlanta | NL | 50 | 172 | 40 | 8 | 1 | 1 | (1 | 0) | 53 | 21 | 10 | 15 | 1 | 17 | 0 | 3 | 3 | 1 | 3 | .25 | 4 | .233 | .289 | .308 |
| 1988 Atlanta | NL | 120 | 422 | 117 | 20 | 4 | 3 | (1 | 2) | 154 | 42 | 40 | 32 | 6 | 28 | 2 | 5 | 8 | 4 | 5 | .44 | 6 | .277 | .325 | .365 |
| Pittsburgh | NL | 20 | 54 | 12 | 2 | 0 | 0 | (0 | 0) | 14 | 7 | 2 | 5 | 1 | 6 | 0 | 1 | 0 | 0 | 0 | .00 | 2 | .222 | .288 | .259 |
| 1989 Pittsburgh | NL | 14 | 40 | 5 | 1 | 0 | 0 | (0 | 0) | 6 | 2 | 2 | 2 | 0 | 2 | 0 | 1 | 1 | 0 | 0 | .00 | 0 | .125 | .163 | .150 |
| San Francisco | NL | 83 | 116 | 37 | 5 | 1 | 2 | (1 | 1) | 50 | 17 | 15 | 8 | 0 | 8 | 2 | 1 | 2 | 0 | 1 | .00 | 4 | .319 | .367 | .431 |
| 14 ML YEARS | | 1508 | 4713 | 1314 | 232 | 44 | 29 | (11 | 18) | 1721 | 545 | 422 | 524 | 62 | 343 | 23 | 43 | 40 | 62 | 46 | .57 | 111 | .279 | .351 | .365 |

## Ron Oester

**Bats:** Both **Throws:** Right **Pos:** 2B **Ht:** 6' 2" **Wt:** 190 **Born:** 05/05/56 **Age:** 35

| BATTING | | | | | | | | | | | | | | | | | | | BASERUNNING | | | | PERCENTAGES | | |
|---|---|---|---|---|---|---|---|---|---|---|---|---|---|---|---|---|---|---|---|---|---|---|---|---|---|
| Year Team | Lg | G | AB | H | 2B | 3B | HR | (Hm | Rd) | TB | R | RBI | TBB | IBB | SO | HBP | SH | SF | SB | CS | SB% | GDP | Avg | OBP | SLG |
| 1978 Cincinnati | NL | 6 | 8 | 3 | 0 | 0 | 0 | (0 | 0) | 3 | 1 | 1 | 0 | 0 | 2 | 0 | 1 | 0 | 0 | 0 | .00 | 0 | .375 | .375 | .375 |
| 1979 Cincinnati | NL | 6 | 3 | 0 | 0 | 0 | 0 | (0 | 0) | 0 | 0 | 0 | 0 | 0 | 1 | 0 | 0 | 0 | 0 | 0 | .00 | 0 | .000 | .000 | .000 |
| 1980 Cincinnati | NL | 100 | 303 | 84 | 16 | 2 | 2 | (0 | 2) | 110 | 40 | 20 | 26 | 7 | 44 | 1 | 5 | 0 | 6 | 2 | .75 | 7 | .277 | .336 | .363 |
| 1981 Cincinnati | NL | 105 | 354 | 96 | 16 | 7 | 5 | (3 | 2) | 141 | 45 | 42 | 42 | 8 | 49 | 0 | 5 | 7 | 2 | 5 | .29 | 8 | .271 | .342 | .398 |
| 1982 Cincinnati | NL | 151 | 549 | 143 | 19 | 4 | 9 | (4 | 5) | 197 | 63 | 47 | 35 | 8 | 82 | 0 | 8 | 3 | 5 | 6 | .45 | 16 | .260 | .303 | .359 |
| 1983 Cincinnati | NL | 157 | 549 | 145 | 23 | 5 | 11 | (6 | 5) | 211 | 63 | 58 | 49 | 14 | 106 | 1 | 7 | 6 | 2 | 2 | .50 | 17 | .264 | .322 | .384 |
| 1984 Cincinnati | NL | 150 | 553 | 134 | 26 | 3 | 3 | (2 | 1) | 175 | 54 | 38 | 41 | 7 | 97 | 1 | 5 | 1 | 7 | 2 | .78 | 16 | .242 | .295 | .316 |
| 1985 Cincinnati | NL | 152 | 526 | 155 | 26 | 3 | 1 | (0 | 1) | 190 | 59 | 34 | 51 | 17 | 65 | 0 | 2 | 5 | 5 | 0 | 1.00 | 13 | .295 | .354 | .361 |
| 1986 Cincinnati | NL | 153 | 523 | 135 | 23 | 2 | 8 | (6 | 2) | 186 | 52 | 44 | 52 | 16 | 84 | 1 | 7 | 3 | 9 | 2 | .82 | 18 | .258 | .325 | .356 |
| 1987 Cincinnati | NL | 69 | 237 | 60 | 9 | 6 | 2 | (0 | 2) | 87 | 28 | 23 | 22 | 4 | 51 | 0 | 2 | 0 | 2 | 3 | .40 | 8 | .253 | .317 | .367 |
| 1988 Cincinnati | NL | 54 | 150 | 42 | 7 | 0 | 0 | (0 | 0) | 49 | 20 | 10 | 9 | 3 | 24 | 0 | 3 | 1 | 0 | 2 | .00 | 2 | .280 | .319 | .327 |
| 1989 Cincinnati | NL | 109 | 305 | 75 | 15 | 0 | 1 | (1 | 0) | 93 | 23 | 14 | 32 | 8 | 47 | 0 | 0 | 0 | 1 | 0 | 1.00 | 10 | .246 | .318 | .305 |
| 1990 Cincinnati | NL | 64 | 154 | 46 | 10 | 1 | 0 | (0 | 0) | 58 | 10 | 13 | 10 | 1 | 29 | 0 | 6 | 1 | 1 | 2 | .33 | 1 | .299 | .339 | .377 |
| 13 ML YEARS | | 1276 | 4214 | 1118 | 190 | 33 | 42 | (22 | 20) | 1500 | 458 | 344 | 369 | 93 | 681 | 4 | 51 | 27 | 40 | 26 | .61 | 116 | .265 | .323 | .356 |

## Jose Offerman

**Bats:** Both **Throws:** Right **Pos:** SS **Ht:** 6' 0" **Wt:** 160 **Born:** 11/08/68 **Age:** 22

| BATTING | | | | | | | | | | | | | | | | | | | BASERUNNING | | | | PERCENTAGES | | |
|---|---|---|---|---|---|---|---|---|---|---|---|---|---|---|---|---|---|---|---|---|---|---|---|---|---|
| Year Team | Lg | G | AB | H | 2B | 3B | HR | (Hm | Rd) | TB | R | RBI | TBB | IBB | SO | HBP | SH | SF | SB | CS | SB% | GDP | Avg | OBP | SLG |
| 1988 Vero Beach | A | 4 | 14 | 4 | 2 | 0 | 0 | -- | -- | 6 | 4 | 2 | 2 | 0 | 0 | 0 | 0 | 0 | 0 | 0 | .00 | 0 | .286 | .375 | .429 |
| Great Falls | R | 60 | 251 | 83 | 11 | 5 | 2 | -- | -- | 110 | 75 | 28 | 38 | 1 | 42 | 2 | 1 | 1 | 57 | 10 | .85 | 3 | .331 | .421 | .438 |
| 1989 Bakersfield | A | 62 | 245 | 75 | 9 | 4 | 2 | -- | -- | 98 | 53 | 22 | 35 | 2 | 48 | 2 | 0 | 1 | 37 | 13 | .74 | 5 | .306 | .396 | .400 |
| San Antonio | AA | 68 | 278 | 80 | 6 | 3 | 2 | -- | -- | 98 | 47 | 22 | 40 | 4 | 39 | 1 | 3 | 0 | 32 | 13 | .71 | 1 | .288 | .379 | .353 |
| 1990 Albuquerque | AAA | 117 | 454 | 148 | 16 | 11 | 0 | -- | -- | 186 | 104 | 56 | 71 | 2 | 81 | 2 | 4 | 4 | 60 | 19 | .76 | 7 | .326 | .416 | .410 |
| 1990 Los Angeles | NL | 29 | 58 | 9 | 0 | 0 | 1 | (1 | 0) | 12 | 7 | 7 | 4 | 1 | 14 | 0 | 1 | 0 | 1 | 0 | 1.00 | 0 | .155 | .210 | .207 |

## Bobby Ojeda

**Pitches:** Left **Bats:** Left **Pos:** RP/SP **Ht:** 6' 1" **Wt:** 195 **Born:** 12/17/57 **Age:** 33

| HOW MUCH HE PITCHED | | | | | | | | WHAT HE GAVE UP | | | | | | | | | | | | THE RESULTS | | | | | |
|---|---|---|---|---|---|---|---|---|---|---|---|---|---|---|---|---|---|---|---|---|---|---|---|---|---|
| Year Team | Lg | G | GS | CG | GF | IP | BFP | H | R | ER | HR | SH | SF | HB | TBB | IBB | SO | WP | Bk | W | L | Pct. | ShO | Sv | ERA |
| 1980 Boston | AL | 7 | 7 | 0 | 0 | 26 | 122 | 39 | 20 | 20 | 2 | 0 | 0 | 0 | 14 | 1 | 12 | 1 | 0 | 1 | 1 | .500 | 0 | 0 | 6.92 |
| 1981 Boston | AL | 10 | 10 | 2 | 0 | 66 | 267 | 50 | 25 | 23 | 6 | 3 | 1 | 2 | 25 | 2 | 28 | 0 | 0 | 6 | 2 | .750 | 0 | 0 | 3.14 |
| 1982 Boston | AL | 22 | 14 | 0 | 6 | 78.1 | 352 | 95 | 53 | 49 | 13 | 0 | 1 | 1 | 29 | 0 | 52 | 5 | 0 | 4 | 6 | .400 | 0 | 0 | 5.63 |
| 1983 Boston | AL | 29 | 28 | 5 | 0 | 173.2 | 746 | 173 | 85 | 78 | 15 | 6 | 11 | 3 | 73 | 2 | 94 | 2 | 0 | 12 | 7 | .632 | 0 | 0 | 4.04 |
| 1984 Boston | AL | 33 | 32 | 8 | 0 | 216.2 | 928 | 211 | 106 | 96 | 17 | 8 | 6 | 2 | 96 | 2 | 137 | 0 | 1 | 12 | 12 | .500 | 5 | 0 | 3.99 |
| 1985 Boston | AL | 39 | 22 | 5 | 10 | 157.2 | 671 | 166 | 74 | 70 | 11 | 10 | 3 | 2 | 48 | 9 | 102 | 3 | 3 | 9 | 11 | .450 | 0 | 1 | 4.00 |
| 1986 New York | NL | 32 | 30 | 7 | 1 | 217.1 | 871 | 185 | 72 | 62 | 15 | 10 | 3 | 2 | 52 | 3 | 148 | 2 | 1 | 18 | 5 | .783 | 2 | 0 | 2.57 |
| 1987 New York | NL | 10 | 7 | 0 | 0 | 46.1 | 192 | 45 | 23 | 20 | 5 | 3 | 1 | 0 | 10 | 1 | 21 | 1 | 0 | 3 | 5 | .375 | 0 | 0 | 3.88 |
| 1988 New York | NL | 29 | 29 | 5 | 0 | 190.1 | 752 | 158 | 74 | 61 | 6 | 6 | 6 | 4 | 33 | 2 | 133 | 4 | 7 | 10 | 13 | .435 | 5 | 0 | 2.88 |
| 1989 New York | NL | 31 | 31 | 5 | 0 | 192 | 824 | 179 | 83 | 74 | 16 | 6 | 7 | 2 | 78 | 5 | 95 | 0 | 2 | 13 | 11 | .542 | 2 | 0 | 3.47 |
| 1990 New York | NL | 38 | 12 | 0 | 9 | 118 | 500 | 123 | 53 | 48 | 10 | 3 | 3 | 2 | 40 | 4 | 62 | 2 | 3 | 7 | 6 | .538 | 0 | 0 | 3.66 |
| 11 ML YEARS | | 280 | 222 | 37 | 26 | 1482.1 | 6225 | 1424 | 668 | 601 | 116 | 55 | 42 | 20 | 498 | 31 | 884 | 20 | 17 | 95 | 79 | .546 | 14 | 1 | 3.65 |

## John Olerud

**Bats:** Left **Throws:** Left **Pos:** DH/1B **Ht:** 6' 5" **Wt:** 205 **Born:** 08/05/68 **Age:** 22

| BATTING | | | | | | | | | | | | | | | | | | | BASERUNNING | | | | PERCENTAGES | | |
|---|---|---|---|---|---|---|---|---|---|---|---|---|---|---|---|---|---|---|---|---|---|---|---|---|---|
| Year Team | Lg | G | AB | H | 2B | 3B | HR | (Hm | Rd) | TB | R | RBI | TBB | IBB | SO | HBP | SH | SF | SB | CS | SB% | GDP | Avg | OBP | SLG |
| 1989 Toronto | AL | 6 | 8 | 3 | 0 | 0 | 0 | (0 | 0) | 3 | 2 | 0 | 0 | 0 | 1 | 0 | 0 | 0 | 0 | 0 | .00 | 0 | .375 | .375 | .375 |
| 1990 Toronto | AL | 111 | 358 | 95 | 15 | 1 | 14 | (11 | 3) | 154 | 43 | 48 | 57 | 6 | 75 | 1 | 1 | 4 | 0 | 2 | .00 | 5 | .265 | .364 | .430 |
| 2 ML YEARS | | 117 | 366 | 98 | 15 | 1 | 14 | (11 | 3) | 157 | 45 | 48 | 57 | 6 | 76 | 1 | 1 | 4 | 0 | 2 | .00 | 5 | .268 | .364 | .429 |

## Steve Olin

**Pitches:** Right **Bats:** Right **Pos:** RP **Ht:** 6' 2" **Wt:** 185 **Born:** 10/10/65 **Age:** 25

| | | | HOW MUCH HE PITCHED | | | | | | WHAT HE GAVE UP | | | | | | | | | | | | THE RESULTS | | | | | |
|---|---|---|---|---|---|---|---|---|---|---|---|---|---|---|---|---|---|---|---|---|---|---|---|---|---|---|
| Year | Team | Lg | G | GS | CG | GF | IP | BFP | H | R | ER | HR | SH | SF | HB | TBB | IBB | SO | WP | Bk | W | L | Pct. | ShO | Sv | ERA |
| 1987 | Burlington | R | 26 | 0 | 0 | 25 | 57.1 | 231 | 42 | 21 | 15 | 0 | 3 | 0 | 1 | 17 | 5 | 75 | 4 | 0 | 4 | 4 | .500 | 0 | 7 | 2.35 |
| 1988 | Waterloo | A | 29 | 0 | 0 | 23 | 39.1 | 163 | 26 | 7 | 6 | 0 | 3 | 1 | 2 | 14 | 3 | 48 | 4 | 2 | 3 | 0 | 1.000 | 0 | 15 | 1.37 |
| | Kinston | A | 33 | 0 | 0 | 22 | 56.2 | 234 | 49 | 23 | 19 | 1 | 0 | 1 | 2 | 15 | 0 | 45 | 0 | 0 | 5 | 2 | .714 | 0 | 8 | 3.02 |
| 1989 | Colo Sprngs | AAA | 42 | 0 | 0 | 38 | 50.1 | 195 | 34 | 18 | 18 | 6 | 2 | 0 | 3 | 15 | 3 | 46 | 0 | 0 | 4 | 1 | .800 | 0 | 24 | 3.22 |
| 1990 | Colo Sprngs | AAA | 14 | 0 | 0 | 8 | 27.1 | 117 | 18 | 9 | 2 | 0 | 1 | 4 | 1 | 15 | 2 | 30 | 0 | 0 | 3 | 1 | .750 | 0 | 2 | 0.66 |
| 1989 | Cleveland | AL | 25 | 0 | 0 | 8 | 36 | 152 | 35 | 16 | 15 | 1 | 1 | 0 | 0 | 14 | 2 | 24 | 2 | 0 | 1 | 4 | .200 | 0 | 1 | 3.75 |
| 1990 | Cleveland | AL | 50 | 1 | 0 | 16 | 92.1 | 394 | 96 | 41 | 35 | 3 | 5 | 2 | 6 | 26 | 2 | 64 | 0 | 0 | 4 | 4 | .500 | 0 | 1 | 3.41 |
| | 2 ML YEARS | | 75 | 1 | 0 | 24 | 128.1 | 546 | 131 | 57 | 50 | 4 | 6 | 2 | 6 | 40 | 4 | 88 | 2 | 0 | 5 | 8 | .385 | 0 | 2 | 3.51 |

## Omar Olivares

**Pitches:** Right **Bats:** Right **Pos:** SP **Ht:** 6' 1" **Wt:** 185 **Born:** 07/06/67 **Age:** 23

| | | | HOW MUCH HE PITCHED | | | | | | WHAT HE GAVE UP | | | | | | | | | | | | THE RESULTS | | | | | |
|---|---|---|---|---|---|---|---|---|---|---|---|---|---|---|---|---|---|---|---|---|---|---|---|---|---|---|
| Year | Team | Lg | G | GS | CG | GF | IP | BFP | H | R | ER | HR | SH | SF | HB | TBB | IBB | SO | WP | Bk | W | L | Pct. | ShO | Sv | ERA |
| 1987 | Chston-Sc | A | 31 | 24 | 5 | 3 | 170.1 | 744 | 182 | 107 | 87 | 9 | 6 | 10 | 7 | 57 | 4 | 86 | 3 | 1 | 4 | 14 | .222 | 0 | 0 | 4.60 |
| 1988 | Chston-Sc | A | 24 | 24 | 10 | 0 | 185.1 | 746 | 166 | 63 | 46 | 3 | 5 | 7 | 3 | 43 | 2 | 94 | 9 | 7 | 13 | 6 | .684 | 3 | 0 | 2.23 |
| | Riverside | A | 4 | 3 | 1 | 0 | 23.1 | 96 | 18 | 9 | 3 | 2 | 1 | 0 | 2 | 9 | 0 | 16 | 1 | 1 | 3 | 0 | 1.000 | 0 | 0 | 1.16 |
| 1989 | Wichita | AA | 26 | 26 | 6 | 0 | 185.2 | 771 | 175 | 87 | 70 | 10 | 3 | 8 | 10 | 61 | 6 | 79 | 10 | 1 | 12 | 11 | .522 | 1 | 0 | 3.39 |
| 1990 | Louisville | AAA | 23 | 23 | 5 | 0 | 159.1 | 643 | 127 | 58 | 50 | 6 | 4 | 2 | 9 | 59 | 1 | 88 | 6 | 2 | 10 | 11 | .476 | 2 | 0 | 2.82 |
| 1990 | St. Louis | NL | 9 | 6 | 0 | 0 | 49.1 | 201 | 45 | 17 | 16 | 2 | 1 | 0 | 2 | 17 | 0 | 20 | 1 | 1 | 1 | 1 | .500 | 0 | 0 | 2.92 |

## Joe Oliver

**Bats:** Right **Throws:** Right **Pos:** C **Ht:** 6' 3" **Wt:** 215 **Born:** 07/24/65 **Age:** 25

| | | | BATTING | | | | | | | | | | | | | | | | | BASERUNNING | | | | PERCENTAGES | | |
|---|---|---|---|---|---|---|---|---|---|---|---|---|---|---|---|---|---|---|---|---|---|---|---|---|---|---|
| Year | Team | Lg | G | AB | H | 2B | 3B | HR | (Hm | Rd) | TB | R | RBI | TBB | IBB | SO | HBP | SH | SF | SB | CS | SB% | GDP | Avg | OBP | SLG |
| 1984 | Cedar Rapds | A | 102 | 335 | 73 | 11 | 0 | 3 | -- | -- | 93 | 34 | 29 | 17 | 1 | 83 | 4 | 4 | 3 | 2 | 2 | .50 | 11 | .218 | .262 | .278 |
| 1985 | Tampa | A | 112 | 386 | 104 | 23 | 2 | 7 | -- | -- | 152 | 38 | 62 | 32 | 3 | 75 | 1 | 4 | 5 | 1 | 5 | .17 | 9 | .269 | .323 | .394 |
| 1986 | Vermont | AA | 84 | 282 | 78 | 18 | 1 | 6 | -- | -- | 116 | 32 | 41 | 21 | 1 | 47 | 0 | 0 | 5 | 2 | 2 | .50 | 12 | .277 | .321 | .411 |
| 1987 | Vermont | AA | 66 | 236 | 72 | 13 | 2 | 10 | -- | -- | 119 | 31 | 60 | 17 | 2 | 30 | 3 | 1 | 7 | 0 | 3 | .00 | 2 | .305 | .350 | .504 |
| 1988 | Nashville | AAA | 73 | 220 | 45 | 7 | 2 | 4 | -- | -- | 68 | 19 | 24 | 18 | 1 | 39 | 3 | 1 | 2 | 0 | 1 | .00 | 9 | .205 | .272 | .309 |
| | Chattanooga | AA | 28 | 105 | 26 | 6 | 0 | 3 | -- | -- | 41 | 9 | 12 | 5 | 0 | 19 | 2 | 0 | 0 | 0 | 0 | .00 | 3 | .248 | .295 | .390 |
| 1989 | Nashville | AAA | 71 | 233 | 68 | 13 | 0 | 6 | -- | -- | 99 | 22 | 31 | 13 | 1 | 35 | 3 | 1 | 5 | 0 | 0 | .00 | 3 | .292 | .331 | .425 |
| 1989 | Cincinnati | NL | 49 | 151 | 41 | 8 | 0 | 3 | (1 | 2) | 58 | 13 | 23 | 6 | 1 | 28 | 1 | 1 | 2 | 0 | 0 | .00 | 3 | .272 | .300 | .384 |
| 1990 | Cincinnati | NL | 121 | 364 | 84 | 23 | 0 | 8 | (3 | 5) | 131 | 34 | 52 | 37 | 15 | 75 | 2 | 5 | 1 | 1 | 1 | .50 | 6 | .231 | .304 | .360 |
| | 2 ML YEARS | | 170 | 515 | 125 | 31 | 0 | 11 | (4 | 7) | 189 | 47 | 75 | 43 | 16 | 103 | 3 | 6 | 3 | 1 | 1 | .50 | 9 | .243 | .303 | .367 |

## Francisco Oliveras

**Pitches:** Right **Bats:** Right **Pos:** RP **Ht:** 5'10" **Wt:** 170 **Born:** 01/31/63 **Age:** 28

| | | | HOW MUCH HE PITCHED | | | | | | WHAT HE GAVE UP | | | | | | | | | | | | THE RESULTS | | | | | |
|---|---|---|---|---|---|---|---|---|---|---|---|---|---|---|---|---|---|---|---|---|---|---|---|---|---|---|
| Year | Team | Lg | G | GS | CG | GF | IP | BFP | H | R | ER | HR | SH | SF | HB | TBB | IBB | SO | WP | Bk | W | L | Pct. | ShO | Sv | ERA |
| 1984 | Charlotte | AA | 19 | 6 | 0 | 4 | 75 | 329 | 68 | 45 | 35 | 8 | 4 | 4 | 4 | 39 | 2 | 52 | 9 | 0 | 3 | 7 | .300 | 0 | 0 | 4.20 |
| | Rochester | AAA | 12 | 7 | 2 | 4 | 40.2 | 195 | 58 | 37 | 36 | 6 | 0 | 0 | 1 | 19 | 1 | 39 | 2 | 0 | 1 | 3 | .250 | 0 | 0 | 7.97 |
| 1985 | Daytona Bch | A | 3 | 3 | 2 | 0 | 23.2 | 89 | 13 | 6 | 5 | 0 | 0 | 3 | 1 | 9 | 0 | 25 | 1 | 0 | 3 | 0 | 1.000 | 0 | 0 | 1.90 |
| | Charlotte | AA | 12 | 7 | 0 | 2 | 40.2 | 201 | 57 | 40 | 30 | 3 | 2 | 6 | 1 | 25 | 0 | 20 | 5 | 0 | 2 | 1 | .667 | 0 | 0 | 6.64 |
| | Beaumont | AA | 7 | 4 | 0 | 0 | 27 | 112 | 23 | 17 | 15 | 2 | 2 | 1 | 1 | 9 | 0 | 24 | 2 | 0 | 3 | 1 | .750 | 0 | 0 | 5.00 |
| 1986 | Charlotte | AA | 33 | 25 | 5 | 3 | 194 | 828 | 185 | 112 | 90 | 27 | 4 | 7 | 5 | 71 | 1 | 127 | 7 | 1 | 12 | 9 | .571 | 1 | 0 | 4.18 |
| 1987 | Charlotte | AA | 23 | 10 | 3 | 6 | 100 | 407 | 99 | 43 | 40 | 9 | 2 | 4 | 5 | 21 | 0 | 67 | 5 | 1 | 6 | 3 | .667 | 1 | 2 | 3.60 |
| | Rochester | AAA | 6 | 4 | 0 | 1 | 27 | 115 | 31 | 14 | 13 | 3 | 0 | 0 | 0 | 7 | 0 | 18 | 0 | 0 | 3 | 0 | 1.000 | 0 | 0 | 4.33 |
| 1988 | Orlando | AA | 7 | 7 | 0 | 0 | 43 | 189 | 44 | 24 | 23 | 8 | 1 | 0 | 1 | 18 | 0 | 42 | 0 | 2 | 3 | 1 | .750 | 0 | 0 | 4.81 |
| | Portland | AAA | 21 | 21 | 4 | 0 | 133.2 | 566 | 134 | 69 | 64 | 10 | 0 | 7 | 2 | 43 | 0 | 95 | 0 | 6 | 11 | 10 | .524 | 0 | 0 | 4.31 |
| 1989 | Portland | AAA | 17 | 13 | 3 | 2 | 97.2 | 414 | 108 | 54 | 54 | 11 | 0 | 3 | 1 | 24 | 1 | 54 | 2 | 2 | 6 | 4 | .600 | 1 | 0 | 4.98 |
| 1990 | Portland | AAA | 11 | 6 | 1 | 1 | 62 | 247 | 44 | 23 | 20 | 2 | 3 | 3 | 3 | 22 | 0 | 56 | 1 | 1 | 3 | 4 | .429 | 0 | 1 | 2.90 |
| | San Jose | A | 1 | 1 | 0 | 0 | 3.2 | 15 | 4 | 2 | 1 | 0 | 0 | 0 | 0 | 1 | 0 | 3 | 0 | 0 | 0 | 0 | .000 | 0 | 0 | 2.45 |
| 1989 | Minnesota | AL | 12 | 8 | 1 | 1 | 55.2 | 239 | 64 | 28 | 28 | 8 | 0 | 1 | 1 | 15 | 0 | 24 | 0 | 2 | 3 | 4 | .429 | 0 | 0 | 4.53 |
| 1990 | San Francisco | NL | 33 | 2 | 0 | 9 | 55.1 | 231 | 47 | 22 | 17 | 5 | 1 | 3 | 2 | 21 | 6 | 41 | 2 | 1 | 2 | 2 | .500 | 0 | 2 | 2.77 |
| | 2 ML YEARS | | 45 | 10 | 1 | 10 | 111 | 470 | 111 | 50 | 45 | 13 | 1 | 4 | 3 | 36 | 6 | 65 | 2 | 3 | 5 | 6 | .455 | 0 | 2 | 3.65 |

## Greg Olson

**Bats:** Right **Throws:** Right **Pos:** C **Ht:** 6' 0" **Wt:** 200 **Born:** 09/06/60 **Age:** 30

| | | | BATTING | | | | | | | | | | | | | | | | | BASERUNNING | | | | PERCENTAGES | | |
|---|---|---|---|---|---|---|---|---|---|---|---|---|---|---|---|---|---|---|---|---|---|---|---|---|---|---|
| Year | Team | Lg | G | AB | H | 2B | 3B | HR | (Hm | Rd) | TB | R | RBI | TBB | IBB | SO | HBP | SH | SF | SB | CS | SB% | GDP | Avg | OBP | SLG |
| 1984 | Jackson | AA | 74 | 234 | 55 | 9 | 0 | 0 | -- | -- | 64 | 27 | 22 | 30 | 5 | 16 | 1 | 5 | 2 | 1 | 1 | .50 | 10 | .235 | .322 | .274 |
| 1985 | Jackson | AA | 69 | 211 | 57 | 7 | 0 | 1 | -- | -- | 67 | 21 | 32 | 23 | 1 | 20 | 1 | 3 | 2 | 1 | 3 | .25 | 4 | .270 | .342 | .318 |
| 1986 | Jackson | AA | 64 | 196 | 39 | 5 | 1 | 2 | -- | -- | 52 | 28 | 16 | 30 | 0 | 16 | 1 | 3 | 1 | 0 | 0 | .00 | 4 | .199 | .307 | .265 |
| | Tidewater | AAA | 19 | 55 | 18 | 1 | 0 | 0 | -- | -- | 19 | 11 | 7 | 5 | 0 | 7 | 0 | 1 | 1 | 1 | 0 | 1.00 | 4 | .327 | .377 | .345 |

| 1987 Tidewater | AAA | 47 | 120 | 34 | 8 | 1 | 2 | -- | -- | 50 | 15 | 15 | 14 | 1 | 13 | 0 | 2 | 2 | 0 | 0 | .00 | 1 | .283 | .353 | .417 |
|---|---|---|---|---|---|---|---|---|---|---|---|---|---|---|---|---|---|---|---|---|---|---|---|---|---|
| 1988 Tidewater | AAA | 115 | 344 | 92 | 19 | 1 | 6 | -- | -- | 131 | 39 | 48 | 42 | 2 | 42 | 4 | 1 | 6 | 0 | 0 | .00 | 12 | .267 | .348 | .381 |
| 1989 Portland | AAA | 79 | 247 | 58 | 8 | 2 | 6 | -- | -- | 88 | 38 | 38 | 45 | 2 | 27 | 3 | 3 | 5 | 3 | 2 | .60 | 10 | .235 | .353 | .356 |
| 1990 Richmond | AAA | 3 | 7 | 0 | 0 | 0 | 0 | -- | -- | 0 | 0 | 0 | 0 | 0 | 0 | 0 | 0 | 0 | 0 | 0 | .00 | 0 | .000 | .000 | .000 |
| 1989 Minnesota | AL | 3 | 2 | 1 | 0 | 0 | 0 | (0 | 0) | 1 | 0 | 0 | 0 | 0 | 0 | 0 | 0 | 0 | 0 | 0 | .00 | 0 | .500 | .500 | .500 |
| 1990 Atlanta | NL | 100 | 298 | 78 | 12 | 1 | 7 | (4 | 3) | 113 | 36 | 36 | 30 | 4 | 51 | 2 | 1 | 1 | 1 | 1 | .50 | 8 | .262 | .332 | .379 |
| 2 ML YEARS | | 103 | 300 | 79 | 12 | 1 | 7 | (4 | 3) | 114 | 36 | 36 | 30 | 4 | 51 | 2 | 1 | 1 | 1 | 1 | .50 | 8 | .263 | .333 | .380 |

## Gregg Olson

**Pitches:** Right **Bats:** Right **Pos:** RP **Ht:** 6' 4" **Wt:** 211 **Born:** 10/11/66 **Age:** 24

| HOW MUCH HE PITCHED | | | | | | | | WHAT HE GAVE UP | | | | | | | | | | | | THE RESULTS | | | | | |
|---|---|---|---|---|---|---|---|---|---|---|---|---|---|---|---|---|---|---|---|---|---|---|---|---|---|
| Year Team | Lg | G | GS | CG | GF | IP | BFP | H | R | ER | HR | SH | SF | HB | TBB | IBB | SO | WP | Bk | W | L | Pct. | ShO | Sv | ERA |
| 1988 Baltimore | AL | 10 | 0 | 0 | 4 | 11 | 51 | 10 | 4 | 4 | 1 | 0 | 0 | 0 | 10 | 1 | 9 | 0 | 1 | 1 | 1 | .500 | 0 | 0 | 3.27 |
| 1989 Baltimore | AL | 64 | 0 | 0 | 52 | 85 | 356 | 57 | 17 | 16 | 1 | 4 | 1 | 1 | 46 | 10 | 90 | 9 | 3 | 5 | 2 | .714 | 0 | 27 | 1.69 |
| 1990 Baltimore | AL | 64 | 0 | 0 | 58 | 74.1 | 305 | 57 | 20 | 20 | 3 | 1 | 2 | 3 | 31 | 3 | 74 | 5 | 0 | 6 | 5 | .545 | 0 | 37 | 2.42 |
| 3 ML YEARS | | 138 | 0 | 0 | 114 | 170.1 | 712 | 124 | 41 | 40 | 5 | 5 | 3 | 4 | 87 | 14 | 173 | 14 | 4 | 12 | 8 | .600 | 0 | 64 | 2.11 |

## Steve Ontiveros

**Pitches:** Right **Bats:** Right **Pos:** RP **Ht:** 6' 0" **Wt:** 180 **Born:** 03/05/61 **Age:** 30

| HOW MUCH HE PITCHED | | | | | | | | WHAT HE GAVE UP | | | | | | | | | | | | THE RESULTS | | | | | |
|---|---|---|---|---|---|---|---|---|---|---|---|---|---|---|---|---|---|---|---|---|---|---|---|---|---|
| Year Team | Lg | G | GS | CG | GF | IP | BFP | H | R | ER | HR | SH | SF | HB | TBB | IBB | SO | WP | Bk | W | L | Pct. | ShO | Sv | ERA |
| 1985 Oakland | AL | 39 | 0 | 0 | 18 | 74.2 | 284 | 45 | 17 | 16 | 4 | 2 | 2 | 2 | 19 | 2 | 36 | 1 | 0 | 1 | 3 | .250 | 0 | 8 | 1.93 |
| 1986 Oakland | AL | 46 | 0 | 0 | 27 | 72.2 | 305 | 72 | 40 | 38 | 10 | 1 | 6 | 1 | 25 | 3 | 54 | 4 | 0 | 2 | 2 | .500 | 0 | 10 | 4.71 |
| 1987 Oakland | AL | 35 | 22 | 2 | 6 | 150.2 | 645 | 141 | 78 | 67 | 19 | 6 | 2 | 4 | 50 | 3 | 97 | 4 | 1 | 10 | 8 | .556 | 1 | 1 | 4.00 |
| 1988 Oakland | AL | 10 | 10 | 0 | 0 | 54.2 | 241 | 57 | 32 | 28 | 4 | 5 | 0 | 0 | 21 | 1 | 30 | 5 | 5 | 3 | 4 | .429 | 0 | 0 | 4.61 |
| 1989 Philadelphia | NL | 6 | 5 | 0 | 0 | 30.2 | 134 | 34 | 15 | 13 | 2 | 1 | 0 | 0 | 15 | 1 | 12 | 2 | 0 | 2 | 1 | .667 | 0 | 0 | 3.82 |
| 1990 Philadelphia | NL | 5 | 0 | 0 | 1 | 10 | 43 | 9 | 3 | 3 | 1 | 0 | 0 | 0 | 3 | 0 | 6 | 0 | 0 | 0 | 0 | .000 | 0 | 0 | 2.70 |
| 6 ML YEARS | | 141 | 37 | 2 | 52 | 393.1 | 1652 | 358 | 185 | 165 | 40 | 15 | 10 | 7 | 133 | 10 | 235 | 16 | 6 | 18 | 18 | .500 | 1 | 19 | 3.78 |

## Jose Oquendo

**Bats:** Both **Throws:** Right **Pos:** 2B **Ht:** 5'10" **Wt:** 156 **Born:** 07/04/63 **Age:** 27

| BATTING | | | | | | | | | | | | | | | | | | | BASERUNNING | | | | PERCENTAGES | | |
|---|---|---|---|---|---|---|---|---|---|---|---|---|---|---|---|---|---|---|---|---|---|---|---|---|---|
| Year Team | Lg | G | AB | H | 2B | 3B | HR | (Hm | Rd) | TB | R | RBI | TBB | IBB | SO | HBP | SH | SF | SB | CS | SB% | GDP | Avg | OBP | SLG |
| 1983 New York | NL | 120 | 328 | 70 | 7 | 0 | 1 | (0 | 1) | 80 | 29 | 17 | 19 | 2 | 60 | 2 | 3 | 1 | 8 | 9 | .47 | 10 | .213 | .260 | .244 |
| 1984 New York | NL | 81 | 189 | 42 | 5 | 0 | 0 | (0 | 0) | 47 | 23 | 10 | 15 | 2 | 26 | 2 | 3 | 2 | 10 | 1 | .91 | 2 | .222 | .284 | .249 |
| 1986 St. Louis | NL | 76 | 138 | 41 | 4 | 1 | 0 | (0 | 0) | 47 | 20 | 13 | 15 | 4 | 20 | 0 | 2 | 3 | 2 | 3 | .40 | 3 | .297 | .359 | .341 |
| 1987 St. Louis | NL | 116 | 248 | 71 | 9 | 0 | 1 | (0 | 1) | 83 | 43 | 24 | 54 | 6 | 29 | 0 | 6 | 4 | 4 | 4 | .50 | 6 | .286 | .408 | .335 |
| 1988 St. Louis | NL | 148 | 451 | 125 | 10 | 1 | 7 | (4 | 3) | 158 | 36 | 46 | 52 | 7 | 40 | 0 | 12 | 3 | 4 | 6 | .40 | 8 | .277 | .350 | .350 |
| 1989 St. Louis | NL | 163 | 556 | 162 | 28 | 7 | 1 | (0 | 1) | 207 | 59 | 48 | 79 | 7 | 59 | 0 | 7 | 8 | 3 | 5 | .38 | 12 | .291 | .375 | .372 |
| 1990 St. Louis | NL | 156 | 469 | 118 | 17 | 5 | 1 | (1 | 0) | 148 | 38 | 37 | 74 | 8 | 46 | 0 | 5 | 5 | 1 | 1 | .50 | 7 | .252 | .350 | .316 |
| 7 ML YEARS | | 860 | 2379 | 629 | 80 | 14 | 11 | (5 | 6) | 770 | 248 | 195 | 308 | 36 | 280 | 4 | 38 | 26 | 32 | 29 | .52 | 48 | .264 | .346 | .324 |

## Jesse Orosco

**Pitches:** Left **Bats:** Right **Pos:** RP **Ht:** 6' 2" **Wt:** 185 **Born:** 04/21/57 **Age:** 34

| HOW MUCH HE PITCHED | | | | | | | | WHAT HE GAVE UP | | | | | | | | | | | | THE RESULTS | | | | | |
|---|---|---|---|---|---|---|---|---|---|---|---|---|---|---|---|---|---|---|---|---|---|---|---|---|---|
| Year Team | Lg | G | GS | CG | GF | IP | BFP | H | R | ER | HR | SH | SF | HB | TBB | IBB | SO | WP | Bk | W | L | Pct. | ShO | Sv | ERA |
| 1979 New York | NL | 18 | 2 | 0 | 6 | 35 | 154 | 33 | 20 | 19 | 4 | 3 | 0 | 2 | 22 | 0 | 22 | 0 | 0 | 1 | 2 | .333 | 0 | 0 | 4.89 |
| 1981 New York | NL | 8 | 0 | 0 | 4 | 17 | 69 | 13 | 4 | 3 | 2 | 2 | 0 | 0 | 6 | 2 | 18 | 0 | 1 | 0 | 1 | .000 | 0 | 1 | 1.59 |
| 1982 New York | NL | 54 | 2 | 0 | 22 | 109.1 | 451 | 92 | 37 | 33 | 7 | 5 | 4 | 2 | 40 | 2 | 89 | 3 | 2 | 4 | 10 | .286 | 0 | 4 | 2.72 |
| 1983 New York | NL | 62 | 0 | 0 | 42 | 110 | 432 | 76 | 27 | 18 | 3 | 4 | 3 | 1 | 38 | 7 | 84 | 1 | 2 | 13 | 7 | .650 | 0 | 17 | 1.47 |
| 1984 New York | NL | 60 | 0 | 0 | 52 | 87 | 355 | 58 | 29 | 25 | 7 | 3 | 3 | 2 | 34 | 6 | 85 | 1 | 1 | 10 | 6 | .625 | 0 | 31 | 2.59 |
| 1985 New York | NL | 54 | 0 | 0 | 39 | 79 | 331 | 66 | 26 | 24 | 6 | 1 | 1 | 0 | 34 | 7 | 68 | 4 | 0 | 8 | 6 | .571 | 0 | 17 | 2.73 |
| 1986 New York | NL | 58 | 0 | 0 | 40 | 81 | 338 | 64 | 23 | 21 | 6 | 2 | 3 | 3 | 35 | 3 | 62 | 2 | 0 | 8 | 6 | .571 | 0 | 21 | 2.33 |
| 1987 New York | NL | 58 | 0 | 0 | 41 | 77 | 335 | 78 | 41 | 38 | 5 | 5 | 4 | 2 | 31 | 9 | 78 | 2 | 0 | 3 | 9 | .250 | 0 | 16 | 4.44 |
| 1988 Los Angeles | NL | 55 | 0 | 0 | 21 | 53 | 229 | 41 | 18 | 16 | 4 | 3 | 3 | 2 | 30 | 3 | 43 | 1 | 0 | 3 | 2 | .600 | 0 | 9 | 2.72 |
| 1989 Cleveland | AL | 69 | 0 | 0 | 29 | 78 | 312 | 54 | 20 | 18 | 7 | 8 | 3 | 2 | 26 | 4 | 79 | 0 | 0 | 3 | 4 | .429 | 0 | 3 | 2.08 |
| 1990 Cleveland | AL | 55 | 0 | 0 | 28 | 64.2 | 289 | 58 | 35 | 28 | 9 | 5 | 3 | 0 | 38 | 7 | 55 | 1 | 0 | 5 | 4 | .556 | 0 | 2 | 3.90 |
| 11 ML YEARS | | 551 | 4 | 0 | 324 | 791 | 3295 | 633 | 280 | 243 | 60 | 41 | 27 | 16 | 334 | 50 | 683 | 15 | 6 | 58 | 57 | .504 | 0 | 121 | 2.76 |

## Joe Orsulak

**Bats:** Left **Throws:** Left **Pos:** RF/LF **Ht:** 6' 1" **Wt:** 186 **Born:** 05/31/62 **Age:** 29

| BATTING | | | | | | | | | | | | | | | | | | | BASERUNNING | | | | PERCENTAGES | | |
|---|---|---|---|---|---|---|---|---|---|---|---|---|---|---|---|---|---|---|---|---|---|---|---|---|---|
| Year Team | Lg | G | AB | H | 2B | 3B | HR | (Hm | Rd) | TB | R | RBI | TBB | IBB | SO | HBP | SH | SF | SB | CS | SB% | GDP | Avg | OBP | SLG |
| 1983 Pittsburgh | NL | 7 | 11 | 2 | 0 | 0 | 0 | (0 | 0) | 2 | 0 | 1 | 0 | 0 | 2 | 0 | 0 | 1 | 0 | 1 | .00 | 0 | .182 | .167 | .182 |
| 1984 Pittsburgh | NL | 32 | 67 | 17 | 1 | 2 | 0 | (0 | 0) | 22 | 12 | 3 | 1 | 0 | 7 | 1 | 3 | 1 | 3 | 1 | .75 | 0 | .254 | .271 | .328 |

| Year Team | Lg | G | AB | H | 2B | 3B | HR | (Hm | Rd) | TB | R | RBI | TBB | IBB | SO | HBP | SH | SF | SB | CS | SB% | GDP | Avg | OBP | SLG |
|---|---|---|---|---|---|---|---|---|---|---|---|---|---|---|---|---|---|---|---|---|---|---|---|---|---|
| 1985 Pittsburgh | NL | 121 | 397 | 119 | 14 | 6 | 0 | (0 | 0) | 145 | 54 | 21 | 26 | 3 | 27 | 1 | 9 | 3 | 24 | 11 | .69 | 5 | .300 | .342 | .365 |
| 1986 Pittsburgh | NL | 138 | 401 | 100 | 19 | 6 | 2 | (0 | 2) | 137 | 60 | 19 | 28 | 2 | 38 | 1 | 6 | 1 | 24 | 11 | .69 | 4 | .249 | .299 | .342 |
| 1988 Baltimore | AL | 125 | 379 | 109 | 21 | 3 | 8 | (3 | 5) | 160 | 48 | 27 | 23 | 2 | 30 | 3 | 8 | 3 | 9 | 8 | .53 | 7 | .288 | .331 | .422 |
| 1989 Baltimore | AL | 123 | 390 | 111 | 22 | 5 | 7 | (0 | 7) | 164 | 59 | 55 | 41 | 6 | 35 | 2 | 7 | 6 | 5 | 3 | .63 | 8 | .285 | .351 | .421 |
| 1990 Baltimore | AL | 124 | 413 | 111 | 14 | 3 | 11 | (9 | 2) | 164 | 49 | 57 | 46 | 9 | 48 | 1 | 4 | 1 | 6 | 8 | .43 | 7 | .269 | .343 | .397 |
| 7 ML YEARS | | 670 | 2058 | 569 | 91 | 25 | 28 | (12 | 16) | 794 | 282 | 183 | 165 | 22 | 187 | 9 | 37 | 16 | 71 | 43 | .62 | 31 | .276 | .331 | .386 |

## Javier Ortiz

**Bats:** Right **Throws:** Right **Pos:** LF **Ht:** 6' 4" **Wt:** 220 **Born:** 01/22/63 **Age:** 28

| | | BATTING | | | | | | | | | | | | | | | | | BASERUNNING | | | | PERCENTAGES | | |
|---|---|---|---|---|---|---|---|---|---|---|---|---|---|---|---|---|---|---|---|---|---|---|---|---|---|
| Year Team | Lg | G | AB | H | 2B | 3B | HR | (Hm | Rd) | TB | R | RBI | TBB | IBB | SO | HBP | SH | SF | SB | CS | SB% | GDP | Avg | OBP | SLG |
| 1983 Burlington | A | 101 | 378 | 133 | 23 | 4 | 16 | -- | -- | 212 | 72 | 79 | 42 | 3 | 94 | 2 | 2 | 3 | 10 | 6 | .63 | 14 | .352 | .416 | .561 |
| 1984 Tulsa | AA | 94 | 325 | 97 | 21 | 3 | 8 | -- | -- | 148 | 42 | 53 | 47 | 2 | 67 | 5 | 4 | 4 | 4 | 5 | .44 | 8 | .298 | .391 | .455 |
| 1985 Tulsa | AA | 86 | 304 | 75 | 12 | 3 | 5 | -- | -- | 108 | 47 | 31 | 52 | 2 | 75 | 4 | 0 | 1 | 11 | 3 | .79 | 10 | .247 | .363 | .355 |
| 1986 Tulsa | AA | 110 | 378 | 114 | 29 | 3 | 14 | -- | -- | 191 | 52 | 65 | 54 | 2 | 94 | 7 | 3 | 1 | 15 | 10 | .60 | 7 | .302 | .398 | .505 |
| 1987 Okla City | AAA | 119 | 381 | 105 | 23 | 7 | 15 | -- | -- | 187 | 58 | 69 | 58 | 2 | 99 | 4 | 1 | 10 | 5 | 2 | .71 | 6 | .276 | .369 | .491 |
| 1988 San Antonio | AA | 51 | 182 | 53 | 13 | 2 | 8 | -- | -- | 94 | 35 | 33 | 22 | 0 | 38 | 5 | 0 | 5 | 6 | 3 | .67 | 5 | .291 | .374 | .516 |
| 1989 Albuquerque | AAA | 70 | 220 | 59 | 10 | 0 | 11 | -- | -- | 102 | 42 | 36 | 34 | 1 | 54 | 4 | 1 | 0 | 2 | 2 | .50 | 4 | .268 | .376 | .464 |
| Tucson | AAA | 11 | 40 | 7 | 0 | 0 | 0 | -- | -- | 7 | 5 | 0 | 2 | 0 | 9 | 0 | 0 | 0 | 0 | 0 | .00 | 1 | .175 | .214 | .175 |
| 1990 Tucson | AAA | 49 | 179 | 63 | 16 | 2 | 5 | -- | -- | 98 | 36 | 39 | 22 | 1 | 36 | 1 | 0 | 3 | 2 | 3 | .40 | 6 | .352 | .420 | .547 |
| 1990 Houston | NL | 30 | 77 | 21 | 5 | 1 | 1 | (1 | 0) | 31 | 7 | 10 | 12 | 0 | 11 | 0 | 0 | 1 | 1 | 1 | .50 | 1 | .273 | .367 | .403 |

## Junior Ortiz

**Bats:** Right **Throws:** Right **Pos:** C **Ht:** 5'11" **Wt:** 176 **Born:** 10/24/59 **Age:** 31

| | | BATTING | | | | | | | | | | | | | | | | | BASERUNNING | | | | PERCENTAGES | | |
|---|---|---|---|---|---|---|---|---|---|---|---|---|---|---|---|---|---|---|---|---|---|---|---|---|---|
| Year Team | Lg | G | AB | H | 2B | 3B | HR | (Hm | Rd) | TB | R | RBI | TBB | IBB | SO | HBP | SH | SF | SB | CS | SB% | GDP | Avg | OBP | SLG |
| 1982 Pittsburgh | NL | 7 | 15 | 3 | 1 | 0 | 0 | (0 | 0) | 4 | 1 | 0 | 1 | 0 | 3 | 0 | 0 | 0 | 0 | 0 | .00 | 1 | .200 | .250 | .267 |
| 1983 2 ML Teams | | 73 | 193 | 48 | 5 | 0 | 0 | (0 | 0) | 53 | 11 | 12 | 4 | 0 | 34 | 1 | 2 | 0 | 1 | 0 | 1.00 | 1 | .249 | .268 | .275 |
| 1984 New York | NL | 40 | 91 | 18 | 3 | 0 | 0 | (0 | 0) | 21 | 6 | 11 | 5 | 0 | 15 | 0 | 0 | 2 | 1 | 0 | 1.00 | 2 | .198 | .235 | .231 |
| 1985 Pittsburgh | NL | 23 | 72 | 21 | 2 | 0 | 1 | (0 | 1) | 26 | 4 | 5 | 3 | 1 | 17 | 0 | 1 | 0 | 1 | 0 | 1.00 | 1 | .292 | .320 | .361 |
| 1986 Pittsburgh | NL | 49 | 110 | 37 | 6 | 0 | 0 | (0 | 0) | 43 | 11 | 14 | 9 | 0 | 13 | 0 | 1 | 2 | 0 | 1 | .00 | 4 | .336 | .380 | .391 |
| 1987 Pittsburgh | NL | 75 | 192 | 52 | 8 | 1 | 1 | (0 | 1) | 65 | 16 | 22 | 15 | 1 | 23 | 0 | 5 | 1 | 0 | 2 | .00 | 6 | .271 | .322 | .339 |
| 1988 Pittsburgh | NL | 49 | 118 | 33 | 6 | 0 | 2 | (1 | 1) | 45 | 8 | 18 | 9 | 0 | 9 | 2 | 1 | 2 | 1 | 4 | .20 | 6 | .280 | .336 | .381 |
| 1989 Pittsburgh | NL | 91 | 230 | 50 | 6 | 1 | 1 | (0 | 1) | 61 | 16 | 22 | 20 | 4 | 20 | 2 | 3 | 3 | 2 | 2 | .50 | 9 | .217 | .282 | .265 |
| 1990 Minnesota | AL | 71 | 170 | 57 | 7 | 1 | 0 | (0 | 0) | 66 | 18 | 18 | 12 | 0 | 16 | 2 | 2 | 1 | 0 | 4 | .00 | 4 | .335 | .384 | .388 |
| 1983 Pittsburgh | NL | 5 | 8 | 1 | 0 | 0 | 0 | (0 | 0) | 1 | 1 | 0 | 1 | 0 | 0 | 0 | 1 | 0 | 0 | 0 | .00 | 0 | .125 | .222 | .125 |
| New York | NL | 68 | 185 | 47 | 5 | 0 | 0 | (0 | 0) | 52 | 10 | 12 | 3 | 0 | 34 | 1 | 1 | 0 | 1 | 0 | 1.00 | 1 | .254 | .270 | .281 |
| 9 ML YEARS | | 478 | 1191 | 319 | 44 | 3 | 5 | (1 | 4) | 384 | 91 | 122 | 78 | 6 | 150 | 7 | 15 | 11 | 6 | 13 | .32 | 34 | .268 | .314 | .322 |

## John Orton

**Bats:** Right **Throws:** Right **Pos:** C **Ht:** 6' 1" **Wt:** 195 **Born:** 12/08/65 **Age:** 25

| | | BATTING | | | | | | | | | | | | | | | | | BASERUNNING | | | | PERCENTAGES | | |
|---|---|---|---|---|---|---|---|---|---|---|---|---|---|---|---|---|---|---|---|---|---|---|---|---|---|
| Year Team | Lg | G | AB | H | 2B | 3B | HR | (Hm | Rd) | TB | R | RBI | TBB | IBB | SO | HBP | SH | SF | SB | CS | SB% | GDP | Avg | OBP | SLG |
| 1987 Salem | A | 51 | 176 | 46 | 8 | 1 | 8 | -- | -- | 80 | 31 | 36 | 32 | 1 | 61 | 7 | 1 | 2 | 6 | 2 | .75 | 5 | .261 | .392 | .455 |
| Midland | AA | 5 | 13 | 2 | 1 | 0 | 0 | -- | -- | 3 | 1 | 0 | 2 | 0 | 3 | 1 | 0 | 0 | 0 | 0 | .00 | 0 | .154 | .313 | .231 |
| 1988 Palm Sprngs | A | 68 | 230 | 46 | 6 | 1 | 1 | -- | -- | 57 | 42 | 28 | 45 | 0 | 79 | 10 | 2 | 0 | 5 | 2 | .71 | 4 | .200 | .354 | .248 |
| 1989 Midland | AA | 99 | 344 | 80 | 20 | 6 | 10 | -- | -- | 142 | 51 | 53 | 37 | 1 | 102 | 7 | 6 | 7 | 2 | 1 | .67 | 5 | .233 | .314 | .413 |
| 1990 Edmonton | AAA | 50 | 174 | 42 | 8 | 0 | 6 | -- | -- | 68 | 29 | 26 | 19 | 1 | 63 | 0 | 1 | 1 | 4 | 2 | .67 | 7 | .241 | .314 | .391 |
| 1989 California | AL | 16 | 39 | 7 | 1 | 0 | 0 | (0 | 0) | 8 | 4 | 4 | 2 | 0 | 17 | 0 | 1 | 0 | 0 | 0 | .00 | 0 | .179 | .220 | .205 |
| 1990 California | AL | 31 | 84 | 16 | 5 | 0 | 1 | (0 | 1) | 24 | 8 | 6 | 5 | 0 | 31 | 1 | 2 | 0 | 0 | 1 | .00 | 2 | .190 | .244 | .286 |
| 2 ML YEARS | | 47 | 123 | 23 | 6 | 0 | 1 | (0 | 1) | 32 | 12 | 10 | 7 | 0 | 48 | 1 | 3 | 0 | 0 | 1 | .00 | 2 | .187 | .237 | .260 |

## Al Osuna

**Pitches:** Left **Bats:** Right **Pos:** RP **Ht:** 6' 3" **Wt:** 200 **Born:** 08/10/65 **Age:** 25

| | | HOW MUCH HE PITCHED | | | | | | WHAT HE GAVE UP | | | | | | | | | | | | THE RESULTS | | | | | |
|---|---|---|---|---|---|---|---|---|---|---|---|---|---|---|---|---|---|---|---|---|---|---|---|---|---|
| Year Team | Lg | G | GS | CG | GF | IP | BFP | H | R | ER | HR | SH | SF | HB | TBB | IBB | SO | WP | Bk | W | L | Pct. | ShO | Sv | ERA |
| 1987 Auburn | A | 8 | 0 | 0 | 3 | 15.2 | 75 | 16 | 16 | 10 | 1 | 0 | 0 | 0 | 14 | 2 | 20 | 0 | 2 | 1 | 0 | 1.000 | 0 | 0 | 5.74 |
| Asheville | A | 14 | 0 | 0 | 7 | 19.2 | 81 | 20 | 6 | 6 | 1 | 0 | 0 | 0 | 6 | 0 | 20 | 0 | 3 | 2 | 0 | 1.000 | 0 | 2 | 2.75 |
| 1988 Osceola | A | 8 | 0 | 0 | 2 | 11.2 | 58 | 12 | 9 | 9 | 1 | 0 | 1 | 0 | 9 | 1 | 5 | 0 | 0 | 0 | 1 | .000 | 0 | 0 | 6.94 |
| Asheville | A | 31 | 0 | 0 | 19 | 50 | 212 | 41 | 19 | 11 | 1 | 1 | 0 | 2 | 25 | 2 | 41 | 4 | 9 | 6 | 1 | .857 | 0 | 3 | 1.98 |
| 1989 Osceola | A | 46 | 0 | 0 | 26 | 67.2 | 283 | 50 | 27 | 20 | 2 | 7 | 2 | 2 | 27 | 4 | 62 | 5 | 5 | 3 | 4 | .429 | 0 | 7 | 2.66 |
| 1990 Columbus | AA | 60 | 0 | 0 | 26 | 69.1 | 289 | 57 | 30 | 26 | 4 | 3 | 1 | 3 | 33 | 2 | 82 | 4 | 1 | 7 | 5 | .583 | 0 | 6 | 3.37 |
| 1990 Houston | NL | 12 | 0 | 0 | 2 | 11.1 | 48 | 10 | 6 | 6 | 1 | 0 | 2 | 3 | 6 | 1 | 6 | 3 | 0 | 2 | 0 | 1.000 | 0 | 0 | 4.76 |

## Dave Otto

**Pitches:** Left **Bats:** Left **Pos:** RP **Ht:** 6' 7" **Wt:** 210 **Born:** 11/12/64 **Age:** 26

| | | HOW MUCH HE PITCHED | | | | | | WHAT HE GAVE UP | | | | | | | | | | | | THE RESULTS | | | | | |
|---|---|---|---|---|---|---|---|---|---|---|---|---|---|---|---|---|---|---|---|---|---|---|---|---|---|
| Year Team | Lg | G | GS | CG | GF | IP | BFP | H | R | ER | HR | SH | SF | HB | TBB | IBB | SO | WP | Bk | W | L | Pct. | ShO | Sv | ERA |
| 1987 Oakland | AL | 3 | 0 | 0 | 3 | 6 | 24 | 7 | 6 | 6 | 1 | 0 | 0 | 0 | 1 | 0 | 3 | 0 | 0 | 0 | 0 | .000 | 0 | 0 | 9.00 |
| 1988 Oakland | AL | 3 | 2 | 0 | 1 | 10 | 43 | 9 | 2 | 2 | 0 | 0 | 0 | 0 | 6 | 0 | 7 | 0 | 1 | 0 | 0 | .000 | 0 | 0 | 1.80 |
| 1989 Oakland | AL | 1 | 1 | 0 | 0 | 6.2 | 26 | 6 | 2 | 2 | 0 | 1 | 0 | 0 | 2 | 0 | 4 | 0 | 0 | 0 | 0 | .000 | 0 | 0 | 2.70 |
| 1990 Oakland | AL | 2 | 0 | 0 | 2 | 2.1 | 13 | 3 | 3 | 2 | 0 | 0 | 0 | 0 | 3 | 0 | 2 | 0 | 0 | 0 | 0 | .000 | 0 | 0 | 7.71 |
| 4 ML YEARS | | 9 | 3 | 0 | 6 | 25 | 106 | 25 | 13 | 12 | 1 | 1 | 0 | 0 | 12 | 0 | 16 | 0 | 1 | 0 | 0 | .000 | 0 | 0 | 4.32 |

## Spike Owen

**Bats:** Both **Throws:** Right **Pos:** SS **Ht:** 5'10" **Wt:** 165 **Born:** 04/19/61 **Age:** 30

| | | BATTING | | | | | | | | | | | | | | | | | BASERUNNING | | | | PERCENTAGES | | |
|---|---|---|---|---|---|---|---|---|---|---|---|---|---|---|---|---|---|---|---|---|---|---|---|---|---|
| Year Team | Lg | G | AB | H | 2B | 3B | HR | (Hm | Rd) | TB | R | RBI | TBB | IBB | SO | HBP | SH | SF | SB | CS | SB% | GDP | Avg | OBP | SLG |
| 1983 Seattle | AL | 80 | 306 | 60 | 11 | 3 | 2 | (1 | 1) | 83 | 36 | 21 | 24 | 0 | 44 | 2 | 5 | 3 | 10 | 6 | .63 | 2 | .196 | .257 | .271 |
| 1984 Seattle | AL | 152 | 530 | 130 | 18 | 8 | 3 | (2 | 1) | 173 | 67 | 43 | 46 | 0 | 63 | 3 | 9 | 2 | 16 | 8 | .67 | 5 | .245 | .308 | .326 |
| 1985 Seattle | AL | 118 | 352 | 91 | 10 | 6 | 6 | (3 | 3) | 131 | 41 | 37 | 34 | 0 | 27 | 0 | 5 | 2 | 11 | 5 | .69 | 5 | .259 | .322 | .372 |
| 1986 2 ML Teams | | 154 | 528 | 122 | 24 | 7 | 1 | (0 | 1) | 163 | 67 | 45 | 51 | 1 | 51 | 2 | 9 | 3 | 4 | 4 | .50 | 13 | .231 | .300 | .309 |
| 1987 Boston | AL | 132 | 437 | 113 | 17 | 7 | 2 | (2 | 0) | 150 | 50 | 48 | 53 | 2 | 43 | 1 | 9 | 4 | 11 | 8 | .58 | 9 | .259 | .337 | .343 |
| 1988 Boston | AL | 89 | 257 | 64 | 14 | 1 | 5 | (2 | 3) | 95 | 40 | 18 | 27 | 0 | 27 | 2 | 7 | 1 | 0 | 1 | .00 | 7 | .249 | .324 | .370 |
| 1989 Montreal | NL | 142 | 437 | 102 | 17 | 4 | 6 | (5 | 1) | 145 | 52 | 41 | 76 | 25 | 44 | 3 | 3 | 3 | 3 | 2 | .60 | 11 | .233 | .349 | .332 |
| 1990 Montreal | NL | 149 | 453 | 106 | 24 | 5 | 5 | (2 | 3) | 155 | 55 | 35 | 70 | 12 | 60 | 0 | 5 | 5 | 8 | 6 | .57 | 6 | .234 | .333 | .342 |
| 1986 Seattle | AL | 112 | 402 | 99 | 22 | 6 | 0 | (0 | 0) | 133 | 46 | 35 | 34 | 1 | 42 | 1 | 7 | 2 | 1 | 3 | .25 | 11 | .246 | .305 | .331 |
| Boston | AL | 42 | 126 | 23 | 2 | 1 | 1 | (0 | 1) | 30 | 21 | 10 | 17 | 0 | 9 | 1 | 2 | 1 | 3 | 1 | .75 | 2 | .183 | .283 | .238 |
| 8 ML YEARS | | 1016 | 3300 | 788 | 135 | 41 | 30 | (17 | 13) | 1095 | 408 | 288 | 381 | 40 | 359 | 13 | 52 | 23 | 63 | 40 | .61 | 58 | .239 | .318 | .332 |

## Mike Pagliarulo

**Bats:** Left **Throws:** Right **Pos:** 3B **Ht:** 6' 2" **Wt:** 195 **Born:** 03/15/60 **Age:** 31

| | | BATTING | | | | | | | | | | | | | | | | | BASERUNNING | | | | PERCENTAGES | | |
|---|---|---|---|---|---|---|---|---|---|---|---|---|---|---|---|---|---|---|---|---|---|---|---|---|---|
| Year Team | Lg | G | AB | H | 2B | 3B | HR | (Hm | Rd) | TB | R | RBI | TBB | IBB | SO | HBP | SH | SF | SB | CS | SB% | GDP | Avg | OBP | SLG |
| 1984 New York | AL | 67 | 201 | 48 | 15 | 3 | 7 | (4 | 3) | 90 | 24 | 34 | 15 | 0 | 46 | 0 | 0 | 3 | 0 | 0 | .00 | 5 | .239 | .288 | .448 |
| 1985 New York | AL | 138 | 380 | 91 | 16 | 2 | 19 | (8 | 11) | 168 | 55 | 62 | 45 | 4 | 86 | 4 | 3 | 3 | 0 | 0 | .00 | 6 | .239 | .324 | .442 |
| 1986 New York | AL | 149 | 504 | 120 | 24 | 3 | 28 | (14 | 14) | 234 | 71 | 71 | 54 | 10 | 120 | 4 | 1 | 2 | 4 | 1 | .80 | 10 | .238 | .316 | .464 |
| 1987 New York | AL | 150 | 522 | 122 | 26 | 3 | 32 | (17 | 15) | 250 | 76 | 87 | 53 | 9 | 111 | 2 | 2 | 3 | 1 | 3 | .25 | 9 | .234 | .305 | .479 |
| 1988 New York | AL | 125 | 444 | 96 | 20 | 1 | 15 | (8 | 7) | 163 | 46 | 67 | 37 | 9 | 104 | 2 | 1 | 6 | 1 | 0 | 1.00 | 5 | .216 | .276 | .367 |
| 1989 2 ML Teams | | 124 | 371 | 73 | 17 | 0 | 7 | (5 | 2) | 111 | 31 | 30 | 37 | 4 | 82 | 3 | 1 | 0 | 3 | 1 | .75 | 5 | .197 | .275 | .299 |
| 1990 San Diego | NL | 128 | 398 | 101 | 23 | 2 | 7 | (1 | 6) | 149 | 29 | 38 | 39 | 3 | 66 | 3 | 2 | 4 | 1 | 3 | .25 | 12 | .254 | .322 | .374 |
| 1989 New York | AL | 74 | 223 | 44 | 10 | 0 | 4 | (3 | 1) | 66 | 19 | 16 | 19 | 0 | 43 | 2 | 0 | 0 | 1 | 1 | .50 | 2 | .197 | .266 | .296 |
| San Diego | NL | 50 | 148 | 29 | 7 | 0 | 3 | (2 | 1) | 45 | 12 | 14 | 18 | 4 | 39 | 1 | 1 | 0 | 2 | 0 | 1.00 | 3 | .196 | .287 | .304 |
| 7 ML YEARS | | 881 | 2820 | 651 | 141 | 14 | 115 | (57 | 58) | 1165 | 332 | 389 | 280 | 39 | 615 | 18 | 10 | 21 | 10 | 8 | .56 | 52 | .231 | .302 | .413 |

## Tom Pagnozzi

**Bats:** Right **Throws:** Right **Pos:** C **Ht:** 6' 1" **Wt:** 190 **Born:** 07/30/62 **Age:** 28

| | | BATTING | | | | | | | | | | | | | | | | | BASERUNNING | | | | PERCENTAGES | | |
|---|---|---|---|---|---|---|---|---|---|---|---|---|---|---|---|---|---|---|---|---|---|---|---|---|---|
| Year Team | Lg | G | AB | H | 2B | 3B | HR | (Hm | Rd) | TB | R | RBI | TBB | IBB | SO | HBP | SH | SF | SB | CS | SB% | GDP | Avg | OBP | SLG |
| 1987 St. Louis | NL | 27 | 48 | 9 | 1 | 0 | 2 | (2 | 0) | 16 | 8 | 9 | 4 | 2 | 13 | 0 | 1 | 0 | 1 | 0 | 1.00 | 0 | .188 | .250 | .333 |
| 1988 St. Louis | NL | 81 | 195 | 55 | 9 | 0 | 0 | (0 | 0) | 64 | 17 | 15 | 11 | 1 | 32 | 0 | 2 | 1 | 0 | 0 | .00 | 5 | .282 | .319 | .328 |
| 1989 St. Louis | NL | 52 | 80 | 12 | 2 | 0 | 0 | (0 | 0) | 14 | 3 | 3 | 6 | 2 | 19 | 1 | 0 | 1 | 0 | 0 | .00 | 7 | .150 | .216 | .175 |
| 1990 St. Louis | NL | 69 | 220 | 61 | 15 | 0 | 2 | (2 | 0) | 82 | 20 | 23 | 14 | 1 | 37 | 1 | 0 | 2 | 1 | 1 | .50 | 0 | .277 | .321 | .373 |
| 4 ML YEARS | | 229 | 543 | 137 | 27 | 0 | 4 | (4 | 0) | 176 | 48 | 50 | 35 | 6 | 101 | 2 | 3 | 4 | 2 | 1 | .67 | 12 | .252 | .298 | .324 |

## Rey Palacios

**Bats:** Right **Throws:** Right **Pos:** C **Ht:** 5'10" **Wt:** 190 **Born:** 11/08/62 **Age:** 28

| | | BATTING | | | | | | | | | | | | | | | | | BASERUNNING | | | | PERCENTAGES | | |
|---|---|---|---|---|---|---|---|---|---|---|---|---|---|---|---|---|---|---|---|---|---|---|---|---|---|
| Year Team | Lg | G | AB | H | 2B | 3B | HR | (Hm | Rd) | TB | R | RBI | TBB | IBB | SO | HBP | SH | SF | SB | CS | SB% | GDP | Avg | OBP | SLG |
| 1988 Kansas City | AL | 5 | 11 | 1 | 0 | 0 | 0 | (0 | 0) | 1 | 2 | 0 | 0 | 0 | 4 | 0 | 0 | 0 | 0 | 0 | .00 | 1 | .091 | .091 | .091 |
| 1989 Kansas City | AL | 55 | 47 | 8 | 2 | 0 | 1 | (0 | 1) | 13 | 12 | 8 | 2 | 0 | 14 | 1 | 2 | 1 | 0 | 1 | .00 | 1 | .170 | .216 | .277 |
| 1990 Kansas City | AL | 41 | 56 | 13 | 3 | 0 | 2 | (1 | 1) | 22 | 8 | 9 | 5 | 0 | 24 | 0 | 0 | 0 | 2 | 2 | .50 | 0 | .232 | .295 | .393 |
| 3 ML YEARS | | 101 | 114 | 22 | 5 | 0 | 3 | (1 | 2) | 36 | 22 | 17 | 7 | 0 | 42 | 1 | 2 | 1 | 2 | 3 | .40 | 2 | .193 | .244 | .316 |

## Vince Palacios

**Pitches:** Right **Bats:** Right **Pos:** RP **Ht:** 6' 3" **Wt:** 180 **Born:** 07/19/63 **Age:** 27

| | | HOW MUCH HE PITCHED | | | | | | WHAT HE GAVE UP | | | | | | | | | | | | THE RESULTS | | | | | |
|---|---|---|---|---|---|---|---|---|---|---|---|---|---|---|---|---|---|---|---|---|---|---|---|---|---|
| Year Team | Lg | G | GS | CG | GF | IP | BFP | H | R | ER | HR | SH | SF | HB | TBB | IBB | SO | WP | Bk | W | L | Pct. | ShO | Sv | ERA |
| 1987 Pittsburgh | NL | 6 | 4 | 0 | 0 | 29.1 | 120 | 27 | 14 | 14 | 1 | 2 | 0 | 1 | 9 | 1 | 13 | 0 | 2 | 2 | 1 | .667 | 0 | 0 | 4.30 |

| Year Team | Lg | G | GS | CG | GF | IP | BFP | H | R | ER | HR | SH | SF | HB | TBB | IBB | SO | WP | Bk | W | L | Pct. | ShO | Sv | ERA |
|---|---|---|---|---|---|---|---|---|---|---|---|---|---|---|---|---|---|---|---|---|---|---|---|---|---|
| 1988 Pittsburgh | NL | 7 | 3 | 0 | 0 | 24.1 | 113 | 28 | 18 | 18 | 3 | 2 | 1 | 0 | 15 | 1 | 15 | 2 | 3 | 1 | 2 | .333 | 0 | 0 | 6.66 |
| 1990 Pittsburgh | NL | 7 | 0 | 0 | 4 | 15 | 50 | 4 | 0 | 0 | 0 | 0 | 0 | 0 | 2 | 0 | 8 | 2 | 0 | 0 | 0 | .000 | 0 | 3 | 0.00 |
| 3 ML YEARS | | 20 | 7 | 0 | 4 | 68.2 | 283 | 59 | 32 | 32 | 4 | 4 | 1 | 1 | 26 | 2 | 36 | 4 | 5 | 3 | 3 | .500 | 0 | 3 | 4.19 |

## Donn Pall

**Pitches:** Right **Bats:** Right **Pos:** RP **Ht:** 6' 1" **Wt:** 180 **Born:** 01/11/62 **Age:** 29

| | | HOW MUCH HE PITCHED | | | | | | WHAT HE GAVE UP | | | | | | | | | | | | THE RESULTS | | | | | |
|---|---|---|---|---|---|---|---|---|---|---|---|---|---|---|---|---|---|---|---|---|---|---|---|---|---|
| Year Team | Lg | G | GS | CG | GF | IP | BFP | H | R | ER | HR | SH | SF | HB | TBB | IBB | SO | WP | Bk | W | L | Pct. | ShO | Sv | ERA |
| 1988 Chicago | AL | 17 | 0 | 0 | 6 | 28.2 | 130 | 39 | 11 | 11 | 1 | 2 | 1 | 0 | 8 | 1 | 16 | 1 | 0 | 0 | 2 | .000 | 0 | 0 | 3.45 |
| 1989 Chicago | AL | 53 | 0 | 0 | 27 | 87 | 370 | 90 | 35 | 32 | 9 | 8 | 2 | 8 | 19 | 3 | 58 | 4 | 1 | 4 | 5 | .444 | 0 | 6 | 3.31 |
| 1990 Chicago | AL | 56 | 0 | 0 | 11 | 76 | 306 | 63 | 33 | 28 | 7 | 4 | 2 | 4 | 24 | 8 | 39 | 2 | 0 | 3 | 5 | .375 | 0 | 2 | 3.32 |
| 3 ML YEARS | | 126 | 0 | 0 | 44 | 191.2 | 806 | 192 | 79 | 71 | 17 | 14 | 5 | 12 | 51 | 12 | 113 | 7 | 1 | 7 | 12 | .368 | 0 | 8 | 3.33 |

## Rafael Palmeiro

**Bats:** Left **Throws:** Left **Pos:** 1B **Ht:** 6' 0" **Wt:** 180 **Born:** 09/24/64 **Age:** 26

| | | BATTING | | | | | | | | | | | | | | | | | BASERUNNING | | | | PERCENTAGES | | |
|---|---|---|---|---|---|---|---|---|---|---|---|---|---|---|---|---|---|---|---|---|---|---|---|---|---|
| Year Team | Lg | G | AB | H | 2B | 3B | HR | (Hm | Rd) | TB | R | RBI | TBB | IBB | SO | HBP | SH | SF | SB | CS | SB% | GDP | Avg | OBP | SLG |
| 1986 Chicago | NL | 22 | 73 | 18 | 4 | 0 | 3 | (1 | 2) | 31 | 9 | 12 | 4 | 0 | 6 | 1 | 0 | 0 | 1 | 1 | .50 | 4 | .247 | .295 | .425 |
| 1987 Chicago | NL | 84 | 221 | 61 | 15 | 1 | 14 | (5 | 9) | 120 | 32 | 30 | 20 | 1 | 26 | 1 | 0 | 2 | 2 | 2 | .50 | 4 | .276 | .336 | .543 |
| 1988 Chicago | NL | 152 | 580 | 178 | 41 | 5 | 8 | (8 | 0) | 253 | 75 | 53 | 38 | 6 | 34 | 3 | 2 | 6 | 12 | 2 | .86 | 11 | .307 | .349 | .436 |
| 1989 Texas | AL | 156 | 559 | 154 | 23 | 4 | 8 | (4 | 4) | 209 | 76 | 64 | 63 | 3 | 48 | 6 | 2 | 2 | 4 | 3 | .57 | 18 | .275 | .354 | .374 |
| 1990 Texas | AL | 154 | 598 | 191 | 35 | 6 | 14 | (9 | 5) | 280 | 72 | 89 | 40 | 6 | 59 | 3 | 2 | 8 | 3 | 3 | .50 | 24 | .319 | .361 | .468 |
| 5 ML YEARS | | 568 | 2031 | 602 | 118 | 16 | 47 | (27 | 20) | 893 | 264 | 248 | 165 | 16 | 173 | 14 | 6 | 18 | 22 | 11 | .67 | 61 | .296 | .351 | .440 |

## Jim Pankovits

**Bats:** Right **Throws:** Right **Pos:** 2B **Ht:** 5'10" **Wt:** 175 **Born:** 08/06/55 **Age:** 35

| | | BATTING | | | | | | | | | | | | | | | | | BASERUNNING | | | | PERCENTAGES | | |
|---|---|---|---|---|---|---|---|---|---|---|---|---|---|---|---|---|---|---|---|---|---|---|---|---|---|
| Year Team | Lg | G | AB | H | 2B | 3B | HR | (Hm | Rd) | TB | R | RBI | TBB | IBB | SO | HBP | SH | SF | SB | CS | SB% | GDP | Avg | OBP | SLG |
| 1984 Houston | NL | 53 | 81 | 23 | 7 | 0 | 1 | (0 | 1) | 33 | 6 | 14 | 2 | 0 | 20 | 0 | 1 | 1 | 2 | 1 | .67 | 1 | .284 | .298 | .407 |
| 1985 Houston | NL | 75 | 172 | 42 | 3 | 0 | 4 | (2 | 2) | 57 | 24 | 14 | 17 | 1 | 29 | 1 | 1 | 0 | 1 | 0 | 1.00 | 3 | .244 | .316 | .331 |
| 1986 Houston | NL | 70 | 113 | 32 | 6 | 1 | 1 | (0 | 1) | 43 | 12 | 7 | 11 | 1 | 25 | 0 | 0 | 0 | 1 | 1 | .50 | 4 | .283 | .347 | .381 |
| 1987 Houston | NL | 50 | 61 | 14 | 2 | 0 | 1 | (0 | 1) | 19 | 7 | 8 | 6 | 1 | 13 | 0 | 0 | 0 | 2 | 0 | 1.00 | 2 | .230 | .299 | .311 |
| 1988 Houston | NL | 68 | 140 | 31 | 7 | 1 | 2 | (0 | 2) | 46 | 13 | 12 | 8 | 0 | 28 | 2 | 2 | 1 | 2 | 1 | .67 | 1 | .221 | .272 | .329 |
| 1990 Boston | AL | 2 | 0 | 0 | 0 | 0 | 0 | (0 | 0) | 0 | 0 | 0 | 0 | 0 | 0 | 0 | 0 | 0 | 0 | 0 | .00 | 0 | .000 | .000 | .000 |
| 6 ML YEARS | | 318 | 567 | 142 | 25 | 2 | 9 | (2 | 7) | 198 | 62 | 55 | 44 | 3 | 115 | 3 | 4 | 2 | 8 | 3 | .73 | 11 | .250 | .307 | .349 |

## Johnny Paredes

**Bats:** Right **Throws:** Right **Pos:** 2B **Ht:** 5'11" **Wt:** 165 **Born:** 09/02/62 **Age:** 28

| | | BATTING | | | | | | | | | | | | | | | | | BASERUNNING | | | | PERCENTAGES | | |
|---|---|---|---|---|---|---|---|---|---|---|---|---|---|---|---|---|---|---|---|---|---|---|---|---|---|
| Year Team | Lg | G | AB | H | 2B | 3B | HR | (Hm | Rd) | TB | R | RBI | TBB | IBB | SO | HBP | SH | SF | SB | CS | SB% | GDP | Avg | OBP | SLG |
| 1988 Montreal | NL | 35 | 91 | 17 | 2 | 0 | 1 | (0 | 1) | 22 | 6 | 10 | 9 | 0 | 17 | 3 | 1 | 0 | 5 | 2 | .71 | 1 | .187 | .282 | .242 |
| 1990 2 ML Teams | | 9 | 14 | 3 | 1 | 0 | 0 | (0 | 0) | 4 | 2 | 1 | 2 | 1 | 0 | 0 | 0 | 0 | 0 | 0 | .00 | 0 | .214 | .313 | .286 |
| 1990 Detroit | AL | 6 | 8 | 1 | 0 | 0 | 0 | (0 | 0) | 1 | 2 | 0 | 1 | 0 | 0 | 0 | 0 | 0 | 0 | 0 | .00 | 0 | .125 | .222 | .125 |
| Montreal | NL | 3 | 6 | 2 | 1 | 0 | 0 | (0 | 0) | 3 | 0 | 1 | 1 | 1 | 0 | 0 | 0 | 0 | 0 | 0 | .00 | 0 | .333 | .429 | .500 |
| 2 ML YEARS | | 44 | 105 | 20 | 3 | 0 | 1 | (0 | 1) | 26 | 8 | 11 | 11 | 1 | 17 | 3 | 1 | 0 | 5 | 2 | .71 | 1 | .190 | .286 | .248 |

## Mark Parent

**Bats:** Right **Throws:** Right **Pos:** C **Ht:** 6' 5" **Wt:** 224 **Born:** 09/16/61 **Age:** 29

| | | BATTING | | | | | | | | | | | | | | | | | BASERUNNING | | | | PERCENTAGES | | |
|---|---|---|---|---|---|---|---|---|---|---|---|---|---|---|---|---|---|---|---|---|---|---|---|---|---|
| Year Team | Lg | G | AB | H | 2B | 3B | HR | (Hm | Rd) | TB | R | RBI | TBB | IBB | SO | HBP | SH | SF | SB | CS | SB% | GDP | Avg | OBP | SLG |
| 1986 San Diego | NL | 8 | 14 | 2 | 0 | 0 | 0 | (0 | 0) | 2 | 1 | 0 | 1 | 0 | 3 | 0 | 0 | 0 | 0 | 0 | .00 | 1 | .143 | .200 | .143 |
| 1987 San Diego | NL | 12 | 25 | 2 | 0 | 0 | 0 | (0 | 0) | 2 | 0 | 2 | 0 | 0 | 9 | 0 | 0 | 0 | 0 | 0 | .00 | 0 | .080 | .080 | .080 |
| 1988 San Diego | NL | 41 | 118 | 23 | 3 | 0 | 6 | (4 | 2) | 44 | 9 | 15 | 6 | 0 | 23 | 0 | 0 | 1 | 0 | 0 | .00 | 1 | .195 | .232 | .373 |
| 1989 San Diego | NL | 52 | 141 | 27 | 4 | 0 | 7 | (6 | 1) | 52 | 12 | 21 | 8 | 2 | 34 | 0 | 1 | 4 | 1 | 0 | 1.00 | 5 | .191 | .229 | .369 |
| 1990 San Diego | NL | 65 | 189 | 42 | 11 | 0 | 3 | (1 | 2) | 62 | 13 | 16 | 16 | 3 | 29 | 0 | 3 | 0 | 1 | 0 | 1.00 | 2 | .222 | .283 | .328 |
| 5 ML YEARS | | 178 | 487 | 96 | 18 | 0 | 16 | (11 | 5) | 162 | 35 | 54 | 31 | 5 | 98 | 0 | 4 | 5 | 2 | 0 | 1.00 | 9 | .197 | .243 | .333 |

## Clay Parker

**Pitches:** Right **Bats:** Right **Pos:** RP/SP **Ht:** 6' 1" **Wt:** 185 **Born:** 12/19/62 **Age:** 28

| | | HOW MUCH HE PITCHED | | | | | | WHAT HE GAVE UP | | | | | | | | | | | | THE RESULTS | | | | | |
|---|---|---|---|---|---|---|---|---|---|---|---|---|---|---|---|---|---|---|---|---|---|---|---|---|---|
| Year Team | Lg | G | GS | CG | GF | IP | BFP | H | R | ER | HR | SH | SF | HB | TBB | IBB | SO | WP | Bk | W | L | Pct. | ShO | Sv | ERA |
| 1987 Seattle | AL | 3 | 1 | 0 | 1 | 7.2 | 43 | 15 | 10 | 9 | 2 | 0 | 1 | 1 | 4 | 0 | 8 | 0 | 0 | 0 | 0 | .000 | 0 | 0 | 10.57 |
| 1989 New York | AL | 22 | 17 | 2 | 1 | 120 | 507 | 123 | 53 | 49 | 12 | 6 | 2 | 2 | 31 | 3 | 53 | 2 | 2 | 4 | 5 | .444 | 0 | 0 | 3.68 |
| 1990 2 ML Teams | | 29 | 3 | 0 | 8 | 73 | 308 | 64 | 29 | 29 | 11 | 3 | 3 | 1 | 32 | 6 | 40 | 4 | 0 | 3 | 3 | .500 | 0 | 0 | 3.58 |
| 1990 New York | AL | 5 | 2 | 0 | 1 | 22 | 91 | 19 | 11 | 11 | 5 | 0 | 1 | 0 | 7 | 1 | 20 | 1 | 0 | 1 | 1 | .500 | 0 | 0 | 4.50 |
| Detroit | AL | 24 | 1 | 0 | 7 | 51 | 217 | 45 | 18 | 18 | 6 | 3 | 2 | 1 | 25 | 5 | 20 | 3 | 0 | 2 | 2 | .500 | 0 | 0 | 3.18 |
| 3 ML YEARS | | 54 | 21 | 2 | 10 | 200.2 | 858 | 202 | 92 | 87 | 25 | 9 | 6 | 4 | 67 | 9 | 101 | 6 | 2 | 7 | 8 | .467 | 0 | 0 | 3.90 |

## Dave Parker

**Bats:** Left **Throws:** Right **Pos:** DH **Ht:** 6' 5" **Wt:** 245 **Born:** 06/09/51 **Age:** 40

| | | | BATTING | | | | | | | | | | | | | | | | | | BASERUNNING | | | | PERCENTAGES | | |
|---|---|---|---|---|---|---|---|---|---|---|---|---|---|---|---|---|---|---|---|---|---|---|---|---|---|---|---|
| Year | Team | Lg | G | AB | H | 2B | 3B | HR | (Hm | Rd) | TB | R | RBI | TBB | IBB | SO | HBP | SH | SF | SB | CS | SB% | GDP | Avg | OBP | SLG |
| 1973 | Pittsburgh | NL | 54 | 139 | 40 | 9 | 1 | 4 | (2 | 2) | 63 | 17 | 14 | 2 | 1 | 27 | 2 | 1 | 0 | 1 | 1 | .50 | 2 | .288 | .308 | .453 |
| 1974 | Pittsburgh | NL | 73 | 220 | 62 | 10 | 3 | 4 | (3 | 1) | 90 | 27 | 29 | 10 | 1 | 53 | 3 | 0 | 0 | 3 | 3 | .50 | 3 | .282 | .322 | .409 |
| 1975 | Pittsburgh | NL | 148 | 558 | 172 | 35 | 10 | 25 | (10 | 15) | 302 | 75 | 101 | 38 | 4 | 89 | 5 | 0 | 1 | 8 | 6 | .57 | 18 | .308 | .357 | .541 |
| 1976 | Pittsburgh | NL | 138 | 537 | 168 | 28 | 10 | 13 | (5 | 8) | 255 | 82 | 90 | 30 | 6 | 80 | 2 | 0 | 4 | 19 | 7 | .73 | 16 | .313 | .349 | .475 |
| 1977 | Pittsburgh | NL | 159 | 637 | 215 | 44 | 8 | 21 | (10 | 11) | 338 | 107 | 88 | 58 | 13 | 107 | 7 | 0 | 4 | 17 | 19 | .47 | 7 | .338 | .397 | .531 |
| 1978 | Pittsburgh | NL | 148 | 581 | 194 | 32 | 12 | 30 | (14 | 16) | 340 | 102 | 117 | 57 | 23 | 92 | 2 | 0 | 2 | 20 | 7 | .74 | 8 | .334 | .394 | .585 |
| 1979 | Pittsburgh | NL | 158 | 622 | 193 | 45 | 7 | 25 | (14 | 11) | 327 | 109 | 94 | 67 | 14 | 101 | 9 | 0 | 9 | 20 | 4 | .83 | 7 | .310 | .380 | .526 |
| 1980 | Pittsburgh | NL | 139 | 518 | 153 | 31 | 1 | 17 | (10 | 7) | 237 | 71 | 79 | 25 | 5 | 69 | 2 | 0 | 5 | 10 | 7 | .59 | 8 | .295 | .327 | .458 |
| 1981 | Pittsburgh | NL | 67 | 240 | 62 | 14 | 3 | 9 | (4 | 5) | 109 | 29 | 48 | 9 | 3 | 25 | 2 | 0 | 3 | 6 | 2 | .75 | 5 | .258 | .287 | .454 |
| 1982 | Pittsburgh | NL | 73 | 244 | 66 | 19 | 3 | 6 | (4 | 2) | 109 | 41 | 29 | 22 | 2 | 45 | 1 | 0 | 3 | 7 | 5 | .58 | 7 | .270 | .330 | .447 |
| 1983 | Pittsburgh | NL | 144 | 552 | 154 | 29 | 4 | 12 | (6 | 6) | 227 | 68 | 69 | 28 | 6 | 89 | 0 | 0 | 6 | 12 | 9 | .57 | 11 | .279 | .311 | .411 |
| 1984 | Cincinnati | NL | 156 | 607 | 173 | 28 | 0 | 16 | (10 | 6) | 249 | 73 | 94 | 41 | 10 | 89 | 1 | 0 | 6 | 11 | 10 | .52 | 8 | .285 | .328 | .410 |
| 1985 | Cincinnati | NL | 160 | 635 | 198 | 42 | 4 | 34 | (16 | 18) | 350 | 88 | 125 | 52 | 24 | 80 | 3 | 0 | 4 | 5 | 13 | .28 | 26 | .312 | .365 | .551 |
| 1986 | Cincinnati | NL | 162 | 637 | 174 | 31 | 3 | 31 | (17 | 14) | 304 | 89 | 116 | 56 | 16 | 126 | 1 | 0 | 6 | 1 | 6 | .14 | 18 | .273 | .330 | .477 |
| 1987 | Cincinnati | NL | 153 | 589 | 149 | 28 | 0 | 26 | (14 | 12) | 255 | 77 | 97 | 44 | 13 | 104 | 8 | 0 | 6 | 7 | 3 | .70 | 14 | .253 | .311 | .433 |
| 1988 | Oakland | AL | 101 | 377 | 97 | 18 | 1 | 12 | (6 | 6) | 153 | 43 | 55 | 32 | 2 | 70 | 0 | 0 | 2 | 0 | 1 | .00 | 3 | .257 | .314 | .406 |
| 1989 | Oakland | AL | 144 | 553 | 146 | 27 | 0 | 22 | (10 | 12) | 239 | 56 | 97 | 38 | 13 | 91 | 1 | 0 | 8 | 0 | 0 | .00 | 21 | .264 | .308 | .432 |
| 1990 | Milwaukee | AL | 157 | 610 | 176 | 30 | 3 | 21 | (9 | 12) | 275 | 71 | 92 | 41 | 11 | 102 | 4 | 0 | 14 | 4 | 7 | .36 | 18 | .289 | .330 | .451 |
| | 18 ML YEARS | | 2334 | 8856 | 2592 | 500 | 73 | 328 | (164 | 164) | 4222 | 1225 | 1434 | 650 | 167 | 1439 | 53 | 1 | 83 | 151 | 110 | .58 | 200 | .293 | .342 | .477 |

## Rick Parker

**Bats:** Right **Throws:** Right **Pos:** RF **Ht:** 6' 0" **Wt:** 185 **Born:** 03/20/63 **Age:** 28

| | | | BATTING | | | | | | | | | | | | | | | | | | BASERUNNING | | | | PERCENTAGES | | |
|---|---|---|---|---|---|---|---|---|---|---|---|---|---|---|---|---|---|---|---|---|---|---|---|---|---|---|---|
| Year | Team | Lg | G | AB | H | 2B | 3B | HR | (Hm | Rd) | TB | R | RBI | TBB | IBB | SO | HBP | SH | SF | SB | CS | SB% | GDP | Avg | OBP | SLG |
| 1985 | Bend | A | 55 | 205 | 51 | 9 | 1 | 2 | -- | -- | 68 | 45 | 20 | 40 | 0 | 42 | 4 | 0 | 3 | 14 | 7 | .67 | 2 | .249 | .377 | .332 |
| 1986 | Spartanburg | A | 62 | 233 | 69 | 7 | 3 | 5 | -- | -- | 97 | 39 | 28 | 36 | 0 | 39 | 2 | 2 | 0 | 14 | 9 | .61 | 7 | .296 | .395 | .416 |
| | Clearwater | A | 63 | 218 | 51 | 10 | 2 | 0 | -- | -- | 65 | 24 | 15 | 21 | 1 | 29 | 2 | 3 | 2 | 8 | 9 | .47 | 2 | .234 | .305 | .298 |
| 1987 | Clearwater | A | 101 | 330 | 83 | 13 | 3 | 3 | -- | -- | 111 | 56 | 34 | 31 | 3 | 36 | 3 | 2 | 3 | 6 | 4 | .60 | 4 | .252 | .319 | .336 |
| 1988 | Reading | AA | 116 | 362 | 93 | 13 | 3 | 3 | -- | -- | 121 | 50 | 47 | 36 | 2 | 50 | 3 | 1 | 6 | 24 | 6 | .80 | 6 | .257 | .324 | .334 |
| 1989 | Reading | AA | 103 | 388 | 92 | 7 | 9 | 3 | -- | -- | 126 | 59 | 32 | 42 | 0 | 62 | 5 | 2 | 3 | 17 | 13 | .57 | 8 | .237 | .317 | .325 |
| | Phoenix | AAA | 18 | 68 | 18 | 2 | 2 | 0 | -- | -- | 24 | 5 | 11 | 2 | 0 | 14 | 1 | 1 | 0 | 1 | 2 | .33 | 1 | .265 | .296 | .353 |
| 1990 | Phoenix | AAA | 44 | 173 | 58 | 7 | 4 | 1 | -- | -- | 76 | 38 | 18 | 22 | 0 | 25 | 0 | 0 | 0 | 18 | 10 | .64 | 1 | .335 | .410 | .439 |
| 1990 | San Francisco | NL | 54 | 107 | 26 | 5 | 0 | 2 | (0 | 2) | 37 | 19 | 14 | 10 | 0 | 15 | 1 | 3 | 0 | 6 | 1 | .86 | 1 | .243 | .314 | .346 |

## Jeff Parrett

**Pitches:** Right **Bats:** Right **Pos:** RP/SP **Ht:** 6' 3" **Wt:** 200 **Born:** 08/26/61 **Age:** 29

| | | | HOW MUCH HE PITCHED | | | | | | WHAT HE GAVE UP | | | | | | | | | | | | THE RESULTS | | | | | |
|---|---|---|---|---|---|---|---|---|---|---|---|---|---|---|---|---|---|---|---|---|---|---|---|---|---|---|
| Year | Team | Lg | G | GS | CG | GF | IP | BFP | H | R | ER | HR | SH | SF | HB | TBB | IBB | SO | WP | Bk | W | L | Pct. | ShO | Sv | ERA |
| 1986 | Montreal | NL | 12 | 0 | 0 | 6 | 20.1 | 91 | 19 | 11 | 11 | 3 | 0 | 1 | 0 | 13 | 0 | 21 | 2 | 0 | 0 | 1 | .000 | 0 | 0 | 4.87 |
| 1987 | Montreal | NL | 45 | 0 | 0 | 26 | 62 | 267 | 53 | 33 | 29 | 8 | 5 | 1 | 0 | 30 | 4 | 56 | 6 | 1 | 7 | 6 | .538 | 0 | 6 | 4.21 |
| 1988 | Montreal | NL | 61 | 0 | 0 | 34 | 91.2 | 369 | 66 | 29 | 27 | 8 | 9 | 6 | 1 | 45 | 9 | 62 | 4 | 1 | 12 | 4 | .750 | 0 | 6 | 2.65 |
| 1989 | Philadelphia | NL | 72 | 0 | 0 | 34 | 105.2 | 444 | 90 | 43 | 35 | 6 | 7 | 5 | 0 | 44 | 13 | 98 | 7 | 3 | 12 | 6 | .667 | 0 | 6 | 2.98 |
| 1990 | 2 ML Teams | | 67 | 5 | 0 | 19 | 108.2 | 479 | 119 | 62 | 56 | 11 | 7 | 5 | 2 | 55 | 10 | 86 | 5 | 1 | 5 | 10 | .333 | 0 | 2 | 4.64 |
| 1990 | Philadelphia | NL | 47 | 5 | 0 | 14 | 81.2 | 355 | 92 | 51 | 47 | 10 | 3 | 1 | 1 | 36 | 8 | 69 | 3 | 1 | 4 | 9 | .308 | 0 | 1 | 5.18 |
| | Atlanta | NL | 20 | 0 | 0 | 5 | 27 | 124 | 27 | 11 | 9 | 1 | 4 | 4 | 1 | 19 | 2 | 17 | 2 | 0 | 1 | 1 | .500 | 0 | 1 | 3.00 |
| | 5 ML YEARS | | 257 | 5 | 0 | 119 | 388.1 | 1650 | 347 | 178 | 158 | 36 | 28 | 18 | 3 | 187 | 36 | 323 | 24 | 6 | 36 | 27 | .571 | 0 | 20 | 3.66 |

## Lance Parrish

**Bats:** Right **Throws:** Right **Pos:** C **Ht:** 6' 3" **Wt:** 220 **Born:** 06/15/56 **Age:** 35

| | | | BATTING | | | | | | | | | | | | | | | | | | BASERUNNING | | | | PERCENTAGES | | |
|---|---|---|---|---|---|---|---|---|---|---|---|---|---|---|---|---|---|---|---|---|---|---|---|---|---|---|---|
| Year | Team | Lg | G | AB | H | 2B | 3B | HR | (Hm | Rd) | TB | R | RBI | TBB | IBB | SO | HBP | SH | SF | SB | CS | SB% | GDP | Avg | OBP | SLG |
| 1977 | Detroit | AL | 12 | 46 | 9 | 2 | 0 | 3 | (2 | 1) | 20 | 10 | 7 | 5 | 0 | 12 | 0 | 0 | 0 | 0 | 0 | .00 | 2 | .196 | .275 | .435 |
| 1978 | Detroit | AL | 85 | 288 | 63 | 11 | 3 | 14 | (7 | 7) | 122 | 37 | 41 | 11 | 0 | 71 | 3 | 1 | 1 | 0 | 0 | .00 | 8 | .219 | .254 | .424 |
| 1979 | Detroit | AL | 143 | 493 | 136 | 26 | 3 | 19 | (8 | 11) | 225 | 65 | 65 | 49 | 2 | 105 | 2 | 3 | 1 | 6 | 7 | .46 | 15 | .276 | .343 | .456 |
| 1980 | Detroit | AL | 144 | 553 | 158 | 34 | 6 | 24 | (7 | 17) | 276 | 79 | 82 | 31 | 3 | 109 | 3 | 2 | 3 | 6 | 4 | .60 | 24 | .286 | .325 | .499 |
| 1981 | Detroit | AL | 96 | 348 | 85 | 18 | 2 | 10 | (8 | 2) | 137 | 39 | 46 | 34 | 6 | 52 | 0 | 1 | 1 | 2 | 3 | .40 | 16 | .244 | .311 | .394 |
| 1982 | Detroit | AL | 133 | 486 | 138 | 19 | 2 | 32 | (22 | 10) | 257 | 75 | 87 | 40 | 5 | 99 | 1 | 0 | 2 | 3 | 4 | .43 | 5 | .284 | .338 | .529 |
| 1983 | Detroit | AL | 155 | 605 | 163 | 42 | 3 | 27 | (12 | 15) | 292 | 80 | 114 | 44 | 7 | 106 | 1 | 0 | 13 | 1 | 3 | .25 | 21 | .269 | .314 | .483 |
| 1984 | Detroit | AL | 147 | 578 | 137 | 16 | 2 | 33 | (13 | 20) | 256 | 75 | 98 | 41 | 6 | 120 | 2 | 2 | 6 | 2 | 3 | .40 | 12 | .237 | .287 | .443 |
| 1985 | Detroit | AL | 140 | 549 | 150 | 27 | 1 | 28 | (11 | 17) | 263 | 64 | 98 | 41 | 5 | 90 | 2 | 3 | 5 | 2 | 6 | .25 | 10 | .273 | .323 | .479 |
| 1986 | Detroit | AL | 91 | 327 | 84 | 6 | 1 | 22 | (8 | 14) | 158 | 53 | 62 | 38 | 3 | 83 | 5 | 1 | 3 | 0 | 0 | .00 | 3 | .257 | .340 | .483 |

| Year Team | Lg | G | AB | H | 2B | 3B | HR | (Hm | Rd) | TB | R | RBI | TBB | IBB | SO | HBP | SH | SF | SB | CS | SB% | GDP | Avg | OBP | SLG |
|---|---|---|---|---|---|---|---|---|---|---|---|---|---|---|---|---|---|---|---|---|---|---|---|---|---|
| 1987 Philadelphia | NL | 130 | 466 | 114 | 21 | 0 | 17 | (5 | 12) | 186 | 42 | 67 | 47 | 2 | 104 | 1 | 1 | 3 | 0 | 1 | .00 | 23 | .245 | .313 | .399 |
| 1988 Philadelphia | NL | 123 | 424 | 91 | 17 | 2 | 15 | (11 | 4) | 157 | 44 | 60 | 47 | 7 | 93 | 2 | 0 | 5 | 0 | 0 | .00 | 11 | .215 | .293 | .370 |
| 1989 California | AL | 124 | 433 | 103 | 12 | 1 | 17 | (8 | 9) | 168 | 48 | 50 | 42 | 6 | 104 | 2 | 1 | 4 | 1 | 1 | .50 | 10 | .238 | .306 | .388 |
| 1990 California | AL | 133 | 470 | 126 | 14 | 0 | 24 | (14 | 10) | 212 | 54 | 70 | 46 | 4 | 107 | 5 | 0 | 2 | 2 | 2 | .50 | 13 | .268 | .338 | .451 |
| 14 ML YEARS | | 1656 | 6066 | 1557 | 265 | 26 | 285 | (136 | 149) | 2729 | 765 | 947 | 516 | 56 | 1255 | 29 | 15 | 49 | 25 | 34 | .42 | 173 | .257 | .316 | .450 |

## Dan Pasqua

**Bats:** Left **Throws:** Left **Pos:** DH/LF/RF **Ht:** 6' 0" **Wt:** 205 **Born:** 10/17/61 **Age:** 29

| | | BATTING | | | | | | | | | | | | | | | | | BASERUNNING | | | | PERCENTAGES | | |
|---|---|---|---|---|---|---|---|---|---|---|---|---|---|---|---|---|---|---|---|---|---|---|---|---|---|
| Year Team | Lg | G | AB | H | 2B | 3B | HR | (Hm | Rd) | TB | R | RBI | TBB | IBB | SO | HBP | SH | SF | SB | CS | SB% | GDP | Avg | OBP | SLG |
| 1985 New York | AL | 60 | 148 | 31 | 3 | 1 | 9 | (7 | 2) | 63 | 17 | 25 | 16 | 4 | 38 | 1 | 0 | 1 | 0 | 0 | .00 | 1 | .209 | .289 | .426 |
| 1986 New York | AL | 102 | 280 | 82 | 17 | 0 | 16 | (9 | 7) | 147 | 44 | 45 | 47 | 3 | 78 | 3 | 1 | 1 | 2 | 0 | 1.00 | 4 | .293 | .399 | .525 |
| 1987 New York | AL | 113 | 318 | 74 | 7 | 1 | 17 | (6 | 11) | 134 | 42 | 42 | 40 | 3 | 99 | 1 | 2 | 1 | 0 | 2 | .00 | 7 | .233 | .319 | .421 |
| 1988 Chicago | AL | 129 | 422 | 96 | 16 | 2 | 20 | (11 | 9) | 176 | 48 | 50 | 46 | 5 | 100 | 3 | 2 | 2 | 1 | 0 | 1.00 | 10 | .227 | .307 | .417 |
| 1989 Chicago | AL | 73 | 246 | 61 | 9 | 1 | 11 | (5 | 6) | 105 | 26 | 47 | 25 | 1 | 58 | 1 | 1 | 4 | 1 | 2 | .33 | 0 | .248 | .315 | .427 |
| 1990 Chicago | AL | 112 | 325 | 89 | 27 | 3 | 13 | (4 | 9) | 161 | 43 | 58 | 37 | 7 | 66 | 2 | 0 | 5 | 1 | 1 | .50 | 4 | .274 | .347 | .495 |
| 6 ML YEARS | | 589 | 1739 | 433 | 79 | 8 | 86 | (42 | 44) | 786 | 220 | 267 | 211 | 23 | 439 | 11 | 6 | 14 | 5 | 5 | .50 | 26 | .249 | .332 | .452 |

## Bob Patterson

**Pitches:** Left **Bats:** Right **Pos:** RP/SP **Ht:** 6' 2" **Wt:** 192 **Born:** 05/16/59 **Age:** 32

| | | HOW MUCH HE PITCHED | | | | | | WHAT HE GAVE UP | | | | | | | | | | | | THE RESULTS | | | | | |
|---|---|---|---|---|---|---|---|---|---|---|---|---|---|---|---|---|---|---|---|---|---|---|---|---|---|
| Year Team | Lg | G | GS | CG | GF | IP | BFP | H | R | ER | HR | SH | SF | HB | TBB | IBB | SO | WP | Bk | W | L | Pct. | ShO | Sv | ERA |
| 1985 San Diego | NL | 3 | 0 | 0 | 2 | 4 | 26 | 13 | 11 | 11 | 2 | 0 | 0 | 0 | 3 | 0 | 1 | 0 | 1 | 0 | 0 | .000 | 0 | 0 | 24.75 |
| 1986 Pittsburgh | NL | 11 | 5 | 0 | 2 | 36.1 | 159 | 49 | 20 | 20 | 0 | 1 | 1 | 0 | 5 | 2 | 20 | 0 | 1 | 2 | 3 | .400 | 0 | 0 | 4.95 |
| 1987 Pittsburgh | NL | 15 | 7 | 0 | 2 | 43 | 201 | 49 | 34 | 32 | 5 | 6 | 3 | 1 | 22 | 4 | 27 | 1 | 0 | 1 | 4 | .200 | 0 | 0 | 6.70 |
| 1989 Pittsburgh | NL | 12 | 3 | 0 | 2 | 26.2 | 109 | 23 | 13 | 12 | 3 | 1 | 1 | 0 | 8 | 2 | 20 | 0 | 0 | 4 | 3 | .571 | 0 | 1 | 4.05 |
| 1990 Pittsburgh | NL | 55 | 5 | 0 | 19 | 94.2 | 386 | 88 | 33 | 31 | 9 | 5 | 3 | 3 | 21 | 7 | 70 | 1 | 2 | 8 | 5 | .615 | 0 | 5 | 2.95 |
| 5 ML YEARS | | 96 | 20 | 0 | 27 | 204.2 | 881 | 222 | 111 | 106 | 19 | 13 | 8 | 4 | 59 | 15 | 138 | 2 | 4 | 15 | 15 | .500 | 0 | 6 | 4.66 |

## Ken Patterson

**Pitches:** Left **Bats:** Left **Pos:** RP **Ht:** 6' 4" **Wt:** 210 **Born:** 07/08/64 **Age:** 26

| | | HOW MUCH HE PITCHED | | | | | | WHAT HE GAVE UP | | | | | | | | | | | | THE RESULTS | | | | | |
|---|---|---|---|---|---|---|---|---|---|---|---|---|---|---|---|---|---|---|---|---|---|---|---|---|---|
| Year Team | Lg | G | GS | CG | GF | IP | BFP | H | R | ER | HR | SH | SF | HB | TBB | IBB | SO | WP | Bk | W | L | Pct. | ShO | Sv | ERA |
| 1988 Chicago | AL | 9 | 2 | 0 | 3 | 20.2 | 92 | 25 | 11 | 11 | 2 | 0 | 0 | 0 | 7 | 0 | 8 | 1 | 1 | 0 | 2 | .000 | 0 | 1 | 4.79 |
| 1989 Chicago | AL | 50 | 1 | 0 | 18 | 65.2 | 284 | 64 | 37 | 33 | 11 | 1 | 4 | 2 | 28 | 3 | 43 | 3 | 1 | 6 | 1 | .857 | 0 | 0 | 4.52 |
| 1990 Chicago | AL | 43 | 0 | 0 | 15 | 66.1 | 283 | 58 | 27 | 25 | 6 | 2 | 5 | 2 | 34 | 1 | 40 | 2 | 0 | 2 | 1 | .667 | 0 | 2 | 3.39 |
| 3 ML YEARS | | 102 | 3 | 0 | 36 | 152.2 | 659 | 147 | 75 | 69 | 19 | 3 | 9 | 4 | 69 | 4 | 91 | 6 | 2 | 8 | 4 | .667 | 0 | 3 | 4.07 |

## Dave Pavlas

**Pitches:** Right **Bats:** Right **Pos:** RP **Ht:** 6' 7" **Wt:** 180 **Born:** 08/12/62 **Age:** 28

| | | HOW MUCH HE PITCHED | | | | | | WHAT HE GAVE UP | | | | | | | | | | | | THE RESULTS | | | | | |
|---|---|---|---|---|---|---|---|---|---|---|---|---|---|---|---|---|---|---|---|---|---|---|---|---|---|
| Year Team | Lg | G | GS | CG | GF | IP | BFP | H | R | ER | HR | SH | SF | HB | TBB | IBB | SO | WP | Bk | W | L | Pct. | ShO | Sv | ERA |
| 1985 Peoria | A | 17 | 15 | 3 | 2 | 110 | 452 | 90 | 40 | 32 | 7 | 3 | 1 | 3 | 32 | 0 | 86 | 6 | 1 | 8 | 3 | .727 | 1 | 1 | 2.62 |
| 1986 Winston-Sal | A | 28 | 26 | 5 | 0 | 173.1 | 739 | 172 | 91 | 74 | 8 | 6 | 4 | 6 | 57 | 2 | 143 | 11 | 1 | 14 | 6 | .700 | 2 | 0 | 3.84 |
| 1987 Pittsfield | AA | 7 | 7 | 0 | 0 | 45 | 199 | 49 | 25 | 19 | 6 | 0 | 3 | 3 | 17 | 0 | 27 | 1 | 1 | 6 | 1 | .857 | 0 | 0 | 3.80 |
| Tulsa | AA | 13 | 12 | 0 | 1 | 59.2 | 280 | 79 | 51 | 51 | 9 | 1 | 0 | 3 | 27 | 0 | 46 | 7 | 0 | 1 | 6 | .143 | 0 | 0 | 7.69 |
| 1988 Tulsa | AA | 26 | 5 | 1 | 9 | 77.1 | 299 | 52 | 26 | 17 | 3 | 6 | 2 | 5 | 18 | 1 | 69 | 4 | 6 | 5 | 2 | .714 | 0 | 2 | 1.98 |
| Okla City | AAA | 13 | 8 | 0 | 2 | 52.1 | 237 | 59 | 29 | 26 | 1 | 1 | 2 | 3 | 28 | 0 | 40 | 2 | 1 | 3 | 1 | .750 | 0 | 0 | 4.47 |
| 1989 Okla City | AAA | 29 | 21 | 4 | 4 | 143.2 | 652 | 175 | 89 | 75 | 7 | 6 | 7 | 7 | 67 | 4 | 94 | 8 | 1 | 2 | 14 | .125 | 0 | 0 | 4.70 |
| 1990 Iowa | AAA | 53 | 3 | 0 | 22 | 99.1 | 421 | 84 | 38 | 36 | 4 | 4 | 3 | 10 | 48 | 6 | 96 | 8 | 1 | 8 | 3 | .727 | 0 | 8 | 3.26 |
| 1990 Chicago | NL | 13 | 0 | 0 | 3 | 21.1 | 93 | 23 | 7 | 5 | 2 | 0 | 2 | 0 | 6 | 2 | 12 | 3 | 0 | 2 | 0 | 1.000 | 0 | 0 | 2.11 |

## Bill Pecota

**Bats:** Right **Throws:** Right **Pos:** 2B/SS **Ht:** 6' 2" **Wt:** 190 **Born:** 02/16/60 **Age:** 31

| | | BATTING | | | | | | | | | | | | | | | | | BASERUNNING | | | | PERCENTAGES | | |
|---|---|---|---|---|---|---|---|---|---|---|---|---|---|---|---|---|---|---|---|---|---|---|---|---|---|
| Year Team | Lg | G | AB | H | 2B | 3B | HR | (Hm | Rd) | TB | R | RBI | TBB | IBB | SO | HBP | SH | SF | SB | CS | SB% | GDP | Avg | OBP | SLG |
| 1986 Kansas City | AL | 12 | 29 | 6 | 2 | 0 | 0 | (0 | 0) | 8 | 3 | 2 | 3 | 0 | 3 | 1 | 0 | 1 | 0 | 2 | .00 | 1 | .207 | .294 | .276 |
| 1987 Kansas City | AL | 66 | 156 | 43 | 5 | 1 | 3 | (0 | 3) | 59 | 22 | 14 | 15 | 0 | 25 | 1 | 0 | 0 | 5 | 0 | 1.00 | 3 | .276 | .343 | .378 |
| 1988 Kansas City | AL | 90 | 178 | 37 | 3 | 3 | 1 | (0 | 1) | 49 | 25 | 15 | 18 | 0 | 34 | 2 | 7 | 1 | 7 | 2 | .78 | 1 | .208 | .286 | .275 |
| 1989 Kansas City | AL | 65 | 83 | 17 | 4 | 2 | 3 | (0 | 3) | 34 | 21 | 5 | 7 | 1 | 9 | 1 | 1 | 0 | 5 | 0 | 1.00 | 4 | .205 | .275 | .410 |
| 1990 Kansas City | AL | 87 | 240 | 58 | 15 | 2 | 5 | (3 | 2) | 92 | 43 | 20 | 33 | 0 | 39 | 1 | 6 | 0 | 8 | 5 | .62 | 5 | .242 | .336 | .383 |
| 5 ML YEARS | | 320 | 686 | 161 | 29 | 8 | 12 | (3 | 9) | 242 | 114 | 56 | 76 | 1 | 110 | 6 | 14 | 2 | 25 | 9 | .74 | 14 | .235 | .316 | .353 |

## Alejandro Pena

**Pitches:** Right **Bats:** Right **Pos:** RP **Ht:** 6' 1" **Wt:** 205 **Born:** 06/25/59 **Age:** 32

| | | HOW MUCH HE PITCHED | | | | | | WHAT HE GAVE UP | | | | | | | | | | | | THE RESULTS | | | | | |
|---|---|---|---|---|---|---|---|---|---|---|---|---|---|---|---|---|---|---|---|---|---|---|---|---|---|
| Year Team | Lg | G | GS | CG | GF | IP | BFP | H | R | ER | HR | SH | SF | HB | TBB | IBB | SO | WP | Bk | W | L | Pct. | ShO | Sv | ERA |
| 1981 Los Angeles | NL | 14 | 0 | 0 | 7 | 25 | 104 | 18 | 8 | 8 | 2 | 0 | 0 | 0 | 11 | 1 | 14 | 0 | 0 | 1 | 1 | .500 | 0 | 2 | 2.88 |
| 1982 Los Angeles | NL | 29 | 0 | 0 | 11 | 35.2 | 160 | 37 | 24 | 19 | 2 | 2 | 0 | 1 | 21 | 7 | 20 | 1 | 1 | 0 | 2 | .000 | 0 | 0 | 4.79 |
| 1983 Los Angeles | NL | 34 | 26 | 4 | 4 | 177 | 730 | 152 | 67 | 54 | 7 | 8 | 5 | 1 | 51 | 7 | 120 | 2 | 1 | 12 | 9 | .571 | 3 | 1 | 2.75 |
| 1984 Los Angeles | NL | 28 | 28 | 8 | 0 | 199.1 | 813 | 186 | 67 | 55 | 7 | 6 | 2 | 3 | 46 | 7 | 135 | 5 | 1 | 12 | 6 | .667 | 4 | 0 | 2.48 |
| 1985 Los Angeles | NL | 2 | 1 | 0 | 0 | 4.1 | 23 | 7 | 5 | 4 | 1 | 0 | 0 | 0 | 3 | 1 | 2 | 0 | 0 | 0 | 1 | .000 | 0 | 0 | 8.31 |
| 1986 Los Angeles | NL | 24 | 10 | 0 | 6 | 70 | 309 | 74 | 40 | 38 | 6 | 3 | 1 | 1 | 30 | 5 | 46 | 1 | 1 | 1 | 2 | .333 | 0 | 1 | 4.89 |
| 1987 Los Angeles | NL | 37 | 7 | 0 | 17 | 87.1 | 377 | 82 | 41 | 34 | 9 | 5 | 6 | 2 | 37 | 5 | 76 | 0 | 1 | 2 | 7 | .222 | 0 | 11 | 3.50 |
| 1988 Los Angeles | NL | 60 | 0 | 0 | 31 | 94.1 | 378 | 75 | 29 | 20 | 4 | 3 | 3 | 1 | 27 | 6 | 83 | 3 | 2 | 6 | 7 | .462 | 0 | 12 | 1.91 |
| 1989 Los Angeles | NL | 53 | 0 | 0 | 28 | 76 | 306 | 62 | 20 | 18 | 6 | 3 | 1 | 2 | 18 | 4 | 75 | 1 | 1 | 4 | 3 | .571 | 0 | 5 | 2.13 |
| 1990 New York | NL | 52 | 0 | 0 | 32 | 76 | 320 | 71 | 31 | 27 | 4 | 1 | 6 | 1 | 22 | 5 | 76 | 0 | 0 | 3 | 3 | .500 | 0 | 5 | 3.20 |
| 10 ML YEARS | | 333 | 72 | 12 | 136 | 845 | 3520 | 764 | 332 | 277 | 48 | 31 | 24 | 12 | 266 | 48 | 647 | 13 | 8 | 41 | 41 | .500 | 7 | 37 | 2.95 |

## Geronimo Pena

**Bats:** Both **Throws:** Right **Pos:** 2B **Ht:** 6' 1" **Wt:** 170 **Born:** 03/29/67 **Age:** 24

| | | BATTING | | | | | | | | | | | | | | | | BASERUNNING | | | | PERCENTAGES | | |
|---|---|---|---|---|---|---|---|---|---|---|---|---|---|---|---|---|---|---|---|---|---|---|---|---|
| Year Team | Lg | G | AB | H | 2B | 3B | HR | (Hm | Rd) | TB | R | RBI | TBB | IBB | SO | HBP | SH | SF | SB | CS | SB% | GDP | Avg | OBP | SLG |
| 1986 Johnson City | R | 56 | 202 | 60 | 7 | 4 | 3 | -- | -- | 84 | 55 | 20 | 46 | 4 | 33 | 7 | 1 | 3 | 27 | 3 | .90 | 1 | .297 | .438 | .416 |
| 1987 Savannah | A | 134 | 505 | 136 | 28 | 3 | 9 | -- | -- | 197 | 95 | 51 | 73 | 6 | 98 | 8 | 1 | 3 | 80 | 21 | .79 | 6 | .269 | .368 | .390 |
| 1988 St. Pete | A | 130 | 484 | 125 | 25 | 10 | 4 | -- | -- | 182 | 82 | 35 | 88 | 3 | 103 | 8 | 8 | 5 | 35 | 18 | .66 | 5 | .258 | .378 | .376 |
| 1989 St.Pete | A | 6 | 21 | 4 | 1 | 0 | 0 | -- | -- | 5 | 2 | 2 | 3 | 0 | 6 | 3 | 0 | 0 | 2 | 3 | .40 | 0 | .190 | .370 | .238 |
| Arkansas | AA | 77 | 267 | 79 | 16 | 8 | 9 | -- | -- | 138 | 61 | 44 | 38 | 3 | 68 | 8 | 3 | 4 | 14 | 6 | .70 | 0 | .296 | .394 | .517 |
| 1990 Louisville | AAA | 118 | 390 | 97 | 24 | 6 | 6 | -- | -- | 151 | 65 | 35 | 69 | 0 | 116 | 18 | 3 | 4 | 24 | 12 | .67 | 3 | .249 | .383 | .387 |
| 1990 St. Louis | NL | 18 | 45 | 11 | 2 | 0 | 0 | (0 | 0) | 13 | 5 | 2 | 4 | 0 | 14 | 1 | 0 | 1 | 1 | 1 | .50 | 0 | .244 | .314 | .289 |

## Tony Pena

**Bats:** Right **Throws:** Right **Pos:** C **Ht:** 6' 0" **Wt:** 184 **Born:** 06/04/57 **Age:** 34

| | | BATTING | | | | | | | | | | | | | | | | BASERUNNING | | | | PERCENTAGES | | |
|---|---|---|---|---|---|---|---|---|---|---|---|---|---|---|---|---|---|---|---|---|---|---|---|---|
| Year Team | Lg | G | AB | H | 2B | 3B | HR | (Hm | Rd) | TB | R | RBI | TBB | IBB | SO | HBP | SH | SF | SB | CS | SB% | GDP | Avg | OBP | SLG |
| 1980 Pittsburgh | NL | 8 | 21 | 9 | 1 | 1 | 0 | (0 | 0) | 12 | 1 | 1 | 0 | 0 | 4 | 0 | 0 | 0 | 0 | 1 | .00 | 1 | .429 | .429 | .571 |
| 1981 Pittsburgh | NL | 66 | 210 | 63 | 9 | 1 | 2 | (1 | 1) | 80 | 16 | 17 | 8 | 2 | 23 | 1 | 2 | 2 | 1 | 2 | .33 | 4 | .300 | .326 | .381 |
| 1982 Pittsburgh | NL | 138 | 497 | 147 | 28 | 4 | 11 | (5 | 6) | 216 | 53 | 63 | 17 | 3 | 57 | 4 | 3 | 2 | 2 | 5 | .29 | 17 | .296 | .323 | .435 |
| 1983 Pittsburgh | NL | 151 | 542 | 163 | 22 | 3 | 15 | (8 | 7) | 236 | 51 | 70 | 31 | 8 | 73 | 0 | 6 | 1 | 6 | 7 | .46 | 13 | .301 | .338 | .435 |
| 1984 Pittsburgh | NL | 147 | 546 | 156 | 27 | 2 | 15 | (7 | 8) | 232 | 77 | 78 | 36 | 5 | 79 | 4 | 4 | 2 | 12 | 8 | .60 | 14 | .286 | .333 | .425 |
| 1985 Pittsburgh | NL | 147 | 546 | 136 | 27 | 2 | 10 | (2 | 8) | 197 | 53 | 59 | 29 | 4 | 67 | 0 | 7 | 5 | 12 | 8 | .60 | 19 | .249 | .284 | .361 |
| 1986 Pittsburgh | NL | 144 | 510 | 147 | 26 | 2 | 10 | (5 | 5) | 207 | 56 | 52 | 53 | 6 | 69 | 1 | 0 | 1 | 9 | 10 | .47 | 21 | .288 | .356 | .406 |
| 1987 St. Louis | NL | 116 | 384 | 82 | 13 | 4 | 5 | (1 | 4) | 118 | 40 | 44 | 36 | 9 | 54 | 1 | 2 | 2 | 6 | 1 | .86 | 19 | .214 | .281 | .307 |
| 1988 St. Louis | NL | 149 | 505 | 133 | 23 | 1 | 10 | (4 | 6) | 188 | 55 | 51 | 33 | 11 | 60 | 1 | 3 | 4 | 6 | 2 | .75 | 12 | .263 | .308 | .372 |
| 1989 St. Louis | NL | 141 | 424 | 110 | 17 | 2 | 4 | (3 | 1) | 143 | 36 | 37 | 35 | 19 | 33 | 2 | 2 | 1 | 5 | 3 | .63 | 19 | .259 | .318 | .337 |
| 1990 Boston | AL | 143 | 491 | 129 | 19 | 1 | 7 | (3 | 4) | 171 | 62 | 56 | 43 | 3 | 71 | 1 | 2 | 3 | 8 | 6 | .57 | 23 | .263 | .322 | .348 |
| 11 ML YEARS | | 1350 | 4676 | 1275 | 212 | 23 | 89 | (39 | 50) | 1800 | 500 | 528 | 321 | 70 | 590 | 15 | 31 | 23 | 67 | 53 | .56 | 162 | .273 | .320 | .385 |

## Terry Pendleton

**Bats:** Both **Throws:** Right **Pos:** 3B **Ht:** 5' 9" **Wt:** 178 **Born:** 07/16/60 **Age:** 30

| | | BATTING | | | | | | | | | | | | | | | | BASERUNNING | | | | PERCENTAGES | | |
|---|---|---|---|---|---|---|---|---|---|---|---|---|---|---|---|---|---|---|---|---|---|---|---|---|
| Year Team | Lg | G | AB | H | 2B | 3B | HR | (Hm | Rd) | TB | R | RBI | TBB | IBB | SO | HBP | SH | SF | SB | CS | SB% | GDP | Avg | OBP | SLG |
| 1984 St. Louis | NL | 67 | 262 | 85 | 16 | 3 | 1 | (0 | 1) | 110 | 37 | 33 | 16 | 3 | 32 | 0 | 0 | 5 | 20 | 5 | .80 | 7 | .324 | .357 | .420 |
| 1985 St. Louis | NL | 149 | 559 | 134 | 16 | 3 | 5 | (3 | 2) | 171 | 56 | 69 | 37 | 4 | 75 | 0 | 3 | 3 | 17 | 12 | .59 | 18 | .240 | .285 | .306 |
| 1986 St. Louis | NL | 159 | 578 | 138 | 26 | 5 | 1 | (0 | 1) | 177 | 56 | 59 | 34 | 10 | 59 | 1 | 6 | 7 | 24 | 6 | .80 | 12 | .239 | .279 | .306 |
| 1987 St. Louis | NL | 159 | 583 | 167 | 29 | 4 | 12 | (5 | 7) | 240 | 82 | 96 | 70 | 6 | 74 | 2 | 3 | 9 | 19 | 12 | .61 | 18 | .286 | .360 | .412 |
| 1988 St. Louis | NL | 110 | 391 | 99 | 20 | 2 | 6 | (3 | 3) | 141 | 44 | 53 | 21 | 4 | 51 | 2 | 4 | 3 | 3 | 3 | .50 | 9 | .253 | .293 | .361 |
| 1989 St. Louis | NL | 162 | 613 | 162 | 28 | 5 | 13 | (8 | 5) | 239 | 83 | 74 | 44 | 3 | 81 | 0 | 2 | 2 | 9 | 5 | .64 | 16 | .264 | .313 | .390 |
| 1990 St. Louis | NL | 121 | 447 | 103 | 20 | 2 | 6 | (6 | 0) | 145 | 46 | 58 | 30 | 8 | 58 | 1 | 0 | 6 | 7 | 5 | .58 | 12 | .230 | .277 | .324 |
| 7 ML YEARS | | 927 | 3433 | 888 | 155 | 24 | 44 | (25 | 19) | 1223 | 404 | 442 | 252 | 38 | 430 | 6 | 18 | 35 | 99 | 48 | .67 | 92 | .259 | .308 | .356 |

## Melido Perez

**Pitches:** Right **Bats:** Right **Pos:** SP **Ht:** 6' 4" **Wt:** 180 **Born:** 02/15/66 **Age:** 25

| | | HOW MUCH HE PITCHED | | | | | | WHAT HE GAVE UP | | | | | | | | | | | | THE RESULTS | | | | | |
|---|---|---|---|---|---|---|---|---|---|---|---|---|---|---|---|---|---|---|---|---|---|---|---|---|---|
| Year Team | Lg | G | GS | CG | GF | IP | BFP | H | R | ER | HR | SH | SF | HB | TBB | IBB | SO | WP | Bk | W | L | Pct. | ShO | Sv | ERA |
| 1987 Kansas City | AL | 3 | 3 | 0 | 0 | 10.1 | 53 | 18 | 12 | 9 | 2 | 0 | 0 | 0 | 5 | 0 | 5 | 0 | 0 | 1 | 1 | .500 | 0 | 0 | 7.84 |
| 1988 Chicago | AL | 32 | 32 | 3 | 0 | 197 | 836 | 186 | 105 | 83 | 26 | 5 | 8 | 2 | 72 | 0 | 138 | 13 | 3 | 12 | 10 | .545 | 1 | 0 | 3.79 |

| | | | | | | | | | | | | | | | | | | | | | | | | | |
|---|---|---|---|---|---|---|---|---|---|---|---|---|---|---|---|---|---|---|---|---|---|---|---|---|---|
| 1989 Chicago | AL | 31 | 31 | 2 | 0 | 183.1 | 810 | 187 | 106 | 102 | 23 | 5 | 4 | 3 | 90 | 3 | 141 | 12 | 5 | 11 | 14 | .440 | 0 | 0 | 5.01 |
| 1990 Chicago | AL | 35 | 35 | 3 | 0 | 197 | 833 | 177 | 111 | 101 | 14 | 4 | 6 | 2 | 86 | 1 | 161 | 8 | 4 | 13 | 14 | .481 | 3 | 0 | 4.61 |
| 4 ML YEARS | | 101 | 101 | 8 | 0 | 587.2 | 2532 | 568 | 334 | 295 | 65 | 14 | 18 | 7 | 253 | 4 | 445 | 33 | 12 | 37 | 39 | .487 | 4 | 0 | 4.52 |

## Mike Perez

**Pitches:** Right **Bats:** Right **Pos:** RP **Ht:** 6' 0" **Wt:** 185 **Born:** 10/19/64 **Age:** 26

| | | HOW MUCH HE PITCHED | | | | | | WHAT HE GAVE UP | | | | | | | | | | | | THE RESULTS | | | | | |
|---|---|---|---|---|---|---|---|---|---|---|---|---|---|---|---|---|---|---|---|---|---|---|---|---|---|
| Year Team | Lg | G | GS | CG | GF | IP | BFP | H | R | ER | HR | SH | SF | HB | TBB | IBB | SO | WP | Bk | W | L | Pct. | ShO | Sv | ERA |
| 1986 Johnson Cty | R | 18 | 8 | 2 | 6 | 72.2 | 314 | 69 | 35 | 24 | 3 | 1 | 2 | 5 | 22 | 0 | 72 | 1 | 0 | 3 | 5 | .375 | 0 | 3 | 2.97 |
| 1987 Springfield | A | 58 | 0 | 0 | 51 | 84.1 | 321 | 47 | 12 | 8 | 2 | 3 | 2 | 2 | 21 | 3 | 119 | 2 | 0 | 6 | 2 | .750 | 0 | 41 | 0.85 |
| 1988 Arkansas | AA | 11 | 0 | 0 | 6 | 14.1 | 75 | 18 | 18 | 18 | 2 | 1 | 2 | 1 | 13 | 2 | 17 | 2 | 3 | 1 | 3 | .250 | 0 | 0 | 11.30 |
| St. Pete | A | 35 | 0 | 0 | 28 | 43.1 | 173 | 24 | 12 | 10 | 0 | 2 | 3 | 4 | 16 | 1 | 45 | 2 | 4 | 2 | 2 | .500 | 0 | 17 | 2.08 |
| 1989 Arkansas | AA | 57 | 0 | 0 | 51 | 76.2 | 329 | 68 | 34 | 31 | 5 | 0 | 2 | 2 | 32 | 2 | 74 | 3 | 1 | 4 | 6 | .400 | 0 | 33 | 3.64 |
| 1990 Louisville | AAA | 57 | 0 | 0 | 50 | 67.1 | 298 | 64 | 34 | 32 | 9 | 4 | 1 | 2 | 33 | 4 | 69 | 3 | 0 | 7 | 7 | .500 | 0 | 31 | 4.28 |
| 1990 St. Louis | NL | 13 | 0 | 0 | 7 | 13.2 | 55 | 12 | 6 | 6 | 0 | 0 | 2 | 0 | 3 | 0 | 5 | 0 | 0 | 1 | 0 | 1.000 | 0 | 1 | 3.95 |

## Pascual Perez

**Pitches:** Right **Bats:** Right **Pos:** SP **Ht:** 6' 3" **Wt:** 180 **Born:** 05/17/57 **Age:** 34

| | | HOW MUCH HE PITCHED | | | | | | WHAT HE GAVE UP | | | | | | | | | | | | THE RESULTS | | | | | |
|---|---|---|---|---|---|---|---|---|---|---|---|---|---|---|---|---|---|---|---|---|---|---|---|---|---|
| Year Team | Lg | G | GS | CG | GF | IP | BFP | H | R | ER | HR | SH | SF | HB | TBB | IBB | SO | WP | Bk | W | L | Pct. | ShO | Sv | ERA |
| 1980 Pittsburgh | NL | 2 | 2 | 0 | 0 | 12 | 51 | 15 | 6 | 5 | 0 | 1 | 2 | 2 | 2 | 0 | 7 | 0 | 0 | 0 | 1 | .000 | 0 | 0 | 3.75 |
| 1981 Pittsburgh | NL | 17 | 13 | 2 | 1 | 86 | 380 | 92 | 50 | 38 | 5 | 6 | 0 | 3 | 34 | 9 | 46 | 5 | 1 | 2 | 7 | .222 | 0 | 0 | 3.98 |
| 1982 Atlanta | NL | 16 | 11 | 0 | 2 | 79.1 | 333 | 85 | 35 | 27 | 4 | 5 | 3 | 0 | 17 | 3 | 29 | 2 | 1 | 4 | 4 | .500 | 0 | 0 | 3.06 |
| 1983 Atlanta | NL | 33 | 33 | 7 | 0 | 215.1 | 889 | 213 | 88 | 82 | 20 | 12 | 4 | 4 | 51 | 5 | 144 | 7 | 0 | 15 | 8 | .652 | 1 | 0 | 3.43 |
| 1984 Atlanta | NL | 30 | 30 | 4 | 0 | 211.2 | 864 | 208 | 96 | 88 | 26 | 6 | 4 | 3 | 51 | 5 | 145 | 4 | 5 | 14 | 8 | .636 | 1 | 0 | 3.74 |
| 1985 Atlanta | NL | 22 | 22 | 0 | 0 | 95.1 | 453 | 115 | 72 | 65 | 10 | 5 | 3 | 1 | 57 | 10 | 57 | 2 | 2 | 1 | 13 | .071 | 0 | 0 | 6.14 |
| 1987 Montreal | NL | 10 | 10 | 2 | 0 | 70.1 | 273 | 52 | 21 | 18 | 5 | 3 | 1 | 1 | 16 | 1 | 58 | 1 | 1 | 7 | 0 | 1.000 | 0 | 0 | 2.30 |
| 1988 Montreal | NL | 27 | 27 | 4 | 0 | 188 | 741 | 133 | 59 | 51 | 15 | 10 | 3 | 7 | 44 | 6 | 131 | 5 | 10 | 12 | 8 | .600 | 2 | 0 | 2.44 |
| 1989 Montreal | NL | 33 | 28 | 2 | 3 | 198.1 | 811 | 178 | 85 | 73 | 15 | 6 | 4 | 4 | 45 | 13 | 152 | 6 | 1 | 9 | 13 | .409 | 0 | 0 | 3.31 |
| 1990 New York | AL | 3 | 3 | 0 | 0 | 14 | 52 | 8 | 3 | 2 | 0 | 0 | 0 | 0 | 3 | 0 | 12 | 1 | 0 | 1 | 2 | .333 | 0 | 0 | 1.29 |
| 10 ML YEARS | | 193 | 179 | 21 | 6 | 1170.1 | 4847 | 1099 | 515 | 449 | 100 | 54 | 24 | 25 | 320 | 52 | 781 | 33 | 21 | 65 | 64 | .504 | 4 | 0 | 3.45 |

## Tony Perezchica

**Bats:** Right **Throws:** Right **Pos:** 2B **Ht:** 5'11" **Wt:** 175 **Born:** 04/20/66 **Age:** 25

| | | BATTING | | | | | | | | | | | | | | | | | BASERUNNING | | | | PERCENTAGES | | |
|---|---|---|---|---|---|---|---|---|---|---|---|---|---|---|---|---|---|---|---|---|---|---|---|---|---|
| Year Team | Lg | G | AB | H | 2B | 3B | HR | (Hm | Rd) | TB | R | RBI | TBB | IBB | SO | HBP | SH | SF | SB | CS | SB% | GDP | Avg | OBP | SLG |
| 1988 San Francisco | NL | 7 | 8 | 1 | 0 | 0 | 0 | (0 | 0) | 1 | 1 | 1 | 2 | 0 | 1 | 0 | 0 | 1 | 0 | 0 | .00 | 0 | .125 | .273 | .125 |
| 1990 San Francisco | NL | 4 | 3 | 1 | 0 | 0 | 0 | (0 | 0) | 1 | 1 | 0 | 1 | 0 | 2 | 0 | 0 | 0 | 0 | 0 | .00 | 0 | .333 | .500 | .333 |
| 2 ML YEARS | | 11 | 11 | 2 | 0 | 0 | 0 | (0 | 0) | 2 | 2 | 1 | 3 | 0 | 3 | 0 | 0 | 1 | 0 | 0 | .00 | 0 | .182 | .333 | .182 |

## Gerald Perry

**Bats:** Left **Throws:** Right **Pos:** DH/1B **Ht:** 6' 0" **Wt:** 190 **Born:** 10/30/60 **Age:** 30

| | | BATTING | | | | | | | | | | | | | | | | | BASERUNNING | | | | PERCENTAGES | | |
|---|---|---|---|---|---|---|---|---|---|---|---|---|---|---|---|---|---|---|---|---|---|---|---|---|---|
| Year Team | Lg | G | AB | H | 2B | 3B | HR | (Hm | Rd) | TB | R | RBI | TBB | IBB | SO | HBP | SH | SF | SB | CS | SB% | GDP | Avg | OBP | SLG |
| 1983 Atlanta | NL | 27 | 39 | 14 | 2 | 0 | 1 | (0 | 1) | 19 | 5 | 6 | 5 | 0 | 4 | 0 | 0 | 1 | 0 | 1 | .00 | 1 | .359 | .422 | .487 |
| 1984 Atlanta | NL | 122 | 347 | 92 | 12 | 2 | 7 | (3 | 4) | 129 | 52 | 47 | 61 | 5 | 38 | 2 | 2 | 7 | 15 | 12 | .56 | 9 | .265 | .372 | .372 |
| 1985 Atlanta | NL | 110 | 238 | 51 | 5 | 0 | 3 | (3 | 0) | 65 | 22 | 13 | 23 | 1 | 28 | 0 | 0 | 1 | 9 | 5 | .64 | 7 | .214 | .282 | .273 |
| 1986 Atlanta | NL | 29 | 70 | 19 | 2 | 0 | 2 | (2 | 0) | 27 | 6 | 11 | 8 | 1 | 4 | 0 | 1 | 1 | 0 | 1 | .00 | 4 | .271 | .342 | .386 |
| 1987 Atlanta | NL | 142 | 533 | 144 | 35 | 2 | 12 | (2 | 10) | 219 | 77 | 74 | 48 | 1 | 63 | 1 | 3 | 5 | 42 | 16 | .72 | 18 | .270 | .329 | .411 |
| 1988 Atlanta | NL | 141 | 547 | 164 | 29 | 1 | 8 | (4 | 4) | 219 | 61 | 74 | 36 | 9 | 49 | 1 | 1 | 10 | 29 | 14 | .67 | 18 | .300 | .338 | .400 |
| 1989 Atlanta | NL | 72 | 266 | 67 | 11 | 0 | 4 | (2 | 2) | 90 | 24 | 21 | 32 | 5 | 28 | 3 | 0 | 2 | 10 | 6 | .63 | 5 | .252 | .337 | .338 |
| 1990 Kansas City | AL | 133 | 465 | 118 | 22 | 2 | 8 | (3 | 5) | 168 | 57 | 57 | 39 | 4 | 56 | 3 | 0 | 5 | 17 | 4 | .81 | 15 | .254 | .313 | .361 |
| 8 ML YEARS | | 776 | 2505 | 669 | 118 | 7 | 45 | (19 | 26) | 936 | 304 | 303 | 252 | 26 | 270 | 10 | 7 | 32 | 122 | 59 | .67 | 77 | .267 | .333 | .374 |

## Pat Perry

**Pitches:** Left **Bats:** Left **Pos:** RP **Ht:** 6' 1" **Wt:** 190 **Born:** 02/04/59 **Age:** 32

| | | HOW MUCH HE PITCHED | | | | | | WHAT HE GAVE UP | | | | | | | | | | | | THE RESULTS | | | | | |
|---|---|---|---|---|---|---|---|---|---|---|---|---|---|---|---|---|---|---|---|---|---|---|---|---|---|
| Year Team | Lg | G | GS | CG | GF | IP | BFP | H | R | ER | HR | SH | SF | HB | TBB | IBB | SO | WP | Bk | W | L | Pct. | ShO | Sv | ERA |
| 1985 St. Louis | NL | 6 | 0 | 0 | 1 | 12.1 | 42 | 3 | 0 | 0 | 0 | 0 | 0 | 0 | 3 | 1 | 6 | 1 | 0 | 1 | 0 | 1.000 | 0 | 0 | 0.00 |
| 1986 St. Louis | NL | 46 | 0 | 0 | 20 | 68.2 | 288 | 59 | 31 | 29 | 5 | 0 | 7 | 0 | 34 | 9 | 29 | 5 | 0 | 2 | 3 | .400 | 0 | 2 | 3.80 |
| 1987 2 ML Teams | | 57 | 0 | 0 | 16 | 81 | 324 | 60 | 34 | 32 | 7 | 3 | 1 | 3 | 25 | 4 | 39 | 3 | 0 | 5 | 2 | .714 | 0 | 2 | 3.56 |
| 1988 2 ML Teams | | 47 | 0 | 0 | 18 | 58.2 | 251 | 61 | 32 | 27 | 9 | 1 | 5 | 1 | 16 | 4 | 35 | 3 | 1 | 4 | 4 | .500 | 0 | 1 | 4.14 |
| 1989 Chicago | NL | 19 | 0 | 0 | 6 | 35.2 | 141 | 23 | 8 | 7 | 2 | 1 | 1 | 0 | 16 | 3 | 20 | 1 | 0 | 0 | 1 | .000 | 0 | 1 | 1.77 |
| 1990 Los Angeles | NL | 7 | 0 | 0 | 2 | 6.2 | 36 | 9 | 7 | 6 | 0 | 0 | 1 | 1 | 5 | 1 | 2 | 2 | 0 | 0 | 0 | .000 | 0 | 0 | 8.10 |
| 1987 St. Louis | NL | 45 | 0 | 0 | 13 | 65.2 | 269 | 54 | 34 | 32 | 7 | 2 | 1 | 2 | 21 | 3 | 33 | 3 | 0 | 4 | 2 | .667 | 0 | 1 | 4.39 |
| Cincinnati | NL | 12 | 0 | 0 | 3 | 15.1 | 55 | 6 | 0 | 0 | 0 | 1 | 0 | 1 | 4 | 1 | 6 | 0 | 0 | 1 | 0 | 1.000 | 0 | 1 | 0.00 |

| Year Team | Lg | G | GS | CG | GF | IP | BFP | H | R | ER | HR | SH | SF | HB | TBB | IBB | SO | WP | Bk | W | L | Pct. | ShO | Sv | ERA |
|---|---|---|---|---|---|---|---|---|---|---|---|---|---|---|---|---|---|---|---|---|---|---|---|---|---|
| 1988 Cincinnati | NL | 12 | 0 | 0 | 5 | 20.2 | 93 | 21 | 17 | 13 | 4 | 1 | 3 | 0 | 9 | 4 | 11 | 1 | 1 | 2 | 2 | .500 | 0 | 0 | 5.66 |
| Chicago | NL | 35 | 0 | 0 | 13 | 38 | 158 | 40 | 15 | 14 | 5 | 0 | 2 | 1 | 7 | 0 | 24 | 2 | 0 | 2 | 2 | .500 | 0 | 1 | 3.32 |
| 6 ML YEARS | | 182 | 0 | 0 | 63 | 263 | 1082 | 215 | 112 | 101 | 23 | 5 | 15 | 5 | 99 | 22 | 131 | 15 | 1 | 12 | 10 | .545 | 0 | 6 | 3.46 |

## Adam Peterson

**Pitches:** Right **Bats:** Right **Pos:** SP/RP **Ht:** 6' 3" **Wt:** 190 **Born:** 12/11/65 **Age:** 25

| | | HOW MUCH HE PITCHED | | | | | | WHAT HE GAVE UP | | | | | | | | | | | | THE RESULTS | | | | | |
|---|---|---|---|---|---|---|---|---|---|---|---|---|---|---|---|---|---|---|---|---|---|---|---|---|---|
| Year Team | Lg | G | GS | CG | GF | IP | BFP | H | R | ER | HR | SH | SF | HB | TBB | IBB | SO | WP | Bk | W | L | Pct. | ShO | Sv | ERA |
| 1987 Chicago | AL | 1 | 1 | 0 | 0 | 4 | 22 | 8 | 6 | 6 | 1 | 0 | 1 | 0 | 3 | 0 | 1 | 0 | 0 | 0 | 0 | .000 | 0 | 0 | 13.50 |
| 1988 Chicago | AL | 2 | 2 | 0 | 0 | 6 | 31 | 6 | 9 | 9 | 0 | 0 | 0 | 0 | 6 | 1 | 5 | 1 | 0 | 0 | 1 | .000 | 0 | 0 | 13.50 |
| 1989 Chicago | AL | 3 | 2 | 0 | 0 | 5.1 | 31 | 13 | 9 | 9 | 1 | 1 | 0 | 0 | 2 | 0 | 3 | 0 | 0 | 0 | 1 | .000 | 0 | 0 | 15.19 |
| 1990 Chicago | AL | 20 | 11 | 2 | 4 | 85 | 357 | 90 | 46 | 43 | 12 | 2 | 3 | 2 | 26 | 0 | 29 | 3 | 0 | 2 | 5 | .286 | 0 | 0 | 4.55 |
| 4 ML YEARS | | 26 | 16 | 2 | 4 | 100.1 | 441 | 117 | 70 | 67 | 14 | 3 | 4 | 2 | 37 | 1 | 38 | 4 | 0 | 2 | 7 | .222 | 0 | 0 | 6.01 |

## Geno Petralli

**Bats:** Left **Throws:** Right **Pos:** C **Ht:** 6' 1" **Wt:** 180 **Born:** 09/25/59 **Age:** 31

| | | BATTING | | | | | | | | | | | | | | | | | BASERUNNING | | | | PERCENTAGES | | |
|---|---|---|---|---|---|---|---|---|---|---|---|---|---|---|---|---|---|---|---|---|---|---|---|---|---|
| Year Team | Lg | G | AB | H | 2B | 3B | HR | (Hm | Rd) | TB | R | RBI | TBB | IBB | SO | HBP | SH | SF | SB | CS | SB% | GDP | Avg | OBP | SLG |
| 1982 Toronto | AL | 16 | 44 | 16 | 2 | 0 | 0 | (0 | 0) | 18 | 3 | 1 | 4 | 0 | 6 | 0 | 1 | 0 | 0 | 0 | .00 | 1 | .364 | .417 | .409 |
| 1983 Toronto | AL | 6 | 4 | 0 | 0 | 0 | 0 | (0 | 0) | 0 | 0 | 0 | 1 | 0 | 1 | 0 | 0 | 0 | 0 | 0 | .00 | 0 | .000 | .200 | .000 |
| 1984 Toronto | AL | 3 | 3 | 0 | 0 | 0 | 0 | (0 | 0) | 0 | 0 | 0 | 0 | 0 | 0 | 0 | 0 | 0 | 0 | 0 | .00 | 0 | .000 | .000 | .000 |
| 1985 Texas | AL | 42 | 100 | 27 | 2 | 0 | 0 | (0 | 0) | 29 | 7 | 11 | 8 | 0 | 12 | 1 | 3 | 4 | 1 | 0 | 1.00 | 4 | .270 | .319 | .290 |
| 1986 Texas | AL | 69 | 137 | 35 | 9 | 3 | 2 | (1 | 1) | 56 | 17 | 18 | 5 | 0 | 14 | 0 | 0 | 0 | 3 | 0 | 1.00 | 7 | .255 | .282 | .409 |
| 1987 Texas | AL | 101 | 202 | 61 | 11 | 2 | 7 | (4 | 3) | 97 | 28 | 31 | 27 | 2 | 29 | 2 | 0 | 1 | 0 | 2 | .00 | 4 | .302 | .388 | .480 |
| 1988 Texas | AL | 129 | 351 | 99 | 14 | 2 | 7 | (1 | 6) | 138 | 35 | 36 | 41 | 5 | 52 | 2 | 1 | 5 | 0 | 1 | .00 | 12 | .282 | .356 | .393 |
| 1989 Texas | AL | 70 | 184 | 56 | 7 | 0 | 4 | (1 | 3) | 75 | 18 | 23 | 17 | 1 | 24 | 2 | 1 | 1 | 0 | 0 | .00 | 5 | .304 | .368 | .408 |
| 1990 Texas | AL | 133 | 325 | 83 | 13 | 1 | 0 | (0 | 0) | 98 | 28 | 21 | 50 | 3 | 49 | 3 | 1 | 3 | 0 | 2 | .00 | 12 | .255 | .357 | .302 |
| 9 ML YEARS | | 569 | 1350 | 377 | 58 | 8 | 20 | (7 | 13) | 511 | 136 | 141 | 153 | 11 | 187 | 10 | 7 | 14 | 4 | 5 | .44 | 45 | .279 | .354 | .379 |

## Dan Petry

**Pitches:** Right **Bats:** Right **Pos:** SP/RP **Ht:** 6' 4" **Wt:** 215 **Born:** 11/13/58 **Age:** 32

| | | HOW MUCH HE PITCHED | | | | | | WHAT HE GAVE UP | | | | | | | | | | | | THE RESULTS | | | | | |
|---|---|---|---|---|---|---|---|---|---|---|---|---|---|---|---|---|---|---|---|---|---|---|---|---|---|
| Year Team | Lg | G | GS | CG | GF | IP | BFP | H | R | ER | HR | SH | SF | HB | TBB | IBB | SO | WP | Bk | W | L | Pct. | ShO | Sv | ERA |
| 1979 Detroit | AL | 15 | 15 | 2 | 0 | 98 | 401 | 90 | 46 | 43 | 11 | 5 | 5 | 4 | 33 | 5 | 43 | 3 | 1 | 6 | 5 | .545 | 0 | 0 | 3.95 |
| 1980 Detroit | AL | 27 | 25 | 4 | 1 | 165 | 716 | 156 | 82 | 72 | 9 | 10 | 5 | 1 | 83 | 14 | 88 | 5 | 2 | 10 | 9 | .526 | 3 | 0 | 3.93 |
| 1981 Detroit | AL | 23 | 22 | 7 | 1 | 141 | 583 | 115 | 53 | 47 | 10 | 9 | 2 | 1 | 57 | 4 | 79 | 3 | 1 | 10 | 9 | .526 | 2 | 0 | 3.00 |
| 1982 Detroit | AL | 35 | 35 | 8 | 0 | 246 | 1031 | 220 | 98 | 88 | 15 | 8 | 8 | 4 | 100 | 5 | 132 | 9 | 0 | 15 | 9 | .625 | 1 | 0 | 3.22 |
| 1983 Detroit | AL | 38 | 38 | 9 | 0 | 266.1 | 1115 | 256 | 126 | 116 | 37 | 5 | 5 | 6 | 99 | 7 | 122 | 12 | 0 | 19 | 11 | .633 | 2 | 0 | 3.92 |
| 1984 Detroit | AL | 35 | 35 | 7 | 0 | 233.1 | 968 | 231 | 94 | 84 | 21 | 5 | 2 | 3 | 66 | 4 | 144 | 7 | 0 | 18 | 8 | .692 | 2 | 0 | 3.24 |
| 1985 Detroit | AL | 34 | 34 | 8 | 0 | 238.2 | 962 | 190 | 98 | 89 | 24 | 0 | 2 | 3 | 81 | 9 | 109 | 6 | 0 | 15 | 13 | .536 | 0 | 0 | 3.36 |
| 1986 Detroit | AL | 20 | 20 | 2 | 0 | 116 | 520 | 122 | 78 | 60 | 15 | 3 | 3 | 5 | 53 | 3 | 56 | 5 | 0 | 5 | 10 | .333 | 0 | 0 | 4.66 |
| 1987 Detroit | AL | 30 | 21 | 0 | 3 | 134.2 | 628 | 148 | 101 | 84 | 22 | 4 | 7 | 10 | 76 | 5 | 93 | 8 | 1 | 9 | 7 | .563 | 0 | 0 | 5.61 |
| 1988 California | AL | 22 | 22 | 4 | 0 | 139.2 | 604 | 139 | 70 | 68 | 18 | 5 | 6 | 6 | 59 | 5 | 64 | 5 | 2 | 3 | 9 | .250 | 1 | 0 | 4.38 |
| 1989 California | AL | 19 | 4 | 0 | 3 | 51 | 223 | 53 | 32 | 31 | 8 | 1 | 5 | 1 | 23 | 0 | 21 | 2 | 0 | 3 | 2 | .600 | 0 | 0 | 5.47 |
| 1990 Detroit | AL | 32 | 23 | 1 | 2 | 149.2 | 655 | 148 | 78 | 74 | 14 | 8 | 6 | 1 | 77 | 7 | 73 | 10 | 0 | 10 | 9 | .526 | 0 | 0 | 4.45 |
| 12 ML YEARS | | 330 | 294 | 52 | 10 | 1979.1 | 8406 | 1868 | 956 | 856 | 204 | 63 | 56 | 45 | 807 | 68 | 1024 | 75 | 7 | 123 | 101 | .549 | 11 | 0 | 3.89 |

## Gary Pettis

**Bats:** Both **Throws:** Right **Pos:** CF **Ht:** 6' 1" **Wt:** 160 **Born:** 04/03/58 **Age:** 33

| | | BATTING | | | | | | | | | | | | | | | | | BASERUNNING | | | | PERCENTAGES | | |
|---|---|---|---|---|---|---|---|---|---|---|---|---|---|---|---|---|---|---|---|---|---|---|---|---|---|
| Year Team | Lg | G | AB | H | 2B | 3B | HR | (Hm | Rd) | TB | R | RBI | TBB | IBB | SO | HBP | SH | SF | SB | CS | SB% | GDP | Avg | OBP | SLG |
| 1982 California | AL | 10 | 5 | 1 | 0 | 0 | 1 | (1 | 0) | 4 | 5 | 1 | 0 | 0 | 2 | 0 | 0 | 0 | 0 | 0 | .00 | 0 | .200 | .200 | .800 |
| 1983 California | AL | 22 | 85 | 25 | 2 | 3 | 3 | (3 | 0) | 42 | 19 | 6 | 7 | 0 | 15 | 0 | 1 | 0 | 8 | 3 | .73 | 1 | .294 | .348 | .494 |
| 1984 California | AL | 140 | 397 | 90 | 11 | 6 | 2 | (1 | 1) | 119 | 63 | 29 | 60 | 1 | 115 | 3 | 5 | 1 | 48 | 17 | .74 | 4 | .227 | .332 | .300 |
| 1985 California | AL | 125 | 443 | 114 | 10 | 8 | 1 | (0 | 1) | 143 | 67 | 32 | 62 | 0 | 125 | 0 | 9 | 2 | 56 | 9 | .86 | 5 | .257 | .347 | .323 |
| 1986 California | AL | 154 | 539 | 139 | 23 | 4 | 5 | (1 | 4) | 185 | 93 | 58 | 69 | 2 | 132 | 0 | 15 | 5 | 50 | 13 | .79 | 7 | .258 | .339 | .343 |
| 1987 California | AL | 133 | 394 | 82 | 13 | 2 | 1 | (1 | 0) | 102 | 49 | 17 | 52 | 0 | 124 | 1 | 1 | 0 | 24 | 5 | .83 | 8 | .208 | .302 | .259 |
| 1988 Detroit | AL | 129 | 458 | 96 | 14 | 4 | 3 | (0 | 3) | 127 | 65 | 36 | 47 | 0 | 85 | 1 | 6 | 0 | 44 | 10 | .81 | 3 | .210 | .285 | .277 |
| 1989 Detroit | AL | 119 | 444 | 114 | 8 | 6 | 1 | (1 | 0) | 137 | 77 | 18 | 84 | 0 | 106 | 0 | 8 | 0 | 43 | 15 | .74 | 14 | .257 | .375 | .309 |
| 1990 Texas | AL | 136 | 423 | 101 | 16 | 8 | 3 | (3 | 0) | 142 | 66 | 31 | 57 | 0 | 118 | 4 | 11 | 3 | 38 | 15 | .72 | 6 | .239 | .333 | .336 |
| 9 ML YEARS | | 968 | 3188 | 762 | 97 | 41 | 20 | (11 | 9) | 1001 | 504 | 228 | 438 | 3 | 822 | 9 | 56 | 11 | 311 | 87 | .78 | 48 | .239 | .332 | .314 |

## Ken Phelps

**Bats:** Left **Throws:** Left **Pos:** DH/1B **Ht:** 6' 1" **Wt:** 204 **Born:** 08/06/54 **Age:** 36

| BATTING | | | | | | | | | | | | | | | | | | | BASERUNNING | | | | PERCENTAGES | | |
|---|---|---|---|---|---|---|---|---|---|---|---|---|---|---|---|---|---|---|---|---|---|---|---|---|---|
| Year Team | Lg | G | AB | H | 2B | 3B | HR | (Hm | Rd) | TB | R | RBI | TBB | IBB | SO | HBP | SH | SF | SB | CS | SB% | GDP | Avg | OBP | SLG |
| 1980 Kansas City | AL | 3 | 4 | 0 | 0 | 0 | 0 | (0 | 0) | 0 | 0 | 0 | 0 | 0 | 2 | 0 | 0 | 0 | 0 | 0 | .00 | 0 | .000 | .000 | .000 |
| 1981 Kansas City | AL | 21 | 22 | 3 | 0 | 1 | 0 | (0 | 0) | 5 | 1 | 1 | 1 | 0 | 13 | 0 | 0 | 0 | 0 | 0 | .00 | 0 | .136 | .174 | .227 |
| 1982 Montreal | NL | 10 | 8 | 2 | 0 | 0 | 0 | (0 | 0) | 2 | 0 | 0 | 0 | 0 | 3 | 1 | 0 | 0 | 0 | 0 | .00 | 0 | .250 | .333 | .250 |
| 1983 Seattle | AL | 50 | 127 | 30 | 4 | 1 | 7 | (6 | 1) | 57 | 10 | 16 | 13 | 0 | 25 | 0 | 1 | 3 | 0 | 0 | .00 | 0 | .236 | .301 | .449 |
| 1984 Seattle | AL | 101 | 290 | 70 | 9 | 0 | 24 | (13 | 11) | 151 | 52 | 51 | 61 | 5 | 73 | 5 | 0 | 4 | 3 | 3 | .50 | 1 | .241 | .378 | .521 |
| 1985 Seattle | AL | 61 | 116 | 24 | 3 | 0 | 9 | (5 | 4) | 54 | 18 | 24 | 24 | 2 | 33 | 0 | 0 | 0 | 2 | 0 | 1.00 | 1 | .207 | .343 | .466 |
| 1986 Seattle | AL | 125 | 344 | 85 | 16 | 4 | 24 | (15 | 9) | 181 | 69 | 64 | 88 | 6 | 96 | 6 | 0 | 3 | 2 | 3 | .40 | 4 | .247 | .406 | .526 |
| 1987 Seattle | AL | 120 | 332 | 86 | 13 | 1 | 27 | (15 | 12) | 182 | 68 | 68 | 80 | 5 | 75 | 8 | 0 | 4 | 1 | 1 | .50 | 7 | .259 | .410 | .548 |
| 1988 2 ML Teams | | 117 | 297 | 78 | 13 | 0 | 24 | (12 | 12) | 163 | 54 | 54 | 70 | 5 | 61 | 1 | 0 | 3 | 1 | 0 | 1.00 | 6 | .263 | .402 | .549 |
| 1989 2 ML Teams | | 97 | 194 | 47 | 4 | 0 | 7 | (4 | 3) | 72 | 26 | 29 | 31 | 2 | 47 | 0 | 0 | 3 | 0 | 0 | .00 | 2 | .242 | .342 | .371 |
| 1990 2 ML Teams | | 56 | 120 | 18 | 2 | 0 | 1 | (1 | 0) | 23 | 10 | 6 | 22 | 3 | 21 | 0 | 0 | 1 | 1 | 0 | 1.00 | 4 | .150 | .280 | .192 |
| 1988 Seattle | AL | 72 | 190 | 54 | 8 | 0 | 14 | (6 | 8) | 104 | 37 | 32 | 51 | 2 | 35 | 1 | 0 | 2 | 1 | 0 | 1.00 | 3 | .284 | .434 | .547 |
| New York | AL | 45 | 107 | 24 | 5 | 0 | 10 | (6 | 4) | 59 | 17 | 22 | 19 | 3 | 26 | 0 | 0 | 1 | 0 | 0 | .00 | 3 | .224 | .339 | .551 |
| 1989 New York | AL | 86 | 185 | 46 | 3 | 0 | 7 | (4 | 3) | 70 | 26 | 29 | 27 | 2 | 47 | 0 | 0 | 3 | 0 | 0 | .00 | 2 | .249 | .340 | .378 |
| Oakland | AL | 11 | 9 | 1 | 1 | 0 | 0 | (0 | 0) | 2 | 0 | 0 | 4 | 0 | 0 | 0 | 0 | 0 | 0 | 0 | .00 | 0 | .111 | .385 | .222 |
| 1990 Oakland | AL | 32 | 59 | 11 | 2 | 0 | 1 | (1 | 0) | 16 | 6 | 6 | 12 | 1 | 10 | 0 | 0 | 1 | 0 | 0 | .00 | 1 | .186 | .319 | .271 |
| Cleveland | AL | 24 | 61 | 7 | 0 | 0 | 0 | (0 | 0) | 7 | 4 | 0 | 10 | 2 | 11 | 0 | 0 | 0 | 1 | 0 | 1.00 | 3 | .115 | .239 | .115 |
| 11 ML YEARS | | 761 | 1854 | 443 | 64 | 7 | 123 | (71 | 52) | 890 | 308 | 313 | 390 | 28 | 449 | 21 | 1 | 21 | 10 | 7 | .59 | 25 | .239 | .374 | .480 |

## Tony Phillips

**Bats:** Both **Throws:** Right **Pos:** 3B/2B/SS **Ht:** 5'10" **Wt:** 175 **Born:** 04/15/59 **Age:** 32

| BATTING | | | | | | | | | | | | | | | | | | | BASERUNNING | | | | PERCENTAGES | | |
|---|---|---|---|---|---|---|---|---|---|---|---|---|---|---|---|---|---|---|---|---|---|---|---|---|---|
| Year Team | Lg | G | AB | H | 2B | 3B | HR | (Hm | Rd) | TB | R | RBI | TBB | IBB | SO | HBP | SH | SF | SB | CS | SB% | GDP | Avg | OBP | SLG |
| 1982 Oakland | AL | 40 | 81 | 17 | 2 | 2 | 0 | (0 | 0) | 23 | 11 | 8 | 12 | 0 | 26 | 2 | 5 | 0 | 2 | 3 | .40 | 0 | .210 | .326 | .284 |
| 1983 Oakland | AL | 148 | 412 | 102 | 12 | 3 | 4 | (1 | 3) | 132 | 54 | 35 | 48 | 1 | 70 | 2 | 11 | 3 | 16 | 5 | .76 | 5 | .248 | .327 | .320 |
| 1984 Oakland | AL | 154 | 451 | 120 | 24 | 3 | 4 | (2 | 2) | 162 | 62 | 37 | 42 | 1 | 86 | 0 | 7 | 5 | 10 | 6 | .63 | 5 | .266 | .325 | .359 |
| 1985 Oakland | AL | 42 | 161 | 45 | 12 | 2 | 4 | (2 | 2) | 73 | 23 | 17 | 13 | 0 | 34 | 0 | 3 | 1 | 3 | 2 | .60 | 1 | .280 | .331 | .453 |
| 1986 Oakland | AL | 118 | 441 | 113 | 14 | 5 | 5 | (3 | 2) | 152 | 76 | 52 | 76 | 0 | 82 | 3 | 9 | 3 | 15 | 10 | .60 | 2 | .256 | .367 | .345 |
| 1987 Oakland | AL | 111 | 379 | 91 | 20 | 0 | 10 | (5 | 5) | 141 | 48 | 46 | 57 | 1 | 76 | 0 | 2 | 3 | 7 | 6 | .54 | 9 | .240 | .337 | .372 |
| 1988 Oakland | AL | 79 | 212 | 43 | 8 | 4 | 2 | (2 | 0) | 65 | 32 | 17 | 36 | 0 | 50 | 1 | 1 | 1 | 0 | 2 | .00 | 6 | .203 | .320 | .307 |
| 1989 Oakland | AL | 143 | 451 | 118 | 15 | 6 | 4 | (2 | 2) | 157 | 48 | 47 | 58 | 2 | 66 | 3 | 5 | 7 | 3 | 8 | .27 | 17 | .262 | .345 | .348 |
| 1990 Detroit | AL | 152 | 573 | 144 | 23 | 5 | 8 | (4 | 4) | 201 | 97 | 55 | 99 | 0 | 85 | 4 | 9 | 2 | 19 | 9 | .68 | 10 | .251 | .364 | .351 |
| 9 ML YEARS | | 987 | 3161 | 793 | 130 | 30 | 41 | (21 | 20) | 1106 | 451 | 314 | 441 | 5 | 575 | 15 | 52 | 25 | 75 | 51 | .60 | 55 | .251 | .343 | .350 |

## Jeff Pico

**Pitches:** Right **Bats:** Right **Pos:** RP/SP **Ht:** 6' 2" **Wt:** 170 **Born:** 02/12/66 **Age:** 25

| HOW MUCH HE PITCHED | | | | | | | | WHAT HE GAVE UP | | | | | | | | | | | | THE RESULTS | | | | | |
|---|---|---|---|---|---|---|---|---|---|---|---|---|---|---|---|---|---|---|---|---|---|---|---|---|---|
| Year Team | Lg | G | GS | CG | GF | IP | BFP | H | R | ER | HR | SH | SF | HB | TBB | IBB | SO | WP | Bk | W | L | Pct. | ShO | Sv | ERA |
| 1988 Chicago | NL | 29 | 13 | 3 | 9 | 112.2 | 472 | 108 | 57 | 52 | 6 | 3 | 4 | 0 | 37 | 6 | 57 | 6 | 1 | 6 | 7 | .462 | 2 | 1 | 4.15 |
| 1989 Chicago | NL | 53 | 5 | 0 | 17 | 90.2 | 394 | 99 | 43 | 38 | 8 | 5 | 2 | 0 | 31 | 10 | 38 | 2 | 0 | 3 | 1 | .750 | 0 | 2 | 3.77 |
| 1990 Chicago | NL | 31 | 8 | 0 | 8 | 92 | 421 | 120 | 53 | 49 | 7 | 7 | 2 | 1 | 37 | 10 | 37 | 2 | 1 | 4 | 4 | .500 | 0 | 2 | 4.79 |
| 3 ML YEARS | | 113 | 26 | 3 | 34 | 295.1 | 1287 | 327 | 153 | 139 | 21 | 15 | 8 | 1 | 105 | 26 | 132 | 10 | 2 | 13 | 12 | .520 | 2 | 5 | 4.24 |

## Phil Plantier

**Bats:** Left **Throws:** Right **Pos:** DH **Ht:** 6' 0" **Wt:** 175 **Born:** 01/27/69 **Age:** 22

| BATTING | | | | | | | | | | | | | | | | | | | BASERUNNING | | | | PERCENTAGES | | |
|---|---|---|---|---|---|---|---|---|---|---|---|---|---|---|---|---|---|---|---|---|---|---|---|---|---|
| Year Team | Lg | G | AB | H | 2B | 3B | HR | (Hm | Rd) | TB | R | RBI | TBB | IBB | SO | HBP | SH | SF | SB | CS | SB% | GDP | Avg | OBP | SLG |
| 1987 Elmira | A | 28 | 80 | 14 | 2 | 0 | 2 | -- | -- | 22 | 7 | 9 | 9 | 0 | 9 | 0 | 1 | 1 | 0 | 0 | .00 | 4 | .175 | .256 | .275 |
| 1988 Winter Havn | A | 111 | 337 | 81 | 13 | 1 | 4 | -- | -- | 108 | 29 | 32 | 51 | 6 | 62 | 5 | 3 | 3 | 0 | 2 | .00 | 4 | .240 | .346 | .320 |
| 1989 Lynchburg | A | 131 | 443 | 133 | 26 | 1 | 27 | -- | -- | 242 | 73 | 105 | 74 | 7 | 122 | 7 | 0 | 4 | 4 | 5 | .44 | 2 | .300 | .405 | .546 |
| 1990 Pawtucket | AAA | 123 | 430 | 109 | 22 | 3 | 33 | -- | -- | 236 | 83 | 79 | 62 | 3 | 148 | 9 | 3 | 3 | 1 | 8 | .11 | 4 | .253 | .357 | .549 |
| 1990 Boston | AL | 14 | 15 | 2 | 1 | 0 | 0 | (0 | 0) | 3 | 1 | 3 | 4 | 0 | 6 | 1 | 0 | 1 | 0 | 0 | .00 | 1 | .133 | .333 | .200 |

## Dan Plesac

**Pitches:** Left **Bats:** Left **Pos:** RP **Ht:** 6' 5" **Wt:** 210 **Born:** 02/04/62 **Age:** 29

| HOW MUCH HE PITCHED | | | | | | | | WHAT HE GAVE UP | | | | | | | | | | | | THE RESULTS | | | | | |
|---|---|---|---|---|---|---|---|---|---|---|---|---|---|---|---|---|---|---|---|---|---|---|---|---|---|
| Year Team | Lg | G | GS | CG | GF | IP | BFP | H | R | ER | HR | SH | SF | HB | TBB | IBB | SO | WP | Bk | W | L | Pct. | ShO | Sv | ERA |
| 1986 Milwaukee | AL | 51 | 0 | 0 | 33 | 91 | 377 | 81 | 34 | 30 | 5 | 6 | 5 | 0 | 29 | 1 | 75 | 4 | 0 | 10 | 7 | .588 | 0 | 14 | 2.97 |
| 1987 Milwaukee | AL | 57 | 0 | 0 | 47 | 79.1 | 325 | 63 | 30 | 23 | 8 | 1 | 2 | 3 | 23 | 1 | 89 | 6 | 0 | 5 | 6 | .455 | 0 | 23 | 2.61 |
| 1988 Milwaukee | AL | 50 | 0 | 0 | 48 | 52.1 | 211 | 46 | 14 | 14 | 2 | 2 | 0 | 0 | 12 | 2 | 52 | 4 | 6 | 1 | 2 | .333 | 0 | 30 | 2.41 |

| Year Team | Lg | G | GS | CG | GF | IP | BFP | H | R | ER | HR | SH | SF | HB | TBB | IBB | SO | WP | Bk | W | L | Pct. | ShO | Sv | ERA |
|---|---|---|---|---|---|---|---|---|---|---|---|---|---|---|---|---|---|---|---|---|---|---|---|---|---|
| 1989 Milwaukee | AL | 52 | 0 | 0 | 51 | 61.1 | 242 | 47 | 16 | 16 | 6 | 0 | 4 | 0 | 17 | 1 | 52 | 0 | 0 | 3 | 4 | .429 | 0 | 33 | 2.35 |
| 1990 Milwaukee | AL | 66 | 0 | 0 | 52 | 69 | 299 | 67 | 36 | 34 | 5 | 2 | 2 | 3 | 31 | 6 | 65 | 2 | 0 | 3 | 7 | .300 | 0 | 24 | 4.43 |
| 5 ML YEARS | | 276 | 0 | 0 | 231 | 353 | 1454 | 304 | 130 | 117 | 26 | 11 | 13 | 6 | 112 | 11 | 333 | 16 | 6 | 22 | 26 | .458 | 0 | 124 | 2.98 |

## Eric Plunk

**Pitches:** Right **Bats:** Right **Pos:** RP **Ht:** 6' 5" **Wt:** 210 **Born:** 09/03/63 **Age:** 27

| | | HOW MUCH HE PITCHED | | | | | | WHAT HE GAVE UP | | | | | | | | | | | | THE RESULTS | | | | | |
|---|---|---|---|---|---|---|---|---|---|---|---|---|---|---|---|---|---|---|---|---|---|---|---|---|---|
| Year Team | Lg | G | GS | CG | GF | IP | BFP | H | R | ER | HR | SH | SF | HB | TBB | IBB | SO | WP | Bk | W | L | Pct. | ShO | Sv | ERA |
| 1986 Oakland | AL | 26 | 15 | 0 | 2 | 120.1 | 537 | 91 | 75 | 71 | 14 | 2 | 3 | 5 | 102 | 2 | 98 | 9 | 6 | 4 | 7 | .364 | 0 | 0 | 5.31 |
| 1987 Oakland | AL | 32 | 11 | 0 | 11 | 95 | 432 | 91 | 53 | 50 | 8 | 3 | 5 | 2 | 62 | 3 | 90 | 5 | 2 | 4 | 6 | .400 | 0 | 2 | 4.74 |
| 1988 Oakland | AL | 49 | 0 | 0 | 22 | 78 | 331 | 62 | 27 | 26 | 6 | 3 | 2 | 1 | 39 | 4 | 79 | 4 | 7 | 7 | 2 | .778 | 0 | 5 | 3.00 |
| 1989 2 ML Teams | | 50 | 7 | 0 | 17 | 104.1 | 445 | 82 | 43 | 38 | 10 | 3 | 4 | 1 | 64 | 2 | 85 | 10 | 3 | 8 | 6 | .571 | 0 | 1 | 3.28 |
| 1990 New York | AL | 47 | 0 | 0 | 16 | 72.2 | 310 | 58 | 27 | 22 | 6 | 7 | 0 | 2 | 43 | 4 | 67 | 4 | 2 | 6 | 3 | .667 | 0 | 0 | 2.72 |
| 1989 Oakland | AL | 23 | 0 | 0 | 12 | 28.2 | 113 | 17 | 7 | 7 | 1 | 1 | 0 | 1 | 12 | 0 | 24 | 4 | 0 | 1 | 1 | .500 | 0 | 1 | 2.20 |
| New York | AL | 27 | 7 | 0 | 5 | 75.2 | 332 | 65 | 36 | 31 | 9 | 2 | 4 | 0 | 52 | 2 | 61 | 6 | 3 | 7 | 5 | .583 | 0 | 0 | 3.69 |
| 5 ML YEARS | | 204 | 33 | 0 | 68 | 470.1 | 2055 | 384 | 225 | 207 | 44 | 18 | 14 | 11 | 310 | 15 | 419 | 32 | 20 | 29 | 24 | .547 | 0 | 8 | 3.96 |

## Gus Polidor

**Bats:** Right **Throws:** Right **Pos:** 3B **Ht:** 6' 0" **Wt:** 184 **Born:** 10/26/61 **Age:** 29

| | | BATTING | | | | | | | | | | | | | | | | BASERUNNING | | | | PERCENTAGES | | |
|---|---|---|---|---|---|---|---|---|---|---|---|---|---|---|---|---|---|---|---|---|---|---|---|---|
| Year Team | Lg | G | AB | H | 2B | 3B | HR | (Hm | Rd) | TB | R | RBI | TBB | IBB | SO | HBP | SH | SF | SB | CS | SB% | GDP | Avg | OBP | SLG |
| 1985 California | AL | 2 | 1 | 1 | 0 | 0 | 0 | (0 | 0) | 1 | 1 | 0 | 0 | 0 | 0 | 0 | 0 | 0 | 0 | 0 | .00 | 0 | 1.000 | 1.000 | 1.000 |
| 1986 California | AL | 6 | 19 | 5 | 1 | 0 | 0 | (0 | 0) | 6 | 1 | 1 | 1 | 0 | 0 | 0 | 0 | 0 | 0 | 0 | .00 | 2 | .263 | .300 | .316 |
| 1987 California | AL | 63 | 137 | 36 | 3 | 0 | 2 | (0 | 2) | 45 | 12 | 15 | 2 | 0 | 15 | 1 | 0 | 1 | 0 | 0 | .00 | 3 | .263 | .277 | .328 |
| 1988 California | AL | 54 | 81 | 12 | 3 | 0 | 0 | (0 | 0) | 15 | 4 | 4 | 3 | 0 | 11 | 0 | 3 | 0 | 0 | 0 | .00 | 2 | .148 | .179 | .185 |
| 1989 Milwaukee | AL | 79 | 175 | 34 | 7 | 0 | 0 | (0 | 0) | 41 | 15 | 14 | 6 | 0 | 18 | 2 | 3 | 0 | 3 | 0 | 1.00 | 6 | .194 | .230 | .234 |
| 1990 Milwaukee | AL | 18 | 15 | 1 | 0 | 0 | 0 | (0 | 0) | 1 | 0 | 1 | 0 | 0 | 1 | 0 | 0 | 0 | 0 | 0 | .00 | 0 | .067 | .067 | .067 |
| 6 ML YEARS | | 222 | 428 | 89 | 14 | 0 | 2 | (0 | 2) | 109 | 33 | 35 | 12 | 0 | 45 | 3 | 6 | 1 | 3 | 0 | 1.00 | 13 | .208 | .234 | .255 |

## Luis Polonia

**Bats:** Left **Throws:** Left **Pos:** LF/CF/DH **Ht:** 5' 8" **Wt:** 155 **Born:** 10/12/64 **Age:** 26

| | | BATTING | | | | | | | | | | | | | | | | BASERUNNING | | | | PERCENTAGES | | |
|---|---|---|---|---|---|---|---|---|---|---|---|---|---|---|---|---|---|---|---|---|---|---|---|---|
| Year Team | Lg | G | AB | H | 2B | 3B | HR | (Hm | Rd) | TB | R | RBI | TBB | IBB | SO | HBP | SH | SF | SB | CS | SB% | GDP | Avg | OBP | SLG |
| 1987 Oakland | AL | 125 | 435 | 125 | 16 | 10 | 4 | (1 | 3) | 173 | 78 | 49 | 32 | 1 | 64 | 0 | 1 | 1 | 29 | 7 | .81 | 4 | .287 | .335 | .398 |
| 1988 Oakland | AL | 84 | 288 | 84 | 11 | 4 | 2 | (1 | 1) | 109 | 51 | 27 | 21 | 0 | 40 | 0 | 2 | 2 | 24 | 9 | .73 | 3 | .292 | .338 | .378 |
| 1989 2 ML Teams | | 125 | 433 | 130 | 17 | 6 | 3 | (1 | 2) | 168 | 70 | 46 | 25 | 1 | 44 | 2 | 2 | 4 | 22 | 8 | .73 | 13 | .300 | .338 | .388 |
| 1990 2 ML Teams | | 120 | 403 | 135 | 7 | 9 | 2 | (2 | 0) | 166 | 52 | 35 | 25 | 1 | 43 | 1 | 3 | 4 | 21 | 14 | .60 | 9 | .335 | .372 | .412 |
| 1989 Oakland | AL | 59 | 206 | 59 | 6 | 4 | 1 | (0 | 1) | 76 | 31 | 17 | 9 | 0 | 15 | 0 | 2 | 1 | 13 | 4 | .76 | 5 | .286 | .315 | .369 |
| New York | AL | 66 | 227 | 71 | 11 | 2 | 2 | (1 | 1) | 92 | 39 | 29 | 16 | 1 | 29 | 2 | 0 | 3 | 9 | 4 | .69 | 8 | .313 | .359 | .405 |
| 1990 New York | AL | 11 | 22 | 7 | 0 | 0 | 0 | (0 | 0) | 7 | 2 | 3 | 0 | 0 | 1 | 0 | 0 | 1 | 1 | 0 | 1.00 | 1 | .318 | .304 | .318 |
| California | AL | 109 | 381 | 128 | 7 | 9 | 2 | (2 | 0) | 159 | 50 | 32 | 25 | 1 | 42 | 1 | 3 | 3 | 20 | 14 | .59 | 8 | .336 | .376 | .417 |
| 4 ML YEARS | | 454 | 1559 | 474 | 51 | 29 | 11 | (5 | 6) | 616 | 251 | 157 | 103 | 3 | 191 | 3 | 8 | 11 | 96 | 38 | .72 | 29 | .304 | .346 | .395 |

## Jim Poole

**Pitches:** Left **Bats:** Left **Pos:** RP **Ht:** 6' 2" **Wt:** 190 **Born:** 04/28/66 **Age:** 25

| | | HOW MUCH HE PITCHED | | | | | | WHAT HE GAVE UP | | | | | | | | | | | | THE RESULTS | | | | | |
|---|---|---|---|---|---|---|---|---|---|---|---|---|---|---|---|---|---|---|---|---|---|---|---|---|---|
| Year Team | Lg | G | GS | CG | GF | IP | BFP | H | R | ER | HR | SH | SF | HB | TBB | IBB | SO | WP | Bk | W | L | Pct. | ShO | Sv | ERA |
| 1988 Vero Beach | A | 10 | 0 | 0 | 6 | 14.1 | 63 | 13 | 7 | 6 | 0 | 1 | 1 | 1 | 9 | 1 | 12 | 1 | 1 | 1 | 1 | .500 | 0 | 0 | 3.77 |
| 1989 Vero Beach | A | 60 | 0 | 0 | 50 | 78.1 | 306 | 57 | 16 | 14 | 0 | 5 | 0 | 2 | 24 | 7 | 93 | 3 | 0 | 11 | 4 | .733 | 0 | 19 | 1.61 |
| Bakersfield | A | 1 | 0 | 0 | 1 | 1.2 | 7 | 2 | 1 | 0 | 0 | 0 | 0 | 0 | 0 | 0 | 1 | 0 | 0 | 0 | 0 | .000 | 0 | 0 | 0.00 |
| 1990 San Antonio | AA | 54 | 0 | 0 | 35 | 63.2 | 278 | 55 | 31 | 17 | 3 | 8 | 0 | 2 | 27 | 5 | 77 | 6 | 0 | 6 | 7 | .462 | 0 | 16 | 2.40 |
| 1990 Los Angeles | NL | 16 | 0 | 0 | 4 | 10.2 | 46 | 7 | 5 | 5 | 1 | 0 | 0 | 0 | 8 | 4 | 6 | 1 | 0 | 0 | 0 | .000 | 0 | 0 | 4.22 |

## Mark Portugal

**Pitches:** Right **Bats:** Right **Pos:** SP **Ht:** 6' 0" **Wt:** 200 **Born:** 10/30/62 **Age:** 28

| | | HOW MUCH HE PITCHED | | | | | | WHAT HE GAVE UP | | | | | | | | | | | | THE RESULTS | | | | | |
|---|---|---|---|---|---|---|---|---|---|---|---|---|---|---|---|---|---|---|---|---|---|---|---|---|---|
| Year Team | Lg | G | GS | CG | GF | IP | BFP | H | R | ER | HR | SH | SF | HB | TBB | IBB | SO | WP | Bk | W | L | Pct. | ShO | Sv | ERA |
| 1985 Minnesota | AL | 6 | 4 | 0 | 0 | 24.1 | 105 | 24 | 16 | 15 | 3 | 0 | 2 | 0 | 14 | 0 | 12 | 1 | 1 | 1 | 3 | .250 | 0 | 0 | 5.55 |
| 1986 Minnesota | AL | 27 | 15 | 3 | 7 | 112.2 | 481 | 112 | 56 | 54 | 10 | 5 | 3 | 1 | 50 | 1 | 67 | 5 | 0 | 6 | 10 | .375 | 0 | 1 | 4.31 |
| 1987 Minnesota | AL | 13 | 7 | 0 | 3 | 44 | 204 | 58 | 40 | 38 | 13 | 0 | 1 | 1 | 24 | 1 | 28 | 2 | 0 | 1 | 3 | .250 | 0 | 0 | 7.77 |
| 1988 Minnesota | AL | 26 | 0 | 0 | 9 | 57.2 | 242 | 60 | 30 | 29 | 11 | 2 | 3 | 1 | 17 | 1 | 31 | 2 | 2 | 3 | 3 | .500 | 0 | 3 | 4.53 |
| 1989 Houston | NL | 20 | 15 | 2 | 1 | 108 | 440 | 91 | 34 | 33 | 7 | 8 | 1 | 2 | 37 | 0 | 86 | 3 | 0 | 7 | 1 | .875 | 1 | 0 | 2.75 |
| 1990 Houston | NL | 32 | 32 | 1 | 0 | 196.2 | 831 | 187 | 90 | 79 | 21 | 7 | 6 | 4 | 67 | 4 | 136 | 6 | 0 | 11 | 10 | .524 | 0 | 0 | 3.62 |
| 6 ML YEARS | | 124 | 73 | 6 | 20 | 543.1 | 2303 | 532 | 266 | 248 | 65 | 22 | 16 | 9 | 209 | 7 | 360 | 19 | 3 | 29 | 30 | .492 | 1 | 4 | 4.11 |

## Dennis Powell

**Pitches:** Left **Bats:** Right **Pos:** SP **Ht:** 6' 3" **Wt:** 200 **Born:** 08/13/63 **Age:** 27

| | | HOW MUCH HE PITCHED | | | | | | WHAT HE GAVE UP | | | | | | | | | | | | THE RESULTS | | | | | |
|---|---|---|---|---|---|---|---|---|---|---|---|---|---|---|---|---|---|---|---|---|---|---|---|---|---|
| Year Team | Lg | G | GS | CG | GF | IP | BFP | H | R | ER | HR | SH | SF | HB | TBB | IBB | SO | WP | Bk | W | L | Pct. | ShO | Sv | ERA |
| 1985 Los Angeles | NL | 16 | 2 | 0 | 6 | 29.1 | 133 | 30 | 19 | 17 | 7 | 4 | 1 | 1 | 13 | 3 | 19 | 3 | 0 | 1 | 1 | .500 | 0 | 1 | 5.22 |
| 1986 Los Angeles | NL | 27 | 6 | 0 | 5 | 65.1 | 272 | 65 | 32 | 31 | 5 | 5 | 2 | 1 | 25 | 7 | 31 | 7 | 2 | 2 | 7 | .222 | 0 | 0 | 4.27 |
| 1987 Seattle | AL | 16 | 3 | 0 | 1 | 34.1 | 147 | 32 | 13 | 12 | 3 | 2 | 2 | 0 | 15 | 0 | 17 | 0 | 0 | 1 | 3 | .250 | 0 | 0 | 3.15 |
| 1988 Seattle | AL | 12 | 2 | 0 | 1 | 18.2 | 95 | 29 | 20 | 18 | 2 | 0 | 2 | 2 | 11 | 2 | 15 | 0 | 0 | 1 | 3 | .250 | 0 | 0 | 8.68 |
| 1989 Seattle | AL | 43 | 1 | 0 | 9 | 45 | 201 | 49 | 25 | 25 | 6 | 3 | 3 | 2 | 21 | 0 | 27 | 1 | 0 | 2 | 2 | .500 | 0 | 2 | 5.00 |
| 1990 2 ML Teams | | 11 | 7 | 0 | 2 | 42.1 | 214 | 64 | 40 | 33 | 0 | 2 | 2 | 2 | 21 | 0 | 23 | 2 | 0 | 0 | 4 | .000 | 0 | 0 | 7.02 |
| 1990 Seattle | AL | 2 | 0 | 0 | 1 | 3 | 17 | 5 | 3 | 3 | 0 | 0 | 0 | 1 | 2 | 0 | 0 | 0 | 0 | 0 | 0 | .000 | 0 | 0 | 9.00 |
| Milwaukee | AL | 9 | 7 | 0 | 1 | 39.1 | 197 | 59 | 37 | 30 | 0 | 2 | 2 | 1 | 19 | 0 | 23 | 2 | 0 | 0 | 4 | .000 | 0 | 0 | 6.86 |
| 6 ML YEARS | | 125 | 21 | 0 | 24 | 235 | 1062 | 269 | 149 | 136 | 23 | 16 | 12 | 8 | 106 | 12 | 132 | 13 | 2 | 7 | 20 | .259 | 0 | 3 | 5.21 |

## Ted Power

**Pitches:** Right **Bats:** Right **Pos:** RP **Ht:** 6' 4" **Wt:** 220 **Born:** 01/31/55 **Age:** 36

| | | HOW MUCH HE PITCHED | | | | | | WHAT HE GAVE UP | | | | | | | | | | | | THE RESULTS | | | | | |
|---|---|---|---|---|---|---|---|---|---|---|---|---|---|---|---|---|---|---|---|---|---|---|---|---|---|
| Year Team | Lg | G | GS | CG | GF | IP | BFP | H | R | ER | HR | SH | SF | HB | TBB | IBB | SO | WP | Bk | W | L | Pct. | ShO | Sv | ERA |
| 1981 Los Angeles | NL | 5 | 2 | 0 | 1 | 14 | 66 | 16 | 6 | 5 | 0 | 0 | 2 | 1 | 7 | 2 | 7 | 0 | 0 | 1 | 3 | .250 | 0 | 0 | 3.21 |
| 1982 Los Angeles | NL | 12 | 4 | 0 | 4 | 33.2 | 160 | 38 | 27 | 25 | 4 | 4 | 1 | 0 | 23 | 1 | 15 | 3 | 3 | 1 | 1 | .500 | 0 | 0 | 6.68 |
| 1983 Cincinnati | NL | 49 | 6 | 1 | 14 | 111 | 480 | 120 | 62 | 56 | 10 | 4 | 6 | 1 | 49 | 3 | 57 | 1 | 0 | 5 | 6 | .455 | 0 | 2 | 4.54 |
| 1984 Cincinnati | NL | 78 | 0 | 0 | 42 | 108.2 | 456 | 93 | 37 | 34 | 4 | 9 | 8 | 0 | 46 | 8 | 81 | 3 | 0 | 9 | 7 | .563 | 0 | 11 | 2.82 |
| 1985 Cincinnati | NL | 64 | 0 | 0 | 50 | 80 | 342 | 65 | 27 | 24 | 2 | 6 | 4 | 1 | 45 | 8 | 42 | 1 | 0 | 8 | 6 | .571 | 0 | 27 | 2.70 |
| 1986 Cincinnati | NL | 56 | 10 | 0 | 30 | 129 | 537 | 115 | 59 | 53 | 13 | 9 | 6 | 1 | 52 | 10 | 95 | 5 | 1 | 10 | 6 | .625 | 0 | 1 | 3.70 |
| 1987 Cincinnati | NL | 34 | 34 | 2 | 0 | 204 | 887 | 213 | 115 | 102 | 28 | 8 | 7 | 3 | 71 | 7 | 133 | 3 | 2 | 10 | 13 | .435 | 1 | 0 | 4.50 |
| 1988 2 ML Teams | | 26 | 14 | 2 | 3 | 99 | 443 | 121 | 67 | 65 | 8 | 2 | 4 | 3 | 38 | 7 | 57 | 4 | 2 | 6 | 7 | .462 | 2 | 0 | 5.91 |
| 1989 St. Louis | NL | 23 | 15 | 0 | 2 | 97 | 407 | 96 | 47 | 40 | 7 | 5 | 3 | 1 | 21 | 3 | 43 | 1 | 0 | 7 | 7 | .500 | 0 | 0 | 3.71 |
| 1990 Pittsburgh | NL | 40 | 0 | 0 | 25 | 51.2 | 218 | 50 | 23 | 21 | 5 | 3 | 2 | 0 | 17 | 6 | 42 | 1 | 0 | 1 | 3 | .250 | 0 | 7 | 3.66 |
| 1988 Kansas City | AL | 22 | 12 | 2 | 3 | 80.1 | 360 | 98 | 54 | 53 | 7 | 2 | 4 | 3 | 30 | 3 | 44 | 3 | 2 | 5 | 6 | .455 | 2 | 0 | 5.94 |
| Detroit | AL | 4 | 2 | 0 | 0 | 18.2 | 83 | 23 | 13 | 12 | 1 | 0 | 0 | 0 | 8 | 4 | 13 | 1 | 0 | 1 | 1 | .500 | 0 | 0 | 5.79 |
| 10 ML YEARS | | 387 | 85 | 5 | 171 | 928 | 3996 | 927 | 470 | 425 | 81 | 50 | 43 | 11 | 369 | 55 | 572 | 22 | 8 | 58 | 59 | .496 | 3 | 48 | 4.12 |

## Jim Presley

**Bats:** Right **Throws:** Right **Pos:** 3B/1B **Ht:** 6' 1" **Wt:** 190 **Born:** 10/23/61 **Age:** 29

| | | BATTING | | | | | | | | | | | | | | | | | BASERUNNING | | | | PERCENTAGES | | |
|---|---|---|---|---|---|---|---|---|---|---|---|---|---|---|---|---|---|---|---|---|---|---|---|---|---|
| Year Team | Lg | G | AB | H | 2B | 3B | HR | (Hm | Rd) | TB | R | RBI | TBB | IBB | SO | HBP | SH | SF | SB | CS | SB% | GDP | Avg | OBP | SLG |
| 1984 Seattle | AL | 70 | 251 | 57 | 12 | 1 | 10 | (5 | 5) | 101 | 27 | 36 | 6 | 1 | 63 | 1 | 0 | 1 | 1 | 1 | .50 | 4 | .227 | .247 | .402 |
| 1985 Seattle | AL | 155 | 570 | 157 | 33 | 1 | 28 | (12 | 16) | 276 | 71 | 84 | 44 | 9 | 100 | 1 | 1 | 9 | 2 | 2 | .50 | 29 | .275 | .324 | .484 |
| 1986 Seattle | AL | 155 | 616 | 163 | 33 | 4 | 27 | (16 | 11) | 285 | 83 | 107 | 32 | 3 | 172 | 4 | 3 | 5 | 0 | 4 | .00 | 18 | .265 | .303 | .463 |
| 1987 Seattle | AL | 152 | 575 | 142 | 23 | 6 | 24 | (11 | 13) | 249 | 78 | 88 | 38 | 1 | 157 | 4 | 1 | 4 | 2 | 0 | 1.00 | 15 | .247 | .296 | .433 |
| 1988 Seattle | AL | 150 | 544 | 125 | 26 | 0 | 14 | (7 | 7) | 193 | 50 | 62 | 36 | 1 | 114 | 4 | 3 | 5 | 3 | 5 | .38 | 14 | .230 | .280 | .355 |
| 1989 Seattle | AL | 117 | 390 | 92 | 20 | 1 | 12 | (7 | 5) | 150 | 42 | 41 | 21 | 2 | 107 | 1 | 3 | 2 | 0 | 0 | .00 | 12 | .236 | .275 | .385 |
| 1990 Atlanta | NL | 140 | 541 | 131 | 34 | 1 | 19 | (10 | 9) | 224 | 59 | 72 | 29 | 0 | 130 | 3 | 0 | 4 | 1 | 1 | .50 | 10 | .242 | .282 | .414 |
| 7 ML YEARS | | 939 | 3487 | 867 | 181 | 14 | 134 | (68 | 66) | 1478 | 410 | 490 | 206 | 17 | 843 | 18 | 11 | 30 | 9 | 13 | .41 | 102 | .249 | .292 | .424 |

## Joe Price

**Pitches:** Left **Bats:** Right **Pos:** RP **Ht:** 6' 4" **Wt:** 215 **Born:** 11/29/56 **Age:** 34

| | | HOW MUCH HE PITCHED | | | | | | WHAT HE GAVE UP | | | | | | | | | | | | THE RESULTS | | | | | |
|---|---|---|---|---|---|---|---|---|---|---|---|---|---|---|---|---|---|---|---|---|---|---|---|---|---|
| Year Team | Lg | G | GS | CG | GF | IP | BFP | H | R | ER | HR | SH | SF | HB | TBB | IBB | SO | WP | Bk | W | L | Pct. | ShO | Sv | ERA |
| 1980 Cincinnati | NL | 24 | 13 | 2 | 3 | 111 | 448 | 95 | 45 | 44 | 10 | 8 | 0 | 1 | 37 | 0 | 44 | 1 | 1 | 7 | 3 | .700 | 0 | 0 | 3.57 |
| 1981 Cincinnati | NL | 41 | 0 | 0 | 13 | 54 | 216 | 42 | 19 | 15 | 3 | 6 | 3 | 0 | 18 | 2 | 41 | 2 | 0 | 6 | 1 | .857 | 0 | 4 | 2.50 |
| 1982 Cincinnati | NL | 59 | 1 | 0 | 17 | 72.2 | 318 | 73 | 26 | 23 | 7 | 3 | 1 | 4 | 32 | 8 | 71 | 1 | 0 | 3 | 4 | .429 | 0 | 3 | 2.85 |
| 1983 Cincinnati | NL | 21 | 21 | 5 | 0 | 144 | 581 | 118 | 46 | 46 | 12 | 6 | 4 | 0 | 46 | 2 | 83 | 0 | 0 | 10 | 6 | .625 | 0 | 0 | 2.88 |
| 1984 Cincinnati | NL | 30 | 30 | 3 | 0 | 171.2 | 748 | 176 | 91 | 80 | 19 | 5 | 5 | 2 | 61 | 5 | 129 | 3 | 0 | 7 | 13 | .350 | 1 | 0 | 4.19 |
| 1985 Cincinnati | NL | 26 | 8 | 0 | 5 | 64.2 | 274 | 59 | 35 | 28 | 10 | 2 | 5 | 0 | 23 | 7 | 52 | 2 | 0 | 2 | 2 | .500 | 0 | 1 | 3.90 |
| 1986 Cincinnati | NL | 25 | 2 | 0 | 2 | 41.2 | 194 | 49 | 30 | 25 | 5 | 0 | 5 | 0 | 22 | 2 | 30 | 1 | 0 | 1 | 2 | .333 | 0 | 0 | 5.40 |
| 1987 San Francisco | NL | 20 | 0 | 0 | 5 | 35 | 137 | 19 | 10 | 10 | 5 | 0 | 0 | 1 | 13 | 2 | 42 | 1 | 0 | 2 | 2 | .500 | 0 | 1 | 2.57 |
| 1988 San Francisco | NL | 38 | 3 | 0 | 14 | 61.2 | 269 | 59 | 33 | 27 | 5 | 4 | 0 | 1 | 27 | 6 | 49 | 1 | 3 | 1 | 6 | .143 | 0 | 4 | 3.94 |
| 1989 2 ML Teams | | 38 | 6 | 0 | 13 | 84.1 | 364 | 87 | 44 | 43 | 11 | 4 | 4 | 0 | 34 | 5 | 62 | 2 | 1 | 3 | 6 | .333 | 0 | 0 | 4.59 |
| 1990 Baltimore | AL | 50 | 0 | 0 | 12 | 65.1 | 273 | 62 | 29 | 26 | 8 | 3 | 1 | 0 | 24 | 2 | 54 | 1 | 0 | 3 | 4 | .429 | 0 | 0 | 3.58 |
| 1989 San Francisco | NL | 7 | 1 | 0 | 3 | 14 | 59 | 16 | 9 | 9 | 3 | 3 | 1 | 0 | 4 | 2 | 10 | 1 | 1 | 1 | 1 | .500 | 0 | 0 | 5.79 |
| Boston | AL | 31 | 5 | 0 | 10 | 70.1 | 305 | 71 | 35 | 34 | 8 | 1 | 3 | 0 | 30 | 3 | 52 | 1 | 0 | 2 | 5 | .286 | 0 | 0 | 4.35 |
| 11 ML YEARS | | 372 | 84 | 10 | 84 | 906 | 3822 | 839 | 408 | 367 | 95 | 41 | 28 | 9 | 337 | 41 | 657 | 15 | 5 | 45 | 49 | .479 | 1 | 13 | 3.65 |

## Tom Prince

**Bats:** Right **Throws:** Right **Pos:** C **Ht:** 5'11" **Wt:** 185 **Born:** 08/13/64 **Age:** 26

| BATTING | | | | | | | | | | | | | | | | | | | BASERUNNING | | | | PERCENTAGES | | |
|---|---|---|---|---|---|---|---|---|---|---|---|---|---|---|---|---|---|---|---|---|---|---|---|---|---|
| Year Team | Lg | G | AB | H | 2B | 3B | HR | (Hm | Rd) | TB | R | RBI | TBB | IBB | SO | HBP | SH | SF | SB | CS | SB% | GDP | Avg | OBP | SLG |
| 1987 Pittsburgh | NL | 4 | 9 | 2 | 1 | 0 | 1 | (0 | 1) | 6 | 1 | 2 | 0 | 0 | 2 | 0 | 0 | 0 | 0 | 0 | .00 | 0 | .222 | .222 | .667 |
| 1988 Pittsburgh | NL | 29 | 74 | 13 | 2 | 0 | 0 | (0 | 0) | 15 | 3 | 6 | 4 | 0 | 15 | 0 | 2 | 0 | 0 | 0 | .00 | 5 | .176 | .218 | .203 |
| 1989 Pittsburgh | NL | 21 | 52 | 7 | 4 | 0 | 0 | (0 | 0) | 11 | 1 | 5 | 6 | 1 | 12 | 0 | 0 | 1 | 1 | 1 | .50 | 1 | .135 | .220 | .212 |
| 1990 Pittsburgh | NL | 4 | 10 | 1 | 0 | 0 | 0 | (0 | 0) | 1 | 1 | 0 | 1 | 0 | 2 | 0 | 0 | 0 | 0 | 1 | .00 | 0 | .100 | .182 | .100 |
| 4 ML YEARS | | 58 | 145 | 23 | 7 | 0 | 1 | (0 | 1) | 33 | 6 | 13 | 11 | 1 | 31 | 0 | 2 | 1 | 1 | 2 | .33 | 6 | .159 | .217 | .228 |

## Kirby Puckett

**Bats:** Right **Throws:** Right **Pos:** CF **Ht:** 5' 8" **Wt:** 210 **Born:** 03/14/61 **Age:** 30

| BATTING | | | | | | | | | | | | | | | | | | | BASERUNNING | | | | PERCENTAGES | | |
|---|---|---|---|---|---|---|---|---|---|---|---|---|---|---|---|---|---|---|---|---|---|---|---|---|---|
| Year Team | Lg | G | AB | H | 2B | 3B | HR | (Hm | Rd) | TB | R | RBI | TBB | IBB | SO | HBP | SH | SF | SB | CS | SB% | GDP | Avg | OBP | SLG |
| 1984 Minnesota | AL | 128 | 557 | 165 | 12 | 5 | 0 | (0 | 0) | 187 | 63 | 31 | 16 | 1 | 69 | 4 | 4 | 2 | 14 | 7 | .67 | 11 | .296 | .320 | .336 |
| 1985 Minnesota | AL | 161 | 691 | 199 | 29 | 13 | 4 | (2 | 2) | 266 | 80 | 74 | 41 | 0 | 87 | 4 | 5 | 3 | 21 | 12 | .64 | 9 | .288 | .330 | .385 |
| 1986 Minnesota | AL | 161 | 680 | 223 | 37 | 6 | 31 | (14 | 17) | 365 | 119 | 96 | 34 | 4 | 99 | 7 | 2 | 0 | 20 | 12 | .63 | 14 | .328 | .366 | .537 |
| 1987 Minnesota | AL | 157 | 624 | 207 | 32 | 5 | 28 | (18 | 10) | 333 | 96 | 99 | 32 | 7 | 91 | 6 | 0 | 6 | 12 | 7 | .63 | 16 | .332 | .367 | .534 |
| 1988 Minnesota | AL | 158 | 657 | 234 | 42 | 5 | 24 | (13 | 11) | 358 | 109 | 121 | 23 | 4 | 83 | 2 | 0 | 9 | 6 | 7 | .46 | 17 | .356 | .375 | .545 |
| 1989 Minnesota | AL | 159 | 635 | 215 | 45 | 4 | 9 | (7 | 2) | 295 | 75 | 85 | 41 | 9 | 59 | 3 | 0 | 5 | 11 | 4 | .73 | 21 | .339 | .379 | .465 |
| 1990 Minnesota | AL | 146 | 551 | 164 | 40 | 3 | 12 | (6 | 6) | 246 | 82 | 80 | 57 | 11 | 73 | 3 | 1 | 3 | 5 | 4 | .56 | 15 | .298 | .365 | .446 |
| 7 ML YEARS | | 1070 | 4395 | 1407 | 237 | 41 | 108 | (60 | 48) | 2050 | 624 | 586 | 244 | 36 | 561 | 29 | 12 | 28 | 89 | 53 | .63 | 103 | .320 | .358 | .466 |

## Terry Puhl

**Bats:** Left **Throws:** Right **Pos:** LF **Ht:** 6' 2" **Wt:** 197 **Born:** 07/08/56 **Age:** 34

| BATTING | | | | | | | | | | | | | | | | | | | BASERUNNING | | | | PERCENTAGES | | |
|---|---|---|---|---|---|---|---|---|---|---|---|---|---|---|---|---|---|---|---|---|---|---|---|---|---|
| Year Team | Lg | G | AB | H | 2B | 3B | HR | (Hm | Rd) | TB | R | RBI | TBB | IBB | SO | HBP | SH | SF | SB | CS | SB% | GDP | Avg | OBP | SLG |
| 1977 Houston | NL | 60 | 229 | 69 | 13 | 5 | 0 | (0 | 0) | 92 | 40 | 10 | 30 | 0 | 31 | 1 | 5 | 0 | 10 | 1 | .91 | 3 | .301 | .385 | .402 |
| 1978 Houston | NL | 149 | 585 | 169 | 25 | 6 | 3 | (1 | 2) | 215 | 87 | 35 | 48 | 5 | 46 | 4 | 3 | 7 | 32 | 14 | .70 | 11 | .289 | .343 | .368 |
| 1979 Houston | NL | 157 | 600 | 172 | 22 | 4 | 8 | (2 | 6) | 226 | 87 | 49 | 58 | 8 | 46 | 4 | 8 | 2 | 30 | 22 | .58 | 7 | .287 | .352 | .377 |
| 1980 Houston | NL | 141 | 535 | 151 | 24 | 5 | 13 | (4 | 9) | 224 | 75 | 55 | 60 | 3 | 52 | 4 | 6 | 3 | 27 | 11 | .71 | 3 | .282 | .357 | .419 |
| 1981 Houston | NL | 96 | 350 | 88 | 19 | 4 | 3 | (1 | 2) | 124 | 43 | 28 | 31 | 5 | 49 | 4 | 4 | 5 | 22 | 4 | .85 | 3 | .251 | .315 | .354 |
| 1982 Houston | NL | 145 | 507 | 133 | 17 | 9 | 8 | (5 | 3) | 192 | 64 | 50 | 51 | 2 | 49 | 2 | 5 | 2 | 17 | 9 | .65 | 6 | .262 | .331 | .379 |
| 1983 Houston | NL | 137 | 465 | 136 | 25 | 7 | 8 | (1 | 7) | 199 | 66 | 44 | 36 | 2 | 48 | 2 | 5 | 4 | 24 | 11 | .69 | 4 | .292 | .343 | .428 |
| 1984 Houston | NL | 132 | 449 | 135 | 19 | 7 | 9 | (2 | 7) | 195 | 66 | 55 | 59 | 12 | 45 | 1 | 6 | 4 | 13 | 8 | .62 | 5 | .301 | .380 | .434 |
| 1985 Houston | NL | 57 | 194 | 55 | 14 | 3 | 2 | (1 | 1) | 81 | 34 | 23 | 18 | 4 | 23 | 1 | 4 | 3 | 6 | 2 | .75 | 0 | .284 | .343 | .418 |
| 1986 Houston | NL | 81 | 172 | 42 | 10 | 0 | 3 | (1 | 2) | 61 | 17 | 14 | 15 | 1 | 24 | 0 | 4 | 2 | 3 | 2 | .60 | 6 | .244 | .302 | .355 |
| 1987 Houston | NL | 90 | 122 | 28 | 5 | 0 | 2 | (1 | 1) | 39 | 9 | 15 | 11 | 0 | 16 | 0 | 1 | 0 | 1 | 1 | .50 | 3 | .230 | .293 | .320 |
| 1988 Houston | NL | 113 | 234 | 71 | 7 | 2 | 3 | (2 | 1) | 91 | 42 | 19 | 35 | 3 | 30 | 1 | 1 | 1 | 22 | 4 | .85 | 0 | .303 | .395 | .389 |
| 1989 Houston | NL | 121 | 354 | 96 | 25 | 4 | 0 | (0 | 0) | 129 | 41 | 27 | 45 | 3 | 39 | 1 | 4 | 2 | 9 | 8 | .53 | 7 | .271 | .353 | .364 |
| 1990 Houston | NL | 37 | 41 | 12 | 1 | 0 | 0 | (0 | 0) | 13 | 5 | 8 | 5 | 0 | 7 | 1 | 1 | 1 | 1 | 2 | .33 | 0 | .293 | .375 | .317 |
| 14 ML YEARS | | 1516 | 4837 | 1357 | 226 | 56 | 62 | (21 | 41) | 1881 | 676 | 432 | 502 | 48 | 505 | 26 | 57 | 36 | 217 | 99 | .69 | 58 | .281 | .349 | .389 |

## Tom Quinlan

**Bats:** Right **Throws:** Right **Pos:** 3B **Ht:** 6' 3" **Wt:** 190 **Born:** 03/27/68 **Age:** 23

| BATTING | | | | | | | | | | | | | | | | | | | BASERUNNING | | | | PERCENTAGES | | |
|---|---|---|---|---|---|---|---|---|---|---|---|---|---|---|---|---|---|---|---|---|---|---|---|---|---|
| Year Team | Lg | G | AB | H | 2B | 3B | HR | (Hm | Rd) | TB | R | RBI | TBB | IBB | SO | HBP | SH | SF | SB | CS | SB% | GDP | Avg | OBP | SLG |
| 1987 Myrtle Bch | A | 132 | 435 | 97 | 20 | 3 | 5 | -- | -- | 138 | 42 | 51 | 34 | 0 | 130 | 6 | 3 | 6 | 0 | 2 | .00 | 4 | .223 | .285 | .317 |
| 1988 Knoxville | AA | 98 | 326 | 71 | 19 | 1 | 8 | -- | -- | 116 | 33 | 47 | 35 | 1 | 99 | 5 | 3 | 2 | 4 | 9 | .31 | 5 | .218 | .302 | .356 |
| 1989 Knoxville | AA | 139 | 452 | 95 | 21 | 3 | 16 | -- | -- | 170 | 62 | 57 | 41 | 0 | 118 | 9 | 3 | 4 | 6 | 4 | .60 | 11 | .210 | .287 | .376 |
| 1990 Knoxville | AA | 141 | 481 | 124 | 24 | 6 | 15 | -- | -- | 205 | 70 | 51 | 49 | 2 | 157 | 14 | 7 | 1 | 8 | 9 | .47 | 5 | .258 | .343 | .426 |
| 1990 Toronto | AL | 1 | 2 | 1 | 0 | 0 | 0 | (0 | 0) | 1 | 0 | 0 | 0 | 0 | 1 | 1 | 0 | 0 | 0 | 0 | .00 | 0 | .500 | .667 | .500 |

## Luis Quinones

**Bats:** Both **Throws:** Right **Pos:** 3B/2B **Ht:** 5'11" **Wt:** 175 **Born:** 04/28/62 **Age:** 29

| BATTING | | | | | | | | | | | | | | | | | | | BASERUNNING | | | | PERCENTAGES | | |
|---|---|---|---|---|---|---|---|---|---|---|---|---|---|---|---|---|---|---|---|---|---|---|---|---|---|
| Year Team | Lg | G | AB | H | 2B | 3B | HR | (Hm | Rd) | TB | R | RBI | TBB | IBB | SO | HBP | SH | SF | SB | CS | SB% | GDP | Avg | OBP | SLG |
| 1983 Oakland | AL | 19 | 42 | 8 | 2 | 1 | 0 | (0 | 0) | 12 | 5 | 4 | 1 | 0 | 4 | 0 | 1 | 1 | 1 | 1 | .50 | 0 | .190 | .205 | .286 |
| 1986 San Francisco | NL | 71 | 106 | 19 | 1 | 3 | 0 | (0 | 0) | 26 | 13 | 11 | 3 | 1 | 17 | 1 | 4 | 1 | 3 | 1 | .75 | 1 | .179 | .207 | .245 |
| 1987 Chicago | NL | 49 | 101 | 22 | 6 | 0 | 0 | (0 | 0) | 28 | 12 | 8 | 10 | 0 | 16 | 0 | 0 | 0 | 0 | 0 | .00 | 0 | .218 | .288 | .277 |
| 1988 Cincinnati | NL | 23 | 52 | 12 | 3 | 0 | 1 | (0 | 1) | 18 | 4 | 11 | 2 | 1 | 11 | 0 | 2 | 1 | 1 | 1 | .50 | 0 | .231 | .255 | .346 |
| 1989 Cincinnati | NL | 97 | 340 | 83 | 13 | 4 | 12 | (5 | 7) | 140 | 43 | 34 | 25 | 0 | 46 | 3 | 8 | 2 | 2 | 4 | .33 | 3 | .244 | .300 | .412 |
| 1990 Cincinnati | NL | 83 | 145 | 35 | 7 | 0 | 2 | (1 | 1) | 48 | 10 | 17 | 13 | 3 | 29 | 1 | 1 | 4 | 1 | 0 | 1.00 | 3 | .241 | .301 | .331 |
| 6 ML YEARS | | 342 | 786 | 179 | 32 | 8 | 15 | (6 | 9) | 272 | 87 | 85 | 54 | 5 | 123 | 5 | 16 | 9 | 8 | 7 | .53 | 7 | .228 | .279 | .346 |

## Carlos Quintana

**Bats:** Right **Throws:** Right **Pos:** 1B **Ht:** 6' 2" **Wt:** 195 **Born:** 08/26/65 **Age:** 25

| BATTING | | | | | | | | | | | | | | | | | | | BASERUNNING | | | | PERCENTAGES | | |
|---|---|---|---|---|---|---|---|---|---|---|---|---|---|---|---|---|---|---|---|---|---|---|---|---|---|
| Year Team | Lg | G | AB | H | 2B | 3B | HR | (Hm | Rd) | TB | R | RBI | TBB | IBB | SO | HBP | SH | SF | SB | CS | SB% | GDP | Avg | OBP | SLG |
| 1988 Boston | AL | 5 | 6 | 2 | 0 | 0 | 0 | (0 | 0) | 2 | 1 | 2 | 2 | 0 | 3 | 0 | 0 | 0 | 0 | 0 | .00 | 0 | .333 | .500 | .333 |
| 1989 Boston | AL | 34 | 77 | 16 | 5 | 0 | 0 | (0 | 0) | 21 | 6 | 6 | 7 | 0 | 12 | 0 | 0 | 0 | 0 | 0 | .00 | 5 | .208 | .274 | .273 |
| 1990 Boston | AL | 149 | 512 | 147 | 28 | 0 | 7 | (3 | 4) | 196 | 56 | 67 | 52 | 0 | 74 | 2 | 4 | 2 | 1 | 2 | .33 | 19 | .287 | .354 | .383 |
| 3 ML YEARS | | 188 | 595 | 165 | 33 | 0 | 7 | (3 | 4) | 219 | 63 | 75 | 61 | 0 | 89 | 2 | 4 | 2 | 1 | 2 | .33 | 24 | .277 | .345 | .368 |

## Jamie Quirk

**Bats:** Left **Throws:** Right **Pos:** C **Ht:** 6' 4" **Wt:** 200 **Born:** 10/22/54 **Age:** 36

| BATTING | | | | | | | | | | | | | | | | | | | BASERUNNING | | | | PERCENTAGES | | |
|---|---|---|---|---|---|---|---|---|---|---|---|---|---|---|---|---|---|---|---|---|---|---|---|---|---|
| Year Team | Lg | G | AB | H | 2B | 3B | HR | (Hm | Rd) | TB | R | RBI | TBB | IBB | SO | HBP | SH | SF | SB | CS | SB% | GDP | Avg | OBP | SLG |
| 1975 Kansas City | AL | 14 | 39 | 10 | 0 | 0 | 1 | (1 | 0) | 13 | 2 | 5 | 2 | 1 | 7 | 0 | 0 | 0 | 0 | 0 | .00 | 1 | .256 | .293 | .333 |
| 1976 Kansas City | AL | 64 | 114 | 28 | 6 | 0 | 1 | (1 | 0) | 37 | 11 | 15 | 2 | 0 | 22 | 0 | 0 | 3 | 0 | 0 | .00 | 5 | .246 | .252 | .325 |
| 1977 Milwaukee | AL | 93 | 221 | 48 | 14 | 1 | 3 | (2 | 1) | 73 | 16 | 13 | 8 | 2 | 47 | 2 | 2 | 0 | 0 | 1 | .00 | 4 | .217 | .251 | .330 |
| 1978 Kansas City | AL | 17 | 29 | 6 | 2 | 0 | 0 | (0 | 0) | 8 | 3 | 2 | 5 | 0 | 4 | 0 | 0 | 0 | 0 | 0 | .00 | 0 | .207 | .324 | .276 |
| 1979 Kansas City | AL | 51 | 79 | 24 | 6 | 1 | 1 | (1 | 0) | 35 | 8 | 11 | 5 | 0 | 13 | 1 | 0 | 0 | 0 | 0 | .00 | 0 | .304 | .353 | .443 |
| 1980 Kansas City | AL | 62 | 163 | 45 | 5 | 0 | 5 | (3 | 2) | 65 | 13 | 21 | 7 | 2 | 24 | 1 | 3 | 3 | 3 | 2 | .60 | 7 | .276 | .305 | .399 |
| 1981 Kansas City | AL | 46 | 100 | 25 | 7 | 0 | 0 | (0 | 0) | 32 | 8 | 10 | 6 | 1 | 17 | 1 | 0 | 0 | 0 | 2 | .00 | 5 | .250 | .299 | .320 |
| 1982 Kansas City | AL | 36 | 78 | 18 | 3 | 0 | 1 | (1 | 0) | 24 | 8 | 5 | 3 | 0 | 15 | 0 | 0 | 1 | 0 | 0 | .00 | 2 | .231 | .256 | .308 |
| 1983 St. Louis | NL | 48 | 86 | 18 | 2 | 1 | 2 | (0 | 2) | 28 | 3 | 11 | 6 | 0 | 27 | 1 | 0 | 0 | 0 | 0 | .00 | 2 | .209 | .269 | .326 |
| 1984 2 ML Teams | | 4 | 3 | 1 | 0 | 0 | 1 | (1 | 0) | 4 | 1 | 2 | 0 | 0 | 2 | 0 | 0 | 1 | 0 | 0 | .00 | 0 | .333 | .250 | 1.333 |
| 1985 Kansas City | AL | 19 | 57 | 16 | 3 | 1 | 0 | (0 | 0) | 21 | 3 | 4 | 2 | 0 | 9 | 0 | 0 | 0 | 0 | 0 | .00 | 1 | .281 | .305 | .368 |
| 1986 Kansas City | AL | 80 | 219 | 47 | 10 | 0 | 8 | (5 | 3) | 81 | 24 | 26 | 17 | 3 | 41 | 1 | 0 | 1 | 0 | 1 | .00 | 4 | .215 | .273 | .370 |
| 1987 Kansas City | AL | 109 | 296 | 70 | 17 | 0 | 5 | (0 | 5) | 102 | 24 | 33 | 28 | 1 | 56 | 4 | 2 | 4 | 1 | 0 | 1.00 | 8 | .236 | .307 | .345 |
| 1988 Kansas City | AL | 84 | 196 | 47 | 7 | 1 | 8 | (2 | 6) | 80 | 22 | 25 | 28 | 2 | 41 | 1 | 4 | 3 | 1 | 5 | .17 | 2 | .240 | .333 | .408 |
| 1989 3 ML Teams | | 47 | 85 | 15 | 2 | 0 | 1 | (0 | 1) | 20 | 6 | 10 | 12 | 0 | 20 | 0 | 1 | 1 | 0 | 2 | .00 | 4 | .176 | .276 | .235 |
| 1990 Oakland | AL | 56 | 121 | 34 | 5 | 1 | 3 | (1 | 2) | 50 | 12 | 26 | 14 | 1 | 34 | 1 | 5 | 3 | 0 | 0 | .00 | 1 | .281 | .353 | .413 |
| 1984 Chicago | AL | 3 | 2 | 0 | 0 | 0 | 0 | (0 | 0) | 0 | 0 | 1 | 0 | 0 | 2 | 0 | 0 | 1 | 0 | 0 | .00 | 0 | .000 | .000 | .000 |
| Cleveland | AL | 1 | 1 | 1 | 0 | 0 | 1 | (1 | 0) | 4 | 1 | 1 | 0 | 0 | 0 | 0 | 0 | 0 | 0 | 0 | .00 | 0 | 1.000 | 1.000 | 4.000 |
| 1989 New York | AL | 13 | 24 | 2 | 0 | 0 | 0 | (0 | 0) | 2 | 0 | 0 | 3 | 0 | 5 | 0 | 0 | 0 | 0 | 1 | .00 | 1 | .083 | .185 | .083 |
| Oakland | AL | 9 | 10 | 2 | 0 | 0 | 1 | (0 | 1) | 5 | 1 | 1 | 0 | 0 | 4 | 0 | 0 | 0 | 0 | 0 | .00 | 0 | .200 | .200 | .500 |
| Baltimore | AL | 25 | 51 | 11 | 2 | 0 | 0 | (0 | 0) | 13 | 5 | 9 | 9 | 0 | 11 | 0 | 1 | 1 | 0 | 1 | .00 | 3 | .216 | .328 | .255 |
| 16 ML YEARS | | 830 | 1886 | 452 | 89 | 6 | 40 | (18 | 22) | 673 | 164 | 219 | 145 | 13 | 379 | 13 | 17 | 20 | 5 | 13 | .28 | 46 | .240 | .296 | .357 |

## Dan Quisenberry

**Pitches:** Right **Bats:** Right **Pos:** RP **Ht:** 6' 2" **Wt:** 185 **Born:** 02/07/53 **Age:** 38

| | | HOW MUCH HE PITCHED | | | | | | WHAT HE GAVE UP | | | | | | | | | | | | THE RESULTS | | | | | |
|---|---|---|---|---|---|---|---|---|---|---|---|---|---|---|---|---|---|---|---|---|---|---|---|---|---|
| Year Team | Lg | G | GS | CG | GF | IP | BFP | H | R | ER | HR | SH | SF | HB | TBB | IBB | SO | WP | Bk | W | L | Pct. | ShO | Sv | ERA |
| 1979 Kansas City | AL | 32 | 0 | 0 | 21 | 40 | 163 | 42 | 16 | 14 | 5 | 3 | 2 | 0 | 7 | 5 | 13 | 1 | 0 | 3 | 2 | .600 | 0 | 5 | 3.15 |
| 1980 Kansas City | AL | 75 | 0 | 0 | 68 | 128 | 528 | 129 | 47 | 44 | 5 | 8 | 5 | 1 | 27 | 15 | 37 | 1 | 0 | 12 | 7 | .632 | 0 | 33 | 3.09 |
| 1981 Kansas City | AL | 40 | 0 | 0 | 35 | 62 | 254 | 59 | 16 | 12 | 1 | 5 | 4 | 1 | 15 | 8 | 20 | 0 | 0 | 1 | 4 | .200 | 0 | 18 | 1.74 |
| 1982 Kansas City | AL | 72 | 0 | 0 | 68 | 136.2 | 529 | 126 | 43 | 39 | 12 | 10 | 7 | 0 | 12 | 2 | 46 | 1 | 0 | 9 | 7 | .563 | 0 | 35 | 2.57 |
| 1983 Kansas City | AL | 69 | 0 | 0 | 62 | 139 | 536 | 118 | 35 | 30 | 6 | 6 | 4 | 0 | 11 | 2 | 48 | 0 | 0 | 5 | 3 | .625 | 0 | 45 | 1.94 |
| 1984 Kansas City | AL | 72 | 0 | 0 | 67 | 129.1 | 506 | 121 | 39 | 38 | 10 | 2 | 3 | 0 | 12 | 4 | 41 | 0 | 0 | 6 | 3 | .667 | 0 | 44 | 2.64 |
| 1985 Kansas City | AL | 84 | 0 | 0 | 76 | 129 | 532 | 142 | 41 | 34 | 8 | 4 | 3 | 1 | 16 | 5 | 54 | 0 | 0 | 8 | 9 | .471 | 0 | 37 | 2.37 |
| 1986 Kansas City | AL | 62 | 0 | 0 | 54 | 81.1 | 352 | 92 | 30 | 25 | 2 | 4 | 5 | 3 | 24 | 12 | 36 | 0 | 0 | 3 | 7 | .300 | 0 | 12 | 2.77 |
| 1987 Kansas City | AL | 47 | 0 | 0 | 39 | 49 | 215 | 58 | 15 | 15 | 3 | 1 | 1 | 1 | 10 | 3 | 17 | 0 | 0 | 4 | 1 | .800 | 0 | 8 | 2.76 |
| 1988 2 ML Teams | | 53 | 0 | 0 | 26 | 63.1 | 278 | 86 | 37 | 36 | 4 | 3 | 2 | 0 | 11 | 3 | 28 | 1 | 3 | 2 | 1 | .667 | 0 | 1 | 5.12 |
| 1989 St. Louis | NL | 63 | 0 | 0 | 35 | 78.1 | 317 | 78 | 25 | 23 | 2 | 3 | 1 | 0 | 14 | 9 | 37 | 0 | 1 | 3 | 1 | .750 | 0 | 6 | 2.64 |
| 1990 San Francisco | NL | 5 | 0 | 0 | 2 | 6.2 | 37 | 13 | 12 | 10 | 1 | 0 | 3 | 0 | 3 | 2 | 2 | 0 | 1 | 0 | 1 | .000 | 0 | 0 | 13.50 |
| 1988 Kansas City | AL | 20 | 0 | 0 | 13 | 25.1 | 110 | 32 | 11 | 10 | 0 | 0 | 0 | 0 | 5 | 2 | 9 | 1 | 1 | 0 | 1 | .000 | 0 | 1 | 3.55 |
| St. Louis | NL | 33 | 0 | 0 | 13 | 38 | 168 | 54 | 26 | 26 | 4 | 3 | 2 | 0 | 6 | 1 | 19 | 0 | 2 | 2 | 0 | 1.000 | 0 | 0 | 6.16 |
| 12 ML YEARS | | 674 | 0 | 0 | 553 | 1042.2 | 4247 | 1064 | 356 | 320 | 59 | 49 | 40 | 7 | 162 | 70 | 379 | 4 | 5 | 56 | 46 | .549 | 0 | 244 | 2.76 |

## Scott Radinsky

**Pitches:** Left **Bats:** Left **Pos:** RP **Ht:** 6' 3" **Wt:** 190 **Born:** 03/03/68 **Age:** 23

| | | HOW MUCH HE PITCHED | | | | | | WHAT HE GAVE UP | | | | | | | | | | | | THE RESULTS | | | | | |
|---|---|---|---|---|---|---|---|---|---|---|---|---|---|---|---|---|---|---|---|---|---|---|---|---|---|
| Year Team | Lg | G | GS | CG | GF | IP | BFP | H | R | ER | HR | SH | SF | HB | TBB | IBB | SO | WP | Bk | W | L | Pct. | ShO | Sv | ERA |
| 1986 White Sox | R | 7 | 7 | 0 | 0 | 26.2 | 122 | 24 | 20 | 10 | 0 | 1 | 3 | 0 | 17 | 0 | 18 | 2 | 1 | 1 | 0 | 1.000 | 0 | 0 | 3.38 |
| 1987 Peninsula | A | 12 | 8 | 0 | 2 | 39 | 187 | 43 | 30 | 25 | 2 | 2 | 2 | 3 | 32 | 0 | 37 | 3 | 1 | 1 | 7 | .125 | 0 | 0 | 5.77 |
| White Sox | R | 11 | 10 | 0 | 0 | 58.1 | 249 | 43 | 23 | 15 | 1 | 0 | 2 | 4 | 39 | 0 | 41 | 5 | 1 | 3 | 3 | .500 | 0 | 0 | 2.31 |
| 1988 White Sox | R | 5 | 0 | 0 | 2 | 3.1 | 17 | 2 | 2 | 2 | 0 | 0 | 0 | 0 | 4 | 0 | 7 | 1 | 2 | 0 | 0 | .000 | 0 | 0 | 5.40 |
| 1989 South Bend | A | 53 | 0 | 0 | 49 | 61.2 | 248 | 39 | 21 | 12 | 1 | 4 | 2 | 5 | 19 | 2 | 83 | 2 | 2 | 7 | 5 | .583 | 0 | 31 | 1.75 |
| 1990 Chicago | AL | 62 | 0 | 0 | 18 | 52.1 | 237 | 47 | 29 | 28 | 1 | 2 | 2 | 2 | 36 | 1 | 46 | 2 | 1 | 6 | 1 | .857 | 0 | 4 | 4.82 |

## Tim Raines

**Bats:** Both **Throws:** Right **Pos:** LF **Ht:** 5' 8" **Wt:** 180 **Born:** 09/16/59 **Age:** 31

| BATTING | | | | | | | | | | | | | | | | | | | BASERUNNING | | | | PERCENTAGES | | |
|---|---|---|---|---|---|---|---|---|---|---|---|---|---|---|---|---|---|---|---|---|---|---|---|---|---|
| Year Team | Lg | G | AB | H | 2B | 3B | HR | (Hm | Rd) | TB | R | RBI | TBB | IBB | SO | HBP | SH | SF | SB | CS | SB% | GDP | Avg | OBP | SLG |
| 1979 Montreal | NL | 6 | 0 | 0 | 0 | 0 | 0 | (0 | 0) | 0 | 3 | 0 | 0 | 0 | 0 | 0 | 0 | 0 | 2 | 0 | 1.00 | 0 | .000 | .000 | .000 |
| 1980 Montreal | NL | 15 | 20 | 1 | 0 | 0 | 0 | (0 | 0) | 1 | 5 | 0 | 6 | 0 | 3 | 0 | 1 | 0 | 5 | 0 | 1.00 | 0 | .050 | .269 | .050 |
| 1981 Montreal | NL | 88 | 313 | 95 | 13 | 7 | 5 | (3 | 2) | 137 | 61 | 37 | 45 | 5 | 31 | 2 | 0 | 3 | 71 | 11 | .87 | 7 | .304 | .391 | .438 |
| 1982 Montreal | NL | 156 | 647 | 179 | 32 | 8 | 4 | (1 | 3) | 239 | 90 | 43 | 75 | 9 | 83 | 2 | 6 | 1 | 78 | 16 | .83 | 6 | .277 | .353 | .369 |
| 1983 Montreal | NL | 156 | 615 | 183 | 32 | 8 | 11 | (5 | 6) | 264 | 133 | 71 | 97 | 9 | 70 | 2 | 2 | 4 | 90 | 14 | .87 | 12 | .298 | .393 | .429 |
| 1984 Montreal | NL | 160 | 622 | 192 | 38 | 9 | 8 | (2 | 6) | 272 | 106 | 60 | 87 | 7 | 69 | 2 | 3 | 4 | 75 | 10 | .88 | 7 | .309 | .393 | .437 |
| 1985 Montreal | NL | 150 | 575 | 184 | 30 | 13 | 11 | (4 | 7) | 273 | 115 | 41 | 81 | 13 | 60 | 3 | 3 | 3 | 70 | 9 | .89 | 9 | .320 | .405 | .475 |
| 1986 Montreal | NL | 151 | 580 | 194 | 35 | 10 | 9 | (4 | 5) | 276 | 91 | 62 | 78 | 9 | 60 | 2 | 1 | 3 | 70 | 9 | .89 | 6 | .334 | .413 | .476 |
| 1987 Montreal | NL | 139 | 530 | 175 | 34 | 8 | 18 | (9 | 9) | 279 | 123 | 68 | 90 | 26 | 52 | 4 | 0 | 3 | 50 | 5 | .91 | 9 | .330 | .429 | .526 |
| 1988 Montreal | NL | 109 | 429 | 116 | 19 | 7 | 12 | (5 | 7) | 185 | 66 | 48 | 53 | 14 | 44 | 2 | 0 | 4 | 33 | 7 | .83 | 8 | .270 | .350 | .431 |
| 1989 Montreal | NL | 145 | 517 | 148 | 29 | 6 | 9 | (6 | 3) | 216 | 76 | 60 | 93 | 18 | 48 | 3 | 0 | 5 | 41 | 9 | .82 | 8 | .286 | .395 | .418 |
| 1990 Montreal | NL | 130 | 457 | 131 | 11 | 5 | 9 | (6 | 3) | 179 | 65 | 62 | 70 | 8 | 43 | 3 | 0 | 8 | 49 | 16 | .75 | 9 | .287 | .379 | .392 |
| 12 ML YEARS | | 1405 | 5305 | 1598 | 273 | 81 | 96 | (45 | 51) | 2321 | 934 | 552 | 775 | 118 | 563 | 25 | 16 | 38 | 634 | 106 | .86 | 81 | .301 | .390 | .438 |

## Rafael Ramirez

**Bats:** Right **Throws:** Right **Pos:** SS **Ht:** 5'11" **Wt:** 190 **Born:** 02/18/59 **Age:** 32

| BATTING | | | | | | | | | | | | | | | | | | | BASERUNNING | | | | PERCENTAGES | | |
|---|---|---|---|---|---|---|---|---|---|---|---|---|---|---|---|---|---|---|---|---|---|---|---|---|---|
| Year Team | Lg | G | AB | H | 2B | 3B | HR | (Hm | Rd) | TB | R | RBI | TBB | IBB | SO | HBP | SH | SF | SB | CS | SB% | GDP | Avg | OBP | SLG |
| 1980 Atlanta | NL | 50 | 165 | 44 | 6 | 1 | 2 | (2 | 0) | 58 | 17 | 11 | 2 | 0 | 33 | 4 | 3 | 0 | 2 | 1 | .67 | 2 | .267 | .292 | .352 |
| 1981 Atlanta | NL | 95 | 307 | 67 | 16 | 2 | 2 | (1 | 1) | 93 | 30 | 20 | 24 | 3 | 47 | 1 | 9 | 1 | 7 | 3 | .70 | 3 | .218 | .276 | .303 |
| 1982 Atlanta | NL | 157 | 609 | 169 | 24 | 4 | 10 | (7 | 3) | 231 | 74 | 52 | 36 | 7 | 49 | 3 | 16 | 5 | 27 | 14 | .66 | 10 | .278 | .319 | .379 |
| 1983 Atlanta | NL | 152 | 622 | 185 | 13 | 5 | 7 | (2 | 5) | 229 | 82 | 58 | 36 | 4 | 48 | 2 | 6 | 2 | 16 | 12 | .57 | 8 | .297 | .337 | .368 |
| 1984 Atlanta | NL | 145 | 591 | 157 | 22 | 4 | 2 | (1 | 1) | 193 | 51 | 48 | 26 | 1 | 70 | 1 | 5 | 6 | 14 | 17 | .45 | 9 | .266 | .295 | .327 |
| 1985 Atlanta | NL | 138 | 568 | 141 | 25 | 4 | 5 | (4 | 1) | 189 | 54 | 58 | 20 | 1 | 63 | 0 | 2 | 5 | 2 | 6 | .25 | 21 | .248 | .272 | .333 |
| 1986 Atlanta | NL | 134 | 496 | 119 | 21 | 1 | 8 | (1 | 7) | 166 | 57 | 33 | 21 | 1 | 60 | 3 | 7 | 3 | 19 | 8 | .70 | 16 | .240 | .273 | .335 |
| 1987 Atlanta | NL | 56 | 179 | 47 | 12 | 0 | 1 | (0 | 1) | 62 | 22 | 21 | 8 | 0 | 16 | 2 | 4 | 1 | 6 | 3 | .67 | 3 | .263 | .300 | .346 |
| 1988 Houston | NL | 155 | 566 | 156 | 30 | 5 | 6 | (2 | 4) | 214 | 51 | 59 | 18 | 6 | 61 | 3 | 4 | 6 | 3 | 2 | .60 | 16 | .276 | .298 | .378 |
| 1989 Houston | NL | 151 | 537 | 132 | 20 | 2 | 6 | (3 | 3) | 174 | 46 | 54 | 29 | 3 | 64 | 0 | 6 | 3 | 3 | 1 | .75 | 8 | .246 | .283 | .324 |
| 1990 Houston | NL | 132 | 445 | 116 | 19 | 3 | 2 | (1 | 1) | 147 | 44 | 37 | 24 | 9 | 46 | 1 | 9 | 1 | 10 | 5 | .67 | 9 | .261 | .299 | .330 |
| 11 ML YEARS | | 1365 | 5085 | 1333 | 208 | 31 | 51 | (24 | 27) | 1756 | 528 | 451 | 244 | 35 | 557 | 20 | 71 | 33 | 109 | 72 | .60 | 105 | .262 | .297 | .345 |

## Domingo Ramos

**Bats:** Right **Throws:** Right **Pos:** 3B/SS **Ht:** 5'10" **Wt:** 154 **Born:** 03/29/58 **Age:** 33

| BATTING | | | | | | | | | | | | | | | | | | | BASERUNNING | | | | PERCENTAGES | | |
|---|---|---|---|---|---|---|---|---|---|---|---|---|---|---|---|---|---|---|---|---|---|---|---|---|---|
| Year Team | Lg | G | AB | H | 2B | 3B | HR | (Hm | Rd) | TB | R | RBI | TBB | IBB | SO | HBP | SH | SF | SB | CS | SB% | GDP | Avg | OBP | SLG |
| 1978 New York | AL | 1 | 0 | 0 | 0 | 0 | 0 | (0 | 0) | 0 | 0 | 0 | 0 | 0 | 0 | 0 | 0 | 0 | 0 | 0 | .00 | 0 | .000 | .000 | .000 |
| 1980 Toronto | AL | 5 | 16 | 2 | 0 | 0 | 0 | (0 | 0) | 2 | 0 | 0 | 2 | 0 | 5 | 0 | 0 | 0 | 0 | 0 | .00 | 0 | .125 | .222 | .125 |
| 1982 Seattle | AL | 8 | 26 | 4 | 2 | 0 | 0 | (0 | 0) | 6 | 3 | 1 | 3 | 0 | 2 | 0 | 1 | 0 | 0 | 0 | .00 | 0 | .154 | .241 | .231 |
| 1983 Seattle | AL | 53 | 127 | 36 | 4 | 0 | 2 | (2 | 0) | 46 | 14 | 10 | 7 | 0 | 12 | 1 | 1 | 0 | 3 | 1 | .75 | 4 | .283 | .326 | .362 |
| 1984 Seattle | AL | 59 | 81 | 15 | 2 | 0 | 0 | (0 | 0) | 17 | 6 | 2 | 5 | 0 | 12 | 0 | 1 | 0 | 2 | 2 | .50 | 4 | .185 | .233 | .210 |
| 1985 Seattle | AL | 75 | 168 | 33 | 6 | 0 | 1 | (0 | 1) | 42 | 19 | 15 | 17 | 0 | 23 | 0 | 3 | 2 | 0 | 1 | .00 | 4 | .196 | .267 | .250 |
| 1986 Seattle | AL | 49 | 99 | 18 | 2 | 0 | 0 | (0 | 0) | 20 | 8 | 5 | 8 | 0 | 13 | 1 | 2 | 0 | 0 | 1 | .00 | 7 | .182 | .250 | .202 |
| 1987 Seattle | AL | 42 | 103 | 32 | 6 | 0 | 2 | (1 | 1) | 44 | 9 | 11 | 3 | 0 | 12 | 1 | 2 | 0 | 0 | 1 | .00 | 1 | .311 | .336 | .427 |
| 1988 2 ML Teams | | 32 | 61 | 14 | 1 | 0 | 0 | (0 | 0) | 15 | 10 | 5 | 3 | 0 | 7 | 1 | 0 | 2 | 0 | 0 | .00 | 2 | .230 | .269 | .246 |
| 1989 Chicago | NL | 85 | 179 | 47 | 6 | 2 | 1 | (1 | 0) | 60 | 18 | 19 | 17 | 4 | 23 | 2 | 6 | 0 | 1 | 1 | .50 | 10 | .263 | .333 | .335 |
| 1990 Chicago | NL | 98 | 226 | 60 | 5 | 0 | 2 | (2 | 0) | 71 | 22 | 17 | 27 | 1 | 29 | 1 | 2 | 3 | 0 | 2 | .00 | 7 | .265 | .342 | .314 |
| 1988 Cleveland | AL | 22 | 46 | 12 | 1 | 0 | 0 | (0 | 0) | 13 | 7 | 5 | 3 | 0 | 7 | 1 | 0 | 2 | 0 | 0 | .00 | 0 | .261 | .308 | .283 |
| California | AL | 10 | 15 | 2 | 0 | 0 | 0 | (0 | 0) | 2 | 3 | 0 | 0 | 0 | 0 | 0 | 0 | 0 | 0 | 0 | .00 | 2 | .133 | .133 | .133 |
| 11 ML YEARS | | 507 | 1086 | 261 | 34 | 2 | 8 | (6 | 2) | 323 | 109 | 85 | 92 | 5 | 138 | 7 | 18 | 7 | 6 | 9 | .40 | 39 | .240 | .302 | .297 |

## Willie Randolph

**Bats:** Right **Throws:** Right **Pos:** 2B **Ht:** 5'11" **Wt:** 163 **Born:** 07/06/54 **Age:** 36

| BATTING | | | | | | | | | | | | | | | | | | | BASERUNNING | | | | PERCENTAGES | | |
|---|---|---|---|---|---|---|---|---|---|---|---|---|---|---|---|---|---|---|---|---|---|---|---|---|---|
| Year Team | Lg | G | AB | H | 2B | 3B | HR | (Hm | Rd) | TB | R | RBI | TBB | IBB | SO | HBP | SH | SF | SB | CS | SB% | GDP | Avg | OBP | SLG |
| 1975 Pittsburgh | NL | 30 | 61 | 10 | 1 | 0 | 0 | (0 | 0) | 11 | 9 | 3 | 7 | 1 | 6 | 0 | 1 | 1 | 1 | 0 | 1.00 | 3 | .164 | .246 | .180 |
| 1976 New York | AL | 125 | 430 | 115 | 15 | 4 | 1 | (0 | 1) | 141 | 59 | 40 | 58 | 5 | 39 | 3 | 6 | 3 | 37 | 12 | .76 | 10 | .267 | .356 | .328 |
| 1977 New York | AL | 147 | 551 | 151 | 28 | 11 | 4 | (2 | 2) | 213 | 91 | 40 | 64 | 1 | 53 | 1 | 2 | 6 | 13 | 6 | .68 | 11 | .274 | .347 | .387 |
| 1978 New York | AL | 134 | 499 | 139 | 18 | 6 | 3 | (2 | 1) | 178 | 87 | 42 | 82 | 1 | 51 | 4 | 6 | 5 | 36 | 7 | .84 | 12 | .279 | .381 | .357 |
| 1979 New York | AL | 153 | 574 | 155 | 15 | 13 | 5 | (2 | 3) | 211 | 98 | 61 | 95 | 5 | 39 | 3 | 5 | 5 | 33 | 12 | .73 | 23 | .270 | .374 | .368 |
| 1980 New York | AL | 138 | 513 | 151 | 23 | 7 | 7 | (2 | 5) | 209 | 99 | 46 | 119 | 4 | 45 | 2 | 5 | 3 | 30 | 5 | .86 | 6 | .294 | .427 | .407 |
| 1981 New York | AL | 93 | 357 | 83 | 14 | 3 | 2 | (1 | 1) | 109 | 59 | 24 | 57 | 0 | 24 | 0 | 5 | 3 | 14 | 5 | .74 | 10 | .232 | .336 | .305 |

| 1982 New York | AL | 144 | 553 | 155 | 21 | 4 | 3 | (1 | 2) | 193 | 85 | 36 | 75 | 3 | 35 | 3 | 10 | 2 | 16 | 9 | .64 | 13 | .280 | .368 | .349 |
|---|---|---|---|---|---|---|---|---|---|---|---|---|---|---|---|---|---|---|---|---|---|---|---|---|---|
| 1983 New York | AL | 104 | 420 | 117 | 21 | 1 | 2 | (1 | 1) | 146 | 73 | 38 | 53 | 0 | 32 | 1 | 3 | 0 | 12 | 4 | .75 | 11 | .279 | .361 | .348 |
| 1984 New York | AL | 142 | 564 | 162 | 24 | 2 | 2 | (1 | 1) | 196 | 86 | 31 | 86 | 4 | 42 | 0 | 7 | 7 | 10 | 6 | .63 | 15 | .287 | .377 | .348 |
| 1985 New York | AL | 143 | 497 | 137 | 21 | 2 | 5 | (3 | 2) | 177 | 75 | 40 | 85 | 3 | 39 | 4 | 5 | 6 | 16 | 9 | .64 | 24 | .276 | .382 | .356 |
| 1986 New York | AL | 141 | 492 | 136 | 15 | 2 | 5 | (2 | 3) | 170 | 76 | 50 | 94 | 0 | 49 | 3 | 8 | 4 | 15 | 2 | .88 | 11 | .276 | .393 | .346 |
| 1987 New York | AL | 120 | 449 | 137 | 24 | 2 | 7 | (3 | 4) | 186 | 96 | 67 | 82 | 1 | 25 | 2 | 5 | 5 | 11 | 1 | .92 | 15 | .305 | .411 | .414 |
| 1988 New York | AL | 110 | 404 | 93 | 20 | 1 | 2 | (1 | 1) | 121 | 43 | 34 | 55 | 2 | 39 | 2 | 8 | 5 | 8 | 4 | .67 | 10 | .230 | .322 | .300 |
| 1989 Los Angeles | NL | 145 | 549 | 155 | 18 | 0 | 2 | (0 | 2) | 179 | 62 | 36 | 71 | 2 | 51 | 4 | 4 | 5 | 7 | 6 | .54 | 10 | .282 | .366 | .326 |
| 1990 2 ML Teams | | 119 | 388 | 101 | 13 | 3 | 2 | (1 | 1) | 126 | 52 | 30 | 45 | 1 | 34 | 2 | 10 | 1 | 7 | 1 | .88 | 14 | .260 | .339 | .325 |
| 1990 Los Angeles | NL | 26 | 96 | 26 | 4 | 0 | 1 | (0 | 1) | 33 | 15 | 9 | 13 | 0 | 9 | 1 | 3 | 0 | 1 | 0 | 1.00 | 3 | .271 | .364 | .344 |
| Oakland | AL | 93 | 292 | 75 | 9 | 3 | 1 | (1 | 0) | 93 | 37 | 21 | 32 | 1 | 25 | 1 | 7 | 1 | 6 | 1 | .86 | 11 | .257 | .331 | .318 |
| 16 ML YEARS | | 1988 | 7301 | 1997 | 291 | 61 | 52 | (22 | 30) | 2566 | 1150 | 618 | 1128 | 33 | 603 | 34 | 90 | 61 | 266 | 89 | .75 | 198 | .274 | .371 | .351 |

## Dennis Rasmussen

**Pitches:** Left **Bats:** Left **Pos:** SP **Ht:** 6' 7" **Wt:** 225 **Born:** 04/18/59 **Age:** 32

| HOW MUCH HE PITCHED | | | | | | | | WHAT HE GAVE UP | | | | | | | | | | | | THE RESULTS | | | | | |
|---|---|---|---|---|---|---|---|---|---|---|---|---|---|---|---|---|---|---|---|---|---|---|---|---|---|
| Year Team | Lg | G | GS | CG | GF | IP | BFP | H | R | ER | HR | SH | SF | HB | TBB | IBB | SO | WP | Bk | W | L | Pct. | ShO | Sv | ERA |
| 1983 San Diego | NL | 4 | 1 | 0 | 1 | 13.2 | 58 | 10 | 5 | 3 | 1 | 0 | 0 | 0 | 8 | 0 | 13 | 1 | 0 | 0 | 0 | .000 | 0 | 0 | 1.98 |
| 1984 New York | AL | 24 | 24 | 1 | 0 | 147.2 | 616 | 127 | 79 | 75 | 16 | 3 | 7 | 4 | 60 | 0 | 110 | 8 | 2 | 9 | 6 | .600 | 0 | 0 | 4.57 |
| 1985 New York | AL | 22 | 16 | 2 | 1 | 101.2 | 429 | 97 | 56 | 45 | 10 | 1 | 5 | 1 | 42 | 1 | 63 | 3 | 1 | 3 | 5 | .375 | 0 | 0 | 3.98 |
| 1986 New York | AL | 31 | 31 | 3 | 0 | 202 | 819 | 160 | 91 | 87 | 28 | 1 | 5 | 2 | 74 | 0 | 131 | 5 | 0 | 18 | 6 | .750 | 1 | 0 | 3.88 |
| 1987 2 ML Teams | | 33 | 32 | 2 | 0 | 191.1 | 814 | 184 | 100 | 97 | 36 | 8 | 6 | 5 | 67 | 1 | 128 | 7 | 2 | 13 | 8 | .619 | 0 | 0 | 4.56 |
| 1988 2 ML Teams | | 31 | 31 | 7 | 0 | 204.2 | 854 | 199 | 84 | 78 | 17 | 10 | 4 | 4 | 58 | 4 | 112 | 7 | 5 | 16 | 10 | .615 | 1 | 0 | 3.43 |
| 1989 San Diego | NL | 33 | 33 | 1 | 0 | 183.2 | 799 | 190 | 100 | 87 | 18 | 9 | 11 | 3 | 72 | 6 | 87 | 4 | 2 | 10 | 10 | .500 | 0 | 0 | 4.26 |
| 1990 San Diego | NL | 32 | 32 | 3 | 0 | 187.2 | 825 | 217 | 110 | 94 | 28 | 14 | 4 | 3 | 62 | 4 | 86 | 9 | 1 | 11 | 15 | .423 | 1 | 0 | 4.51 |
| 1987 New York | AL | 26 | 25 | 2 | 0 | 146 | 627 | 145 | 78 | 77 | 31 | 5 | 5 | 4 | 55 | 1 | 89 | 6 | 0 | 9 | 7 | .563 | 0 | 0 | 4.75 |
| Cincinnati | NL | 7 | 7 | 0 | 0 | 45.1 | 187 | 39 | 22 | 20 | 5 | 3 | 1 | 1 | 12 | 0 | 39 | 1 | 2 | 4 | 1 | .800 | 0 | 0 | 3.97 |
| 1988 Cincinnati | NL | 11 | 11 | 1 | 0 | 56.1 | 255 | 68 | 36 | 36 | 8 | 2 | 2 | 2 | 22 | 4 | 27 | 1 | 5 | 2 | 6 | .250 | 1 | 0 | 5.75 |
| San Diego | NL | 20 | 20 | 6 | 0 | 148.1 | 599 | 131 | 48 | 42 | 9 | 8 | 2 | 2 | 36 | 0 | 85 | 6 | 0 | 14 | 4 | .778 | 0 | 0 | 2.55 |
| 8 ML YEARS | | 210 | 200 | 19 | 2 | 1232.1 | 5214 | 1184 | 625 | 566 | 154 | 46 | 42 | 22 | 443 | 16 | 730 | 44 | 13 | 80 | 60 | .571 | 3 | 0 | 4.13 |

## Johnny Ray

**Bats:** Both **Throws:** Right **Pos:** 2B **Ht:** 5'11" **Wt:** 189 **Born:** 03/01/57 **Age:** 34

| BATTING | | | | | | | | | | | | | | | | | | | BASERUNNING | | | | PERCENTAGES | | |
|---|---|---|---|---|---|---|---|---|---|---|---|---|---|---|---|---|---|---|---|---|---|---|---|---|---|
| Year Team | Lg | G | AB | H | 2B | 3B | HR | (Hm | Rd) | TB | R | RBI | TBB | IBB | SO | HBP | SH | SF | SB | CS | SB% | GDP | Avg | OBP | SLG |
| 1981 Pittsburgh | NL | 31 | 102 | 25 | 11 | 0 | 0 | (0 | 0) | 36 | 10 | 6 | 6 | 2 | 9 | 0 | 0 | 1 | 0 | 0 | .00 | 3 | .245 | .284 | .353 |
| 1982 Pittsburgh | NL | 162 | 647 | 182 | 30 | 7 | 7 | (6 | 1) | 247 | 79 | 63 | 36 | 1 | 34 | 1 | 13 | 5 | 16 | 7 | .70 | 8 | .281 | .318 | .382 |
| 1983 Pittsburgh | NL | 151 | 576 | 163 | 38 | 7 | 5 | (3 | 2) | 230 | 68 | 53 | 35 | 3 | 26 | 0 | 10 | 2 | 18 | 9 | .67 | 11 | .283 | .323 | .399 |
| 1984 Pittsburgh | NL | 155 | 555 | 173 | 38 | 6 | 6 | (3 | 3) | 241 | 75 | 67 | 37 | 2 | 31 | 3 | 2 | 6 | 11 | 6 | .65 | 16 | .312 | .354 | .434 |
| 1985 Pittsburgh | NL | 154 | 594 | 163 | 33 | 3 | 7 | (3 | 4) | 223 | 67 | 70 | 46 | 10 | 24 | 1 | 5 | 6 | 13 | 9 | .59 | 11 | .274 | .325 | .375 |
| 1986 Pittsburgh | NL | 155 | 579 | 174 | 33 | 0 | 7 | (2 | 5) | 228 | 67 | 78 | 58 | 10 | 47 | 3 | 1 | 7 | 6 | 9 | .40 | 21 | .301 | .363 | .394 |
| 1987 2 ML Teams | | 153 | 599 | 173 | 30 | 3 | 5 | (5 | 0) | 224 | 64 | 69 | 44 | 4 | 46 | 0 | 1 | 6 | 4 | 2 | .67 | 22 | .289 | .334 | .374 |
| 1988 California | AL | 153 | 602 | 184 | 42 | 7 | 6 | (4 | 2) | 258 | 75 | 83 | 36 | 2 | 38 | 4 | 9 | 8 | 4 | 1 | .80 | 10 | .306 | .345 | .429 |
| 1989 California | AL | 134 | 530 | 153 | 16 | 3 | 5 | (3 | 2) | 190 | 52 | 62 | 36 | 3 | 30 | 0 | 4 | 12 | 6 | 3 | .67 | 14 | .289 | .327 | .358 |
| 1990 California | AL | 105 | 404 | 112 | 23 | 0 | 5 | (5 | 0) | 150 | 47 | 43 | 19 | 2 | 44 | 0 | 3 | 3 | 2 | 3 | .40 | 10 | .277 | .308 | .371 |
| 1987 Pittsburgh | NL | 123 | 472 | 129 | 19 | 3 | 5 | (5 | 0) | 169 | 48 | 54 | 41 | 4 | 36 | 0 | 0 | 5 | 4 | 2 | .67 | 18 | .273 | .328 | .358 |
| California | AL | 30 | 127 | 44 | 11 | 0 | 0 | (0 | 0) | 55 | 16 | 15 | 3 | 0 | 10 | 0 | 1 | 1 | 0 | 0 | .00 | 4 | .346 | .359 | .433 |
| 10 ML YEARS | | 1353 | 5188 | 1502 | 294 | 36 | 53 | (34 | 19) | 2027 | 604 | 594 | 353 | 39 | 329 | 12 | 48 | 56 | 80 | 49 | .62 | 126 | .290 | .333 | .391 |

## Randy Ready

**Bats:** Right **Throws:** Right **Pos:** LF/2B **Ht:** 5'11" **Wt:** 180 **Born:** 01/08/60 **Age:** 31

| BATTING | | | | | | | | | | | | | | | | | | | BASERUNNING | | | | PERCENTAGES | | |
|---|---|---|---|---|---|---|---|---|---|---|---|---|---|---|---|---|---|---|---|---|---|---|---|---|---|
| Year Team | Lg | G | AB | H | 2B | 3B | HR | (Hm | Rd) | TB | R | RBI | TBB | IBB | SO | HBP | SH | SF | SB | CS | SB% | GDP | Avg | OBP | SLG |
| 1983 Milwaukee | AL | 12 | 37 | 15 | 3 | 2 | 1 | (0 | 1) | 25 | 8 | 6 | 6 | 1 | 3 | 0 | 0 | 0 | 0 | 1 | .00 | 0 | .405 | .488 | .676 |
| 1984 Milwaukee | AL | 37 | 123 | 23 | 6 | 1 | 3 | (3 | 0) | 40 | 13 | 13 | 14 | 0 | 18 | 0 | 3 | 0 | 0 | 0 | .00 | 2 | .187 | .270 | .325 |
| 1985 Milwaukee | AL | 48 | 181 | 48 | 9 | 5 | 1 | (0 | 1) | 70 | 29 | 21 | 14 | 0 | 23 | 1 | 2 | 2 | 0 | 0 | .00 | 6 | .265 | .318 | .387 |
| 1986 2 ML Teams | | 24 | 82 | 15 | 4 | 0 | 1 | (0 | 1) | 22 | 8 | 4 | 9 | 0 | 10 | 0 | 1 | 0 | 2 | 0 | 1.00 | 3 | .183 | .264 | .268 |
| 1987 San Diego | NL | 124 | 350 | 108 | 26 | 6 | 12 | (7 | 5) | 182 | 69 | 54 | 67 | 2 | 44 | 3 | 2 | 1 | 7 | 3 | .70 | 7 | .309 | .423 | .520 |
| 1988 San Diego | NL | 114 | 331 | 88 | 16 | 2 | 7 | (3 | 4) | 129 | 43 | 39 | 39 | 1 | 38 | 3 | 4 | 3 | 6 | 2 | .75 | 3 | .266 | .346 | .390 |
| 1989 2 ML Teams | | 100 | 254 | 67 | 13 | 2 | 8 | (3 | 5) | 108 | 37 | 26 | 42 | 0 | 37 | 2 | 1 | 4 | 4 | 3 | .57 | 4 | .264 | .368 | .425 |
| 1990 Philadelphia | NL | 101 | 217 | 53 | 9 | 1 | 1 | (0 | 1) | 67 | 26 | 26 | 29 | 0 | 35 | 1 | 3 | 3 | 3 | 2 | .60 | 3 | .244 | .332 | .309 |
| 1986 Milwaukee | AL | 23 | 79 | 15 | 4 | 0 | 1 | (0 | 1) | 22 | 8 | 4 | 9 | 0 | 9 | 0 | 1 | 0 | 2 | 0 | 1.00 | 3 | .190 | .273 | .278 |
| San Diego | NL | 1 | 3 | 0 | 0 | 0 | 0 | (0 | 0) | 0 | 0 | 0 | 0 | 0 | 1 | 0 | 0 | 0 | 0 | 0 | .00 | 0 | .000 | .000 | .000 |
| 1989 San Diego | NL | 28 | 67 | 17 | 2 | 1 | 0 | (0 | 0) | 21 | 4 | 5 | 11 | 0 | 6 | 0 | 1 | 1 | 0 | 0 | .00 | 2 | .254 | .354 | .313 |
| Philadelphia | NL | 72 | 187 | 50 | 11 | 1 | 8 | (3 | 5) | 87 | 33 | 21 | 31 | 0 | 31 | 2 | 0 | 3 | 4 | 3 | .57 | 2 | .267 | .372 | .465 |
| 8 ML YEARS | | 560 | 1575 | 417 | 86 | 19 | 34 | (16 | 18) | 643 | 233 | 189 | 220 | 4 | 208 | 10 | 16 | 13 | 22 | 11 | .67 | 28 | .265 | .356 | .408 |

## Jeff Reardon

**Pitches:** Right **Bats:** Right **Pos:** RP **Ht:** 6' 0" **Wt:** 200 **Born:** 10/01/55 **Age:** 35

| | | | HOW MUCH HE PITCHED | | | | | | WHAT HE GAVE UP | | | | | | | | | | | | THE RESULTS | | | | | |
|---|---|---|---|---|---|---|---|---|---|---|---|---|---|---|---|---|---|---|---|---|---|---|---|---|---|---|
| Year | Team | Lg | G | GS | CG | GF | IP | BFP | H | R | ER | HR | SH | SF | HB | TBB | IBB | SO | WP | Bk | W | L | Pct. | ShO | Sv | ERA |
| 1979 | New York | NL | 18 | 0 | 0 | 10 | 21 | 81 | 12 | 7 | 4 | 2 | 2 | 1 | 0 | 9 | 3 | 10 | 2 | 0 | 1 | 2 | .333 | 0 | 2 | 1.71 |
| 1980 | New York | NL | 61 | 0 | 0 | 35 | 110 | 475 | 96 | 36 | 32 | 10 | 8 | 5 | 0 | 47 | 15 | 101 | 2 | 0 | 8 | 7 | .533 | 0 | 6 | 2.62 |
| 1981 | 2 ML Teams | | 43 | 0 | 0 | 33 | 70.1 | 279 | 48 | 17 | 17 | 5 | 3 | 1 | 2 | 21 | 4 | 49 | 1 | 0 | 3 | 0 | 1.000 | 0 | 8 | 2.18 |
| 1982 | Montreal | NL | 75 | 0 | 0 | 53 | 109 | 444 | 87 | 28 | 25 | 6 | 8 | 4 | 2 | 36 | 4 | 86 | 2 | 0 | 7 | 4 | .636 | 0 | 26 | 2.06 |
| 1983 | Montreal | NL | 66 | 0 | 0 | 53 | 92 | 403 | 87 | 34 | 31 | 7 | 8 | 2 | 1 | 44 | 9 | 78 | 2 | 0 | 7 | 9 | .438 | 0 | 21 | 3.03 |
| 1984 | Montreal | NL | 68 | 0 | 0 | 58 | 87 | 363 | 70 | 31 | 28 | 5 | 3 | 2 | 3 | 37 | 7 | 79 | 4 | 0 | 7 | 7 | .500 | 0 | 23 | 2.90 |
| 1985 | Montreal | NL | 63 | 0 | 0 | 50 | 87.2 | 356 | 68 | 31 | 31 | 7 | 3 | 1 | 1 | 26 | 4 | 67 | 2 | 0 | 2 | 8 | .200 | 0 | 41 | 3.18 |
| 1986 | Montreal | NL | 62 | 0 | 0 | 48 | 89 | 368 | 83 | 42 | 39 | 12 | 9 | 1 | 1 | 26 | 2 | 67 | 0 | 0 | 7 | 9 | .438 | 0 | 35 | 3.94 |
| 1987 | Minnesota | AL | 63 | 0 | 0 | 58 | 80.1 | 337 | 70 | 41 | 40 | 14 | 1 | 3 | 3 | 28 | 4 | 83 | 2 | 0 | 8 | 8 | .500 | 0 | 31 | 4.48 |
| 1988 | Minnesota | AL | 63 | 0 | 0 | 58 | 73 | 299 | 68 | 21 | 20 | 6 | 4 | 1 | 2 | 15 | 2 | 56 | 0 | 3 | 2 | 4 | .333 | 0 | 42 | 2.47 |
| 1989 | Minnesota | AL | 65 | 0 | 0 | 61 | 73 | 297 | 68 | 33 | 33 | 8 | 1 | 5 | 3 | 12 | 3 | 46 | 1 | 1 | 5 | 4 | .556 | 0 | 31 | 4.07 |
| 1990 | Boston | AL | 47 | 0 | 0 | 37 | 51.1 | 210 | 39 | 19 | 18 | 5 | 1 | 0 | 1 | 19 | 4 | 33 | 0 | 0 | 5 | 3 | .625 | 0 | 21 | 3.16 |
| 1981 | New York | NL | 18 | 0 | 0 | 14 | 28.2 | 124 | 27 | 11 | 11 | 2 | 0 | 1 | 1 | 12 | 4 | 28 | 0 | 0 | 1 | 0 | 1.000 | 0 | 2 | 3.45 |
| | Montreal | NL | 25 | 0 | 0 | 19 | 41.2 | 155 | 21 | 6 | 6 | 3 | 3 | 0 | 1 | 9 | 0 | 21 | 1 | 0 | 2 | 0 | 1.000 | 0 | 6 | 1.30 |
| | 12 ML YEARS | | 694 | 0 | 0 | 554 | 943.2 | 3912 | 796 | 340 | 318 | 87 | 51 | 26 | 19 | 320 | 61 | 755 | 18 | 4 | 62 | 65 | .488 | 0 | 287 | 3.03 |

## Gary Redus

**Bats:** Right **Throws:** Right **Pos:** 1B **Ht:** 6' 1" **Wt:** 185 **Born:** 11/01/56 **Age:** 34

| | | | BATTING | | | | | | | | | | | | | | | | | BASERUNNING | | | | PERCENTAGES | | |
|---|---|---|---|---|---|---|---|---|---|---|---|---|---|---|---|---|---|---|---|---|---|---|---|---|---|---|
| Year | Team | Lg | G | AB | H | 2B | 3B | HR | (Hm | Rd) | TB | R | RBI | TBB | IBB | SO | HBP | SH | SF | SB | CS | SB% | GDP | Avg | OBP | SLG |
| 1982 | Cincinnati | NL | 20 | 83 | 18 | 3 | 2 | 1 | (1 | 0) | 28 | 12 | 7 | 5 | 0 | 21 | 0 | 0 | 1 | 11 | 2 | .85 | 0 | .217 | .258 | .337 |
| 1983 | Cincinnati | NL | 125 | 453 | 112 | 20 | 9 | 17 | (6 | 11) | 201 | 90 | 51 | 71 | 4 | 111 | 3 | 2 | 2 | 39 | 14 | .74 | 6 | .247 | .352 | .444 |
| 1984 | Cincinnati | NL | 123 | 394 | 100 | 21 | 3 | 7 | (4 | 3) | 148 | 69 | 22 | 52 | 3 | 71 | 1 | 3 | 5 | 48 | 11 | .81 | 4 | .254 | .338 | .376 |
| 1985 | Cincinnati | NL | 101 | 246 | 62 | 14 | 4 | 6 | (4 | 2) | 102 | 51 | 28 | 44 | 2 | 52 | 1 | 2 | 1 | 48 | 12 | .80 | 0 | .252 | .366 | .415 |
| 1986 | Philadelphia | NL | 90 | 340 | 84 | 22 | 4 | 11 | (8 | 3) | 147 | 62 | 33 | 47 | 4 | 78 | 3 | 1 | 1 | 25 | 7 | .78 | 2 | .247 | .343 | .432 |
| 1987 | Chicago | AL | 130 | 475 | 112 | 26 | 6 | 12 | (4 | 8) | 186 | 78 | 48 | 69 | 0 | 90 | 0 | 3 | 7 | 52 | 11 | .83 | 7 | .236 | .328 | .392 |
| 1988 | 2 ML Teams | | 107 | 333 | 83 | 12 | 4 | 8 | (3 | 5) | 127 | 54 | 38 | 48 | 1 | 71 | 3 | 0 | 8 | 31 | 4 | .89 | 6 | .249 | .342 | .381 |
| 1989 | Pittsburgh | NL | 98 | 279 | 79 | 18 | 7 | 6 | (3 | 3) | 129 | 42 | 33 | 40 | 3 | 51 | 1 | 1 | 3 | 25 | 6 | .81 | 5 | .283 | .372 | .462 |
| 1990 | Pittsburgh | NL | 96 | 227 | 56 | 15 | 3 | 6 | (2 | 4) | 95 | 32 | 23 | 33 | 0 | 38 | 2 | 1 | 5 | 11 | 5 | .69 | 1 | .247 | .341 | .419 |
| 1988 | Chicago | AL | 77 | 262 | 69 | 10 | 4 | 6 | (1 | 5) | 105 | 42 | 34 | 33 | 1 | 52 | 2 | 0 | 7 | 26 | 2 | .93 | 5 | .263 | .342 | .401 |
| | Pittsburgh | NL | 30 | 71 | 14 | 2 | 0 | 2 | (2 | 0) | 22 | 12 | 4 | 15 | 0 | 19 | 1 | 0 | 1 | 5 | 2 | .71 | 1 | .197 | .341 | .310 |
| | 9 ML YEARS | | 890 | 2830 | 706 | 151 | 42 | 74 | (35 | 39) | 1163 | 490 | 283 | 409 | 17 | 583 | 14 | 13 | 33 | 290 | 72 | .80 | 31 | .249 | .344 | .411 |

## Darren Reed

**Bats:** Right **Throws:** Right **Pos:** CF **Ht:** 6' 1" **Wt:** 190 **Born:** 10/16/65 **Age:** 25

| | | | BATTING | | | | | | | | | | | | | | | | | BASERUNNING | | | | PERCENTAGES | | |
|---|---|---|---|---|---|---|---|---|---|---|---|---|---|---|---|---|---|---|---|---|---|---|---|---|---|---|
| Year | Team | Lg | G | AB | H | 2B | 3B | HR | (Hm | Rd) | TB | R | RBI | TBB | IBB | SO | HBP | SH | SF | SB | CS | SB% | GDP | Avg | OBP | SLG |
| 1984 | Oneonta | A | 40 | 113 | 26 | 7 | 0 | 2 | -- | -- | 39 | 17 | 9 | 10 | 0 | 19 | 0 | 1 | 1 | 2 | 1 | .67 | 2 | .230 | .290 | .345 |
| 1985 | Ft.Laudrdle | A | 100 | 369 | 117 | 21 | 4 | 10 | -- | -- | 176 | 63 | 61 | 36 | 3 | 56 | 7 | 0 | 7 | 13 | 3 | .81 | 9 | .317 | .382 | .477 |
| 1986 | Albany | AA | 51 | 196 | 45 | 11 | 1 | 4 | -- | -- | 70 | 22 | 27 | 15 | 0 | 24 | 1 | 1 | 5 | 1 | 0 | 1.00 | 2 | .230 | .281 | .357 |
| 1987 | Columbus | AAA | 21 | 79 | 26 | 3 | 3 | 8 | -- | -- | 59 | 15 | 16 | 4 | 0 | 9 | 0 | 0 | 0 | 0 | 2 | .00 | 2 | .329 | .361 | .747 |
| | Albany | AA | 107 | 404 | 129 | 23 | 4 | 20 | -- | -- | 220 | 68 | 79 | 51 | 9 | 50 | 8 | 0 | 3 | 9 | 6 | .60 | 10 | .319 | .403 | .545 |
| 1988 | Tidewater | AAA | 101 | 345 | 83 | 26 | 0 | 9 | -- | -- | 136 | 31 | 47 | 32 | 2 | 66 | 3 | 3 | 4 | 0 | 3 | .00 | 9 | .241 | .307 | .394 |
| 1989 | Tidewater | AAA | 133 | 444 | 119 | 30 | 6 | 4 | -- | -- | 173 | 57 | 50 | 60 | 1 | 70 | 11 | 1 | 4 | 11 | 2 | .85 | 15 | .268 | .366 | .390 |
| 1990 | Tidewater | AAA | 104 | 359 | 95 | 21 | 6 | 17 | -- | -- | 179 | 58 | 74 | 51 | 4 | 62 | 6 | 0 | 4 | 15 | 4 | .79 | 11 | .265 | .362 | .499 |
| 1990 | New York | NL | 26 | 39 | 8 | 4 | 1 | 1 | (1 | 0) | 17 | 5 | 2 | 3 | 0 | 11 | 0 | 0 | 0 | 1 | 0 | 1.00 | 0 | .205 | .262 | .436 |

## Jeff Reed

**Bats:** Left **Throws:** Right **Pos:** C **Ht:** 6' 2" **Wt:** 190 **Born:** 11/12/62 **Age:** 28

| | | | BATTING | | | | | | | | | | | | | | | | | BASERUNNING | | | | PERCENTAGES | | |
|---|---|---|---|---|---|---|---|---|---|---|---|---|---|---|---|---|---|---|---|---|---|---|---|---|---|---|
| Year | Team | Lg | G | AB | H | 2B | 3B | HR | (Hm | Rd) | TB | R | RBI | TBB | IBB | SO | HBP | SH | SF | SB | CS | SB% | GDP | Avg | OBP | SLG |
| 1984 | Minnesota | AL | 18 | 21 | 3 | 3 | 0 | 0 | (0 | 0) | 6 | 3 | 1 | 2 | 0 | 6 | 0 | 1 | 0 | 0 | 0 | .00 | 0 | .143 | .217 | .286 |
| 1985 | Minnesota | AL | 7 | 10 | 2 | 0 | 0 | 0 | (0 | 0) | 2 | 2 | 0 | 0 | 0 | 3 | 0 | 0 | 0 | 0 | 0 | .00 | 0 | .200 | .200 | .200 |
| 1986 | Minnesota | AL | 68 | 165 | 39 | 6 | 1 | 2 | (1 | 1) | 53 | 13 | 9 | 16 | 0 | 19 | 1 | 3 | 0 | 1 | 0 | 1.00 | 2 | .236 | .308 | .321 |
| 1987 | Montreal | NL | 75 | 207 | 44 | 11 | 0 | 1 | (1 | 0) | 58 | 15 | 21 | 12 | 1 | 20 | 1 | 4 | 4 | 0 | 1 | .00 | 8 | .213 | .254 | .280 |
| 1988 | 2 ML Teams | | 92 | 265 | 60 | 9 | 2 | 1 | (1 | 0) | 76 | 20 | 16 | 28 | 1 | 41 | 0 | 1 | 1 | 1 | 0 | 1.00 | 5 | .226 | .299 | .287 |
| 1989 | Cincinnati | NL | 102 | 287 | 64 | 11 | 0 | 3 | (1 | 2) | 84 | 16 | 23 | 34 | 5 | 46 | 2 | 3 | 4 | 0 | 0 | .00 | 6 | .223 | .306 | .293 |
| 1990 | Cincinnati | NL | 72 | 175 | 44 | 8 | 1 | 3 | (2 | 1) | 63 | 12 | 16 | 24 | 5 | 26 | 0 | 5 | 1 | 0 | 0 | .00 | 4 | .251 | .340 | .360 |
| 1988 | Montreal | NL | 43 | 123 | 27 | 3 | 2 | 0 | (0 | 0) | 34 | 10 | 9 | 13 | 1 | 22 | 0 | 1 | 1 | 1 | 0 | 1.00 | 3 | .220 | .292 | .276 |
| | Cincinnati | NL | 49 | 142 | 33 | 6 | 0 | 1 | (1 | 0) | 42 | 10 | 7 | 15 | 0 | 19 | 0 | 0 | 0 | 0 | 0 | .00 | 2 | .232 | .306 | .296 |
| | 7 ML YEARS | | 434 | 1130 | 256 | 48 | 4 | 10 | (6 | 4) | 342 | 81 | 86 | 116 | 12 | 161 | 4 | 17 | 10 | 2 | 1 | .67 | 25 | .227 | .298 | .303 |

## Jerry Reed

**Pitches:** Right **Bats:** Right **Pos:** RP **Ht:** 6' 1" **Wt:** 190 **Born:** 10/08/55 **Age:** 35

| | | HOW MUCH HE PITCHED | | | | | | WHAT HE GAVE UP | | | | | | | | | | | | THE RESULTS | | | | | |
|---|---|---|---|---|---|---|---|---|---|---|---|---|---|---|---|---|---|---|---|---|---|---|---|---|---|
| Year Team | Lg | G | GS | CG | GF | IP | BFP | H | R | ER | HR | SH | SF | HB | TBB | IBB | SO | WP | Bk | W | L | Pct. | ShO | Sv | ERA |
| 1981 Philadelphia | NL | 4 | 0 | 0 | 2 | 5 | 27 | 7 | 4 | 4 | 0 | 0 | 0 | 0 | 6 | 0 | 5 | 0 | 0 | 0 | 1 | .000 | 0 | 0 | 7.20 |
| 1982 2 ML Teams | | 13 | 1 | 0 | 2 | 24.1 | 101 | 26 | 12 | 11 | 1 | 0 | 0 | 1 | 6 | 0 | 11 | 0 | 0 | 2 | 1 | .667 | 0 | 0 | 4.07 |
| 1983 Cleveland | AL | 7 | 0 | 0 | 1 | 21.1 | 95 | 26 | 19 | 17 | 4 | 1 | 1 | 0 | 9 | 1 | 11 | 0 | 0 | 0 | 0 | .000 | 0 | 0 | 7.17 |
| 1985 Cleveland | AL | 33 | 5 | 0 | 19 | 72.1 | 301 | 67 | 41 | 33 | 12 | 2 | 4 | 3 | 19 | 2 | 37 | 4 | 0 | 3 | 5 | .375 | 0 | 8 | 4.11 |
| 1986 Seattle | AL | 11 | 4 | 0 | 4 | 34.2 | 152 | 38 | 13 | 12 | 3 | 0 | 0 | 0 | 13 | 0 | 16 | 1 | 0 | 4 | 0 | 1.000 | 0 | 0 | 3.12 |
| 1987 Seattle | AL | 39 | 1 | 0 | 17 | 81.2 | 340 | 79 | 32 | 31 | 7 | 2 | 1 | 3 | 24 | 3 | 51 | 1 | 0 | 1 | 2 | .333 | 0 | 7 | 3.42 |
| 1988 Seattle | AL | 46 | 0 | 0 | 19 | 86.1 | 363 | 82 | 42 | 38 | 8 | 3 | 5 | 2 | 33 | 7 | 48 | 1 | 7 | 1 | 1 | .500 | 0 | 1 | 3.96 |
| 1989 Seattle | AL | 52 | 1 | 0 | 14 | 101.2 | 432 | 89 | 44 | 36 | 10 | 7 | 2 | 1 | 43 | 10 | 50 | 5 | 1 | 7 | 7 | .500 | 0 | 0 | 3.19 |
| 1990 2 ML Teams | | 33 | 0 | 0 | 16 | 52.1 | 234 | 63 | 31 | 28 | 2 | 2 | 3 | 0 | 19 | 2 | 19 | 7 | 1 | 2 | 2 | .500 | 0 | 2 | 4.82 |
| 1982 Philadelphia | NL | 7 | 0 | 0 | 1 | 8.2 | 38 | 11 | 6 | 5 | 0 | 0 | 0 | 1 | 3 | 0 | 1 | 0 | 0 | 1 | 0 | 1.000 | 0 | 0 | 5.19 |
| Cleveland | AL | 6 | 1 | 0 | 1 | 15.2 | 63 | 15 | 6 | 6 | 1 | 0 | 0 | 0 | 3 | 0 | 10 | 0 | 0 | 1 | 1 | .500 | 0 | 0 | 3.45 |
| 1990 Seattle | AL | 4 | 0 | 0 | 1 | 7.1 | 31 | 8 | 4 | 4 | 1 | 0 | 0 | 0 | 3 | 0 | 2 | 0 | 0 | 0 | 1 | .000 | 0 | 0 | 4.91 |
| Boston | AL | 29 | 0 | 0 | 15 | 45 | 203 | 55 | 27 | 24 | 1 | 2 | 3 | 0 | 16 | 2 | 17 | 7 | 1 | 2 | 1 | .667 | 0 | 2 | 4.80 |
| 9 ML YEARS | | 238 | 12 | 0 | 94 | 479.2 | 2045 | 477 | 238 | 210 | 47 | 17 | 16 | 10 | 172 | 25 | 248 | 19 | 9 | 20 | 19 | .513 | 0 | 18 | 3.94 |

## Jody Reed

**Bats:** Right **Throws:** Right **Pos:** 2B/SS **Ht:** 5' 9" **Wt:** 160 **Born:** 07/26/62 **Age:** 28

| | | BATTING | | | | | | | | | | | | | | | | | BASERUNNING | | | | PERCENTAGES | | |
|---|---|---|---|---|---|---|---|---|---|---|---|---|---|---|---|---|---|---|---|---|---|---|---|---|---|
| Year Team | Lg | G | AB | H | 2B | 3B | HR | (Hm | Rd) | TB | R | RBI | TBB | IBB | SO | HBP | SH | SF | SB | CS | SB% | GDP | Avg | OBP | SLG |
| 1987 Boston | AL | 9 | 30 | 9 | 1 | 1 | 0 | (0 | 0) | 12 | 4 | 8 | 4 | 0 | 0 | 0 | 1 | 0 | 1 | 1 | .50 | 0 | .300 | .382 | .400 |
| 1988 Boston | AL | 109 | 338 | 99 | 23 | 1 | 1 | (1 | 0) | 127 | 60 | 28 | 45 | 1 | 21 | 4 | 11 | 2 | 1 | 3 | .25 | 5 | .293 | .380 | .376 |
| 1989 Boston | AL | 146 | 524 | 151 | 42 | 2 | 3 | (2 | 1) | 206 | 76 | 40 | 73 | 0 | 44 | 4 | 13 | 5 | 4 | 5 | .44 | 12 | .288 | .376 | .393 |
| 1990 Boston | AL | 155 | 598 | 173 | 45 | 0 | 5 | (3 | 2) | 233 | 70 | 51 | 75 | 4 | 65 | 4 | 11 | 3 | 4 | 4 | .50 | 19 | .289 | .371 | .390 |
| 4 ML YEARS | | 419 | 1490 | 432 | 111 | 4 | 9 | (6 | 3) | 578 | 210 | 127 | 197 | 5 | 130 | 12 | 36 | 10 | 10 | 13 | .43 | 36 | .290 | .375 | .388 |

## Rick Reed

**Pitches:** Right **Bats:** Right **Pos:** SP/RP **Ht:** 6' 0" **Wt:** 195 **Born:** 08/16/64 **Age:** 26

| | | HOW MUCH HE PITCHED | | | | | | WHAT HE GAVE UP | | | | | | | | | | | | THE RESULTS | | | | | |
|---|---|---|---|---|---|---|---|---|---|---|---|---|---|---|---|---|---|---|---|---|---|---|---|---|---|
| Year Team | Lg | G | GS | CG | GF | IP | BFP | H | R | ER | HR | SH | SF | HB | TBB | IBB | SO | WP | Bk | W | L | Pct. | ShO | Sv | ERA |
| 1988 Pittsburgh | NL | 2 | 2 | 0 | 0 | 12 | 47 | 10 | 4 | 4 | 1 | 2 | 0 | 0 | 2 | 0 | 6 | 0 | 0 | 1 | 0 | 1.000 | 0 | 0 | 3.00 |
| 1989 Pittsburgh | NL | 15 | 7 | 0 | 2 | 54.2 | 232 | 62 | 35 | 34 | 5 | 2 | 3 | 2 | 11 | 3 | 34 | 0 | 3 | 1 | 4 | .200 | 0 | 0 | 5.60 |
| 1990 Pittsburgh | NL | 13 | 8 | 1 | 2 | 53.2 | 238 | 62 | 32 | 26 | 6 | 2 | 1 | 1 | 12 | 6 | 27 | 0 | 0 | 2 | 3 | .400 | 1 | 1 | 4.36 |
| 3 ML YEARS | | 30 | 17 | 1 | 4 | 120.1 | 517 | 134 | 71 | 64 | 12 | 6 | 4 | 3 | 25 | 9 | 67 | 0 | 3 | 4 | 7 | .364 | 1 | 1 | 4.79 |

## Kevin Reimer

**Bats:** Left **Throws:** Right **Pos:** DH **Ht:** 6' 2" **Wt:** 215 **Born:** 06/28/64 **Age:** 27

| | | BATTING | | | | | | | | | | | | | | | | | BASERUNNING | | | | PERCENTAGES | | |
|---|---|---|---|---|---|---|---|---|---|---|---|---|---|---|---|---|---|---|---|---|---|---|---|---|---|
| Year Team | Lg | G | AB | H | 2B | 3B | HR | (Hm | Rd) | TB | R | RBI | TBB | IBB | SO | HBP | SH | SF | SB | CS | SB% | GDP | Avg | OBP | SLG |
| 1988 Texas | AL | 12 | 25 | 3 | 0 | 0 | 1 | (0 | 1) | 6 | 2 | 2 | 0 | 0 | 6 | 0 | 0 | 1 | 0 | 0 | .00 | 0 | .120 | .115 | .240 |
| 1989 Texas | AL | 3 | 5 | 0 | 0 | 0 | 0 | (0 | 0) | 0 | 0 | 0 | 0 | 0 | 1 | 0 | 0 | 0 | 0 | 0 | .00 | 1 | .000 | .000 | .000 |
| 1990 Texas | AL | 64 | 100 | 26 | 9 | 1 | 2 | (0 | 2) | 43 | 5 | 15 | 10 | 0 | 22 | 1 | 0 | 0 | 0 | 1 | .00 | 3 | .260 | .333 | .430 |
| 3 ML YEARS | | 79 | 130 | 29 | 9 | 1 | 3 | (0 | 3) | 49 | 7 | 17 | 10 | 0 | 29 | 1 | 0 | 1 | 0 | 1 | .00 | 4 | .223 | .282 | .377 |

## Rick Reuschel

**Pitches:** Right **Bats:** Right **Pos:** SP **Ht:** 6' 3" **Wt:** 240 **Born:** 05/16/49 **Age:** 42

| | | HOW MUCH HE PITCHED | | | | | | WHAT HE GAVE UP | | | | | | | | | | | | THE RESULTS | | | | | |
|---|---|---|---|---|---|---|---|---|---|---|---|---|---|---|---|---|---|---|---|---|---|---|---|---|---|
| Year Team | Lg | G | GS | CG | GF | IP | BFP | H | R | ER | HR | SH | SF | HB | TBB | IBB | SO | WP | Bk | W | L | Pct. | ShO | Sv | ERA |
| 1972 Chicago | NL | 21 | 18 | 5 | 1 | 129 | 527 | 127 | 46 | 42 | 3 | 4 | 2 | 2 | 29 | 6 | 87 | 1 | 2 | 10 | 8 | .556 | 4 | 0 | 2.93 |
| 1973 Chicago | NL | 36 | 36 | 7 | 0 | 237 | 1003 | 244 | 95 | 79 | 15 | 5 | 2 | 5 | 62 | 6 | 168 | 10 | 1 | 14 | 15 | .483 | 3 | 0 | 3.00 |
| 1974 Chicago | NL | 41 | 38 | 8 | 2 | 241 | 1061 | 262 | 130 | 115 | 18 | 14 | 8 | 6 | 83 | 12 | 160 | 7 | 1 | 13 | 12 | .520 | 2 | 0 | 4.29 |
| 1975 Chicago | NL | 38 | 37 | 6 | 1 | 234 | 1007 | 244 | 116 | 97 | 17 | 20 | 4 | 7 | 67 | 8 | 155 | 4 | 1 | 11 | 17 | .393 | 0 | 1 | 3.73 |
| 1976 Chicago | NL | 38 | 37 | 9 | 1 | 260 | 1078 | 260 | 117 | 100 | 17 | 11 | 13 | 8 | 64 | 5 | 146 | 7 | 1 | 14 | 12 | .538 | 2 | 1 | 3.46 |
| 1977 Chicago | NL | 39 | 37 | 8 | 2 | 252 | 1030 | 233 | 84 | 78 | 13 | 3 | 4 | 5 | 74 | 11 | 166 | 9 | 1 | 20 | 10 | .667 | 4 | 1 | 2.79 |
| 1978 Chicago | NL | 35 | 35 | 9 | 0 | 243 | 1007 | 235 | 98 | 92 | 16 | 16 | 8 | 5 | 54 | 8 | 115 | 13 | 1 | 14 | 15 | .483 | 1 | 0 | 3.41 |
| 1979 Chicago | NL | 36 | 36 | 5 | 0 | 239 | 1021 | 251 | 104 | 96 | 16 | 13 | 6 | 10 | 75 | 8 | 125 | 5 | 0 | 18 | 12 | .600 | 1 | 0 | 3.62 |
| 1980 Chicago | NL | 38 | 38 | 6 | 0 | 257 | 1094 | 281 | 111 | 97 | 13 | 19 | 14 | 4 | 76 | 10 | 140 | 3 | 1 | 11 | 13 | .458 | 0 | 0 | 3.40 |
| 1981 2 ML Teams | | 25 | 24 | 4 | 1 | 157 | 640 | 162 | 64 | 54 | 8 | 6 | 2 | 5 | 33 | 4 | 75 | 5 | 0 | 8 | 11 | .421 | 0 | 0 | 3.10 |
| 1983 Chicago | NL | 4 | 4 | 0 | 0 | 20.2 | 88 | 18 | 9 | 9 | 1 | 0 | 1 | 0 | 10 | 2 | 9 | 0 | 0 | 1 | 1 | .500 | 0 | 0 | 3.92 |
| 1984 Chicago | NL | 19 | 14 | 1 | 2 | 92.1 | 405 | 123 | 57 | 53 | 7 | 7 | 9 | 3 | 23 | 0 | 43 | 2 | 0 | 5 | 5 | .500 | 0 | 0 | 5.17 |
| 1985 Pittsburgh | NL | 31 | 26 | 9 | 4 | 194 | 773 | 153 | 58 | 49 | 7 | 5 | 3 | 3 | 52 | 10 | 138 | 4 | 0 | 14 | 8 | .636 | 1 | 1 | 2.27 |
| 1986 Pittsburgh | NL | 35 | 34 | 4 | 0 | 215.2 | 930 | 232 | 106 | 95 | 20 | 9 | 10 | 8 | 57 | 2 | 125 | 6 | 1 | 9 | 16 | .360 | 2 | 0 | 3.96 |
| 1987 2 ML Teams | | 34 | 33 | 12 | 0 | 227 | 920 | 207 | 91 | 78 | 13 | 8 | 8 | 8 | 42 | 3 | 107 | 7 | 0 | 13 | 9 | .591 | 4 | 0 | 3.09 |
| 1988 San Francisco | NL | 36 | 36 | 7 | 0 | 245 | 1000 | 242 | 88 | 85 | 11 | 9 | 14 | 6 | 42 | 8 | 92 | 4 | 0 | 19 | 11 | .633 | 2 | 0 | 3.12 |

| Year | Team | Lg | G | GS | CG | GF | IP | BFP | H | R | ER | HR | SH | SF | HB | TBB | IBB | SO | WP | Bk | W | L | Pct. | ShO | Sv | ERA |
|---|---|---|---|---|---|---|---|---|---|---|---|---|---|---|---|---|---|---|---|---|---|---|---|---|---|---|
| 1989 | San Francisco | NL | 32 | 32 | 2 | 0 | 208.1 | 860 | 195 | 75 | 68 | 18 | 7 | 7 | 2 | 54 | 4 | 111 | 1 | 0 | 17 | 8 | .680 | 0 | 0 | 2.94 |
| 1990 | San Francisco | NL | 15 | 13 | 0 | 1 | 87 | 390 | 102 | 40 | 38 | 8 | 10 | 5 | 1 | 31 | 9 | 49 | 1 | 0 | 3 | 6 | .333 | 0 | 1 | 3.93 |
| 1981 | Chicago | NL | 13 | 13 | 1 | 0 | 86 | 358 | 87 | 40 | 33 | 4 | 5 | 0 | 4 | 23 | 4 | 53 | 5 | 0 | 4 | 7 | .364 | 0 | 0 | 3.45 |
| | New York | AL | 12 | 11 | 3 | 1 | 71 | 282 | 75 | 24 | 21 | 4 | 1 | 2 | 1 | 10 | 0 | 22 | 0 | 0 | 4 | 4 | .500 | 0 | 0 | 2.66 |
| 1987 | Pittsburgh | NL | 25 | 25 | 9 | 0 | 177 | 715 | 163 | 63 | 54 | 12 | 4 | 7 | 6 | 35 | 1 | 80 | 5 | 0 | 8 | 6 | .571 | 3 | 0 | 2.75 |
| | San Francisco | NL | 9 | 8 | 3 | 0 | 50 | 205 | 44 | 28 | 24 | 1 | 4 | 1 | 2 | 7 | 2 | 27 | 2 | 0 | 5 | 3 | .625 | 1 | 0 | 4.32 |
| 18 | ML YEARS | | 553 | 528 | 102 | 15 | 3539 | 14834 | 3571 | 1489 | 1325 | 221 | 166 | 120 | 88 | 928 | 116 | 2011 | 89 | 10 | 214 | 189 | .531 | 26 | 5 | 3.37 |

## Jerry Reuss

**Pitches:** Left **Bats:** Left **Pos:** RP **Ht:** 6' 5" **Wt:** 227 **Born:** 06/19/49 **Age:** 42

| | | | HOW MUCH HE PITCHED | | | | | | WHAT HE GAVE UP | | | | | | | | | | | | THE RESULTS | | | | | |
|---|---|---|---|---|---|---|---|---|---|---|---|---|---|---|---|---|---|---|---|---|---|---|---|---|---|---|
| Year | Team | Lg | G | GS | CG | GF | IP | BFP | H | R | ER | HR | SH | SF | HB | TBB | IBB | SO | WP | Bk | W | L | Pct. | ShO | Sv | ERA |
| 1969 | St. Louis | NL | 1 | 1 | 0 | 0 | 7 | 27 | 2 | 0 | 0 | 0 | 0 | 0 | 2 | 3 | 0 | 3 | 0 | 1 | 1 | 0 | 1.000 | 0 | 0 | 0.00 |
| 1970 | St. Louis | NL | 20 | 20 | 5 | 0 | 127 | 548 | 132 | 62 | 58 | 9 | 8 | 3 | 1 | 49 | 2 | 74 | 8 | 1 | 7 | 8 | .467 | 2 | 0 | 4.11 |
| 1971 | St. Louis | NL | 36 | 35 | 7 | 0 | 211 | 952 | 228 | 125 | 112 | 15 | 13 | 5 | 7 | 109 | 11 | 131 | 9 | 2 | 14 | 14 | .500 | 2 | 0 | 4.78 |
| 1972 | Houston | NL | 33 | 30 | 4 | 1 | 192 | 832 | 177 | 101 | 89 | 14 | 12 | 7 | 10 | 83 | 3 | 174 | 7 | 2 | 9 | 13 | .409 | 1 | 1 | 4.17 |
| 1973 | Houston | NL | 41 | 40 | 12 | 1 | 279 | 1198 | 271 | 123 | 116 | 17 | 13 | 8 | 3 | 117 | 6 | 177 | 10 | 1 | 16 | 13 | .552 | 3 | 0 | 3.74 |
| 1974 | Pittsburgh | NL | 35 | 35 | 14 | 0 | 260 | 1125 | 259 | 115 | 101 | 20 | 20 | 9 | 1 | 101 | 16 | 105 | 7 | 1 | 16 | 11 | .593 | 1 | 0 | 3.50 |
| 1975 | Pittsburgh | NL | 32 | 32 | 15 | 0 | 237 | 984 | 224 | 73 | 67 | 10 | 18 | 3 | 0 | 78 | 8 | 131 | 4 | 1 | 18 | 11 | .621 | 6 | 0 | 2.54 |
| 1976 | Pittsburgh | NL | 31 | 29 | 11 | 2 | 209 | 880 | 209 | 98 | 82 | 16 | 9 | 2 | 2 | 51 | 10 | 108 | 7 | 0 | 14 | 9 | .609 | 3 | 2 | 3.53 |
| 1977 | Pittsburgh | NL | 33 | 33 | 8 | 0 | 208 | 894 | 225 | 109 | 95 | 11 | 10 | 5 | 4 | 71 | 2 | 116 | 11 | 1 | 10 | 13 | .435 | 2 | 0 | 4.11 |
| 1978 | Pittsburgh | NL | 23 | 12 | 3 | 3 | 83 | 361 | 97 | 48 | 45 | 5 | 5 | 3 | 3 | 23 | 1 | 42 | 3 | 1 | 3 | 2 | .600 | 1 | 0 | 4.88 |
| 1979 | Los Angeles | NL | 39 | 21 | 4 | 11 | 160 | 712 | 178 | 88 | 63 | 4 | 17 | 0 | 3 | 60 | 7 | 83 | 7 | 0 | 7 | 14 | .333 | 1 | 3 | 3.54 |
| 1980 | Los Angeles | NL | 37 | 29 | 10 | 7 | 229 | 907 | 193 | 74 | 64 | 12 | 10 | 5 | 0 | 40 | 9 | 111 | 3 | 1 | 18 | 6 | .750 | 6 | 3 | 2.52 |
| 1981 | Los Angeles | NL | 22 | 22 | 8 | 0 | 153 | 608 | 138 | 44 | 39 | 6 | 9 | 0 | 4 | 27 | 3 | 51 | 1 | 0 | 10 | 4 | .714 | 2 | 0 | 2.29 |
| 1982 | Los Angeles | NL | 39 | 37 | 8 | 2 | 254.2 | 1036 | 232 | 98 | 88 | 11 | 12 | 4 | 2 | 50 | 10 | 138 | 7 | 3 | 18 | 11 | .621 | 4 | 0 | 3.11 |
| 1983 | Los Angeles | NL | 32 | 31 | 7 | 0 | 223.1 | 935 | 233 | 94 | 73 | 12 | 18 | 6 | 2 | 50 | 5 | 143 | 3 | 2 | 12 | 11 | .522 | 0 | 0 | 2.94 |
| 1984 | Los Angeles | NL | 30 | 15 | 2 | 9 | 99 | 428 | 102 | 51 | 42 | 4 | 11 | 3 | 0 | 31 | 7 | 44 | 4 | 1 | 5 | 7 | .417 | 0 | 1 | 3.82 |
| 1985 | Los Angeles | NL | 34 | 33 | 5 | 0 | 212.2 | 883 | 210 | 78 | 69 | 13 | 8 | 6 | 3 | 58 | 7 | 84 | 5 | 0 | 14 | 10 | .583 | 3 | 0 | 2.92 |
| 1986 | Los Angeles | NL | 19 | 13 | 0 | 3 | 74 | 331 | 96 | 57 | 48 | 13 | 5 | 0 | 2 | 17 | 4 | 29 | 2 | 0 | 2 | 6 | .250 | 0 | 1 | 5.84 |
| 1987 | 3 ML Teams | | 25 | 23 | 1 | 1 | 119 | 539 | 166 | 92 | 79 | 18 | 8 | 2 | 3 | 29 | 3 | 49 | 4 | 1 | 4 | 10 | .286 | 1 | 0 | 5.97 |
| 1988 | Chicago | AL | 32 | 29 | 2 | 1 | 183 | 751 | 183 | 79 | 70 | 15 | 5 | 4 | 3 | 43 | 1 | 73 | 3 | 4 | 13 | 9 | .591 | 0 | 0 | 3.44 |
| 1989 | 2 ML Teams | | 30 | 26 | 1 | 0 | 140.1 | 617 | 171 | 88 | 80 | 19 | 3 | 6 | 4 | 34 | 2 | 40 | 1 | 0 | 9 | 9 | .500 | 1 | 0 | 5.13 |
| 1990 | Pittsburgh | NL | 4 | 1 | 0 | 0 | 7.2 | 34 | 8 | 3 | 3 | 1 | 1 | 0 | 0 | 3 | 1 | 1 | 1 | 0 | 0 | 0 | .000 | 0 | 0 | 3.52 |
| 1987 | Los Angeles | NL | 1 | 0 | 0 | 0 | 2 | 8 | 2 | 1 | 1 | 0 | 1 | 1 | 0 | 0 | 0 | 2 | 0 | 0 | 0 | 0 | .000 | 0 | 0 | 4.50 |
| | Cincinnati | NL | 7 | 7 | 0 | 0 | 34.2 | 163 | 52 | 31 | 30 | 2 | 2 | 0 | 1 | 12 | 2 | 10 | 1 | 1 | 0 | 5 | .000 | 0 | 0 | 7.79 |
| | California | AL | 17 | 16 | 1 | 1 | 82.1 | 368 | 112 | 60 | 48 | 16 | 5 | 1 | 2 | 17 | 1 | 37 | 3 | 0 | 4 | 5 | .444 | 1 | 0 | 5.25 |
| 1989 | Chicago | AL | 23 | 19 | 1 | 0 | 106.2 | 470 | 135 | 65 | 60 | 12 | 2 | 6 | 3 | 21 | 1 | 27 | 1 | 0 | 8 | 5 | .615 | 1 | 0 | 5.06 |
| | Milwaukee | AL | 7 | 7 | 0 | 0 | 33.2 | 147 | 36 | 23 | 20 | 7 | 1 | 0 | 1 | 13 | 1 | 13 | 0 | 0 | 1 | 4 | .200 | 0 | 0 | 5.35 |
| 22 | ML YEARS | | 628 | 547 | 127 | 41 | 3668.2 | 15582 | 3734 | 1700 | 1483 | 245 | 215 | 81 | 59 | 1127 | 118 | 1907 | 107 | 23 | 220 | 191 | .535 | 39 | 11 | 3.64 |

## Harold Reynolds

**Bats:** Both **Throws:** Right **Pos:** 2B **Ht:** 5'11" **Wt:** 165 **Born:** 11/26/60 **Age:** 30

| | | | BATTING | | | | | | | | | | | | | | | | BASERUNNING | | | | PERCENTAGES | | |
|---|---|---|---|---|---|---|---|---|---|---|---|---|---|---|---|---|---|---|---|---|---|---|---|---|---|
| Year | Team | Lg | G | AB | H | 2B | 3B | HR | (Hm | Rd) | TB | R | RBI | TBB | IBB | SO | HBP | SH | SF | SB | CS | SB% | GDP | Avg | OBP | SLG |
| 1983 | Seattle | AL | 20 | 59 | 12 | 4 | 1 | 0 | (0 | 0) | 18 | 8 | 1 | 2 | 0 | 9 | 0 | 1 | 1 | 0 | 2 | .00 | 1 | .203 | .226 | .305 |
| 1984 | Seattle | AL | 10 | 10 | 3 | 0 | 0 | 0 | (0 | 0) | 3 | 3 | 0 | 0 | 0 | 1 | 1 | 1 | 0 | 1 | 1 | .50 | 0 | .300 | .364 | .300 |
| 1985 | Seattle | AL | 67 | 104 | 15 | 3 | 1 | 0 | (0 | 0) | 20 | 15 | 6 | 17 | 0 | 14 | 0 | 1 | 0 | 3 | 2 | .60 | 0 | .144 | .264 | .192 |
| 1986 | Seattle | AL | 126 | 445 | 99 | 19 | 4 | 1 | (1 | 0) | 129 | 46 | 24 | 29 | 0 | 42 | 3 | 9 | 0 | 30 | 12 | .71 | 6 | .222 | .275 | .290 |
| 1987 | Seattle | AL | 160 | 530 | 146 | 31 | 8 | 1 | (1 | 0) | 196 | 73 | 35 | 39 | 0 | 34 | 2 | 8 | 5 | 60 | 20 | .75 | 7 | .275 | .325 | .370 |
| 1988 | Seattle | AL | 158 | 598 | 169 | 26 | 11 | 4 | (4 | 0) | 229 | 61 | 41 | 51 | 1 | 51 | 2 | 10 | 2 | 35 | 29 | .55 | 9 | .283 | .340 | .383 |
| 1989 | Seattle | AL | 153 | 613 | 184 | 24 | 9 | 0 | (0 | 0) | 226 | 87 | 43 | 55 | 1 | 45 | 3 | 3 | 3 | 25 | 18 | .58 | 4 | .300 | .359 | .369 |
| 1990 | Seattle | AL | 160 | 642 | 162 | 36 | 5 | 5 | (0 | 5) | 223 | 100 | 55 | 81 | 3 | 52 | 3 | 5 | 6 | 31 | 16 | .66 | 9 | .252 | .336 | .347 |
| 8 | ML YEARS | | 854 | 3001 | 790 | 143 | 39 | 11 | (6 | 5) | 1044 | 393 | 205 | 274 | 5 | 248 | 14 | 38 | 17 | 185 | 100 | .65 | 36 | .263 | .326 | .348 |

## RJ Reynolds

**Bats:** Both **Throws:** Right **Pos:** CF/LF/RF **Ht:** 6' 0" **Wt:** 180 **Born:** 04/19/60 **Age:** 31

| | | | BATTING | | | | | | | | | | | | | | | | BASERUNNING | | | | PERCENTAGES | | |
|---|---|---|---|---|---|---|---|---|---|---|---|---|---|---|---|---|---|---|---|---|---|---|---|---|---|
| Year | Team | Lg | G | AB | H | 2B | 3B | HR | (Hm | Rd) | TB | R | RBI | TBB | IBB | SO | HBP | SH | SF | SB | CS | SB% | GDP | Avg | OBP | SLG |
| 1983 | Los Angeles | NL | 24 | 55 | 13 | 0 | 0 | 2 | (1 | 1) | 19 | 5 | 11 | 3 | 1 | 11 | 0 | 1 | 2 | 5 | 0 | 1.00 | 1 | .236 | .267 | .345 |
| 1984 | Los Angeles | NL | 73 | 240 | 62 | 12 | 2 | 2 | (1 | 1) | 84 | 24 | 24 | 14 | 0 | 38 | 1 | 4 | 2 | 7 | 5 | .58 | 6 | .258 | .300 | .350 |
| 1985 | 2 ML Teams | | 104 | 337 | 95 | 15 | 7 | 3 | (1 | 2) | 133 | 44 | 42 | 22 | 1 | 49 | 2 | 7 | 3 | 18 | 5 | .78 | 6 | .282 | .327 | .395 |
| 1986 | Pittsburgh | NL | 118 | 402 | 108 | 30 | 2 | 9 | (6 | 3) | 169 | 63 | 48 | 40 | 4 | 78 | 1 | 3 | 2 | 16 | 9 | .64 | 10 | .269 | .335 | .420 |
| 1987 | Pittsburgh | NL | 117 | 335 | 87 | 24 | 1 | 7 | (2 | 5) | 134 | 47 | 51 | 34 | 8 | 80 | 0 | 0 | 6 | 14 | 1 | .93 | 5 | .260 | .323 | .400 |
| 1988 | Pittsburgh | NL | 130 | 323 | 80 | 14 | 2 | 6 | (4 | 2) | 116 | 35 | 51 | 20 | 3 | 62 | 0 | 0 | 4 | 15 | 2 | .88 | 5 | .248 | .288 | .359 |
| 1989 | Pittsburgh | NL | 125 | 363 | 98 | 16 | 2 | 6 | (3 | 3) | 136 | 45 | 48 | 34 | 8 | 66 | 1 | 1 | 4 | 22 | 5 | .81 | 13 | .270 | .331 | .375 |
| 1990 | Pittsburgh | NL | 95 | 215 | 62 | 10 | 1 | 0 | (0 | 0) | 74 | 25 | 19 | 23 | 1 | 35 | 0 | 0 | 2 | 12 | 2 | .86 | 12 | .288 | .354 | .344 |
| 1985 | Los Angeles | NL | 73 | 207 | 55 | 10 | 4 | 0 | (0 | 0) | 73 | 22 | 25 | 13 | 0 | 31 | 1 | 5 | 3 | 6 | 3 | .67 | 3 | .266 | .308 | .353 |

| Year Team | Lg | G | AB | H | 2B | 3B | HR | (Hm | Rd) | TB | R | RBI | TBB | IBB | SO | HBP | SH | SF | SB | CS | SB% | GDP | Avg | OBP | SLG |
|---|---|---|---|---|---|---|---|---|---|---|---|---|---|---|---|---|---|---|---|---|---|---|---|---|---|
| Pittsburgh | NL | 31 | 130 | 40 | 5 | 3 | 3 | (1 | 2) | 60 | 22 | 17 | 9 | 1 | 18 | 1 | 2 | 0 | 12 | 2 | .86 | 3 | .308 | .357 | .462 |
| 8 ML YEARS | | 786 | 2270 | 605 | 121 | 17 | 35 | (18 | 17) | 865 | 288 | 294 | 190 | 26 | 419 | 5 | 16 | 25 | 109 | 29 | .79 | 58 | .267 | .321 | .381 |

## Ronn Reynolds

**Bats:** Right **Throws:** Right **Pos:** C **Ht:** 6' 0" **Wt:** 190 **Born:** 09/28/58 **Age:** 32

| BATTING | | | | | | | | | | | | | | | | | | | BASERUNNING | | | | PERCENTAGES | | |
|---|---|---|---|---|---|---|---|---|---|---|---|---|---|---|---|---|---|---|---|---|---|---|---|---|---|
| Year Team | Lg | G | AB | H | 2B | 3B | HR | (Hm | Rd) | TB | R | RBI | TBB | IBB | SO | HBP | SH | SF | SB | CS | SB% | GDP | Avg | OBP | SLG |
| 1982 New York | NL | 2 | 4 | 0 | 0 | 0 | 0 | (0 | 0) | 0 | 0 | 0 | 1 | 0 | 1 | 0 | 0 | 0 | 0 | 0 | .00 | 0 | .000 | .200 | .000 |
| 1983 New York | NL | 24 | 66 | 13 | 1 | 0 | 0 | (0 | 0) | 14 | 4 | 2 | 8 | 1 | 12 | 0 | 0 | 1 | 0 | 0 | .00 | 2 | .197 | .280 | .212 |
| 1985 New York | NL | 28 | 43 | 9 | 2 | 0 | 0 | (0 | 0) | 11 | 4 | 1 | 0 | 0 | 18 | 1 | 2 | 0 | 0 | 0 | .00 | 1 | .209 | .227 | .256 |
| 1986 Philadelphia | NL | 43 | 126 | 27 | 4 | 0 | 3 | (1 | 2) | 40 | 8 | 10 | 5 | 0 | 30 | 0 | 0 | 1 | 0 | 0 | .00 | 4 | .214 | .242 | .317 |
| 1987 Houston | NL | 38 | 102 | 17 | 4 | 0 | 1 | (0 | 1) | 24 | 5 | 7 | 3 | 0 | 29 | 0 | 1 | 1 | 0 | 1 | .00 | 3 | .167 | .189 | .235 |
| 1990 San Diego | NL | 8 | 15 | 1 | 1 | 0 | 0 | (0 | 0) | 2 | 1 | 1 | 1 | 0 | 6 | 0 | 0 | 0 | 0 | 0 | .00 | 0 | .067 | .125 | .133 |
| 6 ML YEARS | | 143 | 356 | 67 | 12 | 0 | 4 | (1 | 3) | 91 | 22 | 21 | 18 | 1 | 96 | 1 | 3 | 3 | 0 | 1 | .00 | 10 | .188 | .228 | .256 |

## Karl Rhodes

**Bats:** Left **Throws:** Left **Pos:** LF **Ht:** 5'11" **Wt:** 170 **Born:** 08/21/68 **Age:** 22

| BATTING | | | | | | | | | | | | | | | | | | | BASERUNNING | | | | PERCENTAGES | | |
|---|---|---|---|---|---|---|---|---|---|---|---|---|---|---|---|---|---|---|---|---|---|---|---|---|---|
| Year Team | Lg | G | AB | H | 2B | 3B | HR | (Hm | Rd) | TB | R | RBI | TBB | IBB | SO | HBP | SH | SF | SB | CS | SB% | GDP | Avg | OBP | SLG |
| 1986 Astros | R | 62 | 222 | 65 | 10 | 3 | 0 | -- | -- | 81 | 36 | 22 | 32 | 3 | 33 | 0 | 5 | 2 | 14 | 6 | .70 | 1 | .293 | .379 | .365 |
| 1987 Asheville | A | 129 | 413 | 104 | 16 | 4 | 3 | -- | -- | 137 | 62 | 50 | 77 | 6 | 82 | 0 | 3 | 8 | 43 | 14 | .75 | 4 | .252 | .363 | .332 |
| 1988 Osceola | A | 132 | 452 | 128 | 4 | 2 | 1 | -- | -- | 139 | 69 | 34 | 81 | 4 | 58 | 2 | 6 | 5 | 65 | 23 | .74 | 7 | .283 | .391 | .308 |
| 1989 Columbus | AA | 143 | 520 | 134 | 25 | 5 | 4 | -- | -- | 181 | 81 | 63 | 93 | 3 | 105 | 3 | 0 | 3 | 18 | 12 | .60 | 13 | .258 | .372 | .348 |
| 1990 Tucson | AAA | 107 | 385 | 106 | 24 | 11 | 3 | -- | -- | 161 | 68 | 59 | 47 | 2 | 75 | 0 | 3 | 5 | 24 | 4 | .86 | 9 | .275 | .350 | .418 |
| 1990 Houston | NL | 38 | 86 | 21 | 6 | 1 | 1 | (0 | 1) | 32 | 12 | 3 | 13 | 3 | 12 | 0 | 1 | 1 | 4 | 1 | .80 | 1 | .244 | .340 | .372 |

## Rusty Richards

**Pitches:** Right **Bats:** Left **Pos:** RP **Ht:** 6' 4" **Wt:** 200 **Born:** 01/27/65 **Age:** 26

| HOW MUCH HE PITCHED | | | | | | | | WHAT HE GAVE UP | | | | | | | | | | | | THE RESULTS | | | | | |
|---|---|---|---|---|---|---|---|---|---|---|---|---|---|---|---|---|---|---|---|---|---|---|---|---|---|
| Year Team | Lg | G | GS | CG | GF | IP | BFP | H | R | ER | HR | SH | SF | HB | TBB | IBB | SO | WP | Bk | W | L | Pct. | ShO | Sv | ERA |
| 1986 Braves | R | 12 | 0 | 0 | 5 | 19.1 | 83 | 17 | 8 | 5 | 0 | 2 | 1 | 2 | 7 | 2 | 15 | 2 | 0 | 0 | 0 | .000 | 0 | 1 | 2.33 |
| 1987 Sumter | A | 10 | 8 | 1 | 0 | 48 | 200 | 45 | 28 | 17 | 5 | 2 | 1 | 0 | 17 | 1 | 39 | 3 | 0 | 3 | 3 | .500 | 1 | 0 | 3.19 |
| Durham | A | 22 | 20 | 1 | 1 | 125 | 540 | 138 | 73 | 63 | 14 | 9 | 7 | 9 | 50 | 1 | 62 | 3 | 1 | 6 | 10 | .375 | 0 | 0 | 4.54 |
| 1988 Durham | A | 1 | 0 | 0 | 1 | 3.1 | 10 | 0 | 0 | 0 | 0 | 0 | 0 | 0 | 0 | 0 | 3 | 0 | 0 | 1 | 0 | 1.000 | 0 | 0 | 0.00 |
| Greenville | AA | 28 | 20 | 3 | 1 | 147 | 587 | 125 | 46 | 43 | 13 | 2 | 7 | 2 | 42 | 1 | 96 | 5 | 0 | 10 | 7 | .588 | 2 | 0 | 2.63 |
| 1989 Richmond | AAA | 27 | 27 | 0 | 0 | 167.2 | 706 | 178 | 76 | 71 | 4 | 7 | 6 | 5 | 54 | 1 | 85 | 6 | 1 | 11 | 11 | .500 | 0 | 0 | 3.81 |
| 1990 Richmond | AAA | 30 | 26 | 0 | 0 | 140.1 | 641 | 159 | 83 | 71 | 12 | 8 | 8 | 3 | 73 | 5 | 56 | 12 | 0 | 6 | 9 | .400 | 0 | 0 | 4.55 |
| 1989 Atlanta | NL | 2 | 2 | 0 | 0 | 9.1 | 43 | 10 | 5 | 5 | 2 | 0 | 0 | 1 | 6 | 0 | 4 | 1 | 0 | 0 | 0 | .000 | 0 | 0 | 4.82 |
| 1990 Atlanta | NL | 1 | 0 | 0 | 1 | 1 | 6 | 2 | 3 | 3 | 1 | 0 | 0 | 0 | 1 | 0 | 0 | 0 | 0 | 0 | 0 | .000 | 0 | 0 | 27.00 |
| 2 ML YEARS | | 3 | 2 | 0 | 1 | 10.1 | 49 | 12 | 8 | 8 | 3 | 0 | 0 | 1 | 7 | 0 | 4 | 1 | 0 | 0 | 0 | .000 | 0 | 0 | 6.97 |

## Jeff Richardson

**Pitches:** Right **Bats:** Right **Pos:** RP **Ht:** 6' 3" **Wt:** 185 **Born:** 08/29/63 **Age:** 27

| HOW MUCH HE PITCHED | | | | | | | | WHAT HE GAVE UP | | | | | | | | | | | | THE RESULTS | | | | | |
|---|---|---|---|---|---|---|---|---|---|---|---|---|---|---|---|---|---|---|---|---|---|---|---|---|---|
| Year Team | Lg | G | GS | CG | GF | IP | BFP | H | R | ER | HR | SH | SF | HB | TBB | IBB | SO | WP | Bk | W | L | Pct. | ShO | Sv | ERA |
| 1984 Medicne Hat | R | 18 | 7 | 0 | 4 | 70 | 0 | 96 | 67 | 56 | 7 | 0 | 0 | 1 | 32 | 1 | 39 | 8 | 2 | 4 | 6 | .400 | 0 | 0 | 7.20 |
| 1985 Little Fls | A | 11 | 10 | 3 | 1 | 62.1 | 275 | 58 | 32 | 25 | 6 | 1 | 0 | 4 | 32 | 3 | 56 | 4 | 0 | 4 | 3 | .571 | 2 | 0 | 3.61 |
| Columbia | A | 5 | 5 | 3 | 0 | 35.2 | 143 | 25 | 11 | 7 | 1 | 0 | 1 | 3 | 11 | 0 | 33 | 3 | 0 | 3 | 2 | .600 | 0 | 0 | 1.77 |
| 1986 Lynchburg | A | 32 | 21 | 6 | 3 | 171 | 757 | 183 | 96 | 80 | 9 | 4 | 3 | 5 | 82 | 2 | 93 | 18 | 2 | 13 | 5 | .722 | 1 | 1 | 4.21 |
| Jackson | AA | 1 | 1 | 0 | 0 | 3 | 19 | 6 | 8 | 6 | 0 | 0 | 0 | 0 | 4 | 0 | 2 | 2 | 0 | 0 | 1 | .000 | 0 | 0 | 18.00 |
| 1987 Lynchburg | A | 29 | 28 | 3 | 0 | 154 | 703 | 180 | 103 | 84 | 11 | 4 | 3 | 7 | 68 | 2 | 79 | 16 | 2 | 6 | 12 | .333 | 0 | 0 | 4.91 |
| 1988 Palm Sprngs | A | 44 | 0 | 0 | 29 | 69 | 297 | 66 | 24 | 19 | 3 | 3 | 1 | 1 | 27 | 0 | 56 | 9 | 1 | 0 | 4 | .000 | 0 | 5 | 2.48 |
| 1989 Palm Sprngs | A | 24 | 0 | 0 | 19 | 26.2 | 109 | 19 | 15 | 12 | 3 | 0 | 2 | 3 | 9 | 0 | 25 | 5 | 1 | 4 | 2 | .667 | 0 | 5 | 4.05 |
| Midland | AA | 19 | 0 | 0 | 18 | 22.2 | 78 | 9 | 4 | 4 | 1 | 0 | 0 | 0 | 5 | 0 | 12 | 2 | 0 | 0 | 1 | .000 | 0 | 10 | 1.59 |
| 1990 Edmonton | AAA | 38 | 0 | 0 | 26 | 48.1 | 215 | 46 | 17 | 10 | 1 | 2 | 0 | 0 | 27 | 1 | 31 | 0 | 0 | 5 | 0 | 1.000 | 0 | 10 | 1.86 |
| 1990 California | AL | 1 | 0 | 0 | 1 | 0.1 | 2 | 1 | 0 | 0 | 0 | 0 | 0 | 0 | 0 | 0 | 0 | 0 | 0 | 0 | 0 | .000 | 0 | 0 | 0.00 |

## Dave Righetti

**Pitches:** Left **Bats:** Left **Pos:** RP **Ht:** 6' 4" **Wt:** 210 **Born:** 11/28/58 **Age:** 32

| HOW MUCH HE PITCHED | | | | | | | | WHAT HE GAVE UP | | | | | | | | | | | | THE RESULTS | | | | | |
|---|---|---|---|---|---|---|---|---|---|---|---|---|---|---|---|---|---|---|---|---|---|---|---|---|---|
| Year Team | Lg | G | GS | CG | GF | IP | BFP | H | R | ER | HR | SH | SF | HB | TBB | IBB | SO | WP | Bk | W | L | Pct. | ShO | Sv | ERA |
| 1979 New York | AL | 3 | 3 | 0 | 0 | 17 | 67 | 10 | 7 | 7 | 2 | 1 | 1 | 0 | 10 | 0 | 13 | 0 | 0 | 0 | 1 | .000 | 0 | 0 | 3.71 |
| 1981 New York | AL | 15 | 15 | 2 | 0 | 105 | 422 | 75 | 25 | 24 | 1 | 0 | 2 | 0 | 38 | 0 | 89 | 1 | 1 | 8 | 4 | .667 | 0 | 0 | 2.06 |
| 1982 New York | AL | 33 | 27 | 4 | 3 | 183 | 804 | 155 | 88 | 77 | 11 | 8 | 5 | 6 | 108 | 4 | 163 | 9 | 5 | 11 | 10 | .524 | 0 | 1 | 3.79 |
| 1983 New York | AL | 31 | 31 | 7 | 0 | 217 | 900 | 194 | 96 | 83 | 12 | 10 | 4 | 2 | 67 | 2 | 169 | 10 | 1 | 14 | 8 | .636 | 2 | 0 | 3.44 |
| 1984 New York | AL | 64 | 0 | 0 | 53 | 96.1 | 400 | 79 | 29 | 25 | 5 | 4 | 4 | 0 | 37 | 7 | 90 | 0 | 2 | 5 | 6 | .455 | 0 | 31 | 2.34 |

| Year Team | Lg | G | GS | CG | GF | IP | BFP | H | R | ER | HR | SH | SF | HB | TBB | IBB | SO | WP | Bk | W | L | Pct. | ShO | Sv | ERA |
|---|---|---|---|---|---|---|---|---|---|---|---|---|---|---|---|---|---|---|---|---|---|---|---|---|---|
| 1985 New York | AL | 74 | 0 | 0 | 60 | 107 | 452 | 96 | 36 | 33 | 5 | 6 | 3 | 0 | 45 | 3 | 92 | 7 | 0 | 12 | 7 | .632 | 0 | 29 | 2.78 |
| 1986 New York | AL | 74 | 0 | 0 | 68 | 106.2 | 435 | 88 | 31 | 29 | 4 | 5 | 4 | 2 | 35 | 7 | 83 | 1 | 0 | 8 | 8 | .500 | 0 | 46 | 2.45 |
| 1987 New York | AL | 60 | 0 | 0 | 54 | 95 | 419 | 95 | 45 | 37 | 9 | 6 | 5 | 2 | 44 | 4 | 77 | 1 | 3 | 8 | 6 | .571 | 0 | 31 | 3.51 |
| 1988 New York | AL | 60 | 0 | 0 | 41 | 87 | 377 | 86 | 35 | 34 | 5 | 4 | 0 | 1 | 37 | 2 | 70 | 2 | 4 | 5 | 4 | .556 | 0 | 25 | 3.52 |
| 1989 New York | AL | 55 | 0 | 0 | 53 | 69 | 300 | 73 | 32 | 23 | 3 | 7 | 2 | 1 | 26 | 6 | 51 | 0 | 0 | 2 | 6 | .250 | 0 | 25 | 3.00 |
| 1990 New York | AL | 53 | 0 | 0 | 47 | 53 | 235 | 48 | 24 | 21 | 8 | 1 | 1 | 2 | 26 | 2 | 43 | 2 | 0 | 1 | 1 | .500 | 0 | 36 | 3.57 |
| 11 ML YEARS | | 522 | 76 | 13 | 379 | 1136 | 4811 | 999 | 448 | 393 | 65 | 52 | 31 | 16 | 473 | 37 | 940 | 33 | 16 | 74 | 61 | .548 | 2 | 224 | 3.11 |

## Jose Rijo

**Pitches:** Right **Bats:** Right **Pos:** SP **Ht:** 6' 2" **Wt:** 200 **Born:** 05/13/65 **Age:** 26

| | | HOW MUCH HE PITCHED | | | | | | WHAT HE GAVE UP | | | | | | | | | | | | THE RESULTS | | | | | |
|---|---|---|---|---|---|---|---|---|---|---|---|---|---|---|---|---|---|---|---|---|---|---|---|---|---|
| Year Team | Lg | G | GS | CG | GF | IP | BFP | H | R | ER | HR | SH | SF | HB | TBB | IBB | SO | WP | Bk | W | L | Pct. | ShO | Sv | ERA |
| 1984 New York | AL | 24 | 5 | 0 | 8 | 62.1 | 289 | 74 | 40 | 33 | 5 | 6 | 1 | 1 | 33 | 1 | 47 | 2 | 1 | 2 | 8 | .200 | 0 | 2 | 4.76 |
| 1985 Oakland | AL | 12 | 9 | 0 | 1 | 63.2 | 272 | 57 | 26 | 25 | 6 | 5 | 0 | 1 | 28 | 2 | 65 | 0 | 0 | 6 | 4 | .600 | 0 | 0 | 3.53 |
| 1986 Oakland | AL | 39 | 26 | 4 | 9 | 193.2 | 856 | 172 | 116 | 100 | 24 | 10 | 9 | 4 | 108 | 7 | 176 | 6 | 4 | 9 | 11 | .450 | 0 | 1 | 4.65 |
| 1987 Oakland | AL | 21 | 14 | 1 | 3 | 82.1 | 394 | 106 | 67 | 54 | 10 | 0 | 3 | 2 | 41 | 1 | 67 | 5 | 2 | 2 | 7 | .222 | 0 | 0 | 5.90 |
| 1988 Cincinnati | NL | 49 | 19 | 0 | 12 | 162 | 653 | 120 | 47 | 43 | 7 | 8 | 5 | 3 | 63 | 7 | 160 | 1 | 4 | 13 | 8 | .619 | 0 | 0 | 2.39 |
| 1989 Cincinnati | NL | 19 | 19 | 1 | 0 | 111 | 464 | 101 | 39 | 35 | 6 | 3 | 6 | 2 | 48 | 3 | 86 | 4 | 3 | 7 | 6 | .538 | 1 | 0 | 2.84 |
| 1990 Cincinnati | NL | 29 | 29 | 7 | 0 | 197 | 801 | 151 | 65 | 59 | 10 | 8 | 1 | 2 | 78 | 1 | 152 | 2 | 5 | 14 | 8 | .636 | 1 | 0 | 2.70 |
| 7 ML YEARS | | 193 | 121 | 13 | 33 | 872 | 3729 | 781 | 400 | 349 | 68 | 40 | 25 | 15 | 399 | 22 | 753 | 20 | 19 | 53 | 52 | .505 | 2 | 3 | 3.60 |

## Ernest Riles

**Bats:** Left **Throws:** Right **Pos:** 2B/SS **Ht:** 6' 1" **Wt:** 180 **Born:** 10/02/60 **Age:** 30

| | | BATTING | | | | | | | | | | | | | | | | | BASERUNNING | | | | PERCENTAGES | | |
|---|---|---|---|---|---|---|---|---|---|---|---|---|---|---|---|---|---|---|---|---|---|---|---|---|---|
| Year Team | Lg | G | AB | H | 2B | 3B | HR | (Hm | Rd) | TB | R | RBI | TBB | IBB | SO | HBP | SH | SF | SB | CS | SB% | GDP | Avg | OBP | SLG |
| 1985 Milwaukee | AL | 116 | 448 | 128 | 12 | 7 | 5 | (2 | 3) | 169 | 54 | 45 | 36 | 0 | 54 | 2 | 6 | 3 | 2 | 2 | .50 | 16 | .286 | .339 | .377 |
| 1986 Milwaukee | AL | 145 | 524 | 132 | 24 | 2 | 9 | (2 | 7) | 187 | 69 | 47 | 54 | 0 | 80 | 1 | 6 | 3 | 7 | 7 | .50 | 14 | .252 | .321 | .357 |
| 1987 Milwaukee | AL | 83 | 276 | 72 | 11 | 1 | 4 | (1 | 3) | 97 | 38 | 38 | 30 | 1 | 47 | 1 | 3 | 6 | 3 | 4 | .43 | 6 | .261 | .329 | .351 |
| 1988 2 ML Teams | | 120 | 314 | 87 | 13 | 3 | 4 | (4 | 0) | 118 | 33 | 37 | 17 | 2 | 59 | 0 | 1 | 4 | 3 | 4 | .43 | 8 | .277 | .310 | .376 |
| 1989 San Francisco | NL | 122 | 302 | 84 | 13 | 2 | 7 | (5 | 2) | 122 | 43 | 40 | 28 | 3 | 50 | 2 | 1 | 4 | 0 | 6 | .00 | 7 | .278 | .339 | .404 |
| 1990 San Francisco | NL | 92 | 155 | 31 | 2 | 1 | 8 | (7 | 1) | 59 | 22 | 21 | 26 | 3 | 26 | 0 | 2 | 1 | 0 | 0 | .00 | 2 | .200 | .313 | .381 |
| 1988 Milwaukee | AL | 41 | 127 | 32 | 6 | 1 | 1 | (1 | 0) | 43 | 7 | 9 | 7 | 0 | 26 | 0 | 1 | 0 | 2 | 2 | .50 | 3 | .252 | .291 | .339 |
| San Francisco | NL | 79 | 187 | 55 | 7 | 2 | 3 | (3 | 0) | 75 | 26 | 28 | 10 | 2 | 33 | 0 | 0 | 4 | 1 | 2 | .33 | 5 | .294 | .323 | .401 |
| 6 ML YEARS | | 678 | 2019 | 534 | 75 | 16 | 37 | (21 | 16) | 752 | 259 | 228 | 191 | 9 | 316 | 6 | 19 | 21 | 15 | 23 | .39 | 53 | .264 | .327 | .372 |

## Billy Ripken

**Bats:** Right **Throws:** Right **Pos:** 2B **Ht:** 6' 1" **Wt:** 183 **Born:** 12/16/64 **Age:** 26

| | | BATTING | | | | | | | | | | | | | | | | | BASERUNNING | | | | PERCENTAGES | | |
|---|---|---|---|---|---|---|---|---|---|---|---|---|---|---|---|---|---|---|---|---|---|---|---|---|---|
| Year Team | Lg | G | AB | H | 2B | 3B | HR | (Hm | Rd) | TB | R | RBI | TBB | IBB | SO | HBP | SH | SF | SB | CS | SB% | GDP | Avg | OBP | SLG |
| 1987 Baltimore | AL | 58 | 234 | 72 | 9 | 0 | 2 | (0 | 2) | 87 | 27 | 20 | 21 | 0 | 23 | 0 | 1 | 1 | 4 | 1 | .80 | 3 | .308 | .363 | .372 |
| 1988 Baltimore | AL | 150 | 512 | 106 | 18 | 1 | 2 | (0 | 2) | 132 | 52 | 34 | 33 | 0 | 63 | 5 | 6 | 3 | 8 | 2 | .80 | 14 | .207 | .260 | .258 |
| 1989 Baltimore | AL | 115 | 318 | 76 | 11 | 2 | 2 | (0 | 2) | 97 | 31 | 26 | 22 | 0 | 53 | 0 | 19 | 5 | 1 | 2 | .33 | 12 | .239 | .284 | .305 |
| 1990 Baltimore | AL | 129 | 406 | 118 | 28 | 1 | 3 | (2 | 1) | 157 | 48 | 38 | 28 | 2 | 43 | 4 | 17 | 1 | 5 | 2 | .71 | 7 | .291 | .342 | .387 |
| 4 ML YEARS | | 452 | 1470 | 372 | 66 | 4 | 9 | (2 | 7) | 473 | 158 | 118 | 104 | 2 | 182 | 9 | 43 | 10 | 18 | 7 | .72 | 36 | .253 | .304 | .322 |

## Cal Ripken

**Bats:** Right **Throws:** Right **Pos:** SS **Ht:** 6' 4" **Wt:** 225 **Born:** 08/24/60 **Age:** 30

| | | BATTING | | | | | | | | | | | | | | | | | BASERUNNING | | | | PERCENTAGES | | |
|---|---|---|---|---|---|---|---|---|---|---|---|---|---|---|---|---|---|---|---|---|---|---|---|---|---|
| Year Team | Lg | G | AB | H | 2B | 3B | HR | (Hm | Rd) | TB | R | RBI | TBB | IBB | SO | HBP | SH | SF | SB | CS | SB% | GDP | Avg | OBP | SLG |
| 1981 Baltimore | AL | 23 | 39 | 5 | 0 | 0 | 0 | (0 | 0) | 5 | 1 | 0 | 1 | 0 | 8 | 0 | 0 | 0 | 0 | 0 | .00 | 4 | .128 | .150 | .128 |
| 1982 Baltimore | AL | 160 | 598 | 158 | 32 | 5 | 28 | (11 | 17) | 284 | 90 | 93 | 46 | 3 | 95 | 3 | 2 | 6 | 3 | 3 | .50 | 16 | .264 | .317 | .475 |
| 1983 Baltimore | AL | 162 | 663 | 211 | 47 | 2 | 27 | (12 | 15) | 343 | 121 | 102 | 58 | 0 | 97 | 0 | 0 | 5 | 0 | 4 | .00 | 24 | .318 | .371 | .517 |
| 1984 Baltimore | AL | 162 | 641 | 195 | 37 | 7 | 27 | (16 | 11) | 327 | 103 | 86 | 71 | 1 | 89 | 2 | 0 | 2 | 2 | 1 | .67 | 16 | .304 | .374 | .510 |
| 1985 Baltimore | AL | 161 | 642 | 181 | 32 | 5 | 26 | (15 | 11) | 301 | 116 | 110 | 67 | 1 | 68 | 1 | 0 | 8 | 2 | 3 | .40 | 32 | .282 | .347 | .469 |
| 1986 Baltimore | AL | 162 | 627 | 177 | 35 | 1 | 25 | (10 | 15) | 289 | 98 | 81 | 70 | 5 | 60 | 4 | 0 | 6 | 4 | 2 | .67 | 19 | .282 | .355 | .461 |
| 1987 Baltimore | AL | 162 | 624 | 157 | 28 | 3 | 27 | (17 | 10) | 272 | 97 | 98 | 81 | 0 | 77 | 1 | 0 | 11 | 3 | 5 | .38 | 19 | .252 | .333 | .436 |
| 1988 Baltimore | AL | 161 | 575 | 152 | 25 | 1 | 23 | (11 | 12) | 248 | 87 | 81 | 102 | 7 | 69 | 2 | 0 | 10 | 2 | 2 | .50 | 10 | .264 | .372 | .431 |
| 1989 Baltimore | AL | 162 | 646 | 166 | 30 | 0 | 21 | (13 | 8) | 259 | 80 | 93 | 57 | 5 | 72 | 3 | 0 | 6 | 3 | 2 | .60 | 22 | .257 | .317 | .401 |
| 1990 Baltimore | AL | 161 | 600 | 150 | 28 | 4 | 21 | (8 | 13) | 249 | 78 | 84 | 82 | 18 | 66 | 5 | 1 | 7 | 3 | 1 | .75 | 12 | .250 | .341 | .415 |
| 10 ML YEARS | | 1476 | 5655 | 1552 | 294 | 28 | 225 | (113 | 112) | 2577 | 871 | 828 | 635 | 40 | 701 | 21 | 3 | 61 | 22 | 23 | .49 | 174 | .274 | .347 | .456 |

## Kevin Ritz

**Pitches:** Right **Bats:** Right **Pos:** SP **Ht:** 6' 4" **Wt:** 195 **Born:** 06/08/65 **Age:** 26

| | | HOW MUCH HE PITCHED | | | | | | WHAT HE GAVE UP | | | | | | | | | | | | THE RESULTS | | | | | |
|---|---|---|---|---|---|---|---|---|---|---|---|---|---|---|---|---|---|---|---|---|---|---|---|---|---|
| Year Team | Lg | G | GS | CG | GF | IP | BFP | H | R | ER | HR | SH | SF | HB | TBB | IBB | SO | WP | Bk | W | L | Pct. | ShO | Sv | ERA |
| 1986 Gastonia | A | 7 | 7 | 0 | 0 | 36.1 | 155 | 29 | 19 | 17 | 2 | 0 | 1 | 0 | 21 | 0 | 34 | 6 | 0 | 1 | 2 | .333 | 0 | 0 | 4.21 |

| | | | | | | | | | | | | | | | | | | | | | | | | |
|---|---|---|---|---|---|---|---|---|---|---|---|---|---|---|---|---|---|---|---|---|---|---|---|---|
| Lakeland | A | 18 | 15 | 0 | 2 | 85.2 | 393 | 114 | 60 | 53 | 3 | 2 | 2 | 2 | 45 | 1 | 39 | 6 | 0 | 3 | 9 | .250 | 0 | 1 | 5.57 |
| 1987 Glens Falls | AA | 25 | 25 | 1 | 0 | 152.2 | 680 | 171 | 95 | 83 | 5 | 10 | 4 | 4 | 71 | 1 | 78 | 11 | 3 | 8 | 8 | .500 | 0 | 0 | 4.89 |
| 1988 Glens Falls | AA | 26 | 26 | 4 | 0 | 136.2 | 583 | 115 | 68 | 58 | 8 | 2 | 4 | 4 | 70 | 0 | 75 | 6 | 4 | 8 | 10 | .444 | 2 | 0 | 3.82 |
| 1989 Toledo | AAA | 16 | 16 | 1 | 0 | 102.2 | 447 | 95 | 48 | 36 | 3 | 3 | 1 | 8 | 60 | 1 | 74 | 4 | 2 | 7 | 8 | .467 | 0 | 0 | 3.16 |
| 1990 Toledo | AAA | 20 | 18 | 0 | 1 | 89.2 | 418 | 93 | 68 | 52 | 5 | 5 | 4 | 9 | 59 | 3 | 57 | 6 | 3 | 3 | 6 | .333 | 0 | 0 | 5.22 |
| 1989 Detroit | AL | 12 | 12 | 1 | 0 | 74 | 334 | 75 | 41 | 36 | 2 | 1 | 5 | 1 | 44 | 5 | 56 | 6 | 0 | 4 | 6 | .400 | 0 | 0 | 4.38 |
| 1990 Detroit | AL | 4 | 4 | 0 | 0 | 7.1 | 52 | 14 | 12 | 9 | 0 | 3 | 0 | 0 | 14 | 2 | 3 | 3 | 0 | 0 | 4 | .000 | 0 | 0 | 11.05 |
| 2 ML YEARS | | 16 | 16 | 1 | 0 | 81.1 | 386 | 89 | 53 | 45 | 2 | 4 | 5 | 1 | 58 | 7 | 59 | 9 | 0 | 4 | 10 | .286 | 0 | 0 | 4.98 |

## Luis Rivera

**Bats:** Right **Throws:** Right **Pos:** SS **Ht:** 5' 9" **Wt:** 165 **Born:** 01/03/64 **Age:** 27

| | | BATTING | | | | | | | | | | | | | | | | | BASERUNNING | | | | PERCENTAGES | | |
|---|---|---|---|---|---|---|---|---|---|---|---|---|---|---|---|---|---|---|---|---|---|---|---|---|---|
| Year Team | Lg | G | AB | H | 2B | 3B | HR | (Hm | Rd) | TB | R | RBI | TBB | IBB | SO | HBP | SH | SF | SB | CS | SB% | GDP | Avg | OBP | SLG |
| 1986 Montreal | NL | 55 | 166 | 34 | 11 | 1 | 0 | (0 | 0) | 47 | 20 | 13 | 17 | 0 | 33 | 2 | 1 | 1 | 1 | 1 | .50 | 1 | .205 | .285 | .283 |
| 1987 Montreal | NL | 18 | 32 | 5 | 2 | 0 | 0 | (0 | 0) | 7 | 0 | 1 | 1 | 0 | 8 | 0 | 0 | 0 | 0 | 0 | .00 | 0 | .156 | .182 | .219 |
| 1988 Montreal | NL | 123 | 371 | 83 | 17 | 3 | 4 | (2 | 2) | 118 | 35 | 30 | 24 | 4 | 69 | 1 | 3 | 3 | 3 | 4 | .43 | 9 | .224 | .271 | .318 |
| 1989 Boston | AL | 93 | 323 | 83 | 17 | 1 | 5 | (4 | 1) | 117 | 35 | 29 | 20 | 1 | 60 | 1 | 4 | 1 | 2 | 3 | .40 | 7 | .257 | .301 | .362 |
| 1990 Boston | AL | 118 | 346 | 78 | 20 | 0 | 7 | (4 | 3) | 119 | 38 | 45 | 25 | 0 | 58 | 1 | 12 | 1 | 4 | 3 | .57 | 10 | .225 | .279 | .344 |
| 5 ML YEARS | | 407 | 1238 | 283 | 67 | 5 | 16 | (10 | 6) | 408 | 128 | 118 | 87 | 5 | 228 | 5 | 20 | 6 | 10 | 11 | .48 | 27 | .229 | .281 | .330 |

## Bip Roberts

**Bats:** Both **Throws:** Right **Pos:** LF/3B/SS **Ht:** 5' 7" **Wt:** 160 **Born:** 10/27/63 **Age:** 27

| | | BATTING | | | | | | | | | | | | | | | | | BASERUNNING | | | | PERCENTAGES | | |
|---|---|---|---|---|---|---|---|---|---|---|---|---|---|---|---|---|---|---|---|---|---|---|---|---|---|
| Year Team | Lg | G | AB | H | 2B | 3B | HR | (Hm | Rd) | TB | R | RBI | TBB | IBB | SO | HBP | SH | SF | SB | CS | SB% | GDP | Avg | OBP | SLG |
| 1986 San Diego | NL | 101 | 241 | 61 | 5 | 2 | 1 | (0 | 1) | 73 | 34 | 12 | 14 | 1 | 29 | 0 | 2 | 1 | 14 | 12 | .54 | 2 | .253 | .293 | .303 |
| 1988 San Diego | NL | 5 | 9 | 3 | 0 | 0 | 0 | (0 | 0) | 3 | 1 | 0 | 1 | 0 | 2 | 0 | 0 | 0 | 0 | 2 | .00 | 0 | .333 | .400 | .333 |
| 1989 San Diego | NL | 117 | 329 | 99 | 15 | 8 | 3 | (2 | 1) | 139 | 81 | 25 | 49 | 0 | 45 | 1 | 6 | 2 | 21 | 11 | .66 | 3 | .301 | .391 | .422 |
| 1990 San Diego | NL | 149 | 556 | 172 | 36 | 3 | 9 | (4 | 5) | 241 | 104 | 44 | 55 | 1 | 65 | 6 | 8 | 4 | 46 | 12 | .79 | 8 | .309 | .375 | .433 |
| 4 ML YEARS | | 372 | 1135 | 335 | 56 | 13 | 13 | (6 | 7) | 456 | 220 | 81 | 119 | 2 | 141 | 7 | 16 | 7 | 81 | 37 | .69 | 13 | .295 | .364 | .402 |

## Billy Robidoux

**Bats:** Left **Throws:** Right **Pos:** 1B **Ht:** 6' 1" **Wt:** 200 **Born:** 01/13/64 **Age:** 27

| | | BATTING | | | | | | | | | | | | | | | | | BASERUNNING | | | | PERCENTAGES | | |
|---|---|---|---|---|---|---|---|---|---|---|---|---|---|---|---|---|---|---|---|---|---|---|---|---|---|
| Year Team | Lg | G | AB | H | 2B | 3B | HR | (Hm | Rd) | TB | R | RBI | TBB | IBB | SO | HBP | SH | SF | SB | CS | SB% | GDP | Avg | OBP | SLG |
| 1985 Milwaukee | AL | 18 | 51 | 9 | 2 | 0 | 3 | (0 | 3) | 20 | 5 | 8 | 12 | 0 | 16 | 0 | 0 | 0 | 0 | 0 | .00 | 1 | .176 | .333 | .392 |
| 1986 Milwaukee | AL | 56 | 181 | 41 | 8 | 0 | 1 | (0 | 1) | 52 | 15 | 21 | 33 | 1 | 36 | 0 | 0 | 1 | 0 | 0 | .00 | 8 | .227 | .344 | .287 |
| 1987 Milwaukee | AL | 23 | 62 | 12 | 0 | 0 | 0 | (0 | 0) | 12 | 9 | 4 | 8 | 1 | 17 | 0 | 0 | 0 | 0 | 1 | .00 | 0 | .194 | .286 | .194 |
| 1988 Milwaukee | AL | 33 | 91 | 23 | 5 | 0 | 0 | (0 | 0) | 28 | 9 | 5 | 8 | 3 | 14 | 0 | 3 | 2 | 1 | 1 | .50 | 3 | .253 | .307 | .308 |
| 1989 Chicago | AL | 16 | 39 | 5 | 2 | 0 | 0 | (0 | 0) | 7 | 2 | 1 | 4 | 0 | 9 | 0 | 0 | 0 | 0 | 0 | .00 | 0 | .128 | .209 | .179 |
| 1990 Boston | AL | 27 | 44 | 8 | 4 | 0 | 1 | (1 | 0) | 15 | 3 | 4 | 6 | 1 | 14 | 1 | 0 | 1 | 0 | 0 | .00 | 2 | .182 | .288 | .341 |
| 6 ML YEARS | | 173 | 468 | 98 | 21 | 0 | 5 | (1 | 4) | 134 | 43 | 43 | 71 | 6 | 106 | 1 | 3 | 4 | 1 | 2 | .33 | 14 | .209 | .313 | .286 |

## Don Robinson

**Pitches:** Right **Bats:** Right **Pos:** SP **Ht:** 6' 4" **Wt:** 231 **Born:** 06/08/57 **Age:** 34

| | | HOW MUCH HE PITCHED | | | | | | WHAT HE GAVE UP | | | | | | | | | | | | THE RESULTS | | | | | |
|---|---|---|---|---|---|---|---|---|---|---|---|---|---|---|---|---|---|---|---|---|---|---|---|---|---|
| Year Team | Lg | G | GS | CG | GF | IP | BFP | H | R | ER | HR | SH | SF | HB | TBB | IBB | SO | WP | Bk | W | L | Pct. | ShO | Sv | ERA |
| 1978 Pittsburgh | NL | 35 | 32 | 9 | 1 | 228 | 937 | 203 | 98 | 88 | 20 | 8 | 8 | 3 | 57 | 4 | 135 | 9 | 4 | 14 | 6 | .700 | 1 | 1 | 3.47 |
| 1979 Pittsburgh | NL | 29 | 25 | 4 | 1 | 161 | 684 | 171 | 74 | 69 | 12 | 6 | 5 | 4 | 52 | 5 | 96 | 6 | 1 | 8 | 8 | .500 | 0 | 0 | 3.86 |
| 1980 Pittsburgh | NL | 29 | 24 | 3 | 1 | 160 | 671 | 157 | 74 | 71 | 14 | 8 | 3 | 5 | 45 | 5 | 103 | 7 | 2 | 7 | 10 | .412 | 2 | 1 | 3.99 |
| 1981 Pittsburgh | NL | 16 | 2 | 0 | 4 | 38 | 182 | 47 | 27 | 25 | 4 | 7 | 2 | 0 | 23 | 4 | 17 | 3 | 0 | 0 | 3 | .000 | 0 | 2 | 5.92 |
| 1982 Pittsburgh | NL | 38 | 30 | 6 | 3 | 227 | 977 | 213 | 123 | 108 | 26 | 12 | 8 | 3 | 103 | 11 | 165 | 17 | 0 | 15 | 13 | .536 | 0 | 0 | 4.28 |
| 1983• Pittsburgh | NL | 9 | 6 | 0 | 2 | 36.1 | 168 | 43 | 21 | 18 | 5 | 2 | 0 | 0 | 21 | 3 | 28 | 2 | 0 | 2 | 2 | .500 | 0 | 0 | 4.46 |
| 1984 Pittsburgh | NL | 51 | 1 | 0 | 28 | 122 | 500 | 99 | 45 | 41 | 6 | 4 | 9 | 0 | 49 | 4 | 110 | 5 | 0 | 5 | 6 | .455 | 0 | 10 | 3.02 |
| 1985 Pittsburgh | NL | 44 | 6 | 0 | 22 | 95.1 | 418 | 95 | 49 | 41 | 6 | 2 | 0 | 2 | 42 | 11 | 65 | 2 | 0 | 5 | 11 | .313 | 0 | 3 | 3.87 |
| 1986 Pittsburgh | NL | 50 | 0 | 0 | 41 | 69.1 | 295 | 61 | 27 | 26 | 5 | 5 | 4 | 2 | 27 | 3 | 53 | 4 | 1 | 3 | 4 | .429 | 0 | 14 | 3.37 |
| 1987 2 ML Teams | | 67 | 0 | 0 | 54 | 108 | 460 | 105 | 42 | 41 | 7 | 7 | 3 | 0 | 40 | 6 | 79 | 7 | 1 | 11 | 7 | .611 | 0 | 19 | 3.42 |
| 1988 San Francisco | NL | 51 | 19 | 3 | 19 | 176.2 | 725 | 152 | 63 | 48 | 11 | 7 | 8 | 3 | 49 | 12 | 122 | 4 | 2 | 10 | 5 | .667 | 2 | 6 | 2.45 |
| 1989 San Francisco | NL | 34 | 32 | 5 | 2 | 197 | 793 | 184 | 80 | 75 | 22 | 6 | 5 | 2 | 37 | 6 | 96 | 4 | 4 | 12 | 11 | .522 | 1 | 0 | 3.43 |
| 1990 San Francisco | NL | 26 | 25 | 4 | 0 | 157.2 | 667 | 173 | 84 | 80 | 18 | 4 | 3 | 1 | 41 | 8 | 78 | 2 | 0 | 10 | 7 | .588 | 0 | 0 | 4.57 |
| 1987 Pittsburgh | NL | 42 | 0 | 0 | 37 | 65.1 | 276 | 66 | 29 | 28 | 6 | 6 | 1 | 0 | 22 | 3 | 53 | 6 | 1 | 6 | 6 | .500 | 0 | 12 | 3.86 |
| San Francisco | NL | 25 | 0 | 0 | 17 | 42.2 | 184 | 39 | 13 | 13 | 1 | 1 | 2 | 0 | 18 | 3 | 26 | 1 | 0 | 5 | 1 | .833 | 0 | 7 | 2.74 |
| 13 ML YEARS | | 479 | 202 | 34 | 178 | 1776.1 | 7477 | 1703 | 807 | 731 | 156 | 78 | 58 | 25 | 586 | 82 | 1147 | 72 | 15 | 102 | 93 | .523 | 6 | 56 | 3.70 |

## Jeff Robinson

**Pitches:** Right **Bats:** Right **Pos:** RP/SP **Ht:** 6' 4" **Wt:** 200 **Born:** 12/13/60 **Age:** 30

| HOW MUCH HE PITCHED | | | | | | | | | WHAT HE GAVE UP | | | | | | | | | | | | THE RESULTS | | | | | |
|---|---|---|---|---|---|---|---|---|---|---|---|---|---|---|---|---|---|---|---|---|---|---|---|---|---|---|
| Year | Team | Lg | G | GS | CG | GF | IP | BFP | H | R | ER | HR | SH | SF | HB | TBB | IBB | SO | WP | Bk | W | L | Pct. | ShO | Sv | ERA |
| 1984 | San Francisco | NL | 34 | 33 | 1 | 0 | 171.2 | 749 | 195 | 99 | 87 | 12 | 5 | 8 | 7 | 52 | 4 | 102 | 7 | 2 | 7 | 15 | .318 | 1 | 0 | 4.56 |
| 1985 | San Francisco | NL | 8 | 0 | 0 | 0 | 12.1 | 59 | 16 | 11 | 7 | 2 | 0 | 1 | 0 | 10 | 1 | 8 | 1 | 0 | 0 | 0 | .000 | 0 | 0 | 5.11 |
| 1986 | San Francisco | NL | 64 | 1 | 0 | 22 | 104.1 | 431 | 92 | 46 | 39 | 8 | 1 | 3 | 1 | 32 | 7 | 90 | 11 | 0 | 6 | 3 | .667 | 0 | 8 | 3.36 |
| 1987 | 2 ML Teams | | 81 | 0 | 0 | 40 | 123.1 | 495 | 89 | 43 | 39 | 11 | 10 | 4 | 1 | 54 | 11 | 101 | 5 | 2 | 8 | 9 | .471 | 0 | 14 | 2.85 |
| 1988 | Pittsburgh | NL | 75 | 0 | 0 | 35 | 124.2 | 513 | 113 | 44 | 42 | 6 | 2 | 6 | 3 | 39 | 5 | 87 | 11 | 0 | 11 | 5 | .688 | 0 | 9 | 3.03 |
| 1989 | Pittsburgh | NL | 50 | 19 | 0 | 18 | 141.1 | 643 | 161 | 92 | 72 | 14 | 7 | 7 | 1 | 59 | 11 | 95 | 14 | 2 | 7 | 13 | .350 | 0 | 4 | 4.58 |
| 1990 | New York | AL | 54 | 4 | 1 | 12 | 88.2 | 372 | 82 | 35 | 34 | 8 | 5 | 1 | 1 | 34 | 3 | 43 | 2 | 0 | 3 | 6 | .333 | 0 | 0 | 3.45 |
| 1987 | San Francisco | NL | 63 | 0 | 0 | 33 | 96.2 | 395 | 69 | 34 | 30 | 10 | 9 | 4 | 1 | 48 | 10 | 82 | 3 | 2 | 6 | 8 | .429 | 0 | 10 | 2.79 |
| | Pittsburgh | NL | 18 | 0 | 0 | 7 | 26.2 | 100 | 20 | 9 | 9 | 1 | 1 | 0 | 0 | 6 | 1 | 19 | 2 | 0 | 2 | 1 | .667 | 0 | 4 | 3.04 |
| | 7 ML YEARS | | 366 | 57 | 2 | 127 | 766.1 | 3262 | 748 | 370 | 320 | 61 | 30 | 30 | 14 | 280 | 42 | 526 | 51 | 6 | 42 | 51 | .452 | 1 | 35 | 3.76 |

## Jeff M. Robinson

**Pitches:** Right **Bats:** Right **Pos:** SP **Ht:** 6' 6" **Wt:** 210 **Born:** 12/14/61 **Age:** 29

| HOW MUCH HE PITCHED | | | | | | | | | WHAT HE GAVE UP | | | | | | | | | | | | THE RESULTS | | | | | |
|---|---|---|---|---|---|---|---|---|---|---|---|---|---|---|---|---|---|---|---|---|---|---|---|---|---|---|
| Year | Team | Lg | G | GS | CG | GF | IP | BFP | H | R | ER | HR | SH | SF | HB | TBB | IBB | SO | WP | Bk | W | L | Pct. | ShO | Sv | ERA |
| 1987 | Detroit | AL | 29 | 21 | 2 | 2 | 127.1 | 569 | 132 | 86 | 76 | 16 | 2 | 2 | 7 | 54 | 3 | 98 | 4 | 3 | 9 | 6 | .600 | 1 | 0 | 5.37 |
| 1988 | Detroit | AL | 24 | 23 | 6 | 0 | 172 | 698 | 121 | 61 | 57 | 19 | 2 | 6 | 3 | 72 | 5 | 114 | 8 | 1 | 13 | 6 | .684 | 2 | 0 | 2.98 |
| 1989 | Detroit | AL | 16 | 16 | 1 | 0 | 78 | 347 | 76 | 47 | 41 | 10 | 3 | 3 | 1 | 46 | 1 | 40 | 5 | 0 | 4 | 5 | .444 | 1 | 0 | 4.73 |
| 1990 | Detroit | AL | 27 | 27 | 1 | 0 | 145 | 654 | 141 | 101 | 96 | 23 | 3 | 5 | 6 | 88 | 9 | 76 | 16 | 1 | 10 | 9 | .526 | 1 | 0 | 5.96 |
| | 4 ML YEARS | | 96 | 87 | 10 | 2 | 522.1 | 2268 | 470 | 295 | 270 | 68 | 10 | 16 | 17 | 260 | 18 | 328 | 33 | 5 | 36 | 26 | .581 | 5 | 0 | 4.65 |

## Ron Robinson

**Pitches:** Right **Bats:** Right **Pos:** SP **Ht:** 6' 4" **Wt:** 230 **Born:** 03/24/62 **Age:** 29

| HOW MUCH HE PITCHED | | | | | | | | | WHAT HE GAVE UP | | | | | | | | | | | | THE RESULTS | | | | | |
|---|---|---|---|---|---|---|---|---|---|---|---|---|---|---|---|---|---|---|---|---|---|---|---|---|---|---|
| Year | Team | Lg | G | GS | CG | GF | IP | BFP | H | R | ER | HR | SH | SF | HB | TBB | IBB | SO | WP | Bk | W | L | Pct. | ShO | Sv | ERA |
| 1984 | Cincinnati | NL | 12 | 5 | 1 | 2 | 39.2 | 166 | 35 | 18 | 12 | 3 | 1 | 1 | 0 | 13 | 3 | 24 | 0 | 2 | 1 | 2 | .333 | 0 | 0 | 2.72 |
| 1985 | Cincinnati | NL | 33 | 12 | 0 | 9 | 108.1 | 453 | 107 | 53 | 48 | 11 | 3 | 4 | 1 | 32 | 3 | 76 | 3 | 0 | 7 | 7 | .500 | 0 | 1 | 3.99 |
| 1986 | Cincinnati | NL | 70 | 0 | 0 | 32 | 116.2 | 487 | 110 | 44 | 42 | 10 | 4 | 3 | 2 | 43 | 8 | 117 | 3 | 0 | 10 | 3 | .769 | 0 | 14 | 3.24 |
| 1987 | Cincinnati | NL | 48 | 18 | 0 | 14 | 154 | 638 | 148 | 71 | 63 | 14 | 8 | 7 | 1 | 43 | 8 | 99 | 2 | 0 | 7 | 5 | .583 | 0 | 4 | 3.68 |
| 1988 | Cincinnati | NL | 17 | 16 | 0 | 0 | 78.2 | 347 | 88 | 47 | 36 | 5 | 5 | 5 | 2 | 26 | 4 | 38 | 3 | 0 | 3 | 7 | .300 | 0 | 0 | 4.12 |
| 1989 | Cincinnati | NL | 15 | 15 | 0 | 0 | 83.1 | 353 | 80 | 36 | 31 | 8 | 5 | 1 | 2 | 28 | 2 | 36 | 2 | 0 | 5 | 3 | .625 | 0 | 0 | 3.35 |
| 1990 | 2 ML Teams | | 28 | 27 | 7 | 0 | 179.2 | 764 | 194 | 78 | 65 | 7 | 4 | 7 | 6 | 51 | 1 | 71 | 3 | 0 | 14 | 7 | .667 | 2 | 0 | 3.26 |
| 1990 | Cincinnati | NL | 6 | 5 | 0 | 0 | 31.1 | 137 | 36 | 18 | 17 | 2 | 1 | 0 | 0 | 14 | 0 | 14 | 1 | 0 | 2 | 2 | .500 | 0 | 0 | 4.88 |
| | Milwaukee | AL | 22 | 22 | 7 | 0 | 148.1 | 627 | 158 | 60 | 48 | 5 | 3 | 7 | 6 | 37 | 1 | 57 | 2 | 0 | 12 | 5 | .706 | 2 | 0 | 2.91 |
| | 7 ML YEARS | | 223 | 93 | 8 | 57 | 760.1 | 3208 | 762 | 347 | 297 | 58 | 30 | 28 | 14 | 236 | 29 | 461 | 16 | 2 | 47 | 34 | .580 | 2 | 19 | 3.52 |

## Mike Rochford

**Pitches:** Left **Bats:** Left **Pos:** SP **Ht:** 6' 4" **Wt:** 205 **Born:** 03/14/63 **Age:** 28

| HOW MUCH HE PITCHED | | | | | | | | | WHAT HE GAVE UP | | | | | | | | | | | | THE RESULTS | | | | | |
|---|---|---|---|---|---|---|---|---|---|---|---|---|---|---|---|---|---|---|---|---|---|---|---|---|---|---|
| Year | Team | Lg | G | GS | CG | GF | IP | BFP | H | R | ER | HR | SH | SF | HB | TBB | IBB | SO | WP | Bk | W | L | Pct. | ShO | Sv | ERA |
| 1988 | Boston | AL | 2 | 0 | 0 | 0 | 2.1 | 12 | 4 | 0 | 0 | 0 | 0 | 0 | 0 | 1 | 0 | 1 | 0 | 0 | 0 | 0 | .000 | 0 | 0 | 0.00 |
| 1989 | Boston | AL | 4 | 0 | 0 | 4 | 4 | 20 | 4 | 7 | 3 | 1 | 0 | 1 | 0 | 4 | 1 | 1 | 2 | 0 | 0 | 0 | .000 | 0 | 0 | 6.75 |
| 1990 | Boston | AL | 2 | 1 | 0 | 0 | 4 | 25 | 10 | 10 | 8 | 1 | 1 | 1 | 0 | 4 | 0 | 0 | 1 | 0 | 0 | 1 | .000 | 0 | 0 | 18.00 |
| | 3 ML YEARS | | 8 | 1 | 0 | 4 | 10.1 | 57 | 18 | 17 | 11 | 2 | 1 | 2 | 0 | 9 | 1 | 2 | 3 | 0 | 0 | 1 | .000 | 0 | 0 | 9.58 |

## Rich Rodriguez

**Pitches:** Left **Bats:** Left **Pos:** RP **Ht:** 5'10" **Wt:** 194 **Born:** 03/01/63 **Age:** 28

| HOW MUCH HE PITCHED | | | | | | | | | WHAT HE GAVE UP | | | | | | | | | | | | THE RESULTS | | | | | |
|---|---|---|---|---|---|---|---|---|---|---|---|---|---|---|---|---|---|---|---|---|---|---|---|---|---|---|
| Year | Team | Lg | G | GS | CG | GF | IP | BFP | H | R | ER | HR | SH | SF | HB | TBB | IBB | SO | WP | Bk | W | L | Pct. | ShO | Sv | ERA |
| 1984 | Little Fls | A | 25 | 1 | 0 | 6 | 35.1 | 171 | 28 | 21 | 11 | 0 | 4 | 2 | 1 | 36 | 7 | 27 | 3 | 0 | 2 | 1 | .667 | 0 | 0 | 2.80 |
| 1985 | Columbia | A | 49 | 3 | 0 | 19 | 80.1 | 365 | 89 | 41 | 36 | 4 | 6 | 1 | 1 | 36 | 2 | 71 | 7 | 1 | 6 | 3 | .667 | 0 | 6 | 4.03 |
| 1986 | Jackson | AA | 13 | 5 | 1 | 2 | 33 | 161 | 51 | 35 | 33 | 5 | 2 | 2 | 0 | 15 | 2 | 15 | 2 | 0 | 3 | 4 | .429 | 0 | 0 | 9.00 |
| | Lynchburg | A | 36 | 0 | 0 | 16 | 45.1 | 184 | 37 | 20 | 18 | 2 | 1 | 1 | 1 | 19 | 0 | 38 | 4 | 1 | 2 | 1 | .667 | 0 | 3 | 3.57 |
| 1987 | Lynchburg | A | 69 | 0 | 0 | 30 | 68 | 291 | 69 | 23 | 21 | 3 | 1 | 2 | 0 | 26 | 6 | 59 | 8 | 0 | 3 | 1 | .750 | 0 | 5 | 2.78 |
| 1988 | Jackson | AA | 47 | 1 | 0 | 25 | 78.1 | 335 | 66 | 35 | 25 | 3 | 9 | 4 | 1 | 42 | 6 | 68 | 6 | 5 | 2 | 7 | .222 | 0 | 6 | 2.87 |
| 1989 | Wichita | AA | 54 | 0 | 0 | 38 | 74.1 | 319 | 74 | 30 | 30 | 3 | 3 | 1 | 2 | 37 | 11 | 40 | 4 | 1 | 8 | 3 | .727 | 0 | 8 | 3.63 |
| 1990 | Las Vegas | AAA | 27 | 2 | 0 | 13 | 59 | 243 | 50 | 24 | 23 | 5 | 1 | 3 | 1 | 22 | 1 | 46 | 3 | 1 | 3 | 4 | .429 | 0 | 8 | 3.51 |
| 1990 | San Diego | NL | 32 | 0 | 0 | 15 | 47.2 | 201 | 52 | 17 | 15 | 2 | 2 | 1 | 1 | 16 | 4 | 22 | 1 | 1 | 1 | 1 | .500 | 0 | 1 | 2.83 |

## Rick Rodriguez

**Pitches:** Right **Bats:** Right **Pos:** RP **Ht:** 6' 2" **Wt:** 200 **Born:** 09/21/60 **Age:** 30

| | | | HOW MUCH HE PITCHED | | | | | | WHAT HE GAVE UP | | | | | | | | | | | | THE RESULTS | | | | | |
|---|---|---|---|---|---|---|---|---|---|---|---|---|---|---|---|---|---|---|---|---|---|---|---|---|---|---|
| Year | Team | Lg | G | GS | CG | GF | IP | BFP | H | R | ER | HR | SH | SF | HB | TBB | IBB | SO | WP | Bk | W | L | Pct. | ShO | Sv | ERA |
| 1986 | Oakland | AL | 3 | 3 | 0 | 0 | 16.1 | 72 | 17 | 12 | 12 | 4 | 0 | 0 | 0 | 7 | 0 | 2 | 2 | 1 | 1 | 2 | .333 | 0 | 0 | 6.61 |
| 1987 | Oakland | AL | 15 | 0 | 0 | 11 | 24.1 | 112 | 32 | 8 | 8 | 1 | 1 | 0 | 1 | 15 | 1 | 9 | 0 | 0 | 1 | 0 | 1.000 | 0 | 0 | 2.96 |
| 1988 | Cleveland | AL | 10 | 5 | 0 | 4 | 33 | 156 | 43 | 28 | 26 | 4 | 4 | 1 | 1 | 17 | 1 | 9 | 2 | 0 | 1 | 2 | .333 | 0 | 0 | 7.09 |
| 1990 | San Francisco | NL | 3 | 0 | 0 | 0 | 3.1 | 16 | 5 | 3 | 3 | 0 | 0 | 0 | 0 | 2 | 0 | 2 | 0 | 0 | 0 | 0 | .000 | 0 | 0 | 8.10 |
| 4 ML YEARS | | | 31 | 8 | 0 | 15 | 77 | 356 | 97 | 51 | 49 | 9 | 5 | 1 | 2 | 41 | 2 | 22 | 4 | 1 | 3 | 4 | .429 | 0 | 0 | 5.73 |

## Rosario Rodriguez

**Pitches:** Left **Bats:** Right **Pos:** RP **Ht:** 6' 0" **Wt:** 185 **Born:** 07/08/69 **Age:** 21

| | | | HOW MUCH HE PITCHED | | | | | | WHAT HE GAVE UP | | | | | | | | | | | | THE RESULTS | | | | | |
|---|---|---|---|---|---|---|---|---|---|---|---|---|---|---|---|---|---|---|---|---|---|---|---|---|---|---|
| Year | Team | Lg | G | GS | CG | GF | IP | BFP | H | R | ER | HR | SH | SF | HB | TBB | IBB | SO | WP | Bk | W | L | Pct. | ShO | Sv | ERA |
| 1987 | Reds | R | 17 | 10 | 0 | 4 | 64.1 | 271 | 64 | 32 | 22 | 2 | 2 | 2 | 2 | 21 | 5 | 33 | 1 | 3 | 1 | 5 | .167 | 0 | 1 | 3.08 |
| 1988 | Greensboro | A | 23 | 3 | 1 | 13 | 65.1 | 267 | 49 | 15 | 11 | 2 | 5 | 1 | 3 | 24 | 3 | 53 | 4 | 8 | 6 | 4 | .600 | 1 | 2 | 1.52 |
| | Cedar Rapds | A | 13 | 11 | 0 | 0 | 70 | 314 | 73 | 41 | 31 | 4 | 2 | 4 | 5 | 25 | 2 | 47 | 3 | 11 | 3 | 4 | .429 | 0 | 0 | 3.99 |
| 1989 | Chattanooga | AA | 28 | 0 | 0 | 11 | 44.1 | 195 | 48 | 24 | 22 | 6 | 3 | 2 | 4 | 18 | 2 | 36 | 6 | 3 | 3 | 0 | 1.000 | 0 | 2 | 4.47 |
| 1990 | Nashville | AAA | 5 | 0 | 0 | 1 | 4.1 | 19 | 4 | 5 | 5 | 1 | 0 | 1 | 0 | 3 | 0 | 1 | 0 | 1 | 0 | 1 | .000 | 0 | 0 | 10.38 |
| | Chattanooga | AA | 36 | 2 | 1 | 22 | 53.2 | 256 | 52 | 29 | 26 | 5 | 11 | 0 | 6 | 48 | 5 | 39 | 7 | 3 | 2 | 2 | .500 | 0 | 7 | 4.36 |
| 1989 | Cincinnati | NL | 7 | 0 | 0 | 4 | 4.1 | 19 | 3 | 2 | 2 | 0 | 0 | 0 | 0 | 3 | 1 | 0 | 1 | 0 | 1 | 1 | .500 | 0 | 0 | 4.15 |
| 1990 | Cincinnati | NL | 9 | 0 | 0 | 4 | 10.1 | 47 | 15 | 7 | 7 | 3 | 1 | 1 | 1 | 2 | 0 | 8 | 0 | 0 | 0 | 0 | .000 | 0 | 0 | 6.10 |
| 2 ML YEARS | | | 16 | 0 | 0 | 8 | 14.2 | 66 | 18 | 9 | 9 | 3 | 1 | 1 | 1 | 5 | 1 | 8 | 1 | 0 | 1 | 1 | .500 | 0 | 0 | 5.52 |

## Mike Roesler

**Pitches:** Right **Bats:** Right **Pos:** RP **Ht:** 6' 5" **Wt:** 195 **Born:** 09/12/63 **Age:** 27

| | | | HOW MUCH HE PITCHED | | | | | | WHAT HE GAVE UP | | | | | | | | | | | | THE RESULTS | | | | | |
|---|---|---|---|---|---|---|---|---|---|---|---|---|---|---|---|---|---|---|---|---|---|---|---|---|---|---|
| Year | Team | Lg | G | GS | CG | GF | IP | BFP | H | R | ER | HR | SH | SF | HB | TBB | IBB | SO | WP | Bk | W | L | Pct. | ShO | Sv | ERA |
| 1985 | Billings | R | 13 | 13 | 4 | 0 | 88.2 | 0 | 72 | 32 | 23 | 3 | 0 | 0 | 2 | 28 | 0 | 73 | 5 | 1 | 8 | 2 | .800 | 1 | 0 | 2.33 |
| 1986 | Cedar Rapds | A | 32 | 24 | 1 | 4 | 163 | 718 | 165 | 95 | 83 | 16 | 3 | 1 | 5 | 80 | 1 | 135 | 13 | 2 | 9 | 13 | .409 | 0 | 3 | 4.58 |
| 1987 | Tampa | A | 28 | 0 | 0 | 24 | 36.1 | 155 | 30 | 14 | 9 | 0 | 3 | 3 | 0 | 15 | 4 | 29 | 2 | 0 | 7 | 2 | .778 | 0 | 11 | 2.23 |
| | Vermont | AA | 22 | 0 | 0 | 20 | 27.1 | 115 | 28 | 10 | 10 | 1 | 2 | 0 | 0 | 10 | 3 | 19 | 0 | 0 | 4 | 2 | .667 | 0 | 11 | 3.29 |
| 1988 | Nashville | AAA | 32 | 0 | 0 | 17 | 41.1 | 195 | 44 | 25 | 23 | 1 | 2 | 3 | 2 | 27 | 2 | 31 | 3 | 3 | 3 | 2 | .600 | 0 | 1 | 5.01 |
| | Chattanooga | AA | 16 | 0 | 0 | 13 | 20.1 | 83 | 16 | 5 | 5 | 1 | 3 | 0 | 0 | 8 | 0 | 13 | 0 | 0 | 1 | 1 | .500 | 0 | 9 | 2.21 |
| 1989 | Nashville | AAA | 40 | 0 | 0 | 30 | 69.1 | 305 | 63 | 30 | 25 | 2 | 3 | 4 | 1 | 39 | 4 | 53 | 5 | 1 | 6 | 4 | .600 | 0 | 10 | 3.25 |
| 1990 | Buffalo | AAA | 24 | 0 | 0 | 7 | 42 | 198 | 50 | 25 | 20 | 2 | 7 | 1 | 1 | 17 | 6 | 19 | 3 | 0 | 0 | 3 | .000 | 0 | 0 | 4.29 |
| | Harrisburg | AA | 10 | 0 | 0 | 1 | 23.2 | 104 | 29 | 14 | 12 | 3 | 2 | 1 | 0 | 6 | 1 | 10 | 0 | 0 | 2 | 1 | .667 | 0 | 0 | 4.56 |
| 1989 | Cincinnati | NL | 17 | 0 | 0 | 6 | 25 | 102 | 22 | 11 | 11 | 4 | 1 | 0 | 0 | 9 | 1 | 14 | 0 | 0 | 0 | 1 | .000 | 0 | 0 | 3.96 |
| 1990 | Pittsburgh | NL | 5 | 0 | 0 | 1 | 6 | 25 | 5 | 2 | 2 | 1 | 0 | 0 | 0 | 2 | 0 | 4 | 0 | 0 | 1 | 0 | 1.000 | 0 | 0 | 3.00 |
| 2 ML YEARS | | | 22 | 0 | 0 | 7 | 31 | 127 | 27 | 13 | 13 | 5 | 1 | 0 | 0 | 11 | 1 | 18 | 0 | 0 | 1 | 1 | .500 | 0 | 0 | 3.77 |

## Kenny Rogers

**Pitches:** Left **Bats:** Left **Pos:** RP/SP **Ht:** 6' 1" **Wt:** 200 **Born:** 11/10/64 **Age:** 26

| | | | HOW MUCH HE PITCHED | | | | | | WHAT HE GAVE UP | | | | | | | | | | | | THE RESULTS | | | | | |
|---|---|---|---|---|---|---|---|---|---|---|---|---|---|---|---|---|---|---|---|---|---|---|---|---|---|---|
| Year | Team | Lg | G | GS | CG | GF | IP | BFP | H | R | ER | HR | SH | SF | HB | TBB | IBB | SO | WP | Bk | W | L | Pct. | ShO | Sv | ERA |
| 1984 | Burlington | A | 39 | 4 | 1 | 16 | 92.2 | 396 | 87 | 52 | 41 | 9 | 5 | 0 | 4 | 33 | 3 | 93 | 8 | 0 | 4 | 7 | .364 | 1 | 3 | 3.98 |
| 1985 | Daytona Bch | A | 6 | 0 | 0 | 1 | 10 | 54 | 12 | 9 | 8 | 0 | 1 | 1 | 1 | 11 | 1 | 9 | 3 | 0 | 0 | 1 | .000 | 0 | 0 | 7.20 |
| | Burlington | A | 33 | 4 | 2 | 12 | 95 | 411 | 67 | 34 | 30 | 3 | 4 | 6 | 6 | 62 | 9 | 96 | 5 | 1 | 2 | 5 | .286 | 1 | 4 | 2.84 |
| 1986 | Salem | A | 12 | 12 | 0 | 0 | 66 | 297 | 75 | 54 | 46 | 9 | 2 | 2 | 1 | 26 | 0 | 46 | 2 | 1 | 2 | 7 | .222 | 0 | 0 | 6.27 |
| | Tulsa | AA | 10 | 4 | 0 | 2 | 26.1 | 135 | 39 | 30 | 29 | 4 | 0 | 0 | 0 | 18 | 1 | 23 | 3 | 1 | 0 | 3 | .000 | 0 | 0 | 9.91 |
| 1987 | Charlotte | A | 5 | 3 | 0 | 1 | 17 | 76 | 17 | 13 | 9 | 1 | 1 | 0 | 1 | 8 | 0 | 14 | 2 | 0 | 0 | 3 | .000 | 0 | 0 | 4.76 |
| | Tulsa | AA | 28 | 6 | 0 | 8 | 69 | 316 | 80 | 51 | 41 | 5 | 3 | 1 | 2 | 35 | 3 | 59 | 14 | 0 | 1 | 5 | .167 | 0 | 2 | 5.35 |
| 1988 | Charlotte | A | 8 | 6 | 0 | 1 | 35.1 | 138 | 22 | 8 | 5 | 1 | 0 | 2 | 2 | 11 | 0 | 26 | 1 | 2 | 2 | 0 | 1.000 | 0 | 1 | 1.27 |
| | Tulsa | AA | 13 | 13 | 2 | 0 | 83.1 | 354 | 73 | 43 | 37 | 6 | 3 | 1 | 3 | 34 | 0 | 76 | 3 | 4 | 4 | 6 | .400 | 0 | 0 | 4.00 |
| 1989 | Texas | AL | 73 | 0 | 0 | 24 | 73.2 | 314 | 60 | 28 | 24 | 2 | 6 | 3 | 4 | 42 | 9 | 63 | 6 | 0 | 3 | 4 | .429 | 0 | 2 | 2.93 |
| 1990 | Texas | AL | 69 | 3 | 0 | 46 | 97.2 | 428 | 93 | 40 | 34 | 6 | 7 | 4 | 1 | 42 | 5 | 74 | 5 | 0 | 10 | 6 | .625 | 0 | 15 | 3.13 |
| 2 ML YEARS | | | 142 | 3 | 0 | 70 | 171.1 | 742 | 153 | 68 | 58 | 8 | 13 | 7 | 5 | 84 | 14 | 137 | 11 | 0 | 13 | 10 | .565 | 0 | 17 | 3.05 |

## David Rohde

**Bats:** Both **Throws:** Right **Pos:** 2B **Ht:** 6' 2" **Wt:** 182 **Born:** 05/08/64 **Age:** 27

| | | | BATTING | | | | | | | | | | | | | | | | BASERUNNING | | | | PERCENTAGES | | |
|---|---|---|---|---|---|---|---|---|---|---|---|---|---|---|---|---|---|---|---|---|---|---|---|---|---|
| Year | Team | Lg | G | AB | H | 2B | 3B | HR | (Hm | Rd) | TB | R | RBI | TBB | IBB | SO | HBP | SH | SF | SB | CS | SB% | GDP | Avg | OBP | SLG |
| 1986 | Auburn | A | 61 | 207 | 54 | 6 | 4 | 2 | -- | -- | 74 | 41 | 22 | 37 | 1 | 37 | 0 | 1 | 2 | 28 | 9 | .76 | 2 | .261 | .370 | .357 |
| 1987 | Osceola | A | 103 | 377 | 108 | 15 | 1 | 5 | -- | -- | 140 | 57 | 42 | 50 | 1 | 58 | 4 | 10 | 0 | 12 | 6 | .67 | 4 | .286 | .376 | .371 |
| 1988 | Columbus | AA | 142 | 486 | 130 | 20 | 2 | 4 | -- | -- | 166 | 76 | 53 | 81 | 1 | 62 | 5 | 4 | 7 | 36 | 4 | .90 | 14 | .267 | .373 | .342 |
| 1989 | Columbus | AA | 67 | 254 | 71 | 5 | 2 | 2 | -- | -- | 86 | 40 | 27 | 41 | 0 | 25 | 1 | 5 | 2 | 15 | 5 | .75 | 6 | .280 | .379 | .339 |

| Year Team | Lg | G | AB | H | 2B | 3B | HR | (Hm | Rd) | TB | R | RBI | TBB | IBB | SO | HBP | SH | SF | SB | CS | SB% | GDP | Avg | OBP | SLG |
|---|---|---|---|---|---|---|---|---|---|---|---|---|---|---|---|---|---|---|---|---|---|---|---|---|---|
| Tucson | AAA | 75 | 234 | 68 | 7 | 3 | 1 | -- | -- | 84 | 35 | 30 | 32 | 1 | 30 | 1 | 7 | 5 | 11 | 5 | .69 | 4 | .291 | .371 | .359 |
| 1990 Tucson | AAA | 47 | 170 | 60 | 10 | 2 | 0 | -- | -- | 74 | 42 | 20 | 40 | 0 | 20 | 1 | 1 | 0 | 5 | 2 | .71 | 7 | .353 | .479 | .435 |
| 1990 Houston | NL | 59 | 98 | 18 | 4 | 0 | 0 | (0 | 0) | 22 | 8 | 5 | 9 | 2 | 20 | 5 | 4 | 1 | 0 | 0 | .00 | 3 | .184 | .283 | .224 |

## Mel Rojas

**Pitches:** Right **Bats:** Right **Pos:** RP **Ht:** 5'11" **Wt:** 175 **Born:** 12/10/66 **Age:** 24

| HOW MUCH HE PITCHED | | | | | | | | WHAT HE GAVE UP | | | | | | | | | | | | THE RESULTS | | | | | |
|---|---|---|---|---|---|---|---|---|---|---|---|---|---|---|---|---|---|---|---|---|---|---|---|---|---|
| Year Team | Lg | G | GS | CG | GF | IP | BFP | H | R | ER | HR | SH | SF | HB | TBB | IBB | SO | WP | Bk | W | L | Pct. | ShO | Sv | ERA |
| 1986 Expos | R | 13 | 12 | 1 | 1 | 55.1 | 261 | 63 | 39 | 30 | 0 | 3 | 3 | 2 | 37 | 0 | 34 | 4 | 0 | 4 | 5 | .444 | 0 | 0 | 4.88 |
| 1987 Burlington | A | 25 | 25 | 4 | 0 | 158.2 | 686 | 146 | 84 | 67 | 10 | 4 | 6 | 3 | 67 | 1 | 100 | 8 | 0 | 8 | 9 | .471 | 1 | 0 | 3.80 |
| 1988 Rockford | A | 12 | 12 | 3 | 0 | 73.1 | 302 | 52 | 30 | 20 | 3 | 3 | 1 | 2 | 29 | 0 | 72 | 3 | 2 | 6 | 4 | .600 | 0 | 0 | 2.45 |
| Wst Plm Bch | A | 2 | 2 | 0 | 0 | 5 | 19 | 4 | 2 | 2 | 1 | 0 | 0 | 0 | 1 | 0 | 4 | 0 | 0 | 1 | 0 | 1.000 | 0 | 0 | 3.60 |
| 1989 Jacksnville | AA | 34 | 12 | 1 | 17 | 112 | 447 | 62 | 39 | 31 | 1 | 7 | 4 | 5 | 57 | 0 | 104 | 8 | 1 | 10 | 7 | .588 | 1 | 5 | 2.49 |
| 1990 Indianapols | AAA | 17 | 17 | 0 | 0 | 97.2 | 412 | 84 | 42 | 34 | 9 | 5 | 2 | 1 | 47 | 3 | 64 | 3 | 1 | 2 | 4 | .333 | 0 | 0 | 3.13 |
| 1990 Montreal | NL | 23 | 0 | 0 | 5 | 40 | 173 | 34 | 17 | 16 | 5 | 2 | 0 | 2 | 24 | 4 | 26 | 2 | 0 | 3 | 1 | .750 | 0 | 1 | 3.60 |

## Ed Romero

**Bats:** Right **Throws:** Right **Pos:** 3B **Ht:** 5'11" **Wt:** 180 **Born:** 12/09/57 **Age:** 33

| BATTING | | | | | | | | | | | | | | | | | | | BASERUNNING | | | | PERCENTAGES | | |
|---|---|---|---|---|---|---|---|---|---|---|---|---|---|---|---|---|---|---|---|---|---|---|---|---|---|
| Year Team | Lg | G | AB | H | 2B | 3B | HR | (Hm | Rd) | TB | R | RBI | TBB | IBB | SO | HBP | SH | SF | SB | CS | SB% | GDP | Avg | OBP | SLG |
| 1977 Milwaukee | AL | 10 | 25 | 7 | 1 | 0 | 0 | (0 | 0) | 8 | 4 | 2 | 4 | 0 | 3 | 0 | 1 | 0 | 0 | 0 | .00 | 1 | .280 | .379 | .320 |
| 1980 Milwaukee | AL | 42 | 104 | 27 | 7 | 0 | 1 | (1 | 0) | 37 | 20 | 10 | 9 | 0 | 11 | 0 | 2 | 0 | 2 | 0 | 1.00 | 3 | .260 | .319 | .356 |
| 1981 Milwaukee | AL | 44 | 91 | 18 | 3 | 0 | 1 | (0 | 1) | 24 | 6 | 10 | 4 | 0 | 9 | 0 | 1 | 2 | 0 | 2 | .00 | 4 | .198 | .227 | .264 |
| 1982 Milwaukee | AL | 52 | 144 | 36 | 8 | 0 | 1 | (1 | 0) | 47 | 18 | 7 | 8 | 0 | 16 | 0 | 3 | 0 | 0 | 0 | .00 | 4 | .250 | .289 | .326 |
| 1983 Milwaukee | AL | 59 | 145 | 46 | 7 | 0 | 1 | (0 | 1) | 56 | 17 | 18 | 8 | 0 | 8 | 0 | 3 | 2 | 1 | 0 | 1.00 | 2 | .317 | .348 | .386 |
| 1984 Milwaukee | AL | 116 | 357 | 90 | 12 | 0 | 1 | (1 | 0) | 105 | 36 | 31 | 29 | 2 | 25 | 1 | 6 | 4 | 3 | 3 | .50 | 12 | .252 | .307 | .294 |
| 1985 Milwaukee | AL | 88 | 251 | 63 | 11 | 1 | 0 | (0 | 0) | 76 | 24 | 21 | 26 | 0 | 20 | 0 | 5 | 0 | 1 | 1 | .50 | 3 | .251 | .321 | .303 |
| 1986 Boston | AL | 100 | 233 | 49 | 11 | 0 | 2 | (2 | 0) | 66 | 41 | 23 | 18 | 0 | 16 | 2 | 7 | 3 | 2 | 0 | 1.00 | 5 | .210 | .270 | .283 |
| 1987 Boston | AL | 88 | 235 | 64 | 5 | 0 | 0 | (0 | 0) | 69 | 23 | 14 | 18 | 0 | 22 | 0 | 1 | 2 | 0 | 2 | .00 | 9 | .272 | .322 | .294 |
| 1988 Boston | AL | 31 | 75 | 18 | 3 | 0 | 0 | (0 | 0) | 21 | 3 | 5 | 3 | 0 | 8 | 1 | 2 | 2 | 0 | 0 | .00 | 4 | .240 | .272 | .280 |
| 1989 3 ML Teams | | 68 | 182 | 39 | 8 | 0 | 1 | (0 | 1) | 50 | 18 | 10 | 7 | 1 | 17 | 1 | 2 | 2 | 0 | 2 | .00 | 5 | .214 | .245 | .275 |
| 1990 Detroit | AL | 32 | 70 | 16 | 3 | 0 | 0 | (0 | 0) | 19 | 8 | 4 | 6 | 1 | 4 | 0 | 3 | 1 | 0 | 0 | .00 | 0 | .229 | .286 | .271 |
| 1989 Boston | AL | 46 | 113 | 24 | 4 | 0 | 0 | (0 | 0) | 28 | 14 | 6 | 7 | 1 | 7 | 1 | 2 | 2 | 0 | 2 | .00 | 1 | .212 | .260 | .248 |
| Atlanta | NL | 7 | 19 | 5 | 1 | 0 | 1 | (0 | 1) | 9 | 1 | 1 | 0 | 0 | 0 | 0 | 0 | 0 | 0 | 0 | .00 | 1 | .263 | .263 | .474 |
| Milwaukee | AL | 15 | 50 | 10 | 3 | 0 | 0 | (0 | 0) | 13 | 3 | 3 | 0 | 0 | 10 | 0 | 0 | 0 | 0 | 0 | .00 | 3 | .200 | .200 | .260 |
| 12 ML YEARS | | 730 | 1912 | 473 | 79 | 1 | 8 | (5 | 3) | 578 | 218 | 155 | 140 | 4 | 159 | 5 | 36 | 18 | 9 | 10 | .47 | 52 | .247 | .298 | .302 |

## Kevin Romine

**Bats:** Right **Throws:** Right **Pos:** RF/CF **Ht:** 5'11" **Wt:** 185 **Born:** 05/23/61 **Age:** 30

| BATTING | | | | | | | | | | | | | | | | | | | BASERUNNING | | | | PERCENTAGES | | |
|---|---|---|---|---|---|---|---|---|---|---|---|---|---|---|---|---|---|---|---|---|---|---|---|---|---|
| Year Team | Lg | G | AB | H | 2B | 3B | HR | (Hm | Rd) | TB | R | RBI | TBB | IBB | SO | HBP | SH | SF | SB | CS | SB% | GDP | Avg | OBP | SLG |
| 1985 Boston | AL | 24 | 28 | 6 | 2 | 0 | 0 | (0 | 0) | 8 | 3 | 1 | 1 | 0 | 4 | 0 | 2 | 0 | 1 | 0 | 1.00 | 1 | .214 | .241 | .286 |
| 1986 Boston | AL | 35 | 35 | 9 | 2 | 0 | 0 | (0 | 0) | 11 | 6 | 2 | 3 | 0 | 9 | 0 | 1 | 0 | 2 | 0 | 1.00 | 1 | .257 | .316 | .314 |
| 1987 Boston | AL | 9 | 24 | 7 | 2 | 0 | 0 | (0 | 0) | 9 | 5 | 2 | 2 | 0 | 6 | 0 | 0 | 0 | 0 | 0 | .00 | 0 | .292 | .346 | .375 |
| 1988 Boston | AL | 57 | 78 | 15 | 2 | 1 | 1 | (1 | 0) | 22 | 17 | 6 | 7 | 0 | 15 | 0 | 0 | 0 | 2 | 0 | 1.00 | 3 | .192 | .259 | .282 |
| 1989 Boston | AL | 92 | 274 | 75 | 13 | 0 | 1 | (1 | 0) | 91 | 30 | 23 | 21 | 1 | 53 | 2 | 3 | 3 | 1 | 1 | .50 | 11 | .274 | .327 | .332 |
| 1990 Boston | AL | 70 | 136 | 37 | 7 | 0 | 2 | (2 | 0) | 50 | 21 | 14 | 12 | 0 | 27 | 1 | 0 | 2 | 4 | 0 | 1.00 | 7 | .272 | .331 | .368 |
| 6 ML YEARS | | 287 | 575 | 149 | 28 | 1 | 4 | (4 | 0) | 191 | 82 | 48 | 46 | 1 | 114 | 3 | 6 | 5 | 10 | 1 | .91 | 23 | .259 | .315 | .332 |

## Rolando Roomes

**Bats:** Right **Throws:** Right **Pos:** LF **Ht:** 6' 3" **Wt:** 180 **Born:** 02/15/62 **Age:** 29

| BATTING | | | | | | | | | | | | | | | | | | | BASERUNNING | | | | PERCENTAGES | | |
|---|---|---|---|---|---|---|---|---|---|---|---|---|---|---|---|---|---|---|---|---|---|---|---|---|---|
| Year Team | Lg | G | AB | H | 2B | 3B | HR | (Hm | Rd) | TB | R | RBI | TBB | IBB | SO | HBP | SH | SF | SB | CS | SB% | GDP | Avg | OBP | SLG |
| 1988 Chicago | NL | 17 | 16 | 3 | 0 | 0 | 0 | (0 | 0) | 3 | 3 | 0 | 0 | 0 | 4 | 0 | 0 | 0 | 0 | 1 | .00 | 0 | .188 | .188 | .188 |
| 1989 Cincinnati | NL | 107 | 315 | 83 | 18 | 5 | 7 | (5 | 2) | 132 | 36 | 34 | 13 | 0 | 100 | 3 | 0 | 3 | 12 | 8 | .60 | 2 | .263 | .296 | .419 |
| 1990 2 ML Teams | | 46 | 75 | 17 | 0 | 1 | 2 | (2 | 0) | 25 | 6 | 8 | 1 | 1 | 26 | 0 | 0 | 0 | 0 | 2 | .00 | 2 | .227 | .237 | .333 |
| 1990 Cincinnati | NL | 30 | 61 | 13 | 0 | 0 | 2 | (2 | 0) | 19 | 5 | 7 | 0 | 0 | 20 | 0 | 0 | 0 | 0 | 0 | .00 | 2 | .213 | .213 | .311 |
| Montreal | NL | 16 | 14 | 4 | 0 | 1 | 0 | (0 | 0) | 6 | 1 | 1 | 1 | 1 | 6 | 0 | 0 | 0 | 0 | 2 | .00 | 0 | .286 | .333 | .429 |
| 3 ML YEARS | | 170 | 406 | 103 | 18 | 6 | 9 | (7 | 2) | 160 | 45 | 42 | 14 | 1 | 130 | 3 | 0 | 3 | 12 | 11 | .52 | 4 | .254 | .282 | .394 |

## Victor Rosario

**Bats:** Right **Throws:** Right **Pos:** SS **Ht:** 5'11" **Wt:** 145 **Born:** 08/26/66 **Age:** 24

| BATTING | | | | | | | | | | | | | | | | | | | BASERUNNING | | | | PERCENTAGES | | |
|---|---|---|---|---|---|---|---|---|---|---|---|---|---|---|---|---|---|---|---|---|---|---|---|---|---|
| Year Team | Lg | G | AB | H | 2B | 3B | HR | (Hm | Rd) | TB | R | RBI | TBB | IBB | SO | HBP | SH | SF | SB | CS | SB% | GDP | Avg | OBP | SLG |
| 1984 Elmira | A | 23 | 27 | 3 | 0 | 0 | 0 | -- | -- | 3 | 2 | 0 | 3 | 0 | 6 | 0 | 0 | 0 | 0 | 0 | .00 | 0 | .111 | .200 | .111 |

| Year Team | Lg | G | AB | H | 2B | 3B | HR | (Hm | Rd) | TB | R | RBI | TBB | IBB | SO | HBP | SH | SF | SB | CS | SB% | GDP | Avg | OBP | SLG |
|---|---|---|---|---|---|---|---|---|---|---|---|---|---|---|---|---|---|---|---|---|---|---|---|---|---|
| 1985 Elmira | A | 59 | 177 | 36 | 8 | 1 | 1 | -- | -- | 49 | 11 | 14 | 19 | 0 | 47 | 1 | 1 | 1 | 1 | 2 | .33 | 3 | .203 | .283 | .277 |
| 1986 Greensboro | A | 26 | 93 | 28 | 5 | 1 | 4 | -- | -- | 47 | 12 | 19 | 0 | 0 | 14 | 1 | 1 | 2 | 3 | 1 | .75 | 0 | .301 | .302 | .505 |
| Winter Havn | A | 19 | 52 | 12 | 2 | 0 | 0 | -- | -- | 14 | 6 | 5 | 1 | 0 | 10 | 0 | 0 | 0 | 0 | 0 | .00 | 1 | .231 | .245 | .269 |
| 1987 Greensboro | A | 109 | 370 | 81 | 9 | 0 | 10 | -- | -- | 120 | 43 | 48 | 24 | 3 | 60 | 7 | 3 | 1 | 2 | 5 | .29 | 8 | .219 | .279 | .324 |
| 1988 New Britain | AA | 101 | 347 | 90 | 14 | 1 | 1 | -- | -- | 109 | 28 | 26 | 11 | 1 | 56 | 2 | 7 | 2 | 4 | 6 | .40 | 4 | .259 | .285 | .314 |
| 1989 Scr Wil-Bar | AAA | 56 | 151 | 39 | 7 | 0 | 0 | -- | -- | 46 | 16 | 16 | 4 | 0 | 29 | 1 | 3 | 1 | 3 | 1 | .75 | 1 | .258 | .280 | .305 |
| 1990 Scr Wil-Bar | AAA | 143 | 478 | 120 | 23 | 6 | 5 | -- | -- | 170 | 45 | 42 | 12 | 2 | 91 | 1 | 7 | 4 | 8 | 3 | .73 | 4 | .251 | .269 | .356 |
| 1990 Atlanta | NL | 9 | 7 | 1 | 0 | 0 | 0 | (0 | 0) | 1 | 3 | 0 | 1 | 0 | 1 | 0 | 0 | 0 | 0 | 0 | .00 | 0 | .143 | .250 | .143 |

## Bobby Rose

**Bats:** Right **Throws:** Right **Pos:** 3B **Ht:** 5'11" **Wt:** 170 **Born:** 03/15/67 **Age:** 24

| BATTING | | | | | | | | | | | | | | | | | | | BASERUNNING | | | | PERCENTAGES | | |
|---|---|---|---|---|---|---|---|---|---|---|---|---|---|---|---|---|---|---|---|---|---|---|---|---|---|
| Year Team | Lg | G | AB | H | 2B | 3B | HR | (Hm | Rd) | TB | R | RBI | TBB | IBB | SO | HBP | SH | SF | SB | CS | SB% | GDP | Avg | OBP | SLG |
| 1985 Salem | A | 50 | 167 | 37 | 6 | 2 | 0 | -- | -- | 47 | 15 | 16 | 14 | 0 | 43 | 0 | 1 | 0 | 8 | 2 | .80 | 3 | .222 | .282 | .281 |
| 1986 Quad City | A | 129 | 467 | 118 | 21 | 5 | 7 | -- | -- | 170 | 67 | 56 | 66 | 2 | 116 | 0 | 2 | 4 | 13 | 9 | .59 | 11 | .253 | .343 | .364 |
| 1988 Quad City | A | 135 | 483 | 137 | 23 | 3 | 13 | -- | -- | 205 | 75 | 78 | 78 | 3 | 92 | 7 | 3 | 3 | 14 | 7 | .67 | 9 | .284 | .389 | .424 |
| Palm Sprngs | A | 1 | 3 | 1 | 0 | 0 | 0 | -- | -- | 1 | 0 | 1 | 0 | 0 | 1 | 0 | 0 | 0 | 0 | 0 | .00 | 0 | .333 | .333 | .333 |
| 1989 Midland | AA | 99 | 351 | 126 | 21 | 5 | 11 | -- | -- | 190 | 64 | 73 | 50 | 3 | 62 | 6 | 3 | 8 | 3 | 2 | .60 | 6 | .359 | .439 | .541 |
| 1990 Edmonton | AAA | 134 | 502 | 142 | 27 | 10 | 9 | -- | -- | 216 | 84 | 68 | 56 | 0 | 83 | 4 | 7 | 6 | 6 | 2 | .75 | 14 | .283 | .356 | .430 |
| 1989 California | AL | 14 | 38 | 8 | 1 | 2 | 1 | (1 | 0) | 16 | 4 | 3 | 2 | 0 | 10 | 1 | 1 | 0 | 0 | 0 | .00 | 2 | .211 | .268 | .421 |
| 1990 California | AL | 7 | 13 | 5 | 0 | 0 | 1 | (1 | 0) | 8 | 5 | 2 | 2 | 0 | 1 | 0 | 1 | 0 | 0 | 0 | .00 | 0 | .385 | .467 | .615 |
| 2 ML YEARS | | 21 | 51 | 13 | 1 | 2 | 2 | (2 | 0) | 24 | 9 | 5 | 4 | 0 | 11 | 1 | 2 | 0 | 0 | 0 | .00 | 2 | .255 | .321 | .471 |

## Steve Rosenberg

**Pitches:** Left **Bats:** Left **Pos:** RP **Ht:** 6' 0" **Wt:** 185 **Born:** 10/31/64 **Age:** 26

| HOW MUCH HE PITCHED | | | | | | | | WHAT HE GAVE UP | | | | | | | | | | | | THE RESULTS | | | | | |
|---|---|---|---|---|---|---|---|---|---|---|---|---|---|---|---|---|---|---|---|---|---|---|---|---|---|
| Year Team | Lg | G | GS | CG | GF | IP | BFP | H | R | ER | HR | SH | SF | HB | TBB | IBB | SO | WP | Bk | W | L | Pct. | ShO | Sv | ERA |
| 1988 Chicago | AL | 33 | 0 | 0 | 18 | 46 | 203 | 53 | 22 | 22 | 5 | 3 | 3 | 0 | 19 | 0 | 28 | 1 | 0 | 0 | 1 | .000 | 0 | 1 | 4.30 |
| 1989 Chicago | AL | 38 | 21 | 2 | 2 | 142 | 617 | 148 | 92 | 78 | 14 | 7 | 9 | 1 | 58 | 1 | 77 | 7 | 2 | 4 | 13 | .235 | 0 | 0 | 4.94 |
| 1990 Chicago | AL | 6 | 0 | 0 | 3 | 10 | 44 | 10 | 6 | 6 | 2 | 0 | 0 | 0 | 5 | 0 | 4 | 0 | 0 | 1 | 0 | 1.000 | 0 | 0 | 5.40 |
| 3 ML YEARS | | 77 | 21 | 2 | 23 | 198 | 864 | 211 | 120 | 106 | 21 | 10 | 12 | 1 | 82 | 1 | 109 | 8 | 2 | 5 | 14 | .263 | 0 | 1 | 4.82 |

## Mark Ross

**Pitches:** Right **Bats:** Right **Pos:** RP **Ht:** 6' 0" **Wt:** 200 **Born:** 08/08/57 **Age:** 33

| HOW MUCH HE PITCHED | | | | | | | | WHAT HE GAVE UP | | | | | | | | | | | | THE RESULTS | | | | | |
|---|---|---|---|---|---|---|---|---|---|---|---|---|---|---|---|---|---|---|---|---|---|---|---|---|---|
| Year Team | Lg | G | GS | CG | GF | IP | BFP | H | R | ER | HR | SH | SF | HB | TBB | IBB | SO | WP | Bk | W | L | Pct. | ShO | Sv | ERA |
| 1982 Houston | NL | 4 | 0 | 0 | 2 | 6 | 21 | 3 | 1 | 1 | 0 | 0 | 0 | 0 | 0 | 0 | 4 | 0 | 0 | 0 | 0 | .000 | 0 | 0 | 1.50 |
| 1984 Houston | NL | 2 | 0 | 0 | 0 | 2.1 | 8 | 1 | 0 | 0 | 0 | 0 | 0 | 0 | 0 | 0 | 1 | 0 | 0 | 1 | 0 | 1.000 | 0 | 0 | 0.00 |
| 1985 Houston | NL | 8 | 0 | 0 | 4 | 13 | 52 | 12 | 7 | 7 | 2 | 0 | 0 | 0 | 2 | 0 | 3 | 2 | 0 | 0 | 2 | .000 | 0 | 1 | 4.85 |
| 1987 Pittsburgh | NL | 1 | 0 | 0 | 1 | 1 | 4 | 1 | 1 | 1 | 1 | 0 | 0 | 0 | 0 | 0 | 0 | 0 | 0 | 0 | 0 | .000 | 0 | 0 | 9.00 |
| 1988 Toronto | AL | 3 | 0 | 0 | 2 | 7.1 | 32 | 5 | 6 | 4 | 0 | 0 | 1 | 0 | 4 | 1 | 4 | 0 | 0 | 0 | 0 | .000 | 0 | 0 | 4.91 |
| 1990 Pittsburgh | NL | 9 | 0 | 0 | 6 | 12.2 | 50 | 11 | 5 | 5 | 2 | 1 | 0 | 0 | 4 | 2 | 5 | 1 | 0 | 1 | 0 | 1.000 | 0 | 0 | 3.55 |
| 6 ML YEARS | | 27 | 0 | 0 | 15 | 42.1 | 167 | 33 | 20 | 18 | 5 | 1 | 1 | 0 | 10 | 3 | 17 | 3 | 0 | 2 | 2 | .500 | 0 | 1 | 3.83 |

## Rick Rowland

**Bats:** Right **Throws:** Right **Pos:** C **Ht:** 6' 1" **Wt:** 210 **Born:** 02/25/67 **Age:** 24

| BATTING | | | | | | | | | | | | | | | | | | | BASERUNNING | | | | PERCENTAGES | | |
|---|---|---|---|---|---|---|---|---|---|---|---|---|---|---|---|---|---|---|---|---|---|---|---|---|---|
| Year Team | Lg | G | AB | H | 2B | 3B | HR | (Hm | Rd) | TB | R | RBI | TBB | IBB | SO | HBP | SH | SF | SB | CS | SB% | GDP | Avg | OBP | SLG |
| 1988 Bristol | R | 56 | 186 | 51 | 10 | 1 | 4 | -- | -- | 75 | 29 | 41 | 27 | 1 | 39 | 1 | 0 | 3 | 1 | 2 | .33 | 2 | .274 | .364 | .403 |
| 1989 Fayettevlle | A | 108 | 375 | 102 | 17 | 1 | 9 | -- | -- | 148 | 43 | 59 | 54 | 2 | 98 | 3 | 3 | 3 | 4 | 1 | .80 | 8 | .272 | .366 | .395 |
| 1990 London | AA | 47 | 161 | 46 | 10 | 0 | 8 | -- | -- | 80 | 22 | 30 | 20 | 3 | 33 | 3 | 0 | 1 | 1 | 1 | .50 | 7 | .286 | .373 | .497 |
| Toledo | AAA | 62 | 192 | 50 | 12 | 0 | 7 | -- | -- | 83 | 28 | 22 | 15 | 0 | 33 | 1 | 3 | 2 | 2 | 3 | .40 | 3 | .260 | .314 | .432 |
| 1990 Detroit | AL | 7 | 19 | 3 | 1 | 0 | 0 | (0 | 0) | 4 | 3 | 0 | 2 | 1 | 4 | 0 | 0 | 0 | 0 | 0 | .00 | 1 | .158 | .238 | .211 |

## Bruce Ruffin

**Pitches:** Left **Bats:** Right **Pos:** SP/RP **Ht:** 6' 2" **Wt:** 205 **Born:** 10/04/63 **Age:** 27

| HOW MUCH HE PITCHED | | | | | | | | WHAT HE GAVE UP | | | | | | | | | | | | THE RESULTS | | | | | |
|---|---|---|---|---|---|---|---|---|---|---|---|---|---|---|---|---|---|---|---|---|---|---|---|---|---|
| Year Team | Lg | G | GS | CG | GF | IP | BFP | H | R | ER | HR | SH | SF | HB | TBB | IBB | SO | WP | Bk | W | L | Pct. | ShO | Sv | ERA |
| 1986 Philadelphia | NL | 21 | 21 | 6 | 0 | 146.1 | 600 | 138 | 53 | 40 | 6 | 2 | 4 | 1 | 44 | 6 | 70 | 0 | 1 | 9 | 4 | .692 | 0 | 0 | 2.46 |
| 1987 Philadelphia | NL | 35 | 35 | 3 | 0 | 204.2 | 884 | 236 | 118 | 99 | 17 | 8 | 10 | 2 | 73 | 4 | 93 | 6 | 0 | 11 | 14 | .440 | 1 | 0 | 4.35 |
| 1988 Philadelphia | NL | 55 | 15 | 3 | 14 | 144.1 | 646 | 151 | 86 | 71 | 7 | 10 | 3 | 3 | 80 | 6 | 82 | 12 | 0 | 6 | 10 | .375 | 0 | 3 | 4.43 |
| 1989 Philadelphia | NL | 24 | 23 | 1 | 0 | 125.2 | 576 | 152 | 69 | 62 | 10 | 8 | 1 | 0 | 62 | 6 | 70 | 8 | 0 | 6 | 10 | .375 | 0 | 0 | 4.44 |
| 1990 Philadelphia | NL | 32 | 25 | 2 | 1 | 149 | 678 | 178 | 99 | 89 | 14 | 10 | 6 | 1 | 62 | 7 | 79 | 3 | 2 | 6 | 13 | .316 | 1 | 0 | 5.38 |
| 5 ML YEARS | | 167 | 119 | 15 | 15 | 770 | 3384 | 855 | 425 | 361 | 54 | 38 | 24 | 7 | 321 | 29 | 394 | 29 | 3 | 38 | 51 | .427 | 2 | 3 | 4.22 |

## Scott Ruskin

**Pitches:** Left **Bats:** Right **Pos:** RP **Ht:** 6' 2" **Wt:** 185 **Born:** 06/08/63 **Age:** 28

| HOW MUCH HE PITCHED | | | | | | | | WHAT HE GAVE UP | | | | | | | | | | | | THE RESULTS | | | | | |
|---|---|---|---|---|---|---|---|---|---|---|---|---|---|---|---|---|---|---|---|---|---|---|---|---|---|
| Year Team | Lg | G | GS | CG | GF | IP | BFP | H | R | ER | HR | SH | SF | HB | TBB | IBB | SO | WP | Bk | W | L | Pct. | ShO | Sv | ERA |
| 1989 Salem | A | 14 | 13 | 3 | 1 | 84.2 | 359 | 71 | 35 | 21 | 5 | 1 | 1 | 4 | 33 | 0 | 92 | 6 | 4 | 4 | 5 | .444 | 0 | 1 | 2.23 |
| Harrisburg | AA | 12 | 10 | 2 | 0 | 63 | 278 | 64 | 38 | 34 | 5 | 2 | 3 | 1 | 32 | 0 | 56 | 2 | 2 | 2 | 3 | .400 | 0 | 0 | 4.86 |
| 1990 2 ML Teams | | 67 | 0 | 0 | 12 | 75.1 | 336 | 75 | 28 | 23 | 4 | 5 | 2 | 2 | 38 | 6 | 57 | 3 | 1 | 3 | 2 | .600 | 0 | 2 | 2.75 |
| 1990 Pittsburgh | NL | 44 | 0 | 0 | 8 | 47.2 | 221 | 50 | 21 | 16 | 2 | 3 | 2 | 2 | 28 | 3 | 34 | 3 | 1 | 2 | 2 | .500 | 0 | 2 | 3.02 |
| Montreal | NL | 23 | 0 | 0 | 4 | 27.2 | 115 | 25 | 7 | 7 | 2 | 2 | 0 | 0 | 10 | 3 | 23 | 0 | 0 | 1 | 0 | 1.000 | 0 | 0 | 2.28 |

## Jeff Russell

**Pitches:** Right **Bats:** Right **Pos:** RP **Ht:** 6' 3" **Wt:** 210 **Born:** 09/02/61 **Age:** 29

| HOW MUCH HE PITCHED | | | | | | | | WHAT HE GAVE UP | | | | | | | | | | | | THE RESULTS | | | | | |
|---|---|---|---|---|---|---|---|---|---|---|---|---|---|---|---|---|---|---|---|---|---|---|---|---|---|
| Year Team | Lg | G | GS | CG | GF | IP | BFP | H | R | ER | HR | SH | SF | HB | TBB | IBB | SO | WP | Bk | W | L | Pct. | ShO | Sv | ERA |
| 1983 Cincinnati | NL | 10 | 10 | 2 | 0 | 68.1 | 282 | 58 | 30 | 23 | 7 | 6 | 5 | 0 | 22 | 3 | 40 | 1 | 1 | 4 | 5 | .444 | 0 | 0 | 3.03 |
| 1984 Cincinnati | NL | 33 | 30 | 4 | 1 | 181.2 | 787 | 186 | 97 | 86 | 15 | 8 | 3 | 4 | 65 | 8 | 101 | 3 | 3 | 6 | 18 | .250 | 2 | 0 | 4.26 |
| 1985 Texas | AL | 13 | 13 | 0 | 0 | 62 | 295 | 85 | 55 | 52 | 10 | 1 | 3 | 2 | 27 | 1 | 44 | 2 | 0 | 3 | 6 | .333 | 0 | 0 | 7.55 |
| 1986 Texas | AL | 37 | 0 | 0 | 9 | 82 | 338 | 74 | 40 | 31 | 11 | 1 | 2 | 1 | 31 | 2 | 54 | 5 | 0 | 5 | 2 | .714 | 0 | 2 | 3.40 |
| 1987 Texas | AL | 52 | 2 | 0 | 12 | 97.1 | 442 | 109 | 56 | 48 | 9 | 0 | 5 | 2 | 52 | 5 | 56 | 6 | 1 | 5 | 4 | .556 | 0 | 3 | 4.44 |
| 1988 Texas | AL | 34 | 24 | 5 | 1 | 188.2 | 793 | 183 | 86 | 80 | 15 | 4 | 3 | 7 | 66 | 3 | 88 | 5 | 7 | 10 | 9 | .526 | 0 | 0 | 3.82 |
| 1989 Texas | AL | 71 | 0 | 0 | 66 | 72.2 | 278 | 45 | 21 | 16 | 4 | 1 | 3 | 3 | 24 | 5 | 77 | 6 | 0 | 6 | 4 | .600 | 0 | 38 | 1.98 |
| 1990 Texas | AL | 27 | 0 | 0 | 22 | 25.1 | 111 | 23 | 15 | 12 | 1 | 3 | 1 | 0 | 16 | 5 | 16 | 2 | 0 | 1 | 5 | .167 | 0 | 10 | 4.26 |
| 8 ML YEARS | | 277 | 79 | 11 | 111 | 778 | 3326 | 763 | 400 | 348 | 72 | 24 | 25 | 19 | 303 | 32 | 476 | 30 | 12 | 40 | 53 | .430 | 2 | 53 | 4.03 |

## John Russell

**Bats:** Right **Throws:** Right **Pos:** C/DH **Ht:** 6' 0" **Wt:** 195 **Born:** 01/05/61 **Age:** 30

| BATTING | | | | | | | | | | | | | | | | | | | BASERUNNING | | | | PERCENTAGES | | |
|---|---|---|---|---|---|---|---|---|---|---|---|---|---|---|---|---|---|---|---|---|---|---|---|---|---|
| Year Team | Lg | G | AB | H | 2B | 3B | HR | (Hm | Rd) | TB | R | RBI | TBB | IBB | SO | HBP | SH | SF | SB | CS | SB% | GDP | Avg | OBP | SLG |
| 1984 Philadelphia | NL | 39 | 99 | 28 | 8 | 1 | 2 | (1 | 1) | 44 | 11 | 11 | 12 | 2 | 33 | 0 | 0 | 3 | 0 | 1 | .00 | 2 | .283 | .351 | .444 |
| 1985 Philadelphia | NL | 81 | 216 | 47 | 12 | 0 | 9 | (6 | 3) | 86 | 22 | 23 | 18 | 0 | 72 | 0 | 0 | 0 | 2 | 0 | 1.00 | 5 | .218 | .278 | .398 |
| 1986 Philadelphia | NL | 93 | 315 | 76 | 21 | 2 | 13 | (8 | 5) | 140 | 35 | 60 | 25 | 2 | 103 | 3 | 1 | 4 | 0 | 1 | .00 | 6 | .241 | .300 | .444 |
| 1987 Philadelphia | NL | 24 | 62 | 9 | 1 | 0 | 3 | (1 | 2) | 19 | 5 | 8 | 3 | 0 | 17 | 0 | 0 | 0 | 0 | 1 | .00 | 4 | .145 | .185 | .306 |
| 1988 Philadelphia | NL | 22 | 49 | 12 | 1 | 0 | 2 | (1 | 1) | 19 | 5 | 4 | 3 | 0 | 15 | 1 | 0 | 0 | 0 | 0 | .00 | 2 | .245 | .302 | .388 |
| 1989 Atlanta | NL | 74 | 159 | 29 | 2 | 0 | 2 | (1 | 1) | 37 | 14 | 9 | 8 | 1 | 53 | 1 | 0 | 1 | 0 | 0 | .00 | 4 | .182 | .225 | .233 |
| 1990 Texas | AL | 68 | 128 | 35 | 4 | 0 | 2 | (0 | 2) | 45 | 16 | 8 | 11 | 2 | 41 | 0 | 1 | 0 | 1 | 0 | 1.00 | 3 | .273 | .331 | .352 |
| 7 ML YEARS | | 401 | 1028 | 236 | 49 | 3 | 33 | (18 | 15) | 390 | 108 | 123 | 80 | 7 | 334 | 5 | 2 | 8 | 3 | 3 | .50 | 26 | .230 | .286 | .379 |

## Mark Ryal

**Bats:** Left **Throws:** Left **Pos:** LF **Ht:** 6' 1" **Wt:** 197 **Born:** 04/28/60 **Age:** 31

| BATTING | | | | | | | | | | | | | | | | | | | BASERUNNING | | | | PERCENTAGES | | |
|---|---|---|---|---|---|---|---|---|---|---|---|---|---|---|---|---|---|---|---|---|---|---|---|---|---|
| Year Team | Lg | G | AB | H | 2B | 3B | HR | (Hm | Rd) | TB | R | RBI | TBB | IBB | SO | HBP | SH | SF | SB | CS | SB% | GDP | Avg | OBP | SLG |
| 1982 Kansas City | AL | 6 | 13 | 1 | 0 | 0 | 0 | (0 | 0) | 1 | 0 | 0 | 1 | 0 | 3 | 0 | 0 | 0 | 0 | 0 | .00 | 0 | .077 | .143 | .077 |
| 1985 Chicago | AL | 12 | 33 | 5 | 3 | 0 | 0 | (0 | 0) | 8 | 4 | 3 | 3 | 0 | 3 | 0 | 1 | 0 | 0 | 0 | .00 | 2 | .152 | .222 | .242 |
| 1986 California | AL | 13 | 32 | 12 | 0 | 0 | 2 | (1 | 1) | 18 | 6 | 5 | 2 | 1 | 4 | 0 | 0 | 0 | 1 | 0 | 1.00 | 1 | .375 | .412 | .563 |
| 1987 California | AL | 58 | 100 | 20 | 6 | 0 | 5 | (3 | 2) | 41 | 7 | 18 | 3 | 1 | 15 | 0 | 1 | 0 | 0 | 0 | .00 | 4 | .200 | .223 | .410 |
| 1989 Philadelphia | NL | 29 | 33 | 8 | 2 | 0 | 0 | (0 | 0) | 10 | 2 | 5 | 1 | 0 | 6 | 0 | 0 | 0 | 0 | 0 | .00 | 0 | .242 | .265 | .303 |
| 1990 Pittsburgh | NL | 9 | 12 | 1 | 0 | 0 | 0 | (0 | 0) | 1 | 0 | 0 | 0 | 0 | 3 | 0 | 0 | 0 | 0 | 0 | .00 | 0 | .083 | .083 | .083 |
| 6 ML YEARS | | 127 | 223 | 47 | 11 | 0 | 7 | (4 | 3) | 79 | 19 | 31 | 10 | 2 | 34 | 0 | 2 | 0 | 1 | 0 | 1.00 | 7 | .211 | .245 | .354 |

## Nolan Ryan

**Pitches:** Right **Bats:** Right **Pos:** SP **Ht:** 6' 2" **Wt:** 220 **Born:** 01/31/47 **Age:** 44

| HOW MUCH HE PITCHED | | | | | | | | WHAT HE GAVE UP | | | | | | | | | | | | THE RESULTS | | | | | |
|---|---|---|---|---|---|---|---|---|---|---|---|---|---|---|---|---|---|---|---|---|---|---|---|---|---|
| Year Team | Lg | G | GS | CG | GF | IP | BFP | H | R | ER | HR | SH | SF | HB | TBB | IBB | SO | WP | Bk | W | L | Pct. | ShO | Sv | ERA |
| 1966 New York | NL | 2 | 1 | 0 | 0 | 3 | 17 | 5 | 5 | 5 | 1 | 0 | 0 | 0 | 3 | 1 | 6 | 1 | 0 | 0 | 1 | .000 | 0 | 0 | 15.00 |
| 1968 New York | NL | 21 | 18 | 3 | 1 | 134 | 559 | 93 | 50 | 46 | 12 | 12 | 4 | 4 | 75 | 4 | 133 | 7 | 0 | 6 | 9 | .400 | 0 | 0 | 3.09 |
| 1969 New York | NL | 25 | 10 | 2 | 4 | 89 | 375 | 60 | 38 | 35 | 3 | 2 | 2 | 1 | 53 | 3 | 92 | 1 | 3 | 6 | 3 | .667 | 0 | 1 | 3.54 |
| 1970 New York | NL | 27 | 19 | 5 | 4 | 132 | 570 | 86 | 59 | 50 | 10 | 8 | 4 | 4 | 97 | 2 | 125 | 8 | 0 | 7 | 11 | .389 | 2 | 1 | 3.41 |
| 1971 New York | NL | 30 | 26 | 3 | 1 | 152 | 705 | 125 | 78 | 67 | 8 | 3 | 0 | 15 | 116 | 4 | 137 | 6 | 1 | 10 | 14 | .417 | 0 | 0 | 3.97 |
| 1972 California | AL | 39 | 39 | 20 | 0 | 284 | 1154 | 166 | 80 | 72 | 14 | 11 | 3 | 10 | 157 | 4 | 329 | 18 | 0 | 19 | 16 | .543 | 9 | 0 | 2.28 |
| 1973 California | AL | 41 | 39 | 26 | 2 | 326 | 1355 | 238 | 113 | 104 | 18 | 7 | 7 | 7 | 162 | 2 | 383 | 15 | 0 | 21 | 16 | .568 | 4 | 1 | 2.87 |
| 1974 California | AL | 42 | 41 | 26 | 1 | 333 | 1392 | 221 | 127 | 107 | 18 | 12 | 4 | 9 | 202 | 3 | 367 | 9 | 0 | 22 | 16 | .579 | 3 | 0 | 2.89 |
| 1975 California | AL | 28 | 28 | 10 | 0 | 198 | 864 | 152 | 90 | 76 | 13 | 6 | 7 | 7 | 132 | 0 | 186 | 12 | 0 | 14 | 12 | .538 | 5 | 0 | 3.45 |
| 1976 California | AL | 39 | 39 | 21 | 0 | 284 | 1196 | 193 | 117 | 106 | 13 | 13 | 4 | 5 | 183 | 2 | 327 | 5 | 2 | 17 | 18 | .486 | 7 | 0 | 3.36 |
| 1977 California | AL | 37 | 37 | 22 | 0 | 299 | 1272 | 198 | 110 | 92 | 12 | 22 | 10 | 9 | 204 | 7 | 341 | 21 | 3 | 19 | 16 | .543 | 4 | 0 | 2.77 |
| 1978 California | AL | 31 | 31 | 14 | 0 | 235 | 1008 | 183 | 106 | 97 | 12 | 11 | 14 | 3 | 148 | 7 | 260 | 13 | 2 | 10 | 13 | .435 | 3 | 0 | 3.71 |
| 1979 California | AL | 34 | 34 | 17 | 0 | 223 | 937 | 169 | 104 | 89 | 15 | 8 | 10 | 6 | 114 | 3 | 223 | 9 | 0 | 16 | 14 | .533 | 5 | 0 | 3.59 |

| Year Team | Lg | G | GS | CG | GF | IP | BFP | H | R | ER | HR | SH | SF | HB | TBB | IBB | SO | WP | Bk | W | L | Pct. | ShO | Sv | ERA |
|---|---|---|---|---|---|---|---|---|---|---|---|---|---|---|---|---|---|---|---|---|---|---|---|---|---|
| 1980 Houston | NL | 35 | 35 | 4 | 0 | 234 | 982 | 205 | 100 | 87 | 10 | 7 | 7 | 3 | 98 | 1 | 200 | 10 | 1 | 11 | 10 | .524 | 2 | 0 | 3.35 |
| 1981 Houston | NL | 21 | 21 | 5 | 0 | 149 | 605 | 99 | 34 | 28 | 2 | 5 | 3 | 1 | 68 | 1 | 140 | 16 | 2 | 11 | 5 | .688 | 3 | 0 | 1.69 |
| 1982 Houston | NL | 35 | 35 | 10 | 0 | 250.1 | 1050 | 196 | 100 | 88 | 20 | 9 | 3 | 8 | 109 | 3 | 245 | 18 | 2 | 16 | 12 | .571 | 3 | 0 | 3.16 |
| 1983 Houston | NL | 29 | 29 | 5 | 0 | 196.1 | 804 | 134 | 74 | 65 | 9 | 7 | 5 | 4 | 101 | 3 | 183 | 5 | 1 | 14 | 9 | .609 | 2 | 0 | 2.98 |
| 1984 Houston | NL | 30 | 30 | 5 | 0 | 183.2 | 760 | 143 | 78 | 62 | 12 | 4 | 6 | 4 | 69 | 2 | 197 | 6 | 3 | 12 | 11 | .522 | 2 | 0 | 3.04 |
| 1985 Houston | NL | 35 | 35 | 4 | 0 | 232 | 983 | 205 | 108 | 98 | 12 | 11 | 12 | 9 | 95 | 8 | 209 | 14 | 2 | 10 | 12 | .455 | 0 | 0 | 3.80 |
| 1986 Houston | NL | 30 | 30 | 1 | 0 | 178 | 729 | 119 | 72 | 66 | 14 | 5 | 4 | 4 | 82 | 5 | 194 | 15 | 0 | 12 | 8 | .600 | 0 | 0 | 3.34 |
| 1987 Houston | NL | 34 | 34 | 0 | 0 | 211.2 | 873 | 154 | 75 | 65 | 14 | 9 | 1 | 4 | 87 | 2 | 270 | 10 | 2 | 8 | 16 | .333 | 0 | 0 | 2.76 |
| 1988 Houston | NL | 33 | 33 | 4 | 0 | 220 | 930 | 186 | 98 | 86 | 18 | 10 | 8 | 7 | 87 | 6 | 228 | 10 | 7 | 12 | 11 | .522 | 1 | 0 | 3.52 |
| 1989 Texas | AL | 32 | 32 | 6 | 0 | 239.1 | 988 | 162 | 96 | 85 | 17 | 9 | 5 | 9 | 98 | 3 | 301 | 19 | 1 | 16 | 10 | .615 | 2 | 0 | 3.20 |
| 1990 Texas | AL | 30 | 30 | 5 | 0 | 204 | 818 | 137 | 86 | 78 | 18 | 3 | 5 | 7 | 74 | 2 | 232 | 9 | 1 | 13 | 9 | .591 | 2 | 0 | 3.44 |
| 24 ML YEARS | | 740 | 706 | 218 | 13 | 4990.1 | 20926 | 3629 | 1998 | 1754 | 295 | 194 | 128 | 140 | 2614 | 78 | 5308 | 257 | 33 | 302 | 272 | .526 | 59 | 3 | 3.16 |

## Bret Saberhagen

**Pitches:** Right **Bats:** Right **Pos:** SP **Ht:** 6' 1" **Wt:** 185 **Born:** 04/11/64 **Age:** 27

| HOW MUCH HE PITCHED | | | | | | | | WHAT HE GAVE UP | | | | | | | | | | | | THE RESULTS | | | | | |
|---|---|---|---|---|---|---|---|---|---|---|---|---|---|---|---|---|---|---|---|---|---|---|---|---|---|
| Year Team | Lg | G | GS | CG | GF | IP | BFP | H | R | ER | HR | SH | SF | HB | TBB | IBB | SO | WP | Bk | W | L | Pct. | ShO | Sv | ERA |
| 1984 Kansas City | AL | 38 | 18 | 2 | 9 | 157.2 | 634 | 138 | 71 | 61 | 13 | 8 | 5 | 2 | 36 | 4 | 73 | 7 | 1 | 10 | 11 | .476 | 1 | 1 | 3.48 |
| 1985 Kansas City | AL | 32 | 32 | 10 | 0 | 235.1 | 931 | 211 | 79 | 75 | 19 | 9 | 7 | 1 | 38 | 1 | 158 | 1 | 3 | 20 | 6 | .769 | 1 | 0 | 2.87 |
| 1986 Kansas City | AL | 30 | 25 | 4 | 4 | 156 | 652 | 165 | 77 | 72 | 15 | 3 | 3 | 2 | 29 | 1 | 112 | 1 | 1 | 7 | 12 | .368 | 2 | 0 | 4.15 |
| 1987 Kansas City | AL | 33 | 33 | 15 | 0 | 257 | 1048 | 246 | 99 | 96 | 27 | 8 | 5 | 6 | 53 | 2 | 163 | 6 | 1 | 18 | 10 | .643 | 4 | 0 | 3.36 |
| 1988 Kansas City | AL | 35 | 35 | 9 | 0 | 260.2 | 1089 | 271 | 122 | 110 | 18 | 8 | 10 | 4 | 59 | 5 | 171 | 9 | 0 | 14 | 16 | .467 | 0 | 0 | 3.80 |
| 1989 Kansas City | AL | 36 | 35 | 12 | 0 | 262.1 | 1021 | 209 | 74 | 63 | 13 | 9 | 6 | 2 | 43 | 6 | 193 | 8 | 1 | 23 | 6 | .793 | 4 | 0 | 2.16 |
| 1990 Kansas City | AL | 20 | 20 | 5 | 0 | 135 | 561 | 146 | 52 | 49 | 9 | 4 | 4 | 1 | 28 | 1 | 87 | 1 | 0 | 5 | 9 | .357 | 0 | 0 | 3.27 |
| 7 ML YEARS | | 224 | 198 | 57 | 13 | 1464 | 5936 | 1386 | 574 | 526 | 114 | 49 | 40 | 18 | 286 | 20 | 957 | 33 | 7 | 97 | 70 | .581 | 12 | 1 | 3.23 |

## Chris Sabo

**Bats:** Right **Throws:** Right **Pos:** 3B **Ht:** 6' 0" **Wt:** 185 **Born:** 01/19/62 **Age:** 29

| BATTING | | | | | | | | | | | | | | | | | | | BASERUNNING | | | | PERCENTAGES | | |
|---|---|---|---|---|---|---|---|---|---|---|---|---|---|---|---|---|---|---|---|---|---|---|---|---|---|
| Year Team | Lg | G | AB | H | 2B | 3B | HR | (Hm | Rd) | TB | R | RBI | TBB | IBB | SO | HBP | SH | SF | SB | CS | SB% | GDP | Avg | OBP | SLG |
| 1988 Cincinnati | NL | 137 | 538 | 146 | 40 | 2 | 11 | (8 | 3) | 223 | 74 | 44 | 29 | 1 | 52 | 6 | 5 | 4 | 46 | 14 | .77 | 12 | .271 | .314 | .414 |
| 1989 Cincinnati | NL | 82 | 304 | 79 | 21 | 1 | 6 | (3 | 3) | 120 | 40 | 29 | 25 | 2 | 33 | 1 | 4 | 2 | 14 | 9 | .61 | 2 | .260 | .316 | .395 |
| 1990 Cincinnati | NL | 148 | 567 | 153 | 38 | 2 | 25 | (15 | 10) | 270 | 95 | 71 | 61 | 7 | 58 | 4 | 1 | 3 | 25 | 10 | .71 | 8 | .270 | .343 | .476 |
| 3 ML YEARS | | 367 | 1409 | 378 | 99 | 5 | 42 | (26 | 16) | 613 | 209 | 144 | 115 | 10 | 143 | 11 | 10 | 9 | 85 | 33 | .72 | 22 | .268 | .326 | .435 |

## Mark Salas

**Bats:** Left **Throws:** Right **Pos:** C **Ht:** 6' 0" **Wt:** 205 **Born:** 03/08/61 **Age:** 30

| BATTING | | | | | | | | | | | | | | | | | | | BASERUNNING | | | | PERCENTAGES | | |
|---|---|---|---|---|---|---|---|---|---|---|---|---|---|---|---|---|---|---|---|---|---|---|---|---|---|
| Year Team | Lg | G | AB | H | 2B | 3B | HR | (Hm | Rd) | TB | R | RBI | TBB | IBB | SO | HBP | SH | SF | SB | CS | SB% | GDP | Avg | OBP | SLG |
| 1984 St. Louis | NL | 14 | 20 | 2 | 1 | 0 | 0 | (0 | 0) | 3 | 1 | 1 | 0 | 0 | 3 | 0 | 1 | 0 | 0 | 0 | .00 | 0 | .100 | .100 | .150 |
| 1985 Minnesota | AL | 120 | 360 | 108 | 20 | 5 | 9 | (6 | 3) | 165 | 51 | 41 | 18 | 5 | 37 | 1 | 0 | 3 | 0 | 1 | .00 | 7 | .300 | .332 | .458 |
| 1986 Minnesota | AL | 91 | 258 | 60 | 7 | 4 | 8 | (5 | 3) | 99 | 28 | 33 | 18 | 2 | 32 | 1 | 5 | 3 | 3 | 1 | .75 | 8 | .233 | .282 | .384 |
| 1987 2 ML Teams | | 72 | 160 | 40 | 6 | 0 | 6 | (3 | 3) | 64 | 21 | 21 | 15 | 1 | 23 | 3 | 1 | 2 | 0 | 1 | .00 | 2 | .250 | .322 | .400 |
| 1988 Chicago | AL | 75 | 196 | 49 | 7 | 0 | 3 | (2 | 1) | 65 | 17 | 9 | 12 | 2 | 17 | 3 | 0 | 0 | 0 | 0 | .00 | 3 | .250 | .303 | .332 |
| 1989 Cleveland | AL | 30 | 77 | 17 | 4 | 1 | 2 | (1 | 1) | 29 | 4 | 7 | 5 | 1 | 13 | 1 | 0 | 0 | 0 | 0 | .00 | 2 | .221 | .277 | .377 |
| 1990 Detroit | AL | 74 | 164 | 38 | 3 | 0 | 9 | (8 | 1) | 68 | 18 | 24 | 21 | 2 | 28 | 1 | 1 | 0 | 0 | 0 | .00 | 3 | .232 | .323 | .415 |
| 1987 Minnesota | AL | 22 | 45 | 17 | 2 | 0 | 3 | (1 | 2) | 28 | 8 | 9 | 5 | 1 | 6 | 0 | 0 | 1 | 0 | 1 | .00 | 0 | .378 | .431 | .622 |
| New York | AL | 50 | 115 | 23 | 4 | 0 | 3 | (2 | 1) | 36 | 13 | 12 | 10 | 0 | 17 | 3 | 1 | 1 | 0 | 0 | .00 | 2 | .200 | .279 | .313 |
| 7 ML YEARS | | 476 | 1235 | 314 | 48 | 10 | 37 | (25 | 12) | 493 | 140 | 136 | 89 | 13 | 153 | 10 | 8 | 8 | 3 | 3 | .50 | 25 | .254 | .308 | .399 |

## Luis Salazar

**Bats:** Right **Throws:** Right **Pos:** 3B/LF **Ht:** 5' 9" **Wt:** 180 **Born:** 05/19/56 **Age:** 35

| BATTING | | | | | | | | | | | | | | | | | | | BASERUNNING | | | | PERCENTAGES | | |
|---|---|---|---|---|---|---|---|---|---|---|---|---|---|---|---|---|---|---|---|---|---|---|---|---|---|
| Year Team | Lg | G | AB | H | 2B | 3B | HR | (Hm | Rd) | TB | R | RBI | TBB | IBB | SO | HBP | SH | SF | SB | CS | SB% | GDP | Avg | OBP | SLG |
| 1980 San Diego | NL | 44 | 169 | 57 | 4 | 7 | 1 | (0 | 1) | 78 | 28 | 25 | 9 | 1 | 25 | 1 | 3 | 1 | 11 | 2 | .85 | 4 | .337 | .372 | .462 |
| 1981 San Diego | NL | 109 | 400 | 121 | 19 | 6 | 3 | (2 | 1) | 161 | 37 | 38 | 16 | 2 | 72 | 1 | 5 | 2 | 11 | 8 | .58 | 7 | .303 | .329 | .403 |
| 1982 San Diego | NL | 145 | 524 | 127 | 15 | 5 | 8 | (6 | 2) | 176 | 55 | 62 | 23 | 10 | 80 | 2 | 5 | 5 | 32 | 9 | .78 | 10 | .242 | .274 | .336 |
| 1983 San Diego | NL | 134 | 481 | 124 | 16 | 2 | 14 | (10 | 4) | 186 | 52 | 45 | 17 | 8 | 80 | 2 | 8 | 2 | 24 | 9 | .73 | 4 | .258 | .285 | .387 |
| 1984 San Diego | NL | 93 | 228 | 55 | 7 | 2 | 3 | (1 | 2) | 75 | 20 | 17 | 6 | 1 | 38 | 0 | 2 | 0 | 11 | 7 | .61 | 5 | .241 | .261 | .329 |
| 1985 Chicago | AL | 122 | 327 | 80 | 18 | 2 | 10 | (4 | 6) | 132 | 39 | 45 | 12 | 2 | 60 | 0 | 9 | 5 | 14 | 4 | .78 | 5 | .245 | .267 | .404 |
| 1986 Chicago | AL | 4 | 7 | 1 | 0 | 0 | 0 | (0 | 0) | 1 | 1 | 0 | 1 | 0 | 3 | 0 | 0 | 0 | 0 | 0 | .00 | 0 | .143 | .250 | .143 |
| 1987 San Diego | NL | 84 | 189 | 48 | 5 | 0 | 3 | (1 | 2) | 62 | 13 | 17 | 14 | 2 | 30 | 0 | 1 | 2 | 3 | 3 | .50 | 2 | .254 | .302 | .328 |
| 1988 Detroit | AL | 130 | 452 | 122 | 14 | 1 | 12 | (5 | 7) | 174 | 61 | 62 | 21 | 2 | 70 | 3 | 10 | 3 | 6 | 0 | 1.00 | 13 | .270 | .305 | .385 |
| 1989 2 ML Teams | | 121 | 326 | 92 | 12 | 2 | 9 | (6 | 3) | 135 | 34 | 34 | 15 | 3 | 57 | 1 | 7 | 0 | 1 | 4 | .20 | 6 | .282 | .316 | .414 |
| 1990 Chicago | NL | 115 | 410 | 104 | 13 | 3 | 12 | (7 | 5) | 159 | 44 | 47 | 19 | 3 | 59 | 4 | 0 | 1 | 3 | 1 | .75 | 4 | .254 | .293 | .388 |
| 1989 San Diego | NL | 95 | 246 | 66 | 7 | 2 | 8 | (5 | 3) | 101 | 27 | 22 | 11 | 3 | 44 | 1 | 7 | 0 | 1 | 3 | .25 | 4 | .268 | .302 | .411 |

| Year Team | Lg | G | AB | H | 2B | 3B | HR | (Hm | Rd) | TB | R | RBI | TBB | IBB | SO | HBP | SH | SF | SB | CS | SB% | GDP | Avg | OBP | SLG |
|---|---|---|---|---|---|---|---|---|---|---|---|---|---|---|---|---|---|---|---|---|---|---|---|---|---|
| Chicago | NL | 26 | 80 | 26 | 5 | 0 | 1 | (1 | 0) | 34 | 7 | 12 | 4 | 0 | 13 | 0 | 0 | 0 | 0 | 1 | .00 | 2 | .325 | .357 | .425 |
| 11 ML YEARS | | 1101 | 3513 | 931 | 123 | 30 | 75 | (42 | 33) | 1339 | 384 | 392 | 153 | 34 | 574 | 14 | 50 | 21 | 116 | 47 | .71 | 60 | .265 | .297 | .381 |

## Bill Sampen

**Pitches:** Right **Bats:** Right **Pos:** RP/SP **Ht:** 6' 1" **Wt:** 185 **Born:** 01/18/63 **Age:** 28

| | | HOW MUCH HE PITCHED | | | | | | WHAT HE GAVE UP | | | | | | | | | | | | THE RESULTS | | | | | |
|---|---|---|---|---|---|---|---|---|---|---|---|---|---|---|---|---|---|---|---|---|---|---|---|---|---|
| Year Team | Lg | G | GS | CG | GF | IP | BFP | H | R | ER | HR | SH | SF | HB | TBB | IBB | SO | WP | Bk | W | L | Pct. | ShO | Sv | ERA |
| 1985 Watertown | A | 5 | 0 | 0 | 2 | 10 | 48 | 9 | 3 | 2 | 0 | 1 | 1 | 1 | 7 | 0 | 11 | 2 | 0 | 0 | 0 | .000 | 0 | 1 | 1.80 |
| 1986 Watertown | A | 9 | 5 | 0 | 3 | 29.2 | 130 | 27 | 18 | 14 | 0 | 1 | 2 | 1 | 13 | 0 | 29 | 3 | 0 | 0 | 3 | .000 | 0 | 2 | 4.25 |
| 1987 Salem | A | 26 | 26 | 2 | 0 | 152.1 | 650 | 126 | 77 | 65 | 16 | 5 | 5 | 7 | 72 | 1 | 137 | 3 | 2 | 9 | 8 | .529 | 1 | 0 | 3.84 |
| 1988 Salem | A | 8 | 8 | 1 | 0 | 51.1 | 217 | 47 | 22 | 19 | 4 | 1 | 1 | 0 | 14 | 0 | 59 | 1 | 2 | 3 | 3 | .500 | 0 | 0 | 3.33 |
| Harrisburg | AA | 13 | 12 | 3 | 0 | 82.2 | 349 | 72 | 38 | 34 | 3 | 1 | 2 | 2 | 27 | 1 | 65 | 2 | 2 | 6 | 3 | .667 | 0 | 0 | 3.70 |
| 1989 Harrisburg | AA | 26 | 26 | 6 | 0 | 165.2 | 691 | 148 | 75 | 59 | 8 | 7 | 8 | 5 | 40 | 3 | 134 | 6 | 0 | 11 | 9 | .550 | 0 | 0 | 3.21 |
| 1990 Montreal | NL | 59 | 4 | 0 | 26 | 90.1 | 394 | 94 | 34 | 30 | 7 | 5 | 3 | 2 | 33 | 6 | 69 | 4 | 0 | 12 | 7 | .632 | 0 | 2 | 2.99 |

## Juan Samuel

**Bats:** Right **Throws:** Right **Pos:** 2B/CF **Ht:** 5'11" **Wt:** 170 **Born:** 12/09/60 **Age:** 30

| | | BATTING | | | | | | | | | | | | | | | | | BASERUNNING | | | | PERCENTAGES | | |
|---|---|---|---|---|---|---|---|---|---|---|---|---|---|---|---|---|---|---|---|---|---|---|---|---|---|
| Year Team | Lg | G | AB | H | 2B | 3B | HR | (Hm | Rd) | TB | R | RBI | TBB | IBB | SO | HBP | SH | SF | SB | CS | SB% | GDP | Avg | OBP | SLG |
| 1983 Philadelphia | NL | 18 | 65 | 18 | 1 | 2 | 2 | (1 | 1) | 29 | 14 | 5 | 4 | 1 | 16 | 1 | 0 | 1 | 3 | 2 | .60 | 1 | .277 | .324 | .446 |
| 1984 Philadelphia | NL | 160 | 701 | 191 | 36 | 19 | 15 | (8 | 7) | 310 | 105 | 69 | 28 | 2 | 168 | 7 | 0 | 1 | 72 | 15 | .83 | 6 | .272 | .307 | .442 |
| 1985 Philadelphia | NL | 161 | 663 | 175 | 31 | 13 | 19 | (8 | 11) | 289 | 101 | 74 | 33 | 2 | 141 | 6 | 2 | 5 | 53 | 19 | .74 | 8 | .264 | .303 | .436 |
| 1986 Philadelphia | NL | 145 | 591 | 157 | 36 | 12 | 16 | (10 | 6) | 265 | 90 | 78 | 26 | 3 | 142 | 8 | 1 | 7 | 42 | 14 | .75 | 8 | .266 | .302 | .448 |
| 1987 Philadelphia | NL | 160 | 655 | 178 | 37 | 15 | 28 | (15 | 13) | 329 | 113 | 100 | 60 | 5 | 162 | 5 | 0 | 6 | 35 | 15 | .70 | 12 | .272 | .335 | .502 |
| 1988 Philadelphia | NL | 157 | 629 | 153 | 32 | 9 | 12 | (7 | 5) | 239 | 68 | 67 | 39 | 6 | 151 | 12 | 0 | 5 | 33 | 10 | .77 | 8 | .243 | .298 | .380 |
| 1989 2 ML Teams | | 137 | 532 | 125 | 16 | 2 | 11 | (5 | 6) | 178 | 69 | 48 | 42 | 2 | 120 | 11 | 2 | 2 | 42 | 12 | .78 | 7 | .235 | .303 | .335 |
| 1990 Los Angeles | NL | 143 | 492 | 119 | 24 | 3 | 13 | (6 | 7) | 188 | 62 | 52 | 51 | 5 | 126 | 5 | 5 | 5 | 38 | 20 | .66 | 8 | .242 | .316 | .382 |
| 1989 Philadelphia | NL | 51 | 199 | 49 | 3 | 1 | 8 | (3 | 5) | 78 | 32 | 20 | 18 | 1 | 45 | 1 | 0 | 1 | 11 | 3 | .79 | 2 | .246 | .311 | .392 |
| New York | NL | 86 | 333 | 76 | 13 | 1 | 3 | (2 | 1) | 100 | 37 | 28 | 24 | 1 | 75 | 10 | 2 | 1 | 31 | 9 | .78 | 5 | .228 | .299 | .300 |
| 8 ML YEARS | | 1081 | 4328 | 1116 | 213 | 75 | 116 | (60 | 56) | 1827 | 622 | 493 | 283 | 26 | 1026 | 55 | 10 | 32 | 318 | 107 | .75 | 58 | .258 | .309 | .422 |

## Zip Sanchez

**Pitches:** Left **Bats:** Left **Pos:** RP **Ht:** 5' 9" **Wt:** 170 **Born:** 08/20/63 **Age:** 27

| | | HOW MUCH HE PITCHED | | | | | | WHAT HE GAVE UP | | | | | | | | | | | | THE RESULTS | | | | | |
|---|---|---|---|---|---|---|---|---|---|---|---|---|---|---|---|---|---|---|---|---|---|---|---|---|---|
| Year Team | Lg | G | GS | CG | GF | IP | BFP | H | R | ER | HR | SH | SF | HB | TBB | IBB | SO | WP | Bk | W | L | Pct. | ShO | Sv | ERA |
| 1988 Kansas City | AL | 19 | 1 | 0 | 6 | 35.2 | 157 | 36 | 20 | 18 | 0 | 2 | 1 | 0 | 18 | 2 | 14 | 3 | 1 | 3 | 2 | .600 | 0 | 1 | 4.54 |
| 1990 Kansas City | AL | 11 | 0 | 0 | 3 | 9.2 | 47 | 16 | 9 | 9 | 1 | 0 | 1 | 1 | 3 | 0 | 5 | 0 | 0 | 0 | 0 | .000 | 0 | 0 | 8.38 |
| 2 ML YEARS | | 30 | 1 | 0 | 9 | 45.1 | 204 | 52 | 29 | 27 | 1 | 2 | 2 | 1 | 21 | 2 | 19 | 3 | 1 | 3 | 2 | .600 | 0 | 1 | 5.36 |

## Ryne Sandberg

**Bats:** Right **Throws:** Right **Pos:** 2B **Ht:** 6' 2" **Wt:** 180 **Born:** 09/18/59 **Age:** 31

| | | BATTING | | | | | | | | | | | | | | | | | BASERUNNING | | | | PERCENTAGES | | |
|---|---|---|---|---|---|---|---|---|---|---|---|---|---|---|---|---|---|---|---|---|---|---|---|---|---|
| Year Team | Lg | G | AB | H | 2B | 3B | HR | (Hm | Rd) | TB | R | RBI | TBB | IBB | SO | HBP | SH | SF | SB | CS | SB% | GDP | Avg | OBP | SLG |
| 1981 Philadelphia | NL | 13 | 6 | 1 | 0 | 0 | 0 | (0 | 0) | 1 | 2 | 0 | 0 | 0 | 1 | 0 | 0 | 0 | 0 | 0 | .00 | 0 | .167 | .167 | .167 |
| 1982 Chicago | NL | 156 | 635 | 172 | 33 | 5 | 7 | (5 | 2) | 236 | 103 | 54 | 36 | 3 | 90 | 4 | 7 | 5 | 32 | 12 | .73 | 7 | .271 | .312 | .372 |
| 1983 Chicago | NL | 158 | 633 | 165 | 25 | 4 | 8 | (4 | 4) | 222 | 94 | 48 | 51 | 3 | 79 | 3 | 7 | 5 | 37 | 11 | .77 | 8 | .261 | .316 | .351 |
| 1984 Chicago | NL | 156 | 636 | 200 | 36 | 19 | 19 | (11 | 8) | 331 | 114 | 84 | 52 | 3 | 101 | 3 | 5 | 4 | 32 | 7 | .82 | 7 | .314 | .367 | .520 |
| 1985 Chicago | NL | 153 | 609 | 186 | 31 | 6 | 26 | (17 | 9) | 307 | 113 | 83 | 57 | 5 | 97 | 1 | 2 | 4 | 54 | 11 | .83 | 10 | .305 | .364 | .504 |
| 1986 Chicago | NL | 154 | 627 | 178 | 28 | 5 | 14 | (8 | 6) | 258 | 68 | 76 | 46 | 6 | 79 | 0 | 3 | 6 | 34 | 11 | .76 | 11 | .284 | .330 | .411 |
| 1987 Chicago | NL | 132 | 523 | 154 | 25 | 2 | 16 | (8 | 8) | 231 | 81 | 59 | 59 | 4 | 79 | 2 | 1 | 2 | 21 | 2 | .91 | 11 | .294 | .367 | .442 |
| 1988 Chicago | NL | 155 | 618 | 163 | 23 | 8 | 19 | (10 | 9) | 259 | 77 | 69 | 54 | 3 | 91 | 1 | 1 | 5 | 25 | 10 | .71 | 14 | .264 | .322 | .419 |
| 1989 Chicago | NL | 157 | 606 | 176 | 25 | 5 | 30 | (16 | 14) | 301 | 104 | 76 | 59 | 8 | 85 | 4 | 1 | 2 | 15 | 5 | .75 | 9 | .290 | .356 | .497 |
| 1990 Chicago | NL | 155 | 615 | 188 | 30 | 3 | 40 | (25 | 15) | 344 | 116 | 100 | 50 | 8 | 84 | 1 | 0 | 9 | 25 | 7 | .78 | 8 | .306 | .354 | .559 |
| 10 ML YEARS | | 1389 | 5508 | 1583 | 256 | 57 | 179 | (104 | 75) | 2490 | 872 | 649 | 464 | 43 | 786 | 19 | 27 | 42 | 275 | 76 | .78 | 85 | .287 | .342 | .452 |

## Deion Sanders

**Bats:** Left **Throws:** Left **Pos:** LF/CF **Ht:** 6' 1" **Wt:** 195 **Born:** 08/09/67 **Age:** 23

| | | BATTING | | | | | | | | | | | | | | | | | BASERUNNING | | | | PERCENTAGES | | |
|---|---|---|---|---|---|---|---|---|---|---|---|---|---|---|---|---|---|---|---|---|---|---|---|---|---|
| Year Team | Lg | G | AB | H | 2B | 3B | HR | (Hm | Rd) | TB | R | RBI | TBB | IBB | SO | HBP | SH | SF | SB | CS | SB% | GDP | Avg | OBP | SLG |
| 1988 Yankees | R | 17 | 75 | 21 | 4 | 2 | 0 | -- | -- | 29 | 7 | 6 | 2 | 0 | 10 | 1 | 0 | 1 | 11 | 2 | .85 | 1 | .280 | .304 | .387 |
| Ft.Laudrdle | A | 6 | 21 | 9 | 2 | 0 | 0 | -- | -- | 11 | 5 | 2 | 1 | 0 | 3 | 0 | 1 | 0 | 2 | 0 | 1.00 | 1 | .429 | .455 | .524 |
| Columbus | AAA | 5 | 20 | 3 | 1 | 0 | 0 | -- | -- | 4 | 3 | 0 | 1 | 0 | 4 | 2 | 1 | 0 | 1 | 1 | .50 | 1 | .150 | .261 | .200 |
| 1989 Albany | AA | 33 | 119 | 34 | 2 | 2 | 1 | -- | -- | 43 | 28 | 6 | 11 | 1 | 20 | 7 | 1 | 0 | 17 | 5 | .77 | 1 | .286 | .380 | .361 |
| Columbus | AAA | 70 | 259 | 72 | 12 | 7 | 5 | -- | -- | 113 | 38 | 30 | 22 | 1 | 48 | 1 | 4 | 3 | 16 | 7 | .70 | 8 | .278 | .333 | .436 |
| 1990 Columbus | AAA | 22 | 84 | 27 | 7 | 1 | 2 | -- | -- | 42 | 21 | 10 | 17 | 0 | 15 | 2 | 1 | 1 | 9 | 1 | .90 | 1 | .321 | .442 | .500 |
| 1989 New York | AL | 14 | 47 | 11 | 2 | 0 | 2 | (0 | 2) | 19 | 7 | 7 | 3 | 1 | 8 | 0 | 0 | 0 | 1 | 0 | 1.00 | 0 | .234 | .280 | .404 |

| Year | Team | Lg | G | AB | H | 2B | 3B | HR | (Hm | Rd) | TB | R | RBI | TBB | IBB | SO | HBP | SH | SF | SB | CS | SB% | GDP | Avg | OBP | SLG |
|---|---|---|---|---|---|---|---|---|---|---|---|---|---|---|---|---|---|---|---|---|---|---|---|---|---|---|
| 1990 | New York | AL | 57 | 133 | 21 | 2 | 2 | 3 | (1 | 2) | 36 | 24 | 9 | 13 | 0 | 27 | 1 | 1 | 1 | 8 | 2 | .80 | 2 | .158 | .236 | .271 |
| 2 ML YEARS | | | 71 | 180 | 32 | 4 | 2 | 5 | (1 | 4) | 55 | 31 | 16 | 16 | 1 | 35 | 1 | 1 | 1 | 9 | 2 | .82 | 2 | .178 | .247 | .306 |

## Scott Sanderson

**Pitches:** Right **Bats:** Right **Pos:** SP **Ht:** 6' 5" **Wt:** 198 **Born:** 07/22/56 **Age:** 34

| | | | HOW MUCH HE PITCHED | | | | | | WHAT HE GAVE UP | | | | | | | | | | | | | THE RESULTS | | | | | |
|---|---|---|---|---|---|---|---|---|---|---|---|---|---|---|---|---|---|---|---|---|---|---|---|---|---|---|---|
| Year | Team | Lg | G | GS | CG | GF | IP | BFP | H | R | ER | HR | SH | SF | HB | TBB | IBB | SO | WP | Bk | W | L | Pct. | ShO | Sv | ERA |
| 1978 | Montreal | NL | 10 | 9 | 1 | 1 | 61 | 251 | 52 | 20 | 17 | 3 | 3 | 2 | 1 | 21 | 0 | 50 | 2 | 0 | 4 | 2 | .667 | 1 | 0 | 2.51 |
| 1979 | Montreal | NL | 34 | 24 | 5 | 3 | 168 | 696 | 148 | 69 | 64 | 16 | 5 | 7 | 3 | 54 | 4 | 138 | 2 | 3 | 9 | 8 | .529 | 3 | 1 | 3.43 |
| 1980 | Montreal | NL | 33 | 33 | 7 | 0 | 211 | 875 | 206 | 76 | 73 | 18 | 11 | 5 | 3 | 56 | 3 | 125 | 6 | 0 | 16 | 11 | .593 | 3 | 0 | 3.11 |
| 1981 | Montreal | NL | 22 | 22 | 4 | 0 | 137 | 560 | 122 | 50 | 45 | 10 | 7 | 4 | 1 | 31 | 2 | 77 | 2 | 0 | 9 | 7 | .563 | 1 | 0 | 2.96 |
| 1982 | Montreal | NL | 32 | 32 | 7 | 0 | 224 | 922 | 212 | 98 | 86 | 24 | 9 | 6 | 3 | 58 | 5 | 158 | 2 | 1 | 12 | 12 | .500 | 0 | 0 | 3.46 |
| 1983 | Montreal | NL | 18 | 16 | 0 | 1 | 81.1 | 346 | 98 | 50 | 42 | 12 | 2 | 1 | 0 | 20 | 0 | 55 | 0 | 0 | 6 | 7 | .462 | 0 | 1 | 4.65 |
| 1984 | Chicago | NL | 24 | 24 | 3 | 0 | 140.2 | 571 | 140 | 54 | 49 | 5 | 6 | 8 | 2 | 24 | 3 | 76 | 3 | 2 | 8 | 5 | .615 | 0 | 0 | 3.14 |
| 1985 | Chicago | NL | 19 | 19 | 2 | 0 | 121 | 480 | 100 | 49 | 42 | 13 | 7 | 7 | 0 | 27 | 4 | 80 | 1 | 0 | 5 | 6 | .455 | 0 | 0 | 3.12 |
| 1986 | Chicago | NL | 37 | 28 | 1 | 2 | 169.2 | 697 | 165 | 85 | 79 | 21 | 6 | 5 | 2 | 37 | 2 | 124 | 3 | 1 | 9 | 11 | .450 | 1 | 1 | 4.19 |
| 1987 | Chicago | NL | 32 | 22 | 0 | 5 | 144.2 | 631 | 156 | 72 | 69 | 23 | 4 | 5 | 3 | 50 | 5 | 106 | 1 | 0 | 8 | 9 | .471 | 0 | 2 | 4.29 |
| 1988 | Chicago | NL | 11 | 0 | 0 | 3 | 15.1 | 62 | 13 | 9 | 9 | 1 | 0 | 3 | 0 | 3 | 1 | 6 | 0 | 0 | 1 | 2 | .333 | 0 | 0 | 5.28 |
| 1989 | Chicago | NL | 37 | 23 | 2 | 2 | 146.1 | 611 | 155 | 69 | 64 | 16 | 8 | 3 | 2 | 31 | 6 | 86 | 1 | 3 | 11 | 9 | .550 | 0 | 0 | 3.94 |
| 1990 | Oakland | AL | 34 | 34 | 2 | 0 | 206.1 | 885 | 205 | 99 | 89 | 27 | 4 | 8 | 4 | 66 | 2 | 128 | 7 | 1 | 17 | 11 | .607 | 1 | 0 | 3.88 |
| 13 ML YEARS | | | 343 | 286 | 34 | 17 | 1826.1 | 7587 | 1772 | 800 | 728 | 189 | 72 | 64 | 24 | 478 | 37 | 1209 | 30 | 11 | 115 | 100 | .535 | 10 | 5 | 3.59 |

## Andres Santana

**Bats:** Both **Throws:** Right **Pos:** SS **Ht:** 5'11" **Wt:** 160 **Born:** 03/19/68 **Age:** 23

| | | | BATTING | | | | | | | | | | | | | | | | | BASERUNNING | | | | PERCENTAGES | | |
|---|---|---|---|---|---|---|---|---|---|---|---|---|---|---|---|---|---|---|---|---|---|---|---|---|---|---|
| Year | Team | Lg | G | AB | H | 2B | 3B | HR | (Hm | Rd) | TB | R | RBI | TBB | IBB | SO | HBP | SH | SF | SB | CS | SB% | GDP | Avg | OBP | SLG |
| 1987 | Pocatello | R | 67 | 256 | 67 | 2 | 3 | 0 | -- | -- | 75 | 51 | 9 | 36 | 0 | 37 | 1 | 1 | 0 | 45 | 10 | .82 | 2 | .262 | .355 | .293 |
| 1988 | Clinton | A | 118 | 450 | 126 | 4 | 1 | 0 | -- | -- | 132 | 77 | 24 | 42 | 1 | 83 | 3 | 7 | 2 | 88 | 23 | .79 | 2 | .280 | .344 | .293 |
| | Shreveport | AA | 11 | 36 | 6 | 0 | 0 | 0 | -- | -- | 6 | 3 | 3 | 4 | 0 | 9 | 0 | 1 | 0 | 3 | 2 | .60 | 0 | .167 | .250 | .167 |
| 1989 | San Jose | A | 18 | 69 | 18 | 3 | 0 | 0 | -- | -- | 21 | 14 | 3 | 8 | 1 | 16 | 0 | 0 | 1 | 10 | 6 | .63 | 2 | .261 | .333 | .304 |
| 1990 | Shreveport | AA | 92 | 336 | 98 | 5 | 4 | 0 | -- | -- | 111 | 50 | 24 | 31 | 0 | 41 | 1 | 7 | 1 | 31 | 18 | .63 | 3 | .292 | .352 | .330 |
| 1990 | San Francisco | NL | 6 | 2 | 0 | 0 | 0 | 0 | (0 | 0) | 0 | 0 | 1 | 0 | 0 | 0 | 0 | 0 | 0 | 0 | 0 | .00 | 0 | .000 | .000 | .000 |

## Rafael Santana

**Bats:** Right **Throws:** Right **Pos:** SS **Ht:** 6' 1" **Wt:** 160 **Born:** 01/31/58 **Age:** 33

| | | | BATTING | | | | | | | | | | | | | | | | | BASERUNNING | | | | PERCENTAGES | | |
|---|---|---|---|---|---|---|---|---|---|---|---|---|---|---|---|---|---|---|---|---|---|---|---|---|---|---|
| Year | Team | Lg | G | AB | H | 2B | 3B | HR | (Hm | Rd) | TB | R | RBI | TBB | IBB | SO | HBP | SH | SF | SB | CS | SB% | GDP | Avg | OBP | SLG |
| 1983 | St. Louis | NL | 30 | 14 | 3 | 0 | 0 | 0 | (0 | 0) | 3 | 1 | 2 | 2 | 0 | 2 | 1 | 0 | 0 | 0 | 1 | .00 | 0 | .214 | .353 | .214 |
| 1984 | New York | NL | 51 | 152 | 42 | 11 | 1 | 1 | (1 | 0) | 58 | 14 | 12 | 9 | 0 | 17 | 0 | 1 | 0 | 0 | 3 | .00 | 3 | .276 | .317 | .382 |
| 1985 | New York | NL | 154 | 529 | 136 | 19 | 1 | 1 | (0 | 1) | 160 | 41 | 29 | 29 | 12 | 54 | 0 | 4 | 2 | 1 | 0 | 1.00 | 14 | .257 | .295 | .302 |
| 1986 | New York | NL | 139 | 394 | 86 | 11 | 0 | 1 | (0 | 1) | 100 | 38 | 28 | 36 | 12 | 43 | 2 | 1 | 3 | 0 | 0 | .00 | 15 | .218 | .285 | .254 |
| 1987 | New York | NL | 139 | 439 | 112 | 21 | 2 | 5 | (2 | 3) | 152 | 41 | 44 | 29 | 10 | 57 | 1 | 0 | 1 | 1 | 1 | .50 | 11 | .255 | .302 | .346 |
| 1988 | New York | AL | 148 | 480 | 115 | 12 | 1 | 4 | (2 | 2) | 141 | 50 | 38 | 33 | 0 | 61 | 1 | 5 | 2 | 1 | 2 | .33 | 17 | .240 | .289 | .294 |
| 1990 | Cleveland | AL | 7 | 13 | 3 | 0 | 0 | 1 | (0 | 1) | 6 | 3 | 3 | 0 | 0 | 0 | 0 | 0 | 0 | 0 | 0 | .00 | 1 | .231 | .231 | .462 |
| 7 ML YEARS | | | 668 | 2021 | 497 | 74 | 5 | 13 | (5 | 8) | 620 | 188 | 156 | 138 | 34 | 234 | 5 | 11 | 8 | 3 | 7 | .30 | 61 | .246 | .295 | .307 |

## Benito Santiago

**Bats:** Right **Throws:** Right **Pos:** C **Ht:** 6' 1" **Wt:** 185 **Born:** 03/09/65 **Age:** 26

| | | | BATTING | | | | | | | | | | | | | | | | | BASERUNNING | | | | PERCENTAGES | | |
|---|---|---|---|---|---|---|---|---|---|---|---|---|---|---|---|---|---|---|---|---|---|---|---|---|---|---|
| Year | Team | Lg | G | AB | H | 2B | 3B | HR | (Hm | Rd) | TB | R | RBI | TBB | IBB | SO | HBP | SH | SF | SB | CS | SB% | GDP | Avg | OBP | SLG |
| 1986 | San Diego | NL | 17 | 62 | 18 | 2 | 0 | 3 | (2 | 1) | 29 | 10 | 6 | 2 | 0 | 12 | 0 | 0 | 1 | 0 | 1 | .00 | 0 | .290 | .308 | .468 |
| 1987 | San Diego | NL | 146 | 546 | 164 | 33 | 2 | 18 | (11 | 7) | 255 | 64 | 79 | 16 | 2 | 112 | 5 | 1 | 4 | 21 | 12 | .64 | 12 | .300 | .324 | .467 |
| 1988 | San Diego | NL | 139 | 492 | 122 | 22 | 2 | 10 | (3 | 7) | 178 | 49 | 46 | 24 | 2 | 82 | 1 | 5 | 5 | 15 | 7 | .68 | 18 | .248 | .282 | .362 |
| 1989 | San Diego | NL | 129 | 462 | 109 | 16 | 3 | 16 | (8 | 8) | 179 | 50 | 62 | 26 | 6 | 89 | 1 | 3 | 2 | 11 | 6 | .65 | 9 | .236 | .277 | .387 |
| 1990 | San Diego | NL | 100 | 344 | 93 | 8 | 5 | 11 | (5 | 6) | 144 | 42 | 53 | 27 | 2 | 55 | 3 | 1 | 7 | 5 | 5 | .50 | 4 | .270 | .323 | .419 |
| 5 ML YEARS | | | 531 | 1906 | 506 | 81 | 12 | 58 | (29 | 29) | 785 | 215 | 246 | 95 | 12 | 350 | 10 | 10 | 19 | 52 | 31 | .63 | 43 | .265 | .301 | .412 |

## Nelson Santovenia

**Bats:** Right **Throws:** Right **Pos:** C **Ht:** 6' 3" **Wt:** 220 **Born:** 07/27/61 **Age:** 29

| | | | BATTING | | | | | | | | | | | | | | | | | BASERUNNING | | | | PERCENTAGES | | |
|---|---|---|---|---|---|---|---|---|---|---|---|---|---|---|---|---|---|---|---|---|---|---|---|---|---|---|
| Year | Team | Lg | G | AB | H | 2B | 3B | HR | (Hm | Rd) | TB | R | RBI | TBB | IBB | SO | HBP | SH | SF | SB | CS | SB% | GDP | Avg | OBP | SLG |
| 1987 | Montreal | NL | 2 | 1 | 0 | 0 | 0 | 0 | (0 | 0) | 0 | 0 | 0 | 0 | 0 | 0 | 0 | 0 | 0 | 0 | 0 | .00 | 0 | .000 | .000 | .000 |
| 1988 | Montreal | NL | 92 | 309 | 73 | 20 | 2 | 8 | (6 | 2) | 121 | 26 | 41 | 24 | 3 | 77 | 3 | 4 | 4 | 2 | 3 | .40 | 4 | .236 | .294 | .392 |
| 1989 | Montreal | NL | 97 | 304 | 76 | 14 | 1 | 5 | (4 | 1) | 107 | 30 | 31 | 24 | 2 | 37 | 3 | 2 | 4 | 2 | 1 | .67 | 12 | .250 | .307 | .352 |
| 1990 | Montreal | NL | 59 | 163 | 31 | 3 | 1 | 6 | (4 | 2) | 54 | 13 | 28 | 8 | 0 | 31 | 0 | 0 | 5 | 0 | 3 | .00 | 5 | .190 | .222 | .331 |
| 4 ML YEARS | | | 250 | 777 | 180 | 37 | 4 | 19 | (14 | 5) | 282 | 69 | 100 | 56 | 5 | 145 | 6 | 6 | 13 | 4 | 7 | .36 | 21 | .232 | .284 | .363 |

## Mackey Sasser

**Bats:** Left **Throws:** Right **Pos:** C **Ht:** 6' 1" **Wt:** 210 **Born:** 08/03/62 **Age:** 28

| | | BATTING | | | | | | | | | | | | | | | | | BASERUNNING | | | | PERCENTAGES | | |
|---|---|---|---|---|---|---|---|---|---|---|---|---|---|---|---|---|---|---|---|---|---|---|---|---|---|
| Year Team | Lg | G | AB | H | 2B | 3B | HR | (Hm | Rd) | TB | R | RBI | TBB | IBB | SO | HBP | SH | SF | SB | CS | SB% | GDP | Avg | OBP | SLG |
| 1987 2 ML Teams | | 14 | 27 | 5 | 0 | 0 | 0 | (0 | 0) | 5 | 2 | 2 | 0 | 0 | 2 | 0 | 0 | 0 | 0 | 0 | .00 | 1 | .185 | .185 | .185 |
| 1988 New York | NL | 60 | 123 | 35 | 10 | 1 | 1 | (0 | 1) | 50 | 9 | 17 | 6 | 4 | 9 | 0 | 0 | 2 | 0 | 0 | .00 | 4 | .285 | .313 | .407 |
| 1989 New York | NL | 72 | 182 | 53 | 14 | 2 | 1 | (1 | 0) | 74 | 17 | 22 | 7 | 4 | 15 | 0 | 1 | 1 | 0 | 1 | .00 | 3 | .291 | .316 | .407 |
| 1990 New York | NL | 100 | 270 | 83 | 14 | 0 | 6 | (3 | 3) | 115 | 31 | 41 | 15 | 9 | 19 | 1 | 0 | 2 | 0 | 0 | .00 | 7 | .307 | .344 | .426 |
| 1987 San Francisco | NL | 2 | 4 | 0 | 0 | 0 | 0 | (0 | 0) | 0 | 0 | 0 | 0 | 0 | 0 | 0 | 0 | 0 | 0 | 0 | .00 | 0 | .000 | .000 | .000 |
| Pittsburgh | NL | 12 | 23 | 5 | 0 | 0 | 0 | (0 | 0) | 5 | 2 | 2 | 0 | 0 | 2 | 0 | 0 | 0 | 0 | 0 | .00 | 1 | .217 | .217 | .217 |
| 4 ML YEARS | | 246 | 602 | 176 | 38 | 3 | 8 | (4 | 4) | 244 | 59 | 82 | 28 | 17 | 45 | 1 | 1 | 5 | 0 | 1 | .00 | 15 | .292 | .322 | .405 |

## Jack Savage

**Pitches:** Right **Bats:** Right **Pos:** RP **Ht:** 6' 0" **Wt:** 185 **Born:** 04/22/64 **Age:** 27

| | | HOW MUCH HE PITCHED | | | | | | WHAT HE GAVE UP | | | | | | | | | | | | THE RESULTS | | | | | |
|---|---|---|---|---|---|---|---|---|---|---|---|---|---|---|---|---|---|---|---|---|---|---|---|---|---|
| Year Team | Lg | G | GS | CG | GF | IP | BFP | H | R | ER | HR | SH | SF | HB | TBB | IBB | SO | WP | Bk | W | L | Pct. | ShO | Sv | ERA |
| 1987 Los Angeles | NL | 3 | 0 | 0 | 0 | 3.1 | 14 | 4 | 1 | 1 | 0 | 0 | 0 | 0 | 0 | 0 | 0 | 0 | 0 | 0 | 0 | .000 | 0 | 0 | 2.70 |
| 1990 Minnesota | AL | 17 | 0 | 0 | 9 | 26 | 121 | 37 | 26 | 24 | 3 | 0 | 1 | 0 | 11 | 1 | 12 | 4 | 0 | 0 | 2 | .000 | 0 | 1 | 8.31 |
| 2 ML YEARS | | 20 | 0 | 0 | 9 | 29.1 | 135 | 41 | 27 | 25 | 3 | 0 | 1 | 0 | 11 | 1 | 12 | 4 | 0 | 0 | 2 | .000 | 0 | 1 | 7.67 |

## Steve Sax

**Bats:** Right **Throws:** Right **Pos:** 2B **Ht:** 5'11" **Wt:** 185 **Born:** 01/29/60 **Age:** 31

| | | BATTING | | | | | | | | | | | | | | | | | BASERUNNING | | | | PERCENTAGES | | |
|---|---|---|---|---|---|---|---|---|---|---|---|---|---|---|---|---|---|---|---|---|---|---|---|---|---|
| Year Team | Lg | G | AB | H | 2B | 3B | HR | (Hm | Rd) | TB | R | RBI | TBB | IBB | SO | HBP | SH | SF | SB | CS | SB% | GDP | Avg | OBP | SLG |
| 1981 Los Angeles | NL | 31 | 119 | 33 | 2 | 0 | 2 | (0 | 2) | 41 | 15 | 9 | 7 | 1 | 14 | 0 | 1 | 0 | 5 | 7 | .42 | 0 | .277 | .317 | .345 |
| 1982 Los Angeles | NL | 150 | 638 | 180 | 23 | 7 | 4 | (2 | 2) | 229 | 88 | 47 | 49 | 1 | 53 | 2 | 10 | 0 | 49 | 19 | .72 | 10 | .282 | .335 | .359 |
| 1983 Los Angeles | NL | 155 | 623 | 175 | 18 | 5 | 5 | (3 | 2) | 218 | 94 | 41 | 58 | 3 | 73 | 1 | 8 | 2 | 56 | 30 | .65 | 8 | .281 | .342 | .350 |
| 1984 Los Angeles | NL | 145 | 569 | 138 | 24 | 4 | 1 | (1 | 0) | 173 | 70 | 35 | 47 | 3 | 53 | 1 | 2 | 3 | 34 | 19 | .64 | 12 | .243 | .300 | .304 |
| 1985 Los Angeles | NL | 136 | 488 | 136 | 8 | 4 | 1 | (1 | 0) | 155 | 62 | 42 | 54 | 12 | 43 | 3 | 3 | 3 | 27 | 11 | .71 | 15 | .279 | .352 | .318 |
| 1986 Los Angeles | NL | 157 | 633 | 210 | 43 | 4 | 6 | (1 | 5) | 279 | 91 | 56 | 59 | 5 | 58 | 3 | 6 | 3 | 40 | 17 | .70 | 12 | .332 | .390 | .441 |
| 1987 Los Angeles | NL | 157 | 610 | 171 | 22 | 7 | 6 | (2 | 4) | 225 | 84 | 46 | 44 | 5 | 61 | 3 | 5 | 1 | 37 | 11 | .77 | 13 | .280 | .331 | .369 |
| 1988 Los Angeles | NL | 160 | 632 | 175 | 19 | 4 | 5 | (2 | 3) | 217 | 70 | 57 | 45 | 6 | 51 | 1 | 7 | 2 | 42 | 12 | .78 | 11 | .277 | .325 | .343 |
| 1989 New York | AL | 158 | 651 | 205 | 26 | 3 | 5 | (2 | 3) | 252 | 88 | 63 | 52 | 2 | 44 | 1 | 8 | 5 | 43 | 17 | .72 | 19 | .315 | .364 | .387 |
| 1990 New York | AL | 155 | 615 | 160 | 24 | 2 | 4 | (3 | 1) | 200 | 70 | 42 | 49 | 3 | 46 | 4 | 6 | 6 | 43 | 9 | .83 | 13 | .260 | .316 | .325 |
| 10 ML YEARS | | 1404 | 5578 | 1583 | 209 | 40 | 39 | (17 | 22) | 1989 | 732 | 438 | 464 | 41 | 496 | 19 | 56 | 25 | 376 | 152 | .71 | 113 | .284 | .339 | .357 |

## Jeff Schaefer

**Bats:** Right **Throws:** Right **Pos:** 3B/SS **Ht:** 5'10" **Wt:** 170 **Born:** 05/31/60 **Age:** 31

| | | BATTING | | | | | | | | | | | | | | | | | BASERUNNING | | | | PERCENTAGES | | |
|---|---|---|---|---|---|---|---|---|---|---|---|---|---|---|---|---|---|---|---|---|---|---|---|---|---|
| Year Team | Lg | G | AB | H | 2B | 3B | HR | (Hm | Rd) | TB | R | RBI | TBB | IBB | SO | HBP | SH | SF | SB | CS | SB% | GDP | Avg | OBP | SLG |
| 1984 Rochester | AAA | 31 | 91 | 24 | 5 | 1 | 0 | -- | -- | 31 | 10 | 3 | 9 | 0 | 20 | 0 | 3 | 0 | 0 | 0 | .00 | 5 | .264 | .330 | .341 |
| Charlotte | AA | 99 | 383 | 90 | 8 | 0 | 4 | -- | -- | 110 | 47 | 31 | 23 | 1 | 45 | 6 | 6 | 3 | 8 | 3 | .73 | 12 | .235 | .287 | .287 |
| 1985 Charlotte | AA | 49 | 181 | 47 | 7 | 1 | 2 | -- | -- | 62 | 19 | 19 | 12 | 0 | 14 | 0 | 3 | 1 | 6 | 5 | .55 | 2 | .260 | .304 | .343 |
| Rochester | AAA | 68 | 187 | 37 | 4 | 0 | 2 | -- | -- | 47 | 17 | 12 | 6 | 0 | 21 | 0 | 2 | 1 | 1 | 2 | .33 | 5 | .198 | .222 | .251 |
| 1986 Midland | AA | 114 | 406 | 109 | 17 | 1 | 6 | -- | -- | 146 | 50 | 41 | 14 | 0 | 40 | 2 | 4 | 6 | 1 | 4 | .20 | 11 | .268 | .292 | .360 |
| 1987 San Antonio | AA | 101 | 368 | 112 | 18 | 2 | 0 | -- | -- | 134 | 39 | 37 | 13 | 0 | 49 | 3 | 7 | 4 | 2 | 4 | .33 | 8 | .304 | .330 | .364 |
| Albuquerque | AAA | 8 | 27 | 7 | 1 | 0 | 0 | -- | -- | 8 | 3 | 3 | 1 | 0 | 3 | 0 | 0 | 0 | 0 | 0 | .00 | 2 | .259 | .286 | .296 |
| 1988 Vancouver | AAA | 131 | 450 | 111 | 30 | 2 | 1 | -- | -- | 148 | 53 | 59 | 21 | 0 | 53 | 4 | 4 | 6 | 7 | 4 | .64 | 8 | .247 | .283 | .329 |
| 1989 Vancouver | AAA | 88 | 294 | 67 | 13 | 2 | 3 | -- | -- | 93 | 32 | 22 | 21 | 0 | 29 | 1 | 5 | 1 | 10 | 10 | .50 | 4 | .228 | .281 | .316 |
| 1990 Calgary | AAA | 49 | 170 | 41 | 9 | 2 | 0 | -- | -- | 54 | 24 | 19 | 18 | 0 | 15 | 0 | 9 | 2 | 8 | 7 | .53 | 3 | .241 | .311 | .318 |
| 1989 Chicago | AL | 15 | 10 | 1 | 0 | 0 | 0 | (0 | 0) | 1 | 2 | 0 | 0 | 0 | 2 | 0 | 1 | 0 | 1 | 1 | .50 | 0 | .100 | .100 | .100 |
| 1990 Seattle | AL | 55 | 107 | 22 | 3 | 0 | 0 | (0 | 0) | 25 | 11 | 6 | 3 | 0 | 11 | 2 | 2 | 1 | 4 | 1 | .80 | 1 | .206 | .239 | .234 |
| 2 ML YEARS | | 70 | 117 | 23 | 3 | 0 | 0 | (0 | 0) | 26 | 13 | 6 | 3 | 0 | 13 | 2 | 3 | 1 | 5 | 2 | .71 | 1 | .197 | .228 | .222 |

## Dan Schatzeder

**Pitches:** Left **Bats:** Left **Pos:** RP **Ht:** 6' 0" **Wt:** 195 **Born:** 12/01/54 **Age:** 36

| | | HOW MUCH HE PITCHED | | | | | | WHAT HE GAVE UP | | | | | | | | | | | | THE RESULTS | | | | | |
|---|---|---|---|---|---|---|---|---|---|---|---|---|---|---|---|---|---|---|---|---|---|---|---|---|---|
| Year Team | Lg | G | GS | CG | GF | IP | BFP | H | R | ER | HR | SH | SF | HB | TBB | IBB | SO | WP | Bk | W | L | Pct. | ShO | Sv | ERA |
| 1977 Montreal | NL | 6 | 3 | 1 | 0 | 22 | 93 | 16 | 6 | 6 | 0 | 0 | 1 | 0 | 13 | 0 | 14 | 1 | 0 | 2 | 1 | .667 | 1 | 0 | 2.45 |
| 1978 Montreal | NL | 29 | 18 | 2 | 1 | 144 | 586 | 108 | 54 | 49 | 10 | 5 | 4 | 2 | 68 | 5 | 69 | 4 | 3 | 7 | 7 | .500 | 0 | 0 | 3.06 |
| 1979 Montreal | NL | 32 | 21 | 3 | 4 | 162 | 677 | 136 | 57 | 51 | 17 | 10 | 3 | 1 | 59 | 2 | 106 | 6 | 0 | 10 | 5 | .667 | 0 | 1 | 2.83 |
| 1980 Detroit | AL | 32 | 26 | 9 | 2 | 193 | 794 | 178 | 88 | 86 | 23 | 6 | 3 | 3 | 58 | 9 | 94 | 8 | 0 | 11 | 13 | .458 | 2 | 0 | 4.01 |
| 1981 Detroit | AL | 17 | 14 | 1 | 1 | 71 | 318 | 74 | 49 | 48 | 13 | 4 | 4 | 2 | 29 | 1 | 20 | 3 | 0 | 6 | 8 | .429 | 0 | 0 | 6.08 |
| 1982 2 ML Teams | | 39 | 4 | 0 | 11 | 69.1 | 307 | 84 | 46 | 41 | 4 | 3 | 3 | 2 | 24 | 9 | 33 | 4 | 0 | 1 | 6 | .143 | 0 | 0 | 5.32 |
| 1983 Montreal | NL | 58 | 2 | 0 | 23 | 87 | 369 | 88 | 34 | 31 | 3 | 5 | 2 | 5 | 25 | 6 | 48 | 5 | 0 | 5 | 2 | .714 | 0 | 2 | 3.21 |
| 1984 Montreal | NL | 36 | 14 | 1 | 6 | 136 | 547 | 112 | 44 | 41 | 13 | 4 | 4 | 2 | 36 | 1 | 89 | 3 | 1 | 7 | 7 | .500 | 1 | 1 | 2.71 |
| 1985 Montreal | NL | 24 | 15 | 1 | 2 | 104.1 | 431 | 101 | 52 | 44 | 13 | 7 | 3 | 0 | 31 | 0 | 64 | 4 | 0 | 3 | 5 | .375 | 0 | 0 | 3.80 |
| 1986 2 ML Teams | | 55 | 1 | 0 | 19 | 88.1 | 375 | 81 | 43 | 32 | 9 | 5 | 3 | 0 | 35 | 9 | 47 | 1 | 0 | 6 | 5 | .545 | 0 | 2 | 3.26 |

| Year Team | Lg | G | GS | CG | GF | IP | BFP | H | R | ER | HR | SH | SF | HB | TBB | IBB | SO | WP | Bk | W | L | Pct. | ShO | Sv | ERA |
|---|---|---|---|---|---|---|---|---|---|---|---|---|---|---|---|---|---|---|---|---|---|---|---|---|---|
| 1987 2 ML Teams | | 56 | 1 | 0 | 13 | 81.1 | 372 | 104 | 58 | 48 | 12 | 2 | 6 | 1 | 32 | 10 | 58 | 8 | 0 | 6 | 2 | .750 | 0 | 0 | 5.31 |
| 1988 2 ML Teams | | 25 | 0 | 0 | 10 | 26.1 | 121 | 34 | 21 | 19 | 7 | 1 | 0 | 2 | 7 | 1 | 17 | 0 | 0 | 0 | 3 | .000 | 0 | 3 | 6.49 |
| 1989 Houston | NL | 36 | 0 | 0 | 7 | 56.2 | 259 | 64 | 33 | 28 | 2 | 5 | 0 | 3 | 28 | 6 | 46 | 7 | 1 | 4 | 1 | .800 | 0 | 1 | 4.45 |
| 1990 2 ML Teams | | 51 | 2 | 0 | 16 | 69.2 | 283 | 66 | 23 | 17 | 2 | 2 | 5 | 0 | 23 | 4 | 39 | 2 | 0 | 1 | 3 | .250 | 0 | 0 | 2.20 |
| 1982 San Francisco | NL | 13 | 3 | 0 | 1 | 33.1 | 155 | 47 | 30 | 27 | 3 | 1 | 1 | 0 | 12 | 4 | 18 | 2 | 0 | 1 | 4 | .200 | 0 | 0 | 7.29 |
| Montreal | NL | 26 | 1 | 0 | 10 | 36 | 152 | 37 | 16 | 14 | 1 | 2 | 2 | 2 | 12 | 5 | 15 | 2 | 0 | 0 | 2 | .000 | 0 | 0 | 3.50 |
| 1986 Montreal | NL | 30 | 1 | 0 | 9 | 59 | 244 | 53 | 29 | 21 | 6 | 2 | 2 | 0 | 19 | 2 | 33 | 1 | 0 | 3 | 2 | .600 | 0 | 1 | 3.20 |
| Philadelphia | NL | 25 | 0 | 0 | 10 | 29.1 | 131 | 28 | 14 | 11 | 3 | 3 | 1 | 0 | 16 | 7 | 14 | 0 | 0 | 3 | 3 | .500 | 0 | 1 | 3.38 |
| 1987 Philadelphia | NL | 26 | 0 | 0 | 8 | 37.2 | 164 | 40 | 21 | 17 | 4 | 2 | 4 | 0 | 14 | 7 | 28 | 0 | 0 | 3 | 1 | .750 | 0 | 0 | 4.06 |
| Minnesota | AL | 30 | 1 | 0 | 5 | 43.2 | 208 | 64 | 37 | 31 | 8 | 0 | 2 | 1 | 18 | 3 | 30 | 8 | 0 | 3 | 1 | .750 | 0 | 0 | 6.39 |
| 1988 Cleveland | AL | 15 | 0 | 0 | 8 | 16 | 77 | 26 | 19 | 17 | 6 | 0 | 0 | 1 | 2 | 0 | 10 | 0 | 0 | 0 | 2 | .000 | 0 | 3 | 9.56 |
| Minnesota | AL | 10 | 0 | 0 | 2 | 10.1 | 44 | 8 | 2 | 2 | 1 | 1 | 0 | 1 | 5 | 1 | 7 | 0 | 0 | 0 | 1 | .000 | 0 | 0 | 1.74 |
| 1990 Houston | NL | 45 | 2 | 0 | 13 | 64 | 264 | 61 | 23 | 17 | 2 | 2 | 5 | 0 | 23 | 4 | 37 | 2 | 0 | 1 | 3 | .250 | 0 | 0 | 2.39 |
| New York | NL | 6 | 0 | 0 | 3 | 5.2 | 19 | 5 | 0 | 0 | 0 | 0 | 0 | 0 | 0 | 0 | 2 | 0 | 0 | 0 | 0 | .000 | 0 | 0 | 0.00 |
| 14 ML YEARS | | 496 | 121 | 18 | 115 | 1311 | 5532 | 1246 | 608 | 541 | 128 | 59 | 41 | 23 | 468 | 63 | 744 | 56 | 5 | 69 | 68 | .504 | 4 | 10 | 3.71 |

## Curt Schilling

**Pitches:** Right **Bats:** Right **Pos:** RP **Ht:** 6' 4" **Wt:** 215 **Born:** 11/14/66 **Age:** 24

| | | HOW MUCH HE PITCHED | | | | | | WHAT HE GAVE UP | | | | | | | | | | | | THE RESULTS | | | | | |
|---|---|---|---|---|---|---|---|---|---|---|---|---|---|---|---|---|---|---|---|---|---|---|---|---|---|
| Year Team | Lg | G | GS | CG | GF | IP | BFP | H | R | ER | HR | SH | SF | HB | TBB | IBB | SO | WP | Bk | W | L | Pct. | ShO | Sv | ERA |
| 1988 Baltimore | AL | 4 | 4 | 0 | 0 | 14.2 | 76 | 22 | 19 | 16 | 3 | 0 | 3 | 1 | 10 | 1 | 4 | 2 | 0 | 0 | 3 | .000 | 0 | 0 | 9.82 |
| 1989 Baltimore | AL | 5 | 1 | 0 | 0 | 8.2 | 38 | 10 | 6 | 6 | 2 | 0 | 0 | 0 | 3 | 0 | 6 | 1 | 0 | 0 | 1 | .000 | 0 | 0 | 6.23 |
| 1990 Baltimore | AL | 35 | 0 | 0 | 16 | 46 | 191 | 38 | 13 | 13 | 1 | 2 | 4 | 0 | 19 | 0 | 32 | 0 | 0 | 1 | 2 | .333 | 0 | 3 | 2.54 |
| 3 ML YEARS | | 44 | 5 | 0 | 16 | 69.1 | 305 | 70 | 38 | 35 | 6 | 2 | 7 | 1 | 32 | 1 | 42 | 3 | 0 | 1 | 6 | .143 | 0 | 3 | 4.54 |

## Calvin Schiraldi

**Pitches:** Right **Bats:** Right **Pos:** RP/SP **Ht:** 6' 5" **Wt:** 215 **Born:** 06/16/62 **Age:** 29

| | | HOW MUCH HE PITCHED | | | | | | WHAT HE GAVE UP | | | | | | | | | | | | THE RESULTS | | | | | |
|---|---|---|---|---|---|---|---|---|---|---|---|---|---|---|---|---|---|---|---|---|---|---|---|---|---|
| Year Team | Lg | G | GS | CG | GF | IP | BFP | H | R | ER | HR | SH | SF | HB | TBB | IBB | SO | WP | Bk | W | L | Pct. | ShO | Sv | ERA |
| 1984 New York | NL | 5 | 3 | 0 | 0 | 17.1 | 80 | 20 | 13 | 11 | 3 | 0 | 0 | 0 | 10 | 0 | 16 | 0 | 0 | 0 | 2 | .000 | 0 | 0 | 5.71 |
| 1985 New York | NL | 10 | 4 | 0 | 2 | 26.1 | 131 | 43 | 27 | 26 | 4 | 0 | 0 | 3 | 11 | 0 | 21 | 2 | 1 | 2 | 1 | .667 | 0 | 0 | 8.89 |
| 1986 Boston | AL | 25 | 0 | 0 | 21 | 51 | 198 | 36 | 8 | 8 | 5 | 2 | 1 | 1 | 15 | 2 | 55 | 1 | 0 | 4 | 2 | .667 | 0 | 9 | 1.41 |
| 1987 Boston | AL | 62 | 1 | 0 | 52 | 83.2 | 361 | 75 | 45 | 41 | 15 | 5 | 2 | 1 | 40 | 5 | 93 | 5 | 2 | 8 | 5 | .615 | 0 | 6 | 4.41 |
| 1988 Chicago | NL | 29 | 27 | 2 | 2 | 166.1 | 717 | 166 | 87 | 81 | 13 | 2 | 4 | 2 | 63 | 7 | 140 | 6 | 3 | 9 | 13 | .409 | 1 | 1 | 4.38 |
| 1989 2 ML Teams | | 59 | 4 | 0 | 25 | 100 | 429 | 72 | 40 | 39 | 8 | 2 | 2 | 1 | 63 | 2 | 71 | 4 | 1 | 6 | 7 | .462 | 0 | 4 | 3.51 |
| 1990 San Diego | NL | 42 | 8 | 0 | 14 | 104 | 468 | 105 | 59 | 51 | 11 | 7 | 3 | 1 | 60 | 6 | 74 | 3 | 1 | 3 | 8 | .273 | 0 | 1 | 4.41 |
| 1989 Chicago | NL | 54 | 0 | 0 | 24 | 78.2 | 342 | 60 | 34 | 33 | 7 | 2 | 2 | 1 | 50 | 2 | 54 | 3 | 0 | 3 | 6 | .333 | 0 | 4 | 3.78 |
| San Diego | NL | 5 | 4 | 0 | 1 | 21.1 | 87 | 12 | 6 | 6 | 1 | 0 | 0 | 0 | 13 | 0 | 17 | 1 | 1 | 3 | 1 | .750 | 0 | 0 | 2.53 |
| 7 ML YEARS | | 232 | 47 | 2 | 116 | 548.2 | 2384 | 517 | 279 | 257 | 59 | 18 | 12 | 9 | 262 | 22 | 470 | 21 | 8 | 32 | 38 | .457 | 1 | 21 | 4.22 |

## Dave Schmidt

**Pitches:** Right **Bats:** Right **Pos:** RP **Ht:** 6' 1" **Wt:** 194 **Born:** 04/22/57 **Age:** 34

| | | HOW MUCH HE PITCHED | | | | | | WHAT HE GAVE UP | | | | | | | | | | | | THE RESULTS | | | | | |
|---|---|---|---|---|---|---|---|---|---|---|---|---|---|---|---|---|---|---|---|---|---|---|---|---|---|
| Year Team | Lg | G | GS | CG | GF | IP | BFP | H | R | ER | HR | SH | SF | HB | TBB | IBB | SO | WP | Bk | W | L | Pct. | ShO | Sv | ERA |
| 1981 Texas | AL | 14 | 1 | 0 | 8 | 32 | 132 | 31 | 11 | 11 | 1 | 0 | 0 | 1 | 11 | 3 | 13 | 3 | 1 | 0 | 1 | .000 | 0 | 1 | 3.09 |
| 1982 Texas | AL | 33 | 8 | 0 | 14 | 109.2 | 462 | 118 | 45 | 39 | 5 | 6 | 3 | 5 | 25 | 5 | 69 | 2 | 0 | 4 | 6 | .400 | 0 | 6 | 3.20 |
| 1983 Texas | AL | 31 | 0 | 0 | 20 | 46.1 | 191 | 42 | 20 | 20 | 3 | 1 | 1 | 1 | 14 | 1 | 29 | 2 | 0 | 3 | 3 | .500 | 0 | 2 | 3.88 |
| 1984 Texas | AL | 43 | 0 | 0 | 37 | 70.1 | 293 | 69 | 30 | 20 | 3 | 7 | 3 | 0 | 20 | 9 | 46 | 4 | 0 | 6 | 6 | .500 | 0 | 12 | 2.56 |
| 1985 Texas | AL | 51 | 4 | 1 | 35 | 85.2 | 356 | 81 | 36 | 30 | 6 | 3 | 2 | 0 | 22 | 8 | 46 | 2 | 1 | 7 | 6 | .538 | 1 | 5 | 3.15 |
| 1986 Chicago | AL | 49 | 1 | 0 | 21 | 92.1 | 394 | 94 | 37 | 34 | 10 | 3 | 3 | 5 | 27 | 7 | 67 | 5 | 0 | 3 | 6 | .333 | 0 | 8 | 3.31 |
| 1987 Baltimore | AL | 35 | 14 | 2 | 7 | 124 | 515 | 128 | 57 | 52 | 13 | 0 | 1 | 1 | 26 | 2 | 70 | 2 | 0 | 10 | 5 | .667 | 2 | 1 | 3.77 |
| 1988 Baltimore | AL | 41 | 9 | 0 | 11 | 129.2 | 541 | 129 | 58 | 49 | 14 | 5 | 3 | 3 | 38 | 5 | 67 | 3 | 0 | 8 | 5 | .615 | 0 | 2 | 3.40 |
| 1989 Baltimore | AL | 38 | 26 | 2 | 5 | 156.2 | 686 | 196 | 102 | 99 | 24 | 9 | 7 | 2 | 36 | 2 | 46 | 3 | 1 | 10 | 13 | .435 | 0 | 0 | 5.69 |
| 1990 Montreal | NL | 34 | 0 | 0 | 20 | 48 | 213 | 58 | 26 | 23 | 3 | 4 | 1 | 0 | 13 | 5 | 22 | 1 | 0 | 3 | 3 | .500 | 0 | 13 | 4.31 |
| 10 ML YEARS | | 369 | 63 | 5 | 178 | 894.2 | 3783 | 946 | 422 | 377 | 82 | 38 | 24 | 18 | 232 | 47 | 475 | 27 | 3 | 54 | 54 | .500 | 3 | 50 | 3.79 |

## Dick Schofield

**Bats:** Right **Throws:** Right **Pos:** SS **Ht:** 5'10" **Wt:** 175 **Born:** 11/21/62 **Age:** 28

| | | BATTING | | | | | | | | | | | | | | | | | BASERUNNING | | | | PERCENTAGES | | |
|---|---|---|---|---|---|---|---|---|---|---|---|---|---|---|---|---|---|---|---|---|---|---|---|---|---|
| Year Team | Lg | G | AB | H | 2B | 3B | HR | (Hm | Rd) | TB | R | RBI | TBB | IBB | SO | HBP | SH | SF | SB | CS | SB% | GDP | Avg | OBP | SLG |
| 1983 California | AL | 21 | 54 | 11 | 2 | 0 | 3 | (2 | 1) | 22 | 4 | 4 | 6 | 0 | 8 | 1 | 1 | 0 | 0 | 0 | .00 | 2 | .204 | .295 | .407 |
| 1984 California | AL | 140 | 400 | 77 | 10 | 3 | 4 | (0 | 4) | 105 | 39 | 21 | 33 | 0 | 79 | 6 | 13 | 0 | 5 | 2 | .71 | 7 | .193 | .264 | .263 |
| 1985 California | AL | 147 | 438 | 96 | 19 | 3 | 8 | (5 | 3) | 145 | 50 | 41 | 35 | 0 | 70 | 8 | 12 | 3 | 11 | 4 | .73 | 8 | .219 | .287 | .331 |
| 1986 California | AL | 139 | 458 | 114 | 17 | 6 | 13 | (7 | 6) | 182 | 67 | 57 | 48 | 2 | 55 | 5 | 9 | 9 | 23 | 5 | .82 | 8 | .249 | .321 | .397 |
| 1987 California | AL | 134 | 479 | 120 | 17 | 3 | 9 | (4 | 5) | 170 | 52 | 46 | 37 | 0 | 63 | 2 | 10 | 3 | 19 | 3 | .86 | 4 | .251 | .305 | .355 |
| 1988 California | AL | 155 | 527 | 126 | 11 | 6 | 6 | (3 | 3) | 167 | 61 | 34 | 40 | 0 | 57 | 9 | 11 | 2 | 20 | 5 | .80 | 5 | .239 | .303 | .317 |

| | | | | | | | | | | | | | | | | | | | | | | | | | | |
|---|---|---|---|---|---|---|---|---|---|---|---|---|---|---|---|---|---|---|---|---|---|---|---|---|---|---|
| 1989 California | AL | 91 | 302 | 69 | 11 | 2 | 4 | (1 | 3) | 96 | 42 | 26 | 28 | 0 | 47 | 3 | 11 | 2 | 9 | 3 | .75 | 4 | .228 | .299 | .318 |
| 1990 California | AL | 99 | 310 | 79 | 8 | 1 | 1 | (1 | 0) | 92 | 41 | 18 | 52 | 3 | 61 | 2 | 13 | 2 | 3 | 4 | .43 | 3 | .255 | .363 | .297 |
| 8 ML YEARS | | 926 | 2968 | 692 | 95 | 24 | 48 | (23 | 25) | 979 | 356 | 247 | 279 | 5 | 440 | 36 | 80 | 21 | 90 | 26 | .78 | 41 | .233 | .305 | .330 |

## Mike Schooler

**Pitches:** Right **Bats:** Right **Pos:** RP **Ht:** 6' 3" **Wt:** 220 **Born:** 08/10/62 **Age:** 28

| | | HOW MUCH HE PITCHED | | | | | | WHAT HE GAVE UP | | | | | | | | | | | | THE RESULTS | | | | | |
|---|---|---|---|---|---|---|---|---|---|---|---|---|---|---|---|---|---|---|---|---|---|---|---|---|---|
| Year Team | Lg | G | GS | CG | GF | IP | BFP | H | R | ER | HR | SH | SF | HB | TBB | IBB | SO | WP | Bk | W | L | Pct. | ShO | Sv | ERA |
| 1988 Seattle | AL | 40 | 0 | 0 | 33 | 48.1 | 214 | 45 | 21 | 19 | 4 | 2 | 3 | 1 | 24 | 4 | 54 | 4 | 1 | 5 | 8 | .385 | 0 | 15 | 3.54 |
| 1989 Seattle | AL | 67 | 0 | 0 | 60 | 77 | 329 | 81 | 27 | 24 | 2 | 3 | 1 | 2 | 19 | 3 | 69 | 6 | 1 | 1 | 7 | .125 | 0 | 33 | 2.81 |
| 1990 Seattle | AL | 49 | 0 | 0 | 45 | 56 | 229 | 47 | 18 | 14 | 5 | 3 | 2 | 1 | 16 | 5 | 45 | 1 | 0 | 1 | 4 | .200 | 0 | 30 | 2.25 |
| 3 ML YEARS | | 156 | 0 | 0 | 138 | 181.1 | 772 | 173 | 66 | 57 | 11 | 8 | 6 | 4 | 59 | 12 | 168 | 11 | 2 | 7 | 19 | .269 | 0 | 78 | 2.83 |

## Bill Schroeder

**Bats:** Right **Throws:** Right **Pos:** C **Ht:** 6' 2" **Wt:** 200 **Born:** 09/07/58 **Age:** 32

| | | BATTING | | | | | | | | | | | | | | | | | BASERUNNING | | | | PERCENTAGES | | |
|---|---|---|---|---|---|---|---|---|---|---|---|---|---|---|---|---|---|---|---|---|---|---|---|---|---|
| Year Team | Lg | G | AB | H | 2B | 3B | HR | (Hm | Rd) | TB | R | RBI | TBB | IBB | SO | HBP | SH | SF | SB | CS | SB% | GDP | Avg | OBP | SLG |
| 1983 Milwaukee | AL | 23 | 73 | 13 | 2 | 1 | 3 | (2 | 1) | 26 | 7 | 7 | 3 | 0 | 23 | 1 | 2 | 0 | 0 | 1 | .00 | 0 | .178 | .221 | .356 |
| 1984 Milwaukee | AL | 61 | 210 | 54 | 6 | 0 | 14 | (7 | 7) | 102 | 29 | 25 | 8 | 2 | 54 | 2 | 4 | 2 | 0 | 1 | .00 | 6 | .257 | .288 | .486 |
| 1985 Milwaukee | AL | 53 | 194 | 47 | 8 | 0 | 8 | (2 | 6) | 79 | 18 | 25 | 12 | 1 | 61 | 2 | 0 | 2 | 0 | 1 | .00 | 5 | .242 | .290 | .407 |
| 1986 Milwaukee | AL | 64 | 217 | 46 | 14 | 0 | 7 | (2 | 5) | 81 | 32 | 19 | 9 | 0 | 59 | 6 | 4 | 1 | 1 | 0 | 1.00 | 3 | .212 | .262 | .373 |
| 1987 Milwaukee | AL | 75 | 250 | 83 | 12 | 0 | 14 | (5 | 9) | 137 | 35 | 42 | 16 | 0 | 56 | 3 | 1 | 0 | 5 | 2 | .71 | 3 | .332 | .379 | .548 |
| 1988 Milwaukee | AL | 41 | 122 | 19 | 2 | 0 | 5 | (2 | 3) | 36 | 9 | 10 | 6 | 0 | 36 | 2 | 1 | 0 | 0 | 0 | .00 | 6 | .156 | .208 | .295 |
| 1989 California | AL | 41 | 138 | 28 | 2 | 0 | 6 | (2 | 4) | 48 | 16 | 15 | 3 | 0 | 44 | 0 | 3 | 0 | 0 | 0 | .00 | 3 | .203 | .220 | .348 |
| 1990 California | AL | 18 | 58 | 13 | 3 | 0 | 4 | (0 | 4) | 28 | 7 | 9 | 1 | 0 | 10 | 0 | 0 | 0 | 0 | 0 | .00 | 3 | .224 | .237 | .483 |
| 8 ML YEARS | | 376 | 1262 | 303 | 49 | 1 | 61 | (22 | 39) | 537 | 153 | 152 | 58 | 3 | 343 | 16 | 15 | 5 | 6 | 5 | .55 | 29 | .240 | .281 | .426 |

## Rick Schu

**Bats:** Right **Throws:** Right **Pos:** 3B/1B **Ht:** 6' 0" **Wt:** 194 **Born:** 01/26/62 **Age:** 29

| | | BATTING | | | | | | | | | | | | | | | | | BASERUNNING | | | | PERCENTAGES | | |
|---|---|---|---|---|---|---|---|---|---|---|---|---|---|---|---|---|---|---|---|---|---|---|---|---|---|
| Year Team | Lg | G | AB | H | 2B | 3B | HR | (Hm | Rd) | TB | R | RBI | TBB | IBB | SO | HBP | SH | SF | SB | CS | SB% | GDP | Avg | OBP | SLG |
| 1984 Philadelphia | NL | 17 | 29 | 8 | 2 | 1 | 2 | (1 | 1) | 18 | 12 | 5 | 6 | 0 | 6 | 0 | 0 | 1 | 0 | 0 | .00 | 0 | .276 | .389 | .621 |
| 1985 Philadelphia | NL | 112 | 416 | 105 | 21 | 4 | 7 | (2 | 5) | 155 | 54 | 24 | 38 | 3 | 78 | 2 | 1 | 0 | 8 | 6 | .57 | 7 | .252 | .318 | .373 |
| 1986 Philadelphia | NL | 92 | 208 | 57 | 10 | 1 | 8 | (1 | 7) | 93 | 32 | 25 | 18 | 1 | 44 | 2 | 3 | 2 | 2 | 2 | .50 | 1 | .274 | .335 | .447 |
| 1987 Philadelphia | NL | 92 | 196 | 46 | 6 | 3 | 7 | (5 | 2) | 79 | 24 | 23 | 20 | 1 | 36 | 2 | 0 | 1 | 0 | 2 | .00 | 1 | .235 | .311 | .403 |
| 1988 Baltimore | AL | 89 | 270 | 69 | 9 | 4 | 4 | (2 | 2) | 98 | 22 | 20 | 21 | 0 | 49 | 3 | 0 | 0 | 6 | 4 | .60 | 7 | .256 | .316 | .363 |
| 1989 2 ML Teams | | 99 | 266 | 57 | 11 | 0 | 7 | (3 | 4) | 89 | 25 | 21 | 24 | 0 | 37 | 0 | 2 | 1 | 1 | 2 | .33 | 6 | .214 | .278 | .335 |
| 1990 California | AL | 61 | 157 | 42 | 8 | 0 | 6 | (3 | 3) | 68 | 19 | 14 | 11 | 0 | 25 | 0 | 0 | 1 | 0 | 0 | .00 | 4 | .268 | .314 | .433 |
| 1989 Baltimore | AL | 1 | 0 | 0 | 0 | 0 | 0 | (0 | 0) | 0 | 0 | 0 | 0 | 0 | 0 | 0 | 0 | 0 | 0 | 0 | .00 | 0 | .000 | .000 | .000 |
| Detroit | AL | 98 | 266 | 57 | 11 | 0 | 7 | (3 | 4) | 89 | 25 | 21 | 24 | 0 | 37 | 0 | 2 | 1 | 1 | 2 | .33 | 6 | .214 | .278 | .335 |
| 7 ML YEARS | | 562 | 1542 | 384 | 67 | 13 | 41 | (17 | 24) | 600 | 188 | 132 | 138 | 5 | 275 | 9 | 6 | 6 | 17 | 16 | .52 | 26 | .249 | .313 | .389 |

## Jeff Schulz

**Bats:** Left **Throws:** Right **Pos:** RF **Ht:** 6' 1" **Wt:** 190 **Born:** 06/02/61 **Age:** 30

| | | BATTING | | | | | | | | | | | | | | | | | BASERUNNING | | | | PERCENTAGES | | |
|---|---|---|---|---|---|---|---|---|---|---|---|---|---|---|---|---|---|---|---|---|---|---|---|---|---|
| Year Team | Lg | G | AB | H | 2B | 3B | HR | (Hm | Rd) | TB | R | RBI | TBB | IBB | SO | HBP | SH | SF | SB | CS | SB% | GDP | Avg | OBP | SLG |
| 1984 Charleston | A | 69 | 265 | 89 | 14 | 3 | 5 | -- | -- | 124 | 52 | 54 | 34 | 3 | 20 | 1 | 0 | 2 | 4 | 2 | .67 | 1 | .336 | .411 | .468 |
| Ft. Myers | A | 59 | 204 | 64 | 10 | 0 | 0 | -- | -- | 74 | 23 | 26 | 18 | 0 | 23 | 1 | 2 | 2 | 8 | 5 | .62 | 7 | .314 | .369 | .363 |
| 1985 Memphis | AA | 136 | 488 | 149 | 15 | 5 | 4 | -- | -- | 186 | 73 | 53 | 59 | 5 | 42 | 0 | 4 | 8 | 8 | 4 | .67 | 15 | .305 | .375 | .381 |
| 1986 Omaha | AAA | 123 | 400 | 121 | 19 | 4 | 2 | -- | -- | 154 | 40 | 61 | 37 | 9 | 51 | 2 | 2 | 8 | 0 | 2 | .00 | 15 | .303 | .358 | .385 |
| 1987 Omaha | AAA | 99 | 316 | 81 | 12 | 7 | 4 | -- | -- | 119 | 25 | 36 | 24 | 1 | 56 | 2 | 1 | 2 | 1 | 0 | 1.00 | 12 | .256 | .311 | .377 |
| 1988 Omaha | AAA | 101 | 359 | 103 | 20 | 3 | 5 | -- | -- | 144 | 37 | 41 | 17 | 7 | 47 | 0 | 0 | 3 | 1 | 3 | .25 | 8 | .287 | .317 | .401 |
| 1989 Omaha | AAA | 95 | 331 | 92 | 19 | 5 | 2 | -- | -- | 127 | 31 | 37 | 28 | 6 | 47 | 2 | 1 | 1 | 2 | 0 | 1.00 | 10 | .278 | .337 | .384 |
| 1990 Omaha | AAA | 69 | 231 | 69 | 16 | 1 | 4 | -- | -- | 99 | 35 | 27 | 16 | 4 | 46 | 1 | 1 | 3 | 2 | 0 | 1.00 | 4 | .299 | .343 | .429 |
| 1989 Kansas City | AL | 7 | 9 | 2 | 0 | 0 | 0 | (0 | 0) | 2 | 0 | 1 | 0 | 0 | 2 | 0 | 0 | 0 | 0 | 0 | .00 | 0 | .222 | .222 | .222 |
| 1990 Kansas City | AL | 30 | 66 | 17 | 5 | 1 | 0 | (0 | 0) | 24 | 5 | 6 | 6 | 2 | 13 | 0 | 1 | 0 | 0 | 0 | .00 | 2 | .258 | .319 | .364 |
| 2 ML YEARS | | 37 | 75 | 19 | 5 | 1 | 0 | (0 | 0) | 26 | 5 | 7 | 6 | 2 | 15 | 0 | 1 | 0 | 0 | 0 | .00 | 2 | .253 | .309 | .347 |

## Mike Schwabe

**Pitches:** Right **Bats:** Right **Pos:** RP **Ht:** 6' 4" **Wt:** 200 **Born:** 07/12/64 **Age:** 26

| | | HOW MUCH HE PITCHED | | | | | | WHAT HE GAVE UP | | | | | | | | | | | | THE RESULTS | | | | | |
|---|---|---|---|---|---|---|---|---|---|---|---|---|---|---|---|---|---|---|---|---|---|---|---|---|---|
| Year Team | Lg | G | GS | CG | GF | IP | BFP | H | R | ER | HR | SH | SF | HB | TBB | IBB | SO | WP | Bk | W | L | Pct. | ShO | Sv | ERA |
| 1987 Bristol | R | 4 | 1 | 0 | 2 | 12.2 | 50 | 8 | 8 | 6 | 1 | 0 | 1 | 1 | 3 | 0 | 7 | 1 | 0 | 2 | 1 | .667 | 0 | 0 | 4.26 |
| Fayetteville | A | 11 | 0 | 0 | 7 | 22 | 85 | 18 | 10 | 6 | 2 | 0 | 0 | 0 | 2 | 1 | 23 | 1 | 1 | 1 | 1 | .500 | 0 | 3 | 2.45 |
| Lakeland | A | 5 | 2 | 2 | 1 | 18 | 72 | 12 | 6 | 6 | 1 | 0 | 1 | 0 | 8 | 0 | 9 | 0 | 0 | 2 | 1 | .667 | 0 | 1 | 3.00 |
| 1988 Glens Falls | AA | 8 | 0 | 0 | 3 | 18 | 76 | 16 | 9 | 7 | 4 | 0 | 0 | 1 | 5 | 0 | 11 | 0 | 0 | 0 | 2 | .000 | 0 | 0 | 3.50 |
| Lakeland | A | 40 | 5 | 1 | 23 | 111.2 | 443 | 88 | 24 | 20 | 1 | 1 | 2 | 4 | 14 | 2 | 80 | 6 | 2 | 9 | 0 | 1.000 | 1 | 8 | 1.61 |

| Year | Team | Lg | G | GS | CG | GF | IP | BFP | H | R | ER | HR | SH | SF | HB | TBB | IBB | SO | WP | Bk | W | L | Pct. | ShO | Sv | ERA |
|---|---|---|---|---|---|---|---|---|---|---|---|---|---|---|---|---|---|---|---|---|---|---|---|---|---|---|
| 1989 | London | AA | 8 | 2 | 0 | 5 | 25.1 | 111 | 25 | 7 | 3 | 1 | 0 | 0 | 2 | 5 | 2 | 22 | 2 | 0 | 3 | 0 | 1.000 | 0 | 2 | 1.07 |
| | Toledo | AAA | 13 | 5 | 1 | 4 | 62.1 | 255 | 60 | 20 | 18 | 2 | 3 | 2 | 1 | 10 | 4 | 32 | 5 | 0 | 5 | 3 | .625 | 0 | 0 | 2.60 |
| 1990 | Toledo | AAA | 51 | 2 | 0 | 15 | 108 | 459 | 112 | 58 | 46 | 4 | 6 | 6 | 2 | 22 | 1 | 69 | 7 | 0 | 6 | 5 | .545 | 0 | 5 | 3.83 |
| 1989 | Detroit | AL | 13 | 4 | 0 | 6 | 44.2 | 209 | 58 | 33 | 30 | 6 | 0 | 3 | 1 | 16 | 5 | 13 | 1 | 0 | 2 | 4 | .333 | 0 | 0 | 6.04 |
| 1990 | Detroit | AL | 1 | 0 | 0 | 0 | 3.2 | 15 | 5 | 1 | 1 | 0 | 1 | 0 | 0 | 0 | 0 | 1 | 0 | 0 | 0 | 0 | .000 | 0 | 0 | 2.45 |
| | 2 ML YEARS | | 14 | 4 | 0 | 6 | 48.1 | 224 | 63 | 34 | 31 | 6 | 1 | 3 | 1 | 16 | 5 | 14 | 1 | 0 | 2 | 4 | .333 | 0 | 0 | 5.77 |

## Mike Scioscia

**Bats:** Left **Throws:** Right **Pos:** C **Ht:** 6' 2" **Wt:** 219 **Born:** 11/27/58 **Age:** 32

| | | | BATTING | | | | | | | | | | | | | | | | BASERUNNING | | | | PERCENTAGES | | |
|---|---|---|---|---|---|---|---|---|---|---|---|---|---|---|---|---|---|---|---|---|---|---|---|---|---|
| Year | Team | Lg | G | AB | H | 2B | 3B | HR | (Hm | Rd) | TB | R | RBI | TBB | IBB | SO | HBP | SH | SF | SB | CS | SB% | GDP | Avg | OBP | SLG |
| 1980 | Los Angeles | NL | 54 | 134 | 34 | 5 | 1 | 1 | (1 | 0) | 44 | 8 | 8 | 12 | 2 | 9 | 0 | 5 | 1 | 1 | 0 | 1.00 | 2 | .254 | .313 | .328 |
| 1981 | Los Angeles | NL | 93 | 290 | 80 | 10 | 0 | 2 | (0 | 2) | 96 | 27 | 29 | 36 | 8 | 18 | 1 | 4 | 4 | 0 | 2 | .00 | 8 | .276 | .353 | .331 |
| 1982 | Los Angeles | NL | 129 | 365 | 80 | 11 | 1 | 5 | (2 | 3) | 108 | 31 | 38 | 44 | 11 | 31 | 1 | 5 | 4 | 2 | 0 | 1.00 | 8 | .219 | .302 | .296 |
| 1983 | Los Angeles | NL | 12 | 35 | 11 | 3 | 0 | 1 | (0 | 1) | 17 | 3 | 7 | 5 | 1 | 2 | 0 | 0 | 0 | 0 | 0 | .00 | 1 | .314 | .400 | .486 |
| 1984 | Los Angeles | NL | 114 | 341 | 93 | 18 | 0 | 5 | (0 | 5) | 126 | 29 | 38 | 52 | 10 | 26 | 1 | 1 | 4 | 2 | 1 | .67 | 10 | .273 | .367 | .370 |
| 1985 | Los Angeles | NL | 141 | 429 | 127 | 26 | 3 | 7 | (1 | 6) | 180 | 47 | 53 | 77 | 9 | 21 | 5 | 11 | 3 | 3 | 3 | .50 | 10 | .296 | .407 | .420 |
| 1986 | Los Angeles | NL | 122 | 374 | 94 | 18 | 1 | 5 | (2 | 3) | 129 | 36 | 26 | 62 | 4 | 23 | 3 | 6 | 4 | 3 | 3 | .50 | 11 | .251 | .359 | .345 |
| 1987 | Los Angeles | NL | 142 | 461 | 122 | 26 | 1 | 6 | (2 | 4) | 168 | 44 | 38 | 55 | 9 | 23 | 1 | 4 | 2 | 7 | 4 | .64 | 13 | .265 | .343 | .364 |
| 1988 | Los Angeles | NL | 130 | 408 | 105 | 18 | 0 | 3 | (1 | 2) | 132 | 29 | 35 | 38 | 12 | 31 | 0 | 3 | 3 | 0 | 3 | .00 | 14 | .257 | .318 | .324 |
| 1989 | Los Angeles | NL | 133 | 408 | 102 | 16 | 0 | 10 | (4 | 6) | 148 | 40 | 44 | 52 | 14 | 29 | 3 | 7 | 1 | 0 | 2 | .00 | 4 | .250 | .338 | .363 |
| 1990 | Los Angeles | NL | 135 | 435 | 115 | 25 | 0 | 12 | (5 | 7) | 176 | 46 | 66 | 55 | 14 | 31 | 3 | 1 | 4 | 4 | 1 | .80 | 11 | .264 | .348 | .405 |
| | 11 ML YEARS | | 1205 | 3680 | 963 | 176 | 7 | 57 | (18 | 39) | 1324 | 340 | 382 | 488 | 94 | 244 | 18 | 47 | 30 | 22 | 19 | .54 | 92 | .262 | .348 | .360 |

## Mike Scott

**Pitches:** Right **Bats:** Right **Pos:** SP **Ht:** 6' 3" **Wt:** 215 **Born:** 04/26/55 **Age:** 36

| | | | HOW MUCH HE PITCHED | | | | | | WHAT HE GAVE UP | | | | | | | | | | | | THE RESULTS | | | | | |
|---|---|---|---|---|---|---|---|---|---|---|---|---|---|---|---|---|---|---|---|---|---|---|---|---|---|---|
| Year | Team | Lg | G | GS | CG | GF | IP | BFP | H | R | ER | HR | SH | SF | HB | TBB | IBB | SO | WP | Bk | W | L | Pct. | ShO | Sv | ERA |
| 1979 | New York | NL | 18 | 9 | 0 | 0 | 52 | 229 | 59 | 35 | 31 | 4 | 4 | 1 | 0 | 20 | 3 | 21 | 1 | 1 | 1 | 3 | .250 | 0 | 0 | 5.37 |
| 1980 | New York | NL | 6 | 6 | 1 | 0 | 29 | 132 | 40 | 14 | 14 | 1 | 2 | 1 | 0 | 8 | 1 | 13 | 1 | 0 | 1 | 1 | .500 | 1 | 0 | 4.34 |
| 1981 | New York | NL | 23 | 23 | 1 | 0 | 136 | 551 | 130 | 65 | 59 | 11 | 12 | 5 | 1 | 34 | 1 | 54 | 1 | 2 | 5 | 10 | .333 | 0 | 0 | 3.90 |
| 1982 | New York | NL | 37 | 22 | 1 | 10 | 147 | 670 | 185 | 100 | 84 | 13 | 21 | 11 | 2 | 60 | 3 | 63 | 1 | 2 | 7 | 13 | .350 | 0 | 3 | 5.14 |
| 1983 | Houston | NL | 24 | 24 | 2 | 0 | 145 | 612 | 143 | 67 | 60 | 8 | 1 | 5 | 5 | 46 | 0 | 73 | 4 | 4 | 10 | 6 | .625 | 2 | 0 | 3.72 |
| 1984 | Houston | NL | 31 | 29 | 0 | 1 | 154 | 675 | 179 | 96 | 80 | 7 | 8 | 11 | 3 | 43 | 4 | 83 | 2 | 2 | 5 | 11 | .313 | 0 | 0 | 4.68 |
| 1985 | Houston | NL | 36 | 35 | 4 | 1 | 221.2 | 922 | 194 | 91 | 81 | 20 | 6 | 6 | 3 | 80 | 4 | 137 | 7 | 2 | 18 | 8 | .692 | 2 | 0 | 3.29 |
| 1986 | Houston | NL | 37 | 37 | 7 | 0 | 275.1 | 1065 | 182 | 73 | 68 | 17 | 8 | 6 | 2 | 72 | 6 | 306 | 3 | 0 | 18 | 10 | .643 | 5 | 0 | 2.22 |
| 1987 | Houston | NL | 36 | 36 | 8 | 0 | 247.2 | 1010 | 199 | 94 | 89 | 21 | 8 | 3 | 4 | 79 | 6 | 233 | 10 | 2 | 16 | 13 | .552 | 3 | 0 | 3.23 |
| 1988 | Houston | NL | 32 | 32 | 8 | 0 | 218.2 | 875 | 162 | 74 | 71 | 19 | 16 | 4 | 8 | 53 | 6 | 190 | 1 | 1 | 14 | 8 | .636 | 5 | 0 | 2.92 |
| 1989 | Houston | NL | 33 | 32 | 9 | 1 | 229 | 924 | 180 | 87 | 79 | 23 | 7 | 4 | 3 | 62 | 12 | 172 | 7 | 0 | 20 | 10 | .667 | 2 | 0 | 3.10 |
| 1990 | Houston | NL | 32 | 32 | 4 | 0 | 205.2 | 871 | 194 | 102 | 87 | 27 | 7 | 8 | 1 | 66 | 6 | 121 | 1 | 3 | 9 | 13 | .409 | 2 | 0 | 3.81 |
| | 12 ML YEARS | | 345 | 317 | 45 | 13 | 2061 | 8536 | 1847 | 898 | 803 | 171 | 100 | 65 | 32 | 623 | 52 | 1466 | 39 | 19 | 124 | 106 | .539 | 22 | 3 | 3.51 |

## Scott Scudder

**Pitches:** Right **Bats:** Right **Pos:** RP/SP **Ht:** 6' 2" **Wt:** 180 **Born:** 02/14/68 **Age:** 23

| | | | HOW MUCH HE PITCHED | | | | | | WHAT HE GAVE UP | | | | | | | | | | | | THE RESULTS | | | | | |
|---|---|---|---|---|---|---|---|---|---|---|---|---|---|---|---|---|---|---|---|---|---|---|---|---|---|---|
| Year | Team | Lg | G | GS | CG | GF | IP | BFP | H | R | ER | HR | SH | SF | HB | TBB | IBB | SO | WP | Bk | W | L | Pct. | ShO | Sv | ERA |
| 1986 | Billings | R | 12 | 8 | 0 | 1 | 52.2 | 0 | 42 | 34 | 28 | 1 | 0 | 0 | 3 | 36 | 0 | 38 | 8 | 0 | 1 | 3 | .250 | 0 | 0 | 4.78 |
| 1987 | Cedar Rapds | A | 26 | 26 | 0 | 0 | 153.2 | 660 | 129 | 86 | 70 | 16 | 8 | 2 | 7 | 76 | 0 | 128 | 15 | 3 | 7 | 12 | .368 | 0 | 0 | 4.10 |
| 1988 | Cedar Rapds | A | 16 | 15 | 1 | 0 | 102.1 | 405 | 61 | 30 | 23 | 3 | 2 | 1 | 2 | 41 | 0 | 126 | 5 | 0 | 7 | 3 | .700 | 1 | 0 | 2.02 |
| | Chattanooga | AA | 11 | 11 | 0 | 0 | 70 | 290 | 53 | 24 | 23 | 7 | 1 | 3 | 1 | 30 | 0 | 52 | 5 | 0 | 7 | 0 | 1.000 | 0 | 0 | 2.96 |
| 1989 | Nashville | AAA | 12 | 12 | 3 | 0 | 80.2 | 339 | 54 | 27 | 24 | 6 | 2 | 3 | 3 | 48 | 0 | 64 | 1 | 1 | 6 | 2 | .750 | 3 | 0 | 2.68 |
| 1990 | Nashville | AAA | 11 | 11 | 1 | 0 | 80.2 | 315 | 53 | 27 | 21 | 1 | 0 | 1 | 0 | 32 | 0 | 60 | 0 | 3 | 7 | 1 | .875 | 0 | 0 | 2.34 |
| 1989 | Cincinnati | NL | 23 | 17 | 0 | 3 | 100.1 | 451 | 91 | 54 | 50 | 14 | 7 | 2 | 1 | 61 | 11 | 66 | 0 | 1 | 4 | 9 | .308 | 0 | 0 | 4.49 |
| 1990 | Cincinnati | NL | 21 | 10 | 0 | 3 | 71.2 | 316 | 74 | 41 | 39 | 12 | 3 | 1 | 3 | 30 | 4 | 42 | 2 | 2 | 5 | 5 | .500 | 0 | 0 | 4.90 |
| | 2 ML YEARS | | 44 | 27 | 0 | 6 | 172 | 767 | 165 | 95 | 89 | 26 | 10 | 3 | 4 | 91 | 15 | 108 | 2 | 3 | 9 | 14 | .391 | 0 | 0 | 4.66 |

## Rudy Seanez

**Pitches:** Right **Bats:** Right **Pos:** RP **Ht:** 6' 0" **Wt:** 170 **Born:** 10/20/68 **Age:** 22

| | | | HOW MUCH HE PITCHED | | | | | | WHAT HE GAVE UP | | | | | | | | | | | | THE RESULTS | | | | | |
|---|---|---|---|---|---|---|---|---|---|---|---|---|---|---|---|---|---|---|---|---|---|---|---|---|---|---|
| Year | Team | Lg | G | GS | CG | GF | IP | BFP | H | R | ER | HR | SH | SF | HB | TBB | IBB | SO | WP | Bk | W | L | Pct. | ShO | Sv | ERA |
| 1986 | Burlington | R | 13 | 12 | 1 | 1 | 76 | 318 | 59 | 37 | 27 | 5 | 1 | 3 | 3 | 32 | 0 | 56 | 6 | 0 | 5 | 2 | .714 | 1 | 0 | 3.20 |
| 1987 | Waterloo | A | 10 | 10 | 0 | 0 | 34.2 | 159 | 35 | 29 | 26 | 6 | 0 | 2 | 1 | 23 | 0 | 23 | 2 | 2 | 0 | 4 | .000 | 0 | 0 | 6.75 |
| 1988 | Waterloo | A | 22 | 22 | 1 | 0 | 113.1 | 505 | 98 | 69 | 59 | 10 | 2 | 2 | 6 | 68 | 0 | 93 | 14 | 2 | 6 | 6 | .500 | 1 | 0 | 4.69 |
| 1989 | Kinston | A | 25 | 25 | 1 | 0 | 113 | 539 | 94 | 66 | 52 | 0 | 1 | 1 | 5 | 111 | 1 | 149 | 13 | 1 | 8 | 10 | .444 | 0 | 0 | 4.14 |
| | Colo Sprngs | AAA | 1 | 0 | 0 | 1 | 1 | 4 | 1 | 0 | 0 | 0 | 0 | 0 | 0 | 0 | 0 | 0 | 0 | 0 | 0 | 0 | .000 | 0 | 0 | 0.00 |

| Year | Team | Lg | G | GS | CG | GF | IP | BFP | H | R | ER | HR | SH | SF | HB | TBB | IBB | SO | WP | Bk | W | L | Pct. | ShO | Sv | ERA |
|---|---|---|---|---|---|---|---|---|---|---|---|---|---|---|---|---|---|---|---|---|---|---|---|---|---|---|
| 1990 | Canton-Akrn | AA | 15 | 0 | 0 | 11 | 16.2 | 68 | 9 | 4 | 4 | 0 | 2 | 0 | 1 | 12 | 0 | 27 | 0 | 0 | 1 | 0 | 1.000 | 0 | 5 | 2.16 |
| | Colo Sprngs | AAA | 12 | 0 | 0 | 10 | 12 | 59 | 15 | 10 | 9 | 2 | 0 | 1 | 0 | 10 | 0 | 7 | 3 | 0 | 1 | 4 | .200 | 0 | 1 | 6.75 |
| 1989 | Cleveland | AL | 5 | 0 | 0 | 2 | 5 | 20 | 1 | 2 | 2 | 0 | 0 | 2 | 0 | 4 | 1 | 7 | 1 | 1 | 0 | 0 | .000 | 0 | 0 | 3.60 |
| 1990 | Cleveland | AL | 24 | 0 | 0 | 12 | 27.1 | 127 | 22 | 17 | 17 | 2 | 0 | 1 | 1 | 25 | 1 | 24 | 5 | 0 | 2 | 1 | .667 | 0 | 0 | 5.60 |
| | 2 ML YEARS | | 29 | 0 | 0 | 14 | 32.1 | 147 | 23 | 19 | 19 | 2 | 0 | 3 | 1 | 29 | 2 | 31 | 6 | 1 | 2 | 1 | .667 | 0 | 0 | 5.29 |

## Ray Searage

**Pitches:** Left **Bats:** Left **Pos:** RP **Ht:** 6' 1" **Wt:** 180 **Born:** 05/01/55 **Age:** 36

| | | | HOW MUCH HE PITCHED | | | | | | WHAT HE GAVE UP | | | | | | | | | | | | THE RESULTS | | | | | |
|---|---|---|---|---|---|---|---|---|---|---|---|---|---|---|---|---|---|---|---|---|---|---|---|---|---|---|
| Year | Team | Lg | G | GS | CG | GF | IP | BFP | H | R | ER | HR | SH | SF | HB | TBB | IBB | SO | WP | Bk | W | L | Pct. | ShO | Sv | ERA |
| 1981 | New York | NL | 26 | 0 | 0 | 7 | 37 | 156 | 34 | 16 | 15 | 2 | 2 | 2 | 0 | 17 | 3 | 16 | 3 | 0 | 1 | 0 | 1.000 | 0 | 1 | 3.65 |
| 1984 | Milwaukee | AL | 21 | 0 | 0 | 16 | 38.1 | 149 | 20 | 3 | 3 | 0 | 3 | 0 | 1 | 16 | 3 | 29 | 1 | 0 | 2 | 1 | .667 | 0 | 6 | 0.70 |
| 1985 | Milwaukee | AL | 33 | 0 | 0 | 18 | 38 | 189 | 54 | 27 | 25 | 2 | 4 | 1 | 0 | 24 | 4 | 36 | 0 | 0 | 1 | 4 | .200 | 0 | 1 | 5.92 |
| 1986 | 2 ML Teams | | 46 | 0 | 0 | 17 | 51 | 220 | 44 | 20 | 19 | 7 | 1 | 2 | 1 | 28 | 4 | 36 | 1 | 1 | 1 | 1 | .500 | 0 | 1 | 3.35 |
| 1987 | Chicago | AL | 58 | 0 | 0 | 18 | 55.2 | 240 | 56 | 28 | 26 | 9 | 1 | 2 | 1 | 24 | 3 | 33 | 2 | 0 | 2 | 3 | .400 | 0 | 2 | 4.20 |
| 1989 | Los Angeles | NL | 41 | 0 | 0 | 17 | 35.2 | 152 | 29 | 15 | 14 | 1 | 2 | 3 | 0 | 18 | 6 | 24 | 2 | 1 | 3 | 4 | .429 | 0 | 0 | 3.53 |
| 1990 | Los Angeles | NL | 29 | 0 | 0 | 8 | 32.1 | 136 | 30 | 11 | 10 | 1 | 2 | 4 | 0 | 10 | 0 | 19 | 5 | 0 | 1 | 0 | 1.000 | 0 | 0 | 2.78 |
| 1986 | Milwaukee | AL | 17 | 0 | 0 | 8 | 22 | 103 | 29 | 17 | 17 | 6 | 1 | 0 | 1 | 9 | 1 | 10 | 1 | 1 | 0 | 1 | .000 | 0 | 1 | 6.95 |
| | Chicago | AL | 29 | 0 | 0 | 9 | 29 | 117 | 15 | 3 | 2 | 1 | 0 | 2 | 0 | 19 | 3 | 26 | 0 | 0 | 1 | 0 | 1.000 | 0 | 0 | 0.62 |
| | 7 ML YEARS | | 254 | 0 | 0 | 101 | 288 | 1242 | 267 | 120 | 112 | 22 | 15 | 14 | 3 | 137 | 23 | 193 | 14 | 2 | 11 | 13 | .458 | 0 | 11 | 3.50 |

## Steve Searcy

**Pitches:** Left **Bats:** Left **Pos:** SP **Ht:** 6' 1" **Wt:** 185 **Born:** 06/04/64 **Age:** 27

| | | | HOW MUCH HE PITCHED | | | | | | WHAT HE GAVE UP | | | | | | | | | | | | THE RESULTS | | | | | |
|---|---|---|---|---|---|---|---|---|---|---|---|---|---|---|---|---|---|---|---|---|---|---|---|---|---|---|
| Year | Team | Lg | G | GS | CG | GF | IP | BFP | H | R | ER | HR | SH | SF | HB | TBB | IBB | SO | WP | Bk | W | L | Pct. | ShO | Sv | ERA |
| 1988 | Detroit | AL | 2 | 2 | 0 | 0 | 8 | 37 | 8 | 6 | 5 | 3 | 0 | 0 | 0 | 4 | 0 | 5 | 0 | 0 | 0 | 2 | .000 | 0 | 0 | 5.63 |
| 1989 | Detroit | AL | 8 | 2 | 0 | 3 | 22.1 | 100 | 27 | 16 | 15 | 3 | 0 | 0 | 0 | 12 | 1 | 11 | 0 | 0 | 1 | 1 | .500 | 0 | 0 | 6.04 |
| 1990 | Detroit | AL | 16 | 12 | 1 | 2 | 75.1 | 341 | 76 | 44 | 39 | 9 | 2 | 6 | 0 | 51 | 3 | 66 | 3 | 0 | 2 | 7 | .222 | 0 | 0 | 4.66 |
| | 3 ML YEARS | | 26 | 16 | 1 | 5 | 105.2 | 478 | 111 | 66 | 59 | 15 | 2 | 6 | 0 | 67 | 4 | 82 | 3 | 0 | 3 | 10 | .231 | 0 | 0 | 5.03 |

## Bob Sebra

**Pitches:** Right **Bats:** Right **Pos:** RP **Ht:** 6' 2" **Wt:** 195 **Born:** 12/11/61 **Age:** 29

| | | | HOW MUCH HE PITCHED | | | | | | WHAT HE GAVE UP | | | | | | | | | | | | THE RESULTS | | | | | |
|---|---|---|---|---|---|---|---|---|---|---|---|---|---|---|---|---|---|---|---|---|---|---|---|---|---|---|
| Year | Team | Lg | G | GS | CG | GF | IP | BFP | H | R | ER | HR | SH | SF | HB | TBB | IBB | SO | WP | Bk | W | L | Pct. | ShO | Sv | ERA |
| 1985 | Texas | AL | 7 | 4 | 0 | 0 | 20.1 | 102 | 26 | 17 | 17 | 4 | 0 | 2 | 1 | 14 | 2 | 13 | 0 | 0 | 0 | 2 | .000 | 0 | 0 | 7.52 |
| 1986 | Montreal | NL | 17 | 13 | 3 | 4 | 91.1 | 377 | 82 | 39 | 36 | 9 | 3 | 3 | 3 | 25 | 2 | 66 | 2 | 3 | 5 | 5 | .500 | 1 | 0 | 3.55 |
| 1987 | Montreal | NL | 36 | 27 | 4 | 3 | 177.1 | 765 | 184 | 99 | 87 | 15 | 12 | 7 | 3 | 67 | 0 | 156 | 8 | 2 | 6 | 15 | .286 | 1 | 0 | 4.42 |
| 1988 | Philadelphia | NL | 3 | 3 | 0 | 0 | 11.1 | 60 | 15 | 11 | 10 | 0 | 0 | 5 | 0 | 10 | 0 | 7 | 0 | 1 | 1 | 2 | .333 | 0 | 0 | 7.94 |
| 1989 | 2 ML Teams | | 21 | 5 | 0 | 4 | 55.1 | 263 | 65 | 36 | 32 | 8 | 5 | 3 | 7 | 28 | 3 | 35 | 2 | 1 | 2 | 3 | .400 | 0 | 1 | 5.20 |
| 1990 | Milwaukee | AL | 10 | 0 | 0 | 2 | 11 | 59 | 20 | 10 | 10 | 1 | 2 | 2 | 1 | 5 | 1 | 4 | 1 | 0 | 1 | 2 | .333 | 0 | 0 | 8.18 |
| 1989 | Philadelphia | NL | 6 | 5 | 0 | 0 | 34.1 | 157 | 41 | 20 | 17 | 6 | 3 | 1 | 4 | 10 | 2 | 21 | 1 | 0 | 2 | 3 | .400 | 0 | 0 | 4.46 |
| | Cincinnati | NL | 15 | 0 | 0 | 4 | 21 | 106 | 24 | 16 | 15 | 2 | 2 | 2 | 3 | 18 | 1 | 14 | 1 | 1 | 0 | 0 | .000 | 0 | 1 | 6.43 |
| | 6 ML YEARS | | 94 | 52 | 7 | 13 | 366.2 | 1626 | 392 | 212 | 192 | 37 | 22 | 22 | 15 | 149 | 8 | 281 | 13 | 7 | 15 | 29 | .341 | 2 | 1 | 4.71 |

## David Segui

**Bats:** Both **Throws:** Left **Pos:** 1B **Ht:** 6' 1" **Wt:** 170 **Born:** 07/19/66 **Age:** 24

| | | | BATTING | | | | | | | | | | | | | | | | | | BASERUNNING | | | | PERCENTAGES | | |
|---|---|---|---|---|---|---|---|---|---|---|---|---|---|---|---|---|---|---|---|---|---|---|---|---|---|---|---|
| Year | Team | Lg | G | AB | H | 2B | 3B | HR | (Hm | Rd) | TB | R | RBI | TBB | IBB | SO | HBP | SH | SF | SB | CS | SB% | GDP | Avg | OBP | SLG |
| 1988 | Hagerstown | A | 60 | 190 | 51 | 12 | 4 | 3 | -- | -- | 80 | 35 | 31 | 22 | 3 | 23 | 3 | 0 | 4 | 0 | 0 | .00 | 7 | .268 | .347 | .421 |
| 1989 | Frederick | A | 83 | 284 | 90 | 19 | 0 | 10 | -- | -- | 139 | 43 | 50 | 41 | 3 | 32 | 4 | 0 | 3 | 2 | 1 | .67 | 4 | .317 | .407 | .489 |
| | Hagerstown | AA | 44 | 173 | 56 | 14 | 1 | 1 | -- | -- | 75 | 22 | 27 | 16 | 0 | 16 | 2 | 1 | 2 | 0 | 0 | .00 | 6 | .324 | .383 | .434 |
| 1990 | Rochester | AAA | 86 | 307 | 103 | 28 | 0 | 2 | -- | -- | 137 | 55 | 51 | 45 | 4 | 28 | 0 | 0 | 5 | 5 | 4 | .56 | 15 | .336 | .415 | .446 |
| 1990 | Baltimore | AL | 40 | 123 | 30 | 7 | 0 | 2 | (1 | 1) | 43 | 14 | 15 | 11 | 2 | 15 | 1 | 1 | 0 | 0 | 0 | .00 | 12 | .244 | .311 | .350 |

## Kevin Seitzer

**Bats:** Right **Throws:** Right **Pos:** 3B **Ht:** 5'11" **Wt:** 180 **Born:** 03/26/62 **Age:** 29

| | | | BATTING | | | | | | | | | | | | | | | | | | BASERUNNING | | | | PERCENTAGES | | |
|---|---|---|---|---|---|---|---|---|---|---|---|---|---|---|---|---|---|---|---|---|---|---|---|---|---|---|---|
| Year | Team | Lg | G | AB | H | 2B | 3B | HR | (Hm | Rd) | TB | R | RBI | TBB | IBB | SO | HBP | SH | SF | SB | CS | SB% | GDP | Avg | OBP | SLG |
| 1986 | Kansas City | AL | 28 | 96 | 31 | 4 | 1 | 2 | (1 | 1) | 43 | 16 | 11 | 19 | 0 | 14 | 1 | 0 | 0 | 0 | 0 | .00 | 0 | .323 | .440 | .448 |
| 1987 | Kansas City | AL | 161 | 641 | 207 | 33 | 8 | 15 | (7 | 8) | 301 | 105 | 83 | 80 | 0 | 85 | 2 | 1 | 1 | 12 | 7 | .63 | 18 | .323 | .399 | .470 |
| 1988 | Kansas City | AL | 149 | 559 | 170 | 32 | 5 | 5 | (4 | 1) | 227 | 90 | 60 | 72 | 4 | 64 | 6 | 3 | 3 | 10 | 8 | .56 | 15 | .304 | .388 | .406 |
| 1989 | Kansas City | AL | 160 | 597 | 168 | 17 | 2 | 4 | (2 | 2) | 201 | 78 | 48 | 102 | 7 | 76 | 5 | 4 | 7 | 17 | 8 | .68 | 16 | .281 | .387 | .337 |
| 1990 | Kansas City | AL | 158 | 622 | 171 | 31 | 5 | 6 | (5 | 1) | 230 | 91 | 38 | 67 | 2 | 66 | 2 | 4 | 2 | 7 | 5 | .58 | 11 | .275 | .346 | .370 |
| | 5 ML YEARS | | 656 | 2515 | 747 | 117 | 21 | 32 | (19 | 13) | 1002 | 380 | 240 | 340 | 13 | 305 | 16 | 12 | 13 | 46 | 28 | .62 | 60 | .297 | .382 | .398 |

## Mike Sharperson

**Bats:** Right **Throws:** Right **Pos:** 3B/SS **Ht:** 6' 3" **Wt:** 185 **Born:** 10/04/61 **Age:** 29

| BATTING | | | | | | | | | | | | | | | | | | | | BASERUNNING | | | | PERCENTAGES | | |
|---|---|---|---|---|---|---|---|---|---|---|---|---|---|---|---|---|---|---|---|---|---|---|---|---|---|---|
| Year | Team | Lg | G | AB | H | 2B | 3B | HR | (Hm | Rd) | TB | R | RBI | TBB | IBB | SO | HBP | SH | SF | SB | CS | SB% | GDP | Avg | OBP | SLG |
| 1987 | 2 ML Teams | | 42 | 129 | 29 | 6 | 1 | 0 | (0 | 0) | 37 | 11 | 10 | 11 | 1 | 20 | 1 | 1 | 0 | 2 | 1 | .67 | 3 | .225 | .291 | .287 |
| 1988 | Los Angeles | NL | 46 | 59 | 16 | 1 | 0 | 0 | (0 | 0) | 17 | 8 | 4 | 1 | 0 | 12 | 1 | 2 | 1 | 0 | 1 | .00 | 1 | .271 | .290 | .288 |
| 1989 | Los Angeles | NL | 27 | 28 | 7 | 3 | 0 | 0 | (0 | 0) | 10 | 2 | 5 | 4 | 1 | 7 | 0 | 1 | 1 | 0 | 1 | .00 | 1 | .250 | .333 | .357 |
| 1990 | Los Angeles | NL | 129 | 357 | 106 | 14 | 2 | 3 | (1 | 2) | 133 | 42 | 36 | 46 | 6 | 39 | 1 | 8 | 3 | 15 | 6 | .71 | 5 | .297 | .376 | .373 |
| 1987 | Toronto | AL | 32 | 96 | 20 | 4 | 1 | 0 | (0 | 0) | 26 | 4 | 9 | 7 | 0 | 15 | 1 | 1 | 0 | 2 | 1 | .67 | 2 | .208 | .269 | .271 |
| | Los Angeles | NL | 10 | 33 | 9 | 2 | 0 | 0 | (0 | 0) | 11 | 7 | 1 | 4 | 1 | 5 | 0 | 0 | 0 | 0 | 0 | .00 | 1 | .273 | .351 | .333 |
| | 4 ML YEARS | | 244 | 573 | 158 | 24 | 3 | 3 | (1 | 2) | 197 | 63 | 55 | 62 | 8 | 78 | 3 | 12 | 5 | 17 | 9 | .65 | 10 | .276 | .347 | .344 |

## Jeff Shaw

**Pitches:** Right **Bats:** Right **Pos:** SP **Ht:** 6' 2" **Wt:** 185 **Born:** 07/07/66 **Age:** 24

| HOW MUCH HE PITCHED | | | | | | | | | WHAT HE GAVE UP | | | | | | | | | | | THE RESULTS | | | | | |
|---|---|---|---|---|---|---|---|---|---|---|---|---|---|---|---|---|---|---|---|---|---|---|---|---|---|
| Year | Team | Lg | G | GS | CG | GF | IP | BFP | H | R | ER | HR | SH | SF | HB | TBB | IBB | SO | WP | Bk | W | L | Pct. | ShO | Sv | ERA |
| 1986 | Batavia | A | 14 | 12 | 3 | 1 | 88.2 | 367 | 79 | 32 | 24 | 5 | 3 | 4 | 5 | 35 | 0 | 71 | 10 | 0 | 8 | 4 | .667 | 1 | 0 | 2.44 |
| 1987 | Waterloo | A | 28 | 28 | 6 | 0 | 184.1 | 788 | 192 | 89 | 72 | 15 | 4 | 6 | 6 | 56 | 0 | 117 | 8 | 5 | 11 | 11 | .500 | 4 | 0 | 3.52 |
| 1988 | Williamsprt | AA | 27 | 27 | 6 | 0 | 163.2 | 718 | 173 | 94 | 66 | 11 | 10 | 10 | 10 | 75 | 1 | 61 | 12 | 4 | 5 | 19 | .208 | 1 | 0 | 3.63 |
| 1989 | Canton-Akrn | AA | 30 | 22 | 6 | 3 | 154.1 | 661 | 134 | 84 | 62 | 9 | 5 | 7 | 14 | 67 | 3 | 95 | 7 | 0 | 7 | 10 | .412 | 3 | 0 | 3.62 |
| 1990 | Colo Sprngs | AAA | 17 | 16 | 4 | 0 | 98.2 | 438 | 98 | 54 | 47 | 7 | 4 | 5 | 3 | 52 | 0 | 55 | 5 | 0 | 10 | 3 | .769 | 0 | 0 | 4.29 |
| 1990 | Cleveland | AL | 12 | 9 | 0 | 0 | 48.2 | 229 | 73 | 38 | 36 | 11 | 1 | 3 | 0 | 20 | 0 | 25 | 3 | 0 | 3 | 4 | .429 | 0 | 0 | 6.66 |

## Larry Sheets

**Bats:** Left **Throws:** Right **Pos:** LF/RF/DH **Ht:** 6' 3" **Wt:** 236 **Born:** 12/06/59 **Age:** 31

| BATTING | | | | | | | | | | | | | | | | | | | | BASERUNNING | | | | PERCENTAGES | | |
|---|---|---|---|---|---|---|---|---|---|---|---|---|---|---|---|---|---|---|---|---|---|---|---|---|---|---|
| Year | Team | Lg | G | AB | H | 2B | 3B | HR | (Hm | Rd) | TB | R | RBI | TBB | IBB | SO | HBP | SH | SF | SB | CS | SB% | GDP | Avg | OBP | SLG |
| 1984 | Baltimore | AL | 8 | 16 | 7 | 1 | 0 | 1 | (0 | 1) | 11 | 3 | 2 | 1 | 0 | 3 | 0 | 0 | 0 | 0 | 0 | .00 | 0 | .438 | .471 | .688 |
| 1985 | Baltimore | AL | 113 | 328 | 86 | 8 | 0 | 17 | (5 | 12) | 145 | 43 | 50 | 28 | 2 | 52 | 2 | 1 | 1 | 0 | 1 | .00 | 15 | .262 | .323 | .442 |
| 1986 | Baltimore | AL | 112 | 338 | 92 | 17 | 1 | 18 | (10 | 8) | 165 | 42 | 60 | 21 | 3 | 56 | 2 | 1 | 2 | 2 | 0 | 1.00 | 16 | .272 | .317 | .488 |
| 1987 | Baltimore | AL | 135 | 469 | 148 | 23 | 0 | 31 | (21 | 10) | 264 | 74 | 94 | 31 | 1 | 67 | 3 | 0 | 5 | 1 | 1 | .50 | 16 | .316 | .358 | .563 |
| 1988 | Baltimore | AL | 136 | 452 | 104 | 19 | 1 | 10 | (6 | 4) | 155 | 38 | 47 | 42 | 4 | 72 | 6 | 0 | 4 | 1 | 6 | .14 | 11 | .230 | .302 | .343 |
| 1989 | Baltimore | AL | 102 | 304 | 74 | 12 | 1 | 7 | (1 | 6) | 109 | 33 | 33 | 26 | 10 | 58 | 3 | 0 | 5 | 1 | 1 | .50 | 4 | .243 | .305 | .359 |
| 1990 | Detroit | AL | 131 | 360 | 94 | 17 | 2 | 10 | (7 | 3) | 145 | 40 | 52 | 24 | 2 | 42 | 2 | 0 | 4 | 1 | 3 | .25 | 12 | .261 | .308 | .403 |
| | 7 ML YEARS | | 737 | 2267 | 605 | 97 | 5 | 94 | (50 | 44) | 994 | 273 | 338 | 173 | 22 | 350 | 18 | 2 | 21 | 6 | 12 | .33 | 74 | .267 | .321 | .438 |

## Gary Sheffield

**Bats:** Right **Throws:** Right **Pos:** 3B **Ht:** 5'11" **Wt:** 190 **Born:** 11/18/68 **Age:** 22

| BATTING | | | | | | | | | | | | | | | | | | | | BASERUNNING | | | | PERCENTAGES | | |
|---|---|---|---|---|---|---|---|---|---|---|---|---|---|---|---|---|---|---|---|---|---|---|---|---|---|---|
| Year | Team | Lg | G | AB | H | 2B | 3B | HR | (Hm | Rd) | TB | R | RBI | TBB | IBB | SO | HBP | SH | SF | SB | CS | SB% | GDP | Avg | OBP | SLG |
| 1988 | Milwaukee | AL | 24 | 80 | 19 | 1 | 0 | 4 | (1 | 3) | 32 | 12 | 12 | 7 | 0 | 7 | 0 | 1 | 1 | 3 | 1 | .75 | 5 | .238 | .295 | .400 |
| 1989 | Milwaukee | AL | 95 | 368 | 91 | 18 | 0 | 5 | (2 | 3) | 124 | 34 | 32 | 27 | 0 | 33 | 4 | 3 | 3 | 10 | 6 | .63 | 4 | .247 | .303 | .337 |
| 1990 | Milwaukee | AL | 125 | 487 | 143 | 30 | 1 | 10 | (3 | 7) | 205 | 67 | 67 | 44 | 1 | 41 | 3 | 4 | 9 | 25 | 10 | .71 | 11 | .294 | .350 | .421 |
| | 3 ML YEARS | | 244 | 935 | 253 | 49 | 1 | 19 | (6 | 13) | 361 | 113 | 111 | 78 | 1 | 81 | 7 | 8 | 13 | 38 | 17 | .69 | 20 | .271 | .327 | .386 |

## John Shelby

**Bats:** Both **Throws:** Right **Pos:** CF/LF/RF **Ht:** 6' 1" **Wt:** 175 **Born:** 02/23/58 **Age:** 33

| BATTING | | | | | | | | | | | | | | | | | | | | BASERUNNING | | | | PERCENTAGES | | |
|---|---|---|---|---|---|---|---|---|---|---|---|---|---|---|---|---|---|---|---|---|---|---|---|---|---|---|
| Year | Team | Lg | G | AB | H | 2B | 3B | HR | (Hm | Rd) | TB | R | RBI | TBB | IBB | SO | HBP | SH | SF | SB | CS | SB% | GDP | Avg | OBP | SLG |
| 1981 | Baltimore | AL | 7 | 2 | 0 | 0 | 0 | 0 | (0 | 0) | 0 | 2 | 0 | 0 | 0 | 1 | 0 | 0 | 0 | 2 | 0 | 1.00 | 0 | .000 | .000 | .000 |
| 1982 | Baltimore | AL | 26 | 35 | 11 | 3 | 0 | 1 | (1 | 0) | 17 | 8 | 2 | 0 | 0 | 5 | 0 | 0 | 0 | 0 | 1 | .00 | 0 | .314 | .314 | .486 |
| 1983 | Baltimore | AL | 126 | 325 | 84 | 15 | 2 | 5 | (0 | 5) | 118 | 52 | 27 | 18 | 2 | 64 | 0 | 6 | 0 | 15 | 2 | .88 | 2 | .258 | .297 | .363 |
| 1984 | Baltimore | AL | 128 | 383 | 80 | 12 | 5 | 6 | (2 | 4) | 120 | 44 | 30 | 20 | 0 | 71 | 0 | 12 | 0 | 12 | 4 | .75 | 4 | .209 | .248 | .313 |
| 1985 | Baltimore | AL | 69 | 205 | 58 | 6 | 2 | 7 | (4 | 3) | 89 | 28 | 27 | 7 | 0 | 44 | 0 | 2 | 0 | 5 | 1 | .83 | 4 | .283 | .307 | .434 |
| 1986 | Baltimore | AL | 135 | 404 | 92 | 14 | 4 | 11 | (5 | 6) | 147 | 54 | 49 | 18 | 0 | 75 | 2 | 2 | 2 | 18 | 6 | .75 | 3 | .228 | .263 | .364 |
| 1987 | 2 ML Teams | | 141 | 508 | 138 | 26 | 0 | 22 | (8 | 14) | 230 | 65 | 72 | 32 | 2 | 110 | 1 | 2 | 9 | 16 | 7 | .70 | 9 | .272 | .311 | .453 |
| 1988 | Los Angeles | NL | 140 | 494 | 130 | 23 | 6 | 10 | (5 | 5) | 195 | 65 | 64 | 44 | 5 | 128 | 0 | 1 | 6 | 16 | 5 | .76 | 13 | .263 | .320 | .395 |
| 1989 | Los Angeles | NL | 108 | 345 | 63 | 11 | 1 | 1 | (0 | 1) | 79 | 28 | 12 | 25 | 5 | 92 | 0 | 0 | 1 | 10 | 7 | .59 | 6 | .183 | .237 | .229 |
| 1990 | 2 ML Teams | | 103 | 246 | 61 | 10 | 3 | 4 | (3 | 1) | 89 | 24 | 22 | 10 | 0 | 58 | 0 | 6 | 0 | 4 | 5 | .44 | 7 | .248 | .277 | .362 |
| 1987 | Baltimore | AL | 21 | 32 | 6 | 0 | 0 | 1 | (0 | 1) | 9 | 4 | 3 | 1 | 0 | 13 | 0 | 1 | 0 | 0 | 1 | .00 | 0 | .188 | .212 | .281 |
| | Los Angeles | NL | 120 | 476 | 132 | 26 | 0 | 21 | (8 | 13) | 221 | 61 | 69 | 31 | 2 | 97 | 1 | 1 | 9 | 16 | 6 | .73 | 9 | .277 | .317 | .464 |
| 1990 | Los Angeles | NL | 25 | 24 | 6 | 1 | 0 | 0 | (0 | 0) | 7 | 2 | 2 | 0 | 0 | 7 | 0 | 0 | 0 | 1 | 0 | 1.00 | 1 | .250 | .250 | .292 |
| | Detroit | AL | 78 | 222 | 55 | 9 | 3 | 4 | (3 | 1) | 82 | 22 | 20 | 10 | 0 | 51 | 0 | 6 | 0 | 3 | 5 | .38 | 6 | .248 | .280 | .369 |
| | 10 ML YEARS | | 983 | 2947 | 717 | 120 | 23 | 67 | (28 | 39) | 1084 | 370 | 305 | 174 | 14 | 648 | 3 | 31 | 18 | 98 | 38 | .72 | 48 | .243 | .285 | .368 |

## Tim Sherrill

**Pitches:** Left **Bats:** Left **Pos:** RP **Ht:** 5'11" **Wt:** 170 **Born:** 09/10/65 **Age:** 25

| HOW MUCH HE PITCHED | | | | | | | | WHAT HE GAVE UP | | | | | | | | | | | | THE RESULTS | | | | | |
|---|---|---|---|---|---|---|---|---|---|---|---|---|---|---|---|---|---|---|---|---|---|---|---|---|---|
| Year Team | Lg | G | GS | CG | GF | IP | BFP | H | R | ER | HR | SH | SF | HB | TBB | IBB | SO | WP | Bk | W | L | Pct. | ShO | Sv | ERA |
| 1987 Johnson Cty | R | 25 | 0 | 0 | 18 | 42 | 172 | 25 | 18 | 14 | 1 | 1 | 0 | 2 | 18 | 2 | 62 | 0 | 0 | 3 | 4 | .429 | 0 | 8 | 3.00 |
| 1988 Savannah | A | 31 | 0 | 0 | 29 | 45.1 | 173 | 26 | 12 | 9 | 2 | 5 | 2 | 1 | 13 | 2 | 62 | 0 | 1 | 3 | 2 | .600 | 0 | 16 | 1.79 |
| St. Pete | A | 16 | 0 | 0 | 11 | 23.1 | 87 | 14 | 4 | 4 | 0 | 0 | 3 | 1 | 8 | 1 | 25 | 0 | 2 | 2 | 0 | 1.000 | 0 | 6 | 1.54 |
| 1989 Savannah | A | 3 | 0 | 0 | 3 | 3.2 | 16 | 3 | 0 | 0 | 0 | 0 | 1 | 0 | 2 | 0 | 6 | 0 | 0 | 0 | 0 | .000 | 0 | 2 | 0.00 |
| St.Pete | A | 52 | 0 | 0 | 21 | 68 | 269 | 52 | 19 | 16 | 3 | 7 | 2 | 0 | 23 | 3 | 48 | 2 | 0 | 4 | 0 | 1.000 | 0 | 6 | 2.12 |
| 1990 Louisville | AAA | 52 | 0 | 0 | 20 | 61.1 | 253 | 49 | 17 | 17 | 4 | 4 | 1 | 1 | 21 | 2 | 57 | 4 | 0 | 4 | 3 | .571 | 0 | 2 | 2.49 |
| 1990 St. Louis | NL | 8 | 0 | 0 | 2 | 4.1 | 25 | 10 | 5 | 3 | 0 | 1 | 0 | 0 | 3 | 0 | 3 | 1 | 0 | 0 | 0 | .000 | 0 | 0 | 6.23 |

## Eric Show

**Pitches:** Right **Bats:** Right **Pos:** RP/SP **Ht:** 6' 1" **Wt:** 190 **Born:** 05/19/56 **Age:** 35

| HOW MUCH HE PITCHED | | | | | | | | WHAT HE GAVE UP | | | | | | | | | | | | THE RESULTS | | | | | |
|---|---|---|---|---|---|---|---|---|---|---|---|---|---|---|---|---|---|---|---|---|---|---|---|---|---|
| Year Team | Lg | G | GS | CG | GF | IP | BFP | H | R | ER | HR | SH | SF | HB | TBB | IBB | SO | WP | Bk | W | L | Pct. | ShO | Sv | ERA |
| 1981 San Diego | NL | 15 | 0 | 0 | 4 | 23 | 92 | 17 | 9 | 8 | 2 | 2 | 0 | 1 | 9 | 3 | 22 | 0 | 0 | 1 | 3 | .250 | 0 | 3 | 3.13 |
| 1982 San Diego | NL | 47 | 14 | 2 | 12 | 150 | 611 | 117 | 49 | 44 | 10 | 13 | 6 | 5 | 48 | 3 | 88 | 2 | 0 | 10 | 6 | .625 | 2 | 3 | 2.64 |
| 1983 San Diego | NL | 35 | 33 | 4 | 0 | 200.2 | 857 | 201 | 97 | 93 | 25 | 9 | 4 | 6 | 74 | 3 | 120 | 4 | 2 | 15 | 12 | .556 | 2 | 0 | 4.17 |
| 1984 San Diego | NL | 32 | 32 | 3 | 0 | 206.2 | 862 | 175 | 88 | 78 | 18 | 17 | 4 | 4 | 88 | 4 | 104 | 6 | 2 | 15 | 9 | .625 | 1 | 0 | 3.40 |
| 1985 San Diego | NL | 35 | 35 | 5 | 0 | 233 | 977 | 212 | 95 | 80 | 27 | 9 | 5 | 5 | 87 | 7 | 141 | 4 | 0 | 12 | 11 | .522 | 2 | 0 | 3.09 |
| 1986 San Diego | NL | 24 | 22 | 2 | 1 | 136.1 | 569 | 109 | 47 | 45 | 11 | 10 | 1 | 4 | 69 | 4 | 94 | 3 | 2 | 9 | 5 | .643 | 0 | 0 | 2.97 |
| 1987 San Diego | NL | 34 | 34 | 5 | 0 | 206.1 | 887 | 188 | 99 | 88 | 26 | 9 | 5 | 9 | 85 | 7 | 117 | 6 | 5 | 8 | 16 | .333 | 3 | 0 | 3.84 |
| 1988 San Diego | NL | 32 | 32 | 13 | 0 | 234.2 | 936 | 201 | 86 | 85 | 22 | 3 | 5 | 6 | 53 | 5 | 144 | 4 | 5 | 16 | 11 | .593 | 1 | 0 | 3.26 |
| 1989 San Diego | NL | 16 | 16 | 1 | 0 | 106.1 | 464 | 113 | 59 | 50 | 9 | 6 | 5 | 2 | 39 | 3 | 66 | 2 | 2 | 8 | 6 | .571 | 0 | 0 | 4.23 |
| 1990 San Diego | NL | 39 | 12 | 0 | 14 | 106.1 | 482 | 131 | 74 | 68 | 16 | 5 | 4 | 4 | 41 | 9 | 55 | 3 | 3 | 6 | 8 | .429 | 0 | 1 | 5.76 |
| 10 ML YEARS | | 309 | 230 | 35 | 31 | 1603.1 | 6737 | 1464 | 703 | 639 | 166 | 83 | 39 | 46 | 593 | 48 | 951 | 34 | 21 | 100 | 87 | .535 | 11 | 7 | 3.59 |

## Terry Shumpert

**Bats:** Right **Throws:** Right **Pos:** 2B **Ht:** 5'11" **Wt:** 190 **Born:** 08/16/66 **Age:** 24

| BATTING | | | | | | | | | | | | | | | | | | | BASERUNNING | | | | PERCENTAGES | | |
|---|---|---|---|---|---|---|---|---|---|---|---|---|---|---|---|---|---|---|---|---|---|---|---|---|---|
| Year Team | Lg | G | AB | H | 2B | 3B | HR | (Hm | Rd) | TB | R | RBI | TBB | IBB | SO | HBP | SH | SF | SB | CS | SB% | GDP | Avg | OBP | SLG |
| 1987 Eugene | A | 48 | 186 | 54 | 16 | 1 | 4 | -- | -- | 84 | 38 | 21 | 27 | 0 | 41 | 3 | 0 | 2 | 16 | 4 | .80 | 0 | .290 | .385 | .452 |
| 1988 Appleton | A | 114 | 422 | 102 | 37 | 2 | 7 | -- | -- | 164 | 64 | 38 | 56 | 1 | 90 | 3 | 0 | 5 | 36 | 3 | .92 | 1 | .242 | .331 | .389 |
| 1989 Omaha | AAA | 113 | 355 | 88 | 29 | 2 | 4 | -- | -- | 133 | 54 | 22 | 25 | 0 | 63 | 10 | 7 | 1 | 23 | 7 | .77 | 5 | .248 | .315 | .375 |
| 1990 Omaha | AAA | 39 | 153 | 39 | 6 | 4 | 2 | -- | -- | 59 | 24 | 12 | 14 | 0 | 28 | 3 | 4 | 1 | 18 | 0 | 1.00 | 3 | .255 | .327 | .386 |
| 1990 Kansas City | AL | 32 | 91 | 25 | 6 | 1 | 0 | (0 | 0) | 33 | 7 | 8 | 2 | 0 | 17 | 1 | 0 | 2 | 3 | 3 | .50 | 4 | .275 | .292 | .363 |

## Ruben Sierra

**Bats:** Both **Throws:** Right **Pos:** RF **Ht:** 6' 1" **Wt:** 175 **Born:** 10/06/65 **Age:** 25

| BATTING | | | | | | | | | | | | | | | | | | | BASERUNNING | | | | PERCENTAGES | | |
|---|---|---|---|---|---|---|---|---|---|---|---|---|---|---|---|---|---|---|---|---|---|---|---|---|---|
| Year Team | Lg | G | AB | H | 2B | 3B | HR | (Hm | Rd) | TB | R | RBI | TBB | IBB | SO | HBP | SH | SF | SB | CS | SB% | GDP | Avg | OBP | SLG |
| 1986 Texas | AL | 113 | 382 | 101 | 13 | 10 | 16 | (8 | 8) | 182 | 50 | 55 | 22 | 3 | 65 | 1 | 1 | 5 | 7 | 8 | .47 | 8 | .264 | .302 | .476 |
| 1987 Texas | AL | 158 | 643 | 169 | 35 | 4 | 30 | (15 | 15) | 302 | 97 | 109 | 39 | 4 | 114 | 2 | 0 | 12 | 16 | 11 | .59 | 18 | .263 | .302 | .470 |
| 1988 Texas | AL | 156 | 615 | 156 | 32 | 2 | 23 | (15 | 8) | 261 | 77 | 91 | 44 | 10 | 91 | 1 | 0 | 8 | 18 | 4 | .82 | 15 | .254 | .301 | .424 |
| 1989 Texas | AL | 162 | 634 | 194 | 35 | 14 | 29 | (21 | 8) | 344 | 101 | 119 | 43 | 2 | 82 | 2 | 0 | 10 | 8 | 2 | .80 | 7 | .306 | .347 | .543 |
| 1990 Texas | AL | 159 | 608 | 170 | 37 | 2 | 16 | (10 | 6) | 259 | 70 | 96 | 49 | 13 | 86 | 1 | 0 | 8 | 9 | 0 | 1.00 | 15 | .280 | .330 | .426 |
| 5 ML YEARS | | 748 | 2882 | 790 | 152 | 32 | 114 | (69 | 45) | 1348 | 395 | 470 | 197 | 32 | 438 | 7 | 1 | 43 | 58 | 25 | .70 | 63 | .274 | .318 | .468 |

## Mike Simms

**Bats:** Right **Throws:** Right **Pos:** 1B **Ht:** 6' 4" **Wt:** 185 **Born:** 01/12/67 **Age:** 24

| BATTING | | | | | | | | | | | | | | | | | | | BASERUNNING | | | | PERCENTAGES | | |
|---|---|---|---|---|---|---|---|---|---|---|---|---|---|---|---|---|---|---|---|---|---|---|---|---|---|
| Year Team | Lg | G | AB | H | 2B | 3B | HR | (Hm | Rd) | TB | R | RBI | TBB | IBB | SO | HBP | SH | SF | SB | CS | SB% | GDP | Avg | OBP | SLG |
| 1985 Astros | R | 21 | 70 | 19 | 2 | 1 | 3 | -- | -- | 32 | 10 | 18 | 6 | 0 | 26 | 4 | 0 | 3 | 0 | 0 | .00 | 1 | .271 | .349 | .457 |
| 1986 Astros | R | 54 | 181 | 47 | 14 | 1 | 4 | -- | -- | 75 | 33 | 37 | 22 | 1 | 48 | 4 | 0 | 4 | 2 | 1 | .67 | 4 | .260 | .346 | .414 |
| 1987 Asheville | A | 133 | 469 | 128 | 19 | 0 | 39 | -- | -- | 264 | 93 | 100 | 73 | 5 | 167 | 9 | 0 | 3 | 7 | 0 | 1.00 | 4 | .273 | .379 | .563 |
| 1988 Osceola | A | 123 | 428 | 104 | 19 | 1 | 16 | -- | -- | 173 | 63 | 73 | 76 | 3 | 130 | 1 | 0 | 6 | 9 | 6 | .60 | 6 | .243 | .354 | .404 |
| 1989 Columbus | AA | 109 | 378 | 97 | 21 | 3 | 20 | -- | -- | 184 | 64 | 81 | 66 | 4 | 110 | 2 | 0 | 6 | 12 | 6 | .67 | 2 | .257 | .365 | .487 |
| 1990 Tucson | AAA | 124 | 421 | 115 | 34 | 5 | 13 | -- | -- | 198 | 75 | 72 | 74 | 3 | 135 | 8 | 1 | 8 | 3 | 6 | .33 | 5 | .273 | .386 | .470 |
| 1990 Houston | NL | 12 | 13 | 4 | 1 | 0 | 1 | (0 | 1) | 8 | 3 | 2 | 0 | 0 | 4 | 0 | 0 | 0 | 0 | 0 | .00 | 1 | .308 | .308 | .615 |

## Matt Sinatro

**Bats:** Right **Throws:** Right **Pos:** C **Ht:** 5' 9" **Wt:** 174 **Born:** 03/22/60 **Age:** 31

| BATTING | | | | | | | | | | | | | | | | | | | BASERUNNING | | | | PERCENTAGES | | |
|---|---|---|---|---|---|---|---|---|---|---|---|---|---|---|---|---|---|---|---|---|---|---|---|---|---|
| Year Team | Lg | G | AB | H | 2B | 3B | HR | (Hm | Rd) | TB | R | RBI | TBB | IBB | SO | HBP | SH | SF | SB | CS | SB% | GDP | Avg | OBP | SLG |
| 1981 Atlanta | NL | 12 | 32 | 9 | 1 | 1 | 0 | (0 | 0) | 12 | 4 | 4 | 5 | 1 | 4 | 0 | 0 | 0 | 1 | 0 | 1.00 | 0 | .281 | .378 | .375 |

| | | | | | | | | | | | | | | | | | | | | | | | | | |
|---|---|---|---|---|---|---|---|---|---|---|---|---|---|---|---|---|---|---|---|---|---|---|---|---|---|
| 1982 Atlanta | NL | 37 | 81 | 11 | 2 | 0 | 1 | (0 | 1) | 16 | 10 | 4 | 4 | 0 | 9 | 0 | 2 | 0 | 0 | 1 | .00 | 3 | .136 | .176 | .198 |
| 1983 Atlanta | NL | 7 | 12 | 2 | 0 | 0 | 0 | (0 | 0) | 2 | 0 | 2 | 2 | 0 | 1 | 0 | 0 | 0 | 0 | 0 | .00 | 0 | .167 | .286 | .167 |
| 1984 Atlanta | NL | 2 | 4 | 0 | 0 | 0 | 0 | (0 | 0) | 0 | 0 | 0 | 0 | 0 | 0 | 0 | 0 | 0 | 0 | 0 | .00 | 0 | .000 | .000 | .000 |
| 1987 Oakland | AL | 6 | 3 | 0 | 0 | 0 | 0 | (0 | 0) | 0 | 0 | 0 | 0 | 0 | 1 | 0 | 0 | 0 | 0 | 0 | .00 | 1 | .000 | .000 | .000 |
| 1988 Oakland | AL | 10 | 9 | 3 | 2 | 0 | 0 | (0 | 0) | 5 | 1 | 5 | 0 | 0 | 1 | 0 | 0 | 1 | 0 | 0 | .00 | 2 | .333 | .300 | .556 |
| 1989 Detroit | AL | 13 | 25 | 3 | 0 | 0 | 0 | (0 | 0) | 3 | 2 | 1 | 1 | 0 | 3 | 1 | 0 | 0 | 0 | 0 | .00 | 1 | .120 | .185 | .120 |
| 1990 Seattle | AL | 30 | 50 | 15 | 1 | 0 | 0 | (0 | 0) | 16 | 2 | 4 | 4 | 0 | 10 | 0 | 3 | 0 | 1 | 0 | 1.00 | 3 | .300 | .352 | .320 |
| 8 ML YEARS | | 117 | 216 | 43 | 6 | 1 | 1 | (0 | 1) | 54 | 19 | 20 | 16 | 1 | 29 | 1 | 5 | 1 | 2 | 1 | .67 | 10 | .199 | .256 | .250 |

## Doug Sisk

**Pitches:** Right **Bats:** Right **Pos:** RP **Ht:** 6' 2" **Wt:** 210 **Born:** 09/26/57 **Age:** 33

| HOW MUCH HE PITCHED | | | | | | | | WHAT HE GAVE UP | | | | | | | | | | | | THE RESULTS | | | | | |
|---|---|---|---|---|---|---|---|---|---|---|---|---|---|---|---|---|---|---|---|---|---|---|---|---|---|
| Year Team | Lg | G | GS | CG | GF | IP | BFP | H | R | ER | HR | SH | SF | HB | TBB | IBB | SO | WP | Bk | W | L | Pct. | ShO | Sv | ERA |
| 1982 New York | NL | 8 | 0 | 0 | 4 | 8.2 | 34 | 5 | 1 | 1 | 1 | 0 | 0 | 1 | 4 | 2 | 4 | 0 | 0 | 0 | 1 | .000 | 0 | 1 | 1.04 |
| 1983 New York | NL | 67 | 0 | 0 | 39 | 104.1 | 447 | 88 | 38 | 26 | 1 | 6 | 4 | 4 | 59 | 7 | 33 | 5 | 1 | 5 | 4 | .556 | 0 | 11 | 2.24 |
| 1984 New York | NL | 50 | 0 | 0 | 31 | 77.2 | 329 | 57 | 24 | 18 | 1 | 7 | 0 | 3 | 54 | 5 | 32 | 1 | 0 | 1 | 3 | .250 | 0 | 15 | 2.09 |
| 1985 New York | NL | 42 | 0 | 0 | 22 | 73 | 341 | 86 | 48 | 43 | 3 | 3 | 0 | 2 | 40 | 2 | 26 | 1 | 1 | 4 | 5 | .444 | 0 | 2 | 5.30 |
| 1986 New York | NL | 41 | 0 | 0 | 15 | 70.2 | 312 | 77 | 31 | 24 | 0 | 3 | 0 | 5 | 31 | 5 | 31 | 2 | 1 | 4 | 2 | .667 | 0 | 1 | 3.06 |
| 1987 New York | NL | 55 | 0 | 0 | 17 | 78 | 339 | 83 | 38 | 30 | 5 | 5 | 2 | 3 | 22 | 4 | 37 | 2 | 0 | 3 | 1 | .750 | 0 | 3 | 3.46 |
| 1988 Baltimore | AL | 52 | 0 | 0 | 29 | 94.1 | 410 | 109 | 43 | 39 | 3 | 5 | 2 | 2 | 45 | 6 | 26 | 3 | 0 | 3 | 3 | .500 | 0 | 0 | 3.72 |
| 1990 Atlanta | NL | 3 | 0 | 0 | 2 | 2.1 | 13 | 1 | 1 | 1 | 0 | 0 | 2 | 0 | 4 | 0 | 1 | 1 | 0 | 0 | 0 | .000 | 0 | 0 | 3.86 |
| 8 ML YEARS | | 318 | 0 | 0 | 159 | 509 | 2225 | 506 | 224 | 182 | 14 | 29 | 10 | 20 | 259 | 31 | 190 | 15 | 3 | 20 | 19 | .513 | 0 | 33 | 3.22 |

## Joel Skinner

**Bats:** Right **Throws:** Right **Pos:** C **Ht:** 6' 4" **Wt:** 205 **Born:** 02/21/61 **Age:** 30

| | | BATTING | | | | | | | | | | | | | | | | | BASERUNNING | | | | PERCENTAGES | | |
|---|---|---|---|---|---|---|---|---|---|---|---|---|---|---|---|---|---|---|---|---|---|---|---|---|---|
| Year Team | Lg | G | AB | H | 2B | 3B | HR | (Hm | Rd) | TB | R | RBI | TBB | IBB | SO | HBP | SH | SF | SB | CS | SB% | GDP | Avg | OBP | SLG |
| 1983 Chicago | AL | 6 | 11 | 3 | 0 | 0 | 0 | (0 | 0) | 3 | 2 | 1 | 0 | 0 | 1 | 0 | 0 | 0 | 0 | 0 | .00 | 2 | .273 | .273 | .273 |
| 1984 Chicago | AL | 43 | 80 | 17 | 2 | 0 | 0 | (0 | 0) | 19 | 4 | 3 | 7 | 0 | 19 | 0 | 0 | 1 | 1 | 0 | 1.00 | 2 | .213 | .273 | .238 |
| 1985 Chicago | AL | 22 | 44 | 15 | 4 | 1 | 1 | (1 | 0) | 24 | 9 | 5 | 5 | 0 | 13 | 0 | 1 | 0 | 0 | 0 | .00 | 2 | .341 | .408 | .545 |
| 1986 2 ML Teams | | 114 | 315 | 73 | 9 | 1 | 5 | (1 | 4) | 99 | 23 | 37 | 16 | 0 | 83 | 1 | 2 | 2 | 1 | 4 | .20 | 6 | .232 | .269 | .314 |
| 1987 New York | AL | 64 | 139 | 19 | 4 | 0 | 3 | (1 | 2) | 32 | 9 | 14 | 8 | 0 | 46 | 1 | 4 | 2 | 0 | 0 | .00 | 9 | .137 | .187 | .230 |
| 1988 New York | AL | 88 | 251 | 57 | 15 | 0 | 4 | (1 | 3) | 84 | 23 | 23 | 14 | 0 | 72 | 0 | 6 | 1 | 0 | 0 | .00 | 6 | .227 | .267 | .335 |
| 1989 Cleveland | AL | 79 | 178 | 41 | 10 | 0 | 1 | (0 | 1) | 54 | 10 | 13 | 9 | 0 | 42 | 1 | 1 | 0 | 1 | 1 | .50 | 3 | .230 | .271 | .303 |
| 1990 Cleveland | AL | 49 | 139 | 35 | 4 | 1 | 2 | (1 | 1) | 47 | 16 | 16 | 7 | 0 | 44 | 0 | 0 | 0 | 0 | 0 | .00 | 3 | .252 | .288 | .338 |
| 1986 Chicago | AL | 60 | 149 | 30 | 5 | 1 | 4 | (1 | 3) | 49 | 17 | 20 | 9 | 0 | 43 | 1 | 2 | 1 | 1 | 0 | 1.00 | 2 | .201 | .250 | .329 |
| New York | AL | 54 | 166 | 43 | 4 | 0 | 1 | (0 | 1) | 50 | 6 | 17 | 7 | 0 | 40 | 0 | 0 | 1 | 0 | 4 | .00 | 4 | .259 | .287 | .301 |
| 8 ML YEARS | | 465 | 1157 | 260 | 48 | 3 | 16 | (5 | 11) | 362 | 96 | 112 | 66 | 0 | 320 | 3 | 14 | 6 | 3 | 5 | .38 | 33 | .225 | .267 | .313 |

## Don Slaught

**Bats:** Right **Throws:** Right **Pos:** C **Ht:** 6' 1" **Wt:** 190 **Born:** 09/11/58 **Age:** 32

| | | BATTING | | | | | | | | | | | | | | | | | BASERUNNING | | | | PERCENTAGES | | |
|---|---|---|---|---|---|---|---|---|---|---|---|---|---|---|---|---|---|---|---|---|---|---|---|---|---|
| Year Team | Lg | G | AB | H | 2B | 3B | HR | (Hm | Rd) | TB | R | RBI | TBB | IBB | SO | HBP | SH | SF | SB | CS | SB% | GDP | Avg | OBP | SLG |
| 1982 Kansas City | AL | 43 | 115 | 32 | 6 | 0 | 3 | (0 | 3) | 47 | 14 | 8 | 9 | 0 | 12 | 0 | 2 | 0 | 0 | 0 | .00 | 3 | .278 | .331 | .409 |
| 1983 Kansas City | AL | 83 | 276 | 86 | 13 | 4 | 0 | (0 | 0) | 107 | 21 | 28 | 11 | 0 | 27 | 0 | 1 | 2 | 3 | 1 | .75 | 8 | .312 | .336 | .388 |
| 1984 Kansas City | AL | 124 | 409 | 108 | 27 | 4 | 4 | (1 | 3) | 155 | 48 | 42 | 20 | 4 | 55 | 2 | 8 | 7 | 0 | 0 | .00 | 8 | .264 | .297 | .379 |
| 1985 Texas | AL | 102 | 343 | 96 | 17 | 4 | 8 | (4 | 4) | 145 | 34 | 35 | 20 | 1 | 41 | 6 | 1 | 0 | 5 | 4 | .56 | 8 | .280 | .331 | .423 |
| 1986 Texas | AL | 95 | 314 | 83 | 17 | 1 | 13 | (5 | 8) | 141 | 39 | 46 | 16 | 0 | 59 | 5 | 3 | 3 | 3 | 2 | .60 | 8 | .264 | .308 | .449 |
| 1987 Texas | AL | 95 | 237 | 53 | 15 | 2 | 8 | (5 | 3) | 96 | 25 | 16 | 24 | 3 | 51 | 1 | 4 | 0 | 0 | 3 | .00 | 7 | .224 | .298 | .405 |
| 1988 New York | AL | 97 | 322 | 91 | 25 | 1 | 9 | (7 | 2) | 145 | 33 | 43 | 24 | 3 | 54 | 3 | 5 | 4 | 1 | 0 | 1.00 | 10 | .283 | .334 | .450 |
| 1989 New York | AL | 117 | 350 | 88 | 21 | 3 | 5 | (3 | 2) | 130 | 34 | 38 | 30 | 3 | 57 | 5 | 2 | 5 | 1 | 1 | .50 | 9 | .251 | .315 | .371 |
| 1990 Pittsburgh | NL | 84 | 230 | 69 | 18 | 3 | 4 | (1 | 3) | 105 | 27 | 29 | 27 | 2 | 27 | 3 | 3 | 4 | 0 | 1 | .00 | 2 | .300 | .375 | .457 |
| 9 ML YEARS | | 840 | 2596 | 706 | 159 | 22 | 54 | (26 | 28) | 1071 | 275 | 285 | 181 | 16 | 383 | 25 | 29 | 25 | 13 | 12 | .52 | 63 | .272 | .323 | .413 |

## John Smiley

**Pitches:** Left **Bats:** Left **Pos:** SP **Ht:** 6' 4" **Wt:** 195 **Born:** 03/17/65 **Age:** 26

| HOW MUCH HE PITCHED | | | | | | | | WHAT HE GAVE UP | | | | | | | | | | | | THE RESULTS | | | | | |
|---|---|---|---|---|---|---|---|---|---|---|---|---|---|---|---|---|---|---|---|---|---|---|---|---|---|
| Year Team | Lg | G | GS | CG | GF | IP | BFP | H | R | ER | HR | SH | SF | HB | TBB | IBB | SO | WP | Bk | W | L | Pct. | ShO | Sv | ERA |
| 1986 Pittsburgh | NL | 12 | 0 | 0 | 2 | 11.2 | 42 | 4 | 6 | 5 | 2 | 0 | 0 | 0 | 4 | 0 | 9 | 0 | 0 | 1 | 0 | 1.000 | 0 | 0 | 3.86 |
| 1987 Pittsburgh | NL | 63 | 0 | 0 | 19 | 75 | 336 | 69 | 49 | 48 | 7 | 0 | 3 | 0 | 50 | 8 | 58 | 5 | 1 | 5 | 5 | .500 | 0 | 4 | 5.76 |
| 1988 Pittsburgh | NL | 34 | 32 | 5 | 0 | 205 | 835 | 185 | 81 | 74 | 15 | 11 | 8 | 3 | 46 | 4 | 129 | 6 | 6 | 13 | 11 | .542 | 1 | 0 | 3.25 |
| 1989 Pittsburgh | NL | 28 | 28 | 8 | 0 | 205.1 | 835 | 174 | 78 | 64 | 22 | 5 | 7 | 4 | 49 | 5 | 123 | 5 | 2 | 12 | 8 | .600 | 1 | 0 | 2.81 |
| 1990 Pittsburgh | NL | 26 | 25 | 2 | 0 | 149.1 | 632 | 161 | 83 | 77 | 15 | 5 | 4 | 2 | 36 | 1 | 86 | 2 | 2 | 9 | 10 | .474 | 0 | 0 | 4.64 |
| 5 ML YEARS | | 163 | 85 | 15 | 21 | 646.1 | 2680 | 593 | 297 | 268 | 61 | 21 | 22 | 9 | 185 | 18 | 405 | 18 | 11 | 40 | 34 | .541 | 2 | 4 | 3.73 |

## Bryn Smith

**Pitches:** Right **Bats:** Right **Pos:** SP **Ht:** 6' 2" **Wt:** 205 **Born:** 08/11/55 **Age:** 35

| HOW MUCH HE PITCHED | | | | | | | | | WHAT HE GAVE UP | | | | | | | | | | | | THE RESULTS | | | | | |
|---|---|---|---|---|---|---|---|---|---|---|---|---|---|---|---|---|---|---|---|---|---|---|---|---|---|---|
| Year | Team | Lg | G | GS | CG | GF | IP | BFP | H | R | ER | HR | SH | SF | HB | TBB | IBB | SO | WP | Bk | W | L | Pct. | ShO | Sv | ERA |
| 1981 | Montreal | NL | 7 | 0 | 0 | 1 | 13 | 53 | 14 | 4 | 4 | 1 | 0 | 0 | 0 | 3 | 0 | 9 | 2 | 0 | 1 | 0 | 1.000 | 0 | 0 | 2.77 |
| 1982 | Montreal | NL | 47 | 1 | 0 | 16 | 79.1 | 335 | 81 | 43 | 37 | 5 | 1 | 4 | 0 | 23 | 5 | 50 | 5 | 1 | 2 | 4 | .333 | 0 | 3 | 4.20 |
| 1983 | Montreal | NL | 49 | 12 | 5 | 17 | 155.1 | 636 | 142 | 51 | 43 | 13 | 14 | 2 | 5 | 43 | 6 | 101 | 5 | 3 | 6 | 11 | .353 | 3 | 3 | 2.49 |
| 1984 | Montreal | NL | 28 | 28 | 4 | 0 | 179 | 751 | 178 | 72 | 66 | 15 | 7 | 2 | 3 | 51 | 7 | 101 | 2 | 2 | 12 | 13 | .480 | 2 | 0 | 3.32 |
| 1985 | Montreal | NL | 32 | 32 | 4 | 0 | 222.1 | 890 | 193 | 85 | 72 | 12 | 13 | 4 | 1 | 41 | 3 | 127 | 1 | 1 | 18 | 5 | .783 | 2 | 0 | 2.91 |
| 1986 | Montreal | NL | 30 | 30 | 1 | 0 | 187.1 | 807 | 182 | 101 | 82 | 15 | 10 | 3 | 6 | 63 | 6 | 105 | 4 | 2 | 10 | 8 | .556 | 0 | 0 | 3.94 |
| 1987 | Montreal | NL | 26 | 26 | 2 | 0 | 150.1 | 643 | 164 | 81 | 73 | 16 | 7 | 5 | 2 | 31 | 4 | 94 | 2 | 0 | 10 | 9 | .526 | 0 | 0 | 4.37 |
| 1988 | Montreal | NL | 32 | 32 | 1 | 0 | 198 | 791 | 179 | 79 | 66 | 15 | 7 | 6 | 10 | 32 | 2 | 122 | 2 | 5 | 12 | 10 | .545 | 0 | 0 | 3.00 |
| 1989 | Montreal | NL | 33 | 32 | 3 | 0 | 215.2 | 864 | 177 | 76 | 68 | 16 | 7 | 5 | 4 | 54 | 4 | 129 | 3 | 1 | 10 | 11 | .476 | 1 | 0 | 2.84 |
| 1990 | St. Louis | NL | 26 | 25 | 0 | 0 | 141.1 | 605 | 160 | 81 | 67 | 11 | 7 | 5 | 4 | 30 | 1 | 78 | 2 | 0 | 9 | 8 | .529 | 0 | 0 | 4.27 |
| 10 ML YEARS | | | 310 | 218 | 20 | 34 | 1541.2 | 6375 | 1470 | 673 | 578 | 119 | 73 | 36 | 35 | 371 | 38 | 916 | 28 | 15 | 90 | 79 | .533 | 8 | 6 | 3.37 |

## Daryl Smith

**Pitches:** Right **Bats:** Right **Pos:** SP **Ht:** 6' 4" **Wt:** 185 **Born:** 07/29/60 **Age:** 30

| HOW MUCH HE PITCHED | | | | | | | | | WHAT HE GAVE UP | | | | | | | | | | | | THE RESULTS | | | | | |
|---|---|---|---|---|---|---|---|---|---|---|---|---|---|---|---|---|---|---|---|---|---|---|---|---|---|---|
| Year | Team | Lg | G | GS | CG | GF | IP | BFP | H | R | ER | HR | SH | SF | HB | TBB | IBB | SO | WP | Bk | W | L | Pct. | ShO | Sv | ERA |
| 1984 | Tulsa | AA | 7 | 0 | 0 | 1 | 10.2 | 57 | 18 | 17 | 17 | 0 | 1 | 1 | 1 | 9 | 0 | 6 | 3 | 0 | 0 | 1 | .000 | 0 | 0 | 14.34 |
| | Salem | A | 16 | 12 | 0 | 1 | 67 | 297 | 67 | 40 | 32 | 6 | 0 | 1 | 2 | 44 | 1 | 38 | 10 | 0 | 6 | 3 | .667 | 0 | 0 | 4.30 |
| 1985 | Waterloo | A | 1 | 0 | 0 | 0 | 4.2 | 18 | 4 | 1 | 1 | 1 | 0 | 0 | 0 | 2 | 0 | 5 | 0 | 0 | 0 | 0 | .000 | 0 | 0 | 1.93 |
| | Waterbury | AA | 16 | 6 | 1 | 8 | 53.2 | 231 | 42 | 25 | 21 | 5 | 1 | 2 | 1 | 37 | 1 | 38 | 5 | 0 | 2 | 2 | .500 | 0 | 4 | 3.52 |
| 1986 | Waterbury | AA | 21 | 11 | 4 | 4 | 89 | 368 | 71 | 37 | 35 | 8 | 0 | 2 | 3 | 48 | 0 | 55 | 11 | 0 | 4 | 3 | .571 | 1 | 0 | 3.54 |
| 1987 | Williamsprt | AA | 2 | 2 | 0 | 0 | 8 | 37 | 11 | 8 | 7 | 1 | 0 | 1 | 0 | 3 | 0 | 5 | 1 | 0 | 1 | 1 | .500 | 0 | 0 | 7.88 |
| | Reading | AA | 19 | 12 | 1 | 2 | 79.1 | 349 | 75 | 38 | 31 | 5 | 3 | 3 | 4 | 43 | 2 | 53 | 5 | 1 | 6 | 2 | .750 | 0 | 1 | 3.52 |
| | Maine | AAA | 4 | 4 | 0 | 0 | 22.2 | 103 | 21 | 18 | 17 | 4 | 1 | 2 | 2 | 13 | 0 | 16 | 0 | 0 | 1 | 3 | .250 | 0 | 0 | 6.75 |
| 1988 | Birmingham | AA | 40 | 0 | 0 | 33 | 53 | 226 | 42 | 25 | 19 | 0 | 2 | 4 | 0 | 27 | 3 | 44 | 6 | 6 | 1 | 4 | .200 | 0 | 7 | 3.23 |
| 1990 | Memphis | AA | 21 | 0 | 0 | 5 | 48.1 | 211 | 46 | 27 | 17 | 1 | 3 | 6 | 0 | 23 | 0 | 48 | 10 | 0 | 2 | 1 | .667 | 0 | 1 | 3.17 |
| | Omaha | AAA | 11 | 10 | 0 | 0 | 64 | 268 | 59 | 25 | 22 | 5 | 2 | 0 | 2 | 32 | 0 | 56 | 3 | 4 | 6 | 2 | .750 | 0 | 0 | 3.09 |
| 1990 | Kansas City | AL | 2 | 1 | 0 | 1 | 6.2 | 27 | 5 | 3 | 3 | 0 | 0 | 2 | 0 | 4 | 0 | 6 | 0 | 0 | 0 | 1 | .000 | 0 | 0 | 4.05 |

## Dave Smith

**Pitches:** Right **Bats:** Right **Pos:** RP **Ht:** 6' 1" **Wt:** 195 **Born:** 01/21/55 **Age:** 36

| HOW MUCH HE PITCHED | | | | | | | | | WHAT HE GAVE UP | | | | | | | | | | | | THE RESULTS | | | | | |
|---|---|---|---|---|---|---|---|---|---|---|---|---|---|---|---|---|---|---|---|---|---|---|---|---|---|---|
| Year | Team | Lg | G | GS | CG | GF | IP | BFP | H | R | ER | HR | SH | SF | HB | TBB | IBB | SO | WP | Bk | W | L | Pct. | ShO | Sv | ERA |
| 1980 | Houston | NL | 57 | 0 | 0 | 35 | 103 | 422 | 90 | 24 | 22 | 1 | 6 | 1 | 4 | 32 | 7 | 85 | 3 | 1 | 7 | 5 | .583 | 0 | 10 | 1.92 |
| 1981 | Houston | NL | 42 | 0 | 0 | 22 | 75 | 305 | 54 | 26 | 23 | 2 | 6 | 1 | 2 | 23 | 4 | 52 | 4 | 0 | 5 | 3 | .625 | 0 | 8 | 2.76 |
| 1982 | Houston | NL | 49 | 1 | 0 | 29 | 63.1 | 286 | 69 | 30 | 27 | 4 | 9 | 4 | 0 | 31 | 4 | 28 | 2 | 4 | 5 | 4 | .556 | 0 | 11 | 3.84 |
| 1983 | Houston | NL | 42 | 0 | 0 | 24 | 72.2 | 323 | 72 | 32 | 25 | 2 | 3 | 5 | 0 | 36 | 4 | 41 | 1 | 1 | 3 | 1 | .750 | 0 | 6 | 3.10 |
| 1984 | Houston | NL | 53 | 0 | 0 | 24 | 77.1 | 304 | 60 | 22 | 19 | 5 | 2 | 1 | 1 | 20 | 3 | 45 | 1 | 1 | 5 | 4 | .556 | 0 | 5 | 2.21 |
| 1985 | Houston | NL | 64 | 0 | 0 | 46 | 79.1 | 315 | 69 | 26 | 20 | 3 | 3 | 1 | 1 | 17 | 5 | 40 | 4 | 1 | 9 | 5 | .643 | 0 | 27 | 2.27 |
| 1986 | Houston | NL | 54 | 0 | 0 | 51 | 56 | 223 | 39 | 17 | 17 | 5 | 4 | 1 | 1 | 22 | 3 | 46 | 2 | 0 | 4 | 7 | .364 | 0 | 33 | 2.73 |
| 1987 | Houston | NL | 50 | 0 | 0 | 44 | 60 | 240 | 39 | 13 | 11 | 0 | 3 | 1 | 1 | 21 | 8 | 73 | 2 | 2 | 2 | 3 | .400 | 0 | 24 | 1.65 |
| 1988 | Houston | NL | 51 | 0 | 0 | 39 | 57.1 | 249 | 60 | 26 | 17 | 1 | 4 | 1 | 1 | 19 | 8 | 38 | 1 | 3 | 4 | 5 | .444 | 0 | 27 | 2.67 |
| 1989 | Houston | NL | 52 | 0 | 0 | 44 | 58 | 239 | 49 | 20 | 17 | 1 | 8 | 1 | 1 | 19 | 7 | 31 | 2 | 2 | 3 | 4 | .429 | 0 | 25 | 2.64 |
| 1990 | Houston | NL | 49 | 0 | 0 | 42 | 60.1 | 239 | 45 | 18 | 16 | 4 | 4 | 1 | 0 | 20 | 4 | 50 | 5 | 5 | 6 | 6 | .500 | 0 | 23 | 2.39 |
| 11 ML YEARS | | | 563 | 1 | 0 | 400 | 762.1 | 3145 | 646 | 254 | 214 | 28 | 52 | 18 | 12 | 260 | 57 | 529 | 27 | 20 | 53 | 47 | .530 | 0 | 199 | 2.53 |

## Dwight Smith

**Bats:** Left **Throws:** Right **Pos:** LF/RF **Ht:** 5'11" **Wt:** 175 **Born:** 11/08/63 **Age:** 27

| BATTING | | | | | | | | | | | | | | | | | | | BASERUNNING | | | | PERCENTAGES | | |
|---|---|---|---|---|---|---|---|---|---|---|---|---|---|---|---|---|---|---|---|---|---|---|---|---|---|
| Year | Team | Lg | G | AB | H | 2B | 3B | HR | (Hm | Rd) | TB | R | RBI | TBB | IBB | SO | HBP | SH | SF | SB | CS | SB% | GDP | Avg | OBP | SLG |
| 1984 | Pikeville | R | 61 | 195 | 46 | 6 | 2 | 1 | -- | -- | 59 | 42 | 17 | 52 | 1 | 47 | 4 | 2 | 0 | 39 | 7 | .85 | 2 | .236 | .406 | .303 |
| 1985 | Geneva | A | 73 | 232 | 67 | 11 | 2 | 4 | -- | -- | 94 | 44 | 32 | 31 | 3 | 33 | 1 | 0 | 1 | 30 | 10 | .75 | 1 | .289 | .374 | .405 |
| 1986 | Peoria | A | 124 | 471 | 146 | 22 | 11 | 11 | -- | -- | 223 | 92 | 57 | 59 | 2 | 92 | 3 | 2 | 2 | 53 | 19 | .74 | 8 | .310 | .389 | .473 |
| 1987 | Pittsfield | AA | 130 | 498 | 168 | 28 | 10 | 18 | -- | -- | 270 | 111 | 72 | 67 | 6 | 79 | 2 | 2 | 4 | 60 | 18 | .77 | 8 | .337 | .415 | .542 |
| 1988 | Iowa | AAA | 129 | 505 | 148 | 26 | 3 | 9 | -- | -- | 207 | 76 | 48 | 54 | 1 | 90 | 5 | 5 | 0 | 25 | 20 | .56 | 9 | .293 | .367 | .410 |
| 1989 | Iowa | AAA | 21 | 83 | 27 | 7 | 3 | 2 | -- | -- | 46 | 11 | 7 | 7 | 0 | 11 | 0 | 1 | 0 | 6 | 2 | .75 | 2 | .325 | .378 | .554 |
| 1989 | Chicago | NL | 109 | 343 | 111 | 19 | 6 | 9 | (5 | 4) | 169 | 52 | 52 | 31 | 0 | 51 | 2 | 4 | 1 | 9 | 4 | .69 | 4 | .324 | .382 | .493 |
| 1990 | Chicago | NL | 117 | 290 | 76 | 15 | 0 | 6 | (3 | 3) | 109 | 34 | 27 | 28 | 2 | 46 | 2 | 0 | 2 | 11 | 6 | .65 | 7 | .262 | .329 | .376 |
| 2 ML YEARS | | | 226 | 633 | 187 | 34 | 6 | 15 | (8 | 7) | 278 | 86 | 79 | 59 | 2 | 97 | 4 | 4 | 3 | 20 | 10 | .67 | 11 | .295 | .358 | .439 |

## Greg Smith

**Bats:** Both **Throws:** Right **Pos:** 2B **Ht:** 5'11" **Wt:** 170 **Born:** 04/05/67 **Age:** 24

| BATTING | | | | | | | | | | | | | | | | | | | BASERUNNING | | | | PERCENTAGES | | |
|---|---|---|---|---|---|---|---|---|---|---|---|---|---|---|---|---|---|---|---|---|---|---|---|---|---|
| Year Team | Lg | G | AB | H | 2B | 3B | HR | (Hm | Rd) | TB | R | RBI | TBB | IBB | SO | HBP | SH | SF | SB | CS | SB% | GDP | Avg | OBP | SLG |
| 1985 Wytheville | R | 51 | 179 | 42 | 6 | 2 | 0 | -- | -- | 52 | 28 | 15 | 20 | 1 | 27 | 2 | 3 | 1 | 8 | 1 | .89 | 1 | .235 | .317 | .291 |
| 1986 Peoria | A | 53 | 170 | 43 | 6 | 3 | 2 | -- | -- | 61 | 24 | 26 | 19 | 1 | 45 | 1 | 2 | 0 | 9 | 2 | .82 | 2 | .253 | .332 | .359 |
| 1987 Peoria | A | 124 | 444 | 120 | 23 | 5 | 6 | -- | -- | 171 | 69 | 56 | 62 | 5 | 96 | 4 | 7 | 5 | 26 | 9 | .74 | 11 | .270 | .361 | .385 |
| 1988 Winston-Sal | A | 95 | 361 | 101 | 12 | 2 | 4 | -- | -- | 129 | 62 | 29 | 46 | 2 | 50 | 2 | 6 | 3 | 52 | 12 | .81 | 5 | .280 | .362 | .357 |
| 1989 Charlotte | AA | 126 | 467 | 138 | 23 | 6 | 5 | -- | -- | 188 | 59 | 64 | 42 | 1 | 52 | 6 | 9 | 4 | 38 | 13 | .75 | 8 | .296 | .358 | .403 |
| 1990 Iowa | AAA | 105 | 398 | 116 | 19 | 1 | 5 | -- | -- | 152 | 54 | 44 | 37 | 1 | 57 | 2 | 4 | 1 | 26 | 14 | .65 | 8 | .291 | .354 | .382 |
| 1989 Chicago | NL | 4 | 5 | 2 | 0 | 0 | 0 | (0 | 0) | 2 | 1 | 2 | 0 | 0 | 0 | 1 | 0 | 0 | 0 | 0 | .00 | 0 | .400 | .500 | .400 |
| 1990 Chicago | NL | 18 | 44 | 9 | 2 | 1 | 0 | (0 | 0) | 13 | 4 | 5 | 2 | 0 | 5 | 0 | 1 | 1 | 1 | 0 | 1.00 | 1 | .205 | .234 | .295 |
| 2 ML YEARS | | 22 | 49 | 11 | 2 | 1 | 0 | (0 | 0) | 15 | 5 | 7 | 2 | 0 | 5 | 1 | 1 | 1 | 1 | 0 | 1.00 | 1 | .224 | .264 | .306 |

## Lee Smith

**Pitches:** Right **Bats:** Right **Pos:** RP **Ht:** 6' 6" **Wt:** 245 **Born:** 12/04/57 **Age:** 33

| HOW MUCH HE PITCHED | | | | | | | | WHAT HE GAVE UP | | | | | | | | | | | | THE RESULTS | | | | | | |
|---|---|---|---|---|---|---|---|---|---|---|---|---|---|---|---|---|---|---|---|---|---|---|---|---|---|---|
| Year Team | Lg | G | GS | CG | GF | IP | BFP | H | R | ER | HR | SH | SF | HB | TBB | IBB | SO | WP | Bk | W | L | Pct. | ShO | Sv | ERA |
| 1980 Chicago | NL | 18 | 0 | 0 | 6 | 22 | 97 | 21 | 9 | 7 | 0 | 1 | 1 | 0 | 14 | 5 | 17 | 0 | 0 | 2 | 0 | 1.000 | 0 | 0 | 2.86 |
| 1981 Chicago | NL | 40 | 1 | 0 | 12 | 67 | 280 | 57 | 31 | 26 | 2 | 8 | 2 | 1 | 31 | 8 | 50 | 7 | 1 | 3 | 6 | .333 | 0 | 1 | 3.49 |
| 1982 Chicago | NL | 72 | 5 | 0 | 38 | 117 | 480 | 105 | 38 | 35 | 5 | 6 | 5 | 3 | 37 | 5 | 99 | 6 | 1 | 2 | 5 | .286 | 0 | 17 | 2.69 |
| 1983 Chicago | NL | 66 | 0 | 0 | 56 | 103.1 | 413 | 70 | 23 | 19 | 5 | 9 | 2 | 1 | 41 | 14 | 91 | 5 | 2 | 4 | 10 | .286 | 0 | 29 | 1.65 |
| 1984 Chicago | NL | 69 | 0 | 0 | 59 | 101 | 428 | 98 | 42 | 41 | 6 | 4 | 5 | 0 | 35 | 7 | 86 | 6 | 0 | 9 | 7 | .563 | 0 | 33 | 3.65 |
| 1985 Chicago | NL | 65 | 0 | 0 | 57 | 97.2 | 397 | 87 | 35 | 33 | 9 | 3 | 1 | 1 | 32 | 6 | 112 | 4 | 0 | 7 | 4 | .636 | 0 | 33 | 3.04 |
| 1986 Chicago | NL | 66 | 0 | 0 | 59 | 90.1 | 372 | 69 | 32 | 31 | 7 | 6 | 3 | 0 | 42 | 11 | 93 | 2 | 0 | 9 | 9 | .500 | 0 | 31 | 3.09 |
| 1987 Chicago | NL | 62 | 0 | 0 | 55 | 83.2 | 360 | 84 | 30 | 29 | 4 | 4 | 0 | 0 | 32 | 5 | 96 | 4 | 0 | 4 | 10 | .286 | 0 | 36 | 3.12 |
| 1988 Boston | AL | 64 | 0 | 0 | 57 | 83.2 | 363 | 72 | 34 | 26 | 7 | 3 | 2 | 1 | 37 | 6 | 96 | 2 | 0 | 4 | 5 | .444 | 0 | 29 | 2.80 |
| 1989 Boston | AL | 64 | 0 | 0 | 50 | 70.2 | 290 | 53 | 30 | 28 | 6 | 2 | 2 | 0 | 33 | 6 | 96 | 1 | 0 | 6 | 1 | .857 | 0 | 25 | 3.57 |
| 1990 2 ML Teams | | 64 | 0 | 0 | 53 | 83 | 344 | 71 | 24 | 19 | 3 | 2 | 3 | 0 | 29 | 7 | 87 | 2 | 0 | 5 | 5 | .500 | 0 | 31 | 2.06 |
| 1990 Boston | AL | 11 | 0 | 0 | 8 | 14.1 | 64 | 13 | 4 | 3 | 0 | 0 | 0 | 0 | 9 | 2 | 17 | 1 | 0 | 2 | 1 | .667 | 0 | 4 | 1.88 |
| St. Louis | NL | 53 | 0 | 0 | 45 | 68.2 | 280 | 58 | 20 | 16 | 3 | 2 | 3 | 0 | 20 | 5 | 70 | 1 | 0 | 3 | 4 | .429 | 0 | 27 | 2.10 |
| 11 ML YEARS | | 650 | 6 | 0 | 502 | 919.1 | 3824 | 787 | 328 | 294 | 54 | 48 | 26 | 7 | 363 | 80 | 923 | 39 | 4 | 55 | 62 | .470 | 0 | 265 | 2.88 |

## Lonnie Smith

**Bats:** Right **Throws:** Right **Pos:** LF **Ht:** 5' 9" **Wt:** 170 **Born:** 12/22/55 **Age:** 35

| BATTING | | | | | | | | | | | | | | | | | | | BASERUNNING | | | | PERCENTAGES | | |
|---|---|---|---|---|---|---|---|---|---|---|---|---|---|---|---|---|---|---|---|---|---|---|---|---|---|
| Year Team | Lg | G | AB | H | 2B | 3B | HR | (Hm | Rd) | TB | R | RBI | TBB | IBB | SO | HBP | SH | SF | SB | CS | SB% | GDP | Avg | OBP | SLG |
| 1978 Philadelphia | NL | 17 | 4 | 0 | 0 | 0 | 0 | (0 | 0) | 0 | 6 | 0 | 4 | 0 | 3 | 0 | 0 | 0 | 4 | 0 | 1.00 | 0 | .000 | .500 | .000 |
| 1979 Philadelphia | NL | 17 | 30 | 5 | 2 | 0 | 0 | (0 | 0) | 7 | 4 | 3 | 1 | 0 | 7 | 0 | 0 | 0 | 2 | 1 | .67 | 0 | .167 | .194 | .233 |
| 1980 Philadelphia | NL | 100 | 298 | 101 | 14 | 4 | 3 | (2 | 1) | 132 | 69 | 20 | 26 | 2 | 48 | 4 | 1 | 2 | 33 | 13 | .72 | 5 | .339 | .397 | .443 |
| 1981 Philadelphia | NL | 62 | 176 | 57 | 14 | 3 | 2 | (1 | 1) | 83 | 40 | 11 | 18 | 1 | 14 | 5 | 3 | 0 | 21 | 10 | .68 | 1 | .324 | .402 | .472 |
| 1982 St. Louis | NL | 156 | 592 | 182 | 35 | 8 | 8 | (3 | 5) | 257 | 120 | 69 | 64 | 2 | 74 | 9 | 3 | 4 | 68 | 26 | .72 | 11 | .307 | .381 | .434 |
| 1983 St. Louis | NL | 130 | 492 | 158 | 31 | 5 | 8 | (4 | 4) | 223 | 83 | 45 | 41 | 2 | 55 | 9 | 1 | 4 | 43 | 18 | .70 | 11 | .321 | .381 | .453 |
| 1984 St. Louis | NL | 145 | 504 | 126 | 20 | 4 | 6 | (3 | 3) | 172 | 77 | 49 | 70 | 0 | 90 | 9 | 3 | 4 | 50 | 13 | .79 | 7 | .250 | .349 | .341 |
| 1985 2 ML Teams | | 148 | 544 | 140 | 25 | 6 | 6 | (2 | 4) | 195 | 92 | 48 | 56 | 0 | 89 | 7 | 1 | 5 | 52 | 13 | .80 | 4 | .257 | .332 | .358 |
| 1986 Kansas City | AL | 134 | 508 | 146 | 25 | 7 | 8 | (2 | 6) | 209 | 80 | 44 | 46 | 0 | 78 | 10 | 2 | 2 | 26 | 9 | .74 | 10 | .287 | .357 | .411 |
| 1987 Kansas City | AL | 48 | 167 | 42 | 7 | 1 | 3 | (1 | 2) | 60 | 26 | 8 | 24 | 0 | 31 | 4 | 0 | 2 | 9 | 4 | .69 | 1 | .251 | .355 | .359 |
| 1988 Atlanta | NL | 43 | 114 | 27 | 3 | 0 | 3 | (2 | 1) | 39 | 14 | 9 | 10 | 0 | 25 | 0 | 0 | 1 | 4 | 2 | .67 | 0 | .237 | .296 | .342 |
| 1989 Atlanta | NL | 134 | 482 | 152 | 34 | 4 | 21 | (10 | 11) | 257 | 89 | 79 | 76 | 3 | 95 | 11 | 1 | 7 | 25 | 12 | .68 | 7 | .315 | .415 | .533 |
| 1990 Atlanta | NL | 135 | 466 | 142 | 27 | 9 | 9 | (2 | 7) | 214 | 72 | 42 | 58 | 3 | 69 | 6 | 1 | 6 | 10 | 10 | .50 | 2 | .305 | .384 | .459 |
| 1985 St. Louis | NL | 28 | 96 | 25 | 2 | 2 | 0 | (0 | 0) | 31 | 15 | 7 | 15 | 0 | 20 | 3 | 1 | 0 | 12 | 6 | .67 | 2 | .260 | .377 | .323 |
| Kansas City | AL | 120 | 448 | 115 | 23 | 4 | 6 | (2 | 4) | 164 | 77 | 41 | 41 | 0 | 69 | 4 | 0 | 5 | 40 | 7 | .85 | 2 | .257 | .321 | .366 |
| 13 ML YEARS | | 1269 | 4377 | 1278 | 237 | 51 | 77 | (32 | 45) | 1848 | 772 | 427 | 494 | 13 | 678 | 74 | 16 | 37 | 347 | 131 | .73 | 59 | .292 | .371 | .422 |

## Michael Smith

**Pitches:** Right **Bats:** Right **Pos:** RP **Ht:** 6' 3" **Wt:** 180 **Born:** 10/31/63 **Age:** 27

| HOW MUCH HE PITCHED | | | | | | | | WHAT HE GAVE UP | | | | | | | | | | | | THE RESULTS | | | | | | |
|---|---|---|---|---|---|---|---|---|---|---|---|---|---|---|---|---|---|---|---|---|---|---|---|---|---|---|
| Year Team | Lg | G | GS | CG | GF | IP | BFP | H | R | ER | HR | SH | SF | HB | TBB | IBB | SO | WP | Bk | W | L | Pct. | ShO | Sv | ERA |
| 1984 Reds | R | 11 | 11 | 0 | 0 | 67 | 286 | 65 | 33 | 27 | 3 | 1 | 2 | 5 | 24 | 1 | 65 | 7 | 1 | 2 | 4 | .333 | 0 | 0 | 3.63 |
| 1985 Billings | R | 7 | 5 | 1 | 0 | 33.2 | 0 | 24 | 15 | 11 | 0 | 0 | 0 | 2 | 24 | 0 | 24 | 2 | 0 | 2 | 2 | .500 | 1 | 0 | 2.94 |
| Cedar Rapds | A | 8 | 8 | 4 | 0 | 44.1 | 192 | 38 | 20 | 16 | 2 | 3 | 1 | 3 | 22 | 1 | 28 | 4 | 0 | 5 | 1 | .833 | 3 | 0 | 3.25 |
| 1986 Cedar Rapds | A | 28 | 27 | 4 | 1 | 191 | 807 | 155 | 88 | 71 | 12 | 4 | 2 | 6 | 106 | 1 | 172 | 19 | 0 | 10 | 10 | .500 | 1 | 0 | 3.35 |
| 1987 Vermont | AA | 27 | 27 | 6 | 0 | 171.1 | 740 | 152 | 78 | 64 | 5 | 6 | 3 | 3 | 117 | 3 | 104 | 15 | 2 | 8 | 12 | .400 | 2 | 0 | 3.36 |
| 1988 Chattanooga | AA | 28 | 28 | 5 | 0 | 194.1 | 822 | 160 | 90 | 69 | 10 | 5 | 5 | 10 | 98 | 2 | 141 | 10 | 3 | 9 | 10 | .474 | 1 | 0 | 3.20 |
| 1989 Rochester | AAA | 36 | 1 | 0 | 22 | 56 | 234 | 45 | 23 | 20 | 6 | 6 | 6 | 1 | 22 | 1 | 48 | 2 | 0 | 2 | 4 | .333 | 0 | 7 | 3.21 |
| 1990 Rochester | AAA | 29 | 20 | 1 | 3 | 123.1 | 551 | 118 | 76 | 68 | 14 | 3 | 3 | 8 | 73 | 1 | 112 | 12 | 2 | 9 | 6 | .600 | 1 | 0 | 4.96 |

| | | | | | | | | | | | | | | | | | | | | | | | | | |
|---|---|---|---|---|---|---|---|---|---|---|---|---|---|---|---|---|---|---|---|---|---|---|---|---|---|
| 1989 Baltimore | AL | 13 | 1 | 0 | 3 | 20 | 97 | 25 | 19 | 17 | 3 | 2 | 1 | 0 | 14 | 2 | 12 | 2 | 0 | 2 | 0 | 1.000 | 0 | 0 | 7.65 |
| 1990 Baltimore | AL | 2 | 0 | 0 | 1 | 3 | 14 | 4 | 4 | 4 | 2 | 0 | 0 | 0 | 1 | 0 | 2 | 0 | 0 | 0 | 0 | .000 | 0 | 0 | 12.00 |
| 2 ML YEARS | | 15 | 1 | 0 | 4 | 23 | 111 | 29 | 23 | 21 | 5 | 2 | 1 | 0 | 15 | 2 | 14 | 2 | 0 | 2 | 0 | 1.000 | 0 | 0 | 8.22 |

## Ozzie Smith

**Bats:** Both **Throws:** Right **Pos:** SS **Ht:** 5'10" **Wt:** 155 **Born:** 12/26/54 **Age:** 36

| | | BATTING | | | | | | | | | | | | | | | | | | BASERUNNING | | | | PERCENTAGES | | |
|---|---|---|---|---|---|---|---|---|---|---|---|---|---|---|---|---|---|---|---|---|---|---|---|---|---|---|
| Year Team | Lg | G | AB | H | 2B | 3B | HR | (Hm | Rd) | TB | R | RBI | TBB | IBB | SO | HBP | SH | SF | SB | CS | SB% | GDP | Avg | OBP | SLG |
| 1978 San Diego | NL | 159 | 590 | 152 | 17 | 6 | 1 | (0 | 1) | 184 | 69 | 46 | 47 | 0 | 43 | 0 | 28 | 3 | 40 | 12 | .77 | 11 | .258 | .311 | .312 |
| 1979 San Diego | NL | 156 | 587 | 124 | 18 | 6 | 0 | (0 | 0) | 154 | 77 | 27 | 37 | 5 | 37 | 2 | 22 | 1 | 28 | 7 | .80 | 11 | .211 | .260 | .262 |
| 1980 San Diego | NL | 158 | 609 | 140 | 18 | 5 | 0 | (0 | 0) | 168 | 67 | 35 | 71 | 1 | 49 | 5 | 23 | 4 | 57 | 15 | .79 | 9 | .230 | .313 | .276 |
| 1981 San Diego | NL | 110 | 450 | 100 | 11 | 2 | 0 | (0 | 0) | 115 | 53 | 21 | 41 | 1 | 37 | 5 | 10 | 1 | 22 | 12 | .65 | 8 | .222 | .294 | .256 |
| 1982 St. Louis | NL | 140 | 488 | 121 | 24 | 1 | 2 | (0 | 2) | 153 | 58 | 43 | 68 | 12 | 32 | 2 | 4 | 5 | 25 | 5 | .83 | 10 | .248 | .339 | .314 |
| 1983 St. Louis | NL | 159 | 552 | 134 | 30 | 6 | 3 | (1 | 2) | 185 | 69 | 50 | 64 | 9 | 36 | 1 | 7 | 2 | 34 | 7 | .83 | 10 | .243 | .321 | .335 |
| 1984 St. Louis | NL | 124 | 412 | 106 | 20 | 5 | 1 | (1 | 0) | 139 | 53 | 44 | 56 | 5 | 17 | 2 | 11 | 3 | 35 | 7 | .83 | 8 | .257 | .347 | .337 |
| 1985 St. Louis | NL | 158 | 537 | 148 | 22 | 3 | 6 | (2 | 4) | 194 | 70 | 54 | 65 | 11 | 27 | 2 | 9 | 2 | 31 | 8 | .79 | 13 | .276 | .355 | .361 |
| 1986 St. Louis | NL | 153 | 514 | 144 | 19 | 4 | 0 | (0 | 0) | 171 | 67 | 54 | 79 | 13 | 27 | 2 | 11 | 3 | 31 | 7 | .82 | 9 | .280 | .376 | .333 |
| 1987 St. Louis | NL | 158 | 600 | 182 | 40 | 4 | 0 | (0 | 0) | 230 | 104 | 75 | 89 | 3 | 36 | 1 | 12 | 4 | 43 | 9 | .83 | 9 | .303 | .392 | .383 |
| 1988 St. Louis | NL | 153 | 575 | 155 | 27 | 1 | 3 | (2 | 1) | 193 | 80 | 51 | 74 | 2 | 43 | 1 | 12 | 7 | 57 | 9 | .86 | 7 | .270 | .350 | .336 |
| 1989 St. Louis | NL | 155 | 593 | 162 | 30 | 8 | 2 | (1 | 1) | 214 | 82 | 50 | 55 | 3 | 37 | 2 | 11 | 3 | 29 | 7 | .81 | 10 | .273 | .335 | .361 |
| 1990 St. Louis | NL | 143 | 512 | 130 | 21 | 1 | 1 | (0 | 1) | 156 | 61 | 50 | 61 | 4 | 33 | 2 | 7 | 10 | 32 | 6 | .84 | 8 | .254 | .330 | .305 |
| 13 ML YEARS | | 1926 | 7019 | 1798 | 297 | 52 | 19 | (7 | 12) | 2256 | 910 | 600 | 807 | 69 | 454 | 27 | 167 | 48 | 464 | 111 | .81 | 123 | .256 | .333 | .321 |

## Pete Smith

**Pitches:** Right **Bats:** Right **Pos:** SP **Ht:** 6' 2" **Wt:** 185 **Born:** 02/27/66 **Age:** 25

| | | HOW MUCH HE PITCHED | | | | | | WHAT HE GAVE UP | | | | | | | | | | | | THE RESULTS | | | | | |
|---|---|---|---|---|---|---|---|---|---|---|---|---|---|---|---|---|---|---|---|---|---|---|---|---|---|
| Year Team | Lg | G | GS | CG | GF | IP | BFP | H | R | ER | HR | SH | SF | HB | TBB | IBB | SO | WP | Bk | W | L | Pct. | ShO | Sv | ERA |
| 1987 Atlanta | NL | 6 | 6 | 0 | 0 | 31.2 | 143 | 39 | 21 | 17 | 3 | 0 | 2 | 0 | 14 | 0 | 11 | 3 | 1 | 1 | 2 | .333 | 0 | 0 | 4.83 |
| 1988 Atlanta | NL | 32 | 32 | 5 | 0 | 195.1 | 837 | 183 | 89 | 80 | 15 | 12 | 4 | 1 | 88 | 3 | 124 | 5 | 7 | 7 | 15 | .318 | 3 | 0 | 3.69 |
| 1989 Atlanta | NL | 28 | 27 | 1 | 0 | 142 | 613 | 144 | 83 | 75 | 13 | 4 | 5 | 0 | 57 | 2 | 115 | 3 | 7 | 5 | 14 | .263 | 0 | 0 | 4.75 |
| 1990 Atlanta | NL | 13 | 13 | 3 | 0 | 77 | 327 | 77 | 45 | 41 | 11 | 4 | 3 | 0 | 24 | 2 | 56 | 2 | 1 | 5 | 6 | .455 | 0 | 0 | 4.79 |
| 4 ML YEARS | | 79 | 78 | 9 | 0 | 446 | 1920 | 443 | 238 | 213 | 42 | 20 | 14 | 1 | 183 | 7 | 306 | 13 | 16 | 18 | 37 | .327 | 3 | 0 | 4.30 |

## Roy Smith

**Pitches:** Right **Bats:** Right **Pos:** SP/RP **Ht:** 6' 3" **Wt:** 217 **Born:** 09/06/61 **Age:** 29

| | | HOW MUCH HE PITCHED | | | | | | WHAT HE GAVE UP | | | | | | | | | | | | THE RESULTS | | | | | |
|---|---|---|---|---|---|---|---|---|---|---|---|---|---|---|---|---|---|---|---|---|---|---|---|---|---|
| Year Team | Lg | G | GS | CG | GF | IP | BFP | H | R | ER | HR | SH | SF | HB | TBB | IBB | SO | WP | Bk | W | L | Pct. | ShO | Sv | ERA |
| 1984 Cleveland | AL | 22 | 14 | 0 | 1 | 86.1 | 382 | 91 | 49 | 44 | 14 | 1 | 3 | 1 | 40 | 5 | 55 | 3 | 2 | 5 | 5 | .500 | 0 | 0 | 4.59 |
| 1985 Cleveland | AL | 12 | 11 | 1 | 0 | 62.1 | 285 | 84 | 40 | 37 | 8 | 1 | 4 | 1 | 17 | 0 | 28 | 1 | 0 | 1 | 4 | .200 | 0 | 0 | 5.34 |
| 1986 Minnesota | AL | 5 | 0 | 0 | 2 | 10.1 | 50 | 13 | 8 | 8 | 1 | 0 | 0 | 1 | 5 | 1 | 8 | 0 | 0 | 0 | 2 | .000 | 0 | 0 | 6.97 |
| 1987 Minnesota | AL | 7 | 1 | 0 | 1 | 16.1 | 78 | 20 | 10 | 9 | 3 | 0 | 1 | 2 | 6 | 0 | 8 | 0 | 0 | 1 | 0 | 1.000 | 0 | 0 | 4.96 |
| 1988 Minnesota | AL | 9 | 4 | 0 | 1 | 37 | 152 | 29 | 12 | 11 | 3 | 0 | 1 | 1 | 12 | 1 | 17 | 1 | 4 | 3 | 0 | 1.000 | 0 | 0 | 2.68 |
| 1989 Minnesota | AL | 32 | 26 | 2 | 1 | 172.1 | 733 | 180 | 82 | 75 | 22 | 5 | 3 | 5 | 51 | 5 | 92 | 5 | 1 | 10 | 6 | .625 | 0 | 1 | 3.92 |
| 1990 Minnesota | AL | 32 | 23 | 1 | 1 | 153.1 | 671 | 191 | 91 | 82 | 20 | 2 | 11 | 0 | 47 | 4 | 87 | 10 | 0 | 5 | 10 | .333 | 1 | 0 | 4.81 |
| 7 ML YEARS | | 119 | 79 | 4 | 7 | 538 | 2351 | 608 | 292 | 266 | 71 | 9 | 23 | 11 | 178 | 16 | 295 | 20 | 7 | 25 | 27 | .481 | 1 | 1 | 4.45 |

## Zane Smith

**Pitches:** Left **Bats:** Left **Pos:** SP **Ht:** 6' 2" **Wt:** 195 **Born:** 12/28/60 **Age:** 30

| | | HOW MUCH HE PITCHED | | | | | | WHAT HE GAVE UP | | | | | | | | | | | | THE RESULTS | | | | | |
|---|---|---|---|---|---|---|---|---|---|---|---|---|---|---|---|---|---|---|---|---|---|---|---|---|---|
| Year Team | Lg | G | GS | CG | GF | IP | BFP | H | R | ER | HR | SH | SF | HB | TBB | IBB | SO | WP | Bk | W | L | Pct. | ShO | Sv | ERA |
| 1984 Atlanta | NL | 3 | 3 | 0 | 0 | 20 | 87 | 16 | 7 | 5 | 1 | 1 | 0 | 0 | 13 | 2 | 16 | 0 | 0 | 1 | 0 | 1.000 | 0 | 0 | 2.25 |
| 1985 Atlanta | NL | 42 | 18 | 2 | 3 | 147 | 631 | 135 | 70 | 62 | 4 | 16 | 1 | 3 | 80 | 5 | 85 | 2 | 0 | 9 | 10 | .474 | 2 | 0 | 3.80 |
| 1986 Atlanta | NL | 38 | 32 | 3 | 2 | 204.2 | 889 | 209 | 109 | 92 | 8 | 13 | 6 | 5 | 105 | 6 | 139 | 8 | 0 | 8 | 16 | .333 | 1 | 1 | 4.05 |
| 1987 Atlanta | NL | 36 | 36 | 9 | 0 | 242 | 1035 | 245 | 130 | 110 | 19 | 12 | 5 | 5 | 91 | 6 | 130 | 5 | 1 | 15 | 10 | .600 | 3 | 0 | 4.09 |
| 1988 Atlanta | NL | 23 | 22 | 3 | 0 | 140.1 | 609 | 159 | 72 | 67 | 8 | 15 | 2 | 3 | 44 | 4 | 59 | 2 | 2 | 5 | 10 | .333 | 0 | 0 | 4.30 |
| 1989 2 ML Teams | | 48 | 17 | 0 | 10 | 147 | 634 | 141 | 76 | 57 | 7 | 15 | 5 | 3 | 52 | 7 | 93 | 4 | 0 | 1 | 13 | .071 | 0 | 2 | 3.49 |
| 1990 2 ML Teams | | 33 | 31 | 4 | 1 | 215.1 | 860 | 196 | 77 | 61 | 15 | 3 | 3 | 3 | 50 | 4 | 130 | 2 | 0 | 12 | 9 | .571 | 2 | 0 | 2.55 |
| 1989 Atlanta | NL | 17 | 17 | 0 | 0 | 99 | 432 | 102 | 65 | 49 | 5 | 10 | 5 | 2 | 33 | 3 | 58 | 3 | 0 | 1 | 12 | .077 | 0 | 0 | 4.45 |
| Montreal | NL | 31 | 0 | 0 | 10 | 48 | 202 | 39 | 11 | 8 | 2 | 5 | 0 | 1 | 19 | 4 | 35 | 1 | 0 | 0 | 1 | .000 | 0 | 2 | 1.50 |
| 1990 Montreal | NL | 22 | 21 | 1 | 0 | 139.1 | 578 | 141 | 57 | 50 | 11 | 2 | 2 | 3 | 41 | 3 | 80 | 1 | 0 | 6 | 7 | .462 | 0 | 0 | 3.23 |
| Pittsburgh | NL | 11 | 10 | 3 | 1 | 76 | 282 | 55 | 20 | 11 | 4 | 1 | 1 | 0 | 9 | 1 | 50 | 1 | 0 | 6 | 2 | .750 | 2 | 0 | 1.30 |
| 7 ML YEARS | | 223 | 159 | 21 | 16 | 1116.1 | 4745 | 1101 | 541 | 454 | 62 | 75 | 22 | 22 | 435 | 34 | 652 | 23 | 3 | 51 | 68 | .429 | 8 | 3 | 3.66 |

## John Smoltz

**Pitches:** Right **Bats:** Right **Pos:** SP **Ht:** 6' 3" **Wt:** 185 **Born:** 05/15/67 **Age:** 24

| | | | HOW MUCH HE PITCHED | | | | | | WHAT HE GAVE UP | | | | | | | | | | | | THE RESULTS | | | | | |
|---|---|---|---|---|---|---|---|---|---|---|---|---|---|---|---|---|---|---|---|---|---|---|---|---|---|---|
| Year | Team | Lg | G | GS | CG | GF | IP | BFP | H | R | ER | HR | SH | SF | HB | TBB | IBB | SO | WP | Bk | W | L | Pct. | ShO | Sv | ERA |
| 1988 | Atlanta | NL | 12 | 12 | 0 | 0 | 64 | 297 | 74 | 40 | 39 | 10 | 2 | 0 | 2 | 33 | 4 | 37 | 2 | 1 | 2 | 7 | .222 | 0 | 0 | 5.48 |
| 1989 | Atlanta | NL | 29 | 29 | 5 | 0 | 208 | 847 | 160 | 79 | 68 | 15 | 10 | 7 | 2 | 72 | 2 | 168 | 8 | 3 | 12 | 11 | .522 | 0 | 0 | 2.94 |
| 1990 | Atlanta | NL | 34 | 34 | 6 | 0 | 231.1 | 966 | 206 | 109 | 99 | 20 | 9 | 8 | 1 | 90 | 3 | 170 | 14 | 3 | 14 | 11 | .560 | 2 | 0 | 3.85 |
| | 3 ML YEARS | | 75 | 75 | 11 | 0 | 503.1 | 2110 | 440 | 228 | 206 | 45 | 21 | 15 | 5 | 195 | 9 | 375 | 24 | 7 | 28 | 29 | .491 | 2 | 0 | 3.68 |

## Cory Snyder

**Bats:** Right **Throws:** Right **Pos:** RF **Ht:** 6' 3" **Wt:** 185 **Born:** 11/11/62 **Age:** 28

| | | | | | | | BATTING | | | | | | | | | | | | | BASERUNNING | | | | PERCENTAGES | | |
|---|---|---|---|---|---|---|---|---|---|---|---|---|---|---|---|---|---|---|---|---|---|---|---|---|---|---|
| Year | Team | Lg | G | AB | H | 2B | 3B | HR | (Hm | Rd) | TB | R | RBI | TBB | IBB | SO | HBP | SH | SF | SB | CS | SB% | GDP | Avg | OBP | SLG |
| 1986 | Cleveland | AL | 103 | 416 | 113 | 21 | 1 | 24 | (12 | 12) | 208 | 58 | 69 | 16 | 0 | 123 | 0 | 1 | 0 | 2 | 3 | .40 | 8 | .272 | .299 | .500 |
| 1987 | Cleveland | AL | 157 | 577 | 136 | 24 | 2 | 33 | (17 | 16) | 263 | 74 | 82 | 31 | 4 | 166 | 1 | 0 | 6 | 5 | 1 | .83 | 3 | .236 | .273 | .456 |
| 1988 | Cleveland | AL | 142 | 511 | 139 | 24 | 3 | 26 | (11 | 15) | 247 | 71 | 75 | 42 | 7 | 101 | 1 | 0 | 4 | 5 | 1 | .83 | 12 | .272 | .326 | .483 |
| 1989 | Cleveland | AL | 132 | 489 | 105 | 17 | 0 | 18 | (6 | 12) | 176 | 49 | 59 | 23 | 1 | 134 | 2 | 0 | 4 | 6 | 5 | .55 | 11 | .215 | .251 | .360 |
| 1990 | Cleveland | AL | 123 | 438 | 102 | 27 | 3 | 14 | (3 | 11) | 177 | 46 | 55 | 21 | 3 | 118 | 2 | 1 | 6 | 1 | 4 | .20 | 11 | .233 | .268 | .404 |
| | 5 ML YEARS | | 657 | 2431 | 595 | 113 | 9 | 115 | (49 | 66) | 1071 | 298 | 340 | 133 | 15 | 642 | 6 | 2 | 20 | 19 | 14 | .58 | 45 | .245 | .283 | .441 |

## Luis Sojo

**Bats:** Right **Throws:** Right **Pos:** 2B **Ht:** 5'11" **Wt:** 174 **Born:** 01/03/66 **Age:** 25

| | | | | | | | BATTING | | | | | | | | | | | | | BASERUNNING | | | | PERCENTAGES | | |
|---|---|---|---|---|---|---|---|---|---|---|---|---|---|---|---|---|---|---|---|---|---|---|---|---|---|---|
| Year | Team | Lg | G | AB | H | 2B | 3B | HR | (Hm | Rd) | TB | R | RBI | TBB | IBB | SO | HBP | SH | SF | SB | CS | SB% | GDP | Avg | OBP | SLG |
| 1987 | Myrtle Bch | A | 72 | 223 | 47 | 5 | 4 | 2 | -- | -- | 66 | 23 | 15 | 17 | 0 | 18 | 0 | 4 | 1 | 5 | 1 | .83 | 9 | .211 | .266 | .296 |
| 1988 | Myrtle Bch | A | 135 | 536 | 155 | 22 | 5 | 5 | -- | -- | 202 | 83 | 56 | 35 | 1 | 35 | 2 | 7 | 6 | 14 | 9 | .61 | 18 | .289 | .332 | .377 |
| 1989 | Syracuse | AAA | 121 | 482 | 133 | 20 | 5 | 3 | -- | -- | 172 | 54 | 54 | 21 | 0 | 42 | 1 | 4 | 5 | 9 | 14 | .39 | 9 | .276 | .305 | .357 |
| 1990 | Syracuse | AAA | 75 | 297 | 88 | 12 | 3 | 6 | -- | -- | 124 | 39 | 25 | 14 | 0 | 23 | 1 | 3 | 9 | 10 | 2 | .83 | 8 | .296 | .321 | .418 |
| 1990 | Toronto | AL | 33 | 80 | 18 | 3 | 0 | 1 | (0 | 1) | 24 | 14 | 9 | 5 | 0 | 5 | 0 | 0 | 0 | 1 | 1 | .50 | 1 | .225 | .271 | .300 |

## Paul Sorrento

**Bats:** Left **Throws:** Right **Pos:** DH/1B **Ht:** 6' 2" **Wt:** 195 **Born:** 11/17/65 **Age:** 25

| | | | | | | | BATTING | | | | | | | | | | | | | BASERUNNING | | | | PERCENTAGES | | |
|---|---|---|---|---|---|---|---|---|---|---|---|---|---|---|---|---|---|---|---|---|---|---|---|---|---|---|
| Year | Team | Lg | G | AB | H | 2B | 3B | HR | (Hm | Rd) | TB | R | RBI | TBB | IBB | SO | HBP | SH | SF | SB | CS | SB% | GDP | Avg | OBP | SLG |
| 1986 | Quad City | A | 53 | 177 | 63 | 11 | 2 | 6 | -- | -- | 96 | 33 | 34 | 24 | 0 | 40 | 2 | 0 | 1 | 0 | 0 | .00 | 4 | .356 | .436 | .542 |
| | Palm Sprngs | A | 16 | 62 | 15 | 3 | 0 | 1 | -- | -- | 21 | 5 | 7 | 4 | 1 | 15 | 0 | 0 | 0 | 0 | 1 | .00 | 3 | .242 | .288 | .339 |
| 1987 | Palm Sprngs | A | 114 | 370 | 83 | 14 | 2 | 8 | -- | -- | 125 | 66 | 45 | 78 | 7 | 95 | 3 | 0 | 3 | 1 | 2 | .33 | 9 | .224 | .361 | .338 |
| 1988 | Palm Sprngs | A | 133 | 465 | 133 | 30 | 6 | 14 | -- | -- | 217 | 91 | 99 | 110 | 5 | 101 | 2 | 0 | 5 | 3 | 4 | .43 | 10 | .286 | .421 | .467 |
| 1989 | Orlando | AA | 140 | 509 | 130 | 35 | 2 | 27 | -- | -- | 250 | 81 | 112 | 84 | 7 | 119 | 7 | 0 | 4 | 1 | 1 | .50 | 7 | .255 | .366 | .491 |
| 1990 | Portland | AAA | 102 | 354 | 107 | 27 | 1 | 19 | -- | -- | 193 | 59 | 72 | 64 | 2 | 95 | 1 | 0 | 5 | 3 | 0 | 1.00 | 8 | .302 | .406 | .545 |
| 1989 | Minnesota | AL | 14 | 21 | 5 | 0 | 0 | 0 | (0 | 0) | 5 | 2 | 1 | 5 | 1 | 4 | 0 | 0 | 1 | 0 | 0 | .00 | 0 | .238 | .370 | .238 |
| 1990 | Minnesota | AL | 41 | 121 | 25 | 4 | 1 | 5 | (2 | 3) | 46 | 11 | 13 | 12 | 0 | 31 | 1 | 0 | 1 | 1 | 1 | .50 | 3 | .207 | .281 | .380 |
| | 2 ML YEARS | | 55 | 142 | 30 | 4 | 1 | 5 | (2 | 3) | 51 | 13 | 14 | 17 | 1 | 35 | 1 | 0 | 2 | 1 | 1 | .50 | 3 | .211 | .296 | .359 |

## Sammy Sosa

**Bats:** Right **Throws:** Right **Pos:** RF **Ht:** 6' 0" **Wt:** 165 **Born:** 11/10/68 **Age:** 22

| | | | | | | | BATTING | | | | | | | | | | | | | BASERUNNING | | | | PERCENTAGES | | |
|---|---|---|---|---|---|---|---|---|---|---|---|---|---|---|---|---|---|---|---|---|---|---|---|---|---|---|
| Year | Team | Lg | G | AB | H | 2B | 3B | HR | (Hm | Rd) | TB | R | RBI | TBB | IBB | SO | HBP | SH | SF | SB | CS | SB% | GDP | Avg | OBP | SLG |
| 1986 | Rangers | R | 61 | 229 | 63 | 19 | 1 | 4 | -- | -- | 96 | 38 | 28 | 22 | 0 | 51 | 0 | 0 | 2 | 11 | 3 | .79 | 4 | .275 | .336 | .419 |
| 1987 | Gastonia | A | 129 | 519 | 145 | 27 | 4 | 11 | -- | -- | 213 | 73 | 59 | 21 | 0 | 123 | 5 | 0 | 3 | 22 | 8 | .73 | 7 | .279 | .312 | .410 |
| 1988 | Charlotte | A | 131 | 507 | 116 | 13 | 12 | 9 | -- | -- | 180 | 70 | 51 | 35 | 0 | 106 | 4 | 0 | 3 | 42 | 24 | .64 | 14 | .229 | .282 | .355 |
| 1989 | Tulsa | AA | 66 | 273 | 81 | 15 | 4 | 7 | -- | -- | 125 | 45 | 31 | 15 | 0 | 52 | 3 | 2 | 2 | 16 | 11 | .59 | 4 | .297 | .338 | .458 |
| | Okla City | AAA | 10 | 39 | 4 | 2 | 0 | 0 | -- | -- | 6 | 2 | 3 | 2 | 0 | 8 | 0 | 0 | 0 | 4 | 2 | .67 | 2 | .103 | .146 | .154 |
| | Vancouver | AAA | 13 | 49 | 18 | 3 | 0 | 1 | -- | -- | 24 | 7 | 5 | 7 | 0 | 6 | 0 | 0 | 0 | 3 | 1 | .75 | 1 | .367 | .446 | .490 |
| 1989 | 2 ML Teams | | 58 | 183 | 47 | 8 | 0 | 4 | (1 | 3) | 67 | 27 | 13 | 11 | 2 | 47 | 2 | 5 | 2 | 7 | 5 | .58 | 6 | .257 | .303 | .366 |
| 1990 | Chicago | AL | 153 | 532 | 124 | 26 | 10 | 15 | (10 | 5) | 215 | 72 | 70 | 33 | 4 | 150 | 6 | 2 | 6 | 32 | 16 | .67 | 10 | .233 | .282 | .404 |
| 1989 | Texas | AL | 25 | 84 | 20 | 3 | 0 | 1 | (0 | 1) | 26 | 8 | 3 | 0 | 0 | 20 | 0 | 4 | 0 | 0 | 2 | .00 | 3 | .238 | .238 | .310 |
| | Chicago | AL | 33 | 99 | 27 | 5 | 0 | 3 | (1 | 2) | 41 | 19 | 10 | 11 | 2 | 27 | 2 | 1 | 2 | 7 | 3 | .70 | 3 | .273 | .351 | .414 |
| | 2 ML YEARS | | 211 | 715 | 171 | 34 | 10 | 19 | (11 | 8) | 282 | 99 | 83 | 44 | 6 | 197 | 8 | 7 | 8 | 39 | 21 | .65 | 16 | .239 | .288 | .394 |

## Bill Spiers

**Bats:** Left **Throws:** Right **Pos:** SS **Ht:** 6' 2" **Wt:** 190 **Born:** 06/05/66 **Age:** 25

| | | | | | | | BATTING | | | | | | | | | | | | | BASERUNNING | | | | PERCENTAGES | | |
|---|---|---|---|---|---|---|---|---|---|---|---|---|---|---|---|---|---|---|---|---|---|---|---|---|---|---|
| Year | Team | Lg | G | AB | H | 2B | 3B | HR | (Hm | Rd) | TB | R | RBI | TBB | IBB | SO | HBP | SH | SF | SB | CS | SB% | GDP | Avg | OBP | SLG |
| 1987 | Helena | R | 6 | 22 | 9 | 1 | 0 | 0 | -- | -- | 10 | 4 | 3 | 3 | 0 | 3 | 0 | 0 | 0 | 2 | 0 | 1.00 | 0 | .409 | .480 | .455 |

| Year | Team | Lg | G | AB | H | 2B | 3B | HR | (Hm | Rd) | TB | R | RBI | TBB | IBB | SO | HBP | SH | SF | SB | CS | SB% | GDP | Avg | OBP | SLG |
|---|---|---|---|---|---|---|---|---|---|---|---|---|---|---|---|---|---|---|---|---|---|---|---|---|---|---|
| | Beloit | A | 64 | 258 | 77 | 10 | 1 | 3 | -- | -- | 98 | 43 | 26 | 15 | 0 | 38 | 3 | 2 | 0 | 11 | 5 | .69 | 6 | .298 | .344 | .380 |
| 1988 | Stockton | A | 84 | 353 | 95 | 17 | 3 | 5 | -- | -- | 133 | 68 | 52 | 42 | 1 | 41 | 5 | 7 | 2 | 27 | 7 | .79 | 5 | .269 | .353 | .377 |
| | El Paso | AA | 47 | 168 | 47 | 5 | 2 | 3 | -- | -- | 65 | 22 | 21 | 15 | 0 | 20 | 2 | 0 | 1 | 4 | 4 | .50 | 7 | .280 | .344 | .387 |
| 1989 | Denver | AAA | 14 | 47 | 17 | 2 | 1 | 2 | -- | -- | 27 | 9 | 8 | 5 | 0 | 6 | 0 | 1 | 0 | 1 | 0 | 1.00 | 1 | .362 | .423 | .574 |
| 1990 | Denver | AAA | 11 | 38 | 12 | 0 | 0 | 1 | -- | -- | 15 | 6 | 7 | 10 | 0 | 8 | 0 | 0 | 1 | 1 | 1 | .50 | 2 | .316 | .449 | .395 |
| 1989 | Milwaukee | AL | 114 | 345 | 88 | 9 | 3 | 4 | (1 | 3) | 115 | 44 | 33 | 21 | 1 | 63 | 1 | 4 | 2 | 10 | 2 | .83 | 2 | .255 | .298 | .333 |
| 1990 | Milwaukee | AL | 112 | 363 | 88 | 15 | 3 | 2 | (2 | 0) | 115 | 44 | 36 | 16 | 0 | 45 | 1 | 6 | 3 | 11 | 6 | .65 | 12 | .242 | .274 | .317 |
| | 2 ML YEARS | | 226 | 708 | 176 | 24 | 6 | 6 | (3 | 3) | 230 | 88 | 69 | 37 | 1 | 108 | 2 | 10 | 5 | 21 | 8 | .72 | 14 | .249 | .286 | .325 |

## Steve Springer

**Bats:** Right **Throws:** Right **Pos:** 3B **Ht:** 6' 0" **Wt:** 190 **Born:** 02/11/61 **Age:** 30

| | | | BATTING | | | | | | | | | | | | | | | | | BASERUNNING | | | | PERCENTAGES | | |
|---|---|---|---|---|---|---|---|---|---|---|---|---|---|---|---|---|---|---|---|---|---|---|---|---|---|---|
| Year | Team | Lg | G | AB | H | 2B | 3B | HR | (Hm | Rd) | TB | R | RBI | TBB | IBB | SO | HBP | SH | SF | SB | CS | SB% | GDP | Avg | OBP | SLG |
| 1984 | Jackson | AA | 103 | 362 | 99 | 21 | 3 | 5 | -- | -- | 141 | 41 | 40 | 24 | 3 | 50 | 2 | 0 | 0 | 6 | 4 | .60 | 16 | .273 | .322 | .390 |
| 1985 | Tidewater | AAA | 126 | 479 | 125 | 20 | 4 | 7 | -- | -- | 174 | 59 | 56 | 34 | 2 | 72 | 1 | 6 | 5 | 9 | 5 | .64 | 16 | .261 | .308 | .363 |
| 1986 | Tidewater | AAA | 117 | 440 | 120 | 19 | 6 | 4 | -- | -- | 163 | 52 | 46 | 30 | 0 | 74 | 1 | 5 | 0 | 10 | 5 | .67 | 16 | .273 | .321 | .370 |
| 1987 | Tidewater | AAA | 132 | 467 | 131 | 23 | 4 | 7 | -- | -- | 183 | 65 | 54 | 41 | 6 | 78 | 3 | 4 | 5 | 6 | 3 | .67 | 10 | .281 | .339 | .392 |
| 1988 | Tidewater | AAA | 97 | 337 | 88 | 15 | 0 | 2 | -- | -- | 109 | 42 | 25 | 29 | 0 | 66 | 0 | 2 | 1 | 4 | 0 | 1.00 | 7 | .261 | .319 | .323 |
| | Vancouver | AAA | 27 | 105 | 28 | 4 | 1 | 2 | -- | -- | 40 | 15 | 9 | 4 | 1 | 17 | 0 | 2 | 0 | 1 | 2 | .33 | 4 | .267 | .294 | .381 |
| 1989 | Vancouver | AAA | 137 | 520 | 144 | 21 | 3 | 8 | -- | -- | 195 | 61 | 56 | 26 | 1 | 83 | 3 | 7 | 5 | 8 | 8 | .50 | 11 | .277 | .312 | .375 |
| 1990 | Colo Sprngs | AAA | 73 | 252 | 70 | 21 | 5 | 6 | -- | -- | 119 | 39 | 42 | 17 | 1 | 48 | 0 | 0 | 8 | 6 | 3 | .67 | 6 | .278 | .314 | .472 |
| | Las Vegas | AAA | 22 | 72 | 18 | 5 | 0 | 2 | -- | -- | 29 | 7 | 10 | 7 | 0 | 19 | 0 | 1 | 2 | 0 | 1 | .00 | 2 | .250 | .309 | .403 |
| 1990 | Cleveland | AL | 4 | 12 | 2 | 0 | 0 | 0 | (0 | 0) | 2 | 1 | 1 | 0 | 0 | 6 | 0 | 0 | 1 | 0 | 0 | .00 | 0 | .167 | .154 | .167 |

## Mike Stanley

**Bats:** Right **Throws:** Right **Pos:** C **Ht:** 6' 0" **Wt:** 185 **Born:** 06/25/63 **Age:** 28

| | | | BATTING | | | | | | | | | | | | | | | | | BASERUNNING | | | | PERCENTAGES | | |
|---|---|---|---|---|---|---|---|---|---|---|---|---|---|---|---|---|---|---|---|---|---|---|---|---|---|---|
| Year | Team | Lg | G | AB | H | 2B | 3B | HR | (Hm | Rd) | TB | R | RBI | TBB | IBB | SO | HBP | SH | SF | SB | CS | SB% | GDP | Avg | OBP | SLG |
| 1986 | Texas | AL | 15 | 30 | 10 | 3 | 0 | 1 | (0 | 1) | 16 | 4 | 1 | 3 | 0 | 7 | 0 | 0 | 0 | 1 | 0 | 1.00 | 0 | .333 | .394 | .533 |
| 1987 | Texas | AL | 78 | 216 | 59 | 8 | 1 | 6 | (3 | 3) | 87 | 34 | 37 | 31 | 0 | 48 | 1 | 1 | 4 | 3 | 0 | 1.00 | 6 | .273 | .361 | .403 |
| 1988 | Texas | AL | 94 | 249 | 57 | 8 | 0 | 3 | (1 | 2) | 74 | 21 | 27 | 37 | 0 | 62 | 0 | 1 | 5 | 0 | 0 | .00 | 6 | .229 | .323 | .297 |
| 1989 | Texas | AL | 67 | 122 | 30 | 3 | 1 | 1 | (1 | 0) | 38 | 9 | 11 | 12 | 1 | 29 | 2 | 1 | 0 | 1 | 0 | 1.00 | 5 | .246 | .324 | .311 |
| 1990 | Texas | AL | 103 | 189 | 47 | 8 | 1 | 2 | (1 | 1) | 63 | 21 | 19 | 30 | 2 | 25 | 0 | 6 | 1 | 1 | 0 | 1.00 | 4 | .249 | .350 | .333 |
| | 5 ML YEARS | | 357 | 806 | 203 | 30 | 3 | 13 | (6 | 7) | 278 | 89 | 95 | 113 | 3 | 171 | 3 | 9 | 10 | 6 | 0 | 1.00 | 21 | .252 | .342 | .345 |

## Mike Stanton

**Pitches:** Left **Bats:** Left **Pos:** RP **Ht:** 6' 1" **Wt:** 190 **Born:** 06/02/67 **Age:** 24

| | | | HOW MUCH HE PITCHED | | | | | | WHAT HE GAVE UP | | | | | | | | | | | | THE RESULTS | | | | | |
|---|---|---|---|---|---|---|---|---|---|---|---|---|---|---|---|---|---|---|---|---|---|---|---|---|---|---|
| Year | Team | Lg | G | GS | CG | GF | IP | BFP | H | R | ER | HR | SH | SF | HB | TBB | IBB | SO | WP | Bk | W | L | Pct. | ShO | Sv | ERA |
| 1987 | Pulaski | R | 15 | 13 | 3 | 1 | 83.1 | 354 | 64 | 37 | 30 | 7 | 3 | 4 | 3 | 42 | 0 | 82 | 2 | 0 | 4 | 8 | .333 | 2 | 0 | 3.24 |
| 1988 | Burlington | A | 30 | 23 | 1 | 3 | 154 | 675 | 154 | 86 | 62 | 7 | 4 | 3 | 1 | 69 | 2 | 160 | 16 | 1 | 11 | 5 | .688 | 1 | 0 | 3.62 |
| | Durham | A | 2 | 2 | 1 | 0 | 12.1 | 55 | 14 | 3 | 2 | 0 | 0 | 0 | 0 | 5 | 0 | 14 | 1 | 1 | 1 | 0 | 1.000 | 1 | 0 | 1.46 |
| 1989 | Greenville | AA | 47 | 0 | 0 | 36 | 51.1 | 207 | 32 | 10 | 9 | 1 | 5 | 2 | 0 | 31 | 3 | 58 | 4 | 0 | 4 | 1 | .800 | 0 | 19 | 1.58 |
| | Richmond | AAA | 13 | 0 | 0 | 11 | 20 | 77 | 6 | 0 | 0 | 0 | 1 | 0 | 1 | 13 | 2 | 20 | 0 | 0 | 2 | 0 | 1.000 | 0 | 8 | 0.00 |
| 1990 | Greenville | AA | 4 | 4 | 0 | 0 | 5.2 | 27 | 7 | 1 | 1 | 1 | 0 | 0 | 0 | 3 | 0 | 4 | 0 | 0 | 0 | 1 | .000 | 0 | 0 | 1.59 |
| 1989 | Atlanta | NL | 20 | 0 | 0 | 10 | 24 | 94 | 17 | 4 | 4 | 0 | 4 | 0 | 0 | 8 | 1 | 27 | 1 | 0 | 0 | 1 | .000 | 0 | 7 | 1.50 |
| 1990 | Atlanta | NL | 7 | 0 | 0 | 4 | 7 | 42 | 16 | 16 | 14 | 1 | 1 | 0 | 1 | 4 | 2 | 7 | 1 | 0 | 0 | 3 | .000 | 0 | 2 | 18.00 |
| | 2 ML YEARS | | 27 | 0 | 0 | 14 | 31 | 136 | 33 | 20 | 18 | 1 | 5 | 0 | 1 | 12 | 3 | 34 | 2 | 0 | 0 | 4 | .000 | 0 | 9 | 5.23 |

## Matt Stark

**Bats:** Right **Throws:** Right **Pos:** DH **Ht:** 6' 4" **Wt:** 220 **Born:** 01/21/65 **Age:** 26

| | | | BATTING | | | | | | | | | | | | | | | | | BASERUNNING | | | | PERCENTAGES | | |
|---|---|---|---|---|---|---|---|---|---|---|---|---|---|---|---|---|---|---|---|---|---|---|---|---|---|---|
| Year | Team | Lg | G | AB | H | 2B | 3B | HR | (Hm | Rd) | TB | R | RBI | TBB | IBB | SO | HBP | SH | SF | SB | CS | SB% | GDP | Avg | OBP | SLG |
| 1987 | Toronto | AL | 5 | 12 | 1 | 0 | 0 | 0 | (0 | 0) | 1 | 0 | 0 | 0 | 0 | 0 | 0 | 0 | 0 | 0 | 0 | .00 | 2 | .083 | .083 | .083 |
| 1990 | Chicago | AL | 8 | 16 | 4 | 1 | 0 | 0 | (0 | 0) | 5 | 0 | 3 | 1 | 0 | 6 | 0 | 1 | 0 | 0 | 0 | .00 | 2 | .250 | .294 | .313 |
| | 2 ML YEARS | | 13 | 28 | 5 | 1 | 0 | 0 | (0 | 0) | 6 | 0 | 3 | 1 | 0 | 6 | 0 | 1 | 0 | 0 | 0 | .00 | 4 | .179 | .207 | .214 |

## Terry Steinbach

**Bats:** Right **Throws:** Right **Pos:** C/DH **Ht:** 6' 1" **Wt:** 195 **Born:** 03/02/62 **Age:** 29

| | | | BATTING | | | | | | | | | | | | | | | | | BASERUNNING | | | | PERCENTAGES | | |
|---|---|---|---|---|---|---|---|---|---|---|---|---|---|---|---|---|---|---|---|---|---|---|---|---|---|---|
| Year | Team | Lg | G | AB | H | 2B | 3B | HR | (Hm | Rd) | TB | R | RBI | TBB | IBB | SO | HBP | SH | SF | SB | CS | SB% | GDP | Avg | OBP | SLG |
| 1986 | Oakland | AL | 6 | 15 | 5 | 0 | 0 | 2 | (0 | 2) | 11 | 3 | 4 | 1 | 0 | 0 | 0 | 0 | 0 | 0 | 0 | .00 | 0 | .333 | .375 | .733 |
| 1987 | Oakland | AL | 122 | 391 | 111 | 16 | 3 | 16 | (6 | 10) | 181 | 66 | 56 | 32 | 2 | 66 | 9 | 3 | 3 | 1 | 2 | .33 | 10 | .284 | .349 | .463 |
| 1988 | Oakland | AL | 104 | 351 | 93 | 19 | 1 | 9 | (6 | 3) | 141 | 42 | 51 | 33 | 2 | 47 | 6 | 3 | 5 | 3 | 0 | 1.00 | 13 | .265 | .334 | .402 |
| 1989 | Oakland | AL | 130 | 454 | 124 | 13 | 1 | 7 | (5 | 2) | 160 | 37 | 42 | 30 | 2 | 66 | 2 | 2 | 3 | 1 | 2 | .33 | 14 | .273 | .319 | .352 |
| 1990 | Oakland | AL | 114 | 379 | 95 | 15 | 2 | 9 | (3 | 6) | 141 | 32 | 57 | 19 | 1 | 66 | 4 | 5 | 3 | 0 | 1 | .00 | 11 | .251 | .291 | .372 |
| | 5 ML YEARS | | 476 | 1590 | 428 | 63 | 7 | 43 | (20 | 23) | 634 | 180 | 210 | 115 | 7 | 245 | 21 | 13 | 14 | 5 | 5 | .50 | 48 | .269 | .324 | .399 |

## Ray Stephens

**Bats:** Right **Throws:** Right **Pos:** C **Ht:** 6' 0" **Wt:** 190 **Born:** 09/22/62 **Age:** 28

| BATTING | | | | | | | | | | | | | | | | | | | | BASERUNNING | | | | PERCENTAGES | | |
|---|---|---|---|---|---|---|---|---|---|---|---|---|---|---|---|---|---|---|---|---|---|---|---|---|---|---|
| Year | Team | Lg | G | AB | H | 2B | 3B | HR | (Hm | Rd) | TB | R | RBI | TBB | IBB | SO | HBP | SH | SF | SB | CS | SB% | GDP | Avg | OBP | SLG |
| 1985 | Erie | A | 9 | 31 | 9 | 1 | 1 | 1 | -- | -- | 15 | 3 | 5 | 7 | 0 | 6 | 0 | 0 | 0 | 0 | 0 | .00 | 1 | .290 | .421 | .484 |
| | Savannah | A | 39 | 127 | 26 | 6 | 0 | 0 | -- | -- | 32 | 11 | 6 | 14 | 0 | 32 | 1 | 1 | 1 | 1 | 1 | .50 | 3 | .205 | .287 | .252 |
| 1986 | Savannah | A | 95 | 325 | 71 | 10 | 0 | 13 | -- | -- | 120 | 52 | 56 | 57 | 1 | 76 | 3 | 1 | 2 | 2 | 4 | .33 | 6 | .218 | .339 | .369 |
| | Louisville | AAA | 12 | 31 | 6 | 1 | 0 | 1 | -- | -- | 10 | 2 | 2 | 1 | 0 | 13 | 1 | 0 | 1 | 0 | 0 | .00 | 0 | .194 | .235 | .323 |
| 1987 | Arkansas | AA | 100 | 307 | 77 | 20 | 0 | 8 | -- | -- | 121 | 35 | 42 | 37 | 4 | 68 | 3 | 2 | 2 | 6 | 2 | .75 | 10 | .251 | .335 | .394 |
| | Louisville | AAA | 9 | 30 | 4 | 0 | 0 | 0 | -- | -- | 4 | 1 | 2 | 5 | 1 | 9 | 0 | 0 | 1 | 0 | 1 | .00 | 3 | .133 | .250 | .133 |
| 1988 | Louisville | AAA | 115 | 355 | 67 | 13 | 2 | 3 | -- | -- | 93 | 26 | 25 | 45 | 3 | 78 | 1 | 0 | 3 | 2 | 0 | 1.00 | 6 | .189 | .280 | .262 |
| 1989 | Arkansas | AA | 112 | 363 | 95 | 14 | 0 | 7 | -- | -- | 130 | 49 | 44 | 44 | 2 | 61 | 4 | 4 | 3 | 2 | 1 | .67 | 11 | .262 | .345 | .358 |
| 1990 | Louisville | AAA | 98 | 294 | 65 | 8 | 1 | 3 | -- | -- | 84 | 20 | 27 | 27 | 3 | 74 | 4 | 9 | 1 | 0 | 1 | .00 | 12 | .221 | .294 | .286 |
| 1990 | St. Louis | NL | 5 | 15 | 2 | 1 | 0 | 1 | (1 | 0) | 6 | 2 | 1 | 0 | 0 | 3 | 0 | 0 | 0 | 0 | 0 | .00 | 2 | .133 | .133 | .400 |

## Phil Stephenson

**Bats:** Left **Throws:** Left **Pos:** 1B **Ht:** 6' 1" **Wt:** 195 **Born:** 09/19/60 **Age:** 30

| BATTING | | | | | | | | | | | | | | | | | | | | BASERUNNING | | | | PERCENTAGES | | |
|---|---|---|---|---|---|---|---|---|---|---|---|---|---|---|---|---|---|---|---|---|---|---|---|---|---|---|
| Year | Team | Lg | G | AB | H | 2B | 3B | HR | (Hm | Rd) | TB | R | RBI | TBB | IBB | SO | HBP | SH | SF | SB | CS | SB% | GDP | Avg | OBP | SLG |
| 1984 | Tacoma | AAA | 124 | 398 | 120 | 25 | 1 | 10 | -- | -- | 177 | 70 | 69 | 85 | 9 | 54 | 0 | 6 | 3 | 15 | 4 | .79 | 14 | .302 | .422 | .445 |
| 1985 | Tacoma | AAA | 56 | 171 | 36 | 11 | 0 | 5 | -- | -- | 62 | 30 | 24 | 46 | 1 | 32 | 0 | 1 | 2 | 5 | 1 | .83 | 1 | .211 | .374 | .363 |
| | Midland | AA | 50 | 176 | 52 | 14 | 0 | 7 | -- | -- | 87 | 39 | 41 | 35 | 3 | 27 | 1 | 0 | 0 | 5 | 2 | .71 | 4 | .295 | .415 | .494 |
| 1986 | Pittsfield | AA | 140 | 423 | 115 | 29 | 2 | 12 | -- | -- | 184 | 72 | 68 | 129 | 8 | 67 | 2 | 3 | 8 | 30 | 18 | .63 | 9 | .272 | .438 | .435 |
| 1987 | Iowa | AAA | 105 | 298 | 91 | 24 | 2 | 10 | -- | -- | 149 | 53 | 56 | 62 | 2 | 56 | 1 | 2 | 7 | 4 | 6 | .40 | 9 | .305 | .418 | .500 |
| 1988 | Iowa | AAA | 118 | 426 | 125 | 28 | 11 | 22 | -- | -- | 241 | 69 | 81 | 50 | 9 | 76 | 1 | 2 | 5 | 9 | 5 | .64 | 9 | .293 | .365 | .566 |
| 1989 | Iowa | AAA | 84 | 290 | 87 | 17 | 3 | 13 | -- | -- | 149 | 52 | 62 | 58 | 9 | 41 | 1 | 0 | 4 | 28 | 3 | .90 | 4 | .300 | .414 | .514 |
| 1989 | 2 ML Teams | | 27 | 38 | 9 | 0 | 0 | 2 | (2 | 0) | 15 | 4 | 2 | 5 | 0 | 5 | 0 | 2 | 0 | 1 | 0 | 1.00 | 0 | .237 | .326 | .395 |
| 1990 | San Diego | NL | 103 | 182 | 38 | 9 | 1 | 4 | (2 | 2) | 61 | 26 | 19 | 30 | 1 | 43 | 0 | 0 | 1 | 2 | 1 | .67 | 2 | .209 | .319 | .335 |
| 1989 | Chicago | NL | 17 | 21 | 3 | 0 | 0 | 0 | (0 | 0) | 3 | 0 | 0 | 2 | 0 | 3 | 0 | 0 | 0 | 1 | 0 | 1.00 | 0 | .143 | .217 | .143 |
| | San Diego | NL | 10 | 17 | 6 | 0 | 0 | 2 | (2 | 0) | 12 | 4 | 2 | 3 | 0 | 2 | 0 | 2 | 0 | 0 | 0 | .00 | 0 | .353 | .450 | .706 |
| | 2 ML YEARS | | 130 | 220 | 47 | 9 | 1 | 6 | (4 | 2) | 76 | 30 | 21 | 35 | 1 | 48 | 0 | 2 | 1 | 3 | 1 | .75 | 2 | .214 | .320 | .345 |

## Lee Stevens

**Bats:** Left **Throws:** Left **Pos:** 1B **Ht:** 6' 4" **Wt:** 205 **Born:** 07/10/67 **Age:** 23

| BATTING | | | | | | | | | | | | | | | | | | | | BASERUNNING | | | | PERCENTAGES | | |
|---|---|---|---|---|---|---|---|---|---|---|---|---|---|---|---|---|---|---|---|---|---|---|---|---|---|---|
| Year | Team | Lg | G | AB | H | 2B | 3B | HR | (Hm | Rd) | TB | R | RBI | TBB | IBB | SO | HBP | SH | SF | SB | CS | SB% | GDP | Avg | OBP | SLG |
| 1986 | Salem | A | 72 | 267 | 75 | 18 | 2 | 6 | -- | -- | 115 | 45 | 47 | 45 | 3 | 49 | 2 | 0 | 1 | 13 | 6 | .68 | 6 | .281 | .387 | .431 |
| 1987 | Palm Sprngs | A | 140 | 532 | 130 | 29 | 2 | 19 | -- | -- | 220 | 82 | 97 | 61 | 5 | 117 | 4 | 0 | 4 | 1 | 9 | .10 | 18 | .244 | .324 | .414 |
| 1988 | Midland | AA | 116 | 414 | 123 | 26 | 2 | 23 | -- | -- | 222 | 79 | 76 | 58 | 4 | 108 | 5 | 2 | 3 | 0 | 5 | .00 | 16 | .297 | .388 | .536 |
| 1989 | Edmonton | AAA | 127 | 446 | 110 | 29 | 9 | 14 | -- | -- | 199 | 72 | 74 | 61 | 3 | 115 | 4 | 0 | 2 | 5 | 3 | .63 | 14 | .247 | .341 | .446 |
| 1990 | Edmonton | AAA | 90 | 338 | 99 | 31 | 2 | 16 | -- | -- | 182 | 57 | 66 | 55 | 11 | 83 | 1 | 0 | 3 | 1 | 2 | .33 | 10 | .293 | .390 | .538 |
| 1990 | California | AL | 67 | 248 | 53 | 10 | 0 | 7 | (4 | 3) | 84 | 28 | 32 | 22 | 3 | 75 | 0 | 2 | 3 | 1 | 1 | .50 | 8 | .214 | .275 | .339 |

## Dave Stewart

**Pitches:** Right **Bats:** Right **Pos:** SP **Ht:** 6' 2" **Wt:** 200 **Born:** 02/19/57 **Age:** 34

| HOW MUCH HE PITCHED | | | | | | | | | WHAT HE GAVE UP | | | | | | | | | | | | THE RESULTS | | | | | |
|---|---|---|---|---|---|---|---|---|---|---|---|---|---|---|---|---|---|---|---|---|---|---|---|---|---|---|
| Year | Team | Lg | G | GS | CG | GF | IP | BFP | H | R | ER | HR | SH | SF | HB | TBB | IBB | SO | WP | Bk | W | L | Pct. | ShO | Sv | ERA |
| 1978 | Los Angeles | NL | 1 | 0 | 0 | 1 | 2 | 6 | 1 | 0 | 0 | 0 | 0 | 0 | 0 | 0 | 0 | 1 | 0 | 0 | 0 | 0 | .000 | 0 | 0 | 0.00 |
| 1981 | Los Angeles | NL | 32 | 0 | 0 | 14 | 43 | 184 | 40 | 13 | 12 | 3 | 7 | 3 | 0 | 14 | 5 | 29 | 4 | 0 | 4 | 3 | .571 | 0 | 6 | 2.51 |
| 1982 | Los Angeles | NL | 45 | 14 | 0 | 9 | 146.1 | 616 | 137 | 72 | 62 | 14 | 10 | 5 | 2 | 49 | 11 | 80 | 3 | 0 | 9 | 8 | .529 | 0 | 1 | 3.81 |
| 1983 | 2 ML Teams | | 54 | 9 | 2 | 25 | 135 | 565 | 117 | 43 | 39 | 6 | 9 | 4 | 4 | 50 | 7 | 78 | 3 | 0 | 10 | 4 | .714 | 0 | 8 | 2.60 |
| 1984 | Texas | AL | 32 | 27 | 3 | 2 | 192.1 | 847 | 193 | 106 | 101 | 26 | 4 | 5 | 4 | 87 | 3 | 119 | 12 | 0 | 7 | 14 | .333 | 0 | 0 | 4.73 |
| 1985 | 2 ML Teams | | 46 | 5 | 0 | 32 | 85.2 | 383 | 91 | 57 | 52 | 13 | 5 | 2 | 2 | 41 | 5 | 66 | 7 | 1 | 0 | 6 | .000 | 0 | 4 | 5.46 |
| 1986 | 2 ML Teams | | 37 | 17 | 4 | 4 | 161.2 | 700 | 152 | 76 | 71 | 16 | 4 | 7 | 3 | 69 | 0 | 111 | 10 | 3 | 9 | 5 | .643 | 1 | 0 | 3.95 |
| 1987 | Oakland | AL | 37 | 37 | 8 | 0 | 261.1 | 1103 | 224 | 121 | 107 | 24 | 7 | 5 | 6 | 105 | 2 | 205 | 11 | 0 | 20 | 13 | .606 | 1 | 0 | 3.68 |
| 1988 | Oakland | AL | 37 | 37 | 14 | 0 | 275.2 | 1156 | 240 | 111 | 99 | 14 | 7 | 9 | 3 | 110 | 5 | 192 | 14 | 16 | 21 | 12 | .636 | 2 | 0 | 3.23 |
| 1989 | Oakland | AL | 36 | 36 | 8 | 0 | 257.2 | 1081 | 260 | 105 | 95 | 23 | 9 | 10 | 6 | 69 | 0 | 155 | 13 | 0 | 21 | 9 | .700 | 0 | 0 | 3.32 |
| 1990 | Oakland | AL | 36 | 36 | 11 | 0 | 267 | 1088 | 226 | 84 | 76 | 16 | 10 | 10 | 5 | 83 | 1 | 166 | 8 | 0 | 22 | 11 | .667 | 4 | 0 | 2.56 |
| 1983 | Los Angeles | NL | 46 | 1 | 0 | 25 | 76 | 328 | 67 | 28 | 25 | 4 | 7 | 3 | 2 | 33 | 7 | 54 | 2 | 0 | 5 | 2 | .714 | 0 | 8 | 2.96 |
| | Texas | AL | 8 | 8 | 2 | 0 | 59 | 237 | 50 | 15 | 14 | 2 | 2 | 1 | 2 | 17 | 0 | 24 | 1 | 0 | 5 | 2 | .714 | 0 | 0 | 2.14 |
| 1985 | Texas | AL | 42 | 5 | 0 | 29 | 81.1 | 361 | 86 | 53 | 49 | 13 | 5 | 2 | 2 | 37 | 5 | 64 | 5 | 1 | 0 | 6 | .000 | 0 | 4 | 5.42 |
| | Philadelphia | NL | 4 | 0 | 0 | 3 | 4.1 | 22 | 5 | 4 | 3 | 0 | 0 | 0 | 0 | 4 | 0 | 2 | 2 | 0 | 0 | 0 | .000 | 0 | 0 | 6.23 |
| 1986 | Philadelphia | NL | 8 | 0 | 0 | 2 | 12.1 | 56 | 15 | 9 | 9 | 1 | 0 | 3 | 0 | 4 | 0 | 9 | 1 | 3 | 0 | 0 | .000 | 0 | 0 | 6.57 |
| | Oakland | AL | 29 | 17 | 4 | 2 | 149.1 | 644 | 137 | 67 | 62 | 15 | 4 | 4 | 3 | 65 | 0 | 102 | 9 | 0 | 9 | 5 | .643 | 1 | 0 | 3.74 |
| | 11 ML YEARS | | 393 | 218 | 50 | 87 | 1827.2 | 7729 | 1681 | 788 | 714 | 155 | 72 | 60 | 35 | 677 | 39 | 1202 | 85 | 20 | 123 | 85 | .591 | 8 | 19 | 3.52 |

## Dave Stieb

**Pitches:** Right **Bats:** Right **Pos:** SP **Ht:** 6' 0" **Wt:** 195 **Born:** 07/22/57 **Age:** 33

| | | HOW MUCH HE PITCHED | | | | | | WHAT HE GAVE UP | | | | | | | | | | | | THE RESULTS | | | | | |
|---|---|---|---|---|---|---|---|---|---|---|---|---|---|---|---|---|---|---|---|---|---|---|---|---|---|
| Year Team | Lg | G | GS | CG | GF | IP | BFP | H | R | ER | HR | SH | SF | HB | TBB | IBB | SO | WP | Bk | W | L | Pct. | ShO | Sv | ERA |
| 1979 Toronto | AL | 18 | 18 | 7 | 0 | 129 | 563 | 139 | 70 | 62 | 11 | 4 | 4 | 4 | 48 | 3 | 52 | 3 | 1 | 8 | 8 | .500 | 1 | 0 | 4.33 |
| 1980 Toronto | AL | 34 | 32 | 14 | 0 | 243 | 1004 | 232 | 108 | 100 | 12 | 12 | 9 | 6 | 83 | 6 | 108 | 6 | 2 | 12 | 15 | .444 | 4 | 0 | 3.70 |
| 1981 Toronto | AL | 25 | 25 | 11 | 0 | 184 | 748 | 148 | 70 | 65 | 10 | 5 | 7 | 11 | 61 | 2 | 89 | 1 | 2 | 11 | 10 | .524 | 2 | 0 | 3.18 |
| 1982 Toronto | AL | 38 | 38 | 19 | 0 | 288.1 | 1187 | 271 | 116 | 104 | 27 | 10 | 3 | 5 | 75 | 4 | 141 | 3 | 1 | 17 | 14 | .548 | 5 | 0 | 3.25 |
| 1983 Toronto | AL | 36 | 36 | 14 | 0 | 278 | 1141 | 223 | 105 | 94 | 21 | 6 | 9 | 14 | 93 | 6 | 187 | 5 | 1 | 17 | 12 | .586 | 4 | 0 | 3.04 |
| 1984 Toronto | AL | 35 | 35 | 11 | 0 | 267 | 1085 | 215 | 87 | 84 | 19 | 8 | 6 | 11 | 88 | 1 | 198 | 2 | 0 | 16 | 8 | .667 | 2 | 0 | 2.83 |
| 1985 Toronto | AL | 36 | 36 | 8 | 0 | 265 | 1087 | 206 | 89 | 73 | 22 | 14 | 2 | 9 | 96 | 3 | 167 | 4 | 1 | 14 | 13 | .519 | 2 | 0 | 2.48 |
| 1986 Toronto | AL | 37 | 34 | 1 | 2 | 205 | 919 | 239 | 128 | 108 | 29 | 6 | 6 | 15 | 87 | 1 | 127 | 7 | 0 | 7 | 12 | .368 | 1 | 1 | 4.74 |
| 1987 Toronto | AL | 33 | 31 | 3 | 1 | 185 | 789 | 164 | 92 | 84 | 16 | 5 | 5 | 7 | 87 | 4 | 115 | 4 | 0 | 13 | 9 | .591 | 1 | 0 | 4.09 |
| 1988 Toronto | AL | 32 | 31 | 8 | 1 | 207.1 | 844 | 157 | 76 | 70 | 15 | 0 | 4 | 13 | 79 | 0 | 147 | 4 | 5 | 16 | 8 | .667 | 4 | 0 | 3.04 |
| 1989 Toronto | AL | 33 | 33 | 3 | 0 | 206.2 | 850 | 164 | 83 | 77 | 12 | 10 | 3 | 13 | 76 | 2 | 101 | 3 | 1 | 17 | 8 | .680 | 2 | 0 | 3.35 |
| 1990 Toronto | AL | 33 | 33 | 2 | 0 | 208.2 | 861 | 179 | 73 | 68 | 11 | 6 | 3 | 10 | 64 | 0 | 125 | 5 | 0 | 18 | 6 | .750 | 2 | 0 | 2.93 |
| 12 ML YEARS | | 390 | 382 | 101 | 4 | 2667 | 11078 | 2337 | 1097 | 989 | 205 | 86 | 61 | 118 | 937 | 32 | 1557 | 47 | 14 | 166 | 123 | .574 | 30 | 1 | 3.34 |

## Kurt Stillwell

**Bats:** Both **Throws:** Right **Pos:** SS **Ht:** 5'11" **Wt:** 175 **Born:** 06/04/65 **Age:** 26

| | | BATTING | | | | | | | | | | | | | | | | BASERUNNING | | | | PERCENTAGES | | |
|---|---|---|---|---|---|---|---|---|---|---|---|---|---|---|---|---|---|---|---|---|---|---|---|---|
| Year Team | Lg | G | AB | H | 2B | 3B | HR | (Hm | Rd) | TB | R | RBI | TBB | IBB | SO | HBP | SH | SF | SB | CS | SB% | GDP | Avg | OBP | SLG |
| 1986 Cincinnati | NL | 104 | 279 | 64 | 6 | 1 | 0 | (0 | 0) | 72 | 31 | 26 | 30 | 1 | 47 | 2 | 4 | 0 | 6 | 2 | .75 | 5 | .229 | .309 | .258 |
| 1987 Cincinnati | NL | 131 | 395 | 102 | 20 | 7 | 4 | (3 | 1) | 148 | 54 | 33 | 32 | 2 | 50 | 2 | 2 | 2 | 4 | 6 | .40 | 5 | .258 | .316 | .375 |
| 1988 Kansas City | AL | 128 | 459 | 115 | 28 | 5 | 10 | (4 | 6) | 183 | 63 | 53 | 47 | 0 | 76 | 3 | 6 | 3 | 6 | 5 | .55 | 7 | .251 | .322 | .399 |
| 1989 Kansas City | AL | 130 | 463 | 121 | 20 | 7 | 7 | (2 | 5) | 176 | 52 | 54 | 42 | 2 | 64 | 3 | 5 | 3 | 9 | 6 | .60 | 3 | .261 | .325 | .380 |
| 1990 Kansas City | AL | 144 | 506 | 126 | 35 | 4 | 3 | (3 | 0) | 178 | 60 | 51 | 39 | 1 | 60 | 4 | 4 | 7 | 0 | 2 | .00 | 11 | .249 | .304 | .352 |
| 5 ML YEARS | | 637 | 2102 | 528 | 109 | 24 | 24 | (12 | 12) | 757 | 260 | 217 | 190 | 6 | 297 | 14 | 21 | 15 | 25 | 21 | .54 | 31 | .251 | .315 | .360 |

## Jeff Stone

**Bats:** Left **Throws:** Right **Pos:** DH **Ht:** 6' 0" **Wt:** 180 **Born:** 12/26/60 **Age:** 30

| | | BATTING | | | | | | | | | | | | | | | | BASERUNNING | | | | PERCENTAGES | | |
|---|---|---|---|---|---|---|---|---|---|---|---|---|---|---|---|---|---|---|---|---|---|---|---|---|
| Year Team | Lg | G | AB | H | 2B | 3B | HR | (Hm | Rd) | TB | R | RBI | TBB | IBB | SO | HBP | SH | SF | SB | CS | SB% | GDP | Avg | OBP | SLG |
| 1983 Philadelphia | NL | 9 | 4 | 3 | 0 | 2 | 0 | (0 | 0) | 7 | 2 | 3 | 0 | 0 | 1 | 0 | 0 | 0 | 4 | 0 | 1.00 | 0 | .750 | .750 | 1.750 |
| 1984 Philadelphia | NL | 51 | 185 | 67 | 4 | 6 | 1 | (1 | 0) | 86 | 27 | 15 | 9 | 0 | 26 | 2 | 1 | 2 | 27 | 5 | .84 | 2 | .362 | .394 | .465 |
| 1985 Philadelphia | NL | 88 | 264 | 70 | 4 | 3 | 3 | (2 | 1) | 89 | 36 | 11 | 15 | 0 | 50 | 1 | 2 | 0 | 15 | 5 | .75 | 3 | .265 | .307 | .337 |
| 1986 Philadelphia | NL | 82 | 249 | 69 | 6 | 4 | 6 | (4 | 2) | 101 | 32 | 19 | 20 | 0 | 52 | 4 | 2 | 0 | 19 | 6 | .76 | 3 | .277 | .341 | .406 |
| 1987 Philadelphia | NL | 66 | 125 | 32 | 7 | 1 | 1 | (1 | 0) | 44 | 19 | 16 | 8 | 0 | 38 | 3 | 0 | 0 | 3 | 1 | .75 | 2 | .256 | .316 | .352 |
| 1988 Baltimore | AL | 26 | 61 | 10 | 1 | 0 | 0 | (0 | 0) | 11 | 4 | 1 | 4 | 0 | 11 | 0 | 1 | 0 | 4 | 1 | .80 | 3 | .164 | .215 | .180 |
| 1989 2 ML Teams | | 40 | 51 | 9 | 1 | 2 | 0 | (0 | 0) | 14 | 8 | 6 | 4 | 1 | 7 | 1 | 1 | 1 | 3 | 1 | .75 | 3 | .176 | .246 | .275 |
| 1990 Boston | AL | 10 | 2 | 1 | 0 | 0 | 0 | (0 | 0) | 1 | 1 | 1 | 0 | 0 | 1 | 0 | 0 | 0 | 0 | 1 | .00 | 0 | .500 | .500 | .500 |
| 1989 Texas | AL | 22 | 36 | 6 | 1 | 2 | 0 | (0 | 0) | 11 | 5 | 5 | 3 | 0 | 5 | 1 | 1 | 0 | 2 | 1 | .67 | 2 | .167 | .250 | .306 |
| Boston | AL | 18 | 15 | 3 | 0 | 0 | 0 | (0 | 0) | 3 | 3 | 1 | 1 | 1 | 2 | 0 | 0 | 1 | 1 | 0 | 1.00 | 1 | .200 | .235 | .200 |
| 8 ML YEARS | | 372 | 941 | 261 | 23 | 18 | 11 | (8 | 3) | 353 | 129 | 72 | 60 | 1 | 186 | 11 | 7 | 3 | 75 | 20 | .79 | 16 | .277 | .327 | .375 |

## Mel Stottlemyre

**Pitches:** Right **Bats:** Right **Pos:** RP **Ht:** 6' 0" **Wt:** 190 **Born:** 12/28/63 **Age:** 27

| | | HOW MUCH HE PITCHED | | | | | | WHAT HE GAVE UP | | | | | | | | | | | | THE RESULTS | | | | | |
|---|---|---|---|---|---|---|---|---|---|---|---|---|---|---|---|---|---|---|---|---|---|---|---|---|---|
| Year Team | Lg | G | GS | CG | GF | IP | BFP | H | R | ER | HR | SH | SF | HB | TBB | IBB | SO | WP | Bk | W | L | Pct. | ShO | Sv | ERA |
| 1985 Asheville | A | 14 | 13 | 1 | 0 | 78.2 | 330 | 65 | 33 | 24 | 4 | 3 | 3 | 2 | 38 | 0 | 70 | 4 | 4 | 5 | 4 | .556 | 0 | 0 | 2.75 |
| 1986 Osceola | A | 9 | 8 | 0 | 0 | 35.2 | 178 | 48 | 38 | 31 | 3 | 4 | 2 | 1 | 26 | 0 | 25 | 5 | 1 | 0 | 7 | .000 | 0 | 0 | 7.82 |
| Asheville | A | 7 | 7 | 2 | 0 | 34.1 | 152 | 32 | 13 | 8 | 3 | 3 | 2 | 3 | 12 | 0 | 28 | 2 | 0 | 3 | 1 | .750 | 1 | 0 | 2.10 |
| 1987 Columbus | AA | 19 | 19 | 4 | 0 | 123.2 | 527 | 121 | 66 | 59 | 10 | 11 | 3 | 7 | 40 | 2 | 83 | 1 | 2 | 7 | 6 | .538 | 1 | 0 | 4.29 |
| Memphis | AA | 1 | 1 | 0 | 0 | 3.2 | 17 | 4 | 2 | 2 | 2 | 0 | 0 | 1 | 1 | 0 | 2 | 1 | 0 | 0 | 0 | .000 | 0 | 0 | 4.91 |
| 1988 Memphis | AA | 7 | 7 | 1 | 0 | 45 | 186 | 41 | 18 | 12 | 1 | 5 | 0 | 1 | 14 | 0 | 29 | 1 | 5 | 3 | 2 | .600 | 0 | 0 | 2.40 |
| 1989 Baseball Cy | A | 13 | 2 | 0 | 6 | 23.2 | 111 | 30 | 14 | 13 | 1 | 1 | 1 | 1 | 9 | 2 | 25 | 3 | 2 | 1 | 2 | .333 | 0 | 4 | 4.94 |
| Memphis | AA | 16 | 0 | 0 | 11 | 22.2 | 91 | 15 | 4 | 4 | 0 | 0 | 0 | 0 | 9 | 0 | 18 | 1 | 3 | 3 | 0 | 1.000 | 0 | 6 | 1.59 |
| Omaha | AAA | 7 | 0 | 0 | 6 | 7.2 | 33 | 6 | 4 | 2 | 1 | 0 | 0 | 0 | 3 | 0 | 9 | 1 | 2 | 1 | 1 | .500 | 0 | 1 | 2.35 |
| 1990 Omaha | AAA | 29 | 0 | 0 | 19 | 41.2 | 160 | 26 | 9 | 7 | 0 | 5 | 1 | 0 | 11 | 1 | 33 | 1 | 4 | 2 | 1 | .667 | 0 | 13 | 1.51 |
| 1990 Kansas City | AL | 13 | 2 | 0 | 3 | 31.1 | 138 | 35 | 18 | 17 | 3 | 1 | 0 | 0 | 12 | 1 | 14 | 0 | 0 | 0 | 1 | .000 | 0 | 0 | 4.88 |

## Todd Stottlemyre

**Pitches:** Right **Bats:** Left **Pos:** SP **Ht:** 6' 0" **Wt:** 190 **Born:** 05/20/65 **Age:** 26

| | | HOW MUCH HE PITCHED | | | | | | WHAT HE GAVE UP | | | | | | | | | | | | THE RESULTS | | | | | |
|---|---|---|---|---|---|---|---|---|---|---|---|---|---|---|---|---|---|---|---|---|---|---|---|---|---|
| Year Team | Lg | G | GS | CG | GF | IP | BFP | H | R | ER | HR | SH | SF | HB | TBB | IBB | SO | WP | Bk | W | L | Pct. | ShO | Sv | ERA |
| 1988 Toronto | AL | 28 | 16 | 0 | 2 | 98 | 443 | 109 | 70 | 62 | 15 | 5 | 3 | 4 | 46 | 5 | 67 | 2 | 3 | 4 | 8 | .333 | 0 | 0 | 5.69 |
| 1989 Toronto | AL | 27 | 18 | 0 | 4 | 127.2 | 545 | 137 | 56 | 55 | 11 | 3 | 7 | 5 | 44 | 4 | 63 | 4 | 1 | 7 | 7 | .500 | 0 | 0 | 3.88 |

| | | | | | | | | | | | | | | | | | | | | | | | |
|---|---|---|---|---|---|---|---|---|---|---|---|---|---|---|---|---|---|---|---|---|---|---|---|
| 1990 Toronto | AL | 33 | 33 | 4 | 0 | 203 | 866 | 214 | 101 | 98 | 18 | 3 | 5 | 8 | 69 | 4 | 115 | 6 | 1 | 13 | 17 | .433 | 0 | 0 | 4.34 |
| 3 ML YEARS | | 88 | 67 | 4 | 6 | 428.2 | 1854 | 460 | 227 | 215 | 44 | 11 | 15 | 17 | 159 | 13 | 245 | 12 | 5 | 24 | 32 | .429 | 0 | 0 | 4.51 |

## Darryl Strawberry

**Bats:** Left **Throws:** Left **Pos:** RF **Ht:** 6' 6" **Wt:** 195 **Born:** 03/12/62 **Age:** 29

| BATTING | | | | | | | | | | | | | | | | | | | | | BASERUNNING | | | | PERCENTAGES | | |
|---|---|---|---|---|---|---|---|---|---|---|---|---|---|---|---|---|---|---|---|---|---|---|---|---|---|---|---|
| Year Team | Lg | G | AB | H | 2B | 3B | HR | (Hm | Rd) | TB | R | RBI | TBB | IBB | SO | HBP | SH | SF | SB | CS | SB% | GDP | Avg | OBP | SLG |
| 1983 New York | NL | 122 | 420 | 108 | 15 | 7 | 26 | (10 | 16) | 215 | 63 | 74 | 47 | 9 | 128 | 4 | 0 | 2 | 19 | 6 | .76 | 5 | .257 | .336 | .512 |
| 1984 New York | NL | 147 | 522 | 131 | 27 | 4 | 26 | (8 | 18) | 244 | 75 | 97 | 75 | 15 | 131 | 0 | 1 | 4 | 27 | 8 | .77 | 8 | .251 | .343 | .467 |
| 1985 New York | NL | 111 | 393 | 109 | 15 | 4 | 29 | (14 | 15) | 219 | 78 | 79 | 73 | 13 | 96 | 1 | 0 | 3 | 26 | 11 | .70 | 9 | .277 | .389 | .557 |
| 1986 New York | NL | 136 | 475 | 123 | 27 | 5 | 27 | (11 | 16) | 241 | 76 | 93 | 72 | 9 | 141 | 6 | 0 | 9 | 28 | 12 | .70 | 4 | .259 | .358 | .507 |
| 1987 New York | NL | 154 | 532 | 151 | 32 | 5 | 39 | (20 | 19) | 310 | 108 | 104 | 97 | 13 | 122 | 7 | 0 | 4 | 36 | 12 | .75 | 4 | .284 | .398 | .583 |
| 1988 New York | NL | 153 | 543 | 146 | 27 | 3 | 39 | (21 | 18) | 296 | 101 | 101 | 85 | 21 | 127 | 3 | 0 | 9 | 29 | 14 | .67 | 6 | .269 | .366 | .545 |
| 1989 New York | NL | 134 | 476 | 107 | 26 | 1 | 29 | (15 | 14) | 222 | 69 | 77 | 61 | 13 | 105 | 1 | 0 | 3 | 11 | 4 | .73 | 4 | .225 | .312 | .466 |
| 1990 New York | NL | 152 | 542 | 150 | 18 | 1 | 37 | (24 | 13) | 281 | 92 | 108 | 70 | 15 | 110 | 4 | 0 | 5 | 15 | 8 | .65 | 5 | .277 | .361 | .518 |
| 8 ML YEARS | | 1109 | 3903 | 1025 | 187 | 30 | 252 | (123 | 129) | 2028 | 662 | 733 | 580 | 108 | 960 | 26 | 1 | 39 | 191 | 75 | .72 | 45 | .263 | .359 | .520 |

## Franklin Stubbs

**Bats:** Left **Throws:** Left **Pos:** 1B/LF **Ht:** 6' 2" **Wt:** 218 **Born:** 10/21/60 **Age:** 30

| BATTING | | | | | | | | | | | | | | | | | | | | | BASERUNNING | | | | PERCENTAGES | | |
|---|---|---|---|---|---|---|---|---|---|---|---|---|---|---|---|---|---|---|---|---|---|---|---|---|---|---|---|
| Year Team | Lg | G | AB | H | 2B | 3B | HR | (Hm | Rd) | TB | R | RBI | TBB | IBB | SO | HBP | SH | SF | SB | CS | SB% | GDP | Avg | OBP | SLG |
| 1984 Los Angeles | NL | 87 | 217 | 42 | 2 | 3 | 8 | (4 | 4) | 74 | 22 | 17 | 24 | 3 | 63 | 0 | 3 | 1 | 2 | 2 | .50 | 0 | .194 | .273 | .341 |
| 1985 Los Angeles | NL | 10 | 9 | 2 | 0 | 0 | 0 | (0 | 0) | 2 | 0 | 2 | 0 | 0 | 3 | 0 | 0 | 0 | 0 | 0 | .00 | 0 | .222 | .222 | .222 |
| 1986 Los Angeles | NL | 132 | 420 | 95 | 11 | 1 | 23 | (12 | 11) | 177 | 55 | 58 | 37 | 11 | 107 | 2 | 4 | 2 | 7 | 1 | .88 | 9 | .226 | .291 | .421 |
| 1987 Los Angeles | NL | 129 | 386 | 90 | 16 | 3 | 16 | (6 | 10) | 160 | 48 | 52 | 31 | 9 | 85 | 1 | 3 | 2 | 8 | 1 | .89 | 7 | .233 | .290 | .415 |
| 1988 Los Angeles | NL | 115 | 242 | 54 | 13 | 0 | 8 | (3 | 5) | 91 | 30 | 34 | 23 | 3 | 61 | 1 | 2 | 5 | 11 | 3 | .79 | 4 | .223 | .288 | .376 |
| 1989 Los Angeles | NL | 69 | 103 | 30 | 6 | 0 | 4 | (1 | 3) | 48 | 11 | 15 | 16 | 2 | 27 | 0 | 1 | 0 | 3 | 2 | .60 | 3 | .291 | .387 | .466 |
| 1990 Houston | NL | 146 | 448 | 117 | 23 | 2 | 23 | (9 | 14) | 213 | 59 | 71 | 48 | 3 | 114 | 2 | 1 | 2 | 19 | 6 | .76 | 4 | .261 | .334 | .475 |
| 7 ML YEARS | | 688 | 1825 | 430 | 71 | 9 | 82 | (35 | 47) | 765 | 225 | 249 | 179 | 31 | 460 | 6 | 14 | 12 | 50 | 15 | .77 | 27 | .236 | .304 | .419 |

## B.J. Surhoff

**Bats:** Left **Throws:** Right **Pos:** C **Ht:** 6' 1" **Wt:** 190 **Born:** 08/04/64 **Age:** 26

| BATTING | | | | | | | | | | | | | | | | | | | | | BASERUNNING | | | | PERCENTAGES | | |
|---|---|---|---|---|---|---|---|---|---|---|---|---|---|---|---|---|---|---|---|---|---|---|---|---|---|---|---|
| Year Team | Lg | G | AB | H | 2B | 3B | HR | (Hm | Rd) | TB | R | RBI | TBB | IBB | SO | HBP | SH | SF | SB | CS | SB% | GDP | Avg | OBP | SLG |
| 1987 Milwaukee | AL | 115 | 395 | 118 | 22 | 3 | 7 | (5 | 2) | 167 | 50 | 68 | 36 | 1 | 30 | 0 | 5 | 9 | 11 | 10 | .52 | 13 | .299 | .350 | .423 |
| 1988 Milwaukee | AL | 139 | 493 | 121 | 21 | 0 | 5 | (2 | 3) | 157 | 47 | 38 | 31 | 9 | 49 | 3 | 11 | 3 | 21 | 6 | .78 | 12 | .245 | .292 | .318 |
| 1989 Milwaukee | AL | 126 | 436 | 108 | 17 | 4 | 5 | (3 | 2) | 148 | 42 | 55 | 25 | 1 | 29 | 3 | 3 | 10 | 14 | 12 | .54 | 8 | .248 | .287 | .339 |
| 1990 Milwaukee | AL | 135 | 474 | 131 | 21 | 4 | 6 | (4 | 2) | 178 | 55 | 59 | 41 | 5 | 37 | 1 | 7 | 7 | 18 | 7 | .72 | 8 | .276 | .331 | .376 |
| 4 ML YEARS | | 515 | 1798 | 478 | 81 | 11 | 23 | (14 | 9) | 650 | 194 | 220 | 133 | 16 | 145 | 7 | 26 | 29 | 64 | 35 | .65 | 41 | .266 | .314 | .362 |

## Rick Sutcliffe

**Pitches:** Right **Bats:** Left **Pos:** SP **Ht:** 6' 7" **Wt:** 215 **Born:** 06/21/56 **Age:** 35

| HOW MUCH HE PITCHED | | | | | | | | WHAT HE GAVE UP | | | | | | | | | | | | THE RESULTS | | | | | |
|---|---|---|---|---|---|---|---|---|---|---|---|---|---|---|---|---|---|---|---|---|---|---|---|---|---|
| Year Team | Lg | G | GS | CG | GF | IP | BFP | H | R | ER | HR | SH | SF | HB | TBB | IBB | SO | WP | Bk | W | L | Pct. | ShO | Sv | ERA |
| 1976 Los Angeles | NL | 1 | 1 | 0 | 0 | 5 | 17 | 2 | 0 | 0 | 0 | 0 | 0 | 0 | 1 | 0 | 3 | 0 | 0 | 0 | 0 | .000 | 0 | 0 | 0.00 |
| 1978 Los Angeles | NL | 2 | 0 | 0 | 0 | 2 | 9 | 2 | 0 | 0 | 0 | 0 | 0 | 1 | 1 | 0 | 0 | 0 | 0 | 0 | 0 | .000 | 0 | 0 | 0.00 |
| 1979 Los Angeles | NL | 39 | 30 | 5 | 2 | 242 | 1016 | 217 | 104 | 93 | 16 | 16 | 9 | 2 | 97 | 6 | 117 | 8 | 6 | 17 | 10 | .630 | 1 | 0 | 3.46 |
| 1980 Los Angeles | NL | 42 | 10 | 1 | 19 | 110 | 491 | 122 | 73 | 68 | 10 | 4 | 3 | 1 | 55 | 2 | 59 | 4 | 5 | 3 | 9 | .250 | 1 | 5 | 5.56 |
| 1981 Los Angeles | NL | 14 | 6 | 0 | 5 | 47 | 197 | 41 | 24 | 21 | 5 | 1 | 2 | 2 | 20 | 2 | 16 | 0 | 0 | 2 | 2 | .500 | 0 | 0 | 4.02 |
| 1982 Cleveland | AL | 34 | 27 | 6 | 3 | 216 | 887 | 174 | 81 | 71 | 16 | 7 | 8 | 4 | 98 | 2 | 142 | 6 | 1 | 14 | 8 | .636 | 1 | 1 | 2.96 |
| 1983 Cleveland | AL | 36 | 35 | 10 | 0 | 243.1 | 1061 | 251 | 131 | 116 | 23 | 8 | 9 | 6 | 102 | 5 | 160 | 7 | 3 | 17 | 11 | .607 | 2 | 0 | 4.29 |
| 1984 2 ML Teams | | 35 | 35 | 9 | 0 | 244.2 | 1030 | 234 | 113 | 99 | 16 | 5 | 4 | 3 | 85 | 3 | 213 | 6 | 3 | 20 | 6 | .769 | 3 | 0 | 3.64 |
| 1985 Chicago | NL | 20 | 20 | 6 | 0 | 130 | 549 | 119 | 51 | 46 | 12 | 3 | 4 | 3 | 44 | 3 | 102 | 6 | 0 | 8 | 8 | .500 | 3 | 0 | 3.18 |
| 1986 Chicago | NL | 28 | 27 | 4 | 0 | 176.2 | 764 | 166 | 92 | 91 | 18 | 6 | 2 | 1 | 96 | 8 | 122 | 13 | 1 | 5 | 14 | .263 | 1 | 0 | 4.64 |
| 1987 Chicago | NL | 34 | 34 | 6 | 0 | 237.1 | 1012 | 223 | 106 | 97 | 24 | 9 | 8 | 4 | 106 | 14 | 174 | 9 | 4 | 18 | 10 | .643 | 1 | 0 | 3.68 |
| 1988 Chicago | NL | 32 | 32 | 12 | 0 | 226 | 958 | 232 | 97 | 97 | 18 | 17 | 5 | 2 | 70 | 9 | 144 | 11 | 4 | 13 | 14 | .481 | 2 | 0 | 3.86 |
| 1989 Chicago | NL | 35 | 34 | 5 | 0 | 229 | 938 | 202 | 98 | 93 | 18 | 15 | 10 | 2 | 69 | 8 | 153 | 12 | 6 | 16 | 11 | .593 | 1 | 0 | 3.66 |
| 1990 Chicago | NL | 5 | 5 | 0 | 0 | 21.1 | 97 | 25 | 14 | 14 | 2 | 1 | 2 | 0 | 12 | 0 | 7 | 4 | 0 | 0 | 2 | .000 | 0 | 0 | 5.91 |
| 1984 Cleveland | AL | 15 | 15 | 2 | 0 | 94.1 | 428 | 111 | 60 | 54 | 7 | 4 | 3 | 2 | 46 | 3 | 58 | 3 | 1 | 4 | 5 | .444 | 0 | 0 | 5.15 |
| Chicago | NL | 20 | 20 | 7 | 0 | 150.1 | 602 | 123 | 53 | 45 | 9 | 1 | 1 | 1 | 39 | 0 | 155 | 3 | 2 | 16 | 1 | .941 | 3 | 0 | 2.69 |
| 14 ML YEARS | | 357 | 296 | 64 | 29 | 2130.1 | 9026 | 2010 | 984 | 906 | 178 | 92 | 66 | 31 | 856 | 62 | 1412 | 86 | 33 | 133 | 105 | .559 | 16 | 6 | 3.83 |

## Glenn Sutko

**Bats:** Right **Throws:** Right **Pos:** C **Ht:** 6' 3" **Wt:** 225 **Born:** 05/09/68 **Age:** 23

| BATTING | | | | | | | | | | | | | | | | | | | BASERUNNING | | | | PERCENTAGES | | |
|---|---|---|---|---|---|---|---|---|---|---|---|---|---|---|---|---|---|---|---|---|---|---|---|---|---|
| Year Team | Lg | G | AB | H | 2B | 3B | HR | (Hm | Rd) | TB | R | RBI | TBB | IBB | SO | HBP | SH | SF | SB | CS | SB% | GDP | Avg | OBP | SLG |
| 1988 Billings | R | 30 | 84 | 13 | 2 | 1 | 1 | -- | -- | 20 | 3 | 8 | 14 | 0 | 38 | 1 | 3 | 2 | 3 | 1 | .75 | 2 | .155 | .277 | .238 |
| 1989 Greensboro | A | 109 | 333 | 78 | 21 | 0 | 7 | -- | -- | 120 | 44 | 41 | 47 | 1 | 105 | 4 | 0 | 3 | 1 | 3 | .25 | 5 | .234 | .333 | .360 |
| 1990 Cedar Rapds | A | 4 | 10 | 3 | 0 | 0 | 0 | -- | -- | 3 | 0 | 0 | 0 | 0 | 2 | 1 | 0 | 0 | 0 | 0 | .00 | 1 | .300 | .364 | .300 |
| Chattanooga | AA | 53 | 174 | 29 | 7 | 1 | 2 | -- | -- | 44 | 12 | 11 | 8 | 1 | 66 | 1 | 0 | 0 | 1 | 1 | .50 | 2 | .167 | .208 | .253 |
| 1990 Cincinnati | NL | 1 | 1 | 0 | 0 | 0 | 0 | (0 | 0) | 0 | 0 | 0 | 0 | 0 | 1 | 0 | 0 | 0 | 0 | 0 | .00 | 0 | .000 | .000 | .000 |

## Dale Sveum

**Bats:** Both **Throws:** Right **Pos:** 3B/2B **Ht:** 6' 3" **Wt:** 185 **Born:** 11/23/63 **Age:** 27

| BATTING | | | | | | | | | | | | | | | | | | | BASERUNNING | | | | PERCENTAGES | | |
|---|---|---|---|---|---|---|---|---|---|---|---|---|---|---|---|---|---|---|---|---|---|---|---|---|---|
| Year Team | Lg | G | AB | H | 2B | 3B | HR | (Hm | Rd) | TB | R | RBI | TBB | IBB | SO | HBP | SH | SF | SB | CS | SB% | GDP | Avg | OBP | SLG |
| 1986 Milwaukee | AL | 91 | 317 | 78 | 13 | 2 | 7 | (4 | 3) | 116 | 35 | 35 | 32 | 0 | 63 | 1 | 5 | 1 | 4 | 3 | .57 | 7 | .246 | .316 | .366 |
| 1987 Milwaukee | AL | 153 | 535 | 135 | 27 | 3 | 25 | (9 | 16) | 243 | 86 | 95 | 40 | 4 | 133 | 1 | 5 | 5 | 2 | 6 | .25 | 11 | .252 | .303 | .454 |
| 1988 Milwaukee | AL | 129 | 467 | 113 | 14 | 4 | 9 | (2 | 7) | 162 | 41 | 51 | 21 | 0 | 122 | 1 | 3 | 3 | 1 | 0 | 1.00 | 6 | .242 | .274 | .347 |
| 1990 Milwaukee | AL | 48 | 117 | 23 | 7 | 0 | 1 | (1 | 0) | 33 | 15 | 12 | 12 | 0 | 30 | 2 | 0 | 2 | 0 | 1 | .00 | 2 | .197 | .278 | .282 |
| 4 ML YEARS | | 421 | 1436 | 349 | 61 | 9 | 42 | (16 | 26) | 554 | 177 | 193 | 105 | 4 | 348 | 5 | 13 | 11 | 7 | 10 | .41 | 26 | .243 | .295 | .386 |

## Russ Swan

**Pitches:** Left **Bats:** Left **Pos:** SP **Ht:** 6' 4" **Wt:** 210 **Born:** 01/03/64 **Age:** 27

| | | HOW MUCH HE PITCHED | | | | | | WHAT HE GAVE UP | | | | | | | | | | | | THE RESULTS | | | | | |
|---|---|---|---|---|---|---|---|---|---|---|---|---|---|---|---|---|---|---|---|---|---|---|---|---|---|
| Year Team | Lg | G | GS | CG | GF | IP | BFP | H | R | ER | HR | SH | SF | HB | TBB | IBB | SO | WP | Bk | W | L | Pct. | ShO | Sv | ERA |
| 1986 Everett | A | 7 | 7 | 2 | 0 | 46 | 0 | 30 | 17 | 11 | 2 | 0 | 0 | 1 | 22 | 0 | 45 | 1 | 1 | 5 | 0 | 1.000 | 0 | 0 | 2.15 |
| Clinton | A | 7 | 7 | 2 | 0 | 43.2 | 179 | 36 | 18 | 15 | 2 | 0 | 2 | 1 | 8 | 0 | 37 | 1 | 1 | 3 | 3 | .500 | 1 | 0 | 3.09 |
| 1987 Fresno | A | 12 | 12 | 0 | 0 | 64 | 274 | 54 | 40 | 27 | 5 | 4 | 0 | 1 | 29 | 0 | 59 | 4 | 0 | 6 | 3 | .667 | 0 | 0 | 3.80 |
| 1988 San Jose | A | 11 | 11 | 2 | 0 | 76.2 | 301 | 53 | 28 | 19 | 2 | 7 | 0 | 1 | 26 | 0 | 62 | 2 | 0 | 7 | 0 | 1.000 | 1 | 0 | 2.23 |
| 1989 Shreveport | AA | 11 | 11 | 0 | 0 | 75.1 | 304 | 62 | 25 | 22 | 2 | 1 | 1 | 1 | 22 | 1 | 56 | 3 | 2 | 2 | 3 | .400 | 0 | 0 | 2.63 |
| Phoenix | AAA | 14 | 13 | 1 | 0 | 83 | 348 | 75 | 37 | 31 | 8 | 5 | 2 | 3 | 29 | 0 | 49 | 2 | 3 | 4 | 3 | .571 | 0 | 0 | 3.36 |
| 1990 Phoenix | AAA | 6 | 6 | 0 | 0 | 33.2 | 153 | 41 | 17 | 13 | 1 | 1 | 1 | 2 | 15 | 0 | 21 | 1 | 1 | 2 | 4 | .333 | 0 | 0 | 3.48 |
| Calgary | AAA | 5 | 5 | 0 | 0 | 23 | 105 | 28 | 18 | 15 | 0 | 1 | 0 | 0 | 12 | 0 | 14 | 3 | 0 | 1 | 2 | .333 | 0 | 0 | 5.87 |
| 1989 San Francisco | NL | 2 | 2 | 0 | 0 | 6.2 | 34 | 11 | 10 | 8 | 4 | 2 | 0 | 0 | 4 | 0 | 2 | 0 | 0 | 0 | 2 | .000 | 0 | 0 | 10.80 |
| 1990 2 ML Teams | | 13 | 9 | 0 | 0 | 49.1 | 213 | 48 | 26 | 20 | 3 | 2 | 3 | 0 | 22 | 2 | 16 | 1 | 1 | 2 | 4 | .333 | 0 | 0 | 3.65 |
| 1990 San Francisco | NL | 2 | 1 | 0 | 0 | 2.1 | 18 | 6 | 4 | 1 | 0 | 0 | 0 | 0 | 4 | 0 | 1 | 1 | 0 | 0 | 1 | .000 | 0 | 0 | 3.86 |
| Seattle | AL | 11 | 8 | 0 | 0 | 47 | 195 | 42 | 22 | 19 | 3 | 2 | 3 | 0 | 18 | 2 | 15 | 0 | 1 | 2 | 3 | .400 | 0 | 0 | 3.64 |
| 2 ML YEARS | | 15 | 11 | 0 | 0 | 56 | 247 | 59 | 36 | 28 | 7 | 4 | 3 | 0 | 26 | 2 | 18 | 1 | 1 | 2 | 6 | .250 | 0 | 0 | 4.50 |

## Bill Swift

**Pitches:** Right **Bats:** Right **Pos:** RP/SP **Ht:** 6' 0" **Wt:** 180 **Born:** 10/27/61 **Age:** 29

| | | HOW MUCH HE PITCHED | | | | | | WHAT HE GAVE UP | | | | | | | | | | | | THE RESULTS | | | | | |
|---|---|---|---|---|---|---|---|---|---|---|---|---|---|---|---|---|---|---|---|---|---|---|---|---|---|
| Year Team | Lg | G | GS | CG | GF | IP | BFP | H | R | ER | HR | SH | SF | HB | TBB | IBB | SO | WP | Bk | W | L | Pct. | ShO | Sv | ERA |
| 1985 Seattle | AL | 23 | 21 | 0 | 0 | 120.2 | 532 | 131 | 71 | 64 | 8 | 6 | 3 | 5 | 48 | 5 | 55 | 5 | 3 | 6 | 10 | .375 | 0 | 0 | 4.77 |
| 1986 Seattle | AL | 29 | 17 | 1 | 3 | 115.1 | 534 | 148 | 85 | 70 | 5 | 5 | 3 | 7 | 55 | 2 | 55 | 2 | 1 | 2 | 9 | .182 | 0 | 0 | 5.46 |
| 1988 Seattle | AL | 38 | 24 | 6 | 4 | 174.2 | 757 | 199 | 99 | 89 | 10 | 5 | 3 | 8 | 65 | 3 | 47 | 6 | 2 | 8 | 12 | .400 | 1 | 0 | 4.59 |
| 1989 Seattle | AL | 37 | 16 | 0 | 7 | 130 | 551 | 140 | 72 | 64 | 7 | 4 | 3 | 2 | 38 | 4 | 45 | 4 | 1 | 7 | 3 | .700 | 0 | 1 | 4.43 |
| 1990 Seattle | AL | 55 | 8 | 0 | 18 | 128 | 533 | 135 | 46 | 34 | 4 | 5 | 4 | 7 | 21 | 6 | 42 | 8 | 3 | 6 | 4 | .600 | 0 | 6 | 2.39 |
| 5 ML YEARS | | 182 | 86 | 7 | 32 | 668.2 | 2907 | 753 | 373 | 321 | 34 | 25 | 16 | 29 | 227 | 20 | 244 | 25 | 10 | 29 | 38 | .433 | 1 | 7 | 4.32 |

## Greg Swindell

**Pitches:** Left **Bats:** Both **Pos:** SP **Ht:** 6' 3" **Wt:** 225 **Born:** 01/02/65 **Age:** 26

| | | HOW MUCH HE PITCHED | | | | | | WHAT HE GAVE UP | | | | | | | | | | | | THE RESULTS | | | | | |
|---|---|---|---|---|---|---|---|---|---|---|---|---|---|---|---|---|---|---|---|---|---|---|---|---|---|
| Year Team | Lg | G | GS | CG | GF | IP | BFP | H | R | ER | HR | SH | SF | HB | TBB | IBB | SO | WP | Bk | W | L | Pct. | ShO | Sv | ERA |
| 1986 Cleveland | AL | 9 | 9 | 1 | 0 | 61.2 | 255 | 57 | 35 | 29 | 9 | 3 | 1 | 1 | 15 | 0 | 46 | 3 | 2 | 5 | 2 | .714 | 0 | 0 | 4.23 |
| 1987 Cleveland | AL | 16 | 15 | 4 | 0 | 102.1 | 441 | 112 | 62 | 58 | 18 | 4 | 3 | 1 | 37 | 1 | 97 | 0 | 1 | 3 | 8 | .273 | 1 | 0 | 5.10 |
| 1988 Cleveland | AL | 33 | 33 | 12 | 0 | 242 | 988 | 234 | 97 | 86 | 18 | 9 | 5 | 1 | 45 | 3 | 180 | 5 | 0 | 18 | 14 | .563 | 4 | 0 | 3.20 |
| 1989 Cleveland | AL | 28 | 28 | 5 | 0 | 184.1 | 749 | 170 | 71 | 69 | 16 | 4 | 4 | 0 | 51 | 1 | 129 | 3 | 1 | 13 | 6 | .684 | 2 | 0 | 3.37 |
| 1990 Cleveland | AL | 34 | 34 | 3 | 0 | 214.2 | 912 | 245 | 110 | 105 | 27 | 8 | 6 | 1 | 47 | 2 | 135 | 3 | 2 | 12 | 9 | .571 | 0 | 0 | 4.40 |
| 5 ML YEARS | | 120 | 119 | 25 | 0 | 805 | 3345 | 818 | 375 | 347 | 88 | 28 | 19 | 4 | 195 | 7 | 587 | 14 | 6 | 51 | 39 | .567 | 7 | 0 | 3.88 |

## Pat Tabler

**Bats:** Right **Throws:** Right **Pos:** RF/LF/DH **Ht:** 6' 2" **Wt:** 200 **Born:** 02/02/58 **Age:** 33

| BATTING | | | | | | | | | | | | | | | | | | | BASERUNNING | | | | PERCENTAGES | | |
|---|---|---|---|---|---|---|---|---|---|---|---|---|---|---|---|---|---|---|---|---|---|---|---|---|---|
| Year Team | Lg | G | AB | H | 2B | 3B | HR | (Hm | Rd) | TB | R | RBI | TBB | IBB | SO | HBP | SH | SF | SB | CS | SB% | GDP | Avg | OBP | SLG |
| 1981 Chicago | NL | 35 | 101 | 19 | 3 | 1 | 1 | (1 | 0) | 27 | 11 | 5 | 13 | 0 | 26 | 0 | 3 | 0 | 0 | 1 | .00 | 4 | .188 | .281 | .267 |
| 1982 Chicago | NL | 25 | 85 | 20 | 4 | 2 | 1 | (0 | 1) | 31 | 9 | 7 | 6 | 0 | 20 | 1 | 0 | 2 | 0 | 0 | .00 | 3 | .235 | .287 | .365 |

| Year Team | Lg | G | AB | H | 2B | 3B | HR | (Hm | Rd) | TB | R | RBI | TBB | IBB | SO | HBP | SH | SF | SB | CS | SB% | GDP | Avg | OBP | SLG |
|---|---|---|---|---|---|---|---|---|---|---|---|---|---|---|---|---|---|---|---|---|---|---|---|---|---|
| 1983 Cleveland | AL | 124 | 430 | 125 | 23 | 5 | 6 | (3 | 3) | 176 | 56 | 65 | 56 | 1 | 63 | 1 | 0 | 5 | 2 | 4 | .33 | 18 | .291 | .370 | .409 |
| 1984 Cleveland | AL | 144 | 473 | 137 | 21 | 3 | 10 | (5 | 5) | 194 | 66 | 68 | 47 | 2 | 62 | 3 | 0 | 5 | 3 | 1 | .75 | 16 | .290 | .354 | .410 |
| 1985 Cleveland | AL | 117 | 404 | 111 | 18 | 3 | 5 | (5 | 0) | 150 | 47 | 59 | 27 | 2 | 55 | 2 | 2 | 3 | 0 | 6 | .00 | 15 | .275 | .321 | .371 |
| 1986 Cleveland | AL | 130 | 473 | 154 | 29 | 2 | 6 | (5 | 1) | 205 | 61 | 48 | 29 | 3 | 75 | 3 | 2 | 1 | 3 | 1 | .75 | 11 | .326 | .368 | .433 |
| 1987 Cleveland | AL | 151 | 553 | 170 | 34 | 3 | 11 | (5 | 6) | 243 | 66 | 86 | 51 | 6 | 84 | 6 | 3 | 5 | 5 | 2 | .71 | 6 | .307 | .369 | .439 |
| 1988 2 ML Teams | | 130 | 444 | 125 | 22 | 3 | 2 | (0 | 2) | 159 | 53 | 66 | 46 | 1 | 68 | 3 | 0 | 5 | 3 | 3 | .50 | 9 | .282 | .349 | .358 |
| 1989 Kansas City | AL | 123 | 390 | 101 | 11 | 1 | 2 | (2 | 0) | 120 | 36 | 42 | 37 | 0 | 42 | 2 | 3 | 2 | 0 | 0 | .00 | 14 | .259 | .325 | .308 |
| 1990 2 ML Teams | | 92 | 238 | 65 | 15 | 1 | 2 | (1 | 1) | 88 | 18 | 29 | 23 | 2 | 29 | 2 | 0 | 3 | 0 | 2 | .00 | 8 | .273 | .338 | .370 |
| 1988 Cleveland | AL | 41 | 143 | 32 | 5 | 1 | 1 | (0 | 1) | 42 | 16 | 17 | 23 | 1 | 27 | 1 | 0 | 1 | 1 | 0 | 1.00 | 3 | .224 | .333 | .294 |
| Kansas City | AL | 89 | 301 | 93 | 17 | 2 | 1 | (0 | 1) | 117 | 37 | 49 | 23 | 0 | 41 | 2 | 0 | 4 | 2 | 3 | .40 | 6 | .309 | .358 | .389 |
| 1990 Kansas City | AL | 75 | 195 | 53 | 14 | 0 | 1 | (0 | 1) | 70 | 12 | 19 | 20 | 2 | 21 | 1 | 0 | 3 | 0 | 2 | .00 | 8 | .272 | .338 | .359 |
| New York | NL | 17 | 43 | 12 | 1 | 1 | 1 | (1 | 0) | 18 | 6 | 10 | 3 | 0 | 8 | 1 | 0 | 0 | 0 | 0 | .00 | 0 | .279 | .340 | .419 |
| 10 ML YEARS | | 1071 | 3591 | 1027 | 180 | 24 | 46 | (27 | 19) | 1393 | 423 | 475 | 335 | 17 | 524 | 23 | 13 | 31 | 16 | 20 | .44 | 104 | .286 | .348 | .388 |

## Frank Tanana

**Pitches:** Left **Bats:** Left **Pos:** SP/RP **Ht:** 6' 3" **Wt:** 195 **Born:** 07/03/53 **Age:** 37

| | | HOW MUCH HE PITCHED | | | | | | WHAT HE GAVE UP | | | | | | | | | | | | THE RESULTS | | | | | |
|---|---|---|---|---|---|---|---|---|---|---|---|---|---|---|---|---|---|---|---|---|---|---|---|---|---|
| Year Team | Lg | G | GS | CG | GF | IP | BFP | H | R | ER | HR | SH | SF | HB | TBB | IBB | SO | WP | Bk | W | L | Pct. | ShO | Sv | ERA |
| 1973 California | AL | 4 | 4 | 2 | 0 | 26 | 108 | 20 | 11 | 9 | 2 | 0 | 0 | 0 | 8 | 0 | 22 | 2 | 0 | 2 | 2 | .500 | 1 | 0 | 3.12 |
| 1974 California | AL | 39 | 35 | 12 | 2 | 269 | 1127 | 262 | 104 | 93 | 27 | 10 | 4 | 8 | 77 | 4 | 180 | 4 | 2 | 14 | 19 | .424 | 4 | 0 | 3.11 |
| 1975 California | AL | 34 | 33 | 16 | 1 | 257 | 1029 | 211 | 80 | 75 | 21 | 13 | 4 | 7 | 73 | 6 | 269 | 8 | 1 | 16 | 9 | .640 | 5 | 0 | 2.63 |
| 1976 California | AL | 34 | 34 | 23 | 0 | 288 | 1142 | 212 | 88 | 78 | 24 | 14 | 3 | 9 | 73 | 5 | 261 | 5 | 0 | 19 | 10 | .655 | 2 | 0 | 2.44 |
| 1977 California | AL | 31 | 31 | 20 | 0 | 241 | 973 | 201 | 72 | 68 | 19 | 8 | 7 | 12 | 61 | 2 | 205 | 8 | 1 | 15 | 9 | .625 | 7 | 0 | 2.54 |
| 1978 California | AL | 33 | 33 | 10 | 0 | 239 | 1014 | 239 | 108 | 97 | 26 | 8 | 10 | 9 | 60 | 7 | 137 | 5 | 8 | 18 | 12 | .600 | 4 | 0 | 3.65 |
| 1979 California | AL | 18 | 17 | 2 | 0 | 90 | 382 | 93 | 44 | 39 | 9 | 1 | 2 | 2 | 25 | 0 | 46 | 6 | 1 | 7 | 5 | .583 | 1 | 0 | 3.90 |
| 1980 California | AL | 32 | 31 | 7 | 1 | 204 | 870 | 223 | 107 | 94 | 18 | 8 | 4 | 8 | 45 | 0 | 113 | 3 | 1 | 11 | 12 | .478 | 0 | 0 | 4.15 |
| 1981 Boston | AL | 24 | 23 | 5 | 0 | 141 | 596 | 142 | 70 | 63 | 17 | 9 | 4 | 4 | 43 | 4 | 78 | 2 | 0 | 4 | 10 | .286 | 2 | 0 | 4.02 |
| 1982 Texas | AL | 30 | 30 | 7 | 0 | 194.1 | 832 | 199 | 102 | 91 | 16 | 13 | 4 | 7 | 55 | 10 | 87 | 0 | 1 | 7 | 18 | .280 | 0 | 0 | 4.21 |
| 1983 Texas | AL | 29 | 22 | 3 | 1 | 159.1 | 667 | 144 | 70 | 56 | 14 | 7 | 3 | 7 | 49 | 5 | 108 | 6 | 1 | 7 | 9 | .438 | 0 | 0 | 3.16 |
| 1984 Texas | AL | 35 | 35 | 9 | 0 | 246.1 | 1054 | 234 | 117 | 89 | 30 | 6 | 5 | 6 | 81 | 3 | 141 | 12 | 4 | 15 | 15 | .500 | 1 | 0 | 3.25 |
| 1985 2 ML Teams | | 33 | 33 | 4 | 0 | 215 | 907 | 220 | 112 | 102 | 28 | 5 | 8 | 3 | 57 | 8 | 159 | 5 | 1 | 12 | 14 | .462 | 0 | 0 | 4.27 |
| 1986 Detroit | AL | 32 | 31 | 3 | 1 | 188.1 | 812 | 196 | 95 | 87 | 23 | 8 | 5 | 3 | 65 | 9 | 119 | 7 | 1 | 12 | 9 | .571 | 1 | 0 | 4.16 |
| 1987 Detroit | AL | 34 | 34 | 5 | 0 | 218.2 | 924 | 216 | 106 | 95 | 27 | 8 | 11 | 5 | 56 | 5 | 146 | 6 | 0 | 15 | 10 | .600 | 3 | 0 | 3.91 |
| 1988 Detroit | AL | 32 | 32 | 2 | 0 | 203 | 876 | 213 | 105 | 95 | 25 | 6 | 3 | 4 | 64 | 7 | 127 | 6 | 0 | 14 | 11 | .560 | 0 | 0 | 4.21 |
| 1989 Detroit | AL | 33 | 33 | 6 | 0 | 223.2 | 955 | 227 | 105 | 89 | 21 | 7 | 10 | 8 | 74 | 8 | 147 | 8 | 0 | 10 | 14 | .417 | 1 | 0 | 3.58 |
| 1990 Detroit | AL | 34 | 29 | 1 | 4 | 176.1 | 763 | 190 | 104 | 104 | 25 | 3 | 7 | 9 | 66 | 7 | 114 | 5 | 1 | 9 | 8 | .529 | 0 | 1 | 5.31 |
| 1985 Texas | AL | 13 | 13 | 0 | 0 | 77.2 | 340 | 89 | 53 | 51 | 15 | 2 | 4 | 1 | 23 | 2 | 52 | 3 | 0 | 2 | 7 | .222 | 0 | 0 | 5.91 |
| Detroit | AL | 20 | 20 | 4 | 0 | 137.1 | 567 | 131 | 59 | 51 | 13 | 3 | 4 | 2 | 34 | 6 | 107 | 2 | 1 | 10 | 7 | .588 | 0 | 0 | 3.34 |
| 18 ML YEARS | | 541 | 520 | 137 | 10 | 3580 | 15031 | 3442 | 1600 | 1424 | 372 | 134 | 94 | 111 | 1032 | 90 | 2459 | 98 | 23 | 207 | 196 | .514 | 32 | 1 | 3.58 |

## Kevin Tapani

**Pitches:** Right **Bats:** Right **Pos:** SP **Ht:** 6' 0" **Wt:** 180 **Born:** 02/18/64 **Age:** 27

| | | HOW MUCH HE PITCHED | | | | | | WHAT HE GAVE UP | | | | | | | | | | | | THE RESULTS | | | | | |
|---|---|---|---|---|---|---|---|---|---|---|---|---|---|---|---|---|---|---|---|---|---|---|---|---|---|
| Year Team | Lg | G | GS | CG | GF | IP | BFP | H | R | ER | HR | SH | SF | HB | TBB | IBB | SO | WP | Bk | W | L | Pct. | ShO | Sv | ERA |
| 1986 Medford | A | 2 | 2 | 0 | 0 | 8.1 | 0 | 6 | 3 | 0 | 0 | 0 | 0 | 0 | 3 | 0 | 9 | 0 | 0 | 1 | 0 | 1.000 | 0 | 0 | 0.00 |
| Tacoma | AAA | 1 | 1 | 0 | 0 | 2.1 | 14 | 5 | 6 | 4 | 1 | 0 | 0 | 0 | 1 | 0 | 1 | 1 | 0 | 0 | 1 | .000 | 0 | 0 | 15.43 |
| Modesto | A | 11 | 11 | 1 | 0 | 69 | 293 | 74 | 26 | 19 | 2 | 2 | 0 | 1 | 22 | 1 | 44 | 1 | 0 | 6 | 1 | .857 | 0 | 0 | 2.48 |
| Huntsville | AA | 1 | 1 | 0 | 0 | 6 | 26 | 8 | 4 | 4 | 0 | 0 | 1 | 0 | 1 | 0 | 2 | 0 | 0 | 1 | 0 | 1.000 | 0 | 0 | 6.00 |
| 1987 Modesto | A | 24 | 24 | 6 | 0 | 148.1 | 627 | 122 | 74 | 62 | 14 | 6 | 1 | 5 | 60 | 2 | 121 | 21 | 0 | 10 | 7 | .588 | 1 | 0 | 3.76 |
| 1988 St. Lucie | A | 3 | 3 | 0 | 0 | 19 | 76 | 17 | 5 | 3 | 1 | 0 | 0 | 0 | 4 | 0 | 11 | 2 | 0 | 1 | 0 | 1.000 | 0 | 0 | 1.42 |
| Jackson | AA | 24 | 5 | 0 | 9 | 62.1 | 248 | 46 | 23 | 19 | 1 | 5 | 2 | 0 | 19 | 2 | 35 | 1 | 3 | 5 | 1 | .833 | 0 | 3 | 2.74 |
| 1989 Tidewater | AAA | 17 | 17 | 2 | 0 | 109 | 459 | 113 | 49 | 42 | 6 | 1 | 2 | 1 | 25 | 2 | 63 | 3 | 1 | 7 | 5 | .583 | 1 | 0 | 3.47 |
| Portland | AAA | 6 | 6 | 1 | 0 | 41 | 170 | 38 | 15 | 10 | 4 | 1 | 0 | 0 | 12 | 1 | 30 | 0 | 1 | 4 | 2 | .667 | 0 | 0 | 2.20 |
| 1989 2 ML Teams | | 8 | 5 | 0 | 1 | 40 | 169 | 39 | 18 | 17 | 3 | 1 | 2 | 0 | 12 | 1 | 23 | 0 | 1 | 2 | 2 | .500 | 0 | 0 | 3.83 |
| 1990 Minnesota | AL | 28 | 28 | 1 | 0 | 159.1 | 659 | 164 | 75 | 72 | 12 | 3 | 4 | 2 | 29 | 2 | 101 | 1 | 0 | 12 | 8 | .600 | 1 | 0 | 4.07 |
| 1989 New York | NL | 3 | 0 | 0 | 1 | 7.1 | 31 | 5 | 3 | 3 | 1 | 0 | 1 | 0 | 4 | 0 | 2 | 0 | 1 | 0 | 0 | .000 | 0 | 0 | 3.68 |
| Minnesota | AL | 5 | 5 | 0 | 0 | 32.2 | 138 | 34 | 15 | 14 | 2 | 1 | 1 | 0 | 8 | 1 | 21 | 0 | 0 | 2 | 2 | .500 | 0 | 0 | 3.86 |
| 2 ML YEARS | | 36 | 33 | 1 | 1 | 199.1 | 828 | 203 | 93 | 89 | 15 | 4 | 6 | 2 | 41 | 3 | 124 | 1 | 1 | 14 | 10 | .583 | 1 | 0 | 4.02 |

## Danny Tartabull

**Bats:** Right **Throws:** Right **Pos:** RF/DH **Ht:** 6' 1" **Wt:** 205 **Born:** 10/30/62 **Age:** 28

| | | BATTING | | | | | | | | | | | | | | | | | BASERUNNING | | | | PERCENTAGES | | |
|---|---|---|---|---|---|---|---|---|---|---|---|---|---|---|---|---|---|---|---|---|---|---|---|---|---|
| Year Team | Lg | G | AB | H | 2B | 3B | HR | (Hm | Rd) | TB | R | RBI | TBB | IBB | SO | HBP | SH | SF | SB | CS | SB% | GDP | Avg | OBP | SLG |
| 1984 Seattle | AL | 10 | 20 | 6 | 1 | 0 | 2 | (1 | 1) | 13 | 3 | 7 | 2 | 0 | 3 | 1 | 0 | 1 | 0 | 0 | .00 | 0 | .300 | .375 | .650 |
| 1985 Seattle | AL | 19 | 61 | 20 | 7 | 1 | 1 | (0 | 1) | 32 | 8 | 7 | 8 | 0 | 14 | 0 | 0 | 0 | 1 | 0 | 1.00 | 1 | .328 | .406 | .525 |
| 1986 Seattle | AL | 137 | 511 | 138 | 25 | 6 | 25 | (13 | 12) | 250 | 76 | 96 | 61 | 2 | 157 | 1 | 2 | 3 | 4 | 8 | .33 | 10 | .270 | .347 | .489 |
| 1987 Kansas City | AL | 158 | 582 | 180 | 27 | 3 | 34 | (15 | 19) | 315 | 95 | 101 | 79 | 2 | 136 | 1 | 0 | 5 | 9 | 4 | .69 | 14 | .309 | .390 | .541 |
| 1988 Kansas City | AL | 146 | 507 | 139 | 38 | 3 | 26 | (15 | 11) | 261 | 80 | 102 | 76 | 4 | 119 | 4 | 0 | 6 | 8 | 5 | .62 | 10 | .274 | .369 | .515 |

| Year Team | Lg | G | AB | H | 2B | 3B | HR | (Hm | Rd) | TB | R | RBI | TBB | IBB | SO | HBP | SH | SF | SB | CS | SB% | GDP | Avg | OBP | SLG |
|---|---|---|---|---|---|---|---|---|---|---|---|---|---|---|---|---|---|---|---|---|---|---|---|---|---|
| 1989 Kansas City | AL | 133 | 441 | 118 | 22 | 0 | 18 | (9 | 9) | 194 | 54 | 62 | 69 | 2 | 123 | 3 | 0 | 2 | 4 | 2 | .67 | 12 | .268 | .369 | .440 |
| 1990 Kansas City | AL | 88 | 313 | 84 | 19 | 0 | 15 | (5 | 10) | 148 | 41 | 60 | 36 | 0 | 93 | 0 | 0 | 3 | 1 | 1 | .50 | 9 | .268 | .341 | .473 |
| 7 ML YEARS | | 691 | 2435 | 685 | 139 | 13 | 121 | (58 | 63) | 1213 | 357 | 435 | 331 | 10 | 645 | 10 | 2 | 20 | 27 | 20 | .57 | 56 | .281 | .367 | .498 |

## Dorn Taylor

**Pitches:** Right **Bats:** Right **Pos:** RP **Ht:** 6' 2" **Wt:** 180 **Born:** 08/11/58 **Age:** 32

| | | HOW MUCH HE PITCHED | | | | | | WHAT HE GAVE UP | | | | | | | | | | | | THE RESULTS | | | | | |
|---|---|---|---|---|---|---|---|---|---|---|---|---|---|---|---|---|---|---|---|---|---|---|---|---|---|
| Year Team | Lg | G | GS | CG | GF | IP | BFP | H | R | ER | HR | SH | SF | HB | TBB | IBB | SO | WP | Bk | W | L | Pct. | ShO | Sv | ERA |
| 1987 Pittsburgh | NL | 14 | 8 | 0 | 0 | 53.1 | 226 | 48 | 35 | 34 | 10 | 1 | 2 | 1 | 28 | 1 | 37 | 3 | 0 | 2 | 3 | .400 | 0 | 0 | 5.74 |
| 1989 Pittsburgh | NL | 9 | 0 | 0 | 5 | 10.2 | 47 | 14 | 6 | 6 | 0 | 0 | 0 | 0 | 5 | 2 | 3 | 0 | 0 | 1 | 1 | .500 | 0 | 0 | 5.06 |
| 1990 Baltimore | AL | 4 | 0 | 0 | 2 | 3.2 | 18 | 4 | 3 | 1 | 0 | 0 | 0 | 0 | 2 | 0 | 4 | 1 | 0 | 0 | 1 | .000 | 0 | 0 | 2.45 |
| 3 ML YEARS | | 27 | 8 | 0 | 7 | 67.2 | 291 | 66 | 44 | 41 | 10 | 1 | 2 | 1 | 35 | 3 | 44 | 4 | 0 | 3 | 5 | .375 | 0 | 0 | 5.45 |

## Anthony Telford

**Pitches:** Right **Bats:** Right **Pos:** SP **Ht:** 6' 0" **Wt:** 175 **Born:** 03/06/66 **Age:** 25

| | | HOW MUCH HE PITCHED | | | | | | WHAT HE GAVE UP | | | | | | | | | | | | THE RESULTS | | | | | |
|---|---|---|---|---|---|---|---|---|---|---|---|---|---|---|---|---|---|---|---|---|---|---|---|---|---|
| Year Team | Lg | G | GS | CG | GF | IP | BFP | H | R | ER | HR | SH | SF | HB | TBB | IBB | SO | WP | Bk | W | L | Pct. | ShO | Sv | ERA |
| 1987 Newark | A | 6 | 2 | 0 | 3 | 17.2 | 72 | 16 | 2 | 2 | 0 | 0 | 0 | 0 | 3 | 0 | 27 | 0 | 0 | 1 | 0 | 1.000 | 0 | 0 | 1.02 |
| Hagerstown | A | 2 | 2 | 0 | 0 | 11.1 | 46 | 9 | 2 | 2 | 0 | 0 | 0 | 1 | 5 | 0 | 10 | 0 | 0 | 1 | 0 | 1.000 | 0 | 0 | 1.59 |
| Rochester | AAA | 1 | 0 | 0 | 0 | 2 | 9 | 0 | 0 | 0 | 0 | 0 | 0 | 0 | 3 | 0 | 3 | 1 | 0 | 0 | 0 | .000 | 0 | 0 | 0.00 |
| 1988 Hagerstown | A | 1 | 1 | 0 | 0 | 7 | 24 | 3 | 0 | 0 | 0 | 0 | 0 | 0 | 0 | 0 | 10 | 0 | 0 | 1 | 0 | 1.000 | 0 | 0 | 0.00 |
| 1989 Frederick | A | 9 | 5 | 0 | 2 | 25.2 | 116 | 25 | 15 | 12 | 1 | 1 | 2 | 2 | 12 | 0 | 19 | 2 | 0 | 2 | 1 | .667 | 0 | 1 | 4.21 |
| 1990 Frederick | A | 8 | 8 | 1 | 0 | 53.2 | 207 | 35 | 15 | 10 | 1 | 0 | 0 | 4 | 11 | 1 | 49 | 4 | 0 | 4 | 2 | .667 | 0 | 0 | 1.68 |
| Hagerstown | AA | 14 | 13 | 3 | 1 | 96 | 384 | 80 | 26 | 21 | 3 | 5 | 3 | 3 | 25 | 1 | 73 | 4 | 0 | 10 | 2 | .833 | 1 | 0 | 1.97 |
| 1990 Baltimore | AL | 8 | 8 | 0 | 0 | 36.1 | 168 | 43 | 22 | 20 | 4 | 0 | 2 | 1 | 19 | 0 | 20 | 1 | 0 | 3 | 3 | .500 | 0 | 0 | 4.95 |

## Garry Templeton

**Bats:** Both **Throws:** Right **Pos:** SS **Ht:** 5'11" **Wt:** 190 **Born:** 03/24/56 **Age:** 35

| | | BATTING | | | | | | | | | | | | | | | | | BASERUNNING | | | | PERCENTAGES | | |
|---|---|---|---|---|---|---|---|---|---|---|---|---|---|---|---|---|---|---|---|---|---|---|---|---|---|
| Year Team | Lg | G | AB | H | 2B | 3B | HR | (Hm | Rd) | TB | R | RBI | TBB | IBB | SO | HBP | SH | SF | SB | CS | SB% | GDP | Avg | OBP | SLG |
| 1976 St. Louis | NL | 53 | 213 | 62 | 8 | 2 | 1 | (1 | 0) | 77 | 32 | 17 | 7 | 0 | 33 | 1 | 2 | 2 | 11 | 7 | .61 | 1 | .291 | .314 | .362 |
| 1977 St. Louis | NL | 153 | 621 | 200 | 19 | 18 | 8 | (2 | 6) | 279 | 94 | 79 | 15 | 3 | 70 | 1 | 2 | 5 | 28 | 24 | .54 | 9 | .322 | .336 | .449 |
| 1978 St. Louis | NL | 155 | 647 | 181 | 31 | 13 | 2 | (1 | 1) | 244 | 82 | 47 | 22 | 3 | 87 | 1 | 2 | 3 | 34 | 11 | .76 | 7 | .280 | .303 | .377 |
| 1979 St. Louis | NL | 154 | 672 | 211 | 32 | 19 | 9 | (2 | 7) | 308 | 105 | 62 | 18 | 4 | 91 | 1 | 2 | 3 | 26 | 10 | .72 | 8 | .314 | .331 | .458 |
| 1980 St. Louis | NL | 118 | 504 | 161 | 19 | 9 | 4 | (1 | 3) | 210 | 83 | 43 | 18 | 6 | 43 | 0 | 1 | 1 | 31 | 15 | .67 | 13 | .319 | .342 | .417 |
| 1981 St. Louis | NL | 80 | 333 | 96 | 16 | 8 | 1 | (1 | 0) | 131 | 47 | 33 | 14 | 3 | 55 | 0 | 1 | 2 | 8 | 12 | .40 | 4 | .288 | .315 | .393 |
| 1982 San Diego | NL | 141 | 563 | 139 | 25 | 8 | 6 | (2 | 4) | 198 | 76 | 64 | 26 | 7 | 82 | 1 | 6 | 5 | 27 | 16 | .63 | 19 | .247 | .279 | .352 |
| 1983 San Diego | NL | 126 | 460 | 121 | 20 | 2 | 3 | (1 | 2) | 154 | 39 | 40 | 21 | 7 | 57 | 0 | 7 | 2 | 16 | 6 | .73 | 16 | .263 | .294 | .335 |
| 1984 San Diego | NL | 148 | 493 | 127 | 19 | 3 | 2 | (2 | 0) | 158 | 40 | 35 | 39 | 23 | 81 | 1 | 0 | 2 | 8 | 3 | .73 | 10 | .258 | .312 | .320 |
| 1985 San Diego | NL | 148 | 546 | 154 | 30 | 2 | 6 | (4 | 2) | 206 | 63 | 55 | 41 | 24 | 88 | 1 | 5 | 3 | 16 | 6 | .73 | 5 | .282 | .332 | .377 |
| 1986 San Diego | NL | 147 | 510 | 126 | 21 | 2 | 2 | (1 | 1) | 157 | 42 | 44 | 35 | 21 | 86 | 1 | 1 | 2 | 10 | 5 | .67 | 12 | .247 | .296 | .308 |
| 1987 San Diego | NL | 148 | 510 | 113 | 13 | 5 | 5 | (2 | 3) | 151 | 42 | 48 | 42 | 11 | 92 | 1 | 5 | 3 | 14 | 3 | .82 | 15 | .222 | .281 | .296 |
| 1988 San Diego | NL | 110 | 362 | 90 | 15 | 7 | 3 | (3 | 0) | 128 | 35 | 36 | 20 | 10 | 50 | 0 | 7 | 3 | 8 | 2 | .80 | 6 | .249 | .286 | .354 |
| 1989 San Diego | NL | 142 | 506 | 129 | 26 | 3 | 6 | (5 | 1) | 179 | 43 | 40 | 23 | 12 | 80 | 0 | 4 | 3 | 1 | 3 | .25 | 15 | .255 | .286 | .354 |
| 1990 San Diego | NL | 144 | 505 | 125 | 25 | 3 | 9 | (6 | 3) | 183 | 45 | 59 | 24 | 7 | 59 | 0 | 8 | 4 | 1 | 4 | .20 | 17 | .248 | .280 | .362 |
| 15 ML YEARS | | 1967 | 7445 | 2035 | 319 | 104 | 67 | (34 | 33) | 2763 | 868 | 702 | 365 | 141 | 1054 | 9 | 53 | 43 | 239 | 127 | .65 | 157 | .273 | .306 | .371 |

## Walt Terrell

**Pitches:** Right **Bats:** Left **Pos:** SP **Ht:** 6' 2" **Wt:** 205 **Born:** 05/11/58 **Age:** 33

| | | HOW MUCH HE PITCHED | | | | | | WHAT HE GAVE UP | | | | | | | | | | | | THE RESULTS | | | | | |
|---|---|---|---|---|---|---|---|---|---|---|---|---|---|---|---|---|---|---|---|---|---|---|---|---|---|
| Year Team | Lg | G | GS | CG | GF | IP | BFP | H | R | ER | HR | SH | SF | HB | TBB | IBB | SO | WP | Bk | W | L | Pct. | ShO | Sv | ERA |
| 1982 New York | NL | 3 | 3 | 0 | 0 | 21 | 97 | 22 | 12 | 8 | 2 | 1 | 0 | 0 | 14 | 2 | 8 | 1 | 1 | 0 | 3 | .000 | 0 | 0 | 3.43 |
| 1983 New York | NL | 21 | 20 | 4 | 1 | 133.2 | 561 | 123 | 57 | 53 | 7 | 9 | 5 | 2 | 55 | 7 | 59 | 5 | 0 | 8 | 8 | .500 | 2 | 0 | 3.57 |
| 1984 New York | NL | 33 | 33 | 3 | 0 | 215 | 926 | 232 | 99 | 84 | 16 | 11 | 8 | 4 | 80 | 1 | 114 | 6 | 0 | 11 | 12 | .478 | 1 | 0 | 3.52 |
| 1985 Detroit | AL | 34 | 34 | 5 | 0 | 229 | 983 | 221 | 107 | 98 | 9 | 11 | 7 | 4 | 95 | 5 | 130 | 5 | 0 | 15 | 10 | .600 | 3 | 0 | 3.85 |
| 1986 Detroit | AL | 34 | 33 | 9 | 1 | 217.1 | 918 | 199 | 116 | 110 | 30 | 2 | 3 | 3 | 98 | 5 | 93 | 5 | 0 | 15 | 12 | .556 | 2 | 0 | 4.56 |
| 1987 Detroit | AL | 35 | 35 | 10 | 0 | 244.2 | 1057 | 254 | 123 | 110 | 30 | 3 | 10 | 3 | 94 | 7 | 143 | 8 | 0 | 17 | 10 | .630 | 1 | 0 | 4.05 |
| 1988 Detroit | AL | 29 | 29 | 11 | 0 | 206.1 | 870 | 199 | 101 | 91 | 20 | 13 | 6 | 2 | 78 | 8 | 84 | 7 | 2 | 7 | 16 | .304 | 1 | 0 | 3.97 |
| 1989 2 ML Teams | | 32 | 32 | 5 | 0 | 206.1 | 882 | 236 | 117 | 103 | 23 | 10 | 4 | 2 | 50 | 1 | 93 | 6 | 0 | 11 | 18 | .379 | 2 | 0 | 4.49 |
| 1990 2 ML Teams | | 29 | 28 | 0 | 0 | 158 | 710 | 184 | 98 | 92 | 20 | 9 | 3 | 12 | 57 | 4 | 64 | 7 | 2 | 8 | 11 | .421 | 0 | 0 | 5.24 |
| 1989 San Diego | NL | 19 | 19 | 4 | 0 | 123.1 | 520 | 134 | 65 | 55 | 14 | 8 | 2 | 0 | 26 | 1 | 63 | 4 | 0 | 5 | 13 | .278 | 1 | 0 | 4.01 |
| New York | AL | 13 | 13 | 1 | 0 | 83 | 362 | 102 | 52 | 48 | 9 | 2 | 2 | 2 | 24 | 0 | 30 | 2 | 0 | 6 | 5 | .545 | 1 | 0 | 5.20 |
| 1990 Pittsburgh | NL | 16 | 16 | 0 | 0 | 82.2 | 377 | 98 | 59 | 54 | 13 | 6 | 2 | 4 | 33 | 1 | 34 | 7 | 2 | 2 | 7 | .222 | 0 | 0 | 5.88 |
| Detroit | AL | 13 | 12 | 0 | 0 | 75.1 | 333 | 86 | 39 | 38 | 7 | 3 | 1 | 8 | 24 | 3 | 30 | 0 | 0 | 6 | 4 | .600 | 0 | 0 | 4.54 |
| 9 ML YEARS | | 250 | 247 | 47 | 2 | 1631.1 | 7004 | 1670 | 830 | 749 | 157 | 69 | 46 | 32 | 621 | 40 | 788 | 50 | 5 | 92 | 100 | .479 | 12 | 0 | 4.13 |

## Scott Terry

**Pitches:** Right **Bats:** Right **Pos:** RP **Ht:** 5'11" **Wt:** 195 **Born:** 11/21/59 **Age:** 31

| | | HOW MUCH HE PITCHED | | | | | | WHAT HE GAVE UP | | | | | | | | | | | | THE RESULTS | | | | | |
|---|---|---|---|---|---|---|---|---|---|---|---|---|---|---|---|---|---|---|---|---|---|---|---|---|---|
| Year Team | Lg | G | GS | CG | GF | IP | BFP | H | R | ER | HR | SH | SF | HB | TBB | IBB | SO | WP | Bk | W | L | Pct. | ShO | Sv | ERA |
| 1986 Cincinnati | NL | 28 | 3 | 0 | 7 | 55.2 | 258 | 66 | 40 | 38 | 8 | 5 | 1 | 0 | 32 | 3 | 32 | 2 | 0 | 1 | 2 | .333 | 0 | 0 | 6.14 |
| 1987 St. Louis | NL | 11 | 0 | 0 | 2 | 13.1 | 59 | 13 | 5 | 5 | 0 | 1 | 0 | 0 | 8 | 2 | 9 | 0 | 0 | 0 | 0 | .000 | 0 | 0 | 3.38 |
| 1988 St. Louis | NL | 51 | 11 | 1 | 14 | 129.1 | 524 | 119 | 48 | 42 | 5 | 6 | 3 | 0 | 34 | 6 | 65 | 1 | 2 | 9 | 6 | .600 | 0 | 3 | 2.92 |
| 1989 St. Louis | NL | 31 | 24 | 1 | 5 | 148.2 | 619 | 142 | 65 | 59 | 14 | 8 | 4 | 3 | 43 | 6 | 69 | 2 | 2 | 8 | 10 | .444 | 0 | 2 | 3.57 |
| 1990 St. Louis | NL | 50 | 2 | 0 | 26 | 72 | 323 | 75 | 45 | 38 | 7 | 3 | 5 | 4 | 27 | 5 | 35 | 2 | 0 | 2 | 6 | .250 | 0 | 2 | 4.75 |
| 5 ML YEARS | | 171 | 40 | 2 | 54 | 419 | 1783 | 415 | 203 | 182 | 34 | 23 | 13 | 7 | 144 | 22 | 210 | 7 | 4 | 20 | 24 | .455 | 0 | 7 | 3.91 |

## Mickey Tettleton

**Bats:** Both **Throws:** Right **Pos:** C/DH **Ht:** 6' 2" **Wt:** 214 **Born:** 09/16/60 **Age:** 30

| | | BATTING | | | | | | | | | | | | | | | | | BASERUNNING | | | | PERCENTAGES | | |
|---|---|---|---|---|---|---|---|---|---|---|---|---|---|---|---|---|---|---|---|---|---|---|---|---|---|
| Year Team | Lg | G | AB | H | 2B | 3B | HR | (Hm | Rd) | TB | R | RBI | TBB | IBB | SO | HBP | SH | SF | SB | CS | SB% | GDP | Avg | OBP | SLG |
| 1984 Oakland | AL | 33 | 76 | 20 | 2 | 1 | 1 | (1 | 0) | 27 | 10 | 5 | 11 | 0 | 21 | 0 | 0 | 1 | 0 | 0 | .00 | 3 | .263 | .352 | .355 |
| 1985 Oakland | AL | 78 | 211 | 53 | 12 | 0 | 3 | (1 | 2) | 74 | 23 | 15 | 28 | 0 | 59 | 2 | 5 | 0 | 2 | 2 | .50 | 6 | .251 | .344 | .351 |
| 1986 Oakland | AL | 90 | 211 | 43 | 9 | 0 | 10 | (4 | 6) | 82 | 26 | 35 | 39 | 0 | 51 | 1 | 7 | 4 | 7 | 1 | .88 | 3 | .204 | .325 | .389 |
| 1987 Oakland | AL | 82 | 211 | 41 | 3 | 0 | 8 | (5 | 3) | 68 | 19 | 26 | 30 | 0 | 65 | 0 | 5 | 2 | 1 | 1 | .50 | 3 | .194 | .292 | .322 |
| 1988 Baltimore | AL | 86 | 283 | 74 | 11 | 1 | 11 | (7 | 4) | 120 | 31 | 37 | 28 | 2 | 70 | 2 | 1 | 2 | 0 | 1 | .00 | 9 | .261 | .330 | .424 |
| 1989 Baltimore | AL | 117 | 411 | 106 | 21 | 2 | 26 | (15 | 11) | 209 | 72 | 65 | 73 | 4 | 117 | 1 | 1 | 3 | 3 | 2 | .60 | 8 | .258 | .369 | .509 |
| 1990 Baltimore | AL | 135 | 444 | 99 | 21 | 2 | 15 | (8 | 7) | 169 | 68 | 51 | 106 | 3 | 160 | 5 | 0 | 4 | 2 | 4 | .33 | 7 | .223 | .376 | .381 |
| 7 ML YEARS | | 621 | 1847 | 436 | 79 | 6 | 74 | (41 | 33) | 749 | 249 | 234 | 315 | 9 | 543 | 11 | 19 | 16 | 15 | 11 | .58 | 39 | .236 | .348 | .406 |

## Tim Teufel

**Bats:** Right **Throws:** Right **Pos:** 2B/1B **Ht:** 6' 0" **Wt:** 175 **Born:** 07/07/58 **Age:** 32

| | | BATTING | | | | | | | | | | | | | | | | | BASERUNNING | | | | PERCENTAGES | | |
|---|---|---|---|---|---|---|---|---|---|---|---|---|---|---|---|---|---|---|---|---|---|---|---|---|---|
| Year Team | Lg | G | AB | H | 2B | 3B | HR | (Hm | Rd) | TB | R | RBI | TBB | IBB | SO | HBP | SH | SF | SB | CS | SB% | GDP | Avg | OBP | SLG |
| 1983 Minnesota | AL | 21 | 78 | 24 | 7 | 1 | 3 | (3 | 0) | 42 | 11 | 6 | 2 | 0 | 8 | 0 | 2 | 0 | 0 | 0 | .00 | 1 | .308 | .325 | .538 |
| 1984 Minnesota | AL | 157 | 568 | 149 | 30 | 3 | 14 | (9 | 5) | 227 | 76 | 61 | 76 | 8 | 73 | 2 | 2 | 4 | 1 | 3 | .25 | 18 | .262 | .349 | .400 |
| 1985 Minnesota | AL | 138 | 434 | 113 | 24 | 3 | 10 | (6 | 4) | 173 | 58 | 50 | 48 | 2 | 70 | 3 | 7 | 4 | 4 | 2 | .67 | 14 | .260 | .335 | .399 |
| 1986 New York | NL | 93 | 279 | 69 | 20 | 1 | 4 | (2 | 2) | 103 | 35 | 31 | 32 | 1 | 42 | 1 | 3 | 3 | 1 | 2 | .33 | 6 | .247 | .324 | .369 |
| 1987 New York | NL | 97 | 299 | 92 | 29 | 0 | 14 | (4 | 10) | 163 | 55 | 61 | 44 | 2 | 53 | 2 | 3 | 2 | 3 | 2 | .60 | 7 | .308 | .398 | .545 |
| 1988 New York | NL | 90 | 273 | 64 | 20 | 0 | 4 | (1 | 3) | 96 | 35 | 31 | 29 | 1 | 41 | 1 | 2 | 4 | 0 | 1 | .00 | 6 | .234 | .306 | .352 |
| 1989 New York | NL | 83 | 219 | 56 | 7 | 2 | 2 | (1 | 1) | 73 | 27 | 15 | 32 | 1 | 50 | 1 | 0 | 2 | 1 | 3 | .25 | 4 | .256 | .350 | .333 |
| 1990 New York | NL | 80 | 175 | 43 | 11 | 0 | 10 | (4 | 6) | 84 | 28 | 24 | 15 | 1 | 33 | 0 | 1 | 1 | 0 | 0 | .00 | 5 | .246 | .304 | .480 |
| 8 ML YEARS | | 759 | 2325 | 610 | 148 | 10 | 61 | (30 | 31) | 961 | 325 | 279 | 278 | 16 | 370 | 10 | 20 | 20 | 10 | 13 | .43 | 61 | .262 | .341 | .413 |

## Bob Tewksbury

**Pitches:** Right **Bats:** Right **Pos:** SP/RP **Ht:** 6' 4" **Wt:** 200 **Born:** 11/30/60 **Age:** 30

| | | HOW MUCH HE PITCHED | | | | | | WHAT HE GAVE UP | | | | | | | | | | | | THE RESULTS | | | | | |
|---|---|---|---|---|---|---|---|---|---|---|---|---|---|---|---|---|---|---|---|---|---|---|---|---|---|
| Year Team | Lg | G | GS | CG | GF | IP | BFP | H | R | ER | HR | SH | SF | HB | TBB | IBB | SO | WP | Bk | W | L | Pct. | ShO | Sv | ERA |
| 1986 New York | AL | 23 | 20 | 2 | 0 | 130.1 | 558 | 144 | 58 | 48 | 8 | 4 | 7 | 5 | 31 | 0 | 49 | 3 | 2 | 9 | 5 | .643 | 0 | 0 | 3.31 |
| 1987 2 ML Teams | | 15 | 9 | 0 | 4 | 51.1 | 242 | 79 | 41 | 38 | 6 | 5 | 1 | 1 | 20 | 3 | 22 | 1 | 2 | 1 | 8 | .111 | 0 | 0 | 6.66 |
| 1988 Chicago | NL | 1 | 1 | 0 | 0 | 3.1 | 18 | 6 | 5 | 3 | 1 | 0 | 1 | 0 | 2 | 0 | 1 | 0 | 0 | 0 | 0 | .000 | 0 | 0 | 8.10 |
| 1989 St. Louis | NL | 7 | 4 | 1 | 2 | 30 | 125 | 25 | 12 | 11 | 2 | 1 | 1 | 2 | 10 | 3 | 17 | 0 | 0 | 1 | 0 | 1.000 | 1 | 0 | 3.30 |
| 1990 St. Louis | NL | 28 | 20 | 3 | 1 | 145.1 | 595 | 151 | 67 | 56 | 7 | 5 | 7 | 3 | 15 | 3 | 50 | 2 | 0 | 10 | 9 | .526 | 2 | 1 | 3.47 |
| 1987 New York | AL | 8 | 6 | 0 | 1 | 33.1 | 149 | 47 | 26 | 25 | 5 | 2 | 0 | 1 | 7 | 0 | 12 | 0 | 0 | 1 | 4 | .200 | 0 | 0 | 6.75 |
| Chicago | NL | 7 | 3 | 0 | 3 | 18 | 93 | 32 | 15 | 13 | 1 | 3 | 1 | 0 | 13 | 3 | 10 | 1 | 2 | 0 | 4 | .000 | 0 | 0 | 6.50 |
| 5 ML YEARS | | 74 | 54 | 6 | 7 | 360.1 | 1538 | 405 | 183 | 156 | 24 | 15 | 17 | 11 | 78 | 9 | 139 | 6 | 4 | 21 | 22 | .488 | 3 | 1 | 3.90 |

## Bobby Thigpen

**Pitches:** Right **Bats:** Right **Pos:** RP **Ht:** 6' 3" **Wt:** 195 **Born:** 07/17/63 **Age:** 27

| | | HOW MUCH HE PITCHED | | | | | | WHAT HE GAVE UP | | | | | | | | | | | | THE RESULTS | | | | | |
|---|---|---|---|---|---|---|---|---|---|---|---|---|---|---|---|---|---|---|---|---|---|---|---|---|---|
| Year Team | Lg | G | GS | CG | GF | IP | BFP | H | R | ER | HR | SH | SF | HB | TBB | IBB | SO | WP | Bk | W | L | Pct. | ShO | Sv | ERA |
| 1986 Chicago | AL | 20 | 0 | 0 | 14 | 35.2 | 142 | 26 | 7 | 7 | 1 | 1 | 1 | 1 | 12 | 0 | 20 | 0 | 0 | 2 | 0 | 1.000 | 0 | 7 | 1.77 |
| 1987 Chicago | AL | 51 | 0 | 0 | 37 | 89 | 369 | 86 | 30 | 27 | 10 | 6 | 0 | 3 | 24 | 5 | 52 | 0 | 0 | 7 | 5 | .583 | 0 | 16 | 2.73 |
| 1988 Chicago | AL | 68 | 0 | 0 | 59 | 90 | 398 | 96 | 38 | 33 | 6 | 4 | 5 | 4 | 33 | 3 | 62 | 6 | 2 | 5 | 8 | .385 | 0 | 34 | 3.30 |
| 1989 Chicago | AL | 61 | 0 | 0 | 56 | 79 | 336 | 62 | 34 | 33 | 10 | 5 | 5 | 1 | 40 | 3 | 47 | 2 | 1 | 2 | 6 | .250 | 0 | 34 | 3.76 |
| 1990 Chicago | AL | 77 | 0 | 0 | 73 | 88.2 | 347 | 60 | 20 | 18 | 5 | 4 | 3 | 1 | 32 | 3 | 70 | 2 | 0 | 4 | 6 | .400 | 0 | 57 | 1.83 |
| 5 ML YEARS | | 277 | 0 | 0 | 239 | 382.1 | 1592 | 330 | 129 | 118 | 32 | 20 | 14 | 10 | 141 | 14 | 251 | 10 | 3 | 20 | 25 | .444 | 0 | 148 | 2.78 |

## Andres Thomas

**Bats:** Right **Throws:** Right **Pos:** SS **Ht:** 6' 1" **Wt:** 185 **Born:** 11/10/63 **Age:** 27

| | | BATTING | | | | | | | | | | | | | | | | | BASERUNNING | | | | PERCENTAGES | | |
|---|---|---|---|---|---|---|---|---|---|---|---|---|---|---|---|---|---|---|---|---|---|---|---|---|---|
| Year Team | Lg | G | AB | H | 2B | 3B | HR | (Hm | Rd) | TB | R | RBI | TBB | IBB | SO | HBP | SH | SF | SB | CS | SB% | GDP | Avg | OBP | SLG |
| 1985 Atlanta | NL | 15 | 18 | 5 | 0 | 0 | 0 | (0 | 0) | 5 | 6 | 2 | 0 | 0 | 2 | 0 | 1 | 0 | 0 | 0 | .00 | 1 | .278 | .278 | .278 |

| | | | | | | | | | | | | | | | | | | | | | | | | | |
|---|---|---|---|---|---|---|---|---|---|---|---|---|---|---|---|---|---|---|---|---|---|---|---|---|---|
| 1986 Atlanta | NL | 102 | 323 | 81 | 17 | 2 | 6 | (1 | 5) | 120 | 26 | 32 | 8 | 2 | 49 | 0 | 2 | 2 | 4 | 6 | .40 | 14 | .251 | .267 | .372 |
| 1987 Atlanta | NL | 82 | 324 | 75 | 11 | 0 | 5 | (4 | 1) | 101 | 29 | 39 | 14 | 0 | 50 | 2 | 3 | 0 | 6 | 5 | .55 | 7 | .231 | .268 | .312 |
| 1988 Atlanta | NL | 153 | 606 | 153 | 22 | 2 | 13 | (6 | 7) | 218 | 54 | 68 | 14 | 6 | 95 | 1 | 0 | 6 | 7 | 3 | .70 | 17 | .252 | .268 | .360 |
| 1989 Atlanta | NL | 141 | 554 | 118 | 18 | 0 | 13 | (5 | 8) | 175 | 41 | 57 | 12 | 3 | 62 | 0 | 1 | 4 | 3 | 3 | .50 | 17 | .213 | .228 | .316 |
| 1990 Atlanta | NL | 84 | 278 | 61 | 8 | 0 | 5 | (1 | 4) | 84 | 26 | 30 | 11 | 2 | 43 | 0 | 0 | 1 | 2 | 1 | .67 | 10 | .219 | .248 | .302 |
| 6 ML YEARS | | 577 | 2103 | 493 | 76 | 4 | 42 | (17 | 25) | 703 | 182 | 228 | 59 | 13 | 301 | 3 | 7 | 13 | 22 | 18 | .55 | 66 | .234 | .255 | .334 |

## Frank Thomas

**Bats:** Right **Throws:** Right **Pos:** 1B **Ht:** 6' 5" **Wt:** 240 **Born:** 05/27/68 **Age:** 23

| BATTING | | | | | | | | | | | | | | | | | | | BASERUNNING | | | | PERCENTAGES | | |
|---|---|---|---|---|---|---|---|---|---|---|---|---|---|---|---|---|---|---|---|---|---|---|---|---|---|
| Year Team | Lg | G | AB | H | 2B | 3B | HR | (Hm | Rd) | TB | R | RBI | TBB | IBB | SO | HBP | SH | SF | SB | CS | SB% | GDP | Avg | OBP | SLG |
| 1989 White Sox | R | 17 | 52 | 19 | 5 | 0 | 1 | -- | -- | 27 | 8 | 11 | 11 | 0 | 3 | 1 | 0 | 2 | 1 | 0 | 1.00 | 0 | .365 | .470 | .519 |
| Sarasota | A | 55 | 188 | 52 | 9 | 1 | 4 | -- | -- | 75 | 27 | 30 | 31 | 0 | 33 | 3 | 0 | 1 | 0 | 1 | .00 | 6 | .277 | .386 | .399 |
| 1990 Birmingham | AA | 109 | 353 | 114 | 27 | 5 | 18 | -- | -- | 205 | 85 | 71 | 112 | 2 | 74 | 5 | 0 | 4 | 7 | 5 | .58 | 13 | .323 | .487 | .581 |
| 1990 Chicago | AL | 60 | 191 | 63 | 11 | 3 | 7 | (2 | 5) | 101 | 39 | 31 | 44 | 0 | 54 | 2 | 0 | 3 | 0 | 1 | .00 | 5 | .330 | .454 | .529 |

## Milt Thompson

**Bats:** Left **Throws:** Right **Pos:** RF/LF/CF **Ht:** 5'11" **Wt:** 170 **Born:** 01/05/59 **Age:** 32

| BATTING | | | | | | | | | | | | | | | | | | | BASERUNNING | | | | PERCENTAGES | | |
|---|---|---|---|---|---|---|---|---|---|---|---|---|---|---|---|---|---|---|---|---|---|---|---|---|---|
| Year Team | Lg | G | AB | H | 2B | 3B | HR | (Hm | Rd) | TB | R | RBI | TBB | IBB | SO | HBP | SH | SF | SB | CS | SB% | GDP | Avg | OBP | SLG |
| 1984 Atlanta | NL | 25 | 99 | 30 | 1 | 0 | 2 | (0 | 2) | 37 | 16 | 4 | 11 | 1 | 11 | 0 | 1 | 0 | 14 | 2 | .88 | 1 | .303 | .373 | .374 |
| 1985 Atlanta | NL | 73 | 182 | 55 | 7 | 2 | 0 | (0 | 0) | 66 | 17 | 6 | 7 | 0 | 36 | 3 | 1 | 0 | 9 | 4 | .69 | 1 | .302 | .339 | .363 |
| 1986 Philadelphia | NL | 96 | 299 | 75 | 7 | 1 | 6 | (4 | 2) | 102 | 38 | 23 | 26 | 1 | 62 | 1 | 4 | 2 | 19 | 4 | .83 | 4 | .251 | .311 | .341 |
| 1987 Philadelphia | NL | 150 | 527 | 159 | 26 | 9 | 7 | (3 | 4) | 224 | 86 | 43 | 42 | 2 | 87 | 0 | 3 | 3 | 46 | 10 | .82 | 5 | .302 | .351 | .425 |
| 1988 Philadelphia | NL | 122 | 378 | 109 | 16 | 2 | 2 | (1 | 1) | 135 | 53 | 33 | 39 | 6 | 59 | 1 | 2 | 3 | 17 | 9 | .65 | 8 | .288 | .354 | .357 |
| 1989 St. Louis | NL | 155 | 545 | 158 | 28 | 8 | 4 | (2 | 2) | 214 | 60 | 68 | 39 | 5 | 91 | 4 | 0 | 3 | 27 | 8 | .77 | 12 | .290 | .340 | .393 |
| 1990 St. Louis | NL | 135 | 418 | 91 | 14 | 7 | 6 | (3 | 3) | 137 | 42 | 30 | 39 | 5 | 60 | 5 | 1 | 0 | 25 | 5 | .83 | 4 | .218 | .292 | .328 |
| 7 ML YEARS | | 756 | 2448 | 677 | 99 | 29 | 27 | (13 | 14) | 915 | 312 | 207 | 203 | 20 | 406 | 14 | 12 | 11 | 157 | 42 | .79 | 35 | .277 | .334 | .374 |

## Rich Thompson

**Pitches:** Right **Bats:** Both **Pos:** RP **Ht:** 5'11" **Wt:** 170 **Born:** 11/01/58 **Age:** 32

| HOW MUCH HE PITCHED | | | | | | | | WHAT HE GAVE UP | | | | | | | | | | | | THE RESULTS | | | | | |
|---|---|---|---|---|---|---|---|---|---|---|---|---|---|---|---|---|---|---|---|---|---|---|---|---|---|
| Year Team | Lg | G | GS | CG | GF | IP | BFP | H | R | ER | HR | SH | SF | HB | TBB | IBB | SO | WP | Bk | W | L | Pct. | ShO | Sv | ERA |
| 1985 Cleveland | AL | 57 | 0 | 0 | 24 | 80 | 379 | 95 | 63 | 56 | 8 | 5 | 6 | 6 | 48 | 6 | 30 | 6 | 2 | 3 | 8 | .273 | 0 | 5 | 6.30 |
| 1989 Montreal | NL | 19 | 1 | 0 | 9 | 33 | 129 | 27 | 11 | 8 | 2 | 2 | 2 | 2 | 11 | 2 | 15 | 0 | 1 | 0 | 2 | .000 | 0 | 0 | 2.18 |
| 1990 Montreal | NL | 1 | 0 | 0 | 1 | 1 | 4 | 1 | 0 | 0 | 0 | 0 | 0 | 0 | 0 | 0 | 0 | 0 | 0 | 0 | 0 | .000 | 0 | 0 | 0.00 |
| 3 ML YEARS | | 77 | 1 | 0 | 34 | 114 | 512 | 123 | 74 | 64 | 10 | 7 | 8 | 8 | 59 | 8 | 45 | 6 | 3 | 3 | 10 | .231 | 0 | 5 | 5.05 |

## Robbie Thompson

**Bats:** Right **Throws:** Right **Pos:** 2B **Ht:** 5'11" **Wt:** 170 **Born:** 05/10/62 **Age:** 29

| BATTING | | | | | | | | | | | | | | | | | | | BASERUNNING | | | | PERCENTAGES | | |
|---|---|---|---|---|---|---|---|---|---|---|---|---|---|---|---|---|---|---|---|---|---|---|---|---|---|
| Year Team | Lg | G | AB | H | 2B | 3B | HR | (Hm | Rd) | TB | R | RBI | TBB | IBB | SO | HBP | SH | SF | SB | CS | SB% | GDP | Avg | OBP | SLG |
| 1986 San Francisco | NL | 149 | 549 | 149 | 27 | 3 | 7 | (0 | 7) | 203 | 73 | 47 | 42 | 0 | 112 | 5 | 18 | 1 | 12 | 15 | .44 | 11 | .271 | .328 | .370 |
| 1987 San Francisco | NL | 132 | 420 | 110 | 26 | 5 | 10 | (7 | 3) | 176 | 62 | 44 | 40 | 3 | 91 | 8 | 6 | 0 | 16 | 11 | .59 | 8 | .262 | .338 | .419 |
| 1988 San Francisco | NL | 138 | 477 | 126 | 24 | 6 | 7 | (3 | 4) | 183 | 66 | 48 | 40 | 0 | 111 | 4 | 14 | 5 | 14 | 5 | .74 | 7 | .264 | .323 | .384 |
| 1989 San Francisco | NL | 148 | 547 | 132 | 26 | 11 | 13 | (7 | 6) | 219 | 91 | 50 | 51 | 0 | 133 | 13 | 9 | 0 | 12 | 2 | .86 | 6 | .241 | .321 | .400 |
| 1990 San Francisco | NL | 144 | 498 | 122 | 22 | 3 | 15 | (8 | 7) | 195 | 67 | 56 | 34 | 1 | 96 | 6 | 8 | 3 | 14 | 4 | .78 | 9 | .245 | .299 | .392 |
| 5 ML YEARS | | 711 | 2491 | 639 | 125 | 28 | 52 | (25 | 27) | 976 | 359 | 245 | 207 | 4 | 543 | 36 | 55 | 9 | 68 | 37 | .65 | 41 | .257 | .322 | .392 |

## Dickie Thon

**Bats:** Right **Throws:** Right **Pos:** SS **Ht:** 5'11" **Wt:** 175 **Born:** 06/20/58 **Age:** 33

| BATTING | | | | | | | | | | | | | | | | | | | BASERUNNING | | | | PERCENTAGES | | |
|---|---|---|---|---|---|---|---|---|---|---|---|---|---|---|---|---|---|---|---|---|---|---|---|---|---|
| Year Team | Lg | G | AB | H | 2B | 3B | HR | (Hm | Rd) | TB | R | RBI | TBB | IBB | SO | HBP | SH | SF | SB | CS | SB% | GDP | Avg | OBP | SLG |
| 1979 California | AL | 35 | 56 | 19 | 3 | 0 | 0 | (0 | 0) | 22 | 6 | 8 | 5 | 0 | 10 | 0 | 1 | 0 | 0 | 0 | .00 | 2 | .339 | .393 | .393 |
| 1980 California | AL | 80 | 267 | 68 | 12 | 2 | 0 | (0 | 0) | 84 | 32 | 15 | 10 | 0 | 28 | 1 | 5 | 2 | 7 | 5 | .58 | 5 | .255 | .282 | .315 |
| 1981 Houston | NL | 49 | 95 | 26 | 6 | 0 | 0 | (0 | 0) | 32 | 13 | 3 | 9 | 1 | 13 | 0 | 1 | 0 | 6 | 1 | .86 | 3 | .274 | .337 | .337 |
| 1982 Houston | NL | 136 | 496 | 137 | 31 | 10 | 3 | (1 | 2) | 197 | 73 | 36 | 37 | 2 | 48 | 1 | 5 | 1 | 37 | 8 | .82 | 4 | .276 | .327 | .397 |
| 1983 Houston | NL | 154 | 619 | 177 | 28 | 9 | 20 | (4 | 16) | 283 | 81 | 79 | 54 | 10 | 73 | 2 | 3 | 8 | 34 | 16 | .68 | 12 | .286 | .341 | .457 |
| 1984 Houston | NL | 5 | 17 | 6 | 0 | 1 | 0 | (0 | 0) | 8 | 3 | 1 | 0 | 0 | 4 | 1 | 0 | 0 | 0 | 1 | .00 | 1 | .353 | .389 | .471 |
| 1985 Houston | NL | 84 | 251 | 63 | 6 | 1 | 6 | (3 | 3) | 89 | 26 | 29 | 18 | 4 | 50 | 0 | 1 | 2 | 8 | 3 | .73 | 2 | .251 | .299 | .355 |
| 1986 Houston | NL | 106 | 278 | 69 | 13 | 1 | 3 | (0 | 3) | 93 | 24 | 21 | 29 | 5 | 49 | 0 | 1 | 1 | 6 | 5 | .55 | 8 | .248 | .318 | .335 |
| 1987 Houston | NL | 32 | 66 | 14 | 1 | 0 | 1 | (0 | 1) | 18 | 6 | 3 | 16 | 3 | 13 | 0 | 1 | 0 | 3 | 0 | 1.00 | 1 | .212 | .366 | .273 |
| 1988 San Diego | NL | 95 | 258 | 68 | 12 | 2 | 1 | (0 | 1) | 87 | 36 | 18 | 33 | 0 | 49 | 1 | 2 | 2 | 19 | 4 | .83 | 4 | .264 | .347 | .337 |
| 1989 Philadelphia | NL | 136 | 435 | 118 | 18 | 4 | 15 | (8 | 7) | 189 | 45 | 60 | 33 | 6 | 81 | 0 | 1 | 3 | 6 | 3 | .67 | 6 | .271 | .321 | .434 |
| 1990 Philadelphia | NL | 149 | 552 | 141 | 20 | 4 | 8 | (3 | 5) | 193 | 54 | 48 | 37 | 10 | 77 | 3 | 1 | 2 | 12 | 5 | .71 | 14 | .255 | .305 | .350 |
| 12 ML YEARS | | 1061 | 3390 | 906 | 150 | 34 | 57 | (19 | 38) | 1295 | 399 | 321 | 281 | 41 | 495 | 9 | 22 | 21 | 138 | 51 | .73 | 62 | .267 | .323 | .382 |

## Lou Thornton

**Bats:** Left **Throws:** Right **Pos:** CF **Ht:** 6' 0" **Wt:** 175 **Born:** 04/26/63 **Age:** 28

| BATTING | | | | | | | | | | | | | | | | | | | BASERUNNING | | | | PERCENTAGES | | |
|---|---|---|---|---|---|---|---|---|---|---|---|---|---|---|---|---|---|---|---|---|---|---|---|---|---|
| Year Team | Lg | G | AB | H | 2B | 3B | HR | (Hm | Rd) | TB | R | RBI | TBB | IBB | SO | HBP | SH | SF | SB | CS | SB% | GDP | Avg | OBP | SLG |
| 1985 Toronto | AL | 56 | 72 | 17 | 1 | 1 | 1 | (1 | 0) | 23 | 18 | 8 | 2 | 0 | 24 | 1 | 0 | 0 | 1 | 0 | 1.00 | 2 | .236 | .267 | .319 |
| 1987 Toronto | AL | 12 | 2 | 1 | 0 | 0 | 0 | (0 | 0) | 1 | 5 | 0 | 1 | 1 | 0 | 0 | 0 | 0 | 0 | 1 | .00 | 1 | .500 | .667 | .500 |
| 1988 Toronto | AL | 11 | 2 | 0 | 0 | 0 | 0 | (0 | 0) | 0 | 1 | 0 | 0 | 0 | 0 | 0 | 0 | 0 | 0 | 0 | .00 | 0 | .000 | .000 | .000 |
| 1989 New York | NL | 13 | 13 | 4 | 1 | 0 | 0 | (0 | 0) | 5 | 5 | 1 | 0 | 0 | 1 | 0 | 0 | 0 | 2 | 0 | 1.00 | 0 | .308 | .308 | .385 |
| 1990 New York | NL | 3 | 0 | 0 | 0 | 0 | 0 | (0 | 0) | 0 | 0 | 0 | 0 | 0 | 0 | 0 | 0 | 0 | 0 | 0 | .00 | 0 | .000 | .000 | .000 |
| 5 ML YEARS | | 95 | 89 | 22 | 2 | 1 | 1 | (1 | 0) | 29 | 29 | 9 | 3 | 1 | 25 | 1 | 0 | 0 | 3 | 1 | .75 | 3 | .247 | .280 | .326 |

## Gary Thurman

**Bats:** Right **Throws:** Right **Pos:** RF **Ht:** 5'10" **Wt:** 175 **Born:** 11/12/64 **Age:** 26

| BATTING | | | | | | | | | | | | | | | | | | | BASERUNNING | | | | PERCENTAGES | | |
|---|---|---|---|---|---|---|---|---|---|---|---|---|---|---|---|---|---|---|---|---|---|---|---|---|---|
| Year Team | Lg | G | AB | H | 2B | 3B | HR | (Hm | Rd) | TB | R | RBI | TBB | IBB | SO | HBP | SH | SF | SB | CS | SB% | GDP | Avg | OBP | SLG |
| 1987 Kansas City | AL | 27 | 81 | 24 | 2 | 0 | 0 | (0 | 0) | 26 | 12 | 5 | 8 | 0 | 20 | 0 | 1 | 0 | 7 | 2 | .78 | 1 | .296 | .360 | .321 |
| 1988 Kansas City | AL | 35 | 66 | 11 | 1 | 0 | 0 | (0 | 0) | 12 | 6 | 2 | 4 | 0 | 20 | 0 | 0 | 0 | 5 | 1 | .83 | 0 | .167 | .214 | .182 |
| 1989 Kansas City | AL | 72 | 87 | 17 | 2 | 1 | 0 | (0 | 0) | 21 | 24 | 5 | 15 | 0 | 26 | 0 | 2 | 1 | 16 | 0 | 1.00 | 0 | .195 | .311 | .241 |
| 1990 Kansas City | AL | 23 | 60 | 14 | 3 | 0 | 0 | (0 | 0) | 17 | 5 | 3 | 2 | 0 | 12 | 0 | 1 | 0 | 1 | 1 | .50 | 2 | .233 | .258 | .283 |
| 4 ML YEARS | | 157 | 294 | 66 | 8 | 1 | 0 | (0 | 0) | 76 | 47 | 15 | 29 | 0 | 78 | 0 | 4 | 1 | 29 | 4 | .88 | 3 | .224 | .293 | .259 |

## Mark Thurmond

**Pitches:** Left **Bats:** Left **Pos:** RP **Ht:** 6' 0" **Wt:** 190 **Born:** 09/12/56 **Age:** 34

| HOW MUCH HE PITCHED | | | | | | | | WHAT HE GAVE UP | | | | | | | | | | | | THE RESULTS | | | | | |
|---|---|---|---|---|---|---|---|---|---|---|---|---|---|---|---|---|---|---|---|---|---|---|---|---|---|
| Year Team | Lg | G | GS | CG | GF | IP | BFP | H | R | ER | HR | SH | SF | HB | TBB | IBB | SO | WP | Bk | W | L | Pct. | ShO | Sv | ERA |
| 1983 San Diego | NL | 21 | 18 | 2 | 2 | 115.1 | 466 | 104 | 40 | 34 | 7 | 9 | 3 | 2 | 33 | 2 | 49 | 0 | 1 | 7 | 3 | .700 | 0 | 0 | 2.65 |
| 1984 San Diego | NL | 32 | 29 | 1 | 1 | 178.2 | 750 | 174 | 70 | 59 | 12 | 11 | 3 | 0 | 55 | 3 | 57 | 2 | 2 | 14 | 8 | .636 | 1 | 0 | 2.97 |
| 1985 San Diego | NL | 36 | 23 | 1 | 4 | 138.1 | 592 | 154 | 70 | 61 | 9 | 12 | 4 | 3 | 44 | 5 | 57 | 0 | 0 | 7 | 11 | .389 | 1 | 2 | 3.97 |
| 1986 2 ML Teams | | 42 | 19 | 2 | 5 | 122.1 | 537 | 140 | 71 | 62 | 14 | 7 | 3 | 0 | 44 | 7 | 49 | 1 | 1 | 7 | 8 | .467 | 1 | 3 | 4.56 |
| 1987 Detroit | AL | 48 | 0 | 0 | 23 | 61.2 | 280 | 83 | 32 | 29 | 5 | 1 | 4 | 0 | 24 | 4 | 21 | 4 | 0 | 0 | 1 | .000 | 0 | 5 | 4.23 |
| 1988 Baltimore | AL | 43 | 6 | 0 | 15 | 74.2 | 322 | 80 | 43 | 38 | 10 | 0 | 4 | 2 | 27 | 3 | 29 | 0 | 0 | 1 | 8 | .111 | 0 | 3 | 4.58 |
| 1989 Baltimore | AL | 49 | 2 | 0 | 12 | 90 | 375 | 102 | 43 | 39 | 6 | 2 | 1 | 1 | 17 | 2 | 34 | 1 | 0 | 2 | 4 | .333 | 0 | 4 | 3.90 |
| 1990 San Francisco | NL | 43 | 0 | 0 | 16 | 56.2 | 238 | 53 | 26 | 21 | 6 | 8 | 6 | 0 | 18 | 3 | 24 | 1 | 0 | 2 | 3 | .400 | 0 | 4 | 3.34 |
| 1986 San Diego | NL | 17 | 15 | 2 | 0 | 70.2 | 328 | 96 | 58 | 51 | 7 | 4 | 2 | 0 | 27 | 5 | 32 | 0 | 1 | 3 | 7 | .300 | 1 | 0 | 6.50 |
| Detroit | AL | 25 | 4 | 0 | 5 | 51.2 | 209 | 44 | 13 | 11 | 7 | 3 | 1 | 0 | 17 | 2 | 17 | 1 | 0 | 4 | 1 | .800 | 0 | 3 | 1.92 |
| 8 ML YEARS | | 314 | 97 | 6 | 78 | 837.2 | 3560 | 890 | 395 | 343 | 69 | 50 | 28 | 8 | 262 | 29 | 320 | 9 | 4 | 40 | 46 | .465 | 3 | 21 | 3.69 |

## Jay Tibbs

**Pitches:** Right **Bats:** Right **Pos:** SP/RP **Ht:** 6' 1" **Wt:** 175 **Born:** 01/04/62 **Age:** 29

| HOW MUCH HE PITCHED | | | | | | | | WHAT HE GAVE UP | | | | | | | | | | | | THE RESULTS | | | | | |
|---|---|---|---|---|---|---|---|---|---|---|---|---|---|---|---|---|---|---|---|---|---|---|---|---|---|
| Year Team | Lg | G | GS | CG | GF | IP | BFP | H | R | ER | HR | SH | SF | HB | TBB | IBB | SO | WP | Bk | W | L | Pct. | ShO | Sv | ERA |
| 1984 Cincinnati | NL | 14 | 14 | 3 | 0 | 100.2 | 403 | 87 | 34 | 32 | 4 | 5 | 0 | 0 | 33 | 1 | 40 | 2 | 0 | 6 | 2 | .750 | 1 | 0 | 2.86 |
| 1985 Cincinnati | NL | 35 | 34 | 5 | 0 | 218 | 928 | 216 | 111 | 95 | 14 | 11 | 8 | 0 | 83 | 10 | 98 | 12 | 1 | 10 | 16 | .385 | 2 | 0 | 3.92 |
| 1986 Montreal | NL | 35 | 31 | 3 | 2 | 190.1 | 797 | 181 | 96 | 84 | 12 | 13 | 4 | 3 | 70 | 3 | 117 | 7 | 2 | 7 | 9 | .438 | 2 | 0 | 3.97 |
| 1987 Montreal | NL | 19 | 12 | 0 | 2 | 83 | 366 | 95 | 55 | 46 | 10 | 2 | 1 | 0 | 34 | 2 | 54 | 1 | 1 | 4 | 5 | .444 | 0 | 0 | 4.99 |
| 1988 Baltimore | AL | 30 | 24 | 1 | 1 | 158.2 | 708 | 184 | 103 | 95 | 18 | 6 | 7 | 3 | 63 | 2 | 82 | 8 | 3 | 4 | 15 | .211 | 0 | 0 | 5.39 |
| 1989 Baltimore | AL | 10 | 8 | 1 | 0 | 54.1 | 238 | 62 | 17 | 17 | 2 | 0 | 2 | 0 | 20 | 0 | 30 | 3 | 1 | 5 | 0 | 1.000 | 0 | 0 | 2.82 |
| 1990 2 ML Teams | | 15 | 10 | 0 | 3 | 57.2 | 244 | 62 | 36 | 34 | 8 | 2 | 2 | 0 | 16 | 1 | 27 | 2 | 0 | 3 | 7 | .300 | 0 | 0 | 5.31 |
| 1990 Baltimore | AL | 10 | 10 | 0 | 0 | 50.2 | 215 | 55 | 34 | 32 | 8 | 2 | 2 | 0 | 14 | 1 | 23 | 2 | 0 | 2 | 7 | .222 | 0 | 0 | 5.68 |
| Pittsburgh | NL | 5 | 0 | 0 | 3 | 7 | 29 | 7 | 2 | 2 | 0 | 0 | 0 | 0 | 2 | 0 | 4 | 0 | 0 | 1 | 0 | 1.000 | 0 | 0 | 2.57 |
| 7 ML YEARS | | 158 | 133 | 13 | 8 | 862.2 | 3684 | 887 | 452 | 403 | 68 | 39 | 24 | 6 | 319 | 19 | 448 | 35 | 8 | 39 | 54 | .419 | 5 | 0 | 4.20 |

## Ron Tingley

**Bats:** Right **Throws:** Right **Pos:** C **Ht:** 6' 2" **Wt:** 180 **Born:** 05/27/59 **Age:** 32

| BATTING | | | | | | | | | | | | | | | | | | | BASERUNNING | | | | PERCENTAGES | | |
|---|---|---|---|---|---|---|---|---|---|---|---|---|---|---|---|---|---|---|---|---|---|---|---|---|---|
| Year Team | Lg | G | AB | H | 2B | 3B | HR | (Hm | Rd) | TB | R | RBI | TBB | IBB | SO | HBP | SH | SF | SB | CS | SB% | GDP | Avg | OBP | SLG |
| 1982 San Diego | NL | 8 | 20 | 2 | 0 | 0 | 0 | (0 | 0) | 2 | 0 | 0 | 0 | 0 | 7 | 0 | 1 | 0 | 0 | 0 | .00 | 0 | .100 | .100 | .100 |
| 1988 Cleveland | AL | 9 | 24 | 4 | 0 | 0 | 1 | (0 | 1) | 7 | 1 | 2 | 2 | 0 | 8 | 0 | 0 | 0 | 0 | 0 | .00 | 1 | .167 | .231 | .292 |
| 1989 California | AL | 4 | 3 | 1 | 0 | 0 | 0 | (0 | 0) | 1 | 0 | 0 | 1 | 0 | 0 | 0 | 0 | 0 | 0 | 0 | .00 | 0 | .333 | .500 | .333 |
| 1990 California | AL | 5 | 3 | 0 | 0 | 0 | 0 | (0 | 0) | 0 | 0 | 0 | 1 | 0 | 1 | 0 | 0 | 0 | 0 | 0 | .00 | 1 | .000 | .250 | .000 |
| 4 ML YEARS | | 26 | 50 | 7 | 0 | 0 | 1 | (0 | 1) | 10 | 1 | 2 | 4 | 0 | 16 | 0 | 1 | 0 | 0 | 0 | .00 | 2 | .140 | .204 | .200 |

## Wayne Tolleson

**Bats:** Both **Throws:** Right **Pos:** SS **Ht:** 5' 9" **Wt:** 160 **Born:** 09/22/55 **Age:** 35

| | | | BATTING | | | | | | | | | | | | | | | | | | BASERUNNING | | | | PERCENTAGES | | |
|---|---|---|---|---|---|---|---|---|---|---|---|---|---|---|---|---|---|---|---|---|---|---|---|---|---|---|---|
| Year | Team | Lg | G | AB | H | 2B | 3B | HR | (Hm | Rd) | TB | R | RBI | TBB | IBB | SO | HBP | SH | SF | SB | CS | SB% | GDP | Avg | OBP | SLG |
| 1981 | Texas | AL | 14 | 24 | 4 | 0 | 0 | 0 | (0 | 0) | 4 | 6 | 1 | 1 | 0 | 5 | 0 | 0 | 0 | 2 | 0 | 1.00 | 0 | .167 | .200 | .167 |
| 1982 | Texas | AL | 38 | 70 | 8 | 1 | 0 | 0 | (0 | 0) | 9 | 6 | 2 | 5 | 0 | 14 | 0 | 3 | 0 | 1 | 1 | .50 | 1 | .114 | .173 | .129 |
| 1983 | Texas | AL | 134 | 470 | 122 | 13 | 2 | 3 | (2 | 1) | 148 | 64 | 20 | 40 | 0 | 68 | 2 | 7 | 2 | 33 | 10 | .77 | 8 | .260 | .319 | .315 |
| 1984 | Texas | AL | 118 | 338 | 72 | 9 | 2 | 0 | (0 | 0) | 85 | 35 | 9 | 27 | 0 | 47 | 3 | 9 | 1 | 22 | 4 | .85 | 12 | .213 | .276 | .251 |
| 1985 | Texas | AL | 123 | 323 | 101 | 9 | 5 | 1 | (0 | 1) | 123 | 45 | 18 | 21 | 0 | 46 | 0 | 9 | 2 | 21 | 12 | .64 | 6 | .313 | .353 | .381 |
| 1986 | 2 ML Teams | | 141 | 475 | 126 | 16 | 5 | 3 | (1 | 2) | 161 | 61 | 43 | 52 | 0 | 76 | 2 | 13 | 4 | 17 | 10 | .63 | 6 | .265 | .338 | .339 |
| 1987 | New York | AL | 121 | 349 | 77 | 4 | 0 | 1 | (0 | 1) | 84 | 48 | 22 | 43 | 0 | 72 | 0 | 6 | 0 | 5 | 3 | .63 | 3 | .221 | .306 | .241 |
| 1988 | New York | AL | 21 | 59 | 15 | 2 | 0 | 0 | (0 | 0) | 17 | 8 | 5 | 8 | 0 | 12 | 0 | 1 | 1 | 1 | 0 | 1.00 | 1 | .254 | .338 | .288 |
| 1989 | New York | AL | 79 | 140 | 23 | 5 | 2 | 1 | (0 | 1) | 35 | 16 | 9 | 16 | 0 | 23 | 1 | 3 | 0 | 5 | 1 | .83 | 3 | .164 | .255 | .250 |
| 1990 | New York | AL | 73 | 74 | 11 | 1 | 1 | 0 | (0 | 0) | 14 | 12 | 4 | 6 | 0 | 21 | 0 | 2 | 1 | 1 | 0 | 1.00 | 0 | .149 | .210 | .189 |
| 1986 | Chicago | AL | 81 | 260 | 65 | 7 | 3 | 3 | (1 | 2) | 87 | 39 | 29 | 38 | 0 | 43 | 0 | 9 | 3 | 13 | 6 | .68 | 3 | .250 | .342 | .335 |
| | New York | AL | 60 | 215 | 61 | 9 | 2 | 0 | (0 | 0) | 74 | 22 | 14 | 14 | 0 | 33 | 2 | 4 | 1 | 4 | 4 | .50 | 3 | .284 | .332 | .344 |
| 10 ML YEARS | | | 862 | 2322 | 559 | 60 | 17 | 9 | (3 | 6) | 680 | 301 | 133 | 219 | 0 | 384 | 8 | 53 | 11 | 108 | 41 | .72 | 40 | .241 | .307 | .293 |

## Randy Tomlin

**Pitches:** Left **Bats:** Left **Pos:** SP **Ht:** 5'11" **Wt:** 179 **Born:** 06/14/66 **Age:** 25

| | | | HOW MUCH HE PITCHED | | | | | | WHAT HE GAVE UP | | | | | | | | | | | | THE RESULTS | | | | | |
|---|---|---|---|---|---|---|---|---|---|---|---|---|---|---|---|---|---|---|---|---|---|---|---|---|---|---|
| Year | Team | Lg | G | GS | CG | GF | IP | BFP | H | R | ER | HR | SH | SF | HB | TBB | IBB | SO | WP | Bk | W | L | Pct. | ShO | Sv | ERA |
| 1988 | Watertown | A | 15 | 15 | 5 | 0 | 103.1 | 407 | 75 | 31 | 25 | 4 | 3 | 3 | 6 | 25 | 1 | 87 | 4 | 2 | 7 | 5 | .583 | 2 | 0 | 2.18 |
| 1989 | Salem | A | 21 | 21 | 3 | 0 | 138.2 | 582 | 131 | 60 | 50 | 11 | 2 | 2 | 3 | 43 | 0 | 99 | 7 | 0 | 12 | 6 | .667 | 2 | 0 | 3.25 |
| | Harrisburg | AA | 5 | 5 | 1 | 0 | 32 | 119 | 18 | 6 | 3 | 0 | 1 | 3 | 1 | 6 | 0 | 31 | 0 | 0 | 2 | 2 | .500 | 0 | 0 | 0.84 |
| 1990 | Buffalo | AAA | 3 | 1 | 0 | 1 | 8 | 33 | 12 | 3 | 3 | 1 | 0 | 1 | 0 | 1 | 0 | 3 | 0 | 0 | 0 | 0 | .000 | 0 | 0 | 3.38 |
| | Harrisburg | AA | 19 | 18 | 4 | 1 | 126.1 | 521 | 101 | 43 | 32 | 3 | 2 | 4 | 6 | 34 | 6 | 92 | 2 | 1 | 9 | 6 | .600 | 3 | 0 | 2.28 |
| 1990 | Pittsburgh | NL | 12 | 12 | 2 | 0 | 77.2 | 297 | 62 | 24 | 22 | 5 | 2 | 2 | 1 | 12 | 1 | 42 | 1 | 3 | 4 | 4 | .500 | 0 | 0 | 2.55 |

## Kelvin Torve

**Bats:** Left **Throws:** Right **Pos:** 1B **Ht:** 6' 3" **Wt:** 185 **Born:** 01/10/60 **Age:** 31

| | | | BATTING | | | | | | | | | | | | | | | | | | BASERUNNING | | | | PERCENTAGES | | |
|---|---|---|---|---|---|---|---|---|---|---|---|---|---|---|---|---|---|---|---|---|---|---|---|---|---|---|---|
| Year | Team | Lg | G | AB | H | 2B | 3B | HR | (Hm | Rd) | TB | R | RBI | TBB | IBB | SO | HBP | SH | SF | SB | CS | SB% | GDP | Avg | OBP | SLG |
| 1988 | Minnesota | AL | 12 | 16 | 3 | 0 | 0 | 1 | (0 | 1) | 6 | 1 | 2 | 1 | 0 | 2 | 0 | 0 | 0 | 0 | 1 | .00 | 0 | .188 | .235 | .375 |
| 1990 | New York | NL | 20 | 38 | 11 | 4 | 0 | 0 | (0 | 0) | 15 | 0 | 2 | 4 | 0 | 9 | 2 | 0 | 0 | 0 | 0 | .00 | 1 | .289 | .386 | .395 |
| 2 ML YEARS | | | 32 | 54 | 14 | 4 | 0 | 1 | (0 | 1) | 21 | 1 | 4 | 5 | 0 | 11 | 2 | 0 | 0 | 0 | 1 | .00 | 1 | .259 | .344 | .389 |

## Alan Trammell

**Bats:** Right **Throws:** Right **Pos:** SS **Ht:** 6' 0" **Wt:** 175 **Born:** 02/21/58 **Age:** 33

| | | | BATTING | | | | | | | | | | | | | | | | | | BASERUNNING | | | | PERCENTAGES | | |
|---|---|---|---|---|---|---|---|---|---|---|---|---|---|---|---|---|---|---|---|---|---|---|---|---|---|---|---|
| Year | Team | Lg | G | AB | H | 2B | 3B | HR | (Hm | Rd) | TB | R | RBI | TBB | IBB | SO | HBP | SH | SF | SB | CS | SB% | GDP | Avg | OBP | SLG |
| 1977 | Detroit | AL | 19 | 43 | 8 | 0 | 0 | 0 | (0 | 0) | 8 | 6 | 0 | 4 | 0 | 12 | 0 | 1 | 0 | 0 | 0 | .00 | 1 | .186 | .255 | .186 |
| 1978 | Detroit | AL | 139 | 448 | 120 | 14 | 6 | 2 | (0 | 2) | 152 | 49 | 34 | 45 | 0 | 56 | 2 | 6 | 3 | 3 | 1 | .75 | 12 | .268 | .335 | .339 |
| 1979 | Detroit | AL | 142 | 460 | 127 | 11 | 4 | 6 | (4 | 2) | 164 | 68 | 50 | 43 | 0 | 55 | 0 | 12 | 5 | 17 | 14 | .55 | 6 | .276 | .335 | .357 |
| 1980 | Detroit | AL | 146 | 560 | 168 | 21 | 5 | 9 | (5 | 4) | 226 | 107 | 65 | 69 | 2 | 63 | 3 | 13 | 7 | 12 | 12 | .50 | 10 | .300 | .376 | .404 |
| 1981 | Detroit | AL | 105 | 392 | 101 | 15 | 3 | 2 | (2 | 0) | 128 | 52 | 31 | 49 | 2 | 31 | 3 | 16 | 3 | 10 | 3 | .77 | 10 | .258 | .342 | .327 |
| 1982 | Detroit | AL | 157 | 489 | 126 | 34 | 3 | 9 | (5 | 4) | 193 | 66 | 57 | 52 | 0 | 47 | 0 | 9 | 6 | 19 | 8 | .70 | 5 | .258 | .325 | .395 |
| 1983 | Detroit | AL | 142 | 505 | 161 | 31 | 2 | 14 | (8 | 6) | 238 | 83 | 66 | 57 | 2 | 64 | 0 | 15 | 4 | 30 | 10 | .75 | 7 | .319 | .385 | .471 |
| 1984 | Detroit | AL | 139 | 555 | 174 | 34 | 5 | 14 | (7 | 7) | 260 | 85 | 69 | 60 | 2 | 63 | 3 | 6 | 2 | 19 | 13 | .59 | 8 | .314 | .382 | .468 |
| 1985 | Detroit | AL | 149 | 605 | 156 | 21 | 7 | 13 | (7 | 6) | 230 | 79 | 57 | 50 | 4 | 71 | 2 | 11 | 9 | 14 | 5 | .74 | 6 | .258 | .312 | .380 |
| 1986 | Detroit | AL | 151 | 574 | 159 | 33 | 7 | 21 | (8 | 13) | 269 | 107 | 75 | 59 | 4 | 57 | 5 | 11 | 4 | 25 | 12 | .68 | 7 | .277 | .347 | .469 |
| 1987 | Detroit | AL | 151 | 597 | 205 | 34 | 3 | 28 | (13 | 15) | 329 | 109 | 105 | 60 | 8 | 47 | 3 | 2 | 6 | 21 | 2 | .91 | 11 | .343 | .402 | .551 |
| 1988 | Detroit | AL | 128 | 466 | 145 | 24 | 1 | 15 | (7 | 8) | 216 | 73 | 69 | 46 | 8 | 46 | 4 | 0 | 7 | 7 | 4 | .64 | 14 | .311 | .373 | .464 |
| 1989 | Detroit | AL | 121 | 449 | 109 | 20 | 3 | 5 | (2 | 3) | 150 | 54 | 43 | 45 | 1 | 45 | 4 | 3 | 5 | 10 | 2 | .83 | 9 | .243 | .314 | .334 |
| 1990 | Detroit | AL | 146 | 559 | 170 | 37 | 1 | 14 | (9 | 5) | 251 | 71 | 89 | 68 | 7 | 55 | 1 | 3 | 6 | 12 | 10 | .55 | 11 | .304 | .377 | .449 |
| 14 ML YEARS | | | 1835 | 6702 | 1929 | 329 | 50 | 152 | (77 | 75) | 2814 | 1009 | 810 | 707 | 40 | 712 | 30 | 108 | 67 | 199 | 96 | .67 | 117 | .288 | .355 | .420 |

## Brian Traxler

**Bats:** Left **Throws:** Left **Pos:** 1B **Ht:** 5'10" **Wt:** 203 **Born:** 09/26/67 **Age:** 23

| | | | BATTING | | | | | | | | | | | | | | | | | | BASERUNNING | | | | PERCENTAGES | | |
|---|---|---|---|---|---|---|---|---|---|---|---|---|---|---|---|---|---|---|---|---|---|---|---|---|---|---|---|
| Year | Team | Lg | G | AB | H | 2B | 3B | HR | (Hm | Rd) | TB | R | RBI | TBB | IBB | SO | HBP | SH | SF | SB | CS | SB% | GDP | Avg | OBP | SLG |
| 1988 | Vero Beach | A | 72 | 260 | 76 | 14 | 0 | 2 | -- | -- | 96 | 30 | 34 | 30 | 0 | 35 | 0 | 0 | 1 | 1 | 1 | .50 | 6 | .292 | .364 | .369 |
| 1989 | San Antonio | AA | 63 | 228 | 79 | 7 | 0 | 9 | -- | -- | 113 | 37 | 44 | 22 | 1 | 20 | 0 | 3 | 4 | 1 | 0 | 1.00 | 4 | .346 | .398 | .496 |
| | Albuquerque | AAA | 64 | 239 | 72 | 10 | 3 | 3 | -- | -- | 97 | 33 | 30 | 17 | 2 | 17 | 1 | 0 | 3 | 0 | 2 | .00 | 4 | .301 | .346 | .406 |
| 1990 | Albuquerque | AAA | 98 | 318 | 88 | 23 | 0 | 7 | -- | -- | 132 | 43 | 53 | 39 | 1 | 39 | 0 | 2 | 7 | 4 | 0 | 1.00 | 7 | .277 | .349 | .415 |
| 1990 | Los Angeles | NL | 9 | 11 | 1 | 1 | 0 | 0 | (0 | 0) | 2 | 0 | 0 | 0 | 0 | 4 | 0 | 0 | 0 | 0 | 0 | .00 | 0 | .091 | .091 | .182 |

## Jeff Treadway

**Bats:** Left **Throws:** Right **Pos:** 2B **Ht:** 5'11" **Wt:** 170 **Born:** 01/22/63 **Age:** 28

| BATTING | | | | | | | | | | | | | | | | | | | BASERUNNING | | | | PERCENTAGES | | |
|---|---|---|---|---|---|---|---|---|---|---|---|---|---|---|---|---|---|---|---|---|---|---|---|---|---|
| Year Team | Lg | G | AB | H | 2B | 3B | HR | (Hm | Rd) | TB | R | RBI | TBB | IBB | SO | HBP | SH | SF | SB | CS | SB% | GDP | Avg | OBP | SLG |
| 1987 Cincinnati | NL | 23 | 84 | 28 | 4 | 0 | 2 | (2 | 0) | 38 | 9 | 4 | 2 | 0 | 6 | 1 | 3 | 0 | 1 | 0 | 1.00 | 1 | .333 | .356 | .452 |
| 1988 Cincinnati | NL | 103 | 301 | 76 | 19 | 4 | 2 | (2 | 0) | 109 | 30 | 23 | 27 | 7 | 30 | 3 | 4 | 6 | 2 | 0 | 1.00 | 4 | .252 | .315 | .362 |
| 1989 Atlanta | NL | 134 | 473 | 131 | 18 | 3 | 8 | (2 | 6) | 179 | 58 | 40 | 30 | 3 | 38 | 0 | 6 | 5 | 3 | 2 | .60 | 9 | .277 | .317 | .378 |
| 1990 Atlanta | NL | 128 | 474 | 134 | 20 | 2 | 11 | (5 | 6) | 191 | 56 | 59 | 25 | 1 | 42 | 3 | 5 | 4 | 3 | 4 | .43 | 10 | .283 | .320 | .403 |
| 4 ML YEARS | | 388 | 1332 | 369 | 61 | 9 | 23 | (11 | 12) | 517 | 153 | 126 | 84 | 11 | 116 | 7 | 18 | 15 | 9 | 6 | .60 | 24 | .277 | .320 | .388 |

## Alex Trevino

**Bats:** Right **Throws:** Right **Pos:** C **Ht:** 5'11" **Wt:** 179 **Born:** 08/26/57 **Age:** 33

| BATTING | | | | | | | | | | | | | | | | | | | BASERUNNING | | | | PERCENTAGES | | |
|---|---|---|---|---|---|---|---|---|---|---|---|---|---|---|---|---|---|---|---|---|---|---|---|---|---|
| Year Team | Lg | G | AB | H | 2B | 3B | HR | (Hm | Rd) | TB | R | RBI | TBB | IBB | SO | HBP | SH | SF | SB | CS | SB% | GDP | Avg | OBP | SLG |
| 1978 New York | NL | 6 | 12 | 3 | 0 | 0 | 0 | (0 | 0) | 3 | 3 | 0 | 1 | 0 | 2 | 0 | 0 | 0 | 0 | 0 | .00 | 1 | .250 | .308 | .250 |
| 1979 New York | NL | 79 | 207 | 56 | 11 | 1 | 0 | (0 | 0) | 69 | 24 | 20 | 20 | 2 | 27 | 1 | 4 | 0 | 2 | 2 | .50 | 8 | .271 | .338 | .333 |
| 1980 New York | NL | 106 | 355 | 91 | 11 | 2 | 0 | (0 | 0) | 106 | 26 | 37 | 13 | 1 | 41 | 1 | 2 | 5 | 0 | 3 | .00 | 11 | .256 | .281 | .299 |
| 1981 New York | NL | 56 | 149 | 39 | 2 | 0 | 0 | (0 | 0) | 41 | 17 | 10 | 13 | 0 | 19 | 1 | 1 | 1 | 3 | 0 | 1.00 | 4 | .262 | .323 | .275 |
| 1982 Cincinnati | NL | 120 | 355 | 89 | 10 | 3 | 1 | (0 | 1) | 108 | 24 | 33 | 34 | 11 | 34 | 3 | 5 | 4 | 3 | 1 | .75 | 16 | .251 | .318 | .304 |
| 1983 Cincinnati | NL | 74 | 167 | 36 | 8 | 1 | 1 | (0 | 1) | 49 | 14 | 13 | 17 | 6 | 20 | 0 | 1 | 2 | 0 | 0 | .00 | 3 | .216 | .285 | .293 |
| 1984 2 ML Teams | | 85 | 272 | 66 | 16 | 0 | 3 | (1 | 2) | 91 | 36 | 28 | 16 | 1 | 29 | 1 | 5 | 1 | 5 | 2 | .71 | 4 | .243 | .286 | .335 |
| 1985 San Francisco | NL | 57 | 157 | 34 | 10 | 1 | 6 | (3 | 3) | 64 | 17 | 19 | 20 | 0 | 24 | 0 | 1 | 1 | 0 | 0 | .00 | 5 | .217 | .303 | .408 |
| 1986 Los Angeles | NL | 89 | 202 | 53 | 13 | 0 | 4 | (2 | 2) | 78 | 31 | 26 | 27 | 2 | 35 | 1 | 2 | 1 | 0 | 0 | .00 | 6 | .262 | .351 | .386 |
| 1987 Los Angeles | NL | 72 | 144 | 32 | 7 | 1 | 3 | (2 | 1) | 50 | 16 | 16 | 6 | 2 | 28 | 4 | 1 | 1 | 1 | 0 | 1.00 | 7 | .222 | .271 | .347 |
| 1988 Houston | NL | 78 | 193 | 48 | 17 | 0 | 2 | (0 | 2) | 71 | 19 | 13 | 24 | 4 | 29 | 3 | 3 | 0 | 5 | 2 | .71 | 8 | .249 | .341 | .368 |
| 1989 Houston | NL | 59 | 131 | 38 | 7 | 1 | 2 | (1 | 1) | 53 | 15 | 16 | 7 | 0 | 18 | 1 | 1 | 1 | 0 | 0 | .00 | 3 | .290 | .329 | .405 |
| 1990 3 ML Teams | | 58 | 86 | 19 | 5 | 0 | 1 | (1 | 0) | 27 | 3 | 13 | 7 | 1 | 11 | 3 | 1 | 3 | 0 | 1 | .00 | 2 | .221 | .293 | .314 |
| 1984 Cincinnati | NL | 6 | 6 | 1 | 0 | 0 | 0 | (0 | 0) | 1 | 0 | 0 | 0 | 0 | 2 | 0 | 0 | 0 | 0 | 0 | .00 | 0 | .167 | .167 | .167 |
| Atlanta | NL | 79 | 266 | 65 | 16 | 0 | 3 | (1 | 2) | 90 | 36 | 28 | 16 | 1 | 27 | 1 | 5 | 1 | 5 | 2 | .71 | 4 | .244 | .289 | .338 |
| 1990 Houston | NL | 42 | 69 | 13 | 3 | 0 | 1 | (1 | 0) | 19 | 3 | 10 | 6 | 1 | 11 | 2 | 1 | 2 | 0 | 1 | .00 | 2 | .188 | .266 | .275 |
| New York | NL | 9 | 10 | 3 | 1 | 0 | 0 | (0 | 0) | 4 | 0 | 2 | 1 | 0 | 0 | 0 | 0 | 1 | 0 | 0 | .00 | 0 | .300 | .333 | .400 |
| Cincinnati | NL | 7 | 7 | 3 | 1 | 0 | 0 | (0 | 0) | 4 | 0 | 1 | 0 | 0 | 0 | 1 | 0 | 0 | 0 | 0 | .00 | 0 | .429 | .500 | .571 |
| 13 ML YEARS | | 939 | 2430 | 604 | 117 | 10 | 23 | (10 | 13) | 810 | 245 | 244 | 205 | 30 | 317 | 19 | 27 | 20 | 19 | 11 | .63 | 78 | .249 | .310 | .333 |

## John Tudor

**Pitches:** Left **Bats:** Left **Pos:** SP **Ht:** 6' 0" **Wt:** 185 **Born:** 02/02/54 **Age:** 37

| HOW MUCH HE PITCHED | | | | | | | | WHAT HE GAVE UP | | | | | | | | | | | | THE RESULTS | | | | | |
|---|---|---|---|---|---|---|---|---|---|---|---|---|---|---|---|---|---|---|---|---|---|---|---|---|---|
| Year Team | Lg | G | GS | CG | GF | IP | BFP | H | R | ER | HR | SH | SF | HB | TBB | IBB | SO | WP | Bk | W | L | Pct. | ShO | Sv | ERA |
| 1979 Boston | AL | 6 | 6 | 1 | 0 | 28 | 128 | 39 | 23 | 20 | 2 | 3 | 3 | 0 | 9 | 1 | 11 | 0 | 0 | 1 | 2 | .333 | 0 | 0 | 6.43 |
| 1980 Boston | AL | 16 | 13 | 5 | 0 | 92 | 382 | 81 | 35 | 31 | 4 | 4 | 3 | 3 | 31 | 1 | 45 | 1 | 0 | 8 | 5 | .615 | 0 | 0 | 3.03 |
| 1981 Boston | AL | 18 | 11 | 2 | 3 | 79 | 331 | 74 | 44 | 40 | 11 | 2 | 4 | 3 | 28 | 1 | 44 | 1 | 1 | 4 | 3 | .571 | 0 | 1 | 4.56 |
| 1982 Boston | AL | 32 | 30 | 6 | 1 | 195.2 | 847 | 215 | 90 | 79 | 20 | 8 | 5 | 8 | 59 | 3 | 146 | 0 | 2 | 13 | 10 | .565 | 1 | 0 | 3.63 |
| 1983 Boston | AL | 34 | 34 | 7 | 0 | 242 | 1022 | 236 | 122 | 110 | 32 | 5 | 5 | 4 | 81 | 3 | 136 | 8 | 2 | 13 | 12 | .520 | 2 | 0 | 4.09 |
| 1984 Pittsburgh | NL | 32 | 32 | 6 | 0 | 212 | 881 | 200 | 81 | 77 | 19 | 10 | 6 | 1 | 56 | 2 | 117 | 1 | 1 | 12 | 11 | .522 | 1 | 0 | 3.27 |
| 1985 St. Louis | NL | 36 | 36 | 14 | 0 | 275 | 1062 | 209 | 68 | 59 | 14 | 4 | 3 | 5 | 49 | 4 | 169 | 4 | 0 | 21 | 8 | .724 | 10 | 0 | 1.93 |
| 1986 St. Louis | NL | 30 | 30 | 3 | 0 | 219 | 879 | 197 | 81 | 71 | 22 | 9 | 8 | 1 | 53 | 5 | 107 | 2 | 1 | 13 | 7 | .650 | 0 | 0 | 2.92 |
| 1987 St. Louis | NL | 16 | 16 | 0 | 0 | 96 | 405 | 100 | 43 | 41 | 11 | 3 | 2 | 1 | 32 | 1 | 54 | 1 | 0 | 10 | 2 | .833 | 0 | 0 | 3.84 |
| 1988 2 ML Teams | | 30 | 30 | 5 | 0 | 197.2 | 794 | 189 | 60 | 51 | 10 | 12 | 5 | 1 | 41 | 7 | 87 | 0 | 3 | 10 | 8 | .556 | 1 | 0 | 2.32 |
| 1989 Los Angeles | NL | 6 | 3 | 0 | 1 | 14.1 | 62 | 17 | 5 | 5 | 1 | 1 | 0 | 0 | 6 | 0 | 9 | 0 | 0 | 0 | 0 | .000 | 0 | 0 | 3.14 |
| 1990 St. Louis | NL | 25 | 22 | 1 | 0 | 146.1 | 575 | 120 | 48 | 39 | 10 | 8 | 1 | 2 | 30 | 4 | 63 | 0 | 0 | 12 | 4 | .750 | 1 | 0 | 2.40 |
| 1988 St. Louis | NL | 21 | 21 | 4 | 0 | 145.1 | 578 | 131 | 44 | 37 | 5 | 10 | 5 | 1 | 31 | 7 | 55 | 0 | 1 | 6 | 5 | .545 | 1 | 0 | 2.29 |
| Los Angeles | NL | 9 | 9 | 1 | 0 | 52.1 | 216 | 58 | 16 | 14 | 5 | 2 | 0 | 0 | 10 | 0 | 32 | 0 | 2 | 4 | 3 | .571 | 0 | 0 | 2.41 |
| 12 ML YEARS | | 281 | 263 | 50 | 5 | 1797 | 7368 | 1677 | 700 | 623 | 156 | 69 | 45 | 29 | 475 | 32 | 988 | 18 | 10 | 117 | 72 | .619 | 16 | 1 | 3.12 |

## Jose Uribe

**Bats:** Both **Throws:** Right **Pos:** SS **Ht:** 5'10" **Wt:** 165 **Born:** 01/21/60 **Age:** 31

| BATTING | | | | | | | | | | | | | | | | | | | BASERUNNING | | | | PERCENTAGES | | |
|---|---|---|---|---|---|---|---|---|---|---|---|---|---|---|---|---|---|---|---|---|---|---|---|---|---|
| Year Team | Lg | G | AB | H | 2B | 3B | HR | (Hm | Rd) | TB | R | RBI | TBB | IBB | SO | HBP | SH | SF | SB | CS | SB% | GDP | Avg | OBP | SLG |
| 1984 St. Louis | NL | 8 | 19 | 4 | 0 | 0 | 0 | (0 | 0) | 4 | 4 | 3 | 0 | 0 | 2 | 0 | 1 | 0 | 1 | 0 | 1.00 | 1 | .211 | .211 | .211 |
| 1985 San Francisco | NL | 147 | 476 | 113 | 20 | 4 | 3 | (2 | 1) | 150 | 46 | 26 | 30 | 8 | 57 | 2 | 5 | 0 | 8 | 2 | .80 | 5 | .237 | .285 | .315 |
| 1986 San Francisco | NL | 157 | 453 | 101 | 15 | 1 | 3 | (1 | 2) | 127 | 46 | 43 | 61 | 19 | 76 | 0 | 3 | 0 | 22 | 11 | .67 | 2 | .223 | .315 | .280 |
| 1987 San Francisco | NL | 95 | 309 | 90 | 16 | 5 | 5 | (4 | 1) | 131 | 44 | 30 | 24 | 9 | 35 | 1 | 5 | 1 | 12 | 2 | .86 | 1 | .291 | .343 | .424 |
| 1988 San Francisco | NL | 141 | 493 | 124 | 10 | 7 | 3 | (1 | 2) | 157 | 47 | 35 | 36 | 10 | 69 | 0 | 4 | 2 | 14 | 10 | .58 | 3 | .252 | .301 | .318 |
| 1989 San Francisco | NL | 151 | 453 | 100 | 12 | 6 | 1 | (0 | 1) | 127 | 34 | 30 | 34 | 12 | 74 | 0 | 6 | 4 | 6 | 6 | .50 | 7 | .221 | .273 | .280 |
| 1990 San Francisco | NL | 138 | 415 | 103 | 8 | 6 | 1 | (0 | 1) | 126 | 35 | 24 | 29 | 13 | 49 | 0 | 4 | 0 | 5 | 9 | .36 | 8 | .248 | .297 | .304 |
| 7 ML YEARS | | 837 | 2618 | 635 | 81 | 29 | 16 | (8 | 8) | 822 | 256 | 191 | 214 | 71 | 362 | 3 | 28 | 7 | 68 | 40 | .63 | 27 | .243 | .300 | .314 |

## Efrain Valdez

**Pitches:** Left **Bats:** Left **Pos:** RP **Ht:** 5'11" **Wt:** 170 **Born:** 06/11/66 **Age:** 25

| HOW MUCH HE PITCHED | | | | | | | | WHAT HE GAVE UP | | | | | | | | | | | | THE RESULTS | | | | | |
|---|---|---|---|---|---|---|---|---|---|---|---|---|---|---|---|---|---|---|---|---|---|---|---|---|---|
| Year Team | Lg | G | GS | CG | GF | IP | BFP | H | R | ER | HR | SH | SF | HB | TBB | IBB | SO | WP | Bk | W | L | Pct. | ShO | Sv | ERA |
| 1984 Spokane | A | 13 | 1 | 0 | 6 | 16.2 | 0 | 26 | 18 | 14 | 1 | 0 | 0 | 0 | 8 | 0 | 15 | 0 | 0 | 1 | 2 | .333 | 0 | 0 | 7.56 |
| 1986 Tulsa | AA | 4 | 2 | 0 | 1 | 12.1 | 52 | 12 | 8 | 8 | 1 | 1 | 0 | 1 | 6 | 0 | 4 | 0 | 1 | 0 | 1 | .000 | 0 | 0 | 5.84 |
| 1987 Tulsa | AA | 11 | 8 | 1 | 1 | 49.1 | 235 | 62 | 44 | 39 | 9 | 1 | 3 | 2 | 24 | 3 | 38 | 3 | 0 | 1 | 4 | .200 | 1 | 0 | 7.11 |
| Charlotte | A | 17 | 8 | 0 | 2 | 70.1 | 301 | 67 | 32 | 29 | 6 | 2 | 3 | 1 | 28 | 2 | 45 | 3 | 2 | 3 | 6 | .333 | 0 | 0 | 3.71 |
| 1988 Tulsa | AA | 43 | 3 | 0 | 21 | 63.1 | 276 | 63 | 37 | 32 | 6 | 3 | 2 | 4 | 24 | 2 | 52 | 3 | 1 | 6 | 5 | .545 | 0 | 6 | 4.55 |
| 1989 Canton-Akrn | AA | 44 | 2 | 0 | 18 | 75.1 | 318 | 60 | 26 | 18 | 1 | 6 | 3 | 4 | 33 | 3 | 55 | 4 | 0 | 2 | 4 | .333 | 0 | 1 | 2.15 |
| 1990 Colo Sprngs | AAA | 46 | 1 | 0 | 17 | 75.2 | 330 | 72 | 38 | 32 | 6 | 4 | 5 | 4 | 30 | 8 | 52 | 4 | 2 | 4 | 2 | .667 | 0 | 6 | 3.81 |
| 1990 Cleveland | AL | 13 | 0 | 0 | 4 | 23.2 | 104 | 20 | 10 | 8 | 2 | 1 | 3 | 0 | 14 | 3 | 13 | 1 | 0 | 1 | 1 | .500 | 0 | 0 | 3.04 |

## Rafael Valdez

**Pitches:** Right **Bats:** Right **Pos:** RP **Ht:** 5'11" **Wt:** 165 **Born:** 12/17/68 **Age:** 22

| HOW MUCH HE PITCHED | | | | | | | | WHAT HE GAVE UP | | | | | | | | | | | | THE RESULTS | | | | | |
|---|---|---|---|---|---|---|---|---|---|---|---|---|---|---|---|---|---|---|---|---|---|---|---|---|---|
| Year Team | Lg | G | GS | CG | GF | IP | BFP | H | R | ER | HR | SH | SF | HB | TBB | IBB | SO | WP | Bk | W | L | Pct. | ShO | Sv | ERA |
| 1988 Chston-Sc | A | 28 | 17 | 4 | 6 | 152.1 | 603 | 117 | 42 | 38 | 6 | 3 | 3 | 1 | 46 | 4 | 100 | 9 | 6 | 11 | 4 | .733 | 1 | 0 | 2.25 |
| 1989 Riverside | A | 21 | 21 | 5 | 0 | 143.1 | 567 | 89 | 40 | 36 | 6 | 2 | 1 | 4 | 58 | 1 | 137 | 6 | 0 | 10 | 5 | .667 | 3 | 0 | 2.26 |
| Wichita | AA | 6 | 6 | 2 | 0 | 41.2 | 172 | 28 | 10 | 9 | 1 | 0 | 1 | 1 | 24 | 2 | 26 | 1 | 1 | 5 | 0 | 1.000 | 0 | 0 | 1.94 |
| 1990 Las Vegas | AAA | 17 | 17 | 0 | 0 | 86 | 401 | 82 | 58 | 47 | 6 | 5 | 3 | 2 | 65 | 0 | 79 | 4 | 3 | 4 | 7 | .364 | 0 | 0 | 4.92 |
| 1990 San Diego | NL | 3 | 0 | 0 | 2 | 5.2 | 30 | 11 | 7 | 7 | 4 | 0 | 0 | 0 | 2 | 0 | 3 | 0 | 0 | 0 | 1 | .000 | 0 | 0 | 11.12 |

## Sergio Valdez

**Pitches:** Right **Bats:** Right **Pos:** RP/SP **Ht:** 6' 1" **Wt:** 190 **Born:** 09/07/65 **Age:** 25

| HOW MUCH HE PITCHED | | | | | | | | WHAT HE GAVE UP | | | | | | | | | | | | THE RESULTS | | | | | |
|---|---|---|---|---|---|---|---|---|---|---|---|---|---|---|---|---|---|---|---|---|---|---|---|---|---|
| Year Team | Lg | G | GS | CG | GF | IP | BFP | H | R | ER | HR | SH | SF | HB | TBB | IBB | SO | WP | Bk | W | L | Pct. | ShO | Sv | ERA |
| 1986 Montreal | NL | 5 | 5 | 0 | 0 | 25 | 120 | 39 | 20 | 19 | 2 | 0 | 0 | 1 | 11 | 0 | 20 | 2 | 0 | 0 | 4 | .000 | 0 | 0 | 6.84 |
| 1989 Atlanta | NL | 19 | 1 | 0 | 8 | 32.2 | 145 | 31 | 24 | 22 | 5 | 2 | 0 | 0 | 17 | 3 | 26 | 2 | 0 | 1 | 2 | .333 | 0 | 0 | 6.06 |
| 1990 2 ML Teams | | 30 | 13 | 0 | 7 | 107.2 | 466 | 115 | 66 | 58 | 17 | 5 | 5 | 1 | 38 | 2 | 66 | 4 | 0 | 6 | 6 | .500 | 0 | 0 | 4.85 |
| 1990 Atlanta | NL | 6 | 0 | 0 | 3 | 5.1 | 26 | 6 | 4 | 4 | 0 | 1 | 0 | 0 | 3 | 0 | 3 | 1 | 0 | 0 | 0 | .000 | 0 | 0 | 6.75 |
| Cleveland | AL | 24 | 13 | 0 | 4 | 102.1 | 440 | 109 | 62 | 54 | 17 | 4 | 5 | 1 | 35 | 2 | 63 | 3 | 0 | 6 | 6 | .500 | 0 | 0 | 4.75 |
| 3 ML YEARS | | 54 | 19 | 0 | 15 | 165.1 | 731 | 185 | 110 | 99 | 24 | 7 | 5 | 2 | 66 | 5 | 112 | 8 | 0 | 7 | 12 | .368 | 0 | 0 | 5.39 |

## Fernando Valenzuela

**Pitches:** Left **Bats:** Left **Pos:** SP **Ht:** 5'11" **Wt:** 202 **Born:** 11/01/60 **Age:** 30

| HOW MUCH HE PITCHED | | | | | | | | WHAT HE GAVE UP | | | | | | | | | | | | THE RESULTS | | | | | |
|---|---|---|---|---|---|---|---|---|---|---|---|---|---|---|---|---|---|---|---|---|---|---|---|---|---|
| Year Team | Lg | G | GS | CG | GF | IP | BFP | H | R | ER | HR | SH | SF | HB | TBB | IBB | SO | WP | Bk | W | L | Pct. | ShO | Sv | ERA |
| 1980 Los Angeles | NL | 10 | 0 | 0 | 4 | 18 | 66 | 8 | 2 | 0 | 0 | 1 | 1 | 0 | 5 | 0 | 16 | 0 | 1 | 2 | 0 | 1.000 | 0 | 1 | 0.00 |
| 1981 Los Angeles | NL | 25 | 25 | 11 | 0 | 192 | 758 | 140 | 55 | 53 | 11 | 9 | 3 | 1 | 61 | 4 | 180 | 4 | 0 | 13 | 7 | .650 | 8 | 0 | 2.48 |
| 1982 Los Angeles | NL | 37 | 37 | 18 | 0 | 285 | 1156 | 247 | 105 | 91 | 13 | 19 | 6 | 2 | 83 | 12 | 199 | 4 | 0 | 19 | 13 | .594 | 4 | 0 | 2.87 |
| 1983 Los Angeles | NL | 35 | 35 | 9 | 0 | 257 | 1094 | 245 | 122 | 107 | 16 | 27 | 5 | 3 | 99 | 10 | 189 | 12 | 1 | 15 | 10 | .600 | 4 | 0 | 3.75 |
| 1984 Los Angeles | NL | 34 | 34 | 12 | 0 | 261 | 1078 | 218 | 109 | 88 | 14 | 11 | 7 | 2 | 106 | 4 | 240 | 11 | 1 | 12 | 17 | .414 | 2 | 0 | 3.03 |
| 1985 Los Angeles | NL | 35 | 35 | 14 | 0 | 272.1 | 1109 | 211 | 92 | 74 | 14 | 13 | 8 | 1 | 101 | 5 | 208 | 10 | 1 | 17 | 10 | .630 | 5 | 0 | 2.45 |
| 1986 Los Angeles | NL | 34 | 34 | 20 | 0 | 269.1 | 1102 | 226 | 104 | 94 | 18 | 15 | 3 | 1 | 85 | 5 | 242 | 13 | 0 | 21 | 11 | .656 | 3 | 0 | 3.14 |
| 1987 Los Angeles | NL | 34 | 34 | 12 | 0 | 251 | 1116 | 254 | 120 | 111 | 25 | 18 | 2 | 4 | 124 | 4 | 190 | 14 | 1 | 14 | 14 | .500 | 1 | 0 | 3.98 |
| 1988 Los Angeles | NL | 23 | 22 | 3 | 1 | 142.1 | 626 | 142 | 71 | 67 | 11 | 15 | 5 | 0 | 76 | 4 | 64 | 7 | 1 | 5 | 8 | .385 | 0 | 1 | 4.24 |
| 1989 Los Angeles | NL | 31 | 31 | 3 | 0 | 196.2 | 852 | 185 | 89 | 75 | 11 | 7 | 7 | 2 | 98 | 6 | 116 | 6 | 4 | 10 | 13 | .435 | 0 | 0 | 3.43 |
| 1990 Los Angeles | NL | 33 | 33 | 5 | 0 | 204 | 900 | 223 | 112 | 104 | 19 | 11 | 4 | 0 | 77 | 4 | 115 | 13 | 1 | 13 | 13 | .500 | 2 | 0 | 4.59 |
| 11 ML YEARS | | 331 | 320 | 107 | 5 | 2348.2 | 9857 | 2099 | 981 | 864 | 152 | 146 | 51 | 16 | 915 | 58 | 1759 | 94 | 11 | 141 | 116 | .549 | 29 | 2 | 3.31 |

## Julio Valera

**Pitches:** Right **Bats:** Right **Pos:** SP **Ht:** 6' 2" **Wt:** 185 **Born:** 10/13/68 **Age:** 22

| HOW MUCH HE PITCHED | | | | | | | | WHAT HE GAVE UP | | | | | | | | | | | | THE RESULTS | | | | | |
|---|---|---|---|---|---|---|---|---|---|---|---|---|---|---|---|---|---|---|---|---|---|---|---|---|---|
| Year Team | Lg | G | GS | CG | GF | IP | BFP | H | R | ER | HR | SH | SF | HB | TBB | IBB | SO | WP | Bk | W | L | Pct. | ShO | Sv | ERA |
| 1986 Kingsport | R | 13 | 13 | 2 | 0 | 76.1 | 356 | 91 | 58 | 44 | 5 | 4 | 0 | 0 | 29 | 2 | 64 | 4 | 1 | 3 | 10 | .231 | 1 | 0 | 5.19 |
| 1987 Columbia | A | 22 | 22 | 2 | 0 | 125.1 | 522 | 114 | 53 | 39 | 7 | 2 | 1 | 4 | 31 | 0 | 97 | 6 | 0 | 8 | 7 | .533 | 2 | 0 | 2.80 |
| 1988 Columbia | A | 30 | 27 | 8 | 3 | 191 | 775 | 171 | 77 | 68 | 8 | 5 | 7 | 4 | 51 | 3 | 144 | 9 | 6 | 15 | 11 | .577 | 0 | 1 | 3.20 |
| 1989 St.Lucie | A | 6 | 6 | 3 | 0 | 45 | 173 | 34 | 5 | 5 | 1 | 2 | 0 | 0 | 6 | 1 | 45 | 0 | 0 | 4 | 2 | .667 | 2 | 0 | 1.00 |
| Jackson | AA | 19 | 19 | 6 | 0 | 137.1 | 566 | 123 | 47 | 38 | 4 | 7 | 3 | 8 | 36 | 2 | 107 | 10 | 0 | 10 | 6 | .625 | 2 | 0 | 2.49 |
| Tidewater | AAA | 2 | 2 | 0 | 0 | 13 | 52 | 8 | 3 | 3 | 1 | 0 | 0 | 1 | 5 | 0 | 10 | 1 | 0 | 1 | 1 | .500 | 0 | 0 | 2.08 |
| 1990 Tidewater | AAA | 24 | 24 | 9 | 0 | 158 | 648 | 146 | 66 | 53 | 12 | 6 | 5 | 5 | 39 | 3 | 133 | 7 | 5 | 10 | 10 | .500 | 2 | 0 | 3.02 |
| 1990 New York | NL | 3 | 3 | 0 | 0 | 13 | 64 | 20 | 11 | 10 | 1 | 0 | 0 | 0 | 7 | 0 | 4 | 0 | 0 | 1 | 1 | .500 | 0 | 0 | 6.92 |

## Dave Valle

**Bats:** Right **Throws:** Right **Pos:** C **Ht:** 6' 2" **Wt:** 200 **Born:** 10/30/60 **Age:** 30

| BATTING | | | | | | | | | | | | | | | | | | | BASERUNNING | | | | PERCENTAGES | | |
|---|---|---|---|---|---|---|---|---|---|---|---|---|---|---|---|---|---|---|---|---|---|---|---|---|---|
| Year Team | Lg | G | AB | H | 2B | 3B | HR | (Hm | Rd) | TB | R | RBI | TBB | IBB | SO | HBP | SH | SF | SB | CS | SB% | GDP | Avg | OBP | SLG |
| 1984 Seattle | AL | 13 | 27 | 8 | 1 | 0 | 1 | (1 | 0) | 12 | 4 | 4 | 1 | 0 | 5 | 0 | 0 | 0 | 0 | 0 | .00 | 0 | .296 | .321 | .444 |
| 1985 Seattle | AL | 31 | 70 | 11 | 1 | 0 | 0 | (0 | 0) | 12 | 2 | 4 | 1 | 0 | 17 | 1 | 1 | 0 | 0 | 0 | .00 | 1 | .157 | .181 | .171 |
| 1986 Seattle | AL | 22 | 53 | 18 | 3 | 0 | 5 | (4 | 1) | 36 | 10 | 15 | 7 | 0 | 7 | 0 | 0 | 0 | 0 | 0 | .00 | 2 | .340 | .417 | .679 |
| 1987 Seattle | AL | 95 | 324 | 83 | 16 | 3 | 12 | (8 | 4) | 141 | 40 | 53 | 15 | 2 | 46 | 3 | 0 | 4 | 2 | 0 | 1.00 | 13 | .256 | .292 | .435 |
| 1988 Seattle | AL | 92 | 290 | 67 | 15 | 2 | 10 | (5 | 5) | 116 | 29 | 50 | 18 | 0 | 38 | 9 | 3 | 2 | 0 | 1 | .00 | 13 | .231 | .295 | .400 |
| 1989 Seattle | AL | 94 | 316 | 75 | 10 | 3 | 7 | (1 | 6) | 112 | 32 | 34 | 29 | 2 | 32 | 6 | 1 | 3 | 0 | 0 | .00 | 13 | .237 | .311 | .354 |
| 1990 Seattle | AL | 107 | 308 | 66 | 15 | 0 | 7 | (1 | 6) | 102 | 37 | 33 | 45 | 0 | 48 | 7 | 4 | 0 | 1 | 2 | .33 | 11 | .214 | .328 | .331 |
| 7 ML YEARS | | 454 | 1388 | 328 | 61 | 8 | 42 | (20 | 22) | 531 | 154 | 193 | 116 | 4 | 193 | 26 | 9 | 9 | 3 | 3 | .50 | 53 | .236 | .305 | .383 |

## Andy Van Slyke

**Bats:** Left **Throws:** Right **Pos:** CF **Ht:** 6' 2" **Wt:** 190 **Born:** 12/21/60 **Age:** 30

| BATTING | | | | | | | | | | | | | | | | | | | BASERUNNING | | | | PERCENTAGES | | |
|---|---|---|---|---|---|---|---|---|---|---|---|---|---|---|---|---|---|---|---|---|---|---|---|---|---|
| Year Team | Lg | G | AB | H | 2B | 3B | HR | (Hm | Rd) | TB | R | RBI | TBB | IBB | SO | HBP | SH | SF | SB | CS | SB% | GDP | Avg | OBP | SLG |
| 1983 St. Louis | NL | 101 | 309 | 81 | 15 | 5 | 8 | (3 | 5) | 130 | 51 | 38 | 46 | 5 | 64 | 1 | 2 | 3 | 21 | 7 | .75 | 4 | .262 | .357 | .421 |
| 1984 St. Louis | NL | 137 | 361 | 88 | 16 | 4 | 7 | (3 | 4) | 133 | 45 | 50 | 63 | 9 | 71 | 0 | 0 | 2 | 28 | 5 | .85 | 5 | .244 | .354 | .368 |
| 1985 St. Louis | NL | 146 | 424 | 110 | 25 | 6 | 13 | (5 | 8) | 186 | 61 | 55 | 47 | 6 | 54 | 2 | 1 | 1 | 34 | 6 | .85 | 7 | .259 | .335 | .439 |
| 1986 St. Louis | NL | 137 | 418 | 113 | 23 | 7 | 13 | (6 | 7) | 189 | 48 | 61 | 47 | 5 | 85 | 1 | 1 | 3 | 21 | 8 | .72 | 2 | .270 | .343 | .452 |
| 1987 Pittsburgh | NL | 157 | 564 | 165 | 36 | 11 | 21 | (11 | 10) | 286 | 93 | 82 | 56 | 4 | 122 | 4 | 3 | 3 | 34 | 8 | .81 | 6 | .293 | .359 | .507 |
| 1988 Pittsburgh | NL | 154 | 587 | 169 | 23 | 15 | 25 | (16 | 9) | 297 | 101 | 100 | 57 | 2 | 126 | 1 | 1 | 13 | 30 | 9 | .77 | 8 | .288 | .345 | .506 |
| 1989 Pittsburgh | NL | 130 | 476 | 113 | 18 | 9 | 9 | (4 | 5) | 176 | 64 | 53 | 47 | 3 | 100 | 3 | 1 | 4 | 16 | 4 | .80 | 13 | .237 | .308 | .370 |
| 1990 Pittsburgh | NL | 136 | 493 | 140 | 26 | 6 | 17 | (6 | 11) | 229 | 67 | 77 | 66 | 2 | 89 | 1 | 3 | 4 | 14 | 4 | .78 | 6 | .284 | .367 | .465 |
| 8 ML YEARS | | 1098 | 3632 | 979 | 182 | 63 | 113 | (54 | 59) | 1626 | 530 | 516 | 429 | 36 | 711 | 13 | 12 | 33 | 198 | 51 | .80 | 51 | .270 | .346 | .448 |

## Gary Varsho

**Bats:** Left **Throws:** Right **Pos:** LF **Ht:** 5'11" **Wt:** 190 **Born:** 06/20/61 **Age:** 30

| BATTING | | | | | | | | | | | | | | | | | | | BASERUNNING | | | | PERCENTAGES | | |
|---|---|---|---|---|---|---|---|---|---|---|---|---|---|---|---|---|---|---|---|---|---|---|---|---|---|
| Year Team | Lg | G | AB | H | 2B | 3B | HR | (Hm | Rd) | TB | R | RBI | TBB | IBB | SO | HBP | SH | SF | SB | CS | SB% | GDP | Avg | OBP | SLG |
| 1988 Chicago | NL | 46 | 73 | 20 | 3 | 0 | 0 | (0 | 0) | 23 | 6 | 5 | 1 | 0 | 6 | 0 | 0 | 1 | 5 | 0 | 1.00 | 0 | .274 | .280 | .315 |
| 1989 Chicago | NL | 61 | 87 | 16 | 4 | 2 | 0 | (0 | 0) | 24 | 10 | 6 | 4 | 1 | 13 | 0 | 0 | 0 | 3 | 0 | 1.00 | 0 | .184 | .220 | .276 |
| 1990 Chicago | NL | 46 | 48 | 12 | 4 | 0 | 0 | (0 | 0) | 16 | 10 | 1 | 1 | 1 | 6 | 0 | 0 | 0 | 2 | 0 | 1.00 | 1 | .250 | .265 | .333 |
| 3 ML YEARS | | 153 | 208 | 48 | 11 | 2 | 0 | (0 | 0) | 63 | 26 | 12 | 6 | 2 | 25 | 0 | 0 | 1 | 10 | 0 | 1.00 | 1 | .231 | .251 | .303 |

## Jim Vatcher

**Bats:** Right **Throws:** Right **Pos:** RF **Ht:** 5' 9" **Wt:** 165 **Born:** 05/27/66 **Age:** 25

| BATTING | | | | | | | | | | | | | | | | | | | BASERUNNING | | | | PERCENTAGES | | |
|---|---|---|---|---|---|---|---|---|---|---|---|---|---|---|---|---|---|---|---|---|---|---|---|---|---|
| Year Team | Lg | G | AB | H | 2B | 3B | HR | (Hm | Rd) | TB | R | RBI | TBB | IBB | SO | HBP | SH | SF | SB | CS | SB% | GDP | Avg | OBP | SLG |
| 1987 Utica | A | 67 | 249 | 67 | 15 | 2 | 3 | -- | -- | 95 | 44 | 21 | 28 | 0 | 31 | 2 | 2 | 1 | 10 | 5 | .67 | 5 | .269 | .346 | .382 |
| 1988 Spartanburg | A | 137 | 496 | 150 | 32 | 2 | 12 | -- | -- | 222 | 90 | 72 | 89 | 1 | 73 | 8 | 9 | 3 | 26 | 13 | .67 | 10 | .302 | .414 | .448 |
| 1989 Clearwater | A | 92 | 349 | 105 | 30 | 5 | 4 | -- | -- | 157 | 51 | 46 | 41 | 0 | 49 | 2 | 0 | 2 | 7 | 3 | .70 | 11 | .301 | .376 | .450 |
| Reading | AA | 48 | 171 | 56 | 11 | 3 | 4 | -- | -- | 85 | 27 | 32 | 26 | 1 | 29 | 1 | 0 | 4 | 2 | 0 | 1.00 | 8 | .327 | .411 | .497 |
| 1990 Scr Wil-Bar | AAA | 55 | 181 | 46 | 12 | 4 | 5 | -- | -- | 81 | 30 | 22 | 32 | 1 | 33 | 0 | 1 | 2 | 1 | 4 | .20 | 4 | .254 | .363 | .448 |
| 1990 2 ML Teams | | 57 | 73 | 19 | 2 | 1 | 1 | (1 | 0) | 26 | 7 | 7 | 5 | 0 | 15 | 0 | 0 | 0 | 0 | 0 | .00 | 1 | .260 | .308 | .356 |
| 1990 Philadelphia | NL | 36 | 46 | 12 | 1 | 0 | 1 | (1 | 0) | 16 | 5 | 4 | 4 | 0 | 6 | 0 | 0 | 0 | 0 | 0 | .00 | 1 | .261 | .320 | .348 |
| Atlanta | NL | 21 | 27 | 7 | 1 | 1 | 0 | (0 | 0) | 10 | 2 | 3 | 1 | 0 | 9 | 0 | 0 | 0 | 0 | 0 | .00 | 0 | .259 | .286 | .370 |

## Greg Vaughn

**Bats:** Right **Throws:** Right **Pos:** LF **Ht:** 6' 1" **Wt:** 175 **Born:** 07/03/65 **Age:** 25

| BATTING | | | | | | | | | | | | | | | | | | | BASERUNNING | | | | PERCENTAGES | | |
|---|---|---|---|---|---|---|---|---|---|---|---|---|---|---|---|---|---|---|---|---|---|---|---|---|---|
| Year Team | Lg | G | AB | H | 2B | 3B | HR | (Hm | Rd) | TB | R | RBI | TBB | IBB | SO | HBP | SH | SF | SB | CS | SB% | GDP | Avg | OBP | SLG |
| 1986 Helena | R | 66 | 258 | 75 | 13 | 2 | 16 | -- | -- | 140 | 64 | 54 | 30 | 1 | 69 | 2 | 5 | 5 | 23 | 5 | .82 | 1 | .291 | .363 | .543 |
| 1987 Beloit | A | 139 | 492 | 150 | 31 | 6 | 33 | -- | -- | 292 | 120 | 105 | 102 | 2 | 115 | 5 | 3 | 6 | 36 | 9 | .80 | 8 | .305 | .425 | .593 |
| 1988 El Paso | AA | 131 | 505 | 152 | 39 | 2 | 28 | -- | -- | 279 | 104 | 105 | 63 | 3 | 120 | 3 | 4 | 4 | 22 | 5 | .81 | 11 | .301 | .379 | .552 |
| 1989 Denver | AAA | 110 | 387 | 107 | 17 | 5 | 26 | -- | -- | 212 | 74 | 92 | 62 | 4 | 94 | 0 | 2 | 1 | 20 | 3 | .87 | 10 | .276 | .376 | .548 |
| 1989 Milwaukee | AL | 38 | 113 | 30 | 3 | 0 | 5 | (1 | 4) | 48 | 18 | 23 | 13 | 0 | 23 | 0 | 0 | 2 | 4 | 1 | .80 | 0 | .265 | .336 | .425 |
| 1990 Milwaukee | AL | 120 | 382 | 84 | 26 | 2 | 17 | (9 | 8) | 165 | 51 | 61 | 33 | 1 | 91 | 1 | 7 | 6 | 7 | 4 | .64 | 11 | .220 | .280 | .432 |
| 2 ML YEARS | | 158 | 495 | 114 | 29 | 2 | 22 | (10 | 12) | 213 | 69 | 84 | 46 | 1 | 114 | 1 | 7 | 8 | 11 | 5 | .69 | 11 | .230 | .293 | .430 |

## Randy Velarde

**Bats:** Right **Throws:** Right **Pos:** 3B/SS **Ht:** 6' 0" **Wt:** 185 **Born:** 11/24/62 **Age:** 28

| BATTING | | | | | | | | | | | | | | | | | | | BASERUNNING | | | | PERCENTAGES | | |
|---|---|---|---|---|---|---|---|---|---|---|---|---|---|---|---|---|---|---|---|---|---|---|---|---|---|
| Year Team | Lg | G | AB | H | 2B | 3B | HR | (Hm | Rd) | TB | R | RBI | TBB | IBB | SO | HBP | SH | SF | SB | CS | SB% | GDP | Avg | OBP | SLG |
| 1987 New York | AL | 8 | 22 | 4 | 0 | 0 | 0 | (0 | 0) | 4 | 1 | 1 | 0 | 0 | 6 | 0 | 0 | 0 | 0 | 0 | .00 | 1 | .182 | .182 | .182 |
| 1988 New York | AL | 48 | 115 | 20 | 6 | 0 | 5 | (2 | 3) | 41 | 18 | 12 | 8 | 0 | 24 | 2 | 0 | 0 | 1 | 1 | .50 | 3 | .174 | .240 | .357 |

| Year Team | Lg | G | AB | H | 2B | 3B | HR | (Hm | Rd) | TB | R | RBI | TBB | IBB | SO | HBP | SH | SF | SB | CS | SB% | GDP | Avg | OBP | SLG |
|---|---|---|---|---|---|---|---|---|---|---|---|---|---|---|---|---|---|---|---|---|---|---|---|---|---|
| 1989 New York | AL | 33 | 100 | 34 | 4 | 2 | 2 | (1 | 1) | 48 | 12 | 11 | 7 | 0 | 14 | 1 | 3 | 0 | 0 | 3 | .00 | 0 | .340 | .389 | .480 |
| 1990 New York | AL | 95 | 229 | 48 | 6 | 2 | 5 | (1 | 4) | 73 | 21 | 19 | 20 | 0 | 53 | 1 | 2 | 1 | 0 | 3 | .00 | 6 | .210 | .275 | .319 |
| 4 ML YEARS | | 184 | 466 | 106 | 16 | 4 | 12 | (4 | 8) | 166 | 52 | 43 | 35 | 0 | 97 | 4 | 5 | 1 | 1 | 7 | .13 | 10 | .227 | .287 | .356 |

## Max Venable

**Bats:** Left **Throws:** Right **Pos:** CF/LF **Ht:** 5'10" **Wt:** 185 **Born:** 06/06/57 **Age:** 34

| BATTING | | | | | | | | | | | | | | | | | | | BASERUNNING | | | | PERCENTAGES | | |
|---|---|---|---|---|---|---|---|---|---|---|---|---|---|---|---|---|---|---|---|---|---|---|---|---|---|
| Year Team | Lg | G | AB | H | 2B | 3B | HR | (Hm | Rd) | TB | R | RBI | TBB | IBB | SO | HBP | SH | SF | SB | CS | SB% | GDP | Avg | OBP | SLG |
| 1979 San Francisco | NL | 55 | 85 | 14 | 1 | 1 | 0 | (0 | 0) | 17 | 12 | 3 | 10 | 1 | 18 | 1 | 1 | 0 | 3 | 3 | .50 | 0 | .165 | .260 | .200 |
| 1980 San Francisco | NL | 64 | 138 | 37 | 5 | 0 | 0 | (0 | 0) | 42 | 13 | 10 | 15 | 0 | 22 | 0 | 1 | 3 | 8 | 2 | .80 | 3 | .268 | .333 | .304 |
| 1981 San Francisco | NL | 18 | 32 | 6 | 0 | 2 | 0 | (0 | 0) | 10 | 2 | 1 | 4 | 0 | 3 | 0 | 0 | 0 | 3 | 1 | .75 | 0 | .188 | .278 | .313 |
| 1982 San Francisco | NL | 71 | 125 | 28 | 2 | 1 | 1 | (1 | 0) | 35 | 17 | 7 | 7 | 0 | 16 | 0 | 0 | 0 | 9 | 3 | .75 | 2 | .224 | .265 | .280 |
| 1983 San Francisco | NL | 94 | 228 | 50 | 7 | 4 | 6 | (3 | 3) | 83 | 28 | 27 | 22 | 1 | 34 | 3 | 2 | 1 | 15 | 2 | .88 | 3 | .219 | .295 | .364 |
| 1984 Montreal | NL | 38 | 71 | 17 | 2 | 0 | 2 | (0 | 2) | 25 | 7 | 7 | 3 | 1 | 7 | 1 | 0 | 1 | 1 | 0 | 1.00 | 0 | .239 | .276 | .352 |
| 1985 Cincinnati | NL | 77 | 135 | 39 | 12 | 3 | 0 | (0 | 0) | 57 | 21 | 10 | 6 | 0 | 17 | 0 | 3 | 2 | 11 | 3 | .79 | 2 | .289 | .315 | .422 |
| 1986 Cincinnati | NL | 108 | 147 | 31 | 7 | 1 | 2 | (1 | 1) | 46 | 17 | 15 | 17 | 2 | 24 | 0 | 2 | 2 | 7 | 2 | .78 | 0 | .211 | .289 | .313 |
| 1987 Cincinnati | NL | 7 | 7 | 1 | 0 | 0 | 0 | (0 | 0) | 1 | 2 | 2 | 0 | 0 | 0 | 0 | 0 | 0 | 0 | 0 | .00 | 0 | .143 | .143 | .143 |
| 1989 California | AL | 20 | 53 | 19 | 4 | 0 | 0 | (0 | 0) | 23 | 7 | 4 | 1 | 0 | 16 | 0 | 3 | 0 | 0 | 0 | .00 | 0 | .358 | .370 | .434 |
| 1990 California | AL | 93 | 189 | 49 | 9 | 3 | 4 | (3 | 1) | 76 | 26 | 21 | 24 | 2 | 31 | 0 | 7 | 2 | 5 | 1 | .83 | 3 | .259 | .340 | .402 |
| 11 ML YEARS | | 645 | 1210 | 291 | 49 | 15 | 15 | (8 | 7) | 415 | 152 | 107 | 109 | 7 | 188 | 5 | 19 | 11 | 62 | 17 | .78 | 13 | .240 | .303 | .343 |

## Robin Ventura

**Bats:** Left **Throws:** Right **Pos:** 3B **Ht:** 6' 1" **Wt:** 185 **Born:** 07/14/67 **Age:** 23

| BATTING | | | | | | | | | | | | | | | | | | | BASERUNNING | | | | PERCENTAGES | | |
|---|---|---|---|---|---|---|---|---|---|---|---|---|---|---|---|---|---|---|---|---|---|---|---|---|---|
| Year Team | Lg | G | AB | H | 2B | 3B | HR | (Hm | Rd) | TB | R | RBI | TBB | IBB | SO | HBP | SH | SF | SB | CS | SB% | GDP | Avg | OBP | SLG |
| 1989 Birmingham | AA | 129 | 454 | 126 | 25 | 2 | 3 | -- | -- | 164 | 75 | 67 | 93 | 12 | 51 | 6 | 4 | 6 | 9 | 7 | .56 | 9 | .278 | .403 | .361 |
| 1989 Chicago | AL | 16 | 45 | 8 | 3 | 0 | 0 | (0 | 0) | 11 | 5 | 7 | 8 | 0 | 6 | 1 | 1 | 3 | 0 | 0 | .00 | 1 | .178 | .298 | .244 |
| 1990 Chicago | AL | 150 | 493 | 123 | 17 | 1 | 5 | (2 | 3) | 157 | 48 | 54 | 55 | 2 | 53 | 1 | 13 | 3 | 1 | 4 | .20 | 5 | .249 | .324 | .318 |
| 2 ML YEARS | | 166 | 538 | 131 | 20 | 1 | 5 | (2 | 3) | 168 | 53 | 61 | 63 | 2 | 59 | 2 | 14 | 6 | 1 | 4 | .20 | 6 | .243 | .322 | .312 |

## Randy Veres

**Pitches:** Right **Bats:** Right **Pos:** RP **Ht:** 6' 3" **Wt:** 190 **Born:** 11/25/65 **Age:** 25

| HOW MUCH HE PITCHED | | | | | | | | WHAT HE GAVE UP | | | | | | | | | | | | THE RESULTS | | | | | |
|---|---|---|---|---|---|---|---|---|---|---|---|---|---|---|---|---|---|---|---|---|---|---|---|---|---|
| Year Team | Lg | G | GS | CG | GF | IP | BFP | H | R | ER | HR | SH | SF | HB | TBB | IBB | SO | WP | Bk | W | L | Pct. | ShO | Sv | ERA |
| 1985 Helena | R | 13 | 13 | 3 | 0 | 77.1 | 0 | 66 | 43 | 33 | 3 | 0 | 0 | 2 | 36 | 0 | 67 | 9 | 2 | 7 | 4 | .636 | 2 | 0 | 3.84 |
| 1986 Beloit | A | 23 | 22 | 3 | 0 | 113.1 | 519 | 132 | 78 | 49 | 6 | 2 | 4 | 4 | 52 | 1 | 87 | 13 | 4 | 4 | 12 | .250 | 1 | 0 | 3.89 |
| 1987 Beloit | A | 21 | 21 | 6 | 0 | 127 | 558 | 132 | 63 | 44 | 5 | 3 | 0 | 4 | 52 | 2 | 98 | 8 | 2 | 10 | 6 | .625 | 0 | 0 | 3.12 |
| 1988 Stockton | A | 20 | 19 | 1 | 0 | 110 | 486 | 94 | 54 | 41 | 2 | 4 | 7 | 4 | 77 | 0 | 96 | 16 | 1 | 8 | 4 | .667 | 1 | 0 | 3.35 |
| El Paso | AA | 6 | 6 | 0 | 0 | 39.1 | 167 | 35 | 18 | 16 | 4 | 2 | 1 | 4 | 12 | 1 | 31 | 1 | 0 | 3 | 2 | .600 | 0 | 0 | 3.66 |
| 1989 El Paso | AA | 8 | 8 | 0 | 0 | 43.1 | 193 | 43 | 29 | 23 | 3 | 1 | 2 | 1 | 25 | 1 | 41 | 4 | 0 | 2 | 3 | .400 | 0 | 0 | 4.78 |
| Denver | AAA | 17 | 17 | 2 | 0 | 107 | 469 | 108 | 57 | 47 | 6 | 3 | 3 | 4 | 38 | 0 | 80 | 4 | 2 | 6 | 7 | .462 | 1 | 0 | 3.95 |
| 1990 Denver | AAA | 16 | 7 | 0 | 7 | 50.1 | 230 | 60 | 36 | 29 | 5 | 5 | 1 | 1 | 27 | 2 | 36 | 11 | 2 | 1 | 6 | .143 | 0 | 2 | 5.19 |
| 1989 Milwaukee | AL | 3 | 1 | 0 | 1 | 8.1 | 36 | 9 | 5 | 4 | 0 | 0 | 1 | 0 | 4 | 0 | 8 | 0 | 0 | 0 | 1 | .000 | 0 | 0 | 4.32 |
| 1990 Milwaukee | AL | 26 | 0 | 0 | 12 | 41.2 | 175 | 38 | 17 | 17 | 5 | 2 | 2 | 1 | 16 | 3 | 16 | 3 | 0 | 0 | 3 | .000 | 0 | 1 | 3.67 |
| 2 ML YEARS | | 29 | 1 | 0 | 13 | 50 | 211 | 47 | 22 | 21 | 5 | 2 | 3 | 1 | 20 | 3 | 24 | 3 | 0 | 0 | 4 | .000 | 0 | 1 | 3.78 |

## Hector Villanueva

**Bats:** Right **Throws:** Right **Pos:** C/1B **Ht:** 6' 1" **Wt:** 210 **Born:** 10/02/64 **Age:** 26

| BATTING | | | | | | | | | | | | | | | | | | | BASERUNNING | | | | PERCENTAGES | | |
|---|---|---|---|---|---|---|---|---|---|---|---|---|---|---|---|---|---|---|---|---|---|---|---|---|---|
| Year Team | Lg | G | AB | H | 2B | 3B | HR | (Hm | Rd) | TB | R | RBI | TBB | IBB | SO | HBP | SH | SF | SB | CS | SB% | GDP | Avg | OBP | SLG |
| 1985 Peoria | A | 65 | 193 | 45 | 7 | 0 | 1 | -- | -- | 55 | 22 | 19 | 27 | 0 | 36 | 3 | 2 | 1 | 0 | 2 | .00 | 7 | .233 | .335 | .285 |
| 1986 Winston-Sal | A | 125 | 412 | 131 | 20 | 2 | 13 | -- | -- | 194 | 58 | 100 | 81 | 3 | 42 | 2 | 2 | 12 | 6 | 4 | .60 | 12 | .318 | .422 | .471 |
| 1987 Pittsfield | AA | 109 | 391 | 107 | 31 | 0 | 14 | -- | -- | 180 | 59 | 70 | 43 | 1 | 38 | 1 | 2 | 3 | 3 | 4 | .43 | 8 | .274 | .345 | .460 |
| 1988 Pittsfield | AA | 127 | 436 | 137 | 24 | 3 | 10 | -- | -- | 197 | 50 | 75 | 71 | 6 | 58 | 4 | 2 | 8 | 5 | 4 | .56 | 9 | .314 | .408 | .452 |
| 1989 Iowa | AAA | 120 | 444 | 112 | 25 | 1 | 12 | -- | -- | 175 | 46 | 57 | 32 | 2 | 95 | 1 | 1 | 2 | 1 | 1 | .50 | 6 | .252 | .303 | .394 |
| 1990 Iowa | AAA | 52 | 177 | 47 | 7 | 1 | 8 | -- | -- | 80 | 20 | 34 | 19 | 2 | 36 | 1 | 1 | 0 | 0 | 1 | .00 | 4 | .266 | .340 | .452 |
| 1990 Chicago | NL | 52 | 114 | 31 | 4 | 1 | 7 | (2 | 5) | 58 | 14 | 18 | 4 | 2 | 27 | 2 | 0 | 0 | 1 | 0 | 1.00 | 3 | .272 | .308 | .509 |

## Frank Viola

**Pitches:** Left **Bats:** Left **Pos:** SP **Ht:** 6' 4" **Wt:** 209 **Born:** 04/19/60 **Age:** 31

| HOW MUCH HE PITCHED | | | | | | | | WHAT HE GAVE UP | | | | | | | | | | | | THE RESULTS | | | | | |
|---|---|---|---|---|---|---|---|---|---|---|---|---|---|---|---|---|---|---|---|---|---|---|---|---|---|
| Year Team | Lg | G | GS | CG | GF | IP | BFP | H | R | ER | HR | SH | SF | HB | TBB | IBB | SO | WP | Bk | W | L | Pct. | ShO | Sv | ERA |
| 1982 Minnesota | AL | 22 | 22 | 3 | 0 | 126 | 543 | 152 | 77 | 73 | 22 | 2 | 0 | 0 | 38 | 2 | 84 | 4 | 1 | 4 | 10 | .286 | 1 | 0 | 5.21 |
| 1983 Minnesota | AL | 35 | 34 | 4 | 0 | 210 | 949 | 242 | 141 | 128 | 34 | 5 | 2 | 8 | 92 | 7 | 127 | 6 | 2 | 7 | 15 | .318 | 0 | 0 | 5.49 |
| 1984 Minnesota | AL | 35 | 35 | 10 | 0 | 257.2 | 1047 | 225 | 101 | 92 | 28 | 1 | 5 | 4 | 73 | 1 | 149 | 6 | 1 | 18 | 12 | .600 | 4 | 0 | 3.21 |
| 1985 Minnesota | AL | 36 | 36 | 9 | 0 | 250.2 | 1059 | 262 | 136 | 114 | 26 | 5 | 5 | 2 | 68 | 3 | 135 | 6 | 2 | 18 | 14 | .563 | 0 | 0 | 4.09 |

| | | | | | | | | | | | | | | | | | | | | | | | | |
|---|---|---|---|---|---|---|---|---|---|---|---|---|---|---|---|---|---|---|---|---|---|---|---|---|
| 1986 Minnesota | AL | 37 | 37 | 7 | 0 | 245.2 | 1053 | 257 | 136 | 123 | 37 | 4 | 5 | 3 | 83 | 0 | 191 | 12 | 0 | 16 | 13 | .552 | 1 | 0 | 4.51 |
| 1987 Minnesota | AL | 36 | 36 | 7 | 0 | 251.2 | 1037 | 230 | 91 | 81 | 29 | 7 | 3 | 6 | 66 | 1 | 197 | 1 | 1 | 17 | 10 | .630 | 1 | 0 | 2.90 |
| 1988 Minnesota | AL | 35 | 35 | 7 | 0 | 255.1 | 1031 | 236 | 80 | 75 | 20 | 6 | 6 | 3 | 54 | 2 | 193 | 5 | 1 | 24 | 7 | .774 | 2 | 0 | 2.64 |
| 1989 2 ML Teams | | 36 | 36 | 9 | 0 | 261 | 1082 | 246 | 115 | 106 | 22 | 12 | 6 | 4 | 74 | 4 | 211 | 8 | 1 | 13 | 17 | .433 | 2 | 0 | 3.66 |
| 1990 New York | NL | 35 | 35 | 7 | 0 | 249.2 | 1016 | 227 | 83 | 74 | 15 | 13 | 3 | 2 | 60 | 2 | 182 | 11 | 0 | 20 | 12 | .625 | 3 | 0 | 2.67 |
| 1989 Minnesota | AL | 24 | 24 | 7 | 0 | 175.2 | 731 | 171 | 80 | 74 | 17 | 9 | 4 | 3 | 47 | 1 | 138 | 5 | 1 | 8 | 12 | .400 | 1 | 0 | 3.79 |
| New York | NL | 12 | 12 | 2 | 0 | 85.1 | 351 | 75 | 35 | 32 | 5 | 3 | 2 | 1 | 27 | 3 | 73 | 3 | 0 | 5 | 5 | .500 | 1 | 0 | 3.38 |
| 9 ML YEARS | | 307 | 306 | 63 | 0 | 2107.2 | 8817 | 2077 | 960 | 866 | 233 | 55 | 35 | 32 | 608 | 22 | 1469 | 59 | 9 | 137 | 110 | .555 | 14 | 0 | 3.70 |

## Ozzie Virgil

**Bats:** Right **Throws:** Right **Pos:** C **Ht:** 6' 1" **Wt:** 195 **Born:** 12/07/56 **Age:** 34

| BATTING | | | | | | | | | | | | | | | | | | BASERUNNING | | | | PERCENTAGES | | |
|---|---|---|---|---|---|---|---|---|---|---|---|---|---|---|---|---|---|---|---|---|---|---|---|---|
| Year Team | Lg | G | AB | H | 2B | 3B | HR | (Hm | Rd) | TB | R | RBI | TBB | IBB | SO | HBP | SH | SF | SB | CS | SB% | GDP | Avg | OBP | SLG |
| 1980 Philadelphia | NL | 1 | 5 | 1 | 1 | 0 | 0 | (0 | 0) | 2 | 1 | 0 | 0 | 0 | 1 | 0 | 0 | 0 | 0 | 0 | .00 | 0 | .200 | .200 | .400 |
| 1981 Philadelphia | NL | 6 | 6 | 0 | 0 | 0 | 0 | (0 | 0) | 0 | 0 | 0 | 0 | 0 | 2 | 0 | 0 | 0 | 0 | 0 | .00 | 0 | .000 | .000 | .000 |
| 1982 Philadelphia | NL | 49 | 101 | 24 | 6 | 0 | 3 | (1 | 2) | 39 | 11 | 8 | 10 | 0 | 26 | 0 | 0 | 0 | 0 | 1 | .00 | 3 | .238 | .306 | .386 |
| 1983 Philadelphia | NL | 55 | 140 | 30 | 7 | 0 | 6 | (2 | 4) | 55 | 11 | 23 | 8 | 0 | 34 | 3 | 0 | 0 | 0 | 2 | .00 | 8 | .214 | .272 | .393 |
| 1984 Philadelphia | NL | 141 | 456 | 119 | 21 | 2 | 18 | (10 | 8) | 198 | 61 | 68 | 45 | 5 | 91 | 5 | 1 | 5 | 1 | 1 | .50 | 19 | .261 | .331 | .434 |
| 1985 Philadelphia | NL | 131 | 426 | 105 | 16 | 3 | 19 | (7 | 12) | 184 | 47 | 55 | 49 | 6 | 85 | 5 | 1 | 2 | 0 | 0 | .00 | 14 | .246 | .330 | .432 |
| 1986 Atlanta | NL | 114 | 359 | 80 | 9 | 0 | 15 | (6 | 9) | 134 | 45 | 48 | 63 | 5 | 73 | 4 | 2 | 3 | 1 | 0 | 1.00 | 9 | .223 | .343 | .373 |
| 1987 Atlanta | NL | 123 | 429 | 106 | 13 | 1 | 27 | (15 | 12) | 202 | 57 | 72 | 47 | 4 | 81 | 7 | 2 | 1 | 0 | 1 | .00 | 18 | .247 | .331 | .471 |
| 1988 Atlanta | NL | 107 | 320 | 82 | 10 | 0 | 9 | (5 | 4) | 119 | 23 | 31 | 22 | 1 | 54 | 5 | 2 | 1 | 2 | 0 | 1.00 | 10 | .256 | .313 | .372 |
| 1989 Toronto | AL | 9 | 11 | 2 | 1 | 0 | 1 | (1 | 0) | 6 | 2 | 2 | 4 | 0 | 3 | 0 | 0 | 0 | 0 | 0 | .00 | 0 | .182 | .400 | .545 |
| 1990 Toronto | AL | 3 | 5 | 0 | 0 | 0 | 0 | (0 | 0) | 0 | 0 | 0 | 0 | 0 | 3 | 0 | 0 | 0 | 0 | 0 | .00 | 0 | .000 | .000 | .000 |
| 11 ML YEARS | | 739 | 2258 | 549 | 84 | 6 | 98 | (47 | 51) | 939 | 258 | 307 | 248 | 21 | 453 | 29 | 8 | 12 | 4 | 5 | .44 | 81 | .243 | .324 | .416 |

## Jose Vizcaino

**Bats:** Both **Throws:** Right **Pos:** SS **Ht:** 6' 1" **Wt:** 150 **Born:** 03/26/68 **Age:** 23

| BATTING | | | | | | | | | | | | | | | | | | BASERUNNING | | | | PERCENTAGES | | |
|---|---|---|---|---|---|---|---|---|---|---|---|---|---|---|---|---|---|---|---|---|---|---|---|---|
| Year Team | Lg | G | AB | H | 2B | 3B | HR | (Hm | Rd) | TB | R | RBI | TBB | IBB | SO | HBP | SH | SF | SB | CS | SB% | GDP | Avg | OBP | SLG |
| 1987 Dodgers | R | 49 | 150 | 38 | 5 | 1 | 0 | -- | -- | 45 | 26 | 12 | 22 | 1 | 24 | 0 | 2 | 1 | 8 | 5 | .62 | 1 | .253 | .347 | .300 |
| 1988 Bakersfield | A | 122 | 433 | 126 | 11 | 4 | 0 | -- | -- | 145 | 77 | 38 | 50 | 1 | 54 | 7 | 10 | 2 | 13 | 14 | .48 | 6 | .291 | .372 | .335 |
| 1989 Albuquerque | AAA | 129 | 434 | 123 | 10 | 4 | 1 | -- | -- | 144 | 60 | 44 | 33 | 2 | 41 | 1 | 12 | 3 | 16 | 14 | .53 | 10 | .283 | .333 | .332 |
| 1990 Albuquerque | AAA | 81 | 276 | 77 | 10 | 2 | 2 | -- | -- | 97 | 46 | 38 | 30 | 3 | 33 | 0 | 3 | 3 | 13 | 6 | .68 | 6 | .279 | .346 | .351 |
| 1989 Los Angeles | NL | 7 | 10 | 2 | 0 | 0 | 0 | (0 | 0) | 2 | 2 | 0 | 0 | 0 | 1 | 0 | 1 | 0 | 0 | 0 | .00 | 0 | .200 | .200 | .200 |
| 1990 Los Angeles | NL | 37 | 51 | 14 | 1 | 1 | 0 | (0 | 0) | 17 | 3 | 2 | 4 | 1 | 8 | 0 | 0 | 0 | 1 | 1 | .50 | 1 | .275 | .327 | .333 |
| 2 ML YEARS | | 44 | 61 | 16 | 1 | 1 | 0 | (0 | 0) | 19 | 5 | 2 | 4 | 1 | 9 | 0 | 1 | 0 | 1 | 1 | .50 | 1 | .262 | .308 | .311 |

## Omar Vizquel

**Bats:** Both **Throws:** Right **Pos:** SS **Ht:** 5' 9" **Wt:** 155 **Born:** 04/24/67 **Age:** 24

| BATTING | | | | | | | | | | | | | | | | | | BASERUNNING | | | | PERCENTAGES | | |
|---|---|---|---|---|---|---|---|---|---|---|---|---|---|---|---|---|---|---|---|---|---|---|---|---|
| Year Team | Lg | G | AB | H | 2B | 3B | HR | (Hm | Rd) | TB | R | RBI | TBB | IBB | SO | HBP | SH | SF | SB | CS | SB% | GDP | Avg | OBP | SLG |
| 1984 Butte | R | 15 | 45 | 14 | 2 | 0 | 0 | -- | -- | 16 | 7 | 4 | 3 | 0 | 8 | 0 | 0 | 1 | 2 | 0 | 1.00 | 0 | .311 | .347 | .356 |
| 1985 Bellingham | A | 50 | 187 | 42 | 9 | 0 | 5 | -- | -- | 66 | 24 | 17 | 12 | 1 | 27 | 0 | 4 | 1 | 4 | 3 | .57 | 0 | .225 | .270 | .353 |
| 1986 Wausau | A | 105 | 352 | 75 | 13 | 2 | 4 | -- | -- | 104 | 60 | 28 | 64 | 1 | 56 | 2 | 2 | 5 | 19 | 6 | .76 | 6 | .213 | .333 | .295 |
| 1987 Salinas | A | 114 | 407 | 107 | 12 | 8 | 0 | -- | -- | 135 | 61 | 38 | 57 | 1 | 56 | 0 | 6 | 4 | 25 | 19 | .57 | 5 | .263 | .350 | .332 |
| 1988 Vermont | AA | 103 | 374 | 95 | 18 | 2 | 2 | -- | -- | 123 | 54 | 35 | 42 | 1 | 44 | 3 | 3 | 8 | 30 | 11 | .73 | 6 | .254 | .328 | .329 |
| Calgary | AAA | 33 | 107 | 24 | 2 | 3 | 1 | -- | -- | 35 | 10 | 12 | 5 | 1 | 14 | 0 | 1 | 0 | 2 | 4 | .33 | 1 | .224 | .259 | .327 |
| 1989 Calgary | AAA | 7 | 28 | 6 | 2 | 0 | 0 | -- | -- | 8 | 3 | 3 | 3 | 0 | 4 | 1 | 0 | 0 | 0 | 2 | .00 | 1 | .214 | .313 | .286 |
| 1990 San Berndno | A | 5 | 22 | 6 | 0 | 0 | 0 | -- | -- | 6 | 4 | 3 | 3 | 0 | 0 | 0 | 0 | 0 | 1 | 2 | .33 | 0 | .273 | .360 | .273 |
| Calgary | AAA | 48 | 150 | 35 | 6 | 2 | 0 | -- | -- | 45 | 18 | 8 | 13 | 0 | 10 | 2 | 9 | 2 | 4 | 3 | .57 | 3 | .233 | .299 | .300 |
| 1989 Seattle | AL | 143 | 387 | 85 | 7 | 3 | 1 | (1 | 0) | 101 | 45 | 20 | 28 | 0 | 40 | 1 | 13 | 2 | 1 | 4 | .20 | 6 | .220 | .273 | .261 |
| 1990 Seattle | AL | 81 | 255 | 63 | 3 | 2 | 2 | (0 | 2) | 76 | 19 | 18 | 18 | 0 | 22 | 0 | 10 | 2 | 4 | 1 | .80 | 7 | .247 | .295 | .298 |
| 2 ML YEARS | | 224 | 642 | 148 | 10 | 5 | 3 | (1 | 2) | 177 | 64 | 38 | 46 | 0 | 62 | 1 | 23 | 4 | 5 | 5 | .50 | 13 | .231 | .281 | .276 |

## Ed Vosberg

**Pitches:** Left **Bats:** Left **Pos:** RP **Ht:** 6' 1" **Wt:** 190 **Born:** 09/28/61 **Age:** 29

| HOW MUCH HE PITCHED | | | | | | | | WHAT HE GAVE UP | | | | | | | | | | | | THE RESULTS | | | | | |
|---|---|---|---|---|---|---|---|---|---|---|---|---|---|---|---|---|---|---|---|---|---|---|---|---|---|
| Year Team | Lg | G | GS | CG | GF | IP | BFP | H | R | ER | HR | SH | SF | HB | TBB | IBB | SO | WP | Bk | W | L | Pct. | ShO | Sv | ERA |
| 1986 San Diego | NL | 5 | 3 | 0 | 0 | 13.2 | 65 | 17 | 11 | 10 | 1 | 0 | 0 | 0 | 9 | 1 | 8 | 0 | 1 | 0 | 1 | .000 | 0 | 0 | 6.59 |
| 1990 San Francisco | NL | 18 | 0 | 0 | 5 | 24.1 | 104 | 21 | 16 | 15 | 3 | 2 | 0 | 0 | 12 | 2 | 12 | 0 | 0 | 1 | 1 | .500 | 0 | 0 | 5.55 |
| 2 ML YEARS | | 23 | 3 | 0 | 5 | 38 | 169 | 38 | 27 | 25 | 4 | 2 | 0 | 0 | 21 | 3 | 20 | 0 | 1 | 1 | 2 | .333 | 0 | 0 | 5.92 |

## Hector Wagner

**Pitches:** Right **Bats:** Right **Pos:** SP **Ht:** 6' 3" **Wt:** 185 **Born:** 11/26/68 **Age:** 22

| | | HOW MUCH HE PITCHED | | | | | | WHAT HE GAVE UP | | | | | | | | | | | | THE RESULTS | | | | | |
|---|---|---|---|---|---|---|---|---|---|---|---|---|---|---|---|---|---|---|---|---|---|---|---|---|---|
| Year Team | Lg | G | GS | CG | GF | IP | BFP | H | R | ER | HR | SH | SF | HB | TBB | IBB | SO | WP | Bk | W | L | Pct. | ShO | Sv | ERA |
| 1987 Royals | R | 13 | 12 | 0 | 0 | 53 | 226 | 63 | 26 | 18 | 0 | 2 | 2 | 2 | 12 | 0 | 28 | 0 | 0 | 1 | 3 | .250 | 0 | 0 | 3.06 |
| 1988 Eugene | A | 15 | 15 | 0 | 0 | 85.2 | 365 | 76 | 46 | 35 | 3 | 0 | 1 | 4 | 28 | 0 | 67 | 3 | 1 | 4 | 9 | .308 | 0 | 0 | 3.68 |
| 1989 Appleton | A | 24 | 23 | 3 | 1 | 130.1 | 557 | 149 | 79 | 66 | 9 | 5 | 1 | 6 | 29 | 1 | 71 | 6 | 1 | 6 | 11 | .353 | 0 | 0 | 4.56 |
| 1990 Memphis | AA | 40 | 11 | 1 | 8 | 133.1 | 538 | 114 | 37 | 30 | 7 | 5 | 1 | 2 | 41 | 0 | 63 | 3 | 0 | 12 | 4 | .750 | 1 | 1 | 2.03 |
| 1990 Kansas City | AL | 5 | 5 | 0 | 0 | 23.1 | 112 | 32 | 24 | 21 | 4 | 0 | 2 | 0 | 11 | 1 | 14 | 3 | 0 | 0 | 2 | .000 | 0 | 0 | 8.10 |

## Jim Walewander

**Bats:** Both **Throws:** Right **Pos:** 2B **Ht:** 5'10" **Wt:** 160 **Born:** 05/02/61 **Age:** 30

| | | BATTING | | | | | | | | | | | | | | | | | BASERUNNING | | | | PERCENTAGES | | |
|---|---|---|---|---|---|---|---|---|---|---|---|---|---|---|---|---|---|---|---|---|---|---|---|---|---|
| Year Team | Lg | G | AB | H | 2B | 3B | HR | (Hm | Rd) | TB | R | RBI | TBB | IBB | SO | HBP | SH | SF | SB | CS | SB% | GDP | Avg | OBP | SLG |
| 1987 Detroit | AL | 53 | 54 | 13 | 3 | 1 | 1 | (1 | 0) | 21 | 24 | 4 | 7 | 0 | 6 | 0 | 2 | 0 | 2 | 1 | .67 | 2 | .241 | .328 | .389 |
| 1988 Detroit | AL | 88 | 175 | 37 | 5 | 0 | 0 | (0 | 0) | 42 | 23 | 6 | 12 | 0 | 26 | 0 | 10 | 1 | 11 | 4 | .73 | 1 | .211 | .261 | .240 |
| 1990 New York | AL | 9 | 5 | 1 | 1 | 0 | 0 | (0 | 0) | 2 | 1 | 1 | 0 | 0 | 0 | 0 | 0 | 0 | 1 | 1 | .50 | 0 | .200 | .200 | .400 |
| 3 ML YEARS | | 150 | 234 | 51 | 9 | 1 | 1 | (1 | 0) | 65 | 48 | 11 | 19 | 0 | 32 | 0 | 12 | 1 | 14 | 6 | .70 | 3 | .218 | .276 | .278 |

## Bob Walk

**Pitches:** Right **Bats:** Right **Pos:** SP **Ht:** 6' 4" **Wt:** 217 **Born:** 11/26/56 **Age:** 34

| | | HOW MUCH HE PITCHED | | | | | | WHAT HE GAVE UP | | | | | | | | | | | | THE RESULTS | | | | | |
|---|---|---|---|---|---|---|---|---|---|---|---|---|---|---|---|---|---|---|---|---|---|---|---|---|---|
| Year Team | Lg | G | GS | CG | GF | IP | BFP | H | R | ER | HR | SH | SF | HB | TBB | IBB | SO | WP | Bk | W | L | Pct. | ShO | Sv | ERA |
| 1980 Philadelphia | NL | 27 | 27 | 2 | 0 | 152 | 673 | 163 | 82 | 77 | 8 | 5 | 5 | 2 | 71 | 2 | 94 | 6 | 3 | 11 | 7 | .611 | 0 | 0 | 4.56 |
| 1981 Atlanta | NL | 12 | 8 | 0 | 1 | 43 | 189 | 41 | 25 | 22 | 6 | 2 | 0 | 0 | 23 | 0 | 16 | 1 | 0 | 1 | 4 | .200 | 0 | 0 | 4.60 |
| 1982 Atlanta | NL | 32 | 27 | 3 | 1 | 164.1 | 717 | 179 | 101 | 89 | 19 | 8 | 5 | 6 | 59 | 2 | 84 | 7 | 0 | 11 | 9 | .550 | 1 | 0 | 4.87 |
| 1983 Atlanta | NL | 1 | 1 | 0 | 0 | 3.2 | 20 | 7 | 3 | 3 | 0 | 1 | 0 | 0 | 2 | 0 | 4 | 0 | 0 | 0 | 0 | .000 | 0 | 0 | 7.36 |
| 1984 Pittsburgh | NL | 2 | 2 | 0 | 0 | 10.1 | 44 | 8 | 5 | 3 | 1 | 0 | 0 | 0 | 4 | 1 | 10 | 0 | 0 | 1 | 1 | .500 | 0 | 0 | 2.61 |
| 1985 Pittsburgh | NL | 9 | 9 | 1 | 0 | 58.2 | 248 | 60 | 27 | 24 | 3 | 3 | 1 | 0 | 18 | 2 | 40 | 2 | 3 | 2 | 3 | .400 | 1 | 0 | 3.68 |
| 1986 Pittsburgh | NL | 44 | 15 | 1 | 7 | 141.2 | 592 | 129 | 66 | 59 | 14 | 6 | 5 | 3 | 64 | 7 | 78 | 12 | 1 | 7 | 8 | .467 | 1 | 2 | 3.75 |
| 1987 Pittsburgh | NL | 39 | 12 | 1 | 6 | 117 | 498 | 107 | 52 | 43 | 11 | 6 | 2 | 3 | 51 | 2 | 78 | 7 | 3 | 8 | 2 | .800 | 1 | 0 | 3.31 |
| 1988 Pittsburgh | NL | 32 | 32 | 1 | 0 | 212.2 | 881 | 183 | 75 | 64 | 6 | 14 | 5 | 2 | 65 | 5 | 81 | 13 | 9 | 12 | 10 | .545 | 1 | 0 | 2.71 |
| 1989 Pittsburgh | NL | 33 | 31 | 2 | 1 | 196 | 843 | 208 | 106 | 96 | 15 | 4 | 2 | 4 | 65 | 1 | 83 | 7 | 4 | 13 | 10 | .565 | 0 | 0 | 4.41 |
| 1990 Pittsburgh | NL | 26 | 24 | 1 | 1 | 129.2 | 549 | 136 | 59 | 54 | 17 | 3 | 3 | 4 | 36 | 2 | 73 | 5 | 3 | 7 | 5 | .583 | 1 | 1 | 3.75 |
| 11 ML YEARS | | 257 | 188 | 12 | 17 | 1229 | 5254 | 1221 | 601 | 534 | 100 | 52 | 28 | 24 | 458 | 24 | 641 | 60 | 26 | 73 | 59 | .553 | 6 | 3 | 3.91 |

## Greg Walker

**Bats:** Left **Throws:** Right **Pos:** DH **Ht:** 6' 3" **Wt:** 210 **Born:** 10/06/59 **Age:** 31

| | | BATTING | | | | | | | | | | | | | | | | | BASERUNNING | | | | PERCENTAGES | | |
|---|---|---|---|---|---|---|---|---|---|---|---|---|---|---|---|---|---|---|---|---|---|---|---|---|---|
| Year Team | Lg | G | AB | H | 2B | 3B | HR | (Hm | Rd) | TB | R | RBI | TBB | IBB | SO | HBP | SH | SF | SB | CS | SB% | GDP | Avg | OBP | SLG |
| 1982 Chicago | AL | 11 | 17 | 7 | 2 | 1 | 2 | (1 | 1) | 17 | 3 | 7 | 2 | 0 | 3 | 0 | 0 | 0 | 0 | 0 | .00 | 0 | .412 | .474 | 1.000 |
| 1983 Chicago | AL | 118 | 307 | 83 | 16 | 3 | 10 | (4 | 6) | 135 | 32 | 55 | 28 | 3 | 57 | 2 | 0 | 3 | 2 | 1 | .67 | 3 | .270 | .332 | .440 |
| 1984 Chicago | AL | 136 | 442 | 130 | 29 | 2 | 24 | (16 | 8) | 235 | 62 | 75 | 35 | 3 | 66 | 2 | 0 | 3 | 8 | 5 | .62 | 9 | .294 | .346 | .532 |
| 1985 Chicago | AL | 163 | 601 | 155 | 38 | 4 | 24 | (11 | 13) | 273 | 77 | 92 | 44 | 6 | 100 | 2 | 0 | 3 | 5 | 2 | .71 | 16 | .258 | .309 | .454 |
| 1986 Chicago | AL | 78 | 282 | 78 | 10 | 6 | 13 | (6 | 7) | 139 | 37 | 51 | 29 | 4 | 44 | 2 | 0 | 3 | 1 | 2 | .33 | 4 | .277 | .345 | .493 |
| 1987 Chicago | AL | 157 | 566 | 145 | 33 | 2 | 27 | (12 | 15) | 263 | 85 | 94 | 75 | 7 | 112 | 5 | 1 | 5 | 2 | 1 | .67 | 12 | .256 | .346 | .465 |
| 1988 Chicago | AL | 99 | 377 | 93 | 22 | 1 | 8 | (2 | 6) | 141 | 45 | 42 | 29 | 3 | 77 | 3 | 1 | 2 | 0 | 1 | .00 | 7 | .247 | .304 | .374 |
| 1989 Chicago | AL | 77 | 233 | 49 | 14 | 0 | 5 | (4 | 1) | 78 | 25 | 26 | 23 | 2 | 50 | 3 | 1 | 3 | 0 | 0 | .00 | 8 | .210 | .286 | .335 |
| 1990 2 ML Teams | | 16 | 39 | 6 | 0 | 0 | 0 | (0 | 0) | 6 | 2 | 2 | 3 | 0 | 11 | 1 | 0 | 0 | 1 | 0 | 1.00 | 2 | .154 | .233 | .154 |
| 1990 Chicago | AL | 2 | 5 | 1 | 0 | 0 | 0 | (0 | 0) | 1 | 0 | 0 | 0 | 0 | 2 | 0 | 0 | 0 | 0 | 0 | .00 | 0 | .200 | .200 | .200 |
| Baltimore | AL | 14 | 34 | 5 | 0 | 0 | 0 | (0 | 0) | 5 | 2 | 2 | 3 | 0 | 9 | 1 | 0 | 0 | 1 | 0 | 1.00 | 2 | .147 | .237 | .147 |
| 9 ML YEARS | | 855 | 2864 | 746 | 164 | 19 | 113 | (56 | 57) | 1287 | 368 | 444 | 268 | 28 | 520 | 20 | 3 | 22 | 19 | 12 | .61 | 61 | .260 | .326 | .449 |

## Larry Walker

**Bats:** Left **Throws:** Right **Pos:** RF **Ht:** 6' 2" **Wt:** 185 **Born:** 12/01/66 **Age:** 24

| | | BATTING | | | | | | | | | | | | | | | | | BASERUNNING | | | | PERCENTAGES | | |
|---|---|---|---|---|---|---|---|---|---|---|---|---|---|---|---|---|---|---|---|---|---|---|---|---|---|
| Year Team | Lg | G | AB | H | 2B | 3B | HR | (Hm | Rd) | TB | R | RBI | TBB | IBB | SO | HBP | SH | SF | SB | CS | SB% | GDP | Avg | OBP | SLG |
| 1985 Utica | A | 62 | 215 | 48 | 8 | 2 | 2 | -- | -- | 66 | 24 | 26 | 18 | 4 | 57 | 5 | 2 | 1 | 12 | 6 | .67 | 1 | .223 | .297 | .307 |
| 1986 Burlington | A | 95 | 332 | 96 | 12 | 6 | 29 | -- | -- | 207 | 67 | 74 | 46 | 1 | 112 | 9 | 0 | 3 | 16 | 8 | .67 | 4 | .289 | .387 | .623 |
| Wst Plm Bch | A | 38 | 113 | 32 | 7 | 5 | 4 | -- | -- | 61 | 20 | 16 | 26 | 2 | 32 | 2 | 0 | 1 | 2 | 2 | .50 | 2 | .283 | .423 | .540 |
| 1987 Jacksnville | AA | 128 | 474 | 136 | 25 | 7 | 26 | -- | -- | 253 | 91 | 83 | 67 | 5 | 120 | 9 | 0 | 3 | 24 | 3 | .89 | 6 | .287 | .383 | .534 |
| 1989 Indianapols | AAA | 114 | 385 | 104 | 18 | 2 | 12 | -- | -- | 162 | 68 | 59 | 50 | 8 | 87 | 9 | 5 | 7 | 36 | 6 | .86 | 8 | .270 | .361 | .421 |
| 1989 Montreal | NL | 20 | 47 | 8 | 0 | 0 | 0 | (0 | 0) | 8 | 4 | 4 | 5 | 0 | 13 | 1 | 3 | 0 | 1 | 1 | .50 | 0 | .170 | .264 | .170 |
| 1990 Montreal | NL | 133 | 419 | 101 | 18 | 3 | 19 | (9 | 10) | 182 | 59 | 51 | 49 | 5 | 112 | 5 | 3 | 2 | 21 | 7 | .75 | 8 | .241 | .326 | .434 |
| 2 ML YEARS | | 153 | 466 | 109 | 18 | 3 | 19 | (9 | 10) | 190 | 63 | 55 | 54 | 5 | 125 | 6 | 6 | 2 | 22 | 8 | .73 | 8 | .234 | .320 | .408 |

## Mike Walker

**Pitches:** Right **Bats:** Right **Pos:** SP/RP **Ht:** 6' 1" **Wt:** 175 **Born:** 10/04/66 **Age:** 24

| HOW MUCH HE PITCHED | | | | | | | | | WHAT HE GAVE UP | | | | | | | | | | | | THE RESULTS | | | | | |
|---|---|---|---|---|---|---|---|---|---|---|---|---|---|---|---|---|---|---|---|---|---|---|---|---|---|---|
| Year | Team | Lg | G | GS | CG | GF | IP | BFP | H | R | ER | HR | SH | SF | HB | TBB | IBB | SO | WP | Bk | W | L | Pct. | ShO | Sv | ERA |
| 1988 | Cleveland | AL | 3 | 1 | 0 | 0 | 8.2 | 42 | 8 | 7 | 7 | 0 | 1 | 0 | 0 | 10 | 0 | 7 | 0 | 0 | 0 | 1 | .000 | 0 | 0 | 7.27 |
| 1990 | Cleveland | AL | 18 | 11 | 0 | 2 | 75.2 | 350 | 82 | 49 | 41 | 6 | 4 | 2 | 6 | 42 | 4 | 34 | 3 | 1 | 2 | 6 | .250 | 0 | 0 | 4.88 |
| | 2 ML YEARS | | 21 | 12 | 0 | 2 | 84.1 | 392 | 90 | 56 | 48 | 6 | 5 | 2 | 6 | 52 | 4 | 41 | 3 | 1 | 2 | 7 | .222 | 0 | 0 | 5.12 |

## Tim Wallach

**Bats:** Right **Throws:** Right **Pos:** 3B **Ht:** 6' 3" **Wt:** 200 **Born:** 09/14/57 **Age:** 33

| BATTING | | | | | | | | | | | | | | | | | | | | BASERUNNING | | | | PERCENTAGES | | |
|---|---|---|---|---|---|---|---|---|---|---|---|---|---|---|---|---|---|---|---|---|---|---|---|---|---|---|
| Year | Team | Lg | G | AB | H | 2B | 3B | HR | (Hm | Rd) | TB | R | RBI | TBB | IBB | SO | HBP | SH | SF | SB | CS | SB% | GDP | Avg | OBP | SLG |
| 1980 | Montreal | NL | 5 | 11 | 2 | 0 | 0 | 1 | (0 | 1) | 5 | 1 | 2 | 1 | 0 | 5 | 0 | 0 | 0 | 0 | 0 | .00 | 0 | .182 | .250 | .455 |
| 1981 | Montreal | NL | 71 | 212 | 50 | 9 | 1 | 4 | (1 | 3) | 73 | 19 | 13 | 15 | 2 | 37 | 4 | 0 | 0 | 0 | 1 | .00 | 3 | .236 | .299 | .344 |
| 1982 | Montreal | NL | 158 | 596 | 160 | 31 | 3 | 28 | (11 | 17) | 281 | 89 | 97 | 36 | 4 | 81 | 4 | 5 | 4 | 6 | 4 | .60 | 15 | .268 | .313 | .471 |
| 1983 | Montreal | NL | 156 | 581 | 156 | 33 | 3 | 19 | (9 | 10) | 252 | 54 | 70 | 55 | 8 | 97 | 6 | 0 | 5 | 0 | 3 | .00 | 9 | .269 | .335 | .434 |
| 1984 | Montreal | NL | 160 | 582 | 143 | 25 | 4 | 18 | (4 | 14) | 230 | 55 | 72 | 50 | 6 | 101 | 7 | 0 | 4 | 3 | 7 | .30 | 12 | .246 | .311 | .395 |
| 1985 | Montreal | NL | 155 | 569 | 148 | 36 | 3 | 22 | (9 | 13) | 256 | 70 | 81 | 38 | 8 | 79 | 5 | 0 | 5 | 9 | 9 | .50 | 17 | .260 | .310 | .450 |
| 1986 | Montreal | NL | 134 | 480 | 112 | 22 | 1 | 18 | (6 | 12) | 190 | 50 | 71 | 44 | 8 | 72 | 10 | 0 | 5 | 8 | 4 | .67 | 16 | .233 | .308 | .396 |
| 1987 | Montreal | NL | 153 | 593 | 177 | 42 | 4 | 26 | (13 | 13) | 305 | 89 | 123 | 37 | 5 | 98 | 7 | 0 | 7 | 9 | 5 | .64 | 6 | .298 | .343 | .514 |
| 1988 | Montreal | NL | 159 | 592 | 152 | 32 | 5 | 12 | (3 | 9) | 230 | 52 | 69 | 38 | 7 | 88 | 3 | 0 | 7 | 2 | 6 | .25 | 19 | .257 | .302 | .389 |
| 1989 | Montreal | NL | 154 | 573 | 159 | 42 | 0 | 13 | (6 | 7) | 240 | 76 | 77 | 58 | 10 | 81 | 1 | 0 | 7 | 3 | 7 | .30 | 21 | .277 | .341 | .419 |
| 1990 | Montreal | NL | 161 | 626 | 185 | 37 | 5 | 21 | (9 | 12) | 295 | 69 | 98 | 42 | 11 | 80 | 3 | 0 | 7 | 6 | 9 | .40 | 12 | .296 | .339 | .471 |
| | 11 ML YEARS | | 1466 | 5415 | 1444 | 309 | 29 | 182 | (71 | 111) | 2357 | 624 | 773 | 414 | 69 | 819 | 50 | 5 | 51 | 46 | 55 | .46 | 130 | .267 | .322 | .435 |

## Denny Walling

**Bats:** Left **Throws:** Right **Pos:** 3B **Ht:** 6' 1" **Wt:** 185 **Born:** 04/17/54 **Age:** 37

| BATTING | | | | | | | | | | | | | | | | | | | | BASERUNNING | | | | PERCENTAGES | | |
|---|---|---|---|---|---|---|---|---|---|---|---|---|---|---|---|---|---|---|---|---|---|---|---|---|---|---|
| Year | Team | Lg | G | AB | H | 2B | 3B | HR | (Hm | Rd) | TB | R | RBI | TBB | IBB | SO | HBP | SH | SF | SB | CS | SB% | GDP | Avg | OBP | SLG |
| 1975 | Oakland | AL | 6 | 8 | 1 | 1 | 0 | 0 | (0 | 0) | 2 | 0 | 2 | 0 | 0 | 4 | 0 | 0 | 0 | 0 | 0 | .00 | 0 | .125 | .125 | .250 |
| 1976 | Oakland | AL | 3 | 11 | 3 | 0 | 0 | 0 | (0 | 0) | 3 | 1 | 0 | 0 | 0 | 3 | 0 | 0 | 0 | 0 | 0 | .00 | 0 | .273 | .273 | .273 |
| 1977 | Houston | NL | 6 | 21 | 6 | 0 | 1 | 0 | (0 | 0) | 8 | 1 | 6 | 2 | 0 | 4 | 0 | 0 | 0 | 0 | 1 | .00 | 0 | .286 | .348 | .381 |
| 1978 | Houston | NL | 120 | 247 | 62 | 11 | 3 | 3 | (2 | 1) | 88 | 30 | 36 | 30 | 3 | 24 | 1 | 0 | 2 | 9 | 2 | .82 | 2 | .251 | .332 | .356 |
| 1979 | Houston | NL | 82 | 147 | 48 | 8 | 4 | 3 | (3 | 0) | 73 | 21 | 31 | 17 | 2 | 21 | 0 | 0 | 1 | 3 | 2 | .60 | 2 | .327 | .394 | .497 |
| 1980 | Houston | NL | 100 | 284 | 85 | 6 | 5 | 3 | (1 | 2) | 110 | 30 | 29 | 35 | 4 | 26 | 0 | 0 | 2 | 4 | 3 | .57 | 2 | .299 | .374 | .387 |
| 1981 | Houston | NL | 65 | 158 | 37 | 6 | 0 | 5 | (2 | 3) | 58 | 23 | 23 | 28 | 1 | 17 | 0 | 1 | 2 | 2 | 1 | .67 | 3 | .234 | .346 | .367 |
| 1982 | Houston | NL | 85 | 146 | 30 | 4 | 1 | 1 | (1 | 0) | 39 | 22 | 14 | 23 | 3 | 19 | 0 | 0 | 1 | 4 | 2 | .67 | 6 | .205 | .312 | .267 |
| 1983 | Houston | NL | 100 | 135 | 40 | 5 | 3 | 3 | (1 | 2) | 60 | 24 | 19 | 15 | 1 | 16 | 0 | 1 | 1 | 2 | 2 | .50 | 1 | .296 | .364 | .444 |
| 1984 | Houston | NL | 87 | 249 | 70 | 11 | 5 | 3 | (0 | 3) | 100 | 37 | 31 | 16 | 2 | 28 | 1 | 0 | 2 | 7 | 1 | .88 | 4 | .281 | .325 | .402 |
| 1985 | Houston | NL | 119 | 345 | 93 | 20 | 1 | 7 | (2 | 5) | 136 | 44 | 45 | 25 | 2 | 26 | 0 | 0 | 4 | 5 | 2 | .71 | 8 | .270 | .316 | .394 |
| 1986 | Houston | NL | 130 | 382 | 119 | 23 | 1 | 13 | (5 | 8) | 183 | 54 | 58 | 36 | 5 | 31 | 0 | 0 | 4 | 1 | 1 | .50 | 8 | .312 | .367 | .479 |
| 1987 | Houston | NL | 110 | 325 | 92 | 21 | 4 | 5 | (2 | 3) | 136 | 45 | 33 | 39 | 1 | 37 | 0 | 2 | 4 | 5 | 1 | .83 | 9 | .283 | .356 | .418 |
| 1988 | 2 ML Teams | | 84 | 234 | 56 | 13 | 2 | 1 | (0 | 1) | 76 | 22 | 21 | 17 | 3 | 25 | 0 | 1 | 0 | 2 | 0 | 1.00 | 3 | .239 | .291 | .325 |
| 1989 | St. Louis | NL | 69 | 79 | 24 | 7 | 0 | 1 | (0 | 1) | 34 | 9 | 11 | 14 | 2 | 12 | 0 | 0 | 0 | 0 | 0 | .00 | 1 | .304 | .409 | .430 |
| 1990 | St. Louis | NL | 78 | 127 | 28 | 5 | 0 | 1 | (1 | 0) | 36 | 7 | 19 | 8 | 0 | 15 | 0 | 1 | 1 | 0 | 0 | .00 | 5 | .220 | .265 | .283 |
| 1988 | Houston | NL | 65 | 176 | 43 | 10 | 2 | 1 | (0 | 1) | 60 | 19 | 20 | 15 | 3 | 18 | 0 | 1 | 0 | 1 | 0 | 1.00 | 2 | .244 | .304 | .341 |
| | St. Louis | NL | 19 | 58 | 13 | 3 | 0 | 0 | (0 | 0) | 16 | 3 | 1 | 2 | 0 | 7 | 0 | 0 | 0 | 1 | 0 | 1.00 | 1 | .224 | .250 | .276 |
| | 16 ML YEARS | | 1244 | 2898 | 794 | 141 | 30 | 49 | (20 | 29) | 1142 | 370 | 378 | 305 | 29 | 308 | 2 | 6 | 24 | 44 | 18 | .71 | 54 | .274 | .341 | .394 |

## David Walsh

**Pitches:** Left **Bats:** Left **Pos:** RP **Ht:** 6' 1" **Wt:** 185 **Born:** 09/25/60 **Age:** 30

| HOW MUCH HE PITCHED | | | | | | | | | WHAT HE GAVE UP | | | | | | | | | | | | THE RESULTS | | | | | |
|---|---|---|---|---|---|---|---|---|---|---|---|---|---|---|---|---|---|---|---|---|---|---|---|---|---|---|
| Year | Team | Lg | G | GS | CG | GF | IP | BFP | H | R | ER | HR | SH | SF | HB | TBB | IBB | SO | WP | Bk | W | L | Pct. | ShO | Sv | ERA |
| 1982 | Medicine Hat | R | 13 | 0 | 0 | 7 | 26 | 0 | 35 | 30 | 16 | 4 | 0 | 0 | 2 | 18 | 0 | 22 | 0 | 0 | 1 | 2 | .333 | 0 | 2 | 5.54 |
| 1983 | Florence | A | 41 | 3 | 1 | 14 | 100 | 0 | 95 | 53 | 37 | 9 | 0 | 0 | 5 | 34 | 0 | 90 | 0 | 0 | 10 | 2 | .833 | 1 | 3 | 3.33 |
| 1984 | Kinston | A | 3 | 0 | 0 | 1 | 7.2 | 33 | 8 | 2 | 2 | 0 | 0 | 0 | 0 | 2 | 0 | 9 | 0 | 0 | 1 | 1 | .500 | 0 | 1 | 2.35 |
| | Syracuse | AAA | 9 | 4 | 0 | 3 | 28.2 | 140 | 40 | 23 | 21 | 3 | 1 | 4 | 0 | 15 | 0 | 15 | 4 | 1 | 1 | 1 | .500 | 0 | 0 | 6.59 |
| | Knoxville | AA | 23 | 19 | 4 | 2 | 119.1 | 513 | 111 | 54 | 43 | 6 | 5 | 5 | 0 | 64 | 0 | 60 | 8 | 3 | 5 | 8 | .385 | 1 | 0 | 3.24 |
| 1985 | Knoxville | AA | 38 | 25 | 3 | 6 | 154 | 688 | 147 | 89 | 77 | 11 | 1 | 4 | 5 | 89 | 0 | 103 | 14 | 6 | 11 | 8 | .579 | 1 | 0 | 4.50 |
| 1986 | Knoxville | AA | 11 | 2 | 0 | 4 | 28.2 | 144 | 30 | 21 | 18 | 3 | 1 | 1 | 0 | 32 | 0 | 15 | 4 | 2 | 2 | 0 | 1.000 | 0 | 0 | 5.65 |
| | Ventura | A | 15 | 9 | 0 | 4 | 59.1 | 270 | 65 | 41 | 34 | 4 | 0 | 3 | 3 | 26 | 0 | 43 | 5 | 1 | 6 | 3 | .667 | 0 | 0 | 5.16 |
| 1987 | Knoxville | AA | 24 | 8 | 0 | 7 | 67.2 | 319 | 72 | 52 | 41 | 8 | 4 | 5 | 4 | 46 | 1 | 42 | 8 | 1 | 2 | 4 | .333 | 0 | 0 | 5.45 |
| 1988 | Syracuse | AAA | 3 | 2 | 0 | 0 | 10 | 43 | 8 | 9 | 9 | 2 | 1 | 0 | 0 | 9 | 0 | 10 | 1 | 0 | 0 | 1 | .000 | 0 | 0 | 8.10 |
| 1989 | Albuquerque | AAA | 6 | 6 | 0 | 0 | 27 | 123 | 27 | 15 | 15 | 1 | 1 | 1 | 1 | 17 | 0 | 18 | 2 | 2 | 1 | 2 | .333 | 0 | 0 | 5.00 |
| | San Antonio | AA | 38 | 0 | 0 | 15 | 55.2 | 237 | 47 | 26 | 23 | 4 | 4 | 1 | 2 | 30 | 5 | 63 | 7 | 0 | 2 | 6 | .250 | 0 | 2 | 3.72 |

| Year Team | Lg | G | GS | CG | GF | IP | BFP | H | R | ER | HR | SH | SF | HB | TBB | IBB | SO | WP | Bk | W | L | Pct. | ShO | Sv | ERA |
|---|---|---|---|---|---|---|---|---|---|---|---|---|---|---|---|---|---|---|---|---|---|---|---|---|---|
| 1990 Albuquerque | AAA | 47 | 0 | 0 | 28 | 62 | 255 | 50 | 21 | 18 | 2 | 2 | 1 | 0 | 31 | 1 | 66 | 4 | 3 | 6 | 0 | 1.000 | 0 | 12 | 2.61 |
| 1990 Los Angeles | NL | 20 | 0 | 0 | 7 | 16.1 | 70 | 15 | 12 | 7 | 1 | 1 | 1 | 0 | 6 | 1 | 15 | 1 | 1 | 1 | 0 | 1.000 | 0 | 1 | 3.86 |

## Jerome Walton

**Bats:** Right **Throws:** Right **Pos:** CF **Ht:** 6' 1" **Wt:** 175 **Born:** 07/08/65 **Age:** 25

| BATTING | | | | | | | | | | | | | | | | | | | | BASERUNNING | | | | PERCENTAGES | | |
|---|---|---|---|---|---|---|---|---|---|---|---|---|---|---|---|---|---|---|---|---|---|---|---|---|---|---|
| Year Team | Lg | G | AB | H | 2B | 3B | HR | (Hm | Rd) | TB | R | RBI | TBB | IBB | SO | HBP | SH | SF | SB | CS | SB% | GDP | Avg | OBP | SLG |
| 1986 Wytheville | R | 62 | 229 | 66 | 7 | 4 | 5 | -- | -- | 96 | 48 | 34 | 28 | 0 | 40 | 6 | 3 | 3 | 21 | 3 | .88 | 3 | .288 | .376 | .419 |
| 1987 Peoria | A | 128 | 472 | 158 | 24 | 11 | 6 | -- | -- | 222 | 102 | 38 | 91 | 2 | 91 | 11 | 5 | 1 | 49 | 25 | .66 | 9 | .335 | .452 | .470 |
| 1988 Pittsfield | AA | 120 | 414 | 137 | 26 | 2 | 3 | -- | -- | 176 | 64 | 49 | 41 | 1 | 69 | 8 | 4 | 3 | 42 | 13 | .76 | 6 | .331 | .399 | .425 |
| 1989 Iowa | AAA | 4 | 18 | 6 | 1 | 0 | 1 | -- | -- | 10 | 4 | 3 | 1 | 0 | 5 | 0 | 0 | 0 | 2 | 1 | .67 | 0 | .333 | .368 | .556 |
| 1990 Iowa | AAA | 4 | 16 | 3 | 0 | 0 | 1 | -- | -- | 6 | 3 | 1 | 2 | 0 | 4 | 0 | 0 | 0 | 0 | 0 | .00 | 0 | .188 | .278 | .375 |
| 1989 Chicago | NL | 116 | 475 | 139 | 23 | 3 | 5 | (3 | 2) | 183 | 64 | 46 | 27 | 1 | 77 | 6 | 2 | 5 | 24 | 7 | .77 | 6 | .293 | .335 | .385 |
| 1990 Chicago | NL | 101 | 392 | 103 | 16 | 2 | 2 | (2 | 0) | 129 | 63 | 21 | 50 | 1 | 70 | 4 | 1 | 2 | 14 | 7 | .67 | 4 | .263 | .350 | .329 |
| 2 ML YEARS | | 217 | 867 | 242 | 39 | 5 | 7 | (5 | 2) | 312 | 127 | 67 | 77 | 2 | 147 | 10 | 3 | 7 | 38 | 14 | .73 | 10 | .279 | .342 | .360 |

## Steve Wapnick

**Pitches:** Right **Bats:** Right **Pos:** RP **Ht:** 6' 2" **Wt:** 196 **Born:** 09/25/65 **Age:** 25

| HOW MUCH HE PITCHED | | | | | | | | WHAT HE GAVE UP | | | | | | | | | | | | THE RESULTS | | | | | |
|---|---|---|---|---|---|---|---|---|---|---|---|---|---|---|---|---|---|---|---|---|---|---|---|---|---|
| Year Team | Lg | G | GS | CG | GF | IP | BFP | H | R | ER | HR | SH | SF | HB | TBB | IBB | SO | WP | Bk | W | L | Pct. | ShO | Sv | ERA |
| 1987 St.Cathrnes | A | 20 | 6 | 0 | 4 | 65.2 | 272 | 53 | 28 | 22 | 5 | 1 | 1 | 2 | 21 | 0 | 63 | 3 | 1 | 3 | 4 | .429 | 0 | 1 | 3.02 |
| 1988 Myrtle Bch | A | 54 | 0 | 0 | 27 | 60.1 | 252 | 44 | 18 | 15 | 2 | 2 | 2 | 0 | 31 | 5 | 69 | 3 | 3 | 4 | 3 | .571 | 0 | 12 | 2.24 |
| 1989 Dunedin | A | 24 | 1 | 0 | 11 | 66 | 262 | 48 | 19 | 15 | 2 | 0 | 1 | 3 | 22 | 1 | 59 | 9 | 1 | 4 | 0 | 1.000 | 0 | 7 | 2.05 |
| Knoxville | AA | 12 | 0 | 0 | 9 | 18.1 | 73 | 12 | 1 | 1 | 1 | 1 | 0 | 0 | 7 | 0 | 20 | 0 | 1 | 1 | 0 | 1.000 | 0 | 2 | 0.49 |
| Syracuse | AAA | 6 | 1 | 0 | 4 | 13 | 51 | 9 | 1 | 1 | 0 | 1 | 0 | 1 | 5 | 0 | 10 | 0 | 0 | 1 | 0 | 1.000 | 0 | 0 | 0.69 |
| 1990 Syracuse | AAA | 11 | 1 | 0 | 6 | 16 | 70 | 16 | 9 | 9 | 2 | 1 | 1 | 1 | 6 | 0 | 19 | 1 | 0 | 0 | 1 | .000 | 0 | 2 | 5.06 |
| 1990 Detroit | AL | 4 | 0 | 0 | 1 | 7 | 37 | 8 | 5 | 5 | 0 | 0 | 0 | 0 | 10 | 0 | 6 | 0 | 0 | 0 | 0 | .000 | 0 | 0 | 6.43 |

## Colby Ward

**Pitches:** Right **Bats:** Right **Pos:** RP **Ht:** 6' 2" **Wt:** 185 **Born:** 01/02/64 **Age:** 27

| HOW MUCH HE PITCHED | | | | | | | | WHAT HE GAVE UP | | | | | | | | | | | | THE RESULTS | | | | | |
|---|---|---|---|---|---|---|---|---|---|---|---|---|---|---|---|---|---|---|---|---|---|---|---|---|---|
| Year Team | Lg | G | GS | CG | GF | IP | BFP | H | R | ER | HR | SH | SF | HB | TBB | IBB | SO | WP | Bk | W | L | Pct. | ShO | Sv | ERA |
| 1986 Salem | A | 27 | 0 | 0 | 24 | 53.1 | 0 | 43 | 24 | 19 | 3 | 0 | 0 | 1 | 22 | 0 | 74 | 5 | 0 | 4 | 6 | .400 | 0 | 9 | 3.21 |
| 1987 Palm Sprngs | A | 54 | 0 | 0 | 44 | 88.2 | 393 | 75 | 37 | 26 | 1 | 6 | 3 | 6 | 42 | 7 | 85 | 16 | 0 | 7 | 7 | .500 | 0 | 18 | 2.64 |
| 1988 Midland | AA | 26 | 0 | 0 | 14 | 40.1 | 183 | 42 | 17 | 12 | 4 | 3 | 1 | 0 | 19 | 2 | 32 | 5 | 5 | 9 | 2 | .818 | 0 | 2 | 2.68 |
| Edmonton | AAA | 22 | 0 | 0 | 9 | 31 | 134 | 23 | 13 | 11 | 2 | 1 | 3 | 1 | 16 | 2 | 17 | 5 | 0 | 0 | 2 | .000 | 0 | 4 | 3.19 |
| 1989 Edmonton | AAA | 27 | 0 | 0 | 13 | 40.1 | 191 | 49 | 28 | 23 | 1 | 3 | 0 | 5 | 25 | 4 | 34 | 1 | 0 | 3 | 2 | .600 | 0 | 2 | 5.13 |
| Colo Sprngs | AAA | 14 | 1 | 0 | 5 | 37.2 | 174 | 50 | 28 | 22 | 4 | 0 | 3 | 1 | 15 | 0 | 23 | 1 | 2 | 1 | 0 | 1.000 | 0 | 0 | 5.26 |
| 1990 Colo Sprngs | AAA | 43 | 0 | 0 | 28 | 63 | 265 | 45 | 23 | 14 | 2 | 3 | 1 | 0 | 30 | 3 | 56 | 2 | 0 | 4 | 3 | .571 | 0 | 9 | 2.00 |
| 1990 Cleveland | AL | 22 | 0 | 0 | 7 | 36 | 158 | 31 | 17 | 17 | 3 | 4 | 2 | 1 | 21 | 4 | 23 | 6 | 0 | 1 | 3 | .250 | 0 | 1 | 4.25 |

## Duane Ward

**Pitches:** Right **Bats:** Right **Pos:** RP **Ht:** 6' 4" **Wt:** 205 **Born:** 05/28/64 **Age:** 27

| HOW MUCH HE PITCHED | | | | | | | | WHAT HE GAVE UP | | | | | | | | | | | | THE RESULTS | | | | | |
|---|---|---|---|---|---|---|---|---|---|---|---|---|---|---|---|---|---|---|---|---|---|---|---|---|---|
| Year Team | Lg | G | GS | CG | GF | IP | BFP | H | R | ER | HR | SH | SF | HB | TBB | IBB | SO | WP | Bk | W | L | Pct. | ShO | Sv | ERA |
| 1986 2 ML Teams | | 12 | 1 | 0 | 7 | 18 | 88 | 25 | 17 | 16 | 2 | 2 | 0 | 1 | 12 | 0 | 9 | 1 | 1 | 0 | 2 | .000 | 0 | 0 | 8.00 |
| 1987 Toronto | AL | 12 | 1 | 0 | 4 | 11.2 | 57 | 14 | 9 | 9 | 0 | 1 | 1 | 0 | 12 | 2 | 10 | 0 | 0 | 1 | 0 | 1.000 | 0 | 0 | 6.94 |
| 1988 Toronto | AL | 64 | 0 | 0 | 32 | 111.2 | 487 | 101 | 46 | 41 | 5 | 4 | 5 | 5 | 60 | 8 | 91 | 10 | 3 | 9 | 3 | .750 | 0 | 15 | 3.30 |
| 1989 Toronto | AL | 66 | 0 | 0 | 39 | 114.2 | 494 | 94 | 55 | 48 | 4 | 12 | 11 | 5 | 58 | 11 | 122 | 13 | 0 | 4 | 10 | .286 | 0 | 15 | 3.77 |
| 1990 Toronto | AL | 73 | 0 | 0 | 39 | 127.2 | 508 | 101 | 51 | 49 | 9 | 6 | 2 | 1 | 42 | 10 | 112 | 5 | 0 | 2 | 8 | .200 | 0 | 11 | 3.45 |
| 1986 Atlanta | NL | 10 | 0 | 0 | 6 | 16 | 73 | 22 | 13 | 13 | 2 | 2 | 0 | 0 | 8 | 0 | 8 | 0 | 1 | 0 | 1 | .000 | 0 | 0 | 7.31 |
| Toronto | AL | 2 | 1 | 0 | 1 | 2 | 15 | 3 | 4 | 3 | 0 | 0 | 0 | 1 | 4 | 0 | 1 | 1 | 0 | 0 | 1 | .000 | 0 | 0 | 13.50 |
| 5 ML YEARS | | 227 | 2 | 0 | 121 | 383.2 | 1634 | 335 | 178 | 163 | 20 | 25 | 19 | 12 | 184 | 31 | 344 | 29 | 4 | 16 | 23 | .410 | 0 | 41 | 3.82 |

## Gary Ward

**Bats:** Right **Throws:** Right **Pos:** LF/RF **Ht:** 6' 2" **Wt:** 202 **Born:** 12/06/53 **Age:** 37

| BATTING | | | | | | | | | | | | | | | | | | | | BASERUNNING | | | | PERCENTAGES | | |
|---|---|---|---|---|---|---|---|---|---|---|---|---|---|---|---|---|---|---|---|---|---|---|---|---|---|---|
| Year Team | Lg | G | AB | H | 2B | 3B | HR | (Hm | Rd) | TB | R | RBI | TBB | IBB | SO | HBP | SH | SF | SB | CS | SB% | GDP | Avg | OBP | SLG |
| 1979 Minnesota | AL | 10 | 14 | 4 | 0 | 0 | 0 | (0 | 0) | 4 | 2 | 1 | 3 | 0 | 3 | 0 | 0 | 0 | 0 | 1 | .00 | 0 | .286 | .412 | .286 |
| 1980 Minnesota | AL | 13 | 41 | 19 | 6 | 2 | 1 | (0 | 1) | 32 | 11 | 10 | 3 | 1 | 6 | 0 | 1 | 1 | 0 | 0 | .00 | 0 | .463 | .489 | .780 |
| 1981 Minnesota | AL | 85 | 295 | 78 | 7 | 6 | 3 | (2 | 1) | 106 | 42 | 29 | 28 | 4 | 48 | 0 | 0 | 3 | 5 | 2 | .71 | 10 | .264 | .325 | .359 |
| 1982 Minnesota | AL | 152 | 570 | 165 | 33 | 7 | 28 | (16 | 12) | 296 | 85 | 91 | 37 | 4 | 105 | 1 | 1 | 7 | 13 | 1 | .93 | 16 | .289 | .330 | .519 |
| 1983 Minnesota | AL | 157 | 623 | 173 | 34 | 5 | 19 | (7 | 12) | 274 | 76 | 88 | 44 | 2 | 98 | 3 | 1 | 5 | 8 | 1 | .89 | 24 | .278 | .326 | .440 |
| 1984 Texas | AL | 155 | 602 | 171 | 21 | 7 | 21 | (7 | 14) | 269 | 97 | 79 | 55 | 3 | 95 | 0 | 1 | 1 | 7 | 5 | .58 | 22 | .284 | .343 | .447 |
| 1985 Texas | AL | 154 | 593 | 170 | 28 | 7 | 15 | (10 | 5) | 257 | 77 | 70 | 39 | 3 | 97 | 1 | 0 | 5 | 26 | 7 | .79 | 19 | .287 | .329 | .433 |
| 1986 Texas | AL | 105 | 380 | 120 | 15 | 2 | 5 | (3 | 2) | 154 | 54 | 51 | 31 | 3 | 72 | 4 | 1 | 2 | 12 | 8 | .60 | 10 | .316 | .372 | .405 |
| 1987 New York | AL | 146 | 529 | 131 | 22 | 1 | 16 | (7 | 9) | 203 | 65 | 78 | 33 | 2 | 101 | 1 | 2 | 4 | 9 | 1 | .90 | 20 | .248 | .291 | .384 |

| | | | | | | | | | | | | | | | | | | | | | | | | | |
|---|---|---|---|---|---|---|---|---|---|---|---|---|---|---|---|---|---|---|---|---|---|---|---|---|---|
| 1988 New York | AL | 91 | 231 | 52 | 8 | 0 | 4 | (3 | 1) | 72 | 26 | 24 | 24 | 4 | 41 | 2 | 4 | 1 | 0 | 1 | .00 | 8 | .225 | .302 | .312 |
| 1989 2 ML Teams | | 113 | 292 | 74 | 11 | 2 | 9 | (6 | 3) | 116 | 27 | 30 | 24 | 2 | 59 | 0 | 1 | 4 | 1 | 3 | .25 | 11 | .253 | .306 | .397 |
| 1990 Detroit | AL | 106 | 309 | 79 | 11 | 2 | 9 | (2 | 7) | 121 | 32 | 46 | 30 | 0 | 50 | 1 | 2 | 2 | 2 | 0 | 1.00 | 12 | .256 | .322 | .392 |
| 1989 New York | AL | 8 | 17 | 5 | 1 | 0 | 0 | (0 | 0) | 6 | 3 | 1 | 3 | 1 | 5 | 0 | 0 | 0 | 0 | 0 | .00 | 1 | .294 | .400 | .353 |
| Detroit | AL | 105 | 275 | 69 | 10 | 2 | 9 | (6 | 3) | 110 | 24 | 29 | 21 | 1 | 54 | 0 | 1 | 4 | 1 | 3 | .25 | 10 | .251 | .300 | .400 |
| 12 ML YEARS | | 1287 | 4479 | 1236 | 196 | 41 | 130 | (63 | 67) | 1904 | 594 | 597 | 351 | 28 | 775 | 13 | 14 | 35 | 83 | 30 | .73 | 152 | .276 | .328 | .425 |

## Turner Ward

**Bats:** Both **Throws:** Right **Pos:** RF **Ht:** 6' 2" **Wt:** 200 **Born:** 04/11/65 **Age:** 26

| BATTING | | | | | | | | | | | | | | | | | | | BASERUNNING | | | | PERCENTAGES | | |
|---|---|---|---|---|---|---|---|---|---|---|---|---|---|---|---|---|---|---|---|---|---|---|---|---|---|
| Year Team | Lg | G | AB | H | 2B | 3B | HR | (Hm | Rd) | TB | R | RBI | TBB | IBB | SO | HBP | SH | SF | SB | CS | SB% | GDP | Avg | OBP | SLG |
| 1986 Oneonta | A | 63 | 221 | 62 | 4 | 1 | 1 | -- | -- | 71 | 42 | 19 | 31 | 1 | 39 | 2 | 2 | 3 | 6 | 6 | .50 | 4 | .281 | .370 | .321 |
| 1987 Ft.Laudrdle | A | 130 | 493 | 145 | 15 | 2 | 7 | -- | -- | 185 | 83 | 55 | 64 | 4 | 83 | 6 | 7 | 3 | 25 | 3 | .89 | 8 | .294 | .380 | .375 |
| 1988 Columbus | AAA | 134 | 490 | 123 | 24 | 1 | 7 | -- | -- | 170 | 55 | 50 | 48 | 5 | 100 | 3 | 8 | 2 | 28 | 5 | .85 | 7 | .251 | .320 | .347 |
| 1989 Indians | R | 4 | 15 | 3 | 0 | 0 | 0 | -- | -- | 3 | 2 | 1 | 2 | 0 | 2 | 0 | 0 | 0 | 1 | 0 | 1.00 | 1 | .200 | .294 | .200 |
| Canton-Akrn | AA | 30 | 93 | 28 | 5 | 1 | 0 | -- | -- | 35 | 19 | 3 | 15 | 0 | 16 | 0 | 0 | 0 | 1 | 2 | .33 | 2 | .301 | .398 | .376 |
| 1990 Colo Sprngs | AAA | 133 | 495 | 148 | 24 | 9 | 6 | -- | -- | 208 | 89 | 65 | 72 | 1 | 70 | 4 | 5 | 9 | 22 | 15 | .59 | 16 | .299 | .386 | .420 |
| 1990 Cleveland | AL | 14 | 46 | 16 | 2 | 1 | 1 | (0 | 1) | 23 | 10 | 10 | 3 | 0 | 8 | 0 | 0 | 0 | 3 | 0 | 1.00 | 1 | .348 | .388 | .500 |

## Claudell Washington

**Bats:** Left **Throws:** Left **Pos:** LF/RF **Ht:** 6' 2" **Wt:** 195 **Born:** 08/31/54 **Age:** 36

| BATTING | | | | | | | | | | | | | | | | | | | BASERUNNING | | | | PERCENTAGES | | |
|---|---|---|---|---|---|---|---|---|---|---|---|---|---|---|---|---|---|---|---|---|---|---|---|---|---|
| Year Team | Lg | G | AB | H | 2B | 3B | HR | (Hm | Rd) | TB | R | RBI | TBB | IBB | SO | HBP | SH | SF | SB | CS | SB% | GDP | Avg | OBP | SLG |
| 1974 Oakland | AL | 73 | 221 | 63 | 10 | 5 | 0 | (0 | 0) | 83 | 16 | 19 | 13 | 1 | 44 | 1 | 1 | 1 | 6 | 8 | .43 | 6 | .285 | .326 | .376 |
| 1975 Oakland | AL | 148 | 590 | 182 | 24 | 7 | 10 | (7 | 3) | 250 | 86 | 77 | 32 | 9 | 80 | 5 | 1 | 7 | 40 | 15 | .73 | 12 | .308 | .345 | .424 |
| 1976 Oakland | AL | 134 | 490 | 126 | 20 | 6 | 5 | (1 | 4) | 173 | 65 | 53 | 30 | 1 | 90 | 3 | 3 | 4 | 37 | 20 | .65 | 13 | .257 | .302 | .353 |
| 1977 Texas | AL | 129 | 521 | 148 | 31 | 2 | 12 | (6 | 6) | 219 | 63 | 68 | 25 | 9 | 112 | 3 | 1 | 4 | 21 | 8 | .72 | 10 | .284 | .318 | .420 |
| 1978 2 ML Teams | | 98 | 356 | 90 | 16 | 5 | 6 | (3 | 3) | 134 | 34 | 33 | 13 | 2 | 69 | 1 | 2 | 4 | 5 | 6 | .45 | 8 | .253 | .278 | .376 |
| 1979 Chicago | AL | 131 | 471 | 132 | 33 | 5 | 13 | (10 | 3) | 214 | 79 | 66 | 28 | 7 | 93 | 3 | 2 | 4 | 19 | 11 | .63 | 10 | .280 | .322 | .454 |
| 1980 2 ML Teams | | 111 | 374 | 104 | 20 | 6 | 11 | (5 | 6) | 169 | 53 | 54 | 25 | 5 | 82 | 2 | 1 | 1 | 21 | 7 | .75 | 10 | .278 | .326 | .452 |
| 1981 Atlanta | NL | 85 | 320 | 93 | 22 | 3 | 5 | (3 | 2) | 136 | 37 | 37 | 15 | 1 | 47 | 4 | 8 | 2 | 12 | 6 | .67 | 6 | .291 | .328 | .425 |
| 1982 Atlanta | NL | 150 | 563 | 150 | 24 | 6 | 16 | (8 | 8) | 234 | 94 | 80 | 50 | 9 | 107 | 6 | 1 | 6 | 33 | 10 | .77 | 9 | .266 | .330 | .416 |
| 1983 Atlanta | NL | 134 | 496 | 138 | 24 | 8 | 9 | (4 | 5) | 205 | 75 | 44 | 35 | 6 | 103 | 0 | 1 | 6 | 31 | 9 | .78 | 8 | .278 | .322 | .413 |
| 1984 Atlanta | NL | 120 | 416 | 119 | 21 | 2 | 17 | (12 | 5) | 195 | 62 | 61 | 59 | 8 | 77 | 1 | 0 | 3 | 21 | 9 | .70 | 11 | .286 | .374 | .469 |
| 1985 Atlanta | NL | 122 | 398 | 110 | 14 | 6 | 15 | (4 | 11) | 181 | 62 | 43 | 40 | 11 | 66 | 1 | 0 | 2 | 14 | 4 | .78 | 11 | .276 | .342 | .455 |
| 1986 2 ML Teams | | 94 | 272 | 69 | 16 | 0 | 11 | (7 | 4) | 118 | 36 | 30 | 21 | 0 | 59 | 2 | 1 | 1 | 10 | 8 | .56 | 7 | .254 | .311 | .434 |
| 1987 New York | AL | 102 | 312 | 87 | 17 | 0 | 9 | (5 | 4) | 131 | 42 | 44 | 27 | 2 | 54 | 0 | 0 | 0 | 10 | 1 | .91 | 3 | .279 | .336 | .420 |
| 1988 New York | AL | 126 | 455 | 140 | 22 | 3 | 11 | (6 | 5) | 201 | 62 | 64 | 24 | 2 | 74 | 2 | 0 | 4 | 15 | 6 | .71 | 7 | .308 | .342 | .442 |
| 1989 California | AL | 110 | 418 | 114 | 18 | 4 | 13 | (9 | 4) | 179 | 53 | 42 | 27 | 3 | 84 | 2 | 3 | 1 | 13 | 5 | .72 | 7 | .273 | .319 | .428 |
| 1990 2 ML Teams | | 45 | 114 | 19 | 2 | 1 | 1 | (0 | 1) | 26 | 7 | 9 | 4 | 1 | 25 | 0 | 0 | 1 | 4 | 1 | .80 | 2 | .167 | .193 | .228 |
| 1978 Texas | AL | 12 | 42 | 7 | 0 | 0 | 0 | (0 | 0) | 7 | 1 | 2 | 1 | 0 | 12 | 0 | 0 | 0 | 0 | 1 | .00 | 1 | .167 | .186 | .167 |
| Chicago | AL | 86 | 314 | 83 | 16 | 5 | 6 | (3 | 3) | 127 | 33 | 31 | 12 | 2 | 57 | 1 | 2 | 4 | 5 | 5 | .50 | 7 | .264 | .290 | .404 |
| 1980 Chicago | AL | 32 | 90 | 26 | 4 | 2 | 1 | (0 | 1) | 37 | 15 | 12 | 5 | 0 | 19 | 1 | 1 | 0 | 4 | 2 | .67 | 5 | .289 | .333 | .411 |
| New York | NL | 79 | 284 | 78 | 16 | 4 | 10 | (5 | 5) | 132 | 38 | 42 | 20 | 5 | 63 | 1 | 0 | 1 | 17 | 5 | .77 | 5 | .275 | .324 | .465 |
| 1986 Atlanta | NL | 40 | 137 | 37 | 11 | 0 | 5 | (3 | 2) | 63 | 17 | 14 | 14 | 0 | 26 | 0 | 1 | 1 | 4 | 7 | .36 | 4 | .270 | .336 | .460 |
| New York | AL | 54 | 135 | 32 | 5 | 0 | 6 | (4 | 2) | 55 | 19 | 16 | 7 | 0 | 33 | 2 | 0 | 0 | 6 | 1 | .86 | 3 | .237 | .285 | .407 |
| 1990 California | AL | 12 | 34 | 6 | 1 | 0 | 1 | (0 | 1) | 10 | 3 | 3 | 2 | 0 | 8 | 0 | 0 | 0 | 1 | 0 | 1.00 | 1 | .176 | .222 | .294 |
| New York | AL | 33 | 80 | 13 | 1 | 1 | 0 | (0 | 0) | 16 | 4 | 6 | 2 | 1 | 17 | 0 | 0 | 1 | 3 | 1 | .75 | 1 | .163 | .181 | .200 |
| 17 ML YEARS | | 1912 | 6787 | 1884 | 334 | 69 | 164 | (90 | 74) | 2848 | 926 | 824 | 468 | 77 | 1266 | 36 | 25 | 51 | 312 | 134 | .70 | 140 | .278 | .325 | .420 |

## Gary Wayne

**Pitches:** Left **Bats:** Left **Pos:** RP **Ht:** 6' 3" **Wt:** 185 **Born:** 11/30/62 **Age:** 28

| HOW MUCH HE PITCHED | | | | | | | | WHAT HE GAVE UP | | | | | | | | | | | | THE RESULTS | | | | | |
|---|---|---|---|---|---|---|---|---|---|---|---|---|---|---|---|---|---|---|---|---|---|---|---|---|---|
| Year Team | Lg | G | GS | CG | GF | IP | BFP | H | R | ER | HR | SH | SF | HB | TBB | IBB | SO | WP | Bk | W | L | Pct. | ShO | Sv | ERA |
| 1984 Wst Plm Bch | A | 13 | 12 | 2 | 0 | 74.1 | 342 | 70 | 38 | 32 | 1 | 3 | 2 | 3 | 49 | 0 | 46 | 9 | 2 | 3 | 5 | .375 | 0 | 0 | 3.87 |
| 1985 Jacksnville | AA | 21 | 20 | 2 | 0 | 102 | 471 | 108 | 67 | 60 | 3 | 2 | 4 | 1 | 70 | 3 | 62 | 11 | 1 | 3 | 12 | .200 | 0 | 0 | 5.29 |
| Wst Plm Bch | A | 8 | 4 | 0 | 1 | 30.2 | 147 | 37 | 23 | 19 | 1 | 5 | 1 | 0 | 22 | 0 | 18 | 5 | 0 | 2 | 2 | .500 | 0 | 0 | 5.58 |
| 1986 Wst Plm Bch | A | 47 | 0 | 0 | 41 | 61.1 | 255 | 48 | 16 | 11 | 1 | 2 | 2 | 1 | 25 | 2 | 55 | 3 | 1 | 2 | 5 | .286 | 0 | 25 | 1.61 |
| 1987 Jacksnville | AA | 56 | 0 | 0 | 28 | 80.1 | 324 | 56 | 23 | 21 | 4 | 2 | 2 | 0 | 35 | 0 | 78 | 2 | 1 | 5 | 1 | .833 | 0 | 10 | 2.35 |
| 1988 Indianapols | AAA | 8 | 0 | 0 | 2 | 7.1 | 33 | 9 | 5 | 5 | 0 | 0 | 1 | 0 | 3 | 0 | 6 | 3 | 1 | 0 | 0 | .000 | 0 | 1 | 6.14 |
| 1990 Portland | AAA | 22 | 0 | 0 | 13 | 31.2 | 134 | 29 | 14 | 12 | 1 | 0 | 1 | 0 | 13 | 1 | 30 | 3 | 1 | 2 | 4 | .333 | 0 | 5 | 3.41 |
| 1989 Minnesota | AL | 60 | 0 | 0 | 21 | 71 | 302 | 55 | 28 | 26 | 4 | 4 | 2 | 1 | 36 | 4 | 41 | 7 | 0 | 3 | 4 | .429 | 0 | 1 | 3.30 |
| 1990 Minnesota | AL | 38 | 0 | 0 | 12 | 38.2 | 166 | 38 | 19 | 18 | 5 | 1 | 2 | 1 | 13 | 0 | 28 | 4 | 0 | 1 | 1 | .500 | 0 | 1 | 4.19 |
| 2 ML YEARS | | 98 | 0 | 0 | 33 | 109.2 | 468 | 93 | 47 | 44 | 9 | 5 | 4 | 2 | 49 | 4 | 69 | 11 | 0 | 4 | 5 | .444 | 0 | 2 | 3.61 |

## Lenny Webster

**Bats:** Right **Throws:** Right **Pos:** C **Ht:** 6' 1" **Wt:** 185 **Born:** 02/10/65 **Age:** 26

| BATTING | | | | | | | | | | | | | | | | | | | | BASERUNNING | | | | PERCENTAGES | | |
|---|---|---|---|---|---|---|---|---|---|---|---|---|---|---|---|---|---|---|---|---|---|---|---|---|---|---|
| Year | Team | Lg | G | AB | H | 2B | 3B | HR | (Hm | Rd) | TB | R | RBI | TBB | IBB | SO | HBP | SH | SF | SB | CS | SB% | GDP | Avg | OBP | SLG |
| 1986 | Kenosha | A | 22 | 65 | 10 | 2 | 0 | 0 | -- | -- | 12 | 2 | 8 | 10 | 0 | 12 | 0 | 1 | 0 | 0 | 0 | .00 | 3 | .154 | .267 | .185 |
| | Elizabethtn | R | 48 | 152 | 35 | 4 | 0 | 3 | -- | -- | 48 | 29 | 14 | 22 | 0 | 21 | 2 | 0 | 0 | 1 | 0 | 1.00 | 6 | .230 | .335 | .316 |
| 1987 | Kenosha | A | 52 | 140 | 35 | 7 | 0 | 3 | -- | -- | 51 | 17 | 17 | 17 | 0 | 20 | 0 | 0 | 3 | 2 | 0 | 1.00 | 8 | .250 | .325 | .364 |
| 1988 | Kenosha | A | 129 | 465 | 134 | 23 | 2 | 11 | -- | -- | 194 | 82 | 87 | 71 | 5 | 47 | 1 | 2 | 7 | 3 | 2 | .60 | 13 | .288 | .379 | .417 |
| 1989 | Visalia | A | 63 | 231 | 62 | 7 | 0 | 5 | -- | -- | 84 | 36 | 39 | 27 | 1 | 27 | 1 | 0 | 5 | 2 | 1 | .67 | 9 | .268 | .341 | .364 |
| | Orlando | AA | 59 | 191 | 45 | 7 | 0 | 2 | -- | -- | 58 | 29 | 17 | 44 | 1 | 20 | 3 | 2 | 2 | 2 | 0 | 1.00 | 3 | .236 | .383 | .304 |
| 1990 | Orlando | AA | 126 | 455 | 119 | 31 | 0 | 8 | -- | -- | 174 | 69 | 71 | 68 | 5 | 57 | 0 | 0 | 3 | 0 | 0 | .00 | 11 | .262 | .356 | .382 |
| 1989 | Minnesota | AL | 14 | 20 | 6 | 2 | 0 | 0 | (0 | 0) | 8 | 3 | 1 | 3 | 0 | 2 | 0 | 0 | 0 | 0 | 0 | .00 | 0 | .300 | .391 | .400 |
| 1990 | Minnesota | AL | 2 | 6 | 2 | 1 | 0 | 0 | (0 | 0) | 3 | 1 | 0 | 1 | 0 | 1 | 0 | 0 | 0 | 0 | 0 | .00 | 0 | .333 | .429 | .500 |
| | 2 ML YEARS | | 16 | 26 | 8 | 3 | 0 | 0 | (0 | 0) | 11 | 4 | 1 | 4 | 0 | 3 | 0 | 0 | 0 | 0 | 0 | .00 | 0 | .308 | .400 | .423 |

## Mitch Webster

**Bats:** Both **Throws:** Left **Pos:** CF/LF **Ht:** 6' 1" **Wt:** 185 **Born:** 05/16/59 **Age:** 32

| BATTING | | | | | | | | | | | | | | | | | | | | BASERUNNING | | | | PERCENTAGES | | |
|---|---|---|---|---|---|---|---|---|---|---|---|---|---|---|---|---|---|---|---|---|---|---|---|---|---|---|
| Year | Team | Lg | G | AB | H | 2B | 3B | HR | (Hm | Rd) | TB | R | RBI | TBB | IBB | SO | HBP | SH | SF | SB | CS | SB% | GDP | Avg | OBP | SLG |
| 1983 | Toronto | AL | 11 | 11 | 2 | 0 | 0 | 0 | (0 | 0) | 2 | 2 | 0 | 1 | 0 | 1 | 0 | 0 | 0 | 0 | 0 | .00 | 0 | .182 | .250 | .182 |
| 1984 | Toronto | AL | 26 | 22 | 5 | 2 | 1 | 0 | (0 | 0) | 9 | 9 | 4 | 1 | 0 | 7 | 0 | 0 | 0 | 0 | 0 | .00 | 1 | .227 | .261 | .409 |
| 1985 | 2 ML Teams | | 78 | 213 | 58 | 8 | 2 | 11 | (3 | 8) | 103 | 32 | 30 | 20 | 3 | 33 | 0 | 1 | 1 | 15 | 10 | .60 | 3 | .272 | .333 | .484 |
| 1986 | Montreal | NL | 151 | 576 | 167 | 31 | 13 | 8 | (2 | 6) | 248 | 89 | 49 | 57 | 4 | 78 | 4 | 3 | 5 | 36 | 15 | .71 | 9 | .290 | .355 | .431 |
| 1987 | Montreal | NL | 156 | 588 | 165 | 30 | 8 | 15 | (9 | 6) | 256 | 101 | 63 | 70 | 5 | 95 | 6 | 8 | 4 | 33 | 10 | .77 | 6 | .281 | .361 | .435 |
| 1988 | 2 ML Teams | | 151 | 523 | 136 | 16 | 8 | 6 | (3 | 3) | 186 | 69 | 39 | 55 | 2 | 87 | 8 | 5 | 4 | 22 | 14 | .61 | 5 | .260 | .337 | .356 |
| 1989 | Chicago | NL | 98 | 272 | 70 | 12 | 4 | 3 | (1 | 2) | 99 | 40 | 19 | 30 | 5 | 55 | 1 | 3 | 2 | 14 | 2 | .88 | 3 | .257 | .331 | .364 |
| 1990 | Cleveland | AL | 128 | 437 | 110 | 20 | 6 | 12 | (6 | 6) | 178 | 58 | 55 | 20 | 1 | 61 | 3 | 11 | 6 | 22 | 6 | .79 | 5 | .252 | .285 | .407 |
| 1985 | Toronto | AL | 4 | 1 | 0 | 0 | 0 | 0 | (0 | 0) | 0 | 0 | 0 | 0 | 0 | 0 | 0 | 0 | 0 | 0 | 1 | .00 | 0 | .000 | .000 | .000 |
| | Montreal | NL | 74 | 212 | 58 | 8 | 2 | 11 | (3 | 8) | 103 | 32 | 30 | 20 | 3 | 33 | 0 | 1 | 1 | 15 | 9 | .63 | 3 | .274 | .335 | .486 |
| 1988 | Montreal | NL | 81 | 259 | 66 | 5 | 2 | 2 | (0 | 2) | 81 | 33 | 13 | 36 | 2 | 37 | 5 | 4 | 2 | 12 | 10 | .55 | 3 | .255 | .354 | .313 |
| | Chicago | NL | 70 | 264 | 70 | 11 | 6 | 4 | (3 | 1) | 105 | 36 | 26 | 19 | 0 | 50 | 3 | 1 | 2 | 10 | 4 | .71 | 2 | .265 | .319 | .398 |
| | 8 ML YEARS | | 799 | 2642 | 713 | 119 | 42 | 55 | (24 | 31) | 1081 | 400 | 259 | 254 | 20 | 417 | 22 | 31 | 22 | 142 | 57 | .71 | 32 | .270 | .336 | .409 |

## Bill Wegman

**Pitches:** Right **Bats:** Right **Pos:** SP **Ht:** 6' 5" **Wt:** 200 **Born:** 12/19/62 **Age:** 28

| HOW MUCH HE PITCHED | | | | | | | | | WHAT HE GAVE UP | | | | | | | | | | | | THE RESULTS | | | | | |
|---|---|---|---|---|---|---|---|---|---|---|---|---|---|---|---|---|---|---|---|---|---|---|---|---|---|---|
| Year | Team | Lg | G | GS | CG | GF | IP | BFP | H | R | ER | HR | SH | SF | HB | TBB | IBB | SO | WP | Bk | W | L | Pct. | ShO | Sv | ERA |
| 1985 | Milwaukee | AL | 3 | 3 | 0 | 0 | 17.2 | 73 | 17 | 8 | 7 | 3 | 0 | 1 | 0 | 3 | 0 | 6 | 0 | 1 | 2 | 0 | 1.000 | 0 | 0 | 3.57 |
| 1986 | Milwaukee | AL | 35 | 32 | 2 | 1 | 198.1 | 836 | 217 | 120 | 113 | 32 | 4 | 5 | 7 | 43 | 2 | 82 | 5 | 2 | 5 | 12 | .294 | 0 | 0 | 5.13 |
| 1987 | Milwaukee | AL | 34 | 33 | 7 | 0 | 225 | 934 | 229 | 113 | 106 | 31 | 4 | 6 | 6 | 53 | 2 | 102 | 0 | 2 | 12 | 11 | .522 | 0 | 0 | 4.24 |
| 1988 | Milwaukee | AL | 32 | 31 | 4 | 0 | 199 | 847 | 207 | 104 | 91 | 24 | 3 | 10 | 4 | 50 | 5 | 84 | 1 | 1 | 13 | 13 | .500 | 1 | 0 | 4.12 |
| 1989 | Milwaukee | AL | 11 | 8 | 0 | 1 | 51 | 240 | 69 | 44 | 38 | 6 | 0 | 4 | 0 | 21 | 2 | 27 | 2 | 0 | 2 | 6 | .250 | 0 | 0 | 6.71 |
| 1990 | Milwaukee | AL | 8 | 5 | 1 | 0 | 29.2 | 132 | 37 | 21 | 16 | 6 | 1 | 1 | 0 | 6 | 1 | 20 | 0 | 0 | 2 | 2 | .500 | 1 | 0 | 4.85 |
| | 6 ML YEARS | | 123 | 112 | 14 | 2 | 720.2 | 3062 | 776 | 410 | 371 | 102 | 12 | 27 | 17 | 176 | 12 | 321 | 8 | 6 | 36 | 44 | .450 | 2 | 0 | 4.63 |

## Walt Weiss

**Bats:** Both **Throws:** Right **Pos:** SS **Ht:** 6' 0" **Wt:** 175 **Born:** 11/28/63 **Age:** 27

| BATTING | | | | | | | | | | | | | | | | | | | | BASERUNNING | | | | PERCENTAGES | | |
|---|---|---|---|---|---|---|---|---|---|---|---|---|---|---|---|---|---|---|---|---|---|---|---|---|---|---|
| Year | Team | Lg | G | AB | H | 2B | 3B | HR | (Hm | Rd) | TB | R | RBI | TBB | IBB | SO | HBP | SH | SF | SB | CS | SB% | GDP | Avg | OBP | SLG |
| 1987 | Oakland | AL | 16 | 26 | 12 | 4 | 0 | 0 | (0 | 0) | 16 | 3 | 1 | 2 | 0 | 2 | 0 | 1 | 0 | 1 | 2 | .33 | 0 | .462 | .500 | .615 |
| 1988 | Oakland | AL | 147 | 452 | 113 | 17 | 3 | 3 | (0 | 3) | 145 | 44 | 39 | 35 | 1 | 56 | 9 | 8 | 7 | 4 | 4 | .50 | 9 | .250 | .312 | .321 |
| 1989 | Oakland | AL | 84 | 236 | 55 | 11 | 0 | 3 | (2 | 1) | 75 | 30 | 21 | 21 | 0 | 39 | 1 | 5 | 0 | 6 | 1 | .86 | 5 | .233 | .298 | .318 |
| 1990 | Oakland | AL | 138 | 445 | 118 | 17 | 1 | 2 | (1 | 1) | 143 | 50 | 35 | 46 | 5 | 53 | 4 | 6 | 4 | 9 | 3 | .75 | 8 | .265 | .337 | .321 |
| | 4 ML YEARS | | 385 | 1159 | 298 | 49 | 4 | 8 | (3 | 5) | 379 | 127 | 96 | 104 | 6 | 150 | 14 | 20 | 11 | 20 | 10 | .67 | 22 | .257 | .323 | .327 |

## Bob Welch

**Pitches:** Right **Bats:** Right **Pos:** SP **Ht:** 6' 3" **Wt:** 195 **Born:** 11/03/56 **Age:** 34

| HOW MUCH HE PITCHED | | | | | | | | | WHAT HE GAVE UP | | | | | | | | | | | | THE RESULTS | | | | | |
|---|---|---|---|---|---|---|---|---|---|---|---|---|---|---|---|---|---|---|---|---|---|---|---|---|---|---|
| Year | Team | Lg | G | GS | CG | GF | IP | BFP | H | R | ER | HR | SH | SF | HB | TBB | IBB | SO | WP | Bk | W | L | Pct. | ShO | Sv | ERA |
| 1978 | Los Angeles | NL | 23 | 13 | 4 | 6 | 111 | 439 | 92 | 28 | 25 | 6 | 4 | 6 | 1 | 26 | 2 | 66 | 2 | 2 | 7 | 4 | .636 | 3 | 3 | 2.03 |
| 1979 | Los Angeles | NL | 25 | 12 | 1 | 10 | 81 | 349 | 82 | 42 | 36 | 7 | 4 | 1 | 3 | 32 | 4 | 64 | 0 | 0 | 5 | 6 | .455 | 0 | 5 | 4.00 |
| 1980 | Los Angeles | NL | 32 | 32 | 3 | 0 | 214 | 889 | 190 | 85 | 78 | 15 | 12 | 10 | 3 | 79 | 6 | 141 | 7 | 5 | 14 | 9 | .609 | 2 | 0 | 3.28 |
| 1981 | Los Angeles | NL | 23 | 23 | 2 | 0 | 141 | 601 | 141 | 56 | 54 | 11 | 9 | 4 | 3 | 41 | 0 | 88 | 2 | 0 | 9 | 5 | .643 | 1 | 0 | 3.45 |
| 1982 | Los Angeles | NL | 36 | 36 | 9 | 0 | 235.2 | 965 | 199 | 94 | 88 | 19 | 7 | 4 | 5 | 81 | 5 | 176 | 5 | 1 | 16 | 11 | .593 | 3 | 0 | 3.36 |
| 1983 | Los Angeles | NL | 31 | 31 | 4 | 0 | 204 | 828 | 164 | 73 | 60 | 13 | 8 | 7 | 3 | 72 | 4 | 156 | 4 | 6 | 15 | 12 | .556 | 3 | 0 | 2.65 |
| 1984 | Los Angeles | NL | 31 | 29 | 3 | 0 | 178.2 | 771 | 191 | 86 | 75 | 11 | 10 | 2 | 2 | 58 | 7 | 126 | 4 | 2 | 13 | 13 | .500 | 1 | 0 | 3.78 |
| 1985 | Los Angeles | NL | 23 | 23 | 8 | 0 | 167.1 | 675 | 141 | 49 | 43 | 16 | 6 | 2 | 6 | 35 | 2 | 96 | 7 | 4 | 14 | 4 | .778 | 3 | 0 | 2.31 |

| Year Team | Lg | G | GS | CG | GF | IP | BFP | H | R | ER | HR | SH | SF | HB | TBB | IBB | SO | WP | Bk | W | L | Pct. | ShO | Sv | ERA |
|---|---|---|---|---|---|---|---|---|---|---|---|---|---|---|---|---|---|---|---|---|---|---|---|---|---|
| 1986 Los Angeles | NL | 33 | 33 | 7 | 0 | 235.2 | 981 | 227 | 95 | 86 | 14 | 7 | 8 | 7 | 55 | 6 | 183 | 2 | 1 | 7 | 13 | .350 | 3 | 0 | 3.28 |
| 1987 Los Angeles | NL | 35 | 35 | 6 | 0 | 251.2 | 1027 | 204 | 94 | 90 | 21 | 10 | 6 | 4 | 86 | 6 | 196 | 4 | 4 | 15 | 9 | .625 | 4 | 0 | 3.22 |
| 1988 Oakland | AL | 36 | 36 | 4 | 0 | 244.2 | 1034 | 237 | 107 | 99 | 22 | 12 | 8 | 10 | 81 | 1 | 158 | 3 | 13 | 17 | 9 | .654 | 2 | 0 | 3.64 |
| 1989 Oakland | AL | 33 | 33 | 1 | 0 | 209.2 | 884 | 191 | 82 | 70 | 13 | 3 | 4 | 6 | 78 | 3 | 137 | 5 | 0 | 17 | 8 | .680 | 0 | 0 | 3.00 |
| 1990 Oakland | AL | 35 | 35 | 2 | 0 | 238 | 979 | 214 | 90 | 78 | 26 | 6 | 5 | 5 | 77 | 4 | 127 | 2 | 2 | 27 | 6 | .818 | 2 | 0 | 2.95 |
| 13 ML YEARS | | 396 | 371 | 54 | 16 | 2512.1 | 10422 | 2273 | 981 | 882 | 194 | 98 | 67 | 58 | 801 | 50 | 1714 | 47 | 40 | 176 | 109 | .618 | 27 | 8 | 3.16 |

## David Wells

**Pitches:** Left **Bats:** Left **Pos:** SP/RP **Ht:** 6' 4" **Wt:** 225 **Born:** 05/20/63 **Age:** 28

| | | HOW MUCH HE PITCHED | | | | | | WHAT HE GAVE UP | | | | | | | | | | | | THE RESULTS | | | | | |
|---|---|---|---|---|---|---|---|---|---|---|---|---|---|---|---|---|---|---|---|---|---|---|---|---|---|
| Year Team | Lg | G | GS | CG | GF | IP | BFP | H | R | ER | HR | SH | SF | HB | TBB | IBB | SO | WP | Bk | W | L | Pct. | ShO | Sv | ERA |
| 1987 Toronto | AL | 18 | 2 | 0 | 6 | 29.1 | 132 | 37 | 14 | 13 | 0 | 1 | 0 | 0 | 12 | 0 | 32 | 4 | 0 | 4 | 3 | .571 | 0 | 1 | 3.99 |
| 1988 Toronto | AL | 41 | 0 | 0 | 15 | 64.1 | 279 | 65 | 36 | 33 | 12 | 2 | 2 | 2 | 31 | 9 | 56 | 6 | 2 | 3 | 5 | .375 | 0 | 4 | 4.62 |
| 1989 Toronto | AL | 54 | 0 | 0 | 19 | 86.1 | 352 | 66 | 25 | 23 | 5 | 3 | 2 | 0 | 28 | 7 | 78 | 6 | 3 | 7 | 4 | .636 | 0 | 2 | 2.40 |
| 1990 Toronto | AL | 43 | 25 | 0 | 8 | 189 | 759 | 165 | 72 | 66 | 14 | 9 | 2 | 2 | 45 | 3 | 115 | 7 | 1 | 11 | 6 | .647 | 0 | 3 | 3.14 |
| 4 ML YEARS | | 156 | 27 | 0 | 48 | 369 | 1522 | 333 | 147 | 135 | 31 | 15 | 6 | 4 | 116 | 19 | 281 | 23 | 6 | 25 | 18 | .581 | 0 | 10 | 3.29 |

## Terry Wells

**Pitches:** Left **Bats:** Left **Pos:** SP **Ht:** 6' 3" **Wt:** 205 **Born:** 09/10/63 **Age:** 27

| | | HOW MUCH HE PITCHED | | | | | | WHAT HE GAVE UP | | | | | | | | | | | | THE RESULTS | | | | | |
|---|---|---|---|---|---|---|---|---|---|---|---|---|---|---|---|---|---|---|---|---|---|---|---|---|---|
| Year Team | Lg | G | GS | CG | GF | IP | BFP | H | R | ER | HR | SH | SF | HB | TBB | IBB | SO | WP | Bk | W | L | Pct. | ShO | Sv | ERA |
| 1985 Auburn | A | 13 | 9 | 0 | 2 | 62.1 | 260 | 35 | 19 | 19 | 3 | 4 | 1 | 1 | 51 | 1 | 46 | 1 | 0 | 4 | 4 | .500 | 0 | 1 | 2.74 |
| 1986 Asheville | A | 26 | 26 | 1 | 0 | 136.2 | 606 | 125 | 87 | 69 | 20 | 4 | 1 | 2 | 83 | 0 | 125 | 15 | 1 | 12 | 6 | .667 | 0 | 0 | 4.54 |
| 1987 Osceola | A | 26 | 23 | 2 | 1 | 130.1 | 590 | 118 | 74 | 69 | 7 | 2 | 5 | 4 | 82 | 0 | 93 | 13 | 0 | 7 | 9 | .438 | 0 | 0 | 4.76 |
| 1988 Columbus | AA | 37 | 8 | 1 | 12 | 108.1 | 496 | 92 | 58 | 55 | 11 | 1 | 2 | 0 | 85 | 4 | 109 | 14 | 2 | 5 | 5 | .500 | 1 | 1 | 4.57 |
| 1989 Columbus | AA | 23 | 1 | 0 | 5 | 46.2 | 211 | 44 | 25 | 24 | 4 | 2 | 1 | 1 | 31 | 1 | 38 | 5 | 0 | 2 | 3 | .400 | 0 | 2 | 4.63 |
| Tucson | AAA | 26 | 4 | 0 | 9 | 48.1 | 232 | 57 | 32 | 31 | 2 | 1 | 2 | 1 | 36 | 0 | 47 | 3 | 2 | 0 | 5 | .000 | 0 | 0 | 5.77 |
| 1990 Albuquerque | AAA | 24 | 19 | 1 | 2 | 115 | 507 | 83 | 64 | 59 | 6 | 5 | 5 | 0 | 87 | 0 | 86 | 17 | 0 | 8 | 6 | .571 | 1 | 1 | 4.62 |
| 1990 Los Angeles | NL | 5 | 5 | 0 | 0 | 20.2 | 102 | 25 | 23 | 18 | 4 | 1 | 0 | 0 | 14 | 0 | 18 | 1 | 0 | 1 | 2 | .333 | 0 | 0 | 7.84 |

## David West

**Pitches:** Left **Bats:** Left **Pos:** SP **Ht:** 6' 6" **Wt:** 220 **Born:** 09/01/64 **Age:** 26

| | | HOW MUCH HE PITCHED | | | | | | WHAT HE GAVE UP | | | | | | | | | | | | THE RESULTS | | | | | |
|---|---|---|---|---|---|---|---|---|---|---|---|---|---|---|---|---|---|---|---|---|---|---|---|---|---|
| Year Team | Lg | G | GS | CG | GF | IP | BFP | H | R | ER | HR | SH | SF | HB | TBB | IBB | SO | WP | Bk | W | L | Pct. | ShO | Sv | ERA |
| 1988 New York | NL | 2 | 1 | 0 | 0 | 6 | 25 | 6 | 2 | 2 | 0 | 0 | 0 | 0 | 3 | 0 | 3 | 0 | 2 | 1 | 0 | 1.000 | 0 | 0 | 3.00 |
| 1989 2 ML Teams | | 21 | 7 | 0 | 4 | 63.2 | 294 | 73 | 49 | 48 | 9 | 2 | 3 | 3 | 33 | 3 | 50 | 2 | 0 | 3 | 4 | .429 | 0 | 0 | 6.79 |
| 1990 Minnesota | AL | 29 | 27 | 2 | 0 | 146.1 | 646 | 142 | 88 | 83 | 21 | 6 | 4 | 4 | 78 | 1 | 92 | 4 | 1 | 7 | 9 | .438 | 0 | 0 | 5.10 |
| 1989 New York | NL | 11 | 2 | 0 | 0 | 24.1 | 112 | 25 | 20 | 20 | 4 | 0 | 1 | 1 | 14 | 2 | 19 | 1 | 0 | 0 | 2 | .000 | 0 | 0 | 7.40 |
| Minnesota | AL | 10 | 5 | 0 | 4 | 39.1 | 182 | 48 | 29 | 28 | 5 | 2 | 2 | 2 | 19 | 1 | 31 | 1 | 0 | 3 | 2 | .600 | 0 | 0 | 6.41 |
| 3 ML YEARS | | 52 | 35 | 2 | 4 | 216 | 965 | 221 | 139 | 133 | 30 | 8 | 7 | 7 | 114 | 4 | 145 | 6 | 3 | 11 | 13 | .458 | 0 | 0 | 5.54 |

## Mickey Weston

**Pitches:** Right **Bats:** Right **Pos:** RP **Ht:** 6' 1" **Wt:** 180 **Born:** 03/26/61 **Age:** 30

| | | HOW MUCH HE PITCHED | | | | | | WHAT HE GAVE UP | | | | | | | | | | | | THE RESULTS | | | | | |
|---|---|---|---|---|---|---|---|---|---|---|---|---|---|---|---|---|---|---|---|---|---|---|---|---|---|
| Year Team | Lg | G | GS | CG | GF | IP | BFP | H | R | ER | HR | SH | SF | HB | TBB | IBB | SO | WP | Bk | W | L | Pct. | ShO | Sv | ERA |
| 1984 Columbia | A | 32 | 2 | 0 | 20 | 63.2 | 272 | 58 | 27 | 13 | 2 | 6 | 1 | 2 | 27 | 6 | 40 | 5 | 0 | 6 | 5 | .545 | 0 | 2 | 1.84 |
| 1985 Lynchburg | A | 49 | 3 | 1 | 24 | 100.1 | 407 | 81 | 29 | 24 | 4 | 3 | 2 | 0 | 22 | 2 | 62 | 4 | 1 | 6 | 5 | .545 | 1 | 10 | 2.15 |
| 1986 Jackson | AA | 34 | 4 | 0 | 7 | 70.2 | 308 | 73 | 40 | 34 | 9 | 3 | 2 | 4 | 27 | 3 | 36 | 3 | 0 | 4 | 4 | .500 | 0 | 2 | 4.33 |
| 1987 Jackson | AA | 58 | 1 | 0 | 21 | 82 | 346 | 96 | 39 | 31 | 4 | 0 | 1 | 1 | 18 | 5 | 50 | 6 | 1 | 8 | 4 | .667 | 0 | 3 | 3.40 |
| 1988 Jackson | AA | 30 | 14 | 1 | 4 | 125.1 | 507 | 127 | 50 | 31 | 3 | 8 | 5 | 0 | 20 | 4 | 61 | 4 | 0 | 8 | 5 | .615 | 0 | 0 | 2.23 |
| Tidewater | AAA | 4 | 4 | 2 | 0 | 29.2 | 115 | 21 | 6 | 5 | 0 | 3 | 0 | 1 | 5 | 1 | 16 | 1 | 0 | 2 | 1 | .667 | 1 | 0 | 1.52 |
| 1989 Rochester | AAA | 23 | 14 | 2 | 7 | 112 | 445 | 103 | 30 | 26 | 6 | 2 | 2 | 1 | 19 | 0 | 51 | 1 | 0 | 8 | 3 | .727 | 1 | 4 | 2.09 |
| 1990 Rochester | AAA | 29 | 12 | 2 | 13 | 109.1 | 432 | 93 | 36 | 24 | 3 | 1 | 2 | 0 | 22 | 0 | 58 | 3 | 0 | 11 | 1 | .917 | 0 | 6 | 1.98 |
| 1989 Baltimore | AL | 7 | 0 | 0 | 2 | 13 | 55 | 18 | 8 | 8 | 1 | 0 | 0 | 1 | 2 | 0 | 7 | 0 | 0 | 1 | 0 | 1.000 | 0 | 1 | 5.54 |
| 1990 Baltimore | AL | 9 | 2 | 0 | 4 | 21 | 94 | 28 | 20 | 18 | 6 | 1 | 0 | 0 | 6 | 1 | 9 | 1 | 0 | 0 | 1 | .000 | 0 | 0 | 7.71 |
| 2 ML YEARS | | 16 | 2 | 0 | 6 | 34 | 149 | 46 | 28 | 26 | 7 | 1 | 0 | 1 | 8 | 1 | 16 | 1 | 0 | 1 | 1 | .500 | 0 | 1 | 6.88 |

## John Wetteland

**Pitches:** Right **Bats:** Right **Pos:** RP/SP **Ht:** 6' 2" **Wt:** 195 **Born:** 08/21/66 **Age:** 24

| | | HOW MUCH HE PITCHED | | | | | | WHAT HE GAVE UP | | | | | | | | | | | | THE RESULTS | | | | | |
|---|---|---|---|---|---|---|---|---|---|---|---|---|---|---|---|---|---|---|---|---|---|---|---|---|---|
| Year Team | Lg | G | GS | CG | GF | IP | BFP | H | R | ER | HR | SH | SF | HB | TBB | IBB | SO | WP | Bk | W | L | Pct. | ShO | Sv | ERA |
| 1989 Los Angeles | NL | 31 | 12 | 0 | 7 | 102.2 | 411 | 81 | 46 | 43 | 8 | 4 | 2 | 0 | 34 | 4 | 96 | 16 | 1 | 5 | 8 | .385 | 0 | 1 | 3.77 |
| 1990 Los Angeles | NL | 22 | 5 | 0 | 7 | 43 | 190 | 44 | 28 | 23 | 6 | 1 | 1 | 4 | 17 | 3 | 36 | 8 | 0 | 2 | 4 | .333 | 0 | 0 | 4.81 |
| 2 ML YEARS | | 53 | 17 | 0 | 14 | 145.2 | 601 | 125 | 74 | 66 | 14 | 5 | 3 | 4 | 51 | 7 | 132 | 24 | 1 | 7 | 12 | .368 | 0 | 1 | 4.08 |

## Lou Whitaker

**Bats:** Left **Throws:** Right **Pos:** 2B **Ht:** 5'11" **Wt:** 160 **Born:** 05/12/57 **Age:** 34

| | | BATTING | | | | | | | | | | | | | | | | | BASERUNNING | | | | PERCENTAGES | | |
|---|---|---|---|---|---|---|---|---|---|---|---|---|---|---|---|---|---|---|---|---|---|---|---|---|---|
| Year Team | Lg | G | AB | H | 2B | 3B | HR | (Hm | Rd) | TB | R | RBI | TBB | IBB | SO | HBP | SH | SF | SB | CS | SB% | GDP | Avg | OBP | SLG |
| 1977 Detroit | AL | 11 | 32 | 8 | 1 | 0 | 0 | (0 | 0) | 9 | 5 | 2 | 4 | 0 | 6 | 0 | 1 | 0 | 2 | 2 | .50 | 0 | .250 | .333 | .281 |
| 1978 Detroit | AL | 139 | 484 | 138 | 12 | 7 | 3 | (2 | 1) | 173 | 71 | 58 | 61 | 0 | 65 | 1 | 13 | 8 | 7 | 7 | .50 | 9 | .285 | .361 | .357 |
| 1979 Detroit | AL | 127 | 423 | 121 | 14 | 8 | 3 | (3 | 0) | 160 | 75 | 42 | 78 | 2 | 66 | 1 | 14 | 4 | 20 | 10 | .67 | 10 | .286 | .395 | .378 |
| 1980 Detroit | AL | 145 | 477 | 111 | 19 | 1 | 1 | (1 | 0) | 135 | 68 | 45 | 73 | 0 | 79 | 0 | 12 | 6 | 8 | 4 | .67 | 9 | .233 | .331 | .283 |
| 1981 Detroit | AL | 109 | 335 | 88 | 14 | 4 | 5 | (4 | 1) | 125 | 48 | 36 | 40 | 3 | 42 | 1 | 3 | 3 | 5 | 3 | .63 | 5 | .263 | .340 | .373 |
| 1982 Detroit | AL | 152 | 560 | 160 | 22 | 8 | 15 | (9 | 6) | 243 | 76 | 65 | 48 | 4 | 58 | 1 | 6 | 4 | 11 | 3 | .79 | 8 | .286 | .341 | .434 |
| 1983 Detroit | AL | 161 | 643 | 206 | 40 | 6 | 12 | (7 | 5) | 294 | 94 | 72 | 67 | 8 | 70 | 0 | 2 | 8 | 17 | 10 | .63 | 9 | .320 | .380 | .457 |
| 1984 Detroit | AL | 143 | 558 | 161 | 25 | 1 | 13 | (8 | 5) | 227 | 90 | 56 | 62 | 5 | 63 | 0 | 4 | 5 | 6 | 5 | .55 | 9 | .289 | .357 | .407 |
| 1985 Detroit | AL | 152 | 609 | 170 | 29 | 8 | 21 | (11 | 10) | 278 | 102 | 73 | 80 | 9 | 56 | 2 | 5 | 5 | 6 | 4 | .60 | 3 | .279 | .362 | .456 |
| 1986 Detroit | AL | 144 | 584 | 157 | 26 | 6 | 20 | (8 | 12) | 255 | 95 | 73 | 63 | 5 | 70 | 0 | 0 | 4 | 13 | 8 | .62 | 20 | .269 | .338 | .437 |
| 1987 Detroit | AL | 149 | 604 | 160 | 38 | 6 | 16 | (10 | 6) | 258 | 110 | 59 | 71 | 2 | 108 | 1 | 4 | 4 | 13 | 5 | .72 | 5 | .265 | .341 | .427 |
| 1988 Detroit | AL | 115 | 403 | 111 | 18 | 2 | 12 | (8 | 4) | 169 | 54 | 55 | 66 | 5 | 61 | 0 | 6 | 2 | 2 | 0 | 1.00 | 8 | .275 | .376 | .419 |
| 1989 Detroit | AL | 148 | 509 | 128 | 21 | 1 | 28 | (17 | 11) | 235 | 77 | 85 | 89 | 6 | 59 | 3 | 1 | 9 | 6 | 3 | .67 | 7 | .251 | .361 | .462 |
| 1990 Detroit | AL | 132 | 472 | 112 | 22 | 2 | 18 | (8 | 10) | 192 | 75 | 60 | 74 | 7 | 71 | 0 | 1 | 5 | 8 | 2 | .80 | 10 | .237 | .338 | .407 |
| 14 ML YEARS | | 1827 | 6693 | 1831 | 301 | 60 | 167 | (96 | 71) | 2753 | 1040 | 781 | 876 | 56 | 874 | 10 | 72 | 67 | 124 | 66 | .65 | 112 | .274 | .355 | .411 |

## Devon White

**Bats:** Both **Throws:** Right **Pos:** CF **Ht:** 6' 2" **Wt:** 178 **Born:** 12/29/62 **Age:** 28

| | | BATTING | | | | | | | | | | | | | | | | | BASERUNNING | | | | PERCENTAGES | | |
|---|---|---|---|---|---|---|---|---|---|---|---|---|---|---|---|---|---|---|---|---|---|---|---|---|---|
| Year Team | Lg | G | AB | H | 2B | 3B | HR | (Hm | Rd) | TB | R | RBI | TBB | IBB | SO | HBP | SH | SF | SB | CS | SB% | GDP | Avg | OBP | SLG |
| 1985 California | AL | 21 | 7 | 1 | 0 | 0 | 0 | (0 | 0) | 1 | 7 | 0 | 1 | 0 | 3 | 1 | 0 | 0 | 3 | 1 | .75 | 0 | .143 | .333 | .143 |
| 1986 California | AL | 29 | 51 | 12 | 1 | 1 | 1 | (0 | 1) | 18 | 8 | 3 | 6 | 0 | 8 | 0 | 0 | 0 | 6 | 0 | 1.00 | 0 | .235 | .316 | .353 |
| 1987 California | AL | 159 | 639 | 168 | 33 | 5 | 24 | (11 | 13) | 283 | 103 | 87 | 39 | 2 | 135 | 2 | 14 | 2 | 32 | 11 | .74 | 8 | .263 | .306 | .443 |
| 1988 California | AL | 122 | 455 | 118 | 22 | 2 | 11 | (3 | 8) | 177 | 76 | 51 | 23 | 1 | 84 | 2 | 5 | 1 | 17 | 8 | .68 | 5 | .259 | .297 | .389 |
| 1989 California | AL | 156 | 636 | 156 | 18 | 13 | 12 | (9 | 3) | 236 | 86 | 56 | 31 | 3 | 129 | 2 | 7 | 2 | 44 | 16 | .73 | 12 | .245 | .282 | .371 |
| 1990 California | AL | 125 | 443 | 96 | 17 | 3 | 11 | (5 | 6) | 152 | 57 | 44 | 44 | 5 | 116 | 3 | 10 | 3 | 21 | 6 | .78 | 6 | .217 | .290 | .343 |
| 6 ML YEARS | | 612 | 2231 | 551 | 91 | 24 | 59 | (28 | 31) | 867 | 337 | 241 | 144 | 11 | 475 | 10 | 36 | 8 | 123 | 42 | .75 | 31 | .247 | .295 | .389 |

## Frank White

**Bats:** Right **Throws:** Right **Pos:** 2B **Ht:** 5'11" **Wt:** 190 **Born:** 09/04/50 **Age:** 40

| | | BATTING | | | | | | | | | | | | | | | | | BASERUNNING | | | | PERCENTAGES | | |
|---|---|---|---|---|---|---|---|---|---|---|---|---|---|---|---|---|---|---|---|---|---|---|---|---|---|
| Year Team | Lg | G | AB | H | 2B | 3B | HR | (Hm | Rd) | TB | R | RBI | TBB | IBB | SO | HBP | SH | SF | SB | CS | SB% | GDP | Avg | OBP | SLG |
| 1973 Kansas City | AL | 51 | 139 | 31 | 6 | 1 | 0 | (0 | 0) | 39 | 20 | 5 | 8 | 0 | 23 | 0 | 2 | 2 | 3 | 1 | .75 | 1 | .223 | .262 | .281 |
| 1974 Kansas City | AL | 99 | 204 | 45 | 6 | 3 | 1 | (1 | 0) | 60 | 19 | 18 | 5 | 0 | 33 | 0 | 5 | 0 | 3 | 4 | .43 | 4 | .221 | .239 | .294 |
| 1975 Kansas City | AL | 111 | 304 | 76 | 10 | 2 | 7 | (4 | 3) | 111 | 43 | 36 | 20 | 0 | 39 | 1 | 2 | 2 | 11 | 3 | .79 | 4 | .250 | .297 | .365 |
| 1976 Kansas City | AL | 152 | 446 | 102 | 17 | 6 | 2 | (0 | 2) | 137 | 39 | 46 | 19 | 0 | 42 | 3 | 18 | 3 | 20 | 11 | .65 | 4 | .229 | .263 | .307 |
| 1977 Kansas City | AL | 152 | 474 | 116 | 21 | 5 | 5 | (3 | 2) | 162 | 59 | 50 | 25 | 0 | 67 | 2 | 11 | 2 | 23 | 5 | .82 | 4 | .245 | .284 | .342 |
| 1978 Kansas City | AL | 143 | 461 | 127 | 24 | 6 | 7 | (3 | 4) | 184 | 66 | 50 | 26 | 1 | 59 | 3 | 9 | 2 | 13 | 10 | .57 | 2 | .275 | .317 | .399 |
| 1979 Kansas City | AL | 127 | 467 | 124 | 26 | 4 | 10 | (5 | 5) | 188 | 73 | 48 | 25 | 3 | 54 | 1 | 3 | 7 | 28 | 8 | .78 | 11 | .266 | .300 | .403 |
| 1980 Kansas City | AL | 154 | 560 | 148 | 23 | 4 | 7 | (1 | 6) | 200 | 70 | 60 | 19 | 0 | 69 | 2 | 9 | 4 | 19 | 6 | .76 | 11 | .264 | .289 | .357 |
| 1981 Kansas City | AL | 94 | 364 | 91 | 17 | 1 | 9 | (4 | 5) | 137 | 35 | 38 | 19 | 0 | 50 | 0 | 4 | 3 | 4 | 2 | .67 | 10 | .250 | .285 | .376 |
| 1982 Kansas City | AL | 145 | 524 | 156 | 45 | 6 | 11 | (7 | 4) | 246 | 71 | 56 | 16 | 1 | 65 | 2 | 7 | 5 | 10 | 7 | .59 | 12 | .298 | .318 | .469 |
| 1983 Kansas City | AL | 146 | 549 | 143 | 35 | 6 | 11 | (8 | 3) | 223 | 52 | 77 | 20 | 4 | 51 | 0 | 4 | 6 | 13 | 5 | .72 | 18 | .260 | .283 | .406 |
| 1984 Kansas City | AL | 129 | 479 | 130 | 22 | 5 | 17 | (6 | 11) | 213 | 58 | 56 | 27 | 3 | 72 | 2 | 4 | 3 | 5 | 5 | .50 | 11 | .271 | .311 | .445 |
| 1985 Kansas City | AL | 149 | 563 | 140 | 25 | 1 | 22 | (9 | 13) | 233 | 62 | 69 | 28 | 2 | 86 | 1 | 5 | 3 | 10 | 4 | .71 | 8 | .249 | .284 | .414 |
| 1986 Kansas City | AL | 151 | 566 | 154 | 37 | 3 | 22 | (12 | 10) | 263 | 76 | 84 | 43 | 5 | 88 | 2 | 2 | 7 | 4 | 4 | .50 | 10 | .272 | .322 | .465 |
| 1987 Kansas City | AL | 154 | 563 | 138 | 32 | 2 | 17 | (6 | 11) | 225 | 67 | 78 | 51 | 5 | 86 | 2 | 4 | 4 | 1 | 3 | .25 | 16 | .245 | .308 | .400 |
| 1988 Kansas City | AL | 150 | 537 | 126 | 25 | 1 | 8 | (3 | 5) | 177 | 48 | 58 | 21 | 3 | 67 | 4 | 7 | 6 | 7 | 3 | .70 | 16 | .235 | .266 | .330 |
| 1989 Kansas City | AL | 135 | 418 | 107 | 22 | 1 | 2 | (1 | 1) | 137 | 34 | 36 | 30 | 0 | 52 | 2 | 5 | 3 | 3 | 2 | .60 | 7 | .256 | .307 | .328 |
| 1990 Kansas City | AL | 82 | 241 | 52 | 14 | 1 | 2 | (2 | 0) | 74 | 20 | 21 | 10 | 0 | 32 | 3 | 0 | 3 | 1 | 0 | 1.00 | 7 | .216 | .253 | .307 |
| 18 ML YEARS | | 2324 | 7859 | 2006 | 407 | 58 | 160 | (75 | 85) | 3009 | 912 | 886 | 412 | 27 | 1035 | 30 | 101 | 65 | 178 | 83 | .68 | 156 | .255 | .293 | .383 |

## Wally Whitehurst

**Pitches:** Right **Bats:** Right **Pos:** RP **Ht:** 6' 3" **Wt:** 180 **Born:** 04/11/64 **Age:** 27

| | | HOW MUCH HE PITCHED | | | | | | WHAT HE GAVE UP | | | | | | | | | | | | THE RESULTS | | | | | |
|---|---|---|---|---|---|---|---|---|---|---|---|---|---|---|---|---|---|---|---|---|---|---|---|---|---|
| Year Team | Lg | G | GS | CG | GF | IP | BFP | H | R | ER | HR | SH | SF | HB | TBB | IBB | SO | WP | Bk | W | L | Pct. | ShO | Sv | ERA |
| 1985 Medford | A | 14 | 14 | 2 | 0 | 88 | 0 | 92 | 51 | 35 | 6 | 0 | 0 | 7 | 29 | 1 | 91 | 11 | 2 | 7 | 5 | .583 | 0 | 0 | 3.58 |
| Modesto | A | 2 | 2 | 0 | 0 | 10 | 0 | 10 | 3 | 2 | 1 | 0 | 0 | 1 | 5 | 0 | 5 | 0 | 0 | 1 | 0 | 1.000 | 0 | 0 | 1.80 |
| 1986 Madison | A | 8 | 8 | 5 | 0 | 61 | 234 | 42 | 8 | 4 | 1 | 1 | 0 | 1 | 16 | 0 | 57 | 4 | 0 | 6 | 1 | .857 | 4 | 0 | 0.59 |
| Huntsville | AA | 19 | 19 | 2 | 0 | 104.2 | 468 | 114 | 66 | 54 | 4 | 5 | 2 | 7 | 46 | 3 | 54 | 12 | 3 | 9 | 5 | .643 | 0 | 0 | 4.64 |
| 1987 Huntsville | AA | 28 | 28 | 5 | 0 | 183.1 | 766 | 192 | 104 | 81 | 12 | 6 | 6 | 2 | 42 | 3 | 106 | 9 | 0 | 11 | 10 | .524 | 3 | 0 | 3.98 |

| Year Team | Lg | G | GS | CG | GF | IP | BFP | H | R | ER | HR | SH | SF | HB | TBB | IBB | SO | WP | Bk | W | L | Pct. | ShO | Sv | ERA |
|---|---|---|---|---|---|---|---|---|---|---|---|---|---|---|---|---|---|---|---|---|---|---|---|---|---|
| 1988 Tidewater | AAA | 26 | 26 | 3 | 0 | 165 | 664 | 145 | 65 | 56 | 7 | 8 | 4 | 8 | 32 | 3 | 113 | 10 | 9 | 10 | 11 | .476 | 1 | 0 | 3.05 |
| 1989 Tidewater | AAA | 21 | 20 | 3 | 1 | 133 | 551 | 123 | 54 | 48 | 5 | 3 | 2 | 1 | 32 | 2 | 95 | 3 | 2 | 8 | 7 | .533 | 1 | 0 | 3.25 |
| 1990 Tidewater | AAA | 2 | 2 | 0 | 0 | 9 | 34 | 7 | 2 | 2 | 0 | 0 | 0 | 1 | 1 | 0 | 10 | 0 | 0 | 1 | 0 | 1.000 | 0 | 0 | 2.00 |
| 1989 New York | NL | 9 | 1 | 0 | 4 | 14 | 64 | 17 | 7 | 7 | 2 | 0 | 1 | 0 | 5 | 0 | 9 | 1 | 0 | 0 | 1 | .000 | 0 | 0 | 4.50 |
| 1990 New York | NL | 38 | 0 | 0 | 16 | 65.2 | 263 | 63 | 27 | 24 | 5 | 3 | 0 | 0 | 9 | 2 | 46 | 2 | 0 | 1 | 0 | 1.000 | 0 | 2 | 3.29 |
| 2 ML YEARS | | 47 | 1 | 0 | 20 | 79.2 | 327 | 80 | 34 | 31 | 7 | 3 | 1 | 0 | 14 | 2 | 55 | 3 | 0 | 1 | 1 | .500 | 0 | 2 | 3.50 |

## Mark Whiten

**Bats:** Both **Throws:** Right **Pos:** RF **Ht:** 6' 3" **Wt:** 215 **Born:** 11/25/66 **Age:** 24

| BATTING | | | | | | | | | | | | | | | | | | | | BASERUNNING | | | | PERCENTAGES | | |
|---|---|---|---|---|---|---|---|---|---|---|---|---|---|---|---|---|---|---|---|---|---|---|---|---|---|---|
| Year Team | Lg | G | AB | H | 2B | 3B | HR | (Hm | Rd) | TB | R | RBI | TBB | IBB | SO | HBP | SH | SF | | SB | CS | SB% | GDP | Avg | OBP | SLG |
| 1986 Medicne Hat | R | 70 | 270 | 81 | 16 | 3 | 10 | -- | -- | 133 | 53 | 44 | 29 | 2 | 56 | 6 | 1 | 2 | | 22 | 3 | .88 | 2 | .300 | .378 | .493 |
| 1987 Myrtle Bch | A | 139 | 494 | 125 | 22 | 5 | 15 | -- | -- | 202 | 90 | 64 | 76 | 10 | 149 | 16 | 0 | 1 | | 49 | 14 | .78 | 1 | .253 | .370 | .409 |
| 1988 Dunedin | A | 99 | 385 | 97 | 8 | 5 | 7 | -- | -- | 136 | 61 | 37 | 41 | 6 | 69 | 3 | 2 | 3 | | 17 | 14 | .55 | 8 | .252 | .326 | .353 |
| Knoxville | AA | 28 | 108 | 28 | 3 | 1 | 2 | -- | -- | 39 | 20 | 9 | 12 | 1 | 20 | 1 | 0 | 0 | | 6 | 0 | 1.00 | 5 | .259 | .339 | .361 |
| 1989 Knoxville | AA | 129 | 423 | 109 | 13 | 6 | 12 | -- | -- | 170 | 75 | 47 | 60 | 1 | 114 | 11 | 0 | 2 | | 11 | 10 | .52 | 7 | .258 | .363 | .402 |
| 1990 Syracuse | AAA | 104 | 390 | 113 | 19 | 4 | 14 | -- | -- | 182 | 65 | 48 | 37 | 5 | 72 | 3 | 0 | 4 | | 14 | 5 | .74 | 8 | .290 | .353 | .467 |
| 1990 Toronto | AL | 33 | 88 | 24 | 1 | 1 | 2 | (1 | 1) | 33 | 12 | 7 | 7 | 0 | 14 | 0 | 0 | 1 | | 2 | 0 | 1.00 | 2 | .273 | .323 | .375 |

## Ed Whitson

**Pitches:** Right **Bats:** Right **Pos:** SP **Ht:** 6' 3" **Wt:** 195 **Born:** 05/19/55 **Age:** 36

| HOW MUCH HE PITCHED | | | | | | | | WHAT HE GAVE UP | | | | | | | | | | | | THE RESULTS | | | | | |
|---|---|---|---|---|---|---|---|---|---|---|---|---|---|---|---|---|---|---|---|---|---|---|---|---|---|
| Year Team | Lg | G | GS | CG | GF | IP | BFP | H | R | ER | HR | SH | SF | HB | TBB | IBB | SO | WP | Bk | W | L | Pct. | ShO | Sv | ERA |
| 1977 Pittsburgh | NL | 5 | 2 | 0 | 1 | 16 | 66 | 11 | 6 | 6 | 0 | 1 | 2 | 0 | 9 | 1 | 10 | 0 | 0 | 1 | 0 | 1.000 | 0 | 0 | 3.38 |
| 1978 Pittsburgh | NL | 43 | 0 | 0 | 14 | 74 | 318 | 66 | 31 | 27 | 5 | 3 | 4 | 2 | 37 | 5 | 64 | 1 | 0 | 5 | 6 | .455 | 0 | 4 | 3.28 |
| 1979 2 ML Teams | | 37 | 24 | 2 | 5 | 158 | 702 | 151 | 83 | 72 | 11 | 10 | 3 | 5 | 75 | 9 | 93 | 5 | 2 | 7 | 11 | .389 | 0 | 1 | 4.10 |
| 1980 San Francisco | NL | 34 | 34 | 6 | 0 | 212 | 898 | 222 | 88 | 73 | 7 | 10 | 9 | 4 | 56 | 7 | 90 | 1 | 1 | 11 | 13 | .458 | 2 | 0 | 3.10 |
| 1981 San Francisco | NL | 22 | 22 | 2 | 0 | 123 | 534 | 130 | 61 | 55 | 10 | 6 | 2 | 2 | 47 | 5 | 65 | 3 | 2 | 6 | 9 | .400 | 1 | 0 | 4.02 |
| 1982 Cleveland | AL | 40 | 9 | 1 | 18 | 107.2 | 467 | 91 | 43 | 39 | 6 | 7 | 8 | 0 | 58 | 3 | 61 | 4 | 1 | 4 | 2 | .667 | 1 | 2 | 3.26 |
| 1983 San Diego | NL | 31 | 21 | 2 | 4 | 144.1 | 617 | 143 | 73 | 69 | 23 | 3 | 4 | 1 | 50 | 1 | 81 | 2 | 0 | 5 | 7 | .417 | 0 | 1 | 4.30 |
| 1984 San Diego | NL | 31 | 31 | 1 | 0 | 189 | 773 | 181 | 72 | 68 | 16 | 10 | 7 | 3 | 42 | 1 | 103 | 3 | 1 | 14 | 8 | .636 | 0 | 0 | 3.24 |
| 1985 New York | AL | 30 | 30 | 2 | 0 | 158.2 | 705 | 201 | 100 | 86 | 19 | 3 | 7 | 2 | 43 | 0 | 89 | 1 | 0 | 10 | 8 | .556 | 2 | 0 | 4.88 |
| 1986 2 ML Teams | | 31 | 16 | 0 | 6 | 112.2 | 526 | 139 | 85 | 78 | 13 | 4 | 5 | 0 | 60 | 1 | 73 | 3 | 0 | 6 | 9 | .400 | 0 | 0 | 6.23 |
| 1987 San Diego | NL | 36 | 34 | 3 | 0 | 205.2 | 858 | 197 | 113 | 108 | 36 | 4 | 2 | 3 | 64 | 3 | 135 | 2 | 1 | 10 | 13 | .435 | 1 | 0 | 4.73 |
| 1988 San Diego | NL | 34 | 33 | 3 | 0 | 205.1 | 846 | 202 | 93 | 86 | 17 | 13 | 8 | 1 | 45 | 1 | 118 | 2 | 2 | 13 | 11 | .542 | 1 | 0 | 3.77 |
| 1989 San Diego | NL | 33 | 33 | 5 | 0 | 227 | 914 | 198 | 77 | 67 | 22 | 12 | 8 | 5 | 48 | 6 | 117 | 2 | 3 | 16 | 11 | .593 | 1 | 0 | 2.66 |
| 1990 San Diego | NL | 32 | 32 | 6 | 0 | 228.2 | 918 | 215 | 73 | 66 | 13 | 9 | 6 | 1 | 47 | 8 | 127 | 2 | 0 | 14 | 9 | .609 | 3 | 0 | 2.60 |
| 1979 Pittsburgh | NL | 19 | 7 | 0 | 4 | 58 | 263 | 53 | 36 | 28 | 6 | 3 | 0 | 1 | 36 | 3 | 31 | 2 | 1 | 2 | 3 | .400 | 0 | 1 | 4.34 |
| San Francisco | NL | 18 | 17 | 2 | 1 | 100 | 439 | 98 | 47 | 44 | 5 | 7 | 3 | 4 | 39 | 6 | 62 | 3 | 1 | 5 | 8 | .385 | 0 | 0 | 3.96 |
| 1986 New York | AL | 14 | 4 | 0 | 6 | 37 | 189 | 54 | 37 | 31 | 5 | 2 | 3 | 0 | 23 | 1 | 27 | 2 | 0 | 5 | 2 | .714 | 0 | 0 | 7.54 |
| San Diego | NL | 17 | 12 | 0 | 0 | 75.2 | 337 | 85 | 48 | 47 | 8 | 2 | 2 | 0 | 37 | 0 | 46 | 1 | 0 | 1 | 7 | .125 | 0 | 0 | 5.59 |
| 14 ML YEARS | | 439 | 321 | 33 | 48 | 2162 | 9142 | 2147 | 998 | 900 | 198 | 95 | 75 | 29 | 681 | 51 | 1226 | 31 | 13 | 122 | 117 | .510 | 12 | 8 | 3.75 |

## Ernie Whitt

**Bats:** Left **Throws:** Right **Pos:** C **Ht:** 6' 2" **Wt:** 200 **Born:** 06/13/52 **Age:** 39

| BATTING | | | | | | | | | | | | | | | | | | | BASERUNNING | | | | PERCENTAGES | | |
|---|---|---|---|---|---|---|---|---|---|---|---|---|---|---|---|---|---|---|---|---|---|---|---|---|---|
| Year Team | Lg | G | AB | H | 2B | 3B | HR | (Hm | Rd) | TB | R | RBI | TBB | IBB | SO | HBP | SH | SF | SB | CS | SB% | GDP | Avg | OBP | SLG |
| 1976 Boston | AL | 8 | 18 | 4 | 2 | 0 | 1 | (1 | 0) | 9 | 4 | 3 | 2 | 0 | 2 | 0 | 0 | 0 | 0 | 0 | .00 | 0 | .222 | .300 | .500 |
| 1977 Toronto | AL | 23 | 41 | 7 | 3 | 0 | 0 | (0 | 0) | 10 | 4 | 6 | 2 | 0 | 12 | 0 | 0 | 2 | 0 | 0 | .00 | 1 | .171 | .200 | .244 |
| 1978 Toronto | AL | 2 | 4 | 0 | 0 | 0 | 0 | (0 | 0) | 0 | 0 | 0 | 1 | 0 | 1 | 0 | 0 | 0 | 0 | 0 | .00 | 0 | .000 | .200 | .000 |
| 1980 Toronto | AL | 106 | 295 | 70 | 12 | 2 | 6 | (2 | 4) | 104 | 23 | 34 | 22 | 0 | 30 | 0 | 5 | 3 | 1 | 3 | .25 | 11 | .237 | .288 | .353 |
| 1981 Toronto | AL | 74 | 195 | 46 | 9 | 0 | 1 | (0 | 1) | 58 | 16 | 16 | 20 | 3 | 30 | 0 | 7 | 0 | 5 | 2 | .71 | 2 | .236 | .307 | .297 |
| 1982 Toronto | AL | 105 | 284 | 74 | 14 | 2 | 11 | (8 | 3) | 125 | 28 | 42 | 26 | 5 | 34 | 0 | 1 | 5 | 3 | 1 | .75 | 5 | .261 | .317 | .440 |
| 1983 Toronto | AL | 123 | 344 | 88 | 15 | 2 | 17 | (11 | 6) | 158 | 53 | 56 | 50 | 5 | 55 | 0 | 1 | 5 | 1 | 1 | .50 | 9 | .256 | .346 | .459 |
| 1984 Toronto | AL | 124 | 315 | 75 | 12 | 1 | 15 | (5 | 10) | 134 | 35 | 46 | 43 | 7 | 49 | 1 | 0 | 5 | 0 | 3 | .00 | 7 | .238 | .327 | .425 |
| 1985 Toronto | AL | 139 | 412 | 101 | 21 | 2 | 19 | (7 | 12) | 183 | 55 | 64 | 47 | 9 | 59 | 1 | 3 | 2 | 3 | 6 | .33 | 7 | .245 | .323 | .444 |
| 1986 Toronto | AL | 131 | 395 | 106 | 19 | 2 | 16 | (7 | 9) | 177 | 48 | 56 | 35 | 3 | 39 | 0 | 0 | 3 | 0 | 1 | .00 | 11 | .268 | .326 | .448 |
| 1987 Toronto | AL | 135 | 446 | 120 | 24 | 1 | 19 | (11 | 8) | 203 | 57 | 75 | 44 | 4 | 50 | 1 | 0 | 3 | 0 | 1 | .00 | 17 | .269 | .334 | .455 |
| 1988 Toronto | AL | 127 | 398 | 100 | 11 | 2 | 16 | (9 | 7) | 163 | 63 | 70 | 61 | 4 | 38 | 1 | 2 | 6 | 4 | 2 | .67 | 9 | .251 | .348 | .410 |
| 1989 Toronto | AL | 129 | 385 | 101 | 24 | 1 | 11 | (8 | 3) | 160 | 42 | 53 | 52 | 2 | 53 | 0 | 1 | 2 | 5 | 4 | .56 | 9 | .262 | .349 | .416 |
| 1990 Atlanta | NL | 67 | 180 | 31 | 8 | 0 | 2 | (2 | 0) | 45 | 14 | 10 | 23 | 2 | 27 | 0 | 0 | 1 | 0 | 2 | .00 | 6 | .172 | .265 | .250 |
| 14 ML YEARS | | 1293 | 3712 | 923 | 174 | 15 | 134 | (71 | 63) | 1529 | 442 | 531 | 428 | 44 | 479 | 4 | 20 | 37 | 22 | 26 | .46 | 94 | .249 | .324 | .412 |

## Kevin Wickander

**Pitches:** Left **Bats:** Left **Pos:** RP **Ht:** 6' 2" **Wt:** 202 **Born:** 01/04/65 **Age:** 26

| | | HOW MUCH HE PITCHED | | | | | | WHAT HE GAVE UP | | | | | | | | | | | | THE RESULTS | | | | | |
|---|---|---|---|---|---|---|---|---|---|---|---|---|---|---|---|---|---|---|---|---|---|---|---|---|---|
| Year Team | Lg | G | GS | CG | GF | IP | BFP | H | R | ER | HR | SH | SF | HB | TBB | IBB | SO | WP | Bk | W | L | Pct. | ShO | Sv | ERA |
| 1986 Batavia | A | 11 | 9 | 0 | 2 | 46.1 | 194 | 30 | 19 | 14 | 4 | 0 | 0 | 1 | 27 | 0 | 63 | 2 | 0 | 3 | 4 | .429 | 0 | 0 | 2.72 |
| 1987 Kinston | A | 25 | 25 | 2 | 0 | 147.1 | 621 | 128 | 69 | 56 | 7 | 5 | 6 | 7 | 75 | 2 | 118 | 14 | 0 | 9 | 6 | .600 | 1 | 0 | 3.42 |
| 1988 Williamsprt | AA | 24 | 0 | 0 | 24 | 28.2 | 113 | 14 | 3 | 2 | 0 | 1 | 0 | 4 | 9 | 0 | 33 | 0 | 1 | 1 | 0 | 1.000 | 0 | 16 | 0.63 |
| Colo Sprngs | AAA | 19 | 0 | 0 | 9 | 32.2 | 167 | 44 | 30 | 26 | 4 | 1 | 1 | 2 | 27 | 3 | 22 | 5 | 0 | 0 | 2 | .000 | 0 | 0 | 7.16 |
| 1989 Colo Sprngs | AAA | 45 | 0 | 0 | 26 | 42.2 | 200 | 40 | 14 | 14 | 2 | 3 | 5 | 4 | 27 | 5 | 41 | 1 | 2 | 1 | 3 | .250 | 0 | 11 | 2.95 |
| 1989 Cleveland | AL | 2 | 0 | 0 | 1 | 2.2 | 15 | 6 | 1 | 1 | 0 | 0 | 0 | 0 | 2 | 1 | 0 | 0 | 0 | 0 | 0 | .000 | 0 | 0 | 3.38 |
| 1990 Cleveland | AL | 10 | 0 | 0 | 3 | 12.1 | 53 | 14 | 6 | 5 | 0 | 0 | 2 | 1 | 4 | 0 | 10 | 0 | 0 | 0 | 1 | .000 | 0 | 0 | 3.65 |
| 2 ML YEARS | | 12 | 0 | 0 | 4 | 15 | 68 | 20 | 7 | 6 | 0 | 0 | 2 | 1 | 6 | 1 | 10 | 0 | 0 | 0 | 1 | .000 | 0 | 0 | 3.60 |

## Curt Wilkerson

**Bats:** Both **Throws:** Right **Pos:** 3B/2B **Ht:** 5' 9" **Wt:** 160 **Born:** 04/26/61 **Age:** 30

| | | BATTING | | | | | | | | | | | | | | | | | BASERUNNING | | | | PERCENTAGES | | |
|---|---|---|---|---|---|---|---|---|---|---|---|---|---|---|---|---|---|---|---|---|---|---|---|---|---|
| Year Team | Lg | G | AB | H | 2B | 3B | HR | (Hm | Rd) | TB | R | RBI | TBB | IBB | SO | HBP | SH | SF | SB | CS | SB% | GDP | Avg | OBP | SLG |
| 1983 Texas | AL | 16 | 35 | 6 | 0 | 1 | 0 | (0 | 0) | 8 | 7 | 1 | 2 | 0 | 5 | 0 | 0 | 0 | 3 | 0 | 1.00 | 0 | .171 | .216 | .229 |
| 1984 Texas | AL | 153 | 484 | 120 | 12 | 0 | 1 | (0 | 1) | 135 | 47 | 26 | 22 | 0 | 72 | 2 | 12 | 2 | 12 | 10 | .55 | 7 | .248 | .282 | .279 |
| 1985 Texas | AL | 129 | 360 | 88 | 11 | 6 | 0 | (0 | 0) | 111 | 35 | 22 | 22 | 0 | 63 | 4 | 6 | 3 | 14 | 7 | .67 | 7 | .244 | .293 | .308 |
| 1986 Texas | AL | 110 | 236 | 56 | 10 | 3 | 0 | (0 | 0) | 72 | 27 | 15 | 11 | 0 | 42 | 1 | 0 | 1 | 9 | 7 | .56 | 2 | .237 | .273 | .305 |
| 1987 Texas | AL | 85 | 138 | 37 | 5 | 3 | 2 | (1 | 1) | 54 | 28 | 14 | 6 | 0 | 16 | 2 | 0 | 0 | 6 | 3 | .67 | 2 | .268 | .308 | .391 |
| 1988 Texas | AL | 117 | 338 | 99 | 12 | 5 | 0 | (0 | 0) | 121 | 41 | 28 | 26 | 3 | 43 | 2 | 3 | 2 | 9 | 4 | .69 | 7 | .293 | .345 | .358 |
| 1989 Chicago | NL | 77 | 160 | 39 | 4 | 2 | 1 | (1 | 0) | 50 | 18 | 10 | 8 | 0 | 33 | 0 | 1 | 1 | 4 | 2 | .67 | 3 | .244 | .278 | .313 |
| 1990 Chicago | NL | 77 | 186 | 41 | 5 | 1 | 0 | (0 | 0) | 48 | 21 | 16 | 7 | 2 | 36 | 0 | 3 | 0 | 2 | 2 | .50 | 4 | .220 | .249 | .258 |
| 8 ML YEARS | | 764 | 1937 | 486 | 59 | 21 | 4 | (2 | 2) | 599 | 224 | 132 | 104 | 5 | 310 | 11 | 25 | 9 | 59 | 35 | .63 | 32 | .251 | .292 | .309 |

## Dean Wilkins

**Pitches:** Right **Bats:** Right **Pos:** RP **Ht:** 6' 1" **Wt:** 170 **Born:** 08/24/66 **Age:** 24

| | | HOW MUCH HE PITCHED | | | | | | WHAT HE GAVE UP | | | | | | | | | | | | THE RESULTS | | | | | |
|---|---|---|---|---|---|---|---|---|---|---|---|---|---|---|---|---|---|---|---|---|---|---|---|---|---|
| Year Team | Lg | G | GS | CG | GF | IP | BFP | H | R | ER | HR | SH | SF | HB | TBB | IBB | SO | WP | Bk | W | L | Pct. | ShO | Sv | ERA |
| 1986 Oneonta | A | 15 | 12 | 1 | 3 | 83.1 | 337 | 64 | 32 | 29 | 5 | 5 | 1 | 8 | 24 | 0 | 80 | 4 | 1 | 9 | 0 | 1.000 | 0 | 1 | 3.13 |
| 1987 Albany | AA | 2 | 2 | 0 | 0 | 12 | 55 | 18 | 11 | 9 | 3 | 0 | 1 | 1 | 1 | 0 | 8 | 0 | 0 | 0 | 0 | .000 | 0 | 0 | 6.75 |
| Ft.Laudrdle | A | 15 | 14 | 5 | 1 | 105.2 | 435 | 95 | 41 | 32 | 2 | 1 | 1 | 1 | 39 | 1 | 76 | 7 | 4 | 8 | 5 | .615 | 2 | 0 | 2.73 |
| Winston-Sal | A | 13 | 6 | 3 | 1 | 50.1 | 224 | 49 | 31 | 23 | 3 | 2 | 3 | 1 | 24 | 0 | 29 | 1 | 0 | 4 | 4 | .500 | 0 | 1 | 4.11 |
| 1988 Pittsfield | AA | 59 | 0 | 0 | 49 | 71.2 | 295 | 53 | 25 | 13 | 0 | 6 | 1 | 2 | 30 | 5 | 59 | 9 | 0 | 5 | 7 | .417 | 0 | 26 | 1.63 |
| 1989 Iowa | AAA | 38 | 16 | 0 | 17 | 138 | 604 | 149 | 74 | 65 | 5 | 3 | 4 | 4 | 58 | 5 | 82 | 15 | 1 | 8 | 11 | .421 | 0 | 3 | 4.24 |
| 1990 Iowa | AAA | 52 | 2 | 0 | 33 | 73 | 325 | 75 | 37 | 30 | 4 | 2 | 3 | 6 | 38 | 5 | 61 | 10 | 2 | 6 | 2 | .750 | 0 | 11 | 3.70 |
| 1989 Chicago | NL | 11 | 0 | 0 | 1 | 15.2 | 67 | 13 | 9 | 9 | 2 | 1 | 0 | 0 | 9 | 2 | 14 | 0 | 0 | 1 | 0 | 1.000 | 0 | 0 | 5.17 |
| 1990 Chicago | NL | 7 | 0 | 0 | 3 | 7.1 | 41 | 11 | 8 | 8 | 1 | 0 | 0 | 1 | 7 | 0 | 3 | 3 | 0 | 0 | 0 | .000 | 0 | 1 | 9.82 |
| 2 ML YEARS | | 18 | 0 | 0 | 4 | 23 | 108 | 24 | 17 | 17 | 3 | 1 | 0 | 1 | 16 | 2 | 17 | 3 | 0 | 1 | 0 | 1.000 | 0 | 1 | 6.65 |

## Jerry Willard

**Bats:** Left **Throws:** Right **Pos:** C **Ht:** 6' 2" **Wt:** 195 **Born:** 03/14/60 **Age:** 31

| | | BATTING | | | | | | | | | | | | | | | | | BASERUNNING | | | | PERCENTAGES | | |
|---|---|---|---|---|---|---|---|---|---|---|---|---|---|---|---|---|---|---|---|---|---|---|---|---|---|
| Year Team | Lg | G | AB | H | 2B | 3B | HR | (Hm | Rd) | TB | R | RBI | TBB | IBB | SO | HBP | SH | SF | SB | CS | SB% | GDP | Avg | OBP | SLG |
| 1984 Cleveland | AL | 87 | 246 | 55 | 8 | 1 | 10 | (5 | 5) | 95 | 21 | 37 | 26 | 0 | 55 | 0 | 0 | 3 | 1 | 0 | 1.00 | 6 | .224 | .295 | .386 |
| 1985 Cleveland | AL | 104 | 300 | 81 | 13 | 0 | 7 | (4 | 3) | 115 | 39 | 36 | 28 | 1 | 59 | 1 | 4 | 1 | 0 | 0 | .00 | 3 | .270 | .333 | .383 |
| 1986 Oakland | AL | 75 | 161 | 43 | 7 | 0 | 4 | (2 | 2) | 62 | 17 | 26 | 22 | 0 | 28 | 2 | 4 | 4 | 0 | 1 | .00 | 4 | .267 | .354 | .385 |
| 1987 Oakland | AL | 7 | 6 | 1 | 0 | 0 | 0 | (0 | 0) | 1 | 1 | 0 | 2 | 0 | 1 | 0 | 0 | 0 | 0 | 0 | .00 | 0 | .167 | .375 | .167 |
| 1990 Chicago | AL | 3 | 3 | 0 | 0 | 0 | 0 | (0 | 0) | 0 | 0 | 0 | 0 | 0 | 2 | 0 | 0 | 0 | 0 | 0 | .00 | 0 | .000 | .000 | .000 |
| 5 ML YEARS | | 276 | 716 | 180 | 28 | 1 | 21 | (11 | 10) | 273 | 78 | 99 | 78 | 1 | 145 | 3 | 8 | 8 | 1 | 1 | .50 | 13 | .251 | .324 | .381 |

## Eddie Williams

**Bats:** Right **Throws:** Right **Pos:** 3B **Ht:** 6' 0" **Wt:** 175 **Born:** 11/01/64 **Age:** 26

| | | BATTING | | | | | | | | | | | | | | | | | BASERUNNING | | | | PERCENTAGES | | |
|---|---|---|---|---|---|---|---|---|---|---|---|---|---|---|---|---|---|---|---|---|---|---|---|---|---|
| Year Team | Lg | G | AB | H | 2B | 3B | HR | (Hm | Rd) | TB | R | RBI | TBB | IBB | SO | HBP | SH | SF | SB | CS | SB% | GDP | Avg | OBP | SLG |
| 1986 Cleveland | AL | 5 | 7 | 1 | 0 | 0 | 0 | (0 | 0) | 1 | 2 | 1 | 0 | 0 | 3 | 0 | 0 | 0 | 0 | 0 | .00 | 0 | .143 | .143 | .143 |
| 1987 Cleveland | AL | 22 | 64 | 11 | 4 | 0 | 1 | (0 | 1) | 18 | 9 | 4 | 9 | 0 | 19 | 1 | 0 | 1 | 0 | 0 | .00 | 2 | .172 | .280 | .281 |
| 1988 Cleveland | AL | 10 | 21 | 4 | 0 | 0 | 0 | (0 | 0) | 4 | 3 | 1 | 0 | 0 | 3 | 1 | 1 | 0 | 0 | 0 | .00 | 1 | .190 | .227 | .190 |
| 1989 Chicago | AL | 66 | 201 | 55 | 8 | 0 | 3 | (2 | 1) | 72 | 25 | 10 | 18 | 3 | 31 | 4 | 3 | 3 | 1 | 2 | .33 | 4 | .274 | .341 | .358 |
| 1990 San Diego | NL | 14 | 42 | 12 | 3 | 0 | 3 | (1 | 2) | 24 | 5 | 4 | 5 | 2 | 6 | 0 | 0 | 0 | 0 | 1 | .00 | 1 | .286 | .362 | .571 |
| 5 ML YEARS | | 117 | 335 | 83 | 15 | 0 | 7 | (3 | 4) | 119 | 44 | 20 | 32 | 5 | 62 | 6 | 4 | 4 | 1 | 3 | .25 | 8 | .248 | .321 | .355 |

## Ken Williams

**Bats:** Right **Throws:** Right **Pos:** RF/LF/CF **Ht:** 6' 1" **Wt:** 187 **Born:** 04/06/64 **Age:** 27

| | | BATTING | | | | | | | | | | | | | | | | | BASERUNNING | | | | PERCENTAGES | | |
|---|---|---|---|---|---|---|---|---|---|---|---|---|---|---|---|---|---|---|---|---|---|---|---|---|---|
| Year Team | Lg | G | AB | H | 2B | 3B | HR | (Hm | Rd) | TB | R | RBI | TBB | IBB | SO | HBP | SH | SF | SB | CS | SB% | GDP | Avg | OBP | SLG |
| 1986 Chicago | AL | 15 | 31 | 4 | 0 | 0 | 1 | (1 | 0) | 7 | 2 | 1 | 1 | 0 | 11 | 1 | 0 | 0 | 1 | 1 | .50 | 1 | .129 | .182 | .226 |
| 1987 Chicago | AL | 116 | 391 | 110 | 18 | 2 | 11 | (4 | 7) | 165 | 48 | 50 | 10 | 0 | 83 | 9 | 3 | 1 | 21 | 10 | .68 | 5 | .281 | .314 | .422 |
| 1988 Chicago | AL | 73 | 220 | 35 | 4 | 2 | 8 | (3 | 5) | 67 | 18 | 28 | 10 | 0 | 64 | 8 | 3 | 2 | 6 | 5 | .55 | 2 | .159 | .221 | .305 |
| 1989 Detroit | AL | 94 | 258 | 53 | 5 | 1 | 6 | (3 | 3) | 78 | 29 | 23 | 18 | 0 | 63 | 5 | 2 | 2 | 9 | 4 | .69 | 6 | .205 | .269 | .302 |
| 1990 2 ML Teams | | 106 | 155 | 25 | 8 | 1 | 0 | (0 | 0) | 35 | 23 | 13 | 10 | 0 | 42 | 2 | 0 | 2 | 9 | 4 | .69 | 1 | .161 | .219 | .226 |
| 1990 Detroit | AL | 57 | 83 | 11 | 2 | 0 | 0 | (0 | 0) | 13 | 10 | 5 | 3 | 0 | 24 | 1 | 0 | 1 | 2 | 2 | .50 | 0 | .133 | .170 | .157 |
| Toronto | AL | 49 | 72 | 14 | 6 | 1 | 0 | (0 | 0) | 22 | 13 | 8 | 7 | 0 | 18 | 1 | 0 | 1 | 7 | 2 | .78 | 1 | .194 | .272 | .306 |
| 5 ML YEARS | | 404 | 1055 | 227 | 35 | 6 | 26 | (11 | 15) | 352 | 120 | 115 | 49 | 0 | 263 | 25 | 8 | 7 | 46 | 24 | .66 | 15 | .215 | .265 | .334 |

## Matt D. Williams

**Bats:** Right **Throws:** Right **Pos:** 3B **Ht:** 6' 2" **Wt:** 205 **Born:** 11/28/65 **Age:** 25

| | | BATTING | | | | | | | | | | | | | | | | | BASERUNNING | | | | PERCENTAGES | | |
|---|---|---|---|---|---|---|---|---|---|---|---|---|---|---|---|---|---|---|---|---|---|---|---|---|---|
| Year Team | Lg | G | AB | H | 2B | 3B | HR | (Hm | Rd) | TB | R | RBI | TBB | IBB | SO | HBP | SH | SF | SB | CS | SB% | GDP | Avg | OBP | SLG |
| 1987 San Francisco | NL | 84 | 245 | 46 | 9 | 2 | 8 | (5 | 3) | 83 | 28 | 21 | 16 | 4 | 68 | 1 | 3 | 1 | 4 | 3 | .57 | 5 | .188 | .240 | .339 |
| 1988 San Francisco | NL | 52 | 156 | 32 | 6 | 1 | 8 | (7 | 1) | 64 | 17 | 19 | 8 | 0 | 41 | 2 | 3 | 1 | 0 | 1 | .00 | 7 | .205 | .251 | .410 |
| 1989 San Francisco | NL | 84 | 292 | 59 | 18 | 1 | 18 | (10 | 8) | 133 | 31 | 50 | 14 | 1 | 72 | 2 | 1 | 2 | 1 | 2 | .33 | 5 | .202 | .242 | .455 |
| 1990 San Francisco | NL | 159 | 617 | 171 | 27 | 2 | 33 | (20 | 13) | 301 | 87 | 122 | 33 | 9 | 138 | 7 | 2 | 5 | 7 | 4 | .64 | 13 | .277 | .319 | .488 |
| 4 ML YEARS | | 379 | 1310 | 308 | 60 | 6 | 67 | (42 | 25) | 581 | 163 | 212 | 71 | 14 | 319 | 12 | 9 | 9 | 12 | 10 | .55 | 30 | .235 | .279 | .444 |

## Mitch Williams

**Pitches:** Left **Bats:** Left **Pos:** RP **Ht:** 6' 4" **Wt:** 200 **Born:** 11/17/64 **Age:** 26

| | | HOW MUCH HE PITCHED | | | | | | WHAT HE GAVE UP | | | | | | | | | | | | THE RESULTS | | | | | |
|---|---|---|---|---|---|---|---|---|---|---|---|---|---|---|---|---|---|---|---|---|---|---|---|---|---|
| Year Team | Lg | G | GS | CG | GF | IP | BFP | H | R | ER | HR | SH | SF | HB | TBB | IBB | SO | WP | Bk | W | L | Pct. | ShO | Sv | ERA |
| 1986 Texas | AL | 80 | 0 | 0 | 38 | 98 | 435 | 69 | 39 | 39 | 8 | 1 | 3 | 11 | 79 | 8 | 90 | 5 | 5 | 8 | 6 | .571 | 0 | 8 | 3.58 |
| 1987 Texas | AL | 85 | 1 | 0 | 32 | 108.2 | 469 | 63 | 47 | 39 | 9 | 4 | 3 | 7 | 94 | 7 | 129 | 4 | 2 | 8 | 6 | .571 | 0 | 6 | 3.23 |
| 1988 Texas | AL | 67 | 0 | 0 | 51 | 68 | 296 | 48 | 38 | 35 | 4 | 3 | 4 | 6 | 47 | 3 | 61 | 5 | 6 | 2 | 7 | .222 | 0 | 18 | 4.63 |
| 1989 Chicago | NL | 76 | 0 | 0 | 61 | 81.2 | 365 | 71 | 27 | 24 | 6 | 2 | 5 | 8 | 52 | 4 | 67 | 6 | 4 | 4 | 4 | .500 | 0 | 36 | 2.64 |
| 1990 Chicago | NL | 59 | 2 | 0 | 39 | 66.1 | 310 | 60 | 38 | 29 | 4 | 5 | 3 | 1 | 50 | 6 | 55 | 4 | 2 | 1 | 8 | .111 | 0 | 16 | 3.93 |
| 5 ML YEARS | | 367 | 3 | 0 | 221 | 422.2 | 1875 | 311 | 189 | 166 | 31 | 15 | 18 | 33 | 322 | 28 | 402 | 24 | 19 | 23 | 31 | .426 | 0 | 84 | 3.53 |

## Mark Williamson

**Pitches:** Right **Bats:** Right **Pos:** RP **Ht:** 6' 0" **Wt:** 171 **Born:** 07/21/59 **Age:** 31

| | | HOW MUCH HE PITCHED | | | | | | WHAT HE GAVE UP | | | | | | | | | | | | THE RESULTS | | | | | |
|---|---|---|---|---|---|---|---|---|---|---|---|---|---|---|---|---|---|---|---|---|---|---|---|---|---|
| Year Team | Lg | G | GS | CG | GF | IP | BFP | H | R | ER | HR | SH | SF | HB | TBB | IBB | SO | WP | Bk | W | L | Pct. | ShO | Sv | ERA |
| 1987 Baltimore | AL | 61 | 2 | 0 | 36 | 125 | 520 | 122 | 59 | 56 | 12 | 5 | 3 | 3 | 41 | 15 | 73 | 3 | 0 | 8 | 9 | .471 | 0 | 3 | 4.03 |
| 1988 Baltimore | AL | 37 | 10 | 2 | 11 | 117.2 | 507 | 125 | 70 | 64 | 14 | 4 | 2 | 2 | 40 | 8 | 69 | 5 | 3 | 5 | 8 | .385 | 0 | 2 | 4.90 |
| 1989 Baltimore | AL | 65 | 0 | 0 | 38 | 107.1 | 445 | 105 | 35 | 35 | 4 | 7 | 3 | 2 | 30 | 9 | 55 | 0 | 0 | 10 | 5 | .667 | 0 | 9 | 2.93 |
| 1990 Baltimore | AL | 49 | 0 | 0 | 15 | 85.1 | 343 | 65 | 25 | 21 | 8 | 6 | 7 | 0 | 28 | 2 | 60 | 1 | 0 | 8 | 2 | .800 | 0 | 1 | 2.21 |
| 4 ML YEARS | | 212 | 12 | 2 | 100 | 435.1 | 1815 | 417 | 189 | 176 | 38 | 22 | 15 | 7 | 139 | 34 | 257 | 9 | 3 | 31 | 24 | .564 | 0 | 15 | 3.64 |

## Frank Wills

**Pitches:** Right **Bats:** Right **Pos:** RP/SP **Ht:** 6' 2" **Wt:** 200 **Born:** 10/26/58 **Age:** 32

| | | HOW MUCH HE PITCHED | | | | | | WHAT HE GAVE UP | | | | | | | | | | | | THE RESULTS | | | | | |
|---|---|---|---|---|---|---|---|---|---|---|---|---|---|---|---|---|---|---|---|---|---|---|---|---|---|
| Year Team | Lg | G | GS | CG | GF | IP | BFP | H | R | ER | HR | SH | SF | HB | TBB | IBB | SO | WP | Bk | W | L | Pct. | ShO | Sv | ERA |
| 1983 Kansas City | AL | 6 | 4 | 0 | 1 | 34.2 | 152 | 35 | 17 | 16 | 2 | 0 | 2 | 0 | 15 | 0 | 23 | 3 | 0 | 2 | 1 | .667 | 0 | 0 | 4.15 |
| 1984 Kansas City | AL | 10 | 5 | 0 | 2 | 37 | 161 | 39 | 21 | 21 | 3 | 0 | 4 | 0 | 13 | 0 | 21 | 2 | 0 | 2 | 3 | .400 | 0 | 0 | 5.11 |
| 1985 Seattle | AL | 24 | 18 | 1 | 2 | 123 | 541 | 122 | 85 | 82 | 18 | 4 | 8 | 3 | 68 | 3 | 67 | 9 | 1 | 5 | 11 | .313 | 0 | 1 | 6.00 |
| 1986 Cleveland | AL | 26 | 0 | 0 | 16 | 40.1 | 182 | 43 | 23 | 22 | 6 | 6 | 2 | 0 | 16 | 4 | 32 | 2 | 0 | 4 | 4 | .500 | 0 | 4 | 4.91 |
| 1987 Cleveland | AL | 6 | 0 | 0 | 4 | 5.1 | 26 | 3 | 3 | 3 | 0 | 1 | 1 | 0 | 7 | 0 | 4 | 0 | 0 | 0 | 1 | .000 | 0 | 1 | 5.06 |
| 1988 Toronto | AL | 10 | 0 | 0 | 4 | 20.2 | 89 | 22 | 12 | 12 | 2 | 1 | 1 | 0 | 6 | 2 | 19 | 1 | 0 | 0 | 0 | .000 | 0 | 0 | 5.23 |
| 1989 Toronto | AL | 24 | 4 | 0 | 6 | 71.1 | 302 | 65 | 31 | 29 | 4 | 1 | 1 | 1 | 30 | 2 | 41 | 4 | 0 | 3 | 1 | .750 | 0 | 0 | 3.66 |
| 1990 Toronto | AL | 44 | 4 | 0 | 6 | 99 | 422 | 101 | 54 | 52 | 13 | 2 | 1 | 1 | 38 | 7 | 72 | 1 | 0 | 6 | 4 | .600 | 0 | 0 | 4.73 |
| 8 ML YEARS | | 150 | 35 | 1 | 41 | 431.1 | 1875 | 430 | 246 | 237 | 48 | 15 | 20 | 5 | 193 | 18 | 279 | 22 | 1 | 22 | 25 | .468 | 0 | 6 | 4.95 |

## Craig Wilson

**Bats:** Right **Throws:** Right **Pos:** 3B **Ht:** 5'11" **Wt:** 175 **Born:** 11/28/64 **Age:** 26

| | | BATTING | | | | | | | | | | | | | | | | | BASERUNNING | | | | PERCENTAGES | | |
|---|---|---|---|---|---|---|---|---|---|---|---|---|---|---|---|---|---|---|---|---|---|---|---|---|---|
| Year Team | Lg | G | AB | H | 2B | 3B | HR | (Hm | Rd) | TB | R | RBI | TBB | IBB | SO | HBP | SH | SF | SB | CS | SB% | GDP | Avg | OBP | SLG |
| 1984 Erie | A | 72 | 282 | 83 | 18 | 4 | 7 | -- | -- | 130 | 53 | 46 | 29 | 0 | 27 | 4 | 1 | 2 | 10 | 4 | .71 | 8 | .294 | .366 | .461 |
| 1985 Springfield | A | 133 | 504 | 132 | 16 | 4 | 8 | -- | -- | 180 | 64 | 52 | 47 | 0 | 67 | 1 | 4 | 6 | 33 | 14 | .70 | 12 | .262 | .323 | .357 |
| 1986 Springfield | A | 127 | 496 | 136 | 17 | 6 | 1 | -- | -- | 168 | 106 | 49 | 65 | 0 | 49 | 1 | 9 | 4 | 44 | 12 | .79 | 11 | .274 | .357 | .339 |
| 1987 St. Pete | A | 38 | 162 | 58 | 6 | 4 | 0 | -- | -- | 72 | 35 | 28 | 14 | 0 | 5 | 0 | 0 | 0 | 12 | 8 | .60 | 3 | .358 | .409 | .444 |

| | Louisville | AAA | 21 | 70 | 15 | 2 | 0 | 1 | -- | -- | 20 | 10 | 8 | 3 | 0 | 5 | 0 | 2 | 1 | 0 | 2 | .00 | 1 | .214 | .243 | .286 |
|---|---|---|---|---|---|---|---|---|---|---|---|---|---|---|---|---|---|---|---|---|---|---|---|---|---|---|
| | Arkansas | AA | 66 | 238 | 69 | 13 | 1 | 1 | -- | -- | 87 | 37 | 26 | 30 | 1 | 19 | 1 | 3 | 2 | 9 | 6 | .60 | 5 | .290 | .369 | .366 |
| 1988 | Louisville | AAA | 133 | 497 | 127 | 27 | 2 | 1 | -- | -- | 161 | 59 | 46 | 54 | 1 | 46 | 0 | 6 | 4 | 6 | 4 | .60 | 13 | .256 | .326 | .324 |
| 1989 | Arkansas | AA | 55 | 224 | 71 | 12 | 1 | 1 | -- | -- | 88 | 41 | 40 | 21 | 1 | 14 | 1 | 3 | 1 | 8 | 5 | .62 | 4 | .317 | .377 | .393 |
| | Louisville | AAA | 75 | 278 | 81 | 18 | 3 | 1 | -- | -- | 108 | 37 | 30 | 14 | 0 | 25 | 2 | 3 | 1 | 1 | 3 | .25 | 5 | .291 | .329 | .388 |
| 1990 | Louisville | AAA | 57 | 204 | 57 | 9 | 2 | 2 | -- | -- | 76 | 30 | 23 | 28 | 0 | 15 | 1 | 5 | 6 | 5 | 3 | .63 | 3 | .279 | .360 | .373 |
| 1989 | St. Louis | NL | 6 | 4 | 1 | 0 | 0 | 0 | (0 | 0) | 1 | 1 | 1 | 1 | 0 | 2 | 0 | 0 | 0 | 0 | 0 | .00 | 0 | .250 | .400 | .250 |
| 1990 | St. Louis | NL | 55 | 121 | 30 | 2 | 0 | 0 | (0 | 0) | 32 | 13 | 7 | 8 | 0 | 14 | 0 | 0 | 2 | 0 | 2 | .00 | 7 | .248 | .290 | .264 |
| | 2 ML YEARS | | 61 | 125 | 31 | 2 | 0 | 0 | (0 | 0) | 33 | 14 | 8 | 9 | 0 | 16 | 0 | 0 | 2 | 0 | 2 | .00 | 7 | .248 | .294 | .264 |

## Glenn Wilson

**Bats:** Right **Throws:** Right **Pos:** RF/LF **Ht:** 6' 1" **Wt:** 190 **Born:** 12/22/58 **Age:** 32

| BATTING | | | | | | | | | | | | | | | | | | | | BASERUNNING | | | | PERCENTAGES | | |
|---|---|---|---|---|---|---|---|---|---|---|---|---|---|---|---|---|---|---|---|---|---|---|---|---|---|---|
| Year | Team | Lg | G | AB | H | 2B | 3B | HR | (Hm | Rd) | TB | R | RBI | TBB | IBB | SO | HBP | SH | SF | SB | CS | SB% | GDP | Avg | OBP | SLG |
| 1982 | Detroit | AL | 84 | 322 | 94 | 15 | 1 | 12 | (9 | 3) | 147 | 39 | 34 | 15 | 0 | 51 | 0 | 3 | 2 | 2 | 3 | .40 | 8 | .292 | .322 | .457 |
| 1983 | Detroit | AL | 144 | 503 | 135 | 25 | 6 | 11 | (9 | 2) | 205 | 55 | 65 | 25 | 1 | 79 | 3 | 0 | 2 | 1 | 1 | .50 | 9 | .268 | .306 | .408 |
| 1984 | Philadelphia | NL | 132 | 341 | 82 | 21 | 3 | 6 | (5 | 1) | 127 | 28 | 31 | 17 | 1 | 56 | 1 | 1 | 3 | 7 | 1 | .88 | 12 | .240 | .276 | .372 |
| 1985 | Philadelphia | NL | 161 | 608 | 167 | 39 | 5 | 14 | (7 | 7) | 258 | 73 | 102 | 35 | 1 | 117 | 0 | 0 | 7 | 7 | 4 | .64 | 24 | .275 | .311 | .424 |
| 1986 | Philadelphia | NL | 155 | 584 | 158 | 30 | 4 | 15 | (7 | 8) | 241 | 70 | 84 | 42 | 1 | 91 | 4 | 0 | 9 | 5 | 1 | .83 | 15 | .271 | .319 | .413 |
| 1987 | Philadelphia | NL | 154 | 569 | 150 | 21 | 2 | 14 | (5 | 9) | 217 | 55 | 54 | 38 | 2 | 82 | 1 | 0 | 6 | 3 | 6 | .33 | 18 | .264 | .308 | .381 |
| 1988 | 2 ML Teams | | 115 | 410 | 105 | 18 | 1 | 5 | (2 | 3) | 140 | 39 | 32 | 18 | 1 | 70 | 1 | 3 | 4 | 1 | 1 | .50 | 17 | .256 | .286 | .341 |
| 1989 | 2 ML Teams | | 128 | 432 | 115 | 26 | 4 | 11 | (4 | 7) | 182 | 50 | 64 | 37 | 5 | 53 | 1 | 0 | 6 | 1 | 5 | .17 | 11 | .266 | .321 | .421 |
| 1990 | Houston | NL | 118 | 368 | 90 | 14 | 0 | 10 | (5 | 5) | 134 | 42 | 55 | 26 | 1 | 64 | 1 | 0 | 4 | 0 | 3 | .00 | 16 | .245 | .293 | .364 |
| 1988 | Seattle | AL | 78 | 284 | 71 | 10 | 1 | 3 | (2 | 1) | 92 | 28 | 17 | 15 | 0 | 52 | 0 | 1 | 2 | 1 | 1 | .50 | 13 | .250 | .286 | .324 |
| | Pittsburgh | NL | 37 | 126 | 34 | 8 | 0 | 2 | (0 | 2) | 48 | 11 | 15 | 3 | 1 | 18 | 1 | 2 | 2 | 0 | 0 | .00 | 4 | .270 | .288 | .381 |
| 1989 | Pittsburgh | NL | 100 | 330 | 93 | 20 | 4 | 9 | (2 | 7) | 148 | 42 | 49 | 32 | 5 | 39 | 1 | 0 | 5 | 1 | 4 | .20 | 8 | .282 | .342 | .448 |
| | Houston | NL | 28 | 102 | 22 | 6 | 0 | 2 | (2 | 0) | 34 | 8 | 15 | 5 | 0 | 14 | 0 | 0 | 1 | 0 | 1 | .00 | 3 | .216 | .250 | .333 |
| | 9 ML YEARS | | 1191 | 4137 | 1096 | 209 | 26 | 98 | (53 | 45) | 1651 | 451 | 521 | 253 | 13 | 663 | 12 | 7 | 43 | 27 | 25 | .52 | 130 | .265 | .306 | .399 |

## Mookie Wilson

**Bats:** Both **Throws:** Right **Pos:** CF **Ht:** 5'10" **Wt:** 170 **Born:** 02/09/56 **Age:** 35

| BATTING | | | | | | | | | | | | | | | | | | | | BASERUNNING | | | | PERCENTAGES | | |
|---|---|---|---|---|---|---|---|---|---|---|---|---|---|---|---|---|---|---|---|---|---|---|---|---|---|---|
| Year | Team | Lg | G | AB | H | 2B | 3B | HR | (Hm | Rd) | TB | R | RBI | TBB | IBB | SO | HBP | SH | SF | SB | CS | SB% | GDP | Avg | OBP | SLG |
| 1980 | New York | NL | 27 | 105 | 26 | 5 | 3 | 0 | (0 | 0) | 37 | 16 | 4 | 12 | 0 | 19 | 0 | 2 | 0 | 7 | 7 | .50 | 0 | .248 | .325 | .352 |
| 1981 | New York | NL | 92 | 328 | 89 | 8 | 8 | 3 | (2 | 1) | 122 | 49 | 14 | 20 | 3 | 59 | 2 | 0 | 0 | 24 | 12 | .67 | 3 | .271 | .317 | .372 |
| 1982 | New York | NL | 159 | 639 | 178 | 25 | 9 | 5 | (2 | 3) | 236 | 90 | 55 | 32 | 4 | 102 | 2 | 1 | 3 | 58 | 16 | .78 | 5 | .279 | .314 | .369 |
| 1983 | New York | NL | 152 | 638 | 176 | 25 | 6 | 7 | (4 | 3) | 234 | 91 | 51 | 18 | 3 | 103 | 4 | 2 | 1 | 54 | 16 | .77 | 6 | .276 | .300 | .367 |
| 1984 | New York | NL | 154 | 587 | 162 | 28 | 10 | 10 | (7 | 3) | 240 | 88 | 54 | 26 | 2 | 90 | 2 | 2 | 2 | 46 | 9 | .84 | 5 | .276 | .308 | .409 |
| 1985 | New York | NL | 93 | 337 | 93 | 16 | 8 | 6 | (2 | 4) | 143 | 56 | 26 | 28 | 6 | 52 | 0 | 1 | 1 | 24 | 9 | .73 | 9 | .276 | .331 | .424 |
| 1986 | New York | NL | 123 | 381 | 110 | 17 | 5 | 9 | (4 | 5) | 164 | 61 | 45 | 32 | 5 | 72 | 1 | 0 | 1 | 25 | 7 | .78 | 5 | .289 | .345 | .430 |
| 1987 | New York | NL | 124 | 385 | 115 | 19 | 7 | 9 | (5 | 4) | 175 | 58 | 34 | 35 | 8 | 85 | 2 | 2 | 1 | 21 | 6 | .78 | 2 | .299 | .359 | .455 |
| 1988 | New York | NL | 112 | 378 | 112 | 17 | 5 | 8 | (1 | 7) | 163 | 61 | 41 | 27 | 2 | 63 | 2 | 1 | 2 | 15 | 4 | .79 | 12 | .296 | .345 | .431 |
| 1989 | 2 ML Teams | | 134 | 487 | 122 | 19 | 2 | 5 | (2 | 3) | 160 | 54 | 35 | 13 | 3 | 84 | 3 | 3 | 3 | 19 | 5 | .79 | 5 | .251 | .273 | .329 |
| 1990 | Toronto | AL | 147 | 588 | 156 | 36 | 4 | 3 | (0 | 3) | 209 | 81 | 51 | 31 | 0 | 102 | 0 | 6 | 4 | 23 | 4 | .85 | 10 | .265 | .300 | .355 |
| 1989 | New York | NL | 80 | 249 | 51 | 10 | 1 | 3 | (1 | 2) | 72 | 22 | 18 | 10 | 3 | 47 | 1 | 0 | 2 | 7 | 4 | .64 | 0 | .205 | .237 | .289 |
| | Toronto | AL | 54 | 238 | 71 | 9 | 1 | 2 | (1 | 1) | 88 | 32 | 17 | 3 | 0 | 37 | 2 | 3 | 1 | 12 | 1 | .92 | 5 | .298 | .311 | .370 |
| | 11 ML YEARS | | 1317 | 4853 | 1339 | 215 | 67 | 65 | (29 | 36) | 1883 | 705 | 410 | 274 | 36 | 831 | 18 | 20 | 18 | 316 | 95 | .77 | 62 | .276 | .316 | .388 |

## Steve Wilson

**Pitches:** Left **Bats:** Left **Pos:** RP/SP **Ht:** 6' 4" **Wt:** 195 **Born:** 12/13/64 **Age:** 26

| HOW MUCH HE PITCHED | | | | | | | | | WHAT HE GAVE UP | | | | | | | | | | | | THE RESULTS | | | | | |
|---|---|---|---|---|---|---|---|---|---|---|---|---|---|---|---|---|---|---|---|---|---|---|---|---|---|---|
| Year | Team | Lg | G | GS | CG | GF | IP | BFP | H | R | ER | HR | SH | SF | HB | TBB | IBB | SO | WP | Bk | W | L | Pct. | ShO | Sv | ERA |
| 1988 | Texas | AL | 3 | 0 | 0 | 1 | 7.2 | 31 | 7 | 5 | 5 | 1 | 0 | 0 | 0 | 4 | 1 | 1 | 0 | 0 | 0 | 0 | .000 | 0 | 0 | 5.87 |
| 1989 | Chicago | NL | 53 | 8 | 0 | 9 | 85.2 | 364 | 83 | 43 | 40 | 6 | 5 | 4 | 1 | 31 | 5 | 65 | 0 | 1 | 6 | 4 | .600 | 0 | 2 | 4.20 |
| 1990 | Chicago | NL | 45 | 15 | 1 | 5 | 139 | 597 | 140 | 77 | 74 | 17 | 9 | 3 | 2 | 43 | 6 | 95 | 2 | 1 | 4 | 9 | .308 | 0 | 1 | 4.79 |
| | 3 ML YEARS | | 101 | 23 | 1 | 15 | 232.1 | 992 | 230 | 125 | 119 | 24 | 14 | 7 | 3 | 78 | 12 | 161 | 2 | 2 | 10 | 13 | .435 | 0 | 3 | 4.61 |

## Trevor Wilson

**Pitches:** Left **Bats:** Left **Pos:** SP/RP **Ht:** 6' 0" **Wt:** 175 **Born:** 06/07/66 **Age:** 25

| HOW MUCH HE PITCHED | | | | | | | | | WHAT HE GAVE UP | | | | | | | | | | | | THE RESULTS | | | | | |
|---|---|---|---|---|---|---|---|---|---|---|---|---|---|---|---|---|---|---|---|---|---|---|---|---|---|---|
| Year | Team | Lg | G | GS | CG | GF | IP | BFP | H | R | ER | HR | SH | SF | HB | TBB | IBB | SO | WP | Bk | W | L | Pct. | ShO | Sv | ERA |
| 1988 | San Francisco | NL | 4 | 4 | 0 | 0 | 22 | 96 | 25 | 14 | 10 | 1 | 3 | 1 | 0 | 8 | 0 | 15 | 0 | 1 | 0 | 2 | .000 | 0 | 0 | 4.09 |
| 1989 | San Francisco | NL | 14 | 4 | 0 | 2 | 39.1 | 167 | 28 | 20 | 19 | 2 | 3 | 1 | 4 | 24 | 0 | 22 | 0 | 1 | 2 | 3 | .400 | 0 | 0 | 4.35 |
| 1990 | San Francisco | NL | 27 | 17 | 3 | 3 | 110.1 | 457 | 87 | 52 | 49 | 11 | 6 | 2 | 1 | 49 | 3 | 66 | 5 | 2 | 8 | 7 | .533 | 2 | 0 | 4.00 |
| | 3 ML YEARS | | 45 | 25 | 3 | 5 | 171.2 | 720 | 140 | 86 | 78 | 14 | 12 | 4 | 5 | 81 | 3 | 103 | 5 | 4 | 10 | 12 | .455 | 2 | 0 | 4.09 |

## Willie Wilson

**Bats:** Both **Throws:** Right **Pos:** LF/CF **Ht:** 6' 3" **Wt:** 195 **Born:** 07/09/55 **Age:** 35

| | | | | | BATTING | | | | | | | | | | | | | | BASERUNNING | | | | PERCENTAGES | | |
|---|---|---|---|---|---|---|---|---|---|---|---|---|---|---|---|---|---|---|---|---|---|---|---|---|---|
| Year Team | Lg | G | AB | H | 2B | 3B | HR | (Hm | Rd) | TB | R | RBI | TBB | IBB | SO | HBP | SH | SF | SB | CS | SB% | GDP | Avg | OBP | SLG |
| 1976 Kansas City | AL | 12 | 6 | 1 | 0 | 0 | 0 | (0 | 0) | 1 | 0 | 0 | 0 | 0 | 2 | 0 | 0 | 0 | 2 | 1 | .67 | 0 | .167 | .167 | .167 |
| 1977 Kansas City | AL | 13 | 34 | 11 | 2 | 0 | 0 | (0 | 0) | 13 | 10 | 1 | 1 | 0 | 8 | 0 | 2 | 0 | 6 | 3 | .67 | 1 | .324 | .343 | .382 |
| 1978 Kansas City | AL | 127 | 198 | 43 | 8 | 2 | 0 | (0 | 0) | 55 | 43 | 16 | 16 | 0 | 33 | 2 | 5 | 2 | 46 | 12 | .79 | 2 | .217 | .280 | .278 |
| 1979 Kansas City | AL | 154 | 588 | 185 | 18 | 13 | 6 | (3 | 3) | 247 | 113 | 49 | 28 | 3 | 92 | 7 | 13 | 4 | 83 | 12 | .87 | 1 | .315 | .351 | .420 |
| 1980 Kansas City | AL | 161 | 705 | 230 | 28 | 15 | 3 | (2 | 1) | 297 | 133 | 49 | 28 | 3 | 81 | 6 | 5 | 1 | 79 | 10 | .89 | 4 | .326 | .357 | .421 |
| 1981 Kansas City | AL | 102 | 439 | 133 | 10 | 7 | 1 | (0 | 1) | 160 | 54 | 32 | 18 | 3 | 42 | 4 | 3 | 1 | 34 | 8 | .81 | 5 | .303 | .335 | .364 |
| 1982 Kansas City | AL | 136 | 585 | 194 | 19 | 15 | 3 | (2 | 1) | 252 | 87 | 46 | 26 | 2 | 81 | 6 | 2 | 2 | 37 | 11 | .77 | 4 | .332 | .365 | .431 |
| 1983 Kansas City | AL | 137 | 576 | 159 | 22 | 8 | 2 | (2 | 0) | 203 | 90 | 33 | 33 | 2 | 75 | 1 | 1 | 0 | 59 | 8 | .88 | 4 | .276 | .316 | .352 |
| 1984 Kansas City | AL | 128 | 541 | 163 | 24 | 9 | 2 | (1 | 1) | 211 | 81 | 44 | 39 | 2 | 56 | 3 | 2 | 3 | 47 | 5 | .90 | 7 | .301 | .350 | .390 |
| 1985 Kansas City | AL | 141 | 605 | 168 | 25 | 21 | 4 | (1 | 3) | 247 | 87 | 43 | 29 | 3 | 94 | 5 | 2 | 1 | 43 | 11 | .80 | 6 | .278 | .316 | .408 |
| 1986 Kansas City | AL | 156 | 631 | 170 | 20 | 7 | 9 | (5 | 4) | 231 | 77 | 44 | 31 | 1 | 97 | 9 | 3 | 1 | 34 | 8 | .81 | 6 | .269 | .313 | .366 |
| 1987 Kansas City | AL | 146 | 610 | 170 | 18 | 15 | 4 | (0 | 4) | 230 | 97 | 30 | 32 | 2 | 88 | 6 | 4 | 1 | 59 | 11 | .84 | 9 | .279 | .320 | .377 |
| 1988 Kansas City | AL | 147 | 591 | 155 | 17 | 11 | 1 | (0 | 1) | 197 | 81 | 37 | 22 | 1 | 106 | 2 | 8 | 5 | 35 | 7 | .83 | 5 | .262 | .289 | .333 |
| 1989 Kansas City | AL | 112 | 383 | 97 | 17 | 7 | 3 | (1 | 2) | 137 | 58 | 43 | 27 | 0 | 78 | 1 | 6 | 6 | 24 | 6 | .80 | 8 | .253 | .300 | .358 |
| 1990 Kansas City | AL | 115 | 307 | 89 | 13 | 3 | 2 | (1 | 1) | 114 | 49 | 42 | 30 | 1 | 57 | 2 | 3 | 3 | 24 | 6 | .80 | 4 | .290 | .354 | .371 |
| 15 ML YEARS | | 1787 | 6799 | 1968 | 241 | 133 | 40 | (18 | 22) | 2595 | 1060 | 509 | 360 | 23 | 990 | 54 | 59 | 30 | 612 | 119 | .84 | 66 | .289 | .329 | .382 |

## Dave Winfield

**Bats:** Right **Throws:** Right **Pos:** RF **Ht:** 6' 6" **Wt:** 220 **Born:** 10/03/51 **Age:** 39

| | | | | | BATTING | | | | | | | | | | | | | | BASERUNNING | | | | PERCENTAGES | | |
|---|---|---|---|---|---|---|---|---|---|---|---|---|---|---|---|---|---|---|---|---|---|---|---|---|---|
| Year Team | Lg | G | AB | H | 2B | 3B | HR | (Hm | Rd) | TB | R | RBI | TBB | IBB | SO | HBP | SH | SF | SB | CS | SB% | GDP | Avg | OBP | SLG |
| 1973 San Diego | NL | 56 | 141 | 39 | 4 | 1 | 3 | (2 | 1) | 54 | 9 | 12 | 12 | 1 | 19 | 0 | 0 | 1 | 0 | 0 | .00 | 5 | .277 | .331 | .383 |
| 1974 San Diego | NL | 145 | 498 | 132 | 18 | 4 | 20 | (12 | 8) | 218 | 57 | 75 | 40 | 2 | 96 | 1 | 0 | 5 | 9 | 7 | .56 | 14 | .265 | .318 | .438 |
| 1975 San Diego | NL | 143 | 509 | 136 | 20 | 2 | 15 | (7 | 8) | 205 | 74 | 76 | 69 | 14 | 82 | 3 | 3 | 7 | 23 | 4 | .85 | 11 | .267 | .354 | .403 |
| 1976 San Diego | NL | 137 | 492 | 139 | 26 | 4 | 13 | (4 | 9) | 212 | 81 | 69 | 65 | 8 | 78 | 3 | 2 | 5 | 26 | 7 | .79 | 14 | .283 | .366 | .431 |
| 1977 San Diego | NL | 157 | 615 | 169 | 29 | 7 | 25 | (12 | 13) | 287 | 104 | 92 | 58 | 10 | 75 | 0 | 0 | 5 | 16 | 7 | .70 | 12 | .275 | .335 | .467 |
| 1978 San Diego | NL | 158 | 587 | 181 | 30 | 5 | 24 | (11 | 13) | 293 | 88 | 97 | 55 | 20 | 81 | 2 | 0 | 5 | 21 | 9 | .70 | 13 | .308 | .367 | .499 |
| 1979 San Diego | NL | 159 | 597 | 184 | 27 | 10 | 34 | (16 | 18) | 333 | 97 | 118 | 85 | 24 | 71 | 2 | 0 | 2 | 15 | 9 | .63 | 9 | .308 | .395 | .558 |
| 1980 San Diego | NL | 162 | 558 | 154 | 25 | 6 | 20 | (7 | 13) | 251 | 89 | 87 | 79 | 14 | 83 | 2 | 0 | 4 | 23 | 7 | .77 | 13 | .276 | .365 | .450 |
| 1981 New York | AL | 105 | 388 | 114 | 25 | 1 | 13 | (4 | 9) | 180 | 52 | 68 | 43 | 3 | 41 | 1 | 1 | 7 | 11 | 1 | .92 | 13 | .294 | .360 | .464 |
| 1982 New York | AL | 140 | 539 | 151 | 24 | 8 | 37 | (14 | 23) | 302 | 84 | 106 | 45 | 7 | 64 | 0 | 5 | 8 | 5 | 3 | .63 | 20 | .280 | .331 | .560 |
| 1983 New York | AL | 152 | 598 | 169 | 26 | 8 | 32 | (13 | 19) | 307 | 99 | 116 | 58 | 2 | 77 | 2 | 0 | 6 | 15 | 6 | .71 | 30 | .283 | .345 | .513 |
| 1984 New York | AL | 141 | 567 | 193 | 34 | 4 | 19 | (9 | 10) | 292 | 106 | 100 | 53 | 9 | 71 | 0 | 0 | 6 | 6 | 4 | .60 | 14 | .340 | .393 | .515 |
| 1985 New York | AL | 155 | 633 | 174 | 34 | 6 | 26 | (15 | 11) | 298 | 105 | 114 | 52 | 8 | 96 | 0 | 0 | 4 | 19 | 7 | .73 | 17 | .275 | .328 | .471 |
| 1986 New York | AL | 154 | 565 | 148 | 31 | 5 | 24 | (12 | 12) | 261 | 90 | 104 | 77 | 9 | 106 | 2 | 2 | 6 | 6 | 5 | .55 | 20 | .262 | .349 | .462 |
| 1987 New York | AL | 156 | 575 | 158 | 22 | 1 | 27 | (11 | 16) | 263 | 83 | 97 | 76 | 5 | 96 | 0 | 1 | 3 | 5 | 6 | .45 | 20 | .275 | .358 | .457 |
| 1988 New York | AL | 149 | 559 | 180 | 37 | 2 | 25 | (12 | 13) | 296 | 96 | 107 | 69 | 10 | 88 | 2 | 0 | 1 | 9 | 4 | .69 | 19 | .322 | .398 | .530 |
| 1990 2 ML Teams | | 132 | 475 | 127 | 21 | 2 | 21 | (13 | 8) | 215 | 70 | 78 | 52 | 3 | 81 | 2 | 1 | 7 | 0 | 1 | .00 | 18 | .267 | .338 | .453 |
| 1990 New York | AL | 20 | 61 | 13 | 3 | 0 | 2 | (0 | 2) | 22 | 7 | 6 | 4 | 0 | 13 | 1 | 0 | 1 | 0 | 0 | .00 | 2 | .213 | .269 | .361 |
| California | AL | 112 | 414 | 114 | 18 | 2 | 19 | (13 | 6) | 193 | 63 | 72 | 48 | 3 | 68 | 1 | 1 | 6 | 0 | 1 | .00 | 16 | .275 | .348 | .466 |
| 17 ML YEARS | | 2401 | 8896 | 2548 | 433 | 76 | 378 | (174 | 204) | 4267 | 1384 | 1516 | 988 | 149 | 1305 | 22 | 15 | 82 | 209 | 87 | .71 | 262 | .286 | .356 | .480 |

## Herm Winningham

**Bats:** Left **Throws:** Right **Pos:** CF **Ht:** 5'11" **Wt:** 175 **Born:** 12/01/61 **Age:** 29

| | | | | | BATTING | | | | | | | | | | | | | | BASERUNNING | | | | PERCENTAGES | | |
|---|---|---|---|---|---|---|---|---|---|---|---|---|---|---|---|---|---|---|---|---|---|---|---|---|---|
| Year Team | Lg | G | AB | H | 2B | 3B | HR | (Hm | Rd) | TB | R | RBI | TBB | IBB | SO | HBP | SH | SF | SB | CS | SB% | GDP | Avg | OBP | SLG |
| 1984 New York | NL | 14 | 27 | 11 | 1 | 1 | 0 | (0 | 0) | 14 | 5 | 5 | 1 | 0 | 7 | 0 | 0 | 0 | 2 | 1 | .67 | 0 | .407 | .429 | .519 |
| 1985 Montreal | NL | 125 | 312 | 74 | 6 | 5 | 3 | (0 | 3) | 99 | 30 | 21 | 28 | 3 | 72 | 0 | 1 | 4 | 20 | 9 | .69 | 1 | .237 | .297 | .317 |
| 1986 Montreal | NL | 90 | 185 | 40 | 6 | 3 | 4 | (1 | 3) | 64 | 23 | 11 | 18 | 3 | 51 | 0 | 1 | 0 | 12 | 7 | .63 | 4 | .216 | .286 | .346 |
| 1987 Montreal | NL | 137 | 347 | 83 | 20 | 3 | 4 | (2 | 2) | 121 | 34 | 41 | 34 | 7 | 68 | 0 | 1 | 4 | 29 | 10 | .74 | 10 | .239 | .304 | .349 |
| 1988 2 ML Teams | | 100 | 203 | 47 | 3 | 4 | 0 | (0 | 0) | 58 | 16 | 21 | 17 | 1 | 45 | 0 | 3 | 2 | 12 | 8 | .60 | 2 | .232 | .288 | .286 |
| 1989 Cincinnati | NL | 115 | 251 | 63 | 11 | 3 | 3 | (1 | 2) | 89 | 40 | 13 | 24 | 1 | 50 | 0 | 3 | 0 | 14 | 5 | .74 | 5 | .251 | .316 | .355 |
| 1990 Cincinnati | NL | 84 | 160 | 41 | 8 | 5 | 3 | (0 | 3) | 68 | 20 | 17 | 14 | 1 | 31 | 0 | 2 | 1 | 6 | 4 | .60 | 0 | .256 | .314 | .425 |
| 1988 Montreal | NL | 47 | 90 | 21 | 2 | 1 | 0 | (0 | 0) | 25 | 10 | 6 | 12 | 1 | 18 | 0 | 0 | 1 | 4 | 5 | .44 | 2 | .233 | .320 | .278 |
| Cincinnati | NL | 53 | 113 | 26 | 1 | 3 | 0 | (0 | 0) | 33 | 6 | 15 | 5 | 0 | 27 | 0 | 3 | 1 | 8 | 3 | .73 | 0 | .230 | .261 | .292 |
| 7 ML YEARS | | 665 | 1485 | 359 | 55 | 24 | 17 | (4 | 13) | 513 | 168 | 129 | 136 | 16 | 324 | 0 | 11 | 11 | 95 | 44 | .68 | 22 | .242 | .303 | .345 |

## Bobby Witt

**Pitches:** Right **Bats:** Right **Pos:** SP **Ht:** 6' 2" **Wt:** 205 **Born:** 05/11/64 **Age:** 27

| | | HOW MUCH HE PITCHED | | | | | | WHAT HE GAVE UP | | | | | | | | | | | THE RESULTS | | | | |
|---|---|---|---|---|---|---|---|---|---|---|---|---|---|---|---|---|---|---|---|---|---|---|---|
| Year Team | Lg | G | GS | CG | GF | IP | BFP | H | R | ER | HR | SH | SF | HB | TBB | IBB | SO | WP | Bk | W | L | Pct. | ShO | Sv | ERA |
| 1986 Texas | AL | 31 | 31 | 0 | 0 | 157.2 | 741 | 130 | 104 | 96 | 18 | 3 | 9 | 3 | 143 | 2 | 174 | 22 | 3 | 11 | 9 | .550 | 0 | 0 | 5.48 |

| 1987 | Texas | AL | 26 | 25 | 1 | 0 | 143 | 673 | 114 | 82 | 78 | 10 | 5 | 5 | 3 | 140 | 1 | 160 | 7 | 2 | 8 | 10 | .444 | 0 | 0 | 4.91 |
|---|---|---|---|---|---|---|---|---|---|---|---|---|---|---|---|---|---|---|---|---|---|---|---|---|---|---|
| 1988 | Texas | AL | 22 | 22 | 13 | 0 | 174.1 | 736 | 134 | 83 | 76 | 13 | 7 | 6 | 1 | 101 | 2 | 148 | 16 | 8 | 8 | 10 | .444 | 2 | 0 | 3.92 |
| 1989 | Texas | AL | 31 | 31 | 5 | 0 | 194.1 | 869 | 182 | 123 | 111 | 14 | 11 | 8 | 2 | 114 | 3 | 166 | 7 | 4 | 12 | 13 | .480 | 1 | 0 | 5.14 |
| 1990 | Texas | AL | 33 | 32 | 7 | 1 | 222 | 954 | 197 | 98 | 83 | 12 | 5 | 6 | 4 | 110 | 3 | 221 | 11 | 2 | 17 | 10 | .630 | 1 | 0 | 3.36 |
| | 5 ML YEARS | | 143 | 141 | 26 | 1 | 891.1 | 3973 | 757 | 490 | 444 | 67 | 31 | 34 | 13 | 608 | 11 | 869 | 63 | 19 | 56 | 52 | .519 | 4 | 0 | 4.48 |

## Mike Witt

**Pitches:** Right **Bats:** Right **Pos:** SP/RP **Ht:** 6' 7" **Wt:** 198 **Born:** 07/20/60 **Age:** 30

| HOW MUCH HE PITCHED | | | | | | | | | WHAT HE GAVE UP | | | | | | | | | | | | THE RESULTS | | | | | |
|---|---|---|---|---|---|---|---|---|---|---|---|---|---|---|---|---|---|---|---|---|---|---|---|---|---|---|
| Year | Team | Lg | G | GS | CG | GF | IP | BFP | H | R | ER | HR | SH | SF | HB | TBB | IBB | SO | WP | Bk | W | L | Pct. | ShO | Sv | ERA |
| 1981 | California | AL | 22 | 21 | 7 | 1 | 129 | 555 | 123 | 60 | 47 | 9 | 3 | 4 | 11 | 47 | 4 | 75 | 2 | 0 | 8 | 9 | .471 | 1 | 0 | 3.28 |
| 1982 | California | AL | 33 | 26 | 5 | 2 | 179.2 | 748 | 177 | 77 | 70 | 8 | 8 | 5 | 7 | 47 | 2 | 85 | 8 | 1 | 8 | 6 | .571 | 1 | 0 | 3.51 |
| 1983 | California | AL | 43 | 19 | 2 | 15 | 154 | 683 | 173 | 90 | 84 | 14 | 5 | 7 | 6 | 75 | 7 | 77 | 8 | 0 | 7 | 14 | .333 | 0 | 5 | 4.91 |
| 1984 | California | AL | 34 | 34 | 9 | 0 | 246.2 | 1032 | 227 | 103 | 95 | 17 | 7 | 7 | 5 | 84 | 3 | 196 | 7 | 1 | 15 | 11 | .577 | 2 | 0 | 3.47 |
| 1985 | California | AL | 35 | 35 | 6 | 0 | 250 | 1049 | 228 | 115 | 99 | 22 | 4 | 5 | 4 | 98 | 6 | 180 | 11 | 1 | 15 | 9 | .625 | 1 | 0 | 3.56 |
| 1986 | California | AL | 34 | 34 | 14 | 0 | 269 | 1071 | 218 | 95 | 85 | 22 | 3 | 5 | 3 | 73 | 2 | 208 | 6 | 0 | 18 | 10 | .643 | 3 | 0 | 2.84 |
| 1987 | California | AL | 36 | 36 | 10 | 0 | 247 | 1065 | 252 | 128 | 110 | 34 | 6 | 6 | 4 | 84 | 4 | 192 | 6 | 0 | 16 | 14 | .533 | 0 | 0 | 4.01 |
| 1988 | California | AL | 34 | 34 | 12 | 0 | 249.2 | 1080 | 263 | 130 | 115 | 14 | 11 | 10 | 5 | 87 | 7 | 133 | 9 | 2 | 13 | 16 | .448 | 2 | 0 | 4.15 |
| 1989 | California | AL | 33 | 33 | 5 | 0 | 220 | 937 | 252 | 119 | 111 | 26 | 10 | 13 | 2 | 48 | 1 | 123 | 7 | 0 | 9 | 15 | .375 | 0 | 0 | 4.54 |
| 1990 | 2 ML Teams | | 26 | 16 | 2 | 4 | 117 | 498 | 106 | 62 | 52 | 9 | 1 | 6 | 5 | 47 | 4 | 74 | 7 | 0 | 5 | 9 | .357 | 1 | 1 | 4.00 |
| 1990 | California | AL | 10 | 0 | 0 | 4 | 20.1 | 92 | 19 | 9 | 4 | 1 | 1 | 1 | 1 | 13 | 2 | 14 | 1 | 0 | 0 | 3 | .000 | 0 | 1 | 1.77 |
| | New York | AL | 16 | 16 | 2 | 0 | 96.2 | 406 | 87 | 53 | 48 | 8 | 0 | 5 | 4 | 34 | 2 | 60 | 6 | 0 | 5 | 6 | .455 | 1 | 0 | 4.47 |
| | 10 ML YEARS | | 330 | 288 | 72 | 22 | 2062 | 8718 | 2019 | 979 | 868 | 175 | 58 | 68 | 52 | 690 | 40 | 1343 | 71 | 5 | 114 | 113 | .502 | 11 | 6 | 3.79 |

## Craig Worthington

**Bats:** Right **Throws:** Right **Pos:** 3B **Ht:** 6' 0" **Wt:** 190 **Born:** 04/17/65 **Age:** 26

| BATTING | | | | | | | | | | | | | | | | | | | | BASERUNNING | | | | PERCENTAGES | | |
|---|---|---|---|---|---|---|---|---|---|---|---|---|---|---|---|---|---|---|---|---|---|---|---|---|---|---|
| Year | Team | Lg | G | AB | H | 2B | 3B | HR | (Hm | Rd) | TB | R | RBI | TBB | IBB | SO | HBP | SH | SF | SB | CS | SB% | GDP | Avg | OBP | SLG |
| 1988 | Baltimore | AL | 26 | 81 | 15 | 2 | 0 | 2 | (0 | 2) | 23 | 5 | 4 | 9 | 0 | 24 | 0 | 0 | 0 | 1 | 0 | 1.00 | 2 | .185 | .267 | .284 |
| 1989 | Baltimore | AL | 145 | 497 | 123 | 23 | 0 | 15 | (12 | 3) | 191 | 57 | 70 | 61 | 2 | 114 | 4 | 3 | 1 | 1 | 2 | .33 | 10 | .247 | .334 | .384 |
| 1990 | Baltimore | AL | 133 | 425 | 96 | 17 | 0 | 8 | (3 | 5) | 137 | 46 | 44 | 63 | 2 | 96 | 3 | 7 | 3 | 1 | 2 | .33 | 13 | .226 | .328 | .322 |
| | 3 ML YEARS | | 304 | 1003 | 234 | 42 | 0 | 25 | (15 | 10) | 351 | 108 | 118 | 133 | 4 | 234 | 7 | 10 | 4 | 3 | 4 | .43 | 25 | .233 | .326 | .350 |

## Rick Wrona

**Bats:** Right **Throws:** Right **Pos:** C **Ht:** 6' 0" **Wt:** 180 **Born:** 12/10/63 **Age:** 27

| BATTING | | | | | | | | | | | | | | | | | | | | BASERUNNING | | | | PERCENTAGES | | |
|---|---|---|---|---|---|---|---|---|---|---|---|---|---|---|---|---|---|---|---|---|---|---|---|---|---|---|
| Year | Team | Lg | G | AB | H | 2B | 3B | HR | (Hm | Rd) | TB | R | RBI | TBB | IBB | SO | HBP | SH | SF | SB | CS | SB% | GDP | Avg | OBP | SLG |
| 1988 | Chicago | NL | 4 | 6 | 0 | 0 | 0 | 0 | (0 | 0) | 0 | 0 | 0 | 0 | 0 | 1 | 0 | 0 | 0 | 0 | 0 | .00 | 0 | .000 | .000 | .000 |
| 1989 | Chicago | NL | 38 | 92 | 26 | 2 | 1 | 2 | (0 | 2) | 36 | 11 | 14 | 2 | 1 | 21 | 1 | 0 | 2 | 0 | 0 | .00 | 1 | .283 | .299 | .391 |
| 1990 | Chicago | NL | 16 | 29 | 5 | 0 | 0 | 0 | (0 | 0) | 5 | 3 | 0 | 2 | 1 | 11 | 0 | 1 | 0 | 1 | 0 | 1.00 | 0 | .172 | .226 | .172 |
| | 3 ML YEARS | | 58 | 127 | 31 | 2 | 1 | 2 | (0 | 2) | 41 | 14 | 14 | 4 | 2 | 33 | 1 | 1 | 2 | 1 | 0 | 1.00 | 1 | .244 | .269 | .323 |

## Marvell Wynne

**Bats:** Left **Throws:** Left **Pos:** CF/LF **Ht:** 5'11" **Wt:** 185 **Born:** 12/17/59 **Age:** 31

| BATTING | | | | | | | | | | | | | | | | | | | | BASERUNNING | | | | PERCENTAGES | | |
|---|---|---|---|---|---|---|---|---|---|---|---|---|---|---|---|---|---|---|---|---|---|---|---|---|---|---|
| Year | Team | Lg | G | AB | H | 2B | 3B | HR | (Hm | Rd) | TB | R | RBI | TBB | IBB | SO | HBP | SH | SF | SB | CS | SB% | GDP | Avg | OBP | SLG |
| 1983 | Pittsburgh | NL | 103 | 366 | 89 | 16 | 2 | 7 | (3 | 4) | 130 | 66 | 26 | 38 | 0 | 52 | 3 | 7 | 1 | 12 | 10 | .55 | 3 | .243 | .319 | .355 |
| 1984 | Pittsburgh | NL | 154 | 653 | 174 | 24 | 11 | 0 | (0 | 0) | 220 | 77 | 39 | 42 | 0 | 81 | 0 | 5 | 2 | 24 | 19 | .56 | 8 | .266 | .310 | .337 |
| 1985 | Pittsburgh | NL | 103 | 337 | 69 | 6 | 3 | 2 | (1 | 1) | 87 | 21 | 18 | 18 | 2 | 48 | 1 | 7 | 0 | 10 | 5 | .67 | 8 | .205 | .247 | .258 |
| 1986 | San Diego | NL | 137 | 288 | 76 | 19 | 2 | 7 | (5 | 2) | 120 | 34 | 37 | 15 | 2 | 45 | 1 | 1 | 3 | 11 | 11 | .50 | 5 | .264 | .300 | .417 |
| 1987 | San Diego | NL | 98 | 188 | 47 | 8 | 2 | 2 | (2 | 0) | 65 | 17 | 24 | 20 | 1 | 37 | 0 | 4 | 1 | 11 | 6 | .65 | 5 | .250 | .321 | .346 |
| 1988 | San Diego | NL | 128 | 333 | 88 | 13 | 4 | 11 | (6 | 5) | 142 | 37 | 42 | 31 | 2 | 62 | 0 | 3 | 2 | 3 | 4 | .43 | 3 | .264 | .325 | .426 |
| 1989 | 2 ML Teams | | 125 | 342 | 83 | 13 | 2 | 7 | (3 | 4) | 121 | 27 | 39 | 13 | 2 | 48 | 2 | 7 | 1 | 6 | 1 | .86 | 3 | .243 | .274 | .354 |
| 1990 | Chicago | NL | 92 | 186 | 38 | 8 | 2 | 4 | (2 | 2) | 62 | 21 | 19 | 14 | 3 | 25 | 1 | 1 | 0 | 3 | 2 | .60 | 4 | .204 | .264 | .333 |
| 1989 | San Diego | NL | 105 | 294 | 74 | 11 | 1 | 6 | (3 | 3) | 105 | 19 | 35 | 12 | 1 | 41 | 1 | 6 | 1 | 4 | 1 | .80 | 3 | .252 | .282 | .357 |
| | Chicago | NL | 20 | 48 | 9 | 2 | 1 | 1 | (0 | 1) | 16 | 8 | 4 | 1 | 1 | 7 | 1 | 1 | 0 | 2 | 0 | 1.00 | 0 | .188 | .220 | .333 |
| | 8 ML YEARS | | 940 | 2693 | 664 | 107 | 28 | 40 | (22 | 18) | 947 | 300 | 244 | 191 | 12 | 398 | 8 | 35 | 10 | 80 | 58 | .58 | 39 | .247 | .297 | .352 |

## Eric Yelding

**Bats:** Right **Throws:** Right **Pos:** CF/SS **Ht:** 6' 1" **Wt:** 170 **Born:** 02/22/65 **Age:** 26

| BATTING | | | | | | | | | | | | | | | | | | | | BASERUNNING | | | | PERCENTAGES | | |
|---|---|---|---|---|---|---|---|---|---|---|---|---|---|---|---|---|---|---|---|---|---|---|---|---|---|---|
| Year | Team | Lg | G | AB | H | 2B | 3B | HR | (Hm | Rd) | TB | R | RBI | TBB | IBB | SO | HBP | SH | SF | SB | CS | SB% | GDP | Avg | OBP | SLG |
| 1984 | Medicne Hat | R | 67 | 304 | 94 | 14 | 6 | 4 | -- | -- | 132 | 61 | 29 | 26 | 0 | 46 | 0 | 0 | 2 | 31 | 11 | .74 | 3 | .309 | .361 | .434 |
| 1985 | Kinston | A | 135 | 526 | 137 | 14 | 4 | 2 | -- | -- | 165 | 59 | 31 | 33 | 0 | 70 | 4 | 5 | 3 | 62 | 26 | .70 | 4 | .260 | .307 | .314 |
| 1986 | Ventura | A | 131 | 560 | 157 | 14 | 7 | 4 | -- | -- | 197 | 83 | 40 | 33 | 3 | 84 | 0 | 6 | 2 | 41 | 18 | .69 | 6 | .280 | .319 | .352 |
| 1987 | Knoxville | AA | 39 | 150 | 30 | 6 | 1 | 0 | -- | -- | 38 | 23 | 7 | 12 | 0 | 25 | 1 | 1 | 1 | 10 | 5 | .67 | 4 | .200 | .262 | .253 |
| | Myrtle Bch | A | 88 | 357 | 109 | 12 | 2 | 1 | -- | -- | 128 | 53 | 31 | 18 | 0 | 30 | 4 | 1 | 4 | 73 | 13 | .85 | 5 | .305 | .342 | .359 |

| Year Team | Lg | G | AB | H | 2B | 3B | HR | (Hm | Rd) | TB | R | RBI | TBB | IBB | SO | HBP | SH | SF | SB | CS | SB% | GDP | Avg | OBP | SLG |
|---|---|---|---|---|---|---|---|---|---|---|---|---|---|---|---|---|---|---|---|---|---|---|---|---|---|
| 1988 Syracuse | AAA | 138 | 556 | 139 | 15 | 2 | 1 | -- | -- | 161 | 69 | 38 | 36 | 3 | 102 | 0 | 2 | 0 | 59 | 23 | .72 | 4 | .250 | .296 | .290 |
| 1989 Houston | NL | 70 | 90 | 21 | 2 | 0 | 0 | (0 | 0) | 23 | 19 | 9 | 7 | 0 | 19 | 1 | 2 | 2 | 11 | 5 | .69 | 2 | .233 | .290 | .256 |
| 1990 Houston | NL | 142 | 511 | 130 | 9 | 5 | 1 | (0 | 1) | 152 | 69 | 28 | 39 | 1 | 87 | 0 | 4 | 5 | 64 | 25 | .72 | 12 | .254 | .305 | .297 |
| 2 ML YEARS | | 212 | 601 | 151 | 11 | 5 | 1 | (0 | 1) | 175 | 88 | 37 | 46 | 1 | 106 | 1 | 6 | 7 | 75 | 30 | .71 | 14 | .251 | .302 | .291 |

## Richard Yett

**Pitches:** Right **Bats:** Right **Pos:** RP **Ht:** 6' 2" **Wt:** 187 **Born:** 10/06/62 **Age:** 28

| | | HOW MUCH HE PITCHED | | | | | | WHAT HE GAVE UP | | | | | | | | | | | | THE RESULTS | | | | | |
|---|---|---|---|---|---|---|---|---|---|---|---|---|---|---|---|---|---|---|---|---|---|---|---|---|---|
| Year Team | Lg | G | GS | CG | GF | IP | BFP | H | R | ER | HR | SH | SF | HB | TBB | IBB | SO | WP | Bk | W | L | Pct. | ShO | Sv | ERA |
| 1985 Minnesota | AL | 1 | 1 | 0 | 0 | 0.1 | 5 | 1 | 1 | 1 | 0 | 0 | 0 | 0 | 2 | 0 | 0 | 1 | 0 | 0 | 0 | .000 | 0 | 0 | 27.00 |
| 1986 Cleveland | AL | 39 | 3 | 1 | 17 | 78.2 | 350 | 84 | 48 | 45 | 10 | 2 | 4 | 1 | 37 | 4 | 50 | 8 | 0 | 5 | 3 | .625 | 1 | 1 | 5.15 |
| 1987 Cleveland | AL | 37 | 11 | 2 | 13 | 97.2 | 432 | 96 | 63 | 57 | 21 | 4 | 2 | 3 | 49 | 3 | 59 | 9 | 0 | 3 | 9 | .250 | 0 | 1 | 5.25 |
| 1988 Cleveland | AL | 23 | 22 | 0 | 0 | 134.1 | 590 | 146 | 72 | 69 | 11 | 2 | 1 | 1 | 55 | 1 | 71 | 4 | 3 | 9 | 6 | .600 | 0 | 0 | 4.62 |
| 1989 Cleveland | AL | 32 | 12 | 1 | 5 | 99 | 446 | 111 | 56 | 55 | 10 | 2 | 3 | 2 | 47 | 1 | 47 | 7 | 0 | 5 | 6 | .455 | 0 | 0 | 5.00 |
| 1990 Minnesota | AL | 4 | 0 | 0 | 0 | 4.1 | 19 | 6 | 2 | 1 | 1 | 1 | 0 | 0 | 1 | 1 | 2 | 0 | 0 | 0 | 0 | .000 | 0 | 0 | 2.08 |
| 6 ML YEARS | | 136 | 49 | 4 | 35 | 414.1 | 1842 | 444 | 242 | 228 | 53 | 11 | 10 | 7 | 191 | 10 | 229 | 29 | 3 | 22 | 24 | .478 | 1 | 2 | 4.95 |

## Mike York

**Pitches:** Right **Bats:** Right **Pos:** RP **Ht:** 6' 1" **Wt:** 192 **Born:** 09/06/64 **Age:** 26

| | | HOW MUCH HE PITCHED | | | | | | WHAT HE GAVE UP | | | | | | | | | | | | THE RESULTS | | | | | |
|---|---|---|---|---|---|---|---|---|---|---|---|---|---|---|---|---|---|---|---|---|---|---|---|---|---|
| Year Team | Lg | G | GS | CG | GF | IP | BFP | H | R | ER | HR | SH | SF | HB | TBB | IBB | SO | WP | Bk | W | L | Pct. | ShO | Sv | ERA |
| 1984 White Sox | R | 5 | 1 | 0 | 0 | 14.2 | 70 | 18 | 9 | 6 | 1 | 1 | 0 | 0 | 9 | 0 | 19 | 0 | 0 | 1 | 0 | 1.000 | 0 | 0 | 3.68 |
| 1985 Bristol | R | 21 | 0 | 0 | 18 | 38 | 168 | 24 | 12 | 10 | 1 | 5 | 2 | 2 | 34 | 2 | 31 | 6 | 1 | 9 | 2 | .818 | 0 | 2 | 2.37 |
| 1986 Lakeland | A | 16 | 0 | 0 | 13 | 40.2 | 214 | 49 | 42 | 29 | 2 | 1 | 3 | 3 | 43 | 0 | 29 | 9 | 0 | 1 | 3 | .250 | 0 | 1 | 6.42 |
| Gastonia | A | 22 | 0 | 0 | 20 | 34 | 153 | 26 | 15 | 13 | 0 | 3 | 6 | 2 | 27 | 1 | 27 | 5 | 0 | 2 | 2 | .500 | 0 | 9 | 3.44 |
| 1987 Macon | A | 28 | 28 | 3 | 0 | 165.2 | 700 | 129 | 71 | 56 | 11 | 5 | 3 | 2 | 88 | 1 | 169 | 9 | 3 | 17 | 6 | .739 | 2 | 0 | 3.04 |
| 1988 Salem | A | 13 | 13 | 2 | 0 | 84 | 360 | 65 | 31 | 25 | 3 | 2 | 2 | 1 | 52 | 0 | 77 | 5 | 4 | 9 | 2 | .818 | 1 | 0 | 2.68 |
| Harrisburg | AA | 13 | 13 | 2 | 0 | 82.1 | 381 | 92 | 43 | 34 | 5 | 5 | 5 | 1 | 45 | 2 | 61 | 3 | 2 | 0 | 5 | .000 | 0 | 0 | 3.72 |
| 1989 Harrisburg | AA | 18 | 18 | 3 | 0 | 121 | 492 | 105 | 37 | 31 | 6 | 1 | 5 | 2 | 40 | 2 | 106 | 8 | 0 | 11 | 5 | .688 | 2 | 0 | 2.31 |
| Buffalo | AAA | 8 | 8 | 0 | 0 | 41 | 193 | 48 | 29 | 27 | 3 | 2 | 0 | 1 | 25 | 0 | 28 | 1 | 0 | 1 | 3 | .250 | 0 | 0 | 5.93 |
| 1990 Buffalo | AAA | 27 | 26 | 3 | 0 | 158.2 | 707 | 165 | 87 | 74 | 6 | 7 | 2 | 5 | 78 | 2 | 130 | 7 | 5 | 8 | 7 | .533 | 1 | 0 | 4.20 |
| 1990 Pittsburgh | NL | 4 | 1 | 0 | 0 | 12.2 | 56 | 13 | 5 | 4 | 0 | 2 | 1 | 1 | 5 | 0 | 4 | 0 | 1 | 1 | 1 | .500 | 0 | 0 | 2.84 |

## Cliff Young

**Pitches:** Left **Bats:** Left **Pos:** RP **Ht:** 6' 4" **Wt:** 200 **Born:** 08/02/64 **Age:** 26

| | | HOW MUCH HE PITCHED | | | | | | WHAT HE GAVE UP | | | | | | | | | | | | THE RESULTS | | | | | |
|---|---|---|---|---|---|---|---|---|---|---|---|---|---|---|---|---|---|---|---|---|---|---|---|---|---|
| Year Team | Lg | G | GS | CG | GF | IP | BFP | H | R | ER | HR | SH | SF | HB | TBB | IBB | SO | WP | Bk | W | L | Pct. | ShO | Sv | ERA |
| 1984 Gastonia | A | 24 | 24 | 7 | 0 | 144.1 | 614 | 117 | 77 | 67 | 10 | 7 | 7 | 1 | 68 | 2 | 121 | 9 | 0 | 8 | 10 | .444 | 2 | 0 | 4.18 |
| 1985 Wst Plm Bch | A | 25 | 25 | 7 | 0 | 153.2 | 664 | 149 | 77 | 68 | 13 | 3 | 6 | 6 | 57 | 0 | 112 | 6 | 4 | 15 | 5 | .750 | 0 | 0 | 3.98 |
| 1986 Knoxville | AA | 31 | 31 | 1 | 0 | 203.2 | 880 | 232 | 111 | 88 | 25 | 3 | 4 | 2 | 71 | 1 | 121 | 3 | 5 | 12 | 14 | .462 | 0 | 0 | 3.89 |
| 1987 Knoxville | AA | 42 | 12 | 0 | 10 | 119.1 | 541 | 148 | 76 | 59 | 15 | 5 | 4 | 3 | 43 | 5 | 81 | 12 | 2 | 8 | 9 | .471 | 0 | 1 | 4.45 |
| 1988 Syracuse | AAA | 33 | 18 | 4 | 7 | 147.1 | 608 | 133 | 68 | 56 | 13 | 2 | 5 | 3 | 32 | 0 | 75 | 3 | 4 | 9 | 6 | .600 | 1 | 1 | 3.42 |
| 1989 Edmonton | AAA | 31 | 21 | 2 | 3 | 139 | 591 | 158 | 80 | 74 | 16 | 6 | 4 | 5 | 32 | 1 | 89 | 3 | 4 | 8 | 9 | .471 | 1 | 0 | 4.79 |
| 1990 Edmonton | AAA | 30 | 0 | 0 | 14 | 52 | 208 | 45 | 15 | 14 | 1 | 6 | 1 | 1 | 10 | 1 | 30 | 0 | 2 | 7 | 4 | .636 | 0 | 4 | 2.42 |
| 1990 California | AL | 17 | 0 | 0 | 5 | 30.2 | 137 | 40 | 14 | 12 | 2 | 2 | 4 | 1 | 7 | 1 | 19 | 1 | 0 | 1 | 1 | .500 | 0 | 0 | 3.52 |

## Curt Young

**Pitches:** Left **Bats:** Right **Pos:** SP/RP **Ht:** 6' 1" **Wt:** 175 **Born:** 04/16/60 **Age:** 31

| | | HOW MUCH HE PITCHED | | | | | | WHAT HE GAVE UP | | | | | | | | | | | | THE RESULTS | | | | | |
|---|---|---|---|---|---|---|---|---|---|---|---|---|---|---|---|---|---|---|---|---|---|---|---|---|---|
| Year Team | Lg | G | GS | CG | GF | IP | BFP | H | R | ER | HR | SH | SF | HB | TBB | IBB | SO | WP | Bk | W | L | Pct. | ShO | Sv | ERA |
| 1983 Oakland | AL | 8 | 2 | 0 | 0 | 9 | 50 | 17 | 17 | 16 | 1 | 0 | 0 | 1 | 5 | 0 | 5 | 1 | 0 | 0 | 1 | .000 | 0 | 0 | 16.00 |
| 1984 Oakland | AL | 20 | 17 | 2 | 0 | 108.2 | 475 | 118 | 53 | 49 | 9 | 1 | 4 | 8 | 31 | 0 | 41 | 3 | 0 | 9 | 4 | .692 | 1 | 0 | 4.06 |
| 1985 Oakland | AL | 19 | 7 | 0 | 5 | 46 | 214 | 57 | 38 | 37 | 15 | 0 | 1 | 1 | 22 | 0 | 19 | 1 | 0 | 0 | 4 | .000 | 0 | 0 | 7.24 |
| 1986 Oakland | AL | 29 | 27 | 5 | 0 | 198 | 826 | 176 | 88 | 76 | 19 | 8 | 9 | 7 | 57 | 1 | 116 | 7 | 2 | 13 | 9 | .591 | 2 | 0 | 3.45 |
| 1987 Oakland | AL | 31 | 31 | 6 | 0 | 203 | 828 | 194 | 102 | 92 | 38 | 6 | 4 | 3 | 44 | 0 | 124 | 2 | 1 | 13 | 7 | .650 | 0 | 0 | 4.08 |
| 1988 Oakland | AL | 26 | 26 | 1 | 0 | 156.1 | 651 | 162 | 77 | 72 | 23 | 3 | 5 | 4 | 50 | 3 | 69 | 3 | 6 | 11 | 8 | .579 | 0 | 0 | 4.14 |
| 1989 Oakland | AL | 25 | 20 | 1 | 2 | 111 | 495 | 117 | 56 | 46 | 10 | 1 | 0 | 3 | 47 | 2 | 55 | 4 | 4 | 5 | 9 | .357 | 0 | 0 | 3.73 |
| 1990 Oakland | AL | 26 | 21 | 0 | 0 | 124.1 | 527 | 124 | 70 | 67 | 17 | 4 | 2 | 2 | 53 | 1 | 56 | 3 | 0 | 9 | 6 | .600 | 0 | 0 | 4.85 |
| 8 ML YEARS | | 184 | 151 | 15 | 7 | 956.1 | 4066 | 965 | 501 | 455 | 132 | 23 | 25 | 29 | 309 | 7 | 485 | 24 | 13 | 60 | 48 | .556 | 3 | 0 | 4.28 |

## Gerald Young

**Bats:** Both **Throws:** Right **Pos:** CF **Ht:** 6' 2" **Wt:** 185 **Born:** 10/22/64 **Age:** 26

| | | BATTING | | | | | | | | | | | | | | | | | BASERUNNING | | | | PERCENTAGES | | |
|---|---|---|---|---|---|---|---|---|---|---|---|---|---|---|---|---|---|---|---|---|---|---|---|---|---|
| Year Team | Lg | G | AB | H | 2B | 3B | HR | (Hm | Rd) | TB | R | RBI | TBB | IBB | SO | HBP | SH | SF | SB | CS | SB% | GDP | Avg | OBP | SLG |
| 1987 Houston | NL | 71 | 274 | 88 | 9 | 2 | 1 | (0 | 1) | 104 | 44 | 15 | 26 | 0 | 27 | 1 | 0 | 2 | 26 | 9 | .74 | 1 | .321 | .380 | .380 |
| 1988 Houston | NL | 149 | 576 | 148 | 21 | 9 | 0 | (0 | 0) | 187 | 79 | 37 | 66 | 1 | 66 | 3 | 5 | 5 | 65 | 27 | .71 | 10 | .257 | .334 | .325 |

| | | | | | | | | | | | | | | | | | | | | | | | | | | |
|---|---|---|---|---|---|---|---|---|---|---|---|---|---|---|---|---|---|---|---|---|---|---|---|---|---|---|
| 1989 Houston | NL | 146 | 533 | 124 | 17 | 3 | 0 | (0 | 0) | 147 | 71 | 38 | 74 | 4 | 60 | 2 | 6 | 5 | 34 | 25 | .58 | 7 | .233 | .326 | .276 |
| 1990 Houston | NL | 57 | 154 | 27 | 4 | 1 | 1 | (1 | 0) | 36 | 15 | 4 | 20 | 0 | 23 | 0 | 4 | 1 | 6 | 3 | .67 | 3 | .175 | .269 | .234 |
| 4 ML YEARS | | 423 | 1537 | 387 | 51 | 15 | 2 | (1 | 1) | 474 | 209 | 94 | 186 | 5 | 176 | 6 | 15 | 13 | 131 | 64 | .67 | 21 | .252 | .332 | .308 |

## Matt Young

**Pitches:** Left **Bats:** Left **Pos:** SP **Ht:** 6' 3" **Wt:** 205 **Born:** 08/09/58 **Age:** 32

| HOW MUCH HE PITCHED | | | | | | | | WHAT HE GAVE UP | | | | | | | | | | | | THE RESULTS | | | | | |
|---|---|---|---|---|---|---|---|---|---|---|---|---|---|---|---|---|---|---|---|---|---|---|---|---|---|
| Year Team | Lg | G | GS | CG | GF | IP | BFP | H | R | ER | HR | SH | SF | HB | TBB | IBB | SO | WP | Bk | W | L | Pct. | ShO | Sv | ERA |
| 1983 Seattle | AL | 33 | 32 | 5 | 0 | 203.2 | 851 | 178 | 86 | 74 | 17 | 4 | 8 | 7 | 79 | 2 | 130 | 4 | 2 | 11 | 15 | .423 | 2 | 0 | 3.27 |
| 1984 Seattle | AL | 22 | 22 | 1 | 0 | 113.1 | 524 | 141 | 81 | 72 | 11 | 1 | 5 | 1 | 57 | 3 | 73 | 3 | 1 | 6 | 8 | .429 | 0 | 0 | 5.72 |
| 1985 Seattle | AL | 37 | 35 | 5 | 2 | 218.1 | 951 | 242 | 135 | 119 | 23 | 7 | 3 | 7 | 76 | 3 | 136 | 6 | 2 | 12 | 19 | .387 | 2 | 1 | 4.91 |
| 1986 Seattle | AL | 65 | 5 | 1 | 32 | 103.2 | 458 | 108 | 50 | 44 | 9 | 4 | 3 | 8 | 46 | 2 | 82 | 7 | 1 | 8 | 6 | .571 | 0 | 13 | 3.82 |
| 1987 Los Angeles | NL | 47 | 0 | 0 | 31 | 54.1 | 234 | 62 | 30 | 27 | 3 | 1 | 1 | 0 | 17 | 5 | 42 | 3 | 0 | 5 | 8 | .385 | 0 | 11 | 4.47 |
| 1989 Oakland | AL | 26 | 4 | 0 | 1 | 37.1 | 183 | 42 | 31 | 28 | 2 | 4 | 1 | 0 | 31 | 2 | 27 | 5 | 0 | 1 | 4 | .200 | 0 | 0 | 6.75 |
| 1990 Seattle | AL | 34 | 33 | 7 | 0 | 225.1 | 963 | 198 | 106 | 88 | 15 | 7 | 7 | 6 | 107 | 7 | 176 | 16 | 0 | 8 | 18 | .308 | 1 | 0 | 3.51 |
| 7 ML YEARS | | 264 | 131 | 19 | 66 | 956 | 4164 | 971 | 519 | 452 | 80 | 28 | 28 | 29 | 413 | 24 | 666 | 44 | 6 | 51 | 78 | .395 | 5 | 25 | 4.26 |

## Robin Yount

**Bats:** Right **Throws:** Right **Pos:** CF **Ht:** 6' 0" **Wt:** 180 **Born:** 09/16/55 **Age:** 35

| BATTING | | | | | | | | | | | | | | | | | | | BASERUNNING | | | | PERCENTAGES | | |
|---|---|---|---|---|---|---|---|---|---|---|---|---|---|---|---|---|---|---|---|---|---|---|---|---|---|
| Year Team | Lg | G | AB | H | 2B | 3B | HR | (Hm | Rd) | TB | R | RBI | TBB | IBB | SO | HBP | SH | SF | SB | CS | SB% | GDP | Avg | OBP | SLG |
| 1974 Milwaukee | AL | 107 | 344 | 86 | 14 | 5 | 3 | (3 | 0) | 119 | 48 | 26 | 12 | 0 | 46 | 1 | 5 | 2 | 7 | 7 | .50 | 4 | .250 | .276 | .346 |
| 1975 Milwaukee | AL | 147 | 558 | 149 | 28 | 2 | 8 | (4 | 4) | 205 | 67 | 52 | 33 | 3 | 69 | 1 | 10 | 5 | 12 | 4 | .75 | 8 | .267 | .307 | .367 |
| 1976 Milwaukee | AL | 161 | 638 | 161 | 19 | 3 | 2 | (1 | 1) | 192 | 59 | 54 | 38 | 3 | 69 | 0 | 8 | 6 | 16 | 11 | .59 | 13 | .252 | .292 | .301 |
| 1977 Milwaukee | AL | 154 | 605 | 174 | 34 | 4 | 4 | (2 | 2) | 228 | 66 | 49 | 41 | 1 | 80 | 2 | 11 | 4 | 16 | 7 | .70 | 11 | .288 | .333 | .377 |
| 1978 Milwaukee | AL | 127 | 502 | 147 | 23 | 9 | 9 | (5 | 4) | 215 | 66 | 71 | 24 | 1 | 43 | 1 | 13 | 5 | 16 | 5 | .76 | 5 | .293 | .323 | .428 |
| 1979 Milwaukee | AL | 149 | 577 | 154 | 26 | 5 | 8 | (4 | 4) | 214 | 72 | 51 | 35 | 3 | 52 | 1 | 10 | 3 | 11 | 8 | .58 | 15 | .267 | .308 | .371 |
| 1980 Milwaukee | AL | 143 | 611 | 179 | 49 | 10 | 23 | (13 | 10) | 317 | 121 | 87 | 26 | 1 | 67 | 1 | 6 | 3 | 20 | 5 | .80 | 8 | .293 | .321 | .519 |
| 1981 Milwaukee | AL | 96 | 377 | 103 | 15 | 5 | 10 | (1 | 9) | 158 | 50 | 49 | 22 | 1 | 37 | 2 | 4 | 6 | 4 | 1 | .80 | 4 | .273 | .312 | .419 |
| 1982 Milwaukee | AL | 156 | 635 | 210 | 46 | 12 | 29 | (9 | 20) | 367 | 129 | 114 | 54 | 2 | 63 | 1 | 4 | 10 | 14 | 3 | .82 | 19 | .331 | .379 | .578 |
| 1983 Milwaukee | AL | 149 | 578 | 178 | 42 | 10 | 17 | (6 | 11) | 291 | 102 | 80 | 72 | 6 | 58 | 3 | 1 | 8 | 12 | 5 | .71 | 11 | .308 | .383 | .503 |
| 1984 Milwaukee | AL | 160 | 624 | 186 | 27 | 7 | 16 | (8 | 8) | 275 | 105 | 80 | 67 | 7 | 67 | 1 | 1 | 9 | 14 | 4 | .78 | 22 | .298 | .362 | .441 |
| 1985 Milwaukee | AL | 122 | 466 | 129 | 26 | 3 | 15 | (11 | 4) | 206 | 76 | 68 | 49 | 3 | 56 | 2 | 1 | 9 | 10 | 4 | .71 | 8 | .277 | .342 | .442 |
| 1986 Milwaukee | AL | 140 | 522 | 163 | 31 | 7 | 9 | (4 | 5) | 235 | 82 | 46 | 62 | 7 | 73 | 4 | 5 | 2 | 14 | 5 | .74 | 9 | .312 | .388 | .450 |
| 1987 Milwaukee | AL | 158 | 635 | 198 | 25 | 9 | 21 | (12 | 9) | 304 | 99 | 103 | 76 | 10 | 94 | 1 | 6 | 5 | 19 | 9 | .68 | 9 | .312 | .384 | .479 |
| 1988 Milwaukee | AL | 162 | 621 | 190 | 38 | 11 | 13 | (7 | 6) | 289 | 92 | 91 | 63 | 10 | 63 | 3 | 2 | 7 | 22 | 4 | .85 | 21 | .306 | .369 | .465 |
| 1989 Milwaukee | AL | 160 | 614 | 195 | 38 | 9 | 21 | (14 | 7) | 314 | 101 | 103 | 63 | 9 | 71 | 6 | 3 | 4 | 19 | 3 | .86 | 9 | .318 | .384 | .511 |
| 1990 Milwaukee | AL | 158 | 587 | 145 | 17 | 5 | 17 | (8 | 9) | 223 | 98 | 77 | 78 | 6 | 89 | 6 | 4 | 8 | 15 | 8 | .65 | 7 | .247 | .337 | .380 |
| 17 ML YEARS | | 2449 | 9494 | 2747 | 498 | 116 | 225 | (112 | 113) | 4152 | 1433 | 1201 | 815 | 73 | 1097 | 36 | 94 | 96 | 241 | 93 | .72 | 183 | .289 | .345 | .437 |

## Todd Zeile

**Bats:** Right **Throws:** Right **Pos:** C/1B/3B **Ht:** 6' 1" **Wt:** 190 **Born:** 09/09/65 **Age:** 25

| BATTING | | | | | | | | | | | | | | | | | | | BASERUNNING | | | | PERCENTAGES | | |
|---|---|---|---|---|---|---|---|---|---|---|---|---|---|---|---|---|---|---|---|---|---|---|---|---|---|
| Year Team | Lg | G | AB | H | 2B | 3B | HR | (Hm | Rd) | TB | R | RBI | TBB | IBB | SO | HBP | SH | SF | SB | CS | SB% | GDP | Avg | OBP | SLG |
| 1986 Erie | A | 70 | 248 | 64 | 14 | 1 | 14 | -- | -- | 122 | 40 | 63 | 37 | 1 | 52 | 2 | 1 | 6 | 5 | 1 | .83 | 3 | .258 | .352 | .492 |
| 1987 Springfield | A | 130 | 487 | 142 | 24 | 4 | 25 | -- | -- | 249 | 94 | 106 | 70 | 7 | 85 | 1 | 0 | 3 | 1 | 3 | .25 | 10 | .292 | .380 | .511 |
| 1988 Arkansas | AA | 129 | 430 | 117 | 33 | 2 | 19 | -- | -- | 211 | 95 | 75 | 83 | 8 | 64 | 1 | 0 | 4 | 6 | 5 | .55 | 11 | .272 | .388 | .491 |
| 1989 Louisville | AAA | 118 | 453 | 131 | 26 | 3 | 19 | -- | -- | 220 | 71 | 85 | 45 | 1 | 78 | 1 | 0 | 7 | 0 | 1 | .00 | 10 | .289 | .350 | .486 |
| 1989 St. Louis | NL | 28 | 82 | 21 | 3 | 1 | 1 | (0 | 1) | 29 | 7 | 8 | 9 | 1 | 14 | 0 | 1 | 1 | 0 | 0 | .00 | 1 | .256 | .326 | .354 |
| 1990 St. Louis | NL | 144 | 495 | 121 | 25 | 3 | 15 | (8 | 7) | 197 | 62 | 57 | 67 | 3 | 77 | 2 | 0 | 6 | 2 | 4 | .33 | 11 | .244 | .333 | .398 |
| 2 ML YEARS | | 172 | 577 | 142 | 28 | 4 | 16 | (8 | 8) | 226 | 69 | 65 | 76 | 4 | 91 | 2 | 1 | 7 | 2 | 4 | .33 | 12 | .246 | .332 | .392 |

# 1990 Team Stats

## American League Batting

| BATTING | | | | | | | | | | | | | | | | | | BASERUNNING | | | | PERCENTAGES | | |
|---|---|---|---|---|---|---|---|---|---|---|---|---|---|---|---|---|---|---|---|---|---|---|---|---|
| Team | G | AB | H | 2B | 3B | HR | (Hm | Rd) | TB | R | RBI | TBB | IBB | SO | HBP | SH | SF | SB | CS | SB% | GDP | Avg | OBP | SLG |
| Toronto | 162 | 5589 | 1479 | 263 | 50 | 167 | (93 | 74) | 2343 | 767 | 729 | 526 | 35 | 970 | 28 | 18 | 62 | 111 | 52 | .68 | 125 | .265 | .328 | .419 |
| Detroit | 162 | 5479 | 1418 | 241 | 32 | 172 | (92 | 80) | 2239 | 750 | 714 | 634 | 44 | 952 | 34 | 36 | 41 | 82 | 57 | .59 | 139 | .259 | .337 | .409 |
| Oakland | 162 | 5433 | 1379 | 209 | 22 | 164 | (69 | 95) | 2124 | 733 | 693 | 651 | 38 | 992 | 46 | 60 | 48 | 141 | 54 | .72 | 123 | .254 | .336 | .391 |
| Cleveland | 162 | 5485 | 1465 | 266 | 41 | 110 | (52 | 58) | 2143 | 732 | 675 | 458 | 33 | 836 | 29 | 54 | 61 | 107 | 52 | .67 | 123 | .267 | .324 | .391 |
| Milwaukee | 162 | 5503 | 1408 | 247 | 36 | 128 | (60 | 68) | 2111 | 732 | 680 | 519 | 46 | 821 | 33 | 59 | 71 | 164 | 72 | .69 | 101 | .256 | .320 | .384 |
| Kansas City | 161 | 5488 | 1465 | 316 | 44 | 100 | (42 | 58) | 2169 | 707 | 660 | 498 | 32 | 879 | 27 | 31 | 54 | 107 | 62 | .63 | 132 | .267 | .328 | .395 |
| Boston | 162 | 5516 | 1502 | 298 | 31 | 106 | (61 | 45) | 2180 | 699 | 660 | 598 | 59 | 795 | 28 | 48 | 44 | 53 | 52 | .50 | 174 | .272 | .344 | .395 |
| California | 162 | 5570 | 1448 | 237 | 27 | 147 | (89 | 58) | 2180 | 690 | 646 | 566 | 41 | 1000 | 28 | 58 | 45 | 69 | 43 | .62 | 144 | .260 | .329 | .391 |
| Chicago | 162 | 5402 | 1393 | 251 | 44 | 106 | (41 | 65) | 2050 | 682 | 637 | 478 | 50 | 903 | 36 | 75 | 47 | 140 | 90 | .61 | 112 | .258 | .320 | .379 |
| Texas | 162 | 5469 | 1416 | 257 | 27 | 110 | (64 | 46) | 2057 | 676 | 641 | 575 | 45 | 1054 | 34 | 54 | 44 | 115 | 48 | .71 | 142 | .259 | .331 | .376 |
| Baltimore | 161 | 5410 | 1328 | 234 | 22 | 132 | (74 | 58) | 2002 | 669 | 623 | 660 | 50 | 962 | 40 | 72 | 41 | 94 | 52 | .64 | 132 | .245 | .330 | .370 |
| Minnesota | 162 | 5499 | 1458 | 281 | 39 | 100 | (46 | 54) | 2117 | 666 | 625 | 445 | 32 | 749 | 53 | 40 | 49 | 96 | 53 | .64 | 149 | .265 | .324 | .385 |
| Seattle | 162 | 5474 | 1419 | 251 | 26 | 107 | (49 | 58) | 2043 | 640 | 610 | 596 | 41 | 749 | 40 | 41 | 54 | 105 | 51 | .67 | 140 | .259 | .333 | .373 |
| New York | 162 | 5483 | 1322 | 208 | 19 | 147 | (64 | 83) | 2009 | 603 | 561 | 427 | 41 | 1027 | 53 | 37 | 36 | 119 | 45 | .73 | 114 | .241 | .300 | .366 |
| American | 2266 | 76800 | 19900 | 3559 | 460 | 1796 | (896 | 900) | 29767 | 9746 | 9154 | 7631 | 587 | 12689 | 509 | 683 | 697 | 1503 | 783 | .66 | 1850 | .259 | .327 | .388 |

## American League Pitching

| HOW MUCH THEY PITCHED | | | | | | | WHAT THEY GAVE UP | | | | | | | | | | | | THE RESULTS | | | | | |
|---|---|---|---|---|---|---|---|---|---|---|---|---|---|---|---|---|---|---|---|---|---|---|---|---|
| Team | G | GS | CG | GF | IP | BFP | H | R | ER | HR | SH | SF | HB | TBB | IBB | SO | WP | Bk | W | L | Pct. | ShO | Sv | ERA |
| Oakland | 162 | 162 | 18 | 162 | 1456 | 6020 | 1287 | 570 | 514 | 123 | 40 | 50 | 27 | 494 | 19 | 831 | 50 | 7 | 103 | 59 | .636 | 16 | 64 | 3.18 |
| Chicago | 162 | 162 | 17 | 162 | 1449.1 | 6073 | 1313 | 633 | 581 | 106 | 52 | 46 | 39 | 548 | 27 | 914 | 35 | 11 | 94 | 68 | .580 | 10 | 68 | 3.61 |
| Toronto | 162 | 162 | 6 | 162 | 1454 | 6092 | 1434 | 661 | 620 | 143 | 48 | 38 | 37 | 445 | 44 | 892 | 43 | 5 | 86 | 76 | .531 | 9 | 48 | 3.84 |
| Boston | 162 | 162 | 15 | 162 | 1442 | 6174 | 1439 | 664 | 596 | 92 | 47 | 46 | 45 | 519 | 47 | 997 | 62 | 6 | 88 | 74 | .543 | 13 | 44 | 3.72 |
| Seattle | 162 | 162 | 21 | 162 | 1443.1 | 6165 | 1319 | 680 | 592 | 120 | 48 | 50 | 41 | 606 | 55 | 1064 | 69 | 12 | 77 | 85 | .475 | 7 | 41 | 3.69 |
| Texas | 162 | 162 | 25 | 162 | 1444.2 | 6181 | 1343 | 696 | 615 | 113 | 37 | 57 | 44 | 623 | 39 | 997 | 61 | 6 | 83 | 79 | .512 | 9 | 36 | 3.83 |
| Baltimore | 161 | 161 | 10 | 161 | 1435.1 | 6141 | 1445 | 698 | 644 | 161 | 52 | 56 | 16 | 537 | 43 | 776 | 34 | 10 | 76 | 85 | .472 | 5 | 43 | 4.04 |
| California | 162 | 162 | 21 | 162 | 1454 | 6223 | 1482 | 706 | 613 | 106 | 47 | 46 | 38 | 544 | 25 | 944 | 50 | 6 | 80 | 82 | .494 | 13 | 42 | 3.79 |
| Kansas City | 161 | 161 | 18 | 161 | 1420.2 | 6193 | 1449 | 709 | 621 | 116 | 48 | 44 | 46 | 560 | 45 | 1006 | 59 | 5 | 75 | 86 | .466 | 8 | 33 | 3.93 |
| Minnesota | 162 | 162 | 13 | 162 | 1435.2 | 6140 | 1509 | 729 | 658 | 134 | 47 | 46 | 27 | 489 | 40 | 872 | 55 | 5 | 74 | 88 | .457 | 13 | 43 | 4.12 |
| Cleveland | 162 | 162 | 12 | 162 | 1427.1 | 6184 | 1491 | 737 | 676 | 163 | 50 | 50 | 40 | 518 | 38 | 860 | 50 | 8 | 77 | 85 | .475 | 10 | 47 | 4.26 |
| New York | 162 | 162 | 15 | 162 | 1444.2 | 6227 | 1430 | 749 | 676 | 144 | 60 | 48 | 26 | 618 | 40 | 909 | 83 | 6 | 67 | 95 | .414 | 6 | 41 | 4.21 |
| Detroit | 162 | 162 | 15 | 162 | 1430.1 | 6230 | 1401 | 754 | 697 | 154 | 57 | 57 | 45 | 661 | 86 | 856 | 76 | 7 | 79 | 83 | .488 | 12 | 45 | 4.39 |
| Milwaukee | 162 | 162 | 23 | 162 | 1445 | 6284 | 1558 | 760 | 655 | 121 | 50 | 63 | 38 | 469 | 39 | 771 | 47 | 7 | 74 | 88 | .457 | 13 | 42 | 4.08 |
| American | 2266 | 2266 | 229 | 2266 | 20182.1 | 86327 | 19900 | 9746 | 8758 | 1796 | 683 | 697 | 509 | 7631 | 587 | 12689 | 774 | 101 | 1133 | 1133 | .500 | 144 | 637 | 3.91 |

## National League Batting

| | BATTING | | | | | | | | | | | | | | | | | | BASERUNNING | | | | PERCENTAGES | | |
|---|---|---|---|---|---|---|---|---|---|---|---|---|---|---|---|---|---|---|---|---|---|---|---|---|---|
| Team | G | AB | H | 2B | 3B | HR | (Hm | Rd) | TB | R | RBI | TBB | IBB | SO | HBP | SH | SF | SB | CS | SB% | GDP | Avg | OBP | SLG |
| New York | 162 | 5504 | 1410 | 278 | 21 | 172 | (85 | 87) | 2246 | 775 | 734 | 536 | 65 | 851 | 32 | 54 | 56 | 110 | 33 | .77 | 89 | .256 | .323 | .408 |
| Pittsburgh | 162 | 5388 | 1395 | 288 | 42 | 138 | (59 | 79) | 2181 | 733 | 693 | 582 | 64 | 914 | 24 | 96 | 66 | 137 | 52 | .72 | 114 | .259 | .330 | .405 |
| Los Angeles | 162 | 5491 | 1436 | 222 | 27 | 129 | (53 | 76) | 2099 | 728 | 669 | 538 | 78 | 952 | 31 | 71 | 48 | 141 | 65 | .68 | 111 | .262 | .328 | .382 |
| San Francisco | 162 | 5573 | 1459 | 221 | 35 | 152 | (81 | 71) | 2206 | 719 | 681 | 488 | 61 | 973 | 33 | 76 | 45 | 109 | 56 | .66 | 84 | .262 | .323 | .396 |
| Cincinnati | 162 | 5525 | 1466 | 284 | 40 | 125 | (70 | 55) | 2205 | 693 | 644 | 466 | 73 | 913 | 42 | 88 | 42 | 166 | 66 | .72 | 99 | .265 | .325 | .399 |
| Chicago | 162 | 5600 | 1474 | 240 | 36 | 136 | (75 | 61) | 2194 | 690 | 649 | 406 | 68 | 869 | 30 | 61 | 51 | 151 | 50 | .75 | 100 | .263 | .314 | .392 |
| Atlanta | 162 | 5504 | 1376 | 263 | 26 | 162 | (83 | 79) | 2177 | 682 | 636 | 473 | 37 | 1010 | 27 | 49 | 31 | 92 | 55 | .63 | 102 | .250 | .311 | .396 |
| San Diego | 162 | 5554 | 1429 | 243 | 35 | 123 | (63 | 60) | 2111 | 673 | 628 | 509 | 75 | 902 | 28 | 79 | 48 | 138 | 59 | .70 | 117 | .257 | .320 | .380 |
| Montreal | 162 | 5452 | 1363 | 227 | 43 | 114 | (48 | 66) | 2018 | 662 | 607 | 576 | 67 | 1024 | 26 | 88 | 47 | 235 | 99 | .70 | 96 | .250 | .322 | .370 |
| Philadelphia | 162 | 5535 | 1410 | 237 | 27 | 103 | (47 | 56) | 2010 | 646 | 619 | 582 | 92 | 915 | 30 | 59 | 39 | 108 | 35 | .76 | 115 | .255 | .327 | .363 |
| St. Louis | 162 | 5462 | 1398 | 255 | 41 | 73 | (43 | 30) | 1954 | 599 | 554 | 517 | 54 | 844 | 21 | 77 | 50 | 221 | 74 | .75 | 101 | .256 | .320 | .358 |
| Houston | 162 | 5379 | 1301 | 209 | 32 | 94 | (35 | 59) | 1856 | 573 | 536 | 548 | 64 | 997 | 28 | 79 | 41 | 179 | 83 | .68 | 107 | .242 | .313 | .345 |
| National | 1944 | 65967 | 16917 | 2967 | 405 | 1521 | (742 | 779) | 25257 | 8173 | 7650 | 6221 | 798 | 11164 | 352 | 877 | 564 | 1787 | 727 | .71 | 1235 | .256 | .321 | .383 |

## National League Pitching

| | HOW MUCH THEY PITCHED | | | | | | WHAT THEY GAVE UP | | | | | | | | | | | | THE RESULTS | | | | | |
|---|---|---|---|---|---|---|---|---|---|---|---|---|---|---|---|---|---|---|---|---|---|---|---|---|
| Team | G | GS | CG | GF | IP | BFP | H | R | ER | HR | SH | SF | HB | TBB | IBB | SO | WP | Bk | W | L | Pct. | ShO | Sv | ERA |
| Cincinnati | 162 | 162 | 14 | 162 | 1456.1 | 6128 | 1338 | 597 | 549 | 124 | 64 | 37 | 34 | 543 | 61 | 1029 | 48 | 26 | 91 | 71 | .562 | 12 | 50 | 3.39 |
| Montreal | 162 | 162 | 18 | 162 | 1473.1 | 6173 | 1349 | 598 | 551 | 127 | 69 | 48 | 38 | 510 | 76 | 991 | 27 | 13 | 85 | 77 | .525 | 11 | 50 | 3.37 |
| New York | 162 | 162 | 18 | 162 | 1440 | 6009 | 1339 | 613 | 548 | 119 | 53 | 41 | 27 | 444 | 35 | 1217 | 51 | 14 | 91 | 71 | .562 | 14 | 41 | 3.43 |
| Pittsburgh | 162 | 162 | 18 | 162 | 1447 | 5997 | 1367 | 619 | 546 | 135 | 68 | 38 | 30 | 413 | 48 | 848 | 42 | 22 | 95 | 67 | .586 | 8 | 43 | 3.40 |
| Houston | 162 | 162 | 12 | 162 | 1450 | 6143 | 1396 | 656 | 581 | 130 | 67 | 61 | 38 | 496 | 74 | 854 | 36 | 15 | 75 | 87 | .463 | 6 | 37 | 3.61 |
| San Diego | 162 | 162 | 21 | 162 | 1461.2 | 6208 | 1437 | 673 | 597 | 147 | 79 | 37 | 19 | 507 | 69 | 928 | 39 | 19 | 75 | 87 | .463 | 12 | 35 | 3.68 |
| Los Angeles | 162 | 162 | 29 | 162 | 1442 | 6082 | 1364 | 685 | 596 | 137 | 56 | 42 | 28 | 478 | 49 | 1021 | 63 | 10 | 86 | 76 | .531 | 12 | 29 | 3.72 |
| St. Louis | 162 | 162 | 8 | 162 | 1443.1 | 6132 | 1432 | 698 | 621 | 98 | 70 | 64 | 34 | 475 | 72 | 833 | 45 | 5 | 70 | 92 | .432 | 13 | 39 | 3.87 |
| San Francisco | 162 | 162 | 14 | 162 | 1446.1 | 6235 | 1477 | 710 | 655 | 131 | 70 | 50 | 21 | 553 | 84 | 788 | 37 | 19 | 85 | 77 | .525 | 6 | 45 | 4.08 |
| Philadelphia | 162 | 162 | 18 | 162 | 1449 | 6259 | 1381 | 729 | 655 | 124 | 80 | 48 | 29 | 651 | 81 | 840 | 69 | 15 | 77 | 85 | .475 | 7 | 35 | 4.07 |
| Chicago | 162 | 162 | 13 | 162 | 1442.2 | 6320 | 1510 | 774 | 695 | 121 | 107 | 44 | 28 | 572 | 85 | 877 | 62 | 14 | 77 | 85 | .475 | 7 | 42 | 4.34 |
| Atlanta | 162 | 162 | 17 | 162 | 1429.2 | 6303 | 1527 | 821 | 727 | 128 | 94 | 54 | 26 | 579 | 64 | 938 | 61 | 15 | 65 | 97 | .401 | 8 | 30 | 4.58 |
| National | 1944 | 1944 | 200 | 1944 | 17381.1 | 73989 | 16917 | 8173 | 7321 | 1521 | 877 | 564 | 352 | 6221 | 798 | 11164 | 580 | 187 | 972 | 972 | .500 | 116 | 476 | 3.79 |

# 1990 Fielding Stats

Fielding statistics and the weather. Everyone complains about 'em, but no one ever does anything about 'em. Well, the least we could do is give 'em to you, so here they are.

All of the positions are listed, and outfielders are broken down by Left-, Center- and Right-field. We've included all of the traditional categories: Games (G), Putouts (PO), Assists (A), Errors (E), Double Plays (DP) and Passed Balls (PB). Two categories you may not be familiar with are Innings Played (Inn) and Range Factor (Rng). Innings Played is self-explanatory, while Range Factor constitutes the number of Chances per Nine Innings Played. A more complete explanation is given in the Glossary.

The fielding statistics in this section are, of course, unofficial. Unlike the Batting and Pitching statistics, our schedule for double and triple checking fielding stats comes after the deadline for handing this manuscript to the printer. There will be differences between the data here and what is printed as "official" in December, but we felt that the difference between a shortstop having 588 chances rather than 589 chances wasn't great enough to prevent publishing the data.

## First Basemen

| Player | Tm | Inn | G | PO | A | E | DP | PB | Pct. | Rng |
|---|---|---|---|---|---|---|---|---|---|---|
| Aldrete,M | Mon | 103.1 | 18 | 108 | 8 | 0 | 16 | -- | 1.000 | --- |
| Anderson,D | SF | 9.0 | 3 | 9 | 0 | 0 | 2 | -- | 1.000 | --- |
| Balboni,S | NYA | 186.0 | 28 | 183 | 7 | 3 | 23 | -- | .984 | --- |
| Bell,M | Atl | 86.2 | 24 | 97 | 9 | 2 | 7 | -- | .981 | --- |
| Benzinger,T | Cin | 746.0 | 95 | 706 | 52 | 6 | 57 | -- | .992 | --- |
| Bergman,D | Det | 198.0 | 27 | 203 | 14 | 1 | 19 | -- | .995 | --- |
| Blankenship,L | Oak | 1.0 | 1 | 0 | 0 | 0 | 0 | -- | .000 | --- |
| Bonilla,B | Pit | 19.2 | 3 | 16 | 1 | 0 | 0 | -- | 1.000 | --- |
| Bradley,S | Sea | 1.0 | 1 | 2 | 0 | 0 | 0 | -- | 1.000 | --- |
| Bream,S | Pit | 975.2 | 142 | 970 | 107 | 8 | 82 | -- | .993 | --- |
| Brett,G | KC | 877.0 | 102 | 865 | 65 | 7 | 88 | -- | .993 | --- |
| Brewer,R | StL | 44.0 | 9 | 46 | 4 | 1 | 5 | -- | .980 | --- |
| Brock,G | Mil | 899.2 | 115 | 886 | 62 | 5 | 88 | -- | .995 | --- |
| Brookens,T | Cle | 7.1 | 2 | 3 | 1 | 0 | 1 | -- | 1.000 | --- |
| Buckner,B | Bos | 81.1 | 15 | 75 | 6 | 0 | 6 | -- | 1.000 | --- |
| Bush,R | Min | 17.0 | 6 | 12 | 2 | 0 | 1 | -- | 1.000 | --- |
| Cabrera,F | Atl | 266.2 | 48 | 263 | 19 | 3 | 16 | -- | .989 | --- |
| Calderon,I | ChA | 4.0 | 2 | 1 | 0 | 0 | 0 | -- | 1.000 | --- |
| Canale,G | Mil | 41.0 | 6 | 32 | 4 | 0 | 1 | -- | 1.000 | --- |
| Carter,G | SF | 25.0 | 3 | 25 | 0 | 0 | 3 | -- | 1.000 | --- |
| Carter,J | SD | 111.0 | 14 | 107 | 3 | 6 | 15 | -- | .948 | --- |
| Clark,Jack | SD | 888.2 | 111 | 854 | 67 | 6 | 72 | -- | .994 | --- |
| Clark,Jerald | SD | 78.0 | 15 | 77 | 6 | 0 | 3 | -- | 1.000 | --- |
| Clark,W | SF | 1338.1 | 153 | 1460 | 113 | 12 | 119 | -- | .992 | --- |
| Cochrane,D | Sea | 10.0 | 3 | 7 | 1 | 0 | 0 | -- | 1.000 | --- |
| Coles,D | Sea | 22.0 | 4 | 19 | 3 | 1 | 1 | -- | .957 | --- |
| Collins,D | StL | 86.0 | 49 | 79 | 0 | 0 | 5 | -- | 1.000 | --- |
| Conine,J | KC | 46.0 | 9 | 39 | 4 | 1 | 7 | -- | .977 | --- |
| Daugherty,J | Tex | 162.0 | 30 | 174 | 17 | 2 | 20 | -- | .990 | --- |
| Davis,A | Sea | 446.1 | 52 | 432 | 32 | 3 | 41 | -- | .994 | --- |
| Davis,G | Hou | 774.1 | 91 | 797 | 54 | 4 | 55 | -- | .995 | --- |
| Davis,J | Atl | 37.2 | 6 | 45 | 5 | 0 | 4 | -- | 1.000 | --- |
| Deer,R | Mil | 140.1 | 21 | 127 | 12 | 2 | 11 | -- | .986 | --- |
| Esasky,N | Atl | 78.0 | 9 | 79 | 5 | 5 | 7 | -- | .944 | --- |
| Fielder,C | Det | 1225.1 | 143 | 1197 | 109 | 14 | 140 | -- | .989 | --- |
| Foley,T | Mon | 1.0 | 1 | 0 | 0 | 0 | 0 | -- | .000 | --- |
| Francona,T | Mil | 8.0 | 2 | 6 | 0 | 0 | 1 | -- | 1.000 | --- |
| Gaetti,G | Min | 15.2 | 2 | 23 | 0 | 0 | 0 | -- | 1.000 | --- |
| Galarraga,A | Mon | 1318.1 | 154 | 1304 | 86 | 10 | 93 | -- | .993 | --- |
| Goff,J | Mon | 17.1 | 3 | 19 | 0 | 0 | 1 | -- | 1.000 | --- |
| Gonzalez,L | Hou | 10.2 | 2 | 17 | 0 | 0 | 0 | -- | 1.000 | --- |
| Grace,M | ChN | 1315.1 | 153 | 1322 | 178 | 12 | 116 | -- | .992 | --- |
| Gregg,T | Atl | 349.0 | 50 | 336 | 32 | 5 | 31 | -- | .987 | --- |
| Griffey Sr,K | Cin | 43.2 | 9 | 42 | 4 | 1 | 2 | -- | .979 | --- |
| Guerrero,P | StL | 1083.1 | 132 | 1084 | 74 | 13 | 74 | -- | .989 | --- |
| Harper,B | Min | 17.0 | 2 | 13 | 3 | 0 | 0 | -- | 1.000 | --- |
| Hassey,R | Oak | 4.0 | 3 | 5 | 0 | 0 | 1 | -- | 1.000 | --- |
| Hatcher,M | LA | 99.0 | 25 | 73 | 7 | 0 | 10 | -- | 1.000 | --- |
| Hayes,C | Phi | 28.0 | 4 | 28 | 2 | 0 | 0 | -- | 1.000 | --- |
| Heep,D | Bos | 27.0 | 5 | 24 | 3 | 1 | 2 | -- | .964 | --- |
| Hernandez,K | Cle | 320.0 | 43 | 340 | 20 | 2 | 28 | -- | .994 | --- |
| Hill,D | Cal | 21.0 | 3 | 24 | 2 | 0 | 5 | -- | 1.000 | --- |
| Hoiles,C | Bal | 43.1 | 6 | 41 | 2 | 0 | 5 | -- | 1.000 | --- |
| Hollins,D | Phi | 7.0 | 1 | 8 | 1 | 0 | 0 | -- | 1.000 | --- |
| Horn,S | Bal | 76.1 | 10 | 58 | 6 | 2 | 7 | -- | .970 | --- |
| Howell,J | Cal | 1.0 | 1 | 2 | 0 | 0 | 0 | -- | 1.000 | --- |
| Howitt,D | Oak | 19.0 | 5 | 18 | 1 | 0 | 3 | -- | 1.000 | --- |
| Hrbek,K | Min | 1021.0 | 120 | 1055 | 77 | 3 | 102 | -- | .997 | --- |

## First Basemen

| Player | Tm | Inn | G | PO | A | E | DP | PB | Pct. | Rng |
|---|---|---|---|---|---|---|---|---|---|---|
| Hudler,R | StL | 45.0 | 6 | 54 | 4 | 0 | 6 | -- | 1.000 | --- |
| Jacoby,B | Cle | 561.2 | 79 | 583 | 30 | 2 | 62 | -- | .997 | --- |
| James,D | Cle | 250.0 | 35 | 230 | 15 | 1 | 21 | -- | .996 | --- |
| Jennings,D | Oak | 25.1 | 4 | 28 | 0 | 0 | 5 | -- | 1.000 | --- |
| Johnson,W | Mon | 33.1 | 7 | 39 | 0 | 0 | 7 | -- | 1.000 | --- |
| Jordan,R | Phi | 690.2 | 84 | 742 | 37 | 4 | 64 | -- | .995 | --- |
| Joyner,W | Cal | 725.0 | 83 | 734 | 61 | 4 | 78 | -- | .995 | --- |
| Justice,D | Atl | 535.2 | 69 | 487 | 37 | 10 | 43 | -- | .981 | --- |
| King,J | Pit | 2.1 | 1 | 3 | 0 | 0 | 0 | -- | 1.000 | --- |
| Kittle,R | ChA | 164.2 | 25 | 150 | 5 | 2 | 18 | -- | .987 | --- |
| Kittle,R | Bal | 28.0 | 5 | 26 | 1 | 0 | 1 | -- | 1.000 | --- |
| Kruk,J | Phi | 411.1 | 61 | 400 | 44 | 2 | 34 | -- | .996 | --- |
| Laga,M | SF | 43.0 | 10 | 33 | 5 | 0 | 4 | -- | 1.000 | --- |
| Lancellotti,R | Bos | 16.0 | 2 | 20 | 2 | 0 | 3 | -- | 1.000 | --- |
| Lansford,C | Oak | 27.0 | 5 | 28 | 1 | 0 | 2 | -- | 1.000 | --- |
| Larkin,G | Min | 227.0 | 28 | 222 | 12 | 2 | 27 | -- | .992 | --- |
| Leach,R | SF | 31.0 | 6 | 37 | 2 | 0 | 4 | -- | 1.000 | --- |
| Lee,T | Cin | 33.0 | 6 | 28 | 3 | 0 | 1 | -- | 1.000 | --- |
| Lindeman,J | Det | 3.0 | 1 | 5 | 0 | 0 | 0 | -- | 1.000 | --- |
| Lopez,L | LA | 4.0 | 1 | 4 | 0 | 0 | 1 | -- | 1.000 | --- |
| Lyons,S | ChA | 224.1 | 61 | 206 | 18 | 2 | 26 | -- | .991 | --- |
| Maas,K | NYA | 480.1 | 57 | 485 | 34 | 9 | 47 | -- | .983 | --- |
| Magadan,D | NYN | 900.1 | 114 | 829 | 72 | 2 | 51 | -- | .998 | --- |
| Manto,J | Cle | 173.1 | 25 | 180 | 19 | 2 | 18 | -- | .990 | --- |
| Marshall,M | NYN | 337.0 | 42 | 277 | 24 | 2 | 20 | -- | .993 | --- |
| Marshall,M | Bos | 52.0 | 8 | 42 | 7 | 0 | 5 | -- | 1.000 | --- |
| Martinez,Carlos | ChA | 626.0 | 82 | 634 | 37 | 8 | 50 | -- | .988 | --- |
| Martinez,Carml. | Phi | 312.0 | 43 | 319 | 21 | 2 | 31 | -- | .994 | --- |
| Martinez,Carml. | Pit | 23.0 | 5 | 22 | 4 | 0 | 4 | -- | 1.000 | --- |
| Martinez,T | Sea | 163.0 | 23 | 155 | 12 | 0 | 25 | -- | 1.000 | --- |
| Mattingly,D | NYA | 778.1 | 89 | 800 | 77 | 3 | 82 | -- | .997 | --- |
| McClendon,L | ChN | 51.1 | 8 | 58 | 7 | 0 | 5 | -- | 1.000 | --- |
| McGriff,F | Tor | 1299.0 | 147 | 1246 | 125 | 6 | 120 | -- | .996 | --- |
| McGwire,M | Oak | 1334.2 | 154 | 1332 | 93 | 5 | 127 | -- | .997 | --- |
| McKnight,J | Bal | 112.0 | 15 | 89 | 11 | 0 | 10 | -- | 1.000 | --- |
| Melvin,B | Bal | 2.0 | 1 | 1 | 1 | 0 | 0 | -- | 1.000 | --- |
| Milligan,R | Bal | 846.2 | 99 | 844 | 86 | 9 | 95 | -- | .990 | --- |
| Molitor,P | Mil | 311.0 | 37 | 324 | 25 | 5 | 27 | -- | .986 | --- |
| Morman,R | KC | 20.0 | 3 | 19 | 3 | 0 | 1 | -- | 1.000 | --- |
| Morris,H | Cin | 632.2 | 80 | 585 | 54 | 3 | 50 | -- | .995 | --- |
| Moses,J | Min | 9.0 | 6 | 5 | 0 | 0 | 0 | -- | 1.000 | --- |
| Mulliniks,R | Tor | 11.0 | 3 | 11 | 0 | 0 | 1 | -- | 1.000 | --- |
| Murray,E | LA | 1286.0 | 150 | 1182 | 110 | 10 | 90 | -- | .992 | --- |
| Nichols,C | Hou | 25.0 | 3 | 22 | 1 | 2 | 1 | -- | .920 | --- |
| O'Brien,P | Sea | 800.0 | 97 | 852 | 73 | 5 | 69 | -- | .995 | --- |
| O'Malley,T | NYN | 12.2 | 3 | 15 | 0 | 1 | 0 | -- | .938 | --- |
| Oberkfell,K | Hou | 64.2 | 11 | 69 | 7 | 1 | 7 | -- | .987 | --- |
| Olerud,J | Tor | 144.0 | 18 | 133 | 9 | 2 | 10 | -- | .986 | --- |
| Pagnozzi,T | StL | 8.0 | 2 | 11 | 0 | 0 | 0 | -- | 1.000 | --- |
| Palacios,R | KC | 11.0 | 7 | 8 | 0 | 0 | 1 | -- | 1.000 | --- |
| Palmeiro,R | Tex | 1255.2 | 147 | 1214 | 91 | 7 | 123 | -- | .995 | --- |
| Parker,D | Mil | 25.0 | 3 | 24 | 0 | 1 | 4 | -- | .960 | --- |
| Parrish,L | Cal | 33.0 | 4 | 34 | 2 | 0 | 6 | -- | 1.000 | --- |
| Pecota,B | KC | 13.0 | 4 | 19 | 1 | 0 | 2 | -- | 1.000 | --- |
| Pena,T | Bos | 1.1 | 1 | 2 | 0 | 0 | 0 | -- | 1.000 | --- |
| Perry,G | KC | 420.2 | 51 | 398 | 38 | 6 | 39 | -- | .986 | --- |
| Phelps,K | Oak | 20.0 | 5 | 24 | 3 | 1 | 3 | -- | .964 | --- |
| Phelps,K | Cle | 97.0 | 14 | 88 | 7 | 0 | 4 | -- | 1.000 | --- |

## First Basemen

| Player | Tm | Inn | G | PO | A | E | DP | PB | Pct. | Rng |
|---|---|---|---|---|---|---|---|---|---|---|
| Presley,J | Atl | 76.0 | 17 | 78 | 10 | 1 | 10 | -- | .989 | --- |
| Puhl,T | Hou | 1.0 | 1 | 1 | 0 | 0 | 0 | -- | 1.000 | --- |
| Quinones,L | Cin | 1.0 | 1 | 2 | 0 | 0 | 0 | -- | 1.000 | --- |
| Quintana,C | Bos | 1201.1 | 148 | 1188 | 137 | 17 | 117 | -- | .987 | --- |
| Quirk,J | Oak | 20.0 | 8 | 13 | 0 | 0 | 0 | -- | 1.000 | --- |
| Redus,G | Pit | 426.1 | 72 | 446 | 34 | 6 | 28 | -- | .988 | --- |
| Robidoux,B | Bos | 63.0 | 11 | 49 | 4 | 1 | 4 | -- | .981 | --- |
| Russell,J | Tex | 12.0 | 3 | 8 | 0 | 0 | 0 | -- | 1.000 | --- |
| Sasser,M | NYN | 1.1 | 1 | 4 | 0 | 0 | 0 | -- | 1.000 | --- |
| Schroeder,B | Cal | 24.0 | 3 | 26 | 3 | 0 | 0 | -- | 1.000 | --- |
| Schu,R | Cal | 78.0 | 14 | 82 | 5 | 1 | 6 | -- | .989 | --- |
| Segui,D | Bal | 292.0 | 36 | 284 | 26 | 3 | 24 | -- | .990 | --- |
| Sharperson,M | LA | 43.0 | 6 | 55 | 2 | 1 | 5 | -- | .983 | --- |
| Simms,M | Hou | 21.0 | 6 | 20 | 1 | 0 | 2 | -- | 1.000 | --- |
| Sorrento,P | Min | 129.0 | 15 | 118 | 7 | 1 | 14 | -- | .992 | --- |
| Stanley,M | Tex | 15.0 | 6 | 14 | 1 | 0 | 1 | -- | 1.000 | --- |
| Steinbach,T | Oak | 5.0 | 3 | 5 | 0 | 0 | 0 | -- | 1.000 | --- |
| Stephenson,P | SD | 384.0 | 60 | 345 | 35 | 1 | 34 | -- | .997 | --- |
| Stevens,L | Cal | 572.0 | 67 | 602 | 34 | 4 | 62 | -- | .994 | --- |
| Stubbs,F | Hou | 543.1 | 72 | 496 | 40 | 5 | 42 | -- | .991 | --- |
| Sveum,D | Mil | 20.0 | 5 | 17 | 0 | 0 | 1 | -- | 1.000 | --- |
| Tabler,P | KC | 33.0 | 5 | 29 | 1 | 0 | 6 | -- | 1.000 | --- |
| Tettleton,M | Bal | 35.0 | 5 | 32 | 2 | 1 | 1 | -- | .971 | --- |
| Teufel,T | NYN | 120.0 | 24 | 106 | 9 | 1 | 11 | -- | .991 | --- |
| Thomas,F | ChA | 421.1 | 51 | 427 | 27 | 5 | 54 | -- | .989 | --- |
| Torve,K | NYN | 68.2 | 9 | 65 | 0 | 0 | 6 | -- | 1.000 | --- |
| Traxler,B | LA | 10.0 | 3 | 6 | 2 | 0 | 0 | -- | 1.000 | --- |
| Trevino,A | Hou | 8.0 | 1 | 14 | 1 | 1 | 0 | -- | .938 | --- |
| Valle,D | Sea | 1.0 | 1 | 2 | 0 | 0 | 0 | -- | 1.000 | --- |
| Ventura,R | ChA | 1.0 | 1 | 0 | 0 | 0 | 0 | -- | .000 | --- |
| Villanueva,H | ChN | 76.0 | 14 | 63 | 4 | 1 | 4 | -- | .985 | --- |
| Walker,G | ChA | 8.0 | 1 | 14 | 1 | 0 | 2 | -- | 1.000 | --- |
| Walling,D | StL | 80.1 | 15 | 86 | 6 | 0 | 4 | -- | 1.000 | --- |
| Ward,G | Det | 4.0 | 2 | 7 | 0 | 0 | 0 | -- | 1.000 | --- |
| Webster,M | Cle | 18.0 | 3 | 15 | 2 | 2 | 2 | -- | .895 | --- |
| Wilson,G | Hou | 2.0 | 1 | 2 | 0 | 0 | 0 | -- | 1.000 | --- |
| Zeile,T | StL | 96.2 | 11 | 104 | 8 | 1 | 7 | -- | .991 | --- |

## Second Basemen

| Player | Tm | Inn | G | PO | A | E | DP | PB | Pct. | Rng |
|---|---|---|---|---|---|---|---|---|---|---|
| Alomar,R | SD | 1226.1 | 137 | 312 | 394 | 17 | 74 | -- | .976 | 5.31 |
| Anderson,D | SF | 53.2 | 13 | 7 | 20 | 1 | 3 | -- | .964 | 4.70 |
| Anderson,K | Cal | 27.0 | 5 | 10 | 11 | 1 | 2 | -- | .955 | 7.33 |
| Backman,W | Pit | 106.0 | 15 | 23 | 32 | 0 | 5 | -- | 1.000 | 4.67 |
| Baerga,C | Cle | 70.0 | 8 | 22 | 22 | 5 | 8 | -- | .898 | 6.30 |
| Baker,D | Min | 5.0 | 3 | 1 | 2 | 0 | 0 | -- | 1.000 | 5.40 |
| Barrett,M | Bos | 423.1 | 60 | 91 | 146 | 2 | 27 | -- | .992 | 5.08 |
| Bates,B | Mil | 87.0 | 14 | 18 | 33 | 2 | 5 | -- | .962 | 5.48 |
| Bates,B | Cin | 9.0 | 1 | 0 | 1 | 0 | 0 | -- | 1.000 | 1.00 |
| Belliard,R | Pit | 65.2 | 21 | 23 | 16 | 0 | 5 | -- | 1.000 | 5.35 |
| Blankenship,L | Oak | 85.0 | 20 | 20 | 32 | 0 | 7 | -- | 1.000 | 5.51 |
| Blauser,J | Atl | 101.2 | 14 | 22 | 26 | 0 | 6 | -- | 1.000 | 4.25 |
| Booker,R | Phi | 88.1 | 23 | 16 | 22 | 1 | 5 | -- | .974 | 3.97 |
| Bordick,M | Oak | 12.2 | 7 | 2 | 4 | 0 | 0 | -- | 1.000 | 4.26 |
| Brookens,T | Cle | 153.1 | 21 | 40 | 48 | 1 | 14 | -- | .989 | 5.22 |
| Brown,M | Bal | 6.0 | 3 | 1 | 1 | 0 | 0 | -- | 1.000 | 3.00 |

## Second Basemen

| Player | Tm | Inn | G | PO | A | E | DP | PB | Pct. | Rng |
|---|---|---|---|---|---|---|---|---|---|---|
| Browne,J | Cle | 1180.0 | 139 | 288 | 383 | 10 | 69 | -- | .985 | 5.19 |
| Brumley,M | Sea | 14.0 | 6 | 3 | 7 | 0 | 3 | -- | 1.000 | 6.43 |
| Buechele,S | Tex | 13.2 | 4 | 2 | 3 | 0 | 0 | -- | 1.000 | 3.29 |
| Candaele,C | Hou | 315.2 | 50 | 74 | 107 | 2 | 17 | -- | .989 | 5.22 |
| Cerone,R | NYA | 2.0 | 1 | 2 | 0 | 0 | 0 | -- | 1.000 | 9.00 |
| Coachman,P | Cal | 11.0 | 2 | 1 | 5 | 1 | 1 | -- | .857 | 5.73 |
| Cora,J | SD | 110.0 | 15 | 43 | 32 | 5 | 12 | -- | .938 | 6.55 |
| DeShields,D | Mon | 1115.0 | 128 | 236 | 376 | 12 | 64 | -- | .981 | 5.04 |
| Diaz,E | Mil | 74.0 | 15 | 23 | 29 | 3 | 7 | -- | .945 | 6.69 |
| Diaz,M | NYN | 1.0 | 1 | 0 | 0 | 0 | 0 | -- | .000 | .00 |
| Disarcina,G | Cal | 19.0 | 3 | 3 | 8 | 0 | 1 | -- | 1.000 | 5.21 |
| Doran,B | Hou | 827.1 | 99 | 170 | 263 | 5 | 42 | -- | .989 | 4.76 |
| Doran,B | Cin | 104.2 | 12 | 28 | 37 | 1 | 6 | -- | .985 | 5.68 |
| Duncan,M | Cin | 924.2 | 115 | 246 | 287 | 15 | 51 | -- | .973 | 5.33 |
| Espy,C | Tex | 1.0 | 1 | 0 | 0 | 0 | 0 | -- | .000 | .00 |
| Faries,P | SD | 60.0 | 7 | 20 | 18 | 0 | 3 | -- | 1.000 | 5.70 |
| Felder,M | Mil | 3.0 | 1 | 2 | 0 | 0 | 0 | -- | 1.000 | 6.00 |
| Fermin,F | Cle | 4.0 | 1 | 1 | 2 | 0 | 0 | -- | 1.000 | 6.75 |
| Fletcher,S | ChA | 1321.1 | 151 | 304 | 440 | 9 | 115 | -- | .988 | 5.13 |
| Foley,T | Mon | 128.2 | 20 | 18 | 29 | 3 | 4 | -- | .940 | 3.50 |
| Franco,J | Tex | 1308.2 | 152 | 308 | 444 | 19 | 100 | -- | .975 | 5.30 |
| Gallego,M | Oak | 661.1 | 84 | 151 | 257 | 4 | 47 | -- | .990 | 5.61 |
| Gantner,J | Mil | 675.2 | 80 | 167 | 220 | 7 | 53 | -- | .982 | 5.25 |
| Giles,B | Sea | 18.0 | 2 | 6 | 5 | 0 | 2 | -- | 1.000 | 5.50 |
| Gonzales,R | Bal | 249.0 | 43 | 61 | 92 | 1 | 19 | -- | .994 | 5.57 |
| Grebeck,C | ChA | 31.0 | 6 | 6 | 12 | 0 | 2 | -- | 1.000 | 5.23 |
| Green,G | Tex | 16.0 | 2 | 5 | 6 | 0 | 1 | -- | 1.000 | 6.19 |
| Hale,C | Min | 9.0 | 1 | 2 | 6 | 0 | 2 | -- | 1.000 | 8.00 |
| Harris,L | LA | 275.2 | 44 | 63 | 70 | 2 | 14 | -- | .985 | 4.41 |
| Hayes,C | Phi | 8.0 | 1 | 2 | 3 | 0 | 1 | -- | 1.000 | 5.63 |
| Hemond,S | Oak | 1.0 | 1 | 0 | 0 | 0 | 0 | -- | .000 | .00 |
| Herr,T | Phi | 946.2 | 114 | 239 | 292 | 5 | 79 | -- | .991 | 5.10 |
| Herr,T | NYN | 223.1 | 26 | 35 | 59 | 2 | 15 | -- | .979 | 3.87 |
| Hill,D | Cal | 467.2 | 60 | 127 | 174 | 3 | 46 | -- | .990 | 5.85 |
| Hudler,R | StL | 51.2 | 10 | 10 | 26 | 2 | 3 | -- | .947 | 6.62 |
| Hulett,T | Bal | 105.1 | 16 | 27 | 45 | 1 | 11 | -- | .986 | 6.24 |
| Huson,J | Tex | 38.0 | 10 | 10 | 14 | 0 | 4 | -- | 1.000 | 5.68 |
| Infante,A | Atl | 42.0 | 11 | 14 | 13 | 1 | 3 | -- | .964 | 6.00 |
| Jefferies,G | NYN | 996.1 | 118 | 216 | 275 | 12 | 47 | -- | .976 | 4.54 |
| Jeltz,S | KC | 158.1 | 34 | 28 | 57 | 2 | 12 | -- | .977 | 4.95 |
| Jones,T | StL | 71.0 | 19 | 16 | 28 | 1 | 3 | -- | .978 | 5.70 |
| Kunkel,J | Tex | 60.0 | 13 | 12 | 18 | 0 | 3 | -- | 1.000 | 4.50 |
| Kutcher,R | Bos | 25.0 | 5 | 8 | 11 | 0 | 2 | -- | 1.000 | 6.84 |
| Lawless,T | Tor | 3.0 | 1 | 4 | 1 | 0 | 1 | -- | 1.000 | 15.00 |
| Lee,M | Tor | 956.2 | 112 | 259 | 285 | 4 | 65 | -- | .993 | 5.16 |
| Lemke,M | Atl | 295.2 | 44 | 71 | 122 | 3 | 22 | -- | .985 | 5.97 |
| Lind,J | Pit | 1275.1 | 152 | 332 | 450 | 7 | 77 | -- | .991 | 5.57 |
| Liriano,N | Tor | 422.1 | 49 | 93 | 132 | 4 | 27 | -- | .983 | 4.88 |
| Liriano,N | Min | 407.2 | 50 | 83 | 128 | 7 | 27 | -- | .968 | 4.81 |
| Litton,G | SF | 83.2 | 18 | 19 | 25 | 0 | 7 | -- | 1.000 | 4.73 |
| Lyons,S | ChA | 97.0 | 15 | 28 | 29 | 3 | 6 | -- | .950 | 5.57 |
| Manrique,F | Min | 486.1 | 67 | 105 | 156 | 7 | 41 | -- | .974 | 4.96 |
| McKnight,J | Bal | 28.0 | 5 | 8 | 8 | 0 | 1 | -- | 1.000 | 5.14 |
| McLemore,M | Cal | 59.0 | 8 | 13 | 16 | 0 | 3 | -- | 1.000 | 4.42 |
| McLemore,M | Cle | 20.0 | 3 | 7 | 7 | 0 | 3 | -- | 1.000 | 6.30 |
| Miller,K | NYN | 57.1 | 11 | 19 | 16 | 1 | 5 | -- | .972 | 5.65 |
| Molitor,P | Mil | 503.1 | 60 | 135 | 190 | 4 | 35 | -- | .988 | 5.88 |
| Morandini,M | Phi | 198.2 | 25 | 37 | 61 | 1 | 10 | -- | .990 | 4.48 |

## Second Basemen

| Player | Tm | Inn | G | PO | A | E | DP | PB | Pct. | Rng |
|---|---|---|---|---|---|---|---|---|---|---|
| Naehring,T | Bos | 1.0 | 1 | 0 | 0 | 0 | 0 | -- | .000 | .00 |
| Newman,A | Min | 527.1 | 89 | 118 | 173 | 2 | 48 | -- | .993 | 5.00 |
| Noboa,J | Mon | 211.2 | 31 | 31 | 45 | 0 | 9 | -- | 1.000 | 3.23 |
| Oberkfell,K | Hou | 66.2 | 11 | 12 | 14 | 0 | 6 | -- | 1.000 | 3.51 |
| Oester,R | Cin | 338.1 | 50 | 79 | 88 | 3 | 13 | -- | .982 | 4.52 |
| Oquendo,J | StL | 1202.2 | 150 | 284 | 393 | 3 | 65 | -- | .996 | 5.09 |
| Pankovits,J | Bos | 3.0 | 2 | 0 | 0 | 0 | 0 | -- | .000 | .00 |
| Paredes,J | Det | 21.0 | 4 | 4 | 7 | 1 | 2 | -- | .917 | 5.14 |
| Paredes,J | Mon | 18.0 | 2 | 1 | 7 | 1 | 2 | -- | .889 | 4.50 |
| Parker,R | SF | 2.0 | 2 | 0 | 0 | 0 | 0 | -- | .000 | .00 |
| Pecota,B | KC | 347.2 | 50 | 82 | 120 | 3 | 21 | -- | .985 | 5.31 |
| Pena,G | StL | 83.2 | 11 | 24 | 29 | 1 | 7 | -- | .981 | 5.81 |
| Perezchica,T | SF | 6.0 | 2 | 2 | 0 | 0 | 0 | -- | 1.000 | 3.00 |
| Petralli,G | Tex | 7.1 | 5 | 3 | 3 | 0 | 2 | -- | 1.000 | 7.36 |
| Phillips,T | Det | 372.0 | 47 | 91 | 135 | 1 | 37 | -- | .996 | 5.49 |
| Polidor,G | Mil | 7.0 | 2 | 1 | 2 | 0 | 0 | -- | 1.000 | 3.86 |
| Puckett,K | Min | 0.1 | 1 | 0 | 0 | 0 | 0 | -- | .000 | .00 |
| Quinones,L | Cin | 79.2 | 13 | 22 | 31 | 2 | 12 | -- | .964 | 6.21 |
| Ramos,D | ChN | 0.2 | 1 | 0 | 0 | 0 | 0 | -- | .000 | .00 |
| Randolph,W | LA | 224.0 | 26 | 50 | 73 | 4 | 10 | -- | .969 | 5.10 |
| Randolph,W | Oak | 696.0 | 84 | 147 | 239 | 7 | 62 | -- | .982 | 5.08 |
| Ray,J | Cal | 854.1 | 100 | 235 | 297 | 7 | 81 | -- | .987 | 5.68 |
| Ready,R | Phi | 207.1 | 28 | 46 | 84 | 2 | 17 | -- | .985 | 5.73 |
| Reed,J | Bos | 984.2 | 118 | 212 | 372 | 6 | 80 | -- | .990 | 5.39 |
| Reynolds,H | Sea | 1406.1 | 160 | 325 | 496 | 19 | 109 | -- | .977 | 5.38 |
| Riles,E | SF | 134.0 | 24 | 28 | 48 | 2 | 6 | -- | .974 | 5.24 |
| Ripken,B | Bal | 1047.0 | 127 | 249 | 364 | 8 | 84 | -- | .987 | 5.34 |
| Rivera,L | Bos | 5.0 | 4 | 1 | 0 | 0 | 0 | -- | 1.000 | 1.80 |
| Roberts,B | SD | 65.1 | 8 | 10 | 25 | 3 | 6 | -- | .921 | 5.23 |
| Rohde,D | Hou | 175.1 | 32 | 28 | 63 | 0 | 11 | -- | 1.000 | 4.67 |
| Rosario,V | Atl | 1.0 | 1 | 0 | 0 | 0 | 0 | -- | .000 | .00 |
| Rose,B | Cal | 8.0 | 4 | 1 | 2 | 0 | 0 | -- | 1.000 | 3.38 |
| Samuel,J | LA | 881.2 | 108 | 194 | 257 | 13 | 49 | -- | .972 | 4.74 |
| Sandberg,R | ChN | 1315.0 | 154 | 284 | 472 | 8 | 85 | -- | .990 | 5.23 |
| Sax,S | NYA | 1355.2 | 154 | 290 | 457 | 10 | 103 | -- | .987 | 5.03 |
| Schaefer,J | Sea | 5.0 | 3 | 1 | 1 | 0 | 1 | -- | 1.000 | 3.60 |
| Schu,R | Cal | 8.0 | 1 | 3 | 3 | 2 | 0 | -- | .750 | 9.00 |
| Seitzer,K | KC | 57.0 | 10 | 18 | 19 | 1 | 5 | -- | .974 | 6.00 |
| Sharperson,M | LA | 41.2 | 9 | 10 | 12 | 1 | 1 | -- | .957 | 4.97 |
| Shumpert,T | KC | 230.0 | 27 | 55 | 74 | 3 | 15 | -- | .977 | 5.17 |
| Smith,G | ChN | 43.0 | 7 | 10 | 16 | 0 | 3 | -- | 1.000 | 5.44 |
| Sojo,L | Tor | 72.0 | 15 | 15 | 15 | 1 | 3 | -- | .968 | 3.88 |
| Sveum,D | Mil | 95.0 | 16 | 24 | 31 | 1 | 7 | -- | .982 | 5.31 |
| Teufel,T | NYN | 162.0 | 24 | 30 | 34 | 2 | 5 | -- | .970 | 3.67 |
| Thompson,R | SF | 1167.0 | 142 | 284 | 440 | 8 | 94 | -- | .989 | 5.65 |
| Tolleson,W | NYA | 65.0 | 13 | 14 | 14 | 0 | 4 | -- | 1.000 | 3.88 |
| Treadway,J | Atl | 989.1 | 122 | 240 | 360 | 15 | 73 | -- | .976 | 5.59 |
| Velarde,R | NYA | 10.0 | 3 | 0 | 5 | 1 | 1 | -- | .833 | 5.40 |
| Vizcaino,J | LA | 19.0 | 6 | 4 | 3 | 0 | 1 | -- | 1.000 | 3.32 |
| Walewander,J | NYA | 12.0 | 2 | 3 | 2 | 0 | 0 | -- | 1.000 | 3.75 |
| Whitaker,L | Det | 1037.1 | 131 | 282 | 372 | 6 | 98 | -- | .991 | 5.73 |
| White,F | KC | 627.2 | 79 | 142 | 221 | 8 | 49 | -- | .978 | 5.32 |
| Wilkerson,C | ChN | 84.0 | 14 | 24 | 29 | 3 | 3 | -- | .946 | 6.00 |
| Wilson,C | StL | 34.1 | 9 | 6 | 8 | 0 | 3 | -- | 1.000 | 3.67 |
| Yelding,E | Hou | 65.0 | 10 | 20 | 20 | 2 | 3 | -- | .952 | 5.82 |

## Third Basemen

| Player | Tm | Inn | G | PO | A | E | DP | PB | Pct. | Rng |
|---|---|---|---|---|---|---|---|---|---|---|
| Anderson,D | SF | 5.2 | 2 | 0 | 1 | 0 | 0 | -- | 1.000 | 1.59 |
| Anderson,K | Cal | 127.0 | 16 | 12 | 38 | 3 | 3 | -- | .943 | 3.76 |
| Backman,W | Pit | 517.2 | 71 | 34 | 101 | 12 | 5 | -- | .918 | 2.56 |
| Baerga,C | Cle | 396.2 | 50 | 33 | 101 | 8 | 9 | -- | .944 | 3.22 |
| Barrett,M | Bos | 2.0 | 1 | 0 | 1 | 0 | 1 | -- | 1.000 | 4.50 |
| Belliard,R | Pit | 8.2 | 5 | 3 | 3 | 0 | 0 | -- | 1.000 | 6.23 |
| Berry,S | KC | 62.0 | 8 | 7 | 10 | 1 | 2 | -- | .944 | 2.61 |
| Blankenship,L | Oak | 177.0 | 29 | 17 | 36 | 3 | 2 | -- | .946 | 2.85 |
| Blauser,J | Atl | 39.0 | 10 | 5 | 5 | 0 | 1 | -- | 1.000 | 2.31 |
| Blowers,M | NYA | 366.2 | 45 | 26 | 63 | 10 | 4 | -- | .899 | 2.43 |
| Boggs,W | Bos | 1340.2 | 152 | 110 | 241 | 20 | 18 | -- | .946 | 2.49 |
| Bonilla,B | Pit | 80.0 | 14 | 10 | 27 | 3 | 1 | -- | .925 | 4.50 |
| Booker,R | Phi | 29.2 | 10 | 5 | 4 | 1 | 0 | -- | .900 | 3.03 |
| Bordick,M | Oak | 18.0 | 10 | 2 | 3 | 0 | 0 | -- | 1.000 | 2.50 |
| Bradley,S | Sea | 21.0 | 5 | 3 | 6 | 0 | 0 | -- | 1.000 | 3.86 |
| Brett,G | KC | 1.0 | 1 | 1 | 0 | 0 | 0 | -- | 1.000 | 9.00 |
| Brookens,T | Cle | 184.2 | 35 | 9 | 51 | 5 | 4 | -- | .923 | 3.17 |
| Brown,M | Bal | 12.0 | 2 | 0 | 2 | 0 | 0 | -- | 1.000 | 1.50 |
| Brumley,M | Sea | 20.0 | 3 | 1 | 5 | 2 | 0 | -- | .750 | 3.60 |
| Buechele,S | Tex | 685.2 | 91 | 71 | 156 | 8 | 6 | -- | .966 | 3.08 |
| Caminiti,K | Hou | 1249.1 | 149 | 118 | 243 | 21 | 22 | -- | .945 | 2.75 |
| Candaele,C | Hou | 3.0 | 1 | 0 | 1 | 0 | 0 | -- | 1.000 | 3.00 |
| Coachman,P | Cal | 76.0 | 9 | 5 | 17 | 1 | 2 | -- | .957 | 2.72 |
| Cochrane,D | Sea | 16.0 | 3 | 1 | 8 | 0 | 0 | -- | 1.000 | 5.06 |
| Coles,D | Sea | 53.0 | 6 | 2 | 20 | 5 | 0 | -- | .815 | 4.58 |
| Coles,D | Det | 57.0 | 8 | 6 | 19 | 2 | 2 | -- | .926 | 4.26 |
| Coolbaugh,S | Tex | 482.0 | 66 | 43 | 116 | 10 | 12 | -- | .941 | 3.16 |
| Diaz,E | Mil | 20.0 | 7 | 1 | 5 | 0 | 0 | -- | 1.000 | 2.70 |
| Doran,B | Cin | 22.0 | 4 | 0 | 4 | 2 | 0 | -- | .667 | 2.45 |
| Faries,P | SD | 9.0 | 1 | 1 | 6 | 1 | 1 | -- | .875 | 8.00 |
| Felder,M | Mil | 2.0 | 1 | 0 | 1 | 0 | 0 | -- | 1.000 | 4.50 |
| Foley,T | Mon | 17.1 | 7 | 0 | 5 | 0 | 0 | -- | 1.000 | 2.60 |
| Fryman,T | Det | 388.0 | 48 | 23 | 95 | 11 | 12 | -- | .915 | 2.99 |
| Gaetti,G | Min | 1291.0 | 151 | 104 | 320 | 18 | 37 | -- | .959 | 3.08 |
| Gallego,M | Oak | 166.0 | 27 | 10 | 35 | 6 | 4 | -- | .882 | 2.77 |
| Gantner,J | Mil | 74.2 | 9 | 3 | 20 | 2 | 1 | -- | .920 | 3.01 |
| Giles,B | Sea | 3.0 | 1 | 0 | 3 | 0 | 1 | -- | 1.000 | 9.00 |
| Goff,J | Mon | 14.0 | 3 | 1 | 4 | 1 | 0 | -- | .833 | 3.86 |
| Gomez,L | Bal | 107.0 | 12 | 11 | 20 | 4 | 2 | -- | .886 | 2.94 |
| Gonzales,R | Bal | 43.0 | 15 | 3 | 10 | 1 | 1 | -- | .929 | 2.93 |
| Gonzalez,L | Hou | 28.0 | 4 | 5 | 10 | 0 | 1 | -- | 1.000 | 4.82 |
| Grebeck,C | ChA | 233.1 | 35 | 17 | 60 | 1 | 3 | -- | .987 | 3.01 |
| Gruber,K | Tor | 1267.2 | 145 | 124 | 278 | 19 | 21 | -- | .955 | 2.99 |
| Hamilton,J | LA | 54.0 | 7 | 3 | 12 | 0 | 2 | -- | 1.000 | 2.50 |
| Hansen,D | LA | 10.0 | 2 | 0 | 1 | 1 | 0 | -- | .500 | 1.80 |
| Harper,B | Min | 3.0 | 3 | 1 | 2 | 0 | 0 | -- | 1.000 | 9.00 |
| Harris,L | LA | 639.1 | 94 | 78 | 130 | 9 | 11 | -- | .959 | 3.05 |
| Hatcher,M | LA | 48.2 | 10 | 3 | 11 | 3 | 0 | -- | .824 | 3.14 |
| Hayes,C | Phi | 1236.2 | 146 | 121 | 324 | 20 | 31 | -- | .957 | 3.38 |
| Hemond,S | Oak | 34.0 | 7 | 2 | 5 | 0 | 0 | -- | 1.000 | 1.85 |
| Hill,D | Cal | 137.0 | 21 | 8 | 33 | 5 | 4 | -- | .891 | 3.02 |
| Hollins,D | Phi | 182.2 | 30 | 19 | 36 | 4 | 0 | -- | .932 | 2.91 |
| Howell,J | Cal | 817.0 | 102 | 70 | 193 | 17 | 16 | -- | .939 | 3.08 |
| Howitt,D | Oak | 1.0 | 1 | 0 | 0 | 0 | 0 | -- | .000 | .00 |
| Hrbek,K | Min | 1.0 | 1 | 0 | 2 | 0 | 0 | -- | 1.000 | 18.00 |
| Hudler,R | StL | 34.0 | 6 | 5 | 8 | 1 | 0 | -- | .929 | 3.71 |
| Hulett,T | Bal | 199.0 | 24 | 17 | 55 | 3 | 4 | -- | .960 | 3.39 |
| Huson,J | Tex | 130.1 | 36 | 12 | 30 | 2 | 2 | -- | .955 | 3.04 |

## Third Basemen

| Player | Tm | Inn | G | PO | A | E | DP | PB | Pct. | Rng |
|---|---|---|---|---|---|---|---|---|---|---|
| Infante,A | Atl | 9.0 | 4 | 0 | 3 | 0 | 0 | -- | 1.000 | 3.00 |
| Jacoby,B | Cle | 772.2 | 99 | 44 | 158 | 4 | 14 | -- | .981 | 2.40 |
| Jefferies,G | NYN | 286.1 | 34 | 24 | 61 | 4 | 5 | -- | .955 | 2.80 |
| Jeltz,S | KC | 6.0 | 3 | 1 | 1 | 0 | 0 | -- | 1.000 | 3.00 |
| Johnson,H | NYN | 771.2 | 93 | 53 | 158 | 20 | 11 | -- | .913 | 2.69 |
| Jones,T | StL | 15.1 | 6 | 0 | 3 | 0 | 0 | -- | 1.000 | 1.76 |
| King,J | Pit | 840.2 | 115 | 58 | 215 | 18 | 16 | -- | .938 | 3.12 |
| Kunkel,J | Tex | 105.0 | 15 | 10 | 28 | 2 | 3 | -- | .950 | 3.43 |
| Kutcher,R | Bos | 61.1 | 11 | 6 | 15 | 0 | 0 | -- | 1.000 | 3.08 |
| Lansford,C | Oak | 1032.0 | 127 | 101 | 195 | 9 | 23 | -- | .970 | 2.66 |
| Lawless,T | Tor | 15.0 | 4 | 2 | 4 | 1 | 1 | -- | .857 | 4.20 |
| Leius,S | Min | 1.0 | 1 | 0 | 0 | 0 | 0 | -- | .000 | .00 |
| Lemke,M | Atl | 259.2 | 45 | 21 | 71 | 1 | 7 | -- | .989 | 3.22 |
| Leyritz,J | NYA | 580.0 | 69 | 43 | 101 | 11 | 6 | -- | .929 | 2.41 |
| Litton,G | SF | 14.2 | 5 | 2 | 3 | 0 | 0 | -- | 1.000 | 3.07 |
| Lyons,S | ChA | 6.0 | 5 | 0 | 4 | 0 | 1 | -- | 1.000 | 6.00 |
| Magadan,D | NYN | 123.1 | 19 | 7 | 28 | 1 | 1 | -- | .972 | 2.63 |
| Manto,J | Cle | 38.0 | 5 | 6 | 6 | 0 | 0 | -- | 1.000 | 2.84 |
| Martinez,E | Sea | 1196.1 | 143 | 88 | 257 | 27 | 16 | -- | .927 | 2.80 |
| McLemore,M | Cle | 12.1 | 4 | 0 | 3 | 0 | 1 | -- | 1.000 | 2.19 |
| Molitor,P | Mil | 18.0 | 2 | 2 | 7 | 1 | 1 | -- | .900 | 5.00 |
| Mulliniks,R | Tor | 138.0 | 22 | 13 | 25 | 2 | 4 | -- | .950 | 2.61 |
| Naehring,T | Bos | 35.0 | 5 | 3 | 9 | 1 | 1 | -- | .923 | 3.34 |
| Newman,A | Min | 139.0 | 29 | 14 | 38 | 3 | 8 | -- | .945 | 3.56 |
| Noboa,J | Mon | 16.1 | 8 | 3 | 2 | 2 | 0 | -- | .714 | 3.86 |
| O'Malley,T | NYN | 192.2 | 38 | 26 | 33 | 1 | 4 | -- | .983 | 2.80 |
| Oberkfell,K | Hou | 142.0 | 24 | 13 | 30 | 3 | 3 | -- | .935 | 2.92 |
| Oester,R | Cin | 15.0 | 3 | 0 | 2 | 1 | 0 | -- | .667 | 1.80 |
| Olson,G | Atl | 1.0 | 1 | 0 | 0 | 0 | 0 | -- | .000 | .00 |
| Pagliarulo,M | SD | 950.0 | 116 | 78 | 198 | 13 | 16 | -- | .955 | 2.74 |
| Palacios,R | KC | 6.0 | 3 | 1 | 1 | 0 | 0 | -- | 1.000 | 3.00 |
| Parker,R | SF | 4.0 | 1 | 1 | 0 | 1 | 0 | -- | .500 | 4.50 |
| Pecota,B | KC | 61.0 | 11 | 5 | 15 | 0 | 2 | -- | 1.000 | 2.95 |
| Pendleton,T | StL | 1010.0 | 117 | 91 | 248 | 19 | 17 | -- | .947 | 3.19 |
| Petralli,G | Tex | 16.2 | 9 | 1 | 1 | 0 | 0 | -- | 1.000 | 1.08 |
| Phillips,T | Det | 793.1 | 106 | 68 | 198 | 20 | 15 | -- | .930 | 3.24 |
| Polidor,G | Mil | 41.2 | 14 | 1 | 9 | 0 | 0 | -- | 1.000 | 2.16 |
| Presley,J | Atl | 1095.0 | 133 | 102 | 230 | 25 | 19 | -- | .930 | 2.93 |
| Puckett,K | Min | 0.2 | 1 | 0 | 0 | 0 | 0 | -- | .000 | .00 |
| Quinlan,T | Tor | 8.0 | 1 | 0 | 1 | 0 | 0 | -- | 1.000 | 1.13 |
| Quinones,L | Cin | 150.1 | 22 | 12 | 41 | 1 | 0 | -- | .981 | 3.23 |
| Quirk,J | Oak | 28.0 | 8 | 4 | 1 | 1 | 1 | -- | .833 | 1.93 |
| Ramos,D | ChN | 402.2 | 67 | 23 | 46 | 5 | 2 | -- | .932 | 1.65 |
| Riles,E | SF | 49.1 | 10 | 4 | 8 | 0 | 0 | -- | 1.000 | 2.19 |
| Rivera,L | Bos | 3.0 | 1 | 0 | 0 | 0 | 0 | -- | .000 | .00 |
| Roberts,B | SD | 399.2 | 56 | 32 | 90 | 6 | 8 | -- | .953 | 2.88 |
| Rohde,D | Hou | 21.1 | 4 | 0 | 5 | 0 | 0 | -- | 1.000 | 2.11 |
| Romero,E | Det | 191.0 | 27 | 15 | 40 | 1 | 9 | -- | .982 | 2.64 |
| Rose,B | Cal | 26.0 | 3 | 2 | 5 | 0 | 1 | -- | 1.000 | 2.42 |
| Russell,J | Tex | 1.0 | 1 | 0 | 0 | 0 | 0 | -- | .000 | .00 |
| Sabo,C | Cin | 1269.0 | 146 | 71 | 270 | 12 | 17 | -- | .966 | 2.50 |
| Salas,M | Det | 1.0 | 1 | 0 | 1 | 0 | 0 | -- | 1.000 | 9.00 |
| Salazar,L | ChN | 727.0 | 93 | 54 | 137 | 10 | 12 | -- | .950 | 2.49 |
| Schaefer,J | Sea | 134.0 | 26 | 17 | 39 | 4 | 6 | -- | .933 | 4.03 |
| Schu,R | Cal | 271.0 | 38 | 17 | 71 | 8 | 9 | -- | .917 | 3.19 |
| Seitzer,K | KC | 1257.2 | 152 | 101 | 263 | 18 | 30 | -- | .953 | 2.73 |
| Sharperson,M | LA | 690.0 | 106 | 70 | 155 | 12 | 11 | -- | .949 | 3.09 |
| Sheffield,G | Mil | 1069.0 | 125 | 98 | 253 | 25 | 15 | -- | .934 | 3.17 |

## Third Basemen

| Player | Tm | Inn | G | PO | A | E | DP | PB | Pct. | Rng |
|---|---|---|---|---|---|---|---|---|---|---|
| Sojo,L | Tor | 25.1 | 4 | 2 | 5 | 1 | 1 | -- | .875 | 2.84 |
| Springer,S | Cle | 23.0 | 3 | 2 | 3 | 0 | 0 | -- | 1.000 | 1.96 |
| Stanley,M | Tex | 24.0 | 8 | 3 | 4 | 0 | 0 | -- | 1.000 | 2.63 |
| Surhoff,B | Mil | 58.1 | 11 | 4 | 9 | 2 | 1 | -- | .867 | 2.31 |
| Sveum,D | Mil | 161.1 | 22 | 17 | 28 | 4 | 1 | -- | .918 | 2.73 |
| Tabler,P | KC | 27.0 | 6 | 2 | 5 | 1 | 0 | -- | .875 | 2.67 |
| Teufel,T | NYN | 66.0 | 10 | 6 | 14 | 1 | 0 | -- | .952 | 2.86 |
| Thomas,A | Atl | 26.0 | 5 | 1 | 7 | 0 | 2 | -- | 1.000 | 2.77 |
| Tolleson,W | NYA | 3.2 | 3 | 0 | 0 | 0 | 0 | -- | .000 | .00 |
| Velarde,R | NYA | 491.1 | 74 | 43 | 130 | 10 | 11 | -- | .945 | 3.35 |
| Ventura,R | ChA | 1210.0 | 147 | 115 | 262 | 25 | 32 | -- | .938 | 2.99 |
| Walewander,J | NYA | 3.0 | 2 | 1 | 1 | 0 | 0 | -- | 1.000 | 6.00 |
| Wallach,T | Mon | 1425.2 | 161 | 129 | 306 | 21 | 23 | -- | .954 | 2.88 |
| Walling,D | StL | 83.0 | 11 | 6 | 18 | 0 | 1 | -- | 1.000 | 2.60 |
| Wilkerson,C | ChN | 313.0 | 52 | 25 | 61 | 11 | 4 | -- | .887 | 2.79 |
| Williams,E | SD | 103.0 | 13 | 5 | 21 | 3 | 2 | -- | .897 | 2.53 |
| Williams,M | SF | 1372.2 | 159 | 142 | 305 | 19 | 33 | -- | .959 | 3.06 |
| Wilson,C | StL | 98.0 | 13 | 13 | 20 | 1 | 1 | -- | .971 | 3.12 |
| Worthington,C | Bal | 1074.1 | 131 | 90 | 217 | 18 | 28 | -- | .945 | 2.72 |
| Yelding,E | Hou | 6.1 | 3 | 0 | 2 | 1 | 0 | -- | .667 | 4.26 |
| Zeile,T | StL | 203.0 | 24 | 11 | 42 | 7 | 2 | -- | .883 | 2.66 |

## Shortstops

| Player | Tm | Inn | G | PO | A | E | DP | PB | Pct. | Rng |
|---|---|---|---|---|---|---|---|---|---|---|
| Alomar,R | SD | 41.0 | 5 | 5 | 12 | 2 | 4 | -- | .895 | 4.17 |
| Anderson,D | SF | 123.1 | 29 | 18 | 37 | 0 | 5 | -- | 1.000 | 4.01 |
| Anderson,K | Cal | 233.0 | 29 | 53 | 78 | 5 | 21 | -- | .963 | 5.25 |
| Baerga,C | Cle | 171.0 | 48 | 25 | 43 | 4 | 11 | -- | .944 | 3.79 |
| Baez,K | NYN | 27.0 | 4 | 5 | 7 | 0 | 1 | -- | 1.000 | 4.00 |
| Bell,Jay | Pit | 1377.0 | 159 | 260 | 461 | 22 | 86 | -- | .970 | 4.86 |
| Bell,Juan | Bal | 4.0 | 1 | 1 | 1 | 0 | 0 | -- | 1.000 | 4.50 |
| Belliard,R | Pit | 61.0 | 10 | 11 | 17 | 2 | 3 | -- | .933 | 4.43 |
| Benjamin,M | SF | 137.1 | 21 | 30 | 53 | 1 | 10 | -- | .988 | 5.50 |
| Blauser,J | Atl | 778.2 | 93 | 140 | 258 | 16 | 49 | -- | .961 | 4.79 |
| Booker,R | Phi | 187.0 | 27 | 35 | 47 | 2 | 11 | -- | .976 | 4.04 |
| Bordick,M | Oak | 18.0 | 9 | 5 | 1 | 0 | 0 | -- | 1.000 | 3.00 |
| Brookens,T | Cle | 10.0 | 3 | 5 | 4 | 0 | 1 | -- | 1.000 | 8.10 |
| Brumley,M | Sea | 353.1 | 47 | 59 | 110 | 3 | 23 | -- | .983 | 4.38 |
| Candaele,C | Hou | 33.1 | 13 | 6 | 11 | 1 | 2 | -- | .944 | 4.86 |
| Cedeno,A | Hou | 16.0 | 3 | 3 | 2 | 1 | 0 | -- | .833 | 3.38 |
| Cochrane,D | Sea | 5.0 | 5 | 0 | 1 | 0 | 0 | -- | 1.000 | 1.80 |
| Cora,J | SD | 105.2 | 21 | 13 | 17 | 6 | 3 | -- | .833 | 3.07 |
| Diaz,E | Mil | 497.1 | 65 | 100 | 163 | 14 | 35 | -- | .949 | 5.01 |
| Diaz,M | NYN | 42.1 | 10 | 5 | 18 | 1 | 1 | -- | .958 | 5.10 |
| Disarcina,G | Cal | 125.0 | 14 | 14 | 50 | 4 | 8 | -- | .941 | 4.90 |
| Duncan,M | Cin | 65.0 | 12 | 16 | 16 | 3 | 4 | -- | .914 | 4.85 |
| Dunston,S | ChN | 1247.2 | 145 | 250 | 389 | 20 | 79 | -- | .970 | 4.75 |
| Elster,K | NYN | 795.2 | 92 | 157 | 250 | 17 | 41 | -- | .960 | 4.80 |
| Espinoza,A | NYA | 1209.1 | 150 | 270 | 447 | 17 | 103 | -- | .977 | 5.46 |
| Faries,P | SD | 28.0 | 4 | 0 | 10 | 1 | 4 | -- | .909 | 3.54 |
| Fermin,F | Cle | 1180.0 | 147 | 212 | 419 | 16 | 82 | -- | .975 | 4.93 |
| Fernandez,T | Tor | 1384.0 | 161 | 294 | 484 | 9 | 92 | -- | .989 | 5.12 |
| Foley,T | Mon | 262.1 | 45 | 63 | 87 | 2 | 22 | -- | .987 | 5.21 |
| Fryman,T | Det | 139.0 | 17 | 24 | 49 | 3 | 9 | -- | .961 | 4.92 |
| Gaetti,G | Min | 2.0 | 2 | 0 | 1 | 0 | 0 | -- | 1.000 | 4.50 |
| Gagne,G | Min | 1074.0 | 135 | 182 | 376 | 14 | 63 | -- | .976 | 4.79 |

## Shortstops

| Player | Tm | Inn | G | PO | A | E | DP | PB | Pct. | Rng |
|---|---|---|---|---|---|---|---|---|---|---|
| Gallego,M | Oak | 284.0 | 38 | 44 | 85 | 3 | 26 | -- | .977 | 4.18 |
| Garcia,C | Pit | 9.0 | 3 | 0 | 4 | 0 | 1 | -- | 1.000 | 4.00 |
| Giles,B | Sea | 253.0 | 37 | 51 | 80 | 3 | 26 | -- | .978 | 4.77 |
| Gonzales,R | Bal | 25.0 | 9 | 4 | 10 | 0 | 3 | -- | 1.000 | 5.04 |
| Grebeck,C | ChA | 86.0 | 16 | 13 | 28 | 2 | 5 | -- | .953 | 4.50 |
| Green,G | Tex | 283.0 | 56 | 57 | 104 | 5 | 24 | -- | .970 | 5.28 |
| Griffin,A | LA | 1153.2 | 139 | 221 | 384 | 26 | 63 | -- | .959 | 4.92 |
| Guillen,O | ChA | 1361.1 | 159 | 253 | 472 | 17 | 100 | -- | .977 | 4.91 |
| Harris,L | LA | 1.0 | 1 | 0 | 2 | 0 | 0 | -- | 1.000 | 18.00 |
| Heath,M | Det | 1.0 | 1 | 1 | 0 | 0 | 0 | -- | 1.000 | 9.00 |
| Hill,D | Cal | 158.1 | 24 | 35 | 48 | 3 | 7 | -- | .965 | 4.89 |
| Howell,J | Cal | 11.0 | 1 | 4 | 3 | 1 | 0 | -- | .875 | 6.55 |
| Hudler,R | StL | 1.1 | 1 | 1 | 1 | 0 | 0 | -- | 1.000 | 13.50 |
| Huson,J | Tex | 795.1 | 121 | 157 | 261 | 17 | 70 | -- | .961 | 4.92 |
| Infante,A | Atl | 27.0 | 3 | 8 | 8 | 1 | 1 | -- | .941 | 5.67 |
| Jeltz,S | KC | 126.0 | 23 | 24 | 38 | 2 | 9 | -- | .969 | 4.57 |
| Johnson,H | NYN | 563.1 | 73 | 98 | 179 | 8 | 28 | -- | .972 | 4.55 |
| Jones,T | StL | 205.2 | 29 | 28 | 74 | 6 | 12 | -- | .944 | 4.73 |
| Kunkel,J | Tex | 366.1 | 67 | 78 | 125 | 9 | 27 | -- | .958 | 5.21 |
| Larkin,B | Cin | 1344.0 | 156 | 255 | 467 | 17 | 86 | -- | .977 | 4.95 |
| Lee,M | Tor | 43.0 | 9 | 6 | 15 | 0 | 1 | -- | 1.000 | 4.40 |
| Leius,S | Min | 76.0 | 12 | 20 | 25 | 0 | 10 | -- | 1.000 | 5.33 |
| Lemke,M | Atl | 1.0 | 1 | 0 | 1 | 0 | 0 | -- | 1.000 | 9.00 |
| Liriano,N | Min | 0.1 | 1 | 0 | 0 | 0 | 0 | -- | .000 | .00 |
| Litton,G | SF | 18.0 | 7 | 9 | 9 | 0 | 2 | -- | 1.000 | 9.00 |
| Lyons,S | ChA | 2.0 | 1 | 0 | 1 | 0 | 0 | -- | 1.000 | 4.50 |
| McKnight,J | Bal | 2.0 | 1 | 1 | 1 | 0 | 1 | -- | 1.000 | 9.00 |
| McLemore,M | Cal | 61.1 | 8 | 14 | 15 | 4 | 3 | -- | .879 | 4.84 |
| Miller,K | NYN | 11.2 | 4 | 3 | 4 | 0 | 2 | -- | 1.000 | 5.40 |
| Naehring,T | Bos | 164.0 | 19 | 32 | 58 | 8 | 12 | -- | .918 | 5.38 |
| Newman,A | Min | 283.1 | 48 | 56 | 92 | 8 | 26 | -- | .949 | 4.96 |
| Nixon,O | Mon | 0.2 | 1 | 0 | 1 | 0 | 1 | -- | 1.000 | 13.50 |
| Noboa,J | Mon | 16.0 | 7 | 4 | 4 | 0 | 1 | -- | 1.000 | 4.50 |
| Offerman,J | LA | 149.0 | 27 | 29 | 40 | 4 | 6 | -- | .945 | 4.41 |
| Oquendo,J | StL | 33.0 | 4 | 9 | 10 | 1 | 2 | -- | .950 | 5.45 |
| Owen,S | Mon | 1194.1 | 148 | 215 | 340 | 6 | 52 | -- | .989 | 4.23 |
| Parker,R | SF | 1.1 | 1 | 0 | 2 | 0 | 0 | -- | 1.000 | 13.50 |
| Pecota,B | KC | 156.0 | 22 | 44 | 57 | 2 | 18 | -- | .981 | 5.94 |
| Perezchica,T | SF | 1.1 | 2 | 0 | 0 | 0 | 0 | -- | .000 | .00 |
| Phillips,T | Det | 77.0 | 11 | 11 | 33 | 1 | 9 | -- | .978 | 5.26 |
| Polidor,G | Mil | 3.0 | 2 | 0 | 1 | 0 | 0 | -- | 1.000 | 3.00 |
| Puckett,K | Min | 0.0 | 1 | 0 | 0 | 0 | 0 | -- | .000 | .00 |
| Quinones,L | Cin | 47.1 | 9 | 8 | 13 | 3 | 3 | -- | .875 | 4.56 |
| Ramirez,R | Hou | 1058.0 | 129 | 190 | 321 | 25 | 58 | -- | .953 | 4.56 |
| Ramos,D | ChN | 139.2 | 21 | 37 | 54 | 5 | 15 | -- | .948 | 6.19 |
| Reed,J | Bos | 349.1 | 50 | 61 | 107 | 10 | 21 | -- | .944 | 4.59 |
| Riles,E | SF | 119.2 | 26 | 21 | 49 | 1 | 8 | -- | .986 | 5.34 |
| Ripken,C | Bal | 1404.1 | 161 | 241 | 433 | 3 | 95 | -- | .996 | 4.34 |
| Rivera,L | Bos | 928.2 | 111 | 186 | 310 | 18 | 71 | -- | .965 | 4.98 |
| Roberts,B | SD | 121.1 | 18 | 23 | 38 | 1 | 8 | -- | .984 | 4.60 |
| Rohde,D | Hou | 6.0 | 2 | 1 | 2 | 0 | 0 | -- | 1.000 | 4.50 |
| Rosario,V | Atl | 17.0 | 3 | 3 | 4 | 0 | 0 | -- | 1.000 | 3.71 |
| Santana,A | SF | 9.0 | 3 | 2 | 1 | 0 | 1 | -- | 1.000 | 3.00 |
| Santana,R | Cle | 33.0 | 7 | 2 | 9 | 0 | 2 | -- | 1.000 | 3.00 |
| Schaefer,J | Sea | 152.0 | 24 | 35 | 47 | 1 | 13 | -- | .988 | 4.91 |
| Schofield,D | Cal | 865.1 | 99 | 170 | 321 | 17 | 77 | -- | .967 | 5.28 |
| Sharperson,M | LA | 65.1 | 15 | 17 | 26 | 1 | 7 | -- | .977 | 6.06 |
| Smith,G | ChN | 52.1 | 7 | 10 | 21 | 3 | 5 | -- | .912 | 5.85 |

## Shortstops

| Player | Tm | Inn | G | PO | A | E | DP | PB | Pct. | Rng |
|---|---|---|---|---|---|---|---|---|---|---|
| Smith,O | StL | 1203.1 | 140 | 212 | 376 | 12 | 67 | -- | .980 | 4.49 |
| Snyder,C | Cle | 33.1 | 5 | 5 | 7 | 1 | 2 | -- | .923 | 3.51 |
| Sojo,L | Tor | 27.0 | 5 | 6 | 10 | 3 | 3 | -- | .842 | 6.33 |
| Spiers,B | Mil | 929.2 | 111 | 159 | 327 | 12 | 72 | -- | .976 | 4.82 |
| Stillwell,K | KC | 1138.2 | 141 | 179 | 350 | 24 | 80 | -- | .957 | 4.37 |
| Sveum,D | Mil | 15.0 | 5 | 3 | 5 | 1 | 1 | -- | .889 | 5.40 |
| Templeton,G | SD | 1165.2 | 135 | 216 | 364 | 26 | 73 | -- | .957 | 4.68 |
| Thomas,A | Atl | 606.0 | 72 | 103 | 194 | 10 | 41 | -- | .967 | 4.56 |
| Thon,D | Phi | 1262.0 | 148 | 223 | 437 | 25 | 86 | -- | .964 | 4.89 |
| Tolleson,W | NYA | 161.0 | 45 | 43 | 71 | 2 | 22 | -- | .983 | 6.48 |
| Trammell,A | Det | 1213.1 | 142 | 232 | 406 | 14 | 103 | -- | .979 | 4.84 |
| Uribe,J | SF | 1036.1 | 134 | 180 | 371 | 20 | 74 | -- | .965 | 4.96 |
| Velarde,R | NYA | 73.1 | 15 | 21 | 26 | 1 | 6 | -- | .979 | 5.89 |
| Vizcaino,J | LA | 73.0 | 11 | 18 | 25 | 2 | 5 | -- | .956 | 5.55 |
| Vizquel,O | Sea | 680.0 | 81 | 106 | 243 | 7 | 51 | -- | .980 | 4.71 |
| Walewander,J | NYA | 1.0 | 1 | 0 | 2 | 0 | 0 | -- | 1.000 | 18.00 |
| Weiss,W | Oak | 1154.0 | 137 | 193 | 373 | 12 | 79 | -- | .979 | 4.51 |
| Wilkerson,C | ChN | 3.0 | 1 | 0 | 2 | 0 | 0 | -- | 1.000 | 6.00 |
| Yelding,E | Hou | 336.2 | 40 | 64 | 98 | 7 | 16 | -- | .959 | 4.52 |

## Left Fielders

| Player | Tm | Inn | G | PO | A | E | DP | PB | Pct. | Rng |
|---|---|---|---|---|---|---|---|---|---|---|
| Abner,S | SD | 103.2 | 23 | 30 | 1 | 1 | 0 | -- | .969 | 2.78 |
| Aldrete,M | Mon | 177.1 | 26 | 38 | 3 | 1 | 0 | -- | .976 | 2.13 |
| Alou,M | Pit | 12.0 | 2 | 3 | 0 | 0 | 0 | -- | 1.000 | 2.25 |
| Alou,M | Mon | 1.0 | 1 | 0 | 0 | 0 | 0 | -- | .000 | .00 |
| Anderson,B | Bal | 323.0 | 44 | 101 | 2 | 1 | 0 | -- | .990 | 2.90 |
| Anthony,E | Hou | 94.1 | 13 | 20 | 1 | 1 | 0 | -- | .955 | 2.10 |
| Azocar,O | NYA | 358.0 | 47 | 88 | 4 | 1 | 1 | -- | .989 | 2.34 |
| Baldwin,J | Hou | 5.0 | 2 | 1 | 0 | 0 | 0 | -- | 1.000 | 1.80 |
| Belcher,K | Tex | 2.0 | 2 | 1 | 0 | 0 | 0 | -- | 1.000 | 4.50 |
| Bell,G | Tor | 922.0 | 106 | 224 | 4 | 5 | 1 | -- | .979 | 2.27 |
| Belle,J | Cle | 2.0 | 1 | 0 | 0 | 0 | 0 | -- | .000 | .00 |
| Benzinger,T | Cin | 74.0 | 10 | 26 | 0 | 0 | 0 | -- | 1.000 | 3.16 |
| Bergman,D | Det | 5.1 | 5 | 0 | 0 | 0 | 0 | -- | .000 | .00 |
| Berroa,G | Atl | 5.0 | 3 | 1 | 0 | 0 | 0 | -- | 1.000 | 1.80 |
| Bichette,D | Cal | 342.1 | 51 | 70 | 3 | 6 | 1 | -- | .924 | 2.08 |
| Biggio,C | Hou | 87.2 | 18 | 20 | 2 | 1 | 0 | -- | .957 | 2.36 |
| Blankenship,L | Oak | 36.0 | 10 | 5 | 0 | 1 | 0 | -- | .833 | 1.50 |
| Bonds,B | Pit | 1275.0 | 149 | 333 | 14 | 6 | 3 | -- | .983 | 2.49 |
| Bosley,T | Tex | 27.2 | 7 | 2 | 0 | 0 | 0 | -- | 1.000 | 0.65 |
| Boston,D | NYN | 9.0 | 1 | 4 | 0 | 0 | 0 | -- | 1.000 | 4.00 |
| Bradley,P | Bal | 596.0 | 70 | 150 | 3 | 2 | 0 | -- | .987 | 2.34 |
| Bradley,P | ChA | 132.1 | 23 | 35 | 1 | 1 | 0 | -- | .973 | 2.52 |
| Braggs,G | Mil | 102.0 | 13 | 26 | 1 | 1 | 0 | -- | .964 | 2.47 |
| Braggs,G | Cin | 214.0 | 26 | 46 | 7 | 2 | 1 | -- | .964 | 2.31 |
| Brett,G | KC | 16.1 | 2 | 5 | 1 | 0 | 0 | -- | 1.000 | 3.31 |
| Briley,G | Sea | 279.0 | 43 | 56 | 4 | 1 | 1 | -- | .984 | 1.97 |
| Brumley,M | Sea | 1.0 | 1 | 0 | 0 | 0 | 0 | -- | .000 | .00 |
| Bush,R | Min | 9.0 | 2 | 2 | 0 | 0 | 0 | -- | 1.000 | 2.00 |
| Calderon,I | ChA | 1113.0 | 132 | 267 | 7 | 7 | 1 | -- | .975 | 2.27 |
| Campusano,S | Phi | 40.1 | 16 | 4 | 0 | 0 | 0 | -- | 1.000 | 0.89 |
| Candaele,C | Hou | 131.0 | 36 | 36 | 1 | 0 | 0 | -- | 1.000 | 2.54 |
| Cangelosi,J | Pit | 18.0 | 3 | 8 | 0 | 0 | 0 | -- | 1.000 | 4.00 |
| Canseco,O | Oak | 8.0 | 1 | 3 | 0 | 0 | 0 | -- | 1.000 | 3.38 |
| Carr,C | NYN | 1.0 | 1 | 0 | 0 | 0 | 0 | -- | .000 | .00 |

## Left Fielders

| Player | Tm | Inn | G | PO | A | E | DP | PB | Pct. | Rng |
|---|---|---|---|---|---|---|---|---|---|---|
| Carreon,M | NYN | 100.0 | 16 | 18 | 0 | 0 | 0 | -- | 1.000 | 1.62 |
| Carter,J | SD | 358.0 | 53 | 92 | 5 | 2 | 1 | -- | .980 | 2.49 |
| Carter,S | Pit | 1.0 | 1 | 0 | 0 | 0 | 0 | -- | .000 | .00 |
| Castillo,C | Min | 7.0 | 2 | 4 | 0 | 0 | 0 | -- | 1.000 | 5.14 |
| Chamberlain,W | Phi | 79.0 | 10 | 22 | 0 | 0 | 0 | -- | 1.000 | 2.51 |
| Clark,D | ChN | 275.0 | 39 | 62 | 1 | 0 | 0 | -- | 1.000 | 2.06 |
| Clark,J | SD | 19.0 | 4 | 4 | 0 | 1 | 0 | -- | .800 | 2.37 |
| Coleman,V | StL | 1008.0 | 118 | 240 | 10 | 5 | 1 | -- | .980 | 2.28 |
| Coles,D | Det | 16.0 | 4 | 4 | 0 | 0 | 0 | -- | 1.000 | 2.25 |
| Collins,D | StL | 27.2 | 4 | 4 | 0 | 0 | 0 | -- | 1.000 | 1.30 |
| Cotto,H | Sea | 227.1 | 41 | 66 | 0 | 1 | 0 | -- | .985 | 2.65 |
| Daniels,K | LA | 985.0 | 127 | 207 | 13 | 3 | 3 | -- | .987 | 2.04 |
| Dascenzo,D | ChN | 225.2 | 63 | 54 | 1 | 0 | 1 | -- | 1.000 | 2.19 |
| Daugherty,J | Tex | 275.2 | 39 | 45 | 4 | 1 | 1 | -- | .980 | 1.63 |
| Davidson,M | Hou | 151.2 | 26 | 50 | 0 | 2 | 0 | -- | .962 | 3.09 |
| Davis,C | Cal | 365.2 | 46 | 69 | 5 | 3 | 1 | -- | .961 | 1.90 |
| Davis,E | Cin | 480.1 | 56 | 97 | 9 | 1 | 0 | -- | .991 | 2.00 |
| Ducey,R | Tor | 149.0 | 19 | 37 | 0 | 0 | 0 | -- | 1.000 | 2.23 |
| Duncan,M | Cin | 6.0 | 1 | 4 | 0 | 0 | 0 | -- | 1.000 | 6.00 |
| Dwyer,J | Min | 1.0 | 1 | 1 | 0 | 0 | 0 | -- | 1.000 | 9.00 |
| Eisenreich,J | KC | 493.2 | 71 | 110 | 2 | 0 | 1 | -- | 1.000 | 2.04 |
| Espy,C | Tex | 9.0 | 4 | 2 | 0 | 0 | 0 | -- | 1.000 | 2.00 |
| Felder,M | Mil | 271.1 | 63 | 78 | 2 | 2 | 2 | -- | .976 | 2.72 |
| Finley,S | Bal | 99.2 | 22 | 25 | 0 | 0 | 0 | -- | 1.000 | 2.26 |
| Fitzgerald,M | Mon | 9.0 | 1 | 3 | 0 | 0 | 0 | -- | 1.000 | 3.00 |
| Gallagher,D | ChA | 33.1 | 14 | 7 | 1 | 1 | 1 | -- | .889 | 2.43 |
| Gallagher,D | Bal | 107.0 | 17 | 36 | 2 | 0 | 1 | -- | 1.000 | 3.20 |
| Gant,R | Atl | 289.2 | 38 | 78 | 0 | 3 | 0 | -- | .963 | 2.52 |
| Gibson,K | LA | 91.0 | 11 | 30 | 1 | 1 | 0 | -- | .969 | 3.16 |
| Gilkey,B | StL | 144.0 | 19 | 47 | 1 | 2 | 0 | -- | .960 | 3.13 |
| Gladden,D | Min | 1100.0 | 134 | 284 | 12 | 6 | 2 | -- | .980 | 2.47 |
| Gonzalez,Jose | LA | 115.2 | 43 | 31 | 1 | 0 | 0 | -- | 1.000 | 2.49 |
| Gonzalez,Juan | Tex | 1.0 | 1 | 1 | 0 | 0 | 0 | -- | 1.000 | 9.00 |
| Greenwell,M | Bos | 1381.0 | 159 | 287 | 12 | 7 | 1 | -- | .977 | 1.99 |
| Gregg,T | Atl | 38.0 | 7 | 8 | 0 | 0 | 0 | -- | 1.000 | 1.89 |
| Griffey Sr,K | Cin | 31.2 | 5 | 12 | 0 | 0 | 0 | -- | 1.000 | 3.41 |
| Griffey Sr,K | Sea | 151.0 | 20 | 25 | 1 | 1 | 0 | -- | .963 | 1.61 |
| Grissom,M | Mon | 108.1 | 18 | 23 | 0 | 1 | 0 | -- | .958 | 1.99 |
| Gwynn,C | LA | 135.0 | 32 | 25 | 1 | 0 | 0 | -- | 1.000 | 1.73 |
| Hall,M | NYA | 280.2 | 36 | 51 | 2 | 1 | 0 | -- | .981 | 1.73 |
| Hamilton,D | Mil | 237.1 | 41 | 74 | 0 | 1 | 0 | -- | .987 | 2.84 |
| Hatcher,B | Cin | 525.1 | 76 | 134 | 6 | 1 | 1 | -- | .993 | 2.42 |
| Hatcher,M | LA | 57.0 | 10 | 10 | 0 | 0 | 0 | -- | 1.000 | 1.58 |
| Hayes,V | Phi | 407.2 | 46 | 92 | 2 | 4 | 0 | -- | .959 | 2.16 |
| Heep,D | Bos | 2.0 | 1 | 1 | 0 | 0 | 0 | -- | 1.000 | 4.50 |
| Henderson,D | Oak | 7.0 | 1 | 1 | 0 | 0 | 0 | -- | 1.000 | 1.29 |
| Henderson,R | Oak | 993.1 | 119 | 291 | 5 | 5 | 0 | -- | .983 | 2.73 |
| Hill,G | Tor | 204.0 | 27 | 48 | 2 | 0 | 0 | -- | 1.000 | 2.21 |
| Howard,S | Oak | 18.0 | 4 | 4 | 0 | 0 | 0 | -- | 1.000 | 2.00 |
| Howard,T | SD | 53.2 | 9 | 13 | 0 | 1 | 0 | -- | .929 | 2.35 |
| Howitt,D | Oak | 1.0 | 1 | 0 | 0 | 0 | 0 | -- | .000 | .00 |
| Hudler,R | StL | 122.0 | 17 | 40 | 3 | 1 | 0 | -- | .977 | 3.25 |
| Hughes,K | NYN | 10.0 | 4 | 4 | 0 | 0 | 0 | -- | 1.000 | 3.60 |
| Incaviglia,P | Tex | 1080.1 | 136 | 252 | 11 | 7 | 3 | -- | .974 | 2.25 |
| Jackson,B | KC | 313.0 | 36 | 83 | 3 | 6 | 1 | -- | .935 | 2.65 |
| Jackson,D | SD | 2.2 | 2 | 1 | 0 | 0 | 0 | -- | 1.000 | 3.38 |
| James,C | Cle | 96.0 | 12 | 20 | 1 | 0 | 0 | -- | 1.000 | 1.97 |
| James,D | Cle | 174.1 | 25 | 40 | 0 | 2 | 0 | -- | .952 | 2.17 |

## Left Fielders

| Player | Tm | Inn | G | PO | A | E | DP | PB | Pct. | Rng |
|---|---|---|---|---|---|---|---|---|---|---|
| Javier,S | Oak | 6.2 | 4 | 0 | 0 | 0 | 0 | -- | .000 | .00 |
| Javier,S | LA | 44.0 | 9 | 10 | 0 | 0 | 0 | -- | 1.000 | 2.05 |
| Jefferson,S | Cle | 153.1 | 23 | 32 | 2 | 0 | 0 | -- | 1.000 | 2.00 |
| Jelic,C | NYN | 21.0 | 4 | 1 | 0 | 0 | 0 | -- | 1.000 | 0.43 |
| Jeltz,S | KC | 0.1 | 1 | 0 | 0 | 0 | 0 | -- | .000 | .00 |
| Jennings,D | Oak | 197.1 | 32 | 46 | 0 | 1 | 0 | -- | .979 | 2.14 |
| Johnson,L | ChA | 14.0 | 9 | 2 | 0 | 0 | 0 | -- | 1.000 | 1.29 |
| Jones,R | Phi | 56.0 | 8 | 9 | 1 | 0 | 0 | -- | 1.000 | 1.61 |
| Jones,T | Det | 170.0 | 27 | 37 | 3 | 2 | 0 | -- | .952 | 2.22 |
| Jones,T | Sea | 148.0 | 18 | 31 | 0 | 0 | 0 | -- | 1.000 | 1.89 |
| Jose,F | Oak | 182.2 | 26 | 52 | 1 | 2 | 0 | -- | .964 | 2.71 |
| Jose,F | StL | 8.0 | 1 | 4 | 0 | 0 | 0 | -- | 1.000 | 4.50 |
| Justice,D | Atl | 2.0 | 1 | 0 | 0 | 0 | 0 | -- | .000 | .00 |
| Kelly,R | NYA | 95.1 | 11 | 19 | 0 | 1 | 0 | -- | .950 | 1.89 |
| Kingery,M | SF | 73.1 | 15 | 13 | 2 | 0 | 1 | -- | 1.000 | 1.84 |
| Komminsk,B | SF | 7.0 | 2 | 1 | 0 | 0 | 0 | -- | 1.000 | 1.29 |
| Komminsk,B | Bal | 20.2 | 6 | 5 | 0 | 0 | 0 | -- | 1.000 | 2.18 |
| Kruk,J | Phi | 497.1 | 69 | 98 | 1 | 1 | 0 | -- | .990 | 1.81 |
| Kunkel,J | Tex | 1.0 | 1 | 0 | 0 | 0 | 0 | -- | .000 | .00 |
| Kutcher,R | Bos | 4.0 | 2 | 0 | 0 | 0 | 0 | -- | .000 | .00 |
| Lancaster,L | ChN | 0.0 | 1 | 0 | 0 | 0 | 0 | -- | .000 | .00 |
| Lawless,T | Tor | 13.0 | 2 | 6 | 0 | 0 | 0 | -- | 1.000 | 4.15 |
| Leach,R | SF | 79.0 | 13 | 18 | 0 | 0 | 0 | -- | 1.000 | 2.05 |
| Leonard,J | Sea | 600.0 | 74 | 107 | 0 | 1 | 0 | -- | .991 | 1.62 |
| Leonard,M | SF | 8.0 | 2 | 0 | 0 | 0 | 0 | -- | .000 | .00 |
| Lewis,D | Oak | 6.0 | 3 | 1 | 0 | 0 | 0 | -- | 1.000 | 1.50 |
| Leyritz,J | NYA | 69.0 | 10 | 14 | 2 | 1 | 0 | -- | .941 | 2.22 |
| Litton,G | SF | 46.0 | 14 | 6 | 0 | 1 | 0 | -- | .857 | 1.37 |
| Lusader,S | Det | 31.0 | 12 | 3 | 0 | 0 | 0 | -- | 1.000 | 0.87 |
| Lynn,F | SD | 314.0 | 42 | 64 | 1 | 0 | 0 | -- | 1.000 | 1.86 |
| Lyons,S | ChA | 14.0 | 2 | 2 | 0 | 0 | 0 | -- | 1.000 | 1.29 |
| Mack,S | Min | 124.2 | 23 | 31 | 3 | 0 | 1 | -- | 1.000 | 2.45 |
| Maldonado,C | Cle | 837.1 | 104 | 202 | 8 | 1 | 1 | -- | .995 | 2.27 |
| Martinez,Carlos | ChA | 1.2 | 1 | 0 | 0 | 0 | 0 | -- | .000 | .00 |
| Martinez,Carml. | Phi | 128.0 | 20 | 31 | 1 | 0 | 0 | -- | 1.000 | 2.25 |
| Martinez,Carml. | Pit | 9.0 | 2 | 2 | 0 | 0 | 0 | -- | 1.000 | 2.00 |
| Mattingly,D | NYA | 1.0 | 1 | 0 | 0 | 0 | 0 | -- | .000 | .00 |
| May,D | ChN | 130.2 | 17 | 34 | 1 | 1 | 0 | -- | .972 | 2.48 |
| McClendon,L | ChN | 167.0 | 23 | 50 | 0 | 1 | 0 | -- | .980 | 2.75 |
| McClendon,L | Pit | 1.0 | 1 | 0 | 0 | 0 | 0 | -- | .000 | .00 |
| McCray,R | ChA | 5.0 | 2 | 2 | 0 | 0 | 0 | -- | 1.000 | 3.60 |
| McDowell,O | Atl | 97.1 | 12 | 14 | 0 | 0 | 0 | -- | 1.000 | 1.29 |
| McKnight,J | Bal | 26.1 | 4 | 3 | 0 | 0 | 0 | -- | 1.000 | 1.03 |
| McReynolds,K | NYN | 1238.0 | 144 | 237 | 14 | 3 | 2 | -- | .988 | 1.85 |
| Meadows,L | Hou | 24.1 | 7 | 7 | 0 | 0 | 0 | -- | 1.000 | 2.59 |
| Meadows,L | Phi | 8.0 | 3 | 0 | 0 | 0 | 0 | -- | .000 | .00 |
| Meulens,H | NYA | 197.1 | 23 | 49 | 3 | 2 | 1 | -- | .963 | 2.46 |
| Miller,K | NYN | 37.0 | 7 | 4 | 0 | 1 | 0 | -- | .800 | 1.22 |
| Mitchell,K | SF | 1180.0 | 138 | 293 | 9 | 9 | 3 | -- | .971 | 2.37 |
| Morman,R | KC | 59.0 | 8 | 8 | 1 | 0 | 0 | -- | 1.000 | 1.37 |
| Morris,H | Cin | 30.1 | 6 | 6 | 0 | 1 | 0 | -- | .857 | 2.08 |
| Moseby,L | Det | 108.0 | 14 | 25 | 1 | 0 | 0 | -- | 1.000 | 2.17 |
| Moses,J | Min | 92.0 | 17 | 24 | 1 | 0 | 0 | -- | 1.000 | 2.45 |
| Munoz,P | Min | 14.0 | 3 | 0 | 0 | 1 | 0 | -- | .000 | 0.64 |
| Newman,A | Min | 11.0 | 3 | 2 | 0 | 0 | 0 | -- | 1.000 | 1.64 |
| Nichols,C | Hou | 1.0 | 1 | 0 | 0 | 0 | 0 | -- | .000 | .00 |
| Nixon,D | Bal | 29.0 | 4 | 5 | 0 | 0 | 0 | -- | 1.000 | 1.55 |
| Nixon,O | Mon | 99.0 | 21 | 29 | 1 | 0 | 0 | -- | 1.000 | 2.73 |

## Left Fielders

| Player | Tm | Inn | G | PO | A | E | DP | PB | Pct. | Rng |
|---|---|---|---|---|---|---|---|---|---|---|
| Noboa,J | Mon | 2.0 | 2 | 1 | 0 | 0 | 0 | -- | 1.000 | 4.50 |
| O'Brien,P | Sea | 37.0 | 6 | 2 | 0 | 0 | 0 | -- | 1.000 | 0.49 |
| Orsulak,J | Bal | 233.2 | 29 | 59 | 3 | 1 | 1 | -- | .984 | 2.43 |
| Ortiz,J | Hou | 138.2 | 20 | 34 | 1 | 0 | 0 | -- | 1.000 | 2.27 |
| Parker,R | SF | 53.0 | 13 | 13 | 0 | 0 | 0 | -- | 1.000 | 2.21 |
| Pasqua,D | ChA | 136.0 | 21 | 37 | 3 | 3 | 0 | -- | .930 | 2.85 |
| Pecota,B | KC | 31.0 | 4 | 8 | 0 | 0 | 0 | -- | 1.000 | 2.32 |
| Phillips,T | Det | 17.0 | 4 | 4 | 0 | 1 | 0 | -- | .800 | 2.65 |
| Plantier,P | Bos | 1.0 | 1 | 0 | 0 | 0 | 0 | -- | .000 | .00 |
| Polonia,L | Cal | 576.2 | 73 | 116 | 3 | 3 | 2 | -- | .975 | 1.90 |
| Puckett,K | Min | 77.0 | 9 | 20 | 0 | 1 | 0 | -- | .952 | 2.45 |
| Puhl,T | Hou | 37.0 | 6 | 5 | 0 | 0 | 0 | -- | 1.000 | 1.22 |
| Raines,T | Mon | 1059.2 | 123 | 239 | 3 | 6 | 1 | -- | .976 | 2.11 |
| Ready,R | Phi | 195.2 | 30 | 32 | 2 | 0 | 0 | -- | 1.000 | 1.56 |
| Redus,G | Pit | 27.0 | 4 | 6 | 1 | 0 | 0 | -- | 1.000 | 2.33 |
| Reed,D | NYN | 6.0 | 2 | 1 | 0 | 0 | 0 | -- | 1.000 | 1.50 |
| Reimer,K | Tex | 26.0 | 5 | 5 | 0 | 0 | 0 | -- | 1.000 | 1.73 |
| Reynolds,R | Pit | 91.0 | 13 | 24 | 0 | 1 | 0 | -- | .960 | 2.47 |
| Rhodes,K | Hou | 122.1 | 20 | 37 | 0 | 2 | 0 | -- | .949 | 2.87 |
| Roberts,B | SD | 610.2 | 75 | 161 | 8 | 3 | 1 | -- | .983 | 2.53 |
| Romine,K | Bos | 54.0 | 16 | 15 | 0 | 2 | 0 | -- | .882 | 2.83 |
| Roomes,R | Cin | 82.0 | 12 | 20 | 1 | 0 | 0 | -- | 1.000 | 2.30 |
| Roomes,R | Mon | 17.0 | 3 | 4 | 0 | 0 | 0 | -- | 1.000 | 2.12 |
| Russell,J | Tex | 22.0 | 6 | 5 | 0 | 0 | 0 | -- | 1.000 | 2.05 |
| Ryal,M | Pit | 13.0 | 3 | 3 | 0 | 0 | 0 | -- | 1.000 | 2.08 |
| Salazar,L | ChN | 169.2 | 28 | 42 | 1 | 2 | 0 | -- | .956 | 2.39 |
| Sanders,D | NYA | 195.2 | 29 | 39 | 1 | 1 | 1 | -- | .976 | 1.89 |
| Schu,R | Cal | 11.0 | 4 | 0 | 0 | 0 | 0 | -- | .000 | .00 |
| Schulz,J | KC | 60.0 | 8 | 15 | 0 | 1 | 0 | -- | .938 | 2.40 |
| Sheets,L | Det | 379.0 | 56 | 71 | 5 | 1 | 0 | -- | .987 | 1.83 |
| Shelby,J | LA | 14.1 | 7 | 4 | 0 | 0 | 0 | -- | 1.000 | 2.51 |
| Shelby,J | Det | 125.0 | 24 | 27 | 2 | 1 | 1 | -- | .967 | 2.16 |
| Smith,D | ChN | 426.1 | 59 | 107 | 2 | 1 | 1 | -- | .991 | 2.32 |
| Smith,L | Atl | 992.2 | 122 | 252 | 6 | 12 | 2 | -- | .956 | 2.45 |
| Sojo,L | Tor | 36.0 | 5 | 10 | 2 | 0 | 0 | -- | 1.000 | 3.00 |
| Stubbs,F | Hou | 479.1 | 67 | 108 | 1 | 1 | 0 | -- | .991 | 2.07 |
| Tabler,P | KC | 67.0 | 11 | 12 | 1 | 1 | 0 | -- | .929 | 1.88 |
| Tabler,P | NYN | 16.0 | 3 | 2 | 0 | 0 | 0 | -- | 1.000 | 1.13 |
| Thompson,M | StL | 72.1 | 12 | 15 | 2 | 2 | 0 | -- | .895 | 2.36 |
| Thurman,G | KC | 21.0 | 5 | 6 | 0 | 0 | 0 | -- | 1.000 | 2.57 |
| Torve,K | NYN | 2.0 | 1 | 0 | 0 | 0 | 0 | -- | .000 | .00 |
| Varsho,G | ChN | 2.0 | 2 | 0 | 0 | 0 | 0 | -- | .000 | .00 |
| Vatcher,J | Phi | 37.0 | 12 | 8 | 0 | 0 | 0 | -- | 1.000 | 1.95 |
| Vatcher,J | Atl | 5.0 | 2 | 1 | 0 | 0 | 0 | -- | 1.000 | 1.80 |
| Vaughn,G | Mil | 834.1 | 106 | 196 | 8 | 7 | 0 | -- | .967 | 2.28 |
| Velarde,R | NYA | 20.1 | 5 | 6 | 0 | 0 | 0 | -- | 1.000 | 2.66 |
| Venable,M | Cal | 158.1 | 41 | 42 | 2 | 1 | 0 | -- | .978 | 2.56 |
| Walling,D | StL | 17.0 | 3 | 4 | 1 | 0 | 0 | -- | 1.000 | 2.65 |
| Ward,G | Det | 546.0 | 76 | 136 | 1 | 2 | 1 | -- | .986 | 2.29 |
| Washington,C | NYA | 145.0 | 19 | 36 | 2 | 0 | 0 | -- | 1.000 | 2.36 |
| Webster,M | Cle | 164.1 | 25 | 44 | 0 | 1 | 0 | -- | .978 | 2.46 |
| Whiten,M | Tor | 13.0 | 3 | 1 | 1 | 0 | 0 | -- | 1.000 | 1.38 |
| Wilkerson,C | ChN | 0.1 | 1 | 0 | 0 | 0 | 0 | -- | .000 | .00 |
| Williams,K | Det | 33.0 | 17 | 6 | 0 | 0 | 0 | -- | 1.000 | 1.64 |
| Williams,K | Tor | 49.0 | 15 | 14 | 0 | 0 | 0 | -- | 1.000 | 2.57 |
| Wilson,C | StL | 43.0 | 7 | 13 | 2 | 0 | 1 | -- | 1.000 | 3.14 |
| Wilson,G | Hou | 142.1 | 21 | 35 | 0 | 1 | 0 | -- | .972 | 2.28 |
| Wilson,M | Tor | 68.0 | 8 | 17 | 0 | 0 | 0 | -- | 1.000 | 2.25 |

## Left Fielders

| Player | Tm | Inn | G | PO | A | E | DP | PB | Pct. | Rng |
|---|---|---|---|---|---|---|---|---|---|---|
| Wilson,W | KC | 359.1 | 54 | 90 | 1 | 0 | 0 | -- | 1.000 | 2.28 |
| Winfield,D | NYA | 82.1 | 12 | 12 | 0 | 0 | 0 | -- | 1.000 | 1.31 |
| Winningham,H | Cin | 12.2 | 5 | 3 | 0 | 0 | 0 | -- | 1.000 | 2.13 |
| Wynne,M | ChN | 46.0 | 13 | 13 | 1 | 0 | 0 | -- | 1.000 | 2.74 |
| Yelding,E | Hou | 35.1 | 11 | 12 | 0 | 0 | 0 | -- | 1.000 | 3.06 |
| Zeile,T | StL | 1.1 | 1 | 0 | 0 | 0 | 0 | -- | .000 | .00 |

## Center Fielders

| Player | Tm | Inn | G | PO | A | E | DP | PB | Pct. | Rng |
|---|---|---|---|---|---|---|---|---|---|---|
| Abner,S | SD | 254.2 | 36 | 72 | 0 | 0 | 0 | -- | 1.000 | 2.54 |
| Allred,B | Cle | 21.0 | 3 | 4 | 0 | 1 | 0 | -- | .800 | 2.14 |
| Alou,M | Mon | 4.0 | 2 | 0 | 0 | 0 | 0 | -- | .000 | .00 |
| Anderson,B | Bal | 150.1 | 21 | 47 | 1 | 1 | 1 | -- | .980 | 2.93 |
| Barfield,J | NYA | 27.0 | 4 | 8 | 0 | 1 | 0 | -- | .889 | 3.00 |
| Belcher,K | Tex | 31.0 | 5 | 9 | 0 | 0 | 0 | -- | 1.000 | 2.61 |
| Bichette,D | Cal | 113.0 | 16 | 35 | 1 | 0 | 1 | -- | 1.000 | 2.87 |
| Biggio,C | Hou | 283.0 | 34 | 91 | 4 | 3 | 0 | -- | .969 | 3.12 |
| Blankenship,L | Oak | 2.0 | 1 | 1 | 0 | 0 | 0 | -- | 1.000 | 4.50 |
| Blauser,J | Atl | 2.2 | 1 | 0 | 0 | 0 | 0 | -- | .000 | .00 |
| Bonds,B | Pit | 12.0 | 2 | 3 | 0 | 0 | 0 | -- | 1.000 | 2.25 |
| Bosley,T | Tex | 1.0 | 1 | 1 | 0 | 0 | 0 | -- | 1.000 | 9.00 |
| Boston,D | NYN | 796.1 | 108 | 199 | 3 | 3 | 1 | -- | .985 | 2.32 |
| Bradley,P | ChA | 102.0 | 14 | 29 | 0 | 1 | 0 | -- | .967 | 2.65 |
| Brumley,M | Sea | 1.0 | 1 | 1 | 0 | 0 | 0 | -- | 1.000 | 9.00 |
| Brunansky,T | Bos | 1.0 | 1 | 0 | 0 | 0 | 0 | -- | .000 | .00 |
| Buhner,J | Sea | 8.0 | 1 | 2 | 0 | 1 | 0 | -- | .667 | 3.38 |
| Burks,E | Bos | 1267.1 | 143 | 322 | 7 | 2 | 0 | -- | .994 | 2.35 |
| Butler,B | SF | 1391.1 | 159 | 418 | 4 | 6 | 0 | -- | .986 | 2.77 |
| Campusano,S | Phi | 128.0 | 25 | 32 | 1 | 1 | 0 | -- | .971 | 2.39 |
| Candaele,C | Hou | 58.0 | 12 | 18 | 0 | 0 | 0 | -- | 1.000 | 2.79 |
| Cangelosi,J | Pit | 80.0 | 9 | 16 | 0 | 0 | 0 | -- | 1.000 | 1.80 |
| Carreon,M | NYN | 230.1 | 36 | 61 | 1 | 0 | 0 | -- | 1.000 | 2.42 |
| Carter,J | SD | 950.0 | 111 | 294 | 9 | 3 | 3 | -- | .990 | 2.90 |
| Carter,S | Pit | 7.0 | 2 | 3 | 0 | 0 | 0 | -- | 1.000 | 3.86 |
| Cole,A | Cle | 492.1 | 59 | 145 | 3 | 6 | 1 | -- | .961 | 2.82 |
| Collins,D | StL | 1.1 | 1 | 0 | 0 | 1 | 0 | -- | .000 | 6.75 |
| Cotto,H | Sea | 100.2 | 18 | 26 | 1 | 0 | 1 | -- | 1.000 | 2.41 |
| Cuyler,M | Det | 139.0 | 17 | 38 | 2 | 1 | 0 | -- | .976 | 2.65 |
| Dascenzo,D | ChN | 265.0 | 38 | 75 | 1 | 0 | 1 | -- | 1.000 | 2.58 |
| Davidson,M | Hou | 9.2 | 1 | 3 | 0 | 0 | 0 | -- | 1.000 | 2.79 |
| Davis,E | Cin | 566.0 | 66 | 161 | 2 | 1 | 1 | -- | .994 | 2.61 |
| Devereaux,M | Bal | 845.1 | 104 | 279 | 4 | 5 | 2 | -- | .983 | 3.07 |
| Dykstra,L | Phi | 1287.2 | 149 | 439 | 8 | 6 | 5 | -- | .987 | 3.17 |
| Eisenreich,J | KC | 144.1 | 19 | 44 | 0 | 0 | 0 | -- | 1.000 | 2.74 |
| Espy,C | Tex | 132.0 | 28 | 47 | 1 | 0 | 0 | -- | 1.000 | 3.27 |
| Felder,M | Mil | 68.1 | 15 | 20 | 1 | 0 | 0 | -- | 1.000 | 2.77 |
| Felix,J | Tor | 238.0 | 28 | 62 | 3 | 0 | 2 | -- | 1.000 | 2.46 |
| Finley,S | Bal | 337.1 | 44 | 115 | 0 | 1 | 0 | -- | .991 | 3.09 |
| Gagne,G | Min | 2.0 | 1 | 0 | 0 | 0 | 0 | -- | .000 | .00 |
| Gallagher,D | ChA | 146.2 | 22 | 42 | 0 | 0 | 0 | -- | 1.000 | 2.58 |
| Gallagher,D | Bal | 14.1 | 2 | 8 | 0 | 1 | 0 | -- | .889 | 5.65 |
| Gant,R | Atl | 950.0 | 113 | 279 | 6 | 5 | 2 | -- | .983 | 2.75 |
| Gibson,K | LA | 576.1 | 70 | 161 | 3 | 0 | 1 | -- | 1.000 | 2.56 |
| Gilkey,B | StL | 4.0 | 1 | 0 | 1 | 0 | 0 | -- | 1.000 | 2.25 |
| Gladden,D | Min | 2.0 | 1 | 2 | 0 | 0 | 0 | -- | 1.000 | 9.00 |
| Gonzalez,Jose | LA | 75.2 | 19 | 20 | 0 | 0 | 0 | -- | 1.000 | 2.38 |

## Center Fielders

| Player | Tm | Inn | G | PO | A | E | DP | PB | Pct. | Rng |
|---|---|---|---|---|---|---|---|---|---|---|
| Gonzalez,Juan | Tex | 99.0 | 12 | 30 | 0 | 0 | 0 | -- | 1.000 | 2.73 |
| Griffey Jr,K | Sea | 1332.2 | 151 | 331 | 9 | 7 | 1 | -- | .980 | 2.34 |
| Grissom,M | Mon | 258.0 | 36 | 85 | 2 | 1 | 0 | -- | .989 | 3.07 |
| Gwynn,C | LA | 26.0 | 5 | 5 | 0 | 0 | 0 | -- | 1.000 | 1.73 |
| Hamilton,D | Mil | 14.0 | 6 | 4 | 0 | 0 | 0 | -- | 1.000 | 2.57 |
| Harris,L | LA | 2.0 | 1 | 1 | 0 | 0 | 0 | -- | 1.000 | 4.50 |
| Hatcher,B | Cin | 555.1 | 69 | 173 | 4 | 0 | 0 | -- | 1.000 | 2.87 |
| Hayes,V | Phi | 20.1 | 4 | 4 | 0 | 0 | 0 | -- | 1.000 | 1.77 |
| Henderson,D | Oak | 943.1 | 110 | 310 | 4 | 4 | 2 | -- | .987 | 3.03 |
| Hill,G | Tor | 7.0 | 1 | 3 | 0 | 0 | 0 | -- | 1.000 | 3.86 |
| Howard,S | Oak | 7.0 | 3 | 0 | 0 | 0 | 0 | -- | .000 | .00 |
| Howard,T | SD | 16.0 | 2 | 6 | 0 | 0 | 0 | -- | 1.000 | 3.38 |
| Hudler,R | StL | 19.2 | 3 | 1 | 0 | 0 | 0 | -- | 1.000 | 0.46 |
| Hughes,K | NYN | 1.2 | 1 | 1 | 0 | 0 | 0 | -- | 1.000 | 5.40 |
| Incaviglia,P | Tex | 147.2 | 27 | 38 | 1 | 1 | 1 | -- | .975 | 2.44 |
| Jackson,B | KC | 531.2 | 61 | 147 | 4 | 6 | 1 | -- | .962 | 2.66 |
| Jackson,D | SD | 195.0 | 32 | 55 | 1 | 0 | 1 | -- | 1.000 | 2.58 |
| James,C | Cle | 6.0 | 1 | 3 | 0 | 0 | 0 | -- | 1.000 | 4.50 |
| James,D | Cle | 63.0 | 8 | 14 | 0 | 1 | 0 | -- | .933 | 2.14 |
| Javier,S | Oak | 30.0 | 4 | 15 | 0 | 0 | 0 | -- | 1.000 | 4.50 |
| Javier,S | LA | 492.0 | 70 | 172 | 1 | 0 | 1 | -- | 1.000 | 3.16 |
| Jefferson,S | Bal | 7.0 | 3 | 2 | 0 | 0 | 0 | -- | 1.000 | 2.57 |
| Jefferson,S | Cle | 72.0 | 11 | 26 | 1 | 1 | 0 | -- | .964 | 3.50 |
| Jeltz,S | KC | 3.0 | 1 | 1 | 0 | 0 | 0 | -- | 1.000 | 3.00 |
| Johnson,L | ChA | 1169.2 | 150 | 351 | 5 | 10 | 3 | -- | .973 | 2.82 |
| Jones,T | Sea | 1.0 | 1 | 0 | 0 | 0 | 0 | -- | .000 | .00 |
| Jose,F | Oak | 161.2 | 24 | 64 | 1 | 1 | 0 | -- | .985 | 3.67 |
| Jose,F | StL | 12.0 | 2 | 8 | 0 | 0 | 0 | -- | 1.000 | 6.00 |
| Kelly,R | NYA | 1294.1 | 151 | 400 | 4 | 4 | 0 | -- | .990 | 2.84 |
| Kingery,M | SF | 23.0 | 9 | 6 | 0 | 0 | 0 | -- | 1.000 | 2.35 |
| Komminsk,B | SF | 3.0 | 2 | 0 | 0 | 0 | 0 | -- | .000 | .00 |
| Komminsk,B | Bal | 81.0 | 12 | 24 | 0 | 0 | 0 | -- | 1.000 | 2.67 |
| Kunkel,J | Tex | 2.0 | 2 | 0 | 0 | 0 | 0 | -- | .000 | .00 |
| Kutcher,R | Bos | 48.0 | 9 | 12 | 0 | 0 | 0 | -- | 1.000 | 2.25 |
| Lankford,R | StL | 273.1 | 35 | 91 | 1 | 1 | 0 | -- | .989 | 3.06 |
| Lemon,C | Det | 18.0 | 3 | 4 | 0 | 0 | 0 | -- | 1.000 | 2.00 |
| Lewis,D | Oak | 85.0 | 16 | 25 | 0 | 0 | 0 | -- | 1.000 | 2.65 |
| Lusader,S | Det | 21.0 | 5 | 12 | 0 | 1 | 0 | -- | .923 | 5.57 |
| Lynn,F | SD | 46.0 | 6 | 12 | 0 | 0 | 0 | -- | 1.000 | 2.35 |
| Lyons,S | ChA | 18.0 | 3 | 6 | 0 | 0 | 0 | -- | 1.000 | 3.00 |
| Mack,S | Min | 315.1 | 44 | 111 | 4 | 0 | 0 | -- | 1.000 | 3.28 |
| Martinez,D | Mon | 788.2 | 105 | 247 | 5 | 3 | 1 | -- | .988 | 2.91 |
| McCray,R | ChA | 12.0 | 8 | 5 | 0 | 0 | 0 | -- | 1.000 | 3.75 |
| McDowell,O | Atl | 477.0 | 60 | 120 | 2 | 4 | 0 | -- | .968 | 2.38 |
| McGee,W | StL | 1041.0 | 118 | 329 | 12 | 16 | 4 | -- | .955 | 3.09 |
| McGee,W | Oak | 227.0 | 28 | 71 | 1 | 1 | 1 | -- | .986 | 2.89 |
| McRae,B | KC | 383.2 | 45 | 119 | 1 | 0 | 0 | -- | 1.000 | 2.81 |
| Meadows,L | Phi | 4.0 | 2 | 1 | 0 | 0 | 0 | -- | 1.000 | 2.25 |
| Miller,K | NYN | 362.2 | 53 | 130 | 1 | 2 | 1 | -- | .985 | 3.30 |
| Morris,J | StL | 4.0 | 1 | 0 | 0 | 0 | 0 | -- | .000 | .00 |
| Moseby,L | Det | 862.2 | 104 | 265 | 6 | 5 | 5 | -- | .982 | 2.88 |
| Moses,J | Min | 74.0 | 21 | 27 | 0 | 0 | 0 | -- | 1.000 | 3.28 |
| Murphy,D | Phi | 9.0 | 1 | 3 | 0 | 0 | 0 | -- | 1.000 | 3.00 |
| Nixon,O | Mon | 413.2 | 71 | 120 | 4 | 1 | 0 | -- | .992 | 2.72 |
| O'Neill,P | Cin | 1.0 | 1 | 0 | 0 | 0 | 0 | -- | .000 | .00 |
| Ortiz,J | Hou | 2.0 | 1 | 1 | 0 | 0 | 0 | -- | 1.000 | 4.50 |
| Parker,R | SF | 29.0 | 5 | 9 | 0 | 0 | 0 | -- | 1.000 | 2.79 |
| Pettis,G | Tex | 1032.0 | 128 | 287 | 9 | 2 | 3 | -- | .993 | 2.60 |

## Center Fielders

| Player | Tm | Inn | G | PO | A | E | DP | PB | Pct. | Rng |
|---|---|---|---|---|---|---|---|---|---|---|
| Phillips,T | Det | 2.0 | 1 | 1 | 0 | 0 | 0 | -- | 1.000 | 4.50 |
| Polonia,L | Cal | 104.1 | 13 | 26 | 0 | 0 | 0 | -- | 1.000 | 2.24 |
| Puckett,K | Min | 1042.1 | 126 | 319 | 6 | 3 | 0 | -- | .991 | 2.83 |
| Puhl,T | Hou | 12.0 | 2 | 3 | 0 | 0 | 0 | -- | 1.000 | 2.25 |
| Redus,G | Pit | 9.0 | 1 | 3 | 0 | 2 | 0 | -- | .600 | 5.00 |
| Reed,D | NYN | 46.0 | 8 | 14 | 0 | 1 | 0 | -- | .933 | 2.93 |
| Reynolds,R | Pit | 204.1 | 24 | 48 | 2 | 1 | 0 | -- | .980 | 2.25 |
| Rhodes,K | Hou | 71.0 | 9 | 18 | 2 | 1 | 0 | -- | .952 | 2.66 |
| Romine,K | Bos | 125.2 | 18 | 32 | 0 | 0 | 0 | -- | 1.000 | 2.29 |
| Roomes,R | Mon | 9.0 | 2 | 2 | 0 | 0 | 0 | -- | 1.000 | 2.00 |
| Samuel,J | LA | 269.0 | 31 | 79 | 4 | 3 | 0 | -- | .965 | 2.88 |
| Sanders,D | NYA | 123.1 | 15 | 31 | 1 | 1 | 0 | -- | .970 | 2.41 |
| Shelby,J | LA | 1.0 | 1 | 1 | 0 | 0 | 0 | -- | 1.000 | 9.00 |
| Shelby,J | Det | 286.2 | 35 | 79 | 1 | 3 | 0 | -- | .964 | 2.61 |
| Smith,D | ChN | 11.0 | 4 | 3 | 0 | 0 | 0 | -- | 1.000 | 2.45 |
| Sosa,S | ChA | 1.0 | 3 | 1 | 0 | 0 | 0 | -- | 1.000 | 9.00 |
| Thompson,M | StL | 88.0 | 14 | 30 | 0 | 0 | 0 | -- | 1.000 | 3.07 |
| Thornton,L | NYN | 3.0 | 1 | 0 | 0 | 0 | 0 | -- | .000 | .00 |
| Thurman,G | KC | 8.0 | 2 | 1 | 0 | 0 | 0 | -- | 1.000 | 1.13 |
| Van Slyke,A | Pit | 1134.2 | 133 | 325 | 7 | 8 | 1 | -- | .976 | 2.70 |
| Venable,M | Cal | 223.0 | 33 | 61 | 1 | 2 | 1 | -- | .969 | 2.58 |
| Walton,J | ChN | 850.0 | 99 | 249 | 3 | 6 | 0 | -- | .977 | 2.73 |
| Webster,M | Cle | 773.0 | 95 | 287 | 1 | 2 | 0 | -- | .993 | 3.38 |
| White,D | Cal | 1013.2 | 122 | 302 | 11 | 9 | 3 | -- | .972 | 2.86 |
| Williams,K | Det | 101.0 | 13 | 42 | 4 | 0 | 1 | -- | 1.000 | 4.10 |
| Williams,K | Tor | 38.0 | 9 | 7 | 0 | 0 | 0 | -- | 1.000 | 1.66 |
| Wilson,M | Tor | 1171.0 | 133 | 352 | 5 | 3 | 2 | -- | .992 | 2.77 |
| Wilson,W | KC | 350.0 | 48 | 91 | 1 | 0 | 1 | -- | 1.000 | 2.37 |
| Winningham,H | Cin | 334.0 | 58 | 86 | 3 | 0 | 0 | -- | 1.000 | 2.40 |
| Wynne,M | ChN | 316.2 | 53 | 88 | 3 | 1 | 3 | -- | .989 | 2.61 |
| Yelding,E | Hou | 662.0 | 84 | 215 | 5 | 7 | 1 | -- | .969 | 3.09 |
| Young,G | Hou | 352.1 | 50 | 99 | 4 | 1 | 1 | -- | .990 | 2.66 |
| Yount,R | Mil | 1362.2 | 157 | 422 | 3 | 4 | 0 | -- | .991 | 2.83 |

## Right Fielders

| Player | Tm | Inn | G | PO | A | E | DP | PB | Pct. | Rng |
|---|---|---|---|---|---|---|---|---|---|---|
| Abner,S | SD | 34.0 | 6 | 7 | 0 | 0 | 0 | -- | 1.000 | 1.85 |
| Aldrete,M | Mon | 53.0 | 14 | 14 | 1 | 0 | 0 | -- | 1.000 | 2.55 |
| Allred,B | Cle | 8.0 | 1 | 1 | 0 | 0 | 0 | -- | 1.000 | 1.13 |
| Alou,M | Mon | 18.0 | 2 | 6 | 1 | 0 | 0 | -- | 1.000 | 3.50 |
| Anderson,B | Bal | 8.0 | 2 | 1 | 0 | 0 | 0 | -- | 1.000 | 1.13 |
| Anthony,E | Hou | 468.0 | 59 | 104 | 3 | 3 | 0 | -- | .973 | 2.12 |
| Azocar,O | NYA | 90.0 | 12 | 16 | 0 | 0 | 0 | -- | 1.000 | 1.60 |
| Baines,H | Tex | 12.0 | 2 | 5 | 0 | 1 | 0 | -- | .833 | 4.50 |
| Baldwin,J | Hou | 1.1 | 1 | 0 | 0 | 0 | 0 | -- | .000 | .00 |
| Barfield,J | NYA | 1193.1 | 152 | 299 | 17 | 8 | 3 | -- | .975 | 2.44 |
| Bass,K | SF | 457.0 | 55 | 89 | 2 | 3 | 0 | -- | .968 | 1.85 |
| Belcher,K | Tex | 4.0 | 2 | 2 | 0 | 0 | 0 | -- | 1.000 | 4.50 |
| Bichette,D | Cal | 352.2 | 53 | 78 | 9 | 1 | 2 | -- | .989 | 2.25 |
| Biggio,C | Hou | 1.1 | 2 | 1 | 0 | 0 | 0 | -- | 1.000 | 6.75 |
| Blankenship,L | Oak | 91.0 | 17 | 23 | 0 | 1 | 0 | -- | .958 | 2.37 |
| Bonilla,B | Pit | 1300.0 | 149 | 290 | 8 | 12 | 1 | -- | .961 | 2.15 |
| Bosley,T | Tex | 3.0 | 1 | 0 | 0 | 0 | 0 | -- | .000 | .00 |
| Boston,D | ChA | 1.0 | 1 | 0 | 0 | 0 | 0 | -- | .000 | .00 |
| Bradley,P | ChA | 33.1 | 6 | 6 | 0 | 0 | 0 | -- | 1.000 | 1.62 |
| Braggs,G | Mil | 149.1 | 20 | 55 | 0 | 2 | 0 | -- | .965 | 3.44 |

## Right Fielders

| Player | Tm | Inn | G | PO | A | E | DP | PB | Pct. | Rng |
|---|---|---|---|---|---|---|---|---|---|---|
| Braggs,G | Cin | 248.0 | 35 | 64 | 3 | 2 | 2 | -- | .971 | 2.50 |
| Brett,G | KC | 53.0 | 7 | 9 | 0 | 0 | 0 | -- | 1.000 | 1.53 |
| Briley,G | Sea | 497.0 | 66 | 120 | 0 | 1 | 0 | -- | .992 | 2.19 |
| Brooks,H | LA | 1252.0 | 151 | 255 | 9 | 10 | 2 | -- | .964 | 1.97 |
| Brunansky,T | StL | 142.2 | 17 | 37 | 1 | 2 | 1 | -- | .950 | 2.52 |
| Brunansky,T | Bos | 1037.1 | 121 | 268 | 5 | 5 | 1 | -- | .982 | 2.41 |
| Buhner,J | Sea | 304.0 | 39 | 53 | 1 | 1 | 0 | -- | .982 | 1.63 |
| Bush,R | Min | 200.2 | 31 | 50 | 1 | 0 | 0 | -- | 1.000 | 2.29 |
| Calderon,I | ChA | 2.2 | 5 | 1 | 0 | 0 | 0 | -- | 1.000 | 3.38 |
| Campusano,S | Phi | 13.1 | 7 | 4 | 0 | 0 | 0 | -- | 1.000 | 2.70 |
| Candaele,C | Hou | 36.2 | 13 | 12 | 0 | 0 | 0 | -- | 1.000 | 2.95 |
| Canseco,J | Oak | 742.0 | 88 | 183 | 6 | 1 | 2 | -- | .995 | 2.30 |
| Canseco,O | Oak | 6.0 | 1 | 0 | 0 | 0 | 0 | -- | .000 | .00 |
| Carreon,M | NYN | 55.0 | 13 | 8 | 0 | 0 | 0 | -- | 1.000 | 1.31 |
| Carter,S | Pit | 1.0 | 1 | 1 | 0 | 0 | 0 | -- | 1.000 | 9.00 |
| Castillo,C | Min | 89.0 | 20 | 20 | 0 | 2 | 0 | -- | .909 | 2.22 |
| Chamberlain,W | Phi | 6.1 | 2 | 1 | 0 | 1 | 0 | -- | .500 | 2.84 |
| Clark,J | SD | 70.0 | 9 | 22 | 0 | 0 | 0 | -- | 1.000 | 2.83 |
| Coleman,V | StL | 20.0 | 2 | 3 | 2 | 0 | 1 | -- | 1.000 | 2.25 |
| Coles,D | Sea | 154.0 | 20 | 32 | 0 | 1 | 0 | -- | .970 | 1.93 |
| Coles,D | Det | 32.1 | 9 | 7 | 0 | 0 | 0 | -- | 1.000 | 1.95 |
| Collins,D | StL | 14.1 | 8 | 5 | 0 | 0 | 0 | -- | 1.000 | 3.14 |
| Cotto,H | Sea | 437.1 | 67 | 103 | 3 | 1 | 0 | -- | .991 | 2.20 |
| Cuyler,M | Det | 0.0 | 1 | 0 | 0 | 0 | 0 | -- | .000 | .00 |
| Dascenzo,D | ChN | 106.1 | 22 | 37 | 0 | 0 | 0 | -- | 1.000 | 3.13 |
| Daugherty,J | Tex | 23.0 | 4 | 5 | 0 | 0 | 0 | -- | 1.000 | 1.96 |
| Davidson,M | Hou | 153.2 | 27 | 50 | 1 | 0 | 0 | -- | 1.000 | 2.99 |
| Davis,C | Cal | 49.0 | 6 | 8 | 0 | 0 | 0 | -- | 1.000 | 1.47 |
| Dawson,A | ChN | 1164.1 | 140 | 249 | 11 | 5 | 4 | -- | .981 | 2.05 |
| Deer,R | Mil | 912.2 | 118 | 242 | 14 | 8 | 7 | -- | .970 | 2.60 |
| Dwyer,J | Min | 2.0 | 1 | 1 | 0 | 0 | 0 | -- | 1.000 | 4.50 |
| Eisenreich,J | KC | 487.2 | 78 | 107 | 4 | 1 | 2 | -- | .991 | 2.07 |
| Espy,C | Tex | 33.0 | 9 | 7 | 0 | 0 | 0 | -- | 1.000 | 1.91 |
| Felder,M | Mil | 246.0 | 44 | 66 | 4 | 3 | 3 | -- | .959 | 2.67 |
| Felix,J | Tor | 860.1 | 99 | 183 | 9 | 9 | 1 | -- | .955 | 2.10 |
| Finley,S | Bal | 567.2 | 72 | 160 | 4 | 6 | 2 | -- | .965 | 2.70 |
| Fitzgerald,M | Mon | 27.0 | 5 | 2 | 1 | 0 | 0 | -- | 1.000 | 1.00 |
| Ford,C | Phi | 5.0 | 3 | 2 | 0 | 0 | 0 | -- | 1.000 | 3.60 |
| Gallagher,D | ChA | 9.0 | 1 | 2 | 0 | 0 | 0 | -- | 1.000 | 2.00 |
| Gallagher,D | Bal | 9.0 | 1 | 2 | 0 | 0 | 0 | -- | 1.000 | 2.00 |
| Gallego,M | Oak | 1.0 | 1 | 1 | 0 | 0 | 0 | -- | 1.000 | 9.00 |
| Gant,R | Atl | 5.0 | 2 | 0 | 0 | 0 | 0 | -- | .000 | .00 |
| Gonzales,R | Bal | 1.0 | 1 | 0 | 0 | 0 | 0 | -- | .000 | .00 |
| Gonzalez,Jose | LA | 61.2 | 26 | 11 | 0 | 0 | 0 | -- | 1.000 | 1.61 |
| Gonzalez,Juan | Tex | 28.0 | 4 | 3 | 0 | 0 | 0 | -- | 1.000 | 0.96 |
| Gregg,T | Atl | 72.1 | 13 | 14 | 0 | 1 | 0 | -- | .933 | 1.87 |
| Griffey Sr,K | Cin | 1.0 | 1 | 0 | 0 | 0 | 0 | -- | .000 | .00 |
| Grissom,M | Mon | 263.1 | 40 | 57 | 2 | 0 | 0 | -- | 1.000 | 2.02 |
| Gruber,K | Tor | 41.0 | 6 | 7 | 0 | 0 | 0 | -- | 1.000 | 1.54 |
| Gwynn,C | LA | 38.0 | 8 | 8 | 0 | 0 | 0 | -- | 1.000 | 1.89 |
| Gwynn,T | SD | 1265.2 | 141 | 327 | 11 | 5 | 2 | -- | .985 | 2.44 |
| Hall,M | NYA | 105.0 | 15 | 18 | 0 | 1 | 0 | -- | .947 | 1.63 |
| Hamilton,D | Mil | 137.0 | 25 | 42 | 1 | 0 | 0 | -- | 1.000 | 2.82 |
| Harris,L | LA | 3.0 | 1 | 0 | 0 | 0 | 0 | -- | .000 | .00 |
| Hayes,V | Phi | 677.1 | 80 | 175 | 6 | 2 | 0 | -- | .989 | 2.43 |
| Heath,M | Det | 7.0 | 3 | 2 | 0 | 0 | 0 | -- | 1.000 | 2.57 |
| Heep,D | Bos | 63.0 | 13 | 18 | 1 | 0 | 1 | -- | 1.000 | 2.71 |
| Henderson,D | Oak | 32.0 | 5 | 8 | 1 | 0 | 0 | -- | 1.000 | 2.53 |

## Right Fielders

| Player | Tm | Inn | G | PO | A | E | DP | PB | Pct. | Rng |
|---|---|---|---|---|---|---|---|---|---|---|
| Hill,G | Tor | 290.2 | 34 | 64 | 2 | 2 | 0 | -- | .971 | 2.11 |
| Howard,S | Oak | 55.0 | 8 | 10 | 0 | 1 | 0 | -- | .909 | 1.80 |
| Howard,T | SD | 12.0 | 2 | 0 | 0 | 0 | 0 | -- | .000 | .00 |
| Howitt,D | Oak | 31.0 | 10 | 16 | 0 | 0 | 0 | -- | 1.000 | 4.65 |
| Hudler,R | StL | 188.2 | 27 | 49 | 0 | 1 | 0 | -- | .980 | 2.39 |
| Incaviglia,P | Tex | 1.0 | 1 | 0 | 0 | 0 | 0 | -- | .000 | .00 |
| Jackson,D | SD | 26.1 | 5 | 7 | 0 | 1 | 0 | -- | .875 | 2.73 |
| James,C | Cle | 7.0 | 1 | 2 | 0 | 0 | 0 | -- | 1.000 | 2.57 |
| Javier,S | Oak | 15.0 | 5 | 3 | 0 | 0 | 0 | -- | 1.000 | 1.80 |
| Javier,S | LA | 74.1 | 12 | 21 | 1 | 0 | 0 | -- | 1.000 | 2.66 |
| Jefferson,S | Bal | 31.0 | 5 | 7 | 0 | 0 | 0 | -- | 1.000 | 2.03 |
| Jefferson,S | Cle | 8.0 | 1 | 3 | 0 | 0 | 0 | -- | 1.000 | 3.38 |
| Jeltz,S | KC | 19.0 | 12 | 5 | 1 | 0 | 0 | -- | 1.000 | 2.84 |
| Jennings,D | Oak | 77.0 | 15 | 16 | 1 | 0 | 0 | -- | 1.000 | 1.99 |
| Johnson,L | ChA | 0.0 | 1 | 0 | 0 | 0 | 0 | -- | .000 | .00 |
| Jones,R | Phi | 67.2 | 8 | 16 | 0 | 0 | 0 | -- | 1.000 | 2.13 |
| Jose,F | Oak | 392.0 | 53 | 98 | 3 | 2 | 1 | -- | .981 | 2.36 |
| Jose,F | StL | 168.1 | 21 | 30 | 0 | 0 | 0 | -- | 1.000 | 1.60 |
| Justice,D | Atl | 508.2 | 60 | 116 | 4 | 4 | 1 | -- | .968 | 2.19 |
| Kingery,M | SF | 374.1 | 74 | 105 | 4 | 3 | 1 | -- | .973 | 2.69 |
| Komminsk,B | SF | 10.0 | 3 | 2 | 0 | 0 | 0 | -- | 1.000 | 1.80 |
| Komminsk,B | Bal | 149.1 | 25 | 37 | 2 | 0 | 0 | -- | 1.000 | 2.35 |
| Kruk,J | Phi | 155.0 | 21 | 43 | 1 | 1 | 0 | -- | .978 | 2.61 |
| Kunkel,J | Tex | 5.0 | 2 | 2 | 0 | 0 | 0 | -- | 1.000 | 3.60 |
| Kutcher,R | Bos | 99.1 | 23 | 29 | 0 | 0 | 0 | -- | 1.000 | 2.63 |
| Larkin,G | Min | 367.0 | 47 | 77 | 5 | 0 | 1 | -- | 1.000 | 2.01 |
| Leach,R | SF | 241.0 | 40 | 71 | 2 | 1 | 0 | -- | .986 | 2.76 |
| Lemon,C | Det | 765.0 | 94 | 204 | 7 | 6 | 1 | -- | .972 | 2.55 |
| Leonard,J | Sea | 51.0 | 6 | 9 | 0 | 1 | 0 | -- | .900 | 1.76 |
| Leonard,M | SF | 28.0 | 5 | 10 | 0 | 0 | 0 | -- | 1.000 | 3.21 |
| Lewis,D | Oak | 13.0 | 5 | 5 | 0 | 0 | 0 | -- | 1.000 | 3.46 |
| Leyritz,J | NYA | 16.1 | 4 | 5 | 0 | 0 | 0 | -- | 1.000 | 2.76 |
| Lindeman,J | Det | 2.0 | 1 | 0 | 0 | 0 | 0 | -- | .000 | .00 |
| Litton,G | SF | 226.1 | 42 | 54 | 6 | 0 | 1 | -- | 1.000 | 2.39 |
| Lusader,S | Det | 188.2 | 26 | 38 | 1 | 0 | 0 | -- | 1.000 | 1.86 |
| Lynn,F | SD | 53.2 | 8 | 14 | 0 | 0 | 0 | -- | 1.000 | 2.35 |
| Lyons,S | ChA | 3.0 | 3 | 1 | 0 | 0 | 0 | -- | 1.000 | 3.00 |
| Mack,S | Min | 324.0 | 51 | 88 | 1 | 3 | 0 | -- | .967 | 2.56 |
| Maldonado,C | Cle | 324.2 | 41 | 90 | 1 | 1 | 0 | -- | .989 | 2.55 |
| Marshall,M | NYN | 5.0 | 1 | 0 | 0 | 0 | 0 | -- | .000 | .00 |
| Marshall,M | Bos | 61.0 | 8 | 13 | 0 | 1 | 0 | -- | .929 | 2.07 |
| Martinez,C | Phi | 7.0 | 1 | 1 | 0 | 0 | 0 | -- | 1.000 | 1.29 |
| Martinez,D | Mon | 60.2 | 22 | 11 | 0 | 0 | 0 | -- | 1.000 | 1.63 |
| McCray,R | ChA | 5.1 | 4 | 1 | 0 | 0 | 0 | -- | 1.000 | 1.69 |
| McDowell,O | Atl | 5.0 | 1 | 1 | 0 | 0 | 0 | -- | 1.000 | 1.80 |
| McGee,W | StL | 53.0 | 6 | 12 | 2 | 0 | 1 | -- | 1.000 | 2.38 |
| McKnight,J | Bal | 22.0 | 4 | 5 | 0 | 0 | 0 | -- | 1.000 | 2.05 |
| Meadows,L | Hou | 2.1 | 2 | 0 | 0 | 0 | 0 | -- | .000 | .00 |
| Merced,O | Pit | 1.0 | 1 | 0 | 0 | 0 | 0 | -- | .000 | .00 |
| Miller,K | NYN | 23.0 | 5 | 12 | 0 | 0 | 0 | -- | 1.000 | 4.70 |
| Morris,J | StL | 14.1 | 5 | 4 | 0 | 0 | 0 | -- | 1.000 | 2.51 |
| Moses,J | Min | 216.0 | 54 | 52 | 1 | 0 | 0 | -- | 1.000 | 2.21 |
| Munoz,P | Min | 161.0 | 19 | 34 | 1 | 0 | 1 | -- | 1.000 | 1.96 |
| Murphy,D | Atl | 820.1 | 97 | 208 | 3 | 4 | 0 | -- | .981 | 2.36 |
| Murphy,D | Phi | 469.0 | 54 | 110 | 4 | 1 | 1 | -- | .991 | 2.21 |
| Noboa,J | Mon | 46.2 | 7 | 8 | 1 | 0 | 0 | -- | 1.000 | 1.74 |
| Nokes,M | NYA | 12.0 | 2 | 1 | 0 | 0 | 0 | -- | 1.000 | 0.75 |
| O'Neill,P | Cin | 1165.1 | 141 | 272 | 12 | 2 | 0 | -- | .993 | 2.21 |

## Right Fielders

| Player | Tm | Inn | G | PO | A | E | DP | PB | Pct. | Rng |
|---|---|---|---|---|---|---|---|---|---|---|
| Orsulak,J | Bal | 643.1 | 81 | 209 | 2 | 2 | 1 | -- | .991 | 2.98 |
| Ortiz,J | Hou | 39.1 | 9 | 9 | 0 | 1 | 0 | -- | .900 | 2.29 |
| Palacios,R | KC | 2.0 | 1 | 0 | 0 | 0 | 0 | -- | .000 | .00 |
| Parker,R | SF | 109.2 | 23 | 23 | 1 | 1 | 0 | -- | .960 | 2.05 |
| Pasqua,D | ChA | 142.0 | 22 | 34 | 2 | 0 | 1 | -- | 1.000 | 2.28 |
| Pecota,B | KC | 8.0 | 3 | 2 | 0 | 0 | 0 | -- | 1.000 | 2.25 |
| Phillips,T | Det | 13.1 | 4 | 3 | 0 | 0 | 0 | -- | 1.000 | 2.03 |
| Puckett,K | Min | 76.0 | 9 | 15 | 3 | 0 | 3 | -- | 1.000 | 2.13 |
| Quintana,C | Bos | 12.1 | 3 | 2 | 0 | 0 | 0 | -- | 1.000 | 1.46 |
| Quirk,J | Oak | 1.0 | 1 | 0 | 0 | 0 | 0 | -- | .000 | .00 |
| Redus,G | Pit | 10.0 | 2 | 5 | 0 | 0 | 0 | -- | 1.000 | 4.50 |
| Reed,D | NYN | 30.0 | 6 | 5 | 1 | 0 | 0 | -- | 1.000 | 1.80 |
| Reimer,K | Tex | 27.0 | 5 | 7 | 0 | 2 | 0 | -- | .778 | 3.00 |
| Reynolds,R | Pit | 133.0 | 26 | 31 | 1 | 1 | 0 | -- | .970 | 2.23 |
| Rhodes,K | Hou | 19.2 | 6 | 6 | 0 | 0 | 0 | -- | 1.000 | 2.75 |
| Romine,K | Bos | 169.0 | 30 | 35 | 0 | 0 | 0 | -- | 1.000 | 1.86 |
| Roomes,R | Cin | 40.2 | 7 | 13 | 0 | 0 | 0 | -- | 1.000 | 2.88 |
| Roomes,R | Mon | 1.1 | 1 | 0 | 0 | 0 | 0 | -- | .000 | .00 |
| Ryal,M | Pit | 2.0 | 2 | 1 | 0 | 0 | 0 | -- | 1.000 | 4.50 |
| Schulz,J | KC | 87.0 | 16 | 18 | 0 | 1 | 0 | -- | .947 | 1.97 |
| Sheets,L | Det | 131.0 | 23 | 27 | 2 | 1 | 0 | -- | .967 | 2.06 |
| Shelby,J | LA | 13.0 | 4 | 3 | 0 | 0 | 0 | -- | 1.000 | 2.08 |
| Shelby,J | Det | 95.0 | 13 | 31 | 2 | 0 | 2 | -- | 1.000 | 3.13 |
| Sierra,R | Tex | 1308.2 | 151 | 282 | 7 | 10 | 1 | -- | .967 | 2.06 |
| Smith,D | ChN | 140.0 | 22 | 33 | 1 | 1 | 1 | -- | .971 | 2.25 |
| Snyder,C | Cle | 984.1 | 120 | 222 | 11 | 6 | 2 | -- | .975 | 2.19 |
| Sosa,S | ChA | 1253.0 | 154 | 313 | 14 | 13 | 1 | -- | .962 | 2.44 |
| Strawberry,D | NYN | 1263.0 | 149 | 268 | 11 | 3 | 3 | -- | .989 | 2.01 |
| Stubbs,F | Hou | 25.0 | 5 | 3 | 0 | 0 | 0 | -- | 1.000 | 1.08 |
| Tabler,P | KC | 219.0 | 31 | 57 | 3 | 0 | 0 | -- | 1.000 | 2.47 |
| Tabler,P | NYN | 63.0 | 8 | 18 | 1 | 0 | 1 | -- | 1.000 | 2.71 |
| Tartabull,D | KC | 416.0 | 52 | 82 | 1 | 3 | 0 | -- | .965 | 1.86 |
| Tettleton,M | Bal | 4.0 | 1 | 1 | 0 | 0 | 0 | -- | 1.000 | 2.25 |
| Thompson,M | StL | 772.2 | 96 | 187 | 2 | 5 | 0 | -- | .974 | 2.26 |
| Thornton,L | NYN | 1.0 | 1 | 1 | 0 | 0 | 0 | -- | 1.000 | 9.00 |
| Thurman,G | KC | 113.2 | 15 | 25 | 0 | 0 | 0 | -- | 1.000 | 1.98 |
| Varsho,G | ChN | 8.0 | 1 | 2 | 0 | 0 | 0 | -- | 1.000 | 2.25 |
| Vatcher,J | Phi | 48.1 | 12 | 12 | 0 | 0 | 0 | -- | 1.000 | 2.23 |
| Vatcher,J | Atl | 18.1 | 4 | 6 | 0 | 0 | 0 | -- | 1.000 | 2.95 |
| Venable,M | Cal | 59.2 | 9 | 10 | 0 | 0 | 0 | -- | 1.000 | 1.51 |
| Walker,L | Mon | 1003.1 | 123 | 247 | 11 | 4 | 6 | -- | .985 | 2.35 |
| Walling,D | StL | 20.1 | 5 | 7 | 0 | 0 | 0 | -- | 1.000 | 3.10 |
| Ward,G | Det | 97.0 | 16 | 21 | 1 | 0 | 0 | -- | 1.000 | 2.04 |
| Ward,T | Cle | 95.1 | 13 | 20 | 3 | 1 | 0 | -- | .958 | 2.27 |
| Washington,C | Cal | 71.0 | 9 | 19 | 1 | 0 | 0 | -- | 1.000 | 2.54 |
| Washington,C | NYA | 28.0 | 4 | 6 | 0 | 0 | 0 | -- | 1.000 | 1.93 |
| White,F | KC | 0.0 | 1 | 0 | 0 | 0 | 0 | -- | .000 | .00 |
| Whiten,M | Tor | 203.0 | 27 | 60 | 1 | 0 | 0 | -- | 1.000 | 2.70 |
| Williams,K | Det | 99.0 | 19 | 19 | 1 | 0 | 0 | -- | 1.000 | 1.82 |
| Williams,K | Tor | 59.0 | 8 | 15 | 0 | 0 | 0 | -- | 1.000 | 2.29 |
| Wilson,C | StL | 49.0 | 7 | 13 | 0 | 0 | 0 | -- | 1.000 | 2.39 |
| Wilson,G | Hou | 681.1 | 93 | 190 | 11 | 5 | 6 | -- | .976 | 2.72 |
| Wilson,W | KC | 15.1 | 4 | 6 | 0 | 0 | 0 | -- | 1.000 | 3.52 |
| Winfield,D | Cal | 921.2 | 108 | 164 | 7 | 2 | 1 | -- | .988 | 1.69 |
| Winningham,H | Cin | 1.1 | 1 | 0 | 0 | 0 | 0 | -- | .000 | .00 |
| Wynne,M | ChN | 24.0 | 4 | 6 | 0 | 0 | 0 | -- | 1.000 | 2.25 |
| Yelding,E | Hou | 21.1 | 6 | 3 | 0 | 0 | 0 | -- | 1.000 | 1.27 |

## Catchers

| Player | Tm | Inn | G | PO | A | E | DP | PB | Pct. | Rng |
|---|---|---|---|---|---|---|---|---|---|---|
| Afenir,T | Oak | 33.0 | 12 | 13 | 0 | 0 | 0 | 2 | 1.000 | --- |
| Alomar Jr,S | Cle | 1052.1 | 129 | 686 | 45 | 14 | 6 | 11 | .981 | --- |
| Bailey,M | SF | 4.0 | 1 | 3 | 0 | 0 | 0 | 0 | 1.000 | --- |
| Bathe,B | SF | 21.0 | 8 | 11 | 1 | 0 | 1 | 0 | 1.000 | --- |
| Berryhill,D | ChN | 127.0 | 15 | 87 | 3 | 2 | 0 | 2 | .978 | --- |
| Biggio,C | Hou | 904.2 | 113 | 547 | 51 | 9 | 4 | 7 | .985 | --- |
| Bilardello,D | Pit | 109.2 | 19 | 69 | 9 | 0 | 0 | 2 | 1.000 | --- |
| Boone,B | KC | 335.0 | 40 | 243 | 18 | 4 | 0 | 4 | .985 | --- |
| Borders,P | Tor | 799.2 | 115 | 516 | 46 | 4 | 6 | 6 | .993 | --- |
| Bradley,S | Sea | 448.1 | 63 | 349 | 24 | 2 | 4 | 8 | .995 | --- |
| Cabrera,F | Atl | 5.2 | 3 | 5 | 0 | 0 | 0 | 0 | 1.000 | --- |
| Carter,G | SF | 534.2 | 80 | 322 | 31 | 3 | 2 | 4 | .992 | --- |
| Cerone,R | NYA | 256.2 | 35 | 177 | 14 | 1 | 1 | 6 | .995 | --- |
| Cochrane,D | Sea | 1.0 | 1 | 0 | 0 | 0 | 0 | 0 | .000 | --- |
| Cora,J | SD | 2.0 | 1 | 3 | 0 | 0 | 0 | 0 | 1.000 | --- |
| Daulton,D | Phi | 1115.0 | 139 | 683 | 67 | 8 | 11 | 6 | .989 | --- |
| Davis,J | Atl | 22.0 | 4 | 19 | 1 | 0 | 0 | 0 | 1.000 | --- |
| Decker,S | SF | 124.0 | 15 | 76 | 10 | 1 | 2 | 1 | .989 | --- |
| Dempsey,R | LA | 314.2 | 53 | 213 | 27 | 2 | 3 | 4 | .992 | --- |
| Diaz,C | Tor | 13.1 | 10 | 13 | 3 | 0 | 0 | 0 | 1.000 | --- |
| Dorsett,B | NYA | 48.0 | 9 | 31 | 0 | 0 | 1 | 0 | 1.000 | --- |
| Fisk,C | ChA | 970.0 | 116 | 661 | 62 | 4 | 14 | 11 | .994 | --- |
| Fitzgerald,M | Mon | 778.2 | 98 | 559 | 42 | 6 | 9 | 3 | .990 | --- |
| Fletcher,D | LA | 1.0 | 1 | 0 | 0 | 0 | 0 | 0 | .000 | --- |
| Fletcher,D | Phi | 50.0 | 6 | 31 | 2 | 0 | 0 | 0 | 1.000 | --- |
| Gedman,R | Bos | 50.1 | 9 | 27 | 5 | 1 | 1 | 0 | .970 | --- |
| Gedman,R | Hou | 281.2 | 39 | 180 | 24 | 0 | 5 | 8 | 1.000 | --- |
| Geren,B | NYA | 750.2 | 107 | 487 | 54 | 4 | 5 | 10 | .993 | --- |
| Girardi,J | ChN | 1070.1 | 133 | 652 | 60 | 11 | 5 | 16 | .985 | --- |
| Goff,J | Mon | 286.1 | 38 | 197 | 12 | 8 | 2 | 12 | .963 | --- |
| Harper,B | Min | 985.2 | 120 | 673 | 52 | 11 | 5 | 5 | .985 | --- |
| Haselman,B | Tex | 4.0 | 1 | 8 | 0 | 0 | 0 | 0 | 1.000 | --- |
| Hassey,R | Oak | 489.2 | 59 | 307 | 17 | 1 | 2 | 5 | .997 | --- |
| Heath,M | Det | 890.1 | 117 | 588 | 53 | 13 | 7 | 8 | .980 | --- |
| Hernandez,C | LA | 52.1 | 10 | 37 | 2 | 0 | 1 | 1 | 1.000 | --- |
| Hoiles,C | Bal | 48.0 | 7 | 21 | 4 | 0 | 1 | 0 | 1.000 | --- |
| Hundley,T | NYN | 186.1 | 36 | 162 | 8 | 2 | 2 | 6 | .988 | --- |
| Karkovice,R | ChA | 478.1 | 64 | 297 | 31 | 2 | 4 | 2 | .994 | --- |
| Kennedy,T | SF | 727.1 | 103 | 387 | 38 | 4 | 3 | 5 | .991 | --- |
| Kremers,J | Atl | 173.1 | 27 | 107 | 10 | 1 | 2 | 2 | .992 | --- |
| Kreuter,C | Tex | 81.0 | 20 | 39 | 4 | 1 | 0 | 1 | .977 | --- |
| Lake,S | Phi | 195.0 | 28 | 115 | 19 | 1 | 1 | 2 | .993 | --- |
| Lampkin,T | SD | 144.1 | 20 | 91 | 9 | 3 | 0 | 2 | .971 | --- |
| LaValliere,M | Pit | 751.0 | 95 | 478 | 36 | 5 | 5 | 3 | .990 | --- |
| Leyritz,J | NYA | 74.0 | 11 | 55 | 4 | 1 | 0 | 4 | .983 | --- |
| Liddell,D | NYN | 1.0 | 1 | 1 | 0 | 0 | 0 | 0 | 1.000 | --- |
| Lyons,B | NYN | 190.1 | 23 | 181 | 11 | 4 | 1 | 2 | .980 | --- |
| Lyons,B | LA | 5.0 | 2 | 3 | 0 | 0 | 0 | 0 | 1.000 | --- |
| Macfarlane,M | KC | 910.2 | 112 | 660 | 23 | 6 | 9 | 7 | .991 | --- |
| Mann,K | Atl | 66.0 | 10 | 40 | 3 | 0 | 2 | 3 | 1.000 | --- |
| Manwaring,K | SF | 35.1 | 8 | 21 | 3 | 0 | 1 | 1 | 1.000 | --- |
| Marzano,J | Bos | 205.2 | 32 | 153 | 14 | 0 | 3 | 1 | 1.000 | --- |
| Mayne,B | KC | 35.0 | 5 | 29 | 3 | 1 | 0 | 1 | .970 | --- |
| McClendon,L | ChN | 16.0 | 8 | 13 | 2 | 0 | 0 | 1 | 1.000 | --- |
| McGriff,T | Cin | 9.0 | 1 | 4 | 2 | 0 | 1 | 0 | 1.000 | --- |
| McGriff,T | Hou | 16.0 | 4 | 9 | 0 | 1 | 0 | 0 | .900 | --- |
| McIntosh,T | Mil | 15.0 | 4 | 6 | 1 | 1 | 0 | 3 | .875 | --- |
| Melvin,B | Bal | 633.2 | 76 | 364 | 25 | 1 | 2 | 1 | .997 | --- |

## Catchers

| Player | Tm | Inn | G | PO | A | E | DP | PB | Pct. | Rng |
|---|---|---|---|---|---|---|---|---|---|---|
| Mercado,O | NYN | 242.0 | 40 | 213 | 8 | 2 | 2 | 4 | .991 | --- |
| Mercado,O | Mon | 29.2 | 8 | 26 | 1 | 0 | 0 | 0 | 1.000 | --- |
| Merced,O | Pit | 1.0 | 1 | 0 | 0 | 0 | 0 | 0 | .000 | --- |
| Myers,G | Tor | 635.0 | 87 | 411 | 30 | 3 | 4 | 8 | .993 | --- |
| Nichols,C | Hou | 90.0 | 15 | 64 | 9 | 1 | 2 | 2 | .986 | --- |
| Nieto,T | Phi | 89.0 | 17 | 57 | 5 | 1 | 1 | 0 | .984 | --- |
| Nokes,M | Det | 119.0 | 19 | 55 | 7 | 1 | 1 | 1 | .984 | --- |
| Nokes,M | NYA | 315.1 | 46 | 181 | 26 | 1 | 5 | 7 | .995 | --- |
| O'Brien,C | Mil | 381.2 | 46 | 218 | 23 | 2 | 5 | 3 | .992 | --- |
| O'Brien,C | NYN | 211.0 | 28 | 191 | 20 | 3 | 1 | 1 | .986 | --- |
| Oliver,J | Cin | 943.0 | 118 | 686 | 59 | 6 | 8 | 16 | .992 | --- |
| Olson,G | Atl | 718.1 | 97 | 502 | 42 | 7 | 3 | 2 | .987 | --- |
| Ortiz,J | Min | 432.0 | 68 | 248 | 25 | 0 | 7 | 6 | 1.000 | --- |
| Orton,J | Cal | 222.0 | 31 | 139 | 15 | 2 | 0 | 1 | .987 | --- |
| Pagnozzi,T | StL | 520.0 | 63 | 334 | 39 | 4 | 4 | 0 | .989 | --- |
| Palacios,R | KC | 140.0 | 27 | 113 | 5 | 1 | 1 | 1 | .992 | --- |
| Parent,M | SD | 473.2 | 60 | 324 | 30 | 3 | 6 | 1 | .992 | --- |
| Parrish,L | Cal | 1098.0 | 131 | 760 | 88 | 6 | 13 | 12 | .993 | --- |
| Pena,T | Bos | 1186.0 | 142 | 864 | 70 | 5 | 13 | 7 | .995 | --- |
| Petralli,G | Tex | 827.2 | 118 | 600 | 40 | 6 | 5 | 20 | .991 | --- |
| Prince,T | Pit | 22.2 | 3 | 16 | 1 | 0 | 0 | 0 | 1.000 | --- |
| Quirk,J | Oak | 252.0 | 37 | 151 | 17 | 4 | 3 | 1 | .977 | --- |
| Reed,J | Cin | 490.1 | 70 | 358 | 26 | 5 | 1 | 3 | .987 | --- |
| Reynolds,R | SD | 42.0 | 8 | 26 | 2 | 0 | 1 | 0 | 1.000 | --- |
| Rowland,R | Det | 37.0 | 5 | 29 | 0 | 1 | 0 | 0 | .967 | --- |
| Russell,J | Tex | 171.1 | 31 | 135 | 10 | 3 | 0 | 4 | .980 | --- |
| Salas,M | Det | 384.0 | 56 | 225 | 20 | 3 | 3 | 6 | .988 | --- |
| Santiago,B | SD | 799.2 | 98 | 541 | 50 | 12 | 6 | 6 | .980 | --- |
| Santovenia,N | Mon | 378.2 | 51 | 264 | 24 | 6 | 8 | 6 | .980 | --- |
| Sasser,M | NYN | 583.1 | 87 | 499 | 42 | 14 | 4 | 5 | .975 | --- |
| Schroeder,B | Cal | 117.0 | 15 | 73 | 8 | 0 | 2 | 1 | 1.000 | --- |
| Scioscia,M | LA | 1069.0 | 132 | 843 | 56 | 10 | 9 | 5 | .989 | --- |
| Sinatro,M | Sea | 151.0 | 28 | 113 | 15 | 1 | 1 | 1 | .992 | --- |
| Skinner,J | Cle | 375.0 | 49 | 222 | 16 | 1 | 4 | 3 | .996 | --- |
| Slaught,D | Pit | 562.2 | 78 | 344 | 37 | 8 | 4 | 4 | .979 | --- |
| Stanley,M | Tex | 360.2 | 63 | 244 | 20 | 4 | 0 | 10 | .985 | --- |
| Steinbach,T | Oak | 681.1 | 84 | 398 | 29 | 5 | 1 | 6 | .988 | --- |
| Stephens,R | StL | 39.0 | 5 | 31 | 2 | 0 | 0 | 1 | 1.000 | --- |
| Surhoff,B | Mil | 1048.1 | 125 | 616 | 53 | 10 | 9 | 5 | .985 | --- |
| Sutko,G | Cin | 4.0 | 1 | 3 | 0 | 0 | 0 | 0 | 1.000 | --- |
| Tettleton,M | Bal | 753.2 | 90 | 426 | 36 | 4 | 3 | 4 | .991 | --- |
| Tingley,R | Cal | 17.0 | 5 | 12 | 0 | 0 | 0 | 1 | 1.000 | --- |
| Trevino,A | Hou | 157.2 | 30 | 124 | 7 | 1 | 0 | 1 | .992 | --- |
| Trevino,A | NYN | 26.0 | 7 | 25 | 1 | 2 | 0 | 2 | .929 | --- |
| Trevino,A | Cin | 10.0 | 2 | 9 | 0 | 0 | 0 | 0 | 1.000 | --- |
| Valle,D | Sea | 843.0 | 104 | 632 | 43 | 2 | 8 | 9 | .997 | --- |
| Villanueva,H | ChN | 143.1 | 23 | 110 | 6 | 1 | 2 | 4 | .991 | --- |
| Virgil,O | Tor | 6.0 | 2 | 1 | 0 | 0 | 0 | 0 | 1.000 | --- |
| Webster,L | Min | 18.0 | 2 | 9 | 0 | 0 | 0 | 0 | 1.000 | --- |
| Whitt,E | Atl | 444.1 | 59 | 296 | 41 | 3 | 1 | 8 | .991 | --- |
| Willard,J | ChA | 1.0 | 1 | 0 | 0 | 0 | 0 | 0 | .000 | --- |
| Wrona,R | ChN | 86.0 | 16 | 56 | 9 | 2 | 2 | 1 | .970 | --- |
| Zeile,T | StL | 884.1 | 105 | 533 | 55 | 7 | 5 | 10 | .988 | --- |

## Pitchers

| Player | Tm | Inn | G | PO | A | E | DP | PB | Pct. | Rng |
|---|---|---|---|---|---|---|---|---|---|---|
| Aase,D | LA | 38.0 | 32 | 1 | 3 | 0 | 0 | -- | 1.000 | --- |
| Abbott,J | Cal | 211.2 | 33 | 8 | 35 | 1 | 4 | -- | .977 | --- |
| Abbott,P | Min | 34.2 | 7 | 2 | 2 | 1 | 1 | -- | .800 | --- |
| Acker,J | Tor | 91.2 | 59 | 6 | 19 | 0 | 0 | -- | 1.000 | --- |
| Adkins,S | NYA | 24.0 | 5 | 0 | 3 | 0 | 0 | -- | 1.000 | --- |
| Agosto,J | Hou | 92.1 | 82 | 11 | 18 | 0 | 1 | -- | 1.000 | --- |
| Aguilera,R | Min | 65.1 | 56 | 2 | 4 | 0 | 0 | -- | 1.000 | --- |
| Akerfelds,D | Phi | 87.0 | 68 | 3 | 13 | 1 | 0 | -- | .941 | --- |
| Aldred,S | Det | 13.2 | 3 | 0 | 2 | 0 | 0 | -- | 1.000 | --- |
| Aldrich,J | Bal | 12.0 | 7 | 2 | 1 | 0 | 0 | -- | 1.000 | --- |
| Alexander,G | Tex | 7.0 | 3 | 1 | 0 | 0 | 1 | -- | 1.000 | --- |
| Andersen,L | Hou | 73.2 | 50 | 11 | 12 | 1 | 1 | -- | .958 | --- |
| Andersen,L | Bos | 22.0 | 15 | 2 | 0 | 1 | 0 | -- | .667 | --- |
| Anderson,A | Min | 188.2 | 31 | 7 | 37 | 0 | 4 | -- | 1.000 | --- |
| Anderson,S | Mon | 18.0 | 4 | 0 | 2 | 0 | 0 | -- | 1.000 | --- |
| Appier,K | KC | 185.2 | 32 | 15 | 21 | 3 | 3 | -- | .923 | --- |
| Aquino,L | KC | 68.1 | 20 | 4 | 10 | 0 | 2 | -- | 1.000 | --- |
| Armstrong,J | Cin | 166.0 | 29 | 15 | 22 | 0 | 2 | -- | 1.000 | --- |
| Arnsberg,B | Tex | 62.2 | 53 | 6 | 11 | 0 | 2 | -- | 1.000 | --- |
| Assenmacher,P | ChN | 103.0 | 72 | 2 | 18 | 0 | 0 | -- | 1.000 | --- |
| August,D | Mil | 11.0 | 5 | 1 | 2 | 1 | 0 | -- | .750 | --- |
| Avery,S | Atl | 99.0 | 21 | 4 | 23 | 2 | 1 | -- | .931 | --- |
| Bailes,S | Cal | 35.1 | 27 | 2 | 10 | 1 | 0 | -- | .923 | --- |
| Bair,D | Pit | 24.1 | 22 | 2 | 4 | 1 | 1 | -- | .857 | --- |
| Ballard,J | Bal | 133.1 | 44 | 11 | 20 | 1 | 1 | -- | .969 | --- |
| Baller,J | KC | 2.1 | 3 | 0 | 0 | 0 | 0 | -- | .000 | --- |
| Bankhead,S | Sea | 13.0 | 4 | 0 | 0 | 0 | 0 | -- | .000 | --- |
| Barfield,J | Tex | 44.1 | 33 | 4 | 6 | 0 | 0 | -- | 1.000 | --- |
| Barnes,B | Mon | 28.0 | 4 | 2 | 3 | 1 | 0 | -- | .833 | --- |
| Bautista,J | Bal | 26.2 | 22 | 1 | 2 | 0 | 0 | -- | 1.000 | --- |
| Bearse,K | Cle | 7.2 | 3 | 0 | 1 | 0 | 0 | -- | 1.000 | --- |
| Bedrosian,S | SF | 79.1 | 68 | 9 | 11 | 1 | 1 | -- | .952 | --- |
| Belcher,T | LA | 146.0 | 23 | 11 | 10 | 0 | 1 | -- | 1.000 | --- |
| Belinda,S | Pit | 58.1 | 55 | 2 | 4 | 0 | 0 | -- | 1.000 | --- |
| Benes,A | SD | 192.1 | 32 | 14 | 9 | 1 | 1 | -- | .958 | --- |
| Berenguer,J | Min | 100.1 | 51 | 3 | 5 | 0 | 0 | -- | 1.000 | --- |
| Bielecki,M | ChN | 168.0 | 36 | 17 | 33 | 3 | 2 | -- | .943 | --- |
| Birtsas,T | Cin | 51.1 | 29 | 4 | 8 | 0 | 0 | -- | 1.000 | --- |
| Bitker,J | Oak | 3.0 | 1 | 0 | 1 | 0 | 1 | -- | 1.000 | --- |
| Bitker,J | Tex | 9.0 | 5 | 1 | 2 | 0 | 0 | -- | 1.000 | --- |
| Black,B | Cle | 191.0 | 29 | 7 | 27 | 1 | 3 | -- | .971 | --- |
| Black,B | Tor | 15.2 | 3 | 0 | 6 | 0 | 0 | -- | 1.000 | --- |
| Blair,W | Tor | 68.2 | 27 | 3 | 6 | 0 | 0 | -- | 1.000 | --- |
| Blankenship,K | ChN | 12.1 | 3 | 1 | 1 | 1 | 0 | -- | .667 | --- |
| Blyleven,B | Cal | 134.0 | 23 | 3 | 24 | 1 | 0 | -- | .964 | --- |
| Boddicker,M | Bos | 228.0 | 34 | 29 | 28 | 2 | 6 | -- | .966 | --- |
| Boever,J | Atl | 42.1 | 33 | 1 | 2 | 2 | 1 | -- | .600 | --- |
| Boever,J | Phi | 46.0 | 34 | 5 | 5 | 0 | 0 | -- | 1.000 | --- |
| Bohanon,B | Tex | 34.0 | 11 | 1 | 10 | 0 | 2 | -- | 1.000 | --- |
| Bolton,T | Bos | 119.2 | 21 | 4 | 21 | 1 | 1 | -- | .962 | --- |
| Booker,G | SF | 2.0 | 2 | 0 | 0 | 0 | 0 | -- | .000 | --- |
| Boone,D | Bal | 9.2 | 4 | 0 | 2 | 0 | 0 | -- | 1.000 | --- |
| Bosio,C | Mil | 132.2 | 20 | 12 | 24 | 1 | 2 | -- | .973 | --- |
| Boskie,S | ChN | 97.2 | 15 | 13 | 12 | 0 | 2 | -- | 1.000 | --- |
| Boyd,O | Mon | 190.2 | 31 | 6 | 24 | 3 | 1 | -- | .909 | --- |
| Brantley,J | SF | 86.2 | 55 | 6 | 11 | 1 | 1 | -- | .944 | --- |
| Brown,Keith | Cin | 11.1 | 8 | 1 | 2 | 0 | 0 | -- | 1.000 | --- |
| Brown,Kevin | Tex | 180.0 | 26 | 15 | 25 | 3 | 0 | -- | .930 | --- |

## Pitchers

| Player | Tm | Inn | G | PO | A | E | DP | PB | Pct. | Rng |
|---|---|---|---|---|---|---|---|---|---|---|
| Brown,KevinD | NYN | 1.0 | 1 | 0 | 1 | 0 | 0 | -- | 1.000 | --- |
| Brown,KevinD | Mil | 21.0 | 5 | 2 | 5 | 0 | 0 | -- | 1.000 | --- |
| Browning,T | Cin | 227.2 | 35 | 8 | 27 | 3 | 1 | -- | .921 | --- |
| Burba,D | Sea | 8.0 | 6 | 1 | 2 | 1 | 0 | -- | .750 | --- |
| Burke,T | Mon | 75.0 | 58 | 3 | 20 | 0 | 1 | -- | 1.000 | --- |
| Burkett,J | SF | 204.0 | 33 | 12 | 24 | 1 | 4 | -- | .973 | --- |
| Burns,T | Oak | 78.2 | 43 | 2 | 7 | 0 | 1 | -- | 1.000 | --- |
| Cadaret,G | NYA | 121.1 | 54 | 7 | 26 | 1 | 1 | -- | .971 | --- |
| Camacho,E | SF | 10.0 | 8 | 0 | 0 | 0 | 0 | -- | .000 | --- |
| Camacho,E | StL | 5.2 | 6 | 0 | 1 | 0 | 0 | -- | 1.000 | --- |
| Campbell,J | KC | 9.2 | 2 | 1 | 0 | 0 | 0 | -- | 1.000 | --- |
| Candelaria,J | Min | 58.1 | 34 | 3 | 3 | 0 | 0 | -- | 1.000 | --- |
| Candelaria,J | Tor | 21.1 | 13 | 1 | 6 | 0 | 0 | -- | 1.000 | --- |
| Candiotti,T | Cle | 202.0 | 31 | 21 | 36 | 2 | 1 | -- | .966 | --- |
| Capel,M | Mil | 0.1 | 2 | 0 | 0 | 0 | 0 | -- | .000 | --- |
| Carman,D | Phi | 86.2 | 59 | 5 | 12 | 1 | 1 | -- | .944 | --- |
| Carpenter,C | StL | 8.0 | 4 | 0 | 0 | 1 | 0 | -- | .000 | --- |
| Cary,C | NYA | 156.2 | 28 | 8 | 13 | 1 | 1 | -- | .955 | --- |
| Casian,L | Min | 22.1 | 5 | 0 | 3 | 0 | 1 | -- | 1.000 | --- |
| Castillo,T | Atl | 76.2 | 52 | 5 | 13 | 0 | 1 | -- | 1.000 | --- |
| Cerutti,J | Tor | 140.0 | 30 | 11 | 18 | 0 | 3 | -- | 1.000 | --- |
| Charlton,N | Cin | 154.1 | 56 | 6 | 23 | 1 | 3 | -- | .967 | --- |
| Chiamparino,S | Tex | 37.2 | 6 | 3 | 1 | 0 | 0 | -- | 1.000 | --- |
| Chitren,S | Oak | 17.2 | 8 | 1 | 2 | 0 | 0 | -- | 1.000 | --- |
| Clancy,J | Hou | 76.0 | 33 | 4 | 13 | 0 | 1 | -- | 1.000 | --- |
| Clark,B | Sea | 11.0 | 12 | 1 | 3 | 0 | 1 | -- | 1.000 | --- |
| Clark,T | Hou | 4.0 | 1 | 0 | 0 | 0 | 0 | -- | .000 | --- |
| Clarke,S | StL | 3.1 | 2 | 0 | 0 | 0 | 0 | -- | .000 | --- |
| Clary,M | Atl | 101.2 | 33 | 6 | 19 | 1 | 0 | -- | .962 | --- |
| Clear,M | Cal | 7.2 | 4 | 0 | 0 | 0 | 0 | -- | .000 | --- |
| Clemens,R | Bos | 228.1 | 31 | 23 | 26 | 2 | 1 | -- | .961 | --- |
| Clements,P | SD | 13.0 | 9 | 1 | 3 | 0 | 0 | -- | 1.000 | --- |
| Codiroli,C | KC | 10.1 | 6 | 1 | 0 | 0 | 0 | -- | 1.000 | --- |
| Coffman,K | ChN | 18.1 | 8 | 3 | 4 | 0 | 0 | -- | 1.000 | --- |
| Combs,P | Phi | 183.1 | 32 | 9 | 25 | 0 | 2 | -- | 1.000 | --- |
| Comstock,K | Sea | 56.0 | 60 | 2 | 11 | 1 | 0 | -- | .929 | --- |
| Cone,D | NYN | 211.2 | 31 | 16 | 19 | 3 | 1 | -- | .921 | --- |
| Cook,D | Phi | 148.2 | 44 | 9 | 20 | 0 | 1 | -- | 1.000 | --- |
| Cook,D | LA | 14.1 | 5 | 3 | 2 | 0 | 1 | -- | 1.000 | --- |
| Corbett,S | Cal | 5.0 | 4 | 0 | 0 | 0 | 0 | -- | .000 | --- |
| Costello,J | StL | 4.1 | 4 | 0 | 0 | 0 | 0 | -- | .000 | --- |
| Costello,J | Mon | 6.1 | 4 | 0 | 0 | 0 | 0 | -- | .000 | --- |
| Crawford,S | KC | 80.0 | 46 | 8 | 14 | 0 | 0 | -- | 1.000 | --- |
| Crews,T | LA | 107.1 | 66 | 8 | 7 | 1 | 0 | -- | .938 | --- |
| Crim,C | Mil | 85.2 | 67 | 8 | 12 | 1 | 1 | -- | .952 | --- |
| Cummings,S | Tor | 12.1 | 6 | 1 | 1 | 0 | 0 | -- | 1.000 | --- |
| Darling,R | NYN | 126.0 | 33 | 8 | 21 | 2 | 0 | -- | .935 | --- |
| Darwin,D | Hou | 162.2 | 48 | 11 | 15 | 1 | 1 | -- | .963 | --- |
| Dascenzo,D | ChN | 1.0 | 1 | 0 | 0 | 0 | 0 | -- | .000 | --- |
| Davis,J | SD | 9.1 | 6 | 0 | 1 | 0 | 0 | -- | 1.000 | --- |
| Davis,M | KC | 68.2 | 53 | 1 | 6 | 1 | 0 | -- | .875 | --- |
| Davis,S | KC | 112.0 | 21 | 2 | 10 | 1 | 2 | -- | .923 | --- |
| Dayley,K | StL | 73.1 | 58 | 5 | 7 | 1 | 0 | -- | .923 | --- |
| DeJesus,J | Phi | 130.0 | 22 | 9 | 15 | 2 | 1 | -- | .923 | --- |
| DeLeon,J | StL | 182.2 | 32 | 8 | 14 | 2 | 0 | -- | .917 | --- |
| Delucia,R | Sea | 36.0 | 5 | 3 | 2 | 1 | 0 | -- | .833 | --- |
| Deshaies,J | Hou | 209.1 | 34 | 3 | 32 | 2 | 1 | -- | .946 | --- |
| Dewey,M | SF | 22.2 | 14 | 2 | 2 | 0 | 1 | -- | 1.000 | --- |

## Pitchers

| Player | Tm | Inn | G | PO | A | E | DP | PB | Pct. | Rng |
|---|---|---|---|---|---|---|---|---|---|---|
| Dibble,R | Cin | 98.0 | 68 | 5 | 9 | 0 | 0 | -- | 1.000 | --- |
| Dickson,L | ChN | 13.2 | 3 | 1 | 5 | 0 | 1 | -- | 1.000 | --- |
| DePino,F | StL | 81.0 | 62 | 2 | 15 | 0 | 1 | -- | 1.000 | --- |
| Dopson,J | Bos | 17.2 | 4 | 1 | 4 | 0 | 0 | -- | 1.000 | --- |
| Dotson,R | KC | 28.2 | 8 | 2 | 3 | 0 | 1 | -- | 1.000 | --- |
| Downs,K | SF | 63.0 | 13 | 6 | 12 | 1 | 0 | -- | .947 | --- |
| Drabek,D | Pit | 231.1 | 33 | 25 | 36 | 1 | 2 | -- | .984 | --- |
| Drummond,T | Min | 87.2 | 34 | 5 | 7 | 1 | 1 | -- | .923 | --- |
| DuBois,B | Det | 58.1 | 12 | 1 | 3 | 1 | 1 | -- | .800 | --- |
| Dunne,M | SD | 28.2 | 10 | 4 | 5 | 0 | 1 | -- | 1.000 | --- |
| Eave,G | Sea | 30.0 | 8 | 1 | 5 | 0 | 1 | -- | 1.000 | --- |
| Eckersley,D | Oak | 73.1 | 63 | 3 | 1 | 0 | 0 | -- | 1.000 | --- |
| Edens,T | Mil | 89.0 | 35 | 7 | 11 | 3 | 1 | -- | .857 | --- |
| Edwards,W | ChA | 95.0 | 42 | 6 | 14 | 1 | 1 | -- | .952 | --- |
| Eichhorn,M | Cal | 84.2 | 60 | 7 | 16 | 0 | 0 | -- | 1.000 | --- |
| Eiland,D | NYA | 30.1 | 5 | 1 | 3 | 0 | 0 | -- | 1.000 | --- |
| Elvira,N | Mil | 5.0 | 4 | 0 | 1 | 0 | 0 | -- | 1.000 | --- |
| Encarnacion,L | KC | 10.1 | 4 | 1 | 0 | 0 | 0 | -- | 1.000 | --- |
| Erickson,S | Min | 113.0 | 19 | 10 | 13 | 0 | 0 | -- | 1.000 | --- |
| Farmer,H | Mon | 23.0 | 6 | 1 | 7 | 0 | 1 | -- | 1.000 | --- |
| Farr,S | KC | 127.0 | 57 | 7 | 17 | 2 | 1 | -- | .923 | --- |
| Farrell,J | Cle | 96.2 | 17 | 8 | 12 | 2 | 1 | -- | .909 | --- |
| Fernandez,A | ChA | 87.2 | 13 | 3 | 12 | 2 | 0 | -- | .882 | --- |
| Fernandez,S | NYN | 179.1 | 30 | 1 | 16 | 2 | 0 | -- | .895 | --- |
| Fetters,M | Cal | 67.2 | 26 | 7 | 11 | 1 | 0 | -- | .947 | --- |
| Filer,T | Mil | 22.0 | 7 | 1 | 1 | 0 | 0 | -- | 1.000 | --- |
| Filson,P | KC | 35.0 | 8 | 2 | 2 | 0 | 0 | -- | 1.000 | --- |
| Finley,C | Cal | 236.0 | 32 | 14 | 21 | 5 | 2 | -- | .875 | --- |
| Fisher,B | Hou | 5.0 | 4 | 0 | 0 | 0 | 0 | -- | .000 | --- |
| Flanagan,M | Tor | 20.1 | 5 | 0 | 6 | 1 | 0 | -- | .857 | --- |
| Fossas,T | Mil | 29.1 | 32 | 1 | 4 | 3 | 0 | -- | .625 | --- |
| Franco,J | NYN | 75.1 | 56 | 4 | 13 | 1 | 0 | -- | .944 | --- |
| Fraser,W | Cal | 76.0 | 45 | 2 | 6 | 0 | 0 | -- | 1.000 | --- |
| Freeman,M | Phi | 32.1 | 16 | 1 | 4 | 0 | 1 | -- | 1.000 | --- |
| Freeman,M | Atl | 15.2 | 9 | 0 | 2 | 1 | 0 | -- | .667 | --- |
| Frey,S | Mon | 57.2 | 52 | 4 | 7 | 1 | 0 | -- | .917 | --- |
| Frohwirth,T | Phi | 1.0 | 5 | 0 | 1 | 1 | 0 | -- | .500 | --- |
| Garces,R | Min | 5.2 | 5 | 0 | 1 | 0 | 0 | -- | 1.000 | --- |
| Gardiner,M | Sea | 12.2 | 5 | 1 | 2 | 0 | 0 | -- | 1.000 | --- |
| Gardner,M | Mon | 152.2 | 27 | 9 | 24 | 0 | 5 | -- | 1.000 | --- |
| Gardner,W | Bos | 77.1 | 34 | 9 | 7 | 1 | 1 | -- | .941 | --- |
| Garrelts,S | SF | 182.0 | 31 | 5 | 26 | 3 | 0 | -- | .912 | --- |
| Gibson,P | Det | 97.1 | 61 | 9 | 10 | 0 | 1 | -- | 1.000 | --- |
| Gideon,B | Mon | 1.0 | 1 | 0 | 1 | 0 | 0 | -- | 1.000 | --- |
| Gilles,T | Tor | 1.1 | 2 | 0 | 1 | 0 | 0 | -- | 1.000 | --- |
| Glavine,T | Atl | 214.1 | 33 | 18 | 33 | 1 | 1 | -- | .981 | --- |
| Gleaton,J | Det | 82.2 | 57 | 0 | 10 | 1 | 0 | -- | .909 | --- |
| Gooden,D | NYN | 225.0 | 33 | 15 | 35 | 4 | 5 | -- | .926 | --- |
| Gordon,T | KC | 195.1 | 32 | 17 | 24 | 1 | 1 | -- | .976 | --- |
| Gott,J | LA | 62.0 | 50 | 6 | 5 | 0 | 0 | -- | 1.000 | --- |
| Gozzo,M | Cle | 3.0 | 2 | 0 | 0 | 0 | 0 | -- | .000 | --- |
| Grahe,J | Cal | 43.1 | 8 | 2 | 10 | 0 | 2 | -- | 1.000 | --- |
| Grant,M | SD | 39.0 | 26 | 1 | 10 | 0 | 1 | -- | 1.000 | --- |
| Grant,M | Atl | 52.1 | 33 | 5 | 4 | 1 | 0 | -- | .900 | --- |
| Gray,J | Bos | 50.2 | 41 | 2 | 6 | 0 | 2 | -- | 1.000 | --- |
| Greene,T | Atl | 12.1 | 5 | 0 | 2 | 0 | 0 | -- | 1.000 | --- |
| Greene,T | Phi | 41.0 | 11 | 3 | 5 | 1 | 0 | -- | .889 | --- |
| Grimsley,J | Phi | 57.1 | 11 | 13 | 8 | 1 | 2 | -- | .955 | --- |

## Pitchers

| Player | Tm | Inn | G | PO | A | E | DP | PB | Pct. | Rng |
|---|---|---|---|---|---|---|---|---|---|---|
| Gross,Kevin | Mon | 163.1 | 31 | 6 | 13 | 1 | 0 | -- | .950 | --- |
| Gross,Kip | Cin | 6.1 | 5 | 0 | 0 | 0 | 0 | -- | .000 | --- |
| Guante,C | Cle | 46.2 | 26 | 3 | 5 | 0 | 2 | -- | 1.000 | --- |
| Gubicza,M | KC | 94.0 | 16 | 9 | 10 | 1 | 3 | -- | .950 | --- |
| Guetterman,L | NYA | 93.0 | 64 | 6 | 19 | 2 | 1 | -- | .926 | --- |
| Gullickson,B | Hou | 193.1 | 32 | 11 | 13 | 0 | 1 | -- | 1.000 | --- |
| Gunderson,E | SF | 19.2 | 7 | 0 | 4 | 0 | 0 | -- | 1.000 | --- |
| Guthrie,M | Min | 144.2 | 24 | 5 | 21 | 1 | 1 | -- | .963 | --- |
| Habyan,J | NYA | 8.2 | 6 | 2 | 0 | 0 | 0 | -- | 1.000 | --- |
| Hall,D | Mon | 56.1 | 41 | 2 | 11 | 1 | 1 | -- | .929 | --- |
| Hammaker,A | SF | 67.1 | 25 | 4 | 6 | 0 | 2 | -- | 1.000 | --- |
| Hammaker,A | SD | 19.1 | 9 | 2 | 1 | 0 | 0 | -- | 1.000 | --- |
| Hammond,C | Cin | 11.1 | 3 | 0 | 3 | 2 | 0 | -- | .600 | --- |
| Hanson,E | Sea | 236.0 | 33 | 31 | 21 | 4 | 0 | -- | .929 | --- |
| Harkey,M | ChN | 173.2 | 27 | 18 | 16 | 1 | 0 | -- | .971 | --- |
| Harnisch,P | Bal | 188.2 | 31 | 12 | 14 | 1 | 0 | -- | .963 | --- |
| Harris,Gene | Sea | 35.2 | 24 | 4 | 2 | 0 | 1 | -- | 1.000 | --- |
| Harris,Greg | Bos | 184.1 | 34 | 24 | 36 | 4 | 1 | -- | .938 | --- |
| Harris,GW | SD | 117.1 | 73 | 3 | 17 | 0 | 1 | -- | 1.000 | --- |
| Harris,R | Oak | 41.1 | 16 | 2 | 3 | 0 | 1 | -- | 1.000 | --- |
| Hartley,M | LA | 79.1 | 32 | 3 | 8 | 1 | 1 | -- | .917 | --- |
| Harvey,B | Cal | 64.1 | 54 | 3 | 5 | 0 | 1 | -- | 1.000 | --- |
| Hawkins,A | NYA | 157.2 | 28 | 12 | 9 | 0 | 3 | -- | 1.000 | --- |
| Heaton,N | Pit | 146.0 | 30 | 5 | 22 | 2 | 1 | -- | .931 | --- |
| Heep,D | Bos | 1.0 | 1 | 0 | 0 | 0 | 0 | -- | .000 | --- |
| Henke,T | Tor | 74.2 | 61 | 5 | 5 | 0 | 0 | -- | 1.000 | --- |
| Henneman,M | Det | 96.1 | 70 | 7 | 16 | 3 | 2 | -- | .885 | --- |
| Hennis,R | Hou | 9.2 | 3 | 2 | 0 | 0 | 0 | -- | 1.000 | --- |
| Henry,D | Atl | 37.0 | 33 | 4 | 1 | 0 | 0 | -- | 1.000 | --- |
| Hernandez,X | Hou | 62.1 | 34 | 3 | 5 | 0 | 0 | -- | 1.000 | --- |
| Hershiser,O | LA | 25.1 | 4 | 1 | 3 | 0 | 0 | -- | 1.000 | --- |
| Hesketh,J | Mon | 3.0 | 2 | 1 | 0 | 0 | 0 | -- | 1.000 | --- |
| Hesketh,J | Atl | 31.0 | 31 | 3 | 3 | 1 | 0 | -- | .857 | --- |
| Hesketh,J | Bos | 25.2 | 12 | 0 | 3 | 1 | 0 | -- | .750 | --- |
| Hetzel,E | Bos | 35.0 | 9 | 2 | 3 | 0 | 0 | -- | 1.000 | --- |
| Hibbard,G | ChA | 211.0 | 33 | 7 | 29 | 0 | 2 | -- | 1.000 | --- |
| Hickey,K | Bal | 26.1 | 37 | 1 | 4 | 0 | 0 | -- | 1.000 | --- |
| Higuera,T | Mil | 170.0 | 27 | 7 | 19 | 2 | 2 | -- | .929 | --- |
| Hill,D | Cal | 1.0 | 1 | 0 | 0 | 0 | 0 | -- | .000 | --- |
| Hill,K | StL | 78.2 | 17 | 7 | 11 | 1 | 1 | -- | .947 | --- |
| Hillegas,S | ChA | 11.1 | 7 | 2 | 2 | 0 | 0 | -- | 1.000 | --- |
| Hilton,H | StL | 3.0 | 2 | 0 | 0 | 0 | 0 | -- | .000 | --- |
| Holman,B | Sea | 189.2 | 28 | 16 | 16 | 1 | 0 | -- | .970 | --- |
| Holmes,D | LA | 17.1 | 14 | 1 | 1 | 0 | 0 | -- | 1.000 | --- |
| Holton,B | Bal | 58.0 | 33 | 6 | 10 | 1 | 0 | -- | .941 | --- |
| Honeycutt,R | Oak | 66.0 | 64 | 0 | 15 | 1 | 1 | -- | .938 | --- |
| Hoover,J | Tex | 4.2 | 2 | 0 | 0 | 0 | 0 | -- | .000 | --- |
| Horton,R | StL | 42.0 | 32 | 2 | 13 | 0 | 2 | -- | 1.000 | --- |
| Hough,C | Tex | 218.2 | 32 | 11 | 30 | 2 | 3 | -- | .953 | --- |
| Howell,J | LA | 73.0 | 46 | 3 | 10 | 0 | 0 | -- | 1.000 | --- |
| Howell,K | Phi | 106.2 | 18 | 7 | 10 | 2 | 0 | -- | .895 | --- |
| Huismann,M | Pit | 3.0 | 2 | 0 | 0 | 0 | 0 | -- | .000 | --- |
| Hurst,B | SD | 223.2 | 33 | 7 | 36 | 1 | 4 | -- | .977 | --- |
| Innis,J | NYN | 26.1 | 18 | 4 | 3 | 0 | 0 | -- | 1.000 | --- |
| Irvine,D | Bos | 17.1 | 11 | 1 | 3 | 0 | 0 | -- | 1.000 | --- |
| Jackson,D | Cin | 117.1 | 22 | 4 | 13 | 1 | 0 | -- | .944 | --- |
| Jackson,M | Sea | 76.1 | 62 | 3 | 12 | 0 | 3 | -- | 1.000 | --- |
| Jeffcoat,M | Tex | 102.2 | 43 | 4 | 10 | 1 | 3 | -- | .933 | --- |

## Pitchers

| Player | Tm | Inn | G | PO | A | E | DP | PB | Pct. | Rng |
|---|---|---|---|---|---|---|---|---|---|---|
| Johnson,D | Bal | 180.0 | 30 | 13 | 10 | 2 | 1 | -- | .920 | --- |
| Johnson,R | Sea | 219.2 | 33 | 6 | 24 | 5 | 2 | -- | .857 | --- |
| Jones,B | ChA | 74.0 | 65 | 4 | 20 | 0 | 1 | -- | 1.000 | --- |
| Jones,D | Cle | 84.1 | 66 | 0 | 9 | 2 | 0 | -- | .818 | --- |
| Jones,J | NYA | 50.0 | 17 | 1 | 4 | 1 | 1 | -- | .833 | --- |
| Jones,T | StL | 1.1 | 1 | 0 | 0 | 0 | 0 | -- | .000 | --- |
| Kaiser,J | Cle | 12.2 | 5 | 3 | 1 | 0 | 0 | -- | 1.000 | --- |
| Kerfeld,C | Hou | 3.1 | 5 | 0 | 0 | 1 | 0 | -- | .000 | --- |
| Kerfeld,C | Atl | 30.2 | 25 | 2 | 2 | 2 | 0 | -- | .667 | --- |
| Key,J | Tor | 154.2 | 27 | 9 | 21 | 1 | 3 | -- | .968 | --- |
| Kiecker,D | Bos | 152.0 | 32 | 18 | 28 | 2 | 1 | -- | .958 | --- |
| Kilgus,P | Tor | 16.1 | 11 | 1 | 3 | 0 | 0 | -- | 1.000 | --- |
| King,E | ChA | 151.0 | 25 | 8 | 15 | 0 | 1 | -- | 1.000 | --- |
| Kinzer,M | Det | 1.2 | 1 | 0 | 0 | 0 | 0 | -- | .000 | --- |
| Kipper,B | Pit | 62.2 | 41 | 5 | 8 | 0 | 1 | -- | 1.000 | --- |
| Klink,J | Oak | 39.2 | 40 | 1 | 1 | 0 | 0 | -- | 1.000 | --- |
| Knackert,B | Sea | 37.1 | 24 | 4 | 3 | 2 | 0 | -- | .778 | --- |
| Knepper,B | SF | 44.1 | 12 | 1 | 8 | 0 | 0 | -- | 1.000 | --- |
| Knudson,M | Mil | 168.1 | 30 | 14 | 16 | 2 | 2 | -- | .938 | --- |
| Kraemer,J | ChN | 25.0 | 18 | 2 | 4 | 1 | 1 | -- | .857 | --- |
| Kramer,R | Pit | 25.2 | 12 | 4 | 5 | 0 | 1 | -- | 1.000 | --- |
| Kramer,R | ChN | 20.1 | 10 | 4 | 1 | 0 | 0 | -- | 1.000 | --- |
| Krueger,B | Mil | 129.0 | 30 | 2 | 17 | 0 | 2 | -- | 1.000 | --- |
| Kutzler,J | ChA | 31.1 | 7 | 2 | 2 | 0 | 0 | -- | 1.000 | --- |
| LaCoss,M | SF | 77.2 | 13 | 5 | 8 | 1 | 1 | -- | .929 | --- |
| Lamp,D | Bos | 105.2 | 47 | 12 | 15 | 0 | 0 | -- | 1.000 | --- |
| Lancaster,L | ChN | 115.0 | 57 | 8 | 21 | 0 | 2 | -- | 1.000 | --- |
| Landrum,B | Pit | 71.2 | 54 | 11 | 6 | 0 | 0 | -- | 1.000 | --- |
| Langston,M | Cal | 223.0 | 33 | 7 | 41 | 3 | 0 | -- | .941 | --- |
| LaPoint,D | NYA | 157.2 | 28 | 7 | 23 | 2 | 5 | -- | .938 | --- |
| Layana,T | Cin | 79.0 | 54 | 10 | 9 | 0 | 1 | -- | 1.000 | --- |
| Leach,T | Min | 81.2 | 55 | 11 | 11 | 1 | 0 | -- | .957 | --- |
| Leary,T | NYA | 208.0 | 31 | 14 | 37 | 4 | 4 | -- | .927 | --- |
| Lee,M | Mil | 21.1 | 11 | 1 | 1 | 0 | 0 | -- | 1.000 | --- |
| Lefferts,C | SD | 78.2 | 56 | 6 | 9 | 0 | 2 | -- | 1.000 | --- |
| Leibrandt,C | Atl | 162.1 | 24 | 10 | 27 | 0 | 2 | -- | 1.000 | --- |
| Leister,J | Bos | 5.2 | 2 | 0 | 0 | 0 | 0 | -- | .000 | --- |
| Leiter,A | Tor | 6.1 | 4 | 1 | 1 | 0 | 0 | -- | 1.000 | --- |
| Leiter,M | NYA | 26.1 | 8 | 0 | 8 | 0 | 1 | -- | 1.000 | --- |
| Lewis,S | Cal | 16.1 | 2 | 0 | 1 | 0 | 0 | -- | 1.000 | --- |
| Lilliquist,D | Atl | 61.2 | 12 | 3 | 4 | 0 | 0 | -- | 1.000 | --- |
| Lilliquist,D | SD | 60.1 | 16 | 1 | 3 | 0 | 1 | -- | 1.000 | --- |
| Long,B | ChA | 5.2 | 4 | 1 | 2 | 0 | 0 | -- | 1.000 | --- |
| Long,B | ChN | 55.2 | 43 | 5 | 9 | 1 | 0 | -- | .933 | --- |
| Lovelace,V | Sea | 2.1 | 5 | 0 | 0 | 0 | 0 | -- | .000 | --- |
| Luecken,R | Atl | 53.0 | 36 | 5 | 7 | 0 | 0 | -- | 1.000 | --- |
| Luecken,R | Tor | 1.0 | 1 | 0 | 0 | 0 | 0 | -- | .000 | --- |
| Lugo,U | Det | 24.1 | 13 | 0 | 7 | 0 | 0 | -- | 1.000 | --- |
| Lyons,S | ChA | 2.0 | 1 | 0 | 1 | 0 | 0 | -- | 1.000 | --- |
| MacDonald,B | Tor | 2.1 | 4 | 0 | 0 | 0 | 0 | -- | .000 | --- |
| Machado,J | NYN | 34.1 | 27 | 1 | 3 | 0 | 0 | -- | 1.000 | --- |
| Machado,J | Mil | 13.0 | 10 | 1 | 1 | 0 | 0 | -- | 1.000 | --- |
| Maddux,G | ChN | 237.0 | 35 | 40 | 53 | 0 | 7 | -- | 1.000 | --- |
| Maddux,M | LA | 20.2 | 11 | 0 | 3 | 0 | 0 | -- | 1.000 | --- |
| Magrane,J | StL | 203.1 | 31 | 8 | 37 | 1 | 2 | -- | .978 | --- |
| Mahler,R | Cin | 134.2 | 35 | 12 | 17 | 1 | 1 | -- | .967 | --- |
| Maldonado,C | KC | 6.0 | 4 | 0 | 0 | 0 | 0 | -- | .000 | --- |
| Malloy,B | Mon | 2.0 | 1 | 0 | 0 | 0 | 0 | -- | .000 | --- |

## Pitchers

| Player | Tm | Inn | G | PO | A | E | DP | PB | Pct. | Rng |
|---|---|---|---|---|---|---|---|---|---|---|
| Malone,C | Phi | 7.1 | 7 | 0 | 0 | 0 | 0 | -- | .000 | --- |
| Manon,R | Tex | 2.0 | 1 | 2 | 0 | 0 | 0 | -- | 1.000 | --- |
| Marak,P | Atl | 39.0 | 7 | 6 | 9 | 0 | 1 | -- | 1.000 | --- |
| Martinez,Dave | Mon | 0.1 | 1 | 0 | 0 | 0 | 0 | -- | .000 | --- |
| Martinez,Dennis | Mon | 226.0 | 32 | 16 | 34 | 1 | 2 | -- | .980 | --- |
| Martinez,R | LA | 234.1 | 33 | 16 | 26 | 1 | 1 | -- | .977 | --- |
| Mathews,G | StL | 50.2 | 11 | 3 | 14 | 1 | 2 | -- | .944 | --- |
| McCament,R | SF | 6.0 | 3 | 1 | 0 | 0 | 0 | -- | 1.000 | --- |
| McCaskill,K | Cal | 174.1 | 29 | 20 | 29 | 3 | 2 | -- | .942 | --- |
| McClellan,P | SF | 7.2 | 4 | 1 | 2 | 0 | 1 | -- | 1.000 | --- |
| McClure,B | Cal | 7.0 | 11 | 0 | 1 | 0 | 0 | -- | 1.000 | --- |
| McCullers,L | NYA | 15.0 | 11 | 1 | 2 | 0 | 0 | -- | 1.000 | --- |
| McCullers,L | Det | 29.2 | 9 | 3 | 0 | 0 | 0 | -- | 1.000 | --- |
| McDonald,B | Bal | 118.2 | 21 | 15 | 14 | 1 | 1 | -- | .967 | --- |
| McDowell,J | ChA | 205.0 | 33 | 17 | 20 | 1 | 3 | -- | .974 | --- |
| McDowell,R | Phi | 88.1 | 73 | 1 | 23 | 5 | 2 | -- | .828 | --- |
| McElroy,C | Phi | 14.0 | 16 | 1 | 0 | 1 | 0 | -- | .500 | --- |
| McGaffigan,A | SF | 4.2 | 4 | 0 | 0 | 0 | 0 | -- | .000 | --- |
| McGaffigan,A | KC | 78.2 | 24 | 5 | 6 | 1 | 0 | -- | .917 | --- |
| McMurtry,C | Tex | 41.2 | 23 | 1 | 8 | 0 | 2 | -- | 1.000 | --- |
| McWilliams,L | KC | 8.1 | 13 | 0 | 3 | 0 | 0 | -- | 1.000 | --- |
| Medvin,S | Sea | 4.1 | 5 | 1 | 2 | 1 | 0 | -- | .750 | --- |
| Melendez,J | Sea | 5.1 | 3 | 0 | 0 | 0 | 0 | -- | .000 | --- |
| Mercker,K | Atl | 49.2 | 37 | 2 | 2 | 1 | 0 | -- | .800 | --- |
| Mesa,J | Bal | 46.2 | 7 | 3 | 5 | 1 | 1 | -- | .889 | --- |
| Meyer,B | Hou | 22.1 | 15 | 2 | 7 | 0 | 0 | -- | 1.000 | --- |
| Mielke,G | Tex | 41.0 | 33 | 2 | 7 | 0 | 0 | -- | 1.000 | --- |
| Milacki,B | Bal | 135.1 | 27 | 21 | 16 | 1 | 2 | -- | .974 | --- |
| Mills,A | NYA | 41.2 | 36 | 3 | 10 | 2 | 0 | -- | .867 | --- |
| Minton,G | Cal | 15.1 | 11 | 0 | 3 | 0 | 0 | -- | 1.000 | --- |
| Minutelli,G | Cin | 1.0 | 2 | 0 | 0 | 0 | 0 | -- | .000 | --- |
| Mirabella,P | Mil | 59.0 | 44 | 4 | 7 | 1 | 1 | -- | .917 | --- |
| Mitchell,J | Bal | 114.1 | 24 | 7 | 20 | 2 | 4 | -- | .931 | --- |
| Mohorcic,D | Mon | 53.0 | 34 | 2 | 9 | 0 | 2 | -- | 1.000 | --- |
| Monteleone,R | NYA | 7.1 | 5 | 1 | 1 | 0 | 0 | -- | 1.000 | --- |
| Montgomery,J | KC | 94.1 | 73 | 3 | 13 | 0 | 0 | -- | 1.000 | --- |
| Moore,B | Phi | 2.2 | 3 | 0 | 1 | 0 | 0 | -- | 1.000 | --- |
| Moore,M | Oak | 199.1 | 33 | 21 | 30 | 1 | 1 | -- | .981 | --- |
| Morgan,M | LA | 211.0 | 33 | 24 | 40 | 1 | 3 | -- | .985 | --- |
| Morris,J | Det | 249.2 | 36 | 37 | 14 | 2 | 2 | -- | .962 | --- |
| Moses,J | Min | 8.0 | 4 | 1 | 0 | 0 | 0 | -- | 1.000 | --- |
| Moyer,J | Tex | 102.1 | 33 | 6 | 15 | 0 | 3 | -- | 1.000 | --- |
| Mulholland,T | Phi | 180.2 | 33 | 8 | 17 | 3 | 0 | -- | .893 | --- |
| Munoz,M | LA | 5.2 | 8 | 0 | 0 | 0 | 0 | -- | .000 | --- |
| Murphy,R | Bos | 57.0 | 68 | 4 | 7 | 1 | 2 | -- | .917 | --- |
| Musselman,J | NYN | 32.0 | 28 | 5 | 5 | 0 | 0 | -- | 1.000 | --- |
| Myers,R | Cin | 87.2 | 67 | 1 | 12 | 0 | 0 | -- | 1.000 | --- |
| Nabholz,C | Mon | 70.0 | 11 | 3 | 11 | 1 | 1 | -- | .933 | --- |
| Nagy,C | Cle | 45.2 | 9 | 3 | 8 | 1 | 2 | -- | .917 | --- |
| Navarro,J | Mil | 149.1 | 32 | 10 | 19 | 1 | 2 | -- | .967 | --- |
| Neidlinger,J | LA | 74.0 | 12 | 8 | 5 | 0 | 0 | -- | 1.000 | --- |
| Nelson,G | Oak | 72.0 | 50 | 4 | 8 | 1 | 0 | -- | .923 | --- |
| Nichols,R | Cle | 16.0 | 4 | 0 | 4 | 0 | 0 | -- | 1.000 | --- |
| Niedenfuer,T | StL | 65.0 | 52 | 3 | 8 | 2 | 0 | -- | .846 | --- |
| Nipper,A | Cle | 24.0 | 9 | 1 | 1 | 0 | 1 | -- | 1.000 | --- |
| Noboa,J | Mon | 0.2 | 1 | 0 | 0 | 0 | 0 | -- | .000 | --- |
| Noles,D | Phi | 0.1 | 1 | 0 | 0 | 0 | 0 | -- | .000 | --- |
| Norris,M | Oak | 27.0 | 14 | 3 | 3 | 0 | 0 | -- | 1.000 | --- |

## Pitchers

| Player | Tm | Inn | G | PO | A | E | DP | PB | Pct. | Rng |
|---|---|---|---|---|---|---|---|---|---|---|
| Nosek,R | Det | 7.0 | 3 | 0 | 0 | 0 | 0 | -- | .000 | --- |
| Novoa,R | SF | 18.2 | 7 | 0 | 0 | 0 | 0 | -- | .000 | --- |
| Nunez,E | Det | 78.1 | 41 | 7 | 5 | 1 | 1 | -- | .923 | --- |
| Nunez,J | ChN | 60.2 | 21 | 11 | 7 | 2 | 1 | -- | .900 | --- |
| O'Neal,R | SF | 47.0 | 26 | 1 | 8 | 0 | 1 | -- | 1.000 | --- |
| Ojeda,B | NYN | 118.0 | 38 | 8 | 31 | 2 | 1 | -- | .951 | --- |
| Olin,S | Cle | 92.1 | 50 | 3 | 24 | 3 | 1 | -- | .900 | --- |
| Olivares,O | StL | 49.1 | 9 | 7 | 8 | 0 | 0 | -- | 1.000 | --- |
| Oliveras,F | SF | 55.1 | 33 | 1 | 5 | 0 | 1 | -- | 1.000 | --- |
| Olson,G | Bal | 74.1 | 64 | 5 | 4 | 0 | 1 | -- | 1.000 | --- |
| Ontiveros,S | Phi | 10.0 | 5 | 2 | 3 | 0 | 0 | -- | 1.000 | --- |
| Orosco,J | Cle | 64.2 | 55 | 1 | 14 | 1 | 1 | -- | .938 | --- |
| Osuna,A | Hou | 9.1 | 11 | 1 | 1 | 0 | 0 | -- | 1.000 | --- |
| Otto,D | Oak | 2.1 | 2 | 0 | 2 | 0 | 1 | -- | 1.000 | --- |
| Palacios,V | Pit | 15.0 | 7 | 2 | 0 | 0 | 0 | -- | 1.000 | --- |
| Pall,D | ChA | 76.0 | 56 | 1 | 11 | 0 | 2 | -- | 1.000 | --- |
| Parker,C | NYA | 22.0 | 5 | 0 | 2 | 0 | 0 | -- | 1.000 | --- |
| Parker,C | Det | 51.0 | 24 | 5 | 8 | 0 | 1 | -- | 1.000 | --- |
| Parrett,J | Phi | 76.2 | 46 | 1 | 13 | 3 | 1 | -- | .824 | --- |
| Parrett,J | Atl | 27.0 | 20 | 0 | 6 | 1 | 0 | -- | .857 | --- |
| Patterson,B | Pit | 94.2 | 55 | 9 | 10 | 0 | 0 | -- | 1.000 | --- |
| Patterson,K | ChA | 66.1 | 43 | 2 | 12 | 1 | 0 | -- | .933 | --- |
| Pavlas,D | ChN | 21.1 | 13 | 1 | 2 | 0 | 0 | -- | 1.000 | --- |
| Pena,A | NYN | 77.0 | 53 | 2 | 4 | 0 | 0 | -- | 1.000 | --- |
| Perez,Melido | ChA | 197.0 | 35 | 4 | 21 | 1 | 1 | -- | .962 | --- |
| Perez,Mike | StL | 13.2 | 13 | 3 | 2 | 0 | 0 | -- | 1.000 | --- |
| Perez,P | NYA | 14.0 | 3 | 0 | 0 | 0 | 0 | -- | .000 | --- |
| Perry,P | LA | 6.2 | 7 | 0 | 1 | 2 | 0 | -- | .333 | --- |
| Peterson,A | ChA | 85.0 | 20 | 4 | 7 | 1 | 0 | -- | .917 | --- |
| Petry,D | Det | 150.1 | 33 | 19 | 23 | 0 | 3 | -- | 1.000 | --- |
| Pico,J | ChN | 92.0 | 32 | 12 | 16 | 1 | 2 | -- | .966 | --- |
| Plesac,D | Mil | 69.0 | 66 | 1 | 7 | 0 | 1 | -- | 1.000 | --- |
| Plunk,E | NYA | 72.2 | 47 | 3 | 17 | 2 | 2 | -- | .909 | --- |
| Poole,J | LA | 10.2 | 16 | 0 | 1 | 0 | 0 | -- | 1.000 | --- |
| Portugal,M | Hou | 196.2 | 32 | 22 | 19 | 1 | 2 | -- | .976 | --- |
| Powell,D | Sea | 3.0 | 2 | 0 | 0 | 0 | 0 | -- | .000 | --- |
| Powell,D | Mil | 39.1 | 9 | 2 | 9 | 0 | 0 | -- | 1.000 | --- |
| Power,T | Pit | 51.2 | 40 | 3 | 4 | 0 | 0 | -- | 1.000 | --- |
| Price,J | Bal | 65.1 | 50 | 1 | 8 | 2 | 0 | -- | .818 | --- |
| Quisenberry,D | SF | 6.2 | 5 | 0 | 1 | 0 | 0 | -- | 1.000 | --- |
| Radinsky,S | ChA | 52.1 | 62 | 7 | 4 | 0 | 0 | -- | 1.000 | --- |
| Rasmussen,D | SD | 187.2 | 32 | 8 | 32 | 3 | 2 | -- | .930 | --- |
| Reardon,J | Bos | 51.1 | 47 | 1 | 4 | 1 | 0 | -- | .833 | --- |
| Reed,J | Sea | 7.1 | 4 | 2 | 1 | 0 | 1 | -- | 1.000 | --- |
| Reed,J | Bos | 45.0 | 29 | 6 | 4 | 0 | 1 | -- | 1.000 | --- |
| Reed,R | Pit | 53.2 | 13 | 7 | 3 | 1 | 0 | -- | .909 | --- |
| Reuschel,R | SF | 87.0 | 15 | 2 | 16 | 1 | 1 | -- | .947 | --- |
| Reuss,J | Pit | 7.2 | 4 | 1 | 2 | 0 | 0 | -- | 1.000 | --- |
| Richards,R | Atl | 1.0 | 1 | 0 | 0 | 0 | 0 | -- | .000 | --- |
| Richardson,J | Cal | 0.1 | 1 | 0 | 1 | 0 | 0 | -- | 1.000 | --- |
| Righetti,D | NYA | 53.0 | 53 | 3 | 2 | 1 | 0 | -- | .833 | --- |
| Rijo,J | Cin | 197.0 | 29 | 19 | 26 | 2 | 0 | -- | .957 | --- |
| Ritz,K | Det | 7.1 | 4 | 2 | 3 | 1 | 0 | -- | .833 | --- |
| Robinson,D | SF | 157.2 | 26 | 4 | 18 | 0 | 0 | -- | 1.000 | --- |
| Robinson,Jeff | NYA | 88.2 | 54 | 5 | 23 | 3 | 1 | -- | .903 | --- |
| Robinson,JeffM | Det | 145.0 | 27 | 14 | 15 | 3 | 1 | -- | .906 | --- |
| Robinson,R | Cin | 31.1 | 6 | 2 | 4 | 0 | 0 | -- | 1.000 | --- |
| Robinson,R | Mil | 148.1 | 22 | 17 | 17 | 0 | 0 | -- | 1.000 | --- |

## Pitchers

| Player | Tm | Inn | G | PO | A | E | DP | PB | Pct. | Rng |
|---|---|---|---|---|---|---|---|---|---|---|
| Rochford,M | Bos | 4.0 | 2 | 0 | 0 | 0 | 0 | -- | .000 | --- |
| Rodriguez,Rich | SD | 47.2 | 32 | 1 | 10 | 0 | 1 | -- | 1.000 | --- |
| Rodriguez,Rick | SF | 3.1 | 3 | 1 | 0 | 0 | 0 | -- | 1.000 | --- |
| Rodriguez,Rosa. | Cin | 10.1 | 9 | 0 | 3 | 0 | 0 | -- | 1.000 | --- |
| Roesler,M | Pit | 6.0 | 5 | 0 | 0 | 0 | 0 | -- | .000 | --- |
| Rogers,K | Tex | 97.2 | 69 | 5 | 22 | 2 | 1 | -- | .931 | --- |
| Rojas,M | Mon | 40.0 | 23 | 2 | 4 | 1 | 0 | -- | .857 | --- |
| Rosenberg,S | ChA | 10.0 | 6 | 1 | 2 | 0 | 0 | -- | 1.000 | --- |
| Ross,M | Pit | 12.2 | 9 | 1 | 3 | 0 | 0 | -- | 1.000 | --- |
| Ruffin,B | Phi | 149.0 | 32 | 5 | 23 | 0 | 2 | -- | 1.000 | --- |
| Ruskin,S | Pit | 47.2 | 44 | 1 | 8 | 2 | 1 | -- | .818 | --- |
| Ruskin,S | Mon | 27.2 | 23 | 0 | 6 | 0 | 1 | -- | 1.000 | --- |
| Russell,J | Tex | 25.1 | 27 | 1 | 5 | 1 | 0 | -- | .857 | --- |
| Ryan,N | Tex | 204.0 | 30 | 7 | 12 | 0 | 0 | -- | 1.000 | --- |
| Saberhagen,B | KC | 135.0 | 20 | 16 | 28 | 1 | 3 | -- | .978 | --- |
| Sampen,B | Mon | 90.1 | 59 | 4 | 9 | 0 | 0 | -- | 1.000 | --- |
| Sanchez,Z | KC | 9.2 | 11 | 1 | 1 | 1 | 0 | -- | .667 | --- |
| Sanderson,S | Oak | 206.1 | 34 | 11 | 18 | 2 | 2 | -- | .935 | --- |
| Savage,J | Min | 26.0 | 17 | 0 | 4 | 0 | 0 | -- | 1.000 | --- |
| Schatzeder,D | Hou | 64.0 | 45 | 1 | 10 | 1 | 0 | -- | .917 | --- |
| Schatzeder,D | NYN | 5.2 | 6 | 0 | 0 | 0 | 0 | -- | .000 | --- |
| Schilling,C | Bal | 46.0 | 35 | 1 | 4 | 0 | 0 | -- | 1.000 | --- |
| Schiraldi,C | SD | 104.0 | 42 | 6 | 11 | 3 | 0 | -- | .850 | --- |
| Schmidt,D | Mon | 48.0 | 34 | 2 | 10 | 2 | 0 | -- | .857 | --- |
| Schooler,M | Sea | 59.1 | 51 | 4 | 9 | 1 | 0 | -- | .929 | --- |
| Schwabe,M | Det | 3.2 | 1 | 0 | 3 | 0 | 0 | -- | 1.000 | --- |
| Scott,M | Hou | 205.2 | 32 | 10 | 20 | 1 | 0 | -- | .968 | --- |
| Scudder,S | Cin | 71.2 | 21 | 5 | 5 | 1 | 0 | -- | .909 | --- |
| Seanez,R | Cle | 27.1 | 24 | 1 | 1 | 0 | 0 | -- | 1.000 | --- |
| Searage,R | LA | 32.1 | 29 | 2 | 8 | 0 | 0 | -- | 1.000 | --- |
| Searcy,S | Det | 75.1 | 16 | 3 | 7 | 0 | 0 | -- | 1.000 | --- |
| Sebra,B | Mil | 11.0 | 10 | 2 | 4 | 0 | 1 | -- | 1.000 | --- |
| Shaw,J | Cle | 48.2 | 12 | 4 | 7 | 0 | 0 | -- | 1.000 | --- |
| Sherrill,T | StL | 4.1 | 8 | 1 | 0 | 0 | 0 | -- | 1.000 | --- |
| Show,E | SD | 106.1 | 39 | 7 | 12 | 1 | 1 | -- | .950 | --- |
| Sisk,D | Atl | 2.1 | 3 | 0 | 1 | 0 | 0 | -- | 1.000 | --- |
| Smiley,J | Pit | 149.1 | 26 | 8 | 24 | 2 | 2 | -- | .941 | --- |
| Smith,B | StL | 134.0 | 24 | 10 | 16 | 1 | 2 | -- | .963 | --- |
| Smith,Daryl | KC | 6.2 | 2 | 0 | 0 | 0 | 0 | -- | .000 | --- |
| Smith,Dave | Hou | 60.1 | 49 | 1 | 3 | 1 | 1 | -- | .800 | --- |
| Smith,L | Bos | 14.1 | 11 | 0 | 2 | 0 | 0 | -- | 1.000 | --- |
| Smith,L | StL | 76.0 | 55 | 2 | 1 | 1 | 0 | -- | .750 | --- |
| Smith,M | Bal | 3.0 | 2 | 0 | 0 | 0 | 0 | -- | .000 | --- |
| Smith,P | Atl | 77.0 | 13 | 5 | 6 | 0 | 0 | -- | 1.000 | --- |
| Smith,R | Min | 153.1 | 32 | 10 | 9 | 1 | 0 | -- | .950 | --- |
| Smith,Z | Mon | 139.1 | 22 | 4 | 26 | 3 | 3 | -- | .909 | --- |
| Smith,Z | Pit | 76.0 | 11 | 6 | 8 | 0 | 2 | -- | 1.000 | --- |
| Smoltz,J | Atl | 231.1 | 34 | 26 | 28 | 3 | 4 | -- | .947 | --- |
| Stanton,M | Atl | 7.0 | 7 | 0 | 2 | 0 | 0 | -- | 1.000 | --- |
| Stewart,D | Oak | 267.0 | 36 | 23 | 25 | 0 | 3 | -- | 1.000 | --- |
| Stieb,D | Tor | 208.2 | 33 | 23 | 40 | 4 | 3 | -- | .940 | --- |
| Stottlemyre,M | KC | 31.1 | 13 | 1 | 5 | 0 | 0 | -- | 1.000 | --- |
| Stottlemyre,T | Tor | 203.0 | 33 | 17 | 30 | 1 | 5 | -- | .979 | --- |
| Sutcliffe,R | ChN | 21.1 | 5 | 3 | 3 | 0 | 0 | -- | 1.000 | --- |
| Swan,R | SF | 2.1 | 2 | 0 | 1 | 0 | 0 | -- | 1.000 | --- |
| Swan,R | Sea | 47.0 | 11 | 3 | 7 | 0 | 0 | -- | 1.000 | --- |
| Swift,B | Sea | 128.0 | 55 | 10 | 20 | 2 | 1 | -- | .938 | --- |
| Swindell,G | Cle | 214.2 | 34 | 8 | 20 | 1 | 1 | -- | .966 | --- |

## Pitchers

| Player | Tm | Inn | G | PO | A | E | DP | PB | Pct. | Rng |
|---|---|---|---|---|---|---|---|---|---|---|
| Tanana,F | Det | 176.1 | 34 | 8 | 26 | 0 | 0 | -- | 1.000 | --- |
| Tapani,K | Min | 159.1 | 28 | 14 | 20 | 1 | 1 | -- | .971 | --- |
| Taylor,D | Bal | 3.2 | 4 | 0 | 0 | 0 | 0 | -- | .000 | --- |
| Telford,A | Bal | 36.1 | 8 | 3 | 5 | 0 | 0 | -- | 1.000 | --- |
| Terrell,W | Pit | 82.2 | 16 | 10 | 15 | 0 | 1 | -- | 1.000 | --- |
| Terrell,W | Det | 75.1 | 13 | 3 | 9 | 1 | 1 | -- | .923 | --- |
| Terry,S | StL | 72.0 | 50 | 2 | 14 | 1 | 0 | -- | .941 | --- |
| Tewksbury,B | StL | 145.1 | 28 | 6 | 20 | 1 | 2 | -- | .963 | --- |
| Thigpen,B | ChA | 88.2 | 77 | 9 | 8 | 1 | 2 | -- | .944 | --- |
| Thompson,R | Mon | 1.0 | 1 | 0 | 0 | 0 | 0 | -- | .000 | --- |
| Thurmond,M | SF | 56.2 | 43 | 4 | 15 | 1 | 3 | -- | .950 | --- |
| Tibbs,J | Bal | 50.2 | 10 | 6 | 8 | 0 | 0 | -- | 1.000 | --- |
| Tibbs,J | Pit | 7.0 | 5 | 1 | 1 | 0 | 0 | -- | 1.000 | --- |
| Tomlin,R | Pit | 77.2 | 12 | 2 | 18 | 0 | 0 | -- | 1.000 | --- |
| Tudor,J | StL | 146.1 | 25 | 10 | 29 | 1 | 2 | -- | .975 | --- |
| Valdez,E | Cle | 23.2 | 13 | 2 | 3 | 1 | 0 | -- | .833 | --- |
| Valdez,R | SD | 5.2 | 3 | 0 | 0 | 0 | 0 | -- | .000 | --- |
| Valdez,S | Atl | 5.1 | 6 | 2 | 1 | 0 | 0 | -- | 1.000 | --- |
| Valdez,S | Cle | 102.1 | 24 | 8 | 11 | 2 | 1 | -- | .905 | --- |
| Valenzuela,F | LA | 204.0 | 33 | 5 | 31 | 3 | 3 | -- | .923 | --- |
| Valera,J | NYN | 13.0 | 3 | 1 | 0 | 1 | 0 | -- | .500 | --- |
| Veres,R | Mil | 41.2 | 26 | 2 | 10 | 0 | 2 | -- | 1.000 | --- |
| Viola,F | NYN | 249.2 | 35 | 11 | 34 | 1 | 1 | -- | .978 | --- |
| Vosberg,E | SF | 24.1 | 18 | 1 | 5 | 0 | 0 | -- | 1.000 | --- |
| Wagner,H | KC | 23.1 | 5 | 3 | 3 | 0 | 1 | -- | 1.000 | --- |
| Walk,B | Pit | 129.2 | 26 | 12 | 11 | 3 | 0 | -- | .885 | --- |
| Walker,M | Cle | 75.2 | 18 | 4 | 9 | 0 | 1 | -- | 1.000 | --- |
| Walsh,D | LA | 16.1 | 20 | 2 | 3 | 0 | 0 | -- | 1.000 | --- |
| Wapnick,S | Det | 7.0 | 4 | 1 | 0 | 1 | 0 | -- | .500 | --- |
| Ward,C | Cle | 36.0 | 22 | 2 | 3 | 0 | 0 | -- | 1.000 | --- |
| Ward,D | Tor | 127.2 | 73 | 9 | 18 | 1 | 0 | -- | .964 | --- |
| Wayne,G | Min | 36.0 | 37 | 1 | 4 | 0 | 1 | -- | 1.000 | --- |
| Wegman,B | Mil | 29.2 | 8 | 1 | 3 | 2 | 0 | -- | .667 | --- |
| Welch,B | Oak | 238.0 | 35 | 19 | 32 | 0 | 2 | -- | 1.000 | --- |
| Wells,D | Tor | 189.0 | 43 | 7 | 31 | 0 | 1 | -- | 1.000 | --- |
| Wells,T | LA | 20.2 | 5 | 1 | 0 | 2 | 0 | -- | .333 | --- |
| West,D | Min | 146.1 | 29 | 3 | 17 | 2 | 2 | -- | .909 | --- |
| Weston,M | Bal | 21.0 | 9 | 3 | 0 | 0 | 0 | -- | 1.000 | --- |
| Wetteland,J | LA | 43.0 | 22 | 1 | 3 | 1 | 0 | -- | .800 | --- |
| Whitehurst,W | NYN | 65.2 | 38 | 4 | 10 | 0 | 1 | -- | 1.000 | --- |
| Whitson,E | SD | 228.2 | 32 | 17 | 41 | 0 | 3 | -- | 1.000 | --- |
| Wickander,K | Cle | 12.1 | 10 | 0 | 1 | 0 | 0 | -- | 1.000 | --- |
| Wilkins,D | ChN | 7.1 | 6 | 0 | 0 | 0 | 0 | -- | .000 | --- |
| Williams,M | ChN | 66.1 | 59 | 1 | 5 | 0 | 0 | -- | 1.000 | --- |
| Williamson,M | Bal | 85.1 | 49 | 14 | 13 | 2 | 2 | -- | .931 | --- |
| Wills,F | Tor | 99.0 | 44 | 9 | 10 | 0 | 2 | -- | 1.000 | --- |
| Wilson,S | ChN | 133.0 | 44 | 4 | 14 | 2 | 1 | -- | .900 | --- |
| Wilson,T | SF | 110.1 | 27 | 9 | 22 | 0 | 1 | -- | 1.000 | --- |
| Witt,B | Tex | 230.0 | 34 | 18 | 18 | 5 | 3 | -- | .878 | --- |
| Witt,M | Cal | 20.1 | 10 | 2 | 4 | 0 | 1 | -- | 1.000 | --- |
| Witt,M | NYA | 96.2 | 16 | 7 | 14 | 1 | 0 | -- | .955 | --- |
| Yett,R | Min | 4.1 | 4 | 2 | 1 | 1 | 1 | -- | .750 | --- |
| York,M | Pit | 12.2 | 4 | 1 | 3 | 0 | 0 | -- | 1.000 | --- |
| Young,Cliff | Cal | 30.2 | 17 | 0 | 5 | 1 | 0 | -- | .833 | --- |
| Young,Curt | Oak | 124.1 | 26 | 6 | 25 | 1 | 4 | -- | .969 | --- |
| Young,M | Sea | 225.1 | 34 | 12 | 32 | 9 | 1 | -- | .830 | --- |

# 1990 Lefty-Righty Stats

# **Batters** vs. Left-Handed and Right-Handed Pitchers

| Batter | | vs. Left-Handed Pitchers | | | | | | | | | | | vs. Right-Handed Pitchers | | | | | | | | | | |
|---|---|---|---|---|---|---|---|---|---|---|---|---|---|---|---|---|---|---|---|---|---|---|---|
| | | Avg | AB | H | 2B | 3B | HR | RBI | BB | SO | OBP | SLG | Avg | AB | H | 2B | 3B | HR | RBI | BB | SO | OBP | SLG |
| Abner,Shawn | R | .228 | 101 | 23 | 5 | 0 | 0 | 10 | 3 | 18 | .255 | .277 | .265 | 83 | 22 | 4 | 0 | 1 | 5 | 6 | 10 | .322 | .349 |
| Afenir,Troy | R | .111 | 9 | 1 | 0 | 0 | 0 | 1 | 0 | 2 | .100 | .111 | .200 | 5 | 1 | 0 | 0 | 0 | 1 | 0 | 4 | .200 | .200 |
| Aldrete,Mike | L | .000 | 9 | 0 | 0 | 0 | 0 | 0 | 3 | 2 | .250 | .000 | .257 | 152 | 39 | 7 | 1 | 1 | 18 | 34 | 29 | .394 | .336 |
| Allred,Beau | L | .000 | 0 | 0 | 0 | 0 | 0 | 0 | 0 | 0 | .000 | .000 | .188 | 16 | 3 | 1 | 0 | 1 | 2 | 2 | 3 | .278 | .438 |
| Alomar,Roberto | B | .260 | 204 | 53 | 13 | 1 | 3 | 17 | 21 | 38 | .330 | .377 | .301 | 382 | 115 | 14 | 4 | 3 | 43 | 27 | 34 | .345 | .382 |
| Alomar Jr,Sandy | R | .376 | 117 | 44 | 5 | 0 | 2 | 18 | 8 | 13 | .403 | .470 | .259 | 328 | 85 | 21 | 2 | 7 | 48 | 17 | 33 | .298 | .399 |
| Alou,Moises | R | .176 | 17 | 3 | 0 | 1 | 0 | 0 | 0 | 2 | .176 | .294 | .333 | 3 | 1 | 0 | 0 | 0 | 0 | 0 | 1 | .333 | .333 |
| Anderson,Brady | L | .152 | 46 | 7 | 1 | 0 | 0 | 4 | 5 | 11 | .250 | .174 | .250 | 188 | 47 | 4 | 2 | 3 | 20 | 26 | 35 | .347 | .340 |
| Anderson,Dave | R | .389 | 54 | 21 | 3 | 0 | 1 | 5 | 2 | 11 | .411 | .500 | .304 | 46 | 14 | 2 | 1 | 0 | 1 | 1 | 9 | .319 | .391 |
| Anderson,Kent | R | .333 | 57 | 19 | 2 | 1 | 1 | 1 | 4 | 4 | .377 | .456 | .291 | 86 | 25 | 4 | 0 | 0 | 4 | 9 | 15 | .365 | .337 |
| Anthony,Eric | L | .214 | 84 | 18 | 3 | 0 | 3 | 10 | 8 | 23 | .284 | .357 | .181 | 155 | 28 | 5 | 0 | 7 | 19 | 21 | 55 | .276 | .348 |
| Azocar,Oscar | L | .200 | 60 | 12 | 2 | 0 | 1 | 7 | 1 | 2 | .210 | .283 | .266 | 154 | 41 | 6 | 0 | 4 | 12 | 1 | 13 | .276 | .383 |
| Backman,Wally | B | .194 | 31 | 6 | 1 | 0 | 0 | 3 | 7 | 9 | .359 | .226 | .303 | 284 | 86 | 20 | 3 | 2 | 25 | 35 | 44 | .376 | .415 |
| Baerga,Carlos | B | .243 | 103 | 25 | 4 | 0 | 2 | 16 | 1 | 22 | .250 | .340 | .268 | 209 | 56 | 13 | 2 | 5 | 31 | 15 | 35 | .323 | .421 |
| Baez,Kevin | R | .286 | 7 | 2 | 1 | 0 | 0 | 0 | 0 | 0 | .286 | .429 | .000 | 5 | 0 | 0 | 0 | 0 | 0 | 0 | 0 | .000 | .000 |
| Bailey,Mark | B | .000 | 1 | 0 | 0 | 0 | 0 | 0 | 0 | 1 | .000 | .000 | .167 | 6 | 1 | 0 | 0 | 1 | 3 | 0 | 1 | .167 | .667 |
| Baines,Harold | L | .253 | 91 | 23 | 3 | 0 | 3 | 15 | 12 | 22 | .330 | .385 | .293 | 324 | 95 | 12 | 1 | 13 | 50 | 55 | 58 | .392 | .457 |
| Baker,Doug | B | .000 | 0 | 0 | 0 | 0 | 0 | 0 | 0 | 0 | .000 | .000 | .000 | 1 | 0 | 0 | 0 | 0 | 0 | 0 | 0 | .000 | .000 |
| Balboni,Steve | R | .211 | 161 | 34 | 4 | 0 | 14 | 27 | 30 | 53 | .340 | .497 | .162 | 105 | 17 | 2 | 0 | 3 | 7 | 5 | 38 | .205 | .267 |
| Baldwin,Jeff | L | .000 | 1 | 0 | 0 | 0 | 0 | 0 | 1 | 0 | .500 | .000 | .000 | 7 | 0 | 0 | 0 | 0 | 0 | 0 | 2 | .000 | .000 |
| Barfield,Jesse | R | .259 | 162 | 42 | 7 | 0 | 13 | 25 | 33 | 51 | .394 | .543 | .239 | 314 | 75 | 14 | 2 | 12 | 53 | 49 | 99 | .341 | .411 |
| Barrett,Marty | R | .243 | 37 | 9 | 2 | 0 | 0 | 3 | 9 | 2 | .383 | .297 | .221 | 122 | 27 | 2 | 0 | 0 | 10 | 6 | 11 | .262 | .238 |
| Bass,Kevin | B | .256 | 90 | 23 | 4 | 0 | 5 | 16 | 4 | 10 | .302 | .467 | .250 | 124 | 31 | 5 | 1 | 2 | 16 | 10 | 16 | .304 | .355 |
| Bates,Billy | L | .600 | 5 | 3 | 1 | 0 | 0 | 1 | 0 | 1 | .600 | .800 | .000 | 29 | 0 | 0 | 0 | 0 | 1 | 4 | 8 | .118 | .000 |
| Bathe,Bill | R | .310 | 29 | 9 | 0 | 1 | 3 | 10 | 5 | 5 | .400 | .690 | .105 | 19 | 2 | 0 | 0 | 0 | 2 | 2 | 7 | .190 | .105 |
| Belcher,Kevin | R | .000 | 8 | 0 | 0 | 0 | 0 | 0 | 2 | 5 | .200 | .000 | .286 | 7 | 2 | 1 | 0 | 0 | 0 | 0 | 1 | .286 | .429 |
| Bell,George | R | .248 | 149 | 37 | 6 | 0 | 5 | 22 | 15 | 17 | .315 | .389 | .271 | 413 | 112 | 19 | 0 | 16 | 64 | 17 | 63 | .298 | .433 |
| Bell,Jay | R | .275 | 251 | 69 | 13 | 4 | 2 | 17 | 34 | 42 | .359 | .382 | .238 | 332 | 79 | 15 | 3 | 5 | 35 | 31 | 67 | .305 | .346 |
| Bell,Juan | B | .000 | 0 | 0 | 0 | 0 | 0 | 0 | 0 | 0 | .000 | .000 | .000 | 2 | 0 | 0 | 0 | 0 | 0 | 0 | 1 | .000 | .000 |
| Bell,Mike | L | .000 | 6 | 0 | 0 | 0 | 0 | 0 | 0 | 1 | .143 | .000 | .282 | 39 | 11 | 5 | 1 | 1 | 5 | 2 | 8 | .317 | .538 |
| Belle,Joey | R | .222 | 9 | 2 | 0 | 0 | 1 | 2 | 0 | 1 | .222 | .556 | .143 | 14 | 2 | 0 | 0 | 0 | 1 | 1 | 5 | .200 | .143 |
| Belliard,Rafael | R | .190 | 21 | 4 | 2 | 0 | 0 | 5 | 2 | 4 | .261 | .286 | .212 | 33 | 7 | 1 | 0 | 0 | 1 | 3 | 9 | .297 | .242 |
| Benjamin,Mike | R | .154 | 26 | 4 | 0 | 1 | 0 | 0 | 1 | 5 | .185 | .231 | .267 | 30 | 8 | 3 | 0 | 2 | 3 | 2 | 5 | .313 | .567 |
| Benzinger,Todd | B | .285 | 172 | 49 | 7 | 0 | 2 | 17 | 6 | 15 | .306 | .360 | .225 | 204 | 46 | 7 | 2 | 3 | 29 | 13 | 54 | .279 | .324 |
| Bergman,Dave | L | .231 | 13 | 3 | 2 | 0 | 0 | 2 | 1 | 3 | .286 | .385 | .281 | 192 | 54 | 8 | 1 | 2 | 24 | 32 | 14 | .381 | .365 |
| Berroa,Geronimo | R | .000 | 3 | 0 | 0 | 0 | 0 | 0 | 1 | 1 | .250 | .000 | .000 | 1 | 0 | 0 | 0 | 0 | 0 | 0 | 0 | .000 | .000 |
| Berry,Sean | R | .231 | 13 | 3 | 0 | 1 | 0 | 3 | 1 | 2 | .286 | .385 | .200 | 10 | 2 | 1 | 0 | 0 | 1 | 1 | 3 | .273 | .300 |
| Berryhill,Damon | B | .250 | 16 | 4 | 1 | 0 | 1 | 3 | 1 | 3 | .294 | .500 | .162 | 37 | 6 | 3 | 0 | 0 | 6 | 4 | 11 | .238 | .243 |
| Bichette,Dante | R | .274 | 146 | 40 | 8 | 1 | 5 | 21 | 7 | 30 | .312 | .445 | .241 | 203 | 49 | 7 | 0 | 10 | 32 | 9 | 49 | .278 | .424 |
| Biggio,Craig | R | .229 | 218 | 50 | 6 | 1 | 2 | 13 | 27 | 27 | .316 | .294 | .306 | 337 | 103 | 18 | 1 | 2 | 29 | 26 | 52 | .359 | .383 |
| Bilardello,Dann | R | .056 | 18 | 1 | 0 | 0 | 0 | 1 | 2 | 6 | .150 | .056 | .053 | 19 | 1 | 0 | 0 | 0 | 2 | 2 | 4 | .143 | .053 |
| Blankenship,Lance | R | .176 | 68 | 12 | 1 | 0 | 0 | 8 | 8 | 10 | .263 | .191 | .206 | 68 | 14 | 2 | 0 | 0 | 2 | 12 | 13 | .325 | .235 |
| Blauser,Jeff | R | .294 | 136 | 40 | 12 | 1 | 3 | 17 | 16 | 20 | .373 | .463 | .256 | 250 | 64 | 12 | 2 | 5 | 22 | 19 | 50 | .319 | .380 |
| Blowers,Mike | R | .286 | 49 | 14 | 3 | 0 | 2 | 9 | 7 | 11 | .375 | .469 | .137 | 95 | 13 | 1 | 0 | 3 | 12 | 5 | 39 | .188 | .242 |
| Boggs,Wade | L | .274 | 230 | 63 | 14 | 2 | 1 | 30 | 21 | 39 | .332 | .365 | .319 | 389 | 124 | 30 | 3 | 5 | 33 | 66 | 29 | .415 | .450 |
| Bonds,Barry | L | .304 | 240 | 73 | 14 | 2 | 17 | 58 | 31 | 41 | .386 | .592 | .297 | 279 | 83 | 18 | 1 | 16 | 56 | 62 | 42 | .422 | .541 |
| Bonilla,Bobby | B | .261 | 280 | 73 | 19 | 2 | 14 | 48 | 20 | 32 | .303 | .493 | .296 | 345 | 102 | 20 | 5 | 18 | 72 | 25 | 71 | .338 | .539 |
| Booker,Rod | L | .214 | 14 | 3 | 0 | 1 | 0 | 2 | 1 | 5 | .267 | .357 | .222 | 117 | 26 | 5 | 1 | 0 | 8 | 14 | 21 | .305 | .282 |
| Boone,Bob | R | .250 | 40 | 10 | 1 | 0 | 0 | 3 | 6 | 4 | .348 | .275 | .234 | 77 | 18 | 2 | 0 | 0 | 6 | 11 | 8 | .330 | .260 |
| Borders,Pat | R | .285 | 186 | 53 | 16 | 2 | 10 | 27 | 15 | 29 | .337 | .554 | .288 | 160 | 46 | 8 | 0 | 5 | 22 | 3 | 28 | .297 | .431 |

# **Batters** vs. Left-Handed and Right-Handed Pitchers

| Batter | | vs. Left-Handed Pitchers Avg | AB | H | 2B | 3B | HR | RBI | BB | SO | OBP | SLG | vs. Right-Handed Pitchers Avg | AB | H | 2B | 3B | HR | RBI | BB | SO | OBP | SLG |
|---|---|---|---|---|---|---|---|---|---|---|---|---|---|---|---|---|---|---|---|---|---|---|---|
| Bordick,Mike | R | .000 | 6 | 0 | 0 | 0 | 0 | 0 | 0 | 2 | .000 | .000 | .125 | 8 | 1 | 0 | 0 | 0 | 0 | 1 | 2 | .222 | .125 |
| Bosley,Thad | L | .000 | 0 | 0 | 0 | 0 | 0 | 0 | 0 | 0 | .000 | .000 | .138 | 29 | 4 | 0 | 0 | 1 | 3 | 4 | 7 | .242 | .241 |
| Boston,Daryl | L | .262 | 61 | 16 | 3 | 0 | 0 | 8 | 7 | 11 | .338 | .311 | .275 | 306 | 84 | 18 | 2 | 12 | 37 | 21 | 39 | .325 | .464 |
| Bradley,Phil | R | .236 | 161 | 38 | 7 | 2 | 2 | 9 | 22 | 24 | .339 | .342 | .268 | 261 | 70 | 7 | 0 | 2 | 22 | 28 | 37 | .356 | .318 |
| Bradley,Scott | L | .160 | 25 | 4 | 0 | 0 | 0 | 4 | 3 | 2 | .233 | .160 | .231 | 208 | 48 | 9 | 0 | 1 | 24 | 12 | 18 | .268 | .288 |
| Braggs,Glenn | R | .289 | 149 | 43 | 5 | 1 | 6 | 19 | 26 | 26 | .399 | .456 | .273 | 165 | 45 | 9 | 0 | 3 | 22 | 12 | 38 | .332 | .382 |
| Bream,Sid | L | .260 | 96 | 25 | 8 | 1 | 2 | 12 | 6 | 16 | .308 | .427 | .273 | 293 | 80 | 15 | 1 | 13 | 55 | 42 | 49 | .362 | .464 |
| Brett,George | L | .316 | 187 | 59 | 11 | 3 | 5 | 28 | 16 | 26 | .366 | .487 | .336 | 357 | 120 | 34 | 4 | 9 | 59 | 40 | 37 | .398 | .529 |
| Brewer,Rod | L | .250 | 4 | 1 | 0 | 0 | 0 | 2 | 0 | 0 | .250 | .250 | .238 | 21 | 5 | 1 | 0 | 0 | 0 | 0 | 4 | .238 | .286 |
| Briley,Greg | L | .212 | 33 | 7 | 1 | 0 | 0 | 3 | 4 | 7 | .297 | .242 | .250 | 304 | 76 | 17 | 2 | 5 | 26 | 33 | 41 | .322 | .368 |
| Brock,Greg | L | .209 | 86 | 18 | 5 | 0 | 2 | 17 | 10 | 12 | .283 | .337 | .260 | 281 | 73 | 18 | 0 | 5 | 33 | 33 | 33 | .336 | .377 |
| Brookens,Tom | R | .258 | 93 | 24 | 6 | 1 | 1 | 11 | 12 | 15 | .340 | .376 | .279 | 61 | 17 | 1 | 1 | 0 | 9 | 2 | 10 | .292 | .328 |
| Brooks,Hubie | R | .240 | 217 | 52 | 12 | 0 | 9 | 34 | 17 | 41 | .294 | .419 | .282 | 351 | 99 | 16 | 1 | 11 | 57 | 16 | 67 | .316 | .427 |
| Brown,Marty | R | .000 | 7 | 0 | 0 | 0 | 0 | 0 | 1 | 2 | .125 | .000 | .375 | 8 | 3 | 0 | 0 | 0 | 0 | 0 | 5 | .375 | .375 |
| Browne,Jerry | B | .281 | 139 | 39 | 9 | 3 | 0 | 14 | 26 | 8 | .392 | .388 | .262 | 374 | 98 | 17 | 2 | 6 | 36 | 46 | 38 | .337 | .366 |
| Brumley,Mike | B | .176 | 34 | 6 | 0 | 1 | 0 | 0 | 0 | 6 | .176 | .235 | .239 | 113 | 27 | 5 | 3 | 0 | 7 | 10 | 16 | .298 | .336 |
| Brunansky,Tom | R | .285 | 179 | 51 | 11 | 3 | 6 | 29 | 16 | 32 | .333 | .480 | .239 | 339 | 81 | 16 | 2 | 10 | 44 | 50 | 83 | .341 | .386 |
| Buckner,Bill | L | .000 | 1 | 0 | 0 | 0 | 0 | 0 | 0 | 1 | .000 | .000 | .190 | 42 | 8 | 0 | 0 | 1 | 3 | 3 | 1 | .239 | .262 |
| Buechele,Steve | R | .275 | 80 | 22 | 5 | 0 | 4 | 12 | 12 | 18 | .372 | .488 | .187 | 171 | 32 | 5 | 0 | 3 | 18 | 15 | 45 | .255 | .269 |
| Buhner,Jay | R | .357 | 56 | 20 | 8 | 0 | 4 | 15 | 7 | 13 | .438 | .714 | .234 | 107 | 25 | 4 | 0 | 3 | 18 | 10 | 37 | .314 | .355 |
| Bullock,Eric | L | .000 | 0 | 0 | 0 | 0 | 0 | 0 | 0 | 0 | .000 | .000 | .500 | 2 | 1 | 0 | 0 | 0 | 0 | 0 | 0 | .500 | .500 |
| Burks,Ellis | R | .298 | 188 | 56 | 10 | 2 | 5 | 24 | 20 | 26 | .365 | .452 | .295 | 400 | 118 | 23 | 6 | 16 | 65 | 28 | 56 | .341 | .503 |
| Bush,Randy | L | .250 | 4 | 1 | 1 | 0 | 0 | 1 | 0 | 1 | .333 | .500 | .243 | 177 | 43 | 7 | 0 | 6 | 17 | 21 | 26 | .338 | .384 |
| Butler,Brett | L | .302 | 245 | 74 | 6 | 2 | 1 | 20 | 33 | 28 | .389 | .355 | .313 | 377 | 118 | 14 | 7 | 2 | 24 | 57 | 34 | .403 | .403 |
| Cabrera,Francisco | R | .294 | 109 | 32 | 4 | 1 | 6 | 21 | 3 | 11 | .310 | .514 | .214 | 28 | 6 | 1 | 0 | 1 | 4 | 2 | 10 | .267 | .357 |
| Calderon,Ivan | R | .295 | 227 | 67 | 19 | 2 | 6 | 27 | 21 | 25 | .353 | .476 | .261 | 380 | 99 | 25 | 0 | 8 | 47 | 30 | 54 | .311 | .389 |
| Caminiti,Ken | B | .246 | 240 | 59 | 9 | 1 | 2 | 23 | 13 | 35 | .280 | .317 | .239 | 301 | 72 | 11 | 1 | 2 | 28 | 35 | 62 | .318 | .302 |
| Campusano,Sil | R | .207 | 58 | 12 | 1 | 1 | 1 | 8 | 5 | 11 | .277 | .310 | .222 | 27 | 6 | 0 | 0 | 1 | 1 | 1 | 5 | .250 | .333 |
| Canale,George | L | .000 | 5 | 0 | 0 | 0 | 0 | 0 | 1 | 2 | .167 | .000 | .125 | 8 | 1 | 1 | 0 | 0 | 0 | 1 | 4 | .222 | .250 |
| Candaele,Casey | B | .341 | 126 | 43 | 3 | 2 | 2 | 10 | 14 | 12 | .407 | .444 | .235 | 136 | 32 | 5 | 4 | 1 | 12 | 17 | 30 | .325 | .353 |
| Cangelosi,John | B | .214 | 42 | 9 | 1 | 0 | 0 | 0 | 3 | 8 | .283 | .238 | .176 | 34 | 6 | 1 | 0 | 0 | 1 | 8 | 4 | .333 | .206 |
| Canseco,Jose | R | .276 | 123 | 34 | 3 | 1 | 12 | 28 | 15 | 41 | .362 | .610 | .274 | 358 | 98 | 11 | 1 | 25 | 73 | 57 | 117 | .374 | .520 |
| Canseco,Ozzie | R | .143 | 14 | 2 | 1 | 0 | 0 | 1 | 1 | 7 | .200 | .214 | .000 | 5 | 0 | 0 | 0 | 0 | 0 | 0 | 3 | .000 | .000 |
| Carr,Chuck | B | .000 | 1 | 0 | 0 | 0 | 0 | 0 | 0 | 1 | .000 | .000 | .000 | 1 | 0 | 0 | 0 | 0 | 0 | 0 | 1 | .000 | .000 |
| Carreon,Mark | R | .259 | 116 | 30 | 9 | 0 | 7 | 17 | 9 | 20 | .312 | .517 | .236 | 72 | 17 | 3 | 0 | 3 | 9 | 6 | 9 | .313 | .403 |
| Carter,Gary | R | .236 | 127 | 30 | 7 | 0 | 3 | 11 | 16 | 13 | .322 | .362 | .274 | 117 | 32 | 3 | 0 | 6 | 16 | 9 | 18 | .325 | .453 |
| Carter,Joe | R | .197 | 203 | 40 | 7 | 0 | 7 | 32 | 17 | 27 | .258 | .335 | .248 | 431 | 107 | 20 | 1 | 17 | 83 | 31 | 66 | .305 | .418 |
| Carter,Steve | L | .500 | 2 | 1 | 0 | 0 | 0 | 0 | 0 | 0 | .500 | .500 | .000 | 3 | 0 | 0 | 0 | 0 | 0 | 0 | 1 | .000 | .000 |
| Castillo,Carmen | R | .236 | 110 | 26 | 4 | 0 | 0 | 11 | 3 | 20 | .261 | .273 | .148 | 27 | 4 | 0 | 0 | 0 | 1 | 0 | 3 | .148 | .148 |
| Cedeno,Andujar | R | .000 | 4 | 0 | 0 | 0 | 0 | 0 | 0 | 2 | .000 | .000 | .000 | 4 | 0 | 0 | 0 | 0 | 0 | 0 | 3 | .000 | .000 |
| Cerone,Rick | R | .277 | 47 | 13 | 2 | 0 | 1 | 5 | 1 | 4 | .286 | .383 | .315 | 92 | 29 | 4 | 0 | 1 | 6 | 4 | 9 | .344 | .391 |
| Chamberlain,Wes | R | .280 | 25 | 7 | 1 | 0 | 1 | 2 | 0 | 7 | .280 | .440 | .286 | 21 | 6 | 2 | 0 | 1 | 2 | 1 | 2 | .318 | .524 |
| Clark,Dave | L | .200 | 5 | 1 | 0 | 0 | 0 | 0 | 0 | 2 | .200 | .200 | .277 | 166 | 46 | 4 | 2 | 5 | 20 | 8 | 38 | .307 | .416 |
| Clark,Jack | R | .377 | 114 | 43 | 4 | 1 | 9 | 21 | 41 | 29 | .541 | .667 | .209 | 220 | 46 | 8 | 0 | 16 | 41 | 63 | 62 | .386 | .464 |
| Clark,Jerald | R | .189 | 53 | 10 | 1 | 1 | 2 | 2 | 2 | 14 | .218 | .358 | .354 | 48 | 17 | 3 | 0 | 3 | 9 | 3 | 10 | .385 | .604 |
| Clark,Will | L | .317 | 249 | 79 | 7 | 4 | 9 | 47 | 22 | 35 | .372 | .486 | .279 | 351 | 98 | 18 | 1 | 10 | 48 | 40 | 62 | .347 | .422 |
| Coachman,Pete | R | .308 | 13 | 4 | 0 | 0 | 0 | 2 | 0 | 4 | .357 | .308 | .313 | 32 | 10 | 3 | 0 | 0 | 3 | 1 | 3 | .353 | .406 |
| Cochrane,Dave | B | .000 | 6 | 0 | 0 | 0 | 0 | 0 | 0 | 3 | .000 | .000 | .214 | 14 | 3 | 0 | 0 | 0 | 0 | 0 | 5 | .214 | .214 |
| Cole,Alex | L | .250 | 52 | 13 | 0 | 1 | 0 | 4 | 10 | 11 | .381 | .288 | .314 | 175 | 55 | 5 | 3 | 0 | 9 | 18 | 27 | .378 | .377 |
| Coleman,Vince | B | .262 | 191 | 50 | 13 | 4 | 5 | 18 | 9 | 37 | .297 | .450 | .310 | 306 | 95 | 5 | 5 | 1 | 21 | 26 | 51 | .366 | .369 |

# Batters vs. Left-Handed and Right-Handed Pitchers

| Batter | | vs. Left-Handed Pitchers | | | | | | | | | | | vs. Right-Handed Pitchers | | | | | | | | | | |
|---|---|---|---|---|---|---|---|---|---|---|---|---|---|---|---|---|---|---|---|---|---|---|---|
| | | Avg | AB | H | 2B | 3B | HR | RBI | BB | SO | OBP | SLG | Avg | AB | H | 2B | 3B | HR | RBI | BB | SO | OBP | SLG |
| Coles,Darnell | R | .215 | 121 | 26 | 4 | 1 | 1 | 11 | 13 | 18 | .287 | .289 | .202 | 94 | 19 | 3 | 0 | 2 | 9 | 3 | 20 | .235 | .298 |
| Collins,Dave | B | .194 | 36 | 7 | 1 | 0 | 0 | 1 | 5 | 3 | .293 | .222 | .273 | 22 | 6 | 0 | 0 | 0 | 2 | 8 | 7 | .467 | .273 |
| Conine,Jeff | R | .364 | 11 | 4 | 1 | 0 | 0 | 2 | 2 | 3 | .462 | .455 | .111 | 9 | 1 | 1 | 0 | 0 | 0 | 0 | 2 | .111 | .222 |
| Coolbaugh,Scott | R | .315 | 54 | 17 | 4 | 0 | 0 | 7 | 6 | 6 | .377 | .389 | .151 | 126 | 19 | 2 | 0 | 2 | 6 | 9 | 41 | .213 | .214 |
| Cooper,Scott | L | .000 | 0 | 0 | 0 | 0 | 0 | 0 | 0 | 0 | .000 | .000 | .000 | 1 | 0 | 0 | 0 | 0 | 0 | 0 | 1 | .000 | .000 |
| Cora,Joey | B | .250 | 28 | 7 | 0 | 0 | 0 | 0 | 2 | 3 | .300 | .250 | .278 | 72 | 20 | 3 | 0 | 0 | 2 | 4 | 6 | .316 | .319 |
| Cotto,Henry | R | .260 | 192 | 50 | 7 | 2 | 2 | 19 | 13 | 25 | .308 | .349 | .258 | 163 | 42 | 7 | 1 | 2 | 14 | 9 | 27 | .307 | .350 |
| Cuyler,Milt | B | .333 | 12 | 4 | 1 | 0 | 0 | 3 | 0 | 0 | .308 | .417 | .231 | 39 | 9 | 2 | 1 | 0 | 5 | 5 | 10 | .318 | .333 |
| Daniels,Kal | L | .285 | 151 | 43 | 6 | 0 | 6 | 30 | 25 | 33 | .393 | .444 | .301 | 299 | 90 | 17 | 1 | 21 | 64 | 43 | 71 | .387 | .575 |
| Dascenzo,Doug | B | .274 | 135 | 37 | 9 | 0 | 1 | 19 | 9 | 11 | .317 | .363 | .219 | 105 | 23 | 0 | 5 | 0 | 7 | 12 | 7 | .300 | .314 |
| Daugherty,Jack | B | .273 | 77 | 21 | 3 | 0 | 0 | 10 | 7 | 20 | .337 | .312 | .309 | 233 | 72 | 17 | 2 | 6 | 37 | 15 | 29 | .351 | .476 |
| Daulton,Darren | L | .257 | 113 | 29 | 8 | 0 | 1 | 9 | 22 | 23 | .378 | .354 | .272 | 346 | 94 | 22 | 1 | 11 | 48 | 50 | 49 | .363 | .436 |
| Davidson,Mark | R | .327 | 98 | 32 | 3 | 1 | 1 | 7 | 6 | 11 | .362 | .408 | .188 | 32 | 6 | 2 | 0 | 0 | 4 | 4 | 7 | .278 | .250 |
| Davis,Alvin | L | .256 | 168 | 43 | 7 | 0 | 6 | 29 | 28 | 24 | .360 | .405 | .298 | 326 | 97 | 14 | 0 | 11 | 39 | 57 | 44 | .401 | .442 |
| Davis,Chili | B | .254 | 126 | 32 | 5 | 0 | 4 | 20 | 18 | 29 | .345 | .389 | .269 | 286 | 77 | 12 | 1 | 8 | 38 | 43 | 60 | .363 | .402 |
| Davis,Eric | R | .287 | 150 | 43 | 11 | 0 | 8 | 36 | 19 | 32 | .365 | .520 | .248 | 303 | 75 | 15 | 2 | 16 | 50 | 41 | 68 | .339 | .469 |
| Davis,Glenn | R | .252 | 123 | 31 | 6 | 0 | 11 | 27 | 21 | 11 | .378 | .569 | .250 | 204 | 51 | 9 | 4 | 11 | 37 | 25 | 43 | .343 | .495 |
| Davis,Jody | R | .105 | 19 | 2 | 0 | 0 | 0 | 0 | 3 | 2 | .227 | .105 | .000 | 9 | 0 | 0 | 0 | 0 | 1 | 0 | 1 | .000 | .000 |
| Dawson,Andre | R | .298 | 181 | 54 | 10 | 2 | 8 | 25 | 14 | 19 | .343 | .508 | .316 | 348 | 110 | 18 | 3 | 19 | 75 | 28 | 46 | .366 | .549 |
| Decker,Steve | R | .348 | 23 | 8 | 1 | 0 | 1 | 2 | 1 | 2 | .375 | .522 | .258 | 31 | 8 | 1 | 0 | 2 | 6 | 0 | 8 | .258 | .484 |
| Deer,Rob | R | .293 | 140 | 41 | 5 | 0 | 16 | 34 | 25 | 40 | .399 | .671 | .170 | 300 | 51 | 10 | 1 | 11 | 35 | 39 | 107 | .271 | .320 |
| Dempsey,Rick | R | .170 | 94 | 16 | 3 | 0 | 2 | 9 | 19 | 17 | .310 | .266 | .265 | 34 | 9 | 2 | 0 | 0 | 6 | 4 | 12 | .342 | .324 |
| DeShields,Delino | L | .264 | 193 | 51 | 9 | 3 | 2 | 17 | 26 | 48 | .356 | .373 | .304 | 306 | 93 | 19 | 3 | 2 | 28 | 40 | 48 | .387 | .405 |
| Devereaux,Mike | R | .231 | 160 | 37 | 7 | 0 | 7 | 22 | 10 | 15 | .273 | .406 | .246 | 207 | 51 | 11 | 1 | 5 | 27 | 18 | 33 | .304 | .382 |
| Diaz,Carlos | R | .000 | 2 | 0 | 0 | 0 | 0 | 0 | 0 | 2 | .000 | .000 | 1.000 | 1 | 1 | 0 | 0 | 0 | 0 | 0 | 0 | 1.000 | 1.000 |
| Diaz,Edgar | R | .284 | 95 | 27 | 2 | 0 | 0 | 2 | 9 | 11 | .346 | .305 | .260 | 123 | 32 | 0 | 2 | 0 | 12 | 12 | 21 | .331 | .293 |
| Diaz,Mario | R | .200 | 10 | 2 | 0 | 0 | 0 | 1 | 0 | 1 | .182 | .200 | .083 | 12 | 1 | 1 | 0 | 0 | 0 | 0 | 2 | .083 | .167 |
| Disarcina,Gary | R | .000 | 12 | 0 | 0 | 0 | 0 | 0 | 1 | 1 | .077 | .000 | .178 | 45 | 8 | 1 | 1 | 0 | 0 | 2 | 9 | .213 | .244 |
| Doran,Billy | B | .268 | 142 | 38 | 12 | 1 | 2 | 12 | 35 | 19 | .408 | .408 | .318 | 261 | 83 | 17 | 1 | 5 | 25 | 44 | 39 | .412 | .448 |
| Dorsett,Brian | R | .176 | 17 | 3 | 1 | 0 | 0 | 0 | 0 | 1 | .176 | .235 | .111 | 18 | 2 | 1 | 0 | 0 | 0 | 2 | 3 | .200 | .167 |
| Downing,Brian | R | .345 | 119 | 41 | 8 | 1 | 5 | 16 | 25 | 14 | .466 | .555 | .232 | 211 | 49 | 10 | 1 | 9 | 35 | 25 | 31 | .318 | .417 |
| Ducey,Rob | L | .333 | 6 | 2 | 1 | 0 | 0 | 2 | 1 | 1 | .429 | .500 | .298 | 47 | 14 | 4 | 0 | 0 | 5 | 6 | 14 | .382 | .383 |
| Duncan,Mariano | B | .410 | 188 | 77 | 17 | 4 | 4 | 27 | 10 | 22 | .437 | .606 | .227 | 247 | 56 | 5 | 7 | 6 | 28 | 14 | 45 | .276 | .377 |
| Dunston,Shawon | R | .287 | 188 | 54 | 6 | 4 | 9 | 23 | 3 | 24 | .295 | .505 | .249 | 357 | 89 | 16 | 4 | 8 | 43 | 12 | 63 | .277 | .384 |
| Dwyer,Jim | L | .000 | 2 | 0 | 0 | 0 | 0 | 1 | 0 | 1 | .000 | .000 | .197 | 61 | 12 | 0 | 0 | 1 | 4 | 12 | 6 | .329 | .246 |
| Dykstra,Lenny | L | .290 | 200 | 58 | 6 | 1 | 1 | 17 | 29 | 20 | .385 | .345 | .344 | 390 | 134 | 29 | 2 | 8 | 43 | 60 | 28 | .434 | .490 |
| Eisenreich,Jim | L | .224 | 156 | 35 | 9 | 2 | 1 | 16 | 10 | 18 | .268 | .327 | .306 | 340 | 104 | 20 | 5 | 4 | 35 | 32 | 33 | .365 | .429 |
| Elster,Kevin | R | .233 | 120 | 28 | 7 | 0 | 2 | 10 | 10 | 16 | .286 | .342 | .191 | 194 | 37 | 13 | 1 | 7 | 35 | 20 | 38 | .266 | .376 |
| Eppard,Jim | L | .000 | 0 | 0 | 0 | 0 | 0 | 0 | 0 | 0 | .000 | .000 | .200 | 5 | 1 | 0 | 0 | 0 | 0 | 0 | 2 | .333 | .200 |
| Esasky,Nick | R | .400 | 10 | 4 | 0 | 0 | 0 | 0 | 1 | 3 | .455 | .400 | .080 | 25 | 2 | 0 | 0 | 0 | 0 | 3 | 11 | .179 | .080 |
| Espinoza,Alvaro | R | .250 | 144 | 36 | 2 | 1 | 1 | 9 | 9 | 13 | .294 | .299 | .211 | 294 | 62 | 10 | 1 | 1 | 11 | 7 | 41 | .240 | .262 |
| Espy,Cecil | B | .174 | 23 | 4 | 0 | 0 | 0 | 1 | 3 | 6 | .269 | .174 | .104 | 48 | 5 | 0 | 0 | 0 | 0 | 7 | 14 | .218 | .104 |
| Evans,Dwight | R | .265 | 147 | 39 | 10 | 2 | 3 | 16 | 25 | 29 | .375 | .422 | .242 | 298 | 72 | 8 | 1 | 10 | 47 | 42 | 44 | .335 | .376 |
| Faries,Paul | R | .357 | 14 | 5 | 1 | 0 | 0 | 2 | 1 | 1 | .375 | .429 | .087 | 23 | 2 | 0 | 0 | 0 | 0 | 3 | 6 | .222 | .087 |
| Felder,Mike | B | .275 | 80 | 22 | 2 | 2 | 3 | 14 | 6 | 5 | .315 | .463 | .274 | 157 | 43 | 5 | 0 | 0 | 13 | 16 | 12 | .337 | .306 |
| Felix,Junior | B | .211 | 152 | 32 | 8 | 1 | 9 | 22 | 15 | 41 | .282 | .454 | .289 | 311 | 90 | 15 | 6 | 6 | 43 | 30 | 58 | .351 | .434 |
| Fermin,Felix | R | .262 | 130 | 34 | 3 | 0 | 0 | 15 | 9 | 4 | .303 | .285 | .254 | 284 | 72 | 10 | 2 | 1 | 25 | 17 | 18 | .294 | .313 |
| Fernandez,Tony | B | .238 | 202 | 48 | 6 | 2 | 1 | 13 | 31 | 18 | .340 | .302 | .293 | 433 | 127 | 21 | 15 | 3 | 53 | 40 | 52 | .358 | .432 |
| Fielder,Cecil | R | .371 | 178 | 66 | 11 | 0 | 25 | 54 | 37 | 47 | .479 | .854 | .235 | 395 | 93 | 14 | 1 | 26 | 78 | 53 | 135 | .330 | .473 |
| Finley,Steve | L | .193 | 114 | 22 | 2 | 0 | 1 | 9 | 2 | 15 | .202 | .237 | .277 | 350 | 97 | 14 | 4 | 2 | 28 | 30 | 38 | .336 | .357 |

## Batters vs. Left-Handed and Right-Handed Pitchers

| Batter | | vs. Left-Handed Pitchers | | | | | | | | | | | vs. Right-Handed Pitchers | | | | | | | | | | |
|---|---|---|---|---|---|---|---|---|---|---|---|---|---|---|---|---|---|---|---|---|---|---|---|
| Batter | | Avg | AB | H | 2B | 3B | HR | RBI | BB | SO | OBP | SLG | Avg | AB | H | 2B | 3B | HR | RBI | BB | SO | OBP | SLG |
| Fisk,Carlton | R | .315 | 165 | 52 | 10 | 0 | 9 | 30 | 21 | 23 | .397 | .539 | .268 | 287 | 77 | 11 | 0 | 9 | 35 | 40 | 50 | .367 | .401 |
| Fitzgerald,Mike | R | .225 | 138 | 31 | 4 | 0 | 5 | 20 | 30 | 21 | .359 | .362 | .257 | 175 | 45 | 14 | 1 | 4 | 21 | 30 | 39 | .370 | .417 |
| Fletcher,Darrin | L | .250 | 4 | 1 | 0 | 0 | 0 | 0 | 0 | 0 | .250 | .250 | .105 | 19 | 2 | 1 | 0 | 0 | 1 | 1 | 6 | .150 | .158 |
| Fletcher,Scott | R | .283 | 173 | 49 | 4 | 0 | 1 | 13 | 21 | 16 | .365 | .324 | .220 | 336 | 74 | 14 | 3 | 3 | 43 | 24 | 47 | .271 | .307 |
| Foley,Tom | L | .278 | 18 | 5 | 0 | 0 | 0 | 1 | 0 | 3 | .278 | .278 | .205 | 146 | 30 | 2 | 1 | 0 | 11 | 12 | 19 | .264 | .233 |
| Ford,Curt | L | .000 | 1 | 0 | 0 | 0 | 0 | 0 | 0 | 1 | .000 | .000 | .118 | 17 | 2 | 0 | 0 | 0 | 0 | 1 | 4 | .167 | .118 |
| Franco,Julio | R | .296 | 179 | 53 | 9 | 0 | 3 | 19 | 31 | 25 | .398 | .397 | .295 | 403 | 119 | 18 | 1 | 8 | 50 | 51 | 58 | .376 | .404 |
| Francona,Terry | L | .000 | 1 | 0 | 0 | 0 | 0 | 0 | 0 | 0 | .000 | .000 | .000 | 3 | 0 | 0 | 0 | 0 | 0 | 0 | 0 | .000 | .000 |
| Fryman,Travis | R | .318 | 88 | 28 | 7 | 0 | 5 | 12 | 8 | 16 | .375 | .568 | .285 | 144 | 41 | 4 | 1 | 4 | 15 | 9 | 35 | .331 | .410 |
| Gaetti,Gary | R | .223 | 166 | 37 | 8 | 0 | 5 | 18 | 14 | 28 | .283 | .361 | .231 | 411 | 95 | 19 | 5 | 11 | 67 | 22 | 73 | .270 | .382 |
| Gagne,Greg | R | .298 | 124 | 37 | 12 | 1 | 3 | 18 | 10 | 27 | .353 | .484 | .205 | 264 | 54 | 10 | 2 | 4 | 20 | 14 | 49 | .244 | .303 |
| Galarraga,Andres | R | .226 | 217 | 49 | 9 | 0 | 9 | 35 | 11 | 62 | .260 | .392 | .273 | 362 | 99 | 20 | 0 | 11 | 52 | 29 | 107 | .332 | .420 |
| Gallagher,Dave | R | .248 | 101 | 25 | 3 | 1 | 0 | 6 | 6 | 11 | .296 | .297 | .280 | 25 | 7 | 1 | 0 | 0 | 1 | 1 | 1 | .296 | .320 |
| Gallego,Mike | R | .180 | 128 | 23 | 5 | 0 | 1 | 9 | 9 | 19 | .234 | .242 | .218 | 261 | 57 | 8 | 2 | 2 | 25 | 26 | 31 | .297 | .287 |
| Gant,Ron | R | .299 | 204 | 61 | 15 | 0 | 10 | 32 | 21 | 20 | .361 | .520 | .305 | 371 | 113 | 19 | 3 | 22 | 52 | 29 | 66 | .355 | .550 |
| Gantner,Jim | L | .307 | 88 | 27 | 2 | 0 | 0 | 9 | 12 | 6 | .390 | .330 | .247 | 235 | 58 | 6 | 5 | 0 | 16 | 17 | 13 | .303 | .315 |
| Garcia,Carlos | R | .500 | 2 | 1 | 0 | 0 | 0 | 0 | 0 | 1 | .500 | .500 | .500 | 2 | 1 | 0 | 0 | 0 | 0 | 0 | 1 | .500 | .500 |
| Gedman,Rich | L | .111 | 9 | 1 | 0 | 0 | 0 | 2 | 0 | 3 | .111 | .111 | .209 | 110 | 23 | 7 | 0 | 1 | 8 | 20 | 27 | .333 | .300 |
| Geren,Bob | R | .254 | 114 | 29 | 4 | 0 | 4 | 10 | 7 | 25 | .309 | .395 | .184 | 163 | 30 | 3 | 0 | 4 | 21 | 6 | 48 | .224 | .276 |
| Gibson,Kirk | L | .255 | 102 | 26 | 7 | 0 | 3 | 15 | 12 | 30 | .347 | .412 | .263 | 213 | 56 | 13 | 0 | 5 | 23 | 27 | 35 | .344 | .394 |
| Giles,Brian | R | .245 | 49 | 12 | 2 | 0 | 3 | 5 | 9 | 14 | .362 | .469 | .217 | 46 | 10 | 4 | 0 | 1 | 6 | 6 | 10 | .308 | .370 |
| Gilkey,Bernard | R | .276 | 29 | 8 | 2 | 2 | 0 | 0 | 4 | 2 | .364 | .483 | .314 | 35 | 11 | 3 | 0 | 1 | 3 | 4 | 3 | .385 | .486 |
| Girardi,Joe | R | .326 | 141 | 46 | 15 | 1 | 1 | 16 | 3 | 11 | .336 | .468 | .241 | 278 | 67 | 9 | 1 | 0 | 22 | 14 | 39 | .283 | .281 |
| Gladden,Dan | R | .270 | 163 | 44 | 8 | 0 | 2 | 16 | 5 | 18 | .297 | .356 | .278 | 371 | 103 | 19 | 6 | 3 | 24 | 21 | 49 | .322 | .385 |
| Goff,Jerry | L | .091 | 11 | 1 | 0 | 0 | 0 | 0 | 0 | 4 | .091 | .091 | .241 | 108 | 26 | 1 | 0 | 3 | 7 | 21 | 32 | .364 | .333 |
| Gomez,Leo | R | .278 | 18 | 5 | 0 | 0 | 0 | 0 | 1 | 1 | .316 | .278 | .190 | 21 | 4 | 0 | 0 | 0 | 1 | 7 | 6 | .393 | .190 |
| Gonzales,Rene | R | .222 | 27 | 6 | 1 | 1 | 0 | 5 | 8 | 3 | .400 | .333 | .211 | 76 | 16 | 2 | 0 | 1 | 7 | 4 | 11 | .250 | .276 |
| Gonzalez,Jose | R | .214 | 70 | 15 | 2 | 2 | 0 | 5 | 6 | 17 | .282 | .300 | .276 | 29 | 8 | 3 | 1 | 2 | 3 | 0 | 10 | .276 | .655 |
| Gonzalez,Juan | R | .292 | 24 | 7 | 3 | 0 | 1 | 3 | 2 | 5 | .333 | .542 | .288 | 66 | 19 | 4 | 1 | 3 | 9 | 0 | 13 | .309 | .515 |
| Gonzalez,Luis | L | .000 | 1 | 0 | 0 | 0 | 0 | 0 | 0 | 0 | .000 | .000 | .200 | 20 | 4 | 2 | 0 | 0 | 0 | 2 | 5 | .273 | .300 |
| Grace,Mark | L | .308 | 185 | 57 | 12 | 0 | 3 | 33 | 20 | 21 | .378 | .422 | .309 | 404 | 125 | 20 | 1 | 6 | 49 | 39 | 33 | .369 | .408 |
| Grebeck,Craig | R | .148 | 88 | 13 | 3 | 1 | 0 | 4 | 6 | 18 | .198 | .205 | .226 | 31 | 7 | 0 | 0 | 1 | 5 | 2 | 6 | .306 | .323 |
| Green,Gary | R | .179 | 39 | 7 | 2 | 0 | 0 | 3 | 3 | 7 | .233 | .231 | .245 | 49 | 12 | 1 | 0 | 0 | 5 | 3 | 11 | .288 | .265 |
| Greenwell,Mike | L | .257 | 202 | 52 | 8 | 2 | 3 | 22 | 17 | 19 | .326 | .361 | .316 | 408 | 129 | 22 | 4 | 11 | 51 | 48 | 24 | .386 | .471 |
| Gregg,Tommy | L | .105 | 19 | 2 | 0 | 0 | 0 | 0 | 3 | 6 | .227 | .105 | .277 | 220 | 61 | 13 | 1 | 5 | 32 | 17 | 33 | .331 | .414 |
| Griffey Jr,Ken | L | .306 | 219 | 67 | 14 | 1 | 5 | 22 | 17 | 45 | .357 | .447 | .296 | 378 | 112 | 14 | 6 | 17 | 58 | 46 | 36 | .371 | .500 |
| Griffey Sr,Ken | L | .267 | 15 | 4 | 0 | 0 | 0 | 4 | 2 | 4 | .353 | .267 | .304 | 125 | 38 | 4 | 0 | 4 | 22 | 10 | 4 | .353 | .432 |
| Griffin,Alfredo | B | .207 | 169 | 35 | 2 | 0 | 1 | 12 | 11 | 30 | .257 | .237 | .212 | 292 | 62 | 9 | 3 | 0 | 23 | 18 | 35 | .259 | .264 |
| Grissom,Marquis | R | .243 | 181 | 44 | 11 | 2 | 2 | 16 | 20 | 20 | .317 | .359 | .280 | 107 | 30 | 3 | 0 | 1 | 13 | 7 | 20 | .325 | .336 |
| Gruber,Kelly | R | .295 | 166 | 49 | 11 | 4 | 8 | 34 | 16 | 27 | .349 | .554 | .265 | 426 | 113 | 25 | 2 | 23 | 84 | 32 | 67 | .322 | .495 |
| Guerrero,Pedro | R | .274 | 168 | 46 | 17 | 0 | 4 | 30 | 13 | 28 | .319 | .446 | .285 | 330 | 94 | 14 | 1 | 9 | 50 | 31 | 42 | .341 | .415 |
| Guillen,Ozzie | L | .267 | 206 | 55 | 8 | 1 | 0 | 28 | 6 | 19 | .288 | .316 | .287 | 310 | 89 | 13 | 3 | 1 | 30 | 20 | 18 | .327 | .358 |
| Gwynn,Chris | L | .118 | 17 | 2 | 0 | 0 | 0 | 2 | 1 | 6 | .167 | .118 | .306 | 124 | 38 | 2 | 1 | 5 | 20 | 6 | 22 | .331 | .460 |
| Gwynn,Tony | L | .281 | 228 | 64 | 8 | 2 | 3 | 28 | 8 | 10 | .307 | .373 | .328 | 345 | 113 | 21 | 8 | 1 | 44 | 36 | 13 | .388 | .443 |
| Hale,Chip | L | .000 | 1 | 0 | 0 | 0 | 0 | 0 | 0 | 1 | .000 | .000 | .000 | 1 | 0 | 0 | 0 | 0 | 2 | 0 | 0 | .000 | .000 |
| Hall,Mel | L | .207 | 58 | 12 | 3 | 0 | 1 | 5 | 0 | 11 | .203 | .310 | .268 | 302 | 81 | 20 | 2 | 11 | 41 | 6 | 35 | .285 | .457 |
| Hamilton,Daryl | L | .111 | 9 | 1 | 1 | 0 | 0 | 0 | 2 | 1 | .273 | .222 | .306 | 147 | 45 | 4 | 0 | 1 | 18 | 7 | 11 | .338 | .354 |
| Hamilton,Jeff | R | .125 | 8 | 1 | 0 | 0 | 0 | 1 | 0 | 0 | .125 | .125 | .125 | 16 | 2 | 0 | 0 | 0 | 0 | 0 | 3 | .125 | .125 |
| Hansen,Dave | L | .000 | 1 | 0 | 0 | 0 | 0 | 0 | 0 | 1 | .000 | .000 | .167 | 6 | 1 | 0 | 0 | 0 | 1 | 0 | 2 | .167 | .167 |
| Harper,Brian | R | .315 | 146 | 46 | 19 | 1 | 4 | 20 | 8 | 10 | .357 | .541 | .285 | 333 | 95 | 23 | 2 | 2 | 34 | 11 | 17 | .315 | .384 |

# **Batters** vs. Left-Handed and Right-Handed Pitchers

| Batter | | vs. Left-Handed Pitchers | | | | | | | | | | | vs. Right-Handed Pitchers | | | | | | | | | | |
|---|---|---|---|---|---|---|---|---|---|---|---|---|---|---|---|---|---|---|---|---|---|---|---|
| | | Avg | AB | H | 2B | 3B | HR | RBI | BB | SO | OBP | SLG | Avg | AB | H | 2B | 3B | HR | RBI | BB | SO | OBP | SLG |
| Harris,Lenny | L | .238 | 42 | 10 | 0 | 1 | 0 | 6 | 3 | 5 | .304 | .286 | .311 | 389 | 121 | 16 | 3 | 2 | 23 | 26 | 26 | .353 | .383 |
| Haselman,Bill | R | .200 | 10 | 2 | 0 | 0 | 0 | 3 | 1 | 3 | .273 | .200 | .000 | 3 | 0 | 0 | 0 | 0 | 0 | 0 | 2 | .000 | .000 |
| Hassey,Ron | L | .091 | 33 | 3 | 0 | 0 | 0 | 1 | 1 | 4 | .143 | .091 | .231 | 221 | 51 | 7 | 0 | 5 | 21 | 26 | 25 | .308 | .330 |
| Hatcher,Billy | R | .246 | 207 | 51 | 10 | 1 | 1 | 8 | 16 | 16 | .299 | .319 | .296 | 297 | 88 | 18 | 4 | 4 | 17 | 17 | 26 | .347 | .424 |
| Hatcher,Mickey | R | .225 | 102 | 23 | 2 | 1 | 0 | 11 | 6 | 17 | .273 | .265 | .167 | 30 | 5 | 1 | 0 | 0 | 2 | 0 | 5 | .161 | .200 |
| Hayes,Charlie | R | .295 | 193 | 57 | 10 | 0 | 5 | 22 | 8 | 26 | .324 | .425 | .239 | 368 | 88 | 10 | 0 | 5 | 35 | 20 | 65 | .277 | .307 |
| Hayes,Von | L | .274 | 179 | 49 | 6 | 1 | 6 | 28 | 24 | 36 | .365 | .419 | .253 | 288 | 73 | 8 | 2 | 11 | 45 | 63 | 45 | .381 | .410 |
| Heath,Mike | R | .228 | 149 | 34 | 6 | 0 | 3 | 15 | 8 | 28 | .264 | .329 | .299 | 221 | 66 | 12 | 2 | 4 | 23 | 11 | 43 | .342 | .425 |
| Heep,Danny | L | .000 | 1 | 0 | 0 | 0 | 0 | 0 | 1 | 0 | .500 | .000 | .176 | 68 | 12 | 1 | 1 | 0 | 8 | 6 | 14 | .250 | .221 |
| Hemond,Scott | R | .143 | 7 | 1 | 0 | 0 | 0 | 0 | 0 | 3 | .143 | .143 | .167 | 6 | 1 | 0 | 0 | 0 | 1 | 0 | 2 | .167 | .167 |
| Henderson,Dave | R | .353 | 133 | 47 | 7 | 0 | 11 | 23 | 10 | 22 | .400 | .654 | .237 | 317 | 75 | 21 | 0 | 9 | 40 | 30 | 83 | .302 | .388 |
| Henderson,Rickey | R | .313 | 134 | 42 | 12 | 0 | 9 | 17 | 24 | 22 | .421 | .604 | .330 | 355 | 117 | 21 | 3 | 19 | 44 | 73 | 38 | .446 | .566 |
| Hernandez,Carlos | R | .286 | 14 | 4 | 1 | 0 | 0 | 1 | 0 | 1 | .286 | .357 | .000 | 6 | 0 | 0 | 0 | 0 | 0 | 0 | 1 | .000 | .000 |
| Hernandez,Keith | L | .148 | 27 | 4 | 0 | 0 | 0 | 2 | 3 | 3 | .233 | .148 | .214 | 103 | 22 | 2 | 0 | 1 | 6 | 11 | 14 | .296 | .262 |
| Herr,Tommy | B | .264 | 208 | 55 | 8 | 1 | 1 | 20 | 20 | 19 | .329 | .327 | .260 | 339 | 88 | 18 | 2 | 4 | 40 | 30 | 39 | .322 | .360 |
| Hill,Donnie | B | .235 | 98 | 23 | 8 | 0 | 1 | 12 | 12 | 10 | .315 | .347 | .276 | 254 | 70 | 10 | 2 | 2 | 20 | 17 | 17 | .320 | .354 |
| Hill,Glenallen | R | .224 | 143 | 32 | 5 | 3 | 5 | 12 | 10 | 36 | .275 | .406 | .239 | 117 | 28 | 6 | 0 | 7 | 20 | 8 | 26 | .288 | .470 |
| Hoiles,Chris | R | .121 | 33 | 4 | 0 | 0 | 0 | 0 | 1 | 5 | .147 | .121 | .267 | 30 | 8 | 3 | 0 | 1 | 6 | 4 | 7 | .353 | .467 |
| Hollins,Dave | B | .174 | 46 | 8 | 0 | 0 | 3 | 7 | 2 | 12 | .208 | .370 | .191 | 68 | 13 | 0 | 0 | 2 | 8 | 8 | 16 | .278 | .279 |
| Horn,Sam | L | .059 | 17 | 1 | 0 | 0 | 0 | 0 | 0 | 7 | .059 | .059 | .262 | 229 | 60 | 13 | 0 | 14 | 45 | 32 | 55 | .350 | .502 |
| Howard,Steve | R | .240 | 25 | 6 | 3 | 0 | 0 | 0 | 4 | 7 | .345 | .360 | .222 | 27 | 6 | 1 | 0 | 0 | 1 | 0 | 10 | .222 | .259 |
| Howard,Thomas | B | .188 | 16 | 3 | 0 | 0 | 0 | 0 | 0 | 6 | .188 | .188 | .321 | 28 | 9 | 2 | 0 | 0 | 0 | 0 | 5 | .321 | .393 |
| Howell,Jack | L | .177 | 62 | 11 | 2 | 0 | 0 | 5 | 9 | 16 | .292 | .210 | .240 | 254 | 61 | 17 | 1 | 8 | 28 | 37 | 45 | .334 | .409 |
| Howitt,Dann | L | .000 | 4 | 0 | 0 | 0 | 0 | 0 | 0 | 2 | .000 | .000 | .167 | 18 | 3 | 0 | 1 | 0 | 1 | 3 | 10 | .286 | .278 |
| Hrbek,Kent | L | .287 | 129 | 37 | 3 | 0 | 2 | 17 | 17 | 13 | .377 | .357 | .287 | 363 | 104 | 23 | 0 | 20 | 62 | 52 | 32 | .376 | .515 |
| Hudler,Rex | R | .234 | 137 | 32 | 5 | 1 | 5 | 11 | 9 | 22 | .281 | .394 | .361 | 83 | 30 | 6 | 1 | 2 | 11 | 3 | 10 | .393 | .530 |
| Hughes,Keith | L | .000 | 1 | 0 | 0 | 0 | 0 | 0 | 0 | 1 | .000 | .000 | .000 | 8 | 0 | 0 | 0 | 0 | 0 | 0 | 3 | .000 | .000 |
| Hulett,Tim | R | .211 | 57 | 12 | 2 | 1 | 3 | 9 | 6 | 16 | .286 | .439 | .281 | 96 | 27 | 5 | 0 | 0 | 7 | 9 | 25 | .343 | .333 |
| Hundley,Todd | B | .238 | 21 | 5 | 2 | 0 | 0 | 0 | 2 | 8 | .304 | .333 | .196 | 46 | 9 | 4 | 0 | 0 | 2 | 4 | 10 | .260 | .283 |
| Huson,Jeff | L | .261 | 46 | 12 | 1 | 0 | 0 | 3 | 4 | 9 | .327 | .283 | .237 | 350 | 83 | 11 | 2 | 0 | 25 | 42 | 45 | .319 | .280 |
| Incaviglia,Pete | R | .249 | 169 | 42 | 9 | 0 | 8 | 30 | 21 | 36 | .347 | .444 | .225 | 360 | 81 | 18 | 0 | 16 | 55 | 24 | 110 | .279 | .408 |
| Infante,Alex | R | .056 | 18 | 1 | 1 | 0 | 0 | 0 | 0 | 3 | .105 | .111 | .000 | 10 | 0 | 0 | 0 | 0 | 0 | 0 | 4 | .000 | .000 |
| Jackson,Bo | R | .273 | 143 | 39 | 4 | 0 | 10 | 24 | 16 | 46 | .348 | .510 | .271 | 262 | 71 | 12 | 1 | 18 | 54 | 28 | 82 | .339 | .531 |
| Jackson,Darrin | R | .277 | 65 | 18 | 1 | 0 | 2 | 5 | 4 | 11 | .314 | .385 | .229 | 48 | 11 | 2 | 0 | 1 | 4 | 1 | 13 | .245 | .333 |
| Jacoby,Brook | R | .316 | 158 | 50 | 4 | 1 | 3 | 18 | 16 | 13 | .383 | .411 | .284 | 395 | 112 | 20 | 3 | 11 | 57 | 47 | 45 | .358 | .433 |
| James,Chris | R | .302 | 162 | 49 | 7 | 1 | 4 | 22 | 15 | 25 | .361 | .432 | .298 | 366 | 109 | 25 | 3 | 8 | 48 | 16 | 46 | .332 | .448 |
| James,Dion | L | .111 | 9 | 1 | 1 | 0 | 0 | 1 | 1 | 0 | .200 | .222 | .280 | 239 | 67 | 14 | 2 | 1 | 21 | 26 | 23 | .352 | .368 |
| Javier,Stan | B | .315 | 124 | 39 | 2 | 3 | 1 | 10 | 18 | 14 | .401 | .403 | .286 | 185 | 53 | 7 | 3 | 2 | 17 | 22 | 36 | .359 | .389 |
| Jefferies,Gregg | B | .266 | 222 | 59 | 15 | 2 | 5 | 23 | 14 | 17 | .311 | .419 | .293 | 382 | 112 | 25 | 1 | 10 | 45 | 32 | 23 | .352 | .442 |
| Jefferson,Stan | B | .229 | 35 | 8 | 2 | 0 | 0 | 2 | 1 | 10 | .250 | .286 | .232 | 82 | 19 | 6 | 0 | 2 | 8 | 9 | 16 | .313 | .378 |
| Jelic,Chris | R | .000 | 8 | 0 | 0 | 0 | 0 | 0 | 0 | 2 | .000 | .000 | .333 | 3 | 1 | 0 | 0 | 1 | 1 | 0 | 1 | .333 | 1.333 |
| Jeltz,Steve | B | .250 | 32 | 8 | 2 | 0 | 0 | 4 | 2 | 2 | .294 | .313 | .113 | 71 | 8 | 2 | 0 | 0 | 6 | 4 | 19 | .158 | .141 |
| Jennings,Doug | L | .231 | 13 | 3 | 0 | 1 | 0 | 0 | 0 | 2 | .231 | .385 | .189 | 143 | 27 | 7 | 1 | 2 | 14 | 17 | 46 | .279 | .294 |
| Johnson,Howard | B | .211 | 223 | 47 | 12 | 0 | 7 | 27 | 29 | 50 | .298 | .359 | .264 | 367 | 97 | 25 | 3 | 16 | 63 | 40 | 50 | .332 | .480 |
| Johnson,Lance | L | .321 | 156 | 50 | 3 | 3 | 0 | 19 | 9 | 18 | .353 | .378 | .270 | 385 | 104 | 15 | 6 | 1 | 32 | 24 | 27 | .313 | .348 |
| Johnson,Wallace | B | .182 | 22 | 4 | 0 | 0 | 1 | 3 | 2 | 3 | .250 | .318 | .148 | 27 | 4 | 1 | 0 | 0 | 2 | 5 | 3 | .303 | .185 |
| Jones,Ron | L | .286 | 7 | 2 | 0 | 0 | 0 | 0 | 3 | 1 | .500 | .286 | .275 | 51 | 14 | 2 | 0 | 3 | 7 | 6 | 8 | .351 | .490 |
| Jones,Tim | L | .048 | 21 | 1 | 0 | 0 | 0 | 2 | 3 | 3 | .200 | .048 | .250 | 104 | 26 | 6 | 1 | 1 | 9 | 9 | 17 | .310 | .356 |
| Jones,Tracy | R | .259 | 112 | 29 | 4 | 0 | 4 | 13 | 6 | 11 | .308 | .402 | .261 | 92 | 24 | 4 | 1 | 2 | 11 | 3 | 14 | .306 | .391 |
| Jordan,Ricky | R | .246 | 118 | 29 | 9 | 0 | 2 | 12 | 10 | 9 | .313 | .373 | .238 | 206 | 49 | 12 | 0 | 3 | 32 | 3 | 30 | .256 | .340 |

# **Batters** vs. Left-Handed and Right-Handed Pitchers

| Batter | | vs. Left-Handed Pitchers | | | | | | | | | | | vs. Right-Handed Pitchers | | | | | | | | | | |
|---|---|---|---|---|---|---|---|---|---|---|---|---|---|---|---|---|---|---|---|---|---|---|---|
| | | Avg | AB | H | 2B | 3B | HR | RBI | BB | SO | OBP | SLG | Avg | AB | H | 2B | 3B | HR | RBI | BB | SO | OBP | SLG |
| Jose,Felix | B | .301 | 103 | 31 | 5 | 1 | 2 | 16 | 7 | 21 | .348 | .427 | .254 | 323 | 82 | 11 | 0 | 9 | 36 | 17 | 60 | .299 | .372 |
| Joyner,Wally | L | .226 | 106 | 24 | 2 | 0 | 2 | 17 | 10 | 15 | .291 | .302 | .289 | 204 | 59 | 13 | 0 | 6 | 24 | 31 | 19 | .379 | .441 |
| Justice,Dave | L | .366 | 131 | 48 | 8 | 0 | 10 | 32 | 18 | 22 | .443 | .656 | .247 | 308 | 76 | 15 | 2 | 18 | 46 | 46 | 70 | .344 | .484 |
| Karkovice,Ron | R | .219 | 64 | 14 | 4 | 0 | 2 | 9 | 6 | 24 | .282 | .375 | .261 | 119 | 31 | 6 | 0 | 4 | 11 | 10 | 28 | .323 | .412 |
| Kelly,Roberto | R | .304 | 181 | 55 | 10 | 0 | 5 | 17 | 12 | 46 | .352 | .442 | .278 | 460 | 128 | 22 | 4 | 10 | 44 | 21 | 102 | .311 | .409 |
| Kennedy,Terry | L | .188 | 32 | 6 | 1 | 0 | 0 | 1 | 3 | 4 | .257 | .219 | .288 | 271 | 78 | 21 | 0 | 2 | 25 | 28 | 34 | .352 | .387 |
| King,Jeff | R | .264 | 231 | 61 | 13 | 1 | 9 | 36 | 14 | 24 | .303 | .446 | .214 | 140 | 30 | 4 | 0 | 5 | 17 | 7 | 26 | .248 | .350 |
| Kingery,Mike | L | .400 | 25 | 10 | 1 | 0 | 0 | 4 | 1 | 1 | .444 | .440 | .280 | 182 | 51 | 6 | 1 | 0 | 20 | 11 | 18 | .320 | .324 |
| Kittle,Ron | R | .225 | 151 | 34 | 6 | 0 | 13 | 25 | 13 | 38 | .291 | .523 | .235 | 187 | 44 | 10 | 0 | 5 | 21 | 13 | 53 | .294 | .369 |
| Komminsk,Brad | R | .250 | 64 | 16 | 4 | 0 | 2 | 6 | 8 | 20 | .342 | .406 | .214 | 42 | 9 | 0 | 0 | 1 | 2 | 7 | 11 | .340 | .286 |
| Kremers,Jimmy | L | .250 | 4 | 1 | 0 | 0 | 0 | 0 | 0 | 0 | .250 | .250 | .101 | 69 | 7 | 1 | 1 | 1 | 2 | 6 | 27 | .173 | .188 |
| Kreuter,Chad | R | .067 | 15 | 1 | 1 | 0 | 0 | 2 | 5 | 6 | .286 | .133 | .000 | 7 | 0 | 0 | 0 | 0 | 0 | 3 | 3 | .300 | .000 |
| Kruk,John | L | .222 | 117 | 26 | 2 | 2 | 2 | 15 | 14 | 20 | .303 | .325 | .316 | 326 | 103 | 23 | 6 | 5 | 52 | 55 | 50 | .415 | .469 |
| Kunkel,Jeff | R | .229 | 118 | 27 | 8 | 1 | 2 | 14 | 8 | 39 | .278 | .364 | .085 | 82 | 7 | 3 | 0 | 1 | 3 | 3 | 27 | .138 | .159 |
| Kutcher,Randy | R | .143 | 28 | 4 | 2 | 0 | 1 | 1 | 3 | 6 | .226 | .321 | .283 | 46 | 13 | 2 | 1 | 0 | 4 | 10 | 12 | .411 | .370 |
| Laga,Mike | L | .600 | 5 | 3 | 1 | 0 | 1 | 2 | 0 | 0 | .667 | 1.400 | .091 | 22 | 2 | 0 | 0 | 1 | 2 | 1 | 7 | .130 | .227 |
| Lake,Steve | R | .280 | 50 | 14 | 2 | 0 | 0 | 5 | 1 | 6 | .308 | .320 | .200 | 30 | 6 | 0 | 0 | 0 | 1 | 2 | 6 | .250 | .200 |
| Lampkin,Tom | L | .333 | 9 | 3 | 0 | 0 | 0 | 2 | 0 | 4 | .333 | .333 | .204 | 54 | 11 | 0 | 1 | 1 | 2 | 4 | 5 | .259 | .296 |
| Lancellotti,Rick | L | .000 | 0 | 0 | 0 | 0 | 0 | 0 | 0 | 0 | .000 | .000 | .000 | 8 | 0 | 0 | 0 | 0 | 1 | 0 | 3 | .000 | .000 |
| Lankford,Ray | L | .311 | 45 | 14 | 3 | 1 | 0 | 1 | 4 | 12 | .367 | .422 | .272 | 81 | 22 | 7 | 0 | 3 | 11 | 9 | 15 | .344 | .469 |
| Lansford,Carney | R | .345 | 119 | 41 | 5 | 1 | 1 | 11 | 19 | 13 | .439 | .429 | .245 | 388 | 95 | 10 | 0 | 2 | 39 | 26 | 37 | .298 | .286 |
| Larkin,Barry | R | .266 | 203 | 54 | 10 | 3 | 4 | 21 | 23 | 10 | .344 | .404 | .319 | 411 | 131 | 15 | 3 | 3 | 46 | 26 | 39 | .365 | .392 |
| Larkin,Gene | B | .248 | 121 | 30 | 6 | 2 | 0 | 12 | 10 | 14 | .303 | .331 | .279 | 280 | 78 | 20 | 2 | 5 | 30 | 32 | 41 | .359 | .418 |
| LaValliere,Mike | L | .375 | 56 | 21 | 3 | 0 | 2 | 11 | 9 | 6 | .470 | .536 | .229 | 223 | 51 | 12 | 0 | 1 | 20 | 35 | 14 | .335 | .296 |
| Lawless,Tom | R | .111 | 9 | 1 | 0 | 0 | 0 | 1 | 0 | 1 | .111 | .111 | .000 | 3 | 0 | 0 | 0 | 0 | 0 | 0 | 0 | .000 | .000 |
| Leach,Rick | L | .231 | 13 | 3 | 1 | 0 | 0 | 0 | 2 | 3 | .375 | .308 | .298 | 161 | 48 | 12 | 0 | 2 | 16 | 19 | 17 | .372 | .410 |
| Lee,Manny | B | .242 | 178 | 43 | 8 | 2 | 6 | 20 | 6 | 41 | .265 | .410 | .244 | 213 | 52 | 4 | 2 | 0 | 21 | 20 | 49 | .306 | .282 |
| Lee,Terry | R | .235 | 17 | 4 | 1 | 0 | 0 | 3 | 2 | 2 | .300 | .294 | .000 | 2 | 0 | 0 | 0 | 0 | 0 | 0 | 0 | .000 | .000 |
| Leius,Scott | R | .267 | 15 | 4 | 1 | 0 | 1 | 4 | 2 | 1 | .353 | .533 | .200 | 10 | 2 | 0 | 0 | 0 | 0 | 0 | 1 | .200 | .200 |
| Lemke,Mark | B | .268 | 97 | 26 | 8 | 0 | 0 | 11 | 9 | 6 | .330 | .351 | .197 | 142 | 28 | 5 | 0 | 0 | 10 | 12 | 16 | .256 | .232 |
| Lemon,Chet | R | .283 | 138 | 39 | 4 | 3 | 3 | 12 | 21 | 22 | .375 | .420 | .239 | 184 | 44 | 12 | 1 | 2 | 20 | 27 | 39 | .347 | .348 |
| Leonard,Jeff | R | .309 | 175 | 54 | 9 | 0 | 6 | 40 | 15 | 28 | .361 | .463 | .218 | 303 | 66 | 11 | 0 | 4 | 35 | 22 | 69 | .272 | .294 |
| Leonard,Mark | L | .250 | 4 | 1 | 0 | 0 | 0 | 1 | 0 | 3 | .250 | .250 | .154 | 13 | 2 | 1 | 0 | 1 | 1 | 3 | 5 | .313 | .462 |
| Lewis,Darren | R | .375 | 8 | 3 | 0 | 0 | 0 | 0 | 2 | 1 | .500 | .375 | .185 | 27 | 5 | 0 | 0 | 0 | 1 | 5 | 3 | .333 | .185 |
| Leyritz,Jim | R | .291 | 103 | 30 | 7 | 1 | 2 | 7 | 15 | 15 | .392 | .437 | .240 | 200 | 48 | 6 | 0 | 3 | 18 | 12 | 36 | .298 | .315 |
| Liddell,Dave | R | 1.000 | 1 | 1 | 0 | 0 | 0 | 0 | 0 | 0 | 1.000 | 1.000 | .000 | 0 | 0 | 0 | 0 | 0 | 0 | 0 | 0 | .000 | .000 |
| Lind,Jose | R | .231 | 216 | 50 | 12 | 3 | 1 | 19 | 18 | 21 | .285 | .329 | .282 | 298 | 84 | 16 | 2 | 0 | 29 | 17 | 31 | .321 | .349 |
| Lindeman,Jim | R | .231 | 26 | 6 | 1 | 0 | 2 | 8 | 2 | 12 | .286 | .500 | .167 | 6 | 1 | 0 | 0 | 0 | 0 | 0 | 1 | .167 | .167 |
| Liriano,Nelson | B | .194 | 67 | 13 | 1 | 3 | 0 | 6 | 11 | 12 | .308 | .299 | .243 | 288 | 70 | 11 | 6 | 1 | 22 | 27 | 32 | .308 | .333 |
| Litton,Greg | R | .281 | 139 | 39 | 9 | 1 | 1 | 15 | 5 | 25 | .306 | .381 | .169 | 65 | 11 | 0 | 0 | 0 | 9 | 6 | 20 | .243 | .169 |
| Lombardozzi,Steve | R | .000 | 0 | 0 | 0 | 0 | 0 | 0 | 1 | 0 | 1.000 | .000 | .000 | 1 | 0 | 0 | 0 | 0 | 0 | 0 | 1 | .000 | .000 |
| Lopez,Luis | R | .000 | 6 | 0 | 0 | 0 | 0 | 0 | 0 | 2 | .000 | .000 | .000 | 0 | 0 | 0 | 0 | 0 | 0 | 0 | 0 | .000 | .000 |
| Lusader,Scott | L | .333 | 12 | 4 | 1 | 0 | 0 | 2 | 1 | 4 | .385 | .417 | .227 | 75 | 17 | 1 | 0 | 2 | 14 | 11 | 4 | .315 | .320 |
| Lynn,Fred | L | .250 | 20 | 5 | 0 | 0 | 0 | 1 | 3 | 6 | .348 | .250 | .239 | 176 | 42 | 3 | 1 | 6 | 22 | 19 | 38 | .312 | .369 |
| Lyons,Barry | R | .167 | 36 | 6 | 0 | 0 | 1 | 3 | 0 | 4 | .167 | .250 | .286 | 49 | 14 | 0 | 0 | 2 | 6 | 2 | 6 | .327 | .408 |
| Lyons,Steve | L | .080 | 25 | 2 | 0 | 0 | 0 | 4 | 2 | 11 | .143 | .080 | .215 | 121 | 26 | 6 | 1 | 1 | 7 | 8 | 30 | .267 | .306 |
| Maas,Kevin | L | .164 | 67 | 11 | 1 | 0 | 3 | 8 | 10 | 28 | .273 | .313 | .283 | 187 | 53 | 8 | 0 | 18 | 33 | 33 | 48 | .399 | .615 |
| Macfarlane,Mike | R | .245 | 147 | 36 | 8 | 3 | 2 | 12 | 9 | 26 | .300 | .381 | .261 | 253 | 66 | 16 | 1 | 4 | 46 | 16 | 43 | .309 | .379 |
| Mack,Shane | R | .370 | 146 | 54 | 9 | 1 | 5 | 27 | 15 | 26 | .439 | .548 | .287 | 167 | 48 | 1 | 3 | 3 | 17 | 14 | 43 | .350 | .383 |
| Magadan,Dave | L | .254 | 169 | 43 | 6 | 2 | 2 | 27 | 20 | 22 | .333 | .349 | .372 | 282 | 105 | 22 | 4 | 4 | 45 | 54 | 33 | .464 | .521 |

# **Batters** vs. Left-Handed and Right-Handed Pitchers

| | | vs. Left-Handed Pitchers | | | | | | | | | | | vs. Right-Handed Pitchers | | | | | | | | | | |
|---|---|---|---|---|---|---|---|---|---|---|---|---|---|---|---|---|---|---|---|---|---|---|---|
| Batter | | Avg | AB | H | 2B | 3B | HR | RBI | BB | SO | OBP | SLG | Avg | AB | H | 2B | 3B | HR | RBI | BB | SO | OBP | SLG |
| Maldonado,Candy | R | .331 | 175 | 58 | 7 | 0 | 10 | 34 | 16 | 32 | .387 | .543 | .248 | 415 | 103 | 25 | 2 | 12 | 61 | 33 | 102 | .306 | .405 |
| Mann,Kelly | R | .100 | 10 | 1 | 0 | 0 | 1 | 1 | 0 | 1 | .100 | .400 | .167 | 18 | 3 | 1 | 0 | 0 | 1 | 0 | 5 | .167 | .222 |
| Manrique,Fred | R | .246 | 61 | 15 | 2 | 0 | 1 | 8 | 1 | 13 | .254 | .328 | .234 | 167 | 39 | 8 | 0 | 4 | 21 | 3 | 22 | .254 | .353 |
| Manto,Jeff | R | .259 | 27 | 7 | 2 | 0 | 0 | 3 | 11 | 6 | .474 | .333 | .204 | 49 | 10 | 3 | 1 | 2 | 11 | 10 | 12 | .339 | .429 |
| Manwaring,Kirt | R | .250 | 8 | 2 | 0 | 1 | 0 | 1 | 0 | 1 | .250 | .500 | .000 | 5 | 0 | 0 | 0 | 0 | 0 | 0 | 2 | .000 | .000 |
| Marshall,Mike | R | .219 | 96 | 21 | 6 | 0 | 4 | 9 | 5 | 27 | .257 | .406 | .279 | 179 | 50 | 8 | 2 | 6 | 30 | 6 | 39 | .313 | .447 |
| Martinez,Carlos | R | .221 | 140 | 31 | 2 | 2 | 2 | 7 | 5 | 20 | .248 | .307 | .227 | 132 | 30 | 4 | 3 | 2 | 17 | 5 | 20 | .255 | .348 |
| Martinez,Carmelo | R | .233 | 90 | 21 | 5 | 0 | 5 | 16 | 15 | 15 | .343 | .456 | .244 | 127 | 31 | 4 | 0 | 5 | 19 | 15 | 27 | .324 | .394 |
| Martinez,Dave | L | .244 | 78 | 19 | 0 | 1 | 1 | 11 | 11 | 15 | .333 | .308 | .288 | 313 | 90 | 13 | 4 | 10 | 28 | 13 | 33 | .317 | .450 |
| Martinez,Edgar | R | .308 | 156 | 48 | 8 | 1 | 6 | 24 | 27 | 21 | .412 | .487 | .299 | 331 | 99 | 19 | 1 | 5 | 25 | 47 | 41 | .390 | .408 |
| Martinez,Tino | L | .267 | 15 | 4 | 1 | 0 | 0 | 1 | 3 | 1 | .368 | .333 | .208 | 53 | 11 | 3 | 0 | 0 | 4 | 6 | 8 | .288 | .264 |
| Marzano,John | R | .226 | 31 | 7 | 1 | 0 | 0 | 3 | 1 | 6 | .242 | .258 | .250 | 52 | 13 | 3 | 0 | 0 | 3 | 4 | 4 | .304 | .308 |
| Mattingly,Don | L | .262 | 126 | 33 | 6 | 0 | 0 | 17 | 7 | 8 | .301 | .310 | .254 | 268 | 68 | 10 | 0 | 5 | 25 | 21 | 12 | .312 | .347 |
| May,Derrick | L | .400 | 5 | 2 | 0 | 0 | 0 | 1 | 1 | 0 | .500 | .400 | .232 | 56 | 13 | 3 | 0 | 1 | 10 | 1 | 7 | .246 | .339 |
| Mayne,Brent | L | .000 | 0 | 0 | 0 | 0 | 0 | 0 | 0 | 0 | .000 | .000 | .231 | 13 | 3 | 0 | 0 | 0 | 1 | 3 | 3 | .375 | .231 |
| McClendon,Lloyd | R | .170 | 88 | 15 | 2 | 0 | 2 | 11 | 10 | 14 | .253 | .261 | .136 | 22 | 3 | 1 | 0 | 0 | 1 | 4 | 8 | .269 | .182 |
| McCray,Rodney | R | .000 | 4 | 0 | 0 | 0 | 0 | 0 | 0 | 3 | .000 | .000 | .000 | 2 | 0 | 0 | 0 | 0 | 0 | 1 | 1 | .333 | .000 |
| McDowell,Oddibe | L | .103 | 39 | 4 | 0 | 0 | 0 | 1 | 5 | 8 | .222 | .103 | .263 | 266 | 70 | 14 | 0 | 7 | 24 | 16 | 45 | .306 | .395 |
| McGee,Willie | B | .324 | 225 | 73 | 11 | 3 | 2 | 27 | 10 | 43 | .352 | .427 | .324 | 389 | 126 | 24 | 4 | 1 | 50 | 38 | 61 | .385 | .414 |
| McGriff,Fred | L | .257 | 202 | 52 | 5 | 1 | 8 | 30 | 21 | 48 | .324 | .411 | .324 | 355 | 115 | 16 | 0 | 27 | 58 | 73 | 60 | .440 | .597 |
| McGriff,Terry | R | .000 | 5 | 0 | 0 | 0 | 0 | 0 | 0 | 1 | .000 | .000 | .000 | 4 | 0 | 0 | 0 | 0 | 0 | 0 | 0 | .000 | .000 |
| McGwire,Mark | R | .258 | 132 | 34 | 3 | 0 | 11 | 38 | 29 | 19 | .387 | .530 | .228 | 391 | 89 | 13 | 0 | 28 | 70 | 81 | 97 | .364 | .476 |
| McIntosh,Tim | R | .200 | 5 | 1 | 0 | 0 | 1 | 1 | 0 | 2 | .200 | .800 | .000 | 0 | 0 | 0 | 0 | 0 | 0 | 0 | 0 | .000 | .000 |
| McKnight,Jeff | B | .294 | 34 | 10 | 1 | 0 | 0 | 3 | 2 | 4 | .333 | .324 | .122 | 41 | 5 | 1 | 0 | 1 | 1 | 3 | 13 | .200 | .220 |
| McLemore,Mark | B | .227 | 22 | 5 | 1 | 0 | 0 | 2 | 0 | 3 | .227 | .273 | .105 | 38 | 4 | 1 | 0 | 0 | 0 | 4 | 12 | .190 | .132 |
| McRae,Brian | B | .361 | 72 | 26 | 4 | 0 | 1 | 13 | 3 | 7 | .382 | .458 | .229 | 96 | 22 | 4 | 3 | 1 | 10 | 6 | 22 | .272 | .365 |
| McReynolds,Kevin | R | .231 | 195 | 45 | 11 | 0 | 4 | 15 | 38 | 20 | .356 | .349 | .291 | 326 | 95 | 12 | 1 | 20 | 67 | 33 | 41 | .351 | .518 |
| Meadows,Louie | L | .000 | 0 | 0 | 0 | 0 | 0 | 0 | 0 | 0 | .000 | .000 | .107 | 28 | 3 | 0 | 0 | 0 | 0 | 3 | 6 | .194 | .107 |
| Melvin,Bob | R | .276 | 152 | 42 | 11 | 0 | 3 | 16 | 6 | 18 | .298 | .408 | .208 | 149 | 31 | 3 | 1 | 2 | 21 | 5 | 35 | .234 | .282 |
| Mercado,Orlando | R | .200 | 70 | 14 | 1 | 0 | 3 | 6 | 7 | 8 | .282 | .343 | .250 | 28 | 7 | 0 | 0 | 0 | 1 | 1 | 4 | .300 | .250 |
| Merced,Orlando | B | .125 | 8 | 1 | 0 | 0 | 0 | 0 | 0 | 5 | .125 | .125 | .250 | 16 | 4 | 1 | 0 | 0 | 0 | 1 | 4 | .294 | .313 |
| Meulens,Hensley | R | .290 | 31 | 9 | 3 | 0 | 1 | 4 | 2 | 9 | .333 | .484 | .212 | 52 | 11 | 4 | 0 | 2 | 6 | 7 | 16 | .339 | .404 |
| Miller,Keith | R | .289 | 149 | 43 | 7 | 0 | 0 | 8 | 12 | 27 | .340 | .336 | .202 | 84 | 17 | 1 | 0 | 1 | 4 | 11 | 19 | .306 | .250 |
| Milligan,Randy | R | .330 | 100 | 33 | 9 | 1 | 8 | 22 | 28 | 14 | .473 | .680 | .240 | 262 | 63 | 11 | 0 | 12 | 38 | 60 | 54 | .382 | .420 |
| Mitchell,Kevin | R | .306 | 170 | 52 | 11 | 0 | 10 | 29 | 27 | 24 | .395 | .547 | .282 | 354 | 100 | 13 | 2 | 25 | 64 | 31 | 63 | .342 | .542 |
| Molitor,Paul | R | .313 | 112 | 35 | 9 | 2 | 5 | 14 | 9 | 16 | .364 | .563 | .275 | 306 | 84 | 18 | 4 | 7 | 31 | 28 | 35 | .335 | .428 |
| Morandini,Mickey | L | .133 | 15 | 2 | 1 | 0 | 0 | 0 | 1 | 5 | .188 | .200 | .266 | 64 | 17 | 3 | 0 | 1 | 3 | 5 | 14 | .319 | .359 |
| Morman,Russ | R | .364 | 22 | 8 | 3 | 1 | 1 | 2 | 0 | 1 | .364 | .727 | .133 | 15 | 2 | 1 | 1 | 0 | 1 | 3 | 2 | .263 | .333 |
| Morris,Hal | L | .224 | 76 | 17 | 0 | 0 | 0 | 5 | 6 | 13 | .280 | .224 | .378 | 233 | 88 | 22 | 3 | 7 | 31 | 15 | 19 | .414 | .588 |
| Morris,John | L | .000 | 1 | 0 | 0 | 0 | 0 | 0 | 0 | 1 | .000 | .000 | .118 | 17 | 2 | 0 | 0 | 0 | 0 | 3 | 5 | .250 | .118 |
| Moseby,Lloyd | L | .182 | 132 | 24 | 2 | 0 | 2 | 9 | 10 | 26 | .264 | .242 | .278 | 299 | 83 | 14 | 5 | 12 | 42 | 38 | 51 | .358 | .478 |
| Moses,John | B | .381 | 21 | 8 | 0 | 0 | 0 | 2 | 2 | 1 | .435 | .381 | .197 | 147 | 29 | 3 | 1 | 1 | 12 | 17 | 18 | .286 | .252 |
| Mulliniks,Rance | L | .429 | 7 | 3 | 1 | 0 | 0 | 1 | 4 | 3 | .636 | .571 | .278 | 90 | 25 | 3 | 0 | 2 | 15 | 18 | 16 | .394 | .378 |
| Munoz,Pedro | R | .391 | 23 | 9 | 1 | 1 | 0 | 2 | 1 | 1 | .385 | .522 | .226 | 62 | 14 | 3 | 0 | 0 | 3 | 1 | 15 | .238 | .274 |
| Murphy,Dale | R | .311 | 180 | 56 | 11 | 1 | 14 | 38 | 31 | 22 | .410 | .617 | .214 | 383 | 82 | 12 | 0 | 10 | 45 | 30 | 108 | .271 | .324 |
| Murray,Eddie | B | .316 | 206 | 65 | 7 | 0 | 8 | 36 | 25 | 22 | .387 | .466 | .338 | 352 | 119 | 15 | 3 | 18 | 59 | 57 | 42 | .429 | .551 |
| Myers,Greg | L | .174 | 23 | 4 | 0 | 0 | 0 | 2 | 3 | 4 | .259 | .174 | .242 | 227 | 55 | 7 | 1 | 5 | 20 | 19 | 29 | .297 | .348 |
| Naehring,Tim | R | .414 | 29 | 12 | 3 | 0 | 1 | 7 | 5 | 4 | .500 | .621 | .196 | 56 | 11 | 3 | 0 | 1 | 5 | 3 | 11 | .237 | .304 |
| Nelson,Rob | L | .000 | 0 | 0 | 0 | 0 | 0 | 0 | 0 | 0 | .000 | .000 | .000 | 5 | 0 | 0 | 0 | 0 | 0 | 0 | 4 | .000 | .000 |
| Newman,Al | B | .252 | 123 | 31 | 6 | 0 | 0 | 6 | 15 | 14 | .333 | .301 | .238 | 265 | 63 | 8 | 0 | 0 | 24 | 18 | 20 | .289 | .268 |

## **Batters** vs. Left-Handed and Right-Handed Pitchers

| | | vs. Left-Handed Pitchers | | | | | | | | | | | vs. Right-Handed Pitchers | | | | | | | | | | |
|---|---|---|---|---|---|---|---|---|---|---|---|---|---|---|---|---|---|---|---|---|---|---|---|
| Batter | | Avg | AB | H | 2B | 3B | HR | RBI | BB | SO | OBP | SLG | Avg | AB | H | 2B | 3B | HR | RBI | BB | SO | OBP | SLG |
| Nichols,Carl | R | .200 | 40 | 8 | 3 | 0 | 0 | 11 | 7 | 8 | .306 | .275 | .222 | 9 | 2 | 0 | 0 | 0 | 0 | 1 | 3 | .364 | .222 |
| Nieto,Tom | R | .120 | 25 | 3 | 0 | 0 | 0 | 1 | 1 | 10 | .185 | .120 | .400 | 5 | 2 | 0 | 0 | 0 | 3 | 2 | 1 | .571 | .400 |
| Nixon,Donell | R | .214 | 14 | 3 | 2 | 0 | 0 | 2 | 0 | 7 | .214 | .357 | .333 | 6 | 2 | 0 | 0 | 0 | 0 | 1 | 0 | .429 | .333 |
| Nixon,Otis | B | .238 | 151 | 36 | 3 | 2 | 1 | 11 | 15 | 14 | .307 | .305 | .275 | 80 | 22 | 3 | 0 | 0 | 9 | 13 | 19 | .372 | .313 |
| Noboa,Junior | R | .279 | 122 | 34 | 4 | 1 | 0 | 7 | 6 | 10 | .305 | .328 | .212 | 33 | 7 | 3 | 1 | 0 | 6 | 1 | 4 | .250 | .364 |
| Noce,Paul | R | 1.000 | 1 | 1 | 0 | 0 | 0 | 0 | 0 | 0 | 1.000 | 1.000 | .000 | 0 | 0 | 0 | 0 | 0 | 0 | 0 | 0 | .000 | .000 |
| Nokes,Matt | L | .143 | 14 | 2 | 0 | 0 | 0 | 2 | 0 | 5 | .200 | .143 | .252 | 337 | 85 | 9 | 1 | 11 | 38 | 24 | 42 | .311 | .383 |
| O'Brien,Charlie | R | .143 | 112 | 16 | 7 | 1 | 0 | 7 | 9 | 18 | .211 | .223 | .218 | 101 | 22 | 3 | 1 | 0 | 13 | 12 | 16 | .310 | .267 |
| O'Brien,Pete | L | .200 | 130 | 26 | 2 | 0 | 1 | 12 | 16 | 13 | .291 | .238 | .237 | 236 | 56 | 16 | 0 | 4 | 15 | 28 | 20 | .317 | .356 |
| O'Malley,Tom | L | .261 | 23 | 6 | 3 | 0 | 0 | 3 | 3 | 4 | .346 | .391 | .214 | 98 | 21 | 4 | 0 | 3 | 11 | 8 | 16 | .271 | .347 |
| O'Neill,Paul | L | .259 | 143 | 37 | 12 | 0 | 3 | 25 | 11 | 45 | .310 | .406 | .275 | 360 | 99 | 16 | 0 | 13 | 53 | 42 | 58 | .351 | .428 |
| Oberkfell,Ken | L | .059 | 17 | 1 | 0 | 0 | 0 | 0 | 2 | 4 | .158 | .059 | .226 | 133 | 30 | 6 | 1 | 1 | 12 | 13 | 13 | .297 | .308 |
| Oester,Ron | B | .300 | 40 | 12 | 3 | 0 | 0 | 2 | 3 | 9 | .349 | .375 | .298 | 114 | 34 | 7 | 1 | 0 | 11 | 7 | 20 | .336 | .377 |
| Offerman,Jose | B | .192 | 26 | 5 | 0 | 0 | 0 | 2 | 0 | 4 | .192 | .192 | .125 | 32 | 4 | 0 | 0 | 1 | 5 | 4 | 10 | .222 | .219 |
| Olerud,John | L | .342 | 73 | 25 | 5 | 0 | 3 | 15 | 15 | 18 | .444 | .534 | .246 | 285 | 70 | 10 | 1 | 11 | 33 | 42 | 57 | .342 | .404 |
| Oliver,Joe | R | .283 | 180 | 51 | 13 | 0 | 5 | 28 | 18 | 34 | .350 | .439 | .179 | 184 | 33 | 10 | 0 | 3 | 24 | 19 | 41 | .260 | .283 |
| Olson,Greg | R | .312 | 154 | 48 | 9 | 1 | 5 | 25 | 15 | 26 | .374 | .481 | .208 | 144 | 30 | 3 | 0 | 2 | 11 | 15 | 25 | .288 | .271 |
| Oquendo,Jose | B | .220 | 164 | 36 | 4 | 2 | 1 | 7 | 24 | 13 | .319 | .287 | .269 | 305 | 82 | 13 | 3 | 0 | 30 | 50 | 33 | .367 | .331 |
| Orsulak,Joe | L | .250 | 72 | 18 | 0 | 1 | 0 | 7 | 8 | 8 | .325 | .278 | .273 | 341 | 93 | 14 | 2 | 11 | 50 | 38 | 40 | .346 | .422 |
| Ortiz,Javier | R | .333 | 39 | 13 | 4 | 1 | 1 | 5 | 4 | 5 | .386 | .564 | .211 | 38 | 8 | 1 | 0 | 0 | 5 | 8 | 6 | .348 | .237 |
| Ortiz,Junior | R | .360 | 50 | 18 | 1 | 0 | 0 | 7 | 7 | 6 | .441 | .380 | .325 | 120 | 39 | 6 | 1 | 0 | 11 | 5 | 10 | .357 | .392 |
| Orton,John | R | .167 | 24 | 4 | 1 | 0 | 0 | 0 | 2 | 8 | .231 | .208 | .200 | 60 | 12 | 4 | 0 | 1 | 6 | 3 | 23 | .250 | .317 |
| Owen,Spike | B | .259 | 201 | 52 | 16 | 2 | 3 | 17 | 23 | 25 | .330 | .403 | .214 | 252 | 54 | 8 | 3 | 2 | 18 | 47 | 35 | .336 | .294 |
| Pagliarulo,Mike | L | .248 | 101 | 25 | 3 | 0 | 4 | 13 | 15 | 21 | .353 | .396 | .256 | 297 | 76 | 20 | 2 | 3 | 25 | 24 | 45 | .311 | .367 |
| Pagnozzi,Tom | R | .293 | 82 | 24 | 6 | 0 | 1 | 9 | 7 | 17 | .356 | .402 | .268 | 138 | 37 | 9 | 0 | 1 | 14 | 7 | 20 | .299 | .355 |
| Palacios,Rey | R | .176 | 17 | 3 | 0 | 0 | 1 | 1 | 1 | 9 | .222 | .353 | .256 | 39 | 10 | 3 | 0 | 1 | 8 | 4 | 15 | .326 | .410 |
| Palmeiro,Rafael | L | .339 | 189 | 64 | 9 | 1 | 5 | 32 | 8 | 17 | .361 | .476 | .311 | 409 | 127 | 26 | 5 | 9 | 57 | 32 | 42 | .360 | .465 |
| Pankovits,Jim | R | .000 | 0 | 0 | 0 | 0 | 0 | 0 | 0 | 0 | .000 | .000 | .000 | 0 | 0 | 0 | 0 | 0 | 0 | 0 | 0 | .000 | .000 |
| Paredes,Johnny | R | .182 | 11 | 2 | 1 | 0 | 0 | 0 | 1 | 0 | .250 | .273 | .333 | 3 | 1 | 0 | 0 | 0 | 1 | 1 | 0 | .500 | .333 |
| Parent,Mark | R | .306 | 85 | 26 | 7 | 0 | 2 | 7 | 10 | 12 | .379 | .459 | .154 | 104 | 16 | 4 | 0 | 1 | 9 | 6 | 17 | .200 | .221 |
| Parker,Dave | L | .259 | 185 | 48 | 6 | 0 | 6 | 24 | 5 | 35 | .282 | .389 | .301 | 425 | 128 | 24 | 3 | 15 | 68 | 36 | 67 | .350 | .478 |
| Parker,Rick | R | .263 | 80 | 21 | 4 | 0 | 2 | 10 | 8 | 11 | .330 | .388 | .185 | 27 | 5 | 1 | 0 | 0 | 4 | 2 | 4 | .267 | .222 |
| Parrish,Lance | R | .304 | 125 | 38 | 2 | 0 | 7 | 17 | 13 | 27 | .370 | .488 | .255 | 345 | 88 | 12 | 0 | 17 | 53 | 33 | 80 | .327 | .438 |
| Pasqua,Dan | L | .194 | 31 | 6 | 3 | 0 | 0 | 4 | 2 | 8 | .265 | .290 | .282 | 294 | 83 | 24 | 3 | 13 | 54 | 35 | 58 | .355 | .517 |
| Pecota,Bill | R | .290 | 100 | 29 | 11 | 1 | 2 | 6 | 13 | 12 | .372 | .480 | .207 | 140 | 29 | 4 | 1 | 3 | 14 | 20 | 27 | .311 | .314 |
| Pena,Geronimo | B | .308 | 13 | 4 | 0 | 0 | 0 | 1 | 2 | 3 | .412 | .308 | .219 | 32 | 7 | 2 | 0 | 0 | 1 | 2 | 11 | .265 | .281 |
| Pena,Tony | R | .290 | 155 | 45 | 4 | 0 | 5 | 22 | 12 | 14 | .341 | .413 | .250 | 336 | 84 | 15 | 1 | 2 | 34 | 31 | 57 | .313 | .318 |
| Pendleton,Terry | B | .209 | 158 | 33 | 12 | 0 | 4 | 23 | 6 | 15 | .235 | .361 | .242 | 289 | 70 | 8 | 2 | 2 | 35 | 24 | 43 | .299 | .304 |
| Perezchica,Tony | R | .000 | 1 | 0 | 0 | 0 | 0 | 0 | 0 | 1 | .000 | .000 | .500 | 2 | 1 | 0 | 0 | 0 | 0 | 1 | 1 | .667 | .500 |
| Perry,Gerald | L | .209 | 134 | 28 | 5 | 0 | 1 | 14 | 7 | 19 | .252 | .269 | .272 | 331 | 90 | 17 | 2 | 7 | 43 | 32 | 37 | .336 | .399 |
| Petralli,Geno | L | .300 | 20 | 6 | 0 | 0 | 0 | 3 | 8 | 1 | .483 | .300 | .252 | 305 | 77 | 13 | 1 | 0 | 18 | 42 | 48 | .347 | .302 |
| Pettis,Gary | B | .217 | 152 | 33 | 6 | 3 | 0 | 7 | 23 | 38 | .320 | .296 | .251 | 271 | 68 | 10 | 5 | 3 | 24 | 34 | 80 | .340 | .358 |
| Phelps,Ken | L | .000 | 4 | 0 | 0 | 0 | 0 | 0 | 1 | 0 | .200 | .000 | .155 | 116 | 18 | 2 | 0 | 1 | 6 | 21 | 21 | .283 | .198 |
| Phillips,Tony | B | .248 | 202 | 50 | 11 | 2 | 2 | 19 | 27 | 22 | .341 | .351 | .253 | 371 | 94 | 12 | 3 | 6 | 36 | 72 | 63 | .377 | .350 |
| Plantier,Phil | L | .000 | 0 | 0 | 0 | 0 | 0 | 0 | 0 | 0 | .000 | .000 | .133 | 15 | 2 | 1 | 0 | 0 | 3 | 4 | 6 | .333 | .200 |
| Polidor,Gus | R | .000 | 4 | 0 | 0 | 0 | 0 | 0 | 0 | 1 | .000 | .000 | .091 | 11 | 1 | 0 | 0 | 0 | 1 | 0 | 0 | .091 | .091 |
| Polonia,Luis | L | .294 | 51 | 15 | 0 | 2 | 0 | 3 | 4 | 11 | .345 | .373 | .341 | 352 | 120 | 7 | 7 | 2 | 32 | 21 | 32 | .376 | .418 |
| Presley,Jim | R | .267 | 180 | 48 | 15 | 0 | 6 | 28 | 16 | 38 | .330 | .450 | .230 | 361 | 83 | 19 | 1 | 13 | 44 | 13 | 92 | .257 | .396 |
| Prince,Tom | R | .143 | 7 | 1 | 0 | 0 | 0 | 0 | 0 | 2 | .143 | .143 | .000 | 3 | 0 | 0 | 0 | 0 | 0 | 1 | 0 | .250 | .000 |
| Puckett,Kirby | R | .299 | 164 | 49 | 11 | 1 | 4 | 22 | 22 | 21 | .382 | .451 | .297 | 387 | 115 | 29 | 2 | 8 | 58 | 35 | 52 | .357 | .444 |

# **Batters** vs. Left-Handed and Right-Handed Pitchers

| Batter | | vs. Left-Handed Pitchers | | | | | | | | | | | vs. Right-Handed Pitchers | | | | | | | | | | |
|---|---|---|---|---|---|---|---|---|---|---|---|---|---|---|---|---|---|---|---|---|---|---|---|
| | | Avg | AB | H | 2B | 3B | HR | RBI | BB | SO | OBP | SLG | Avg | AB | H | 2B | 3B | HR | RBI | BB | SO | OBP | SLG |
| Puhl,Terry | L | .667 | 3 | 2 | 0 | 0 | 0 | 0 | 0 | 0 | .667 | .667 | .263 | 38 | 10 | 1 | 0 | 0 | 8 | 5 | 7 | .356 | .289 |
| Quinlan,Tom | R | .500 | 2 | 1 | 0 | 0 | 0 | 0 | 0 | 1 | .667 | .500 | .000 | 0 | 0 | 0 | 0 | 0 | 0 | 0 | 0 | .000 | .000 |
| Quinones,Luis | B | .266 | 64 | 17 | 4 | 0 | 2 | 12 | 7 | 15 | .333 | .422 | .222 | 81 | 18 | 3 | 0 | 0 | 5 | 6 | 14 | .273 | .259 |
| Quintana,Carlos | R | .352 | 182 | 64 | 12 | 0 | 3 | 27 | 16 | 24 | .407 | .467 | .252 | 330 | 83 | 16 | 0 | 4 | 40 | 36 | 50 | .325 | .336 |
| Quirk,Jamie | L | .448 | 29 | 13 | 2 | 0 | 0 | 13 | 2 | 6 | .455 | .517 | .228 | 92 | 21 | 3 | 1 | 3 | 13 | 12 | 28 | .321 | .380 |
| Raines,Tim | B | .289 | 180 | 52 | 0 | 2 | 3 | 27 | 21 | 13 | .357 | .361 | .285 | 277 | 79 | 11 | 3 | 6 | 35 | 49 | 30 | .393 | .412 |
| Ramirez,Rafael | R | .260 | 192 | 50 | 9 | 1 | 1 | 15 | 13 | 17 | .306 | .333 | .261 | 253 | 66 | 10 | 2 | 1 | 22 | 11 | 29 | .294 | .328 |
| Ramos,Domingo | R | .255 | 102 | 26 | 2 | 0 | 0 | 6 | 12 | 10 | .331 | .275 | .274 | 124 | 34 | 3 | 0 | 2 | 11 | 15 | 19 | .353 | .347 |
| Randolph,Willie | R | .353 | 116 | 41 | 8 | 1 | 0 | 12 | 10 | 5 | .405 | .440 | .221 | 272 | 60 | 5 | 2 | 2 | 18 | 35 | 29 | .313 | .276 |
| Ray,Johnny | B | .300 | 120 | 36 | 5 | 0 | 0 | 15 | 3 | 14 | .317 | .342 | .268 | 284 | 76 | 18 | 0 | 5 | 28 | 16 | 30 | .304 | .384 |
| Ready,Randy | R | .250 | 128 | 32 | 8 | 1 | 1 | 15 | 17 | 18 | .336 | .352 | .236 | 89 | 21 | 1 | 0 | 0 | 11 | 12 | 17 | .327 | .247 |
| Redus,Gary | R | .262 | 202 | 53 | 15 | 3 | 6 | 23 | 27 | 29 | .345 | .455 | .120 | 25 | 3 | 0 | 0 | 0 | 0 | 6 | 9 | .313 | .120 |
| Reed,Darren | R | .214 | 28 | 6 | 3 | 1 | 1 | 2 | 1 | 8 | .241 | .500 | .182 | 11 | 2 | 1 | 0 | 0 | 0 | 2 | 3 | .308 | .273 |
| Reed,Jeff | L | .360 | 25 | 9 | 2 | 0 | 2 | 4 | 5 | 6 | .467 | .680 | .233 | 150 | 35 | 6 | 1 | 1 | 12 | 19 | 20 | .318 | .307 |
| Reed,Jody | R | .299 | 184 | 55 | 16 | 0 | 0 | 14 | 23 | 17 | .376 | .386 | .285 | 414 | 118 | 29 | 0 | 5 | 37 | 52 | 48 | .368 | .391 |
| Reimer,Kevin | L | .000 | 5 | 0 | 0 | 0 | 0 | 0 | 0 | 2 | .000 | .000 | .274 | 95 | 26 | 9 | 1 | 2 | 15 | 10 | 20 | .349 | .453 |
| Reynolds,Harold | B | .285 | 207 | 59 | 15 | 2 | 1 | 22 | 17 | 7 | .335 | .391 | .237 | 435 | 103 | 21 | 3 | 4 | 33 | 64 | 45 | .337 | .326 |
| Reynolds,RJ | B | .295 | 112 | 33 | 4 | 0 | 0 | 8 | 14 | 13 | .373 | .330 | .282 | 103 | 29 | 6 | 1 | 0 | 11 | 9 | 22 | .333 | .359 |
| Reynolds,Ronn | R | .000 | 3 | 0 | 0 | 0 | 0 | 0 | 1 | 0 | .250 | .000 | .083 | 12 | 1 | 1 | 0 | 0 | 1 | 0 | 6 | .083 | .167 |
| Rhodes,Karl | L | .000 | 12 | 0 | 0 | 0 | 0 | 0 | 0 | 4 | .000 | .000 | .284 | 74 | 21 | 6 | 1 | 1 | 3 | 13 | 8 | .386 | .432 |
| Riles,Ernest | L | .250 | 8 | 2 | 0 | 0 | 1 | 3 | 3 | 3 | .455 | .625 | .197 | 147 | 29 | 2 | 1 | 7 | 18 | 23 | 23 | .304 | .367 |
| Ripken,Billy | R | .314 | 140 | 44 | 9 | 0 | 2 | 11 | 12 | 16 | .370 | .421 | .278 | 266 | 74 | 19 | 1 | 1 | 27 | 16 | 27 | .326 | .368 |
| Ripken,Cal | R | .264 | 182 | 48 | 9 | 1 | 9 | 24 | 30 | 17 | .363 | .473 | .244 | 418 | 102 | 19 | 3 | 12 | 60 | 52 | 49 | .332 | .390 |
| Rivera,Luis | R | .172 | 116 | 20 | 5 | 0 | 2 | 15 | 8 | 24 | .226 | .267 | .252 | 230 | 58 | 15 | 0 | 5 | 30 | 17 | 34 | .305 | .383 |
| Roberts,Bip | B | .294 | 221 | 65 | 17 | 0 | 4 | 16 | 16 | 26 | .350 | .425 | .319 | 335 | 107 | 19 | 3 | 5 | 28 | 39 | 39 | .391 | .439 |
| Robidoux,Billy | L | .000 | 1 | 0 | 0 | 0 | 0 | 0 | 0 | 1 | .000 | .000 | .186 | 43 | 8 | 4 | 0 | 1 | 4 | 6 | 13 | .294 | .349 |
| Rohde,David | B | .233 | 43 | 10 | 3 | 0 | 0 | 3 | 5 | 10 | .333 | .302 | .145 | 55 | 8 | 1 | 0 | 0 | 2 | 4 | 10 | .242 | .164 |
| Romero,Ed | R | .289 | 45 | 13 | 3 | 0 | 0 | 3 | 5 | 3 | .360 | .356 | .120 | 25 | 3 | 0 | 0 | 0 | 1 | 1 | 1 | .148 | .120 |
| Romine,Kevin | R | .295 | 61 | 18 | 1 | 0 | 1 | 9 | 3 | 8 | .328 | .361 | .253 | 75 | 19 | 6 | 0 | 1 | 5 | 9 | 19 | .333 | .373 |
| Roomes,Rolando | R | .239 | 71 | 17 | 0 | 1 | 2 | 8 | 1 | 24 | .250 | .352 | .000 | 4 | 0 | 0 | 0 | 0 | 0 | 0 | 2 | .000 | .000 |
| Rosario,Victor | R | .000 | 1 | 0 | 0 | 0 | 0 | 0 | 0 | 1 | .000 | .000 | .167 | 6 | 1 | 0 | 0 | 0 | 0 | 1 | 0 | .286 | .167 |
| Rose,Bobby | R | .444 | 9 | 4 | 0 | 0 | 1 | 2 | 1 | 1 | .500 | .778 | .250 | 4 | 1 | 0 | 0 | 0 | 0 | 1 | 0 | .400 | .250 |
| Rowland,Rick | R | .250 | 12 | 3 | 1 | 0 | 0 | 0 | 1 | 1 | .308 | .333 | .000 | 7 | 0 | 0 | 0 | 0 | 0 | 1 | 3 | .125 | .000 |
| Russell,John | R | .258 | 89 | 23 | 3 | 0 | 1 | 6 | 8 | 30 | .320 | .326 | .308 | 39 | 12 | 1 | 0 | 1 | 2 | 3 | 11 | .357 | .410 |
| Ryal,Mark | L | .000 | 0 | 0 | 0 | 0 | 0 | 0 | 0 | 0 | .000 | .000 | .083 | 12 | 1 | 0 | 0 | 0 | 0 | 0 | 3 | .083 | .083 |
| Sabo,Chris | R | .327 | 214 | 70 | 12 | 1 | 14 | 33 | 27 | 12 | .408 | .589 | .235 | 353 | 83 | 26 | 1 | 11 | 38 | 34 | 46 | .303 | .408 |
| Salas,Mark | L | .235 | 34 | 8 | 1 | 0 | 1 | 6 | 4 | 7 | .316 | .353 | .231 | 130 | 30 | 2 | 0 | 8 | 18 | 17 | 21 | .324 | .431 |
| Salazar,Luis | R | .293 | 157 | 46 | 7 | 1 | 6 | 22 | 6 | 18 | .319 | .465 | .229 | 253 | 58 | 6 | 2 | 6 | 25 | 13 | 41 | .277 | .340 |
| Samuel,Juan | R | .289 | 187 | 54 | 10 | 2 | 10 | 25 | 17 | 43 | .350 | .524 | .213 | 305 | 65 | 14 | 1 | 3 | 27 | 34 | 83 | .297 | .295 |
| Sandberg,Ryne | R | .252 | 214 | 54 | 13 | 0 | 10 | 23 | 21 | 34 | .319 | .453 | .334 | 401 | 134 | 17 | 3 | 30 | 77 | 29 | 50 | .373 | .616 |
| Sanders,Deion | L | .182 | 22 | 4 | 0 | 1 | 0 | 1 | 1 | 5 | .217 | .273 | .153 | 111 | 17 | 2 | 1 | 3 | 8 | 12 | 22 | .240 | .270 |
| Santana,Andres | B | .000 | 2 | 0 | 0 | 0 | 0 | 1 | 0 | 0 | .000 | .000 | .000 | 0 | 0 | 0 | 0 | 0 | 0 | 0 | 0 | .000 | .000 |
| Santana,Rafael | R | .333 | 3 | 1 | 0 | 0 | 1 | 2 | 0 | 0 | .333 | 1.333 | .200 | 10 | 2 | 0 | 0 | 0 | 1 | 0 | 0 | .200 | .200 |
| Santiago,Benito | R | .276 | 116 | 32 | 3 | 0 | 1 | 12 | 9 | 21 | .323 | .328 | .268 | 228 | 61 | 5 | 5 | 10 | 41 | 18 | 34 | .323 | .465 |
| Santovenia,Nelson | R | .164 | 67 | 11 | 2 | 1 | 1 | 7 | 2 | 10 | .181 | .269 | .208 | 96 | 20 | 1 | 0 | 5 | 21 | 6 | 21 | .250 | .375 |
| Sasser,Mackey | L | .204 | 54 | 11 | 3 | 0 | 1 | 7 | 3 | 10 | .246 | .315 | .333 | 216 | 72 | 11 | 0 | 5 | 34 | 12 | 9 | .368 | .454 |
| Sax,Steve | R | .249 | 177 | 44 | 7 | 1 | 0 | 11 | 20 | 10 | .325 | .299 | .265 | 438 | 116 | 17 | 1 | 4 | 31 | 29 | 36 | .312 | .336 |
| Schaefer,Jeff | R | .290 | 31 | 9 | 1 | 0 | 0 | 2 | 2 | 3 | .324 | .323 | .171 | 76 | 13 | 2 | 0 | 0 | 4 | 1 | 8 | .203 | .197 |
| Schofield,Dick | R | .281 | 89 | 25 | 2 | 0 | 1 | 6 | 18 | 14 | .404 | .337 | .244 | 221 | 54 | 6 | 1 | 0 | 12 | 34 | 47 | .346 | .281 |
| Schroeder,Bill | R | .300 | 20 | 6 | 0 | 0 | 3 | 6 | 0 | 3 | .300 | .750 | .184 | 38 | 7 | 3 | 0 | 1 | 3 | 1 | 7 | .205 | .342 |

# Batters vs. Left-Handed and Right-Handed Pitchers

| | | vs. Left-Handed Pitchers | | | | | | | | | | | vs. Right-Handed Pitchers | | | | | | | | | | |
|---|---|---|---|---|---|---|---|---|---|---|---|---|---|---|---|---|---|---|---|---|---|---|---|
| Batter | | Avg | AB | H | 2B | 3B | HR | RBI | BB | SO | OBP | SLG | Avg | AB | H | 2B | 3B | HR | RBI | BB | SO | OBP | SLG |
| Schu,Rick | R | .265 | 83 | 22 | 4 | 0 | 5 | 9 | 5 | 11 | .303 | .494 | .270 | 74 | 20 | 4 | 0 | 1 | 5 | 6 | 14 | .325 | .365 |
| Schulz,Jeff | L | .250 | 4 | 1 | 0 | 0 | 0 | 0 | 0 | 2 | .250 | .250 | .258 | 62 | 16 | 5 | 1 | 0 | 6 | 6 | 11 | .324 | .371 |
| Sciosda,Mike | L | .235 | 119 | 28 | 5 | 0 | 2 | 18 | 10 | 11 | .295 | .328 | .275 | 316 | 87 | 20 | 0 | 10 | 48 | 45 | 20 | .367 | .434 |
| Segui,David | B | .250 | 40 | 10 | 4 | 0 | 1 | 6 | 1 | 5 | .268 | .425 | .241 | 83 | 20 | 3 | 0 | 1 | 9 | 10 | 10 | .330 | .313 |
| Seitzer,Kevin | R | .278 | 209 | 58 | 17 | 4 | 4 | 23 | 22 | 22 | .345 | .455 | .274 | 413 | 113 | 14 | 1 | 2 | 15 | 45 | 44 | .347 | .327 |
| Sharperson,Mike | R | .322 | 208 | 67 | 8 | 1 | 1 | 17 | 25 | 23 | .396 | .385 | .262 | 149 | 39 | 6 | 1 | 2 | 19 | 21 | 16 | .349 | .356 |
| Sheets,Larry | L | .235 | 17 | 4 | 0 | 0 | 0 | 1 | 1 | 3 | .278 | .235 | .262 | 343 | 90 | 17 | 2 | 10 | 51 | 23 | 39 | .309 | .411 |
| Sheffield,Gary | R | .274 | 135 | 37 | 12 | 1 | 3 | 18 | 14 | 15 | .338 | .444 | .301 | 352 | 106 | 18 | 0 | 7 | 49 | 30 | 26 | .355 | .412 |
| Shelby,John | B | .179 | 78 | 14 | 2 | 1 | 2 | 6 | 3 | 21 | .210 | .308 | .280 | 168 | 47 | 8 | 2 | 2 | 16 | 7 | 37 | .309 | .387 |
| Shumpert,Terry | R | .367 | 30 | 11 | 3 | 0 | 0 | 3 | 0 | 3 | .355 | .467 | .230 | 61 | 14 | 3 | 1 | 0 | 5 | 2 | 14 | .262 | .311 |
| Sierra,Ruben | B | .324 | 216 | 70 | 16 | 0 | 3 | 31 | 14 | 25 | .361 | .440 | .255 | 392 | 100 | 21 | 2 | 13 | 65 | 35 | 61 | .314 | .418 |
| Simms,Mike | R | .286 | 7 | 2 | 1 | 0 | 1 | 1 | 0 | 3 | .286 | .857 | .333 | 6 | 2 | 0 | 0 | 0 | 1 | 0 | 1 | .333 | .333 |
| Sinatro,Matt | R | .300 | 30 | 9 | 0 | 0 | 0 | 1 | 3 | 4 | .364 | .300 | .300 | 20 | 6 | 1 | 0 | 0 | 3 | 1 | 6 | .333 | .350 |
| Skinner,Joel | R | .234 | 47 | 11 | 2 | 0 | 0 | 4 | 2 | 16 | .265 | .277 | .261 | 92 | 24 | 2 | 1 | 2 | 12 | 5 | 28 | .299 | .370 |
| Slaught,Don | R | .317 | 164 | 52 | 13 | 2 | 2 | 17 | 22 | 20 | .393 | .457 | .258 | 66 | 17 | 5 | 1 | 2 | 12 | 5 | 7 | .329 | .455 |
| Smith,Dwight | L | .222 | 36 | 8 | 2 | 0 | 1 | 3 | 1 | 11 | .263 | .361 | .268 | 254 | 68 | 13 | 0 | 5 | 24 | 27 | 35 | .338 | .378 |
| Smith,Greg | B | .125 | 8 | 1 | 0 | 0 | 0 | 0 | 0 | 2 | .125 | .125 | .222 | 36 | 8 | 2 | 1 | 0 | 5 | 2 | 3 | .256 | .333 |
| Smith,Lonnie | R | .294 | 197 | 58 | 14 | 3 | 6 | 18 | 21 | 22 | .365 | .487 | .312 | 269 | 84 | 13 | 6 | 3 | 24 | 37 | 47 | .397 | .439 |
| Smith,Ozzie | B | .289 | 201 | 58 | 12 | 1 | 1 | 23 | 21 | 11 | .350 | .373 | .232 | 311 | 72 | 9 | 0 | 0 | 27 | 40 | 22 | .318 | .260 |
| Snyder,Cory | R | .222 | 135 | 30 | 6 | 1 | 4 | 14 | 12 | 36 | .291 | .370 | .238 | 303 | 72 | 21 | 2 | 10 | 41 | 9 | 82 | .256 | .419 |
| Sojo,Luis | R | .222 | 36 | 8 | 2 | 0 | 0 | 2 | 3 | 3 | .282 | .278 | .227 | 44 | 10 | 1 | 0 | 1 | 7 | 2 | 2 | .261 | .318 |
| Sorrento,Paul | L | .000 | 3 | 0 | 0 | 0 | 0 | 0 | 2 | 2 | .400 | .000 | .212 | 118 | 25 | 4 | 1 | 5 | 13 | 10 | 29 | .277 | .390 |
| Sosa,Sammy | R | .262 | 233 | 61 | 14 | 3 | 12 | 37 | 20 | 59 | .316 | .502 | .211 | 299 | 63 | 12 | 7 | 3 | 33 | 13 | 91 | .255 | .328 |
| Spiers,Bill | L | .235 | 81 | 19 | 3 | 1 | 0 | 7 | 5 | 13 | .279 | .296 | .245 | 282 | 69 | 12 | 2 | 2 | 29 | 11 | 32 | .273 | .323 |
| Springer,Steve | R | .400 | 5 | 2 | 0 | 0 | 0 | 0 | 0 | 1 | .400 | .400 | .000 | 7 | 0 | 0 | 0 | 0 | 1 | 0 | 5 | .000 | .000 |
| Stanley,Mike | R | .277 | 137 | 38 | 6 | 1 | 2 | 17 | 24 | 18 | .385 | .380 | .173 | 52 | 9 | 2 | 0 | 0 | 2 | 6 | 7 | .254 | .212 |
| Stark,Matt | R | .286 | 14 | 4 | 1 | 0 | 0 | 3 | 1 | 5 | .333 | .357 | .000 | 2 | 0 | 0 | 0 | 0 | 0 | 0 | 1 | .000 | .000 |
| Steinbach,Terry | R | .284 | 109 | 31 | 6 | 1 | 3 | 16 | 8 | 15 | .336 | .440 | .237 | 270 | 64 | 9 | 1 | 6 | 41 | 11 | 51 | .273 | .344 |
| Stephens,Ray | R | .143 | 7 | 1 | 0 | 0 | 1 | 1 | 0 | 2 | .143 | .571 | .125 | 8 | 1 | 1 | 0 | 0 | 0 | 0 | 1 | .125 | .250 |
| Stephenson,Phil | L | .250 | 32 | 8 | 3 | 1 | 0 | 5 | 4 | 9 | .333 | .406 | .200 | 150 | 30 | 6 | 0 | 4 | 14 | 26 | 34 | .316 | .320 |
| Stevens,Lee | L | .204 | 54 | 11 | 1 | 0 | 1 | 9 | 5 | 19 | .267 | .278 | .216 | 194 | 42 | 9 | 0 | 6 | 23 | 17 | 56 | .277 | .356 |
| Stillwell,Kurt | B | .211 | 128 | 27 | 9 | 2 | 0 | 20 | 17 | 15 | .302 | .313 | .262 | 378 | 99 | 26 | 2 | 3 | 31 | 22 | 45 | .305 | .365 |
| Stone,Jeff | L | .000 | 0 | 0 | 0 | 0 | 0 | 0 | 0 | 0 | .000 | .000 | .500 | 2 | 1 | 0 | 0 | 0 | 1 | 0 | 1 | .500 | .500 |
| Strawberry,Darryl | L | .248 | 218 | 54 | 8 | 0 | 9 | 29 | 17 | 51 | .303 | .408 | .296 | 324 | 96 | 10 | 1 | 28 | 79 | 53 | 59 | .397 | .593 |
| Stubbs,Franklin | L | .258 | 159 | 41 | 10 | 1 | 7 | 23 | 10 | 41 | .300 | .465 | .263 | 289 | 76 | 13 | 1 | 16 | 48 | 38 | 73 | .352 | .481 |
| Surhoff,B.J. | L | .317 | 104 | 33 | 4 | 1 | 2 | 17 | 8 | 9 | .353 | .433 | .265 | 370 | 98 | 17 | 3 | 4 | 42 | 33 | 28 | .324 | .359 |
| Sutko,Glenn | R | .000 | 1 | 0 | 0 | 0 | 0 | 0 | 0 | 1 | .000 | .000 | .000 | 0 | 0 | 0 | 0 | 0 | 0 | 0 | 0 | .000 | .000 |
| Sveum,Dale | B | .190 | 58 | 11 | 4 | 0 | 1 | 3 | 2 | 16 | .226 | .310 | .203 | 59 | 12 | 3 | 0 | 0 | 9 | 10 | 14 | .324 | .254 |
| Tabler,Pat | R | .333 | 105 | 35 | 7 | 1 | 1 | 14 | 11 | 13 | .393 | .448 | .226 | 133 | 30 | 8 | 0 | 1 | 15 | 12 | 16 | .295 | .308 |
| Tartabull,Danny | R | .321 | 106 | 34 | 5 | 0 | 5 | 17 | 21 | 28 | .426 | .509 | .242 | 207 | 50 | 14 | 0 | 10 | 43 | 15 | 65 | .291 | .454 |
| Templeton,Garry | B | .254 | 189 | 48 | 8 | 1 | 4 | 29 | 9 | 21 | .286 | .370 | .244 | 316 | 77 | 17 | 2 | 5 | 30 | 15 | 38 | .275 | .358 |
| Tettleton,Mickey | B | .234 | 128 | 30 | 8 | 0 | 5 | 18 | 24 | 50 | .351 | .414 | .218 | 316 | 69 | 13 | 2 | 10 | 33 | 82 | 110 | .385 | .367 |
| Teufel,Tim | R | .241 | 108 | 26 | 7 | 0 | 5 | 10 | 12 | 16 | .317 | .444 | .254 | 67 | 17 | 4 | 0 | 5 | 14 | 3 | 17 | .282 | .537 |
| Thomas,Andres | R | .225 | 102 | 23 | 2 | 0 | 4 | 15 | 5 | 15 | .259 | .363 | .216 | 176 | 38 | 6 | 0 | 1 | 15 | 6 | 28 | .242 | .267 |
| Thomas,Frank | R | .408 | 71 | 29 | 6 | 1 | 5 | 12 | 21 | 17 | .538 | .732 | .283 | 120 | 34 | 5 | 2 | 2 | 19 | 23 | 37 | .401 | .408 |
| Thompson,Milt | L | .175 | 120 | 21 | 3 | 2 | 0 | 4 | 5 | 26 | .227 | .233 | .235 | 298 | 70 | 11 | 5 | 6 | 26 | 34 | 34 | .317 | .366 |
| Thompson,Robbie | R | .273 | 183 | 50 | 11 | 1 | 8 | 27 | 13 | 34 | .325 | .475 | .229 | 315 | 72 | 11 | 2 | 7 | 29 | 21 | 62 | .284 | .343 |
| Thon,Dickie | R | .262 | 202 | 53 | 9 | 1 | 5 | 21 | 14 | 25 | .310 | .391 | .251 | 350 | 88 | 11 | 3 | 3 | 27 | 23 | 52 | .302 | .326 |
| Thornton,Lou | L | .000 | 0 | 0 | 0 | 0 | 0 | 0 | 0 | 0 | .000 | .000 | .000 | 0 | 0 | 0 | 0 | 0 | 0 | 0 | 0 | .000 | .000 |
| Thurman,Gary | R | .364 | 33 | 12 | 3 | 0 | 0 | 3 | 1 | 5 | .382 | .455 | .074 | 27 | 2 | 0 | 0 | 0 | 0 | 1 | 7 | .107 | .074 |

# Batters vs. Left-Handed and Right-Handed Pitchers

| | | vs. Left-Handed Pitchers | | | | | | | | | | | vs. Right-Handed Pitchers | | | | | | | | | | |
|---|---|---|---|---|---|---|---|---|---|---|---|---|---|---|---|---|---|---|---|---|---|---|---|
| Batter | | Avg | AB | H | 2B | 3B | HR | RBI | BB | SO | OBP | SLG | Avg | AB | H | 2B | 3B | HR | RBI | BB | SO | OBP | SLG |
| Tingley,Ron | R | .000 | 1 | 0 | 0 | 0 | 0 | 0 | 1 | 0 | .500 | .000 | .000 | 2 | 0 | 0 | 0 | 0 | 0 | 0 | 1 | .000 | .000 |
| Tolleson,Wayne | B | .167 | 12 | 2 | 0 | 0 | 0 | 2 | 0 | 4 | .167 | .167 | .145 | 62 | 9 | 1 | 1 | 0 | 2 | 6 | 17 | .217 | .194 |
| Torve,Kelvin | L | .500 | 2 | 1 | 1 | 0 | 0 | 0 | 2 | 0 | .750 | 1.000 | .278 | 36 | 10 | 3 | 0 | 0 | 2 | 2 | 9 | .350 | .361 |
| Trammell,Alan | R | .289 | 173 | 50 | 11 | 1 | 7 | 27 | 23 | 14 | .367 | .486 | .311 | 386 | 120 | 26 | 0 | 7 | 62 | 45 | 41 | .382 | .433 |
| Traxler,Brian | L | .000 | 0 | 0 | 0 | 0 | 0 | 0 | 0 | 0 | .000 | .000 | .091 | 11 | 1 | 1 | 0 | 0 | 0 | 0 | 4 | .091 | .182 |
| Treadway,Jeff | L | .303 | 119 | 36 | 5 | 0 | 4 | 20 | 10 | 10 | .359 | .445 | .276 | 355 | 98 | 15 | 2 | 7 | 39 | 15 | 32 | .307 | .389 |
| Trevino,Alex | R | .267 | 60 | 16 | 4 | 0 | 1 | 10 | 6 | 6 | .357 | .383 | .115 | 26 | 3 | 1 | 0 | 0 | 3 | 1 | 5 | .138 | .154 |
| Uribe,Jose | B | .282 | 142 | 40 | 4 | 1 | 0 | 7 | 9 | 13 | .325 | .324 | .231 | 273 | 63 | 4 | 5 | 1 | 17 | 20 | 36 | .283 | .293 |
| Valle,Dave | R | .202 | 104 | 21 | 4 | 0 | 2 | 10 | 14 | 17 | .308 | .298 | .221 | 204 | 45 | 11 | 0 | 5 | 23 | 31 | 31 | .338 | .348 |
| Van Slyke,Andy | L | .261 | 188 | 49 | 3 | 2 | 5 | 28 | 26 | 35 | .349 | .378 | .298 | 305 | 91 | 23 | 4 | 12 | 49 | 40 | 54 | .378 | .518 |
| Varsho,Gary | L | .000 | 2 | 0 | 0 | 0 | 0 | 0 | 0 | 1 | .000 | .000 | .261 | 46 | 12 | 4 | 0 | 0 | 1 | 1 | 5 | .277 | .348 |
| Vatcher,Jim | R | .294 | 51 | 15 | 2 | 1 | 1 | 5 | 4 | 11 | .345 | .431 | .182 | 22 | 4 | 0 | 0 | 0 | 2 | 1 | 4 | .217 | .182 |
| Vaughn,Greg | R | .197 | 127 | 25 | 10 | 1 | 4 | 12 | 10 | 29 | .254 | .386 | .231 | 255 | 59 | 16 | 1 | 13 | 49 | 23 | 62 | .292 | .455 |
| Velarde,Randy | R | .277 | 65 | 18 | 2 | 1 | 1 | 2 | 4 | 15 | .314 | .385 | .183 | 164 | 30 | 4 | 1 | 4 | 17 | 16 | 38 | .260 | .293 |
| Venable,Max | L | .240 | 25 | 6 | 2 | 0 | 0 | 4 | 3 | 6 | .321 | .320 | .262 | 164 | 43 | 7 | 3 | 4 | 17 | 21 | 25 | .342 | .415 |
| Ventura,Robin | L | .221 | 154 | 34 | 2 | 1 | 0 | 12 | 22 | 26 | .315 | .247 | .263 | 339 | 89 | 15 | 0 | 5 | 42 | 33 | 27 | .329 | .351 |
| Villanueva,Hector | R | .254 | 63 | 16 | 2 | 1 | 6 | 14 | 3 | 14 | .288 | .603 | .294 | 51 | 15 | 2 | 0 | 1 | 4 | 1 | 13 | .333 | .392 |
| Virgil,Ozzie | R | .000 | 4 | 0 | 0 | 0 | 0 | 0 | 0 | 2 | .000 | .000 | .000 | 1 | 0 | 0 | 0 | 0 | 0 | 0 | 1 | .000 | .000 |
| Vizcaino,Jose | B | .368 | 19 | 7 | 0 | 0 | 0 | 1 | 4 | 2 | .478 | .368 | .219 | 32 | 7 | 1 | 1 | 0 | 1 | 0 | 6 | .219 | .313 |
| Vizquel,Omar | B | .235 | 81 | 19 | 2 | 0 | 1 | 8 | 5 | 8 | .279 | .296 | .253 | 174 | 44 | 1 | 2 | 1 | 10 | 13 | 14 | .302 | .299 |
| Walewander,Jim | B | .000 | 0 | 0 | 0 | 0 | 0 | 0 | 0 | 0 | .000 | .000 | .200 | 5 | 1 | 1 | 0 | 0 | 1 | 0 | 0 | .200 | .400 |
| Walker,Greg | L | .000 | 3 | 0 | 0 | 0 | 0 | 0 | 0 | 2 | .000 | .000 | .167 | 36 | 6 | 0 | 0 | 0 | 2 | 3 | 9 | .250 | .167 |
| Walker,Larry | L | .207 | 116 | 24 | 6 | 0 | 6 | 18 | 8 | 30 | .264 | .414 | .254 | 303 | 77 | 12 | 3 | 13 | 33 | 41 | 82 | .349 | .442 |
| Wallach,Tim | R | .289 | 204 | 59 | 12 | 2 | 6 | 29 | 21 | 23 | .355 | .456 | .299 | 422 | 126 | 25 | 3 | 15 | 69 | 21 | 57 | .331 | .479 |
| Walling,Denny | L | .000 | 7 | 0 | 0 | 0 | 0 | 0 | 0 | 1 | .000 | .000 | .233 | 120 | 28 | 5 | 0 | 1 | 19 | 8 | 14 | .279 | .300 |
| Walton,Jerome | R | .288 | 146 | 42 | 7 | 1 | 1 | 12 | 19 | 20 | .369 | .370 | .248 | 246 | 61 | 9 | 1 | 1 | 9 | 31 | 50 | .339 | .305 |
| Ward,Gary | R | .257 | 152 | 39 | 6 | 2 | 5 | 20 | 14 | 22 | .315 | .421 | .255 | 157 | 40 | 5 | 0 | 4 | 26 | 16 | 28 | .328 | .363 |
| Ward,Turner | B | .333 | 12 | 4 | 0 | 0 | 0 | 1 | 0 | 1 | .333 | .333 | .353 | 34 | 12 | 2 | 1 | 1 | 9 | 3 | 7 | .405 | .559 |
| Washington,Claudell | L | .333 | 12 | 4 | 0 | 0 | 0 | 2 | 0 | 3 | .308 | .333 | .147 | 102 | 15 | 2 | 1 | 1 | 7 | 4 | 22 | .179 | .216 |
| Webster,Lenny | R | .000 | 1 | 0 | 0 | 0 | 0 | 0 | 1 | 0 | .500 | .000 | .400 | 5 | 2 | 1 | 0 | 0 | 0 | 0 | 1 | .400 | .600 |
| Webster,Mitch | B | .292 | 192 | 56 | 11 | 2 | 8 | 33 | 7 | 14 | .320 | .495 | .220 | 245 | 54 | 9 | 4 | 4 | 22 | 13 | 47 | .259 | .339 |
| Weiss,Walt | B | .261 | 115 | 30 | 5 | 0 | 0 | 12 | 8 | 10 | .306 | .304 | .267 | 330 | 88 | 12 | 1 | 2 | 23 | 38 | 43 | .347 | .327 |
| Whitaker,Lou | L | .162 | 99 | 16 | 1 | 1 | 2 | 7 | 16 | 19 | .278 | .253 | .257 | 373 | 96 | 21 | 1 | 16 | 53 | 58 | 52 | .353 | .448 |
| White,Devon | B | .246 | 130 | 32 | 5 | 0 | 3 | 10 | 12 | 22 | .315 | .354 | .204 | 313 | 64 | 12 | 3 | 8 | 34 | 32 | 94 | .280 | .339 |
| White,Frank | R | .194 | 93 | 18 | 5 | 0 | 1 | 6 | 6 | 15 | .240 | .280 | .230 | 148 | 34 | 9 | 1 | 1 | 15 | 4 | 17 | .261 | .324 |
| Whiten,Mark | B | .316 | 38 | 12 | 1 | 1 | 1 | 4 | 3 | 9 | .357 | .474 | .240 | 50 | 12 | 0 | 0 | 1 | 3 | 4 | 5 | .296 | .300 |
| Whitt,Ernie | L | .118 | 17 | 2 | 0 | 0 | 0 | 2 | 1 | 5 | .167 | .118 | .178 | 163 | 29 | 8 | 0 | 2 | 8 | 22 | 22 | .274 | .264 |
| Wilkerson,Curt | B | .241 | 58 | 14 | 1 | 1 | 0 | 7 | 3 | 11 | .279 | .293 | .211 | 128 | 27 | 4 | 0 | 0 | 9 | 4 | 25 | .235 | .242 |
| Willard,Jerry | L | .000 | 0 | 0 | 0 | 0 | 0 | 0 | 0 | 0 | .000 | .000 | .000 | 3 | 0 | 0 | 0 | 0 | 0 | 0 | 2 | .000 | .000 |
| Williams,Eddie | R | .321 | 28 | 9 | 3 | 0 | 2 | 2 | 5 | 4 | .424 | .643 | .214 | 14 | 3 | 0 | 0 | 1 | 2 | 0 | 2 | .214 | .429 |
| Williams,Ken | R | .186 | 113 | 21 | 7 | 1 | 0 | 12 | 8 | 28 | .242 | .265 | .095 | 42 | 4 | 1 | 0 | 0 | 1 | 2 | 14 | .156 | .119 |
| Williams,Matt D. | R | .284 | 208 | 59 | 9 | 0 | 12 | 48 | 13 | 40 | .332 | .500 | .274 | 409 | 112 | 18 | 2 | 21 | 74 | 20 | 98 | .312 | .482 |
| Wilson,Craig | R | .264 | 72 | 19 | 1 | 0 | 0 | 7 | 6 | 8 | .313 | .278 | .224 | 49 | 11 | 1 | 0 | 0 | 0 | 2 | 6 | .255 | .245 |
| Wilson,Glenn | R | .262 | 164 | 43 | 10 | 0 | 2 | 25 | 13 | 27 | .311 | .360 | .230 | 204 | 47 | 4 | 0 | 8 | 30 | 13 | 37 | .279 | .368 |
| Wilson,Mookie | B | .245 | 188 | 46 | 10 | 2 | 2 | 21 | 14 | 36 | .294 | .351 | .275 | 400 | 110 | 26 | 2 | 1 | 30 | 17 | 66 | .303 | .358 |
| Wilson,Willie | B | .272 | 103 | 28 | 6 | 1 | 0 | 17 | 5 | 19 | .306 | .350 | .299 | 204 | 61 | 7 | 2 | 2 | 25 | 25 | 38 | .377 | .382 |
| Winfield,Dave | R | .288 | 156 | 45 | 9 | 2 | 5 | 32 | 20 | 22 | .365 | .468 | .257 | 319 | 82 | 12 | 0 | 16 | 46 | 32 | 59 | .324 | .445 |
| Winningham,Herm | L | .143 | 28 | 4 | 1 | 0 | 1 | 3 | 0 | 6 | .138 | .286 | .280 | 132 | 37 | 7 | 5 | 2 | 14 | 14 | 25 | .349 | .455 |
| Worthington,Craig | R | .254 | 126 | 32 | 7 | 0 | 2 | 12 | 27 | 21 | .387 | .357 | .214 | 299 | 64 | 10 | 0 | 6 | 32 | 36 | 75 | .301 | .308 |
| Wrona,Rick | R | .200 | 15 | 3 | 0 | 0 | 0 | 0 | 2 | 6 | .294 | .200 | .143 | 14 | 2 | 0 | 0 | 0 | 0 | 0 | 5 | .143 | .143 |

# **Batters** vs. Left-Handed and Right-Handed Pitchers

| Batter | | vs. Left-Handed Pitchers | | | | | | | | | | | vs. Right-Handed Pitchers | | | | | | | | | | |
|---|---|---|---|---|---|---|---|---|---|---|---|---|---|---|---|---|---|---|---|---|---|---|---|
| | | Avg | AB | H | 2B | 3B | HR | RBI | BB | SO | OBP | SLG | Avg | AB | H | 2B | 3B | HR | RBI | BB | SO | OBP | SLG |
| Wynne,Marvell | L | .176 | 17 | 3 | 0 | 0 | 1 | 2 | 2 | 2 | .263 | .353 | .207 | 169 | 35 | 8 | 2 | 3 | 17 | 12 | 23 | .264 | .331 |
| Yelding,Eric | R | .281 | 235 | 66 | 6 | 3 | 0 | 16 | 16 | 31 | .324 | .332 | .232 | 276 | 64 | 3 | 2 | 1 | 12 | 23 | 56 | .288 | .268 |
| Young,Gerald | B | .174 | 46 | 8 | 2 | 1 | 1 | 4 | 6 | 11 | .264 | .326 | .176 | 108 | 19 | 2 | 0 | 0 | 0 | 14 | 12 | .270 | .194 |
| Yount,Robin | R | .269 | 156 | 42 | 5 | 1 | 5 | 20 | 23 | 27 | .359 | .410 | .239 | 431 | 103 | 12 | 4 | 12 | 57 | 55 | 62 | .329 | .369 |
| Zeile,Todd | R | .266 | 173 | 46 | 12 | 1 | 6 | 22 | 21 | 21 | .347 | .451 | .233 | 322 | 75 | 13 | 2 | 9 | 35 | 46 | 56 | .326 | .370 |

# **Pitchers** vs. Left-Handed and Right-Handed Batters

| | | vs. Left-Handed Batters | | | | | | | | | | | vs. Right-Handed Batters | | | | | | | | | | |
|---|---|---|---|---|---|---|---|---|---|---|---|---|---|---|---|---|---|---|---|---|---|---|---|
| Pitcher | | Avg | AB | H | 2B | 3B | HR | RBI | BB | SO | OBP | SLG | Avg | AB | H | 2B | 3B | HR | RBI | BB | SO | OBP | SLG |
| Aase,Don | R | .197 | 76 | 15 | 1 | 0 | 3 | 7 | 10 | 14 | .291 | .329 | .273 | 66 | 18 | 2 | 1 | 2 | 13 | 9 | 10 | .360 | .424 |
| Abbott,Jim | L | .318 | 110 | 35 | 4 | 0 | 3 | 20 | 15 | 20 | .398 | .436 | .292 | 723 | 211 | 32 | 2 | 13 | 76 | 57 | 85 | .345 | .396 |
| Abbott,Paul | R | .237 | 76 | 18 | 1 | 1 | 0 | 10 | 19 | 18 | .392 | .276 | .345 | 55 | 19 | 8 | 1 | 0 | 7 | 9 | 7 | .438 | .527 |
| Acker,Jim | R | .289 | 149 | 43 | 10 | 1 | 2 | 16 | 14 | 13 | .355 | .409 | .276 | 217 | 60 | 11 | 0 | 7 | 37 | 16 | 41 | .329 | .424 |
| Adkins,Steve | L | .125 | 16 | 2 | 0 | 0 | 0 | 1 | 7 | 5 | .391 | .125 | .250 | 68 | 17 | 4 | 2 | 4 | 13 | 22 | 9 | .429 | .544 |
| Agosto,Juan | L | .227 | 110 | 25 | 3 | 0 | 1 | 15 | 7 | 24 | .303 | .282 | .276 | 239 | 66 | 12 | 2 | 3 | 24 | 32 | 26 | .364 | .381 |
| Aguilera,Rick | R | .219 | 114 | 25 | 2 | 0 | 0 | 5 | 12 | 29 | .299 | .237 | .229 | 131 | 30 | 7 | 0 | 5 | 21 | 7 | 32 | .284 | .397 |
| Akerfelds,Darrel | R | .195 | 159 | 31 | 7 | 1 | 7 | 30 | 25 | 19 | .300 | .384 | .206 | 165 | 34 | 6 | 1 | 3 | 18 | 29 | 23 | .332 | .309 |
| Aldred,Scott | L | .444 | 9 | 4 | 0 | 0 | 0 | 1 | 1 | 0 | .500 | .444 | .225 | 40 | 9 | 2 | 0 | 0 | 4 | 9 | 7 | .373 | .275 |
| Aldrich,Jay | R | .320 | 25 | 8 | 0 | 0 | 1 | 7 | 6 | 2 | .452 | .440 | .333 | 27 | 9 | 1 | 0 | 0 | 5 | 1 | 3 | .357 | .370 |
| Alexander,Gerald | R | .353 | 17 | 6 | 0 | 0 | 0 | 3 | 3 | 6 | .455 | .353 | .533 | 15 | 8 | 1 | 1 | 0 | 3 | 2 | 2 | .588 | .733 |
| Andersen,Larry | R | .280 | 168 | 47 | 4 | 1 | 2 | 23 | 17 | 26 | .347 | .351 | .178 | 180 | 32 | 4 | 0 | 0 | 15 | 10 | 67 | .219 | .200 |
| Anderson,Allan | L | .257 | 109 | 28 | 2 | 0 | 2 | 13 | 7 | 11 | .297 | .330 | .294 | 632 | 186 | 39 | 3 | 18 | 84 | 32 | 71 | .330 | .451 |
| Anderson,Scott | R | .189 | 37 | 7 | 1 | 1 | 1 | 4 | 4 | 8 | .262 | .351 | .185 | 27 | 5 | 4 | 0 | 0 | 4 | 1 | 8 | .214 | .333 |
| Appier,Kevin | R | .260 | 311 | 81 | 9 | 1 | 7 | 32 | 35 | 50 | .331 | .363 | .246 | 399 | 98 | 8 | 0 | 6 | 27 | 19 | 77 | .286 | .311 |
| Aquino,Luis | R | .241 | 116 | 28 | 7 | 0 | 3 | 13 | 16 | 17 | .346 | .379 | .233 | 133 | 31 | 7 | 0 | 3 | 14 | 11 | 11 | .295 | .353 |
| Armstrong,Jack | R | .256 | 386 | 99 | 21 | 4 | 6 | 46 | 40 | 51 | .327 | .378 | .218 | 238 | 52 | 9 | 2 | 3 | 18 | 19 | 59 | .285 | .311 |
| Arnsberg,Brad | R | .225 | 89 | 20 | 4 | 0 | 2 | 12 | 10 | 12 | .310 | .337 | .242 | 149 | 36 | 7 | 0 | 2 | 17 | 23 | 32 | .343 | .329 |
| Assenmacher,Paul | L | .223 | 121 | 27 | 2 | 1 | 1 | 19 | 6 | 30 | .262 | .281 | .247 | 255 | 63 | 6 | 1 | 9 | 23 | 30 | 65 | .325 | .384 |
| August,Don | R | .200 | 20 | 4 | 3 | 0 | 0 | 2 | 1 | 0 | .238 | .350 | .375 | 24 | 9 | 0 | 1 | 0 | 3 | 4 | 2 | .464 | .458 |
| Avery,Steve | L | .262 | 61 | 16 | 1 | 1 | 0 | 12 | 5 | 19 | .318 | .311 | .309 | 340 | 105 | 24 | 2 | 7 | 55 | 40 | 56 | .381 | .453 |
| Bailes,Scott | L | .286 | 49 | 14 | 1 | 0 | 1 | 10 | 5 | 6 | .345 | .367 | .330 | 97 | 32 | 2 | 2 | 7 | 19 | 15 | 10 | .412 | .608 |
| Bair,Doug | R | .333 | 45 | 15 | 2 | 1 | 1 | 6 | 4 | 7 | .388 | .489 | .283 | 53 | 15 | 3 | 0 | 2 | 6 | 7 | 12 | .367 | .453 |
| Ballard,Jeff | L | .294 | 136 | 40 | 4 | 0 | 4 | 15 | 9 | 23 | .342 | .412 | .287 | 390 | 112 | 30 | 0 | 18 | 52 | 33 | 27 | .344 | .503 |
| Baller,Jay | R | .400 | 5 | 2 | 1 | 0 | 0 | 2 | 2 | 0 | .571 | .600 | .333 | 6 | 2 | 0 | 0 | 1 | 3 | 0 | 1 | .429 | .833 |
| Bankhead,Scott | R | .250 | 28 | 7 | 2 | 0 | 0 | 7 | 0 | 7 | .241 | .321 | .423 | 26 | 11 | 2 | 1 | 2 | 4 | 7 | 3 | .529 | .808 |
| Barfield,John | L | .340 | 47 | 16 | 2 | 0 | 0 | 5 | 4 | 4 | .404 | .383 | .236 | 110 | 26 | 6 | 1 | 2 | 23 | 9 | 13 | .285 | .364 |
| Barnes,Brian | L | .238 | 21 | 5 | 1 | 0 | 2 | 3 | 0 | 2 | .238 | .571 | .235 | 85 | 20 | 2 | 0 | 0 | 6 | 7 | 21 | .293 | .259 |
| Bautista,Jose | R | .405 | 37 | 15 | 3 | 2 | 4 | 11 | 3 | 1 | .450 | .919 | .197 | 66 | 13 | 1 | 1 | 0 | 7 | 4 | 14 | .239 | .242 |
| Bearse,Kevin | L | .444 | 9 | 4 | 1 | 1 | 0 | 4 | 2 | 0 | .545 | .778 | .414 | 29 | 12 | 3 | 0 | 2 | 7 | 3 | 2 | .500 | .724 |
| Bedrosian,Steve | R | .265 | 170 | 45 | 6 | 1 | 4 | 24 | 26 | 25 | .369 | .382 | .209 | 129 | 27 | 4 | 0 | 2 | 12 | 18 | 18 | .304 | .287 |
| Belcher,Tim | R | .225 | 302 | 68 | 11 | 2 | 8 | 27 | 30 | 58 | .294 | .354 | .258 | 264 | 68 | 8 | 3 | 9 | 40 | 18 | 44 | .305 | .413 |
| Belinda,Stan | R | .176 | 91 | 16 | 5 | 0 | 1 | 10 | 13 | 22 | .274 | .264 | .267 | 120 | 32 | 4 | 2 | 3 | 14 | 16 | 33 | .358 | .408 |
| Benes,Andy | R | .251 | 431 | 108 | 16 | 7 | 9 | 41 | 40 | 68 | .313 | .383 | .231 | 299 | 69 | 8 | 2 | 9 | 30 | 29 | 72 | .297 | .361 |
| Berenguer,Juan | R | .264 | 159 | 42 | 7 | 2 | 3 | 19 | 23 | 34 | .361 | .390 | .207 | 208 | 43 | 4 | 0 | 6 | 21 | 35 | 43 | .321 | .313 |
| Bielecki,Mike | R | .275 | 403 | 111 | 20 | 5 | 8 | 51 | 45 | 62 | .349 | .409 | .307 | 251 | 77 | 15 | 4 | 5 | 36 | 25 | 41 | .375 | .458 |
| Birtsas,Tim | L | .275 | 80 | 22 | 4 | 0 | 3 | 10 | 6 | 19 | .326 | .438 | .356 | 132 | 47 | 9 | 1 | 4 | 17 | 18 | 22 | .434 | .530 |
| Bitker,Joe | R | .207 | 29 | 6 | 1 | 2 | 0 | 2 | 1 | 6 | .233 | .379 | .154 | 13 | 2 | 1 | 0 | 0 | 2 | 3 | 2 | .333 | .231 |
| Black,Bud | L | .283 | 145 | 41 | 4 | 0 | 7 | 20 | 11 | 12 | .327 | .455 | .221 | 633 | 140 | 26 | 2 | 12 | 49 | 50 | 94 | .282 | .325 |
| Blair,Willie | R | .246 | 126 | 31 | 6 | 2 | 2 | 14 | 14 | 18 | .317 | .373 | .254 | 138 | 35 | 9 | 2 | 2 | 18 | 14 | 25 | .323 | .391 |
| Blankenship,Kevin | R | .267 | 30 | 8 | 1 | 1 | 0 | 5 | 5 | 3 | .361 | .367 | .263 | 19 | 5 | 1 | 0 | 1 | 4 | 1 | 2 | .286 | .474 |
| Blyleven,Bert | R | .311 | 270 | 84 | 13 | 3 | 8 | 35 | 14 | 27 | .346 | .470 | .295 | 268 | 79 | 20 | 1 | 7 | 38 | 11 | 42 | .331 | .455 |
| Boddicker,Mike | R | .261 | 464 | 121 | 20 | 4 | 7 | 44 | 33 | 51 | .317 | .366 | .254 | 409 | 104 | 18 | 1 | 9 | 33 | 36 | 92 | .321 | .369 |
| Boever,Joe | R | .182 | 176 | 32 | 7 | 0 | 1 | 24 | 34 | 41 | .314 | .239 | .290 | 155 | 45 | 13 | 0 | 5 | 21 | 17 | 34 | .356 | .471 |
| Bohanon,Brian | L | .200 | 25 | 5 | 0 | 1 | 0 | 4 | 3 | 5 | .276 | .280 | .318 | 110 | 35 | 6 | 0 | 6 | 20 | 15 | 10 | .403 | .536 |
| Bolton,Tom | L | .242 | 99 | 24 | 2 | 0 | 1 | 9 | 6 | 11 | .283 | .293 | .253 | 344 | 87 | 17 | 1 | 5 | 36 | 41 | 54 | .334 | .352 |
| Booker,Greg | R | .429 | 7 | 3 | 1 | 0 | 0 | 2 | 0 | 1 | .429 | .571 | .667 | 6 | 4 | 2 | 0 | 0 | 2 | 0 | 0 | .667 | 1.000 |
| Boone,Dan | L | .200 | 5 | 1 | 0 | 0 | 0 | 1 | 0 | 0 | .200 | .200 | .324 | 34 | 11 | 3 | 0 | 1 | 4 | 3 | 2 | .395 | .500 |
| Bosio,Chris | R | .286 | 273 | 78 | 11 | 4 | 10 | 37 | 19 | 25 | .336 | .465 | .226 | 235 | 53 | 12 | 1 | 5 | 23 | 19 | 51 | .282 | .349 |
| Boskie,Shawn | R | .272 | 213 | 58 | 15 | 2 | 2 | 16 | 28 | 23 | .354 | .390 | .256 | 160 | 41 | 6 | 0 | 6 | 17 | 3 | 26 | .274 | .406 |

# Pitchers vs. Left-Handed and Right-Handed Batters

| Pitcher | | vs. Left-Handed Batters | | | | | | | | | | | vs. Right-Handed Batters | | | | | | | | | | |
|---|---|---|---|---|---|---|---|---|---|---|---|---|---|---|---|---|---|---|---|---|---|---|---|
| | | Avg | AB | H | 2B | 3B | HR | RBI | BB | SO | OBP | SLG | Avg | AB | H | 2B | 3B | HR | RBI | BB | SO | OBP | SLG |
| Boyd,Oil Can | R | .227 | 432 | 98 | 22 | 1 | 10 | 33 | 35 | 67 | .288 | .352 | .244 | 271 | 66 | 17 | 1 | 9 | 27 | 17 | 46 | .287 | .413 |
| Brantley,Jeff | R | .268 | 190 | 51 | 7 | 0 | 1 | 13 | 20 | 29 | .335 | .321 | .198 | 131 | 26 | 1 | 0 | 2 | 9 | 13 | 32 | .286 | .252 |
| Brown,Keith | R | .250 | 20 | 5 | 0 | 0 | 1 | 3 | 2 | 4 | .318 | .400 | .318 | 22 | 7 | 0 | 0 | 1 | 3 | 1 | 4 | .348 | .455 |
| Brown,Kevin | R | .249 | 337 | 84 | 18 | 1 | 6 | 35 | 30 | 47 | .309 | .362 | .261 | 348 | 91 | 16 | 0 | 7 | 36 | 30 | 41 | .321 | .368 |
| Brown,Kevin D. | L | .136 | 22 | 3 | 0 | 0 | 0 | 1 | 2 | 1 | .208 | .136 | .206 | 63 | 13 | 2 | 0 | 1 | 6 | 6 | 11 | .282 | .286 |
| Browning,Tom | L | .253 | 162 | 41 | 8 | 0 | 5 | 15 | 13 | 30 | .309 | .395 | .269 | 720 | 194 | 36 | 6 | 19 | 73 | 39 | 69 | .309 | .415 |
| Burba,Dave | R | .111 | 9 | 1 | 0 | 0 | 0 | 0 | 1 | 2 | .273 | .111 | .333 | 21 | 7 | 0 | 0 | 0 | 2 | 1 | 2 | .364 | .333 |
| Burke,Tim | R | .285 | 144 | 41 | 8 | 0 | 3 | 18 | 10 | 19 | .329 | .403 | .210 | 143 | 30 | 0 | 1 | 3 | 20 | 11 | 28 | .272 | .287 |
| Burkett,John | R | .254 | 464 | 118 | 19 | 1 | 10 | 50 | 36 | 64 | .308 | .364 | .262 | 317 | 83 | 14 | 1 | 8 | 28 | 25 | 54 | .319 | .388 |
| Burns,Todd | R | .268 | 127 | 34 | 6 | 4 | 3 | 13 | 17 | 11 | .354 | .449 | .259 | 170 | 44 | 11 | 0 | 5 | 23 | 15 | 32 | .314 | .412 |
| Cadaret,Greg | L | .252 | 119 | 30 | 5 | 0 | 3 | 15 | 15 | 17 | .333 | .370 | .274 | 328 | 90 | 22 | 5 | 5 | 42 | 49 | 63 | .367 | .418 |
| Camacho,Ernie | R | .250 | 36 | 9 | 2 | 0 | 0 | 7 | 6 | 10 | .341 | .306 | .320 | 25 | 8 | 2 | 0 | 3 | 4 | 3 | 5 | .393 | .760 |
| Campbell,Jim | L | .286 | 7 | 2 | 1 | 0 | 0 | 1 | 0 | 1 | .286 | .429 | .361 | 36 | 13 | 6 | 0 | 1 | 7 | 1 | 1 | .378 | .611 |
| Candelaria,John | L | .253 | 79 | 20 | 4 | 1 | 0 | 7 | 3 | 21 | .274 | .329 | .284 | 236 | 67 | 13 | 2 | 11 | 34 | 17 | 42 | .332 | .496 |
| Candiotti,Tom | R | .256 | 403 | 103 | 13 | 0 | 9 | 38 | 32 | 52 | .311 | .355 | .270 | 385 | 104 | 17 | 0 | 14 | 48 | 23 | 76 | .318 | .423 |
| Capel,Mike | R | 1.000 | 3 | 3 | 0 | 0 | 0 | 1 | 1 | 0 | 1.000 | 1.000 | .750 | 4 | 3 | 1 | 0 | 0 | 2 | 0 | 1 | .800 | 1.000 |
| Carman,Don | L | .175 | 103 | 18 | 3 | 0 | 7 | 22 | 10 | 19 | .250 | .408 | .239 | 213 | 51 | 12 | 1 | 6 | 24 | 28 | 39 | .333 | .390 |
| Carpenter,Cris | R | .167 | 12 | 2 | 0 | 0 | 2 | 3 | 1 | 3 | .231 | .667 | .167 | 18 | 3 | 0 | 0 | 0 | 2 | 1 | 3 | .211 | .167 |
| Cary,Chuck | L | .292 | 113 | 33 | 5 | 2 | 4 | 12 | 10 | 16 | .344 | .478 | .252 | 484 | 122 | 28 | 3 | 17 | 58 | 45 | 118 | .315 | .428 |
| Casian,Larry | L | .333 | 9 | 3 | 0 | 0 | 0 | 1 | 1 | 3 | .364 | .333 | .303 | 76 | 23 | 7 | 0 | 2 | 7 | 3 | 8 | .329 | .474 |
| Castillo,Tony | L | .284 | 95 | 27 | 2 | 0 | 2 | 18 | 6 | 25 | .330 | .368 | .310 | 213 | 66 | 13 | 0 | 3 | 32 | 14 | 39 | .348 | .413 |
| Cerutti,John | L | .277 | 112 | 31 | 5 | 2 | 3 | 14 | 6 | 7 | .317 | .438 | .302 | 434 | 131 | 21 | 3 | 20 | 59 | 43 | 42 | .366 | .502 |
| Charlton,Norm | L | .224 | 116 | 26 | 6 | 0 | 4 | 19 | 17 | 25 | .338 | .379 | .233 | 451 | 105 | 14 | 2 | 6 | 27 | 53 | 92 | .314 | .313 |
| Chiamparino,Scott | R | .219 | 73 | 16 | 2 | 0 | 0 | 6 | 7 | 9 | .288 | .247 | .282 | 71 | 20 | 5 | 0 | 1 | 7 | 5 | 10 | .342 | .394 |
| Chitren,Steve | R | .148 | 27 | 4 | 1 | 0 | 0 | 2 | 2 | 7 | .207 | .185 | .091 | 33 | 3 | 1 | 0 | 0 | 1 | 2 | 12 | .143 | .121 |
| Clancy,Jim | R | .361 | 166 | 60 | 9 | 4 | 1 | 32 | 21 | 14 | .432 | .482 | .276 | 145 | 40 | 9 | 3 | 3 | 26 | 12 | 30 | .335 | .441 |
| Clark,Bryan | L | .316 | 19 | 6 | 1 | 0 | 0 | 3 | 4 | 1 | .435 | .368 | .158 | 19 | 3 | 0 | 0 | 0 | 0 | 6 | 2 | .360 | .158 |
| Clark,Terry | R | .533 | 15 | 8 | 2 | 0 | 0 | 4 | 3 | 1 | .611 | .667 | .167 | 6 | 1 | 0 | 0 | 0 | 1 | 0 | 1 | .167 | .167 |
| Clarke,Stan | L | .200 | 5 | 1 | 1 | 0 | 0 | 1 | 0 | 2 | .200 | .400 | .143 | 7 | 1 | 0 | 0 | 0 | 0 | 0 | 1 | .143 | .143 |
| Clary,Martin | R | .325 | 240 | 78 | 10 | 3 | 7 | 29 | 23 | 19 | .381 | .479 | .284 | 176 | 50 | 11 | 1 | 2 | 22 | 16 | 25 | .342 | .392 |
| Clear,Mark | R | .000 | 4 | 0 | 0 | 0 | 0 | 0 | 3 | 1 | .500 | .000 | .238 | 21 | 5 | 1 | 1 | 0 | 8 | 6 | 5 | .400 | .381 |
| Clemens,Roger | R | .242 | 443 | 107 | 20 | 2 | 7 | 28 | 27 | 97 | .288 | .343 | .213 | 404 | 86 | 15 | 3 | 0 | 18 | 27 | 112 | .267 | .265 |
| Clements,Pat | L | .296 | 27 | 8 | 2 | 1 | 1 | 7 | 3 | 3 | .367 | .556 | .414 | 29 | 12 | 5 | 0 | 0 | 6 | 4 | 3 | .485 | .586 |
| Codiroli,Chris | R | .409 | 22 | 9 | 2 | 0 | 1 | 8 | 15 | 4 | .675 | .636 | .222 | 18 | 4 | 0 | 0 | 0 | 1 | 2 | 4 | .333 | .222 |
| Coffman,Kevin | R | .348 | 46 | 16 | 1 | 3 | 0 | 16 | 13 | 4 | .483 | .500 | .333 | 30 | 10 | 2 | 0 | 0 | 4 | 6 | 5 | .444 | .400 |
| Combs,Pat | L | .259 | 135 | 35 | 3 | 1 | 5 | 20 | 16 | 25 | .338 | .407 | .257 | 561 | 144 | 33 | 4 | 7 | 61 | 70 | 83 | .340 | .367 |
| Comstock,Keith | L | .250 | 72 | 18 | 1 | 0 | 0 | 11 | 8 | 13 | .313 | .264 | .180 | 122 | 22 | 5 | 0 | 4 | 20 | 18 | 37 | .286 | .320 |
| Cone,David | R | .214 | 473 | 101 | 22 | 7 | 14 | 36 | 38 | 128 | .272 | .378 | .244 | 311 | 76 | 9 | 0 | 7 | 33 | 27 | 105 | .301 | .341 |
| Cook,Dennis | L | .296 | 135 | 40 | 8 | 2 | 4 | 20 | 16 | 15 | .373 | .474 | .252 | 456 | 115 | 15 | 1 | 16 | 56 | 40 | 49 | .310 | .395 |
| Corbett,Sherman | L | .500 | 6 | 3 | 1 | 0 | 0 | 1 | 0 | 1 | .429 | .667 | .313 | 16 | 5 | 2 | 0 | 0 | 2 | 3 | 1 | .421 | .438 |
| Costello,John | R | .364 | 22 | 8 | 3 | 0 | 2 | 5 | 2 | 1 | .417 | .773 | .190 | 21 | 4 | 2 | 0 | 1 | 5 | 0 | 1 | .217 | .429 |
| Crawford,Steve | R | .347 | 124 | 43 | 11 | 1 | 3 | 20 | 12 | 11 | .407 | .524 | .193 | 187 | 36 | 5 | 0 | 4 | 23 | 11 | 43 | .241 | .283 |
| Crews,Tim | R | .259 | 220 | 57 | 10 | 3 | 3 | 15 | 11 | 34 | .293 | .373 | .215 | 191 | 41 | 6 | 0 | 6 | 22 | 13 | 42 | .266 | .340 |
| Crim,Chuck | R | .252 | 131 | 33 | 6 | 0 | 1 | 15 | 7 | 16 | .288 | .321 | .267 | 206 | 55 | 6 | 2 | 6 | 26 | 16 | 23 | .322 | .403 |
| Cummings,Steve | R | .545 | 22 | 12 | 1 | 0 | 2 | 3 | 2 | 0 | .583 | .864 | .345 | 29 | 10 | 2 | 0 | 2 | 3 | 3 | 4 | .424 | .621 |
| Darling,Ron | R | .260 | 288 | 75 | 9 | 1 | 9 | 40 | 30 | 56 | .334 | .392 | .290 | 207 | 60 | 9 | 4 | 11 | 27 | 14 | 43 | .339 | .531 |
| Darwin,Danny | R | .264 | 363 | 96 | 22 | 0 | 7 | 24 | 23 | 68 | .312 | .383 | .165 | 242 | 40 | 9 | 0 | 4 | 20 | 8 | 41 | .197 | .252 |
| Davis,John | R | .250 | 16 | 4 | 0 | 0 | 1 | 1 | 2 | 4 | .333 | .438 | .263 | 19 | 5 | 1 | 0 | 0 | 5 | 2 | 3 | .333 | .316 |
| Davis,Mark | L | .200 | 55 | 11 | 3 | 0 | 0 | 7 | 11 | 19 | .362 | .255 | .274 | 219 | 60 | 13 | 1 | 9 | 42 | 41 | 54 | .388 | .466 |
| Davis,Storm | R | .294 | 235 | 69 | 14 | 2 | 4 | 29 | 22 | 32 | .353 | .421 | .268 | 224 | 60 | 13 | 0 | 5 | 26 | 13 | 30 | .305 | .393 |

# **Pitchers** vs. Left-Handed and Right-Handed Batters

| Pitcher | | vs. Left-Handed Batters | | | | | | | | | | | vs. Right-Handed Batters | | | | | | | | | | |
|---|---|---|---|---|---|---|---|---|---|---|---|---|---|---|---|---|---|---|---|---|---|---|---|
| | | Avg | AB | H | 2B | 3B | HR | RBI | BB | SO | OBP | SLG | Avg | AB | H | 2B | 3B | HR | RBI | BB | SO | OBP | SLG |
| Dayley,Ken | L | .283 | 106 | 30 | 3 | 0 | 3 | 15 | 8 | 22 | .330 | .396 | .201 | 164 | 33 | 8 | 1 | 2 | 23 | 22 | 29 | .289 | .299 |
| DeJesus,Jose | R | .190 | 300 | 57 | 9 | 2 | 4 | 20 | 54 | 57 | .315 | .273 | .252 | 159 | 40 | 7 | 0 | 6 | 28 | 19 | 30 | .335 | .409 |
| DeLeon,Jose | R | .286 | 405 | 116 | 22 | 5 | 8 | 56 | 59 | 69 | .376 | .425 | .187 | 278 | 52 | 8 | 0 | 7 | 30 | 27 | 95 | .264 | .291 |
| Delucia,Rich | R | .257 | 70 | 18 | 1 | 2 | 1 | 2 | 5 | 6 | .307 | .371 | .190 | 63 | 12 | 3 | 0 | 1 | 3 | 4 | 14 | .239 | .286 |
| Deshaies,Jim | L | .304 | 115 | 35 | 7 | 2 | 1 | 14 | 23 | 20 | .429 | .426 | .234 | 645 | 151 | 27 | 3 | 20 | 69 | 61 | 99 | .301 | .378 |
| Dewey,Mark | R | .315 | 54 | 17 | 3 | 2 | 1 | 7 | 3 | 2 | .351 | .500 | .161 | 31 | 5 | 0 | 0 | 0 | 1 | 2 | 9 | .212 | .161 |
| Dibble,Rob | R | .185 | 173 | 32 | 7 | 1 | 1 | 19 | 24 | 69 | .282 | .254 | .181 | 166 | 30 | 6 | 0 | 2 | 19 | 10 | 67 | .225 | .253 |
| Dickson,Lance | L | 1.000 | 4 | 4 | 1 | 0 | 2 | 5 | 0 | 0 | 1.000 | 2.750 | .320 | 50 | 16 | 4 | 0 | 0 | 4 | 4 | 4 | .364 | .400 |
| DePino,Frank | L | .293 | 133 | 39 | 5 | 1 | 2 | 18 | 12 | 18 | .349 | .391 | .294 | 180 | 53 | 13 | 2 | 6 | 40 | 19 | 31 | .354 | .489 |
| Dopson,John | R | .148 | 27 | 4 | 0 | 0 | 1 | 4 | 4 | 4 | .250 | .259 | .237 | 38 | 9 | 1 | 0 | 1 | 2 | 5 | 5 | .326 | .342 |
| Dotson,Rich | R | .357 | 56 | 20 | 5 | 1 | 3 | 15 | 4 | 1 | .393 | .643 | .354 | 65 | 23 | 7 | 2 | 0 | 12 | 10 | 8 | .423 | .523 |
| Downs,Kelly | R | .243 | 152 | 37 | 10 | 0 | 1 | 16 | 11 | 16 | .297 | .329 | .216 | 88 | 19 | 4 | 0 | 1 | 8 | 9 | 15 | .296 | .295 |
| Drabek,Doug | R | .243 | 538 | 131 | 29 | 4 | 10 | 47 | 35 | 70 | .289 | .368 | .192 | 308 | 59 | 8 | 0 | 5 | 18 | 21 | 61 | .249 | .266 |
| Drummond,Tim | R | .302 | 149 | 45 | 9 | 1 | 5 | 28 | 14 | 15 | .355 | .477 | .289 | 204 | 59 | 7 | 1 | 3 | 21 | 22 | 34 | .358 | .377 |
| DuBois,Brian | L | .379 | 29 | 11 | 1 | 0 | 0 | 4 | 1 | 1 | .387 | .414 | .299 | 197 | 59 | 12 | 3 | 9 | 29 | 21 | 33 | .365 | .528 |
| Dunne,Mike | R | .193 | 57 | 11 | 2 | 0 | 1 | 5 | 12 | 5 | .333 | .281 | .288 | 59 | 17 | 2 | 0 | 3 | 9 | 5 | 10 | .344 | .475 |
| Eave,Gary | R | .256 | 43 | 11 | 3 | 1 | 1 | 5 | 8 | 7 | .373 | .442 | .232 | 69 | 16 | 1 | 0 | 4 | 8 | 12 | 9 | .361 | .420 |
| Eckersley,Dennis | R | .168 | 119 | 20 | 4 | 1 | 1 | 10 | 2 | 22 | .180 | .244 | .152 | 138 | 21 | 5 | 0 | 1 | 2 | 2 | 51 | .164 | .210 |
| Edens,Tom | R | .275 | 142 | 39 | 4 | 1 | 2 | 15 | 14 | 16 | .338 | .359 | .253 | 198 | 50 | 8 | 0 | 6 | 27 | 19 | 24 | .326 | .384 |
| Edwards,Wayne | L | .183 | 93 | 17 | 0 | 1 | 1 | 12 | 14 | 16 | .287 | .237 | .253 | 253 | 64 | 13 | 0 | 5 | 28 | 27 | 47 | .331 | .364 |
| Eichhorn,Mark | R | .290 | 155 | 45 | 4 | 1 | 1 | 19 | 10 | 29 | .353 | .348 | .288 | 184 | 53 | 10 | 0 | 1 | 31 | 13 | 40 | .332 | .359 |
| Eiland,Dave | R | .238 | 80 | 19 | 4 | 3 | 1 | 7 | 4 | 7 | .274 | .400 | .286 | 42 | 12 | 4 | 0 | 1 | 6 | 1 | 9 | .302 | .452 |
| Elvira,Narciso | L | .000 | 2 | 0 | 0 | 0 | 0 | 0 | 2 | 1 | .500 | .000 | .333 | 18 | 6 | 3 | 0 | 0 | 3 | 3 | 5 | .429 | .500 |
| Encarnacion,Luis | R | .333 | 18 | 6 | 1 | 0 | 1 | 2 | 1 | 2 | .368 | .556 | .296 | 27 | 8 | 1 | 0 | 0 | 6 | 3 | 6 | .367 | .333 |
| Erickson,Scott | R | .246 | 224 | 55 | 9 | 1 | 4 | 27 | 27 | 16 | .329 | .348 | .268 | 198 | 53 | 7 | 1 | 5 | 17 | 24 | 37 | .356 | .389 |
| Farmer,Howard | R | .316 | 38 | 12 | 2 | 0 | 4 | 7 | 7 | 6 | .413 | .684 | .292 | 48 | 14 | 3 | 0 | 5 | 10 | 3 | 8 | .333 | .667 |
| Farr,Steve | R | .225 | 204 | 46 | 6 | 1 | 2 | 14 | 27 | 34 | .319 | .294 | .215 | 247 | 53 | 6 | 1 | 4 | 24 | 21 | 60 | .286 | .296 |
| Farrell,John | R | .278 | 205 | 57 | 11 | 1 | 4 | 23 | 19 | 19 | .336 | .400 | .297 | 172 | 51 | 13 | 2 | 6 | 21 | 14 | 25 | .353 | .500 |
| Fernandez,Alex | R | .273 | 176 | 48 | 6 | 1 | 3 | 12 | 17 | 29 | .340 | .369 | .256 | 160 | 41 | 4 | 1 | 3 | 21 | 17 | 32 | .335 | .350 |
| Fernandez,Sid | L | .222 | 126 | 28 | 6 | 1 | 3 | 22 | 16 | 44 | .317 | .357 | .195 | 524 | 102 | 19 | 5 | 15 | 46 | 51 | 137 | .268 | .336 |
| Fetters,Mike | R | .328 | 128 | 42 | 5 | 1 | 7 | 26 | 6 | 13 | .368 | .547 | .250 | 140 | 35 | 1 | 0 | 2 | 14 | 14 | 22 | .318 | .300 |
| Filer,Tom | R | .200 | 30 | 6 | 0 | 0 | 0 | 3 | 4 | 3 | .294 | .200 | .333 | 60 | 20 | 3 | 0 | 2 | 7 | 5 | 5 | .385 | .483 |
| Filson,Pete | L | .207 | 29 | 6 | 1 | 1 | 0 | 2 | 1 | 2 | .233 | .310 | .300 | 120 | 36 | 10 | 4 | 6 | 21 | 12 | 7 | .370 | .600 |
| Finley,Chuck | L | .256 | 121 | 31 | 2 | 0 | 0 | 6 | 14 | 15 | .333 | .273 | .241 | 743 | 179 | 34 | 3 | 17 | 57 | 67 | 162 | .304 | .363 |
| Fisher,Brian | R | .500 | 12 | 6 | 0 | 1 | 1 | 4 | 0 | 0 | .429 | .917 | .300 | 10 | 3 | 0 | 0 | 0 | 2 | 0 | 1 | .300 | .300 |
| Flanagan,Mike | L | .300 | 10 | 3 | 0 | 0 | 1 | 1 | 1 | 1 | .364 | .600 | .333 | 75 | 25 | 3 | 0 | 2 | 7 | 7 | 4 | .390 | .453 |
| Fossas,Tony | L | .300 | 40 | 12 | 0 | 0 | 1 | 8 | 3 | 12 | .349 | .375 | .344 | 93 | 32 | 6 | 1 | 4 | 28 | 7 | 12 | .386 | .559 |
| Franco,John | L | .228 | 57 | 13 | 2 | 1 | 0 | 9 | 8 | 16 | .323 | .298 | .259 | 205 | 53 | 9 | 0 | 4 | 19 | 13 | 40 | .301 | .361 |
| Fraser,Willie | R | .207 | 121 | 25 | 5 | 0 | 1 | 12 | 14 | 16 | .287 | .273 | .267 | 165 | 44 | 8 | 1 | 3 | 23 | 10 | 16 | .305 | .382 |
| Freeman,Marvin | R | .269 | 78 | 21 | 2 | 2 | 2 | 10 | 11 | 10 | .374 | .423 | .190 | 105 | 20 | 1 | 0 | 3 | 10 | 6 | 28 | .254 | .286 |
| Frey,Steve | L | .274 | 62 | 17 | 2 | 0 | 2 | 8 | 9 | 11 | .361 | .403 | .194 | 139 | 27 | 6 | 0 | 2 | 6 | 20 | 18 | .298 | .281 |
| Frohwirth,Todd | R | 1.000 | 1 | 1 | 0 | 0 | 0 | 0 | 1 | 0 | 1.000 | 1.000 | .400 | 5 | 2 | 0 | 0 | 0 | 1 | 5 | 1 | .700 | .400 |
| Garces,Rich | R | .231 | 13 | 3 | 0 | 0 | 0 | 0 | 3 | 0 | .375 | .231 | .143 | 7 | 1 | 0 | 0 | 0 | 1 | 1 | 1 | .250 | .143 |
| Gardiner,Mike | R | .385 | 26 | 10 | 2 | 1 | 1 | 6 | 2 | 4 | .414 | .654 | .375 | 32 | 12 | 1 | 1 | 0 | 7 | 3 | 2 | .459 | .469 |
| Gardner,Mark | R | .231 | 321 | 74 | 10 | 4 | 9 | 33 | 47 | 70 | .327 | .371 | .229 | 240 | 55 | 11 | 0 | 4 | 23 | 14 | 65 | .291 | .325 |
| Gardner,Wes | R | .282 | 149 | 42 | 7 | 0 | 1 | 20 | 21 | 25 | .366 | .349 | .236 | 148 | 35 | 6 | 1 | 5 | 16 | 14 | 33 | .311 | .392 |
| Garrelts,Scott | R | .300 | 397 | 119 | 22 | 4 | 8 | 44 | 42 | 34 | .369 | .436 | .236 | 301 | 71 | 12 | 1 | 8 | 34 | 28 | 46 | .299 | .362 |
| Gibson,Paul | L | .263 | 118 | 31 | 5 | 0 | 2 | 15 | 11 | 11 | .321 | .356 | .272 | 250 | 68 | 19 | 2 | 8 | 31 | 33 | 45 | .356 | .460 |
| Gideon,Brett | R | .667 | 3 | 2 | 0 | 0 | 0 | 0 | 2 | 0 | .800 | .667 | .000 | 1 | 0 | 0 | 0 | 0 | 0 | 2 | 0 | .667 | .000 |
| Gilles,Tom | R | .000 | 2 | 0 | 0 | 0 | 0 | 0 | 0 | 1 | .000 | .000 | .500 | 4 | 2 | 1 | 0 | 0 | 1 | 0 | 0 | .500 | .750 |

# Pitchers vs. Left-Handed and Right-Handed Batters

| Pitcher | | vs. Left-Handed Batters Avg | AB | H | 2B | 3B | HR | RBI | BB | SO | OBP | SLG | vs. Right-Handed Batters Avg | AB | H | 2B | 3B | HR | RBI | BB | SO | OBP | SLG |
|---|---|---|---|---|---|---|---|---|---|---|---|---|---|---|---|---|---|---|---|---|---|---|---|
| Glavine,Tom | L | .212 | 151 | 32 | 3 | 0 | 2 | 11 | 20 | 33 | .304 | .272 | .296 | 676 | 200 | 42 | 4 | 16 | 83 | 58 | 96 | .351 | .441 |
| Gleaton,Jerry Don | L | .242 | 91 | 22 | 2 | 0 | 1 | 16 | 3 | 13 | .276 | .297 | .200 | 200 | 40 | 5 | 0 | 4 | 22 | 22 | 43 | .280 | .285 |
| Gooden,Dwight | R | .260 | 520 | 135 | 24 | 4 | 6 | 58 | 44 | 130 | .317 | .356 | .256 | 367 | 94 | 9 | 3 | 4 | 36 | 26 | 93 | .313 | .330 |
| Gordon,Tom | R | .252 | 365 | 92 | 12 | 2 | 6 | 30 | 55 | 75 | .352 | .345 | .262 | 381 | 100 | 19 | 5 | 11 | 49 | 44 | 100 | .340 | .425 |
| Gott,Jim | R | .291 | 134 | 39 | 7 | 1 | 1 | 9 | 20 | 22 | .378 | .381 | .208 | 96 | 20 | 2 | 0 | 4 | 16 | 14 | 22 | .304 | .354 |
| Gozzo,Mauro | R | .333 | 6 | 2 | 1 | 0 | 0 | 0 | 0 | 1 | .333 | .500 | .000 | 5 | 0 | 0 | 0 | 0 | 0 | 2 | 1 | .286 | .000 |
| Grahe,Joe | R | .370 | 81 | 30 | 6 | 2 | 3 | 16 | 7 | 8 | .427 | .605 | .226 | 93 | 21 | 6 | 0 | 0 | 10 | 16 | 17 | .351 | .290 |
| Grant,Mark | R | .312 | 199 | 62 | 16 | 3 | 4 | 29 | 21 | 42 | .378 | .482 | .282 | 163 | 46 | 6 | 0 | 5 | 38 | 16 | 27 | .339 | .411 |
| Gray,Jeff | R | .276 | 98 | 27 | 3 | 1 | 2 | 11 | 8 | 26 | .330 | .388 | .260 | 100 | 26 | 4 | 1 | 1 | 13 | 7 | 24 | .312 | .350 |
| Greene,Tommy | R | .314 | 105 | 33 | 7 | 1 | 4 | 14 | 19 | 9 | .424 | .514 | .189 | 90 | 17 | 3 | 1 | 4 | 13 | 7 | 12 | .247 | .378 |
| Grimsley,Jason | R | .203 | 128 | 26 | 3 | 1 | 0 | 9 | 27 | 24 | .348 | .242 | .266 | 79 | 21 | 3 | 0 | 1 | 7 | 16 | 17 | .389 | .342 |
| Gross,Kevin | R | .296 | 371 | 110 | 21 | 1 | 7 | 52 | 49 | 73 | .375 | .415 | .237 | 257 | 61 | 8 | 1 | 2 | 21 | 16 | 38 | .287 | .300 |
| Gross,Kip | R | .111 | 9 | 1 | 0 | 0 | 0 | 0 | 0 | 2 | .111 | .111 | .385 | 13 | 5 | 0 | 0 | 0 | 3 | 2 | 1 | .438 | .385 |
| Guante,Cecilio | R | .183 | 71 | 13 | 3 | 0 | 4 | 11 | 8 | 7 | .284 | .394 | .245 | 102 | 25 | 4 | 1 | 6 | 18 | 10 | 23 | .313 | .480 |
| Gubicza,Mark | R | .266 | 158 | 42 | 7 | 0 | 3 | 11 | 24 | 30 | .371 | .367 | .296 | 199 | 59 | 12 | 2 | 2 | 30 | 14 | 41 | .341 | .407 |
| Guetterman,Lee | L | .253 | 99 | 25 | 2 | 3 | 1 | 11 | 9 | 21 | .315 | .364 | .229 | 240 | 55 | 6 | 2 | 5 | 31 | 17 | 27 | .277 | .333 |
| Gullickson,Bill | R | .316 | 471 | 149 | 24 | 4 | 12 | 55 | 43 | 30 | .373 | .461 | .242 | 298 | 72 | 13 | 5 | 9 | 35 | 18 | 43 | .282 | .409 |
| Gunderson,Eric | L | .294 | 17 | 5 | 0 | 0 | 0 | 4 | 2 | 2 | .368 | .294 | .292 | 65 | 19 | 3 | 0 | 2 | 10 | 9 | 12 | .378 | .431 |
| Guthrie,Mark | L | .343 | 99 | 34 | 4 | 0 | 1 | 10 | 3 | 13 | .363 | .414 | .262 | 458 | 120 | 24 | 0 | 7 | 40 | 36 | 88 | .317 | .360 |
| Habyan,John | R | .333 | 21 | 7 | 2 | 1 | 0 | 2 | 1 | 1 | .364 | .524 | .231 | 13 | 3 | 2 | 0 | 0 | 1 | 1 | 3 | .333 | .385 |
| Hall,Drew | L | .270 | 63 | 17 | 3 | 1 | 1 | 7 | 9 | 13 | .356 | .397 | .230 | 152 | 35 | 9 | 3 | 5 | 18 | 20 | 27 | .314 | .428 |
| Hammaker,Atlee | L | .194 | 67 | 13 | 3 | 0 | 2 | 5 | 7 | 12 | .267 | .328 | .276 | 261 | 72 | 9 | 2 | 6 | 31 | 20 | 32 | .324 | .395 |
| Hammond,Chris | L | .385 | 13 | 5 | 1 | 0 | 2 | 3 | 4 | 1 | .529 | .923 | .267 | 30 | 8 | 2 | 0 | 0 | 4 | 8 | 3 | .421 | .333 |
| Hanson,Erik | R | .222 | 465 | 103 | 21 | 2 | 5 | 33 | 41 | 114 | .283 | .308 | .244 | 418 | 102 | 14 | 2 | 10 | 42 | 27 | 97 | .291 | .359 |
| Harkey,Mike | R | .238 | 411 | 98 | 21 | 3 | 7 | 35 | 38 | 57 | .303 | .355 | .227 | 242 | 55 | 8 | 2 | 7 | 26 | 21 | 37 | .302 | .364 |
| Harnisch,Pete | R | .287 | 435 | 125 | 26 | 5 | 10 | 50 | 49 | 59 | .358 | .439 | .222 | 288 | 64 | 7 | 1 | 7 | 30 | 37 | 63 | .310 | .326 |
| Harris,Gene | R | .192 | 52 | 10 | 4 | 0 | 1 | 6 | 16 | 15 | .382 | .327 | .231 | 91 | 21 | 6 | 1 | 4 | 23 | 14 | 28 | .333 | .451 |
| Harris,Greg | R | .239 | 352 | 84 | 18 | 1 | 5 | 29 | 37 | 52 | .312 | .338 | .291 | 351 | 102 | 19 | 2 | 8 | 42 | 40 | 65 | .364 | .425 |
| Harris,Greg W. | R | .278 | 223 | 62 | 11 | 1 | 2 | 26 | 28 | 38 | .357 | .363 | .153 | 196 | 30 | 5 | 1 | 4 | 21 | 21 | 59 | .241 | .250 |
| Harris,Reggie | R | .209 | 67 | 14 | 2 | 0 | 3 | 8 | 10 | 16 | .312 | .373 | .147 | 75 | 11 | 2 | 0 | 2 | 8 | 11 | 15 | .267 | .253 |
| Hartley,Mike | R | .213 | 155 | 33 | 4 | 3 | 2 | 10 | 24 | 40 | .322 | .316 | .185 | 135 | 25 | 4 | 0 | 5 | 19 | 6 | 36 | .224 | .326 |
| Harvey,Bryan | R | .208 | 106 | 22 | 4 | 1 | 1 | 14 | 21 | 42 | .331 | .292 | .195 | 118 | 23 | 3 | 0 | 3 | 11 | 14 | 40 | .278 | .297 |
| Hawkins,Andy | R | .294 | 313 | 92 | 13 | 3 | 8 | 37 | 55 | 31 | .398 | .431 | .224 | 286 | 64 | 17 | 0 | 12 | 45 | 27 | 43 | .291 | .409 |
| Heaton,Neal | L | .311 | 90 | 28 | 7 | 0 | 4 | 9 | 10 | 13 | .376 | .522 | .254 | 453 | 115 | 19 | 2 | 13 | 48 | 28 | 55 | .297 | .391 |
| Henke,Tom | R | .210 | 138 | 29 | 6 | 1 | 4 | 17 | 11 | 42 | .267 | .355 | .216 | 134 | 29 | 3 | 0 | 4 | 7 | 8 | 33 | .266 | .328 |
| Henneman,Mike | R | .278 | 144 | 40 | 7 | 0 | 0 | 10 | 18 | 14 | .364 | .326 | .236 | 212 | 50 | 8 | 1 | 4 | 24 | 15 | 36 | .288 | .340 |
| Hennis,Randy | R | .056 | 18 | 1 | 1 | 0 | 0 | 0 | 2 | 2 | .150 | .111 | .000 | 12 | 0 | 0 | 0 | 0 | 0 | 1 | 2 | .143 | .000 |
| Henry,Dwayne | R | .275 | 69 | 19 | 4 | 1 | 1 | 12 | 14 | 15 | .393 | .406 | .272 | 81 | 22 | 5 | 0 | 2 | 15 | 11 | 19 | .359 | .407 |
| Hernandez,Xavier | R | .289 | 114 | 33 | 4 | 0 | 4 | 15 | 18 | 5 | .391 | .430 | .225 | 120 | 27 | 7 | 0 | 4 | 18 | 6 | 19 | .271 | .383 |
| Hershiser,Orel | R | .189 | 53 | 10 | 1 | 0 | 1 | 3 | 2 | 9 | .218 | .264 | .340 | 47 | 16 | 3 | 0 | 0 | 5 | 2 | 7 | .380 | .404 |
| Hesketh,Joe | L | .260 | 73 | 19 | 1 | 1 | 3 | 10 | 9 | 19 | .349 | .425 | .296 | 169 | 50 | 13 | 0 | 4 | 31 | 16 | 31 | .355 | .444 |
| Hetzel,Eric | R | .348 | 66 | 23 | 5 | 0 | 2 | 13 | 12 | 7 | .443 | .515 | .219 | 73 | 16 | 3 | 1 | 1 | 12 | 9 | 13 | .313 | .329 |
| Hibbard,Greg | L | .209 | 91 | 19 | 6 | 0 | 0 | 7 | 8 | 10 | .270 | .275 | .261 | 701 | 183 | 28 | 6 | 11 | 59 | 47 | 82 | .309 | .365 |
| Hickey,Kevin | L | .261 | 46 | 12 | 4 | 1 | 1 | 7 | 4 | 8 | .314 | .457 | .269 | 52 | 14 | 1 | 1 | 2 | 7 | 9 | 9 | .377 | .442 |
| Higuera,Ted | L | .246 | 126 | 31 | 3 | 0 | 1 | 12 | 7 | 23 | .291 | .294 | .258 | 527 | 136 | 27 | 1 | 15 | 61 | 43 | 106 | .314 | .398 |
| Hill,Ken | R | .265 | 185 | 49 | 9 | 3 | 4 | 21 | 25 | 31 | .347 | .411 | .263 | 114 | 30 | 8 | 0 | 3 | 18 | 8 | 27 | .312 | .412 |
| Hillegas,Shawn | R | .214 | 14 | 3 | 0 | 0 | 0 | 0 | 1 | 1 | .267 | .214 | .045 | 22 | 1 | 0 | 1 | 0 | 3 | 4 | 4 | .185 | .136 |
| Hilton,Howard | R | .250 | 4 | 1 | 0 | 0 | 0 | 1 | 1 | 1 | .400 | .250 | .143 | 7 | 1 | 0 | 0 | 0 | 0 | 2 | 1 | .333 | .143 |
| Holman,Brian | R | .280 | 379 | 106 | 20 | 1 | 10 | 37 | 38 | 49 | .346 | .417 | .238 | 345 | 82 | 14 | 1 | 7 | 42 | 28 | 72 | .299 | .345 |
| Holmes,Darren | R | .273 | 33 | 9 | 2 | 0 | 0 | 1 | 3 | 9 | .333 | .333 | .200 | 30 | 6 | 1 | 0 | 1 | 7 | 8 | 10 | .350 | .333 |

# Pitchers vs. Left-Handed and Right-Handed Batters

| Pitcher | | vs. Left-Handed Batters | | | | | | | | | | | vs. Right-Handed Batters | | | | | | | | | | |
|---|---|---|---|---|---|---|---|---|---|---|---|---|---|---|---|---|---|---|---|---|---|---|---|
| | | Avg | AB | H | 2B | 3B | HR | RBI | BB | SO | OBP | SLG | Avg | AB | H | 2B | 3B | HR | RBI | BB | SO | OBP | SLG |
| Holton,Brian | R | .250 | 100 | 25 | 5 | 0 | 1 | 13 | 10 | 13 | .315 | .330 | .323 | 133 | 43 | 8 | 0 | 6 | 25 | 11 | 14 | .372 | .519 |
| Honeycutt,Rick | L | .163 | 86 | 14 | 2 | 0 | 1 | 7 | 5 | 17 | .204 | .221 | .230 | 139 | 32 | 6 | 1 | 1 | 18 | 17 | 21 | .311 | .309 |
| Hoover,John | R | .500 | 8 | 4 | 0 | 0 | 0 | 2 | 1 | 0 | .556 | .500 | .286 | 14 | 4 | 0 | 0 | 0 | 4 | 2 | 0 | .375 | .286 |
| Horton,Ricky | L | .279 | 68 | 19 | 2 | 0 | 0 | 5 | 9 | 10 | .372 | .309 | .340 | 97 | 33 | 7 | 0 | 3 | 18 | 13 | 8 | .414 | .505 |
| Hough,Charlie | R | .241 | 349 | 84 | 12 | 2 | 7 | 34 | 56 | 48 | .346 | .347 | .231 | 458 | 106 | 16 | 2 | 17 | 60 | 63 | 66 | .331 | .386 |
| Howell,Jay | R | .235 | 153 | 36 | 5 | 1 | 3 | 14 | 10 | 41 | .299 | .340 | .253 | 91 | 23 | 3 | 0 | 2 | 11 | 10 | 18 | .340 | .352 |
| Howell,Ken | R | .300 | 257 | 77 | 18 | 2 | 7 | 43 | 37 | 34 | .386 | .467 | .193 | 150 | 29 | 8 | 0 | 5 | 10 | 12 | 36 | .267 | .347 |
| Huismann,Mark | R | .286 | 7 | 2 | 0 | 0 | 1 | 1 | 1 | 2 | .375 | .714 | .667 | 6 | 4 | 1 | 0 | 1 | 2 | 0 | 0 | .714 | 1.333 |
| Hurst,Bruce | L | .230 | 165 | 38 | 3 | 2 | 7 | 23 | 17 | 43 | .302 | .400 | .228 | 658 | 150 | 32 | 2 | 14 | 49 | 46 | 119 | .279 | .347 |
| Innis,Jeff | R | .270 | 37 | 10 | 1 | 0 | 3 | 5 | 4 | 5 | .349 | .541 | .167 | 54 | 9 | 1 | 0 | 1 | 2 | 6 | 7 | .246 | .241 |
| Irvine,Daryl | R | .296 | 27 | 8 | 0 | 0 | 0 | 6 | 4 | 3 | .353 | .296 | .206 | 34 | 7 | 2 | 0 | 0 | 4 | 6 | 6 | .325 | .265 |
| Jackson,Danny | L | .241 | 79 | 19 | 3 | 1 | 2 | 5 | 11 | 13 | .341 | .380 | .271 | 369 | 100 | 10 | 3 | 9 | 44 | 29 | 63 | .322 | .388 |
| Jackson,Mike | R | .257 | 105 | 27 | 4 | 0 | 5 | 18 | 21 | 9 | .375 | .438 | .213 | 174 | 37 | 5 | 0 | 3 | 31 | 23 | 60 | .307 | .293 |
| Jeffcoat,Mike | L | .233 | 90 | 21 | 3 | 0 | 0 | 10 | 2 | 13 | .263 | .267 | .296 | 341 | 101 | 21 | 1 | 12 | 44 | 26 | 45 | .345 | .469 |
| Johnson,Dave | R | .297 | 347 | 103 | 29 | 2 | 15 | 37 | 24 | 24 | .340 | .522 | .263 | 353 | 93 | 14 | 0 | 15 | 36 | 19 | 44 | .303 | .431 |
| Johnson,Randy | L | .195 | 82 | 16 | 3 | 0 | 0 | 4 | 7 | 23 | .256 | .232 | .218 | 724 | 158 | 23 | 4 | 26 | 76 | 113 | 171 | .326 | .369 |
| Jones,Barry | R | .304 | 112 | 34 | 5 | 0 | 2 | 19 | 13 | 13 | .364 | .402 | .184 | 152 | 28 | 4 | 0 | 0 | 14 | 20 | 32 | .282 | .211 |
| Jones,Doug | R | .200 | 165 | 33 | 8 | 1 | 3 | 18 | 11 | 26 | .249 | .315 | .239 | 138 | 33 | 5 | 1 | 2 | 16 | 11 | 29 | .303 | .333 |
| Jones,Jimmy | R | .327 | 101 | 33 | 6 | 0 | 1 | 11 | 10 | 10 | .389 | .416 | .361 | 108 | 39 | 7 | 0 | 7 | 29 | 13 | 15 | .419 | .620 |
| Kaiser,Jeff | L | .353 | 17 | 6 | 0 | 0 | 0 | 3 | 5 | 4 | .500 | .353 | .286 | 35 | 10 | 2 | 0 | 2 | 6 | 2 | 5 | .316 | .514 |
| Kerfeld,Charlie | R | .258 | 66 | 17 | 3 | 0 | 0 | 8 | 17 | 15 | .405 | .303 | .348 | 66 | 23 | 5 | 1 | 2 | 15 | 12 | 16 | .443 | .545 |
| Key,Jimmy | L | .182 | 88 | 16 | 1 | 0 | 0 | 5 | 4 | 14 | .213 | .193 | .298 | 514 | 153 | 30 | 2 | 20 | 61 | 18 | 74 | .320 | .481 |
| Kiecker,Dana | R | .318 | 299 | 95 | 18 | 2 | 4 | 34 | 29 | 21 | .375 | .431 | .183 | 273 | 50 | 13 | 1 | 3 | 26 | 25 | 72 | .272 | .271 |
| Kilgus,Paul | L | .294 | 17 | 5 | 0 | 0 | 1 | 4 | 2 | 1 | .350 | .471 | .311 | 45 | 14 | 2 | 1 | 1 | 7 | 5 | 6 | .377 | .467 |
| King,Eric | R | .216 | 268 | 58 | 7 | 3 | 5 | 27 | 25 | 30 | .286 | .321 | .255 | 302 | 77 | 10 | 1 | 5 | 27 | 15 | 40 | .300 | .344 |
| Kinzer,Matt | R | .250 | 4 | 1 | 0 | 0 | 0 | 1 | 1 | 0 | .400 | .250 | .500 | 4 | 2 | 1 | 0 | 0 | 3 | 2 | 1 | .667 | .750 |
| Kipper,Bob | L | .225 | 80 | 18 | 4 | 0 | 0 | 7 | 9 | 12 | .323 | .275 | .178 | 146 | 26 | 5 | 0 | 7 | 19 | 17 | 23 | .261 | .356 |
| Klink,Joe | L | .255 | 51 | 13 | 2 | 0 | 1 | 4 | 8 | 8 | .356 | .353 | .221 | 95 | 21 | 2 | 1 | 0 | 4 | 10 | 11 | .295 | .263 |
| Knackert,Brent | R | .392 | 79 | 31 | 5 | 0 | 2 | 15 | 11 | 9 | .462 | .532 | .235 | 81 | 19 | 2 | 1 | 3 | 18 | 10 | 19 | .330 | .395 |
| Knepper,Bob | L | .200 | 25 | 5 | 1 | 0 | 0 | 2 | 1 | 2 | .231 | .240 | .329 | 155 | 51 | 7 | 6 | 7 | 26 | 18 | 22 | .398 | .587 |
| Knudson,Mark | R | .279 | 340 | 95 | 19 | 3 | 6 | 29 | 23 | 29 | .320 | .406 | .284 | 324 | 92 | 20 | 2 | 8 | 39 | 17 | 27 | .323 | .432 |
| Kraemer,Joe | L | .273 | 33 | 9 | 2 | 0 | 1 | 12 | 6 | 3 | .400 | .424 | .328 | 67 | 22 | 4 | 1 | 1 | 14 | 8 | 13 | .397 | .463 |
| Kramer,Randy | R | .314 | 86 | 27 | 4 | 1 | 3 | 14 | 15 | 14 | .416 | .488 | .217 | 92 | 20 | 1 | 1 | 3 | 13 | 6 | 13 | .287 | .348 |
| Krueger,Bill | L | .237 | 93 | 22 | 3 | 1 | 1 | 13 | 4 | 14 | .265 | .323 | .285 | 403 | 115 | 19 | 4 | 9 | 53 | 50 | 50 | .361 | .419 |
| Kutzler,Jerry | R | .297 | 64 | 19 | 7 | 3 | 0 | 11 | 8 | 11 | .370 | .500 | .311 | 61 | 19 | 3 | 1 | 2 | 7 | 6 | 10 | .373 | .492 |
| LaCoss,Mike | R | .246 | 179 | 44 | 7 | 0 | 3 | 16 | 28 | 20 | .346 | .335 | .279 | 111 | 31 | 5 | 0 | 2 | 16 | 11 | 19 | .336 | .378 |
| Lamp,Dennis | R | .299 | 194 | 58 | 10 | 2 | 3 | 26 | 17 | 24 | .354 | .418 | .262 | 214 | 56 | 12 | 1 | 7 | 47 | 13 | 25 | .309 | .425 |
| Lancaster,Les | R | .282 | 227 | 64 | 12 | 0 | 3 | 23 | 29 | 30 | .362 | .374 | .285 | 200 | 57 | 8 | 1 | 8 | 39 | 11 | 35 | .319 | .455 |
| Landrum,Bill | R | .275 | 138 | 38 | 1 | 2 | 2 | 16 | 13 | 16 | .333 | .355 | .248 | 125 | 31 | 2 | 1 | 2 | 13 | 8 | 23 | .291 | .328 |
| Langston,Mark | L | .246 | 138 | 34 | 9 | 1 | 1 | 15 | 15 | 27 | .318 | .348 | .262 | 691 | 181 | 31 | 7 | 12 | 89 | 89 | 168 | .348 | .379 |
| LaPoint,Dave | L | .295 | 95 | 28 | 1 | 2 | 2 | 9 | 9 | 7 | .349 | .411 | .291 | 522 | 152 | 31 | 4 | 9 | 61 | 48 | 60 | .347 | .418 |
| Layana,Tim | R | .256 | 133 | 34 | 12 | 0 | 3 | 17 | 25 | 22 | .375 | .414 | .234 | 158 | 37 | 7 | 0 | 4 | 17 | 19 | 31 | .317 | .354 |
| Leach,Terry | R | .270 | 126 | 34 | 8 | 3 | 0 | 11 | 11 | 9 | .331 | .381 | .267 | 187 | 50 | 10 | 0 | 2 | 28 | 10 | 37 | .303 | .353 |
| Leary,Tim | R | .260 | 408 | 106 | 22 | 1 | 10 | 47 | 46 | 61 | .338 | .392 | .255 | 377 | 96 | 17 | 0 | 8 | 37 | 32 | 77 | .318 | .363 |
| Lee,Mark | L | .304 | 23 | 7 | 2 | 0 | 0 | 6 | 2 | 3 | .333 | .391 | .236 | 55 | 13 | 4 | 1 | 1 | 2 | 2 | 11 | .263 | .400 |
| Lefferts,Craig | L | .207 | 87 | 18 | 0 | 0 | 1 | 5 | 8 | 18 | .281 | .241 | .237 | 211 | 50 | 7 | 0 | 9 | 28 | 14 | 42 | .283 | .398 |
| Leibrandt,Charlie | L | .212 | 99 | 21 | 2 | 0 | 3 | 14 | 6 | 14 | .269 | .323 | .270 | 529 | 143 | 36 | 3 | 6 | 51 | 29 | 62 | .308 | .384 |
| Leister,John | R | .364 | 11 | 4 | 1 | 1 | 0 | 3 | 2 | 1 | .462 | .636 | .250 | 12 | 3 | 1 | 0 | 0 | 1 | 2 | 2 | .333 | .333 |
| Leiter,Al | L | .000 | 5 | 0 | 0 | 0 | 0 | 0 | 0 | 2 | .000 | .000 | .067 | 15 | 1 | 0 | 0 | 0 | 0 | 2 | 3 | .176 | .067 |
| Leiter,Mark | R | .308 | 52 | 16 | 3 | 0 | 2 | 9 | 6 | 11 | .373 | .481 | .321 | 53 | 17 | 3 | 0 | 3 | 9 | 3 | 10 | .379 | .547 |

# Pitchers vs. Left-Handed and Right-Handed Batters

| Pitcher | | vs. Left-Handed Batters | | | | | | | | | | | vs. Right-Handed Batters | | | | | | | | | | |
|---|---|---|---|---|---|---|---|---|---|---|---|---|---|---|---|---|---|---|---|---|---|---|---|
| | | Avg | AB | H | 2B | 3B | HR | RBI | BB | SO | OBP | SLG | Avg | AB | H | 2B | 3B | HR | RBI | BB | SO | OBP | SLG |
| Lewis,Scott | R | .132 | 38 | 5 | 0 | 0 | 1 | 2 | 2 | 4 | .175 | .211 | .250 | 20 | 5 | 3 | 0 | 1 | 2 | 0 | 5 | .250 | .550 |
| Lilliquist,Derek | L | .326 | 92 | 30 | 5 | 0 | 3 | 8 | 9 | 23 | .392 | .478 | .275 | 386 | 106 | 20 | 0 | 13 | 51 | 33 | 40 | .331 | .427 |
| Long,Bill | R | .328 | 122 | 40 | 6 | 2 | 5 | 14 | 14 | 17 | .397 | .533 | .267 | 120 | 32 | 2 | 0 | 5 | 21 | 9 | 17 | .323 | .408 |
| Lovelace,Vance | L | .500 | 2 | 1 | 0 | 0 | 0 | 3 | 3 | 1 | .833 | .500 | .250 | 8 | 2 | 1 | 0 | 0 | 5 | 3 | 0 | .455 | .375 |
| Luecken,Rick | R | .345 | 113 | 39 | 4 | 0 | 1 | 15 | 16 | 16 | .431 | .407 | .333 | 108 | 36 | 3 | 0 | 5 | 25 | 15 | 19 | .421 | .500 |
| Lugo,Urbano | R | .371 | 35 | 13 | 5 | 0 | 3 | 8 | 7 | 5 | .500 | .771 | .279 | 61 | 17 | 1 | 0 | 6 | 11 | 6 | 7 | .353 | .590 |
| MacDonald,Bob | L | .000 | 2 | 0 | 0 | 0 | 0 | 0 | 1 | 0 | .333 | .000 | .000 | 4 | 0 | 0 | 0 | 0 | 0 | 1 | 0 | .200 | .000 |
| Machado,Julio | R | .195 | 77 | 15 | 3 | 2 | 1 | 11 | 13 | 19 | .312 | .325 | .263 | 99 | 26 | 4 | 1 | 3 | 15 | 12 | 20 | .345 | .414 |
| Maddux,Greg | R | .291 | 564 | 164 | 26 | 2 | 6 | 70 | 54 | 80 | .352 | .376 | .223 | 349 | 78 | 16 | 1 | 5 | 28 | 17 | 64 | .265 | .318 |
| Maddux,Mike | R | .279 | 43 | 12 | 2 | 0 | 1 | 7 | 2 | 5 | .319 | .395 | .308 | 39 | 12 | 1 | 0 | 2 | 5 | 2 | 6 | .341 | .487 |
| Magrane,Joe | L | .287 | 150 | 43 | 7 | 2 | 1 | 14 | 16 | 25 | .363 | .380 | .258 | 624 | 161 | 29 | 7 | 9 | 56 | 43 | 75 | .309 | .370 |
| Mahler,Rick | R | .278 | 295 | 82 | 14 | 1 | 9 | 34 | 22 | 33 | .329 | .424 | .237 | 219 | 52 | 7 | 1 | 7 | 25 | 17 | 35 | .294 | .374 |
| Maldonado,Carlos | R | .417 | 12 | 5 | 1 | 1 | 0 | 2 | 3 | 4 | .500 | .667 | .286 | 14 | 4 | 2 | 0 | 0 | 2 | 1 | 5 | .333 | .429 |
| Malloy,Bob | R | .000 | 3 | 0 | 0 | 0 | 0 | 0 | 1 | 0 | .250 | .000 | .250 | 4 | 1 | 0 | 0 | 0 | 0 | 0 | 1 | .250 | .250 |
| Malone,Chuck | R | .091 | 11 | 1 | 0 | 0 | 1 | 2 | 8 | 2 | .474 | .364 | .167 | 12 | 2 | 0 | 0 | 0 | 1 | 3 | 5 | .333 | .167 |
| Manon,Ramon | R | .167 | 6 | 1 | 1 | 0 | 0 | 1 | 2 | 0 | .375 | .333 | .667 | 3 | 2 | 1 | 0 | 0 | 2 | 1 | 0 | .750 | 1.000 |
| Marak,Paul | R | .347 | 95 | 33 | 6 | 0 | 2 | 11 | 16 | 8 | .446 | .474 | .118 | 51 | 6 | 0 | 2 | 0 | 2 | 3 | 7 | .193 | .196 |
| Martinez,Dennis | R | .226 | 499 | 113 | 19 | 2 | 9 | 46 | 28 | 91 | .267 | .327 | .229 | 340 | 78 | 11 | 4 | 7 | 30 | 21 | 65 | .285 | .347 |
| Martinez,Ramon | R | .247 | 515 | 127 | 26 | 5 | 13 | 56 | 54 | 119 | .320 | .392 | .183 | 350 | 64 | 12 | 2 | 9 | 29 | 13 | 104 | .213 | .306 |
| Mathews,Greg | L | .326 | 43 | 14 | 3 | 2 | 1 | 7 | 6 | 4 | .408 | .558 | .264 | 148 | 39 | 8 | 2 | 1 | 17 | 24 | 14 | .369 | .365 |
| McCament,Randy | R | .375 | 8 | 3 | 1 | 0 | 0 | 3 | 4 | 2 | .538 | .500 | .313 | 16 | 5 | 2 | 0 | 0 | 1 | 1 | 3 | .353 | .438 |
| McCaskill,Kirk | R | .251 | 334 | 84 | 11 | 5 | 6 | 35 | 34 | 30 | .322 | .368 | .236 | 326 | 77 | 8 | 1 | 3 | 32 | 38 | 48 | .318 | .294 |
| McClellan,Paul | R | .318 | 22 | 7 | 5 | 0 | 0 | 3 | 2 | 1 | .375 | .545 | .500 | 14 | 7 | 1 | 0 | 3 | 7 | 4 | 1 | .632 | 1.214 |
| McClure,Bob | L | .333 | 12 | 4 | 0 | 0 | 0 | 2 | 1 | 4 | .385 | .333 | .214 | 14 | 3 | 0 | 0 | 0 | 1 | 2 | 2 | .313 | .214 |
| McCullers,Lance | R | .200 | 70 | 14 | 3 | 0 | 1 | 5 | 7 | 9 | .269 | .286 | .191 | 94 | 18 | 3 | 1 | 3 | 21 | 12 | 22 | .278 | .340 |
| McDonald,Ben | R | .181 | 216 | 39 | 6 | 0 | 2 | 8 | 17 | 38 | .236 | .236 | .230 | 213 | 49 | 8 | 0 | 7 | 23 | 18 | 27 | .289 | .366 |
| McDowell,Jack | R | .243 | 408 | 99 | 15 | 4 | 11 | 37 | 34 | 76 | .302 | .380 | .245 | 368 | 90 | 17 | 3 | 9 | 46 | 43 | 89 | .330 | .380 |
| McDowell,Roger | R | .328 | 183 | 60 | 8 | 1 | 2 | 35 | 28 | 16 | .414 | .415 | .230 | 139 | 32 | 7 | 1 | 0 | 15 | 7 | 23 | .270 | .295 |
| McElroy,Charlie | L | .286 | 21 | 6 | 3 | 0 | 0 | 4 | 3 | 4 | .360 | .429 | .409 | 44 | 18 | 4 | 0 | 0 | 8 | 7 | 12 | .490 | .500 |
| McGaffigan,Andy | R | .266 | 169 | 45 | 6 | 1 | 6 | 31 | 18 | 24 | .333 | .420 | .256 | 156 | 40 | 5 | 1 | 2 | 15 | 14 | 29 | .326 | .340 |
| McMurtry,Craig | R | .326 | 46 | 15 | 2 | 2 | 2 | 12 | 12 | 7 | .450 | .587 | .262 | 107 | 28 | 4 | 0 | 2 | 12 | 18 | 7 | .373 | .355 |
| McWilliams,Larry | L | .385 | 13 | 5 | 1 | 0 | 1 | 3 | 4 | 3 | .556 | .692 | .263 | 19 | 5 | 2 | 1 | 1 | 8 | 5 | 4 | .417 | .632 |
| Medvin,Scott | R | .400 | 5 | 2 | 0 | 0 | 0 | 2 | 1 | 0 | .500 | .400 | .357 | 14 | 5 | 1 | 0 | 0 | 3 | 1 | 1 | .438 | .429 |
| Melendez,Jose | R | .364 | 11 | 4 | 1 | 0 | 0 | 1 | 3 | 3 | .500 | .455 | .308 | 13 | 4 | 0 | 0 | 2 | 6 | 0 | 4 | .357 | .769 |
| Mercker,Kent | L | .250 | 48 | 12 | 2 | 0 | 1 | 2 | 8 | 11 | .351 | .354 | .231 | 134 | 31 | 3 | 1 | 5 | 20 | 16 | 28 | .320 | .381 |
| Mesa,Jose | R | .220 | 91 | 20 | 3 | 0 | 0 | 10 | 16 | 15 | .339 | .253 | .215 | 79 | 17 | 6 | 0 | 2 | 9 | 11 | 9 | .308 | .367 |
| Meyer,Brian | R | .217 | 46 | 10 | 1 | 0 | 1 | 1 | 3 | 1 | .265 | .304 | .200 | 30 | 6 | 1 | 0 | 2 | 3 | 3 | 5 | .273 | .433 |
| Mielke,Gary | R | .292 | 48 | 14 | 1 | 3 | 2 | 7 | 6 | 3 | .370 | .563 | .262 | 107 | 28 | 4 | 1 | 2 | 17 | 9 | 10 | .331 | .374 |
| Milacki,Bob | R | .276 | 261 | 72 | 17 | 0 | 6 | 26 | 35 | 31 | .358 | .410 | .271 | 262 | 71 | 13 | 0 | 12 | 41 | 26 | 29 | .334 | .458 |
| Mills,Alan | R | .293 | 75 | 22 | 4 | 0 | 1 | 6 | 16 | 13 | .424 | .387 | .302 | 86 | 26 | 6 | 2 | 3 | 20 | 17 | 11 | .413 | .523 |
| Minton,Greg | R | .222 | 18 | 4 | 0 | 0 | 0 | 0 | 3 | 2 | .333 | .222 | .206 | 34 | 7 | 0 | 0 | 1 | 1 | 4 | 2 | .308 | .294 |
| Minutelli,Gino | L | .000 | 0 | 0 | 0 | 0 | 0 | 0 | 2 | 0 | 1.000 | .000 | .000 | 3 | 0 | 0 | 0 | 0 | 0 | 0 | 0 | .250 | .000 |
| Mirabella,Paul | L | .235 | 68 | 16 | 2 | 0 | 0 | 8 | 10 | 13 | .333 | .265 | .299 | 167 | 50 | 6 | 2 | 9 | 30 | 17 | 15 | .368 | .521 |
| Mitchell,John | R | .317 | 202 | 64 | 16 | 0 | 4 | 23 | 29 | 16 | .397 | .455 | .285 | 242 | 69 | 18 | 0 | 3 | 33 | 19 | 27 | .338 | .397 |
| Mohorcic,Dale | R | .320 | 97 | 31 | 2 | 0 | 5 | 14 | 7 | 14 | .368 | .495 | .253 | 99 | 25 | 4 | 0 | 1 | 13 | 11 | 15 | .333 | .323 |
| Monteleone,Rich | R | .200 | 15 | 3 | 2 | 0 | 0 | 1 | 0 | 3 | .200 | .333 | .357 | 14 | 5 | 1 | 0 | 0 | 3 | 2 | 5 | .438 | .429 |
| Montgomery,Jeff | R | .278 | 176 | 49 | 10 | 1 | 4 | 22 | 21 | 27 | .357 | .415 | .179 | 179 | 32 | 7 | 0 | 2 | 20 | 13 | 67 | .249 | .251 |
| Moore,Brad | R | .333 | 3 | 1 | 0 | 1 | 0 | 3 | 1 | 0 | .400 | 1.000 | .429 | 7 | 3 | 1 | 0 | 0 | 0 | 1 | 1 | .500 | .571 |
| Moore,Mike | R | .260 | 404 | 105 | 23 | 4 | 5 | 53 | 47 | 34 | .333 | .374 | .275 | 360 | 99 | 18 | 4 | 9 | 43 | 37 | 39 | .346 | .422 |
| Morgan,Mike | R | .289 | 461 | 133 | 29 | 1 | 9 | 46 | 34 | 54 | .339 | .414 | .237 | 350 | 83 | 8 | 3 | 10 | 40 | 26 | 52 | .294 | .363 |

# Pitchers vs. Left-Handed and Right-Handed Batters

| | | vs. Left-Handed Batters | | | | | | | | | | | vs. Right-Handed Batters | | | | | | | | | | |
|---|---|---|---|---|---|---|---|---|---|---|---|---|---|---|---|---|---|---|---|---|---|---|---|
| Pitcher | | Avg | AB | H | 2B | 3B | HR | RBI | BB | SO | OBP | SLG | Avg | AB | H | 2B | 3B | HR | RBI | BB | SO | OBP | SLG |
| Morris,Jack | R | .268 | 466 | 125 | 19 | 1 | 13 | 60 | 58 | 70 | .350 | .397 | .218 | 487 | 106 | 23 | 2 | 13 | 64 | 39 | 92 | .277 | .353 |
| Moyer,Jamie | L | .222 | 81 | 18 | 4 | 1 | 1 | 12 | 4 | 9 | .267 | .333 | .308 | 315 | 97 | 29 | 2 | 5 | 39 | 35 | 49 | .376 | .460 |
| Mulholland,Terry | L | .277 | 101 | 28 | 3 | 0 | 2 | 12 | 3 | 13 | .299 | .366 | .247 | 582 | 144 | 37 | 4 | 13 | 61 | 39 | 62 | .291 | .392 |
| Munoz,Mike | L | .333 | 9 | 3 | 0 | 0 | 0 | 2 | 1 | 1 | .400 | .333 | .273 | 11 | 3 | 0 | 0 | 0 | 3 | 2 | 1 | .385 | .273 |
| Murphy,Rob | L | .241 | 83 | 20 | 4 | 0 | 0 | 6 | 12 | 19 | .340 | .289 | .404 | 161 | 65 | 12 | 1 | 10 | 43 | 20 | 35 | .462 | .677 |
| Musselman,Jeff | L | .229 | 48 | 11 | 2 | 0 | 1 | 4 | 4 | 5 | .288 | .333 | .358 | 81 | 29 | 2 | 0 | 2 | 14 | 7 | 9 | .407 | .457 |
| Myers,Randy | L | .181 | 72 | 13 | 0 | 0 | 2 | 5 | 12 | 32 | .294 | .264 | .197 | 234 | 46 | 7 | 1 | 4 | 21 | 26 | 66 | .284 | .286 |
| Nabholz,Chris | L | .116 | 43 | 5 | 1 | 0 | 1 | 3 | 9 | 12 | .283 | .209 | .188 | 202 | 38 | 7 | 2 | 5 | 16 | 23 | 41 | .272 | .317 |
| Nagy,Charles | R | .321 | 106 | 34 | 3 | 0 | 3 | 16 | 12 | 18 | .392 | .434 | .308 | 78 | 24 | 6 | 0 | 4 | 13 | 9 | 8 | .379 | .538 |
| Navarro,Jaime | R | .299 | 321 | 96 | 12 | 0 | 4 | 33 | 25 | 37 | .348 | .374 | .287 | 279 | 80 | 13 | 4 | 7 | 32 | 16 | 38 | .330 | .437 |
| Neidlinger,Jim | R | .273 | 172 | 47 | 3 | 1 | 1 | 14 | 11 | 23 | .314 | .320 | .189 | 106 | 20 | 2 | 0 | 3 | 11 | 4 | 23 | .223 | .292 |
| Nelson,Gene | R | .236 | 110 | 26 | 4 | 0 | 2 | 8 | 5 | 17 | .263 | .327 | .187 | 155 | 29 | 7 | 0 | 3 | 11 | 12 | 21 | .256 | .290 |
| Nichols,Rod | R | .387 | 31 | 12 | 2 | 1 | 1 | 6 | 2 | 0 | .457 | .613 | .308 | 39 | 12 | 4 | 3 | 4 | 8 | 4 | 3 | .372 | .872 |
| Niedenfuer,Tom | R | .330 | 103 | 34 | 5 | 2 | 1 | 13 | 18 | 8 | .416 | .447 | .225 | 142 | 32 | 7 | 3 | 2 | 12 | 7 | 24 | .260 | .359 |
| Nipper,Al | R | .351 | 37 | 13 | 1 | 0 | 1 | 9 | 5 | 5 | .426 | .459 | .355 | 62 | 22 | 4 | 0 | 1 | 11 | 14 | 7 | .462 | .468 |
| Noles,Dickie | R | .000 | 1 | 0 | 0 | 0 | 0 | 0 | 0 | 0 | .000 | .000 | 1.000 | 2 | 2 | 1 | 0 | 0 | 1 | 0 | 0 | 1.000 | 1.500 |
| Norris,Mike | R | .226 | 53 | 12 | 1 | 0 | 0 | 5 | 4 | 9 | .300 | .245 | .261 | 46 | 12 | 0 | 1 | 0 | 3 | 5 | 7 | .333 | .304 |
| Nosek,Randy | R | .125 | 8 | 1 | 1 | 0 | 0 | 0 | 7 | 0 | .533 | .250 | .353 | 17 | 6 | 0 | 0 | 1 | 5 | 2 | 3 | .400 | .529 |
| Novoa,Rafael | L | .071 | 14 | 1 | 0 | 0 | 0 | 1 | 2 | 5 | .188 | .071 | .333 | 60 | 20 | 0 | 1 | 3 | 13 | 11 | 9 | .431 | .517 |
| Nunez,Edwin | R | .209 | 110 | 23 | 6 | 0 | 2 | 10 | 17 | 29 | .313 | .318 | .223 | 188 | 42 | 9 | 0 | 2 | 18 | 20 | 37 | .305 | .303 |
| Nunez,Jose | R | .277 | 137 | 38 | 9 | 1 | 2 | 26 | 20 | 21 | .363 | .401 | .258 | 89 | 23 | 5 | 0 | 3 | 11 | 14 | 19 | .359 | .416 |
| O'Neal,Randy | R | .308 | 91 | 28 | 3 | 0 | 2 | 11 | 10 | 11 | .376 | .407 | .319 | 94 | 30 | 4 | 0 | 1 | 16 | 8 | 19 | .365 | .394 |
| Ojeda,Bobby | L | .168 | 113 | 19 | 5 | 1 | 1 | 7 | 7 | 20 | .230 | .257 | .307 | 339 | 104 | 21 | 3 | 9 | 42 | 33 | 42 | .365 | .466 |
| Olin,Steve | R | .300 | 140 | 42 | 7 | 0 | 1 | 15 | 11 | 19 | .357 | .371 | .251 | 215 | 54 | 6 | 1 | 2 | 36 | 15 | 45 | .311 | .316 |
| Olivares,Omar | R | .193 | 88 | 17 | 2 | 0 | 0 | 6 | 13 | 11 | .304 | .216 | .301 | 93 | 28 | 5 | 1 | 2 | 8 | 4 | 9 | .337 | .441 |
| Oliveras,Francisco | R | .222 | 117 | 26 | 4 | 3 | 3 | 17 | 14 | 20 | .304 | .385 | .241 | 87 | 21 | 1 | 0 | 2 | 10 | 7 | 21 | .305 | .322 |
| Olson,Gregg | R | .200 | 145 | 29 | 4 | 0 | 1 | 13 | 19 | 34 | .298 | .248 | .228 | 123 | 28 | 4 | 0 | 2 | 14 | 12 | 40 | .301 | .309 |
| Ontiveros,Steve | R | .217 | 23 | 5 | 0 | 0 | 0 | 1 | 3 | 4 | .308 | .217 | .235 | 17 | 4 | 0 | 0 | 1 | 2 | 0 | 2 | .235 | .412 |
| Orosco,Jesse | L | .224 | 67 | 15 | 3 | 0 | 2 | 12 | 12 | 16 | .338 | .358 | .244 | 176 | 43 | 7 | 2 | 7 | 26 | 26 | 39 | .338 | .426 |
| Osuna,Al | L | .188 | 16 | 3 | 0 | 0 | 0 | 0 | 3 | 4 | .409 | .188 | .333 | 21 | 7 | 3 | 1 | 1 | 4 | 3 | 2 | .385 | .714 |
| Otto,Dave | L | .000 | 1 | 0 | 0 | 0 | 0 | 0 | 1 | 0 | .500 | .000 | .333 | 9 | 3 | 0 | 0 | 0 | 4 | 2 | 2 | .455 | .333 |
| Palacios,Vince | R | .045 | 22 | 1 | 0 | 0 | 0 | 0 | 0 | 3 | .045 | .045 | .115 | 26 | 3 | 0 | 0 | 0 | 0 | 2 | 5 | .179 | .115 |
| Pall,Donn | R | .278 | 115 | 32 | 6 | 3 | 1 | 17 | 12 | 17 | .344 | .409 | .197 | 157 | 31 | 5 | 1 | 6 | 19 | 12 | 22 | .270 | .357 |
| Parker,Clay | R | .208 | 96 | 20 | 3 | 0 | 1 | 11 | 17 | 12 | .319 | .271 | .254 | 173 | 44 | 8 | 2 | 10 | 27 | 15 | 28 | .317 | .497 |
| Parrett,Jeff | R | .268 | 213 | 57 | 8 | 4 | 7 | 32 | 39 | 37 | .380 | .441 | .315 | 197 | 62 | 9 | 2 | 4 | 28 | 16 | 49 | .364 | .442 |
| Patterson,Bob | L | .204 | 103 | 21 | 2 | 1 | 1 | 8 | 6 | 29 | .252 | .272 | .267 | 251 | 67 | 13 | 0 | 8 | 28 | 15 | 41 | .311 | .414 |
| Patterson,Ken | L | .194 | 67 | 13 | 0 | 0 | 0 | 8 | 10 | 15 | .291 | .194 | .260 | 173 | 45 | 9 | 1 | 6 | 29 | 24 | 25 | .351 | .428 |
| Pavlas,Dave | R | .326 | 46 | 15 | 3 | 1 | 2 | 6 | 4 | 4 | .365 | .565 | .205 | 39 | 8 | 2 | 0 | 0 | 2 | 2 | 8 | .244 | .256 |
| Pena,Alejandro | R | .248 | 133 | 33 | 4 | 1 | 1 | 16 | 14 | 40 | .318 | .316 | .242 | 157 | 38 | 7 | 1 | 3 | 17 | 8 | 36 | .275 | .357 |
| Perez,Melido | R | .250 | 380 | 95 | 15 | 7 | 6 | 47 | 42 | 81 | .322 | .374 | .231 | 355 | 82 | 16 | 3 | 8 | 36 | 44 | 80 | .318 | .361 |
| Perez,Mike | R | .259 | 27 | 7 | 3 | 0 | 0 | 2 | 3 | 2 | .323 | .370 | .217 | 23 | 5 | 0 | 0 | 0 | 5 | 0 | 3 | .208 | .217 |
| Perez,Pascual | R | .130 | 23 | 3 | 1 | 0 | 0 | 1 | 3 | 6 | .231 | .174 | .192 | 26 | 5 | 0 | 1 | 0 | 0 | 0 | 6 | .192 | .269 |
| Perry,Pat | L | .250 | 8 | 2 | 0 | 0 | 0 | 1 | 2 | 1 | .417 | .250 | .333 | 21 | 7 | 3 | 1 | 0 | 2 | 3 | 1 | .417 | .571 |
| Peterson,Adam | R | .354 | 147 | 52 | 7 | 3 | 6 | 21 | 6 | 5 | .383 | .565 | .215 | 177 | 38 | 3 | 2 | 6 | 19 | 20 | 24 | .294 | .356 |
| Petry,Dan | R | .249 | 245 | 61 | 16 | 0 | 3 | 24 | 37 | 32 | .345 | .351 | .274 | 318 | 87 | 15 | 3 | 11 | 41 | 40 | 41 | .353 | .443 |
| Pico,Jeff | R | .372 | 199 | 74 | 11 | 2 | 3 | 28 | 25 | 13 | .441 | .492 | .263 | 175 | 46 | 8 | 3 | 4 | 30 | 12 | 24 | .310 | .411 |
| Plesac,Dan | L | .161 | 62 | 10 | 2 | 1 | 0 | 13 | 6 | 18 | .254 | .226 | .286 | 199 | 57 | 11 | 0 | 5 | 34 | 25 | 47 | .367 | .417 |
| Plunk,Eric | R | .286 | 91 | 26 | 0 | 3 | 1 | 9 | 17 | 25 | .404 | .385 | .192 | 167 | 32 | 6 | 0 | 5 | 27 | 26 | 42 | .304 | .317 |
| Poole,Jim | L | .182 | 11 | 2 | 1 | 0 | 1 | 3 | 0 | 2 | .182 | .545 | .185 | 27 | 5 | 1 | 0 | 0 | 3 | 8 | 4 | .371 | .222 |
| Portugal,Mark | R | .227 | 427 | 97 | 13 | 1 | 10 | 41 | 44 | 88 | .301 | .333 | .281 | 320 | 90 | 15 | 0 | 11 | 39 | 23 | 48 | .329 | .431 |

# Pitchers vs. Left-Handed and Right-Handed Batters

| Pitcher | | vs. Left-Handed Batters | | | | | | | | | | | vs. Right-Handed Batters | | | | | | | | | | |
|---|---|---|---|---|---|---|---|---|---|---|---|---|---|---|---|---|---|---|---|---|---|---|---|
| | | Avg | AB | H | 2B | 3B | HR | RBI | BB | SO | OBP | SLG | Avg | AB | H | 2B | 3B | HR | RBI | BB | SO | OBP | SLG |
| Powell,Dennis | L | .256 | 43 | 11 | 3 | 1 | 0 | 10 | 2 | 6 | .283 | .372 | .368 | 144 | 53 | 8 | 3 | 0 | 23 | 19 | 17 | .446 | .465 |
| Power,Ted | R | .272 | 81 | 22 | 1 | 1 | 3 | 12 | 14 | 18 | .375 | .420 | .243 | 115 | 28 | 6 | 0 | 2 | 13 | 3 | 24 | .261 | .348 |
| Price,Joe | L | .267 | 90 | 24 | 2 | 0 | 1 | 6 | 9 | 18 | .333 | .322 | .245 | 155 | 38 | 7 | 0 | 7 | 22 | 15 | 36 | .310 | .426 |
| Quisenberry,Dan | R | .727 | 11 | 8 | 2 | 1 | 0 | 5 | 1 | 0 | .600 | 1.091 | .250 | 20 | 5 | 0 | 0 | 1 | 5 | 2 | 2 | .318 | .400 |
| Radinsky,Scott | L | .177 | 62 | 11 | 1 | 1 | 0 | 8 | 7 | 20 | .268 | .226 | .271 | 133 | 36 | 5 | 0 | 1 | 19 | 29 | 26 | .402 | .331 |
| Rasmussen,Dennis | L | .333 | 108 | 36 | 5 | 1 | 5 | 17 | 7 | 12 | .385 | .537 | .285 | 634 | 181 | 25 | 1 | 23 | 77 | 55 | 74 | .341 | .437 |
| Reardon,Jeff | R | .143 | 91 | 13 | 3 | 0 | 1 | 6 | 12 | 12 | .243 | .209 | .265 | 98 | 26 | 8 | 0 | 4 | 19 | 7 | 21 | .321 | .469 |
| Reed,Jerry | R | .278 | 97 | 27 | 9 | 1 | 1 | 16 | 12 | 5 | .348 | .423 | .319 | 113 | 36 | 8 | 2 | 1 | 21 | 7 | 14 | .358 | .451 |
| Reed,Rick | R | .228 | 145 | 33 | 8 | 0 | 3 | 14 | 10 | 16 | .277 | .345 | .377 | 77 | 29 | 5 | 0 | 3 | 11 | 2 | 11 | .395 | .558 |
| Reuschel,Rick | R | .325 | 206 | 67 | 17 | 1 | 6 | 23 | 22 | 21 | .384 | .505 | .255 | 137 | 35 | 6 | 0 | 2 | 15 | 9 | 28 | .304 | .343 |
| Reuss,Jerry | L | .125 | 8 | 1 | 1 | 0 | 0 | 2 | 2 | 0 | .300 | .250 | .318 | 22 | 7 | 2 | 0 | 1 | 2 | 1 | 1 | .348 | .545 |
| Richards,Rusty | R | 1.000 | 2 | 2 | 0 | 0 | 1 | 3 | 0 | 0 | 1.000 | 2.500 | .000 | 3 | 0 | 0 | 0 | 0 | 0 | 1 | 0 | .250 | .000 |
| Richardson,Jeff | R | .000 | 0 | 0 | 0 | 0 | 0 | 0 | 0 | 0 | .000 | .000 | .500 | 2 | 1 | 0 | 1 | 0 | 3 | 0 | 0 | .500 | 1.500 |
| Righetti,Dave | L | .244 | 41 | 10 | 1 | 0 | 2 | 8 | 2 | 10 | .295 | .415 | .232 | 164 | 38 | 5 | 2 | 6 | 18 | 24 | 33 | .332 | .396 |
| Rijo,Jose | R | .218 | 409 | 89 | 16 | 2 | 7 | 32 | 58 | 83 | .316 | .318 | .205 | 303 | 62 | 18 | 2 | 3 | 21 | 20 | 69 | .255 | .307 |
| Ritz,Kevin | R | .455 | 11 | 5 | 1 | 0 | 0 | 3 | 6 | 1 | .647 | .545 | .375 | 24 | 9 | 1 | 0 | 0 | 5 | 8 | 2 | .531 | .417 |
| Robinson,Don | R | .285 | 369 | 105 | 24 | 1 | 12 | 43 | 32 | 40 | .342 | .453 | .273 | 249 | 68 | 12 | 1 | 6 | 35 | 9 | 38 | .296 | .402 |
| Robinson,Jeff | R | .221 | 140 | 31 | 4 | 0 | 3 | 13 | 10 | 14 | .273 | .314 | .267 | 191 | 51 | 11 | 2 | 5 | 26 | 24 | 29 | .350 | .424 |
| Robinson,Jeff M. | R | .244 | 254 | 62 | 13 | 3 | 10 | 32 | 39 | 35 | .348 | .437 | .265 | 298 | 79 | 21 | 1 | 13 | 54 | 49 | 41 | .372 | .473 |
| Robinson,Ron | R | .265 | 370 | 98 | 18 | 0 | 4 | 31 | 30 | 32 | .320 | .346 | .294 | 326 | 96 | 18 | 1 | 3 | 37 | 21 | 39 | .342 | .383 |
| Rochford,Mike | L | .400 | 5 | 2 | 0 | 0 | 1 | 2 | 0 | 0 | .400 | 1.000 | .571 | 14 | 8 | 1 | 0 | 0 | 6 | 4 | 0 | .632 | .643 |
| Rodriguez,Rich | L | .231 | 65 | 15 | 1 | 0 | 0 | 7 | 6 | 12 | .296 | .246 | .319 | 116 | 37 | 9 | 0 | 2 | 15 | 10 | 10 | .375 | .448 |
| Rodriguez,Rick | R | .444 | 9 | 4 | 1 | 0 | 0 | 2 | 2 | 1 | .545 | .556 | .200 | 5 | 1 | 0 | 0 | 0 | 1 | 0 | 1 | .200 | .200 |
| Rodriguez,Rosario | L | .368 | 19 | 7 | 0 | 0 | 1 | 2 | 0 | 4 | .368 | .526 | .348 | 23 | 8 | 0 | 1 | 2 | 5 | 2 | 4 | .407 | .696 |
| Roesler,Mike | R | .200 | 10 | 2 | 1 | 0 | 0 | 1 | 0 | 3 | .200 | .300 | .231 | 13 | 3 | 0 | 0 | 1 | 1 | 2 | 1 | .333 | .462 |
| Rogers,Kenny | L | .219 | 96 | 21 | 6 | 1 | 1 | 10 | 6 | 19 | .272 | .333 | .259 | 278 | 72 | 16 | 2 | 5 | 36 | 36 | 55 | .340 | .385 |
| Rojas,Mel | R | .207 | 92 | 19 | 4 | 0 | 3 | 10 | 19 | 14 | .342 | .348 | .283 | 53 | 15 | 3 | 0 | 2 | 8 | 5 | 12 | .367 | .453 |
| Rosenberg,Steve | L | .400 | 10 | 4 | 0 | 1 | 2 | 5 | 2 | 1 | .500 | 1.200 | .207 | 29 | 6 | 0 | 0 | 0 | 4 | 3 | 3 | .281 | .207 |
| Ross,Mark | R | .167 | 24 | 4 | 1 | 0 | 2 | 3 | 2 | 3 | .231 | .458 | .333 | 21 | 7 | 1 | 0 | 0 | 3 | 2 | 2 | .391 | .381 |
| Ruffin,Bruce | L | .292 | 120 | 35 | 8 | 0 | 0 | 29 | 12 | 19 | .351 | .358 | .299 | 479 | 143 | 37 | 4 | 14 | 61 | 50 | 60 | .363 | .480 |
| Ruskin,Scott | L | .281 | 114 | 32 | 2 | 0 | 3 | 13 | 13 | 26 | .354 | .377 | .246 | 175 | 43 | 9 | 1 | 1 | 14 | 25 | 31 | .343 | .326 |
| Russell,Jeff | R | .128 | 39 | 5 | 1 | 0 | 1 | 4 | 4 | 7 | .209 | .231 | .346 | 52 | 18 | 6 | 0 | 0 | 12 | 12 | 9 | .462 | .462 |
| Ryan,Nolan | R | .218 | 362 | 79 | 10 | 8 | 8 | 31 | 43 | 92 | .305 | .356 | .158 | 367 | 58 | 10 | 4 | 10 | 41 | 31 | 140 | .230 | .289 |
| Saberhagen,Bret | R | .275 | 222 | 61 | 6 | 4 | 5 | 25 | 16 | 42 | .318 | .405 | .281 | 302 | 85 | 14 | 1 | 4 | 23 | 12 | 45 | .311 | .374 |
| Sampen,Bill | R | .254 | 177 | 45 | 6 | 0 | 1 | 19 | 18 | 26 | .320 | .305 | .282 | 174 | 49 | 6 | 0 | 6 | 20 | 15 | 43 | .344 | .420 |
| Sanchez,Zip | L | .250 | 12 | 3 | 2 | 0 | 0 | 2 | 2 | 2 | .357 | .417 | .433 | 30 | 13 | 2 | 0 | 1 | 6 | 1 | 3 | .455 | .600 |
| Sanderson,Scott | R | .234 | 402 | 94 | 14 | 5 | 13 | 46 | 39 | 54 | .300 | .391 | .277 | 401 | 111 | 25 | 2 | 14 | 45 | 27 | 74 | .325 | .454 |
| Savage,Jack | R | .370 | 46 | 17 | 2 | 2 | 2 | 14 | 5 | 5 | .423 | .630 | .317 | 63 | 20 | 3 | 0 | 1 | 12 | 6 | 7 | .377 | .413 |
| Schatzeder,Dan | L | .261 | 88 | 23 | 2 | 1 | 1 | 13 | 8 | 17 | .316 | .341 | .261 | 165 | 43 | 7 | 0 | 1 | 15 | 15 | 22 | .317 | .321 |
| Schilling,Curt | R | .308 | 65 | 20 | 4 | 0 | 0 | 7 | 8 | 7 | .378 | .369 | .178 | 101 | 18 | 5 | 0 | 1 | 15 | 11 | 25 | .252 | .257 |
| Schiraldi,Calvin | R | .266 | 207 | 55 | 7 | 3 | 7 | 33 | 40 | 31 | .383 | .430 | .263 | 190 | 50 | 11 | 3 | 4 | 30 | 20 | 43 | .333 | .416 |
| Schmidt,Dave | R | .309 | 110 | 34 | 6 | 2 | 2 | 14 | 9 | 10 | .358 | .455 | .289 | 83 | 24 | 3 | 1 | 1 | 9 | 4 | 12 | .322 | .386 |
| Schooler,Mike | R | .209 | 110 | 23 | 5 | 1 | 2 | 15 | 13 | 19 | .294 | .327 | .247 | 97 | 24 | 3 | 1 | 3 | 6 | 3 | 26 | .270 | .392 |
| Schwabe,Mike | R | .167 | 6 | 1 | 0 | 0 | 0 | 1 | 0 | 0 | .167 | .167 | .500 | 8 | 4 | 0 | 0 | 0 | 0 | 0 | 1 | .500 | .500 |
| Scott,Mike | R | .240 | 450 | 108 | 21 | 3 | 11 | 52 | 43 | 55 | .303 | .373 | .254 | 339 | 86 | 12 | 2 | 16 | 41 | 23 | 66 | .301 | .442 |
| Scudder,Scott | R | .297 | 158 | 47 | 9 | 3 | 4 | 20 | 17 | 17 | .369 | .468 | .223 | 121 | 27 | 5 | 0 | 8 | 18 | 13 | 25 | .307 | .463 |
| Seanez,Rudy | R | .302 | 43 | 13 | 0 | 1 | 1 | 10 | 11 | 3 | .446 | .419 | .158 | 57 | 9 | 1 | 0 | 1 | 8 | 14 | 21 | .324 | .228 |
| Searage,Ray | L | .255 | 47 | 12 | 1 | 0 | 0 | 6 | 4 | 9 | .308 | .277 | .247 | 73 | 18 | 4 | 0 | 1 | 11 | 6 | 10 | .293 | .342 |
| Searcy,Steve | L | .326 | 46 | 15 | 3 | 0 | 1 | 9 | 7 | 3 | .407 | .457 | .258 | 236 | 61 | 10 | 1 | 8 | 32 | 44 | 63 | .368 | .411 |
| Sebra,Bob | R | .294 | 17 | 5 | 1 | 1 | 0 | 1 | 2 | 2 | .368 | .471 | .469 | 32 | 15 | 5 | 0 | 1 | 10 | 3 | 2 | .500 | .719 |

# **Pitchers** vs. Left-Handed and Right-Handed Batters

| Pitcher | | vs. Left-Handed Batters | | | | | | | | | | | vs. Right-Handed Batters | | | | | | | | | | |
|---|---|---|---|---|---|---|---|---|---|---|---|---|---|---|---|---|---|---|---|---|---|---|---|
| | | Avg | AB | H | 2B | 3B | HR | RBI | BB | SO | OBP | SLG | Avg | AB | H | 2B | 3B | HR | RBI | BB | SO | OBP | SLG |
| Shaw,Jeff | R | .356 | 118 | 42 | 9 | 0 | 4 | 13 | 11 | 13 | .408 | .534 | .356 | 87 | 31 | 7 | 1 | 7 | 16 | 9 | 12 | .408 | .701 |
| Sherrill,Tim | L | .444 | 9 | 4 | 2 | 0 | 0 | 5 | 1 | 2 | .500 | .667 | .500 | 12 | 6 | 1 | 0 | 0 | 2 | 2 | 1 | .571 | .583 |
| Show,Eric | R | .316 | 234 | 74 | 7 | 4 | 8 | 34 | 31 | 25 | .393 | .483 | .294 | 194 | 57 | 8 | 0 | 8 | 38 | 10 | 30 | .338 | .459 |
| Sisk,Doug | R | .000 | 2 | 0 | 0 | 0 | 0 | 2 | 3 | 1 | .429 | .000 | .200 | 5 | 1 | 0 | 0 | 0 | 0 | 1 | 0 | .333 | .200 |
| Smiley,John | L | .301 | 93 | 28 | 4 | 2 | 3 | 14 | 7 | 9 | .350 | .484 | .270 | 492 | 133 | 25 | 5 | 12 | 55 | 29 | 77 | .311 | .415 |
| Smith,Bryn | R | .301 | 339 | 102 | 14 | 4 | 3 | 41 | 18 | 35 | .339 | .392 | .264 | 220 | 58 | 9 | 0 | 8 | 32 | 12 | 43 | .302 | .414 |
| Smith,Daryl | R | .167 | 6 | 1 | 0 | 0 | 0 | 2 | 4 | 1 | .417 | .167 | .267 | 15 | 4 | 0 | 0 | 0 | 2 | 0 | 5 | .267 | .267 |
| Smith,Dave | R | .230 | 113 | 26 | 3 | 0 | 1 | 8 | 10 | 23 | .293 | .283 | .188 | 101 | 19 | 2 | 2 | 3 | 12 | 10 | 27 | .259 | .337 |
| Smith,Lee | R | .233 | 180 | 42 | 10 | 1 | 3 | 19 | 24 | 54 | .320 | .350 | .223 | 130 | 29 | 6 | 0 | 0 | 7 | 5 | 33 | .250 | .269 |
| Smith,Michael | R | .500 | 6 | 3 | 1 | 0 | 1 | 1 | 1 | 0 | .571 | 1.167 | .143 | 7 | 1 | 0 | 0 | 1 | 3 | 0 | 2 | .143 | .571 |
| Smith,Pete | R | .295 | 166 | 49 | 8 | 0 | 3 | 18 | 17 | 19 | .357 | .398 | .215 | 130 | 28 | 2 | 0 | 8 | 19 | 7 | 37 | .254 | .415 |
| Smith,Roy | R | .369 | 287 | 106 | 18 | 4 | 9 | 47 | 31 | 36 | .423 | .554 | .262 | 324 | 85 | 16 | 0 | 11 | 38 | 16 | 51 | .293 | .414 |
| Smith,Zane | L | .164 | 116 | 19 | 5 | 0 | 1 | 8 | 10 | 28 | .230 | .233 | .258 | 685 | 177 | 20 | 7 | 14 | 60 | 40 | 102 | .301 | .369 |
| Smoltz,John | R | .269 | 510 | 137 | 20 | 4 | 10 | 51 | 63 | 76 | .347 | .382 | .198 | 348 | 69 | 11 | 1 | 10 | 44 | 27 | 94 | .255 | .322 |
| Stanton,Mike | L | .250 | 8 | 2 | 0 | 0 | 0 | 2 | 1 | 3 | .400 | .250 | .500 | 28 | 14 | 1 | 0 | 1 | 11 | 3 | 4 | .548 | .643 |
| Stewart,Dave | R | .207 | 478 | 99 | 19 | 2 | 8 | 39 | 48 | 80 | .280 | .305 | .253 | 502 | 127 | 20 | 1 | 8 | 43 | 35 | 86 | .303 | .345 |
| Stieb,Dave | R | .253 | 403 | 102 | 14 | 2 | 8 | 39 | 40 | 47 | .326 | .357 | .205 | 375 | 77 | 17 | 1 | 3 | 29 | 24 | 78 | .263 | .280 |
| Stottlemyre,Mel | R | .316 | 57 | 18 | 1 | 0 | 3 | 11 | 8 | 6 | .400 | .491 | .250 | 68 | 17 | 5 | 0 | 0 | 6 | 4 | 8 | .292 | .324 |
| Stottlemyre,Todd | R | .300 | 393 | 118 | 22 | 5 | 8 | 52 | 37 | 42 | .365 | .443 | .247 | 388 | 96 | 14 | 3 | 10 | 44 | 32 | 73 | .309 | .376 |
| Sutcliffe,Rick | R | .319 | 47 | 15 | 3 | 0 | 0 | 7 | 10 | 4 | .431 | .383 | .286 | 35 | 10 | 2 | 0 | 2 | 5 | 2 | 3 | .316 | .514 |
| Swan,Russ | L | .231 | 39 | 9 | 1 | 0 | 0 | 7 | 2 | 2 | .256 | .256 | .265 | 147 | 39 | 8 | 1 | 3 | 20 | 20 | 14 | .351 | .395 |
| Swift,Bill | R | .287 | 216 | 62 | 12 | 0 | 4 | 27 | 8 | 15 | .317 | .398 | .261 | 280 | 73 | 15 | 0 | 0 | 27 | 13 | 27 | .302 | .314 |
| Swindell,Greg | L | .294 | 126 | 37 | 5 | 0 | 4 | 15 | 6 | 18 | .326 | .429 | .287 | 724 | 208 | 36 | 8 | 23 | 84 | 41 | 117 | .324 | .454 |
| Tanana,Frank | L | .230 | 113 | 26 | 4 | 0 | 1 | 10 | 7 | 15 | .290 | .292 | .290 | 565 | 164 | 36 | 1 | 24 | 89 | 59 | 99 | .360 | .485 |
| Tapani,Kevin | R | .284 | 317 | 90 | 16 | 7 | 6 | 30 | 21 | 53 | .328 | .435 | .243 | 304 | 74 | 12 | 1 | 6 | 32 | 8 | 48 | .263 | .349 |
| Taylor,Dorn | R | .333 | 6 | 2 | 1 | 0 | 0 | 1 | 2 | 1 | .500 | .500 | .200 | 10 | 2 | 0 | 0 | 0 | 1 | 0 | 3 | .200 | .200 |
| Telford,Anthony | R | .309 | 68 | 21 | 4 | 0 | 3 | 12 | 5 | 9 | .351 | .500 | .282 | 78 | 22 | 5 | 0 | 1 | 5 | 14 | 11 | .394 | .385 |
| Terrell,Walt | R | .323 | 341 | 110 | 22 | 1 | 16 | 53 | 37 | 34 | .390 | .534 | .257 | 288 | 74 | 14 | 3 | 4 | 26 | 20 | 30 | .326 | .368 |
| Terry,Scott | R | .269 | 130 | 35 | 9 | 1 | 4 | 26 | 15 | 20 | .342 | .446 | .260 | 154 | 40 | 11 | 0 | 3 | 23 | 12 | 15 | .322 | .390 |
| Tewksbury,Bob | R | .277 | 339 | 94 | 21 | 1 | 4 | 37 | 13 | 22 | .301 | .381 | .252 | 226 | 57 | 15 | 2 | 3 | 22 | 2 | 28 | .264 | .376 |
| Thigpen,Bobby | R | .215 | 158 | 34 | 4 | 1 | 3 | 12 | 18 | 35 | .294 | .310 | .174 | 149 | 26 | 4 | 1 | 2 | 13 | 14 | 35 | .247 | .255 |
| Thompson,Rich | R | .500 | 2 | 1 | 1 | 0 | 0 | 0 | 0 | 0 | .500 | 1.000 | .000 | 2 | 0 | 0 | 0 | 0 | 0 | 0 | 0 | .000 | .000 |
| Thurmond,Mark | L | .233 | 60 | 14 | 1 | 1 | 3 | 10 | 6 | 8 | .299 | .433 | .267 | 146 | 39 | 8 | 2 | 3 | 22 | 12 | 16 | .313 | .411 |
| Tibbs,Jay | R | .268 | 112 | 30 | 5 | 0 | 3 | 11 | 9 | 16 | .320 | .393 | .286 | 112 | 32 | 4 | 1 | 5 | 22 | 7 | 11 | .325 | .473 |
| Tomlin,Randy | L | .267 | 45 | 12 | 2 | 0 | 2 | 5 | 1 | 11 | .283 | .444 | .213 | 235 | 50 | 15 | 1 | 3 | 15 | 11 | 31 | .249 | .323 |
| Tudor,John | L | .214 | 126 | 27 | 5 | 0 | 1 | 7 | 5 | 23 | .244 | .278 | .228 | 408 | 93 | 20 | 1 | 9 | 32 | 25 | 40 | .275 | .348 |
| Valdez,Efrain | L | .188 | 32 | 6 | 2 | 0 | 0 | 5 | 4 | 4 | .270 | .250 | .259 | 54 | 14 | 3 | 0 | 2 | 6 | 10 | 9 | .364 | .426 |
| Valdez,Rafael | R | .615 | 13 | 8 | 1 | 0 | 4 | 7 | 2 | 1 | .667 | 1.615 | .200 | 15 | 3 | 2 | 0 | 0 | 0 | 0 | 2 | .200 | .333 |
| Valdez,Sergio | R | .208 | 192 | 40 | 10 | 1 | 6 | 19 | 21 | 29 | .284 | .365 | .333 | 225 | 75 | 17 | 0 | 11 | 40 | 17 | 37 | .379 | .556 |
| Valenzuela,Fernando | L | .315 | 130 | 41 | 6 | 0 | 4 | 18 | 15 | 19 | .381 | .454 | .268 | 678 | 182 | 45 | 1 | 15 | 86 | 62 | 96 | .329 | .404 |
| Valera,Julio | R | .361 | 36 | 13 | 4 | 0 | 0 | 4 | 4 | 1 | .425 | .472 | .333 | 21 | 7 | 1 | 0 | 1 | 5 | 3 | 3 | .417 | .524 |
| Veres,Randy | R | .262 | 61 | 16 | 3 | 0 | 2 | 7 | 7 | 5 | .333 | .410 | .237 | 93 | 22 | 2 | 0 | 3 | 15 | 9 | 11 | .308 | .355 |
| Viola,Frank | L | .257 | 183 | 47 | 10 | 0 | 1 | 12 | 14 | 47 | .317 | .328 | .238 | 755 | 180 | 26 | 2 | 14 | 60 | 46 | 135 | .281 | .334 |
| Vosberg,Ed | L | .192 | 26 | 5 | 1 | 1 | 0 | 5 | 6 | 3 | .344 | .308 | .250 | 64 | 16 | 2 | 1 | 3 | 12 | 6 | 9 | .314 | .453 |
| Wagner,Hector | R | .270 | 63 | 17 | 2 | 0 | 1 | 7 | 6 | 10 | .329 | .349 | .417 | 36 | 15 | 3 | 0 | 3 | 11 | 5 | 4 | .476 | .750 |
| Walk,Bob | R | .260 | 300 | 78 | 10 | 1 | 9 | 32 | 26 | 37 | .323 | .390 | .286 | 203 | 58 | 12 | 0 | 8 | 19 | 10 | 36 | .321 | .463 |
| Walker,Mike | R | .250 | 140 | 35 | 6 | 1 | 3 | 16 | 20 | 20 | .350 | .371 | .301 | 156 | 47 | 9 | 1 | 3 | 21 | 22 | 14 | .399 | .429 |
| Walsh,David | L | .222 | 27 | 6 | 0 | 0 | 1 | 8 | 2 | 5 | .267 | .333 | .257 | 35 | 9 | 3 | 1 | 0 | 6 | 4 | 10 | .333 | .400 |
| Wapnick,Steve | R | .455 | 11 | 5 | 1 | 0 | 0 | 2 | 1 | 1 | .500 | .545 | .188 | 16 | 3 | 1 | 0 | 0 | 1 | 9 | 5 | .480 | .250 |
| Ward,Colby | R | .222 | 54 | 12 | 2 | 0 | 0 | 4 | 12 | 7 | .368 | .259 | .250 | 76 | 19 | 5 | 0 | 3 | 15 | 9 | 16 | .326 | .434 |

# **Pitchers** vs. Left-Handed and Right-Handed Batters

| | | vs. Left-Handed Batters | | | | | | | | | | | vs. Right-Handed Batters | | | | | | | | | | |
|---|---|---|---|---|---|---|---|---|---|---|---|---|---|---|---|---|---|---|---|---|---|---|---|
| Pitcher | | Avg | AB | H | 2B | 3B | HR | RBI | BB | SO | OBP | SLG | Avg | AB | H | 2B | 3B | HR | RBI | BB | SO | OBP | SLG |
| Ward,Duane | R | .259 | 189 | 49 | 7 | 1 | 5 | 26 | 33 | 49 | .372 | .386 | .194 | 268 | 52 | 6 | 2 | 4 | 27 | 9 | 63 | .219 | .276 |
| Wayne,Gary | L | .174 | 46 | 8 | 1 | 0 | 2 | 8 | 5 | 8 | .245 | .326 | .291 | 103 | 30 | 7 | 0 | 3 | 19 | 8 | 20 | .348 | .447 |
| Wegman,Bill | R | .286 | 56 | 16 | 2 | 1 | 2 | 3 | 2 | 7 | .310 | .464 | .309 | 68 | 21 | 5 | 0 | 4 | 13 | 4 | 13 | .342 | .559 |
| Welch,Bob | R | .258 | 465 | 120 | 20 | 6 | 12 | 39 | 43 | 55 | .325 | .404 | .223 | 421 | 94 | 22 | 0 | 14 | 42 | 34 | 72 | .281 | .375 |
| Wells,David | L | .264 | 110 | 29 | 11 | 1 | 2 | 15 | 8 | 12 | .319 | .436 | .230 | 591 | 136 | 28 | 6 | 12 | 50 | 37 | 103 | .276 | .359 |
| Wells,Terry | L | .600 | 5 | 3 | 1 | 0 | 0 | 3 | 2 | 0 | .714 | .800 | .268 | 82 | 22 | 5 | 0 | 4 | 16 | 12 | 18 | .362 | .476 |
| West,David | L | .244 | 90 | 22 | 3 | 2 | 1 | 13 | 12 | 14 | .333 | .356 | .259 | 464 | 120 | 32 | 3 | 20 | 70 | 66 | 78 | .353 | .470 |
| Weston,Mickey | R | .350 | 40 | 14 | 0 | 0 | 3 | 8 | 5 | 4 | .422 | .575 | .298 | 47 | 14 | 2 | 0 | 3 | 13 | 1 | 5 | .313 | .532 |
| Wetteland,John | R | .292 | 89 | 26 | 3 | 0 | 3 | 19 | 11 | 15 | .394 | .427 | .231 | 78 | 18 | 3 | 0 | 3 | 15 | 6 | 21 | .282 | .385 |
| Whitehurst,Wally | R | .238 | 126 | 30 | 4 | 1 | 0 | 8 | 6 | 29 | .273 | .286 | .264 | 125 | 33 | 4 | 0 | 5 | 21 | 3 | 17 | .281 | .416 |
| Whitson,Ed | R | .271 | 527 | 143 | 26 | 1 | 6 | 37 | 30 | 73 | .310 | .359 | .220 | 328 | 72 | 15 | 0 | 7 | 29 | 17 | 54 | .256 | .329 |
| Wickander,Kevin | L | .400 | 15 | 6 | 1 | 0 | 0 | 1 | 3 | 2 | .474 | .467 | .258 | 31 | 8 | 1 | 1 | 0 | 3 | 1 | 8 | .294 | .355 |
| Wilkins,Dean | R | .294 | 17 | 5 | 4 | 0 | 0 | 2 | 3 | 2 | .400 | .529 | .375 | 16 | 6 | 1 | 0 | 1 | 6 | 4 | 1 | .524 | .625 |
| Williams,Mitch | L | .227 | 66 | 15 | 5 | 1 | 2 | 14 | 16 | 18 | .369 | .424 | .243 | 185 | 45 | 15 | 2 | 2 | 30 | 34 | 37 | .362 | .378 |
| Williamson,Mark | R | .223 | 139 | 31 | 4 | 2 | 6 | 19 | 7 | 25 | .257 | .410 | .209 | 163 | 34 | 9 | 0 | 2 | 18 | 21 | 35 | .291 | .301 |
| Wills,Frank | R | .250 | 172 | 43 | 10 | 0 | 4 | 14 | 17 | 18 | .319 | .378 | .279 | 208 | 58 | 9 | 1 | 9 | 39 | 21 | 54 | .345 | .462 |
| Wilson,Steve | L | .219 | 137 | 30 | 6 | 1 | 3 | 20 | 8 | 34 | .267 | .343 | .273 | 403 | 110 | 17 | 5 | 14 | 52 | 35 | 61 | .330 | .444 |
| Wilson,Trevor | L | .219 | 64 | 14 | 3 | 0 | 1 | 8 | 5 | 12 | .275 | .313 | .218 | 335 | 73 | 10 | 0 | 10 | 36 | 44 | 54 | .309 | .337 |
| Witt,Bobby | R | .232 | 396 | 92 | 16 | 2 | 5 | 42 | 54 | 98 | .323 | .321 | .242 | 433 | 105 | 15 | 1 | 7 | 41 | 56 | 123 | .332 | .330 |
| Witt,Mike | R | .267 | 217 | 58 | 10 | 1 | 3 | 28 | 23 | 29 | .339 | .364 | .216 | 222 | 48 | 9 | 2 | 6 | 25 | 24 | 45 | .298 | .356 |
| Yett,Richard | R | .500 | 6 | 3 | 1 | 0 | 0 | 0 | 1 | 0 | .571 | .667 | .273 | 11 | 3 | 2 | 0 | 1 | 1 | 0 | 2 | .273 | .727 |
| York,Mike | R | .333 | 27 | 9 | 0 | 0 | 0 | 3 | 2 | 0 | .367 | .333 | .200 | 20 | 4 | 0 | 0 | 0 | 2 | 3 | 4 | .333 | .200 |
| Young,Cliff | L | .394 | 33 | 13 | 2 | 0 | 0 | 8 | 2 | 7 | .417 | .455 | .300 | 90 | 27 | 5 | 1 | 2 | 14 | 5 | 12 | .333 | .444 |
| Young,Curt | L | .260 | 96 | 25 | 4 | 0 | 1 | 12 | 6 | 13 | .311 | .333 | .268 | 370 | 99 | 16 | 0 | 16 | 45 | 47 | 43 | .350 | .441 |
| Young,Matt | L | .158 | 101 | 16 | 1 | 0 | 0 | 7 | 7 | 27 | .218 | .168 | .248 | 735 | 182 | 24 | 3 | 15 | 79 | 100 | 149 | .339 | .350 |

This page intentionally left blank.

# Leader Boards

A good list is always fun to look at. It's got that "Wow, I didn't know that!" quality. It follows then, that many good lists are even more fun to look at.

This section of the book contains a lot of lists: 12 pages worth, to be exact. Section One consists of 1990 Batting Leaders, Section Two contains 1990 Pitching Leaders, Section Three has Special Batting and Pitching Leaders, Section Four holds Active Career Leaders, and Section Five shows Bill James Leaders. Some of the more unorthodox lists are explained more fully in the Glossary.

We've tried to cram almost every list we could think of onto these pages, but there are still a couple hundred we had to leave on the cutting room floor. Knowledge is power, and isn't it a powerful feeling to stump your friends with such gems as "Guess who led the American League last year in Games Finished?"

# 1990 American League Batting Leaders

## Batting Average

| Player, Team | AB | H | AVG |
|---|---|---|---|
| **G BRETT, KC** | **544** | **179** | **.329** |
| R Henderson, Oak | 489 | 159 | .325 |
| R Palmeiro, Tex | 598 | 191 | .319 |
| A Trammell, Det | 559 | 170 | .304 |
| W Boggs, Bos | 619 | 187 | .302 |
| E Martinez, Sea | 487 | 147 | .302 |
| K Griffey Jr, Sea | 597 | 179 | .300 |
| F McGriff, Tor | 557 | 167 | .300 |
| C James, Cle | 528 | 158 | .299 |
| K Puckett, Min | 551 | 164 | .298 |

## On-Base Percentage

| Player, Team | PA* | OB | OBP |
|---|---|---|---|
| **R HENDERSON,Oak** | **592** | **260** | **.439** |
| F McGriff, Tor | 657 | 263 | .400 |
| E Martinez, Sea | 569 | 226 | .397 |
| G Brett, KC | 607 | 235 | .387 |
| A Davis, Sea | 592 | 229 | .387 |
| W Boggs, Bos | 713 | 275 | .386 |
| J Franco, Tex | 668 | 256 | .383 |
| C Fisk, ChA | 521 | 197 | .378 |
| C Fielder, Det | 673 | 254 | .377 |
| A Trammell, Det | 634 | 239 | .377 |

## Slugging Percentage

| Player, Team | AB | TB | SLG |
|---|---|---|---|
| **C FIELDER, Det** | **573** | **339** | **.592** |
| R Henderson, Oak | 489 | 282 | .577 |
| J Canseco, Oak | 481 | 261 | .543 |
| F McGriff, Tor | 557 | 295 | .530 |
| G Brett, KC | 544 | 280 | .515 |
| K Gruber, Tor | 592 | 303 | .512 |
| M McGwire, Oak | 523 | 256 | .489 |
| E Burks, Bos | 588 | 286 | .486 |
| K Griffey Jr, Sea | 597 | 287 | .481 |
| K Hrbek, Min | 492 | 233 | .474 |

## Games

| | |
|---|---|
| **R KELLY, NYA** | **162** |
| T Fernandez, Tor | 161 |
| C Ripken, Bal | 161 |
| O Guillen, ChA | 160 |
| H Reynolds, Sea | 160 |

## Plate Appearances

| | |
|---|---|
| **H REYNOLDS, Sea** | **737** |
| T Fernandez, Tor | 721 |
| W Boggs, Bos | 713 |
| K Seitzer, KC | 697 |
| C Ripken, Bal | 695 |

## At Bats

| | |
|---|---|
| **H REYNOLDS, Sea** | **642** |
| R Kelly, NYA | 641 |
| T Fernandez, Tor | 635 |
| K Seitzer, KC | 622 |
| W Boggs, Bos | 619 |

## Hits

| | |
|---|---|
| **R PALMEIRO, Tex** | **191** |
| W Boggs, Bos | 187 |
| R Kelly, NYA | 183 |
| M Greenwell, Bos | 181 |
| 2 Players with | 179 |

## Singles

| | |
|---|---|
| **R PALMEIRO, Tex** | **136** |
| J Franco, Tex | 133 |
| W Boggs, Bos | 132 |
| R Kelly, NYA | 132 |
| M Greenwell, Bos | 131 |

## Doubles

| | |
|---|---|
| **J REED, Bos** | **45** |
| **G BRETT, KC** | **45** |
| W Boggs, Bos | 44 |
| I Calderon, ChA | 44 |
| B Harper, Min | 42 |

## Triples

| | |
|---|---|
| **T FERNANDEZ, Tor** | **17** |
| S Sosa, ChA | 10 |
| L Johnson, ChA | 9 |
| N Liriano, Min | 9 |
| L Polonia, Cal | 9 |

## Home Runs

| | |
|---|---|
| **C FIELDER, Det** | **51** |
| M McGwire, Oak | 39 |
| J Canseco, Oak | 37 |
| F McGriff, Tor | 35 |
| K Gruber, Tor | 31 |

## Total Bases

| | |
|---|---|
| **C FIELDER, Det** | **339** |
| K Gruber, Tor | 303 |
| F McGriff, Tor | 295 |
| K Griffey Jr, Sea | 287 |
| E Burks, Bos | 286 |

## Runs Scored

| | |
|---|---|
| **R HENDERSON, Oak** | **119** |
| C Fielder, Det | 104 |
| H Reynolds, Sea | 100 |
| R Yount, Mil | 98 |
| T Phillips, Det | 97 |

## Runs Batted In

| | |
|---|---|
| **C FIELDER, Det** | **132** |
| K Gruber, Tor | 118 |
| M McGwire, Oak | 108 |
| J Canseco, Oak | 101 |
| R Sierra, Tex | 96 |

## Ground Double Play

| | |
|---|---|
| **I CALDERON, ChA** | **26** |
| R Palmeiro, Tex | 24 |
| T Pena, Bos | 23 |
| G Gaetti, Min | 22 |
| 3 Players with | 20 |

## Sacrifice Hits

| | |
|---|---|
| **M GALLEGO, Oak** | **17** |
| **B RIPKEN, Bal** | **17** |
| O Guillen, ChA | 15 |
| 3 Players with | 13 |

## Sacrifice Flies

| | |
|---|---|
| **D PARKER, Mil** | **14** |
| K Gruber, Tor | 13 |
| G Bell, Tor | 11 |
| J Browne, Cle | 11 |
| 3 Players with | 9 |

## Stolen Bases

| | |
|---|---|
| **R HENDERSON, Oak** | **65** |
| S Sax, NYA | 43 |
| R Kelly, NYA | 42 |
| A Cole, Cle | 40 |
| G Pettis, Tex | 38 |

## Caught Stealing

| | |
|---|---|
| **L JOHNSON, ChA** | **22** |
| R Kelly, NYA | 17 |
| O Guillen, ChA | 17 |
| 3 Players with | 16 |

## Walks

| | |
|---|---|
| **M MCGWIRE, Oak** | **110** |
| M Tettleton, Bal | 106 |
| T Phillips, Det | 99 |
| R Henderson, Oak | 97 |
| F McGriff, Tor | 94 |

## Intentional Walks

| | |
|---|---|
| **W BOGGS, Bos** | **19** |
| C Ripken, Bal | 18 |
| G Brett, KC | 14 |
| D Mattingly, NYA | 13 |
| R Sierra, Tex | 13 |

## Hit by Pitch

| | |
|---|---|
| **P BRADLEY, ChA** | **11** |
| P Incaviglia, Tex | 9 |
| K Gruber, Tor | 8 |
| 8 Players with | 7 |

## Strikeouts

| | |
|---|---|
| **C FIELDER, Det** | **182** |
| M Tettleton, Bal | 160 |
| J Canseco, Oak | 158 |
| S Sosa, ChA | 150 |
| J Barfield, NYA | 150 |

# 1990 National League Batting Leaders

### Batting Average

| Player, Team | AB | H | AVG |
|---|---|---|---|
| **W MCGEE, StL** | **501** | **168** | **.335** |
| E Murray, LA | 558 | 184 | .330 |
| D Magadan, NYN | 451 | 148 | .328 |
| L Dykstra, Phi | 590 | 192 | .325 |
| A Dawson, ChN | 529 | 164 | .310 |
| B Roberts, SD | 556 | 172 | .309 |
| M Grace, ChN | 589 | 182 | .309 |
| T Gwynn, SD | 573 | 177 | .309 |
| B Butler, SF | 622 | 192 | .309 |
| R Sandberg, ChN | 615 | 188 | .306 |

### On-Base Percentage

| Player, Team | PA* | OB | OBP |
|---|---|---|---|
| **L DYKSTRA, Phi** | **689** | **288** | **.418** |
| D Magadan, NYN | 537 | 224 | .417 |
| E Murray, LA | 645 | 267 | .414 |
| B Bonds, Pit | 621 | 252 | .406 |
| B Butler, SF | 725 | 288 | .397 |
| K Daniels, LA | 524 | 204 | .389 |
| J Kruk, Phi | 513 | 198 | .386 |
| L Smith, Atl | 536 | 206 | .384 |
| W McGee, StL | 542 | 207 | .382 |
| T Raines, Mon | 538 | 204 | .379 |

### Slugging Percentage

| Player, Team | AB | TB | SLG |
|---|---|---|---|
| **B BONDS, Pit** | **519** | **293** | **.564** |
| R Sandberg, ChN | 615 | 344 | .559 |
| K Mitchell, SF | 524 | 285 | .544 |
| R Gant, Atl | 575 | 310 | .539 |
| D Justice, Atl | 439 | 235 | .535 |
| A Dawson, ChN | 529 | 283 | .535 |
| K Daniels, LA | 450 | 239 | .531 |
| E Murray, LA | 558 | 290 | .520 |
| B Bonilla, Pit | 625 | 324 | .518 |
| D Strawberry, NYN | 542 | 281 | .518 |

### Games

| | |
|---|---|
| **J CARTER, SD** | **162** |
| T Wallach, Mon | 161 |
| B Butler, SF | 160 |
| B Bonilla, Pit | 160 |
| 2 Players with | 159 |

### Plate Appearances

| | |
|---|---|
| **B BUTLER, SF** | **732** |
| J Carter, SD | 697 |
| J Bell, Pit | 696 |
| L Dykstra, Phi | 691 |
| B Bonilla, Pit | 686 |

### At Bats

| | |
|---|---|
| **J CARTER, SD** | **634** |
| T Wallach, Mon | 626 |
| B Bonilla, Pit | 625 |
| B Butler, SF | 622 |
| M Williams, SF | 617 |

### Hits

| | |
|---|---|
| **B BUTLER, SF** | **192** |
| **L DYKSTRA, Phi** | **192** |
| R Sandberg, ChN | 188 |
| T Wallach, Mon | 185 |
| B Larkin, Cin | 185 |

### Singles

| | |
|---|---|
| **B BUTLER, SF** | **160** |
| B Larkin, Cin | 147 |
| L Dykstra, Phi | 145 |
| M Grace, ChN | 140 |
| T Gwynn, SD | 134 |

### Doubles

| | |
|---|---|
| **G JEFFERIES, NYN** | **40** |
| B Bonilla, Pit | 39 |
| C Sabo, Cin | 38 |
| T Wallach, Mon | 37 |
| H Johnson, NYN | 37 |

### Triples

| | |
|---|---|
| **M DUNCAN, Cin** | **11** |
| T Gwynn, SD | 10 |
| V Coleman, StL | 9 |
| B Butler, SF | 9 |
| L Smith, Atl | 9 |

### Home Runs

| | |
|---|---|
| **R SANDBERG, ChN** | **40** |
| D Strawberry, NYN | 37 |
| K Mitchell, SF | 35 |
| B Bonds, Pit | 33 |
| M Williams, SF | 33 |

### Total Bases

| | |
|---|---|
| **R SANDBERG, ChN** | **344** |
| B Bonilla, Pit | 324 |
| R Gant, Atl | 310 |
| M Williams, SF | 301 |
| T Wallach, Mon | 295 |

### Runs Scored

| | |
|---|---|
| **R SANDBERG, ChN** | **116** |
| B Bonilla, Pit | 112 |
| B Butler, SF | 108 |
| R Gant, Atl | 107 |
| L Dykstra, Phi | 106 |

### Runs Batted In

| | |
|---|---|
| **M WILLIAMS, SF** | **122** |
| B Bonilla, Pit | 120 |
| J Carter, SD | 115 |
| B Bonds, Pit | 114 |
| D Strawberry, NYN | 108 |

### Ground Double Play

| | |
|---|---|
| **D MURPHY, Phi** | **22** |
| J Lind, Pit | 20 |
| E Murray, LA | 19 |
| G Templeton, SD | 17 |
| 2 Players with | 16 |

### Sacrifice Bunts

| | |
|---|---|
| **J BELL, Pit** | **39** |
| D Gooden, NYN | 14 |
| J Armstrong, Cin | 13 |
| E Whitson, SD | 13 |
| 2 Players with | 12 |

### Sacrifice Flies

| | |
|---|---|
| **B BONILLA, Pit** | **15** |
| W Clark, SF | 13 |
| P Guerrero, StL | 11 |
| H Brooks, LA | 11 |
| 3 Players with | 10 |

### Stolen Bases

| | |
|---|---|
| **V COLEMAN, StL** | **77** |
| E Yelding, Hou | 64 |
| B Bonds, Pit | 52 |
| B Butler, SF | 51 |
| O Nixon, Mon | 50 |

### Caught Stealing

| | |
|---|---|
| **E YELDING, Hou** | **25** |
| D DeShields, Mon | 22 |
| J Samuel, LA | 20 |
| B Butler, SF | 19 |
| V Coleman, StL | 17 |

### Walks

| | |
|---|---|
| **J CLARK, SD** | **104** |
| B Bonds, Pit | 93 |
| B Butler, SF | 90 |
| L Dykstra, Phi | 89 |
| V Hayes, Phi | 87 |

### Intentional Walks

| | |
|---|---|
| **E MURRAY, LA** | **21** |
| **A DAWSON, ChN** | **21** |
| T Gwynn, SD | 20 |
| J Lind, Pit | 19 |
| J Carter, SD | 18 |

### Hit by Pitch

| | |
|---|---|
| **G DAVIS, Hou** | **8** |
| L Dykstra, Phi | 7 |
| J Carter, SD | 7 |
| B Larkin, Cin | 7 |
| M Williams, SF | 7 |

### Strikeouts

| | |
|---|---|
| **A GALARRAGA, Mon** | **169** |
| M Williams, SF | 138 |
| J Presley, Atl | 130 |
| D Murphy, Phi | 130 |
| J Samuel, LA | 126 |

# 1990 American League Pitching Leaders

## Earned Run Average

| Pitcher, Team | IP | ER | ERA |
|---|---|---|---|
| **R CLEMENS, Bos** | **228.1** | **49** | **1.93** |
| C Finley, Cal | 236.0 | 63 | 2.40 |
| D Stewart, Oak | 267.0 | 76 | 2.56 |
| K Appier, KC | 185.2 | 57 | 2.76 |
| D Stieb, Tor | 208.2 | 68 | 2.93 |
| B Welch, Oak | 238.0 | 78 | 2.95 |
| D Wells, Tor | 189.0 | 66 | 3.14 |
| G Hibbard, ChA | 211.0 | 74 | 3.16 |
| E Hanson, Sea | 236.0 | 85 | 3.24 |
| K McCaskill, Cal | 174.1 | 63 | 3.25 |

## Win-Loss Percentage

| Pitcher, Team | W | L | WL% |
|---|---|---|---|
| **B WELCH, Oak** | **27** | **6** | **.818** |
| R Clemens, Bos | 21 | 6 | .778 |
| D Stieb, Tor | 18 | 6 | .750 |
| E King, ChA | 12 | 4 | .750 |
| B Jones, ChA | 11 | 4 | .733 |
| R Robinson, Mil | 12 | 5 | .706 |
| M Boddicker, Bos | 17 | 8 | .680 |
| D Stewart, Oak | 22 | 11 | .667 |
| C Finley, Cal | 18 | 9 | .667 |
| E Hanson, Sea | 18 | 9 | .667 |

## Opponent Batting Average

| Pitcher, Team | AB | H | AVG |
|---|---|---|---|
| **N RYAN, Tex** | **729** | **137** | **.188** |
| R Johnson, Sea | 806 | 174 | .216 |
| R Clemens, Bos | 847 | 193 | .228 |
| D Stieb, Tor | 778 | 179 | .230 |
| D Stewart, Oak | 980 | 226 | .231 |
| E Hanson, Sea | 883 | 205 | .232 |
| B Black, Tor | 778 | 181 | .233 |
| D Wells, Tor | 701 | 165 | .235 |
| C Hough, Tex | 807 | 190 | .235 |
| M Young, Sea | 836 | 198 | .237 |

## Games

| | |
|---|---|
| **B THIGPEN, ChA** | **77** |
| D Ward, Tor | 73 |
| J Montgomery, KC | 73 |
| M Henneman, Det | 69 |
| K Rogers, Tex | 69 |

## Games Started

| | |
|---|---|
| **J MORRIS, Det** | **36** |
| **D STEWART, Oak** | **36** |
| B Welch, Oak | 35 |
| M Perez, ChA | 35 |
| 3 Players with | 34 |

## Complete Games

| | |
|---|---|
| **J MORRIS, Det** | **11** |
| **D STEWART, Oak** | **11** |
| 5 Players with | 7 |

## Games Finished

| | |
|---|---|
| **B THIGPEN, ChA** | **73** |
| D Jones, Cle | 64 |
| D Eckersley, Oak | 61 |
| J Montgomery, KC | 59 |
| 2 Players with | 58 |

## Wins

| | |
|---|---|
| **B WELCH, Oak** | **27** |
| D Stewart, Oak | 22 |
| R Clemens, Bos | 21 |
| C Finley, Cal | 18 |
| D Stieb, Tor | 18 |
| E Hanson, Sea | 18 |

## Losses

| | |
|---|---|
| **T LEARY, NYA** | **19** |
| J Morris, Det | 18 |
| M Young, Sea | 18 |
| A Anderson, Min | 18 |
| 2 Players with | 17 |

## Saves

| | |
|---|---|
| **B THIGPEN, ChA** | **57** |
| D Eckersley, Oak | 48 |
| D Jones, Cle | 43 |
| G Olson, Bal | 37 |
| D Righetti, NYA | 36 |

## Shutouts

| | |
|---|---|
| **D STEWART, Oak** | **4** |
| **R CLEMENS, Bos** | **4** |
| J Morris, Det | 3 |
| M Perez, ChA | 3 |
| K Appier, KC | 3 |

## Hits Allowed

| | |
|---|---|
| **J ABBOTT, Cal** | **246** |
| G Swindell, Cle | 245 |
| J Morris, Det | 231 |
| D Stewart, Oak | 226 |
| M Boddicker, Bos | 225 |

## Doubles Off

| | |
|---|---|
| **D JOHNSON, Bal** | **43** |
| J Morris, Det | 42 |
| B Welch, Oak | 42 |
| 3 Players with | 41 |

## Triples Off

| | |
|---|---|
| **N RYAN, Tex** | **12** |
| M Perez, ChA | 10 |
| 5 Players with | 8 |

## Home Runs Allowed

| | |
|---|---|
| **D JOHNSON, Bal** | **30** |
| G Swindell, Cle | 27 |
| S Sanderson, Oak | 27 |
| B Welch, Oak | 26 |
| R Johnson, Sea | 26 |
| J Morris, Det | 26 |

## Batters Faced

| | |
|---|---|
| **D STEWART, Oak** | **1088** |
| J Morris, Det | 1073 |
| B Welch, Oak | 979 |
| E Hanson, Sea | 964 |
| M Young, Sea | 963 |

## Innings Pitched

| | |
|---|---|
| **D STEWART, Oak** | **267.0** |
| J Morris, Det | 249.2 |
| B Welch, Oak | 238.0 |
| C Finley, Cal | 236.0 |
| E Hanson, Sea | 236.0 |

## Runs Allowed

| | |
|---|---|
| **J MORRIS, Det** | **144** |
| M Langston, Cal | 120 |
| J Abbott, Cal | 116 |
| M Moore, Oak | 113 |
| M Perez, ChA | 111 |

## Strikeouts

| | |
|---|---|
| **N RYAN, Tex** | **232** |
| B Witt, Tex | 221 |
| E Hanson, Sea | 211 |
| R Clemens, Bos | 209 |
| M Langston, Cal | 195 |

## Walks Allowed

| | |
|---|---|
| **R JOHNSON, Sea** | **120** |
| C Hough, Tex | 119 |
| B Witt, Tex | 110 |
| M Young, Sea | 107 |
| M Langston, Cal | 104 |

## Hit Batters

| | |
|---|---|
| **C HOUGH, Tex** | **11** |
| M Boddicker, Bos | 10 |
| D Stieb, Tor | 10 |
| F Tanana, Det | 9 |
| D Kiecker, Bos | 9 |

## Wild Pitches

| | |
|---|---|
| **T LEARY, NYA** | **23** |
| J Morris, Det | 16 |
| M Young, Sea | 16 |
| J Robinson, Det | 16 |
| G Cadaret, NYA | 14 |

## Balks

| | |
|---|---|
| **J NAVARRO, Mil** | **5** |
| M Perez, ChA | 4 |
| 5 Players with | 3 |

# 1990 National League Pitching Leaders

## Earned Run Average

| Pitcher, Team | IP | ER | ERA |
|---|---|---|---|
| **D DARWIN, Hou** | **162.2** | **40** | **2.21** |
| Z Smith, Mon-Pit | 215.1 | 61 | 2.55 |
| E Whitson, SD | 228.2 | 66 | 2.60 |
| F Viola, NYN | 249.2 | 74 | 2.67 |
| J Rijo, Cin | 197.0 | 59 | 2.70 |
| D Drabek, Pit | 231.1 | 71 | 2.76 |
| R Martinez, LA | 234.1 | 76 | 2.92 |
| O Boyd, Mon | 190.2 | 62 | 2.93 |
| D Martinez, Mon | 226.0 | 74 | 2.95 |
| B Hurst, SD | 223.2 | 78 | 3.14 |

## Win-Loss Percentage

| Pitcher, Team | W | L | WL% |
|---|---|---|---|
| **D DRABEK, Pit** | **22** | **6** | **.786** |
| R Martinez, LA | 20 | 6 | .769 |
| J Tudor, StL | 12 | 4 | .750 |
| D Gooden, NYN | 19 | 7 | .731 |
| D Darwin, Hou | 11 | 4 | .733 |
| J Burkett, SF | 14 | 7 | .667 |
| M Harkey, ChN | 12 | 6 | .667 |
| J Rijo, Cin | 14 | 8 | .636 |
| B Sampen, Mon | 12 | 7 | .632 |
| F Viola, NYN | 20 | 12 | .625 |

## Opponent Batting Average

| Pitcher, Team | AB | H | AVG |
|---|---|---|---|
| **S FERNANDEZ, NYN** | **650** | **130** | **.200** |
| J Rijo, Cin | 712 | 151 | .212 |
| R Martinez, LA | 866 | 191 | .221 |
| D Drabek, Pit | 846 | 190 | .225 |
| D Darwin, Hou | 605 | 136 | .225 |
| D Cone, NYN | 784 | 177 | .226 |
| D Martinez, Mon | 839 | 191 | .228 |
| B Hurst, SD | 823 | 188 | .228 |
| O Boyd, Mon | 702 | 164 | .234 |
| M Harkey, ChN | 653 | 153 | .234 |

## Games

| | |
|---|---|
| **J AGOSTO, Hou** | **82** |
| P Assenmacher, ChN | 74 |
| G Harris, SD | 73 |
| R McDowell, Phi | 72 |
| D Akerfelds, Phi | 71 |

## Wins

| | |
|---|---|
| **D DRABEK, Pit** | **22** |
| R Martinez, LA | 20 |
| F Viola, NYN | 20 |
| D Gooden, NYN | 19 |
| T Browning, Cin | 15 |
| G Maddux, ChN | 15 |

## Hits Allowed

| | |
|---|---|
| **G MADDUX, ChN** | **242** |
| T Browning, Cin | 235 |
| T Glavine, Atl | 232 |
| D Gooden, NYN | 229 |
| F Viola, NYN | 227 |

## Batters Faced

| | |
|---|---|
| **F VIOLA, NYN** | **1016** |
| G Maddux, ChN | 1011 |
| D Gooden, NYN | 983 |
| J Smoltz, Atl | 966 |
| T Browning, Cin | 957 |

## Walks Allowed

| | |
|---|---|
| J Smoltz, Atl | 90 |
| P Combs, Phi | 86 |
| J DeLeon, StL | 86 |
| J Deshaies, Hou | 84 |
| 2 Players with | 78 |

## Games Started

| | |
|---|---|
| **F VIOLA, NYN** | **35** |
| **T BROWNING, Cin** | **35** |
| **G MADDUX, ChN** | **35** |
| 4 Players with | 34 |

## Losses

| | |
|---|---|
| **J DeLeon, StL** | **19** |
| J Magrane, StL | 17 |
| G Maddux, ChN | 15 |
| M Morgan, LA | 15 |
| D Rasmussen, SD | 15 |

## Doubles Off

| | |
|---|---|
| **F VALENZUELA, LA** | **51** |
| B Ruffin, Phi | 45 |
| T Glavine, Atl | 45 |
| T Browning, Cin | 44 |
| G Maddux, ChN | 42 |

## Innings Pitched

| | |
|---|---|
| **F VIOLA, NYN** | **249.2** |
| G Maddux, ChN | 237.0 |
| R Martinez, LA | 234.1 |
| D Gooden, NYN | 232.2 |
| D Drabek, Pit | 231.1 |
| J Smoltz, Atl | 231.1 |

## Hit Batters

| | |
|---|---|
| **M GARDNER, Mon** | **9** |
| J Magrane, StL | 8 |
| J Deshaies, Hou | 8 |
| 3 Players with | 7 |

## Complete Games

| | |
|---|---|
| **R MARTINEZ, LA** | **12** |
| B Hurst, SD | 9 |
| D Drabek, Pit | 9 |
| G Maddux, ChN | 8 |
| 3 Players with | 7 |

## Saves

| | |
|---|---|
| **J FRANCO, NYN** | **33** |
| R Myers, Cin | 31 |
| L Smith, StL | 27 |
| D Smith, Hou | 23 |
| C Lefferts, SD | 23 |

## Triples Off

| | |
|---|---|
| **M BIELECKI, ChN** | **9** |
| **A BENES, SD** | **9** |
| **B GULLICKSON, Hou** | **9** |
| **J MAGRANE, StL** | **9** |
| 6 Players with | 7 |

## Runs Allowed

| | |
|---|---|
| **G MADDUX, ChN** | **116** |
| F Valenzuela, LA | 112 |
| T Glavine, Atl | 111 |
| D Rasmussen, SD | 110 |
| J Smoltz, Atl | 109 |

## Wild Pitches

| | |
|---|---|
| **J SMOLTZ, Atl** | **14** |
| F Valenzuela, LA | 13 |
| J Magrane, StL | 11 |
| F Viola, NYN | 11 |
| M Bielecki, ChN | 11 |

## Games Finished

| | |
|---|---|
| **R MCDOWELL, Phi** | **60** |
| R Myers, Cin | 59 |
| S Bedrosian, SF | 53 |
| J Franco, NYN | 48 |
| L Smith, StL | 45 |

## Shutouts

| | |
|---|---|
| **B HURST, SD** | **4** |
| **M MORGAN, LA** | **4** |
| 6 Players with | 3 |

## Home Runs Allowed

| | |
|---|---|
| **D RASMUSSEN, SD** | **28** |
| M Scott, Hou | 27 |
| T Browning, Cin | 24 |
| R Martinez, LA | 22 |
| 5 Players with | 21 |

## Strikeouts

| | |
|---|---|
| **D CONE, NYN** | **233** |
| R Martinez, LA | 223 |
| D Gooden, NYN | 223 |
| F Viola, NYN | 182 |
| S Fernandez, NYN | 181 |

## Balks

| | |
|---|---|
| **D SMITH, Hou** | **5** |
| **A BENES, SD** | **5** |
| **J ARMSTRONG, Cin** | **5** |
| **B KIPPER, Pit** | **5** |
| **J RIJO, Cin** | **5** |

# 1990 American League Special Batting Leaders

## Scoring Position

| Player, Team | AB | H | AVG |
|---|---|---|---|
| **A TRAMMELL, Det** | **145** | **55** | **.379** |
| G Brett, KC | 136 | 49 | .360 |
| L Johnson, ChA | 116 | 40 | .345 |
| K Puckett, Min | 138 | 47 | .341 |
| W Boggs, Bos | 139 | 47 | .338 |
| G Sheffield, Mil | 125 | 42 | .336 |
| O Guillen, ChA | 133 | 44 | .331 |
| I Calderon, ChA | 131 | 43 | .328 |
| R Palmeiro, Tex | 148 | 48 | .324 |
| C James, Cle | 145 | 47 | .324 |

## Leadoff On-Base%

| Player, Team | PA* | OB | OBP |
|---|---|---|---|
| **R HENDERSON, Oak** | **586** | **257** | **.439** |
| W Boggs, Bos | 418 | 168 | .402 |
| B Downing, Cal | 152 | 58 | .382 |
| A Cole, Cle | 256 | 97 | .379 |
| L Polonia, Cal | 374 | 141 | .377 |
| J Reed, Bos | 306 | 111 | .363 |
| L Whitaker, Det | 290 | 105 | .362 |
| P Bradley, ChA | 357 | 126 | .353 |
| T Phillips, Det | 450 | 157 | .349 |
| P Molitor, Mil | 408 | 142 | .348 |

## Cleanup Slugging%

| Player, Team | AB | TB | SLG |
|---|---|---|---|
| **C FIELDER, Det** | **424** | **248** | **.585** |
| M McGwire, Oak | 349 | 190 | .544 |
| B Jackson, KC | 285 | 147 | .516 |
| D Pasqua, ChA | 269 | 136 | .506 |
| F McGriff, Tor | 139 | 69 | .496 |
| D Tartabull, KC | 207 | 101 | .488 |
| K Hrbek, Min | 325 | 156 | .480 |
| D Winfield, Cal | 288 | 132 | .458 |
| T Brunansky, Bos | 245 | 112 | .457 |
| R Kittle, Bal | 192 | 87 | .453 |

## Vs LHP

| | |
|---|---|
| **S ALOMAR JR, Cle** | **.376** |
| C Fielder, Det | .371 |
| S Mack, Min | .370 |
| D Henderson, Oak | .353 |
| C Quintana, Bos | .352 |

## Vs RHP

| | |
|---|---|
| **L POLONIA, Cal** | **.341** |
| G Brett, KC | .336 |
| R Henderson, Oak | .330 |
| F McGriff, Tor | .324 |
| W Boggs, Bos | .319 |

## Late & Close

| | |
|---|---|
| **R HENDERSON, Oak** | **.426** |
| W Weiss, Oak | .405 |
| G Sheffield, Mil | .397 |
| G Gagne, Min | .385 |
| H Baines, Oak | .373 |

## Bases Loaded

| | |
|---|---|
| **L RIVERA, Bos** | **.600** |
| T Steinbach, Oak | .579 |
| J Ray, Cal | .556 |
| G Ward, Det | .539 |
| T Fernandez, Tor | .500 |

## OBP off LHP

| | |
|---|---|
| **C FIELDER, Det** | **.479** |
| R Milligan, Bal | .473 |
| B Downing, Cal | .466 |
| S Mack, Min | .439 |
| C Lansford, Oak | .439 |

## OBP off RHP

| | |
|---|---|
| **R HENDERSON, Oak** | **.446** |
| F McGriff, Tor | .440 |
| W Boggs, Bos | .415 |
| A Davis, Sea | .400 |
| G Brett, KC | .398 |

## BA at Home

| | |
|---|---|
| **W BOGGS, Bos** | **.359** |
| K Puckett, Min | .344 |
| T Brunansky, Bos | .340 |
| A Trammell, Det | .340 |
| G Brett, KC | .319 |

## BA on the Road

| | |
|---|---|
| **R PALMEIRO, Tex** | **.350** |
| R Henderson, Oak | .342 |
| G Brett, KC | .340 |
| F McGriff, Tor | .321 |
| G Sheffield, Mil | .315 |

## SLG off LHP

| | |
|---|---|
| **C FIELDER, Det** | **.854** |
| R Milligan, Bal | .680 |
| R Deer, Mil | .671 |
| D Henderson, Oak | .654 |
| J Canseco, Oak | .610 |

## SLG off RHP

| | |
|---|---|
| **F McGriff, Tor** | **.597** |
| R Henderson, Oak | .566 |
| G Brett, KC | .529 |
| J Canseco, Oak | .520 |
| K Hrbek, Min | .515 |

## SB Success %

| | |
|---|---|
| **H COTTO, Sea** | **87.5** |
| R Henderson, Oak | 86.7 |
| P Molitor, Mil | 85.7 |
| J Gantner, Mil | 85.7 |
| M Wilson, Tor | 85.2 |

## SB Att/On 1st Base

| | |
|---|---|
| **S SOSA, ChA** | **.43** |
| R Henderson, Oak | .38 |
| L Johnson, ChA | .36 |
| R Kelly, NYA | .35 |
| I Calderon, ChA | .30 |

## AB Per HR

| | |
|---|---|
| **C FIELDER, Det** | **11.2** |
| J Canseco, Oak | 13.0 |
| M McGwire, Oak | 13.4 |
| F McGriff, Tor | 15.9 |
| R Deer, Mil | 16.3 |

## Ground/Fly Ratio

| | |
|---|---|
| **S SAX, NYA** | **2.83** |
| T Pena, Bos | 2.49 |
| K Puckett, Min | 2.38 |
| L Johnson, ChA | 2.26 |
| M Wilson, Tor | 2.19 |

## AB per GDP

| | |
|---|---|
| **R DEER, Mil (440 ab)** | **∞** |
| J Felix, Tor | 92.6 |
| R Ventura, ChA | 82.2 |
| R Kelly, NYA | 80.1 |
| O Guillen, ChA | 73.7 |

## % CS by Catchers

| | |
|---|---|
| **L PARRISH, Cal** | **47.0** |
| B Geren, NYA | 43.3 |
| P Borders, Tor | 42.6 |
| G Petralli, Tex | 37.6 |
| C Fisk, ChA | 37.2 |

## Pitches Seen

| | |
|---|---|
| **W BOGGS, Bos** | **3067** |
| T Phillips, Det | 2784 |
| C Fielder, Det | 2749 |
| H Reynolds, Sea | 2686 |
| J Reed, Bos | 2666 |

## Pitches per PA

| | |
|---|---|
| **M TETTLETON, Bal** | **4.44** |
| W Boggs, Bos | 4.30 |
| R Henderson, Oak | 4.28 |
| J Barfield, NYA | 4.16 |
| R Deer, Mil | 4.12 |

## BA on 3-1 Count

| | |
|---|---|
| **S HORN, Bal** | **1.000** |
| C O'Brien, NYN | .800 |
| C Snyder, Cle | .750 |
| F Jose, StL | .750 |
| H Baines, Oak | .647 |

## BA on 0-2 Count

| | |
|---|---|
| **C DAVIS, Cal** | **.409** |
| L Polonia, Cal | .353 |
| S Alomar jr, Cle | .351 |
| G Sheffield, Mil | .333 |
| R Henderson, Oak | .304 |

# 1990 National League Special Batting Leaders

## Scoring Position

| Player, Team | AB | H | AVG |
|---|---|---|---|
| **L DYKSTRA, Phi** | **110** | **47** | **.427** |
| D Magadan, NYN | 110 | 42 | .382 |
| B Bonds, Pit | 138 | 52 | .377 |
| J Treadway, Atl | 123 | 42 | .342 |
| R Alomar, SD | 139 | 47 | .338 |
| M Williams, SF | 157 | 52 | .331 |
| M Grace, ChN | 170 | 56 | .329 |
| E Murray, LA | 150 | 49 | .327 |
| D Justice, Atl | 113 | 36 | .319 |
| W McGee, Oak | 151 | 48 | .318 |

## Leadoff On-Base%

| Player, Team | PA* | OB | OBP |
|---|---|---|---|
| **L DYKSTRA, Phi** | **687** | **288** | **.419** |
| L Smith, Atl | 363 | 152 | .419 |
| B Butler, SF | 724 | 288 | .398 |
| D DeShields, Mon | 458 | 174 | .380 |
| B Roberts, SD | 560 | 211 | .377 |
| W Backman, Pit | 337 | 125 | .371 |
| C Sabo, Cin | 328 | 120 | .366 |
| G Redus, Pit | 156 | 56 | .359 |
| L Harris, LA | 343 | 123 | .359 |
| J Walton, ChN | 441 | 153 | .347 |

## Cleanup Slugging%

| Player, Team | AB | TB | SLG |
|---|---|---|---|
| **D JUSTICE, Atl** | **147** | **83** | **.565** |
| J Clark, SD | 215 | 120 | .558 |
| K Mitchell, SF | 522 | 284 | .544 |
| A Dawson, ChN | 501 | 271 | .541 |
| D Strawberry, NYN | 477 | 253 | .530 |
| E Murray, LA | 554 | 290 | .524 |
| G Davis, Hou | 326 | 170 | .521 |
| B Bonilla, Pit | 624 | 324 | .519 |
| E Davis, Cin | 387 | 189 | .488 |
| F Stubbs, Hou | 150 | 68 | .453 |

## Vs LHP

| | |
|---|---|
| **M DUNCAN, Cin** | .410 |
| J Clark, SD | .377 |
| D Justice, Atl | .366 |
| C Candaele, Hou | .341 |
| G Braggs, Cin | .339 |

## Vs RHP

| | |
|---|---|
| **L DYKSTRA, Phi** | .344 |
| E Murray, LA | .338 |
| R Sandberg, ChN | .334 |
| T Gwynn, SD | .327 |
| B Roberts, SD | .319 |

## Late & Close

| | |
|---|---|
| **B SANTIAGO, SD** | .433 |
| R Ready, Phi | .407 |
| D Magadan, NYN | .391 |
| W McGee,StL | .380 |
| T Kennedy, SF | .378 |

## Bases Loaded

| | |
|---|---|
| **K MCREYN'LDS,NY** | .800 |
| O Smith, StL | .571 |
| T Gwynn, SD | .556 |
| K Caminiti, Hou | .533 |
| T Pendleton, StL | .500 |

## OBP off LHP

| | |
|---|---|
| **J CLARK, SD** | .541 |
| D Justice, Atl | .443 |
| M Duncan, Cin | .437 |
| G Braggs, Cin | .437 |
| D Murphy, Phi | .410 |

## OBP off RHP

| | |
|---|---|
| **L DYKSTRA, Phi** | .435 |
| E Murray, LA | .429 |
| J Kruk, Phi | .415 |
| B Butler, SF | .403 |
| D Strawberry, NYN | .397 |

## BA at Home

| | |
|---|---|
| **R SANDBERG, ChN** | .357 |
| W McGee, StL | .348 |
| E Murray, LA | .343 |
| L Dykstra, Phi | .339 |
| B Butler, SF | .336 |

## BA on the Road

| | |
|---|---|
| **D MAGADAN, NYN** | .372 |
| B Roberts, SD | .338 |
| B Larkin, Cin | .326 |
| B Bonds, Pit | .321 |
| E Murray, LA | .317 |

## SLG off LHP

| | |
|---|---|
| **J CLARK, SD** | .667 |
| D Justice, Atl | .656 |
| D Murphy, Phi | .617 |
| M Duncan, Cin | .606 |
| B Bonds, Pit | .592 |

## SLG off RHP

| | |
|---|---|
| **R SANDBERG, ChN** | .616 |
| D Strawberry, NYN | .593 |
| E Murray, LA | .551 |
| R Gant, Atl | .550 |
| A Dawson, ChN | .549 |

## SB Success %

| | |
|---|---|
| **K GIBSON, LA** | **92.9** |
| M Grissom, Mon | 91.7 |
| E Davis, Cin | 87.5 |
| L Dykstra, Phi | 86.8 |
| B Larkin, Cin | 85.7 |

## SB Att/On 1st Base

| | |
|---|---|
| **V COLEMAN, StL** | **0.63** |
| E Yelding, Hou | 0.58 |
| J Samuel, LA | 0.43 |
| D DeShields, Mon | 0.36 |
| T Raines, Mon | 0.36 |

## AB Per HR

| | |
|---|---|
| **D STRAWB'Y, NYN** | **14.7** |
| K Mitchell, SF | 15.0 |
| R Sandberg, ChN | 15.4 |
| D Justice, Atl | 15.7 |
| B Bonds, Pit | 15.7 |

## Ground/Fly Ratio

| | |
|---|---|
| **W MCGEE, StL** | **3.29** |
| B Butler, SF | 2.19 |
| D DeShields, Mon | 2.15 |
| O Smith, StL | 2.12 |
| T Gwynn, SD | 2.10 |

## AB per GDP

| | |
|---|---|
| **B BUTLER, SF** | 155.5 |
| L Smith, Atl | 155.3 |
| D Justice, Atl | 146.3 |
| B Hatcher, Cin | 100.8 |
| L Dykstra, Phi | 98.3 |

## % CS by Catchers

| | |
|---|---|
| **J OLIVER, Cin** | **40.2** |
| J Girardi, ChN | 37.0 |
| D Daulton, Phi | 35.0 |
| M LaValliere, Pit | 34.6 |
| B Santiago, SD | 34.1 |

## Pitches Seen

| | |
|---|---|
| **B BUTLER, SF** | **2902** |
| J Bell, Pit | 2671 |
| L Dykstra, Phi | 2551 |
| J Carter, SD | 2528 |
| W Clark, SF | 2480 |

## Pitches Seen/PA

| | |
|---|---|
| **K DANIELS, LA** | **4.09** |
| D Magadan, NYN | 4.07 |
| D DeShields, Mon | 4.01 |
| T Zeile, StL | 3.97 |
| B Butler, SF | 3.96 |

## BA on 3-1 Count

| | |
|---|---|
| **H BROOKS, LA** | .750 |
| J Presley, Atl | .667 |
| F Stubbs, Hou | .636 |
| M Lemke, Atl | .625 |
| W McGee,StL | .611 |

## BA on 0-2 Count

| | |
|---|---|
| **T GWYNN, SD** | .435 |
| L Smith, Atl | .381 |
| R Ramirez, Hou | .314 |
| T Benzinger, Cin | .310 |
| G Jefferies, NYN | .308 |

# 1990 American League Special Pitching Leaders

### Baserunners Per 9 IP

| Player, Team | IP | BR | BR/9 |
|---|---|---|---|
| **N RYAN, Tex** | **204** | **218** | **9.62** |
| R Clemens, Bos | 228 | 254 | 10.01 |
| D Wells, Tor | 189 | 212 | 10.10 |
| E Hanson, Sea | 236 | 275 | 10.49 |
| D Stewart, Oak | 267 | 314 | 10.58 |
| B Black, Tor | 206 | 247 | 10.76 |
| D Stieb, Tor | 208 | 253 | 10.91 |
| C Finley, Cal | 236 | 293 | 11.17 |
| B Welch, Oak | 238 | 296 | 11.19 |
| G Hibbard, ChA | 211 | 263 | 11.22 |

### Run Support Per 9 IP

| Player, Team | IP | R | R/9 |
|---|---|---|---|
| **B WELCH, Oak** | **238** | **156** | **5.90** |
| T Stottlemyre, Tor | 203 | 131 | 5.81 |
| P Harnisch, Bal | 188 | 121 | 5.77 |
| M Boddicker, Bos | 228 | 137 | 5.41 |
| T Candiotti, Cle | 202 | 119 | 5.30 |
| J Morris, Det | 249 | 145 | 5.23 |
| J McDowell, ChA | 205 | 119 | 5.22 |
| K Brown, Tex | 180 | 104 | 5.20 |
| D Stewart, Oak | 267 | 149 | 5.02 |
| T Gordon, KC | 195 | 109 | 5.02 |

### Save Percentage

| Player, Team | OP | SV | SV% |
|---|---|---|---|
| **D ECKERSLEY, Oak** | **50** | **48** | **96** |
| D Righetti, NYA | 39 | 36 | 92 |
| M Schooler, Sea | 34 | 30 | 88 |
| G Olson, Bal | 42 | 37 | 88 |
| B Thigpen, ChA | 65 | 57 | 88 |
| D Jones, Cle | 51 | 43 | 84 |
| T Henke, Tor | 38 | 32 | 84 |
| R Aguilera, Min | 39 | 32 | 82 |
| B Harvey, Cal | 31 | 25 | 81 |
| M Henneman, Det | 28 | 22 | 79 |

### Hits Per 9 IP

| | |
|---|---|
| **N RYAN, Tex** | **6.04** |
| R Johnson, Sea | 7.13 |
| R Clemens, Bos | 7.61 |
| D Stewart, Oak | 7.62 |
| D Stieb, Tor | 7.72 |

### Homeruns Per 9 IP

| | |
|---|---|
| **R CLEMENS, Bos** | **.28** |
| K McCaskill, Cal | .46 |
| G Hibbard, ChA | .47 |
| D Stieb, Tor | .47 |
| B Witt, Tex | .49 |

### Strikeouts Per 9 IP

| | |
|---|---|
| **N RYAN, Tex** | **10.24** |
| B Witt, Tex | 8.96 |
| R Clemens, Bos | 8.24 |
| T Gordon, KC | 8.06 |
| E Hanson, Sea | 8.05 |

### GDP Per 9 IP

| | |
|---|---|
| **K BROWN, Tex** | **1.20** |
| J Abbott, Cal | 1.15 |
| M Young, Sea | 1.08 |
| G Hibbard, ChA | 1.07 |
| M Moore, Oak | 1.04 |

### Vs LHB

| | |
|---|---|
| **B McDonald, Bal** | .181 |
| D Jones, Cle | .200 |
| G Olson, Bal | .200 |
| W Fraser, Cal | .207 |
| S Valdez, Cle | .207 |

### Vs RHB

| | |
|---|---|
| **N RYAN, Tex** | .158 |
| D Stieb, Tor | .205 |
| R Clemens, Bos | .213 |
| J Morris, Det | .218 |
| R Johnson, Sea | .218 |

### OBP Leadoff Inning

| | |
|---|---|
| **N RYAN, Tex** | .230 |
| K Tapani, Min | .241 |
| E Hanson, Sea | .244 |
| G Hibbard, ChA | .247 |
| D Stieb, Tor | .250 |

### BA ScPos Allowed

| | |
|---|---|
| **N RYAN, Tex** | .157 |
| S Farr, KC | .157 |
| R Clemens, Bos | .172 |
| R Johnson, Sea | .181 |
| D Stewart, Oak | .206 |

### SLG Allowed

| | |
|---|---|
| **R CLEMENS, Bos** | .306 |
| D Stieb, Tor | .320 |
| N Ryan, Tex | .322 |
| D Stewart, Oak | .326 |
| B Witt, Tex | .326 |

### OBP Allowed

| | |
|---|---|
| **N RYAN, Tex** | .268 |
| R Clemens, Bos | .278 |
| D Wells, Tor | .283 |
| E Hanson, Sea | .287 |
| B Black, Tor | .290 |

### PkOf Throw/Runner

| | |
|---|---|
| **C HOUGH, Tex** | **2.34** |
| R Clemens, Bos | 1.55 |
| K Brown, Tex | 1.47 |
| F Tanana, Det | 1.43 |
| J McDowell, ChA | 1.38 |

### SB% Allowed

| | |
|---|---|
| **G SWINDELL, Cle** | **20** |
| D Johnson, Bal | 20 |
| F Tanana, Det | 38 |
| K McCaskill, Cal | 38 |
| D Stieb, Tor | 43 |

### Pitches Per Batter

| | |
|---|---|
| **K BROWN, Tex** | **3.40** |
| D Johnson, Bal | 3.42 |
| A Anderson, Min | 3.45 |
| G Swindell, Cle | 3.49 |
| J Morris, Det | 3.50 |

### Grd/Fly Ratio Off

| | |
|---|---|
| **K BROWN, Tex** | **3.44** |
| M Young, Sea | 2.23 |
| J Abbott, Cal | 1.95 |
| T Leary, NYA | 1.87 |
| G Harris, Bos | 1.74 |

### K/BB Ratio

| | |
|---|---|
| **R CLEMENS, Bos** | **3.87** |
| N Ryan, Tex | 3.14 |
| E Hanson, Sea | 3.10 |
| G Swindell, Cle | 2.87 |
| T Higuera, Mil | 2.58 |

### Wins In Relief

| | |
|---|---|
| L GUETTERMAN, NYA | 11 |
| B JONES, ChA | 11 |
| K Rogers, Tex | 9 |
| 4 Players with | 8 |

### Holds

| | |
|---|---|
| **B JONES, ChA** | **30** |
| R Honeycutt, Oak | 27 |
| C Crim, Mil | 19 |
| G Nelson, Oak | 18 |
| R Murphy | 17 |

### Blown Saves

| | |
|---|---|
| **D PLESAC, Mil** | **10** |
| **J MONTGOMERY, KC** | **10** |
| M Jackson, Sea | 9 |
| D Jones, Cle | 8 |
| K Rogers, Tex | 8 |
| B Thigpen, ChA | 8 |

### % Inherited Scored

| | |
|---|---|
| **J KLINK, Oak** | **12.9** |
| K Hickey, Bal | 17.1 |
| B Thigpen, ChA | 17.6 |
| J Price, Bal | 18.0 |
| T Henke, Tor | 18.8 |

### 1st Batter OBP

| | |
|---|---|
| **D WARD, Tor** | **.164** |
| D Schatzeder, Min | .167 |
| R Honeycutt, Oak | .177 |
| T Leach, KC | .189 |
| D Eckersley, Oak | .206 |

# 1990 National League Special Pitching Leaders

### Baserunners Per 9 IP

| Player, Team | IP | BR | BR/9 |
|---|---|---|---|
| **D DARWIN, Hou** | **162** | **171** | **9.46** |
| D Drabek, Pit | 231 | 249 | 9.69 |
| D Martinez, Mon | 226 | 246 | 9.80 |
| R Martinez, LA | 234 | 262 | 10.06 |
| S Fernandez, NYN | 179 | 202 | 10.14 |
| B Hurst, SD | 223 | 252 | 10.14 |
| D Cone, NYN | 211 | 243 | 10.33 |
| O Boyd, Mon | 190 | 219 | 10.34 |
| E Whitson, SD | 228 | 263 | 10.35 |
| Z Smith, Pit | 215 | 249 | 10.41 |

### Run Support Per 9 IP

| Player, Team | IP | R | R/9 |
|---|---|---|---|
| **D GOODEN, NYN** | **232** | **175** | **6.77** |
| D Drabek, Pit | 231 | 152 | 5.91 |
| D Rasmussen, SD | 187 | 118 | 5.66 |
| F Valenzuela, LA | 204 | 128 | 5.65 |
| J Burkett, SF | 204 | 127 | 5.60 |
| R Martinez, LA | 234 | 141 | 5.42 |
| J Smoltz, Atl | 231 | 132 | 5.14 |
| P Combs, Phi | 183 | 101 | 4.96 |
| F Viola, NYN | 249 | 137 | 4.94 |
| D Cone, NYN | 211 | 111 | 4.72 |

### Save Percentage

| Player, Team | OP | SV | SV% |
|---|---|---|---|
| **J FRANCO, NYN** | **39** | **33** | **85** |
| L Smith, StL | 32 | 27 | 84 |
| R Myers, Cin | 37 | 31 | 84 |
| D Smith, Hou | 28 | 23 | 82 |
| T Burke, Mon | 25 | 20 | 80 |
| M Williams, ChN | 20 | 16 | 80 |
| J Brantley, SF | 24 | 19 | 79 |
| R McDowell, Phi | 28 | 22 | 79 |
| S Bedrosian, SF | 22 | 17 | 77 |
| C Lefferts, SD | 30 | 23 | 77 |

### Hits Per 9 IP

| | |
|---|---|
| **S FERNANDEZ, NY** | **6.48** |
| J Rijo, Cin | 6.93 |
| R Martinez, LA | 7.38 |
| D Drabek, Pit | 7.38 |
| D Darwin, Hou | 7.56 |

### Homeruns per 9 IP

| | |
|---|---|
| **D GOODEN, NYN** | **.39** |
| G Maddux, ChN | .42 |
| J Magrane, StL | .44 |
| J Rijo, Cin | .46 |
| J Armstrong, Cin | .49 |

### Strikeouts Per 9 IP

| | |
|---|---|
| **D CONE, NYN** | **9.91** |
| S Fernandez, NYN | 9.08 |
| D Gooden, NYN | 8.63 |
| R Martinez, LA | 8.56 |
| J DeLeon, StL | 8.08 |

### GDP Per 9 IP

| | |
|---|---|
| **Z SMITH, Pit** | **1.42** |
| S Garrelts, SF | 1.09 |
| G Maddux, ChN | 1.03 |
| T Glavine, Atl | 0.97 |
| B Hurst, SD | 0.85 |

### Vs LHB

| | |
|---|---|
| **Z SMITH, Pit** | .164 |
| J Boever, Phi | .182 |
| R Dibble, Cin | .185 |
| J DeJesus, Phi | .190 |
| D Akerfelds, Phi | .195 |

### Vs RHB

| | |
|---|---|
| **S FERNANDEZ, NY** | .194 |
| J Smoltz, Atl | .198 |
| T Wilson, SF | .218 |
| G Maddux, ChN | .223 |
| B Hurst, SD | .228 |

### OBP Leadoff Inning

| | |
|---|---|
| **M GARDNER, Mon** | .219 |
| D Drabek, Pit | .242 |
| D Darwin, Hou | .247 |
| B Tewksbury, StL | .248 |
| M Harkey, ChN | .254 |

### BA ScPos Allowed

| | |
|---|---|
| **O BOYD, Mon** | .169 |
| D Cone, NYN | .183 |
| D Darwin, Hou | .200 |
| A Benes, SD | .208 |
| D Martinez, Mon | .209 |

### SLG Allowed

| | |
|---|---|
| **J RIJO, Cin** | .313 |
| D Darwin, Hou | .331 |
| D Drabek, Pit | .331 |
| F Viola, NYN | .333 |
| D Martinez, Mon | .335 |

### OBP Allowed

| | |
|---|---|
| **D DARWIN, Hou** | .266 |
| D Drabek, Pit | .274 |
| D Martinez, Mon | .274 |
| S Fernandez, NYN | .278 |
| R Martinez, LA | .278 |

### PkOf Throw/Runner

| | |
|---|---|
| **J DESHAIES, Hou** | **2.42** |
| J Burkett, SF | 1.69 |
| J Rijo, Cin | 1.61 |
| J Armstrong, Cin | 1.58 |
| D Cone, NYN | 1.56 |

### SB% Allowed

| | |
|---|---|
| **T MULHOL'ND,Phi** | **50** |
| P Combs, Phi | 52 |
| T Browning, Cin | 55 |
| M Morgan, LA | 55 |
| J Magrane, StL | 57 |

### Pitches Per Batter

| | |
|---|---|
| **E WHITSON, SD** | **3.20** |
| T Browning, Cin | 3.21 |
| B Gullickson, Hou | 3.31 |
| T Mulholland, Phi | 3.33 |
| O Boyd, Mon | 3.38 |

### Grd/Fly Ratio Off

| | |
|---|---|
| **M MORGAN, LA** | **2.65** |
| G Maddux, ChN | 2.59 |
| Z Smith, Pit | 2.14 |
| D Gooden, NYN | 1.88 |
| D Martinez, Mon | 1.77 |

### K/BB Ratio

| | |
|---|---|
| **D CONE, NYN** | **3.58** |
| D Darwin, Hou | 3.52 |
| R Martinez, LA | 3.33 |
| D Gooden, NYN | 3.19 |
| D Martinez, Mon | 3.18 |

### Wins in Relief

| | |
|---|---|
| B SAMPEN, Mon | 11 |
| S Bedrosian, SF | 9 |
| J Agosto, Hou | 9 |
| 3 Players with | 8 |

### Holds

| | |
|---|---|
| **R DIBBLE,Cin** | **17** |
| J Agosto, Hou | 16 |
| S Ruskin, Pit | 15 |
| K Dayley, StL | 14 |
| J Parrett, Mon | 11 |

### Blown Saves

| | |
|---|---|
| **P ASSENMACHER, Ch** | **10** |
| J Howell, LA | 8 |
| C Lefferts, SD | 7 |
| G Harris, SD | 7 |
| 6 Players with | 6 |

### % Inherited Scored

| | |
|---|---|
| **R MYERS, Cin** | **9.4** |
| J Agosto, Hou | 16.9 |
| S Belinda, Pit | 22.0 |
| C Lefferts, SD | 22.2 |
| S Bedrosian, SF | 22.6 |

### 1st Batter OBP

| | |
|---|---|
| D DARWIN, Hou | .097 |
| B Kipper, Pit | .175 |
| L Andersen, Hou | .180 |
| S Wilson, ChN | .200 |
| D Schmidt, Mon | .206 |

# Active Career Batting Leaders

## Batting Average

| Player | AB | H | AVG |
|---|---|---|---|
| **W BOGGS** | **5153** | **1784** | **.346** |
| T Gwynn | 4651 | 1531 | .329 |
| K Puckett | 4395 | 1407 | .320 |
| D Mattingly | 4416 | 1401 | .317 |
| M Greenwell | 2256 | 707 | .313 |
| G Brett | 8692 | 2707 | .311 |
| M Grace | 1585 | 486 | .307 |
| P Guerrero | 4819 | 1470 | .305 |
| D Magadan | 1349 | 411 | .305 |
| L Polonia | 1559 | 474 | .304 |

## On-Base Percentage

| Player | PA | OB | OBP |
|---|---|---|---|
| **W BOGGS** | **6061** | **2643** | **.436** |
| R Henderson | 7178 | 2892 | .403 |
| K Daniels | 1966 | 791 | .402 |
| D Magadan | 1580 | 624 | .395 |
| A Davis | 4362 | 1705 | .391 |
| T Raines | 6143 | 2398 | .390 |
| F McGriff | 2320 | 903 | .389 |
| J Kruk | 2229 | 864 | .388 |
| T Gwynn | 5115 | 1969 | .385 |
| M Greenwell | 2546 | 980 | .385 |

## Slugging Percentage

| Player | AB | TB | SLG |
|---|---|---|---|
| **C FIELDER** | **1079** | **578** | **.536** |
| F McGriff | 1944 | 1030 | .530 |
| E Davis | 2572 | 1343 | .522 |
| D Strawberry | 3903 | 2028 | .520 |
| K Mitchell | 2378 | 1229 | .517 |
| K Daniels | 1665 | 856 | .514 |
| M McGwire | 2173 | 1112 | .512 |
| J Canseco | 2644 | 1348 | .510 |
| W Clark | 2700 | 1370 | .507 |
| D Mattingly | 4416 | 2226 | .504 |

## Games

| | |
|---|---|
| **B BUCKNER** | **2517** |
| D Evans | 2505 |
| R Yount | 2449 |
| D Winfield | 2401 |
| D Parker | 2334 |

## Plate Appearances

| | |
|---|---|
| **R YOUNT** | **10535** |
| D Evans | 10240 |
| B Buckner | 10033 |
| D Winfield | 10003 |
| G Brett | 9803 |

## Hits

| | |
|---|---|
| **R YOUNT** | **2747** |
| B Buckner | 2715 |
| G Brett | 2707 |
| D Parker | 2592 |
| D Winfield | 2548 |

## Home Runs

| | |
|---|---|
| **D EVANS** | **379** |
| **E MURRAY** | **379** |
| D Winfield | 378 |
| D Murphy | 378 |
| C Fisk | 354 |

## Runs Scored

| | |
|---|---|
| **D EVANS** | **1435** |
| R Yount | 1433 |
| D Winfield | 1384 |
| G Brett | 1382 |
| R Henderson | 1290 |

## Runs Batted In

| | |
|---|---|
| **D WINFIELD** | **1516** |
| D Parker | 1434 |
| G Brett | 1398 |
| E Murray | 1373 |
| D Evans | 1346 |

## Doubles

| | |
|---|---|
| **G BRETT** | **559** |
| D Parker | 500 |
| R Yount | 498 |
| B Buckner | 498 |
| D Evans | 474 |

## Triples

| | |
|---|---|
| **W WILSON** | **133** |
| G Brett | 127 |
| R Yount | 116 |
| G Templeton | 104 |
| A Dawson | 88 |

## Walks

| | |
|---|---|
| **D EVANS** | **1337** |
| W Randolph | 1128 |
| J Clark | 1110 |
| R Henderson | 1093 |
| B Downing | 1077 |

## Intentional Walks

| | |
|---|---|
| **G BRETT** | **204** |
| E Murray | 176 |
| D Parker | 167 |
| D Murphy | 155 |
| D Winfield | 149 |

## Strikeouts

| | |
|---|---|
| **D EVANS** | **1643** |
| D Murphy | 1627 |
| D Parker | 1439 |
| D Winfield | 1305 |
| C Washington | 1266 |

## K/BB Ratio

| | |
|---|---|
| **W BOGGS** | **.48** |
| M Scioscia | .50 |
| W Randolph | .53 |
| O Smith | .56 |
| T Gwynn | .60 |

## Stolen Bases

| | |
|---|---|
| **R HENDERSON** | **936** |
| T Raines | 634 |
| W Wilson | 612 |
| V Coleman | 549 |
| O Smith | 464 |

## Hit by Pitch

| | |
|---|---|
| **C LEMON** | **151** |
| C Fisk | 134 |
| B Downing | 113 |
| A Dawson | 76 |
| L Smith | 74 |

## Sacrifice Hits

| | |
|---|---|
| **O SMITH** | **167** |
| B Boone | 142 |
| A Griffin | 122 |
| A Trammell | 108 |
| M Barrett | 102 |

## Sacrifice Flies

| | |
|---|---|
| **G BRETT** | **98** |
| B Buckner | 97 |
| R Yount | 96 |
| A Dawson | 95 |
| G Carter | 93 |

## AB Per HR

| | |
|---|---|
| **C FIELDER** | **13.16** |
| M McGwire | 13.93 |
| K Phelps | 15.07 |
| R Kittle | 15.29 |
| D Strawberry | 15.49 |

## SB Success %

| | |
|---|---|
| **E DAVIS** | **86.9** |
| T Raines | 85.7 |
| W Wilson | 83.7 |
| V Coleman | 82.7 |
| B Larkin | 82.6 |

## AB Per GDP

| | |
|---|---|
| **B HARPER** | **25.8** |
| D Valle | 26.2 |
| J Franco | 26.5 |
| D Ramos | 27.8 |
| O Virgil | 27.9 |

## AB Per RBI

| | |
|---|---|
| **C FIELDER** | **5.00** |
| J Canseco | 5.04 |
| M McGwire | 5.07 |
| E Davis | 5.15 |
| D Strawberry | 5.32 |

# Active Career Pitching Leaders

## Earned Run Average

| Player | IP | ER | ERA |
|---|---|---|---|
| **D SMITH** | **762** | **214** | **2.53** |
| O Hershiser | 1482 | 447 | 2.71 |
| D Quisenberry | 1042 | 320 | 2.76 |
| J Orosco | 791 | 243 | 2.76 |
| D Gooden | 1523 | 478 | 2.82 |
| L Smith | 919 | 294 | 2.88 |
| R Clemens | 1513 | 486 | 2.89 |
| A Pena | 845 | 277 | 2.95 |
| C Lefferts | 762 | 250 | 2.95 |
| J Reardon | 943 | 318 | 3.03 |

## Winning Percentage

| Player | W | L | W% |
|---|---|---|---|
| **D GOODEN** | **119** | **46** | **.721** |
| R Clemens | 116 | 51 | .695 |
| T Higuera | 89 | 54 | .622 |
| J Tudor | 117 | 72 | .619 |
| B Welch | 176 | 109 | .618 |
| J Key | 87 | 56 | .608 |
| J Candelaria | 174 | 113 | .606 |
| D Drabek | 69 | 45 | .605 |
| T Browning | 93 | 61 | .604 |
| O Hershiser | 99 | 65 | .604 |

## Opponent Batting Average

| Player | AB | H | AVG |
|---|---|---|---|
| **N RYAN** | **17850** | **3629** | **.203** |
| S FERNANDEZ | 4385 | 894 | .204 |
| J Orosco | 2877 | 633 | .220 |
| J DeLeon | 5170 | 1142 | .221 |
| D Cone | 2900 | 654 | .226 |
| D Gooden | 5643 | 1282 | .227 |
| R Clemens | 5636 | 1281 | .227 |
| J Reardon | 3496 | 796 | .228 |
| M Clear | 2950 | 674 | .228 |
| S Bedrosian | 3671 | 841 | .229 |

## Hits Per 9 Innings

| Player | H | IP | H/9 |
|---|---|---|---|
| **N RYAN** | **3629** | **4990** | **6.54** |
| S Fernandez | 894 | 1212 | 6.64 |
| J Orosco | 633 | 791 | 7.20 |
| J DeLeon | 1142 | 1417 | 7.25 |
| D Cone | 654 | 784 | 7.50 |

## Homeruns Per 9 Innings

| Player | HR | IP | HR/9 |
|---|---|---|---|
| **D SMITH** | **28** | **762** | **0.33** |
| G Minton | 43 | 1131 | 0.34 |
| J Magrane | 30 | 773 | 0.35 |
| D Gooden | 75 | 1523 | 0.44 |
| O Hershiser | 76 | 1482 | 0.46 |

## Baserunners Per 9 Innings

| Player | BR | IP | BR/9 |
|---|---|---|---|
| **D GOODEN** | **1756** | **1523** | **10.37** |
| R Clemens | 1745 | 1513 | 10.38 |
| B Saberhagen | 1690 | 1464 | 10.39 |
| S Fernandez | 1415 | 1212 | 10.50 |
| O Hershiser | 1736 | 1482 | 10.54 |

## Walks per 9 Innings

| Player | BB | IP | BB/9 |
|---|---|---|---|
| **D Quisenberry** | **162** | **1042** | **1.40** |
| B Saberhagen | 286 | 1464 | 1.76 |
| J Candelaria | 559 | 2447 | 2.06 |
| D Eckersley | 659 | 2815 | 2.11 |
| J Key | 301 | 1269 | 2.13 |

## Strikeouts per 9 Innings

| Player | K | IP | K/9 |
|---|---|---|---|
| **N RYAN** | **5308** | **4990** | **9.57** |
| L Smith | 923 | 919 | 9.04 |
| M Clear | 804 | 804 | 9.00 |
| B Witt | 869 | 891 | 8.77 |
| S Fernandez | 1153 | 1212 | 8.56 |

## Strikeout to Walk Ratio

| Player | K | BB | K/BB |
|---|---|---|---|
| **R CLEMENS** | **1424** | **425** | **3.35** |
| B Saberhagen | 957 | 286 | 3.35 |
| D Gooden | 1391 | 449 | 3.10 |
| G Swindell | 587 | 195 | 3.01 |
| D Eckersley | 1938 | 659 | 2.94 |

## Wins

| | |
|---|---|
| **N RYAN** | **302** |
| B Blyleven | 279 |
| J Reuss | 220 |
| R Reuschel | 214 |
| F Tanana | 207 |

## Losses

| | |
|---|---|
| **N RYAN** | **272** |
| B Blyleven | 238 |
| F Tanana | 196 |
| J Reuss | 191 |
| R Reuschel | 189 |

## Saves

| | |
|---|---|
| **J REARDON** | **287** |
| L Smith | 265 |
| D Quisenberry | 244 |
| D Righetti | 224 |
| D Smith | 199 |

## Shutouts

| | |
|---|---|
| **B BLYLEVEN** | **60** |
| N Ryan | 59 |
| J Reuss | 39 |
| F Tanana | 32 |
| B Knepper | 30 |
| D Stieb | 30 |

## Games

| | |
|---|---|
| **C HOUGH** | **745** |
| N Ryan | 740 |
| G Minton | 710 |
| J Reardon | 694 |
| D Quisenberry | 674 |

## Games Started

| | |
|---|---|
| **N RYAN** | **706** |
| B Blyleven | 661 |
| J Reuss | 547 |
| R Reuschel | 528 |
| F Tanana | 520 |

## Batters Faced

| | |
|---|---|
| **N RYAN** | **20607** |
| B Blyleven | 19681 |
| J Reuss | 15582 |
| F Tanana | 15023 |
| R Reuschel | 14834 |

## Innings

| | |
|---|---|
| **N RYAN** | **4990** |
| B Blyleven | 4836 |
| J Reuss | 3668 |
| F Tanana | 3580 |
| R Reuschel | 3539 |

## CG Per GS

| | |
|---|---|
| **J MORRIS** | **.38** |
| B Blyleven | .36 |
| F Valenzuela | .33 |
| M Norris | .33 |
| R Clemens | .32 |

## Hit Batters

| | |
|---|---|
| **B BLYLEVEN** | **150** |
| N Ryan | 140 |
| C Hough | 138 |
| D Stieb | 118 |
| F Tanana | 111 |

## Wild Pitches

| | |
|---|---|
| **N RYAN** | **257** |
| J Morris | 155 |
| C Hough | 144 |
| B Blyleven | 111 |
| J Reuss | 107 |

## Balks

| | |
|---|---|
| **B WELCH** | **40** |
| R Sutcliffe | 33 |
| N Ryan | 33 |
| C Hough | 32 |
| B McClure | 29 |

# Bill James Leaders: American League

## Top Game Scores of the Year

| Pitcher | Date | Opp | IP | H | R | ER | BB | K | SC |
|---|---|---|---|---|---|---|---|---|---|
| **N Ryan, Tex** | **8/17** | **Cha** | **10.0** | **3** | **0** | **0** | **0** | **15** | **101** |
| N Ryan, Tex | 4/26 | Cha | 9.0 | 1 | 0 | 0 | 2 | 16 | 99 |
| N Ryan, Tex | 6/11 | Oak | 9.0 | 0 | 0 | 0 | 2 | 14 | 99 |
| E Hanson, Sea | 8/1 | Oak | 10.0 | 2 | 0 | 0 | 0 | 11 | 99 |
| D Stewart , Oak | 6/29 | Tor | 9.0 | 0 | 0 | 0 | 3 | 12 | 96 |

## Top Game Scores of the Year

| Pitcher | Date | Opp | IP | H | R | ER | BB | K | SC |
|---|---|---|---|---|---|---|---|---|---|
| D Stieb, Tor | 9/2 | Cle | 9.0 | 0 | 0 | 0 | 4 | 9 | 92 |
| J Morris, Det | 7/6 | KC | 9.0 | 1 | 0 | 0 | 0 | 6 | 91 |
| M Young, Sea | 6/16 | Tex | 9.0 | 3 | 0 | 0 | 2 | 11 | 90 |
| K Appier, KC | 7/20 | Bos | 9.0 | 3 | 0 | 0 | 1 | 10 | 90 |

## Offensive Winning%

| | |
|---|---|
| **R Henderson, Oak** | **.853** |
| F McGriff, Tor | .786 |
| C Fielder, Det | .775 |
| G Brett, KC | .745 |
| J Canseco, Oak | .733 |
| M McGwire, Oak | .691 |
| E Martinez, Sea | .689 |
| A Davis, Sea | .683 |
| C Fisk, Chi | .681 |
| K Hrbek, Min | .681 |
| K Griffey Jr, Sea | .680 |

## Runs Created

| | |
|---|---|
| **R Henderson, Oak** | **137** |
| C Fielder, Det | 129 |
| F McGriff, Tor | 124 |
| G Brett, KC | 106 |
| W Boggs, Bos | 103 |
| K Griffey Jr, Sea | 103 |
| M McGwire, Oak | 101 |
| K Gruber, Tor | 101 |
| J Canseco, Oak | 98 |
| J Franco, Tex | 95 |
| A Trammell, Det | 95 |

## Isolated Power

| | |
|---|---|
| **C Fielder, Det** | **.314** |
| J Canseco, Oak | .268 |
| M McGwire, Oak | .254 |
| R Henderson, Oak | .252 |
| K Gruber, Tor | .238 |
| F McGriff, Tor | .230 |
| R Deer, Mil | .223 |
| J Barfield, NY | .210 |
| E Burks, Bos | .190 |
| P Incaviglia, Tex | .187 |
| K Hrbek, Min | .187 |

## Power/Speed

| | |
|---|---|
| **R Henderson, Oak** | **39.1** |
| J Canseco, Oak | 25.1 |
| R Kelly, NY | 22.1 |
| S Sosa, Chi | 20.4 |
| I Calderon, Chi | 19.5 |
| K Gruber, Tor | 19.3 |
| K Griffey Jr, Sea | 18.5 |
| J Franco, Tex | 16.2 |
| R Yount, Mil | 15.9 |
| D White, Cal | 14.4 |
| G Sheffield, Mil | 14.3 |

## Secondary Average

| | |
|---|---|
| **R Henderson, Oak** | **.583** |
| C Fielder, Det | .471 |
| M McGwire, Oak | .468 |
| J Canseco, Oak | .457 |
| F McGriff, Tor | .408 |
| M Tettleton, Bal | .401 |
| J Barfield, NY | .391 |
| R Deer, Mil | .373 |
| K Gruber, Tor | .343 |
| L Whitaker, Det | .343 |
| K Hrbek, Min | .337 |

## Cheap Wins

| | |
|---|---|
| **J Morris, Det** | **6** |
| **S Sanderson, Oak** | **6** |
| J Cerutti, Tor | 5 |
| B Welch, Oak | 5 |
| C Hough, Tex | 4 |
| D Johnson, Bal | 4 |
| J Key, Tor | 4 |
| J Robinson, Det | 4 |
| T Stottlemyre, Tor | 4 |
| 12 Players with | 3 |

## Tough Losses

| | |
|---|---|
| **M Langston, Cal** | **9** |
| **M Young, Sea** | **9** |
| T Stottlemyre, Tor | 8 |
| C Cary, NY | 7 |
| C Hough, Tex | 7 |
| T Leary, NY | 7 |

## Slow Hooks

| | |
|---|---|
| **Tigers** | **18** |
| Athletics | 16 |
| Rangers | 14 |
| Yankees | 14 |
| Brewers | 14 |
| Angels | 13 |
| Twins | 10 |
| Indians | 10 |
| Royals | 10 |
| Mariners | 9 |
| White Sox | 7 |
| Red Sox | 3 |
| Orioles | 3 |
| Blue Jays | 3 |

## Quick Hooks

| | |
|---|---|
| **Blue Jays** | **29** |
| **Yankees** | **29** |
| Red Sox | 27 |
| White Sox | 26 |
| Royals | 26 |
| Brewers | 25 |
| Tigers | 25 |
| Indians | 24 |
| Orioles | 23 |
| Athletics | 22 |
| Twins | 21 |
| Rangers | 17 |
| Mariners | 17 |
| Angels | 9 |

# Bill James Leaders: National League

## Top Game Scores of the Year

| Pitcher | Date | Opp | IP | H | R | ER | BB | K | SC |
|---|---|---|---|---|---|---|---|---|---|
| **R Martinez, La** | **6/4** | **Atl** | **9.0** | **3** | **0** | **0** | **1** | **18** | **98** |
| M Scott, Hou | 6/8 | Cin | 10.0 | 3 | 1 | 1 | 1 | 15 | 96 |
| T Mulhollnd, Phi | 8/15 | SF | 9.0 | 0 | 0 | 0 | 0 | 8 | 95 |
| T Wilson, SF | 6/13 | SD | 9.0 | 1 | 0 | 0 | 0 | 9 | 94 |

## Top Game Scores of the Year

| Pitcher | Date | Opp | IP | H | R | ER | BB | K | SC |
|---|---|---|---|---|---|---|---|---|---|
| J Rijo, Cin | 9/17 | SF | 9.0 | 2 | 0 | 0 | 2 | 12 | 93 |
| F Valenzuela, La | 6/29 | StL | 9.0 | 0 | 0 | 0 | 3 | 7 | 92 |
| Z Smith, Pit | 9/05 | NY | 9.0 | 1 | 0 | 0 | 1 | 7 | 91 |
| T Belcher, La | 7/21 | Pit | 9.0 | 1 | 0 | 0 | 1 | 6 | 90 |

## Offensive Winning%

| | |
|---|---|
| **B Bonds, Pit** | **.816** |
| L Dykstra, Phi | .780 |
| E Murray, LA | .779 |
| K Daniels, LA | .769 |
| D Justice, Atl | .768 |
| D Magadan, NYN | .763 |
| R Sandberg, ChN | .756 |
| A Dawson, ChN | .736 |
| K Mitchell, SF | .731 |
| R Gant, Atl | .727 |
| D Strawberry, NYN | .727 |

## Runs Created

| | |
|---|---|
| **B Bonds, Pit** | **128** |
| R Sandberg, ChN | 124 |
| L Dykstra, Phi | 121 |
| E Murray, LA | 118 |
| R Gant, Atl | 109 |
| B Butler, SF | 108 |
| B Bonilla, Pit | 104 |
| D Strawberry, NYN | 104 |
| A Dawson, ChN | 101 |
| K Mitchell, SF | 101 |
| W Clark, SF | 101 |

## Isolated Power

| | |
|---|---|
| **B Bonds, Pit** | **.264** |
| K Mitchell, SF | .254 |
| R Sandberg, Chi | .254 |
| D Justice, Atl | .253 |
| D Strawberry, NY | .242 |
| B Bonilla, Pit | .238 |
| R Gant, Atl | .237 |
| K Daniels, LA | .236 |
| A Dawson, Chi | .225 |
| E Davis, Cin | .225 |

## Power/Speed

| | |
|---|---|
| **B Bonds, Pit** | **40.4** |
| R Gant, Atl | 32.5 |
| R Sandberg, Chi | 30.8 |
| H Johnson, NY | 27.4 |
| C Sabo, Cin | 25.0 |
| J Carter, SD | 23.0 |
| E Davis, Cin | 22.4 |
| D Strawberry, NY | 21.3 |
| S Dunston, Chi | 20.2 |
| A Dawson, Chi | 20.1 |
| J Samuel, LA | 19.4 |

## Secondary Average

| | |
|---|---|
| **B Bonds, Pit** | **.543** |
| D Justice, Atl | .424 |
| E Davis, Cin | .404 |
| D Strawberry, NY | .399 |
| K Daniels, LA | .396 |
| R Gant, Atl | .381 |
| R Sandberg, Chi | .376 |
| V Hayes, Phi | .373 |
| K Mitchell, SF | .372 |
| T Raines, Mon | .365 |
| H Johnson, NY | .364 |

## Cheap Wins

| | |
|---|---|
| **T Browning, Cin** | **5** |
| D Gooden, NY | 4 |
| D Rasmussen, SD | 3 |
| J Smiley, Pit | 3 |
| B Tewksbury, StL | 3 |
| 15 Players with | 2 |

## Tough Losses

| | |
|---|---|
| **J DeLeon, StL** | **8** |
| D Martinez, Mon | 8 |
| S Fernandez, NY | 7 |
| J Magrane, StL | 7 |
| D Cone, NY | 5 |
| E Whitson, SD | 5 |
| 8 Players with | 4 |

## Slow Hooks

| | |
|---|---|
| **Braves** | **15** |
| **Dodgers** | **15** |
| Cubs | 12 |
| Mets | 10 |
| Phillies | 10 |
| Giants | 10 |
| Reds | 9 |
| Astros | 9 |
| Cardinals | 8 |
| Padres | 6 |
| Expos | 5 |
| Pirates | 3 |

## Quick Hooks

| | |
|---|---|
| **Phillies** | **34** |
| Pirates | 30 |
| Giants | 29 |
| Expos | 23 |
| Reds | 22 |
| Astros | 22 |
| Cubs | 20 |
| Padres | 17 |
| Cardinals | 17 |
| Braves | 15 |
| Dodgers | 14 |
| Mets | 12 |

# Player Profiles

Whew! It's been a long book. Glad you made it all the way back here.

In the first edition of this book, we published "player profiles" on twenty-five of baseball's biggest stars. Each one consisted of about fifty "splits," or breakdowns, both batting and pitching. They were a big hit, so we made them available via our on-line computer service.

This year, we decided to feed our computer four names, then wait and see what it spit out. The results are on the twenty pages that follow. It was difficult to pick only four, but we've got four good ones: Carlton Fisk, who had the best season of any catcher in baseball in 1990; Dennis Eckersley, whose Earned Run Average seems to have disappeared; Ryne Sandberg, whose bat is actually beginning to get more attention than his glove; and Doug Drabek, probable Cy Young Award winner and almost a White Sox (drat!).

For Fisk and Sandberg, the statistics are grouped by Batting, Baserunning, and Fielding. For Eckersley and Drabek, by Pitching and Fielding. You'll notice that each major section is divided into smaller sections, i.e. "Vs. Each Team," "By Park," "On Base," etc., to lend a little more organization to the whole affair.

Again, we'd have liked to show more than these four, but our book was getting too big. Plus, what looks like everything you can think of about a player is only about part of what actually IS everything you can think of about a player. So, if you tell us you want to see more in the next book and drop us a line saying how great the expanded player profiles were, we'll feed the computer a little more next year.

Player Profile Defintions:

- **AVG, OBP** and **SLG** are Batting Average, On-Base Percentage and Slugging Percentage, respectively.
- **FLY** is the number of Flyballs exluding line drives (not just outs).

- **GDP Opp** indicates a record of performance in plate appearances in which there was a Double Play Opportunity (Runner on 1st and less than 2 outs).
- **GRD** indicates the number of Groundballs.
- **HD** indicates Holds.
- **OP** indicates Save Opportunities.
- **RF** indicates the total number of Runs scored For a pitcher.
- **SB Atd** indicates a record of performance in plate appearances in which there was a Stolen Base Attempt.
- **SB Opp** indicates a record of performance in plate appearances in which there was a Stolen Base Opportunity.
- **SUP** indicates Run Support Per 9 Innings Pitched.
- **#Pit** is the number of Pitches Thrown.
- **#PKO** is the number of Pickoff Throws Made.

Player Profile Notes:

- You may notice some walks being given up with less than a 3-ball count. These are intentional walks. We don't count pitches as true pitches if they are intentional.
- There are two sets of count information. The first set shows performance when the play happens on that pitch. For example, a .231 Avg on the **0-1** line indicate a batting average when hitting that exact pitch. The second set of count info would show performance anytime after that count. For example, **After (0-1)** would tell you what a guy does after he receives a first pitch strike, whether or not he actually hits the ball on the very next pitch or any subsequent pitch in that at bat.
- In the Rankings section, a "ranking" is listed if the player cracked the Top 10 when compared to players in his league. For Team and Postion rankings we only show the ranking if he ranked first. His Rank, the Stat, and a Minimum Requirement, if there was one, are listed.

# Doug Drabek – Pittsburgh Pirates

| 1990 | W | L | S | ERA | SUP | G | GS | CG | SO | GF | OP | HD | IP | H | HR | BFP | R | ER | RF |
|---|---|---|---|---|---|---|---|---|---|---|---|---|---|---|---|---|---|---|---|
| Total | 22 | 6 | 0 | 2.76 | 5.91 | 33 | 33 | 9 | 3 | 0 | 0 | 0 | 231.1 | 190 | 15 | 918 | 78 | 71 | 152 |

| vs. Teams | W | L | S | ERA | SUP | G | GS | CG | SO | GF | OP | HD | IP | H | HR | BFP | R | ER | RF |
|---|---|---|---|---|---|---|---|---|---|---|---|---|---|---|---|---|---|---|---|
| vs.Atl | 3 | 0 | 0 | 0.82 | 6.95 | 3 | 3 | 2 | 1 | 0 | 0 | 0 | 22.0 | 12 | 2 | 78 | 2 | 2 | 17 |
| vs.ChN | 3 | 1 | 0 | 3.90 | 6.51 | 4 | 4 | 2 | 0 | 0 | 0 | 0 | 27.2 | 22 | 2 | 107 | 13 | 12 | 20 |
| vs.Cin | 1 | 0 | 0 | 2.63 | 5.27 | 2 | 2 | 0 | 0 | 0 | 0 | 0 | 13.2 | 15 | 1 | 57 | 4 | 4 | 8 |
| vs.Hou | 1 | 0 | 0 | 3.07 | 3.68 | 2 | 2 | 0 | 0 | 0 | 0 | 0 | 14.2 | 12 | 1 | 58 | 5 | 5 | 6 |
| vs.LA | 1 | 0 | 0 | 2.57 | 9.00 | 1 | 1 | 0 | 0 | 0 | 0 | 0 | 7.0 | 6 | 0 | 28 | 2 | 2 | 7 |
| vs.Mon | 2 | 3 | 0 | 3.38 | 3.63 | 5 | 5 | 0 | 0 | 0 | 0 | 0 | 34.2 | 36 | 1 | 147 | 17 | 13 | 14 |
| vs.NYN | 1 | 1 | 0 | 8.36 | 7.71 | 3 | 3 | 0 | 0 | 0 | 0 | 0 | 14.0 | 16 | 5 | 66 | 13 | 13 | 12 |
| vs.Phi | 3 | 0 | 0 | 0.67 | 5.67 | 3 | 3 | 3 | 1 | 0 | 0 | 0 | 27.0 | 7 | 1 | 94 | 2 | 2 | 17 |
| vs.StL | 2 | 1 | 0 | 2.28 | 4.23 | 4 | 4 | 1 | 1 | 0 | 0 | 0 | 27.2 | 24 | 0 | 111 | 9 | 7 | 13 |
| vs.SD | 2 | 0 | 0 | 2.37 | 6.63 | 3 | 3 | 0 | 0 | 0 | 0 | 0 | 19.0 | 19 | 0 | 79 | 5 | 5 | 14 |
| vs.SF | 3 | 0 | 0 | 2.25 | 9.00 | 3 | 3 | 1 | 0 | 0 | 0 | 0 | 24.0 | 21 | 2 | 93 | 6 | 6 | 24 |

| By Park | W | L | S | ERA | SUP | G | GS | CG | SO | GF | OP | HD | IP | H | HR | BFP | R | ER | RF |
|---|---|---|---|---|---|---|---|---|---|---|---|---|---|---|---|---|---|---|---|
| at Atl | 1 | 0 | 0 | 0.00 | 15.00 | 1 | 1 | 1 | 1 | 0 | 0 | 0 | 6.0 | 2 | 0 | 20 | 0 | 0 | 10 |
| at ChN | 1 | 0 | 0 | 6.14 | 9.82 | 1 | 1 | 0 | 0 | 0 | 0 | 0 | 7.1 | 7 | 0 | 30 | 5 | 5 | 8 |
| at Cin | 1 | 0 | 0 | 1.35 | 6.75 | 1 | 1 | 0 | 0 | 0 | 0 | 0 | 6.2 | 8 | 0 | 28 | 1 | 1 | 5 |
| at Hou | 0 | 0 | 0 | 2.84 | 2.84 | 1 | 1 | 0 | 0 | 0 | 0 | 0 | 6.1 | 7 | 1 | 27 | 2 | 2 | 2 |
| at LA | 1 | 0 | 0 | 2.57 | 9.00 | 1 | 1 | 0 | 0 | 0 | 0 | 0 | 7.0 | 6 | 0 | 28 | 2 | 2 | 7 |
| at Mon | 1 | 1 | 0 | 2.03 | 4.05 | 2 | 2 | 0 | 0 | 0 | 0 | 0 | 13.1 | 11 | 0 | 55 | 6 | 3 | 6 |
| at NYN | 1 | 1 | 0 | 7.00 | 8.00 | 2 | 2 | 0 | 0 | 0 | 0 | 0 | 9.0 | 8 | 3 | 39 | 7 | 7 | 8 |
| at Phi | 1 | 0 | 0 | 0.00 | 11.00 | 1 | 1 | 1 | 1 | 0 | 0 | 0 | 9.0 | 1 | 0 | 29 | 0 | 0 | 11 |
| at Pit | 11 | 3 | 0 | 3.00 | 5.18 | 16 | 16 | 6 | 0 | 0 | 0 | 0 | 120.0 | 96 | 11 | 473 | 42 | 40 | 69 |
| at StL | 2 | 1 | 0 | 2.28 | 4.23 | 4 | 4 | 1 | 1 | 0 | 0 | 0 | 27.2 | 24 | 0 | 111 | 9 | 7 | 13 |
| at SD | 1 | 0 | 0 | 3.00 | 7.50 | 2 | 2 | 0 | 0 | 0 | 0 | 0 | 12.0 | 12 | 0 | 51 | 4 | 4 | 10 |
| at SF | 1 | 0 | 0 | 0.00 | 3.86 | 1 | 1 | 0 | 0 | 0 | 0 | 0 | 7.0 | 8 | 0 | 27 | 0 | 0 | 3 |

| By Month | W | L | S | ERA | SUP | G | GS | CG | SO | GF | OP | HD | IP | H | HR | BFP | R | ER | RF |
|---|---|---|---|---|---|---|---|---|---|---|---|---|---|---|---|---|---|---|---|
| April | 4 | 1 | 0 | 2.37 | 6.82 | 5 | 5 | 0 | 0 | 0 | 0 | 0 | 30.1 | 26 | 2 | 124 | 9 | 8 | 23 |
| May | 3 | 0 | 0 | 2.93 | 5.87 | 4 | 4 | 1 | 0 | 0 | 0 | 0 | 30.2 | 22 | 4 | 117 | 10 | 10 | 20 |
| June | 1 | 3 | 0 | 4.29 | 4.54 | 6 | 6 | 1 | 0 | 0 | 0 | 0 | 35.2 | 44 | 4 | 161 | 22 | 17 | 18 |
| July | 5 | 0 | 0 | 2.23 | 6.29 | 6 | 6 | 1 | 0 | 0 | 0 | 0 | 44.1 | 33 | 1 | 177 | 12 | 11 | 31 |
| August | 4 | 1 | 0 | 2.23 | 6.70 | 6 | 6 | 3 | 2 | 0 | 0 | 0 | 44.1 | 34 | 2 | 170 | 11 | 11 | 33 |
| September | 5 | 1 | 0 | 2.74 | 5.28 | 6 | 6 | 3 | 1 | 0 | 0 | 0 | 46.0 | 31 | 2 | 169 | 14 | 14 | 27 |

| Conditions | W | L | S | ERA | SUP | G | GS | CG | SO | GF | OP | HD | IP | H | HR | BFP | R | ER | RF |
|---|---|---|---|---|---|---|---|---|---|---|---|---|---|---|---|---|---|---|---|
| Home | 11 | 3 | 0 | 3.00 | 5.18 | 16 | 16 | 6 | 0 | 0 | 0 | 0 | 120.0 | 96 | 11 | 473 | 42 | 40 | 69 |
| Away | 11 | 3 | 0 | 2.51 | 6.71 | 17 | 17 | 3 | 3 | 0 | 0 | 0 | 111.1 | 94 | 4 | 445 | 36 | 31 | 83 |
| Day | 9 | 1 | 0 | 2.30 | 6.01 | 10 | 10 | 3 | 1 | 0 | 0 | 0 | 70.1 | 49 | 4 | 272 | 19 | 18 | 47 |
| Night | 13 | 5 | 0 | 2.96 | 5.87 | 23 | 23 | 6 | 2 | 0 | 0 | 0 | 161.0 | 141 | 11 | 646 | 59 | 53 | 105 |
| Grass | 6 | 1 | 0 | 3.35 | 8.57 | 8 | 8 | 1 | 1 | 0 | 0 | 0 | 48.1 | 43 | 3 | 195 | 18 | 18 | 46 |
| Turf | 16 | 5 | 0 | 2.61 | 5.21 | 25 | 25 | 8 | 2 | 0 | 0 | 0 | 183.0 | 147 | 12 | 723 | 60 | 53 | 106 |

| Days Rest | W | L | S | ERA | SUP | G | GS | CG | SO | GF | OP | HD | IP | H | HR | BFP | R | ER | RF |
|---|---|---|---|---|---|---|---|---|---|---|---|---|---|---|---|---|---|---|---|
| 4 | 16 | 4 | 0 | 2.69 | 6.29 | 24 | 24 | 7 | 3 | 0 | 0 | 0 | 167.1 | 141 | 8 | 665 | 53 | 50 | 117 |
| 5 | 4 | 1 | 0 | 3.18 | 4.99 | 5 | 5 | 2 | 0 | 0 | 0 | 0 | 39.2 | 31 | 3 | 154 | 16 | 14 | 22 |
| 6+ | 2 | 1 | 0 | 2.59 | 4.81 | 4 | 4 | 0 | 0 | 0 | 0 | 0 | 24.1 | 18 | 4 | 99 | 9 | 7 | 13 |

| 1990 | 2B | 3B | RBI | SH | SF | BB | IW | HB | K | WP | SB | CS | DP | FLY | GRD | #PIT | #PKO | AVG | OBP | SLG |
|---|---|---|---|---|---|---|---|---|---|---|---|---|---|---|---|---|---|---|---|---|
| Total | 37 | 4 | 65 | 10 | 3 | 56 | 2 | 3 | 131 | 6 | 18 | 9 | 11 | 212 | 364 | 3360 | 90 | .225 | .274 | .331 |

| vs. Teams | 2B | 3B | RBI | SH | SF | BB | IW | HB | K | WP | SB | CS | DP | FLY | GRD | #PIT | #PKO | AVG | OBP | SLG |
|---|---|---|---|---|---|---|---|---|---|---|---|---|---|---|---|---|---|---|---|---|
| vs.Atl | 0 | 0 | 2 | 0 | 0 | 2 | 0 | 1 | 9 | 0 | 0 | 2 | 1 | 27 | 29 | 289 | 3 | .160 | .192 | .240 |
| vs.ChN | 4 | 0 | 10 | 1 | 0 | 7 | 0 | 1 | 16 | 0 | 3 | 2 | 2 | 25 | 35 | 363 | 14 | .224 | .283 | .327 |
| vs.Cin | 2 | 0 | 3 | 0 | 1 | 2 | 0 | 0 | 13 | 1 | 2 | 0 | 1 | 12 | 23 | 206 | 13 | .278 | .298 | .370 |
| vs.Hou | 1 | 1 | 2 | 1 | 0 | 5 | 0 | 0 | 8 | 0 | 1 | 1 | 1 | 10 | 26 | 229 | 4 | .231 | .298 | .346 |
| vs.LA | 2 | 0 | 2 | 0 | 0 | 1 | 0 | 0 | 3 | 0 | 0 | 0 | 0 | 6 | 14 | 97 | 2 | .222 | .250 | .296 |
| vs.Mon | 8 | 2 | 13 | 2 | 0 | 9 | 0 | 1 | 20 | 1 | 2 | 1 | 2 | 32 | 67 | 546 | 12 | .267 | .317 | .378 |
| vs.NYN | 2 | 0 | 13 | 0 | 0 | 8 | 0 | 0 | 3 | 2 | 1 | 0 | 0 | 16 | 23 | 259 | 9 | .276 | .364 | .569 |
| vs.Phi | 2 | 0 | 2 | 1 | 0 | 8 | 1 | 0 | 19 | 0 | 1 | 1 | 0 | 22 | 36 | 368 | 5 | .082 | .161 | .141 |
| vs.StL | 6 | 1 | 9 | 3 | 1 | 7 | 1 | 0 | 10 | 2 | 5 | 1 | 1 | 21 | 50 | 351 | 16 | .240 | .287 | .320 |
| vs.SD | 6 | 0 | 3 | 1 | 0 | 5 | 0 | 0 | 14 | 0 | 1 | 0 | 1 | 19 | 23 | 325 | 7 | .260 | .308 | .342 |
| vs.SF | 4 | 0 | 6 | 1 | 1 | 2 | 0 | 0 | 16 | 0 | 2 | 1 | 2 | 22 | 38 | 327 | 5 | .236 | .250 | .348 |

| By Park | 2B | 3B | RBI | SH | SF | BB | IW | HB | K | WP | SB | CS | DP | FLY | GRD | #PIT | #PKO | AVG | OBP | SLG |
|---|---|---|---|---|---|---|---|---|---|---|---|---|---|---|---|---|---|---|---|---|
| at Atl | 0 | 0 | 0 | 0 | 0 | 0 | 0 | 1 | 5 | 0 | 0 | 1 | 0 | 8 | 4 | 79 | 0 | .105 | .150 | .105 |
| at ChN | 2 | 0 | 3 | 0 | 0 | 2 | 0 | 0 | 6 | 0 | 1 | 1 | 0 | 5 | 11 | 106 | 0 | .250 | .300 | .321 |
| at Cin | 1 | 0 | 0 | 0 | 0 | 2 | 0 | 0 | 5 | 0 | 0 | 0 | 1 | 7 | 8 | 108 | 7 | .308 | .357 | .346 |
| at Hou | 1 | 0 | 2 | 1 | 0 | 3 | 0 | 0 | 4 | 0 | 1 | 1 | 1 | 3 | 12 | 109 | 3 | .304 | .385 | .478 |
| at LA | 2 | 0 | 2 | 0 | 0 | 1 | 0 | 0 | 3 | 0 | 0 | 0 | 0 | 6 | 14 | 97 | 2 | .222 | .250 | .296 |
| at Mon | 3 | 0 | 3 | 1 | 0 | 4 | 0 | 0 | 8 | 1 | 0 | 1 | 0 | 14 | 22 | 222 | 2 | .220 | .278 | .280 |
| at NYN | 0 | 0 | 7 | 0 | 0 | 4 | 0 | 0 | 0 | 1 | 1 | 0 | 0 | 7 | 16 | 156 | 8 | .229 | .308 | .486 |
| at Phi | 0 | 0 | 0 | 0 | 0 | 1 | 0 | 0 | 5 | 0 | 0 | 0 | 0 | 6 | 14 | 112 | 0 | .036 | .069 | .036 |
| at Pit | 17 | 3 | 36 | 3 | 2 | 28 | 1 | 2 | 72 | 2 | 8 | 3 | 7 | 118 | 190 | 1711 | 45 | .219 | .268 | .347 |
| at StL | 6 | 1 | 9 | 3 | 1 | 7 | 1 | 0 | 10 | 2 | 5 | 1 | 1 | 21 | 50 | 351 | 16 | .240 | .287 | .320 |
| at SD | 5 | 0 | 3 | 1 | 0 | 4 | 0 | 0 | 7 | 0 | 1 | 0 | 0 | 12 | 15 | 214 | 3 | .261 | .320 | .370 |
| at SF | 0 | 0 | 0 | 1 | 0 | 0 | 0 | 0 | 6 | 0 | 1 | 1 | 1 | 5 | 8 | 95 | 4 | .308 | .308 | .308 |

| By Month | 2B | 3B | RBI | SH | SF | BB | IW | HB | K | WP | SB | CS | DP | FLY | GRD | #PIT | #PKO | AVG | OBP | SLG |
|---|---|---|---|---|---|---|---|---|---|---|---|---|---|---|---|---|---|---|---|---|
| April | 1 | 0 | 8 | 2 | 1 | 9 | 0 | 1 | 16 | 2 | 7 | 1 | 1 | 26 | 45 | 467 | 22 | .234 | .295 | .297 |
| May | 2 | 1 | 7 | 1 | 1 | 7 | 0 | 0 | 16 | 0 | 1 | 1 | 3 | 28 | 50 | 440 | 6 | .204 | .250 | .352 |
| June | 12 | 2 | 19 | 4 | 0 | 13 | 1 | 1 | 16 | 3 | 3 | 1 | 2 | 41 | 56 | 564 | 19 | .308 | .369 | .503 |
| July | 12 | 0 | 9 | 1 | 0 | 13 | 1 | 0 | 29 | 0 | 3 | 1 | 1 | 41 | 74 | 687 | 12 | .202 | .261 | .294 |
| August | 6 | 1 | 10 | 0 | 1 | 6 | 0 | 1 | 30 | 1 | 2 | 2 | 2 | 41 | 71 | 625 | 19 | .210 | .241 | .296 |
| September | 4 | 0 | 12 | 2 | 0 | 8 | 0 | 0 | 24 | 0 | 2 | 3 | 2 | 35 | 68 | 577 | 12 | .195 | .234 | .258 |

| Conditions | 2B | 3B | RBI | SH | SF | BB | IW | HB | K | WP | SB | CS | DP | FLY | GRD | #PIT | #PKO | AVG | OBP | SLG |
|---|---|---|---|---|---|---|---|---|---|---|---|---|---|---|---|---|---|---|---|---|
| Home | 17 | 3 | 36 | 3 | 2 | 28 | 1 | 2 | 72 | 2 | 8 | 3 | 7 | 118 | 190 | 1711 | 45 | .219 | .268 | .347 |
| Away | 20 | 1 | 29 | 7 | 1 | 28 | 1 | 1 | 59 | 4 | 10 | 6 | 4 | 94 | 174 | 1649 | 45 | .230 | .281 | .314 |
| Day | 9 | 0 | 15 | 3 | 0 | 20 | 1 | 1 | 37 | 1 | 5 | 3 | 2 | 64 | 103 | 998 | 32 | .198 | .260 | .282 |
| Night | 28 | 4 | 50 | 7 | 3 | 36 | 1 | 2 | 94 | 5 | 13 | 6 | 9 | 148 | 261 | 2362 | 58 | .236 | .280 | .351 |
| Grass | 9 | 0 | 15 | 2 | 0 | 11 | 0 | 1 | 27 | 1 | 4 | 3 | 1 | 43 | 68 | 747 | 17 | .238 | .285 | .337 |
| Turf | 28 | 4 | 50 | 8 | 3 | 45 | 2 | 2 | 104 | 5 | 14 | 6 | 10 | 169 | 296 | 2613 | 73 | .221 | .271 | .329 |

| Days Rest | 2B | 3B | RBI | SH | SF | BB | IW | HB | K | WP | SB | CS | DP | FLY | GRD | #PIT | #PKO | AVG | OBP | SLG |
|---|---|---|---|---|---|---|---|---|---|---|---|---|---|---|---|---|---|---|---|---|
| 4 | 30 | 3 | 46 | 7 | 3 | 38 | 2 | 2 | 98 | 4 | 14 | 4 | 8 | 151 | 263 | 2417 | 74 | .229 | .275 | .327 |
| 5 | 4 | 1 | 12 | 1 | 0 | 8 | 0 | 1 | 23 | 0 | 2 | 3 | 1 | 40 | 59 | 556 | 7 | .215 | .261 | .319 |
| 6+ | 3 | 0 | 7 | 2 | 0 | 10 | 0 | 0 | 10 | 2 | 2 | 2 | 2 | 21 | 42 | 387 | 9 | .207 | .289 | .379 |

| Batter Types | IP | H | HR | BFP | - | - | 2B | 3B | RBI | SH | SF | BB | IW | HB | K | WP | SB | CS | DP | FLY | GRD | AVG | OBP | SLG |
|---|---|---|---|---|---|---|---|---|---|---|---|---|---|---|---|---|---|---|---|---|---|---|---|---|
| vs. Left | 143.1 | 131 | 10 | 579 | - | - | 29 | 4 | 47 | 4 | 2 | 35 | 2 | 0 | 70 | 4 | 12 | 6 | 7 | 128 | 246 | .243 | .289 | .368 |
| vs. Right | 88.0 | 59 | 5 | 339 | - | - | 8 | 0 | 18 | 6 | 1 | 21 | 0 | 3 | 61 | 2 | 6 | 3 | 4 | 84 | 118 | .192 | .249 | .266 |

| Inning | IP | H | HR | BFP | R | ER | 2B | 3B | RBI | SH | SF | BB | IW | HB | K | WP | SB | CS | DP | FLY | GRD | AVG | OBP | SLG |
|---|---|---|---|---|---|---|---|---|---|---|---|---|---|---|---|---|---|---|---|---|---|---|---|---|
| Inning 1-6 | 191.0 | 157 | 11 | 751 | 59 | 52 | 32 | 3 | 52 | 9 | 2 | 45 | 2 | 3 | 107 | 6 | 15 | 9 | 10 | 169 | 301 | .227 | .276 | .329 |
| Inning 7+ | 40.1 | 33 | 4 | 167 | 19 | 19 | 5 | 1 | 13 | 1 | 1 | 11 | 0 | 0 | 24 | 0 | 3 | 0 | 1 | 43 | 63 | .214 | .265 | .338 |

| Game Situation | IP | H | HR | BFP | R | ER | 2B | 3B | RBI | SH | SF | BB | IW | HB | K | WP | SB | CS | DP | FLY | GRD | AVG | OBP | SLG |
|---|---|---|---|---|---|---|---|---|---|---|---|---|---|---|---|---|---|---|---|---|---|---|---|---|
| Close & Late | 20.1 | 11 | 1 | 78 | 10 | 10 | 1 | 0 | 2 | 1 | 0 | 5 | 0 | 0 | 15 | 0 | 2 | 0 | 0 | 23 | 22 | .153 | .208 | .208 |
| Close | 64.2 | 52 | 5 | 259 | 25 | 24 | 11 | 1 | 18 | 3 | 0 | 18 | 0 | 1 | 46 | 0 | 7 | 4 | 2 | 67 | 87 | .219 | .277 | .338 |
| Not Close | 166.2 | 138 | 10 | 659 | 53 | 47 | 26 | 3 | 47 | 7 | 3 | 38 | 2 | 2 | 85 | 6 | 11 | 5 | 9 | 145 | 277 | .227 | .273 | .328 |

| Bases Empty | IP | H | HR | BFP | - | - | 2B | 3B | RBI | SH | SF | BB | IW | HB | K | WP | SB | CS | DP | FLY | GRD | AVG | OBP | SLG |
|---|---|---|---|---|---|---|---|---|---|---|---|---|---|---|---|---|---|---|---|---|---|---|---|---|
| 0 on | 143.0 | 120 | 11 | 588 | - | - | 22 | 3 | 11 | 0 | 0 | 32 | 0 | 1 | 92 | 0 | 0 | 0 | 0 | 142 | 227 | .216 | .260 | .326 |
| 0 on, 0 out | 60.1 | 49 | 5 | 244 | - | - | 12 | 1 | 5 | 0 | 0 | 10 | 0 | 0 | 33 | 0 | 0 | 0 | 0 | 60 | 93 | .209 | .242 | .333 |
| 0 on, 1-2 out | 82.2 | 71 | 6 | 344 | - | - | 10 | 2 | 6 | 0 | 0 | 22 | 0 | 1 | 59 | 0 | 0 | 0 | 0 | 82 | 134 | .221 | .273 | .321 |

| On Base | IP | H | HR | BFP | - | - | 2B | 3B | RBI | SH | SF | BB | IW | HB | K | WP | SB | CS | DP | FLY | GRD | AVG | OBP | SLG |
|---|---|---|---|---|---|---|---|---|---|---|---|---|---|---|---|---|---|---|---|---|---|---|---|---|
| Runners on | 88.1 | 70 | 4 | 330 | - | - | 15 | 1 | 54 | 10 | 3 | 24 | 2 | 2 | 39 | 6 | 18 | 9 | 11 | 70 | 137 | .241 | .300 | .340 |
| Scoring Posn | 49.1 | 37 | 2 | 191 | - | - | 7 | 1 | 49 | 3 | 3 | 16 | 2 | 1 | 25 | 5 | 3 | 1 | 3 | 34 | 83 | .220 | .287 | .310 |
| SB Opp | 46.1 | 35 | 2 | 157 | - | - | 8 | 0 | 9 | 7 | 0 | 8 | 0 | 1 | 17 | 2 | 18 | 9 | 10 | 40 | 62 | .248 | .293 | .348 |
| SB Atd | 11.0 | 4 | 0 | 38 | - | - | 0 | 0 | 1 | 3 | 0 | 3 | 0 | 0 | 6 | 0 | 0 | 1 | 0 | 6 | 16 | .125 | .200 | .125 |
| GDP Opp | 35.2 | 30 | 3 | 124 | - | - | 7 | 0 | 17 | 7 | 0 | 7 | 0 | 1 | 16 | 4 | 11 | 4 | 11 | 22 | 52 | .275 | .325 | .422 |

| At Count | IP | H | HR | BFP | - | - | 2B | 3B | RBI | SH | SF | BB | IW | HB | K | WP | SB | CS | DP | FLY | GRD | AVG | OBP | SLG |
|---|---|---|---|---|---|---|---|---|---|---|---|---|---|---|---|---|---|---|---|---|---|---|---|---|
| 0-0 count | 38.1 | 39 | 2 | 142 | - | - | 9 | 0 | 12 | 2 | 0 | 2 | 2 | 2 | 0 | 4 | 8 | 4 | 5 | 33 | 76 | .287 | .307 | .397 |
| 0-1 Count | 19.2 | 19 | 0 | 77 | - | - | 6 | 1 | 6 | 2 | 1 | 0 | 0 | 0 | 0 | 0 | 1 | 0 | 1 | 24 | 38 | .257 | .253 | .365 |
| 0-2 Count | 16.2 | 10 | 0 | 59 | - | - | 1 | 0 | 2 | 2 | 1 | 0 | 0 | 0 | 23 | 0 | 2 | 1 | 0 | 9 | 17 | .179 | .175 | .196 |
| 1-0 Count | 20.0 | 15 | 2 | 74 | - | - | 3 | 1 | 8 | 0 | 1 | 0 | 0 | 0 | 0 | 0 | 3 | 2 | 1 | 22 | 39 | .205 | .203 | .356 |
| 1-1 Count | 22.0 | 15 | 2 | 79 | - | - | 2 | 1 | 5 | 0 | 0 | 0 | 0 | 0 | 0 | 0 | 2 | 1 | 2 | 19 | 47 | .190 | .190 | .316 |
| 1-2 Count | 31.1 | 18 | 2 | 112 | - | - | 5 | 0 | 5 | 1 | 0 | 0 | 0 | 1 | 53 | 1 | 0 | 0 | 0 | 12 | 29 | .164 | .171 | .264 |
| 2-0 Count | 7.1 | 12 | 2 | 34 | - | - | 3 | 1 | 9 | 1 | 0 | 0 | 0 | 0 | 0 | 0 | 0 | 0 | 0 | 11 | 16 | .364 | .364 | .697 |
| 2-1 Count | 17.2 | 18 | 2 | 69 | - | - | 0 | 0 | 5 | 2 | 0 | 0 | 0 | 0 | 0 | 0 | 1 | 0 | 1 | 22 | 30 | .269 | .269 | .358 |
| 2-2 Count | 30.0 | 22 | 1 | 110 | - | - | 3 | 0 | 3 | 0 | 0 | 0 | 0 | 0 | 34 | 1 | 1 | 1 | 1 | 23 | 41 | .200 | .200 | .255 |
| 3-0 Count | 1.1 | 0 | 0 | 17 | - | - | 0 | 0 | 2 | 0 | 0 | 13 | 0 | 0 | 0 | 0 | 0 | 0 | 0 | 2 | 2 | .000 | .765 | .000 |
| 3-1 Count | 6.2 | 5 | 1 | 41 | - | - | 2 | 0 | 4 | 0 | 0 | 17 | 0 | 0 | 0 | 0 | 0 | 0 | 0 | 16 | 4 | .208 | .537 | .417 |
| 3-2 Count | 20.0 | 16 | 1 | 102 | - | - | 3 | 0 | 3 | 0 | 0 | 24 | 0 | 0 | 21 | 0 | 0 | 0 | 0 | 19 | 24 | .205 | .392 | .282 |

| After Count | IP | H | HR | BFP | - | - | 2B | 3B | RBI | SH | SF | BB | IW | HB | K | WP | SB | CS | DP | FLY | GRD | AVG | OBP | SLG |
|---|---|---|---|---|---|---|---|---|---|---|---|---|---|---|---|---|---|---|---|---|---|---|---|---|
| After (0-1) | 97.0 | 74 | 5 | 379 | - | - | 15 | 2 | 21 | 6 | 2 | 19 | 0 | 1 | 77 | 1 | 5 | 2 | 2 | 86 | 133 | .211 | .252 | .308 |
| After (0-2) | 36.1 | 26 | 1 | 140 | - | - | 6 | 0 | 6 | 2 | 1 | 5 | 0 | 1 | 48 | 0 | 3 | 1 | 0 | 23 | 42 | .198 | .232 | .267 |
| After (1-0) | 96.0 | 77 | 8 | 397 | - | - | 13 | 2 | 32 | 2 | 1 | 35 | 0 | 0 | 54 | 1 | 5 | 3 | 4 | 93 | 155 | .214 | .284 | .329 |
| After (1-1) | 87.2 | 63 | 7 | 347 | - | - | 9 | 1 | 17 | 3 | 0 | 24 | 0 | 0 | 73 | 2 | 3 | 1 | 3 | 69 | 128 | .197 | .253 | .297 |
| After (1-2) | 53.2 | 37 | 2 | 211 | - | - | 8 | 0 | 8 | 1 | 0 | 11 | 0 | 1 | 79 | 1 | 1 | 0 | 0 | 30 | 62 | .187 | .233 | .258 |
| After (2-0) | 29.1 | 28 | 3 | 138 | - | - | 4 | 1 | 16 | 1 | 0 | 25 | 0 | 0 | 10 | 0 | 0 | 1 | 1 | 41 | 41 | .250 | .387 | .384 |
| After (2-1) | 49.1 | 38 | 4 | 204 | - | - | 4 | 0 | 10 | 2 | 0 | 22 | 0 | 0 | 28 | 1 | 1 | 1 | 2 | 56 | 65 | .211 | .297 | .300 |
| After (2-2) | 43.2 | 35 | 1 | 180 | - | - | 6 | 0 | 5 | 0 | 0 | 14 | 0 | 0 | 50 | 1 | 1 | 1 | 1 | 32 | 61 | .211 | .272 | .265 |
| After (3-0) | 4.1 | 5 | 1 | 38 | - | - | 1 | 0 | 5 | 0 | 0 | 21 | 0 | 0 | 1 | 0 | 0 | 0 | 0 | 8 | 4 | .294 | .684 | .529 |
| After (3-1) | 14.0 | 9 | 2 | 77 | - | - | 2 | 0 | 6 | 0 | 0 | 27 | 0 | 0 | 5 | 0 | 0 | 0 | 0 | 27 | 10 | .180 | .468 | .340 |
| After (3-2) | 20.0 | 17 | 1 | 103 | - | - | 3 | 0 | 3 | 0 | 0 | 24 | 0 | 0 | 21 | 0 | 0 | 0 | 0 | 19 | 24 | .215 | .398 | .291 |

| Pitch Level | IP | H | HR | BFP | R | ER | 2B | 3B | RBI | SH | SF | BB | IW | HB | K | WP | SB | CS | DP | FLY | GRD | AVG | OBP | SLG |
|---|---|---|---|---|---|---|---|---|---|---|---|---|---|---|---|---|---|---|---|---|---|---|---|---|
| Pitch 1-15 | 33.0 | 23 | 2 | 122 | 19 | 19 | 6 | 0 | 8 | 0 | 1 | 2 | 0 | 0 | 15 | 0 | 2 | 1 | 0 | 23 | 62 | .193 | .205 | .294 |
| Pitch 16-30 | 35.2 | 32 | 4 | 142 | 9 | 9 | 4 | 0 | 8 | 2 | 1 | 9 | 0 | 0 | 16 | 0 | 2 | 1 | 3 | 34 | 57 | .246 | .293 | .369 |
| Pitch 31-45 | 39.0 | 30 | 2 | 144 | 10 | 8 | 5 | 0 | 8 | 3 | 0 | 5 | 1 | 0 | 28 | 1 | 0 | 3 | 2 | 35 | 59 | .221 | .248 | .301 |
| Pitch 46-60 | 31.1 | 30 | 1 | 136 | 14 | 11 | 6 | 3 | 13 | 0 | 0 | 15 | 1 | 0 | 18 | 3 | 3 | 1 | 3 | 31 | 45 | .248 | .331 | .372 |
| Pitch 61-75 | 33.2 | 24 | 1 | 130 | 9 | 8 | 8 | 0 | 10 | 3 | 0 | 7 | 0 | 2 | 19 | 2 | 5 | 1 | 0 | 26 | 51 | .203 | .260 | .297 |
| Pitch 76-90 | 30.1 | 16 | 1 | 111 | 8 | 7 | 2 | 1 | 2 | 0 | 0 | 6 | 0 | 1 | 19 | 0 | 1 | 2 | 3 | 25 | 50 | .154 | .207 | .221 |
| Pitch 91-105 | 19.0 | 26 | 3 | 91 | 4 | 4 | 4 | 0 | 14 | 1 | 0 | 7 | 0 | 0 | 12 | 0 | 5 | 0 | 0 | 22 | 31 | .313 | .367 | .470 |
| Pitch 106-20 | 7.1 | 9 | 1 | 33 | 3 | 3 | 1 | 0 | 2 | 1 | 0 | 2 | 0 | 0 | 3 | 0 | 0 | 0 | 0 | 13 | 8 | .300 | .344 | .433 |
| Pitch 121-35 | 1.2 | 1 | 0 | 8 | 2 | 2 | 1 | 0 | 1 | 0 | 1 | 2 | 0 | 0 | 0 | 0 | 0 | 0 | 0 | 3 | 1 | .200 | .375 | .400 |
| Pitch 136-50 | 0.2 | 0 | 0 | 3 | 0 | 0 | 0 | 0 | 0 | 0 | 0 | 1 | 0 | 0 | 1 | 0 | 0 | 0 | 0 | 0 | 1 | .000 | .333 | .000 |

Results At Each Pitch

| Result | 0-0 | 0-1 | 0-2 | 1-0 | 1-1 | 1-2 | 2-0 | 2-1 | 2-2 | 3-0 | 3-1 | 3-2 |
|---|---|---|---|---|---|---|---|---|---|---|---|---|
| Ball | 402 | 162 | 81 | 139 | 138 | 100 | 38 | 54 | 68 | 14 | 17 | 24 |
| Taken Strike | 242 | 47 | 3 | 93 | 40 | 9 | 40 | 15 | 9 | 22 | 15 | 9 |
| Swung | 49 | 28 | 17 | 25 | 35 | 44 | 6 | 15 | 28 | 1 | 5 | 12 |
| Fouled | 88 | 65 | 24 | 68 | 55 | 56 | 21 | 52 | 73 | 1 | 16 | 40 |
| In Play | 140 | 77 | 36 | 74 | 79 | 58 | 34 | 69 | 76 | 4 | 24 | 57 |

Drabek's Pitching Record with Each Pirates Catcher

| Catcher | ERA | IP | H | BFP | R | ER | HR | SH | SF | BB | IW | HB | K | WP | BK | 2B | 3B | RBI | SB | CS | DP | GRD | FLY |
|---|---|---|---|---|---|---|---|---|---|---|---|---|---|---|---|---|---|---|---|---|---|---|---|
| Dann BILARDELLO | 1.50 | 30.0 | 20 | 115 | 5 | 5 | 2 | 0 | 0 | 9 | 1 | 0 | 20 | 0 | 0 | 6 | 0 | 4 | 1 | 1 | 2 | 43 | 28 |
| Mike LAVALLIERE | 4.01 | 92.0 | 95 | 385 | 44 | 41 | 7 | 4 | 1 | 22 | 1 | 2 | 54 | 2 | 0 | 16 | 3 | 37 | 11 | 2 | 5 | 151 | 85 |
| Don SLAUGHT | 2.06 | 109.1 | 75 | 418 | 29 | 25 | 6 | 6 | 2 | 25 | 0 | 1 | 57 | 4 | 0 | 15 | 1 | 24 | 6 | 6 | 4 | 170 | 99 |

Opponent Baserunning

| | Which Pitch | | | Which Count | | | | |
|---|---|---|---|---|---|---|---|---|
| Event | Pitch 1 | Pitch 2 | Other | Even | Ahead | Behind | 3-2 | 2 Strikes |
| Stolen Bases | 7 | 5 | 6 | 11 | 3 | 4 | 0 | 3 |
| Pitcher Caught Stealing | 1 | 0 | 0 | 1 | 0 | 0 | 0 | 0 |
| Catcher Caught Stealing | 3 | 2 | 3 | 5 | 1 | 2 | 0 | 2 |
| Pitcher Pickoffs | 2 | 1 | 0 | 2 | 1 | 0 | 0 | 0 |

Outs and Men on at time of Pitching Change (Outs, men on)

| | (0,1) | (0,2) | (0,3) | (1,1) | (1,2) | (1,3) | (2,1) | (2,2) | (2,3) | Total | Scored |
|---|---|---|---|---|---|---|---|---|---|---|---|
| Runners Inherited | 0 | 0 | 0 | 0 | 0 | 0 | 0 | 0 | 0 | 0 | 0 |
| Runners Bequeathed | 2 | 0 | 0 | 2 | 2 | 1 | 2 | 1 | 1 | 18 | 6 |

Fielding

| Pos | G | Inn | PO | A | E | DP |
|---|---|---|---|---|---|---|
| P | 33 | 231.1 | 25 | 36 | 1 | 2 |

Compared to Other National Leaguers

| Category | Rank | Stat | Minimum |
|---|---|---|---|
| Wins | 1 | 22 | |
| Win Loss % | 1 | .786 | 15 Dec |
| Complete Games | 2 | 9 | |
| Most Run Support per 9 IP | 2 | 5.91 | 162 IP |
| Fewest Baserunners per 9 IP | 2 | 9.69 | 162 IP |
| Lowest On-Base Average Allowed | 2 | .274 | 162 IP |
| OBP Allowed, Leading Off Inning | 2 | .242 | 150 PA |
| Shutouts | 3 | 3 | |
| ERA on the Road | 3 | 2.51 | 81 IP |
| Slugging Pct Allowed | 3 | .331 | 162 IP |
| Fewest Hits/Inning | 4 | .821 | 162 IP |
| Batting Average Allowed | 4 | .225 | 162 IP |
| Innings | 5 | 231 | |
| Earned Run Average | 6 | 2.76 | 162 IP |
| Games Started | 7 | 33 | |
| Batters Faced | 8 | 918 | |
| Pitches Thrown | 9 | 3360 | |
| BA Allowed, Scoring Position | 9 | .220 | 150 PA |
| K/BB Ratio | 10 | 2.34 | 162 IP |
| Fewest HR's Off per 9 inning | 10 | .584 | 162 IP |
| Doubles Off | 11 | 37 | |
| Caught Stealing Off | 13 | 9 | |

Compared to Other Pirates Players

| Category | Rank | Stat | Minimum |
|---|---|---|---|
| Wins | 1 | 22 | |
| W/L Pct | 1 | .786 | 15 Dec |
| Hits/IP | 1 | .821 | 162 IP |
| Innings | 1 | 231 | |
| Shutouts | 1 | 3 | |
| K/BB Ratio | 1 | 2.34 | 162 IP |
| Strikeouts | 1 | 131 | |
| Doubles Off | 1 | 37 | |
| Hits Allowed | 1 | 190 | |
| Games Started | 1 | 33 | |
| Batters Faced | 1 | 918 | |
| Pitches Thrown | 1 | 3360 | |
| Complete Games | 1 | 9 | |
| ERA on the Road | 1 | 2.51 | 81 IP |
| Earned Run Average | 1 | 2.76 | 162 IP |
| Slugging Pct Allowed | 1 | .331 | 162 IP |
| Baserunners per 9 IP | 1 | 9.69 | 162 IP |
| Run Support per 9 IP | 1 | 5.91 | 162 IP |
| HR's Off per 9 inning | 1 | .584 | 162 IP |
| Batting Average Allowed | 1 | .225 | 162 IP |
| On-Base Average Allowed | 1 | .274 | 162 IP |
| BA Allowed, Scoring Position | 1 | .220 | 150 PA |
| OBA Allowed, Leading Off Inning | 1 | .242 | 150 PA |

Active Batters vs. Doug Drabek
(10 or more At Bats since 1985)

| Batter | AVG | AB | H | 2B | 3B | HR | RBI | W | K | SF | SB | CS |
|---|---|---|---|---|---|---|---|---|---|---|---|---|
| BACKMAN, Wally | .533 | 15 | 8 | 0 | 0 | 0 | 0 | 1 | 2 | 0 | 0 | 0 |
| GRACE, Mark | .471 | 34 | 16 | 2 | 0 | 1 | 5 | 2 | 1 | 0 | 0 | 2 |
| MURRAY, Eddie | .462 | 13 | 6 | 0 | 0 | 0 | 0 | 3 | 1 | 0 | 0 | 0 |
| BUTLER, Brett | .455 | 22 | 10 | 2 | 0 | 0 | 0 | 2 | 2 | 0 | 1 | 1 |
| DESHIELDS, Deli | .438 | 16 | 7 | 1 | 1 | 0 | 1 | 0 | 2 | 0 | 1 | 0 |
| JAMES, Dion | .417 | 12 | 5 | 0 | 0 | 0 | 1 | 1 | 0 | 0 | 0 | 0 |
| DAVIS, Glenn | .407 | 27 | 11 | 2 | 0 | 1 | 2 | 2 | 3 | 0 | 0 | 0 |
| ESASKY, Nick | .400 | 10 | 4 | 2 | 0 | 0 | 1 | 1 | 0 | 0 | 0 | 0 |
| ASHBY, Alan | .400 | 10 | 4 | 1 | 0 | 1 | 5 | 1 | 3 | 0 | 0 | 0 |
| GWYNN, Tony | .400 | 25 | 10 | 5 | 1 | 0 | 2 | 1 | 1 | 0 | 2 | 1 |
| SAX, Steve | .400 | 10 | 4 | 0 | 0 | 1 | 3 | 1 | 0 | 0 | 2 | 1 |
| ELSTER, Kevin | .391 | 23 | 9 | 1 | 1 | 1 | 6 | 3 | 3 | 0 | 0 | 0 |
| DANIELS, Kal | .389 | 18 | 7 | 3 | 0 | 1 | 4 | 1 | 2 | 0 | 2 | 0 |
| BRADLEY, Phil | .389 | 18 | 7 | 0 | 1 | 0 | 0 | 2 | 3 | 0 | 1 | 0 |
| LARKIN, Barry | .379 | 29 | 11 | 2 | 1 | 0 | 0 | 1 | 3 | 0 | 3 | 0 |
| MAGADAN, Dave | .375 | 32 | 12 | 2 | 0 | 0 | 3 | 3 | 0 | 0 | 0 | 0 |
| MCGEE, Willie | .370 | 27 | 10 | 1 | 2 | 1 | 5 | 2 | 2 | 0 | 1 | 0 |
| WHITT, Ernie | .357 | 14 | 5 | 1 | 0 | 1 | 1 | 1 | 1 | 0 | 0 | 1 |
| PENA, Tony | .353 | 17 | 6 | 2 | 0 | 0 | 2 | 0 | 1 | 0 | 0 | 0 |
| SAMUEL, Juan | .341 | 41 | 14 | 4 | 0 | 2 | 2 | 2 | 6 | 0 | 3 | 1 |
| WINNINGHAM, Her | .333 | 18 | 6 | 3 | 0 | 0 | 1 | 0 | 3 | 0 | 0 | 0 |
| WYNNE, Marvell | .333 | 21 | 7 | 0 | 0 | 1 | 2 | 2 | 2 | 0 | 3 | 1 |
| WILSON, Mookie | .333 | 12 | 4 | 0 | 0 | 1 | 1 | 0 | 1 | 0 | 1 | 0 |
| DAVIS, Eric | .333 | 24 | 8 | 2 | 1 | 2 | 5 | 2 | 6 | 0 | 2 | 0 |
| BIGGIO, Craig | .333 | 15 | 5 | 1 | 0 | 0 | 0 | 1 | 3 | 0 | 0 | 1 |
| GUERRERO, Pedro | .333 | 27 | 9 | 2 | 0 | 2 | 7 | 2 | 6 | 0 | 0 | 0 |
| OQUENDO, Jose | .320 | 25 | 8 | 0 | 0 | 0 | 1 | 3 | 1 | 0 | 0 | 1 |
| JAMES, Chris | .318 | 22 | 7 | 3 | 0 | 1 | 4 | 0 | 2 | 0 | 0 | 0 |
| JEFFERIES, Greg | .318 | 22 | 7 | 3 | 0 | 0 | 2 | 4 | 2 | 0 | 2 | 0 |
| JELTZ, Steve | .304 | 23 | 7 | 0 | 2 | 0 | 1 | 3 | 3 | 0 | 0 | 0 |
| MITCHELL, Kevin | .304 | 23 | 7 | 0 | 1 | 3 | 8 | 1 | 4 | 0 | 0 | 0 |
| ALOMAR, Roberto | .300 | 20 | 6 | 1 | 0 | 0 | 2 | 2 | 3 | 1 | 0 | 1 |
| GARCIA, Damaso | .300 | 10 | 3 | 1 | 0 | 0 | 0 | 0 | 1 | 0 | 0 | 0 |
| PARENT, Mark | .300 | 10 | 3 | 0 | 0 | 1 | 4 | 0 | 1 | 1 | 0 | 0 |
| DUNSTON, Shawon | .297 | 37 | 11 | 0 | 0 | 3 | 5 | 1 | 8 | 0 | 2 | 3 |
| STRAWBERRY, Dar | .297 | 37 | 11 | 2 | 0 | 5 | 11 | 4 | 2 | 0 | 2 | 0 |
| GALARRAGA, Andr | .295 | 44 | 13 | 3 | 0 | 1 | 2 | 3 | 14 | 0 | 1 | 2 |
| CLARK, Jack | .294 | 17 | 5 | 1 | 0 | 2 | 4 | 8 | 3 | 0 | 0 | 0 |
| TREADWAY, Jeff | .292 | 24 | 7 | 2 | 0 | 1 | 2 | 1 | 1 | 0 | 0 | 0 |
| YOUNG, Gerald | .292 | 24 | 7 | 0 | 0 | 0 | 0 | 3 | 2 | 0 | 2 | 3 |
| DORAN, Billy | .292 | 24 | 7 | 0 | 0 | 0 | 1 | 2 | 0 | 0 | 2 | 0 |
| WEBSTER, Mitch | .286 | 21 | 6 | 1 | 0 | 0 | 0 | 1 | 3 | 0 | 0 | 0 |
| GREGG, Tommy | .286 | 14 | 4 | 1 | 0 | 0 | 0 | 1 | 1 | 0 | 0 | 1 |
| SMITH, Ozzie | .280 | 25 | 7 | 1 | 0 | 0 | 0 | 1 | 1 | 0 | 5 | 0 |
| RILES, Ernest | .278 | 18 | 5 | 0 | 0 | 1 | 2 | 1 | 3 | 1 | 0 | 0 |
| MCDOWELL, Oddib | .278 | 18 | 5 | 0 | 0 | 2 | 3 | 2 | 1 | 0 | 1 | 0 |
| LAW, Vance | .276 | 29 | 8 | 1 | 0 | 0 | 1 | 3 | 4 | 0 | 0 | 0 |
| SANDBERG, Ryne | .275 | 51 | 14 | 1 | 0 | 1 | 4 | 2 | 4 | 0 | 4 | 0 |
| PALMEIRO, Rafae | .273 | 22 | 6 | 2 | 0 | 1 | 1 | 1 | 2 | 0 | 0 | 0 |
| BLAUSER, Jeff | .273 | 11 | 3 | 1 | 0 | 0 | 1 | 0 | 2 | 0 | 0 | 0 |
| HAMILTON, Jeff | .273 | 11 | 3 | 1 | 0 | 0 | 0 | 0 | 1 | 0 | 0 | 0 |
| NOCE, Paul | .273 | 11 | 3 | 0 | 0 | 0 | 0 | 1 | 2 | 0 | 1 | 2 |
| COLEMAN, Vince | .269 | 26 | 7 | 2 | 0 | 0 | 3 | 1 | 4 | 0 | 3 | 0 |
| STUBBS, Frankli | .267 | 15 | 4 | 1 | 1 | 1 | 1 | 0 | 3 | 0 | 0 | 0 |
| O'NEILL, Paul | .263 | 19 | 5 | 0 | 0 | 0 | 1 | 1 | 2 | 0 | 0 | 1 |
| BRUNANSKY, Tom | .263 | 19 | 5 | 0 | 0 | 0 | 1 | 1 | 4 | 0 | 0 | 0 |
| BASS, Kevin | .261 | 23 | 6 | 1 | 0 | 2 | 7 | 2 | 3 | 2 | 0 | 0 |
| BERRYHILL, Damo | .261 | 23 | 6 | 1 | 0 | 0 | 2 | 2 | 7 | 0 | 0 | 0 |
| SALAZAR, Luis | .250 | 16 | 4 | 0 | 0 | 1 | 2 | 1 | 2 | 0 | 0 | 0 |

| Batter | AVG | AB | H | 2B | 3B | HR | RBI | W | K | SF | SB | CS |
|---|---|---|---|---|---|---|---|---|---|---|---|---|
| RAINES, Tim | .250 | 36 | 9 | 3 | 0 | 3 | 11 | 4 | 2 | 0 | 1 | 0 |
| WALTON, Jerome | .250 | 28 | 7 | 2 | 0 | 0 | 1 | 1 | 6 | 0 | 0 | 0 |
| MARTINEZ, Dave | .250 | 56 | 14 | 2 | 1 | 1 | 5 | 2 | 9 | 0 | 1 | 0 |
| SMITH, Dwight | .240 | 25 | 6 | 1 | 0 | 0 | 2 | 1 | 2 | 0 | 1 | 1 |
| TEMPLETON, Garr | .238 | 21 | 5 | 3 | 0 | 0 | 1 | 0 | 1 | 0 | 0 | 0 |
| SCIOSCIA, Mike | .235 | 17 | 4 | 2 | 0 | 0 | 2 | 4 | 2 | 0 | 0 | 0 |
| RAMIREZ, Rafael | .235 | 17 | 4 | 0 | 0 | 0 | 0 | 1 | 2 | 0 | 0 | 0 |
| HERR, Tommy | .231 | 26 | 6 | 2 | 0 | 0 | 3 | 1 | 4 | 0 | 0 | 0 |
| PENDLETON, Terr | .231 | 26 | 6 | 1 | 0 | 0 | 2 | 2 | 2 | 1 | 0 | 0 |
| DURHAM, Leon | .222 | 18 | 4 | 2 | 0 | 1 | 3 | 1 | 5 | 0 | 0 | 0 |
| ALDRETE, Mike | .222 | 18 | 4 | 0 | 0 | 1 | 3 | 3 | 3 | 0 | 0 | 1 |
| BROOKS, Hubie | .219 | 32 | 7 | 1 | 0 | 0 | 1 | 2 | 3 | 0 | 0 | 1 |
| DAWSON, Andre | .214 | 42 | 9 | 2 | 0 | 1 | 3 | 3 | 7 | 0 | 0 | 0 |
| WALLING, Denny | .208 | 24 | 5 | 0 | 0 | 1 | 3 | 3 | 2 | 0 | 0 | 0 |
| OWEN, Spike | .208 | 24 | 5 | 1 | 1 | 0 | 4 | 3 | 1 | 0 | 0 | 0 |
| JOHNSON, Howard | .206 | 34 | 7 | 2 | 0 | 3 | 3 | 4 | 5 | 0 | 0 | 1 |
| SHELBY, John | .200 | 15 | 3 | 1 | 0 | 1 | 6 | 2 | 3 | 0 | 0 | 0 |
| PERRY, Gerald | .200 | 10 | 2 | 2 | 0 | 0 | 0 | 0 | 2 | 0 | 0 | 0 |
| MARSHALL, Mike | .200 | 15 | 3 | 0 | 0 | 1 | 1 | 1 | 2 | 0 | 0 | 0 |
| READY, Randy | .200 | 15 | 3 | 0 | 0 | 2 | 2 | 2 | 2 | 0 | 0 | 0 |
| SMITH, Lonnie | .200 | 20 | 4 | 1 | 0 | 0 | 1 | 2 | 2 | 0 | 0 | 1 |
| THOMAS, Andres | .200 | 20 | 4 | 1 | 0 | 1 | 2 | 0 | 1 | 0 | 0 | 0 |
| HAYES, Von | .195 | 41 | 8 | 2 | 1 | 2 | 5 | 4 | 5 | 0 | 2 | 0 |
| CLARK, Will | .190 | 21 | 4 | 0 | 0 | 0 | 1 | 2 | 4 | 1 | 0 | 0 |
| WALLACH, Tim | .186 | 43 | 8 | 2 | 1 | 1 | 6 | 3 | 7 | 0 | 0 | 0 |
| MURPHY, Dale | .182 | 22 | 4 | 2 | 0 | 0 | 0 | 0 | 5 | 0 | 0 | 0 |
| GRIFFIN, Alfred | .182 | 11 | 2 | 0 | 0 | 0 | 0 | 2 | 1 | 0 | 1 | 1 |
| CANDAELE, Casey | .182 | 11 | 2 | 0 | 0 | 0 | 0 | 0 | 0 | 0 | 0 | 0 |
| DAVIS, Mike | .182 | 11 | 2 | 0 | 0 | 0 | 0 | 1 | 4 | 0 | 0 | 0 |
| COLLINS, Dave | .182 | 11 | 2 | 0 | 0 | 0 | 2 | 1 | 1 | 1 | 1 | 0 |
| ROBERTS, Bip | .182 | 11 | 2 | 0 | 0 | 0 | 0 | 0 | 1 | 0 | 1 | 0 |
| BOOKER, Rod | .182 | 11 | 2 | 1 | 0 | 0 | 0 | 0 | 2 | 0 | 0 | 0 |
| THOMPSON, Milt | .179 | 39 | 7 | 1 | 0 | 1 | 2 | 3 | 8 | 0 | 3 | 2 |
| WILSON, Glenn | .176 | 17 | 3 | 0 | 1 | 0 | 3 | 0 | 4 | 1 | 0 | 0 |
| DAULTON, Darren | .174 | 23 | 4 | 0 | 0 | 1 | 1 | 0 | 3 | 0 | 0 | 0 |
| SABO, Chris | .167 | 18 | 3 | 0 | 0 | 1 | 2 | 1 | 0 | 1 | 1 | 0 |
| REED, Jeff | .167 | 18 | 3 | 0 | 0 | 0 | 1 | 2 | 2 | 0 | 0 | 0 |
| HATCHER, Billy | .167 | 18 | 3 | 0 | 0 | 1 | 1 | 0 | 0 | 0 | 0 | 0 |
| DYKSTRA, Lenny | .167 | 42 | 7 | 1 | 0 | 0 | 2 | 3 | 7 | 0 | 1 | 0 |
| CAMINITI, Ken | .167 | 12 | 2 | 0 | 0 | 0 | 1 | 3 | 4 | 0 | 0 | 0 |
| GIBSON, Kirk | .167 | 18 | 3 | 0 | 0 | 0 | 1 | 1 | 1 | 0 | 0 | 0 |
| PARRISH, Lance | .160 | 25 | 4 | 0 | 0 | 0 | 0 | 1 | 6 | 0 | 0 | 0 |
| KRUK, John | .143 | 14 | 2 | 0 | 0 | 0 | 1 | 4 | 1 | 0 | 0 | 1 |
| WALKER, Larry | .133 | 15 | 2 | 0 | 0 | 0 | 1 | 0 | 3 | 0 | 0 | 0 |
| FITZGERALD, Mik | .130 | 23 | 3 | 0 | 0 | 0 | 1 | 1 | 6 | 0 | 1 | 0 |
| GANT, Ron | .125 | 16 | 2 | 0 | 0 | 0 | 2 | 0 | 7 | 0 | 0 | 0 |
| CARTER, Gary | .125 | 24 | 3 | 0 | 0 | 0 | 0 | 1 | 2 | 0 | 0 | 0 |
| FOLEY, Tom | .115 | 26 | 3 | 0 | 0 | 0 | 1 | 3 | 1 | 0 | 0 | 1 |
| JONES, Tim | .100 | 10 | 1 | 0 | 0 | 0 | 1 | 0 | 1 | 0 | 0 | 0 |
| HAYES, Charlie | .100 | 10 | 1 | 0 | 0 | 1 | 1 | 2 | 2 | 0 | 0 | 0 |
| KENNEDY, Terry | .100 | 10 | 1 | 1 | 0 | 0 | 0 | 0 | 2 | 0 | 0 | 0 |
| DUNCAN, Mariano | .091 | 11 | 1 | 0 | 0 | 0 | 0 | 0 | 1 | 0 | 1 | 0 |
| MCREYNOLDS, Kev | .091 | 33 | 3 | 0 | 0 | 2 | 6 | 5 | 3 | 0 | 0 | 0 |
| SANTIAGO, Benit | .071 | 14 | 1 | 0 | 1 | 0 | 3 | 1 | 1 | 0 | 0 | 0 |
| THOMPSON, Robbi | .071 | 14 | 1 | 0 | 0 | 0 | 0 | 2 | 4 | 0 | 1 | 0 |
| DIAZ, Bo | .071 | 14 | 1 | 0 | 0 | 0 | 0 | 0 | 0 | 0 | 0 | 0 |
| MARTINEZ, Carme | .067 | 15 | 1 | 0 | 0 | 0 | 0 | 3 | 4 | 0 | 0 | 0 |
| URIBE, Jose | .067 | 15 | 1 | 0 | 0 | 0 | 0 | 1 | 3 | 0 | 0 | 1 |
| JORDAN, Ricky | .000 | 13 | 0 | 0 | 0 | 0 | 1 | 0 | 6 | 0 | 0 | 0 |
| NIXON, Otis | .000 | 11 | 0 | 0 | 0 | 0 | 0 | 1 | 3 | 0 | 0 | 0 |
| WILKERSON, Curt | .000 | 11 | 0 | 0 | 0 | 0 | 0 | 0 | 4 | 0 | 0 | 0 |

# Dennis Eckersley – Oakland A's

| 1990 | W | L | S | ERA | SUP | G | GS | CG | SO | GF | OP | HD | IP | H | HR | BFP | R | ER | RF |
|---|---|---|---|---|---|---|---|---|---|---|---|---|---|---|---|---|---|---|---|
| Total | 4 | 2 | 48 | 0.61 | 1.47 | 63 | 0 | 0 | 0 | 61 | 50 | 0 | 73.1 | 41 | 2 | 262 | 9 | 5 | 12 |

| Vs. Teams | W | L | S | ERA | SUP | G | GS | CG | SO | GF | OP | HD | IP | H | HR | BFP | R | ER | RF |
|---|---|---|---|---|---|---|---|---|---|---|---|---|---|---|---|---|---|---|---|
| vs.Bal | 0 | 0 | 5 | 0.00 | 1.29 | 6 | 0 | 0 | 0 | 6 | 5 | 0 | 7.0 | 1 | 0 | 23 | 0 | 0 | 1 |
| vs.Bos | 0 | 0 | 2 | 0.00 | 0.00 | 3 | 0 | 0 | 0 | 3 | 2 | 0 | 3.1 | 0 | 0 | 10 | 0 | 0 | 0 |
| vs.Cal | 0 | 1 | 6 | 2.16 | 0.00 | 7 | 0 | 0 | 0 | 7 | 6 | 0 | 8.1 | 4 | 1 | 30 | 2 | 2 | 0 |
| vs.ChA | 0 | 0 | 2 | 0.00 | 4.15 | 4 | 0 | 0 | 0 | 4 | 2 | 0 | 4.1 | 2 | 0 | 15 | 0 | 0 | 2 |
| vs.Cle | 1 | 0 | 4 | 1.29 | 5.14 | 6 | 0 | 0 | 0 | 6 | 4 | 0 | 7.0 | 5 | 0 | 25 | 1 | 1 | 4 |
| vs.Det | 0 | 0 | 4 | 0.00 | 0.00 | 5 | 0 | 0 | 0 | 5 | 4 | 0 | 6.2 | 5 | 0 | 25 | 0 | 0 | 0 |
| vs.KC | 1 | 0 | 5 | 2.25 | 1.13 | 6 | 0 | 0 | 0 | 6 | 6 | 0 | 8.0 | 8 | 1 | 32 | 2 | 2 | 1 |
| vs.Mil | 0 | 0 | 2 | 0.00 | 0.00 | 2 | 0 | 0 | 0 | 2 | 2 | 0 | 2.0 | 0 | 0 | 6 | 0 | 0 | 0 |
| vs.Min | 1 | 0 | 3 | 0.00 | 1.59 | 5 | 0 | 0 | 0 | 4 | 3 | 0 | 5.2 | 3 | 0 | 20 | 0 | 0 | 1 |
| vs.NYA | 0 | 0 | 2 | 0.00 | 3.86 | 4 | 0 | 0 | 0 | 3 | 2 | 0 | 4.2 | 2 | 0 | 16 | 0 | 0 | 2 |
| vs.Sea | 1 | 0 | 3 | 0.00 | 2.08 | 4 | 0 | 0 | 0 | 4 | 3 | 0 | 4.1 | 1 | 0 | 14 | 0 | 0 | 1 |
| vs.Tex | 0 | 1 | 6 | 0.00 | 0.00 | 7 | 0 | 0 | 0 | 7 | 7 | 0 | 7.0 | 8 | 0 | 30 | 4 | 0 | 0 |
| vs.Tor | 0 | 0 | 4 | 0.00 | 0.00 | 4 | 0 | 0 | 0 | 4 | 4 | 0 | 5.0 | 2 | 0 | 16 | 0 | 0 | 0 |

| By Park | W | L | S | ERA | SUP | G | GS | CG | SO | GF | OP | HD | IP | H | HR | BFP | R | ER | RF |
|---|---|---|---|---|---|---|---|---|---|---|---|---|---|---|---|---|---|---|---|
| at Bal | 0 | 0 | 3 | 0.00 | 1.93 | 4 | 0 | 0 | 0 | 4 | 3 | 0 | 4.2 | 1 | 0 | 15 | 0 | 0 | 1 |
| at Bos | 0 | 0 | 1 | 0.00 | 0.00 | 2 | 0 | 0 | 0 | 2 | 1 | 0 | 2.1 | 0 | 0 | 7 | 0 | 0 | 0 |
| at Cal | 0 | 0 | 4 | 0.00 | 0.00 | 4 | 0 | 0 | 0 | 4 | 4 | 0 | 4.2 | 3 | 0 | 17 | 0 | 0 | 0 |
| at ChA | 0 | 0 | 2 | 0.00 | 6.75 | 3 | 0 | 0 | 0 | 3 | 2 | 0 | 2.2 | 1 | 0 | 9 | 0 | 0 | 2 |
| at Cle | 1 | 0 | 0 | 0.00 | 6.00 | 2 | 0 | 0 | 0 | 2 | 0 | 0 | 3.0 | 2 | 0 | 10 | 0 | 0 | 2 |
| at Det | 0 | 0 | 1 | 0.00 | 0.00 | 2 | 0 | 0 | 0 | 2 | 1 | 0 | 3.0 | 2 | 0 | 11 | 0 | 0 | 0 |
| at KC | 0 | 0 | 3 | 2.45 | 0.00 | 3 | 0 | 0 | 0 | 3 | 3 | 0 | 3.2 | 3 | 0 | 14 | 1 | 1 | 0 |
| at Min | 0 | 0 | 1 | 0.00 | 0.00 | 1 | 0 | 0 | 0 | 1 | 1 | 0 | 0.1 | 0 | 0 | 1 | 0 | 0 | 0 |
| at NYA | 0 | 0 | 2 | 0.00 | 4.50 | 3 | 0 | 0 | 0 | 3 | 2 | 0 | 4.0 | 2 | 0 | 14 | 0 | 0 | 2 |
| at Oak | 3 | 2 | 22 | 1.02 | 1.27 | 30 | 0 | 0 | 0 | 28 | 24 | 0 | 35.1 | 20 | 2 | 131 | 8 | 4 | 5 |
| at Sea | 0 | 0 | 2 | 0.00 | 0.00 | 2 | 0 | 0 | 0 | 2 | 2 | 0 | 2.0 | 1 | 0 | 7 | 0 | 0 | 0 |
| at Tex | 0 | 0 | 4 | 0.00 | 0.00 | 4 | 0 | 0 | 0 | 4 | 4 | 0 | 3.2 | 4 | 0 | 13 | 0 | 0 | 0 |
| at Tor | 0 | 0 | 3 | 0.00 | 0.00 | 3 | 0 | 0 | 0 | 3 | 3 | 0 | 4.0 | 2 | 0 | 13 | 0 | 0 | 0 |

| By Month | W | L | S | ERA | SUP | G | GS | CG | SO | GF | OP | HD | IP | H | HR | BFP | R | ER | RF |
|---|---|---|---|---|---|---|---|---|---|---|---|---|---|---|---|---|---|---|---|
| April | 1 | 0 | 7 | 0.00 | 1.80 | 8 | 0 | 0 | 0 | 8 | 7 | 0 | 10.0 | 5 | 0 | 35 | 0 | 0 | 2 |
| May | 1 | 0 | 8 | 0.77 | 3.09 | 10 | 0 | 0 | 0 | 9 | 8 | 0 | 11.2 | 7 | 0 | 41 | 1 | 1 | 4 |
| June | 0 | 1 | 9 | 0.77 | 1.54 | 11 | 0 | 0 | 0 | 11 | 10 | 0 | 11.2 | 10 | 0 | 47 | 5 | 1 | 2 |
| July | 0 | 1 | 8 | 1.64 | 0.00 | 10 | 0 | 0 | 0 | 10 | 8 | 0 | 11.0 | 2 | 1 | 35 | 2 | 2 | 0 |
| August | 1 | 0 | 8 | 0.64 | 0.64 | 11 | 0 | 0 | 0 | 11 | 9 | 0 | 14.0 | 8 | 1 | 51 | 1 | 1 | 1 |
| September | 1 | 0 | 7 | 0.00 | 1.93 | 12 | 0 | 0 | 0 | 11 | 7 | 0 | 14.0 | 9 | 0 | 50 | 0 | 0 | 3 |
| October | 0 | 0 | 1 | 0.00 | 0.00 | 1 | 0 | 0 | 0 | 1 | 1 | 0 | 1.0 | 0 | 0 | 3 | 0 | 0 | 0 |

| Conditions | W | L | S | ERA | SUP | G | GS | CG | SO | GF | OP | HD | IP | H | HR | BFP | R | ER | RF |
|---|---|---|---|---|---|---|---|---|---|---|---|---|---|---|---|---|---|---|---|
| Home | 3 | 2 | 22 | 1.02 | 1.27 | 30 | 0 | 0 | 0 | 28 | 24 | 0 | 35.1 | 20 | 2 | 131 | 8 | 4 | 5 |
| Away | 1 | 0 | 26 | 0.24 | 1.66 | 33 | 0 | 0 | 0 | 33 | 26 | 0 | 38.0 | 21 | 0 | 131 | 1 | 1 | 7 |
| Day | 3 | 2 | 20 | 1.04 | 2.08 | 29 | 0 | 0 | 0 | 28 | 22 | 0 | 34.2 | 19 | 2 | 127 | 8 | 4 | 8 |
| Night | 1 | 0 | 28 | 0.23 | 0.93 | 34 | 0 | 0 | 0 | 33 | 28 | 0 | 38.2 | 22 | 0 | 135 | 1 | 1 | 4 |
| Grass | 4 | 2 | 39 | 0.57 | 1.71 | 54 | 0 | 0 | 0 | 52 | 41 | 0 | 63.1 | 35 | 2 | 227 | 8 | 4 | 12 |
| Turf | 0 | 0 | 9 | 0.90 | 0.00 | 9 | 0 | 0 | 0 | 9 | 9 | 0 | 10.0 | 6 | 0 | 35 | 1 | 1 | 0 |

| Days Rest | W | L | S | ERA | SUP | G | GS | CG | SO | GF | OP | HD | IP | H | HR | BFP | R | ER | RF |
|---|---|---|---|---|---|---|---|---|---|---|---|---|---|---|---|---|---|---|---|
| 0 | 1 | 0 | 14 | 0.52 | 1.04 | 16 | 0 | 0 | 0 | 16 | 14 | 0 | 17.1 | 13 | 0 | 64 | 1 | 1 | 2 |
| 1 | 0 | 2 | 14 | 0.84 | 0.84 | 17 | 0 | 0 | 0 | 17 | 15 | 0 | 21.1 | 14 | 1 | 82 | 6 | 2 | 2 |
| 2 | 0 | 0 | 6 | 1.04 | 2.08 | 9 | 0 | 0 | 0 | 8 | 6 | 0 | 8.2 | 4 | 0 | 30 | 1 | 1 | 2 |
| 3-5 | 2 | 0 | 13 | 0.43 | 1.71 | 18 | 0 | 0 | 0 | 17 | 14 | 0 | 21.0 | 6 | 1 | 68 | 1 | 1 | 4 |
| 6+ | 1 | 0 | 1 | 0.00 | 3.60 | 3 | 0 | 0 | 0 | 3 | 1 | 0 | 5.0 | 4 | 0 | 18 | 0 | 0 | 2 |

| 1990 | 2B | 3B | RBI | SH | SF | BB | IW | HB | K | WP | BK | SB | CS | DP | FLY | GRD | #PIT | #PKO | AVG | OBP | SLG |
|---|---|---|---|---|---|---|---|---|---|---|---|---|---|---|---|---|---|---|---|---|---|
| Total | 9 | 1 | 12 | 0 | 1 | 4 | 1 | 0 | 73 | 0 | 0 | 1 | 2 | 3 | 87 | 64 | 1004 | 6 | .160 | .172 | .226 |

| Vs. Teams | 2B | 3B | RBI | SH | SF | BB | IW | HB | K | WP | BK | SB | CS | DP | FLY | GRD | #PIT | #PKO | AVG | OBP | SLG |
|---|---|---|---|---|---|---|---|---|---|---|---|---|---|---|---|---|---|---|---|---|---|
| vs.Bal | 0 | 0 | 0 | 0 | 0 | 0 | 0 | 0 | 5 | 0 | 0 | 0 | 0 | 0 | 10 | 6 | 83 | 1 | .043 | .043 | .043 |
| vs.Bos | 0 | 0 | 0 | 0 | 0 | 0 | 0 | 0 | 3 | 0 | 0 | 0 | 0 | 0 | 4 | 3 | 38 | 0 | .000 | .000 | .000 |
| vs.Cal | 1 | 0 | 2 | 0 | 0 | 1 | 0 | 0 | 8 | 0 | 0 | 0 | 0 | 0 | 13 | 5 | 116 | 0 | .138 | .167 | .276 |
| vs.ChA | 1 | 0 | 0 | 0 | 0 | 0 | 0 | 0 | 4 | 0 | 0 | 0 | 0 | 0 | 7 | 3 | 55 | 0 | .133 | .133 | .200 |
| vs.Cle | 1 | 0 | 0 | 0 | 0 | 0 | 0 | 0 | 6 | 0 | 0 | 0 | 0 | 1 | 8 | 6 | 95 | 0 | .200 | .200 | .240 |
| vs.Det | 1 | 0 | 2 | 0 | 0 | 0 | 0 | 0 | 7 | 0 | 0 | 0 | 0 | 0 | 6 | 8 | 92 | 0 | .200 | .200 | .240 |
| vs.KC | 1 | 1 | 2 | 0 | 0 | 0 | 0 | 0 | 11 | 0 | 0 | 0 | 0 | 0 | 10 | 8 | 116 | 2 | .250 | .250 | .438 |
| vs.Mil | 0 | 0 | 0 | 0 | 0 | 0 | 0 | 0 | 2 | 0 | 0 | 0 | 0 | 0 | 1 | 2 | 37 | 0 | .000 | .000 | .000 |
| vs.Min | 0 | 0 | 2 | 0 | 1 | 1 | 0 | 0 | 5 | 0 | 0 | 0 | 1 | 0 | 9 | 4 | 70 | 1 | .167 | .200 | .167 |
| vs.NYA | 0 | 0 | 0 | 0 | 0 | 0 | 0 | 0 | 5 | 0 | 0 | 0 | 0 | 0 | 2 | 7 | 57 | 0 | .125 | .125 | .125 |
| vs.Sea | 1 | 0 | 0 | 0 | 0 | 0 | 0 | 0 | 3 | 0 | 0 | 0 | 0 | 0 | 6 | 4 | 63 | 0 | .071 | .071 | .143 |
| vs.Tex | 2 | 0 | 4 | 0 | 0 | 2 | 1 | 0 | 7 | 0 | 0 | 1 | 1 | 1 | 8 | 4 | 123 | 2 | .286 | .333 | .357 |
| vs.Tor | 1 | 0 | 0 | 0 | 0 | 0 | 0 | 0 | 7 | 0 | 0 | 0 | 0 | 1 | 3 | 4 | 59 | 0 | .125 | .125 | .188 |

| By Park | 2B | 3B | RBI | SH | SF | BB | IW | HB | K | WP | BK | SB | CS | DP | FLY | GRD | #PIT | #PKO | AVG | OBP | SLG |
|---|---|---|---|---|---|---|---|---|---|---|---|---|---|---|---|---|---|---|---|---|---|
| at Bal | 0 | 0 | 0 | 0 | 0 | 0 | 0 | 0 | 4 | 0 | 0 | 0 | 0 | 0 | 6 | 3 | 61 | 0 | .067 | .067 | .067 |
| at Bos | 0 | 0 | 0 | 0 | 0 | 0 | 0 | 0 | 1 | 0 | 0 | 0 | 0 | 0 | 3 | 3 | 24 | 0 | .000 | .000 | .000 |
| at Cal | 1 | 0 | 0 | 0 | 0 | 0 | 0 | 0 | 4 | 0 | 0 | 0 | 0 | 0 | 8 | 4 | 63 | 0 | .176 | .176 | .235 |
| at ChA | 0 | 0 | 0 | 0 | 0 | 0 | 0 | 0 | 2 | 0 | 0 | 0 | 0 | 0 | 4 | 2 | 30 | 0 | .111 | .111 | .111 |
| at Cle | 0 | 0 | 0 | 0 | 0 | 0 | 0 | 0 | 1 | 0 | 0 | 0 | 0 | 1 | 3 | 3 | 39 | 0 | .200 | .200 | .200 |
| at Det | 1 | 0 | 0 | 0 | 0 | 0 | 0 | 0 | 4 | 0 | 0 | 0 | 0 | 0 | 1 | 4 | 45 | 0 | .182 | .182 | .273 |
| at KC | 1 | 0 | 1 | 0 | 0 | 0 | 0 | 0 | 5 | 0 | 0 | 0 | 0 | 0 | 6 | 2 | 48 | 0 | .214 | .214 | .286 |
| at Min | 0 | 0 | 0 | 0 | 0 | 0 | 0 | 0 | 0 | 0 | 0 | 0 | 0 | 0 | 0 | 1 | 6 | 0 | .000 | .000 | .000 |
| at NYA | 0 | 0 | 0 | 0 | 0 | 0 | 0 | 0 | 5 | 0 | 0 | 0 | 0 | 0 | 2 | 5 | 54 | 0 | .143 | .143 | .143 |
| at Oak | 4 | 1 | 11 | 0 | 1 | 4 | 1 | 0 | 35 | 0 | 0 | 1 | 1 | 0 | 50 | 30 | 498 | 4 | .159 | .183 | .254 |
| at Sea | 1 | 0 | 0 | 0 | 0 | 0 | 0 | 0 | 3 | 0 | 0 | 0 | 0 | 0 | 1 | 2 | 38 | 0 | .143 | .143 | .286 |
| at Tex | 0 | 0 | 0 | 0 | 0 | 0 | 0 | 0 | 3 | 0 | 0 | 0 | 1 | 1 | 1 | 2 | 55 | 2 | .308 | .308 | .308 |
| at Tor | 1 | 0 | 0 | 0 | 0 | 0 | 0 | 0 | 6 | 0 | 0 | 0 | 0 | 1 | 2 | 3 | 43 | 0 | .154 | .154 | .231 |

| By Month | 2B | 3B | RBI | SH | SF | BB | IW | HB | K | WP | BK | SB | CS | DP | FLY | GRD | #PIT | #PKO | AVG | OBP | SLG |
|---|---|---|---|---|---|---|---|---|---|---|---|---|---|---|---|---|---|---|---|---|---|
| April | 2 | 0 | 2 | 0 | 1 | 0 | 0 | 0 | 9 | 0 | 0 | 0 | 0 | 0 | 19 | 4 | 135 | 0 | .147 | .143 | .206 |
| May | 2 | 0 | 0 | 0 | 0 | 0 | 0 | 0 | 15 | 0 | 0 | 0 | 0 | 1 | 9 | 11 | 155 | 0 | .171 | .171 | .220 |
| June | 3 | 0 | 5 | 0 | 0 | 2 | 1 | 0 | 8 | 0 | 0 | 1 | 1 | 0 | 17 | 12 | 166 | 2 | .222 | .255 | .289 |
| July | 0 | 0 | 2 | 0 | 0 | 1 | 0 | 0 | 12 | 0 | 0 | 0 | 0 | 1 | 9 | 9 | 154 | 0 | .059 | .086 | .147 |
| August | 1 | 1 | 1 | 0 | 0 | 0 | 0 | 0 | 13 | 0 | 0 | 0 | 0 | 0 | 18 | 13 | 191 | 3 | .157 | .157 | .275 |
| September | 1 | 0 | 2 | 0 | 0 | 1 | 0 | 0 | 16 | 0 | 0 | 0 | 1 | 1 | 12 | 15 | 196 | 1 | .184 | .200 | .204 |
| October | 0 | 0 | 0 | 0 | 0 | 0 | 0 | 0 | 0 | 0 | 0 | 0 | 0 | 0 | 3 | 0 | 7 | 0 | .000 | .000 | .000 |

| Conditions | 2B | 3B | RBI | SH | SF | BB | IW | HB | K | WP | BK | SB | CS | DP | FLY | GRD | #PIT | #PKO | AVG | OBP | SLG |
|---|---|---|---|---|---|---|---|---|---|---|---|---|---|---|---|---|---|---|---|---|---|
| Home | 4 | 1 | 11 | 0 | 1 | 4 | 1 | 0 | 35 | 0 | 0 | 1 | 1 | 0 | 50 | 30 | 498 | 4 | .159 | .183 | .254 |
| Away | 5 | 0 | 1 | 0 | 0 | 0 | 0 | 0 | 38 | 0 | 0 | 0 | 1 | 3 | 37 | 34 | 506 | 2 | .160 | .160 | .198 |
| Day | 6 | 1 | 7 | 0 | 0 | 4 | 1 | 0 | 40 | 0 | 0 | 1 | 1 | 1 | 43 | 27 | 503 | 3 | .154 | .181 | .268 |
| Night | 3 | 0 | 5 | 0 | 1 | 0 | 0 | 0 | 33 | 0 | 0 | 0 | 1 | 2 | 44 | 37 | 501 | 3 | .164 | .163 | .187 |
| Grass | 6 | 1 | 11 | 0 | 1 | 4 | 1 | 0 | 59 | 0 | 0 | 1 | 2 | 2 | 78 | 56 | 869 | 6 | .158 | .172 | .221 |
| Turf | 3 | 0 | 1 | 0 | 0 | 0 | 0 | 0 | 14 | 0 | 0 | 0 | 0 | 1 | 9 | 8 | 135 | 0 | .171 | .171 | .257 |

| Days Rest | 2B | 3B | RBI | SH | SF | BB | IW | HB | K | WP | BK | SB | CS | DP | FLY | GRD | #PIT | #PKO | AVG | OBP | SLG |
|---|---|---|---|---|---|---|---|---|---|---|---|---|---|---|---|---|---|---|---|---|---|
| 0 | 3 | 0 | 1 | 0 | 0 | 1 | 0 | 0 | 21 | 0 | 0 | 0 | 2 | 0 | 21 | 12 | 251 | 3 | .206 | .219 | .254 |
| 1 | 4 | 0 | 8 | 0 | 0 | 3 | 1 | 0 | 24 | 0 | 0 | 1 | 0 | 1 | 21 | 25 | 331 | 1 | .177 | .207 | .266 |
| 2 | 2 | 0 | 0 | 0 | 0 | 0 | 0 | 0 | 6 | 0 | 0 | 0 | 0 | 0 | 13 | 9 | 102 | 0 | .133 | .133 | .200 |
| 3-5 | 0 | 1 | 1 | 0 | 0 | 0 | 0 | 0 | 19 | 0 | 0 | 0 | 0 | 1 | 25 | 15 | 256 | 2 | .088 | .088 | .162 |
| 6+ | 0 | 0 | 2 | 0 | 1 | 0 | 0 | 0 | 3 | 0 | 0 | 0 | 0 | 1 | 7 | 3 | 64 | 0 | .235 | .222 | .235 |

| Batter Types | IP | H | HR | BFP | - | - | 2B | 3B | RBI | SH | SF | BB | IW | HB | K | WP | BK | SB | CS | DP | FLY | GRD | AVG | OBP | SLG |
|---|---|---|---|---|---|---|---|---|---|---|---|---|---|---|---|---|---|---|---|---|---|---|---|---|---|
| vs. Left | 33.2 | 20 | 1 | 122 | - | - | 4 | 1 | 10 | 0 | 1 | 2 | 1 | 0 | 22 | 0 | 0 | 1 | 2 | 1 | 41 | 40 | .168 | .180 | .244 |
| vs. Right | 39.2 | 21 | 1 | 140 | - | - | 5 | 0 | 2 | 0 | 0 | 2 | 0 | 0 | 51 | 0 | 0 | 0 | 0 | 2 | 46 | 24 | .152 | .164 | .210 |

| Inning | IP | H | HR | BFP | R | ER | 2B | 3B | RBI | SH | SF | BB | IW | HB | K | WP | BK | SB | CS | DP | FLY | GRD | AVG | OBP | SLG |
|---|---|---|---|---|---|---|---|---|---|---|---|---|---|---|---|---|---|---|---|---|---|---|---|---|---|
| Inning 1-6 | 0.0 | 0 | 0 | 0 | 0 | 0 | 0 | 0 | 0 | 0 | 0 | 0 | 0 | 0 | 0 | 0 | 0 | 0 | 0 | 0 | 0 | 0 | - | - | - |
| Inning 7+ | 73.1 | 41 | 2 | 262 | 9 | 5 | 9 | 1 | 12 | 0 | 1 | 4 | 1 | 0 | 73 | 0 | 0 | 1 | 2 | 3 | 87 | 64 | .160 | .172 | .226 |

| Game Situation | IP | H | HR | BFP | R | ER | 2B | 3B | RBI | SH | SF | BB | IW | HB | K | WP | BK | SB | CS | DP | FLY | GRD | AVG | OBP | SLG |
|---|---|---|---|---|---|---|---|---|---|---|---|---|---|---|---|---|---|---|---|---|---|---|---|---|---|
| Close & Late | 55.1 | 32 | 2 | 197 | 7 | 3 | 6 | 1 | 12 | 0 | 1 | 4 | 1 | 0 | 56 | 0 | 0 | 1 | 2 | 3 | 70 | 42 | .167 | .183 | .240 |
| Close | 63.1 | 34 | 2 | 225 | 9 | 5 | 7 | 1 | 11 | 0 | 1 | 4 | 1 | 0 | 65 | 0 | 0 | 1 | 2 | 3 | 77 | 50 | .155 | .169 | .223 |
| Not Close | 10.0 | 7 | 0 | 37 | 0 | 0 | 2 | 0 | 1 | 0 | 0 | 0 | 0 | 0 | 8 | 0 | 0 | 0 | 0 | 0 | 10 | 14 | .189 | .189 | .243 |

| Bases Empty | IP | H | HR | BFP | - | - | 2B | 3B | RBI | SH | SF | BB | IW | HB | K | WP | BK | SB | CS | DP | FLY | GRD | AVG | OBP | SLG |
|---|---|---|---|---|---|---|---|---|---|---|---|---|---|---|---|---|---|---|---|---|---|---|---|---|---|
| 0 on | 44.0 | 26 | 1 | 161 | - | - | 7 | 1 | 1 | 0 | 0 | 1 | 0 | 0 | 50 | 0 | 0 | 0 | 0 | 0 | 50 | 40 | .162 | .168 | .237 |
| 0 on/0 out | 17.0 | 8 | 0 | 60 | - | - | 3 | 0 | 0 | 0 | 0 | 0 | 0 | 0 | 18 | 0 | 0 | 0 | 0 | 0 | 18 | 17 | .133 | .133 | .183 |
| 0 on/1-2 out | 27.0 | 18 | 1 | 101 | - | - | 4 | 1 | 1 | 0 | 0 | 1 | 0 | 0 | 32 | 0 | 0 | 0 | 0 | 0 | 32 | 23 | .180 | .188 | .270 |

| On Base | IP | H | HR | BFP | - | - | 2B | 3B | RBI | SH | SF | BB | IW | HB | K | WP | BK | SB | CS | DP | FLY | GRD | AVG | OBP | SLG |
|---|---|---|---|---|---|---|---|---|---|---|---|---|---|---|---|---|---|---|---|---|---|---|---|---|---|
| Runners on | 29.1 | 15 | 1 | 101 | - | - | 2 | 0 | 11 | 0 | 1 | 3 | 1 | 0 | 23 | 0 | 0 | 1 | 2 | 3 | 37 | 24 | .155 | .178 | .206 |
| Scoring Posn | 13.2 | 11 | 0 | 52 | - | - | 1 | 0 | 8 | 0 | 1 | 2 | 1 | 0 | 9 | 0 | 0 | 0 | 1 | 1 | 19 | 16 | .224 | .250 | .245 |
| SB Opp | 17.0 | 4 | 1 | 53 | - | - | 1 | 0 | 3 | 0 | 0 | 1 | 0 | 0 | 16 | 0 | 0 | 1 | 1 | 2 | 19 | 8 | .077 | .094 | .154 |
| SB Atd | 1.0 | 0 | 0 | 3 | - | - | 0 | 0 | 0 | 0 | 0 | 1 | 0 | 0 | 1 | 0 | 0 | 0 | 1 | 0 | 1 | 0 | .000 | .333 | .000 |
| GDP Opp | 12.0 | 6 | 0 | 39 | - | - | 0 | 0 | 4 | 0 | 1 | 1 | 0 | 0 | 9 | 0 | 0 | 0 | 1 | 3 | 13 | 7 | .162 | .179 | .162 |

| At Count | IP | H | HR | BFP | - | - | 2B | 3B | RBI | SH | SF | BB | IW | HB | K | WP | BK | SB | CS | DP | FLY | GRD | AVG | OBP | SLG |
|---|---|---|---|---|---|---|---|---|---|---|---|---|---|---|---|---|---|---|---|---|---|---|---|---|---|
| 0-0 count | 8.1 | 9 | 1 | 35 | - | - | 1 | 0 | 3 | 0 | 0 | 1 | 1 | 0 | 0 | 0 | 0 | 1 | 0 | 0 | 19 | 7 | .265 | .286 | .382 |
| 0-1 Count | 6.2 | 9 | 1 | 29 | - | - | 3 | 0 | 3 | 0 | 0 | 0 | 0 | 0 | 0 | 0 | 0 | 0 | 0 | 0 | 9 | 11 | .310 | .310 | .517 |
| 0-2 Count | 14.0 | 1 | 0 | 42 | - | - | 1 | 0 | 0 | 0 | 0 | 0 | 0 | 0 | 24 | 0 | 0 | 0 | 1 | 0 | 9 | 5 | .024 | .024 | .048 |
| 1-0 Count | 3.1 | 3 | 0 | 13 | - | - | 0 | 0 | 2 | 0 | 1 | 0 | 0 | 0 | 0 | 0 | 0 | 0 | 0 | 0 | 8 | 3 | .250 | .231 | .250 |
| 1-1 Count | 5.0 | 2 | 0 | 16 | - | - | 0 | 0 | 0 | 0 | 0 | 0 | 0 | 0 | 0 | 0 | 0 | 0 | 1 | 1 | 7 | 7 | .125 | .125 | .125 |
| 1-2 Count | 18.0 | 6 | 0 | 59 | - | - | 2 | 0 | 0 | 0 | 0 | 0 | 0 | 0 | 29 | 0 | 0 | 0 | 0 | 2 | 16 | 13 | .102 | .102 | .136 |
| 2-0 Count | 1.0 | 1 | 0 | 4 | - | - | 0 | 0 | 0 | 0 | 0 | 0 | 0 | 0 | 0 | 0 | 0 | 0 | 0 | 0 | 2 | 2 | .250 | .250 | .250 |
| 2-1 Count | 1.2 | 4 | 0 | 9 | - | - | 1 | 0 | 1 | 0 | 0 | 0 | 0 | 0 | 0 | 0 | 0 | 0 | 0 | 0 | 5 | 2 | .444 | .444 | .556 |
| 2-2 Count | 10.1 | 3 | 0 | 34 | - | - | 0 | 0 | 1 | 0 | 0 | 0 | 0 | 0 | 15 | 0 | 0 | 0 | 0 | 0 | 5 | 10 | .088 | .088 | .088 |
| 3-0 Count | 0.0 | 0 | 0 | 1 | - | - | 0 | 0 | 0 | 0 | 0 | 1 | 0 | 0 | 0 | 0 | 0 | 0 | 0 | 0 | 0 | 0 | - | 1.000 | - |
| 3-1 Count | 0.2 | 1 | 0 | 4 | - | - | 0 | 1 | 0 | 0 | 0 | 1 | 0 | 0 | 0 | 0 | 0 | 0 | 0 | 0 | 3 | 0 | .333 | .500 | 1.000 |
| 3-2 Count | 4.1 | 2 | 0 | 16 | - | - | 1 | 0 | 2 | 0 | 0 | 1 | 0 | 0 | 5 | 0 | 0 | 0 | 0 | 0 | 4 | 4 | .133 | .188 | .200 |

| After Count | IP | H | HR | BFP | - | - | 2B | 3B | RBI | SH | SF | BB | IW | HB | K | WP | BK | SB | CS | DP | FLY | GRD | AVG | OBP | SLG |
|---|---|---|---|---|---|---|---|---|---|---|---|---|---|---|---|---|---|---|---|---|---|---|---|---|---|
| After (0-1) | 43.1 | 21 | 1 | 151 | - | - | 7 | 0 | 7 | 0 | 0 | 0 | 0 | 0 | 53 | 0 | 0 | 0 | 1 | 1 | 41 | 37 | .139 | .139 | .205 |
| After (0-2) | 25.1 | 6 | 0 | 82 | - | - | 4 | 0 | 2 | 0 | 0 | 0 | 0 | 0 | 41 | 0 | 0 | 0 | 1 | 0 | 20 | 17 | .073 | .073 | .122 |
| After (1-0) | 21.2 | 11 | 0 | 76 | - | - | 1 | 1 | 2 | 0 | 1 | 3 | 0 | 0 | 20 | 0 | 0 | 0 | 1 | 2 | 27 | 20 | .153 | .184 | .194 |
| After (1-1) | 26.1 | 12 | 0 | 88 | - | - | 0 | 1 | 2 | 0 | 0 | 0 | 0 | 0 | 29 | 0 | 0 | 0 | 1 | 3 | 27 | 22 | .136 | .136 | .159 |
| After (1-2) | 27.2 | 9 | 0 | 91 | - | - | 3 | 0 | 3 | 0 | 0 | 0 | 0 | 0 | 42 | 0 | 0 | 0 | 0 | 2 | 24 | 20 | .099 | .099 | .132 |
| After (2-0) | 3.1 | 2 | 0 | 15 | - | - | 1 | 0 | 0 | 0 | 0 | 3 | 0 | 0 | 3 | 0 | 0 | 0 | 0 | 0 | 4 | 4 | .167 | .333 | .250 |
| After (2-1) | 7.0 | 7 | 0 | 30 | - | - | 1 | 1 | 1 | 0 | 0 | 2 | 0 | 0 | 7 | 0 | 0 | 0 | 0 | 0 | 8 | 9 | .250 | .300 | .357 |
| After (2-2) | 14.2 | 5 | 0 | 50 | - | - | 1 | 0 | 3 | 0 | 0 | 1 | 0 | 0 | 20 | 0 | 0 | 0 | 0 | 0 | 9 | 14 | .102 | .120 | .122 |
| After (3-0) | 0.1 | 0 | 0 | 2 | - | - | 0 | 0 | 0 | 0 | 0 | 1 | 0 | 0 | 0 | 0 | 0 | 0 | 0 | 0 | 1 | 0 | .000 | .500 | .000 |
| After (3-1) | 0.2 | 1 | 0 | 4 | - | - | 0 | 1 | 0 | 0 | 0 | 1 | 0 | 0 | 0 | 0 | 0 | 0 | 0 | 0 | 3 | 0 | .333 | .500 | 1.000 |
| After (3-2) | 4.1 | 2 | 0 | 16 | - | - | 1 | 0 | 2 | 0 | 0 | 1 | 0 | 0 | 5 | 0 | 0 | 0 | 0 | 0 | 4 | 4 | .133 | .188 | .200 |

| Pitch Level | IP | H | HR | BFP | R | ER | 2B | 3B | RBI | SH | SF | BB | IW | HB | K | WP | BK | SB | CS | DP | FLY | GRD | AVG | OBP | SLG |
|---|---|---|---|---|---|---|---|---|---|---|---|---|---|---|---|---|---|---|---|---|---|---|---|---|---|
| Pitch 1-15 | 56.2 | 32 | 1 | 201 | 0 | 0 | 6 | 1 | 5 | 0 | 1 | 1 | 0 | 0 | 52 | 0 | 0 | 0 | 1 | 2 | 72 | 49 | .161 | .164 | .216 |
| Pitch 16-30 | 15.0 | 8 | 1 | 53 | 3 | 3 | 2 | 0 | 5 | 0 | 0 | 1 | 0 | 0 | 19 | 0 | 0 | 1 | 1 | 1 | 12 | 14 | .154 | .170 | .250 |
| Pitch 31-45 | 1.2 | 1 | 0 | 8 | 6 | 2 | 1 | 0 | 2 | 0 | 0 | 2 | 1 | 0 | 2 | 0 | 0 | 0 | 0 | 0 | 3 | 1 | .167 | .375 | .333 |

Results At Each Pitch

| Result | 0-0 | 0-1 | 0-2 | 1-0 | 1-1 | 1-2 | 2-0 | 2-1 | 2-2 | 3-0 | 3-1 | 3-2 |
|---|---|---|---|---|---|---|---|---|---|---|---|---|
| | Count | | | | | | | | | | | |
| Ball | 76 | 40 | 41 | 15 | 21 | 32 | 2 | 3 | 16 | 1 | 1 | 1 |
| Taken Strike | 80 | 22 | 7 | 20 | 12 | 8 | 4 | 5 | 3 | 1 | 0 | 2 |
| Swung | 39 | 25 | 17 | 8 | 8 | 21 | 2 | 7 | 12 | 0 | 0 | 3 |
| Fouled | 33 | 36 | 30 | 20 | 32 | 39 | 3 | 6 | 28 | 0 | 0 | 13 |
| In Play | 34 | 29 | 18 | 13 | 15 | 30 | 4 | 9 | 19 | 0 | 3 | 10 |

Eckersley's Pitching Record with Each A's Catcher

| Catcher | ERA | IP | H | BFP | R | ER | HR | SH | SF | BB | IW | HB | K | WP | BK | 2B | 3B | RBI | SB | CS | DP | GRD | FLY |
|---|---|---|---|---|---|---|---|---|---|---|---|---|---|---|---|---|---|---|---|---|---|---|---|
| Troy AFENIR | 0.00 | 1.2 | 0 | 5 | 0 | 0 | 0 | 0 | 0 | 0 | 0 | 0 | 1 | 0 | 0 | 0 | 0 | 0 | 0 | 0 | 0 | 2 | 2 |
| Ron HASSEY | 0.00 | 29.2 | 16 | 108 | 4 | 0 | 0 | 0 | 1 | 2 | 1 | 0 | 32 | 0 | 0 | 4 | 0 | 6 | 1 | 0 | 0 | 23 | 34 |
| Jamie QUIRK | 1.54 | 11.2 | 7 | 42 | 2 | 2 | 1 | 0 | 0 | 1 | 0 | 0 | 11 | 0 | 0 | 0 | 0 | 4 | 0 | 0 | 1 | 14 | 9 |
| Terry STEINBACH | 0.89 | 30.1 | 18 | 107 | 3 | 3 | 1 | 0 | 0 | 1 | 0 | 0 | 29 | 0 | 0 | 5 | 1 | 2 | 0 | 2 | 2 | 25 | 42 |

Opponent Baserunning

| | Which Pitch | | | Which Count | | | | |
|---|---|---|---|---|---|---|---|---|
| Event | Pitch 1 | Pitch 2 | Other | Even | Ahead | Behind | 3-2 | 2 Strikes |
| Stolen Base | 0 | 1 | 0 | 1 | 0 | 0 | 0 | 0 |
| Catcher Caught Stealing | 0 | 0 | 2 | 1 | 1 | 0 | 0 | 1 |

Outs and Men on Base at time of Pitching Change (Outs, men on)

| | (0,1) | (0,2) | (0,3) | (1,1) | (1,2) | (1,3) | (2,1) | (2,2) | (2,3) | Total | Scored |
|---|---|---|---|---|---|---|---|---|---|---|---|
| Runners Inherited | 1 | 1 | 0 | 4 | 4 | 0 | 5 | 3 | 1 | 29 | 4 |
| Runners Bequeathed | 0 | 0 | 0 | 0 | 0 | 0 | 0 | 0 | 0 | 0 | 0 |

Active Batters vs. Dennis Eckersley
(10 or more At Bats since 1985)

| Batter | AVG | AB | H | 2B | 3B | HR | RBI | W | K | SF | SB | CS |
|---|---|---|---|---|---|---|---|---|---|---|---|---|
| REYNOLDS, Harol | .400 | 10 | 4 | 2 | 0 | 0 | 0 | 0 | 1 | 0 | 0 | 0 |
| WINFIELD, Dave | .385 | 13 | 5 | 1 | 0 | 0 | 1 | 0 | 3 | 0 | 0 | 0 |
| TRAMMELL, Alan | .364 | 11 | 4 | 2 | 0 | 0 | 1 | 1 | 5 | 0 | 0 | 0 |
| TARTABULL, Dann | .333 | 12 | 4 | 2 | 0 | 0 | 3 | 0 | 5 | 0 | 0 | 0 |
| SEITZER, Kevin | .333 | 12 | 4 | 0 | 0 | 0 | 1 | 0 | 2 | 0 | 0 | 0 |
| BOGGS, Wade | .308 | 13 | 4 | 2 | 0 | 0 | 1 | 0 | 1 | 1 | 0 | 0 |
| LARKIN, Gene | .300 | 10 | 3 | 2 | 0 | 0 | 1 | 0 | 0 | 0 | 0 | 0 |
| EVANS, Dwight | .250 | 12 | 3 | 0 | 0 | 1 | 5 | 3 | 3 | 0 | 0 | 0 |
| INCAVIGLIA, Pet | .200 | 10 | 2 | 1 | 0 | 0 | 0 | 0 | 3 | 0 | 0 | 0 |
| BARRETT, Marty | .200 | 15 | 3 | 0 | 0 | 0 | 0 | 0 | 1 | 0 | 0 | 0 |
| GREENWELL, Mike | .200 | 10 | 2 | 0 | 0 | 0 | 1 | 0 | 0 | 0 | 0 | 0 |
| JACOBY, Brook | .200 | 10 | 2 | 0 | 0 | 1 | 1 | 1 | 3 | 0 | 0 | 0 |
| BERGMAN, Dave | .182 | 11 | 2 | 0 | 0 | 0 | 2 | 0 | 4 | 0 | 0 | 0 |
| BELL, George | .167 | 12 | 2 | 1 | 0 | 1 | 2 | 0 | 3 | 0 | 0 | 0 |
| SNYDER, Cory | .167 | 12 | 2 | 1 | 0 | 0 | 0 | 0 | 6 | 0 | 0 | 0 |
| BALBONI, Steve | .154 | 13 | 2 | 0 | 0 | 1 | 3 | 0 | 6 | 0 | 0 | 0 |
| DOWNING, Brian | .100 | 10 | 1 | 0 | 0 | 1 | 1 | 0 | 3 | 0 | 0 | 0 |
| WHITE, Frank | .100 | 10 | 1 | 0 | 0 | 0 | 0 | 1 | 4 | 0 | 1 | 0 |
| BARFIELD, Jesse | .100 | 10 | 1 | 0 | 0 | 0 | 0 | 0 | 2 | 0 | 0 | 0 |
| GAETTI, Gary | .100 | 10 | 1 | 0 | 0 | 0 | 0 | 1 | 2 | 0 | 0 | 0 |
| BURKS, Ellis | .077 | 13 | 1 | 1 | 0 | 0 | 0 | 0 | 4 | 0 | 0 | 0 |
| LEONARD, Jeff | .000 | 10 | 0 | 0 | 0 | 0 | 0 | 0 | 5 | 0 | 0 | 0 |

Compared to Other American Leaguers

| Category | Rank | Stat | Minimum |
|---|---|---|---|
| Save Percentage | 1 | 96.0 | 20 Opp |
| Saves | 2 | 48 | |
| Save Opportunities | 3 | 50 | |
| Games Finished | 3 | 61 | |
| Games Pitched | 13 | 63 | |

Compared to Other Athletics Players

| Category | Rank | Stat | Minimum |
|---|---|---|---|
| Saves | 1 | 48 | |
| Games Pitched | 1 | 63 | |
| Save Opportunities | 1 | 50 | |

Fielding

| Pos | G | Inn | PO | A | E | DP | TP |
|---|---|---|---|---|---|---|---|
| P | 63 | 73.1 | 3 | 1 | 0 | 0 | 0 |

# Carlton Fisk – Chicago White Sox

## Batting

| 1990 | AVG | G | AB | R | H | 2B | 3B | HR | RBI | SB | CS | SH | SF | BB | IW | HP | K | GRD | FLY | DP | #PIT | OBP | SLG |
|---|---|---|---|---|---|---|---|---|---|---|---|---|---|---|---|---|---|---|---|---|---|---|---|
| Total | .285 | 137 | 452 | 65 | 129 | 21 | 0 | 18 | 65 | 7 | 2 | 0 | 1 | 61 | 8 | 7 | 73 | 144 | 166 | 12 | 1897 | .378 | .451 |

| Vs. Teams | AVG | G | AB | R | H | 2B | 3B | HR | RBI | SB | CS | SH | SF | BB | IW | HP | K | GRD | FLY | DP | #PIT | OBP | SLG |
|---|---|---|---|---|---|---|---|---|---|---|---|---|---|---|---|---|---|---|---|---|---|---|---|
| vs.Bal | .233 | 10 | 30 | 3 | 7 | 0 | 0 | 1 | 6 | 1 | 0 | 0 | 0 | 8 | 1 | 0 | 3 | 7 | 18 | 1 | 132 | .395 | .333 |
| vs.Bos | .300 | 11 | 40 | 3 | 12 | 4 | 0 | 1 | 5 | 0 | 0 | 0 | 0 | 5 | 0 | 1 | 10 | 10 | 12 | 1 | 174 | .391 | .475 |
| vs.Cal | .294 | 10 | 34 | 2 | 10 | 2 | 0 | 2 | 5 | 0 | 0 | 0 | 0 | 4 | 1 | 0 | 7 | 10 | 9 | 1 | 144 | .368 | .529 |
| vs.Cle | .366 | 11 | 41 | 8 | 15 | 2 | 0 | 3 | 8 | 1 | 0 | 0 | 0 | 2 | 0 | 1 | 5 | 8 | 20 | 1 | 151 | .409 | .634 |
| vs.Det | .419 | 11 | 31 | 6 | 13 | 2 | 0 | 2 | 6 | 3 | 0 | 0 | 1 | 5 | 1 | 1 | 8 | 6 | 12 | 0 | 147 | .500 | .677 |
| vs.KC | .293 | 12 | 41 | 6 | 12 | 3 | 0 | 2 | 4 | 1 | 0 | 0 | 0 | 4 | 0 | 1 | 3 | 17 | 18 | 2 | 158 | .370 | .512 |
| vs.Mil | .333 | 10 | 36 | 8 | 12 | 3 | 0 | 2 | 3 | 0 | 1 | 0 | 0 | 5 | 0 | 0 | 6 | 11 | 9 | 0 | 152 | .415 | .583 |
| vs.Min | .171 | 9 | 35 | 4 | 6 | 0 | 0 | 1 | 3 | 0 | 0 | 0 | 0 | 1 | 0 | 0 | 10 | 11 | 11 | 1 | 121 | .194 | .257 |
| vs.NYA | .147 | 11 | 34 | 8 | 5 | 1 | 0 | 1 | 6 | 1 | 0 | 0 | 0 | 7 | 2 | 1 | 2 | 16 | 14 | 1 | 149 | .310 | .265 |
| vs.Oak | .364 | 11 | 33 | 8 | 12 | 1 | 0 | 0 | 5 | 0 | 0 | 0 | 0 | 5 | 0 | 0 | 1 | 17 | 11 | 0 | 143 | .447 | .394 |
| vs.Sea | .229 | 11 | 35 | 6 | 8 | 1 | 0 | 2 | 7 | 0 | 1 | 0 | 0 | 6 | 0 | 0 | 7 | 16 | 6 | 2 | 168 | .341 | .429 |
| vs.Tex | .200 | 10 | 30 | 2 | 6 | 1 | 0 | 1 | 3 | 0 | 0 | 0 | 0 | 4 | 2 | 1 | 6 | 8 | 11 | 1 | 138 | .314 | .333 |
| vs.Tor | .344 | 10 | 32 | 1 | 11 | 1 | 0 | 0 | 4 | 0 | 0 | 0 | 0 | 5 | 1 | 1 | 5 | 7 | 15 | 1 | 120 | .447 | .375 |

| By Park | AVG | G | AB | R | H | 2B | 3B | HR | RBI | SB | CS | SH | SF | BB | IW | HP | K | GRD | FLY | DP | #PIT | OBP | SLG |
|---|---|---|---|---|---|---|---|---|---|---|---|---|---|---|---|---|---|---|---|---|---|---|---|
| at Bal | .333 | 5 | 15 | 1 | 5 | 0 | 0 | 0 | 1 | 1 | 0 | 0 | 0 | 3 | 0 | 0 | 2 | 4 | 8 | 1 | 58 | .444 | .333 |
| at Bos | .273 | 6 | 22 | 2 | 6 | 3 | 0 | 1 | 1 | 0 | 0 | 0 | 0 | 3 | 0 | 0 | 5 | 9 | 4 | 0 | 107 | .360 | .545 |
| at Cal | .400 | 4 | 15 | 2 | 6 | 0 | 0 | 2 | 2 | 0 | 0 | 0 | 0 | 2 | 0 | 0 | 4 | 6 | 4 | 1 | 67 | .471 | .800 |
| at ChA | .288 | 69 | 219 | 28 | 63 | 13 | 0 | 5 | 37 | 2 | 2 | 0 | 1 | 33 | 7 | 3 | 30 | 70 | 82 | 3 | 920 | .387 | .416 |
| at Cle | .364 | 6 | 22 | 5 | 8 | 1 | 0 | 2 | 5 | 0 | 0 | 0 | 0 | 1 | 0 | 1 | 2 | 5 | 11 | 1 | 73 | .417 | .682 |
| at Det | .308 | 6 | 13 | 4 | 4 | 1 | 0 | 1 | 2 | 2 | 0 | 0 | 0 | 4 | 1 | 1 | 5 | 1 | 4 | 0 | 73 | .500 | .615 |
| at KC | .350 | 6 | 20 | 3 | 7 | 2 | 0 | 1 | 1 | 1 | 0 | 0 | 0 | 3 | 0 | 1 | 2 | 9 | 8 | 0 | 82 | .458 | .600 |
| at Mil | .250 | 4 | 16 | 4 | 4 | 0 | 0 | 1 | 1 | 0 | 0 | 0 | 0 | 1 | 0 | 0 | 5 | 4 | 4 | 0 | 59 | .294 | .438 |
| at Min | .125 | 4 | 16 | 2 | 2 | 0 | 0 | 1 | 1 | 0 | 0 | 0 | 0 | 0 | 0 | 0 | 4 | 3 | 8 | 1 | 56 | .125 | .313 |
| at NYA | .200 | 6 | 20 | 5 | 4 | 0 | 0 | 1 | 5 | 1 | 0 | 0 | 0 | 2 | 0 | 0 | 1 | 8 | 10 | 1 | 86 | .273 | .350 |
| at Oak | .353 | 4 | 17 | 4 | 6 | 0 | 0 | 0 | 0 | 0 | 0 | 0 | 0 | 1 | 0 | 0 | 0 | 7 | 7 | 0 | 59 | .389 | .353 |
| at Sea | .143 | 6 | 21 | 3 | 3 | 0 | 0 | 2 | 5 | 0 | 0 | 0 | 0 | 5 | 0 | 0 | 5 | 10 | 4 | 2 | 104 | .308 | .429 |
| at Tex | .316 | 6 | 19 | 2 | 6 | 1 | 0 | 1 | 3 | 0 | 0 | 0 | 0 | 1 | 0 | 0 | 6 | 2 | 6 | 1 | 90 | .350 | .526 |
| at Tor | .294 | 5 | 17 | 0 | 5 | 0 | 0 | 0 | 1 | 0 | 0 | 0 | 0 | 2 | 0 | 1 | 2 | 6 | 6 | 1 | 63 | .400 | .294 |

| By Month | AVG | G | AB | R | H | 2B | 3B | HR | RBI | SB | CS | SH | SF | BB | IW | HP | K | GRD | FLY | DP | #PIT | OBP | SLG |
|---|---|---|---|---|---|---|---|---|---|---|---|---|---|---|---|---|---|---|---|---|---|---|---|
| April | .309 | 15 | 55 | 5 | 17 | 4 | 0 | 0 | 5 | 1 | 0 | 0 | 0 | 4 | 2 | 0 | 10 | 9 | 25 | 1 | 199 | .356 | .382 |
| May | .250 | 25 | 84 | 8 | 21 | 1 | 0 | 3 | 13 | 3 | 0 | 0 | 0 | 13 | 2 | 2 | 15 | 27 | 34 | 1 | 345 | .364 | .369 |
| June | .278 | 18 | 54 | 9 | 15 | 1 | 0 | 3 | 6 | 0 | 1 | 0 | 0 | 11 | 1 | 0 | 5 | 29 | 13 | 1 | 248 | .400 | .463 |
| July | .300 | 23 | 70 | 13 | 21 | 5 | 0 | 3 | 10 | 3 | 1 | 0 | 1 | 11 | 1 | 1 | 6 | 24 | 28 | 1 | 318 | .398 | .500 |
| August | .247 | 27 | 85 | 13 | 21 | 5 | 0 | 4 | 13 | 0 | 0 | 0 | 0 | 10 | 2 | 2 | 19 | 22 | 32 | 0 | 364 | .340 | .447 |
| September | .333 | 26 | 93 | 17 | 31 | 4 | 0 | 5 | 18 | 0 | 0 | 0 | 0 | 10 | 0 | 2 | 14 | 29 | 33 | 8 | 364 | .410 | .538 |
| October | .273 | 3 | 11 | 0 | 3 | 1 | 0 | 0 | 0 | 0 | 0 | 0 | 0 | 2 | 0 | 0 | 4 | 4 | 1 | 0 | 59 | .385 | .364 |

| By Fielding Pos | AVG | G | AB | R | H | 2B | 3B | HR | RBI | SB | CS | SH | SF | BB | IW | HP | K | GRD | FLY | DP | #PIT | OBP | SLG |
|---|---|---|---|---|---|---|---|---|---|---|---|---|---|---|---|---|---|---|---|---|---|---|---|
| As ph | .222 | 12 | 9 | 0 | 2 | 2 | 0 | 0 | 4 | 0 | 0 | 0 | 0 | 3 | 0 | 0 | 2 | 4 | 1 | 0 | 56 | .417 | .444 |
| As c | .300 | 114 | 397 | 0 | 119 | 18 | 0 | 17 | 56 | 0 | 0 | 0 | 1 | 53 | 7 | 6 | 59 | 125 | 149 | 9 | 1643 | .389 | .474 |
| As dh | .174 | 12 | 46 | 0 | 8 | 1 | 0 | 1 | 5 | 0 | 0 | 0 | 0 | 5 | 1 | 1 | 12 | 15 | 16 | 3 | 198 | .269 | .261 |

| By Lineup Posit | AVG | G | AB | R | H | 2B | 3B | HR | RBI | SB | CS | SH | SF | BB | IW | HP | K | GRD | FLY | DP | #PIT | OBP | SLG |
|---|---|---|---|---|---|---|---|---|---|---|---|---|---|---|---|---|---|---|---|---|---|---|---|
| Batting #3 | .257 | 20 | 74 | 11 | 19 | 3 | 0 | 1 | 10 | 0 | 0 | 0 | 0 | 11 | 2 | 2 | 16 | 24 | 22 | 3 | 317 | .368 | .338 |
| Batting #4 | .216 | 14 | 37 | 4 | 8 | 1 | 0 | 2 | 3 | 0 | 0 | 0 | 0 | 4 | 0 | 1 | 10 | 9 | 13 | 0 | 159 | .310 | .405 |
| Batting #5 | .297 | 92 | 323 | 46 | 96 | 14 | 0 | 15 | 47 | 7 | 2 | 0 | 1 | 43 | 6 | 4 | 45 | 103 | 126 | 9 | 1345 | .385 | .480 |
| Batting #6 | .286 | 6 | 14 | 3 | 4 | 1 | 0 | 0 | 1 | 0 | 0 | 0 | 0 | 2 | 0 | 0 | 1 | 7 | 4 | 0 | 60 | .375 | .357 |
| Batting #7 | .000 | 1 | 1 | 0 | 0 | 0 | 0 | 0 | 0 | 0 | 0 | 0 | 0 | 0 | 0 | 0 | 0 | 1 | 0 | 0 | 3 | .000 | .000 |
| Batting #8 | .667 | 4 | 3 | 1 | 2 | 2 | 0 | 0 | 4 | 0 | 0 | 0 | 0 | 1 | 0 | 0 | 1 | 0 | 1 | 0 | 13 | .750 | 1.333 |

| Conditions | AVG | G | AB | R | H | 2B | 3B | HR | RBI | SB | CS | SH | SF | BB | IW | HP | K | GRD | FLY | DP | #PIT | OBP | SLG |
|---|---|---|---|---|---|---|---|---|---|---|---|---|---|---|---|---|---|---|---|---|---|---|---|
| Home | .288 | 69 | 219 | 28 | 63 | 13 | 0 | 5 | 37 | 2 | 2 | 0 | 1 | 33 | 7 | 3 | 30 | 70 | 82 | 3 | 920 | .387 | .416 |
| Away | .283 | 68 | 233 | 37 | 66 | 8 | 0 | 13 | 28 | 5 | 0 | 0 | 0 | 28 | 1 | 4 | 43 | 74 | 84 | 9 | 977 | .370 | .485 |
| Day | .266 | 27 | 79 | 8 | 21 | 3 | 0 | 2 | 3 | 1 | 1 | 0 | 0 | 8 | 1 | 0 | 11 | 28 | 26 | 4 | 304 | .333 | .380 |
| Night | .290 | 110 | 373 | 57 | 108 | 18 | 0 | 16 | 62 | 6 | 1 | 0 | 1 | 53 | 7 | 7 | 62 | 116 | 140 | 8 | 1593 | .387 | .466 |
| Grass | .296 | 116 | 378 | 57 | 112 | 19 | 0 | 14 | 57 | 6 | 2 | 0 | 1 | 51 | 8 | 5 | 60 | 116 | 140 | 8 | 1592 | .386 | .458 |
| Turf | .230 | 21 | 74 | 8 | 17 | 2 | 0 | 4 | 8 | 1 | 0 | 0 | 0 | 10 | 0 | 2 | 13 | 28 | 26 | 4 | 305 | .337 | .419 |

| Pitcher Types | AVG | G | AB | R | H | 2B | 3B | HR | RBI | SB | CS | SH | SF | BB | IW | HP | K | GRD | FLY | DP | #PIT | OBP | SLG |
|---|---|---|---|---|---|---|---|---|---|---|---|---|---|---|---|---|---|---|---|---|---|---|---|
| vs. Left | .315 | 76 | 165 | 25 | 52 | 10 | 0 | 9 | 30 | 3 | 1 | 0 | 1 | 21 | 2 | 2 | 23 | 56 | 61 | 6 | 674 | .397 | .539 |
| vs. Right | .268 | 120 | 287 | 40 | 77 | 11 | 0 | 9 | 35 | 4 | 1 | 0 | 0 | 40 | 6 | 5 | 50 | 88 | 105 | 6 | 1223 | .367 | .401 |
| Groundball | .301 | 39 | 73 | 12 | 22 | 3 | 0 | 2 | 6 | 0 | 0 | 0 | 0 | 8 | 1 | 2 | 6 | 23 | 34 | 2 | 280 | .386 | .425 |
| Flyball | .302 | 79 | 126 | 15 | 38 | 5 | 0 | 7 | 19 | 1 | 1 | 0 | 0 | 19 | 3 | 2 | 28 | 37 | 41 | 4 | 563 | .401 | .508 |
| Ave Grd/Fly | .273 | 100 | 253 | 38 | 69 | 13 | 0 | 9 | 40 | 6 | 1 | 0 | 1 | 34 | 4 | 3 | 39 | 84 | 91 | 6 | 1054 | .364 | .431 |
| Finesse | .231 | 56 | 104 | 12 | 24 | 4 | 0 | 2 | 14 | 0 | 1 | 0 | 0 | 11 | 3 | 3 | 14 | 30 | 46 | 5 | 420 | .322 | .327 |
| Power | .359 | 48 | 78 | 15 | 28 | 4 | 0 | 6 | 14 | 1 | 0 | 0 | 0 | 13 | 1 | 0 | 16 | 26 | 22 | 0 | 324 | .451 | .641 |
| Ave Fin/Pow | .285 | 105 | 270 | 38 | 77 | 13 | 0 | 10 | 37 | 6 | 1 | 0 | 1 | 37 | 4 | 4 | 43 | 88 | 98 | 7 | 1153 | .378 | .444 |

| Inning | AVG | G | AB | R | H | 2B | 3B | HR | RBI | SB | CS | SH | SF | BB | IW | HP | K | GRD | FLY | DP | #PIT | OBP | SLG |
|---|---|---|---|---|---|---|---|---|---|---|---|---|---|---|---|---|---|---|---|---|---|---|---|
| Inning 1-6 | .291 | 126 | 313 | 52 | 91 | 12 | 0 | 12 | 47 | 6 | 1 | 0 | 1 | 39 | 1 | 7 | 39 | 107 | 118 | 9 | 1312 | .381 | .444 |
| Inning 7+ | .273 | 127 | 139 | 13 | 38 | 9 | 0 | 6 | 18 | 1 | 1 | 0 | 0 | 22 | 7 | 0 | 34 | 37 | 48 | 3 | 585 | .373 | .468 |

| Game Situation | AVG | G | AB | R | H | 2B | 3B | HR | RBI | SB | CS | SH | SF | BB | IW | HP | K | GRD | FLY | DP | #PIT | OBP | SLG |
|---|---|---|---|---|---|---|---|---|---|---|---|---|---|---|---|---|---|---|---|---|---|---|---|
| Close & Late | .229 | 65 | 70 | 7 | 16 | 5 | 0 | 3 | 12 | 1 | 1 | 0 | 0 | 10 | 5 | 0 | 19 | 21 | 19 | 2 | 277 | .325 | .429 |
| Close | .242 | 118 | 186 | 18 | 45 | 8 | 0 | 6 | 20 | 3 | 1 | 0 | 0 | 31 | 8 | 0 | 43 | 50 | 62 | 6 | 794 | .350 | .382 |
| Not Close | .316 | 126 | 266 | 47 | 84 | 13 | 0 | 12 | 45 | 4 | 1 | 0 | 1 | 30 | 0 | 7 | 30 | 94 | 104 | 6 | 1103 | .398 | .500 |

| Bases Empty | AVG | G | AB | R | H | 2B | 3B | HR | RBI | SB | CS | SH | SF | BB | IW | HP | K | GRD | FLY | DP | #PIT | OBP | SLG |
|---|---|---|---|---|---|---|---|---|---|---|---|---|---|---|---|---|---|---|---|---|---|---|---|
| 0 on | .313 | 124 | 262 | 14 | 82 | 12 | 0 | 14 | 14 | 0 | 0 | 0 | 0 | 30 | 0 | 4 | 42 | 102 | 76 | 0 | 1084 | .392 | .519 |
| 0 on, 0 out | .349 | 94 | 106 | 7 | 37 | 7 | 0 | 7 | 7 | 0 | 0 | 0 | 0 | 11 | 0 | 1 | 14 | 41 | 33 | 0 | 418 | .415 | .613 |
| 0 on, 1-2 out | .288 | 104 | 156 | 7 | 45 | 5 | 0 | 7 | 7 | 0 | 0 | 0 | 0 | 19 | 0 | 3 | 28 | 61 | 43 | 0 | 666 | .376 | .455 |

| On Base | AVG | G | AB | R | H | 2B | 3B | HR | RBI | SB | CS | SH | SF | BB | IW | HP | K | GRD | FLY | DP | #PIT | OBP | SLG |
|---|---|---|---|---|---|---|---|---|---|---|---|---|---|---|---|---|---|---|---|---|---|---|---|
| Runners on | .247 | 123 | 190 | 51 | 47 | 9 | 0 | 4 | 51 | 7 | 2 | 0 | 1 | 31 | 8 | 3 | 31 | 42 | 90 | 12 | 813 | .360 | .358 |
| Scoring Posn | .221 | 110 | 131 | 47 | 29 | 6 | 0 | 3 | 47 | 0 | 0 | 0 | 1 | 26 | 8 | 3 | 21 | 26 | 67 | 4 | 607 | .360 | .336 |
| OnBase: 2 | .146 | 56 | 48 | 8 | 7 | 2 | 0 | 0 | 6 | 0 | 0 | 0 | 0 | 13 | 4 | 0 | 11 | 8 | 26 | 0 | 220 | .328 | .188 |
| OnBase: 3 | .294 | 22 | 17 | 4 | 5 | 1 | 0 | 1 | 8 | 0 | 0 | 0 | 0 | 2 | 1 | 0 | 4 | 3 | 8 | 0 | 76 | .368 | .529 |
| OnBase: 12 | .235 | 42 | 34 | 11 | 8 | 1 | 0 | 0 | 8 | 0 | 0 | 0 | 0 | 0 | 0 | 1 | 4 | 8 | 15 | 3 | 130 | .257 | .265 |
| OnBase: 13 | .286 | 24 | 14 | 11 | 4 | 0 | 0 | 2 | 9 | 0 | 0 | 0 | 1 | 5 | 1 | 1 | 0 | 5 | 7 | 0 | 90 | .476 | .714 |
| OnBase: 23 | .300 | 17 | 10 | 3 | 3 | 0 | 0 | 0 | 5 | 0 | 0 | 0 | 0 | 4 | 2 | 0 | 2 | 2 | 4 | 0 | 52 | .500 | .300 |
| Bases Loaded | .250 | 21 | 8 | 10 | 2 | 2 | 0 | 0 | 11 | 0 | 0 | 0 | 0 | 2 | 0 | 1 | 0 | 0 | 7 | 1 | 39 | .455 | .500 |
| SB Opp | .301 | 69 | 73 | 15 | 22 | 3 | 0 | 3 | 13 | 7 | 2 | 0 | 1 | 10 | 1 | 1 | 10 | 21 | 30 | 8 | 296 | .388 | .466 |
| SB Atd | .235 | 22 | 17 | 0 | 4 | 0 | 0 | 1 | 4 | 0 | 0 | 0 | 0 | 6 | 2 | 0 | 5 | 4 | 4 | 0 | 101 | .435 | .412 |
| GDP Opp | .274 | 66 | 62 | 19 | 17 | 2 | 0 | 0 | 12 | 2 | 0 | 0 | 1 | 8 | 1 | 2 | 8 | 15 | 30 | 12 | 249 | .370 | .306 |

| At Count | AVG | G | AB | H | 2B | 3B | HR | RBI | SB | CS | SH | SF | BB | IW | HP | K | GRD | FLY | DP | #PIT | OBP | SLG |
|---|---|---|---|---|---|---|---|---|---|---|---|---|---|---|---|---|---|---|---|---|---|---|
| 0-0 count | .373 | 52 | 59 | 22 | 3 | 0 | 2 | 5 | 0 | 0 | 0 | 0 | 0 | 0 | 1 | 0 | 19 | 29 | 4 | 60 | .383 | .525 |
| 0-1 Count | .422 | 46 | 45 | 19 | 3 | 0 | 4 | 10 | 1 | 0 | 0 | 0 | 0 | 0 | 3 | 0 | 12 | 23 | 1 | 96 | .458 | .756 |
| 0-2 Count | .100 | 28 | 30 | 3 | 1 | 0 | 1 | 5 | 1 | 0 | 0 | 0 | 0 | 0 | 0 | 16 | 6 | 7 | 0 | 98 | .100 | .233 |
| 1-0 Count | .415 | 38 | 41 | 17 | 4 | 0 | 2 | 8 | 1 | 0 | 0 | 0 | 0 | 0 | 0 | 0 | 17 | 14 | 1 | 82 | .415 | .659 |
| 1-1 Count | .327 | 46 | 49 | 16 | 2 | 0 | 3 | 7 | 0 | 0 | 0 | 0 | 0 | 0 | 0 | 0 | 20 | 19 | 2 | 147 | .327 | .551 |
| 1-2 Count | .167 | 65 | 72 | 12 | 2 | 0 | 2 | 3 | 2 | 0 | 0 | 0 | 0 | 0 | 2 | 30 | 17 | 16 | 0 | 326 | .189 | .278 |
| 2-0 Count | .348 | 22 | 23 | 8 | 2 | 0 | 1 | 6 | 0 | 0 | 0 | 0 | 0 | 0 | 0 | 0 | 11 | 11 | 0 | 69 | .348 | .565 |
| 2-1 Count | .250 | 31 | 32 | 8 | 2 | 0 | 0 | 2 | 0 | 0 | 0 | 1 | 0 | 0 | 1 | 0 | 14 | 15 | 1 | 136 | .265 | .313 |
| 2-2 Count | .222 | 47 | 54 | 12 | 1 | 0 | 1 | 9 | 1 | 1 | 0 | 0 | 0 | 0 | 0 | 17 | 11 | 19 | 1 | 305 | .222 | .296 |
| 3-0 Count | .667 | 18 | 3 | 2 | 0 | 0 | 1 | 5 | 0 | 0 | 0 | 0 | 16 | 0 | 0 | 0 | 1 | 0 | 0 | 76 | .947 | 1.667 |
| 3-1 Count | .300 | 23 | 10 | 3 | 0 | 0 | 1 | 2 | 0 | 0 | 0 | 0 | 15 | 0 | 0 | 0 | 6 | 3 | 1 | 125 | .720 | .600 |
| 3-2 Count | .206 | 48 | 34 | 7 | 1 | 0 | 0 | 3 | 0 | 0 | 0 | 0 | 22 | 0 | 0 | 10 | 10 | 10 | 1 | 376 | .518 | .235 |

| After Count | AVG | G | AB | H | 2B | 3B | HR | RBI | SB | CS | SH | SF | BB | IW | HP | K | GRD | FLY | DP | #PIT | OBP | SLG |
|---|---|---|---|---|---|---|---|---|---|---|---|---|---|---|---|---|---|---|---|---|---|---|
| After (0-1) | .261 | 121 | 184 | 48 | 9 | 0 | 6 | 27 | 5 | 1 | 0 | 1 | 10 | 0 | 4 | 41 | 52 | 63 | 2 | 781 | .312 | .408 |
| After (0-2) | .153 | 53 | 59 | 9 | 2 | 0 | 1 | 7 | 3 | 0 | 0 | 0 | 3 | 0 | 1 | 28 | 14 | 11 | 0 | 281 | .206 | .237 |
| After (1-0) | .282 | 126 | 209 | 59 | 9 | 0 | 10 | 33 | 1 | 0 | 0 | 0 | 43 | 0 | 2 | 32 | 73 | 74 | 6 | 1055 | .409 | .469 |
| After (1-1) | .224 | 113 | 183 | 41 | 7 | 0 | 6 | 19 | 1 | 1 | 0 | 1 | 18 | 0 | 2 | 36 | 55 | 66 | 5 | 941 | .299 | .361 |
| After (1-2) | .165 | 91 | 115 | 19 | 4 | 0 | 3 | 7 | 3 | 0 | 0 | 0 | 5 | 0 | 2 | 45 | 26 | 28 | 1 | 629 | .213 | .278 |
| After (2-0) | .323 | 79 | 65 | 21 | 2 | 0 | 3 | 16 | 0 | 0 | 0 | 0 | 32 | 0 | 0 | 9 | 27 | 23 | 1 | 436 | .546 | .492 |
| After (2-1) | .265 | 80 | 83 | 22 | 2 | 0 | 1 | 11 | 0 | 1 | 0 | 1 | 26 | 0 | 1 | 11 | 31 | 34 | 3 | 581 | .441 | .325 |
| After (2-2) | .221 | 74 | 77 | 17 | 2 | 0 | 1 | 10 | 1 | 1 | 0 | 0 | 17 | 0 | 0 | 22 | 18 | 27 | 2 | 575 | .362 | .286 |
| After (3-0) | .429 | 27 | 7 | 3 | 0 | 0 | 1 | 6 | 0 | 0 | 0 | 0 | 22 | 0 | 0 | 1 | 2 | 1 | 0 | 134 | .862 | .857 |
| After (3-1) | .238 | 37 | 21 | 5 | 0 | 0 | 1 | 4 | 0 | 0 | 0 | 0 | 20 | 0 | 0 | 5 | 9 | 5 | 1 | 231 | .610 | .381 |
| After (3-2) | .206 | 48 | 34 | 7 | 1 | 0 | 0 | 3 | 0 | 0 | 0 | 0 | 22 | 0 | 0 | 10 | 10 | 10 | 1 | 376 | .518 | .235 |

At Each Pitch

| | Count | | | | | | | | | | | |
|---|---|---|---|---|---|---|---|---|---|---|---|---|
| Result | 0-0 | 0-1 | 0-2 | 1-0 | 1-1 | 1-2 | 2-0 | 2-1 | 2-2 | 3-0 | 3-1 | 3-2 |
| Ball | 244 | 92 | 36 | 96 | 63 | 52 | 28 | 32 | 42 | 16 | 15 | 23 |
| Taken Strike | 119 | 24 | 6 | 57 | 28 | 6 | 23 | 16 | 4 | 6 | 11 | 1 |
| Swung | 25 | 19 | 11 | 18 | 21 | 24 | 6 | 6 | 13 | 0 | 1 | 8 |
| Fouled | 57 | 23 | 17 | 36 | 38 | 50 | 16 | 24 | 28 | 4 | 4 | 21 |
| In Play | 59 | 45 | 15 | 41 | 49 | 42 | 23 | 33 | 37 | 3 | 10 | 24 |

Baserunning

| | Which Pitch? | | | Which Count? | | | | |
|---|---|---|---|---|---|---|---|---|
| Basestealing | Pitch 1 | Pitch 2 | Other | Even | Ahead | Behind | 3-2 | 2 Strikes |
| Stolen Base | 1 | 2 | 4 | 2 | 4 | 1 | 0 | 4 |
| Catcher Caught Stealing | 1 | 0 | 1 | 2 | 0 | 0 | 0 | 1 |
| Pitcher Pickoffs | 0 | 1 | 0 | 0 | 0 | 1 | 0 | 0 |
| Catcher Pickoffs | 0 | 0 | 1 | 0 | 0 | 1 | 0 | 0 |

## Pitcher Performance with Fisk Catching

| Pitcher | ERA | IP | H | BFP | R | ER | HR | SH | SF | BB | IW | HB | K | WP | BK | 2B | 3B | RBI | SB | CS | DP | GRD | FLY |
|---|---|---|---|---|---|---|---|---|---|---|---|---|---|---|---|---|---|---|---|---|---|---|---|
| Fisk Catching | 3.70 | 970.0 | 894 | 4070 | 436 | 399 | 68 | 30 | 28 | 361 | 14 | 25 | 642 | 26 | 6 | 138 | 32 | 409 | 71 | 42 | 95 | 1294 | 1036 |
| Other Catchers | 3.44 | 479.0 | 419 | 2003 | 197 | 183 | 38 | 22 | 18 | 187 | 13 | 14 | 272 | 9 | 5 | 64 | 17 | 187 | 18 | 18 | 45 | 644 | 528 |
| | | | | | | | | | | | | | | | | | | | | | | | |
| Wayne EDWARDS | 3.71 | 60.2 | 56 | 258 | 30 | 25 | 5 | 3 | 2 | 24 | 1 | 1 | 44 | 0 | 0 | 9 | 1 | 33 | 7 | 2 | 8 | 100 | 50 |
| Alex FERNANDEZ | 4.39 | 69.2 | 76 | 306 | 36 | 34 | 4 | 3 | 0 | 27 | 0 | 3 | 47 | 1 | 0 | 9 | 2 | 29 | 1 | 4 | 3 | 105 | 76 |
| Greg HIBBARD | 3.50 | 131.0 | 135 | 551 | 55 | 51 | 6 | 6 | 8 | 35 | 2 | 4 | 58 | 2 | 0 | 24 | 5 | 49 | 10 | 6 | 14 | 202 | 143 |
| Shawn HILLEGAS | 0.00 | 10.0 | 3 | 36 | 0 | 0 | 0 | 1 | 0 | 3 | 0 | 0 | 4 | 2 | 0 | 0 | 0 | 0 | 1 | 0 | 0 | 14 | 10 |
| Barry JONES | 2.56 | 45.2 | 38 | 191 | 13 | 13 | 1 | 5 | 2 | 21 | 6 | 1 | 24 | 0 | 0 | 7 | 0 | 19 | 1 | 0 | 5 | 67 | 45 |
| Eric KING | 3.52 | 84.1 | 81 | 356 | 35 | 33 | 6 | 4 | 0 | 23 | 0 | 4 | 48 | 1 | 3 | 10 | 2 | 32 | 6 | 2 | 6 | 128 | 97 |
| Jerry KUTZLER | 5.46 | 28.0 | 32 | 125 | 19 | 17 | 1 | 0 | 1 | 14 | 1 | 0 | 20 | 1 | 0 | 9 | 3 | 15 | 2 | 3 | 1 | 34 | 28 |
| Bill LONG | 6.35 | 5.2 | 6 | 26 | 5 | 4 | 2 | 1 | 0 | 2 | 0 | 0 | 2 | 0 | 0 | 1 | 0 | 8 | 0 | 0 | 0 | 10 | 4 |
| Jack MCDOWELL | 3.74 | 139.2 | 131 | 592 | 64 | 58 | 13 | 1 | 3 | 55 | 0 | 4 | 116 | 4 | 0 | 19 | 5 | 54 | 22 | 9 | 9 | 162 | 136 |
| Donn PALL | 3.46 | 52.0 | 37 | 197 | 22 | 20 | 5 | 1 | 1 | 12 | 1 | 3 | 32 | 1 | 0 | 8 | 2 | 26 | 6 | 2 | 10 | 88 | 38 |
| Ken PATTERSON | 3.11 | 46.1 | 40 | 197 | 18 | 16 | 5 | 0 | 3 | 21 | 1 | 2 | 30 | 2 | 0 | 5 | 1 | 23 | 4 | 2 | 3 | 49 | 57 |
| Melido PEREZ | 4.35 | 138.2 | 124 | 585 | 75 | 67 | 6 | 2 | 3 | 57 | 0 | 2 | 122 | 6 | 2 | 21 | 4 | 56 | 7 | 8 | 15 | 154 | 158 |
| Adam PETERSON | 4.14 | 67.1 | 68 | 278 | 34 | 31 | 7 | 2 | 3 | 20 | 0 | 1 | 23 | 2 | 0 | 10 | 5 | 33 | 1 | 4 | 9 | 72 | 111 |
| Scott RADINSKY | 4.70 | 30.2 | 23 | 134 | 16 | 16 | 1 | 1 | 1 | 24 | 0 | 0 | 26 | 2 | 1 | 3 | 1 | 12 | 1 | 0 | 3 | 41 | 23 |
| Steve ROSENBERG | 2.35 | 7.2 | 6 | 31 | 2 | 2 | 2 | 0 | 0 | 3 | 0 | 0 | 3 | 0 | 0 | 0 | 0 | 5 | 0 | 0 | 1 | 8 | 11 |
| Bobby THIGPEN | 2.05 | 52.2 | 38 | 207 | 12 | 12 | 4 | 0 | 1 | 20 | 2 | 0 | 43 | 2 | 0 | 3 | 1 | 15 | 2 | 0 | 8 | 60 | 49 |

### Opponent Base Stealers

| -----By Fisk----- | | | | -By Pitchers- | | |
|---|---|---|---|---|---|---|
| SB | CS | PkOf | PkOE | CS | PkOf | PkOE |
| 71 | 35 | 1 | 2 | 7 | 8 | 3 |

### Fielding By Position

| Pos | G | Inn | PO | A | E | DP | TP | PB |
|---|---|---|---|---|---|---|---|---|
| C | 116 | 970.0 | 661 | 62 | 4 | 14 | 0 | 11 |

### Pitchouts By Count

| | ------------------------Count------------------------ | | | | | | | | |
|---|---|---|---|---|---|---|---|---|---|
| Total | (0-0) | (0-1) | (0-2) | (1-0) | (1-1) | (1-2) | (2-0) | (2-1) | (2-2) |
| 39 | 14 | 5 | 5 | 6 | 5 | 4 | 0 | 0 | 0 |

### Rankings

#### Compared to Other American Leaguers

| Category | Rank | Stat | Minimum |
|---|---|---|---|
| Hit by Pitch | 4 | 7 | |
| On-Base Average | 8 | .378 | 502 PA |
| % CS by Catchers | 5 | .372 | 75 Attpt |
| Errors by Catcher | 10 | 4 | |
| Offensive Win Pct | 10 | .680 | 502 PA |
| Fielding Pct by Catcher | 3 | .994 | 90 Games |

#### Compared to Other American League Catchers

| Category | Rank | Stat | Minimum |
|---|---|---|---|
| SLG | 1 | .451 | 502 PA |
| Hit by Pitch | 1 | 7 | |
| Runs Created | 1 | 78 | |
| On-Base Average | 1 | .378 | 502 PA |
| Power/Speed Mix | 1 | 10 | |
| Offensive Win Pct | 1 | .680 | 502 PA |
| Intentional Walks | 1 | 8 | |

#### Compared to Other White Sox Players

| Category | Rank | Stat | Minimum |
|---|---|---|---|
| SLG | 1 | .451 | 502 PA |
| Walks | 1 | 61 | |
| Home Runs | 1 | 18 | |
| Hit by Pitch | 1 | 7 | |
| Runs Created | 1 | 78 | |
| On-Base Average | 1 | .378 | 502 PA |
| Intentional Walks | 1 | 8 | |
| Offensive Win Pct | 1 | .680 | 502 PA |
| Secondary Average | 1 | .312 | 502 PA |

Active Pitchers vs. Carlton Fisk

(10 or more At Bats Since 1985)

| Pitcher | AVG | AB | H | 2B | 3B | HR | RBI | W | K | SB | CS |
|---|---|---|---|---|---|---|---|---|---|---|---|
| BAILES, Scott | .455 | 11 | 5 | 1 | 0 | 0 | 1 | 0 | 1 | 0 | 0 |
| PLUNK, Eric | .455 | 11 | 5 | 0 | 0 | 2 | 6 | 1 | 2 | 0 | 0 |
| SWINDELL, Gre | .438 | 16 | 7 | 0 | 0 | 3 | 5 | 1 | 2 | 0 | 0 |
| CANDELARIA, J | .417 | 12 | 5 | 0 | 0 | 3 | 9 | 3 | 1 | 0 | 0 |
| REARDON, Jeff | .400 | 10 | 4 | 2 | 0 | 2 | 4 | 0 | 3 | 0 | 0 |
| O'NEAL, Randy | .400 | 10 | 4 | 0 | 0 | 2 | 2 | 1 | 3 | 0 | 0 |
| CERUTTI, John | .400 | 10 | 4 | 1 | 0 | 0 | 2 | 4 | 2 | 0 | 0 |
| SWIFT, Bill | .381 | 21 | 8 | 2 | 0 | 0 | 3 | 4 | 0 | 0 | 1 |
| LEIBRANDT, Ch | .375 | 32 | 12 | 2 | 0 | 2 | 6 | 2 | 5 | 0 | 1 |
| LAPOINT, Dave | .364 | 11 | 4 | 2 | 0 | 0 | 1 | 0 | 0 | 0 | 0 |
| WEGMAN, Bill | .357 | 14 | 5 | 1 | 0 | 2 | 2 | 0 | 4 | 0 | 0 |
| PETRY, Dan | .357 | 28 | 10 | 3 | 0 | 3 | 6 | 1 | 3 | 1 | 0 |
| SABERHAGEN, B | .344 | 32 | 11 | 1 | 0 | 3 | 9 | 1 | 4 | 0 | 1 |
| MONTGOMERY, J | .333 | 12 | 4 | 2 | 0 | 0 | 2 | 0 | 2 | 0 | 0 |
| JOHNSON, Rand | .333 | 12 | 4 | 1 | 0 | 1 | 4 | 1 | 0 | 0 | 0 |
| HURST, Bruce | .321 | 28 | 9 | 3 | 0 | 3 | 6 | 2 | 8 | 0 | 1 |
| JACKSON, Dann | .321 | 28 | 9 | 0 | 0 | 2 | 5 | 2 | 5 | 0 | 0 |
| STIEB, Dave | .320 | 25 | 8 | 0 | 0 | 0 | 5 | 5 | 5 | 0 | 2 |
| FINLEY, Chuck | .320 | 25 | 8 | 2 | 0 | 2 | 5 | 2 | 5 | 0 | 0 |
| MCCASKILL, Ki | .318 | 22 | 7 | 2 | 0 | 0 | 2 | 3 | 1 | 0 | 1 |
| WITT, Mike | .316 | 38 | 12 | 3 | 0 | 2 | 3 | 1 | 7 | 0 | 0 |
| HIGUERA, Ted | .313 | 32 | 10 | 1 | 0 | 2 | 6 | 0 | 5 | 1 | 0 |
| NIEKRO, Phil | .308 | 13 | 4 | 0 | 0 | 0 | 0 | 0 | 2 | 0 | 1 |
| LANGSTON, Mar | .308 | 39 | 12 | 1 | 0 | 4 | 8 | 2 | 5 | 0 | 0 |
| CRIM, Chuck | .300 | 10 | 3 | 1 | 0 | 0 | 1 | 1 | 1 | 0 | 0 |
| BALLARD, Jeff | .300 | 10 | 3 | 1 | 0 | 0 | 3 | 2 | 0 | 0 | 0 |
| WITT, Bobby | .278 | 18 | 5 | 1 | 0 | 1 | 3 | 2 | 6 | 0 | 0 |
| YOUNG, Matt | .278 | 18 | 5 | 0 | 0 | 1 | 4 | 3 | 2 | 0 | 1 |
| MORRIS, Jack | .276 | 29 | 8 | 3 | 0 | 2 | 4 | 3 | 3 | 2 | 0 |
| RASMUSSEN, De | .273 | 11 | 3 | 0 | 0 | 0 | 0 | 1 | 1 | 0 | 0 |
| ABBOTT, Jim | .273 | 11 | 3 | 1 | 0 | 0 | 3 | 1 | 1 | 0 | 0 |
| WELCH, Bob | .273 | 11 | 3 | 0 | 0 | 0 | 2 | 4 | 1 | 0 | 0 |
| NICHOLS, Rod | .273 | 11 | 3 | 1 | 0 | 0 | 1 | 1 | 0 | 0 | 0 |
| ATHERTON, Kei | .273 | 11 | 3 | 0 | 0 | 0 | 4 | 2 | 2 | 0 | 0 |
| BOYD, Oil Can | .267 | 15 | 4 | 0 | 0 | 2 | 3 | 2 | 1 | 0 | 0 |
| TANANA, Frank | .259 | 27 | 7 | 2 | 2 | 0 | 3 | 3 | 3 | 1 | 0 |
| VIOLA, Frank | .258 | 31 | 8 | 2 | 0 | 0 | 2 | 2 | 5 | 0 | 0 |
| BLYLEVEN, Bert | .235 | 34 | 8 | 0 | 0 | 2 | 5 | 3 | 3 | 1 | 0 |
| ANDERSON, Allan | .231 | 26 | 6 | 0 | 0 | 2 | 2 | 1 | 2 | 0 | 0 |
| ROBINSON, Jeff | .231 | 13 | 3 | 1 | 0 | 0 | 0 | 0 | 2 | 0 | 0 |
| RIGHETTI, Dave | .222 | 18 | 4 | 1 | 0 | 0 | 1 | 0 | 4 | 1 | 0 |
| TERRELL, Walt | .217 | 23 | 5 | 1 | 0 | 0 | 1 | 2 | 2 | 0 | 0 |
| NELSON, Gene | .214 | 14 | 3 | 1 | 0 | 1 | 1 | 0 | 3 | 0 | 0 |
| DAVIS, Storm | .214 | 14 | 3 | 1 | 1 | 1 | 2 | 2 | 2 | 0 | 0 |
| JONES, Doug | .214 | 14 | 3 | 0 | 0 | 0 | 2 | 1 | 2 | 0 | 0 |
| STEWART, Dave | .207 | 29 | 6 | 1 | 0 | 0 | 3 | 3 | 6 | 1 | 0 |
| HUDSON, Charlie | .200 | 10 | 2 | 1 | 0 | 0 | 1 | 1 | 3 | 0 | 0 |
| PLESAC, Dan | .200 | 10 | 2 | 1 | 0 | 0 | 0 | 3 | 3 | 0 | 0 |
| CLEMENS, Roger | .194 | 31 | 6 | 1 | 0 | 4 | 6 | 3 | 10 | 0 | 0 |
| CARY, Chuck | .182 | 11 | 2 | 0 | 0 | 0 | 1 | 2 | 1 | 0 | 0 |
| BERENGUER, Juan | .182 | 11 | 2 | 1 | 0 | 0 | 0 | 1 | 4 | 0 | 0 |
| CANDIOTTI, Tom | .176 | 17 | 3 | 0 | 0 | 1 | 2 | 4 | 1 | 0 | 0 |
| BODDICKER, Mike | .174 | 23 | 4 | 1 | 0 | 1 | 3 | 3 | 6 | 1 | 1 |
| CODIROLI, Chris | .167 | 12 | 2 | 1 | 0 | 0 | 1 | 3 | 1 | 0 | 0 |
| GUTHRIE, Mark | .167 | 12 | 2 | 0 | 0 | 0 | 2 | 2 | 6 | 0 | 0 |
| GUBICZA, Mark | .167 | 18 | 3 | 2 | 0 | 0 | 2 | 1 | 2 | 0 | 0 |
| KRUEGER, Bill | .154 | 13 | 2 | 0 | 0 | 0 | 2 | 3 | 1 | 2 | 0 |
| NIEVES, Juan | .150 | 20 | 3 | 1 | 0 | 0 | 1 | 0 | 7 | 0 | 0 |
| REED, Jerry | .143 | 14 | 2 | 1 | 0 | 0 | 1 | 1 | 2 | 0 | 0 |
| KEY, Jimmy | .143 | 35 | 5 | 0 | 0 | 2 | 7 | 3 | 4 | 0 | 0 |
| SMITHSON, Mike | .143 | 14 | 2 | 0 | 0 | 0 | 0 | 4 | 4 | 0 | 0 |
| HEATON, Neal | .143 | 14 | 2 | 1 | 0 | 1 | 2 | 2 | 3 | 1 | 0 |
| MOORE, Mike | .130 | 23 | 3 | 0 | 0 | 0 | 2 | 0 | 7 | 0 | 0 |
| HOUGH, Charlie | .121 | 33 | 4 | 0 | 0 | 2 | 3 | 1 | 8 | 1 | 0 |
| BLACK, Bud | .121 | 33 | 4 | 0 | 0 | 2 | 6 | 3 | 8 | 1 | 0 |
| FRASER, Willie | .118 | 17 | 2 | 0 | 0 | 2 | 3 | 0 | 5 | 0 | 0 |
| MINTON, Greg | .091 | 11 | 1 | 0 | 0 | 0 | 1 | 1 | 5 | 0 | 0 |
| YOUNG, Curt | .080 | 25 | 2 | 0 | 0 | 0 | 1 | 1 | 4 | 0 | 0 |
| BROWN, Kevin | .077 | 13 | 1 | 0 | 0 | 0 | 1 | 0 | 3 | 0 | 0 |
| FARR, Steve | .000 | 13 | 0 | 0 | 0 | 0 | 0 | 0 | 7 | 0 | 0 |
| RUSSELL, Jeff | .000 | 10 | 0 | 0 | 0 | 0 | 0 | 3 | 4 | 0 | 0 |

# Ryne Sandberg – Chicago Cubs

Batting

| 1990 | AVG | G | AB | R | H | 2B | 3B | HR | RBI | SB | CS | SH | SF | BB | IW | HP | K | GRD | FLY | DP | #PIT | OBP | SLG |
|---|---|---|---|---|---|---|---|---|---|---|---|---|---|---|---|---|---|---|---|---|---|---|---|
| Total | .306 | 155 | 615 | 116 | 188 | 30 | 3 | 40 | 100 | 25 | 7 | 0 | 9 | 50 | 8 | 1 | 84 | 204 | 219 | 8 | 2378 | .354 | .559 |

| Vs. Teams | AVG | G | AB | R | H | 2B | 3B | HR | RBI | SB | CS | SH | SF | BB | IW | HP | K | GRD | FLY | DP | #PIT | OBP | SLG |
|---|---|---|---|---|---|---|---|---|---|---|---|---|---|---|---|---|---|---|---|---|---|---|---|
| vs.Atl | .279 | 11 | 43 | 8 | 12 | 3 | 0 | 3 | 6 | 3 | 0 | 0 | 0 | 3 | 0 | 0 | 4 | 17 | 17 | 1 | 150 | .326 | .558 |
| vs.Cin | .212 | 12 | 52 | 6 | 11 | 2 | 0 | 3 | 7 | 2 | 0 | 0 | 0 | 4 | 1 | 0 | 11 | 22 | 13 | 0 | 183 | .268 | .423 |
| vs.Hou | .360 | 12 | 50 | 11 | 18 | 4 | 0 | 4 | 12 | 1 | 0 | 0 | 2 | 4 | 0 | 0 | 8 | 15 | 19 | 2 | 196 | .393 | .680 |
| vs.LA | .208 | 12 | 48 | 4 | 10 | 3 | 0 | 1 | 7 | 0 | 0 | 0 | 2 | 2 | 0 | 0 | 8 | 13 | 19 | 0 | 209 | .231 | .333 |
| vs.Mon | .308 | 17 | 65 | 18 | 20 | 2 | 0 | 5 | 8 | 3 | 0 | 0 | 0 | 5 | 2 | 0 | 8 | 22 | 24 | 1 | 239 | .357 | .569 |
| vs.NYN | .342 | 18 | 76 | 13 | 26 | 2 | 1 | 7 | 22 | 3 | 4 | 0 | 2 | 7 | 2 | 0 | 15 | 21 | 30 | 0 | 322 | .388 | .671 |
| vs.Phi | .356 | 15 | 59 | 13 | 21 | 4 | 0 | 4 | 7 | 1 | 1 | 0 | 0 | 2 | 1 | 0 | 8 | 18 | 18 | 2 | 226 | .377 | .627 |
| vs.Pit | .275 | 18 | 69 | 11 | 19 | 4 | 0 | 3 | 8 | 5 | 1 | 0 | 1 | 1 | 0 | 0 | 6 | 25 | 22 | 0 | 209 | .282 | .464 |
| vs.StL | .328 | 17 | 67 | 16 | 22 | 2 | 0 | 7 | 13 | 3 | 1 | 0 | 0 | 11 | 0 | 0 | 4 | 26 | 26 | 1 | 305 | .423 | .672 |
| vs.SD | .238 | 12 | 42 | 7 | 10 | 2 | 1 | 0 | 5 | 2 | 0 | 0 | 2 | 5 | 0 | 0 | 6 | 11 | 15 | 1 | 165 | .306 | .333 |
| vs.SF | .432 | 11 | 44 | 9 | 19 | 2 | 1 | 3 | 5 | 2 | 0 | 0 | 0 | 6 | 2 | 1 | 6 | 14 | 16 | 0 | 174 | .510 | .727 |

| By Park | AVG | G | AB | R | H | 2B | 3B | HR | RBI | SB | CS | SH | SF | BB | IW | HP | K | GRD | FLY | DP | #PIT | OBP | SLG |
|---|---|---|---|---|---|---|---|---|---|---|---|---|---|---|---|---|---|---|---|---|---|---|---|
| at Atl | .238 | 5 | 21 | 2 | 5 | 1 | 0 | 1 | 1 | 2 | 0 | 0 | 0 | 1 | 0 | 0 | 1 | 9 | 9 | 1 | 79 | .273 | .429 |
| at ChN | .357 | 78 | 305 | 67 | 109 | 21 | 1 | 25 | 62 | 12 | 4 | 0 | 5 | 27 | 7 | 1 | 44 | 93 | 100 | 3 | 1158 | .405 | .679 |
| at Cin | .200 | 6 | 25 | 3 | 5 | 0 | 0 | 2 | 3 | 1 | 0 | 0 | 0 | 2 | 1 | 0 | 3 | 14 | 5 | 0 | 84 | .259 | .440 |
| at Hou | .308 | 6 | 26 | 5 | 8 | 2 | 0 | 1 | 4 | 0 | 0 | 0 | 1 | 3 | 0 | 0 | 5 | 4 | 12 | 1 | 108 | .367 | .500 |
| at LA | .208 | 6 | 24 | 1 | 5 | 0 | 0 | 0 | 2 | 0 | 0 | 0 | 2 | 0 | 0 | 0 | 5 | 8 | 11 | 0 | 107 | .192 | .208 |
| at Mon | .222 | 9 | 36 | 6 | 8 | 0 | 0 | 2 | 5 | 1 | 0 | 0 | 0 | 1 | 0 | 0 | 4 | 16 | 14 | 1 | 126 | .243 | .389 |
| at NYN | .231 | 9 | 39 | 4 | 9 | 1 | 1 | 2 | 7 | 2 | 2 | 0 | 0 | 4 | 0 | 0 | 7 | 11 | 16 | 0 | 183 | .302 | .462 |
| at Phi | .222 | 7 | 27 | 2 | 6 | 1 | 0 | 1 | 2 | 1 | 0 | 0 | 0 | 0 | 0 | 0 | 7 | 7 | 10 | 1 | 98 | .222 | .370 |
| at Pit | .303 | 9 | 33 | 7 | 10 | 2 | 0 | 2 | 4 | 2 | 1 | 0 | 0 | 0 | 0 | 0 | 0 | 13 | 13 | 0 | 99 | .303 | .545 |
| at StL | .242 | 9 | 33 | 9 | 8 | 0 | 0 | 3 | 6 | 2 | 0 | 0 | 0 | 8 | 0 | 0 | 1 | 14 | 13 | 1 | 167 | .390 | .515 |
| at SD | .217 | 6 | 23 | 4 | 5 | 0 | 1 | 0 | 2 | 1 | 0 | 0 | 1 | 3 | 0 | 0 | 4 | 5 | 7 | 0 | 90 | .296 | .304 |
| at SF | .435 | 5 | 23 | 6 | 10 | 2 | 0 | 1 | 2 | 1 | 0 | 0 | 0 | 1 | 0 | 0 | 3 | 10 | 9 | 0 | 79 | .458 | .652 |

| By Month | AVG | G | AB | R | H | 2B | 3B | HR | RBI | SB | CS | SH | SF | BB | IW | HP | K | GRD | FLY | DP | #PIT | OBP | SLG |
|---|---|---|---|---|---|---|---|---|---|---|---|---|---|---|---|---|---|---|---|---|---|---|---|
| April | .250 | 19 | 76 | 8 | 19 | 3 | 0 | 1 | 7 | 3 | 1 | 0 | 1 | 2 | 0 | 0 | 11 | 25 | 28 | 0 | 270 | .266 | .329 |
| May | .373 | 28 | 118 | 22 | 44 | 10 | 0 | 9 | 21 | 6 | 0 | 0 | 1 | 12 | 3 | 0 | 13 | 38 | 45 | 1 | 441 | .427 | .686 |
| June | .377 | 29 | 114 | 32 | 43 | 3 | 1 | 14 | 25 | 6 | 1 | 0 | 1 | 13 | 4 | 0 | 16 | 34 | 36 | 1 | 446 | .438 | .789 |
| July | .204 | 25 | 98 | 14 | 20 | 4 | 1 | 1 | 10 | 1 | 0 | 0 | 3 | 6 | 0 | 1 | 15 | 31 | 38 | 2 | 402 | .250 | .296 |
| August | .280 | 26 | 107 | 19 | 30 | 5 | 1 | 6 | 16 | 6 | 1 | 0 | 2 | 8 | 0 | 0 | 16 | 45 | 31 | 2 | 416 | .325 | .514 |
| September | .310 | 27 | 100 | 20 | 31 | 5 | 0 | 8 | 19 | 3 | 4 | 0 | 1 | 9 | 1 | 0 | 12 | 30 | 41 | 2 | 398 | .364 | .600 |
| October | .500 | 1 | 2 | 1 | 1 | 0 | 0 | 1 | 2 | 0 | 0 | 0 | 0 | 0 | 0 | 0 | 1 | 1 | 0 | 0 | 5 | .500 | 2.000 |

| By Fielding Pos | AVG | G | AB | R | H | 2B | 3B | HR | RBI | SB | CS | SH | SF | BB | IW | HP | K | GRD | FLY | DP | #PIT | OBP | SLG |
|---|---|---|---|---|---|---|---|---|---|---|---|---|---|---|---|---|---|---|---|---|---|---|---|
| As ph | .000 | 4 | 2 | 0 | 0 | 0 | 0 | 0 | 1 | 0 | 0 | 0 | 1 | 1 | 0 | 0 | 0 | 3 | 0 | 0 | 17 | .250 | .000 |
| As 2b | .307 | 152 | 613 | 0 | 188 | 30 | 3 | 40 | 100 | 0 | 0 | 0 | 9 | 50 | 8 | 1 | 84 | 202 | 219 | 8 | 2374 | .355 | .561 |

| By Lineup Posit | AVG | G | AB | R | H | 2B | 3B | HR | RBI | SB | CS | SH | SF | BB | IW | HP | K | GRD | FLY | DP | #PIT | OBP | SLG |
|---|---|---|---|---|---|---|---|---|---|---|---|---|---|---|---|---|---|---|---|---|---|---|---|
| Batting #2 | .306 | 153 | 614 | 116 | 188 | 30 | 3 | 40 | 100 | 25 | 7 | 0 | 9 | 50 | 8 | 1 | 84 | 203 | 219 | 8 | 2376 | .355 | .560 |
| Batting #8 | .000 | 1 | 1 | 0 | 0 | 0 | 0 | 0 | 0 | 0 | 0 | 0 | 0 | 0 | 0 | 0 | 0 | 1 | 0 | 0 | 2 | .000 | .000 |
| Batting #9 | .000 | 1 | 0 | 0 | 0 | 0 | 0 | 0 | 0 | 0 | 0 | 0 | 0 | 0 | 0 | 0 | 0 | 0 | 0 | 0 | 0 | - | - |

| Conditions | AVG | G | AB | R | H | 2B | 3B | HR | RBI | SB | CS | SH | SF | BB | IW | HP | K | GRD | FLY | DP | #PIT | OBP | SLG |
|---|---|---|---|---|---|---|---|---|---|---|---|---|---|---|---|---|---|---|---|---|---|---|---|
| Home | .357 | 78 | 305 | 67 | 109 | 21 | 1 | 25 | 62 | 12 | 4 | 0 | 5 | 27 | 7 | 1 | 44 | 93 | 100 | 3 | 1158 | .405 | .679 |
| Away | .255 | 77 | 310 | 49 | 79 | 9 | 2 | 15 | 38 | 13 | 3 | 0 | 4 | 23 | 1 | 0 | 40 | 111 | 119 | 5 | 1220 | .303 | .442 |
| Day | .319 | 80 | 320 | 66 | 102 | 17 | 1 | 22 | 57 | 13 | 4 | 0 | 5 | 29 | 6 | 1 | 45 | 107 | 110 | 3 | 1264 | .372 | .584 |
| Night | .292 | 75 | 295 | 50 | 86 | 13 | 2 | 18 | 43 | 12 | 3 | 0 | 4 | 21 | 2 | 0 | 39 | 97 | 109 | 5 | 1114 | .334 | .532 |
| Grass | .329 | 109 | 435 | 84 | 143 | 25 | 3 | 29 | 76 | 18 | 6 | 0 | 8 | 36 | 7 | 1 | 64 | 136 | 152 | 4 | 1696 | .375 | .600 |
| Turf | .250 | 46 | 180 | 32 | 45 | 5 | 0 | 11 | 24 | 7 | 1 | 0 | 1 | 14 | 1 | 0 | 20 | 68 | 67 | 4 | 682 | .303 | .461 |

| Pitcher Types | AVG | G | AB | R | H | 2B | 3B | HR | RBI | SB | CS | SH | SF | BB | IW | HP | K | GRD | FLY | DP | #PIT | OBP | SLG |
|---|---|---|---|---|---|---|---|---|---|---|---|---|---|---|---|---|---|---|---|---|---|---|---|
| vs. Left | .252 | 91 | 214 | 38 | 54 | 13 | 0 | 10 | 23 | 7 | 1 | 0 | 0 | 21 | 6 | 0 | 34 | 69 | 76 | 4 | 857 | .319 | .453 |
| vs. Right | .334 | 138 | 401 | 78 | 134 | 17 | 3 | 30 | 77 | 18 | 6 | 0 | 9 | 29 | 2 | 1 | 50 | 135 | 143 | 4 | 1521 | .373 | .616 |
| Groundball | .355 | 52 | 124 | 26 | 44 | 6 | 1 | 10 | 21 | 8 | 1 | 0 | 0 | 3 | 1 | 0 | 10 | 43 | 42 | 0 | 407 | .370 | .661 |
| Flyball | .278 | 94 | 209 | 38 | 58 | 10 | 1 | 12 | 38 | 10 | 4 | 0 | 6 | 22 | 2 | 0 | 32 | 81 | 68 | 3 | 838 | .338 | .507 |
| Ave Grd/Fly | .305 | 109 | 282 | 52 | 86 | 14 | 1 | 18 | 41 | 7 | 2 | 0 | 3 | 25 | 5 | 1 | 42 | 80 | 109 | 5 | 1133 | .360 | .553 |
| Finesse | .318 | 77 | 201 | 33 | 64 | 10 | 0 | 12 | 31 | 6 | 5 | 0 | 2 | 16 | 3 | 0 | 24 | 62 | 85 | 4 | 763 | .365 | .547 |
| Power | .254 | 79 | 185 | 36 | 47 | 12 | 2 | 11 | 31 | 9 | 0 | 0 | 1 | 17 | 1 | 0 | 26 | 71 | 55 | 2 | 745 | .315 | .519 |
| Ave Fin/Pow | .336 | 99 | 229 | 47 | 77 | 8 | 1 | 17 | 38 | 10 | 2 | 0 | 6 | 17 | 4 | 1 | 34 | 71 | 79 | 2 | 870 | .375 | .603 |

| Inning | AVG | G | AB | R | H | 2B | 3B | HR | RBI | SB | CS | SH | SF | BB | IW | HP | K | GRD | FLY | DP | #PIT | OBP | SLG |
|---|---|---|---|---|---|---|---|---|---|---|---|---|---|---|---|---|---|---|---|---|---|---|---|
| Inning 1-6 | .294 | 152 | 436 | 83 | 128 | 26 | 2 | 27 | 62 | 19 | 6 | 0 | 3 | 35 | 7 | 0 | 61 | 145 | 150 | 7 | 1669 | .344 | .548 |
| Inning 7+ | .335 | 141 | 179 | 33 | 60 | 4 | 1 | 13 | 38 | 6 | 1 | 0 | 6 | 15 | 1 | 1 | 23 | 59 | 69 | 1 | 709 | .378 | .587 |

| Game Situation | AVG | G | AB | R | H | 2B | 3B | HR | RBI | SB | CS | SH | SF | BB | IW | HP | K | GRD | FLY | DP | #PIT | OBP | SLG |
|---|---|---|---|---|---|---|---|---|---|---|---|---|---|---|---|---|---|---|---|---|---|---|---|
| Close & Late | .323 | 80 | 96 | 19 | 31 | 3 | 1 | 6 | 19 | 3 | 1 | 0 | 4 | 8 | 1 | 1 | 12 | 31 | 42 | 1 | 382 | .367 | .563 |
| Close | .289 | 116 | 211 | 42 | 61 | 8 | 1 | 16 | 35 | 6 | 1 | 0 | 6 | 18 | 3 | 1 | 36 | 65 | 78 | 2 | 827 | .339 | .564 |
| Not Close | .314 | 152 | 404 | 74 | 127 | 22 | 2 | 24 | 65 | 19 | 6 | 0 | 3 | 32 | 5 | 0 | 48 | 139 | 141 | 6 | 1551 | .362 | .557 |

| Bases Empty | AVG | G | AB | R | H | 2B | 3B | HR | RBI | SB | CS | SH | SF | BB | IW | HP | K | GRD | FLY | DP | #PIT | OBP | SLG |
|---|---|---|---|---|---|---|---|---|---|---|---|---|---|---|---|---|---|---|---|---|---|---|---|
| None on | .267 | 148 | 378 | 24 | 101 | 20 | 0 | 24 | 24 | 0 | 0 | 0 | 0 | 23 | 0 | 1 | 55 | 122 | 130 | 0 | 1447 | .311 | .511 |
| None on/0 Out | .267 | 100 | 120 | 14 | 32 | 3 | 0 | 14 | 14 | 0 | 0 | 0 | 0 | 10 | 0 | 0 | 22 | 43 | 33 | 0 | 464 | .323 | .642 |
| None on/1,2 Out | .267 | 137 | 258 | 10 | 69 | 17 | 0 | 10 | 10 | 0 | 0 | 0 | 0 | 13 | 0 | 1 | 33 | 79 | 97 | 0 | 983 | .305 | .450 |

| On Base | AVG | G | AB | R | H | 2B | 3B | HR | RBI | SB | CS | SH | SF | BB | IW | HP | K | GRD | FLY | DP | #PIT | OBP | SLG |
|---|---|---|---|---|---|---|---|---|---|---|---|---|---|---|---|---|---|---|---|---|---|---|---|
| Runners on | .367 | 146 | 237 | 92 | 87 | 10 | 3 | 16 | 76 | 25 | 7 | 0 | 9 | 27 | 8 | 0 | 29 | 82 | 89 | 8 | 931 | .418 | .637 |
| Scoring Posn | .298 | 122 | 124 | 81 | 37 | 3 | 2 | 9 | 56 | 8 | 0 | 0 | 9 | 20 | 8 | 0 | 19 | 47 | 51 | 2 | 539 | .373 | .573 |
| OnBase: 2 | .341 | 54 | 41 | 20 | 14 | 0 | 1 | 3 | 10 | 0 | 0 | 0 | 0 | 9 | 2 | 0 | 7 | 11 | 18 | 0 | 201 | .460 | .610 |
| OnBase: 3 | .176 | 36 | 17 | 11 | 3 | 0 | 0 | 1 | 6 | 0 | 0 | 0 | 2 | 7 | 2 | 0 | 5 | 7 | 7 | 0 | 108 | .385 | .353 |
| OnBase: 12 | .286 | 45 | 42 | 17 | 12 | 1 | 1 | 4 | 18 | 1 | 0 | 0 | 0 | 0 | 0 | 0 | 5 | 16 | 14 | 1 | 135 | .286 | .643 |
| OnBase: 13 | .333 | 32 | 12 | 18 | 4 | 1 | 0 | 1 | 10 | 7 | 0 | 0 | 1 | 0 | 0 | 0 | 1 | 4 | 7 | 0 | 31 | .308 | .667 |
| OnBase: 23 | .500 | 12 | 4 | 3 | 2 | 0 | 0 | 0 | 4 | 0 | 0 | 0 | 1 | 4 | 4 | 0 | 1 | 3 | 0 | 0 | 18 | .667 | .500 |
| Bases Loaded | .250 | 24 | 8 | 12 | 2 | 1 | 0 | 0 | 8 | 0 | 0 | 0 | 5 | 0 | 0 | 0 | 0 | 6 | 5 | 1 | 46 | .154 | .375 |
| SB Opp | .432 | 111 | 125 | 29 | 54 | 8 | 1 | 8 | 30 | 24 | 7 | 0 | 1 | 7 | 0 | 0 | 11 | 39 | 45 | 6 | 423 | .459 | .704 |
| SB Atd | .318 | 28 | 22 | 0 | 7 | 1 | 0 | 2 | 7 | 1 | 0 | 0 | 2 | 5 | 0 | 0 | 5 | 8 | 10 | 0 | 143 | .414 | .636 |
| GDP Opp | .423 | 106 | 123 | 44 | 52 | 7 | 2 | 11 | 47 | 13 | 4 | 0 | 6 | 3 | 0 | 0 | 9 | 50 | 41 | 8 | 420 | .417 | .780 |

| At Count | AVG | G | AB | H | 2B | 3B | HR | RBI | SB | CS | SH | SF | BB | IW | HP | K | GRD | FLY | DP | #PIT | OBP | SLG |
|---|---|---|---|---|---|---|---|---|---|---|---|---|---|---|---|---|---|---|---|---|---|---|
| 0-0 count | .427 | 64 | 75 | 32 | 3 | 1 | 8 | 20 | 5 | 1 | 0 | 1 | 0 | 0 | 0 | 0 | 30 | 25 | 1 | 76 | .421 | .813 |
| 0-1 Count | .250 | 56 | 60 | 15 | 2 | 0 | 4 | 10 | 5 | 1 | 0 | 1 | 0 | 0 | 0 | 0 | 25 | 25 | 1 | 122 | .246 | .483 |
| 0-2 Count | .214 | 38 | 42 | 9 | 2 | 0 | 3 | 8 | 1 | 0 | 0 | 0 | 0 | 0 | 1 | 16 | 12 | 10 | 1 | 139 | .233 | .476 |
| 1-0 Count | .395 | 62 | 76 | 30 | 11 | 0 | 6 | 14 | 4 | 0 | 0 | 1 | 0 | 0 | 0 | 0 | 33 | 28 | 2 | 154 | .390 | .776 |
| 1-1 Count | .382 | 60 | 68 | 26 | 3 | 1 | 5 | 18 | 4 | 1 | 0 | 3 | 0 | 0 | 0 | 0 | 27 | 28 | 1 | 213 | .366 | .676 |
| 1-2 Count | .228 | 66 | 79 | 18 | 1 | 0 | 4 | 9 | 1 | 0 | 0 | 1 | 0 | 0 | 0 | 35 | 14 | 20 | 0 | 338 | .225 | .392 |
| 2-0 Count | .357 | 32 | 28 | 10 | 2 | 0 | 3 | 6 | 2 | 1 | 0 | 0 | 2 | 2 | 0 | 0 | 9 | 12 | 0 | 90 | .400 | .750 |
| 2-1 Count | .333 | 39 | 39 | 13 | 2 | 1 | 1 | 3 | 1 | 1 | 0 | 1 | 0 | 0 | 0 | 0 | 14 | 17 | 1 | 160 | .325 | .513 |
| 2-2 Count | .192 | 64 | 78 | 15 | 1 | 0 | 1 | 5 | 1 | 0 | 0 | 0 | 0 | 0 | 0 | 25 | 16 | 28 | 0 | 439 | .192 | .244 |
| 3-0 Count | .000 | 17 | 2 | 0 | 0 | 0 | 0 | 0 | 0 | 0 | 0 | 0 | 15 | 0 | 0 | 0 | 1 | 0 | 0 | 68 | .882 | .000 |
| 3-1 Count | .300 | 30 | 20 | 6 | 1 | 0 | 2 | 2 | 0 | 0 | 0 | 0 | 10 | 0 | 0 | 0 | 8 | 7 | 1 | 150 | .533 | .650 |
| 3-2 Count | .277 | 55 | 47 | 13 | 2 | 0 | 3 | 4 | 0 | 0 | 0 | 0 | 16 | 0 | 0 | 8 | 14 | 18 | 0 | 412 | .460 | .511 |

| After Count | AVG | G | AB | H | 2B | 3B | HR | RBI | SB | CS | SH | SF | BB | IW | HP | K | GRD | FLY | DP | #PIT | OBP | SLG |
|---|---|---|---|---|---|---|---|---|---|---|---|---|---|---|---|---|---|---|---|---|---|---|
| After (0-1) | .244 | 134 | 266 | 65 | 8 | 1 | 13 | 35 | 8 | 2 | 0 | 4 | 6 | 0 | 1 | 57 | 81 | 88 | 3 | 1104 | .260 | .429 |
| After (0-2) | .222 | 77 | 99 | 22 | 3 | 0 | 5 | 15 | 2 | 0 | 0 | 1 | 2 | 0 | 1 | 37 | 28 | 23 | 1 | 460 | .243 | .404 |
| After (1-0) | .332 | 139 | 274 | 91 | 19 | 1 | 19 | 45 | 11 | 2 | 0 | 4 | 38 | 2 | 0 | 27 | 93 | 106 | 4 | 1198 | .408 | .617 |
| After (1-1) | .278 | 141 | 230 | 64 | 7 | 2 | 12 | 30 | 6 | 2 | 0 | 4 | 14 | 0 | 0 | 41 | 67 | 87 | 2 | 1104 | .315 | .483 |
| After (1-2) | .219 | 102 | 151 | 33 | 2 | 0 | 4 | 11 | 2 | 0 | 0 | 1 | 4 | 0 | 0 | 56 | 29 | 49 | 0 | 804 | .237 | .311 |
| After (2-0) | .333 | 79 | 75 | 25 | 4 | 0 | 5 | 11 | 2 | 1 | 0 | 1 | 28 | 2 | 0 | 6 | 21 | 31 | 1 | 462 | .510 | .587 |
| After (2-1) | .283 | 94 | 99 | 28 | 4 | 1 | 6 | 11 | 1 | 1 | 0 | 2 | 18 | 0 | 0 | 11 | 32 | 37 | 2 | 606 | .387 | .525 |
| After (2-2) | .212 | 92 | 113 | 24 | 2 | 0 | 2 | 6 | 1 | 0 | 0 | 0 | 11 | 0 | 0 | 31 | 26 | 41 | 0 | 743 | .282 | .283 |
| After (3-0) | .313 | 35 | 16 | 5 | 1 | 0 | 1 | 2 | 0 | 0 | 0 | 0 | 20 | 0 | 0 | 1 | 7 | 5 | 0 | 174 | .694 | .563 |
| After (3-1) | .313 | 47 | 32 | 10 | 2 | 0 | 4 | 6 | 0 | 0 | 0 | 1 | 16 | 0 | 0 | 2 | 13 | 12 | 1 | 271 | .531 | .750 |
| After (3-2) | .283 | 54 | 46 | 13 | 2 | 0 | 3 | 4 | 0 | 0 | 0 | 0 | 16 | 0 | 0 | 7 | 14 | 18 | 0 | 407 | .468 | .522 |

At Each Pitch

| Result | Count | | | | | | | | | | | |
|---|---|---|---|---|---|---|---|---|---|---|---|---|
| | 0-0 | 0-1 | 0-2 | 1-0 | 1-1 | 1-2 | 2-0 | 2-1 | 2-2 | 3-0 | 3-1 | 3-2 |
| Ball | 326 | 116 | 60 | 105 | 86 | 75 | 37 | 30 | 45 | 17 | 11 | 16 |
| Taken Strike | 187 | 28 | 8 | 68 | 25 | 10 | 22 | 8 | 7 | 19 | 5 | 3 |
| Swung | 42 | 31 | 11 | 27 | 30 | 25 | 6 | 10 | 20 | 0 | 1 | 4 |
| Fouled | 54 | 46 | 19 | 50 | 41 | 31 | 12 | 31 | 44 | 1 | 12 | 20 |
| In Play | 76 | 61 | 27 | 77 | 71 | 45 | 27 | 40 | 53 | 2 | 20 | 39 |

## Baserunning

Basestealing

| Event | Which Pitch? | | | Which Count? | | | | |
|---|---|---|---|---|---|---|---|---|
| | Pitch 1 | Pitch 2 | Other | Even | Ahead | Behind | 3-2 | 2 Strikes |
| Stolen Bases | 6 | 9 | 10 | 11 | 7 | 8 | 0 | 3 |
| Pitcher Caught Stealing | 2 | 0 | 0 | 2 | 0 | 0 | 0 | 0 |
| Catcher Caught Stealing | 1 | 1 | 3 | 2 | 1 | 2 | 0 | 0 |
| Pitcher Pickoffs | 0 | 0 | 1 | 0 | 0 | 1 | 0 | 0 |
| Pitcher Pickoff Errors | 0 | 0 | 2 | 2 | 0 | 0 | 0 | 2 |

Base Stealing By Base and Pitcher

| --3rd Base-- | | | ----LHP---- | | | ----RHP---- | | | Attempts -by Out- | | | Attempts by Pitch | | | |
|---|---|---|---|---|---|---|---|---|---|---|---|---|---|---|---|
| Att | SB | Pct | Att | SB | Pct | Att | SB | Pct | 0 | 1 | 2 | 1 | 2 | 3+ | Picked Off |
| 0 | 0 | 0.0 | 8 | 1 | 87.5 | 24 | 18 | 75.0 | 4 | 13 | 15 | 9 | 10 | 13 | 1 |

On the Bases

| Extra Bases | Opportunities | Pct% |
|---|---|---|
| 69 | 132 | 52.3 |

Fielding By Position

| Pos | G | Inn | PO | A | E | DP | TP |
|---|---|---|---|---|---|---|---|
| 2B | 154 | 3945 | 284 | 472 | 8 | 85 | 0 |

## Rankings

### Compared to Other National Leaguers

| Category | Rank | Stat | Minimum |
|---|---|---|---|
| Home Runs | 1 | 40 | |
| BA at Home | 1 | .357 | 252 BFP |
| Runs Scored | 1 | 116 | |
| SLG off RHP | 1 | .616 | 377 PA |
| Total Bases | 1 | 344 | |
| SLG | 2 | .559 | 502 PA |
| Runs Created | 2 | 123 | |
| Hits | 3 | 188 | |
| AB/HR | 3 | 15.380 | 502 PA |
| Isolated Power | 3 | .254 | 502 PA |
| Power/Speed Mix | 3 | 30 | |
| BA vs RH Pitchers | 3 | .334 | 377 PA |
| Fielding Pct by Second Base | 3 | .989 | 100 Games |
| At Bats | 6 | 615 | |
| Runs Batted In | 6 | 100 | |
| Secondary Average | 6 | .364 | 502 PA |
| Offensive Win Pct | 7 | .756 | 502 PA |
| Errors by Second Base | 7 | 8 | |
| OBA off RHP | 8 | .373 | 377 PA |
| Sacrifice Flies | 8 | 9 | |
| Batter Plate Appearances | 9 | 675 | |
| Pitches Seen | 10 | 2378 | |
| Games Played | 10 | 155 | |
| Batting Average | 10 | .306 | 502 PA |

### Compared to Other Cubs Players

| Category | Rank | Stat | Minimum |
|---|---|---|---|
| SLG | 1 | .559 | 502 PA |
| Hits | 1 | 188 | |
| AB/HR | 1 | 15.380 | 502 PA |
| At Bats | 1 | 615 | |
| OBA off RHP | 1 | .373 | 377 PA |
| Stolen Bases | 1 | 25 | |
| Pitches Seen | 1 | 2378 | |
| Runs Created | 1 | 123 | |
| Isolated Power | 1 | .254 | 502 PA |
| Runs Batted In | 1 | 100 | |
| Sacrifice Flies | 1 | 9 | |
| Caught Stealing | 1 | 7 | |
| Power/Speed Mix | 1 | 30 | |
| BA vs RH Pitchers | 1 | .334 | 377 PA |
| Secondary Average | 1 | .364 | 502 PA |
| Offensive Win Pct | 1 | .756 | 502 PA |
| BA after 6th Inning | 1 | .335 | 150 PA |
| Errors by Second Base | 1 | 8 | |
| Batter Plate Appearances | 1 | 675 | |
| Fielding Pct by Second Base | 1 | .989 | 100 Gm |

### Compared to Other National League Players At Second Base

| Category | Rank | Stat | Minimum |
|---|---|---|---|
| SLG | 1 | .559 | 502 PA |
| Hits | 1 | 188 | |
| AB/HR | 1 | 15.38 | 502 PA |
| At Bats | 1 | 615 | |
| OBA off RHP | 1 | .373 | 377 PA |
| Runs Created | 1 | 123 | |
| Isolated Power | 1 | .254 | 502 PA |
| Runs Batted In | 1 | 100 | |
| Batting Average | 1 | .306 | 502 PA |
| Sacrifice Flies | 1 | 9 | |
| Power/Speed Mix | 1 | 30 | |
| BA vs RH Pitchers | 1 | .334 | 377 PA |
| Offensive Win Pct | 1 | .756 | 502 PA |
| Secondary Average | 1 | .364 | 502 PA |
| BA after 6th Inning | 1 | .335 | 150 PA |
| Batter Plate Appearances | 1 | 675 | |

## Active Pitchers vs. Ryne Sandberg

(10 or more At Bats Since 1985)

| Pitcher | AVG | AB | H | 2B | 3B | HR | RBI | W | K | SB | CS |
|---|---|---|---|---|---|---|---|---|---|---|---|
| GULLICKSON, Bi | .484 | 31 | 15 | 2 | 0 | 2 | 10 | 1 | 4 | 5 | 0 |
| LACOSS, Mike | .481 | 27 | 13 | 2 | 0 | 3 | 3 | 3 | 0 | 1 | 3 |
| OJEDA, Bobby | .458 | 24 | 11 | 0 | 0 | 3 | 8 | 2 | 1 | 4 | 0 |
| HUDSON, Charli | .444 | 18 | 8 | 0 | 0 | 3 | 5 | 3 | 2 | 1 | 0 |
| KNEPPER, Bob | .421 | 19 | 8 | 1 | 0 | 1 | 3 | 3 | 1 | 1 | 0 |
| TOLIVER, Fred | .417 | 12 | 5 | 0 | 0 | 1 | 1 | 0 | 3 | 1 | 1 |
| SEBRA, Bob | .417 | 12 | 5 | 0 | 0 | 0 | 2 | 3 | 0 | 2 | 0 |
| HEATON, Neal | .412 | 17 | 7 | 3 | 0 | 1 | 3 | 1 | 0 | 0 | 0 |
| CARMAN, Don | .412 | 17 | 7 | 1 | 1 | 2 | 5 | 4 | 3 | 2 | 0 |
| YOUMANS, Floyd | .400 | 30 | 12 | 3 | 0 | 3 | 5 | 7 | 1 | 5 | 0 |
| KRUKOW, Mike | .393 | 28 | 11 | 0 | 0 | 1 | 1 | 0 | 4 | 2 | 0 |
| JACKSON, Danny | .385 | 13 | 5 | 2 | 0 | 0 | 4 | 0 | 3 | 0 | 0 |
| HILL, Ken | .385 | 13 | 5 | 0 | 0 | 1 | 1 | 3 | 0 | 3 | 1 |
| MULHOLLAND, Te | .381 | 21 | 8 | 0 | 1 | 3 | 6 | 2 | 2 | 0 | 0 |
| GROSS, Kevin | .378 | 45 | 17 | 1 | 1 | 1 | 4 | 2 | 7 | 5 | 0 |
| WELCH, Bob | .375 | 24 | 9 | 2 | 0 | 0 | 1 | 2 | 1 | 1 | 0 |
| ROBINSON, Don | .375 | 32 | 12 | 0 | 2 | 1 | 4 | 2 | 4 | 3 | 0 |
| VIOLA, Frank | .375 | 16 | 6 | 0 | 0 | 2 | 2 | 4 | 6 | 0 | 1 |
| MARTINEZ, Denn | .370 | 46 | 17 | 2 | 1 | 4 | 9 | 0 | 3 | 1 | 0 |
| DAWLEY, Bill | .364 | 11 | 4 | 1 | 0 | 1 | 2 | 1 | 2 | 0 | 0 |
| PENA, Alejandr | .364 | 22 | 8 | 3 | 0 | 1 | 5 | 1 | 2 | 1 | 0 |
| WALK, Bob | .360 | 25 | 9 | 2 | 0 | 2 | 6 | 3 | 3 | 1 | 1 |
| HONEYCUTT, Ric | .360 | 25 | 9 | 2 | 0 | 1 | 2 | 2 | 3 | 1 | 0 |
| BEDROSIAN, Ste | .357 | 28 | 10 | 2 | 0 | 0 | 3 | 1 | 4 | 1 | 1 |
| MAHLER, Rick | .356 | 45 | 16 | 1 | 0 | 4 | 10 | 7 | 3 | 1 | 1 |
| DUNNE, Mike | .353 | 17 | 6 | 1 | 0 | 0 | 0 | 0 | 1 | 1 | 0 |
| PORTUGAL, Mark | .350 | 20 | 7 | 0 | 0 | 1 | 4 | 2 | 2 | 1 | 0 |
| TERRY, Scott | .346 | 26 | 9 | 2 | 0 | 5 | 9 | 0 | 3 | 0 | 1 |
| RASMUSSEN, Den | .345 | 29 | 10 | 3 | 0 | 1 | 5 | 3 | 3 | 1 | 1 |
| GOODEN, Dwight | .342 | 73 | 25 | 3 | 0 | 1 | 7 | 3 | 12 | 5 | 3 |
| NIEDENFUER, To | .333 | 12 | 4 | 0 | 0 | 0 | 1 | 0 | 0 | 0 | 0 |
| BROWNING, Tom | .333 | 57 | 19 | 4 | 0 | 2 | 9 | 6 | 8 | 3 | 1 |
| MADDUX, Mike | .333 | 21 | 7 | 2 | 0 | 0 | 2 | 2 | 3 | 1 | 0 |
| WORRELL, Todd | .333 | 18 | 6 | 2 | 0 | 0 | 4 | 1 | 3 | 0 | 0 |
| SMITH, Zane | .321 | 28 | 9 | 0 | 0 | 0 | 1 | 5 | 5 | 0 | 1 |
| POWER, Ted | .318 | 22 | 7 | 0 | 0 | 1 | 1 | 2 | 1 | 3 | 0 |
| LEARY, Tim | .316 | 19 | 6 | 0 | 1 | 1 | 3 | 0 | 3 | 1 | 0 |
| ROBINSON, Ron | .316 | 19 | 6 | 1 | 0 | 2 | 6 | 1 | 3 | 0 | 0 |
| TERRELL, Walt | .316 | 19 | 6 | 0 | 0 | 2 | 2 | 1 | 1 | 0 | 0 |
| MORGAN, Mike | .316 | 19 | 6 | 0 | 0 | 0 | 1 | 0 | 1 | 1 | 0 |
| MCGAFFIGAN, An | .310 | 29 | 9 | 3 | 0 | 1 | 5 | 1 | 7 | 3 | 0 |
| LILLIQUIST, De | .308 | 13 | 4 | 1 | 0 | 0 | 0 | 0 | 0 | 0 | 0 |
| LEFFERTS, Crai | .308 | 13 | 4 | 2 | 0 | 0 | 0 | 0 | 3 | 0 | 1 |
| DARWIN, Danny | .300 | 20 | 6 | 0 | 0 | 3 | 4 | 3 | 4 | 0 | 0 |
| SCOTT, Mike | .295 | 44 | 13 | 2 | 1 | 4 | 8 | 4 | 12 | 3 | 1 |
| VALENZUELA, Fe | .294 | 34 | 10 | 2 | 0 | 2 | 10 | 9 | 7 | 0 | 1 |
| DESHAIES, Jim | .294 | 17 | 5 | 1 | 0 | 0 | 3 | 1 | 2 | 0 | 0 |
| CONE, David | .290 | 31 | 9 | 1 | 2 | 1 | 8 | 3 | 8 | 0 | 1 |
| MCCULLERS, Lan | .286 | 14 | 4 | 2 | 1 | 0 | 0 | 1 | 2 | 0 | 0 |
| GARRELTS, Scot | .286 | 35 | 10 | 1 | 0 | 1 | 2 | 1 | 4 | 3 | 0 |
| HAMMAKER, Atle | .286 | 21 | 6 | 1 | 0 | 0 | 0 | 1 | 4 | 1 | 0 |
| LEACH, Terry | .280 | 25 | 7 | 0 | 0 | 0 | 1 | 0 | 2 | 2 | 1 |
| RUFFIN, Bruce | .279 | 43 | 12 | 4 | 0 | 0 | 2 | 5 | 4 | 1 | 0 |
| GLAVINE, Tom | .278 | 18 | 5 | 3 | 1 | 1 | 3 | 0 | 1 | 1 | 0 |
| AGUILERA, Rick | .278 | 18 | 5 | 0 | 0 | 0 | 3 | 1 | 5 | 0 | 0 |
| DRABEK, Doug | .275 | 51 | 14 | 1 | 0 | 1 | 4 | 2 | 4 | 4 | 0 |
| MCDOWELL, Roge | .273 | 33 | 9 | 1 | 0 | 1 | 8 | 0 | 4 | 1 | 0 |
| GUANTE, Cecili | .273 | 11 | 3 | 0 | 1 | 0 | 2 | 0 | 3 | 0 | 0 |
| CARPENTER, Cri | .273 | 11 | 3 | 1 | 0 | 0 | 0 | 1 | 2 | 0 | 0 |
| RAWLEY, Shane | .268 | 41 | 11 | 2 | 0 | 1 | 2 | 2 | 7 | 3 | 0 |
| HAWKINS, Andy | .258 | 31 | 8 | 0 | 1 | 1 | 4 | 2 | 1 | 1 | 0 |
| PEREZ, Pascual | .250 | 12 | 3 | 0 | 0 | 0 | 0 | 1 | 6 | 1 | 1 |
| GOTT, Jim | .250 | 20 | 5 | 1 | 0 | 1 | 2 | 0 | 6 | 0 | 0 |
| DELEON, Jose | .235 | 51 | 12 | 1 | 0 | 3 | 5 | 7 | 12 | 2 | 1 |
| WHITSON, Ed | .235 | 34 | 8 | 1 | 0 | 2 | 5 | 0 | 8 | 0 | 0 |
| REUSCHEL, Rick | .234 | 47 | 11 | 1 | 0 | 0 | 2 | 3 | 8 | 0 | 0 |
| BURKE, Tim | .231 | 26 | 6 | 1 | 0 | 1 | 1 | 3 | 7 | 2 | 0 |
| COX, Danny | .226 | 31 | 7 | 2 | 0 | 1 | 4 | 5 | 2 | 2 | 0 |
| MAGRANE, Joe | .222 | 27 | 6 | 1 | 0 | 1 | 3 | 4 | 3 | 0 | 0 |
| DRAVECKY, Dave | .222 | 18 | 4 | 0 | 0 | 0 | 3 | 1 | 1 | 0 | 0 |
| TUDOR, John | .217 | 46 | 10 | 1 | 1 | 1 | 3 | 3 | 2 | 0 | 0 |
| HERSHISER, Ore | .214 | 28 | 6 | 2 | 0 | 0 | 2 | 2 | 6 | 3 | 0 |
| PARRETT, Jeff | .214 | 14 | 3 | 0 | 0 | 0 | 0 | 1 | 1 | 0 | 0 |
| SMILEY, John | .214 | 28 | 6 | 1 | 0 | 1 | 2 | 0 | 6 | 1 | 0 |
| KRAMER, Randy | .214 | 14 | 3 | 1 | 0 | 0 | 1 | 0 | 3 | 0 | 0 |
| ROBINSON, Jeff | .214 | 28 | 6 | 3 | 0 | 1 | 3 | 4 | 4 | 1 | 1 |
| FRANCO, John | .214 | 14 | 3 | 0 | 0 | 0 | 3 | 5 | 3 | 0 | 0 |
| BELCHER, Tim | .214 | 28 | 6 | 2 | 0 | 1 | 4 | 1 | 1 | 0 | 0 |
| DARLING, Ron | .213 | 61 | 13 | 4 | 1 | 2 | 7 | 11 | 18 | 4 | 4 |
| FERNANDEZ, Sid | .192 | 52 | 10 | 3 | 0 | 2 | 5 | 6 | 8 | 2 | 1 |
| RYAN, Nolan | .192 | 26 | 5 | 0 | 0 | 2 | 2 | 4 | 7 | 2 | 2 |
| TIBBS, Jay | .190 | 21 | 4 | 0 | 0 | 0 | 0 | 3 | 3 | 1 | 0 |
| SHOW, Eric | .190 | 21 | 4 | 0 | 0 | 2 | 5 | 2 | 4 | 2 | 0 |
| ACKER, Jim | .188 | 16 | 3 | 0 | 0 | 0 | 0 | 1 | 4 | 0 | 0 |
| SMOLTZ, John | .188 | 16 | 3 | 0 | 0 | 1 | 1 | 2 | 2 | 1 | 0 |
| RHODEN, Rick | .185 | 27 | 5 | 1 | 0 | 2 | 2 | 2 | 4 | 1 | 0 |
| SCHATZEDER, Da | .182 | 11 | 2 | 0 | 0 | 0 | 1 | 2 | 3 | 0 | 0 |
| MYERS, Randy | .182 | 11 | 2 | 0 | 0 | 1 | 1 | 0 | 2 | 0 | 0 |
| SMITH, Bryn | .154 | 52 | 8 | 2 | 0 | 2 | 4 | 9 | 8 | 4 | 0 |
| MATHEWS, Greg | .154 | 13 | 2 | 0 | 0 | 1 | 2 | 2 | 0 | 0 | 0 |
| GRANT, Mark | .143 | 14 | 2 | 0 | 0 | 1 | 2 | 2 | 2 | 0 | 0 |
| SMITH, Pete | .136 | 22 | 3 | 0 | 0 | 1 | 2 | 1 | 3 | 0 | 0 |
| HOWELL, Ken | .136 | 22 | 3 | 1 | 0 | 0 | 3 | 1 | 7 | 0 | 2 |
| BIELECKI, Mike | .133 | 15 | 2 | 0 | 1 | 1 | 1 | 2 | 1 | 0 | 1 |
| ANDERSEN, Larr | .125 | 24 | 3 | 0 | 0 | 0 | 2 | 0 | 6 | 0 | 0 |
| MCWILLIAMS, La | .111 | 18 | 2 | 1 | 0 | 1 | 2 | 2 | 2 | 0 | 0 |
| KIPPER, Bob | .111 | 18 | 2 | 1 | 0 | 0 | 0 | 1 | 1 | 0 | 0 |
| GARDNER, Mark | .100 | 10 | 1 | 1 | 0 | 0 | 0 | 2 | 3 | 1 | 0 |
| BOYD, Oil Can | .100 | 10 | 1 | 0 | 0 | 1 | 1 | 0 | 1 | 1 | 0 |
| DAVIS, Mark | .100 | 10 | 1 | 0 | 0 | 0 | 0 | 2 | 0 | 1 | 0 |
| RIJO, Jose | .077 | 13 | 1 | 0 | 0 | 0 | 0 | 0 | 4 | 0 | 0 |
| MARTINEZ, Ramo | .000 | 11 | 0 | 0 | 0 | 0 | 0 | 0 | 3 | 0 | 0 |

This page intentionally left blank.

# 1991 Projections

When John Dewan asked me, a year ago, if I wanted to include projected player stats for next season in this Handbook, my reaction wasn't very positive. I didn't think we could make the projections accurately enough for them to have real value, but John persisted, and eventually I agreed to work with him on them.

To be frank, after the first year I'm shocked at how well we did. We projected many, many players to do almost exactly what they did, while encountering, of course, a certain number of bloops, twists, and unexpected injuries. The way I evaluate predictions is by similarity scorers; if the predicted season is similar to the actual season, the system has scored a success. Similarity scores compare seasons on a scale of zero to a thousand; if two players had identical stats in a season, the score would be 1000.

We didn't score any 1,000s—in fact, there probably aren't any 1,000s. There probably aren't any two seasons in baseball history which are statistically identical in more than about 50 at bats. But we came remarkably close a number of times. The best prediction in this chart last season was for Rick Dempsey. The first line below shows what we projected Dempsey would do, the second line what he actually did. The similarity is scored at 980:

| **Rick Dempsey** | Avg | G | AB | R | H | 2B | 3B | HR | RBI | BB | SO | SB | CS |
|---|---|---|---|---|---|---|---|---|---|---|---|---|---|
| Projected | .189 | 58 | 143 | 15 | 27 | 6 | 0 | 2 | 13 | 25 | 37 | 0 | 0 |
| Actual | .195 | 62 | 128 | 13 | 25 | 5 | 0 | 2 | 15 | 23 | 29 | 1 | 0 |

Slugging Percentage and on-base percentage, though not displayed here, are also among the elements of similarity which are evaluated.

The second-best match was for Ozzie Smith (974), followed by Kent Hrbek (971). These are the stats for Hrbek:

| **Kent Hrbek** | Avg | G | AB | R | H | 2B | 3B | HR | RBI | BB | SO | SB | CS |
|---|---|---|---|---|---|---|---|---|---|---|---|---|---|
| Projected | .288 | 130 | 468 | 75 | 135 | 25 | 1 | 22 | 79 | 74 | 51 | 2 | 1 |
| Actual | .287 | 143 | 492 | 61 | 141 | 26 | 0 | 22 | 79 | 69 | 45 | 5 | 2 |

Damn, I could have sworn he was going to stretch that double on August 8 into a triple. A few other players that we hit pretty good include B.J. Surhoff, Jose Lind, Jody Reed, Julio Franco, Tony Pena and Dale Murphy:

| **B.J.Surhoff** | Avg | G | AB | R | H | 2B | 3B | HR | RBI | BB | SO | SB | CS |
|---|---|---|---|---|---|---|---|---|---|---|---|---|---|
| Projected | .268 | 136 | 471 | 51 | 126 | 21 | 2 | 6 | 58 | 34 | 34 | 21 | 13 |
| Actual | .278 | 135 | 474 | 55 | 131 | 21 | 4 | 6 | 59 | 41 | 37 | 18 | 7 |

Do you know what the B.J. in B.J. Surhoff stands for, by the way. It stands for Bill James—his name is William James Surhoff.

| **Jose Lind** | Avg | G | AB | R | H | 2B | 3B | HR | RBI | BB | SO | SB | CS |
|---|---|---|---|---|---|---|---|---|---|---|---|---|---|
| Projected | .262 | 141 | 549 | 65 | 144 | 22 | 4 | 1 | 47 | 38 | 56 | 16 | 5 |
| Actual | .261 | 152 | 514 | 46 | 134 | 28 | 5 | 1 | 48 | 35 | 52 | 8 | 0 |

| **Jody Reed** | Avg | G | AB | R | H | 2B | 3B | HR | RBI | BB | SO | SB | CS |
|---|---|---|---|---|---|---|---|---|---|---|---|---|---|
| Projected | .291 | 155 | 550 | 86 | 160 | 37 | 2 | 2 | 50 | 79 | 36 | 6 | 6 |
| Actual | .289 | 155 | 598 | 70 | 173 | 45 | 0 | 5 | 51 | 75 | 65 | 4 | 4 |

| **Julio Franco** | Avg | G | AB | R | H | 2B | 3B | HR | RBI | BB | SO | SB | CS |
|---|---|---|---|---|---|---|---|---|---|---|---|---|---|
| Projected | .299 | 153 | 595 | 89 | 178 | 27 | 4 | 8 | 67 | 68 | 70 | 23 | 8 |
| Actual | .296 | 157 | 582 | 96 | 172 | 27 | 1 | 11 | 69 | 82 | 83 | 31 | 10 |

| **Tony Pena** | Avg | G | AB | R | H | 2B | 3B | HR | RBI | BB | SO | SB | CS |
|---|---|---|---|---|---|---|---|---|---|---|---|---|---|
| Projected | .257 | 137 | 474 | 48 | 122 | 21 | 1 | 8 | 50 | 38 | 55 | 4 | 2 |
| Actual | .263 | 143 | 491 | 62 | 129 | 19 | 1 | 7 | 56 | 43 | 71 | 8 | 6 |

| **Dale Murphy** | Avg | G | AB | R | H | 2B | 3B | HR | RBI | BB | SO | SB | CS |
|---|---|---|---|---|---|---|---|---|---|---|---|---|---|
| Projected | .245 | 143 | 527 | 73 | 129 | 21 | 1 | 23 | 76 | 79 | 128 | 4 | 2 |
| Actual | .245 | 154 | 563 | 60 | 138 | 23 | 1 | 24 | 83 | 61 | 130 | 9 | 3 |

All of these similarity scores are over 950. The scale that I use for interpreting similarity scores is this:

**below 750:** the two seasons compared cannot be considered similar in any significant sense.

**750-799:** the two seasons have slight similarities.

**800-849:** the seasons have significant similarities but also important differences.

**850-899:** the season have some differences but important similarities.

**900 or higher:** the seasons are truly similar.

**950 or above:** the true similarities of the players have been emphasized by coincidental likenesses.

There were 382 projections printed in the book last year. Of those 382, an astonishing 47 scored at 950 or above, and essentially one-half (49%) scored at 900 or better. The median was 898. This is the spread of scores:

| 950+ | 900-949 | 850-899 | 800-849 | 750-799 | 700-749 | Below 700 |
|---|---|---|---|---|---|---|
| 47 | 140 | 83 | 45 | 14 | 8 | 45 |

Having shown you the best projections, I am honor bound now to acquaint you with the worst. The system of similarity scores, however, is not as good at calibrating difference as it is similarity: how "different" two things are is harder to say than how similar.

The lowest similarity scores result when a player is projected to play but didn't. The lowest similarity score between projected and actual performance in 1990 is for Rob Richie, a Detroit prospect whom we projected to hit .289 with 14 homers, 66 RBI. Instead, he joined Jehovah's Witnesses, quit baseball and spent his summer harassing shut-ins or whatever they do; in any case, it wasn't very similar to .289 with 14 homers and 66 RBI. The similarity was scored at 115.

All of the lowest scores are like that—players who were projected to play but didn't for one reason or another, like Joey Meyer, Benny Distefano and Jim Rice. Even if you're projected to play only a few games and don't, as the system is currently written, it results in a very low similarity score.

So 71% of the players were projected with an accuracy of 850 or better, but if you leave out the guys who were projected to play but didn't—Jeff Richardson—it's well over 80%. I'm amazed that we did that well.

Among players who were projected to play and did, the worst projections are for two groups of players: those who had great years, and those who had terrible years. The lowest similarity score for a player projected to play in 100 games who did play in 100 games was Don Mattingly, at 665:

| **Don Mattingly** | Avg | G | AB | R | H | 2B | 3B | HR | RBI | BB | SO | SB | CS |
|---|---|---|---|---|---|---|---|---|---|---|---|---|---|
| Projected | .320 | 155 | 615 | 95 | 197 | 42 | 2 | 25 | 111 | 51 | 33 | 1 | 1 |
| Actual | .256 | 102 | 394 | 40 | 101 | 16 | 0 | 5 | 42 | 28 | 20 | 1 | 0 |

Mattingly was the king of the disappointments of 1990; he was followed by Jerome Walton (802), Pete O'Brien (812), Dwight Smith (816), and Oddibe McDowell (834), all of whom, I am perversely proud to say, were on my

Fantasy League team for a good part of the summer (can I pick a winner, or what?).

On the other side, the player who most exceeded expectations was Ronnie Gant:

| Ronnie Gant | Avg | G | AB | R | H | 2B | 3B | HR | RBI | BB | SO | SB | CS |
|---|---|---|---|---|---|---|---|---|---|---|---|---|---|
| Projected | .247 | 107 | 392 | 55 | 97 | 18 | 3 | 14 | 47 | 36 | 70 | 16 | 9 |
| Actual | .303 | 152 | 575 | 107 | 174 | 34 | 3 | 32 | 84 | 50 | 86 | 33 | 16 |

The score is 735. Next to him are Darren Daulton (789) and Rickey Henderson (800). This is Rickey:

| Rickey Henderson | Avg | G | AB | R | H | 2B | 3B | HR | RBI | BB | SO | SB | CS |
|---|---|---|---|---|---|---|---|---|---|---|---|---|---|
| Projected | .284 | 135 | 504 | 104 | 143 | 24 | 2 | 12 | 49 | 103 | 60 | 52 | 9 |
| Actual | .325 | 136 | 489 | 119 | 159 | 33 | 3 | 28 | 61 | 97 | 60 | 65 | 10 |

He's something, isn't he? It's not like we projected him to hit .207. We projected him to be great, and we projected his playing time almost perfectly. He was just twice as great as he had been before. Other leading over-achievers included Matt Williams, Lenny Dykstra, Kelly Gruber, Candy Maldonado, Ryne Sandberg, Eddie Murray and Franklin Stubbs.

The system could still work a lot better than it does, and in fact we have made a dozen or more changes to the projection system for this year's book. Last year we radically over-projected stolen base totals for younger players, for example, and under-projected them for veterans. We had the batting averages of younger players too high, and those of older players too low. We projected way too much playing time for certain types of over-the-hill veterans. There are some other changes in the system that we're working on, and the system will be a little different—and a little better—next year.

Statistically, we won't do as well on the average next year as we did this year because we're trying to do more. Last year we projected 382 players; this year I think it will be at least a hundred more than that. Many of those extra players won't play at all, and will show up in the evaluation with very low scores. But after all, we're not trying to build up a score. We're trying to show you what we think these guys can do if they play. We think that if Andy Tomberlin plays, there is a heck of a chance he'll hit .300; we also know there is a good chance he won't play. We think that if Francisco Cabrera is a regular, he'll put up some good numbers; we realize that the Braves may continue to diddle around with him. If Jeff Conine plays, on the basis of what we know we think he will hit like Mark Grace. We certainly recognize that he may spend the summer on the beaches on Omaha. What you want to know, presumably, is this: If Milt Cuyler plays, how will he do?

The real value of this information, in all likelihood, is the young players. Most of you, I suspect, can evaluate what Brett Butler will do this year about as well as I can, or make about as good a guess whether Don Mattingly can come back from his injury. What we can do better than most of you is evaluate minor league performance and project it into a major league setting.

I would have thought, because we think of the young as unpredictable, that the projections for younger players would tend to be less accurate than those for veterans. In fact, the opposite was true; our projections for young players were somewhat better than those for veterans. Among the young players that we projected accurately last year, based primarily on their minor league stats, were Sammie Sosa (900), Greg Jeffries (954), Robin Ventura (921), Omar Vizquel (955), Carlos Quintana (910), Bill Spiers (932), Greg Vaughn (932) and Todd Zeile (949). Of course we also hit a few clinkers, like Eric Anthony (777), Joey Belle (688), Scott Coolbaugh (733) and Mark Lemke (740), but all of those, without any exception, were for players who batted less that 250 times in the major leagues. My experience has always been that within two or three years, virtually all of those players will have the seasons that we projected for them.

Hope you like them. Here's my advice for next year: Don't Draft Darren Daulton.

# Projections for 1991 Batters

| Batter | Age | Avg | G | AB | R | H | 2B | 3B | HR | RBI | BB | SO | SB | CS | OBP | SLG |
|---|---|---|---|---|---|---|---|---|---|---|---|---|---|---|---|---|
| Abner,Shawn | 25 | .227 | 80 | 216 | 21 | 49 | 9 | 2 | 4 | 22 | 10 | 42 | 2 | 2 | .261 | .343 |
| Aldrete,Mike | 30 | .255 | 93 | 216 | 26 | 55 | 11 | 1 | 3 | 26 | 37 | 40 | 3 | 3 | .364 | .356 |
| Alomar,Roberto | 23 | .292 | 154 | 600 | 87 | 175 | 28 | 4 | 9 | 58 | 53 | 72 | 32 | 12 | .349 | .397 |
| Alomar Jr,Sandy | 25 | .271 | 135 | 450 | 56 | 122 | 23 | 4 | 10 | 64 | 27 | 45 | 2 | 1 | .312 | .407 |
| Alou,Moises | 24 | .270 | 104 | 400 | 55 | 108 | 8 | 4 | 7 | 41 | 39 | 64 | 15 | 11 | .335 | .363 |
| Anderson,Brady | 27 | .236 | 87 | 259 | 34 | 61 | 9 | 2 | 4 | 23 | 34 | 47 | 14 | 6 | .324 | .332 |
| Anderson,Dave | 30 | .237 | 92 | 211 | 23 | 50 | 8 | 1 | 2 | 17 | 22 | 37 | 3 | 2 | .309 | .313 |
| Anderson,Kent | 27 | .234 | 87 | 244 | 26 | 57 | 9 | 1 | 1 | 19 | 17 | 40 | 3 | 2 | .284 | .291 |
| Anthony,Eric | 23 | .247 | 155 | 550 | 73 | 136 | 17 | 1 | 27 | 81 | 53 | 163 | 14 | 7 | .313 | .429 |
| Azocar,Oscar | 26 | .270 | 106 | 370 | 43 | 100 | 17 | 4 | 5 | 46 | 9 | 28 | 10 | 5 | .288 | .378 |
| Backman,Wally | 31 | .266 | 111 | 335 | 49 | 89 | 14 | 1 | 1 | 25 | 43 | 54 | 6 | 4 | .349 | .322 |
| Baerga,Carlos | 22 | .248 | 94 | 310 | 36 | 77 | 18 | 1 | 6 | 38 | 14 | 54 | 2 | 2 | .281 | .371 |
| Baines,Harold | 32 | .272 | 146 | 537 | 61 | 146 | 27 | 3 | 17 | 76 | 75 | 95 | 1 | 1 | .361 | .428 |
| Balboni,Steve | 34 | .223 | 82 | 247 | 26 | 55 | 10 | 1 | 13 | 39 | 22 | 64 | 0 | 0 | .286 | .429 |
| Barfield,Jesse | 31 | .243 | 147 | 490 | 70 | 119 | 23 | 2 | 23 | 68 | 72 | 136 | 6 | 4 | .340 | .439 |
| Barrett,Marty | 33 | .269 | 62 | 201 | 24 | 54 | 10 | 0 | 1 | 20 | 16 | 11 | 2 | 1 | .323 | .333 |
| Bass,Kevin | 32 | .263 | 99 | 315 | 36 | 83 | 16 | 2 | 8 | 43 | 26 | 40 | 13 | 4 | .320 | .403 |
| Bell,George | 31 | .276 | 144 | 550 | 72 | 152 | 29 | 3 | 23 | 93 | 31 | 63 | 3 | 2 | .315 | .465 |
| Bell,Jay | 25 | .257 | 157 | 571 | 86 | 147 | 24 | 5 | 12 | 66 | 65 | 106 | 13 | 8 | .333 | .380 |
| Bell,Mike | 23 | .260 | 60 | 100 | 14 | 26 | 12 | 1 | 1 | 13 | 11 | 16 | 1 | 1 | .333 | .430 |
| Benjamin,Mike | 25 | .219 | 72 | 114 | 16 | 25 | 9 | 2 | 1 | 11 | 6 | 24 | 2 | 1 | .258 | .360 |
| Benzinger,Todd | 28 | .254 | 103 | 351 | 41 | 89 | 18 | 1 | 10 | 48 | 22 | 61 | 3 | 3 | .298 | .396 |
| Bergman,Dave | 38 | .253 | 103 | 190 | 19 | 48 | 7 | 1 | 3 | 20 | 25 | 22 | 1 | 1 | .340 | .347 |
| Berroa,Geronimo | 26 | .271 | 66 | 129 | 16 | 35 | 11 | 1 | 4 | 21 | 10 | 23 | 1 | 1 | .324 | .465 |
| Berry,Sean | 25 | .264 | 80 | 250 | 31 | 66 | 13 | 3 | 5 | 33 | 19 | 47 | 7 | 4 | .316 | .400 |
| Berryhill,Damon | 27 | .258 | 110 | 380 | 34 | 98 | 19 | 0 | 7 | 47 | 22 | 62 | 1 | 0 | .299 | .363 |
| Bichette,Dante | 27 | .237 | 106 | 350 | 37 | 83 | 16 | 2 | 11 | 45 | 17 | 60 | 5 | 3 | .272 | .389 |
| Biggio,Craig | 25 | .271 | 155 | 550 | 70 | 149 | 25 | 3 | 10 | 56 | 56 | 77 | 27 | 9 | .338 | .382 |
| Blankenship,Lance | 27 | .219 | 59 | 146 | 23 | 32 | 6 | 1 | 1 | 12 | 23 | 27 | 8 | 3 | .325 | .295 |
| Blauser,Jeff | 25 | .271 | 134 | 487 | 63 | 132 | 26 | 3 | 11 | 49 | 40 | 89 | 6 | 5 | .326 | .405 |
| Blowers,Mike | 26 | .256 | 35 | 90 | 9 | 23 | 5 | 1 | 3 | 12 | 10 | 21 | 1 | 0 | .330 | .433 |
| Boggs,Wade | 33 | .328 | 151 | 579 | 101 | 190 | 39 | 3 | 7 | 55 | 103 | 51 | 2 | 2 | .430 | .442 |
| Bonds,Barry | 26 | .278 | 156 | 564 | 106 | 157 | 35 | 6 | 28 | 83 | 93 | 86 | 36 | 13 | .381 | .511 |
| Bonilla,Bobby | 28 | .278 | 161 | 576 | 92 | 160 | 34 | 6 | 26 | 95 | 68 | 88 | 6 | 5 | .354 | .493 |
| Boone,Bob | 43 | .235 | 41 | 102 | 8 | 24 | 4 | 0 | 1 | 10 | 11 | 10 | 1 | 0 | .310 | .304 |
| Borders,Pat | 28 | .272 | 127 | 372 | 36 | 101 | 21 | 2 | 12 | 49 | 21 | 59 | 1 | 1 | .310 | .435 |
| Boston,Daryl | 28 | .251 | 126 | 347 | 55 | 87 | 17 | 3 | 11 | 40 | 31 | 50 | 14 | 6 | .312 | .412 |
| Bradley,Phil | 32 | .277 | 116 | 411 | 60 | 114 | 20 | 3 | 8 | 40 | 48 | 72 | 13 | 7 | .353 | .399 |
| Bradley,Scott | 31 | .252 | 98 | 266 | 24 | 67 | 13 | 1 | 3 | 32 | 17 | 19 | 1 | 1 | .297 | .342 |
| Braggs,Glenn | 28 | .257 | 131 | 459 | 62 | 118 | 20 | 3 | 13 | 61 | 41 | 98 | 13 | 7 | .318 | .399 |
| Bream,Sid | 30 | .256 | 119 | 352 | 36 | 90 | 22 | 1 | 10 | 50 | 45 | 55 | 8 | 7 | .340 | .409 |
| Brett,George | 38 | .282 | 133 | 503 | 67 | 142 | 29 | 5 | 13 | 76 | 64 | 56 | 10 | 4 | .363 | .437 |
| Briley,Greg | 26 | .262 | 125 | 420 | 52 | 110 | 21 | 4 | 9 | 46 | 41 | 66 | 17 | 8 | .328 | .395 |
| Brock,Greg | 34 | .242 | 92 | 277 | 34 | 67 | 12 | 0 | 9 | 40 | 38 | 37 | 4 | 2 | .333 | .383 |
| Brookens,Tom | 37 | .231 | 70 | 182 | 21 | 42 | 9 | 1 | 3 | 17 | 17 | 33 | 1 | 1 | .296 | .341 |

# Projections for 1991 Batters

| Batter | Age | Avg | G | AB | R | H | 2B | 3B | HR | RBI | BB | SO | SB | CS | OBP | SLG |
|---|---|---|---|---|---|---|---|---|---|---|---|---|---|---|---|---|
| Brooks,Hubie | 34 | .255 | 136 | 509 | 52 | 130 | 25 | 2 | 16 | 71 | 33 | 101 | 5 | 5 | .301 | .407 |
| Browne,Jerry | 25 | .282 | 149 | 524 | 81 | 148 | 25 | 5 | 4 | 47 | 69 | 55 | 14 | 8 | .366 | .372 |
| Brumley,Mike | 28 | .232 | 89 | 250 | 33 | 58 | 9 | 3 | 2 | 17 | 20 | 50 | 11 | 6 | .289 | .316 |
| Brunansky,Tom | 30 | .241 | 154 | 552 | 70 | 133 | 26 | 3 | 24 | 83 | 74 | 106 | 10 | 9 | .331 | .429 |
| Buechele,Steve | 29 | .231 | 109 | 321 | 41 | 74 | 14 | 1 | 11 | 38 | 35 | 64 | 1 | 1 | .306 | .383 |
| Buhner,Jay | 26 | .262 | 81 | 263 | 39 | 69 | 14 | 1 | 14 | 44 | 33 | 74 | 3 | 4 | .345 | .483 |
| Burks,Ellis | 26 | .302 | 159 | 593 | 101 | 179 | 35 | 6 | 22 | 96 | 60 | 84 | 22 | 11 | .366 | .492 |
| Bush,Randy | 32 | .249 | 96 | 241 | 31 | 60 | 13 | 2 | 8 | 29 | 32 | 37 | 4 | 4 | .337 | .419 |
| Butler,Brett | 34 | .276 | 150 | 551 | 92 | 152 | 20 | 6 | 4 | 36 | 78 | 63 | 37 | 17 | .366 | .356 |
| Cabrera,Francisco | 24 | .284 | 156 | 560 | 69 | 159 | 27 | 3 | 24 | 82 | 29 | 89 | 5 | 3 | .319 | .471 |
| Calderon,Ivan | 29 | .270 | 159 | 585 | 84 | 158 | 38 | 4 | 19 | 80 | 53 | 94 | 17 | 9 | .331 | .446 |
| Caminiti,Ken | 28 | .243 | 141 | 497 | 52 | 121 | 23 | 2 | 7 | 55 | 40 | 82 | 7 | 3 | .300 | .340 |
| Candaele,Casey | 30 | .243 | 138 | 371 | 37 | 90 | 17 | 4 | 1 | 29 | 40 | 49 | 8 | 6 | .316 | .318 |
| Canseco,Jose | 26 | .287 | 140 | 520 | 97 | 149 | 25 | 1 | 36 | 108 | 72 | 136 | 26 | 13 | .373 | .546 |
| Carreon,Mark | 27 | .265 | 99 | 287 | 42 | 76 | 15 | 1 | 8 | 37 | 28 | 40 | 7 | 5 | .330 | .408 |
| Carter,Gary | 37 | .247 | 79 | 271 | 25 | 67 | 12 | 1 | 10 | 31 | 23 | 34 | 1 | 1 | .306 | .410 |
| Carter,Joe | 31 | .253 | 152 | 584 | 75 | 148 | 28 | 2 | 25 | 96 | 38 | 88 | 20 | 6 | .299 | .437 |
| Cerone,Rick | 37 | .226 | 77 | 221 | 19 | 50 | 10 | 1 | 3 | 24 | 19 | 29 | 0 | 0 | .288 | .321 |
| Chamberlain,Wes | 25 | .276 | 110 | 370 | 44 | 102 | 22 | 2 | 12 | 54 | 25 | 59 | 10 | 10 | .322 | .443 |
| Clark,Dave | 28 | .257 | 108 | 296 | 30 | 76 | 12 | 1 | 10 | 37 | 30 | 62 | 5 | 4 | .325 | .405 |
| Clark,Jack | 35 | .224 | 134 | 456 | 72 | 102 | 22 | 2 | 18 | 75 | 126 | 139 | 4 | 3 | .392 | .399 |
| Clark,Jerald | 27 | .253 | 100 | 300 | 36 | 76 | 14 | 2 | 11 | 38 | 13 | 63 | 2 | 2 | .284 | .423 |
| Clark,Will | 27 | .304 | 157 | 576 | 100 | 175 | 33 | 5 | 26 | 105 | 81 | 108 | 8 | 3 | .390 | .514 |
| Cole,Alex | 25 | .259 | 155 | 580 | 78 | 150 | 9 | 6 | 0 | 36 | 65 | 92 | 56 | 24 | .333 | .295 |
| Coleman,Vince | 29 | .263 | 139 | 556 | 79 | 146 | 17 | 8 | 2 | 36 | 47 | 96 | 79 | 21 | .320 | .333 |
| Coles,Darnell | 29 | .243 | 81 | 251 | 28 | 61 | 12 | 1 | 7 | 32 | 18 | 36 | 2 | 2 | .294 | .382 |
| Conine,Jeff | 25 | .297 | 133 | 465 | 71 | 138 | 27 | 7 | 9 | 75 | 74 | 86 | 14 | 5 | .393 | .443 |
| Coolbaugh,Scott | 25 | .242 | 51 | 149 | 16 | 36 | 6 | 0 | 4 | 17 | 15 | 28 | 0 | 0 | .311 | .362 |
| Cooper,Scott | 23 | .270 | 40 | 100 | 13 | 27 | 7 | 0 | 2 | 11 | 11 | 18 | 0 | 0 | .342 | .400 |
| Cora,Joey | 26 | .257 | 69 | 210 | 24 | 54 | 7 | 2 | 0 | 14 | 14 | 14 | 11 | 5 | .304 | .310 |
| Cotto,Henry | 30 | .255 | 115 | 275 | 35 | 70 | 12 | 1 | 5 | 27 | 16 | 40 | 15 | 4 | .296 | .360 |
| Cuyler,Milt | 22 | .251 | 125 | 450 | 77 | 113 | 11 | 6 | 5 | 43 | 54 | 82 | 36 | 11 | .331 | .336 |
| Daniels,Kal | 27 | .294 | 125 | 435 | 85 | 128 | 25 | 2 | 22 | 71 | 81 | 90 | 8 | 3 | .405 | .513 |
| Dascenzo,Doug | 27 | .250 | 90 | 280 | 34 | 70 | 12 | 2 | 2 | 24 | 25 | 25 | 16 | 9 | .311 | .329 |
| Daugherty,Jack | 31 | .267 | 114 | 326 | 38 | 87 | 21 | 1 | 4 | 38 | 32 | 44 | 5 | 3 | .332 | .374 |
| Daulton,Darren | 29 | .237 | 145 | 410 | 45 | 97 | 19 | 1 | 12 | 50 | 63 | 60 | 4 | 2 | .338 | .376 |
| Davidson,Mark | 30 | .244 | 77 | 135 | 17 | 33 | 6 | 1 | 2 | 14 | 47 | 25 | 2 | 2 | .440 | .348 |
| Davis,Alvin | 30 | .287 | 146 | 523 | 77 | 150 | 28 | 1 | 21 | 82 | 105 | 61 | 1 | 1 | .406 | .465 |
| Davis,Chili | 31 | .257 | 138 | 499 | 67 | 128 | 23 | 2 | 16 | 73 | 58 | 100 | 4 | 4 | .334 | .407 |
| Davis,Eric | 29 | .270 | 137 | 456 | 80 | 123 | 20 | 3 | 30 | 92 | 67 | 112 | 25 | 6 | .363 | .524 |
| Davis,Glenn | 30 | .254 | 145 | 515 | 72 | 131 | 26 | 2 | 27 | 83 | 62 | 89 | 6 | 3 | .334 | .470 |
| Dawson,Andre | 36 | .271 | 136 | 520 | 64 | 141 | 26 | 4 | 20 | 78 | 39 | 74 | 11 | 4 | .322 | .452 |
| Decker,Steve | 25 | .289 | 135 | 485 | 56 | 140 | 17 | 1 | 16 | 75 | 39 | 76 | 5 | 8 | .342 | .427 |
| Deer,Rob | 30 | .226 | 135 | 446 | 65 | 101 | 17 | 1 | 26 | 71 | 59 | 146 | 6 | 5 | .317 | .444 |
| DeShields,Delino | 22 | .277 | 156 | 577 | 84 | 160 | 28 | 9 | 5 | 55 | 84 | 128 | 52 | 25 | .369 | .383 |

# Projections for 1991 Batters

| Batter | Age | Avg | G | AB | R | H | 2B | 3B | HR | RBI | BB | SO | SB | CS | OBP | SLG |
|---|---|---|---|---|---|---|---|---|---|---|---|---|---|---|---|---|
| Devereaux,Mike | 28 | .254 | 119 | 398 | 54 | 101 | 17 | 2 | 10 | 48 | 32 | 55 | 19 | 11 | .309 | .382 |
| Doran,Billy | 33 | .254 | 135 | 489 | 65 | 124 | 21 | 3 | 7 | 51 | 73 | 66 | 22 | 7 | .351 | .352 |
| Downing,Brian | 40 | .244 | 119 | 393 | 48 | 96 | 16 | 1 | 11 | 43 | 55 | 62 | 1 | 1 | .337 | .374 |
| Ducey,Rob | 26 | .265 | 80 | 200 | 25 | 53 | 13 | 3 | 3 | 24 | 26 | 44 | 5 | 3 | .350 | .405 |
| Duncan,Mariano | 28 | .261 | 127 | 445 | 60 | 116 | 17 | 4 | 7 | 44 | 20 | 78 | 21 | 10 | .292 | .364 |
| Dunston,Shawon | 28 | .258 | 155 | 550 | 68 | 142 | 27 | 5 | 13 | 64 | 22 | 97 | 25 | 10 | .287 | .396 |
| Dykstra,Lenny | 28 | .284 | 152 | 578 | 88 | 164 | 31 | 4 | 10 | 51 | 71 | 54 | 37 | 11 | .362 | .403 |
| Eisenreich,Jim | 32 | .273 | 120 | 370 | 46 | 101 | 23 | 3 | 5 | 40 | 27 | 36 | 15 | 8 | .322 | .392 |
| Elster,Kevin | 26 | .226 | 124 | 359 | 41 | 81 | 18 | 1 | 9 | 43 | 32 | 49 | 2 | 1 | .289 | .357 |
| Espinoza,Alvaro | 29 | .249 | 134 | 405 | 36 | 101 | 12 | 2 | 2 | 29 | 11 | 50 | 2 | 2 | .269 | .304 |
| Evans,Dwight | 39 | .257 | 109 | 369 | 54 | 95 | 18 | 2 | 13 | 62 | 60 | 68 | 2 | 2 | .361 | .423 |
| Faries,Paul | 26 | .245 | 70 | 200 | 26 | 49 | 10 | 2 | 2 | 18 | 17 | 24 | 11 | 5 | .304 | .345 |
| Felder,Mike | 28 | .247 | 122 | 300 | 49 | 74 | 7 | 4 | 2 | 27 | 22 | 28 | 26 | 9 | .298 | .317 |
| Felix,Junior | 23 | .266 | 132 | 488 | 76 | 130 | 22 | 8 | 12 | 57 | 41 | 103 | 27 | 15 | .323 | .418 |
| Fermin,Felix | 27 | .246 | 151 | 483 | 51 | 119 | 11 | 2 | 0 | 35 | 35 | 28 | 7 | 5 | .297 | .277 |
| Fernandez,Tony | 29 | .277 | 156 | 599 | 73 | 166 | 30 | 8 | 6 | 65 | 49 | 60 | 22 | 9 | .332 | .384 |
| Fielder,Cecil | 27 | .272 | 155 | 544 | 95 | 148 | 18 | 1 | 45 | 110 | 80 | 156 | 1 | 1 | .365 | .557 |
| Finley,Steve | 26 | .275 | 112 | 360 | 44 | 99 | 12 | 3 | 3 | 37 | 24 | 41 | 18 | 8 | .320 | .350 |
| Fisk,Carlton | 43 | .249 | 120 | 409 | 48 | 102 | 18 | 1 | 13 | 58 | 52 | 71 | 2 | 1 | .334 | .394 |
| Fitzgerald,Mike | 30 | .237 | 121 | 337 | 36 | 80 | 15 | 1 | 7 | 40 | 53 | 64 | 6 | 4 | .341 | .350 |
| Fletcher,Darrin | 24 | .258 | 125 | 400 | 45 | 103 | 22 | 1 | 10 | 51 | 35 | 46 | 2 | 2 | .317 | .393 |
| Fletcher,Scott | 32 | .255 | 131 | 427 | 51 | 109 | 19 | 2 | 2 | 41 | 47 | 43 | 3 | 2 | .329 | .323 |
| Foley,Tom | 31 | .243 | 66 | 152 | 13 | 37 | 8 | 1 | 2 | 16 | 15 | 21 | 1 | 1 | .311 | .349 |
| Franco,Julio | 29 | .293 | 157 | 604 | 90 | 177 | 28 | 4 | 9 | 71 | 74 | 78 | 27 | 10 | .370 | .397 |
| Fryman,Travis | 22 | .261 | 152 | 575 | 70 | 150 | 32 | 2 | 19 | 78 | 30 | 107 | 7 | 6 | .298 | .423 |
| Gaetti,Gary | 32 | .248 | 124 | 448 | 53 | 111 | 23 | 2 | 17 | 69 | 29 | 79 | 5 | 2 | .294 | .422 |
| Gagne,Greg | 29 | .243 | 145 | 428 | 57 | 104 | 24 | 5 | 9 | 44 | 23 | 87 | 11 | 7 | .282 | .386 |
| Galarraga,Andres | 30 | .265 | 143 | 520 | 69 | 138 | 30 | 2 | 18 | 73 | 39 | 142 | 10 | 4 | .317 | .435 |
| Gallagher,Dave | 30 | .273 | 74 | 227 | 31 | 62 | 9 | 1 | 1 | 19 | 18 | 25 | 3 | 2 | .327 | .335 |
| Gallego,Mike | 30 | .220 | 118 | 255 | 30 | 56 | 10 | 1 | 2 | 22 | 27 | 36 | 4 | 3 | .294 | .290 |
| Gant,Ron | 26 | .263 | 156 | 560 | 89 | 147 | 29 | 4 | 23 | 67 | 52 | 104 | 25 | 15 | .325 | .452 |
| Gantner,Jim | 37 | .261 | 111 | 376 | 42 | 98 | 15 | 1 | 3 | 31 | 25 | 33 | 15 | 5 | .307 | .330 |
| Gedman,Rich | 31 | .236 | 43 | 106 | 11 | 25 | 7 | 0 | 3 | 12 | 10 | 20 | 0 | 0 | .302 | .387 |
| Geren,Bob | 29 | .251 | 101 | 279 | 30 | 70 | 9 | 1 | 9 | 33 | 22 | 60 | 0 | 0 | .306 | .387 |
| Gibson,Kirk | 34 | .258 | 112 | 392 | 69 | 101 | 18 | 2 | 16 | 50 | 53 | 88 | 23 | 5 | .346 | .436 |
| Gilkey,Bernard | 24 | .267 | 152 | 585 | 91 | 156 | 29 | 6 | 4 | 52 | 70 | 57 | 46 | 28 | .345 | .357 |
| Girardi,Joe | 26 | .267 | 122 | 378 | 38 | 101 | 19 | 1 | 5 | 39 | 23 | 50 | 7 | 4 | .309 | .362 |
| Gladden,Dan | 33 | .272 | 116 | 427 | 57 | 116 | 20 | 2 | 6 | 38 | 26 | 55 | 21 | 7 | .313 | .370 |
| Goff,Jerry | 27 | .221 | 67 | 154 | 19 | 34 | 7 | 1 | 6 | 19 | 19 | 42 | 2 | 2 | .306 | .396 |
| Gomez,Leo | 24 | .264 | 140 | 450 | 78 | 119 | 23 | 2 | 22 | 78 | 84 | 96 | 2 | 2 | .380 | .471 |
| Gonzales,Rene | 29 | .217 | 73 | 138 | 12 | 30 | 4 | 0 | 1 | 11 | 11 | 19 | 2 | 2 | .275 | .268 |
| Gonzalez,Juan | 21 | .263 | 151 | 551 | 74 | 145 | 30 | 4 | 26 | 90 | 30 | 114 | 3 | 4 | .301 | .474 |
| Grace,Mark | 27 | .310 | 155 | 565 | 77 | 175 | 30 | 3 | 11 | 78 | 74 | 45 | 12 | 6 | .390 | .432 |
| Greenwell,Mike | 27 | .314 | 156 | 554 | 79 | 174 | 35 | 4 | 19 | 93 | 68 | 39 | 12 | 7 | .389 | .495 |
| Gregg,Tommy | 27 | .279 | 116 | 305 | 31 | 85 | 14 | 1 | 6 | 35 | 26 | 40 | 6 | 6 | .335 | .390 |

## Projections for 1991 Batters

| Batter | Age | Avg | G | AB | R | H | 2B | 3B | HR | RBI | BB | SO | SB | CS | OBP | SLG |
|---|---|---|---|---|---|---|---|---|---|---|---|---|---|---|---|---|
| Griffey Jr,Ken | 21 | .292 | 156 | 558 | 84 | 163 | 28 | 4 | 23 | 80 | 60 | 79 | 18 | 11 | .361 | .480 |
| Griffey Sr,Ken | 41 | .269 | 78 | 249 | 28 | 67 | 12 | 2 | 4 | 31 | 25 | 36 | 3 | 2 | .336 | .382 |
| Griffin,Alfredo | 34 | .229 | 102 | 349 | 35 | 80 | 13 | 3 | 1 | 26 | 23 | 43 | 6 | 4 | .277 | .292 |
| Grissom,Marquis | 24 | .270 | 111 | 359 | 52 | 97 | 16 | 4 | 4 | 29 | 52 | 47 | 24 | 7 | .363 | .370 |
| Gruber,Kelly | 29 | .269 | 158 | 580 | 81 | 156 | 25 | 4 | 22 | 86 | 41 | 84 | 16 | 5 | .317 | .440 |
| Guerrero,Pedro | 35 | .292 | 126 | 435 | 42 | 127 | 22 | 2 | 17 | 83 | 52 | 67 | 2 | 1 | .368 | .469 |
| Guillen,Ozzie | 27 | .269 | 159 | 561 | 63 | 151 | 21 | 6 | 1 | 53 | 23 | 42 | 26 | 17 | .298 | .333 |
| Gwynn,Chris | 26 | .267 | 99 | 146 | 19 | 39 | 4 | 1 | 3 | 18 | 7 | 24 | 1 | 1 | .301 | .370 |
| Gwynn,Tony | 31 | .317 | 146 | 562 | 73 | 178 | 27 | 5 | 6 | 67 | 51 | 31 | 28 | 13 | .374 | .415 |
| Hall,Mel | 30 | .277 | 99 | 318 | 44 | 88 | 17 | 2 | 10 | 47 | 15 | 34 | 2 | 1 | .309 | .437 |
| Hamilton,Daryl | 26 | .261 | 130 | 425 | 56 | 111 | 15 | 2 | 1 | 35 | 33 | 44 | 21 | 11 | .314 | .313 |
| Hansen,Dave | 22 | .270 | 80 | 200 | 26 | 54 | 9 | 1 | 3 | 23 | 21 | 20 | 2 | 1 | .339 | .370 |
| Harper,Brian | 31 | .290 | 125 | 400 | 44 | 116 | 21 | 1 | 9 | 50 | 18 | 21 | 3 | 3 | .321 | .415 |
| Harris,Lenny | 26 | .271 | 138 | 446 | 46 | 121 | 17 | 2 | 2 | 36 | 28 | 35 | 26 | 16 | .314 | .332 |
| Haselman,Bill | 25 | .288 | 60 | 160 | 19 | 46 | 12 | 0 | 5 | 22 | 15 | 38 | 2 | 2 | .349 | .456 |
| Hassey,Ron | 38 | .239 | 86 | 234 | 21 | 56 | 11 | 0 | 4 | 25 | 23 | 35 | 1 | 0 | .307 | .338 |
| Hatcher,Billy | 30 | .258 | 136 | 484 | 66 | 125 | 23 | 3 | 6 | 43 | 34 | 51 | 28 | 11 | .307 | .355 |
| Hayes,Charlie | 26 | .262 | 149 | 543 | 54 | 142 | 27 | 1 | 12 | 62 | 26 | 97 | 5 | 4 | .295 | .381 |
| Hayes,Von | 32 | .254 | 133 | 464 | 67 | 118 | 25 | 2 | 13 | 61 | 82 | 82 | 22 | 9 | .366 | .401 |
| Heath,Mike | 36 | .233 | 114 | 356 | 34 | 83 | 15 | 1 | 6 | 31 | 22 | 68 | 5 | 3 | .278 | .331 |
| Henderson,Dave | 32 | .257 | 142 | 460 | 68 | 118 | 26 | 1 | 16 | 67 | 43 | 98 | 4 | 3 | .320 | .422 |
| Henderson,Rickey | 32 | .288 | 143 | 531 | 111 | 153 | 26 | 3 | 14 | 53 | 104 | 61 | 80 | 14 | .405 | .427 |
| Herr,Tommy | 35 | .258 | 129 | 465 | 48 | 120 | 22 | 2 | 2 | 36 | 50 | 57 | 9 | 4 | .330 | .327 |
| Hill,Donnie | 30 | .246 | 72 | 207 | 20 | 51 | 8 | 1 | 2 | 20 | 21 | 21 | 2 | 1 | .316 | .324 |
| Hill,Glenallen | 26 | .263 | 81 | 266 | 42 | 70 | 14 | 4 | 12 | 37 | 20 | 65 | 9 | 4 | .315 | .481 |
| Hoiles,Chris | 26 | .268 | 100 | 280 | 43 | 75 | 17 | 1 | 13 | 47 | 34 | 49 | 2 | 2 | .347 | .475 |
| Horn,Sam | 27 | .241 | 88 | 261 | 29 | 63 | 12 | 0 | 13 | 40 | 37 | 68 | 0 | 0 | .336 | .437 |
| Howard,Thomas | 26 | .258 | 50 | 120 | 14 | 31 | 8 | 2 | 1 | 11 | 9 | 24 | 5 | 3 | .310 | .383 |
| Howell,Jack | 29 | .234 | 109 | 329 | 39 | 77 | 18 | 2 | 12 | 39 | 39 | 81 | 2 | 2 | .315 | .410 |
| Hrbek,Kent | 31 | .290 | 136 | 487 | 67 | 141 | 26 | 1 | 23 | 82 | 68 | 47 | 3 | 2 | .377 | .489 |
| Hudler,Rex | 30 | .268 | 110 | 261 | 37 | 70 | 13 | 2 | 7 | 24 | 12 | 37 | 24 | 11 | .300 | .414 |
| Hughes,Keith | 27 | .267 | 70 | 150 | 24 | 40 | 10 | 1 | 3 | 21 | 22 | 27 | 3 | 2 | .360 | .407 |
| Hulett,Tim | 31 | .230 | 57 | 139 | 13 | 32 | 7 | 1 | 2 | 15 | 11 | 32 | 1 | 0 | .287 | .338 |
| Hundley,Todd | 22 | .240 | 110 | 350 | 32 | 84 | 18 | 1 | 1 | 33 | 36 | 66 | 4 | 2 | .311 | .306 |
| Huson,Jeff | 26 | .249 | 119 | 325 | 45 | 81 | 13 | 2 | 1 | 24 | 38 | 31 | 21 | 8 | .328 | .311 |
| Incaviglia,Pete | 27 | .248 | 140 | 491 | 61 | 122 | 25 | 2 | 26 | 80 | 43 | 153 | 6 | 5 | .309 | .466 |
| Jackson,Bo | 28 | .255 | 130 | 463 | 76 | 118 | 17 | 3 | 29 | 83 | 39 | 152 | 24 | 9 | .313 | .492 |
| Jackson,Darrin | 27 | .254 | 86 | 209 | 27 | 53 | 10 | 1 | 8 | 25 | 11 | 36 | 4 | 3 | .291 | .426 |
| Jacoby,Brook | 31 | .270 | 151 | 537 | 61 | 145 | 25 | 2 | 15 | 65 | 58 | 82 | 3 | 3 | .341 | .408 |
| James,Chris | 28 | .264 | 144 | 512 | 59 | 135 | 25 | 3 | 16 | 68 | 30 | 69 | 5 | 3 | .304 | .418 |
| James,Dion | 28 | .277 | 109 | 332 | 38 | 92 | 18 | 3 | 3 | 33 | 45 | 41 | 6 | 6 | .363 | .377 |
| Javier,Stan | 25 | .267 | 130 | 326 | 49 | 87 | 12 | 3 | 2 | 30 | 35 | 49 | 15 | 4 | .338 | .340 |
| Jefferies,Gregg | 23 | .284 | 152 | 560 | 84 | 159 | 38 | 3 | 15 | 70 | 42 | 42 | 20 | 6 | .334 | .443 |
| Jefferson,Stan | 28 | .243 | 77 | 226 | 32 | 55 | 9 | 3 | 4 | 22 | 20 | 38 | 13 | 7 | .305 | .363 |
| Jennings,Doug | 26 | .245 | 63 | 159 | 22 | 39 | 9 | 1 | 3 | 17 | 24 | 34 | 2 | 3 | .344 | .371 |

# Projections for 1991 Batters

| Batter | Age | Avg | G | AB | R | H | 2B | 3B | HR | RBI | BB | SO | SB | CS | OBP | SLG |
|---|---|---|---|---|---|---|---|---|---|---|---|---|---|---|---|---|
| Johnson,Howard | 30 | .250 | 156 | 516 | 85 | 129 | 26 | 2 | 24 | 75 | 76 | 103 | 33 | 9 | .346 | .448 |
| Johnson,Lance | 27 | .278 | 155 | 550 | 79 | 153 | 18 | 7 | 2 | 45 | 47 | 58 | 42 | 21 | .335 | .347 |
| Jones,Tim | 28 | .254 | 75 | 126 | 11 | 32 | 7 | 0 | 1 | 12 | 12 | 17 | 4 | 3 | .319 | .333 |
| Jones,Tracy | 30 | .269 | 81 | 212 | 24 | 57 | 9 | 1 | 4 | 27 | 16 | 21 | 7 | 4 | .320 | .377 |
| Jordan,Ricky | 26 | .281 | 86 | 302 | 36 | 85 | 17 | 1 | 8 | 41 | 11 | 35 | 3 | 1 | .307 | .424 |
| Jose,Felix | 26 | .273 | 145 | 495 | 59 | 135 | 25 | 2 | 11 | 63 | 37 | 86 | 12 | 8 | .323 | .398 |
| Joyner,Wally | 29 | .281 | 122 | 455 | 61 | 128 | 24 | 1 | 16 | 66 | 45 | 43 | 4 | 2 | .346 | .444 |
| Justice,Dave | 25 | .264 | 155 | 560 | 80 | 148 | 28 | 2 | 27 | 85 | 88 | 105 | 15 | 9 | .364 | .466 |
| Karkovice,Ron | 27 | .239 | 92 | 234 | 29 | 56 | 11 | 0 | 7 | 27 | 17 | 59 | 3 | 2 | .291 | .376 |
| Kelly,Roberto | 26 | .296 | 156 | 628 | 91 | 186 | 25 | 4 | 15 | 68 | 43 | 134 | 48 | 20 | .341 | .420 |
| Kennedy,Terry | 35 | .252 | 86 | 282 | 20 | 71 | 14 | 0 | 6 | 26 | 25 | 47 | 1 | 1 | .313 | .365 |
| King,Jeff | 26 | .242 | 141 | 467 | 60 | 113 | 22 | 2 | 16 | 64 | 41 | 73 | 7 | 5 | .303 | .400 |
| Kingery,Mike | 30 | .249 | 86 | 201 | 27 | 50 | 11 | 2 | 2 | 20 | 22 | 29 | 4 | 4 | .323 | .353 |
| Kittle,Ron | 33 | .232 | 65 | 185 | 21 | 43 | 7 | 0 | 11 | 29 | 17 | 52 | 0 | 0 | .297 | .449 |
| Komminsk,Brad | 30 | .222 | 72 | 203 | 26 | 45 | 9 | 1 | 6 | 24 | 22 | 56 | 4 | 2 | .298 | .365 |
| Kruk,John | 30 | .284 | 140 | 416 | 58 | 118 | 19 | 4 | 10 | 56 | 72 | 67 | 7 | 4 | .389 | .421 |
| Kunkel,Jeff | 29 | .224 | 92 | 241 | 26 | 54 | 12 | 2 | 6 | 24 | 13 | 59 | 3 | 2 | .264 | .365 |
| Lankford,Ray | 24 | .272 | 151 | 585 | 76 | 159 | 31 | 8 | 11 | 80 | 67 | 84 | 32 | 11 | .347 | .409 |
| Lansford,Carney | 34 | .286 | 122 | 461 | 63 | 132 | 21 | 2 | 9 | 50 | 38 | 33 | 21 | 10 | .341 | .399 |
| Larkin,Barry | 27 | .304 | 156 | 556 | 81 | 169 | 24 | 5 | 11 | 60 | 42 | 35 | 29 | 8 | .353 | .424 |
| Larkin,Gene | 28 | .269 | 114 | 353 | 43 | 95 | 22 | 2 | 5 | 42 | 45 | 40 | 3 | 2 | .352 | .385 |
| LaValliere,Mike | 30 | .265 | 106 | 291 | 23 | 77 | 14 | 0 | 2 | 33 | 46 | 28 | 2 | 2 | .365 | .333 |
| Leach,Rick | 34 | .261 | 104 | 211 | 25 | 55 | 12 | 1 | 2 | 21 | 25 | 29 | 1 | 1 | .339 | .355 |
| Lee,Manny | 26 | .271 | 130 | 410 | 42 | 111 | 11 | 3 | 4 | 43 | 29 | 74 | 4 | 3 | .319 | .341 |
| Lee,Terry | 29 | .287 | 80 | 230 | 30 | 66 | 17 | 1 | 10 | 39 | 23 | 35 | 2 | 1 | .352 | .500 |
| Lemke,Mark | 25 | .256 | 68 | 203 | 25 | 52 | 10 | 1 | 3 | 23 | 21 | 23 | 3 | 2 | .326 | .360 |
| Lemon,Chet | 36 | .249 | 116 | 390 | 45 | 97 | 22 | 2 | 10 | 45 | 49 | 67 | 2 | 2 | .333 | .392 |
| Leonard,Jeff | 35 | .248 | 106 | 367 | 38 | 91 | 16 | 2 | 9 | 54 | 24 | 76 | 6 | 3 | .294 | .376 |
| Leonard,Mark | 26 | .300 | 90 | 150 | 25 | 45 | 14 | 1 | 7 | 30 | 23 | 30 | 1 | 1 | .393 | .547 |
| Leyritz,Jim | 27 | .268 | 135 | 440 | 53 | 118 | 20 | 2 | 9 | 57 | 60 | 64 | 4 | 3 | .356 | .384 |
| Lind,Jose | 27 | .257 | 154 | 540 | 59 | 139 | 25 | 4 | 2 | 49 | 39 | 55 | 12 | 3 | .307 | .330 |
| Liriano,Nelson | 27 | .257 | 119 | 381 | 49 | 98 | 16 | 5 | 4 | 39 | 35 | 45 | 14 | 8 | .320 | .357 |
| Litton,Greg | 26 | .251 | 77 | 215 | 22 | 54 | 11 | 2 | 5 | 27 | 15 | 41 | 1 | 1 | .300 | .391 |
| Lynn,Fred | 39 | .239 | 61 | 155 | 18 | 37 | 10 | 1 | 5 | 21 | 17 | 35 | 1 | 0 | .314 | .413 |
| Lyons,Steve | 31 | .252 | 52 | 115 | 14 | 29 | 6 | 1 | 1 | 11 | 9 | 18 | 1 | 1 | .306 | .348 |
| Maas,Kevin | 26 | .284 | 140 | 450 | 77 | 128 | 23 | 2 | 24 | 74 | 76 | 114 | 4 | 3 | .388 | .504 |
| Macfarlane,Mike | 27 | .254 | 120 | 343 | 34 | 87 | 20 | 2 | 6 | 45 | 25 | 54 | 0 | 0 | .304 | .376 |
| Mack,Shane | 27 | .296 | 134 | 311 | 46 | 92 | 11 | 3 | 6 | 40 | 33 | 59 | 12 | 5 | .363 | .408 |
| Magadan,Dave | 28 | .302 | 150 | 500 | 70 | 151 | 25 | 3 | 5 | 63 | 84 | 52 | 1 | 1 | .402 | .394 |
| Maldonado,Candy | 30 | .246 | 154 | 540 | 62 | 133 | 24 | 2 | 17 | 73 | 49 | 110 | 5 | 4 | .309 | .393 |
| Mann,Kelly | 23 | .264 | 110 | 330 | 36 | 87 | 19 | 0 | 10 | 45 | 37 | 53 | 3 | 2 | .338 | .412 |
| Manrique,Fred | 29 | .258 | 92 | 240 | 28 | 62 | 11 | 2 | 4 | 29 | 11 | 35 | 3 | 3 | .291 | .371 |
| Manto,Jeff | 26 | .249 | 80 | 201 | 33 | 50 | 13 | 1 | 9 | 33 | 32 | 40 | 2 | 2 | .352 | .458 |
| Marshall,Mike | 31 | .267 | 101 | 337 | 38 | 90 | 16 | 1 | 14 | 47 | 20 | 67 | 2 | 2 | .308 | .445 |
| Martinez,Carlos | 25 | .260 | 73 | 235 | 25 | 61 | 10 | 1 | 4 | 24 | 13 | 36 | 5 | 3 | .298 | .362 |

## Projections for 1991 Batters

| Batter | Age | Avg | G | AB | R | H | 2B | 3B | HR | RBI | BB | SO | SB | CS | OBP | SLG |
|---|---|---|---|---|---|---|---|---|---|---|---|---|---|---|---|---|
| Martinez,Carmelo | 30 | .237 | 104 | 300 | 35 | 71 | 14 | 1 | 11 | 46 | 36 | 54 | 1 | 1 | .318 | .400 |
| Martinez,Dave | 26 | .277 | 131 | 397 | 52 | 110 | 14 | 6 | 7 | 40 | 31 | 64 | 21 | 9 | .329 | .395 |
| Martinez,Edgar | 28 | .294 | 152 | 554 | 79 | 163 | 29 | 2 | 11 | 68 | 83 | 70 | 6 | 4 | .386 | .413 |
| Martinez,Tino | 23 | .260 | 100 | 315 | 35 | 82 | 20 | 1 | 10 | 42 | 38 | 31 | 3 | 2 | .340 | .425 |
| Mattingly,Don | 30 | .307 | 135 | 525 | 74 | 161 | 35 | 2 | 19 | 87 | 41 | 26 | 1 | 1 | .357 | .490 |
| McCray,Rodney | 27 | .190 | 69 | 21 | 4 | 4 | 0 | 0 | 0 | 1 | 3 | 6 | 3 | 1 | .292 | .190 |
| McDowell,Oddibe | 28 | .257 | 130 | 443 | 70 | 114 | 21 | 4 | 13 | 44 | 42 | 76 | 26 | 11 | .322 | .411 |
| McGee,Willie | 32 | .285 | 124 | 481 | 65 | 137 | 21 | 5 | 5 | 49 | 32 | 78 | 27 | 8 | .329 | .380 |
| McGriff,Fred | 27 | .285 | 157 | 550 | 99 | 157 | 27 | 2 | 38 | 90 | 103 | 130 | 6 | 3 | .398 | .549 |
| McGwire,Mark | 27 | .251 | 154 | 550 | 92 | 138 | 21 | 1 | 41 | 112 | 99 | 115 | 1 | 1 | .365 | .516 |
| McIntosh,Tim | 26 | .256 | 60 | 160 | 20 | 41 | 9 | 1 | 5 | 22 | 7 | 25 | 1 | 1 | .287 | .419 |
| McKnight,Jeff | 28 | .244 | 50 | 90 | 15 | 22 | 7 | 0 | 1 | 10 | 12 | 12 | 1 | 0 | .333 | .356 |
| McRae,Brian | 23 | .258 | 149 | 565 | 76 | 146 | 29 | 8 | 8 | 68 | 41 | 84 | 18 | 10 | .309 | .381 |
| McReynolds,Kevin | 31 | .268 | 148 | 541 | 74 | 145 | 26 | 3 | 22 | 85 | 53 | 64 | 14 | 4 | .333 | .449 |
| Melvin,Bob | 29 | .237 | 82 | 228 | 20 | 54 | 10 | 1 | 5 | 26 | 11 | 37 | 1 | 1 | .272 | .355 |
| Meulens,Hensley | 24 | .262 | 140 | 500 | 76 | 131 | 14 | 2 | 20 | 74 | 67 | 140 | 5 | 4 | .349 | .418 |
| Miller,Keith | 28 | .250 | 96 | 272 | 40 | 68 | 11 | 1 | 2 | 21 | 22 | 40 | 13 | 7 | .306 | .320 |
| Milligan,Randy | 29 | .269 | 130 | 420 | 69 | 113 | 24 | 2 | 17 | 59 | 93 | 78 | 8 | 6 | .402 | .457 |
| Mitchell,Kevin | 29 | .273 | 149 | 513 | 80 | 140 | 28 | 4 | 34 | 96 | 66 | 94 | 5 | 5 | .356 | .542 |
| Molitor,Paul | 34 | .290 | 136 | 549 | 82 | 159 | 29 | 4 | 11 | 50 | 59 | 60 | 28 | 9 | .359 | .417 |
| Morandini,Mickey | 25 | .277 | 145 | 520 | 76 | 144 | 21 | 5 | 5 | 43 | 59 | 93 | 16 | 13 | .351 | .365 |
| Morris,Hal | 26 | .312 | 135 | 490 | 67 | 153 | 23 | 3 | 10 | 59 | 38 | 62 | 8 | 4 | .362 | .433 |
| Moseby,Lloyd | 31 | .246 | 134 | 487 | 76 | 120 | 23 | 4 | 14 | 50 | 62 | 94 | 26 | 8 | .332 | .396 |
| Moses,John | 33 | .262 | 64 | 122 | 17 | 32 | 5 | 1 | 1 | 11 | 11 | 13 | 5 | 3 | .323 | .344 |
| Munoz,Pedro | 22 | .285 | 140 | 480 | 61 | 137 | 26 | 4 | 17 | 71 | 30 | 90 | 15 | 7 | .327 | .463 |
| Murphy,Dale | 35 | .245 | 138 | 507 | 59 | 124 | 21 | 2 | 22 | 76 | 60 | 121 | 5 | 3 | .325 | .424 |
| Murray,Eddie | 35 | .279 | 150 | 560 | 74 | 156 | 28 | 1 | 23 | 84 | 79 | 75 | 6 | 3 | .368 | .455 |
| Myers,Greg | 25 | .245 | 88 | 257 | 31 | 63 | 11 | 1 | 7 | 29 | 19 | 36 | 1 | 1 | .297 | .377 |
| Naehring,Tim | 24 | .277 | 155 | 570 | 74 | 158 | 28 | 1 | 19 | 76 | 62 | 93 | 3 | 2 | .348 | .430 |
| Newman,Al | 31 | .231 | 118 | 299 | 37 | 69 | 11 | 1 | 0 | 23 | 34 | 31 | 13 | 6 | .309 | .274 |
| Nixon,Otis | 32 | .229 | 115 | 236 | 40 | 54 | 7 | 1 | 1 | 17 | 31 | 34 | 38 | 15 | .318 | .280 |
| Noboa,Junior | 26 | .291 | 86 | 179 | 20 | 52 | 7 | 2 | 0 | 18 | 8 | 13 | 4 | 3 | .321 | .352 |
| Nokes,Matt | 27 | .258 | 130 | 392 | 42 | 101 | 14 | 1 | 19 | 57 | 31 | 56 | 1 | 1 | .312 | .444 |
| O'Brien,Charlie | 30 | .211 | 69 | 180 | 18 | 38 | 10 | 1 | 3 | 20 | 17 | 19 | 0 | 0 | .279 | .328 |
| O'Brien,Pete | 33 | .254 | 101 | 342 | 38 | 87 | 16 | 1 | 10 | 38 | 47 | 37 | 1 | 1 | .344 | .395 |
| O'Malley,Tom | 30 | .263 | 69 | 194 | 22 | 51 | 9 | 1 | 3 | 24 | 19 | 26 | 1 | 0 | .329 | .366 |
| O'Neill,Paul | 28 | .267 | 155 | 550 | 65 | 147 | 28 | 2 | 19 | 86 | 56 | 82 | 17 | 10 | .335 | .429 |
| Oberkfell,Ken | 35 | .261 | 46 | 115 | 12 | 30 | 6 | 1 | 1 | 11 | 9 | 9 | 1 | 1 | .315 | .357 |
| Oester,Ron | 35 | .250 | 84 | 260 | 22 | 65 | 12 | 1 | 2 | 16 | 22 | 44 | 1 | 1 | .309 | .327 |
| Offerman,Jose | 22 | .270 | 155 | 600 | 91 | 162 | 9 | 3 | 2 | 51 | 62 | 98 | 53 | 32 | .338 | .305 |
| Olerud,John | 22 | .275 | 135 | 440 | 56 | 121 | 18 | 1 | 19 | 61 | 72 | 83 | 1 | 1 | .377 | .450 |
| Oliver,Joe | 25 | .250 | 113 | 348 | 32 | 87 | 19 | 1 | 9 | 47 | 27 | 59 | 1 | 1 | .304 | .388 |
| Olson,Greg | 30 | .251 | 91 | 259 | 31 | 65 | 11 | 1 | 5 | 32 | 33 | 33 | 1 | 1 | .336 | .359 |
| Oquendo,Jose | 27 | .275 | 155 | 510 | 45 | 140 | 15 | 2 | 3 | 44 | 74 | 50 | 4 | 4 | .366 | .329 |
| Orsulak,Joe | 29 | .273 | 133 | 406 | 52 | 111 | 18 | 4 | 6 | 45 | 40 | 39 | 8 | 7 | .339 | .382 |

## Projections for 1991 Batters

| Batter | Age | Avg | G | AB | R | H | 2B | 3B | HR | RBI | BB | SO | SB | CS | OBP | SLG |
|---|---|---|---|---|---|---|---|---|---|---|---|---|---|---|---|---|
| Ortiz,Javier | 28 | .261 | 90 | 280 | 40 | 73 | 15 | 1 | 7 | 36 | 29 | 59 | 4 | 3 | .330 | .396 |
| Ortiz,Junior | 31 | .274 | 91 | 212 | 17 | 58 | 8 | 0 | 1 | 23 | 17 | 17 | 2 | 3 | .328 | .325 |
| Owen,Spike | 30 | .232 | 151 | 487 | 61 | 113 | 20 | 5 | 4 | 40 | 77 | 56 | 5 | 4 | .337 | .318 |
| Pagliarulo,Mike | 31 | .225 | 128 | 405 | 37 | 91 | 20 | 1 | 16 | 52 | 39 | 84 | 2 | 1 | .293 | .398 |
| Pagnozzi,Tom | 28 | .259 | 120 | 390 | 31 | 101 | 14 | 0 | 3 | 34 | 26 | 63 | 1 | 1 | .305 | .318 |
| Palmeiro,Rafael | 26 | .304 | 157 | 559 | 74 | 170 | 33 | 4 | 14 | 72 | 48 | 44 | 6 | 3 | .359 | .453 |
| Parent,Mark | 29 | .213 | 83 | 239 | 18 | 51 | 10 | 0 | 5 | 25 | 17 | 42 | 1 | 0 | .266 | .318 |
| Parker,Dave | 40 | .263 | 120 | 448 | 46 | 118 | 23 | 2 | 13 | 67 | 33 | 83 | 2 | 2 | .314 | .411 |
| Parker,Rick | 28 | .277 | 70 | 130 | 23 | 36 | 5 | 1 | 1 | 13 | 13 | 20 | 9 | 4 | .343 | .354 |
| Parrish,Lance | 35 | .234 | 127 | 461 | 50 | 108 | 20 | 1 | 18 | 62 | 48 | 110 | 1 | 1 | .306 | .399 |
| Pasqua,Dan | 29 | .249 | 115 | 333 | 40 | 83 | 15 | 1 | 17 | 52 | 38 | 75 | 1 | 1 | .326 | .453 |
| Pecota,Bill | 31 | .232 | 99 | 198 | 35 | 46 | 9 | 2 | 3 | 15 | 23 | 30 | 8 | 4 | .312 | .343 |
| Pena,Geronimo | 24 | .253 | 70 | 170 | 29 | 43 | 13 | 3 | 3 | 19 | 22 | 46 | 7 | 4 | .339 | .418 |
| Pena,Tony | 34 | .261 | 141 | 487 | 52 | 127 | 22 | 2 | 8 | 51 | 39 | 58 | 6 | 4 | .316 | .363 |
| Pendleton,Terry | 30 | .249 | 117 | 430 | 51 | 107 | 19 | 3 | 5 | 51 | 30 | 56 | 6 | 4 | .298 | .342 |
| Perry,Gerald | 30 | .262 | 96 | 302 | 33 | 79 | 14 | 1 | 5 | 35 | 27 | 31 | 13 | 6 | .322 | .364 |
| Petralli,Geno | 31 | .272 | 121 | 279 | 26 | 76 | 12 | 1 | 4 | 26 | 36 | 41 | 0 | 0 | .356 | .366 |
| Pettis,Gary | 33 | .234 | 122 | 393 | 60 | 92 | 12 | 3 | 2 | 25 | 57 | 95 | 37 | 13 | .331 | .295 |
| Phillips,Tony | 32 | .247 | 152 | 555 | 77 | 137 | 20 | 3 | 7 | 52 | 88 | 90 | 11 | 9 | .350 | .332 |
| Plantier,Phil | 22 | .244 | 90 | 250 | 44 | 61 | 14 | 1 | 15 | 43 | 33 | 91 | 1 | 3 | .332 | .488 |
| Polonia,Luis | 26 | .311 | 132 | 453 | 74 | 141 | 16 | 8 | 3 | 46 | 33 | 51 | 31 | 18 | .358 | .402 |
| Presley,Jim | 29 | .243 | 137 | 507 | 54 | 123 | 27 | 2 | 19 | 65 | 31 | 121 | 2 | 2 | .286 | .416 |
| Puckett,Kirby | 30 | .318 | 153 | 628 | 86 | 200 | 34 | 5 | 15 | 92 | 43 | 73 | 8 | 5 | .362 | .460 |
| Quinones,Luis | 29 | .239 | 94 | 255 | 25 | 61 | 13 | 3 | 6 | 29 | 17 | 36 | 2 | 3 | .287 | .384 |
| Quintana,Carlos | 25 | .291 | 155 | 550 | 73 | 160 | 26 | 2 | 14 | 78 | 64 | 76 | 4 | 3 | .365 | .422 |
| Quirk,Jamie | 36 | .210 | 55 | 100 | 9 | 21 | 5 | 0 | 2 | 13 | 14 | 26 | 1 | 1 | .307 | .320 |
| Raines,Tim | 31 | .291 | 134 | 501 | 75 | 146 | 26 | 5 | 9 | 61 | 79 | 48 | 46 | 13 | .388 | .417 |
| Ramirez,Rafael | 32 | .251 | 144 | 534 | 46 | 134 | 22 | 2 | 5 | 49 | 25 | 59 | 5 | 3 | .284 | .328 |
| Ramos,Domingo | 33 | .236 | 76 | 144 | 15 | 34 | 5 | 0 | 1 | 12 | 15 | 19 | 1 | 1 | .308 | .292 |
| Randolph,Willie | 36 | .253 | 120 | 431 | 48 | 109 | 17 | 2 | 3 | 32 | 56 | 43 | 6 | 4 | .339 | .323 |
| Ray,Johnny | 34 | .277 | 131 | 498 | 53 | 138 | 28 | 2 | 5 | 58 | 30 | 38 | 4 | 2 | .318 | .371 |
| Ready,Randy | 31 | .257 | 88 | 230 | 31 | 59 | 13 | 2 | 5 | 27 | 32 | 32 | 4 | 2 | .347 | .396 |
| Redus,Gary | 34 | .243 | 97 | 296 | 43 | 72 | 16 | 3 | 7 | 31 | 44 | 59 | 22 | 6 | .341 | .389 |
| Reed,Jeff | 28 | .229 | 102 | 258 | 17 | 59 | 11 | 1 | 2 | 21 | 32 | 37 | 0 | 0 | .314 | .302 |
| Reed,Jody | 28 | .288 | 155 | 586 | 83 | 169 | 42 | 1 | 4 | 50 | 81 | 47 | 5 | 5 | .375 | .384 |
| Reimer,Kevin | 27 | .264 | 115 | 330 | 37 | 87 | 24 | 3 | 8 | 45 | 22 | 59 | 2 | 1 | .310 | .427 |
| Reynolds,Harold | 30 | .264 | 159 | 557 | 73 | 147 | 27 | 7 | 2 | 42 | 59 | 45 | 28 | 19 | .334 | .348 |
| Reynolds,RJ | 31 | .261 | 125 | 356 | 41 | 93 | 19 | 2 | 5 | 47 | 31 | 64 | 18 | 5 | .320 | .368 |
| Rhodes,Karl | 22 | .245 | 40 | 110 | 15 | 27 | 6 | 1 | 1 | 12 | 14 | 21 | 4 | 2 | .331 | .345 |
| Riles,Ernest | 30 | .254 | 117 | 343 | 42 | 87 | 13 | 2 | 6 | 40 | 33 | 60 | 3 | 3 | .319 | .356 |
| Ripken,Billy | 26 | .255 | 134 | 432 | 48 | 110 | 20 | 1 | 3 | 37 | 30 | 51 | 5 | 3 | .303 | .326 |
| Ripken,Cal | 30 | .267 | 162 | 619 | 88 | 165 | 32 | 3 | 24 | 93 | 86 | 70 | 3 | 2 | .356 | .444 |
| Rivera,Luis | 27 | .241 | 121 | 382 | 42 | 92 | 21 | 1 | 5 | 38 | 26 | 66 | 5 | 5 | .289 | .340 |
| Roberts,Bip | 27 | .293 | 155 | 550 | 99 | 161 | 22 | 5 | 6 | 45 | 59 | 75 | 41 | 17 | .361 | .384 |
| Rohde,David | 27 | .253 | 115 | 340 | 46 | 86 | 10 | 1 | 1 | 29 | 48 | 43 | 14 | 6 | .345 | .297 |

# Projections for 1991 Batters

| Batter | Age | Avg | G | AB | R | H | 2B | 3B | HR | RBI | BB | SO | SB | CS | OBP | SLG |
|---|---|---|---|---|---|---|---|---|---|---|---|---|---|---|---|---|
| Romine,Kevin | 30 | .270 | 99 | 252 | 34 | 68 | 13 | 1 | 4 | 28 | 20 | 42 | 3 | 1 | .324 | .377 |
| Rose,Bobby | 24 | .269 | 130 | 450 | 58 | 121 | 20 | 4 | 10 | 54 | 41 | 79 | 3 | 2 | .330 | .398 |
| Rowland,Rick | 24 | .252 | 80 | 230 | 32 | 58 | 13 | 0 | 9 | 30 | 21 | 47 | 2 | 2 | .315 | .426 |
| Russell,John | 30 | .230 | 93 | 230 | 28 | 53 | 11 | 1 | 7 | 23 | 16 | 68 | 0 | 0 | .280 | .378 |
| Sabo,Chris | 29 | .267 | 156 | 561 | 84 | 150 | 39 | 2 | 16 | 59 | 48 | 52 | 36 | 15 | .325 | .430 |
| Salas,Mark | 30 | .246 | 85 | 211 | 20 | 52 | 8 | 2 | 6 | 22 | 19 | 26 | 0 | 0 | .309 | .389 |
| Salazar,Luis | 35 | .255 | 110 | 341 | 37 | 87 | 12 | 2 | 7 | 37 | 16 | 56 | 3 | 2 | .289 | .364 |
| Samuel,Juan | 30 | .245 | 146 | 584 | 75 | 143 | 29 | 9 | 15 | 66 | 49 | 140 | 40 | 16 | .303 | .402 |
| Sandberg,Ryne | 31 | .279 | 154 | 610 | 92 | 170 | 28 | 4 | 24 | 76 | 55 | 86 | 22 | 9 | .338 | .456 |
| Santiago,Benito | 26 | .268 | 123 | 436 | 51 | 117 | 19 | 3 | 14 | 59 | 27 | 74 | 11 | 7 | .311 | .422 |
| Santovenia,Nelson | 29 | .235 | 75 | 226 | 21 | 53 | 11 | 1 | 7 | 29 | 17 | 38 | 2 | 2 | .288 | .385 |
| Sasser,Mackey | 28 | .293 | 109 | 259 | 25 | 76 | 17 | 1 | 4 | 35 | 13 | 18 | 0 | 0 | .327 | .413 |
| Sax,Steve | 31 | .279 | 155 | 614 | 72 | 171 | 23 | 3 | 4 | 51 | 48 | 46 | 41 | 13 | .331 | .345 |
| Schofield,Dick | 28 | .237 | 113 | 355 | 47 | 84 | 12 | 3 | 6 | 28 | 39 | 51 | 10 | 4 | .312 | .338 |
| Schu,Rick | 29 | .247 | 96 | 255 | 25 | 63 | 11 | 2 | 7 | 24 | 22 | 41 | 3 | 2 | .307 | .388 |
| Schulz,Jeff | 30 | .269 | 70 | 160 | 16 | 43 | 13 | 2 | 1 | 17 | 10 | 23 | 1 | 0 | .312 | .394 |
| Scioscia,Mike | 32 | .251 | 136 | 411 | 36 | 103 | 20 | 1 | 11 | 50 | 49 | 30 | 2 | 2 | .330 | .384 |
| Segui,David | 24 | .295 | 80 | 200 | 28 | 59 | 14 | 0 | 2 | 27 | 23 | 19 | 2 | 1 | .368 | .395 |
| Seitzer,Kevin | 29 | .288 | 160 | 611 | 92 | 176 | 29 | 5 | 8 | 55 | 87 | 71 | 12 | 8 | .377 | .391 |
| Sharperson,Mike | 29 | .273 | 112 | 304 | 43 | 83 | 12 | 2 | 1 | 30 | 35 | 37 | 12 | 7 | .348 | .336 |
| Sheets,Larry | 31 | .253 | 117 | 352 | 36 | 89 | 15 | 1 | 14 | 47 | 30 | 54 | 2 | 2 | .312 | .420 |
| Sheffield,Gary | 22 | .276 | 145 | 540 | 71 | 149 | 28 | 2 | 15 | 73 | 44 | 52 | 19 | 10 | .330 | .419 |
| Shelby,John | 33 | .221 | 104 | 298 | 31 | 66 | 12 | 2 | 6 | 27 | 22 | 80 | 8 | 5 | .275 | .336 |
| Shumpert,Terry | 24 | .249 | 100 | 325 | 41 | 81 | 23 | 4 | 2 | 26 | 20 | 53 | 19 | 7 | .293 | .363 |
| Sierra,Ruben | 25 | .286 | 161 | 618 | 85 | 177 | 33 | 7 | 27 | 107 | 48 | 84 | 11 | 3 | .338 | .494 |
| Skinner,Joel | 30 | .228 | 85 | 202 | 17 | 46 | 8 | 0 | 3 | 19 | 11 | 51 | 0 | 0 | .268 | .312 |
| Slaught,Don | 32 | .263 | 112 | 334 | 33 | 88 | 21 | 2 | 7 | 38 | 31 | 51 | 1 | 1 | .326 | .401 |
| Smith,Dwight | 27 | .293 | 119 | 386 | 53 | 113 | 20 | 3 | 10 | 45 | 37 | 61 | 14 | 10 | .355 | .438 |
| Smith,Lonnie | 35 | .286 | 111 | 371 | 56 | 106 | 20 | 3 | 9 | 40 | 58 | 73 | 16 | 8 | .382 | .429 |
| Smith,Ozzie | 36 | .243 | 142 | 514 | 61 | 125 | 21 | 2 | 1 | 42 | 59 | 38 | 33 | 8 | .321 | .298 |
| Snyder,Cory | 28 | .244 | 117 | 426 | 51 | 104 | 20 | 1 | 21 | 60 | 27 | 105 | 4 | 3 | .289 | .444 |
| Sojo,Luis | 25 | .268 | 70 | 220 | 27 | 59 | 11 | 2 | 3 | 23 | 10 | 17 | 5 | 4 | .300 | .377 |
| Sorrento,Paul | 25 | .266 | 102 | 297 | 42 | 79 | 22 | 1 | 16 | 54 | 46 | 74 | 1 | 1 | .364 | .508 |
| Sosa,Sammy | 22 | .259 | 153 | 525 | 76 | 136 | 26 | 7 | 16 | 63 | 31 | 123 | 30 | 21 | .300 | .427 |
| Spiers,Bill | 25 | .251 | 119 | 371 | 44 | 93 | 12 | 3 | 4 | 36 | 20 | 50 | 11 | 8 | .289 | .332 |
| Stanley,Mike | 28 | .251 | 109 | 239 | 23 | 60 | 9 | 1 | 4 | 26 | 35 | 45 | 1 | 0 | .347 | .347 |
| Stark,Matt | 26 | .284 | 65 | 190 | 23 | 54 | 10 | 0 | 6 | 38 | 25 | 26 | 1 | 1 | .367 | .432 |
| Steinbach,Terry | 29 | .267 | 130 | 430 | 42 | 115 | 17 | 2 | 12 | 57 | 31 | 59 | 2 | 1 | .317 | .400 |
| Stephenson,Phil | 30 | .250 | 63 | 164 | 22 | 41 | 8 | 2 | 6 | 22 | 22 | 29 | 5 | 2 | .339 | .433 |
| Stevens,Lee | 23 | .238 | 70 | 240 | 30 | 57 | 13 | 1 | 9 | 32 | 26 | 63 | 1 | 1 | .312 | .413 |
| Stillwell,Kurt | 26 | .258 | 145 | 476 | 59 | 123 | 25 | 5 | 6 | 53 | 45 | 65 | 6 | 5 | .322 | .370 |
| Strawberry,Darryl | 29 | .265 | 155 | 550 | 95 | 146 | 26 | 4 | 36 | 101 | 80 | 120 | 21 | 10 | .359 | .524 |
| Stubbs,Franklin | 30 | .236 | 131 | 343 | 41 | 81 | 13 | 2 | 15 | 48 | 40 | 87 | 14 | 6 | .316 | .417 |
| Surhoff,B.J. | 26 | .267 | 140 | 484 | 52 | 129 | 22 | 3 | 7 | 56 | 35 | 39 | 19 | 10 | .316 | .368 |
| Tabler,Pat | 33 | .277 | 80 | 220 | 23 | 61 | 13 | 1 | 3 | 31 | 22 | 30 | 1 | 1 | .343 | .386 |

# Projections for 1991 Batters

| Batter | Age | Avg | G | AB | R | H | 2B | 3B | HR | RBI | BB | SO | SB | CS | OBP | SLG |
|---|---|---|---|---|---|---|---|---|---|---|---|---|---|---|---|---|
| Tartabull,Danny | 28 | .276 | 135 | 460 | 66 | 127 | 28 | 2 | 23 | 83 | 69 | 122 | 5 | 3 | .371 | .496 |
| Templeton,Garry | 35 | .255 | 126 | 470 | 41 | 120 | 20 | 4 | 4 | 44 | 23 | 67 | 4 | 3 | .290 | .340 |
| Tettleton,Mickey | 30 | .232 | 137 | 405 | 59 | 94 | 17 | 1 | 16 | 50 | 77 | 124 | 2 | 2 | .355 | .398 |
| Teufel,Tim | 32 | .244 | 85 | 242 | 33 | 59 | 16 | 1 | 6 | 26 | 28 | 45 | 1 | 1 | .322 | .393 |
| Thomas,Andres | 27 | .235 | 105 | 375 | 32 | 88 | 14 | 1 | 8 | 41 | 10 | 52 | 3 | 2 | .255 | .341 |
| Thomas,Frank | 23 | .312 | 155 | 525 | 105 | 164 | 34 | 7 | 25 | 87 | 121 | 133 | 5 | 5 | .441 | .547 |
| Thompson,Milt | 32 | .268 | 107 | 336 | 38 | 90 | 14 | 3 | 3 | 32 | 30 | 53 | 18 | 6 | .328 | .354 |
| Thompson,Robbie | 29 | .247 | 150 | 522 | 77 | 129 | 27 | 5 | 11 | 53 | 45 | 117 | 14 | 5 | .307 | .381 |
| Thon,Dickie | 33 | .250 | 148 | 545 | 55 | 136 | 20 | 3 | 8 | 50 | 46 | 94 | 15 | 6 | .308 | .341 |
| Thurman,Gary | 26 | .270 | 115 | 307 | 50 | 83 | 10 | 4 | 1 | 24 | 26 | 57 | 26 | 9 | .327 | .339 |
| Torve,Kelvin | 31 | .277 | 85 | 130 | 18 | 36 | 20 | 1 | 3 | 19 | 14 | 15 | 1 | 1 | .347 | .515 |
| Trammell,Alan | 33 | .275 | 134 | 484 | 61 | 133 | 23 | 2 | 10 | 62 | 53 | 50 | 9 | 6 | .346 | .393 |
| Treadway,Jeff | 28 | .274 | 138 | 463 | 55 | 127 | 24 | 3 | 8 | 48 | 32 | 41 | 3 | 2 | .321 | .391 |
| Uribe,Jose | 31 | .235 | 136 | 421 | 35 | 99 | 13 | 3 | 2 | 27 | 31 | 59 | 8 | 7 | .288 | .295 |
| Valle,Dave | 30 | .232 | 117 | 354 | 39 | 82 | 16 | 2 | 11 | 46 | 37 | 42 | 1 | 1 | .304 | .381 |
| Van Slyke,Andy | 30 | .263 | 141 | 464 | 69 | 122 | 23 | 7 | 14 | 66 | 53 | 94 | 18 | 6 | .338 | .433 |
| Vatcher,Jim | 25 | .285 | 90 | 130 | 19 | 37 | 9 | 2 | 3 | 18 | 18 | 22 | 1 | 1 | .372 | .454 |
| Vaughn,Greg | 25 | .243 | 130 | 448 | 62 | 109 | 24 | 2 | 20 | 71 | 43 | 105 | 13 | 5 | .310 | .440 |
| Velarde,Randy | 28 | .262 | 70 | 210 | 30 | 55 | 12 | 2 | 5 | 26 | 20 | 47 | 3 | 3 | .326 | .410 |
| Venable,Max | 34 | .219 | 82 | 151 | 17 | 33 | 6 | 1 | 1 | 13 | 16 | 31 | 3 | 1 | .293 | .291 |
| Ventura,Robin | 23 | .257 | 149 | 490 | 61 | 126 | 22 | 1 | 4 | 58 | 76 | 52 | 5 | 5 | .357 | .331 |
| Villanueva,Hector | 26 | .275 | 67 | 207 | 21 | 57 | 10 | 1 | 7 | 30 | 22 | 37 | 1 | 1 | .345 | .435 |
| Vizcaino,Jose | 23 | .246 | 135 | 350 | 36 | 86 | 8 | 2 | 1 | 29 | 21 | 36 | 10 | 8 | .288 | .289 |
| Vizquel,Omar | 24 | .235 | 103 | 306 | 35 | 72 | 9 | 2 | 1 | 23 | 27 | 29 | 9 | 6 | .297 | .288 |
| Walker,Larry | 24 | .255 | 130 | 415 | 64 | 106 | 19 | 3 | 18 | 57 | 51 | 97 | 25 | 9 | .337 | .446 |
| Wallach,Tim | 33 | .261 | 153 | 563 | 58 | 147 | 31 | 2 | 18 | 85 | 44 | 81 | 4 | 6 | .315 | .419 |
| Walling,Denny | 37 | .256 | 62 | 90 | 8 | 23 | 6 | 1 | 1 | 12 | 8 | 12 | 0 | 0 | .316 | .378 |
| Walton,Jerome | 25 | .302 | 140 | 530 | 81 | 160 | 27 | 3 | 5 | 51 | 51 | 84 | 32 | 12 | .363 | .392 |
| Ward,Gary | 37 | .253 | 88 | 288 | 29 | 73 | 13 | 2 | 7 | 36 | 28 | 57 | 1 | 1 | .320 | .385 |
| Ward,Turner | 26 | .261 | 80 | 230 | 30 | 60 | 10 | 3 | 2 | 23 | 22 | 35 | 8 | 5 | .325 | .357 |
| Webster,Mitch | 32 | .258 | 128 | 418 | 56 | 108 | 19 | 5 | 8 | 39 | 36 | 69 | 19 | 8 | .317 | .385 |
| Weiss,Walt | 27 | .257 | 131 | 389 | 44 | 100 | 17 | 1 | 3 | 35 | 37 | 46 | 7 | 3 | .322 | .329 |
| Whitaker,Lou | 34 | .254 | 132 | 480 | 68 | 122 | 21 | 3 | 15 | 65 | 81 | 69 | 5 | 2 | .362 | .404 |
| White,Devon | 28 | .242 | 132 | 476 | 70 | 115 | 20 | 5 | 13 | 50 | 32 | 102 | 26 | 10 | .289 | .387 |
| White,Frank | 40 | .236 | 82 | 258 | 21 | 61 | 12 | 1 | 4 | 26 | 13 | 35 | 2 | 1 | .273 | .337 |
| Whiten,Mark | 24 | .268 | 110 | 325 | 53 | 87 | 11 | 3 | 10 | 36 | 37 | 69 | 10 | 8 | .343 | .412 |
| Whitt,Ernie | 39 | .234 | 47 | 107 | 13 | 25 | 5 | 0 | 3 | 15 | 15 | 14 | 1 | 1 | .328 | .364 |
| Wilkerson,Curt | 30 | .246 | 58 | 134 | 15 | 33 | 4 | 1 | 0 | 11 | 8 | 22 | 3 | 2 | .289 | .291 |
| Willard,Jerry | 31 | .265 | 65 | 200 | 29 | 53 | 10 | 0 | 11 | 34 | 39 | 36 | 1 | 2 | .385 | .480 |
| Williams,Ken | 27 | .205 | 77 | 190 | 24 | 39 | 6 | 1 | 5 | 21 | 12 | 46 | 8 | 5 | .252 | .326 |
| Williams,Matt D. | 25 | .251 | 160 | 605 | 78 | 152 | 26 | 2 | 32 | 98 | 33 | 130 | 8 | 6 | .290 | .460 |
| Wilson,Craig | 26 | .253 | 70 | 170 | 21 | 43 | 10 | 1 | 1 | 17 | 15 | 14 | 2 | 2 | .314 | .341 |
| Wilson,Glenn | 32 | .255 | 102 | 341 | 37 | 87 | 18 | 1 | 8 | 43 | 23 | 53 | 1 | 2 | .302 | .384 |
| Wilson,Mookie | 35 | .263 | 121 | 438 | 56 | 115 | 19 | 4 | 5 | 37 | 22 | 78 | 16 | 5 | .298 | .358 |
| Wilson,Willie | 35 | .258 | 121 | 453 | 63 | 117 | 16 | 6 | 2 | 41 | 29 | 89 | 28 | 8 | .303 | .333 |

# Projections for 1991 Batters

| Batter | Age | Avg | G | AB | R | H | 2B | 3B | HR | RBI | BB | SO | SB | CS | OBP | SLG |
|---|---|---|---|---|---|---|---|---|---|---|---|---|---|---|---|---|
| Winfield,Dave | 39 | .259 | 128 | 467 | 63 | 121 | 21 | 2 | 16 | 70 | 56 | 83 | 4 | 2 | .338 | .415 |
| Winningham,Herm | 29 | .244 | 111 | 242 | 30 | 59 | 9 | 4 | 3 | 22 | 23 | 50 | 13 | 7 | .309 | .351 |
| Worthington,Craig | 26 | .238 | 133 | 442 | 49 | 105 | 19 | 0 | 12 | 56 | 54 | 100 | 2 | 2 | .321 | .362 |
| Wynne,Marvell | 31 | .236 | 75 | 195 | 18 | 46 | 8 | 1 | 3 | 20 | 13 | 31 | 3 | 2 | .284 | .333 |
| Yelding,Eric | 26 | .248 | 143 | 521 | 69 | 129 | 10 | 2 | 1 | 36 | 39 | 88 | 60 | 25 | .300 | .280 |
| Young,Gerald | 26 | .257 | 94 | 331 | 46 | 85 | 11 | 3 | 0 | 25 | 46 | 35 | 29 | 17 | .347 | .308 |
| Yount,Robin | 35 | .269 | 149 | 576 | 84 | 155 | 30 | 5 | 12 | 75 | 66 | 73 | 16 | 5 | .344 | .401 |
| Zeile,Todd | 25 | .256 | 145 | 500 | 72 | 128 | 28 | 3 | 17 | 68 | 63 | 75 | 3 | 3 | .339 | .426 |

# These Guys Can Play Too And Might Get A Shot

| Batter | Age | Avg | G | AB | R | H | 2B | 3B | HR | RBI | BB | SO | SB | CS | OBP | SLG |
|---|---|---|---|---|---|---|---|---|---|---|---|---|---|---|---|---|
| Amaral,Richie | 29 | .280 | 101 | 217 | 38 | 61 | 11 | 2 | 2 | 24 | 38 | 30 | 17 | 5 | .388 | .378 |
| Amaro,Ruben | 26 | .274 | 64 | 161 | 23 | 44 | 8 | 1 | 2 | 46 | 14 | 22 | 8 | 3 | .331 | .373 |
| Bagwell,Jeff | 23 | .318 | 140 | 500 | 65 | 159 | 34 | 6 | 3 | 62 | 68 | 64 | 3 | 5 | .400 | .436 |
| Bell,Juan | 23 | .257 | 150 | 541 | 74 | 139 | 17 | 4 | 8 | 52 | 44 | 113 | 18 | 8 | .313 | .348 |
| Bierley,Brad | 28 | .264 | 62 | 134 | 18 | 35 | 9 | 1 | 3 | 17 | 17 | 23 | 2 | 1 | .344 | .410 |
| Brosius,Scott | 24 | .244 | 71 | 244 | 28 | 55 | 12 | 0 | 5 | 26 | 26 | 33 | 3 | 1 | .300 | .336 |
| Colbrun,Greg | 21 | .279 | 74 | 218 | 23 | 61 | 15 | 1 | 5 | 29 | 17 | 38 | 4 | 2 | .332 | .427 |
| Crabbe,Bruce | 29 | .260 | 40 | 110 | 13 | 29 | 6 | 0 | 2 | 12 | 10 | 15 | 1 | 1 | .325 | .373 |
| Fariss,Monte | 23 | .266 | 71 | 260 | 38 | 69 | 14 | 3 | 4 | 31 | 31 | 59 | 4 | 2 | .344 | .388 |
| Jones,Barry | 26 | .272 | 65 | 130 | 15 | 35 | 5 | 1 | 4 | 17 | 12 | 16 | 3 | 2 | .331 | .415 |
| Lewis,Mark | 21 | .256 | 139 | 503 | 59 | 129 | 26 | 4 | 9 | 66 | 26 | 61 | 7 | 4 | .287 | .377 |
| Ramos,John | 25 | .282 | 52 | 171 | 24 | 48 | 11 | 0 | 3 | 25 | 20 | 26 | 2 | 2 | .356 | .398 |
| Tromberlin,Andy | 24 | .314 | 61 | 219 | 31 | 69 | 14 | 1 | 4 | 27 | 29 | 33 | 7 | 3 | .395 | .443 |
| Vaughn,Mo | 23 | .299 | 129 | 402 | 57 | 120 | 31 | 1 | 18 | 70 | 43 | 80 | 3 | 2 | .366 | .515 |
| Whited,Ed | 27 | .249 | 43 | 112 | 18 | 28 | 5 | 1 | 3 | 13 | 17 | 21 | 3 | 1 | .349 | .393 |

This page intentionally left blank.

# About STATS, Inc.

It all starts with the **system**. The STATS scoring method, which includes pitch-by-pitch information and the direction, distance, and velocity of each ball hit into play, yields an immense amount of information. Sure, we have all the statistics you're used to seeing, but where other statistic sources quit, STATS is just getting started.

Then, there's the **network**. Our information is timely because our game reporters send their information by computer as soon as the game is over. Statistics are checked, rechecked, updated, and are available daily.

**Analysis** comes next. STATS constantly searches for new ways to use this wealth of information to open windows into the workings of Baseball. Accurate numbers, intelligent computer programming, and a large dose of imagination all help coax the most valuable information from its elusive cover.

Finally, distribution!

STATS has served Major League teams for 11 years now including the Athletics, Yankees, and White Sox. The boxscores that STATS provides exclusively to *USA Today* have revolutionized what Baseball fans expect from a boxscore. *The National*, *Sports Illustrated*, and *The Sporting News* regularly feature STATS, Inc. *ESPN's* nightly baseball coverage is supported by a full-time STATS statistician and supplemented by on-site assistance for their Sunday night broadcasts. We provide statistics for *Earl Weaver Baseball*, *Rotisserie Baseball*, the nationally syndicated newspaper game *Dugout Derby*, and other baseball games and fantasy leagues all over the country.

For the baseball fan, STATS publishes monthly and year-end reports on each Major League team. We offer a host of year-end statistical breakdowns on paper or disk that cover hitting, pitching, catching, baserunning, throwing, and more. STATS produces custom reports on request.

Computer users with modems can access the STATS computer for information with **STATS On-line**. If you own a computer with a modem, there is no other source with the scope of baseball information that STATS can offer.

STATS and Bill James enjoy an on-going affiliation that has produced the handbook you are now holding. We also administer *Bill James Fantasy Baseball*, the ultimate baseball game written by Bill James himself which allows you to manage your own team and compete with other team owners around the country.

Keep an eye out for other exciting future projects.

It is the purpose of STATS, Inc. to make the best possible Baseball information available to all Baseball interests: fans, players, teams, or media. Write to:

STATS, Inc.
7366 North Lincoln Ave.
Lincolnwood, IL 60646

. . . or call us at 1-708-676-3322. We can send you a STATS brochure, a free Bill James Fantasy Baseball information kit, and/or information on STATS On-line.

To maintain its information, STATS hires people around the country to cover games using STATS scoring method. If you are interested in applying for a game reporter's position, please write or call STATS.

Also available from STATS, Inc. is ***The STATS 1991 Baseball Scoreboard***. The first edition of this book in 1990 took the nation's Baseball fans by storm. This all new edition, available for order directly from STATS, is back with the same great writing, great graphics and stats you won't find anywhere else. In addition, STATS continues a tradition with ***The Scouting Report:1991***, available in book stores in the Spring of 1991. You'll find scouting reports on over 700 players in this book, backed by statistical findings you can only get from STATS, Inc.

# Glossary

### % Inherited Scored
The number of runners allowed by a relief pitcher to score out of the number of runners on base at the time he entered the game.

### 1st Batter OBP
The On-Base Percentage Allowed by a relief pitcher to the first batter he faces upon entering a game.

### Active Career Batting Leaders
Minimum of 1,000 At Bats required for Batting Average, On-Base Percentage, Slugging Percentage, At Bats Per HR, At Bats Per GDP, At Bats Per RBI, and K/BB Ratio. One hundred (100) Stolen Base Attempts required for Stolen Base Success %. Any player who appeared in 1990 eligible for inclusion provided he meets the category's minimum requirements.

### Active Career Pitching Leaders
Minimum 750 Innings Pitched required for Earned Run Average, Opponent Batting Average, all of the "Per 9 Innings" categories, and Strikeout to Walk Ratio. Two hundred fifty (250) Games Started required for Complete Game Frequency. One hunderd (100) decisions required for Win-Loss Percentage. Any player who appeared in 1990 eligible for inclusion provided he meets the category's minimum requirements.

### BA ScPos Allowed
Batting Average Allowed with Runners in Scoring Position.

### Batting Average
Hits divided by At Bats.

### Cheap Wins/Tough Losses/Top Game Scores
First determine the starting pitcher's Game Score as follows: (1)Start with 50. (2)Add 1 point for each out recorded by the starting pitcher. (3)Add 2 points for each inning the pitcher completes afer the fourth inning. (4)Add 1 point for each strikeout. (5)Subtract 2 points for each hit allowed. (6)Subtract 4 points for each earned run allowed. (7)Subtract 2 points for an unearned run. (8)Subtract 1 point for each walk.

If the starting pitcher scores over 50 and loses, it's a Tough Loss. If he wins with a game score under 50, it's a Cheap Win. All Game Scores of 90 or above are listed.

### Cleanup Slugging%
The Slugging Percentage of a player batting fourth in the batting order.

### Complete Game Frequency
Complete Games divided by Games Started.

### Earned Run Average
(Earned Runs times 9) divided by Innings Pitched.

### Hold
A Save Situation successfully passed on to the next reliever. A pitcher cannot finish the game and get credit with a Hold.

### Isolated Power
Slugging Percentage minus Batting Average.

### K/BB Ratio
Strikeouts divided by Walks.

### Late & Close
In the seventh inning or later, with either team ahead by 3 runs or less.

### Leadoff On Base%
The On-Base Percentage of a player batting first in the batting order.

### Offensive Winning Percentage
The Winning Percentage a team of nine Will Clarks (or anybody) would compile against average pitching and defense. The formula: (Runs Created per 27 outs) divided by the League average of runs scored per game. Square the result and divide it by (1+itself).

### On Base Percentage
(Hits plus Walks plus Hit by Pitcher) divided by (At Bats plus Walks plus Hit by Pitcher plus Sacrifice Flies).

### Opponent Batting Average
Hits Allowed divided by (Batters Faced minus Walks minus Hit Batsmen minus Sacrifice Hits minus Sacrifice Flies minus Catcher's Interfernce).

### PA*
Denotes the divisor for On Base Percentage, which is At Bats plus Walks plus Hit By Pitcher plus Sacrifice Flies; or Plate Appearances minus Sacrifice Hits and Times Reached Base on Defensive Interference.

### PkOf Throw/Runner
The number of pickoff throws made by a pitcher divided by the number of runners on first base.

### Plate Apperances
At Bats plus Walks plus Hit By Pitcher plus Sacrifice Hits plus Sacrifice Flies plus Times Reached on Defensive Interference.

### Power/Speed Number
A way to look at power and speed in one number. A player must score high in both areas to earn a high Power/Speed Number. The formula: (HR x SB x 2) divided by (HR + SB).

### Quick Hooks and Slow Hooks
A Quick Hook is the removal of a pitcher who has pitched less than 6 innings and given up 3 runs or less. A Slow Hook goes to a pitcher who pitches more than 9 innings, or allows 7 or more runs, or who's combined innings pitched and runs allowed totals 13 or more.

## Range Factor

The number of Chances (Putouts plus Assists plus Errors) times nine divided by the number of Defensive Innings Played. The average for each position in 1990:

| | |
|---|---|
| Second Base: 5.21 | Left Field: 2.23 |
| Third Base: 2.90 | Center Right: 2.79 |
| Shortstop: 4.81 | Right Field: 2.27 |

## Run Support Per 9 IP

(The number of runs scored by a pitcher's team while he was still in the game times nine) divided by his Innings Pitched.

## Runs Created

A way to combine a batter's total offensive contributions into one number. The formula: (H + BB + HBP - CS - GIDP) times (Total Bases + .26(TBB - IBB + HBP) + .52(SH + SF + SB)) divided by (AB + TBB + HBP +SH + SF).

## Save Percentage

Saves (SV) divided by Save Opportunities (OP).

## SB Att/On 1st Base

A ratio representing the number of times time a player attempted to steal second per the number of times he was on first base.

## SB Success%

Stolen Bases divided by (Stolen Bases plus Caught Stealing).

## Secondary Average

A way to look at a player's extra bases gained, independently of Batting Average. The formula: (Total Bases - Hits + BB + SB) divided by At Bats.

## Slugging Percentage

Total Bases divided by At Bats.

## Total Bases

Hits plus Doubles plus (2 times Triples) plus (3 times Homeruns).

## Win-Loss Percentage or Winning Percentage

Wins divided by (Wins plus Losses).